Official Gazette Of The United States Patent Office, Volume 270

CONTENTS.

ANNOUNCEMENTS.

ALPHABETICAL LIST OF PATENTEES

TO WHOM

PATENTS WERE ISSUED DURING THE MONTH OF JANUARY, 1920.

NOTE.—Arranged in accordance with the first significant character or word of the name. (In accordance with city and telephone directory practice.)

Aaron, Solomon E., Boston, Mass. Pliers. No. 1,329,155; Jan. 27; v. 270; p. 554.

Abbott, Herbert E., and E. Enz, Oakville, Iowa. Tractor steering device. No. 1,327,511; Jan. 6; v. 270; p. 118.

Abbott, William T., et al. (See Soule, Charles E., assignor.)

Abercrombie, Jamie, Horton, and N. M. Dunman, West Columbia, Tex. Combination well-packer and setting-tool. No. 1,327,077; Jan. 6; v. 270; p. 37.

Aberg, Carl J., Stenstorp, Sweden. Road-making. No. 1,327,131; Jan. 6; v. 270; p. 47.

Abraham, Herbert, New York, N. Y., assignor to The Standard Paint Company. Strip-shingle. No. 1,326,899; Jan. 6; v. 270; p. 3.

Abram Cox Stove Company. (See Mott and Kinsley, assignors.)

Acker, Julius J. (See Goodwin and Acker.)

Acme Card System Company. (See Anthony, Stanley, assignor.)

Adams, Joseph H., Brooklyn, N. Y., assignor to The Texas Company, Houston, Tex. Conversion of liquids, fluids, and oils. No. 1,327,263; Jan. 6; v. 270; p. 72.

Adams, Reed, Lapeer, Mich. Printing-press. No. 1,328,253; Jan. 20; v. 270; p. 355.

Adler, Stella, St. Louis, Mo. Doll. No. 1,328,254; Jan. 20; v. 270; p. 255.

Aeolian Company, The. (See Callender, Romaine, assignor.)

Aeroplane Railway Patents Corporation. (See Williams, Franklin M., assignor.)

Affelder, Harry F., Cleveland, Ohio. Envelop-clasping machine. No. 1,328,472; Jan. 20; v. 270; p. 397.

Ahana, William W. L., Honolulu, Hawaii. Envelop. No. 1,328,028; Jan. 13; v. 270; p. 276.

Ajax Metal Company, The. (See Northrup, Edwin F., assignor.)

Aktiebolaget Carlit. (See Carlson, Oscar B., assignor.)

Aktiebolaget Lidköpings Mekaniska Verkstad. (See Soderlund, Carl G., assignor.)

Aktiebolaget Svenska Kullagerfabriken. (See Olsson, Niles J., assignor.)

Aktiebolaget Vaporackumulator. (See Ruths, Johannes K., assignor.)

Albers, Ulfert L., Rico, Colo. Toothbrush. No. 1,326,900; Jan. 6; v. 270; p. 3.

Alcock, Frederick T., Kamloops, British Columbia, Canada. Tool-holder. No. 1,327,934; Jan. 13; v. 270; p. 258.

Alderman, L. R., & Co. (See Walker, Roy S., assignor.)

Aldrich Pump Company. (See Aldrich, Roscoe H., assignor.)

Aldrich, Roscoe H., assignor to Aldrich Pump Company, Allentown, Pa. Reinforced pump-casing. No. 1,327,512; Jan. 6; v. 270; p. 118.

Aldridge, James G. W., Westminster, London, England. Machine for charging and discharging retorts. No. 1,327,582; Jan. 6; v. 270; p. 131.

Alexander, Francis H., Jesmond, Newcastle-upon-Tyne, England. Clutch-coupling for transmission of power by shafting. No. 1,327,935; Jan. 13; v. 270; p. 258.

Alexanderson, Ernst F. W., Schenectady, N. Y., assignor to General Electric Company. Means for controlling alternating currents. No. 1,328,473; Jan. 20; v. 270; p. 397.

Alexanderson, Ernst F. W., Schenectady, N. Y., assignor to General Electric Company. Method of and means for controlling high-frequency alternating currents. No. 1,328,610; Jan. 20; v. 270; p. 423.

Alexanderson, Ernst F. W., Schenectady, N. Y., assignor to General Electric Company. Means for controlling alternating currents. No. 1,328,797; Jan. 20; v. 270; p. 457.

Alfano, Giuseppe, New York, N. Y. Safety device for elevators. No. 1,327,513; Jan. 6; v. 270; p. 118.

Allegretti, Benedetto E., Chicago, Ill. Candy-making machine. No. 1,329,282; Jan. 27; v. 270; p. 578.

Allen, Claude E., Kenosha, Wis., assignor to C. M. Hall Lamp Company, Detroit, Mich. Automatic air-brush machine for coating lamps, &c. No. 1,327,973; Jan. 13; v. 270; p. 265.

Allen, George W., assignor to B. F. Sturtevant Company, Boston, Mass. Pneumatic cleaner. No. 1,326,901; Jan. 6; v. 270; p. 3.

Allesina, John, Portland, Oreg. Umbrella. No. 1,329,219; Jan. 27; v. 270; p. 566.

Allman, William H., Blythedale, Mo. Flying-machine. No. 1,327,514; Jan. 6; v. 270; p. 118.

Allsteelequip Company, The. (See Erickson, Axel F., assignor.)

Almond, T. R., Manufacturing Company. (See Hubbell, Henry S., assignor.)

Alpen, Henry, Hempstead, N. Y. Holder attachment for ladders. No. 1,328,705; Jan. 20; v. 270; p. 440.

Alpern, Maxwell, assignor to American Engineering Company, Philadelphia, Pa. Stoker. No. 1,328,611; Jan. 20; v. 270; p. 423.

Alsten, Alfred O., Worcester, Mass. Pneumatic vulcanizing-core. No. 1,327,264; Jan. 6; v. 270; p. 72.

Altmann, Jakob, Weesen, Switzerland. Machine for truing loom-shuttles. No. 1,327,515; Jan. 6; v. 270; p. 119.

American Bank Note Company. (See Marquardt, Frank C., assignor.)

American Blower Company. (See Cunliffe, Cicero M., assignor.)

American Bosch Magneto Corporation. (See Honold and Krauss, assignors.)

American Brake Company, The. (See Burton, Thomas L., assignor.)

American Brake Company, The. (See Schwentler, Francis E., assignor.)

American Brake Shoe and Foundry Company, The. (See Sargent, Fitz William, assignor.)

American Brass Company. (See Coe, James R., assignor.)

American Can Company. (See Augensen, August M., assignor.)

American Can Company. (See Gray, James A., assignor.)

American Can Company. (See Rudolphi, Frank, assignor.)

American Can Company. (See Stewart, Thomas H., assignor.)

American Can Company. (See Symonds, Clarence M., assignor.)

American Dressler Tunnel Kilns. (See Meehan, Paul A., assignor.)

American Engineering Company. (See Alpern, Maxwell, assignor.)

American Grain Deodorizing Co. (See Moore, Payton J. H., assignor.)

American Lacing Hook Co. (See Havener, Arthur R., assignor.)

American Lacing Hook Co. (See Rhodes, Austin D., assignor.)

American Laundry Machinery Company, The. (See Andrée, William E., assignor.)

American Laundry Machinery Company, The. (See Benjamin, Dana H., assignor.)

American Manganese Steel Company. (See Exton, Alfred H., assignor.)

American Marine Equipment Corporation. (See Row and Davis, assignors.)

American Metal Cap Company. (See Hammer, Charles, assignor.)

American Potash Corporation. (See Charlton, Harry W., assignor.)

American Steel Foundries. (See Peycke, Armand H., assignor.)

American Tap Bush Co. (See Rice, Frank E., assignor.)

American Thermophone Company. (See de Lange and van Lynden, assignors.)

American Tool Company. (See Beaudreau, Edward H., assignor.)

American Train Control Co., The. (See Scott, Thomas W., assignor.)

American Warp Drawing Machine Company. (See Lea, Charles, assignor.)

Anchor Cap & Closure Corporation. (See Ramsey, George, assignor.)

Anchor Cap & Closure Corporation. (See Wieland, Frederick G., assignor.)

Anderfuhren, Louis, Baltimore, Md. Pneumatic-tire alarm. No. 1,327,416; Jan. 6; v. 270; p. 99.

Andersen, Peter C., Medford, Wis. Crushing-machine. No. 1,328,806; Jan. 27; v. 270; p. 487.

Anderson, Anton D., Harrison, N. Y. Talking-machine. No. 1,327,516; Jan. 6; v. 270; p. 119.

Anderson, Arvid R., assignor to The Automatic Reclosing Circuit Breaker Company, Columbus, Ohio. Attachment for electric controllers. No. 1,328,804; Jan. 27; v. 270; p. 487.

Anderson, Carl E., East Orange, assignor to Eastern Tool & Mfg. Company, Bloomfield, N. J. Binder. No. 1,327,186; Jan. 6; p. 270; p. 58.

Anderson, Charles A., assignor to G. E. Sundstrom, Chicago, Ill. Fluid-pump. (Reissue.) No. 14,789; Jan. 13; v. 270; p. 319.

Anderson, Charles H., Lexington, Ky. Apparatus for feeding liquid fuel to carbureters. No. 1,328,354; Jan. 20; v. 270; p. 374.

Anderson, Clarence S., Lake Geneva, Wis. Radiator. No. 1,327,797; Jan. 13; v. 270; p. 233.

Anderson, Edward, Brooklyn, N. Y. Adjustable and knockdown window-seat. No. 1,328,706; Jan. 20; v. 270; p. 440.

Anderson, Ernst G. K. (See Benjamin and Anderson.)

Anderson, Frank, Denver, Colo., and A. Wild, Loveland, Colo. Dumping-body for automobile-trucks, wagons, freight-cars, and other vehicles. No. 1,328,805; Jan. 27; v. 270; p. 487.

Anderson, Gideon, assignor to W. West, New York, N. Y. Tilting bed. No. 1,328,802; Jan. 27; v. 270; p. 487.

Anderson, Gustaf A., assignor to Landis Machine Company, Waynesboro, Pa. Cutter-head. No. 1,327,007; Jan. 6; v. 270; p. 24.

Anderson, Gustaf A., assignor to Landis Machine Company, Waynesboro, Pa. Cutter-head. No. 1,327,008; Jan. 6; v. 270; p. 25.

Anderson, Harry T., Butler, Pa., assignor to Harry Vissering & Company, Chicago, Ill. Manufacture of railway draft-gear yokes. No. 1,328,975; Jan. 27; v. 270; p. 521.

Anderson, Harry T., Crafton, Pa., assignor to Harry Vissering & Company, Chicago, Ill. Draft-gear yoke. No. 1,329,318; Jan. 27; v. 270; p. 584.

Anderson, Lee S., Detroit, Mich. Device for turning sheet-music. No. 1,328,976; Jan. 27; v. 270; p. 521.

Anderson, Lemuel O., assignor of one-half to F. P. Armstrong, Miami, Fla. Sash-fastener. No. 1,328,029; Jan. 13; v. 270; p. 276.

Anderson, Per A., New York, N. Y. Fan. No. 1,328,255; Jan. 20; v. 270; p. 255.

Anderson, William S., Victorville, Calif. Valve-truing device. No. 1,327,187; Jan. 6; v. 270; p. 58.

Andrée, William E., Chicago, Ill., assignor to The American Laundry Machinery Company, Cincinnati, Ohio. Electric switch. No. 1,327,009; Jan. 6; v. 270; p. 25.

Andregg, Louis A. (See Krannich, Emil A., assignor.)

Andrew, William P., Mount Pleasant, Pa. Nut-lock. No. 1,328,939; Jan. 27; v. 270; p. 514.

Andrews, Moril V., and S. W. Holman, assignors to Mors Pump Company, Marmarth, N. D. Rotary water-pump. No. 1,327,517; Jan. 6; v. 270; p. 119.

Andrews, Shellie. (See May, Walter P., assignor.)

Animated Target Company, Inc. (See Franklin, Hubert F., assignor.)

Ansonia Manufacturing Company. (See Malby, Seth G., assignor.)

Anthony, Marcus O., assignor to A. Kimball Company, New York, N. Y. Pin-ticket. No. 1,327,010; Jan. 6; v. 270; p. 25.

Anthony, Stanley, Boston, Mass., assignor to Acme Card System Company, Chicago, Ill. Card-index. No. 1,327,936; Jan. 13; v. 270; p. 258.

Apostoloff. Serge, New York, N. Y. Anti-friction device. No. 1,327,895; Jan. 13; v. 270; p. 251.

Aranar Company, The. (See Roberts, Fred T., assignor.)

Arbon, Paul, assignor to R. Gulberson, Tulsa, Okla. Sand-trap. No. 1,327,583; Jan. 6; v. 270; p. 131.

Archibald, James G., et al. (See Schott, John H., assignor.)

Armour Grain Company. (See Remmers, Bernhard, assignor.)

Armstrong, Franklin P. (See Anderson, Lemuel O., assignor.)

Armstrong, Ira, Merkel, assignor to Dixieland Motor Truck Company, Bowie county, Tex. Power-driven-implement frame. No. 1,328,222; Jan. 13; v. 270; p. 313.

Arndt, Franklin E., Galion, Ohio. Clamp for burial-vaults. No. 1,327,011; Jan. 6; v. 270; p. 25.

Arndt, Franklin E., assignor to D. C. Boyd, Galion, Ohio. Locking mechanism for vault-doors. No. 1,328,355; Jan. 20; v. 270; p. 374.

Arndt, Richard L., assignor to Union Tractor Company, San Francisco, Calif. Traction-belt. No. 1,328,643; Jan. 20; v. 270; p. 429.

Arnold, Harold D., Maplewood, N. J., assignor to Western Electric Company, Incorporated, New York, N. Y. Thermionic amplifier. No. 1,329,283; Jan. 27; v. 270; p. 578.

Arquint, Hans, Richterswil, Switzerland. Car-frame. No. 1,327,367; Jan. 6; v. 270; p. 90.

Asche, Evert, Clara City, Minn. Ratchet-brace. No. 1,328,111; Jan. 13; v. 270; p. 292.

Ashby, Bert, El Paso, Tex. Packet-holder. No. 1,328,869; Jan. 27; v. 270; p. 500.

Ashby, Bert A., El Paso, Tex. Spark-arrester. No. 1,328,808; Jan. 27; v. 270; p. 500.

Asmondis, Rocco, Zellenople, Pa. Saw-sharpening machine. No. 1,327,012; Jan. 6; v. 270; p. 26.

Aspronet Company. (See Young, James H., assignor.)

Associate Company, The. (See Taft, Walter R., assignor.)

Astrom, John, assignor to Fort Wayne Engineering & Manufacturing Co., Fort Wayne, Ind. Pump. No. 1,328,474; Jan. 20; v. 270; p. 397.

Atlas Process Company. (See von Groeling, Albrecht F. G. C. P. J., assignor.)

Atterbury, Grosvenor, New York, N. Y. Process of and apparatus for making concrete slabs. No. 1,326,902; Jan. 6; v. 270; p. 3.

Aubert, Albert M., Billancourt, France. Firearm. No. 1,328,475; Jan. 20; v. 270; p. 397.

Aubry-Schaltenbrandt, Francis, La Chaux-de-Fonds, Switzerland. Night-watchman's checking apparatus. No. 1,328,223; Jan. 13; v. 270; p. 313.

Auerbach, Julia H., Hollywood, Calif. Corset-fastening. No. 1,327,078; Jan. 6; v. 270; p. 38.

Augensen, August M., Maywood, Ill., assignor to American Can Company, New York, N. Y. Can-feeding mechanism. No. 1,326,903; Jan. 6; v. 270; p. 3.

Austin, Frederick C. (See Bentson, Hans J., assignor.)

Austin, Herbert, Bromsgrove, England. Mounting an aeroplane-propeller and carrying a gun which fires axially through the propeller. No. 1,329,156; Jan. 27; v. 270; p. 555.

Austin, Leslie W., San Jose, Calif. Treating manganese silver ores. No. 1,327,974; Jan. 13; v. 270; p. 266.

Austral Window Company. (See Myers, Winter W., assignor.)

Auto-Ordnance Corporation. (See Eickhoff and Tunks, assignors.)

Automatic Electric Company. (See Campbell, Wilson L., assignor.)

Automatic Reclosing Circuit Breaker Company, The. (See Anderson, Arvid R., assignor.)

Automatic Sprinkler Company of America. (See Hamilton, John R., assignor.)

Automatic Straight Air Brake Company. (See Neal, Spencer G., assignor.)

Automotive Development Co. (See Huggins, Merion J., assignor.)

Averill, William H., assignor to Owl Supply Company, Boston, Mass. Copy-holder. No. 1,328,476; Jan. 20; v. 270; p. 397.

Avery Company. (See Bartholomew, John B., assignor.)

Ayres, Richard S., Brookline, Mass. Manufacture of boot and shoe heels. No. 1,327,851; Jan. 13; v. 270; p. 243.

Ayres, Walter W. (See Cassingham and Ayres.)

Ayrton, Hertha, Hyde Park, London, England. Propulsion of air and other gases or fluids. No. 1,327,975; Jan. 13; v. 270; p. 266.

Baader, Stephan. (See Hough and Baader.)

Babcock & Wilcox Company, The. (See Jacobus, David S., assignor.)

Babendreer, Albert, Ocean Springs, Miss., assignor to Whole Grain Wheat Company, Phoenix, Ariz. Treating food. No. 1,327,220; Jan. 6; v. 270; p. 64.

Bacharach, Samuel, Philadelphia, Pa. Finger-ring. No. 1,327,606; Jan. 13; v. 270; p. 197.

Bache-Wiig, Carl, Portland, Me. Preparing pulp. No. 1,327,221; Jan. 6; v. 270; p. 65.

Backstrom, Fridolf F., assignor to Western Felt Works, Chicago, Ill. Belt-fastener. No. 1,327,798; Jan. 13; v. 270; p. 233.

Badger Meter Manufacturing Company. (See Krueger, Emil M., assignor.)

Badoian, Vartan K., Lawrence, Mass. Shuttle-guard for looms. No. 1,329,157; Jan. 27; v. 270; p. 555.

Baender, Charles L., Oakland, Calif., assignor, by mesne assignments, to The Torrington Company, Torrington, Conn. Can-teat-sweeping appliance. No. 1,327,456; Jan. 6; v. 270; p. 107.

Bagley, Charles H. F., Stockton-upon-Tees, England. Making basic steel in open-hearth steel-furnaces. No. 1,328,803; Jan. 27; v. 270; p. 487.

Baker, A. T., & Company. (See Ott, Frederick, assignor.)

Baker, Arthur F., Sedro Woolley, assignor to The Perfecto Gear Differential Co., Seattle, Wash. Driving mechanism for motor-cars. No. 1,329,319; Jan. 27; v. 270; p. 584.

Baker, Erle K., assignor to Baker Wheel & Rim Company, Chicago, Ill. Dual-tired wheel. No. 1,327,607; Jan. 13; v. 270; p. 197.

Baker, Joseph, & Sons. (See Hewitt, Harry, assignor.)

Baker, Malcolm H., deceased, Braintree; M. H. Baker, administratrix, assignor to K. W. Crosby, trustee, Boston, Mass. Time-retarded cut-off switch. No. 1,328,477; Jan. 20; v. 270; p. 398.

Baker, Malcolm H., deceased, Braintree; M. H. Baker, administratrix, assignor to K. W. Crosby, trustee, Boston, Mass. Thermodynamically-controlled socket-switch for electric lights. No. 1,328,478; Jan. 20; v. 270; p. 398.

Baker, Malcolm H., deceased, Braintree; M. H. Baker, administratrix, assignor to K. W. Crosby, trustee, Boston, Mass. Thermodynamically-controlled socket-switch for electric lights. No. 1,328,479; Jan. 20; v. 270; p. 398.

Baker, Malcolm H., deceased, Braintree; M. H. Baker, administratrix, assignor to K. W. Crosby, trustee, Boston, Mass. Thermodynamically-controlled pendent switch for electric circuits. No. 1,328,480; Jan. 20; v. 270; p. 398.

Baker, Malcolm H., deceased, Braintree; M. H. Baker, administratrix, assignor to K. W. Crosby, trustee, Boston, Mass. Flush push-button switch for electric circuits. No. 1,328,481; Jan. 20; v. 270; p. 399.

Baker, Malcolm H., deceased, Braintree; M. H. Baker, administratrix, assignor to K. W. Crosby, trustee, Boston, Mass. Thermodynamically - controlled electric switch. No. 1,328,482; Jan. 20; v. 270; p. 399.

Baker, Marie H., administratrix. (See Baker, Malcolm H.)

Baker, Thomas W. (See Magee, Frederick W., assignor.)

Baker-Vawter Company. (See Manny, Fred L., assignor.)

Baker Wheel & Rim Company. (See Baker, Earle K., assignor.)

Bakke, Bjarne, assignor to Norsk Hydro-Elektrisk Kvaelstofaktieselskab, Christiania, Norway. Treatment of liquids to effect crystallization therefrom while the liquid is kept in motion. No. 1,329,158; Jan. 27; v. 270; p. 555.

Baldon, J. L., et al. (See Shreibman, Abram, assignor.)

Baldwin, Arthur S., Baltimore, Md. Gun. No. 1,327,897; Jan 13; v. 270; p. 251.

Baldwin, Frank G., assignor to The Sechler & Company, Cincinnati, Ohio. Rolling military kitchen. No. 1,328,071; Jan. 13; v. 270; p. 284.

Baldwin Locomotive Works, The. (See Rushton, Kenneth, assignor.)

Balkwill, Wesley J. (See Schweiger and Balkwill.)

Ball & Ball Carburetor Company. (See Ball, Frederick O., assignor.) (Reissue.)

Ball, Frederick O., assignor to Ball & Ball Carburetor Company, Detroit, Mich. Carbureter. (Reissue.) No. 14,790; Jan. 13; v. 270; p. 320.

Ballard, Albert M., Drumright, Okla., assignor to Sun Company, Philadelphia, Pa. Apparatus for separating oil and gas direct from wells. No. 1,327,691; Jan. 13; v. 270; p. 213.

Ballard, James W., Fairfax, Va. Repeating rifle. No. 1,328,856; Jan. 20; v. 270; p. 375.

Ballin, Hugo, New York, N. Y. Bird-house. No. 1,329,104; Jan. 27; v. 270; p. 545.

Balogh, George W., Buffalo, N. Y. Heater. No. 1,327,896; Jan. 13; v. 270; p. 251.

Balster, Frederick W., Wilmington, Del. Steam-boiler. No. 1,327,188; Jan. 6; v. 270; p. 58.

Balthasar, Harry G., assignor to Interstate Tool and Manufacturing Company, St. Louis, Mo. Dial-indicator for combination-locks. No. 1,327,457; Jan. 6; v. 270; p. 107.

Balzer, Fritz, assignor to Troy Laundry Machinery Company, Ltd., Chicago, Ill. Shirt-bosom-ironing machine. No. 1,328,807; Jan. 27; v. 270; p. 488.

Bancroft, John S., and A. L. Knight, assignors to Lanston Monotype Machine Company, Philadelphia, Pa. Multiple-blade type-mold. No. 1,328,256; Jan. 20; v. 270; p. 355.

Bancroft, John S., and M. C. Indahl, assignors to Lanston Monotype Machine Company, Philadelphia, Pa. Typographic composing-machine. No. 1,328,257; Jan. 20; v. 270; p. 356.

Barbee, James B., Central City, and O. J. Cross, Nederland, Colo. Jig. No. 1,328,778; Jan. 20; v. 270; p. 453.

Barbet, E., & Fils & Cie. (See Barbet, Emile A., assignor.)

Barbet, Emile A., assignor to E. Barbet & Fils & Cie., Paris, France. Continuous production of ether. No. 1,328,258; Jan. 20; v. 270; p. 356.

Barbet, Emile A., Paris, France. Cooling-plate for continuous rectification apparatus. No. 1,328,259; Jan. 20; v. 270; p. 356.

Barchi, Giovanni, New York, N. Y. Drawer attachment. No. 1,328,112; Jan. 13; v. 270; p. 292.

Bard, George P., Youngstown, Ohio. Pressed corrugated sheet-metal annealing-box. No. 1,328,030; Jan. 13; v. 270; p. 276.

Barger, Bernard J., El Paso, Tex. Saw gaging and setting tool. No. 1,328,554; Jan. 20; v. 270; p. 412.

Barhoff, Fred W., assignor to The Hartford Storage Battery Manufacturing Company, Hartford, Conn. Method of and means for sealing storage-battery connectors and posts. No. 1,328,357; Jan. 20; v. 270; p. 375.

Barhoff, Fred W., assignor to The Hartford Storage Battery Manufacturing Company, Hartford, Conn. Means for sealing storage-battery covers in cells. No. 1,328,358; Jan. 20; v. 270; p. 375.

Barhoff, Fred W., assignor to The Hartford Storage Battery Manufacturing Company, Hartford, Conn. Method of and means for sealing terminal posts in storage-battery covers. No. 1,328,359; Jan. 20; v. 270; p. 375.

Barker, George R., Chicago, Ill. Cushioned wheel. No. 1,328,779; Jan. 20; v. 270; p. 454.

Barker, George S., Denver, Colo. Valve. No. 1,328,780; Jan. 20; v. 270; p. 454.

Barnard, Elmer, Cleburne, Tex. Mirror - holder. No. 1,327,808; Jan. 13; v. 270; p. 197.

Barnard, Hugh A., Houstonville, N. C. Folding chicken-coop. No. 1,327,868; Jan. 6; v. 270; p. 91.

Barnes, Frank R., Dupree, S. D. Centrifugal gun. No. 1,327,518; Jan. 6; v. 270; p. 119.

Barnes, James W., assignor to Estey Piano Co., New York, N. Y. Tracking device. No. 1,328,260; Jan. 20; v. 270; p. 356.

Barnes, Peter, et al. (See de Esparya, Timoteo R., assignor.)

Barr, John U., New York, N. Y. Advertising-clock. No. 1,327,898; Jan. 13; v. 270; p. 251.

Barraclough, Horatio L., London, England. Construction of reinforced-concrete floors. No. 1,328,555; Jan. 20; v. 270; p. 413.

Barrell, Charles S., Boston, Mass. Swivel device. No. 1,327,013; Jan. 6; v. 270; p. 26.

Barrett Company, The. (See Perry, Ray P., assignor.)

Bartholomew, John B., assignor to Avery Company, Peoria, Ill. Steering mechanism for tractors. No. 1,328,808; Jan. 27; v. 270; p. 488.

Bartholomew, William, assignor to Troy Laundry Machinery Company, Ltd., Chicago, Ill. Drying-tumbler. No. 1,327,609; Jan. 13; v. 270; p. 197.

Barton, Charles N., assignor of one-third to J. W. Langley and one-third to W. Peck, Indianapolis, Ind. Sectional machinery-repair washer. No. 1,327,417; Jan. 6; v. 270; p. 100.

Bartz, Adolph J., Crandall, Tex. Stalk - chopper. No. 1,329,220; Jan. 27; v. 270; p. 566.

Basford, Harold R., San Francisco, Calif. Foldable bed. No. 1,328,977; Jan. 27; v. 270; p. 521.

Bassett, Preston R., assignor to E. A. Sperry, Brooklyn, N. Y. Operating flaming-arc lights for projectors. No. 1,328,811; Jan. 20; v. 270; p. 366.

Bassett, Robert N., Company. (See Cocker, Frederick, assignor.)

Bastian, Charles L., Chicago, Ill. Soda-fountain apparatus. No. 1,327,189; Jan. 6; v. 270; p. 58.

Bateman, Ernest, Madison, Wis. Bleaching wood. No. 1,329,284; Jan. 27; v. 270; p. 578.

Bateman Manufacturing Company. (See Willis and Woodworth, assignors.)

Bates, Albert J., Chicago, Ill., assignor to Bates Expanded Steel Truss Co., Wilmington, Del. Discharging mechanism. No. 1,328,809; Jan. 27; v. 270; p. 488.

Bates, Albert J. Jr., assignor, by mesne assignments, to D. S. Gardner, Chicago, Ill. Crimping-machine. No. 1,328,411; Jan. 20; v. 270; p. 385.

Bates, Arthur, Leicester, England, assignor, by mesne assignments, to United Shoe Machinery Corporation, Paterson, N. J. Wax-applying device. No. 1,327,014; Jan. 6; v. 270; p. 26.

Bates, Ben M., Baltimore, Md. Rail-joint. No. 1,328,113; Jan. 13; v. 270; p. 292.

Bates Expanded Steel Truss Co. (See Bates, Albert J., assignor.)

Baum, William F. (See Greco, Vito B., assignor.)

Bausman, Alonzo L., Chicopee, assignor to National Equipment Company, Springfield, Mass. Shaking-table. No. 1,328,483; Jan. 20; v. 270; p. 399.

Bayer, Alois, and A. Klingele, Lorain, Ohio. Flytrap. No. 1,328,114; Jan. 13; v. 270; p. 292.

Beach, Milo D., Litchfield, Conn. Wheel-indicator. No. 1,328,978; Jan. 27; v. 270; p. 521.

Beaman, Albert W., Pittsboro, Ind. Pig-brooder. No. 1,328,810; Jan. 27; v. 270; p. 488.

Benn, Albert M., Colville, Wash. Harness-hanger. No. 1,328,312; Jan. 20; v. 270; p. 367.

Bean Spray Pump Co. (See Crummey. Frederick E., assignor.)

Beardsley, Edson L., Columbus, Ohio. Valve-lifter. No. 1,327,015; Jan. 6; v. 270; p. 26.

Bearse, Frank P., et al. (See Soule, Charles E., assignor.)

Beatty, Harry W., Oilfields, Calif. Casing-cutter. No. 1,328,940; Jan. 27; v. 270; p. 514.

Beaudreau, Edward H., assignor to American Tool Company, Meriden, Conn. Automobile non-skid chain. No. 1,327,369; Jan. 6; v. 270; p. 91.

Beaven, Leslie W., Chicago, Ill. Hydraulic dredging apparatus. No. 1,327,651; Jan. 13; v. 270; p. 205.

Beccari, Giuseppe, Florence, Italy. Apparatus for working garbage and refuse of towns. No. 1,329,105; Jan. 27; v. 270; p. 545.

Bechoff, Ferdinand, New York, N. Y. Electrical circuit-controller. No. 1,328,072; Jan. 13; v. 270; p. 284.

Bechoff, Ferdinand, New York, N. Y. Indicator for controlling switches. No. 1,328,073; Jan. 13; v. 270; p. 285.

Beck, John L., Newark, N. J. Fishing rod and reel. No. 1,327,751; Jan. 13; v. 270; p. 224.

Becker, Benjamin, St. Louis, Mo. Door - opener. No. 1,328,979; Jan. 27; v. 270; p. 522.

Becker, Robert A., assignor of one-half to C. Tremain. Poughkeepsie, N. Y. Connector. No. 1,328,612; Jan. 20; v. 270; p. 423.

Beckett, John R., Somerville, Mass. Universal angle-fixture. No. 1,327,370; Jan. 6; v. 270; p. 91.

Beckwith, William C., Urbana, Ill. Phonograph-resonator. No. 1,328,412; Jan. 20; v. 270; p. 385.

Beckworth, Otto Q. (See Hobson. Oliver J., assignor.)

Beede, Herbert G., Pawtucket, R. I. Work-holder for metal-working machines. No. 1,327,799; Jan. 13; v. 270; p. 233.

Beede, Neal M., assignor to A. R. Brewster, Boston, Mass. Glass-washing apparatus. No. 1,328,360; Jan. 20; v. 270; p. 376.

Beesley, Frank M. (See Lockhart and Ord, assignors.)

Beighlee, Henry E., assignor, by mesne assignments, to The Cleveland Instrument Company, Cleveland, Ohio. Compensating pyrometer system and apparatus. No. 1,327,800; Jan. 13; v. 270; p. 233.

Beinhart, Ernest G., Washington, D. C. Curing tobacco. No. 1,327,692; Jan. 13; v. 270; p. 213.

Belcher, Leon K., New York, N. Y. Heat-distributer. No. 1,326,904; Jan. 6; v. 270; p. 4.

Belding, Harlow H., West Chicago, Ill. Laundry-wringer. No. 1,328,361; Jan. 20; v. 270; p. 376.

Belrose, Thomas H. (See Funk, James M., assignor.)

Bemisderfer, Harvey O., Fostoria, Ohio, assignor to Central Railway Signal Company, Pittsburgh, Pa. Bonnet for railway - signal fusee - caps and making it. No. 1,327,899 ; Jan. 13 ; v. 270 ; p. 252.

Bender, David G., Blue Island, Ill. Wall construction. No. 1,327,584 ; Jan. 6 ; v. 270 ; p. 132.

Bendix, Vincent, Chicago, Ill. Engine-starter. No. 1,327,132 ; Jan. 6 ; v. 270 ; p. 47.

Bendix, Vincent, Chicago, Ill. Engine-starter. No. 1,327,302 ; Jan. 6 ; v. 270 ; p. 79.

Bendix, Vincent, Chicago, Ill. Engine-starter. No. 1,327,303 ; Jan. 6 ; v. 270 ; p. 79.

Bendix, Vincent, Chicago, Ill. Engine-starter. No. 1,327,304 ; Jan. 6 ; v. 270 ; p. 79.

Benedict, Henry I., New Orleans, La. Jack-base. No. 1,328,115 ; Jan. 13 ; v. 270 ; p. 292.

Benjamin, Bert R., and C. A. Hagadone, Oak Park, Ill., assignors, by mesne assignments, to International Harvester Company. Pivoted discharge-arm. No. 1,327,305 ; Jan. 6 ; v. 270 ; p. 79.

Benjamin, Bert R., Oak Park, Ill., assignor, by mesne assignments, to International Harvester Company. Bundle-carrier for harvesters. No. 1,328,781 ; Jan. 20 ; v. 270 ; p. 454.

Benjamin, Dana H., Cleveland Heights, assignor to The American Laundry Machinery Company, Cincinnati, Ohio. Pressing-machine. No. 1,327,976 ; Jan. 13 ; v. 270 ; p. 266.

Benjamin, Edward O., Newark, N. J. Closure and tap for tanks, &c. No. 1,328,980 ; Jan. 27 ; v. 270 ; p. 522.

Benjamin, Edward O., Newark, N. J. Electrolytic apparatus. No. 1,328,981 ; Jan. 27 ; v. 270 ; p. 522.

Benjamin Electric Manufacturing Company. (See Benjamin, Reuben B., assignor.)

Benjamin Electric Manufacturing Company. (See Benjamin and Anderson, assignors.)

Benjamin Electric Manufacturing Company. (See Curless, James M., assignor.)

Benjamin Electric Manufacturing Company. (See Tregoning, William C., assignor.)

Benjamin, Reuben B., assignor to Benjamin Electric Manufacturing Company, Chicago, Ill. Receptacle. No. 1,328,224 ; Jan. 13 ; v. 270 ; p. 313.

Benjamin, Reuben B., assignor to Benjamin Electric Manufacturing Company, Chicago, Ill. Fuse-plug. No. 1,328,782 ; Jan. 20 ; v. 270 ; p. 454.

Benjamin, Reuben B., assignor to Benjamin Electric Manufacturing Company, Chicago, Ill. Attachment-plug. No. 1,328,783 ; Jan. 20 ; v. 270 ; p. 454.

Benjamin, Reuben B., and E. G. K. Anderson, assignors to Benjamin Electric Manufacturing Company, Chicago, Ill. Binding terminal. No. 1,328,784 ; Jan. 20 ; v. 270 ; p. 455.

Benjamin, Reuben B., assignor to Benjamin Electric Manufacturing Company, Chicago, Ill. Electrical receptacle. No. 1,328,785 ; Jan. 20 ; v. 270 ; p. 455.

Bennett, Andrew P. (See Parsons, Cook, and Bennett.)

Bennett, Ashley C., Minneapolis, Minn. Explosive-engine. No. 1,328,484 ; Jan. 20 ; v. 270 ; p. 399.

Bennett, Edward O., Oakland, Calif., assignor of fifty per cent to H. Ruhl, San Francisco, Calif., and Chicago, Ill. Key-lock. No. 1,328,074 ; Jan. 13 ; v. 270 ; p. 285.

Bennett, Samuel. (See Calow, Stanley C., assignor.)

Bennington, Wesley H., Cleveland, Ohio. Phonograph-cabinet. No. 1,327,977 ; Jan. 13 ; v. 270 ; p. 266.

Benton, Henry, Elizabeth, N. J. Furnace. No. 1,328,116 ; Jan. 13 ; v. 270 ; p. 293.

Benton, Hans J., Winthrop Harbor, assignor to F. C. Austin, Chicago, Ill. Trenching-machine. No. 1,327,418 ; Jan. 6 ; v. 270 ; p. 100.

Berg, Louis H. (See Marburger and Berg.)

Berger, Isidore S., New York, N. Y. Tooth-shade guide. No. 1,327,306 ; Jan. 6 ; v. 270 ; p. 79.

Berger, Joseph, Utica, N. Y., assignor to Union Special Machine Company, Chicago, Ill. Sewing - machine. No. 1,329,221 ; Jan. 27 ; v. 270 ; p. 567.

Berghaus, John H., Jr. (See Lamkin and Berghaus.)

Bernier, Henry N., Iroquois Falls, Ontario, assignor of one-half to J. De Froy, Timmins, Canada. Lamp-burner. No. 1,329,222 ; Jan. 27 ; v. 270 ; p. 567.

Berry, Edward R., Malden, Mass., assignor to General Electric Company. Explosion-arrester. No. 1,328,485 ; Jan. 20 ; v. 270 ; p. 400.

Berry, Ora, Princeton, Ind. Automatic pump. No. 1,327,371 ; Jan. 6 ; v. 270 ; p. 91.

Berthelote, Joseph T., Havre, Mont. Animal-exterminator. No. 1,328,117 ; Jan. 13 ; v. 270 ; p. 293.

Beshenich, Matija, Beatty, assignor of one-fourth to J. Throdor and one-fourth to M. Mohanec, Greensburg, Pa. Non-refillable bottle. No. 1,327,133 ; Jan. 6 ; v. 270 ; p. 47.

Bessière, Gustave, Neuilly-sur-Seine, France. Projectile. No. 1,327,372 ; Jan. 6 ; v. 270 ; p. 91.

Bethlehem Shipbuilding Corporation, Ltd. (See Essner, Eugene F., assignor.)

Bethlehem Steel Company. (See Lukens, William L., assignor.)

Betts, Arthur L. (See Davis and Betts.)

Beugler, Chas. E., et al. (See Coates, Frank E., assignor.)

Bevier, Henry R., assignor to Johnson Automatic Sealer Co., Ltd., Battle Creek, Mich. Wrapping-machine. No. 1,329,069 ; Jan. 27 ; v. 270 ; p. 588.

Bevin, William S. H., and J. S. Rawsthorne, Liverpool, England. Mixing apparatus for granular, powdered, or like material. No. 1,328,486 ; Jan. 20 ; v. 270 ; p. 400.

Bewan, James O., Roanoke, Ala. Thermos-tank and valve therefor. No. 1,327,693 ; Jan. 13 ; v. 270 ; p. 213.

Biagini, Ray. (See Di Grazia and Biakini.)

Bigoney, Thomas W., New York, N. Y. Container and making same. No. 1,327,190 ; Jan. 6 ; v. 270 ; p. 58.

Bilderback, Bart, Rockville, Ind. Metallic smokehouse. No. 1,327,937 ; Jan. 13 ; v. 270 ; p. 258.

Billings, Frank, Cleveland, Ohio. Mine-loading machine. No. 1,328,487 ; Jan. 20 ; v. 270 ; p. 400.

Billow, Milton O., Harrisburg, Pa. Class record-book. No. 1,327,610 ; Jan. 13 ; v. 270 ; p. 198.

Billson, Edward F. (See Lippincott and Billson.) (Re-issue.)

Binder, Richard L., Philadelphia, Pa. Chain. No. 1,329,034 ; Jan. 27 ; v. 270 ; p. 532.

Birch, Joseph F., Jr., assignor to Musher and Company, Inc., Baltimore, Md. Fish-cleaning machine. No. 1,326,905 ; Jan. 6 ; v. 270 ; p. 4.

Birchard, Eslie R., Toronto, Ontario, Canada, assignor to The Department of Soldiers Civil Re-Establishment, Invalided Soldiers' Commission of The Dominion of Canada. Artificial arm. No. 1,327,938 ; Jan. 13 ; v. 270 ; p. 259.

Bird, Charles S. (See Cowan, Clarence P., assignor.)

Birkigt, Marc, Bois-Colombes, France. Mechanism for synchronizing machine-gun fire. No. 1,328,811 ; Jan. 27 ; v. 270 ; p. 488.

Bissinger, John B., Jr., Lancaster, Pa. Means for carrying out systems for savings-accounts. No. 1,329,106 ; Jan. 27 ; v. 270 ; p. 545.

Bitler, Frederic C., Brooklyn, N. Y., assignor of one-half to L. V. Jones, Norwalk, Conn. Bottle-stopper. No. 1,327,519 ; Jan. 6 ; v. 270 ; p. 119.

Bixby, Allan S., Indianapolis, Ind., assignor to The National Malleable Castings Company, Cleveland, Ohio. Molding-machine. No. 1,327,419 ; Jan. 6 ; v. 270 ; p. 100.

Blache, Hans H., Copenhagen, Denmark. Scraper-ring for scraping oil from cylinders, piston-rods, or the like. No. 1,327,801 ; Jan. 13 ; v. 270 ; p. 234.

Black, Mathew, Brooklyn, N. Y. Beverage-mixer. No. 1,327,900 ; Jan. 13 ; v. 270 ; p. 252.

Blackburn, Arthur H., Downers Grove, and F. E. Fleming, assignors to The Underfeed Stoker Company of America, Chicago, Ill. The Underfeed furnace. No. 1,326,906 ; Jan. 6 ; v. 270 ; p. 4.

Blackburn, Harold, Doncaster, England. Parachute. No. 1,328,413 ; Jan. 20 ; v. 270 ; p. 386.

Blacker, William, Stalybridge, England. Machine or apparatus for breaking up or pulverizing caustic soda and the like. No. 1,327,901 ; Jan. 13 ; v. 270 ; p. 252.

Blackmer Rotary Pump Co. (See Oldham, John H., assignor.)

Blackstone Manufacturing Company. (See More, Glenn, assignor.)

Blaisdell, Sidney S. (See Cook and Blaisdell.)

Blake, C. C., Incorporated. (See Foster, Edward E., assignor.)

Blake, John R., Rolling Prairie, Ind. Shock-absorber. No. 1,328,812 ; Jan. 27 ; v. 270 ; p. 489.

Blake, William F., assignor of fifty-one per cent. to H. W. Duvendack, Toledo, Ohio. Can-opener. No. 1,327,184 ; Jan. 6 ; v. 270 ; p. 48.

Blakely, William W., Detroit, Mich. Manufacturing securing devices. No. 1,327,852 ; Jan. 13 ; v. 270 ; p. 243.

Blakemore, James R., assignor to G. B. Sawyer, Murfreesboro, Tenn. Egg-tester. No. 1,329,223 ; Jan. 27 ; v. 270 ; p. 567.

Blanfield, Charles, Boston, Mass. Pistol-light. No. 1,327,585 ; Jan. .6 ; v. 270 ; p. 132.

Blanchard, Herbert C., assignor to The A. I. Root Company, Medina, Ohio. Honeycomb-foundation machine. No. 1,328,813 ; Jan. 27 ; v. 270 ; p. 489.

Blankenburg, Wilhelm A. C., Amsterdam, Netherlands. Machine with rotary and self-controlling cylinders. No. 1,328,261 ; Jan. 20 ; v. 270 ; p. 356.

Blardone, George, New Orleans, La. Regeneration of decolorizing-carbons. No. 1,327,222 ; Jan. 6 ; v. 270 ; p. 65.

Blasdale, Frederick W. (See Muschenheim and Blasdale.)

Blast, Joseph, Brooklyn, N. Y., assignor to the Singer Manufacturing Company. Sewing on garment-hooks. No. 1,327,191 ; Jan. 6 ; v. 270 ; p. 59.

Blessmeyer, Fred D., Pittsburgh, Pa. Stabilizing device. No. 1,327,586 ; Jan. 6 ; v. 270 ; p. 132.

Blettner, George H., Chicago, Ill. Making piston-rings. No. 1,328,414 ; Jan. 20 ; v. 270 ; p. 386.

Bliss, John, London, England. Key-operated rotatable part of valves, faucets, locking devices, or other articles. No. 1,327,587 ; Jan. 6 ; v. 270 ; p. 132.

Bliss, William L., assignor to U. S. Light & Heat Corporation, Niagara Falls, N. Y. Rheostat. No. 1,327,185 ; Jan. 6 ; v. 270 ; p. 48.

Bloch, Flora W., Milwaukee, Wis. Coating composition for kitchen utensils. No. 1,328,556 ; Jan. 20 ; v. 270 ; p. 413.

Blondeau, Eugene H., Marquette, Mich. Horseshoe. No. 1,328,708 ; Jan. 20 ; v. 270 ; p. 440.

Blood, Burr B., assignor of one-half to G. Heidman and N. A. Street, Chicago, Ill. Cover-support. No. 1,327,978; Jan. 13; v. 270; p.266.

Bloom, Randolph, Germantown, N. Y. Horseshoe-calk. No. 1,327,853; Jan. 13; v. 270; p. 243.

Bludworth, William D., Fairoaks, Calif. Gold-saving device. No. 1,327,854; Jan. 13; v. 270; p. 243.

Blye, Harold, assignor to National Brass Company, Grand Rapids, Mich. Hasp-staple. No. 1,327,694; Jan. 13; v. 270; p. 214.

Blye, Harold, assignor to National Brass Company, Grand Rapids, Mich. Latch set. No. 1,327,695; Jan. 13; v. 270; p. 214.

Boardman, C. H., et al. (See Coates, Frank E., assignor.)

Bobroff, Bornett L., assignor, by mesne assignments, to E. Dillmann and H. J. Turck, trustees, Milwaukee, Wis. Indicating device for voting-machines. No. 1,328,613; Jan. 20; v. 270; p. 423.

Bobst, Charles A., Brooklyn, assignor to National Binding Machine Company, New York, N. Y. Label-detaching device. No. 1,328,814; Jan. 27; v. 270; p. 489.

Boedicker, Herman C., Minneapolis, Minn. Combination-machine for making photoprints on printing-plates by direct contact or projection printing. No. 1,327,752; Jan. 13; v. 270; p. 225.

Boehmig, Edwin C., Hammond, Ind. Lock for automobiles. No. 1,327,979; Jan. 13; v. 270; p. 267.

Böhn, Ingebret, Sörumsanden, Norway. Tunneling-machine. No. 1,328,118; Jan. 13; v. 270; p. 293.

Boles, Clarence, Hugoton, Kans. Leaf-spring. No. 1,327,016; Jan. 6; v. 270; p. 26.

Bolthoff, Henry, Denver, Colo. Concentrator. No. 1,327,902; Jan. 13; v. 270; p. 252.

Bolton, James, Council Bluffs, Iowa. Road-maintainer. No. 1,328,910; Jan. 27; v. 270; p. 509.

Boltshauser, Conrad, assignor to Company Phoebus, E. G., Zurich, Switzerland. Electric pocket - lamp. No. 1,327,017; Jan. 6; v. 270; p. 26.

Bombardie, Charles H., South Bend, Ind., assignor to Wirebounds Patents Company, Kittery, Me. Box. No. 1,329,332; Jan. 27; v. 270; p. 586.

Bombardie, Charles H., South Bend, Ind., assignor to Wirebounds Patents Company, Kittery, Me. Box. No. 1,329,333; Jan. 27; v. 270; p. 586.

Bond, James W., Columbia, S. C. Rim-tool. No. 1,326,907; Jan. 6; v. 270; p. 4.

Boosey, Edward W., Detroit, Mich. Cover for floor-sumps. No. 1,328,262; Jan. 20; v. 270; p. 356.

Booth, Augustus C., Los Angeles, Calif. Vertically-adjustable engine-lathe. No. 1,327,604; Jan. 6; v. 270; p. 135.

Booth, William N., Detroit, Mich. Trailer draft connection. No. 1,327,265; Jan. 6; v. 270; p. 72.

Booth, William S., Owosso, Mich. Automobile-bumper. No. 1,328,786; Jan. 20; v. 270; p. 455.

Boozer, Arthur G., Providence, R. I., assignor of one-half to G. Hill, Tucapau, S. C. Stripping mechanism for carding-machines. No. 1,327,696; Jan. 13; v. 270; p. 214.

Borchert, Ralph W., St. Louis, Mo. Marine-motor attachment. No. 1,328,313; Jan. 20; v. 270; p. 367.

Bordeaux, Pearl, Mount Desert, Me. Device for removing valves and their seats or cages. No. 1,328,362; Jan. 20; v. 270; p. 376.

Borener, Albert J., Chicago, Ill. Oil-burning furnace. No. 1,328,075; Jan. 13; v. 270; p. 285.

Borgarello, Octavio E., Buenos Aires, Argentina. Machine for securing the felts to piano-hammers. No. 1,327,018; Jan. 6; v. 270; p. 27.

Borglin, Hans W., Streator, Ill. Pencil attachment. No. 1,328,076; Jan. 13; v. 270; p. 285.

Borst, William E., and C. C. Gilleo, Grand Rapids, Mich. Crucible-mouthpiece for linotype-machines. No. 1,327,697; Jan. 13; v. 270; p. 214.

Bosch, Robert, Aktiengesellschaft. (See Kratz, Franz, assignor.)

Boston Pressed Metal Co. (See Needham, William H., assignor.)

Both, Tonjes A., Stratford, Conn., assignor to The Connecticut Electric Manufacturing Company. Mechanical movement. No. 1,327,192; Jan. 6; v. 270; p. 59.

Boulton, William W. (See McClure and Boulton.)

Bowden, George, Malden, Mass. End-gate fastener. No. 1,327,079; Jan. 6; v. 270; p. 38.

Bowden, Junius A., Los Angeles, Calif. Dust-cap and attaching means therefor. No. 1,328,488; Jan. 20; v. 270; p. 400.

Bowden, Junius A., Los Angeles, Calif. Dust-cap and attaching means therefor. No. 1,328,801; Jan. 20; v. 270; p. 468.

Bowen, Charles, assignor of one-third to F. Gaskins and one-third to A. G. Niebergall, Fort Wayne, Ind. Bumper for automobiles. No. 1,329,334; Jan. 27; v. 270; p. 586.

Bowles, John A., Richmond, Va. Locomotive-driving-box lubricator. No. 1,327,186; Jan. 6; v. 270; p. 48.

Bowman, George. (See Graham and Bowman.)

Bowman, James W., Morley, Mo. Harrow. No. 1,328,363; Jan. 20; v. 270; p. 376.

Bowerman, Joseph A., assignor to The Fiske Rubber Company, Chicopee Falls, Mass. Method and apparatus for manufacture of tires. No. 1,327,802; Jan. 13; v. 270; p. 234.

Bowness, George A. (See Jardine, Dickie, and Bowness.)

Boyd, Alexander J. (See Smith, John F., assignor.)

Boyd, David C. (See Arndt, Franklin E., assignor.)

Boyer, Lewis E., Easton, Pa., assignor to Ingersoll-Rand Company, Jersey City, N. J. Method of and apparatus for forming rifled bores in metal. No. 1,328,077; Jan. 13; v. 270; p. 285.

Boylan, Samuel H., Joplin, Mo. Classifier. No. 1,326,908; Jan. 6; v. 270; p. 4.

Boyle, Louis M., Los Angeles, Calif. Supply outfit for vehicles, &c. No. 1,327,223; Jan. 6; v. 270; p. 65.

Boyle, William P., Springfield, Mass. Burner for gas-furnaces. No. 1,328,225; Jan. 13; v. 270; p. 314.

Bozard, Harrison B., Hamilton, Ontario, Canada, assignor to International Harvester Company of Canada, Limited. Steel bearing for disks. No. 1,328,787; Jan. 20; v. 270; p. 455.

Brady, Clyde E., Pineblaff, Wyo. Grain-separator. No. 1,327,193; Jan. 6; v. 270; p. 59.

Braden, Albert R., Beverly, Mass., assignor to United Shoe Machinery Corporation, Paterson, N. J. Die and joining its ends. No. 1,327,652; Jan. 13; v. 270; p. 205.

Bradley, George M., Lansing, Mich. Auto burglar-alarm. No. 1,327,266; Jan. 6; v. 270; p. 72.

Bradley, John M., and C. F. Pike, Philadelphia, Pa., assignors to The Safety Eyeglass Company, Wilmington, Del. Eyeglass-case. No. 1,328,644; Jan. 20; v. 270; p. 429.

Bradley, John M., and C. F. Pike, Philadelphia, Pa., assignors to The Safety Eyeglass Company, Wilmington, Del. Eyeglass-case. No. 1,328,645; Jan. 20; v. 270; p. 429.

Bradley, John M., and C. F. Pike, Philadelphia, Pa., assignors to The Safety Eyeglass Company, Wilmington, Del. Eyeglass-case. No. 1,328,646; Jan. 20; v. 270; p. 429.

Brady, Francis M. (See Richard and Brady.)

Braly, Norman B., Butte, Mont. Record-card. No. 1,327,855; Jan. 13; v. 270; p. 243.

Brandenstein, Daniel, New York, N. Y., and J. Fischer, Roseville, N. J. Pedal-operated mechanism. No. 1,327,187; Jan. 6; v. 270; p. 48.

Branson, Samuel J., Chicago, Ill., and E. C. Strathmann, assignors to The Concrete Forms Company, Indianapolis, Ind. False work for concrete floors. No. 1,327,081; Jan. 6; v. 270; p. 38.

Bray, Michael J., Upland, Pa. Splicing-thimble. No. 1,327,856; Jan. 13; v. 270; p. 244.

Bray, Nelson H., San Francisco, Calif. Automatic igniter for orchard-heaters. No. 1,328,788; Jan. 20; v. 270; p. 455.

Brauer, Otto M., Gothenburg, Nebr. Toy car. No. 1,328,557; Jan. 20; v. 270; p. 418.

Brayman, Louis M., Westville, N. H. Mixer. No. 1,328,119; Jan. 13; v. 270; p. 293.

Brazil, David H., Montgomery, Ala. Fluid - fuel burner. No. 1,329,224; Jan. 27; v. 270; p. 567.

Brennan, John S., Milwaukee, Wis. Means for lifting burner-drums. No. 1,327,857; Jan. 13; v. 270; p. 244.

Brennan, John S., Milwaukee, Wis. Wick. No. 1,327,858; Jan. 13; v. 270; p. 244.

Brenner, Ralph F. (See Scholes and Brenner.)

Bressler, Robert E., Hammond, assignor to O. F. Jordan Company, East Chicago, Ind. Railway way construction and maintenance car. No. 1,328,489; Jan. 20; v. 270; p. 400.

Brewer, Griffith, London, England. Adjustable dial for pressure-gages and like dial instruments. No. 1,328,941; Jan. 27; v. 270; p. 515.

Brewster, Albert R. (See Reede, Neal M., assignor.)

Brewster, Leon B., and F. Weisehan, assignors to The Ferro Machine and Foundry Company, Cleveland, Ohio. Welding. No. 1,327,267; Jan. 6; v. 270; p. 73.

Bricker, Grace L., Anderson, Ind. Combination comb and brush. No. 1,328,120; Jan. 13; v. 270; p. 293.

Bridgeport Brass Company. (See Clark, Walter R., assignor.)

Bright, Fred E., Philadelphia, Pa. Chuck. No. 1,327,194; Jan. 6; v. 270; p. 59.

Brightman, Joseph F., Syracuse, N. Y. Steam-trap. No. 1,327,939; Jan. 13; v. 270; p. 259.

Brinkhaus, Hugo, Brooklyn, N. Y. Hair-dressing device. No. 1,327,980; Jan. 13; v. 270; p. 267.

Brinkman, Louis H., Glen Ridge, N. J., assignor to Titeflex Metal Hose Corporation. Tube. No. 1,327,195; Jan. 6; v. 270; p. 59.

British Ever Ready Company, The. (See Dewick and Caddy, assignors.)

British Westinghouse Electric and Manufacturing Company. (See Scanes, Arthur E. L., assignor.)

Britton, Coozie, Moline, Ill. Educational playing-cards. No. 1,327,019; Jan. 6; v. 270; p. 27.

Britz, John S., Port Huron, Mich. Stamp-canceler and fountain-brush. No. 1,328,031; Jan. 13; v. 270; p. 276.

Brock, Matthias, Boston, Mass., assignor, by mesne assignments, to United Shoe Machinery Corporation, Paterson, N. J. Staple-lasting machine. No. 1,327,196; Jan. 6; v. 270; p. 59.

Brock, Matthias, Boston, Mass., assignor, by mesne assignments, to United Shoe Machinery Corporation, Paterson, N. J. Working uppers over lasts. No. 1,328,314; Jan. 20; v. 270; p. 367.

Brockett, Bluford W., Cleveland, Ohio. Cooling-system control. No. 1,328,815; Jan. 27; v. 270; p. 489.

Butterfield, Percy F., Toronto, Ontario, Canada. Nail. No. 1,326,910; Jan. 6; v. 270; p. 5.

Butters Camp Mfg. Co., The. (See Butters, Robert H., assignor.)

Butters, Robert H., Atlanta, Ga., assignor to The Butters Camp Mfg. Co. Machine for forming or renewing and sharpening the teeth of gin or linter saws. No. 1,329,036; Jan. 27; v. 270; p. 532.

Byers, Joseph J., Brookline, assignor to Products Syndicate Inc., Boston, Mass. Material treated with cellulose derivatives. No. 1,327,197; Jan. 6; v. 270; p. 60.

Byron Jackson Iron Works, Inc. (See Paulsmeier, Albert C., assignor.)

Cabot, Godfrey L., Boston, Mass. Supply means for aircraft. No. 1,328,560; Jan. 20; v. 270; p. 214.

Caddy, Donald B. (See Dewick and Caddy.)

Cade, Charles W., Bellevue, assignor to McKinney Manufacturing Company, Pittsburgh, Pa. Door-holder. No. 1,327,754; Jan. 13; v. 270; p. 225.

Calkins, Bert L., Detroit, Mich. Hacksaw - blade. No. 1,328,982; Jan. 27; v. 270; p. 522.

Calkins, Herbert V., Longmont, Colo. Agricultural implement. No. 1,328,124; Jan. 13; v. 270; p. 294.

Call, Franklin H., Portland, Oreg. Cabinet for phonographic records. No. 1,327,142; Jan. 6; v. 270; p. 49.

Call, Franklin H., Portland, Oreg. Cabinet for phonographic records. No. 1,327,143; Jan. 6; v. 270; p. 49.

Callender, Romaine, Philadelphia, Pa., assignor to The Aeolian Company. Music-sheet. No. 1,329,286; Jan. 27; v. 270; p. 578.

Callow, John M., Salt Lake City, Utah, assignor, by mesne assignments, to Pneumatic Process Flotation Company, New York, N. Y. Method of and apparatus for concentrating ores. No. 1,329,335; Jan. 27; v. 270; p 587.

Calow, Stanley C., assignor of one-half to S. Bennett, Calgary, Alberta, Canada. Incubator. No. 1,328,032; Jan. 13; v. 270; p. 277.

Camelinat, Eugene G., Birmingham, England. Means for supporting lamps. No. 1,328,125; Jan. 13; v. 270; p. 294.

Cameron, William W., assignor of one-half to H. J. Hirshheimer, La Crosse, Wis. Luggage - carrier. No. 1,328,316; Jan. 20; v. 270; p. 367.

Camp, Ernest. San Diego, Calif. Mixer for gaseous fuel. No. 1,327,699; Jan. 13; v. 270; p. 214.

Camp. Harriette M., Boston, Mass. Cabinet-couch. No. 1,327,941; Jan. 13; v. 270; p. 259.

Campbell, Donald F. (See Gow and Campbell.)

Campbell, Frank M., South Bend, Wash. Brake. No. 1,328,491; Jan. 20; v. 270; p 401.

Campbell, Robert E., Berkeley, Calif. Valve. No. 1,327,984; Jan. 13; v. 270; p. 267.

Campbell, Wilson L., Chicago, Ill., assignor, by mesne assignments, to Automatic Electric Company. Automatic party-line telephone system. No. 1,329,287; Jan. 27; v. 270; p. 579.

Carbon Destroyer Corporation. (See Millard, William, assignor.)

Carborundum Company, The. (See MacGregor, William, assignor.)

Carden, Luther W., Cherokee, Ala. Nut-lock. No. 1,327,373; Jan. 6; v. 270; p. 92.

Carl, Reinhold A., Elgin, Tex. Combination-flue. No. 1,328,647; Jan. 20; v. 270; p. 430.

Carlson, C. A., administrator. (See Carlson, John A.)

Carlson, Charles G., Chicago, Ill. Clothespole. No. 1,326,911; Jan. 6; v. 270; p. 5.

Carlson, Emilia A. (See Carlson, John A., assignor.)

Carlson, John A., deceased; C. A. Carlson, administrator, assignor to E. A. Carlson, Idaho Falls, Idaho. Linesquare. No. 1,327,198; Jan. 6; v. 270; p. 60.

Carlson, Oscar B., Mänsbo, Avesta, assignor to Aktiebolaget Carlit, Stockholm, Sweden. Ammonium perchlorate explosive. No. 1,327,985; Jan. 13; v. 270; p. 268.

Carman, Frank V., Oakland, Calif. Work-holding cradle for spike-hole-plug machine. No. 1,328,492; Jan. 20; v. 270; p. 401.

Carney, James A., Aurora, Ill. Hand-brake-operating mechanism. No. 1,328,493; Jan. 20; v. 270; p. 401.

Carney, James A., Aurora, Ill. Brake-operating mechanism. No. 1,328,494; Jan. 20; v. 270; p. 401.

Carney, Joseph, assignor to Paragon Binder Corporation, Newark, N. J. Loose-leaf binder. No. 1,328,561; Jan. 20; v. 270; p. 414.

Carney, Wilbur O. (See Lingle, George W., assignor.)

Carpenter, Francis W., Greenwich, Conn. Feed - holder. No. 1,329,288; Jan. 27; v. 270; p. 579.

Carpenter, Henry W., Key West. Fla., assignor, by mesne assignments, to P. Wilson. Spark-plug. No. 1,329,320; Jan. 27; v. 270; p. 584.

Carr, Charles B., New York, N. Y. Game device. No. 1,328,711; Jan. 20; v. 270; p. 441.

Carr, Oma, New York, N. Y. Tube suspension. No. 1,327,144; Jan. 6; v. 270; p. 50.

Carroll, Basil M., Rising Star, Tex. Snap - hook. No. 1,329,071; Jan. 27; v. 270; p. 539.

Carson, Alexander A., Braintree, Mass. Flushing-valve. No. 1,329,109; Jan. 27; v. 270; p. 546.

Carson, Wilfred P., Greensboro, Calif. Attachment for grain or grist mills. No. 1,327,700; Jan. 13; v. 270; p. 215.

Carswell, William W., et al. (See Golata and Roberts, assignors.)

Carter, Charlie O., Anderson, assignor to Draper Corporation, Hopedale, Mass. Tension for spoolers. No. 1,327,022; Jan. 6; v. 270; p. 27.

Carter, Clarence W., Minneapolis, Minn. Machine for separating wild peas from wheat, &c. No. 1,328,819; Jan. 27; v. 270; p. 490.

Carter, Douglass R., Washington, D. C. Demountable rim. No. 1,329,289; Jan. 27; v. 270; p. 579.

Carter, Horace J., and C. Taylor, Wilmington, Del. Piling-machine. No. 1,328,615; Jan. 20; v. 270; p. 424.

Carter, John T., Jefferson City, Mo. Dish-washing device. No. 1,328,942; Jan. 27; v. 270; p. 515.

Carter, William C., Radnor, assignor to The Goodyear Tire & Rubber Company, Akron, Ohio. Treating fabric. No. 1,327,904; Jan. 13; v. 270; p. 253.

Carvalho, Leslie R. N., et al. (See Russell, Robert A., assignor.)

Cary, Spencer C., Brooklyn, N. Y. Welding. No. 1,326,912; Jan. 6; v. 270; p. 5.

Cary, Spencer C., Brooklyn, N. Y. Means for cleaning metal preparatory to welding. No. 1,326,913; Jan. 6; v. 270; p. 5.

Cary, Spencer C., Brooklyn, N. Y. Divergent saw-tooth fastener. No. 1,328,911; Jan. 27; v. 270; p. 509.

Cassidy, Wade L., Hamlet, N. C. Automatic railway-gate. No. 1,327,860; Jan. 13; v. 270; p. 244.

Cassingham, John R., and W. W. Ayres, assignors of one-half to H. W. Morrison and J. W. Morrison, Oklahoma, Okla. Auto-fuel-supply lock. No. 1,328,616; Jan. 20; v. 270; p. 424.

Cater, Theodore T., Aurora, Mo. Electric controller. No. 1,328,126; Jan. 13; v. 270; p. 295.

Caunt, Hubert, East Calgary, Alberta, Canada. Internal-combustion engine. No. 1,328,265; Jan. 20; v. 270; p. 357.

Cavanagh, John F., assignor to The Connecticut Telephone & Electric Company, Inc., Meriden, Conn. Electric switch. No. 1,328,562; Jan. 20; v. 270; p. 414.

Celane, Jacob L., New York, N. Y. Folding chair. No. 1,329,261; Jan. 27; v. 270; p. 574.

Central Railway Signal Company. (See Bemisderfer, Harvey O., assignor.)

Cervenka, Frank L., Granger, Tex. Wire - straightening tool. No. 1,329,226; Jan. 27; v. 270; p. 568.

Cesar, Ervin N., Ponca City, Okla. Cranking mechanism for explosive-engines. No. 1,328,127; Jan. 13; v. 270; p 295.

Chagnon, Alexandre. (See Lafrance, Joseph, assignor.)

Challenge Refrigerator Company. (See Hillman, Herbert H., assignor.)

Chamberlain, Chauncey C., assignor to Ypsilanti Reed Furniture Company, Ionia. Mich. Cord-burnishing device. No. 1,328,943; Jan. 27; v. 270; p. 515.

Chamberlain, Rufus N., Chicago, Ill Separator. No. 1,328,420; Jan. 20; v. 270; p. 387.

Champion Engineering Company, The. (See Valls, Raphael W., assignor.)

Champlin, James M., South Coventry, Conn. Adjustable trestle. No. 1,329,290; Jan. 27; v. 270; p. 579.

Chapman. Otto. Mordialloc. Victoria, Australia. Game of skill. No. 1,329,291; Jan 27; v. 270; p. 579.

Charles, Mario C., Jersey City, N. J. Package-tie holder. No. 1,327,591; Jan. 6; v. 270; p. 133.

Charlton, Harry W. (See Meadows, Hauber, and Charlton.)

Charlton, Harry W., Jones Point, N. Y., assignor to American Potash Corporation. Cementing material obtained from greensand. No. 1,327,145; Jan. 6; v. 270; p. 50.

Charter. James A., Chicago, Ill. Wheel. No. 1,327,310; Jan. 6; v. 270; p. 80.

Chase, George C., Providence, R. I. Calculating-machine. No. 1,329,262; Jan. 27; v. 270; p. 575.

Chase. George L., Seattle, Wash. Engine. No. 1,328,033; Jan. 13; v. 270; p. 277.

Chase, Wallace S., Lakewood, Ohio, assignor, by mesne assignments, to National Carbon Company, Inc. Obtaining calcium-fluorid precipitate. No. 1,329,072; Jan. 27; v. 270; p. 539.

Chernack Manufacturing Company. (See Kennedy, Joseph A., assignor.)

Cherry, Louis B., Kansas City, Mo. Electrical apparatus for the electrochemical treatment of liquid hydrocarbon and other compounds. No. 1,327,023; Jan. 6; v. 270; p. 27.

Cheshire, Robert G., Birmingham, England. Hinge for trestles and the like. No. 1,327,808; Jan. 13; v. 270; p 235.

Chesnutt, Ralph C., Pottstown, Pa. Manifold for internal-combustion engines. No. 1,327,311; Jan. 6; v. 270; p. 80.

Chicago Manufacturing and Distributing Co. (See Buckius, Albert O., Jr., assignor.)

Chojnacki, Stephen. (See Korzeniewski and Chojnacki.)

Chojnacki, Leon, Vawn, Saskatchewan, Canada. Gate. No. 1,329,263; Jan. 27; v. 270; p. 575.

Christ, Benjamin F., Idagrove, Iowa. Watch-holder. No. 1,327,701; Jan. 13; v. 270; p. 215.

Christen, Victor H., Toledo, Ohio. Glass-cleaner. No. 1,327,146; Jan. 6; v. 270; p. 50.

Christensen, Harold G., New York, N. Y. Apparatus and process for producing motion-pictures. No. 1,328,266; Jan. 20; v. 270; p. 357.

Christenson, John O., Wilson, Fla. Combined shaving-brush and shaving-stick holder. No. 1,326,914; Jan. 6; v. 270; p. 6.

Cotoli, Antonio, Habana, Cuba. Method of and means for distributing pigments. No. 1,328,368 ; Jan. 20 ; v. 270 ; p. 377.

Cott-a-lap Co. (See Stirling, Charles P., assignor.)

Coulson, Edward, Lake Forest, Ill. Combined self-locking clip and shield. No. 1,328,422 ; Jan. 20 ; v. 270 ; p. 387.

Coultas, Fred, Bradford, and A. Pick, Eldwick, Bingley, England. Lifting apparatus for motor road-vehicles and the like. No. 1,327,905 ; Jan. 13 ; v. 270 ; p. 253.

Coulter, Holbrook W., trustee. (See Merritt, Frank W., assignor.)

Couse, Frederick A. (See Rosebourne and Couse.)

Cousino, Walter P., Curtice, Ohio. Spot-light-mounting device. No. 1,327,945 ; Jan. 13 ; v. 270 ; p. 260.

Covar, George P., Chester, S. C. Combined rolling-pin and culinary holder. No. 1,327,461 ; Jan. 6 ; v. 270 ; p. 108.

Cowan, Clarence P., Pont Rouge, Quebec, Canada, assignor to C. S. Bird, Walpole, Mass. Felt paper. No. 1,328,267 ; Jan. 20 ; v. 270 ; p. 358.

Cowan, Frank. (See Kellogg, Neff, Rogers, and Cowan.)

Cowan Truck Company. (See Hennessy, Daniel E., assignor.)

Cowles, Ida S., Waverly, Pa. Drawer or shelf lining. No. 1,327,755 ; Jan. 13 ; v. 270 ; p. 225.

Cox, Charles B., Jr., Stafford Springs, Conn. Self-feeder for Bock-cutters. No. 1,327,612 ; Jan. 13 ; v. 270 ; p. 198.

Cox, Charles D., Los Angeles, Calif. Pneumatic shock-absorber. No. 1,328,496 ; Jan. 20 ; v. 270 ; p. 402.

Cox, Ernest. (See Gower, Owen, and Cox.)

Coyle, Joseph L., Vancouver, British Columbia, assignor of one-fourth to F. D. Todd, Victoria, Canada. Egg-box. No. 1,327,946 ; Jan. 13 ; v. 270 ; p. 260.

Cramer, Stuart W., and W. B. Hodge, Charlotte, N. C., assignors to Parks-Cramer Company, Fitchburg, Mass. Hygrometer for regulating humidifying and heating systems. No 1,329,112 ; Jan. 27 ; v. 270 ; p. 546.

Cramer, William V. T., Cincinnati, Ohio. Roadway. No. 1,329,264 ; Jan. 27 ; v. 270 ; p. 575.

Crandall, Floyd A., Flint, Mich. Truck-body. No. 1,328,130 ; Jan. 13 ; v. 270 ; p. 295.

Crane, Samuel G., assignor to Toledo Scale Company, Toledo, Ohio. Automatic weighing-scale. No. 1,328,319 ; Jan. 20 ; v. 270 ; p. 368.

Crane, Samuel G., assignor to Toledo Scale Company, Toledo. Ohio. Electric automatic scale. No. 1,328,320 ; Jan. 20 ; v. 270 ; p. 368.

Crawford, Alex S., Cannonsville, N. Y. Horseshoe. No. 1,327,523 ; Jan. 6 ; v. 270 ; p. 120.

Crawford, George M., et al. (See London, Jacob M., assignor.)

Crecelius, Lawrence P., assignor to The Electric Railway Improvement Company, Cleveland, Ohio. System of bonding rails. No. 1,327,947 ; Jan. 13 ; v. 270 ; p. 260.

Crehan, Hubert, Pittsburgh, Pa. Bolt-threading machine. No. 1,327,312 ; Jan. 6 ; v. 270 ; p. 80.

Creveling, John L., White Plains, N. Y., assignor to Gould Coupler Company. Electric system. No. 1,328,321 ; Jan. 20 ; v. 270 ; p. 368.

Crombie, Louis A., Hicksville, N. Y. Wrench. No. 1,327,524 ; Jan. 6 ; v. 270 ; p. 120.

Crookshank, Samuel M. (See Dobson and Crookshank.)

Crosby, Kenneth W., trustee. (See Baker, Malcolm H., assignor.)

Cross, Andrew B., Denver, Colo. Apparatus for recovering gasoline from natural gases. No. 1,327,906 ; Jan. 13 ; v. 270 ; p. 253.

Cross, Otto J. (See Barbee and Cross.)

Cross Paper Feeder Company. (See Upham, Burt F., assignor.)

Crossen, Edgar H., Franklin, Pa. Piston for internal-combustion motors. No. 1,327,462 ; Jan. 6 ; v. 270 ; p. 108.

Crouse-Hinds Company. (See Schneider, August H., assignor.)

Crowley, Joseph P., Toledo, Ohio, assignor to The Libbey Owens Sheet Glass Company, Charleston, W. Va. Method of and apparatus for drawing continuous sheets of glass. No. 1,328,268 ; Jan. 20 ; v. 270 ; p. 358.

Crowther, Henry M., Kingman, Ariz. Aeroplane safety-parachute and means of launching same from aeroplanes. No. 1,327,592 ; Jan. 6 ; v. 270 ; p. 133.

Crozier, John A., Knoxville, Iowa. Window - bracket. No. 1,327,025 ; Jan. 6 ; v. 270 ; p. 28.

Cru Patents Corporation. (See Uebelmesser, Charles, assignor.)

Crummey, Frederick E., assignor to Bean Spray Pump Co., San Jose, Calif. Spray-gun. No. 1,328,721 ; Jan. 20 ; v 270 ; p. 443.

Cryder, Floyd E., Chicago, Ill. Milk-sterilizing apparatus. No. 1,328,722 ; Jan. 20 ; v. 270 ; p. 443.

Culling, Merritt A., assignor to Buffum Tool Company, Louisiana, Mo. Taper-turning tool. No. 1,329,065 ; Jan. 27 ; v. 270 ; p. 575.

Cullman, Otto, Chicago, Ill. Holder for phonographic disk records. No. 1,327,949 ; Jan. 13 ; v. 270 ; p. 261.

Cunliffe, Cicero M., assignor to American Blower Company, Detroit, Mich. Apparatus for treating painted or varnished articles. No. 1,327,313 ; Jan. 6 ; v. 270 ; p. 80.

Cunliffe, Cicero M., assignor to American Blower Company, Detroit, Mich. Treating painted or varnished articles. No. 1,327,314 ; Jan. 6 ; v. 270 ; p. 81.

Curless, James M., assignor to Benjamin Electric Manufacturing Company, Chicago, Ill. Electric heater. No. 1,328,723 ; Jan. 20 ; v. 270 ; p. 443.

Currie, Alfred C., St. John, New Brunswick, Canada. Game-board. No. 1,327,907 ; Jan. 13 ; v. 270 ; p. 253.

Currier, Howard S., Detroit, Mich. Transmission - lock. No. 1,328,724 ; Jan. 20 ; v. 270 ; p. 443.

Curtis, Walter L., Springfield, Mass. Die for making double-ended rivets. No. 1,327,525 ; Jan. 6 ; v. 270 ; p. 121.

Curtiss Aeroplane and Motor Corporation. (See Curtiss, Glenn H., assignor.)

Curtiss Aeroplane and Motor Corporation. (See Kleckler, Henry, assignor.)

Curtiss, Glenn H., Hammondsport, assignor, by mesne assignments, to Curtiss Aeroplane and Motor Corporation, Buffalo, N. Y. Lubricating system for traveling motors. No. 1,329,038 ; Jan. 27 ; v. 270 ; p. 532.

Curtiss, Glenn H., Buffalo, N. Y., assignor to Curtiss Aeroplane and Motor Corporation. Flying-boat hull. No. 1,329,336 ; Jan. 27 ; v. 270 ; p. 587.

Curttright, George L., Olin, Iowa. Hog-oiler. No. 1,327,088 ; Jan. 6 ; v. 270 ; p. 39.

Cushman, Edward L., Miami, Fla. Slug. No. 1,328,725 ; Jan. 20 ; v. 270 ; p. 444.

Cusick, Patrick H., Oregon, Wis. Radiator. No. 1,328,789 ; Jan. 20 ; v. 270 ; p. 456.

Cutler-Hammer Mfg. Co. (See Reisbach, Gustave B., assignor.)

Cutler-Hammer Mfg. Co., The. (See Stevens, William C., assignor.)

Cutler, William C., North Glendale, Calif. Card-receptacle. No. 1,328,035 ; Jan. 13 ; v. 270 ; p. 277.

Czicziriga, Szilard, Coatesville, Pa. Swimming apparatus. No. 1,329,073 ; Jan. 27 ; v. 270 ; p. 539.

Dabbs, Albert E., S. W. Savage, Manchester, and A. H. Hindle, Birmingham, assignors of one-eighth to A. Liddle, Manchester, and one-half to J. G. W. Gruban, Kingsway, London, England. Roller or ball bearing. No. 1,327,026 ; Jan. 6 ; v. 270 ; p. 28.

Daccord, Auguste, New York, N. Y. Bottle-closure. No. 1,327,899 ; Jan. 13 ; v. 270 ; p. 235.

Dalton Adding Machine Company. (See Dalton and Magnus, assignors.)

Dalton, James L., and J. Magnus, Poplar Bluff, assignors to Dalton Adding Machine Company, St. Louis, Mo. Adding and recording machine. No. 1,328,822 ; Jan. 27 ; v. 270 ; p. 491.

Damitz, Rinehold H., Kennedy, Minn. Milk-pail. No. 1,327,704 ; Jan. 13 ; v. 270 ; p. 215.

Damon, William H., Los Angeles, Calif. Automobile-lock. No. 1,328,619 ; Jan. 20 ; v. 270 ; p. 424.

Dansk Varmekedel Syndikat System Lange Fabrikant-Firma. (See Lange, Jens, assignor.)

Darby, James K., Chillicothe, Ohio. Press-roll arrangement for paper-making machines. No. 1,327,225 ; Jan. 6 ; v. 270 ; p. 65.

Darier, Georges E., Chêne, near Geneva, Switzerland. Gas and liquid contact apparatus. No. 1,327,422 ; Jan. 6 ; v. 270 ; p. 101.

Davenport, Eugene F., Melrose, Mass., assignor to United Shoe Machinery Corporation, Paterson, N. J. Skiving-machine. No. 1,329,294 ; Jan. 27 ; v. 270 ; p. 580.

Davenport Manufacturing Company. (See Hemsing, Maurice A., assignor.)

Davies, Daniel L., Pasadena, Calif. Waterproofing composition. No. 1,329,162 ; Jan. 27 ; v. 270 ; p. 556.

Davies, Evan W., Dowlais, Wales. Apparatus for manipulation of metal ingots and the like. No. 1,327,315 ; Jan. 6 ; v. 270 ; p. 81.

Davies, Llewelyn, Sisson, Calif. Wire-binding tool. No. 1,328,423 ; Jan. 20 ; v. 270 ; p. 387.

Davis, Augustine, assignor to Davis-Bournonville Company, New York, N. Y. Variable-pressure acetylene-generator. No. 1,328,227 ; Jan. 13 ; v. 270 ; p. 314.

Davis, Augustine, Jr., Covington, Ky., and A. L. Betts, Cincinnati, Ohio; said Betts assignor to said Davis. Mounting for vehicle-tanks. No. 1,329,039 ; Jan. 27 ; v. 270 ; p. 533.

Davis, Augustine, Jr., Covington, Ky. Manhole. No. 1,329,040 ; Jan. 27 ; v. 270 ; p. 533.

Davis, Benjamin W., Chicago, Ill. Signal system for controlling street traffic. No. 1,328,269 ; Jan. 20 ; v. 270 ; p. 358.

Davis-Bournonville Company. (See Davis, Augustine, assignor.)

Davis, Calvin R., assignor to Emerson & Brantingham Company, Rockford, Ill. Fertilizer-distributer. No. 1,327,654 ; Jan. 13 ; v. 270 ; p. 206.

Davis, Charles B., New York, N. Y. Mashing. No. 1,328,036 ; Jan. 13 ; v. 270 ; p. 286.

Davis, Claude B., Richmond, assignor of one-half to J. W. Keeling, Danville, Va. Wringer attachment for tubs. No. 1,327,526 ; Jan. 6 ; v. 270 ; p. 121.

Davis, Claude B., Richmond, assignor of one-half to J. W. Keeling, Danville, Va. Wringer attachment for tubs. No. 1,327,527 ; Jan. 6 ; v. 270 ; p. 121.

Davis, David J., Haverfordwest, Wales. Permutation-lock. No. 1,329,041 ; Jan. 27 ; v. 270 ; p. 533.

Davis, Earl J., Appleton, Wis. Railway-rail-securing device. No. 1,329,163 ; Jan. 27 ; v. 270 ; p. 556.

Davis, Frank B., Erie, Pa. Dental instrument. No. 1,328,131 ; Jan. 13 ; v. 270 ; p. 296.

Davis, George P., McIntosh, N. Mex. Pump-pipe lifter. No. 1,328,648 ; Jan. 20 ; v. 270 ; p. 430.

ALPHABETICAL LIST OF PATENTEES.

Davis, Harry W., Edgewood Park, Pa. Section-switch. No. 1,327,463; Jan. 6; v. 270; p. 108.
Davis, Howard C. (See Row and Davis.)
Davis, J. G. (See Wylie, Arthur E., assignor.)
Davis, Thomas A., San Antonio, Tex. Antifreezing appliance for water-pipes. No. 1,328,649; Jan. 20; v. 270; p. 430.
Dawkins, Stephen F., Fayette, Miss. Seed-pan. No. 1,329,266; Jan. 27; v. 270; p. 575.
Dawson, Alva K., Jacksonville, Fla. Combined headcovering and hair-comb. No. 1,327,528; Jan. 6; v. 270; p. 121.
Dawson, Arthur T., and G. T. Buckham, Westminster, London, assignors to Vickers Limited, Westminster, England. Gun-mounting. No. 1,327,084; Jan. 6; v. 270; p. 39.
Dawson, Arthur T., and G. T. Buckham, London, assignors to Vickers Limited, Westminster, England. Gun-mounting. No. 1,327,085; Jan. 6; v. 270; p. 39.
Dawson, Arthur T., and G. T. Buckham, London, assignors to Vickers Limited, Westminster, England. Machine-gun. No. 1,327,086; Jan. 6; v. 270; p. 39.
Dawson, Arthur T., and G. T. Buckham, London, assignors to Vickers Limited, Westminster, England. Breech-loading ordnance. No. 1,327,087; Jan. 6; v. 270; p. 39.
Dawson, Arthur T. and G. T. Buckham, assignors to Vickers Limited, Westminster, London, England. Ordnance-sighting apparatus. No. 1,328,914; Jan. 27; v. 270; p. 509.
Dayton Engineering Laboratories Company, The. (See Hans, Nelson R., assignor.)
Dayton Engineering Laboratories Company, The. (See Midgley, Thomas, Jr., assignor.)
Deak, Alexander and J. Brooklyn, N. Y. Aerial vessel. No. 1,327,529; Jan. 6; v. 270; p. 121.
Deak, Joseph. (See Deak, Alexander and J.)
Dean, James H., assignor to Cole Manufacturing Company, Chicago, Ill. Draft attachment for stoves. No. 1,327,988; Jan. 13; v. 270; p. 268.
Dean, John S., Winkinsburg, Pa., assignor to Westinghouse Electric and Manufacturing Company. Commutator-cylinder. No. 1,329,267; Jan. 27; v. 270; p. 575.
Dean, William W., Stamford, Conn., assignor to Splitdorf Electrical Company, Newark, N. J. Ignition-generator. No. 1,327,375; Jan. 6; v. 270; p. 92.
Deere & Company. (See Dooley, Harry L., assignor.)
Deere and Company. (See Paul, William L., assignor.)
De Esparza, Timoteo R., assignor of two-fifths to F. Barnes and one-tenth to F. Defoy, Calexico, Calif. Marine propulsion. No. 1,329,228; Jan. 27; v. 270; p. 568.
Defoy, Fred, et al. (See de Esparza, Timoteo R., assignor.)
De Froy, Jules. (See Bernier, Henry N., assignor.)
Dehuff, Walter F., Glen Rock, Pa. Dough-mixer. No. 1,329,164; Jan. 27; v. 270; p. 556.
De Kalb, J. Emmons, et al. (See Schott, John H., assignor.)
De Lange, Pieter, and R. A. van Lynden, Utrecht, Netherlands, assignors, by mesne assignments, to American Thermophone Company, Boston, Mass. Sounding-chamber for thermic telephones and other apparatus. No. 1,328,620; Jan. 20; v. 270; p. 425.
De Laval Separator Company, The. (See Wright, Bert R., assignor.)
Delaporte, Maurice, Paris, France. Steam-ejector. No. 1,328,270; Jan. 20; v. 270; p. 358.
De Lavaud, Dimitri S., New York, N. Y. Rotary casting. No. 1,329,295; Jan. 27; v. 270; p. 580.
De Lavaud, Dimitri S., New York, N. Y. Rotary casting. No. 1,329,296; Jan. 27; v. 270; p. 580.
De La Vergne Machine Company. (See Doelling, Louis K., assignor.)
Delleuvin, Paul A. M., Neuilly-sur-Seine, France. Device for increasing the adherence of agricultural tractors to the soil. No. 1,327,376; Jan. 6; v. 270; p. 92.
Dellgren, Karl, Västervik, Sweden. Liquid-pump. No. 1,327,272; Jan. 6; v. 270; p. 73.
De Long, Charles E., New York, N. Y. Watch-escapement. No. 1,327,226; Jan. 6; v. 270; p. 65.
De Long, Cyrus W., Gainesville, Fla. Vaginal douche and medicator. No. 1,327,705; Jan. 13; v. 270; p. 216.
Denis, Albert D., et al. (See Genin, John B., assignor.)
Dennis, Ernest A., Glenroy, New Zealand. Picnic and other food-holder. No. 1,327,948; Jan. 13; v. 270; p. 261.
Dennis, Samuel K., Chicago, Ill., assignor, by mesne assignments, to International Harvester Company. Seed-planter. No. 1,327,089; Jan. 6; v. 270; p. 40.
Dennis, Samuel K., Chicago, Ill., assignor, by mesne assignments, to International Harvester Company. Clutch mechanism for corn-planters and like machines. No. 1,327,090; Jan. 6; v. 270; p. 40.
Dennis, William K. (See Goodwin, James D., assignor.)
Dennison, Herbert J. S. (See Thompson and Dennison.)
Dennison, William L., Columbus, Ohio. Holder for bedcovers. No. 1,328,621; Jan. 20; v. 270; p. 425.
Dentists' Supply Company, The. (See Whiteley, George H., Jr., assignor.)
Department of Soldiers Civil Re-Establishment, Invalided Soldiers' Commission, The. (See Birchard, Eslie R., assignor.)
Deposited Metal Products Company. (See Hart, Austin H., assignor.)
Derrom, Donald L., Chicago, Ill. Lathe. No. 1,329,042; Jan. 27; v. 270; p. 533.

De Sibour, Jules H., Washington, D. C. Hatband. No. 1,328,823; Jan. 27; v. 270; p. 491.
De Smet, Edgard C., assignor to S. C. Pandolfo, St. Cloud, Minn. Collapsible footrest. No. 1,327,706; Jan. 13; v. 270; p. 216.
Detmer Woolen Company. (See Kaiser, Richard C., assignor.)
De Waele, René E., Paris, France. Submarine toy. No. 1,328,867; Jan. 27; v. 270; p. 500.
Dewes, A., Company, The. (See Schieman, Paul W., assignor.)
Dewick, Bernard, and D. B. Caddy, London, assignors to The British Ever Ready Company Limited, Holloway, London, England. Apparatus for playing a game of skill. No. 1,327,464; Jan. 6; v. 270; p. 108.
Dezendorf, Richard L., Richmond Hill, N. Y. Apparatus for and method of clearing service-pipes. No. 1,328,726; Jan. 20; v. 270; p. 444.
Diamond, James K., assignor to Clipper Belt Lacer Company, Grand Rapids, Mich. Belt-fastener-setting machine. No. 1,328,424; Jan. 20; v. 270; p. 387.
Diamond Expansion Bolt Company. (See Hiss, William J., assignor.)
Diamond Match Company, The. (See Paridon, Michael, assignor.)
Dick, Joseph, assignor to The Joseph Dick Manufacturing Company, Canton, Ohio. Pipe-door. No. 1,327,377; Jan. 6; v. 270; p. 92.
Dick, Joseph, Manufacturing Company. (See Dick, Joseph, assignor.)
Dickelmann, Lawrence H., and J. Kuchler, Milwaukee, Wis. Pipe-clip and forming same. No. 1,329,268; Jan. 27; v. 270; p. 576.
Dickelman, Lizzie H., Forest, Ohio. Ventilated grainstorehouse. No. 1,328,132; Jan. 13; v. 270; p. 296.
Dickie, James. (See Jardine, Dickie, and Bowness.)
Dickinson, Edgar D., Schenectady, N. Y., assignor to General Electric Company. Turbine installation for ships. No. 1,328,497; Jan. 20; v. 270; p. 402.
Dickinson, Sanford B., Bath, N. Y. Steel track. No. 1,328,780; Jan. 20; v. 270; p. 456.
Dieckmann, Adolf, Cincinnati, Ohio. Sheet-metal-elbowforming machine. No. 1,326,916; Jan. 6; v. 270; p. 6.
Diemer, Charles P., Sapulpa, Okla. Indicating device for vehicles. No. 1,329,043; Jan. 27; v. 270; p. 533.
Diffenbaugh, Harry G., Salt Lake City, Utah. Airpressure liquid-transfer device. No. 1,328,133; Jan. 13; v. 270; p. 296.
Di Grazia, Archie, and R. Biagini, Charleroi, Pa. Self-propelling aerial bomb. No. 1,327,810; Jan. 13; v. 270; p. 235.
Dillmann, Edward, et al., trustees. (See Bobroff, Bornett L., assignor.)
Dings, Ralph E., and L. Schuster, New York, N. Y. Waterproof varnish. No. 1,326,917; Jan. 6; v. 270; p. 7.
Distefano, Quirino V., Waterbury, Conn. Airship. No. 1,328,369; Jan. 20; v. 270; p. 377.
Diver, Daniel, Calgary, Alberta, Canada. Machine for the separation of gold, silver, and platinum from sand. No. 1,329,113; Jan. 27; v. 270; p. 547.
Dixie Fruit Products Corporation. (See Colbert, Clarence F., assignor.)
Dixieland Motor Truck Company. (See Armstrong, Ira, assignor.)
Dixon, Amos F., Newark, N. J., assignor to Western Electric Company, incorporated, New York, N. Y. Selecting system. No. 1,328,986; Jan. 27; v. 270; p. 528.
Dixon, Russell A. (See Mason and Dixon.)
Djidics, Alexander, New York, N. Y. Nurling-tool. No. 1,328,498; Jan. 20; v. 270; p. 402.
Dmitrieff, Vasily N., New York, N. Y., assignor of forty per cent. to R. Kliavin, Seattle, Wash. Combined pendulous table and chairs. No. 1,328,727; Jan. 20; v. 270; p. 444.
Dobson, John E., and S. M. Crookshank, Knoxville, Tenn. Device for packing silage. No. 1,328,728; Jan. 20; v. 270; p. 444.
Doelling, Louis K., New Rochelle, assignor to De La Vergne Machine Company, New York, N. Y. Oil-engine. No. 1,328,499; Jan. 20; v. 270; p. 402.
Doherty, Henry L. (See Laird, Wilbur G., assignor.)
Dolan, George E., and S. Miller; said Dolan assignor of one-half of his right to W. T. Lloyd, San Francisco, Calif. Electric permutation-lock. No. 1,328,729; Jan. 20; v. 270; p. 444.
Dombkowski, Kazimer, Stanhope, N. J. Safeguard-lamp for automobiles. No. 1,326,918; Jan. 6; v. 270; p. 7.
Dombkowski, Kazimer, Stanhope, N. J. Sanitary cuspidor or refuse-receptacle. No. 1,326,919; Jan. 6; v. 270; p. 7.
Donaldson, Harry R. (See Donaldson, Robert M. and H. R.)
Donaldson, Robert M. and H. R., Claysville, Pa. Carbureter-adjuster. No. 1,328,946; Jan. 27; v. 270; p. 515.
Donovan, Michael L., Omaha, Nebr. Lubricator. No. 1,329,229; Jan. 27; v. 270; p. 568.
Doelckner, Max A., Louisville, Ky. Toy flying-machine. No. 1,328,134; Jan. 13; v. 270; p. 296.
Donaldson, William M., Portland, Oreg. Scaffold. No. 1,328,500; Jan. 20; v. 170; p. 402.
Doner, Hugh H., New York, N. Y. Signal and guide light. No. 1,328,135; Jan. 13; v. 270; p. 296.
Donovan, Jerome J., Oakland, Calif. Combination bath-spray. No. 1,328,650; Jan. 20; v. 270; p. 430.

Dooley, Harry L., Rock Island, assignor to Deere & Company. Moline, Ill. Planter. No. 1,328,730; Jan. 20; v. 270; p. 444.

Dorrell, Harry, Peoria, Ill. Violin peg. No. 1,328,824; Jan. 27; v. 270; p. 491.

Dorsey, David J., Baton Rouge, La. Shade and curtain hanger. No. 1,328,136; Jan. 13; v. 270; p. 297.

Doud, Arthur N., Winthrop, N. Y. Dumping-wagon. No. 1,328,137; Jan. 13; v. 270; p. 297.

Dougan, Kennedy, Minneapolis, Minn. Projectile. No. 1,327,655; Jan. 13; v. 270; p. 206.

Dover, George W., Cranston, R. I. Lathe tool. No. 1,328,947; Jan. 27; v. 270; p. 516.

Dover, George W., Cranston, R. I. Setting for jewelry. No. 1,328,948; Jan. 27; v. 270; p. 516.

Dover, George W., Cranston, R. I. Setting for jewelry. No. 1,328,949; Jan. 27; v. 270; p. 516.

Dover, George W., Incorporated. (See Peterson, Erick B., assignor.)

Dowell, Archie G. (See Clark, Charles E., assignor.)

Drake, Harcourt C., and A. Slagenhauf, Brooklyn, N. Y. Headstock-brake. No. 1,327,656; Jan. 13; v. 270; p. 206.

Drane, Merritt, Lyndon, Ky. Direction-signal. No. 1,327,027; Jan. 6; v. 270; p. 28.

Draper Corporation. (See Carter, Charlie O., assignor.)

Draper Corporation. (See Rhoades, Alonzo E., assignor.)

Draper Corporation. (See Stimpson, Edward S., assignor.)

Drew, Herbert H., Edgerton, Wis. Stock-watering apparatus. No. 1,328,036; Jan. 13; v. 270; p. 277.

Drew, John W., assignor to Moon Brothers Manufacturing Company, St. Louis, Mo. Pump-packing. No. 1,329,165; Jan. 27; v. 270; p. 556.

Drinkwater, James F., Willard, Ohio. Railway-brake appliance. No. 1,328,138; Jan. 13; v. 270; p. 297.

Drolet, Benjamin. (See Plante, Albert E., assignor.)

Druar, Frank J., assignor to Packard Motor Car Company, Detroit, Mich. Hydrocarbon-motor. No. 1,327,148; Jan. 6; v. 270; p. 50.

Dryen, Achille, Londerzeel, Belgium. Pump. No. 1,327,423; Jan. 6; v. 270; p. 101.

Drysdale, Charles V., Dumbartonshire, Scotland. Alternating-current relay. No. 1,328,825; Jan. 27; v. 270; p. 491.

Dubilier, William, New York, N. Y. Series condenser. No. 1,327,593; Jan. 6; v. 270; p. 133.

Dudley, Howard M., Philadelphia, Pa. Dyeing-machine. No. 1,327,200; Jan. 6; v. 270; p. 60.

Dudley, Howard M., Philadelphia, Pa. Skein-dyeing machine. No. 1,327,657; Jan. 13; v. 270; p. 206.

Dudley, Howard M., Philadelphia, Pa. Dyeing-machine. No. 1,327,658; Jan. 13; v. 270; p. 206.

Dudley, Howard M., Philadelphia, Pa. Fabric-treating device. No. 1,327,659. Jan. 13; v. 270; p. 207.

Dudley, Howard M., Philadelphia, Pa. Dyeing-machine. No. 1,327,660; Jan. 13; v. 270; p. 207.

Dudley, Howard M., Philadelphia, Pa. Dyeing device. No. 1,327,661; Jan. 13; v. 270; p. 207.

Dudley, Howard M., Philadelphia, Pa. Dyeing-machine. No. 1,327,662; Jan. 13; v. 270; p. 207.

Dudley, Howard M., Philadelphia, Pa. Fiber-treating machine. No. 1,327,663; Jan. 13; v. 270; p. 208.

Dudley, Howard M., Philadelphia, Pa. Hosiery-dyeing machine. No. 1,327,756; Jan. 13; v. 270; p. 225.

Dudley, Howard M., Philadelphia, Pa. Fiber-treating machine. No. 1,328,987; Jan. 27; v. 270; p. 523.

Duffy, Charles H., Chevy Chase, Md. Parachute. No. 1,328,425; Jan. 20; v. 270; p. 387.

Dummer, Horace B., New York, N. Y. Toy aeroplane. No. 1,327,530; Jan. 6; v. 270; p. 121.

Duncan, De Lloyd O., Rockford, Ill. Reservoir-broach. No. 1,327,149; Jan. 6; v. 270; p. 50.

Duncombe, Tyrrell H., Romeo, Mich. Change-speed-power-transmitting mechanism. No. 1,329,297; Jan. 27; v. 270; p. 580.

Dunham, George W., Detroit, Mich., assignor to Graham Brothers, Evansville, Ind. Stabilizer. No. 1,327,811; Jan. 13; v. 270; p. 236.

Dun Lany, William P., assignor to Sears, Roebuck and Company, Chicago, Ill. Sample-affixing machine. No. 1,327,664; Jan. 13; v. 270; p. 208.

Dun Lany, William P., assignor to Sears, Roebuck and Company, Chicago, Ill. Machine for affixing samples to sheets. No. 1,327,665; Jan. 13; v. 270; p. 208.

Dunman, Nesbit M. (See Abercrombie and Dunman.)

Dupler, Raymond R., Toledo, Ohio. Wheeled harrow No. 1,327,424; Jan. 6; v. 270; p. 101.

Du Pont, E. I., de Nemours & Company. (See Bryan and Swint, assignors.)

Du Pont, E. I., de Nemours & Company. (See Marshall, John, assignor.)

Durham, Charles, Chicago, Ill. Projectile. No. 1,327,531; Jan. 6; v. 270; p. 122.

Dürsteler, Wilhelm, assignor to Weidmann Dyeing Co., Ld., Thalwil, Switzerland. Apparatus for treating hanks of textile fabrics with liquids. No. 1,329,166; Jan. 27; v. 270; p. 556.

Dutchess Tool Company. (See Van Houten, Frank H., Jr., assignor.)

Dutemple, William R., Auburn, R. I. Oil-cup holder. No. 1,328,271; Jan. 20; v. 270; p. 358.

Dutton, Abraham L., Otis, Colo. Leveling device for threshing-machines, &c. No. 1,328,370; Jan. 20; v. 270; p. 378.

Duvall, Flora, Chicago, Ill. Strainer. No. 1,327,532. Jan. 6; v. 270; p. 122.

Duvendack, Henry W. (See Blake, William F., assignor.)

Dyer, Frank L., Montclair, N. J. Talking-machine. No. 1,326,920; Jan. 6; v. 270; p. 7.

Dyer, Newell V., Holbrook, Mass., assignor, by mesne assignments, to United Shoe Machinery Corporation, Paterson, N. J. Skiving-machine. No. 1,327,028; Jan. 6; v. 270; p. 28.

Dzimitowicz, Waclaw, Pittsburgh, Pa. Baby-walker. No. 1,326,921; Jan. 6; v. 270; p. 7.

Eades, Rodger, Winchester, Ky. Hemp-brake. No. 1,327,533; Jan. 6; v. 270; p. 122.

Eames, Robert, Detroit, Mich. Calipers. No. 1,328,651; Jan. 20; v. 270; p. 430.

Early, William F., Marion, N. C. Flexible ladder. No. 1,328,037; Jan. 13; v. 270; p. 278.

Eastern Tool & Mfg. Company. (See Anderson, Carl E., assignor.)

Eaton, George M., Pittsburgh, Pa., assignor to Westinghouse Electric & Manufacturing Company. Locomotive-transmission system. No. 1,329,269; Jan. 27; v. 270; p. 576.

Eaton, John, Schenectady, N. Y., assignor to General Electric Company. Control of electric motors. No. 1,328,501; Jan. 20; v. 270; p. 403.

Ebeling, Robert W., Oakland, Calif., assignor to R. W. Ebeling Company, Incorporated. Multiple - circuit - resistance control. No. 1,329,168; Jan. 27; v. 270; p. 557.

Ebeling, R. W., Company. (See Ebeling, Robert W., assignor.)

Ebeling, Robert W., Oakland, Calif., assignor to R. W. Ebeling Company, Incorporated. Rheostat. No. 1,329,167; Jan. 27; v. 270; p. 557.

Eberle, John A., St. Louis, Mo. Baby-walker. No. 1,328,826; Jan. 27; v. 270; p. 491.

Eckert, Carl J., and P. J. Richman, Chicago, Ill. Water-proof combination cigarette, match, and coin case. No. 1,328,988; Jan. 27; v. 270; p. 523.

Eckert, Joseph, Dayton, Ohio. Bottle-cap remover. No. 1,328,827; Jan. 27; v. 270; p. 492.

Ecks, Fred, New York, Y. Air-relief valve for sprinkler systems. No. 1,326,922; Jan. 6; v. 270; p. 7.

Eclipse Stove Company. (See Robinson, Harry A., assignor.)

Edmon, Elmer A. (See Christie and Edmon.)

Edward Valve & Manufacturing Co., The. (See Oleson, Olaf E., assignor.)

Edwards, Josiah H., Los Angeles, Calif. Sash-fastener. No. 1,327,594; Jan. 6; v. 270; p. 133.

Eells, Albert F., Rochester, N. Y. Anchor. No. 1,327,201; Jan. 6; v. 270; p. 60.

Egerton, Henry C., Ridgewood, N. J. Shank-stiffener. No. 1,327,091; Jan. 6; v. 270; p. 40.

Eggers, William J., Brooklyn, N. Y. Rubber toothbrush. No. 1,327,757; Jan. 13; v. 270; p. 226.

Eggleston, Claude M., Searcy, Ark. Gasolene-dispenser. No. 1,327,425; Jan. 6; v. 270; p. 101.

Eggleston, William H., Grandville, assignor of one-half to D. Ritzema, Grand Rapids, Mich. Extension angle-square. No. 1,329,337; Jan. 27; v. 270; p. 587.

Ehlers, Lillie, Stickney, S. D. Pot-lid. No. 1,328,652; Jan. 20; v. 270; p. 430.

Ehrhart, Raymond N., Edgewood Park, Pa., assignor to Westinghouse Electric & Manufacturing Co. Condenser. No. 1,328,828; Jan. 27; v. 270; p. 492.

Eichmeier, Herman C., St. Maries, Idaho. Brake. No. 1,327,534; Jan. 6; v. 270; p. 122.

Eichstedt, John A., Akron, Ohio. Key-ring holder. No. 1,327,534; Jan. 6; v. 270; p. 122.

Eickhoff, Theodore H., and C. A. Tunks, Cleveland, Ohio, assignors to Auto-Ordnance Corporation, New York, N. Y. Ammunition lubrication. No. 1,327,378; Jan. 6; v. 270; p. 93.

Einfeldt, Ernest E., assignor to French & Hecht, Davenport, Iowa. Metal wheel. No. 1,327,227; Jan. 6; v. 270; p. 65.

Eisenhauer, Charles P., assignor to The Burnett-Larsh Manufacturing Company, Dayton, Ohio. Water-pumping system. No. 1,328,989; Jan. 27; v. 270; p. 523.

Eisinger, Ludwig W., Bronxville, N. Y. Railway-link. No. 1,327,535; Jan. 6; v. 270; p. 122.

Ekvall, Arvid P., and H. Stake, Worcester, Mass. Can-labeling machine. No. 1,327,465; Jan. 6; v. 270; p. 108.

Electric Auto Lite Corporation. (See Post, Truman W., assignor.)

Electric Boat Company. (See Grieshaber, Hugo E., assignor.)

Electric Railway Improvement Company, The. (See Crecelius, Lawrence P., assignor.)

Electro-Thermophore Company. (See Lidberg, Tiodolf, assignor.)

Elevator Supplies Company. (See Parsons, Levi L., assignor.)

Elevator Supply & Repair Company. (See Parsons, Levi L., assignor.)

Elgin National Watch Company. (See Hulburd, De Forest, assignor.)

Elias, Perfecto M., and F. F. Llera, Tucson, Ariz. Soldering and melting apparatus. No. 1,329,270; Jan. 27; v. 270; p. 576.

Ellinger, William H., Bonita, Tex. Well-drill wrench. No. 1,327,379; Jan. 6; v. 270; p. 93.

Elliott, Alexander T., assignor of one-tenth to L. M. Freeman, Los Angeles, Calif. Chemical separation of ores. No. 1,327,536; Jan. 6; v. 270; p. 122.

Elliott, William S., Jr., New York, N. Y. Hydraulic water-forcing apparatus. No. 1,328,139; Jan. 13; v. 270; p. 297.

Elliot, William D., Big Timber, Mont. Paper-bag holder. No. 1,328,950; Jan. 27; v. 270; p. 516.

Ellis, Arthur L., et al. (See Golata and Roberts, assignors.)

Ellis, Arthur T., assignor of one-half to H. A. Hands, London, England. Valve of internal-combustion engines. No. 1,329,321; Jan. 27; v. 270; p. 584.

Ellis, Carleton, Montclair, N. J., assignor to C. S. Lutkins, Rye, N.Y. Making a mixture of nitrogen and hydrogen. No. 1,327,029; Jan. 6; v. 270; p. 28.

Ellis, Carleton, Montclair, N. J. Paint and varnish remover. No. 1,328,080; Jan. 13; v. 270; p. 286.

Ellis, Carleton, Montclair, N. J. Making powdered metals and reduced metallic compounds. No. 1,329,322; Jan. 27; v. 270; p. 584.

Ellis, Carleton, Montclair, N. J. Making catalytic material. No. 1,329,323; Jan. 27; v. 270; p. 585.

Ellis Drier & Elevator Company. (See Ellis, Hubert C., assignor.)

Ellis, Hubert C., Evanston, assignor to Ellis Drier & Elevator Company, Chicago, Ill. Grain-drier. No. 1,327,863; Jan. 13; v. 270; p. 245.

Elmore, Guy H., Swarthmore, Pa. Jig. No. 1,327,537; Jan. 6; v. 270; p. 123.

Ely, Frank D., Tientsin, China. Firearm control. No. 1,329,230; Jan. 27; v. 270; p. 568.

Emerson & Brantingham Company. (See Davis, Calvin R., assignor.)

Emerson Phonograph Company. (See Emerson and Pierman, assignors.)

Emerson, Victor H., New York, N. Y., and A. N. Pierman, Newark, N. J., assignors to Emerson Phonograph Company, Inc., New York, N. Y. Record-surfacing and production thereof. No. 1,328,371; Jan. 20; v. 270; p. 378.

Emery, Plato G., Chicago, Ill. Holding device for window-shades. No. 1,327,150; Jan. 6; v. 270; p. 51.

Emmert, Gus. (See Tischer, Edward R., assignor.)

Enders, Gustav A., Boston, Mass. Cornet, trumpet, and the like. No. 1,328,038; Jan. 13; v. 270; p. 278.

Engle, Eugene W. (See White, Fred G., assignor.)

Engle, Isaiah G., Philadelphia, Pa. Valve. No. 1,329,231; Jan. 27; v. 270; p. 569.

Engel, John, Green Bay, Wis. Machine for applying paint to embossed designs. No. 1,328,081; Jan. 13; v. 270; p. 286.

Enochs, C. D., trustee. (See Thomasson, Hiram S., assignor.)

Enslin, Herbert E., Malden, Mass., assignor to United Shoe Machinery Corporation, Paterson, N. J. Lacing-machine. No. 1,329,298; Jan. 27; v. 270; p. 580.

Enz, Ezra. (See Abbott and Enz.)

Eppler, John, Philadelphia, Pa. Machine for knitting lace-work. No. 1,327,228; Jan. 6; v. 270; p. 66.

Erdahl, Sivert A., Madison, Minn. Apple cutter and corer. No. 1,328,503; Jan. 20; v. 270; p. 403.

Erhardt, Oscar P., West Haven, Conn., assignor to The A. C. Gilbert Company, New Haven, Conn. Electric switch. No. 1,328,622; Jan. 20; v. 270; p. 425.

Erickson, Axel F., assignor to The Allsteelequip Company, Aurora, Ill. Lock-mounting plate. No. 1,327,426; Jan. 6; v. 270; p. 101.

Erickson, Carl A. S., Norcross, Minn. Animal-trap. No. 1,327,229; Jan. 6; v. 270; p. 66.

Erler, William C., Terre Haute, Ind. Bituminous composition. No. 1,329,232; Jan. 27; v. 270; p. 569.

Erti, Lorenz, Ivanhoe, Minn. Operating-table. No. 1,328,140; Jan. 13; v. 270; p. 297.

Eschholz, Otto H., Wilkinsburg, Pa., assignor to Westinghouse Electric & Manufacturing Company. Arc-welding system. No. 1,329,233; Jan. 27; v. 270; p. 569.

Eskilson, Sven A., Stockholm, Sweden. Apparatus for flinging off superfluous coating when tinning, painting, or the like. No. 1,327,273; Jan. 6; v. 270; p. 74.

Essex Motors. (See Fekete, Stephen I., assignor.)

Essner, Eugene F., San Francisco, Calif., assignor to Bethlehem Shipbuilding Corporation, Ltd., Bethlehem, Pa. Machine for cutting off condenser-tubes. No. 1,328,039; Jan. 13; v. 270; p. 278.

Estberg, William T., assignor to Penn Pressed Metal Co., Camden, N. J. Automobile-lock. No. 1,329,114; Jan. 27; v. 270; p. 547.

Estève, Felix. (See Labrosse and Estève.)

Estey Organ Company. (See Haskell, William E., assignor.)

Estey Piano Co. (See Barnes, James W., assignor.)

Etter, Harry C., Chambersburg, Pa. Non-skid device. No. 1,327,538; Jan. 6; v. 270; p. 123.

Etzel, John, East Pittsburgh, Pa. Garment-supporter. No. 1,328,504; Jan. 20; v. 270; p. 403.

Evans, Edgar A., Victoria, British Columbia, Canada. Spark arrester and quencher. No. 1,329,115; Jan. 27; v. 270; p. 547.

Evans, Franklin J., West Hazleton, Pa. Positioning-button. No. 1,329,234; Jan. 27; v. 270; p. 569.

Evans, Henry S., East Chicago, Ind. Street-indicator for tramcars. No. 1,327,274; Jan. 6; v. 270; p. 74.

Evans, Isaac, et al. (See McLeod and Quirk, assignors.)

Evans, S. C. (See Markwell, Andrew E., assignor.)

Everingham, John H., Manchester, England. Portable carriage for children. No. 1,327,864; Jan. 13; v. 270; p. 245.

Exley, William H. (See Leitner, Henry, assignor.)

Exley, William H. (See Leitner and Exley.)

Exton, Alfred H., Chicago Heights, Ill., assignor to American Manganese Steel Company, Augusta, Me. Sectional shoe for the runner-vanes of centrifugal pumps. No. 1,327,812; Jan. 13; v. 270; p. 236.

Eyles, Anton G., Cedar Rapids, Iowa, assignor of one-half to J. H. Lee, Oak Park, Ill. Tempo-control device. No. 1,328,870; Jan. 27; v. 270; p. 501.

Fagan, James P. V., H. G. Spear, and R. B. Wolf; said Fagan and said Spear assignors to Brown Company, Berlin, N. H. Manufacturing sulfite fiber and recovering sulfur dioxid. No. 1,327,666; Jan. 13; v. 270; p. 208.

Fairbanks Company. (See Mattern, Frank C., assignor.)

Fairbanks, James J., Gardner, Mass., assignor to The U. S. Toy & Novelties Mfg. Co., Templeton, Mass. Toy Ferris wheel. No. 1,328,829; Jan. 27; v. 270; p. 492.

Fairbanks, Luke J., Los Angeles, Calif. Insect-poison-supply container. No. 1,327,230; Jan. 6; v. 270; p. 66.

Fairbanks, Morse & Co. (See Thompson, Harry E., assignor.)

Fairmont Gas Engine & Railway Motor Car Co. (See Kasper, Walter F., assignor.)

Falcke, Philip. (See Bumpas and Falcke.)

Farley, Henry G., Portland, Me. Machine for grinding the edges of glass plates. No. 1,328,242; Jan. 1; v. 270; p. 317.

Farnam, John, Los Angeles, Calif. Scarecrow. No. 1,329,044; Jan. 27; v. 270; p. 534.

Fausse, Joseph, Brockton, Mass., assignor to United Shoe Machinery Corporation, Paterson, N. J. Making shoes. No. 1,328,322; Jan. 20; v. 270; p. 369.

Fawcett, Charles H., assignor to Interstate Ever-license Company, Independence, Iowa. License-holder for motor-vehicles. No. 1,328,915; Jan. 27; v. 270; p. 510.

Feary, Neville A. T. N., Peterborough, England. Fabric for aircraft and making same. No. 1,327,707; Jan. 13; v. 270; p. 216.

Feazel, Clarence E., Columbus, Ohio. Air-heater. No. 1,328,272; Jan. 20; v. 270; p. 358.

Fedders, John M., assignor to Fedders Manufacturing Company, Inc., Buffalo, N. Y. Radiator-core. No. 1,327,380; Jan. 6; v. 270; p. 93.

Fedders, John M., assignor to Fedders Manufacturing Company, Inc., Buffalo, N. Y. Radiator-core. No. 1,328,323; Jan. 20; v. 270; p. 369.

Fedders Manufacturing Company. (See Fedders, John M., assignor.)

Fehan, John, Buffalo, N. Y. Reserve device for fuel-tanks. No. 1,329,074; Jan. 27; v. 270; p. 579.

Feilbach, Arthur O., North Milwaukee, Wis. Tool for lifting valve-springs. No. 1,328,228; Jan. 13; v. 270; p. 314.

Fekete, Stephen I., assignor, by mesne assignments, to Essex Motors, Detroit, Mich. Fuel-supply mechanism for internal-combustion engines. No. 1,328,142; Jan. 13; v. 270; p. 298.

Felten & Guilleaume Fabrik Elektrischer Kabel, Stahl- und Kupferwerke Aktiengesellschaft. (See Knaur, Richard, assignor.)

Fenton, Walter, Manchester, England, assignor to Underwood Typewriter Company, New York, N. Y. Typewriting-machine. No. 1,327,908; Jan. 13; v. 270; p. 253.

Ferguson, Louis A., Evanston, and H. S. Sines, Oak Park, Ill.; said Sines assignor to said Ferguson. Gas-metering apparatus. No. 1,327,989; Jan. 13; v. 270; p. 268.

Ferguson, Marie A., Newark, N. J. Water-closet seat. No. 1,327,275; Jan. 6; v. 270; p. 74.

Ferguson, Milford N., and E. Haas, Brooklyn, N. Y. Wrapping mechanism for candy. No. 1,329,236; Jan. 27; v. 270; p. 569.

Fergusson, Sterling P., Washington, D. C. Kite-frame or like structure. No. 1,328,143; Jan. 13; v. 270; p. 298.

Fernald, Mark E., Saugus, Mass. Automatic machine. No. 1,328,144; Jan. 13; v. 270; p. 298.

Ferngren, Enoch T., Kansas City, Mo. Glass-molding apparatus. No. 1,328,273; Jan. 20; v. 270; p. 359.

Ferris, Walton C., assignor to National Manufacturing Company, Lincoln, Nebr. Safety-valve for pressure-coolers. No. 1,328,853; Jan. 20; v. 270; p. 481.

Ferro Machine and Foundry Company, The. (See Brewster and Weisehan, assignors.)

Figenshu, William L., assignor of one-half to O. Heymann, Philadelphia, Pa. Bowling-alley. No. 1,329,235; Jan. 27; v. 270; p. 569.

Filkins, George H., Watervliet, assignor of one-half to J. F. Murray, Troy, N. Y. Automobile device. No. 1,328,654; Jan 20; v. 270; p. 431.

Finley, Thomas M., Oran, Mo. Aerocruiser. No. 1,328,040; Jan. 13; v. 270; p. 278.

Finney, Curtiss W., Spokane, Wash. Valve-spring retainer. No. 1,327,539; Jan. 6; v. 270; p. 123.

Fischer, Jacob. (See Brandenstein and Fischer.)

Fischer, Keno, Berlin-Charlottenburg, assignor to Siemens Schuckert Werke, G. m. b. H., Berlin, Germany. Electric relay and the like. No. 1,328,041; Jan. 13; v. 270; p. 278.

Fischer, Martin, Zurich, Switzerland. Device for igniting gas-jets. No. 1,327,813; Jan. 13; v. 270; p. 236.

Fish, Ambrose D., Portland, Oreg. Metal-separator. No. 1,327,667; Jan. 13; v. 270; p. 208.

Fish, Frederick K., Jr., assignor to Lumber Tie and Timber Vulcanizing Company, New York, N. Y. Drying lumber. No. 1,328,505; Jan. 20; v. 270; p. 403.

Fish, Frederick K., Jr., assignor to Lumber Tie and Timber Vulcanizing Company, New York, N. Y. Sterilized wood. No. 1,328,506; Jan. 20; v. 270; p. 404.

Fish, Frederick K., Jr., New York, N. Y. Drying lumber. No. 1,328,507; Jan. 20; v. 270; p. 404.

Fish, Frederick K., Jr., New York, N. Y. Drying lumber. No. 1,328,655; Jan. 20; v. 270; p. 431.

Fish, Frederick K., Jr., New York, N. Y. Sapless composite wood. No. 1,328,656; Jan. 20; v. 270; p. 431.

Fish, Frederick K., Jr., New York, N. Y. Treating and drying wood. No. 1,328,657; Jan. 20; v. 270; p. 431.

Fish, Frederick K., Jr., assignor to Lumber Tie & Timber Vulcanizing Company, New York, N. Y. Drying lumber. No. 1,328,658; Jan. 20; v. 270; p. 431.

Fish, Frederick K., Jr., assignor to Lumber Tie and Timber Vulcanizing Company, New York, N. Y. Drying lumber. No. 1,328,659; Jan. 20; v. 270; p. 432.

Fish, Frederick K., Jr., assignor to Lumber Tie and Timber Vulcanizing Company, New York, N. Y. Drying lumber. No. 1,328,660; Jan. 20; v. 270; p. 432.

Fish, Frederick K., Jr., assignor to Lumber Tie & Timber Vulcanizing Company, New York, N. Y. Drying lumber. No. 1,328,661; Jan. 20; v. 270; p. 432.

Fish, Frederick K., Jr., New York, N. Y. Drying lumber. No. 1,328,662; Jan. 20; v. 270; p. 432.

Fisher, Alva J., Evanston, assignor to Hurley Machine Company, Chicago, Ill. Ironing-machine. No. 1,327,613; Jan. 13; v. 270; p. 198.

Fiske Rubber Company, The. (See Bowerman, Joseph A., assignor.)

Fiske Rubber Company, The. (See Jameson, William, assignor.)

Fisk Rubber Company, The. (See Naylor, Ralph B., assignor.)

Fitzgerald Manufacturing Company, The. (See Fitzgerald, Patrick J., assignor.)

Fitzgerald, Patrick J., assignor to The Fitzgerald Manufacturing Company, Torrington, Conn. Massage-vibrator. No. 1,327,466; Jan. 6; v. 270; p. 109.

Flanagan, James U., assignor of three-fourths to F. F. Slocomb & Co., Incorporated, Wilmington, Del. Apparatus for treating skins, fabric, tobacco, and the like. No. 1,327,668; Jan. 13; v. 270; p. 209.

Flanagan, John, Davenport, Iowa. Lifting-jack. No. 1,329,116; Jan. 27; v. 270; p. 547.

Flannery Bolt Company. (See Mennie, Robert S., assignor.) (Reissue.)

Flaxbaum, Samuel, New York, N. Y. Pocket-mirror. No. 1,327,865; Jan. 13; v. 270; p. 245.

Fleming, Frank E. (See Blackburn and Fleming.)

Fleming, James C., Denver, Colo. Key system for clarinets. No. 1,328,831; Jan. 27; v. 270; p. 492.

Fleming, Wills M., Holyoke, Mass., assignor by mesne assignments, to Worthington Pump and Machinery Corporation, New York, N. Y. Valve. No. 1,328,274; Jan. 20; v. 270; p. 359.

Flury, Georges, Bienne, Switzerland. Belt-fastener. No. 1,328,426; Jan. 20; v. 270; p. 388.

Fogg, Donald E. (See Hunt and Fogg.)

Foley, Dollner S., Montrose, Colo. Potato-cutting machine. No. 1,327,316; Jan. 6; v. 270; p. 81.

Folks, Robert L., Waycross, Ga. Internal-combustion engine. No. 1,328,141; Jan. 13; v. 270; p. 298.

Fooks, Nelson H., Preston, Md. Valve. No. 1,327,540; Jan. 6; v. 270; p. 123.

Forbes, Philip J., et al. (See Rendano, Emil, assignor.)

Forester, Herbert, assignor of one-half to A. M. Skibinsky, Cleveland, Ohio. Burner for gas or oil. No. 1,327,092; Jan. 6; v. 270; p. 40.

Fornonzini, Gervaso, Lanzada, Italy. Sighting means for firearms, optical apparatus, and the like. No. 1,329,075; Jan. 27; v. 270; p. 539.

Forster, Andrew, and J. H. Brown, Cowes, assignors to J. Samuel White & Company, Limited, East Cowes, Isle of Wight, England. Air-valve. No. 1,328,951; Jan. 27; v. 270; p. 516.

Fort Wayne Engineering & Manufacturing Co. (See Astrom, John, assignor.)

Fortescue, Charles L., Pittsburgh, Pa., assignor to Westinghouse Electric and Manufacturing Company. Method of and apparatus for spot-welding. No. 1,327,814; Jan. 13; v. 270; p. 236.

Foss-Hughes Company. (See Noonan, Albert S., assignor.)

Foster Bros. Mfg. Co. (See Frank, William E., assignor.)

Foster, Edward E., Beverly, assignor to C. C. Blake, Incorporated, Boston, Mass. Stop mechanism. No. 1,328,145; Jan. 13; v. 270; p. 298.

Foster, George D., assignor to Union Land & Power Company, North Yakima, Wash. Power-windmill. No. 1,329,299; Jan. 27; v. 270; p. 581.

Foster, George W., assignor of one-half to G. Mayer, New York, N. Y. Flush-valve. No. 1,329,169; Jan. 27; v. 270; p. 557.

Foster, Stephen A., Toledo, Ohio. Advertising weather-shelter. No. 1,327,427; Jan. 6; v. 270; p. 102.

Fourneaux, Emile A., Manchester, England. Production of black upon vegetable textile fibers, silk fibers, or mixtures of same. No. 1,329,117; Jan. 27; v. 270; p. 548.

Fow, Raymond S. C., assignor of seventy-nine one-hundredths to R. T. Frush and twenty-one one-hundredths to W. Thompson, Philadelphia, Pa. Slicing-machine. No. 1,328,916; Jan. 27; v. 270; p. 510.

Fox, Frank H. (See Wallace and Fox.)

Frame, Frank W. (See Spurr and Randall, assignors.)

Francis, Harry G., Rushville, Ind. Veneer-press. No. 1,327,815; Jan. 13; v. 270; p. 236.

Frank, William E., assignor to Foster Bros, Mfg. Co., St. Louis, Mo. Spiral bed-spring. No. 1,327,231; Jan. 6; v. 270; p. 66.

Frankamp, Ernest H., Republic, Kans. Ice-cutting machine. No. 1,328,372; Jan. 20; v. 270; p. 378.

Franke, Johan F., Santa Ana, Calif. Toy. No. 1,329,045; Jan. 27; v. 270; p. 534.

Franklin, Hubert F., Brooklyn, assignor, by mesne assignments, to Animated Target Company, Inc., New York, N. Y. Cinematographic target. No. 1,328,275; Jan. 20; v. 270; p. 359.

Fraser, Alexander, Renfrew, Ontario, Canada. Repeating device for talking-machines. No. 1,327,816; Jan. 13; v. 270; p. 236.

Frazier, Philip L., Rockbury, Conn. Jointer-tool. No. 1,327,151; Jan. 6; v. 270; p. 51.

Frech, Charles, Sault Ste. Marie, Ontario, Canada. Valve for blowing-engines and the like. No. 1,326,923; Jan. 6; v. 270; p. 8.

Freeland, Charles E. (See Klug and Freeland.)

Freeman, E. H., Electric Company. (See Freeman, E. H., assignor.)

Freeman, Edgar H., Trenton, N. J., assignor to E. H. Freeman Electric Company. Lamp-locking construction. No. 1,326,924; Jan. 6; v. 270; p. 8.

Freeman, L. M. (See Elliott, Alexander T., assignor.)

Freimart, Otto, Martin, Ohio. Rail-joint. No. 1,327,541; Jan. 6; v. 270; p. 124.

French, Alfred W., Piqua, Ohio. Expressing apparatus. No. 1,327,093; Jan. 6; v. 270; p. 40.

French, Charles L., Cambridge, Mass. Storage apparatus for liquids. No. 1,327,990; Jan. 13; v. 270; p. 269.

French & Hecht. (See Einfeldt, Ernest E., assignor.)

French, Herman R., assignor to Intertype Corporation, Brooklyn, N. Y. Matrix for typographical machines. No. 1,328,146; Jan. 13; v. 270; p. 299.

Frey, George E., Steubenville, assignor of one-half to R. E. Snider, Mingo Junction, Ohio. Rail-chair. No. 1,328,917; Jan. 27; v. 270; p. 510.

Frey, Peter F., assignor to U. S. Light & Heat Corporation, Niagara Falls, N. Y. Electric conductor. No. 1,327,542; Jan. 6; v. 270; p. 124.

Fricke, Gilbert V. B. (See Henry and Fricke.)

Fried, Marcus, Lawrence, Mass. Tipping hand-tool. No. 1,328,508; Jan. 20; v. 270; p. 404.

Friedman, Mitchell J., Washington, D. C. Calendar. No. 1,328,830; Jan. 27; v. 270; p. 492.

Frisbie, Howard I., Anaconda, Mont. Electric precipitator. No. 1,329,237; Jan. 27; v. 270; p. 569.

Frisz, George E., and J. D. Wiltshire, Indianapolis, Ind. Wheel-puller. No. 1,328,663; Jan. 20; v. 270; p. 432.

Fritsche, John, Philadelphia, Pa. Dispensing-cabinet. No. 1,328,664; Jan. 20; v. 270; p. 432.

Fritzsche, George G. H., Brooklyn, N. Y. Binder. No. 1,327,992; Jan. 13; v. 270; p. 269.

Frohman, Edward D., Pittsburgh, Pa. Refractory material. No. 1,327,768; Jan. 13; v. 270; p. 226.

Frohner, Edward H., Youngstown, Ohio, assignor to Standard Oilcloth Co., New York, N. Y. Method of and apparatus for treating oil and obtaining by-products therefrom. No. 1,329,076; Jan. 27; v. 270; p. 539.

Fronczak, Antoni, Wilkes-Barre, Pa. Harrow. No. 1,329,118; Jan. 27; v. 270; p. 548.

Frush, Rolland T., et al. (See Fow, Raymond S. C., assignor.)

Fry, David F., and C. R. Whitton, Northampton, England. Fabric. No. 1,328,623; Jan. 20; v. 270; p. 425.

Fry, H. C., Glass Company. (See Samuel, Samuel R., assignor.)

Fry, J. Howard. (See Scholes and Brenner, assignors.)

Fuchs, Ernest, Paris, assignor to L. Renault, Billancourt, France. Forging cylinders of engines and similar structures. No. 1,328,276; Jan. 20; v. 270; p. 359.

Fugina, Arthur R., Louisville, Ky. Renitent railway-rail support. No. 1,329,077; Jan. 27; v. 270; p. 540.

Fuld, Katherine B., Baltimore, Md. Toy. No. 1,329,338; Jan. 27; v. 270; p. 587.

Fulda, Edward, New York, N. Y. Metal door construction. No. 1,328,918; Jan. 27; v. 270; p. 510.

Fulda, Edward, New York, N. Y. Uniting vertical plates by electric welding. No. 1,328,919; Jan. 27; v. 270; p. 510.

Fuller, Duane P., Carlisle, Wash. Operating mechanism for whistles. No. 1,328,252; Jan. 13; v. 270; p. 319.

Fuller, Franz A., assignor to The J. E. Mergott Company, Newark, N. J. Perpetual calendar. No. 1,327,317; Jan. 6; v. 270; p. 81.

Fulton Company, The. (See Fulton, Weston M., assignor.)

Fulton, Robert H., Los Angeles, Calif. Pipe-wrench. No. 1,327,595; Jan. 6; v. 270; p. 133.

Fulton, Weston M., assignor to The Fulton Company, Knoxville, Tenn. Tank-regulator. No. 1,328,277; Jan. 20; v. 270; p. 360.

Funahashi, Jo, Kobe, Japan. Manufacture of floor-covering. No. 1,329,170; Jan. 27; p. 270; p. 557.

Funk, James M., assignor of one-half to T. H. Belrose, Ottawa, Ill. Aeroplane. No. 1,327,543; Jan. 6; v. 270; p. 124.

Furber, Frederick M., Revere, Mass. Temperature-controlling mechanism for internal-combustion engines. No. 1,327,381; Jan. 6; v. 270; p. 93.

Furlong, Martin, Seattle, Wash. Mine safety apparatus. No. 1,327,596; Jan. 6; v. 270; p. 133.

Furstenberg, Paul W., New York, N. Y. Advertising device or the like. No. 1,329,078; Jan. 27; v. 270; p. 540.

Fynn, Valère A., assignor to Wagner Electric Manufacturing Company, St. Louis, Mo. Ignition-switch. No. 1,328,990; Jan. 27; v. 270; p. 523.

Gage, Mattie A., New York, N. Y. Alarm mechanism for clocks. No. 1,327,669; Jan. 13; v. 270; p. 209.

Gallup, Edward E., Pittsfield, Mass. Bill-posting device. No. 1,327,544; Jan. 6; v. 270; p. 124.

Gamble, William A., Macon, Ga. Planting-stick. No. 1,327,030; Jan. 6; v. 270) p. 29.

Gammeter, John R., Akron, Ohio, assignor to The B. F. Goodrich Company, New York, N. Y. Bumper. No. 1,329,339; Jan. 27; v. 270; p. 587.

Ganster, Joseph A., Philadelphia, Pa. Forming rings from solid bars. No. 1,328,509; Jan. 20; v. 270; p. 404.

Garber, Harvey C., Columbus, Ohio. Spark-plug. No. 1,327,882; Jan. 6; v. 270; p. 93.

Gardiner, Robert F., Clarendon, Va. Production of synthetic ammonia from the air or nitrogen. No. 1,328,082; Jan. 13; v. 270; p. 286.

Gardner, Davis S. (See Bates, Albert J., Jr., assignor.)

Gardner, Florinda, Salt Lake City, Utah. Speed-indicator. No. 1,329,046; Jan. 27; v. 270; p. 534.

Garfield, Elva R., New York, N. Y. Method and apparatus for teaching manuscript-form. No. 1,328,952; Jan. 27; v. 270; p. 516.

Garford Manufacturing Company, The. (See Manson, Ray H., assignor.)

Garnier, Ernest L., Neuilly-sur-Seine, France. Device for increasing the efficiency of firearms and the like. No. 1,327,545; Jan. 6; v. 270; p. 124.

Garrison, Orlando, Dayton, Ohio. Grinding-machine. No. 1,328,958; Jan. 27; v. 270; p. 517.

Garry, Jerome G. (See Garry, Robert S. and J. G.)

Garry, Robert S. and J. G., Jenks, Okla. Strainer for pumps. No. 1,329,171; Jan. 27; v. 270; p. 557.

Garzoni, Chinto A., De Lancey, Pa. Air-hose coupling. No. 1,328,373; Jan. 20; v. 270; p. 378.

Gaskins, Fred, et al. (See Bowen, Charles, assignor.)

Gatchell, George S., Roselle Park, N. J., assignor to The Singer Manufacturing Company. Thread-nipper-releasing device for sewing-machines. No. 1,327,232; Jan. 6; v. 270; p. 66.

Gatewood, Frank A., Sylvan Grove, Kans. Wrench. No. 1,327,991; Jan. 13; v. 270; p. 269.

Gavin, Mary M., executrix. (See Gavin, Norman A.)

Gavin, Norman A., deceased, Kinshasha, Belgian Congo; M. M. Gavin, executrix, assignor to Lever Brothers Limited, Port Sunlight, England. Extraction of oil from vegetable fruits. No. 1,328,278; Jan. 20; v. 270; p. 360.

Gehring, Walter E., Milwaukee, Wis. Suspended arch for boilers and the like. No. 1,328,511; Jan. 20; v. 270; p. 404.

Geiger, William H., Oakland, Calif. Gearing for egg-beaters, cream-whippers, and the like. No. 1,327,960; Jan. 13; v. 270; p. 261.

Gelatt, Walter B., Seymour, Iowa. Corn-harvester. No. 1,328,791; Jan. 20; v. 270; p. 456.

General Electric Company. (See Alexanderson, Ernst F. W., assignor.)

General Electric Company. (See Berry, Edward R., assignor.)

General Electric Company. (See Coolidge, William D., assignor.)

General Electric Company. (See Dickinson, Edgar D., assignor.)

General Electric Company. (See Eaton, John, assignor.)
General Electric Company. (See Hull, John I., assignor.)
General Electric Company. (See Korthals-Altes, Willem. C., assignor.)

General Electric Company. (See Reichold, Ludwig, assignor.)

General Electric Company. (See Sanborn, Arthur R., assignor.)

General Electric Company. (See Treat, Robert, assignor.)
General Electric Company. (See Van Aller, Tycho, assignor.)

General Electric Company. (See Welch, Alfred F., assignor.)

General Fire Extinguisher Company. (See Loepsinger, Albert J., assignor.)

General Fireproofing Company, The. (See Herbert, Arthur W., assignor.)

General Lead Batteries Company. (See Handler, Eugene, assignor.)

General Machine Works. (See Swartz and Richards, assignors.)

General Motors Company. (See Sweet, Ernest E., assignor.)

General Railway Signal Company. (See Lindner, John C., assignor.)

Genett, Levi E. (See Miles, Edward L., assignor.)

Genin, John B., St. Albans, Vt., assignor of one-eighth to A. D. Denis, Montreal, Canada, and one-eighth to J. O. Goyette, Rouses Point, N. Y. Train-pipe coupling. No. 1,327,031; Jan. 6; v. 270; p. 29.

Genn, John E., assignor to Stewart-Warner Speedometer Corporation, Chicago, Ill. Spark-plug. No. 1,328,147; Jan. 13; v. 270; p. 299.

Gent, Wm., Vending Machine Company, The. (See Larsen, Arnold, assignor.)

Geoghegan, Edward A., Chicago, Ill., assignor to M. Kraemer and E. J. Talbott, trustees. Superheater. No. 1,327,032; Jan. 6; v. 270; p. 29.

George, Maude S., St. Louis, Mo. Baby-pants. No. 1,329,119; Jan. 27; v. 270; p. 548.

Gerhard, Werner, Chicago, Ill. Impact-machine. No. 1,327,817; Jan. 13; v. 270; p. 237.

German-American Button Co. (See Hastings, Herbert, assignor.)

Gesell, Frank A., Los Angeles, Calif. Controlling means for saving systems combined with insurance protection. No. 1,329,120; Jan. 27; v. 270; p. 548.

Getchell, Benjamin E., assignor to The Trumbull Electric Manufacturing Company, Plainville, Conn. Electric switch. No. 1,327,383; Jan. 6; v. 270; p. 94.

Geyer, Hobart W. (See Van Valer, De Witt C., assignor.)

Gibson, Bedell, Nicholls, Ga. Automatic nut-tightening device. No. 1,327,152; Jan. 6; v. 270; p. 51.

Gilbert, A. C., Company, The. (See Erhardt, Oscar P., assignor.)

Gillenwaters, Joseph T. B., Cave City, Ky. Shoe. No. 1,328,665; Jan. 20; v. 270; p. 433.

Gilleo, Clarence C. (See Borst and Gilleo.)

Gillette Safety Razor Company. (See Wharton, Edward R., assignor.)

Gilson, John P. (See Gilson, Michael and J. P.) (Reissue.)

Gilson, Michael and J. P., Fredonia, Wis. Concrete-mixer. (Reissue.) No. 14,795; Jan. 27; v. 270; p. 590.

Ginter, Christian, Jr. (See Burns, John A., assignor.)

Glass, William C., Jamaica Plain, Mass. Sheet-feeding mechanism. No. 1,327,546; Jan. 6; v. 270; p. 124.

Gluck, Marcus, New York, N. Y. Spoon. No. 1,329,172; Jan. 27; v. 270; p. 558.

Goddard, Charles F. (See Stockton and Goddard.)

Godfrey, Warren P. (See Watts, Ben, assignor.) (Reissue.)

Golata, Andrew J., and L. L. Roberts, assignors of one-tenth to W. W. Carswell and one-tenth to A. L. Ellis, Detroit, Mich. Piston. No. 1,329,238; Jan. 27; v. 270; p. 570.

Goldberg, Maximilian M., assignor to The National Cash Register Company, Dayton, Ohio. Registering and recording mechanism. No. 1,327,153; Jan. 6; v. 270; p. 51.

Goldberg, Maximilian M., Dayton, Ohio. Speed-transformer. No. 1,328,083; Jan. 13; v. 270; p. 286.

Goldberg, Solomon H., assignor to The Hump Hairpin Manufacturing Company, Chicago, Ill. Machine for counting and arranging hairpins or like articles. No. 1,326,925; Jan. 6; v. 270; p. 8.

Goldblatt, Albert A., Brooklyn, N. Y. Alarm device for automobiles. No. 1,327,993; Jan. 13; v. 270; p. 269.

Golden, Charles F., Denver, Ind. Compass. No. 1,327,154; Jan. 6; v. 270; p. 51.

Goldthwaite, Helen A., Saco, Me. Conducting-cord holder. No. 1,329,173; Jan. 27; v. 270; p. 558.

Golstein, Albert, assignor to S. B. Hess, New York, N. Y. Electrical thermostat. No. 1,328,427; Jan. 20; v. 270; p. 388.

Gooch, Claiborne W., assignor to Burroughs Adding Machine Company, Detroit, Mich. Adding and subtracting machine. No. 1,327,318; Jan. 6; v. 270; p. 81.

Gooch, Claiborne W., assignor to Burroughs Adding Machine Company, Detroit, Mich. Adding-machine. No. 1,327,319; Jan. 6; v. 270; p. 81.

Gooch, Claiborne W., assignor to Burroughs Adding Machine Company, Detroit, Mich. Adding-machine. No. 1,327,320; Jan. 6; v. 270; p. 81.

Goodrich, B. F., Company, The. (See Gammeter, John R., assignor.)

Goodrich, B. F., Company, The. (See Wagenhorst, James H., assignor.)

Goodwin, George S., and J. J. Acker, Chicago, Ill. Clear-vision window. No. 1,327,321; Jan. 6; v. 270; p. 82.

Goodwin, James D., Richmond, Va., assignor of one-half to W. K. Dennis. Safety-razor. No. 1,327,547; Jan. 6; v. 270; p. 125.

Goodyear Tire & Rubber Company, The. (See Carter, William C., assignor.)

Goodyear Tire & Rubber Company, The. (See Harsel, William B., assignor.)

Goodyear Tire & Rubber Company, The. (See Upson, Ralph H., assignor.)

Gookin, Sylvester L., Boston, Mass., assignor to United Shoe Machinery Corporation, Paterson, N. J. Setting eyelets. No. 1,327,033; Jan. 6; v. 270; p. 29.

Gordon, Hayner H., Washington, D. C. Electrical system. No. 1,328,374; Jan. 20; v. 270; p. 378.

Gottschalk, Charles, St. Paul, Minn. Scraper. No. 1,327,155; Jan. 6; v. 270; p. 52.

Gould Coupler Company. (See Creveling, John L., assignor.)

Goulet, Delphine. (See Goulet, Omer C., assignor.)

Goulet, Omer C., assignor to D. Goulet, Fall River, Mass. Lever-chocking device. No. 1,329,079; Jan. 27; v. 270; p. 540.

Gow, Colin C., and D. F. Campbell, London, England. Control of power absorbed in electric furnaces. No. 1,327,548; Jan. 6; v. 270; p. 125.

Gower, Francis W., H. J. Owen, and E. Cox, Birmingham, England. Insulated handle for aluminum saucepans. No. 1,328,510; Jan. 20; v. 270; p. 404.

Goyette, J. O., et al. (See Genin, John B., assignor.)

Graham Brothers. (See Dunham, George W., assignor.)

Graham, David F., assignor to The Graham Roller Bearing Company, Coudersport, Pa. Socket-wrench. No. 1,328,428; Jan. 20; v. 270; p. 388.

Graham, Edmund, and G. Bowman, Belfast, Ireland. Liquid jacking apparatus for motor-vehicles. No. 1,327,670; Jan. 13; v. 270; p. 209.

Graham, Frank B., Kansas City, Mo. Dilator. No. 1,328,624; Jan. 20; v. 270; p. 425.

Graham, Joshua S., Detroit, Mich. Hatpin-guard. No. 1,328,954; Jan. 27; v. 270; p. 517.

Graham Roller Bearing Company, The. (See Graham, David F., assignor.)

Grand Rapids Show Case Co. (See Vanderveld, Anthony, assignor.)

Granger, William S., Duluth, Minn. Gas-mixer. No. 1,329,324; Jan. 27; v. 270; p. 585.

Grant, William W., Brooklyn, N. Y. Carbureter. No. 1,327,233; Jan. 6; v. 270; p. 66.

Graphoscope Company, The. (See Jenkins, Charles F., assignor.)

Grauer, Joseph, Brooklyn, N. Y. Die-holder. No. 1,328,279; Jan. 20; v. 270; p. 360.

Gray, David E., Highland Park, Ill. Mechanism for winding films. No. 1,327,034; Jan. 6; v. 270; p. 29.

Gray, Harry A., assignor of one-half to G. R. Wright, Milwaukee, Wis. Card-holder. No. 1,326,926; Jan. 6; v. 270; p. 8.

Gray, James A., assignor to American Can Company, San Francisco, Calif. Mechanism for seaming ends to can-bodies. No. 1,327,994; Jan. 13; v. 270; p. 269.

Graybill, Bird M., Chicago, Ill., assignor to S. W. Cook, Brookline, Mass. Apparatus for indicating fuel consumption. No. 1,328,920; Jan. 27; v. 270; p. 511.

Grayson, Iona, Tulsa, Okla. Fish-scaler. No. 1,328,148; Jan. 13; v. 270; p. 299.

Greco, Vito B., assignor of one-half to W. F. Baum, Waterloo, Iowa. Heel for boots and shoes. No. 1,328,991; Jan. 27; v. 270; p. 524.

Green, George W. A., O. Wanas, and F. H. Livens, assignors to Ruston and Hornsby, Limited, Lincoln, England. Reversing mechanism for internal-combustion engines. No. 1,327,995; Jan. 13; v. 270; p. 270.

Green, Walter R., Chicago, Ill. Extra-tire carrier. No. 1,329,174; Jan. 27; v. 270; p. 558.

Greenawalt, William E., Denver, Colo. Metallurgical process. No. 1,328,666; Jan. 20; v. 270; p. 433.

Greene, Richard T., South Pasadena, Calif. Brush-handle. No. 1,327,597; Jan. 6; v. 270; p. 134.

Greenison, Nelson J., New York, N. Y. Shoe-shining stand. No. 1,328,667; Jan. 20; v. 270; p. 433.

Greenwald, Charles E., Spokane, Wash. Belt. No. 1,327,035; Jan. 6; v. 270; p. 30.

Gregory, George H., East Orange, N. J. Adjustable shower-spray device. No. 1,327,428; Jan. 6; v. 270; p. 102.

Greist Manufacturing Company, The. (See Lent, Wilmar F., assignor.)

Grieshaber, Hugo E., New London, Conn., assignor to Electric Boat Company. Torpedo-launching apparatus. No. 1,327,614; Jan. 13; v. 270; p. 198.

Griffice, George D., Big Spring, Tex. Planter attachment. No. 1,328,375; Jan. 20; v. 270; p. 378.

Griffin, Alvah M., Kansas City, Mo. Electrolytic cell. No. 1,327,094; Jan. 6; v. 270; p. 41.

Griffin Wheel Company. (See Vial, Frederick K., assignor.)

Griffith, Graves, San Francisco, Calif. Internal-combustion hydraulic pump. No. 1,327,036; Jan. 6; v. 270; p. 30.

Griner, Alvah A., Bayside, assignor to Renaissance Corset Co., Inc., New York, N. Y. Machine for making fabricated wire. No. 1,327,467; Jan. 6; v. 270; p. 109.

Griscom-Russell Company. (See Jones, Russell C., assignor.)

Gruban, John G. W., et al. (See Dabbs, Savage, and Hindle, assignors.)

Gruhl, Irvin W., Los Angeles, Calif. Signaling device. No. 1,327,818; Jan. 13; v. 270; p. 237.

Gruschka, Max, and F. Marjanko, Prague, Austria. Manufacturing press-button parts. No. 1,327,322; Jan. 6; v. 270; p. 82.

Guaranteed Tractors. (See Phillips, Walter C., assignor.)

Guerritore, Orazio, Rome, Italy. Percussion-fuse. No. 1,327,037; Jan. 6; v. 270; p. 30.

Guett, Monroe, assignor to The Hart & Hegeman Manufacturing Company, Hartford, Conn. Electric switch. No. 1,327,615; Jan. 13; v. 270; p. 199.

Guggenbuehler, Carl, Newark, N. J. Tool for facilitating the positioning of driving-shoes in driving-box bearings of locomotives. No. 1,327,468; Jan. 6; v. 270; p. 109.

Gulberson, Richard. (See Arbon, Paul, assignor.)

Gunchick, Frank, Blanchard, Idaho. Combined card-container and table. No. 1,329,080; Jan. 27; v. 270; p. 540.

Gund Manufacturing Company, The. (See Pieper, Chester R., assignor.)

Gunnarson, Frederick, Ogden, Utah. Roller-skate. No. 1,327,549; Jan. 6; v. 270; p. 125.

Gurney Scale Company, The. (See Sweet, Charles M., assignor.)

Guthrie, William S., Terrell, Tex. Carbureter. No. 1,328,042; Jan. 13; v. 270; p. 279.

Guy, Frederick M., Jackson, assignor of one-third to L. J. Moeller, Detroit, Mich., and one-third to F. R. Sunderman, New York, N. Y. Internal-combustion engine. No. 1,327,202; Jan. 6; v. 270; p. 60.

Guy, Joseph, Humbermouth, Newfoundland. Strainer for water-supply pipes of locomotives. No. 1,327,708; Jan. 13; v. 270; p. 216.

Gwyer, Herbert J., Yonkers N. Y. Refrigerator construction. No. 1,328,324; Jan. 20; v. 270; p. 369.

Gyp Steel Products Company. (See Shuman, Cleo G., assignor.)

H-K Toy & Novelty Co., The. (See McDaniel, Walter O., assignor.)

Haas, Edward. (See Ferguson and Haas.)

Hachmann, Frederick, St. Louis, assignor of one-half to D. M. Hutchinson, Ferguson, Mo. Hose-mender. No. 1,329,121; Jan. 27; v. 270; p. 548.

Hackett, Charles H., assignor to W. W. Marsh, Waterloo, Iowa. Liner for centrifugal cream-separators. No. 1,328,084; Jan. 13; v. 270; p. 287.

Hackleman, William H., Appleton, Wis. Gear-cutting attachment. No. 1,329,175; Jan. 27; v. 270; p. 558.

Hadjisky, Joseph N. (See Heideman and Hadjisky.)

Haefely, Emil, Basel, Switzerland. Winding-machine for the manufacture of hollow insulating-cylinders for electrotechnical purposes. No. 1,328,792; Jan. 20; v. 270; p. 456

Haessly, Stephen B., Faribault, Minn. Internal-combustion engine. No. 1,327,384; Jan. 6; v. 270; p. 94.

Hafner, Edward P., and J. T. Roberts, St. Louis, Mo. Tire-peeling machine. No. 1,329,239; Jan. 27; v. 270; p. 570.

Hagadone, Clinton A. (See Benjamin and Hagadone.)

Hagadone, Clinton A., Western Springs, Ill., assignor, by mesne assignments, to International Harvester Company. Corn-harvester. No. 1,328,668; Jan. 20; v. 270; p. 443.

Hagstrom, Curt W., Wilmette, Ill. Foldable bathtub. No. 1,327,866; Jan. 13; v. 270; p. 245.

Hague, Clifford P., Hartford, Conn. Vapor croup-kettle. No. 1,327,550; Jan. 6; v. 270; p. 125.

Hahn, Louis C., Cincinnati, Ohio. Drafting device. No. 1,328,871; Jan. 27; v. 270; p. 501.

Hainsworth, Arthur F., Leeds, England. Crane. No. 1,328,793; Jan. 20; v. 270; p. 456.

Hakes, Hudson W., Millbury, Mass. Automatically-threading shuttle. No. 1,327,709; Jan. 13; v. 270; p. 216.

Haldeman, James C., assignor to The Silver Manufacturing Company, Salem, Ohio. Arm-binder and elevating control-shaft lock. No. 1,328,429; Jan. 20; v. 270; p. 388.

Hall, C. M., Lamp Company. (See Allen, Claude E., assignor.)

Hall, Edward L., New York, N. Y. Fire-extinguisher. No. 1,326,927; Jan. 6; v. 270; p. 8.

Hall, George F., assignor to E. W. Kaiser, Newark, N. J. Whistle. No. 1,327,323; Jan. 6; v. 270; p. 82.

Hall, William B., Chicago, Ill., assignor to Union Railway Equipment Co. Railway-car. No. 1,327,095; Jan. 6; v. 270; p. 41.

Haller, Hans K., Copenhagen, Denmark. Transport system for postage and other goods. No. 1,327,952; Jan. 13; v. 270; p. 261.

Hamilton, Clifford C. (See Hutchinson and Hamilton.)

Hamilton, James C., Arlington Heights, Mass. Pencil. No. 1,327,038; Jan. 6; v. 270; p. 30.

Hamilton, John R., Yonkers, assignor to Automatic Sprinkler Company of America, New York, N. Y. Water-motor. No. 1,327,953; Jan. 13; v. 270; p. 261.

Hamlyn, George A. (See Weizmann and Hamlyn.)

Hammer, Charles, Queens, assignor to American Metal Cap Company, Brooklyn, N. Y. Bottle-closure. No. 1,328,280; Jan. 20; v. 270; p. 360.

Hammer, Willie A., Eufaula, Okla. Combined grinder and shaker. No. 1,327,385; Jan. 6; v. 270; p. 94.

Hammerstrom, Arthur, Deerfield, N. H. Sled-brake. No. 1,329,047; Jan. 27; v. 270; p. 534.

Hancq, John B., Jamestown, N. Y. Shuttle. No. 1,327,954; Jan. 13; v. 270; p. 262.

Handlan Buck Manufacturing Company. (See Rolfes, George H., assignor.)

Handlan, William C. (See Roe, William C., assignor.)

Handler, Eugene, Newark, assignor to General Lead Batteries Company, Delaware, N. J. Storage-battery element. No. 1,327,234; Jan. 6; v. 270; p. 67.

Hands, Harry A. (See Ellis, Arthur T., assignor.)

Hanes, Cyrus E., Armington, Ill. Oil-measure. No. 1,327,156; Jan. 6; v. 270; p. 52.

Hankee, Harry J., Minneapolis, Minn. Traffic-signal for autos. No. 1,327,671; Jan. 13; v. 270; p. 209.

Hanks, John C., Russell, Ky. Safety-hanger for brake-beams. No. 1,327,909; Jan. 13; v. 270; p. 254.

Hanlon & Goodman Co. (See Hecht, Charles E., assignor.)

Hanrath, Theodore W., Chicago, Ill. Baby-carrier. No. 1,328,832; Jan. 27; v. 270; p. 493.

Hansen, Hans C., Seattle, Wash. Oven attachment for stoves. No. 1,327,203; Jan. 6; v. 270; p. 61.
Hansen, Karl H., Sewickley, assignor, by mesne assignments, to Koppel Industrial Car and Equipment Company, Pittsburgh, Pa. Axle-bearing. No. 1,328,512; Jan. 20; v. 270; p. 405.
Haugen, Andrew J., and E. G. Oversmith, Denver, Colo. Gas-saver for internal-combustion engines. No. 1,327,551; Jan. 6; v. 270; p. 125.
Hanson, Henry L., Worcester, Mass. Broaching-machine. No. 1,328,281; Jan. 20; v. 270; p. 360.
Hanson, John Z., Fort Worth, Tex. Advertising device. No. 1,327,552; Jan. 6; v. 270; p. 126.
Hanson, Samuel L., Albert Lea, Minn. Adjustable cattle-stall. No. 1,327,386; Jan. 6; v. 270; p. 94.
Hanlon, Pater S., Kew, Victoria, Australia. Mixing-valve for steam-heated water-supply systems. No. 1,327,235; Jan. 6; v. 270; p. 67.
Harada, Yotaro, Stockton, Calif. Iron. No. 1,326,928; Jan. 6; v. 270; p. 9.
Harbridge, Chester C., Detroit, Mich. Demountable rim. No. 1,328,731; Jan. 20; v. 270; p. 445.
Hard Manufacturing Company. (See McKay, John, assignor.)
Hardee, Robert E., Savannah, Ga. Violin sound-post. No. 1,327,157; Jan. 6; v. 270; p. 52.
Harley-Davidson Motor Co. (See Harley, William S., assignor.)
Harley, Melvin G., South Bend, Ind. Headlight. No. 1,328,902; Jan. 27; v. 270; p. 524.
Harley, William S., assignor to Harley-Davidson Motor Co., Milwaukee, Wis. Automatic voltage control. No. 1,328,149; Jan. 13; v. 270; p. 299.
Harley, William S., assignor to Harley-Davidson Motor Company, Milwaukee, Wis. Combined intake and exhaust manifold. No. 1,328,150; Jan. 13; v. 270; p. 299.
Harm, Frederick H., St. Paul Minn. Optical trial-frame holder. No. 1,328,669; Jan. 20; v. 270; p. 434.
Harms, Rhinehart W., Chicago, Ill., assignor to The R. Thomas and Sons Company, East Liverpool, Ohio. Insulator-pin. No. 1,328,732; Jan. 20; v. 270; p. 445.
Harpman, Albert J., Owatonna, Minn. Propeller-drive for aeroplanes. No. 1,329,081; Jan. 27; v. 270; p. 540.
Harriman National Bank of the City of New York. (See Vassell, Anthony, assignor.)
Harris, Harold H., Wilmington, N. C. Drain-board. No. 1,327,039; Jan. 6; v. 270; p. 30.
Harris, James W., Turbeville, S. C. Corn-cleaner. No. 1,328,872; Jan. 27; v. 270; p. 501.
Harriss, James B., Newark, N. J. Method of and apparatus for separating leaves. No. 1,328,733; Jan. 20; v. 270; p. 445.
Harriss, James B., Newark, N. J. Method and apparatus for separating leaves from packages. No. 1,328,734; Jan. 20; v. 270; p. 446.
Harriss, James B., Newark, N. J. Method and apparatus for separating leaves from packages. No. 1,328,735; Jan. 20; v. 270; p. 446.
Harsel, William B., assignor to The Goodyear Tire & Rubber Company, Akron, Ohio. Tire-making machine. No. 1,327,010; Jan. 13; v. 270; p. 254.
Hart, Austin H., Bronxville, N. Y., assignor to Deposited Metal Products Company. Radiator. No. 1,328,151; Jan. 13; v. 270; p. 300.
Hart, Harry S., assignor to National Dump Car Co., Chicago, Ill. Door-operating mechanism. (Reissue.) No. 14,785; Jan. 6; v. 270; p. 136.
Hart & Hegeman Manufacturing Company, The. (See Guett, Monroe, assignor.)
Hart & Hegeman Manufacturing Company, The. (See Stirling, Clarence C., assignor.)
Hartford, Edward V. (See Ruggles, William G., assignor.)
Hartford-Fairmont Company. (See Peiler, Karl E., assignor.)
Hartford Storage Battery Manufacturing Company, The. (See Barhoff, Fred W., assignor.)
Hartley, Arthur J., Peoria, Ill. Support and gearing for swinging conveyers. No. 1,327,469; Jan. 6; v. 270; p. 109.
Hartog, S. D., Manufacturing Company. (See Hartog, Stephen D., assignor.)
Hartog, Stephen D., assignor to S. D. Hartog Manufacturing Company, St. Louis, Mo. Manufacturing piston-rings. No. 1,329,271; Jan. 27; v. 270; p. 576.
Harvey, Herbert, Oakland, Calif. Weighing-machine. No. 1,327,553; Jan. 6; v. 270; p. 126.
Hasbrouck, Louis B., Elmira, N. Y. Starter for internal-combustion engines. No. 1,327,276; Jan. 6; v. 270; p 74.
Hasburg, John W., Chicago, Ill. Staining glass. No. 1,328,833; Jan. 27; v. 270; p. 493.
Haschke, Feodor G., assignor of one-half to J. C. Wall, Austin, Tex. Live-bait bucket. No. 1,327,040; Jan. 6; v. 270; p. 31.
Haskell, William E., assignor to Estey Organ Company, Brattleboro, Vt. Speaking-pipe. No. 1,327,906; Jan. 13; v. 270; p. 270
Hass, Nelson R., Dayton, Ohio, assignor to The Dayton Engineering Laboratories Company. Cut-out relay. No. 1,327,951; Jan. 13; v. 270; p. 261.
Hastings, Herbert, assignor to German-American Button Co., Rochester, N. Y. Button-inspecting machine. No. 1,327,672; Jan. 13; v. 270; p. 209.

Hastings Manufacturing Co. (See Johnson, Aben E., assignor.)
Hathaway, Edgar F., Dorchester, Mass. Loom reed cleaning and polishing machine. No. 1,328,563; Jan. 20; v. 270; p. 414.
Hathaway, Hosea, Brookline, Mass. Boring and slotting tool. No. 1,328,430; Jan. 20; v. 270; p. 388.
Hauber, Mathias, Jr. (See Meadows, Hauber, and Charlton.)
Haugen, Henry, Stoughton, Wis. Lawn-edge trimmer. No. 1,329,176; Jan. 27; v. 270; p. 558.
Haugh, Frank A., Winfield, Kans. Underreamer. No. 1,328,955; Jan. 27; v. 270; p. 517.
Hausberg, Ernest, Charles City, Iowa. Electrically-operated typewriter. No. 1,328,736; Jan. 20; v. 270; p. 446.
Havener, Arthur R., Waltham, Mass., assignor to American Lacing Hook Co. Lacing-hook-setting machine. No. 1,327,911; Jan. 13; v. 270; p. 254.
Hawkesworth, Arthur L., Butte, Mont. Drill. No. 1,328,325; Jan. 20; v. 270; p. 369.
Hawkins, Edgar M., assignor to M. D. Knowlton Company, Rochester, N. Y. Machine for making corrugated paper-board. No. 1,327,158; Jan. 6; v. 270; p. 52.
Hawkins, James E., Glendale, Calif. Refrigerator. No. 1,328,625; Jan. 20; v. 270; p. 425.
Hawley, Burton S., Sparta, Wis. Bedstead. No. 1,327,554; Jan. 6; v. 270; p. 126.
Hawn, William L., assignor of one-half to A. Kavanagh, Kansas City, Mo. Mattress. No. 1,328,248; Jan. 13; v. 270; p. 318.
Hayden, Don H., Cleveland, Ohio. Switch-box. No. 1,328,993; Jan. 27; v. 270; p. 524.
Hayes, Peter T. (See Jeans and Hayes.)
Hayes, Robert D., assignor to Index Visible, Incorporated, New Haven, Conn. Index or file. No. 1,328,956; Jan. 27; v. 270; p. 517.
Hays, Charles F., Cottagegrove, Tenn. Grass-rope reel. No. 1,329,240; Jan. 27; v. 270; p. 570.
Head, Ernest C., Van Wert, Ohio, assignor to Colburn Machine Tool Company, Franklin, Pa. Final adjusting device for machine-tools. No. 1,328,670; Jan. 20; v. 270; p. 434.
Heany, John A., Jersey City, N. J., assignor, by mesne assignments, to Industrial Research Corporation. Dynamo-electric starting, lighting, and ignition mechanism for automobiles. No. 1,328,873; Jan. 27; v. 270; p. 501.
Heath, Henry A., Newark, N. J. Combined multiple suspenders and brace. No. 1,327,041; Jan. 6; v. 270; p. 31.
Heath, Wilfrid P. (See Kirkpatrick, Swordling, and Heath.)
Hecht, Charles E., Irvington, N. J., assignor to Hanlon & Goodman Co., New York, N. Y. Brush-holder. No. 1,328,162; Jan. 13; v. 270; p. 301.
Hecker, Arthur S., Cleveland, Ohio. Loading and unloading apparatus. No. 1,327,324; Jan. 6; v. 270; p. 82.
Heckler, Winfeld T. (See Maltry and Heckler.)
Heckman, James, Clarendon, Tex. Pipe-holder. No. 1,327,673; Jan. 13; v. 270; p. 209.
Heideman, Fred J., and J. N. Hadjisky, Detroit, Mich., assignors to Kelvinator Corporation, Wilmington, Del. Means and method of regulating automatic mechanical refrigerators. No. 1,329,350; Jan. 27; v. 270; p. 589.
Heideman, Fred J., and J. N. Hadjisky, Detroit, Mich., assignors to Kelvinator Corporation, Wilmington, Del. Pressure-operated-regulating apparatus. No. 1,329,351; Jan. 27; v. 270; p. 589.
Heidman, George, et al. (See Blood, Burr B., assignor.)
Heindrich, Frank K., et al. (See Carbi, Joseph L., assignor.)
Heinecke, Fredrich G., Gaylord, Minn. Cornstalk-cutter. No. 1,327,997; Jan. 13; v. 270; p. 270.
Heller, Eugene H. (See Jaeger and Heller.)
Hellmund, Rudolf E., Pittsburgh, Pa., assignor to Westinghouse Electric and Manufacturing Company. System of control. No. 1,327,819; Jan. 13; v. 270; p. 237.
Hellmund, Rudolf E., Pittsburgh, Pa., assignor to Westinghouse Electric and Manufacturing Company. Dynamo-electric machine. No. 1,327,820; Jan. 13; v. 270; p. 237.
Hellmund, Rudolf E., Pittsburgh, Pa., assignor to Westinghouse Electric and Manufacturing Company. System of control. No. 1,329,243; Jan. 27; v. 270; p. 571.
Hellmund, Rudolf E., Swissvale, Pa., assignor to Westinghouse Electric & Manufacturing Company. Dynamo-electric machine. No. 1,327,821; Jan. 13; v. 270; p. 237.
Hellmund, Rudolf E., Swissvale, Pa., assignor to Westinghouse Electric and Manufacturing Company. System of control. No. 1,327,822; Jan. 13; v. 270; p. 238.
Hellmund, Rudolf E., Swissvale, Pa., assignor to Westinghouse Electric and Manufacturing Company. System of control. No. 1,327,823; Jan. 13; v. 270; p. 238.
Hellmund, Rudolf E., Swissvale, Pa., assignor to Westinghouse Electric and Manufacturing Company. System of control. No. 1,328,513; Jan. 20; v. 270; p. 405.
Hellmund, Rudolf E., Swissvale, Pa., assignor to Westinghouse Electric & Manufacturing Company. System of control. No. 1,328,514; Jan. 20; v. 270; p. 405.
Hellmund, Rudolf E., Swissvale, Pa., assignor to Westinghouse Electric & Manufacturing Company. System of control. No. 1,328,515; Jan. 20; v. 270; p. 405.

Hellmund, Rudolf E., Swissvale, and B. S. Moore, Wilkinsburg, Pa., assignors to Westinghouse Electric and Manufacturing Company. Shaft-bearing. No. 1,329,241; Jan. 27; v. 270; p. 570.

Hellmund, Rudolf E., Swissvale, Pa., assignor to Westinghouse Electric and Manufacturing Company. Coil-supporting device for dynamo - electric machines. No. 1,329,242; Jan. 27; v. 270; p. 570.

Helmond, William F., Hartford, Conn., assignor to Underwood Typewriter Company, New York, N. Y. Typewriting-machine. No. 1,328,626; Jan. 20; v. 270; p. 426.

Heltzel, John N., Warren, Ohio. Concrete-form. No. 1,329,177; Jan. 27; v. 270; p. 559.

Hemsing, Maurice A., assignor to Davenport Manufacturing Company, Davenport, Iowa. Cigar-lighter. No. 1,328,516; Jan. 20; v. 270; p. 405.

Hemstreet, George P., Hastings-upon-Hudson, N. Y., assignor to The International Pavement Company, Hartford, Conn. Making anchor-blocks. No. 1,327,710; Jan. 13; v. 270; p. 217.

Henault, Lewis N., Albany, N. Y. Deck-sash support. No. 1,328,874; Jan. 27; v. 270; p. 501.

Henderson, James B., Lee, England. Controlling guns. No. 1,327,204; Jan. 6; v. 270; p. 61.

Hendricks, Adam C., Martinsburg, W. Va. Automatic phonograph-stop. No. 1,327,955; Jan. 13; v. 270; p. 262.

Henkmann, August, Bokoshe, Okla. Target. No. 1,327,998; Jan. 13; v. 270; p. 270.

Hennessy, Daniel E., Holyoke, Mass., assignor to Cowan Truck Company. Hydraulic jack. No. 1,327,470; Jan. 6; v. 270; p. 109.

Henning, August H., Milwaukee, Wis. Brush and making same. No. 1,326,929; Jan. 6; v. 270; p. 9.

Henriksen, Lars J., Käflinge, Sweden. Shoe-heel and producing same. No. 1,328,249; Jan. 13; v. 270; p. 318.

Henry, Abner E., Greensburg, Pa. Demountable wheel-rim. No. 1,327,759; Jan. 13; v. 270; p. 226.

Henry, Albert, and G. V. R. Fricke, Hoboken, N. J. Shoe-protector. No. 1,328,957; Jan. 27; v. 270; p. 518.

Henry, Nelson B., assignor, by mesne assignments, to M. H. Miller, Atlanta, Ga. Baling fibrous materials. No. 1,327,471; Jan. 6; v. 270; p. 109.

Henry, Nelson B., assignor, by mesne assignments, to M. H. Miller, Atlanta, Ga. Compress. No. 1,327,472; Jan. 6; v. 270; p. 110.

Hensal, Elmer A., Panora, Iowa. Extension-table. No. 1,328,243; Jan. 13; v. 270; p. 317.

Hensel, John S., Stevens Point, Wis. Traction-lug. No. 1,327,867; Jan. 13; v. 270; p. 246.

Hepburn, Charles J., et al. (See Matthiessen, Conrad S., assignor.)

Herbert, Arthur W., Youngstown, Ohio, assignor to The General Fireproofing Company. Safety-tread structure. No. 1,328,875; Jan. 27; v. 270; p. 502.

Herdman, William J., Toronto, Ontario, Canada. Thermostatic valve. No. 1,327,277; Jan. 6; v. 270; p. 74.

Herpst, Herman A., Norway, Mich. Pump. No. 1,327,868; Jan. 13; v. 270; p. 246.

Heslewood, William R., assignor of one-third to P. J. Rowland, Oakland, Calif. Carbureter. No. 1,327,205; Jan. 6; v. 270; p. 61.

Hess, Henry, Philadelphia, Pa. Pencil. No. 1,327,236; Jan. 6; v. 270; p. 67.

Hess, Simon B. (See Goldstein, Albert, assignor.)

Hewitt, Frank W., Arlington, assignor to Simplex Electric Heating Company, Cambridge, Mass. Electric heating unit. No. 1,328,229; Jan. 13; v. 270; p. 314.

Hewitt, Fred L., assignor to M. E. Converse & Son Co., Winchendon, Mass. Refrigerator. No. 1,327,473; Jan. 6; v. 270; p. 110.

Hewitt, Harry, Manchester, assignor of one-half to Joseph Baker & Sons Limited, London, England. Dividing dough. No. 1,326,930; Jan. 6; v. 270; p. 9.

Hewitt, Peter C., Ringwood Manor, N. J. Electric circuit. No. 1,328,326; Jan. 20; v. 270; p. 369.

Hewitt, Peter C., Ringwood Manor, N. J. Electric circuit. No. 1,328,327; Jan. 20; v. 270; p. 370.

Heymann, Oscar. (See Figenshu, William L., assignor.)

Hezmalhalch, Thomas, et al. (See Yeats, Samuel W., assignor.)

Hill, Alfred N., Lund, Sweden. Measuring instrument. No. 1,328,876; Jan. 27; v. 270; p. 502.

Hill, George. (See Boozer, Arthur G., assignor.)

Hill, John, Jr., Dandridge, Tenn. Sawmill-knee-adjusting mechanism. No. 1,327,555; Jan. 6; v. 270; p. 126.

Hill Pump Valve Company, The. (See Jaeger and Heller, assignors.)

Hill, Raymond I., assignor to The Hill Rubber Heel Company, Elyria, Ohio. Resilient heel or heel-lift. No. 1,328,564; Jan. 20; v. 270; p. 414.

Hill Rubber Heel Company, The. (See Hill, Raymond I., assignor.)

Hill, Thomas A., Brooklyn, N. Y., assignor, by mesne assignments, to The J. G. Wilson Corporation. Roller for partitions and doors. No. 1,328,043; Jan. 13; v. 270; p. 279.

Hill, William G., Brooklyn, N. Y. Male urinal device. No. 1,327,042; Jan. 6; v. 270; p. 31.

Hill, William W., Sarona, Wis. Regulator for engines. No. 1,327,999; Jan. 13; v. 270; p. 270.

270 O. G.—ii

Hilley, William P., Des Moines, Iowa. Operating device for window-sashes. No. 1,329,178; Jan. 27; v. 270; p. 559.

Hilliard, John M., assignor of one-half to C. W. Lott, Waco, Tex. Shear-trimmer. No. 1,328,671; Jan. 20; v. 270; p. 434.

Hilliman, Herbert H., assignor to Challenge Refrigerator Company, Grand Haven, Mich. Refrigerator. No. 1,329,310; Jan. 27; v. 270; p. 588.

Hills, Henry A., Grand Rapids, Mich. Hydrocarbon-filter. No. 1,328,044; Jan. 13; v. 270; p. 279.

Hills, Henry A., Grand Rapids, Mich. Multistage adjustable filtering apparatus. No. 1,328,045; Jan. 13; v. 270; p. 279.

Hills, Henry A., Grand Rapids, Mich. Unitary multistage filter apparatus. No. 1,328,046; Jan. 13; v. 270; p. 279.

Hilty, Frederick, Waukegan, assignor to L. R. Wilder, Chicago, Ill. Centrifugal valve-casting machine. No. 1,329,179; Jan. 27; v. 270; p. 559.

Himes, Orville J., Oswego, N. Y. Umbrella-staff. No. 1,326,931; Jan. 6; v. 270; p. 9.

Hinchey, Charlotte, Buffalo, N. Y. Denture. No. 1,327,674; Jan. 13; v. 270; p. 210.

Hindle, Alfred H. (See Dabbs, Savage, and Hindle.)

Hirshleimer, Harry J. (See Cameron, William W., assignor.)

Hirsohn, Isaac, New York, N. Y. Bucket-closure. No. 1,328,672; Jan. 20; v. 270; p. 434.

Hirst, Franklin G., Philadelphia, Pa. Lubricator. No. 1,327,043; Jan. 6; v. 270; p. 31.

Hiss, William J., assignor to Diamond Expansion Bolt Company, New York, N. Y. Cable - clamp. No. 1,328,376; Jan. 20; v. 270; p. 379.

Hiss, William J., assignor to Diamond Expansion Bolt Company, New York, N. Y. Cable - clamp. No. 1,328,377; Jan. 20; v. 270; p. 379.

Hitchcock, Halbert K., Pittsburgh, Pa., assignor to Pittsburgh Plate Glass Company. Glass-drawing apparatus. No. 1,328,673; Jan. 20; v. 270; p. 434.

Hobbs Wall & Co. (See Burrows, Robert W., assignor.)

Hobbs, William I. (See Hudgins, Iverson D., assignor.)

Hobson & Motzer Co., The. (See Motzer, Alfred, assignor.)

Hobson, Oliver J., assignor of one-half to O. Q. Beckworth, Chicago, Ill. Tire-tread for pneumatic-tire casings and making and attaching same. No. 1,327,912; Jan. 13; v. 270; p. 254.

Hockaday, Frank W., Wichita, Kans. Highway-marker. No. 1,327,387; Jan. 6; v. 270; p. 94.

Hodge, William B. (See Cramer and Hodge.)

Hodgman, Willis K., Taunton, Mass. Apparatus for operating alarms or other devices. No. 1,328,994; Jan. 27; v. 270; p. 524.

Hoe, Robert, New York, N. Y. Sheet-feeding mechanism for printing-presses. No. 1,328,877; Jan. 27; v. 270; p. 502.

Hofer, Joseph L., Bridgewater, S. D. Steering-gear. No. 1,327,616; Jan. 13; v. 270; p. 199.

Hoffay, Jose, South Kensington, London, England. Gramophone, phonograph, and the like. No. 1,326,932; Jan. 6; v. 270; p. 10.

Hoffman, Daniel E., Plymouth, Ohio. Sieve for threshing-machines. No. 1,327,325; Jan. 6; v. 270; p. 83.

Hoffman, Louis F., and W. J. Unkel, Kinder, La. Steam-boiler. No. 1,327,159; Jan. 6; v. 270; p. 52.

Hoffmann, Frank F., Los Angeles, Calif. Direction-indicator. No. 1,327,605; Jan. 6; v. 270; p. 135.

Hogan, Donald P. (See Rendahl, George A., assignor.)

Hoge, Joseph F. D., New York, N. Y. Thermostat. No. 1,329,122; Jan. 27; v. 270; p. 548.

Hoge Manufacturing Company, The. (See Saunders, William M., assignor.)

Holczer, Mike, Norfolk, Va. Tractor-hitch. No. 1,327,617; Jan. 13; v. 270; p. 199.

Holdaway, William S., Jr., Salt Lake City, Utah. Power-transmission machine. No. 1,328,517; Jan. 20; v. 270; p. 406.

Holen, John O., Tono, Wash. Vise. No. 1,326,933; Jan. 6; v. 270; p. 10.

Holland, Nellie G., Boston, Mass. Sheet, blanket, or the like. No. 1,327,824; Jan. 13; v. 270; p. 238.

Holland, Walter E., and J. M. Skinner, assignors to Philadelphia Storage Battery Company, Philadelphia, Pa. Storage-battery separator. No. 1,329,180; Jan. 27; v. 270; p. 559.

Holland, Walter E., Philadelphia, and L. J. Pearson, Wyncote, assignors to Philadelphia Storage Battery Company, Philadelphia, Pa. Storage battery and preparing same. No. 1,329,181; Jan. 27; v. 270; p. 560.

Hollander, Erik E., Newark, N. J. Tool for making holes non-circular. No. 1,328,085; Jan. 13; v. 270; p. 287.

Holman, Daniel F., Farmersville, Ohio. Appliance for the protection and preservation of drains and small sewers. No. 1,327,278; Jan. 6; v. 270; p. 75.

Holman, Stephen W. (See Andrews and Holman.)

Holmes, Thomas J., Chicago, Ill. Car-journal lubricator. No. 1,327,429; Jan. 6; v. 270; p. 102.

Holt Auto Devices Company. (See Holt, Edward E., assignor.)

Holt, Benjamin, Stockton, Calif. Link tread-track. No. 1,327,556; Jan. 6; v. 270; p. 126.

Holt, Edward E., assignor to Holt Auto Devices Company, Chicago, Ill. Valve-cap. No. 1,329,182; Jan. 27; v. 270; p. 560.

Holt, Frederick B., Antrobus, near Northwich, England, assignor to Westinghouse Electric and Manufacturing Company. Circuit-interrupter. No. 1,327,825; Jan. 13; v. 270; p. 238.

Holt Manufacturing Company, The. (See Norelius, Emil F., assignor.)

Holt Manufacturing Company, The. (See Turnbull, William, assignor.)

Holt Manufacturing Company, The. (See Wickersham, Elmer E., assignor.)

Holt, Pliny E., Stockton, Calif. Draft-rigging. No. 1,327,557; Jan. 6; v. 270; p. 126.

Holtom, Albert O., New York, N. Y. Vehicle-body. No. 1,327,558; Jan. 6; v. 270; p. 127.

Holzapfel, Albert C., and P. Walther, New York, N. Y. Composition for coating new iron and steel. No. 1,328,282; Jan. 20; v. 270; p. 360.

Honold, Gottlob, Stuttgart, and A. Krauss, Cannstatt, Germany, assignors, by mesne assignments, to American Bosch Magneto Corporation, New York, N. Y. Priming system for internal-combustion engines. No. 1,327,430; Jan. 6; v. 270; p. 102.

Hook, Charles B., Muncie, Ind. Cultivator-fender. No. 1,328,518; Jan. 20; v. 270; p. 406.

Hoover, Howard E., Chicago, Ill., assignor to The Hoover Suction Sweeper Company, New Berlin, Ohio. Cleaner. No. 1,328,737; Jan. 20; v. 270; p. 446.

Hoover, Howard E., Chicago, Ill., assignor to Hoover Suction Sweeper Company, New Berlin, Ohio. Cleaner. No. 1,329,048; Jan. 27; v. 270; p. 534.

Hoover Suction Sweeper Company, The. (See Hoover, Howard E., assignor.)

Hopedale Manufacturing Company. (See Northrop, Jonas, assignor.)

Hopkins, Alfred, Boston, Mass. Curtain-stretcher. No. 1,328,695; Jan. 27; v. 270; p. 524.

Hopkins, James L., St. Louis, Mo. Street-cleaner. No. 1,328,738; Jan. 20; v. 270; p. 446.

Hopkins, Nevil M., Washington, D. C. Antiskid device for motor-propelled vehicles. No. 1,328,739; Jan. 20; v. 270; p. 447.

Hornung, John C., Chicago, Ill. Valve mechanism. No. 1,327,675; Jan. 13; v. 270; p. 210.

Horschmann, Mary E., Springfield, Mo. Belt or girdle support. No. 1,328,958; Jan. 27; v. 270; p. 518.

Horton, Charles M., Elizabeth, N. J., assignor to The Singer Manufacturing Company. Mechanism for fastening together nested tire-casings. No. 1,327,237; Jan. 6; v. 270; p. 67.

Hosch, Annie M., administratrix. (See Hosch, Walter E.)

Hosch, Walter E., deceased; A. M. Hosch, administratrix, assignor to The Measuregraph Company, St. Louis, Mo. Calculating apparatus. No. 1,327,044; Jan. 6; v. 270; p. 31.

Hosier, Abel R., Toronto, Ontario, Canada. Hinge. No. 1,327,431; Jan. 6; v. 270; p. 102.

Hough, Samuel, Atco, N. J., and S. Baader, Philadelphia, Pa. Grease-cup. No. 1,327,239; Jan. 6; v. 270; p. 67.

Houskeeper, William G., Philadelphia, Pa., assignor to Western Electric Company, Incorporated, New York, N. Y. Transmitter. No. 1,328,906; Jan. 27; v. 270; p. 525.

Howard, Albert L., Montello, Mass. Apparatus for teaching projection. No. 1,327,474; Jan. 6; v. 270; p. 110.

Howard, Lawrence W., Manchester, N. H. Draft-controller for smoke-conduits. No. 1,328,563; Jan. 20; v. 270; p. 415.

Howe, Dale E., assignor of one-half to J. M. Newton, Sioux Falls, S. D. Toy-furniture set. No. 1,328,921; Jan. 27; v. 270; p. 511.

Howe, Earl W., Norfolk, Va. Collapsible steam-chest and oven. No. 1,328,152; Jan. 13; v. 270; p. 300.

Howell, Austin W., Hanover, Ohio. Chair. No. 1,327,475; Jan. 6; v. 270; p. 111.

Howell, Robert R., Minneapolis, Minn. Device for grinding-mills. No. 1,328,834; Jan. 27; v. 270; p. 493.

Howland, Ephraim, Pontiac, Mich. Army-trailer. No. 1,327,326; Jan. 6; v. 270; p. 83.

Höyberg, Hans M., Frederiksberg, near Copenhagen, Denmark. Ascertaining the quantity of fat in milk and cream. No. 1,329,183; Jan. 27; v. 270; p. 560.

Hubbard, Fred, Humboldt, Ariz. Brake for conveyers. No. 1,327,559; Jan. 6; v. 270; p. 127.

Hubbell, Henry S., assignor to T. R. Almond Manufacturing Company, Ashburnham, Mass. Chuck. No. 1,328,627; Jan. 20; v. 270; p. 426.

Hudgins, Iverson D., Kirkwood, assignor of one-third to W. I. Hobbs, Gainesville, Ga. Water-motor. No. 1,329,244; Jan. 27; v. 270; p. 571.

Hudson, David W., assignor to Hudson-Sharp Machine Company, Green Bay, Wis. Machine for perforating, slitting, and rewinding paper. No. 1,328,431; Jan. 20; v. 270; p. 389.

Hudson-Sharp Machine Company. (See Hudson, David W., assignor.)

Hufschmidt, Louis A., San Francisco, Calif. Lighting-fixture bowl-hook. No. 1,327,598; Jan. 6; v. 270; p. 134.

Huggins, Charlie T., Hemingway, S. C. Cultivator. No. 1,328,740; Jan. 20; v. 270; p. 446.

Huggins, Merion J., assignor to Automotive Development Co., Inc., New York, N. Y. Speed-controlling mechanism for automobiles. No. 1,326,935; Jan. 6; v. 270; p. 10.

Hughes, Arthur S., Mansfield, Ohio. Gravity-hinge. No. 1,327,045; Jan. 6; v. 270; p. 32.

Hughes, Edward. (See Hughes, George, assignor.)

Hughes, George, assignor of one-half to E. Hughes, St. Louis, Mo. Resilient wheel. No. 1,327,096; Jan. 6; v. 270; p. 41.

Hughes, Howard R., Houston, Tex. Rotary boring-drill. No. 1,327,913; Jan. 13; v. 270; p. 254.

Hughes, Robert R., Jr., New York, N. Y., assignor to Union Special Machine Company, Chicago, Ill. Sewing-machine. No. 1,329,245; Jan. 27; v. 270; p. 571.

Hulburd, De Forest, Chicago, Ill., assignor to Elgin National Watch Company. Wrist-watch case and clamp. No. 1,326,984; Jan. 6; v. 270; p. 10.

Hulett, Frank E. (See Hulett, George H. and F. E.)

Hulett, George H. and F. E., Cleveland, Ohio. System and apparatus for loading vessels. No. 1,327,327; Jan. 6; v. 270; p. 83.

Hull, John L., Schenectady, N. Y., assignor to General Electric Company. Reactance-shunt for commutator-machines. No. 1,328,519; Jan. 20; v. 270; p. 406.

Humason, Granville A., Houston, Tex. Pump-piston. No. 1,327,914; Jan. 13; v. 270; p. 255.

Hump Hairpin Manufacturing Company, The. (See Goldberg, Solomon H., assignor.)

Humphrey, Frank L., Enid, Okla. Clothes-basket carrier. No. 1,328,163; Jan. 13; v. 270; p. 302.

Hunt, Andrew M., Berkeley, and D. E. Fogg, Oakland, Calif. Apparatus for cooling and scrubbing gases. No. 1,327,599; Jan. 6; v. 270; p. 134.

Hunt, Louis J., Sandycroft, Wales. Alternating-current dynamo-electric machine adapted for synchronous working. No. 1,328,520; Jan. 20; v. 270; p. 406.

Hunt, William H. (See Macintosh and Hunt.)

Huntley Manufacturing Company. (See Leonard, George S., assignor.)

Hurley Machine Company. (See Fisher, Alva J., assignor.)

Hurley, Nell C. (See Wood, James J., assignor.)

Hurst, William, Winnipeg, Manitoba, Canada. Electrical radiator-heater. No. 1,327,279; Jan. 6; v. 270; p. 75.

Hurt, Henry H., Yonkers, assignor to Robeson Process Company, New York, N. Y. Burning fuel. No. 1,329,300; Jan. 27; v. 270; p. 581.

Hurtig, Josef, Rochester, N. Y. Electrically-driven spindle. No. 1,327,160; Jan. 6; v. 270; p. 52.

Hurwitz, Joseph, New York, N. Y. Shirt. No. 1,327,476; Jan. 6; v. 270; p. 111.

Hutchinson, David M. (See Hachmann, Frederick, assignor.)

Hutchinson, Job, Brooklyn, N. Y. Means for cooling liquids. No. 1,327,560; Jan. 6; v. 270; p. 127.

Hutchinson, Joseph, and C. C. Hamilton, Gull Lake, Saskatchewan, Canada. Wheel-lubricator. No. 1,328,959; Jan. 27; v. 270; p. 518.

Hyams, Herbert B., St. Paul, Minn. Dispensing-receptacle. No. 1,329,184; Jan. 27; v. 270; p. 560.

Hyde, Claude C., Otisville, N. Y. Snowplow. No. 1,329,123; Jan. 27; v. 270; p. 548.

Illinois Engineering Company. (See MacDonald, John E., assignor.)

Illinois Tool Works. (See Olson, Carl G., assignor.)

Ince, Frank L., Maplewood, Mo. Puzzle. No. 1,327,388; Jan. 6; v. 270; p. 95.

Indahl, Mauritz C. (See Bancroft and Indahl.)

Index Visible. (See Hayes, Robert D., assignor.)

Industrial Electric Furnace Company. (See Snyder, Frederick T., assignor.)

Industrial Research Corporation. (See Heany, John A., assignor.)

Ingersoll-Rand Company. (See Boyer, Lewis E., assignor.)

Ingham, Emanuel, San Diego, Calif. Method and apparatus for weaving textile fabrics. No. 1,328,794; Jan. 20; v. 270; p. 457.

Ingle, Arthur H. (See Putnam, Salmon W., 3d., assignor.)

International Harvester Company. (See Benjamin, Bert R., assignor.)

International Harvester Company. (See Benjamin and Hagadone, assignors.)

International Harvester Company. (See Burgess, Edward W., assignor.)

International Harvester Company. (See Dennis, Samuel K., assignor.)

International Harvester Company. (See Hagadone, Clinton A., assignor.)

International Harvester Company. (See Merwin, George M., assignor.)

International Harvester Company. (See Mott, Carl W., assignor.)

International Harvester Company. (See Raney, Clemma R., assignor.)

International Harvester Company of Canada. (See Bozard, Harrison B., assignor.)

International Motor Company. (See Leipert, August H., assignor.)

International Nitrogen Company. (See Reid, James H., assignor.)

International Pavement Company, The. (See Hemstreet, George P., assignor.)

International Precipitation Company. (See Welch, Harry V., assignor.)

International Time Recording Company of New York. (See Larabee, Clinton E., assignor.)

Interstate Ever-license Company. (See Fawcett, Charles H., assignor.)

Interstate Tool and Manufacturing Company. (See Balthasar, Harry G., assignor.)

Kops, Daniel. New York, N. Y. Apparel - corset. No. 1,328,086 ; Jan. 13 ; v. 270 ; p. 287.

Kops, Daniel. New York, N. Y. Apparel-corset. No. 1,328,675 ; Jan. 20 ; v. 270 ; p. 435.

Korhonen, John, Englewood, N. J. Snowplow. No. 1,328,157 ; Jan. 13 ; v. 270 ; p. 301.

Kornstein, Ulrich, New York, N. Y. Hair-drying comb. No. 1,329,301 ; Jan. 27 ; v. 270 ; p. 581.

Korthals-Altes, Willem C., Schenectady, N. Y., assignor to General Electric Company. Alternating-current motor. No. 1,328,525 ; Jan. 20 ; v. 270 ; p. 407.

Kory, Joseph N., Denver, Colo. Sample - carrier. No. 1,328,167 ; Jan. 13 ; v. 270 ; p. 302.

Korzeniewski, Czeslaw, and S. Chojnacki, Cleveland, Ohio. Fuel-oil burner. No. 1,327,763 ; Jan. 13 ; v. 270 ; p. 227.

Kossmann, Max, Brooklyn, N. Y. Lamp-shade holder. No. 1,328,331 ; Jan. 20 ; v. 270 ; p. 370.

Kousnetzoff, Nicholas, and E. M. Kouzmin, New York, N. Y. Typewriting-machine. No. 1,328,158 ; Jan. 13 ; v. 270 ; p. 301.

Kouzmin, Eugene M. (See Kousnetzoff and Kouzmin.)

Kozik, Stanislaw, Indian Head, Md. Furniture-caster. No. 1,327,920 ; Jan. 13 ; v. 270 ; p. 256.

Kraemer, Milton, trustee, et al. (See Geoghegan, Edward A., assignor.)

Krag, Nils A. (See Rösholt, Nils, assignor.)

Kramer, William H., Newcastle, Ind. Saw-filing device. No. 1,328,159 ; Jan. 13 ; v. 270 ; p. 301.

Krannich, Emil A., Columbiana, Ohio, assignor of one-half to L. A. Andregg, Mansfield, Ohio. Tire-core. No. 1,328,676 ; Jan. 20 ; v. 270 ; p. 435.

Krasa, Albert, Chicago, Ill. Yarn-dyer. No. 1,328,435 ; Jan. 20 ; v. 270 ; p. 389.

Kratz, Franz, assignor to Robert Bosch Aktiengesellschaft, Stuttgart, Germany. Rolled condenser for sparking apparatus. No. 1,328,925 ; Jan. 27 ; v. 270 ; p. 512.

Kratz, Roy G., Omaha, assignor to L. C. Sharp, Plattsmouth, Nebr. Releasing cup-pastry from molds. No. 1,329,086 ; Jan. 27 ; v. 270 ; p. 541.

Krause, William P., assignor to Mumford Molding Machine Company, Chicago, Ill. Plunger-guide construction. No. 1,328,526 ; Jan. 20 ; v. 270 ; p. 407.

Krause, William P., Chicago, Ill., assignor to Mumford Molding Machine Company, Jersey City, N. J. Molding-machine. No. 1,328,527 ; Jan. 20 ; v. 270 ; p. 408.

Krauss, Adolf. (See Honold and Krauss.)

Kremer, Franklin W., Rutherford, N. J. Tire. No. 1,328,632 ; Jan. 20 ; v. 270 ; p. 427.

Kretek, Frank F. (See Jezik, Joseph J., assignor.)

Kring, Levi, Westerville, Ohio. Tractor. No. 1,328,839 ; Jan. 27 ; v. 270 ; p. 494.

Krogh, Ferdinand W., San Francisco, Calif. Sand-protecting device for turbine-pumps. No. 1,328,234 ; Jan. 13 ; v. 270 ; p. 315.

Krohn, Alfred, Spokane, Wash. Fireless chicken-brooder. No. 1,327,104 ; Jan. 6 ; v. 270 ; p. 84.

Kroon, Arthur W., Glenellyn, Ill. Gate. No. 1,328,168 ; Jan. 13 ; v. 270 ; p. 303.

Kropacz, John, assignor of one-third to J. Jakubecz, Calgary, Alberta, Canada. Rail-support. No. 1,328,002 ; Jan. 13 ; v. 270 ; p. 271.

Krueger, Emil M., assignor to Badger Meter Manufacturing Company, Milwaukee, Wis. Water-meter spindle. No. 1,328,879 ; Jan. 27 ; v. 270 ; p. 503.

Kuchler, John. (See Dickelmann and Kuchler.)

Kuehlhorn, Arnold A., Chicago, Ill. Elevator attachment. No. 1,328,633 ; Jan. 20 ; v. 270 ; p. 427.

Kuhstek, Albert J. H., Richmond, Hill, N. Y. Forming piston-rings No. 1,328,436 ; Jan. 20 ; v. 270 ; p. 390.

Kulow, William J., Pine Bluff, Ark. Concrete-chimney form. No. 1,327,481 ; Jan. 6 ; v. 270 ; p. 112.

Kurtz, Benjamin F., Avalon, Pa. Nut-lock. No. 1,327,435 ; Jan. 6 ; v. 270 ; p. 103.

Kurtz, Stewart S., Sr. (See Leahy, William P., assignor.)

Kusuda, Takejiro, Osaka, Japan. Belt. No. 1,329,190 ; Jan. 27 ; v. 270 ; p. 561.

Kutil, Louis J. (See Ross, John, assignor.)

Kuyser, Jan A., Sale, England, assignor to Westinghouse Electric and Manufacturing Company. Dynamo-electric machine. No. 1,329,247 ; Jan. 27 ; v. 270 ; p. 571.

La Bar, Bert G., Turtle Creek, Pa., assignor to Westinghouse Electric and Manufacturing Company. Gearing for electrical measuring instruments. No. 1,327,832 ; Jan. 13 ; v. 270 ; p. 239.

Labrosse, Paul, and F. Estève, Lyon, France. Circuit-breaker for magnetos. No. 1,327,284 ; Jan. 6 ; v. 270 ; p. 75.

Lachman, Maurice, assignor to Universal Electric Welding Company, New York, N. Y. Fencepost. No. 1,328,926 ; Jan. 27 ; v. 270 ; p. 512.

Lachman, Maurice, assignor to Universal Electric Welding Company, New York, N. Y. Pole or post. No. 1,328,927 ; Jan. 27 ; v. 270 ; p. 512.

Lafrance, Joseph, assignor of one-half to A. Chagnon, Montreal, Quebec, Canada. Air-pump. No. 1,327,833 ; Jan. 13 ; v. 270 ; p. 239.

La Hodny, William, Buffalo, N. Y. Adjustable bracket for mirrors and other objects. No. 1,328,677 ; Jan. 20 ; v. 270 ; p. 435.

Laird, Wilbur G., assignor to H. L. Doherty, New York, N. Y. Refractory lining. No. 1,328,380 ; Jan. 20 ; v. 270 ; p. 370.

Lallié, Norbert, Nantes, France. Typewriter. No. 1,329,087 ; Jan. 27 ; v. 270 ; p. 541.

La May, Arthur C. (See Todd and La May.)

Lamkin, Lorenzo O., and J. H. Berghaus, Jr., Louisville, Ky. Collapsible form. No. 1,327,333 ; Jan. 6 ; v. 270 ; p. 84.

Lammers, Matthew, Sheboygan Falls, Wis. Milker-head. No. 1,328,880 ; Jan. 27 ; v. 270 ; p. 503.

Lampe, Fred E., Newark, N. J. Soldering composition. No. 1,327,620 ; Jan. 13 ; v. 270 ; p. 199.

Lams, William R. (See Snelling and Lams.)

Landers, David L., Estill, S. C. Railway-switch. No. 1,328,003 ; Jan. 13 ; v. 270 ; p. 271.

Landis Machinery Company. (See Anderson, Gustaf A., assignor.)

Landmark, Hans B., Drammen, Norway. Production of tanning extract from waste sulfite lye. No. 1,327,105 ; Jan. 6 ; v. 270 ; p. 43.

Lane, Harry L., Venice, Calif. Air-valve attachment for carbureters. No. 1,328,235 ; Jan. 13 ; v. 270 ; p. 316.

Lang, Lincoln A., assignor to The Northern Trust Company, Chicago, Ill. Power-shift mechanism. No. 1,328,437 ; Jan. 20 ; v. 270 ; p. 390.

Lange, Jens, Hellerup, Denmark, assignor to Dansk Varmekedel Syndikat System Lange, Fabrikant-Firma, Copenhagen, Denmark. Radiator for steam and water. No. 1,327,870 ; Jan. 13 ; v. 270 ; p. 246.

Langley, John W., et al. (See Barton, Charles N., assignor.)

Lanston Monotype Machine Company. (See Bancroft and Indahl, assignors.)

Lanston Monotype Machine Company. (See Bancroft and Knight, assignors.)

Lantz, Eugene, Jersey City, N. J. Releasable bearing. No. 1,327,285 ; Jan. 6 ; v. 270 ; p. 76.

Lantz, Eugene, Jersey City, N. J. Releasable bearing. No. 1,327,286 ; Jan. 6 ; v. 270 ; p. 76.

Lanum, Walter R., Savannah, Ga. Heater. No. 1,328,743 ; Jan. 20 ; v. 270 ; p. 447.

Lanz, Andrew, Pittsburgh, Pa. Fuel-feeding apparatus. No. 1,327,764 ; Jan. 13 ; v. 270 ; p. 227.

Lanz, Andrew, Pittsburgh, Pa. Apparatus for burning solid fuel. No. 1,327,765 ; Jan. 13 ; v. 270 ; p. 227.

Lanzetta, Francesco, Brooklyn, N. Y. Vise attachment. No. 1,328,049 ; Jan. 13 ; v. 270 ; p. 280.

Lard, Allan E. (See Buckley and Lard.)

Larkin, Francis C., Rutherford, N. J. Closure for milk-bottles. No. 1,329,248 ; Jan. 27 ; v. 270 ; p. 572.

Larrabee, Clinton E., Binghamton, N. Y., assignor to International Time Recording Company of New York. Recorder and registering locks. No. 1,327,334 ; Jan. 6 ; v. 270 ; p. 84.

Larsen, Arnold, assignor to The Wm. Gent Vending Machine Company, Cleveland, Ohio. Apportioning device. No. 1,327,678 ; Jan. 13 ; v. 270 ; p. 210.

Larson, Anna J., Sherburn, Minn. Loading device. No. 1,327,436 ; Jan. 6 ; v. 270 ; p. 103.

Larson, Louis H., Santiago, Minn. Tile-trench digger. No. 1,327,335 ; Jan. 6 ; v. 270 ; p. 84.

La Rue, Eugene C. and M. E., South Pasadena, Calif. Infant's bath-wagon. No. 1,327,242 ; Jan. 6 ; v. 270 ; p. 68.

La Rue, Mabel E. (See La Rue, Eugene C. and M. E.)

Lathrop, Edward K. (See Myers, Charles D., assignor.)

Lavoisier, Lucien, Paris, France. Ignition-plug for internal-combustion engines. No. 1,327,482 ; Jan. 6 ; v. 270 ; p. 112.

Lawes, William F., Bedford, N. H. Dumping device. No. 1,328,928 ; Jan. 27 ; v. 270 ; p. 512.

Lawler, William T., Jersey City, N. J. Railway-switch heater. No. 1,327,483 ; Jan. 6 ; v. 270 ; p. 112.

Lawn, William E., Rochester, N. Y. External-explosion engine. No. 1,328,160 ; Jan. 13 ; v. 270 ; p. 301.

Lawson, William C., Roanoke, Va. Locomotive. No. 1,327,243 ; Jan. 6 ; v. 270 ; p. 68.

Layne, Mahlon E., Memphis, Tenn. Well-screen. No. 1,328,438 ; Jan. 20 ; v. 270 ; p. 390.

Layne, Olym A., Los Angeles, Calif. Impact device. No. 1,328,569 ; Jan. 20 ; v. 270 ; p. 415.

Lazarus, Willis H., assignor to S. Pfeiffer Manufacturing Company, St. Louis, Mo. Can or container. No. 1,328,881 ; Jan. 27 ; v. 270 ; p. 503.

Lea, Charles, Boston, Mass., assignor, by mesne assignments, to McCleary, Wallin and Crouse, Amsterdam, N. Y. Mechanism for and process of constructing chenille. No. 1,328,570 ; Jan. 20 ; v. 270 ; p. 416.

Lea, Charles, assignor to American Warp Drawing Machine Company, Boston, Mass. Tube-frame for looms. No. 1,329,302 ; Jan. 27 ; v. 270 ; p. 581.

Lea, Charles, assignor to American Warp Drawing Machine Company, Boston, Mass. Tube-frame. No. 1,329,303 ; Jan. 27 ; v. 270 ; p. 581.

Lea, Frank D., Findlay, Ohio. Piano-lifting truck. No. 1,328,634 ; Jan. 20 ; v. 270 ; p. 427.

Leach, Frank, Detroit, Mich. Soap-holder. No. 1,328,528 ; Jan. 20 ; v. 270 ; p. 408.

Leach, William F., Childress, Tex. Shade-roller and curtain-pole bracket. No. 1,329,249 ; Jan. 27 ; v. 270 ; p. 572.

Leahy, Bernard, Bridgeport, Conn. Trunk-harness. No. 1,327,680 ; Jan. 13 ; v. 270 ; p. 211.

Leahy, William P., Canton, Ohio, assignor, by mesne assignments, of one-half to S. S. Kurtz, Sr. Compression-coupling. No. 1,327,106 ; Jan. 6 ; v. 270 ; p. 43.

Leatherman, Robert L., and F. Pfrogner, Mount Pleasant, Pa. Combination desk and chair. No. 1,328,169 ; Jan. 13 ; v. 270 ; p. 303.

Leavitt, Benjamin F., assignor to The Leavitt Diving Armor Company, Toledo, Ohio. Diving apparatus. No. 1,327,679; Jan. 13; v. 270; p. 211.

Leavitt Diving Armor Company, The. (See Leavitt, Benjamin F., assignor.)

Lebby, States L., Charleston, S. C. No-glare headlight. No. 1,327,563; Jan. 6; v. 270; p. 128.

Le Cho1, Charles C., Akron, Ohio. Ratchet socket-wrench. No. 1,328,087; Jan. 13; v. 270; p. 287.

Lee, Bernard S., Beverly, Mass., assignor, by mesne assignments, to, United Shoe Machinery Corporation, Paterson, N. J. Stamping-machine. No. 1,327,050; Jan. 6; v. 270; p. 33.

Lee, Ira, Suction Cleaner Corporation. (See Sheffler, Ira L., assignor.) (Reissue.)

Lee, John H. (See Eyles, Anton G., assignor.)

Lee, William, New Bedford, Mass. Splice-bar. No. 1,328,170; Jan. 13; v. 270; p. 3

Lee, William H., assignor to Syracuse Chilled Plow Company, Syracuse, N. Y. Plow construction (detachable share.) No. 1,327,921; Jan. 13; v. 270; p. 256.

Lee, William K. (See Renfro, Albert L., assignor.)

Lees, Edgar, assignor to The Whitehead Torpedo Works (Weymouth) Limited, Weymouth, England. Gyroscopic steering mechanism of automobile-torpedoes. No. 1,328,571; Jan. 20; v. 270; p. 416.

Lees, Kenneth F., New Haven, Conn. Pneumatic-tire pressure-gage. No. 1,328,572; Jan. 20; v. 270; p. 416.

Lefax. (See Parker, John C., assignor.)

Lehmann, Karl A. A., Biel, and C. Schindler, Pfäfers, Switzerland. Machine for stamping workmen's individual cards. No. 1,328,840; Jan. 27; v. 270; p. 495.

Lehr, Nicholas P., Fremont, Ohio. Clod crusher and packer. No. 1,328,171; Jan. 13; v. 270; p. 303.

Leighty, William J., Chicago, Ill. Cutting device. No. 1,327,715; Jan. 13; v. 270; p. 217.

Leipert, August H., Brooklyn, assignor to International Motor Company, New York, N. Y. Pressed-steel transmission-case. No. 1,327,681; Jan. 13; v. 270; p. 211.

Leitner, Emil, Hoboken, N. J., assignor to Powers Photo Engraving Company, New York, N. Y. Making printing-plates. No. 1,329,088; Jan. 27; v. 270; p. 541.

Leitner, Henry, Westminster, London, England. Screw-propeller. No. 1,328,004; Jan. 13; v. 270; p. 271.

Leitner, Henry, Westminster, London, England. Screw-propeller. No. 1,328,005; Jan. 13; v. 270; p. 271.

Leitner, Henry, Westminster, London, and W. H. Exley, Harehills, Leeds, England. Manufacture of electric accumulators. No. 1,327,336; Jan. 6; v. 270; p. 85.

Leitner, Henry, London, and W. H. Exley, Pontefract, England. Manufacture of electric accumulators. No. 1,329,125; Jan. 27; v. 270; p. 549.

Lemieux, Thomas D., Lakewood, Ohio. Cable-pulling device. No. 1,328,678; Jan. 20; v. 270; p. 435.

Lemily, John B., Brooklyn, N. Y. Clothes-cabinet. No. 1,326,940; Jan. 6; v. 270; p. 11.

Leming, Frank, Hingham, Mass. Adjustable dust-cap for valve-stems. No. 1,329,126; Jan. 27; v. 270; p. 549.

Lenholt, John E., Leete Island, assignor of one-half to C. R. Painter, Guilford, Conn. Pipe-wrench. No. 1,328,744; Jan. 20; v. 270; p. 447.

Lent, Orlando D., Peekskill, N. Y. Harrow. No. 1,327,337; Jan. 6; v. 270; p. 85.

Lent, Wilmar F., New Haven, Conn., assignor to The Greist Manufacturing Company. Grease-cup. No. 1,328,573; Jan. 20; v. 270; p. 416.

Leonard, George S., Minneapolis, Minn., assignor to Huntley Manufacturing Company, Silver Creek. Fan or blower. No. 1,328,679; Jan. 20; v. 270; p. 435.

Leonard, Goldstone D., New York, N. Y. Brassière. No. 1,328,439; Jan. 20; v. 270; p. 390.

Letre. Philip H., Attleboro Falls, Mass. Match-strike. No. 1,327,244; Jan. 6; v. 270; p. 68.

Leventy, Joseph, Johnstown, Pa. Metallic railway crosstie. No. 1,328,574; Jan. 20; v. 270; p. 416.

Lever Brothers Limited. (See Gavin, Norman A., assignor.)

Levin, Max, Chicago, Ill. Manure-box. No. 1,327,397; Jan. 6; v. 270; p. 96.

Levine, William. (See Rubin and Levine.)

Levinson, Harry B., Brooklyn, N. Y., and W. H. Westfall, Rutherford, N. J. Trailer-truck. No. 1,327,338; Jan. 6; v. 270; p. 85.

Lewis, Charles A., Toronto, Ontario, Canada. Pickle-fork holder. No. 1,327,437; Jan. 6; v. 270; p. 103.

Lewis, Charles A., Toronto, Ontario, Canada. Pickle-fork. No. 1,327,438; Jan. 6; v. 270; p. 104.

Lewis, Charles A., Toronto, Ontario, Canada. Pickle-fork holder. No. 1,327,439; Jan. 6; v. 270; p. 104.

Lewis, David O., Detroit, Mich. Window-latch. No. 1,328,284; Jan. 20; v. 270; p. 361.

Lewis, Frank M., Chicago, Ill. Differential mechanism. No. 1,328,440; Jan. 20; v. 270; p. 390.

Lewis, George W., Grinnell, Iowa, assignor to Lovell Manufacturing Company, Erie, Pa. Wringer. No. 1,327,766; Jan. 13; v. 270; p. 227.

Lewis, Lloyd V., Edgewood borough, assignor to The Union Switch & Signal Company, Swissvale, Pa. Railway-signal. No. 1,328,960; Jan. 27; v. 270; p. 518.

Lewis, Seneca G., Greensburg, Pa. Watch-support. No. 1,327,051; Jan. 6; v. 270; p. 33.

Libbey-Owens Sheet Glass Company, The. (See Colburn, Irving W., assignor.) (Reissue.)

Libbey Owens Sheet Glass Company, The. (See Crowley, Joseph P., assignor.)

Libby-Owens Sheet Glass Company, The. (See Owens, Michael J., assignor.)

Libbey-Owens Sheet Glass Company, The. (See Whittemore, James, assignor.)

Lichtenberg, Erich H., assignor to Koehring Machine Company, Milwaukee, Wis. Clutch and brake control mechanism. No. 1,328,635; Jan. 20; v. 270; p. 427.

Lidberg, Tlodolf, assignor to Electro-Thermophore Company, Chicago, Ill. Controlling temperatures. No. 1,327,207; Jan. 6; v. 270; p. 61.

Liddle, Absalom, et al. (See Dabbs, Savage, and Hindle, assignors.)

Liebegott, George H. (See Miller and Liebegott.)

Liebler, Frederick, New York, N. Y. Signal, indicator, and recorder. No. 1,328,245; Jan. 13; v. 270; p. 318.

Lietz, Paul S., assignor to The Brunswick-Balke-Collender Company, Chicago, Ill. Bed for game-tables and making same. No. 1,328,332; Jan. 20; v. 270; p. 370.

Lillos, Charles G., Minneapolis, Minn. Air-pump. No. 1,328,529; Jan. 20; v. 270; p. 408.

Linch, William H., Bellaire, Ohio. Window-shade appliance. No. 1,326,941; Jan. 6; v. 270; p. 11.

Lind, Anna, Bridgeport, Conn. Spring-fan. No. 1,328,172; Jan. 13; v. 270; p. 303.

Lindblad, Axel R., Stockholm, Sweden. Synthetic production of cyanids and nitrids. No. 1,328,575; Jan. 20; v. 270; p. 417.

Lindman, Konrad W., assignor, by mesne assignments, to Nordiska Kullager Aktiebolaget, Gottenborg, Sweden. Ball-holder for ball-bearings. No. 1,329,089; Jan. 27; v. 270; p. 542.

Lindner, John C., Rochester, N. Y., assignor to General Railway Signal Company, Gates, N. Y. Semaphore-signal-operating mechanism. No. 1,328,381; Jan. 20; v. 270; p. 379.

Lindquist, Knut O. W., Chicago, Ill. Leaf-turner. No. 1,327,621; Jan. 13; v. 270; p. 200.

Lindsay, William, Chicago, Ill. Agitating device. No. 1,328,576; Jan. 20; v. 270; p. 417.

Lindström, Carl, Berlin, Germany. Stamp-affixing machine. No. 1,329,090; Jan. 27; v. 270; p. 542.

Lingle, George W., Silver Lake, Wis., assignor of two-fifths to W. O. Carney, Chicago, Ill. Wheel-rim and sprocket-teeth therefor. No. 1,327,107; Jan. 6; v. 270; p. 43.

Link, Louis, New York, N. Y. Lens-mounting. No. 1,328,441; Jan. 20; v. 270; p. 390.

Lippincott, Fisher II., Philadelphia, Pa. Variable-speed clutch. No. 1,327,767; Jan. 13; v. 270; p. 227.

Lippincott, Roy A., and E. F. Billson, Melbourne, Victoria, Australia. Fastener for hinged structures. (Reissue.) No. 14,793; Jan. 20; v. 270; p. 458.

Lippitt, Sargent V. L., San Juan, Porto Rico. Apparatus for separating fiber. No. 1,327,484; Jan. 6; v. 270; p. 112.

Lisenby Manufacturing Company. (See Quade, Frank H., Jr., assignor.)

Little, Lenard, Gainesville, Ga. Drain cut-off. No. 1,327,831; Jan. 13; v. 270; p. 239.

Little, Thomas R., Liverpool, England. Steel or iron structural work. No. 1,328,841; Jan. 27; v. 270; p. 495.

Livens, Frederick H. (See Green, Wans, and Livens.)

Llera, Felix F. (See Elias and Llera.)

Lloyd, William T. (See Dolan and Miller. assignors.)

Lobe, N. B., & Co. (See Norwood, Harry G., assignor.)

Lochner, Adam F., Chandler, Okla. Attachment for cooking utensils. No. 1,326,942; Jan. 6; v. 270; p. 12.

Lockhart, Frederick R., and H. J. Ord, assignors to F. M. Beesley, Toronto, Ontario, Canada. Motion-picture-film-feed mechanism. No. 1,328,382; Jan. 20; v. 270; p. 379.

Lockwood, Alfred A., Merton Park, England. Separation of ores. No. 1,329,127; Jan. 27; v. 270; p. 549.

Locomotive Superheater Company. (See Broido, Benjamin, assignor.)

Loepsinger, Albert J., Providence, R. I., assignor to General Fire Extinguisher Company, New York, N. Y. Sealing glass bulbs. No. 1,328,530; Jan. 20; v. 270; p. 408.

Logan, Anna E., Ridgewood, N. J. Protective hood for aeroplane-pilots. No. 1,327,339; Jan. 6; v. 270; p. 85.

Loke, Johannes J. and W. A., The Hague, Netherlands. Direct production of refined iron and refined steel from titaniferous iron ores. No. 1,328,636; Jan. 20; v. 270; p. 428.

Loke, Willem A. (See Loke, Johannes J. and W. A.)

London, Jacob M., Tunnelton, assignor of one-fourth to G. M. Crawford and one-half to E. M. Reflor, Pittsburgh, Pa. Coal mining and loading machine. No. 1,327,052; Jan. 6; v. 270; p. 33.

London, Jacob M., Tunnelton, assignor, by mesne assignments, of one-fourth to G. M. Crawford and one-half to E. M. Reflor, Pittsburgh, Pa. Excavating and loading apparatus. No. 1,327,053; Jan. 6; v. 270; p. 33.

Long, George R., New York, assignor to The G. Piel Company, Inc., Long Island City, N. Y. Horn. No. 1,328,772; Jan. 20; v. 270; p. 452.

Long, Leslie R., Tipton, Iowa. Sheaf-loader. No. 1,328,834; Jan. 13; v. 270; p. 240.

Longstreth, William M., et al. (See Matthiessen, Conrad S., assignor.)

Lonson, Albert, Callaway, Minn. Traveler's check. No. 1,329,250; Jan. 27; v. 270; p. 572.

Macy, Alfred J., Chicago, Ill., assignor to Macy Engineering Company, Franklin, Pa. Stabilizing control for aeroplanes. No. 1,326,945; Jan. 6; v. 270; p. 12.

Macy, Alfred J., Chicago, Ill., assignor to Macy Engineering Company, Franklin, Pa. Automatic control for vehicles. No. 1,326,946; Jan. 6; v. 270; p. 13.

Macy, Alfred J., Chicago, Ill., assignor to Macy Engineering Company, Franklin, Pa. Stabilizer. No. 1,327,055; Jan. 6; v. 270; p. 33.

Macy Engineering Company. (See Macy, Alfred J., assignor.)

Madden, Michael. (See Sourbier and Madden.)

Madsen, Francis M., San Francisco, Calif., assignor to The Rudolph Wurlitzer Manufacturing Company, North Tonawanda, N. Y. Double Tracker Musical Instrument. No. 1,327,342; Jan. 6; v. 270; p. 85.

Magee Carpet Co., The. (See McCollum, Alfred F., assignor.)

Magee, Frederick W., assignor of one-half to T. W. Baker, London, Ontario, Canada. Hot-water heater. No. 1,328,682; Jan. 20; v. 270; p. 436.

Magnus, John. (See Dalton and Magnus.)

Maguire, Walter J., Portland, Oreg. Address-matcher. No. 1,328,534; Jan. 20; v. 270; p. 409.

Mahaffey, Florence C., Toledo, Ohio. Egg-candler. No. 1,328,091; Jan. 13; v. 270; p. 288.

Mahler, Ernst, assignor to Kimberly Clark Company, Neenah, Wis. Apparatus for making ornamental paper. No. 1,329,130; Jan. 27; v. 270; p. 550.

Main, Daniel T., Winnipeg, Manitoba, Canada. Casting steel. No. 1,327,398; Jan. 6; v. 270; p. 96.

Makruzin, Hyman, Philadelphia, Pa. Frame for suitcases. No. 1,329,194; Jan. 27; v. 270; p. 562.

Malby, Seth G., Derby, assignor to Ansonia Manufacturing Company, Ansonia, Conn. Gas-valve. No. 1,328,578; Jan. 20; v. 270; p. 417.

Malcom, Robert, Chicago, Ill. Eye-protector. No. 1,328,287; Jan. 20; v. 270; p. 361.

Mallinson, Joseph, Glasgow, Scotland. Chain-grate for furnaces. No. 1,327,399; Jan. 6; v. 270; p. 96.

Maltry, Peter, and W. T. Heckler, Blue Island, Ill. Piston-push-rod holder. No. 1,328,092; Jan. 13; v. 270; p. 288.

Manahan, Michael J., assignor of one-third to E. H. Remick, Indianapolis, Ind. Curtain-bracket. No. 1,328,570; Jan. 20; v. 270; p. 417.

Mann, William L., Georgetown, Tex. Shoe. No. 1,328,333; Jan. 20; v. 270; p. 370.

Mannon, Homer, H. M. Brown and R. G. Perkins, Huntington, W. Va. Indicating device. No. 1,328,007; Jan. 13; v. 270; p. 272.

Manny, Fred L., assignor to Baker-Vawter Company, Benton Harbor, Mich. Loose-leaf binder. No. 1,327,624; Jan. 13; v. 270; p. 200.

Mansfield, Clarence R., El Paso, Tex. Film-winding attachment. No. 1,327,245; Jan. 6; v. 270; p. 69.

Mansfield, Warren M., Davenport, Iowa. Vehicle-wheel. No. 1,327,343; Jan. 6; v. 270; p. 86.

Manson, Ray H., assignor to The Garford Manufacturing Company, Elyria, Ohio. Automobile or motorcycle horn. No. 1,328,093; Jan. 13; v. 270; p. 288.

Maranville, Harvey F., Akron, Ohio. Ventilator. No. 1,328,094; Jan. 13; v. 270; p. 288.

Marburger, Henry L., Baltimore, and L. H. Berg, Baltimore county, Md. Nut-lock. No. 1,328,443; Jan. 20; v. 270; p. 391.

Margolis, David S., et al. (See Corbi, Joseph L., assignor.)

Maril, Harry A., Minneapolis, Minn. Garment. No. 1,327,625; Jan. 13; v. 270; p. 200.

Marino, Algeri, Venice, Italy. Spinthermometer for radiotelegraphic plants. No. 1,328,288; Jan. 20; v. 270; p. 362.

Marion Foundry Corporation. (See Close, Leonard L. assignor.)

Marjanko, Ferdinand. (See Gruschka and Marjanko.)

Markham, James W., Armstrong, Ind. Steering-wheel lock. No. 1,328,882; Jan. 27; v. 270; p. 503.

Markwell, Andrew E., assignor of one-half to S. C. Evans, Fort Worth, Tex. Matrix molding device. No. 1,328,050; Jan. 13; v. 270; p. 280.

Marquardt, Frank C., Brooklyn, assignor to American Bank Note Company, New York, N. Y. Registering mechanism for form or plate cylinders of multicolor-printing machines. No. 1,328,842; Jan. 27; v. 270; p. 495.

Marsden, Mark W., Philadelphia, Pa. Utilizing Spanish moss. No. 1,327,873; Jan. 13; v. 270; p. 247.

Marsh, Elmer E. (See Marsh, Sargent P. and E. E.)

Marsh, Sargent P. and E. E., Cincinnati, Ohio. Detection-signal. No. 1,329,053; Jan. 27; v. 270; p. 535.

Marsh, Wilbur W. (See Hackett, Charles H., assignor.)

Marshall Dobbins & Co. (See Butcher, James M., assignor.)

Marshall, John, Swarthmore, Pa., assignor to E. I. du Pont de Nemours & Company, Wilmington, Del. Making Hexanitrodiphenylamin. No. 1,326,947; Jan. 6; v. 270; p. 13.

Martin, Anna, Cincinnati, Ohio. School-desk. No. 1,328,444; Jan. 20; v. 270; p. 391.

Martin, Charles W., Brooklyn, N. Y. Umbrella. No. 1,328,178; Jan. 13; v. 270; p. 304.

Martin, Robert L., Thomas, W. Va. Nut-locking device. No. 1,327,836; Jan. 13; v. 270; p. 240.

Martin, Stevie L., Snyder, Okla. Automatic lubricant-supply system for internal-combustion engines. No. 1,328,845; Jan. 27; v. 270; p. 495.

Martin, William P., Nashua, Iowa. Door-spring. No. 1,328,961; Jan. 27; v. 270; p. 518.

Martinka, Joseph J., Newark, N. J. Surgical appliance for women. No. 1,328,176; Jan. 13; v. 270; p. 304.

Martinka, Joseph J., Newark, N. J. Catamenial sack. No. 1,329,195; Jan. 27; v. 270; p. 562.

Martucci, Francesco, Jersey City, N. J. Sanitary soap-holder. No. 1,328,177; Jan. 13; v. 270; p. 304.

Mascord, George W., Barnes, London, England. Printing-machine. No. 1,329,325; Jan. 27; v. 270; p. 585.

Mason, Charles F., and R. A. Dixon, Pittsburgh, Pa. Game. No. 1,327,056; Jan. 6; v. 270; p. 34.

Mason, Charles T., Sumter, S. C., assignor to Splitdorf Electrical Company, Newark, N. J. Interrupter for ignition devices. No. 1,327,844; Jan. 6; v. 270; p. 86.

Masterson, Patrick, South Porcupine, Ontario, Canada. Punching-machine. No. 1,327,720; Jan. 13; v. 270; p. 218.

Mathews, Charley B., Andalusia, Ala. Chipper's guide-marker. No. 1,327,874; Jan. 13; v. 270; p. 247.

Mathews Gravity Carrier Company. (See Buck, Herman J., assignor.) (Reissue.)

Mathewson, Henry B., and K. Knutsen, San Francisco, Calif. Interpupillary-distance-measuring instrument. No. 1,327,163; Jan. 6; v. 270; p. 53.

Matoha, Hisashi, Whitefish, Mont. Track-level. No. 1,329,196; Jan. 27; v. 270; p. 562.

Matoha, Hisashi, Whitefish, Mont. Track gage and level. No. 1,329,197; Jan. 27; v. 270; p. 562.

Mattern, Frank C., Great Neck, N. Y., assignor to Fairbanks Company. Cotton-seed-weighing apparatus. No. 1,328,747; Jan. 20; v. 270; p. 448.

Matthews, Zhetley V., Charleston, Wash. Kitchen-fixture. No. 1,327,489; Jan. 6; v. 270; p. 113.

Matthiessen, Conrad S., assignor of one-tenth to C. J. Hepburn, one-fifth to W. M. Longstreth, Philadelphia, Pa., and one-tenth to W. F. Sprenkel, New York, N. Y. Cotton-picker. No. 1,328,385; Jan. 20; v. 270; p. 380.

Matthiessen, Conrad S., Philadelphia, Pa. Nozzle for pneumatic cotton-pickers. No. 1,328,386; Jan. 20; v. 270; p. 380.

Mattison, Richard V., Jr., Upper Dublin township, Montgomery county, Pa. Manufacturing fibrous cement products. No. 1,327,721; Jan. 13; v. 270; p. 219.

Maurer, John F., West New York, N. J. Crate for bottles. No. 1,328,748; Jan. 20; v. 270; p. 448.

Maxwell, Ross R. (See Lowe, Albert H., assignor.)

Maxwell, William, Bloomington, Ill. Railway-gate. No. 1,329,054; Jan. 27; v. 270; p. 535.

May, Daniel T. (See McAnency and May.)

May, Walter P., assignor of one-half to S. Andrews, St. Louis, Mo. Bracelet. No. 1,326,948; Jan. 6; v. 270; p. 13.

Mayer, Fred G., assignor to The Starr Piano Company, Richmond, Ind. Matrix for sound-records. No. 1,327,722; Jan. 13; v. 270; p. 219.

Mayer, George. (See Foster, George W., assignor.)

Mayer, Samuel, New York, N. Y. Dictionary. No. 1,328,178; Jan. 13; v. 270; p. 304.

Mayers, Lewis, New York, N. Y. Internal-combustion engine. No. 1,327,345; Jan. 6; v. 270; p. 86.

Meadows, Thomas C., New York, M. Hauber, Jr., West Haverstraw, and H. W. Charlton, New York, N. Y. Obtaining combined potassium from greensand. No. 1,327,164; Jan. 6; v. 270; p. 53.

Measuregraph Company, The. (See Hosch, Walter E., assignor.)

Mecklenburg, Herman A., Gilby, N. D. Currycomb. No. 1,327,246; Jan. 6; v. 270; p. 69.

Meehan, Paul A., New Castle, Pa., assignor to American Dressler Tunnel Kilns, Inc., New York, N. Y. Car-mover for tunnel-kilns. No. 1,326,949; Jan. 6; v. 270; p. 13.

Meehan, Paul A., New Castle, Pa., assignor to American Dressler Tunnel Kilns, Inc., New York, N. Y. Car for tunnel-kilns. No. 1,328,749; Jan. 20; v. 270; p. 448.

Meeley, George G. (See Parkin, Henry, assignor.)

Meeder, Philip, Jr., Pittsburgh, Pa. Apparatus for feeding pulverized fuel. No. 1,328,750; Jan. 20; v. 270; p. 448.

Meier, Erling, Christiania, Norway. Roller-bearing. No. 1,328,179; Jan. 13; v. 270; p. 304.

Meier, Konrad, Winterthur, Switzerland. Radiator. No. 1,329,198; Jan. 27; v. 270; p. 562.

Meischke-Smith, William, San Francisco, Calif., assignor to Shell Company of California. Evaporator. No. 1,327,247; Jan. 6; v. 270; p. 69.

Mellor, Arthur, Brighouse, England. Machine for dressing silk. No. 1,328,535; Jan. 20; v. 270; p. 409.

Menco-Elma Syndicate Limited, The. (See Pollard, George, assignor.)

Mennie, Robert S., Chicago, Ill., assignor to Flannery Bolt Company, Pittsburgh, Pa. Staybolt. (Reissue.) No. 14,796; Jan. 27; v. 270; p. 590.

Mepsted, Ernest, Pentonville, London, England. Locking means for joint-pins, hinge-pins, coupling-pins, and the like. No. 1,329,131; Jan. 27; v. 270; p. 550.

Mergott, J. E. Company. (See Fuller, Franz A., assignor.)

Merrill, Alfred P., San Diego, Calif. Rotary shaft and coupling for electric dental engines. No. 1,328,095; Jan. 13; v. 270; p. 288.

Merriman, Thurston C., New Haven, Conn., assignor to Winchester Repeating Arms Co. Surface-colored article of copper alloy. No. 1,327,400; Jan. 6; v. 270; p. 97.

Merriman, Thurston C., New Haven, Conn., assignor to Winchester Repeating Arms Co. Surface-coloring articles of copper alloy. No. 1,327,401; Jan. 6; v. 270; p. 97.

Merritt, Frank W., assignor to H. W. Coulter, trustee, Duluth, Minn. Radiator. No. 1,327,165; Jan. 6; v. 270; p. 53.

Merry, Whiting P., Sharpsville, Pa. Heater. No. 1,328,246; Jan. 13; v. 270; p. 318.

Merwin, George M., Berwyn, Ill., assignor, by mesne assignments, to International Harvester Company. Ensilage-cutter. No. 1,327,346; Jan. 6; v. 270; p. 86.

Mesker, Bernard T., and C. E. Smith, assignors to Mesker Brothers Iron Company, St. Louis, Mo. Metallic window construction. No. 1,327,441; Jan. 6; v. 270; p. 104.

Mesker Brothers Iron Company. (See Mesker and Smith, assignors.)

Mesker Brothers Iron Company. (See Mesker, Frank, assignor.)

Mesker, Frank, assignor to Mesker Brothers Iron Company, St. Louis, Mo. Metallic casket. No. 1,327,442; Jan. 6; v. 270; p. 104.

Mester, Robert H., Webster Groves, Mo. Wrapper. No. 1,329,056; Jan. 27; v. 270; p. 536.

Metal Separation Company, The. (See Stockton and Goddard, assignors.)

Metesser, Lewis, New Orleans, La. Furnace. No. 1,328,883; Jan. 27; v. 270; p. 503.

Metropolitan Sewing Machine Corporation. (See Weis, John P., assignor.)

Metz, Herman A. (See Riethmüller, Richard H., assignor.)

Mezzatesta, Gaspare, Hampton, Va. Carbureter. No. 1,328,180; Jan. 13; v. 270; p. 305.

Midgley, Thomas, Jr., Dayton, Ohio, assignor to The Dayton Engineering Laboratories Company. Mercury-cooling system. No. 1,328,051; Jan. 13; v. 270; p. 280.

Midyett, Zacariah M., Jackson, Tenn. Toy popgun. No. 1,327,723; Jan. 13; v. 270; p. 219.

Mikimoto, Kokichi, Tokyo, Japan. Causing oysters to produce pearls. No. 1,328,008; Jan. 13; v. 270; p. 272.

Miler, Mollie H. (See Henry, Nelson B., assignor.)

Miles, Edward L., assignor of one-half to L. E. Genett, Stevens Point, Wis. Antislipping attachment for gangplanks. No. 1,329,057; Jan. 27; v. 270; p. 536.

Miles, William C., assignor of one-fourth to N. T. Whitaker, Washington, D. C. Device for winding and re-winding motors. No. 1,327,567; Jan. 6; v. 270; p. 128.

Millard, William, assignor to Carbon Destroyer Corporation, New York, N. Y. Apparatus for moistening carbureted mixtures for gas-engines. No. 1,329,252; Jan. 27; v. 270; p. 573.

Miller, Alfred W., et al. (See Brooks, Samuel A., assignor.)

Miller, Cyrus M., Jr., assignor to Wheeler & Motter Mercantile Company, St. Joseph, Mo. Safety-pocket for garments. No. 1,328,884; Jan. 27; v. 270; p. 504.

Miller, Edwin L., Kansas City, Mo. Safety cranking device for automobiles. No. 1,327,109; Jan. 6; v. 270; p. 43.

Miller, Frederick W., Los Angeles, Calif. Electric-arc lamp. No. 1,329,132; Jan. 27; v. 270; p. 550.

Miller, John D., San Diego, Calif. Animal-trap. No. 1,327,490; Jan. 6; v. 270; p. 113.

Miller, Max C., Providence, assignor to Jenckes Knitting Machine Company, Pawtucket, R. I. Circular-knitting machine. No. 1,328,580; Jan. 20; v. 270; p. 417.

Miller, Norman H., Meadville, Pa. Swing-chair. No. 1,328,181; Jan. 13; v. 270; p. 305.

Miller, Robert E., Altoona, and G. H. Liebegott, Duncansville, Pa. Air-filtering system for cooling the motors of electrically-driven railway-cars. No. 1,327,287; Jan. 6; v. 270; p. 76.

Miller, Sigwald. (See Dolan and Miller.)

Miller, William J., Goose Creek, Tex. Piston. No. 1,328,182; Jan. 13; v. 270; p. 305.

Millis, Chester B., East McKeesport, Pa., and J. P. Nikonow, New York, N. Y., assignors to Westinghouse Electric and Manufacturing Company Wheel-brake. (Reissue.) No. 14,797; Jan. 27; v. 270; p. 591.

Mills, James S. (See Mills, Samuel J. and J. S.)

Mills, Mortimer B., assignor to Mills Novelty Company, Chicago, Ill. Weighing-scale. No. 1,327,208; Jan. 6; v. 270; p. 62.

Mills Novelty Company. (See Mills, Mortimer B., assignor.)

Mills, Samuel J. and J. S., Fleming, Saskatchewan, Canada. Grinding-mill. No. 1,327,347; Jan. 6; v. 270; p. 87.

Milton, William, Guelph, Ontario, Canada. Tension-evener for yarn-winding machines. No. 1,326,950; Jan. 6; v. 270; p. 13.

Milwaukee Paper Box Company. (See Wade, Frank M., assignor.)

Mine Safety Appliance Company, The. (See Ryan, John T., assignor.)

Mirra, Addieco, et al. (See Morelli and Solimeo, assignors.)

Mirra, Emilio, et al. (See Morelli and Solimeo, assignors.)

Mitchell, Henry A., deceased, Shepherd, Tex.; E. W. Love, administrator. Apparatus for heating and ripening honey. No. 1,327,166; Jan. 6; v. 270; p. 54.

Mitchell, Joseph K., Memphis, Tenn. Double-current syringe. No. 1,327,167; Jan. 6; v. 270; p. 54.

Mickush, Francis, Rankin, Pa. Smoker. No. 1,328,183; Jan. 13; v. 270; p. 305.

Moeller, Leonard J., et al. (See Guy, Frederick M., assignor.)

Moffatt, James R., assignor to Union Special Machine Company, Chicago, Ill. Cross-thread-laying mechanism for sewing-machines. No. 1,327,348; Jan. 6; v. 270; p. 87.

Moffatt, James R., assignor to Union Special Machine Company, Chicago, Ill. Ruffling mechanism for sewing-machines. No. 1,328,885; Jan. 27; v. 270; p. 504.

Mohanec, Mike, et al. (See Beshenich, Matija, assignor.)

Molas, Edouard E., Paris, France. Apparatus for preparation of inert gases. No. 1,327,769; Jan. 13; v. 270; p. 228.

Molina, Ynocente J., Douglas, Ariz. Safety indicator and alarm. No. 1,328,387; Jan. 20; v. 270; p. 381.

Moline Plow Company. (See Cook, Willard J., assignor.)

Moller, Carl E., Jamestown, N. Y. Sash-rod for curtains. No. 1,326,951; Jan. 6; v. 270; p. 13.

Monarch Tag Company, The. (See Kohnle, Frederick, assignor.)

Monroe, George A. C., Geneva, Ill. Knockdown bed-spring. No. 1,328,751; Jan. 20; v. 270; p. 449.

Montgomery, Robert E., Lawton, Okla. Cotton-seed linter. No. 1,327,724; Jan. 13; v. 270; p. 219.

Moody, Daniel W., Chicago, Ill. Occupant-operated vehicle and steering apparatus. No. 1,327,960; Jan. 13; v. 270; p. 268.

Moody, Herbert A., Turners Falls, Mass. Gate-valve. No. 1,328,752; Jan. 20; v. 270; p. 449.

Moody, Jason B., Houston, Tex. Dispensing-vehicle. No. 1,327,248; Jan. 6; v. 270; p. 69.

Moon Brothers Manufacturing Company. (See Drew, John W., assignor.)

Moon Brothers Manufacturing Company. (See Zingsheim, Frederick W., assignor.)

Moore, Benjamin S. (See Hellmund and Moore.)

Moore, Charles E., Terre Haute, Ind. Rim, tire, and wheel carrier for automobiles. No. 1,327,626; Jan. 13; v. 270; p. 200.

Moore, Charles W., Indianapolis, Ind. Piston-ring. No. 1,328,289; Jan. 20; v. 270; p. 362.

Moore, Harlan, New York, N. Y. Bottle or jar closure device. No. 1,328,536; Jan. 20; v. 270; p. 409.

Moore, Payton J. H., assignor to American Grain Deodorizing Co., Chicago, Ill. Ozonizing apparatus. No. 1,326,952; Jan. 6; v. 270; p. 13.

Moore, Warren, Ladysmith, Wis. Self-measuring dispensing vessel. No. 1,328,184; Jan. 13; v. 270; p. 305.

Moors, Walter C., assignor of one-third to W. P. Pedley and one-third to E. Norris, Owensboro, Ky. Shade-roller lock. No. 1,329,092; Jan. 27; v. 270; p. 542.

Mora Pump Company. (See Andrews and Holmon, assignors.)

Morano, Sam., assignor to Sam Morano & Company, Wendel, W. Va. Rail adjusting and gaging device. No. 1,326,953; Jan. 6; v. 270; p. 14.

Morano, Sam, & Company. (See Morano, Sam. assignor.)

More, Glenn, assignor to Blackstone Manufacturing Company, Jamestown, N. Y. Bench. No. 1,328,753; Jan. 20; v. 270; p. 449.

Moore, Glenn, assignor to Blackstone Manufacturing Company, Jamestown, N. Y. Removable wringer mechanism. No. 1,328,754; Jan. 20; v. 270; p. 449.

Moreland, Everett R., Carrollton, Mo. Draftsman's fountain ruling-pen. No. 1,327,922; Jan. 13; v. 270; p. 256.

Morelli, Raffaele, and J. Solimeo, assignors of one-fifth to A. Mirra, one-fifth to E. Mirra, and one-fifth to D. Inzalato, Brooklyn, N. Y. Cleaning apparatus. No. 1,327,110; Jan. 6; v. 270; p. 43.

Morey, Harry J., Syracuse, assignor to Pass & Seymour, Inc., Solvay, N. Y. Candle-socket. No. 1,328,581; Jan. 20; v. 270; p. 418.

Morgan, Edmund C., Chicago, Ill. Mining-machine. No. 1,328,755; Jan. 20; v. 270; p. 449.

Morgan, William, Los Angeles, Calif. Electric flatiron. No. 1,327,602; Jan. 6; v. 270; p. 135.

Mork, Albert C., Minneapolis, Minn. Valve-grinding machine. No. 1,327,875; Jan. 13; v. 270; p. 247.

Moross, William P. D., and J. C. Costello, Chattanooga, Tenn. Apparatus for extracting lye from wood-ashes. No. 1,328,096; Jan. 13; v. 270; p. 289.

Morral, Samuel E. and W. W., Morral, Ohio. Machine for cutting green corn from the cob. No. 1,327,402; Jan. 6; v. 270; p. 97.

Morral, Samuel E., Morral, Ohio. Wheel. No. 1,328,052; Jan. 13; v. 270; p. 281.

Morrall, William W. (See Morrall, Samuel E. and W. W.)

Morris, Charles E., assignor to C. W. Parker, Leavenworth, Kans. Carousel. No. 1,327,725; Jan. 13; v. 270; p. 219.

Morris, Edward, Oakland, Calif. Tool. No. 1,327,566; Jan. 6; v. 270; p. 128.

Morris, William G., Cairo, Egypt. Valve. No. 1,328,009; Jan. 13; v. 270; p. 272.

Morrison, Henry W., et al. (See Cassingham and Ayres, assignors.)

Morrison, Jesse A., Mountainair, N. Mex. Combination-rig for drilling. No. 1,327,403; Jan. 6; v. 270; p. 97.

Morrison, John W., et al. (See Cassingham and Ayres, assignors.)

Morrow, Thomas J. (See Pence and Morrow.)

Morse, Robert V., Ithaca, N. Y. Homopolar magnetic circuit. No. 1,327,349; Jan. 6; v. 270; p. 87.
Morse, Robert V., Ithaca, N. Y. Cooling system for homopolar machines. No. 1,327,350; Jan. 6; v. 270; p. 87.
Morton, William B., Beatrice, Nebr. Store - case. No. 1,328,185; Jan. 13; v. 270; p. 306.
Moscini, John, Brooklyn, N. Y. Paper-match machine. No. 1,327,627; Jan. 13; v. 270; p. 201.
Motor-Compressor Company, The. (See Van Vleck, Horace R., assignor.)
Motsenbocker, James A., assignor of one-half to E. F. Burkle, Indianapolis, Ind. Amusement apparatus. No. 1,326,954; Jan. 6; v. 270; p. 14.
Mott, Abram C., Jr., and L. Kinsley, assignors to Abram Cox Stove Company, Philadelphia, Pa. Means for forming recesses in sand molds. No. 1,328,582; Jan. 20; v. 270; p. 418.
Mott, Carl W., Chicago, Ill., assignor, by mesne assignments, to International Harvester Company. Plow. No. 1,328,756; Jan. 20; v. 270; p. 450.
Motzer, Alfred, assignor to The Hobson & Motzer Co., Meriden, Conn. Auxiliary oiling system for Ford cars. No. 1,328,388; Jan. 20; v. 270; p. 381.
Mueller, Elmer F. E., Chicago, Ill. Musical instrument. No. 1,326,955; Jan. 6; v. 270; p. 14.
Mullen, Charles P. (See Plummer and Mullen.)
Mullikin, Brooks J., New York, N. Y. Overshoe for tires. No. 1,328,757; Jan. 20; v. 270; p. 450.
Multipost Company. (See Schweiger and Balkwill, assignors.)
Mumford Molding Machine Company. (See Krause, William P., assignor.)
Munhall, John, Pittsburgh, Pa. Staybolt structure. No. 1,328,053; Jan. 13; v. 270; p. 281.
Muntz, Otto S., Dubuque, Iowa. Shock-absorbing container. No. 1,328,758; Jan. 20; v. 270; p. 450.
Murmann, Eugene O., Glendale, Calif. Can-opener. No. 1,329,133; Jan. 27; v. 270; p. 550.
Murray, John F. (See Filkins, George H., assignor.)
Murray, Joseph B. (See Murray, Thomas E., Jr., and J. B.)
Murray, Samuel R., Indianapolis, Ind. Composition for paving and other purposes. No. 1,327,726; Jan. 13; v. 270; p. 220.
Murray, Thomas E. (See Christians, George W., assignor.)
Murray, Thomas E. (See Rypinski, Albert B., assignor.)
Murray, Thomas E., Jr., Brooklyn, N. Y. Elongated cylindrical projectile-shell. No. 1,329,134; Jan. 27; v. 270; p. 551.
Murray, Thomas E., Jr., and J. B., Brooklyn, N. Y. Electric welding. No. 1,329,135; Jan. 27; v. 270; p. 551.
Murray, Thomas E., Jr., and J. B., Brooklyn, N. Y. Electrical welding. No. 1,329,136; Jan. 27; v. 270; p. 551.
Muschenheim, Frederick A., and F. W. Blasdale, New York, N. Y. Electrical indicator. No. 1,327,837; Jan. 13; v. 270; p. 240.
Musher and Company. (See Birch, Joseph F., Jr., assignor.)
Myers, Charles D., Ware, assignor of one-half to E. K. Lathrop, Springfield, Mass. Soap-dispensing apparatus. No. 1,329,199; Jan. 27; v. 270; p. 563.
Myers, Edmund T. D., Jr., Richmond, Va. Smoke-control and drift-valve mechanism. No. 1,327,404; Jan. 6; v. 270; p. 97.
Myers, Winter W., Brooklyn, assignor to Austral Window Company, New York, N. Y. Fastening means for windows. No. 1,326,956; Jan. 6; v. 270; p. 14.
N. V. Machinefabriek Brons. (See Brons, Derk, assignor.)
Naamlooze Vennootschap Weduwe J. Ahrend & Zoons Industries- en Handelsvereeniging. (See Koechlin, Emile R., assignor.)
Nainka, Anthony, Janesville, Wis. Shampooing apparatus. No. 1,329,058; Jan. 27; v. 270; p. 536.
National Aniline & Chemical Company. (See Taggesell, Richard, assignor.)
National Binding Machine Company. (See Bobst, Charles A., assignor.)
National Brass Company. (See Blye, Harold, assignor.)
National Candy Company. (See Bunde, Claude W., assignor.)
National Carbon Company. (See Chase, Wallace S., assignor.)
National Carbon Company. (See Spiers, Frederick G., assignor.)
National Cash Register Company. (See Goldberg, Maximilian M., assignor.)
National Dump Car Co. (See Hart, Harry S., assignor.) (Reissue.)
National Equipment Company. (See Bausman, Alonzo L., assignor.)
National Machinery Co., The. (See Clouse, William L., assignor.)
National Malleable Castings Company, The. (See Bixby, Allan S., assignor.)
National Manufacturing Company. (See Ferris, Walton C., assignor.)
National Oil Machinery Corporation. (See Ryan, Henry D., assignor.)
Nayer, Carl F., assignor to Packer's Machinery & Equipment Company, Chicago, Ill. Hog-scraper. No. 1,328,637; Jan. 20; v. 270; p. 428.
Naylor, Jesse R., Sacramento, Calif. Traffic-signal. No. 1,328,097; Jan. 13; v. 270; p. 289.

Naylor, Ralph B., Springfield, assignor to The Fisk Rubber Company, Chicopee Falls, Mass. Testing device for determining the viscosity of rubber. No. 1,327,888; Jan. 13; v. 270; p. 240.
Neal, Spencer G., New York, N. Y., assignor, by mesne assignments, to Automatic Straight Air Brake Company, Wilmington, Del. Diaphragm check - valve. No. 1,328,886; Jan. 27; v. 270; p. 504.
Needham, William H., assignor to Boston Pressed Metal Co., Worcester, Mass. Last-thimble. No. 1,327,839; Jan. 13; v. 270; p. 241.
Neelin, Thomas A., Winnipeg, Manitoba, Canada. Bootbrush. No. 1,327,288; Jan. 6; v. 270; p. 76.
Neff, Arthur P. (See Kellogg, Neff, Rogers, and Cowan.)
Nelson, Elnathan K., Takoma Park, Md. Vanillyl amin, vanillyl acyl amid, &c. No. 1,329,272; Jan. 27; v. 270; p. 576.
Nelson, Swan, Winnifred, Alberta, Canada. Pump. No. 1,328,010; Jan. 13; v. 270; p. 272.
Németh, Joseph, New York, N. Y. Doll. No. 1,327,168; Jan. 6; v. 270; p. 54.
Neukirchen, Peter, assignor to J. H. Wald, Chicago, Ill. Egg-beater. No. 1,327,568; Jan. 6; v. 270; p. 129.
Neumaier, John, Dayton, Ohio. Protractor. No. 1,329,005; Jan. 27; v. 270; p. 526.
Neuman, David, Albany, Ga. Hoe with knife attachment. No. 1,328,587; Jan. 20; v. 270; p. 409.
Nevers, Lester, and F. Whitbeck, Grand Rapids, Mich. Boiler-setting. No. 1,327,727; Jan. 13; v. 270; p. 220.
Newberg, Charles A., and E. I. Weisberger, Brooklyn, N. Y. Conformator. No. 1,328,588; Jan. 20; v. 270; p. 409.
Newhall, Henry B., Jr., executor. (See Pleister, Henry W., assignor.)
Newhope, Alfred, Jacksonville, Fla. Attachment for motor-vehicles. No. 1,329,200; Jan. 27; v. 270; p. 563.
Newton, Charles, Buffalo, N. Y., assignor to P. N. Stone, Cleveland, Ohio. Projectile. No. 1,328,334; Jan. 20; v. 270; p. 371.
Newton, Dudley, Berkeley, Calif. Apparatus for flushing urinals. No. 1,328,445; Jan. 20; v. 270; p. 391.
Newton, J. M. (See Howe, Dale E., assignor.)
Neyd'hart, Francis S., West Hoboken, N. J. Jumping toy. No. 1,329,201; Jan. 27; v. 270; p. 563.
Nicholas, Arthur D. (See Nicholson and Lowery.)
Nicholson, Arthur D., et al. (See Nicholson, Howard M., assignor.)
Nicholson, George B. (See Nicholson and Lowery.)
Nicholson, George B., et al. (See Nicholson, Howard M., assignor.)
Nicholson, Herbert, Chicago, Ill. Pneumatic tire. No. 1,328,054; Jan. 13; v. 270; p. 281.
Nicholson, Howard M., assignor of one-fourth to G. B. Nicholson, one-fourth to A. D. Nicholson, and one-fourth to W. T. Lowery, Pittsburgh, Pa. Automatic dispensing apparatus. No. 1,327,111; Jan. 6; v. 270; p. 44.
Nicholson, Howard M., A. D. Nicholson, G. B. Nicholson, and W. T. Lowery, Pittsburgh, Pa. Vacuum dispensing apparatus. No. 1,327,112; Jan. 6; v. 270; p. 44.
Nickol, Alphonse M., and C. T. Schein, Batesville, Ind. Hinge. No. 1,329,059; Jan. 27; v. 270; p. 536.
Niebergall, Arthur G., et al. (See Bowen, Charles, assignor.)
Nied, Edward H., Akron, Ohio. Lock. No. 1,328,186; Jan. 13; v. 270; p. 306.
Niks, Nickolas J., Kalamazoo, Mich. Paper-making machine. No. 1,327,289; Jan. 6; v. 270; p. 76.
Niles, Waldo E., North Abington, Mass. Tire-protector. No. 1,328,539; Jan. 20; v. 270; p. 410.
Nilson, John L., and J. Prince, Chicago, Ill. Multiplespark plug. No. 1,327,057; Jan. 6; v. 270; p. 34.
Nilson, Leonard. (See Nilson, Nils and L.)
Nilson, Nils and L. Wayzata. Minn. Tractor. No. 1,328,335; Jan. 20; v. 270; p. 371.
Nitrogen Products Company. (See Williams, Roger, assignor.)
Nitzgen, Joseph, New York, N. Y. Molding apparatus. No. 1,328,887; Jan. 27; v. 270; p. 504.
Niva, William J., Minneapolis, Minn. Barn-door hinge. No. 1,328,583; Jan. 20; v. 270; p. 418.
Noble, F. H., & Company. (See Shields, John M., assignor.)
Noerther, Charles, & Cie. (See Nörther, Charles, assignor.)
Noonan, Albert S., assignor to Foss-Hughes Company, Philadelphia, Pa. Door - operating mechanism. No. 1,328,584; Jan. 20; v. 270; p. 418.
Nordiska Kullager Aktiebolaget. (See Lindman, Konrad W., assignor.)
Norelius, Emil F., Peoria, Ill., assignor to The Holt Manufacturing Company, Stockton, Calif. Gun-carriage. No. 1,327,605; Jan. 6; v. 270; p. 135.
Norelius, Emil F., Peoria, Ill., assignor to The Holt Manufacturing Company, Stockton, Calif. Trailer-wagon. No. 1,329,307; Jan. 27; v. 270; p. 582.
Norris, Ernest. (See Moors, Walter C., assignor.)
Norsk Hydro-Elektrisk Kvaelstofaktieselskab. (See Bakke, Bjarne, assignor.)
Nörther, Charles, assignor to Charles Noerther & Cie., Turin, Italy. Music-typewriter. No. 1,327,840; Jan. 13; v. 270; p. 241.
Northern Trust Company, The. (See Lang, Lincoln A., assignor.)
Northrop, Jonas, Hopedale, assignor to Hopedale Manufacturing Company, Milford, Mass. Automatic loom. No. 1,328,585; Jan. 20; v. 270; p. 418.

Northrup, Edwin F., Princeton, N. J., assignor to The Ajax Metal Company, Philadelphia, Pa. Artificially-cooled high-frequency coil. No. 1,328,336 ; Jan. 20 ; v. 270 ; p. 371.

Norton, Joseph C., Cleveland, Ohio. Roof-edging. No. 1,327,770 ; Jan. 13 ; v. 270 ; p. 228.

Norton, Roy H., Dedham, Mass. Bung-hole closure. No. 1,327,351 ; Jan. 6 ; v. 270 ; p. 88.

Norwood, Harry G., assignor, by mesne assignments, to N. B. Lobe & Co., Baltimore, Md. Alligator-wrench. No. 1,328,389 ; Jan. 20 ; v. 270 ; p. 381.

Norwood, Harry Y., assignor to Taylor Instrument Companies, Rochester, N. Y. Thermometer. No. 1,326,957 ; Jan. 6 ; v. 270 ; p. 15.

Novick, Abraham, New York, N. Y., assignor, by mesne assignments, to United States Envelope Company, Springfield, Mass. Envelop-machine. No. 1,328,011 ; Jan. 13 ; v. 270 ; p. 272.

Novick, Max, New York, N. Y. Bed-spring. No. 1,329,202 ; Jan. 27 ; v. 270 ; p. 563.

Nowak, Carl A., St. Louis, Mo. Brewing beer and low-alcoholic malt beverages. No. 1,328,888 ; Jan. 27 ; v. 270 ; p. 504.

Nugent, Adam, Nutley, N. J. Game. No. 1,328,390 ; Jan. 20 ; v. 270 ; p. 381.

Nute, James E., Portland, Me. Waste-heat radiator. No. 1,328,540 ; Jan. 20 ; v. 270 ; p. 410.

Nyblad, Axel L., Newport, England. Hoisting device. No. 1,327,876 ; Jan. 13 ; v. 270 ; p. 247.

Nyström, Knut, Stockholm, Sweden. Holder for balls in ball-bearings. No. 1,327,169 ; Jan. 6 ; v. 270 ; p. 54.

O. K. Giant Battery Co. (See Rabe, Paul B., assignor.)

Oakley, Henry D., Syracuse, N. Y. Device for indicating magnetic polarity. No. 1,328,187 ; Jan. 13 ; v. 270 ; p. 306.

Oberreich, Louie H., Indianapolis, Ind. Carbureter. No 1,328,844 ; Jan. 27 ; v. 270 ; p. 495.

O'Bryan, James P., Hog Island, Pa. Hoisting device. No. 1,329,107 ; Jan. 27 ; v. 270 ; p. 545.

O'Connor, John B., assignor to Lyon Metallic Manufacturing Company, Aurora, Ill. Shelving. No. 1,327,628 ; Jan. 13 ; v. 270 ; p. 201.

Odam, Eugène, Paris, France. Process and apparatus for atomizing materials in a melted state. No. 1,328,446 ; Jan. 20 ; v. 270 ; p. 391.

Oehler, Richard, St. Louis, Mo. Overhead conveyer system. No. 1,327,249 ; Jan. 6 ; v. 270 ; p. 69.

Oehler, Richard, St. Louis, Mo. Overhead roller conveyer system. No. 1,327,290 ; Jan. 6 ; v. 270 ; p. 77.

Oehm, William N., Michigan City, Ind. Car-underframe. No. 1,328,683 ; Jan. 20 ; v. 270 ; p. 436.

Oehm, William N., Michigan City, Ind. Car-end sheet. No. 1,328,684 ; Jan. 20 ; v. 270 ; p. 436.

Oehm, William N., Michigan City, Ind. Car-body. No. 1,329,006 ; Jan. 27 ; v. 270 ; p. 526.

Ogden, Carlton N., Houston, Tex. Vending-machine. No. 1,327,058 ; Jan. 6 ; v. 270 ; p. 34.

Ogden, Carlton N., Houston, Tex. Display and vending device. No. 1,327,771 ; Jan. 13 ; v. 270 ; p. 228.

Ogden, Clarence E., Cincinnati, Ohio. Switchboard for charging storage batteries. No. 1,327,682 ; Jan. 13 ; v. 270 ; p. 211.

Ogden, James D., Crawford, Tex. Cotton-chopper. No. 1,328,638 ; Jan. 20 ; v. 270 ; p. 428.

Ogden, John E. (See Tomkinson, Charles C., assignor.)

Ogle, Percy J., London, England, assignor to Ventiheta Limited. Warming and ventilating gas - stove. No. 1,328,012 ; Jan. 13 ; v. 270 ; p. 273.

Ohashi, Hydesaburo, deceased, New York, N. Y.; M. V. Ohashi, administratrix. Carbon-paper and ink composition therefor. No. 1,328,188 ; Jan. 13 ; v. 270 ; p. 306.

Ohashi, Marie V., administratrix. (See Ohashi, Hydesaburo.)

Ohnell, Ernst J. (See Olhovsky, Vladimir, assignor.)

Old Dominion Specialty Co., The. (See Sanford, Crocker H., assignor.)

Oldham, John II., Detroit, assignor to Blackmer Rotary Pump Co., Petoskey, Mich. Hand-operating attachment for pumps. No. 1,329,137 ; Jan. 27 ; v. 270 ; p. 551.

O'Leary, Marguerite V. (See O'Leary, William J., assignor.)

O'Leary, William J., assignor to M. V. O'Leary, Montreal, Quebec, Canada. Oscillating motor. No. 1,327,250 ; Jan. 6 ; v. 270 ; p. 69.

Oleson, Olaf E., assignor to The Edward Valve & Manufacturing Co., Chicago, Ill. Separator for steam and oil. No. 1,328,889 ; Jan. 27 ; v. 270 ; p. 505.

Olhovsky, Vladimir, New York, assignor to E. J. Ohnell, Brooklyn, N. Y. Tachometer. No. 1,327,629 ; Jan. 13 ; v. 270 ; p. 201.

Ollard, James C. (See Seabury and Ollard.)

Olleo, Ralph, assignor to Frederick Osann Company, New York, N. Y. Dust-collector for beating-machines. No. 1,329,138 ; Jan. 27 ; v. 270 ; p. 551.

Olsen, Simon D., Leeds, England. Machine for making hollow glassware. No. 1,329,253 ; Jan. 27 ; v. 270 ; p. 573.

Olson, Bertha C., New York, N. Y. Brassière. No. 1,328,586 ; Jan. 20 ; v. 270 ; p. 419.

Olson, Carl G., assignor to Illinois Tool Works, Chicago, Ill. Quenching apparatus. No. 1,327,443 ; Jan. 6 ; v. 270 ; p. 104.

Olson, Walter E., Chicago, Ill. Support for rugs in dyeing the same. No. 1,326,958 ; Jan. 6 ; v. 270 ; p. 15.

Olsson, Nils J., assignor to Aktiebolaget Svenska Kullagerfabriken, Gottenborg, Sweden. Means for automatically cutting off the feed-motion of machine-tools. No. 1,328,337 ; Jan. 20 ; v. 270 ; p. 371.

Omen, Charles A., Princeton, Ill. Automobile dump-body. No. 1,328,890 ; Jan. 27 ; v. 270 ; p. 505.

Ord, Harry J. (See Lockhart and Ord.)

Ormiston, John A., Calgary, Alberta, assignor of one-third to A. G. Slaght and one-third to W. P. St. Charles, Toronto, Canada. Locomotive exhaust-nozzle. No. 1,329,093 ; Jan. 27 ; v. 270 ; p. 543.

Ortman, William H., Milwaukee, Wis. Clothesline-support. No. 1,327,059 ; Jan. 6 ; v. 270 ; p. 34.

Ory, Gaston C., Paris, France. Scouring apparatus with sand-throw. No. 1,327,630 ; Jan. 13 ; v. 270 ; p. 201.

Osann, Frederick, Company. (See Olleo, Ralph, assignor.)

Osborn, John F., Ludington, Mich. Combination phonograph and moving-picture machine. No. 1,328,189 ; Jan. 13 ; v. 270 ; p. 306.

Osgood, Samuel W., assignor, by mesne assignments, to N. C. Kenner, Chicago, Ill. Producing flake graphite. No. 1,328,845 ; Jan. 27 ; v. 270 ; p. 496.

Ostius, Frederick J., Racine, Wis. Machine-motor. No. 1,327,209 ; Jan. 6 ; v. 270 ; p. 62.

Ostius, Frederick J., Racine, Wis. Sewing-machine motor. No. 1,327,210 ; Jan. 6 ; v. 270 ; p. 62.

O'Shea, Dennis C., Chicago, Ill. Knitted garment. No. 1,328,545 ; Jan. 20 ; v. 270 ; p. 411.

Ostendorf, Edward, Portland, Oreg. Automobile-jack. No. 1,327,060 ; Jan. 6 ; v. 270 ; p. 34.

Ostrowiecki, Marcin. (See Wanielista and Ostrowiecki.)

Ott, Frederick, Norristown, assignor to A. T. Baker & Company, Manayunk, Pa. Woven pile fabric. No. 1,327,683 ; Jan. 13 ; v. 270 ; p. 211.

Ott, Frederick, Norristown, assignor to A. T. Baker & Company, Manayunk, Pa. Woven pile fabric. No. 1,327,684 ; Jan. 13 ; v. 270 ; p. 212.

Otterson, George W., Seattle, Wash. Apparatus for removing sediment from catch-basins of sewers. No. 1,327,211 ; Jan. 6 ; v. 270 ; p. 62.

Ouzoun-Boghossian, Sissak K., Washington, D. C. Workbench for watchmakers and jewelers. No. 1,328,891 ; Jan. 27 ; v. 270 ; p. 505.

Overbagh, Donald C., Chicago, Ill. Connector for armored conductors. No. 1,328,290 ; Jan. 20 ; v. 270 ; p. 362.

Overbeck, William J., Cincinnati, Ohio. Treatment of candies and the like and the product obtained thereby. No. 1,327,113 ; Jan. 6 ; v. 270 ; p. 44.

Overgaard, Christen, Skovshoved, near Copenhagen, Denmark. Lathe. No. 1,328,962 ; Jan. 27 ; v. 270 ; p. 518.

Overmeyer, Fred, Toledo, Ohio. Puncture-tester. No. 1,327,251 ; Jan. 6 ; v. 270 ; p. 70.

Oversmith, Earl G. (See Hansgen and Oversmith.)

Owen, Hugh R. (See Gower, Owen, and Cox.)

Owens, Michael J., assignor to The Libby-Owens Sheet Glass Company, Toledo, Ohio. Furnace for continuous sheet-glass drawing. No. 1,327,405 ; Jan. 6 ; v. 270 ; p. 97.

Owl Supply Company. (See Averill, William H., assignor.)

Pacific Radiator Shield Co. (See Parmelee, Charles H., assignor.)

Packard Motor Car Company. (See Church, Harold D., assignor.)

Packard Motor Car Company. (See Druar, Frank J., assignor.)

Packard Motor Car Company. (See Tibbetts, Milton, assignor.)

Packer's Machinery & Equipment Company. (See Nayer, Carl F., assignor.)

Page, Frederick H., assignor to Handley Page Limited, London, England. Connection for members of aircraft-frames. No. 1,328,963 ; Jan. 27 ; v. 270 ; p. 519.

Page, George H., Richmond, Mo. Lifting-jack. No. 1,327,685 ; Jan. 13 ; v. 270 ; p. 212.

Page, Handley, Limited. (See Page, Frederick H., assignor.)

Page, John W., Chicago, Ill. Excavating-shovel. No. 1,328,013 ; Jan. 13 ; v. 270 ; p. 273.

Pageau, Louis, Montreal, Quebec, Canada. Boot or shoe. No. 1,327,772 ; Jan. 13 ; v. 270 ; p. 228.

Pagenhardt, Leonard C., Westernport, Md. Shutter-adjusting device. No. 1,328,759 ; Jan. 20 ; v. 270 ; p. 450.

Paige, Jean, Chicago, Ill. Track-switch. No. 1,329,007 ; Jan. 27 ; v. 270 ; p. 527.

Paine Company. (See Paine and Williams, assignors.)

Paine, Mathew H., Glenellyn, and W. S. Williams, Chicago, Ill., assignors to Paine Company. Box-hanger. No. 1,326,959 ; Jan. 6 ; v. 270 ; p. 15.

Palmer, Eli J., Chicago, Ill. Condiment-stopper. No. 1,328,447 ; Jan. 20 ; v. 270 ; p. 392.

Palmer, Elias H., Ladson, S. C. Internal-combustion engine. No. 1,328,685 ; Jan. 20 ; v. 270 ; p. 436.

Palmer, John F., St. Joseph, Mich. Impregnating fibrous materials. No. 1,328,541 ; Jan. 20 ; v. 270 ; p. 410.

Palmer, John M., Chicago, Ill. Valve. No. 1,328,098 ; Jan. 13 ; v. 270 ; p. 289.

Pandolfo, Samuel C. (See De Smet, Edgard C., assignor.)

Paragon Binder Corporation. (See Carney, Joseph, assignor.)

Paragon Metal Cap Company et al. (See Russell, Robert A., assignor.)

Paridon, Michael, Barberton, Ohio, assignor to The Diamond Match Company, Chicago, Ill. Assembling-machine for matches and splints. No. 1,329,060 ; Jan. 27 ; v. 270 ; p. 536.

Paridon, Michael, Barberton, Ohio, assignor to The Diamond Match Company, Chicago, Ill. Assembling-machine for matches and splints. No. 1,329,061; Jan. 27; v. 270; p. 537.

Parizek, Frank, Chicago, Ill. Whistle. No. 1,328,639; Jan. 20; v. 270; p. 428.

Parker, Arthur M., Georgetown, S. C. Machine for making coil-springs. No. 1,327,728; Jan. 13; v. 270; p. 220.

Parker, Charles W. (See Morris, Charles E., assignor.)

Parker, Edward C. S., U. S. Navy. Method of and apparatus for producing photographs and projecting the same in natural colors. No. 1,328,291; Jan. 20; v. 270; p. 362.

Parker, Edward C. S., U. S. Navy. Photographic apparatus. No. 1,328,292; Jan. 20; v. 270; p. 360.

Parker, Edward C. S., U. S. Navy. Photographic apparatus. No. 1,328,293; Jan. 20; v. 270; p. 362.

Parker, Edward C. S., U. S. Navy. Photographic apparatus. No. 1,328,294; Jan. 20; v. 270; p. 363.

Parker, John C., assignor to Lefax, Philadelphia, Pa. Filing-case. No. 1,329,139; Jan. 27; v. 270; p. 551.

Parkes, Bertrand A., assignor to The Philadelphia Drying Machinery Company, Philadelphia, Pa. Conveyer. No. 1,328,099; Jan. 13; v. 270; p. 289.

Parkin, Henry, assignor of one-half to G. G. Meeley, Philadelphia, Pa. Starter applicable to magnetos. No. 1,328,892; Jan. 27; v. 270; p. 505.

Parks-Cramer Company. (See Cramer and 'Hodge, assignors.)

Parmelee, Charles H., assignor, by mesne assignments, to Pacific Radiator Shield Co., Seattle, Wash. Radiator-shield. No. 1,327,877; Jan. 13; v. 270; p. 247.

Parrott, Arthur, Port Orchard, Wash. Handle attachment. No. 1,329,203; Jan. 27; v. 270; p. 563.

Parsons, Charles A., S. S. Cook, and A. P. Bennett, Newcastle-upon-Tyne, England; said Cook and said Bennett assignors to said Parsons. Turbine-blade attachment. No. 1,328,640; Jan. 20; v. 270; p. 428.

Parsons, Levi L., New York, N. Y., assignor to Elevator Supply & Repair Company. Door-hanger. No. 1,329,326; Jan. 27; v. 270; p. 585.

Parsons, Levi L., New York, N. Y., assignor to Elevator Supplies Company, Inc. Door-hanger. No. 1,329,327; Jan. 27; v. 270; p. 585.

Paschall, Benjamin S., New York, N. Y. Fountain-pen. No 1,327,729; Jan. 13; v. 270; p. 220.

Pass & Seymour. (See Morey, Harry J., assignor.)

Patrick, Robert A., assignor to Columbian Bronze Corporation, Freeport, N. Y. Flexible coupling for propeller-shafts. No. 1,328,893; Jan. 27; v. 270; p. 505.

Patterson, Ralph J., Berlin, N. H. Electrical water-heater. No. 1,329,204; Jan. 27; v. 270; p. 564.

Patterson, Warren C., Tamaqua, Pa. Metallic railway-tie. No. 1,329,205; Jan. 27; v. 270; p. 564.

Paul, William L., Berkeley, Calif., assignor to Deere and Company, Moline, Ill. Cultivator. No. 1,327,212; Jan. 6; v. 270; p. 62.

Paulin, Georges A., Asnières, France. Manufacture of cleansing material. No. 1,327,681; Jan. 13; v. 270; p. 201.

Paulsmeier, Albert C., Alameda, assignor to Byron Jackson Iron Works, Inc., San Francisco, Calif. Automatic stuffing-box. No. 1,328,190; Jan. 13; v. 270; p. 307.

Paulson, Andrew J., Salt Lake City, Utah. Controlling-valve for multiple fuel-supply pipes. No. 1,327,252; Jan. 6; v. 270; p. 70.

Paulson, John E., Minneapolis, Minn. Seed spacing and dropping mechanism for planters. No. 1,328,846; Jan. 27; v. 270; p. 496.

Pavlik, Joseph, New York, N. Y. Support for furnace-pokers, &c. No. 1,328,686; Jan. 20; v. 270; p. 437.

Payne, Edward W., Kansas City, Mo. Radiator-shield. No. 1,327,730; Jan. 13; v. 270; p. 220.

Pearson, Arthur E., Muskegon, Mich. Grinding-machine. No. 1,328,894; Jan. 27; v. 270; p. 506.

Pearson, Lawrence J. (See Holland and Pearson.)

Pease, Charles H., Canaan, Conn. License-tag bracket. No. 1,329,206; Jan. 27; v. 270; p. 564.

Pedley, W. P. (See Moors, Walter C., assignor.)

Peek, Will, et al. (See Barton, Charles N., assignor.)

Peelle Company, The. (See Wexler, Benjamin, assignor.)

Peerenboom, Willard, Appleton, Wis. Show-case. No. 1,328,542; Jan. 20; v. 270; p. 410.

Peerless Album Company. (See Uffner, Hyman, assignor.)

Peiler, Karl E., Hartford, Conn., assignor to Hartford-Fairmont Company, Canajoharie, N. Y. Paddle or plunger for molten glass. No. 1,328,799; Jan. 20; v. 270; p. 458.

Peirce, William E., Newark, N. J. Telegraph-receptor. No. 1,327,352; Jan. 6; v. 270; p. 88.

Pence, Alonzo H., and T. J. Morrow, Somerville, Ala. Fertilizer-distributer. No. 1,327,353; Jan. 6; v. 270; p. 88.

Penn, Harry J., Madison, N. C. Tobacco-extractor. No. 1,328,964; Jan. 27; v. 270; p. 519

Penn Pressed Metal Co. (See Estberg, William T., assignor.)

Penniman, Russell S., Jr., and N. M. Zoph, Berkeley, Calif., assignors to West Coast Kalsomine Company. Manufacturing iron compounds. No. 1,327,061; Jan. 6; v. 270; p. 35.

Pentecost, Arthur, East Orange, N. J., assignor to Wales Adding Machine Company, Wilkes-Barre, Pa. Calculating-machine. No. 1,328,847; Jan. 27; v. 270; p. 496.

Peppers, Thomas H., Nashville, Ark. Display-basket. No. 1,329,207; Jan. 27; v. 270; p. 564.

Peregrine, Clarence R., Charleroi, Pa., assignor to Macbeth-Evans Glass Company. Glass. No. 1,327,569; Jan. 6; v. 270; p. 129.

Perfecto Gear Differential Co., The. (See Baker, Arthur F., assignor.)

Perkins, B. F., & Son. (See Senna, Samuel N., assignor.)

Perkins, Robert G. (See Mannon, Brown, and Perkins.)

Perlman, Jacques M., New York, N. Y. Vehicle-body. No. 1,328,391; Jan. 20; v. 270; p. 381.

Pernot, Henri A., assignor to Compagnie des Bouchages Hermatiques Simplex, Paris, France. Apparatus for closing containers by pressure. No. 1,329,140; Jan. 27; v. 270; p. 552.

Perry, Ray P., Montclair, N. J., assignor to The Barrett Company, New York, N. Y. Molded form of bitumen. No. 1,327,354; Jan. 6; v. 270; p. 88.

Peter, Bernard H., Westminster, England, assignor, by mesne assignments, to The Union Switch & Signal Company, Swissvale, Pa. Signaling system. No. 1,327,570; Jan. 6; v. 270; p. 129.

Peters, Frank A., Chicago, Ill. Curtain-support. No. 1,327,061; Jan. 13; v. 270; p. 263.

Peters Machine and Manufacturing Company, The. (See Thiemer, William H., assignor.)

Peterson, Claus E., Worcester, assignor to Iverson Piano Player Company, Boston, Mass. Pneumatic motor for piano players. No. 1,327,731; Jan. 13; v. 270; p. 221.

Peterson, Eldon L., Tacoma, Wash. Garden-tool. No. 1,328,191; Jan. 13; v. 270; p. 307.

Peterson, Erick B., assignor to George W. Dover, Incorporated, Providence, R. I. Ball safety-catch for brooches and articles of a similar nature. No. 1,328,965; Jan. 27; v. 270; p. 519.

Petrie, Robert E., Chicago, Ill. Engine-attaching means for vehicles. No. 1,326,960; Jan. 6; v. 270; p. 15.

Petroske, John J. (See Starkenberg, Karl R., assignor.)

Petterson, Bertill C. (See Petterson, Simon G. and B. C.)

Petterson, Simon G. and B. C., Pine Bluff, Ark. Toy wagon. No. 1,328,760; Jan. 20; v. 270; p. 450.

Pettis, Edson S., Mill Valley, Calif. Drum-filter wiring No. 1,327,962; Jan. 13; v. 270; p. 263.

Peycke, Armand H., assignor to American Steel Foundries, Chicago, Ill. Slack-adjuster. No. 1,329,008; Jan. 27; v. 270; p. 527.

Peycke, Armand H., assignor to American Steel Foundries, Chicago, Ill. Brake mechanism. No. 1,329,009; Jan. 27; v. 270; p. 527.

Peycke, Armand H., assignor to American Steel Foundries, Chicago, Ill. Brake mechanism. No. 1,329,010; Jan. 27; v. 270; p. 527.

Pfeiffer, Fred B., Akron, Ohio. Tire-vulcanizing device. No. 1,327,841; Jan. 13; v. 270; p. 241.

Pfeiffer, S., Manufacturing Company. (See Lazarus, Willis H., assignor.)

Pfell, Frank L. H. (See Steigerwald and Pfell.)

Pflaster, Simon, New York, N. Y. Exhibiting device. No. 1,328,312; Jan. 13; v. 270; p. 307.

Pflueger, John L., New Orleans, La. Parachute and launching device for aeroplanes. No. 1,327,355; Jan. 6; v. 270; p. 88.

Pfrogner, Frank. (See Leatherman and Pfrogner.)

Phelps, Lucius J., San Diego, Calif. Irreversible steering-machine. No. 1,328,761; Jan. 20; v. 270; p. 450.

Phelps, Theophilus J., Lewiston, N. C. Peanut-picking machine. No. 1,328,295; Jan. 20; v. 270; p. 363.

Philadelphia Drying Machinery Company, The. (See Parkes, Bertrand A., assignor.)

Philadelphia Storage Battery Company. (See Holland and Pearson, assignors.)

Philadelphia Storage Battery Company. (See Holland and Skinner, assignors.)

Phillips, Francis L., Tugaske, Saskatchewan, Canada. Grain-pickler. No. 1,327,444; Jan. 6; v. 270; p. 105.

Phillips & Slack, Inc. (See Phillips. Frank A., assignor.)

Phillips, Frank A., assignor to Phillips & Slack, Inc., Northfield, Vt. Edge-lining machine. No. 1,327,928; Jan. 13; v. 270; p. 256.

Phillips, Frank G., Vancouver, British Columbia, Canada. Means for salvaging submerged vessels. No. 1,328,014; Jan. 13; v. 270; p. 273.

Phillips, John E., Birmingham, England. Guard for power-presses. No. 1,329,011; Jan. 27; v. 270; p. 527.

Phillips, John H., Jr., Jackson, Mich. Flexible pipe. No. 1,327,632; Jan. 13; v. 270; p. 202.

Phillips, Walter C., assignor to Guaranteed Tractors, Inc., Chicago, Ill. Tractor attachment for automobiles. No. 1,327,773; Jan. 13; v. 270; p. 228.

Phillipson, Emil, assignor to Plant & Company, New York, N. Y. Electric fan. No. 1,328,055; Jan. 13; v. 270; p. 281.

Phoebus E. G., Company. (See Boltshauser, Conrad, as signor.)

Pick, Albert, & Company. (See Pick, Hugo, assignor.)

Pick, Arthur. (See Coultas and Pick.)

Pick, Hugo, assignor to Albert Pick & Company, Chicago, Ill. Match-box. No. 1,329,012; Jan. 27; v. 270; p. 527.

Piel, G., Company, The. (See Long, George F., assignor.)

Pieper, Alphonse F. (See Pieper, Oscar H. and A. F.)

Pieper, Chester R., assignor to The Gund Manufacturing Company, La Crosse, Wis. Automatic ratchet. No. 1,328,448; Jan. 20; v. 270; p. 392.

Pieper, Oscar H. and A. F., Rochester, N. Y. Indicator mechanism. No. 1,328,895; Jan. 27: v. 270; p. 506.

Pierce, Percy, Philadelphia, Pa. Toy. No. 1,329,062; Jan. 27; v. 270; p. 537.

Pierce, William B. (See Johnson, Arthur E., assignor.)

Pierce, William S., Franklin, Pa. Swage for use in oil-wells. No. 1,327,491; Jan. 6; v. 270; p. 114.

Pierman, Alexander N. (See Emerson and Pierman.)

Pike, Charles F. (See Bradley and Pike.)

Pilon, Eugene, Farmpoint. Ontario, Canada. Spring-hook. No. 1,328,193; Jan. 13; v. 270; p. 307.

Pilsbry-Becker Engineering & Supply Company. (See McGinnis, Walter R., assignor.)

Pittsburgh Plate Glass Company. (See Hitchcock, Halbert K., assignor.)

Place, James F., Glen Ridge, N. J. Apparatus for liquefying air. No. 1,326,961; Jan. 6; v. 270; p. 15.

Placette, Theodore. (See Trahan, Clair A., assignor.)

Plant & Company. (See Phillipson, Emil, assignor.)

Plante, Albert E., assignor of one-half to B. Drolet, Montreal, Quebec, Canada. Electric water-heater. No. 1,327,774; Jan. 13; v. 270; p. 228.

Platt, Benjamin N., Chicago, Ill. Block. No. 1,327,775; Jan. 13; v. 270; p. 229.

Pleister, Henry W., Westfield, N. J., assignor to H. B. Newhall, Jr., executor. Cable-clamp. No. 1,328,543; Jan. 20; v. 270; p. 410.

Plimpton, Bentley A., Victor, N. Y. Insulator-support. No. 1,328,687; Jan. 20; v. 270; p. 437.

Plummer, Allen H., and C. P. Mullen, Conshohocken, Pa. Oil-deflector for engine-cylinders. No. 1,328,544; Jan. 20; v. 270; p. 410.

Pneumatic Process Flotation Company. (See Callow, John M., assignor.)

Poetz, John C., Wenatchee, Wash. Climbing device. No. 1,328,251; Jan. 13; v. 270; p. 319.

Pogue, Homer C., Chicago, Ill. Spark-gap attachment for spark-plugs. No. 1,329,013; Jan. 27; v. 270; p. 527.

Poindexter, Alfred M., Denver, Colo. Sectional non-rotative insulating-knob for supporting electric wires. No. 1,326,962; Jan. 6; v. 270; p. 16.

Pollard, George, assignor to The Menco-Elma Syndicate Limited, London, England. Electromagnetic brake for motor road-vehicles. No. 1,328,966; Jan. 27; v. 270; p. 519.

Pollmiller, August V., Marceline, Mo. Semaphore-signal. No. 1,328,194; Jan. 13; v. 270; p. 307.

Pond, Frank J., Tulsa, Okla. Shaft-clamp. No. 1,328,688; Jan. 20; v. 270; p. 437.

Pool, Elmer C., New Castle, Pa., assignor to Toledo Scale Company, Toledo, Ohio. Pendulum-scale. No. 1,326,963; Jan. 6; v. 270; p. 16.

Poole, Arthur F., Chicago, Ill. Electric-clock system. No. 1,328,247; Jan. 13; v. 270; p. 318.

Poole, Arthur F., Kenilworth, Ill., assignor to The Wahl Company, Wilmington, Del. Gear-shift for cross-actuators. No. 1,329,014; Jan. 27; v. 270; p. 528.

Poole, Fred, Jewell, Kans. Water-heater. No. 1,826,964; Jan. 6; v. 270; p. 16.

Poore, John C., Boston, Mass. Dirigible-eye structure for dolls. No. 1,328,100; Jan. 13; v. 270; p. 290.

Porch, James W., Hurricane Mills, Tenn. Pulling implement. No. 1,326,965; Jan. 6; v. 270; p. 16.

Port, Samuel R., Martinsville. Ind. Collapsible barrel. No. 1,328,587; Jan. 20; v. 270; p. 419.

Porter, J. E., Company. (See Jordan, Burton S., assignor.)

Posson, Edward, Chicago, Ill. Trap and drain for railway-cars. No. 1,329,015; Jan. 27; v. 270; p. 528.

Post, Truman W., Brooklyn, N. Y., assignor to Electric Auto-Lite Corporation, Toledo, Ohio. Headlight. No. 1,327,732; Jan. 13; v. 270; p. 221.

Potter, Henry K., Somerville, Mass. Sweeping streets. No. 1,328,237; Jan. 13; v. 270; p. 316.

Potts, Warren W., Elkhart, Ind. Adjustable illuminating-fixture. No. 1,327,733; Jan. 13; v. 270; p. 221.

Powell, Peter, assignor of one-half to J. Rosenfield, Boston, Mass. Air-bag. No. 1,329,208; Jan. 27; v. 270; p. 564.

Powers Photo Engraving Company. (See Leitner, Emil, assignor.)

Prather, Arthur, Skidmore, Mo. Wheel. No. 1,327,253; Jan. 6; v. 270; p. 70.

Pratt, Alphonso C., Deep River, Conn. Apparatus for making grommets. No. 1,327,170; Jan. 6; v. 270; p. 54.

Pratte, Alphonsine P. (See Pratte, François J. A., assignor.)

Pratte, François J. A., assignor to A. P. Pratte, Montreal, Quebec. Canada. Talking-machine. No. 1,327,776; Jan. 13; v. 270; p. 229.

Prentiss, Augustin M., Fort Caswell, N. C., assignor of one-half to D. E. Bulloch, Washington, D. C. Carbureter. No. 1,329,308; Jan. 27; v. 270; p. 582.

Prentiss, Augustin M., Rock Island. Ill., assignor of one-half to D. E. Bulloch, Washington, D. C. Carbureter. No. 1,329,309; Jan. 27; v. 270; p. 582.

Pressed Steel Car Company. (See Reeder, Nathaniel S., assignor.)

Pressler, Charles F., Fort Wayne, Ind. Liquid-measuring pump. No. 1,328,101; Jan. 13; v. 270; p. 290.

Preston, Albert F., Boston, Mass. Adjustable blank-holder for pattern-grading and other machines. No. 1,328,689; Jan. 20; v. 270; p. 437.

Prince, John. (See Nilson and Prince.)

Pritchard, Albert R., New York, N. Y. Heating apparatus. No. 1,327,213; Jan. 6; v. 270; p. 63.

Products Syndicate Inc. (See Byers, Joseph J., assignor.)

Pruden, Allan K., St. Paul, Minn. Ventilator and ventilating system. No. 1,327,879; Jan. 13; v. 270; p. 248.

Psilander, Charles A., assignor to William Wharton, Jr. & Co., Easton, Pa. Hard-center crossing-frog. No. 1,327,842; Jan. 13; v. 270; p. 241.

Pulliam, Oswald S., New York, N. Y. Steering-gear attachment. No. 1,328,762; Jan. 20; v. 270; p. 541.

Purdy, Fred P., Sharon, Mass. Bowling game. No. 1,329,254; Jan. 27; v. 270; p. 573.

Putnam, Salmon W., 3d, assignor to A. H. Ingle, Rochester, N. Y. Tailstock-clamping mechanism. No. 1,327,356; Jan. 6; v. 270; p. 88.

Putnam, Salmon W., 3d, assignor to A. H. Ingle, Rochester, N. Y. Journal-bushing. No. 1,328,195; Jan. 13; v. 270; p. 308.

Putnam, Salmon W., 3d, assignor to A. H. Ingle, Rochester. N. Y. Tire-lathe. No. 1,328,763; Jan. 20; v. 270; p. 451.

Pytlewski, Steve, Minneapolis, Minn. Reinforced tread for spring-wheels. No. 1,327,843; Jan. 13; v. 270; p. 241.

Quade. Frank H., Jr., assignor to Lisenby Manufacturing Company. Fresno, Calif. Electric snap-switch. No. 1,328,338; Jan. 20; v. 270; p. 371.

Quaill, Francis H. (See Knudsen, Jacob B., assignor.)

Quigley Furnace Specialties Co. (See Renken, William O., assignor.)

Quinn, Michael R., Kent, Ohio. Handkerchief. No. 1,327,062; Jan. 6; v. 270; p. 35.

Quirk, Michael F. (See McLeod and Quirk.)

Raba, Ernest, Valley, Okla. Combined gasket and oil-gasifier. No. 1,329,343; Jan. 27; v. 270; p. 588.

Rabe, Paul B., Chicago, Ill., assignor to O. K. Giant Battery Co., Gary, Ind. Grid-plate for storage batteries. No. 1 328,392; Jan. 20; v. 270; p. 382.

Rabe, Paul B., Chicago, Ill., assignor to O. K. Giant Battery Co. Gary, Ind. Storage battery. No. 1,328,393; Jan. 20; v. 270; p. 382.

Rabe, Paul B., Chicago, Ill., assignor to O. K. Giant Battery Co., Gary. Ind. Storage battery. No. 1,328,394; Jan. 20; v. 270; p. 382.

R. & C. Engineering Company, The. (See Reed, Chase C., assignor.)

Racow, Joseph, New Haven, Conn. Combination-lock for the steering-posts of automobiles. No. 1,327,406; Jan. 6; v. 270; p. 97.

Rail, Napoleon, Lowell. Mass. Automatic cutting-off device for thread-winders. No. 1,328,196; Jan. 13; v. 270; p. 308.

Railway Automatic Safety Appliance Company, The. (See Stafford, Earl C., assignor.)

Railway and Industrial Engineering Company. (See Koppitz, Carl G., assignor.)

Ramauge, Adalberto, Buenos Aires, Argentina. Parachute comprising pneumatic means. No. 1,328,848; Jan. 27; v. 270; p. 496.

Ramsey, George, assignor to Anchor Cap & Closure Corporation, Brooklyn, N. Y. Side-seal closure. No. 1,327,963; Jan. 13; v. 270; p. 263.

Rand, Frederick B., Sanford. Me. Lug-strap holder. No. 1,327,964; Jan. 13; v. 270; p. 264.

Rand, Harry M., Westville, N. J. Valve-grinder. No. 1,328,197; Jan. 13; v. 270; p. 308.

Randall, Herman P. (See Spurr and Randall.)

Randall, Karl C., Edgewood Park, Pa., assignor to Westinghouse Electric & Manufacturing Company. Circuit-interrupter. No. 1,327,777; Jan. 13; v. 270; p. 229.

Raney, Clemma R., Chicago, Ill., assignor, by mesne assignments, to International Harvester Company. Auxiliary buffer for shockers. No. 1,328,795; Jan. 20; v. 270; p. 457.

Rassmann, F., Manufacturing Company. (See Rassmann, Hugo C., assignor.)

Rassmann, Hugo C., Beaver Dam, Wis. Watering device for stock. No. 1,327,734; Jan. 13; v. 270; p. 221.

Rassmann, Hugo C., assignor to F. Rassmann Manufacturing Company. Beaver Dam, Wis. Supporting and alining means for stanchions. No. 1,327,735; Jan. 13; v. 270; p. 221.

Rawsthorne, John S. (See Bevin and Rawsthorne.)

Ray, William R., San Francisco, Calif. Oil-burner. No. 1,327,571; Jan. 6; v. 270; p. 129.

Ray, William R., San Francisco, Calif. Burner-mounting. No. 1,328,198; Jan. 13; v. 270; p. 308.

Raymond, Alonzo C., Detroit, Mich. Wall construction. No. 1,327,292; Jan. 6; v. 270; p. 77.

Rea, Robert, and F. W. Waters. Portland. Oreg. Conveying and steam and water bleaching apparatus for dehydrating plants. No. 1,328,395; Jan. 20; v. 270; p. 382.

Rea, Robert, and F. W. Waters, Portland, Oreg. Fruit, vegetable, and other food dehydrating furnace and its cooperating apparatus. No. 1,328,396; Jan. 20; v. 270; p. 382.

Rea, Robert, and F. W. Waters. Portland, Oreg. Steam bleaching apparatus. No. 1,328,397; Jan. 20; v. 270; p. 382.

Rea, Robert, and E. W. Waters, Portland. Oreg. Heat-regulating adjustable-shutter mechanism for food-dehydrating plants. No. 1,328,398; Jan. 20; v. 270; p. 383.

Reaben, George B., New York, N. Y. Arrow. No. 1,328,967; Jan. 27; v. 270; p. 519.

Ream, Fred H., Kansas City, Mo. Universal joint. No. 1,328,449; Jan. 20; v. 270; p. 392.

Rector, Floyd D. and W. Q., Louisville, Ky. Charge-forming device. No. 1,328,199; Jan. 13; v. 270; p. 308.

Rector, William Q. (See Rector, Floyd D. and W. Q.)

Reddin, Thomas P., Bridgeport, Conn. Power transmission. No. 1,328,588; Jan. 20; v. 270; p. 419.

Reddy, Frederick, Ottawa, Ontario, Canada. Nut-lock. No. 1,328,899; Jan. 20; v. 270; p. 383.

Redfield, Casper L., trustee. (See Lundquist, Frank A., assignor.)

Reed, Chase C., assignor to The R. & C. Engineering Company, Toledo, Ohio. Plowing-machine. No. 1,328,896; Jan. 27; v. 270; p. 506.

Reeder, Nathaniel S., New York, N. Y., assignor to Pressed Steel Car Company, Pittsburgh, Pa. Car-roof construction. No. 1,328,200; Jan. 13; v. 270; p. 309.

Reeves, George C., Oak Park, Ill. Respirator-valve. No. 1,326,966; Jan. 6; v. 270; p. 17.

Refior, Emil M., et al. (See London, Jacob M., assignor.)

Reich, Henry C., New York, N. Y. Extension-pedal. No. 1,328,400; Jan. 20; v. 270; p. 383.

Reichman, Harry, and A. R. Spangenberg, Cincinnati, Ohio. Combined package and trash receptacle. No. 1,327,778; Jan. 13; v. 270; p. 229.

Reichold, Ludwig, Pittsfield, Mass., assignor to General Electric Company. Electric fuel-heater. No. 1,328,546; Jan. 20; v. 270; p. 411.

Reid, James H., Newark, N. J., assignor to International Nitrogen Company. Producing carbid. No. 1,327,736; Jan. 13; v. 270; p. 222.

Reid, James H., Newark, N. J., assignor, by mesne assignments, to International Nitrogen Co. Procuring and securing products from carbohydrates. No. 1,327,787; Jan. 13; v. 270; p. 222.

Reid, James H., Newark, N. J., assignor, by mesne assignments, to International Nitrogen Co. Means actuated by alternating electric current for controlling or operating electric furnaces or other mechanisms. No. 1,327,738; Jan. 13; v. 270; p. 222.

Reisbach, Gustave B., assignor to The Cutler-Hammer Mfg. Co., Milwaukee, Wis. Contact device. No. 1,328,450; Jan. 20; v. 270; p. 392.

Remick, Elmer H. (See Manahan, Michael J., assignor.)

Remington, Joseph P., assignor to Remington Manufacturing Company, Philadelphia, Pa. Air control for internal-combustion engines. No. 1,328,102; Jan. 13; v. 270; p. 290.

Remington Manufacturing Company. (See Remington, Joseph P., assignor.)

Remmers, Bernhard, Philadelphia, Pa., assignor, by mesne assignments, to Armour Grain Company, Chicago, Ill. Apparatus for preparing potatoes. No. 1,327,254; Jan. 6; v. 270; p. 70.

Renaissance Corset Co. (See Griner, Alvah A., assignor.)

Renault Louis. (See Fuchs, Ernest, assignor.)

Rendahl, George A., assignor to D. P. Hogan, Denver, Colo. Oil-baffle for automobile-engines. No. 1,327,779; Jan. 13; v. 270; p. 229.

Rendano, Emil, Brooklyn, assignor of one-half to E. Rendano and N. Rendano, New York, and one-half to P. J. Forbes, Brooklyn, N. Y. Fastening device. No. 1,328,201; Jan. 13; v. 270; p. 273.

Rendano, Nicholas, et al. (See Rendano, Emil, assignor.)

Renfro, Albert L., assignor of one-half to W. K. Lee, Bakersfield, Calif. Sack-holder. No. 1,328,690; Jan. 20; v. 270; p. 437.

Renkin, William O., Oradell, N. J., assignor to Quigley Furnace Specialties Co., Inc. Valve. No. 1,329,016; Jan. 27; v. 270; p. 528.

Renkin, William O., Oradell, N. J., assignor to Quigley Furnace Specialties Co., Inc. Valve-operating mechanism. No. 1,329,017; Jan. 27; v. 270; p. 528.

Renkin, William O., Oradell, N. J., assignor to Quigley Furnace Specialties Co., Inc. Apparatus for automatically controlling flowing materials. No. 1,329,018; Jan. 27; v. 270; p. 528.

Resch, Charles H., Youngstown, Ohio. Steering-wheel lock for motor-vehicles. No. 1,328,691; Jan. 20; v. 270; p. 438.

Revere Rubber Company. (See Brogden, Joseph T., assignor.)

Reynolds, William B., Roundup, Mont. Dump-car. No. 1,327,255; Jan. 6; v. 270; p. 70.

Rhein, Meyer L., New York, N. Y. Gage for dental and surgical instruments. No. 1,327,114; Jan. 6; v. 270; p. 44.

Rhoades, Alonzo E., assignor to Draper Corporation, Hopedale, Mass. Shaft-bearing construction for warpers. No. 1,328,451; Jan. 20; v. 270; p. 392.

Rhoades, Alonzo E., assignor to Draper Corporation, Hopedale, Mass. Filling-replenishing loom. No. 1,328,452; Jan. 20; v. 270; p. 393.

Rhodes, Austin D., Waltham, Mass., assignor to American Lacing Hook Co. Gage for positioning sheet material. No. 1,328,764; Jan. 20; v. 270; p. 451.

Ricardo, Harry R., London, England. Lubricating mechanism. No. 1,328,015; Jan. 13; v. 270; p. 273.

Riccio, Pasquale A., Brooklyn, N. Y. Foot-operated valve. No. 1,329,209; Jan. 27; v. 270; p. 564.

Rice, Frank E., assignor to American Tap Bush Co., Detroit, Mich. Tap-attaching thimble. No. 1,329,141; Jan. 27; v. 270; p. 552.

Rice, Otis D., Winthrop, Mass. Method of and apparatus for drying material. No. 1,328,897; Jan. 27; v. 270; p. 506.

Richard Auto Mfg. Co., The. (See Richard, François, assignor.)

Richard, Charles D., New York, N. Y. Hub-odometer. No. 1,326,967; Jan. 6; v. 270; p. 17.

Richard, François, assignor to The Richard Auto Mfg. Company, Cleveland, Ohio. Headlight. No. 1,328,692; Jan. 20; v. 270; p. 438.

Richard, François, and F. M. Brady, Cleveland, Ohio. Plastic composition. No. 1,329,094; Jan. 27; v. 270; p. 543.

Richards, Oscar B. (See Swartz and Richards.)

Richardson, Alan C., Silver Spring, Md. Processing apparatus for canned products. No. 1,328,202; Jan. 13; v. 270; p. 309.

Richardson, John R., Madera, Calif. Mold for constructing hollow walls of concrete. No. 1,329,095; Jan. 27; v. 270; p. 543.

Richardson, Robert N., Los Angeles, Calif. Cooling device for beds and sleeping-compartments. No. 1,327,214; Jan. 6; v. 270; p. 63.

Richley, Alfred, Cleveland, Ohio, assignor of one-half to W. C. Cone, Toronto, Ontario, Canada. Building concrete ships. No. 1,327,739; Jan. 13; v. 270; p. 222.

Richman, Philip J. (See Eckert and Richman.)

Ricketts, William C., Dayton, Ohio. Scouring soap cake, to be used in general scouring and cleaning purposes. No. 1,328,898; Jan. 27; v. 270; p. 506.

Rickon, Harold J., assignor of one-half to J. A. Sandal, San Francisco, Calif. Automatic air-release. No. 1,329,210; Jan. 27; v. 270; p. 565.

Ridderstedt, Charles H., Pittsburgh, Pa. Combustion of fuel. No. 1,328,296; Jan. 20; v. 270; p. 363.

Rider, Ernest G., assignor to Schwerdtle Machine Company, Philadelphia, Pa. Expansion-mandrel. No. 1,327,445; Jan. 6; v. 270; p. 105.

Riedele, Philip, Los Angeles, Calif. Bumper-bracket holder. No. 1,329,019; Jan. 27; v. 270; p. 529.

Riethmiller, Richard H., Montclair, N. J., assignor to H. A. Metz, New York, N. Y. Hypodermic syringe. No. 1,328,203; Jan. 13; v. 270; p. 309.

Rigby, George E. Manchester, England. Spring suspension. No. 1,327,063; Jan. 6; v. 270; p. 35.

Rinn, Michael M., et al. (See Schott, John H., assignor.)

Ripple, John W., Baltimore, Md. Sewer-trap. No. 1,328,103; Jan. 13; v. 270; p. 290.

Ritter, Thomas J., Jr., and B. M. Warn, Lairdsville, Pa. Lever-holding mechanism for automobiles. No. 1,328,899; Jan. 27; v. 270; p. 506.

Ritter, Thomas J., Jr., and B. M. Warn, Lairdsville, Pa. Lever-holding mechanism for automobiles. No. 1,329,142; Jan. 27; v. 270; p. 552.

Rittman, Walter F. (See Whitaker and Rittman.)

Ritzema, David. (See Eggleston, William H., assignor.)

Robb, John F., Washington, D. C., assignor to Koehring Machine Company, Milwaukee, Wis. Control mechanism for mixing-machines. No. 1,328,765; Jan. 20; v. 270; p. 451.

Roberts, Clarence V., assignor to Roberts & Mander Stove Company, Philadelphia, Pa. Oven-burner for gas-ranges. No. 1,328,580; Jan. 20; v. 270; p. 419.

Roberts, Fred T., assignor to The Aranar Company, Cleveland, Ohio. Inflated golf-ball and making. No. 1,329,310; Jan. 27; v. 270; p. 583.

Roberts, Fred T., Cleveland Heights, assignor to The Aranar Company, Cleveland, Ohio. Making balls. No. 1,329,311; Jan. 27; v. 270; p. 583.

Roberts, Fred T., Cleveland, Ohio. Mold for making rubber articles. No. 1,329,312; Jan. 27; v. 270; p. 583.

Roberts, John T. (See Hafner and Roberts.)

Roberts, Louis L. (See Golata and Roberts.)

Roberts & Mander Stove Company. (See Roberts, Clarence V., assignor.)

Robertson, Stephen, et al. (See Yeats, Samuel W., assignor.)

Robertson, William F., Malta, Mont. Fence-wire fastener. No. 1,328,693; Jan. 20; v. 270; p. 438.

Robeson Process Company. (See Hurt, Henry H., assignor.)

Robinson, Harry A., assignor to Eclipse Stove Company, Mansfield, Ohio. Gas burner. No. 1,329,096; Jan. 27; v. 270; p. 543.

Robinson, William H., Schenectady, N. Y. Knockdown stove. No. 1,327,115; Jan. 6; v. 270; p. 44.

Rockford Milling Machine Company. (See Sundstrand, Gustaf D., assignor.)

Roderick Lean Manufacturing Company. (See Warne, Frederick C., assignor.)

Rodger, Joseph B., Independence, Mo. Automatic time-controlled trip mechanism. No. 1,329,020; Jan. 27; v. 270; p. 529.

Roe, William C., Pittsburgh, Pa., assignor of one-half to W. C. Handlan, Wheeling, W. Va. Train-control system for toy railways. No. 1,327,215; Jan. 6; v. 270; p. 63.

Roesch, Daniel, Chicago, Ill. Automatic spark-controlling device. No. 1,328,453; Jan. 20; v. 270; p. 393.

Rogers, Frank J., Detroit, Mich. Device for the prevention of stammering. No. 1,327,407; Jan. 6; v. 270; p. 98.

Rogers, George D., Gloucester, Mass. Extracting oils from fatty substances. No. 1,326,968; Jan. 6; v. 270; p. 17.

Rogers, Harry M., Petersburg, Va. Humidifier. No. 1,329,143 ; Jan. 27 ; v. 270 ; p. 552.

Rogers, James E., assignor of one-third to P. U. Sunderland, Danbury, Conn. Antiskid device. No. 1,328,297 ; Jan. 20 ; v. 270 ; p. 363.

Rogers, James E., assignor of one-third to P. U. Sunderland, Danbury, Conn. Antiskid device. No. 1,328,298 ; Jan. 20 ; v. 270 ; p. 364.

Rogers, John A., Atlanta, assignor to H. S. Cohen, Marietta, Ga. Coin-assorter. No. 1,327,357 ; Jan. 6 ; v. 270 ; p. 89.

Rogers, John R., Brooklyn, N. Y. Clutch. No. 1,327,880 ; Jan. 13 ; v. 270 ; p. 248.

Rogers, William A. (See Kellogg, Neff, Rogers, and Cowan.)

Rolfes, George H., assignor to Handlan Buck Manufacturing Company, St. Louis, Mo. Lantern-bail. No. 1,327,293 ; Jan. 6 ; v. 270 ; p. 77.

Rolls-Royce Limited. (See Royce, Frederick H., assignor.)

Root, A. I., Company, The. (See Blanchard, Herbert C., assignor.)

Root, Ralph R., Cleveland, Ohio. Electric signaling device. No. 1,328,454 ; Jan. 20 ; v. 270 ; p. 393.

Rose, William, Chicago, Ill. Liquid-measuring device. No. 1,327,686 ; Jan. 13 ; v. 270 ; p. 212.

Rosebourne, Mostyn, Manchester, and F. A. Couse, Urmston, England, assignors to Westinghouse Electric and Manufacturing Company. Automatic protective gear for electrical systems. No. 1,329,255 ; Jan. 27 ; v. 270 ; p. 573.

Roseman, Joseph A., Glenview, Ill. Grass-mowing machine. No. 1,327,924 ; Jan. 13 ; v. 270 ; p. 256.

Rosenfeld, Maurice S., assignor, by mesne assignments, to J. Schechter, New York, N. Y. Apparatus for repairing moving-picture films. No. 1,328,056 ; Jan. 13 ; v 270 ; p. 281.

Rosenfield, James. (See Powell, Peter, assignor.)

Rosenthal, Levi M., assignor to S. Rosenthal, New York, N. Y. Bottle-cap. No. 1,328,455 ; Jan. 20 ; v. 270 ; p. 393.

Rosenthal, Samuel. (See Rosenthal, Levi M., assignor.)

Rösholt, Nils, assignor to N. A. Krag, Christiania, Norway. Locking mechanism for switch-points. No. 1,327,358 ; Jan. 6 ; v. 270 ; p. 89.

Ross, James D., Seattle, Wash. Process and apparatus for ore separation. No. 1,328,456 ; Jan. 20 ; v. 270 ; p. 393.

Ross, John, assignor of one-half to L. J. Kutil, Ironwood, Mich. Non-siphoning trap. No. 1,327,116 ; Jan. 6 ; v. 270 ; p. 45.

Ross, William H., Washington, D. C. Removal of Hydrofluoric acid from phosphoric acid. No. 1,329,273 ; Jan. 27 ; v. 270 ; p. 576.

Rossell, Thomas J., New Smyrna, Fla. Flue-cleaner. No. 1,327,740 ; Jan. 13 ; v. 270 ; p. 222.

Rotary Tire and Rubber Company. (See Sterns, Edward O., assignor.)

Roth, Carl H., Newark, N. J. Tool or cutter head. No. 1,327,881 ; Jan. 13 ; v. 270 ; p. 248.

Rotter, Max, assignor to Busch-Sulzer Bros.-Diesel Engine Company, St. Louis, Mo. Packing or gasket construction. No. 1,327,965 ; Jan. 13 ; v. 270 ; p. 264.

Rouanet, Louis, assignor to Compagnie D'Applications Mecaniques, Ivry-Port, France. Double-jaw calipers. No. 1,327,216 ; Jan. 6 ; v. 270 ; p. 63.

Rounds, Robert, Conde, S. D. Engine-handling device. No. 1,326,969 ; Jan. 6 ; v. 270 ; p. 17.

Row, Reuben R., and H. C. Davis, Elizabeth, N. J., assignors to American Marine Equipment Corporation, New York, N. Y. Coupling and the like. No. 1,326,970 ; Jan. 6 ; v. 270 ; p. 17.

Rowe, William A., Eau Claire, Wis. Floor-cleaning machine. No. 1,328,339 ; Jan. 20 ; v. 270 ; p. 372.

Rowland, Phillip J. (See Heslewood, William R., assignor.)

Rownd, Annie K., Rochester, N. Y. Nursery-seat. No. 1,328,900 ; Jan. 20 ; v. 270 ; p. 507.

Royal Metalware Manufacturing Co. (See Snider, John L., assignor.)

Royce, Frederick H., assignor to Rolls-Royce Limited, Derby, England. Carbureter for internal-combustion engines. No. 1,328,590 ; Jan. 20 ; v. 270 ; p. 419.

Rubenstein, Nathan, New York, N. Y. Sadiron. No. 1,328,766 ; Jan. 20 ; v. 270 ; p. 451.

Rubin, Morris, and W. Levine, New York, N. Y. Soapholder. No. 1,329,097 ; Jan. 27 ; v. 270 ; p. 543

Rudkin, William P., Oklahoma, Okla. Generator. No. 1,328,016 ; Jan. 13 ; v. 270 ; p. 274.

Rudolphi, Frank, New York, N. Y., assignor to American Can Company. Can-closing machine. No. 1,327,966 ; Jan. 13 ; v. 270 ; p. 264.

Ruggles, William G., assignor to E. V. Hartford, New York, N. Y. Golf-stick. No. 1,327,171 ; Jan. 6 ; v. 270 ; p. 55.

Ruhl, Hepburn. (See Bennett, Edward O., assignor.)

Rumsey, Ernest. (See Upp, William M., assignor.)

Rushton, Kenneth, assignor to The Baldwin Locomotive Works, Philadelphia, Pa. Stub-end bearing for locomotive-rods. No. 1,328,591 ; Jan. 20 ; v. 270 ; p. 420.

Rushton, Kenneth, assignor to The Baldwin Locomotive Works, Philadelphia, Pa. Railway-truck. No. 1,328,592 ; Jan. 20 ; v. 270 ; p. 420.

Russell, Bertrom R., Sheridan, Nev. Match-safe. No. 1,328,968 ; Jan. 27 ; v. 270 ; p. 519.

Russell, Robert A., New York, assignor of one-third to Paragon Metal Cap Company, Inc., Brooklyn, one-third to M. King, New York, and one-third to L. R. N. Carvalho, Brooklyn, N. Y. Cap for bottles or jars. No. 1,327,967 ; Jan. 13 ; v. 270 ; p. 264.

Ruston and Hornsby. (See Green, Wans, and Livens, assignors.)

Ruths, Johannes K., Djursholm, Sweden, assignor to Aktiebolaget Vaporackumulator, Stockholm, Sweden. Steam-accumulator. No. 1,328,593 ; Jan. 20 ; v. 270 ; p. 420.

Ryan, Henry D., Boulder, Colo., assignor, by mesne assignments, to National Oil Machinery Corporation, New York, N. Y. Recovering bituminous matter from shale. No. 1,327,572 ; Jan. 6 ; v. 270 ; p. 129.

Ryan, John H., assignor to D. R. Seaman, Chicago, Ill. Grinding calcium carbonate and product thereof. No. 1,328,299 ; Jan. 20 ; v. 270 ; p. 364.

Ryan, John T., Pittsburgh, Pa., assignor to The Mine Safety Appliance Company. Mouthpiece for breathing apparatus. No. 1,328,057 ; Jan. 13 ; v. 270 ; p. 281.

Ryan, John T., assignor to Mine Safety Appliance Company, Pittsburgh, Pa. Regenerator for breathing apparatus. No. 1,328,058 ; Jan. 13 ; v. 270 ; p. 282.

Ryder, Ambrose, New York, N. Y. Umbrella. No. 1,328,901 ; Jan. 27 ; v. 270 ; p. 507.

Ryder, Ambrose, New York, N. Y. Umbrella. No. 1,328,902 ; Jan. 27 ; v. 270 ; p. 507.

Rypinski, Albert B., Brooklyn, assignor to T. E. Murray, New York, N. Y. Connecting plates by electrical riveting. No. 1,329,144 ; Jan. 27 ; v. 270 ; p. 552.

Sabey, William D. (See Smith, Henry A., assignor.)

Safety Eyeglass Company, The. (See Bradley and Pike, assignors.)

Sala, Earl V., Toledo, Ohio. Engine. No. 1,327,172 ; Jan. 6 ; v. 270 ; p. 55.

Salm, John, assignor to C. L. A. Whitney, Albany, N. Y. Making solder. No. 1,326,971 ; Jan. 6 ; v. 270 ; p. 18.

Samelson, Bernard. (See Smith and Samelson.)

Sanborn, Arthur R., Schenectady, N. Y., assignors to General Electric Company. Overload device. No. 1,328,457 ; Jan. 20 ; v. 270 ; p. 394.

Sandal, John A. (See Rickon, Harold J., assignor.)

Sanders, J. Wofford, et al. (See Theriot, Charles, assignor.)

Sanford, Crocker H., assignor to The Old Dominion Specialty Co., Inc., Baltimore, Md. Mixing device. No. 1,328,204 ; Jan. 13 ; v. 270 ; p. 309.

Santoro, Harry, New York, N. Y. Chenille scarf. No. 1,328,903 ; Jan. 27 ; v. 270 ; p. 507.

Sapper, Charles H. (See Wilson and Sapper.)

Sargent, Fitz William, Mahwah. N. J., assignor to The American Brake Shoe and Foundry Company, Wilmington, Del. Brake-shoe. No. 1,328,594 ; Jan. 20 ; v. 270 ; p. 420.

Sargent, Fitz William, Mahwah, N. J., assignor to The American Brake Shoe and Foundry Company, Wilmington, Del. Brake-shoe. No. 1,328,595 ; Jan. 20 ; v. 270 ; p. 420.

Sargent, Fitz William, Mahwah, N. J., assignor to The American Brake Shoe and Foundry Company, Wilmington, Del. Brake-shoe. No. 1,328,596 ; Jan. 20 ; v. 270 ; p. 420.

Sartain, Isaac M., Tracy City, Tenn. Spring-tire. No. 1,329,145 ; Jan. 27 ; v. 270 ; p. 529.

Satterstein, Jesse, New York, N. Y. Book-cover-making machine. No. 1,328,767 ; Jan. 20 ; v. 270 ; p. 452.

Saunders, Lawrence D., Wilkinsburg, assignor to The Westinghouse Air Brake Company, Wilmerding, Pa. Motor-driven compressor. No. 1,328,340 ; Jan. 20 ; v. 270 ; p 372

Saunders, William M., Waterbury, Conn., assignor to The Hoge Manufacturing Company, New York, N. Y. Pencil. No. 1,328,800 ; Jan. 20 ; v. 270 ; p. 364.

Saurer, Hippolyt, Arbon, Switzerland. Embroidering-machine. No. 1,328,969 ; Jan. 27 ; v. 270 ; p. 520.

Savage, Stanley W. (See Dabbs, Savage, and Hinde.)

Savidge, William G., Northumberland, Pa. Nut-lock. No. 1,328,401 ; Jan. 20 ; v. 270 ; p. 383.

Sawyer, Green B. (See Blakemore, James R., assignor.)

Scanes, Arthur E. L., Ashton-on-Mersey, England, assignor to The British Westinghouse Electric and Manufacturing Company Limited. Pump or compressor. No. 1,327,294 ; Jan. 6 ; v. 270 ; p. 77.

Scanlan, Thomas J., Montreal, Quebec, Canada. Crossover. No. 1,327,882 ; Jan. 13 ; v. 270 ; p. 248.

Schaefer, George A., Chicago, Ill. Connector-clip. No. 1,327,844 ; Jan. 13 ; v. 270 ; p. 241.

Schaefer, William J., Ontario, Calif. Cooker. No. 1,328,239 ; Jan. 13 ; v. 270 ; p. 316.

Scharffenberg, Jean H., assignor to J. H. Stewart, Lynn, Mass. Counter-flanging machine. No. 1,327,780 ; Jan. 13 ; v. 270 ; p. 230

Schechter, Jacob. (See Rosenfeld, Maurice S., assignor.)

Schein, Charles T. (See Nickol and Schein.)

Scheminger, John, Jr., Providence, R. I. Atomizing device for rotary oil-burners. No. 1,327,256 ; Jan. 6 ; v. 270 ; p. 70.

Schenck, John F. Jr., Shelby, N. C. Attachment for cotton-pickers. No. 1,328,904 ; Jan. 27 ; v. 270 ; p. 507.

Schenkel, Moritz, Charlottenburg, near Berlin, Germany, assignor to Siemens-Schuckert-Werke G. m. b. H., Berlin, Germany. Anode for electric vacuum apparatus. No. 1,326,972 ; Jan. 6 ; v. 270 ; p. 18.

Schenkel, Moritz, Charlottenburg, near Berlin, Germany, assignor to Siemens-Schuckert-Werke, G. m. b. H., Berlin, Germany. Electrical vacuum apparatus. No. 1,328,597; Jan. 20; v. 270; p. 421.

Schiek, Louis and W., Chicago, Ill. Bucket. No. 1,328,458; Jan. 20; v. 270; p. 304.

Schiek, William. (See Schiek, Louis and W., assignors.)

Schleman, Paul W., Rockville Center, N. Y., assignor to The A. Dewes Company, New York, N. Y. Jack. No. 1,329,098; Jan. 27; v. 270; p. 543.

Schiffi, Charles, Montclair, N. J. Spring-motor. No. 1,328,402; Jan. 20; v. 270; p. 384.

Schilling, Frederick W., Louisville, Ohio. Bottle-closure. No. 1,328,205; Jan. 13; v. 270; p. 310.

Schilling, Frederick W., Louisville, Ohio. Surgical splint. No. 1,328,598; Jan. 20; v. 270; p. 421.

Schindler, Conrad. (See Lehmann and Schindler.)

Schleicher, William A., Cleveland, Ohio. Blanket-fastener. No. 1,328,206; Jan. 13; v. 270; p. 310.

Schloss, Meyer W., New York, N. Y., assignor to Treo Company, Inc. Brassière. No. 1,327,408; Jan. 6; v. 270; p. 98.

Schluter, William M., Orange, N. J. Interchangeable vehicle. No. 1,327,883; Jan. 13; v. 270; p. 249.

Schmidt, Christ, Everett, Wash. Trough. No. 1,328,207; Jan. 13; v. 270; p. 310.

Schmidt, Ludwig, Munich, Germany. Preparation of pyrocatechin aldehyde. No. 1,326,973; Jan. 6; v. 270; p. 18.

Schmidt, William C., Richmond, Va. Indicating-bottle. No. 1,326,974; Jan. 6; v. 270; p. 18.

Schneider, August H., assignor to Crouse-Hinds Company, Syracuse, N. Y. Conduit outlet-box. No. 1,327,409; Jan. 6; v. 270; p. 98.

Schneider & Cie. (See Schneider, Eugene, assignor.)

Schneider, Eberhard, deceased, New York, N. Y.; S. Schneider, administratrix. Chain. No. 1,327,925; Jan. 13; v. 270; p. 257.

Schneider, Eugene, assignor to Schneider & Cie., Paris, France. Apparatus for shifting trail gun-carriages for the purpose of training the guns. No. 1,326,975; Jan. 6; v. 270; p. 18.

Schneider, Eugene, assignor to Schneider & Cie., Paris, France. Mechanism for disengaging and engaging the main governors in steam hoisting-engines. No. 1,327,633; Jan. 13; v. 270; p. 202.

Schneider, Eugene, assignor to Schneider & Cie., Paris, France. Gun - carriage with endless tracks. No. 1,328,849; Jan. 27; v. 270; p. 496.

Schneider, Michael J. N., Black River Falls, Wis. Railway-gate. No. 1,329,022; Jan. 27; v. 270; p. 529.

Schneider, Stanislawa, administratrix. (See Schneider, Eberhard.)

Schnurr, Charles A. B., Brooklyn, N. Y. Captive ball for golf-practice. No. 1,326,976; Jan. 6; v. 270; p. 18.

Scholes, Samuel R., Beaver, and R. F. Brenner, assignors to J. Howard Fry, Rochester, Pa. Extracting potassium from potash bearing silicate minerals. No. 1,327,781; Jan. 13; v. 270; p. 230.

Scholes, Samuel R., Beaver, assignor to H. C. Fry Glass Company, Rochester, Pa. Obtaining combined potassium from minerals. No. 1,327,782; Jan. 13; v. 270; p. 230.

Schonk, Edward P., Wilkes-Barre, Pa. Reamer. No. 1,328,208; Jan. 13; v. 270; p. 310.

Schott, John H., assignor of one-fifth to J. G. Archibald, one-fifth to J. E. De Kalb, and one-fifth to M. M. Rinn, Boulder, Colo. Pulling-machine. No. 1,327,492; Jan. 6; v. 270; p. 114.

Schreiner, Arthur W., Brooklyn, assignor to Standard Scientific Company, New York, N. Y. Resonator. No. 1,328,059; Jan. 13; v. 270; p. 282.

Schumacher, John, and J. E., Los Angeles, Calif. Plasterboard or the like. No. 1,327,446; Jan. 6; v. 270; p. 105.

Schumacher, Joseph E. (See Schumacher, John and J. E.)

Schuster, Lionel. (See Dings and Schuster.)

Schwartzman, Abraham, St. Louis, Mo. Finger-ring. No. 1,326,977; Jan. 6; v. 270; p. 19.

Schweiger, William F., and W. J. Balkwill, assignors to Multipost Company, Rochester, N. Y. Stamp or label affixer. No. 1,326,978; Jan. 6; v. 270; p. 19.

Schwentler, Francis E., assignor to The American Brake Company, St. Louis, Mo. Manually-operated slack-adjuster. No. 1,328,341; Jan. 20; v. 270; p. 372.

Schwerdtle Machine Company. (See Rider, Ernest G., assignor.)

Schwoyer, Levi, Pottstown, Pa. Antislipping attachment for horseshoes. No. 1,327,493; Jan. 6; v. 270; p. 114.

Scott, Barton W., San Jose, Calif. Prune-pitting machine. No. 1,329,023; Jan. 27; v. 270; p. 529.

Scott, Oliver L., San Francisco, Calif. Theft-alarm for automobiles. No. 1,327,573; Jan. 6; v. 270; p. 129.

Scott, Robert W., Boston, Mass., assignor, by mesne assignments, to Scott & Williams, Incorporated. Stocking and making same. No. 1,327,217; Jan. 6; v. 270; p. 64.

Scott, Thomas W., assignor to The American Train Control Co., Baltimore, Md. Air-brake-controlling mechanism. No. 1,327,968; Jan. 13; v. 270; p. 264.

Scott, William D., Martins Ferry, Ohio. Air collecting and delivering apparatus. No. 1,327,926; Jan. 13; v. 270; p. 257.

Scott, William M., Sullivan, Ill. Hen's nest. No. 1,329,024; Jan. 27; v. 270; p. 530.

Scott & Williams. (See Scott, Robert W., assignor.)

Seabury, Benjamin H., and J. C. Ollard, Tacoma, Wash. Buffer for doors. No. 1,329,313; Jan. 27; v. 270; p. 583.

Seaman, Duncan R. (See Ryan, John H., assignor.)

Searle, Harry A., Council Bluffs, Iowa. Grease-drum. No. 1,328,768; Jan. 20; v. 270; p. 452.

Sears, Roebuck and Company. (See Dun Lany, William P., assignor.)

Sebring, Cecil F., Laurel, Nebr. Self-opening gate. No. 1,327,257; Jan. 6; v. 270; p. 71.

Sebring, Frank H., Jr., Salem, Ohio. Coating device. No. 1,326,979; Jan. 6; v. 270; p. 19.

Sechler & Company, The. (See Baldwin, Frank G., assignor.)

Sechler & Company, The. (See Knapp, Jacob, assignor.)

Seelig, Joseph, Lead, S. D. Metallic bed - bottom. No. 1,329,145; Jan. 27; v. 270; p. 553.

Seemuller, Otto, Detroit, Mich. Air-gun. No. 1,327,064; Jan. 6; v. 270; p. 35.

Séguier, Jean J., Castres, France. Gridiron. No. 1,327,258; Jan. 6; v. 270; p. 71.

Segura, Julian, New York, N. Y. Solder for aluminum. No. 1,328,694; Jan. 20; v. 270; p. 438.

Seiss, George J., Toledo, Ohio. Mechanically - operated horn. No. 1,329,275; Jan. 27; v. 270; p. 576.

Sellers, J. E., et al. (See Ehrcibman, Abram, assignor.)

Senna, Samuel N., assignor to B. F. Perkins & Son, Inc., Holyoke, Mass. Lubricated fan-mounting. No. 1,328,017; Jan. 13; v. 270; p. 274.

Serrell, Lemuel W., New York, N. Y. Bread-board. No. 1,328,301; Jan. 13; v. 270; p. 364.

Servis, Fred T., Ontario, N. Y. Pouring-spout for cans. No. 1,328,104; Jan. 13; v. 270; p. 290.

Settiage, August C., New Bremen, Ohio. Dumping mechanism for trucks and the like. No. 1,328,240; Jan. 13; v. 270; p. 317.

Severson, Melvin, Galesville, Wis. Wire-stretcher. No. 1,328,599; Jan. 20; v. 270; p. 421.

Sexton, Isaac E., Boston, Mass. Riveting-machine. No. 1,328,905; Jan. 27; v. 270; p. 508.

Sexton Manufacturing Corporation. (See Knapp, Clyde S., assignor.)

Sharp, L. C. (See Kratz, Roy G., assignor.)

Sharp, Samuel J., assignor to J. L. Stifel & Sons, Wheeling, W. va. Lubricator. No. 1,328,209; Jan. 13; v. 270; p. 310.

Sharpless Specialty Company, The. (See Jones, Leo D., assignor.)

Shaw, James E., Trinidad, Colo. Tool for cutting tire-treads. No. 1,328,547; Jan. 20; v. 270; p. 411.

Shaw, Lloyd D., Higgins, Tex. Electricity-dispelling device for paper-printing apparatus. No. 1,328,403; Jan. 20; v. 270; p. 384.

Shay, James M., et al. (See Brooks, Samuel A., assignor.)

Sheasley, Charles H., Franklin, Pa. Variable gas-port for gas-engines. No. 1,327,927; Jan. 13; v. 270; p. 257.

Sheffier, Ira L, Detroit, Mich., assignor to Ira Lee Suction Cleaner Corporation. Vacuum-cleaner. (Reissue. No. 14,786; Jan. 6; v. 270; p. 136.

Shell Company of California. (See Melschke-Smith, William, assignor.)

Shelton, Carl L., Greenfield, Tenn., assignor of one-half to Vermont Box Company, Bristol, Vt. Cover-fastener for boxes. No. 1,328,302; Jan. 20; v. 270; p. 364.

Sherrod, William H., Seattle, Wash. Soil-pulverizer. No. 1,328,800; Jan. 20; v. 270; p. 458.

Shields, John M., assignor to F. H. Noble & Company, Chicago, Ill. Spring-hinge. No. 1,327,065; Jan. 6; v. 270; p. 35.

Shinn, Bessie. (See Shinn, Lita and B.)

Shinn, Charles. (See Shinn, William, assignor.)

Shinn, Lita and B., Muskogee, Okla. Hand-painted rag doll. No. 1,327,884; Jan. 13; v. 270; p. 249.

Shinn, William, assignor of one-half to C. Shinn, Grandin, Mo. Locomotive-boiler. No. 1,328,303; Jan. 20; v. 270; p. 364.

Shires, George M., Houston, Tex. Apparatus for extracting minerals from ores. No. 1,328,210; Jan. 13; v. 270; p. 311.

Shodron, John G., assignor to James Manufacturing Company, Fort Atkinson, Wis. Feed-trough for pigs and other animals. No. 1,328,970; Jan. 27; v. 270; p. 520.

Short, Samuel B., Humboldt, Tenn. Adjustable bulkhead for freight-cars. No. 1,327,634; Jan. 13; v. 270; p. 202.

Showers, Ernest S., Calumet, Mich. Propeller. No. 1,327,066; Jan. 6; v. 270; p. 35.

Shreibman, Abram, Keokuk, Iowa, assignor of one-third to J. L. Baldon and one-third to J. E. Sellers, Elvaston, Ill. Radiator. No. 1,329,256; Jan. 27; v. 270; p. 573.

Shuman, Cleo G., assignor to Gyp Steel Products Company, Chicago, Ill. Means for fastening plaster-boards and the like. No. 1,327,741; Jan. 13; v. 270; p. 222.

Siemens, Schuckert Werke, G. m. b. H. (See Fischer, Kuno, assignor.)

Siemens - Schuckert - Werke G. m. b. H. (See Schenkel, Moritz, assignor.)

Silver Manufacturing Company, The. (See Haldeman, James C., assignor.)

Silverman, Wulf, New York, N. Y. Bottle-closure. No. 1,328,240; Jan. 13; v. 270; p. 282.

Simeone, Eugene, Webster, Mass. Turning-tool. No. 1,327,410; Jan. 6; v. 270; p. 98.

Simplex Electric Heating Company. (See Hewitt, Frank W., assignor.)
Sims, Wilson E., Greeneville, Tenn. Auxiliary air-valve. No. 1,327,494; Jan. 6; v. 270; p. 114.
Sines, Harold S. (See Ferguson, Louis A., assignor.)
Singer Manufacturing Company, The. (See Blasi, Joseph, assignor.)
Singer Manufacturing Company, The. (See Corrall, Herbert, assignor.)
Singer Manufacturing Company, The. (See Gatchell, George S., assignor.)
Singer Manufacturing Company, The. (See Horton, Charles M., assignor.)
Sinkovich, John, Youngstown, Ohio. Rail joint and fastener. No. 1,328,695; Jan. 20; v. 270; p. 438.
Siqueira, Edward C., Oakland, Calif. Change-making machine. No. 1,327,969; Jan. 13; v. 270; p. 264.
Skarnulis, William, New Britain, Conn. Automobile-signal. No. 1,328,404; Jan. 20; v. 270; p. 384.
Skelton, John W., Douglas, Ariz. Flytrap. No. 1,328,850; Jan. 27; v. 270; p. 497.
Skibinsky, Alexander M. (See Forester, Herbert, assignor.)
Skinner, James M. (See Holland and Skinner.)
Skinner Machinery Company. (See McIntyre, Allen H., assignor.)
Skinner, Perry R., Amsterdam, N. Y. Dental tool. No. 1,329,274; Jan. 27; v. 270; p. 576.
Skinner, Stephen G., Chicago, Ill. Air-pump. No. 1,327,788; Jan. 13; v. 270; p. 230.
Slagenhauf, August. (See Drake and Slagenhauf.)
Slaght, Arthur G., et al. (See Ormiston, John A., assignor.)
Slater, Horace G., Los Angeles, Calif. Dust-cap valve. No. 1,329,146; Jan. 27; v. 270; p. 553.
Slick, Edwin E., Westmont borough, Pa. Wheel-mill. No. 1,327,635; Jan. 13; v. 270; p. 202.
Sloan, Ira L., North Yakima, Wash. Flying-machine. No. 1,328,211; Jan. 13; v. 270; p. 311.
Slocomb, F. F., & Co. (See Flanagan, James U., assignor.)
Sloss, William A., Toledo, Ohio. Production of ammonium sulfate. No. 1,328,342; Jan. 20; v. 270; p. 372.
Smigielski, Stanley, Detroit, Mich. Figure toy. No. 1,327,359; Jan. 6; v. 270; p. 89.
Smigielski, Stanley, Detroit, Mich. Whirligig. No. 1,327,360; Jan. 6; v. 270; p. 89.
Smith, Arthur E., Chicago, Ill. Instrument for producing intra-osseous anesthesia. No. 1,328,459; Jan. 20; v. 270; p. 304.
Smith, Burns L., Syracuse, N. Y. Heat treatment for castings. No. 1,328,851; Jan. 27; v. 270; p. 497.
Smith, Burns L., Syracuse, N. Y. Apparatus for casting hollow one-piece spoke-wheels. No. 1,328,852; Jan. 27; v. 270; p. 497.
Smith, Charles M., Bellingham, Wash. Auxiliary automobile-seat. No. 1,328,105; Jan. 13; v. 270; p. 291.
Smith, Clarence E. (See Mesker and Smith.)
Smith and Coventry. (See Walker, Malcolm, assignor.)
Smith, David J., London, England. Gas-producer for propelling vehicles. No. 1,327,495; Jan. 6; v. 270; p. 115.
Smith, Earl R., Pittsburgh, Pa. Bathing-platform for infants. No. 1,327,295; Jan. 6; v. 270; p. 77.
Smith, Gerald F., Braddock township, Allegheny county, Pa., assignor to Westinghouse Electric & Manufacturing Company. System of control. No. 1,327,784; Jan. 13; v. 270; p. 230.
Smith, Gilbert A., Des Moines, Iowa. Grease-detaining device. No. 1,327,173; Jan. 6; v. 270; p. 55.
Smith, Henry A., assignor of one-fourth to W. D. Sabey, West Albany, N. Y. Station-indicator. No. 1,326,980; Jan. 6; v. 270; p. 19.
Smith, Irwin J., Menands, N. Y. Garment. No. 1,329,025; Jan. 27; v. 270; p. 530.
Smith, John F., assessor to A. J. Boyd, Seattle, Wash. Gas-generator. No. 1,327,117; Jan. 6; v. 270; p. 45.
Smith, Joseph I., The Dalles, Oreg. Fishing-reel. No 1,328,696; Jan. 20; v. 270; p. 438.
Smith, Karl D., Battle Creek, Mich., and B. Samelson, New York, N. Y., assignors to Union Steam Pump Company, Battle Creek, Mich. Rotary pump. No. 1,328,061; Jan. 13; v. 270; p. 282.
Smith, Oscar A., Cleveland, Ohio. Priming and testing cup. No. 1,327,687; Jan. 13; v. 270; p. 212.
Smith, Philocter, Rochester, N. Y. Vehicle. No. 1,328,843; Jan. 20; v. 270; p. 372.
Smith, Raymond D., Arlington, Mass. Automatic circuit-breaker. No. 1,328,460; Jan. 20; v. 270; p. 394.
Smith, Walter S., Brooklyn, N. Y. Ball-crank connection. No. 1,328,600; Jan. 20; v. 270; p. 421.
Smolens, Abraham M., New York, N. Y. Toy. No. 1,328,344; Jan. 20; v. 270; p. 372.
Snead & Co. Iron Works, The. (See Macdonald, Angus S. and H. P., assignors.)
Snelling, Walter O., and W. R. Lams, Allentown, Pa., assignors, by mesne assignments, to Trojan Powder Company, New York, N. Y. Nitrostarch explosive and manufacturing same. No. 1,329,211; Jan. 27; v. 270; p. 565.
Snelling, Walter O., and W. R. Lams, assignors to Trojan Powder Company, Allentown, Pa. Manufacturing nitro-starch explosives. No. 1,329,212; Jan. 27; v. 270; p. 565.

270 O. G.—iii

Snider, Garnett, Bruces Mines, Ontario, Canada. Electric-lamp socket. No. 1,327,496; Jan. 6; v. 270; p. 115.
Snider, John L., assignor to Royal Metalware Manufacturing Co., Denton, N. C. Fireless cooker. No. 1,328,304; Jan. 20; v. 270; p. 365.
Snider, R. E. (See Frey, George E., assignor.)
Snow, Isaac., Lawrence, Mass. Picker-check. No. 1,328,018; Jan. 13; v. 270; p. 274.
Snyder, Daniel H., Snyderville, Ohio. Post. No. 1,329,026; Jan. 27; v. 270; p. 530.
Snyder, Edith L., Johnstown, Pa. Oil water-color paint. No. 1,327,928; Jan. 13; v. 270; p. 257.
Snyder, Frederick T., Oak Park, assignor to Industrial Electric Furnace Company, Chicago, Ill. Three-phase electric furnace. No. 1,327,174; Jan. 6; v. 270; p. 55.
Snyder, Simon, and L. C. Winegardner, Muncy, Pa. Bolting-machine. No. 1,327,636; Jan. 13; v. 270; p. 202.
Söderlund, Carl G., Gottenborg, assignor to Aktiebolaget Lidköpings Mekaniska Verkstad, Lidköping, Sweden. Method and machine for straightening of metal wire. No. 1,326,981; Jan. 6; v. 270; p. 20.
Soemer, Joseph C., Newark, N. J. Desk-basket paper holder and clip. No. 1,328,971; Jan. 27; v. 270; p. 520.
Soisalon-Soininen, Juhani L., Boxbacka, Finland. Paper-knife. No. 1,328,548; Jan. 20; v. 270; p. 411.
Solem, Peter A., Cincinnati, Ohio. Traction-block. No. 1,327,296; Jan. 6; v. 270; p. 78.
Solimeo, Joseph. (See Morelli and Solimeo.)
Sommerhof, William A., Erie, Pa. Sound-controller. No. 1,327,118; Jan. 6; v. 270; p. 45.
Sonner, William I., Blaine, Idaho. Hay gatherer and stacker. No. 1,327,637; Jan. 13; v. 270; p. 202.
Sordillo, Fortunato, Boston, Mass. Mouthpiece for musical instruments. No. 1,327,970; Jan. 13; v. 270; p. 265.
Soule, Charles E., Somerville, assigner of one-third to F. P. Bearse and one-third to W. T. Abbott, Winchester, Mass. Antirattling device. No. 1,327,291; Jan. 6; v. 270; p. 77.
Sourbier, Edward V., and M Madden, Harrisburg, Pa. Railway-rail. No. 1,328,405; Jan. 20; v. 270; p. 384.
Spangenberg, Arthur R (See Reichman and Spangenberg.)
Spangler, William A. (See Burrows and Spangler.)
Sparmaker, Frank P. J., Audubon, N. J. Burial-casket attachment. No. 1,328,345; Jan. 20; v. 270; p. 373.
Sparrow, Simon, assignor to Wagner Electric Manufacturing Company, St. Louis, Mo. Coil for dynamo-electric machines. No. 1,329,027; Jan. 27; v. 270; p. 530.
Spear, Herbert G. (See Fagan, Spear and Wolf.)
Spence, Henry, Kearney, N. J. Automatic tapping-head. No. 1,327,497; Jan. 6; v. 270; p. 115.
Spencer, Carroll K., River Forest, Ill. Sealing-wax applier. No. 1,328,769; Jan. 20; v. 270; p. 452.
Spencer, Ira H., West Hartford, assignor to The Spencer Turbine Company, Hartford, Conn. Valve. No. 1,329,099; Jan. 27; v. 270; p. 544.
Spencer, James B., assignor to United States Hoff-man Machinery Company, Inc., Syracuse, N. J. Machine for pressing garments. No. 1,326,982; Jan. 6; v. 270; p. 20.
Spencer Turbine Company, The. (See Spencer, Ira H., assignor.)
Sperry, Elmer A. (See Bassett, Preston R., assignor.)
Spethmann, Peter H., New Effington, S. D. Burglar-alarm. No. 1,327,785; Jan. 13; v. 270; p. 230.
Spiers, Frederick G. Jamaica, assignor to National Carbon Company, Inc., New York, N. Y. Portable electric light. No. 1,326,983; Jan. 6; v. 270; p. 20.
Splitdorf Electrical Company. (See Dean, William W., assignor.)
Splitdorf Electrical Company. (See Mason, Charles T., assignor.)
Splitdorf Electric Company. (See Van Deventer, Harry R., assignor.)
Spong, Frank, Glendale, Calif. Dirigible headlight. No. 1,327,574; Jan. 6; v. 270; p. 130.
Spreckels, Diedrich H., Dexter, Minn. Poultry-crate. No. 1,329,344; Jan. 27; v. 270; p. 588.
Sprenkel, Ward F., et al. (See Matthiessen, Conrad S., assignor.)
Spring. Frederick L., Indianapolis, Ind. Spring shock-absorber. No. 1,328,601; Jan. 20; v. 270; p. 421.
Sprong, Severn D., Brooklyn, N. Y. Apparatus for adding to the output of a main power station, the output of one or more distant sources. No. 1,329,276; Jan. 27; v. 270; p. 577.
Sproul, John J., New Haven, Conn. Elevator. No. 1,326,984; Jan 6; v. 270; p. 20.
Spurr, Charles S., Los Angeles, and H. P. Randall, Pasadena, assignors of one-half to F. W. Frame, Los Angeles, Calif. Fuel-package. No. 1,327,175; Jan. 6; v. 270; p. 55.
St. Charles, William P., et al. (See Ormiston, John A., assignor.)
St. John, Justin M., Cedar Rapids, Iowa. Weeder. No. 1,328,063; Jan. 13; v. 270; p. 283.
Stach, Carl T. (See Connell and Stach.)
Stafford, Earl C., assignor to The Railway Automatic Safety Appliance Company, Philadelphia, Pa. Train-stop system. No. 1,327,176; Jan. 6; v. 270; p. 55.
Stake, Herman. (See Ekvall and Stake.)
Stalker, James W. (See Comber and Stalker.)

Stalter, Andrew C., Flanagan, Ill. Ridge-plowing attachment for harrows. No. 1,327,119; Jan. 6; v. 270; p. 45.

Standard Oil Company. (See Burns and Winger, assignors.)

Standard Oilcloth Co. (See Frohner, Edward H., assignor.)

Standard Paint Company, The. (See Abraham, Herbert, assignor.)

Standard Parts Company, The. (See McIntyre, Michael M., assignor.)

Standard Scientific Company. (See Schreiner, Arthur W., assignor.)

Stanifer, William D., Chickasha, Okla. Gin-saw cleaner, tooth straightener and sharpener. No. 1,328,212; Jan. 13; v. 270; p. 311.

Starcke, Eugene P., Port Arthur, Tex. Can-closure. No. 1,327,067; Jan. 6; v. 270; p. 35.

Starkenberg, Karl R., Andover, assignor to J. J. Petroske, Methuen, Mass. Centering device. No. 1,328,213; Jan. 13; v. 270; p. 311.

Starr Piano Company, The. (See Mayer, Fred G., assignor.)

Steel, Charles C., and T. H. Lynn, Williamsport, Pa. Tire-carrier for automobiles. No. 1,327,742; Jan. 13; v. 270; p. 223.

Steen, Buford J., Goose Creek, Tex. Elevator. No. 1,328,602; Jan. 20; v. 270; p. 421.

Steere, William J., Rockwood, Tenn. Looping-machine. No. 1,327,638; Jan. 13; v. 270; p. 203.

Stefferud, Leonard C., Brandt, S. D. Steam-jacket for oil-pumps. No. 1,328,906; Jan. 27; v. 270; p. 508.

Steigerwald, Edward, and F. L. H. Pfeil, Philadelphia, Pa. Score-keeping apparatus. No. 1,327,177; Jan. 6; v. 270; p. 56.

Stein, Noah S., Bristol, Ind. Engine. No. 1,328,972; Jan. 27; v. 270; p. 520.

Stephan, Charles H., Springfield, Ohio. Medical appliance. No. 1,327,786; Jan. 13; v. 270; p. 231.

Stephan, Jacob, Cleveland, Ohio. Furniture. No. 1,327,178; Jan. 6; v. 270; p. 56.

Stephens, Richard, Clevedon, England. Drum-brake with internal shoes. No. 1,327,068; Jan. 6; v. 270; p. 36.

Stephenson, Leigh J., assignor of one-half to G. H. Burrage, Chicago, Ill. Dynamo-electric machinery. (Reissue.) No. 14,787; Jan. 6; v. 270; p. 136.

Stepisleh, Dominick W. (See Johnson, Joseph F., assignor.)

Stern, Louis J., Boston, Mass. Mirror-mounting. No. 1,328,930; Jan. 27; v. 270; p. 512.

Sterner, Frank F., Harnedsville, Pa. Car - mover. No. 1,328,770; Jan. 20; v. 270; p. 452.

Sterns, Edward O., assignor to Rotary Tire and Rubber Company, Columbus, Ohio. Sign. No. 1,326,985; Jan. 6; v. 270; p. 20.

Stevens, George B., Granite City, Ill. Roll-polisher. No. 1,327,639; Jan. 13; v. 270; p. 203.

Stevens, Herbert C. M. (See Coatalen and Stevens, assignors.)

Stevens, William C., assignor to The Cutler-Hammer Mfg. Co., Milwaukee, Wis. Motor-controller. No. 1,327,787; Jan. 13; v. 270; p. 231.

Stevens, William H., New York, N. Y. Garter. No. 1,328,931; Jan. 27; v. 270; p. 513.

Steward, Archie L., Chicago, Ill. Strainer for vacuum gasolene systems. No. 1,328,853; Jan. 27; v. 270; p. 497.

Stewart, Alexander, Clintonville, Wis. Selective speed-transmission mechanism. No. 1,328,062; Jan. 13; v. 270; p. 282.

Stewart, Alexander W., Glasgow, Scotland. System of ventilation. No. 1,327,120; Jan. 6; v. 270; p. 45.

Stewart, John H. (See Scharffenberg, Jean H., assignor.)

Stewart, Thomas H., Atlanta, Ga., assignor to American Can Company, New York, N. Y. Label for bale-ties. No. 1,328,019; Jan. 13; v. 270; p. 274.

Stewart-Warner Speedometer Corporation. (See Genn, John E., assignor.)

Stewart, William C., Swampscott, Mass., assignor to United Shoe Machinery Corporation, Paterson, N. J. Sole-pressing machine. No. 1,327,179; Jan. 6; v. 270; p. 56.

Stifel, J. L., & Sons. (See Sharp, Samuel J., assignor.)

Stimpson, Edward S., assignor to Draper Corporation, Hopedale, Mass. Feeler-motion for looms. No. 1,327,069; Jan. 6; v. 270; p. 36.

Stimpson, Edward S., assignor to Draper Corporation, Hopedale, Mass. Feeler-motion for looms. No. 1,327,070; Jan. 6; v. 270; p. 36.

Stimpson, Edward S., assignor to Draper Corporation, Hopedale, Mass. Feeler mechanism for looms. No. 1,327,788; Jan. 13; v. 270; p. 231.

Stimpson, Edward S., assignor to Draper Corporation, Hopedale, Mass. Feeler-motion for looms. No. 1,328,907; Jan. 27; v. 270; p. 508.

Stimpson, Edward S., assignor to Draper Corporation, Hopedale, Mass. Feeler-motion for looms. No. 1,328,908; Jan. 27; v. 270; p. 508.

Stimpson, Edward S., assignor to Draper Corporation, Hopedale, Mass. Feeler with concave teeth. No. 1,329,328; Jan. 27; v. 270; p. 585.

Stimpson, Edwin B., Brooklyn, N. Y. Cartridge-belt. No. 1,329,346; Jan. 27; v. 270; p. 589.

Stinemetts, Henry, Calgary, Alberta, Canada. Tire-rim. No. 1,327,180; Jan. 6; v. 270; p. 56.

Stirling, Charles P., assignor to Cott-a-lap Co., Somerville, N. J. Machine for graining lithographic cylinders. No. 1,328,603; Jan. 20; v. 270; p. 422.

Stirling, Clarence C., assignor to The Hart & Hegeman Manufacturing Company, Hartford, Conn. Electric switch. No. 1,327,640; Jan. 13; v. 270; p. 203.

Stites, Townsend, and E. L. Knoedler, assignors to Weisbach Company, Gloucester City, N. J. Gas-lighting device. No. 1,327,447; Jan. 6; v. 270; p. 105.

Stockton, Lincoln C., and C. F. Goddard, assignors to The Metal Separation Company, Denver, Colo. Apparatus for saving metallic values. No. 1,327,885; Jan. 13; v. 270; p. 249.

Stoll, Frank M., Denver, Colo. Collapsible bed. No. 1,327,886; Jan. 13; v. 270; p. 249.

Stoll, Frank M., Denver, Colo. Tent-bed. No. 1,327,887; Jan. 13; v. 270; p. 249.

Stolp, Frank H., Geneva, N. Y. Machine for forming metal tubes. No. 1,327,461; Jan. 13; v. 270; p. 203.

Stone, Ben M., Chicago, Ill. Lock. No. 1,328,106; Jan. 13; v. 270; p. 291.

Stone, Frank N. (See Newton, Charles, assignor.)

Stonebraker, Harold E., Brooklyn, N. Y. Friction-gearing for motor-vehicles. No. 1,328,846; Jan. 20; v. 270; p. 373.

Storer, Norman W., Pittsburgh, Pa., assignor to Westinghouse Electric & Manufacturing Company. System of control. No. 1,327,789; Jan. 13; v. 270; p. 231.

Stowell, Edward R., Oden, Mich. Making a refractory plastic. No. 1,327,448; Jan. 6; v. 270; p. 105.

Stowell, Lawrence H., Litchville, N. D. Snowplow. No. 1,328,973; Jan. 27; v. 270; p. 521.

Strahan, Ida W., Montclair, N. J. Hair - curler. No. 1,328,771; Jan. 20; v. 270; p. 452.

Strathmann, Edward C. (See Branson and Strathmann.)

Straub, Anselm, Jr., Magnolia, N. J., assignor of one-half to W. F. Tosney, Philadelphia, Pa. Union-suit. No. 1,329,329; Jan. 27; v. 270; p. 585.

Straubel, Louis A., Green Bay, Wis. Machine for cutting and interfolding sheets of paper. No. 1,326,986; Jan. 6; v. 270; p. 21.

Straubel, Louis A., Green Bay, Wis. Machine for interfolding sheets of paper. No. 1,326,987; Jan. 6; v. 270; p. 21.

Strauss, Ernest H., Chicago, Ill. Lamp-shade and light-diffuser. No. 1,329,147; Jan. 27; v. 270; p. 553.

Strauss, Joseph B., Chicago, Ill. Observation-tower. No. 1,328,461; Jan. 20; v. 270; p. 394.

Street, Norman A., et al. (See Blood, Burr B., assignor.)

Strey, Walter F. A., Neenah, Wis. Quack-grass destroyer. No. 1,328,697; Jan. 20; v. 270; p. 439.

Strobel, Carl W. F., Lima, Ohio. Railway-crossing signal. No. 1,328,854; Jan. 27; v. 270; p. 497.

Sturges, Norman D., Bellerose Queens, N. Y. Self-filling storage battery. No. 1,327,121; Jan. 6; v. 270; p. 45.

Sturtevant, B. F., Company. (See Allen, George W., assignor.)

Stynkowic, Ignacy, East Hammond, Ind. Combined folding chair and table. No. 1,328,462; Jan. 20; v. 270; p. 395.

Sullivan, Martin, Kimberly, Idaho. Multiple-cylinder-pump attachment. No. 1,327,449; Jan. 6; v. 270; p. 105.

Sulzberger, Nathan, New York, N. Y. Iodin dusting-powder and making same. No. 1,329,148; Jan. 27; v. 270; p. 553.

Summerbell, William, Washington, D. C., assignor of one-half to F. A. Sutton, Oakhurst, Ashford, England. Honing device or holder for safety-razors. No. 1,327,498; Jan. 6; v. 270; p. 115.

Summers, Bertrand S., Port Huron, Mich. Flax-threshing machine. No. 1,327,297; Jan. 6; v. 270; p. 78.

Sun Company. (See Ballard, Albert M., assignor.)

Sunderland, Paul U. (See Rogers, James E., assignor.)

Sunderman, Frederick R., et al. (See Guy, Frederick M., assignor.)

Sundh, August, Hastings-upon-Hudson, N. Y. Flexible tubing. No. 1,326,988; Jan. 6; v. 270; p. 21.

Sundh, August, Hastings-upon-Hudson, N. Y. Automatic blocking mechanism for strip-mills. No. 1,326,989; Jan. 6; v. 270; p. 21.

Sundh, August, Hastings-upon-Hudson, N. Y. Strip-blocking mechanism. No. 1,326,990; Jan. 6; v. 270; p. 21.

Sundstrand, Gustaf D., assignor to Rockford Milling Machine Company, Rockford, Ill. Listing and adding machine. No. 1,329,028; Jan. 27; v. 270; p. 530.

Sundstrom, G. E. (See Anderson, Charles A., assignor.) (Reissue.)

Sussman, Samuel J., Brooklyn, N. Y. Photographic developing-machine. No. 1,328,805; Jan. 20; v. 270; p. 365.

Sutton, Francis A. (See Summerbell, William, assignor.)

Suursalmi, Onni, assignor to Kangas Pappersbruks Aktiebolag, Jyväskylä, Finland. Making lines and watermarks on paper and apparatus therefor. No. 1,329,100; Jan. 27; v. 270; p. 544.

Swartz, William H., and O. B. Richards, assignors to General Machine Works, York, Pa. Knitting-machine. No. 1,327,122; Jan. 6; v. 270; p. 46.

Sweet, Charles M., assignor to The Gurney Scale Company, Hamilton, Ontario, Canada. Attachment for dial-scales. No. 1,327,450; Jan. 6; v. 270; p. 106.

Sweet, Ernest E., assignor to General Motors Company, Detroit, Mich. Hydrocarbon-motor. No. 1,328,855; Jan. 27; v. 270; p. 498.

Swinehart, James A., Akron, Ohio. Making rubber tires. No. 1,326,991; Jan. 6; v. 270; p. 21.

Swint, Wendell R. (See Bryan and Swint.)

Swordling, Severn M. (See Kirkpatrick, Swordling, and Heath.)

Sykes, George, assignor to Sykes Standard Fruit Wrap Company, Penryn, Calif. Packing device. No. 1,327,888; Jan. 13; v. 270; p. 250.

Sykes, Leonard, Fort Wayne, Ind. Electric regulator. No. 1,327,642; Jan. 13; v. 270; p. 203.

Sykes Standard Fruit Wrap Company. (See Sykes, George, assignor.)

Symes, Henry, Dunedin, New Zealand. Telephone set. No. 1,327,500; Jan. 6; v. 270; p. 115.

Symonds, Clarence M., San Anselmo, assignor to American Can Company, San Francisco, Calif. Apparatus for cutting and applying ring-liners to the flanges of can ends. No. 1,328,020; Jan. 13; v. 270; p. 274.

Synthetic Hydro-Carbon Company. (See Whitaker and Rittman, assignors.)

Syracuse Chilled Plow Company. (See Lee, William H., assignor.)

Taft, Walter E., Providence, R. I., assignor to The Associate Company, Boston, Mass. Spark-plug for internal-combustion engines. No. 1,328,463; Jan. 20; v. 270; p. 395.

Taggart, George H., New York, N. Y. Automatic stop for phonographs. No. 1,327,501; Jan. 6; v. 270; p. 116.

Taggesell, Richard, Buffalo, assignor to National Aniline & Chemical Company, Inc., New York, N. Y. Azo dyes and making same. No. 1,327,688; Jan. 13; v. 270; p. 213.

Tainter, Charles R. (See Lenholt, John E., assignor.)

Talbott, Edward J., et al., trustees. (See Geoghegan, Edward A., assignor.)

Tamura, Shinkichi, Kobe, and M. Watanabe, Tokyo, Japan; said Watanabe assignor to said Tamura. Motor-car of small type. No. 1,328,909; Jan. 27; v. 270; p. 508.

Tarn, Thomas R., Brooklyn, N. Y. Combined steering and handling system for tow-boats and their vessels. No. 1,327,643; Jan. 13; v. 270; p. 204.

Tartrais, Eugène H., Maisons-Laffitte, France. Atomizer for liquid-fuel engines. No. 1,327,744; Jan. 13; v. 270; p. 223.

Taussig, Oskar, Vienna, Austria. Crane or similar lifting device. No. 1,327,181; Jan. 6; v. 270; p. 57.

Taylor, Charles. (See Carter and Taylor.)

Taylor, Ernest W., assignor to The Brown Hoisting Machinery Company, Cleveland, Ohio. Hoisting and conveying machine. No. 1,327,071; Jan. 6; v. 270; p. 36.

Taylor, George H., Richmond, Va. Label-holder. No. 1,327,298; Jan. 6; v. 270; p. 78.

Taylor, Harry H., Fresno, Calif. Hopper for filling cartons with raisins and similar articles of merchandise. No. 1,327,644; Jan. 13; v. 270; p. 204.

Taylor, Horace V. S., Pittsburgh, Pa., assignor to Westinghouse Electric and Manufacturing Company. Ignition system. No. 1,327,790; Jan. 13; v. 270; p. 231.

Taylor Instrument Companies. (See Norwood, Harry Y., assignor.)

Taylor, Walter M., London, England. Gas-fired water-heater or steam-generator. No. 1,328,856; Jan. 27; v. 270; p. 498.

Tebbetts, Lewis B., 2d, St. Louis, Mo. Making powdered or granulated aluminum. No. 1,327,743; Jan. 13; v. 270; p. 223.

Telautograph Corporation. (See Tiffany, George S., assignor.)

Templeton, Walter B., Chicago, Ill. Lifting-jack. No. 1,328,306; Jan. 20; v. 270; p. 365.

Terry, Ellis L., Los Angeles, Calif. Folding ironing-board. No. 1,329,257; Jan. 27; v. 270; p. 574.

Texas Company, The. (See Adams, Joseph H., assignor.)

Thamm, Rosie, Berkeley, Calif. Napkin-fastener. No. 1,329,149; Jan. 27; v. 270; p. 553.

Tharp, Wilber H., Lewiston, Idaho. Current-motor. No. 1,327,745; Jan. 13; v. 270; p. 223.

Theemling, Jakob, Los Angeles, Calif. Rotary engine. No. 1,327,575; Jan. 6; v. 270; p. 130.

Theriot, Charles, assignor of one-third to J. W. Sanders and one-third to P. R. Burke, New Iberia, La. Railway-crossing signal. No. 1,328,932; Jan. 27; v. 270; p. 513.

Thibert, Napoleon R., Worcester, Mass. Lock-nut. No. 1,326,992; Jan. 6; v. 270; p. 22.

Thiemer, William H., assignor to The Peters Machine and Manufacturing Company, Cleveland, Ohio. Universal joint. No. 1,327,791; Jan. 13; v. 270; p. 232.

Thomas, Bertha E., Erie, Pa. Flexible shaft-coupling. No. 1,326,993; Jan. 6; v. 270; p. 22.

Thomas, Elbert F. (See Kees and Thomas.)

Thomas, Frank M., Catskill, N. Y. Cartridge. No. 1,328,807; Jan. 20; v. 270; p. 365.

Thomas, Fred, Roanoke, Va. Coaster. No. 1,327,123; Jan. 6; v. 270; p. 46.

Thomas, George B., assignor to The Bryant Electric Company, Bridgeport, Conn. Electric fitting. No. 1,329,330; Jan. 27; v. 270; p. 586.

Thomas, R., and Sons Company, The. (See Harms, Rhinehart W., assignor.)

Thomas, Raymond G., Monticello, Iowa. Method of and apparatus for measuring the heights of superposed liquids of varying specific gravities. No. 1,329,150; Jan. 27; v. 270; p. 553.

Thomas, William M., Los Angeles, Calif. Concrete structure. No. 1,327,884; Jan. 13; v. 270; p. 250.

Thomasson, Hiram S., assignor, by mesne assignments, of two-thirds to C. D. Enochs, trustee, Minneapolis, Minn. Tank-heater. No. 1,329,063; Jan. 27; v. 270; p. 537.

Thommen, Adolph A., Chicago, Ill. Blower. No. 1,327,218; Jan. 6; v. 270; p. 64.

Thompson, Arnold, and H. J. S. Dennison, Toronto, Ontario, Canada. Hand-grenade. No. 1,327,451; Jan. 6; v. 270; p. 106.

Thompson, Earl A., Gresham, Oreg. Hydraulic engine. No. 1,328,974; Jan. 27; v. 270; p. 521.

Thompson, Fredrick B., Chicago, Ill. Film-treating apparatus. No. 1,328,464; Jan. 20; v. 270; p. 395.

Thompson, Harry E., Three Rivers, Mich., assignor to Fairbanks, Morse & Co., Chicago, Ill. Standpipe. No. 1,328,857; Jan. 27; v. 270; p. 498.

Thompson, Henry A., Manchester, England. Actuating signals on and communicating with trains. No. 1,327,441; Jan. 6; v. 270; p. 98.

Thompson, Oliver H., Brookings, S. D. Torpedo-guard. No. 1,328,549; Jan. 20; v. 270; p. 411.

Thompson, Roy E., New York, N. Y. Radio-receiving apparatus. No. 1,328,933; Jan. 27; v. 270; p. 513.

Thompson, William, et al. (See Fow, Raymond S. C., assignor.)

Thornton, Frank, Jr., Mansfield, Ohio, assignor to Westinghouse Electric & Manufacturing Company. Spot-welding apparatus. No. 1,327,792; Jan. 13; v. 270; p. 232.

Thornycroft, John E. (See Thornycroft, Tom and J. E.)

Thornycroft, Tom and J. E., Westminster, England. Gun for discharging bombs, shells, and other projectiles. No. 1,328,021; Jan. 13; v. 270; p. 275.

Thorward, Benjamin F. H., Cleveland, Ohio. Game apparatus. No. 1,327,072; Jan. 6; v. 270; p. 37.

Tibbetts, Milton, assignor to Packard Motor Car Company, Detroit, Mich. Signaling device for motor-vehicles. No. 1,327,124; Jan. 6; v. 270; p. 46.

Tiernan, Martin F. (See Wallace, Charles F., assignor.)

Tietz, William, Toledo, Ohio. Dehairing apparatus. No. 1,327,073; Jan. 6; v. 270; p. 37.

Tiffany, George S., Summit, N. J., assignor to Telautograph Corporation, Richmond, Va. Telautographic apparatus. No. 1,326,994; Jan. 6; v. 270; p. 22.

Timmons, John S., New York, N. Y. Telephone apparatus. No. 1,329,029; Jan. 27; v. 270; p. 531.

Timpany, Lewis J., Taco Taco, Cuba. Voting-machine. No. 1,328,550; Jan. 20; v. 270; p. 412.

Tinius Olsen Testing Machine Company. (See McAdam, Dunlap J., Jr., assignor.)

Tirodor, John, et al. (See Beshenich, Matija, assignor.)

Tischer, Edward B., assignor of forty-five per cent. to G. Emmert, Houston, Tex. Gin. No. 1,327,845; Jan. 13; v. 270; p. 242.

Titeflex Metal Hose Corporation. (See Brinkham, Louis H., assignor.)

Todd, Evander, Winn, Ala. Boiler-patch. No. 1,327,846; Jan. 13; v. 270; p. 242.

Todd, Frederick D. (See Coyle, Joseph L., assignor.)

Todd, James T. A., Fort Worth, Tex. Bale-tie buckle. No. 1,328,698; Jan. 20; v. 270; p. 439.

Todd, Libanus M., and A. C. La May, assignors, by mesne assignments, to Todd Protectograph Company, Rochester, N. Y. Checkwriter. No. 1,328,773; Jan. 20; v. 270; p. 453.

Todd Protectograph Company. (See Todd and La May, assignors.)

Toledo Scale Company. (See Crane, Samuel G., assignor.)

Toledo Scale Co. (See Pool, Elmer C., assignor.)

Toledo Standard Commutator Company, The. (See Van Dusen, Charles A., assignor.)

Tompkinson, Charles C., Plainfield, N. J., assignor to J. F. Ogden, Mountainville, N. Y. Motor-door. No. 1,326,995; Jan. 6; v. 270; p. 22.

Tonge, James L., Appenaug, R. I. Short-circuiting mechanism. No. 1,327,269; Jan. 6; v. 270; p. 71.

Torrent, John, Jr., Muskegon, Mich. Resilient hub. No. 1,328,858; Jan. 27; v. 270; p. 498.

Torrington Company, The. (See Baender, Charles L., assignor.)

Tosney, William F. (See Straub, Anselm, Jr., assignor.)

Tourtier, Paul A., New Orleans, La. Wheel. No. 1,329,213; Jan. 27; v. 270; p. 565.

Towne, William R., San Francisco, Calif. Potato-seed planter. No. 1,327,971; Jan. 13; v. 270; p. 265.

Townill, George and P., Plainfield, Ill. Steel grain-car door. No. 1,328,214; Jan. 13; v. 270; p. 311.

Townill, Peter. (See Townill, George and P.)

Trahan, Clair A., Beaumont, assignor of one-half to T. Placette, Port Arthur, Tex. Burner. No. 1,326,996; Jan. 6; v. 270; p. 22.

Treat, Robert, Schenectady, N. Y., assignor to General Electric Company. System of power transmission. No. 1,328,465; Jan. 20; v. 270; p. 395.

Tregoning, William C., Cleveland, Ohio, assignor, by mesne assignments, to Benjamin Electric Manufacturing Company, Chicago, Ill. Electrical attachment - plug. No. 1,328,774; Jan. 20; v. 270; p. 453.

Tremain, Charles. (See Becker, Robert A., assignor.)

Treo Company. (See Schloss, Meyer W., assignor.)

Trohon, William G., Danvers, Mass., assignor to United Shoe Machinery Corporation, Paterson, N. J. Die. No. 1,328,347; Jan. 20; v. 270; p. 373.

Tripke, Paul, Jersey City, N. J. Combined egg-separator and juice-extractor. No. 1,327,929; Jan. 13; v. 270; p. 257.
Trojan Powder Company. (See Snelling and Lams, assignors.)
Trolle-Bonde, Gustaf, Trolleholm, Sweden. Sack and the like. No. 1,328,859; Jan. 27; v. 270; p. 498.
Trott, Rolland S., Denver, Colo. Vehicle spring suspension. No. 1,327,746; Jan. 13; v. 270; p. 223.
Trout, Silas E., Philadelphia, Pa. Filing device. No. 1,328,604; Jan. 20; v. 270; p. 422.
Troy Laundry Machinery Company. (See Balzer, Fritz, assignor.)
Troy Laundry Machinery Company. (See Bartholomew, William, assignor.)
Trumbull Electric Manufacturing Company. The. (See Getchell, Benjamin E., assignor.)
Trumbull Electric Manufacturing Company, The. (See Knudsen, Knud, assignor.)
Tubular-Rivet & Stud Company. (See Wakefield, Edward E., assignor.)
Tunks, Charles A. (See Eickhoff and Tunks.)
Turck, Henry J., et al., trustees. (See Bobroff, Bornett L., assignor.)
Turnbull, William, assignor to The Holt Manufacturing Company, Stockton, Calif. Multiple-disk clutch. No. 1,327,576; Jan. 6; v. 270; p. 130.
Turnbull, William, assignor to The Holt Manufacturing Company, Stockton, Calif. Self-propelled vehicle. No. 1,329,314; Jan. 27; v. 270; p. 563.
Turner, Joseph S., Los Angeles, Calif. Surgical-needle holder. No. 1,327,577; Jan. 6; v. 270; p. 130.
Turner, Walter E., Piqua, Ohio. Automatic liquid weigher. No. 1,329,151; Jan. 27; v. 270; p. 554.
Twitchell, Myron A., Elk Point, S. D. Animal-trap. No. 1,327,890; Jan. 13; v. 270; p. 250.
Ude, William C., West Haven, Conn. Telephone. No. 1,327,412; Jan. 6; v. 270; p. 98.
Uebelmesser, Charles, New York, N. Y., assignor to Cru Patents Corporation. Automatic winding and reversing machine. No. 1,326,997; Jan. 6; v. 270; p. 22.
Uffner, Hyman, Brooklyn, N. Y., assignor to Peerless Album Company. Phonographic-record container. No. 1,329,030; Jan. 27; v. 270; p. 531.
Ufford, Morrell J., Kansas, Ill. Firecracker-gun. No. 1,327,747; Jan. 13; v. 270; p. 224.
Ullrich, Alexander L., Chicago, Ill. Antislipping attachment for shoes. No. 1,329,064; Jan. 27; v. 270; p. 537.
Underfeed Stoker Company of America, The. (See Blackburn and Fleming, assignors.)
Underwood Typewriter Company. (See Fenton, Walter, assignor.)
Underwood Typewriter Company. (See Helmond, William F., assignor.)
Union Land & Power Company. (See Foster, George D., assignor.)
Union Railway Equipment Company. (See Hall, William B., assignor.)
Union Special Machine Company. (See Berger, Joseph, assignor.)
Union Special Machine Company. (See Hughes, Robert R., Jr., assignor.)
Union Special Machine Company. (See Moffatt, James R., assignor.)
Union Steam Pump Company. (See Smith and Samelson, assignors.)
Union Switch & Signal Company, The. (See Lewis, Lloyd V., assignor.)
Union Switch & Signal Company, The. (See Peter, Bernard H., assignor.)
Union Switch & Signal Company, The. (See Young, John V., assignor.)
Union Tractor Company. (See Arndt, Richard L., assignor.)
United Mines and Manufacturing Company, The. (See Kohler, Ernest, assignor.)
United Shoe Machinery Corporation. (See Bates, Arthur, assignor.)
United Shoe Machinery Corporation. (See Braden, Albert R., assignor.)
United Shoe Machinery Corporation. (See Brock, Matthias, assignor.)
United Shoe Machinery Corporation. (See Brogan, Michael F., assignor.)
United Shoe Machinery Corporation. (See Davenport, Eugene F., assignor.)
United Shoe Machinery Corporation. (See Dyer, Newell V., assignor.)
United Shoe Machinery Corporation. (See Enslin, Herbert E., assignor.)
United Shoe Machinery Corporation. (See Fausse, Joseph, assignor.)
United Shoe Machinery Corporation. (See Gookin, Sylvester L., assignor.)
United Shoe Machinery Corporation. (See Lee, Bernard S., assignor.)
United Shoe Machinery Corporation. (See Lund, Thomas, assignor.)
United Shoe Machinery Corporation. (See Stewart, William C., assignor.)
United Shoe Machinery Corporation. (See Trohon, William G., assignor.)
United States Envelope Company. (See Novick, Abraham, assignor.)

United States Hoffman Machinery Company. (See Spencer, James B., assignor.)
U. S. Light & Heat Corporation. (See Bliss, William L., assignor.)
U. S. Light & Heat Corporation. (See Frey, Peter F., assignor.)
United States Ordnance Company. (See Bumpas and Falcke, assignors.)
United States Tire Company, The. (See Jury, Alfred E., assignor.)
U. S. Toy & Novelties Manufacturing Co., The. (See Fairbanks, James J., assignor.)
Universal Draft Gear Attachment Co. (See Wrigley, Henry I., assignor.)
Universal Electric Welding Company. (See Lachman, Maurice, assignor.)
Universal Elevated Railway Co. (See McClure and Boulton, assignors.)
Unkel, Winnie J. (See Hoffman and Unkel.)
Upham, Burt F., Brookline, Mass., assignor, by mesne assignments, to Cross Paper Feeder Company, Portland, Me. Mechanism for controlling the feeding and printing of sheets. No. 1,327,182; Jan. 6; v. 270; p. 57.
Upp, William M., assignor of one-half to E. Rumsey, Kansas City, Mo. Electric primer. No. 1,329,345; Jan. 27; v. 270; p. 588.
Upson, Ralph H., assignor to The Goodyear Tire & Rubber Company, Akron, Ohio. Engine-hood and radiator cover. No. 1,327,891; Jan. 13; v. 270; p. 250.
Vagneux, Edmond F. L., Dijon, France. Understructure for supporting railway-tracks. No. 1,327,219; Jan. 6; v. 270; p. 64.
Valley Mould and Iron Corporation. (See Coates, Ray G., assignor.)
Vallier, Wilfred F., Pontiac, Mich. Governor for internal-combustion engines. No. 1,327,847; Jan. 13; v. 270; p. 242.
Valls, Raphael W., assignor to The Champion Engineering Company, Kenton, Ohio. Driving mechanism for overhead traveling bridge-cranes. No. 1,328,934; Jan. 27; v. 270; p. 513.
Van Allen, Frederic L., Toronto, Ontario, Canada. Control for dual-control aeroplanes. No. 1,327,183; Jan. 6; v. 270; p. 57.
Van Aller, Tycho, Schnectady, N. Y., assignor to General Electric Company. Cigar-lighter. No. 1,328,466; Jan. 20; v. 270; p. 396.
Van Alstyn, Albert T., Grand Rapids, Mich. Supporter. No. 1,328,406; Jan. 20; v. 270; p. 384.
Van Briggle, Lilburn H., Indianapolis, Ind. Shock-absorber. No. 1,328,641; Jan. 20; v. 270; p. 428.
Vanderveld, Anthony, assignor to Grand Rapids Show Case Co., Grand Rapids, Mich. Shelving-support. No. 1,327,748; Jan. 13; v. 270; p. 224.
Van Deventer, Harry R., Sumter, S. C. assignor to Splitdorf Electrical Company, Newark, N. J. Ignition device. No. 1,327,361; Jan. 6; v. 270; p. 89.
Van Deventer, Harry R., Sumter, S. C. assignor to Splitdorf Electrical Company, Newark, N. J. Ignition device. No. 1,327,502; Jan. 6; v. 270; p. 116.
Van Dusen, Charles A., Toledo, Ohio, assignor, by mesne assignments, to The Toledo Standard Commutator Company. Commutator and producing same. No. 1,329,277; Jan. 27; v. 270; p. 577.
Vang, Peder C., Omaha, Nebr. Valve-spring remover. No. 1,328,776; Jan. 20; v. 270; p. 453.
Van Houten, Frank H., Jr., Beacon, assignor to Dutchess Tool Company, New York, N. Y. Oiling hoppers. No. 1,328,308; Jan. 20; v. 270; p. 365.
Van Lynden, Robert A. (See de Lange and van Lynden.)
Van Meter, George F., Indianapolis, Ind. Adjustable caster. No. 1,328,775; Jan. 20; v. 270; p. 453.
Van Valer, De Witt C., assignor of one-half to H. W. Geyer, New York, N. Y. Lever-filler for fountain-pens No. 1,328,215; Jan. 13; v. 270; p. 312.
Van Valkenburg, Burt R., Oakland, Calif. Valve-chest. No. 1,328,796; Jan. 20; v. 270; p. 457.
Van Vleck, Horace R., Montclair, N. J., assignor to The Motor-Compressor Company. Starting mechanism for internal-combustion engines. No. 1,329,152; Jan. 27; v. 270; p. 554.
Varner, William I., Athens, Ga. Automobile-tire. No. 1,327,503; Jan. 6; v. 270; p. 116.
Vasselli, Anthony, Newark, N. J., assignor, by mesne assignments, to Harriman National Bank of the City of New York. Fastening device. No. 1,328,064; Jan. 18; v. 270; p. 283.
Vasselli, Anthony, Newark, N. J., assignor, by mesne assignments, to Harriman National Bank of the City of New York. Shaft for talking-machines. No. 1,328,065; Jan. 13; v. 270; p. 283.
Vasselli, Anthony, Newark, N. J., assignor, by mesne assignments, to Harriman National Bank of the City of New York. Level-winder. No. 1,328,066; Jan. 13; v. 270; p. 283.
Vavra, Frank P., Congress Park. Ill. Paraffining-machine. No. 1,327,299; Jan. 6; v. 270; p. 78.
Vavra, Frank P., Cicero. Ill. Machine for coating blanks with paraffin. No. 1,327,300; Jan. 6; v. 270; p. 78.
Ventibeta Limited. (See Ogle, Percy J., assignor.)
Vermont Box Company. (See Shelton, Carl L., assignor.)
Verran, H. E. Company. (See Clauss, Max O., assignor.)
Vessey, Frank D., Spokane, Wash. Wheelbarrow. No. 1,327,578; Jan. 6; v. 270; p. 130.

Vial, Frederick K., assignor to Griffin Wheel Company, Chicago, Ill. Process and apparatus for cooling car-wheels. No. 1,328,278; Jan. 27; v. 270; p. 577.
Vickers Limited. (See Dawson and Buckham, assignors.)
Viertels, Ephraim, New York, N. Y. Tip-fastener for shoe-laces. No. 1,327,892; Jan. 13; v. 270; p. 250.
Virkus, Frederick A., La Grange, Ill., assignor to Wood, Nathan & Virkus Company, New York, N. Y. Machine for embossing without dies. No. 1,328,407; Jan. 20; v. 270; p. 384.
Vissering, Harry, & Company. (See Anderson, Harry T., assignor.)
Vogt, Ernst W., Silverton, Ohio. Downspout cut off. No. 1,328,348; Jan. 20; v. 270; p. 373.
Vogt, Joseph, Richmond, Minn. Self-sharpening adjustable packer-head plate for tile-machines. No. 1,328,699; Jan. 20; v. 270; p. 439.
Vogts, Walter D., Waunakee, Wis. Automobile pump attachment. No. 1,327,798; Jan. 13; v. 270; p. 232.
Von Groeling, Albrecht F. G. C. P. J., assignor to Atlas Process Company, Inc., New York, N. Y. Fractional distillation of crude petroleum and other hydrocarbons. No. 1,327,184; Jan. 6; v. 270; p. 57.
Voorheis, Joseph T., Philadelphia, Pa. Air-regulating device for oil-burners. No. 1,329,279; Jan. 27; v. 270; p. 577.
Voorhees, Sheldon, Syracuse, N. Y. Abdominal support. No. 1,327,930; Jan. 13; v. 270; p. 257.
Voraceh, Frank B., Tillamook, Oreg. Flying-machine. No. 1,327,125; Jan. 6; v. 270; p. 46.
Wade, Frank M., Wauwatosa, assignor to Milwaukee Paper Box Company, Milwaukee, Wis. Paper box. No. 1,328,935; Jan. 27; v. 270; p. 513.
Wadham, Frank L., Detroit, Mich. Tire. No. 1,327,794; Jan. 13; v. 270; p. 232.
Wagenhorst, James H., Akron, Ohio, assignor to The B. F. Goodrich Company, New York, N. Y. Demountable split rim. No. 1,328,605; Jan. 20; v. 270; p. 422.
Wagner, Albert F., New York, N. Y. Gearing for generators and distributers. No. 1,327,504; Jan. 6; v. 270; p. 116.
Wagner Electric Manufacturing Company. (See Fynn, Valère A., assignor.)
Wagner Electric Manufacturing Company. (See Sparrow, Simon, assignor.)
Wagoner, Joseph F., Danville, Ill. Shock-absorber. No. 1,328,700; Jan. 20; v. 270; p. 489.
Wahl Company, The. (See Poole, Arthur F., assignor.)
Wahlstrom, John F., Minneapolis, Minn. Selective circuit-closer. No. 1,327,505; Jan. 6; v. 270; p. 116.
Waitt, George L., Buffalo, N. Y. Chaplet. No. 1,327,689; Jan. 13; v. 270; p. 213.
Wakefield, Edward E., assignor to Tubular Rivet & Stud Company, Providence, R. I. Lacing-stud-setting machine. No. 1,328,701; Jan. 20; v. 270; p. 489.
Wald, Julius H. (See Neukirchen, Peter, assignor.)
Walden, Alfred, London, England, assignor of one-half to H. J. Walsh, Bexhill-on-Sea, England. Construction of hampers. No. 1,327,362; Jan. 6; v. 270; p. 90.
Waldron, Fred D., Brooklyn, assignor to Western Electric Company, Incorporated, New York, N. Y. Transmitter-support. No. 1,329,031; Jan. 27; v. 270; p. 531.
Wales Adding Machine Company. (See Pentecost, Arthur, assignor.)
Walker, Malcolm, Glasgow, Scotland, assignor to Smith and Coventry Limited, Salford, England. Magnetic clutch. No. 1,327,506; Jan. 6; v. 270; p. 117.
Walker, Moses F., Cadiz, Ohio. Film-end fastener for motion-picture-film reels. No. 1,328,408; Jan. 20; v. 270; p. 385.
Walker, Roy S., assignor to L. R. Alderman & Co., Pasadena, Calif. Snail and slug trap. No. 1,327,579; Jan. 6; v. 270; p. 131.
Wall, John C. (See Haschke, Feodor G., assignor.)
Wallace, Charles F., New York, assignor of one-half to M. F. Tiernan, Jamaica, N. Y. Variable-orifice valve. No. 1,326,998; Jan. 6; v. 270; p. 23.
Wallace, Peter, Vancouver, British Columbia, Canada. Means for separating small from large fish. No. 1,328,551; Jan. 20; v. 270; p. 412.
Wallace, Philip B., Burlingame, and F. H. Fox, San Francisco, Calif. Work-holder. No. 1,326,999; Jan. 6; v. 270; p. 23.
Walsh, Edward J., Jersey City, N. J. Shelf-tongs. No. 1,328,860; Jan. 27; v. 270; p. 499.
Walsh, Harry J. (See Walden, Alfred, assignor.)
Walsh, William R., New Haven, Conn. Automatic train-stop. No. 1,329,258; Jan. 27; v. 270; p. 574.
Walter, Erwin, Mellingen, Switzerland. Braiding-machine. No. 1,328,216; Jan. 13; v. 270; p. 312.
Walter, Hugo J., assignor to Consolidated Machine Company, Bradford, Pa. Apparatus for drawing glass cylinders. No. 1,329,065; Jan. 27; v. 270; p. 537.
Walther, Fred, Omaha, Nebr. Internal-combustion-engine water-heater. No. 1,327,507; Jan. 6; v. 270; p. 117.
Walther, Paul. (See Holzapfel and Walther.)
Wandel, Kurt, New York, N. Y. Pulp-screen. No. 1,327,126; Jan. 6; v. 270; p. 46.
Wanielista, Anton, and M. Ostrowiecki, Chicago, Ill. Wall-papering machine. No. 1,327,127; Jan. 6; v. 270; p. 46.
Wans, Oswald. (See Green, Wans, and Livens.)
Ward Leonard Electric Co. (See Kebler, Leonard, assignor.)

Waring, Swinton B., Wallingford, assignor to The Waring-Underwood Company, Philadelphia, Pa. Expansion-joint strip. No. 1,328,107; Jan. 13; v. 270; p. 291.
Waring-Underwood Company, The. (Waring, Swinton B., assignor.)
Warme, Ivar F., assignor to Continental Can Company, Incorporated, Syracuse, N. Y. Can-end clencher. No. 1,329,259; Jan. 27; v. 270; p. 574.
Warn, Benjamin M. (See Ritter and Warn.)
Warne, Frederick C., assignor to Roderick Lean Manufacturing Company, Mansfield, Ohio. Cultivator. No. 1,327,413; Jan. 6; v. 270; p. 99.
Warner, Douglas K., New Haven, Conn. Snow-removal apparatus. No. 1,327,645; Jan. 13; v. 270; p. 204.
Warrington, John E., Brooklyn, Ill. Poultry-roost. No. 1,328,861; Jan. 27; v. 270; p. 499.
Watanabe, Masanori. (See Tamura and Watanabe.)
Waterloo, John, New Eagle, assignor to Window Glass Machine Company, Pittsburgh, Pa. Glass-cutting machine. (Reissue.) No. 14,788; Jan. 6; v. 270; p. 136.
Waters, Frank W. (See Rea and Waters.)
Waters, Sydney J., Esher, England. Reproducing manuscript, typewritten or printed matter, drawings, photographs, or the like. No. 1,327,931; Jan. 13; v. 270; p. 258.
Watkins, Evan, assignor to The Columbian Hardware Company, Cleveland, Ohio. Screw-clamp. No. 1,328,862; Jan. 27; v. 270; p. 499.
Watkins, Leigh, Oakland, Calif. Differential. No. 1,328,217; Jan. 13; v. 270; p. 312.
Watrous, Earl G., Chicago, Ill. Slow-closing faucet. No. 1,327,000; Jan. 6; v. 270; p. 23.
Watson, Edward L., Dallas, S. D. Fly-poisoning device. No. 1,328,936; Jan. 27; v. 270; p. 514.
Watson, James A., Silver Spring, Md. Clutch. No. 1,328,022; Jan. 13; v. 270; p. 275.
Watson, James B., Detroit, Mich. Bearing. No. 1,327,301; Jan. 6; v. 270; p. 79.
Watts, Ben, assignor of forty-nine per cent. to W. P. Godfrey, Jarbidge, Nev. Pipe-wrench. (Reissue.) No. 14,791; Jan. 13; v. 270; p. 320.
Weaver Company. (See Weaver, Victor M., assignor.)
Weaver, Horace E., Bryan, Ohio. Variable-pitch propeller. No. 1,328,241; Jan. 13; v. 270; p. 317.
Weaver, Victor M., Harrisburg, Pa., assignor to Weaver Company. Electrolytic apparatus. No. 1,329,315; Jan. 27; v. 270; p. 583.
Webb, John W., assignor, by mesne assignments, to Webb Tester Incorporated, Chicago, Ill. Device for testing corrugated paper-board and corrugated-paper-board boxes. No. 1,328,849; Jan. 20; v. 270; p. 373.
Webb Tester Incorporated. (See Webb, John W., assignor.)
Weed, Howard L., Detroit, Mich. Cylinder-forming machine. No. 1,328,409; Jan. 20; v. 270; p. 385.
Weed, Howard L., Detroit, Mich. Rotary engine. No. 1,328,410; Jan. 20; v. 270; p. 385.
Weidmann Dyeing Co. (See Dürsteler, Wilhelm, assignor.)
Weinhardt, Robert A., Chicago, Ill., assignor, by mesne assignments, to Continental Motors Corporation, Detroit, Mich. Crank-shaft. No. 1,328,350; Jan. 20; v. 270; p. 373.
Weis, John P., Nyack, N. Y., assignor, by mesne assignments, to Metropolitan Sewing Machine Corporation, Dover, Del. Shoulder-strap-sewing machine. No. 1,327,646; Jan. 13; v. 270; p. 204.
Weis, John P., assignor to Metropolitan Sewing Machine Corporation, Nyack, N. Y. Combined looper and feeding mechanism for sewing-machines. No. 1,327,647; Jan. 13; v. 270; p. 204.
Weis, John P., Nyack, N. Y., assignor to Metropolitan Sewing Machine Corporation. Thread-controlling means for sewing-machines. No. 1,328,023; Jan. 13; v. 270; p. 275.
Weis, John P., Nyack, N. Y., assignor to Metropolitan Sewing Machine Corporation. Sewing-machine. No. 1,328,108; Jan. 13; v. 270; p. 291.
Weisberger, Edward I. (See Newberg and Weisberger.)
Weisehan, Frank. (See Brewster and Weisehan.)
Weizmann, Charles, and G. A. Hamlyn, London, England. Fermentation process for the production of acetone and butyl alcohol. No. 1,329,214; Jan. 27; v. 270; p. 565.
Welch, Alfred F., Fort Wayne, Ind., assignor to General Electric Company. Universal motor. No. 1,328,467; Jan. 20; v. 270; p. 396.
Welch, Harry V., assignor to International Precipitation Company, Los Angeles, Calif. Apparatus for making sulfuric acid. No. 1,328,552; Jan. 20; v. 270; p. 412.
Wellman, Frank E., assignor to The Kansas City Gasoline Company, Kansas City, Kans. Furnace for oil-cracking stills. No. 1,328,468; Jan. 20; v. 270; p. 396.
Welsbach Company. (See Stites and Knoedler, assignors.)
Welsh, Clyde L., Pittsburgh, Pa. Parachute. No. 1,327,932; Jan. 13; v. 270; p. 258.
Wendtland, William, New York, N. Y. Screw-grinding machine. No. 1,328,469; Jan. 20; v. 270; p. 396.
Wentworth, Frank T., Bloomfield, N. J. Luggage-carrier. No. 1,328,843; Jan. 27; v. 270; p. 499.
Wert, Cyrus S., Kendallville, Ind. Cushion-tire. No. 1,329,331; Jan. 27; v. 270; p. 586.
Wesson, Laurence G., Cleveland, and Z. Jeffries, East Cleveland, Ohio. Strop-dressing. No. 1,327,648; Jan. 13; v. 270; p. 205.

West Coast Kalsomine Company. (See Benniman and Zoph, assignors.)
West, William. (See Anderson, Gideon, assignor.)
Westergaard, Peter J., Reinbeck, Iowa. Resilient tire. No. 1,329,215; Jan. 27; v. 270; p. 565.
Western Electric Company. (See Arnold, Harold D., assignor.)
Western Electric Company. (See Bullard, Albert M., assignor.)
Western Electric Company. (See Dixon, Amos F., assignor.)
Western Electric Company. (See Whiting, Donald F., assignor.)
Western Electric Company. (See Houskeeper, William G., assignor.)
Western Electric Company. (See Lundius, Eric R., assignor.)
Western Electric Company. (See MacDougall, Harry W., assignor.)
Western Electric Company. (See Waldron, Fred D., assignor.)
Western Felt Works. (See Backstrom, Fridolf F., assignor.)
Western Hog Oiler Co. (See Busby, Harley S., assignor.)
Western Tire & Rubber Works. (See Brooks, Roscoe A., assignor.)
Western Wheeled Scraper Company. (See McKnight, Thomas R., assignor.)
Westfall, Will H. (See Levinson and Westfall.)
Westinghouse Air Brake Company, The. (See Saunders, Lawrence D., assignor.)
Westinghouse Electric and Manufacturing Company. (See Dean, John S., assignor.)
Westinghouse Electric & Manufacturing Company. (See Eaton, George M., assignor.)
Westinghouse Electric & Manufacturing Co. (See Ehrhart, Raymond N., assignor.)
Westinghouse Electric & Manufacturing Company. (See Eschholz, Otto H., assignor.)
Westinghouse Electric and Manufacturing Company. (See Fortescue, Charles L., assignor.)
Westinghouse Electric and Manufacturing Company. (See Hellmund, Rudolf E., assignor.)
Westinghouse Electric and Manufacturing Company. (See Hellmund and Moore, assignors.)
Westinghouse Electric and Manufacturing Company. (See Holt, Frederick B., assignor.)
Westinghouse Electric & Manufacturing Company. (See Kasley, Alexander T., assignor.)
Westinghouse Electric and Manufacturing Company. (See Kuyser, Jan A., assignor.)
Westinghouse Electric and Manufacturing Company. (See La Bar, Bert G., assignor.)
Westinghouse Electric and Manufacturing Company. (See MacGahan, Paul, assignor.)
Westinghouse Electric and Manufacturing Company. (See Mills and Nikonow, assignors.) (Reissue.)
Westinghouse Electric & Manufacturing Company. (See Randall, Karl C., assignor.)
Westinghouse Electric and Manufacturing Company. (See Roschourne and Couse, assignors.)
Westinghouse Electric & Manufacturing Company. (See Smith, Gerald F., assignor.)
Westinghouse Electric & Manufacturing Company. (See Storer, Norman W., assignor.)
Westinghouse Electric and Manufacturing Company. (See Taylor, Horace V. S., assignor.)
Westinghouse Electric & Manufacturing Company. (See Thornton, Frank, Jr., assignor.)
Westinghouse Electric & Manufacturing Company. (See Whittaker, Charles C., assignor.)
Wexler, Benjamin, assignor to The Peelle Company, Brooklyn, N. Y. Electric interlock for counterbalanced elevator-doors. No. 1,328,309; Jan. 20; v. 270; p. 366.
Wharton, Edward R., Medford, assignor to Gillette Safety Razor Company, Boston, Mass. Safety-razor. No. 1,328,024; Jan. 13; v. 270; p. 275.
Wharton, William, Jr., & Co. (See Pallander, Charles A., assignor.)
Wheary, George H., Racine, Wis. Garment-retainer for trunks. No. 1,328,470; Jan. 20; v. 270; p. 396.
Wheeler, Alvin S., Chapel Hill, N. C. Dyestuffs and making. No. 1,327,260; Jan. 6; v. 270; p. 71.
Wheeler, Charles M., Bellingham, Wash. Machine for forming and cutting doughnuts and other cakes. No. 1,328,025; Jan. 13; v. 270; p. 275.
Wheeler & Motter Mercantile Company. (See Miller, Cyrus M., Jr., assignor.)
Whipp, John W., Wade, Okla. Tack-holder. No. 1,327,749; Jan. 13; v. 270; p. 224.
Whitaker, Milton C., and W. F. Rittman, New York, N. Y., assignors to Synthetic Hydro-Carbon Company, Pittsburgh, Pa. Manufacture of gas. No. 1,327,001; Jan. 6; v. 270; p. 23.
Whitaker, Norman L., et al. (See Miles, William C., assignor.)
Whitaker, Norman T., New York, N. Y. Motion-picture apparatus. No. 1,329,216; Jan. 27; v. 270; p. 566.
Whitbeck, Frank. (See Nevers and Whitbeck.)
White, Fred G., assignor of one-half to E. W. Engle, Kansas City, Mo. Electric switch-box. No. 1,328,606; Jan. 20; v. 270; p. 422.
White, Gus J. (See Joyner and White.)
White, J. Samuel, & Company. (See Forster and Brown, assignors.)

Whitehead Torpedo Works (Weymouth) Limited, The. (See Lees, Edgar, assignor.)
Whitehorn, Lee H., Eureka, Colo. Heater. No. 1,327,508; Jan. 6; v. 270; p. 117.
Whitehurst, John L., assignor, by mesne assignments, to J. T. Whitehurst, Baltimore, Md. Labeling-machine. No. 1,329,260; Jan. 27; v. 270; p. 574.
Whitehurst, John T. (See Whitehurst, John L., assignor.)
Whitelaw, James, St. Louis, Mo. Hat-sewing machine. No. 1,327,972; Jan. 13; v. 270; p. 265.
Whiteley, George H., Jr., York, Pa., assignor to The Dentists' Supply Company. Mold for molding artificial teeth. No. 1,328,351; Jan. 20; v. 270; p. 374.
Whiting, Donald F., assignor to Western Electric Company, Incorporated, New York, N. Y. Telephone system. No. 1,327,185; Jan. 6; v. 270; p. 57.
Whitlock, Robert G., Los Angeles, Calif. Lock for electric switches. No. 1,328,109; Jan. 13; v. 270; p. 291.
Whitney, Charles L. A. (See Salm, John, assignor.)
Whittaker, Charles C., Wilkinsburg, Pa., assignor to Westinghouse Electric & Manufacturing Company. System of control. No. 1,327,795; Jan. 13; v. 270; p. 232.
Whittemore, James, Detroit, Mich., assignor to The Libbey-Owens Sheet Glass Company, Toledo, Ohio. Apparatus for making sheet-glass. No. 1,328,864; Jan. 27; v. 270; p. 499.
Whitton, Charles R. (See Fry and Whitton.)
Whole Grain Wheat Company. (See Babendreer, Albert, assignor.)
Wickersham, Elmer E., assignor to The Holt Manufacturing Company, Stockton, Calif. Self-laying-track vehicle. No. 1,329,316; Jan. 27; v. 270; p. 583.
Wilhelm, Joseph G., Fremont, Nebr. Vapor-burner. No. 1,329,066; Jan. 27; v. 270; p. 537.
Wiegner, William. (See Kirkpatrick and Wiegner.)
Wieland, Frederick G., assignor to Anchor Cap & Closure Corporation, Brooklyn, N. Y. Screw-cap. No. 1,327,453; Jan. 6; v. 270; p. 106.
Wieland, Frederick G., assignor to Anchor Cap & Closure Corporation, Brooklyn, N. Y. Making closure-caps. No. 1,327,454; Jan. 6; v. 270; p. 106.
Wigman, William J., Manitowoc, Wis. Automobile-signal. No. 1,327,128; Jan. 6; v. 270; p. 47.
Wilbur, Burt, assignor of one-half to G. H. Jones, Syracuse, N. Y. Sanitary milk-carrier. No. 1,328,937; Jan. 27; v. 270; p. 514.
Wild, Alfred. (See Anderson and Wild.)
Wilder, Lawrence R. (See Hilty, Frederick, assignor.)
Willard Storage Battery Company. (See Willard, Theodore A., assignor.)
Willard, Theodore A., East Cleveland, assignor to Willard Storage Battery Company, Cleveland, Ohio. Storage-battery jar. No. 1,327,649; Jan. 13; v. 270; p. 205.
Willard, Theodore A., East Cleveland, assignor to Willard Storage Battery Company, Cleveland, Ohio. Storage battery adapted particularly for aeroplanes. No. 1,327,650; Jan. 13; v. 270; p. 205.
Willcox, Walter D., Upper Darby, Pa. Ice-making apparatus. No. 1,327,414; Jan. 6; v. 270; p. 99.
Williams, Edward T., New York, N. Y. Shaft-sealing device. No. 1,327,002; Jan. 6; v. 270; p. 23.
Williams, Franklin M., assignor to Aeroplane Railway Patents Corporation, New York, N. Y. Aeroplane pleasure-railway. No. 1,328,238; Jan. 13; v. 270; p. 316.
Williams, Henry J., Mobile, Ala. Shipping-case. No. 1,329,032; Jan. 27; v. 270; p. 531.
Williams, J. H. & Company. (See Bufford, George W., assignor.)
Williams, Joseph S., Riverton, N. J. Subaqueous tunnel. No. 1,329,317; Jan. 27; v. 270; p. 584.
Williams, Milton F., assignor to Williams Patent Crusher and Pulverizer Company, St. Louis, Mo. Suction-nozzle and material-separator for reducing-machines. No. 1,327,452; Jan. 6; v. 270; p. 106.
Williams Patent Crusher and Pulverizer Company. (See Williams, Milton F., assignor.)
Williams, Roger, assignor to Nitrogen Products Company, Providence, R. I. Producing alkali-metal ferricyanids and the like. No. 1,328,938; Jan. 27; v. 270; p. 514.
Williams, William R., Owensboro, Ky. Toy or display device. No. 1,327,415; Jan. 6; v. 270; p. 99.
Williams, Winfield S. (See Paine and Williams.)
Willis, Harry E., Waterford, assignor to Willite Road Construction Company of America, New York, N. Y. Asphaltic pavement and foundation for pavements. No. 1,328,310; Jan. 20; v. 270; p. 366.
Willis, Leland, and O. F. Woodworth, assignors to Bateman Manufacturing Company, Grenloch, N. J. Seed-planter. No. 1,327,455; Jan. 6; v. 270; p. 106.
Willite Road Construction Company of America. (See Willis, Harry P., assignor.)
Wilson, George, Algona, Iowa. Base-lock for reciprocating engines. No. 1,328,110; Jan. 13; v. 270; p. 292.
Wilson, J. G. Corporation, The. (See Hill, Thomas A, assignor.)
Wilson, Luloff, Chicago, Ill. Roller-bearing. No. 1,327,003; Jan. 6; v. 270; p. 24.
Wilson, Luloff, Chicago, Ill. Tire-carrier. No. 1,327,261; Jan. 6; v. 270; p. 71.
Wilson, Paul J., Grimes, Iowa. Double-acting-pump-operating mechanism. No. 1,328,218; Jan. 13; v. 270; p. 312.

ALPHABETICAL LIST OF PATENTEES OF DESIGNS.

ALPHABETICAL LIST OF REGISTRANTS OF TRADE-MARKS.

Aberdeen Packing Co., Aberdeen, Wash. Canned salmon. No. 128,587; Jan. 13; v. 270; p. 335.
Aborno Laboratory, Lancaster, Wis. Remedy for promoting fertility of live stock. No. 128,274; Jan. 6; v. 270; p. 177.
Acherman, Joseph, & Co., Monroe, Wis. Limburger cheese. No. 129,110; Jan. 27; v. 270; p. 613.
Acme Packing Co., Chicago, Ill. Meat patties. No. 128,588; Jan. 13; v. 270; p. 335.
Adams, Cushing & Foster, Inc., Boston, Mass. Writing and printing paper and writing-tablets. No. 128,275; Jan. 6; v. 270; p. 177.
Adrian Neckwear Co., Portland, Oreg. Neckties. No. 128,589; Jan. 13; v. 270; p. 335.
Advance-Rumely Company, Laporte, Ind. Threshing-machines and grain-separators. No. 128,276; Jan. 6; v. 270; p. 177.
Air Reduction Company, Incorporated, New York, N. Y. Calcium carbid. No. 128,590; Jan. 13; v. 270; p. 335.
Akerlund & Semmes, Inc., New York, N. Y. Gas-producer apparatus. No. 128,913; Jan. 20; v. 270; p. 471.
Aladdin Products Company. (See Robinson, Clinton S., assignor.)
Alan Wood Iron & Steel Company, Philadelphia, Pa. Iron and steel plates, billets, slabs. No. 129,111; Jan. 27; v. 270; p. 613.
Alaska Refrigerator Company, Muskegon Heights, Mich. Refrigerators. No. 128,277; Jan. 6; v. 270; p. 177.
Alban, John A., & Co. Inc., New York, N. Y. Olive-oil. No. 128,591; Jan. 13; v. 270; p. 335.
Albany Shoe Repairing Company, Boston, Mass. Dyes for leather goods. No. 128,278; Jan. 6; v. 270; p. 177.
Albaugh-Dover Co., Chicago, Ill., assignor to Square Turn Tractor Co., Norfolk, Nebr. Tractors. No. 128,279; Jan. 6; v. 270; p. 177.
Albemarle Paper Mfg. Co., Richmond, Va. Blotting-paper. No. 128,592; Jan. 13; v. 270; p. 335.
Alexander Drug Co., Oklahoma, Okla. Medicine for colds, croup, &c. No. 128,280; Jan. 6; v. 270; p. 177.
Alford, Henry N., Atlanta, Ga. Medicine for colds, influenza, &c. No. 128,915; Jan. 20; v. 270; p. 471.
Alfred Brothers, Whitinsville, Mass. Medicine for colds, asthma, &c. No. 128,914; Jan. 20; v. 270; p. 471.
Allan, Joseph W., New York, N. Y. Motor-trucks. No. 128,281; Jan. 6; v. 270; p. 177.
Alling & Cory Company, The, Rochester, N. Y. Printing and writing paper. No. 128,282; Jan. 6; v. 270; p. 177.
Allen & Hanburys, Ltd., London, England. Pepton for bacteriological use. No. 128,593; Jan. 13; v. 270; p. 335.
Ambridge Knitting Co., Ambridge, Pa. Hosiery. No. 129,112; Jan. 27; v. 270; p. 613.
American Abrasive Metals Co., New York, N. Y. Treads and panels for stairways, floors, &c. No. 128,594; Jan. 13; v. 270; p. 335
American Factories, Limited, Honolulu, Hawaii. Canned salmon and vegetables, &c. No. 128,596; Jan. 13; v. 270; p. 335.
American Factories, Limited, Honolulu, Hawaii. Coffee, canned fruits, lemons. No. 128,595; Jan. 13; v. 270; p. 335.
American Flour Corporation, New York, N. Y. Wheat-flour. No. 128,916; Jan. 20; v. 270; p. 471.
American Grinder Manufacturing Company, Milwaukee, Wis. Socket-wrenches. No. 128,597; Jan. 13; v. 270; p. 335
American Harmonica & Accordion Manufacturing Co., New York, N. Y. Harmonicas. No. 128,917; Jan. 20; v. 270; p. 471.
American Laboratories, Indianapolis, Ind. Pharmaceutical preparation for colds and congestions. No. 128,918; Jan. 20; v. 270; p. 471.
American Laboratories Incorporated, Richmond, Va. Antiseptic, disinfectant, &c. No. 128,599; Jan. 13; v. 270; p. 335.
American Laboratories Incorporated, Richmond, Va. Food-flavoring extracts. No. 128,600; Jan. 13; v. 270; p. 335.
American Laboratories Incorporated Richmond, Va. Hair-dressing preparation. No. 128,598; Jan. 13; v. 270; p. 335.
American Lead Pencil Company, New York, N. Y. Lead-pencils. No. 128,601; Jan. 13; v. 270; p. 335.
American Metal Company, Limited, The, New York, N. Y. White arsenic. No. 128,602; Jan. 13; v. 270; p. 335.
American Mustard Co Inc., New York N Y Mustard. No. 128,603; Jan. 13; v. 270; p. 335.
American Mutual Seed Company, Chicago, Ill. Seeds. No. 129,113; Jan. 27; v. 270; p. 613.
American Standard Food Assn., Milwaukee, Wis. Coffee. No. 128,919; Jan. 20; v. 270; p 471.
American Steel Export Company, New York, N. Y. Iron, steel, and sheet-metal products and forgings. No. 129,114; Jan. 27; v. 270; p. 613.

American Steel Export Company, New York, N. Y. Machinery and tools and parts thereof. No. 129,115; Jan. 27; v. 270; p. 613.
American Tobacco Company, The, New York, N. Y. Cigarettes. No. 128,284; Jan. 6; v. 270; p. 177.
American Tobacco Company, The, New York, N. Y. Cigarettes. No. 128,920; Jan. 20; v. 270; p. 471.
American Tobacco Co., New York, N. Y. Cigarettes and tobacco. No. 128,921; Jan. 20; v. 270; p. 471.
American Trading Company, New York, N. Y. Hosiery. Nos. 129,116-17; Jan. 27; v. 270; p. 613.
American Trading Co. of the Pacific Coast, San Francisco, Calif. Canned foods, dried fruits, &c. No. 128,285; Jan. 6; v. 270; p. 177.
American Writing Paper Company, Holyoke, Mass. Printing and writing paper. No. 128,283; Jan. 6; v. 270; p. 177.
American Writing Paper Company, Holyoke, Mass. Printing and writing paper. No. 128,286; Jan. 6; v. 270; p. 177.
American Writing Paper Co., Holyoke, Mass. Printing and writing paper. No. 128,604; Jan. 13; v. 270; p. 335.
Amory, Browne & Co., New York, N. Y. Cotton piece goods. No. 128,605; Jan. 13; v. 270; p. 335.
Andersen, A. O. & Co., Portland, Oreg. Canned salmon. Nos. 128,606-8; Jan. 13; v. 270; p. 335.
Angier Mechanical Laboratories, Framingham, Mass. Wrapping and lining paper. No. 128,287; Jan. 6; v. 270; p. 177.
Ansbacher, A. B. & Company, Inc., New York, N. Y. Insecticides and fungicides. No. 128,609; Jan. 13; v. 270; p. 335.
Ansehl, Benjamin, St. Louis, Mo. Preparation for beautifying the hands, arms, and neck. No. 128,288; Jan. 6; v. 270; p. 177.
Apex Hosiery Company, Philadelphia, Pa. Hosiery. No. 129,118; Jan. 27; v. 270; p. 613.
Apex Steel Co. Ltd., The, Sheffield, England. Steel. Nos. 129,119-20; Jan. 27; v. 270; p. 613.
Apperson Bros. Automobile Co., Kokomo, Ind. Pleasure-automobiles and motor-trucks. No. 128,922; Jan. 20; v. 270; p. 471.
Apsley Rubber Company, Hudson, Mass. Shoes and rubber footwear. No. 128,610-11; Jan. 13; v. 270; p. 335.
Arcadian Waukesha Spring Company, Waukesha, Wis. Non-alcoholic beverages. No. 128,289; Jan. 6; v. 270; p. 177.
Armor-Clad Boy's Clothes Co., New York, N. Y. Children's and boys' clothes, suits, overcoats, and pants. No. 129,109; Jan. 20; v. 270; p. 477.
Armstrong Cork Company, Pittsburgh, Pa. Bottle and prescription corks. No. 128,290; Jan. 6; v. 270; p. 177.
Armstrong Cork Company, Pittsburgh, Pa. Corks. No. 128,612; Jan. 13; v. 270; p. 335.
Armstrong Cork Company, Pittsburgh, Pa. Oiled duck. No. 128,924; Jan. 20; v. 270; p. 471.
Arons, Louis, Chicago, Ill. Garment-supports. No. 128,923; Jan. 20; v. 270; p. 471.
Arrol-Johnston Limited, Heathhall, Dumfries, Scotland. Internal-combustion engines. No. 129,121; Jan. 27; v. 270; p. 613.
A/S, Herman A. Kähler, Næstved, Denmark. Crockery, earthenware, porcelain. No. 129,007; Jan. 20; v. 270; p. 474.
Aterite, M. H., Company Inc., New York, N. Y. Pipe-fittings, valves, &c. No. 129,122; Jan. 27; v. 270; p. 613.
Atlanta Barbers' Supply Co., The, Atlanta, Ga. Hair-tonic, &c. Nos. 128,291-2; Jan. 6; v. 270; p. 177.
Atlanta Paper Company, Atlanta, Ga. Paper bags. Nos. 128,293-4; Jan. 6; v. 270; p. 177.
Atterbury Motor Car Company, Buffalo, N. Y. Motor-trucks and parts. No. 128,925; Jan. 20; v. 270; p. 471.
Auto-Ordnance Corporation, New York, N. Y. Shoulder-rifles. No. 128,926; Jan. 20; v. 270; p. 471.
Automotive Supply Company, Dallas, Tex. Adhesives. No. 128,295; Jan. 6; v. 270; p. 177.
Aydelotte, William M., New York, N. Y. Temporary letter-files and loose-leaf binders and sheet-holding attachments therefor. No. 128,296; Jan. 6; v. 270; p. 177.
Ayotte, Joseph R., Chicago, Ill. Spark-plug. No. 128,613; Jan. 13; v. 270; p. 335.
Back Creek Valley Orchard Company, Hedgesville, W. Va. Fresh peaches, canned apples, peaches, tomatoes, and beans. No. 128,927; Jan. 20; v 270; p. 471.
Badenoch, J. J., Co., Chicago, Ill. Cattle food. No. 129,123; Jan. 27; v. 270; p. 613.
Bahr, Leopold, Brooklyn, N. Y. Antiseptic for cleansing the teeth. No. 128,614; Jan. 13; v. 270; p. 335.

Baker-Overton Company, Dallas, Tex. Waterproof dressing for textiles, &c. No. 128,928; Jan. 20; v. 270; p. 471.
Baker, R. & L., Company, The, Cleveland, Ohio. Automobiles. No. 128,297; Jan. 6; v. 270; p. 177.
Balinky, Abraham, New York, N. Y. Embroidering-machines. No. 128,298; Jan. 6; v. 270; p. 177.
Baltimore Bargain House, Baltimore and Cumberland, Md. Work-shirts. No. 128,615; Jan. 13; v. 270; p. 335.
Bankers Supply Co., The, Denver, Colo., and Chicago, Ill. Safety-paper. Nos. 128,299-300; Jan. 6; v. 270; p. 177.
Barber, Bessie L., Los Angeles, Calif. Toilet creams, face-bleach, &c. No. 128,616; Jan. 13; v. 270; p. 336.
Barbour Brothers Co., Paterson, N. J. Linen thread. No. 128,617; Jan. 13; v 270; p. 336.
Baron, Alexander, Brooklyn, N. Y. Toy-watch dials and cases. No. 128,301; Jan. 6; v. 270; p. 177.
Barr, F. E. & Company, Chicago, Ill. Antiseptic liquid. No. 128,618; Jan. 13; v. 270; p. 336.
Barrett Company, New York, N. Y. Ready-mixed paint. No. 128,929; Jan. 20; v. 270; p. 471.
Bartlett, Stephen L., Company, Boston, Mass. Cocoa and chocolate. No. 128,302; Jan. 6; v. 270; p. 178.
Basket Stores Company, Omaha, Nebr. Coffee. No. 128,305; Jan. 6; v. 270; p. 178.
Basket Stores Co., Omaha, Nebr. Foods. Nos. 128,303-4; Jan. 6; v. 270; p. 178.
Bass, Rubin, New York, N. Y. Press-boards. No. 128,306; Jan. 6; v. 270; p. 178.
Baum, W. A., Co., Inc., New York, N. Y. Sphygmomanometers. No. 128,307; Jan. 6; v. 270; p. 178.
Bear-Cat Products Co., Inc., The, Oklahoma, Okla. Radiator-connection. No. 128,619; Jan. 13; v. 270; p. 336.
Beaudette & Graham Engineering Co., Boston, Mass. Electric-lighting plants. No. 128,620; Jan. 13; v. 270; p. 336.
Beddoes, Joseph G., Birmingham, England. Locks. No. 128,930; Jan. 20; v. 270; p. 471.
Beech-Nut Packing Corporation, Canajoharie, N. Y. Gingerale. No. 128,621; Jan. 13; v. 270; p. 336.
Bell & Howell Co., Chicago, Ill. Motion-picture-producing apparatus. No. 129,124; Jan. 27; v. 270; p. 613.
Bell Pump & Manufacturing Co., Detroit, Mich. Automobile air-pumps and oil-pumps and grease-cups. No. 128,622; Jan. 13; v. 270; p. 336.
Benekos, William J., Chicago, Ill. Non-alcoholic beverages. No. 128,308; Jan. 6; v. 270; p. 178.
Benn, Joseph, & Sons Inc., Greystone, R. I., and New York, N. Y. Cotton and mohair piece goods, &c. No. 128,623; Jan. 13; v. 270; p. 336.
Benson, Nina D., Memphis, Tenn. Laxative medicine. No 128,624; Jan. 13; v. 270; p. 336.
Berlault, Joseph B., Seattle, Wash. Hair-tonic. No. 128,625; Jan 13; v. 270; p. 336.
Berry & Lewis, New York, N. Y. Fuel control for internal-combustion engines. No. 128,627; Jan. 13; v. 270; p. 336.
Berry, Joseph, Binghamton, N. Y. Cream or salve for congestion and inflammation. No. 128,626; Jan. 13; v. 270; p. 336.
Berthe May, Inc., New York, N. Y. Obstetric belts. No. 128,454; Jan. 6; v. 270; p. 182.
Bickell, David A., assignor to San-tro-pas Manufacturing Company, Limited, Lethbridge, Alberta, Canada. Healing compounds. No. 128,628; Jan. 13; v. 270; p. 336.
Binghamton Candy Co., Binghamton, N. Y. Confectionery. No. 128,629; Jan. 13; v. 270; p. 336.
Birrell Silent Motor Co. Inc., Chicago, Ill. Valves for internal-combustion engines. No. 128,630; Jan. 13; v. 270; p. 336.
Bitrose Co., Milwaukee, Wis. Candies. No. 128,309; Jan. 6; v. 270; p. 178.
Black Cat Textile Company, Kenosha, Wis. Knitted underwear. No. 128,585; Jan. 6; v. 270; p. 186.
Blair, J. C., Company, Huntington, Pa. Paper, envelops, tablets, blank books. No. 128,311; Jan. 6; v. 270; p. 178.
Blair, J. C., Company, Huntington, Pa. Paper for writing, envelops for correspondence and writing-tablets. No. 128,310; Jan. 6; v. 270; p. 178.
Blatchford Calf Meal Company, Waukegan, Ill. Compound ground feed for rabbits, &c. No. 128,631; Jan. 13; v. 270; p. 336.
Blatchford Calf Meal Company, Waukegan, Ill. Feeds for animals and poultry. No. 128,632; Jan. 13; v. 270; p. 336.
Blemo Company, The, Canton, Ohio. Ointment for pimples, blackheads, tetter, itch, &c. No. 128,315; Jan. 6; v. 270; p. 178.
Block & Drexler, New York, N. Y.; said Drexler assignor to said Block. Men's neckties and scarfs. No. 128,633; Jan. 13; v. 270; p. 336.
Bloom, Abram, Co., Inc., Paterson, N. J. Thrown silk. No. 128,634; Jan. 13; v. 270; p. 336.
Blubuck Manufacturing Co., Hopkinsville, Ky. Overalls and work-shirts. No. 129,125; Jan. 27; v. 270; p. 613.
Bludwine Company, Athens, Ga. Non-alcoholic beverages and flavoring and syrups for making same. No. 128,312; Jan. 6; v. 270; p. 178.
Blum Brothers, Chicago, Ill. Clothing. No. 129,126; Jan. 27; v. 270; p. 613.
Bodinson-Terrell Candy Co., Chicago, Ill. Candy. No. 128,635; Jan. 13; v. 270; p. 336.

Bommer, Emil, Brooklyn, N. Y. Builders' hardware. No. 129,127; Jan. 27; v. 270; p. 613.
Bonheur Co. Inc., Syracuse, N. Y. Toilet water. No. 128,636; Jan. 13; v. 270; p. 336.
Booth & Platt Co., Bridgeport, Conn. Ginger-beer. No. 128,637; Jan. 13; v. 270; p. 336.
Borden Company, The, New York, N. Y. Condensed milk. Nos. 128,931-2; Jan. 20; v. 270; p. 471.
Borden Company, The, New York, N. Y. Condensed milk. Nos. 128,934-41; Jan. 20; v. 270; pp. 471-2.
Borden Company, The, New York, N. Y. Confectionery. No. 128,933; Jan. 20; v. 270; p. 471.
Borden's Condensed Milk Company, New York, N. Y. Condensed milk. No. 128,313; Jan. 6; v. 270; p. 178.
Borden's Farm Products Company, Inc., Wassaic and New York, N. Y. Foods and ingredients of food. No. 128,942; Jan. 20; v. 270; p. 472.
Bowers, Otho D., Richmond, Ind. Spark-plugs. No. 128,638; Jan. 13; v. 270; p. 336.
Bowman, W. P., Leeds, England. Sauce for fish, game, &c. No. 128,943; Jan. 20; v. 270; p. 472.
Bradford, Albert S., Placentia, Calif. Fresh citrus fruits. No. 128,944; Jan. 20; v. 270; p. 472.
Bradley, Milton, Company, Springfield, Miss. Games of jack-straws. No. 128,945; Jan. 20; v. 270; p. 472.
Bradley & Vrooman Company, Chicago, Ill. Germicide. No. 128,640; Jan. 13; v. 270; p. 336.
Bradley, Willis C., Marshfield, Oreg. Medicinal preparation for the treatment of catarrh, &c. No. 128,639; Jan. 13; v. 270; p. 336.
Brener, J., Co., Boston, Mass. Ladies' petticoats. No. 128,641; Jan. 13; v. 270; p. 336.
Brigham-Hopkins Company, Baltimore, Md. Men's hats. No. 128,648; Jan. 13; v. 270; p. 336.
Britton, Cutadore, Tampa, Fla. Blood-purifier. No. 128,314; Jan. 6; v. 270; p. 178.
Brohard, Georgie M., Philadelphia, Pa. Rouge. No. 128,643; Jan. 13; v. 270; p. 336.
Brooklyn, Shield & Rubber Co., Brooklyn, N. Y. Women's dress-shields. No. 128,644; Jan. 13; v. 270; p. 336.
Brooks, D. E., & Co., Newburgh, N. Y. Foods. No. 128,316; Aug. 19; v. 270; p. 178.
Brooks Tomato Products Company, Collinsville, Ill. Tabasco-flavor catsup. No. 128,946; Jan. 20; v. 270; p. 472.
Brown Instrument Company, The, Philadelphia, Pa. Protecting-tubes for pyrometers. No. 129,129; Jan. 27; v. 270; p. 613.
Brown, L. L., Paper Company, Adams, Mass. Paper. No. 128,318; Jan. 6; v. 270; p. 178.
Browne, Henry V., Tonkawa, Okla. Tractor-cabs. No. 129,128; Jan. 27; v. 270; p. 613.
Buell, George C., & Company, Rochester, N. Y. Tea. No. 128,319; Jan. 6; v. 270; p. 178.
Bullen, Joseph W., Folcroft, Pa. Disinfectant. Nos. 128,947-8; Jan. 20; v. 270; p. 472.
Burns, William S., Grand Rapids, Mich. Laundry soap. No. 128,320; Jan. 6; v. 270; p. 178.
Burton, Frederick D., New York, N. Y. Incense. No. 128,321; Jan. 6; v. 270; p. 178.
Byron Weston Co., Dalton, Mass. Writing-paper. No. 128,949; Jan. 20; v. 270; p. 472.
C and E Shoe Company, The, Columbus, Ohio. Leather shoes. No. 129,130; Jan. 27; v. 270; p. 613.
Cable Draper Baking Co., Detroit, Mich. Bread. No. 128,322; Jan. 6; v. 270; p. 178.
Cadwallader, Harry, Jr., Philadelphia, Pa. Steel forgings and castings. No. 128,645; Jan. 13; v. 270; p. 336.
Cadwallader, Harry, Jr., Philadelphia, Pa. Cutlery, machinery, tools, and parts. No. 128,950; Jan. 20; v. 270; p. 472.
California Packing Corporation, San Francisco, Calif. Canned vegetables and fruits, &c. No. 128,951; Jan. 20; v. 270; p. 472.
California Packing Corporation, San Francisco, Calif. Canned vegetables and fruits, dried cruities, jellies, &c. No. 129,131; Jan. 27; v. 270; p. 613.
Campbell, John, & Co., New York, N. Y. Aniline colors and coal-tar dyes. No. 128,952; Jan. 20; v. 270; p. 472.
Car-Bo-Thymol Company, Atlanta, Ga. Medicated oil for catarrhal conditions of the nose, throat, and bronchi. No. 128,323; Jan. 6; v. 270; p. 178.
Carner, George T., Fulton, N. Y. Salve. No. 128,954; Jan. 20; v. 270; p. 472.
Cascade Cider Company, Springville, N. Y. Vinegar. No. 128,646; Jan. 13; v. 270; p. 336.
Castello, Edward B., Chicago, Ill. Liniment. No. 128,955; Jan. 20; v. 270; p. 472.
Castine Bay Company, Castine, Me. Sardines. No. 128,324; Jan. 6; v. 270; p. 178.
Cataract Chemical Company, Inc., Buffalo, N. Y. Chemicals for use in the manufacture of leather. No. 128,647; Jan. 13; v. 270; p. 337.
Caumont, Leon F., New York, N. Y. Necktie former and holder. No. 129,132; Jan. 27; v. 270; p. 613.
Cement-Gun Company, Inc., Allentown, Pa., and New York, N. Y. Certain named machines and parts thereof. No. 128,325; Jan. 6; v. 270; p. 178.
Chain Shirt Shops, Inc., New York, N. Y. Men's shirts, underwear, &c. No. 128,648; Jan. 13; v. 270; p. 337.
Challoner Company, Oshkosh, Wis. Bars, plates, and bolts for securing antiskid-chains to vehicle wheels. No. 129,133; Jan. 27; v. 270; p. 613.

Chaney Manufacturing Company, The, Springfield, Ohio. Thermometers, barometers, rain-gages. No. 128,956; Jan. 20; v. 270; p. 472.

Chapin & Company, Hammond, Ind., and Chicago, Ill. Mixed live-stock feed. No. 128,326; Jan. 6; v. 270; p. 178.

Chapin & Company, Hammond, Ind., and Chicago, Ill. Dairy and stock feed. No. 128,327; Jan. 6; v. 270; p. 178.

Chaplin, Ivan C., Indianapolis, Ind. Non-alcoholic syrup and beverage made therefrom. No. 128,328; Jan. 6; v. 270; p. 178.

Chapman, Frank, Providence, R. I. Soldering kits. No. 128,329; Jan. 6; v. 270; p. 178.

Chattanooga Medicine Co., Chattanooga, Tenn. Medicine for female diseases. No. 128,649; Jan. 13; v. 270; p. 337.

Chemische Werke vorm. Dr. Heinrich Byk, Oranienburg, near Berlin, Germany. Medicinal preparations. No. 128,330; Jan. 6; v. 270; p. 178.

Chinook Lumber & Shingle Co., Seattle, Wash. Shingles. No. 128,650; Jan. 13; v. 270; p. 337.

Chipman Knitting Mills, Easton, Pa. Hosiery. No. 128,331; Jan. 6; v. 270; p. 178.

Chipman Knitting Mills, Easton, Pa. Hosiery. No. 129,134; Jan. 27; v. 270; p. 613.

Christenson, Hanify & Weatherwax, San Francisco, Calif. Canned pears, salmon, and tomatoes. No. 128,652; Jan. 13; v. 270; p. 337.

Christenson, Hanify & Weatherwax, San Francisco, Calif. Canned salmon, peaches, and tomatoes. No. 128,651; Jan. 13; v. 270; p. 337.

City Consumers Co., Paducah, Ky. Ice-cream, butter, milk, &c. No. 128,653; Jan. 13; v. 270; p. 337.

Cleveland Brass Manufacturing Co., The, Cleveland, Ohio. Castings and forgings. No. 129,135; Jan. 27; v. 270; p. 613.

Cleveland Metal Products Company, Cleveland, Ohio. Enameled steel ware. No. 129,136; Jan. 27; v. 270; p. 613.

Cleveland Osborn Manufacturing Company, Cleveland, Ohio. Wire brushes. No. 128,332; Jan. 6; v. 270; p. 178.

Cifuzzi, Ralph, New York, N. Y. Perfumes, powders, &c. No. 128,957; Jan. 20; v. 270; p. 472.

Cobden Co. Inc., New York, N. Y. Ladies' blouses. No. 129,137; Jan. 27; v. 270; p. 614.

Coe - Stapley Manufacturing Corporation, Bridgeport, Conn. Automobile and bicycle pumps. No. 128,333; Jan. 6; v. 270; p. 178.

Cohen, Charles S., Newark, N. J. Preparation for the amelioration of pyorrhea, &c. No. 128,654; Jan. 13; v. 270; p. 337.

Cohen, Nathan B., Scranton, Pa. Veils. No. 128,958; Jan. 20; v. 270; p. 472.

Collins, A. M., Manufacturing Company, Philadelphia, Pa. Printing coated paper, &c. No. 128,334; Jan. 6; v. 270; p. 178.

Colorado Milling & Elevator Co., Denver, Colo., and Weiser, Idaho. Wheat-flour. No. 128,655; Jan. 13; v. 270; p. 337.

Columbia Produce Company, Columbia, Nashville, Waverly, McEwen, Dickson, Loretto, Lawrenceburg, Fayetteville, Petersburg, Chapel Hill, and Lewisburg, Tenn. Dressed poultry, butter, eggs. No. 128,856; Jan. 13; v. 270; p. 337.

Columbian Rope Company, Auburn, N. Y. Twine. No. 128,335; Jan. 6; v. 270; p. 178.

Colwell Cooperage Company, Inc., New York, N. Y. Barrels, kegs, tubs, &c. No. 128,336; Jan. 6; v. 270; p. 179.

Colwell Cooperage Company, Inc., New York, N. Y. Receptacles and parts thereof. No. 128,337; Jan. 6; v. 270; p. 179.

Commercial Shirt Company, New York, N. Y. Cotton and silk piece goods. No. 128,338; Jan. 6; v. 270; p. 179.

Community Furnace Company, Covington, Ky. Hot-air furnaces. No. 128,657; Jan. 13; v. 270; p. 337.

Consolidated Wafer Company, New York, N. Y., and Chicago, Ill. Ice-cream cones. No. 128,959; Jan. 20; v. 270; p. 472.

Continental Drug Corporation, St. Louis, Mo. Hypophosphites compound and a non-alcoholic tonic. No. 128,658; Jan. 13; v. 270; p. 337.

Cook, C. R., Paint Company, Kansas City, Mo. Creosote-oil used as a wood-preservative. No. 128,339; Jan. 6; v. 270; p. 179.

Coonan, John. (See Roche, John, assignor.)

Cooper, Coate & Casey Dry Goods Co., Los Angeles, Calif., and New York, N. Y. Garments. No. 128,659; Jan. 13; v. 270; p. 337.

Coppus Engineering and Equipment Company, Worcester, Mass. Hydraulic and centrifugal pumps and turbines. No. 128,660; Jan. 13; v. 270; p. 337.

Corn Belt Packing Company, Dubuque, Iowa. Ham, bacon, &c. No. 128,960; Jan. 20; v. 270; p. 472.

Cornwell, G. G., & Son, Inc., Washington, D. C. Ice-cream cones. No. 128,340; Jan. 6; v. 270; p. 179.

Coward, Albert T. H., Sheffield, England. Cutlery, machinery, and tools, and parts. No. 128,962; Jan. 20; v. 270; p. 472.

Cox, Irwin W., Chicago, Ill. Cleanser and polish. No. 128,961; Jan. 20; v. 270; p. 472.

Cramer, John F., Freeport, Ill. Canned fruits and vegetables, tea, &c. No. 128,341; Jan. 6; v. 270; p. 179.

Crane, Clarence A., Cleveland, Ohio. Candy. No. 128,661; Jan. 13; v. 270; p. 337.

Crane & Co., Dalton and Westfield, Mass. Writing-paper. No. 128,342; Jan. 6; v. 270; p. 179.

Crawford, James J., Los Angeles, Calif. Dried parts of ephedra-plant. No. 128,662; Jan. 13; v. 270; p. 337.

Crawford, McGregor & Canby Company, The, Dayton, Ohio. Golf-clubs. No. 128,963; Jan. 20; v. 270; p. 472.

Creotina Chemical Company, St. Louis, Mo. Remedy for cuts, bruises, burns, sprains, &c. No. 128,666; Jan. 13; v. 270; p. 337.

Cresca Company, New York, N. Y. Foods. No. 128,964; Jan. 20; v. 270; p. 472.

Crescent Coffee Mills, Inc., New Orleans, La. Coffee. No. 128,343; Jan. 6; v. 270; p. 179.

Crescent Coffee Mills, Inc., New Orleans, La. Coffee. Nos. 128,663-4; Jan. 13; v. 270; p. 337.

Crescent Coffee Mills, Inc., New Orleans, La. Tea. No. 128,665; Jan. 13; v. 270; p. 337.

Crescent Coffee Mills, Inc., New Orleans, La. Coffee. No. 128,667; Jan. 13; v. 270; p. 337.

Crescent Oil Co., Indianapolis, Ind. Cutting oils. No. 128,344; Jan. 6; v. 270; p. 179.

Crescent-Refractories Company, Curwensville, Pa. Fire-brick and tile for metallurgical furnaces. No. 128,345; Jan. 6; v. 270; p. 179.

Crocker Broom & Brush Co., Chicago, Ill. Brooms. Nos. 129,346-9; Jan. 6; v. 270; p. 179.

Crooks, Abe, Toledo, Ohio. Transparent coating preparations for glass, &c. No. 128,350; Jan. 6; v. 270; p. 179.

Crown Overall Manufacturing Company, Cincinnati, Ohio. Overalls. No. 128,351; Jan. 6; v. 270; p. 179.

Crucible Steel Company of America, Pittsburgh, Pa. Steel bars, rods, billets, &c. Nos. 129,138-42; Jan. 27; v. 270; p. 614.

Crusellas, Alberto, Habana, Cuba. Perfumes. No. 128,668; Jan. 13; v. 270; p. 337.

Curtin, John, Corp., New York, N. Y. Ice, coal, workmen's kit, &c., bags. No. 128,353; Jan. 6; v. 270; p. 179.

Curtin, John, Corp., New York, N. Y. Finished sails, truck and auto covers. No. 129,143; Jan. 27; v. 270; p. 614.

Cushman, Wm. C., New York, N. Y. Chocolate syrup. No. 128,352; Jan. 6; v. 270; p. 179.

Cyclone Grate-Bar Co., Buffalo, N. Y. Grate-bar for use with furnaces and stoves. No. 129,144; Jan. 27; v. 270; p. 614.

Damaske, William, Seattle, Wash. Insecticides. No. 128,672; Jan. 13; v. 270; p. 337.

Dannenhirsch, Max, Philadelphia, Pa. Compound for stopping leaks in radiators, boilers, &c. No. 128,669; Jan. 13; v. 270; p. 337.

Darwin & Milner, Inc., New York, N. Y. Compound anhydrous salts. No. 128,354; Jan. 6; v. 270; p. 179.

Darwin & Milner, Inc., New York, N. Y. Bar-steel and steel castings. No. 129,145; Jan. 27; v. 270; p. 614.

Dash, Allan J., Olean, N. Y. Medicinal balm for inflammations. No. 128,673; Jan. 13; v. 270; p. 337.

Davidson, Arthur C., New York, N. Y. Steel. No. 128,670; Jan. 13; v. 270; p. 337.

Davies, William, Company, Limited, Chicago, Ill. Bacon, hams, lard, &c. No. 128,355; Jan. 6; v. 270; p. 179.

Davies, William, Company, Chicago, Ill. Foods and ingredients of food. No. 128,965; Jan. 20; v. 270; p. 472.

Davies, William, Company, Chicago, Ill. Bacon, sausage, and canned lunch-tongue, &c. No. 128,966; Jan. 20; v. 270; p. 472.

Davies, William, Company, Limited, Chicago, Ill. Foods and ingredients of food. No. 128,967; Jan. 20; v. 270; p. 472.

De Laval Separator Company, New York, N. Y. Pneumatic pumps. No. 128,671; Jan. 13; v. 270; p. 337.

Denney Tag Company, West Chester, Pa. Shipping-tags. Nos. 128,356-60; Jan. 6; v. 270; p. 179.

De Nordiske Fabriker De-No-Fa Aktieselskab, Christiania, Norway. Fats. No. 128,861; Jan. 6; v. 270; p. 179.

Dery, George M., South Bethlehem, Pa. Cigarettes. No. 128,362; Jan. 6; v. 270; p. 179.

Des Moines Glove & Mfg. Company, Inc., Des Moines, Iowa. Gloves and mittens made of horsehide. No. 128,363; Jan. 6; v. 270; p. 179.

Detroit Automatic Scale Company, Detroit, Mich. Weighing-scales. No. 128,364; Jan. 6; v. 270; p. 179.

Detroit Heating & Lighting Company, Detroit, Mich. Bunsen burners. No. 128,674; Jan. 13; v. 270; p. 337.

Dexter, Eugene A., Springfield, Mass. Bread. No. 129,146; Jan. 27; v. 270; p. 614.

Dickinson Drug Co., Los Angeles, Calif. Tonic, powders, ointment, and cream. No. 128,675; Jan. 13; v. 270; p. 337.

Diebolt Brewing Co., Cleveland, Ohio. Non-intoxicating beverage. No. 128,365; Jan. 6; v. 270; p. 179.

Dittlinger, H., Roller Mills Company, New Braunfels, Tex. Wheat-flour. No. 128,676; Jan. 13; v. 270; p. 337.

Dittlinger, H., Roller Mills Company, New Braunfels, Tex. Wheat-flour. No. 128,968; Jan. 20; v. 270; p. 472.

Dollfus-Mieg & Cie. Societe Anonyme, Mulhouse, Germany. Threads and yarns made of wool. No. 129,147; Jan. 27; v. 270; p. 614.

Domestic Engineering Company, The, Dayton, Ohio. Current generating and distributing system for lighting and power purposes. No. 129,148; Jan. 27; v. 270; p. 614.

Donmeyer, Gardner Co., Peoria, Ill. Wheat-flour. No. 129,149 ; Jan. 27 ; v. 270 ; p. 614.

Dothan Syrup Co., Dothan, Ala. Corn and cane syrup. No. 128,866 ; Jan. 6 ; v. 270 ; p. 179.

Douglass Barnes Corporation, New York, N. Y. Ladies' sport-coats, sweaters, slip-ons, &c. No. 128,969 ; Jan. 20 ; v. 270 ; p. 472.

Dourde et Cie., Paris, France. Barometers. No. 129,150 ; Jan. 27 ; v. 270 ; p. 614.

Drobinski, Felix L., Brooklyn, N. Y. Eye-wash. No. 128,677 ; Jan. 13 ; v. 270 ; p. 337.

Dugas-Hundley Corporation, New York, N. Y. Dyes. No. 128,678 ; Jan. 13 ; v. 270 ; p. 338.

Duplex Engine-Governor Company, Inc., Brooklyn, N. Y. Governors for engines. No. 129,970 ; Jan. 20 ; v. 270 ; p. 472.

East Iron & Machine Co., The, Lima, Ohio. Dough-mixers. No. 129,151 ; Jan. 27 ; v. 270 ; p. 614.

Eastern Felt Company, Winchester, Mass. Felt polishing-wheels. No. 128,367 ; Jan. 6 ; v. 270 ; p. 179.

Eastman Kodak Company, Rochester, N. Y. Adjustable camera-supporting clamps and tripod-adapters. No. 128,368 ; Jan. 6 ; v. 270 ; p. 179.

Eastwood Wire Manufacturing Company, Belleville, N. J. Ingots of bronze, Babbitt metal, &c. No. 129,152 ; Jan. 27 ; v. 270 ; p. 614.

Eckerson Company, Jersey City, N. J. Oleomargarin. No. 128,369 ; Jan. 6 ; v. 270 ; p. 179.

Edgerton Salt Brick Company, Goldsboro, N. C., and Atlanta, Ga. Salt brick. No. 128,973 ; Jan. 13 ; v. 270 ; p. 338.

Ehrlick, H., & Sons Mfg. Co., St. Joseph, Mo. Pickling compound for meats. No. 128,680 ; Jan. 13 ; v. 270 ; p. 338.

Electric & Ordnance Accessories Company Limited, Birmingham, England. Electric heaters, cookers, &c. No. 128,681 ; Jan. 13 ; v. 270 ; p. 338.

Electric Phonograph Corporation, New York, N. Y. Combination phonograph and lamp-stand. No. 128,971 ; Jan. 20 ; v. 270 ; p. 472.

Electropure Dairy Company, Wilmington, Del., and Chicago, Ill. Milk. No. 128,972 ; Jan. 20 ; v. 270 ; p. 472.

Elgin Stove & Oven Co., Elgin, Ill. Gas, coal, and oil stoves or ovens. No. 128,370 ; Jan. 6 ; v. 270 ; p. 180.

Ely & Walker D. G. Co., St. Louis, Mo. Hosiery, underwear, &c. No. 128,973 ; Jan. 20 ; v. 270 ; p. 473.

Embalmers' Supply Co., Westport, Conn. Embalming fluid. No. 128,371 ; Jan. 6 ; v. 270 ; p. 180.

Emmerling Products Company, Johnstown, Pa. Ginger-ale. No. 128,974 ; Jan. 20 ; v. 270 ; p. 473.

Empire Rolling Screen Co., Inc., Rochester, N. Y. Window-screens. No. 128,682 ; Jan. 13 ; v. 270 ; p. 338.

Enders, Wm., Manufacturing Company, Walden, N. J. Sadirons, laundry-washing machines, and clothes-wringers. No. 128,372 ; Jan. 6 ; v. 270 ; p. 180.

Enlow Co., Inc., New York, N. Y. Stationery. No. 128,683 ; Jan. 13 ; v. 270 ; p. 338.

Entire Wheat Bread Company, St. Louis, Mo. Bread. No. 128,684 ; Jan. 13 ; v. 270 ; p. 338.

Eppolito, Frank, Chicago, Ill. Hair-tonic. No. 128,685 ; Jan. 13 ; v. 270 ; p. 338.

Esleeck Manufacturing Co., Turners Falls, Mass. Bond-paper, non-carbonized type-writer and manifold papers, &c. No. 128,686 ; Jan. 13 ; v. 270 ; p. 338.

Esleeck Manufacturing Co., Turners Falls, Mass. Bond, &c., paper. No. 128,687 ; Jan. 13 ; v. 270 ; p. 338.

Esleeck Manufacturing Company, Turners Falls, Mass. Bond, typewriter, &c., paper. No. 128,373 ; Jan. 6 ; v. 270 ; p. 180.

Essex Chemical Works, Inc., Belleville, N. J. Fur black, &c., dyes. No. 128,688 ; Jan. 13 ; v. 270 ; p. 338.

Essex Laboratories Inc., Newark, N. J. Cleaning compound. No. 128,689 ; Jan. 13 ; v. 270 ; p. 338.

Everlastik, Incorporated, Boston, Mass. Elastic bandages. No. 128,374 ; Jan. 6 ; v. 270 ; p. 180.

Everwear Mfg. Co., San Francisco, Calif. Children's play-suits, men's overalls and overshirts. No. 128,690 ; Jan. 13 ; v. 270 ; p. 338.

Express Spark Plug Corporation, Washington, D. C. Spark-plugs. No. 128,691 ; Jan. 13 ; v. 270 ; p. 338.

Farmers Cotton Oil Co., Wilson, N. C. Prepared feed for stock. No. 128,375 ; Jan. 6 ; v. 270 ; p. 180.

Febeco Leather Corporation, Wilmington, Del., and New York, N. Y. Leather. No. 128,692 ; Jan. 13 ; v. 270 ; p. 338.

Federal Milling Company, Lockport, N. Y. Wheat-flour. No. 128,376 ; Jan. 6 ; v. 270 ; p.180.

Federal Snap Fastener Corporation, New York, N. Y. Snap and placket fasteners. No. 128,693 ; Jan. 13 ; v. 270 ; p. 338.

Fiat Metal Manufacturing Company, Chicago, Ill. Steel toilet partitions and drainage-fittings. No. 129,154 ; Jan. 27 ; v. 270 ; p. 614.

Fidelity Chocolate Company, Boston, Mass. Chocolates, bonbons, &c. No. 128,377 ; Jan. 6 ; v. 270 ; p. 180.

Filletin & Chochkoff Company, Milwaukee, Wis. Salve for sweaty feet. No. 128,975 ; Jan. 20 ; v. 270 ; p. 473.

Finch, Van Slyck & McConville, St. Paul, Minn. Men's overalls. No. 129,155 ; Jan. 27 ; v. 270 ; p. 614.

Finlay, Thomas, Auckland, New Zealand. Guide-rulers for scholastic purposes. No. 128,378 ; Jan. 6 ; v. 270 ; p. 180.

First Aid Extinguisher Co., New York, N. Y. Chemical fire-extinguishing compound. No. 128,379 ; Jan. 6 ; v. 270 ; p. 180.

Fisher, Frank J., Oconto, Wis. Non-alcoholic beverages. No. 129,156 ; Jan. 27 ; v. 270 ; p. 614.

Fisher, Lee, Mount Sterling, Ky. Medicine for scars, croup, &c. No. 128,694 ; Jan. 13 ; v. 270 ; p. 338.

Fisher, Robert J., Athens, Tenn. Hosiery. No. 128,695 ; Jan. 13 ; v. 270 ; p. 338.

Flaherty & Urbanowski Co., Peru, Ill. Canned foods and vanilla and lemon extracts. No. 129,157 ; Jan. 27 ; v. 270 ; p. 614.

Fleischmann's Vienna Model Bakery, (Inc.,) New York, N. Y. Doughnuts. No. 128,380 ; Jan. 6 ; v. 270 ; p. 180.

Fleitmann, Watjen & Co. Inc., New York, N. Y. Dried fruits, evaporated milk, canned fish, lard, &c. No. 128,381 ; Jan. 6 ; v. 270 ; p. 180.

Florein, Annie T., Cincinnati, Ohio. Preparation for treatment of female irregularities, &c. No. 128,696 ; Jan. 13 ; v. 270 ; p. 338.

Florin, Philip, New York, N. Y. Wallets, bill-folds, and three-folds of leather. No. 128,976 ; Jan. 20 ; v. 270 ; p. 473.

Foley & Company, Chicago, Ill. Medicines, salves, &c. No. 128,697 ; Jan. 13 ; v. 270 ; p. 338.

Foote Company, The, Nunda, N. Y. Caterpillar type of paving-mixers. No. 129,158 ; Jan. 27 ; v. 270 ; p. 614.

Forest Paper Company, Inc., New York, N. Y. Writing and printing bond-paper, &c. No. 128,977 ; Jan. 20 ; v. 270 ; p. 473.

Forest & Stream Publishing Co. Inc., New York, N. Y. Fishing rods and hooks. No. 128,382 ; Jan. 6 ; v. 270 ; p. 180.

Forged Products Co., Chicago, Ill. Unfinished and machined iron and steel forgings. No. 128,698 ; Jan. 13 ; v. 270 ; p. 338.

Francis, Frank L., Newark, N. J. Hair-tonics. No. 128,699 ; Jan. 13 ; v. 270 ; p. 338.

Frederick & Nelson, Seattle, Wash. Women's shoes. No. 128,700 ; Jan. 13 ; v. 270 ; p. 338.

French Valley Springs, Incorporated, Meadville, Pa. Ginger-ale. No. 128,701 ; Jan. 13 ; v. 270 ; p. 338.

Freund Bros. & Company, Inc., New York, N. Y. Pocket-books. No. 128,383 ; Jan. 6 ; v. 270 ; p. 180.

Fritz, Geo. H., & Sons, Inc., Newark, N. J. Fruit-flavored sugar candies. No. 128,384 ; Jan. 6 ; v. 270 ; p. 180.

Fulton Bros. Mfg. Co., Waukegan, Ill. Phonographs, motors for same, tone-arms, &c. No. 128,978 ; Jan. 20 ; v. 270 ; p. 473.

Fulton, W. G., Washington, D. C. Ironing-boards. No. 128,885 ; Jan. 6 ; v. 270 ; p. 180.

Funke, Jos. B., Company, La Crosse, Wis. Candy. No. 128,702 ; Jan. 13 ; v. 270 ; p. 338.

Fuqua, John B., Altus, Okla. Medicinal preparation for venereal diseases. No. 128,703 ; Jan. 13 ; v. 270 ; p. 338.

Gaillard, Ella M., New York, N. Y., and Washington, D. C. Dress-shields. No. 128,704 ; Jan. 13 ; v. 270 ; p. 338.

Galeton Dairy Products Co., Galeton, Pa. Condensed milk. No. 128,705 ; Jan. 13 ; v. 270 ; p. 338.

Gardner Bros., Memphis, Tenn. Dental casting-machines and parts of same, &c. No. 128,979 ; Jan. 20 ; v. 270 ; p. 473.

Gartenlaub, Eve, New York, N. Y. Corn cure. No. 128,706 ; Jan. 13 ; v. 270 ; p. 338.

Gas Products Co., Columbus, Ohio. Acetylene gas. No. 128,708 ; Jan. 13 ; v. 270 ; p. 338.

Gaskill Chemical Corporation, Brooklyn, N. Y. Fur-dyes. No. 128,707 ; Jan. 13 ; v. 270 ; p. 338.

Gates, William H., Norfolk, Va. Home-made candies and chocolates. No. 128,709 ; Jan. 13 ; v. 270 ; p. 338.

Gault, Herbert M., Baltimore, Md. Monuments and tombstones. No. 128,980 ; Jan. 20 ; v. 270 ; p. 473.

Gelarie, Saul, & Company, Brooklyn and New York, N. Y. Bloomers. No. 129,215 ; Jan. 27 ; v. 270 ; p. 616.

General Manufacturing Co., Sioux City, Iowa. Fountain-pens. No. 128,710 ; Jan. 6 ; v. 270 ; p. 180.

General Motors Corporation, Detroit, Mich. Electricity-generating units. No. 128,710 ; Jan. 13 ; v. 270 ; p. 338.

General Motors Corporation, New York, N. Y., and Harrison, N. J. Machinery and tools and parts. No. 128,981 ; Jan. 20 ; v. 270 ; p. 473.

General Ordnance Company, Derby, Conn. Tractors and parts thereof. No. 128,387 ; Jan. 6 ; v. 270 ; p. 180.

Geneva Cutlery Corporation, Geneva, N. Y. Razors. No. 128,388 ; Jan. 6 ; v. 270 ; p. 180.

Gerhold, Charles M., Philadelphia, Pa. Insecticides, disinfectants, and deodorizers. No. 128,711 ; Jan. 13 ; v. 270 ; p. 339.

Gibson, H. B., Co., Inc., New York, N. Y. Vessels for heating beverages. No. 128,712 ; Jan. 13 ; v. 270 ; p. 339.

Gilman, A., & Son, New York, N. Y. Infants' and children's garments. No. 128,889 ; Jan. 6 ; v. 270 ; p. 180.

Gilman, Theodore, Jr., New York, N. Y. Salicylic ointment. No. 128,982 ; Jan. 20 ; v. 270 ; p. 473.

Gilson, Bert D., Chicago, Ill. Automobile circulating-pumps. No. 128,890 ; Jan. 6 ; v. 270 ; p. 180.

Gimble Brothers, New York, N. Y. Talking-machines, violins, harps, &c. No. 128,983 ; Jan. 20 ; v. 270 ; p. 473.

Glantz, Charles, Arkville, N. Y. Camp, folding, and invalid chairs, &c. No. 128,984 ; Jan. 20 ; v. 270 ; p. 473.

Globe Grocery Stores, Inc., Brooklyn, N. Y. Foods and ingredients of food. No. 128,985 ; Jan. 20 ; v. 270 ; p. 473.

Goerz Flour Mills Co., Newton, Kans. Wheat-flour. No. 129,160 ; Jan. 27 ; v. 270 ; p. 614.

Golden Seal Laboratories, Inc., Parkensburg, W. Va. Effervescent salt combined with fruit derivatives. No. 128,713; Jan. 13; v. 270; p. 339.

Goldsmith, Charles A., New York, N. Y. Dolls. No. 128,891; Jan. 6; v. 270; p. 180.

Gonzalez Padin Co., San Juan, Porto Rico. Men's and boys' outer garments. No. 129,159; Jan. 27; v. 270; p. 614.

Goodman & Beer Company, Inc., New Orleans, La. Eggs. No. 128,714; Jan. 13; v. 270; p. 339.

Gould, Wilbert E., Denver, Colo. Non-alcoholic non-cereal maltless beverage. No. 129,161; Jan. 27; v. 270; p. 614.

Gouvea, A. S., & Co., New York, N. Y. Canned sardines. No. 128,392; Jan. 6; v. 270; p. 180.

Grace, W. R., & Co., New York, N. Y. Leather. No. 128,893; Jan. 6; v. 270; p. 180.

Grace, W. R. & Co., New York, N. Y. Boots and shoes. No. 127,715; Jan. 13; v. 270; p. 339.

Grace, W. R. & Co., New York, N. Y., and San Francisco, Calif. Dyes. No. 128,716; Jan. 13; v. 270; p. 339.

Graf, John, Co., Milwaukee, Wis. Non-alcoholic non-intoxicating soft drink. No. 128,986; Jan. 20; v. 270; p. 473.

Grand River Canning Company, Markesan, Wis. Canned vegetables. No. 128,987; Jan. 20; v. 270; p. 473.

Great Eastern Fisheries Corporation, Rockland, Me. Preserved or prepared codfish. No. 128,394; Jan. 6; v. 270; p. 180.

Great Western Alfalfa Milling Company, The, Denver, Colo. Live-stock and poultry feeds. No. 128,395; Jan. 6; v. 270; p. 180.

Greene, S. & M., Brooklyn, N. Y. Hair dressings and gloss, shampoo. No. 128,717; Jan. 13; v. 270; p. 339.

Grewen Fabric Co., Inc., Johnstown, N. Y. Dress-skirts. No. 128,718; Jan. 13; v. 270; p. 339.

Griffin, W. H., Company, Manchester, N. H. Men's, boys', and youths' leather shoes. No. 128,719; Jan. 13; v. 270; p. 389.

Hazemeyer Trading Company, New York, N. Y. Lubricating oils and greases. No. 128,896; Jan. 6; v. 270; p. 180.

Hall, G. Batcheller, Co., Seattle, Wash. Evaporated milk. No. 128,989; Jan. 20; v. 270; p. 473.

Hall, Hartwell & Co., Troy, N. Y. Clothing. No. 129,162; Jan. 27; v. 270; p. 614.

Hannibal Pharmacal Company, St. Louis, Mo. Antiseptic lotion for use as a depilatory. No. 128,897; Jan. 6; v. 270; p. 180.

Hansen Livestock & Feeding Company, Ogden, Utah. Foods for hogs, cattle, sheep, and poultry. No. 128,398; Jan. 6; v. 270; p. 180.

Hansen, O. C. M'f'g Co., Milwaukee, Wis. Gloves and mittens. No. 128,990; Jan. 20; v. 270; p. 473.

Hare, William L., New York, N. Y. Weeding-trowels. No. 128,720; Jan. 13; v. 270; p. 339.

Harrison, Levy, Philadelphia, Pa. Suits, coats, skirts, dresses. No. 128,721; Jan. 13; v. 270; p. 339.

Hart, Charles S., Film Company, New York, N. Y. Motion-picture films. No. 128,722; Jan. 13; v. 270; p. 339.

Hart, Louis H. C., St. Louis, Mo. White lead, zinc, and colors in oil, dry red lead. Nos. 128,991–5; Jan. 20; v. 270; p. 473.

Harvard Brewing Co., (now by change of name Harvard Company.) Lowell, Mass. Ginger-ale. No. 128,724; Jan. 13; v. 270; p. 339.

Harvard Company. (See Harvard Brewing Co.)

Harvard Company, Lowell, Mass. Cereal non-intoxicating malt beverage. No. 128,723; Jan. 13; v. 270; p. 339.

Harvard Company, Lowell, Mass. Cereal non-intoxicating malt beverage. No. 129,163; Jan. 27; v. 270; p. 614.

Harwood Counter Company, Lynn, Mass. Shoe-counters. No. 128,996; Jan. 20; v. 270; p. 473.

Hassler, Fred H., Manning, Iowa. Live hogs. No. 128,725; Jan. 13; v. 270; p. 339.

Hastings, Matthew R., New York Mills, N. Y. Bee-escapes. No. 128,399; Jan. 6; v. 270; p. 180.

Haynes Chemical Corporation, Richmond, Va. Insecticides, deodorizers, &c. No. 128,726; Jan. 13; v. 270; p. 339.

Haysson, E. R., Seneca Falls, N. Y. Goiter preparations. No. 128,400; Jan. 6; v. 270; p. 180.

Health Food Baking Co., Inc., Newport News, Va. Bread and cake. No. 128,727; Jan. 13; v. 270; p. 339.

Hearn, James A., & Son Inc., New York, N. Y. Ladies' hats. No. 129,164; Jan. 27; v. 270; p 614.

Heidelbauch, William W., Lancaster, Pa. Coal. No. 129,165; Jan 27; v. 270; p. 614.

Heine, Frederick W., New York, N. Y. Essential oils. No. 128,997; Jan. 20; v. 270; p. 473.

Heinrichs, Richard H., New York, N. Y. Ointment for external cancers, eczema, ulcers, &c. No. 128,586; Jan. 6; v. 270; p. 186.

Hendler Creamery Co., The, Baltimore, Md. Ice-cream, frozen custards, ices. No. 128,401; Jan. 6; v. 270; p. 180.

Hendry, Oscar W., Toronto, Ontario, Canada. Polish for furniture, &c. No. 128,998; Jan. 20; v. 270; p. 473.

Herbert, William U., Washington, D. C. Salve and ointment. No. 128,402; Jan. 6; v. 270; p. 180.

Herdman, W. H., Portland, Oreg. Medicine for indigestion. No. 128,999; Jan. 20; v. 270; p. 473.

Heywood Brothers and Wakefield Company, Gardner, Mass. Furniture. No. 128,728; Jan. 13; v. 270; p. 339.

High Rock Knitting Company, Philmont, N. Y. Underwear. No. 128,729; Jan. 13; v. 270; p. 339.

Hill, R. & J., Limited, London, England. Cigars, cigarettes, smoking-tobacco. No. 129,000; Jan. 20; v. 270; p. 473.

Hipolite Company, St. Louis, Mo. Marshmallow powder and lemon, &c., flavoring extracts. No. 128,730; Jan. 13; v. 270; p. 339.

Hoberg, John, Co., The, Green Bay, Wis. Toilet-paper, paper toweling. No. 128,403; Jan. 6; v. 270; p. 180.

Hoberg, John, Co., The, Green Bay, Wis. Toilet and wrapping paper, paper napkins and toweling. No. 128,404; Jan. 6; v. 270; p. 181.

Hoberg, John, Co., Green Bay, Wis. Toilet-paper, &c. No. 128,731; Jan. 13; p. 270; p. 339.

Hoberg, John, Co., The, Green Bay, Wis. Toilet and tissue paper, paper toweling and napkins. No. 129,001; Jan. 20; v. 270; p. 473.

Horbie & Johnson, Inc., Boston, Mass. Candies. No. 128,732; Jan. 13; v. 270; p. 339.

Holland Food Corporation, New York, N. Y. Condensed milk. No. 129,166; Jan. 27; v. 270; p. 614.

Holmes and Barnes, Ltd., Baton Rouge, La. Wheat-flour. No. 129,002; Jan. 20; v. 270; p. 473.

Holyoke Braiding Company, Holyoke, Mass. Shoe-laces. Nos. 128,733–4; Jan. 13; v. 270; p. 339.

Hoover Medicine Co., Des Moines, Iowa. Remedy for rheumatism, neuritis, &c. No. 128,735; Jan. 13; v. 270; p. 339.

Horowitz, Joseph, & Sons, Inc., New York, N. Y. Work-shirts. No. 128,736; Jan. 13; v. 270; p. 330.

Hoskins Manufacturing Company, Detroit, Mich. Alloys. Nos. 128,405–6; Jan. 6; v. 270; p. 181.

Hoskins Manufacturing Company, Detroit, Mich. Alloys containing nickel and aluminum. Nos. 128,737–8; Jan. 13; v. 270; p. 339.

Houlton, William L., Uneedus Farms, La. Dairy products—butter. No. 129,003; Jan. 20; v. 270; p. 473.

Howard, R. S., Company, New York, N. Y. Pianos and player-pianos. No. 129,004; Jan. 20; v. 270; p. 474.

Hutnikow, Theodore, Brooklyn, N. Y. Waterproof hand-bags and purses. No. 129,005; Jan. 20; v. 270; p. 474.

Ilex Optical Company, Rochester, N. Y. Photographic shutters and lenses. No. 129,167; Jan. 27; v. 270; p. 614.

Independent Pneumatic Tool Company, Chicago, Ill. Hose-couplings. No. 129,168; Jan. 27; v. 270; p. 614.

India Refining Company, Philadelphia, Pa. Cocoanut-oil. No. 128,739; Jan. 13; v. 270; p. 339.

Ingersoll-Rand Company, Jersey City, N. J., and New York, N. Y. Core-drills. No. 128,407; Jan. 6; v. 270; p. 181.

International Nickel Co., Constable Hook, N. J. Nickel and alloys containing nickel. No. 128,408; Jan. 6; v. 270; p. 181.

Irving Drew Co., Portsmouth, Ohio. Footwear. No. 129,169; Jan. 27; v. 270; p. 615.

Israel Underwear Co., Worcester, Mass. Underwear. No. 128,409; Jan. 6; v. 270; p. 181.

Iten Biscuit Co., Clinton, Iowa, and Omaha, Nebr. Cookies. No. 129,006; Jan. 20; v. 270; p. 474.

Jackoway and Katz Cap Co., St. Louis, Mo. Caps. No. 129,170; Jan. 27; v. 270; p. 615.

Jackson, Chas. H., Philadelphia, Pa. Metal roll-screens for windows, &c. No. 129,171; Jan. 27; v. 270; p. 615.

Jacobs Candy Company Ltd., New Orleans, La. Candy. No. 128,953; Jan. 20; v. 270; p. 472.

Jahn, W. K., Co., Brooklyn, N. Y. Flavoring for foods. No. 128,740; Jan. 13; v. 270; p. 339.

Jensen & Sons Milling & Grain Co., Nelson, Nebr. Wheat-flour. No. 128,741; Jan. 13; v. 270; p. 339.

Jimmy Quick Products Co., San Francisco, Calif. Cleansing compounds. No. 129,053; Jan. 20; v. 270; p. 475.

Johnson, B. L., & Co., Knoxville, Tenn. Caramels, chocolates, cream candies, &c. No. 128,410; Jan. 6; v. 270; p. 181.

Johnson, Charles H., Salem, Ohio. Medicine for tuberculosis. No. 128,742; Jan. 13; v. 270; p. 339.

Johnson, Mead. & Co., Evansville, Ind. Preparation for treating acidity and infant ailments. No. 128,743; Jan. 13; v. 270; p. 340.

Juster, Avram, New York, N. Y. Medicines for use as a stomach compound. No. 128,744; Jan. 13; v. 270; p. 340.

Justrite Mfg. Co., Chicago, Ill. Water-flow-controlling valves for carbid-lamps. No. 129,173; Jan. 27; v. 270; p. 615.

Kane, Henry, Brooklyn, N. Y. Ladies', misses', and children's hats. No. 129,174; Jan. 27; v. 270; p. 615.

Kane, Robert, Pittsburgh, Pa. Pharmaceutical preparation, blood-tea. No. 128,411; Jan. 6; v. 270; p. 180.

Kaplan, Charles M., Philadelphia, Pa. Leather shoes. No. 128,745; Jan. 13; v. 270; p. 340.

Kaut, Wm., Footwear Company, Carthage, Mo. Leather boots and shoes. No. 128,412; Jan. 6; v. 270; p. 181.

Kehlor Flour Mills Co., St. Louis, Mo. Wheat-flour. No. 128,413; Jan. 6; v. 270; p. 181.

Keller-Clifton Co., Seattle, Wash. Coatings for candies and cake. No. 128,746; Jan. 13; v. 270; p. 340.

Kellner Bros., New York, N. Y. Children's dresses. No. 128,747; Jan. 13; v. 270; p. 340.

Kemper, Charles H., Westport, Conn. Sheepskin, skivers, roans, and patent-leather. No. 128,414; Jan. 6; v. 270; p. 181.

Kennedy, Gussie M., Los Angeles, Calif. Sheet-metal-shaping machines. No. 129,008; Jan. 20; v. 270; p. 474.

Kettleman, Edward H., Independence, Kans. Salve. No. 128,748; Jan. 13; v. 270; p. 340.

Keystone Macaroni Company, Lebanon, Pa. Macaroni. No. 128,415; Jan. 6; v. 270; p. 181.

Kil-Tone Company, Vineland, N. J. Insecticide. No. 128,749; Jan. 13; v. 270; p. 340.

Kimberly-Clark Company, Neenah, Wis. Sanitary napkins. No. 128,416; Jan. 6; v. 270; p. 181.

King, Joseph S., Chicago, Ill. Ointment for treatment of skin diseases and piles. No. 128,750; Jan. 13; v. 270; p. 340.

Kingman, Russell B., West Orange, N. J. Ginger-ale. No. 129,175; Jan. 27; v. 270; p. 615.

Kirchheimer Bros. Co., Chicago, Ill. Wrapping-paper. No. 128,751; Jan. 13; v. 270; p. 340.

Kienaseptic Manufacturing Company, Columbus, Ohio. wall-paper-cleaner compounds. Nos. 128,417-18; Jan. 6; v. 270; p. 181.

Klor Early Co., Inc., Bluefield, W. Va. Aspirin. No. 128,419; Jan. 6; v. 270; p. 181.

Knudsen Laboratory, Los Angeles, Calif. Culture of *Bacillus bulgaricus* and milk fermented with same. No. 128,420; Jan. 6; v. 270; p. 181.

Koken Barbers' Supply Company, St. Louis, Mo. Barbers' chairs. No. 129,009; Jan. 20; v. 270; p. 474.

Koppel Industrial Car & Equipment Company, Koppel and Pittsburgh, Pa. Steam-locomotives, bucket excavators, &c. No. 128,752; Jan. 13; v. 270; p. 340.

Kouri, Michel J., New York, N. Y. Wheat-flour. No. 129,010; Jan. 20; v. 270; p. 474.

Kramer, Louis W., Denver, Colo. Chemical compound to be placed in bowl of tobacco-pipe to counteract nicotin. No. 129,011; Jan. 20; v. 270; p. 474.

Krause, Chas. A., Milling Co., Greenfield, Wis. Stock feed. No. 128,753; Jan. 13; v. 270; p. 340.

Krause, Chas. A., Milling Co., Greenfield, Wis. Poultry feed. No. 129,012; Jan. 20; v. 270; p. 474.

Krieg Wallace & McQuaide, Charleston, W. Va. Stomach and liver tablets. No. 128,754; Jan. 13; v. 270; p. 340.

Kuhlman & Chambliss Co., Inc., Knoxville, Tenn. Chemicals, medicines, &c. No. 129,013; Jan. 20; v. 270; p. 474.

Kuppenheimer, B., & Co., Chicago, Ill. Men's and boys' suits, overcoats, &c. No. 128,755; Jan. 13; v. 270; p. 340.

Kushiro, Manzaburo, South Pasadena, Calif. Packed miso, &c. No. 129,014; Jan 20; v. 270; p. 474.

Kwick-Bath Mfg. Corporation, Wilson, N. C. Canning apparatus. No. 128,756; Jan 13; v. 270; p. 340.

L. & S. Products Co., Washington, D. C., assignor to Purity Creamery Company, Baltimore, Md. Coffee and peanut-butter. No. 128,489; Jan. 6; v. 270; p. 183.

La Dora Toilet Preparations, Inc., New York, N. Y. Toilet preparations. No. 128,421; Jan. 6; v. 270; p. 181.

Landenberger, Franklin L., Philadelphia, Pa. Hosiery. No. 128,422; Jan. 6; v. 270; p. 181.

Landers, Frary & Clark, New Britain, Conn. Electrically-driven apparatus. No. 128,757; Jan. 13; v. 270; p. 340.

Lange, H. T., Company, Eau Claire, Wis. Canned fruits and vegetables, &c. No. 129,015; Jan. 20; v. 270; p. 474.

Langerre Sales Co., Inc., New York, N. Y. Yarns. No. 128,423; Jan. 6; v. 270; p. 181.

Larus & Brother Company, Richmond, Va. Smoking and chewing tobacco. No. 128,424; Jan. 6; v. 270; p. 181.

Latta-Martin Pump Co., Hickory, N. C. Certain named cutlery, machinery, tools, and parts thereof. Nos. 128,758-60; Jan. 13; v. 270; p. 340.

Latty, John W., St. Louis, Mo. Remedy for cuts, burns, &c. No. 128,761; Jan. 13; v. 270; p. 340.

Lawden Company, The, New York, N. Y. Non-alcoholic non-cereal maltless syrups. No. 129,016; Jan. 20; v. 270; p. 474.

Lawless, Robert L., Danville, Va. Preparation for treatment of cancers, tumors, &c. No. 128,762; Jan. 13; v. 270; p. 340.

Lawrence Knitting Company, Wilmington, Del., and Philadelphia, Pa. Knitted underwear. No. 128,763; Jan. 13; v. 270; p. 340.

Leader Plow Co. Inc., The, Staunton, Va. Garden-plows. No. 128,425; Jan. 6; v. 270; p. 181.

Lee, H. D., Mercantile Co., The, Salina, Kans. and Kansas City, Mo. Work-clothes. No. 129,176; Jan. 27; v. 270; p. 615.

Lee, Harry C. & Company, New York, N. Y. Tennis-rackets, golf clubs and balls, skates. No. 128,426; Jan. 6; v. 270; p. 181.

Lee, Harry C., & Company, New York, N. Y. Golf-balls. No. 128,427; Jan. 6; v. 270; p. 181.

Lefler, Dr. Edmund S., Hot Springs, Ark. Preparation for the treatment of rheumatism, &c. No. 128,428; Jan. 6; v. 270; p. 181.

Leggett, Francis H., & Co., New York, N. Y. Flours. No. 129,017; Jan. 20; v. 270; p. 474.

Lehn & Fink, Inc., New York, N. Y. Antiseptic and disinfectant. No. 128,764; Jan. 13; v. 270; p. 340.

Lemp, William J., Sappington, Mo. Butter, milk, hams, &c. No. 129,018; Jan 20; v. 270; p. 474.

Lever Brothers Company, Cambridge, Mass. Soap dyes. No. 128,429; Jan. 6; v. 270; p. 181.

Liggett & Myers Tobacco Company, New York, N. Y. Cigarettes. No. 128,430; Jan. 6; v. 270; p. 181.

Lindner Shoe Co., Carlisle, Pa. Boots, shoes, &c. No. 128,765; Jan. 13; v. 270; p. 340.

Lippitt, Thomas P., Washington, D. C., and San Juan, Porto Rico. Fresh fruits. No. 128,431; Jan. 6; v. 270; p. 181.

Locke, H. E., & Company, Inc., Boston, Mass. Threads and yarn. No. 129,177; Jan. 27; v. 270; p. 615.

Lockhart Corundum & Lens Corporation, Southbridge, Mass. Emery and corundum for abrasive and polishing purposes. No. 128,432; Jan. 6; v. 270; p. 181.

Loeb, Herbert A., New York, N. Y. Nurses' uniforms and elements thereof. No. 129,178; Jan. 27; v. 270; p. 615.

Loeb & Schoenfeld Company, Wilmington, Del.; Camden, N. J., and New York, N. Y. Handkerchiefs. No. 128,433; Jan. 6; v. 270; p. 181.

Loose-Wiles Biscuit Company, Chicago, Ill. Cookies. No. 129,179; Jan. 27; v. 270; p. 615.

Loughridge, Matthew H., Bogota, N. J. Tubular tags used on insulated wires. No. 128,766; Jan. 13; v. 270; p. 340.

Louis Drug Co., The, Bay City, Mich. Solvent for removal of corns, &c. No. 128,767; Jan. 13; v. 270; p. 340.

Lowe & Lowe, Washington, D. C. Decorated hand-painted garment-hangers, shoe-trees, &c. No. 129,180; Jan. 27; v. 270; p. 615.

Lowenstein Radio Company, Inc., Brooklyn, N. Y., and Newark and Elizabeth, N. J. Photographic developers. No. 128,768; Jan. 13; v. 270; p. 340.

Lubec Sardine Co., Lubec, Me. Canned sardines. No. 128,434; Jan. 6; v. 270; p. 181.

Lubec Sardine Company, Lubec, Me. Canned sardines. No. 129,019; Jan. 20; v. 270; p. 474.

Lubrite Refining Company, St. Louis, Mo. Petroleum products. No. 128,435; Jan. 6; v. 270; p. 182.

Lundstrom, C. J., Mfg. Co., Little Falls, N. Y. Talking-machine cabinets. No. 128,436; Jan. 6; v. 270; p. 182.

Lunkenheimer Company, Cincinnati, Ohio. Pipe-fittings, valves, and nozzles. No. 129,181; Jan. 27; v. 270; p. 615.

Lyons Ignition Company, Paterson, N. J. Spark-plugs. No. 128,769; Jan. 13; v. 270; p. 340.

Lyster Chemical Company, Augusta, Me., and New York, N. Y. Preservative preparation for vegetable fibers. No. 128,770; Jan. 13; v. 270; p. 340.

Lyster Chemical Company, Augusta, Me., and New York, N. Y. Spray for animals. No. 128,771; Jan. 13; v. 270; p. 340.

McAdam, Charles, Company, Chicago, Ill. Cleanser for fabrics. No. 128,437; Jan. 6; v. 270; p. 182.

McAdam, Charles, Company, Chicago, Ill. Glove-bleach. No. 128,438; Jan. 6; v. 270; p. 182.

McDonald, J. G., Chocolate Co., Salt Lake City, Utah. Chocolates. No. 128,772; Jan. 13; v. 270; p. 340.

McElwain, W. H., Company, Boston, Mass. Boots and shoes. No. 128,773; Jan. 13; v. 270; p. 340.

McEwen, Thomas C., Belleville, N. J., assignor to McEwen Tire Ventilator Company, Inc., New York, N. Y. Tire-ventilating valves. No. 129,182; Jan. 27; v. 270; p. 615.

McEwen Tire Ventilator Company, Inc. (See McEwen, Thomas C., assignor.)

McGovern, Edward B., Seattle, Wash. Canned salmon. No. 128,774; Jan. 13; v. 270; p. 341.

McKiernan-Terry Drill Company, Dover, N. J., and New York, N. Y. Lifting-jacks. No. 129,020; Jan. 20; v. 270; p. 474.

McLean, Dr. J. H., Medicine Co., St. Louis, Mo. Medical preparations and products. No. 128,775; Jan. 13; v. 270; p. 341.

McLean, Dr. J. H., Medicine Co., St. Louis, Mo. Purgative pills. No. 128,776; Jan. 13; v. 270; p. 341.

McMillen, Robert M., New York, N. Y. Sugar. No. 128,777; Jan. 13; v. 270; p. 341.

McNell, B. W., New York, N. Y. Hair-tonic. No. 128,489; Jan. 6; v. 270; p. 182.

MacMorris Drug Co., Newark, N. J. Cough remedy and reconstructive tonic. No. 128,778; Jan. 13; v. 270; p. 341.

Macon Woolen Mills, Bibb county, Ga. Pants and overalls. No. 128,440; Jan. 6; v. 270; p. 182.

Macon Woolen Mills, Macon, Ga. Pants and overalls. No. 128,441; Jan. 6; v. 270; p. 182.

Macy, R. H., & Co., New York, N. Y. Hats, Infants', &c. No. 129,021; Jan. 20; v. 270; p. 474

Madelether Company, Saugus, Mass. Soles made of artificial leather. No. 128,442; Jan. 6; v. 270; p. 182.

Magic-Keller Soap Works, Louisville, Ky. Soaps. No. 129,022; Jan. 20; v. 270; p. 474.

Majestic Mills Paper Company Inc., The, New York, N. Y. Writing-paper, printing-paper, envelops, &c. No. 128,443; Jan. 6; v. 270; p. 182.

Major, Joseph, Detroit, Mich. Preparation for consumption. No. 128,444; Jan. 6; v. 270; p. 182.

Major, Joseph, Detroit, Mich. Nerve medicine. No. 128,445; Jan. 6; v. 270; p. 182.

Malin's, H., Sons, Brooklyn, N. Y. Leather, canvas, and fabric shoes. No. 128,446; Jan. 6; v. 270; p. 182.

Malouf, Abraham M., Salt Lake City, Utah. Canned fruit, teas, &c. No. 129,023; Jan. 20; v. 270; p. 474.

Mandel Mfg. Company, Chicago, Ill. Talking-machines, grafonolas, &c. No. 129,024; Jan. 20; v. 270; p. 474.

Maple Grove Candies, St. Johnsbury, Vt. Candies. No. 128,447; Jan. 6; v. 270; p. 182.
Marathon Fishing & Packing Co., Seattle, Wash. Canned salmon. No. 128,448; Jan. 6; v. 270; p. 182.
Marine Decking & Supply Co., Philadelphia and Eastern, Pa. Construction materials. No. 128,779; Jan. 13; v. 270; p. 341.
Marshall Canning Company, Marshalltown, Iowa. Canned beans. No. 129,025; Jan. 20; v. 270; p. 474.
Marshall, Warren, Kansas City, Kans. Ointment for burns, cuts, &c. No. 128,780; Jan. 13; v. 270; p. 341.
Martin-Copeland Company, Providence, R. I. Spectacles, frames, and mountings for eyeglasses. No. 128,449; Jan. 6; v. 270; p. 182.
Martin-Laskin Company, Milwaukee, Wis. Fur-bearing skins. No. 128,781; Jan. 13; v. 270; p. 341.
Marymont, Max J., New York, N. Y. Containers for toilet articles. No. 128,450; Jan. 6; v. 270; p. 182.
Mason, Au & Magenheimer Conf. Mfg. Co., Brooklyn, N. Y. Candies and chocolate. No. 128,451; Jan. 6; v. 270; p. 182.
Mason, Blanche M., Chicago, Ill. Lip-rouge, face-powder, &c. No. 128,782; Jan. 13; v. 270; p. 341.
Mason, Davis & Company, Chicago, Ill. Weighing-scales. No. 129,183; Jan. 27; v. 270; p. 615.
Master Helps Co., Brooklyn, N. Y. Cleansing compound. No. 128,452; Jan. 6; v. 270; p. 182.
Matchless Metal Polish Co., Chicago, Ill., and Glen Ridge, N. J. Buffing or polishing composition. No. 128,453; Jan. 6; v. 270; p. 182.
Mather, Harold H., Albany, N. Y. Cocoa-palm shampoo. No. 129,026; Jan. 20; v. 270; p. 474.
Mayflower Rubber Works Company, Braintree, Mass. Rubber soles and heels. No. 128,783; Jan. 13; v. 270; p. 341.
Mayos Chemical Co., New Orleans, La. Liquid aspirin compound. No. 128,455; Jan. 6; v. 270; p. 182.
Melvin Candy Co., Chicago, Ill. Candy. Nos. 128,456-7; Jan. 6; v. 270; p. 182.
Merrell, William S., Company, Cincinnati, Ohio. Laxatives and cathartics. No. 128,458; Jan. 6; v. 270; p. 182.
Merrell, William S., Company, Cincinnati, Ohio. Concentrated form of Echinacea angustifolia. No. 128,784; Jan. 13; v. 270; p. 341.
Messmer, Fred, Mfg. Co., St. Louis, Mo. Non-alcoholic non-cereal maltless beverages. No. 129,184; Jan. 27; v. 270; p. 615.
Metcalf, D. D., Greenville, Ala. Shortening compound. No. 129,027; Jan. 20; v. 270; p. 474.
Metropolitan Electric Mfg. Co., Long Island City, N. Y. Electric panel-boards. No. 128,785; Jan. 13; v. 270; p. 341.
Michigan Lubricator Company, Detroit, Mich. Watergages, &c. Nos. 128,786-7; Jan. 13; v. 270; p. 341.
Michigan Washing Machine Company, Muskegon, Mich. Laundry-washing machines. No. 128,459; Jan. 6; v. 270; p. 182.
Midwest Engine Company, Indianapolis, Ind. Turbines and tractors. No. 128,460; Jan. 6; v. 270; p. 182.
Midwest Engine Company, Indianapolis, Ind. Tractors. No. 129,185; Jan. 27; v. 270; p. 615.
Migel, J. A., Inc., New York, N. Y. Women's and misses' garments. No. 128,788; Jan. 13; v. 270; p. 341.
Miller, Charles N., Co., Boston, Mass. Candy. No. 128,789; Jan. 13; v. 270; p. 341.
Miller, Charles N., Company, Boston, Mass. Candies. No. 128,790; Jan. 13; v. 270; p. 341.
Miller Cloak Co., The, Cleveland, Ohio. Auto-coats, raincoats, dress-coats, utility-coats. No. 129,186; Jan. 27; v. 270; p. 615.
Miller, Edward S., New York, N. Y., assignor to California Fruit Products Co., Inc. Non-alcoholic beverages and syrups for making same. No. 128,461; Jan. 6; v. 270; p. 182.
Miller, Vincent F., San Antonio Tex. Cordial, skin-cream, &c. No. 128,912; Jan. 13; v. 270; p. 345.
Millhauser, David, New York, N. Y. Chewing-gum. No. 129,028; Jan. 20; v. 270; p. 474.
Milton, Michael, New York, N. Y. Writing-paper. No. 128,791; Jan. 13; v. 270; p. 341.
Milwaukee Air Power Pump Company, Milwaukee, Wis. Pneumatic water pumping and supply systems. No. 128,792; Jan. 13; v. 270; p. 341.
Mint Products Company, Inc., New York, N. Y. Chewing-gum and candy. No. 128,462; Jan. 6; v. 270; p. 182.
Miyauchi, Kiichi, Nodasam-Mura, Nodasam-Gun, Japan. Canned lobster, crabs, fish, and shell-fish. No. 128,463; Jan. 6; v. 270; p. 182.
Moline Heat, Moline, Ill. Heating and ventilating apparatus. No. 128,793; Jan. 13; v. 270; p. 341.
Monopole Vineyards Corp., New York, N. Y. Maltless non-alcoholic fruit beverages. Nos. 129,187-8; Jan. 27; v. 270; p. 615.
Monroe Calculating Machine Company, Orange, N. J. Calculating and adding machines. No. 129,029; Jan. 20; v. 270; p. 474.
Morgenthal, Otto, Dayton, Ohio. Fuel-ignition substance. No. 128,794; Jan. 13; v. 270; p. 341.
Morningstar, Chas., & Co. Inc., New York, N. Y. Flour and food starches from whatever base produced. No. 128,464; Jan. 6; v. 270; p. 182.
Morrell, John, & Company, Ottumwa, Iowa. Breakfast-bacon. No. 128,795; Jan. 13; v. 270; p. 341.

Morris, Harvey D., Port Arthur, Tex. Germicide, &c., preparation. No. 128,465; Jan. 6; v. 270; p. 182.
Morris, Rashkis, Inc., New York, N. Y. Fabric puttees. No. 128,494; Jan. 6; v. 270; p. 183.
Moshontz Bros. & Co., Cleveland, Ohio. Women's dresses. No. 128,796; Jan. 13; v. 270; p. 341.
Murray Company, Dallas, Tex. Machinery and parts thereof. No. 129,189; Jan. 27; v. 270; p. 615.
Musher & Company Incorporated, New York, N. Y.; Baltimore, Md.; San Diego, Calif., and Washington, D. C. Peanut-oil. No. 128,797; Jan. 13; v. 270; p. 341.
Musher & Company, Incorporated, New York, N. Y.; Baltimore, Md.; San Diego, Calif., and Washington, D. C. Table and cooking oils, sauces, dressings. No. 129,030; Jan. 20; v. 270; p. 474.
Musher & Company Inc., New York, N. Y. Sesame-oil. No. 128,798; Jan. 13; v. 270; p. 341.
Myers, W. F., Cambridge, Ohio. Chemical carbon-solvent and fuel-saver. No. 128,466; Jan. 6; v. 270; p. 182.
Napoleon, Mrs. Mary, Albuquerque, N. Mex. Ointments for burns, warts, &c. No. 128,799; Jan. 13; v. 270; p. 341.
Nash Engineering Co., South Norwalk, Conn. Steam-engineering appliances, &c. No. 129,191; Jan. 27; v. 270; p. 615.
Nash Engineering Company, South Norwalk, Conn. Air-compressors, vacuum heating-pumps, &c. No. 129,190; Jan. 27; v. 270; p. 615.
National Aniline & Chemical Company, Incorporated, New York, N. Y. Oil of peppermint used as a flavor for soft drinks. No. 129,192; Jan. 27; v. 270; p. 615.
National Blue Ribbon Remedy Company, St. Louis, Mo. Poultry-powder, lice-killer, preparation for treatment of chicken-cholera and roup. No. 128,800; Jan. 13; v. 270; p. 341.
National Chain Company, New York, N. Y. Antiskid-chains. No. 128,801; Jan. 13; v. 270; p. 341.
National Dairy Co., Todelo and Pioneer, Ohio, and Ennis and Morenci, Mich. Sterilized milk in containers. No. 128,467; Jan. 6; v. 270; p. 182.
National Enameling & Stamping Co., New York, N. Y. Enameled metal ware. No. 129,193; Jan. 27; v. 270; p. 615.
National Fruit Products Company, Inc., Alexandria, Va. Apple jam. No. 128,802; Jan. 13; v. 270; p. 341.
National Jack Co., The, Cincinnati, Ohio. Jacks. No. 128,468; Jan. 6; v. 270; p. 182.
National Twist Drill & Tool Co., Detroit, Mich. Counterboring-tools, saws, &c. No. 128,469; Jan. 6; v. 270; p. 182.
Navy Knitting Mills, Inc., New York, N. Y. Sweaters, bathing-suits, underwear, and hosiery made of knitted material. No. 129,031; Jan. 20; v. 270; p. 474.
Nestor Johnson Manufacturing Company, Chicago, Ill. Ice-skates. No. 128,470; Jan. 6; v. 270; p. 183.
New England Tool Co. Inc., Boston, Mass. Hacksaws and screw-drivers. No. 129,194; Jan. 27; v. 270; p. 615.
New York Chair Company, New York, N. Y. Upholstered dining-room chairs. No. 128,471; Jan. 6; v. 270; p. 183.
Newell, George R., & Co., Minneapolis, Minn. Molasses, olives, &c. No. 128,803; Jan. 13; v. 270; p. 341.
Nicholas Power Company, Inc., New York, N. Y. Arc-lamps and parts. No. 128,805; Jan. 13; v. 270; p. 341.
Nicholas Power Company, Inc., New York, N. Y. Electric-light-projecting equipment for motion-picture machines, &c. No. 128,804; Jan. 13; v. 270; p. 341.
Nitrate Agencies Company, New York, N. Y. Fertilizer materials. No. 129,037; Jan. 20; v. 270; p. 475.
Noonan, T., & Sons Company, Boston, Mass. Hair-tonic. No. 128,472; Jan. 6; v. 270; p. 183.
No-Ouch Mfg. Co., Sioux Falls, S. D. Corn-remover compounds. No. 128,806; Jan. 13; v. 270; p. 342.
Norcross, C. S., & Sons, Bushnell, Ill. Hand garden implements. No. 128,473; Jan. 6; v. 270; p. 183.
Normandie Company, Norfolk, Va. Non-alcoholic fruit-juices. Nos. 129,032-33; Jan. 20; v. 270; p. 474.
Northwestern Chemical Co., Marietta, Ohio. Paste cement for use in radiators. No. 129,034; Jan. 20; v. 270; p. 474.
Northwestern Chemical Co., Marietta Ohio. Adhesives. No. 129,035; Jan. 20; v. 270; p. 475.
Northwestern Consolidated Milling Company, The, Minneapolis, Minn. and New York, N. Y. Wheat-flour. No. 129,036; Jan. 20; v. 270; p. 475.
Norton Company, Worcester. Mass. Abrasive products. No. 128,474; Jan. 6; v. 270; p. 183.
Oceanus Laboratories, Rockaway Beach, N. Y. Antiseptic powder. No. 128,475; Jan. 6; v. 270; p. 183.
Olive Tablet Company, Columbus, Ohio. Olive-oil tablets. No. 128,807; Jan. 13; v. 270; p. 342.
Omaha Flour Mills Co., Omaha, Nebr. Wheat-flour. Nos. 129,038-40; Jan. 20; v. 270; p. 475.
Omo Mfg. Co., Middletown, Conn. Gum tissue. No. 128,477; Jan. 6; v. 270; p. 183.
Omo Mfg. Co., Middletown, Conn. Hospital-sheeting. Nos. 128,808-9; Jan. 13; v. 270; p. 342.
Omo Mfg. Co., Middletown, Conn. Gum tissue. No. 128,810; Jan. 13; v. 270; p. 342.
Omo Mfg. Co., Middletown, Conn. Bias seam-tape. Nos. 129 195-6; Jan. 27; v. 270; p. 615.
Oppelt, Alvin F., Elma, Wash. Preserved salmon-eggs. No. 128,811; Jan. 13; v. 270; p. 342.

Orange City Mineral Spring Company, Orange City, Fla. Mineral water. No. 129,197; Jan. 27; v. 270; p. 615.

O'Reilly, William E., London, England. Safety-razors and razor-blades. No. 129,198; Jan. 27; v. 270; p. 615.

O'Riely, Cornelius J., Los Angeles, Calif. Bicycles. No. 129,041; Jan. 20; v. 270; p. 475.

Ottawa Milling Company, Kansas City, Mo., and Ottawa, Kans. Wheat-flour. No. 129,199; Jan. 27; v. 270; p. 615.

Pace, Bitts, Ironton, Ala. Electrical intensifiers. No. 128,812; Jan. 13; v. 270; p. 342.

Pacific Export Lumber Co., Portland, Oreg. Peanuts. No. 128,813; Jan. 13; v. 270; p. 342.

Palatine Aniline & Chemical Corporation, Poughkeepsie, N. Y. Dyes. No. 128,478; Jan. 6; v. 270; p. 183.

Pan-America Supply Company, Inc., New York, N. Y. Malt, hops, pitch. No. 128,479; Jan. 6; v. 270; p. 183.

Parmenter, Frank D., Toronto, Ontario, Canada. Metal connections. No. 129,042; Jan. 20; v. 270; p. 475.

Parmoline Co., Richmond, Va. Hair-tonic. No. 128,814; Jan. 13; v. 270; p. 342.

Parsons & Whittemore, Incorporated, New York, N. Y. Writing, printing, blotting, and wrapping paper. No. 129,043; Jan. 20; v. 270; p. 475.

Patent Cereals Co., Geneva and New York, N. Y. Cereal breakfast food. No. 128,815; Jan. 13; v. 270; p. 342.

Patent Cereals Company, Geneva and New York, N. Y. Cereal breakfast food. No. 129,044; Jan. 20; v. 270; p. 475.

Pavania Oil Company, Warren, Pa. Gasolene, naphtha, &c. No. 128,480; Jan. 6; v. 270; p. 183.

Peck, Samuel W., & Co., Brooklyn, N. Y. Knitted and flat underwear for men. No. 128,816; Jan. 13; v. 270; p. 342.

Peerless Musical Instruments Mfg. Co., Meriden, Conn. Mouth-harmonicas. No. 129,045; Jan. 20; v. 270; p. 475.

Peppers, Thomas H., Los Angeles, Calif. Fresh citrus and deciduous fruits. No. 128,817; Jan. 13; v. 270; p. 342.

Perkins Glue Company, Lansdale, Pa. Starch-glue material. No. 129,200; Jan. 27; v. 270; p. 615.

Perkins, Jonathan, San Diego, Calif. Germicide and insecticide. No. 128,481; Jan. 6; v. 270; p. 183.

Perlberg & Halpin, New York, N. Y. Mandolins, banjos, &c. No. 129,046; Jan. 20; v. 270; p. 475.

Perry, Adelaide E., Buffalo, N. Y. Remedy for neuralgia and headache. No. 129,047; Jan. 20; v. 270; p. 475.

Petersen's, J. H. C., Sons Company, Davenport, Iowa. Dresses and dress-aprons. No. 128,482; Jan. 6; v. 270; p. 183.

Petroleum Products Company, San Francisco, Calif. Petroleum products, &c. No. 128,483; Jan. 6; v. 270; p. 183.

Phoenix-Hermetic Co., Chicago, Ill. Metal caps for jars or bottles. No. 128,818; Jan. 13; v. 270; p. 342.

Pidgeon, William, Beloit, Ohio. Hoof-dressing, &c. No. 129,048; Jan. 20; v. 270; p. 475.

Pietzuch, Joseph, Cincinnati, Ohio. Rubber shoe-heels. No. 128,484; Jan. 6; v. 270; p. 183.

Pinder, Carlotta, Chicago, Ill. Raisins, sugar-coated and chocolate-coated peanuts. No. 128,485; Jan. 6; v. 270; p. 183.

Pittsburgh Brewing Company, Pittsburgh, Pa. Malt beverage. No. 129,049; Jan. 20; v. 270; p. 475.

Pittsburgh Brewing Company, Pittsburgh, Pa. Malt beverage. No. 129,201; Jan. 27; v. 270; p. 616.

Polk County Citrus Sub-Exchange, Bartow, Fla. Citrus fruits. No. 128,819; Jan. 13; v. 270; p. 342.

Polk County Citrus Sub-Exchange, Bartow, Fla. Fresh citrus fruits. No. 129,202; Jan. 27; v. 270; p. 616.

Pollak Steel Company, Cincinnati, Ohio. Locomotive and machinery axles. No. 128,820; Jan. 13; v. 270; p. 342.

Pollak Steel Company, Cincinnati, Ohio. Bars of open-hearth steel. No. 129,050; Jan. 20; v. 270; p. 475.

Poole, Clyde W., Los Angeles, Calif. Marmalade. No. 128,486; Jan. 6; v. 270; p. 183.

Popper, E., & Co., New York, N. Y. Cigars. No. 129,051; Jan. 20; v. 270; p. 475.

Portland Flouring Mills Company, Portland, Oreg. Wheat-flour, cake and pastry flour, &c. No. 128,487; Jan. 6; v. 270; p. 183.

Postum Cereal Company, Battle Creek, Mich. Hominy feed. No. 128,821; Jan. 13; v. 270; p. 342.

Powell & Campbell, New York, N. Y. Shoes. No. 128,822; Jan. 13; v. 270; p. 342.

Powerol Chemical Company, Pittsburgh, Pa. Eczema-ointment. No. 128,823; Jan. 13; v. 270; p. 342.

Powers Manufacturing Company, The, Waterloo, Iowa. Overalls and one-piece garments. No. 129,203; Jan. 27; v. 270; p. 616.

Pressed Metal Radiator Company, Pittsburgh, Pa. Welded steel and iron tubing. No. 129,052; Jan. 20; v. 270; p. 475.

Price, Lawrence T., Richmond, Va. Liquid for the treatment of gonorrhea. No. 128,824; Jan. 13; v. 270; p. 342.

Prime Shirt Co., Inc., New York, N. Y. Outer shirts and pajamas. No. 128,825; Jan. 13; v. 270; p. 342.

Procter and Gamble Company, Cincinnati, Ohio. Cooking-fat. No. 128,488; Jan. 6; v. 270; p. 183.

Producer's Paper Company, St. Paul, Minn. Novelty paper coverings for boxes. No. 128,826; Jan. 13; v. 270; p. 342.

Proper Antiseptic Laboratory, Cincinnati, Ohio. Antiseptic, germicide, &c. No. 128,827; Jan. 13; v. 270; p. 342.

Providence Needle Co., Providence, R. I. Metal knitting-machine needles. No. 128,490; Jan. 6; v. 270; p. 183.

Purity Creamery Company. (See L. & S. Products Co., assignor.)

Purity Cross, Inc., West Orange, N. J. Food products in tins, &c. No. 128,828; Jan. 13; v. 270; p. 342.

Putnam, Alfred, & Company, New York, N. Y. Canned fruits and canned vegetables. No. 129,204; Jan. 27; v. 270; p. 616.

Putnam Overall Mfg. Co., Cookeville, Tenn. Men's and boys' coats, pants, &c. No. 129,205; Jan. 27; v. 270; p. 616.

Quaker City Corporation, Philadelphia, Pa. Leather. No. 128,491; Jan. 6; v. 270; p. 183.

Quaker City Flour Mills Co., Philadelphia, Pa. Wheat-flour. No. 128,829; Jan. 13; v. 270; p. 342.

Quaker City Flour Mills Company, Philadelphia, Pa. Self-rising wheat-flour. No. 129,206; Jan. 27; v. 270; p. 616.

Qualitas Patent Leather Corporation, Wilmington, Del., and New York, N. Y. Leather. No. 128,492; Jan. 6; v. 270; p. 183.

Rabinowitz, Isidore, Apparel Co. Inc., New York, N. Y. Women's dresses, skirts, &c. No. 129,054; Jan. 20; v. 270; p. 475.

Rada-Solvt Co., Los Angeles, Calif. Chemical solution to clean out radiators and boilers. No. 128,830; Jan. 13; v. 270; p. 342.

Ragenowich, Dano P., San Francisco, Calif. Consumption cure. No. 128,493; Jan. 6; v. 270; p. 183.

Randall-McLoughlin Co., Seattle, Wash. Stock foods, poultry and dog foods. No. 129,207; Jan. 27; v. 270; p. 616.

Rawleigh, W. T., Company, Freeport, Ill. Sewing-machine oil. No. 128,495; Jan. 6; v. 270; p. 183.

Rawleigh, W. T., Company, Freeport, Ill. Toilet soaps, shaving-cream, washing compounds, &c. No. 128,496; Jan. 6; v. 270; p. 183.

Rawleigh, W. T., Company, Freeport, Ill. Furniture-polish. No. 129,056; Jan. 20; v. 270; p. 475.

Raymond Phonograph Co. Inc., Atlanta, Va. Phonographs, records, and needles. No. 129,055; Jan. 20; v. 270; p. 475.

Red Star Milling Company, Wichita, Kans. Wheat-flour. No. 129,059; Jan. 20; v. 270; p. 475.

Reed Tobacco Company, Richmond, Va. Cigarettes. Nos. 129,057-8; Jan. 20; v. 270; p. 475.

Reeder, Oliver, & Son, Incorporated, Baltimore, Md. Metal-polish. No. 128,476; Jan. 6; v. 270; p. 183.

Reese Chemical Co., Cleveland, Ohio. Remedy for skin eruptions, &c. No. 128,497; Jan. 6; v. 270; p. 183.

Regan, Jas. J., Mfg. Co., Rockville, Me. Woolen and worsted suitings. No. 128,498; Jan. 6; v. 270; p. 183.

Reid Bros., Inc., San Francisco, Calif., and Seattle, Wash. General medical and surgical supplies. No. 129,060; Jan. 20; v. 270; p. 475.

Reno Flour Mills Company, Hutchinson, Kans. Wheat-flour. No. 128,831; Jan. 13; v. 270; p. 342.

Republic Doll & Toy Corporation, New York, N. Y. Dolls. No. 128,499; Jan. 6; v. 270; p. 183.

Restoria Chemical Company, Phoenix, Ariz., and Kansas City, Mo. Medicine for blood diseases, &c. No. 128,500; Jan. 6; v. 270; p. 183.

Reusche, L., & Company, New York, N. Y. Finishing for glass, china, &c. No. 128,832; Jan. 13; v. 270; p. 342.

Reynolds-Lindheim Cigar Company, Nashville, Tenn. Candy. No. 129,208; Jan. 27; v. 270; p. 616.

Rich, Ralph E., Chicago, Ill. Centrifugal pumps. No. 128,501; Jan. 6; v. 270; p. 183.

Richards, A. R., Medicine Co. Inc., Sherman, Tex. Salve and liniment. No. 128,833; Jan. 13; v. 270; p. 342.

Richmond, John S., Philadelphia, Pa. Women's and children's knitted and woven underwear. No. 129,061; Jan. 20; v. 270; p. 475.

Richter, F. Ad., & Co., New York, N. Y. Tonics. No. 128,834; Jan. 13; v. 270; p. 342.

Ricker, Howard H., Minneapolis, Minn. Liniment. No. 128,835; Jan. 13; v. 270; p. 342.

Ridgely Trimmer Company, The, Springfield, Ohio. Rack-exhibitors for wall-paper. No. 128,502; Jan. 6; v. 270; p. 183.

Ries, Jacob, Bottling Works, Inc., Shakopee, Minn. Still and effervescent table-water. No. 129,172; Jan. 27; v. 270; p. 615.

Ringler, Geo., & Co., New York, N. Y. Non-intoxicating beverages. No. 128,836; Jan. 13; v. 270; p. 342.

Roanoke City Mills, Roanoke, Va. Wheat-flour. No. 129,062; Jan. 20; v. 270; p. 475.

Robinson, Clinton S., Chicago, Ill. assignor to Aladdin Products Company. Dyes combined with soap. No. 128,503; Jan. 6; v. 270; p. 184.

Roche, John, assignor to himself and J. Coonan, Buffalo, N. Y. Cream substitute. No. 128,504; Jan. 6; v. 270; p. 184.

Rockfall Cigar Company, New York, N. Y. Tobacco, cigars, &c. No. 128,505; Jan. 6; v. 270; p. 184.

Rodent Exterminator Laboratories, Chicago, Ill. Preparation for exterminating rodents. No. 128,839; Jan. 13; v. 270; p. 343.

Roe, A. V., & Co. Ltd., Manchester, England. Turnbuckles, metal name-plates, &c. Nos. 129,209-10; Jan. 27; v. 270; p. 616.

Rohrman-Cooper Company, Chicago, Ill. Ventilators for roofs and skylights. No. 128,837; Jan. 13; v. 270; p. 342.

Romort Manufacturing Company, Oakfield, Wis. Automobile, &c., accessories. No. 129,211; Jan. 27; v. 270; p. 616.

Rose, D. E., Trunk Company, Topeka, Kans. Trunks. No. 129,063; Jan. 20; v. 270; p. 475.

Rosenstein, J., New York, N. Y. Wheat-flour. No. 128,838; Jan. 13; v. 270; p. 343.

Rosenstein, Jacob, New York, N. Y. Wheat-flour. No. 129,212; Jan. 27; v. 270; p. 616.

Rosman & Laveson, Philadelphia, Pa. Boots and shoes, rubber overshoes, hosiery. No. 129,064; Jan. 20; v. 270; p. 475.

Roth, Charles, New York, N. Y. Ladies' hats. No. 129,213; Jan. 27; v. 270; p. 616.

Roulette, J. C., and Sons, Hagerstown, Md. Underwear. No. 128,506; Jan. 6; v. 270; p. 184.

Roulette, J. C., and Sons, Hagerstown, Md. Underwear. No. 129,214; Jan. 27; v. 270; p. 616.

Ruppert, Jacob, New York, N. Y. Near beer. No. 128,507; Jan. 6; v. 270; p. 184.

Rushworth, Finch, Fenay Bridge, near Huddersfield England. Cloths and stuffs of wool, &c. No. 128,508; Jan 6; v. 270; p. 184.

Ruttenberg, Sam, Chicago, Ill. Caramel bars. No. 128,509; Jan. 6; v. 270; p. 184.

Rythmodik Music Corporation, Belleville, N. J., and New York, N. Y. Note-sheets for player-pianos, &c. No. 129,065; Jan. 20; v. 270; p. 475.

Saberton Mfg. Co., Tampa, Fla. Soap. No. 128,840; Jan. 13; v. 270; p. 343.

Sainberg, Louis, New York, N. Y. Desk-pads and pad-corners, sand and ordinary paper, &c. No. 128,510; Jan. 6; v. 270; p. 184.

Salwen, David, New York, N. Y. Hosiery. No. 128,511; Jan. 6; v. 270; p. 184.

Salz Brothers, New York, N. Y. Fountain-pens. No. 128,817; Jan. 6; v. 270; p. 178.

Salz Brothers, New York, N. Y. Magazine-pencils. No. 128,841; Jan. 13; v. 270; p. 343.

San-tro-pas Manufacturing Company, Limited. (See Bickell, David A., assignor.)

Sanford, Franklin, Cincinnati, Ohio. Disinfectants. No. 129,066; Jan. 20; v. 270; p. 475.

Santiago Orange Growers Association, Orange, Calif. Fresh oranges. No. 128,842; Jan. 13; v. 270; p. 343.

Sauer, C. F., Co., Richmond, Va. Food-flavoring extracts. No. 128,843; Jan. 13; v. 270; p. 343.

Sauer, C. F., Company, Richmond, Va. Food-flavoring extracts. No. 128,512; Jan. 6; v. 270; p. 184.

Sayre Creamery Cold Storage Co., Sayre, Pa. Ice-cream. No. 128,513; Jan. 6; v. 270; p. 184.

Schaefer, F. & M., Brewing Co., New York, N. Y. Soft drink. No. 128,514; Jan. 6; v. 270; p. 184.

Schaffer, William H., Cumberland, Md. Cleaning preparation for removing tar, &c., from automobiles, &c. No. 128,844; Jan. 13; v. 270; p. 343.

Scheidt, Adam, Beverage Co., Norristown, Pa. Sarsaparilla, ginger-ale, lemon-soda. No. 128,845; Jan. 13; v. 270; p. 343.

Schlar, Herman, Philadelphia, Pa. Hair and scalp preparation. No. 128,846; Jan. 13; v. 270; p. 343.

Schlesinger, Harry, Brooklyn, N. Y. Remedy for corns, warts, &c. No. 128,847; Jan. 13; v. 270; p. 343.

Schmid, Roost Jakob, Oerlikon, Switzerland. Ball and roller bearings and ports. No. 129,216; Jan. 27; v. 270; p. 616.

Schmitz, Charles A., Boston, Mass. Puzzles. No. 129,067; Jan. 20; v. 270; p. 475.

Schoenhoffen Company, Chicago, Ill. Non-alcoholic non-cereal maltless beverage. No. 129,217; Jan. 27; v. 270; p. 616.

Schuldenberg, George, Highlandtown and Baltimore, Md. Lard compounds. No. 129,069; Jan. 20; v. 270; p. 476.

Schulemann, F., Co., New York, N. Y. Floss for embroidery and cotton for crocheting. No. 128,849; Jan. 13; v. 270; p. 343.

Schuller, Frederick A., Boston, Mass. Muffins. No. 129,218; Jan. 27; v. 270; p. 616.

Scotch-Tone Company, Oklahoma, Okla. Callous-removing preparations. No. 129,068; Jan. 20; v. 270; p. 476.

Screen Letter Box, Inc., New York, N. Y. Motion-picture films. No. 128,848; Jan. 13; v. 270; p. 343.

Senoret Chemical Co., St. Louis, Mo. Medicinal preparation useful as external treatment for congestion, &c. No. 128,850; Jan. 13; v. 270; p. 343.

Shaller, Paul R., Washington, D. C. Candies. No. 128,515; Jan. 6; v. 270; p. 184.

Shapleigh Hardware Company, St. Louis, Mo. Prepared roofing. No. 129,070; Jan. 20; v. 270; p. 476.

Sheahan, Kohn & Co., Chicago, Ill. Outer garments for boys. No. 128,851; Jan. 13; v. 270; p. 343.

Shepard, Abraham D., Chicago, Ill. Charged table-water. No. 128,852; Jan. 13; v. 270; p. 343.

Sherman, Louis, Cincinnati, Ohio. Cigars, cigarettes, tobacco. No. 128,516; Jan. 6; v. 270; p. 184.

Shiley Chemical Co., Missouri Valley, Iowa. Insecticide. No. 128,853; Jan. 13; v. 270; p. 343.

Shirck & Hirsch, New York, N. Y. Men's and boys' clothing. No. 129,071; Jan. 20; v. 270; p. 476.

Shireman, Nancye L., Birmingham, Ala. Face-rouge. No. 128,854; Jan. 13; v. 270; p. 343.

Shults, Herbert O., Chicago, Ill. Dolls. No. 129,072; Jan. 20; v. 270; p. 476.

Sidney Canning Co., Ltd., Sidney, British Columbia, Canada. Canned fish and clams. No. 129,219; Jan. 27; v. 270; p. 616.

Siegel, Charles, assignor to Victory Confectionery Co., New York, N. Y. Candies, chocolates, and caramels. No. 129,073; Jan. 20; v. 270; p. 476.

Siemon & Eiting, New York, N. Y. Wash-blue. No. 128,855; Jan. 13; v. 270; p. 343.

Simcox, Edward C., Columbus, Ohio. Games and game-boards of a checker or chess like variety. No. 129,074; Jan. 20; v. 270; p. 476.

Simmons Hardware Company, St. Louis, Mo. Lead-pencils and wrapping-paper. No. 128,518; Jan. 6; v. 270; p. 184.

Simmons Hardware Company, St. Louis, Mo. Scales. No. 129,075; Jan. 20; v. 270; p. 476.

Simmons Hardware Company, St. Louis, Mo. Measuring and scientific appliances. No. 129,076; Jan. 20; v. 270; p. 476.

Simmons Hardware Company, St. Louis, Mo. Harness, riding-saddles, &c. No. 129,077; Jan. 20; v. 270; p. 476.

Simmons Hardware Company, St. Louis, Mo. Bicycles. No. 129,220; Jan. 27; v. 270; p. 616.

Simmons Milling Company, The, Cincinnati, Ohio. Stock and poultry feeds. No. 129,078; Jan. 20; v. 270; p. 476.

Simon Bros. Company, Omaha, Nebr. Canned fruits, vegetables, and fish, coffee. No. 128,517; Jan. 6; v. 270; p. 184.

Simpson-Walther Lens Company, Incorporated, Rochester, N. Y. Ophthalmic-lens blanks and ophthalmic lenses. No. 128,519; Jan. 6; v. 270; p. 184.

Simpson-Walther Lens Company, Inc., Rochester, N. Y. Ophthalmic-lens blanks and ophthalmic lenses. No. 129,221; Jan. 27; v. 270; p. 616.

Skin Remedies Company, Celina, Tex. Ointment for skin diseases, &c. No. 128,856; Jan. 13; v. 270; p. 343.

Skinner, Paul F., Omaha, Nebr. Bread, pies, ice-cream. No. 129,079; Jan. 20; v. 270; p. 476.

Sloan, F. A., Albemarle, N. C. Preparation for relief of constipation and indigestion. No. 128,857; Jan. 13; v. 270; p. 343.

Smith, Dayton D., Philadelphia, Pa. Chemical preparation for preserving eggs. No. 129,081; Jan. 20; v. 270; p. 476.

Smith-Frank Packing Co., Sacramento, Calif. Canned fruits and vegetables. No. 129,080; Jan. 20; v. 270; p. 476.

Smith & Nichols, Incorporated, New York, N. Y. Beeswax, stearic acid, spermaceti. No. 128,858; Jan. 13; v. 270; p. 343.

Snovel, Harry H., Van Wert, Ohio. Cigars. No. 129,082; Jan. 20; v. 270; p. 476.

Soifer, Morris S., Philadelphia, Pa. Headache-pills, blood, liver, and stomach tablets, &c. No. 128,859; Jan. 13; v. 270; p. 343.

Sorenson, David, Fortuna, Calif. Hog-cholera medicine. No. 128,860; Jan. 13; v. 270; p. 343.

South & Central American Commercial Co. Inc., New York, N. Y. Cotton, wool, and silk piece goods, &c. No. 128,520; Jan. 6; v. 270; p. 184.

South Lake Apopka Citrus Growers Assn., Oakland and Tildenville, Fla. Fresh citrus fruits. No. 128,861; Jan. 13; v. 270; p. 343.

Southern Beverage Company, Galveston, Tex. Non-alcoholic beverages. No. 129,083; Jan. 20; v. 270; p. 476.

Southern Cotton Oil Company, Jersey City and Bayonne, N. J.; New York, N. Y.; Gretna, La.; Savannah, Ga., and Chicago, Ill. Cotton-seed-oil shortening compound. No. 129,222; Jan. 27; v. 270; p. 616.

Southern Feed Company, Inc., Newport News, Va. Stock feeds. No. 128,862; Jan. 13; v. 270; p. 343.

Southern Fertilizer & Chemical Co., Savannah, Ga. Fertilizers. No. 128,521; Jan. 6; v. 270; p. 184.

Spang, Chalfant & Co. Incorporated, Pittsburgh, Pa. Iron and steel tubes. No. 129,223; Jan. 27; v. 270; p. 616.

Sperry Flour Company, San Francisco, Calif. Stock food. No. 128,522; Jan. 6; v. 270; p. 184.

Sperry Flour Company, San Francisco, Calif. Poultry food. Nos. 128,523–4; Jan. 6; v. 270; p. 184.

Spiegelberg, L. & Sons, New York, N. Y. Slip-covers. No. 128,525; Jan. 6; v. 270; p. 184.

Standard Cooper-Bell Co., Chicago, Ill. Enamel and oil paints, stains, &c. No. 129,084; Jan. 20; v. 270; p. 476.

Standard Oil Company of New York, New York, N. Y. Refined oils. No. 128,526; Jan. 6; v. 270; p. 184.

Standard Optical Co., Geneva, N. Y. Spectacle and eye-glass frames, &c. No. 128,863; Jan. 13; v. 270; p. 343.

Standard Ultramarine Co., The, Huntington, W. Va. Laundry blue. No. 128,527; Jan. 6; v. 270; p. 184. Preparation for treatment of consumption and tuberculosis. No. 128,988; Jan. 20; v. 270; p. 473.

Star Bedding Company, St. Louis, Mo. Feather pillows. No. 128,528; Jan. 6; v. 270; p. 184.

Stearns, Frederick, & Co., Detroit, Mich. Medicated soap. No. 128,864; Jan. 13; v. 270; p. 343.

Stearns, Frederick, & Co., Detroit, Mich. Talcum powders, perfumes, &c. No. 128,865; Jan. 13; v. 270; p. 343.

Stearns-Hollingshead Co., Portland, Oreg. Candles of all kinds. No. 128,869; Jan. 13; v. 270; p. 344.

Steele Packing Co., San Diego, Calif. Canned sardines. No. 128,529; Jan. 6; v. 270; p. 184.

Steele Wedeles Company, Chicago, Ill. Peanut-oil. No. 128,870; Jan. 13; v. 270; p. 344.

Stein-Hall Manufacturing Co., Wilmington, Del., and Chicago, Ill. Starch product used in baking. No. 128,866; Jan. 13; v. 270; p. 343.

Stein-Hall Manufacturing Company, Wilmington, Del., and Chicago, Ill. Starch product for an ingredient in baking. No. 129,085; Jan. 20; v. 270; p. 476.

Steinwender-Stoffregen Coffee Company, St. Louis, Mo. Food-flavoring extracts, roasted coffee. No 129,086; Jan. 20; v. 270; p. 476.

Sterling Potato Brittle Co., Wilkes-Barre, Pa. Potato chips. No. 128,530; Jan. 6; v. 270; p. 184.

Sterling Products, (Incorporated,) Wheeling, W. Va. Hair and scalp tonic. No. 128,871; Jan. 13; v. 270; p. 344.

Sterling Varnish Company, Pittsburgh, Pa. Varnish for the surface of rubber tires. No. 129,087; Jan. 20; v. 270; p. 476.

Stern, Charles, & Sons Inc., Los Angeles, Calif. Canned fruits. No. 128,531; Jan. 6; v. 270; p. 184.

Stern, Charles, & Sons Inc., Los Angeles, Calif. Canned peaches and canned apricots. Nos. 128,867-8; Jan. 13; v. 270; p. 343.

Stern, Charles, Sons Inc., Los Angeles, Calif. Canned fruits. Nos. 128,872-3; Jan. 13; v. 270; p. 344.

Stern, Charles, & Sons Inc., Los Angeles, Calif. Canned fruits. No. 129,225; Jan. 27; v. 270; p. 616.

Stevenson, E. A., & Company. Wilmington. Del. Cocoanut-butter. No. 128,532; Jan. 6; v. 270; p. 184.

Stewart Bros. & Company, Glasgow, Scotland. Trouserings, saxonies, and piece goods. No. 128,533; Jan. 6; v. 270; p. 184.

Stiles-Pellens Coffee Co., Cincinnati, Ohio. Baking-powder. No. 128,534; Jan. 6; v. 270; p. 184.

Stone & Andrew Inc., Boston, Mass. Writing and printing paper. No. 129,088; Jan. 20; v. 270; p. 476.

Stone, Chas. D., & Co., Chicago, Ill. Hosiery. No. 128,874; Jan. 13; v. 270; p. 344.

Stopshok Wheel Co. Inc., Washington, D. C. Vehicle-wheels. No. 129,224; Jan. 27; v. 270; p. 616.

Stuttgart Rice Mill Company, Stuttgart, Ark. Rice. Nos. 129,089-90; Jan. 20; v. 270; p. 476.

Sulfron Medicine Company, Birmingham, Ala. Medicine for indigestion, pellagra, &c. No. 128,875; Jan. 13; v. 270; p. 344.

Sun Company, Philadelphia, Pa. Wool washing and treating oils. No. 128,876; Jan. 13; v. 270; p. 344.

Superior Cone Company, St. Louis, Mo. Ice-cream cones. No. 129,226; Jan. 27; v. 270; p. 616.

Swift & Company, Chicago, Ill. Soap. No. 128,535; Jan. 6; v. 270; p. 184.

Tagliabue, C. J., Mfg. Co., Brooklyn, N. Y. Thermometers, gages, &c. Nos. 128,877-8; Jan. 13; v. 270; p. 344.

Tapo Citrus Ass'n., Santa Susana, Calif. Fresh citrus fruits. No. 128,536; Jan. 6; v. 270; p. 185.

Tatom, Eric, & Co., Nashville, Tenn. Cigars. No. 128,540; Jan. 6; v. 270; p. 185.

Taylor, E. E. Company, Boston, Mass. Rubber heels and soles. No. 128,537; Jan. 6; v. 270; p. 185.

Taylor, E. E., Company, Boston, Mass. Leather boots and shoes. No. 129,091; Jan. 20; v. 270; p. 476.

Taylor, Milton M., Tampa, Fla. Remedy for inactive liver. No. 128,538; Jan. 6; v. 270; p. 185.

Taylor, Milton M., Tampa, Fla. Antiseptic preparation. No. 128,539; Jan. 6; v. 270; p. 185.

Tenenbaum, J., & Sons, New York, N. Y. Ladies' hats. No. 129,227; Jan. 27; v. 270; p. 616.

Terre Haute Brewing Company, Terre Haute. Ind. Cereal malt beverage. No. 129,228; Jan. 27; v. 270; p. 616.

Texoleum Co. of N. Y. Inc., New York, N. Y. Oil-cloth, linoleums, &c. No. 129,229; Jan. 27; v. 270; p. 616.

Thomas, Louis, Chicago, Ill. Liquid for scalds and burns. No. 128,541; Jan. 6; v. 270; p. 185.

Thomson Machine Company, Belleville, N. J. Dough balling and proofing machine, rounding-up machines. No. 129,230; Jan. 27; v. 270; p. 616.

Thorndike and Gerrish Company, Boston, Mass. Dressed poultry. No. 128,542; Jan. 6; v. 270; p. 185.

Todd, George W., Omaha, Nebr. Chewing-gum No. 129,092; Jan. 20; v. 270; p. 476.

Todd, Peyton H., & Son, Atlanta, Ga. General reconstructive tonic and tissue-builder. No. 128,543; Jan. 6; v. 270; p. 185.

Toth, Illes, Washington, D. C. Medicinal jelly for sore throat, &c. No. 129,241; Jan. 13; v. 270; p. 344.

Towle Maple Products Company, Wilmington, Del., and St. Paul. Minn. Confection paste. No. 128,544; Jan. 6; v. 270; p. 185.

Traub, Lazar M., Boston, Mass. Men's, women's, and children's shoes. No. 128,545; Jan. 6; v. 270; p. 185.

Trent, Lorenzo D., Ironton, Ohio. Preparation for treatment of certain named diseases. No. 129,093; Jan. 20; v. 270; p. 476.

Trexler Rim Compressor Co., Philadelphia, Pa. Tire-removing tools. No. 129,231; Jan. 27; v. 270; p. 616.

Trommer, John F., Evergreen Brewery, Brooklyn, N. Y. Non-alcoholic malt beverage. No. 128,880; Jan. 13; v. 270; p. 344.

Troth, Ernest A., Philadelphia, Pa. Liquid preparation for use as a mouth-wash and nasal douche. No. 128,881; Jan. 13; v. 270; p. 344.

Trovillo, Lottie S., Blanchester, Ohio. Canned vegetables and fruits, jellies, &c. No. 128,546; Jan. 6; v. 270; p. 185.

Truman, Charles H. J., San Francisco, Calif. Partially-printed sheets for keeping funeral-records. No. 128,547; Jan. 6; v. 270; p. 185.

Tunnell, F. W., & Company, Inc., Philadelphia, Pa. Vegetable adhesive. No. 128,548; Jan. 6; v. 270; p. 185.

Tushak, Gerald. New York, N. Y. Toy guns. No. 128,549; Jan. 6; v. 270; p. 185.

Tyson, B. E., Newark, N. J. Medicinal preparation for influenza, rheumatism, &c. No. 128,550; Jan. 6; v. 270; p. 185.

U. S. Industrial Co., New York, N. Y. Chemicals. No. 129,234; Jan. 27; v. 270; p. 617.

Ulmer Leather Co., Norwich, Conn. Belt-dressing. No. 128,551; Jan. 6; v. 270; p. 185.

Underwood, Frederick D., New York, N. Y. Fresh milk and cream, eggs, and butter. No. 128,552; Jan. 6; v. 270; p. 185.

Union Tool Company, Torrance, Calif. Tractors, steam and gas engines. No. 128,553; Jan. 6; v. 270; p. 185.

United American Metals Corporation, Brooklyn, N. Y. Babbitt metal. No. 128,882; Jan. 13; v. 270; p. 344.

United American Metals Corporation, Brooklyn, N. Y. Babbitt metal. No. 129,232; Jan. 27; v. 270; p. 617.

United Drug Company, Boston, Mass. Writing-tablets. No. 128,554; Jan. 6; v. 270; p. 185.

United Hosiery Mills Corporation, East Chattanooga, Tenn. Hosiery. Nos. 128,883-5; Jan. 13; v. 270; p. 344.

United Hosiery Mills Corporation, East Chattanooga, Tenn. Hosiery. No. 129,233; Jan. 27; v. 270; p. 617.

United Shoe Machinery Company, Paterson, N. J., and Boston, Mass. Hand shoe-knives and knives and groovers for shoe machinery. No. 128,886; Jan. 13; v. 270; p. 344.

United States Rubber Company, New Brunswick, N. J., and New York, N. Y. Leather shoes. No. 128,555; Jan. 6; v. 270; p. 185.

United States Rubber Company, New Brunswick, N. J., and New York, N. Y. Leather shoes. No. 129,094; Jan. 20; v. 270; p. 476.

United States Rubber Company, New Brunswick, N. J., and New York, N. Y. Rubber mats and mattings. No. 129,235; Jan. 27; v. 270; p. 617.

Universal Film Manufacturing Company, Inc., New York, N. Y. Moving-picture films. Nos. 128,887-8; Jan. 13; v. 270; p. 344.

Universal Tool Co., Detroit, Mich. Cylinder-reboring tools and kits, &c. No. 129,236; Jan. 27; v. 270; p. 617.

Vacuum Oil Company, Rochester, N. Y. Lubricating-oils. No. 129,237; Jan. 27; v. 270; p. 617.

Vacuumeter Co., Columbus, Ga. Registers for recording the amount of fuel consumed by internal-combustion engines. No. 128,556; Jan. 6; v. 270; p. 185.

Vail. Ed. S., Butterine Co., Chicago, Ill. Oleomargarin. No. 128,889; Jan. 13; v. 270; p. 344.

Van Briggle Motor Device Company, Indianapolis, Ind. Carbureters. No. 128,557; Jan. 6; v. 270; p. 185.

Vanity Yarn Company, Boston, Mass. Worsted fingering-yarn. No. 128,890; Jan. 13; v. 270; p. 344.

Vaporine Chemical Company, Savannah, Tenn. Ointment. No. 128,562; Jan. 6; v. 270; p. 185.

Vesuvius Crucible Company, Swissvale, Pa. Crucibles. No. 128,558; Jan. 6; v. 270; p. 185.

Victor Adding Machine Co., Chicago, Ill. Adding and calculating machines. No. 128,891; Jan. 13; v. 270; p. 344.

Victory Bag & Paper Co., Chicago, Ill. Paper bags. No. 128,559; Jan. 6; v. 270; p. 185.

Voigt Milling Company, Grand Rapids, Mich. Stock and poultry feed. No. 129,238; Jan. 27; v. 270; p. 617.

Volt, Leo G., Denver, Colo. Compound flour and syrup. No. 128,560; Jan. 6; v. 270; p. 185.

Voorsanger, Jennie, Chicago, Ill. Steel pens. No. 128,561; Jan. 6; v. 270; p. 185.

Vulcan Proofing Company, Brooklyn, N. Y. Rubber offset-blankets. No. 128,892; Jan. 13; v. 270; p. 344.

Wachusett Shirt Co., Leominster, Mass. Sleeping-garments—viz., night-dresses. No. 129,239; Jan. 27; v. 270; p. 617.

Wade, R. M., & Co., Portland, Oreg. Power drag-saws. No. 129,095; Jan. 20; v. 270; p. 476.

Wahlert & Guntzler, St. Louis, Mo. Feathers. No. 129,240; Jan. 27; v. 270; p. 617.

Walcoff, Phil., & Co., Inc., New York, N. Y. Boys' outer clothing. No. 129,241; Jan. 27; v. 270; p. 617.

Walker, Ella, Manufacturing Company, Sioux City, Iowa. Hair and scalp preparation. No. 128,893; Jan. 13; v. 270; p. 344.

Walker-Matteson Co., Joliet, Ill. Canned goods, mustard, catsup, &c. No. 129,096; Jan. 20; v. 270; p. 476.

Ward, Samuel, Manufacturing Company, Boston, Mass. Fountain and steel pens, lead-pencils, &c. No. 128,563; Jan. 6; v. 270; p. 185.

Warner-Godfrey Co., New York, N. Y. Silk, cotton and silk, wool, &c., piece goods. No. 128,564; Jan. 6; v. 270; p. 185.

Warner-Godfrey Co., New York, N. Y. Silk, cotton, &c., piece goods. No. 128,565; Jan. 6; v. 270; p. 185.

Warshavsky, David, New York, N. Y. Snap-fasteners. No. 129,242; Jan. 27; v. 270; p. 617.

Wash-Co. Alfalfa Milling Co., Riverton, Wyo., and Fort Calhoun and Nebraska City, Nebr. Mixed live-stock feed. No. 128,566; Jan. 6; v. 270; p. 185.

Washington Fruit & Produce Co., Yakima, Wash. Fresh apples. No. 128,567; Jan. 6; v. 270; p. 186.

Wathen Milling Company, Louisville, Ky. Fine grits, pearl-hominy, &c. No. 129,243; Jan. 27; v. 270; p. 617.

Weber, E., & Co., Philadelphia, Pa. Skin-balm. No. 128,894; Jan. 13; v. 270; p. 344.

Webster, Frank B., Los Angeles, Calif. Polishing and cleansing compound for automobiles, &c. No. 129,097; Jan. 20; v. 270; p. 476.

Weihenmayer, William J., Philadelphia, Pa. Worsted knitting-yarns. No. 128,895; Jan. 13; v. 270; p. 344.

Weisberg, Benjamin C., New York, N. Y. Butter-scotch candy. No. 128,568; Jan. 6; v. 270; p. 186.

Weiss, Frederic H., Cincinnati, Ohio. Candy. No. 128,569; Jan. 6; v. 270; p. 186.

Weller Manufacturing Company, Chicago, Ill. Grain-handling machinery. No. 128,896; Jan. 13; v. 270; p. 344.

Wellman-Seaver-Morgan Company, Cleveland, Ohio. Tractors. No. 129,245; Jan. 27; v. 270; p. 617.

Wells, Henry M., London, England. Heating-oils, illuminating-oils, and lubricating-oils. No. 128,570; Jan. 6; v. 270; p. 186.

Wenzelmann, Gustave, Galesburg, Ill. Powdered substance for cleaning purposes. No. 128,571; Jan. 6; v. 270; p. 186.

Werth Mor Mfg. Co., Barberton, Ohio. Laundry tablets. No. 128,572; Jan. 6; v. 270; p. 186.

West Coast Soap Co., Oakland, Calif. Laundry soap. No. 128,573; Jan. 6; v. 270; p. 186.

West Virginia Pulp & Paper Company, New York, N. Y. Bond-paper. No. 128,575; Jan. 6; v. 270; p. 186.

Westcott Motor Car Company, Springfield, Ohio. Automobiles. No. 129,099; Jan. 20; v. 270; p. 476.

Western Boiler Pipe Company, Monmouth, Ill. Road-drags. No. 129,098; Jan. 20; v. 270; p. 476.

Western Fisheries Company, The, Seattle, Wash. Canned salmon. No. 128,574; Jan. 6; v. 270; p. 186.

Western Fisheries Company, Seattle, Wash. Canned salmon. Nos. 128,897-8; Jan. 13; v. 270; p. 344.

Western Hair Goods Company, Chicago, Ill. Face cream and powder, toilet waters. No. 128,899; Jan. 13; v. 270; p. 344.

Westinghouse Electric & Manufacturing Company, East Pittsburgh, Pa. Electric heaters. No. 128,900; Jan. 13; v. 270; p. 344.

Wharton, William, Jr., & Co., Incorporated, Philadelphia and Easton, Pa. Tractor-wheels. No. 129,246; Jan. 27; v. 270; p. 617.

What Cheer Braid Company, Providence, R. I. Shoe strings and lacings, tapes, galloons. No. 129,248; Jan. 27; v. 270; p. 617.

White Star Refining Co., Detroit, Mich. Asphalt shingles, roofing papers and cements. No. 129,101; Jan. 20; v. 270; p. 477.

White-Stokes Co., Inc., Chicago, Ill. Cocoa, icing, cake-filler, &c. No. 128,576; Jan. 6; v. 270; p. 186.

White Stokes Co., Chicago, Ill. Marshmallow inner layers or filling, toppings for cakes, &c. No. 128,901; Jan. 13; v. 270; p. 345.

White, Theodore H., Los Angeles, Calif. Planchette-boards. No. 129,100; Jan. 20; v. 270; p. 477.

Whitney, Rowena L., Springfield, Mass. Fabric shoes for children. No. 129,249; Jan. 27; v. 270; p. 617.

Whittier Citrus Association, Whittier, Calif. Fresh citrus fruits. No. 128,577; Jan. 6; v. 270; p. 186.

Widen Lord Tanning Co., Boston, Mass. Upper-leather for boots and shoes. No. 128,578; Jan. 6; v. 270; p. 186.

Wilbur, H. O., & Sons, Inc., Philadelphia, Pa. Covering used to coat candy. No. 129,102; Jan. 20; v. 270; p. 477.

Williams, Bettie, New York, N. Y. Scalp preparation and hair-grower. No. 129,103; Jan. 20; v. 270; p. 477.

Williams Chocolate Co., Scranton, Pa. Cough-drops. No. 129,104; Jan. 20; v. 270; p. 477.

Williams, Hebron & Herd, Mmes., Baltimore, Md. Hair-pomade. No. 128,579; Jan. 6; v. 270; p. 186.

Williams Patent Crusher and Pulverizer Company, New York, N. Y. Grinding, crushing, and pulverizing machines. No. 129,250; Jan. 27; v. 270; p. 617.

Willis, Joseph V., New York, N. Y. Ginger-beer. No. 129,247; Jan. 27; v. 270; p. 617.

Wilson Brothers, Chicago, Ill. Neckties. No. 129,251; Jan. 27; v. 270; p. 617.

Wilson, Raymond K., Gloversville, N. Y. Gloves and mittens. No. 129,252; Jan. 27; v. 270; p. 617.

Wimpfheimer, A., & Bro. Inc., New York, N. Y. Ribbons of pile fabrics. No. 129,105; Jan. 20; v. 270; p. 477.

Winchenbaugh, Lester F., Co., Boston, Mass. Cover-papers. No. 128,902; Jan. 13; v. 270; p. 345.

Wite-Kat Soap Company, San Francisco, Calif. Waterless soap. No. 128,580; Jan. 6; v. 270; p. 186.

Wolters, Wm., Winfield, S. D. Medicinal preparation. No. 128,903; Jan. 13; v. 270; p. 345.

Wood, W. B., Mfg. Co., St. Louis, Mo. Non-alcoholic non-cereal maltless beverage and syrup for making same. Nos. 129,253-4; Jan. 27; v. 270; p. 617.

Woodruff, Viola Y. N., Flushing, N. Y. Edible nut-meats. No. 128,581; Jan. 6; v. 270; p. 186.

Woodward, John G., & Co., Council Bluffs, Iowa. Candy. No. 128,904; Jan. 13; v. 270; p. 345.

Wortendyke Manufacturing Company, Richmond, Va. Paper bags. No. 128,582; Jan. 6; v. 270; p. 186

Wright Mfg. Co., Lisbon, Ohio. Hoists and trolleys. No. 128,905; Jan. 13; v. 270; p. 345.

Wyatt Bros., Chicago, Ill. Cotton-seed-oil stearin. No. 129,106; Jan. 20; v. 270; p. 477.

Wyeth Chemical Co., Dover, Del., and New York, N. Y. Hair remedy. No. 128,583; Jan. 6; v. 270; p. 186.

Wynne Paper Co., New York, N. Y. Writing-tablets, &c. No. 129,107; Jan. 20; v. 270; p. 477

Wyoming Shovel Works, Wyoming, Pa. Agricultural and earthworking implements. No. 128,584; Jan. 6; v. 270; p. 186.

Yonkers Brewery, assignor to Bittersweet Products Corporation, Yonkers, N. Y. Carbonated beverage. No. 129,255; Jan. 27; v. 270; p. 617.

Young, Corley & Dolan. Inc., New York, N. Y. Hacksaws. No. 129,256; Jan. 27; v. 270; p. 617.

Young & Egan, Inc., New York, N. Y. Globes, shades, and reflectors of glass. No. 129,108; Jan. 20; v. 270; p. 477.

Young, Giles T., Philadelphia, Pa. Hair tonic and pomade, &c. No. 128,906; Jan. 13; v. 270; p. 345.

Young, J. S., & Company, Hanover, Pa. Dyes and dye-stuffs. No. 128,907; Jan. 13; v. 270; p. 345.

Youngsma, Theodore S., Chicago, Ill. Coated book and label paper. No. 128,908; Jan. 13; v. 270; p. 345.

Zeh, L., San Francisco, Calif. Preparations for coughs, colds, neuralgia, &c. No. 128,909; Jan. 13; v. 270; p. 345.

Zelenko & Moskowitz, New York, N. Y. Clothing. No. 128,911; Jan. 13; v. 270; p. 345.

Zeman, Otto, Chicago, Ill. Healing-ointment. No. 128,910; Jan. 13; v. 270; p. 345.

ALPHABETICAL LIST OF REGISTRANTS OF LABELS.

Arnold Bluing Company, Portland, Oreg. "Arnold's Strip Bluing." (For Bluing.) No. 21,617; Jan. 6; v. 270; p. 187.

Blatz, Val. Jr. Candy Co., Milwaukee, Wis. "Buttery Bitter Sweets." (For Candy.) No. 21,643; Jan. 6; v. 270; p. 187.

Bruehn, Louis, Chicago, Ill. "Bruehn's Rose E Ola." (For a Laxative.) No. 21,619; Jan. 6; v. 270; p. 187.

Buck, A. A., Santa Maria, Calif. "Buck's Vulcantite Patch." (For Tire-Patches.) No. 21,618; Jan. 6; v. 270; p. 187.

California Chocolate Shops Co., Los Angeles, Calif. "Quinby's." (For Chocolates.) No. 21,620; Jan. 6; v. 270; p. 187.

Continental Paper Bag Co., New York, N. Y. "Continental Peanut Bag." (For Paper Bags.) No. 21,646; Jan. 27; v. 270; p. 618.

Drew, Arthur E., Lynn, Mass. "Drews." (For Storage Batteries.) No. 21,621; Jan. 6; v. 270; p. 187.

Emmerling Products Company, Johnstown, Pa. "Red Goose." (For a Beverage.) No. 21,622; Jan. 6; v. 270; p. 187.

Happ Brothers Co., Macon, Ga. "Kuver Suit." (For Overalls.) No. 21,623; Jan. 6; v. 270; p. 187.

Ideal Yeast Company Cedar Rapids, Iowa. "Ideal Special Prepared Malt Products." (For Malt Products.) No. 21,624; Jan. 6; v. 270; p. 187.

Levor, Victor, Attica, Ind. "La Roulette." (For Cigars.) No. 21,625; Jan. 6; v. 270; p. 187.

Lyriotakis Bros., New York, N. Y. "Vittoria." (For Olive-Oil.) No. 21,626; Jan. 6; v. 270; p. 187.

Major, Joseph, Detroit, Mich. "Major's Consumption Relief." (For a Preparation for the Relief of Consumption.) No. 21,627; Jan. 6; v. 270; p. 187.

Major, Joseph, Detroit, Mich. "Major's Cholera Medicine." (For a Treatment for Cholera.) No. 21,628; Jan. 6; v. 270; p. 187.

Major, Joseph, Detroit, Mich. "Major's Nerve Medicine." (For a Nerve Medicine.) No. 21,629; Jan. 6; v. 270; p. 187.

Mandabach, Peter A., Chicago, Ill. "Malt Phosphate." (For Malt Phosphate.) No. 21,630; Jan. 6; v. 270; p. 187.

Mangan & Co., New York, N. Y. "Hairforever." (For a Hair-Tonic.) No. 21,647; Jan. 27; v. 270; p. 618.

Milwaukee Paper Box Company, Milwaukee, Wis. "Milk Chocolates." (For Chocolate Candy.) No. 21,631; Jan. 6; v. 270; p. 187.

Oppenheim, Oberndorf & Co., Inc., Baltimore, Md. "'Buddy' and 'Dolly' Vindex Undersuits." (For Underwear.) No. 21,632; Jan. 6; v. 270; p. 187.

Pasbach-Voice Litho. Co., Inc., New York, N. Y. "Nichel Smoke." For Cigars.) No. 21,633; Jan. 6; v. 270; p. 187.

Phillips, M. & Co., San Francisco, Calif. "Phillips . Brand." (For Canned Salmon.) No. 21,634; Jan. 6; v. 270; p. 187.

Price, N., Son & Co., Philadelphia, Pa. "Price Tailored Headwear." (For Headwear.) No. 21,635; Jan. 6; v. 270; p. 187.

Rock Island Brewing Company, Rock Island, Ill. "Lily." (For a Beverage.) No. 21,636; Jan. 6; v. 270; p. 187.

Roth, Joseph S., Carroll township, Washington county, Pa. "Neupro." (For Ginger-Ale.) No. 21,648; Jan. 27; v. 270; p. 618.

Runyan Chemical Products Co., Omaha, Nebr. "Palzo The Great American Cleaner." (For a Cleaner.) No. 21,637; Jan. 6; v. 270; p. 187.

Southern California Products Company, Orange, Calif. "Golden Shreds." (For Orange Marmalade.) No. 21,640; Jan. 6; v. 270; p. 187.

St. Joe Canning Co., St. Joseph, Mich. "Shipmate." (For Canned Strawberries.) No. 21,638; Jan. 6; v. 270; p. 187.

St. Joe Canning Co., St. Joseph, Mich. "Trisum." (For Canned Strawberries.) No. 21,639; Jan. 6; v. 270; p. 187.

Standard Export-Import Co. Ltd., Stavanger, Norway. "Seaside." (For Canned Sardines.) No. 21,649; Jan. 27; v. 270; p. 618.

Steele Packing Co., San Diego, Calif. "Kenilworth." (For Canned Tomatoes.) No. 21,641; Jan. 6; v. 270; p. 187.

Tip-It, (Inc.,) New York, N. Y. "Tip It, Patent Welding Compound. Permanent Weld Guaranteed." (For Welding Compounds.) No. 21,642; Jan. 6; v. 270; p. 187.

White & Wyckoff Mfg. Co., Holyoke, Mass. "Heather Lawn." (For Stationery.) No. 21,644; Jan. 6; v. 270; p. 187.

Windsor Locks Macaroni Mfg. Co., Windsor Locks, Conn. "Victory Star Brand Macaroni." (For Macaroni.) No. 21,645; Jan. 6; v. 270; p. 187.

ALPHABETICAL LIST OF REGISTRANTS OF PRINTS.

B. V. D. Company, The, New York, N. Y. "Wear B. V. D. On Your Vacation." (For Athletic Underwear.) No. 5,194; Jan. 27; v. 270; p. 618.

Braender Rubber & Tire Co., Rutherford, N. J. "The Tyre to Tie To." (For Tires and Tubes.) No. 5,187; Jan. 6; v. 270; p. 187.

Derryvale Linen Company, New York, N. Y. "Derryvale." (For Linen Piece Goods.) No. 5,189; Jan. 6; v. 270; p. 187.

Fairbank, N. K., Company, The, Chicago, Ill. "The glory of a woman is her skin." (For Toilet Soap.) No. 5,190; Jan. 6; v. 270; p. 187.

Great Southern Producing & Refining Co., Indianapolis, Ind. "Samson Motor Fuel." (For Motor-Fuel.) No. 5,195; Jan. 27; v. 270; p. 618.

Hays, Daniel, Company, The, Gloversville, N. Y. "Hays Gloves." (For Leather Gloves.) No. 5,188; Jan. 6; v. 270; p. 187.

King Car Corporation of New York, New York, N. Y. "King '8' 'Limoudan.'" (For Automobiles.) No. 5,191; Jan. 6; v. 270; p. 187.

Reynolds, R. J., Tobacco Company, Winston-Salem, N. C. "P. A. lets the cat out of the smoke-bag." (For Smoking-Tobacco.) No. 5,192; Jan. 6; v. 270; p. 187.

Sunbeam Chemical Company, Chicago, Ill. "Stylish Colors Everywhere 'Rit' ed with Rit." (For Dye-Soap.) No. 5,193; Jan. 6; v. 270; p. 187.

Sunbeam Chemical Company, Chicago, Ill. "Astounding Growth of The World Wide Rit Industry." (For Rit Dye-Soap.) No. 5,196; Jan. 27; v. 270; p. 618.

Sunbeam Chemical Company, Chicago, Ill. "Make Your Own Colors Successfully." (For Rit Dye-Soap.) No. 5,197; Jan. 27; v. 270; p. 618.

Sunbeam Chemical Company, Chicago, Ill. "Try Her Beauty Secret." (For Rit Dye-Soap.) No. 5,198; Jan. 27; v. 270; p. 618.

DISCLAIMERS.

Casgrain, Louis A., Winchester, Mass.; disclaimer filed by assignee, United Shoe Machinery Corporation. Machine for inserting fastenings. No. 864,951; disclaimer filed Dec. 31, 1919; v. 270; p. 1.

Rodman, Hugh, Edgewood, Pa.; disclaimer filed by assignee, Rodman Chemical Company. Method of making case-hardening material. No. 1,076,453; disclaimer filed Dec. 20, 1919; v. 270; p. 1.

ALPHABETICAL LIST OF INVENTIONS

FOR WHICH

PATENTS WERE ISSUED DURING THE MONTH OF JANUARY, 1920.

NOTE.—Arranged in accordance with the first significant character or word of the name. (In accordance with city and telephone directory practice.)

Abdominal support. S. Voorhees. No. 1,327,930; Jan. 13; v. 270; p. 257.

Acetylene-generator, Variable-pressure. A. Davis. No. 1,328,227; Jan. 13; v. 270; p. 314.

Acid, Apparatus for making sulfuric. H. V. Welch. No. 1,328,552; Jan. 20; v. 270; p. 412.

Acid from phosphoric acid, Removal of hydrofluoric. W. H. Ross. No. 1,329,273; Jan. 27; v. 270; p. 576.

Acquaintance-promoting machine. C. J. Witzoreck. No. 1,329,218; Jan. 27; v. 270; p. 566.

Adding and recording machine. J. L. Dalton and J. Magnus. No. 1,328,822; Jan. 27; v. 270; p. 491.

Adding and subtracting machine. C. W. Gooch. No. 1,327,318; Jan. 6; v. 270; p. 81.

Adding-machine. C. W. Gooch. No. 1,327,319; Jan. 6; v. 270; p. 81.

Adding-machine. C. W. Gooch. No. 1,327,320; Jan. 6; v. 270; p. 82.

Address-matcher. W. J. Maguire. No. 1,328,534; Jan. 20; v. 270; p. 409.

Advertising device. P. W. Furstenberg. No. 1,329,078; Jan. 27; v. 270; p. 540.

Advertising device. J. Z. Hanson. No. 1,327,552; Jan. 6; v. 270; p. 126.

Advertising weather-shelter. S. A. Foster. No. 1,327,427; Jan. 6; v. 270; p. 102.

Aerial bomb. J. J. McIntyre. No. 1,327,487; Jan. 6; v. 270; p. 113.

Aerial bomb, Self-propelling. A. Di Grazia and E. Biagini. No. 1,327,810; Jan. 13; v. 270; p. 235.

Aerocruiser. T. M. Finley. No. 1,328,040; Jan. 13; v. 270; p. 278.

Aeroplane. J. L. Cochennet. No. 1,328,421; Jan. 20; v. 270; p. 387.

Aeroplane. J. M. Funk. No. 1,327,543; Jan. 6; v. 270; p. 124.

Aeroplane. E. B. Jaeger and E. H. Heller. No. 1,327,869; Jan. 13; v. 270; p. 246.

Aeroplane construction. H. Kleckler. No. 1,329,342; Jan. 27; v. 270; p. 588.

Aeroplane-motor. F. Wood. No. 1,329,033; Jan. 27; v. 270; p. 531.

Aeroplane-pilots, Protective hood for. A. E. Logan. No. 1,327,339; Jan. 6; v. 270; p. 85.

Aeroplane-propeller and carrying a gun which fires axially through the propeller, Mounting an. H. Austin. No. 1,329,156; Jan. 27; v. 270; p. 555.

Aeroplane propeller-drive. A. J. Harpman. No. 1,329,081; Jan. 27; v. 270; p. 540.

Aeroplane safety-parachute and means of launching same from aeroplanes. H. M. Crowther. No. 1,327,592; Jan. 6; v. 270; p. 133.

Aeroplanes, Control for dual-control. F. L. van Allen. No. 1,327,183; Jan. 6; Gaz. vol. 270; p. 57.

Aeroplanes, Parachute and launching device for. J. L. Pflueger. No. 1,327,355; Jan. 6; v. 270; p. 88.

Aeroplanes, Stabilizing control for. A. J. Macy. No. 1,326,945; Jan. 6; v. 270; p. 12.

Aeroplanes, Storage battery adapted particularly for. T. A. Willard. No. 1,327,650; Jan. 13; v. 270; p. 205.

Agitating device. W. Lindsay. No. 1,328,576; Jan. 20; v. 270; p. 417.

Agricultural implement. H. V. Calkins. No. 1,328,124; Jan. 13; v. 270; p. 294.

Agricultural tractors to the soil, Device for increasing the adherence of. P. A. M. Delieuvin. No. 1,327,376; Jan. 6; v. 270; p. 92.

Air and other gases or fluids, Propulsion of. H. Ayrton. No. 1,327,975; Jan. 13; v. 270; p. 266.

Air, Apparatus for liquefying. J. F. Place. No. 1,326,961; Jan. 6; v. 270; p. 15.

Air-bag. P. Powell. No. 1,329,208; Jan. 27; v. 270; p. 564.

Air-brake-controlling mechanism. T. W. Scott. No. 1,327,968; Jan. 13; v. 270; p. 264.

Air collecting and delivering apparatus. W. D. Scott. No. 1,327,926; Jan. 13; v. 270; p. 257.

Air-heater. C. E. Feazel. No. 1,328,272; Jan. 20; v. 270; p. 358.

Air-pressure liquid-transfer device. H. G. Diffenbaugh. No. 1,328,133; Jan. 13; v. 270; p. 296.

Air-release, Automatic. H. J. Rickon. No. 1,329,210; Jan. 27; v. 270; p. 565.

Aircraft and making the same, Fabric for. N. A. T. N. Feary. No. 1,327,707; Jan. 13; v. 270; p. 216.

Aircraft-frames, Connection for members of. F. H. Page. No. 1,328,963; Jan. 27; v. 270; p. 519.

Aircraft, Supply means for. G. L. Cabot. No. 1,328,560; Jan. 20; v. 270; p. 414.

Airship. Q. Y. Distefano. No. 1,328,369; Jan. 20; v. 270; p. 377.

Alarm : See—

Auto burglar-alarm.   Door-knob alarm.
Automobile theft-alarm. Tire-alarm.
Burglar-alarm.   Vehicle-alarm.

Alarms. Apparatus for operating. W. K. Hodgman. No. 1,328,994; Jan. 27; v. 270; p. 524.

Alcohol, Fermentation process for the production of acetone and butyl. C. Weizmann and G. A. Hamlyn. No. 1,329,214; Jan. 27; v. 270; p. 565.

Aldehyde, Preparation of pyrocatechin. L. Schmidt. No. 1,326,973; Jan. 6; v. 270; p. 18.

Alligator-wrench. H. G. Norwood. No. 1,328,389; Jan. 20; v. 270; p. 381.

Alloy, Surface-colored articles of copper. T. C. Merriman. No. 1,327,400; Jan. 6; v. 270; p. 97.

Alloy, Surface-coloring articles of copper. T. C. Merriman. No. 1,327,401; Jan. 6; v. 270; p. 97.

Aluminum, Making powdered or granulated. L. B. Tebbetts, 2d. No. 1,327,743; Jan. 13; v. 270; p. 223.

Aluminum, Solder for. J. Segura. No. 1,328,694; Jan. 20; v. 270; p. 438.

Alternating-current motor. W. C. Korthals-Altes. No. 1,328,525; Jan. 20; v. 270; p. 407.

Ammonia from the air or nitrogen, Production of synthetic. R. F. Gardiner. No. 1,328,082; Jan. 13; v. 270; p. 286.

Ammonium sulfate, Production of. W. A. Sloss. No. 1,328,342; Jan. 20; v. 270; p. 372.

Ammunition lubrication. T. H. Eickhoff and C. A. Tunks. No. 1,327,378; Jan. 6; v. 270; p. 93.

Amusement apparatus. J. A. Motsenbocker. No. 1,326,954; Jan. 6; v. 270; p. 14.

Amusement device. E. Kohler. No. 1,328,166; Jan. 13; v. 270; p. 302.

Anchor. A. F. Eells. No. 1,327,201; Jan. 6; v. 270; p. 60.

Anesthesia, Instrument for producing intra-osseous. A. E. Smith. No. 1,328,459; Jan. 20; v. 270; p. 394.

Angle-fixture, Universal. J. R. Beckett. No. 1,327,370; Jan. 6; v. 270; p. 66.

Animal-trap. C. A. S. Erickson. No. 1,327,229; Jan. 6; v. 270; p. 66.

Animal-trap. J. D. Miller. No. 1,327,490; Jan. 6; v. 270; p. 113.

Animal-trap. M. A. Twitchell. No. 1,327,890; Jan. 13; v. 270; p. 250.

Annealing-box, Pressed corrugated sheet-metal. G. P. Bard. No. 1,328,030; Jan. 13; v. 270; p. 276.

Antifriction device. S. Apostoloff. No. 1,327,895; Jan. 13; v. 270; p. 251.

Antirattling device. C. E. Soule. No. 1,327,291; Jan. 6; v. 270; p. 77.

Antiskid device. J. E. Rogers. No. 1,328,297; Jan. 20; v. 270; p. 363.

Antiskid device. J. E. Rogers. No. 1,328,298; Jan. 20; v. 270; p. 364.

Apple cutter and corer. S. A. Erdahl. No. 1,328,503; Jan. 20; v. 270; p. 403.

Apportioning device. A. Larsen. No. 1,327,678; Jan. 13; v. 270; p. 210.

Arm, Artificial. E. R Birchard. No. 1,327,938; Jan. 13; v. 270; p. 259.

Army-trailer. E Howland. No. 1,327,326; Jan. 6; v. 270; p. 83.

Arrow. G. B. Reaben. No. 1,328,967; Jan. 27; v. 270; p. 519.

Article-stand. M. Cohen. No. 1,327,943; Jan. 13; v. 270; p. 260.

Asbestos-flange mold. J. Budinich. No. 1,328,817; Jan. 27; v 270; p. 490.

Ash-sifter. T. J. MacIvor. No. 1,328,174; Jan. 13; v. 270; p. 304.

Atomizing materials in a melted state, Process of and apparatus for. E. Odam. No. 1,328,446; Jan. 20; v. 270; p. 391.

Egg-beater. P. Neukirchen. No. 1,327,568; Jan. 6; v. 270; p. 129.

Egg-box. J. L. Coyle. No. 1,327,946; Jan. 13; v. 270; p. 260.

Egg-candler. F. C. Mahaffey. No. 1,328,091; Jan. 13; v. 270; p. 288.

Egg-separator and juice-extractor, Combined. P. Tripke. No. 1,327,929; Jan. 13; v. 270; p. 257.

Egg-tester. J. R. Blakemore. No. 1,329,223; Jan. 27; v. 270; p. 567.

Electric accumulators, Manufacture of. H. Leitner and W. H. Westfall. No. 1,327,336; Jan. 6; v. 270; p. 85.

Electric accumulators, Manufacture of. H. Leitner and W. H. Exley. No. 1,329,125; Jan. 27; v. 270; p. 549.

Electric circuit. P. C. Hewitt. No. 1,328,327; Jan. 20; v. 270; p. 370.

Electric circuits and electroresponsive apparatus, Saline-operated. H. Wygodsky. No. 1,327,262; Jan. 6; v. 270; p. 72.

Electric circuits, Flush push-button switch for. M. H. Baker. No. 1,328,481; Jan. 20; v. 270; p. 399.

Electric circuits, Thermodynamically-controlled pendent switch for. M. H. Baker. No. 1,328,480; Jan. 20; v. 270; p. 398.

Electric conductor. P. F. Frey. No. 1,327,542; Jan. 6; v. 270; p. 124.

Electric controller. T. T. Cater. No. 1,328,126; Jan. 13; v. 270; p. 295.

Electric controllers, Attachment for. A. R. Anderson. No. 1,328,804; Jan. 27; v. 270; p. 487.

Electric fitting. G. B. Thomas. No. 1,329,330; Jan. 27; v. 270; p. 586.

Electric furnace. W. R. Clark. No. 1,328,713; Jan. 20; v. 270; p. 441.

Electric furnace, Three-phase. F. T. Snyder. No. 1,327,174; Jan. 6; v. 270; p. 55.

Electric heater. C. E. Clark and A. G. Dowell. No. 1,327,986; Jan. 13; v. 270; p. 268.

Electric heater. J. M. Curless. No. 1,328,723; Jan. 20; v. 270; p. 443.

Electric light, Portable. F. G. Spiers. No. 1,326,983; Jan. 6; v. 270; p. 20.

Electric lights, Thermodynamically-controlled socket-switch for. M. H. Baker. No. 1,328,478; Jan. 20; v. 270; p. 398.

Electric lights, Thermodynamically-controlled socket-switch for. M. H. Baker. No. 1,328,479; Jan. 20; v. 270; p. 398.

Electric machine adapted for synchronous working, Alternating-current dynamo- J. L. Hunt. No. 1,328,520; Jan. 20; v. 270; p. 406.

Electric machine, Dynamo-. R. E. Hellmund. No. 1,327,820; Jan. 13; v. 270; p. 237.

Electric machine, Dynamo-. R. E. Hellmund. No. 1,327,821; Jan. 13; v. 270; p. 237.

Electric machine, Dynamo-. J. A. Kuyser. No. 1,329,247; Jan. 27; v. 270; p. 571.

Electric machines, Coil for dynamo-. S. Sparrow. No. 1,329,027; Jan. 27; v. 270; p. 530.

Electric machines, Coil-supporting device for dynamo-. R. E. Hellmund. No. 1,329,242; Jan. 27; v. 270; p. 570.

Electric machinery, Dynamo-. L. J. Stephenson. (Reissue.) No. 14,787; Jan. 6; v. 270; p. 186.

Electric-motor control. J. Eaton. No. 1,328,501; Jan. 20; v. 270; p. 403.

Electric precipitator. H. I. Frisbie. No. 1,329,237; Jan. 27; v. 270; p. 569.

Electric primer. W. M. Upp. No. 1,329,345; Jan. 27; v. 270; p. 588.

Electric regulator. L. Sykes. No. 1,327,642; Jan. 13; v. 270; p. 203.

Electrical riveting, Connecting plates by. A. B. Rypinski. No. 1,329,144; Jan. 27; v. 270; p. 552.

Electric switch. W. E. Andrée. No. 1,327,009; Jan. 6; v. 270; p. 25.

Electric switch. J. F. Cavanagh. No. 1,328,562; Jan. 20; v. 270; p. 414.

Electric switch. O. P. Erhardt. No. 1,328,622; Jan. 20; v. 270; p. 425.

Electric switch. B. E. Getchell. No. 1,327,383; Jan. 6; v. 270; p. 94.

Electric switch. M. Guett. No. 1,327,615; Jan. 13; v. 270; p. 199.

Electric switch. K. Knudsen. No. 1,328,798; Jan. 20; v. 270; p. 457.

Electric switch. C. C. Stirling. No. 1,327,640; Jan. 13; v. 270; p. 203.

Electric-switch lock. R. G. Whitlock. No. 1,328,109; Jan. 13; v. 270; p. 291.

Electric switch, Thermodynamically-controlled. M. H. Baker. No. 1,328,482; Jan. 20; v. 270; p. 399.

Electric system. J. L. Creveling. No. 1,328,321; Jan. 20; v. 270; p. 368.

Electric terminals, Governor to control. A. J. Brookins. No. 1,328,490; Jan. 20; v. 270; p. 401.

Electric wires, Sectional non-rotative insulating-knob for supporting. A. M. Poindexter. No. 1,326,962; Jan. 6; v. 270; p. 16.

Electrical circuit-controller. F. Bechoff. No. 1,328,072; Jan. 13; v. 270; p. 284.

Electrical comb. J. M. Brooks. No. 1,327,804; Jan. 13; v. 270; p. 234.

Electrical indicator. F. A. Muschenheim and F. W. Blasdale. No. 1,327,837; Jan. 13; v. 270; p. 240.

Electrical receptacle. R. B.- Benjamin. No. 1,328,785; Jan. 20; v. 270; p. 455.

Electrical system. H. H. Gordon. No. 1,328,374; Jan. 20; v. 270; p. 378.

Electrical systems, Automatic protective gear for. M. Rosebourne and F. A. Couse. No. 1,329,255; Jan. 27; v. 270; p. 573.

Electrolytic apparatus. E. O. Benjamin. No. 1,328,981; Jan. 27; v. 270; p. 522.

Electrolytic apparatus. V. M. Weaver. No. 1,329,315; Jan. 27; v. 270; p. 583.

Electrolytic cell. A. M. Griffin. No. 1,327,094; Jan. 6; v. 270; p. 41.

Electromagnetic brake. H. V. James. No. 1,327,046; Jan. 6; v. 270; p. 32.

Elevator. See— Portable elevator.

Elevator. J. J. Sproul. No. 1,326,984; Jan. 6; v. 270; p. 20.

Elevator. B. J. Steen. No. 1,328,602; Jan. 20; v. 270; p. 421.

Elevator attachment. A. A. Kuchlhorn. No. 1,328,633; Jan. 20; v. 270; p. 427.

Elevator-controlling system, Electric. C. S. Brown. No. 1,327,421; Jan. 6; v. 270; p. 100.

Elevator safety device. G. Alfano. No. 1,327,513; Jan. 6; v. 270; p. 118.

Embossing without dies, Machine for. F. A. Virkus. No. 1,328,407; Jan. 20; v. 270; p. 384.

Embroidering-machine. H. Saurer. No. 1,328,969; Jan. 27; v. 270; p. 520.

Embroidering-machines, Pantograph equipment for. H. Corrall. No. 1,328,821; Jan. 27; v. 270; p. 490.

Engine. See— Explosive-engine. Oil-engine. External-explosion engine. Rotary engine. Hydraulic engine. Internal-combustion engine.

Engine. G. L. Chase. No. 1,328,033; Jan. 13; v. 270; p. 277.

Engine. E. V. Snia. No. 1,327,172; Jan. 6; v. 270; p. 55.

Engine. N. S. Stein. No. 1,328,972; Jan. 27; v. 270; p. 520.

Engine-cylinders, Oil-deflector for. A. H. Plummer and C. P. Mullen. No. 1,328,544; Jan. 20; v. 270; p. 410.

Engine-handling device. R. Rounds. No. 1,326,969; Jan. 6; v. 270; p. 17.

Engine-hood and radiator cover. R. H. Upson. No. 1,327,891; Jan. 13; v. 270; p. 250.

Engine-regulator. W. W. Hill. No. 1,327,999; Jan. 13; v. 270; p. 270.

Engine-starter. V. Bendix. No. 1,327,132; Jan. 6; v. 270; p. 47.

Engine-starter. V. Bendix. No. 1,327,302; Jan. 6; v. 270; p. 79.

Engine-starter. V. Bendix. No. 1,327,303; Jan. 6; v. 270; p. 79.

Engine-starter. V. Bendix. No. 1,327,304; Jan. 6; v. 270; p. 79.

Engine-starter. W. E. Burrows and W. A. Spangler. No. 1,327,753; Jan. 13; v. 270; p. 325.

Engines, Air control for internal-combustion. J. P. Remington. No. 1,328,102; Jan. 13; v. 270; p. 290.

Engines, Atomizer for liquid-fuel. E. H. Tartrais. No. 1,327,744; Jan. 13; v. 270; p. 223.

Engines, Automatic lubricant-supply system for internal-combustion. S. L. Martin. No. 1,328,843; Jan. 27; v. 270; p. 495.

Engines, Base-lock for reciprocating. G. Wilson. No. 1,328,110; Jan. 13; v. 270; p. 291.

Engines, Carbureter for internal-combustion. F. H. Royce. No. 1,328,590; Jan. 20; v. 270; p. 419.

Engines, Cranking mechanism for explosive-. E. N. Cesar. No. 1,328,127; Jan. 13; v. 270; p. 295.

Engines, &c., Forging cylinders of. E. Fuchs. No. 1,328,276; Jan. 20; v. 270; p. 359.

Engines, Fuel-supply for internal-combustion. S. I. Fekete. No. 1,328,142; Jan. 13; v. 270; p. 298.

Engines, Gas-saver for internal-combustion. A. J. Hansgen and E. C. Oversmith. No. 1,327,551; Jan. 6; v. 270; p. 125.

Engines, Governor for internal-combustion. W. F. Vallier. No. 1,327,847; Jan. 13; v. 270; p. 242.

Engines, Ignition-plug for internal-combustion. L. Lavoisier. No. 1,327,482; Jan. 6; v. 270; p. 112.

Engines, Manifold for internal-combustion. B. C. Chesnutt. No. 1,327,311; Jan. 6; v. 270; p. 80.

Engines, Mechanism for disengaging and engaging the main governors in steam hoisting-. E. Schneider. No. 1,327,683; Jan. 13; v. 270; p. 202.

Engines, Oil-baffle for automobile-. G. A. Rendahl. No. 1,327,779; Jan. 13; v. 270; p. 229.

Engines, Priming system for internal-combustion. G. Honold and A. Krauss. No. 1,327,430; Jan. 6; v. 270; p. 102.

Engines, Reversing mechanism for internal-combustion. G. W. A. Green, O. Wans, and F. H. Livens. No. 1,327,995; Jan. 13; v. 270; p. 270.

Engines, Rotary shaft and coupling for electric dental. A. P. Merrill. No. 1,328,095; Jan. 13; v. 270; p. 288.

Engines, Spark-plug for internal-combustion. W. E. Taft. No. 1,328,463; Jan. 20; v. 270; p. 395.

Engines, Starter for internal-combustion. L. B. Hasbrouck. No. 1,327,276; Jan. 6; v. 270; p. 74.

ALPHABETICAL LIST OF DESIGNS.

ALPHABETICAL LIST OF TRADE-MARKS.

Cotton and silk piece goods. Commercial Shirt Company. No. 128,838; Jan. 6; v. 270; p. 179.

Cotton piece goods. Amory, Browne & Co. No. 128,605; Jan 13; v. 270; p. 335.

Cotton, wool, silk, and linen piece goods. South & Central American Commercial Co. No. 128,520; Jan. 6; v. 270; p. 184.

Cough-drops. Williams Chocolate Co. No. 129,104; Jan. 20; v. 270; p. 477.

Cough remedy and reconstructive tonic. MacMorris Drug Co. No. 128,778; Jan. 13; v. 270; p. 341.

Counterboring-tools, saws, &c. National Twist Drill & Tool Co. No. 128,469; Jan. 6; v. 270; p. 182.

Covers, Slip-. L. Spiegelberg & Sons. No. 128,525; Jan. 6; v. 270; p. 184.

Cream and powder, &c., Face. Western Hair Goods Company. No. 128,899; Jan. 13; v. 270; p. 344.

Cream or salve for congestion and inflammation. J. Berry. No. 128,626; v. 270; p. 336.

Cream substitute. J. Roche. No. 128,504; Jan. 6; v. 270; p. 184.

Creams and face powders. B. L. Barber. No. 128,616; Jan. 13; v. 270; p. 336.

Crockery, earthenware, porcelain. A/S. Herman A. Kähler. No. 129,007; Jan. 20; v. 270; p. 474.

Crucibles. Vesuvius Crucible Company. No. 128,558; Jan. 6; v. 270; p. 185.

Culture of *Bacillus Bulgaricus* and milk fermented with same. Knudsen Laboratory. No. 128,420; Jan. 6; v. 270; p. 181.

Cutlery—viz., razors. Geneva Cutlery Corporation. No. 128,388; Jan. 6; v. 270; p. 180.

Cylinder-reboring tools and kits. Universal Tool Co. No. 129,236; Jan. 27; v. 270; p. 617.

Dental casting-machines, &c. Gardner Bros. No. 128,979; Jan. 20; v. 270; p. 473.

Disinfectant. J. W. Bullen. Nos. 128,947-8; Jan. 20; v. 270; p. 472.

Disinfectants. F. Sanford No. 129,066; Jan. 20; v. 270; p. 475.

Dolls. C. A. Goldsmith. No. 128,391; Jan. 6; v. 270; p. 180.

Dolls. Republic Doll & Toy Corporation. No. 128,499; Jan. 6; v. 270; p. 183.

Dolls. H. O. Shults. No. 129,072; Jan. 20; v. 270; p. 476.

Dough balling and proofing machine, &c. Thomson Machine Company. No. 129,230; Jan. 27; v. 270; p. 616.

Dough-mixers. The East Iron & Machine Co. No. 129,151; Jan. 27; v. 270; p. 614.

Doughnuts. Fleischmann's Vienna Model Bakery. No. 128,380; Jan. 6; v. 270; p. 180.

Dress-shields. E. N. Gaillard. No. 128,704; Jan. 13; v. 270; p. 338.

Dress-shields, Women's. Brooklyn Shield & Rubber Co. No. 128,644; Jan. 13; v. 270; p. 336.

Dresses and dress-aprons. J. H. C. Petersen's Sons Company. No. 128,482; Jan. 6; v. 270; p. 183.

Dresses, Children's. Kellner Bros. No. 128,747; Jan. 13; v. 270; p. 340.

Dresses, coats, &c. Women's. Isidore Rabinowitz Apparel Co. No. 129,054; Jan. 20; v. 270; p. 475.

Dresses, Women's. Moshontz Bros. & Co. No. 128,796; Jan. 13; v. 270; p. 344.

Drills, Core-. Ingersoll-Rand Company. No. 128,407; Jan. 6; v. 270; p. 181.

Drink, Soft. F. & M. Schaefer Brewing Co. No. 128,514; Jan. 6; v. 270; p. 184.

Drinks, Soft. John Graf Co. No. 128,986; Jan. 20; v. 270; p. 473.

Duck, Oiled. Armstrong Cork Company. No. 128,924; Jan. 20; v. 270; p. 471.

Dyes. Dugas-Hundley Corporation. No. 128,678; Jan 13; v. 270; p. 338.

Dyes. Essex Chemical Works. No. 128,688; Jan. 13; v. 270; p. 338.

Dyes. W. R. Grace & Company. No. 128,716; Jan. 13; v. 270; p. 339.

Dyes. Palatine Aniline & Chemical Corporation. No. 128,478; Jan. 6; v. 270; p. 183.

Dyes and dyestuffs. J. S. Young & Company. No. 128,907; Jan. 13; v. 270; p. 345.

Dyes combined with soap. C. S. Robison. No. 128,503; Jan. 6; v. 270; p. 184.

Dyes for leather goods. Albany Shoe Repairing Company. No. 128,278; Jan. 6; v. 270; p. 177.

Dyes, Fur-. Gaskill Chemical Corporation. No. 128,707; Jan. 13; v. 270; p. 338.

Dyes, Soap. Lever Brothers Company. No. 128,429; Jan. 6; v. 270; p. 181.

Echinacea Angustifolia, Concentrated form of. William S. Merrell Company. No. 128,784; Jan. 13; v. 270; p. 341.

Effervescent salt combined with fruit derivatives. Golden Seal Laboratories. No. 128,713; Jan. 13; v. 270; p. 339.

Egg-preserving preparation. D. D. Smith. No. 129,081; Jan. 20; v. 270; p. 476.

Eggs. Goodman & Beer Company. No. 128,714; Jan. 13; v. 270; p. 339.

Electric-light fixtures, Metal connections for. F. D. Parmenter. No. 129,042; Jan. 20; v. 270; p. 475.

Electric-lighting plants. Beaudette & Graham Engineering Co. No. 128,620; Jan. 13; v. 270; p. 336.

Electric panel-board. Metropolitan Electric Mfg. Co. No. 128,785; Jan. 13; v. 270; p. 341.

Electrical intensifiers for spark-plugs. B. Pace. No. 128,812; Jan. 13; v. 270; p. 342.

Electrically-driven apparatus. Landers, Frary & Clark. No. 128,757; Jan. 13; v. 270; p. 340.

Electrically-generated units. General Motors Corporation. No. 128,710; Jan. 13; v. 270; p. 338.

Embalming fluid. Embalmers' Supply Co. No. 128,371; Jan. 6; v. 270; p. 180.

Embroidering-machines. A. Balinky. No. 128,298; Jan. 6; v. 270; p. 177.

Emery and corundum for abrasive and polishing purposes. Lockhart Corundum & Lens Company. No. 128,432; Jan. 6; v. 270; p. 181.

Enameled metal ware. National Enameling & Stamping Co. No. 129,193; Jan. 27; v. 270; p. 615.

Enameled steelware. Cleveland Metal Products Company. No. 129,136; Jan. 27; v. 270; p. 613.

Engine-governor. Duplex Engine-Governor Company. No. 128,970; Jan. 20; v. 270; p. 472.

Engines, internal-combustion. Arrol-Johnston. No. 129,121; Jan. 27; v. 270; p. 613.

Ephedra-plant, Dried parts of. J. J. Crawford. No. 128,662; Jan. 13; v. 270; p. 337.

Extracts and syrups for non-alcoholic beverages. W. J. Benekos. No. 128,308; Jan. 6; v. 270; p. 178.

Eye-wash. F. I. Drobinski. No. 128,677; Jan. 13; v. 270; p. 337.

Fat, Cooking-. Procter and Gamble Company. No. 128,488; Jan. 6; v. 270; p. 183.

Fats. De Nordiske Fabriker De-No-Fa Aktieselskab. No. 128,361; Jan. 6; v. 270; p. 179.

Feathers. Wahlert & Guntzler. No. 129,240; Jan. 27; v. 270; p. 617.

Feed. Voigt Milling Company. No. 129,238; Jan. 27; v. 270; p. 617.

Feed. Wash-Co. Alfalfa Milling Co. No. 128,566; Jan. 6; v. 270; p. 185.

Feed, Dairy and stock. Chapin & Company. No. 128,327; Jan. 6; v. 270; p. 178.

Feed for rabbits, &c. Blatchford Calf Meal Company. No. 128,631; Jan. 13; v. 270; p. 336.

Feed for stock. Farmers Cotton Oil Co. No. 128,375; Jan. 6; v. 270; p. 180.

Feed, Hominy. Postum Cereal Company. No. 128,821; Jan. 13; v. 270; p. 342.

Feed, Mixed live-stock. Chapin & Company. No. 128,326; Jan. 6; v. 270; p. 178.

Feed, Poultry. Chas. A. Krause Milling Co. No. 129,012; Jan. 20; v. 270; p. 474.

Feed, Stock. Chas. A. Krause Milling Co. No. 128,753; Jan. 13; v. 270; p. 340.

Feeds. The Great Western Alfalfa Milling Company. No. 128,395; Jan. 6; v. 270; p. 180.

Feeds for animals and poultry. Blatchford Calf Meal Company. No. 128,632; Jan. 13; v. 270; p. 336.

Feeds, Stock. Southern Feed Company. No. 128,862; Jan. 13; v. 270; p. 343.

Feeds, Stock and poultry. Simmons Milling Company. No. 129,078; Jan. 20; v. 270; p. 476.

Fertilizer materials. Nitrate Agencies Company. No. 129,037; Jan. 20; v. 270; p. 475.

Fertilizers. Southern Fertilizer & Chemical Co. No. 128,521; Jan. 6; v. 270; p. 184.

Files and loose-leaf binders and sheet-holding attachments therefor, Temporary. W. M. Aydelotte. No. 128,296; Jan. 6; v. 270; p. 177.

Films, Moving-picture. Universal Film Manufacturing Company. No. 128,887; Jan. 13; v. 370; p. 344.

Fire-bricks and tile for metallurgical furnaces. Crescent Refractories Company. No. 128,345; Jan. 6; v. 270; p. 179.

Fire-extinguishing compound. First Aid Extinguisher Co. No. 128,379; Jan. 6; v. 270; p. 180.

Fish, game, &c., Sauce for. W. P. Bowman. No. 128,943; Jan. 20; v. 270; p. 472.

Fishing rods and hooks. Forest & Stream Publishing Co. No. 128,382; Jan. 6; v. 270; p. 186.

Flavoring extracts. C. F. Sauer Company. No. 128,512; Jan. 6; v. 270; p. 184.

Flavoring extracts, Food-. American Laboratories. No. 128,600; Jan. 13; v. 270; p. 335.

Flavoring extracts, Food-. C. F. Sauer Company. No. 128,843; Jan. 13; v. 270; p. 343.

Flavoring extracts, roasted coffee, Food-. Steinwender-Stoffregen Coffee Company. No. 129,086; Jan. 20; v. 270; p. 476.

Flavoring for foods. W. K. Jahn Co. No. 128,740; Jan. 13; v. 270; p. 339.

Flooring, Wood. Mason-Donaldson Lumber Co. No. 128,574; Jan. 6; v. 270; p. 186.

Floss and crocheting cotton. F. Schulemann Co. No. 128,849; Jan. 13; v. 270; p. 343.

Flour and food starches, Arrowroot. Chas. Morningstar & Co. No. 128,464; Jan. 6; v. 270; p. 182.

Flour, Self-rising wheat-. Quaker City Flour Mills Company. No. 129,206; Jan. 27; v. 270; p. 616.

Flour, syrup, Compound. L. G. Voll. No. 128,560; Jan. 6; v. 270; p. 185.

Flour, Wheat-. American Flour Corporation. No. 128,916; Jan. 20; v. 270; p. 471.

Flour, Wheat-. Colorado Milling & Elevator Co. No. 128,655; Jan. 13; v. 270; p. 337.

Flour, Wheat-. H, Dittlinger Roller Mills Company. No. 128,676; Jan. 13; v. 270; p. 337.
Flour, Wheat-. H. Dittlinger Roller Mills Company. No. 128,968; Jan. 20; v. 270; p. 472.
Flour, Wheat-. Donmeyer, Gardner Co. No. 129,149; Jan. 27; v. 270; p. 614.
Flour, Wheat-. Federal Milling Company. No. 128,376; Jan. 6; v. 270; p. 180.
Flour, Wheat-. Goerz Flour Mills Co. No. 129,160; Jan. 27; v. 270; p. 614.
Flour, Wheat-. Holmes and Barnes. No. 129,002; Jan. 20; v. 270; p. 473.
Flour, Wheat-. Jensen & Sons Milling & Grain Co. No. 128,741; Jan. 13; v. 270; p. 339.
Flour, Wheat-. Kehlor Flour Mills Co. No. 128,413; Jan. 6; v. 270; p. 181.
Flour, Wheat-. M. J. Kouri. No. 129,010; Jan. 20; v. 270; p. 474.
Flour, Wheat-. Northwestern Consolidated Milling Company. No. 129,036; Jan. 20; v. 270; p. 475.
Flour, Wheat-. Omaha Flour Mills Co. Nos. 129,038-40; Jan. 20; v. 270; p. 475.
Flour, Wheat-. Ottawa Milling Company. No. 129,199; Jan. 27; v. 270; p. 615.
Flour, Wheat-. Quaker City Flour Mills Company. No. 128,829; Jan. 13; v. 270; p. 342.
Flour, Wheat-. Red Star Milling Company. No. 129,059; Jan. 20; v. 270; p. 475.
Flour, Wheat-. Reno Flour Mills Company. No. 128,831; Jan. 13; v. 270; p. 342.
Flour, Wheat-. Roanoke City Mills. No. 129,062; Jan. 20; v. 270; p. 475.
Flour, Wheat-. J. Rosenstein. No. 128,838; Jan. 13; v. 270; p. 343.
Flour, Wheat-. J. Rosenstein. No. 129,212; Jan. 27; v. 270; p. 616.
Flours. Francis H. Leggett & Co. No. 129,017; Jan. 20; v. 270; p. 474.
Flours and cereal breakfast foods. Portland Flouring Mills Company. No. 128,487; Jan. 6; v. 270; p. 183.
Food, Cattle. J. J. Badenoch Co. No. 129,123; Jan. 27; v. 270; p. 613.
Food, Cereal breakfast. Patent Cereals Company. No. 128,815; Jan. 13; v. 270; p. 342.
Food, Cereal breakfast. Patent Cereals Company. No. 129,044; Jan. 20; v. 270; p. 475.
Food, Poultry. Sperry Flour Company. Nos. 128,523-4; Jan. 6; v. 270; p. 184.
Food products. Fleitmann, Watjen & Co. No. 128,381; Jan. 6; v. 270; p. 180.
Food products in tins, &c. Purity Cross, Inc. No. 128,828; Jan. 13; v. 270; p. 342.
Food, Stock. Sperry Flour Company. No. 128,522; Jan. 6; v. 270; p. 184.
Foods. The Basket Stores Co. Nos. 128,303-4; Jan. 6; v. 270; p. 178.
Foods. D. E. Brooks & Co. No. 128,316; Jan. 6; v. 270; p. 178.
Foods. Cresca Company. No. 128,964; Jan. 20; v. 270; p. 472.
Foods and ingredients of food. Borden's Farm Products Company. No. 128,942; Jan. 20; v. 270; p. 472.
Foods and ingredients of foods. William Davies Company. No. 128,965; Jan. 20; v. 270; p. 472.
Foods and ingredients of food. William Davies Company. No. 128,967; Jan. 20; v. 270; p. 472.
Foods and ingredients of food. Globe Grocery Stores. No. 128,985; Jan. 20; v. 270; p. 473.
Foods for hogs, cattle, sheep, and poultry. Hansen Livestock & Feeding Company. No. 128,398; Jan. 6; v. 270; p. 180.
Foods, Stock, poultry, and dog. Randall-McLoughlin Co. No. 129,027; Jan. 27; v. 270; p. 616.
Footwear. The Irving Drew Company. No. 129,169; Jan. 27; v. 270; p. 615.
Forging and castings, Steel. II. Cadwallader, Jr. No. 128,645; Jan. 13; v. 270; p. 336.
Forgings, Iron and steel. Forged Products Co. No. 128,698; Jan. 13; v. 270; p. 338.
Frosting for glass, china, &c. L. Reusche & Company. No. 128,832; Jan. 13; v. 270; p. 342.
Fruit-juices. Normandie Company. Nos. 129,032-33; Jan. 20; v. 270; p. 474.
Fruits, Citrus. Polk County Citrus Sub-Exchange. No. 128,819; Jan. 13; v. 270; p. 342.
Fruits, Fresh. T. P. Lippitt. No. 128,431; Jan. 6; v. 270; p. 181.
Fruits, Fresh citrus. A. S. Bradford. No. 128,944; Jan. 20; v. 270; p. 472.
Fruits, Fresh citrus. T. H. Peppers. No. 128,817; Jan. 13; v. 270; p. 342.
Fruits, Fresh citrus. Polk County Citrus Sub-Exchange. No. 129,202; Jan. 27; v. 270; p. 616.
Fruits, Fresh citrus. South Lake Apopka Citrus Growers Assn. No. 128,861; Jan. 13; v. 270; p. 343.
Fruits, Fresh citrus. Tapo Citrus Ass'n. No. 128,536; Jan. 6; v. 270; p. 185.
Fruits, Fresh citrus. Whittier Citrus Association. No. 128,577; Jan. 6; v. 270; p. 186.
Fuel control for internal-combustion engines. Berry & Lewis. No. 128,627; Jan. 13; v. 270; p. 336.
Fuel-ignition substance. O. Morgenthal. No. 128,794; Jan. 13; v. 270; p. 341.
Fuel-registers of internal-combustion engines. Vacuumeter Co. No. 128,556; Jan. 6; v. 270; p. 185.

Furnaces, Hot-air. Community Furnace Company. No. 128,657; Jan. 13; v. 270; p. 337.
Furniture. Heywood Brothers and Wakefield Company. No. 128,728; Jan. 13; v. 270; p. 339.
Furniture, &c., polish. O. W. Hendry. No. 128,998; Jan. 20; v. 270; p. 473.
Furniture-polish. W. T. Rawleigh Company. No. 129,056; Jan. 20; v. 270; p. 475.
Gages and oil-level indicators, Water-. Michigan Lubricator Company. Nos. 128,786-7; Jan. 13; v. 270; p. 341.
Games and game-boards. E. C. Simcox. No. 129,074; Jan. 20; v. 270; p. 476.
Games, Jack-straws. Milton Bradley Company. No. 128,945; Jan. 20; v. 270; p. 472.
Garden implements, Hand. C. S. Norcross & Sons. No. 128,473; Jan. 6; v. 270; p. 183.
Garment-hangers, shoe-trees, &c., Decorated hand-painted. Lowe & Lowe. No. 129,180; Jan. 27; v. 270; p. 615.
Garment-supports. L. Arons. No. 128,923; Jan. 20; v. 270; p. 471.
Garments. Cooper, Coate & Casey Dry Goods Co. No. 128,659; Jan. 13; v. 270; p. 337.
Garments for boys, Outer. Sheahan, Kohn & Co. No. 128,857; Jan. 13; v. 270; p. 343.
Garments, Infants' and children's. A. Gilman & Son. No. 128,389; Jan. 6; v. 270; p. 180.
Garments, Men's and boys' outer. Gonzalez Padin Co. No. 129,150; Jan. 27, v. 270; p. 614.
Garments, Women's and misses'. J. A. Migel, Inc. No. 128,788; Jan. 13; v. 270; p. 341.
Gas-producer apparatus. Akerlund & Semmes. No. 128,913; Jan. 20; v. 270; p. 471.
Gasolene. Pavania Oil Company. No. 128,480; Jan. 6; v. 270; p. 183.
Germicide. Bradley & Vrooman. No. 128,640; Jan. 13; v. 270; p. 336.
Germicide and antiseptic preparation. H. D. Morris. No. 128,465; Jan. 6; v. 270; p. 182.
Germicide and insecticide. J. Perkins. No. 128,481; Jan. 6; v. 270; p. 183.
Ginger-ale. Beech-Nut Packing Company. No. 128,621; Jan. 13; v. 270; p. 336.
Ginger-ale. Emmerling Products Company. No. 128,974; Jan. 20; v. 270; p. 473.
Ginger-ale. French Valley Springs, Incorporated. No. 128,701; Jan. 13; v. 270; p. 338.
Ginger-ale. Harvard Brewing Co., (now by change of name Harvard Company.) No. 128,724; Jan. 13; v. 270; p. 339.
Ginger-ale. R. B. Kingman. No. 129,175; Jan. 27; v. 270; p. 615.
Ginger-beer. J. V. Willis. No. 129,247; Jan. 27; v. 270; p. 617.
Glass globes, shades, and reflectors. Young & Egan. No. 129,108; Jan. 20; v. 270; p. 477.
Glove-bleach. Charles McAdam Company. No. 128,488; Jan. 6; v. 270; p. 182.
Gloves and mittens. Des Moines Glove & Mfg. Company. No. 128,363; Jan. 6; v. 270; p. 179.
Gloves and mittens. O. C. Hansen Mfg. Co. No. 128,990; Jan. 20; v. 270; p. 473.
Gloves and mittens. R. K. Wilson. No. 129,252; Jan. 27; v. 270; p. 617.
Goiter preparations. E. R. Hayssen. No. 128,400; Jan. 6; v. 270; p. 180.
Golf-clubs. Crawford, McGregor & Canby Company. No. 128,968; Jan. 20; v. 270; p. 472.
Grain-bundling machinery. Weller Manufacturing Company. No. 128,896; Jan. 13; v. 270; p. 344.
Grate-bar for furnaces and stoves. Cyclone Grate-Bar Co. No. 129,144; Jan. 27; v. 270; p. 614.
Grinding, crushing, and pulverizing machines. Williams Patent Crusher and Pulverizer Company. No. 129,250; Jan. 27; v. 270; p. 617.
Grits, pearl-hominy, &c. Wathen Milling Company. No. 129,243; Jan. 27; v. 270; p. 617.
Gum and candy, Chewing-. Mint Products Company. No. 128,462; Jan. 6; v. 270; p. 182.
Gum, Chewing-. D. Millhauser. No. 129,028; Jan. 20; v. 270; p. 474.
Gum, Chewing-. G. W. Todd. No. 129,092; Jan. 20; v. 270; p. 476.
Gum tissue. Omo Mfg. Co. No. 128,477; Jan. 6; v. 270; p. 183.
Gum tissue. Omo Mfg. Co. No. 128,810; Jan. 13; v. 270; p. 342.
Hacksaws. Young, Corley & Dolan. No. 129,256; Jan. 27; v. 270; p. 617.
Hacksaws and screw-drivers. New England Tool Co. Inc. No. 129,194; Jan. 27; v. 270; p. 615.
Hair and scalp preparation. H. Schlar. No. 128,846; Jan. 13; v. 270; p. 343.
Hair and scalp preparation. Ella Walker Manufacturing Company. No. 128,893; Jan. 13; v. 270; p. 344.
Hair and scalp preparation and cleansers. Sterling Products. No. 128,871; Jan. 13; v. 270; p. 344.
Hair-dressing. American Laboratories. No. 128,598; Jan. 13; v. 270; p. 335.
Hair-dressings, &c. S. & M. Greene. No. 128,717; Jan. 13; v. 270; p. 339.
Hair-pomade. Mmes. Williams, Hebron & Herd. No. 128,579; Jan. 6; v. 270; p. 186.

Medicinal preparation. J. B. Fuqua. No. 128,703 ; Jan. 13 ; v. 270 ; p. 338.
Medicinal preparation. Dr. J. H. McLean Medicine Co. No. 128,776 ; Jan. 13 ; v. 270 ; p. 341.
Medicinal preparation. Senoret Chemical Company. No. 128,850 ; Jan. 13 ; v. 270 ; p. 343.
Medicinal preparation. B. E. Tyson. No. 128,550 ; Jan. 6 ; v. 270 ; p. 185.
Medicinal preparation for catarrh, &c. W. C. Bradley. No. 128,639 ; Jan. 13 ; v. 270 ; p. 336.
Medicinal preparation for hog diseases. W. Wolters. No. 128,903 ; Jan. 13 ; v. 270 ; p. 345.
Medicinal preparations. Chemische Werke vorm. Dr. Heinrich Byk. No. 128,330 ; Jan. 6 ; v. 270 ; p. 178.
Medicinal preparations and products. Dr. J. H. McLean Medicine Co. No. 128,775 ; Jan. 13 ; v. 270 ; p. 341.
Medicine for blood diseases, &c. Restoria Chemical Company. No. 128,500 ; Jan. 6 ; v. 270 ; p. 183.
Medicine for colds, &c. Alexander Drug Co. No. 128,280 ; Jan. 6 ; v. 270 ; p. 177.
Medicine for colds, la grippe, &c. H. N. Alford. No. 128,915 ; Jan. 20 ; v. 270 ; p. 471.
Medicine for colds, la grippe, &c. Alfred Brothers. No. 128,914 ; Jan. 20 ; v. 270 ; p. 471.
Medicine for indigestion. W. H. Herdman. No. 128,999 ; Jan. 20 ; v. 270 ; p. 473.
Medicine for indigestion, pellagra, &c. Sulfiron Medicine Company. No. 128,875 ; Jan. 13 ; v. 270 ; p. 344.
Medicine for rheumatism, &c. Hoover Medicine Co. No. 128,735 ; Jan. 13 ; v. 270 ; p. 339.
Medicine for scars, croup, &c. L. Fisher. No. 128,694 ; Jan. 13 ; v. 270 ; p. 338.
Medicine for tuberculosis. C. H. Johnson. No. 128,742 ; Jan. 13 ; v. 270 ; p. 339.
Medicine, Laxative. N. B. Benson. No. 128,624 ; Jan. 13 ; v. 270 ; p. 336.
Medicine, Nerve. J. Major. No. 128,445 ; Jan. 6 ; v. 270 ; p. 182.
Medicines for female diseases. Chattanooga Medicine Co. No. 128,649 ; Jan. 13 ; v. 270 ; p. 337.
Medicines for use as a stomach compound. A. Juster. No. 128,744 ; Jan. 13 ; v. 270 ; p. 340.
Medicines, salves, &c. Foley & Company. No. 128,697 ; Jan. 13 ; v. 270 ; p. 338.
Metal-polish. Oliver Reeder & Son. No. 128,476 ; Jan. 6 ; v. 270 ; p. 183.
Milk. Electropure Dairy Company. No. 128,972 ; Jan. 20 ; v. 270 ; p. 472.
Milk and cream, eggs, butter, Fresh. F. D. Underwood. No. 128,552 ; Jan. 6 ; v. 270 ; p. 185.
Milk, Condensed. The Borden Company. Nos. 128,931–2 ; Jan. 20 ; v. 270 ; p. 471.
Milk, Condensed. The Borden Company. Nos. 128,934–41 ; Jan. 20 ; v. 270 ; pp. 471–2.
Milk, Condensed. Borden's Condensed Milk Company. No. 128,813 ; Jan. 6 ; v. 270 ; p. 178.
Milk, Condensed. Galeton Dairy Products Co. No. 128,705 ; Jan. 13 ; v. 270 ; p. 338.
Milk, Condensed. Holland Food Corporation. No. 129,166 ; Jan. 27 ; v. 270 ; p. 614.
Milk, Evaporated. G. Batcheller Hall Co. No. 128,989 ; Jan. 20 ; v. 270 ; p. 473.
Milk, Sterilized. National Dairy Co. No. 128,467 ; Jan. 6 ; v. 270 ; p. 182.
Molasses, olives, &c. Geo. R. Newell & Co. No. 128,803 ; Jan. 13 ; v. 270 ; p. 341.
Monuments and tombstones. H. M. Gault. No. 128,980 ; Jan. 20 ; v. 270 ; p. 473.
Mouth-wash and nasal douche. E. A. Troth. No. 128,881 ; Jan. 13 ; v. 270 ; p. 344.
Muffins. F. A. Schuller. No. 129,218 ; Jan. 27 ; v. 270 ; p. 616.
Mustard. American Mustard Co. No. 128,603 ; Jan. 13 ; v. 270 ; p. 335.
Napkins, Sanitary. Kimberly-Clark Company. No. 128,416 ; Jan. 6 ; v. 270 ; p. 181.
Necktie former and holder. L. F. Caumont. No. 129,132 ; Jan. 27 ; v. 270 ; p. 613.
Neckties. Adrian Neckwear Co. No. 128,589 ; Jan. 13 ; v. 270 ; p. 335.
Neckties. Wilson Brothers. No. 129,251 ; Jan. 27 ; v. 270 ; p. 617.
Neckties and scarfs, Men's. Block & Drexler. No. 128,633 ; Jan. 13 ; v. 270 ; p. 336.
Nickel and alloys containing nickel. The International Nickel Co. No. 128,408 ; Jan. 6 ; v. 270 ; p. 181.
Night-dresses. Wachusett Shirt Co. No. 129,239 ; Jan. 27 ; v. 270 ; p. 617.
Nut-meats. V. V. N. Woodruff. No. 128,581 ; Jan. 6 ; v. 270 ; p. 186.
Oil-cloth, &c. Texoleum Co. of N. Y. No. 129,229 ; Jan. 27 ; v. 270 ; p. 616.
Oil, Cocoanut-. India Refining Company. No. 128,739 ; Jan. 13 ; v. 270 ; p. 339.
Oil, Creosote. C. R. Cook Paint Company. No. 128,339 ; Jan. 6 ; v. 270 ; p. 179.
Oil, Medicated. Car-Bo-Thymol Company. No. 128,323 ; Jan. 6 ; v. 270 ; p. 178.
Oil of peppermint. National Aniline & Chemical Company. No. 129,192 ; Jan. 27 ; v. 270 ; p. 615.
Oil, Olive-. John A. Alban & Co. No. 128,891 ; Jan. 13 ; v. 270 ; p. 335.
Oil, Peanut-. Steele Wedeles Company. No. 128,870 ; Jan. 13 ; v. 270 ; p. 344.

Oil, Sesame-. Musher & Company. No. 128,798 ; Jan. 13 ; v. 270 ; p. 341.
Oil, Sewing-machine. W. T. Rawleigh Company. No. 128,495 ; Jan. 6 ; v. 270 ; p. 183.
Oil stearin, Cotton-seed-. Wyatt Bros. No. 129,106 ; Jan. 20 ; v. 270 ; p. 477.
Oil tablets, Olive-. Olive Tablet Company. No. 128,807 ; Jan. 13 ; v. 270 ; p. 342.
Oils and greases, Lubricating. Hagemeyer Trading Company. No. 128,396 ; Jan. 0 ; v. 270 ; p. 180.
Oils, Cutting-. Crescent Oil Co. No. 128,344 ; Jan. 6 ; v. 270 ; p. 179.
Oils, Essential. F. W. Heinc. No. 128,997 ; Jan. 20 ; v. 270 ; p. 473.
Oils, Heating, illuminating, and lubricating. H. M. Wells. No. 128,570 ; Jan. 6 ; v. 270 ; p. 186.
Oils, Lubricating-. Vacuum Oil Company. No. 129,237 ; Jan. 27 ; v. 270 ; p. 617.
Oils, Refined. Standard Oil Company of New York. No. 128,526 ; Jan. 6 ; v. 270 ; p. 184.
Oils, sauces, dressings, Table and cooking. Musher & Company. No. 129,030 ; Jan. 20 ; v. 270 ; p. 471.
Oils, Wool washing and treating. Sun Company. No. 128,876 ; Jan. 13 ; v. 270 ; p. 341.
Ointment. Skin Remedies Company. No. 128,856 ; Jan. 13 ; v. 270 ; p. 343.
Ointment. Vaporine Chemical Company. No. 128,562 ; Jan. 6 ; v. 270 ; p. 185.
Ointment, Eczema-. Powerol Chemical Company. No. 128,823 ; Jan. 13 ; v. 270 ; p. 342.
Ointment for burns, cuts. &c. W. Marshall. No. 128,780 ; Jan. 13 ; v. 270 ; p. 341.
Ointment for external cancers, eczema, ulcers, &c. R. H. Heinrichs. No. 128,586 ; Jan. 6 ; v. 270 ; p. 186.
Ointment for pimples, &c. The Blemo Company. No. 128,315 ; Jan. 6 ; v. 270 ; p. 178.
Ointment for treatment of skin diseases and piles. J. S. King. No. 128,750 ; Jan. 13 ; v. 270 ; p. 340.
Ointment, Healing-. O. Zeman. No. 128,910 ; Jan. 13 ; v. 270 ; p. 345.
Ointment, Salicylic. T. Gilman, Jr. No. 128,982 ; Jan. 20 ; v. 270 ; p. 473.
Ointments for burns, &c. Mrs. M. Napoleon. No. 128,799 ; Jan. 13 ; v. 270 ; p. 341.
Oleomargarin. Eckerson Company. No. 128,369 ; Jan. 6 ; v. 270 ; p. 179.
Oleomargarin. Ed S. Vail Butterine Co. No. 128,889 ; Jan. 13 ; v. 270 ; p. 344.
Oranges, Fresh. Santiago Orange Growers Association. No. 128,842 ; Jan. 13 ; v. 270 ; p. 343.
Overalls. Crown Overall Manufacturing Company. No. 128,351 ; Jan. 6 ; v. 270 ; p. 179.
Overalls and one-piece garments. The Powers Manufacturing Company. No. 129,203 ; Jan. 27 ; v. 270 ; p. 616.
Overalls and work-shirts. Blubuck Manufacturing Co. No. 129,125 ; Jan. 27 ; v. 270 ; p. 613.
Overalls, Men's. Finch, Van Slyck & McConville. No. 129,155 ; Jan. 27 ; v. 270 ; p. 614.
Packed miso, &c. M. Kushiro. No. 129,014 ; Jan. 20 ; v. 270 ; p. 474.
Pads, board clips, &c., Desk-. L. Sainberg. No. 128,510 ; Jan. 6 ; v. 270 ; p. 184.
Paint, Ready-mixed. The Barrett Company. No. 128,929 ; Jan. 20 ; v. 270 ; p. 471.
Paints, &c. Standard Cooper-Bell Co. No. 129,084 ; Jan. 20 ; v. 270 ; p. 476.
Pants and overalls. Macon Woolen Mills. Nos. 128,440–1 ; Jan. 6 ; v. 270 ; p. 182.
Paper. Ailing & Cory Company. No. 128,282 ; Jan. 6 ; v. 270 ; p. 177.
Paper. American Writing Paper Company. No. 128,604 ; Jan. 13 ; v. 270 ; p. 335.
Paper. Crane & Co. No. 128,342 ; Jan. 6 ; v. 270 ; p. 179.
Paper. Esleeck Manufacturing Company. No. 128,873 ; Jan. 6 ; v. 270 ; p. 180.
Paper. Esleeck Manufacturing Co. No. 128,687 ; Jan. 13 ; v. 270 ; p. 338.
Paper. Stone & Andrew. No. 129,088 ; Jan. 20 ; v. 270 ; p. 476.
Paper and envelops. Forest Paper Company. No. 128,977 ; Jan. 20 ; v. 270 ; p. 473.
Paper and envelops. Majestic Mills Paper Company Inc. No. 128,443 ; Jan. 6 ; v. 270 ; p. 182.
Paper and toweling, Toilet. The John Hoberg Co. No. 128,403 ; Jan. 6 ; v. 270 ; p. 180.
Paper and writing-tablets. Adams, Cushing & Foster. No. 128,275 ; Jan. 6 ; v. 270 ; p. 177.
Paper bags. Atlanta Paper Company. Nos. 128,293–4 ; Jan. 6 ; v. 270 ; p. 177.
Paper bags. Victory Bag & Paper Co. No. 128,559 ; Jan. 6 ; v. 270 ; p. 185.
Paper bags. Wortendyke Manufacturing Company. No. 128,582 ; Jan. 6 ; v. 270 ; p. 186.
Paper, Blotting-. Albemarle Paper Mfg. Co. No. 128,592 ; Jan. 13 ; v. 270 ; p. 335.
Paper, Bond-. West Virginia Pulp & Paper Company. No. 128,575 ; Jan. 6 ; v. 270 ; p. 186.
Paper-cleaner compound, Wall-. Klenaseptic Manufacturing Company. Nos. 128,417–8 ; Jan. 6 ; v. 270 ; p. 181.
Paper, Coated book and label. T. S. Youngsma. No. 128,908 ; Jan. 13 ; v. 270 ; p. 345.
Paper, &c., Coated printing-. A. M. Collins Manufacturing Company. No. 128,334 ; Jan. 6 ; v. 270 ; p. 178.

Paper covering for boxes. Producer's Paper Company. No. 128,826; Jan. 13; v. 270; p. 342.
Paper, envelops, and tablets, Writing-. J. C. Blair Company. No. 128,310; Jan. 6; v. 270; p. 178.
Paper, envelops, tablets, and blank books. J. C. Blair Company. No. 128,311; Jan. 6; v. 270; p. 178.
Paper, paper napkins and toweling, Toilet and wrapping. John Hoberg Co. No. 128,404; Jan. 6; v. 270; p. 181.
Paper, paper toweling and napkins, Toilet-. John Hoberg Co. No. 128,731; Jan. 13; v. 270; p. 339.
Paper, paper toweling and napkins, Toilet and tissue. The John Hoberg Co. No. 129,001; Jan. 20; v. 270; p. 473.
Paper, Printing and writing. American Writing Paper Company. No. 128,283; Jan. 6; v. 270; p. 177.
Paper, Printing and writing. American Writing Paper Company. No. 128,286; Jan. 6; v. 270; p. 177.
Paper, Rack-exibitors for wall-. Ridgely Trimmer Company. No. 128,502; Jan. 6; v. 270; p. 183.
Paper, Safety-. The Bankers Supply Co. Nos. 128,299–300; Jan. 6; v. 270; p. 177.
Paper, Wrapping-. Kirchheimer Bros. Co. No. 128,751; Jan. 13; v. 270; p. 340.
Paper, Wrapping and lining. Angier Mechanical Laboratories. No. 128,287; Jan. 6; v. 270; p. 177.
Paper, Writing-. M. Milton. No. 128,791; Jan. 13, v. 270; p. 341.
Paper, Writing-. Byron Weston Co. No. 128,949; Jan. 20; v. 270; p. 472.
Papers. Parsons & Whittemore. No. 129,043; Jan. 20; v. 270; p. 475.
Papers, Cover-. Lester P. Winchenbaugh Co. No. 128,902; Jan. 13; v. 270; p. 345.
Papers, Linen, ledger, record, &c. L. L. Brown Paper Company. No. 128,318; Jan. 6; v. 270; p. 178.
Paving-mixers. The Foote Company. No. 129,158; Jan. 27; v. 270; p. 614.
Peaches, canned apples, peaches, &c., Fresh. Back Creek Valley Orchard Company. No. 128,927; Jan. 20; v. 270; p. 471.
Peanut-oil. Musher & Company. No. 128,797; Jan. 13; v. 270; p. 341.
Peanuts. Pacific Export Lumber Co. No. 128,813; Jan. 13; v. 270; p. 342.
Pencils and wrapping-paper, Lead-. Simmons Hardware Company. No. 128,518; Jan. 6; v. 270; p. 184.
Pencils, Lead-. American Lead Pencil Company. No. 128,601; Jan. 13; v. 270; p. 335.
Pencils, Magazine-. Salz Brothers. No. 128,841; Jan. 13; v. 270; p. 343.
Pens, Fountain-. General Manufacturing Co. No. 128,386; Jan. 6; v. 270; p. 180.
Pens, Fountain-. Salz Brothers. No. 128,317; Jan. 6; v. 270; p. 178.
Pens, lead-pencils, &c., Fountain and steel. Samuel Ward Manufacturing Company. No. 128,563; Jan. 6; v. 270; p. 185.
Pens, Steel. J. Voorsanger. No. 128,561; Jan. 6; v. 270; p. 185.
Peptone. Allen & Hanburys. No. 128,593; Jan. 13; v. 270; p. 335.
Perfumes. A. Crusellas. No. 128,668; Jan. 13; v. 270; p. 337.
Perfumes, powders, &c. R. Ciluzzi. No. 128,957; Jan. 20; v. 270; p. 472.
Petroleum products. Lubrite Refining Company. No 128,435; Jan. 6; v. 270; p. 181.
Petroleum products. Petroleum Products Company. No. 128,483; Jan. 6; v. 270; p. 183.
Petticoats. J. Brener Co. No. 128,641; Jan. 13; v. 270; p. 336.
Pharmaceutical preparation American Laboratories No. 128,918; Jan. 20; v. 270; p. 471.
Pharmaceutical preparation. R. Kane. No. 128,411; Jan. 6; v. 270; p. 181.
Phonograph and lamp-stand, Combination. Electric Phonograph Corporation. No. 128,971; Jan. 20; v. 270; p. 472.
Phonographs, &c. Fulton Bros. Mfg. Co. No. 128,978; Jan. 20; v. 270; p. 473.
Phonographs, records, and needles. Raymond Phonograph Co. No. 129,055; Jan. 20; v. 270; p. 475.
Photographic developers. Lowenstein Radio Company. No. 128,768; Jan. 13; v. 270; p. 340.
Photographic shutters and lenses. Ilex Optical Company. No. 129,167; Jan. 27; v. 270; p. 614.
Pianos and player-pianos. R. S. Howard Company. No. 129,004; Jan. 20; v. 270; p. 474.
Pianos, &c., Note-sheets for player-. Rythmodik Music Corp. No. 129,065; Jan. 20; v. 270; p. 475.
Pickling compound for curing meats. H. Ehrlich & Sons Mfg. Co. No. 128,680; Jan. 13; v. 270; p. 338.
Picture-films. C. S. Hart Film Company. No. 128,722; Jan. 13; v. 270; p. 339.
Picture-films. Universal Film Manufacturing Company. No. 128,888; Jan. 13; v. 270; p. 344.
Picture films, Motion-. Screen Letter Box. No. 128,848; Jan. 13; v. 270; p. 343.
Picture machines, &c., Projecting equipment for motion-. Nicholas Power Company. No. 128,804; Jan. 13; v. 270; p. 341.
Picture-producing apparatus, Motion-. Bell & Howell Co. No. 129,124; Jan. 27; v. 270; p. 618.
Piece goods. Warner-Godfrey Co. No. 128,565; Jan. 6; v. 270; p. 185.

Pillows, Feather. Star Bedding Company. No. 128,528; Jan. 6; v. 270; p. 184.
Pills, tablets, balsam, &c. M. S. Solfer. No. 128,859; Jan. 13; v. 270; p. 343.
Pipe fittings, valves, &c. M H-Aterite Company. No. 129,122; Jan. 27; v. 270; p. 613.
Pipe-fittings, valves, nozzles, cocks, &c. The Lukenheimer Company. No. 129,181; Jan. 27; v. 270; p. 615.
Planchette-boards. T. H. White. No. 129,100; Jan. 20; v. 270; p. 477.
Play-suits, men's overalls and overshirts. Everwear Mfg. Co. No. 128,690; Jan. 13; v. 270; p. 338.
Plows, Garden-. Leader Plow Co. No. 128,425; Jan. 6; v. 270; p. 181.
Pocket-books. Freund Bros. & Company. No. 128,383; Jan. 6; v. 270; p. 180.
Polishing and cleansing compound. F. B. Webster. No. 129,097; Jan. 20; v. 270; p. 476.
Polishing-wheels, Felt. Eastern Felt Company. No. 128,367; Jan. 6; v. 270; p. 179.
Potato chips. Sterling Potato Brittle Co. No. 128,530; Jan. 6; v. 270; p. 184.
Poultry, butter, &c. Columbia Produce Co. No. 128,856; Jan. 13; v. 270; p. 337.
Poultry, Dressed. Thorndike and Gerrish Company. No. 128,542; Jan. 6; v. 270; p. 185.
Poultry-powder, &c. National Blue Ribbon Remedy Company. No. 128,800; Jan. 13; v. 270; p. 341.
Powders, perfumes, &c., Talcum. Frederick Stearns & Co. No. 128,865; Jan. 13; v. 270; p. 343.
Preparation for beautifying the hands, arms, and neck. B. Ansehl. No. 128,288; Jan. 6; v. 270; p. 177.
Preparation for consumption. J. Major. No. 128,444; Jan. 6; v. 270; p. 182.
Preparation for the amelioration of pyorrhea, &c. C. S. Cohen. No. 128,654; Jan. 13; v. 270; p. 337.
Preparation for the relief of constipation and indigestion. F. A. Sloan. No. 128,857; Jan. 13; v. 270; p. 343.
Preparation for the treatment of cancers, &c. R. L. Lawless. No. 128,762; Jan. 13; v. 270; p. 340.
Preparation for the treatment of certain named diseases. E. D. Trent. No. 129,093; Jan. 20; v. 270; p. 476.
Preparation for the treatment of consumption and tuberculosis. Stanley & Griffin. No. 128,988; Jan. 20; v. 270; p. 473.
Preparation for the treatment of menstrual irregularities, &c. A. T. Florein. No. 128,696; Jan. 13; v. 270; p. 338.
Preparation for the treatment of rheumatism, &c. Dr. E. S. Lefler. No. 128,428; Jan. 6; v. 270; p. 181.
Preparation for treating acidity and infant ailments. Mead, Johnson & Co. No. 128,743; Jan. 16; v. 270; p. 340.
Preparations for headaches, coughs, &c. L. Zeh. No. 128,909; Jan. 13; v. 270; p. 345.
Preservative for vegetable fibers. Lyster Chemical Company. No 128,770; Jan. 13; v. 270; p. 340.
Press-boards. R. Bass. No. 128,306; Jan. 6; v. 270; p. 178.
Pumping systems, &c. Latta-Martin Pump Co. Nos. 128,758–60; Jan. 13; v. 270; p. 340.
Pumps and grease-guns, Automobile air and oil. Bell Pump & Manufacturing Co. No. 128,622; Jan. 13; v. 270; p. 336.
Pumps and turbines. Coppus Engineering and Equipment Company. No. 128,660; Jan. 13; v. 270; p. 337.
Pumps, Automobile and bicycle. Coe-Stapley Manufacturing Corporation. No. 128,333; Jan. 6; v. 270; p. 178.
Pumps, Automobile circulating-. B. D. Gilson. No 128,390; Jan. 6; v. 270; p. 180.
Pumps, Centrifugal. R. E. Rich. No. 128,501; Jan. 6; v. 270; p. 183.
Pumps, Pneumatic. De Laval Separator Company. No. 128,071; Jan. 13; v. 270; p. 337.
Puttees. Morris Rashkis, Inc. No. 128,494; Jan. 6; v. 270; p. 183.
Puzzles. C. A. Schmitz. No. 129,067; Jan. 20; v. 270; p. 475.
Radiator-seal. Bear-Cat Products Co. No. 128,619; Jan. 13; v. 270; p. 336.
Radiators and boilers, Solution to clean out. Rada-Solvt Co. No. 128,830; Jan. 13; v. 270; p. 342.
Radiators, boilers, &c., Compound for stopping leaks in. M. Dannenhirsch. No. 128,669; Jan. 13; v. 270; p. 337.
Raisins, sugar-coated and chocolate-coated peanuts. C. Pinder. No. 128,485; Jan. 6; v. 270; p. 183.
Razors and razor-blades, Safety. W. E. O'Reilly. No. 129,198; Jan. 27; v. 270; p. 615.
Receptacles and parts thereof. Colwell Cooperage Company, Inc. No. 128,357; Jan. 6; v. 270; p. 179.
Refrigerators. Alaska Refrigerator Company. No. 128,277; Jan. 6; v. 270; p. 177.
Remedy for corns, warts, &c. H. Schlesinger. No. 128,847; Jan. 13; v. 270; p. 343.
Remedy for cuts, burns, &c. Creotina Chemical Company. No. 128,666; Jan. 13; v. 270; p. 337.
Remedy for cuts, burns, &c. J. W. Latty. No. 128,761; Jan. 13; v. 270; p. 340.
Remedy for inactive liver. M. M. Taylor. No. 128,538; Jan. 6; v. 270; p. 185.
Remedy for neuralgia and headache. A. R. Perry. No. 129,047; Jan. 20; v. 270; p. 475.
Remedy for promoting fertility of live stock. Aborno Laboratory. No. 128,274; Jan. 6; v. 270; p. 177.

Remedy for skin eruptions, &c. Reese Chemical Co. No. 128,497; Jan. 6; v. 270; p. 183.
Ribbons of pile fabrics. A. Wimpfhelmer & Bro. No. 129,105; Jan. 20; v. 270; p. 477.
Rice. Stuttgart Rice Mill Company. Nos. 129,089-90; Jan. 20; v. 270; p. 476.
Rifles, Shoulder-. Auto-Ordnance Corporation. No. 128,926; Jan. 20; v. 270; p. 471.
Road-drags. Western Boiler Pipe Company. No. 129,098; Jan. 20; v. 270; p. 476.
Rodent-exterminating preparation. Rodent Exterminator Laboratories. No. 128,839; Jan. 13; v. 270; p. 343.
Roofing, Prepared. Shapleigh Hardware Company. No. 129,070; Jan. 20; v. 270; p. 476.
Rouge. G. M. Brohard. No. 128,643; Jan. 13; v. 270; p. 336.
Rouge, Face-. N. L. Shireman. No. 128,854; Jan. 13; v. 270; p. 343.
Rouge, face-powder, &c. Lip-. B. M. Mason. No. 128,782; Jan. 13; v. 270; p. 341.
Rubber heels and soles. E. E. Taylor Company. No. 128,537; Jan. 6; v. 270; p. 185.
Rubber mats and mattings. United States Rubber Company. No. 129,235; Jan. 27; v. 270; p. 617.
Rubber offset-blankets. Vulcan Proofing Company. No. 128,892; Jan. 13; v. 270; p. 344.
Rubber shoe-heels. J. Pietzuch. No. 128,484; Jan. 6; v. 270; p. 183.
Rubber soles and heels. Mayflower Rubber Works Company. No. 128,783; Jan. 13; v. 270; p. 341.
Rulers for scholastic purposes, Guide-. T. Finlay. No. 128,378; Jan. 6; v. 270; p. 180.
Sad-irons, laundry-washing machines, and wringers. Wm. Endus Manufacturing Company. No. 128,372; Jan. 6; v. 270; p. 180.
Sails and truck and auto covers, Finished. John Curtain Corp. No. 129,143; Jan. 27; v. 270; p. 614.
Salmon-eggs, Preserved. A. F. Oppelt. No. 128,811; Jan. 13; v. 270; p. 342.
Salt brick. Edgerton Salt Brick Company. No. 128,679; Jan. 13; v. 270; p. 338.
Salve. G. T. Carner. No. 128,954; Jan. 20; v. 270; p. 472.
Salve. E. H. Kettleman. No. 128,748; Jan. 13; v. 270; p. 340.
Salve and liniment. A. B. Richards Medicine Co. No. 128,833; Jan. 13; v. 270; p. 342.
Salve and ointment. W. U. Herbert. No. 128,402; Jan. 6; v. 270; p. 180.
Salve for sweaty feet. Filletin & Chochkoff Company. No. 128,975; Jan. 20; v. 270; p. 473.
Sardines. Castine Bay Company. No. 128,324; Jan. 6; v. 270; p. 178.
Sarsaparilla, ginger-ale, lemon-soda. Adam Scheidt Beverage Co. No. 128,845; Jan. 13; v. 270; p. 343.
Saws, Power drag-. R. M. Wade & Co. No. 129,095; Jan. 20; v. 270; p. 476.
Scalds and burns, Liquid for. L. Thomas. No. 128,541; Jan. 6; v. 270; p. 185.
Scales for weighing. Simmons Hardware Company. No. 129,075; Jan. 20; v. 270; p. 476.
Scales, Weighing-. Detroit Automatic Scale Company. No. 128,364; Jan. 6; v. 270; p. 179.
Scales, Weighing-. Mason, Davis & Company. No. 129,183; Jan. 27; v. 270; p. 615.
Scalp preparation and hair-grower. B. Williams. No. 129,093; Jan. 20; v. 270; p. 477.
Screens for windows, &c. Metal roll-. C. H. Jackson. No. 129,171; Jan. 27; v. 270; p. 615.
Seeds. American Mutual Seed Company. No. 129,113; Jan. 27; v. 270; p. 613.
Shampoo, Cocoa-palm. H. H. Mather. No. 129,026; Jan. 20; v. 270; p. 474.
Sheepskins, skivers, roans, patent-leather. C. H. Kemper. No. 128,414; Jan. 6; v. 270; p. 181.
Sheet-metal-shaping machines. G. M. Kennedy. No. 129,008; Jan. 20; v. 270; p. 474.
Sheets for keeping funeral-records, Partially-printed C. H. J. Truman. No. 128,547; Jan. 6; v. 270; p. 185.
Sheeting, Hospital-. Omo Mfg. Co. Nos. 128,808-9; Jan. 13; v. 270; p. 342.
Shingles. Chinook Lumber & Shingle Co. No. 128,650; Jan. 13; v. 270; p. 337.
Shirts and pajamas. Prime Shirt Co. No. 128,825; Jan. 13; v. 270; p. 342.
Shirts, underwear, &c., Men's. Chain Shirt Shops. No. 128,648; Jan. 13; v. 270; p. 337.
Shirts, Work-. Baltimore Bargain House. No. 128,615; Jan. 13; v. 270; p. 335.
Shirts, Work-. Joseph Horowitz & Sons. No. 128,736; Jan. 13; v. 270; p. 339.
Shoe-counters. Harwood Counter Company. No. 128,996; Jan. 20; v. 270; p. 473.
Shoe strings and lacings, tapes, galloons. What Cheer Braid Company. No. 129,248; Jan. 27; v. 270; p. 617.
Shoes. Powell & Campbell. No. 128,822; Jan. 13; v. 270; p. 342.
Shoes. United States Rubber Company. No. 128,555; Jan. 6; v. 270; p. 185.
Shoes and rubber footwear. Apsley Rubber Company, Nos. 128,610-11; Jan. 13; v. 270; p. 335.
Shoes for children, Fabric. R. L. Whitney. No. 129,249; Jan. 27; v. 270; p. 617.
Shoes, Leather. The C and E Shoe Company. No. 129,130; Jan. 27; v. 270; p. 613.

Shoes, Leather. Frederick & Nelson. No. 128,700; Jan. 13; v. 270; p. 338.
Shoes, Leather. C. M. Kaplan. No. 128,745; Jan. 13; v. 270; p. 340.
Shoes, Leather. United States Rubber Company. No. 129,094; Jan. 20; v. 270; p. 476.
Shoes, Leather, canvas, and fabric. H. Malkin's Sons. No. 128,446; Jan. 6; v. 270; p. 182.
Shoes, Men's, boys', and youths'. W. H. Griffin Company. No. 128,719; Jan. 13; v. 270; p. 339.
Shoes, Men's, women's, and children's. L. M. Traub. No. 128,545; Jan. 6; v. 270; p. 185.
Shortening compound. Southern Cotton Oil Company. No. 129,222; Jan. 27; v. 270; p. 616.
Silk, Thrown. Abram Bloom Co. No. 128,634; Jan. 13; v. 270; p. 336.
Silk, wool, &c., piece goods. Warner-Godfrey Co. No. 128,564; Jan. 6; v. 270; p. 185.
Skates, Ice-. Nestor Johnson Manufacturing Company. No. 128,470; Jan. 6; v. 270; p. 183.
Skins, Fur-bearing. Martin-Laskin Company. No. 128,781; Jan. 13; v. 270; p. 341.
Skirts, Dress-. Grewen Fabric Co. No. 128,718; Jan. 13; v. 270; p. 339.
Snap and placket fasteners. Federal Snap Fastener Corporation. No. 128,693; Jan. 13; v. 270; p. 338.
Snap-fasteners. D. Warshavsky. No. 129,242; Jan. 27; v. 270; p. 617.
Soap. Saberton Mfg. Co. No. 128,840; Jan. 13; v. 270; p. 343.
Soap. Swift & Company. No. 128,535; Jan. 6; v. 270; p. 184.
Soap, Laundry. W. S. Burns. No. 128,320; Jan. 6; v. 270; p. 178.
Soap, Laundry. West Coast Soap Co. No. 128,573; Jan. 6; v. 270; p. 186.
Soap, Medicated. Frederick Stearns & Co. No. 128,864; Jan. 13; v. 270; p. 343.
Soap, Waterless. Wite-Kat Soap Company. No. 128,580; Jan. 6; v. 270; p. 186.
Soaps. Magic-Keller Soap Works. No. 129,022; Jan. 20 v. 270; p. 474.
Soldering-kits. F. Chapman. No. 128,320; Jan. 6; v. 270; p. 178.
Spark-plugs. J. R. Ayotte. No. 128,613; Jan. 13; v. 270; p. 335.
Spark-plugs. O. D. Bowers. No. 128,638; Jan. 13; v. 270; p. 336.
Spark-plugs. Express Spark Plug Corporation. No. 128,691; Jan. 13; v. 270; p. 338.
Spark-plugs. Lyons Ignition Company. No. 128,769; Jan. 13; v. 270; p. 340.
Spectacle and eyeglass frames, &c. Standard Optical Co. No. 128,863; Jan. 13; v. 270; p. 343.
Spectacles, &c. Martin-Copeland Company. No. 128,449; Jan. 6; v. 270; p. 182.
Sphygmomanometers. W. A. Baum Co. No. 128,307; Jan. 6; v. 270; p. 178.
Spray for animals. Lyster Chemical Company. No. 128,771; Jan. 13; v. 270; p. 340.
Stairway treads and panels, floors, &c. American Abrasive Metals Co. No. 128,594; Jan. 13; v. 270; p. 335.
Starch-glue material. Perkins Glue Company. No. 129,200; Jan. 27; v. 270; p. 615.
Starch product. Stein-Hall Manufacturing Company. No. 128,866; Jan. 13; v. 270; p. 343.
Starch product for an ingredient in baking. Stein-Hall Manufacturing Company No. 129,085; Jan. 20; v. 270; p. 476.
Stationery. Enlow Co. No. 128,683; Jan. 13; v. 270; p. 338.
Steam-engineering appliances, &c. Nash Engineering Co. No. 129,191; Jan. 27; v. 270; p. 615.
Steel. The Apex Steel Co. Nos. 129,119-20; Jan. 27; v. 270; p. 613.
Steel. A. C. Davidson. No. 128,670; Jan. 13; v. 270; p. 337.
Steel and steel castings, Bar-. Darwin & Milner. No. 129,145; Jan. 27; v. 270; p. 614.
Steel, Bars of open-hearth. Pollak Steel Company. No. 129,050; Jan. 20; v. 270; p. 475.
Steel bars, rods, &c. Crucible Steel Company of America. Nos. 128,439-42; Jan. 27; v. 270; p. 614.
Stoves or ovens, Gas, coal, and oil. Elgin Stove & Oven Co. No. 128,370; Jan. 6; v. 270; p. 180.
Sugar. R. M. McMullen. No. 128,777; Jan. 13; v. 270; p. 341.
Suitings in the piece. Jas. J. Regan Mfg. Co. No. 128,498; Jan. 6; v. 270; p. 183.
Suits, coats, skirts, dresses, L. Harrison. No. 128,721; Jan. 13; v. 270; p. 339.
Suits, overcoats, and pants for children and boys. Armor-Clad Boy's Clothes Co. No. 129,109; Jan. 20; v. 270; p. 477.
Sweaters, bathing-suits, underwear, and hosiery. Navy Knitting Mills, Inc. No. 129,031; Jan. 20; v. 270; p. 474.
Syrup and beverage, Non-alcoholic. I. C. Chaplin. No. 128,328; Jan. 6; v. 270; p. 178.
Syrup, Chocolate. W. C. Cushman. No. 128,352; Jan. 6; v. 270; p. 179.
Syrup, Corn and cane. Dotham Syrup Co. No. 128,366; Jan. 6; v. 270; p. 179.
Syrups manufactured from cocoa and sugar. Lawden Company. No. 129,016; Jan. 20; v. 270; p. 474.

ALPHABETICAL LIST OF LABELS.

"Kuver Suit." (For Overalls.) Happ Brothers Co. No. 21,623; Jan. 6; v. 270; p. 187.

"La Roulette." (For Cigars.) V. Levor. No. 21,625; Jan. 6; v. 270; p. 187.

"Lilly." (For a Beverage.) The Rock Island Brewing Company. No. 21,636; Jan. 6; v. 270; p. 187.

"Major's Cholera Medicine." (For a Treatment for Cholera.) J. Major. No. 21,628; Jan. 6; v. 270; p. 187.

"Major's Consumption Relief." (For a Preparation for the Relief of Consumption.) J. Major. No. 21,627; Jan. 6; v. 270; p. 187.

"Major's Nerve Medicine." (For a Nerve Medicine.) J. Major. No. 21,629; Jan. 6; v. 270; p. 187.

"Malt Phosphate." (For Malt Phosphate.) P. A. Mandabach. No. 21,630; Jan. 6; v. 270; p. 187.

"Milk Chocolates." (For Chocolate Candy.) Milwaukee Paper Box Company. No. 21,631; Jan. 6; v. 270; p. 187.

"Neupro." (For Ginger-Ale.) J. S. Roth. No. 21,648; Jan. 27; v. 270; p. 618.

"Nickel Smoke." (For Cigars.) Pasbach-Voice Litho Co., Inc. No. 21,633; Jan. 6; v. 270; p. 187.

"Palzo The Great American Cleaner." (For a Cleaner.) Runyan Chemical Products Co. No. 21,637; Jan. 6; v. 270; p. 187.

"Phillips Brand." (For Canned Salmon.) M. Phillips & Co. No. 21,634; Jan. 6; v. 270; p. 187.

"Price Tailored Headwear." (For Headwear.) N. Price, Son & Co. No. 21,635; Jan. 6; v. 270; p. 187.

"Quimby's." (For Chocolates.) California Chocolate Shops Co. No. 21,620; Jan. 6; v. 270; p. 187.

"Red Goose." (For a Beverage.) Emmerling Products Company. No. 21,622; Jan. 6; v. 270; p. 187.

"Seaside." (For Canned Sardines.) Standard Export-Import Co. Ltd. No. 21,649; Jan. 27; v. 270; p. 618.

"Shipmate." (For Canned Strawberries.) St. Joe Canning Co. No. 21,638; Jan. 6; v. 270; p. 187.

"Tip-It, Patent Welding Compound, Permanent Weld Guaranteed." (For Welding Compounds.) Tip-It, (Inc.) No. 21,642; Jan. 6; v. 270; p. 187.

"Trisum." (For Canned Strawberries.) St. Joe Canning Co. No. 21,639; Jan. 6; v. 270; p. 187.

"Victory Star Brand Macaroni." (For Macaroni.) Windsor Locks Macaroni Mfg. Co. No. 21,645; Jan. 6; v. 270; p. 187.

"Vittoria." (For Olive - Oil.) Lyriotakis Bros. No. 21,626; Jan. 6; v. 270; p. 187.

ALPHABETICAL LIST OF PRINTS.

"Astounding Growth of The World Wide Rit Industry." (For Rit Dye-Soap.) Sunbeam Chemical Company. No. 5,196; Jan. 27; v. 270; p. 618.

"Derryvale." (For Linen Piece Goods.) Derryvale Linen Company. No. 5,189; Jan. 6; v. 270; p. 187.

"Hays Gloves. (For Leather Gloves.) The Daniel Hays Company. No. 5,188; Jan. 6; v. 270; p. 187.

"King '8' 'Limoudan.'" (For Automobiles.) King Car Corporation of New York. No. 5,191; Jan. 6; v. 270; p. 187.

"Make Your Own Colors Successfully." (For Rit Dye-Soap.) Sunbeam Chemical Company. No. 5,197; Jan. 27; v. 270; p. 618.

"P. A. lets the cat out of the smoke-bag." (For Smoking-Tobacco.) R. J. Reynolds Tobacco Company. No. 5,192; Jan. 6; v. 270; p. 187.

"Samson Motor Fuel." (For Motor-Fuel.) Great Southern Producing & Refining Co. No. 5,195; Jan. 27; v. 270; p. 618.

"Stylish Colors Everywhere 'Rit' ed with Rit." (For Dye-Soap.) Sunbeam Chemical Company. No. 5,193; Jan. 6; v. 270; p. 187.

"The glory of a woman is her skin." (For Toilet Soap.) The N. K. Fairbank Company. No. 5,190; Jan. 6; v. 270; p. 187.

"The Tyre to Tie To." (For Tires and Tubes.) Braender Rubber & Tire Co. No. 5,187; Jan. 6; v. 270; p. 187.

"Try Her Beauty Secret." (For Rit Dye-Soap.) Sunbeam Chemical Company. No. 5,198; Jan. 27; v. 270; p. 618.

"Wear B. V. D. On Your Vacation." (For Athletic Underwear.) The B. V. D Company. No. 5,194; Jan. 27; v. 270; p. 618.

DISCLAIMERS.

Case-hardening Material, Method of making. H. Rodman. No. 1,076,453; date of patent Oct. 21, 1913; disclaimer filed Dec. 20, 1919; v. 270; p. 1.

Fastenings, Machine for inserting. L. A. Casgrain. No. 864,951; date of patent Sept. 3, 1907; disclaimer filed Dec. 20, 1919; v. 270; p. 1.

CLASSIFICATION OF PATENTS

JANUARY, 1920.

NOTE.—First number=class, second number=subclass, third number=patent number.

1— 50: 1,328,424	13— 7 1,327,845	22— 57: 1,32 ,236	29— 69: 1,3 8,039	37— 49: 1,328,2 8
2— 9: 1,328,078	15: 1,328,212	65: 1,329,179	81: 1,328,034	54: 1,328,013
15: 1,328,884	17: 1,327,724	1,329 206	84: 1,327,468	57: 1,328,157
41: 1,327,476	22: 1,327,612	70: 1,327,697	85: 1,328,663	1,329,123
42: 1,328,958	15— 2: 1,327,943	80: 1,327,015	87.1: 1,327,015	58: 1,328,489
54: 1,327,062	8: 1,327,110	112: 1,327,224	1,328,228	62: 1,327,645
62: 1,326,915	14: 1,328,339	130: 1,328,832	1,328,776	1,328,973
73: 1,327,408	16: 1,327,288	184: 1,327,689	88.2: 1,328,362	63: 1,328,026
1,318,086	17: 1,328,237	209: 1,329,293	89: 1,328,264	38— 22: 1,328,850
1,328,675	1,328,521	216: 1,327,987	96: 1,327,410	39— 1: 1,329,022
94: 1,328,545	28: 1,326,929	23— 1: 1,329,273	99: 1,328,947	18: 1,327,860
98: 1,328,439	37: 1,326,900	3: 1,328,096	148: 1,328,276	34: 1,327,257
106: 1,327,528	39: 1,327,807	1,328,210	156: 1,328,509	66: 1,329,263
109: 1,328,823	41: 1,328,164	1,329,258	156.1: 1,328,414	57: 1,328,168
131: 1,329,119	52: 1,327,757	1,329,183	1,328,436	7: 1,328,207
144: 1,327,625	58: 1,328,667	10: 1,327,029	1,329,271	40— 10: 1,328,915
1,329,025	59: 1,327,146	13: 1,327,536	167: 1,328,975	11: 1,327,298
1,329,329	60: R.14,786	1,328,614	3: 1,327,134	13: 1,327,544
149: 1,328,287	1,328,456	1,328,938	30— 1,329,133	20: 1,328,019
173: 1,328,586	1,328,737	1,329,072	5: 1,327,438	25: 1,327,019
3— 12: 1,327,938	1,329,048	21— 1,328,082	12: 1,327,547	53: 1,329,916
4— 1: 1,327,768	16— 7: 1,328,043	1,328,342	1,328,024	59: 1,327,274
2: 1,329,058	1,328,442	22: 1,327,164	22: 1,329,172	64: 1,327,552
5: 1,327,262	25: 1,327,065	1,327,781	31— 14: 1,327,704	70: 1,328,613
1,329,109	77: 1,329,313	1,327,782	98: 1,328,880	77: 1,329,218
12: 1,327,042	90: 1,329,326	1,328,416	32— 4: 1,327,674	86: 1,328,178
18: 1,327,275	1,329,327	1,328,417	10: 1,327,140	91: 1,326,980
1,328,445	100: 1,327,431	24: 1,326,947	1,327,477	107: 1,328,830
1,328,900	104: 1,328,961	1,326,973	1,328,121	113: 1,327,317
1,329,339	106: 1,328,583	1,327,714	33— 1: 1,328,871	125: 1,327,387
26: 1,327,428	1,329,059	1,328,258	23: 1,328,689	125.6: 1,329,206
27: 1,327,295	142: 1,328,874	1,329,214	26: 1,327,154	130: 1,328,135
1,327,866	151: 1,327,920	1,326,972	32: R.14,788	132: 1,326,985
39: 1,326,919	163: 1,327,045	28: 1,327,996	42: 1,327,874	145: 1,327,427
1,329,124	169: 1,328,510	1,329,322	48: 1,328,911	152: 1,329,073
5— 3: 1,327,824	17— 10: 1,326,905	1,329,323	52: 1,329,071	41— 38.5: 1,327,931
4: 1,327,103	1,328,148	24— 3: 1,327,701	57: 1,327,141	42— 3: 1,327,897
1,327,554	1,328,551	1,328,644	73: 1,329,005	4: 1,328,475
5: 1,328,977	11: 1,327,073	1,327,534	98: 1,329,347	53: 1,327,747
8: 1,329,202	1,328,637	7: 1,328,149	137: 1,327,198	70: 1,329,230
12: 1,328,802	19: 1,328,226	11: 1,328,076	145: 1,329,196	74: 1,328,700
13: 1,328,248	24: 1,328,916	12: 1,327,762	1,329,197	1,328,924
25: 1,327,221	18— 5: 1,328,887	13: 1,328,645	147: 1,328,378	43— 1: 1,328,114
1,328,878	5.3: 1,327,722	1,328,646	148: 1,328,007	5: 1,328,117
40: 1,329,145	6: 1,327,830	16: 1,327,591	1,328,651	19: 1,327,229
43: 1,327,108	18: 1,327,307	18: 1,328,869	153: 1,328,566	20: 1,329,128
46: 1,327,178	38: 1,327,841	23: 1,328,698	163: 1,327,266	21: 1,327,800
64: 1,328,751	42: 1,328,351	33: 1,327,798	166: 1,328,138	22: 1,327,290
72: 1,327,886	45: 1,327,264	35: 1,328,426	169: 1,327,114	1,327,579
1,327,887	1,328,676	73: 1,327,434	1,329,234	1,328,936
6— 11: 1,328,813	1,329,108	77: 1,329,085	180: 1,328,144	26: 1,327,490
8— 1: 1,327,260	47: 1,329,312	84: 1,328,621	191: 1,328,213	28: 1,327,040
1,327,688	48.3: 1,328,371	104: 1,327,719	215: 1,328,370	36: 1,327,751
2: 1,327,394	55: 1,327,651	34— 5: 1,327,602	12: 1,327,486	44— 1: 1,327,175
1,329,284	56: 1,326,991	155: 1,328,954	1,329,082	1,329,300
5: 1,329,117	19— 6: 1,328,635	156: 1,328,955	15: 1,326,909	2: 1,329,139
6: 1,327,862	8: 1,328,904	191: 1,328,617	19: 1,327,313	45— 6: 1,328,444
17: 1,327,659	15: 1,327,696	201: 1,328,915	1,327,668	9: 1,327,878
1,327,661	20— 11: 1,327,653	225: 1,328,206	1,328,887	1,328,243
18: 1,327,200	16: 1,329,340	226: 1,328,628	24: 1,328,314	17: 1,327,242
1,327,687	19: 1,328,653	234: 1,329,071	1,328,507	18: 1,327,865
1,327,658	40.5: 1,327,321	242: 1,328,193	26: 1,329,064	21: 1,328,995
1,327,660	52: 1,327,594	245: 1,327,959	39: 1,328,398	28: 1,328,528
1,327,662	69: 1,329,003	248: 1,327,673	46: 1,328,396	1,329,097
1,327,663	79: 1,328,875	249: 1,328,602	35— 12: 1,327,474	31: 1,328,462
1,327,756	81.6: 1,328,500	1,328,648	1,326,904	32: 1,328,664
1,328,487	83: 1,329,290	257: 1,329,186	1,328,819	37: 1,326,940
19: 1,326,958	85: 1,328,705	259: 1,327,761	1,328,820	47: 1,328,000
1,328,435	87: 1,327,025	261: 1,328,504	16: 1,327,306	51: 1,328,753
1,328,615	1,328,706	266: 1,327,078	17: 1,327,071	52: 1,327,977
1,329,166	21— 31: 1,327,227	25— 36: 1,328,699	36— 1: 1,328,665	54: 1,327,718
9— 3: 1,328,746	43: 1,328,105	42: 1,327,721	34: 1,328,239	71: 1,328,324
21: 1,329,074	46: 1,329,047	84: 1,327,710	35: 1,328,564	1,328,625
10— 16: 1,328,128	62: 1,327,310	118: 1,327,481	36: 1,328,817	77: 1,328,512
22: 1,327,008	69: 1,327,607	1,328,817	38: 1,328,816	93: 1,328,891
100: 1,327,007	1,328,052	1,329,177	40: 1,328,000	97: 1,327,608
123: 1,328,279	1,328,067	121: 1,326,902	50: 1,328,333	1,328,677
138: 1,327,497	1,329,210	1,327,006	62: 1,329,064	119: 1,329,070
11— 2: 1,328,767	78: 1,327,871	123: 1,328,367	63: 1,328,057	131: 1,327,956
12— 2: 1,327,196	148: 1,328,383	130: 1,327,739	76: 1,327,091	136: 1,328,177
21: 1,327,179	180: 1,327,556	131: 1,329,095	37— 1: 1,327,047	46— 1: 1,326,976
66: 1,327,782	1,328,543	131.5: 1,327,081	6: 1,327,412	1,327,171
88: 1,328,531	1,329,307	27— 6: 1,327,412	9: 1,327,651	12: 1,328,332
125: 1,327,020	1,329,316	28— 2: 1,327,972	14: 1,327,324	14: 1,327,360
139: 1,327,839	162: 1,327,253	4: 1,328,216	1,328,487	1,328,131
142: 1,328,322	215: 1,327,867	21: 1,328,948	24: 1,327,418	1,329,044
145: 1,328,314	22— 19: 1,328,433	29— 2: 1,327,336	33: 1,327,578	21: 1,327,056
13— 2: 1,327,484	48: 1,328,582	32: 1,328,250	39: 1,327,335	1,327,907
6: 1,327,533		48: 1,327,551		24: 1,327,072

46— 25: 1,327,019
27: 1,327,725
35: 1,328,921
37: 1,328,867
40: 1,327,168
1,327,359
1,327,415
1,327,884
1,328,100
1,328,254
1,329,201
41: 1,327,883
45: 1,328,829
1,329,045
1,329,338
46: 1,327,723
51: 1,327,540
54: 1,328,760
59: 1,326,954
1,327,464
1,329,291
63: 1,328,390
1,328,711
66: 1,329,235
1,329,254
48— 4: 1,328,553
11: 1,327,001
41: 1,328,016
52: 1,328,227
83.2: 1,327,861
86 1,327,893
104: 1,327,117
171: 1,329,129
180: 1,327,699
1,328,102
1,328,199
1,329,324
192: 1,328,485
49— 5: 1,328,273
9: 1,329,253
12: 1,328,864
14: 1,328,799
17: R.14,794
1,328,268
17.1: 1,328,673
1,329,065
56: 1,327,406
77: 1,328,530
1,327,618
51— 4: 1,327,639
1,327,875
1,328,337
1,328,469
1,328,803
1,328,804
1,328,953
5: 1,328,563
11: 1,327,440
1,328,242
52— 12: 1,328,913
16: 1,327,498
20: 1,327,244
3: 1,327,859
1,329,211
1,329,212
53— 1: 1,326,942
3: 1,327,532
5: 1,327,258
1,328,702
8: 1,328,001
1,328,558
1,328,662
11: 1,328,304
54— 1,328,992
84: 1,328,312
9: 1,328,231
55— 11: 1,328,363
18: 1,327,020
19: 1,327,424
1,328,156
31: 1,327,337
38: 1,328,124
39: 1,328,171
1,328,537
1,328,642
61: 1,329,154
63: 1,328,063
77: 1,328,171

55—	80: 1,329,118	67—	98: 1,327,447	74—	59: 1,328,754	84—	44: 1,327,157	97—	13: 1,328,518	105—	133: 1,328,163

55— 80: 1,329,118
82: 1,327,119
107: 1,327,760
118: 1,329,220
134: 1,328,697
56— 7: 1,327,924
16: 1,328,791
31: 1,328,385
32: 1,328,386
1,329,067
63: 1,327,997
68: 1,327,305
120: 1,328,668
207: 1,329,266
232: 1,328,836
407: 1,328,795
417: 1,328,674
480: 1,328,781
57— 9: 1,326,969
18: 1,329,057
34: 1,327,059
58— 16: 1,327,669
26: 1,328,247
28: 1,329,083
56: 1,327,051
66: 1,327,391
121: 1,327,226
138: 1,327,392
59— 69: 1,327,853
78: 1,327,365
95: 1,327,013
60— 15: 1,328,685
18: 1,327,753
29: 1,327,769
39: 1,327,159
44: 1,328,088
1,328,160
54: 1,327,080
66: 1,328,951
70: 1,327,510
1,328,497
94: 1,328,502
61— 36: 1,327,263
1,327,269
42: 1,329,317
66: 1,327,285
1,327,286
71: 1,327,679
62— 9: 1,329,350
90: 1,327,214
106: 1,327,414
122: 1,326,961
1,327,906
136: 1,327,560
63— 15: 1,326,977
1,327,606
28: 1,328,948
1,328,949
64— 10: 1,327,301
1,328,451
1,328,591
22: 1,327,173
1,327,429
24: 1,327,136
1,327,429
1,328,209
26: 1,328,787
30: 1,328,983
36: R.14,792
39: 1,327,026
1,328,179
49: 1,328,017
1,328,716
52: 1,329,217
59: 1,327,169
1,329,089
62: 1,327,003
79: 1,328,879
89: 1,328,065
1,328,095
91: 1,328,449
96: 1,328,993
1,328,366
1,328,893
1,328,688
102: 1,327,791
65— 12: 1,327,929
13: 1,329,203
45: 1,328,568
47: 1,328,827
57: 1,328,447
65: 1,327,437
1,327,982
66— 4: 1,328,217
22: 1,327,122
24: 1,328,580
33: 1,327,228
67— 3: 1,328,788
6: 1,327,585
6.1: 1,327,813
50: 1,327,161
69: 1,327,858
70: 1,327,048
79: 1,329,222

67— 98: 1,327,447
68— 9: 1,326,982
1,327,613
1,327,976
1,328,807
10: 1,329,257
12: 1,326,911
26: 1,326,928
1,328,786
32: 1,327,526
1,327,527
1,327,690
1,327,766
1,328,361
69— 9.5: 1,329,294
16: 1,327,028
70— 17: 1,327,426
18: 1,327,406
1,327,601
45: 1,327,916
46: 1,328,074
53: 1,327,140
55: 1,329,041
56: 1,327,457
90: 1,328,619
115: 1,328,106
122: 1,328,109
126: 1,327,979
129: 1,328,186
1,328,591
1,328,582
1,329,114
131: 1,327,432
71— 1: 1,329,105
72— 30: 1,327,584
46: 1,327,292
56: 1,327,589
66: 1,328,555
68: 1,329,292
118: 1,327,741
1,328,201
124: 1,327,448
138: 1,327,151
73— 32: 1,327,800
51: 1,327,251
1,329,160
52: 1,326,957
54: 1,329,150
109: 1,328,895
110: 1,328,876
111: 1,328,572
74— 5: 1,327,793
1,328,252
1,328,350
7: 1,327,276
1,327,302
1,327,303
1,327,304
1,327,504
1,327,950
1,328,217
1,328,440
1,328,670
1,328,934
1,329,159
8: 1,328,064
13: 1,327,559
1,327,656
1,328,502
14: 1,327,192
1,328,379
16: 1,328,493
17: 1,328,600
21: 1,328,834
26: 1,327,209
1,327,210
31: 1,327,925
34: 1,328,517
1,328,588
1,329,297
39: 1,328,761
1,328,899
1,329,079
1,329,142
41: 1,327,107
43: 1,328,172
1,329,050
46: 1,328,501
1,327,955
1,328,145
1,328,253
1,328,635
1,329,011
54: 1,327,942
1,329,000
55: 1,327,250
56: 1,327,681
1,327,891
58: 1,326,935
1,327,832
1,328,724
59: 1,328,062
1,328,220

74— 59: 1,328,754
63: 1,329,190
70: R.14,797
1,327,046
1,328,966
79: 1,327,616
81: 1,327,137
1,328,400
85: 1,327,147
86: 1,328,526
99: 1,329,319
106: 1,329,037
108: 1,327,895
75— 1: 1,326,971
1,327,398
1,328,694
14: 1,328,636
1,329,065
18: 1,327,974
197: 1,327,743
76— 5: 1,327,720
26: 1,327,713
33: 1,327,012
36: 1,328,159
40: 1,329,036
46: 1,328,554
101: 1,327,099
1,327,100
1,327,101
107: 1,327,652
77— 1: 1,328,409
7: 1,328,111
28: 1,328,429
73: 1,327,934
1,328,208
73.5: 1,327,506
28: 1,327,817
30: 1,327,331
49: 1,328,905
79— 3: 1,327,322
16: 1,328,742
80— 1: 1,327,919
5.1: 1,328,498
16: 1,327,635
20: 1,327,225
48: 1,327,315
81— 1: 1,328,197
9.5: 1,329,155
15: 1,326,907
1,327,802
1,328,508
19: 1,326,999
23: 1,326,933
42: 1,328,049
53: 1,328,087
57: 1,327,991
65: 1,328,744
66: 1,327,309
92: 1,328,389
112: 1,327,702
114: 1,327,524
119: 1,327,879
121: 1,328,428
126: 1,327,505
134: R.14,791
179: 1,329,161
195: 1,328,940
82— 1: 1,327,187
2: 1,328,962
8: 1,328,763
11: 1,329,042
28: 1,327,604
31: 1,327,356
35: 1,329,265
83— 8: 1,327,347
9: 1,328,299
13: 1,327,385
26: 1,328,692
27: 1,327,444
38: 1,327,636
53: 1,328,806
60: 1,328,174
64: 1,327,740
67: 1,327,667
1,329,113
73: R.14,795
1,328,486
1,328,765
79: 1,327,537
80: 1,328,778
82: 1,326,908
1,327,885
1,327,903
85: 1,328,456
1,329,127
88: 1,327,554
1,327,902
91: 1,328,446
84— 7: 1,328,831
8: 1,328,038
17: 1,327,621
1,328,976
22: 1,327,996
43: 1,328,838

84— 44: 1,327,157
48: 1,328,718
72: 1,327,433
78: 1,328,524
79: 1,327,970
156: 1,328,796
160: 1,328,870
161: 1,327,342
1,328,260
162: 1,329,298
85— 1.5: R.14,796
1,328,053
1,328,532
5: 1,329,131
11: 1,328,911
20: 1,328,010
51: 1,327,417
86— 19: 1,327,378
48: 1,327,698
87— 5: 1,327,631
1,328,080
1,328,898
6: 1,328,047
1,328,278
12: 1,329,076
19: 1,327,166
88— 1: 1,328,292
1,328,293
14: 1,327,005
16: 1,328,296
16.2: 1,328,189
16.4: 1,328,291
1,328,352
17: 1,326,997
1,328,741
18.6: 1,328,382
18.7: 1,327,934
19.3: 1,328,759
20: 1,327,163
1,328,609
24: 1,327,204
1,327,752
27: 1,327,898
1,328,192
39: 1,328,441
89— 1: 1,327,086
1,328,728
4: 1,327,087
10: 1,327,518
12: 1,328,269
33: 1,328,356
35: 1,329,346
36: 1,327,326
38: 1,327,084
1,327,085
40: 1,326,975
1,327,603
1,328,811
1,328,849
90— 1: 1,329,175
28.1: 1,328,077
33: 1,328,085
1,328,281
53: 1,328,334
58: 1,327,370
60: 1,327,799
91— 14: 1,327,127
14.5: 1,328,841
36: 1,327,420
42: 1,327,014
45: 1,327,014
46: 1,326,979
49: 1,327,300
51: 1,327,299
1,328,081
59: 1,328,407
59.1: 1,327,273
68: 1,327,197
1,328,541
70: 1,327,407
72: 1,328,833
92— 3: 1,327,590
1,327,873
11: 1,327,291
1,327,666
35: 1,327,126
38: 1,329,130
48: 1,329,100
49: 1,327,225
1,327,329
93— 2: 1,329,069
1,329,236
59.1: 1,327,333
61: 1,328,011
81: 1,328,792
1,328,912
94— 3: 1,328,310
18: 1,328,107
44: 1,327,131
95— 1.1: 1,327,383
5.7: 1,328,088
89: 1,328,305
97— 11: 1,328,740

97— 13: 1,328,518
18: 1,327,562
1,327,921
25: 1,328,913
28: 1,329,176
35: 1,327,212
1,327,413
36: 1,328,756
48: 1,328,638
63: 1,328,800
67: 1,327,828
72: 1,328,896
81: 1,328,710
1,328,808
98— 2: 1,328,879
3: 1,328,094
26: 1,327,130
1,328,132
27: 1,327,630
1,327,120
30: 1,328,547
99— 2: 1,327,937
1,328,183
1,328,395
1,328,397
6: 1,328,091
1,329,223
8: 1,329,246
11: 1,327,113
1,328,220
1,328,556
12: 1,328,506
1,328,655
1,328,657
1,328,658
1,328,650
1,328,660
1,328,661
1,328,662
15: 1,327,308
123: 1,328,505
19: 1,327,471
28: 1,327,472
47: 1,327,254
1,328,090
51: 1,327,093
56: 1,328,728
100— 50: 1,328,534
115: 1,328,368
216: 1,329,325
248: 1,328,842
292: 1,327,341
351: 1,327,580
371: 1,328,031
396: 1,328,725
102— 2: 1,327,487
1,327,488
20: 1,327,899
21: 1,328,307
26: 1,327,372
1,327,545
1,327,655
1,328,967
28: 1,328,334
29: 1,327,451
1,327,531
1,329,134
39: 1,327,187
1,327,600
1,327,968
103— 8: 1,327,968
43: 1,328,061
44: 1,327,517
61: 1,327,512
1,328,165
62: 1,329,187
63: 1,327,914
1,328,162
64: 1,327,583
1,329,171
65: 1,328,084
1,329,281
67: 1,328,965
75: 1,327,449
1,328,274
1,328,474
76: 1,327,423
82: 1,328,218
85: 1,327,272
104— 13: 1,329,049
23: 1,328,238
28: 1,327,533
59: 1,328,166
91: 1,327,071
101: 1,327,249
1,327,290
109: 1,328,523
118: 1,329,304
1,329,305
130: 1,329,306
151: 1,327,215
162: 1,326,949
235: 1,327,243
105— 49: 1,329,269
107: 1,328,110

105— 133: 1,328,163
180: 1,328,749
190: 1,328,592
224: 1,328,512
244: R.14,785
271: 1,327,623
354: 1,327,586
374: 1,327,894
376: 1,327,634
400: 1,327,367
406: 1,328,684
1,329,006
414: 1,328,683
106— 9: 1,327,448
10: 1,327,758
21: 1,329,094
24: 1,327,145
31: 1,327,726
1,329,232
36.1: 1,327,569
107— 8: 1,328,483
15: 1,326,930
1,328,308
17: 1,327,806
27: 1,328,603
50: 1,327,461
58: 1,329,086
59: 1,328,745
67: 1,327,328
108— 5.6: 1,327,005
1,328,300
7: 1,328,800
26: 1,327,770
24: 1,328,116
28: 1,328,296
36: 1,327,765
40: 1,327,309
44: 1,328,406
1,328,011
1,328,883
45: 1,327,764
60: 1,327,727
110— 21: 1,327,090
38: 1,328,730
40: 1,328,846
52: 1,328,222
76: 1,327,353
83: 1,328,375
111— 2: 1,327,237
5: 1,328,821
7: 1,328,972
12: 1,327,972
86: 1,328,969
100: 1,327,348
1,327,646
1,328,108
1,329,221
1,329,245
135: 1,328,885
208: 1,327,647
241: 1,328,023
252: 1,327,618
254: 1,327,282
266: 1,327,191
112— 14: 1,329,259
23: 1,327,994
24: 1,327,966
30: 1,329,140
33: 1,327,641
80: 1,328,020
112: 1,327,968
116: 1,327,484
1,329,268
113— 16: 1,327,509
24: 1,328,571
51: 1,328,014
1,328,434
1,329,225
68: 1,328,122
79: 1,328,841
163: 1,327,643
195: 1,328,727
208: 1,327,201
218: 1,328,985
222: 1,327,522
225: 1,327,856
238: 1,327,614
240: 1,328,549
114— 17: 1,328,313
28: 1,329,228
115— 17: 1,328,313
116— 1: 1,327,306
1,327,328
1,327,416
1,327,573
1,327,993
1,328,093
1,328,639
1,328,529
1,328,772
1,329,053
1,329,275
31: 1,327,027
1,327,128
1,327,605
1,328,073

Column 1

116— 31: 1,328,097
1,328,387
1,328,404
1,328,782
1,328,978
42: 1,328,559
44: 1,327,021
1,327,785
49: 1,328,041
65: 1,329,046
118— 11: 1,326,950
119— 4: 1,328,008
16: 1,328,810
23: 1,329,104
25: 1,328,861
27: 1,327,386
33: 1,327,104
37: 1,328,032
48: 1,329,024
61: 1,329,288
63: 1,328,970
74: 1,328,036
75: 1,328,207
90: 1,327,734
84: 1,328,256
88: 1,327,246
99: 1,327,374
103: 1,328,140
147: 1,327,735
157: 1,327,088
120— 1: 1,328,548
15: 1,327,038
18: 1,328,300
28: 1,328,476
43: 1,327,922
46: 1,328,215
50: 1,327,729
52: 1,327,236
85: 1,327,459
128: 1,328,318
121— 14: 1,327,419
1,328,527
41: 1,328,437
60: 1,328,033
63: 1,328,972
108: 1,328,289
122— 32: 1,328,808
65: 1,328,303
209: 1,327,188
250: 1,328,856
462: 1,328,364
473: 1,328,365
485: 1,327,032
123— 3: 1,327,495
11: 1,328,410
14: 1,327,575
25: 1,327,551
31: 1,328,142
32: 1,327,744
1,328,499
33: 1,329,343
41: 1,327,995
43: 1,328,261
44: 1,328,484
52: 1,327,311
58: 1,329,023
59: 1,327,172
1,327,345
65: 1,328,141
74: 1,327,462
76: 1,328,265
80: 1,327,202
104: 1,327,927
117: 1,328,483
122: 1,327,384
131: 1,328,844
148: 1,327,790
1,328,374
1,329,152
149: 1,327,861
1,327,502
1,328,149
1,328,892
163: 1,328,900
166: 1,327,284
1,327,344
169: 1,327,087
1,327,382
1,327,482
1,328,051
1,328,147
1,328,463
1,329,013
174: 1,328,815
1,328,875
178: 1,327,148
1,327,381
1,328,089
1,329,345
185: 1,327,109
1,328,127
187.5: 1,327,687
191: 1,328,544

Column 2

123— 193: 1,329,238
124— 10: 1,327,064
13: 1,328,929
15: 1,327,998
1,328,275
1,328,344
125— 13: 1,327,923
126— 9: 1,327,115
18: 1,327,203
60: 1,328,743
70: 1,328,246
77: 1,327,988
90: 1,328,012
173: 1,328,686
176: 1,327,270
215: 1,326,904
256: 1,327,508
260: 1,328,161
272: 1,328,202
1,328,239
1,328,722
275: 1,328,152
276: 1,328,071
292: 1,328,565
307: 1,327,377
359: 1,328,682
360: 1,328,630
1,329,063
367: 1,329,035
127— 2: 1,327,222
128— 49: 1,327,466
87: 1,328,598
105: 1,328,944
137: 1,327,407
138: 1,328,176
147: 1,328,057
167: 1,327,930
191: 1,328,058
218: 1,328,203
239: 1,327,167
241: 1,327,705
269: 1,327,499
286: 1,329,195
305: 1,328,459
340: 1,327,577
345: 1,328,624
129— 1: 1,327,624
1,328,971
16: 1,327,818
1,328,604
1,328,956
20: 1,329,080
23: 1,328,561
38: 1,327,186
40: 1,327,092
130— 9: 1,327,402
13: 1,327,297
15: 1,327,700
16: 1,328,872
18: 1,328,819
19: 1,327,325
23: 1,327,193
30: 1,328,295
131— 6: 1,327,692
30: 1,324,143
52: 1,327,139
59: 1,328,964
60: 1,328,733
1,328,734
1,328,735
132— 19: 1,327,980
1,328,422
1,328,771
35: 1,328,170
133— 3: 1,327,357
134— 4: 1,327,969
15: 1,327,239
26: 1,328,917
1,327,332
31: 1,328,188
50: 1,327,928
51: 1,328,282
59: 1,327,061
79: 1,327,933
135— 20: 1,328,901
23: 1,326,902
29: 1,328,175
31: 1,329,219
46: 1,326,931
137— 9: 1,328,348
21: 1,327,693
1,328,857
1,329,169
35: 1,328,649
53: 1,328,653
68: 1,327,283
1,327,999
1,328,009
71: 1,328,726
75: 1,328,988
1,327,195
1,329,285
79: 1,327,831

Column 3

137— 93: 1,327,000
99: 1,327,846
101: 1,327,939
103: 1,327,691
139: 1,328,590
1,328,946
1,329,017
152: 1,327,847
138— 9: 1,327,417
1,327,670
139— 7: 1,327,676
1,328,794
9: 1,328,903
1,329,170
22: 1,328,018
23: 1,329,251
27: 1,327,954
30: 1,329,157
40: 1,328,570
46: 1,327,709
48: 1,327,964
66: 1,329,302
1,329,303
71: 1,327,683
1,327,684
85: 1,327,069
1,327,070
1,327,788
1,328,452
1,328,585
1,328,907
1,328,908
1,329,328
140— 2: 1,327,852
105: 1,327,467
121: 1,328,423
123: 1,329,226
141— 7: 1,328,380
11: 1,327,089
143— 114: 1,327,555
133: 1,328,882
163: 1,327,054
144— 1: 1,327,390
12: 1,328,492
29: 1,327,018
42: 1,327,983
51: 1,327,627
61: 1,329,061
114: 1,327,515
191: 1,329,060
193: 1,328,471
240: 1,328,430
281: 1,327,815
304: 1,328,862
145— 47: 1,327,155
121: 1,327,049
146— 5: 1,329,023
6: 1,327,083
1,328,503
7: 1,327,316
12: 1,328,301
26: 1,327,346
148— 6: 1,327,400
1,327,401
13: 1,328,851
25: 1,327,020
149— 5: 1,327,105
1,328,088
150— 8: 1,328,859
151— 2: 1,327,373
8: 1,328,893
18: 1,327,336
19: 1,328,401
25: 1,326,992
28: 1,328,399
1,328,443
47: 1,327,152
53: 1,327,435
152— 2: 1,327,369
5: 1,327,717
6: 1,328,632
8: 1,327,478
1,327,813
1,329,021
1,329,215
1,329,331
11: 1,328,371
2: 1,328,488
1,329,126
1,329,146
14: 1,327,582
1,328,297
1,328,298
1,329,200
16: 1,328,539
17: 1,328,054
18: 1,327,503
21: 1,327,180
1,327,759
1,328,605
1,328,731
1,329,289
1,327,096

Column 4

152— 31: 1,329,213
32: 1,327,343
36: 1,328,779
44: 1,328,858
30: 1,328,244
1,329,111
117: 1,328,757
153— 37: 1,326,981
67: 1,327,728
69.5: 1,328,916
80.5: 1,327,491
154— 1: 1,327,826
6: 1,327,677
9: 1,329,239
10: 1,327,910
14: 1,327,802
1,327,912
1,328,006
17: 1,329,310
1,329,311
31: 1,327,158
42: 1,328,056
46: 1,327,707
1,328,623
51: 1,33,267
53: 1,327,281
155— 8: 1,329,261
9: 1,327,706
18: 1,327,475
20: 1,327,941
23: 1,328,943
34: 1,328,181
35: 1,328,181
45: 1,326,921
1,328,826
156— 16: 1,327,363
1,327,364
19: 1,326,961
22: 1,327,961
23: 1,327,460
24: 1,328,575
1,329,249
26: 1,327,150
27: 1,326,941
1,328,136
35: 1,329,092
37: 1,328,577
158— 1: 1,328,075
1,329,052
1.5: 1,329,279
2: 1,328,198
11.1: 1,327,092
27.4: 1,328,326
27.5: 1,329,270
28: 1,327,256
36: 1,328,354
1,328,920
46.5: 1,329,074
56: 1,329,054
65: 1,327,763
1,329,224
77: 1,327,571
78: 1,326,996
90: 1,327,837
91: 1,328,419
105: 1,328,289
110: 1,328,225
116: 1,3?9,096
179: 1,329,068
160— 1: 1,327,035
161— 8: 1,329,020
162— 1: 1,327,404
1,328,139
4: 1,329,093
163— 8: 1,326,925
164— 29: 1,328,347
43: 1,328,671
49: 1,327,915
68: 1,326,986
71: 1,327,082
80: 1,328,547
166— 8: 1,328,438
20: 1,328,569
167— 3: 1,327,550
9: 1,329,118
1,329,349
168— 13: 1,327,493
1,327,716
18: 1,328,708
35: 1,327,523
169— 20: 1,328,922
23: 1,328,994
31: 1,326,907
67: 1,329,299
117: 1,327,745
150: 1,329,081
159: 1,328,046
1,328,241
169: 1,327,964
171— 119: 1,328,473
1,328,797
206: 1,329,027

Column 5

171— 209: 1,327,160
212: 1,327,349
1,327,350
225: R. 14,787
1,327,795
228: 1,327,820
252: 1,327,375
1,327,619
1,327,621
1,329,242
1,329,247
312: 1,327,819
313: 1,328,321
314: 1,327,682
321: 1,328,267
1,329,277
172— 120: 1,328,465
152: 1,327,421
179: 1,327,784
1,327,789
1,327,822
1,328,513
1,328,514
1,328,515
1,328,631
1,328,804
239: 1,327,129
274: 1,328,519
1,328,520
1,329,243
276: 1,328,467
280: 1,328,525
288: 1,327,787
1,328,501
173— 72: 1,327,803
259: 1,328,784
278: 1,327,947
314: 1,326,962
321: 1,328,687
1,328,732
331: 1,328,224
356: 1,326,924
358: 1,327,496
359: 1,328,774
1,328,783
362: 1,328,581
89: 1,327,786
174— 30: 1,328,720
175— 183: 1,327,341
1,328,187
264: 1,328,403
284: 1,327,009
294: 1,327,777
1,328,457
1,329,193
1,329,255
296: 1,328,516
337: 1,327,671
345: 1,327,540
354: 1,326,972
1,328,597
364: 1,327,521
1,328,311
176— 103: 1,327,289
1,329,132
177— 7: 1,327,194
1,328,454
100.1: 1,326,955
329: 1,327,818
337: 1,329,043
339: 1,327,837
1,328,245
1,328,269
178— 17: 1,328,986
44: 1,328,326
88: 1,327,352
179— 17: 1,329,287
18: 1,327,805
1,329,004
81: 1,327,412
84: 1,329,001
90: 1,327,500
1,327,622
156: 1,329,029
157: 1,328,061
170: 1,327,185
171: 1,328,327
182: 1,328,620
190: 1,328,996
180— 9: 1,329,314
14: 1,327,876
16: 1,327,773
17: 1,327,206
21: 1,327,485
53: 1,328,839
64: 1,326,960
70: 1,327,811
1,328,846
181— 80: 1,327,811
89: 1,328,909
0.5: 1,329,059
27: 1,327,118
1,328,412

Column 6

182— 12: 1,327,116
13: 1,329,015
14: 1,328,103
183— 7: 1,329,237
10: 1,329,115
37: 1,327,287
40: 1,327,494
58: 1,326,901
72: 1,329,138
74: 1,328,868
103: 1,328,642
111: 1,328,889
184— 6: 1,327,565
1,328,015
1,329,088
11: 1,327,779
21: 1,327,043
38: 1,328,573
45: 1,327,238
48: 1,328,959
55: 1,328,388
104: 1,328,906
185— 5: 1,328,384
9: 1,328,402
40: 1,327,567
187— 11: 1,327,513
17: 1,328,964
31: 1,328,399
188— 1: 1,328,886
3: 1,328,491
4: 1,327,823
24: 1,328,092
1,329,010
49: 1,328,341
51: 1,328,008
57: 1,328,494
58: 1,328,138
70: 1,327,909
1,328,315
82: 1,328,584
1,328,596
189— 15: 1,328,461
24: 1,328,926
1,328,927
28: 1,329,026
46: 1,328,314
1,328,918
76: 1,327,441
81: 1,327,711
190— 12: 1,329,080
36: 1,328,470
49: 1,329,194
191— 39: 1,327,463
192— 1: 1,327,890
1,327,993
6: 1,327,080
7: 1,327,506
10: 1,327,576
1,328,022
11: 1,327,767
193— 1: 1,328,903
2: 1,326,099
1,328,464
8: 1,327,053
1,327,438
10: 1,328,750
1,329,018
14: 1,327,469
24: 1,327,672
26: 1,327,296
46: 1,328,747
63: 1,327,058
194— 13: 1,328,289
32: 1,329,079
195— 3: 1,328,522
8: 1,327,247
16: 1,327,184
21: 1,327,572
22: 1,327,344
196— 31: 1,327,263
1,328,680
28: 1,327,271
197— 6.1: 1,329,057
6.2: 1,328,773
8: 1,327,540
14: 1,328,786
33: 1,328,826
46: 1,328,158
60: 1,327,908
199— 63: 1,328,060
64: 1,328,146
77: 1,328,257
81: 1,328,729
200— 44: 1,327,259
50: 1,328,072
1,328,606
52: 1,327,602

Column 1

200—
- 67: 1,328,448
- 72: 1,327,640
- 80: 1,328,490
- 87: 1,327,951
- 91: 1,328,825
- 109: 1,327,383
- 1,328,798
- 116: 1,328,460
- 122: 1,328,477
- 1,328,478
- 1,328,479
- 1,328,480
- 1,328,481
- 1,328,482
- 125: 1,328,782
- 140: 1,328,427
- 142: 1,327,505
- 1,329,122
- 153: 1,329,347
- 154: 1,328,622
- 159: 1,328,562
- 166: 1,327,615
- 1,327,825
- 1,327,844
- 1,328,450

204—
- 3: 1,329,315
- 5: 1,327,094
- 1,328,981
- 8: 1,328,552
- 15: 1,328,666
- 24: 1,326,968
- 29: 1,327,121
- 1,327,234
- 1,327,542
- 1,327,649
- 1,327,650
- 1,328,027
- 1,328,357
- 1,328,358
- 1,328,359
- 1,328,392
- 1,328,393
- 1,328,394
- 1,328,420
- 1,329,125
- 1,329,180
- 1,329,181
- 31: 1,326,952
- 1,327,023
- 1,328,575
- 62: 1,327,736
- 1,327,737
- 64: 1,327,174
- 1,327,282
- 1,327,548
- 1,327,738
- 1,328,336
- 1,328,712
- 1,328,713
- 1,328,714

206—
- 20: 1,328,968
- 21: 1,328,703
- 28: 1,329,012
- 30: 1,327,458
- 40: 1,329,926
- 1,328,035
- 46: 1,329,056
- 56: 1,326,914

207—
208—
- 22: 1,328,748
- 114: 1,327,960
- 165: 1,327,240
- 1,328,343
- 1,328,557
- 1,328,719

210—
- 5: 1,327,211
- 1,327,744
- 1,328,262
- 11: 1,328,221
- 14: 1,327,962
- 16: 1,327,708
- 1,328,044
- 1,328,853
- 18: 1,328,045
- 1,328,046

211—
- 2: 1,328,950
- 6: 1,327,489
- 8: 1,327,712
- 9: 1,328,185
- 16: 1,327,142
- 1,327,143
- 1,327,949
- 20: 1,327,771
- 25: 1,328,542
- 27: 1,327,628
- 34: 1,328,167

212—
213—
- 42: 1,327,074
- 1,329,318
- 67: 1,327,265
- 1,327,480
- 1,327,617
- 1,327,827
- 1,328,335

214—
- 14: 1,328,327
- 17: 1,327,540

Column 2

214—
- 32: 1,329,293
- 38: 1,327,952
- 46: 1,329,084
- 47: 1,328,255
- 77: 1,328,923
- 80: 1,327,834
- 91: 1,328,809
- 105: 1,327,637

215—
- 1: 1,327,439
- 8: 1,327,519
- 9: 1,328,205
- 10: 1,328,455
- 13: 1,327,967
- 1,328,280
- 14: 1,327,809
- 1,328,536
- 52: 1,329,348
- 55: 1,328,060
- 67: 1,327,133
- 81: 1,327,963
- 84: 1,327,453
- 100: 1,328,866
- 112: 1,328,074

216—
- 14: 1,327,664
- 1,327,665
- 44: 1,329,260
- 47: 1,328,465
- 62: 1,328,302
- 64: 1,329,344
- 122: 1,327,362

217—
- 3: 1,327,755
- 12: 1,327,473
- 1,328,328
- 1,329,032
- 1,329,332
- 1,329,333
- 44: 1,328,587
- 47: 1,327,868
- 62: 1,328,302
- 64: 1,329,344
- 122: 1,327,362

218—
- 14: 1,328,033
- 17: 1,327,911
- 17.2: 1,328,764
- 28: 1,327,888
- 58: 1,327,872
- 60: 1,327,978

219—
- 2: 1,329,144
- 4: 1,327,792
- 10: 1,326,912
- 1,327,814
- 1,328,919
- 1,329,135
- 1,329,136
- 12: 1,327,267
- 15: 1,329,233
- 19: 1,327,050
- 1,327,207
- 1,328,126
- 21: 1,327,804
- 1,328,769
- 32: 1,328,466
- 34: 1,327,986
- 36: 1,327,102
- 38: 1,327,279
- 1,327,319
- 1,327,507
- 1,328,068
- 1,328,546
- 39: 1,326,964
- 1,329,204
- 40: 1,327,774
- 44: 1,328,723
- 46: 1,328,249
- 49: 1,327,642
- 55: 1,329,167
- 56: 1,329,168
- 62: 1,327,135

220—
- 1: 1,327,778
- 1,327,917
- 9: 1,328,758
- 15: 1,328,758
- 20: 1,327,948
- 39: 1,329,040
- 56: 1,328,672
- 81: 1,327,965
- 94: 1,327,293
- 98: 1,327,397

221—
- 11: 1,328,704
- 15: 1,327,186
- 1,327,389
- 1,329,184
- 23: 1,328,104
- 1,328,881
- 27: 1,327,067
- 47: 1,329,229
- 60: 1,327,190
- 77: 1,328,077
- 78: 1,329,199
- 79: 1,329,153
- 80: 1,328,768
- 95: 1,327,112
- 1,327,686
- 98: 1,328,184
- 99: 1,327,425
- 100: 1,327,111
- 101: 1,328,101

Column 3

221—
- 103: 1,327,990
- 118: 1,327,455
- 127: 1,327,971

223—
224—
- 57: 1,327,581
- 4: 1,326,934
- 6: 1,328,832
- 21: 1,327,355
- 29: 1,327,097
- 1,327,223
- 1,327,261
- 1,327,626
- 1,327,742
- 1,328,316
- 1,328,863
- 1,329,174
- 40: 1,327,680

225—
- 2: 1,328,980
- 21: 1,327,180
- 26: 1,327,162

226—
- 19: 1,329,110

227—
- 81: 1,328,251

228—
- 40: 1,328,037
- 68: 1,327,303

229—
- 4: 1,328,317
- 15: 1,328,524
- 29: 1,327,946
- 39: 1,328,935
- 86: 1,328,028

230—
- 1: 1,328,055
- 1,328,355
- 7: 1,328,353
- 11: 1,327,218
- 1,327,926
- 1,328,285
- 1,328,679
- 13: 1,327,294
- 1,328,770
- 24: 1,328,984
- 27: 1,327,787
- 1,327,833
- 1,328,232
- 1,328,340
- 1,328,529
- 1,329,165
- 1,329,348
- 33: 1,327,975
- 34: R. 14,789
- 36: 1,327,731
- 19: 1,327,957
- 41: 1,328,084
- 46: 1,327,004

234-34.5: 1,327,989
- 39: 1,328,223
- 43: 1,328,840
- 44: 1,327,334

235—
- 2: 1,327,153
- 50: 1,328,550
- 59: 1,329,014
- 60: 1,328,822
- 1,328,847
- 1,329,028
- 82: 1,327,219
- 1,327,319
- 1,327,320
- 1,327,329
- 83: 1,327,177
- 86: 1,327,044
- 91: 1,326,978
- 1,329,090
- 92: 1,328,368
- 95: 1,326,967

236—
- 16: 1,327,796
- 18: 1,328,277
- 32: 1,328,997
- 44: 1,329,112
- 48: 1,327,277
- 80: 1,327,675

237-12.3: 1,327,869
- 32: 1,328,820
- 68: 1,326,944
- 79: 1,327,877

238—
- 3: 1,329,264
- 26: 1,328,002
- 27: 1,327,219
- 38: 1,328,574
- 46: 1,328,113
- 145: 1,327,541
- 180: 1,328,170
- 250: 1,328,155
- 262: 1,329,227
- 272: 1,328,917
- 286: 1,329,206
- 295: 1,329,163
- 298: 1,328,695
- 302: 1,329,077
- 304: 1,329,533
- 311: 1,329,153
- 319: 1,328,405

240—
- 1: 1,327,978
- 7: 1,327,732
- 8.5: 1,328,968
- 1,327,017
- 45: 1,328,129

Column 4

240—
- 45: 1,328,153
- 48.2: 1,327,563
- 48.6: 1,328,607
- 53: 1,329,051
- 57: 1,328,125
- 60: 1,327,479
- 61: 1,327,945
- 1,328,992
- 62: 1,328,918
- 1,327,574
- 67: 1,327,733
- 78: 1,329,330
- 81: 1,328,785
- 91: 1,327,598
- 93: 1,329,147
- 108: 1,328,331
- 1,329,187
- 115: 1,329,280
- 163: 1,328,415

241—
- 6: 1,328,931
- 8: 1,327,035
- 17: 1,327,041
- 18: 1,327,199

242—
- 19: 1,328,196
- 71: 1,327,245
- 72: 1,327,445
- 74: 1,328,408
- 77: 1,329,240
- 78: 1,326,989
- 1,326,990
- 84.1: 1,328,696
- 84.4: 1,328,066
- 128: 1,328,777
- 151: 1,327,022
- 155: 1,329,341

243—
244—
- 14: 1,327,718
- 1: 1,327,810
- 2: 1,329,336
- 6: 1,328,040
- 12: 1,327,530
- 1,328,421
- 1,329,062
- 14: 1,327,126
- 1,329,342
- 15: 1,327,529
- 1,328,211
- 19: 1,327,514
- 21: 1,327,592
- 1,327,932
- 1,328,413
- 1,328,425
- 1,328,848
- 23: 1,328,143
- 25: 1,328,336
- 1,329,154
- 29: 1,328,945
- 1,326,946
- 1,327,055
- 1,327,183
- 1,327,543
- 30: 1,327,334
- 31: 1,328,963
- 8: 1,329,189

245—
246—
- 34: 1,328,865
- 37: 1,327,570
- 62: 1,327,329
- 110: 1,328,070
- 125: 1,329,184
- 126: 1,328,854
- 187: 1,327,968
- 181: 1,327,176
- 194: 1,327,411
- 200: 1,329,258
- 223: 1,328,381
- 1,328,272
- 294: 1,328,932
- 301: 1,329,034
- 318: 1,327,358
- 381: 1,328,003
- 387: 1,327,877
- 428: 1,327,483
- 1,329,007
- 460: 1,327,812
- 479: 1,328,191

247—
- 5: 1,328,993
- 12: 1,327,409

248—
- 3: 1,327,719
- 6: 1,328,418
- 20: 1,328,271
- 1,328,930
- 30: 1,329,173
- 32: 1,327,981
- 35: 1,326,959
- 36: 1,328,376
- 1,328,543
- 50: 1,328,118

249—
- 27: 1,329,151
- 65: 1,327,644

250—
- 19: 1,328,610
- 20: 1,328,933
- 27: 1,329,101
- 1,329,283
- 34: 1,328,495

Column 5

250—
- 38: 1,328,288
- 41: 1,327,593
- 1,328,925

251—
- 6: 1,328,616
- 19: 1,327,351
- 34: 1,326,998
- 43: 1,328,780
- 47: 1,326,938
- 48: 1,328,578
- 51: 1,329,099
- 56: 1,328,752
- 70: 1,328,098
- 100: 1,328,587
- 107: 1,327,252
- 104: 1,329,016
- 113: 1,327,984
- 122: 1,326,966
- 137: 1,329,209
- 144: 1,326,923
- 1,327,539
- 1,329,321
- 146: 1,327,564
- 159: 1,329,231
- 1,328,845

252—
253—
- 19: 1,329,244
- 65: 1,328,835
- 77: 1,328,640
- 136: 1,327,953
- 179: 1,328,010
- 194: 1,327,812
- 199: 1,328,190

254—
- 1: 1,328,115
- 35: 1,328,770
- 43: 1,326,953
- 1,329,185
- 51: 1,327,492
- 61: 1,327,024
- 72: 1,326,965
- 1,328,599
- 86: 1,327,905
- 89: 1,327,060
- 110: 1,328,306
- 111: 1,329,098
- 123: 1,328,809
- 130: 1,327,685
- 131: 1,328,116
- 135: 1,327,582
- 1,329,034
- 167: 1,327,181
- 176: 1,329,107
- 177: 1,328,678
- 188: 1,328,717
- 190: 1,327,876

255—
- 3: 1,327,403
- 50: 1,328,707
- 71: 1,327,913
- 73: 1,327,986

256—
257—
- 56: 1,328,693
- 24: 1,328,828
- 30: 1,328,908
- 80: 1,327,863
- 125: 1,327,165
- 129: 1,327,787
- 1,328,151
- 1,329,256
- 130: 1,327,380
- 132: 1,327,730
- 134: 1,327,213
- 151: 1,327,877
- 1,328,780
- 1,329,198
- 165: 1,327,806
- 167: 1,328,540
- 241: 1,328,150
- 1,328,272

258—
259—
- 1: 1,328,560
- 72: 1,328,576
- 81: 1,328,119
- 83: 1,327,901
- 126: 1,327,568
- 133: 1,327,900
- 144: 1,329,164
- 11: 1,327,599
- 16: 1,329,300
- 19: 1,328,042
- 41: R. 14,790

261—
- 52: 1,327,233
- 1,329,308
- 62: 1,327,703
- 75: 1,328,204
- 95: 1,327,422
- 99: 1,327,205
- 121: 1,328,552
- 1,328,543
- 6: 1,328,118

262—
- 20: 1,328,372
- 30: 1,328,755

263—
- 5: 1,328,330
- 9: 1,328,468
- 44: 1,329,278
- 46: 1,328,511

Column 6

263—
- 42: 1,328,030

264—
- 3: 1,327,633
- 20: 1,327,629

265—
- 2: 1,327,393
- 11: 1,327,838
- 12: 1,328,349
- 13: 1,329,192
- 27: 1,327,553
- 56: 1,328,319
- 1,328,320
- 62: 1,326,963
- 1,327,208
- 1,327,450

266—
- 6: 1,327,443
- 23: 1,327,715
- 37: 1,328,803
- 43: 1,328,380

267—
- 9: 1,328,641
- 19: 1,327,076
- 27: 1,327,958
- 1,328,601
- 1,328,812
- 33: 1,327,016
- 34: 1,327,750
- 87: 1,327,063
- 50: 1,328,496
- 52: 1,327,746

268—
- 4: 1,329,178
- 8: 1,328,095
- 9: 1,328,584
- 1,328,979
- 15: R. 14,793

270—
- 17: 1,328,219
- 39: 1,328,987
- 41: 1,328,411

271—
- 2: 1,329,108
- 52: 1,328,877
- 55: 1,327,546
- 56: 1,327,182
- 87: 1,327,588

273—
274—
- 2: 1,326,920
- 1,327,616
- 1,327,776
- 15: 1,327,816
- 35: 1,326,932

275—
- 1: 1,328,709
- 5: 1,328,618

277—
- 37: 1,327,235
- 45: 1,328,235
- 57: 1,327,850
- 69: 1,327,366

279—
- 8: 1,327,194
- 55: 1,328,195
- 71: 1,328,627
- 77: 1,327,917
- 93: 1,327,567

280—
- 5: 1,327,039
- 13: 1,328,629
- 1,328,715
- 33.2: 1,327,338
- 33.5: 1,327,557
- 1,328,048
- 1,328,684
- 44: 1,328,634
- 60: 1,327,864
- 61: 1,328,458
- 87.5: 1,327,123
- 94: 1,328,881
- 97: 1,327,829
- 103: 1,327,854

281—
283—
- 14: 1,326,948
- 29: 1,329,250
- 51: 1,327,855
- 56: 1,329,002
- 59: 1,329,120
- 63: 1,327,610

284—
- 6: 1,327,031
- 12: 1,328,373

285—
- 9: 1,327,632
- 26: 1,328,290
- 37: 1,327,144
- 40: 1,329,141
- 77: 1,329,121
- 87: 1,327,106
- 94: 1,326,939
- 120: 1,326,970
- 197: 1,328,650

286—
- 8: 1,328,288
- 11: 1,327,002
- 18: 1,327,801

287—
- 1: 1,329,191
- 17: 1,328,191
- 23: 1,327,611
- 58: 1,327,611
- 116: 1,328,612

290—
- 4: 1,329,276
- 23: 1,328,083
- 37: 1,328,873
- 38: 1,327,132

291—
- 23: 1,328,739

292—
- 52: 1,328,284

292—	62: 1,326,937	292—	265: 1,327,751	293—	55: 1,329,334	296—	21: 1,327,248	298—	13: 1,328,805	298—	30: 1,329,101
	67: 1,327,291		337: 1,327,605	294—	22: 1,328,8:0		23: 1,327,589		17: 1,328,137	299—	36: 1,328,738
	75: 1,328,0:9		340: 1,327,694	295—	9: 1,327,849		26: 1,327,883		1,328,890		83: 1,328,942
	76: 1,328,345	293—	55: 1,326,283		122: 1,327,395		56: 1,327,079		19: 1,328,240		97: 1,329,103
	182: 1,326,956		1,328,786	296—	10: 1,328,999		108: 1,328,391		1,328,837		117: 1,328,721
	212: 1,327,011		1,329,019		14: 1,328,130	297—	8: 1,329,351		1,328,928		135: 1,327,452

Patents Nos. 1,326,899 to 1,327,605.

THE
OFFICIAL GAZETTE

OF THE

United States Patent Office.

Vol. 270—No. 1.   TUESDAY, JANUARY 6, 1920.   Price—$5 per year.

[PUBLISHED JANUARY 8, 1920.]

The OFFICIAL GAZETTE is mailed under the direction of the Superintendent of Documents, Government Printing Office, to whom all subscriptions should be made payable and all communications respecting the Gazette should be addressed. Issued weekly. Subscriptions, $5.00 per annum; single numbers, 10 cents each.

Printed copies of patents are furnished by the Patent Office at 10 cents each. For the latter, address the Commissioner of Patents, Washington, D. C.

CONTENTS

Issue of January 6, 1920.

It is to your best interest to put your Liberty bond interest in W. S. S.

Alphabetical Arrangement of Names in Indexes.

The names in the indexes issued by the Patent Office will hereafter be placed in alphabetical order in accordance with the first significant character or name, as customary with city-directory arrangement.

Interference Notices.

DEPARTMENT OF THE INTERIOR,
UNITED STATES PATENT OFFICE,
Washington, D. C., December 16, 1919.

Davis and Day Engineering Company, its assigns or legal representatives, take notice:

An interference having been declared by this Office between the application of The Northwestern Chemical Co., State street, Marietta, Ohio, for registration of a trade-mark and trade-mark registered March 19, 1907, No. 61,403, to Davis and Day Engineering Company, 309 East Ninth street, Muscatine, Iowa, and a notice of such declaration sent by registered mail to said Davis and Day Engineering Company at the said address having been returned by the post-office undeliverable, notice is hereby given that unless said Davis and Day Engineering Company, its assigns or legal representatives, shall enter an appearance therein within thirty days from the first publication of this order the interference will be proceeded with as in case of default.

This notice will be published in the OFFICIAL GAZETTE for three consecutive weeks.

R. F. WHITEHEAD,
First Assistant Commissioner.

DEPARTMENT OF THE INTERIOR,
UNITED STATES PATENT OFFICE,
Washington, D. C., December 15, 1919.

Southern Substitute Turpentine Company, its assigns or legal representatives, take notice:

An interference having been declared by this Office between the application of Thomas Sealy, of 142 Front street, New York, N. Y., for registration of a trade-mark and trade-mark registered December 24, 1907, No. 66,773, to Southern Substitute Turpentine Company, of Highland-town, Md., and a notice of such declaration sent by registered mail to said Southern Substitute Turpentine Company at the said address having been returned by the post-office undeliverable, notice is hereby given that unless said Southern Substitute Turpentine Company, its assigns or legal representatives, shall enter an appearance therein within thirty days from the first publication of this order the interference will be proceeded with as in case of default.

This notice will be published in the OFFICIAL GAZETTE for three consecutive weeks.

R. F. WHITEHEAD,
First Assistant Commissioner.

Adverse Decisions in Interference.

PATENT No. 1,252,104.

On December 2, 1919, a decision was rendered that Charles W. Girvin was not the first inventor of the subject-matter covered by claims 1, 2, 3, 4, 5, and 6 of his Patent No. 1,252,104, subject, "Art of electrical precipitation of particles from fluid streams," and no appeal having been taken within the time allowed such decision has become final.

Disclaimers.

864,951.—*Louis A. Casgrain*, Winchester, Mass. MACHINE FOR INSERTING FASTENINGS. Patent dated September 3, 1907. Disclaimer filed December 31, 1919, by the assignee, by mesne assignments, *United Shoe Machinery Corporation.*

Enters this disclaimer—

" To said claim 4 of said Letters Patent, which is in the following words, to wit:

" In a machine for inserting fastenings, a horn or work-support, a main driving shaft, mechanism controlled thereby to depress the horn periodically, a clutch for the said shaft, controlling means to throw said clutch into or out of operation, a treadle, operating connections between it and said means, to start the machine, and positive connections between the treadle and the horn, to raise the latter manually when the machine is started."

1,076,453.—*Hugh Rodman*, Edgewood, Pa. METHOD OF MAKING CASE-HARDENING MATERIAL. Patent dated October 21, 1913. Disclaimer filed December 20, 1919, by the assignee, *Rodman Chemical Company.*

" Enters its disclaimer, under claim 10 of said patent, any method or process of manufacturing dry packing for use as carbonizing material consisting in mixing finely divided material with a binding agent and separating the resulting mass into relatively small masses of appreciable size which does not produce small masses that retain their identities under heat."

APPLICATIONS UNDER EXAMINATION.

Condition at Close of Business January 2, 1920.

Room No.	Divisions and subjects of invention.	Oldest new application and oldest action by applicant awaiting office action. New.	Amended.	No. of applications awaiting action.
314	1. Closure Operators; Fences; Gates; Harrows and Diggers; Plows; Planting; Scattering Unloaders; Trees, Plants, and Flowers.	Sept. 23	Aug. 25	421
128	2. Bee Culture; Curtains, Shades, and Screens; Dairy; Medicines; Pneumatics; Preserving; Presses; Tents, Canopies, Umbrellas, and Canes: Tobacco.	June 3	July 25	921
175	3. Electric Heating and Rheostats; Electrochemistry; Heating; Metal-Founding; Metallurgical Apparatus; Metallurgy; Metal Treatment; Plastic Metal Working.	Sept. 11	Sept. 3	307
234	4. Conveyers; Elevators; Excavating; Handling—Hand and Hoist-Line Implements; Hoisting; Material or Article Handling; Pneumatic Despatch; Pushing and Pulling Implements; Railway Mail Delivery; Store-Service; Traversing Hoists.	June 7	Aug. 11	763
167	5. Book-Making; Books, Strips and Leaves; Harvesters; Jewelry; Manifolding; Music; Printed Matter; Tying Cords or Strands.	Aug. 17	Aug. 26	233
318	6. Bleaching and Dyeing; Chemicals; Explosives; Fertilizers; Liquid Coating Compositions; Plastic Compositions; Substance Preparation.	Aug. 13	Oct. 15	494
312	7. Games and Toys; Optics; Velocipedes.	Oct. 2	Nov. 3	555
131	8. Beds; Chairs; Flexible-Sheet Securing Devices; Furniture; Kitchen and Table Articles; Store Furniture; Supports.	Oct. 6	Oct. 7	410
221	9. Air and Gas Pumps; Hydraulic Motors; Injectors and Ejectors; Motors, Fluid; Motors, Fluid-Current; Pumps.	Sept. 8	Oct. 1	227
235	10. Carriages and Wagons; Land-Vehicles; Land-Vehicles—Bodies and Tops; Land-Vehicles—Dumping; Motor Vehicles.	July 23	Sept. 29	939
151	11. Boot and Shoe Making; Boots, Shoes, and Leggings; Button, Eyelet, and Rivet Setting; Harness; Leather Manufactures; Nailing and Stapling; Spring Devices; Whips and Whip Apparatus.	July 3	Oct. 31	491
222	12. Machine Elements.	June 14	Sept. 18	1,015
329	13. Bolt, Nail, Nut, Rivet, and Screw Making; Button Making; Chain, Staple, and Horseshoe Making; Driven, Headed, and Screw-Threaded Fastenings; Gear Cutting, Milling, and Planing; Metal Drawing; Metal Forging and Welding; Metal Rolling; Metal Tools and Implements, Making; Metal Working; Needle and Pin Making; Turning.	June 21	Oct. 1	940
323	14. Compound Tools; Cutting and Punching Sheets and Bars; Farriery; Metal-Bending; Sheet-Metal Ware, Making; Tools; Wire Fabrics and Structure; Wire-Working.	June 7	Sept. 6	417
308	15. Bread, Pastry, and Confection Making; Coating; Fuel; Glass; Laminated Fabrics and Analogous Manufactures; Paper-Making and Fiber Liberation; Photography; Plastic Block and Earthenware Apparatus; Plastics.	June 6	Sept. 27	850
111	16. Radiant Energy; Telegraphy; Telephony.	June 12	June 21	857
307	17. Label Pasting and Paper Hanging; Nut and Bolt Locks; Ornamentation; Paper Manufactures; Printing; Type Casting; Sheet Material Associating or Folding; Sheet Feeding or Delivering, Type Setting.	Sept. 12	Nov. 1	237
229	18. Fluid-Pressure Regulators; Liquid Heaters and Vaporizers; Motors, Expansible Chamber Type; Power Plants; Speed Responsive Devices; Steam and Vacuum Pumps.	Aug. 11	Aug. 16	644
236	19. Automatic Temperature and Humidity Regulation; Furnaces; Heating Systems; Stoves and Furnaces; Domestic Cooking Vessels, Thermostats and Humidostats.	June 5	July 18	563
179	20. Artificial Body Members; Builders' Hardware, Closure-Fasteners; Cutlery; Dentistry; Locks and Latches; Safes; Undertaking.	Oct. 1	Sept. 18	629
212	21. Brakes and Gins; Carding; Cloth-Finishing; Continuous-Strip Feeding; Cordage; Felt and Fur, Knitting and Netting; Silk; Spinning; Weaving; Winding and Reeling.	May 24	Oct. 4	373
219	22. Aeronautics; Firearms; Ordnance.	Sept. 5	Oct. 22	306
217	23. Acoustics; Coin-Handling; Horology; Recorders; Registers; Sound Recording and Reproducing; Time-Controlling Mechanism.	June 24	Sept. 19	596
114	24. Apparel; Apparel Apparatus; Garment Supporters, Sewing-Machines.	June 7	Oct. 4	608
315	25. Agitating; Butchering; Centrifugal Bowl Separators; Mills, Threshing, Vegetable Cutters and Crushers; Gas Separation.	Nov. 17	Nov. 10	246
105	26. Electricity, Generation, Motive Power; Prime Mover Dynamo Plants.	Apr. 24	July 9	723
214	27. Brushing and Scrubbing; Grinding and Polishing; Laundry, Washing Apparatus.	Sept. 2	Nov. 3	504
225	28. Internal-Combustion Engines	Sept. 2	Sept. 22	591
147	29. Boring and Drilling; Chucks or Sockets, Coopering, Rod Joints or Couplings; Wheelwright-Machines; Wood-Sawing; Wood-Turning; Woodworking; Woodworking Tools.	Apr. 1	Aug. 1	626
132	30. Illuminating-Burners; Illumination; Liquid and Gaseous Fuel Burners; Type-Writing Machines.	July 9	Sept. 25	867
172	31. Alcohol; Ammonia, Water, and Wood Distillation, Charcoal and Coke; Gas, Heating and Illuminating; Hides, Skins, and Leather; Hydraulic Cement and Lime; Mineral Oils; Oils, Fats, and Glue. Sugar and Salt.	June 17	July 3	773
278	32. Gas and Liquid Contact Apparatus; Heat Exchange; Refrigeration	June 7	Nov. 3	833
70	33. Bridges, Hydraulic and Earth Engineering; Masonry and Concrete Structures; Metallic Building Structures; Roads and Pavements, Roofs.	Aug. 5	Oct. 3	349
301	34. Railways; Railway Rolling Stock, Railway Switches and Signals; Railways, Surface Track, Railway Wheels and Axles; Track-Sanders; Vehicle-Fenders.	Nov. 4	Nov. 15	240
57	35. Buckles, Buttons, Clasps, Etc.; Card, Picture, and Sign Exhibiting; Signals; Toilet.	Nov. 10	Nov. 24	374
204	36. Automatic Weighers; Driers; Geometrical Instruments; Measuring Instruments; Force Measuring.	Sept. 17	Sept. 20	903
107	37. Electric Lamps; Electricity, Circuit Makers and Breakers; Electricity, General Applications.	July 11	July 19	962
378	38. Animal Husbandry; Earth Boring; Fishing and Trapping, Mining, Quarrying, and Ice-Harvesting; Stationery; Stone-Working; Wells.	Nov. 12	Nov. 18	258
220	39. Joint Packings; Multiple Valves; Packed Shaft or Rod Joints; Pipe Joints or Couplings; Valved Pipe Joints or Couplings; Valves; Water Distribution.	Apr. 7	June 10	922
273	40. Baggage; Bottles and Jars, Check-Controlled Apparatus; Cloth, Leather, and Rubber Receptacles; Deposit and Collection Receptacles; Metallic Receptacles, Package and Article Carriers; Paper Receptacles; Special Receptacles and Packages; Wooden Receptacles.	July 7	Oct. 25	535
125	41. Resilient Tires and Wheels	July 14	Oct. 20	771
114	42. Electricity, Conductors; Electricity-Transmission to Vehicles; Electricity, Conduits; Electric Signaling	July 11	July 19	726
382	43. Baths and Closets; Dispensing, Dispensing Beverages; Electricity, Medical and Surgical; Fire-Extinguishers; Sewerage, Surgery, Water Purification.	Sept. 6	Oct. 31	431
253	44. Air-Guns, Catapults, and Targets; Ammunition and Explosive Devices; Ammunition and Explosive Charge Making; Boats and Buoys; Filling and Closing Portable Receptacles; Marine Propulsion; Railway Draft Appliances; Ships.	July 2	Oct. 8	305
379	45. Clutches, Journal-Boxes, Pulleys, and Shafting; Lubrication; Motors.	June 17	Oct. 24	751
332	46. Educational Appliances; Fire-Escapes; Ladders; Paper Files and Binders; Railway-Brakes; Wooden Buildings.	May 13	Oct. 22	574

Oldest new case, Apr. 1; oldest amended, June 10.
Total number of applications awaiting action.. 27,060

163	TRADE-MARKS, DESIGNS, LABELS AND PRINTS			
	Trade-Marks	Sept. 22	Nov. 1	2,379
	Designs	Aug. 15	Sept. 22	1,199
	Labels and Prints	Sept. 22	Sept. 20	588

2

PATENTS

GRANTED JANUARY 6, 1920.

1,326,899. STRIP-SHINGLE. Herbert Abraham, New York, N. Y., assignor to The Standard Paint Company, a Corporation of New Jersey. Filed Oct. 18, 1918. Serial No. 258,703. 1 Claim. (Cl. 108—7.)

A multiple shingle-strip, having spaced nailing tabs along its upper edge, and having its lower edge formed of a series of straight lines extending parallel to the major axis of the strip, with intervening cut-out portions corresponding substantially in shape to the nailing tabs and disposed in staggered relation thereto, whereby, when the strips are laid as described, not more than two square feet of shingle material are required to waterproof each square foot of roof surface.

1,326,900. TOOTHBRUSH. Ulfert L. Albers. Rico, Colo. Filed Feb. 1, 1918. Serial No. 214,874. 1 Claim. (Cl. 15—37.)

In a tooth brush, the combination with a casing having spaced parallel shafts extending therefrom and brushes on the ends of the shafts, of a pivoted handle and a mounting for said handle eccentrically located on the face side of the casing at a point opposite the shafts of said brushes which allows the handle to be folded between said shafts when not in use.

1,326,901. PNEUMATIC CLEANER. George W. Alles, Boston, Mass., assignor to B. F. Sturtevant Company, Boston, Mass., a Corporation of Massachusetts. Filed Sept. 11, 1914. Serial No. 861,223. 6 Claims. (Cl. 183—58.)

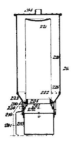

4. A pneumatic cleaner having, in combination, a casing having a dust bag chamber with an inlet and an outlet for the air, a dust bag having a downwardly opening

mouth mounted in said chamber and interposed between the inlet and outlet, said bag being upwardly distensible and having a weight member attached, adapted to cause an abrupt collapse of the bag upon a substantial reduction in air pressure, and a blower attached to the outlet of the casnig and operative to move pulsating currents of air through the bag, the weight on the bag acting automatically to shake the bag as the latter is intermittently inflated by the pulsating current.

1,326,902. PROCESS OF AND APPARATUS FOR MAKING CONCRETE SLABS. Grosvenor Atterbury, New York, N. Y. Filed Mar. 15, 1919. Serial No. 282,772. 7 Claims. (Cl. 25—121.)

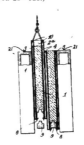

1. A method of simultaneously casting a plurality of cementitious slabs composing pouring, into mold spaces separated by pairs of jackets bearing against one another, the cementitious material in such manner as to maintain the level of the material substantially the same in all said spaces.

1,326,903. CAN-FEEDING MECHANISM. August M Augensen, Maywood, Ill., assignor to American Can Company, New York, N. Y., a Corporation of New Jersey. Filed Apr. 15, 1915. Serial No. 21,545. 10 Claims. (Cl. 193—1.)

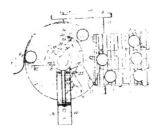

8. A can-feeding mechanism comprising a rotating table upon which the cans are received and supported, a can holding device which is fixed relative to and is rotatable

3

with said table, means for ejecting cans from said device at a predetermined point, a second outwardly movable can holding device rotatable with the table, and means for ejecting cans from said second can holding device at a different predetermined point.

1,326,904. HEAT-DISTRIBUTER. LEON K. BELCHER, New York, N. Y. Filed Jan. 16, 1919. Serial No. 271,374. 2 Claims. (Cl. 126—215.)

1. A heat distributer comprising a casing having an opening in its bottom to be arranged over a burner and a plurality of openings in its top, one of said openings in the top being in vertical alinement with the opening in the bottom and the other out of alinement therewith, and an inclined partition in the casing over the opening in the bottom and having restricted openings therein arranged in alinement with said bottom opening for allowing part of the heat from the burner to pass through the partition to the opening in the top of the casing above it while part of the heat is diverted by said partition to the other openings in the top.

1,326,905. FISH-CLEANING MACHINE. JOSEPH F. BIRCH, Jr., Baltimore, Md., assignor, by direct and mesne assignments, to Musher and Company, Inc., Baltimore, Md., a Corporation of Delaware. Filed May 28, 1918. Serial No. 237,064. 15 Claims. (Cl. 17—10.)

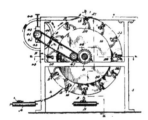

15. A fish eviscerating apparatus comprising a movable fish carrying member, means for clamping the fish in said member, a cutter for partially severing the heads from the fish, means for removing the head and viscera from said firsh while clamped, and means for releasing said clamping means.

1,326,906. UNDERFEED FURNACE. ARTHUR H. BLACKBURN, Downers Grove, and FRANK E. FLEMING, Chicago, Ill., assignors to The Underfeed Stoker Company of America, Chicago, Ill., a Corporation of New Jersey. Filed Mar. 22, 1919. Serial No. 284,396. 6 Claims. (Cl. 110—44.)

1. In an underfeed furnace, the combination with a retort, and ash-disposal means laterally spaced from said retort, of an intervening side-floor structure comprising plates respectively pivoted adjacent each the retort and

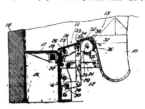

the ash disposal means, and means for raising and lowering the proximate free edges of said plates.

1,326,907. RIM-TOOL. JAMES W. BOND, Columbia, S. C. Filed Apr. 14, 1919. Serial No. 289,937. 1 Claim. (Cl. 81—15.)

The herein described tool for bending wheel rim flanges, the same comprising a handle, and a head secured at its inner end to the handle in line therewith and having its working portion deflected out of said line and notched in its extremity to produce a short upper jaw and a long lower jaw, the jaws and the notch curving outward and upward, the walls of the notch being substantially parallel, and the lower face of said long jaw being rounded and merging into the lower side of the head to constitute a fulcrum rocker, as described.

1,326,908. CLASSIFIER. SAMUEL H. BOYLAN, Joplin, Mo. Filed June 21, 1918. Serial No. 241,206. 3 Claims. (Cl. 83—82.)

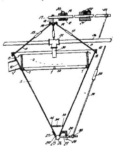

1. An automatic classifier of the character described, comprising a casing provided at its lower end with an outlet opening, a single vertically swinging lever arranged

above the casing, means for pivotally supporting the single lever at a point arranged near and spaced from the forward end thereof, suspension means connecting the forward end of the lever with the casing, a weight longitudinally adjustably mounted upon the rear portion of the lever, means for supplying material to be classified into the upper end of the casing, a valve to cover and uncover the outlet opening from the exterior of the casing, a vertically swinging lever carrying the valve and pivoted to the lower end of the casing to be supported thereby, and a rod pivotally connected with the two levers, said levers and rod lying entirely outside of said casing.

1,326,909. APPARATUS FOR DRYING VEGETABLES AND THE LIKE. DERK BRONS, Zuidbroek, Netherlands, assignor to N. V. Machinefabriek Brons, Zuidbroek, Groningen, Netherlands, a Limited Liability Company of the Netherlands. Filed May 28, 1919. Serial No. 300,417. 1 Claim. (Cl. 34—15.)

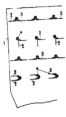

In a device for drying material, the combination of a hurdle comprising like sections, an axle upon which said hurdle sections are symmetrically mounted, means for moving said hurdle sections individually to extend in the same plane or in a plane at right angles to each other, and means for moving said sections jointly in spaced parallel relation.

1,326,910. NAIL. PERCY FREDERICK BUTTERFIELD, Toronto, Ontario, Canada. Filed Feb. 10, 1919. Serial No. 275,974. 3 Claims. (Cl. 85—20.)

3. A nail having a spiral groove extending longitudinally thereof V-shaped in form and having a sharpened rib extending from each edge of the groove, the inner face of each rib forming a continuation of the corresponding face of the groove.

1,326,911. CLOTHESPOLE. CHARLES G. CARLSON, Chicago, Ill. Filed Dec. 26, 1917. Serial No. 208,989. 2 Claims. (Cl. 68—12.)

1. A clothes line prop, comprising of a staff member, having a narrow longitudinally disposed slot extending inwardly from one end thereof so as to form a pair of jaws integral with said member and yieldable relative to each other, said jaws each being provided with a recess substantially semi-circular and the same size formed in the opposed faces thereof inwardly from the end of said slot, said recesses coacting to form a seat adapted to receive and retain a clothes line, and an abutment extending across said slot adjacent to and slightly removed from the bottom of said recesses so as to prevent the clothes line from passing into said slot beyond said seat.

2. A clothes line prop, comprising a staff member having a narrow longitudinally disposed slot extending inwardly from one end thereof so as to form a pair of jaws integral with said member and yieldable relative to each other, said jaws each being provided with a recess substantially semi-circular and the same size formed in the opposed faces thereof inwardly from the end of said slot, said recesses coacting to form a seat adapted to receive and retain a clothes line, and a pin carried by one of said jaws and slidably passing through the other, said pin being located transversely to and immediately beneath said seat so as to prevent a clothes line from passing into said slot below said seat.

1,326,912. METHOD OF WELDING. SPENCER C. CARY, Brooklyn, N. Y. Filed Apr. 6, 1916. Serial No. 89,289. 2 Claims. (Cl. 219—10.)

1. The process of welding metallic sheets to form a continuous sheet, consisting in sand blasting both sides of the edges of the sheets, lapping the edges of the two sheets, pressing the lapped edges and passing a current through the sand blasted portions of the sheets to continuously weld the lapped portions.

1,326,913. MEANS FOR CLEANING METAL PREPARATORY TO WELDING. SPENCER C. CARY, Brooklyn, N. Y. Filed Mar. 2, 1917. Serial No. 151,951. 19 Claims. (Cl. 51—12.)

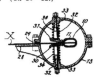

6. In an apparatus of the class described, a substantially tubular chamber of flattened cross sectional dimen-

sions and the length of which chamber exceeds the diameter thereof, said chamber being provided in one wall with a longitudinal slot which is positioned substantially centrally between the flattened walls of said chamber, combined with means for feeding a sand blast into the chamber substantially at one end portion thereof and substantially beyond the end of the slot therein, so as to direct the flow of said sand blast longitudinally of the chamber.

1,326,914. COMBINED SHAVING-BRUSH AND SHAVING-STICK HOLDER. JOHN O. CHRISTENSON, Wilson, Fla. Filed Feb. 14, 1918. Serial No. 217,154. Renewed Nov. 3, 1919. Serial No. 335,474. 1 Claim. (Cl. 206—56.)

A shaving stick holder including a tubular handle, a cap detachably associated with said handle, said cap being provided with a recess, the upper walls of which are provided with threads for engagement with one end of a stick of shaving soap to secure the same to the cap, the lower walls of said recess being smooth without threads or securing means of any kind, the lower portion of the recess being of slightly greater diameter than the upper threaded portion for snugly embracing a portion of the stick of soap below the portion of the stick engaged by the threaded portion of the recess, to prevent the stick from breaking at the point where the lowermost threads of the recess bite into the stick and adapted to form a guide for properly securing the stick of soap to the cap.

1,326,915. FASTENING DEVICE FOR COLLARS. JOSEPH L. CORBI, Washington, D. C., assignor of one-third to Frank K. Heindrich and one-third to David S. Margolis, Washington, D. C. Filed Oct. 10, 1918. Serial No. 258,369. 3 Claims. (Cl. 2—62.)

3. The combination with a collar having an interior lining, of a pair of stiffening plates disposed near the ends of the collar, transversely thereof, the stiffening plate at one end being provided with a plurality of integral hooks, and the other plate being provided with a plurality of integral eyes arranged to register with the hooks, each of said plates being provided with prongs punched therefrom and extending into the lining, said prongs being in the line of direct pull between the hooks and eyes.

1,326,916. SHEET-METAL-ELBOW-FORMING MACHINE. ADOLF DIECKMANN, Cincinnati, Ohio. Filed June 2, 1915. Serial No. 31,769. 7 Claims. (Cl. 153—69.5.)
1. A sheet metal elbow forming machine comprising a mandrel having on its exterior a non-cylindrical pattern,

a frame encircling the free end of said mandrel, an exteriorly supported and inwardly movable crimp former located close to the free end of said mandrel, a series of segmental jaws the counterpart of the pattern of said mandrel mounted upon said frame and movable to and from said mandrel to shape and clamp an elbow blank upon said mandrel during the formation of a crimp, a main plunger having its exterior of the same pattern as that of the mandrel, located inside of the elbow blank and between the crimp former and the free end of the mandrel and movable endwise to and from the free end of the mandrel, and an auxiliary plunger of the pattern of the mandrel jointedly connected to said main plunger and movable therewith to a position outside of said crimp former.

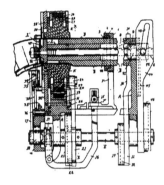

2. A sheet metal elbow forming machine comprising a mandrel a frame encircling the free end of said mandrel, an exteriorly supported and inwardly movable crimp former located close to the free end of said mandrel, a series of segmental jaws pivotally mounted upon said encircling frame with their free ends movable to and from said mandrel to clamp an elbow blank upon said mandrel during the formation of a crimp, an annular shaped member rotatably mounted upon said encircling frame and provided with members to engage cam faces on said jaws to move said jaws to and from said mandrel, a main plunger located between said crimp former and the free end of said mandrel and movable endwise to and from said mandrel, and an auxiliary plunger jointedly connected to and movable with said main plunger and located outside of said crimp former.
3. A machine for forming sheet metal elbows comprising a mandrel to support the elbow blank, clamping jaws overhanging the end of said mandrel to clamp the elbow blank to the mandrel, mechanism to successively form inwardly projecting eccentric crimps in the elbow blank outside of said jaws, and a plunger reciprocating endwise within the elbow blank and movable into the overhanging portion of the clamping jaws.
4. A machine for forming sheet metal elbows comprising a supporting mandrel having a cylindrical section and a non-cylindrical section, clamping jaws opposite said non-cylindrical mandrel section and overhanging the end of said mandrel to form longitudinal corrugations in the cylindrical elbow blank, means at the overhanging end of said jaws operating from the exterior to successively press inwardly, projecting eccentric crimps at intervals in the elbow blank, and a plunger reciprocating endwise within the elbow blank and movable into the overhanging portion of the clamping jaws.
5. A sheet metal elbow forming machine comprising a base, a hollow stationary mandrel carried thereby and having at its exterior a non-cylindrical pattern desired in the elbow, means to feed an elbow blank longitudinally of said mandrel step by step, a series of segmental jaws

assembled about the free end of said mandrel to compress the elbow blank to the exterior pattern of said mandrel, an annular shaped frame carried by said base and encircling the free end of said mandrel upon which said jaws are pivotally mounted, means carried by said loop shaped frame to periodically open and close said jaws, a plurality of crimp forming blades located forward of the free end of the mandrel and movable periodically toward and from the elbow blank to form inwardly projecting eccentric crimps in the elbow blank, a main plunger guided by and movable within said hollow mandrel and of an external pattern to correspond with the external pattern of the mandrel, an auxiliary plunger having an external pattern to correspond with that of the main plunger and jointedly connected with said main plunger, means to periodically reciprocate said plungers endwise relative to said mandrel, and a main driving shaft to actuate said movable members in synchronism.

1,326,917. WATERPROOF VARNISH. RALPH E. DINGS and LIONEL SCHUSTER, New York, N. Y. Filed Nov. 22, 1918. Serial No. 263,676. 4 Claims. (Cl. 134—26.)

4. A varnish suitable as a substitute for liquid shellac, comprising a mixed solution composed substantially of 200 pounds of Manila gum to 40 gallons of alcohol with 100 ounces of carnauba wax to 4 gallons of spirits of turpentine.

1,326,918. SAFEGUARD-LAMP FOR AUTOMOBILES. KAZIMER DOMBKOWSKI, Stanhope, N. J. Filed June 16, 1919. Serial No. 304,512. 2 Claims. (Cl. 240—62.)

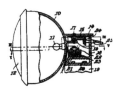

1. In combination with a pivotally mounted headlight and the steering shaft of an automobile, a gear carried by the headlight, a clutch member splined upon the shaft, a pinion journaled concentric with said shaft adapted for clutching engagement with said clutch member, flexible shaft connections in constant operative engagement with said pinion and gear, a casing inclosing the pinion and clutch member and operating means for said clutch member supported on said casing.

1,326,919. SANITARY CUSPIDOR OR REFUSE-RECEPTACLE. KAZIMER DOMBKOWSKI, Stanhope, N. J. Filed July 9, 1919. Serial No. 309,605. 4 Claims. (Cl. 4—39.)

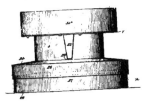

1. A cuspidor or other refuse receptacle comprising an upper receptacle section and a lower receptacle section detachably connected, said upper receptacle section having an outwardly directed horizontal annular flange, a

ring mounted above the flange for limited rotation, partial closure members pivoted to the ring and having link connection with said flange, yieldable means to normally maintain the ring positioned with the partial closure members closing the open top of the upper receptacle section, and foot operated means disposed beneath said flange and operatively connected to said ring to effect partial rotation of the latter to cause the swinging opening movement of the partial closure members.

1,326,920. TALKING-MACHINE. FRANK L. DYER, Montclair, N. J. Filed Dec. 29, 1916. Serial No. 139,476. 7 Claims. (Cl. 274—2.)

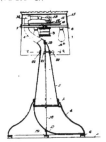

1. A talking machine in the form of a lamp, the record and sound box being carried within the lamp shade and the horn opening into the base of the lamp, substantially as and for the purposes set forth.

1,326,921. BABY-WALKER. WACLAW DZIMITOWICZ, Pittsburgh, Pa. Filed Jan. 30, 1919. Serial No. 274,060. 3 Claims. (Cl. 155—45.)

1. A device of the class described comprising a rectangular frame, supporting legs, hinges connected between said legs and frame retaining latches for the legs when folded and when unfolded pivoted at one of their ends to the frame, a table ring, sockets upon the bottom of said ring, springs extending into said sockets, studs upon the free ends of said legs adapted for detachable connection with said sockets and springs, and a seat board resiliently suspended from said ring.

1,326,922. AIR-RELIEF VALVE FOR SPRINKLER SYSTEMS. FRED ECKS, New York, N. Y. Filed May 21, 1919. Serial No. 298,689. 9 Claims. (Cl. 169—20.)

1. A relief valve of the class described, comprising a cylinder having a cylinder head, a float chamber in com-

munication with said cylinder, a piston movably mounted in one end portion of the cylinder, a valve seat in the other end portion of the cylinder, a shaft connected with and movable with said piston, a valve mounted on said

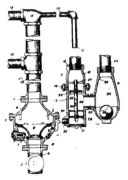

shaft and adapted to operate in connection with said valve seat, a pipe communicating with the bottom portion of the cylinder below the piston therein, and a pipe communicating with the cylinder head.

1,326,923. VALVE FOR BLOWING-ENGINES AND THE LIKE. CHARLES FRECH. Sault Ste. Marie, Ontario, Canada. Filed Apr. 2, 1919. Serial No. 286,881. 5 Claims. (Cl. 251—144.)

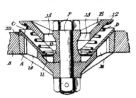

1. In a valve of the character described and in combination a valve seat having a port therein formed with a conical seating surface, a conical valve member, a conical follower member supported from the valve seat and spaced therefrom, and a spiral spring extending from the follower member to the valve member.

1,326,924. LAMP-LOCKING CONSTRUCTION. EDGAR H. FREEMAN, Trenton, N. J., assignor to E. H. Freeman Electric Company, a Corporation of New Jersey. Filed July 2, 1918. Serial No. 243,008. 7 Claims. (Cl. 173—356.)

1. A lamp locking device comprising, in combination with the socket member, a helical snubbing coil arranged within the socket member, a coil holder and guide within the socket member, and a key actuated operating device operatively engaging the coil to contract and expand the same.

1,326,925. MACHINE FOR COUNTING AND ARRANGING HAIRPINS OR LIKE ARTICLES. SOLOMON H. GOLDBERG, Chicago, Ill., assignor to The Hump Hairpin Manufacturing Company, Chicago, Ill., a Corporation of West Virginia. Filed Feb. 23, 1918. Serial No. 218,627. 5 Claims. (Cl. 163—8.)

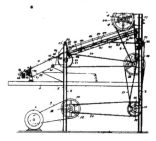

1. In a machine for handling hairpins or like articles the combination with feeding mechanism for advancing the plurality of hairpins or like articles, a main stop normally pressed into the path of movement of such articles, an auxiliary stop normally spring pressed out of the path of such articles, and a movable member adapted in one position of adjustment to force the auxiliary stop into the path of the articles, and a spring for automatically withdrawing the main stop out of the path of the said articles when the auxiliary stop is adjusted into their path.

1,326,926. CARD-HOLDER. HARRY A. GRAY, Milwaukee, Wis., assignor of one-half to George R. Wright, Milwaukee, Wis. Filed May 21, 1918. Serial No. 235,773. 1 Claim. (Cl. 206—40.)

A card holder comprising a receptacle provided with a slot extending through one end of the receptacle adjacent one side thereof, said side of the receptacle being provided with a longitudinally extending slot in its central portion, a dog slidably mounted in said slot and adapted for gripping engagement with cards in the receptacle and a spring in said receptacle bearing against the other side of the receptacle and having a portion engageable directly against the substantially central portion of a pack of cards in the receptacle at a point approximately in transverse alinement with the initial point of engagement of the dog with the pack of cards and a spring for ejecting cards from the receptacle, said spring being otherwise free from connection with the pack of cards, whereby the spring pressure exerted through the pack of cards is progressively reduced from the center of the pack toward the ends of the pack by reason of flexibility of said pack of cards.

1,326,927. FIRE-EXTINGUISHER. EDWARD L. HALL, New York, N. Y. Filed May 27, 1918. Serial No. 236,769. 4 Claims. (Cl. 169—31.)

1. A fire extinguisher including a container for a liquid, a discharge therefor, a valve chamber with closed ends and intermediate ports located within said chamber, a delivery pipe connecting said chamber with said discharge, intakes conveying the liquid to said ports at points remote from the adjacent ends of the container respectively, and a longitudinally grooved valve member bearing circumferentially upon the inner walls of the chamber, the

ends of said member controlling the ports in said chamber from the interior thereof, one port being opened and the other port being closed alternatively.

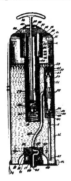

4. A fire extinguisher including a container for a liquid, a stationary valve chamber positioned within said container near one side, a discharge arranged to convey the liquid from said chamber to an outlet of the container, a lever at one end of the container operable on the same side thereof as the valve chamber so as to control said discharge, and a sight on the container diametrically disposed with relation to said lever.

1,326,928. IRON. YOTARO HARADA, Stockton, Calif. Filed July 29, 1918. Serial No. 247,181. 1 Claim. (Cl. 68—26.)

A flat iron having a hollow body adapted to be filled with water and subjected to heat, a bleed hole provided in the top of the body, and a spring closure normally closing said bleed hole but allowing steam generated by the heat to escape therethrough when the steam pressure exceeds the strength of the spring of the closing member, the latter being pivoted to the body and provided with a finger piece whereby the closing member may be turned to one side of the bleed-hole to allow the steam to escape freely therefrom.

1,326,929. BRUSH AND METHOD OF MAKING THE SAME. AUGUST H. HENNING, Milwaukee, Wis. Filed Dec. 4, 1917. Serial No. 205,289. 2 Claims. (Cl. 15—28.)

2. A brush comprising a head formed of a sheet metal strip having outer and inner integral binding portions,

the terminal parts of the strip forming the inner, and the intermediate part the outer binding portion, said portions having central longitudinal bends and having between them a space which is U-shaped in cross section, said terminal parts being tapered and overlapping at their ends, and bristles clamped at their mid portions between said binding portions, the lower edges of said outer binding portion extending inward below the tapered parts firmly against the bristles.

1,326,930. DIVIDING DOUGH. HARRY HEWITT, Manchester, England, assignor of one-half to Joseph Baker & Sons Limited, London, England. Filed May 12, 1914. Serial No. 838,098. 6 Claims. (Cl. 107—15.)

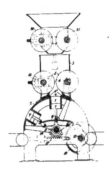

5. A dough-dividing apparatus including in combination, dividing means comprising measuring cells and a pair of rotating rollers arranged with respect to said measuring cells in such juxtaposition that the dough is fed directly into the measuring cell with an unrestricted space between the rollers and the cell.

1,326,931. UMBRELLA - STAFF. ORVILLE J. HIMES, Oswego, N. Y. Original application filed Feb. 8, 1917, Serial No. 147,442. Divided and this application filed Dec. 4, 1917. Serial No. 205,363. 3 Claims. (Cl. 135—46.)

3. A staff for an umbrella comprising an intermediate hollow section, a core slidably mounted in the intermediate section, a link connected with one end portion of the core, an end section having a reduced end connected with the link and fitting into the hollow intermediate section, a handle section fitting into the opposite end portion of the intermediate section, a link connected with the handle section and positioned in the intermediate section, a latch block pivotally connected with the last mentioned link, the inner end portion of the core being provided with a tongue extension having a socket therein, a latch holding pin extending from the block through a longitudinally extending slot in the intermediate section, and a latch carried by the latch pin and provided with a bill

extending through the slot and through an opening in the block to engage the socket of the tongue and releasably hold the sections against longitudinal movement.

1,326,932. GRAMOPHONE, PHONOGRAPH, AND THE LIKE. JOSE HOFFAY, South Kensington, London, England. Filed Feb. 26, 1915. Serial No. 10,698. 4 Claims. (Cl. 274—35.)

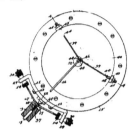

1. In a reproducer for a gramophone, phonograph or the like, the combination with a diaphragm and a support therefor, of a stylus lever connected at one end to said diaphragm, a single universal bearing for said lever upon said support, and means for yieldingly maintaining said lever in a predetermined position upon said bearing constructed to offer greater resistance to movements oblique or parallel to said diaphragm than to movements normal to said diaphragm.

1,326,933. VISE. JOHN O. HOLEN, Tono, Wash. Filed Apr. 5, 1919. Serial No. 287,701. 2 Claims. (Cl. 81—23.)

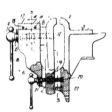

1. A vise comprising a stationary jaw, a relatively fixed bearing in front thereof, a movable jaw between the fixed jaw and the bearing, having a downwardly extending tail pivotally supported at its lower end, a nut pivoted at the upper end of the tail, a feed-screw rotatably supported at one end in the bearing and having its free end working in the nut, and means for holding the screw against longitudinal movement.

1,326,934. WRIST-WATCH CASE AND CLAMP. DE FOREST HULBURD, Chicago, Ill., assignor to Elgin National Watch Company, a Corporation of Illinois. Filed July 29, 1918. Serial No. 247,142. 5 Claims. (Cl. 224—4.)

1. A wrist watch holder comprising a case, an outwardly extending ear carried by one edge of the watch case having an obliquely extending outer end provided with a slot, an ear carried by the opposite edge of the case and having an obliquely extending outer end, a clamp

in said obliquely extending end, and an attaching strap having an enlarged portion forming a guard for the lower

face of the case and having a strap portion passing through the slot in the ear and adapted to be passed through the clamp as shown.

1,326,935. SPEED-CONTROLLING MECHANISM FOR AUTOMOBILES. MERION J. HUGGINS, New York. N. Y., assignor to Automotive Development Co., Inc., New York, N. Y., a Corporation of New York. Filed Dec. 27, 1915, Serial No. 68,751. Renewed Sept. 10, 1919. Serial No. 322,983. 34 Claims. (Cl. 74—58.)

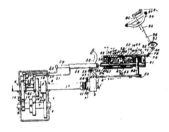

1. In an automobile, the combination with shiftable gears for a variable speed transmission, of shifting devices for said gears, a movable member, means to move said member, locking means for each of said devices to lock it to said member in one position of said locking means and in another position to unlock it from said member and locking the shifting device against movement, and a movable member to operate any one of said locking means.

1,326,936. APPARATUS FOR AUTOMATICALLY FEEDING MELTING-POTS OF TYPE-BAR-MAKING MACHINES. ALLAN EDGAR JEANS and PETER THOMAS HAYES, Liverpool, England. Filed June 24, 1919. Serial No. 306,498. 4 Claims. (Cl. 22—80.)

1. In apparatus for automatically feeding the melting pots of type bar making machines, the combination with

a non-swinging melting pot, of a magazine for holding a plurality of type bars in a pile, a sliding carriage at the bottom thereof in the form of a sliding plate having one part off-set from another part so as to form an abutment adapted to act against one or more lines or bars of type at a time in the magazine to deliver them to a chute feeding the melting pot.

1,326,937. SASH-LOCK. CHRISTIAN J. KASPER, Rochester, N. Y. Filed May 15, 1917. Serial No. 168,717. 2 Claims. (Cl. 292—62.)

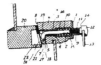

1. A sash lock comprising a casing having a bolt receiving opening and a recess extending downwardly from the inner end of said opening, a locking bolt mounted to rotate in either direction and to move longitudinally in the bolt receiving opening of the casing, said locking bolt having at its inner end a beveled portion on one side and a lateral lug on its other side adapted to depend in the recess of the casing when the locking bolt is withdrawn, said locking bolt also having a shoulder adapted to engage with the casing, and an anchor plate of uniform thickness supported at an angle other than a right angle to the axis of the bolt, said plate having an elongated opening, the top wall of which is so arranged that the beveled end of the bolt will engage therewith to cause the sashes to register.

1,326,938. VALVE. JACOB B. KNUDSEN, Chicago, Ill., assignor of one-half to Francis H. Quail, Chicago, Ill. Filed Jan. 19, 1916. Serial No. 73,005. 3 Claims. (Cl. 251—47.)

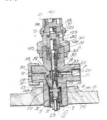

3. In a pressure tank valve, the combination with a valve casing having an enlarged recess in its lower end communicating with an exit passage, a valve member mounted in said enlarged recess and having a frusto-conical portion extending into the exit passage, a shoulder on said valve, a closing plug for said recess having apertures for the passage of the tank contents, a downwardly extending stem projecting through said plug and guiding said valve member, a coiled spring interposed between the shoulder on said valve and said plug for holding the valve in position, an upwardly projecting extension on said valve member, a threaded stem mounted in said casing having its lower end bearing upon said extension and having an irregular shaped upper end, a bonnet for said casing, a rotatable member in said bonnet having a shoulder at its upper end seating against an interior shoulder in said bonnet and provided with an irregular shaped socket for the reception of the irregular shaped end of the threaded stem, a coiled spring holding the shoulder on said rotatable member in seated position, said rotatable member

having an irregular shaped projection extending through the bonnet and a vertically stationary rotatable operating member mounted on said bonnet and having an irregular shaped socket for the reception of said irregular shaped projection on the rotatable member.

1,326,939. UNIVERSAL PIPE-JOINT. JACOB B. KNUDSEN, Chicago, Ill. Filed May 29, 1917. Serial No. 171,620. 1 Claim. (Cl. 285—94.)

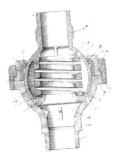

In a ball-and-socket pipe coupling, the combination with a hemispherical socket member, of a retaining ring, a ball member fitting said socket member and a ring interiorly and held movably against withdrawal by said ring, an abutment ring mounted within said socket member and having an edge-engaging seat for the open end of said ball member, and a coil spring within said ball interposed between said abutment ring and ball member.

1,326,940. CLOTHES-CABINET. JOHN B. LEMILY, Brooklyn, N. Y. Filed July 26, 1919. Serial No. 313,605. 5 Claims. (Cl. 45—37.)

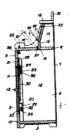

1. A cabinet of the class described comprising main and supplemental compartments, a large door forming a closure for the front of the main compartment, a lift door forming a closure for the top of the main compartment, another lift door forming a closure for said supplemental compartment, and a supplemental door detachably mounted in the cabinet rearwardly of said first named door.

1,326,941. WINDOW-SHADE APPLIANCE. WILLIAM HENRY LYNCH, Bellaire, Ohio. Filed July 24, 1919. Serial No. 313,089. 1 Claim. (Cl. 156—27.)

A window shade support including a vertically arranged slotted tube having its upper end attached to a window frame, a hollow rectangular casing secured to the window frame and supporting the lower end of said tube, a vertical rod slidably arranged in said tube, a pair of locking arms arranged in said rectangular casing and having openings receiving the said rod, a coil spring surrounding said

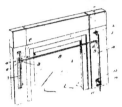

rod and confined between said locking arms, a bracket extended through the slot in said tube and connected to the upper end of said rod, a transverse rod connected to said bracket, a second bracket connected to said transverse rod, and a guide for the second-named bracket.

1,326,942. ATTACHMENT FOR COOKING UTENSILS. ADAM F. LOCHNER, Chandler, Okla. Filed Feb. 15, 1919. Serial No. 277,209. 1 Claim. (Cl. 53—1.)

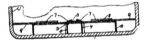

A device including a perforated plate having an integral marginal support, there being parallel slots in the plate adjacent the center thereof, a strip bearing upon the central portions of the plate and having end portions extending through the slots and constituting central supports for the plate, said end portions engaging the walls of the slots to hold said portions against upward displacement relative to the plate, pairs of guide flanges extending approximately radially upon the plate, said flanges being struck upwardly therefrom and constituting guides, arcuate perforated extension plates and tongues extending inwardly from the central portions of the extension plates, and detachably and slidably engaging the flanges of the respective pairs.

1,326,943. TREATMENT-STOOL. JOHN V. McMANIS, Dayton, Ohio. Filed Mar. 7, 1917. Serial No. 153,146. 10 Claims. (Cl. 155—23.)

1. A treatment stool comprising a base, a vertically adjustable standard mounted upon said base to non-rotatably support a seat, a backless patient's seat mounted upon said standard and tiltable fore-and aft relative thereto to different positions of inclination, and means carried by and at the rear of the stool to support the

feet of an operator, the foot-engaging parts thereof lying in a plane above the base and below the seat to enable the operator to bring his knees to bear against the back of the patient.

1,326,944. HEATING SYSTEM. JOHN E. MacDONALD, River Forest, Ill., assignor to Illinois Engineering Company, Chicago, Ill., a Corporation of Illinois. Filed Mar. 11, 1915. Serial No. 13,765. 1 Claim. (Cl. 237—68.)

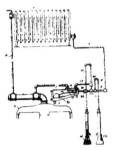

In an apparatus for use with low pressure vacuum heating systems, the combination with a boiler and a heating unit, live steam connections from the boiler to one end of the heating unit, exhaust steam connections from the other end of the heating unit to the boiler, said connections extending above the boiler so that the condensed steam will return to the latter by gravity, a return tank interposed in said exhaust steam connections, a pipe for admitting live steam into said tank, a valve controlling the admission of steam from the pipe, an air vent leading from said tank, a second valve for controlling communication between the tank and air vent, float operated leverage mechanism for moving one of said valves into closed position and simultaneously opening the other of said valves, a check valve interposed in the exhaust steam connections between the heating unit and return tank, connections between the air vent and that side of the check valve remote from the return tank, and an air seal connected to said air vent.

1,326,945. STABILIZING CONTROL FOR AEROPLANES. ALFRED J. MACY, Chicago, Ill., assignor to Macy Engineering Company, Franklin, Pa., a Corporation of Maine. Filed Mar. 25, 1916. Serial No. 86,612. 34 Claims. (Cl. 244—29.)

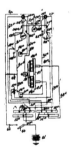

1. In a device of the class described, the combination with an aeroplane and lateral controlling means therefor, of an instrument board mounted transversely of the

aeroplane, a plurality of gravity acting levers thereon, electrical contacts on said instrument board, means associated with said board for movement therewith, and relatively movable with respect thereto, electrical circuits adapted to be closed and opened by said levers and by said means and electrical·mechanisms connected to the controlling means of the aeroplane adapted to be set in operation by a closure of said electrical circuits to operate the controlling means and correct deflections in the flight of the aeroplane.

1,326,946. METHOD OF AUTOMATIC CONTROL FOR VEHICLES. ALFRED J. MACY, Chicago, Ill., assignor to Macy Engineering Company, Franklin, Pa , a Corporation of Maine. Filed Mar. 25, 1916. Serial No. 86,613. 11 Claims. (Cl. 244—29.)

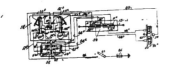

1. The method of automatically controlling an aerial machine comprising adjustment of the controls thereof to restore the same to normal attitude of flight when deflected therefrom, then releasing and returning the controls to normal position before the aerial machine is completely restored to normal flying attitude, and thereby permitting the momentum thereof to continue the movement of the aerial machine to normal flying attitude.

1,326,947. PROCESS OF MAKING HEXANITRODI-PHENYLAMIN. JOHN MARSHALL, Swarthmore, Pa., assignor to E. I. du Pont de Nemours & Company, Wilmington, Del., a Corporation of Delaware. Filed Mar. 20, 1919. Serial No. 283,843. 13 Claims. (Cl. 23—24.)

9. The process which comprises treating 2.4-dinitrodiphenylamin with mixed nitric and sulfuric acids under conditions so regulated as to form 2.4.2'.4'-(tetranitrodiphenylamin, and then nitrating the tetranitrodiphenylamin at an elevated temperature with mixed nitric and sulfuric acids to form 2.4.6.2'.4'.6'-hexanitrodiphenylamin, the mixed acids containing in the first nitration 30% nitric acid and in the second nitration 20% nitric acid.

1,326,948. BRACELET. WALTER P. MAY, St. Louis, Mo., assignor of one-half to Shellie Andrews, St. Louis, Mo. Filed July 17, 1919. Serial No. 311,659. 6 Claims. (Cl. 281—14.)

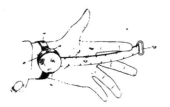

1. A bracelet, a case thereon having a slot, a spring roller in the case, a metal band coiled on the roller and one end leading out the slot, and a handle on said end, the band bearing a writing-surface.

1,326,949. CAR-MOVER FOR TUNNEL-KILNS. PAUL A. MEEHAN, New Castle, Pa., assignor to American Dressler Tunnel Kilns, Inc., New York, N. Y., a Corporation of New York. Filed Oct. 29, 1919. Serial No. 334,352. 5 Claims. (Cl. 104—162.)

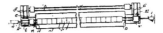

1. In a tunnel kiln comprising a kiln proper, cars movable therethrough and means at one end of a section of the kiln for pushing successively presented cars and thereby a train of cars in the kiln section forward a car length each time a car is presented, the improvement which consists in means at the opposite end of the kiln section for engaging a forward car of the train and moving it away from the preceding cars comprising a car engaging device in the kiln and externally controlled operating mechanism for said device.

1,326,950. TENSION-EVENER FOR YARN-WINDING MACHINES. WILLIAM MILTON, Guelph, Ontario, Canada. Filed June 2, 1919. Serial No. 301,345. 1 Claim. (Cl. 118—11.)

The tension bar suspended from the body of a winding machine so as to rest lightly against the top of the stem of one or any number of unwinding spools set in a line, said pressure bar being composed of an upper rigid portion carrying a semi-flexible flap or feather edge; the whole being suspended by a single adjustable lengthening bar from a suitable point on the machine so as to act by gravity or by means of the springy nature of the material of which the said lengthening bar is composed substantially as hereinbefore described and illustrated in the drawings.

1,326,951. SASH-ROD FOR CURTAINS. CARL EMIL MOLLER, Jamestown, N. Y. Filed Apr. 7, 1919. Serial No. 288,078. 2 Claims. (Cl. 156—19.)

1. In a curtain rod, a pair of telescopic members each having a supporting end, said ends being each formed with a key-hole shaped slot, the outer end wall of the larger part of the slot being turned outwardly to form a lip which lies at an incline and extends toward the slot, and round headed screws having their heads engageable through the larger part of the slot, the inclination of said lips being substantially equal to the curvature of the screw heads whereby the lips act as guides to effect entry of the screws into the slots.

1,326,952. OZONIZING APPARATUS PAYTON J. H. MOORE, Chicago, Ill., assignor to American Grain Deodorizing Co., Chicago, Ill., a Corporation of Illinois. Original application filed Mar. 1, 1917, Serial No. 151,758. Divided and this application field June 19, 1917, Serial No. 175,597. Renewed June 30, 1919. Serial No. 307,783. 2 Claims. (Cl. 204—31.)

1. Ozonizing apparatus comprising a chamber having a transparent top ; a door giving access to the side of said

chamber; a frame in said chamber removable through said door; grooved supporting bars in said chamber, said frame sliding in the grooves in said bars; a plurality of coils

mounted in said frame; means for passing an electric current of high potential through said coils; and means for passing air through said chamber, substantially as described.

1,326,953. RAIL ADJUSTING AND GAGING DEVICE. SAM MORANO, Wendel, W. Va., assignor to Sam Morano & Company, Wendel, W. Va., a Firm. Filed July 16, 1919. Serial No. 311,293. 3 Claims. (Cl. 254—43.)

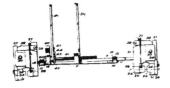

1. A rail adjusting and gaging device including a pair of rail clamps, and means to adjust said clamps toward and away from each other, said clamps each including a pair of opposite rail web engaging members vertically adjustable to accommodate rails of various sizes.

1,326,954. AMUSEMENT APPARATUS. JAMES A. MOTSENBOCKER, Indianapolis, Ind., assignor of one-half to Emil F. Burkle, Indianapolis, Ind. Filed Apr. 21, 1919. Serial No. 291,499. 2 Claims. (Cl. 46—59.)

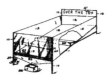

1. An amusement apparatus comprising an inclined field for returning the spent balls to the players, means for disarranging the normal surface plane of the field for deflecting the course of the returning balls, means for inclosing said field and keeping the balls in defined limits, a series of pockets arranged along the foot of the field for receiving the spent balls, a trap door for supporting the spent balls, means for depressing and effecting the discharge of the spent balls from the pockets, a ball chute for receiving the balls discharged from the end of the field and conveying them to a common discharge opening, and means for receiving the collected balls.

1,326,955. MUSICAL INSTRUMENT. ELMER FREDRICK EDMOND MUELLER, Chicago, Ill. Filed May 21, 1917. Serial No. 169,909. 7 Claims. (Cl. 179—100.1.)
2. In a device of the character described, a frame, a carriage mounted reciprocatably thereon, a rotary phono-

graphic record member also mounted thereon and with respect to which said carriage has relative movement, said member having a plurality of parallel records, re-

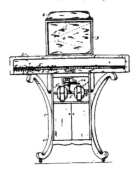

producing means on said carriage, and selector means for adjusting the position of said carriage with respect to the records on said record member.

1,326,956. FASTENING MEANS FOR WINDOWS. WINTER W. MYERS, Brooklyn, N. Y., assignor to Austral Window Company, New York, N. Y., a Corporation of Maine. Filed July 21, 1917. Serial No. 181,944. 11 Claims. (Cl. 292—182.)

1. An improved window latch, comprising a keeper plate adapted to be secured on the meeting rail of one sash, and a bolt member adapted to be supported on the meeting rail of the other sash and normally engaging said keeper plate, in combination with means including means pivoted to the bolt member adapted to move the latter first longitudinally and then vertically with respect to the meeting rails to unlatch the same.
2. An improved window latch, comprising, in combination, a keeper plate adapted to be secured on the meeting rail of one sash, and a spring pressed bolt member adapted to be supported on the meeting rail of the other sash, and normally engaging said keeper plate, in combination with means including means pivoted to the bolt member adapted to move the latter first longitudinally and then vertically with respect to the meeting rails to unlatch the same.
3. An improved window latch comprising a keeper plate located on the meeting rail of one sash, a base member fixed to the meeting rail of the other sash, and a plunger or bolt carried by said base member normally in locking engagement with said keeper plate, an operating lever pivoted to the bolt for oscillating the latter and provided with a cam surface thereon coöperating with said base member for moving the same longitudinally in one direction, and means coöperating with said base member for moving said bolt longitudinally in the other direction.
4. An improved window latch comprising a keeper plate located on the meeting rail of one sash, a base member fixed to the meeting rail of the other sash provided with a pivot bearing and a spring pressed plunger or bolt carried by said base member and adapted to engage said keeper plate, said bolt and base member provided with means for attaching a pivoted or fixed operating member for actuating the same.

5. An improved window latch comprising a keeper plate located on the meeting rail of one sash, a base member fixed to the meeting rail of the other sash, and a spring pressed plunger or bolt operatively connected to said base member, adapted to automatically engage said keeper plate and capable of longitudinal and vertical movement with respect to the base member and means pivoted to said bolt and adapted, when moved in one direction to make a tight joint between the said meeting rails and when moved in the other direction to move the same from the keeper plate.

1,326,957. THERMOMETER. HARRY Y. NORWOOD, Rochester, N. Y., assignor to Taylor Instrument Companies, Rochester, N. Y., a Corporation of New York. Filed Feb. 16, 1916. Serial No. 78,602. 2 Claims. (Cl. 73—32.)

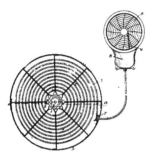

1 In combination with an elongated flexible tube containing heat sensitive fluid and an indicating instrument to be operated thereby, of a support embodying a series of radially arranged arms, each of which arms is slotted at different points forming recesses along its length to receive said tube when coiled on the support.

1,326,958 SUPPORT FOR RUGS IN THE PROCESS OF DYEING THE SAME. WALTER E. OLSON, Chicago, Ill. Original application filed May 20, 1914, Serial No. 839,830. Divided and this application filed Dec. 18, 1915. Serial No. 67,608. 5 Claims. (Cl. 8—19.)

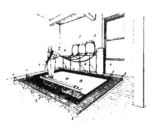

5. A support for rugs or like articles in dyeing the same comprising a foraminated platform; and a foraminated supporting element arranged on said platform, the upper side of said supporting element presenting a plurality of spaced supporting surfaces of small area, substantially as described.

1,326,959. BOX-HANGER. MATHEW H. PAINE, Glenellyn, and WINFIELD S. WILLIAMS, Chicago, Ill., assignors to Paine Company, a Corporation of Illinois. Filed Apr. 3, 1918. Serial No. 226,395. 17 Claims. (Cl. 248—35.)

16. In an anchoring device the combination of a supporting member having a pivotal bearing; two truss members coaxially pivoted upon the bearing; the truss members adapted to swing on the axis by their own weight; said supporting member adapted to act as the center of the truss members and the truss members adapted to coöperate with the stud to form an anchoring truss; automatic means to lock the truss members in an anchoring position.

1,326,960. ENGINE ATTACHING MEANS FOR VEHICLES. ROBERT E. PETRIE, Chicago, Ill. Filed Apr. 2, 1917. Serial No. 159,300. 2 Claims. (Cl. 180—64.)

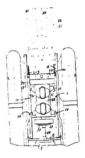

1. The combination with the chassis sills of a vehicle, of angle guide members rigidly secured in said sills and projecting therefrom, grooved sub-frame sills slidably engaged on the projecting portions of said guide members, and a power plant for the vehicle mounted on said sub-frame sills.

2. The combination with the chassis sills of a vehicle, of angle guide members rigidly secured in said channel sills with the horizontal flanges thereof projecting therefrom, grooved sub-frame sills slidable on said horizontal flanges of said guide members, said horizontal flanges of said guide members and said sub frame sills having openings therein, a power plant for the vehicle mounted on said sub-frame sills adapted to be moved longitudinally with said sub-frame sills on said guide members, and pins adapted to engage through the openings in said sub-frame sills and in said horizontal flanges of said guide members when said openings are in register to secure the sub-frame sills and the power plant in position on the vehicle chassis.

1,326,961. APPARATUS FOR LIQUEFYING AIR. JAMES F PLACE, Glen Ridge, N. J. Filed Feb. 14, 1916. Serial No. 78,113. 3 Claims. (Cl. 62—122.)

1. In an apparatus for liquefying atmospheric air, a plurality of expansion chambers, arranged so that into each of which is delivered from a pressure-reducing valve, consecutively, air at an initial high compression, but let down in pressure, and expanded and cooled in steps, from chamber to chamber, successively, until substantially atmospheric pressure and the temperature of liquefica-

tion of said repeatedly expanded air is reached in the last of said chambers; in operative combination with a holder, or low-pressure liquefied-gas reservoir, connected with and below said last expansion chamber; and a liquefier, having a high pressure holder, or liquefied-gas reservoir, below the same and connected therewith; and a delivery spray-head located above said high-pressure reser-

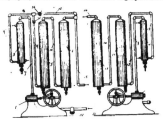

voir, and connected therewith through an upright pipe having a pressure-releasing liquefied-air valve; a low pressure conduit leading from the upper part of said last expansion chamber, and delivering to the outer surfaces of said liquefier; and a pipe connecting said low-pressure reservoir below said last expansion chamber, with said liquefied gas delivery spray-head.

1,326,962. SECTIONAL NON-ROTATIVE INSULATING-KNOB FOR SUPPORTING ELECTRIC WIRES. ALFRED M. POINDEXTER, Denver, Colo. Filed May 1, 1917. Serial No. 165,729. 1 Claim. (Cl. 173—314.)

A wire clamping knob of the character described, comprising a nail which is split centrally for a portion of its length thereby to bulge its sides, head and base clamping sections non-rotatively mounted on said nail, the base section being in frictional engagement with the bulged sides of the nail and being thereby prevented from slipping off the same.

1,326,963. PENDULUM-SCALE. ELMER C. POOL, New Castle, Pa., assignor to Toledo Scale Company, Toledo, Ohio, a Corporation of New Jersey. Filed Mar. 29, 1918. Serial No. 225,476. 5 Claims. (Cl. 265—62.)

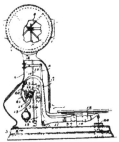

1. In a weighing scale, a pendulum, a main lever, a platform resting upon the lever, connections from the lever to actuate the pendulum, the lever connection with the pendulum being in a plane above that of the lever connections to the platform and the fulcrum pivots, indicating mechanism including a pinion, and a rack rod for driving the pinion connected with the lever in the same horizontal plane as the lever connections to the platform and fulcrum.

1,326,964. WATER-HEATER. FRED POOLE, Jewell, Kans. Filed Feb. 9, 1915. Serial No. 7,172. 2 Claims. (Cl. 219—39.)

1. In a water heater, the combination with a conduit, of a substantially elliptical tubular heating body disposed in the conduit, means arranged on the conduit for facilitating the mounting and removal of the heating body therewithin, an electrical resistance element within the tubular body, an asbestos covering for the element, a coupling member for the tubular body, binding connections having an insulated channel for supporting the tubular body in the conduit, electrical connections passing through the insulated channels and joined with the resistance element, and spring terminals for the electrical connections.

1,326,965. PULLING IMPLEMENT. JAMES W. PORCH, Hurricane Mills, Tenn. Filed May 1, 1919. Serial No. 293,918. 1 Claim. (Cl. 254—72.)

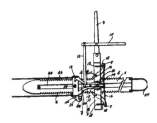

A pulling implement comprising a rack bar having anchoring means, a slide shaped to fit around the rack bar and mounted for travel along the same, said slide having spaced rearwardly extending portions between which the rack bar seats, rollers carried by the slide at the inner faces thereof, the opposite sides of the rack bar having longitudinal grooves in which the rollers seat, means on the slide for anchoring the same to the part to be pulled, pawls engageable with the teeth of the rack bar, an oscillatory carrier for the pawls connected to the rearwardly extending portion of the slide, and operating means for the carrier.

1,326,966. RESPIRATOR-VALVE. GEORGE C. REEVES, Oak Park, Ill. Filed July 15, 1918. Serial No. 245,044. 4 Claims. (Cl. 251—122.)

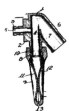

1. A respirator valve having the engaging parts of the valve adapted to simultaneously remain closed and move relatively.

1,326,967. HUB-ODOMETER. CHARLES DONAT RICHARD, New York, N. Y. Filed Dec. 15, 1917. Serial No. 207,304. 3 Claims. (Cl. 235—95.)

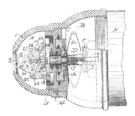

1. A register mechanism for hub odometers including in combination with the rotor element, stator element, and a register carried thereby, register wheel operating means, a driving unit including means for transmitting motion at a right angle consisting of a spindle, a spiral gear loosely mounted on said spindle and having a ratchet face at one end, said spiral gear engaging register wheel operating means, a lever carried by the spindle at right angles thereto and having a ratchet hub for engaging with the ratchet face of the spiral gear, said lever having a part in direct operative engagement with the rotor.

1,326,968. PROCESS OF EXTRACTING OILS FROM FATTY SUBSTANCES. GEORGE D. ROGERS, Gloucester, Mass. Filed Mar. 7, 1919. Serial No. 281,204. 7 Claims. (Cl. 204—24.)

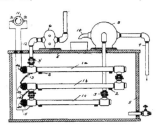

7. The process for liberating oils from the fatty substances originally containing same, which consists in comminuting said fatty substances, mingling the same with a saline electrolyte, causing the said comminuted substances to traverse a conduit provided with electrodes of opposite polarity extending longitudinally thereof, and subjecting said substances during such passage to an electric current discharging between said electrodes through said substances, and of thereafter causing said substances to be passed through a device for effecting the separation of said liberated oil from the residue of said fatty substances.

1,326,969. ENGINE-HANDLING DEVICE. ROBERT ROUNDS, Conde, S. D. Filed July 6, 1918. Serial No. 243,556. 1 Claim. (Cl. 57—9.)

An engine handling device comprising a plate provided with an opening and having a slot which communicates with the opening, chains connected with the opposite side portions of the plate, plugs carried by the said chains, and a third chain adapted to pass through the opening and engage between the edges of the slot and a hook carried by the last mentioned chain.

1,326,970. COUPLING AND THE LIKE. REUBEN R. ROW and HOWARD C. DAVIS, Elizabeth, N. J., assignors to American Marine Equipment Corporation, New York, N. Y., a Corporation of Delaware. Filed Mar. 14, 1917. Serial No. 154,671. 4 Claims. (Cl. 285—120.)

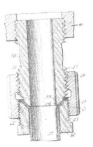

1. A coupling for connecting a pipe to a manifold and the like, comprising, in combination, a manifold having an internally threaded opening, a nipple externally threaded at both ends and at one end screwed into said opening and at the other end having an inwardly extending beveled edge, an internally threaded nut screwed upon said other end of said nipple, an externally threaded bushing screwed into the outer end of said nut and having an inner outwardly extending beveled end edge, and a pipe whose end is within said bushing and whose end edge portions are flared outwardly and held between the opposing beveled surfaces of said nipple and bushing.

2. A coupling for connecting a pipe to a manifold and the like, comprising, in combination, a manifold having an internally threaded opening, a nipple externally threaded at both ends and at one end screwed into said opening and at the other end having an inwardly extending beveled edge, an internally threaded nut screwed upon said other end of said nipple, an externally threaded bushing screwed

into the outer end of said nut and having an inner outwardly extending beveled end edge, and a pipe whose end is within said bushing and whose end edge portions are flared outwardly and held between the opposing beveled surfaces of said nipple and bushing, said end edge of said nipple being beveled on convex lines so as to afford an annular convex bearing surface against which the bushing may bind the flange of the pipe.

3. A pipe joint coupling comprising a nipple having a threaded exterior and beveled end surface, an internally threaded nut screwed on said nipple, an externally threaded bushing screwed on said nut and having a beveled end edge opposing the beveled end edge of the nipple, and a pipe whose end is within said bushing and whose end edge portions are flanged and held between the opposing beveled surfaces of said nipple and bushing, the thread on said nipple and the thread on said bushing being of different pitch and of the same hand and the threads on said nut corresponding therewith, so that the nut on the final tightening of the joint may be given a slight extra turn and thus serve as a lock-nut.

4. A pipe joint coupling comprising a tubular member having a threaded exterior and outer inwardly extending beveled end edge, an internally threaded nut screwed on said member, an externally threaded bushing screwed into said nut and having an inner outwardly extending beveled end edge, and a pipe whose end is within said bushing and whose end edge portions are flared outwardly and held between the opposing beveled surfaces of said member and bushing, said end edge of said member being beveled on convex lines so as to afford an annular convex bearing surface against which the bushing may bind the flange of the pipe, and the thread on said member and the thread on said bushing being of different pitch and of the same hand and the threads on said nut corresponding therewith, so that the nut on the final tightening of the joint may be given a slight extra turn and thus serve as a lock-nut.

1,326,971. METHOD OF MAKING SOLDER. JOHN SALM, Albany, N. Y., assignor to Charles L. A. Whitney, Albany, N. Y. Filed Aug. 3, 1918. Serial No. 248,143. 2 Claims. (Cl. 75—1.)

1. The process of making aluminum solder which consists in melting aluminum, adding thereto a small quantity of salt, adding thereto a relatively large quantity of tin, meanwhile permitting the heat to decrease, covering this product with means for protecting against oxidation and adding zinc in excess of the aluminum and in considerably less quantity than the tin and forming the product into shape for use.

1,326,972. ANODE FOR ELECTRIC VACUUM APPARATUS. MORITZ SCHENKEL, Charlottenburg, near Berlin, Germany, assignor to Siemens-Schuckert-Werke G. M. B. H., Berlin, Germany, a Corporation of Germany. Filed Sept. 13, 1916. Serial No. 119,883. 11 Claims. (Cl. 175—354.)

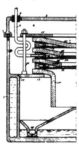

6. Anode for electric vacuum apparatus, composed of a plurality of anode rings of equal diameter and at least one partition separating said rings.

1,326,973. PROCESS FOR THE PREPARATION OF PYROCATECHIN ALDEHYDE. LUDWIG SCHMIDT, Munich, Germany. Filed Mar. 31, 1917. Serial No. 159,035. 2 Claims. (Cl. 28—24.)

1. A process for the preparation of pyrocatechin aldehyde consisting in treating piperonal with thionylchlorid and gaseous chlorin, and then saponifying the dichlorpiperonylchlorid thus formed with water, essentially as described.

1,326,974. INDICATING-BOTTLE. WILLIAM C. SCHMIDT, Richmond, Va. Original application filed Feb. 24, 1909, Serial No. 479,737. Divided and this application filed May 8, 1917. Serial No. 167,266. 7 Claims. (Cl. 215—112.)

1. An indicating bottle of the kind described, having a member in the neck of the bottle provided with a recess forming with the neck of the bottle a chamber, an indicating device provided in said chamber and visible from the exterior of the bottle and comprising layers of suitable material, one layer being provided with an indication and the other layer being impregnated with an acid, and a baffle located adjacent to said chemical carrying materials and acting to prevent return drippings from outflowing liquid from reaching both chemical or materials carrying the chemicals simultaneously.

1,326,975. APPARATUS FOR SHIFTING TRAIL GUN-CARRIAGES FOR THE PURPOSE OF TRAINING THE GUNS. EUGÈNE SCHNEIDER, Paris, France, assignor to Schneider & Cie., Paris, France, a Limited Joint-Stock Company of France. Filed Mar. 31, 1919. Serial No. 286,493. 5 Claims. (Cl. 89—40.)

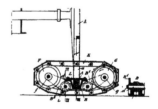

1. The combination of a gun-mounting including carriage-wheels and a trail, with a training apparatus comprising a truck to support each carriage-wheel with the truck operatively positioned to travel the chord of an arc centered at the pivotal point of the trail-tail, and an endless track passing beneath the truck and over the rim of the carriage-wheel supported by the truck when the training apparatus is in operative position.

1,326,976. CAPTIVE BALL FOR GOLF-PRACTICE. CHARLES A. B. SCHNURR, Brooklyn, N. Y. Filed Apr. 19, 1918. Serial No. 229,519. 6 Claims. (Cl. 46—4.)

2. A captive golf ball device consisting of a ball, an eye having a shank secured in the ball, a recess in the

ball to receive the eye, a tethering pin, a tether connected with the eye and tethering pin and comprising a thong

engaging the eye, a cord engaging the thong, and a resilient member engaging the cord and tethering pin.

1,326,977. FINGER-RING. ABRAHAM SCHWARTZMAN, St. Louis, Mo. Filed Mar. 27, 1919. Serial No. 285,412. 3 Claims. (Cl. 63—15.)

1. As a new article of manufacture, a composite ring of the type described formed of a main unit and a second or complementing unit, the main unit consisting of the ring-shaped shank proper of the ring and a collet-section projecting laterally from the shank, the shank being recessed upon one side and at the base of the collet-section, the second unit consisting of an arcuated base and a duplicating collet-section projecting laterally from the base, the base of the second unit fitting in the recess of, and being permanently united to, and completing, the shank of the ring and the collet-sections of the two units completing the entire collet of the ring.

1,326,978. STAMP OR LABEL AFFIXER. WILLIAM F. SCHWEIGER and WESLEY J. BALKWILL, Rochester, N. Y., assignors to Multipost Company, Rochester, N. Y., a Corporation of New York. Filed Nov. 21, 1917. Serial No. 203,199. 6 Claims. (Cl. 235—91.)

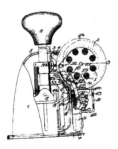

1. In a stamp affixer, the combination with a casing having a chamber for containing a perforated stamp strip, of a support movable in the stamp strip chamber, fingers on the support coöperating with the perforations in the stamp strip, a counter in the casing, connections between the finger support and the counter for actuating the latter as the fingers are carried forward by the perforations in the stamp strip.

1,326,979. COATING DEVICE. FRANK H. SEBRING, Jr., Salem, Ohio. Filed Aug. 21, 1919. Serial No. 318,871. 12 Claims. (Cl. 91—46.)

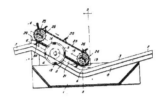

1. A liquid coating device, including a tank containing liquid, a drum containing articles to be coated and means for passing said drum through the tank and rotating the drum as it is passed through the tank.

1,326,980. STATION-INDICATOR. HENRY A. SMITH, West Albany, N. Y., assignor of one-fourth to William D. Sabey, West Albany, N. Y. Filed Dec. 2, 1918. Serial No. 265,006. 10 Claims. (Cl. 40—91.)

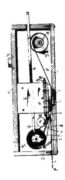

1. A device of the character described including companion rollers, an indicating ribbon connected to said rollers, means constantly tending to wind the ribbon from one of the rollers onto the other, and means for controlling rotation of one of said rollers, said latter means including a lug carried by said last mentioned roller, a pawl normally coacting with the lug for holding such roller against rotation, means for shifting the pawl out of engagement with said lug, and a second pawl independent of the first pawl and shiftable by said last mentioned means into the path of the lug.

1,326,981. METHOD AND MACHINE FOR STRAIGHT-ENING OF METAL WIRE. CARL GUSTAF SÖDERLUND, Gottenborg, Sweden, assignor to Aktiebolaget Lidköpings Mekaniska Verkstad, Lidköping, Sweden. Filed June 7, 1918. Serial No. 238,736. 8 Claims. (Cl. 153—37.)

1. A method for straightening wire, consisting in drawing the wire through helically arranged passageways of successively arranged revolving draw blocks.

1,326,982. MACHINE FOR PRESSING GARMENTS. JAMES B. SPENCER, Syracuse, N. Y., assignor to United States Hoff-man Machinery Company, Inc., Syracuse, N. Y., a Corporation of New York. Filed June 15, 1915. Serial No. 34,130. 7 Claims. (Cl. 68—9.)

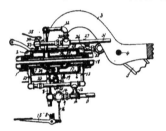

1. A garment pressing machine having a steam chamber communicating with the space between the pressing elements for supplying steam to a garment in said space, a valve for controlling the passage of steam to said chamber, a steam-operated suction device connected to said chamber for removing steam from said garment and a valve for controlling the passage of steam to the suction device.

1,326,983. PORTABLE ELECTRIC LIGHT. FREDERICK G. SPIERS, Jamaica, N. Y., assignor to National Carbon Company, Inc., New York, N. Y., a Corporation of New York. Filed Nov. 29, 1918. Serial No. 264,522. 4 Claims. (Cl. 240—8.5.)

1. A portable electric light having a casing of the kind in which a main body part is permanently provided with a metallic retaining member at the outside of an end or edge thereof for removably holding in place an outer part which has detachable engagement over the outside of said retaining member, characterized by the fact that such retaining member has a reversely turned flange extending over the edge and to the inner side of said body part, said inner flange having a smooth unbroken inner edge and that means coöperative with said inner flange and body part are provided outward in spaced relation from the smooth inner edge of said inner flange for securing the metallic retaining member in place on the body part.

1,326,984. ELEVATOR. JOHN J. SPROUL, New Haven, Conn. Filed Mar. 29, 1917. Serial No. 158,145. 31 Claims. (Cl. 187—17.)

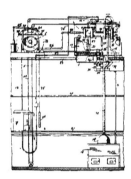

1. In an elevator system, the combination with a car, a motor for driving the same, a non-compressible fluid, reservoirs for said fluid, a pressure supply for forcing the fluid through the motor from one reservoir to the other and vice versa to drive the car in either direction, and means for maintaining the pressure applied to the fluid in both reservoirs when the car is at rest.

1,326,985. SIGN. EDWARD O. STERNS, Columbus, Ohio, assignor to Rotary Tire and Rubber Company, Columbus, Ohio, a Corporation of Ohio. Filed June 19, 1919. Serial No. 305,245. 4 Claims. (Cl. 40—132.)

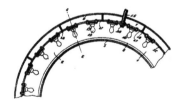

1. A sign of the character described, comprising a pair of spaced glass members of tire resembling contour, the outer peripheral edges of said members being spaced, an outer ring disposed to encircle said members and to bridge the gap therebetween, an inner ring concentric to said outer ring and coöperative with the inner portions of said sign, and clamping means for uniting said rings in assembled relation with said members.

1,326,986. MACHINE FOR CUTTING AND INTER-FOLDING SHEETS OF PAPER. LOUIS ALBERT STRAUBEL, Green Bay, Wis. Filed May 23, 1918. Serial No. 236,117. 7 Claims. (Cl. 164—68.)

1. In a machine of the character described, in combination with a bed roll, a plurality of feed rollers engaging said bed roll at one side thereof, a rotatable transverse cutting means acting on a web of work material fed over the carrier encompassing said bed roll, and guide rollers engaging said bed roll opposite that side in engagement with the feed rollers, said transverse cutting means and said feed and guide rollers having peripheral portions in overlapped relation to guide work material between them and said bed roll.

1,326,987. MACHINE FOR INTERFOLDING SHEETS OF PAPER. LOUIS A. STRAUBEL, Green Bay, Wis. Original application filed May 23, 1918, Serial No. 236,117. Divided and this application filed Mar. 22, 1919. Serial No. 284,252. 9 Claims. (Cl. 270—39.)

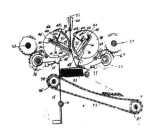

1. In a machine of the character described, a pair of folding members, means for oscillating said members simultaneously in opposite directions, clamping lips carried by said members, said clamping lips and folding members being provided with alined transverse grooves, stripper fingers entering said grooves upon movement of the members to releasing position, and means on said fingers to grip the fold of work material and transfer the same to a stack or pile.

1,326,988. FLEXIBLE TUBING. AUGUST SUNDH, Hastings-upon-Hudson, N. Y. Filed Apr. 25, 1919. Serial No. 292,566. 13 Claims. (Cl. 137—75.)

1. A flexible tubing comprising a helically wound corrugated metal strip with overlapping surfaces and a helically wound relatively rigid member to which the strip is rigidly attached by means of a metallic binder, for the purpose set forth.

1,326,989. AUTOMATIC BLOCKING MECHANISM FOR STRIP-MILLS. AUGUST SUNDH, Hastings-upon-Hudson, N. Y. Filed Nov. 21, 1917. Serial No. 203,267. 90 Claims. (Cl. 242—78.)

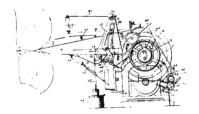

4. In strip-blocking mechanism, the combination of a block, a motor for driving the same, guiding mechanism for the strip, means for actuating the guiding mechanism to inoperative position, an electromagnet controlling said means, a switch for controlling the motor, and a winding for said electromagnet controlled by the motor switch and the strip should the latter buckle in passing through the guiding mechanism.

1,326,990. STRIP-BLOCKING MECHANISM. AUGUST SUNDH, Hastings-upon-Hudson, N. Y. Filed Dec. 27, 1917. Serial No. 209,029. 30 Claims. (Cl. 242—78.)

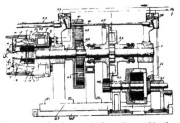

24. In strip blocking mechanism, the combination of a block, driving means therefor, a shaft carrying the block, a gear operatively connected to said shaft, a gear coöperating therewith, a shaft carrying the last-named gear, an electro-magnet, the last-named shaft forming a core therefor, and a second core for said magnet connected to the driving means and adapted to coöperate electrically with the first-named core to drive the block.

1,326,991. METHOD OF MAKING RUBBER TIRES. JAMES A. SWINEHART, Akron, Ohio. Filed July 12, 1918. Serial No. 244,545. 5 Claims. (Cl. 18—56.)

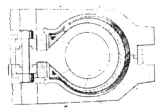

1. A method of making rubber tires, consisting in placing a tire composed of rubber and fabric in a sectional mold

constructed and interconnected to turn its sections toward each other in graduated degree from a pivot point approximately opposite the tread to the base portion of the tire, and in applying pressure axially to the mold at its inner diameter until the mold sections are folded together.

1,326,992. LOCK-NUT. NAPOLEON R. THIBERT, Worcester, Mass. Filed July 14, 1919. Serial No. 310,641. 4 Claims. (Cl. 151—25.)

1. A non-reversible lock nut comprising a screw-threaded nut having a circular grooved recess in one face, a depression located in the bottom of said recess at a distance below the end or face of the nut, a circular wire spring fitting tightly in the groove throughout substantially the whole of its length, one end of said spring having an inwardly extending pawl for engagement with the thread on the bolt, and the other end being bent downwardly at a point near said inwardly engaging pawl for engaging in said depression.

1,326,993. FLEXIBLE SHAFT-COUPLING. BERTHA E. THOMAS, Erie, Pa. Filed May 1, 1918. Serial No. 231,869. 7 Claims. (Cl. 64—96.)

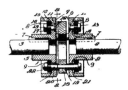

1. A flexible shaft coupling comprising a pair of coupling heads, laminated rings carried by said heads, a coupling ring disposed between said coupling members, and longitudinally disposed members passing through the members of the coupling for alternately connecting said coupling members and ring together and said flexible rings to said heads.

1,326,994. TELAUTOGRAPHIC APPARATUS. GEORGE S. TIFFANY, Summit, N. J., assignor to Telautograph Corporation, Richmond, Va., a Corporation of Virginia. Filed Dec. 15, 1917. Serial No. 207,284. 18 Claims. (Cl. 178—20.)
1. In a telautographic system, the combination with a transmitter, a plurality of receivers, and main line wires from the transmitter, one provided with separate branches to the receivers, of a receiver-selecting switch mechanism effecting the sending of impulses of different quality over the main line wires and unaffected by the writing currents traversing said main line wires, relays connected with and dependent for action upon the quality of the impulses trav-

ersing the main line wires, local circuits controlled by said relays, and other relays in said local circuits controlling

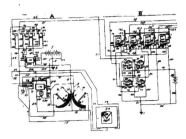

the connection of the branches aforesaid with their main line wire.

1,326,995. MOTOR-DOOR. CHARLES C. TOMKINSON, Plainfield, N. J., assignor to John Edward Ogden, Mountainville, N. Y. Filed Jan. 24, 1918. Serial No. 213,561. 3 Claims. (Cl. 268—8.)

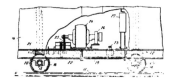

1. A hanger door, a stationary rail, a plurality of wheels with those farthest apart widely separated arranged to run on the track and upon which the door is supported, worm gears connected with a plurality of said wheels, a relatively long driving shaft spanning the distance between said widely separated wheels, worms on said shaft in mesh with said gears, a motor, and a brake therefor, transmission gearing between the motor and the driving shaft, and a manually operated controller for the motor and the brake.

1,326,996. BURNER. CLAIR A. TRAHAN, Beaumont, Tex., assignor of one-half to Theodore Placette, Port Arthur, Tex. Filed June 19, 1918. Serial No. 240,739. 2 Claims. (Cl. 158—78.)

1. A hydrocarbon burner including two coacting sections having their opposed sides provided with recesses and entrance openings communicating with said recesses, a separator disk arranged between the sections, the front portions of said sections being provided with discharge openings having outwardly diverging side walls and upper and lower walls curved inwardly from their ends toward said disk.

1,326,997. AUTOMATIC WINDING AND REVERSING MACHINE. CHARLES UEBELMESSER, New York, N. Y., assignor to Cru Patents Corporation, a Corporation of New York. Filed Mar. 24, 1915. Serial No. 16,699. 10 Claims. (Cl. 88—17.)
1. In combination with a motion picture machine, at least three film reels mounted on shafts located below the

optical axis of the motion picture machine, a supporting frame for the reel shafts, means for rotating one of said

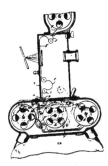

shafts, and means for coincidently rotating either of the other of said shafts.

1,326,998. VARIABLE-ORIFICE VALVE. CHARLES F. WALLACE, New York, N. Y., assignor of one-half to Martin F. Tiernan, Jamaica, Long Island, N. Y. Filed Mar. 27, 1919. Serial No. 285,474. 3 Claims. (Cl. 251—34.)

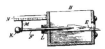

1. In combination, a rigid body having a rectangular slot therein forming an orifice the plane of which is fixed, and means comprising a flat blade movable through said slot for varying the area of said orifice, said blade being of substantially the same thickness as the width of said slot and of sufficient width completely to close said slot.

1,326,999. WORK-HOLDER. PHILIP B. WALLACE, Burlingame, and FRANK H. FOX, San Francisco, Calif. Filed Feb. 5, 1919. Serial No. 275,167. 7 Claims. (C. 81—19.)

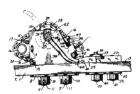

5. A clamping device comprising a block adjustable upon a suitable frame; a chain pivoted at one end thereof; a jaw secured onto said block; an eccentric roller mounted onto said block; an adjustable hook secured onto other end of said block; a mating jaw with an opening therein; said chain extending from its pivoted point, through said opening of the mating jaw over said eccentric roller to said adjustable hook; means to rotate said roller and means to adjust said hook to clamp and hold material disposed between the jaws.

1,327,000. SLOW-CLOSING FAUCET. EARL G. WATROUS, Chicago, Ill. Filed Apr. 5, 1915. Serial No. 19,155. 3 Claims. (Cl. 137—93.)

1. In a slow closing valve mechanism the combination of a piston chamber, a piston therein having a check-valved passage through itself, a valve operated by the piston, said piston being cut away to form two annular portions of different diameters, a piston ring on the portion of the larger diameter, a flat annular plate or washer resting on the portion of the lesser diameter and bearing on the piston ring to hold it in place on the piston, a plunger coöperating with the piston, a cap secured to the piston and coöperating with the washer and with the plunger, and a spring between the cap and washer.

1,327,001. MANUFACTURE OF GAS. MILTON C. WHITAKER and WALTER F. RITTMAN, New York, N. Y., assignors to Synthetic Hydro-Carbon Company, Pittsburgh, Pa., a Corporation of Delaware. Filed Apr. 3, 1914. Serial No. 829,169. 9 Claims. (Cl. 48—211.)

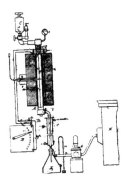

1. The method of increasing the yield of an unsaturated hydrocarbon series from a hydrocarbon oil of the petroleum type, which comprises cracking the hydrocarbon when in a gaseous state under appropriate conditions of temperature, at a pressure lower than two-thirds of an atmosphere absolute, substantially as described.

1,327,002. SHAFT-SEALING DEVICE. EDWARD T. WILLIAMS, New York, N. Y. Filed Jan. 14, 1919. Serial No. 271,043. 6 Claims. (Cl. 286—11.)
1. In a shaft-sealing device of the class described, in combination, a casing, a shaft extending out of the casing, a non-rotating axially expansible sealing device sur-

rounding the shaft and connected at its inner end with the casing and having an axially expansible portion,

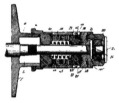

and a cap secured over and inclosing the outer end of the shaft to rotate therewith and coöperating with the outer end of the sealing device to prevent leakage.

1,327,003. ROLLER-BEARING. LULOFF WILSON, Chicago, Ill. Filed Dec. 18, 1918. Serial No. 267,307. 6 Claims. (Cl. 64—62.)

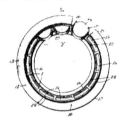

1. A roller bearing having in combination a cage frame, provided with roller-containing openings; a pair of transversely curved wings, pivoted in each said opening, and a roller between wings of each pair.

1,327,004. PROCESS AND APPARATUS FOR STANDARDIZING MILK. BERT R. WRIGHT, Poughkeepsie, N. Y., assignor to The De Laval Separator Company, New York, N. Y., a Corporation of New Jersey. Filed June 3, 1919. Serial No. 301,489. 6 Claims. (Cl. 233—46.)

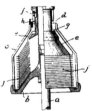

3. In a centrifugal bowl, in combination, a bottom, a top with a milk outlet, and a cream disk with a cream outlet and a supplementary outlet below the milk outlet from the bowl top.

1,327,005. COLOR-CHART. CHESTER A. YOUNG, St. Joseph, Mo. Filed May 19, 1919. Serial No. 297,982. 2 Claims. (Cl. 88—14.)
1. A chart body; an indicator disk rotatably mounted over the central portion of said body; an inner, circular,

marginal line formed on said body adjacent to the edge of said disk; an outer, circular marginal line formed on said body; two intermediate lines formed on said body between said marginal lines, forming three concentric spaces on said body around said disk, the inner one of said spaces being the broadest and the outer one being the narrowest of said three spaces; spacing lines formed radially across said spaces for separating said inner concentric space into a predetermined plurality of spectrum spaces; a plurality of sets of spectrum colors formed on said body in said spectrum spaces; indications formed on said spectrum colors whereby the name of each color can be determined; intermediate lines formed radially between said spacing lines which together with

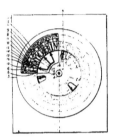

the latter evenly divide the intermediate and outer concentric spaces into a plurality of intermediate and outer spaces; secondary tints formed on said body in said intermediate spaces; complementary tints similarly formed in said outer spaces; secondary indications for indicating the colors of which said secondary tints are composed; complementary tints similarly formed in said outer spaces; complementary indications for indicating the colors of which said complementary tints are composed; a rotatably mounted group of pointers for pointing toward the colors and tints which harmonize; and register points similarly mounted with said pointers whereby said pointers have their proper positions determined.

1,327,006. MOLD FOR SEWER-STRUCTURE INVERT-SECTIONS. JACOB H. ZINN, Indianapolis, Ind. Filed July 11, 1919. Serial No. 310,139. 6 Claims. (Cl. 25—121.)

1. An invert section mold including a flat base, two curved mold walls and end walls on the base, and filling blocks spaced apart on the base against one of the mold walls.

1,327,007. CUTTER-HEAD. GUSTAF ARVID ANDERSON, Waynesboro, Pa., assignor to Landis Machine Company, Waynesboro, Pa., a Corporation of Pennsylvania. Filed Aug. 13, 1918. Serial No. 249,709. 13 Claims. (Cl. 10—100.)
1. A cutter-head comprising pivoted, body members having cutter supports on both faces thereof, means for

supporting said body members either face out, means for mounting cutter-holders on both faces of said body

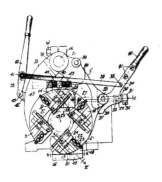

members, and means for opening and closing the die from either side thereof, substantially as set forth.

1,327,008. CUTTER-HEAD. GUSTAF ARVID ANDERSON, Waynesboro, Pa., assignor to Landis Machine Company, Waynesboro, Pa., a Corporation of Pennsylvania. Filed Aug. 14, 1918. Serial No. 249,894. 4 Claims. (Cl. 10—96.)

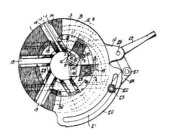

1. A cutter head having a groove formed therein with an underlying narrower groove, a chaser holder having a body proportioned for sliding fit within the groove and a T-rib proportioned for sliding fit in the underlying groove, and gibs rigidly secured within the groove and proportioned for sliding fit between the body and the T-rib.

1,327,009. ELECTRIC SWITCH. WILLIAM E. ANDRÉE, Chicago, Ill., assignor to The American Laundry Machinery Company, Cincinnati, Ohio, a Corporation of Ohio. Original application filed June 7, 1916, Serial No. 102,296. Divided and this application filed June 29, 1916. Serial No. 106,698. 7 Claims. (Cl. 175—284.)

6. An electric switch, comprising two telescoping members, both of which are reciprocable along a line, one of said members carrying two contacts and the other carry-

ing a coöperating bridge, a reciprocating operating device for one of said members, and a yielding lost motion

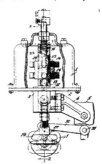

connection in both directions between said device and the member operated thereby.

1,327,010. PIN-TICKET. MARCUS O. ANTHONY, New York, N. Y., assignor to A. Kimball Company, New York, N. Y., a Corporation of New York. Filed May 10, 1917. Serial No. 167,709. 6 Claims. (Cl. 40—25.)

1. A marking ticket comprising a card having a penetrating member passing through the same normal to the face of the card adapted to be inserted through a portion of the article to be marked, the reverse face of said card being provided with means forming a fulcrum located in proximity to the place in which the penetrating member passes through the card about which the penetrating member may be bent to cause its end to engage closely the material to which it is affixed and thereby prevent it from snagging adjacent material.

1,327,011. CLAMP FOR BURIAL-VAULTS. FRANKLIN E. ARNDT, Galion, Ohio. Filed June 14, 1919. Serial No. 304,292. 6 Claims. (Cl. 292—212.)

1. In combination with two parts to be locked together, a bolt carried by one of said parts, a clamp carried by the bolt and engageable with the other part, said clamp being provided with an arm, a stop lock formed with spaced lugs with which said arm is adapted to engage, said stop block having a non-rotative engagement with the first named part, and a spring interposed between the clamp and stop block and holding the stop block in operative position.

1,327,012. SAW - SHARPENING MACHINE. Rocco ASMONDIS, Zelienople, Pa. Original application fied Dec. 10, 1918, Serial No. 266,033. Divided and this application filed June 28, 1919. Serial No. 307,315. 2 Claims. (Cl. 76—33.)

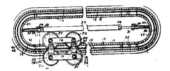

1. A device for the purpose set forth comprising a sharpening element consisting of a rectangular frame having the side bars thereof formed with racks to provide opposed seats, a file mounted in said seats, and a support for the frame.

1,327,013. SWIVEL DEVICE. CHARLES S. BARRELL, Boston, Mass. Filed Mar. 20, 1916, Serial No. 85,300. Renewed May 21, 1919. Serial No. 298,822. 10 Claims. (Cl. 59—95.)

1. A securing member of the character described comprising a member formed of wire bent upon itself, to form a bearing collar for the shank of a link and a pair of hooked members extending at angles from said collar adapted to be bent to grip a side chain of a tire chain.

1,327,014. WAX-APPLYING DEVICE. ARTHUR BATES, Leicester, England, assignor, by mesne assignments, to United Shoe Machinery Corporation, Paterson, N. J., a Corporation of New Jersey. Filed Aug. 15, 1917. Serial No. 186,331. 8 Claims. (Cl. 91—43.)

1. In a wax-applying device, a work-engaging tool having walls converging laterally from the sides of the tool to form an elongated work-engaging projection provided with a furrow extending longitudinally near the apex of said projection, and means for supplying wax to said furrow whereby with relative movement of the work and tool the wax is applied in a ribbon or stripe.

1,327,015. VALVE-LIFTER. EDSON L. BEARDSLEY, Columbus, Ohio. Filed Dec. 23, 1918. Serial No. 267,939. 3 Claims. (Cl. 29—87.1.)
1. In a valve lifter, a yoke structure, means at the top of said structure to cause its elevation, an inwardly

extending leg forming a portion of said structure, said leg having a single valve spring engaging portion, and

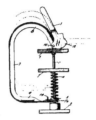

a supplemental element provided with a plurality of spaced valve spring engaging portions seated on said leg.

1,327,016. LEAF-SPRING. CLARENCE BOLES, Hugoton, Kans. Filed Feb. 10, 1917, Serial No. 147,830. Renewed Sept. 19, 1919. Serial No. 325,039. 3 Claims. (Cl. 267—33.)

1. In a spring of the class described, a cap leaf having a pair of rollers at one end, a lower leaf slidably and frictionally disposed between said rollers, a plurality of leaves between said cap and lower leaves, and means for securing said leaves together centrally.

1,327,017. ELECTRIC POCKET-LAMP. CONRAD BOLTSHAUSER, Zurich, Switzerland, assignor to Company, Phoebus, E. G., Zurich, Switzerland, a Swiss Company. Filed Oct. 23, 1917. Serial No. 198,068. 1 Claim. (Cl. 240—8.5.)

An electric pocketlamp having a circular casing with a centrally disposed counter-sunk bulb, in combination with an internal battery composed of loosely superposed couples of flat and equally sized annuli, and insulated springs fast in the casing to form contact and press the said couples against the top wall of the casing, and means for making electrical connection between the lamp and the battery.

1,327,018. MACHINE FOR SECURING THE FELTS TO PIANO-HAMMERS. OCTAVIO EUGENIO BORGARELLO, Buenos Aires, Argentina. Filed June 6, 1917. Serial No. 173,107. 13 Claims. (Cl. 144—29.)

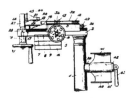

1. In a machine for affixing felts to individual piano hammers, holding elements for engaging the sides of the hammer core and adapted to receive between them the felt, and clamping jaws adapted to close about the felt

---

1,327,019. EDUCATIONAL PLAYING-CARDS. COOZIE BRITTON, Moline, Ill. Filed Mar. 7, 1918. Serial No. 220,997. 1 Claim. (Cl. 46—25.)

A set of educational playing cards comprising a plurality of cards having reversible faces, certain of the faces being line-divided into sections having proverbs and poems, advice, and election of Presidents printed thereon, and the reverse face of the cards being line-divided into sections having questions printed thereon so as to leave a space for answers.

1,327,020. HEEL-CLAMPING DEVICE. MICHAEL F. BROGAN, Lawrence, Mass., assignor, by mesne assignments, to United Shoe Machinery Corporation, Paterson, N. J., a Corporation of New Jersey. Filed June 27, 1916. Serial No. 106,144. 12 Claims. (Cl. 12—125.)

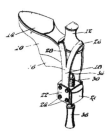

1. A heel clamping device comprising a flexible member shaped to engage the sloping surfaces at the front and rear of a heel, and means for tensioning said member and maintaining it under tension.

1,327,021. DOORKNOB - ALARM. JAMES M. BUTCHER, Chicago, Ill., assignor, by mesne assignments, to Marshall Dobbins & Co., Chicago, Ill., a Corporation of Illinois. Filed Oct. 11, 1918. Serial No..257,750. 16 Claims. (Cl. 116—44.)

2. In an alarm device, the combination of a single mounting member, alarm elements comprising a vibrator, a ratchet wheel controlling said vibrator, and a driving wheel controlling said ratchet wheel; said vibrator, ratchet wheel and driving wheel having each an independent bearing through which is rotatably supported wholly from said single mounting member, and each being assembled into its said bearing by axial movement relative thereto; said elements being assembled in overlapped relation in the order named, whereby one is secured against axial displacement by another; and means being provided for engaging the driving wheel with and securing it against axial separation from its bearing on the mounting member.

1,327,022. TENSION FOR SPOOLERS. CHARLIE O. CARTER, Anderson, Mass., assignor to Draper Corporation, Hopedale, Mass., a Corporation of Maine. Filed Apr. 8, 1918. Serial No. 227,160. 6 Claims. (Cl. 242—151.)

1. Tension mechanism for yarn winding machines comprising a member having a flat weight supporting surface inclined to the horizontal, a weight slidably mounted upon said weight supporting surface and means for guiding the running strand of yarn beneath said weight to cause the running strand partially to support said weight.

1,327,023. ELECTRICAL APPARATUS FOR THE ELECTROCHEMICAL TREATMENT OF LIQUID HYDROCARBON AND OTHER COMPOUNDS. LOUIS BOND CHERRY, Kansas City, Mo. Filed Feb. 26, 1916. Serial No. 80,707. 28 Claims. (Cl. 204—31.)

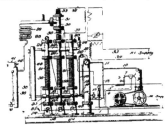

1. Apparatus for treating a liquid hydrocarbon compound, embodying, means for introducing hydrogen carry-

ing gas into said liquid, means for vaporizing said liquid, means for electrically treating the mixture of vapor and gas to produce a compound of different gravity from that of the original liquid, and means for heating said mixture while being thus treated.

1,327,024. APPARATUS FOR HANDLING FENCE-WIRE. WILLIAM H. CONAWAY, Wichita, Kans. Filed Mar. 31, 1919. Serial No. 286,385. 4 Claims. (Cl. 254—64.)

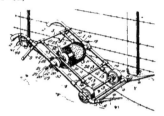

1. In a convertible hand truck and fence-wire handling apparatus, the combination of a frame, having side bars with combined anchors and guards at the forward ends thereof and handles at the rear ends; the said combined anchors and guards having heels at their inner ends disposed at an angle to the side-bars, wheels carried at the forward portion of the frame, and means on the side bars of the frame for the connection thereto of a reel and reel appurtenances.

1,327,025. WINDOW-BRACKET. JOHN A. CROZIER, Knoxville, Iowa. Filed Apr. 10, 1919. Serial No. 288,977. 4 Claims. (Cl. 20—87.)

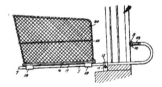

1. In a window bracket, arms having ends overlying the arms proper and terminating in eyes, a bar inserted in the eyes and adapted to engage a window frame, a seat, straps thereon having hooked ends to embrace the bars, means for securing the straps to the seat, and a cage carried by the seat.

1,327,026. ROLLER OR BALL BEARING. ALBERT EDWARD DABBS and STANLEY WHITBY SAVAGE, Manchester, and ALFRED HAROLD HINDLE, Birmingham, England, assignors of one-eighth to Absalom Liddle, Manchester, England, and one-half to John George William Gruban, Kingsway, London, England. Filed Dec. 5, 1918. Serial No. 265,460. 6 Claims. (Cl. 64—39.)

1. In a bearing, rotatable anti-friction members; a close helix forming a race for said members; and a housing for

said helix in contact with parts of the helix, whereby clearance is provided between the helix and its housing and said helix forms a resilient support.

1,327,027. DIRECTION-SIGNAL. MERRITT DRANE, Lyndon, Ky. Filed Aug. 11, 1919. Serial No. 316,771. 1 Claim. (Cl. 116—31.)

A direction signal comprising a double clamping member, a longitudinally adjustable rod carried by one of the clamps of said member, a pivoted indicator carried by the rod, a slidable actuator for the indicator, an operating rod having an adjustable connection with the actuator, a support for the actuator and the operating rod, and an arm extending from the first-mentioned rod and having an adjustable connection with the support.

1,327,028. SKIVING-MACHINE. NEWELL V. DYER, Holbrook, Mass., assignor, by mesne assignments, to United Shoe Machinery Corporation, Paterson, N. J., a Corporation of New Jersey. Filed June 20, 1917. Serial No. 175,966. 16 Claims. (Cl. 69—16.)

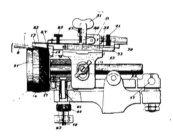

1. A machine of the class described, having, in combination, a knife, a feed roll for advancing the work to the knife, said roll comprising two substantially frusto-conical sections having opposed bases, each section being adapted to permit skiving of work upon it, and an edge gage adjustable longitudinally of the roll, whereby a shoulder scarf and a straight scarf may be produced while maintaining unchanged the relation of the knife and roll.

1,327,029. PROCESS OF MAKING A MIXTURE OF NITROGEN AND HYDROGEN. CARLETON ELLIS, Montclair, N. J., assignor to Clinton S. Lutkins, Rye, N. Y. Filed May 18, 1916. Serial No. 98,421. 2 Claims. (Cl. 23—10.)

1. The process of making a mixture containing hydrogen, and nitrogen in certain proportions, which comprises first producing in a single operation, a mixture containing water gas and producer gas, removing at least the greater part of the carbon monoxid from the gas mixture by liquefaction and passing the resulting gas mixture over lime and an iron compound capable of removing sulfur, to thereby produce a mixture consisting essentially of hydrogen and nitrogen, the H : N ration being lower

than 3 : 1 ; purifying hydrogen gas to remove its content of substances capable of deleteriously affecting catalyzers employed in ammonia synthesis ; and adding such purified hydrogen to the said mixture of gases in such proportions as to produce a 3 : 1 mixture.

1,327,030. PLANTING - STICK. WILLIAM A. GAMBLE, Macon, Ga. Filed Aug. 11, 1919. Serial No. 316,863. 3 Claims. (Cl. 55—18.)

3. In a transplanting implement, a handle, a planting head secured to one end of the handle, a concaved surface forming a part of the planting head, and means for camming a plant into the concaved surface.

1,327,031. TRAIN-PIPE COUPLING. JOHN B. GENIN, St. Albans, Vt., assignor of one-eighth to Albert D. Denis, Montreal, Canada, and one-eighth to J. O. Goyette, Rouses Point, N. Y. Filed June 29, 1918. Serial No. 242,672. 6 Claims. (Cl. 284—6.)

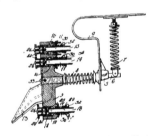

1. In a train pipe coupling device the combination with a casting having a series of recesses formed therein, connecting pipes extending within said recesses, pistons carried by the outer ends of said connecting pipes, valves arranged within said pistons, and means for supplying pneumatic pressure to said pistons substantially as and for the purpose specified.

1,327,032. SUPERHEATER. EDWARD A. GEOGHEGAN, Chicago, Ill., assignor to Milton Kraemer and Edward J. Talbott, trustees. Filed Nov. 8, 1917. Serial No. 200,919. 1 Claim. (Cl. 122—485.)

In an apparatus of the class described, a furnace chamber, a fire-grate therein, a fire-wall behind said grate, an intake return-bend header tube above said fire-grate, a series of succeeding return-bend header tubes on the plane of and behind said intake header, a fire-baffle under said headers, vertical return-bend pipe connections connecting said return-bend headers in alternate pairs, so that the last header becomes a discharge header, a series of return-

bend tube headers under the first named headers and behind said fire-wall, vertical return-bend pipe connections connecting said lower headers in alternate pairs in staggered relation to said upper headers, inclined super-

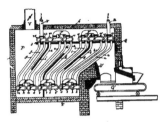

heater tubes connecting the first and succeeding upper headers with the first and succeeding lower headers, and inclined baffles adapted to cause fire-gas to travel a zig-zag course through said furnace chamber, substantially as set forth.

1,327,033. METHOD OF SETTING EYELETS. SYLVESTER LEO GOOKIN, Boston, Mass., assignor to United Shoe Machinery Corporation, Paterson, N. J., a Corporation of New Jersey. Filed June 15, 1918. Serial No. 240,201. 18 Claims. (Cl. 218—14.)

1. The method of setting in telescoping relation, eyelets provided with barrels of different sizes, which consists in guiding the smaller eyelet into a hole in the work, substantially simultaneously inserting the larger eyelet and guiding it into telescoping relation with the smaller eyelet by engagement with the outside of the barrel of the smaller eyelet, and upsetting the larger eyelet by engagement against the inner face of the flange of the smaller eyelet.

14. The method of setting flanged eyelets which consists in inserting two eyelets into a piece of work and in moving the eyelets into telescopic relation therein by continuing the inserting movement while the work remains in one position, and locking the eyelets in telescopic relation in the work by clenching the leading end of the inner eyelet against the flanged end of the outer eyelet.

1,327,034. MECHANISM FOR WINDING FILMS. DAVID E. GRAY, Highland Park, Ill. Filed Nov. 26, 1915. Serial No. 63,370. 20 Claims. (Cl. 88—18.7.)

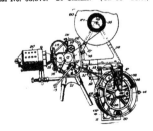

1. In a film winding mechanism, the combination of a hollow drum, devices rotatably supporting said drum,

friction ·mechanism tending to prevent rotation of said drum, and devices for feeding a strip of film into said drum and rotating the latter against said frictional resistance, said drum consisting of two semi-circular parts movable from each other to release the coil of film wound therein.

1,327,035. BELT. CHARLES E. GREENWALD, Spokane, Wash. Filed Sept. 21, 1918. Serial No. 255,023. 1 Claim. (Cl. 241—8.)

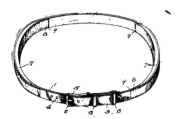

A garment supporting flexible belt for personal wear having attached thereto at its hip portions strips with tapering ends, each of said strips made of relatively rigid material and having a cross sectional area intermediate its ends of substantially greater thickness than the material of the belt, said strips merging into the belt at the points of attachment, and said belt adapted. through the instrumentality of these strips to grip the body only at the sides of the wearer above the hips.

1,327,036. INTERNAL · COMBUSTION HYDRAULIC PUMP. GRAVES GRIFFITH, San Francisco, Calif. Filed Sept. 20, 1918. Serial No. 254,930. 5 Claims. (Cl. 160—1.)

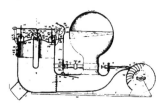

1. In an internal combustion hydraulic apparatus, a body-portion having inlet and outlet conduits, non-return inlet and outlet valves therefor, twin combustion heads communicating freely with the said body-portion, a fuel-chamber common to the said twin combustion heads, passages from said fuel-chamber communicating respectively with the said combustion heads, a valve within the said fuel chamber for closing alternately the said passages, an ignition means communicating with the interior of the said fuel-chamber, and means, dependent on pressure, for rendering the said ignition means operative.

1,327,037. PERCUSSION · FUSE. ORAZIO GUERRITORE, Rome, Italy. Filed Dec. 19, 1918. Serial No. 267,531. 7 Claims. (Cl. 102—89.)

1. In a percussion fuse comprising a body with a cylindrical chamber, a pellet in said chamber, a detonator carried on said pellet, two pivoted members in front of said pellet controlled by a spring, the pellet bearing on the said members when closed, a sleeve surrounding the pellet, projections on said sleeve to engage the two

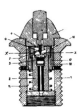

pivoted members, a spring acting on the rear edge of the sleeve and an axial needle in front of the detonator.

1,327,038. PENCIL. JAMES C. HAMILTON, Arlington Heights, Mass. Filed Feb. 26, 1919. Serial No. 279,324. 12 Claims. (Cl. 120—15.)

3. A pencil comprising a barrel, a lead therein adapted to be sharpened by rotation, and an abrasive element arranged within said barrel for sharpening action upon the lead and automatically rotated by the lead during the rotation thereof in sharpening to present different abrasive surfaces to the lead.

1,327,039. DRAIN-BOARD. HAROLD HENRY HARRIS, Wilmington, N. C. Filed Sept. 12, 1918. Serial No. 253,754. 1 Claim. (Cl. 141—11.)

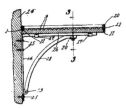

A drain board for sinks having a peripheral flange, comprising a normally inclined board, means for connecting one end of said normally inclined board to the flange of the sink, a plurality of yokes secured to said normally inclined board, a face plate, an arm secured to said face plate. said arm being round in cross section and adapted to be detachably secured within said yokes, a brace having one end pivotally connected to said face plate, the other end being provided with an elongated slot, and a screw passed through said slot and having engagement with said arm.

1,327,040. LIVE-BAIT BUCKET. FEODOR G. HASCHKE, Austin. Tex., assignor of one-half to John C. Wall, Austin, Tex. Filed June 21, 1919. Serial No. 305,750. 2 Claims. (Cl. 43—28.)

1. In a live bait bucket comprising as coöperating parts a float section, a foraminous section and a liquid container, each being provided with interengaging flanges whereby the several sections may be joined together in extended position and nested together in collapsed position, the float section comprising an annular member having an inner side wall inclined from the bottom of said section to the top thereof to define an opening for the removal of bait and a bail secured to the top of the float section whereby the several sections may be bodily transported.

1,327,041. COMBINED MULTIPLE SUSPENDERS AND BRACE. HENRY A. HEATH, Newark, N. J. Filed Aug. 5, 1918, Serial No. 248,387. Renewed Oct. 17, 1919. Serial No. 331,491. 2 Claims. (Cl. 241—17.)

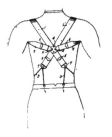

1. In combination with the shoulder straps of suspenders provided in the front and in the rear with elements having oblong openings, under-arm straps provided at their ends with metal pieces provided with oblong headed studs which are adapted to coact with the oblong openings of the metal elements to make detachable connection with the shoulder straps.

1,327,042. MALE URINAL DEVICE. WILLIAM G. HILL, Brooklyn, N. Y. Filed Dec. 9, 1918. Serial No. 265,860. 8 Claims. (Cl. 4—12.)

1. An apparatus of the class described, comprising a stall composed of back and side walls, slabs mounted on the front and back of the top portion of the back wall to form a compartment at the top of the back wall and an aperture formed between the front slab and the back wall

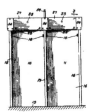

through which flush water discharged into said compartment may be passed downwardly onto the inner face of the back wall.

1,327,043. LUBRICATOR. FRANKLIN G. HIRST, Philadelphia, Pa. Filed May 20, 1919. Serial No. 298,362. 10 Claims. (Cl. 184—21.)

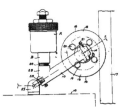

2. In a device of the class described the combination of a yoke having a continuous passage therein, means to connect said yoke with the body of the object to be lubricated to equalize any lateral movement thereof, comprising a T shaped member adapted to be threaded into a threaded opening in said yoke, a bar, extending through the outer arm of said T shaped member, journaled at either end, adjacent to the ends of said outer arm, in supports to be secured to said body, means to rigidly secure said bar in said outer arm, a hollow shaft connected to said yoke, a wheel rotatively mounted on said shaft and communicating outlets in said shaft and the tread of said wheel.

1,327,044. CALCULATING APPARATUS. WALTER E. HOSCH, St. Louis, Mo.; Annie Mae Hosch, administratrix of said Walter E. Hosch, deceased, assignor to The Measuregraph Company, St. Louis, Mo., a Corporation of Missouri. Filed Apr. 24, 1916. Serial No. 93,122. 11 Claims. (Cl. 235—86.)

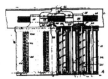

10. In a machine of the class described, a relatively fixed scale having divisions with numbers, a case movable along said scale and carrying fixed scales, and a tabulated member within said case actuated by a movement of the said case along said scale and bearing numbers which are functions of said first named scale and coöperating with said second named scale.

1,327,045. GRAVITY - HINGE. ARTHUR SHERIDAN HUGHES, Mansfield, Ohio. Filed Mar. 25, 1919. Serial No. 285,054. 6 Claims. (Cl. 16—163.)

1. A door hinge structure comprising a track for sustaining the weight of the door and over which the door may swing from the closed to the open position, said track having an intermediate depressed or valley portion and terminal inclines with the incline toward the closed position of the door steeper and shorter than the incline toward the open position of the door so as to serve as a buffer or stop when closing the door.

1,327,046. ELECTROMAGNETIC BRAKE. HENRY VINCENT JAMES, Radlett, England. Filed Sept. 18, 1917. Serial No. 191,979. 9 Claims. (Cl. 74—70.)

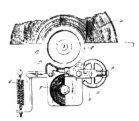

9. Brake mechanism for material feed reels, comprising a brake member on a spindle of a feed reel, a depressibly mounted frame positioned below the said spindle, an electromagnet, a brake shoe connected with said magnet and positioned in close proximity to the aforesaid brake member to contact therewith when the magnet is energized, and flexible means, to permit the lowering of the said brake frame, and brake shoe upon moving the said brake member into and out of its aforesaid normal position in relation to the said brake shoe.

1,327,047. DITCHING AND GRADING MACHINE. CHARLES M. KIMBLEY, Owensboro, Ky. Filed July 17, 1918. Serial No. 245,359. 1 Claim. (Cl. 37—7.)

In a machine of the class described, a substantially rectangular structure composed of an upstanding front plate extending transversely across the machine and having a scraper on its lower edge, longitudinally edgewise curved bars pivotally connected at one end with the ends of said plate and extending rearwardly therefrom and disposed edgewise, wheels carried by the free ends of said bars, upstanding studs carried by the upper edges of said bars intermediately of their ends, an angle bar having apertures

at its ends in one of its flanges said apertures being engaged with said studs, the upper flange having apertures for the attachment of implements, a tongue pivoted intermediate its ends to the upper portion of said plate with its rear

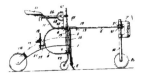

end curved downwardly and forwardly and connected at its terminal with the lower portion of said plate, means detachably connecting said angle bar with the curved portion of said tongue, and means for vertically adjusting said scraper carrying plate and holding it in adjusted position.

1,327,048. KEROSENE-BURNER. JOHN H. KINEALY, Ferguson, Mo. Filed Jan. 10, 1917. Serial No. 141,602. 8 Claims. (Cl. 67—70.)

1. A kerosene burner comprising a well, and a wick portion in said well having an independently removable solid strip of porous refractory material adapted to serve as a wick for a pilot light.

1,327,049. BORING - TOOL. GEORGE KOEHLER, Cincinnati, Ohio. Filed May 1, 1919. Serial No. 294,115. 1 Claim. (Cl. 145—121.)

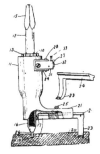

A boring tool comprising a central shank having a long toothed portion, a threaded portion and a lower centering portion, said shank having a limiting shoulder at the upper end of said centering portion, a casing received about said shank, said casing provided with a bore in which said toothed portion is received and with a threaded bore coacting with said threaded portion of said shank, a pawl on said casing coacting with the teeth of said tooth portion, said casing having a radially projecting arm provided with a guideway, a slide adjustable in said guideway, and a cutter-bit on said slide, constructed and arranged whereby axial adjustment of said shank in said casing by means of said screw-threads adjusts the plane of said shoulder with relation to the plane of the cutting edge of said bit, and said shank arranged to be rotated in cutting direction with said casing and in opposite direction relative to said casing.

1,327,050.   STAMPING-MACHINE.   Bernard S. Lee, Beverly, Mass., assignor, by mesne assignments, to United Shoe Machinery Corporation, Paterson, N. J., a Corporation of New Jersey.   Filed Sept. 6, 1917. Serial No. 190,022.   15 Claims.   (Cl. 219—19.)

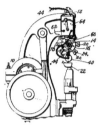

1. In a machine of the class described, a die holder, a die carried by said holder, said die having an opening extending laterally therethrough parallel and in close proximity to its working face, and a heating device adapted to be received in and readily removable from said opening and operating when positioned in the die to conduct heat directly to the working face of said die.

1,327,051.   WATCH - SUPPORT.   Seneca G. Lewis, Greensburg, Pa.   Filed Aug. 21, 1916, Serial No. 116,071. Renewed Aug. 14, 1919.   Serial No. 317,585.   2 Claims. (Cl. 58—56.)

2. A pedestal support for a watch constructed of a single piece of elastic material and consisting of a foot member made of a continuous depending apron having its lower edge terminating in a horizontal plane and forming a pocket extending upwardly from said lower edge, a vertically-disposed member having formed therein a watch pocket open at one side to receive and to retain a watch and to expose the face of such watch, the bottom portion of said body member being provided with a watch-stem receiving opening extending to said pocket, and a flange extending outwardly adjacent to the edge of the open face of said body and encircling said edge.

1,327,052.   COAL MINING AND LOADING MACHINE. Jacob M. London, Tunnelton, Pa., assignor, by direct and mesne assignments, of one-fourth to George M. Crawford and one-half to Emil M. Reflor, Pittsburgh, Pa.   Filed July 25, 1917.   Serial No. 182,658.   13 Claims.   (Cl. 262—30.)

8. A coal cutting machine comprising a supporting frame, a platform mounted on said frame and adapted to have a rocking movement thereon, a carriage composed of two parts adjustably connected together, one of said

270 O. G.—3

parts having sliding pivotal connection with said platform, a coal cutting device mounted on said carriage, means for simultaneously operating said coal cutting mechanism and moving said carriage along said platform, and means coöperating with said last named means for adjusting the parts of said carriage relative to each other.

1,327,053.   EXCAVATING AND LOADING APPARATUS. Jacob M. London, Tunnelton, Pa., assignor, by direct and mesne assignments, of one-fourth to George M. Crawford and one-half to Emil M. Reflor, Pittsburgh, Pa.   Original application filed July 25, 1917, Serial No. 182,658.   Divided and this application filed Mar. 7, 1918.   Serial No. 220,925.   6 Claims.   (Cl. 193—8.)

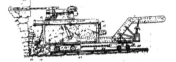

1. In a coal loading apparatus, a carriage mounted for vertical and horizontal movements, and coal feeders swingingly connected to the carriage and each including an upper and a lower rake device of different capacities.

1,327,054.   SAW-GUIDE FOR TIMBER-CUTTERS.   Nils Lundin, Clackamas, Oreg.   Filed Apr. 26, 1919.   Serial No. 292,874.   5 Claims.   (Cl. 143—163.)

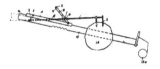

1. A tool for timber cutters comprising a flat metal bar having a longitudinal slot in one edge adapted to receive a saw, a supporting bar capable of positioning said flat metal bar with a tree, links detachably and interchangeably extending from the metal bar to the supporting bar, being pivoted to the lower side of the former and to the upper side of the latter and, by rotation around their respective pivotal points, holding said metal bar either parallelly or transversely to said supporting bar.

1,327,055.   STABILIZER.   Alfred J. Macy, Chicago, Ill., assignor to Macy Engineering Company, Franklin, Pa., a Corporation of Maine.   Filed Mar. 25, 1916.   Serial No. 86,610.   25 Claims.   (Cl. 244—29.)

1. A stabilizing device for aeroplanes comprising a plurality of plumb levers disposed laterally of the aero-

plane to permit relative movement of the aeroplane and plumb levers, and a plurality of plumb levers disposed longitudinally of the aeroplane to permit relative movement between the aeroplane and a plumb levers, each of said plumb levers independently mounted for movement, electrical circuits associated with said plumb levers, a plurality of magnetic clutches adapted to be selectively set in operation when said electrical circuits are operated by the co-action of certain fo said plumb levers and mechanisms adapted to be actuated by said magnetic clutches to operate the controls of the aeroplane.

1,327,056. GAME. CHARLES P. MASON and RUSSELL A. DIXON, Pittsburgh, Pa. Filed Nov. 8, 1918. Serial No. 261,701. 5 Claims. (Cl. 46—21.)

5. A game formed of a board having a map of different opposing countries with a series of pin holes arranged in close spaced relationship for defining continuous lines extending across these countries and having a series of pin holes arranged in like close relationship defining continuous lines extending across the portions of the map representing water, and pins adapted to be placed in said holes.

1,327,057. MULTIPLE-SPARK PLUG. JOHN L. NILSON and JOHN PRINCE, Chicago, Ill. Filed Feb. 19, 1917. Serial No. 149,432. 5 Claims. (Cl. 123—169.)

1. In a spark plug, the combination with its metallic jacket and an insulating core constructed and arranged with a spark gap between said core and jacket and a spark gap bore within said core but open to the exterior of the plug and to the gases to be ignited, of an electrode wire having its ignition end in said bore, and an intermediate electrode piercing the wall of said bore and providing an intensifying spark gap between said wire and said jacket, the latter serving as the "ground" electrode.

1,327,058. VENDING-MACHINE. CARLTON N. OGDEN, Houston, Tex. Filed Jan. 2, 1919. Serial No. 269,227. 2 Claims. (Cl. 194—63.)

1. In a vending machine, a rotatable drum carrying shaft, a coin chute, a pivotally mounted latch support forming one side of said chute, a latch carried by said support and projecting into the chute, a finger projecting laterally from said shaft and provided to engage with said latch to lock the shaft against rotation, said finger being arranged to move said support through a coin when placed in the chute to withdraw said latch to permit the rotation of said shaft.

1,327,059. CLOTHESLINE - SUPPORT. WILLIAM H. ORTMAN, Milwaukee, Wis. Filed Apr. 12, 1919. Serial No. 289,587. 2 Claims. (Cl. 57—34.)

1. A device of the class described comprising in combination, a pulley strap formed in substantially U-shape, one of the arms thereof being longer than the other and provided with attaching means, a sheave pivoted between said arms intermediate their ends and transversely thereof, and a clamp device formed on the base of the U-shaped strap and disposed in the normal path of a cable or the like adapted to be disposed around said sheave whereby to hold said cable or the like against movement in one direction.

1,327,060. AUTOMOBILE-JACK. EDWARD OSTENDORF, Portland, Oreg. Filed Apr. 28, 1919. Serial No. 293,165. 2 Claims. (Cl. 254—89.)

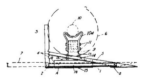

1. In an automobile jack, the combination of a rectangular, horizontal frame having a vertical post pivotally attached to one end, having an inclined runway pivoted to the other end, the free end of the runway being supported by the vertical post, said runway being capable of collapsing when an automobile wheel ascends-

and overturns the vertical post, with a supporting post attached to the side of the horizontal frame and adapted to receive the axle of said automobile wheel when the runway collapses.

1,327,061. PROCESS OF MANUFACTURING IRON COMPOUNDS. RUSSELL S. PENNIMAN, Jr., and NORMAN M. ZOPH, Berkeley, Calif., assignors to West Coast Kalsomine Company, a Corporation of California. Filed June 20, 1917. Serial No. 175,837. 8 Claims. (Cl. 134—59.)

1. A process for manufacturing iron compounds which consists in immersing metallic iron in a solution of a ferrous salt, heating the solution, and introducing an oxidizing agent.

1,327,062. HANDKERCHIEF. MICHAEL R. QUINN, Kent, Ohio. Filed July 10, 1919. Serial No. 309,967. 3 Claims. (Cl. 2—54.)

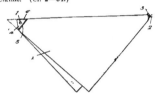

1. A handkerchief or similar sheet folded on a diagonal line and formed at its opposite ends with a knob and eyelet.

1,327,063. SPRING SUSPENSION. GEORGE EDWIN RIGBY, Manchester, England. Original application filed June 11, 1918, Serial No. 237,365. Divided and this application filed June 2, 1919. Serial No. 301,289. 1 Claim. (Cl. 267—87.)

The combination with a leaf spring having an eye in an end thereof, of means forming a roller bearing for said end comprising slotted side plates, a bushing in said eye, a roller in said bushing having its ends supported in the slots of said side plates, and caps secured to said side plates and covering the outer side of the slots therein to hold said roller in position and prevent the entrance of dust to said bearing.

1,327,064. AIR-GUN. OTTO SEEMULLER, Detroit, Mich. Filed June 18, 1919. Serial No. 303,892. 12 Claims. (Cl. 124—10.)

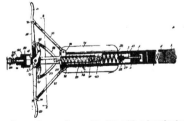

4. In an air gun, the combination with a breech piece, a barrel, and means at said breech adapted for discharg-

ing a projectile from said barrel, of a barrel end plate supporting said barrel relative to said breech piece and adapted to be swung to one side to permit of said barrel being loaded at the inner end thereof.

1,327,065. SPRING-HINGE. JOHN M. SHIELDS, Chicago, Ill., assignor to F. H. Noble & Company, Chicago, Ill., a Corporation of Illinois. Filed Nov. 29, 1918. Serial No. 264,520. 6 Claims. (Cl. 16—25.)

2. In combination with a pair of flat hinged leaves, a spring having opposite outer plane portions pivotally connected at their extremities with the outer portions of such leaves and an intermediate portion extending around the knuckle of the hinge, the plane outer portions of said spring being arranged to stop against the faces of said hinge leaves and the central portion of said spring being out of contact with said knuckle when the hinge is in open position.

1,327,066. PROPELLER. ERNEST SINCLARE SHOWERS, Calumet, Mich. Filed Dec. 20, 1917. Serial No. 208,124. 2 Claims. (Cl. 170—169.)

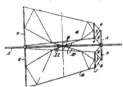

1. A propeller, comprising a shaft, forward and rear cross arms on the shaft, vanes each secured along its forward edge to a cross arm, a rod secured along the rear edge of each vane, cables connecting each rod to a rear cross arm, and cables, affixed to the shaft at a point intermediate the forward and rear cross arms, secured to the vanes and forming a reinforcement and support for the vanes.

1,327,067. CAN-CLOSURE. EUGENE P. STARCKE, Port Arthur, Tex. Filed Dec. 10, 1918. Serial No. 266,080. 1 Claim. (Cl. 221—27.)

A can or container having an opening, a collar in line with the opening and having an inner shoulder at its outer end, a fixed cylinder depending from the inner edge of said shoulder and having its inner end closed and longitudinal slots in its sides, a packing supported on the closed end of the fixed cylinder, a sliding cylinder within the fixed cylinder and having outwardly extending lugs entering the longitudinal slots thereof, a valve at the outer end of the sliding cylinder, a packing supported on the inner shoulder of the collar and in close contact with the outer side of the sliding cylinder, a shell secured to the collar and retaining the packing in position, a sealing member extending over the valve and secured to the shell and a cap threaded on the outer end of the shell.

1,327,068. DRUM-BRAKE WITH INTERNAL SHOES. RICHARD STEPHENS, Clevedon, England. Filed Jan. 23, 1918. Serial No. 213,294. 1 Claim. (Cl. 74—13.)

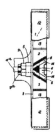

A brake comprising a drum, shoes within the drum, a wedge interposed between one of the ends of said shoes, and movable transversely thereof, wings formed on said wedge, the aforementioned ends of said shoes being pivotal about said wings, a radially disposed arm integral with said wedge and interposed between the adjacent ends of said shoes, and means at the opposite ends of said shoes for forcing the same apart.

1,327,069. FEELER-MOTION FOR LOOMS. EDWARD S. STIMPSON, Hopedale, Mass., assignor to Draper Corporation, Hopedale, Mass., a Corporation of Maine. Filed Feb. 8, 1917. Serial No. 147,468. 15 Claims. (Cl. 139—85.)

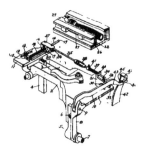

1. In a feeler motion for looms, the combination of a feeler stand having a bearing at its front portion and a slide mounted for lateral movement at its rear portion, a feeler mounted for reciprocating movement in said bearing and slide, and means for moving the slide laterally and swinging the feeler in the front bearing when the filling is exhausted on a detecting beat.

1,327,070. FEELER-MOTION FOR LOOMS. EDWARD S. STIMPSON, Hopedale, Mass., assignor to Draper Corporation, Hopedale, Mass., a Corporation of Maine. Filed Sept. 19, 1917. Serial No. 192,187. 7 Claims. (Cl. 139—85.)

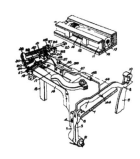

1. In a feeler motion for looms, the combination of a feeler member supported in a position inclined to the longitudinal axis of the shuttle and movable frontwardly on its support in changing angular relation to the longitudinal axis of the shuttle by the frontward push, said feeler member having an end to engage the filling and be held from movement longitudinally of the shuttle by the frontward push until the filling is substantially exhausted, a train of mechanism for effecting replenishment of filling including a rock-shaft, and a finger extending from the rock-shaft and adapted to be actuated by the frontwardly inclined movement of the feeler member on its support when the filling is substantially exhausted.

1,327,071. HOISTING AND CONVEYING MACHINE. ERNEST W. TAYLOR, Cleveland, Ohio, assignor to The Brown Hoisting Machinery Company, Cleveland, Ohio, a Corporation. Filed June 23, 1919. Serial No. 306,215. 3 Claims. (Cl. 104—91.)

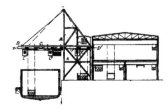

1. In a hoisting and conveying machine, the combination of an overhead I-beam main trackway, a branch trackway therefrom intermediate of the terminals of the main trackway, and trolleys provided with flanged wheels arranged to travel on said trackways, and to hoist, carry and lower loads, the said trackway being interrupted at their junction points for the passage of the trolleys therethrough, and provided in the open space, so formed, with suitable flange-ways to receive and guide the flanges of the trolley-wheels during, and for, their said passage, on and to, the main trackway when the trolleys are traveling in one direction, and on and to the branch trackway, when traveling in the opposite direction, substantially as shown and described.

1,327,072. GAME APPARATUS. BENJAMIN F. H. THOR-
WARD, Cleveland, Ohio. Filed May 31, 1919. Serial
No. 301,064. 2 Claims. (Cl. 46—24.)

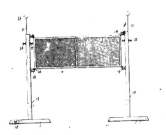

2. In a game apparatus, the combination of a net,
standard between which said net is supported, guide rods
carried by said standards, and means whereby said guide
rods may be adjusted to various heights.

1,327,073. DEHAIRING APPARATUS. WILLIAM TIETZ,
Toledo, Ohio. Filed Dec. 20, 1918. Serial No. 267,567.
7 Claims. (Cl. 17—11.)

1. A rotary driving shaft, a holder mounted thereon
having an arm provided with a tool terminus and an
intermediate resilient section, and means in a resilient
section for limiting the flexing thereof.

1,327,074. DRAFT-RIGGING FOR RAILWAY-CARS.
HENRY I. WRIGLEY, Chicago, Ill., assignor to Universal
Draft Gear Attachment Co., a Corporation of Illinois.
Filed Mar. 29, 1919. Serial No. 285,954. 1 Claim.
(Cl. 213—42.)

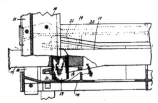

In a draft rigging for railway cars, in combination, a
pair of draft plates, a yoke located between the plates
and having slotted side plates, a draw bar having its butt
provided with a slot of less width than the slots in the
yoke, said draw bar entered and laterally movable between the side plates of the yoke, a key, whose length is
substantially equal to the distance between the draft
plates and whose width is substantially equal to the
width of the slot in the draw bar, setting through the
yoke and draw bar, retained in place solely by the draft
plates and having its ends rounded for engagement therewith.

**1,327,075. PAPER-CLAMP FOR TYPEWRITING-MA-
CHINES.** ALMA A. ZAISS, Kansas City, Mo. Filed
July 21, 1917. Serial No. 183,633. 5 Claims. (Cl.
197—139.)

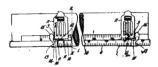

1. The combination in a typewriting machine, of a
platen, a bar parallel to and adjacent the platen at one
side of the line thereof where the type strike in the per-
formance of their printing function, a slidable member
on said bar, a finger hinged to and projecting from said
slidable member to a point at the opposite side of the
line of the platen where the type strike from that occupied by the bar, a spring for snapping and holding the
finger against paper on the platen ,and means for holding
the finger withdrawn from the platen to permit the paper
thereon to be drawn forwardly therefrom.

1,327,076. VEHICLE-SPRING SUSPENSION. GOTT-
LIEB F. ZUCKER, Chicago, Ill. Filed Mar. 17, 1919.
Serial No. 283,195. 3 Claims. (Cl. 267—19.)

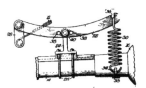

1. In a device of the class described, the combination
of a vehicle axle and its wheel, a vehicle body and its leaf
spring, a lever mechanism lying approximately parallel to
the axle, pivoted intermediate between its ends to a support on the axle, a connection between the portion of said
lever nearest the adjacent wheel and the leaf spring of
said vehicle, and a spring connection between said lever
mechanism and the axle, said spring connection carrying
the pressure of the vehicle load only, and being applied
between the axle and the end portion of the lever which
is nearest the vehicle center.

**1,327,077. COMBINATION WELL-PACKER AND SET-
TING-TOOL.** JAMIE ABERCROMBIE, Houston, and NES-
BIT M. DUNMAN, West Columbia, Tex. Filed Feb. 6,
1919. Serial No. 275,325. 2 Claims. (Cl. 166—10.)

1. A packer for wells, including a pipe section, whose
upper end is externally threaded, an annular member

fixed thereon near the lower end thereof, a longitudinally movable annular member mounted on said section and spaced from said fixed member, and formed into an extended sleeve, the facing sides of said members being formed with annular grooves, a sleevelike packer element surrounding said section and sleeve interposed between said members and whose respective ends are seated in and confined by the corresponding grooves, said sleeve holding said packer element out of contact with said threads and a means whereby said packer element may be expanded.

1,327,078. CORSET-FASTENING. JULIA H. AUERBACH, Hollywood, Calif. Filed Nov. 27, 1918. Serial No. 264,394. 5 Claims. (Cl. 24—266.)

1. A corset fastening comprising a pair of flexible strips each of which is formed with a plurality of parallel longitudinally extending slots arranged in alined pairs and having ribbon engaging bars between the slots, the bars on one strip adapted to be arranged in substantially transverse alinement with the bars on the other strip when the corset is applied.

1,327,079. END-GATE FASTENER. GEORGE BOWDEN, Malden, Mass. Filed Apr. 11, 1919. Serial No. 289,180. 2 Claims. (Cl. 296—56.)

1. A vehicle having in combination, a body, an end-gate hinged at its upper edge to said body and provided with a projecting flange at its lower edge, a fixed support secured at one end to the said body and extending rearwardly to a point underneath and near said flange on said end-gate, a comparatively long lever pivotally mounted at one end on the rear end of said fixed support, said pivotal point being below a straight line drawn from said flange on said end-gate to the point where said fixed support is secured to said body and a latch pivotally mounted on said lever adjacent the pivot point of said lever and having a hooked nose adapted to engage said flange on said end-gate and to hold said end-gate locked when said lever is turned upwardly around its pivot point and into engagement with said fixed support.

1,327,080. HYDRAULIC TRANSMISSION. THOMAS E. BROWN, New York, N. Y. Filed Apr. 7, 1919. Serial No. 288,161. 22 Claims. (Cl. 60—54.)
1. The combination in a hydraulic transmission of an impeller having vanes at each end, a runner centrally placed between said vanes, a casing inclosing said vanes and said runner and an open chamber, formed by said

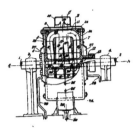

casing, circumferentially surrounding said vanes and said runner.

1,327,081. FALSE WORK FOR CONCRETE FLOORS. SAMUEL J. BRANSON, Chicago, Ill., and EDWARD C. STRATHMANN, Indianapolis, Ind., assignors to The Concrete Forms Company, Indianapolis, Ind., a Corporation of Indiana. Filed Aug. 18, 1916, Serial No. 115,594. Renewed Oct. 27, 1919. Serial No. 333,687. 6 Claims. (Cl. 25—131.5.)

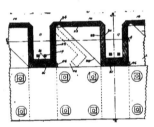

1. A falsework for concrete floor construction, comprising a plurality of centering units each of which is of inverted U-shape in cross-section and at its lower edge has an outwardly projecting flange of sufficient width to reach the adjacent centering unit so that the two centering units comprise a form for the floor slab and the sides and the under face of a concrete joist, each centering unit being formed of hinged parts movable to bring its vertical sides closer together to facilitate removal.

1,327,082. SHEET-METAL-CUTTING MACHINE. CHARLES P. BUCK, Topeka, Kans. Filed Feb. 19, 1918. Serial No. 218,905. 2 Claims. (Cl. 164—71.)

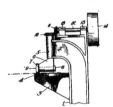

1. A sheet metal cutting machine, comprising a frame, an immovable ring die secured to the frame, a shaft disposed in alinement with the axis of said ring die, a shaft

carried by the first-named shaft and extending parallel with the face and convergingly outward with respect to a radius of said ring die, and a rotatable cutting die mounted on said last-named shaft and bearing a shearing relation to the ring die for coöperating therewith in cutting a segmental opening in a plate resting on said die.

1,327,083. CORING-MACHINE. CLARENCE F. COLBERT, Milwaukee, Wis., assignor to Dixie Fruit Products Corporation, New York, N. Y., a Corporation of Delaware. Filed May 2, 1919. Serial No. 294,145   37 Claims. (Cl. 146—6.)

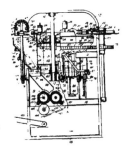

1. In a machine of the character described, the combination of mechanism for gripping a melon-section, an expansible cutter and mechanism for operating the cutter for cutting the core of a melon to enter the melon and to remove the core therefrom.

1,327,084. GUN-MOUNTING. ARTHUR TREVOR DAWSON and GEORGE THOMAS BUCKHAM, Westminster, London, England, assignors to Vickers Limited, Westminster, England. Original application filed Sept. 6, 1916, Serial No. 118,633. Divided and this application filed May 27, 1918. Serial No. 236,918. 3 Claims. (Cl. 89—38.)

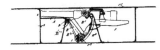

1. The combination with the training and the non-training portions of a gun mounting, of a chamber in which the gun and mounting are adapted to be housed, means for pivoting the non-training portion of the mounting so that during the housing displacement of the mounting as a whole it moves through an angle substantially less than a right angle without the necessity of inverting the gun, and gearing for displacing the mounting about its pivot.

1,327,085. GUN-MOUNTING. ARTHUR TREVOR DAWSON and GEORGE THOMAS BUCKHAM, Westminster, London, England, assignors to Vickers Limited, Westminster, England. Original application filed Sept. 6, 1916, Serial No. 113,633. Divided and this application filed May 27, 1918. Serial No. 236,919. 3 Claims. (Cl. 89—38.)
1. The combination with the training and the non-training portions of a gun mounting, of a chamber in which the gun and mounting are adapted to be housed, means for pivoting the non-training portion of the mounting so that during the housing displacement of the mounting as a whole it moves through an angle substantially less than a right angle without the necessity

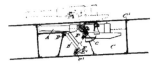

of inverting the gun, and gearing comprising a screw threaded shaft and a nut, for displacing the mounting about its pivot.

1,327,086. MACHINE-GUN. ARTHUR TREVOR DAWSON and GEORGE THOMAS BUCKHAM, Westminster, London, England, assignors to Vickers Limited, Westminster, England. Filed June 19, 1918. Serial No. 240,782. 5 Claims. (Cl. 89—1.)

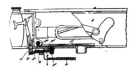

1. The combination with a machine gun, of a heater forming a permanent attachment of the gun for raising the temperature of the working parts when the gun is out of action.

1,327,087. BREECH-LOADING ORDNANCE. ARTHUR TREVOR DAWSON and GEORGE THOMAS BUCKHAM, Westminster, London, England, assignors to Vickers Limited, Westminster, England. Filed June 25, 1918. Serial No. 241,899. 3 Claims. (Cl. 89—4.)

1. In breech loading ordnance of the semi-automatic type, the combination with the breech closing spring, a device for rendering said spring inactive for quick firing working of the gun, means for actuating the breech mechanism automatically during semi-automatic working of the gun and a device for rendering said means inoperative for the quick firing working, of means for connecting said devices together in such manner that a single operation serves to render the spring inactive and the automatic actuating means inoperative for the quick firing working of the gun and a single operation also serves to render the said spring active and the said actuating means operative for the semi-automatic working of the gun.

1,327,088. HOG-OILER. GEORGE L. CURTTRIGHT, Olin, Iowa. Filed Aug. 19, 1916. Serial No. 115,861. 3 Claims. (Cl. 119—157.)
1. A hog oiler including a fixed support, a hollow oil applying member rotatable around said support, a ful-

crum on the support upon which said member is engaged intermediate of its ends for oscillating movement

relative to the support, an oil container having a valve, and means actuated by said oil applying member when the same is oscillated in one direction to open the valve.

1,327,089. SEED-PLANTER. SAMUEL K. DENNIS, Chicago, Ill., assignor, by mesne assignments, to International Harvester Company, a Corporation of New Jersey. Filed Sept. 15, 1913. Serial No. 789,837. 24 Claims. (Cl. 111—21.)

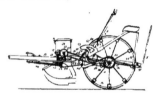

7. In a seed planter, a supporting frame, a furrow opener frame movable with respect thereto, seed dropping mechanism carried on said furrow opener frame, clutch members for said seed dropping mechanism, a laterally shiftable marker carried by said supporting frame, and means controlled by the relative positions of said frames for throwing the clutch members into and out of operative position and for shifting said marker.

1,327,090. CLUTCH MECHANISM FOR CORN-PLANTERS AND LIKE MACHINES. SAMUEL K. DENNIS, Chicago, Ill., assignor, by mesne assignments, to International Harvester Company, a Corporation of New Jersey. Original application filed Sept. 15, 1913, Serial No. 789,837. Divided and this application filed Aug. 4, 1917, Serial No. 184,516. Renewed Oct. 22, 1919. Serial No. 332,546. 5 Claims. (Cl. 192—6.)

1. In a variable clutch mechanism comprising a continuously operating member, a ratchet and a rotatable pawl, a frame, a swinging cam engageable with said pawl, and means whereby said cam may be adjusted comprising a lever pivoted on said cam and engageable with said frame in a plurality of positions, the upper portion of said cam and said lever being disposed in a plane below the upper surface of said continuously operating member.

1,327,091. SHANK-STIFFENER. HENRY C. EGERTON, Ridgewood, N. J. Filed May 2, 1919. Serial No. 294,316. 8 Claims. (Cl. 36—76.)

1. The shank stiffener having longitudinally and transvesely curved surfaces and comprising a single layer of cotton batting material carrying about 40 to 50 per cent. of incorporated cured phenolic condensation cementing material, the rear edge portions of said stiffener being relatively thin and containing less cementing material to render them more yieldable or readily penetrable by attaching devices.

1,327,092. BURNER FOR GAS OR OIL. HERBERT FORESTER, Cleveland, Ohio, assignor of one-half to Alexander M. Skibinsky, Cleveland, Ohio. Filed Mar. 12, 1918. Serial No. 222,022. 2 Claims. (Cl. 158—11.)

1. In a burner, the combination of a casing, the casing having a perforated wall and an opening, a gas generating chamber, means for feeding oil to the gas generating chamber, a tube leading from the gas generating chamber, the tube having a nozzle opposite said opening of the casing, and a valve arranged laterally of said nozzle for directing ordinary gas at an angle across the opening of the casing and against the inner side thereof, substantially as described.

1,327,093. EXPRESSING APPARATUS. ALFRED W. FRENCH, Piqua, Ohio. Filed Jan. 28, 1918. Serial No. 214,071. 17 Claims. (Cl. 100—51.)

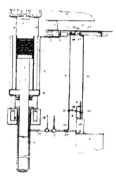

1. The combination of a press cage, a ram movable in said cage to make room for successive charges of material delivered into the cage, a ram cylinder, and mechanism which discharges the ram-operating liquid in successive equal measured quantities from the ram cylinder for causing successive equal movements of the ram.

17. The combination of a cylinder, a member which is moved by the admission and discharge of liquid to and from said cylinder, and means for causing successive equal movements of said member comprising a discharge valve

for the cylinder, and means for causing successive equal movements of said member comprising a device which is actuated by liquid discharging from said cylinder and operates said valve to stop the discharge when a predetermined quantity of liquid has discharged from the cylinder.

1,327,094. ELECTROLYTIC CELL. ALVAH M. GRIFFIN, Kansas City, Mo. Filed Aug. 24, 1918. Serial No. 251,311. 2 Claims. (Cl. 204—5.)

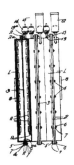

2. An electrolytic cell comprising a pair of flanged pan-members secured together with a gas and water tight relation and insulated from each other, a diaphragm dividing said cell into two compartments and composed of material through which water and electricity may pass, and a plate within each compartment and secured to the adjacent side wall of the cell, each plate being corrugated and in contact at the crests of the corrugations with the adjacent wall of the pan, and provided between the corrugation with openings and with inwardly projecting walls flanking said openings.

1,327,095. RAILWAY-CAR. WILLIAM B. HALL, Chicago, Ill., assignor to Union Railway Equipment Co., a Corporation of Illinois. Filed Aug. 1, 1917. Serial No. 183,860. 1 Claim. (Cl. 108—5.6.)

In a railway car, a carline formed of two metal sections T-shaped in cross-section, the heads of such sections abutting at the median line of the car and their web portions being longitudinally extended and overlapping, such extensions being provided with lateral mating lugs and being secured together.

1,327,096. RESILIENT WHEEL. GEORGE HUGHES, St. Louis, Mo., assignor of one-half to Edward Hughes, St. Louis, Mo. Filed Mar. 25, 1919. Serial No. 284,887. 3 Claims. (Cl. 152—31.)

1. The combination with a rigid hub and inner rim having openings of a deformable outer tire, spokes of resilient metal passed through said inner rim openings and secured to portions of the tire, said spokes being carried by the hub, and having laterally yielding connections with said hub.

---

3. The combination with a hub and deformable tire, of an axle, sleeves surrounding the axle and threaded into the hub, boxings slidable on the sleeves and hub, resilient

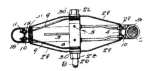

spokes carried by the boxings, and clamp nuts threaded on the boxings for the spokes, there being lateral thrust ball bearings between the boxings and sleeves.

1,327,097. TIRE-CARRIER. ABEN E. JOHNSON, Hastings, Mich., assignor to Hastings Manufacturing Co., Hastings, Mich. Filed June 6, 1919. Serial No. 302,322. 5 Claims. (Cl. 224—29.)

1. In a tire carrier, the combination of a pair of semicircular flat body members disposed in a spaced relation and each adapted to receive a tire, top side pieces extending from end to end of said body members formed of a bar bent into a loop and having inwardly projecting folds in its ends disposed between said body members to support the inner sides of tires arranged in the body members, a U shaped holder embracing the bottoms of said body members and having an upset portion between them providing a pair of tire seats, the rear arm of said holder being secured to the rear top piece, the front arm of said holder members having spaced holes to receive a lock, and a locking bar slotted to receive the arms of said holder and slidably mounted on the rear arm to be detachably engaged with the front arm.

1,327,098. PROCESS OF WELDING. DANIEL P. KELLOGG, ARTHUR P. NEFF, WILLIAM A. ROGERS, and FRANK COWAN, Los Angeles, Calif. Filed Oct. 25, 1915. Serial No. 57,767. 9 Claims. (Cl. 113—112.)

1. The process of applying a facing of a hard metal to a body of softer metal, consisting in heating the surface of the softer metal to or near its welding point and fusing the harder metal and applying it drop by drop to the softer metal to build up a body of the harder metal thereon.

1,327,099. METHOD OF WELDING. DANIEL P. KELLOGG, Los Angeles, Calif. Filed Mar. 30, 1917. Serial No. 158,595. 14 Claims. (Cl. 76—101.)

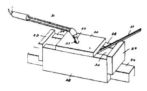

1. The method of uniting a high speed steel facing with a stock of softer steel which consists in reducing to fluidity the high speed steel and the surface of the stock to which it is to be united by means of a flame applied within a space sufficiently inclosed so that the space is filled with flame and air thereby excluded from contact with the work.

1,327,100. METHOD OF MANUFACTURING COMPOSITE TOOLS. DANIEL P. KELLOGG, Los Angeles, Calif. Filed Mar. 30, 1917. Serial No. 158,596. 5 Claims. (Cl. 76—101.)

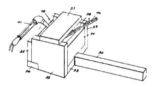

1. The method of manufacturing a composite tool of the character described, comprising forming the stock with a recess, welding a body of high speed steel in said recess, trimming away the soft metal along one edge of the high speed steel body, and dressing said body to a cutting edge.

1,327,101. COMPOSITE TOOL OF THE REVOLUBLE TYPE AND METHOD OF MAKING THE SAME. DANIEL P. KELLOGG, Los Angeles, Calif. Filed Mar. 30, 1917. Serial No. 158,598. 8 Claims. (Cl. 76—101.)

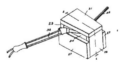

1. The method of manufacturing a composite tool of the type described which consists in forming the stock with grooves, welding bodies of high speed steel into said grooves by fusing the surfaces of the stock and melting the high speed steel to fluidity by means of a gas flame and applying it little by little to the stock, and dressing said bodies of high speed steel to form cutting edges.

1,327,102. SHERARDIZING APPARATUS. CHARLES J. KIRK, New Castle, Pa. Filed Mar. 1, 1919. Serial No. 280,130. 2 Claims. (Cl. 219—36.)

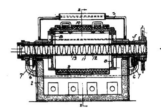

1. In sherardizing apparatus, the combination of a rotary retort, external electric heating units, and an internally aranged electric heating unit.

1,327,103. CREEPER. WILLIAM VICTOR KNOWLES, Hubbard, Iowa. Filed Nov. 12, 1915, Serial No. 61,043. Renewed May 22, 1919. Serial No. 299,078. 9 Claims. (Cl. 5—4.)

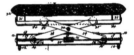

1. A creeper formed with a body, spaced lazy-tongs on one end portion of said body, a pillow frame wholly supported on said lazy-tongs and movable thereon transversely of said body, and a pillow on said frame.

1,327,104. FIRELESS CHICKEN - BROODER. ALFRED KROHN, Spokane, Wash. Filed May 6, 1919. Serial No. 295,118. 7 Claims. (Cl. 119—33.)

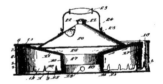

1. A fireless brooder comprising a base having an up-standing outer inclosure portion provided with ingress and egress openings for the chicks passage into and out of said inclosure portion, an inner inclosure portion having a heater supporting section overhanging said base and forming a roof-like top and having a curtain depending from the upper portion of said section in spaced relation interiorly of said inclosure portion and forming therewith a hovering chamber with the space between said curtain and said inclosure portion acting as a ventilating space, and a hot water container shaped to spread over a portion of the upper surface of said supporting section to heat the latter and transmit heat therethrough to said chamber.

1,327,105. PROCESS OF THE PRODUCTION OF TAN-NING EXTRACT FROM WASTE SULFITE LYE. HANS BRUN LANDMARK, Drammen, Norway. Filed Apr. 23, 1915. Serial No. 23,518. 3 Claims. (Cl. 149—5.)

3. A process for the production of tanning-extract from waste sulfite-lye, characterized by evaporating waste sulfite lye to a concentration of about 16° to 18° Baumé; adding to the concentrated solution about 18 grams of carbonate of sodium for each liter of the amount of lye before concentration; separating the liquid from the precipitate thus obtained; and adding to said liquid a quantity of oxalic acid sufficient to precipitate the calcium still remaining in solution; separating the liquid from the precipitate thus obtained and adding a sufficient quantity of formic acid to decompose any saccharate that may be present; and concentrating the solution thus obtained to about 27.5° Baumé.

1,327,106. COMPRESSION - COUPLING. WILLIAM P. LEAHY, Canton, Ohio, assignor, by mesne assignments, of one-half to Stewart S. Kurtz, Sr. Filed Aug. 18, 1915, Serial No. 46,060. Renewed May 26, 1919. Serial No. 299,943. 7 Claims. (Cl. 285—87.)

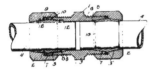

1. A compression coupling for pipe or the like including a thimble for neatly fitting the pipe, a nipple for freely fitting the pipe, and a nut to be screwed upon the end of the nipple, the nut and nipple having internal conical faces, and the thimble having middle peripheral conical faces and end peripheral cylindric faces with rims of substantial thickness adapted to be impigned and compressed into the pipe by the conical faces of the nut and nipple, for bending the thimble and corresponding portion of the pipe into barrel shape and clamping the thimble throughout its length upon the pipe.

1,327,107. WHEEL-RIM AND SPROCKET-TEETH THEREFOR. GEORGE W. LINGLE, Silver Lake, Wis., assignor of two-fifths to Wilbur O. Carney, Chicago, Ill. Filed Nov. 9, 1918. Serial No. 261,822. 7 Claims. (Cl. 74—41.)

1. A sprocket-tooth formed of steel rod and bent to present a central portion and parallel portions, and reinforcing members for said parallel portions.

1,327,108. HEADREST FOR BEDS AND THE LIKE. JOHN MCKAY, Buffalo, N. Y., assignor to Hard Manufacturing Company, Buffalo, N. Y. Filed Feb. 9, 1915. Serial No. 7,022. 1 Claim. (Cl. 5—43.)

The combination with a bedstead frame having side rails and a bed bottom supported by said frame in a plane above the horizontal plane of said side rails, of a head rest having side legs which are offset downwardly from the plane of the head rest and straddle and extend below the bed bottom, means for holding the lower end of said legs at different points on said side rails lengthwise thereof, and a brace pivoted to the head rest and to the head end of said frame, whereby when the head rest is raised and lowered and engaged at different points on the side rails the points at which said offset legs join the main portions of the head rest will move lengthwise of the bed in substantially the plane of said bed bottom so that the lower end of the main part of the head rest will move toward the

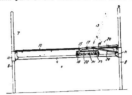

head of the bed as the rest is raised and increase the available area of the bed bottom, and said head rest when lowered is adapted to lie substantially flat on the bed bottom.

1,327,109. SAFETY CRANKING DEVICE FOR AUTO-MOBILES. EDWIN L. MILLER, Kansas City, Mo. Filed Jan. 7, 1919. Serial No. 269,974. 1 Claim. (Cl. 123—185.)

In a safety cranking device for automobiles, the combination with the motor crank shaft of an automobile, of a vertically extending plate provided with a central opening and with an outwardly extending annular flange at the border of the opening and substantially registering with the end of the crank shaft, a hollow cylindrical ratchet member revolubly arranged in the opening in said plate and provided circumferentially with ratchet teeth slidably bearing on the reverse side of the plate and with ratchet teeth extending longitudinally of the ratchet member and presented at the front of said plate, outwardly extending arms adjustably mounted on opposite sides of the reverse side of said plate and provided at their inner ends with fingers extending over said first mentioned ratchet teeth and with bolt holes in their outer end portions, a detent rotatably mounted on the reverse side of said plate and actuated by spring tension to engage said first mentioned ratchet teeth, a crank extending through said ratchet member and adapted for engaging said crank shaft and a split elbow demountably secured on the elbow of said crank and provided with adjustable gripping dogs having beveled projecting end portions adapted for engaging said second mentioned ratchet teeth in one direction and for disengaging the same in the opposite direction.

1,327,110. CLEANING APPARATUS. RAFFAELE MORELLI and JOSEPH SOLIMEO, Brooklyn, N. Y., assignors of one-fifth to Addieco Mirra, one-fifth to Emilio Mirra, and one-fifth to Donato Inzalata, Brooklyn, N. Y. Filed Jan. 5, 1918. Serial No. 210,531. 1 Claim. (Cl. 15—8.)

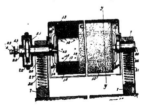

A rotatable brush comprising an outer bristle holding shell, an inner fluid containing tank rotatable within such outer shell, perforations in both the outer shell and the tank, means for bringing such perforations into and out of register, and means to rotate the brush.

1,327,111. AUTOMATIC DISPENSING APPARATUS. HOWARD M. NICHOLSON, Pittsburgh, Pa., assignor of one-fourth to George B. Nicholson, one-fourth to Arthur D. Nicholson, and one-fourth to William T. Lowery, Pittsburgh, Pa. Filed Mar. 28, 1918, Serial No. 225,195. Renewed June 16, 1919. Serial No. 304,739. 6 Claims. (Cl. 221—100.)

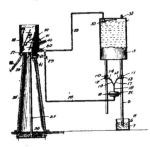

1. In combination, a measuring container, a supply pipe leading thereto, a water tank, supply and waste pipes for the water tank, valves located in the supply and waste pipes, and pressure actuated means operable by pressure created by the movement of the water in the water tank for actuating said valves, and a connection between the tank and the container.

1,327,112. VACUUM DISPENSING APPARATUS. HOWARD M. NICHOLSON, ARTHUR D. NICHOLSON, GEORGE B NICHOLSON, and WILLIAM T. LOWERY, Pittsburgh, Pa. Filed Feb. 23, 1918, Serial No. 218,858. Renewed June 16, 1919. Serial No. 304,740. 3 Claims. (Cl. 221—95.)

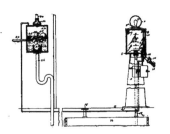

1. In a system of the character described, the combination with a dispensing receptacle, of a storage receptacle, a connection therebetween, a check valve in said connection, a vacuum creating tank, a source of water supply under pressure leading thereto, an outlet therefrom, the movement of the water from the tank acting to create a vacuum therein, a connection between the vacuum tank and the dispensing receptacle, a controlling valve in the last named connection for establishing communication between the vacuum creating tank and the dispensing receptacle, means for admitting air to the interior of the dispensing receptacle and from said receptacle to the tank, and a discharge pipe leading from the dispensing receptacle.

1,327,113. TREATMENT OF CANDIES AND THE LIKE AND THE PRODUCT OBTAINED THEREBY. WILLIAM J. OVERBECK, Cincinnati, Ohio. Filed Oct. 7, 1918. Serial No. 257,209. 2 Claims. (Cl. 99—11.)

1. As a new product, candies coated with hydrogenized oil, in the form of a thin, continuous, even layer of high polish.

1,327,114. GAGE FOR DENTAL AND SURGICAL INSTRUMENTS. MEYER L. RHEIN, New York, N. Y. Filed Oct. 16, 1915. Serial No. 56,310. 8 Claims. (Cl. 33—169.)

1. The combination with a holder provided with means whereby instruments may be used interchangeably therewith, of a gage movable relatively to the instrument, means for mounting the gage on the holder, indicating means whereby the distance intervening between the gage and the extremity of the instrument may be ascertained, and a member movable relatively to said gage and to the indicating means for determining the initial position of the gage with respect to an instrument.

6. A depth gage for dental instruments embodying a member provided with a graduated part and with a gage adapted for contact with a subject the depth of an opening in which is to be ascertained, means for holding a dental instrument and for slidably supporting said first member and the gage thereof whereby said member is operable relatively to the instrument, and a second member movable relatively to the graduated part of the first member and affording means for obtaining a direct reading by aid of the graduated part.

8. The combination with a holder of a member, means whereby said member is supported on the holder for bodily sliding movement directly on said holder, one of said parts being provided with indicating means, an instrument held by said holder and a gage unitary with said sliding member and positioned for surface contact, said gage being movable with the sliding member relatively to said instrument.

1,327,115. KNOCKDOWN STOVE. WILLIAM HORACE ROBINSON, Schenectady, N. Y. Filed Aug. 8, 1919. Serial No. 316,199. 1 Claim. (Cl. 126—9.)

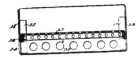

A knock down stove comprising a pair of side walls provided at their upper and lower edges with outwardly extending flanges, said side walls being provided adjacent their lower edges with a series of draft holes, a pair of end walls detachably connected with said side walls and provided at their side edges with spaced lugs frictionally engaging against the outer faces of the side walls and being further provided between said spaced lugs with other lugs frictionally engaging against the inner faces of the side walls, said end walls being slit upwardly from their lower edges to provide tongues, said tongues being bent to extend upwardly in spaced relation to the inner faces of the end walls, and a grate member perforated throughout its area and disposable within the rectangular inclosure formed by said assembled side and end walls, said grate member being provided with depending flanges engaging over said tongues whereby to hold said side and end walls against separation.

1,327,116. NON-SIPHONING TRAP. John Ross, Ironwood, Mich., assignor of one-half to Louis J. Kutil,
Ironwood, Mich. Filed Apr. 18, 1919. Serial No.
290,919. 4 Claims. (Cl. 182—12.)

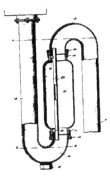

1. In a trap of the character described, a barrel having nipples at its ends adapted for connection with inlet
and outlet elbows, and a vent pipe extending straight
through the barrel at said nipples and supported in place
within the latter.

1,327,117. GAS-GENERATOR. John F. Smith, Seattle,
Wash., assignor, by direct and mesne assignments, to
Alexander J. Boyd, Seattle, Wash. Filed Feb. 17, 1919.
Serial No. 277,515. 1 Claim. (Cl. 48—104.)

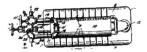

A gas generator of the character described, comprising
a burner having communicating rear and side chambers,
slots provided in the walls of the burner and communicating with said side chambers, a retort disposed above the
burner, an air-and-gas mixing tube extending axially
through the retort and connected from its rear end with
the rear chamber of the burner, an oil supply pipe connected to one end of the retort, a gas outlet provided at
the other end of the retort, and a needle valve provided
on said outlet and disposed in axial relation with and in
front of said tube.

1,327,118. SOUND-CONTROLLER. William A. Sommerhof, Erie, Pa. Filed May 8, 1919. Serial No.
295,683. 1 Claim. (Cl. 181—27.)

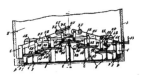

The combination with a casing having an opening and
spaced guides including parallel ribs, of separate panels
having notched ends slidably engaging the ribs, a central
panel, means extending back of the central panel for connecting corresponding panels at opposite sides thereof,
opposed frames mounted for swinging movement, a pivotal
and slidable connection between the frames, and link
connections between the panels and the frames.

1,327,119. RIDGE-PLOWING ATTACHMENT FOR HAR-
ROWS. Andrew C. Stalter, Flanagan, Ill. Filed Aug.
9, 1919. Serial No. 316,344. 2 Claims. (Cl. 55—82.)

1. The combination with a harrow having a longitudinally extending member, of an attachment comprising a
beam downwardly turned at its outer end and provided
with a shovel, the opposite or forward end of the beam
having a transversely extending head, a plate disposed
upon the longitudinal member and attached thereto and
extending downward rearward of the longitudinal member, and a U-shaped yoke disposed against the downwardly
extending portion of said plate and attached thereto for
vertical adjustment, the head being cut out to fit this
yoke and being bolted thereto, and bolts passing through
the head, the yoke and said plate.

1,327,120. SYSTEM OF VENTILATION. Alexander
William Stewart, Glasgow, Scotland. Filed Nov. 20,
1917. Serial No. 202,943. 1 Claim. (Cl. 98—27.)

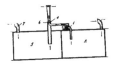

In combination, two compartments, a ventilator for each
compartment, a fan having its intake side in communication with one of said compartments, an air eductor constituted by a double truncated cone in communication
with and projecting from the other compartment and a
nozzle located adjacent to the plane of truncation of said
air eductor and directed away from said last mentioned
compartment, said nozzle communicating with the discharge side of said fan.

1,327,121. SELF-FILLING STORAGE BATTERY. Norman Dexter Sturges, Bellerose Queens, N. Y. Filed
Aug. 6, 1919. Serial No. 315,621. 15 Claims. (Cl.
204—29.)

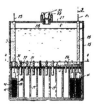

14. In an electric storage battery, the combination of a
plurality of cells, a common reservoir, an insulating partition between said cells and reservoir, electrical connections between said cells and embedded in said partition,
terminal conductors providing communication between
said cells and reservoir, the dimension of said ducts being
such as to substantially preclude current leakage between
said cells when said ducts are filled with liquid.

1,327,122. KNITTING-MACHINE. WILLIAM H. SWARTZ and OSCAR B. RICHARDS, York, Pa., assignors to General Machine Works, York, Pa. Filed June 29, 1918. Serial No. 242,580. 2 Claims. (Cl. 66—22.)

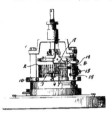

1. In a knitting machine, the combination with a support, of a rotatable shaft mounted upon said support, a needle-actuating, swinging cam carried by said support, means connecting said shaft and cam, a needle-actuating, vertically-movable cam carried by said support, and a bell-crank and eccentric link device mounted upon said support and coöperating with means assembled with the rotatable shaft and the vertically-movable cam for operating the vertically movable cam when said shaft is rotated, whereby both cams are simultaneously actuated.

1,327,123. COASTER. FRED THOMAS, Roanoke, Va. Filed Feb. 1, 1919. Serial No. 274,407. 1 Claim. (Cl. 280—87.5.)

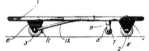

A coaster comprising a body in the form of a plate, a pair of wheels journaled in alinement longitudinally of the plate and centrally thereof, one of the wheels being mounted to swing on an axis perpendicular to the plate to guide the coaster, said wheel having laterally extending foot bars for engagement by the feet of the rider to swing the wheel, and relatively fixed auxiliary wheels arranged on the under side of the plate and spaced apart from the central line and normally spaced above the ground and adapted to come into engagement with the ground when the coaster tilts to either side to support the coaster.

1,327,124. SIGNALING DEVICE FOR MOTOR-VEHICLES. MILTON TIBBETTS, Detroit, Mich., assignor to Packard Motor Car Company, Detroit, Mich., a Corporation of Michigan. Filed Feb. 18, 1916. Serial No. 79,077. 5 Claims. (Cl. 177—7.)

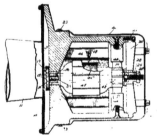

3. In a horn, in combination, a diaphragm, means for vibrating the diaphragm, and means to increase the degree of vibration with the continued operation of the vibrating means at a given speed.

1,327,125. FLYING-MACHINE. FRANK B. VORACEK, Tillamook, Oreg. Filed Aug. 12, 1918. Serial No. 249,447. 2 Claims. (Cl. 244—14.)

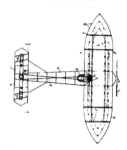

1. In a flying machine, the combination of three transverse, horizontal lifting planes of all metal construction, tapering at each end thereof to a point, said planes decreasing in length from the highest to the lowest, and vertical, metal rods positioned to support and secure said planes to each other and to the fuselage in predetermined positions related to each other and to the fuselage, substantially as described.

1,327,126. PULP-SCREEN. KURT WANDEL, New York, N. Y. Filed Mar. 17, 1916. Serial No. 84,772. 14 Claims. (Cl. 92—35.)

1. A screen or strainer, comprising a material receptacle having a corrugated screening wall, and means for causing a combined rotating and vibrating relative movement of said wall and the material to be screened.

1,327,127. WALL-PAPERING MACHINE. ANTON WANIELISTA and MARCIN OSTROWIECKI, Chicago, Ill. Filed Mar. 28, 1919. Serial No. 285,920. 6 Claims. (Cl. 91—14.)

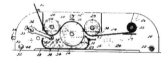

2. A machine comprising sides, a paste roller journaled therebetween, a paste receptacle slidably mounted between said sides with said roller positioned therein, a scraper on one end of the receptacle adjacent said roller, adjusting means for the receptacle outwardly of said sides, and means adapted for guiding paper through the machine in contact with said roller.

1,327,128. AUTOMOBILE-SIGNAL. WILLIAM J. WIGMAN, Manitowoc, Wis. Filed Sept. 26, 1919. Serial No. 326,616. 3 Claims. (Cl. 116—31.)

1. In combination with a vehicle, a signal therefor, means whereby said signal may be pivotally supported on the vehicle, a flexible connection coupled to said signal for moving the same to the indicating position, a rock-shaft journaled on the vehicle and having an arm connected to said flexible connection, means for oscillating said rock-shaft, a spring clip mounted on the signal supporting means and consisting of a single length of wire being substantially U-shaped and providing a pair of spring jaws flared apart at their opened ends to guide the signal between said jaws, and yieldable means for drawing the signal between the jaws when the rock-shaft is released.

1,327,129. DRIVE-GEARING. FAY M. WOLFF, Louisville, Ky. Filed Aug. 23, 1918. Serial No. 251,108. 2 Claims. (Cl. 172—239.)

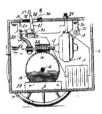

2. The combination of a pair of gear members, a supporting frame, a motor pivoted to said frame and carrying one of said members and driving the same, said member being movable bodily with the motor, a lever for swinging the motor to bring the last-mentioned gear member into and out of mesh with the other gear member, said lever being pivoted to the frame, and the latter having a slot in which one end of the lever works, and an adjustable stop in the slot in the path of the lever for regulating the movement thereof in a direction to mesh the gear member.

1,327,130. SWEET-POTATO-CURING HOUSE. EDGAR MILES WOODS, Gladewater, Tex. Filed Jan. 30, 1919. Serial No. 274,025. 12 Claims. (Cl. 98—26.)

8. In a vegetable curing plant, a building, a plurality of transverse bins therein, aisles being provided between said bins and along one end thereof, the other ends of said bins extending to one side of the building, hollow openwork partitions in said bins extending from end to end thereof, said partition also extending to said side of the building, upper and lower air passages adjacent the tops and bottoms of the bins and located at one end thereof, said passages having outlets for each bin, the outlets of the lower passage discharging into one end of said partitions, and means for forcing air through said passages.

12. The combination with a vegetable curing house having a passage for conducting hot air to different parts of the house, of a pair of passages discharging into said conducting passage at spaced points, means for supplying heated air at different temperatures to said pair of passages and for forcing the two currents of air therethrough into said conducting passage, and a cut-off in said conducting passage between the passages of said pair for either segregating the two currents of heated air for passage to different parts of the house or for allowing such currents to mix in said conducting passage.

1,327,131. ROAD-MAKING. CARL JULIUS ÅBERG, Stenstorp, Sweden. Filed Sept. 26, 1916. Serial No. 122,282. 7 Claims. (Cl. 94—44.)

1. A road making machine comprising a vehicle, means for propelling said vehicle, and means operatively connected with said propelling means for breaking stones and causing the broken stones to be discharged onto the road bed at a speed proportional to the rate of travel of the vehicle, both said means being carried by said vehicle.

1,327,132. ENGINE-STARTER. VINCENT BENDIX, Chicago, Ill. Filed Sept. 25, 1916. Serial No. 121,952. 39 Claims. (Cl. 290—38.)

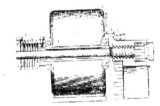

9. In combination with an electric starting motor whose armature shaft is hollow from end to end, a shaft arranged within the armature shaft and operatively connected therewith, and a driving member arranged on the second-named shaft and adapted, as a result of the rotation of the motor, to be automatically engaged with a part of the engine to be started.

1,327,133. NON-REFILLABLE BOTTLE. MATIJA BESHENICH, Beatty, Pa., assignor of one-fourth to John Tirodor and one-fourth to Mike Mohanec, Greensburg, Pa. Filed Sept. 11, 1919. Serial No. 323,107. 4 Claims. (Cl. 215—67.)
1. A device of the class described comprising a bottle, a plug inserted within the bottle, an arm adapted to be transversely positioned relative to said plug after insertion within the bottle to prevent removal of said plug, said arm being curved downwardly and the positioning means therefor including a plurality of cords loosely attached thereto and extending outwardly of the bottle neck.

2. A device of the class described comprising a bottle, a plug insertible within the neck thereof, said plug having a curved transverse opening in its inner end and a curved arm positioned in said plug opening after insertion within said bottle neck to prevent withdrawal thereof, and cords extending outwardly of the bottle neck through the plug.

3. A device of the class described comprising a bottle, a plug insertible within the neck thereof, said plug having a transverse opening in its inner end, a cross arm carried by said plug and adapted to be positioned in said transverse opening, coöperating means at said plug and cross arm to prevent withdrawal of the cross arm from said plug opening, said coöperating means including a spring finger carried by the plug and an engaging recess upon the adjacent face of said cross arm for said spring finger.

4. A device of the class described comprising a bottle, a plug insertible within the neck thereof, said plug having a transverse opening in its inner end, a cross arm carried by said plug and adapted to be positioned in said transverse opening, coöperating means at said plug and cross arm to prevent withdrawal of the cross arm from said plug opening, and means carried by said cross arm adapted to be removed therefrom for placing said cross arm in the plug opening, said means being adapted for removal from said bottle after positioning the arm in said opening.

1,327,134. CAN-OPENER. WILLIAM F. BLAKE, Toledo, Ohio, assignor of fifty-one per cent. to Henry W. Duvendack, Toledo, Ohio. Filed June 25, 1917. Serial No. 176,819. 4 Claims. (Cl. 30—3.)

1. In a can opener, the combination of a handle with a blade guide on one side of the lower portion of said handle, and at right angles from and adjacent thereto a round adjustable fulcrum with a sharp cutting edge to engage the edge of a can.

1,327,135. RHEOSTAT. WILLIAM L. BLISS, Niagara Falls, N. Y., assignor to U. S. Light & Heat Corporation, Niagara Falls, N. Y., a Corporation of New York. Filed May 13, 1918. Serial No. 234,117. 8 Claims. (Cl. 219—62.)

1. A rheostat comprising an exposed resistance element and a contact member, said member comprising a plu-

rality of sections encircling and contacting with said element, and means for yieldingly holding said sections together and pressing them into electrical contact with said resistance element.

1,327,136. LOCOMOTIVE-DRIVING-BOX LUBRICATOR. JOHN A. BOWLES, Richmond, Va. Filed June 16, 1919. Serial No. 304,553. 3 Claims. (Cl. 64—24.)

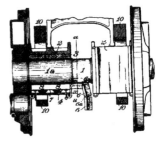

1. The combination, with a "long" driving box, and a lubricant cellar fitted therein, of means for inserting blocks of solid lubricant of aggregate length substantially equal to that of the driving box, at the inner end thereof, without removal of the lubricant cellar.

1,327,137. PEDAL-OPERATED MECHANISM. DANIEL BRANDENSTEIN, New York, N. Y., and JACOB FISCHER, Roseville, N. J. Filed May 6, 1919. Serial No. 295,124. 11 Claims. (Cl. 74—81.)

1. In pedal-operated mechanism, spaced stationary bearings one of which has an open-top socket, and a pedal located between said bearings and having at one side a lug or trunnion adapted for engagement with said open-top bearing, and at the other side a universal joint connection with the other bearing, whereby said pedal may be rocked in said bearings, and also swung up on one bearing and out of the other bearing.

1,327,138. CAMERA ATTACHMENT. HENRY J. BROWN, New York, N. Y. Filed Feb. 6, 1915. Serial No. 6,568. 3 Claims. (Cl. 95—1.1.)

1. An attachment for cameras comprising a casing having an opening therein, a hinged plate for holding a portion of a film over said opening and protecting the same from exposure when the main portion of the film is exposed in taking a picture, means for swinging said hinged plate away from the film to permit adjustment of

the latter, a semi-transparent plate in said opening to receive an inscription, and displaceable means for preventing light from passing through said semi-transparent plate to the unexposed portion of the film for the purpose specified.

1,327,139. SELF-LIGHTING CIGARETTE. MUNRO S. BROWN, Goldfield, Nev. Filed May 8, 1919. Serial No. 295,639. 2 Claims. (Cl. 131—52.)

1. In combination with a cigarette of a tip of igniting material extending into one end of the paper tube or wrapper and slightly penetrating the tobacco filling with a thin film of the igniting material around the outer side of the paper-tube or wrapper whereby the latter and shreds of the tobacco-filling are embedded in said tip.

1,327,140. PERMUTATION-LOCK. JOHN BULANDA, Pullman, Ill. Filed Feb. 21, 1919. Serial No. 278,398. 8 Claims. (Cl. 70—53.)

1. A lock comprising a casing, a cross head shiftable in the casing, a key manipulated slide carried by the cross head, a latch within the casing and a spring pressed latch actuator operatively connected to the head.

1,327,141. SIGHT. JAMES L. BUMPAS and PHILIP FALCKE, Chicago, Ill.; said Bumpas assignor, by direct and mesne assignments, of his right to United States Ordnance Company, Washington, D. C. Filed June 22, 1917. Serial No. 176,444. Renewed June 20, 1919. Serial No. 305,704. 10 Claims. (Cl. 33—57.)

1. A sight comprising a frame connected with a base, a rotatable member disposed therein composed of spiral elements, and means to rotate said member.
5. A sight comprising a frame, a rotatable member formed with a spiral slot extending longitudinally thereof, and whose lateral edges cause a sight hole to be formed transversely of the member, and means to rotate said member.

270 O. G.—4

6. A sight comprising a graduated frame having a base, means to retain the frame in a plurality of positions, a cylindrical member mounted for rotation movement within the frame and composed of spiral elements forming a spiral slot extending longitudinally of the member and producing therein a sighting hole whose position in the frame may be changed by the rotation of the member, means to rotate the slotted member, and means to restrain the movement of the rotatable member.
8. A sight comprising a frame, a cylindrical rotatable member composed of spaced spiral elements so arranged as to form a spiral slot transversely of the member and longitudinally thereof producing a sighting hole, and means to rotate said member to cause said hole to appear to move in a rectilineal path in said frame.
10. A sight comprising a frame, a member rotatable therein having a sight opening therein which apparently moves longitudinally of the frame upon rotation of the member, and means to rotate said member.

1,327,142. CABINET FOR PHONOGRAPHIC RECORDS. FRANKLIN HALE CALL, Portland, Oreg. Filed Apr. 22, 1919. Serial No. 291,947. 3 Claims. (Cl. 211—16.)

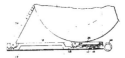

2. In a device of the character described, the combination of, a cabinet provided with partitions, guides between the lower parts of the partitions, a carriage adapted to slide within each guide, an ejector arm pivoted in the guide above the rear end of the carriage, means upon the ejector and carriage whereby each can transmit motion to the other, a retaining arm pivoted in the guide above the forward part of the carriage, means upon said arm and the carriage whereby the carriage may raise and lower said arm, a locking arm pivoted in the guide forward of the retaining arm in a position to be engaged by the retaining arm when it drops to a horizontal position, means in the guide to lock the carriage so it cannot move rearwardly when the retaining arm is raised, and a key formed and arranged to adapt it to engage and raise the locking arm and to engage and move the carriage rearwardly, and through it to cause the ejector to move forwardly, and the retaining arm to move to horizontal position into engagement with the locking arm, and the locking arm to engage the key in a manner that it cannot be withdrawn, substantially as described.

1,327,143. CABINET FOR PHONOGRAPHIC RECORDS. FRANKLIN HALE CALL, Portland, Oreg. Filed May 29, 1919. Serial No. 300,612. 5 Claims. (Cl. 211—16.)

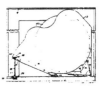

1. In a device of the character described, the combination of a case, a series of cartons pivoted at their lower

parts in the case and in vertical position, a bell crank lever pivoted at its angle upon the case bottom opposite each carton, the lower arm of said lever being longitudinally grooved in its upper part and extending within the carton, the upper lever arm having an angled member, and a thin arm secured at one end upon the rear part of the carton and extending downwardly therefrom, said arm having a curved opening with a series of notches in the upper edge thereof, said opening and notches being formed and arranged to receive the lever angled member through them and the notched parts to engage said member, substantially as described.

1,327,144. TUBE SUSPENSION. OMA CARR, New York, N. Y. Filed Mar. 27, 1917. Serial No. 157,863. 3 Claims. (Cl. 285—37.)

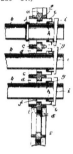

1. In combination with a tube-plate and a tube extending therethrough, means for supporting the tube in the tube-plate consisting wholly of an acid-resisting non-metallic medium, said tube support embodying tiles supported and cemented in the tube-plate.

1,327,145. CEMENTING MATERIAL OBTAINED FROM GREENSAND. HARRY WILLIAMS CHARLTON, Jones Point, N. Y., assignor to American Potash Corporation, a Virginia Company. Filed May 22, 1917. Serial No. 170,332. 1 Claim. (Cl. 106—24.)

The herein described cementing material of a greenish or brownish white color resulting from the digestion of green sand mixed with lime, said material when freshly made consisting of a plastic self hardening mass, and said material containing the silicates of calcium, iron and aluminum, and said material capable when treated with steam of undergoing a still further hardening process, substantially as described.

1,327,146. GLASS-CLEANER. VICTOR H. CHRISTEN, Toledo, Ohio. Filed Dec. 26. 1918. Serial No. 268,411. 1 Claim. (Cl. 15—59.)

In a glass cleaner for automobile wind shields formed of two overlaping parts, a broad strip located between the overlapping portions of the parts, a U-shaped spring member connected to the broad strip, a wiper bar formed of sheet metal bent in the form of a U and located between the legs of the U-shaped member and having a back edge portion extending laterally into proximity to the legs of the U-shaped member to limit rotation of the wiper bar when in use, a wiper strip located between the edges of the wiper bar, the wiper bar having openings near its edges for receiving the ends of the U-shaped spring member.

1,327,147. HYDROCARBON-MOTOR. HAROLD D. CHURCH, Detroit, Mich., assignor to Packard Motor Car Company, Detroit, Mich., a Corporation of Michigan. Filed May 11, 1916. Serial No. 96,880. 3 Claims. (Cl. 74—85.)

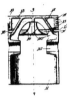

1. A one piece piston comprising upper and lower parts separated at the periphery to form a gap, said piston having a conical web portion connecting its two parts and inclined outwardly toward its lower end and extending directly from adjacent the middle of the upper part to the upper edge of the lower part of the piston.

1,327,148. HYDROCARBON-MOTOR. FRANK J. DRUAR, Detroit, Mich., assignor to Packard Motor Car Company, Detroit, Mich., a Corporation of Michigan. Filed Apr. 29, 1918. Serial No. 231,502. 9 Claims. (Cl. 123—178.)

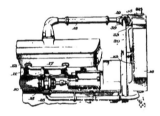

1. The combination with a hydrocarbon motor, and a radiator, of a thermostat unit comprising a body having connections with the motor and the radiator and with a by-pass, said unit having an inlet and a plurality of outlets, balanced valve mechanism controlling said outlets, and a thermostat connected to said mechanism.

1,327,149. RESERVOIR-BROACH. DE LLOYD O. DUNCAN, Rockford, Ill. Filed Mar. 12, 1919. Serial No. 282,108. 3 Claims. (Cl. 32—10.)

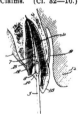

1. An instrument for introducing liquid into a relatively small canal comprising a body shaped to form a

shank having a slender point adapted to be inserted a substantial distance into the canal, the body being formed intermediate the shank and point portions with an open reservoir adapted to hold a quantity of liquid in co-operative relation to the point.

1,327,150. HOLDING DEVICE FOR WINDOW-SHADES. PLATO G. EMERY, Chicago, Ill. Filed Mar. 31, 1915. Serial No. 18,293. 7 Claims. (Cl. 156—26.)

1. The combination with the stick of a shade, of a dog on the end of the stick for engagement with a window frame, means yieldingly pressing said dog outwardly, the outer edge of the dog being in the form of a cam receding from a high portion in opposite directions along said edge, means for supporting the dog so as to permit it to shift from a position in which the high portion of the cam lies on one side of a dead center to a position in which it lies on the opposite side of a dead center, and the parts being so proportioned that a predetermined push or pull on the stick in the same direction as that in which the high portion of the dog lies from the dead center will cause the dog to rock upon the frame and reverse its position.

1,327,151. JOINTER-TOOL. PHILIP L. FRAZIER, Rockbury, Conn. Filed Mar. 12, 1917. Serial No. 154,265. 1 Claim. (Cl. 72—138.)

A pointed tool including a blade which is curved longitudinally and transversely, tapers from one end to the other and which is semi-elliptical in cross section at its broad end and semi-circular in cross section at its narrow end.

1,327,152. AUTOMATIC NUT-TIGHTENING DEVICE. BEDELL GIBSON, Nicholls, Ga. Filed Mar. 7, 1919. Serial No. 281,297. 2 Claims. (Cl. 151—47.)

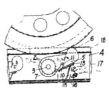

1. An automatic nut tightening device for rails, comprising a bolt; a round nut mounted on the threaded end

of the bolt; a ratchet cut on the nut; a trigger having one end loosely engaging the bolt and the free end projecting up above the tread of the rail; a pawl mounted on the trigger and held in sliding engagement with the ratchet of the nut; and means for holding said pawl in sliding engagement with said ratchet, and for projecting the free end of the trigger up above the tread of the rail.

1,327,153. REGISTERING AND RECORDING MECHANISM. MAXIMILIAN M. GOLDBERG, Dayton, Ohio, assignor to The National Cash Register Company, Dayton, Ohio. Filed July 6, 1915. Serial No. 38,250. 53 Claims. (Cl. 235—2.)

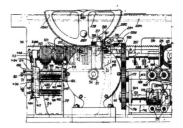

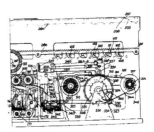

18. In a machine of the class described, the combination with a totalizer, of a differentially movable actuator therefor, operating means normally connected to the actuator, an electro-magnet, and record controlled means for momentarily energizing said electro-magnet at different points in the movement of the operating means to effect the disconnection of the actuator from the operating means.

1,327,154. COMPASS. CHARLES FREMONT GOLDEN, Denver, Ind. Filed Mar. 22, 1919. Serial No. 284.294. 3 Claims. (Cl. 33—26.)

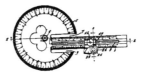

1. The combination with a straight edge, of a slide marking element holder formed from a strip of metal bent to provide a slide, the slide being mounted for longitudinal adjustment on the straight edge, the metal strip being bent upwardly and thence bent at right angles and

disposed above the straight edge, the metal strip terminating into an enlargement a barrel carried by the enlargement and a tube for retaining marking elements carried by the latter.

1,327,155. SCRAPER. CHARLES GOTTSCHALK, St. Paul, Minn. Filed May 24, 1919. Serial No. 299,455. 8 Claims. (Cl. 145—47.)

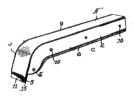

7. A hand scraper having a rectangular handle body portion with smooth engaging sides and means for adjustably holding and concealing a thin, flat, flexible cutting blade in said body portion for the purposes specified.

1,327,156. OIL-MEASURE. CYRUS E. HANES, Armington, Ill. Filed Apr. 11, 1918. Serial No. 227,999. 1 Claim. (Cl. 221—15.)

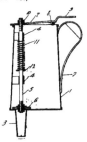

The combination with a measure having an outlet in the bottom thereof near the wall of the measure, and a handle extending radially beyond the wall at a point remote from the outlet, of a tapered nozzle extending downwardly from the outlet, superposed guide brackets extending inwardly from the wall of the measure at points diametrically opposite the handle, a rod slidably mounted in the brackets, a valve disk secured adjustably to the lower end of the rod and adapted to bear upon the bottom of the measure and close the outlet, a spring mounted on the rod and bearing upwardly against one of the brackets and downwardly against the rod, a pin secured upon the upper end of the measure close to the handle, a lever fulcrumed on the pin and having an upwardly offset portion extending over the handle, the remaining portion of the lever being extending diametrically across the top of the measure, its free end engaging the upper end of the rod, and a nut adjustably engaging the upper end of the rod and bearing against the lever, the nut engaging end of said lever being limited in its downward movement by the wall of the measure, the upper end of the rod being slidable upwardly within the lever.

1,327,157. VIOLIN SOUND-POST. ROBERT ERWIN HARDEE, Savannah, Ga. Filed Nov. 23, 1917. Serial No. 203,583. 1 Claim. (Cl. 84—44.)

A sound post for violins comprising a flat substantially rectangular body formed centrally thereof with a transversely extending opening, lugs formed on the upper and lower edges of the body at the corners thereof and having their horizontal surfaces curved to conform to the internal transverse curvature of the belly and back of

the violin, respectively, and kerfs provided in the vertical edges of the body adjacent said lugs to provide weakened portions, the kerfs for the lugs on one edge being reversely formed with respect to the kerfs for the lugs on the other edge.

1,327,158. MACHINE FOR MAKING CORRUGATED PAPER-BOARD. EDGAR M. HAWKINS, Rochester, N. Y., assignor to M. D. Knowlton Company, Rochester, N. Y., a Corporation of New York. Filed Apr. 24, 1918. Serial No. 230,413. 11 Claims. (Cl. 154—31.)

1. The combination with mechanism for lining a web of paper and the like, of a heating bed beneath which the lined web passes, and a supporting bed arranged beneath the heating bed for holding the lined web to said heating bed and being vertically adjustable with respect to the latter, for the purpose described.

1,327,159. STEAM-BOILER. LOUIS F. HOFFMAN and WINNIE J. UNKEL, Kinder, La. Filed Aug. 26, 1919. Serial No. 319,890. 1 Claim. (Cl. 60—39.)

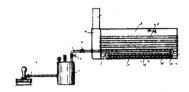

The combination, with a steam boiler, of a perforated pipe arranged in the water space of the boiler, said pipe being provided with a series of folds or convolutions arranged in a vertical plane, a reservoir for compressed air, an outlet pipe provided with a regulating valve and a check valve and connecting the air reservoir with the top convolution of the said perforated pipe, and a pump for forcing compressed air into the reservoir.

1,327,160. ELECTRICALLY-DRIVEN SPINDLE. JOSEF HURTIG, Rochester, N. Y. Filed Jan. 8, 1919. Serial No. 270,145. 4 Claims. (Cl. 171—209.)

1. A high speed spindle having the rotor of a motor securely attached to it, a bearing contiguous to the rotor,

a removable sleeve carrying the bearing, a sustaining yoke or housing into which the removable sleeve and the

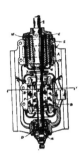

stator of the motor are fitted, whereby the spindle, the motor, the removable sleeve, the main bearing and other attached parts can be readily removed.

1,327,161. VAPORIZER FOR HYDROCARBON-LIGHTS. ADOLPH G. KAUFMAN, New York, N. Y. Filed Feb. 5, 1919. Serial No. 275,158. 3 Claims. (Cl. 67—50.)

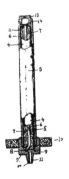

1. A vaporizer filler composed of an outer wall of fibrous material and an inner core of rigid material, said fibrous material being held on said rigid material with fastening means between the fibrous material and the core in a manner whereby longitudinal movement of the fibrous material relative to the rigid material is prevented, and the exterior of the fibrous material is completely exposed.

1,327,162. DISPENSING-FAUCET. STANLEY H. KNIGHT, Chicago, Ill. Filed May 31, 1919. Serial No. 300,808. 16 Claims. (Cl. 225—26.)

1. In a liquid dispensing apparatus of the type described, the combination of an inclosing casing having a bottom outlet, means for introducing a supply of fluid into said casing, a valve controlling said supply, a measuring hopper arranged in said casing and having operative engagement with said valve, said hopper having a valved lower end affording a clear vertical passageway

in its opened condition, means for imparting vertical movement to said hopper, and a liquid dispensing faucet

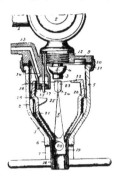

having connection with the upper end of said casing in vertical alinement with the measuring hopper, substantially as set forth.

1,327,163. INTERPUPILARY-DISTANCE-MEASURING INSTRUMENT. HENRY B. MATHEWSON and KNUTE KNUTSEN, San Francisco, Calif. Filed June 19, 1919. Serial No. 305,328. 6 Claims. (Cl. 88—20.)

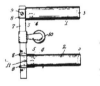

1. A measuring-instrument comprising a pair of projectors for throwing two images in parallel planes; and a graduated bar upon which said projectors are mounted whereby the inter-plane space is indicated.

1,327,164. PROCESS OF OBTAINING COMBINED POTASSIUM FROM GREENSAND. THOMAS C. MEADOWS, New York, MATHIAS HAUBER, Jr., West Haverstraw, and HARRY W. CHARLTON, New York, N. Y. Filed Dec. 6, 1918. Serial No. 265,594. 5 Claims. (Cl. 23—22.)

1. The process of extracting potassium chlorid from green sand which consists in providing a mixture of green sand and lime, digesting said mixture at a pressure exceeding 200 pounds to the square inch, and at a corresponding temperature, with water containing in solution sufficient calcium chlorid to react with substantially all the potassium present in the green sand; and continuing the first digestion until a solution containing more than 2% potassium chlorid and a valuable sludge material is formed, substantially as described.

1,327,165. RADIATOR. FRANK W. MERRITT, Duluth, Minn., assignor to Holbrook W. Coulter, trustee, Duluth, Minn. Filed Sept. 23, 1918. Serial No. 255,282. 9 Claims. (Cl. 257—125.)

1. In a radiator, the combination of two circulation chambers spaced from each other, a series of circulation units interposed between said chambers, one of the

terminal units of said series engaging and communicating with one of said chambers, an adjustable nipple mounted in the other of said chambers and engaging the opposite

terminal of said series, said series and adjustable nipple being adapted to conduct liquid from one of said chambers to the other, each of said units being removably engaged with another of said units.

1,327,166. APPARATUS FOR HEATING AND RIPEN-ING HONEY. HENRY A. MITCHELL, Shepherd, Tex.; E. W. Love administrator of said Henry A. Mitchell, deceased. Filed Sept. 18, 1918. Serial No. 254,687. 1 Claim. (Cl. 87—19.)

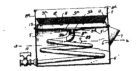

In an apparatus for heating and ripening honey, the combination with a hot water tank, of a carrying-off and discharging coil mounted therein and provided with a faucet controlled discharging means at one end exterior of the tank, a pan corresponding in shape to and telescopically fitting the tank and provided with side and end parts, means upon the walls of the tank for supporting said pan removably and telescopically in the tank, a skeleton honeycomb support removably disposed in the pan and conforming thereto, straining means on the support on which the honey comb rests, the bottom of said pan having a central conical depression, the center of which having an outlet opening, and means for detachably connecting the other end of the coil in said opening, whereby the pan may be removed.

1,327,167. DOUBLE - CURRENT SYRINGE. JOSEPH KINNEY MITCHELL, Memphis, Tenn. Filed May 5, 1919. Serial No. 294,695. 4 Claims. (Cl. 128—239.)

1. A device of the character specified comprising a tubular casing having one end open and having the other provided with a detachable spray head, said casing hav-

ing a branch near the open end extending from the body of the casing toward the spray head at an acute angle with respect to the main casing, said branch being adapted for connnection with a source of liquid supply, the open end of the main casing being adapted to be closed by the thumb to provide either irrigation or drainage, and a web at the junction of the branch with the main casing for deflecting the water entering the branch out at the open end of the tube.

1,327,168. DOLL. JOSEPH NÉMETH, New York, N. Y. Filed Dec. 17, 1918. Serial No. 267,129. 2 Claims. (Cl. 46—40.)

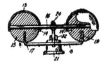

1. An eye mechanism for doll-heads including two eye members, each of which comprises a substantially hemispherical shell constituting the exterior of the eye, and a spherical body over which said shell is drawn, a bridge piece connecting said eyes consisting of a spindle having its ends extending through said shells into the bodies therein, and a clamping piece connecting said spherical bodies.

1,327,169. HOLDER FOR THE BALLS IN BALL-BEARINGS. KNUT NYSTRÖM, Stockholm, Sweden. Filed Aug. 26, 1918. Serial No. 251,544. 2 Claims. (Cl. 64—59.)

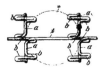

1. A cage for a ball bearing comprising a wire bent to form a series of equidistant circular loops radial to the axis of the bearing and having laterial projections adapted to engage the balls introduced between adjacent loops.

1,327,170. APPARATUS FOR MAKING GROMETS. ALPHONSO COMSTOCK PRATT, Deep River, Conn. Filed Apr. 30, 1918. Serial No. 231,661. 7 Claims. (Cl. 28—2.)

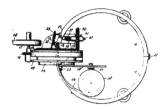

1. The method of making a gromet which consists in bending the end portion of a piece of wire to a circle and supporting the wire against displacement from the position to constitute a core for the gromet and then automatically feeding this circular core continuously about

the axis of the circle of the core while thus supported and at the same time rotating the wire from which the gromet is formed about the core in correspondence with the feeding movement of the core to lay the wire in regular spirals upon the core; substantially as described.

1,327,171. GOLF-STICK. WILLIAM GUY RUGGLES, New York, N. Y., assignor to Edward V. Hartford, New York, N. Y. Filed June 3, 1918. Serial No. 237,872. 3 Claims. (Cl. 46—4.)

1. A golf tool provided with a head having a striking face, a reflector positioned above said face and a ball and socket connection between the reflector and the head providing for universal adjustment of the reflector in all planes relative to the striking surface.

1,327,172. ENGINE. EARL V. SALA, Toledo, Ohio. Filed Mar. 12, 1917. Serial No. 154,127. 3 Claims. (Cl. 123—59.)

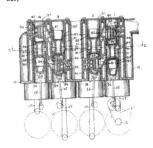

1. In an engine, the combination of an engine cylinder, a pair of piston valves, each piston having heads and a passageway in one of the heads, a valve cylinder for each of the valves, the engine having a port connecting the engine cylinder with one of the valve cylinders intermediate the heads, the passageway to the port controlled by both valve pistons.

1,327,173. GREASE-DETAINING DEVICE. GILBERT A. SMITH, Des Moines, Iowa. Filed Nov. 30, 1917. Serial No. 204,800. 7 Claims. (Cl. 64—22.)

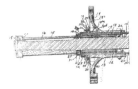

1. A grease-detaining device, comprising an axle housing cap adapted loosely to fit a housing, an elastic washer adapted to surround a housing and receive and engage with one end of said cap, and yielding pressure devices backed by said housing and adapted to apply pressure to said elastic washer toward said cap.

1,327,174. THREE-PHASE ELECTRIC FURNACE. FREDERICK T. SNYDER, Oak Park, Ill., assignor to Industrial Electric Furnace Company, Chicago, Ill., a Corporation of Indiana. Filed Mar. 11, 1918. Serial No. 221,610. 7 Claims. (Cl. 204—64.)

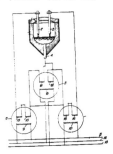

1. The combination with an electric furnace having two upper electrodes and a bottom contact, of three transformers, the secondaries of which are so connected as to produce a phase angle between the voltages existing between the bottom contact and said upper electrodes, greater than 60° and less than 90°.

1,327,175. FUEL-PACKAGE. CHARLES S. SPURR, Los Angeles, and HERMAN P. RANDALL, Pasadena, Calif., assignors of one-half to Frank W. Frame, Los Angeles, Calif. Filed Oct. 23, 1918. Serial No. 259,355. 7 Claims. (Cl. 44—1.)

1. A fuel packet for vulcanizers, embodying a thin flat container of combustible material and a filling of slow burning fuel.

1,327,176. TRAIN-STOP SYSTEM. EARL C. STAFFORD, Philadelphia, Pa., assignor to The Railway Automatic Safety Appliance Company, Philadelphia, Pa., a Corporation of Delaware. Filed Apr. 21, 1915, Serial No. 22,775. Renewed Nov. 3, 1919. Serial No. 335,509. 16 Claims. (Cl. 246—181.)

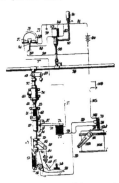

3. A train stop system, comprising an automatic train stop, devices whereby said train stop may be controlled by

the signals at a signal station, said devices including an electrical apparatus for controlling the automatic train stop at intervals when the speed of the train is above a predetermined speed, mechanically operated mechanism for controlling the automatic train stop, between the intervals of control by said electrical apparatus, when said train is traveling above said predetermined speed, and means controlled by the engineer for preventing the release of said automatic train stop at any time when said train is traveling below said predetermined speed.

1,327,177. SCORE - KEEPING APPARATUS. EDWARD STEIGERWALD and FRANK L. H. PFEIL, Philadelphia, Pa. Filed Jan. 29, 1919. Serial No. 273,717. 11 Claims. (Cl. 235—83.)

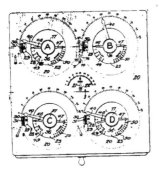

1. A score keeping device comprising a supporting structure; an annularly graduated dial rotatably mounted on said supporting structure; means for registering with the graduations of the dial; plus and minus markings on said supporting structure; a finger movably mounted on said supporting structure; and means attached jointly on said finger and dial, and operative when said dial is rotated a predetermined distance in opposite directions to move said finger alternately to said plus and minus markings and, when said dial is moved in said directions beyond said predetermined distance, to move said finger alternately beyond said plus and minus markings; substantially as described.

6. Apparatus of the character described, including means providing graduations; a pointer for traversing said graduations; a supporting member having a channel arm, one side of said arm having a slot therein; a locking spring having a portion extending into said channel through said slot; a graduated dial; a locking lever pivotally mounted on said arm; said spring having a portion adapted to spring into engagement with said locking lever to hold the latter in locking engagement with the dial; means operatively connecting said traversing means and said supporting means; and means adapted to be engaged by said spring to release said locking lever and permit it to be moved out of locking engagement with the dial; substantially as described.

1,327,178. FURNITURE. JACOB STEPHAN, Cleveland, Ohio. Filed Sept. 29, 1915. Serial No. 53,164. 16 Claims. (Cl. 5—46.)

8. In an article of the class described, a frame or receptacle having side and end members and a plurality of spring sections normally arranged one beneath the other in the receptacle, one of said sections being slidable rearwardly, another being slidable forwardly and upwardly, and a third section adapted to be swung upwardly

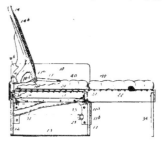

at the front to permit the second section to be given its forward and upward movement.

1,327,179. SOLE-PRESSING MACHINE. WILLIAM C. STEWART, Swampscott, Mass., assignor to United Shoe Machinery Corporation, Paterson, N. J., a Corporation of New Jersey. Filed Apr. 30, 1919. Serial No. 293,828. 7 Claims. (Cl. 12—21.)

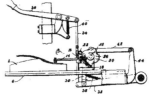

1. A sole pressing machine, having, in combination, co-operating sole pressing forms, mechanism for relatively actuating the forms to move them into and out of alinement, a sole gripper, mechanism under the control of the operator for actuating the gripper to grip and release the sole, and mechanism for automatically actuating the gripper to release the sole.

7. A sole pressing machine, having, in combination, a sole supporting form, a transversely moving slide on which the form is mounted, a reciprocating head on which the slide is mounted, a sole gripper on the slide, a rotary cam on the slide connected to open and close the gripper, a ratchet wheel connected with the cam, and a pawl carried by the head for actuating the ratchet wheel during the transverse movement of the slide.

1,327,180. TIRE-RIM. HENRY STINEMETTS, Calgary, Alberta, Canada. Filed May 24, 1918. Serial No. 236,849. 3 Claims. (Cl. 152—21.)

1. A separable rim comprising an inner section having its inner periphery cylindrical for engagement upon the

outer periphery of a felly, said section being secured to the felly, an inwardly-extending flange formed at one edge of said section and engaging against the side of the felly, an outwardly extending tire engaging flange formed on said edge of said section, the outer periphery of said section being inclined, a plurality of pairs of spaced lugs extending diagonally across said outer periphery, an outer section having its inner periphery inclined and its outer periphery cylindrical, an inwardly extending flange formed on one edge of said outer section and abutting against the ends of said lugs to form a closure for the side of the rim, said last named flange being grooved for the reception of the free edge of said first named section, a gasket within said groove, a tire engaging flange formed on said edge of said outer section, a plurality of lugs extending diagonally across the inner periphery of said outer section and engaging between said pairs of lugs, and means for securing said outer section against movement with respect to said inner section.

1,327,181.   CRANE OR SIMILAR LIFTING DEVICE. Oskar Taussig, Vienna, Austria.   Filed Feb. 12, 1915. Serial No. 7,670.   4 Claims.   (Cl. 254—167.)

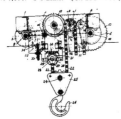

1. In a lifting device, the combination with a device for suspending the load, suspending means for said device and means for hoisting the suspending means, of auxiliary means for hoisting said device and operable at will independently of the first mentioned hoisting means, one of the hoisting means including an eccentric; substantially as described.

1,327,182.   MECHANISM FOR CONTROLLING THE FEEDING AND PRINTING OF SHEETS.   Burt F. Upham, Brookline, Mass., assignor, by mesne assignments, to Cross Paper Feeder Company, Portland, Me., a Corporation of Maine.   Filed Feb. 14, 1917, Serial No. 148,495. Renewed Mar. 31, 1919.   Serial No. 286,621.   15 Claims. (Cl. 271—56.)

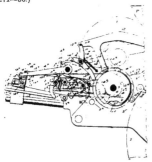

3. In combination mechanism for operating on sheets having sheet taking devices, means for directing sheets to said mechanism, means for detecting misplaced or defective sheets, sheet clamping devices, and co-acting means controlled by the detecting mechanism whereby upon the presentation of a misplaced or defective sheet the clamping devices are permitted to engage and hold the sheet and the sheet taking devices are rendered ineffective.

1,327,183.   CONTROL FOR DUAL-CONTROL AEROPLANES.   Frederic Langtry van Allen, Toronto, Ontario, Canada.   Filed Aug. 30, 1918.   Serial No. 252,127. 5 Claims.   (Cl. 244—29.)

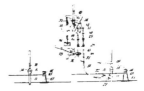

1. In a dual control aeroplane in which each set of controls consists of rudder bars and control stick, lever means for rendering the rudder bar of one set of controls, inoperative while the control stick of the same set remains operative, and lever means for rendering the control stick and rudder bars of the same set simultaneously inoperative.

1,327,184.   FRACTIONAL DISTILLATION OF CRUDE PETROLEUM AND OTHER HYDROCARBONS.   Albrecht Frederich Georg Carl Paul Josef von Groeling, New York, N. Y., assignor to Atlas Process Company, Inc., New York, N. Y., a Corporation of New York. Filed Apr. 22, 1916.   Serial No. 92,807.   3 Claims.   (Cl. 196—16.)

2. An apparatus for distilling crude petroleum, comprising a plurality of stills; condensers connected with the respective stills; receivers connected with the respective condensers; vacuum-producing means connected with the several receivers, for creating a high vacuum in the said stills, condensers and receivers; automatic means for controlling the vacuum-producing means to maintain the vacuum substantially constant in degree; and still-heating means permitting independent control of the distilling temperatures in the several stills.

1,327,185.   TELEPHONE SYSTEM.   Donald F. Whiting, New York, N. Y., assignor to Western Electric Company, Incorporated, New York, N. Y., a Corporation of New York.   Filed Dec. 28, 1918.   Serial No. 268,756.   10 Claims.   (Cl. 179—170.)

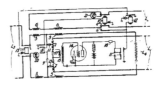

1. In a telephone system, in combination, a transmission line, an amplifier for amplifying signaling currents transmitted over one section of the line, a parallel circuit comprising a condenser and an impedance resonant to signaling current connecting the amplifier with the one line section, a separate source of signaling current, and a relay

responsive to amplified signaling currents for controlling the connection of the separate source with another section of the line.

1,327,186. BINDER. CARL E. ANDERSON, East Orange, N. J., assignor to Eastern Tool & Mfg. Company, Bloomfield, N. J. Filed Apr. 29, 1919. Serial No. 293,378. 7 Claims. (Cl. 129—38.)

1. A binder comprising a long narrow sheet metal backing bent at one end into an eye and at the other end into a member shaped to form a pair of hooks, and a wire doubled so as to form a pair of strands having a connecting part swinging in the eye, the free ends of the strands being adapted to be caught under the hooks.

1,327,187. VALVE-TRUING DEVICE. WILLIAM S. ANDERSON, Victorville, Calif. Filed Apr. 8, 1918. Serial No. 227,212. 1 Claim. (Cl. 82—1.)

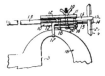

A valve truing device, comprising in combination a plate member having a central longitudinal V-shaped groove therein, a pair of cutter bars disposed longitudinally of the groove and on opposite sides thereof and permanently and rigidly mounted upon and connected with said plate member, said cutter bars being mounted with their respectively opposite faces in a common longitudinal plane, said cutter bars projecting beyond the end of said plate member and having on their ends diagonal cutting edges on their two said co-planer faces ; another plate member having a similar longitudinal V-shaped groove adapted to register over the V-shaped groove in the first mentioned plate member, and means to adjustably hold the second mentioned plate member on the first mentioned plate member and to hold a valve stem rotatable in the two V-shaped grooves, to thus hold the seat surface of a puppet valve in cutting engagement with the cutting edges of said cutter bars.

1,327,188. STEAM - BOILER. FREDERICK W. BALSTER, Wilmington, Del. Filed Aug. 30, 1917. Serial No. 189,021. 21 Claims. (Cl. 122—209.)

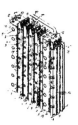

1. In a steam boiler, sections made up of corrugated side walls and corrugated top and bottom walls ; the corrugations in the side walls being offset with respect to the corrugations in the top and bottom walls and disposed in planes parallel thereto.

1,327,189. SODA-FOUNTAIN APPARATUS. CHARLES L. BASTIAN, Chicago, Ill. Filed Apr. 6, 1916. Serial No. 89,291. 19 Claims. (Cl. 225—21.)

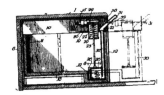

1. A soda fountain apparatus comprising a counter having a plurality of compartments therein, syrup jars removably supported in said compartments, a pump and actuating mechanism therefor in each jar adapted to deliver a measured charge of syrup therefrom, means for supplying fluid under pressure from a single source of supply to actuate the mechanism of said pumps, and means automatically operated by the removal of a jar from its compartment to prevent escape of the fluid pressure.

1,327,190. CONTAINER AND PROCESS FOR MAKING THE SAME. THOMAS WARNOCK BIGONEY, New York. N. Y. Filed Mar. 15, 1917. Serial No. 154,928. 5 Claims. (Cl. 221—60.)

1. A process of making a container which includes first pressing a piece of metal to form the body of the wall with a groove therein constituting a weakened line connecting a detachable part to the encircling body portion of the wall, said detachable part projecting outwardly from

the plane of the outer surface of the body of the wall, and then laterally displacing a portion of the metal of said projecting portion to a point laterally disposed beyond said weakened line, and spaced from said surface.

1,327,191. METHOD OF SEWING ON GARMENT-HOOKS. JOSEPH BLASI, Brooklyn, N. Y., assignor to The Singer Manufacturing Company, a Corporation of New Jersey. Filed May 8, 1918. Serial No. 233,307. 4 Claims. (Cl. 112—265.)

1. The method of attaching a garment-hook to body-fabric material which consists, in positioning the shank of an unbent garment-hook between superposed plies of fabric so that the bill-forming portion of the hook projects beyond an edge of at least one of said plies, presenting said superposed plies of fabric to a sewing machine to form a line of machine made stitches joining said plies along said edge, and lastly bending the bill-forming portion of the hook about the edge of one of said plies and into overhanging relation with said line of stitches.

1,327,192. MECHANICAL MOVEMENT. TONJES A. BOTH, Stratford, Conn., assignor to The Connecticut Electric Manufacturing Company, a Corporation of Connecticut. Filed July 12, 1919. Serial No. 310,333. 11 Claims. (Cl. 74—14.)

1. A mechanical movement comprising a rocker pivoted at one end and provided with a circular opening, an actuating member consisting of a shoe which engages said opening, a head and arms, a crank having a pin lying between the arms, and a spring bearing against the head and the crank pin, movement of the crank causing the shoe to travel around the opening without imparting movement to the rocker, and causing the crank pin to move inward between the arms and compress the spring until the parts are on a dead center, continued movement of the crank causing the spring to expand instantly and the actuating member to throw the rocker to the extreme of its movement with a snap.

1,327,193. GRAIN-SEPARATOR. CLYDE E. BRADDY, Pinebluff, Wyo. Filed Mar. 27, 1919. Serial No. 285,425. 4 Claims. (Cl. 130—23.)

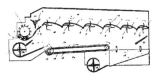

1. In a grain separator, a stationary straw rack formed of a series of grates arranged end to end, each grate com-

prising a series of bars curved upwardly and decreasing in length progressively from the front to the rear of the rack, and revoluble pickers journaled under the front end portions of the grates.

1,327,194. CHUCK. FRED E. BRIGHT, Philadelphia, Pa. Filed Apr. 23, 1917. Serial No. 163,824. 8 Claims. (Cl. 279—8.)

1. In a work holding chuck, the combination of a chuck body provided with a work seat, a jaw carrier sustained by the chuck body and adjustable relatively thereto axially of the chuck, a stem mounted on the jaw carrier and provided with a clamping jaw, said stem being movable back and forth relatively to the carrier to a limited extent axially of the chuck, and a spring sustained by the carrier and acting on the stem to move it relatively to the carrier to clamp the work.

1,327,195. TUBE. LOUIS H. BRINKMAN, Glen Ridge, N. J., assignor to Titeflex Metal Hose Corporation, a Corporation of New York. Filed May 9, 1917. Serial No. 167,510. 4 Claims. (Cl. 137—75.)

1. A tube comprising a helical strip having a central longitudinal groove and a longitudinal groove upon each side of the aforesaid groove, the central groove being much deeper than either of the others, the grooved portion at one edge of the strip nesting within the groove at the other edge, the adjacent edges of convolutions being adapted to be held against relative movement longitudinally of the tube solely by the said nested relationship of the grooved walls.

1,327,196. STAPLE-LASTING MACHINE. MATTHIAS BROCK, Boston, Mass., assignor, by mesne assignments, to United Shoe Machinery Corporation, Paterson, N. J., a Corporation of New Jersey. Filed Mar. 26, 1915. Serial No. 17,182. 22 Claims. (Cl. 12—2.)

2. In a machine of the class described, fastening inserting means, a work support having a sole supporting face provided with an offset substantially in the line of insertion, said support being adjustable about a horizontal axis lying in said offset and being also adjustable horizontally in a direction substantially perpendicular to said axis.

19. In a machine of the class described, fastening inserting mechanism, a work support movable between work receiving position and work supporting position, a treadle for actuating said inserting mechanism, and a second treadle for raising said work support, said two treadles having their treads so located that one may be operated by the ball or toe of the operator's foot while the other is operated by the heel of the same foot.

1,327,197. MATERIAL TREATED WITH CELLULOSE DERIVATIVES. JOSEPH J. BYERS, Brookline, Mass., assignor to Products Syndicate, Inc., Boston, Mass., a Corporation of Massachusetts. Filed Jan. 10, 1917. Serial No. 141,664. 10 Claims. (Cl. 91—68.)

6. As a new article of manufacture, a water-repellant fibrous material impregnated throughout with cement containing a cellulose derivative and non-oxidizing oil, and consisting of initially united fibers charged with said cement and incased with the same.

10. As a new article of manufacture, leather or other fibrous material which has been dried and then impregnated throughout with a cement which includes soluble nitro-cellulose and a non-oxidizing oil.

1,327,198. LINE-SQUARE. JOHN A. CARLSON, Idaho Falls, Idaho; C. A. Carlson, administrator of John A. Carlson, deceased, assignor to Emilia A. Carlson, Idaho Falls, Idaho. Filed June 7, 1918. Serial No. 238,699. 3 Claims. (Cl. 33—137.)

2. A device of the class described comprising a circular member, groove spoke members carried thereby, and string engaging means located above one of the diametrically arranged spoke members.

1,327,199. TWO-PIECE CAST-OFF. EDWARD CLEARY, Bridgeport, Conn., assignor to The Connecticut Web & Buckle Company, Bridgeport, Conn., a Corporation of Connecticut. Filed Sept. 3, 1918. Serial No. 252,333. 1 Claim. (Cl. 241—18.)

A locking cast-off comprising a lower member having an opening and above the opening a ball, and an upper member having an upwardly extending spring socket and provided with a slot extending more than half way around said socket to render it yieldable, the opening in the lower member receiving the spring socket and the latter yielding to receive the ball and permit lateral swinging without detachment.

1,327,200. DYEING-MACHINE. HOWARD M. DUDLEY, Philadelphia, Pa. Filed Nov. 13, 1917. Serial No. 201,759. 9 Claims. (Cl. 8—18.)

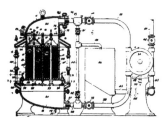

1. In a dyeing machine, in combination, a receptacle, a series of fiber chambers within the receptacle, an imperforate core within each fiber chamber, a series of imperforate hollow members capable of slidable movement over each core and capable of having fiber wound thereon, means at both ends of each fiber chamber for compressing the fiber and means for forcing a liquid through the compressed fiber mass.

1,327,201. ANCHOR. ALBERT F. EELLS, Rochester, N. Y. Filed Mar. 12, 1917. Serial No. 154,212. 8 Claims. (Cl. 114—208.)

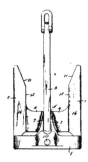

7. An anchor having a head and flukes, webs with cutting edges between the flukes with an opening between the cutting edges, said head having a concavity, a shank loosely received within said opening and having a transverse member in said concavity, and a locking member passed through the head and permitting limited play of said transverse member.

1,327,202. INTERNAL-COMBUSTION ENGINE. FREDERICK M. GUY, Jackson, Mich., assignor, by direct and mesne assignments, of one-third to Leonard J. Moeller, Detroit, Mich., and one-third to Frederick R. Sunderman, Newburgh, N. Y. Filed Aug. 6, 1917. Serial No. 184,694. 8 Claims. (Cl. 123—80.)

1. In an internal combustion engine, the combination of a cylinder; a reciprocating piston within said cylinder; multiple intake ports and multiple exhaust ports in the cylinder head; a rotary valve having multiple ports connected with and operated by the piston; cored out pockets between the ports in the cylinder head arranged to expose

the inner face of the valve to the pressure of the gases on the compression and explosion strokes to equalize the

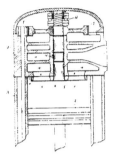

pressure on the said valve, substantially as shown and for the purposes described.

1,327,203. OVEN ATTACHMENT FOR STOVES. HANS C. HANSEN, Seattle, Wash. Filed Jan. 18, 1918. Serial No. 212,521. 4 Claims. (Cl. 126—18.)

1. In combination with a stove and stove pipe, an oven provided above the fire box of said stove, a casing spaced apart from said oven providing a passageway for the circulation of heated air around all sides of said oven, a series of deflectors provided beneath said ovens in said passageway connecting radially with said pipe, and deflectors on the sides of said oven in said passageway for diffusing the heat circulation horizontally over the sides of said oven.

1,327,204. METHOD OF CONTROLLING GUNS. JAMES BLACKLOCK HENDERSON, Lee, England. Filed Sept. 20, 1919. Serial No. 325,174. 8 Claims. (Cl. 88—2.4.)

1. In a director firing system, a gun, a sight mounted to move with the gun, an artificial target adapted to be located through said sight, means operable from a director's station at which the actual target is sighted for causing a relative displacement of said target and sight in accordance with a function of the position of the actual target whereby said gun may be pointed by moving said gun until the target may be again located through the sight.

1,327,205. CARBURETER. WILLIAM R. HESLEWOOD, Oakland, Calif., assignor of one-third to Phillip J. Rowland, Oakland, Calif. Filed Sept. 11, 1916. Serial No. 119,598. 9 Claims. (Cl. 261—99.)

1. In a carbureter, a casing, a capillary pile within said casing formed of superimposed disks having capillary interstices between adjacent surfaces, said pile having capillary feed passages and air passages intersecting said interstices, and a liquid fuel supply having communica-

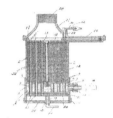

tion with said feed passages and the interstices between said disks whereby fuel is led to the surface of said air passages to be taken up by the passage of air therethrough.

1,327,206. FRICTION TRANSMISSION FOR MOTOR-DRIVEN VEHICLES. GEORGE B. JACKSON, Chicago, Ill. Filed Oct. 23, 1918. Serial No. 259,339. 16 Claims. (Cl. 180—17.)

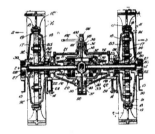

16. Friction power transmission mechanism comprising coaxial disks having opposing friction faces, means to rotate said disks in opposite directions, including means to reverse their directions of rotation, and driven friction wheels engaging friction faces of the disks on opposite sides of the axes thereof through which power is transmitted from said mechanism.

1,327,207. METHOD OF CONTROLLING TEMPERATURES. TIODOLF LIDBERG, Chicago, Ill., assignor to Electro-Thermophore Company, Chicago, Ill., a Corporation of Illinois. Filed Jan. 9, 1919. Serial No. 270,278. 5 Claims. (Cl. 219—19.)

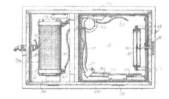

5. The method of maintaining constant the temperature of an electrically heated applicator from which heat is being dispersed which consists in heating an area by electrical means; carrying away the heat from the heated

area in a ratio comparable with that of the applicator and automatically controlling the current supplied to both heating means by a thermo-responsive device affected by said secondary heated area.

1,327,208. WEIGHING-SCALE. MORTIMER B. MILLS, Chicago, Ill., assignor to Mills Novelty Company, Chicago, Ill., a Corporation of Illinois. Filed June 27, 1917. Serial No. 177,201. 13 Claims. (Cl. 265—62.)

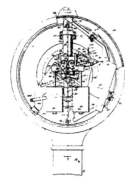

1. In a weighing-scale, the combination of mechanism adapted to be shifted by application of weight to the scale, the movement of which is not directly proportional to increase in weight applied to the scale, weight-indicating means, and means separate from, and controlled by, said mechanism for controlling said weight-indicating means and comprising a cam-device supported by, and movable responsive to, said mechanism and upon which said means rest and against which the latter move, said cam-device being constructed and arranged to cause said weight-indicating means in moving against it to have movement directly proportional to the increase in weight applied to the scale, under the disproportional movement of said mechanism.

1,327,209. MACHINE-MOTOR. FREDERICK J. OSIUS, Racine, Wis. Filed Feb. 5, 1916. Serial No. 76,238. 24 Claims. (Cl. 74—26.)

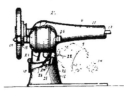

20. A supporting bracket adapted to be attached to a sewing machine frame having an arm, and a motor supporting arm pivoted to said bracket so that the motor may be moved from driving position to a position under the arm of the sewing machine frame.

1,327,210. SEWING-MACHINE MOTOR. FREDERICK J. OSIUS, Racine, Wis. Filed Feb. 26, 1917. Serial No. 151,100. 7 Claims. (Cl. 74—26.)

7. The combination with a sewing machine having a head portion and a wheel to be driven, of a clamping device, a clamping band forming part of said device and extending around a portion of the machine head, a U-

shaped member connected at one end portion to the clamping device, a bearing member fulcrumed on the other end of the U-shaped member, a motor member connected to the bearing member and positioned to have its driving

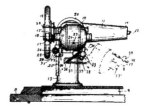

wheel engage the machine wheel and movable to an inoperative position toward the sewing end of the machine, and a spring means for yieldingly maintaining the motor in either one of its positions.

1,327,211. APPARATUS FOR REMOVING SEDIMENT FROM CATCH-BASINS OF SEWERS. GEORGE W. OTTERSON, Seattle, Wash. Filed Feb. 2, 1916. Serial No. 75,849. 6 Claims. (Cl. 210—5.)

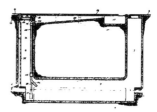

1. The combination with a sewer containing a catch-basin, of a settling bed built in in connection with the sewer at or near the ground level, a hydraulic ejector elevator for removing deposits from the catch-basin upwardly to the settling bed, and a return for water from the settling bed to the sewer.

2. The combination with a sewer catch-basin, and a man-hole opening into the same, of a settling bed built in at or near the ground level adjacent the man-hole, a hydraulic ejector elevator extending within the man-hole for removing the contents of the catch-basin upward to the settling bed, and a return for water from the settling bed to the catch-basin.

3. The combination with a sewer containing a catch-basin, of a settling bed built in in connection with the sewer at or near the ground level, a hydraulic ejector elevator for removing deposits from the catch-basin upwardly to the settling bed, and means for returning water from the settling bed to the catch-basin and for utilizing the return stream to agitate the contents.

1,327,212. CULTIVATOR. WILLIAM L. PAUL, Berkeley, Calif., assignor to Deere and Company, Moline, Ill., a Corporation of Illinois. Filed Apr. 25, 1916. Serial No. 93,403. 2 Claims. (Cl. 97—35.)

1. In a cultivator, the combination of a frame, a gang beam pivotally supported on the frame, a lever pivoted on the frame and operable to raise and lower the gang beam and having an arm extending forwardly from the pivot, a rod pivoted to the free end of said arm and extending

downwardly to connection with the gang beam, a rod pivoted to the free end of said arm and having a sliding

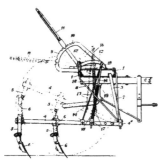

connection with the beam, and a coil spring on said rod exerting its pressure to hold the gang beam down and cooperating with the lever to lift the beam.

1,327,213. HEATING APPARATUS. ALBERT R. PRITCHARD, New York, N. Y. Filed Nov. 28, 1917. Serial No. 204,313. 7 Claims. (Cl. 257—134.)

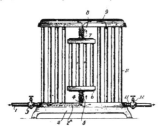

1. In a heating apparatus in combination, a radiator element, inlet connections at the lower part of said element, a second radiator element, a connection intermediate said radiator elements leading from the upper part of said first-mentioned element, a valve in said intermediate connection, a valved inlet to said first element and a valved outlet from said second-mentioned element.

1,327,214. COOLING DEVICE FOR BEDS AND SLEEPING-COMPARTMENTS. ROBERT NEWTON RICHARDSON, Los Angeles, Calif. Filed Aug. 22, 1917. Serial No. 187,633. 4 Claims. (Cl. 62—90.)

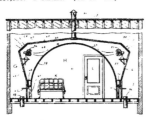

1. A cooling device for compartments including an arched inclosing wall defining the compartment to be cooled, a liquid containing trough extending along one side of the arched inclosing wall, an absorbent thickness fitted over the inclosing wall and having an edge portion thereof extended into the trough, and a guard flange extending inwardly from one of the upper edges of the trough to prevent spilling of the liquid contents of the trough.

2. A cooling device for compartments, including an arched wall defining the compartment to be cooled, liquid containing troughs extending along the sides of the arched inclosing wall at the bottom thereof, an absorbent thickness fitted over the inclosing wall and having the ends thereof extended into the troughs, and guard flanges projecting inwardly from upper edges of the troughs to prevent spilling of the liquid contents thereof.

3. A cooling device for compartments, including arched inclosing walls defining a compartment to be cooled, a housing inclosing the said walls in a spaced relation thereto, air inlets and outlets being provided in the housing, an absorbent layer extending over the inclosing walls, liquid containers receiving portions of the absorbent layer and feeding liquid thereto by capillary attraction, and fans within the space between the inclosing walls and housing to direct a current of air against the absorbent layer to produce a rapid evaporation of the liquid which is distributed thereby over the inclosing walls.

4. An apparatus of the character disclosed, an inclosure, a canopy within the inclosure, a housing within the canopy being spaced therefrom, producing an air space therebetween, said housing having openings therein communicating the air space with the inclosure and means for producing evaporation in intimate association with the canopy; an air outlet for said inclosure and an air inlet communicating with said inclosure.

1,327,215. TRAIN-CONTROL SYSTEM FOR TOY RAILWAYS. WILLIAM C. ROE, Pittsburgh, Pa., assignor of one-half to William C. Handlan, Wheeling, W. Va. Filed Sept. 27, 1919. Serial No. 326,746. 6 Claims. (Cl. 104—151.)

5. The combination with a vehicle of an electric motor carried by said vehicle for driving the latter and embodying a magnet having a differentially wound field, a multipolar armature and a commutator, said armature having a stud fixed upon its shaft adjacent to one end of the latter, a source of electric current, means for conducting current from said current source to said motor, an a fly wheel having a hub provided with a spiral slot therein, said wheel being rotatable upon said armature shaft and having said stud received in the slot of its hub, a pair of separated contacts associated with the differential windings of the magnet, a member disposed for movement between said contacts, said member having a part suitably connected to the fly wheel whereby it is actuated by sliding movement of said fly wheel along said armature shaft to move from engagement with one of said contacts into engagement with the other, said stud and said slot coöperating to cause shifting movement of the fly wheel, when the motor is stopped, through overrunning speed of the fly wheel due to momentum of the latter.

1,327,216. DOUBLE-JAW CALIPERS. LOUIS ROUANET, Ivry-Port, France, assignor to Compagnie D'Applications Mecaniques, Ivry-Port, France. Filed Aug. 4, 1917. Serial No. 184,496. 4 Claims. (Cl. 33—163.)

1. A caliper comprising in combination a support, a jaw fixed on said support, a jaw guided on said support and

movable toward and away from the fixed jaw, yielding means adapted to spread the jaws apart from each other, means for limiting the spreading apart of said jaws, two oppositely disposed contact members one on the fixed jaw and the other on the movable jaw, and two oppositely

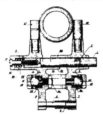

disposed gaging members one on the fixed jaw and the other on the movable jaw, the distance between said gaging members being in a definite relation and preferably equal to the distance between the opposite outer surfaces of the contact members.

1,327,217. STOCKING AND METHOD OF MAKING THE SAME. ROBERT W. SCOTT, Boston, Mass., assignor, by mesne assignments, to Scott & Williams, Incorporated, a Corporation of Massachusetts. Filed July 7, 1916. Serial No. 108,069. 14 Claims. (Cl. 66—4.)

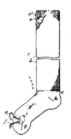

1. A stocking comprising a seamless toe, foot and heel of plain fabric, a tubular leg continuous with foot and heel of multiple-course accordion fabric having a greater number of wales than the foot, and having an integral welt of multiple-course accordion fabric at the top thereof.

1,327,218. BLOWER. ADOLPH A. THOMMEN, Chicago, Ill. Aug. 30, 1917. Serial No. 188,899. 1 Claim. (Cl. 230—11.)

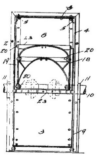

The combination in a blower with a convolute casing having lateral inlets and a tangential outlet, of a rotor

formed with concavo-convex tapered blades having edges converging toward the inlets, spaced side rings connecting the extremities of the blades, transverse braces for the rings and blades, the forward edges of the blades being arranged approximately on line with the rear wall of the preceding blade and each of said transverse braces being connected at its ends to the extremities of one of the ·blades and at its center to the central rear portion of the next foremost blade.

1,327,219. UNDERSTRUCTURE FOR SUPPORTING RAILWAY-TRACKS. EDMOND FRANÇOIS LEOPOLD VAGNEUX, Dijon, France. Filed Apr. 14, 1919. Serial No. 290,023. 1 Claim. (Cl. 238—27.)

Understructure for railway track comprising runner ties including two transversely disposed heads of reinforced concrete, a metallic beam I-shaped in cross section incased within said heads, asymmetrical joint ties each comprising a transversely disposed head similar to the runner tie head on one side and a longitudinally disposed reinforced concrete tie block on the other side below the joint, another metallic beam I-shaped in cross section incased at one end in said last mentioned head and at the other end in said tie block, symmetrical joint ties in a straight alinement also comprising two longitudinally disposed oblong tie blocks of reinforced concrete, another metallic beam I-shaped in cross section incased in said oblong tie blocks, symmetrical joint frames at points at which the track is curved comprising two longitudinally disposed oblong reinforced concrete tie blocks and two additional metallic beams I-shaped in cross section incased in said last mentioned tie blocks.

1,327,220. PROCESS OF TREATING FOOD. ALBERT BABENDREER, Ocean Springs, Miss., assignor to Whole Grain Wheat Company, Phoenix, Ariz., a Corporation of Arizona. Filed Sept. 17, 1917. Serial No. 191,792. 4 Claims. (Cl. 99—11.)

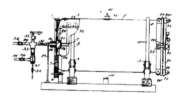

1. The process of treating matured grain to prepare it for food, which consists in partially filling a receptacle with the grain and such amount of liquid that on completion of the process the treated grain will substantially fill the receptacle, sealing the receptacle and heating the receptacle and contents, the receptacle being given movement while being treated, to mix the grain and liquid and cause the heat to permeate the grain and cook it, and cooling the receptacle and grain, whereby the cooked grain is maintained in the sealed receptacle without change and with all food elements retained.

1,327,221. METHOD OF PREPARING PULP. CARL BACHE-WIIG, Portland, Me. Filed Feb. 20, 1919. Serial No. 278,257. 8 Claims. (Cl. 92—11.)

1. The method of preparing pulp from cellulosic material which consists in treating the material with sodium chlorid and subsequently cooking the mass with a bisulfite pulp forming liquor until substantially all the lingeous matter has been freed from the fiber.

1,327,222. PROCESS FOR THE REGENERATION OF DECOLORIZING-CARBONS. GEORGE BLARDONE, New Orleans, La. Filed July 9, 1917. Serial No. 179,577. 3 Claims. (Cl. 127—2.)

1. That process for the regeneration or revivification of decolorizing and deodorizing carbons which consists in washing the said carbon with a solution of sodium bisulfite.

1,327,223. SUPPLY OUTFIT FOR VEHICLES, &c. LOUIS M. BOYLE, Los Angeles, Calif. Filed Nov. 29, 1918. Serial No. 204,717. 9 Claims. (Cl. 224—29.)

1. The combination with a vehicle running board or like support, of spaced and substantially parallel positioning members adjustably mounted upon the running board and movable toward and away from each other, a plurality of independent and similarly shaped containers resting upon the running board between the positioning members and having flat faces which fit closely against each other, the exposed outer sides of the containers presenting a substantially continuous and flush outer surface owing to the similar shape of the containers, a clamping member extending transversely across the top of the several containers, and straps connecting the ends of the clamping member to the respective positioning members on the running board for coöperation therewith to clamp the several containers upon the running board.

1,327,224. ADJUSTABLE JACKET. ROYER S. BUCH, York, Pa. Filed May 19, 1919. Serial No. 298,223. 4 Claims. (Cl. 22—112.)

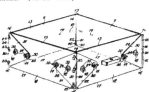

3. A jacket of the character described including side and end sections; staples secured to said sections; corners consisting of plates adjustably secured together, said plates having slots through which the staples on the side and end sections are adapted to respectively project; and securing means extending through the projecting portions of said staples; substantially as described.

1,327,225. PRESS-ROLL ARRANGEMENT FOR PAPER-MAKING MACHINES. JAMES K. DARBY, Chillicothe, Ohio. Filed June 7, 1916. Serial No. 102,194. 4 Claims. (Cl. 92—49.)

1. In a paper making machine, the combination with a pair of press rolls adapted to allow the paper to pass therebetween, and positioned in contact with each other whereby one of said rolls is frictionally rotated by the other and

270 O. G.—5

an auxiliary press roll adapted to coöperate with one of said press rolls to form a second pair of press rolls in the path of travel of the paper all of said rolls being of sub

stantially the same diameter and mechanically operated means coöperating between said auxiliary press roll and one of said first mentioned press rolls for rotating said auxiliary press roll.

1,327,226. WATCH - ESCAPEMENT. CHARLES E. DE LONG, New York, N. Y. Continuation of application Serial No. 18,470, filed Apr. 1, 1915. This application filed July 13, 1916, Serial No. 109,042. Renewed June 12, 1919. Serial No. 303,769. 14 Claims. (Cl. 58—121.)

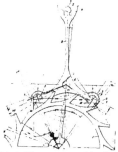

1. In a detached lever escapement for timepieces, an escape wheel having teeth provided with lifting faces, a lever, an entrance and an exit pallet each having a lifting face coöperating with the lifting face of a tooth of the escape wheel to produce thereby the required angular displacement of the lever, each of said pallets traversing the lever at right angles to the face of the lever and interlocked with said lever against displacement of their lifting faces in said lever.

1,327,227. METAL WHEEL. ERNEST E. EINFELDT, Davenport, Iowa, assignor to G. Watson French, Nathaniel French, Joseph L. Hecht, and W. H. Stackhouse, Davenport, Iowa, composing the Firm of French & Hecht, Davenport, Iowa. Filed Apr. 15, 1919. Serial No. 290,275. 3 Claims. (Cl. 21—31.)

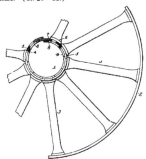

3. In a wheel, the combination of a hub comprising inner and outer layers of material of cylindrical form, the

said inner layer being provided with cavities, and spokes provided with riveting heads and shoulders fastening the spokes to the outer layer, the said heads being seated in the cavities of the inner layer.

1,327,228. MACHINE FOR KNITTING LACEWORK. JOHN EPPLER, Philadelphia, Pa. Filed June 13, 1918. Serial No. 239,746. 13 Claims. (Cl. 66—33.)

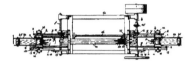

1. In a machine for knitting lace, the combination with a pattern chain drum and means to reciprocate and intermittently rotate the drum, of a sliding lever reciprocable with the drum, means controlled by the lever to lock the drum from turning, means normally retaining the lever in locking position, and means adapted, in the receding movement of the drum and lever, to actuate the lever to release said holding means.

1,327,229. ANIMAL-TRAP. CARL ALBIN SYREJUS ERICKSON, Norcross, Minn. Filed June 5, 1915, Serial No. 32,328. Renewed July 24, 1919. Serial No. 312,981. 1 Claim. (Cl. 43—19.)

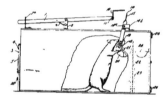

An animal trap, including a cage having pivotally positioned thereon a closure for the entrance-opening thereof, said closure carrying a fixed angular latch with a notch in its lower edge, a bifurcated guide on top of said cage, an automatically engaging lever received by the notch of said latch, a second lever fulcrumed upon said cage and moving in the same direction as the length of the first-referred to lever, said first-referred to lever carrying an angular bracket cut-out and bifurcated to receive said second lever, said second lever having notches in its lateral edges for engagement with the bifurcation of said angular bracket, and a tread-mill member hung in the sides of said cage, said second lever having eccentric and slidable connection with said tread-mill member.

1,327,230. INSECT-POISON-SUPPLY CONTAINER. LUKE J. FAIRBANKS, Los Angeles, Calif. Filed Jan. 7, 1919. Serial No. 270,006. 4 Claims. (Cl. 43—22.)

1. A container of the character described, including a hollow shell having an opening in one of the inclosing walls thereof, a tubular arm extending inwardly within the shell and communicating with the opening, and a guard plate ex-

tending transversely across an end of the arm and held in a spaced relation thereto to provide small passages around the edge of the guard plate through which insects can enter or leave the tubular arm, the said arm terminating in a spaced relation to the walls of the shell so that the level of any contents within the shell will tend to assume a position below the end of the tubular arm, regardless of the position in which the container is supported.

1,327,231. SPIRAL BED-SPRING. WILLIAM E. FRANK, St. Louis, Mo., assignor to Foster Bros. Mfg. Co., St Louis, Mo., a Corporation of Missouri. Filed Mar. 11, 1919. Serial No. 281,902. 1 Claim. (Cl. 5—25.)

In a bed bottom having side pieces connected by transverse members, hook-shaped members adapted to support the bed bottom upon the side rails of a bedstead, said members passing under and affording a rest for said side pieces, and links pivoted to said transverse members and to said hook-shaped members, said links adapted to swing in vertical planes and constituting means whereby said bed bottom is adapted for support on bedsteads of different widths.

1,327,232. THREAD-NIPPER-RELEASING DEVICE FOR SEWING-MACHINES. GEORGE S. GATCHELL, Roselle Park, N. J., assignor to The Singer Manufacturing Company, a Corporation of New Jersey. Filed May 21, 1918. Serial No. 235,772. 15 Claims. (Cl. 112—254.)

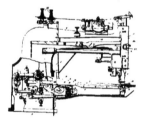

1. In a sewing machine, in combination, stitch-forming mechanism including an eye-pointed needle and a thread-carrying looper coöperating therewith to form stitches, an intermittently acting thread-nipper for arresting the movement of the looper-thread from the supply during a certain period of each stitch-forming cycle, and normally ineffective means acting automatically upon the reversal of the machine to open said nipper and release the looper-thread.

1,327,233. CARBURETER. WILLIAM W. GRANT, Brooklyn, N. Y. Filed Oct. 23, 1916. Serial No. 127,203. 10 Claims. (Cl. 261—52.)

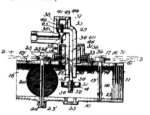

7. In a carbureter construction, a body providing a mixing chamber, an air inlet and a mixture outlet, a fuel sup-

ply pipe leading into the chamber, a drip cup supported in the chamber to receive fuel passing from the pipe into the chamber, a valve mounted in the pipe and opening toward the chamber under suction, and a valve supported by the cup and controlling rate of passage of fuel from the pipe.

1,327,234. STORAGE - BATTERY ELEMENT. EUGENE HANDLER, Newark, N. J., assignor to General Lead Batteries Company, a Corporation of Delaware. Filed May 5, 1916. Serial No. 95,535. 4 Claims. (Cl. 204—29.)

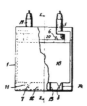

2. A storage battery element comprising a plurality of plates, a terminal structure secured to the said plates near one plate corner and a separating and spacing means corresponding to each of the other plate corners, each corner having one of said means nearer to it than to any other corner.

1,327,235. MIXING - VALVE FOR STEAM - HEATED WATER-SUPPLY SYSTEMS. PETER STEWART HANTON, Kew, Victoria, Australia. Filed Aug. 20, 1917. Serial No. 187,036. 1 Claim. (Cl. 277—18.)

A mixing valve for steam and water comprising a valve casing having a circular seat therein defined by an upstanding circular wall, a steam supply conduit opening centrally on the base of said seat, a water supply conduit surrounding said steam supply conduit and opening on the base of said seat, a circular valve of slightly less diameter than said wall arranged in said seat and forming with said wall a narrow annular passage through which the mixture of steam and water passes and means for moving said valve vertically to control the flow of fluids from said conduits, said valve when raised, being disposed within said wall, whereby the fluids pass through the annular passage in a thin film, said valve having fluid escapement vents formed therethrough and opening above the seat between the steam and water conduits.

1,327,236. PENCIL. HENRY HESS, Philadelphia, Pa. Filed Nov. 27. 1915. Serial No. 63,758. 3 Claims. (Cl. 120—83.)

3. In a pencil, the combination of a marking lead or crayon, a covering applied thereto to reinforce the same and produce a core, and a second covering applied to the

core to form a holding body, the ends of said two coverings sloping backwardly from the end of the lead, the reinforcing covering at a greater slope than the surround-

ing covering, and said two coverings being adaptel to be removed in sections to expose the point of the marking lead.

1,327,237. MECHANISM FOR FASTENING TOGETHER NESTED TIRE-CASINGS. CHARLES M. HORTON, Elizabeth, N. J., assignor to The Singer Manufacturing Company, a Corporation of New Jersey. Filed Oct. 3, 1916. Serial No. 123,582. 19 Claims. (Cl. 112—2.)

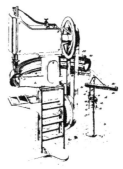

1. The combination with a fastening mechanism for securing together nested tire casings, of work-supporting means sustaining the nested casings internally and externally.

1,327,238. GREASE-CUP. SAMUEL HOUGH, Atco, N. J., and STEPHAN BAADER, Philadelphia, Pa. Filed May 26, 1919. Serial No. 299,780. 7 Claims. (Cl. 184—45.)

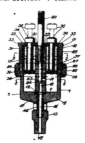

5. A grease cup including a section providing a well and having an outlet passage ; a casing having chambers communicating with said well and a portion having a passage communicating with said outlet passage, said portion including a port communicating with said well and with the passage in said portion ; a valve for cutting off said port to said well passage ; a cap secured to said first section ; rods slidable through said cap and into said chambers ; pistons secured to said rods and operative within said chambers ; and coiled springs operative to move said pistons to force the grease out of said chambers into said well and through said port ; substantially as described.

1,327,239. WATERPROOF COMPOSITION AND METHOD OF MAKING THE SAME. PATRICK W. KIERNAN, Lowell, Mass., assignor to Lowell Bleachery, Lowell, Mass., a Corporation of Massachusetts. Filed July 25, 1918. Serial No. 246,686. 2 Claims. (Cl. 134—15.)

1. A water proof composition consisting of an emulsion of 810 parts of paraffin, 125 parts of petrolatum, the reaction products of 112 parts of a fatty acid and 27 parts of soda ash, and water.

1,327,240. COASTER. WILLIAM KIRKPATRICK and WILLIAM WIEGNER, San Francisco, Calif. Filed May 13, 1919. Serial No. 298,323. 2 Claims. (Cl. 208—165.)

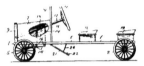

1. A coaster comprising a body; a pair of rear wheels mounted to support the rear end of said body; an axletree pivotally mounted under the front end of the body; a pair of wheels pivotally mounted on the axletree; a hood-housing on the front of the body; a screen secured to the front of the housing to represent a radiator; a windshield mounted upon the back of the housing; a steering post rotatably mounted in the front of the housing and the windshield; means operatively connecting the steering post and the axletree whereby the coaster may be steered; a steering wheel connected to one end of the steering post; and a drag brake pivotally mounted upon the under side of the body and having lateral extensions extending beyond the body to accommodate the feet of an operator; and flexible means for normally elevating the drag brake.

1,327,241. TAG FEEDING AND PRINTING MACHINE. FREDERICK KOHNLE, Dayton, Ohio, assignor to The Monarch Tag Company, Dayton, Ohio, a Corporation of Ohio. Filed Sept. 5, 1916. Serial No. 118,364. 11 Claims. (Cl. 101—292.)

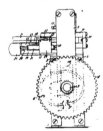

1. A machine of the character described, a support providing a table capable of tracking a gang tag strip, said table longitudinally having a shoulder extending above the plane of the table against which one edge of the tag strip engages, a carriage extending across the table and mounted to reciprocate longitudinally parallel with and over the table, said carriage having a finger pivoted to the carriage and extending forwardly between the carriage and table adapted to engage and advance the tag in one carriage stroke, and release from the tag strip in a reverse stroke, a reciprocating member movable transversely to the carriage for operating upon the tag strip, and means for reciprocating said carriage and member in timed relation.

1,327,242. INFANT'S BATH-WAGON. MABEL ELTON LA RUE and EUGENE C. LA RUE, South Pasadena, Calif. Filed Feb. 11, 1918. Serial No. 216,512. 1 Claim. (Cl. 45—17.)

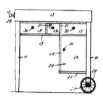

An infant's bath wagon comprising a box-like structure opened at its upper side and having its bottom side covered with a waterproof lining of glass, a pair of short wheeled legs supporting the box like structure at one end and a pair of longer legs supporting the structure at its opposite end, a lifting and guiding handle secured transversely across the latter end of the structure and functioning as a towel rack, and a plurality of compartments carried beneath the structure, the larger compartment space being located at the forward end of the wagon and supported by the wheeled legs, whereby the bulk of the weight will be carried by the latter and whereby unobstructed leg and foot room will be provided beneath the back end of the wagon.

1,327,243. LOCOMOTIVE. WILLIAM C. LAWSON, Roanoke, Va. Filed Mar. 18, 1919. Serial No. 283,350. 30 Claims. (Cl. 104—235.)

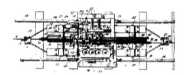

1. In a cable locomotive, the combination with a vehicle member, of a cable drum thereon, means on the member for rotating the drum in either of opposite directions, a propelling cable that moves around the drum, and means constantly engaged with the cable for automatically taking up the slack of the propeller cable in rear of the drum irrespective of the direction of rotation of said drum.

1,327,244. MATCH-STRIKE. PHILIP H. LETTRE, Attleboro Falls, Mass. Filed Aug. 22, 1919. Serial No. 319,168. 2 Claims. (Cl. 51—20.)

1. A match scratching device including a body portion bent intermediate its length to provide a pair of parallel side portions, the edges of said parallel sections forming guideways, and a match engaging prong associated with each guideway.

1,327,245. FILM-WINDING ATTACHMENT. CLARENCE H. MANSFIELD, El Paso, Tex. Filed Oct. 9, 1916. Serial No. 124,661. 4 Claims. (Cl. 242—71.)

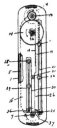

1. In a film winding attachment, a spool upon which the exposed portions of the film are to be wound, a gear mechanism for driving said spool, a bar having a rack at one end in mesh with one of the gears of the mechanism, an operating pin secured to the rack bar, a second rack formed on said bar at or near its lower end, a movable bracket having a rack adjacent to the lower rack of the bar, a means connecting the two oppositely disposed racks and arranged to permit only of the elevation of the bracket during the downward movement of the rack bar and a stop pin carried by the bracket and arranged to limit the downward movement of said rack bar.

1,327,246. CURRYCOMB. HERMAN A. MECKLENBURG, Gilby, N. D. Filed Mar. 17, 1919. Serial No. 283,006. 3 Claims. (Cl. 119—88.)

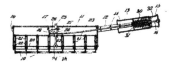

1. A curry comb including a casing, concentric toothed rings mounted in spaced concentric relation within the casing, scraping rings disposed in frictional contact with the toothed rings, a handle carried by the casing, and means carried by the handle and connected with the scraping rings for moving said rings across the faces of the toothed rings.

1,327,247. EVAPORATOR. WILLIAM MEISCHKE-SMITH, San Francisco, Calif., assignor to Shell Company of California, a Corporation of California. Filed Mar. 26, 1918. Serial No. 224,913. 1 Claim. (Cl. 196—8.)

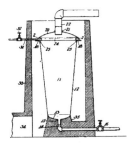

An evaporating apparatus comprising a still having side walls forming an inverted frusto conical shell, means for delivering oil to the inner surface of said walls in a thin film, said oil delivery means consisting of a conduit inclosing the upper edge of the side walls of the still and having an open circular slot on the inside of the side walls forming an opening between the inner walls of the still and the edge of the slot, means for delivering oil to the conduit, means for drawing off vapors from the still, and means for drawing off residuum from the still.

1,327,248. DISPENSING-VEHICLE. JASON B. MOODY, Houston, Tex. Filed June 10, 1918. Serial No. 239,293. 7 Claims. (Cl. 296—21.)

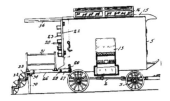

1. In a dispensing vehicle, the combination of a vehicle-body having provision for storing merchandise therein, a counter at one end of the body, doors at the counter end of the body carrying sample display racks, a platform mounted below the doors, and steps leading up to the platform.

1,327,249. OVERHEAD CONVEYER SYSTEM. RICHARD OEHLER, St. Louis, Mo. Filed Sept. 4, 1919. Serial No. 321,529. 4 Claims. (Cl. 104—101.)

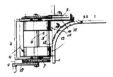

1. In an overhead conveyer system, a stationary rail, a removable rail section, movable into and out of coöperative relationship with the stationary rail, a side rail, a curved rail section movable into and out of coöperative relationship with the stationary rail and the side rail, a pair of shafts supporting the curved rail section and first named rail section, respectively, mechanism for coöperatively turning said shafts to place said rail sections selectively in coöperative relationship as aforesaid, and a stop device to prevent de-railment from the side rail when the curved rail section is out of coöperative relationship with the side rail.

1,327,250. OSCILLATING MOTOR. WILLIAM J. O'LEARY, Montreal, Quebec, Canada, assignor to Marguerite V. O'Leary, Montreal, Quebec, Canada. Filed Feb. 28, 1918. Serial No. 219,627. 13 Claims. (Cl. 74—55.)

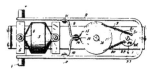

1. A device of the character described, comprising, in combination, a vibrating member, connector means secured to said vibrating member, a pulley to be oscillated, a pair of bands secured to said connector means and extend-

ing in opposite directions on each side of said pulley, anchoring means to which the ends of said bands are secured, and devices for alternately tensioning said bands to cause alternate rotative movement of said pulley.

1,327,251. PUNCTURE-TESTER. FRED OVERMYER, Toledo, Ohio. Filed Mar. 31, 1919. Serial No. 286,542. 2 Claims. (Cl. 73—51.)

1. In a leak detector, a shell, a gasket located in the shell and having a tapering interior surface, means connected to the shell for detecting movement of the air through the gasket.

1,327,252. CONTROLLING-VALVE FOR MULTIPLE FUEL-SUPPLY PIPES. ANDREW J. PAULSON, Salt Lake City, Utah. Filed Mar. 26, 1918. Serial No. 224,910. 2 Claims. (Cl. 251—107.)

1. In a valve of the class described the combination of a casing having a tapered axial bore, and having recesses in its inner wall which open into said bore; centrally bored lugs integral with said casing and extending radially therefrom, and with the bore of each opening into the axial bore of said casing two of which bores open into said recesses; a transversely bored valve operable in said casing the bores of which may be brought into alinement with the bores in said lugs in pairs to conduct liquid fuel from a highly volatile fuel tank to the cylinders of an engine or to the carbureter as desired, also from a less volatile fuel tank to the same carbureter and from a water supply to the carbureter as desired; and means to rotate said valve to open and close said bores.

1,327,253. WHEEL. ARTHUR PRATHER, Skidmore, Mo. Filed Dec. 2, 1918. Serial No. 265,009. 2 Claims. (Cl. 21—162.)

1. A wheel attachment comprising in combination with a tire having notches formed around its inner face, ad-

jacent the edges, and terminating below the outer face, plates engaging the sides of the felly and having their upper ends received in the notches, and means for securing the plates to the felly.

1,327,254. APPARATUS FOR PREPARING POTATOES. BERNHARD REMMERS, Philadelphia, Pa., assignor, by mesne assignments, to Armour Grain Company, Chicago, Ill., a Corporation of New Jersey. Filed June 13, 1916. Serial No. 103,370. 2 Claims. (Cl. 100—47.)

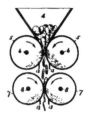

1. A machine for preparing potatoes and the like, comprising a pair of oppositely rotatable hollow cylinders disposed in parallel relation with their axes inclined to the horizontal and having perforated walls spaced a fixed distance apart, said cylinders so mounted relative to each other as to receive the potatoes therebetween and to squeeze the pulp from the skins through the perforations into the cylinder interiors and discharge the same from the lower ends thereof while passing the skins onward between the cylinders.

1,327,255. DUMP-CAR. WILLIAM B. REYNOLDS, Roundup, Mont. Filed May 16, 1919. Serial No. 297,617. 7 Claims. (Cl. 214—47.)

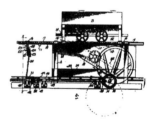

1. A dump comprising a track having a hinged section, a car on said track and provided with a bottom hinged at one end, means for raising and lowering the other end of said track section, and means for supporting the body of the car while its bottom is lowered, substantially as set forth.

1,327,256. ATOMIZING DEVICE FOR ROTARY OIL-BURNERS. JOHN SCHEMINGER, Jr., Providence, R. I. Filed Aug. 27, 1919. Serial No. 320,212. 6 Claims. (Cl. 158—28.)

1. A rotatable spray plate or atomizing device having openings therein of oval form having their axes extending approximately in the plane of the plate at an

angle to its axis, the metal of the plate being pressed into concavo-convex form on opposite sides of said openings

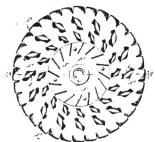

and having the concave surfaces thereof facing at the mouth of the opening.

1,327,257. SELF-OPENING GATE. CECIL FRAY SEBRING, Laurel, Nebr. Filed Apr. 13, 1918. Serial No. 228,395. 1 Claim. (Cl. 39—34.)

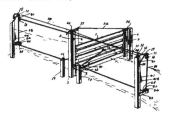

In a gate operating mechanism, the combination, of a gate hinged at one end thereof, a pair of supporting posts positioned on the opposite sides of the gate, a pair of guide posts positioned at each side of the gate adjacent thereto, spaced pulleys carried by each of the supporting posts and arranged in alinement with each other, guide pulleys secured to the guide posts, and a flexible cable extending around the uppermost pulley and then downward around the lowermost pulleys and forming vertical runs and hand operating portions and then inwardly and around the pulleys carried by the guide posts and then having the terminals thereof connected to the opposite sides of the gate, as and for the purpose specified.

1,327,258. GRIDIRON. JEAN JACQUES SÉGUIER, Castres, France. Filed June 20, 1916. Serial No. 104,672. 1 Claim. (Cl. 53—5.)

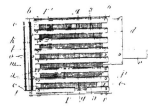

In a grid-iron the combination of a series of grid bars, two side walls parallel with said grid bars forming sup-

porting feet for the grid-iron and extending beyond the extremities of said grid bars, two transverse bars connecting said side walls and upon which the extremities of the grid bars are supported, two transverse rods connecting said walls, a detachable wire gauze sheet of fine mesh substantially level with the bottom edges of said side walls and having its front edge bent upward to rest on one of said transverse rods a hook shaped plate attached to and extending along the rear edge of said wire gauze sheet and adapted to be hooked over the other of said transverse rods a second bent plate attached to and extending along said rear edge of said gauze sheet and forming a handle for detaching the same, a gravy trough extending across the front side of the grid-iron and the handle attached to said gravy trough.

1,327,259. SHORT-CIRCUITING MECHANISM. JAMES LOMAS TONGE, Apponaug, R. I. Filed Feb. 18, 1919. Serial No. 277,713. 2 Claims. (Cl. 200—44.)

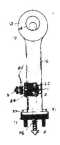

2. A device of the character described comprising a tubular metal standard having a suitable attaching base, a conductor member in said standard and interposed into the electric circuit, insulating material for positively supporting said conductor within said standard, a yieldable member on said conductor in contact with the source of electric energy, a binding post supported on the outside wall of said standard insulated therefrom and connected to said conductor and to which binding post the normal circuit wire may be connected, a key-actuated U-shaped sliding plate having a projection adapted to engage the upper end of said conductor, and means whereby the operating of said plate makes a yielding contact with said conductor to short circuit the current through said standard.

1,327,260. DYESTUFFS AND PROCESS OF MAKING SAME. ALVIN S. WHEELER, Chapel Hill, N. C. Filed Dec. 9, 1918. Serial No. 265,988. 13 Claims. (Cl. 8—1.)
1. The process of preparing dyestuffs which comprises dissolving a hydroxynaphthoquinone having less than three hydroxyl groups in a solvent, treating the solution with a halogen in excess, separating the halogenated product, and forming a salt thereof, substantially as described.

1,327,261. TIRE-CARRIER. LULOFF WILSON, Chicago, Ill. Filed June 21, 1917. Serial No. 176,160. 5 Claims. (Cl. 224—29.)
5. A tire carrier comprising a semi-circular ring segment having a channel shaped leg depending therefrom on each side thereof, a vertical bar adjustably connected to each leg, a channel shaped bracket member adapted to be connected to each side of the vehicle, a longitudinally

extending bar adjustably connected to each bracket member and pivotally connected to each leg and an angular

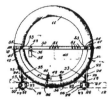

brace member pivotally connected to each leg and each bracket.

1,327,262. SALINE-OPERATED ELECTRIC CIRCUIT AND ELECTRORESPONSIVE APPARATUS. HENRY WYGODSKY, New York, N. Y. Filed Dec. 29, 1916. Serial No. 139,698. 1 Claim. (Cl. 4—5.)

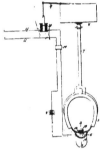

The combination with a urinal and a flushing device; of an electro-magnet in operative connection with said device, a source of electrical energy, a conductive ring arranged in said urinal, an insulator carried by said ring, a conductive convex disk carried by said insulator, and an electrical conductor passed from said ring to said disk through said electro-magnet and said source of energy, said disk and ring being adapted to be electrically connected by a saline fluid interposed therebetween and electrically disconnected by the substitution of water for said saline fluid.

1,327,263. PROCESS FOR THE CONVERSION OF LIQUIDS, FLUIDS, AND OILS. JOSEPH H. ADAMS, Brooklyn, N. Y., assignor to The Texas Company, Houston, Tex., a Corporation of Texas. Filed Mar. 30, 1911, Serial No. 618,011. Renewed Apr. 11, 1919. Serial No. 289,425. 31 Claims. (Cl. 196—25.)

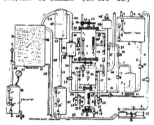

27. A method of converting oils to obtain a relatively large yield of lower boiling oils which consists in heating

the oils to be converted, in liquid form, in a chamber to a cracking temperature while maintaining a vapor pressure on said oils in said chamber solely by the vapors generated therein, and condensing said generated vapors by passing them through connections to a condenser all in open communication so as to insure a substantially uniform pressure from the chamber through the condenser and withdrawing the lower boiling oils from the condenser as the ultimate product.

1,327,264. PNEUMATIC VULCANIZING-CORE. ALFRED O. ALSTEN, Worcester, Mass. Filed May 3, 1916. Serial No. 95,221. 9 Claims. (Cl. 18—45.)

2. As an article of manufacture, a single tube pneumatic vulcanizing core formed entirely of substantially non-expansible but flexible material and having means whereby when inflated its diameter will be increased, said means embodying a flexible joint extending longitudinally of the tube whereby the tube may be bodily expanded notwithstanding the fact that it is made of non-expansible material.

1,327,265. TRAILER DRAFT CONNECTION. WILLIAM N. BOOTH, Detroit, Mich. Original application filed July 23, 1917, Serial No. 182,178. Divided and this application filed Feb. 20, 1919. Serial No. 278,281. 3 Claims. (Cl. 213—67.)

1. A trailer draft connection, comprising a member for connection with the tractor, a member attachable to the trailer, and a universal coupling between said members comprising a ball and socket in permanent engagement with each other, the socket member being attached to one of the members of said draft connection and the ball having a detachable engagement with the other of said members.

1,327,266. AUTO BURGLAR-ALARM. GEORGE M. BRADLEY, Lansing, Mich. Filed Nov. 24, 1917. Serial No. 203,710. 1 Claim. (Cl. 116—1.)

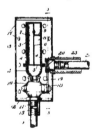

In an alarm device for automobiles, the combination of a dashboard, a motor, an alarm device adapted to be operated by expulsion of fluid products from the motor, an actuating element fitted in the dashboard, a perforated guard casing inclosing the alarm device, a valve inclosed within the guard casing and controlling communication between the alarm device and motor, gearing inclosed within the guard casing for opening and closing the valve, a rod or shaft extending between and connecting said gearing with said actuating element, and a guard tube extending between and connecting the perforated guard casing with the dashboard and inclosing the rod or shaft between the actuating element and the gearing.

1,327,267. PROCESS OF WELDING. LEON B. BREWSTER and FRANK WEISEHAN, Cleveland, Ohio, assignors to The Ferro Machine and Foundry Company, Cleveland. Ohio, a Corporation of Ohio. Filed Dec. 7, 1917. Serial No. 205,926. 4 Claims. (Cl. 219—12.)

1. The process of depositing metal from a fusible electrode having a high temperature point of fusion upon a body of metal having a high temperature point of fusion which consists in making the metal to receive the deposited metal one terminal of a circuit, and a fusible electrode another terminal of the circuit, bringing the fusible electrode into contact with the said metal object and holding the same in contact until the heat generated by the resistance of the current passing from the electrode to the metal object causes a heating and fusion of that portion of the metal object which is directly adjacent the electrode and causes a portion of the electrode to be melted and welded to the metal object and then removing the electrode.

1,327,268. METHOD OF SEALING CREVICES IN ROCK FORMATIONS. GEORGE W. CHRISTIANS, Chattanooga. Tenn. Filed June 9, 1919. Serial No. 302,795. 5 Claims. (Cl. 61—36.)

1. The method of sealing crevices in fissured rock formations consisting in extending a conduit to the place where a crevice occurs, forcing a material which is fluid when heated but nearly solid when cool, through said conduit and into said crevice, generating heat within the conduit, and utilizing the heat generated for maintaining the material in heated condition during its passage through said conduit and into said crevice.

1,327,269. APPARATUS FOR USE IN SEALING CREVICES IN ROCK FORMATIONS. GEORGE W. CHRISTIANS, Chattanooga, Tenn. Filed June 9, 1919. Serial No. 302,796. 11 Claims. (Cl. 61—36.)

1. An apparatus designed for forcing heated fluid material beneath the surface of the earth, comprising a conduit for conducting said material, means in the conduit for maintaining the interior of said conduit in heated condition while the heated material is passing through the same and means for forcing material into said conduit.

1,327,270. MEANS FOR LOCKING GRATE-BARS. LEONARD L. CLOSE, Marion, Ind., assignor to Marion Foundry Corporation, Marion, Ind., a Corporation. Filed Mar. 1, 1919. Serial No. 280,110. 3 Claims. (Cl. 126—176.)

1. In a device of the character described comprising a plurality of supporting rails for grate-bars having a series of spaced recesses, horizontally disposed integral lips formed on both sides of the rails and adjacent the recesses therein, grate-bars arranged to oscillate in said recesses, and locking-blocks having slots terminating in lateral recesses and adapted to be let down over the upper edges of the rail and to one side of the lips, said locking-blocks susceptible of being moved longitudinally to engage the lips and close the mouths of said recesses.

1,327,271. PROCESS OF EXTRACTING OILS FROM COAL-TAR. HUBERT HENRY COMBER and JAMES WRIGHT STALKER, Winnipeg, Manitoba, Canada. Filed June 17, 1918. Serial No. 240,387. 1 Claim. (Cl. 196—28.)

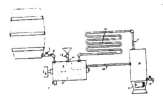

The process of treating coal tar to separate the oils therefrom which consists in thoroughly mixing by agitation in a vessel a quantity of wood alcohol with a quantity of coal tar in the cold state, then draining off the upper layer of liquid comprising the oils and wood alcohol compound, then introducing the liquid drained off from the former vessel into a further vessel containing water to effect the separation of the oils through the compounding of the water with the wood alcohol and finally draining off the oils from the bottom of the latter vessel.

1,327,272. LIQUID-PUMP. KARL DELLGREN, Västervik, Sweden. Filed Nov. 14, 1918. Serial No. 262,570. 4 Claims. (Cl. 103—85.)

1. In a liquid pump, the combination with the pump plunger and a regulating valve for controlling the amount of liquid forced by the pump, of a lever pivotally connected

intermediate its ends with said pump plunger, means connected to one end of said lever to oscillate same, and means engaging with the other end of said lever for forming a stationary fulcrum for said lever when the counter pressure upon the plunger due to the adjustment of said regulating valve does not exceed a certain value, while allowing the lever to swing without imparting any motion to the plunger when said pressure exceeds said certain value.

1,327,273. APPARATUS FOR FLINGING OFF SUPER-FLUOUS COATING WHEN TINNING, PAINTING, OR THE LIKE. SVEN AUGUST ESKILSON, Stockholm, Sweden. Filed Dec. 12, 1917. Serial No. 206,760. 11 Claims. (Cl. 91—59.1.)

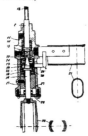

5. In an apparatus of the class described, a fixed driving element, and a portable carrier having a plurality of jaws, and means for transmitting a rotary motion thereto from said driving element.

1,327,274. STREET-INDICATOR FOR TRAMCARS. HENRY S. EVANS, East Chicago, Ind. Filed Apr. 18, 1916. Serial No. 91,897. 1 Claim. (Cl. 40—59.)

A station indicator including a casing having a sight opening, guide rollers in said casing above and below the sight opening, drive rollers in said casing and spaced from and in horizontal alinement with said guide rollers, a web having characters thereon wound on said drive rollers and passing over the guide rollers in rear of the sight opening, a centrally located shaft secured in said casing, means on said shaft for engagement with the web, oppositely directed ratchet wheels secured to said means, a substantially U-shaped frame having the ends of its arms journaled to the outer ends of the shaft, a spring secured to the web portion of said frame and to the casing for normally supporting the frame longitudinally, spring actuated and oppositely disposed dogs pivoted to the arms of the frame and adapted to engage the ratchet wheels, and upper and lower solenoids connected to the web portion of the frame and supported by the casing for swinging the frame upwardly and downwardly.

1,327,275. WATER-CLOSET SEAT. MARIE A. FERGUSON, Newark, N. J. Filed July 21, 1916. Serial No. 110,457. 3 Claims. (Cl. 4—18.)

1. In a device of the class described, the combination with a support, and a relatively fixed water supply pipe, a conduit rotatably mounted in said support, a seat pivot-

ally mounted on said conduit for swinging movement to and from its operative position, a flush pipe carried by the seat and in fluid communication with said conduit

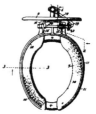

and a swivel connection between said fixed water pipe and said conduit designed to permit relative movement between the pipe and conduit.

1,327,276. STARTER FOR INTERNAL-COMBUSTION ENGINES. LOUIS BENNETT HASBROUCK, Elmira, N. Y. Filed Aug. 24, 1916. Serial No. 116,655. 12 Claims. (Cl. 74—7.)

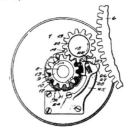

2. A starter for internal combustion engines comprising, in combination with a toothed fly wheel, a shaft, a bracket loosely mounted on the shaft, a gear carried by the bracket adapted to mesh with the fly wheel, a second gear fixed to said shaft and meshing with the first mentioned gear, a toothed disk rotatable with the shaft, a pawl pivotally mounted upon said bracket and normally engaged with the disk, means for releasing the pawl from the disk when the first mentioned gear is brought into mesh with the fly wheel, and means for disengaging said gear from the fly wheel.

1,327,277. THERMOSTATIC VALVE. WILLIAM J. HERDMAN, Toronto, Ontario, Canada. Filed Jan. 22, 1916. Serial No. 78,595. 5 Claims. (Cl. 236—48.)

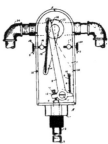

1. In a thermostatic valve, thermostatic elements, a lever operated thereby, a turn valve, a handle for operat-

ing said valve, stops for limiting the motion of said handle, said stops being independently adjustable, and a spring connecting said lever with said handle.

1,327,278. APPLIANCE FOR THE PROTECTION AND PRESERVATION OF DRAINS AND SMALL SEWERS. DANIEL F. HOLMAN, Farmersville, Ohio. Filed May 28, 1919. Serial No. 300,469. 1 Claim. (Cl. 182—9.)

An automatic drain tile protector having an indented metal gate hung at an angle of forty-five degrees or any suitable angle in a square outlet section, and having near the lower under side, a transverse line of points or spikes, resting on the floor of the tile when the gate is not afloat, substantially as described.

1,327,279. ELECTRICAL RADIATOR-HEATER. WILLIAM HURST, Winnipeg, Manitoba, Canada. Filed Jan. 17, 1918. Serial No. 212,302. 2 Claims. (Cl. 219—38.)

1. A device of the kind described comprising an elbow and means to connect the elbow with the water cooling system of an automobile, a horizontal pipe in screw-threaded engagement with the elbow, a detachable cap on the opposite end of the pipe, an electrically energized heating element contained in the pipe in spaced relation to the sides thereof, and having a portion projecting through the cap, and means forming a water tight joint around the projecting portion of the heating element.

1,327,280. PICTURE-PROJECTING APPARATUS. CHARLES FRANCIS JENKINS, Washington, D. C., assignor to The Graphoscope Company, Washington, D. C., a Corporation of Delaware. Filed Oct. 17, 1916. Serial No. 126,063. 3 Claims. (Cl. 176—103.)

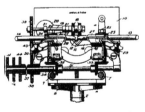

2. The combination with a carbon of two other carbons in the plane of the first, diverging from its end and forming arc gaps therewith, of means whereby the hand of the operator by a single movement may axially adjust one, two, or all of the carbons, as desired.

1,327,281. FLEXIBLE REINFORCED TRANSPARENT SHEET. CHARLES FRANCIS JENKINS, Washington, D. C. Filed Aug. 3, 1918. Serial No. 248,166. 2 Claims. (Cl. 154—53.)

1. The combination with two superposed flexible sheets of transparent material, of non-stretching netting interposed between the sheets and having its mesh forming elements adhering to both sheets, whereby the two sheets are connected only along the interposed reinforcing wires.

1,327,282. HERMETIC UNIT SMELTING SYSTEM. WOOLSEY McA. JOHNSON, Hartford, Conn. Filed Feb. 18, 1913. Serial No. 8,978. 8 Claims. (Cl. 204—64.)

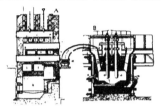

1. In the metallurgical art, the process which comprises heating a charge to form a readily oxidizable between-product, conveying said between-product through air without oxidation, and smelting said between-product to form metallic vapor.

1,327,283. HYDRANT SHUT-OFF. WALTER N. KING, Colorado Springs, Colo. Filed Oct. 8, 1918. Serial No. 257,342. 1 Claim. (Cl. 137—68.)

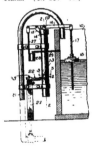

A water controlling supply device for a water tank including a supply pipe having a spring closed valve, a hollow standard supported by the pipe and having an opening in one side, a hook member carried by the stem of the valve and arranged to be engaged in the said opening to hold the valve open, a rocking member carried by the supporting standard, a float on one end of the member and suspended within the tank, and a water receiving receptacle suspended on the other end of the rocking member for receiving overflow water from the side of the tank.

1,327,284. CIRCUIT-BREAKER FOR MAGNETOS. PAUL LABROSSE and FELIX ESTÈVE, Lyon, France. Filed May 9, 1918. Serial No. 233,441. 1 Claim. (Cl. 123—166.)

In a device of the character described, a pawl, a back motion spring therefor, an axle thereon, a disk, an extension thereon provided with a bore into which said axle extends, an annular seating at one end of said bore, a metal ring within said bore in which said axle rotates, a sleeve constructed of insulating material between said ring and the face of said bore, a washer of insulating material between said annular seating and the inner ends

of said metal ring and insulating sleeve, a contact finger constructed of insulating material having an eye, a pivot extending into said eye and a metal ring fixed in said eye and surrounding said pivot.

1,327,285. RELEASABLE BEARING. EUGENE LANTZ, Jersey City, N. J. Filed Mar. 6, 1919. Serial No. 280,938. 3 Claims. (Cl. 61—66.)

1. A releasable bearing comprising a pair of wedges, the inclined faces of which lie in contact with each other, each being stepped to provide a shoulder, and a laterally acting wedge shaped key co-acting with said shoulders.

1,327,286. RELEASABLE BEARING. EUGENE LANTZ, Jersey City, N. J. Original application filed Mar. 6, 1919, Serial No. 280,938. Divided and this application filed May 2, 1919. Serial No. 294,191. 3 Claims. (Cl. 61—66.)

1. A releasable bearing comprising a pair of wedges the inclined faces of which lie in contact with each other, each being stepped to form a shoulder, the shoulder of the upper wedge extending downwardly and the shoulder of the lower wedge extending upwardly and a laterally acting wedge shaped key lying between and co-acting with said shoulders, the shoulder of the upper wedge lying at that side of the key toward the thicker end of the wedge, and the shoulder of the lower wedge lying at the opposite side of said key.

1,327,287. AIR-FILTERING SYSTEM FOR COOLING THE MOTORS OF ELECTRICALLY-DRIVEN RAILWAY-CARS. ROBERT E. MILLER, Altoona, and GEORGE H. LIEBEGOTT, Duncansville, Pa. Filed Jan. 17, 1918. Serial No. 212,299. 4 Claims. (Cl. 183—37.)

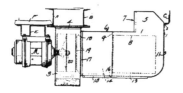

1. In a cooling apparatus of the class described, a combined air filter and blower casing suspended from the bottom of the car and including a relatively large dust collecting box having an air intake hood portion projecting above the plane of the top of the body with its screened open side facing the longitudinal center of the car, a partition wall disposed transversely of the interior dust collecting box and having a plurality of openings therein, and a plurality of bag-like filter elements carried by said wall and having their closed ends disposed toward the air intake opening.

4. In a cooling apparatus, a combined blower and air filter unit having an interior partition wall dividing the same into air filtering and blower compartments, said partition wall having openings and offset flanges surrounding the same, clamping devices for coöperating with said flanges to clamp the filtering units thereto, said clamping devices each including a manipulating member having a clamping foot at one end thereof for coöperating with the said flanges, means for guiding said manipulating member in its movement, and a spring between the guide means and the clamping foot for yieldingly maintaining the latter in clamped relation.

1,327,288. BOOT-BRUSH. THOMAS ADDISON NEELIN, Winnipeg, Manitoba, Canada. Filed May 3, 1919. Serial No. 294,435. 5 Claims. (Cl. 15—16.)

1. The combination with the back of a boot polish brush and an open topped polish box, of a withdrawable drawer receiving the polish box and slidably mounted in the back of the brush and a releasable closure top mounted on the brush back and designed to close the top of the polish box in the closed position of the drawer.

1,327,289. PAPER-MAKING MACHINE. NICKOLAS J. NIES, Kalamazoo, Mich. Filed Sept. 3, 1918. Serial No. 252,293. 6 Claims. (Cl. 92—49.)

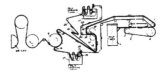

1. In a paper making machine, the combination with a couch roll, press rolls and a drying cylinder, of a press felt extending from said couch roll to said drying cylinder to discharge the web thereto with its forward reach passing between said press rolls, one of said rollers being a suction roll, there being a pair of guiding and supporting rolls for said press felt positioned adjacent said press rolls and so that the press felt is carried over and reversely between said press rolls, a pair of rolls positioned adjacent said drying cylinder supporting said press felt in contact with a substantial arc thereof, the second of such rolls constituting a smoothing roll and being positioned so that the press felt is held to the drying cylinder as it passes over the roll and a second felt guided to pass between said press rolls and over the said guiding and supporting roll at the rear thereof, said second felt being supported and guided to engage the under side of a web on the press felt before it reaches the press rolls, and to leave the same carried on the upper side of the press felt before it reaches the drying cylinder.

1,327,290. OVERHEAD ROLLER CONVEYER SYSTEM. RICHARD OEHLER, St. Louis, Mo. Filed May 5, 1919. Serial No. 294,960. 4 Claims. (Cl. 104—101.)

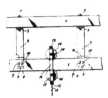

1. In an overhead conveyer system; a rail; straps adapted to be supported by the building construction and having a hook and slot connection at intervals with the rail and being bolted thereto; a conveyer device mounted to move on said rail; and means in said conveyer device to prevent the derailment thereof from said rail.

1,327,291. ANTIRATTLING DEVICE. CHARLES E. SOULE, Somerville, Mass., assignor of one-third to Frank Page Bearse and one-third to William Thomas Abbott, Winchester, Mass. Filed Nov. 25, 1918. Serial No. 263,948. 8 Claims. (Cl. 292—67.)

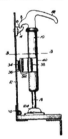

2. The combination with the side of an automobile hood, a fastener for the latter and a member to engage the side of the hood on one side when the hood is closed, of a device to be carried by said fastener comprising means to engage the side of the hood upon the opposite side from that engaged by said member, when said fastener is in operative position, and means whereby said device can be secured to said fastener without removing the latter.

1,327,292. WALL CONSTRUCTION. ALONZO C. RAYMOND, Detroit, Mich. Filed Nov. 8, 1915. Serial No. 60,218. 1 Claim. (Cl. 72—46.)

The method of constructing fireproof partitions, comprising the vertical placing of a metal stud having channels and anchored at top and bottom when so placed, the insertion of a tier of blocks having vertical ribs on their ends, the placing of a second metal stud with a channel portion engaging the ribs on the free ends of the blocks, said stud being anchored in the floor and ceiling, and the repeating of such operation as needed.

1,327,293. LANTERN-BAIL. GEORGE H. ROLFES, St. Louis, Mo., assignor to Handlan Buck Manufacturing Company, St. Louis, Mo., a Corporation of Missouri. Filed Apr. 18, 1919. Serial No. 291,160. 3 Claims. (Cl. 220—94.)

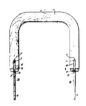

2. A bail comprising a U-shaped grip handle having its legs apertured transversely, grooved longitudinally from the transverse apertures, and provided with end grooves connecting the longitudinal grooves; and wire connection members having loops extending through said transverse apertures and embedded in said longitudinal and transverse grooves.

1,327,294. PUMP OR COMPRESSOR. ARTHUR EDWIN LEIGH SCANES, Ashton-on-Mersey, England, assignor to The British Westinghouse Electric and Manufacturing Company Limited, a Company of Great Britain. Filed Feb. 20, 1917. Serial No. 149,934. 4 Claims. (Cl. 230—13.)

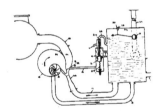

1. In combination with a fluid-ejecting device with liquid as working medium and having a suction inlet for fluid, a seal tank having a gas and vapor outlet and connections whereby said device receives its actuating liquid from said tank and delivers liquid and gaseous fluids thereto, a valved water-over-flow for said tank, the operation of which is dependent upon the opposing pressures existing in the tank and at the fluid inlet of said ejecting device, and means whereby the effective area of said gas and vapor outlet is automatically varied in accordance with the level of water in said tank.

1,327,295. BATHING-PLATFORM FOR INFANTS. EARL R. SMITH, Pittsburgh, Pa. Filed Sept. 3, 1915. Serial No. 48,750. 3 Claims. (Cl. 4—27.)

1. In combination, an infant bathing platform comprising a substantially flat plate adapted to extend longitudinally of a bath tub, and having up-turned side and rear edges with the up-turned side edges inclined toward each

other at their front ends, and having the front edge flat to permit drainage, a removable stopper block lying between the inclined ends of the side edges and engaging

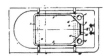

such ends and the upper surface of the plate, and means for supporting the platform adjacent the upper edges of a bath tub.

1,327,296. TRACTION-BLOCK. PETER A. SOLEM, Cincinnati, Ohio. Filed Apr. 16, 1917. Serial No. 162,377. 2 Claims. (Cl. 193—26.)

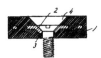

1. A traction block. comprising a centrally apertured elastic body, and a metallic core plate embedded within said body centrally countersink and apertured, the countersink registering with the aperture through said body, said plate being of irregular contour providing a series of tabs, each tab apertured for establishing a union of body material through said plate.
2. A traction block. comprising an elastic body and a metallic core plate embedded within said body, having an opening therethrough and providing a seat for a fastening anchor engaged through the opening in said plate, said plate being of irregular contour providing tabs, each tab apertured for establishing a union of the body material through said tab apertures.

1,327,297. FLAX-THRESHING MACHINE. BERTRAND S. SUMMERS, Port Huron. Mich. Filed Aug. 16, 1915. Serial No. 45,614. 14 Claims. (Cl. 130—13.)

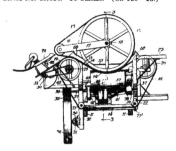

3. In a machine of the class described, a cylindrical stripping drum, means for feeding plants longitudinally thereof and lowering them toward the periphery of the drum.

1,327,298. LABEL-HOLDER. GEORGE H. TAYLOR, Richmond, Va. Filed Apr. 1. 1919. Serial No. 286,691. 8 Claims. (Cl. 40—11.)
2. A label holder comprising a body having a looped portion disposed parallel to the outer face thereof to form

a clasping pocket and its opposite free edges extended at an angle to the body to provide supporting and retaining

flanges connected to tension the pocket toward said body when separated.

1,327,299. PARAFFINING-MACHINE. FRANK P. VAVRA, Congress Park, Ill. Filed July 22, 1918, Serial No. 246,015. Renewed Nov. 1, 1919. Serial No. 335,110. 3 Claims. (Cl. 91—51.)

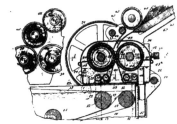

3. In an apparatus of the class described, the combination with a cooling water tank having carton carrying means mounted therein, of a paraffin tank directly over the receiving end of the cooling water tank, a swinging frame pivoted at its outer side to the adjacent end of the cooling water tank frame, a pair of gaging rolls journaled in said pivoted frame in the same or substantially the same hroizontal plane and having their lower sides dipping into the paraffin, gearing carried by said pivoted frame to rotate the rolls in unison, means also carried by the pivoted frame for regulating the pressure between the rollers. the paraffin tank having a discharge passage through the bottom thereof extending from the diverging angle of the rollers to the top of the cooling water tank, and means for securing the pivoted frame in position.

1,327,300. MACHINE FOR COATING BLANKS WITH PARAFFIN. FRANK P. VAVRA, Cicero, Ill. Filed Aug. 9, 1918, Serial No. 249,157. Renewed Nov. 1, 1919. Serial No. 335,111. 4 Claims. (Cl. 91—49.)

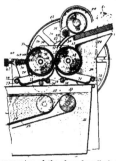

1. In an apparatus of the class described, the combination with a pair of gaging rolls having perforations in

their metallic shells and an external fibrous covering, of means for pressing said rolls into engagement with each other, means for rotating the rolls, and means for supplying the interior of the rolls with the coating liquid.

1,327,301. BEARING. JAMES B. WATSON, Detroit, Mich. Filed Oct. 9, 1918. Serial No. 257,512. 14 Claims. (Cl. 64—10.)

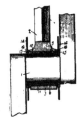

1. In a bearing construction, a main member, a plain bearing of bearing metal carried thereby and including a body portion having an inner surface conforming to and in bearing contact with a shaft, said bearing and shaft having relative angular movement, said bearing also including a thin fin-like element projecting considerably from the body portion and forming a radiating surface of an area at least equal to a large proportion of that of the inner surface of the body portion.

1,327,302. ENGINE-STARTER. VINCENT BENDIX, Chicago, Ill. Filed Mar. 21, 1919. Serial No. 284,052. 25 Claims. (Cl. 74—7.)

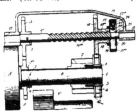

1. In an engine starter, a drive comprising a rotatable driving shaft, a driving member mounted thereon for longitudinal movement thereof for engagement with a part of the engine to be started, and for rotary movement therewith, and means mounted extraneous of such shaft and out of the line of load for automatically moving the driving member longitudinally.

1,327,303. ENGINE-STARTER. VINCENT BENDIX, Chicago, Ill. Filed Mar. 31, 1919. Serial No. 286.386. 10 Claims. (Cl. 74—7.)

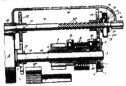

1. In an engine starter, a drive comprising a driving shaft, driving means mounted thereon for longitudinal movement thereof to engage a member of the engine to be started and for rotary movement therewith for rotating such engine member, such driving means including a

yielding driving element, and shifting means mounted extraneous of such shaft and coöperating with the driving means to control the engaging and disengaging movements thereof.

1,327,304. ENGINE-STARTER. VINCENT BENDIX, Chicago, Ill. Filed Mar. 31, 1919. Serial No. 286,387. 11 Claims. (Cl. 74—7.)

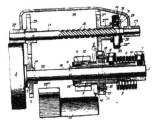

1. In an engine starter, a drive comprising a driving shaft, driving means mounted thereon for longitudinal movement thereof to engage a member of the engine to be started and for rotary movement therewith for rotating such engine member, and shifting means mounted extraneous of such shaft and coöperating with the driving means to control the engaging and disengaging movements thereof, said driving means including an independently longitudinally movable driving member which engages such engine member.

1,327,305. PIVOTED DISCHARGE-ARM. BERT R. BENJAMIN and CLINTON A. HAGADONE, Oak Park, Ill., assignors, by mesne assignments, to International Harvester Company, a Corporation of New Jersey. Filed May 1, 1918. Serial No. 231,901. 6 Claims. (Cl. 56—68.)

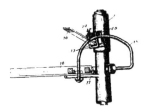

1. In a harvester, a substantially vertically disposed binder shaft, discharging mechanism pivotally carried thereby, and means for lifting said discharging mechanism on its pivot during a portion of its revolution, said discharging mechanism being pivoted to said shaft in such a manner that the pressure of the grain thereagainst tends to force said mechanism downwardly.

1,327,306. TOOTH-SHADE GUIDE. ISIDORE S. BERGER, New York, N. Y. Filed Apr. 29, 1919. Serial No. 293,516. 5 Claims. (Cl. 35—16.)

1. A tooth shade guide embodying a tooth, an arm to which the tooth may be attached and a gold metal surface between the tooth and the arm forming a backing for the tooth.

1,327,307. TIRE-RETREADING APPARATUS. Roscoe A. Brooks, Chicago, Ill., assignor to Western Tire & Rubber Works, Chicago, Ill., a Copartnership comprising Roscoe A. Brooks, Chicago, Ill., and George W. Clark, Oak Park, Ill. Filed Oct. 14, 1918. Serial No. 257,956. 9 Claims. (Cl. 18—18.)

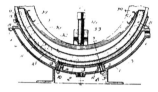

1. In an apparatus of the character described, a mold, a longitudinal spring member, and means for pressing said spring member into the mold.

1,327,308. PROCESS OF TREATING MILK. Hillhouse Buel, Seattle, Wash. Filed Apr. 3, 1916. Serial No. 88,482. 4 Claims. (Cl. 99—15.)

4. In the process of preparing milk products for consumption, the process comprising adding a viable culture of the lactic acid group of bacteria to a fluid milk product which is in a substantially sterile condition, to produce a bacterial content to the desired count per c. c. and sufficient to inhibit the growth of undesirable bacteria without affecting its sweet quality and sufficient to restore to such fluid its qualities of flavor and digestibility, and thereupon maintaining said product under the conditions usually obtained in the milk trade for sweet milk.

1,327,309. CHAIN PIPE-WRENCH. George W. Bufford, Buffalo, N. Y., assignor to J. H. Williams & Company, Brooklyn, N. Y., a Corporation of New York. Filed Mar. 14, 1918. Serial No. 222,329. 2 Claims. (Cl. 81—66.)

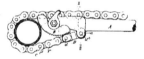

2. A chain pipe wrench comprising a stock, a jaw, a chain, composed of a series of pivoted links, the chain being flexible in one plane and substantially inflexible in a plane transverse of the pivotal axis of the links, and a connection between the chain and stock, said connection having a pivotal connection with the stock and having a swivel therein.

1,327,310. WHEEL. James A. Charter, Chicago, Ill. Filed May 22, 1919. Serial No. 299,022. 3 Claims. (Cl. 21—69.)

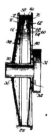

1. A metal vehicle wheel comprising a suitable rim, two disks spaced apart from each other at the rim, and more widely separated from each other as they approach the hub, each of said disks being Z-shaped, the corresponding flanges of said disks being turned in the same direction.

1,327,311. MANIFOLD FOR INTERNAL-COMBUSTION ENGINES. Ralph C. Chesnutt, Pottstown, Pa. Filed Apr. 25, 1919. Serial No. 292,651. 3 Claims. (Cl. 123—52.)

1. In an apparatus of the kind described, the combination of a cylinder block casting, a manifold, said manifold being adapted to be secured to said casting, a groove in the cylinder casting, a groove in said manifold, said grooves being adapted to register with each other and their walls together to form the walls of the intake passage, said manifold being provided with an exhaust passage having a portion of its wall in common with a portion of said intake passage, said exhaust manifold being located at a distance from the joining surface of said manifold and cylinder casting, and so that the outside air shall have access to a large portion of its inclosing wall.

1,327,312. BOLT-THREADING MACHINE. Hubert Crehan, Pittsburgh, Pa. Filed June 5, 1917. Serial No. 172,882. 1 Claim. (Cl. 10—89.)

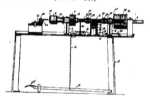

In a machine for threading bolts, the combination of a rotary spindle, devices for imparting a longitudinal movement to the spindle, a die, a bolt-holder having a cavity for the reception of the head of the bolt, and a rib on the face of the bolt-holder to throw the head of the bolt out of the cavity.

1,327,313. APPARATUS FOR TREATING PAINTED OR VARNISHED ARTICLES. Cicero M. Cunliffe, Detroit, Mich., assignor to American Blower Company, Detroit, Mich., a Corporation of New York. Filed Dec. 27, 1916. Serial No. 139,201. 35 Claims. (Cl. 34—19.)

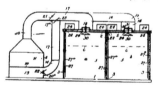

1. In an apparatus for drying varnished articles, the combination of a treating chamber having an air inlet adjacent the top thereof, means within the chamber for introducing air into said chamber through said inlet, and means for deflecting horizontally said air so introduced whereby the same will settle down in mass formation upon the article within the container, the top wall of the container being spaced vertically from the article to be treated and the space below the deflecting means being unobstructed whereby said air after losing substantially all of its velocity contacts with the article.

1,327,314. ART OF TREATING PAINTED OR VARNISHED ARTICLES. CICERO M. CUNLIFFE, Detroit, Mich., assignor to American Blower Company, Detroit, Mich., a Corporation of New York. Filed Dec. 27, 1916. Serial No. 139,202. 20 Claims. (Cl. 34—24.)

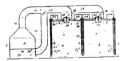

1. The method of drying varnished articles which consists in placing the articles with the varnish applied thereto into the lower portion of an inclosed drying chamber introducing air into the upper portion of the drying chamber so as to be there disseminated into an unoccupied space of considerable area, and removing the air from the lower portion of the chamber whereby the air introduced at the top after it has lost substantially all of its velocity will settle down in mass formation upon and gradually envelop the article.

1,327,315. APPARATUS FOR MANIPULATION OF METAL INGOTS AND THE LIKE. EVAN WALTER DAVIES, Dowlais, Wales. Filed Sept. 19, 1917. Serial No. 192,156. 3 Claims. (Cl. 80—48.)

1. In apparatus for manipulating ingots in rolling mills, a turning member comprising a cross head means for operating said cross head, a lever pivoted to the said cross head, a clutching member, links connecting said clutching member to each end of the said lever substantially as described.

1,327,316. POTATO-CUTTING MACHINE. DOLLNER S. FOLEY, Montrose, Colo. Filed Aug. 7, 1918. Serial No. 248,741. 2 Claims. (Cl. 146—7.)

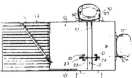

1. A potato quartering machine comprising a table, a track extending transversely of the table and of sufficient width to receive and guide a potato, a knife extending upward from the table between the track and arranged to divide the potato, a longitudinally extending knife transverse of the first named knife and rearward thereof and mounted for vertical movement and arranged to divide the divided portions of the potato, and manually operated means for reciprocating the second named knife.

1,327,317. PERPETUAL CALENDAR. FRANZ A. FULLER, Newark, N. J., assignor to The J. E. Mergott Company, Newark, N. J., a Corporation of New Jersey. Filed Mar. 26, 1917. Serial No. 157,351. 5 Claims. (Cl. 40—113.)

1. In a calendar, the combination with a frame, comprising a front and a rear plate, said rear plate being

provided with integral circular walls extending upwardly therefrom, a pair of day dials, a day-name dial and a month-name dial rotatively secured to the rear plate by means of said integral circular walls, a flat spring, notched

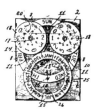

at its ends, interposed between said plates, the notched ends thereof bearing against the circular walls upon which said day dials are rotatively secured, said spring further provided with means engaging with apertures in the day dials for preventing accidental movement of said dials.

1,327,318. ADDING AND SUBTRACTING MACHINE. CLAIBORNE W. GOOCH, Detroit, Mich., assignor to Burroughs Adding Machine Company, Detroit, Mich., a Corporation of Michigan. Filed Mar. 3, 1915. Serial No. 11,758. 5 Claims. (Cl. 235—82.)

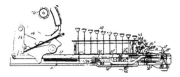

1. In a machine of the class described the combination with racks and rack-carriers having slot and pin and spring connections; of additional racks and rack-carriers also having slot and pin and spring connections; means for moving the additional rack-carriers concurrently with and in the reverse direction to the movement of the first-mentioned rack-carriers; register pinions; means for establishing coöperative relationship between the same and either set of racks; and double acting transfer pawls normally restraining the springs of the rack and carrier connections aforesaid, and adapted to be tripped by the pinions under rotation in either direction.

1,327,319. ADDING-MACHINE. CLAIBORNE W. GOOCH, Detroit, Mich., assignor to Burroughs Adding Machine Company, Detroit, Mich., a Corporation of Michigan. Filed Feb. 15, 1916 Serial No. 78,391. 4 Claims. (Cl. 235—82.)

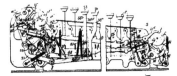

1. The combination of vibrating register actuators; keys which differentially impart movement to said actuators; a plurality of sets of adding wheels, each set having its own carrying mechanism; driving connections between the actuators and said sets of wheels; with settable provisions for causing simultaneous registration of amounts upon both sets of wheels, or upon one set inde-

pendently of the other, by the power imparted through the keys; a zeroizing handle; and separable connections between the same and the sets of wheels for either simultaneously turning the sets of wheels to zero or turning one set only to zero.

1,327,320. ADDING-MACHINE. CLAIBORNE W. GOOCH, Detroit, Mich., assignor to Burroughs Adding Machine Company, Detroit, Mich., a Corporation of Michigan. Filed Feb. 15, 1916. Serial No. 78,392. 11 Claims. (Cl. 235—82.)

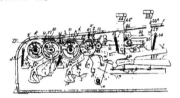

1. The combination of vibrating register actuators; keys for differentially driving said actuators; a set of adding wheels driven by said actuators; a second set of adding wheels; transmission gearing between the two sets of adding wheels; clutches in said transmission gearing; means for operating the clutches to cause simultaneous registration upon said sets of wheels or registration only upon the first-mentioned set, each set of wheels having its own carrying mechanism; zeroizing mechanism for each set of wheels; and a single means for simultaneously actuating said mechanisms, or separately actuating that pertaining to the first-mentioned set of wheels.

1,327,321. CLEAR-VISION WINDOW. GEORGE S. GOODWIN and JULIUS J. ACKER, Chicago, Ill. Filed Oct. 2, 1916. Serial No. 123,231. 2 Claims. (Cl. 20—40.5.)

1. A clear vision window comprising a frame, a fixed glass in said frame having an unobstructed horizontal edge adjacent an opening within said frame, a vertically movable glass adapted to bridge said opening and having an unobstructed horizontal edge opposite the unobstructed edge of said fixed glass, U-shaped metal guides attached to said frame and within which the vertical edges of said movable glass may slide, said guides being inclined downwardly and outwardly to guide said movable glass across the vertical plane of said fixed glass, and means connected to said movable glass for shifting it and holding it in adjusted position.

1,327,322. METHOD OF MANUFACTURING PRESS-BUTTON PARTS. MAX GRUSCHKA and FERDINAND MARJANKO, Prague, Austria. Filed Aug. 3, 1914, Serial No. 854,830. Renewed Nov. 21, 1919. Serial No. 339,681. 4 Claims. (Cl. 79—3.)

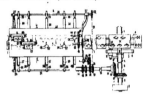

1. A method of manufacturing press-button parts, consisting in stamping out from a metal strip, which has previously been subjected to the operation of drawing from the metal raised cup-shaped portions, each of which has been provided with lateral incisions, groups of circular disks, having said cup-shaped portions in their centers, in drawing the stamped disks into the shape of cylindrical press-button parts, and in immediately transferring the press-button parts in the same groups in which they are stamped out, to the gripping device of a conveyer, progressing at intervals and conveying the press-button parts to spring inserting and securing tools operating on differently located press-button parts in the several groups simultaneously whereby the press-button parts which are operated upon simultaneously will differ in location in their respective groups from one operation stage to the following.

1,327,323. WHISTLE. GEORGE F. HALL, Newark, N. J., assignor to Emanuel W. Kaiser, Newark, N. J. Filed Nov. 4, 1918. Serial No. 260,965. 1 Claim. (Cl. 116—1.)

In a whistle of the character described, the combination of a base piece, an air distributing plate providing an air outlet from the base piece, a pipe-forming member secured to said base piece and plate and providing radial webs or partitions next the base piece and transverse webs at the other ends of said radial webs, a tubular body portion telescoping said pipe-forming means, a set screw working through the end of said tubular body portion against the flat surface of the transverse web of said pipe-forming member farthest from the base piece, and means for adjustably clamping the tubular body portion toward the pipe-forming member to engage said set screw with said web.

1,327,324. LOADING AND UNLOADING APPARATUS. ARTHUR S. HECKER, Cleveland, Ohio. Filed May 26, 1917. Serial No. 171,106. 4 Claims. (Cl. 37—14.)

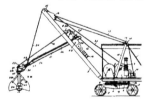

1. In an apparatus of the character described, the combination, with a swinging boom, of a rigid member pivot-

ally supported by said boom, means for moving said member in the direction of its length, a load-carrying device carried by said member, loading means for said device, means for moving said member about its pivotal support, means for operating said loading means, and means operable by the adjustment of said member for imparting a rotary movement to said device.

4. The combination with a rigid supporting arm, of a bucket provided with a head frame, a vertical pivot bolt supporting and directly connecting said head frame to the arm, and means to rotate the head frame and bucket on said pivot.

1,327,325. SIEVE FOR THRESHING-MACHINES. DANIEL EMRY HOFFMAN, Plymouth, Ohio. Filed Oct. 22, 1918. Serial No. 259,176. 24 Claims. (Cl. 130—19.)

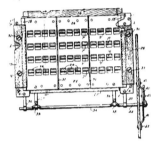

1. In a combined wind guide and brace which is adapted to form a part of a top for threshing machine sieves composed of sheet metal formed to provide a plane smooth top surface and a parallel angularly related flange portion, the ends of the wind guides being provided with an angularly related bent portion with respect to the flange portion of the wind guide.

1,327,326. ARMY-TRAILER. EPHRAIM HOWLAND, Pontiac, Mich. Filed Nov. 18. 1918. Serial No. 262,928. 3 Claims. (Cl. 89—36.)

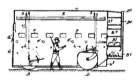

1. A car composed of two side members slidably supported upon traction wheels, means for elevating or lowering it upon said tractor wheels, cross bars intermediate the bottom and roof supporting said sides with respect to each other, pockets in the side walls thereof, perforations in the side walls thereof adjacent to said pockets, a compartment which may be operated as a kitchenette, substantially as and for the purpose described.

1,327,327. SYSTEM AND APPARATUS FOR LOADING VESSELS. GEORGE H. HULETT and FRANK E. HULETT, Cleveland, Ohio. Filed Oct. 29, 1918. Serial No. 260,107. 6 Claims. (Cl. 214—14.)

1 In a system of loading vessels, a pier or dock having an elevated trestle thereon, an inclined up track leading from the shore end of the pier through the trestle to the top thereof, a track located at a side of the trestle, switch connection between the up track and side track, an inclined down track leading from the shore end of the side track down to the starting point of the up track and cars

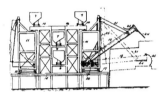

adapted to travel on said tracks and dump their contents into the bins located on the pier and convenient to a vessel moored to the pier.

1,327,328. PEEL. JOHN F. KIEVELL, Hamilton, Ontario, Canada. Filed Oct. 3, 1919. Serial No. 328,103. 2 Claims. (Cl. 107—67.)

2. In a device of the class described, the combination with a peel blade and its handle, of a band extending around the edge of the handle end of the blade, an inner rib integral with said band and occupying a corresponding groove in the periphery of said handle end of the blade, means in the opposed ends of said band for securing it to the blade, a taper pin integral with said band and extending into said blade, an oppositely disposed socket integral with said band and receiving the end of said handle, said socket provided with oppositely disposed lateral inclined ribs, and means for securing said handle against longitudinal and rotative displacement, for the purpose set forth.

1,327,329. AUTOMATIC ELECTRIC RAILWAY BLOCK-SIGNAL SYSTEM. LAWRENCE W. KITE, Barberton, Ohio. Filed Oct. 18, 1919. Serial No. 331,567. 6 Claims. (Cl. 246—62.)

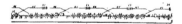

1. In a wiring system of the class described a track, one rail of which is formed of separate rail lengths bonded to form a continuous current carrying element, the other rail of which is composed of a plurality of sections each insulated from the adjacent section and each section composed of a plurality of rail lengths each insulated from the adjacent rail lengths; the alternating rail lengths of each section being connected electrically so as to form a positive and negative element; the negative element of each section being connected to the negative pole of a battery having its positive pole connected to the positive element of an alternating section; the positive element of each section connected to the positive pole of a battery which has its negative pole connected to the negative element of the other alternating section, substantially as described.

1,327,330. SIZING DEVICE FOR EYEGLASS - RIMS. CLARENCE A. KLINE, San Francisco, Calif. Filed Mar. 20, 1919. Serial No. 283,888. 7 Claims. (Cl. 18—6.)

1. A sizing device for eye-glass rims comprising a heating pan; a hollow die secured to the heating pan; a second hollow die movably mounted upon the pan and matching with the first mentioned die, said matched dies being arranged to receive an eye-glass rim externally or internally; and means for moving the second mentioned die relatively to the first mentioned die to alter the size of an eye-glass rim rendered plastic by the application of heat to the heating pan.

1,327,331. DROP-HAMMER. WILLIAM A. KNAPP, Washington, D. C. Filed Nov. 23, 1918. Serial No. 263,917. 8 Claims. (Cl. 78—30.)

1. In combination a drop hammer, a revolving drum, a band passing over the drum connected to the hammer and having a portion to be pulled upon by the operator, and a member mounted to have movement in a direction circumferentially of the drum and engaging the band to normally free it from operative relation with the drum, said member when moved from normal position allowing the band to be operated by its frictional contact with the drum to raise the hammer, substantially as described.

1,327,332. SHELLAC SURROGATE AND PROCESS OF PRODUCING SAME. JOHN ROBERT KÖHLER, Stockholm, Sweden. Filed Apr. 22, 1918. Serial No. 230,081. 9 Claims. (Cl. 134—26.)

4. A shellac-surrogate, consisting essentially of amorphous resin acids separated from the natural resin of conifers and combined with glycerin.

1,327,333. COLLAPSIBLE FORM. LORENZO O. LAMKIN and JOHN H. BERGHAUS, Jr., Louisville, Ky. Filed Dec. 6, 1918. Serial No. 265,622. 56 Claims. (Cl. 93—59.)

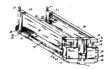

27. In a form as characterized, a base, spaced parallel walls, horizontally disposed pivots on which said walls are mounted and are adapted to turn under prematurely applied pressure, and means operable at a predetermined time to prevent said turning.

1,327,334. RECORDER FOR REGISTERING LOCKS. CLINTON E. LARRABEE, Binghamton, N. Y., assignor to International Time Recording Company of New York, a Corporation of New York. Filed Apr. 7, 1919. Serial No. 288,080. 8 Claims. (Cl. 234—44.)

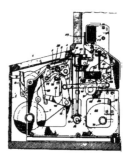

3. A combined time autograph and lock recorder, comprising, in combination, the following: a series of time recording type wheels, a series of lock indicating type wheels, a printing mechanism for taking impressions from either or both series of wheels on a paper strip, two feed mechanisms of different capacity, a manual means for operating the printing mechanism and the feed mechanism of greater capacity, automatic mechanism for setting the indicating wheels and for operating the printing mechanism and the feed mechanism of less capacity.

1,327,335. TILE-TRENCH DIGGER. LOUIS H. LARSON, Santiago, Minn. Filed Oct. 19, 1918. Serial No. 258,840. 11 Claims. (Cl. 37—39.)

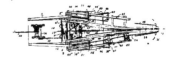

1. An apparatus for digging a trench comprising a frame, inclined ways mounted in said frame and converging from their upper toward their lower ends, excavating buckets mounted in said ways, means for raising one bucket while the other bucket is descending, the spread of said ways providing clearance for the ascending and descending buckets.

1,327,336. MANUFACTURE OF ELECTRIC ACCUMU-
LATORS. HENRY LEITNER, Westminster, London, and
WILLIAM HERBERT EXLEY, Harehills, Leeds, England.
Original application filed Apr. 15, 1919, Serial No.
290,361. Divided and this application filed Aug. 12,
1919. Serial No. 317,038. 4 Claims. (Cl. 29—2.)

1. In the manufacture of electric accumulators, the
method of forming the lead members from a single piece
of sheet lead having parallel side edges, which consists
in slitting the piece longitudinally and transversely to
simultaneously form a plurality of complementary lead
members having collector bars provided on one side with
lugs and on the other side with series of streamers, and
then rolling the streamers to flatten and lengthen the
same.

1,327,337. HARROW. ORLANDO D. LENT, Peekskill,
N. Y. Filed Feb. 7, 1919. Serial No. 275,529. 2
Claims. (Cl. 55—31.)

1. The combination in a harrow of a frame comprising
front and rear bars united by V formed braces, vibrative
beams pivoted between the ends of said cross bars, swinging beams hinged to said vibrative beams, the rear ends
of said beams united by sliding clamping bars, a spring
between the vibrative and swinging beams, buffer wheels
on the outer ends of the swinging beams, handles on the
swinging beams, wheel axle guides on the V braces, an
axle loosely supported within said guides, wheels on the
axle and a driver's seat on the axle.

1,327,338. TRAILER - TRUCK. HARRY B. LEVINSON,
Brooklyn, N. Y., and WILL H. WESTFALL, Rutherford,
N. J. Filed Mar. 16, 1918. Serial No. 222,891. 1
Claim. (Cl. 280—33.2.)

The combination in a pair of hand trucks arranged for
end to end connection, one of said trucks having a lip
provided with an opening centrally arranged, a pair of
eye bolts secured to the adjacent end of the other truck
in spaced relation, a connecting member comprising three
diverging arms, an eye formed upon each of two of said
arms for interlinkage with the eye bolt, the other arm
being bent and curved at right angle, an enlarged head

on said bent end for insertion in the opening of the adjacent truck, and an abutment member extending substantially parallel to the bent portion and located adjacent the point of connection of the arm.

1,327,339. PROTECTIVE HOOD FOR AEROPLANE
PILOTS. ANNA E. LOGAN, Ridgewood, N. J. Filed
Apr. 23, 1918 Serial No. 230,257. 8 Claims. (Cl.
244—30.)

1. The combination of the cock pit of an aeroplane, a
series of leaves pivoted together and to said cock pit
and telescoping to form a hood therefor when extended, in-
terconnections carried by said leaves whereby they open
and close each other, and means for opening or closing the
leaves.

1,327,340. ELECTRIC BELL. WILLIAM D. LUTZ, Allendale, N. J. Filed July 27, 1917. Serial No. 183,086.
5 Claims. (Cl. 175—345.)

1. The combination of an electromagnet, an armature
therefor moved in one direction by the magnet when the
latter is energized, a reciprocating member actuated by
the armature, and an interponent between the armature
and said member placed under tension by said movement
of the armature and operable to return the armature.

1,327,341. METHOD OF DEVELOPING DEFECTS IN
METALLIC OBJECTS. ANGUS S. MACDONALD, Great
Neck Station, N. Y., and HARRY P. MACDONALD, Mont-
clair, N. J., assignors to The Snead & Co. Iron Works,
Jersey City, N. J.. a Corporation of New Jersey. Filed
Apr. 13, 1918. Serial No. 228,371. 3 Claims. (Cl.
175—183.)

1. The herein described process of developing defective
portions in a metallic object without impairing its physical properties which consists in heating the same by its
internal resistance to a current of electricity passed
therethrough, the heat not being carried substantially
beyond the point of decalescence.

1,327,342. DOUBLE - TRACKER MUSICAL INSTRU-
MENT. FRANCIS M. MADSEN, San Francisco, Calif.,
assignor to The Rudolph Wurlitzer Manufacturing Com-
pany, North Tonawanda, N. Y., a Corporation of New
York. Filed Dec. 15, 1915. Serial No. 67,076. 17
Claims. (Cl. 84—161.)

9. In an instrument of the character described, the
combination of an action wind-chest having striker-pneu-

matic valve-mechanism, a plurality of trackers each having note-ducts and a controlling duct adapted to be normally closed by the music sheet, a pneumatic coupler containing independent valve chambers each adapted to be alternately exhausted and flushed, said coupler having a plurality of sets of passages respectively connected with the note-ducts of the trackers and also a single set of passages each common to a plurality of like note-duct

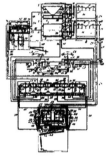

passages and connected with the striker-pneumatic valve-mechanism, coupler valves in each of said chambers connecting or disconnecting said companion tracker and wind-chest passages, independent valves controlling the passage of the air to and from said chambers, and retaining pneumatics governed by said controlling ducts and acting upon said controlling valves to hold them in position to flush said valve-chambers.

1,327,343. VEHICLE-WHEEL. WARREN M. MANSFIELD, Davenport, Iowa. Filed Aug. 5, 1918. Serial No. 248,385. 10 Claims. (Cl. 152—32.)

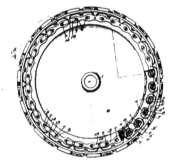

4. A vehicle wheel including an inner rim; a tread rim surrounding the inner rim and movable in the plane of the wheel with respect thereto, one of said rims being of channel formation with two channel walls; a plurality of leaf springs attached to one of said rims, the springs having spirally shaped ends terminating in V-formation; mounting blocks having V-pockets receiving the V-formed ends of the springs, these blocks passing through openings in the aforesaid channel walls; V-shaped tapering assembling keys engaging the V-shaped ends of the springs to maintain them in the V-pockets of the mounting blocks, said keys also passing through the openings that receive said mounting blocks; key retaining clips engaging the outer ends of the keys; and bolts upon one of the channel walls that maintain said clips in engagement with said keys.

1,327,344. INTERRUPTER FOR IGNITION DEVICES. CHARLES THOMAS MASON, Sumter, S. C., assignor to Splitdorf Electrical Company, Newark, N. J., a Corporation of New Jersey. Filed Mar. 27, 1918. Serial No. 225,030. 11 Claims. (Cl. 123—166.)

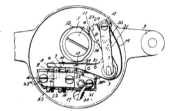

1. An interrupter mechanism for ignition systems comprising a pair of main contacts, one of which is movable for breaking a circuit to produce an ignition spark, a pair of auxiliary contacts in multiple with said main contacts and one of which is movable, said auxiliary contacts being timed so as to open before and close after said main contacts, a lever carrying the movable contacts, said lever being fulcrumed intermediate its ends and carrying the contacts at one end thereof, a fiber block at the other end of said lever from the contacts and a cam adapted to engage the fiber block for moving said lever.

1,327,345. INTERNAL-COMBUSTION ENGINE. LEWIS MAYERS, New York, N. Y. Filed June 15, 1916. Serial No. 103,899. 3 Claims. (Cl. 123—59.)

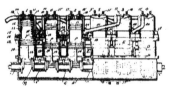

1. In an internal combustion engine, the combination with a plurality of step cylinders, each having a working chamber and a pumping chamber, a step piston for each of said cylinders having a section working in said working chamber and a section working in said pumping chamber, and means for conveying an explosive charge from the pumping chamber of one cylinder to the working chamber of another cylinder where such charge is to be ignited, the compression stroke of each of the pumping sections coinciding with the exhaust stroke of its attached working section, and the connection between each pair of pumping and working chambers communicating with the latter near its outer end, so that a charge is forced from the pumping chamber of one cylinder into the working chamber of another cylinder at approximately the outer dead center of the piston movement and under approximately final pressure whereby reëxpansion of the charge is eliminated.

1,327,346. ENSILAGE-CUTTER. GEORGE M. MERWIN, Berwyn, Ill., assignor, by mesne assignments, to International Harvester Company, a Corporation of New Jersey. Filed Jan. 12, 1918. Serial No. 211,508. 1 Claim. (Cl. 146—26.)

A cutter head for ensilage cutters comprising a journal member having a cylindrical sleeve portion and an outwardly extending flange, a plurality of flat concentric disks of different diameters each of said disks being positioned on said sleeve portion and being secured to said flange, supplementary means connecting said disks together, a plurality of knives secured to said disks and extending from the outer edges of said disks inwardly toward the center thereof, and fan blades having channels therein fitting over the outer circumferential portion of the disk of greatest diameter and having an extension

overlapping a plurality of said disks, and means passing through a plurality of said disks for securing said fan blades to said disks and certain of said disks to each other.

1,327,347. GRINDING-MILL. SAMUEL JOHN MILLS and JAMES SLOAN MILLS, Fleming, Saskatchewan, Canada. Filed Apr. 12, 1919. Serial No. 289,714. 4 Claims. (Cl. 83—8.)

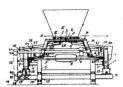

1. In a grinding mill, a support; a horizontal table located above said support and carried thereby and provided with a pair of separated openings therethrough; a hopper supported by said table and provided with two separated horizontally-disposed openings which are in alinement with the openings in said table; a horizontally-disposed cut-off positioned underneath said table and provided with two plates spaced apart which simultaneously control the passage of grain through said openings, and further provided with a handle; means carried by said table to hold said cut-off operatively in place; a pair of chutes located underneath said cut-off to receive grain from said hopper to convey it to point of consumption, and means non-obstructively positioned and carried by said table for pivoting said chutes in place at their inner ends.

1,327,348. CROSS-THREAD-LAYING MECHANISM FOR SEWING-MACHINES. JAMES R. MOFFATT, Chicago, Ill., assignor to Union Special Machine Company, Chicago, Ill., a Corporation of Illinois. Filed Nov. 15, 1916. Serial No. 131,486. 6 Claims. (Cl. 112—100.)

2. The combination of a work support, a pressor foot, a presser bar carrying said foot, a feeding mechanism, a pair of needles arranged in a plane at right angles to the line of feed, a fixed thread guide carried by the presser foot and disposed at one side of the needles and slightly in rear of the plane of the needles, a thread hook carried by the presser bar and movable across the line of feed to engage a cross thread extending through said fixed

thread guide and back across the line of feed for forming a loop in the cross thread, said hook and stationary thread

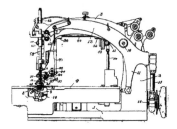

guide being so disposed relative to the needles as to position the loop in the cross thread for the entrance only of the needle farthest removed from the thread guide.

1,327,349. HOMOPOLAR MAGNETIC CIRCUIT. ROBERT V. MORSE, Ithaca, N. Y. Filed Sept. 13, 1917. Serial No. 191,267. 2 Claims. (Cl. 171—212.)

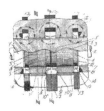

2. In a homopolar dynamo-electric machine, a field structure having a number of ridges and hollows extending in a longitudinal axial direction, the ridges having substantially straight faces on one side and faces extending outwardly from the base on the other side, and electrical conductors extending longitudinally in the hollows between the ridges.

1,327,350. COOLING SYSTEM FOR HOMOPOLAR MACHINES. ROBERT V. MORSE, Ithaca, N. Y. Filed Sept. 13, 1917. Serial No. 191,268. 5 Claims. (Cl. 171—212.)

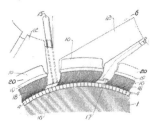

1. In a homopolar dynamo-electric machine, the combination of a homopolar field structure having an annular pole face, an armature having a zone of armature conductors adjacent the pole face but spaced therefrom to form an air gap therebetween, brushes closely spaced circumferentially around the armature and bordering and substantially inclosing the air gap, an air duct passing through the pole face in the region of the trailing tip of

a brush so as to weaken the field where an armature conductor has its connection with a brush interrupted, and means for forcing a current of air through the air duct into the air gap, and from the air gap out between the brushes.

1,327,351. BUNGHOLE-CLOSURE. ROY H. NORTON, Dedham, Mass. Filed Aug. 14, 1919. Serial No. 317,541. 5 Claims. (Cl. 251—19.)

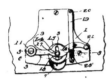

1. In a device of the kind described, comprising a plate having an opening adapted to be secured over the opening of the receptacle, a lever pivotally mounted on said plate, a closure member slidably mounted on said lever, said lever having a cam portion, and an adjustable member arranged in the path of travel of the said cam portion for forcing said plate under pressure.

1,327,352. TELEGRAPH-RECEPTOR. WILLIAM E. PEIRCE, Newark, N. J. Filed Jan. 17, 1917. Serial No. 142,928. 4 Claims. (Cl. 178—88.)

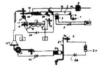

1. In a telegraph receptor having a diaphragm, an amplifying lever in mechanical contact with the same, a support to which said amplifying lever is pivoted, means for adjusting said support, a spiral spring controlling tension of said amplifying lever and means for conveying signals received by said amplifying lever to a Morse circuit substantially as described.

1,327,353. FERTILIZER-DISTRIBUTER. ALONZO H. PENCE and THOMAS J. MORROW, Somerville, Ala. Filed Sept. 6, 1919. Serial No. 322,100. 3 Claims. (Cl. 111—76.)

1. In a fertilizer distributer a wheel, a structure mounted thereon, a hopper carried by said structure, a boot, a pan open at one end and receiving material from the hopper for directing it into the boot, an arm extending from the pan, yielding means for pressing one end of the arm laterally into the path of the spokes of the wheel, an adjusting lever, and a connection between said lever and the arm.

1,327,354. MOLDED FORMS OF BITUMEN. RAY POTTER PERRY, Montclair, N. J., assignor to The Barrett Company, New York, N. Y., a Corporation of West Virginia. Filed Apr. 14, 1916. Serial No. 91,121. 7 Claims. (Cl. 196—22.)

1. The herein described product comprising non-adherent, relatively thin, isolated bodies of bitumen having two substantially parallel faces not more than ⅛ of an inch apart.

1,327,355. PARACHUTE AND LAUNCHING DEVICE FOR AEROPLANES. JOHN LOUIS PFLUEGER, New Orleans, La. Filed July 30, 1919. Serial No. 314,275. 5 Claims. (Cl. 244—21.)

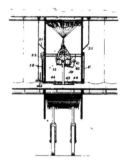

1. The combination of an aeroplane having vertical guide beams, portions of which extend above and below its lower plane, trap doors mounted within the lower plane between the several guide beams, a latch mechanism normally holding the said trap doors in closed position, a lever for releasing said connections, a seat post supported by the said trap doors in closed position, an aviator's seat carried by the seat post, a parachute having telescoping ribs provided with means for engagement with the guide beams when the ribs are collapsed, and connections between the aviator's seat and the said parachute whereby upon the release of the trap doors, the parachute will be carried downwardly along the guide beams with the seat and seat post.

1,327,356. TAILSTOCK-CLAMPING MECHANISM. SALMON W. PUTNAM, 3d, Rochester, N. Y., assignor to Arthur H. Ingle, Rochester, N. Y. Filed Nov. 21, 1918. Serial No. 263,597. 12 Claims. (Cl. 82—31.)

1. Apparatus of the kind described, comprising a bed equipped with ways, a mounting for a tailstock or the like adapted to receive and withstand operative pressure,

slidably fitted on said ways, and means constructed and arranged to clamp said mounting to said bed in a selective adjusted position automatically by operative pressure applied to said mounting and with a force proportional to such pressure.

1,327,357. COIN-ASSORTER. JOHN A. ROGERS, Atlanta, Ga., assignor to Henry S. Cohen, Marietta, Ga. Filed July 28, 1917. Serial No. 183,334. - 4 Claims. (Cl. 133—3.)

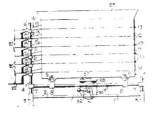

1. In a coin assorter, the combination with a series of inclined perforated courses arranged in vertically spaced relation, each course being adapted to retain coins of a specific denomination, and a plurality of coin depositories coöperating with the several courses; of a carriage supporting said courses, and means for imparting an intermittent gyratory movement to said carriage comprising laterally offset parallelly extending guide members, bearing blocks slidably positioned upon said members, auxiliary guide rods arranged intermediate said bearing blocks and transverse of said guide members, said rods being adapted to support said carriage, and means for alternately sliding said bearing members and carriage, substantially as described.

1,327,358. LOCKING MECHANISM FOR SWITCH-POINTS. NILS RÖSHOLT, Christiania, Norway, assignor to Nils Aall Krag, Christiania, Norway. Filed Nov. 22, 1919. Serial No. 339,929. 4 Claims. (Cl. 246—318.)

1. In a locking mechanism for switch points particularly for tramways or the like, the combination with a connecting member between the points, a stationary cam surface and a yielding member fastened on said connecting member engaging said cam surface.

1,327,359. FIGURE TOY. STANLEY SMIGIELSKI, Detroit, Mich. Filed Sept. 4. 1919. Serial No. 321,572. 1 Claim. (Cl. 46—40.)

A figure toy comprising a platform, an anvil supported thereon, figures mounted on said platform, a longitudinal shaft journaled beneath said platform, crank portions in said shaft adjacent the figures, bell-cranks supported beneath said platform adjacent said figures, connections between said figures and said bell-cranks, link connections between the bell-cranks and the crank portions of the shaft and gear mechanism associated with said shaft for rotating the same, said gear mechanism including a gear

---

wheel fixed to said shaft, a standard secured to the upper face of the platform, a power shaft journaled in said

standard, a crank on the outer end of said power shaft, and a gear fixed to the power shaft in mesh with the aforesaid gear.

1,327,360. WHIRLIGIG. STANLEY SMIGIELSKI, Detroit, Mich. Filed Oct. 15, 1919. Serial No. 330,846. 3 Claims. (Cl. 46—14.)

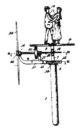

1. A device of the class described comprising a handle, a shank carried thereby, a bracket having a forked end inclosing the shank of said handle, a fan journaled in said bracket, a disk rotatable upon said handle shank, figure toys upon said disk, and means for communicating motion from the fan to the disk.

1,327,361. IGNITION DEVICE. HARRY RANDOLPH VAN DEVENTER, Sumter, S. C., assignor to Splitdorf Electrical Company, Newark, N. J., a Corporation of New Jersey. Filed Oct. 13, 1917. Serial No. 196,371. 3 Claims. (Cl. 123—149.)

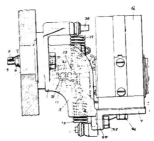

1. An ignition device comprising a two part supporting bracket, ignition electrodes carried by one part of

said bracket, a generator carried by the other part of said bracket, and a trip operated spring actuating device for said generator and electrodes carried by the part of said bracket supporting the electrodes.

1,327,362. CONSTRUCTION OF HAMPERS. Alfred Walden, London, England, assignor of one-half to Harry Joseph Walsh, Bexhill-on-Sea, England. Filed Nov. 15, 1917, Serial No. 202,150. Renewed Nov. 20, 1919. Serial No. 339,316. 8 Claims. (Cl. 217—122.)

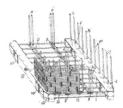

7. In a hamper the combination with a bottom comprising cross canes, vertical canes secured to the end cross canes and extending to the top of the hamper, strengthening canes arranged in pairs interwoven with the cross canes, alternating between the vertical canes and extending up the sides to the top of the hamper.

1,327,363. LOUVRE-BLIND. Percy H. Wilson and Charles H. Sapper, Norfolk, Va. Filed May 1, 1918. Serial No. 231,953. 17 Claims. (Cl. 156—16.)

1. A louvre blind including in combination, a plurality of slats, collapsible means for holding said slats in spaced parallel relation including a jointed metal tape comprising rigid links pivotally connected by rule joints for opening and closing movements in a plane parallel to the plane determined by corresponding longitudinal edges of the slats and each link pivotally connected to a slat.

1,327,364. LOUVRE-BLIND SLAT AND CLIP. Percy H. Wilson and Charles H. Sapper, Norfolk, Va. Filed May 1, 1918. Serial No. 231,954. 5 Claims. (Cl. 156—16.)

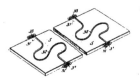

1. As an article of manufacture, a clip for the slats of louvre blinds having a hook at one end adapted to engage the edge of a slat, a part at the other end formed to engage the opposite edge of the slat, and an intermediate spring portion for drawing said hook and part together to clamp the slat.

1,327,365. JOINTED METALLIC TAPE. Percy H. Wilson and Charles H. Sapper, Norfolk, Va. Filed May 1, 1918, Serial No. 231,955. Renewed Nov. 18, 1919. Serial No. 338,826. 8 Claims. (Cl. 59—78.)

1. As an article of manufacture, a tape for louvre blinds comprising a series of rigid flat links pivotally connected end to end with alternate links adapted to swing in the same and adjacent links in opposite directions and means to limit the angle to which adjacent links may open to less than 180°.

1,327,366. MEANS FOR LOCKING AUTOMOBILES. William F. Zink, Garrett, Ind. Filed Nov. 14, 1917. Serial No. 201,978. 5 Claims. (Cl. 277—69.)

1. In a device as set forth, the combination with a plurality of connected valve bodies having a passage therethrough, of a plurality of valves mounted in said bodies, each adapted to control said passage, each valve being movable independently of any other valve and including a valve stem, a pair of elongated bars resting on the upper faces of the valve bodies adjacent their side portions and being in parallelism, means straddling portions of the valve bodies and being secured to said bars, a plurality of dial plates, each disposed concentrically with and rotatably receiving a part of the valve, means for securing the dial plates to the bars, the dial plate being graduated, a pointer mounted on each stem for rotation therewith and coacting with the graduations of the respective dial plate, and means for detachably holding the pointer in engagement with the valve.

1,327,367. CAR-FRAME. Hans Arquint, Richterswil, Switzerland. Filed Dec. 22, 1917. Serial No. 208,404. 4 Claims. (Cl. 105—400.)

1. A car frame of the class described, comprising rigid, closed main supporting frames arranged in the longitudinal direction of the car frame, non-rigid spacing members connecting the main supporting frames, longitudinal elastic draw-members connecting the main sup-

porting frames and the spacing members to a car body, an underframe supporting the car body, and means re-

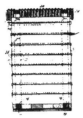

inforcing the cross-section of the lower cross-beams of the main supporting frames at the places where they rest on the underframe.

1,327,368. FOLDING CHICKEN-COOP. HUGH A. BAR-NARD, Houstonville, N. C. Filed Mar. 12, 1917. Serial No. 154,326. 2 Claims. (Cl. 217—47.)

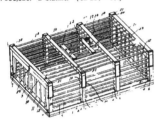

1. A folding coop comprising a bottom wall, cleats secured to the front and rear edges of the bottom wall, end walls pivotally secured to said cleats, front and rear walls hingedly secured to the cleats, a cover resting upon the upper ends of the front and rear walls and loop members having the upper end thereof bent at right angles thereto, the lower portions of said loop members being pivotally secured to the outer faces of the front and rear walls, the angular terminals of the loops being pivotally secured to the cover for permitting the front and rear walls to be folded inwardly over the end walls and permitting the cover to rest flatly upon the front and rear walls and preventing outward movement of the front and rear walls in relation to each other.

1,327,369. AUTOMOBILE NON-SKID CHAIN. EDWARD H. BEAUDREAU, Meriden, Conn., assignor to American Tool Company, Meriden, Conn., a Corporation of Connecticut. Filed Sept. 6, 1918. Serial No. 252,873. 9 Claims. (Cl. 152—2.)

1. An anti-slipping attachment for wheels, comprising a non-skid chain, a pair of relatively short chains per-

manently secured to one end of said chain, and a single fastening device permanently secured upon the other end of said non-skid chain for detachably securing the free ends of said short chains thereto, said pair of chains arranged to straddle one of the spokes of the wheel, whereby said non-skid chain is prevented from creeping about the wheel upon which it is mounted but releasable from the wheel by disengaging said fastening device.

3. A non-skid chain for automobile wheels, and means for securing said chain in place upon the tread of a wheel, comprising a pair of spoke engaging members, each having a portion permanently secured to the same end of said chain, and a safety hook on the other end of said chain for removably securing the free ends of said spoke engaging members thereto.

1,327,370. UNIVERSAL ANGLE-FIXTURE. JOHN R. BECKETT, Somerville, Mass. Filed Oct. 7, 1918, Serial No. 257,202. Renewed Oct. 6, 1919. Serial No. 328,928. 4 Claims. (Cl. 90—58.)

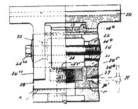

1. A work holding fixture, comprising a base equipped with an upstanding stud, a housing mounted to swivel on said stud, a clamping nut fitted to a seat in said housing and threaded on said stud, said nut having gear teeth on a face thereof to be engaged by an adjusting pinion, and a work holding platen mounted for turning adjustment in said housing on an axis at right angles to said stud.

1,327,371. AUTOMATIC PUMP. ORA BERRY, Princeton, Ind. Filed Mar. 8, 1918. Serial No. 221,281. 3 Claims. (Cl. 152—11.)

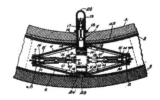

1. An air pump comprising an elastic bulb adapted to be disposed within a pneumatic tire, said bulb having end portions, outer tubular frame members arranged in the ends thereof and provided with check valved outlets, a central annular compressible frame piece arranged centrally within the bulb or sack, rods terminally pivoted to said central and outer frame members, and a filling tube secured to the bulb and to the central frame member thereof.

1,327,372. PROJECTILE. GUSTAVE BESSIÈRE, Neuilly-sur-Seine, France. Filed Dec. 3, 1917. Serial No. 205,131. 1 Claim. (Cl. 102—26.)
A projectile including a message receiving tube, a cylindrical casing enveloping said tube, and being filled with a

smoke producing material, a detonating device positioned in the front of the casing, such detonating device comprising a cap, a striker, a fuse and a soft metal rod, the striker being formed with a transversely extending open-

ing adapted to house the rod which engages the cap member and retains the striker in a position above the cap, the inertia, when such projectile is fired, serving to shield said rod and allow the striker to explode the cap igniting the fuse which fires the smoke producing material.

1,327,373. NUT-LOCK. LUTHER W. CARDEN, Cherokee, Ala. Filed Oct. 31, 1919. Serial No. 334,745. 2 Claims. (Cl. 151—2.)

1 The combination with a bolt having a longitudinal seat, of a nut on the bolt and provided with a transverse opening adapted to communicate with the seat, the opening having a circumferential extension located adjacent to the bolt; and a ball insertible into the seat by way of the opening, the ball being lodged in the seat and the extension when a reverse rotation is imparted to the nut.

1,327,374. ANIMAL-RESTRAINING DEVICE. CHARLES E. CLINE, Abingdon, Ill. Filed Apr. 11, 1919. Serial No. 289,265. 4 Claims. (Cl. 119—99.)

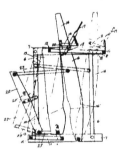

1. In a restraining device, a stall, a pair of coöperating jaws pivoted at the forward end of the same, a lever pivoted at its middle to the stall, a guide bar disposed at the upper end of the stall, one of the jaws being longitudinally movable between the guide and upper part of the stall, a link pivotally connected with one of the jaws, a lever pivotally connected with the link, a loop carried thereby and slidable on the guide adapted to bind thereon when the jaws are in closed or open position, a link opera-

tively connecting one of the jaws and the first mentioned lever together, and a link connecting the latter and the remaining jaw.

1,327,375. IGNITION-GENERATOR. WILLIAM WARREN DEAN, Stamford, Conn., assignor to Splitdorf Electrical Company, Newark, N. J., a Corporation of New Jersey. Filed Aug. 22, 1916. Serial No. 116,358. 5 Claims. (Cl. 171—252.)

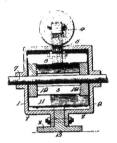

1. An ignition magneto comprising a stationary current generating coil, a core therefor, pole pieces for said core, a rotor comprising a permanent magnet having a plurality of sections extending parallel with the axis of the rotor, said sections being spaced from each other and spaced from the center of said rotor, said pole pieces being located in a plane at right angles to the axis of the rotor and disposed midway between the ends of the respectove magnet sections.

1,327,376. DEVICE FOR INCREASING THE ADHERENCE OF AGRICULTURAL TRACTORS TO THE SOIL. PAUL ALBERT MAURICE DELIEUVIN, Neuilly-sur-Seine, France. Filed Dec. 29, 1917. Serial No. 209,492. 3 Claims. (Cl. 180—14.)

1. The combination with an agricultural tractor provided with front and rear supporting wheels adapted to come in direct contact with the ground of an oscillating frame pivoted to the tractor, a strongly adherent wheel carried by said frame at the rear of the tractor in the space between the vertical planes of the rear wheels of the same, said strongly adherent wheel being adapted to come in direct contact with the ground, means for driving this wheel, means for yoking the oscillating frame to the trailed apparatus so that it may pivot downwardly and thus bring the wheel in contact with the soil through the resistance of the said trailed apparatus and means for pivoting upwardly the oscillating frame and lifting the wheel out of contact with the soil as soon as the strain of the trailed apparatus ceases to be exerted upon the oscillating frame.

1,327,377. PIPE-DOOR. JOSEPH DICK, Canton, Ohio, assignor to The Joseph Dick Manufacturing Company, Canton, Ohio, a Corporation of Ohio. Filed July 5, 1916. Serial No. 107,525. 6 Claims. (Cl. 126—307.)

1. A pipe having an opening therein, and a door plate slightly larger than the opening cut away at each side to

permit its upper portion to be inserted in the opening to underlap the upper portion thereof, there being inter-engag-

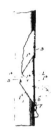

ing shoulders at each side of the opening and the plate, and means for holding the shoulders in engagement.

1,327,378. AMMUNITION LUBRICATION. THEODORE H. EICKHOFF and CHARLES A. TUNKS, Cleveland, Ohio, assignors, by direct and mesne assignments, to Auto-Ordnance Corporation, New York, N. Y., a Corporation of New York. Filed Apr. 13, 1918. Serial No. 228,496. 24 Claims. (Cl. 86—19.)

1. Lubricated ammunition comprising a thin coating of lubricating wax which is substantially non-adhesive at atmospheric temperatures.

1,327,379. WELL-DRILL WRENCH. WILLIAM H. ELLINGER, Bonita, Tex. Filed June 30, 1919. Serial No. 307,664. 1 Claim. (Cl. 81—119.)

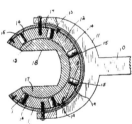

A well drill wrench comprising a shank, a yoke formed on one end of the shank, an open ring swiveled in the yoke, said ring being formed with radial recesses opening through the periphery and the upper face of the ring, a retaining band secured around the periphery of the ring, antifriction rollers in said recesses and partially projecting through the upper portions of the recesses, a second open ring rotatable within the first ring and having upper and lower peripheral flanges engaging the first ring, the upper flange extending over the upper face of the first ring and resting on the antifriction rollers, and band grips on the second ring.

1,327,380. RADIATOR-CORE. JOHN M. FEDDERS, Buffalo, N. Y., assignor to Fedders Manufacturing Company, Inc., Buffalo, N. Y., a Corporation of New York. Filed Sept. 20. 1915. Serial No. 51,548. 2 Claims. (Cl. 257—130.)

1. A radiator core comprising a plurality of water tubes and a plurality of radiating fins arranged between the several water tubes, each of said tubes having two walls each of which is constructed of a corrugated strip of metal and

each of said fins being constructed of a single corrugated strip of metal, and each of said fin strips having the concave faces of its alternate corrugations provided with laterally projecting rows of centering loops which are of sub-

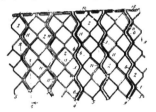

stantially the same form in cross section as the corrugations of the water tube and fin strips and which engage with the concave faces of the corrugations of adjacent strips, and the loops in each row of each fin projecting alternately from opposite sides of the respective strip.

1,327,381. TEMPERATURE - CONTROLLING MECHANISM FOR INTERNAL - COMBUSTION ENGINES. FREDERICK M. FURBER, Revere, Mass. Filed June 8, 1916. Serial No. 102,514. 19 Claims. (Cl. 123—178.)

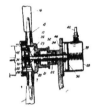

1. The combination with an internal combustion engine and a heat radiating system therefor constructed to radiate heat into the surrounding atmosphere, of means coöperating with said system to facilitate the dissipation of heat therefrom, said means being constructed and arranged to direct waste heat from the engine on to said system to modify the rate at which the heat will be dissipated by said system, and mechanism responsive automatically to changes of temperature in said system for controlling said means.

1,327,382. SPARK-PLUG. HARVEY C. GARBER, Columbus, Ohio. Filed Mar. 25, 1918. Serial No. 224,459. 3 Claims. (Cl. 123—169.)

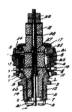

1. In a spark plug, a hollow metallic shell member having a bushing receiving chamber formed therein, and provided with a transverse fluid circulating opening, an electrode bushing of insulating material positioned within.

said chamber and formed with a substantially transverse fluid circulating opening in communication with said former opening, and an electrode positioned within a bore formed in said bushing, said latter bore being of substantially greater diameter than the electrode to permit a cooling fluid passing through said openings to circulate about said electrode.

1,327,383. ELECTRIC SWITCH. BENJAMIN EVERETT GETCHELL, Plainville, Conn., assignor to The Trumbull Electric Manufacturing Company, Plainville, Conn., a Corporation of Connecticut. Filed May 26, 1919. Serial No. 299,931. 10 Claims. (Cl. 200—109.)

1. The combination with the movable element of an electric switch, of a latch lever for holding said movable switch element in one position, a trip lever for securing the latch lever in holding position, an electro-magnet for freeing the trip lever from holding engagement with the latch lever, said trip lever having an arm for engagement with the latch lever and provided with a cam shoulder, and an operating member for said trip lever engaging said cam shoulder.

1,327,384. INTERNAL-COMBUSTION ENGINE. STEPHEN B. HASSLY, Faribault, Minn. Filed Apr. 21, 1916. Serial No. 92,623. 1 Claim. (Cl. 123—122.)

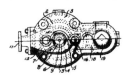

An internal combustion engine comprising a cylinder having its head provided with a gas intake port and a centrally mounted valve therefor, said head having a vaporizing duct formed in its walls extending entirely around said valve and said duct having a port communicating through said valve with the combustion chamber, and a duct on the other side of said valve for connection with the carbureter, the charge entering said duct flowing in opposite directions therein around said valve and being retarded by the mixing of the oppositely flowing currents.

1,327,385. COMBINED GRINDER AND SHAKER. WILLIE A. HAMMER, Eufaula, Okla. Filed Apr. 25, 1919. Serial No. 292,743. 1 Claim. (Cl. 83—13.)

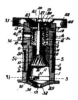

An individual condiment grinder and dispenser, comprising a body-member having communicating chambers at each end thereof, grinding mechanism interposed between the chambers and comprising a grinding sleeve rigidly mounted therein and a grinding cone co-acting with the same, said cone having a shank extending beyond one end of the body-member, a combined base plate and operating member connected to the exposed end of the shank to rotate the same, said base plate and operating member being of greater diameter than the body member and having an upstanding annular wall or flange, and a cap plate mounted on the other end of the body-member to close the chamber at that end, said cap having a dispensing orifice and means for securing the said cap in place.

1,327,386. ADJUSTABLE CATTLE-STALL. SAMUEL L. HANSON, Albert Lea, Minn. Filed Oct. 28, 1918. Serial No. 260,013. 9 Claims. (Cl. 119—27.)

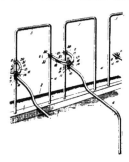

1. In cattle stall construction embodying stanchion supporting frames spaced widthwise of the stalls, a partition bar for dividing one stall from another and approaching but stopping short of the plane of the frames, and means for connecting the bar to adjacent stanchion supporting frames, comprising couplings individual to the frames, separate connecting members, one for each coupling, and a coupling structure common to the connecting members and to the partition bar with the combined length of the connecting members greater than the spacing of the supporting frames.

1,327,387. HIGHWAY-MARKER. FRANK W. HOCKADAY, Wichita, Kans. Filed June 1, 1918. Serial No. 237,783. 6 Claims. (Cl. 40—125.)

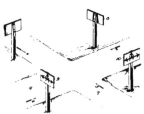

1. The system of marking meeting highways which comprises the use of indicating symbols of different sizes, locating adjacent the highway to be marked and at a point relatively remote from the meeting point of the other highways with the first mentioned highway, a plurality of such symbols being relatively arranged to point in the respective directions to indicate the respective highways to which they bear relation, and proportioning the size of the symbols in accordance with the relative importance of the respective highways.

1,327,388. PUZZLE. FRANK LESLIE INCE, Maplewood, Mo. Filed Sept. 4, 1919. Serial No. 321,680. 3 Claims. (Cl. 46—41.)

1. A puzzle comprising a body member of trefoil form having convoluted lateral loops conjoined by a comparatively narrow median loop, said body member being closed by a movable closing link extending transversely of the body member and movable into position overlying the median loop, a closed keeper permanently interlinked with the body member and closing link, and a removable member retained on the keeper, said removable member being movable from the keeper on to and off of the loops of the body member.

1,327,389. SANITARY MEASURE AND FUNNEL COMBINED. JOSEPH F. JOHNSON, Long Beach, Miss., assignor of one-half to Dominick W. Stepisieh, Long Beach, Miss. Filed Mar. 8, 1918. Serial No 221,233. 2 Claims. (Cl. 221—15.)

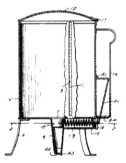

1. A device of the character described including a container having a discharge opening in its bottom, a valve for said opening, a casing secured to the bottom of the container and slidably receiving said valve, a valve rod connected to said valve and extending through said casing, a U-shaped member secured to one side of the container and having a slot in its bottom, an upright flat operating spring disposed within said U-shaped member, said operating spring being secured at its upper end to said container and having its lower end portion extended through the slot in the U-shaped member and connected to said valve rod, and a catch carried by said U-shaped member for locking said operating spring, said operating spring being adapted to be drawn toward said U-shaped member for operating the valve.

1,327,390. COMBINATION SAW-TABLE AND SINGLE-SPINDLE SHAPER. NATHAN JOSIAS, Philadelphia, Pa. Filed Sept. 6, 1919. Serial No. 322,208. 8 Claims. (Cl. 144—1.)

1. In a combination saw table and single spindle shaper, the combination with a hollow standard, of a head slidable therein, the lower portion of the head being bifurcated, means extending transversely of the standard having operative connections with one of the sides of the bifurcation for adjusting the head, the upper part of the head having a bifurcation at right angles to the lower bifurcation, a

spindle holder pivotally mounted in the upper bifurcation, whereby it may be disposed in vertical or horizontal positions, means for securing the holder in either of said

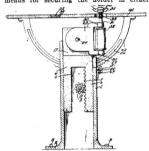

positions, a table tiltably mounted upon the upper end of the standard, and a spindle mounted in the holder and adapted to rotate when in a horizontal position under the table, or in a vertical position passing through the table.

1,327,391. WATCH-SETTING LEVER. WILLIAM W. JORDAN, Delhi, La. Filed Jan. 7, 1918. Serial No. 210,724. 1 Claim. (Cl. 58—66.)

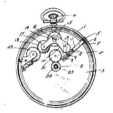

A watch setting device including a bell crank lever having one arm thereof provided at its swinging end with a segmental rack, a pivot pin upon which the bell crank lever is mounted, a shifting gear carried by the other arm of the bell crank lever, a stem operated gear mounted upon the pivot pin and meshing with the shifting gear, a rectilinearly movable slide formed with a rack meshing with the said segmental rack and coöperating therewith to swing the bell crank lever, a spring winding gear arranged to engage the shifting gear at one position of the bell crank lever, and a setting gear arranged to engage the shifting lever at the other position of the bell crank lever.

1,327,392. COMBINED CENTER AND CANNON PINION. WILLIAM W. JORDAN, Delhi, La. Filed Jan. 7, 1918. Serial No. 210,725. 1 Claim. (Cl. 58—138.)

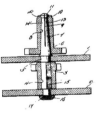

In a device of the character described, the combination with side plates having alined openings of which one is smaller than the other, an arbor journaled within the openings and insertible through the larger opening, the portion of the arbor between the plates having a polygonal formation, a center pinion fitted slidably upon the polygonal portion of the arbor, one end of the arbor projecting beyond the plates, means for locking the arbor against removal, and a cannon pinion fitted upon the projecting end of the arbor.

1,327,393. FABRIC-TESTING MACHINE. ALFRED E. JURY, Newark, N. J., assignor to The United States Tire Company, a Corporation of New York. Filed July 24, 1918. Serial No. 246,473. 8 Claims. (Cl. 265—2.)

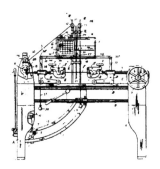

1. In a fabric testing machine, two clamping devices adapted to hold a piece of fabric between them, means for relatively moving said devices, a movable chart and a marker in register therewith, a guide roller carried by each clamping device, and a cord looped about each guide roller, one end of the cord being connected to the chart and the other end being connected to a fixed member.

1,327,394. BLEACHING COMPOSITION. RICHARD B. KADISH and THEODORE W. BUSCHER, Chicago, Ill., assignors to The Kadish Manufacturing Company, Chicago, Ill., a Corporation of South Dakota. Filed Dec. 11, 1917. Serial No. 206,589. (Cl. 8—2.)

1. The chemical composition made by the intermingling of a fluorid, a hydroxid and an acid sulfate of an alkali metal while in a nearly dry state.

1,327,395. HYDROPOWER-BEATER. EDMOND KELLEY, Boston, Mass. Filed Aug. 19, 1918. Serial No. 250,492. 13 Claims. (Cl. 259—122.)

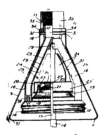

1. A hydromotor attachment for an automatic beating machine comprising a base adapted to be mounted on a

jar to cover the mouth thereof, a pedestal mounted on said base and having a ball race in its upper side, a shaft passing through said pedestal and base adapted to enter the jar, balls in said ball race, a plate resting on said balls and connected to said shaft, vanes mounted upon said shaft, and a conduit rising from said base and extending past said vanes longitudinally, having means for connection with a source of water supply, and having an outlet arranged to direct a jet of water against said vanes, whereby to drive the latter rotatably.

1,327,396. PROCESS FOR PREPARING CATALYTIC AGENT FOR HYDROGENATING HARD OILS. KANESUKE KIMURA, Kobe, Japan. Filed Aug. 1, 1917. Serial No. 183,982. 1 Claim. (Cl. 23—28.)

The process of preparing a nickel catalytic agent for hydrogenating oils, consisting in mixing powdered nickel nitrate with powdered pumice, charging the mixture into a vessel of a material which effects no catalytic action with such mixture, heating said vessel and its contents by heating means applied exteriorly of said vessel, agitating the contents of the vessel, and subjecting the contents of the vessel to the action of the vapor of ammonium chlorid.

1,327,397. MANURE-BOX. MAX LEVIN, Chicago, Ill. Filed Mar. 22, 1915. Serial No. 16,241. 1 Claim. (Cl. 220—98.)

A manure box comprising a body having a bottom, front, back and sides and its top open, a cover hinged to the body to permit material to be discharged into the body through the open top, said body having an opening in one side thereof adjacent the bottom, and a door hinged to the bottom of the body to swing downwardly and outwardly for closing said opening, said door being provided with an extension disposed to swing under the bottom when the door is open.

1,327,398. PROCESS OF CASTING STEEL. DANIEL TODD MAIN, Winnipeg, Manitoba, Canada. Filed June 17, 1918. Serial No. 240,395. 2 Claims. (Cl. 75—1.)

1. The process of casting high speed tools from broken pieces of high speed steel which consists in melting the pieces of steel in a crucible, adding one per cent. of manganese and one-half per cent. of silicon to the molten mass and afterward casting the molten mass in molds previously prepared and of the shape required for the finished tool.

1,327,399. CHAIN GRATE FOR FURNACES. JOSEPH MALLINSON, Glasgow, Scotland. Filed Feb. 13, 1917. Serial No. 148,322. 4 Claims. (Cl. 110—40.)

1. A chain grate link made at one end with a downwardly and rearwardly projecting hook and at the other

end with a downwardly, rearwardly and upwardly projecting hook, said link being retained on the rods of the

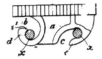

chain grate by elastic compression of the rods between said hooks.

1,327,400. SURFACE-COLORED ARTICLE OF COPPER ALLOY. THURSTON C. MERRIMAN, New Haven, Conn., assignor to Winchester Repeating Arms Co., New Haven, Conn., a Corporation. Filed Aug. 5, 1919. Serial No. 315,448. 3 Claims. (Cl. 148—6.)

1. As a new article of manufacture, an article of copper alloy containing arsenic and having a surface finish of black, or substantially black, color.

1,327,401. PROCESS OF SURFACE-COLORING ARTICLES OF COPPER ALLOY. THURSTON C. MERRIMAN, New Haven, Conn., assignor to Winchester Repeating Arms Co., New Haven, Conn., a Corporation. Filed Aug. 5, 1919. Serial No. 315,449. 4 Claims. (Cl. 148—6.)

1. The process of coloring articles made of alloys containing copper and arsenic which consists in dipping the articles in an acid, oxidizing bath and afterward in an acid solution containing a sulfid and an arsenious compound.

1,327,402. MACHINE FOR CUTTING GREEN CORN FROM THE COB. SAMUEL E. MORRAL and WILLIAM W. MORRAL, Morral, Ohio. Filed July 3, 1916. Serial No. 107,223. 8 Claims. (Cl. 130—9.)

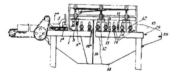

1. In a machine for cutting green corn from the cob including cutters for removing the grain, the combination with means for guiding the ears lengthwise to the cutters, of flexible members for feeding the ears through said guiding means, said flexible members each having a bifurcated spur, the points of which engage the ear circumferentially.

1,327,403. COMBINATION-RIG FOR DRILLING. JESSE A. MORRISON, Mountainair, N. Mex. Filed Dec. 11, 1918. Serial No. 266,256. 1 Claim. (Cl. 255—3.)

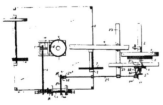

A drill rigging of the class described comprising a band wheel shaft adapted to operate a walking beam, a rotary

carriage, an outfit coacting with the carriage and positioned at one side of the rigging, said outfit including a drive shaft extending longitudinally of the rigging, a line shaft driven by the band wheel shaft, said line shaft also extending longitudinally of the rigging, an operative connection between the line shaft and the drive shaft of the outfit, and means for rendering said last named connection inoperative.

1,327,404. SMOKE-CONTROL AND DRIFT VALVE MECHANISM. EDMUND TROWBRIDGE DANA MYERS, Jr., Richmond, Va. Filed May 26, 1919. Serial No. 299,707. 12 Claims. (Cl. 162—1.)

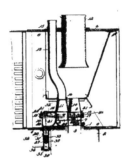

1. In a device of the character described, in combination with the stack, the cylinder saddle and smoke box of a locomotive, a draft device therefor comprising a steam exhaust nozzle adapted to be attached to the cylinder saddle and communicating with the usual cylinder exhaust ports therein, said nozzle including a main nozzle discharging directly into the stack and an auxiliary nozzle, a steam by-pass connection from said auxiliary nozzle to the atmosphere, and separate means for controlling the discharge of steam through each nozzle, said means being operable at will.

1,327,405. FURNACE FOR CONTINUOUS SHEET-GLASS DRAWING. MICHAEL J. OWENS, Toledo, Ohio, assignor to The Libbey-Owens Sheet Glass Company, Toledo, Ohio, a Corporation of Ohio. Filed Nov. 18, 1918. Serial No. 263,024. 11 Claims. (Cl. 49—56.)

1. In combination, a glass melting tank, a refining tank leading therefrom through which molten glass flows from the melting tank toward a sheet drawing source, and regulable means in the refining tank for retarding the flow of hot gases from the melting tank to the outlet end portion of the refining tank over the molten glass therein.

1,327,406. COMBINATION-LOCK FOR THE STEERING-POSTS OF AUTOMOBILES. JOSEPH RACOW, New Haven, Conn. Filed July 31, 1919. Serial No. 314,540. 6 Claims. (Cl. 70—18.)

1. In a combination lock, the combination with a locking sleeve, formed with radial ribs of a series of longitudinally movable tumblers, formed with teeth adapted

to engage with said ribs, a series of screws on which the said tumblers are mounted, said screws each provided

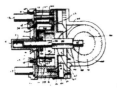

with a knob by which it may be turned for moving said tumblers into and out of engagement with said locking sleeve.

1,327,407. DEVICE FOR THE PREVENTION OF STAM-MERING. FRANK J. ROGERS, Detroit, Mich. Filed Jan. 11, 1917. Serial No. 141,750. 4 Claims. (Cl. 128—137.)

1. A device for the prevention of stammering consisting of a plate of suitable material adapted to be worn between the lower lip and jaw, the plate being substantially ovate in form and curved to conform substantially to the shape of the forward end of the jaw at the base of the teeth, the plate being of greatest thickness at the center to increase the tension of the muscles controlling movement of the lip and jaw, and an insert of soft material adapted to prevent displacement of the plate.

1,327,408. BRASSIÈRE. MEYER W. SCHLOSS, New York, N. Y., assignor to Treo Company, Inc., a Corporation of New York. Filed Mar. 29, 1919. Serial No. 286,035. 2 Claims. (Cl. 2—73.)

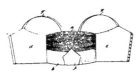

2. A brassière having in combination a breast zone and below the latter and attached thereto, an elastic waist zone provided with an inelastic section of substantial area to form a reducing pad, as set forth.

1,327,409. CONDUIT OUTLET-BOX. AUGUST H. SCHNEIDER, Syracuse, N. Y., assignor to Crouse-Hinds Company, Syracuse, N. Y., a Corporation of New York. Filed Feb. 7, 1916. Serial No. 76,750. 3 Claims. (Cl. 247—12.)

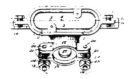

1. A conduit outlet box including a body open at one side and divided into two sections, the dividing line be-tween the sections being located in a plane intersecting the plane of the open side and one of the sections being provided with means individual thereto and remote from the dividing line for connection with a conduit, the sections being provided with flanges at their opposing edges along the dividing line and terminating at the open side, one flange being shaped to house the other and the flanges being shaped to interlock by a sliding movement of one of the sections in a direction parallel to the plane of the dividing line, substantially as and for the purpose set forth.

1,327,410. TURNING-TOOL. EUGENE SIMEONE, Webster, Mass. Filed Mar. 24, 1919. Serial No. 284,757. 4 Claims. (Cl. 29—96.)

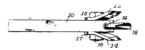

1. A holder for turning tools having, in combination, a shank, and means to secure a plurality of turning tools thereto, said means comprising a fastening device ex-tending transversely through said shank near one end thereof and through a pair of turning tools disposed one on each side thereof, and means on said shank to prevent angular displacement of said tools.

1,327,411. ACTUATING SIGNALS ON AND COMMUNI-CATING WITH TRAINS. HENRY ARTHUR THOMPSON, Manchester, England. Filed Aug. 23, 1916. Serial No. 116,427. 4 Claims. (Cl. 246—194.)

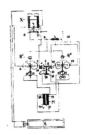

2. In a railway inductive signaling or control system, a normally inoperative valve-operating magnet, a tuned reed relay adapted to send current impulses through the valve-operating magnet, an automatic switch controlled by said reed relay, and a tuned sounder brought into action when said automatic switch is no longer under control.

1,327,412. TELEPHONE. WILLIAM C. UDE, West Haven, Conn. Filed Aug. 1, 1917. Serial No. 183,998. 8 Claims. (Cl. 179—81.)

1. In a telephone, the combination with a talking cir-cuit, of a switch controlling the same, manual means for closing the switch, mechanical locking means for holding the switch in its closed position, a magnetized core ener-

gized by the talking circuit, and an armature released by the said core and co-acting with the said mechanical

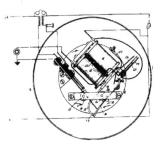

locking means when the talking circuit is opened at central, to open the talking circuit at the telephone.

1,327,413. CULTIVATOR. FREDERICK C. WARNE, Mansfield, Ohio, assignor to Roderick Lean Manufacturing Company, Mansfield, Ohio, a Corporation of New Jersey. Filed Dec. 5, 1914. Serial No. 875,570 18 Claims. (Cl. 97—35.)

16. In an agricultural machine, the combination of steering means, freely movable implements, members movably connected to the steering means and to the implements, and connections between said members constructed to move the steering means when the implements are simultaneously moved in the same direction, and arranged for simultaneous like movement toward and from each other while retaining the steering means motionless.

18. A cultivator provided with pivot axles and wheels, a radius bar pivotally connected to the axles, freely movable cultivator beams, members pivoted on the bar and movably connected to the beams, and connections between the members arranged to allow movement of the beams toward and from each other while retaining the bar motionless, and moving the bar when the beams are simultaneously moved in the same direction.

1,327,414. ICE-MAKING APPARATUS. WALTER D. WILLCOX, Upper Darby, Pa. Filed Aug. 8, 1918. Serial No. 248,977. 8 Claims. (Cl. 62—106.)

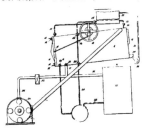

1. A device of the character described including a shell; a can positioned within the shell and spaced therefrom

to provide room for a freezing medium ; a gate for closing one end of the can ; means for continuously admitting water into said can at a position above the bottom of the can and adjacent one end thereof ; and an overflow outlet for the water of said can adjacent the opposite end of the can, said admitted water and overflow effecting the circulation of the water within the can, thereby causing new portions of water to be moved toward the inner surfaces of the can to quicken the freezing of the water ; substantially as described.

1,327,415. TOY OR DISPLAY DEVICE. WILLIAM R. WILLIAMS, Owensboro, Ky. Filed Dec. 11, 1918. Serial No. 266,287. 8 Claims. (Cl. 46—40.)

4. A device of the character described including a base, parallel crank shafts carried thereby, pliable supporting rods upstanding from the base at the outer sides of said shafts and at their upper ends directed inwardly thereover, figures mounted upon the upper ends of said supporting rods and provided with pivoted legs connected to the cranks of said shafts, and means for simultaneously rotating the shafts.

1,327,416. PNEUMATIC-TIRE ALARM. LOUIS ANDER-FUHREN, Baltimore, Md. Filed Sept. 3, 1919. Serial No. 321,342. 2 Claims. (Cl. 116—1.)

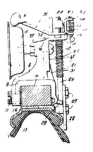

1. A tire alarm comprising a bell, a pivoted clapper for sounding the bell and provided with a stem, a supporting member for the bell and the clapper stem, said member having means for attachment to a wheel, a slidable rod carried by the supporting member and extending radially with respect to the wheel, said rod having a part at its extremity seating adjacent to the tire for engagement thereby when the tire is deflated, an abutment on the rod engaging the clapper stem, a spring for sliding the rod in a direction to actuate the clapper stem, and a spring engageable with the clapper stem for retracting said stem when the aforesaid abutment leaves the same.

1,327,417. SECTIONAL MACHINERY - REPAIR WASHER. CHARLES N. BARTON, Indianapolis, Ind., assignor of one-third to John W. Langley and one-third to Will Peek, Indianapolis, Ind. Filed Oct. 11, 1918. Serial No. 257,761. 2 Claims. (Cl. 85—51.)

2. In a sectional machinery repair washer, the combination of two curved sections, each section being hingedly connected at one end to the other section and being longer circumferentially than a semi-circle but having its inner edge corresponding to the arc of a semi-circle extending from the hinged end of the section, each section adjacent to its opposite end having a relatively thin overlapping portion, each overlapping portion having an inner edge extending tangentially from the opposite end of said arc, the inner side of one of said overlapping portions having a relatively small lug thereon, the lug having an inclined face, the inner side of the remaining one of said overlapping portions having a shallow recess whose bottom is inclined to receive and retain said lug.

1,327,418. TRENCHING-MACHINE. HANS J. BENTSON, Winthrop Harbor, Ill., assignor to Frederick C. Austin, Chicago, Ill. Filed Sept. 15, 1916. Serial No. 120,271. 17 Claims. (Cl. 37—24.)

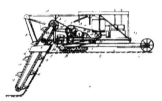

1. An excavating machine comprising an under-frame having traction devices, a body mounted on said under-frame to move bodily sidewise thereon, digging apparatus carried at the rear end of said body, means for operating said digging apparatus while said devices are in operation to move the excavator slowly forward, thereby to produce a forward cut in the ground, mechanism to shift said body laterally during the operation of said apparatus and while said devices are stationary to produce a sidewise cut away from said forward cut, thereby to form a trench the width of which is equal to the width of a forward cut plus the length of the sidewise cut, said apparatus comprising a beam arranged to swing up and down about a horizontal and tranverse axis at the upper end thereof, and means in the trench to propel the beam sidewise in unison with the sidewise movement of said body.

1,327,419. MOLDING-MACHINE. ALLAN S. BIXBY, Indianapolis, Ind., assignor to The National Malleable Castings Company, Cleveland, Ohio, a Corporation of Ohio. Filed July 27, 1915. Serial No. 42,168. 5 Claims. (Cl. 121—14.)

2. In a molding machine, a cylinder, a fluid actuated piston within said cylinder, a valve mounted in one of said members and movable therewith, a plunger in the

other of said members having a valve seat thereon, said valve seat normally holding the valve in open position, the plunger being moved by fluid pressure so that the valve seat follows the valve for a portion of the stroke

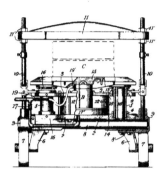

of the piston, the valve moving away from the valve seat during the remainder of the stroke of the piston allowing the valve to close, and providing an outlet for the actuating fluid.

1,327,420. WIND-UP DEVICE FOR SHEETED MATERIAL. JOSEPH T. BROGDEN, Providence, R. I., assignor to Revere Rubber Company, a Corporation of Rhode Island. Filed July 25, 1916. Serial No. 111,121. 1 Claim. (Cl. 91—36.)

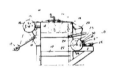

In a machine of the character described a trough open at the top for containing powdered material, a source of rubber-coated fabric supply, a reel for receiving the rubber coated fabric from the fabric supply source, means for guiding the fabric over the top of the trough from the supply source to the reel, winding means for feeding the fabric across the trough, means adapted to raise the powdered material in the trough to maintain it in contact with the rubber-coated surface of said material, and means for removing the surplus powdered material from the said rubber-coated surface.

1,327,421. ELECTRIC ELEVATOR-CONTROLLING SYSTEM. CARL S. BROWN, Portland, Oreg. Filed Nov. 16, 1915. Serial No. 61,783. 14 Claims. (Cl. 172—152.)

1. In an electric elevator system, comprising a main switch magnetically operated, electric circuits controlling said switch, push buttons in said circuits, a plurality of stations, and an elevator car; means whereby should a plurality of said push buttons be operated simultaneously to despatch said elevator car to separate stations, the cir-

cuits set up by one of said simultaneously operated push buttons will operate and control said elevator car, and

the circuits including the other simultaneously operated push buttons will remain dead.

1,327,422. GAS AND LIQUID CONTACT APPARATUS. GEORGES EDMOND DARIER, Chêne, near Geneva, Switzerland. Filed Dec. 30, 1916. Serial No. 139,786. 2 Claims. (Cl. 261—95.)

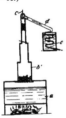

1. A contact body for use as a unit for a filling in a gas and liquid contact apparatus, comprising an open ended cylindrical member having parts spaced so as to permit a liquid by capillary action to extend between the spaced parts and to cover the entire surface of the cylindrical body, thus forming a substantially complete cylindrical wall of the liquid.

1,327,423. PUMP. ACHILLE DRYEN, Londerzeel, Belgium. Filed Feb. 11, 1918. Serial No. 216,643. 3 Claims. (Cl. 103—76.)

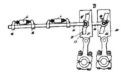

1. In a pump of the kind described, in combination a cylinder, a piston having a reciprocal movement in said cylinder, a distribution chest, a slide valve having a reciprocal movement in said distribution chest, a rod giving the reciprocal movement to the piston, a block provided with a slot driving said rod, said slot being formed at the ends so as to maintain the piston at rest at the end of each stroke.

1,327,424. WHEELED HARROW. RAYMOND R. DUPLER, Toledo, Ohio. Filed Mar. 24, 1919. Serial No. 284,607. 9 Claims. (Cl. 55—19.)

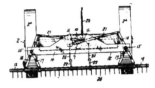

1. In a harrow, a main frame, a tilting frame mounted for tilting movements relative to the main frame, a harrow beam suspended from said tilting frame for longitudinal reciprocatory movements relative thereto, and means for imparting reciprocatory movements to said beam when the machine is operated.

1,327,425. GASOLENE-DISPENSER. CLAUDE M. EGGLESTON, Searcy, Ark. Filed Apr. 7, 1917. Serial No. 160,465. 11 Claims. (Cl. 221—99.)

1. In a fluid dispenser, the combination with a riser, a glass container adapted to receive and display a large quantity of liquid mounted on the upper end of the riser, a pump interposed in the riser for rasing liquid into the container, and discharge means connected to the lower end of the container for withdrawing fluid therefrom, of a casing surrounding the riser and the pump, and a closure member carried by the casing and adapted to be shifted into engagement around said container for inclosing the same.

1,327,426. LOCK-MOUNTING PLATE. AXEL F. ERICKSON, Aurora, Ill., assignor to The Allsteelequip Company, Aurora, Ill., a Corporation of Illinois. Original application filed May 31, 1918. Serial No. 237,590. Divided and this application filed Apr. 26, 1919. Serial No. 292,831. 7 Claims. (Cl. 70—16.)

1. In a structure of the kind described, a wall provided with a lock opening, a lock, and means for mounting said lock consisting of a plate surrounding said lock opening and provided with offset portions that are disposed in opposite directions and to which the lock is removably secured.

1,327,427. ADVERTISING WEATHER-SHELTER. STEPHEN A. FOSTER, Toledo, Ohio. Filed Feb. 19, 1919. Serial No. 277,953. 1 Claim. (Cl. 40—145.)

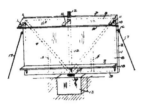

In a weather shelter, an anchored vertical post, a board having a flat plane surface and pivoted along its vertical central axis to the post, a concrete block located in the ground for securing the post, compression members extending diagonally from the concrete block to the corners of the board, the board having a seat extending the length thereof and along the lower edge, a projecting roof extending over the seat, rods secured to the ends of the board having the lower ends of the rods set against the ground for locking the board from rotation.

1,327,428. ADJUSTABLE SHOWER-SPRAY DEVICE. GEORGE H. GREGORY, East Orange, N. J. Filed Aug. 16, 1919. Serial No. 317,866. 4 Claims. (Cl. 4—26.)

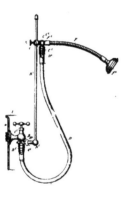

1. In a spraying device of the character set forth, a rod, a clamp thereon adapted to engage a faucet connection and hold said rod vertically, a carrier on said rod having inlet and outlet openings, a hose leading from said faucet connection to said inlet opening, a flexible metal tube connected to such outlet opening, and a delivery nozzle on said tube.

1,327,429. CAR-JOURNAL LUBRICATOR. THOMAS J. HOLMES, Chicago, Ill. Filed Mar. 17, 1919. Serial No. 283,212. 3 Claims. (Cl. 64—24.)

1. In a lubricating device for a journal, the combination of a friction piece having a friction surface substantially conforming to the bearing surface of the journal to be lubricated, means for yieldingly forcing said friction piece against said journal when the device is normally in use, said friction piece having an opening surrounded by said friction surface, walls forming a continuous pipe-like channel for grease extending normally forward longitudinally beneath said friction surface and in communication with said opening, and walls forming a reservoir for grease in communication with said channel, said reservoir

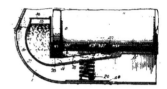

walls extending upward materially above said friction piece opening to provide a hydrostatic head for the grease substantially filling said reservoir.

1,327,430. PRIMING SYSTEM FOR INTERNAL-COMBUSTION ENGINES. GOTTLOB HONOLD, Stuttgart, and ADOLF KRAUSS, Cannstatt, Germany, assignors, by mesne assignments, to American Bosch Magneto Corporation, New York, N. Y., a Corporation of New York. Filed Apr. 13, 1918. Serial No. 228,492. 4 Claims. (Cl. 123—180.)

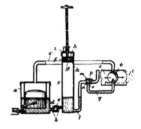

1. In a priming system for internal combustion engines having a fuel inlet and a carbureter, a fuel pump connected between the engine inlet and the fuel float chamber of the carbureter, and valved connections which, when the pump is not operated, maintain in the pump a measured supply of fuel from the carbureter and air from the atmosphere and which, when the pump is operated, closes off the pump from the carbureter and the atmosphere and conducts the measured quantity of fuel and air to the engine inlet in the form of a spray.

1,327,431. HINGE. ABEL ROBERT HOSIER, Toronto, Ontario, Canada. Filed Dec. 2, 1914, Serial No. 875,127. Renewed May 16, 1917. Serial No. 169,113. 2 Claims. (Cl. 16—104.)

2. In a hinge for settees, the combination with the cover and the frame having recesses in the inner sides of the ends, of metal brackets forming slides having horizontal portions arranged within said recesses, said brackets having rounded depressions at the forward ends and end stops at the outer sides of said depressions, and pivot pins rigidly secured to the underside of the cover at the back corners and having rounded portions extending out-

wardly into said slides and adapted to rest in the depressions in said brackets when the cover is raised allowing the seat to incline backwardly against the back.

1,327,432. AUTOMOBILE-LOCK. Avis Jackson, East St. Louis, Ill. Filed Jan. 13, 1919. Serial No. 270,819. 1 Claim. (Cl. 70—131.)

In combination with the change speed lever of an automobile, a lock for the same, comprising two free jaws with right-angled faces to engage the floor and each other, said jaws having prongs to engage the floor plate at each end of the slot therein and one jaw provided with a slot to engage the shank of the change speed lever, a latch pivoted to one of said jaws and having spaced lips adapted to embrace the abutting edges thereof, said latch and jaws formed with alined lock apertures and a padlock for locking said jaws together through said lock apertures.

1,327,433. VIOLIN-BOW. Anton Jelinek, Elizabeth, N. J. Filed Mar. 29, 1919. Serial No. 286,025. 7 Claims. (Cl. 84—72.)

1. In a violin bow, a staff provided with a laterally extending end having a socket therein, said end having an outwardly directed laterally extending toe, a slipper having a toe portion forming a socket for reception of said toe and provided with flanges in interlocking connection with said end, said slipper having an apertured base portion and being provided with a slidable clamping member in opposed relation to one wall of said socket, and means carried by said slipper for adjusting the clamping member toward and away from said socket wall so as to clamp horsehairs within the socket.

1,327,434. BUCKLE. Edwin C. Jones, Toronto, Ontario, Canada. Filed May 6, 1918. Serial No. 232,835. 2 Claims. (Cl. 24—73.)

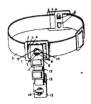

2. A buckle, comprising, a member having a pair of projecting lugs formed with laterally turned outer ends, a keeper member adapted to be placed over said lugs and having a circular hole to rotatably engage the shanks of said lugs, said hole having a recess at one side to allow the placing of the keeper member on said lugs, said keeper having a pair of projecting lugs formed with laterally turned ends, and a suspender buckle having a circular hole adapted to rotatably engage said keeper lugs, the hole in the suspender buckle having a recess at one side of said hole.

1,327,435. NUT-LOCK. Benjamin F. Kurtz, Avalon, Pa. Filed Mar. 12, 1917. Serial No. 154,283. 1 Claim. (Cl. 151—53.)

A device of the character described comprising a metal strip having a longitudinally extending cut out portion for a major portion of its length, the closed end of the cut out portion being rounded to snugly embrace substantially one half of a bolt, the end opposite the rounded end portion of said strip being bent outwardly at right angles to engage with a nut when carried by a bolt, and a pair of arms formed by the cut out portion and adapted to be bent at right angles to said strip in a direction opposite the other right angular bent portion for a purpose specified.

1,327,436. LOADING DEVICE. Anna J. Larson, Sherburn, Minn. Filed Mar. 1, 1918. Serial No. 219,824. 3 Claims. (Cl. 193—8.)

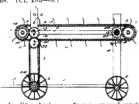

1. In a loading device, a frame, spaced uprights arranged on the forward portion of the frame, conveying means pivotally supported at one end between said uprights, spaced vertically disposed screw threaded shafts arranged upon the remaining end of the frame, the upper and lower extremities of said shafts being formed smooth, screw threaded sleeves rotatable on the smooth extremities of said shafts, rotatable screw threaded boxings secured to the conveying means adjacent the remaining end thereof and receivable over said screw threaded shafts and engageable, at times, with said screw threaded sleeves, means for imparting rotary motion to the conveying means, and other means connected to said motion imparting means and said screw threaded boxings for rotating the same.

1,327,437. PICKLE-FORK HOLDER. Charles A. Lewis, Toronto, Ontario, Canada. Filed Oct. 9, 1917. Serial No. 195,515. 2 Claims. (Cl. 65—65.)

2. A pickle fork holder, comprising, a receptacle having an upright extension formed with longitudinal hook

shaped flanges, spring clips extending forwardly from the top end of said extension, and an elastic band having its looped ends secured in said longitudinal hook flanges and extending around the bottle.

1,327,438. PICKLE-FORK. CHARLES A. LEWIS, Toronto, Ontario, Canada. Filed Oct. 9, 1917. Serial No. 195,516. 2 Claims. (Cl. 30—5.)

1. A pickle fork having rigid tines formed integral with the handle and spaced apart having their flat sides set in angular relation to each other, the upper edges having serrated teeth arranged at the points sloping upwardly toward the handle.

1,327,439. PICKLE-FORK HOLDER. CHARLES AUSTEN LEWIS, Toronto, Ontario, Canada. Filed Dec. 16, 1918. Serial No. 266,975. 4 Claims. (Cl. 215—1.)

1. In a pickle fork holder, the combination with a bottle having grooves formed therein, of a fork holding member having projections adapted to be secured within said grooves, said fork-holding member having a pocket at its lower end.

1,327,440. APPARATUS FOR SMOOTHING AND POLISHING STONE. WILLIAM MACGREGOR, Niagara Falls, N. Y., assignor to The Carborundum Company, Niagara Falls, N. Y., a Corporation of Pennsylvania. Filed Feb. 9, 1918. Serial No. 216,209. 4 Claims. (Cl. 51—11.)

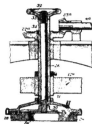

1. A grinding or polishing head having a plurality of concentric rotating grinding or polishing members, and means for moving said members relatively to each other in a direction normal to the planes of their work-engaging faces; substantially as described.

1,327,441. METALLIC WINDOW CONSTRUCTION. BERNARD T. MESKER and CLARENCE E. SMITH, St. Louis, Mo., assignors to Mesker Brothers Iron Company, St. Louis, Mo., a Corporation of Missouri. Filed July 7, 1916. Serial No. 107,942. 4 Claims. (Cl. 189—76.)

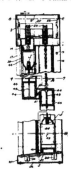

1. In a structure of the class described, hollow jamb and head members disposed in abutting relationship, one of said members being provided with apertures through an outer wall thereof, the other of said members being provided with projections insertible through said apertures, which projections are provided with beveled shoulders, and wedging means slidably mounted within the apertured member and movable into engagement with the beveled shoulders on said projections whereby to draw said members together and secure them in assembled relationship.

1,327,442. METALLIC CASKET. FRANK MESKER, St. Louis, Mo., assignor to Mesker Brothers Iron Company, St. Louis, Mo., a Corporation of Missouri. Filed Mar. 6, 1917. Serial No. 152,815. 9 Claims. (Cl. 27—6.)

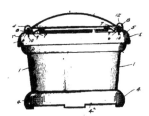

2. In casket construction, a cover formed of sheet metal and having a continuous marginal hollow bead portion of external convex contour, which continuous bead portion forms a stiffening frame for the cover, the outer part of said bead portion terminating in a substantially vertical flange which is adapted to directly engage a suitable support, a reinforcing member arranged within said hollow bead portion, a part of which reinforcing member is disposed substantially at right angles to the vertically disposed outer part of said hollow bead portion, and a sealing strip arranged on the underside of said reinforcing member.

1,327,443. QUENCHING APPARATUS. CARL G. OLSON, Chicago, Ill., assignor to Illinois Tool Works, Chicago, Ill., a Corporation of Illinois. Filed Jan. 31, 1919. Serial No. 274,170. 11 Claims. (Cl. 266—6.)

3. A tempering machine having a bath, two arms movable toward and from each other for engaging and releasing the work, said arms being adapted to rotate about

a horizontal axis for immersing the work, one of the arms
having a cam and the other part having a traveling part
traveling upon said cam for drawing the two arms toward
each other, both the cam and the traveling part being
rotatable relatively to each other and also rotatable ab-

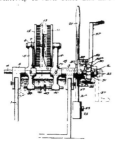

solutely, and means for causing the traveling part to engage the cam after said traveling part has completed a
predetermined portion of its travel to thereafter rotate
the cam for causing its arm to rotate for the purpose of
immersing the work.

1,327,444. GRAIN-PICKLER. FRANCIS LEWELLYN PHIL-
LIPS, Tugaske, Saskatchewan, Canada. Filed Mar. 22,
1918. Serial No. 223,938. 2 Claims. (Cl. 83—27.)

1. In a grain pickler, the combination with a frame
and a hopper supported thereon, of a converging funnel
arranged below said hopper, rods arranged diagonally
across the top of said funnel, a sheet metal cone supported
upon said rods centrally beneath said hopper, means for
regulating the feeding of the grain from the bottom of the
hopper centrally upon the cone, and a spray nozzle arranged below the base of said cone and directing a spray
of pickling fluid laterally outward from beneath said cone
to strike the convergent walls of the funnel and mingle
with the grain.

1,327,445. EXPANSION-MANDREL. ERNEST G. RIDER,
Philadelphia, Pa., assignor to Schwerdtle Machine Com-
pany, Philadelphia, Pa., a Corporation of Pennsylvania.
Filed Jan. 24, 1919. Serial No. 272,847. 7 Claims.
(Cl. 242—72.)

1. The combination, in a mandrel, of a tubular body
slotted to form a spring finger integral with said tubular

body, and means contained within said tubular body and
coacting with said integral spring finger to project the
same outwardly.

1,327,446. PLASTER-BOARD OR THE LIKE. JOHN
SCHUMACHER and JOSEPH E. SCHUMACHER, Los Angeles,
Calif. Filed May 22, 1918. Serial No. 236,040. 10
Claims. (Cl. 72—124.)

1. Plaster board or the like, comprising a body provided
with a surface covering which is in part interrupted, said
body at the zone of such interruption being waterproofed.

1,327,447. GAS-LIGHTING DEVICE. TOWNSEND STITES
and ELMER L. KNOEDLER, Gloucester City, N. J., assignors to Welsbach Company, Gloucester City, N. J., a
Corporation of New Jersey. Filed May 7, 1918. Serial
No. 233,018. 14 Claims. (Cl. 67—98.)

1. As a new article of manufacture, an upright mantle
formed of textile fabric and secured at its lower end to a
carrier shaped to be supported on an upright Bunsen
burner, substantially as described.

1,327,448. PROCESS FOR MAKING A REFRACTORY
PLASTIC. EDWARD R. STOWELL, Oden, Mich. Filed
Apr. 16, 1919. Serial No. 290,463. 1 Claim. (Cl.
106—9.)
A process for making a refractory plastic consisting in
treating silicon carbid containing free silicon with a
caustic alkali solution to generate hydrogen, and after
the evolution of hydrogen has ceased, stirring the mass
down to original volume.

1,327,449. MULTIPLE - CYLINDER - PUMP ATTACH-
MENT. MARTIN SULLIVAN, Kimberly, Idaho. Filed
Mar. 1, 1917. Serial No. 151,756. 1 Claim. (Cl.
103—75.)

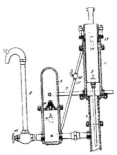

The combination with a pump including a cylinder having a plunger slidably mounted therein and an air cham-

ber in operative communication with the cylinder, of a conduit leading from the lower portion of the air chamber and communicating with the upper portion of the cylinder as and for the purpose set forth.

1,327,450. ATTACHMENT FOR DIAL-SCALES. CHARLES MELVIN SWEET, Hamilton, Ontario, Canada, assignor to The Gurney Scale Company, Hamilton, Ontario, Canada. Filed June 20, 1919. Serial No. 305,470. 4 Claims. (Cl. 265—62.)

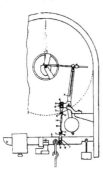

1. In an attachment for dial scales, the combination with the scale beam and pendulum, each having projecting knife edge pivots, of shackles connected to said beam and pendulum through said knife edge pivots, and a link connecting said shackles and having knife edge bearing contact therewith.

1,327,451. HAND-GRENADE. ARNOLD THOMPSON and HERBERT J. S. DENNISON, Toronto, Ontario, Canada. Filed Mar. 11, 1918. Serial No. 221,631. 6 Claims. (Cl. 102—29.)

1. In a grenade, a weighted member pivotally supported to rotate in a fixed plane, an explosive container, and means arranged in the plane of rotation for holding said member stationary and for effecting the detonation of said explosive through the rotation of said weighted member.

1,327,452. SUCTION-NOZZLE AND MATERIAL-SEPARATOR FOR REDUCING-MACHINES. MILTON F. WILLIAMS, St. Louis, Mo., assignor to Williams Patent Crusher and Pulverizer Company, St. Louis, Mo., a Corporation of Missouri. Original application filed July 12, 1915, Serial No. 39,425. Divided and this application filed Aug. 29, 1918. Serial No. 251,905. 2 Claims. (Cl. 299—135.)

1. In a separating and feeding device, the combination with a suction pipe, of a tubular member adjustably and removably connected to said suction pipe, the lower portion of which tubular member is hinged so as to be swung laterally with respect to the upper portion thereof, a suction nozzle connected to the lower end of the hinged portion of

said tubular member, said suction nozzle comprising a pair of oppositely disposed members hinged to said tubular member, means for adjusting the free ends of said hinged members toward or away from each other, and flexible members connecting the side edges of said hinged members.

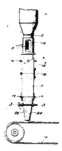

1,327,453. SCREW-CAP. FREDERICK G. WIELAND, Brooklyn, N. Y., assignor to Anchor Cap & Closure Corporation, Brooklyn, N. Y., a Corporation of New York. Filed Feb. 27, 1919. Serial No. 279,499. 14 Claims. (Cl. 215—84.)

1. As an article of manufacture a bottle cap comprising a cover portion, a skirt depending from said cover portion, a thread-engaging projection formed under compression adjacent the lower edge of the skirt, and a continuous rolled edge on the lower edge of the skirt and covering the said projection.

1,327,454. METHOD OF MAKING CLOSURE-CAPS. FREDERICK G. WIELAND, Brooklyn, N. Y., assignor to Anchor Cap & Closure Corporation, Brooklyn, N. Y., a Corporation of New York. Filed Mar. 10, 1919. Serial No. 281,705. 9 Claims. (Cl. 113—116.)

1. The method of manufacturing a closure cap which method comprises forming a blank having excess metal projections adjacent the edge thereof; cupping the said blank to form a cover portion, and a skirt with a flange adjacent the lower edge of the said skirt, the said flange having excess metal projections on the edges thereof; then supporting a portion of the said skirt and applying forces to the edge of the said flange whereby the excess metal is driven radially inwardly and folded upon itself adjacent the edge of the skirt of the cap substantially as specified.

1,327,455. SEED-PLANTER. LELAND WILLIS and OLIN F. WOODWORTH, Grenloch, N. J., assignors to Bateman Manufacturing Company, Grenloch, N. J., a Corporation of New Jersey. Filed Oct. 30, 1917. Serial No. 199,270. 3 Claims. (Cl. 221—118.)

1. The combination, in a seed planter, of the seed hopper having a delivery opening in the bottom, a forwardly

and downwardly inclined and slotted valve for regulating the delivery of seeds through said opening, a rotary brush in the lower portion of the hopper for feeding the seeds to said valve, said brush having its axis above and in advance of the forward edge of the opening in the bottom of the

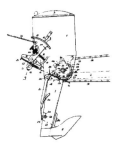

hopper, and means for rotating said brush in such a direction that the outer end of the tuft will swing rearwardly over the valve while also rising so as to prevent said tuft from jamming seeds in the rear end of the slot in the valve or between the tuft and the upper face of said valve.

1,327,456. CARPET-SWEEPING APPLIANCE. CHARLES LEWIS BAENDER, Oakland, Calif., assignor, by mesne assignments, to The Torrington Company, Torrington, Conn., a Corporation of Connecticut. Original application filed June 28, 1909, Serial No. 504,878. Patent No. 1,138,437. Divided and this application filed May 3, 1915. Serial No. 25,568. 2 Claims. (Cl. 15—60.)

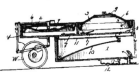

1. A pneumatic cleaner having traction wheels supporting the rear thereof, a dust receptacle, a suction nozzle adapted to support the front end of the receptacle and communicating with the interior thereof, means for creating a suction through the nozzle and dust box, and means for varying the pressure of the nozzle on the surface being swept, said means comprising a shoe adjustably secured to the bottom of the receptacle, said shoe being composed of a corrugated plate.

1,327,457. DIAL-INDICATOR FOR COMBINATION-LOCKS. HARRY G. BALTHASAR, St. Louis, Mo., assignor to Interstate Tool and Manufacturing Company, St. Louis, Mo., a Corporation of Missouri. Original application filed Apr. 16, 1917, Serial No. 162,308. Divided and this application filed Sept. 17, 1917. Serial No. 191,690. 1 Claim. (Cl. 70—56.)

In a combination lock, control and indicating means for use on automobiles, a bearing plate having a portion adapted for attachment to the instrument board of the automobile and an angularly related portion extended from such instrument board to provide a bearing plate through which the lock-shaft is adapted to extend, a dial member secured on the end of the lock-shaft, and rotatably bearing on and within the edge outline of said bearing plate, said dial member being formed in the face engaging the bearing plate with a series of notches, and a spring strip remov-

ably secured to the under side of the bearing plate and concealed thereby, said spring strip being formed at the end remote from its securing means with a detent normally

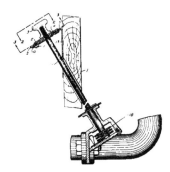

projecting through an opening in the bearing plate and in the path of movement of said notches, whereby said detent will successively engage said notches in the movement of the dial member.

1,327,458. MATCH-SAFE. GUSTAVE C. BROWN, Bridgeport, Conn. Filed Apr. 25, 1919. Serial No. 292,675. 1 Claim. (Cl. 206—30.)

As an article of manufacture, a match safe formed of two sections and comprising a sheet metal body having a plane back wall, a bottom bent at a right angle thereon and extending laterally therefrom, side walls bent at right angles on said back and extending laterally above and adapted to be secured to the bottom to form a receptacle, a right angled metal strip having a tongue on one portion thereof adapted to be projected through the back wall and turned to secure said strip in spaced relation above the bottom, the other portion of said strip acting as a front wall for the safe and apertured to permit access to the scratch surface of a match box supported by the strip, the portion of the receptacle between said bottom and strip adapted to contain an ash receiver therein.

1,327,459. PENCIL-SHARPENER. CLEMENT CLEVELAND, New York, N. Y. Filed Oct. 27, 1916, Serial No. 127,976. Renewed June 11, 1919. Serial No. 303,473. 15 Claims. (Cl. 120—85.)

1. A pencil sharpener for two-stage operation and comprising an expansibly resilient tubular cone having a knife-edge located longitudinally on one side thereof, said knife-

edge being arranged near the smaller end of the cone for sharpening the wood of a pencil, and said cone having at the larger end thereof a support coöperative with the knife-edge and arranged therewith for sharpening the unwooded point of a pencil lead.

1,327,460. CURTAIN AND SHADE FIXTURE. ROY L. COLLINS, Redwood, N. Y. Filed June 24, 1918. Serial No. 241,673. 7 Claims. (Cl. 156—23.)

1. A fixture of the class described having a casing provided with two elongated slots, a hanger mounted by the casing and extending through one of the slots to prevent turning of the hanger relatively to the casing, and a fastening member passing through the other slot and engaging the hanger.

6. A fixture of the class described, comprising a pair of mounting members, cases secured to said members through the medium of clamping nuts, pistons mounted within said casings, expansion springs carried by said pistons, and means connecting the free ends of the piston rods for adjusting the tension of the springs.

1,327,461. COMBINED ROLLING-PIN AND CULINARY HOLDER. GEORGE P. COVAR, Chester, S. C. Filed May 13, 1918. Serial No. 234,285. 1 Claim. (Cl. 107—50.)

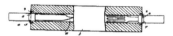

A rolling pin having an axial bore throughout its entire length, handles removably engaged in the bore and provided with annular grooves, one of the edges of the grooves lying flush with the edges of the bore, a plurality of spring clips arranged on the ends of the rolling pin about the bore and disposed radially with respect thereto and the ends of the clips bent to approximate a semicircle and extending within the grooves the termination thereof being coincident with the outer of the edges of the grooves to prevent accidental contact therewith by the hands of the operator.

1,327,462. PISTON FOR INTERNAL - COMBUSTION MOTORS. EDGAR H. CROSSEN, Franklin, Pa. Filed June 17, 1918. Serial No. 240,408. 2 Claims. (Cl. 123—74.)

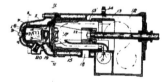

1. The combination with the cylinder of an internal combustion motor having a fuel port arranged to be piston controlled, of a piston of the trunk type, a longitudinally-disposed deflector carried by said piston which is non-continuous with the circumferential walls thereof, the forward end of said deflector projecting beyond the open end of said piston, arranged to over-reach and to coöperate with said port, as, and for the purpose set forth.

1,327,463. SECTION-SWITCH. HARRY W. DAVIS, Edgewood Park, Pa. Filed June 3, 1918. Serial No. 237,842. 8 Claims. (Cl. 191—39.)

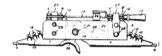

1. A switch for trolley conductors comprising an insulating block having an aperture therein, runner members secured on the end portions of said block and having their inner terminals spaced apart, and a pivoted switch member adapted to close the contact between said runner members having an abruptly concaved terminal for snugly engaging a trolley wheel and providing a positively engaging lever connection therewith.

1,327,464. APPARATUS FOR PLAYING A GAME OF SKILL. BERNARD DEWICK and DONALD BUIST CADDY, London, England, assignors to The British Ever Ready Company Limited, Holloway, London, England. Filed Aug. 28, 1919. Serial No. 320,482. 13 Claims. (Cl. 46—59.)

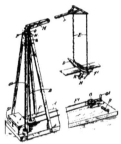

1. In apparatus for playing a game of skill, the combination with a support, of an arm mounted to swing thereon, a projectile-dropping device carried by the arm, and manually-controlled releasing-means operatively connected with the projectile-dropping device for actuating the latter and allowing a projectile to drop therefrom during the movement of the arm.

1,327,465. CAN-LABELING MACHINE. ARVID P. EKVALL and HERMAN STAKE, Worcester, Mass. Filed Apr. 24, 1919. Serial No. 292,401. 9 Claims. (Cl. 216—47.)

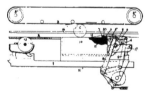

1. In a labeling machine, in combination with a label holder, a run-way for rolling cans over and along said

label holder, and a lap-end gumming mechanism including a gum-applying member that contacts with the rear portion of the upper label, and has backward and upward movement in retreating therefrom, of means for stripping or separating the gummed surface of the label from the face of said gum-applying members, substantially as set forth.

1,327,466. MASSAGE-VIBRATOR. PATRICK J. FITZ-GERALD, Torrington, Conn., assignor to The Fitzgerald Manufacturing Company, Torrington, Conn., a Firm composed of Patrick J. Fitzgerald and Maurice F. Fitzgerald. Filed Jan. 25, 1919. Serial No. 273,070. 3 Claims. (Cl. 128—49.)

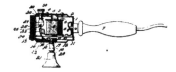

1. In a massage vibrator, the combination of a casing body, a cover fitting loosely thereon, an electro-magnet within the body and adapted to be intermittently energized, a leaf spring secured at one end to said cover with its free end extending into the field of and adapted to be vibrated by said magnet, an applicator secured to said spring and extending through said cover, a spring arranged within the casing and having its opposite ends connected to said leaf spring and the casing wall opposite the cover, and means for adjusting the tension of said spring.

1,327,467. MACHINE FOR MAKING FABRICATED WIRE. ALVAH A. GRINER, Bayside, N. Y., assignor to Renaissance Corset Co., Inc., New York, N. Y., a Corporation of New York. Filed July 17, 1919. Serial No. 311,526. 24 Claims. (Cl. 140—105.)

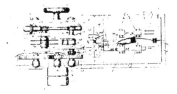

1. In a machine for the purpose set forth, the combination of forming pins, means for raising and lowering said pins, and guiding means through which the wire passes to the pins, said guiding means being actuated by parts of the means for raising and lowering the pins.

1,327,468. TOOL FOR FACILITATING THE POSITIONING OF DRIVING-SHOES IN DRIVING-BOX BEARINGS OF LOCOMOTIVES. CARL GUGGENBUEHLER, Newark, N. J. Filed June 23, 1919. Serial No. 305,951. 5 Claims. (Cl. 29—84.)

1. A tool for facilitating the adjustment of the driving shoes of locomotives when assembling the locomotive and

wheels, said tool including means for temporarily supporting said shoes in position while lowering the locomotive and engaging said driving box of the wheels into its bearing.

1,327,469. SUPPORT AND GEARING FOR SWINGING CONVEYERS. ARTHUR J. HARTLEY, Peoria, Ill. Filed Feb. 3, 1919. Serial No. 274,763. 9 Claims. (Cl. 193—14.)

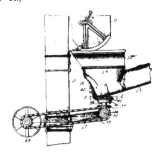

1. In a support and gearing for swinging conveyers, in combination, an extended, stationary, vertically disposed sleeve member, a turntable sleeve member supported therein, fashioned with a flanged member at its upper end provided with lugs thereon, a brake member attached to the turnable sleeve, a suitable brake band related thereto to permit limited brake action thereon, a conveyer member provided with lugs coöperating with the lugs on the turnable sleeve, and a pin connecting the conveyer member, the turnable sleeve, and the brake member, substantially as shown.

1,327,470. HYDRAULIC JACK. DANIEL E. HENNESSY, Holyoke, Mass., assignor to Herbert W. Cowan, J. Lewis Wyckoff, and Edward N. White, trustees, doing business as Cowan Truck Company. Filed June 23, 1914. Serial No. 846,731. Renewed Oct. 3, 1917. Serial No. 194,591. 4 Claims. (Cl. 138—9.)

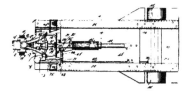

1. In a structure of the class described, a fluid-operated jack comprising a ram and a cylinder, a pump, a reservoir, said jack, pump and reservoir being so connected that said pump may draw fluid from said reservoir and force it into said cylinder behind said ram, and said structure being provided also with a passage leading through the wall of said cylinder upon the pressure side of said ram to said reservoir, a valve in said passage, and means for automatically controlling said valve to prevent over-extension of said jack.

1,327,471. METHOD OF BALING FIBROUS MATERIAL. NELSON B. HENRY, Atlanta, Ga., assignor, by mesne assignments, to Mrs. Mollie H. Miller, Atlanta, Ga. Filed Apr. 24, 1916. Serial No. 93,289. 6 Claims. (Cl. 100—19.)

1. The herein described method of forming material into bales which comprises forming and confining a charge

of material sufficient for a bale and moving the same into compressing position, then exerting a single sustained compressive thrust on the entire charge while confined to compress the same to a reduced and predetermined size and to subject the charge to both longitudinal and transverse compression pressure, holding the charge to said predetermined size and under said longitudinal and transverse compression pressure as developed by said thrust, removing the charge from the compressing position while thus held to said predetermined size and under longitudinal and transverse compression, and tying the charge at said size and while thus held under both longitudinal and transverse compression.

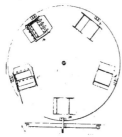

6. The herein described method of forming material into bales which comprises concurrently performing on a plurality of charges of materials the following operations sequential to a single charge, namely, at one station compressing a charge of material sufficient for a bale both longitudinally and transversely by a single sustained thrust and while the charge is confined, and holding the charge under such longitudinal and transverse compression independently of the force which effected compression thereof, at another station applying ties around a charge while thus held under longitudinal and transverse compression, at another station relieving the longitudinal and transverse compression on a charge thus compressed and tied, and at another station making up and confining a charge preparatory to compression at the first mentioned station.

1,327,472. COMPRESS. NELSON B. HENRY, Atlanta, Ga., assignor, by mesne assignments, to Mrs. Mollie H. Miller, Atlanta, Ga. Filed Apr. 24, 1916. Serial No. 93,290. 7 Claims. (Cl. 100—28.)

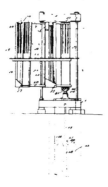

1. A compress comprising a press chamber having sides which are movably connected at one end, means coöpera-

tive with the opposite ends of said sides for relatively moving them inwardly and for locking them in such position, means having a single operative stroke for compressing a charge of material longitudinally within the press chamber, the press chamber and said compressing means being relatively shiftable into and out of coöperative relation, and means located intermediately of the length of the press chamber for maintaining the material under compression therein after the press chamber and said compressing means have been shifted relatively out of coöperative relation.

7. In a compress, a press chamber embodying side members relatively movable laterally of the chamber, a head movable longitudinally of the chamber, and means connecting said head and side members and operative to lock said members and head in fixed relation and also operative to relatively move the side members laterally and to move the head longitudinally of the chamber.

1,327,473. REFRIGERATOR. FRED LINCOLN HEWITT, Winchendon, Mass., assignor to M. E. Converse & Son Co., Winchendon, Mass., a Corporation of Massachusetts. Filed Dec. 31, 1918. Serial No. 269,071. 6 Claims. (Cl. 217—12.)

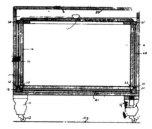

1. A refrigerator, comprising an outer box, an inner box and an insulating box intermediate the said outer and inner boxes, the outer and inner boxes being unitary rigid structures and the insulating box being made of walls, and a sectional frame having means for receiving and holding the said walls whereby the use of nails or the like is obviated, the frame fitting into the outer box and forming a support for the inner box

---

1,327,474. APPARATUS FOR TEACHING PROJECTION. ALBERT L. HOWARD, Montello, Mass. Filed Oct. 3, 1919. Serial No. 328,095. 5 Claims. (Cl. 35—12.)

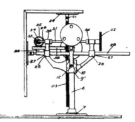

1. In a device for illustrating mechanical projection, an inner member including movable rods, each of said rods supporting a box section, an outer transparent box like structure, and means for moving the rods for moving the box sections into engagement with the outer box like structure.

1,327,475. CHAIR. Austin W. Howell. Hanover, Ohio. Filed Apr. 1. 1919. Serial No. 286,699. 4 Claims. (Cl. 155—18.)

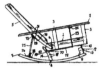

1. A chair of the class described comprising a pair of rockers, front legs carried by said rockers, a seat, hinges connecting the front part of the seat with said legs, means for adjustably connecting the hinges with said front legs, a curved upright member hingedly secured to said rockers, and means for adjustably connecting said upright member with the rear part of the seat.

1,327,476. SHIRT. Joseph Hurwitz, New York, N. Y. Filed May 12, 1919. Serial No. 296,408. 4 Claims. (Cl. 2—41.)

1. In a shirt, a divided front to provide two bosom parts, each having a plurality of superimposed panels and hemstitches along the margins of the outermost panel of each bosom part and adapted to be cut to detach the outermost panel of each bosom part from the shirt and to leave the under panel intact to perform the function of the detached panel.

1,327,477. DENTAL HAND PORT-POLISHER. James W. Ivory, Philadelphia, Pa. Filed Oct. 20, 1919. Serial No. 331,858. 4 Claims. (Cl. 32—10.)

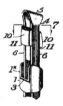

1. In a port polisher, a movable yoke adapted to clamp the pin of said polisher, means for operating said yoke, a stock adapted to receive the sides of said yoke, and a bed adapted to be sustained on said stock within the sides of said yoke, said pin being adapted to be seated on said bed, the polisher being adapted to be seated on said bed and clamped against the same by the crown of said yoke due to the downward movement of the latter.

1,327,478. SHOCK-ABSORBING VEHICLE-TIRE. Ulysses S. James, Newark, N. J. Filed Sept. 4. 1917. Serial No. 189,637. Renewed Nov. 5, 1919. Serial No. 335,946. 20 Claims. (Cl. 152—8.)

19. A tire for vehicle wheels comprising a rubber body having radial ribs extending inwardly from the tread thereof, the inner ends of said ribs at each side of the body being united by a continuous margin, an annular stress-distributing member embedded in the body, a plurality of radial flexible slings looped over the outer periphery of said member and having ends lying within the respective continuous margins of the body, resilient cushions acting to flex and thereby tension said slings, and clamping flanges at opposite sides of the wheel felly operative to secure the slings and said margins of the body to the felly and to hold said cushions in coöperative relation with the slings.

1,327,479. LAMP-BRACKET. Francis Marion Jones, Rosiclare, Ill. Filed May 5, 1919. Serial No. 294,874. 4 Claims. (Cl. 240—60.)

1. A support for miners' lamps including a head encircling ring and an upright frame which are formed from a single length of wire, the upright frame projecting from one side of the ring and being formed with an eye to receive the hook of a miner's lamp and also with spaced sides for engagement with the cross bar of the lamp.

1,327,480. AUTOMATIC-RELEASE CLEVIS CONSTRUCTION. John M. Kahl, Heaton, N. D. Filed June 2, 1919. Serial No. 301,248. 5 Claims. (Cl. 213—67.)

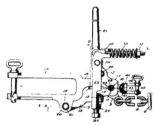

1. In means for the purpose described, jaws mounted to move toward and from each other and one jaw equipped for the connection of draft means, means yieldingly held by the jaws and adapted to be released when one jaw is moved away from the other, a lever pivoted to one jaw, a link pivoted to said lever, and engaged with the other jaw, means connected with the lever and equipped with an abutment, and a spring interposed between the link and said abutment.

1,327,481. CONCRETE-CHIMNEY FORM. WILLIAM J. KULOW, Pine Bluff, Ark. Filed Aug. 12, 1919. Serial No. 316,933. 6 Claims. (Cl. 25—118.)

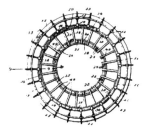

1. A concrete chimney form comprising an annular inner form, an annular outer form spaced from the inner form, means whereby the diameters of both forms may be regulated, an adjustably mounted annular supporting ring and supporting rods slidably connecting the outer form to the annular supporting ring.

1,327,482. IGNITION-PLUG FOR INTERNAL-COMBUSTION ENGINES. LUCIEN LAVOISIER, Paris, France. Filed Jan. 21, 1918. Serial No. 213,015. 2 Claims. (Cl. 123—169.)

1. An ignition plug comprising a seat or bottom, an insulating member fixed on said seat, a bored center rod fixed in the insulating member, said bored rod being open above, closed below by a thin bottom, having lateral apertures relatively large exclusively placed above the insulating member, the interior space of said bored rod being completely free.

1,327,483. RAILWAY-SWITCH HEATER. WILLIAM TALBOT LAWLOR, Jersey City, N. J. Filed May 3, 1919. Serial No. 294,692. 3 Claims. (Cl. 246—428.)

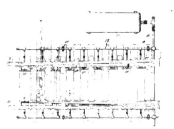

1. In a heating device for railway switches, the combination with a system of pipes, a reservoir from which said pipes are adapted to convey fluid fuel, and means

to regulate the flow of the fuel along the pipes, of a plurality of open topped receptacles located beneath the rails and having communication with said pipes for the delivery of fuel into the receptacles, each receptacle being arranged longitudinally of the rails and being provided with means at its ends to prevent the blowing of the fuel therefrom.

1,327,484. APPARATUS FOR SEPARATING FIBER. SARGENT V. L. LIPPITT, San Juan, Porto Rico. Filed Feb. 2, 1917. Serial No. 146,071. 10 Claims. (Cl. 13—2.)

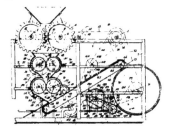

2. An apparatus for separating fiber having a shredder, a toothed belt to which it discharges, a brush coöperating with the belt, and a cleaning and feeding roll coöperating with both the shredder and the belt.

1,327,485. TRACTOR. HENRY W. LUPTON, Los Gatos, Calif. Filed Feb. 24, 1919. Serial No. 278,584. 5 Claims. (Cl. 180—21.)

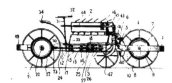

1. A tractor comprising a main frame, a transverse shaft mounted in the main frame and bearing a traction wheel and a miter gear, horizontally disposed spaced annular plates, fixed to the rear portion of the main frame, a central upright post carried by the main frame, a miter gear loosely mounted on said post, a shaft journaled in the main frame and bearing miter gears intermeshed with the miter gear on the shaft of the forward traction wheel and the miter gear on the post, respectively, a motor carried on the main frame, a driving connection intermediate the motor and said shaft, a revoluble frame interposed between the annular plates and having anti-friction wheels engaging said plates, and also having its center of movement about the post, a rear frame fixed with respect to the revoluble frame, a transverse shaft journaled in said rear frame section, and bearing a traction wheel and a miter gear, and a shaft journaled in the rear frame and having a miter gear at one end intermeshed with the loose miter gear on the post, and also having a miter gear intermeshed with the miter gear fixed on the shaft of the rear traction wheel.

1,327,486. FRUIT-DRIER. ALLEN H. McINTYRE, Tampa, Fla., assignor to Skinner Machinery Co., Tampa, Fla., a Corporation. Filed Aug. 6, 1919. Serial No. 315,697. 5 Claims. (Cl. 34—12.)

3. In a fruit drying machine, an endless conveyer made in sections, supports spaced apart and adapted to support

the conveyer during its passage over the supports, the conveyer sections being adapted to swing downward in the opening between the ends of adjacent supports, and

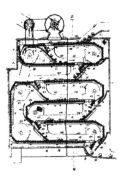

an incline below the said opening and extending in the reverse direction of the travel of the conveyer run passing over the adjacent supports, the said incline leading to another run of the conveyer.

1,327,487. AERIAL BOMB. JOSEPH J. MCINTYRE, Brooklyn, N. Y. Filed Sept. 1, 1917. Serial No. 189,362. 4 Claims. (Cl. 102—2.)

1. An aerial bomb, comprising a casing filled with an explosive charge and provided with a head, a percussion cap held on the said head and extending into the said charge, a screw screwing on the said head and provided with a fan, a detonating plunger slidable in the screw and having a head adapted to strike an object, and limiting means on the said screw to limit the screwing movement thereof and that of the plunger.

1,327,488. MINE. WALTER LAWRENCE MCNULTY, Peace Dale, R. I. Filed Aug. 8, 1919. Serial No. 316,121. 3 Claims. (Cl. 102—2.)
1. The combination with a float, of an explosive member suspended from said float and including a detonator,

270 O. G.—8

a spring pressed plunger, pivoted hook-like elements normally holding the plunger in spaced relation to the

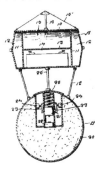

detonator, and electrical means connected in circuit with said receiving apparatus for effecting a release of said elements to permit actuation of said plunger.

1,327,489. KITCHEN-FIXTURE. ZHETLEY V. MATTHEWS, Charleston, Wash. Filed Apr. 12, 1919. Serial No. 289,576. 5 Claims. (Cl. 211—6.)

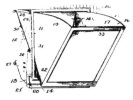

1. A bin comprising a frame; vertically disposed supporting members carried by the inner side of said frame; a transverse hinge rod connecting said vertically disposed supporting members; a bin adapted to be arranged within said frame; hinge bearings carried by the side walls of the bin and adapted to be arranged upon said hinge rod; and adjustable elements carried by the inner lower ends of the side walls of said bin and adapted for regulating the position of the bin when the same is closed.

1,327,490. ANIMAL-TRAP. JOHN DAVID MILLER, San Diego, Calif. Filed June 27, 1919. Serial No. 307,135. 2 Claims. (Cl. 43—26.)

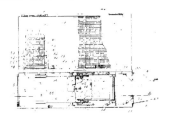

1. An animal trap comprising separable structures forming respectively a trapping compartment and a holding compartment, means detachably uniting the adjacent walls of said structures, registering openings in said

walls for the passage of the animal to the holding compartment, a door affording entrance to the trap compartment, a drop platform in said trap compartment, means tending to raise said platform, connection between the platform and doors to close the doors by a dropping of the platform and open the doors by a raising of the platform, a latch bolt on the platform, means to engage said bolt in the raised and depressed positions of the platform, means on the platform and operable by the animal to release the bolt for the depression of the platform, and means operative by the animal in passing into the holding compartment to release the bolt engaging means for permitting the platform to rise for the resetting of the trap, said last-mentioned means including links extending from the holding compartment through adjacent walls of the two structures to the trap compartment and detachable connections between said links and the bolt-engaging means, the disconnection of said links permitting the same to be removed with the holding compartment.

1,327,491. SWAGE FOR USE IN OIL-WELLS. WILLIAM S. PIERCE, Franklin. Pa. Filed July 31, 1917, Serial No. 183,719. Renewed June 21, 1919. Serial No. 305,872. 1 Claim. (Cl. 153—80.5.)

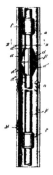

In a device for use in wells of the character described, the combination with a tube composed of a series of sections connected together by coupling rings projecting beyond the outer surface of the tube and forming set collars thereon, of a swage block slidably mounted on said tube between a pair of adjacent collars, the said swage block being substantially in the form of two truncated cones with their bases joined, the maximum transverse diameter of the swage block being slightly less than the inner diameter of the well casing to be expanded, the said swage block having an axial bore slightly larger than the periphery of the member whereon said swage block slides, the ends of said swage block being adapted to be struck by one or the other of said collars as said tube is raised or lowered, substantially as described.

1,327,492. PULLING-MACHINE. JOHN H. SCHOTT, Boulder, Colo., assignor of one-fifth to James G. Archibald, one-fifth to J. Emmons De Kalb, and one-fifth to Michael M. Rinn, Boulder, Colo. Filed May 29, 1919. Serial No. 300,602. 7 Claims. (Cl. 254—51.)

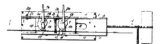

1. A machine of the class described comprising a box-like casing, a guide on said casing having slots, a pair of

slides carried by said guide, a pair of yieldable gripping devices on said slides, a pair of studs on said slides movable in said slots of said guide, a partition in said casing, parallel shafts mounted in said partition, gear wheels mounted on certain of said shafts on the side of the partition adjacent the guide, crank pins on said wheels, links connecting said crank pins and studs and means on the opposite side of the partition for rotating said gear wheels whereby the slides will be simultaneously moved in opposite directions.

1,327,493. ANTISLIPPING ATTACHMENT FOR HORSESHOES. LEVI SCHWOYER, Pottstown, Pa. Filed May 8, 1919. Serial No. 295,682. 2 Claims. (Cl. 168—13.)

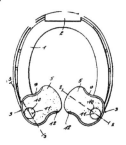

1. An anti-slipping attachment for horseshoes comprising a metal socket member consisting of two vertically offset horizontal portions and a vertical portion connecting them, the lowermost of said horizontal portions being adapted for contact with the lower side of the shoe and said vertical portion being designed to abut the inner edge of the shoe, and a cushion held in said socket member.

1,327,494. AUXILIARY AIR-VALVE. WILSON E. SIMS, Greeneville, Tenn. Filed Nov. 14, 1918. Serial No. 262,518. 1 Claim. (Cl. 183—40.)

In a device of the class described, the combination of a primary casing, a sieve in said primary casing, an auxiliary casing mounted upon said primary casing contiguous to said sieve, said auxiliary casing provided with a reduced extension and with apertures therein around said extension, a stem slidably mounted in said extension, a piston-head secured to the inner end of said stem and being adapted to close the auxiliary casing, a spring engaging the outer end of the primary casing and positioned around the reduced extension of the auxiliary casing, and a clamping nut upon the stem and engaging the spring for causing the spring to exert an outward pressure upon the stem for holding the piston-head seated upon the primary casing.

1,327,495. GAS-PRODUCER FOR PROPELLING VEHICLES. DAVID J. SMITH, London, England. Filed Nov. 29, 1918. Serial No. 264,715. 4 Claims. (Cl. 123—3.)

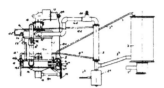

1. The combination with a vehicle having a combustion engine, of a gas producer carried by the vehicle for supplying combustible gas to said engine, including a combustion chamber for solid fuel, a grate therein including a series of movable grate bars, a shaft driven by the engine and extending through the ash pan, and a series of cams on said shaft engaging the said grate bars.

1,327,496. ELECTRIC-LAMP SOCKET. GARNETT SNIDER, Bruces Mines, Ontario, Canada. Filed Sept. 22, 1917. Serial No. 192,785. 2 Claims. (Cl. 173—358.)

1. In a device of the class described, a casing, a body of insulation inclosed thereby and including a plurality of sections, a shell for engaging the threaded base of the lamp and comprising a plurality of segmental members formed with threads, a transversely extending member connecting said segmental members, said sections of the body portion being provided with channeled portions oppositely located for receiving the transversely extending portion of the shell.

2. In a device of the class described, a casing, a body portion of insulation inclosed thereby and including a plurality of sections, each section including a member extending from one end thereof and spaced from the corresponding member of the adjacent section when the sections are secured together, each of said members having an undercut portion, said portions forming together a channel extending transversely of the body portion and in the direction of the line of division between the sections, a shell for engaging the base of a lamp and comprising a plurality of segmental members the walls of which are provided with threads, and a transversely extending member of resilient material connecting the segmental portions and causing the latter to firmly engage the base of the lamp thrust longitudinally between said segmental portions, said transverse member being located within the channel.

1,327,497. AUTOMATIC TRAPPING - HEAD. HENRY SPENCE, Kearney, N. J. Filed July 24, 1918. Serial No. 246,555. 6 Claims. (Cl. 10—138.)

1. The herein described automatic tapping head for drill presses comprising a casing, means to support the casing upon the drill press mandrel, means to prevent rotation of the casing, a tool spindle journaled in the casing, and devices within the casing serving to rotate the

spindle at low speed in either a clockwise or counter-clockwise direction and at high speed in the opposite

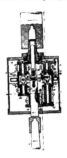

direction while the press mandrel continues to rotate in the same direction.

1,327,498. HONING DEVICE OR HOLDER FOR SAFETY-RAZORS. WILLIAM SUMMERBELL, Washington, D. C., assignor of one-half to Francis Arthur Sutton, Oakhurst, Ashford, England. Filed July 17, 1919. Serial No. 311,434. 6 Claims. (Cl. 51—16.)

4. As a new article of manufacture a reversible blade holder having a ball mounted in the rear portion thereof and protruding outwardly through both sides of such rear portion, said ball being freely revoluble and serving, with the blade being sharpened, as the bearing or support for the holder, whereby the edge of the blade will have a fair and even bearing and may be readily drawn over the sharpening surface in any direction.

1,327,499. [WITHDRAWN.]

1,327,500. TELEPHONE SET. HENRY SYMES, Dunedin, New Zealand. Filed Nov. 9, 1916. Serial No. 130,422. 3 Claims. (Cl. 179—90.)

1. In a telephone of the class specified adapted for automatic telephone work, the combination with an automatic calling device and a transmitter and receiver

mounted on and embodied in the organization of the same, of a bell set, a condenser, an adjustable rheostat, and induction coils all electrically connected to said calling device and the transmitter and receiver, and a switch associated with a weight device automatically movable to press one end of the switch and released for gravitating action by the switch to control the operation of said telephone parts and also to cut off the bell set when receiving messages, the weight device also being automatically operative to cause sounds to pass the user of the telephone when the latter drops away upon the resumption of the latter for use in talking purposes.

1,327,501. AUTOMATIC STOP FOR PHONOGRAPHS. GEORGE H. TAGGART, New York, N. Y. Filed Sept. 3, 1918. Serial No. 252,404. 6 Claims. (Cl. 74—46.)

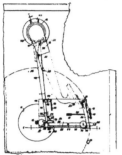

1. The combination with an automatic brake for a phonograph turntable, of means to initiate the setting of the brake automatically when the end of the record is reached, said means including a trigger arm, an arm to which the trigger arm is pivotally connected, means to hold the trigger arm normally substantially at right angles to the arm but permitting it to be swung around its pivot to a different angle, means to reciprocate the trigger arm in opposite directions in alternation continually while the record is being played, the means acting upon the trigger arm to reciprocate it in one direction serving to cause the swinging thereof as aforesaid after the end of the record is reached, and a trip member acted upon by the angular swing of the trigger arm to release the brake.

1,327,502. IGNITION DEVICE. HARRY RANDOLPH VAN DEVENTER, Sumter, S. C., assignor to Splitdorf Electrical Company, Newark, N. J., a Corporation of New Jersey. Filed Oct. 13, 1917. Serial No. 196,372. 5 Claims. (Cl. 123—149.)

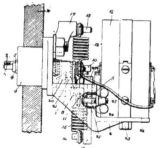

1. An ignition device including in combination a two-part supporting bracket, a fixed and movable electrode

mounted on one of said bracket parts, a generator mounted on the other bracket part, a trip lever carried by the bracket part supporting the electrodes, springs for actuating the trip lever and means whereby the part of the bracket carrying the generator may be adjusted vertically relative to the part of the bracket carrying the trip lever.

1,327,503. AUTOMOBILE-TIRE. WILLIAM I. VARNER, Athens, Ga. Filed Jan. 26, 1918. Serial No. 213,937. 1 Claim. (Cl. 152—18.)

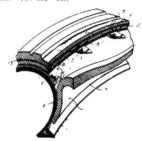

A tire having a plurality of relatively spaced transversely extending fabric strips embedded therein in contact with its carcass, a circumferentially extending fabric strip embedded in the tire and engaging the outer side of said transversely extending strips, a plurality of plates embedded in the tire and engaging the outer side of said circumferentially extending strip and having its ends relatively spaced and overlapping said transversely extending strips, the plates having their ends rolled and embedded in the tread of the tire and having their central portions offset and embedded in the tread, and a fabric strip embedded in the tread in contact with the outer sides of said offset portions.

1,327,504. GEARING FOR GENERATORS AND DISTRIBUTERS. ALBERT F. WAGNER, New York, N. Y. Filed Dec. 1, 1917. Serial No. 204,828. 5 Claims. (Cl. 74—7.)

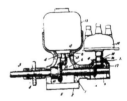

2. A device of the character described, comprising a support having alined shaft bearings and having a gear chamber therein between the bearings, a cup-shaped member on the support adapted to receive a generator therein, said support having a bearing extending from the gear chamber into the cup-shaped member for the reception of the generator shaft, and said support having a second gear chamber therein and adapted to support a distributer adjacent said last-mentioned gear chamber.

1,327,505. SELECTIVE CIRCUIT-CLOSER. JOHN P. WAHLSTROM, Minneapolis, Minn. Filed Oct. 6, 1917. Serial No. 195,103. 9 Claims. (Cl. 200—142.)
3. In a selective circuit closer, the combination with a fixed terminal, a movable terminal pivoted at one end

to the support and having a notch in its rear edge, a spring drawing its free end normally toward the fixed terminal, and a spring retainer whose free arm stands

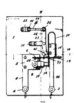

behind the movable terminal; of thermal members fusible at different temperatures, and means for throwing them selectively or jointly into connection with said free arm to hold it out of register with said notch.

1,327,506. MAGNETIC CLUTCH. MALCOLM WALKER, Glasgow, Scotland, assignor to Smith and Coventry Limited, Salford, England. Filed July 11, 1916. Serial No. 108,603. 4 Claims. (Cl. 192—7.)

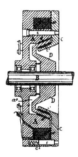

4. A magnetic friction clutch comprising a magnetic friction member having a recess forming a cone face and an energizing electric coil inserted in the body of the member at a distance outwardly from the said recess, the cone face being exterior of the magnetic field, a shaft on which the said magnetic member is loosely mounted, a ring armature suspended close to the polar face of the magnetic member and also provided with a cone friction face at its inner portion which is normally adjacent to the cone face of the magnetic member, the ring armature being movable toward and from and also rotatable with the magnetic member, and a friction member mounted to move between the cone face of the magnetic member and the cone face of the ring armature and having two cone friction faces, one of said faces engaging the cone face of the magnetic friction member and the other the cone face of the ring armature, and means for connecting the friction member with the device to be driven.

1,327,507. INTERNAL-COMBUSTION-ENGINE WATER-HEATER. FRED WALTHER, Omaha, Nebr. Filed Dec. 5, 1918. Serial No. 265,433. 2 Claims. (Cl. 219—88.)

1. A device of the character described, comprising an electric heater suspended horizontally from the bottom of an automobile radiator, said heater consisting of a heating unit inclosed within a case, said case being rigidly secured within a heat insulating jacket and closed at one end by a disk which is overlapped by the end of the case,

and closed at its other end by an insulating plug retained in position by the lapping of the other end of the case, and terminal wires fitting in apertures formed through

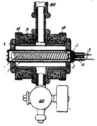

the plug, said wires being covered with non-inflammable material and terminating at a source of electric energy for supplying current to the heating unit.

1,327,508. HEATER. LEE H. WHITEHORN, Eureka, Colo. Filed Aug. 2, 1918. Serial No. 248,008. 2 Claims. (Cl. 126—256.)

1. A heating device designed to be supported on the chimney of a lamp, comprising a receptacle having a dome arranged centrally therein and communicating with the bottom thereof, and concentrically arranged depending legs on the bottom of the said receptacle, disposed outward of the dome and designed to engage with the upper edge of the lamp chimney to support the same thereon and to sustain the same thereabove.

1,327,509. COOLING AIR IN SUBMARINE AND SUBMERSIBLE SHIPS. HAROLD E. YARROW, Scotstoun, Glasgow, Scotland. Filed Mar. 28, 1917. Serial No. 158,081. 3 Claims. (Cl. 114—16.)

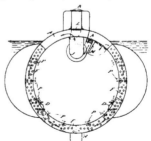

1. In a submersible ship, a chamber extending approximately completely around a transverse section of the

ship and having its outer surface formed at least in part by the external hull of the ship; means for circulating air through said chamber; and means for distributing the air, cooled by its passage through the chamber, to compartments of the ship as may be desired.

1,327,510. PROPULSION OF VESSELS. HAROLD E. YARROW, Glasgow, Scotland. Filed Oct. 30, 1917. Serial No. 199,316. 5 Claims. (Cl. 60—70.)

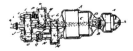

1. In the propulsion of vessels, a plurality of engines normally running at different speeds having their drive shafts arranged coaxially, one of said drive shafts being hollow and surrounding the other drive shaft, a propeller shaft, and gearing between said drive shafts and said propeller shaft for transmitting motion to either or both of said drive shafts to said propeller shaft.

1,327,511. TRACTOR STEERING DEVICE. HERBERT E. ABBOTT and EZRA ENZ, Oakville, Iowa. Filed July 11, 1919. Serial No. 310,031. 1 Claim. (Cl. 180—80.)

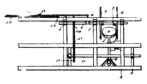

A steering mechanism for tractors comprising an operating shaft driven from the motor power of the tractor and having a frictional wheel, a shifting shaft having opposed friction disks, means for shifting said shaft whereby either disk may be brought into contact with the friction wheel and the shifting shaft rotated in a desired direction, an operating shaft directly connected with the turning mechanism of the tractor and driving connections between the shifting shaft and operating shaft, a lever pivoted upon the frame of the tractor and connected with the shifting shaft, a second lever pivoted upon the frame at right angles to the first mentioned lever, a link providing a connection between the adjacent extremities of said levers, cables having their ends connected with the free ends of the second mentioned lever, and pulleys mounted upon the tractor and over which the cables are trained in a direction to permit shifting of the said shaft from a position remote from the tractor.

1,327,512. REINFORCED PUMP-CASING. ROSCOE H. ALDRICH, Allentown, Pa., assignor to Aldrich Pump Company, Allentown, Pa., a Corporation of Pennsylvania. Filed Mar. 22, 1919, Serial No. 284,245. Renewed Nov. 14, 1919. Serial No. 338,114. 2 Claims. (Cl. 103—61.)

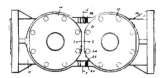

1. A cast metal pump casing having a valve chamber provided with a plurality of entrance openings, adjacent openings being separated by a bridge piece integral with the opposite walls of the casing and provided with a transverse opening extending through the said walls, and a reinforcing member of greater tensile strength than the material of which the pump casing is made, the said reinforcing member fitting into and extending through the said opening and engaging the outer faces of the said walls of the casing, the said reinforcing member being under tension.

1,327,513. SAFETY DEVICE FOR ELEVATORS. GIUSEPPE ALFANO, New York, N. Y. Filed May 25, 1917. Serial No. 171,060. 2 Claims. (Cl. 187—71.)

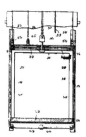

1. In a device of the class described, a car, a main cable supporting the car, a frame within which said car is mounted for unobstructed movement, said frame cooperating with shaft guiding members, cables connected with the frame and adapted to support the car when the main cable is disconnected, a single winding element for all of said cables, said car normally supporting the frame from the upper side thereof, and the frame supporting the car when the latter is released by its normal supporting means.

1,327,514. FLYING-MACHINE. WILLIAM H. ALLMAN, Blythedale, Mo. Filed Oct. 23, 1918. Serial No. 259,443. 1 Claim. (Cl. 244—19.)

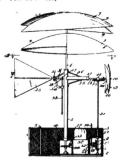

A device of the character described comprising a carrier, a box thereon, a post rising from the box, a vertical shaft journaled through the post and the box and projecting above the post, a pair of super-posed lifting and sustaining propellers connected to the projecting end of the shaft, a prime mover on the carrier, a shaft rotatable by the prime mover, transmission means connected to the shafts and positioned in the box which insure the rotation of the main propellers at all times, a sleeve projecting from the post, a horizontal shaft journaled in the sleeve, an auxiliary propeller connected to the outer end of the horizontal shaft, another vertically disposed shaft journaled in the carrier, means for transmitting motion between the last mentioned vertical shaft and the horizontal shaft, transmission means between the second mentioned shaft and the last mentioned vertical shaft, manually operable clutch means for controlling the transmission of movement between the second mentioned shaft and the last mentioned shaft, and manually operable steering means connected to the post.

1,327,515. MACHINE FOR TRUING LOOM-SHUTTLES. JAKOB ALTMANN, Weesen, Switzerland. Filed Oct. 21, 1918. Serial No. 258,997. 3 Claims. (Cl. 144—114.)

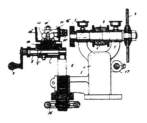

1. In a machine for truing loom shuttles, in combination with a machine upright and a rotatable cutting tool and a grinding and polishing wheel journaled therein, a bracket arm extending from said upright, an internally threaded head to said bracket arm, an externally threaded spindle operating in said head, hand wheel means for causing and limiting the relative displacement between said head and said spindle, a bed supported by said spindle, a slide on said bed and crank handle means for causing and limiting the relative displacement between said bed and said slide axially of said cutting tool, a transverse slide on said axially movable slide adapted to be reciprocated in front of said cutting tool, adjustable means on said transverse slide for supporting a shuttle at its extremities, and adjustable means on said transverse slide for supporting the stock of the shuttle in such manner that the face to be operated upon is always presented to the cutting tool in strictly parallel position.

1,327,516. TALKING-MACHINE. ANTON D. ANDERSON, Harrison, N. Y. Filed June 5, 1919. Serial No. 302,005. 1 Claim. (Cl. 274—2.)

A device of the character described comprising a cabinet, an amplifier rigidly mounted within the cabinet, a washer of pliable material surrounding the opening of the inner end of the amplifier and having an angularly disposed outer face, a motor board pivotally mounted within the cabinet and provided with an opening adapted to register with the inner end of the amplifier when the motor board is within the cabinet, a washer surrounding the opening through the motor board on the side thereof adjacent the amplifier, said washer having an angularly disposed outer face, the angle of which is opposed to the angularly disposed face of the washer surrounding the opening of the inner end of the amplifier, whereby a tight joint is provided between the motor board and the amplifier when the motor board is positioned interiorly of the cabinet.

1,327,517. ROTARY WATER-PUMP. MORIL V. ANDREWS and STEPHEN W. HOLMAN, Marmarth, N. D., assignors to Mora Pump Company, Marmarth, N. D., a Corporation. Filed Sept. 25, 1919. Serial No. 326,187 3 Claims. (Cl. 103—44.)

3. A rotary water pump comprising a rotary disk having peripheral side teeth, a pair of vanes on each side of the disk and diverging outwardly from the axis to the periphery of the disk, a cut-off roller on each side of the disk and having teeth meshing with the disk teeth, said rollers being conical and having lengthwise cut-outs for the vanes and permitting the disk to be revolved therebetween, a casing inclosing the disk, sub-casings inclosing the rollers at an angle to the disk, a water induction pipe and a water eduction pipe connected with the casing respectively on opposite sides of the rollers, and means for revolving the disk.

1,327,518. CENTRIFUGAL GUN. FRANK R. BARNES, Dupree, S. D. Filed June 12, 1917. Serial No. 174,378. 10 Claims. (Cl. 89—10.)

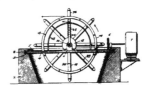

1. In a projector of the type described, the combination with an upright rotor whose shaft is journaled in bearings, and means for rotating said shaft; of means for attaching projectiles to points on the periphery of the rotor, rock shafts extending from the respective means radially inward and carrying pins at different distances from the rotor shaft, and a series of manually operable trippers respectively spaced from the rotor shaft in line with the paths of said pins.

1,327,519. BOTTLE-STOPPER. FREDERIC CLAYTON BITLER, Brooklyn, N. Y., assignor of one-half to Lee Van Jones, Norwalk, Conn. Filed Apr. 1, 1919. Serial No. 286,640. 2 Claims. (Cl. 215—8.)

1. The combination with a bottle having a tapering neck opening of a stopper of glass, formed with a reduced

central part, a ring formed on one end, and a plurality of longitudinal radiating flanges extending from the end of the stopper opposite said ring toward the ring, said ring and said flanges being ground in a common conical surface smaller in diameter at the end opposite the ring so as to fit the tapering neck of the bottle simultaneously.

1,327,520. STRIP - FEEDING MECHANISM. WALTER HENRY BROWNING, Wembley, England. Filed Apr. 14, 1917. Serial No. 162,185. 13 Claims. (Cl. 273.)

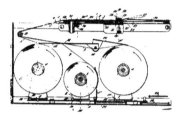

1. Autographic recording apparatus comprising, in combination, a needle operated to perforate and feed forward material in strip form upon which a record is to be made, a needle operated to perforate the material and retain it in position when the first needle is withdrawn, and wedge means for gripping the said strip after the retaining needle has been inserted.

1,327,521. RECTIFIER SYSTEM. HENRY EDWARD BURKET, Kansas City, Mo. Filed Mar. 29, 1917. Serial No. 158,393. 8 Claims. (Cl. 175—364.)

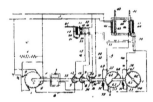

1. In an alternating current rectifying system, a synchronous motor, a rectifying commutator driven by said motor and provided with active and inactive sectors, brushes disposed about said sectors, a condenser and a reactance shunted around said brushes, a transformer having secondary windings connected to certain of the brushes and primary windings connected to the alternating current mains adjustable to certain of the brushes and a direct current circuit connected to certain of the brushes and a neutral point of the secondary windings.

1,327,522. SCRAPER. KUN SUNG CHUNG, Honolulu, Hawaii. Filed Aug. 25, 1919. Serial No. 319,814. 6 Claims. (Cl. 114—222.)

6. A device of the character described comprising a carriage adapted for movement to a selected location upon the deck of a ship, a plurality of wheels rotating in the same vertical plane, a plurality of vertically disposed rods operatively connected with said wheels and movable in a vertical and lateral direction thereby, and a scraper mem-

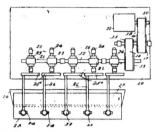

ber carried by said rods and engaging against the hull of a ship.

1,327,523. HORSESHOE. ALEX S. CRAWFORD, Cannonsville, N. Y. Filed Aug. 14, 1918. Serial No. 249,839. 1 Claim. (Cl. 168—35.)

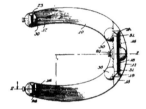

A horse shoe, having a transverse channel in the toe portion and in each heel portion thereof, said channels having undercut walls, calks having grooved and inclined side portions located in said channels, the inclined portions tapering outwardly toward each other, means for securing the calks in position, and reinforcing means on the surface of the shoe adjacent the calks, overlapping the walls of the channels bearing against the inclined faces of the calks and entering the grooves thereof, said reinforcing means comprising thickened portions of metal having rounded surfaces, certain of said thickened portions having undercut inclined edge portions engaging the adjacent calk.

1,327,524. WRENCH. LOUIS A. CROMBIE, Hicksville, N. Y. Filed May 24, 1919. Serial No. 299,618. 2 Claims. (Cl. 81—114.)

1. A wrench comprising handle members having exteriorly-threaded off-set portions presenting crossed jaws on one of their ends, and means engaging and moving in contact with said exteriorly-threaded off-set portions for moving the jaws relatively to each other.

1,327,525. DIE FOR MAKING DOUBLE-ENDED RIVETS. WALTER L. CURTIS, Springfield, Mass. Filed June 6, 1918. Serial No. 238,561. 2 Claims. (Cl. 80—20.)

2. A die plate for forming double ended rivets, said die plate being provided with a longitudinal groove and sets of rolling tables disposed upon opposite sides of the groove, the tables in each set being stepped up progressively, the tables in said sets being arranged in transversely alined pairs, one transverse pair of tables being arranged outwardly with respect to the preceding pair of tables, each table having an inclined edge adapted to sweep the rivet from the starting point to the end thereof, and a plurality of substantially straight fins arranged at the forward ends of the inclined edges of the tables, said fins being arranged in transverse pairs.

1,327,526. WRINGER ATTACHMENT FOR TUBS. CLAUDE B. DAVIS, Richmond, Va., assignor of one-half to J. Walter Keeling, Danville, Va. Filed June 3, 1919. Serial No. 301,386. 5 Claims. (Cl. 68—32.)

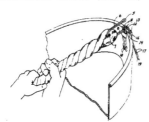

1. A wringer attachment for washtubs comprising a hook having a clamping jaw extending from its stem, in a direction away from its bill and a second clamping jaw pivotally connected with the first jaw for movement into and out of clamping relation thereto and having means for holding it yieldable in clamping relation.

1,327,527. WRINGER ATTACHMENT FOR TUBS. CLAUDE B. DAVIS, Richmond, Va., assignor of one-half to J. Walter Keeling, Danville, Va. Filed Sept. 5, 1919. Serial No. 321,843. 1 Claim. (Cl. 68—32.)

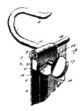

A wringer attachment comprising a clamp including an inverted U-shaped body for engagement over the beaded upper edge of a wash tub, a U-shaped clamping jaw disposed between the arms of the body below its bend with its ends outturned and slidably embracing the side edges of the outer arm, means for adjusting the jaw toward and away from the inner arm, and a hook carried rigidly by such inner arm to receive an article to be wrung.

1,327,528. COMBINED HEAD-COVERING AND HAIR-COMB. ALVA K. DAWSON, Jacksonville, Fla. Filed Dec. 30, 1918. Serial No. 268,843. 4 Claims. (Cl. 2—106.)

1. The combination of a cap having a sweat band and a vizor whose inner edge is arranged adjacent to the lower edge of the sweat band, said vizor having a pocket formed therein with an open mouth adjacent to the sweat band, and a comb carried permanently in the pocket with the points of the teeth adjacent to said pocket mouth and over which the sweat band lies.

1,327,529. AERIAL VESSEL. ALEXANDER DEAK and JOSEPH DEAK, Brooklyn, N. Y. Filed May 3, 1918. Serial No. 232,372. 8 Claims. (Cl. 244—15.)

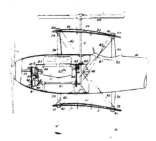

1. In an aerial vessel, a motor, a driving propeller, a clutch between the propeller and motor shafts, a safety propeller disposed horizontally and having its axis approximately at the center of gravity of the vessel, a horizontal shaft having one end geared with the safety propeller shaft, a clutch on the horizontal shaft, gearing between members of the said clutches, and means under the control of the operator for alternately throwing the said clutches into and out of engagement.

1,327,530. TOY AEROPLANE. HORACE BOYLSTON DUMMER, New York, N. Y. Filed Sept. 23, 1919. Serial No. 325,754. 2 Claims. (Cl. 244—12.)

1. A device of the character described comprising a body portion provided with an angularly disposed slot, and

a sustaining plane in the form of a pamphlet having covers and leaves, said pamphlet being removably maintained within said angularly disposed slot by frictional engagement with the defining edges thereof.

1,327,531. PROJECTILE. CHARLES DURHAM, Chicago, Ill. Filed Dec. 6, 1918. Serial No. 265,615. 2 Claims. (Cl. 102—29.)

1. A projectile comprising a body formed with a longitudinal bore flared at one end, longitudinally disposed ribs extending from the flared end of said bore and terminating short of the opposite end defining a shoulder, said ribs having a helical pitch, and a cap loosely fitted in said bore and bearing against said shoulder, said cap including a plate arranged against the bottom of said projectile.

1,327,532. STRAINER. FLORA DUVALL, Chicago, Ill. Filed May 6, 1919. Serial No. 295,155. 3 Claims. (Cl. 53—3.)

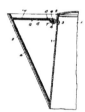

1. A screening attachment for the spouts of coffee or tea pots, comprising a body member frictionally contacting with the inner surface of a spout and a hinged spring influenced screening member supported by the body and frictionally contacting therewith.

1,327,533. HEMP-BRAKE. RODGER EADES, Winchester, Ky. Filed Feb. 26, 1918. Serial No. 219,268. 3 Claims. (Cl. 13—6.)

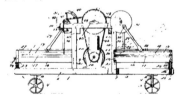

1. In a hemp brake, a portable base frame, a braking bench at each extremity of the frame including a lower

frame held in substantially horizontal position and an upper frame hinged at its inner end to move upwardly from and downwardly toward the lower frame, the frames having coöperating swords, main driving mechanism between the two benches, and independent actuating mechanism for each of the upper frames and connected to the main driving mechanism, each actuating mechanism having an independently operable clutch and clutch wheel, the clutch wheels being connected to the upper hinged frames for causing the said frames to operate either simultaneously or individually and also for permitting the upper frames to be manually raised.

1,327,534. KEY-RING HOLDER. JOHN A. EICHSTEDT, Akron, Ohio. Filed Oct. 10, 1919. Serial No. 329,661. 4 Claims. (Cl. 24—3.)

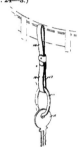

1. A key ring holder consisting of a strip of material, each end of said strip being bent back on itself to form a U-shaped section, and a locking member pivoted to said strip adapted to lock the legs of the U-shaped sections to the strip.

1,327,535. RAILWAY-LINK. LUDWIG W. EISINGER, Bronxville, N. Y. Filed Dec. 26, 1918. Serial No. 268,315. 8 Claims. (Cl. 104—28.)

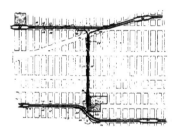

1. In a railway link, two main lines each having double tracks, and additional tracks from the tracks on one of the main lines which cross each other, one over the other, which connect with the tracks on the other main line.

1,327,536. PROCESS FOR CHEMICAL SEPARATION OF ORES. ALEXANDER T. ELLIOTT, Los Angeles, Calif., assignor of one-tenth to L. M. Freeman, Los Angeles, Calif. Filed Feb. 20, 1918. Serial No. 218,210. 2 Claims. (Cl. 23—13.)

1. The process of separation of ores, which consists in leaching the ore with hydrochloric acid, separating the resulting chlorid solution from the residue, treating said solution to obtain a chlorid, subjecting said chlorid to heat to decompose said chlorid and to drive off a vapor containing chlorin and utilizing such chlorin in reproducing the leaching solution.

1,327,537. JIG. GUY H. ELMORE, Swarthmore, Pa. Filed Mar. 28, 1917. Serial No. 158,015. 10 Claims. (Cl. 83—79.)

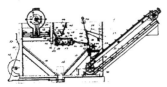

1. In a jig, the combination of a tank; a screen in said tank; means for producing water pulsations through said screen; means for feeding materials to be separated, to said screen; means for separately discharging the separated materials from said screen; and a deflector structure comprising a plurality of separated fixed deflector bars mounted beneath and substantially parallel with that portion of the screen adjacent said pulsation-producing means, for locally checking such pulsations, the deflector bars being transverse to the direction of flow of water and of material on the screen.

2. In a jig, the combination of a tank; a screen in said tank; means for producing water pulsations through said screen; means for feeding materials to be separated, to said screen; means for separately discharging the separated materials from said screen; and a plurality of fixed, transverse deflector bars having steeply inclined top surfaces mounted beneath that portion of the screen adjacent said pulsation producing means for locally checking such pulsations.

3. In a jig, the combination of a tank; a pair of adjacent and vertically offset screens in said tank; means common to both screens for producing water pulsations through said screens; means for feeding materials to be separated, to the higher of said screens; means for discharging the separated materials after passing over the lower of said screens; and a deflector structure comprising a series of separated, fixed, transverse bars arranged beneath and substantially parallel with the higher of said screens, adapted to intensify the pulsations on the lower screen by choking the action upon the upper screen.

4. In a jig, the combination of a tank; a pair of adjacent and vertically offset screens in said tank; means common to both screens for producing water pulsations through said screens; means for feeding materials to be separated, to the higher of said screens; means for discharging the separated materials after passing over the lower of said screens; and a plurality of fixed, transverse deflector bars having steeply inclined top surfaces mounted beneath the higher of said screens, adapted to intensify the pulsations on the lower screen by choking the action upon the upper screen.

5. In a jig, the combination of a tank; a pair of adjacent and vertically offset screens in said tank; a plunger, operative in said tank adjacent the higher of said screens to produce water pulsations through said screens; means for feeding materials to be separated, to the higher of said screens; means for separately discharging the separated materials after passing over the lower of said screens; and a deflector structure comprising a series of separated, fixed, transverse deflector bars arranged beneath and substantially parallel with the higher of said screens.

1,327,538. NON-SKID DEVICE. HARRY C. ETTER, Chambersburg, Pa. Filed Feb. 8, 1919. Serial No. 275,782. 3 Claims. (Cl. 152—14.)

1. In a device of the character described, the combination with an automobile wheel, of a cylinder, means for securing said cylinder to the wheel radially thereof, a rod operable through the outer end of the cylinder and projecting into the same, means for normally forcing said rod inwardly, a traction gripping member carried by the rod at the outer end thereof and adapted to engage about the

tread portion of a tire mounted upon the wheel, and hinge connections between the outer end of said rod and said gripping member adapted to positively limit turning of the

gripping member about its hinge axis in one direction while permitting said member to be folded inwardly in the other direction away from the tire when turned out of engagement therewith.

1,327,539. VALVE-SPRING RETAINER. CURTISS W. FINNEY, Spokane, Wash. Filed Nov. 13, 1918. Serial No. 262,387. 3 Claims. (Cl. 251—144.)

1. The combination with the disk having a central opening and the grooved stem passing therethrough, of a pair of diametrically arranged arms having shoes passed through the opening and engaging the grooved stem, and a spring bearing on the disk and arms.

1,327,540. VALVE. NELSON H. FOOKS, Preston, Md. Filed Apr. 8, 1919. Serial No. 288,588. 19 Claims. (Cl. 214—17.)

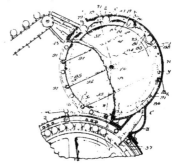

1. A device for conveying material between atmospheres of different pressure and for controlling the flow of fluid

under pressure between the different atmospheres, this device having a carrier with pockets to receive the material, and means for connecting certain pockets in successive steps of their movement to reduce the higher pressure in successive stages toward the lower.

1,327,541. RAIL-JOINT. OTTO FREIMARK, Martin, Ohio. Filed Feb. 7, 1919. Serial No. 275,596. 1 Claim. (Cl. 238—145.)

In a compound rail, a foot section and a head section arranged thereon, said head having its web provided with angular extensions in the nature of plates, the lower edges of which being extended downwardly and outwardly, the base having a central substantially V-shaped rib received between the plates, said base having its upper surface, outward of the rib arranged at opposite inclinations, the edges of the base having upstanding flanges designed to contact with the edges of the outturned portions of the plates, securing elements passing loosely through the plates and rib, spikes arranged upon the outer edges of the base and overlying the flanges thereon, and the angle extensions of the side plates of the web.

1,327,542. ELECTRIC CONDUCTOR. PETER F. FREY, Niagara Falls, N. Y., assignor to U. S. Light & Heat Corporation, Niagara Falls, N. Y., a Corporation of New York. Filed May 27, 1918. Serial No. 236,747. 1 Claim. (Cl. 204—29.)

In a storage battery construction having a cell post extending through the cover, a bushing screw-threaded to both the post and the cover and filling up the space between said post and said cover.

1,327,543. AEROPLANE. JAMES MORRIS FUNK, Ottawa, Ill., assignor of one-half to Thomas H. Belrose, Ottawa, Ill. Filed Oct. 16, 1918. Serial No. 258,363. 10 Claims. (Cl. 244—29.)

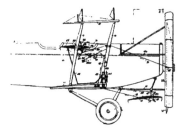

1. In an aeroplane, stabilizing means including a vertically swingable vane, and means extending to swing the vane from a neutral position for functioning, said vane being located rearward of the propeller of the aeroplane

and in such proximity thereto as to be subject to the air current generated by the propeller to such a degree that said current in the normal operation of the propeller will counteract the second-mentioned means to maintain the vane neutral.

1,327,544. BILL-POSTING DEVICE. EDWARD E. GALLUP, Pittsfield, Mass. Filed Nov. 3, 1917. Serial No. 200,160. 4 Claims. (Cl. 40—13.)

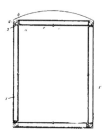

1. A device of the class described, the combination with a substantially rectangular base of brackets located at each corner thereof, spring actuated clamping devices disposed transversely and longitudinally of said base, pintles projecting over each end of said clamping device, said pintles having bearings in said brackets, whereby said clamping device will be arranged in rectangular form and means carried by said brackets and disposed in the path of movement of said clamping device for holding the latter against action of the spring.

1,327,545. DEVICE FOR INCREASING THE EFFICIENCY OF FIREARMS AND THE LIKE. ERNEST LOUIS GARNIER, Neuilly-sur-Seine, France. Filed Mar. 10, 1919. Serial No. 281,720. 4 Claims. (Cl. 102—26.)

1. In a fire-arm, the combination with a bullet having a tapered nose and provided with an annular groove on its exterior transverse to the axis of the bullet, of a metal screw propeller having flexible blades provided with a hollow hub detachably connected to the forward end of the barrel, the forward end of said hub being partly closed and provided with an axial opening of greater diameter than the bore of the fire-arm at the muzzle, a segmental ring housed in said hub between said partly closed end and the muzzle of the fire-arm, and resilient means for attaching said segmental ring to said hub and for causing it to project into engagement with the periphery of the bullet as it leaves the fire-arm.

1,327,546. SHEET-FEEDING MECHANISM. WILLIAM C. GLASS, Jamaica Plain, Mass. Filed Nov. 8, 1912. Serial No. 730,165. 10 Claims. (Cl. 271—55.)

1. A sheet-feeding mechanism for presses having, in combination, sheet-folding means, means to impart a for-

ward and backward motion to said sheet-holding means to carry a sheet into and out of the press, and means for

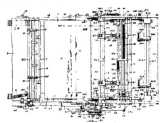

utilizing the forward motion of said sheet-holding means to move the same laterally thereby to position the sheet laterally.

1,327,547. SAFETY-RAZOR. JAMES D. GOODWIN, Richmond, Va., assignor of one-half to William K Dennis. Filed May 28, 1919. Serial No. 300,264. 3 Claims. (Cl. 30—12.)

1. A safety razor comprising a blade holder, a two-part handle, one part of such handle having swiveled connection with the blade holder and formed with a threaded opening, the other part of such handle being wholly separable and provided with a threaded extension to engage the threaded opening and coöperating with the blade holder when in handle forming position to engage the swivel and lock said swivel movement.

1,327,548. CONTROL OF POWER ABSORBED IN ELECTRIC FURNACES. COLIN CLARENCE GOW and DONALD FRASER CAMPBELL, London, England. Filed Apr. 24, 1919. Serial No. 292,438. 6 Claims. (Cl 204—64.)

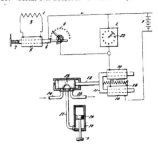

1. Means for maintaining the power absorbed in an electric furnace at a predetermined value, comprising a supply of fluid pressure controlled by an electromagnetic device energized by current from a source independent of the load circuit, the strength of the said current being regulated by means of variable resistances automatically adjusted according to the power supplied to the load circuit.

1,327,549. ROLLER-SKATE. FREDERICK GUNNARSON, Ogden, Utah. Filed Mar. 8, 1919. Serial No. 281,828. 1 Claim. (Cl. 46—51.)

A skate comprising a foot engaging member, a pair of oppositely bowed substantially V-shaped leaf-springs secured transversely upon the underside of said foot engaging member at the forward and rear ends thereof, the free ends of said springs extending vertically downwardly and being formed as bearing members, a wheel disposed between each pair of springs and having its axle journally received within said bearings, a horizontally disposed U-shaped yoke straddling each wheel and having its arms disposed inwardly of said bearing members and journally engaging said axle, the yoke at the forward wheel extending rearwardly and the yoke at the rear wheel extending forwardly, and an inclined resilient strip secured at one end to the bight of each yoke and having its other end secured to said foot engaging member, said resilient strips converging upwardly.

1,327,550. VAPOR CROUP-KETTLE. CLIFFORD P. HAGUE, Hartford, Conn. Filed Jan. 2, 1919. Serial No. 269,223. 2 Claims. (Cl. 167—3.)

1. A device of the character described consisting of a cylindrical support, a kettle seated on the upper edge of the support and formed with an annular rib on the lower edge thereof, catch means carried by the support for engagement with the rib on the kettle to retain the kettle against displacement, an exteriorly threaded collar projecting from the kettle, a cup like strainer formed with an annular flange for seating on the upper edge of the collar, an interiorly threaded nozzle detachably engaged with the exteriorly threaded collar, a handle projecting from the support, and heating means mounted in the support and disposed beneath the kettle.

1,327,551. GAS-SAVER FOR INTERNAL-COMBUSTION ENGINES. ANDREW J. HANSGEN and EARL G. OVERSMITH, Denver, Colo. Filed Aug. 10, 1916. Serial No. 114,235. 1 Claim. (Cl. 123—25.)

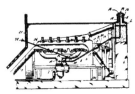

Means for supplying moist air to the manifold of an internal combustion engine comprising in combination a chamber located at the top of a radiator above the normal water level, a conduit connecting said chamber with the manifold, said conduit being provided with an interrupted connection, a nozzle secured upon the extremity of one section of the conduit, and an adjustable disk mounted upon the adjacent extremity of the other section, said nozzle and disk coöperating to supply atmospheric air to the said conduit and to regulate the amount thereof.

1,327,552. ADVERTISING DEVICE. JOHN ZACIOUS HANSON, Fort Worth, Tex. Filed June 5, 1919. Serial No. 301,980. 4 Claims. (Cl. 40—64.)

1. An advertising device, including a receptacle, advertisement holders removably secured to the sides of such receptacle, each advertisement holder including a single sheet of material having its lower and longitudinal side edges bent inwardly and spaced from its body portion, and individually-adjustable advertisement holders applied to said holder and having their outermost ends projecting between the inturned longitudinal edges and body portion of the sheet of material forming the holder.

1,327,553. WEIGHING-MACHINE. HERBERT HARVEY, Oakland, Calif. Filed Jan. 10, 1917. Serial No. 141,901. 7 Claims. (Cl. 265—27.)

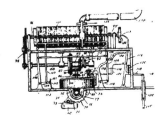

1. The combination of a weighing machine having a weight indicating dial and a pointer, means normally holding said pointer against movement, a phonograph, a spring motor for operating said phonograph, means for normally preventing the operation of said phonograph, a winding lever for said motor and means operable by the movement of said lever for releasing said pointer and said phonograph apparatus.

1,327,554. BEDSTEAD. BURTON S. HAWLEY, Sparta, Wis. Filed Nov. 18, 1918. Serial No. 263,016. 3 Claims. (Cl. 5—4.)

1. A bedstead, comprising in part side rails, a lower part foot member connected thereto, an upper part tubular

foot member hinged to the lower part foot member and having a closed and an open position of rest, means for yieldingly locking said upper part tubular member in open position, and means entirely within the upper part tubular foot member for locking said member in closed position.

1,327,555. SAWMILL-KNEE-ADJUSTING MECHANISM. JOHN HILL, Jr., Dandridge, Tenn. Filed Mar. 11, 1918. Serial No. 221,707. 1 Claim. (Cl. 143—114.)

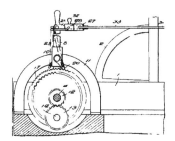

In an advancing and receding device for the knees of saw mill headblocks, an operating shaft, a ratchet wheel fixedly mounted on said shaft, a second ratchet wheel loosely mounted on said shaft, means for effecting connection between the loosely mounted ratchet wheel and the shaft, a lever, pawls pivotally carried upon the opposite sides of said lever adapted to be alternately engaged with said ratchet wheels, a bearing pin carrier upon the upper end of said lever, a pair of rotatable sleeves arranged on said bearing pin, arms formed integral with one of said sleeves, means for directly rotating the latter sleeve, means for connecting said arms to the pivotal pawls, the sleeves being detachably interlocked and a handle rod engaged with the other sleeve.

1,327,556. LINK TREAD-TRACK. BENJAMIN HOLT, Stockton, Calif. Filed Dec. 7, 1916. Serial No. 135,530. 13 Claims. (Cl. 21—150.)

2. A link for endless tracks, comprising a tread plate, pillow blocks conforming thereto, rail sections resting on the pillow blocks, bolts passing through the tread plates, pillow blocks and rail sections, and a paper or equivalent shim member interposed between the pillow blocks and tread plates.

7. A link section for an endless link track embodying parallel side bars having top and bottom flanges lying in a plane with the adjacent longitudinal edges of the bar, a concave shoe for each link, and a cast iron block between each side bar and the shoe completely filling the concavity in the latter.

11. A link section for endless link tracks, embodying parallel side bars, a corrugated shoe carried thereby, fillers between the shoe and side bars, a reinforcing plate on the exterior of the shoe below each filler and side bar and conforming to the curvature of the shoe, and serving also as grousers.

1,327,557. DRAFT-RIGGING. PLINY E. HOLT, Stockton, Calif. Filed Dec. 7, 1916. Serial No. 135,527. 6 Claims. (Cl. 280—33.5.)

1. The combination of a draft vehicle and a drawn element of a draft bar pivotally connected to said vehicle, an axle forming a part of said drawn element and rigidly

secured to the opposite end of said draft bar, steering wheels on the opposite ends of said axle and yieldable means whereby variation in the relation of the draft bar

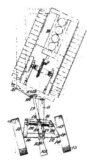

to the vehicle will cause said steering wheels to be disposed to traverse the same path of travel as that described by the draft vehicle and means whereby the steering wheels will be yieldably held in their angular positions.

1,827,558. VEHICLE - BODY. ALBERT OWEN HOLTOM, New York, N. Y. Filed Sept. 10, 1917. Serial No. 190,592. 4 Claims. (Cl. 21—62.)

1. A convertible vehicle body comprising doubled side walls having pockets formed therein, sills hingedly mounted at their ends to said side walls to form covers over said pockets in certain positions thereof and to be swung upright in other positions thereof, top rails hingedly carried by said sill sections extensible to form a superstructure, curtains carried by said side walls in the pockets thereof and fasteners carried by said extensible curtains having engagement with said top rails to reinforce and lock said top rails in fixed position.

1,327,559. BRAKE FOR CONVEYERS. FRED HUBBARD, Humboldt, Ariz. Filed Jan. 7, 1919. Serial No. 269,980. 1 Claim. (Cl. 74—18.)

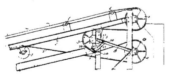

The combination of a frame, rollers rotatably mounted in the frame, a conveyer belt trained over said rollers, a secondary frame carried by the first said frame, the said secondary frame comprising arms in which there forms longitudinal slots, a bar mounted in the first said frame and passing through the slots, and a roller journaled in the secondary frame and bearing upon the belt, whereby the said frame may swing toward or away from one of the first said rollers so that the last said roller may idle upon the belt or jam between it and one of the first said rollers for the useful purpose herein specified.

1,327,560. MEANS FOR COOLING LIQUIDS. JOB HUTCHINSON, Brooklyn, N. Y. Filed Sept. 16, 1918. Serial No. 254,300. 18 Claims. (Cl. 62—136.)

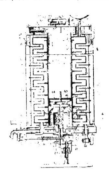

1. A liquid cooler comprising adjacent liquid and gas chambers, automatic means for intermittently delivering successive charges of compressed gases to and expanding them in said gas chamber, and means for expelling each such expanded charge before the delivery of the succeeding charge.

1,327,561. TOOL-HOLDER. ARTHUR E. JOHNSON, Chicago, Ill., assignor of one-half to William B. Pierce, Chicago, Ill. Filed May 14, 1917. Serial No. 168,450. 4 Claims. (Cl. 29—48.)

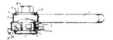

1. In a tool holder of the class described, a shank, a stationary head integrally formed on one end thereof having radial grooves formed in opposite surfaces thereof, an adjustable head having passages therein associated with said stationary head, radially disposed ribs integrally formed on opposite faces thereof, the ribs on one surface of which engage in the grooves in one surface of said stationary head to hold said adjustable head from movement, a threaded bolt adapted to project through said adjustable and stationary heads, a flat head integrally formed on one end of said bolt, grooves formed in the inner surface thereof adapted when said bolt is in position to seat over the ribs on the other surface of said adjustable head to hold said bolt from rotation, a nut threaded on said bolt for securely clamping said movable and stationary heads together, cutter tools disposed in the passages of said movable head, and set screws engaged in said adjustable head for contacting said tools to secure the same in position.

1,327,562. PLOW. ROBERT MARVIN KELLY, Longview, Tex., assignor to G. A. Kelly Plow Company, Longview, Tex., a Corporation of Texas. Filed Aug. 21, 1919. Serial No. 318,972. 3 Claims. (Cl. 97—18.)

1. In a plow, a standard having a frog provided with a projecting nose of trapezium shape in cross section, and which tapers toward its outer end, said nose being defined by one side wall which is a continuation of the landside face of the standard, another side wall which extends out from the front edge of the frog and is inclined toward the landside edge, a top wall which is a continuation of the upper face of the frog, and a bottom wall which is a continuation of the bottom face of the frog, whereby the nose is greater in height or thickness

at the landside end, and the front wall of the nose is beveled rearwardly from the smaller end to the larger end, and is also beveled inwardly from the top wall to the bottom wall, the second-mentioned side wall being also beveled inwardly from the top of the bottom wall, and a

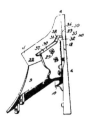

plowpoint having a flange on its underside extending in an inclined line and joined with and forming one wall of a socket provided near the landside edge of the point, said socket having three walls, one of which is the landside flange of the point, the other two walls being undercut and inclined to conform with the walls of the nose.

1,327,563. NO-GLARE HEADLIGHT. STATES LEE LEBBY, Charleston, S. C. Filed Nov. 20, 1917. Serial No. 202,926. 2 Claims. (Cl. 240—48.2.)

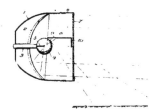

1. A no-glare headlight comprising in combination a casing containing a reflector, a lamp in the axis of said reflector, and a plane auxiliary reflector and screen having an extended flat body supported horizontally above the axis of the lamp in front of the main reflector, and a drop flange on the front edge of said body having its central portion extending downwardly to a point below the axis of the lamp so as to shield the same, and with its lower edges extending obliquely upward in both directions so as to permit a wide dispersion of the light rays.

1,327,564. VALVE. GEORGE F. McDOUGALL, Portland, Oreg. Filed Dec. 11, 1918. Serial No. 266,258. 2 Claims. (Cl. 251—146.)

1. In a valve of the character described, the combination therein of, a valve deck having a seat and a central hub with a series of openings about the hub, a valve having a central opening of pre-determined diameter and ar-

ranged to receive the hub therein and engage the seat in a manner to allow a uniform plane of surface of the deck, the hub and the valve when seated, a disk of resilient material secured upon the upper surface of the valve in a manner to allow the joints of the valve when seated to be sealed, and the valve to carry the substantial pressure load, also at the same time providing a recess in the valve center, of pre-determined dimensions above the hub, and into which recess it is received as the valve is entering its seat, for the purposes indicated.

1,327,565. LUBRICATING DEVICE. JACK B. MacDONALD, Oakland, Calif. Filed Jan. 25, 1918. Serial No. 213,734. 4 Claims. (Cl. 184—6.)

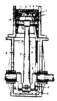

3. In combination with a piston and cylinder and oil sump, said piston being provided with an annular groove, a tube moving with the piston and communicating with said groove, a second tube connected to the piston and telescoping within said first tube and secured in position to communicate with said sump, a check valve in said second tube to prevent escape of oil into the sump on the expansion stroke of the piston, a ring of absorbent material in said piston groove, and said piston being provided with conduits leading from said piston grooves to return the excess oil to the sump.

1,327,566. TOOL. EDWARD MORRIS, Oakland, Calif. Filed Dec. 4, 1918. Serial No. 265,271. 1 Claim. (Cl. 77—73.5.)

A tool of the class described comprising a reamer having a slot in its shank, the lower end of said slot having an inverted tilted V-shaped wall, a countersink tool engaging in said slot and having a recess in its lower end shaped to fit so that it will pass over the V-shaped wall and a key for holding the tool in said slot.

1,327,567. DEVICE FOR WINDING AND REWINDING MOTORS. WILLIAM C. MILES, Washington, D. C., assignor of one-fourth to Norman T. Whitaker, Washington, D. C. Filed Nov. 15, 1917. Serial No. 202,188. 27 Claims. (Cl. 185—40.)

5. A winding device for spring motors comprising an electric motor, means for connecting the electric motor to the spring motor, said means comprising a rotatable element, a second element having a limited rotative movement with respect to the first named element during the winding operation of the prime motor, resilient means opposing

the rotative movement of the second named element with respect to the first named element, and automatically op-

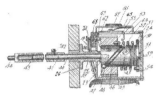

erated means for stopping the electric motor upon the relative movement of the second named element with respect to the first named element.

1,327,568. EGG-BEATER. PETER NEUKIRCHEN, Chicago, Ill., assignor to Julius H. Wald, Chicago, Ill. Filed May 25, 1917, Serial No. 170,802. Renewed Nov. 17, 1919. Serial No. 338,530. 6 Claims. (Cl. 259—126.)

1. In a device of the character described, a beater member having a stem, a perforated beater disk secured thereto, a coiled spring below said disk, and secured thereto, and a second beater disk below said spring and secured thereto.

1,327,569. GLASS. CLARENCE R. PEREGRINE, Charleroi, Pa., assignor to Macbeth-Evans Glass Company, a Corporation of Pennsylvania. Filed Sept. 24, 1917. Serial No. 192,886. 2 Claims. (Cl. 106—36.1.)
1. A glass formed by fusing together a mixture comprising approximately 1500 parts of a foundation batch capable of producing substantially clear glass, with a compound containing from 90 to 150 parts of aluminum and a compound containing from 90 to 140 parts of fluorin.

1,327,570. SIGNALING SYSTEM. BERNARD HARTLEY PETER, Westminster, England, assignor, by mesne assignments, to The Union Switch & Signal Company, Swissvale, Pa., a Corporation of Pennsylvania. Original application filed Oct. 7, 1914, Serial No. 865,495. Divided and this application filed May 16, 1918. Serial No. 235,018. 2 Claims. (Cl. 246—37.)

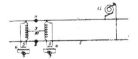

1. In a railway signaling system, the combination of a track section, a source of signaling current connected across the rails of said section, an inductance bond also connected across said track rails, and means associated with the bond which takes a wattless curent leading the voltage, and which wattless current is in multiple with the current required to magnetize the bond.

270 O. G.—9

1,327,571. OIL-BURNER. WILLIAM R. RAY, San Francisco, Calif. Filed Jan. 15, 1919. Serial No. 271,287. 17 Claims. (Cl. 158—77.)

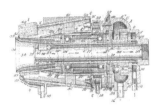

16. In an oil burner, an annular nozzle, an oil spraying cup rotatable in the annular nozzle, means for supplying oil to the cup, and a series of steam actuated air induction nozzles mounted in the mouth of the annular nozzle to induce an air blast therethrough.

1,327,572. PROCESS OF RECOVERING BITUMINOUS MATTER FROM SHALE. HENRY D. RYAN, Boulder, Colo., assignor, by mesne assignments, to National Oil Machinery Corporation, New York, N. Y., a Corporation of Delaware. Filed Mar. 28, 1918. Serial No. 225,344. 17 Claims. (Cl. 196—21.)

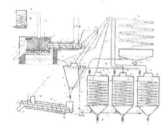

1. A step in the recovery of bitumen from solids which consists in digesting said solids with heavy oil under the action of heat at a temperature insufficiently high to effect substantial distillation of heavy fractions, but high enough to effectively liquefy heavy hydrocarbons contained in said solids.

1,327,573. THEFT-ALARM FOR AUTOMOBILES. OLIVER L. SCOTT, San Francisco, Calif. Filed Dec. 27, 1917. Serial No. 209,065. 6 Claims. (Cl. 116—1.)

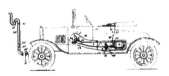

1. A theft alarm for automobiles, comprising a pivotally mounted latch having a hook formed on one end, a pin formed on the clutch pedal of the car, a key-actuated member for raising or lowering the hook-shaped end of the latch into or out of engagement with the pin, a source of air supply, a whistle connected with said source of air supply adapted to be operated thereby, a valve interposed between

the air supply and the whistle, and means connected with the latch for opening the valve and for maintaining it open when the clutch pedal is depressed.

1,327,574. DIRIGIBLE HEADLIGHT. FRANK SPONG, Glendale, Calif. Filed June 17, 1919. Serial No. 304,944. 2 Claims. (Cl. 240—62.)

1. In combination with a vehicle having a front wheel steering apparatus, lamp brackets fixed to the vehicle frame, arms disposed across the tops of the brackets and extending forwardly and backwardly therefrom, the backwardly extending portions being bent downwardly, brace members disposed across below the lamp brackets and extending forwardly and backwardly therefrom, the backwardly extending portions being fixed to the arms, the forwardly extending portions being spaced from the forwardly extending portions of the arms and carrying, together with the arms, vertically disposed lamp holders, said arms and braces being adapted to be pivotally connected with the bracket by vertical pins, a tie rod connecting the two arms whereby the arms will be caused to move in unison, and a reach rod flexibly connecting one of the arms with the steering knuckle of the steering apparatus.

1,327,575. ROTARY ENGINE. JAKOB THEEMLING, Los Angeles, Calif. Filed Dec. 30, 1918. Serial No. 268,889. 15 Claims. (Cl. 123—14.)

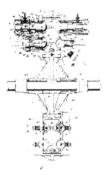

1. In a rotary engine, the combination of a rotor element and a stator element, an annular channel formed in one of said elements, an abutment dividing said channel, a piston abutment slidable into said channel, resilient means tending to hold said piston abutment in said channel with a uniform pressure, and means operated by the impulse pressure of the motive fluid tending to hold said piston abutment in said channel, one of said abutments being fixed to said rotor and the other of said abutments being fixed to said stator, a port on said rotor opening to said channel for the intake of motive fluid, an intake passage in said stator for registration with said port, and an exhaust port on said rotor opening into said channel.

1,327,576. MULTIPLE-DISK CLUTCH. WILLIAM TURNBULL, Stockton, Calif., assignor to The Holt Manufacturing Company, Stockton, Calif., a Corporation of California. Filed Jan. 11, 1917. Serial No. 141,772. 4 Claims. (Cl. 192—10.)

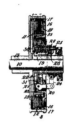

1. A multiple disk clutch including driving and driven members and interposed friction disks, a pressure plate for the disks, an actuating collar for said pressure plate, a plurality of springs acting on said collar at spaced intervals about its circumference, and power increased lever connections between the clutch actuating collar and pressure plate for actuating the latter.

1,327,577. SURGICAL-NEEDLE HOLDER. JOSEPH S. TURNER, Los Angeles, Calif. Filed Mar. 11, 1919. Serial No. 281,998. 2 Claims. (Cl. 128—340.)

1. A surgical needle holder, comprising a pair of pivoted gripping jaws each of which is provided with a groove in its gripping surface opposite a corresponding groove in the other jaw, each of said jaws being provided with side grooves, said side grooves being a continuation of the first mentioned grooves.

1,327,578. WHEELBARROW. FRANK D. VESSEY, Spokane, Wash. Filed Mar. 10, 1919. Serial No. 281,707. 1 Claim. (Cl. 37—33.)

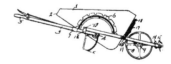

The combination with a barrow body and the handles pivoted thereto, and means rigidly engaging them with respect to the barrow body, of cam shaped legs secured thereto and provided to bodily raise the barrow body and its load from off the ground, pivoted means engaging the handles and supporting between them a supporting wheel frame with the wheel mounted thereupon, of posts secured to the end of said pivoted means and engaging with the ground to push the barrow body forward when the handles are manipulated, and a latch on said pivoted means for releasably engaging the supporting wheel frame to allow contact of the posts with the ground.

1,327,579. SNAIL AND SLUG TRAP. Roy S. Walker, Pasadena, Calif., assignor to L. R. Alderman & Co., Pasadena, Calif., a Partnership consisting of Leighton R. Alderman and Asbury G. Smith. Filed Apr. 3, 1919. Serial No. 287,267. 5 Claims. (Cl. 43—22.)

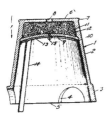

1. A snail and slug trap comprising an inverted pot of porous material having means for keeping the walls of the pot moist, the said pot having an inlet opening at its lower end.

1,327,580. PRINTING-PRESS. Henry A. Wise Wood, New York, N. Y., assignor, by mesne assignments, to Wood Newspaper Machinery Corporation, New York, N. Y., a Corporation of Virginia. Filed Feb. 7, 1912. Serial No. 676,029. Renewed May 16, 1919. Serial No. 297,564. 19 Claims. (Cl. 101—351.)

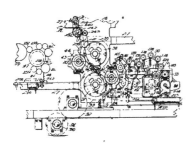

1. In an inking mechanism the combination of a fountain, a fountain roll dipping down from above into the ink therein and running at a slow speed so as to pick up a coating of ink thereon, and a pick-up roll running in coöperation with said fountain roll in a reverse surface direction at a higher speed so as to carry the ink from the surface of said coating in an attenuated continuous film without carrying said film between the rolls.

1,327,581. WORK-STAND. Samuel William Yeats, Monrovia, Calif., assignor of one-third to Thomas Hezmalhalch, Monrovia, Calif., and one-third to Stephen Robertson, Los Angeles, Calif. Filed Apr. 1, 1916. Serial No. 88,394. 1 Claim. (Cl. 223—57.)

The combination with a standard, a heavy base supporting the standard, and a cushion at the top of the standard, of a revoluble tray member centrally disposed on the standard, a circular wall extending upwardly from the tray member, a sleeve concentric with the standard and forming a hub for the revoluble member, radial partition members extending between the sleeve and circular wall and forming a series of receptacles, a plurality of carriers and spool-holding pins projecting upward from the revoluble member and disposed between the circular wall and

the periphery of the revoluble member, swing draw boxes mounted beneath the revoluble member, and a series of

suspension hooks projecting radially from the periphery of the revoluble member and disposed alternately between the swing draw boxes.

1,327,582. MACHINE FOR CHARGING AND DISCHARGING RETORTS. James George Willcox Aldridge, Westminster, London, England. Filed Oct. 26, 1915. Serial No. 58,086. 3 Claims. (Cl. 254—135.)

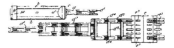

1. The combination in a charging device, of a drum provided with a plurality of annular series of teeth, and a pusher consisting of a plurality of sets of links, one of said sets of links comprising spaced but rigidly united pairs of links which engage with two of said annular series of teeth the spaces between the links of this one of said sets being sufficiently wide to receive the contiguous set of links therein, the links of said contiguous set being engageable with one of said annular series of teeth between those that are engaged by the first said set of links.

1,327,583. SAND-TRAP. Paul Abbon, Tulsa, Okla., assignor to Richard Guiberson, Tulsa, Okla. Filed Apr. 21, 1919. Serial No. 291,582. 2 Claims. (Cl. 103—64.)

2. In an apparatus for pumping wells the combination of a trap section having a greater internal diameter than the tubing, means for connecting said chamber to the tubing, and the anchor section, a removable tube section

of less diameter than the internal diameter of the tubing and projecting up into the trap chamber, a check valve carried by the removable tube section, a movable rod adapted to engage the removable section and adapted to be connected to the working barrel of a well.

1,327,584. WALL CONSTRUCTION. David G. Bender, Blue Island, Ill. Original application filed Mar. 9, 1917, Serial No. 153,697. Divided and this application filed May 15, 1917. Serial No. 168,701. 4 Claims. (Cl. 72—30.)

2. In a wall construction, spaced walls each consisting of individual units laid one upon another, and tie members connecting the said rows, each member being bent angularly in a downward direction adjacent to its end to provide engaging means for a relatively lower unit of one wall, the extremity of the tie being twisted back on the downward bent portion and laterally to provide engaging means for an upper unit of said wall.

1,327,585. PISTOL-LIGHT. Charles Blamfield, Boston, Mass. Filed Mar. 3, 1919. Serial No. 280,483. 6 Claims. (Cl. 67—6.)

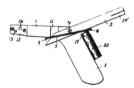

1. A pistol light comprising a body, a hammer consisting of a straight length of material pivoted at an intermediate point to the side of the body, the body having a match-supporting device near its end for holding a match-head in the path of the hammer, and an elastically elongated member attached to the body and the hammer, the points of attachment being disposed to lie below the pivotal point of the hammer when the latter is set, and thereby serving to retain it in such position until released.

1,327,586. STABILIZING DEVICE. Fred D. Blessmeyer, Pittsburgh, Pa. Filed Nov. 30, 1918. Serial No. 264,822. 11 Claims. (Cl. 105—354.)

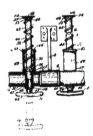

1. In a stabilizing device, in combination with a longitudinal supporting rod, a plurality of stabilizers mounted thereon, and means for placing said series of stabilizers simultaneously into operative positions.

1,327,587. KEY-OPERATED ROTATABLE PART OF VALVES, FAUCETS, LOCKING DEVICES, OR OTHER ARTICLES. John Bliss, London, England. Filed July 3, 1919. Serial No. 308,585. 5 Claims. (Cl. 251—100.)

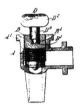

1. The combination, with a support, of a key-operated member mounted to rotate therein, which member has in an outer face a circular recess that is parallel with its axis of rotation and extends into a smaller circular recess that also is parallel with said axis of rotation and is eccentric relatively to the former recess.

1,327,588. PAPER FOLDING AND INTERLEAVING MACHINE. Horace P. Brown and Clarence L. Johnston, Oakland, Calif. Filed Mar. 15, 1916. Serial No. 84,316. 17 Claims. (Cl. 271—87.)

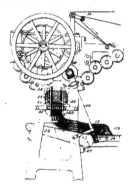

1. A delivery mechanism for a paper folding and interleaving device comprising rotatable, open, spiral coils forming paper receiving spaces extending substantially from the periphery to the center of the coils, said coils being arranged to directly receive between their convolutions the edges of separate folded severed and interleaved sheets, and a delivery device to receive the sheets from the said coils.

1,327,589. CAMPING-AUTOMOBILE. Ward S. Bunker, Waukesha, Wis. Filed Oct. 4, 1917. Serial No. 194,800. 5 Claims. (Cl. 296—23.)

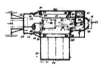

5. An automobile for camping purposes comprising a body having front seats with a passageway leading therefrom to the rear end, a kitchenette at the rear end of

the body at the sides of the passageway, side seats on either side of the passageway between the kitchenette and the front seats, a table in the passageway detachably connected to the front seats and extending down between the side seats, and made up beds forming cushion backs for the side seats and adapted to swing outwardly to a horizontal position.

1,327,590. PROCESS OF REPULPING OLD OR WASTE PAPER. JOHN M. BUBBY, Webster, Mass. Filed Apr. 14, 1916. Serial No. 91,213. 4 Claims. (Cl. 92—3.)

1. The process of converting old paper made from mechanical wood pulp into chemical wood pulp by boiling said paper in a solution containing chemicals effective to act upon the mechanical wood pulp of the old paper and to reduce said wood pulp to the nature of a chemical wood pulp.

1,327,591. PACKAGE-TIE HOLDER. MARIO CIAGLIA CHARLES, Jersey City, N. J. Filed Oct. 4, 1919. Serial No. 328,506. 1 Claim. (Cl. 24—16.)

A device for holding the ends of ropes, comprising an open ended tubular member with a lateral extension at one end thereof, headed pins projecting from said extension, and spaced apart, and a spring hook secured to the extension.

1,327,592. AEROPLANE SAFETY-PARACHUTE AND MEANS OF LAUNCHING SAME FROM AEROPLANES. HENRY M. CROWTHER, Kingman, Ariz. Filed Apr. 4, 1919. Serial No. 287,628. 5 Claims. (Cl. 244—21.)

1. The combination of an aeroplane with a safety parachute, comprising a parachute adapted to be carried on the aeroplane, means attached to a parachute for projecting it away from the aeroplane, and means whereby the projecting means becomes inoperative and detached from the parachute when the parachute is fully drawn out.

1,327,593. SERIES CONDENSER. WILLIAM DUBILIER, New York, N. Y. Filed Apr. 11, 1919. Serial No. 289,263. 7 Claims. (Cl. 250—41.)

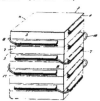

1. A condenser, comprising a plurality of conducting plates interleaved with insulating sheets and assembled into a block, groups of said plates being connected in parallel to form sets of plates of opposite polarity, and terminal connections between said sets of plates extending from different points around the block, said connections which are located at similar points around the block being spaced from each other a distance greater than the thickness of one of said sets of plates.

1,327,594. SASH-FASTENER. JOSIAH H. EDWARDS, Los Angeles, Calif. Filed Oct. 24, 1918. Serial No. 259,546. 1 Claim. (Cl. 20—52.)

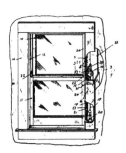

A sash fastener comprising a window casing having a well at the side of the window opening intermediate of the top and bottom and a jamb forming the inner side of the well, an upper and lower sash mounted to slide vertically within the window casing against the jamb, said upper and lower sashes having sockets formed in the marginal edges of adjacent stiles, a cross plate fixed to the back face of the jamb and having tapped holes, thumbscrews mounted in the holes and having elongated shanks to engage in the sockets, and a door opening into said well to provide access to the screws.

1,327,595. PIPE-WRENCH. ROBERT H. FULTON, Los Angeles, Calif. Filed Dec. 30, 1918, Serial No. 268,970. Renewed Oct. 4, 1919. Serial No. 328,586. 3 Claims. (Cl. 81—126.)

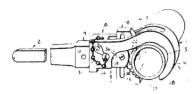

3. In an adjustable pipe wrench, a rigid jaw, a neck extending from the rigid jaw and having a slot, a handle extending from the neck, a jaw plate extending through the slot, means for slidingly connecting the jaw plate to the handle, there being a curved backing behind the jaw plate upon which the jaw plate may rock, and jaws upon the jaw plate in opposition to the rigid jaw.

1,327,596. MINE SAFETY APPARATUS. MARTIN FURLONG, Seattle, Wash. Filed Aug. 7, 1919. Serial No. 315,953. 2 Claims. (Cl. 262—1.)

1. In a safety system for mines, the combination of a main pipe extending from above the surface into a mine, a plurality of auxiliary pipes contained within the main

pipe having openings upon each floor of the mine, **means** for normally closing the auxiliary pipes, and means oper-

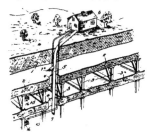

able from the surface for controlling the said closing means.

1,327,597. BRUSH-HANDLE. RICHARD T. GREENE, South Pasadena, Calif. Filed Mar. 24, 1919. Serial·No. 284,784. 2 Claims. (Cl. 279—93.

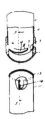

1. In an extension handle, a tube; a locking band fixed in one end of the tube and having a slot between its ends, and the end of the band at one side of the slot being tapered; a ferrule fixed upon the tube and having an opening mating with the opening through the band; a second tube adapted to pass through the first tube and through the band and through the ferrule; a flange extending outwardly from the end of the second tube and adapted to engage the band; and a lug extending outwardly from the second tube and adapted to pass through the slot in the band and to tighten upon the tapered end of the band, so that when tightened the second tube is firmly held in the first tube.

1,327,598. LIGHTING-FIXTURE BOWL-HOOK. LOUIS A. HUFSCHMIDT, San Francisco, Calif. Filed May 19, 1919. Serial No. 297,991. 2 Claims. (Cl. 240—91.)

1. A bowl hook for lighting fixtures comprising a single metal strip bent at one end to form a cylindrical portion

adapted to bear against the inner face of a lighting fixture bowl and further formed with an upwardly and inwardly extending loop portion for receiving a supporting chain, the opposite terminating end of said strip having a V-shaped loop to receive the outer marginal edge of the bowl-lip and continuing downwardly and then outwardly from the lip to form an eye portion to receive an auxiliary lighting fixture chain.

1,327,599. APPARATUS FOR COOLING AND SCRUBBING GASES. ANDREW M. HUNT, Berkeley, and DONALD E. FOGG, Oakland, Calif. Filed May 25, 1914. Serial No. 840,756. 4 Claims. (Cl. 261—11.)

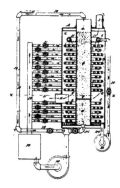

1. An apparatus for cooling and scrubbing hot gases, consisting of a tower having a gas inlet at one side and above the bottom thereof, and a gas outlet at the top, banks of cooling coils in the tower above and below the gas inlet, means for spraying a liquid on the pipes and counter to the currents of gases, a header in the tower with which the cooling pipes connect, and means for maintaining a constant circulation, with intermittent cooling of a second liquid, through said header and pipes.

1,327,600. BASE DETONATING-FUSE. WILLIAM L. LUKENS, Bethlehem, Pa., assignor to Bethlehem Steel Company, Bethlehem, Pa., a Corporation of Pennsylvania. Filed Aug. 19, 1918. Serial No. 250,554. 10 Claims. (Cl. 102—39.)

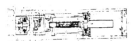

1. In a fuse, the combination with a hollow fuse body, a primer seat therein and a firing pin adapted to coöperate with the primer, of a magazine charge, a channel connecting the primer seat with the magazine charge, a centrally arranged detonator forward of the magazine charge, a holder engaging the rear end of the detonator, a spring normally urging the detonator and holder forward, and means holding said detonator and holder in their rearmost position to seal communication between the magazine charge and the detonator, said means automatically disengaging from the holder on firing the projectile whereby the spring may move the detonator forward.

1,327,601. COMBINATION AUTOMATIC AUTOMOBILE-LOCK. RONALD LUPLOW, Phoenix, Ariz. Filed June 17, 1919. Serial No. 304,940. 6 Claims. (Cl. 70—18.)

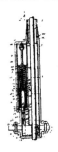

6. In a combination lock, a casing forming a straight square chamber, a series of mixable combination plates stacked in the chamber and forming a tortuous up passage and a straight down passage, an operating bar slidingly and rotatably mounted in the straight down passage, a finger carried by the operating bar and adapted to follow the up passage and raise the operating bar, means for moving the finger out of the tortuous up passage into the straight down passage, and a spring for throwing the operating bar downwardly in the straight passage.

1,327,602. ELECTRIC FLATIRON. WILLIAM MORGAN, Los Angeles, Calif. Filed Mar. 5, 1919. Serial No. 280,794. 2 Claims. (Cl. 200—52.)

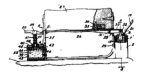

1. The combination with an electric flat iron having a plug socket extending upwardly from the top of its rear end and the terminals of its heating element leading into the socket; of a plug slidingly mounted in the socket and having spring pressed terminals to engage the first terminals; a supplemental handle mounted below the main handle and connected to the plug, so that when the supplemental handle is raised the electricity is turned on, and so that when the supplemental handle is lowered to the limit the electricity is turned off; and timing mechanism for holding the supplemental handle raised to heat the iron for a predetermined time and then release the supplemental handle to stop the heating operation.

1,327,603. GUN-CARRIAGE. EMIL F. NORELIUS, Peoria, Ill., assignor to The Holt Manufacturing Company, Stockton, Calif., a Corporation of California. Filed Nov. 12, 1917. Serial No. 201,581. 10 Claims. (Cl. 89—40.)

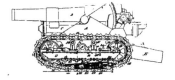

6. In an endless, self-laying track vehicle, the combination of a truck frame provided with truck rollers, an endless, self-laying track enveloping the truck and upon which the truck rollers run, and a jack carried by the truck frame for elevating the truck frame from the track.

1,327,604. VERTICALLY-ADJUSTABLE ENGINE-LATHE. AUGUSTUS C. BOOTH, Los Angeles, Calif. Filed May 13, 1918. Serial No. 234,281. 1 Claim. (Cl. 82—28.)

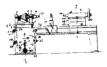

A lathe bed comprising side bars rigidly connected at one end by a crossbar; means forming a vertical slideway comprising channel-shaped clamping bars having portions secured to the crossbar by bolts, the inner faces of the portions being curved, second portions extending from the outer parts of the first portions, third portions extending inwardly from the outer ends of the second portions and having curved inner faces, ears extending from the third portions, and clamping bolts inserted through the ears; and a sliding base fitting in the vertical slideway and having curved end faces fitting the curved inner faces of the first and third portions, so that the base may be moved up or down to a desired position and rigidly held in its adjusted position by tightening the clamping bolts.

1,327,605. DIRECTION-INDICATOR. FRANK F. HOFFMANN, Los Angeles, Calif. Filed Apr. 3, 1917. Serial No. 159,443. 1 Claim. (Cl. 116—31.)

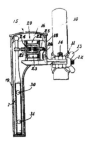

In a direction indicator, a clamp formed in two pieces adapted to fit the side frame of a wind shield, a bolt connecting the two pieces together, a horizontal bearing plate extending from one piece of the clamp, a stud bolt extending vertically from the horizontal bearing plate, a supporting arm resting upon the horizontal bearing plate with the stud bolt passing through the supporting arm, a nut upon the stud bolt to hold the supporting arm and bearing plate hingedly and adjustably together, a case extending from the supporting arm and adapted to form a motor housing extending upwardly from the supporting arm, and a semiphore arm housing extending downwardly from the motor housing.

REISSUES.

14,785. DOOR - OPERATING MECHANISM. HARRY S. HART, Chicago, Ill., assignor to National Dump Car Co., Chicago, Ill., a Corporation of Maine. Filed Nov. 26, 1919. Serial No. 340,938. Original No. 1,318,445, dated Oct. 14, 1919, Serial No. 285,216, filed Mar. 26, 1919. 18 Claims. (Cl. 105—244.)

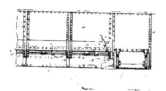

1. In a general service car having a plurality of doors, means for closing said doors individually, and means common to a plurality of the doors and movable lengthwise of the car for releasing said doors.

14,786. VACUUM-CLEANER. IRA L. SHEFFLER, Detroit, Mich., assignor to Ira Lee Suction Cleaner Corporation, a Corporation of Michigan. Filed Jan. 20, 1919. Serial No. 272,203. Original No. 1,231,077, dated June 26, 1917, Serial No. 134,832, filed Dec. 4, 1916. 7 Claims. (Cl. 15—60.)

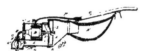

2. In a vacuum cleaner, a wheeled casing provided with a nozzle, a motor having a substantially horizontal shaft located in the casing, the shaft being in a plane at substantially right angles to the nozzle, a gear casing located at one end of the nozzle, a gear mechanism located in the gear casing and connected with the brush, a flexible shaft connected with one of the gears in said gear casing and also with the shaft of the motor, and a suction creating means located in the wheeled casing actuated by the motor.

14,787. DYNAMO-ELECTRIC MACHINERY. LEIGH J. STEPHENSON, Chicago, Ill., assignor of one-half to George H. Burrage, Chicago, Ill. Filed Dec. 10, 1919. Serial No. 343,801. Original No. 1,322,471, dated Nov. 18, 1919, Serial No. 297,420, filed May 15, 1919. 56 Claims. (Cl. 171—225.)

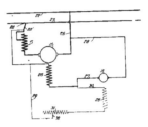

54. The combination with a motor having a magnetic field circuit, of means for causing said motor to have the characteristics of a variable speed motor, comprising means for magnetizing said magnetic field circuit, a regulating dynamo connected to oppose said magnetizing means, means for adjusting the opposition of said regulating dynamo, and means for maintaining the resultant magnetization always greater than zero.

14,788. GLASS-CUTTING MACHINE. JOHN WATERLOO, New Eagle, Pa., assignor to Window Glass Machine Company, Pittsburgh, Pa., a Corporation of New Jersey. Filed Oct. 27, 1919. Serial No. 333,840. Original No. 1,259,688, dated Mar. 19, 1918, Serial No. 169,879, filed May 21, 1917. 10 Claims. (Cl. 33—32.)

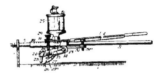

1. Glass cutting apparatus, comprising a cutting table, guides extending transversely over the table, a carriage movable transversely of the table on said guides, a plurality of cutter shafts journaled in said carriage in end to end alinement, a cutting tool carried by each of said shafts, means for imparting proper tension to the cutting tools during their cutting movement, and means for raising the tools, during the return movement of the carriage, substantially as described.

TRADE-MARKS

OFFICIAL GAZETTE, JANUARY 6, 1920.

The following trade-marks are published in compliance with section 6 of the act of February 20, 1905, as amended March 2, 1907. Notice of opposition must be filed within thirty days of this publication.

Marks applied for "under the ten-year proviso" are registrable under the provision in clause (b) of section 5 of said act as amended February 18, 1911.

As provided by section 14 of said act, a fee of ten dollars must accompany each notice of opposition.

Ser. No. 88,376. (CLASS 46. FOODS AND INGREDIENTS OF FOODS.) TOLERTON & WARFIELD Co., Sioux City, Iowa. Filed Aug. 2, 1915. Under ten-year proviso.

The trade-mark consists of the words "First Prize Brand," as shown, no claim being made to the exclusive use of the word "Brand" except as associated with the words "First Prize."

Particular description of goods.—Canned Fruits and Vegetables, Canned Fish, Canned Soups, Pearl-Barley, Corn Flakes, Rolled Oats, Rice, Tapioca, Tea, Coffee, Dried Fruits, Food-Flavoring Extracts, Table Sauce, Peanut-Butter, Spices, Preserved Fruits, Preserved Berries, Preserved Vegetables, Olives, Poultry Food, Corn-Starch, Table-Syrup, and Vinegar.

Claims use since Jan. 1. 1895.

Ser. No. 98,375. (CLASS 36. MUSICAL INSTRUMENTS AND SUPPLIES.) STEWART-WARNER SPEEDOMETER CORPORATION, Chicago, Ill. Filed Oct. 2, 1916.

The trade-mark is a facsimile of the signature of the first president and founder of this corporation.

Particular description of goods.—Warning - Signals of the Type Embodying a Mechanically-Vibrated Diaphragm.

Claims use since Sept. 26, 1914.

Ser. No. 100.464. (CLASS 4. ABRASIVE, DETERGENT, AND POLISHING MATERIALS.) ASUNCIÓN ORTIZ Y PALACIOS, Fuencarral, Spain. Filed Jan. 9, 1917.

Particular description of goods.—Soaps, Not Including Tooth-Soap.

Claims use since Aug. 18, 1909.

Ser. No. 101,590. (CLASS 37. PAPER AND STATIONERY.) BYRON WESTON Co., Dalton, Mass. Filed Feb. 23, 1917.

Particular description of goods.—Machine-Bookkeeping Paper Only.

Claims use since Feb. 15. 1917.

Ser. No. 101,973. (CLASS 46. FOODS AND INGREDIENTS OF FOODS.) THE UNION PACIFIC TEA Co, New York, N. Y. Filed Mar. 7, 1917.

Particular description of goods. — Oat Flakes, Corn Flakes, Tapioca, Shredded Cocoanut, Farina, Flavoring Extracts for Foods, Olive-Oil, Corn-Starch, Rice, Sweet Chocolate, Jelly-Powder, Gelatin, Salad-Dressing, Table Sauce, Chilli Sauce, and Tomato Catsup.

Claims use since January, 1877.

Ser. No. 103,898. (CLASS 46. FOODS AND INGREDIENTS OF FOODS.) NARRAGANSETT BAY OYSTER Co., Providence, R. I. Filed May 17, 1917.

The words "Sea Acre."

Particular description of goods.—Fresh, Dried, and Canned Oysters.

Claims use since Apr. 30, 1917.

Ser. No. 103,899. (CLASS 46. FOODS AND INGREDI-ENTS OF FOODS.) NARRAGANSETT BAY OYSTER CO., Providence, R. I. Filed May 17, 1917.

Particular description of goods.—Fresh, Dried, · and Canned Oysters.

Claims use since Apr. 30, 1917.

Ser. No. 105,630. (CLASS 19. VEHICLES, NOT IN-CLUDING ENGINES.) JOSEPH N. SMITH & COMPANY, Detroit, Mich. Filed Aug. 13, 1917.

Particular description of goods. — Automobile Acces-sories — Namely, Wind - Shields, Wind - Shield Hinges, · Wind-Shield Frames, Robe and Foot Rails.

Claims use since about Feb. 1, 1917.

Ser. No. 105,724. (CLASS 46. FOODS AND INGREDI-ENTS OF FOODS.) TOLERTON & WARFIELD CO., Sioux City, Iowa. Filed Aug. 18, 1917.

Particular description of goods. — Rice, Pickles, and Olives.

Claims use since Jan. 1, 1901.

Ser. No. 106,257. (CLASS 13. HARDWARE AND PLUMBING AND STEAM-FITTING SUPPLIES.) THE BERBECKER & ROWLAND MANUFACTURING COMPANY, Waterville, Conn. Filed Sept. 15,.1917.

Particular description of goods.—Various Metallic Ar-ticles of Upholstery and Cabinet Hardware—Namely, Operating-Handles for Drawers, Doors, &c., for Lifting

Trunks, Boxes, Trays, &c., and for Attachment to Articles Generally Which are to be Grasped by the Hand ; Drawer-Pulls to be Grasped by the Hand in Operating Drawers, Doors, &c. ; Keyhole Escutcheon-Plates ; Label-Holders for Attachment to Boxes, Drawers, &c., to Hold Labels ; Com-bined Label-Holders and Drawer-Pulls ; Sash-Lifts for At-tachment to Sliding Sash, Sliding Doors, &c., to Facili-tate the Manual Operation Thereof ; Metallic and Glass Operating-Knobs for Attachment to and to Facilitate the Manual Operation of Drawers, Doors, Boxes, &c. ; Com-mode-Knobs for Operating Commode, Cupboard, Cabinet, and Similar Doors and Arranged to Rotate to Accomplish the Locking Thereof ; Knob-Bases for Use with Knobs of the Kind Above Referred to to Provide a More Extended Contact Between the Knob and the Article to Which It is Attached ; Garment-Supporting, Drapery, Curtain, Picture, and Like Article Supporting Hooks ; Stationary and Swinging Towel Arms or Supports for Attachment to Washstands, Dressers, Walls, &c., to Support Towels and Similar Articles ; Screen-Guard Brackets for Attachment to the Sides of Screen-Doors, Glass Doors, Windows, &c., to Support the Ends of Rods Extending Across and Pro-tecting the Screen or Glass ; Hinges ; Stay-Joints for Holding Swinging Doors, &c., in an Open Position ; Desk-Slides for Use with Falling-Leaf Desks to Arrest the Movement of the Leaf and Supporting the Same in a Horizontal Position, Desk-Chains for the Purpose Just Above Mentioned, Desk-Posts for Supporting Rods or Railing upon the Upper Ends of Desks ; Caddie-Balls for Use as Supporting-Feet for Boxes, Trays, &c. ; Claw-Feet for Supporting Boxes, Stools, &c. ; Chair-Sockets for At-tachment to the Lower Ends of Chair, Desk, and Similar Legs to Protect the Same ; Shelf-Brackets for Supporting the Ends of Shelves in Cabinets, China-Closets, &c. ; Drawer-Stops for Arresting the Inward Movement of Drawers ; Mirror, Picture, Cabinet, and Like Hanger-Plates for Facilitating the Suspension of Such Devices from Suitable Supports ; Metallic Beading and Molding for Use upon Desks, Cabinets, and other Furniture for Ornamental Effect ; Picture-Frame Ornaments of Metal for Ornamenting and Strengthening the Corners of Picture and Similar Frames ; Box-Corners for Strengthening and Protecting the Corners of Boxes, &c. ; Rosettes or Orna-mental Plates of Metal for Attachment to Furniture, Bed-Bolt Caps for Covering the Heads or Nuts of Bolts Used in Securing Parts of Furniture Together, Plain and Ornamental Head Upholsterers' Nails ; Socket Carpet-Nails for Providing for Removably Securing Carpets, Rugs, &c., to Hardwood, Tile, Cement, or other Floors into Which Tacks Cannot or Ought Not to be Driven ; Screen-Markers to be Attached to Screens, Storm-Win-dows, &c., and Having a Letter, Number, or Character to Show Where the Screen Belongs ; Upholsterers' Fas-teners, Drawer-Slides to Lessen the Friction Between Drawers and the Guides in Which They Move ; Chair-Glides to be Attached to the Lower Ends of Chair-Legs, so That the Chair may be Moved About Easily and with-out Injuring the Floor or Carpet ; Escutcheon Pins or Nails for Securing Escutcheon-Plates in Place, Screws, Sash Curtain-Rods for Attachment to Window-Sash to Support Light-Weight Curtains, Extension-Rods for Sup-porting Heavier Curtains ; Gooseneck or Bent-End Curtain-Supporting Rods to Support Curtains Away from Win-dows, &c. ; Box-Valance Rods for Supporting Curtains or Drapery in Front of Windows, &c., with the Sides of the Curtain Extending Back to the Wall or Casing ; Brass Tubing ; Ornamental Ends or Balls to be Attached to the Ends of Portière, Curtain, Drapery-Supporting, and Like Poles ; Angle-Joints for Use in Connecting Curtain and Similar Poles Extending at an Angle with One Another Together, Curtain-Pole Rings for Slidably Supporting Cur-tains from Curtain Rods or Poles, Vestibule-Curtain Rings for Slidably Supporting Light Sash or Vestibule Indoor Curtains, French Heading-Carriers for Supporting Cur-tains from Poles in Such a Way That the Upper End of the Curtain Extends Above the Pole, Curtain-Rings for Use in Connection with the Manually-Operable Adjust-ing Means Used for Adjusting Spring-Roller and other

Curtains, Pole-Brackets for Supporting the Ends of Curtain-Poles, Extension-Rod Brackets for Supporting the Ends of Rods for Supporting Sash and Similar Light-Weight Curtains; Center-Supports for Supporting Curtain-Supporting Rods, Poles, &c., at Their Middle Portion; Transport-Brackets Having Removable Sockets for Supporting the Ends of Curtain-Poles, &c.; Pole-Sockets for Supporting the Ends of Curtain-Supporting and Similar Poles; Vestibule-Brackets for Supporting the Ends of Rods Used to Support Curtains for Vestibule-Door, Window, and Similar Curtains; Overdrape-Brackets for Supporting the Ends of Curtain-Supporting Rods and for Also Supporting Drapery in Front of the Curtain, Overdrape-Rods for Supporting Drapery in Front of Curtains, Back-Rod Attachments for Supporting the Ends of a Second Curtain-Supporting Rod from Brackets Designed to Support a Single Curtain-Rod; Spring-Operated Rod-Sockets to be Placed upon the Ends of Curtain-Rods, so That the Same may be Supported without Brackets or other Supports at Its Ends; Cord-Cleats for Securing the Free Ends of Curtain-Operating Cords, Wire-Stretchers for Supporting the Ends of and for Adjusting the Tension of Curtain-Supporting Wires, Tassels Made of Metal and Secured to Curtain-Operating Cords to Facilitate the Grasping and Operation of the Same and Incidentally to Serve as Ornaments; Drapery-Hooks for Use in Supporting and Adjusting Drapery, Curtains, &c.; Shower-Bath Rings for Supporting Shower-Bath Curtains; Drapery Ornaments of Metal to be Attached to Drapery, Curtains, &c.; Threaded - Article - Supporting Hooks; Tassel-Hooks for Use with Curtain, Drapery, and Similar Holding-Back Cords; Curtain-Holders for Holding the Lower Ends of Curtains, Drapery, &c., One Side of the Opening Which They Cover; Molding-Hooks for Supporting Pictures, &c., from Molding; Stair-Buttons for Securing Stair-Carpets in Place, Stair-Corners for Keeping Dirt Out of the Corners Between Stair Treads and Risers, Stair-Carpet Rods for Use in Holding Stair-Carpet in Place, Stair-Rod Brackets for Holding the Ends of Stair-Carpet Rods, Shade-Brackets for Supporting the Ends of Spring Curtain - Rollers from Curtain - Pole - Supporting Brackets; Drugget-Pins for Securing Druggets, Rugs, &c., in Place; Shade-Pulls for Use in Operating Curtains Supported by Spring Shade-Supports, Shade-Eyelets for Use with Curtain-Shades, Upholsterers' Pins.

Claims use since about March, 1915.

Ser. No. 106,620.   (CLASS 46.   FOODS AND INGREDIENTS OF FOODS.)   JOHNSON BROS. & ALEXANDER, Chicago, Ill.   Filed Oct. 5, 1917.

OLDFT.DEARBORN

Particular description of goods.—Candles.
Claims use since about August, 1914.

Ser. No. 106,998.   (CLASS 46   FOODS AND INGREDIENTS OF FOODS.)   THE C. F. SAUER CO., Richmond, Va.   Filed Oct. 27, 1917.

F.F.V

Comprising the letters " F. F. V."
Particular description of goods.—Food - Flavoring Extracts.
Claims use since the year 1887.

Ser. No. 107,963.   (CLASS 37.   PAPER AND STATIONERY.)   GEORGE LA MONTE & SON, Nutley, N. J., and New York, N. Y.   Filed Dec. 14, 1917.

Without waiving any common-law right applicant hereby disclaims the word " Check " apart from the words shown.
Particular description of goods.—Safety-Paper Such as is Used for Railroad and other Tickets, Bank-Checks, Bank-Drafts, Pay-Checks, and other Checks and Drafts, Bills of Exchange, Promissory Notes, and All Vouchers of Value.
Claims use since Dec. 3, 1917.

Ser. No. 108,121.   (CLASS 39.   CLOTHING.)   CHIPMAN KNITTING MILLS, Easton, Pa.   Filed Dec. 24, 1917.

Particular description of goods.—Hosiery.
Claims use since Sept. 26, 1917.

Ser. No. 110,022.   (CLASS 46.   FOODS AND INGREDIENTS OF FOODS.)   HAAS, BARUCH & CO., Los Angeles, Calif.   Filed Apr. 6, 1918.

Particular description of goods. — Canned Shrimp, Canned Crab, Canned Minced Clams, Canned Salmon, Canned Tuna Fish, Canned Oysters, Codfish Tablets, Unpopped Popcorn, Dry Split Peas, Lentils, Head-Rice, Pepper Sauce, Chilli Powder, Celery Sauce, Peach Preserves, Honey, Salad-Dressing, and Mince-Meat.
Claims use on honey since June 22, 1914; on peach preserves since Dec. 7, 1915; on mince-meat since Nov. 22, 1917; on salad-dressing since Mar. 30, 1917; on celery-salt since July 3, 1914; on chilli powder since Dec. 5, 1914; on lentils since July 8 and July 28, 1914; on dry split peas since July 28, 1914; on unpopped popcorn since July 28, 1914; on pepper sauce since Dec. 18, 1914; on canned minced clams since Oct. 21, 1914; on canned crabs since Nov. 9, 1914; on canned tuna fish since Oct. 12, 1914; on codfish tablets since Aug. 5, 1914; on canned salmon since July 8, 1914; on canned shrimp since July 16, 1914; on canned oysters since Jan. 10, 1914; on rice since Nov. 25, 1914.

Ser. No. 112,396.   (CLASS 38.   PRINTS AND PUBLICATIONS.)   STANLEY G. MILLER, Chicago, Ill.   Filed July 29, 1918.

E-Z

Particular description of goods.—Yearly Interest-Tables.
Claims use since on or about June 1, 1918.

Ser. No. 112,648. (CLASS 28. JEWELRY AND PRE-CIOUS-METAL WARE.) W. B. KELLOGG CO. INC., New York, N. Y. Filed Aug. 9, 1918.

Particular description of goods.—Set and Unset Pearls and Imitation Pearls.
Claims use since May 20, 1918.

Ser. No. 113,118. (CLASS 46. FOODS AND INGREDI-ENTS OF FOODS.) CLARK & MACKUSICK COMPANY, Boston, Mass. Filed Sept. 11, 1918.

Particular description of goods.—Coffee.
Claims use since about Mar. 1, 1918.

Ser. No. 113,169. (CLASS 14. METALS AND METAL CASTINGS AND FORGINGS.) HIRAM WALKER & SONS METAL PRODUCTS, LIMITED, Walkerville, Ontario, Canada. Filed Sept. 13, 1918.

NICHROLOY

Consisting of the word "Nichroloy."
Particular description of goods.—Heat-Resisting Cast-ings Manufactured from an Alloy of Nickel, Chrome-Iron, Manganese, and Silicon.
Claims use since Jan. 10, 1918.

Ser. No. 113,353. (CLASS 39. CLOTHING.) C. G. FLECKENSTEIN Co., Muskegon, Mich. Filed Sept. 25, 1918.

FLEXOAK

Particular description of goods.—Leather Soles and Heels.
Claims use since Oct. 25, 1911.

Ser. No. 113,388. (CLASS 6. CHEMICALS, MEDI-CINES, AND PHARMACEUTICAL PREPARATIONS.) G. SIEGLE COMPANY, Rosebank, N. Y. Filed Sept. 25, 1918.

Particular description of goods.—Colors for a Combi-nation of Uses.
Claims use since Apr. 1, 1889.

Ser. No. 113,390. (CLASS 43. THREAD AND YARN.) SEARS, ROEBUCK AND Co., Chicago, Ill. Filed Sept. 25, 1918.

No claim being made to the exclusive use of the word "Service" except in association with the mark shown.
Particular description of goods.—Wool Knitting-Yarn.
Claims use since May 4, 1918.

Ser. No. 113,454. (CLASS 39. CLOTHING.) LINEHAN-CONOVER COMPANY, Worcester, Mass. Filed Sept. 27, 1918.

Our trade-mark consists of a rectangular figure contain-ing the words "Wont-Wrust," inclosed within the figure and disposed at an oblique angle to the sides of the figure, said words consisting of script letters and both words beginning with the letter "W," of uniform size and style. No claim is made to the use of the words "Wont-Wrust" aside from the rectangular figure as shown.
Particular description of goods.—Corsets, Corset-Waists, and Brassières,
Claims use since 1905.

Ser. No. 113,491. (CLASS 21. ELECTRICAL APPARA-TUS, MACHINES, AND SUPPLIES.) JOHN P. MENT-ZER, Chicago, Ill. Filed Sept. 30, 1918.

MAXLIFE

Particular description of goods.—Dry Storage Batteries.
Claims use since about July 1, 1918.

Ser. No. 113,636. (CLASS 46. FOODS AND INGREDI-ENTS OF FOODS.) STERLING PRODUCTS Co., Evans-ville, Ind. Filed Oct. 9, 1918.

Particular description of goods.—Catsup, Canned Vege-tables, and Canned Fruits.
Claims use since May, 1918.

Ser. No. 113,682. (CLASS 46. FOODS AND INGREDI-
ENTS OF FOODS.) WATERLOO CANNING ASSOCIATION,
Waterloo, Wis. Filed Oct. 10, 1918.

Particular description of goods.—Canned Corn and
Canned Peas.
Claims use since 1906.

Ser. No. 113,945. (CLASS 6. CHEMICALS, MEDI-
CINES, AND PHARMACEUTICAL PREPARATIONS.)
THE PEPSOTONE COMPANY, Huntington, W. Va. Filed
Oct. 30, 1918.

Particular description of goods.—A Medicated Oil for
the Relief of Rheumatic Pains, Toothache, Neuralgia,
Burns, Scalds, Felons, Cholera Morbus, Cramp, Colic,
Asthma, Heartache, Palpitation, &c.
Claims use since May 31, 1918.

Ser. No. 114,056. (CLASS 15. OILS AND GREASES.)
McCORMICK & Co., Baltimore, Md. Filed Nov. 5, 1918.

The word "Brand" standing alone is disclaimed.
Particular description of goods.—Lubricating-Oils, Rust-
Preventing Oils, and Machine-Oils.
Claims use since 1890.

Ser. No. 114,061. (CLASS 50. MERCHANDISE NOT
OTHERWISE CLASSIFIED.) AUER & TWITCHELL,
INC., Dover, Del., and Philadelphia, Pa. Filed Nov. 6,
1918.

Particular description of goods.—A Certain Coated
Waterproof Fiber Table-Cover.
Claims use since May 1, 1918.

Ser. No. 114,270. (CLASS 39. CLOTHING.) LEOPOLD,
SOLOMON AND EISENDRATH, Chicago, Ill. Filed Nov. 21,
1918.

Particular description of goods.—Men's and Boys' Suits,
Coats, Vests, Trousers, and Overcoats.
Claims use since June 1, 1918.

Ser. No. 114,490. (CLASS 19. VEHICLES, NOT IN-
CLUDING ENGINES.) WINTHER MOTOR TRUCK COM-
PANY, Kenosha, Wis. Filed Dec. 4, 1918.

Particular description of goods.—Motor-Trucks.
Claims use since Apr. 2, 1917.

Ser. No. 114,672. (CLASS 37. PAPER AND STATION-
ERY.) FRANK A. GESELL, Los Angeles, Calif. Filed
Dec. 16, 1918.

The words "Save, Live, Have" are disclaimed.
Particular description of goods.—Bank-Deposit Account-
Books Sold to the Trade.
Claims use since Nov. 26, 1918.

Ser. No. 114,722. (CLASS 40. FANCY GOODS, FUR-
NISHINGS, AND NOTIONS.) TRIFARI & KRUSSMAN,
INC., New York, N. Y. Filed Dec. 19, 1918.

Consisting of a circle and inserted therein the letters
"T, K," the "T" forming an arch over the "K."
Particular description of goods.—Metal Shoe-Buckles,
Combs, and Hairpins Which are Produced in Aluminum,
Celluloid, and Metals other Than the Precious Metals.
Claims use since Nov. 1, 1918.

Ser. No. 114,966. (CLASS 39. CLOTHING.) AMERICAN LA FRANCE FIRE ENGINE CO. INC., Elmira, N. Y. Filed Jan. 3, 1919.

No claim is made to the use of the mark printed in red or on a red background in such manner as to simulate the emblem, sign, or insignia of the Red Cross, referred to in the act to incorporate the American Red Cross, approved January 5, 1905, as amended June 23, 1910.

Particular description of goods.—Asbestos Suits, Asbestos Helmets and Hoods, Asbestos Gloves and Mittens, Asbestos Gauntlet Gloves and Mittens, Rubber Gloves and Mittens, Rubber Gauntlet Gloves and Mittens, Reinforced-Leather-Grip Gloves and Mittens, Rubber Fire-Coats, Asbestos Aprons, Fireproof Duck Aprons, Asbestos Hip-Leggings, Fireproof Duck Hip-Leggings, Leather Leggings, Fiber Leggings, Asbestos Leggings, Fireproof Duck Leggings, Asbestos Coats, Asbestos Trousers, Fireproof Duck Trousers, Fireproof Duck Coats, and Stiff-Leather Helmets.

Claims use since Nov. 22, 1918.

Ser. No. 115,262. (CLASS 46. FOODS AND INGREDIENTS OF FOODS.) THOS. ROULSTON, INC., Brooklyn, N. Y. Filed Jan. 17, 1919.

In which the horizontal lines indicate blue color and the cross-hatching indicates orange color, no claim being made for the representation of the loaf of bread apart from the mark shown in the drawing.

Particular description of goods.—Bread.
Claims use since Jan. 8, 1919.

Ser. No. 115,343. (CLASS 46. FOODS AND INGREDIENTS OF FOODS.) EYE BRAND CONFECTIONERY, INC., Brooklyn, N. Y. Filed Jan. 21, 1919.

 P C.

Particular description of goods.—Candies.
Claims use since Jan. 2, 1914.

Ser. No. 115,403. (CLASS 23. CUTLERY, MACHINERY, AND TOOLS, AND PARTS THEREOF.) THE HARROLD TOOL & FORGE CO., Columbiana, Ohio. Filed Jan. 24, 1919.

BUCKEYE

Consisting of the word "Buckeye."

Particular description of goods.—Wrecking-Bars, Crowbars, Blacksmiths' Cold Cutters, Blacksmiths' Hot Cutters, Automobile-Tools—viz., Combination Screw-Drivers and Gooseneck Tack-Claws, All-Steel Screw-Drivers, Offset Screw-Drivers, and Cotter-Pin Extractors; Box-Chisels, Mechanics' Hammers, Mechanics' Ball-Peen Hammers, Bearing-Scrapers, Cold-Chisels, Mechanics' Sets of Punches and Dies, Automobile Cold-Chisels, Mechanics' Cold-Chisels, Mechanics' Punches, Woodworkers' Chisels; Slaters' Hammers, Rippers, and Stakes; Plumbers' Wood-Chisels and Yarning-Tools, Plumbers' Calking-Tools, Boiler-Makers' Offset Calking-Tools, Boiler-Makers' Beading-Tools, Masons' Brick-Hammers, Masons' Brick-Sketz, Masons' Brick-Chisels; Stone-Cutter's Pitching-Tool, Drafting-Chisel, Plain Chisel, and Drafting Tooth-Chisel; Stone-Cutter's Tooth-Chisel, Stone-Cutters' Points, Stone-Cutters' Mallet-Head Points, Stone-Cutters' Lifters; Grapple Logging-Tools—viz., Swamp-Hooks, Skidding-Tongs; Grab-Hooks, and Round Hooks.

Claims use since November, 1917.

Ser. No. 115,540. (CLASS 6. CHEMICALS, MEDICINES, AND PHARMACEUTICAL PREPARATIONS.) F. AD. RICHTER & CO. OF NEW YORK, New York, N. Y. Filed Jan. 30, 1919. Under ten-year proviso.

ANCHOR

Particular description of goods.—A Liniment for the Treatment of Rheumatism, Neuralgia, Sprains, Bruises, Lameness, and the Like.

Claims use since about Mar. 1, 1869.

Ser. No. 115,576. (CLASS 46. FOODS AND INGREDIENTS OF FOODS.) PARSONS CHEMICAL WORKS, Grand Ledge, Mich. Filed Feb. 1, 1919.

MEDIFEED

Particular description of goods.—Medicated Food for Live Stock.

Claims use since Dec. 12, 1918.

Ser. No. 115,590. (CLASS 37. PAPER AND STATIONERY.) HENRY M. HASTINGS, San Francisco, Calif. Filed Feb. 3, 1919.

The stippling on the drawing indicates shading only.

Particular description of goods.—Printed Forms for Estimates of Printing-Work.

Claims use since Jan. 1, 1919.

Ser. No. 115,634. (CLASS 6. CHEMICALS, MEDI-
CINES, AND PHARMACEUTICAL PREPARATIONS.)
AMERICAN ANILINE PRODUCTS, INC., New York, N. Y.
Filed Feb. 5, 1919.

Particular description of goods.—Dyes.
Claims use since Dec. 31, 1918.

Ser. No. 115,682. (CLASS 16. PAINTS AND PAINT-
ERS' MATERIALS.) TITANINE, INC., New York, N. Y.
Filed Feb. 7, 1919.

>T-I-T-A-N-I-N-E->

Particular description of goods.—A Preparation in the
Nature of Varnish for Preserving, Waterproofing, and
Coloring Textile Fabrics, Leather, and the Like.
Claims use since Dec. 1, 1918.

Ser. No. 115,779. (CLASS 6. CHEMICALS, MEDI-
CINES, AND PHARMACEUTICAL PREPARATIONS.)
F. AD. RICHTER & Co. OF NEW YORK, New York, N. Y.
Filed Feb. 11, 1919.

Particular description of goods.—A Liniment for the
Treatment of Rheumatism, Neuralgia, Lameness, Sprains,
Bruises, and the Like.
Claims use since about 1900.

Ser. No. 115,983. (CLASS 6. CHEMICALS, MEDI-
CINES, AND PHARMACEUTICAL PREPARATIONS.)
KEASBEY & MATTISON COMPANY, Ambler, Pa. Filed
Feb. 19, 1919. Under ten-year proviso.

BROMO CAFFEINE

Particular description of goods.—A Medical Preparation for Headaches and Nervous Diseases.
Claims use since July 26, 1881.

Ser. No. 115,984. (CLASS 6. CHEMICALS, MEDI-
CINES, AND PHARMACEUTICAL PREPARATIONS.)
KEASBEY & MATTISON COMPANY, Ambler, Pa. Filed Feb.
19, 1919. Under ten-year proviso.

ALKALITHIA.

Particular description of goods.—A Preparation for the
Treatment of Rheumatism and Cystitis.
Claims use since Jan. 2, 1891.

Ser. No. 115,985. (CLASS 6. CHEMICALS, MEDI-
CINES, AND PHARMACEUTICAL PREPARATIONS.)
KEASBEY & MATTISON COMPANY, Ambler, Pa. Filed Feb.
19, 1919. Under ten-year proviso.

DEXTRO QUININE

Particular description of goods.—A Medicinal Remedy
for Colds and Malaria.
Claims use since August, 1878.

Ser. No. 115,993. (CLASS 46. FOODS AND INGREDI-
ENTS OF FOODS.) MASON, AU & MAGENHEIMER
CONF. MFG. CO., Brooklyn, N. Y. Filed Feb. 19, 1919.

The words "Orange" and "Bronx" being disclaimed
apart from the other features of the mark.
Particular description of goods.—Candies and Chocolate.
Claims use since Apr. 16, 1918.

Ser. No. 116,023. (CLASS 39. CLOTHING.) DORIS
COHN, New York, N. Y. Filed Feb. 20, 1919.

TENDERFOOT

Particular description of goods.—Ladies' Leather
Shoes.
Claims use since about Feb. 1, 1909.

Ser. No. 116,053. (CLASS 4. ABRASIVE, DETERGENT,
AND POLISHING MATERIALS.) THE IMPORT DRUG
SPECIALTIES COMPANY, Cleveland, Ohio. Filed Feb. 21,
1919.

Particular description of goods.—A Liquid Shoe Dressing and Cleanser.
Claims use since December, 1917.

Ser. No. 116,099. (CLASS 46. FOODS AND INGREDI-ENTS OF FOODS.) OSCAR F. MAYER & BRO., Chicago, Ill. Filed Feb. 24, 1919.

Consists of a red seal resembling in outline a wax seal and mounted upon a triangular wavy-line background. No claim is made to the word "Approved" apart from the mark as shown in the drawing.
Particular description of goods.—Fresh, Dried, and Canned Beef; Fresh, Smoked, and Canned Pork; Ham, Bacon, Sausage, Beef Roll, Pork Roll, and Fresh, Pickled, and Dried Tongue, Pork and Beans, Lard, and Eggs.
Claims use since Apr. 25, 1918.

Ser. No. 116,109. (CLASS 39. CLOTHING.) RELIANCE MANUFACTURING COMPANY, Chicago, Ill. Filed Feb. 24, 1919.

Particular description of goods.—Work-Shirts.
Claims use since Oct. 5, 1918.

Ser. No. 116,110. (CLASS 37. PAPER AND STATION-ERY.) THE SAFE-CABINET COMPANY, Marietta, Ohio. Filed Feb. 24, 1919.

LIBRASTILE

Particular description of goods.—Document-Files.
Claims use since June 20, 1918.

Ser. No. 116,173. (CLASS 33. GLASSWARE.) BENJA-MIN TRIEBER, Chicago, Ill. Filed Feb. 26, 1919.

No claim is made to the word "Lens" apart from the mark shown in the drawing.
Particular description of goods.—Lamp-Lenses.
Claims use since Aug. 1, 1918.

Ser. No. 116,264. (CLASS 39. CLOTHING.) HARRY JACOBSON CO., INC., New York, N. Y. Filed Mar. 3, 1919.

No claim being made to the word "Brand" apart from the mark shown on the drawing.
Particular description of goods.—Men's Clothing, as Follows: Coats, Vests, Trousers, and Overcoats.
Claims use since Jan. 28, 1919.

Ser. No. 116,270. (CLASS 46. FOODS AND INGREDI-ENTS OF FOODS.) LIMPERT BROS. INC., New York, N. Y. Filed Mar. 3, 1919.

Particular description of goods.—An Extract Having a Maple Flavor and Used for Flavoring Desserts, Ice-Cream, Confections, and Syrups Used as Food.
Claims use since Sept. 1, 1917.

Ser. No. 116,324. (CLASS 39. CLOTHING.) JOSEPH F. BYRNE, Omaha, Nebr. Filed Mar. 6, 1919.

Particular description of goods.—Hosiery for Women.
Claims use since October, 1917.

Ser. No. 116,418. (CLASS 21. ELECTRICAL APPA-RATUS, MACHINES, AND SUPPLIES.) LAWSON & COMPANY, INCORPORATED, New York, N. Y. Filed Mar. 8, 1919.

RADBORE

Consisting of the word-symbol " Radbore."
Particular description of goods.—Jigs and Vises on Milling-Machines, Lathes. Planers, and Grinders, and on All Machines in Conjunction with Which Jigs and Vises may be Used ; Heads and Chucks to be Attached to Mill-ing-Machines, Die-Sinkers, and Lathes for Holding Drills : Drills for Boring and Cutting Holes in Metal and other Substances ; Offset Boring-Tools, Grinding Attachments for Holding Drills When They are Being Sharpened. and Vises.
Claims use since Oct. 10, 1916.

Ser. No. 116,517. (CLASS 6. CHEMICALS, MEDI-CINES, AND PHARMACEUTICAL PREPARATIONS.) C. HARRY BONG, Chicago, Ill. Filed Mar. 13, 1919.

GLYROPHOR

Particular description of goods.—Lotions for Soothing and Treating Irritations of the Skin.
Claims use since February, 1914.

Ser. No. 116,644. (CLASS 15. OILS AND GREASES.) CARSON PETROLEUM COMPANY, Chicago, Ill. Filed Mar. 17, 1919.

Particular description of goods.--Petroleum Products—Namely Fuel-Oil, Lubricating-Oil, Lubricating-Greases.
Claims use since about Feb. 20, 1919.

Ser. No. 116,905. (CLASS 5. ADHESIVES.) SIM-MONS HARDWARE COMPANY, St. Louis, Mo. Filed Mar. 25, 1919.

Particular description of goods.—Glue.
Claims use since June 30, 1897.

Ser. No. 116,933. (CLASS 39. CLOTHING.) REGAL MANUFACTURING COMPANY, Knoxville, Tenn. Filed Mar. 26, 1919.

Particular description of goods.—Overalls.
Claims use since Dec. 1, 1918.

270 O. G.—10

Ser. No. 116,938. ((LASS 37. PAPER AND STATION-ERY.) WHITING PAPER COMPANY, Holyoke, Mass. Filed Mar. 26, 1919.

Particular description of goods.—Fine Writing-Paper.
Claims use since Nov. 22, 1904.

Ser. No. 117,143. (CLASS 4. ABRASIVE, DETERGENT, AND POLISHING MATERIALS.) THE SANITARY PROD-UCTS COMPANY, Philadelphia, Pa. Filed Apr. 3, 1919.

"SOAPOLIN"

Particular description of goods.—Liquid Toilet Soap
Claims use since April, 1917.

Ser. No. 117,145. (CLASS 14. METALS AND METAL CASTINGS AND FORGINGS.) UNION SMELTING & REFINING CO. INC., Newark, N. J. Filed Apr. 3, 1919.

Particular description of goods.—Antifriction Bearing Metals.
Claims use since December, 1916.

Ser. No. 117,198. CLASS 17. TOBACCO PRODUCTS.) R. J. SEIDENBERG CO., Buffalo, N. Y. Filed Apr. 5, 1919.

Particular description of goods.—Cigars, Cigarettes, and Smoking and Chewing Tobacco.
Claims use since Mar. 7, 1919.

Ser. No. 117,255. (CLASS 6. CHEMICALS, MEDI-CINES, AND PHARMACEUTICAL PREPARATIONS.) SUNBEAM CHEMICAL COMPANY, Chicago, Ill. Filed Apr. 7, 1919.

NAPHOLAN

Particular description of goods.—A Pharmaceutical Preparation for the Treatment of Skin Diseases.
Claims use since on or about Apr. 2, 1919.

Ser. No. 117,360. (CLASS 6. CHEMICALS, MEDI-CINES, AND PHARMACEUTICAL PREPARATIONS.) USIT MFG. CO. OF AMERICA, INC., New York, N. Y. Filed Apr. 10, 1919.

MARJĀNEH

Particular description of goods.—Cosmetics—Namely, Face-Powders, Wrinkle-Cream, Sunburn-Lotion, Shaving-Lotion to be Applied Before Lathering the Face with Soap and Preventing Irritation, and Facial Beautifier.
Claims use since about Dec. 2, 1918.

Ser. No. 117,463. (CLASS 4. ABRASIVE, DETERGENT, AND POLISHING MATERIALS.) JOHN J. MEYER, New York, N. Y. Filed Apr. 14, 1919.

HIS-MASTERS-CLEANSER
HIS WEDDING DAY

No claim being made to the exclusive use of the word "Cleanser" apart from the mark as shown in the drawing.
Particular description of goods.—A Cleaning Compound.
Claims use since Apr. 3, 1919.

Ser. No. 117,569. (CLASS 46. FOODS AND INGREDI-ENTS OF FOODS.) NATIONAL POULTRY CO., Los Angeles, Calif. Filed Apr. 17, 1919.

The letters "N P Co." being printed in red. The repre-sentation of the turkey is not itself claimed. The word "Nonpareil" is not itself claimed.
Particular description of goods.—Dressed Poultry.
Claims use since Oct. 15, 1913.

Ser. No. 117,874. (CLASS 46. FOODS AND INGREDI-ENTS OF FOODS.) GALBRAITH MILLING COMPANY, Mount Morris, N. Y. Filed Apr. 26, 1919.

No claim is made to the exclusive use of the words "Galbraith Milling Co., Mt. Morris, N. Y." except in con-nection with the mark as shown.
Particular description of goods.—Wheat-Flour.
Claims use since 1881.

Ser. No. 117,958. (CLASS 4. ABRASIVE, DETERGENT, AND POLISHING MATERIALS.) UNITED DRUG COM-PANY, Boston, Mass. Filed Apr. 28, 1919.

Particular description of goods.—A Liquid Chemical Preparation for Polishing Silverware.
Claims use since May 1, 1877.

Ser. No. 117,960. (CLASS 6. CHEMICALS, MEDI-CINES, AND PHARMACEUTICAL PREPARATIONS.) WHEELER OPTICAL COMPANY, Portland, Oreg. Filed Apr. 28, 1919.

Thalmarine

Particular description of goods.—An Eye Remedy.
Claims use since Apr. 1, 1919.

Ser. No. 117,999. (CLASS 32. FURNITURE AND UP-HOLSTERY.) STANDARD STEEL CORP., Milwaukee, Wis. Filed Apr. 29, 1919.

LAV-OLET

Particular description of goods.—Chemical Closets.
Claims use since about Jan. 2, 1919.

Ser. No. 118,102. (CLASS 39. CLOTHING.) THE AMERICAN IMPORT CO., San Francisco, Calif. Filed May 3, 1919.

Le Mérite

Particular description of goods.—Ladies' and Misses' Garments—Namely, Nightgowns, Chemises, Envelop-Chemises, Underskirts, Drawers, and Matinées; Also In-fants' and Children's Garments—Namely, Dresses, Under-skirts, Gertrudes, Rompers, Coats, Hats, and Bibs.
Claims use since January, 1912.

Ser. No. 118,267. (CLASS 38. PRINTS AND PUBLICA-TIONS.) LOS ANGELES EXAMINER, Los Angeles, Calif. Filed May 8, 1919.

WISDOM "O" BLINKEY BEN

The lining on said drawing is intended for the purpose of shading only.
Particular description of goods.—Newspaper-Sections.
Claims use since on or about June 1, 1909.

Ser. No. 118,268. (CLASS 38. PRINTS AND PUBLICA-
TIONS.) Los Angeles Examiner, Los Angeles, Calif.
Filed May 8, 1919.

Particular description of goods.—Newspaper-Sections.
Claims use since on or about May 1, 1914.

Ser. No. 118,323. (CLASS 39. CLOTHING.) National
Mills, Spartanburg, S. C. Filed May 9, 1919.

No claim being made for the word " Service " apart from
the design shown.
Particular description of goods. — Hosiery for Men,
Women, and Children.
Claims use since Apr. 21, 1919.

Ser. No. 118,341. (CLASS 13. HARDWARE AND
PLUMBING AND STEAM - FITTING SUPPLIES.)
American Steel & Wire Company of New Jersey,
Cleveland, Ohio. Filed May 10, 1919.

Particular description of goods.—Oval Fence-Wire and
Wire Fencing.
Claims use since Mar. 26, 1919.

Ser. No. 118,354. (CLASS 39. CLOTHING.) Peter
Sangoff, Worcester, Mass. Filed May 10, 1919.

Disclaiming the use of the representation of a coat.
Particular description of goods.—Coats.
Claims use since July 1, 1918.

Ser. No. 118,431. (CLASS 15. OILS AND GREASES.)
The Denver Powerine Company, Denver, Colo. Filed
May 13, 1919.

Particular description of goods.—Gasolene.
Claims use since January, 1913.

Ser. No. 118,456. (CLASS 23. CUTLERY, MACHINERY,
AND TOOLS, AND PARTS THEREOF.) Axelson Machine Co., Los Angeles, Calif. Filed May 13, 1919.

The trade-mark consists in the letter " A " inside a
circle, the letter and circle being colored red.
Particular description of goods.—Lathes and Metal-
Working Grinders.
Claims use since March, 1917.

Ser. No. 118,484. (CLASS 28. JEWELRY AND PRE-
CIOUS-METAL WARE.) Adolph Simon, London, England. Filed May 14, 1919.

VICTORY

Particular description of goods.—Watch-Wristlets, Not
Including Watches and Bracelets.
Claims use since the 13th day of November, 1918.

Ser. No. 118,493. (CLASS 45. BEVERAGES, NON-
ALCOHOLIC.) Southern Beverage Company, Galveston, Tex. Filed May 14, 1919.

JAVO

Particular description of goods.—A Non-Intoxicating
Beverage Which, as Put Out by Us, is Coffee-Flavored,
Non-Cereal, and Maltless, Contains Not More Than One-
Half of One Per Cent. of Alcohol, and is Sold as a Soft
Drink.
Claims use since some time in March, 1919.

Ser. No. 118,653. (CLASS 35. BELTING, HOSE, MA-CHINERY PACKING, AND NON-METALLIC TIRES.) SPENCER CARROLL COMPANY, Dallas, Tex. **Filed May 19, 1919.**

CARDINAL

The bird being red, with a black portion near the eyes, and the limb blue.
Particular description of goods.—Inner Tubes for Pneumatic Tires.
Claims use since about May 1, 1919.

Ser. No. 118,755. (CLASS 39. CLOTHING.) THE ELASTOWEAR MANUFACTURING COMPANY, Cincinnati, Ohio. Filed May 21, 1919.

Particular description of goods.—Girdles, Brassières, Hip-Reducers, Corsets, and other Reducing and Retaining Garments for Improving the Personal Appearance.
Claims use since Feb. 5, 1918.

Ser. No. 118,756. (CLASS 39. CLOTHING.) MEDORA A. FEEHAN, Haverhill, Mass. Filed May 21, 1919.

No claim is herein made for the words "Gorman's Honest Shoes" apart from the mark as shown in the drawing. The lining on the illustration of the trademark indicates shading only.
Particular description of goods.—Men's, Women's, and Children's Shoes, Boots, and Slippers Made of Leather, Cloth, and other Suitable Fabrics, Rubber, or a Combination of Two or More of These Materials.
Claims use since 1904.

Ser. No. 118,761. (CLASS 26. MEASURING AND SCIENTIFIC APPLIANCES.) JOSEPH LEVY, Boston, Mass. Filed May 21, 1919.

AJAX

Particular description of goods.—Time-Stamps.
Claims use since May 15, 1919.

Ser. No. 118,940. (CLASS 39. CLOTHING.) FRANKLIN SIMON & CO., INC., New York, N. Y. Filed May 26, 1919.

Lochspun

Particular description of goods.—Men's and Boys' Furnishings, Undergarments, and Clothing—Namely, House-Coats, Waistcoats, Bath and Smoking Robes, Smoking-Jackets, Drawers, Pajamas, Dress-Shirts, Undershirts, Night-Shirts, Union-Suits, Bathing-Suits, Swimming-Suits, Dressing-Gowns, Sweaters, Mufflers, Collars, Gloves, Hosiery, Overcoats, Raincoats, Dress-Suits, Golf-Suits, Hunting-Suits, Riding-Suits, Tuxedo-Suits, Walking-Suits, and Sack-Suits, Trousers, Hats, and Caps Made Out of Textile Material and Gloves, Sweaters, Mufflers, Bathing-Suits, Swimming-Suits, Drawers, Undershirts, Hats, and Caps Made Out of Knitted Material and Women's, Girls', and Misses' Furnishings, Undergarments, and Clothing—Namely, Dresses, Corsets, Tailored Suits, Walking-Suits, Sport-Suits, Golf-Suits, Riding-Suits, Skirts, Nightgowns, Petticoats, Bodices, Chemises, Drawers, Combinations, Bath-Robes, Shirt-Waists, Bathing-Suits, Dressing-Gowns, Sweaters, Mufflers, Hosiery, Raincoats, Sport-Coats, Hats, Caps, and Coats Made Out of Textile Material, and Dresses, Corsets, Tailored Suits, Walking-Suits, Sport-Suits, Golf-Suits, Riding-Suits, Skirts, Nightgowns, Petticoats, Bodices, Chemises, Drawers, Combinations, Bath-Robes, Shirt-Waists, Bathing-Suits, Dressing-Gowns, Sweaters, Mufflers, Hosiery, Hats, and Caps Made Out of Knitted Material.
Claims use since the 5th day of May, 1919.

Ser. No. 118,977. (CLASS 39. CLOTHING.) ARMSTRONG CORK COMPANY, Pittsburgh, Pa. Filed May 28, 1919.

Particular description of goods.—Composition Soles and Heels for Boots and Shoes.
Claims use since May 22, 1919.

Ser. No. 118,978. (CLASS 39. CLOTHING.) ARMSTRONG CORK COMPANY, Pittsburgh, Pa. Filed May 28, 1919.

Mountain Goat

Particular description of goods.—Composition Soles and Heels for Boots and Shoes.
Claims use since May 22, 1919.

Ser. No. 119,000. (CLASS 6. CHEMICALS, MEDICINES, AND PHARMACEUTICAL PREPARATIONS.) NATIONAL ANILINE & CHEMICAL COMPANY, INCORPORATED, New York, N. Y. Filed May 28, 1919.

RUBALINE

Particular description of goods.—Food-Colors.
Claims use since July 18, 1918.

Ser. No. 119,004. (CLASS 6. CHEMICALS, MEDI-
CINES, AND PHARMACEUTICAL PREPARATIONS.)
NATIONAL ANILINE & CHEMICAL COMPANY, INCORPORATED,
New York, N. Y. Filed May 28, 1919.

MYRTINE

Particular description of goods.—Food-Colors.
Claims use since July 8, 1918.

Ser. No. 119,015. (CLASS 32. FURNITURE AND UP-
HOLSTERY.) JOHN STOCKTON BLANKINSHIP, Lynchburg, Va. Filed May 29, 1919.

No claim is made for the exclusive use of the word
"Period" apart from the accompanying trade-mark.
Particular description of goods.—Household Tables and
Chairs, Settees, Bedsteads, Music-Cabinets, Desks, Buffets,
Portable China-Closets, Bureaus, Chiffonniers, and Dress-
ing-Tables.
Claims use since Apr. 15, 1919.

Ser. No. 119,071. (CLASS 23. CUTLERY, MACHINERY,
AND TOOLS, AND PARTS THEREOF.) IDEAL ROLLER
COMPANY, Chicago, Ill. Filed May 31, 1919.

No claim being made to the roller illustrated apart
from the mark shown in the drawing.
Particular description of goods.—Rollers for Printing-
Presses; Rollers for Lithographing-Presses; Rollers for
Typewriters; Rollers for Manifolding-Machines; Rollers
for Varnishing-Machines; Rollers for Paper, Textile, and
Metal Coating Machines; Rollers for Paper, Textile, and
Metal Inking Machines; Rollers for Paper, Textile, and
Metal Coloring Machines; Rollers for Paper, Textile, and
Metal Feeding Devices; and Hand-Proofing Rollers Used
in Printing and Lithographing Work.
Claims use since about May 19, 1919.

Ser. No. 119,204. (CLASS 44. DENTAL, MEDICAL,
AND SURGICAL APPLIANCES.) THE OMO MFG. CO.,
Middletown, Conn. Filed June 4, 1919.

Particular description of goods.—Sanitary Belts, Sanitary Aprons, and Gum-Tissue for Surgical Purposes.
Claims use for sanitary belts and sanitary aprons since
1907 and for gum-tissue since 1918.

Ser. No. 119,205. (CLASS 44. DENTAL, MEDICAL,
AND SURGICAL APPLIANCES.) THE OMO MFG. CO.,
Middletown, Conn. Filed June 4, 1919.

Particular description of goods.—Sanitary Belts, Sanitary Aprons, and Gum-Tissue for Surgical Purposes.
Claims use for sanitary belts and sanitary aprons since
1907 and for gum-tissue since 1918.

Ser. No. 119,209. (CLASS 46. FOODS AND INGREDI-
ENTS OF FOODS.) ABRAHAM REZNIKOVE, Sharon, Pa.
Filed June 4, 1919.

The exclusive use of the word "Bread" appearing on
the drawing is hereby disclaimed except in connection
with the other features of the mark.
Particular description of goods.—Bread.
Claims use since Apr. 1, 1919.

Ser. No. 119,367. (CLASS 6. CHEMICALS, MEDI-
CINES, AND PHARMACEUTICAL PREPARATIONS.)
NATIONAL ANILINE & CHEMICAL COMPANY, INCORPORATED,
New York, N. Y. Filed June 9, 1919.

JEROSEE

Particular description of goods.—Food-Colors.
Claims use since May 17, 1919.

Ser. No. 119,389. (CLASS 39. CLOTHING.) LOUIS
BRUN FILS, Arre, France. Filed June 10, 1919.

LYSAR

Particular description of goods.—Stockings and Socks
Claims use since 1916.

Ser. No. 119,399. (CLASS 46. FOODS AND INGREDI-
ENTS OF FOODS.) THE G. E. CONKEY CO., Cleveland,
Ohio. Filed June 10, 1919.

Particular description of goods.—Starting Feed for
Chicks, a Poultry Feed of Meat, Grain, and Bone-Mash.
Claims use since July 1, 1906.

Ser. No. 119,400. (CLASS 46. FOODS AND INGREDI-ENTS OF FOODS.) THE G. E. CONKEY CO., Cleveland, Ohio. Filed June 10, 1919. Under ten-year proviso.

Conkey's

Particular description of goods.—Starting Feed and a Poultry Feed of Meat, Grain, and Bone-Mash.
Claims use since July 1, 1893.

Ser. No. 119,425. (CLASS 6. CHEMICALS, MEDI-CINES, AND PHARMACEUTICAL PREPARATIONS.) HERMAN A. METZ, New York, N. Y. Filed June 10, 1919.

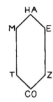

Particular description of goods.—Dyestuffs and Chemicals Used in Dyeing and Printing on Calico or other Textile Fabrics.
Claims use since May 24, 1919.

Ser. No. 119,469. (CLASS 46. FOODS AND INGREDI-ENTS OF FOODS.) CHARMS COMPANY, Newark, N. J. Filed June 11, 1919.

CHARMS

Consisting of the word "Charms."
Particular description of goods.—Candy and Fruit Tablets.
Claims use since its incorporation in October, 1917.

Ser. No. 119,501. (CLASS 23. CUTLERY, MACHINERY, AND TOOLS, AND PARTS THEREOF.) DWIGHT DIVINE & SONS, Ellenville, N. Y. Filed June 12, 1919. Under ten-year proviso.

Ellenville Brand

Consisting of the words "Ellenville Brand," no claim being made to the exclusive use of the word "Brand" apart from the mark as shown in the drawing.
Particular description of goods.—Pocket-Knives and Penknives; Kitchen-Knives; Nursery-Knives; Budding and Pruner Knives; Office-Knives; Knife Erasers; Cotton-Knives; Sugar-Cane Knives, and Skeleton Knives.
Claims use since June, 1876.

Ser. No. 119,502. (CLASS 23. CUTLERY, MACHINERY, AND TOOLS, AND PARTS THEREOF.) DWIGHT DIVINE & SONS, Ellenville, N. Y. Filed June 12, 1919. Under ten-year proviso.

Ellenville Knife Co.

Consisting of the words "Ellenville Knife Co."
Particular description of goods.—Pocket-Knives and Penknives; Kitchen-Knives; Nursery-Knives; Budding and Pruner Knives; Office-Knives; Knife Erasers; Cotton-Knives; Sugar-Cane Knives, and Skeleton Knives.
Claims use since June, 1876.

Ser. No. 119,504. (CLASS 23. CUTLERY, MACHINERY, AND TOOLS, AND PARTS THEREOF.) DWIGHT DIVINE & SONS, Ellenville, N. Y. Filed June 12, 1919. Under ten-year proviso.

Consisting of the word "Ulster" in script, with an underscoring paraph in which appear the words "Knife Co."
Particular description of goods.—Pocket-Knives and Penknives; Kitchen-Knives; Nursery-Knives; Budding and Pruner Knives; Office-Knives; Knife Erasers; Cotton-Knives; Sugar-Cane Knives, and Skeleton Knives.
Claims use since 1876.

Ser. No. 119,561. (CLASS 17. TOBACCO PRODUCTS.) LARUS & BROTHER COMPANY, Richmond, Va. Filed June 13, 1919.

Particular description of goods.—Plug-Tobacco.
Claims use since the year 1910.

Ser. No. 119,593. (CLASS 19. VEHICLES, NOT IN-CLUDING ENGINES.) WILLARD COPE BRINTON, New York, N. Y. Filed June 14, 1919.

T E C

Particular description of goods.—Electric Trucks and Accessories—Namely, Separate Detachable Platforms and Detachable Bodies.
Claims use since Dec. 1, 1918.

Ser. No. 119,620. (CLASS 23. CUTLERY, MACHINERY, AND TOOLS, AND PARTS THEREOF.) ALLIS-CHALMERS MANUFACTURING COMPANY, Milwaukee, Wis. Filed June 14, 1919.

Particular description of goods.—Comminuting Machinery, and Specifically Tube and Ball Mills and Tumbling Comminuting-Bodies Therefor.
Claims use since June 5, 1919.

Ser. No. 119,656. (CLASS 39. CLOTHING.) WM. KAUT FOOTWEAR COMPANY, Carthage, Mo. Filed June 16, 1919.

Particular description of goods.—Boots and Shoes Made of Leather.
Claims use since April, 1919.

Ser. No. 119,682. (CLASS 39. CLOTHING.) SANGER BROTHERS, Dallas and Waco, Tex., and New York, N. Y. Filed June 16, 1919.

BIG BILT

Particular description of goods.—Men's Work-Shirts, Underwear—Namely, Two-Piece Garments of Knitted Material—Overalls, and Jumpers.
Claims use since June 29, 1913.

Ser. No. 119,711. (CLASS 39. CLOTHING.) MARATHON SHOE CO., Wausau, Wis. Filed June 17, 1919.

PIED   PIPER

Particular description of goods.—Shoes, Particularly Children's Shoes. of Leather, Rubber, Fabric, and Combinations of Such Materials.
Claims use since June 9, 1919.

Ser. No. 119,735. (CLASS 35. BELTING, HOSE, MACHINERY PACKING, AND NON-METALLIC TIRES.) JOHN CRANE, Maywood, Ill. Filed June 18, 1919.

The lining on the drawing indicating shading.
Particular description of goods.—Packing Made of Fibrous Material, Fiber and Metal, and Metal and Either Dry or Treated with Lubricant.
Claims use since May 1, 1919.

Ser. No. 119,777. (CLASS 39. CLOTHING.) FRANK M. SCHUMACHER, New Orleans, La. Filed June 19, 1919.

Particular description of goods.—Leather Boots and Shoes for Men.
Claims use since May 1, 1919.

Ser. No. 119,781. (CLASS 39. CLOTHING.) TEXTILE PRODUCTS MANUFACTURING COMPANY, St. Louis, Mo. Filed June 19, 1919.

No claim is made to the words "Better Built" except in connection with the other features of the mark shown.
Particular description of goods.—Overalls, Jumpers, and Work-Shirts.
Claims use since May 15, 1919.

Ser. No. 119,796. (CLASS 21. ELECTRICAL APPARATUS, MACHINES, AND SUPPLIES.) THE DERF MANUFACTURING COMPANY, INC., New York, N. Y. Filed June 20, 1919.

DERF

Particular description of goods.—Spark-Plugs.
Claims use since about Oct. 1, 1917.

Ser. No. 119,802. (CLASS 28. JEWELRY AND PRECIOUS-METAL WARE.) L. HELLER & SON, INC., Providence, R. I. Filed June 20, 1919.

Deltah

Particular description of goods.—Imitation-Pearl Necklaces.
Claims use since June 13, 1919.

Ser. No. 119,810. (CLASS 48. MALT BEVERAGES, EXTRACTS, AND LIQUORS.) THE NATIONAL BREWERS ACADEMY & CONSULTING BUREAU, New York, N. Y. Filed June 20, 1919.

ONYX

Particular description of goods.—A Compound Consisting of Phosphosal, Nectarol, Porterine, Collupulin, Pomax, Lactart, Malto-Dextrin, Burtonizing Salts, and the Like, Used as an Additional Material During Various Stages of Manufacture of Beer or Near Beer in Order to Improve Their Character or Quality.
Claims use since Jan. 1, 1919.

Ser. No. 119,835. (CLASS 39. CLOTHING.) THE LERNER WAIST CO., New York, N. Y. Filed June 21, 1919.

REN-REL

Particular description of goods.—Underwear for Men, Women, and Children, Made of Silk and Textile Fabrics, Both of One and Two Pieced Garments, Aprons as Articles of Clothing, Rubber Coats, Mackintoshes, Overalls, Cloaks; Suits for Men, Women, and Children; Hats and Frame Material-Covered Helmets for Men, Women, and Children; Sleeping-Garments, Gymnasium-Suits, Jackets, Bonnets, Hat-Frames, One-Piece Sashes to be Wound About the Person, Scarfs as Articles of Clothing, Mufflers, Gaiters, Bustles; Dress, Negligée, and Work Shirts; Trousers, Pantalettes, Rubbers; Boots, Shoes, Slippers, Oxfords, Leggings, Puttees, and Sandals of Leather, Rubber, Fabric, and Combinations Thereof for Men, Women, and Children; Shirt-Waists, Blouses, Brassières, Negligées, Toques, Jumpers, Bathing-Suits, Gauntlets, Sweaters, Hoods, Caps, Outer and Under Vests, Capes, Hosiery; Sport and Sporting-Goods Suits and Separate Coats, Vests, and Trousers for Sport and of Sporting Goods; Outing-Shirts, Jerseys, Tights, Camping-Suits, Kimonos, Collars and Neckties, Cuffs, Shawls; Mittens and Gloves of Leather, Fabric, and Knit Material; Bloomers, Petticoats, Corset-Covers, Corsets, and Envelops of All Styles as Undergarments.
Claims use since May 1, 1919.

Ser. No. 119,849. (CLASS 40. FANCY GOODS, FURNISHINGS, AND NOTIONS.) COLUMBIA FASTENER COMPANY, Chicago, Ill. Filed June 23, 1919.

Particular description of goods.—Snap-Fasteners.
Claims use since June 13, 1919.

Ser. No. 119,971. (CLASS 39. CLOTHING.) CONVERSE RUBBER SHOE CO., Malden, Mass. Filed June 26, 1919.

The words "Big Nine."
Particular description of goods.—Boots and Shoes of Rubber, Canvas, or Combination.
Claims use since November, 1916.

Ser. No. 119,985. (CLASS 23. CUTLERY, MACHINERY, AND TOOLS, AND PARTS THEREOF.) CHRIS OSMUNDSON, Webster City, Iowa. Filed June 26, 1919.

Being the word "Queen."
Particular description of goods.—Spades, Shovels.
Claims use since August, 1911.

Ser. No. 120,083. (CLASS 46. FOODS AND INGREDIENTS OF FOODS.) ARCTIC ICE & COAL CO., Greensboro, N. C. Filed June 30, 1919.

THE SMILE FOLLOWS THE SPOON

Particular description of goods.—Ice-Cream and Ices.
Claims use since February, 1913.

Ser. No. 120,222. (CLASS 39. CLOTHING.) A. BUCKLAND PLUMMER, Chicago, Ill. Filed July 2, 1919.

NATURE-TREAD

Particular description of goods.—Foot-Pads in the Nature of Insoles for Use in Boots, Shoes, Slippers, Pumps, and Sandals and Extending for Nearly the Length of the Foot or Less and Affording Support to the Parts of the Foot Requiring Aid.
Claims use since about Mar. 1, 1919.

Ser. No. 120,241. (CLASS 6. CHEMICALS, MEDICINES, AND PHARMACEUTICAL PREPARATIONS.) ALBERT DANVILLE, Sacramento, Calif. Filed July 3, 1919.

Up-Cyl

Particular description of goods.—A Preparation for Improving Gasolene.
Claims use since the 15th day of June, 1916.

Ser. No. 120,303. (CLASS 40. FANCY GOODS, FURNISHINGS, AND NOTIONS.) ELY & WALKER DRY GOODS CO., St. Louis, Mo., and New York, N. Y. Filed July 7, 1919.

No claim being made to the words "Sure," "Hold," and "Garter" or the representation of the goods except in connection with the mark as shown in the drawing.
Particular description of goods.—Hose-Supporter.
Claims use since May 17, 1919.

Ser. No. 120,312. (CLASS 39. CLOTHING.) B. H. LEVY BRO. & CO., Savannah, Ga. Filed July 7, 1919.

No claim is made for the word "Clothes" apart from the mark as shown.
Particular description of goods.—Men's Suits and Overcoats.
Claims use since Sept. 1, 1916.

Ser. No. 120,413. (CLASS 16. PAINTS AND PAINTERS' MATERIALS.) E. I. DU PONT DE NEMOURS & COMPANY, Wilmington, Del. Filed July 10, 1919.

Wonder Lac

No claim is made herein to the word "Lac" as a technical trade-mark apart from the mark shown in the drawing.
Particular description of goods.—Lacquers.
Claims use since July 10, 1913.

Ser. No. 120,421. (CLASS 2. RECEPTACLES.) THE HARTMAN COMPANY, Chicago, Ill. Filed July 10, 1919.

Particular description of goods.—Hog-Waterers of the Nature of Tanks, Serving as a Water-Supply.
Claims use since Jan. 2, 1919.

Ser. No. 120,431. (CLASS 7. CORDAGE.) EMIL A. RUDIN, Toronto, Ontario, Canada. Filed July 10, 1919.

No claim is made to the words "Package Binders."
Particular description of goods.—Package-Binders and Parts Thereof. Comprising a Rigid Fastener and a Flexible Tie.
Claims use since May 31, 1918.

Ser. No. 120,485. (CLASS 13. HARDWARE AND PLUMBING AND STEAM-FITTING SUPPLIES. KOPPEL INDUSTRIAL CAR & EQUIPMENT COMPANY, Koppel and Pittsburgh, Pa. Filed July 12, 1919. Under ten-year proviso.

Particular description of goods.—Welded and Riveted Pipe, Railway-Spikes, and Bolts, Nuts, and Metallic Washers.
Claims use since January, 1888.

Ser. No. 120,514. (CLASS 46. FOODS AND INGREDIENTS OF FOODS.) SAUL D. ABRAMS, Boston, Mass. Filed July 14, 1919.

Particular description of goods.—Tea, Coffee, Cocoa, Spices, Canned Fish, Canned Vegetables, Canned Fruits, Cereal Breakfast Foods, Wheat and Rye Flour, Macaroni, Noodles, Catsup, Vinegar, Olive-Oil, Flavoring Extracts, for Food-Flavoring Purposes, and Candy.
Claims use since June 10, 1919.

Ser. No. 120,572. (CLASS 6. CHEMICALS, MEDICINES, AND PHARMACEUTICAL PREPARATIONS.) THE LUNDBORG COMPANY, New York, N. Y. Filed July 15, 1919.

No claim is made for the registration of the name "Lundborg" as a trade-mark; nor is claim made for the registration of the words "New York" as a trade-mark.
Particular description of goods.—Perfume, Toilet Water, Face-Powder, Talcum Powder, Toilet Cream, and Sachet.
Claims use since January, 1919.

Ser. No. 120,577. (CLASS 46. FOODS AND INGREDIENTS OF FOODS.) THE NULOMOLINE COMPANY, New York, N. Y. Filed July 15, 1919.

NULCO

Particular description of goods.—Table-Syrup.
Claims use since the 26th day of June, 1919.

Ser. No. 120,608. (CLASS 16. PAINTS AND PAINTERS' MATERIALS.) GRAPHITE PRODUCTS LIMITED, London, England. Filed July 16, 1919.

MILCORA

Particular description of goods.—Paints, Varnishes, and Preparations in the Nature of Paints, All for Application to Ships' Bottoms and the Like to Prevent Fouling and Corrosion.
Claims use since the month of October, 1918.

Ser. No. 120,676. (CLASS 28. JEWELRY AND PRE-CIOUS-METAL WARE.) THE M. S. RODENBERG CO., Providence, R. I. Filed July 18, 1919.

Particular description of goods.—Neck-Chains, Watch-Chains, and Swivels for Such Chains, All of Which are Made of or Plated with Precious Metal.
Claims use since June, 1907.

Ser. No. 120,768. (CLASS 29. BROOMS, BRUSHES, AND DUSTERS.) NEWTON BROOM CO., Newton, Ill. Filed July 21, 1919.

The representation of the cat and the words " Blue-Kat " are lined for blue, the background is lined for red, and the outer border is lined for blue and the circle and the inner border are lined for yellow. No claim is made to the representation of the broom or the word " Lime " except as associated with the mark shown.
Particular description of goods.—Brooms.
Claims use since May 1, 1919.

Ser. No. 120,815. (CLASS 40. FANCY GOODS, FUR-NISHINGS, AND NOTIONS.) COLUMBIA FASTENER COMPANY, Chicago, Ill. Filed July 23, 1919.

Particular description of goods.—Snap-Fasteners.
Claims use since July 7, 1919.

Ser. No. 120,827. (CLASS 39. CLOTHING.) INTER-NATIONAL DUPLEX COAT CO. INC., New York, N. Y. Filed July 23, 1919.

Particular description of goods.—Reversible Leather Coats.
Claims use since Apr. 10, 1919.

Ser. No. 120,830. (CLASS 39. CLOTHING.) WM. KAUT FOOTWEAR COMPANY, Carthage, Mo. Filed July 23, 1919.

Particular description of goods.—Boots and Shoes Made of Leather for Misses and Children.
Claims use since May 10, 1919.

Ser. No. 120,831. (CLASS 39. CLOTHING.) WM. KAUT FOOTWEAR COMPANY, Carthage, Mo. Filed July 23, 1919.

Particular description of goods.—Boots and Shoes Made of Leather for Misses and Children.
Claims use since May 10, 1919.

Ser. No. 120,832. (CLASS 39. CLOTHING.) WM. KAUT FOOTWEAR COMPANY, Carthage, Mo. Filed July 23, 1919.

Particular description of goods.—Boots and Shoes Made of Leather for Misses and Children.
Claims use since May 10, 1919.

Ser. No. 120,833. (CLASS 39. CLOTHING.) WM. KAUT FOOTWEAR COMPANY, Carthage, Mo. Filed July 23, 1919.

Particular description of goods.—Boots and Shoes Made of Leather for Misses and Children.
Claims use since May 10, 1919.

Ser. No. 120,893. (CLASS 14. METALS AND METAL CASTINGS AND FORGINGS.) THE VANADIUM-ALLOYS STEEL Co., Latrobe and Pittsburgh, Pa. Filed July 24, 1919.

RED-CUT

Particular description of goods.—Steel.
Claims use since June 1, 1910.

Ser. No. 120,920. (CLASS 40. FANCY GOODS, FURNISHINGS, AND NOTIONS.) INTERNATIONAL BUTTON Co., Rochester, N. Y. Filed July 25, 1919.

ARTIVORY

Particular description of goods.—Buttons Made of Vulcanized Fiber.
Claims use since July 10, 1919.

Ser. No. 120,930. (CLASS 26. MEASURING AND SCIENTIFIC APPLIANCES.) REID BROS., INC., San Francisco, Calif., and Seattle, Wash. Filed July 25, 1919.

Particular description of goods.—Graduates, Infusion-Bottles, Centrifuge-Tubes, Mortars and Pestles, Bath-Thermometers, Microscopic Slides, Albuminometers, Scales, Dynamometers, Cyrtometers, Spirometers, Graduate Cylinders, Sedimentation-Glasses, Mixing-Cylinders, Centrifuges; Medicine-Glasses, (Graduated;) Chemical Thermometers, Urinometers, Pipettes, Measuring-Tapes, Ureometers, Infusion - Jars, Test - Tubes; Drinking - Cups, (Graduated;) Infusion-Thermometers, Saccharometers, Burettes, House-Thermometers, Salvarsan-Tubes.
Claims use since on or about September, 1909.

Ser. No. 121,012. (CLASS 13. HARDWARE AND PLUMBING AND STEAM - FITTING SUPPLIES.) NATIONAL ENAMELING & STAMPING Co., New York, N. Y. Filed July 28, 1919.

Particular description of goods.—Tinware, Galvanized Ware, and Japanned Ware—Namely, Coffee-Boilers, Water-Buckets, Colanders, Dippers, Funnels, Milk-Buckets, Pudding-Molds, Steam-Cookers, Bathtubs, Cooking-Steamers, Cuspidors, Slop-Jars, Dustpans. Water-Pots, Serving-Trays, Dish-Pans, Tea-Kettles, Coffee-Pots, Griddles, Drip-Pans, Coal-Hods, Sap-Pails.
Claims use since 1908.

Ser. No. 121,019. (CLASS 6. CHEMICALS, MEDICINES, AND PHARMACEUTICAL PREPARATIONS.) ARNOLD B. PETERS, San Francisco, Calif. Filed July 28, 1919.

Particular description of goods.—Tooth-Powder.
Claims use since May 22, 1919.

Ser. No. 121,026. (CLASS 6. CHEMICALS, MEDICINES, AND PHARMACEUTICAL PREPARATIONS.) ISIDOR SOLOMOVITZ, St. Louis, Mo. Filed July 28, 1919.

MALARINE

Particular description of goods.—A Preparation for the Treatment of Malaria.
Claims use since about July 10, 1919.

Ser. No. 121,048. (CLASS 39. CLOTHING.) GWLADYS GALE THOMPSON, St. Louis, Mo. Filed July 29, 1919.

Particular description of goods.—Negligées.
Claims use since Dec. 1, 1918.

Ser. No. 121,097. (CLASS 39. CLOTHING.) THE ES-
TELLE COMPANY, Chicago, Ill. Filed July 28, 1919.

No claim being made to the words "Estelle Dress" and
"The Estelle Co." except in the association shown.
Particular description of goods.—Dresses.
Claims use since Oct. 7, 1918.

Ser. No. 121,114. (CLASS 46. FOODS AND INGREDI-
ENTS OF FOODS.) C. F. HATHAWAY & SONS, North
Cambridge, Mass. Filed July 30, 1919.

WIN-SUM

The word "Win-Sum."
Particular description of goods.—Bread.
Claims use since June 27, 1919.

Ser. No. 121,118. (CLASS 36. MUSICAL INSTRU-
MENTS AND SUPPLIES.) MILWAUKEE TALKING MA-
CHINE MANUFACTURING Co., Milwaukee, Wis. Filed
July 30, 1919.

No claim being made to the representation of phono-
graph-records apart from the mark shown.
Particular description of goods.—Phonographs and
Phonograph-Cabinets.
Claims use since Feb. 26, 1919.

Ser. No. 121,149. (CLASS 44. DENTAL, MEDICAL,
AND SURGICAL APPLIANCES.) GEORGE C. LEVY,
New York, N. Y. Filed July 31, 1919.

SANIBAND

Particular description of goods.—Catamenial Bandage.
Claims use since July 17, 1919.

Ser. No. 121,161. (CLASS 40. FANCY GOODS, FUR-
NISHINGS, AND NOTIONS.) UNITED TRIMMING Co.,
New York, N. Y. Filed July 31, 1919.

Particular description of goods.—Snap-Fasteners.
Claims use since Nov. 1, 1918.

Ser. No. 121,171. (CLASS 39. CLOTHING.) JOHN P.
CODY, Evansville, Ind. Filed Aug. 1, 1919.

Particular description of goods.—Caps and Hats for
Men and Children.
Claims use since September, 1918.

Ser. No. 121,179. (CLASS 39. CLOTHING.) MILTON
J. MEYER & Co. INC., New York, N. Y. Filed Aug. 1,
1919.

SEARCHLIGHT

Particular description of goods.—Leather Shoes for
Adults, Boys, and Girls.
Claims use since April, 1916.

Ser. No. 121,249. (CLASS 6. CHEMICALS, MEDI-
CINES, AND PHARMACEUTICAL PREPARATIONS.)
ALEXANDER SEYMOUR MANN, Providence, R. I. Filed
Aug. 4, 1919.

CLEAN-ORAL

Particular description of goods.—Liquid Antiseptic.
Claims use since Apr. 4, 1919.

Ser. No. 121,294. (CLASS 39. CLOTHING.) COWDEN
MANUFACTURING Co., St. Paul, Minn. Filed Aug. 6,
1919.

No claim being made to the exclusive use of the words
"Service Suit" apart from the mark as shown in the
drawing.
Particular description of goods.—Overalls.
Claims use since July 14, 1919.

Ser. No. 121,314. (CLASS 1. RAW OR PARTLY-PRE-
PARED MATERIALS.) A. S. NOWLIN & Co., Lynchburg, Va. Filed Aug. 6, 1919.

KING POCAHONTAS

No claim is made herein for the exclusive use of the
word "Pocahontas" aside from its association with the
word "King."
Particular description of goods.—Coal.
Claims use since 1912.

Ser. No. 121,318. (CLASS 19. · VEHICLES, NOT IN-CLUDING ENGINES.) THE RELIANCE WHEEL Co., Youngstown, Ohio. Filed Aug 6, 1919.

Particular description of goods.—Pressed - Steel Disk Wheels for Automobiles and Aeroplanes.
Claims use since on or about March, 1918.

Ser. No. 121,328. (CLASS 37. PAPER AND STATION-ERY.) LESTER P. WINCHENBAUGH Co., Boston, Mass. Filed Aug. 6, 1919.

WIN-DECO

The word " Win-Deco."
Particular description of goods.--Window-Display Paper.
Claims use since July 1, 1919.

Ser. No. 121,362. (CLASS 39. CLOTHING.) A. STIEG-LITZ & Co. INC., New York, N. Y. Filed Aug. 7, 1919.

"Hosiery With a Conscience"

Particular description of goods.—Hosiery.
Claims use since on or about the 31st day of May, 1919.

Ser. No. 121,406. (CLASS 13. HARDWARE AND PLUMBING AND STEAM-FITTING SUPPLIES.) NASH ENGINEERING Co., South Norwalk, Conn. Filed Aug. 8, 1919.

HYTOR

Particular description of goods.—Relief-Valves for Machinery and Ball Float-Valves for Machinery.
Claims use since June 1, 1919.

Ser. No. 121,409· (CLASS 6. CHEMICALS, MEDI-CINES, AND PHARMACEUTICAL PREPARATIONS.) ORI-ORI COMPANY, New York, N. Y. Filed Aug. 8, 1919.

Particular description of goods.—Hair Dyes and Hair-Shampoo.
Claims use since July 1, 1919.

Ser. No. 121,424. (CLASS 21. ELECTRICAL APPARA-TUS, MACHINES, AND SUPPLIES.) SCHROEDER HEADLIGHT & GENERATOR Co., Evansville, Ind. Filed Aug. 8, 1919.

Particular description of goods.—Electric Headlights (Not Including Lamps Therefor) and Turbo-Generators, Sold Either Separately or as a Combined Unit.
Claims use since Feb. 10, 1919.

Ser. No. 121,457. (CLASS 38. PRINTS AND PUBLICA-TIONS.) COMMERCE PUBLICATIONS COMPANY INC., New York, N. Y. Filed Aug. 9, 1919.

NEW YORK MAGAZINE

Particular description of goods. — Magazines Issued Monthly.
Claims use since the year 1915.

Ser. No. 121,462. (CLASS 39. CLOTHING.) THE EM-ERSON SHOE COMPANY, Rockland, Mass. Filed Aug. 9, 1919. Under ten-year proviso.

Particular description of goods.—Leather Boots and Shoes.
Claims use since about 1889 as to the words "The Emerson Shoe" and about 1890 as to the shoemaker seal design.

Ser. No. 121,463. (CLASS 39. CLOTHING.) THE EM-ERSON SHOE COMPANY, Rockland, Mass. Filed Aug. 9, 1919. Under ten-year proviso.

Particular description of goods.—Leather Boots and Shoes.
Claims use since about 1890.

Ser. No. 121,464. (CLASS 39. CLOTHING.) THE EM-ERSON SHOE COMPANY, Rockland, Mass. Filed Aug. 9, 1919. Under ten-year proviso.

Particular description of goods.—Leather Boots and Shoes.
Claims use since about 1889.

Ser. No. 121,472. (CLASS 39. CLOTHING.) WM. KAUT FOOTWEAR COMPANY, Carthage, Mo. Filed Aug. 9, 1919.

Particular description of goods.—Boots and Shoes Made of Leather.
Claims use since Apr. 19, 1919.

Ser. No. 121,473. (CLASS 39. CLOTHING.) WILLIAM KAUT FOOTWEAR COMPANY, Carthage, Mo. Filed Aug. 9, 1919.

Particular description of goods.—Boots, Shoes, Slippers, and Sandals Made of Leather.
Claims use since June 17, 1919.

Ser. No. 121,495. (CLASS 15. OILS AND GREASES.) VACUUM OIL COMPANY, New York, N. Y. Filed Aug. 9, 1919.

D. T. E.

Particular description of goods.—Oils, Greases, and Waxes of All Kinds and Similar Products for Lubricating, Illuminating, Heating, and Fuel Purposes, Also Gasolene.
Claims use since April, 1910.

Ser. No. 121,564. (CLASS 38. PRINTS AND PUBLICA-TIONS.) CLASS JOURNAL CORPORATION, Seattle, Wash. Filed Aug. 12, 1919.

Particular description of goods.—Monthly Periodical Magazines.
Claims use since June 1, 1915.

Ser. No. 121,565. (CLASS 38. PRINTS AND PUBLICA-TIONS.) CLASS JOURNAL CORPORATION, Seattle, Wash. Filed Aug. 12, 1919.

PACIFIC SHIPPING ILLUSTRATED

Particular description of goods.—Monthly Periodical Magazines.
Claims use since Aug. 1, 1917.

Ser. No. 121,627. (CLASS 7. CORDAGE.) INTERNA-TIONAL HARVESTER COMPANY, Chicago, Ill. Filed Aug. 13, 1919.

BLUE JAY

Particular description of goods.—Rope, Cord, Twine, and Binder-Twine.
Claims use since about the 1st day of January, 1888.

Ser. No. 121,709. (CLASS 39. CLOTHING.) J. BAACH Co., Chicago, Ill. Filed Aug. 16, 1919.

KUMFY UNDYS

Particular description of goods.—Women's One-Piece Underwear of Textile Fabric.
Claims use since about Aug. 1, 1919.

Ser. No. 121,711. (CLASS 39. CLOTHING.) CARTERET SILK COMPANY, Jersey City, N. J. Filed Aug. 16, 1919.

Particular description of goods.—Men's, Women's, and Children's Underwear of Knitted and Textile Fabrics in One and Two Piece Garments, Petticoats, and Outer Waists.
Claims use since the 24th day of July, 1919.

Ser. No. 121,717. (CLASS 35. BELTING, HOSE, MACHINERY PACKING, AND NON-METALLIC TIRES.) HASSEBROCK BROTHERS, St. Peter, Ill. Filed Aug. 16, 1919.

Particular description of goods.—Patches for Wheel-Tire Tubes.
Claims use since July 1, 1919.

Ser. No. 121,728. (CLASS 23. CUTLERY, MACHINERY, AND TOOLS, AND PARTS THEREOF.) SIMONDS MANUFACTURING COMPANY, Fitchburg, Mass. Filed Aug. 16, 1919. Under ten-year proviso.

Particular description of goods.—Saws.
Claims use since 1876.

Ser. No. 121,734. (CLASS 39. CLOTHING.) AMERICAN OVERGAITER Co., Baltimore, Md. Filed Aug. 18, 1919.

No claim is made to the representation of the overgaiter apart from the mark as shown in the drawing. No claim is made for the words "American Brand," "Amco Overgaiter," and "Fit and Wear in Every Pair" apart from the mark shown in the drawing.
Particular description of goods.—Overgaiters.
Claims use since November, 1915.

Ser. No. 121,748. (CLASS 39. CLOTHING.) JAMES T. CARADINE, St. Louis, Mo. Filed Aug. 18, 1919.

ONE-IN-ALL

"IN THE RAIN"

Particular description of goods.—Waterproof Coats and Slickers.
Claims use since about June 16, 1919.

Ser. No. 121,760. (CLASS 14. METALS AND METAL CASTINGS AND FORGINGS.) DRAPER MANUFACTURING COMPANY, Port Huron, Mich. Filed Aug. 18, 1919.

The drawing is lined for the color red, and no exclusive right is claimed to the use of the words "Hollow Balanced" apart from the mark as shown in the drawing.
Particular description of goods.—Hollow Balanced Balls of Brass or other Metal for Use in Making the Working Valves for Steam - Pumps, Globe - Valves, and Check-Valves and other Pump Connections.
Claims use since July 1, 1919.

Ser. No. 121,777. (CLASS 46. FOODS AND INGREDIENTS OF FOODS.) NATIONAL FRUIT FLAVOR Co., New Orleans, La. Filed Aug. 18, 1919.

The trade-mark consists of the word "Cremilla."
Particular description of goods.—Flavoring Extracts for Food.
Claims use since February, 1917.

Ser. No. 121,790. (CLASS 6. CHEMICALS, MEDICINES, AND PHARMACEUTICAL PREPARATIONS.) JOHN D. SHIELDS, Chaplin, Ky. Filed Aug. 18, 1919.

CURTOX

Particular description of goods.—Veterinary Medicine for External Application.
Claims use since Aug. 11, 1919.

Ser. No. 121,816. (CLASS 39. CLOTHING.) S. SCHILLER, New York, N. Y. Filed Aug. 19, 1919.

Applicant makes no claim for the use of the word "Hats" independent of the word "Harmony" used in connection therewith.
Particular description of goods.—Women's Hats, Men's Hats, and Children's Hats.
Claims use since January, 1917.

Ser. No. 121,818. (CLASS 23. CUTLERY, MACHINERY, AND TOOLS, AND PARTS THEREOF.) UNION CUTLERY CO., Olean, N. Y. Filed Aug. 19, 1919.

"WALRUS"

Consisting of the word "Walrus."
Particular description of goods.—Pocket-Cutlery, Razors, Shears, and Butcher-Knives.
Claims use since June 12, 1918.

Ser. No. 121,857. (CLASS 39. CLOTHING.) BEE ESS KNITTING MILLS, INC., New York, N. Y. Filed Aug. 21, 1919.

No claim being made for the words "Knit Goods" and "Brand" apart from the mark shown on the drawing.
Particular description of goods.—Ladies', Misses', Men's, and Boys' Silk, Woolen, and Cotton Sweaters.
Claims use since on or about Mar. 1, 1919.

Ser. No. 121,916. (CLASS 4. ABRASIVE, DETERGENT, AND POLISHING MATERIALS.) ARTHUR W. ZIESENISS, Rolla, Mo. Filed Aug. 22, 1919.

OILPORIA

The trade-mark consists of the word "Oilporia."
Particular description of goods.—Waterproofing-Oils for Leather.
Claims use since Mar. 11, 1919.

Ser. No. 121,921. (CLASS 1. RAW OR PARTLY-PREPARED MATERIALS.) H. K. COCHRAN COMPANY, Little Rock, Ark. Filed Aug. 23, 1919.

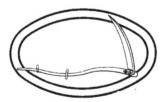

Particular description of goods.—Grain-Seed.
Claims use since Aug. 1, 1919.

Ser. No. 122,005. (CLASS 14. METALS AND METAL CASTINGS AND FORGINGS.) AMERICAN NON-FERROUS METALS CORPORATION, Chester, Pa. Filed Aug. 26, 1919.

COP—LED

Particular description of goods.—Bearing Metal.
Claims use since July 28, 1919.

Ser. No. 122,011. (CLASS 38. PRINTS AND PUBLICATIONS.) FAIRCHILD COMPANY, Chicago, Ill. Filed Aug. 26, 1919.

CHICAGO APPAREL GAZETTE

Particular description of goods.—Semimonthly Publication.
Claims use since November, 1903.

Ser. No. 122,017. (CLASS 39. CLOTHING.) LOCKE SHOE CO., Wheeling, W. Va. Filed Aug. 26, 1919.

FORT HENRY

Particular description of goods.—Leather Boots and Shoes.
Claims use since Apr. 21, 1919.

Ser. No. 122,023. (CLASS 35. BELTING, HOSE, MACHINERY PACKING, AND NON-METALLIC TIRES.) THE POLSON RUBBER CO., Cleveland, Ohio. Filed Aug. 26, 1919.

The picture being fanciful, the lining thereon being for shading only, and the words "Trade Mark Registered" being disclaimed.
Particular description of goods.—Rubber Tires, Inner Tubes, Pneumatic Rubber Tubes, Tube-Patches, Inside Blow-Out Patches, Outside Hook-On Boots, Outside Lace-On Boots, Outside Blow-Out Boots, Floating Flaps, Tire-Treads, Tire-Pads, Valve-Bases, Reliners, Rubber Belting.
Claims use since June 23, 1919.

Ser. No. 122,030. (CLASS 16. PAINTS AND PAINTERS' MATERIALS.) B. LUCAS WEBB, Columbia, S. C. Filed Aug. 26, 1919.

Particular description of goods.—A Wax and Stain Floor-Finish.
Claims use since June, 1919.

Ser. No. 122,066. (CLASS 33. GLASSWARE.) Unique Auto Specialties Co., San Francisco, Calif. Filed Aug. 27, 1919.

Particular description of goods.—Auto-Lenses.
Claims use since Dec. 30, 1918.

Ser. No. 122,073. (CLASS 19. VEHICLES, NOT IN-CLUDING ENGINES.) Commonwealth Steel Company, St. Louis, Mo. Filed Aug. 28, 1919.

COMMONWEALTH

Particular description of goods.—Four-Wheel Railway-Car Truck-Frames, Blind-End Passenger-Car Platforms, Six-Wheel Car Truck-Frames, Center-Bolster for Railway-Car Trucks, Railway-Car Platforms, Upright End Frames for Railway Blind-End and Vestibule Cars, Double Body-Bolsters for Railway-Cars, Transom Draft-Gear for Railway - Cars, Separable Body - Bolsters for Railway - Cars, Cross-Ties for Railway-Cars, Needle-Beams for Railway-Cars, Carry-Irons for Railway-Cars, Striking-Plates for Railway-Cars, Locomotive-Tender Frames, Four-Wheel Locomotive-Tender Truck-Frames, and Locomotive-Tender End Sills.
Claims use since July 25, 1901.

Ser. No. 122,122. (CLASS 46. FOODS AND INGREDI-ENTS OF FOODS.) Franz G. Jensen, Springfield, Mass. Filed Aug. 29, 1919. Under ten-year proviso.

Particular description of goods.—Candied Fruits, Candied Nuts, and Candy.
Claims use since Jan. 1, 1882.

Ser. No. 122,128. (CLASS 39. CLOTHING.) Abe Mill-man, New York, N. Y. Filed Aug. 29, 1919.

No claim is made to the word "Dresses" apart from the mark shown in the drawing.
Particular description of goods.—Infants' and Children's Dresses.
Claims use since the 11th day of July, 1919.

Ser. No. 122,156. (CLASS 19. VEHICLES, NOT IN-CLUDING ENGINES.) Baer Collapsible Rim Cor-poration, San Francisco, Calif. Filed Aug. 30, 1919.

The right to the exclusive use of the words "Baer" and "Trade-Mark" is hereby disclaimed except in connection with the rest of the mark as shown.
Particular description of goods.—Collapsible Rim.
Claims use since Jan. 18, 1919.

Ser. No. 122,164. (CLASS 46. FOODS AND INGREDI-ENTS OF FOODS.) Furry Fruit & Produce Co., Yakima, Wash. Filed Aug. 30, 1919.

FULWORTH

Particular description of goods.—Fresh Fruits—Namely, Cherries, Apples, Pears, Peaches, Berries, Prunes, Plums, Apricots, Yokimines.
Claims use since Apr. 15, 1919.

Ser. No. 122,166. (CLASS 17. TOBACCO PRODUCTS.) Frederick Griswold Gilbert, New Haven, Conn. Filed Aug. 30, 1919.

Comprising an irregular-shaped panel bearing the word "Gilbertmark," together with a fanciful design of a cherub sitting before an open box and with left hand extended in gesture of surprise and pleasure. No claim is made to the exclusive use of the word "Mark" apart from the mark shown in the drawing.
Particular description of goods.—Cigars, Cigarettes, and Tobacco for Pipes and Cigarettes, Packed in Paper, Tin-Foil, Glass, and Tin Containers.
Claims use since Aug. 1, 1916.

Ser. No. 122,184. (CLASS 4. ABRASIVE, DETERGENT, AND POLISHING MATERIALS.) James H. Overton, Quincy, Ill. Filed Aug. 30, 1919.

Particular description of goods.—A Waterproof Coating for Textile Fabrics and Leather.
Claims use since May 5, 1919.

Ser. No. 122,194. (CLASS 6. CHEMICALS, MEDI-CINES, AND PHARMACEUTICAL PREPARATIONS.) H-B. TEMPERING PROCESS CO., Clearbrook, Minn. Filed Aug. 30, 1919.

Particular description of goods.—A Composition for Tempering Steel or other Metals.
Claims use since June 17, 1919.

Ser. No. 122,212. (CLASS 6. CHEMICALS, MEDI-CINES, AND PHARMACEUTICAL PREPARATIONS.) JOHN G. GROSSENBACHER, Apopka, Fla. Filed Sept. 2, 1919.

No claim being made to the words "Insecticides" and "Fla. Insecticide Co." apart from the mark shown on the drawing.
Particular description of goods.—Insecticides.
Claims use since May 29, 1917.

Ser. No. 122,213. (CLASS 46. FOODS AND INGREDI-ENTS OF FOODS.) INTERNATIONAL MERCHANTS IN-CORPORATED, San Francisco, Calif. Filed Sept. 2, 1919.

I. M. I.

Particular description of goods.—Butter.
Claims use since Mar. 20, 1919.

Ser. No. 122,214. (CLASS 38. PRINTS AND PUBLICA-TIONS.) INTERNATIONAL FEATURE SERVICE, INC., New York, N. Y. Filed Sept. 2, 1919.

HON AND DEARIE

Particular description of goods.—A Series or Succession of Comic Drawings or Pictures.
Claims use since May 30, 1919.

Ser. No. 122,216. (CLASS 38. PRINTS AND PUBLICA-TIONS.) INTERNATIONAL FEATURE SERVICE, INC., New York, N. Y. Filed Sept. 2, 1919.

THEN THE FUN BEGAN

Particular description of goods.—A Series of Comic Drawings or Pictures.
Claims use since Jan. 8, 1919.

Ser. No. 122,238. (CLASS 1. RAW OR PARTLY-PRE-PARED MATERIALS.) A/S DET ALMINDELIGE HANDELSKOMPAGNI, Copenhagen, Denmark. Filed Sept. 3, 1919.

ALMINKO

Particular description of goods.—California Hops.
Claims use since Nov. 21, 1917.

Ser. No. 122,292. (CLASS 14. METALS AND METAL CASTINGS AND FORGINGS.) CRUCIBLE STEEL COM-PANY OF AMERICA, Pittsburgh, Pa. Filed Sept. 4, 1919.

ALMO

Particular description of goods.—Steel Bars, Rods, Billets, Blooms, Sheets Plates, Slabs, Strips, Blocks, and Forgings.
Claims use since December, 1918.

Ser. No. 122,293. (CLASS 14. METALS AND METAL CASTINGS AND FORGINGS.) CRUCIBLE STEEL COM-PANY OF AMERICA, Pittsburgh, Pa. Filed Sept. 4, 1919.

AURORA

Particular description of goods.—Steel Bars, Rods, Billets, Blooms, Sheets, Plates, Slabs, Strips, Blocks, and Forgings.
Claims use since June 8, 1907.

Ser. No. 122,327. (CLASS 16. PAINTS AND PAINT-ERS' MATERIALS.) JOSEPH WARREN BULLEN, Folcroft, Pa. Filed Sept. 5, 1919.

Particular description of goods.—Liquid Compounds Which are Used for Floor-Oils.
Claims use since Apr. 7, 1919.

Ser. No. 122,330. (CLASS 38. PRINTS AND PUBLICA-TIONS.) FRED W. BROWN, Columbus, Ohio. Filed Sept. 5, 1919.

Banking In Oil

Particular description of goods.—A Monthly Publication Distributed for Advertising Purposes.
Claims use since Aug. 18, 1919.

Ser. No. 122,350. (CLASS 13. HARDWARE AND PLUMBING AND STEAM - FITTING SUPPLIES.) EASTERN FOUNTAIN Co., Boston, Mass. Filed Sept. 5, 1919.

The word " Uni-Flo."
Particular description of goods.—Drinking-Fountains and Parts Thereof for Human Use—Namely, Coolers and Standards.
Claims use since June, 1919.

Ser. No. 122,362. (CLASS 26. MEASURING AND SCIENTIFIC APPLIANCES.) LEWIS, CONNORS & COMPANY, Chicago, Ill. Filed Sept. 5, 1919.

No claim is made to the words " It divides, multiplies and also figures interest, discounts and all percentages at a glance " aside from the arrangement shown in the drawing.
Particular description of goods.—Logarithmic-Scale Computing Devices.
Claims use since Aug. 23, 1919.

Ser. No. 122,385. (CLASS 21. ELECTRICAL APPARATUS, MACHINES, AND SUPPLIES.) ERIC W. BRANDQUIST, New York, N. Y. Filed Sept. 6, 1919.

No claim being made to the exclusive use of the word " Dual " appearing on the mark as shown in the drawing.
Particular description of goods.—Spark-Plugs for Internal-Combustion Engines.
Claims use since June 15, 1919.

Ser. No. 122,416. (CLASS 23. CUTLERY, MACHINERY, AND TOOLS, AND PARTS THEREOF.) J. D. ADAMS & COMPANY, Indianapolis, Ind. Filed Sept. 8, 1919.

No claim is made to the words " So Does the Adams Adjustable Leaning Wheel Grader " and to the representation of the grader apart from the mark as shown in the drawing.
Particular description of goods.—Road-Graders.
Claims use since Aug. 4, 1919.

Ser. No. 122,423. (CLASS 16. PAINTS AND PAINTERS' MATERIALS.) THE BEAVER VARNISH COMPANY, Buffalo, N. Y. Filed Sept. 8, 1919.

BEAVERTONE

Particular description of goods.—Paste and Ready-Mixed Paints and Varnishes.
Claims use since the 1st day of June, 1917.

Ser. No. 122,427. (CLASS 35. BELTING, HOSE, MACHINERY PACKING, AND NON-METALLIC TIRES.) JOSEPH J. FREADRICH, St. Louis, Mo. Filed Sept. 8, 1919.

CENTERBACK

Particular description of goods.—Leather Belting.
Claims use since December, 1907.

Ser. No. 122,456. (CLASS 22. GAMES, TOYS, AND SPORTING GOODS.) S. ALLCOCK & Co. LIMITED, Redditch, England. Filed Sept. 9, 1919. Under ten-year proviso.

Particular description of goods.—Sproat-Hooks and other Fishhooks.
Claims use since about the month of October, 1873.

Ser. No. 122,489. (CLASS 22. GAMES, TOYS, AND SPORTING GOODS.) JOHN M. LOCKWOOD, Jr., West Hoboken, N. J. Filed Sept. 9, 1919.

CHICIN

Consisting of the word " Chicin."
Particular description of goods.—Dolls.
Claims use since July 2, 1919.

Ser. No. 122,494. (CLASS 23. CUTLERY, MACHINERY, AND TOOLS, AND PARTS THEREOF.) N. & S. ENGINE Co., Seattle, Wash. Filed Sept. 9, 1919.

Particular description of goods.—Internal-Combustion Engines and Parts Thereof, Winches, and Capstans.
Claims use since July 1, 1909.

Ser. No. 122,502. (CLASS 6. CHEMICALS, MEDI-CINES, AND PHARMACEUTICAL PREPARATIONS.) SELECT PRODUCTS SALES CORPORATION, New York, N. Y. Filed Sept. 9, 1919.

Particular description of goods.—Chemical Fire-Extinguishing-Powder Compound.
Claims use since July 19, 1919.

Ser. No. 122,504. (CLASS 1. RAW OR PARTLY-PRE-PARED MATERIALS.) STAR BEDDING COMPANY, St. Louis, Mo. Filed Sept. 9, 1919.

No claim is made to the use of the word "Brand" apart from the trade-mark shown.
Particular description of goods.—Feathers.
Claims use since the month of November, 1884.

Ser. No. 122,505. (CLASS 14. METALS AND METAL CASTINGS AND FORGINGS.) AMERICAN STAMPING COMPANY, Elizabeth, N. J. Filed Sept. 10, 1919.

Particular description of goods.—Decorated Sheet Metal Used for Toys, Advertising-Signs, and Specialties.
Claims use since June 1, 1919.

Ser. No. 122,540. (CLASS 39. CLOTHING.) WM. KAUT FOOTWEAR CO., Carthage, Mo. Filed Sept. 10, 1919.

Particular description of goods.—Leather Boots, Shoes, Slippers, and Sandals.
Claims use since July 8, 1919.

Ser. No. 122,586. (CLASS 39. CLOTHING.) COHEN, GOLDMAN & CO. INC., New York, N. Y. Filed Sept. 12, 1919.

KOVERDINE

Particular description of goods.—Men's and Children's Outer Garments, Consisting of Coats, Pants, Vests, Ulsters, Overcoats, Raincoats, Smoking-Jackets, Mackinaws, and Dusters.
Claims use since Aug. 1, 1919.

Ser. No. 122,599. (CLASS 46. FOODS AND INGREDI-ENTS OF FOODS.) CHARLES HOLLENBACH, Chicago, Ill. Filed Sept. 12, 1919.

No claim being made to the words "Luncheon Sausage" apart from the mark shown.
Particular description of goods.—Fresh Sausage.
Claims use since Jan. 1, 1919.

Ser. No. 122,618. (CLASS 15. OILS AND GREASES.) VACUUM OIL COMPANY, New York, N. Y. Filed Sept. 12, 1919.

KOMO

Particular description of goods.—Oils, Greases, and Waxes of All Kinds and Similar Products for Lubricating, Illuminating, Heating, and Fuel Purposes, also Gasolene.
Claims use since April, 1909.

Ser. No. 122,652. (CLASS 14. METALS AND METAL CASTINGS AND FORGINGS.) EDMUND R. NEBELING, New York, N. Y. Filed Sept. 13, 1919.

ALLIGO

Consisting of the word "Alligo."
Particular description of goods.—Alloyed Platinum.
Claims use since about Mar. 1, 1919.

Ser. No. 122,656. (CLASS 22. GAMES, TOYS, AND SPORTING GOODS.) ROBERT W. PORTER, Mobile, Ala. Filed Sept. 13, 1919.

No claim is made herein to the use of the word "Toys" apart from the mark shown in the drawing.
Particular description of goods.—Toy Furniture.
Claims use since Aug. 1, 1919.

Ser. No. 122,660. (CLASS 38. PRINTS AND PUBLICATIONS.) READY TO WEAR PUBLISHING COMPANY, New York, N. Y. Filed Sept. 13, 1919.

Daily Garment News

Particular description of goods.—A Trade Publication Issued Daily.
Claims use since Aug. 6, 1919.

Ser. No. 122,733. (CLASS 38. PRINTS AND PUBLICATIONS.) WILLIAM A. RADFORD, Chicago, Ill. Filed Sept. 15, 1919.

FARM MECHANICS

Particular description of goods.—A Monthly Magazine.
Claims use since Apr. 1, 1919.

Ser. No. 122,735. (CLASS 23. CUTLERY, MACHINERY, AND TOOLS, AND PARTS THEREOF.) SIMONDS MANUFACTURING COMPANY, Fitchburg, Mass. Filed Sept. 15, 1919.

The pictorial representation of the man is fanciful. No registration rights are claimed for the representation of the saw apart from the mark shown in the drawing.
Particular description of goods.—Saws.
Claims use since January, 1915.

Ser. No. 122,740. (CLASS 9. EXPLOSIVES, FIREARMS, EQUIPMENTS, AND PROJECTILES.) VICTORY SPARKLER COMPANY, Elkton, Md. Filed Sept. 15, 1919.

No claim being made to the word "Safe" apart from the mark on the drawing.
Particular description of goods.—Sparklers.
Claims use since the 1st of June, 1919.

Ser. No. 122,754. (CLASS 23. CUTLERY, MACHINERY, AND TOOLS, AND PARTS THEREOF.) ALSTEEL MANUFACTURING CO., Battle Creek, Mich. Filed Sept. 16, 1919.

AUTO-JAD

Particular description of goods.—A Combination Automobile-Tool Used as a Support for a Jack on Soft Ground, a Shovel for Removing Obstructions, and an Incline or Ladder for the Driving-Wheel.
Claims use since Aug. 11, 1919.

Ser. No. 122,773. (CLASS 45. BEVERAGES, NON-ALCOHOLIC.) ISIDOR BERTHOLD GOETZ, Milwaukee, Wis. Filed Sept. 16, 1919.

RIXIE

Particular description of goods.—Non-Alcoholic Non-Cereal Maltless Beverages Sold as Soft Drinks and the Syrups and Ingredients for the Making of the Same.
Claims use since Apr. 11, 1915.

Ser. No. 122,778. (CLASS 39. CLOTHING.) LEWIS LEVY, Philadelphia, Pa. Filed Sept. 16, 1919.

Phillymaid

Which consists of the word "Phillymaid."
Particular description of goods.—Dresses for Women, Misses, and Children.
Claims use since about Apr. 1, 1919.

Ser. No. 122,796. (CLASS 35. BELTING, HOSE, MACHINERY PACKING, AND NON-METALLIC TIRES.) V-PLEX PISTON RING COMPANY, Chicago, Ill. Filed Sept. 16, 1919.

The picture shown in the mark is fanciful. No claim is made to the exclusive use of the representation of the piston-ring and the words "They Fill the Groove" apart from the mark shown in the drawing.
Particular description of goods.—Piston-Rings.
Claims use since Sept. 28, 1914.

Ser. No. 122,811. (CLASS 33. GLASSWARE.) THE AMERICAN PURE FOOD PROCESS CO., Baltimore, Md. Filed Sept. 18, 1919.

THRIFT

Particular description of goods.—Glass Jars.
Claims use since about July 1, 1918.

Ser. No. 122,828. (CLASS 46. FOODS AND INGREDI-ENTS OF FOODS.) WILLIAM FAEHNDRICH, New York, N. Y. Filed Sept. 18, 1919.

Particular description of goods.—Cheese.
Claims use since Jan. 1, 1918.

Ser. No. 122,835. (CLASS 46. FOODS AND INGREDI-ENTS OF FOODS.) CHAS. HOLLINSHED CO. INC., New York, N. Y. Filed Sept. 18, 1919.

All reading-matter, with the exception of the word "Soyeta," is hereby disclaimed.
Particular description of goods.—Choice Refined De-odorized Soy-Bean Oil.
Claims use since May 16, 1919.

Ser. No. 122,846. (CLASS 38. PRINTS AND PUBLICA-TIONS.) MANUFACTURERS RECORD PUBLISHING COM-PANY, Baltimore, Md. Filed Sept. 18, 1919.

Exponent   of   America

Particular description of goods.—A Weekly Magazine.
Claims use since Jan. 2, 1919.

Ser. No. 122,858. (CLASS 46. FOODS AND INGREDI-ENTS OF FOODS.) RUEPPEL-JONES IMPORTING COM-PANY, INC., New York, N. Y. Filed Sept. 18, 1919.

The word "Brand" being disclaimed apart from the mark shown.
Particular description of goods.—Sardines.
Claims use since Sept. 11, 1919.

Ser. No. 122,862. (CLASS 36. MUSICAL INSTRU-MENTS AND SUPPLIES.) SAMUEL S. SCHIFF, Chi-cago, Ill., assignor to Vitanola Talking Machine Com-pany, Chicago, Ill., a Corporation of Illinois. Filed Sept. 18, 1919.

Particular description of goods.—Talking-Machines and Supplies Therefor, Comprising Tone-Arms, Sound Boxes or Reproducers, and Motors.
Claims use since Feb. 25, 1915.

Ser. No. 122,868. (CLASS 29. BROOMS, BRUSHES, AND DUSTERS.) THE WHITE-VALENTINE COMPANY, Urbana, Ohio. Filed Sept. 18, 1919.

Particular description of goods.—Brooms.
Claims use since about 1890.

Ser. No. 122,882. (CLASS 38. PRINTS AND PUBLICA-TIONS.) CONCRETE-CEMENT AGE PUBLISHING CO., De-troit, Mich. Filed Sept. 19, 1919.

Particular description of goods.—A Monthly Magazine for Building-Supply Dealers.
Claims use since Aug. 18, 1919.

Ser. No. 122,883. (CLASS 21. ELECTRICAL APPARATUS, MACHINES, AND SUPPLIES.) GENSONITE WELDING ELECTRODE CO., Philadelphia, Pa. Filed Sept. 19, 1919.

GENSONITE

Particular description of goods.—Flux or Covered Electrodes.
Claims use since about May 1, 1919.

Ser. No. 122,884. (CLASS 6. CHEMICALS, MEDICINES, AND PHARMACEUTICAL PREPARATIONS.) DUPUIS CHEMICAL CO., Los Angeles, Calif., and El Paso, Tex. Filed Sept. 19, 1919.

Particular description of goods.—Insecticide and Germicide.
Claims use since 1894.

Ser. No. 122,892. (CLASS 46. FOODS AND INGREDIENTS OF FOODS.) HAWAIIAN PINEAPPLE COMPANY, LIMITED, Iwilei, Honolulu, Territory of Hawaii. Filed Sept. 19, 1919.

CORAL REEF

Particular description of goods.—Canned Pineapples.
Claims use since Feb. 10, 1916.

Ser. No. 122,898. (CLASS 46. FOODS AND INGREDIENTS OF FOODS.) LAKE REEDY PACKING CO., Frostproof, Fla. Filed Sept. 19, 1919.

Particular description of goods.—Fresh Citrus Fruits—Namely, Oranges, Grape-Fruit, and Tangerines.
Claims use since July 15, 1919.

Ser. No. 122,912. (CLASS 45. BEVERAGES, NON-ALCOHOLIC.) PEARL CITY FRUIT CO. LTD., Honolulu, Territory of Hawaii. Filed Sept. 19, 1919.

Particular description of goods.—Pineapple-Extract Syrup Used for the Making of Non-Alcoholic Non-Cereal Maltless Beverages Sold as Soft Drinks.
Claims use since May 22, 1919.

Ser. No. 122,913. (CLASS 46. FOODS AND INGREDIENTS OF FOODS.) PEARL CITY FRUIT CO. LTD., Honolulu, Territory of Hawaii. Filed Sept. 19, 1919.

Particular description of goods.—Pineapple Jelly.
Claims use since May 22, 1919.

Ser. No. 122,938. (CLASS 21. ELECTRICAL APPARATUS, MACHINES, AND SUPPLIES.) J. H. FAW, INC., New York, N. Y. Filed Sept. 20, 1919.

FAWSCO

Particular description of goods.—Electrical Wire and Fuses.
Claims use since June, 1916.

Ser. No. 122,943. (CLASS 46. FOODS AND INGREDIENTS OF FOODS.) HENRY KAELIN & SON, Brooklyn, N. Y. Filed Sept. 20, 1919.

ARROW

Particular description of goods.—Fresh Vegetables.
Claims use since July 1, 1919.

Ser. No. 122,951. (CLASS 13. HARDWARE AND PLUMBING AND STEAM-FITTING SUPPLIES.) THE PALNUT CORPORATION, Buffalo, N. Y. Filed Sept. 20, 1919.

No claim being made to the representation of the nut-lock apart from the mark as shown on the drawing.
Particular description of goods.—Nut-Locks.
Claims use since Sept. 18, 1919.

Ser. No. 122,975. (CLASS 42. KNITTED, NETTED, AND TEXTILE FABRICS.) DERRYVALE LINEN COMPANY, New York, N. Y. Filed Sept. 22, 1919.

DERRYVALE

The lining on the drawing is for the purpose of shading only.

Particular description of goods.—Linen and Cotton Piece Goods, Piece Goods of Mixed Linen and Cotton; Towels, Handkerchiefs, Table-Cloths, Napkins, Pillow-Cases, Sheets, Glass-Cloths, and Bedspreads of Linen and Cotton and Mixed Linen and Cotton; Jute, Hemp, Hair, and Wool Piece Goods; Piece Goods of Mixed Jute and Linen, Hair and Wool, Hair and Cotton, Hair and Jute, Hair and Linen, and other Textiles in Which Jute or Hair Forms a Part of the Structural Make-Up of the Goods; Textile Foundations for Wearing-Apparel, Comprising Tailors' Canvas of Linen and Cotton, Mixed Linen and Cotton, and Jute, All in the Piece; Stamped Strips, Forms, Pieces, and Rolls of Linen and Cotton and Mixed Linen and Cotton Goods; Doilies, Scarfs, or Covers for Buffets, Dressers, and other Furniture, and Squares of Linen and Cotton and Mixed Linen and Cotton.

Claims use since January, 1917.

Ser. No. 122,976. (CLASS 42. KNITTED, NETTED, AND TEXTILE FABRICS.) DERRYVALE LINEN COMPANY, New York, N. Y. Filed Sept. 22, 1919.

DERRYVALE
Genuine Irish Linen

The words "Genuine Irish Linen" is disclaimed apart from the mark shown in the drawing. The lining on the drawing is for the purpose of shading only.

Particular description of goods.—Linen and Cotton Piece Goods, Piece Goods of Mixed Linen and Cotton; Towels, Handkerchiefs, Table-Cloths, Napkins, Pillow-Cases, Sheets, Glass-Cloths, and Bedspreads of Linen and Cotton and Mixed Linen and Cotton; Jute, Hemp, Hair, and Wool Piece Goods; Piece Goods of Mixed Jute and Linen, Hair and Wool, Hair and Cotton, Hair and Jute, Hair and Linen, and other Textiles in Which Jute or Hair Forms a Part of the Structural Make-Up of the Goods; Textile Foundations for Wearing-Apparel, Comprising Tailors' Canvas of Linen and Cotton, Mixed Linen and Cotton, and Jute, All in the Piece; Stamped Strips, Forms, Pieces, and Rolls of Linen and Cotton and Mixed Linen and Cotton Goods; Doilies, Scarfs, or Covers for Buffets, Dressers, and other Furniture, and Squares of Linen and Cotton and Mixed Linen and Cotton.

Claims use since January, 1917.

Ser. No. 122,980. (CLASS 39. CLOTHING.) ENTERPRISE MANUFACTURING COMPANY, Atlanta, Ga. Filed Sept. 22, 1919.

Particular description of goods.—Middy-Blouses and Dresses for Children, Misses, and Ladies.

Claims use since July, 1919.

Ser. No. 122,987. (CLASS 6. CHEMICALS, MEDICINES, AND PHARMACEUTICAL PREPARATIONS.) H. KOHNSTAMM & Co., New York, N. Y. Filed Sept. 22, 1919.

Particular description of goods.—Starch for Laundry Purposes and in Treating Textiles.

Claims use since November, 1918.

Ser. No. 123,020. (CLASS 6. CHEMICALS, MEDICINES, AND PHARMACEUTICAL PREPARATIONS.) CLAYTON CHEMICAL CO., New York, N. Y. Filed Sept. 23, 1919.

R-NICO

Particular description of goods.—A Preparation for the Relief of Inflammation and Pain by Cutaneous Absorption.

Claims use since about Sept. 2, 1919.

Ser. No. 123,039. (CLASS 6. CHEMICALS, MEDICINES, AND PHARMACEUTICAL PREPARATIONS.) ROHM & HAAS COMPANY, Philadelphia, Pa. Filed Sept. 23, 1919.

LYKOPON

Particular description of goods.—Anhydrous Sodium Hydrosulfite.

Claims use since on or about June 15, 1919.

Ser. No. 123,040. (CLASS 6. CHEMICALS, MEDICINES, AND PHARMACEUTICAL PREPARATIONS.) ROHM & HAAS COMPANY, Philadelphia, Pa. Filed Sept. 23, 1919.

CRESOTAN

Particular description of goods.—A Chemical Used for Tanning Hides.

Claims use since on or about May 15, 1919.

Ser. No. 123,041. (CLASS 6. CHEMICALS, MEDICINES, AND PHARMACEUTICAL PREPARATIONS.) ROHM & HAAS COMPANY, Philadelphia, Pa. Filed Sept. 23, 1919.

FORMOPON

Particular description of goods.—Sulfoxalate of Sodium Formaldehyde.

Claims use since on or about Aug. 1, 1919.

Ser. No. 123,054. (CLASS 46. FOODS AND INGREDI-ENTS OF FOODS.) HALLER BAKING COMPANY, Pitts-burgh, Pa. Filed Sept. 24, 1919.

HALLER'S
DUTCH
BAKER BOY

Particular description of goods.—Bread, Cakes, and Pastry.
Claims use since about Mar. 1, 1914.

Ser. No. 123,102. (CLASS 6. CHEMICALS, MEDI-CINES, AND PHARMACEUTICAL PREPARATIONS.) GEORGE BORGFELDT & Co., New York, N. Y. Filed Sept. 25, 1919.

Tiss-me

Particular description of goods.—Toilet Powder.
Claims use since Sept. 8, 1919.

Ser. No. 123,104. (CLASS 45. BEVERAGES, NON-ALCOHOLIC.) WILLIAM BACHRACH, Oakland, Calif. Filed Sept. 25, 1919.

Particular description of goods.—Non-Alcoholic Non-Cereal Maltless Beverages, Both Plain and Carbonated, Sold as Soft Drinks and Non-Alcoholic Fruit Syrup for Making the Same.
Claims use since Aug. 26, 1919.

Ser. No. 123,132. (CLASS 6. CHEMICALS, MEDI-CINES, AND PHARMACEUTICAL PREPARATIONS.) THE WILLIAM S. MERRELL COMPANY, Cincinnati, Ohio. Filed Sept. 25, 1919.

IODOLIN

Particular description of goods.—A Compound and Oint-ment of Iodin and Oil.
Claims use since Feb. 22, 1912.

Ser. No. 123,146. (CLASS 6. CHEMICALS, MEDI-CINES, AND PHARMACEUTICAL PREPARATIONS.) UNGERER & COMPANY INC., New York, N. Y. Filed Sept. 25, 1919.

ˈRESINAROME

Particular description of goods.—Resins and Volatile Oils for Imparting Scent to Toilet Preparations.
Claims use since 1906.

Ser. No. 123,163. (CLASS 4, ABRASIVE, DETERGENT, AND POLISHING MATERIALS.) HOWARD BROS. CHEMICAL CO., Buffalo, N. Y. Filed Sept. 26, 1919.

The word "Howard" being the autographic signature of Clarence M. Howard, vice-president of this applicant.
Particular description of goods.—Soap.
Claims use since May 18, 1915.

Ser. No. 123,199. (CLASS 45. BEVERAGES, NON-ALCOHOLIC.) ALPINE CO., INC., New York, N. Y. Filed Sept. 27, 1919.

Particular description of goods.—Ginger-Ale, Cream-Soda, Sarsaparilla, and other Fruit-Flavored Non-Alco-holic Non-Cereal Maltless Carbonated Beverages Sold as Soft Drinks.
Claims use since about Sept. 1, 1919.

Ser. No. 123,201. (CLASS 22. GAMES, TOYS, AND SPORTING GOODS.) THE BRUNSWICK-BALKE-COL-LENDER COMPANY, Wilmington, Del., and Chicago, Ill. Filed Sept. 27, 1919.

DIAMOND

Particular description of goods.—Billiard and Pocket-Billiard Balls.
Claims use since May 15, 1919.

Ser. No. 123,208. (CLASS 46. FOODS AND INGREDI-ENTS OF FOODS.) FREDERICK A. HEROUX, Oakland, Calif. Filed Sept. 27, 1919.

I.KNEAD

Particular description of goods.—Bread.
Claims use since Jan. 1, 1919.

Ser. No. 123,212. (CLASS 46. FOODS AND INGREDI-
ENTS OF FOODS.) JOHN LYNARD, Owatonna, Minn.
Filed Sept. 27, 1919.

Particular description of goods.—Eggs, Poultry, and
Butter.
Claims use since on or about Apr. 1, 1899.

Ser. No. 123,214. (CLASS 6. CHEMICALS, MEDI-
CINES, AND PHARMACEUTICAL PREPARATIONS.)
H. A. METZ LABORATORIES, INC., New York, N. Y. Filed
Sept. 27, 1919.

Parathesin

Particular description of goods.—Anesthetics.
Claims use since Aug. 25, 1919.

Ser. No. 123,215. (CLASS 6. CHEMICALS, MEDI-
CINES, AND PHARMACEUTICAL PREPARATIONS.)
OSWALD M'CARDELL & Co., Manchester, England. Filed
Sept. 27, 1919.

SENTOL

Particular description of goods.—Insecticides.
Claims use since about Apr. 28, 1919.

Ser. No. 123,216. (CLASS 6. CHEMICALS, MEDI-
CINES, AND PHARMACEUTICAL PREPARATIONS.)
OSWALD M'CARDELL & Co., Manchester, England. Filed
Sept. 27, 1919.

ENTOL

Particular description of goods.—Insecticides.
Claims use since about Feb. 26, 1919.

Ser. No. 123,231. (CLASS 19. VEHICLES, NOT IN-
CLUDING ENGINES.) VREELAND MOTOR Co. INC.
Newark, N. J. Filed Sept. 27, 1919.

Particular description of goods.—Automobiles.
Claims use since July, 1919.

Ser. No. 123,238. (CLASS 6. CHEMICALS, MEDI-
CINES, AND PHARMACEUTICAL PREPARATIONS.)
CORRASANTI CHEMICAL Co., INC., Newark, N. J. Filed
Sept. 29, 1919.

CORROSANTI

Particular description of goods.—Boiler Compounds.
Claims use since Jan. 1, 1914.

Ser. No. 123,298. (CLASS 46. FOODS AND INGREDI-
ENTS OF FOODS.) ASPEGREN & Co., New York, N. Y.
Filed Oct. 1, 1919.

Consisting of the word "Fluffo."
Particular description of goods.—A Shortening and a
Frying Medium.
Claims use since July 19, 1919.

Ser. No. 123,316. (CLASS 19. VEHICLES, NOT IN-
CLUDING ENGINES.) KENOSHA WHEEL & AXLE
COMPANY, Kenosha, Wis. Filed Oct. 1, 1919.

SAUCER

Particular description of goods.—Cast-Metal Vehicle-
Wheels.
Claims use since June 15, 1919.

Ser. No. 123,330. (CLASS 39. CLOTHING.) BARVA
HEEL & TIRE FACTORY, INC., Fort Wayne, Ind. Filed
Oct. 2, 1919.

No claim being made to the representation of a rubber
heel apart from the mark shown.
Particular description of goods.—Rubber Heels for
Men's, Women's, and Children's Shoes.
Claims use since Aug. 14, 1919.

Ser. No. 123,361. (CLASS 39. CLOTHING.) Ochs & Frank, Baltimore, Md. Filed Oct. 2, 1919.

Particular description of goods.—Ladies' Waists and Dresses.
Claims use since October, 1909.

Ser. No. 123,363. (CLASS 40. FANCY GOODS, FURNISHINGS, AND NOTIONS.) Parisian Mfg. Company, Philadelphia, Pa. Filed Oct. 2, 1919.

The word "Wavers" being disclaimed apart from the mark shown in the drawing.
Particular description of goods.—Hair-Wavers.
Claims use since Jan. 1, 1916.

Ser. No. 123,365. (CLASS 39. CLOTHING.) Ritter Hosiery Company, Fleetwood, Pa. Filed Oct. 2, 1919.

Particular description of goods.—Men's Hosiery.
Claims use since June 25, 1919.

Ser. No. 123,440½. (CLASS 46. FOODS AND INGREDIENTS OF FOODS.) Stuttgart Rice Mill Company, Stuttgart, Ark. Filed Oct. 4, 1919.

PEKO

Particular description of goods.—Rice.
Claims use since October, 1914.

Ser. No. 123,456. (CLASS 39. CLOTHING.) Rice & Hutchins, Incorporated, Boston, Mass. Filed Oct. 4, 1919.

KNIGHT ERRANT

Particular description of goods.—Men's, Women's, and Children's Boots, Shoes, and Slippers Made Wholly or in Part of Leather.
Claims use since Feb. 15, 1903.

Ser. No. 123,459. (CLASS 40. FANCY GOODS, FURNISHINGS, AND NOTIONS.) Samstag & Hilder Bros., New York, N. Y. Filed Oct. 4, 1919.

Particular description of goods.—Marcel and Water Waver.
Claims use since July 1, 1919.

Ser. No. 123,460. (CLASS 39. CLOTHING.) Samstag & Hilder Bros., New York, N. Y. Filed Oct. 4, 1919.

ROCK A BYE-BABY

Particular description of goods.—Infants' Pants.
Claims use since Sept. 20, 1919.

Ser. No. 123,487. (CLASS 15. OILS AND GREASES.) Lamborn & Co., New York, N. Y. Filed Oct. 6, 1919.

Particular description of goods.—Lubricating-Oils.
Claims use since April, 1918.

Ser. No. 123,507. (CLASS 46. FOODS AND INGREDIENTS OF FOODS.) Victor Vivaudou, New York, N. Y. Filed Oct. 6, 1919.

Particular description of goods.—Candies.
Claims use since 1915.

Ser. No. 123,531. (CLASS 39. CLOTHING.) Apsley Rubber Company, Hudson, Mass. Filed Oct. 8, 1919.

AP-STITCH

Particular description of goods.—Canvas Outing-Shoes. *Claims use* since July 21, 1919.

Ser. No. 123,546. (CLASS 36. MUSICAL INSTRUMENTS AND SUPPLIES.) Kesner & Jerlaw, New York, N. Y. Filed Oct. 8, 1919.

SONATA

Particular description of goods.—Phonographs. *Claims use* since July 1, 1919.

Ser. No. 123,592. (CLASS 38. PRINTS AND PUBLICATIONS.) United Publishers Corporation, New York, N. Y. Filed Oct. 9, 1919.

THE IRON AGE CATALOGUE of AMERICAN EXPORTS

Particular description of goods.—An Annual Publication, Being an Export Catalogue of American Manufacturers of Iron, Steel, Machinery, Tools, Foundry Equipment, Electrical Equipment, Engineering Equipment, Hardware and Cutlery, Sanitary Equipment, Agricultural Implements, Dairy Equipment, Automobiles, Tractors and Trucks, and Accessories.
Claims use since Mar. 1, 1919.

Ser. No. 123,632. (CLASS 21. ELECTRICAL APPARATUS, MACHINES, AND SUPPLIES.) The Electric Controller & Manufacturing Company, Cleveland, Ohio. Filed Oct. 10, 1919.

Particular description of goods.—Electric Controllers, Motor-Starters, Lifting-Magnets, Electric Brakes, Electric-Crane Fittings, Solenoids, Arc-Welders, Electrical Faultfinders, Electric Switches, Float-Switches, Switch-Frames, Switch-Arms, Switch-Contacts, Switch-Brushes, Switch-Magnets, Electromagnets, Magnet - Armatures, Switch Blow-Outs, Switch-Blow-Out Ears, Rheostats, Resistance - Grids, Resistance-Coils, Master-Controllers, Electric Cut-Outs, Overload-Relays, Acceleration-Relays, Limit-Switches, Master-Switches, Automatic Compensators, Alternating-Current Relays, Starting-Switches, Push-Button Switches, Compensator Protective Panels, and Spare Parts for the Above-Named Electrical Apparatus.
Claims use on all the articles down to and including "cut-outs" from July or August, 1908; on overload-relays from July, 1915; on limit-switches from August, 1915; on acceleration-relays from June, 1916; on automatic compensators and master-switches from February, 1918; on compensator protective panels from February, 1919; on alternating-current relays from August, 1919, and on starting-switches and push-button switches from September, 1919.

Ser. No. 123,634. (CLASS 46. FOODS AND INGREDIENTS OF FOODS.) Grand Union Tea Co., Brooklyn, N. Y. Filed Oct. 10, 1919.

Particular description of goods.—Straight Spaghetti and Straight and Elbow Macaroni.
Claims use since about Apr. 2, 1919.

Ser. No. 123,642. (CLASS 46. FOODS AND INGREDIENTS OF FOODS.) The Hale Company, San Francisco, Calif. Filed Oct. 10, 1919.

MIRAFLORES

Particular description of goods.—Canned Fruits—Namely, Canned Peaches and Canned Apricots; Canned Vegetables—Namely, Canned Tomatoes and Canned String-Beans; Canned Fish—Namely, Canned Salmon and Canned Sardines.
Claims use since Aug. 30, 1919.

Ser. No. 123,714. (CLASS 50. MERCHANDISE NOT OTHERWISE CLASSIFIED.) Emile Reizenstein, Waltham, Mass. Filed Oct. 11, 1919.

MODELINE

Particular description of goods.—Plastic Composition for Modeling.
Claims use since June, 1909.

Ser. No. 123,724. (CLASS 26. MEASURING AND SCIENTIFIC APPLIANCES.) American Optical Company, Southbridge, Mass. Filed Oct. 13, 1919.

CRUXITE

Particular description of goods.—Ophthalmic Lenses. *Claims use* Oct. 1, 1919.

Ser. No. 123,755. (CLASS 2. RECEPTACLES.) Riverside Boiler Works, Inc., Cambridgeport, Mass. Filed Oct. 13, 1919.

Particular description of goods.—Tanks and Tanks for Hot Water, Commonly Known as Stand or Range Boilers.
Claims use since Sept. 24, 1919.

Ser. No. 123,756. (CLASS 2. RECEPTACLES.) RIVER-
SIDE BOILER WORKS, INC., Cambridgeport, Mass. Filed
Oct. 13, 1919.

Particular description of goods.—Tanks and Tanks for
Hot Water, Commonly Known as Stand or Range Boilers.
Claims use since Sept. 24, 1919.

Ser. No. 123,796. (CLASS 45. BEVERAGES, NON-
ALCOHOLIC.) EDWARD DIEHL, Nashville, Tenn. Filed
Oct. 15, 1919.

CHERRY CRASH

Particular description of goods.—Non-Alcoholic Non-
Cereal Maltless Beverage Sold as a Soft Drink and Syrup
for Making the Same.
Claims use since Jan. 1. 1919.

Ser. No. 123,923. (CLASS 36. MUSICAL INSTRU-
MENTS AND SUPPLIES.) THOMAS H. DE PEW, Canton,
Ohio. Filed Oct. 18, 1919.

Particular description of goods.—Phonographs and
Records.
Claims use since about Sept. 25, 1919.

Ser. No. 123,944. (CLASS 46. FOODS AND INGREDI-
ENTS OF FOODS.) SHUTTER-JOHNSON CANDY CO.,
Chicago, Ill. Filed Oct. 18, 1919.

Particular description of goods.—Candy.
Claims use since June 1, 1919.

Ser. No. 123,961. (CLASS 45. BEVERAGES, NON-
ALCOHOLIC.) CELRO-KOLA CO., Portland, Oreg. Filed
Oct. 20, 1919.

RUM-ONA

Particular description of goods.—Non-Alcoholic Non-
Intoxicating Maltless Non-Cereal Beverage Sold as a Soft
Drink.
Claims use since Feb. 17, 1919.

Ser. No. 123,986. (CLASS 45. BEVERAGES, NON-
ALCOHOLIC.) JOSEPH KRIEG-FINK CO., INC., Jersey
City, N. J. Filed Oct. 20, 1919.

Particular description of goods.—Non-Intoxicating
Maltless Non-Cereal Beverage Containing Less Than One-
Half of One Per Cent. Alcohol, Sold as a Soft Drink.
Claims use since Dec. 28, 1918.

Ser. No. 124,018. (CLASS 45. BEVERAGES, NON-
ALCOHOLIC.) RICHARD M. SCHLESINGER, New Athens.
Ill. Filed Oct. 20, 1919.

Particular description of goods.—Ginger-Ale.
Claims use since July 5, 1919.

Ser. No. 124,067. (CLASS 38. PRINTS AND PUBLICA-
TIONS.) FRED W. BROWN, Columbus, Ohio. Filed
Oct. 22, 1919.

Security In Oil

Particular description of goods.—A Monthly Publication
Distributed for Advertising Purposes.
Claims use since Oct. 10, 1919.

Ser. No. 124,147. (CLASS 2. RECEPTACLES.) THE
NATIONAL GRAVE VAULT COMPANY, Galion, Ohio. Filed
Oct. 24, 1919.

QUBD

Particular description of goods.—Grave-Vaults.
Claims use since Dec. 1, 1918.

Ser. No. 124,148. (CLASS 46. FOODS AND INGREDI-
ENTS OF FOODS.) NATIONAL BISCUIT COMPANY,
Jersey City, N. J., and New York, N. Y. Filed Oct.
24, 1919.

SALTINA

Particular description of goods.—Biscuit.
Claims use since as early as Oct. 20, 1919.

Ser. No. 124,324. (CLASS 4. ABRASIVE, DETERGENT, AND POLISHING MATERIALS.) THE WASHER MAID COMPANY, Chicago, Ill. Filed Oct. 29, 1919.

Washer Maid

Particular description of goods.—Soap.
Claims use since Aug. 15, 1919.

Ser. No. 124,336. (CLASS 36. MUSICAL INSTRUMENTS AND SUPPLIES.) EMERSON PHONOGRAPH COMPANY, INC., New York, N. Y. Filed Oct. 30, 1919.

Particular description of goods.—Phonograph-Records.
Claims use since May, 1918.

Ser. No. 124,351. (CLASS 38. PRINTS AND PUBLICATIONS.) LOS ANGELES EXAMINER, Los Angeles, Calif. Filed Oct. 30, 1919.

Prudence Penny

Particular description of goods.—Newspaper-Sections.
Claims use since about Feb. 1, 1919.

Ser. No. 124,380. (CLASS 4. ABRASIVE, DETERGENT, AND POLISHING MATERIALS.) THE AGRA COMPANY, Detroit, Mich. Filed Oct. 31, 1919.

Particular description of goods.—Soaps.
Claims use since July 1, 1918.

Ser. No. 124,400. (CLASS 46. FOODS AND INGREDIENTS OF FOODS.) THE HENSCH FOOD COMPANY, Cleveland, Ohio. Filed Oct. 31, 1919. Under ten-year proviso.

HENSCH'S FOOD

Particular description of goods.—Foods for Infants, Invalids, and Convalescents.
Claims use since January, 1865.

Ser. No. 124,469. (CLASS 38. PRINTS AND PUBLICATIONS.) E. J. CLODE, New York, N. Y. Filed Nov. 3, 1919.

HOW TO

No claim is made to the word " Series" apart from the mark shown in the drawing.
Particular description of goods.—Printed Books Published in Series.
Claims use since July, 1919.

Ser. No. 124,593. (CLASS 45. BEVERAGES, NON-ALCOHOLIC.) CALIFORNIA WINE ASSOCIATION, San Francisco, Calif. Filed Nov. 6, 1919.

CALWA

Particular description of goods.—Grape-Juice.
Claims use since Jan. 1, 1916.

Ser. No. 124,595. (CLASS 37. PAPER AND STATIONERY.) JOSEPH DIXON CRUCIBLE COMPANY, Jersey City, N. J. Filed Nov. 6, 1919. Under ten-year proviso.

TICONDEROGA

Particular description of goods.—Pencils.
Claims use since the year 1873.

Ser. No. 124,627. (CLASS 45. BEVERAGES, NON-ALCOHOLIC.) SOUTHWESTERN COCA-COLA BOTTLING Co., Deming, N. Mex. Filed Nov. 6, 1919.

Particular description of goods.—Ginger-Ale.
Claims use since Oct. 5, 1919.

Ser. No. 124,629. (CLASS 36. MUSICAL INSTRUMENTS AND SUPPLIES.) STORY & CLARK PIANO COMPANY, Chicago, Ill. Filed Nov. 6, 1919. Under ten-year proviso.

HAMPTON

Particular description of goods.—Pianos, Piano-Players, and Organs.
Claims use since 1885.

Ser. No. 124,630. (CLASS 36. MUSICAL INSTRUMENTS AND SUPPLIES.) STORY AND CLARK PIANO COMPANY, Chicago, Ill. Filed Nov. 6, 1919. Under ten-year proviso.

STORY & CLARK

Particular description of goods.—Pianos, Piano-Players, and Organs.
Claims use since 1885.

Ser. No. 124,651. (CLASS 37. PAPER AND STATIONERY.) THE ALBERT JACOBS COMPANY, New York, N. Y. Filed Nov. 7, 1919.

Tab-O-Randum

Particular description of goods.—Job and Delivery Tags.
Claims use since May 15, 1919.

TRADE-MARK REGISTRATIONS GRANTED

JANUARY 6, 1920.

128,274. REMEDY FOR PROMOTING FERTILITY OF LIVE STOCK, ESPECIALLY FOR CATTLE. ABORNO LABORATORY, Lancaster, Wis.
Filed June 25, 1919. Serial No. 119,928. PUBLISHED SEPTEMBER 23, 1919.

128,275. WRITING AND PRINTING PAPER AND WRITING-TABLETS. ADAMS, CUSHING & FOSTER, INC., Boston, Mass.
Filed June 1, 1918. Serial No. 111,291. PUBLISHED AUGUST 19, 1919.

128,276. THRESHING MACHINES AND GRAIN-SEPA- RATORS. ADVANCE-RUMELY COMPANY, Laporte, Ind.
Filed April 27, 1918. Serial No. 110,460. PUBLISHED SEPTEMBER 30, 1919.

128,277. REFRIGERATORS. THE ALASKA REFRIGER- ATOR COMPANY, Muskegon Heights, Mich.
Filed February 1, 1919. Serial No. 115,562. PUB- LISHED JULY 29, 1919.

128,278. DYES FOR LEATHER GOODS. ALBANY SHOE REPAIRING COMPANY, Boston, Mass.
Filed August 6, 1919. Serial No. 121,290. PUBLISHED OCTOBER 7, 1919.

128,279 TRACTORS. ALBAUGH-DOVER CO., Chicago, Ill., assignor to Square Turn Tractor Co., Norfolk, Nebr., a Corporation of Delaware.
Filed June 20, 1917. Serial No. 104,538. PUBLISHED AUGUST 26, 1919.

128,280. MEDICINE FOR COLDS, CROUP, PNEUMO- NIA, AND THROAT AFFECTIONS. ALEXANDER DRUG CO., Oklahoma, Okla.
Filed April 25, 1919. Serial No. 117,828. PUBLISHED OCTOBER 7, 1919.

128,281. MOTOR-TRUCKS. JOSEPH W. ALLAN, New York, N. Y.
Filed October 10, 1918. Serial No. 113,639. PUBLISHED SEPTEMBER 23, 1919

128,282. PRINTING AND WRITING PAPER. THE AL- LING & CORY COMPANY, Rochester and Buffalo, N. Y., and Pittsburgh, Pa.
Filed March 19, 1919. Serial No. 116,697. PUBLISHED AUGUST 26, 1919.

128,283. PRINTING AND WRITING PAPER. AMERICAN WRITING PAPER CO., Holyoke, Mass.
Filed April 10, 1919. Serial No. 117,311. PUBLISHED JULY 29, 1919.

128,284. CIGARETTES. THE AMERICAN TOBACCO COM- PANY, New York, N. Y.
Filed June 10, 1919. Serial No. 119,378. PUBLISHED OCTOBER 7, 1919.

128,285. CERTAIN NAMED FOODS. AMERICAN TRAD- ING CO. OF THE PACIFIC COAST, San Francisco, Calif.
Filed May 19, 1919. Serial No. 118,641. PUBLISHED SEPTEMBER 16, 1919.

128,286. PRINTING AND WRITING PAPER. AMERICAN WRITING PAPER COMPANY, Holyoke, Mass.
Filed April 15, 1919. Serial No. 117,475. PUBLISHED JULY 29, 1919.

128,287. WRAPPING AND LINING PAPER. ANGIER MECHANICAL LABORATORIES, Framingham, Mass.
Filed April 22, 1919. Serial No. 117,721. PUBLISHED JULY 29, 1919.

128,288. PREPARATION FOR BEAUTIFYING THE HANDS, ARMS, AND NECK. BENJAMIN ANSEHL, St. Louis, Mo.
Fi'ed May 24, 1919. Serial No. 118,869. PUBLISHED SEPTEMBER 16, 1919.

128,289. CERTAIN NAMED NON-ALCOHOLIC BEVER- AGES. ARCADIAN WAUKESHA SPRING COMPANY, Wau- kesha. Wis.
Filed June 16, 1919. Serial No. 119,622. PUBLISHED SEPTEMBER 16, 1919.

128,290. BOTTLE AND PRESCRIPTION CORKS OF ALL KINDS. ARMSTRONG CORK COMPANY, Pittsburgh, Pa.
Filed July 3, 1919. Serial No. 120,274. PUBLISHED SEPTEMBER 23, 1919.

128,291 HAIR-TONIC, SCALP-STIMULANT, AND DAN- DRUFF-PREVENTIVE. THE ATLANTA BARBERS' SUP- PLY Co., Atlanta, Ga.
Filed August 19, 1918. Serial No. 112,792. PUBLISHED OCTOBER 7, 1919.

128,292. HAIR-TONIC, SCALP-STIMULANT, AND DAN- DRUFF-PREVENTIVE. THE ATLANTA BARBERS' SUP- PLY Co , Atlanta, Ga.
Filed August 23, 1918. Serial No. 112,844. PUBLISHED OCTOBER 7, 1919.

128,293. PAPER BAGS. ATLANTA PAPER COMPANY, At- lanta, Ga.
Filed December 4, 1917. Serial No. 107,743. PUB- LISHED OCTOBER 7. 1919.

128,294. PAPER BAGS ATLANTA PAPER COMPANY, At- lanta, Ga.
Filed December 4, 1917. Serial No. 107,744. PUB- LISHED OCTOBER 7, 1919

128,295. CERTAIN NAMED ADHESIVES. AUTOMOTIVE SUPPLY COMPANY, Dallas. Tex.
Filed May 12, 1919. Serial No. 118,363. PUBLISHED AUGUST 26, 1919.

128,296 TEMPORARY LETTER-FILES AND LOOSE- LEAF BINDERS AND SHEET-HOLDING ATTACH- MENTS THEREFOR. WILLIAM M. AYDELOTTE, New York, N. Y.
Filed April 24, 1919. Serial No. 117,792. PUBLISHED JULY 29, 1919.

128,297. AUTOMOBILES — NAMELY, ELECTRIC PAS- SENGER-VEHICLES. THE BAKER R. & L. COMPANY, Cleveland, Ohio.
Filed June 21, 1919. Serial No. 119,820. PUBLISHED SEPTEMBER 23, 1919.

128,298. EMBROIDERING-MACHINES. ABRAHAM BA- LINKY, New York, N. Y
Filed May 28, 1919. Serial No. 118,981. PUBLISHED SEPTEMBER 16, 1919.

128,299. SAFETY-PAPER. THE BANKERS SUPPLY Co., Denver, Colo., and Chicago, Ill.
Filed April 7, 1919. Serial No. 117,214. PUBLISHED AUGUST 19, 1919.

128,300. SAFETY-PAPER. THE BANKERS SUPPLY Co., Denver, Colo., and Chicago, Ill.
Filed April 7, 1919. Serial No. 117,215. PUBLISHED AUGUST 19, 1919.

128,301. TOY-WATCH DIALS AND CASES. ALEXANDER BARON, Brooklyn, N. Y.
Filed March 29, 1919. Serial No. 117,002. PUBLISHED OCTOBER 7, 1919.

128,302. COCOA AND CHOCOLATE. Stephen L. Bartlett Company, Boston, Mass.
Filed May 24, 1919. Serial No. 118,871. PUBLISHED SEPTEMBER 23, 1919.

128,303. CERTAIN NAMED FOODS. The Basket Stores Co., Omaha, Nebr.
Filed January 18, 1919. Serial No. 115,277. PUBLISHED SEPTEMBER 16, 1919.

128,304. CERTAIN NAMED FOODS. The Basket Stores Co., Omaha, Nebr.
Filed January 18, 1919. Serial No. 115,279. PUBLISHED SEPTEMBER 16, 1919.

128,305. COFFEE. Basket Stores Company, Omaha, Nebr.
Filed June 10, 1919. Serial No. 119,387. PUBLISHED AUGUST 19, 1919.

128,306. PRESS-BOARDS. Rubin Bass, New York, N. Y.
Filed January 12, 1918. Serial No. 108,425. PUBLISHED OCTOBER 7, 1919.

128,307. SPHYGMOMANOMETERS. W. A. Baum Co. Inc., New York, N. Y.
Filed May 27, 1919. Serial No. 118,955. PUBLISHED JULY 15, 1919.

128,308. CERTAIN NAMED NON-ALCOHOLIC BEVERAGES. William J. Benekos, Chicago, Ill.
Filed June 4, 1919. Serial No. 119,182. PUBLISHED SEPTEMBER 16, 1919.

128,309. CANDIES. Bitrose Co., Milwaukee, Wis.
Filed May 14, 1919. Serial No. 118,457. PUBLISHED AUGUST 19, 1919.

128,310. PAPER FOR WRITING, ENVELOPS FOR CORRESPONDENCE, AND WRITING-TABLETS. J. C. Blair Company, Huntingdon, Pa.
Filed December 3, 1918. Serial No. 114,460. PUBLISHED JULY 22, 1919.

128,311. PAPER FOR WRITING AND PRINTING PURPOSES, ENVELOPS. WRITING-TABLETS, AND BLANK BOOKS. J. C. Blair Company, Huntingdon, Pa.
Filed February 26, 1919. Serial No. 116,143. PUBLISHED AUGUST 5, 1919.

128,312. NON-ALCOHOLIC MALTLESS BEVERAGES AND FLAVORINGS AND SYRUPS FOR MAKING THE SAME. Bludwine Company, Athens, Ga.
Filed November 6, 1918. Serial No. 114,062. PUBLISHED OCTOBER 14, 1919.

128,313. CONDENSED MILK. Borden's Condensed Milk Company, New York, N. Y.
Filed June 2, 1919. Serial No. 119,107. PUBLISHED SEPTEMBER 16, 1919.

128,314. BLOOD-PURIFIER. Cutnore Britton, Tampa, Fla.
Filed May 24, 1918. Serial No. 111,167. PUBLISHED SEPTEMBER 30, 1919.

128,315. OINTMENT FOR EXTERNAL USE FOR SKIN DISEASE. The Blemo Company, Canton, Ohio.
Filed June 19, 1919. Serial No 119,761. PUBLISHED AUGUST 19, 1919.

128,316. CERTAIN NAMED FOODS. D. E. Brooks & Co., Newburgh, N. Y.
Filed December 31, 1918. Serial No. 114,896. PUBLISHED AUGUST 19, 1919.

128,317. FOUNTAIN-PENS. Salz Brothers, New York, N. Y.
Filed May 29, 1919. Serial No. 119,051. PUBLISHED AUGUST 26, 1919.

128,318. CERTAIN NAMED PAPER AND STATIONERY. L. L. Brown Paper Company, Adams, Mass.
Filed May 15, 1919. Serial No. 118,504. PUBLISHED AUGUST 26, 1919.

128,319. TEA. George C. Buell & Company, Rochester, N. Y.
Filed June 16, 1919. Serial No. 119,625. PUBLISHED SEPTEMBER 9, 1919.

128,320. LAUNDRY SOAP. Wilbur S. Burns, Grand Rapids, Mich.
Filed March 2, 1918. Serial No. 109,313. PUBLISHED OCTOBER 7, 1919.

128,321. INCENSE. Frederick De Voe Burton, New York, N. Y.
Filed August 5, 1919. Serial No. 121,272. PUBLISHED OCTOBER 7, 1919.

128,322. BREAD. Cable Draper Baking Co., Detroit, Mich.
Filed March 8, 1919. Serial No. 116,407. PUBLISHED AUGUST 19, 1919.

128,323. MEDICATED OIL USED AS A SPRAY. The Car-Bo-Thymol Company, Atlanta, Ga.
Filed June 17, 1919. Serial No. 119,699. PUBLISHED AUGUST 19, 1919.

128,324. SARDINES. Castine Bay Company, Castine, Me.
Filed May 29, 1919. Serial No. 119,026. PUBLISHED SEPTEMBER 23, 1919.

128,325. CERTAIN NAMED MACHINES AND PARTS THEREOF. Cement-Gun Company, Inc., Allentown, Pa., and New York, N. Y.
Filed November 8, 1917. Serial No. 107,224. PUBLISHED SEPTEMBER 16, 1919.

128,326. MIXED LIVE-STOCK FEED. Chapin & Company, Hammond, Ind., and Chicago, Ill.
Filed January 22, 1919. Serial No. 115,371. PUBLISHED OCTOBER 14, 1919.

128,327. DAIRY AND STOCK FEED. Chapin & Company, Hammond, Ind., and Chicago, Ill.
Filed January 22, 1919. Serial No. 115,373. PUBLISHED OCTOBER 14, 1919.

128,328. CERTAIN NON-ALCOHOLIC NON-CEREAL MALTLESS BEVERAGE FLAVORED WITH MINT. Ivan C. Chaplin, Indianapolis, Ind.
Filed July 7, 1919. Serial No. 120,302. PUBLISHED OCTOBER 14, 1919.

128,329. SOLDERING KITS CONSISTING OF BOXES CONTAINING TOOLS AND SUPPLIES FOR SOLDERING-WORK. Frank Chapman, Providence, R. I.
Filed April 19, 1917. Serial No. 103,103. PUBLISHED SEPTEMBER 30, 1919.

128,330. MEDICINAL PREPARATIONS FOR THE DIGESTIVE ORGANS OF HUMAN BEINGS AND ANIMALS. Chemische Werke vorm. Dr. Heinrich Byk, Oranienburg, near Berlin, Germany.
Filed December 8, 1916. Serial No. 99,787. PUBLISHED SEPTEMBER 30, 1919.

128,331. HOSIERY. Chipman Knitting Mills, Easton, Pa.
Filed December 24, 1917. Serial No. 108,119. PUBLISHED OCTOBER 7, 1919.

128,332. WIRE BRUSHES AND BRUSHES MADE FROM WIRE FOR MOUNTING UPON SHAFTING. The Cleveland Osborn Manufacturing Company, Cleveland, Ohio.
Filed May 22, 1918. Serial No. 111,094. PUBLISHED OCTOBER 7, 1919.

128,333. AUTOMOBILE AND BICYCLE PUMPS. Corstapley Manufacturing Corporation, Bridgeport, Conn.
Filed May 17, 1919. Serial No. 118,590. PUBLISHED AUGUST 19, 1919.

128,334. CERTAIN NAMED PAPER AND STATIONERY. A. M. Collins Manufacturing Company, Philadelphia, Pa.
Filed February 26, 1919. Serial No. 116,144. PUBLISHED JULY 22, 1919.

128,335. TWINE COMPOSED OF A MIXTURE OF HEMP AND JUTE. Columbian Rope Company, Auburn, N. Y.
Filed November 2, 1918. Serial No. 114,024. PUBLISHED OCTOBER 7, 1919.

128,336. CERTAIN NAMED RECEPTACLES AND PARTS THEREOF. COLWELL COOPERAGE COMPANY, INC., New York, N. Y.
Filed April 11, 1919. Serial No. 117,371. PUBLISHED OCTOBER 7, 1919.

128,337. CERTAIN NAMED RECPTACLES AND PARTS THEREÓF. COLWELL COOPERAGE COMPANY, INC., New York, N. Y.
Filed April 11, 1919. Serial No. 117,372. PUBLISHED OCTOBER 7, 1919.

128,338. COTTON AND SILK PIECE GOODS COMMERCIAL SHIRT COMPANY, New York, N. Y.
Filed December 19, 1917. Serial No. 108,052. PUBLISHED SEPTEMBER 16, 1919.

128,339. CREOSOTE-OIL USED AS A WOOD-PRESERVATIVE. C. R. COOK PAINT COMPANY, Kansas City, Mo.
Filed July 28, 1917. Serial No. 105,339. PUBLISHED SEPTEMBER 16, 1919.

128,340. ICE-CREAM CONES. G. G. CORNWELL & SON, INC., Washington, D. C.
Filed June 10, 1919. Serial No. 119,407. PUBLISHED AUGUST 19, 1919.

128,341. CERTAIN NAMED FOODS. JOHN P. CRAMER, Freeport, Ill.
Filed June 2, 1913. Serial No. 70,824. PUBLISHED AUGUST 19, 1919.

128,342. WRITING-PAPER. CRANE & CO., Dalton and Westfield, Mass.
Filed April 4, 1919. Serial No. 117,149. PUBLISHED JULY 29, 1919.

128,343. COFFEE. CRESCENT COFFEE MILLS, INC., New Orleans, La.
Filed July 1, 1919. Serial No. 120,155. PUBLISHED SEPTEMBER 23, 1919.

128,344. CUTTING-OILS. CRESCENT OIL COMPANY, Indianapolis, Ind.
Filed May 21, 1919. Serial No. 118,752. PUBLISHED SEPTEMBER 23, 1919.

128,345. FIRE-BRICKS AND TILE MANUFACTURED FROM FIRE-CLAY FOR METALLURGICAL FURNACES. CRESCENT REFRACTORIES COMPANY, Curwensville, Pa.
Filed October 3, 1918. Serial No. 113,556. PUBLISHED SEPTEMBER 23, 1919.

128,346. BROOMS. CROCKER BROOM & BRUSH CO., Chicago, Ill.
Filed May 19, 1919. Serial No. 118,654. PUBLISHED OCTOBER 7, 1919.

128,347. BROOMS. CROCKER BROOM & BRUSH CO, Chicago, Ill.
Filed May 19, 1919. Serial No. 118,655. PUBLISHED OCTOBER 7, 1919.

128,348. BROOMS. CROCKER BROOM & BRUSH CO., Chicago, Ill.
Filed May 19, 1919. Serial No. 118,657. PUBLISHED OCTOBER 7, 1919.

128,349. BROOMS. CROCKER BROOM & BRUSH CO., Chicago, Ill.
Filed May 19, 1919. Serial No. 118,658. PUBLISHED OCTOBER 7, 1919.

128,350. CERTAIN NAMED DETERGENT, ABRASIVE, AND POLISHING MATERIALS. ABE CROOKS, Toledo, Ohio.
Filed March 28, 1919. Serial No. 116,987. PUBLISHED AUGUST 26, 1919.

128,351. OVERALLS. THE CROWN OVERALL MANUFACTURING COMPANY, Cincinnati, Ohio.
Filed May 23, 1919. Serial No. 118,827. PUBLISHED SEPTEMBER 23, 1919.

128,352. CHOCOLATE SYRUP MADE FROM COCOA AND CANE-SUGAR FOR FLAVORING SOFT DRINKS. WM. CRUGER CUSHMAN, New York, N. Y.
Filed March 8, 1919. Serial No. 116,408. PUBLISHED MAY 13, 1919.

128,353. CERTAIN NAMED BAGS. JOHN CURTIN CORP., New York, N. Y.
Filed June 13, 1919. Serial No. 119,551. PUBLISHED SEPTEMBER 16, 1919.

128,354. COMPOUND ANHYDROUS SALTS. DARWIN & MILNER, INC., New York, N. Y.
Filed June 7, 1919. Serial No. 119,294. PUBLISHED AUGUST 19, 1919.

128,355. CERTAIN NAMED FOODS. THE WILLIAM DAVIES COMPANY, LIMITED, Chicago, Ill.
Filed December 7, 1918. Serial No. 114,533. PUBLISHED SEPTEMBER 16, 1919.

128,356. SHIPPING TAGS. THE DENNEY TAG COMPANY, West Chester, Pa.
Filed March 11, 1919. Serial No. 116,458. PUBLISHED JULY 22, 1919.

128,357. SHIPPING-TAGS. THE DENNEY TAG COMPANY, West Chester, Pa.
Filed March 13, 1919. Serial No. 116,534. PUBLISHED JULY 29, 1919.

128,358. SHIPPING-TAGS. THE DENNEY TAG COMPANY, West Chester, Pa.
Filed March 14, 1919. Serial No. 116,564. PUBLISHED JULY 29, 1919.

128,359. SHIPPING-TAGS. THE DENNEY TAG COMPANY, West Chester, Pa.
Filed March 17, 1919. Serial No. 116,648. PUBLISHED JULY 29, 1919.

128,360. SHIPPING-TAGS. THE DENNEY TAG COMPANY, West Chester, Pa.
Filed March 17, 1919. Serial No. 116,649. PUBLISHED JULY 29, 1919.

128,361. REFINED AND UNREFINED FATS AND FATS FOR FUEL, ILLUMINATING, AND LUBRICATING PURPOSES. DE NORDISKE FABRIKER DE-NO-FA AKTIESELSKAB, Christiania, Norway.
Filed March 20. 1917. Serial No. 102,285. PUBLISHED SEPTEMBER 30, 1919.

128,362. CIGARETTES. GEORGE M. DERY, South Bethlehem, Pa.
Filed January 2, 1919. Serial No. 114,948. PUBLISHED SEPTEMBER 16, 1919.

128,363. GLOVES AND MITTENS MADE OF HORSE-HIDE. DES MOINES GLOVE & MFG. COMPANY, INC., Des Moines, Iowa.
Filed June 16, 1919. Serial No. 119,645. PUBLISHED OCTOBER 7, 919.

128,364. WEIGHING-SCALES. DETROIT AUTOMATIC SCALE COMPANY, Detroit, Mich.
Filed January 4, 1919. Serial No. 114,987. PUBLISHED APRIL 15, 1919.

128,365. CERTAIN NAMED NON-ALCOHOLIC BEVERAGES. THE DIEBOLT BREWING CO., Cleveland, Ohio.
Filed July 1, 1919. Serial No. 120,160. PUBLISHED SEPTEMBER 16, 1919.

128,366. CORN AND CANE SYRUP COMBINED AND INTENDED FOR TABLE PURPOSES. DOTHAN SYRUP CO., Dothan, Ala.
Filed March 29, 1919. Serial No. 117,007. PUBLISHED JULY 22, 1919.

128,367. FELT POLISHING-WHEELS. EASTERN FELT COMPANY, Winchester, Mass.
Filed May 6, 1919. Serial No. 118,205. PUBLISHED AUGUST 26, 1919.

128,368. ADJUSTABLE CAMERA - SUPPORTING CLAMPS AND TRIPOD-ADAPTERS. EASTMAN KODAK COMPANY, Rochester, N. Y.
Filed May 8, 1919. Serial No. 118,260. PUBLISHED SEPTEMBER 2, 1919.

128,369. OLEOMARGARIN. ECKERSON COMPANY, Jersey City, N. J.
Filed May 5, 1919. Serial No. 118,140. PUBLISHED AUGUST 26, 1919.

128,370. GAS, COAL, AND OIL STOVES OR OVENS. ELGIN STOVE & OVEN CO., Elgin, Ill.
Filed May 16, 1919. Serial No. 118,545. PUBLISHED SEPTEMBER 23, 1919.

128,371. EMBALMING FLUID. THE EMBALMERS' SUPPLY CO., Westport, Conn.
Filed June 21, 1919. Serial No. 119,826. PUBLISHED AUGUST 19, 1919.

128,372. SAD-IRONS, LAUNDRY-WASHING MACHINES, AND CLOTHES-WRINGERS. WM. ENDERS MANUFACTURING COMPANY, Walden, N. Y.
Filed April 15, 1919. Serial No. 117,482. PUBLISHED JULY 22, 1919.

128,373. CERTAIN NAMED PAPER. ESLEECK MANUFACTURING COMPANY, Turners Falls, Mass.
Filed April 12, 1919. Serial No. 117,399. PUBLISHED AUGUST 19, 1919.

128,374. ELASTIC BANDAGES FOR PERSONAL WEAR. EVERLASTIK, INCORPORATED, Boston, Mass.
Filed April 23, 1918. Serial No. 110,392. PUBLISHED OCTOBER 7, 1919.

128,375. PREPARED FEED FOR STOCK. FARMERS COTTON OIL CO., Wilson, N. C.
Filed July 31, 1918. Serial No. 112,436. PUBLISHED OCTOBER 7, 1919.

128,376. WHEAT-FLOUR. FEDERAL MILLING COMPANY, Lockport, N. Y.
Filed June 21, 1919. Serial No. 119,827. PUBLISHED AUGUST 19, 1919.

128,377. CHOCOLATES, BONBONS, AND OTHER CANDY. FIDELITY CHOCOLATE COMPANY, Boston, Mass.
Filed June 28, 1919. Serial No. 120,050. PUBLISHED OCTOBER 7, 1919.

128,378. GUIDE-RULERS FOR SCHOLASTIC PURPOSES. THOMAS FINLAY, Auckland, New Zealand.
Filed November 10, 1916. Serial No. 99,211. PUBLISHED AUGUST 19, 1919.

128,379. CHEMICAL FIRE-EXTINGUISHING COMPOUND. FIRST AID EXTINGUISHER CO., New York, N. Y.
Filed June 12, 1918. Serial No. 111,516. PUBLISHED SEPTEMBER 30, 1919.

128,380. DOUGHNUTS. FLEISCHMANN'S VIENNA MODEL BAKERY, (INC.,) New York, N. Y.
Filed April 17, 1919. Serial No. 117,563. PUBLISHED AUGUST 19, 1919.

128,381. CERTAIN NAMED FOOD PRODUCTS. FLEITMANN, WATJEN & CO., INC., New York, N. Y.
Filed June 14, 1919. Serial No. 119,599. PUBLISHED AUGUST 19, 1919.

128,382. FISHING-RODS AND FISHING-HOOKS. FOREST & STREAM PUBLISHING CO., INC., New York, N. Y.
Filed May 14, 1918. Serial No. 110,883. PUBLISHED OCTOBER 7, 1919.

128,383. POCKET-BOOKS. FREUND BROS. & COMPANY, INC., New York, N. Y.
Filed April 24, 1919. Serial No. 117,802. PUBLISHED JULY 15, 1919.

128,384. FRUIT-FLAVORED SUGAR CANDIES. GEO. H. FRITZ & SONS, INC., Newark, N. J.
Filed June 15, 1918. Serial No. 111,588. PUBLISHED SEPTEMBER 30, 1919.

128,385. IRONING-BOARDS. WILLIAM G. FULTON, Washington, D. C.
Filed April 8, 1919. Serial No. 117,273. PUBLISHED SEPTEMBER 30, 1919.

128,386. FOUNTAIN-PENS. GENERAL MANUFACTURING CO., Sioux City, Iowa.
Filed October 8, 1918. Serial No. 113,621. PUBLISHED JULY 22, 1919.

128,387. TRACTORS AND PARTS THEREOF. THE GENERAL ORDNANCE COMPANY, Derby, Conn.
Filed May 7, 1919. Serial No. 118,225. PUBLISHED AUGUST 26, 1919.

128,388. CUTLERY—NAMELY, RAZORS. GENEVA CUTLERY CORPORATION, Geneva, N. Y.
Filed October 17, 1918. Serial No. 113,764. PUBLISHED AUGUST 19, 1919.

128,389. CERTAIN NAMED GARMENTS FOR INFANTS AND CHILDREN. A. GILMAN & SON, New York, N. Y.
Filed September 27, 1918. Serial No. 113,448. PUBLISHED SEPTEMBER 16, 1919.

128,390. AUTOMOBILE CIRCULATING-PUMPS. BERT D. GILSON, Chicago, Ill.
Filed April 17, 1919. Serial No. 117,564. PUBLISHED SEPTEMBER 30, 1919.

128,391. DOLLS. CHARLES A. GOLDSMITH, New York, N. Y.
Filed March 8, 1919. Serial No. 116,412. PUBLISHED SEPTEMBER 30, 1919.

128,392. CANNED SARDINES. A. S. GOUVEA & CO., New York, N. Y.
Filed May 17, 1919. Serial No. 118,598. PUBLISHED SEPTEMBER 23, 1919.

128,393. LEATHER. W. R. GRACE & CO., New York. N. Y.
Filed June 5, 1919. Serial No. 119,236. PUBLISHED SEPTEMBER 23, 1919.

128,394. PRESERVED OR PREPARED CODFISH. GREAT EASTERN FISHERIES CORPORATION, Rockland, Me.
Filed May 28, 1919. Serial No. 118,990. PUBLISHED SEPTEMBER 30, 1919.

128,395. LIVE-STOCK FEEDS AND POULTRY FEEDS. THE GREAT WESTERN ALFALFA MILLING COMPANY, Denver, Colo.
Filed May 15, 1919. Serial No. 118,514. PUBLISHED SEPTEMBER 30, 1919.

128,396. LUBRICATING OILS AND GREASES. HAGEMEYER TRADING COMPANY, New York, N. Y.
Filed July 16, 1919. Serial No. 120,610. PUBLISHED SEPTEMBER 16, 1919.

128,397. ANTISEPTIC LOTION FOR USE AS A DEPILATORY. HANNIBAL PHARMACAL COMPANY, St. Louis, Mo.
Filed June 20, 1919. Serial No. 119,801. PUBLISHED AUGUST 19, 1919.

128,398. FOODS FOR HOGS, CATTLE, SHEEP, AND POULTRY. HANSEN LIVESTOCK & FEEDING COMPANY, Ogden, Utah.
Filed June 11, 1918. Serial No. 111,496. PUBLISHED OCTOBER 14, 1919.

128,399. BEE-ESCAPES. MATTHEW E. HASTINGS, New York Mills, N. Y.
Filed October 15, 1918. Serial No. 113,746. PUBLISHED SEPTEMBER 23, 1919.

128,400. GOITER PREPARATIONS. EDWARD R. HAYSSEN, Seneca Falls, N. Y.
Filed March 26, 1919. Serial No. 116,924. PUBLISHED SEPTEMBER 30, 1919.

128,401. ICE-CREAM, FROZEN CUSTARDS, AND ICES. THE HENDLER CREAMERY CO., Baltimore, Md.
Filed April 3, 1919. Serial No. 117,139. PUBLISHED AUGUST 19, 1919.

128,402. SALVE AND OINTMENT USED IN THE TREATMENT OF RECTAL TROUBLES. WILLIAM U. HERBERT, Washington, D. C.
Filed May 7, 1918. Serial No. 110,743. PUBLISHED AUGUST 7, 1919.

128,403. TOILET-PAPER, PAPER TOWELING. THE JOHN HOBERG CO., Green Bay, Wis.
Filed May 12, 1919. Serial No. 118,382. PUBLISHED AUGUST 26, 1919.

128,404. TOILET-PAPER, PAPER NAPKINS, PAPER TOWELING, AND WRAPPING-PAPER. THE JOHN HOBERG CO., Green Bay, Wis.
Filed May 12, 1919. Serial No. 118,383. PUBLISHED SEPTEMBER 9, 1919.

128,405. ALLOYS CONTAINING IRON AND CHROMIUM. HOSKINS MANUFACTURING COMPANY, Detroit, Mich.
Filed December 26, 1917. Serial No. 108,147. PUBLISHED AUGUST 26, 1919.

128,406. ALLOYS CONTAINING NICKEL AND MANGANESE. HOSKINS MANUFACTURING COMPANY, Detroit, Mich.
Filed December 26, 1917. Serial No. 108,149. PUBLISHED AUGUST 26, 1919.

128,407. CORE - DRILLS. INGERSOLL-RAND COMPANY, Jersey City, N. J., and New York, N. Y.
Filed August 1, 1919. Serial No. 121,176. PUBLISHED OCTOBER 7, 1919.

128,408. NICKEL AND ALLOYS CONTAINING NICKEL. THE INTERNATIONAL NICKEL CO., Constable Hook, N. J.
Filed June 6, 1919. Serial No. 119,270. PUBLISHED SEPTEMBER 16, 1919.

128,409. LADIES', MISSES', AND CHILDREN'S ONE-PIECE TEXTILE UNDERWEAR. ISRAEL UNDERWEAR CO., Worcester, Mass.
Filed April 28, 1919. Serial No. 117,936. PUBLISHED AUGUST 26, 1919.

128,410. CERTAIN NAMED FOODS. B. L. JOHNSON & Co., Knoxville, Tenn.
Filed April 22, 1918. Serial No. 110,375. PUBLISHED AUGUST 19, 1919.

128,411. PHARMACEUTICAL PREPARATION ENTITLED BLOOD-TEA. ROBERT KANE, Pittsburgh, Pa.
Filed April 24, 1919. Serial No. 117,807. PUBLISHED SEPTEMBER 23, 1919.

128,412. BOOTS AND SHOES OF LEATHER. WM. KAUT FOOTWEAR COMPANY, Carthage, Mo.
Filed June 16, 1919. Serial No. 119,655. PUBLISHED OCTOBER 7, 1919.

128,413. WHEAT-FLOUR. KEHIOR FIOUR MILLS Co., St. Louis, Mo.
Filed May 15, 1919. Serial No. 118,518. PUBLISHED AUGUST 26, 1919.

128,414. SHEEPSKIN, SKIVERS, ROANS, PATENT-LEATHER. CHARLES H. KEMPER, Westport, Conn.
Filed May 27, 1918. Serial No. 111,217. PUBLISHED SEPTEMBER 23, 1919.

128,415. MACARONI. KEYSTONE MACARONI COMPANY, Lebanon, Pa.
Filed February 14, 1919. Serial No. 115,859. PUBLISHED OCTOBER 7, 1919.

128,416. SANITARY NAPKINS OF TENUOUS AND FIBROUS AND ABSORBENT MATERIAL FOR COMMERCIAL AND HOSPITAL USE. KIMBERLY-CLARK COMPANY, Neenah, Wis.
Filed April 30, 1919. Serial No. 118,017. PUBLISHED AUGUST 19, 1919.

128,417. WALL-PAPER-CLEANER COMPOUNDS. THE KLENASEPTIC MANUFACTURING COMPANY, Columbus, Ohio.
Filed May 14, 1919. Serial No. 118,473. PUBLISHED OCTOBER 7, 1919.

128,418. WALL-PAPER-CLEANER COMPOUNDS. THE KLENASEPTIC MANUFACTURING COMPANY, Columbus, Ohio.
Filed May 14, 1919. Serial No. 118,474. PUBLISHED SEPTEMBER 30, 1919.

128,419. ASPIRIN. THE KLOR EARLY CO., INC., Bluefield, W. Va.
Filed August 7, 1919. Serial No. 121,348. PUBLISHED OCTOBER 7, 1919.

128,420. CULTURE OF BACILLUS BULGARICUS AND MILK FERMENTED WITH BACILLUS BULGARICUS. KNUDSEN LABORATORY, Los Angeles, Calif.
Filed May 26, 1919. Serial No. 118,919. PUBLISHED SEPTEMBER 16, 1919.

128,421. CERTAIN NAMED TOILET PREPARATIONS. LA DORA TOILET PREPARATIONS INC., New York, N. Y.
Filed July 11, 1919. Serial No. 120,463. PUBLISHED SEPTEMBER 23, 1919.

128,422. HOSIERY. FRANKLIN L. LANDENBERGER, Philadelphia, Pa.
Filed May 16, 1918. . Serial No. 110,928. PUBLISHED AUGUST 26, 1919.

128,423. YARNS. LANGERRE SALES CO., INC., New York, N. Y.
Filed June 9, 1919. Serial No. 119,349. PUBLISHED SEPTEMBER 23, 1919.

128,424. SMOKING - TOBACCO AND CHEWING - TOBACCO. LARUS & BROTHER COMPANY, Richmond, Va.
Filed June 13, 1919. Serial No. 119,562. PUBLISHED OCTOBER 7, 1919.

128,425. GARDEN-PLOWS. THE LEADER PLOW CO. INC., Staunton, Va.
Filed June 11, 1919. Serial No. 119,482. PUBLISHED SEPTEMBER 30, 1919.

128,426. TENNIS - RACKETS, GOLF - CLUBS, GOLF-BALLS, AND SKATES. HARRY C. LEE & Co., New York, N. Y.
Filed April 28, 1917. Serial No. 103,392. PUBLISHED OCTOBER 7, 1919.

128,427. GOLF-BALLS. HARRY C. LEE & COMPANY, New York, N. Y.
Filed July 12, 1919. Serial No. 120,492. PUBLISHED SEPTEMBER 16, 1919.

128,428. PREPARATIONS USED INTERNALLY AND EXTERNALLY IN TREATMENT OF CERTAIN NAMED DISEASES. Dr. EDMUND S. LEFLER, Hot Springs, Ark.
Filed May 22, 1919. Serial No. 118,788. PUBLISHED SEPTEMBER 16, 1919.

128,429. SOAP-DYES. LEVER BROTHERS COMPANY, Cambridge. Mass.
Filed June 16, 1919. Serial No. 119,858. PUBLISHED AUGUST 19, 1919.

128,430. CIGARETTES. LIGGETT & MYERS TOBACCO COMPANY, New York, N. Y.
Filed June 16, 1919. Serial No. 119,657. PUBLISHED OCTOBER 7, 1919.

128,431. FRESH FRUITS—NAMELY, ORANGES, BANANAS, PINEAPPLES, GRAPE-FRUIT, AND COCOANUTS. THOMAS P. LIPPITT, Washington, D. C., and San Juan, Porto Rico.
Filed November 16, 1917. Serial No. 107,410. PUBLISHED AUGUST 19, 1919.

128,432. SPECIAL BRANDS OF EMERY AND CORUNDUM IN POWDERED FORM USED FOR ABRASIVE AND POLISHING PURPOSES. LOCKHART CORUNDUM & LFNS CORPORATION, Southbridge, Mass.
Filed February 6, 1919. Serial No. 115,659. PUBLISHED AUGUST 26, 1919.

128,433. HANDKERCHIEFS. LOEB & SCHOENFELD COMPANY, Wilmington, Del.; Camden, N. J., and New York. N. Y.
Filed June 20, 1919 Serial No. 119,805. PUBLISHED AUGUST 26, 1919.

128,434. CANNED SARDINES. LUBEC SARDINE Co., Lubec. Me.
Filed May 19, 1919. Serial No. 118,679. PUBLISHED SEPTEMBER 16, 1919.

128,435. CERTAIN NAMED PETROLEUM PRODUCTS. LUBRITE REFINING COMPANY, St. Louis, Mo.
Filed April 14, 1919. Serial No. 117,462. PUBLISHED OCTOBER 7, 1919.

128,436. TALKING-MACHINE CABINETS. THE C. J. LUNDSTROM MFG. CO., Little Falls, N. Y. Filed May 22, 1918. Serial No. 111,086. PUBLISHED SEPTEMBER 16, 1919.

128,437. CLEANSER FOR REMOVING GREASE AND OTHER SPOTS FROM FABRICS. CHARLES MC-ADAM COMPANY, Chicago, Ill. Filed May 26, 1919. Serial No. 118,928. PUBLISHED SEPTEMBER 30, 1919.

128,438. GLOVE-BLEACH. CHARLES MCADAM COMPANY, Chicago, Ill. Filed May 31, 1919. Serial No. 119,077. PUBLISHED AUGUST 19, 1919.

128,439. HAIR-TONIC. BENJAMIN W. MCNEIL, New York, N. Y. Filed March 18, 1919. Serial No. 116,690. PUBLISHED SEPTEMBER 30, 1919.

128,440. PANTS AND OVERALLS. MACON WOOLEN MILLS, Macon, Ga. Filed November 12, 1917. Serial No. 107,326. PUBLISHED JULY 8, 1919.

128,441. PANTS AND OVERALLS. MACON WOOLEN MILLS, Macon, Ga. Filed November 12, 1917. Serial No. 107,327. PUBLISHED OCTOBER 7, 1919.

128,442. SOLES MADE OF ARTIFICIAL LEATHER. MADELETHER COMPANY, Saugus, Mass. Filed January 22, 1917. Serial No. 100,808. PUBLISHED AUGUST 26, 1919.

128,443. WRITING-PAPER, PRINTING-PAPER, NOTE-PAPER, AND ENVELOPS FOR HOLDING CORRESPONDENCE. THE MAJESTIC MILLS PAPER COMPANY INC., New York, N. Y. Filed November 9, 1918. Serial No. 114,117. PUBLISHED JULY 22, 1919.

128,444. PREPARATION FOR CONSUMPTION. JOSEPH MAJOR, Detroit, Mich. Filed July 31, 1919. Serial No. 121,152. PUBLISHED OCTOBER 7, 1919.

128,445. NERVE MEDICINE. JOSEPH MAJOR, Detroit, Mich. Filed July 31, 1919. Serial No. 121,153. PUBLISHED OCTOBER 7, 1919.

128,446. LEATHER, CANVAS, AND FABRIC SHOES. H. MALKIN'S SONS, Brooklyn, N. Y. Filed May 29, 1919. Serial No. 119,039. PUBLISHED AUGUST 26, 1919.

128,447. CANDIES. MAPLE GROVE CANDIES, St. Johnsbury, Vt. Filed June 5, 1919. Serial No. 119,241. PUBLISHED SEPTEMBER 9, 1919.

128,448. CANNED SALMON. MARATHON FISHING & PACKING CO., Seattle, Wash. Filed June 10, 1919. Serial No. 119,421. PUBLISHED AUGUST 19, 1919.

128,449. SPECTACLES, SPECTACLE - FRAMES, AND MOUNTINGS FOR EYEGLASSES. MARTIN - COPELAND COMPANY, Providence, R. I. Filed May 19, 1919. Serial No. 118,685. PUBLISHED AUGUST 26, 1919.

128,450. CONTAINERS FOR TOILET ARTICLES— NAMELY, KIT - BAGS, AND TRAVELING - CASES MADE OF FABRIC OR LEATHER. MAX J. MARYMONT, New York, N. Y. Filed December 9, 1918. Serial No. 114,567. PUBLISHED OCTOBER 7, 1919.

128,451. CANDIES AND CHOCOLATE. MASON, AU & MAGENHEIMER CONF. MFG. CO., Brooklyn, N. Y. Filed February 19, 1919. Serial No. 115,998. PUBLISHED AUGUST 19, 1919.

128,452. CERTAIN NAMED ABRASIVE, DETERGENT, AND POLISHING MATERIALS. MASTER HELPS CO., Brooklyn, N. Y. Filed May 12, 1919. Serial No. 118,391. PUBLISHED AUGUST 26, 1919.

128,453. CERTAIN NAMED ABRASIVE, DETERGENT, AND POLISHING MATERIALS. THE MATCHLESS METAL POLISH CO., Chicago, Ill., and Glen Ridge, N. J. Filed April 10, 1919. Serial No. 117,347. PUBLISHED AUGUST 26, 1919.

128,454. OBSTETRIC BELTS. BERTHE MAY, INC., New York, N. Y. Filed February 24, 1919. Serial No. 116,097. PUBLISHED JULY 29, 1919.

128,455. LIQUID ASPIRIN COMPOUND. THE MAYOS CHEMICAL CO., New Orleans, La. Filed May 17, 1919. Serial No. 118,606. PUBLISHED SEPTEMBER 23, 1919.

128,456. CANDY. MELVIN CANDY CO., Chicago, Ill. Filed May 26, 1919. Serial No. 118,926. PUBLISHED OCTOBER 14, 1919.

128,457. CANDY. MELVIN CANDY CO., Chicago, Ill. Filed May 26, 1919. Serial No. 118,927. PUBLISHED SEPTEMBER 23, 1919.

128,458. LAXATIVES AND CATHARTICS. THE WILLIAM S. MERRELL COMPANY, Cincinnati, Ohio. Filed July 28, 1919. Serial No. 121,007. PUBLISHED OCTOBER 7, 1919.

128,459. LAUNDRY-WASHING MACHINES. THE MICHIGAN WASHING MACHINE COMPANY, Muskegon, Mich. Filed June 29, 1917. Serial No. 104,755. PUBLISHED SEPTEMBER 23, 1919.

128,460. TURBINES AND TRACTORS. MIDWEST ENGINE COMPANY, Indianapolis, Ind. Filed June 30, 1919. Serial No. 120,121. PUBLISHED OCTOBER 7, 1919.

128,461. NON-ALCOHOLIC MALTLESS NON-CEREAL BEVERAGES AND SYRUPS FOR MAKING SAME. EDWARD S. MILLER, New York, N. Y., assignor to California Fruit Products Co., Inc. Filed April 21, 1919. Serial No. 117,683. PUBLISHED JUNE 10, 1919.

128,462. CHEWING-GUM AND CANDY. MINT PRODUCTS COMPANY, INC., New York, N. Y. Filed February 28, 1918. Serial No. 109,279. PUBLISHED AUGUST 19, 1919.

128,463. CANNED LOBSTER, CANNED CRABS, CANNED FISH, AND CANNED SHELL-FISH. KIUCHI MIYAUCHI, Nodasam, Mura, Nodasam-Gun, Japan. Filed January 18, 1918. Serial No. 108,531. PUBLISHED AUGUST 19, 1919.

128,464. ARROWROOT-FLOUR AND FOOD-STARCHES FROM W H A T E V E R BASE PRODUCED. CHAS. MORNINGSTAR & CO. INC., New York, N. Y. Filed May 1, 1918. Serial No. 110,594. PUBLISHED SEPTEMBER 30, 1918.

128,465. GERMICIDE AND ANTISEPTIC PREPARATION. HARVEY D. MORRIS, Port Arthur, Tex. Filed July 29, 1919. Serial No. 121,046. PUBLISHED OCTOBER 7, 1919.

128,466. CHEMICAL CARBON-SOLVENT AND FUEL-SAVER. W. F. MYERS, Cambridge, Ohio. Filed May 20, 1919. Serial No. 118,737. PUBLISHED SEPTEMBER 23, 1919.

128,467. STERILIZED MILK PUT UP IN SEALED CONTAINERS. THE NATIONAL DAIRY CO., Toledo and Pioneer, Ohio, and Ennis and Morenci, Mich. Filed March 31, 1919. Serial No. 117,059. PUBLISHED AUGUST 19, 1919.

128,468. JACKS. THE NATIONAL JACK COMPANY, Cincinnati, Ohio. Filed June 18, 1919. Serial No. 119,747. PUBLISHED SEPTEMBER 30, 1919.

128,469. COUNTERBORING-TOOLS, SAWS, SPOT-FACERS, TWIST-DRILLS, REAMERS, AND MILL-ING-CUTTERS. NATIONAL TWIST DRILL & TOOL CO., Detroit, Mich. Filed April 16, 1919. Serial No. 117,537. PUBLISHED SEPTEMBER 23, 1919.

128,470. ICE-SKATES, AND MORE PARTICULARLY TUBULAR RACING, FIGURE OR FANCY, AND HOCKEY SKATES. Nestor Johnson Manufactur-ing Company, Chicago, Ill.
Filed July 23, 1919. Serial No. 120,828. PUBLISHED SEPTEMBER 16, 1919.

128,471. UPHOLSTERED DINING-ROOM CHAIRS. New York Chair Company, New York, N. Y.
Filed February 11, 1919. Serial No. 113,774. PUB-LISHED SEPTEMBER 30, 1919.

128,472. HAIR-TONIC. T. Noonan & Sons Company, Boston, Mass.
Filed July 27, 1918. Serial No. 112,364. PUBLISHED SEPTEMBER 16, 1919.

128,473. HAND GARDEN IMPLEMENTS—NAMELY, CULTIVATORS AND WEEDERS. C. S. Norcross & Sons, Bushnell, Ill.
Filed May 19, 1919. Serial No. 118,695. PUBLISHED OCTOBER 7, 1919.

128,474. CERTAIN NAMED ABRASIVE PRODUCTS. Norton Company, Worcester, Mass.
Filed October 3, 1918. Serial No. 113,568. PUBLISHED SEPTEMBER 23, 1919.

128,475. ANTISEPTIC POWDER. Oceanus Labora-tories, Rockaway Beach, N. Y.
Filed June 18, 1919. Serial No. 119,748. PUBLISHED AUGUST 19, 1919.

128,476. METAL-POLISH. Oliver Reeder & Son, Incorporated, Baltimore, Md.
Filed June 23, 1919. Serial No. 119,868. PUBLISHED OCTOBER 7, 1919.

128,477. GUM TISSUE. The Omo Mfc. Co., Middle-town, Conn.
Filed July 23, 1919. Serial No. 120,842. PUBLISHED OCTOBER 14, 1919.

128,478. DYES. Palatine Aniline & Chemical Cor-poration, Poughkeepsie, N. Y.
Filed July 22, 1918. Serial No. 112,266. PUBLISHED SEPTEMBER 30, 1919.

128,479. MALT, HOPS, AND PITCH. Pan-America Supply Company, Inc., New York, N. Y.
Filed June 17, 1919. Serial No. 119,716. PUBLISHED SEPTEMBER 23, 1919.

128,480. CERTAIN NAMED PETROLEUM PRODUCTS. Pavania Oil Company, Warren, Pa.
Filed January 22, 1919. Serial No. 115,380. PUB-LISHED SEPTEMBER 30, 1919.

128,481. GERMICIDE AND INSECTICIDE. Jonathan Perkins, San Diego, Calif.
Filed August 4, 1919. Serial No. 121,260. PUBLISHED OCTOBER 7, 1919.

128,482. DRESSES AND DRESS-APRONS. J. H. C. Petersen's Sons Company, Davenport, Iowa.
Filed June 16, 1919. Serial No. 119,667. PUBLISHED OCTOBER 7, 1919.

128,483. CERTAIN NAMED PETROLEUM PRODUCTS. Petroleum Products Company, San Francisco, Calif.
Filed May 5, 1919. Serial No. 118,179. PUBLISHED SEPTEMBER 23, 1919.

128,484. ATTACHABLE RUBBER OR RUBBER-MATE-RIAL SHOE-HEELS. Joseph Pietzuch, Cincinnati, Ohio.
Filed August 20, 1917. Serial No. 105,754. PUBLISHED OCTOBER 7, 1919.

128,485. RAISINS, SUGAR-COATED PEANUTS, AND CHOCOLATE-COATED PEANUTS. Carlotta Pin-der, Chicago, Ill.
Filed September 25, 1918. Serial No. 113,376. PUB-LISHED AUGUST 19, 1919.

128,486. MARMALADE. Clyde W. Poole, Los Angeles, Calif.
Filed May 10, 1919. Serial No. 118,353. PUBLISHED SEPTEMBER 23, 1919.

128,487. WHEAT - FLOUR, PANCAKE - FLOUR, AND CAKE AND PASTRY FLOUR, ALSO CEREAL BREAKFAST FOODS. The Portland Flouring Mills Company, Portland, Oreg.
Filed February 13, 1919. Serial No. 115,844. PUB-LISHED SEPTEMBER 23, 1919.

128,488. COOKING-FAT—NAMELY, FOR LARD SUB-STITUTES MANUFACTURED FROM COTTON-SEED OIL. The Procter and Gamble Company, Cincinnati, Ohio.
Filed March 29, 1919. Serial No. 117,022. PUBLISHED SEPTEMBER 30, 1919.

128,489. COFFEE AND PEANUT-BUTTER. L. & S. Products Co., Washington, D. C., assignor to Purity Creamery Company, Baltimore, Md., a Copartnership.
Filed May 21, 1919. Serial No. 118,760. PUBLISHED SEPTEMBER 23, 1919.

128,490. METAL KNITTING - MACHINE NEEDLES. Providence Needle Co., Providence, R. I.
Filed June 12, 1919. Serial No. 119,535. PUBLISHED SEPTEMBER 30, 1919.

128,491. LEATHER. The Quaker City Corporation, Philadelphia, Pa.
Filed June 13, 1919. Serial No. 119,579. PUBLISHED SEPTEMBER 23, 1919.

128,492. LEATHER. Qualitas Patent Leather Cor-poration, Wilmington, Del., and New York, N. Y.
Filed July 16, 1918. Serial No. 112,174. PUBLISHED SEPTEMBER 16, 1919.

128,493. CONSUMPTION MEDICATIVE. Dano P. Ragenovich, San Francisco, Calif.
Filed November 26, 1918. Serial No. 114,384. PUB-LISHED SEPTEMBER 30, 1919.

128,494. FABRIC PUTTEES. Morris Rashkis, Inc., New York, N. Y.
Filed May 1, 1919. Serial No. 118,067. PUBLISHED AUGUST 26, 1919.

128,495. SEWING-MACHINE OIL. The W. T. Raw-leigh Company, Freeport, Ill.
Filed April 22, 1919. Serial No. 117,741. PUBLISHED OCTOBER 7, 1919.

128,496. CERTAIN NAMED ABRASIVE, DETERGENT, AND POLISHING MATERIALS. The W. T. Raw-leigh Company, Freeport, Ill.
Filed April 22, 1919. Serial No. 117,745. PUBLISHED SEPTEMBER 23, 1919.

128,497. REMEDY FOR SKIN ERUPTIONS, PIMPLES, AND SALLOW BLOTCHY COMPLEXION. The Reese Chemical Co., Cleveland, Ohio.
Filed December 7, 1918. Serial No. 114,545. PUB-LISHED SEPTEMBER 30, 1919.

128,498. WOOLEN AND WORSTED SUITINGS IN THE PIECE. Jas. J. Regan Mfg. Co., Rockville, Conn.
Filed June 3, 1919. Serial No. 119,963. PUBLISHED SEPTEMBER 23, 1919.

128,499. DOLLS. Republic Doll & Toy Corporation, New York, N. Y.
Filed June 25, 1919. Serial No. 119,961. PUBLISHED SEPTEMBER 16, 1919.

128,500. MEDICINE FOR BLOOD DISEASES AND SKIN DISORDERS RESULTING THEREFROM.. Restoria Chemical Company, Phoenix, Ariz., and Kansas City, Mo.
Filed April 28, 1919. Serial No. 117,784. PUBLISHED SEPTEMBER 16, 1919.

128,501. CENTRIFUGAL PUMPS. Ralph E. Rich, Chicago, Ill.
Filed April 10, 1919. Serial No. 117,355. PUBLISHED OCTOBER 7, 1919.

128,502. RACK-EXHIBITORS FOR WALL-PAPER, DISPLAY-FIXTURES FOR WALL-PAPER. The Ridgely Trimmer Company, Springfield, Ohio.
Filed April 1, 1919. Serial No. 117,094. PUBLISHED JULY 22, 1919.

128,503. DYES COMBINED WITH SOAP. Clinton S. Robison, Chicago, Ill., assignor to Aladdin Products Company, a Corporation of Illinois.
Filed October 25, 1917. Serial No. 106,960. PUBLISHED SEPTEMBER 30, 1919.

128,504. CREAM SUBSTITUTE. John Roche, Buffalo, N. Y., assignor to himself and John Coonan, Buffalo, N. Y.
Filed June 28, 1918. Serial No. 111,872. PUBLISHED SEPTEMBER 16, 1919.

128,505. LEAF-TOBACCO, SCRAP-TOBACCO, CIGARS, CIGARETTES. SNUFF, CHEWING-TOBACCO, AND CHEROOTS. The Rockfall Cigar Company, New York, N. Y.
Filed June 12, 1919. Serial No. 119,536. PUBLISHED OCTOBER 7, 1919.

128,506. CERTAIN NAMED LADIES', MEN'S, AND CHILDREN'S UNDERWEAR. J. C. Roulette and Sons, Hagerstown, Md.
Filed June 5, 1919. Serial No. 119,251. PUBLISHED OCTOBER 7, 1919.

128,507. NEAR BEER. Jacob Ruppert, New York, N. Y.
Filed January 3, 1919. Serial No. 114,979. PUBLISHED SEPTEMBER 16, 1919.

128,508. CLOTHS AND STUFFS OF WOOL, WORSTED, OR HAIR. Finch Rushworth, Fenay Bridge, near Huddersfield, England.
Filed June 25, 1919. Serial No. 119,960. PUBLISHED AUGUST 26, 1919.

128,509. CHOCOLATE-COVERED CARAMEL BARS. Sam Ruttenberg, Chicago, Ill.
Filed May 6, 1919. Serial No. 118,214. PUBLISHED SEPTEMBER 30, 1919.

128,510. CERTAIN NAMED PAPER AND STATIONERY. Louis Sainberg, New York, N. Y.
Filed November 21, 1918. Serial No. 114,278. PUBLISHED AUGUST 26, 1919.

128,511. HOSIERY—NAMELY, FOR MEN, WOMEN, AND CHILDREN. David Salwen, New York, N. Y.
Filed May 19, 1919. Serial No. 118,724. PUBLISHED SEPTEMBER 30, 1919.

128,512. FOOD-FLAVORING EXTRACTS. The C. F. Sauer Company, Richmond, Va.
Filed June 2, 1919. Serial No. 119,135. PUBLISHED OCTOBER 7, 1919.

128,513. ICE-CREAM. Sayre Creamery & Cold Storage Co., Sayre, Pa.
Filed July 14, 1919. Serial No. 120,556. PUBLISHED SEPTEMBER 30, 1919.

128,514. CERTAIN NAMED MALT BEVERAGES, EXTRACTS, AND LIQUORS. The F. & M. Schaefer Brewing Co., New York, N. Y.
Filed April 15, 1918. Serial No. 110,222. PUBLISHED SEPTEMBER 9, 1919.

128,515. CANDIES. Paul R. Shailer, Washington, D. C.
Filed June 14, 1919. Serial No. 119,615. PUBLISHED SEPTEMBER 23, 1919.

128,516. CIGARS, CIGARETTES, AND SMOKING AND CHEWING TOBACCO. Louis Sherman, Cincinnati, Ohio.
Filed June 28, 1919. Serial No. 120,073. PUBLISHED OCTOBER 7, 1919.

128,517. CANNED FRUITS, CANNED VEGETABLES, COFFEE, AND CANNED FISH. Simon Bros. Company, Omaha, Nebr.
Filed May 20, 1919. Serial No. 118,743. PUBLISHED SEPTEMBER 30, 1919.

128,518. LEAD-PENCILS AND WRAPPING-PAPER. Simmons Hardware Company, St. Louis, Mo.
Filed April 26, 1919. Serial No. 117,905. PUBLISHED AUGUST 5, 1919.

128,519. OPHTHALMIC-LENS BLANKS AND OPHTHALMIC LENSES. Simpson-Walther Lens Company, Incorporated, Rochester, N. Y.
Filed May 15, 1919. Serial No. 118,527. PUBLISHED AUGUST 26, 1919.

128,520. COTTON, WOOL, SILK, AND LINEN PIECE GOODS AND MIXTURES OF THE SAME. South & Central American Commercial Co., Inc., New York, N. Y.
Filed June 11, 1919. Serial No. 119,492. PUBLISHED AUGUST 26, 1919.

128,521. FERTILIZERS. Southern Fertilizer & Chemical Co., Savannah, Ga.
Filed March 27, 1919. Serial No. 116,977. PUBLISHED SEPTEMBER 16, 1919.

128,522. STOCK FOOD. Sperry Flour Company, San Francisco, Calif.
Filed June 16, 1919. Serial No. 119,677. PUBLISHED AUGUST 19, 1919.

128,523. POULTRY FOOD. Sperry Flour Company, San Francisco, Calif.
Filed June 16, 1919. Serial No. 119,678. PUBLISHED AUGUST 19, 1919.

128,524. POULTRY FOOD. Sperry Flour Company, San Francisco, Calif.
Filed June 16, 1919. Serial No. 119,679. PUBLISHED AUGUST 19, 1919.

128,525. SLIP-COVERS. L. Spiegelberg & Sons, New York, N. Y.
Filed June 3, 1919. Serial No. 119,172. PUBLISHED AUGUST 26, 1919.

128,526. REFINED OILS FOR ILLUMINATING, HEATING, AND POWER PURPOSES. Standard Oil Company of New York, New York, N. Y.
Filed May 20, 1919. Serial No. 118,744. PUBLISHED OCTOBER 7, 1919.

128,527. LAUNDRY BLUE. The Standard Ultramarine Co., Huntington, W. Va.
Filed February 18, 1919. Serial No. 115,963. PUBLISHED SEPTEMBER 30, 1919.

128,528. FEATHER PILLOWS. Star Bedding Company, St. Louis, Mo.
Filed June 4, 1919. Serial No. 119,217. PUBLISHED OCTOBER 7, 1919.

128,529. CANNED SARDINES. Steele Packing Co., San Diego, Calif.
Filed June 10, 1919. Serial No. 119,449. PUBLISHED AUGUST 19, 1919.

128,530. POTATO CHIPS. The Sterling Potato Brittle Co., Wilkes-Barre, Pa.
Filed June 23, 1919. Serial No. 119,869. PUBLISHED AUGUST 19, 1919.

128,531. CANNED FRUITS—NAMELY, CANNED PEACHES AND CANNED APRICOTS. Charles Stern & Sons Inc., Los Angeles, Calif.
Filed July 1, 1919. Serial No. 120,188. PUBLISHED SEPTEMBER 30, 1919.

128,532. COCOANUT-BUTTER. E. A. Stevenson & Company, Wilmington, Del., and New York, N. Y.
Filed April 15, 1918. Serial No. 110,223. PUBLISHED SEPTEMBER 23, 1919.

128,533. CERTAIN NAMED KNITTED, NETTED, AND TEXTILE FABRICS. Stewart Bros. & Company, Glasgow, Scotland.
Filed March 4, 1919. Serial No. 116,291. PUBLISHED AUGUST 26, 1919.

128,534. BAKING-POWDER. Stiles-Pellens Coffee Co., Cincinnati, Ohio.
Filed June 23, 1919. Serial No. 119,873. PUBLISHED SEPTEMBER 23, 1919 .

128,535. SOAP. Swift & Company, Chicago, Ill.
Filed May 22, 1919. Serial No. 118,797. PUBLISHED AUGUST 26, 1919.

128,536. FRESH CITRUS FRUITS—NAMELY, ORANGES AND LEMONS. Tapo Citrus Ass'n, Santa Susana, Calif.
Filed May 19, 1919. Serial No. 118,716. PUBLISHED AUGUST 19, 1919.

128,537. RUBBER HEELS AND SOLES. E. E. Taylor Company, Boston, Mass.
Filed July 29, 1918. Serial No. 112,419. PUBLISHED OCTOBER 7, 1919.

128,538. REMEDY FOR INACTIVE LIVER. Milton M. Taylor, Tampa, Fla.
Filed May 23, 1919. Serial No. 118,862. PUBLISHED SEPTEMBER 23, 1919.

128,539. ANTISEPTIC PREPARATION. Milton M. Taylor, Tampa, Fla.
Filed May 23, 1919. Serial No. 118,863. PUBLISHED SEPTEMBER 16, 1919.

128,540. CIGARS. Eric Tatom & Co., Nashville. Tenn.
Filed July 1, 1919. Serial No. 120,197. PUBLISHED OCTOBER 7, 1919.

128,541. LIQUID TO BE USED EXTERNALLY FOR SCALDS AND BURNS UPON THE SKIN. Louis Thomas, Chicago, Ill.
Filed June 18, 1919. Serial No. 119,755. PUBLISHED AUGUST 19, 1919.

128,542. DRESSED POULTRY. Thorndike and Gerrish Company, Boston, Mass.
Filed May 8, 1919. Serial No. 118,288. PUBLISHED AUGUST 19, 1919.

128,543. GENERAL RECONSTRUCTIVE TONIC AND TISSUE-BUILDER. Peyton H. Todd & Son, Atlanta, Ga.
Filed August 23, 1918. Serial No. 112,854. PUBLISHED OCTOBER 7, 1919.

128,544. CONFECTION PASTE. The Towle Maple Products Company, Wilmington, Del., and St. Paul. Minn.
Filed August 9, 1915. Serial No. 88,512. PUBLISHED AUGUST 19, 1919.

128,545. MEN'S, WOMEN'S, AND CHILDREN'S SHOES MADE WHOLLY OR IN PART OF LEATHER. Lazar M. Traub, Boston, Mass.
Filed June 3, 1919. Serial No. 119,174. PUBLISHED AUGUST 26, 1919.

128,546. CANNED VEGETABLES, CANNED FRUITS, JELLIES, MARMALADES, PICKLES, FRUIT PRESERVES, CANDY, AND FRUIT BUTTERS. Lottie S. Trovillo, Blanchester, Ohio.
Filed December 31, 1917. Serial No. 108,236. PUBLISHED SEPTEMBER 30, 1919.

128,547. PARTIALLY-PRINTED SHEETS FOR KEEPING FUNERAL-RECORDS. Charles H. J. Truman, San Francisco, Calif.
Filed June 10, 1918. Serial No. 111,467. PUBLISHED JULY 22, 1919.

128,548. VEGETABLE ADHESIVE MADE FROM A STARCH BASIS AND USED AS A SUBSTITUTE FOR ANIMAL GLUE. F. W. Tunnel & Company, Inc., Philadelphia, Pa.
Filed May 22, 1919. Serial No. 118,812. PUBLISHED SEPTEMBER 30, 1919.

128,549. TOY GUNS. Gerald Tushak, New York, N. Y.
Filed June 16, 1919. Serial No. 119,683. PUBLISHED OCTOBER 7, 1919.

128,550. MEDICINAL PREPARATION FOR INFLUENZA, RHEUMATISM, HEADACHE, BACKACHE, AND PAINS CONTAINED IN THE BODY. B. E. Tyson, Newark, N. J.
Filed May 16, 1919. Serial No. 118,575. PUBLISHED SEPTEMBER 23, 1919.

128,551. BELT-DRESSING. The Ulmer Leather Co, Norwich, Conn.
Filed March 25, 1918. Serial No. 109,784. PUBLISHED JUNE 4, 1918

128,552. FRESH MILK AND FRESH CREAM, EGGS, AND BUTTER. Frederick D. Underwood, New York, N. Y.
Filed February 24, 1919. Serial No. 116,115. PUBLISHED SEPTEMBER 23, 1919.

128,553. TRACTORS, STEAM-ENGINES, AND GAS-ENGINES. Union Tool Company, Torrance, Calif.
Filed October 7, 1918. Serial No. 113,615. PUBLISHED AUGUST 26, 1919.

128,554. WRITING-TABLETS. United Drug Company, Boston, Mass.
Filed April 28, 1919. Serial No. 117,957. PUBLISHED AUGUST 26, 1919.

128,555. MEN'S. WOMEN'S, AND CHILDREN'S LEATHER SHOES. United States Rubber Company. New Brunswick, N. J., and New York, N. Y.
Filed July 5, 1918. Serial No. 111,954. PUBLISHED SEPTEMBER 30, 1919.

128,556. REGISTERS FOR INDICATING AND RECORDING THE AMOUNT OF FUEL CONSUMED BY INTERNAL-COMBUSTION ENGINES. The Vacui Meter Co., Columbus, Ga.
Filed August 2, 1919. Serial No. 121,222. PUBLISHED OCTOBER 7, 1919.

128,557. CARBURETERS. Van Briggle Motor Device Company, Indianapolis, Ind.
Filed July 21, 1919. Serial No. 120,783. PUBLISHED OCTOBER 7, 1919.

128,558. CRUCIBLES. Vesuvius Crucible Company, Swissvale, Pa.
Filed October 1, 1918 Serial No. 113,517. PUBLISHED AUGUST 26, 1919.

128,559. PAPER BAGS. Victory Bag & Paper Co., Chicago, Ill.
Filed October 14, 1918. Serial No. 113,726. PUBLISHED OCTOBER 7, 1919.

128,560. COMPOUND FLOUR AND SYRUP WHICH IS A BLEND OF MAPLE, CANE, AND CORN SYRUPS. Leo G. Voll, Denver, Colo.
Filed March 1, 1919. Serial No. 116,243. PUBLISHED AUGUST 19, 1919.

128,561. STEEL PENS. Jennie Voorsanger, Chicago, Ill.
Filed May 10, 1919. Serial No. 118,359. PUBLISHED AUGUST 26, 1919.

128,562. OINTMENT FOR EXTERNAL APPLICATION FOR THE TREATMENT OF DISORDERS OF THE RESPIRATORY ORGANS. Vaporine Chemical Company, Savannah, Tenn.
Filed May 2, 1919. Serial No. 118,099. PUBLISHED SEPTEMBER 23, 1919.

128,563. FOUNTAIN-PENS, STEEL PENS, LEAD-PENCILS, PENHOLDERS, AND RUBBER ERASERS. Samuel Ward Manufacturing Company, Boston, Mass.
Filed March 6, 1919. Serial No. 116,353. PUBLISHED SEPTEMBER 16, 1919.

128,564. SILK, COTTON AND SILK, WOOL, COTTON. AND COTTON AND ARTIFICIAL-SILK PIECE GOODS. Warner-Godfrey Co., New York, N. Y.
Filed June 7, 1919. Serial No. 119,323. PUBLISHED SEPTEMBER 16, 1919.

128,565. SILK, COTTON AND SILK, WOOL, COTTON, AND COTTON AND ARTIFICIAL-SILK PIECE GOODS. Warner-Godfrey Co., New York, N. Y.
Filed June 7, 1919. Serial No. 119,324. PUBLISHED SEPTEMBER 16, 1919.

128,566. MIXED LIVE-STOCK FEED CONTAINING ALFALFA, GRAINS, AND MOLASSES. The Wash-Co. Alfalfa Milling Co., Riverton, Wyo., and Fort Calhoun and Nebraska City, Nebr.
Filed May 19, 1919. Serial No. 118,719. PUBLISHED AUGUST 19, 1919.

128,567. FRESH APPLES. WASHINGTON FRUIT & PRO-
DUCE CO., Yakima, Wash.
Filed June 10, 1919. Serial No. 119,463. PUBLISHED
AUGUST 19, 1919.

128,568. BUTTER - SCOTCH CANDY. BENJAMIN C.
WEISBERG, New York, N. Y.
Filed April 26, 1919. Serial No. 117,914. PUBLISHED
SEPTEMBER 30, 1919.

128,569. CANDY. FREDERIC H. WEISS, Cincinnati, Ohio.
Filed April 12, 1919. Serial No. 117,429. PUBLISHED
SEPTEMBER 23, 1919.

128,570. HEATING-OILS, ILLUMINATING-OILS, AND
LUBRICATING-OILS. HENRY MATTHEW WELLS,
London, England.
Filed June 12, 1919. Serial No. 119,541. PUBLISHED
OCTOBER 7, 1919.

128,571. POWDERED SUBSTANCE FOR CLEANING
PURPOSES. GUSTAVE WENZELMANN, Galesburg, Ill.
Filed August 27, 1918. Serial No. 112,899. PUB-
LISHED AUGUST 26, 1919.

128,572. LAUNDRY TABLETS. WERTH MOR MFG. CO.,
Barberton, Ohio.
Filed April 28, 1919. Serial No. 117,959. PUBLISHED
SEPTEMBER 30, 1919.

128,573. LAUNDRY SOAP. WEST COAST SOAP CO., Oak-
land, Calif.
Filed June 10, 1918. Serial No. 111,470. PUBLISHED
SEPTEMBER 30, 1919.

128,574. CANNED SALMON. THE WESTERN FISHERIES
COMPANY, Seattle, Wash.
Filed July 7, 1919. Serial No. 120,332. PUBLISHED
SEPTEMBER 30, 1919.

128,575. BOND-PAPER FOR PRINTING AND WRIT-
ING PURPOSES. WEST VIRGINIA PULP & PAPER
COMPANY, New York, N. Y.
Filed April 29, 1919. Serial No. 118,005. PUBLISHED
JUNE 17, 1919.

128,576. CERTAIN NAMED FOODS. WHITE-STOKES
CO., INC., Chicago, Ill.
Filed April 10, 1919. Serial No. 117,362. PUBLISHED
AUGUST 19, 1919.

128,577. FRESH CITRUS FRUITS—NAMELY,
ORANGES, LEMONS, AND GRAPE-FRUIT. WHIT-
TIER CITRUS ASSOCIATION, Whittier, Calif.
Filed April 22, 1919. Serial No. 117,757. PUBLISHED
AUGUST 19, 1919.

128,578. UPPER-LEATHER FOR BOOTS AND SHOES,
AND PARTICULARLY SIDE UPPER-LEATHER.
WIDEN-LORD TANNING CO., Boston, Mass.
Filed June 3, 1919. Serial No. 119,179. PUBLISHED
SEPTEMBER 23, 1919.

128,579. HAIR-POMADE. MMES. WILLIAMS, HEBRON &
HERD, Baltimore, Md.
Filed August 6, 1919. Serial No. 121,326. PUBLISHED
OCTOBER 7, 1919.

128,580. WATERLESS SOAP. THE WITE-KAT SOAP
COMPANY, San Francisco, Calif.
Filed June 19, 1918. Serial No. 111,682. PUBLISHED
SEPTEMBER 30, 1919.

128,581. CERTAIN NAMED FOODS AND INGREDI-
ENTS OF FOODS. VIOLA V. N. WOODRUFF, Flushing,
N. Y.
Filed May 21, 1919. Serial No. 118,771. PUBLISHED
SEPTEMBER 30, 1919.

128,582. PAPER BAGS. WORTENDYKE MANUFACTURING
COMPANY, Richmond, Va.
Filed February 7, 1919. Serial No. 115,684. PUB-
LISHED SEPTEMBER 16, 1919.

128,583. HAIR REMEDY AND A RESTORATIVE OF
GRAY HAIR TO ITS NATURAL COLOR. WYETH
CHEMICAL CO., Dover, Del., and New York, N. Y.
Filed June 6, 1919. Serial No. 119,284. PUBLISHED
AUGUST 19, 1919.

128,584. AGRICULTURAL AND EARTHWORKING IM-
PLEMENTS COMPRISING SHOVELS, SPADES,
AND SCOOPS. THE WYOMING SHOVEL WORKS,
Wyoming, Pa.
Filed February 23, 1918. Serial No. 109,185. PUB-
LISHED AUGUST 26, 1919.

128,585. KNITTED UNION-GARMENTS, UNDER-
SHIRTS, AND DRAWERS. BLACK CAT TEXTILES
COMPANY, Kenosha, Wis.
Filed September 10, 1917. Serial No. 106,153. PUB-
LISHED OCTOBER 7, 1919.

128,586. OINTMENT FOR EXTERNAL USE IN TREAT-
ING CERTAIN NAMED AFFECTIONS. RICHARD H.
HEINRICHS, New York, N. Y.
Filed August 17, 1918. Serial No. 112,765. PUB-
LISHED JANUARY 7, 1919.

LABELS

REGISTERED JANUARY 6, 1920.

21,617.—*Title:* "ARNOLD'S STRIP BLUING." (For Bluing.) ARNOLD BLUING COMPANY, Portland, Oreg. Filed August 12, 1919.

21,618.—*Title:* "BUCK'S VULCANTITE PATCH." (For Tire-Patches.) A. A. BUCK, Santa Maria, Calif. Filed June 26, 1919.

21,619.—*Title:* "BRUEHN'S ROSE E OLA." (For a Laxative.) LOUIS BRUEHN, Chicago, Ill. Filed May 12, 1919.

21,620.—*Title:* "QUINBY'S." (For Chocolates.) CALIFORNIA CHOCOLATE SHOPS CO., Los Angeles, Calif. Filed August 23, 1919.

21,621.—*Title:* "DREWS." (For Storage Batteries.) ARTHUR E. DREW, Lynn, Mass. Filed July 28, 1919.

21,622.—*Title:* "RED GOOSE." (For a Beverage.) EMMERLING PRODUCTS COMPANY, Johnstown, Pa. Filed July 31, 1919.

21,623.—*Title:* "KUVER SUIT." (For Overalls.) HAPP BROTHERS CO., Macon, Ga. Filed August 23, 1919.

21,624.—*Title:* "IDEAL SPECIAL PREPARED MALT PRODUCTS." (For Malt Products.) IDEAL YEAST COMPANY, Cedar Rapids, Iowa. Filed August 8, 1919.

21,625.—*Title:* "LA ROULETTE." (For Cigars.) VICTOR LEVOR, Attica, Ind Filed July 14, 1919.

21,626.—*Title:* "VITTORIA." (For Olive-Oil.) LIABIOTAKIS BROS., New York, N. Y. Filed April 3, 1919.

21,627.—*Title:* "MAJOR'S CONSUMPTION RELIEF." (For a Preparation for the Relief of Consumption.) JOSEPH MAJOR, Detroit, Mich. Filed July 31, 1919.

21,628.—*Title:* "MAJOR'S CHOLERA MEDICINE." (For a Treatment for Cholera.) JOSEPH MAJOR, Detroit, Mich. Filed July 31, 1919.

21,629.—*Title:* "MAJOR'S NERVE MEDICINE." (For a Nerve Medicine.) JOSEPH MAJOR, Detroit, Mich. Filed July 31, 1919.

21,630.—*Title:* "MALT PHOSPHATE." (For Malt Phosphate.) PETER A. MANDABACH, Chicago, Ill. Filed July 26, 1919.

21,631.—*Title:* "MILK CHOCOLATES." (For Chocolate Candy.) MILWAUKEE PAPER BOX COMPANY, Milwaukee, Wis. Filed August 14, 1919.

21,632.—*Title:* "'BUDDY' AND 'DOLLY' VINDEX UNDERSUITS." (For Underwear.) OPPENHEIM, OBERNDORF & CO., INC., Baltimore, Md. Filed August 7, 1919.

21,633.—*Title:* "NICKEL SMOKE." (For Cigars.) PASBACH-VOICE LITHO. CO. INC., New York, N. Y. Filed August 7, 1919.

21,634.—*Title:* "PHILLIPS BRAND." (For Canned Salmon.) M. PHILLIPS & CO., San Francisco, Calif. Filed August 8, 1919.

21,635.—*Title:* "PRICE TAILORED HEADWEAR." (For Headwear.) N. PRICE, SON & CO., Philadelphia, Pa. Filed July 25, 1919.

21,636.—*Title:* "LILY." (For a Beverage.) THE ROCK ISLAND BREWING COMPANY, Rock Island, Ill. Filed August 22, 1919.

21,637.—*Title:* "'PALZO' THE GREAT AMERICAN CLEANER." (For a Cleaner.) RUNYAN CHEMICAL PRODUCTS CO., Omaha, Nebr. Filed September 19, 1919.

21,638.—*Title:* "SHIPMATE." (For Canned Strawberries.) ST. JOE CANNING CO., St. Joseph, Mich. Filed September 19, 1919.

21,639.—*Title:* "TRISUM." (For Canned Strawberries.) ST. JOE CANNING CO., St. Joseph, Mich. Filed September 19, 1919.

21,640.—*Title:* "GOLDEN SHREDS" (For Orange Marmalade.) SOUTHERN CALIFORNIA PRODUCTS COMPANY, Orange, Calif. Filed September 19, 1919.

21,641.—*Title:* "KENILWORTH." (For Canned Tomatoes.) STEELE PACKING CO., San Diego, Calif. Filed September 19, 1919.

21,642.—*Title:* "TIP-IT, PATENT WELDING COMPOUND. PERMANENT WELD GUARANTEED." (For Welding Compounds.) TIP-IT, (INC.,) New York, N. Y. Filed June 11, 1919.

21,643.—*Title:* "BUTTERY BITTER SWEETS." (For Candy.) VAL BLATZ JR. CANDY CO., Milwaukee, Wis. Filed August 21, 1919.

21,644.—*Title:* "HEATHER LAWN." (For Stationery.) WHITE & WYCKOFF MFG. CO., Holyoke, Mass. Filed June 10, 1919.

21,645.—*Title:* "VICTORY STAR BRAND MACARONI." (For Macaroni.) WINDSOR LOCKS MACARONI MFG. CO., Windsor Locks, Conn. Filed June 7, 1919.

PRINTS

REGISTERED JANUARY 6, 1920.

5,187.—*Title:* "THE TYRE TO TIE TO." (For Tires and Tubes.) BRAENDER RUBBER & TIRE CO., Rutherford, N. J. Filed July 7, 1919.

5,188.—*Title:* "HAYS GLOVES." (For Leather Gloves.) THE DANIEL HAYS COMPANY, Gloversville, N. Y. Filed April 25, 1919.

5,189.—*Title:* "DERRYVALE." (For Linen Piece Goods.) DERRYVALE LINEN COMPANY, New York, N. Y. Filed December 23, 1919.

5,190.—*Title:* "THE GLORY OF A WOMAN IS HER SKIN." (For Toilet Soap.) THE N. K. FAIRBANK COMPANY, Chicago, Ill. Filed May 15, 1919.

5,191.—*Title:* "KING '8' 'LIMOUDAN'." (For Automobiles.) KING CAR CORPORATION OF NEW YORK, New York, N. Y. Filed July 30, 1919.

5,192.—*Title:* "P. A. LETS THE CAT OUT OF THE SMOKE-BAG." (For Smoking-Tobacco.) R. J. REYNOLDS TOBACCO COMPANY, Winston-Salem, N. C. Filed August 27, 1919.

5,193.—*Title:* "STYLISH COLORS EVERYWHERE 'RIT' ED WITH RIT." (For Dye-Soap.) SUNBEAM CHEMICAL COMPANY, Chicago, Ill. Filed August 15, 1919.

DECISIONS

OF THE

COMMISSIONER OF PATENTS

AND OF

UNITED STATES COURTS IN PATENT CASES.

DECISIONS OF THE U. S. COURTS.

Court of Appeals of the District of Columbia.

IN RE ALVAH BUSHNELL COMPANY.

Decided December 1, 1919.

TRADE-MARKS — DESCRIPTIVENESS — "SAFETSEAL," FOR ENVELOPS.

The mark " SafeTseal " as applied to envelops *Held* descriptive, as indicating either safety-seal envelops or safe-seal envelops.

Mr. E. T. Fenwick, Mr. L. L. Morrill, and *Mr. Charles Allen* for the appellant.

Mr. T. A. Hostetler for the Commissioner of Patents.

VAN ORSDEL, J.:

This appeal is from the decision of the Commissioner of Patents refusing registration of the word-symbol " SafeTseal " as a trade-mark for envelops, wallets, letter-files, jackets, etc.

Counsel for the Commissioner discloses the existence of patent to D'Agostina, dated February 8, 1916, for safety-envelops, and also patent to Halloran. dated July 25, 1905, which is described as relating "to a safety seal for envelops." It must be assumed that the goods of the respective patentees are known to the trade as " safety envelops " or " safety seal envelops." This designation having been established by virtue of the patents, even if arbitrary, would not be available as a trade-mark for either of the patentees for goods of the same class as those patented. It follows that, if by their use, the marks could not be registered as trade-marks by the persons first applying them to the patented articles, a stranger could not adopt either of them as a trade-mark for the same class of goods.

Treating the mark independently, the test here is the impression which it would make upon the public. It is clear that the trade would identify the goods bearing the mark either as safety-seal envelops or safe-seal envelops. In either case the mark is descriptive of the goods and comes within the prohibition of section 5 of the Trade-Mark Act of February 20, 1905.

The decision of the Commissioner of Patents is affirmed, and the clerk is directed to certify these proceedings as required by law.

Affirmed.

Court of Appeals of the District of Columbia.

AMERICAN FEED MILLING CO. *v.* M. C. PETERS MILL CO.

Decided December 1, 1919.

TRADE-MARKS — SIMILARITY.

A mark consisting of the words " Big Chief," associated with the representation of a man on horseback, inclosed within a circle, *Held* deceptively similar to a mark consisting of the word " Arab," associated with the representation of a man on horseback, inclosed within two circles.

Mr. Raymond J. Mawhinney and *Mr. Robert J. Mawhinney* for the appellant.

Mr. T. Walter Fowler for the appellee.

VAN ORSDEL, J.:

This is an appeal from the decision of the Commissioner of Patents in a trade-mark opposition.

The mark of applicant, American Feed Milling Company, a North Carolina corporation, consists of the words " Big Chief," associated with the representation of a man on horseback concentrically inclosed within a single circle. The mark of the opposer, M. C. Peters Mill Company, a Nebraska corporation, consists of the word " Arab," associated with the representation of a man on horseback concentrically inclosed within two circles. The man in the mark of applicant is intended to represent an Indian chief armed with a gun, while the man in opposer's mark represents an Arab armed with a spear.

The sole question presented is the likelihood of confusion in trade. Applicant alleges use of its mark since 1914, while opposer shows use of its mark prior to that date. The dominating feature of each mark is the horse with an armed man mounted upon it. The horse in each mark is similar is size, style and appearance. While the dress of the men is different, they are similar in size, position and the respective manner of holding the spear and gun. These striking similarities bring this case within the rule announced in *Bickmore Gall Cure Co.* v. *Karns Mfg. Co.*, (126 Fed., 573.) where the conflicting marks consisted of representations of horses attached to the same class of goods. In that case the court said:

> Both pictures are used on boxes containing the salve. The complainant's trade-mark cannot confer a monopoly to every representation of a horse upon a medicine of that character. Such a mark would be generic in char-

acter. Its right is restricted to the particular horse designated in the registration, or one of substantially similar appearance, style or position.

Opposer's mark discloses an Arabian horse of unusual appearance, style and position, while the horse of applicant is similar in all its details and dimensions.

The respective marks are used on burlap sacks containing horse feed, displaying at best a dull impression of the mark and forbidding to a large extent the detection of distinguishing features. The similarity of the dimensions and general appearance of the marks emphasizes the improbability of accidental selection by applicant. As was said by Judge Lurton in *Paris Co.* v. *Hill Co.*, (102 Fed., 148, 151:)

When there are found strong resemblances, the natural inquiry for the court is, why do they exist? If no sufficient answer appears, the inference is that they exist for the purpose of misleading. (*Taylor* v. *Taylor*, 2 Eq. Rep., 290.) We are to remember that the average purchaser has seldom the opportunity of making a close comparison; that he is apt to act quickly, and is therefore not expected to exercise a high degree of caution. (*Pillsbury* v. *Flour-Mills Co.*, 12 C. C. A., 432.)

The decision of the Commissioner of Patents sustaining the opposition is affirmed, and the clerk is directed to certify these proceedings as by law required.

Affirmed.

Court of Appeals of the District of Columbia.

B A D E R *v.* B U R R O U G H S .

Decided December 1, 1919.

INTERFERENCE—PRIORITY.

Evidence reviewed and *Held* insufficient to establish that the junior party, on whom the burden of proof rested heavily as an applicant against a patentee, was the first inventor.

Mr. C. S. Davis for the appellant.

Mr. Howard P. Denison for the appellee.

ROBB, *J.*:

Appeal from a decision of an Assistant Commissioner of Patents in an interference proceeding awarding priority of invention to the junior applicant, he having copied the claim of appellant's patent, reading as follows:

In an eye-glass mounting, the combination with a bridge provided with a non-circular opening and a flat surface surrounding the opening, of a pivot stud comprising a portion fitting in and conforming to the non-circular opening, a cylindrical bearing portion, a shoulder at the junction of the bearing portion with the non-circular portion, said shoulder engaging the flat surface of the bridge, and a flange spaced from said flat surface ; a screw engaging the post and the bridge and holding the shoulder against the flat surface, a nose clamp lever pivoted to the stud and engaging the flange and the flat surface of the bridge ; and a spring secured at one end to the stud and at the other end to the nose clamp lever.

At the time the invention was made the parties were in the employ of the Standard Optical Company of Geneva, N. Y., Burroughs as superintendent and Bader as an expert designer of eyeglass-mountings. Burroughs was not an inventor, while Bader had taken out several patents relating to this art. It is conceded that Bader was the inventor of a structure like the device of the issue except that the end of the post supporting the guard was offset and hence not readily removable. In other words, in the device of the issue a screw has been substituted for the offset. For this substitution or change each of the parties claims credit. The Examiner of Inter-
[Vol.. 270

ferences awarded priority to Bader, while the Board and Assistant Commissioner found for Burroughs.

At the time the controversy arose, and thereafter until Bader canceled the license. the company was paying him a royalty on the mounting, minus the screw feature. Some complaint was made because the guard was not removable, and, on the 13th of April, 1915, two representatives of the Geneva Optical Company were in conference with Burroughs at the factory of the Standard Optical Company. During the latter part of this interview, which took place after lunch, some one suggested that by putting a screw in place of the offset or rivet the mounting could be more easily repaired. Burroughs says he made this suggestion. The two representatives of the Geneva Company do not remember who made it. One of them testified, under cross-examination, that most mountings of this character were made with a screw and that the substitution of the screw for the fixed head or offset " was the obvious thing." Bader was called in and the matter discussed. Burroughs at first testified that the interview terminated between 4 and 4.30 in the afternoon and that he thought Bader was there at that time. Later Mr. Dorsey, the attorney who prepared the application for Bader at Rochester, N. Y.—a very frank witness and entirely disinterested at the time of his testimony—produced for Bader a drawing of the invention dated April 13, 1915, and which he testified was on that day sent to his correspondent in Washington for the purpose of a search as to patentability. To the best of Mr. Dorsey's recollection, the drawing was made—

from a description furnished by Mr. Bader at some time before making the search.

Judging from the appearance of the sketch, the witness was certain it had been done when he had plenty of time on his hands, and not in the course of an interview with Bader. The witness was quite sure that the communication from Bader was at a personal interview ; that had the fact been otherwise he, in all probability, would have remembered it. The stenographer to whom the letter accompanying the drawing was dictated by Mr. Dorsey on the date mentioned, stated that her note-book showed she had taken other dictation that day after the letter in question was dictated to her. Following this testimony Mr. Burroughs was recalled to the stand and asked whether he knew where Mr. Bader was in the afternoon of April 13th, and, notwithstanding his former statement that Bader was at the factory when the interview closed at 4 o'clock or later, replied that he did not. He further stated that it was Bader's habit to go to Rochester from Geneva by motorcycle, a distance of approximately forty-six miles. Bader testified positively that he was not in Rochester on the 13th, and that his disclosure to Mr. Dorsey was prior to that time. We do not deem it necessary further to discuss the evidence, save to say that the bill for the filing of Bader's application was paid by the Geneva Company.

Since Bader is a patentee, the burden is heavily on Burroughs, and in our view he has entirely failed to
No. 1.]

sustain it. He does not even claim to have done more than suggest a slight and, according to his own witness, obvious modification of one of the elements of a structure admittedly Bader's. And he really is not corroborated as to that, while the testimony of Mr. Dorsey and the drawing produced by him conclusively establishes, we think, that Bader was in possession of the invention before the interview at which Burroughs says he (Burroughs) first disclosed it. Moreover, this "obvious thing" was more likely to occur to Bader, the expert, than to any one else.

The decision is reversed and priority awarded to Bader.

Reversed.

Court of Appeals of the District of Columbia.

COWLES *v.* RODY.

Decided December 1, 1919.

JURISDICTION—COURT OF APPEALS OF THE DISTRICT OF COLUMBIA—INTERFERENCE PROCEEDING.

The Court of Appeals of the District of Columbia is without authority in an interference proceeding to review the Commissioner's ruling that the claims of one of the parties are not patentable because barred by the statute of public use (or printed publication).

Mr. W. H. Finckel, Jr., for the appellant.

Mr. J. C. Pennie and *Mr. F. E. Barrows* for the appellee.

SMYTH, C. J.:

Cowles appeals from a decision of the Assistant Commissioner of Patents dissolving an interference to which he was a party. The subject-matter, which was a method for treating feldspar and the like, is expressed in nine counts. In view of the conclusion which we have reached it is not necessary to set out any of them.

Rody was granted a patent August 24, 1915, on an application filed October 11, 1913. Cowles's application was not filed until November 20, 1915, nearly three months after Rody's patent had issued. Cowles was therefore the junior party. The Examiner of Interferences awarded priority to Rody on all the counts. This was reversed by the Examiners-in-Chief as to counts 1 to 4 and affirmed as to the remainder. In granting the reversal the Examiners held that while Cowles was prior to Rody with respect ot the first-named claims, he was anticipated by a patent to one Adolf Kayser. and announced that they would so notify the Commissioner of the apparent statutory bar to the granting of a patent to Cowles with claims corresponding to the counts 1 to 4. On appeal by Cowles the Assistant Commissioner held that he had in effect admitted publication of his invention in 1912. or more than two years before he filed his application. He further said:

If the Cowles publications, taken in connection with the previous Kayser patent or otherwise. disclose the invention of Cowles as he claims it, then the possibility of granting a patent to Cowles disappears, and there is no applicant before this Office with allowable claims to this matter, and consequently there is no interference.

The Assistant Commissioner found that the publications disclosed the invention, and he, in consequence dissolved the interference. Rody moves to

dismiss on the ground that the court has no jurisdiction to consider the appeal.

We are without authority in an interference proceeding to reverse the Commissioner's ruling that Cowles's claims are not patentable because barred by the statute of public use. He did not pass upon the question of priority, and that is the only question reviewable by us in this kind of a proceeding. His action in dissolving the interference simply placed the parties back where they were before he had declared the interference, and we have no power to disturb it—it is not a final order. This has been often announced by us. (*In re Fullager,* 32 App. D. D.. 222; *Cosper v. Gold,* 34 App. D. C., 194; *Carlin v. Goldberg,* 45 App. D. C., 540; *Field v. Colman,* 47 App. D. C.. 189.) In the last case it is said:

We have held in many cases that this court is without jurisdiction to entertain an appeal in an interference case except from a judgment of priority. (Citing cases.)

As a result the motion to dismiss in this case for want of jurisdiction must be sustained.

Affirmed.

Court of Appeals of the District of Columbia.

L. OTZEN & CO. *v.* THE J. K. ARMSBY CO.

Decided December 1, 1919.

TRADE-MARKS—SIMILARITY.

A mark consisting of the words "From the Land of Sunshine" Held not deceptively similar to a mark consisting of. the words "Blossom and Sunshine," associated with the representation of blossoms and a sunburst.

Mr. A. P. Greeley for the appellant.

Mr. E. T. Fenwick and *Mr. L. L. Morrill* for the appellee.

VAN ORSDEL, J.:

This is an appeal from the Commissioner of Patents in a trade-mark cancelation proceeding, in which the petitioner, L. Otzen & Company, is seeking the cancelation of the registration of the mark "From the Land of Sunshine," granted to the registrant March 31, 1914.

Petitioner's mark consists of the words "Blossom and Sunshine," associated with the representation of blossoms and a sunburst. Both marks are used on identical goods—dried fruits.

It is contended by petitioner that the word "Sunshine" is the dominating feature of each mark. Registrant, however, answers this by way of a counterclaim that petitioner's registration of the mark in issue in 1906 was illegally secured, because of a prior use by registrant of a mark for fruits consisting of the word "Sunshine" alone. The use of this mark, registrant claims, was prior to any rights acquired by petitioner in its present mark. This would seem to foreclose conclusively petitioner's right to demand cancelation of registrant's mark on the ground that its dominating feature is the word "Sunshine," since prior rights to the use of that word are in the registrant.

This, however, does not decide the issue of probable confusion arising from the use of the marks in question. We agree with the tribunals below that there is nothing inherent in the appearance of the marks, or in the proof adduced by petitioner, to justify an adjudication that the marks are so similar as to be likely to lead to confusion in trade.

The decision of the Commissioner of Patents is affirmed, and the clerk is directed to certify these proceedings as by law required.

Affirmed.

11.	Fountains—		Irrigating and sprinkling—
109.	Bubble-cup,	66.	Systems.
107.	Ornamental—	59.	Nozzle-holders.
108.	Illuminated.	17.	Nozzles—
14.	Irrigating and sprinkling—	110.	Bubble-cup,
63.	Carts,	55.	Compressible,
64.	Heads,	56.	Flexible,
65.	Pipes,	57.	Splasher,
67.	Pumps,	58.	Systems,
62.	Roses and cans,	97.	Tube-cleaners.
61.	Shakers.	80.	Sprayers—
		81.	Cap,

The patents formerly contained in these subclasses have been placed for the most part (with the exception of those in subclasses 97 and 31) in class 299, Fluid Sprinkling, Spraying, and Diffusing, hereinafter established. Those formerly in subclass 97 have been placed in class 122, Liquid Heaters and Vaporizers, subclass 390, Cleaning, Fluid-jet, and the subclasses indented thereunder, and a portion of those formerly in subclass 31 have been placed in class 248, Supports, subclass 28.5, Hose-holders, Rack, hereinafter established.

In class 248, Supports, (Division VIII,) establish subclass—

Changes in Classification.

(ORDER No. 2,537.)

DEPARTMENT OF THE INTERIOR,
UNITED STATES PATENT OFFICE,
Washington, D. C., December 4, 1919.

The following changes in the classification of inventions are hereby directed, to take effect immediately:

In class 137, Water Distribution, (Division XXXIX,) abolish the following subclasses:

	Sprayers—
86.	Centrifugal,
84.	Cutters,
82.	Piston,
83.	Rose,
	Spray-fluid actuated—
155.	Motor,
87.	Reaction,
85.	Terminal cock.
154.	Surface diffusers.
31.	Water-supply hose-holders.

	Hose-holders—
28.5.	Rack.

The patents contained in this subclass have been taken from class 137, Water Distribution, subclass 31, Water-supply hose-holders, hereinbefore abolished.

Establish, in Division XXXIX, class 299, Fluid Sprinkling, Spraying, and Diffusing, with the following subclasses and definitions, the patents contained in this class having been taken for the most part from the subclasses hereinbefore abolished in class 137, Water Distribution:

299.—FLUID SPRINKLING, SPRAYING, AND DIFFUSING.

1.	Miscellaneous.
2.	Fountains—
3.	Ornamental—
4.	Illuminated,
5.	Reversible,
6.	Fluid-pressure feed,
7.	Pump or piston feed,
8.	Drinking—
9.	Combined faucet and fountain—
10.	Single outlet,
11.	Swinging attachment,
12.	Catch-basin and waste-outlet—
13.	Valved,
14.	Liftable bubble-nozzle,
15.	Nozzles or bubble-cups—
16.	Valved,
17.	Portable drinking-tubes.
18.	**Pattern sprayers or sprinklers—**
19.	Roses and pipes.
20.	**Slow diffusers—**
21.	(Withdrawn,)
22.	Drip,
23.	Barometric feed,
24.	Holders.
25.	**Intermittent discharge.**
26.	**Continuously-varied discharge.**
27.	Serial discharges.
28.	Rain-producers.
29.	Ambulant discharge and supply—
30.	Vehicle attachments,
31.	Railroad-sprinklers—
32.	Stock-alarms,
33.	Antirobber,
34.	Street-oilers—
35.	Heated,
36.	Street-flushers,
37.	Reciprocating discharging member,
38.	Rotating discharging member,
39.	Adjustable discharging member—
40.	Fluid-pressure feed,
41.	Liquid-pump feed—
42.	Return by-pass,
43.	Fluid-pressure feed—
44.	Hydrant-charged,
45.	Liquid-pump feed—
46.	Return by-pass.

299.—FLUID SPRINKLING, SPRAYING, AND DIFFUSING— Continued.

47.	Ambulant discharge and stationary supply—
48.	Coke-quenchers,
49.	Spray-fluid propelled—
50.	Reaction,
51.	Intermittent supply,
52.	Open tank or trough supply,
53.	Associated hose-reel,
54.	Revolving,
55.	Reciprocating,
56.	Nozzles—
57.	Adjustable.
58.	Non-ambulant discharge and supply—
59.	Nozzle flushers and cleaners,
60.	Embedded—
61.	Disappearing sprinklers.
62.	Moving discharging member—
63.	Rotating disk or drum,
64.	Spray-fluid actuated—
65.	Wrigglers,
66.	Piston,
67.	Rotor—
68.	External,
69.	Reaction—
70.	Multiple sets,
71.	Oscillatory,
72.	Adjustable discharging member—
73.	Nozzles—
74.	With deflectors,
75.	Nozzles—
76.	With deflectors.
77.	Combined hose-holder and fluid-supply—
78.	Reels—
79.	Automatic valves,
80.	Automatic valves.
81.	Overhead vehicle-washers.
82.	Locomotive-cab squirts.
	Sprayers—
83.	Dissolvers and mixers—
84.	Lateral chamber—
85.	Piston.
86.	Multiple fluid—
87.	Steam,
88.	Hand-pump atomizer type—
89.	Combined with pressure-feed,
90.	Collapsible ejector—
91.	Reservoir-supply,

299.—FLUID SPRINKLING, SPRAYING, AND DIFFUSING— Continued.

	Sprayers—
	Piston-feed—
92.	Threaded rod,
93.	Syringe type,
94.	Fluid-pressure feed—
95.	Air-compressor,
96.	Liquid-pump feed—
97.	Gravity-intake,
98.	Combined receptacle and syringe type,
99.	Receptacle and pump connecting means.
100.	
101.	**Sprinklers, gravity-feed—**
102.	Can-and-rose type.
103.	**Shakers.**
104.	**Sprinkler-pipes—**
105.	Couplings,
106.	Nozzled, and regulable outlet.
107.	**Nozzles—**
108.	Heads,
109.	Air-supply devices for firemen.
110.	Penetrating,
111.	Spray-poles and attachments,
112.	Handled,
113.	Fluid-rotation controllers—
114.	Whirlers—
115.	Centrally and peripherally ported—
116.	Valved,
117.	Convertible solid stream,
118.	Valved,
119.	Adjustable whirler member,
120.	Whirler-inserts.
121.	Deflectors—
122.	Cutters,
123.	Spray-fluid actuated—
124.	Ball,
125.	Nozzle-closures,
126.	Rotating,
127.	Adjustable—
128.	Transversely slidable,
129.	Swinging or pivoted,
130.	Axially movable—
131.	Valve-carried,
132.	Adjustable or variable discharge-port—
133.	Automatic,
134.	Constrictors,
135.	Swinging throttlers,

299.—FLUID SPRINKLING, SPRAYING, AND DIFFUSING— Continued.

Nozzles—
Adjustable or variable discharge-port—
136. Axially - reciprocable throttlers,
137. Interchangeable ported members,
138. Terminal cock,
139. Transversely - movable port - carrying member,
140. Multiple inlet,
141. Multiple outlet—
142. Aspiratory,

299.—FLUID SPRINKLING, SPRAYING, AND DIFFUSING— Continued.

Nozzles—
Multiple outlet—
143. Converging,
144. Valved—
145. Combined central and annular outlets—
146. Compound valve,
147. Rotary plug or disk,
148. Reciprocating valve,

299.—FLUID SPRINKLING, SPRAYING, AND DIFFUSING— Continued.

Nozzles—
149. Valved—
150. Axially movable,
151. Rotary—
152. Disk,
153. Spray-orifice,
154. Tapered and flattened.

J. T. NEWTON, *Commissioner.*

Changes in Classification.

(ORDER No. 2,538.)

DEPARTMENT OF THE INTERIOR,
UNITED STATES PATENT OFFICE,
Washington, D. C., December 10, 1919.

The following changes in the classification of inventions are hereby directed, to take effect immediately:

In class 21, Carriages and Wagons, (Division X,) abolish subclasses:

41. Seat-locks.
42. Seats—
43. Shifting,
44. Spring.

The patents formerly contained in these subclasses have been placed in class 155, Chairs and Seats, subclass 5, Special, Vehicle, and the subclasses indented thereunder, hereinafter established.

In class 45, Furniture, (Division VIII,) establish subclasses—

137. Pads and feet.
138. Upholstery-making.

The patents contained in these subclasses have been taken, respectively, from class 155, Chairs, subclasses 33, Pads and feet, and 43, Upholstery, hereinafter abolished.

In class 155, Chairs, (Division VIII,) change the title of the class to read *Class 155, Chairs and Seats,* abolish the existing subclass titles, and establish in lieu thereof the following subclasses and definitions:

155.—CHAIRS AND SEATS.

1. Miscellaneous.
2. Special—
3. School desk and seat type—
4. Adjustable desk-tops,
5. Vehicle—
6. Convertible seats and berths—
7. Carriage type,
8. Reclining,
9. Shock - absorbing or spring,
10. Auxiliary seats—
11. Seat attachments,
12. Rear—
13. Forwardly - swinging links,
14. Shifting horizontally—
15. Plurality of seats,
16. Grip-handles,
17. Baby-jumpers—
18. Vertically - swinging arms,
19. Horizontally - moving supports,
20. Body-supports,
21. Adjustable backs or leg-rests,
22. Walkers' or skaters' supports—
23. Horizontally - moving supports,
24. Body-supports,
25. Dental or barber—
26. Angularly - adjustable seats,
27. Revolving,
28. Surgical and invalid type—
29. Inclined beds,
30. Rolling,
31. Commode-chairs,
32. Disappearing,
33. Aisle-forming,
34. Duet piano-stools,
35. Shoe salesmen's,
36. Photographers',
37. Body-attached,
38. Convertible high and low—
39. Chair on top of table,
40. Rocking.
41. Convertible—
42. Stepladders,
43. Tables,
44. Cribs,
45. Beds—
46. Extensible laterally,
47. Rearwardly-folding extensible backs,
48. Sectional seats—
49. Rearwardly - folding backs.

270 O. G.—13

155.—CHAIRS AND SEATS—Continued.

50. Spring-supported—
51. Bracket-supported,
52. Pedestal-supported,
53. Backs and seats,
54. Oscillating seats—
55. Pivoted at front or back.
56. Oscillating—
57. Rolling or sliding,
58. Swings—
59. Motor-operated,
60. Oscillating frames,
61. Suspending means below seat,
62. Plurality of seats—
63. Operating means,
64. Separately - suspended seats,
65. Operating means,
66. Sofas, settees, or lounges,
67. Hammock-seats,
68. Adjustable or folding seats,
69. Rocking—
70. Operating means,
71. Platform—
72. Convertible to non-rocking,
73. Convertible to non-rocking—
74. Detachable rockers,
75. Folding—
76. Adjustable,
77. Tilting.
78. Bracket-supported—
79. Auxiliary seats,
80. Vertically - swinging brackets,
81. Horizontally - swinging brackets,
82. Vertically - adjustable brackets,
83. Folding seats—
84. Seats actuating other elements,
85. Opera-chair type—
86. Chairs in row,
87. School desk and seat type.
88. Vertically adjustable—
89. School desk and seat type,
90. Tilting,
91. Toggles or lazy-tongs,
92. Vertical screw—
93. Pedestal,
94. Pedestal.
95. Revolving—
96. Car-seat type—
97. Plurality of seats.

[Vol. 270. No. 1.]

155.—CHAIRS AND SEATS—Continued.

98. Reversible—
99. Interchangeable back and seat,
100. Reclining,
101. Walk-over backs—
102. Foot-rests,
103. Reversible backs—
104. Foot-rests.
105. Reclining—
106. Interconnected back and leg rest—
107. Synchronously - moving head-rest.
108. Stationary seat-frame—
109. Leg-rest operated by moving arm-rests,
110. Leg-rest operated by moving arm-rests,
111. Horizontally-moving leg-rests.
112. Sofas, settees, and lounges—
113. Angularly - adjustable ends,
114. Box-couches.
115. Adjustable seats— (Vertically adjustable, see subs. 88-94)
116. Angularly - adjustable backs—
117. Folding chairs,
118. Independently movable,
119. Flexible back and seat,
120. Angularly—
121. Laterally,
122. Moving laterally,
123. Combined tables and chairs—
124. Table in front of chair—
125. Enlarged arms,
126. Table swinging vertically,
127. Table supported on both chair-arms,
128. Table supported on brackets,
129. Bottoms.
130. Combinations of two or more seats—
131. Auxiliary seating devices—
132. Convertible,
133. Circus-seat type.
134. Pedestal-supported—
135. Folding—
136. Crossed legs,
137. Folding legs,
138. Radiating arms or legs.
139. Folding chairs—
140. Laterally,
141. Integral rear legs and back,

155.—CHAIRS AND SEATS—Continued.
Folding chairs—
142.　　Integral front legs and back—
143.　　Crossed legs—
144.　　　Pivoted back,
145.　　　Arm-rests,
146.　　　Sliding legs,
147.　　Crossed legs,
148.　　Parallel legs.
149. **Folding stools—**
150.　　Crossed legs,
151.　　Parallel legs.
152. **Folding and adjustable backs—**
153.　　Beach-seat type—
154.　　　Angularly adjustable,
155.　　Pivoted on forwardly-extending arms,
156.　　Pivoted above seat,
157.　　Adjustable supporting-post,
158.　　Not pivoted to seat,
159.　　Adjustable arms,
160.　　Adjusting means at pivot,

155.—CHAIRS AND SEATS—Continued.
Folding and adjustable backs—
161.　　Adjusting means below pivot,
162.　　Adjusting means behind back,
163.　　Adjusting means in front of back.
164. **Spring back-supports.**
165. **Foot-rests—**
166.　　Kneeling-stools—
167.　　　Scrubbing,
168.　　Radiator,
169.　　Independent,
170.　　Moving horizontally beneath seat,
171.　　Swinging vertically,
172.　　Adjustable vertically.
173. **Head-rests—**
174.　　Portable—
175.　　　Body-attached,
176.　　Changeable supporting-surfaces,
177.　　Folding or adjustable.

155.—CHAIRS AND SEATS—Continued.
178. **Bottoms and backs—**
179.　　Spring—
180.　　　Upholstery-covering,
181.　　　Upholstery - supporting surfaces,
182.　　Covers and slip-seats,
183.　　Changeable supporting-surfaces,
184.　　Upholstered—
185.　　　Tufted,
186.　　Veneer type,
187.　　Flexible.
188. **Attachments—**
189.　　Guards,
190.　　Garment-holders.
191. **Structural details—**
192.　　Wagon-seat type,
193.　　Bent wood,
194.　　Metal—
195.　　　Car-seat type,
196.　　Fastening means,
197.　　Bracing means,
198.　　Arm-rests.

J. T. NEWTON, *Commissioner.*

Changes in Classification.

(ORDER NO. 2,541.)

DEPARTMENT OF THE INTERIOR,
UNITED STATES PATENT OFFICE,
Washington, D. C., December 22, 1919.

The following changes in the classification of inventions are hereby directed, to take effect immediately :

In class 214, Material or Article Handling, (Division IV,) abolish the following subclass, with its definition :

Roadway vehicle loading or unloading—
　Self loading or unloading vehicles—
　　Elevator—
76.　　　Dumping-body type.

The patents formerly contained in this subclass have been placed for the most part in class 298, Land-Vehicles—Dumping, subclasses 5, Two-wheel ; 7, With load-delivering chute; 9, Rotating and tilting, and 11, Elevating and tilting.

J. T. NEWTON,
Commissioner.

ALPHABETICAL LIST OF PATENTEES

TO WHOM

PATENTS WERE ISSUED ON THE 6TH DAY OF JANUARY, 1920.

NOTE.—Arranged in accordance with the first significant character or word of the name. (In accordance with city and telephone directory practice.)

Abbott, Herbert E., and E. Enz, Oakville, Iowa. Tractor steering device. No. 1,327,511; Jan. 6; v. 270; p. 118.

Abbott, William T., et al. (See Soule, Charles E., assignor.)

Abercrombie, Jamie, Houston, and N. M. Dunman, West Columbia, Tex. Combination well-packer and setting-tool. No. 1,327,077; Jan. 6; v. 270; p. 37.

Åberg, Carl J., Stenstorp, Sweden. Road-making. No. 1,327,131; Jan. 6; v. 270; p. 47.

Abraham, Herbert, New York, N. Y., assignor to The Standard Paint Company. Strip-shingle. No. 1,326,899; Jan. 6; p. 3.

Acker, Julius J. (See Goodwin and Acker.)

Adams, Joseph H., Brooklyn, N. Y., assignor to The Texas Company, Houston, Tex. Conversion of liquids, fluids, and oils. No. 1,327,263; Jan. 6; v. 270; p. 72.

Aktiebolaget Lidköpings Mekaniska Verkstad. (See Soderlund, Carl G., assignor.)

Albers, Ulfert L., Rico, Colo. Toothbrush. No. 1,326,900; Jan. 6; v. 270; p. 3.

Alderman, L. R., & Co. (See Walker, Roy S., assignor.)

Aldrich Pump Company. (See Aldrich, Roscoe H., assignor.)

Aldrich, Roscoe H., assignor to Aldrich Pump Company, Allentown, Pa. Reinforced pump-casing. No. 1,327,512; Jan. 6; v. 270; p. 118.

Aldridge, James G. W., Westminster, London, England. Machine for charging and discharging retorts. No. 1,327,582; Jan. 6; v. 270; p. 131.

Alfano, Giuseppe, New York, N. Y. Safety device for elevators. No. 1,327,513; Jan. 6; v. 270; p. 118.

Allen, George W., assignor to B. F. Sturtevant Company, Boston, Mass. Pneumatic cleaner. No. 1,326,901; Jan. 6; v. 270; p. 3.

Allman, William H., Blythedale, Mo. Flying-machine. No. 1,327,514; Jan. 6; v. 270; p. 118.

Allsteelequip Company, The. (See Erickson, Axel F., assignor.)

Alsten, Alfred O., Worcester, Mass. Pneumatic vulcanizing-core. No. 1,327,264; Jan. 6; v. 270; p. 72.

Altmann, Jakob, Weesen, Switzerland. Machine for truing loom-shuttles. No. 1,327,515; Jan. 6; v. 270; p. 119.

American Blower Company. (See Cunliffe, Cicero M., assignor.)

American Bosch Magneto Corporation. (See Honold and Krauss, assignors.)

American Can Company. (See Augensen, August M., assignor.)

American Dressler Tunnel Kilns. (See Meehan, Paul A., assignor.)

American Grain Deodorizing Co. (See Moore, Payton J. H., assignor.)

American Laundry Machinery Company, The. (See Andrée, William E., assignor.)

American Marine Equipment Corporation. (See Row and Davis, assignors.)

American Potash Corporation. (See Charlton, Harry W., assignor.)

American Tool Company. (See Beaudreau, Edward H., assignor.)

Anchor Cap & Closure Corporation. (See Wieland, Frederick G., assignor.)

Anderfuhren, Louis, Baltimore, Md. Pneumatic-tire alarm. No. 1,327,416; Jan. 6; v. 270; p. 99.

Anderson, Anton D., Harrison, N. Y. Talking-machine. No. 1,327,516; Jan. 6; v. 270; p. 119.

Anderson, Carl E., East Orange, assignor to Eastern Tool & Mfg. Company, Bloomfield, N. J. Binder. No. 1,327,186; Jan. 6; p. 270; p. 58.

Anderson, Gustaf A., assignor to Landis Machine Company, Waynesboro, Pa. Cutter-head. No. 1,327,007; Jan. 6; v. 270; p. 24.

Anderson, Gustaf A., assignor to Landis Machine Company, Waynesboro, Pa. Cutter-head. No. 1,327,008; Jan. 6; v. 270; p. 24.

Anderson, William S., Victorville, Calif. Valve-truing device. No. 1,327,187; Jan. 6; v. 270; p. 58.

Andrée, William E., Chicago, Ill., assignor to The American Laundry Machinery Company, Cincinnati, Ohio. Electric switch. No. 1,327,009; Jan. 6; v. 270; p. 25.

Andrews, Moril V., and S. W. Holman, assignors to Mora Pump Company, Marmarth, N. D. Rotary water-pump. No. 1,327,517; Jan. 6; v. 270; p. 119.

Andrews, Shellie. (See May, Walter P., assignor.)

Anthony, Marcus O., assignor to A. Kimball Company, New York, N. Y. Pin-ticket. No. 1,327,010; Jan. 6; v. 270; p. 25.

Arbon, Paul, assignor to R. Guiberson, Tulsa, Okla. Sand-trap. No. 1,327,583; Jan. 6; v. 270; p. 131.

Archibald, James G., et al. (See Schott, John H., assignor.)

Armour Grain Company. (See Remmers, Bernhard, assignor.)

Arquint, Hans, Richterswil, Switzerland. Car-frame. No. 1,327,367; Jan. 6; v. 270; p. 90.

Arndt, Franklin E., Galion, Ohio. Clamp for burial-vaults. No. 1,327,011; Jan. 6; v. 270; p. 25.

Asmondis, Rocco, Zellenople, Pa. Saw-sharpening machine. No. 1,327,012; Jan. 6; v. 270; p. 26.

Atlass Process Company. (See von Groeling, Albrecht F. G. C. P. J., assignor.)

Atterbury, Grosvenor, New York, N. Y. Process of and apparatus for making concrete slabs. No. 1,326,902; Jan. 6; v. 270; p. 3.

Auerbach, Julia H., Hollywood, Calif. Corset-fastening. No. 1,327,078; Jan. 6; v. 270; p. 38.

Augensen, August M., Maywood, Ill., assignor to American Can Company, New York, N. Y. Can-feeding mechanism. No. 1,326,903; Jan. 6; v. 270; p. 3.

Austin, Frederick C. (See Bentson, Hans J., assignor.)

Austral Window Company. (See Myers, Winter W., assignor.)

Auto-Ordnance Corporation. (See Eickhoff and Tunks, assignors.)

Automotive Development Co. (See Huggins, Merion J., assignor.)

Baader, Stephan. (See Hough and Baader.)

Babendreer, Albert, Ocean Springs, Miss., assignor to Whole Grain Wheat Company, Phoenix, Ariz. Treating food. No. 1,327,220; Jan. 6; v. 270; p. 64.

Bache-Wiig, Carl, Portland, Me. Preparing pulp. No. 1,327,221; Jan. 6; v. 270; p. 65.

Baender, Charles L., Oakland, Calif., assignor, by mesne assignments, to The Torrington Company, Torrington, Conn. Carpet-sweeping appliance. No. 1,327,456; Jan. 6; v. 270; p. 107.

Baker, Joseph, & Sons. (See Hewitt, Harry, assignor.)

Balkwill, Wesley J. (See Schweiger and Balkwill.)

Balster, Frederick W., Wilmington, Del. Steam-boiler. No. 1,327,188; Jan. 6; v. 270; p. 58.

Balthasar, Harry G., assignor to Interstate Tool and Manufacturing Company, St. Louis, Mo. Dial-indicator for combination-locks. No. 1,327,457; Jan. 6; v. 270; p. 107.

Barnard, Hugh A., Houstonville, N. C. Folding chicken-coop. No. 1,327,368; Jan. 6; v. 270; p. 91.

Barnes, Frank R., Dupree, S. D. Centrifugal gun. No. 1,327,518; Jan. 6; v. 270; p. 119.

Barrell, Charles S., Boston, Mass. Swivel device. No. 1,327,013; Jan. 6; v. 270; p. 26.

Barrett Company, The. (See Perry, Ray P., assignor.)

Barton, Charles N., assignor of one-third to J. W. Langley and one-third to W. Peek, Indianapolis, Ind. Sectional machinery-repair washer. No. 1,327,417; Jan. 6; v. 270; p. 100.

Bastian, Charles L., Chicago, Ill. Soda-fountain apparatus. No. 1,327,189; Jan. 6; v. 270; p. 58.

Bateman Manufacturing Company. (See Willis and Woodworth, assignors.)

Bates, Arthur, Leicester, England, assignor, by mesne assignments, to United Shoe Machinery Corporation, Paterson, N. J. Wax-applying device. No. 1,327,014; Jan. 6; v. 270; p. 26.

Beardsley, Edson L., Columbus, Ohio. Valve-lifter. No. 1,327,015; Jan. 6; v. 270; p. 26.

Bearse, Frank P., et al. (See Soule, Charles E., assignor.)

Beaudreau, Edward H., assignor to American Tool Company, Meriden, Conn. Automobile non-skid chain. No. 1,327,369; Jan. 6; v. 270; p. 91.

Beckett, John R., Somerville, Mass. Universal angle fixture. No. 1,327,370; Jan. 6; v. 270; p. 91.

Belcher, Leon K., New York, N. Y. Heat-distributer. No. 1,326,904; Jan. 6; v. 270; p. 4.

Belrose, Thomas H. (See Funk, James M., assignor.)

Bender, David G., Blue Island, Ill. Wall construction. No. 1,327,584; Jan. 6; v. 270; p. 132.

Bendix, Vincent, Chicago, Ill. Engine-starter. No. 1,327,132; Jan. 6; v. 270; p. 47.

Bendix, Vincent, Chicago, Ill. Engine-starter. No. 1,327,302; Jan. 6; v. 270; p. 79.

Bendix, Vincent, Chicago, Ill. Engine-starter. No. 1,327,303; Jan. 6; v. 270; p. 79.

Bendix, Vincent, Chicago, Ill. Engine-starter. No. 1,327,304; Jan. 6; v. 270; p. 79.

Benjamin, Bert R., and C. A. Hagadone, Oak Park, Ill., assignors, by mesne assignments, to International Harvester Company. Pivoted discharge-arm. No. 1,327,305; Jan. 6; v. 270; p. 79.

Bentson, Hans J., Winthrop Harbor, assignor to F. C. Austin, Chicago, Ill. Trenching-machine. No. 1,327,418; Jan. 6; v. 270; p. 100.

Berger, Isidore S., New York, N. Y. Tooth-shade guide. No. 1,327,306; Jan. 6; v. 270; p. 79.

Berghaus, John H., Jr. (See Lamkin and Berghaus.)

Berry, Ora, Princeton, Ind. Automatic pump. No. 1,327,371; Jan. 6; v. 270; p. 91.

Beshenich, Marija, Beatty, assignor of one-fourth to J. Tirodor and one-fourth to M. Mohanec, Greensburg, Pa. Non-refillable bottle. No. 1,327,133; Jan. 6; v. 270; p. 47.

Bessaire, Gustave, Neuilly-sur-Seine, France. Projectile. No. 1,327,372; Jan. 6; v. 270; p. 91.

Bethlehem Steel Company. (See Lukens, William L., assignor.)

Bigoney, Thomas W., New York, N. Y. Container and making same. No. 1,327,190; Jan. 6; v. 270; p. 58.

Birch, Joseph F., Jr., assignor to Musher and Company, Inc., Baltimore, Md. Fish-cleaning machine. No. 1,326,905; Jan. 6; v. 270; p. 4.

Bitler, Frederic C., Brooklyn, N. Y., assignor of one-half to L. V. Jones, Norwalk, Conn. Bottle-stopper. No. 1,327,519; Jan. 6; v. 270; p. 119.

Bixby, Allan S., Indianapolis, Ind., assignor to The National Malleable Castings Company, Cleveland, Ohio. Molding-machine. No. 1,327,419; Jan. 6; v. 270; p. 100.

Blackburn, Arthur H., Downers Grove, and F. E. Fleming, assignors to The Underfeed Stoker Company of America, Chicago, Ill. The Underfeed furnace. No. 1,326,906; Jan. 6; v. 270; p. 4.

Blake, William F., assignor of fifty-one per cent. to H. W. Duvendack, Toledo, Ohio. Can-opener. No. 1,327,184; Jan. 6; v. 270; p. 48.

Blanfield, Charles, Boston, Mass. Pistol-light. No. 1,327,585; Jan. 6; v. 270; p. 132.

Blardone, George, New Orleans, La. Regeneration of decolorizing-carbons. No. 1,327,222; Jan. 6; v. 270; p. 65.

Blasi, Joseph, Brooklyn, N. Y., assignor to the Singer Manufacturing Company. Sewing on garment-hooks. No. 1,327,191; Jan. 6; v. 270; p. 59.

Blessmeyer, Fred D., Pittsburgh, Pa. Stabilizing device. No. 1,327,586; Jan. 6; v. 270; p. 132.

Bliss, John, London, England. Key-operated rotatable part of valves, faucets, locking devices, or other articles. No. 1,327,587; Jan. 6; v. 270; p. 132.

Bliss, William L., assignor to U. S. Light & Heat Corporation, Niagara Falls, N. Y. Rheostat. No. 1,327,135; Jan. 6; v. 270; p. 48.

Boles, Clarence, Hugoton, Kans. Leaf-spring. No. 1,327,016; Jan. 6; v. 270; p. 26.

Boltshauser, Conrad, assignor to Company Phoebus, E. G., Zurich, Switzerland. Electric pocket-lamp. No. 1,327,017; Jan. 6; v. 270; p. 26.

Bond, James W., Columbia, S. C. Rim-tool. No. 1,326,907; Jan. 6; v. 270; p. 4.

Booth, Augustus C., Los Angeles, Calif. Vertically-adjustable engine-lathe. No. 1,327,604; Jan. 6; v. 270; p. 135.

Booth, William N., Detroit, Mich. Trailer draft connection. No. 1,327,265; Jan. 6; v. 270; p. 72.

Borgarello, Octavio E., Buenos Aires, Argentina. Machine for securing the felts to piano-hammers. No. 1,327,015; Jan. 6; v. 270; p. 27.

Both, Tonjes A., Stratford, Conn., assignor to The Connecticut Electric Manufacturing Company. Mechanical movement. No. 1,327,192; Jan. 6; v. 270; p. 59.

Bowden, George, Malden, Mass. End-gate fastener. No. 1,327,079; Jan. 6; v. 270; p. 38.

Bowles, John A., Richmond, Va. Locomotive-driving-box lubricator. No. 1,327,136; Jan. 6; v. 270; p. 48.

Boyd, Alexander J. (See Smith, John F., assignor.)

Boylan, Samuel H., Joplin, Mo. Classifier. No. 1,326,908; Jan. 6; v. 270; p. 4.

Boyle, Louis M., Los Angeles, Calif. Supply outfit for vehicles, &c. No. 1,327,223; Jan. 6; v. 270; p. 65.

Braddy, Clyde E., Pinebluff, Wyo. Grain-separator. No. 1,327,193; Jan. 6; v. 270; p. 59.

Bradley, George M., Lansing, Mich. Auto burglar-alarm. No. 1,327,366; Jan. 6; v. 270; p. 72.

Brandenstein, Daniel, New York, N. Y., and J. Fischer, Roseville, N. J. Pedal-operated mechanism. No. 1,327,187; Jan. 6; v. 270; p. 48.

Branson, Samuel J., Chicago, Ill., and E. C. Strathmann, assignors to The Concrete Forms Company, Indianapolis, Ind. False work for concrete floors. No. 1,327,081; Jan. 6; v. 270; p. 38.

Brewster, Leon B., and F. Weisehan, assignors to The Ferro Machine and Foundry Company, Cleveland, Ohio. Welding. No. 1,327,267; Jan. 6; v. 270; p. 73.

Bright, Fred E., Philadelphia, Pa. Chuck. No. 1,327,194; Jan. 6; v. 270; p. 59.

Brinkman, Louis H., Glen Ridge, N. J., assignor to Titeflex Metal Hose Corporation. Tube. No. 1,327,195; Jan. 6; v. 270; p. 59.

British Ever Ready Company, The. (See Dewick and Caddy, assignors.)

Britton, Coozie, Moline, Ill. Educational playing-cards. No. 1,327,019; Jan. 6; v. 270; p. 27.

British Westinghouse Electric and Manufacturing Company. (See Scanes, Arthur E. L., assignor.)

Brock, Matthias, Boston, Mass. assignor, by mesne assignments, to United Shoe Machinery Corporation, Paterson, N. J. Staple-lasting machine. No. 1,327,196; Jan. 6; v. 270; p. 59.

Brogan, Michael F., Lawrence, Mass., assignor, by mesne assignments, to United Shoe Machinery Corporation, Paterson, N. J. Heel-clamping device. No. 1,327,020; Jan. 6; v. 270; p. 27.

Brogden, Joseph T., Providence, R. I., assignor to Revere Rubber Company. Wind-up device for sheeted material. No. 1,327,420; Jan. 6; v. 270; p. 100.

Brons, Derk, Zuidbroek, Netherlands, assignor to N. V. Machinefabriek Brons, Zuidbroek, Groningen, Netherlands. Apparatus for drying vegetables and the like. No. 1,326,909; Jan. 6; v. 270; p. 5.

Brooks, Roscoe A., assignor to Western Tire & Rubber Works, Chicago, Ill. Tire-retreading apparatus. No. 1,327,807; Jan. 6; v. 270; p. 80.

Brown, Carl S., Portland, Oreg. Electric elevator-controlling system. No. 1,327,421; Jan. 6; v. 270; p. 100.

Brown, Gustave C., Bridgeport, Conn. Match-safe. No. 1,327,458; Jan. 6; v. 270; p. 107.

Brown, Henry J., New York, N. Y. Camera attachment. No. 1,327,138; Jan. 6; v. 270; p. 48.

Brown Hoisting Machinery Company, The. (See Taylor, Ernest W., assignor.)

Brown, Horace P., and C. L. Johnston, Oakland, Calif. Paper folding and interleaving machine. No. 1,327,588; Jan. 6; v. 270; p. 132.

Brown, Munro S., Goldfield, Nev. Self-lighting cigarette. No. 1,327,139; Jan. 6; v. 270; p. 49.

Brown, Thomas E., New York, N. Y. Hydraulic transmission. No. 1,327,080; Jan. 6; v. 270; p. 38.

Browning, Walter H., Wembley, England. Strip-feeding mechanism. No. 1,327,520; Jan. 6; v. 270; p. 120.

Buch, Royer S., York, Pa. Adjustable jacket. No. 1,327,224; Jan. 6; v. 270; p. 65.

Buck, Charles F., Topeka, Kans. Sheet-metal-cutting machine. No. 1,327,082; Jan. 6; v. 270; p. 38.

Buckham, George T. (See Dawson and Buckham.)

Buel, Hillhouse, Seattle, Wash. Treating milk. No. 1,327,308; Jan. 6; v. 270; p. 80.

Bufford, George W., Buffalo, assignor to J. H. Williams & Company, Brooklyn, N. Y. Chain pipe-wrench. No. 1,327,309; Jan. 6; v. 270; p. 80.

Bulanda, John, Pullman, Ill. Permutation-lock. No. 1,327,140; Jan. 6; v. 270; p. 49.

Bumpas, James L., and P. Falcke, Chicago, Ill.; said Bumpas assignor to United States Ordnance Company, Washington, D. C. Sight. No. 1,327,141; Jan. 6; v. 270; p. 49.

Bunker, Ward S., Waukesha, Wis. Camping-automobile. No. 1,327,589; Jan. 6; v. 270; p. 132.

Burby, John M., Webster, Mass. Repulping old or waste paper. No. 1,327,590; Jan. 6; v. 270; p. 133.

Burket, Henry E., Kansas City, Mo. Rectifier system. No. 1,327,521; Jan. 6; v. 270; p. 120.

Burkle, Emil F. (See Mersenbocker, James A., assignor.)

Burrage, George H. (See Stephenson, Leigh J., assignor.) (Reissue.)

Burroughs Adding Machine Company. (See Gooch, Claiborne W., assignor.)

Buscher, Theodore W. (See Kadish and Buscher.)

Butcher, James M., assignor, by mesne assignments, to Marshall Dobbins & Co., Chicago, Ill. Door-knob alarm. No. 1,327,021; Jan. 6; v. 270; p. 27.

Butterfield, Percy F., Toronto, Ontario, Canada. Nail. No. 1,326,910; Jan. 6; v. 270; p. 5.

Byers, Joseph J., Brookline, assignor to Products Syndicate Inc., Boston, Mass. Material treated with cellulose derivatives. No. 1,327,197; Jan. 6; v. 270; p. 60.

Caddy, Donald B. (See Dewick and Caddy.)

Call, Franklin H., Portland, Oreg. Cabinet for phonographic records. No. 1,327,142; Jan. 6; v. 270; p. 49.

Call, Franklin H., Portland, Oreg. Cabinet for phonographic records. No. 1,327,143; Jan. 6; v. 270; p. 49.

Campbell, Donald F. (See Gow and Campbell.)

Carborundum Company, The. (See MacGregor, William, assignor.)

Carden, Luther W., Cherokee, Ala. Nut-lock. No. 1,327,373; Jan. 6; v. 270; p. 92.

Carlson, C. A., administrator. (See Carlson, John A. and C. A.)

Carlson, Emilia A. (See Carlson, John A., assignor.)

Carlson, John A., deceased; C. A. Carlson, administrator, assignor to E. A. Carlson, Idaho Falls, Idaho. Line-square. No. 1,327,198; Jan. 6; v. 270; p. 60.

Carney, Wilbur O. (See Lingle, George W., assignor.)

Carlson, Charles G., Chicago, Ill. Clothespole. No. 1,326,911; Jan. 6; v. 270; p. 5.

Carr, Oma, New York, N. Y. Tube suspension. No. 1,327,144; Jan. 6; v. 270; p. 50.

Carter, Charlie O., Anderson, assignor to Draper Corporation, Hopedale, Mass. Tension for spoolers. No. 1,327,022; Jan. 6; v. 270; p. 27.

Cary, Spencer C., Brooklyn, N. Y. Welding. No. 1,326,912; Jan. 6; v. 270; p. 5.

Cary, Spencer C., Brooklyn, N. Y. Means for cleaning metal preparatory to welding. No. 1,326,913; Jan. 6; v. 270; p. 5.

Charles, Mario C., Jersey City, N. J. Package-tie holder. No. 1,327,591; Jan. 6; v. 270; p. 133.

Charlton, Harry W. (See Meadows, Hauber, and Charlton.)

Charlton, Harry W., Jones Point, N. Y., assignor to American Potash Corporation. Cementing material obtained from greensand. No. 1,327,145; Jan. 6; v. 270; p. 50.

Charter, James A., Chicago, Ill. Wheel. No. 1,327,310; Jan. 6; v. 270; p. 80.

Cherry, Louis B., Kansas City, Mo. Electrical apparatus for the electrochemical treatment of liquid hydrocarbon and other compounds. No. 1,327,023; Jan. 6; v. 270; p. 27.

Chesnutt, Ralph C., Pottstown, Pa. Manifold for internal-combustion engines. No. 1,327,311; Jan. 6; v. 270; p. 80.

Christen, Victor H., Toledo, Ohio. Glass-cleaner. No. 1,327,146; Jan. 6; v 270; p. 50.

Christenson, John O., Wilson, Fla. Combined shaving-brush and shaving-stick holder. No. 1,326,914; Jan. 6; v. 270; p. 6.

Christians, George W., Chattanooga, Tenn. Sealing crevices in rock formations. No. 1,327,268; Jan. 6; v. 270; p. 73.

Christians, George W., Chattanooga, Tenn. Apparatus for use in sealing crevices in rock formations. No. 1,327,269; Jan. 6; v. 270; p. 73.

Chung, Kun S., Honolulu, Hawaii. Scraper. No. 1,327,522; Jan. 6; v. 270; p. 120.

Church, Harold D., assignor to Packard Motor Car Company, Detroit, Mich. Hydrocarbon-motor. No. 1,327,147; Jan. 6; v. 270; p. 50.

Cleary, Edward, assignor to The Connecticut Web & Buckle Company, Bridgeport, Conn. Two-piece cast-off. No. 1,327,199; Jan. 6; v. 270; p. 60.

Cleveland, Clement, New York, N. Y. Pencil-sharpener. No. 1,327,459; Jan. 6; v. 270; p. 107.

Cline, Charles E., Abingdon, Ill. Animal-restraining device. No. 1,327,374; Jan. 6; v. 270; p. 92.

Close, Leonard L., assignor to Marion Foundry Corporation, Marion, Ind. Means for locking grate-bars. No. 1,327,270; Jan. 6; v. 270; p. 73.

Cohen, Henry S. (See Rogers, John A., assignor.)

Colbert, Clarence F., Milwaukee, Wis., assignor to Dixie Fruit Products Corporation, New York, N. Y. Coring-machine. No. 1,327,083; Jan. 6; v. 270; p. 39.

Collins, Roy L., Redwood, N. Y. Curtain and shade fixture. No. 1,327,460; Jan. 6; v. 270; p. 108.

Comber, Hubert H., and J. W. Stalker, Winnipeg, Manitoba, Canada. Extracting oils from coal-tar. No. 1,327,271; Jan. 6; v. 270; p. 73.

Compagnie D'Applications Mecaniques. (See Rouanet, Louis, assignor.)

Conaway, William H., Wichita, Kans. Apparatus for handling fence-wire. No. 1,327,024; Jan. 6; v. 270; p. 28.

Concrete Forms Company, The. (See Branson and Strathmann, assignors.)

Connecticut Electric Manufacturing Company, The. (See Both, Tonjes A., assignor.)

Connecticut Web & Buckle Company, The. (See Cleary, Edward, assignor.)

Converse, M. E., & Son Co. (See Hewitt, Fred L., assignor.)

Corbi, Joseph L., assignor of one-third to F. K. Heindrich, and one-third to D. S. Margolis, Washington, D. C. Fastening device for collars. No. 1,326,915; Jan. 6; v. 270; p. 6.

Coulter, Holbrook W., trustee. (See Merritt, Frank W., assignor.)

Covar, George P., Chester, S. C. Combined rolling-pin and culinary holder. No. 1,327,461; Jan. 6; v. 270; p. 108.

Cowan, Frank. (See Kellogg, Neff, Rogers, and Cowan.)

Cowan Truck Company. (See Hennessy, Daniel E., assignor.)

Crawford, Alex S., Cannonsville, N. Y. Horseshoe. No. 1,327,523; Jan. 6; v. 270; p. 120.

Crawford, George M., et al. (See London, Jacob M., assignor.)

Crehan, Hubert, Pittsburgh, Pa. Bolt-threading machine. No. 1,327,312; Jan. 6; v. 270; p. 80.

Crombie, Louis A., Hicksville, N. Y. Wrench. No. 1,327,524; Jan. 6; v. 270; p. 120.

Cross Paper Feeder Company. (See Upham, Burt F., assignor.)

Crossen, Edgar H., Franklin, Pa. Piston for internal-combustion motors. No. 1,327,462; Jan. 6; v. 270; p. 108.

Crowther, Henry M., Kingman, Ariz. Aeroplane safety-parachute and means of launching same from aeroplanes. No. 1,327,592; Jan. 6; v. 270; p. 133.

Crouse-Hinds Company. (See Schneider, August H., assignor.)

Crozier, John A., Knoxville, Iowa. Window-bracket. No. 1,327,025; Jan. 6; v. 270; p. 28.

Cru Patents Corporation. (See Gellenmesser, Charles, assignor.)

Cunliffe, Cicero M., assignor to American Blower Company, Detroit, Mich. Apparatus for treating painted or varnished articles. No. 1,327,313; Jan. 6; v. 270; p. 80.

Cunliffe, Cicero M., assignor to American Blower Company, Detroit, Mich. Treating painted or varnished articles. No. 1,327,314; Jan. 6; v. 270; p. 81.

Curttright, George L., Olin, Iowa. Hog-oiler. No. 1,327,088; Jan. 6; v. 270; p. 39.

Curtis, Walter L., Springfield, Mass. Die for making double-ended rivets. No. 1,327,525; Jan. 6; v. 270; p. 121.

Dabbs, Albert E., S. W. Savage, Manchester, and A. H. Hindle, Birmingham, assignors of one-eighth to A. Liddle, Manchester, and one-half to J. G. W. Gruban, Kingsway, London, England. Roller or ball bearing. No. 1,327,026; Jan. 6; v. 270; p. 28.

Darby, James K., Chillicothe, Ohio. Press-roll arrangement for paper-making machines. No. 1,327,225; Jan. 6; v. 270; p. 65.

Darier, Georges E., Chêne, near Geneva, Switzerland. Gas and liquid contact apparatus. No. 1,327,422; Jan. 6; v. 270; p. 101.

Davies, Evan W., Dowlais, Wales. Apparatus for manipulation of metal ingots and the like. No. 1,327,315; Jan. 6; v. 270; p. 81.

Davis, Claude B., Richmond, assignor of one-half to J. W. Keeling, Danville, Va. Wringer attachment for tubs. No. 1,327,526; Jan. 6; v. 270; p. 121.

Davis, Claude B., Richmond, assignor of one-half to J. W. Keeling, Danville, Va. Wringer attachment for tubs. No. 1,327,527; Jan. 6; v. 270; p. 121.

Davis, Harry W., Edgewood Park, Pa. Section-switch. No. 1,327,463; Jan. 6; v. 270; p. 108.

Davis, Howard C. (See Row and Davis.)

Dawson, Alva K., Jacksonville, Fla. Combined headcovering and hair-comb. No. 1,327,528; Jan. 6; v. 270; p. 121.

Dawson, Arthur T., and G. T. Buckham, Westminster, London, assignors to Vickers Limited, Westminster, England. Gun-mounting. No. 1,327,084; Jan. 6; v. 270; p. 39.

Dawson, Arthur T., and G. T. Buckham, London, assignors to Vickers Limited, Westminster, England. Gun-mounting. No. 1,327,085; Jan. 6; v. 270; p. 39.

Dawson, Arthur T., and G. T. Buckham, London, assignors to Vickers Limited, Westminster, England. Machine-gun. No. 1,327,086; Jan. 6; v. 270; p. 39.

Dawson, Arthur T., and G. T. Buckham, London, assignors to Vickers Limited, Westminster, England. Breech-loading ordnance. No. 1,327,087; Jan. 6; v. 270; p. 39.

Deak, Alexander and J., Brooklyn, N. Y. Aerial vessel. No. 1,327,529; Jan. 6; v. 270; p. 121.

Deak, Joseph. (See Deak, Alexander and J.)

De Kalb, J. Emmons, et al. (See Schott, John H., assignor.)

Dean, William W., Stamford, Conn., assignor to Splitdorf Electrical Company, Newark, N. J. Ignition-generator. No. 1,327,375; Jan. 6; v. 270; p. 92.

Deere and Company. (See Paul, William L., assignor.)

De Laval Separator Company, The. (See Wright, Bert R., assignor.)

Delieuvin, Paul A. M., Neuilly-sur-Seine, France. Device for increasing the adherence of agricultural tractors to the soil. No. 1,327,376; Jan. 6; v. 270; p. 92.

Dellgren, Karl, Västervik, Sweden. Liquid-pump. No. 1,327,272; Jan. 6; v. 270; p. 73.

De Long, Charles E., New York, N. Y. Watch-escapement. No. 1,327,226; Jan. 6; v. 270; p. 65.

Denis, Albert D., et al. (See Genin, John B., assignor.)

Dennis, Samuel K., Chicago, Ill., assignor, by mesne assignments, to International Harvester Company. Seed-planter. No. 1,327,089; Jan. 6; v. 270; p. 40.

Dennis, Samuel K., Chicago, Ill., assignor, by mesne assignments, to International Harvester Company. Clutch mechanism for corn-planters and like machines. No. 1,327,090; Jan. 6; v. 270; p. 40.

Dennis, William K. (See Goodwin, James D., assignor.)

Dennison, Herbert J. S. (See Thompson and Dennison.)

Dewick, Bernard, and D. B. Caddy, London, assignors to The British Ever Ready Company Limited, Holloway, London, England. Apparatus for playing a game of skill. No. 1,327,464; Jan. 6; v. 270; p. 108.

Dick, Joseph, assignor to The Joseph Dick Manufacturing Company, Canton, Ohio. Pipe-door. No. 1,327,877; Jan. 6; v. 270; p. 92.

Dick, Joseph, Manufacturing Company. (See Dick, Joseph, assignor.)

Dieckmann, Adolf, Cincinnati, Ohio. Sheet-metal-elbow-forming machine. No. 1,326,916; Jan. 6; v. 270; p. 6.

Dings, Ralph E., and L. Schuster, New York, N. Y. Water-proof varnish. No. 1,326,917; Jan. 6; v. 270; p. 7.

Dixie Fruit Products Corporation. (See Colbert, Clarence F., assignor.)

Dixon, Russell A. (See Mason and Dixon.)

Dombkowski, Kazimer, Stanhope, N. J. Safeguard-lamp for automobiles. No. 1,326,918; Jan. 6; v. 270; p. 7.

Dombkowski, Kazimer, Stanhope, N. J. Sanitary cuspidor or refuse-receptacle. No. 1,326,919; Jan. 6; v. 270; p. 7.

Drane, Merritt, Lyndon, Ky. Direction-signal. No. 1,327,027; Jan. 6; v. 270; p. 28.

Draper Corporation. (See Carter, Charlie O., assignor.)

Draper Corporation. (See Stimpson, Edward S., assignor.)

Druar, Frank J., assignor to Packard Motor Car Company, Detroit, Mich. Hydrocarbon-motor. No. 1,327,148; Jan. 6; v. 270; p. 50.

Dryen, Achille, Londerzeel, Belgium. Pump. No. 1,327,423; Jan. 6; v. 270; p. 101.

Dublier, William, New York, N. Y. Series condenser. No. 1,327,593; Jan. 6; v. 270; p. 133.

Dudley, Howard M., Philadelphia, Pa. Dyeing-machine. No. 1,327,200; Jan. 6; v. 270; p. 60.

Dummer, Horace B., New York, N. Y. Toy aeroplane. No. 1,327,530; Jan. 6; v. 270; p. 121.
Duncan, De Lloyd O., Rockford, Ill. Reservoir-broach. No. 1,327,149; Jan. 6; v. 270; p. 50.
Dunman, Nesbit M. (See Abercrombie and Dunman.)
Dupler, Raymond R., Toledo, Ohio. Wheeled harrow. No. 1,327,424; Jan. 6; v. 270; p. 101.
Du Pont, E. I., de Nemours & Company. (See Marshall, John, assignor.)
Durham, Charles, Chicago, Ill. Projectile. No. 1,327,531; Jan. 6; v. 270; p. 122.
Duvall, Flora, Chicago, Ill. Strainer. No. 1,327,532. Jan. 6; v. 270; p. 122.
Duvendack, Henry W. (See Blake, William F., assignor.)
Dyer, Frank L., Montclair, N. J. Talking-machine. No. 1,326,920; Jan. 6; v. 270; p. 7.
Dyer, Newell V., Holbrook, Mass., assignor, by mesne assignments, to United Shoe Machinery Corporation, Paterson, N. J. Sklving-machine. No. 1,327,028; Jan. 6; v. 270; p. 28.
Dzimitowicz, Waclaw, Pittsburgh, Pa. Baby-walker. No. 1,326,921; Jan. 6; v. 270; p. 7.
Eades, Rodger, Winchester, Ky. Hemp-brake. No. 1,327,533; Jan. 6; v. 270; p. 122.
Eastern Tool & Mfg. Company. (See Anderson, Carl E., assignor.)
Ecks, Fred, New York. Y. Air-relief valve for sprinkler systems. No. 1,326,922; Jan. 6; v. 270; p. 7.
Edwards, Josiah H., Los Angeles, Calif. Sash-fastener. No. 1,327,594; Jan. 6; v. 270; p. 133.
Eells, Albert F., Rochester, N. Y. Anchor. No. 1,327,201; Jan. 6; v. 270; p. 60.
Egerton, Henry C., Ridgewood, N. J. Shank-stiffener. No. 1,327091; Jan. 6; v. 270; p. 40.
Eggleston, Claude M., Searcy, Ark. Gasolene-dispenser. No. 1,327,425; Jan. 6; v. 270; p. 101.
Eichstedt, John A., Akron, Ohio. Key-ring holder. No. 1,327,534; Jan. 6; v. 270; p. 122.
Eickhoff, Theodore H., and C. A. Tunks, Cleveland, Ohio, assignors to Auto-Ordnance Corporation, New York, N. Y. Ammunition lubrication. No. 1,327,378; Jan. 6; v. 270; p. 98.
Einfeldt, Ernest E., assignor to French & Hecht, Davenport, Iowa. Metal wheel. No. 1,327,227; Jan. 6; v. 270; p. 65.
Eisinger, Ludwig W., Bronxville, N. Y. Railway-link. No. 1,327,535; Jan. 6; v. 270; p. 122.
Ekvall, Arvid P., and H. Stake, Worcester, Mass. Can-labeling machine. No. 1,327,465; Jan. 6; v. 270; p. 108.
Electro-Thermophore Company. (See Lidberg. Tiodolf, assignor.)
Elgin National Watch Company. (See Hulburd, De Forest, assignor.)
Ellinger, William H., Bonita. Tex. Well-drill wrench. No. 1,327,879; Jan. 6; v. 270; p. 93.
Elliott, Alexander T., assignor of one-tenth to L. M. Freeman, Los Angeles, Calif. Chemical separation of ores. No. 1,327,536; Jan. 6; v. 270; p. 122.
Ellis, Carleton, Montclair, N. J., assignor to C. S. Lutkins, Rye, N.Y. Making a mixture of nitrogen and hydrogen. No. 1,327,029; Jan. 6; v. 270; p. 28.
Elmore, Guy H., Swarthmore, Pa. Jig. No. 1,327,537; Jan. 6; v. 270; p. 123.
Emery, Plato G., Chicago, Ill. Holding device for window-shades. No. 1,327,150; Jan. 6; v. 270; p. 51.
Enz, Ezra. (See Abbott and Enz.)
Eppler, John, Philadelphia, Pa. Machine for knitting lace-work. No. 1,327,228; Jan. 6; v. 270; p. 66.
Erickson, Axel F., assignor to The Allsteelequip Company, Aurora, Ill. Lock-mounting plate. No. 1,327,426; Jan. 6; v. 270; p. 101.
Erickson, Carl A. S., Norcross, Minn. Animal-trap. No. 1,327,229; Jan. 6; v. 270; p. 66.
Eskilson, Sven A., Stockholm, Sweden. Apparatus for flinging off superfluous coating when tinning, painting, or the like. No. 1,327,273; Jan. 6; v. 270; p. 74.
Estève, Felix. (See Labrosse and Estève.)
Etter, Harry C., Chambersburg, Pa. Non-skid device. No. 1,327,538; Jan. 6; v. 270; p. 123.
Evans, Henry S., East Chicago, Ind. Street-indicator for tramcars. No. 1,327,274; Jan. 6; v. 270; p. 74.
Exley, William H. (See Leitner and Exley.)
Fairbanks, Luke J., Los Angeles, Calif. Insect-poison-supply container. No. 1,327,230; Jan. 6; v. 270; p. 66.
Falcke, Philip. (See Bumpas and Falcke.)
Fedders, John M., assignor to Fedders Manufacturing Company, Inc., Buffalo, N. Y. Radiator-core. No. 1,327,380; Jan. 6; v. 270; p. 93.
Fedders Manufacturing Company. (See Fedders, John M., assignor.)
Ferguson, Marie A., Newark, N. J. Water-closet seat. No. 1,327,275; Jan. 6; v. 270; p. 74.
Ferro Machine and Foundry Company, The. (See Brewster and Weisehan, assignors.)
Finney, Curtiss W., Spokane, Wash. Valve-spring retainer. No. 1,327,539; Jan. 6; v. 270; p. 123.
Fischer, Jacob. (See Brandenstein and Fischer.)
Fitzgerald Manufacturing Company, The. (See Fitzgerald, Patrick J., assignor.)
Fitzgerald, Patrick J., assignor to The Fitzgerald Manufacturing Company, Torrington, Conn. Massage-vibrator. No. 1,327,466; Jan. 6; v. 270; p. 109.
Fleming, Frank E. (See Blackburn and Fleming.)
Fogg, Donald E. (See Hunt and Fogg.)

Foley, Dollner S., Montrose. Colo. Potato-cutting machine. No. 1,327,316; Jan. 6; v. 270; p. 81.
Fooks, Nelson H., Preston, Md. Valve. No. 1,327,540; Jan. 6; v. 270; p. 123.
Forester, Herbert, assignor of one-half to A. M. Skibinsky, Cleveland, Ohio. Burner for gas or oil. No. 1,327,092; Jan. 6; v. 270; p. 40.
Foster Bros. Mfg. Co. (See Frank, William E., assignor.)
Foster, Stephen A., Toledo, Ohio. Advertising weather-shelter. No. 1,327,427; Jan. 6; v. 270; p. 102.
Fox, Frank H. (See Wallace and Fox.)
Frame, Frank W. (See Spurr and Randall, assignors.)
Frank, William E., assignor to Foster Bros. Mfg. Co., St. Louis, Mo. Spiral bed-spring. No. 1,327,231; Jan. 6; v. 270; p. 66.
Frazier, Philip L., Rockbury, Conn. Jointer-tool. No. 1,327,151; Jan. 6; v. 270; p. 51.
Frech, Charles, Sault Ste. Marie, Ontario, Canada. Valve for blowing-engines and the like. No. 1,326,923; Jan. 6; v. 270; p. 8.
Freeman, E. H., Electric Company. (See Freeman, E. H., assignor.)
Freeman, Edgar H., Trenton, N. J., assignor to E. H. Freeman Electric Company. Lamp-locking construction. No. 1,326,924; Jan. 6; v. 270; p. 8.
Freeman, L. M. (See Elliott, Alexander T., assignor.)
Freimark, Otto, Martin, Ohio. Rail-joint. No. 1,327,541; Jan. 6; v. 270; p. 124.
French, Alfred W., Piqua, Ohio. Expressing apparatus. No. 1,327,093; Jan. 6; v. 270; p. 40.
French & Hecht. (See Einfeldt, Ernest E., assignor.)
Frey, Peter F., assignor to U. S. Light & Heat Corporation, Niagara Falls, N. Y. Electric conductor. No. 1,327,542; Jan. 6; v. 270; p. 124.
Fuller, Franz A., assignor to The J. E. Mergott Company, Newark, N. J. Perpetual calendar. No. 1,327,317; Jan. 6; v. 270; p. 81.
Fulton, Robert H., Los Angeles, Calif. Pipe-wrench. No. 1,327,595; Jan. 6; v. 270; p. 133.
Funk, James M., assignor of one-half to T. H. Belrose, Ottawa, Ill. Aeroplane. No. 1,327,543; Jan. 6; v. 270; p. 124.
Furber, Frederick M., Revere, Mass. Temperature-controlling mechanism for internal-combustion engines. No. 1,327,381; Jan. 6; v. 270; p. 93.
Furlong, Martin, Seattle, Wash. Mine safety apparatus. No. 1,327,596; Jan. 6; v. 270; p. 133.
Gallup, Edward E., Pittsfield. Mass. Bill-posting device. No. 1,327,544; Jan. 6; v. 270; p. 124.
Gamble, William A., Macon, Ga. Planting-stick. No. 1,327,030; Jan. 6; v. 270; p. 29.
Garber, Harvey C., Columbus, Ohio. Spark-plug. No. 1,327,382; Jan. 6; v. 270; p. 93.
Garnier, Ernest L., Neuilly-sur-Seine, France. Device for increasing the efficiency of firearms and the like. No. 1,327,545; Jan. 6; v. 270; p. 124.
Gatchell, George S., Roselle Park, N. J., assignor to The Singer Manufacturing Company. Thread-nipper-releasing device for sewing-machines. No. 1,327,232; Jan. 6; v. 270; p. 66.
General Lead Batteries Company. (See Handler, Eugene, assignor.)
General Machine Works. (See Swartz and Richards, assignors.)
Genin, John B., St. Albans, Vt., assignor of one-eighth to A. D. Denis, Montreal, Canada, and one-eighth to J. O. Goyette, Rouses Point, N. Y. Train-pipe coupling. No. 1,327,031; Jan. 6; v. 270; p. 29.
Geoghegan, Edward A., Chicago, Ill., assignor to M. Kraemer and E. J. Talbott, trustees. Engine-muffler. No. 1,327,032; Jan. 6; v. 270; p. 29.
Getchell, Benjamin E., assignor to The Trumbull Electric Manufacturing Company, Plainville. Conn. Electric switch. No. 1,327,383; Jan. 6; v. 270; p. 94.
Gibson, Bedell, Nicholls, Ga. Automatic nut-tightening device. No. 1,327,152; Jan. 6; v. 270; p. 51.
Glass, William C., Jamaica Plain, Mass. Sheet-feeding mechanism. No. 1,327,546; Jan. 6; v. 270; p. 124.
Goldberg, Maximilian M., assignor to The National Cash Register Company, Dayton, Ohio. Registering and recording mechanism. No. 1,327,153; Jan. 6; v. 270; p. 51.
Goldberg, Solomon H., assignor to The Hump Hairpin Manufacturing Company, Chicago, Ill. Machine for counting and arranging hairpins or like articles. No. 1,326,925; Jan. 6; v. 270; p. 8.
Golden, Charles F., Denver, Ind. Compass. No. 1,327,154; Jan. 6; v. 270; p. 51.
Gooch, Claiborne W., assignor to Burroughs Adding Machine Company, Detroit, Mich. Adding and subtracting machine. No. 1,327,818; Jan. 6; v. 270; p. 81.
Gooch, Claiborne W., assignor to Burroughs Adding Machine Company, Detroit, Mich. Adding-machine. No. 1,327,319; Jan. 6; v. 270; p. 81.
Gooch, Claiborne W., assignor to Burroughs Adding Machine Company, Detroit, Mich. Adding-machine. No. 1,327,320; Jan. 6; v. 270; p. 81.
Goodwin, George S., and J. Acker, Chicago, Ill. Clear-vision window. No. 1,327,321; Jan. 6; v. 270; p. 82.
Goodwin, James D., Richmond, Va., assignor of one-half to W. R. Dennis. Safety-razor. No. 1,327,547; Jan. 6; v. 270; p. 125.
Gookin, Sylvester L., Boston, Mass., assignor to United Shoe Machinery Corporation, Paterson, N. J. Setting eyelets. No. 1,327,033; Jan. 6; v. 270; p. 29.

Paulson, Andrew J., Salt Lake City, Utah. Controlling-valve for multiple fuel-supply pipes. No. 1,327,252; Jan. 6; v. 270; p. 70.
Peek, Will, et al. (See Barton, Charles N., assignor.)
Peirce, William E., Newark, N. J. Telegraph-receptor. No. 1,327,352; Jan. 6; v. 270; p. 88.
Pence, Alonzo H., and T. J. Morrow, Somerville, Ala. Fertilizer-distributer. No. 1,327,353; Jan. 6; v. 270; p. 88.
Penniman, Russell S., Jr., and N. M. Zoph, Berkeley, Calif., assignors to West Coast Kalsomine Company. Manu-facturing iron compounds. No. 1,327,061; Jan. 6; v. 270; p. 35.
Peregrine, Clarence R., Charleroi, Pa., assignor to Macbeth-Evans Glass Company. Glass. No. 1,327,569; Jan. 6; v. 270; p. 129.
Perry, Ray P., Montclair, N. J., assignor to The Barrett Company, New York, N. Y. Molded form of bitumen. No. 1,327,354; Jan. 6; v. 270; p. 88.
Peter, Bernard H., Westminster, England, assignor, by mesne assignments, to The Union Switch & Signal Com-pany, Swissvale, Pa. Signaling system. No. 1,327,570; Jan. 6; v. 270; p. 129.
Petrie, Robert E., Chicago, Ill. Engine-attaching means for vehicles. No. 1,326,960; Jan. 6; v. 270; p. 15.
Pfeil, Frank L. H. (See Steigerwald and Pfeil.)
Pflueger, John L., New Orleans, La. Parachute and launching device for aeroplanes. No. 1,327,355; Jan. 6; v. 270; p. 88.
Phillips, Francis L., Tugaske, Saskatchewan, Canada. Grain-pickler. No. 1,327,444; Jan. 6; v. 270; p. 105.
Phoebus E. G., Company. (See Boltshauser, Conrad, as signor.)
Pierce, William B. (See Johnson, Arthur E., assignor.)
Pierce, William S., Franklin, Pa. Swage for use in oil-wells. No. 1,327,491; Jan. 6; v. 270; p. 114.
Place, James F., Glen Ridge, N. J. Apparatus for liquefying air. No. 1,326,961; Jan. 6; v. 270; p. 15.
Placetie, Theodore. (See Trahan, Clair A., assignor.)
Poindexter, Alfred M., Denver, Colo. Sectional non-rotative insulating-knob for supporting electric wires. No. 1,326,962; Jan. 6; v. 270; p. 16.
Pool, Elmer C., New Castle, Pa., assignor to Toledo Scale Company, Toledo, Ohio. Pendulum-scale. No. 1,326,963; Jan. 6; v. 270; p. 16.
Poole, Fred, Jewell, Kans. Water-heater. No. 1,326,964; Jan. 6; v. 270; p. 16.
Porcc, James W., Hurricane Mills, Tenn. Pulling im-plement. No. 1,326,965; Jan. 6; v. 270; p. 16.
Prather, Arthur, Skidmore, Mo. Wheel. No. 1,327,253; Jan. 6; v. 270; p. 70.
Pratt, Alphonso C., Deep River, Conn. Apparatus for making gromets. No. 1,327,170; Jan. 6; v. 270; p. 54.
Prince, John. (See Nilson and Prince.)
Pritchard, Albert R., New York, N. Y. Heating apparatus. No. 1,327,213; Jan. 6; v. 270; p. 63.
Products Syndicate Inc. (See Byers, Joseph J., assignor.)
Putnam, Salmon W., 3d, assignor to A. H. Ingle, Rochester, N. Y. Tailstock-clamping mechanism. No. 1,327,356; Jan. 6; v. 270; p. 88.
Quaill, Francis H. (See Knudsen, Jacob B., assignor.)
Quinn, Michael K., Kent, Ohio. Handkerchief. No. 1,327,062; Jan. 6; v. 270; p. 35.
Racow, Joseph, New Haven, Conn. Combination-lock for the steering-posts of automobiles. No. 1,327,406; Jan. 6; v. 270; p. 97.
Railway Automatic Safety Appliance Company, The. (See Stafford, Earl C., assignor.)
Randall, Herman P. (See Spurr and Randall.)
Ray, William R., San Francisco, Calif. Oil-burner. No. 1,327,571; Jan. 6; v. 270; p. 129.
Raymond, Alonzo C., Detroit, Mich. Wall construction. No. 1,327,292; Jan. 6; v. 270; p. 77.
Reeves, George C., Oak Park, Ill. Respirator-valve. No. 1,326,966; Jan. 6; v. 270; p. 17.
Redlor, Emil M., et al. (See London, Jacob M., assignor.)
Remmers, Bernhard, Philadelphia, Pa., assignor, by mesne assignments, to Armour Grain Company, Chicago, Ill. Apparatus for preparing potatoes. No. 1,327,254; Jan. 6; v. 270; p. 70.
Ranaissance Corset Co. (See Griner, Alvah A., assignor.)
Revere Rubber Company. (See Brogden, Joseph T., as signor.)
Reynolds, William B., Roundup, Mont. Dump-car. No. 1,327,255; Jan. 6; v. 270; p. 70.
Rhein, Meyer L., New York, N. Y. Gage for dental and surgical instruments. No. 1,327,114; Jan. 6; v. 270; p. 44.
Richard, Charles D., New York, N. Y. Hub-odometer. No. 1,326,967; Jan. 6; v. 270; p. 17.
Richards, Oscar B. (See Swartz and Richards.)
Richardson, Robert N., Los Angeles, Calif. Cooling de-vice for beds and sleeping-compartments. No. 1,327,214; Jan. 6; v. 270; p. 63.
Rider, Ernest G., assignor to Schwerdtle Machine Com-pany, Philadelphia, Pa. Expansion-mandrel. No. 1,327,445; Jan. 6; v. 270; p. 105.
Rigby, George E., Manchester, England. Spring suspen-sion. No. 1,327,063; Jan. 6; v. 270; p. 35.
Rinn, Michael M., et al. (See Schott, John H., assignor.)
Rittman, Walter F. (See Whitaker and Rittman.)
Robertson, Stephen, et al. (See Yeats, Samuel W., as signor.)
Robinson, William H., Schenectady, N. Y. Knockdown stove. No. 1,327,115; Jan. 6; v. 270; p. 44.

Roderick Lean Manufacturing Company. (See Warne, Frederick C., assignor.)
Roe, William C., Pittsburgh, Pa., assignor of one-half to W. C. Handlan, Wheeling, W. Va. Train-control system for toy railways. No. 1,327,215; Jan. 6; v. 270; p. 63.
Rogers, Frank J., Detroit, Mich. Device for the preven-tion of stammering. No. 1,327,407; Jan. 6; v. 270; p. 98.
Rogers, George D., Gloucester, Mass. Extracting oils from fatty substances. No. 1,326,968; Jan. 6; v. 270; p. 17.
Rogers, John A., Atlanta, assignor to H. S. Cohen, Mari-etta, Ga. Coin-assorter. No. 1,327,357; Jan. 6; v. 270; p. 89.
Rogers, William A. (See Kellogg, Neff, Rogers, and Cowan.)
Rolfes, George H., assignor to Handlan Buck Manufactur-ing Company, St. Louis, Mo. Lantern-bail. No. 1,327,293; Jan. 6; v. 270; p. 77.
Rösholt, Nils, assignor to N. A. Krag, Christiania, Nor-way. Locking mechanism for switch-points. No. 1,327,358; Jan. 6; v. 270; p. 89.
Ross, John, assignor of one-half to L. J. Kutil, Ironwood, Mich. Non-siphoning trap. No. 1,327,116; Jan. 6; v. 270; p. 45.
Rotary Tire and Rubber Company. (See Sterns, Edward O., assignor.)
Rouanet, Louis, assignor to Compagnie D'Applications Mecaniques, Ivry-Port, France. Double-jaw calipers. No. 1,327,216; Jan. 6; v. 270; p. 63.
Rounds, Robert, Conde, S. D. Engine-handling device. No. 1,326,969; Jan. 6; v. 270; p. 17.
Row, Reuben R., and H. C. Davis, Elizabeth, N. J., as-signors to American Marine Equipment Corporation, New York, N. Y. Coupling and the like. No. 1,326,970; Jan. 6; v. 270; p. 17.
Rowland Phillip J. (See Heslewood, William R., as-signor.)
Ruggles, William G., assignor to E. V. Hartford, New York, N. Y. Golf-stick. No. 1,327,171; Jan. 6; v. 270; p. 55.
Ryan, Henry D., Boulder, Colo., assignor, by mesne as-signments, to National Oil Machinery Corporation, New York, N. Y. Recovering bituminous matter from shale. No. 1,327,572; Jan. 6; v. 270; p. 129.
Sabey, William D. (See Smith, Henry A., assignor.)
Sala, Earl V., Toledo, Ohio. Engine. No. 1,327,172; Jan. 6; v. 270; p. 55.
Salm, John, assignor to C. L. A. Whitney, Albany, N. Y. Making solder. No. 1,326,971; Jan. 6; v. 270; p. 18.
Sapper, Charles H. (See Wilson and Sapper.)
Savage, Stanley W. (See Dabbs, Savage, and Hindle.)
Scares, Arthur E. L., Ashton-on-Mersey, England, as-signor to The British Westinghouse Electric and Manu-facturing Company Limited. Pump or compressor. No. 1,327,294; Jan. 6; v. 270; p. 77.
Scheminger, John, Jr., Providence, R. I. Atomizing de-vice for rotary oil-burners. No. 1,327,256; Jan. 6; v. 270; p. 70.
Schenkel, Moritz, Charlottenburg, near Berlin, Germany, assignor to Siemens-Schuckert-Werke G. m. b. H., Ber-lin, Germany. Anode for electric vacuum apparatus. No. 1,326,972; Jan. 6; v. 270; p. 18.
Schloss, Meyer W., New York, N. Y., assignor to Treo Company, Inc. Brassiere. No. 1,327,408; Jan. 6; v. 270; p. 98.
Schmid, Ludwig, Munich, Germany. Preparation of pyrocatechin aldehyde. No. 1,326,973; Jan. 6; v. 270; p. 18.
Schmidt, William C., Richmond, Va. Indicating-bottle. No. 1,326,974; Jan. 6; v. 270; p. 18.
Schneider & Cie. (See Schneider, Eugène, assignor.)
Schneider, August H., assignor to Crouse-Hinds Company, Syracuse, N. Y. Conduit outlet-box. No. 1,327,409; Jan. 6; v. 270; p. 98.
Schneider, Eugène, assignor to Schneider & Cie., Paris, France. Apparatus for shifting trail gun-carriages for the purpose of training the guns. No. 1,326,975; Jan. 6; v. 270; p. 18.
Schnurr, Charles A. B., Brooklyn, N. Y. Captive ball for golf-practice. No. 1,326,976; Jan. 6; v. 270; p. 18.
Schott, John H., assignor of one-fifth to J. G. Archibald, one-fifth to J. E. De Kalb, and one-fifth to M. M. Rinn, Boulder, Colo. Pulling-machine. No. 1,327,492; Jan. 6; v. 270; p. 114.
Schumacher, John, and J. E., Los Angeles, Calif. Plaster-board or the like. No. 1,327,446; Jan. 6; v. 270; p. 105.
Schumacher, Joseph E. (See Schumacher, John and J. E.)
Schuster, Lionel. (See Dings and Schuster.)
Schwartzman, Abraham, St. Louis, Mo. Finger-ring. No. 1,326,977; Jan. 6; v. 270; p. 19.
Schweizer, William F., and W. J. Balkwill, assignors to Multipost Company, Rochester, N. Y. Stamp or label affixer. No. 1,326,978; Jan. 6; v. 270; p. 19.
Schwerdtle Machine Company. (See Rider, Ernest G., assignor.)
Schwoyer, Levi, Pottstown, Pa. Antislipping attach-ment for horseshoes. No. 1,327,493; Jan. 6; v. 270; p. 114.
Scott & Williams. (See Scott, Robert W., assignor.)
Scott, Oliver L., San Francisco, Calif. Theft-alarm for automobiles. No. 1,327,573; Jan. 6; v. 270; p. 129.

ALPHABETICAL LIST OF REGISTRANTS OF TRADE-MARKS.

ALPHABETICAL LIST OF REGISTRANTS OF LABELS.

Arnold Bluing Company, Portland, Oreg. "Arnold's Strip Bluing." (For Bluing.) No. 21,617; Jan. 6; v. 270; p. 187.

Buck, A. A., Santa Maria, Calif. "Buck's Vulcantite Patch." (For Tire-Patches.) No. 21,618; Jan. 6; v. 270; p. 187.

Bruehn, Louis, Chicago, Ill. "Bruehn's Rose E Ola." (For a Laxative.) No. 21,619; Jan. 6; v. 270; p. 187.

California Chocolate Shops Co., Los Angeles, Calif. "Quinby's." (For Chocolates.) No. 21,620; Jan. 6; v. 270; p. 187.

Drew, Arthur E., Lynn, Mass. "Drews." (For Storage Batteries.) No. 21,621; Jan. 6; v. 270; p. 187.

Emmerling Products Company, Johnstown, Pa. "Red Goose." (For a Beverage.) No. 21,622; Jan. 6; v. 270; p. 187.

Happ Brothers Co., Macon, Ga. "Kuver Suit." (For Overalls.) No. 21,623; Jan. 6; v. 270; p. 187.

Ideal Yeast Company Cedar Rapids, Iowa. "Ideal Special Prepared Malt Products." (For Malt Products.) No. 21,624; Jan. 6; v. 270; p. 187.

Levor, Victor, Attica, Ind. "La Roulette." (For Cigars.) No. 21,625; Jan. 6; v. 270; p. 187.

Lyrlotakis Bros., New York, N. Y. "Vittoria." (For Olive-Oil.) No. 21,626; Jan. 6; v. 270; p. 187.

Major, Joseph, Detroit, Mich. "Major's Consumption Relief." (For a Preparation for the Relief of Consumption.) No. 21,627; Jan. 6; v. 270; p. 187.

Major, Joseph, Detroit, Mich. "Major's Cholera Medicine." (For a Treatment for Cholera.) No. 21,628; Jan. 6; v. 270; p. 187.

Major, Joseph, Detroit, Mich. "Major's Nerve Medicine." (For a Nerve Medicine.) No. 21,629; Jan. 6; v. 270; p. 187.

Mandabach, Peter A., Chicago, Ill. "Malt Phosphate." (For Malt Phosphate.) No. 21,630; Jan. 6; v. 270; p. 187.

Milwaukee Paper Box Company, Milwaukee, Wis. "Milk Chocolates." (For Chocolate Candy.) No. 21,631; Jan. 6; v. 270; p. 187.

Oppenheim, Oberndorf & Co., Inc., Baltimore, Md. "'Buddy' and 'Dolly' Vindex Undersuits." (For Underwear.) No. 21,632; Jan. 6; v. 270; p. 187.

Pasbach-Voice Litho. Co., Inc., New York, N. Y. "Nichel Smoke." For Cigars.) No. 21,633; Jan. 6; v. 270; p. 187.

Phillips, M. & Co., San Francisco, Calif. "Phillips Brand." (For Canned Salmon.) No. 21,634; Jan. 6; v. 270; p. 187.

Price, N., Son & Co., Philadelphia, Pa. "Price Tailored Headwear." (For Headwear.) No. 21,635; Jan. 6; v. 270; p. 187.

Rock Island Brewing Company, Rock Island, Ill. "Lily." (For a Beverage.) No. 21,636; Jan. 6; v. 270; p. 187.

Runyan Chemical Products Co., Omaha, Nebr. "Palzo The Great American Cleaner." (For a Cleaner.) No. 21,637; Jan. 6; v. 270; p. 187.

St. Joe Canning Co., St. Joseph, Mich. "Shipmate." (For Canned Strawberries.) No. 21,638; Jan. 6; v. 270; p. 187.

St. Joe Canning Co., St. Joseph, Mich. "Trisum." (For Canned Strawberries.) No. 21,639; Jan. 6; v. 270; p. 187.

Southern California Products Company, Orange, Calif. "Golden Shreds." (For Orange Marmalade.) No. 21,640; Jan. 6; v. 270; p. 187.

Steele Packing Co., San Diego, Calif. "Kenilworth." (For Canned Tomatoes.) No. 21,641; Jan. 6; v. 270; p. 187

Tip-It, (Inc.,) New York, N. Y. "Tip It, Patent Welding Compound. Permanent Weld Guaranteed." (For Welding Compounds.) No. 21,642; Jan. 6; v. 270; p. 187.

Val Blatz J. Candy Co., Milwaukee, Wis. "Buttery Bitter Sweets." (For Candy.) No. 21,643; Jan. 6; v. 270; p. 187.

White & Wyckoff Mfg. Co., Holyoke, Mass. "Heather Lawn." (For Stationery.) No. 21,644; Jan. 6; v. 270; p. 187.

Windsor Locks Macaroni Mfg. Co., Windsor Locks, Conn. "Victory Star Brand Macaroni." (For Macaroni.) No. 21,645; Jan. 6; v. 270; p. 187.

ALPHABETICAL LIST OF REGISTRANTS OF PRINTS.

Braender Rubber & Tire Co., Rutherford, N. J. "The Tyre to Tie To." (For Tires and Tubes.) No. 5,187; Jan. 6; v. 270; p. 187.

Hays, Daniel, Company, The, Gloversville, N. Y. "Hays Gloves." (For Leather Gloves.) No. 5,188; Jan. 6; v. 270; p. 187.

Derryvale Linen Company, New York, N. Y. "Derryvale." (For Linen Piece Goods.) No. 5,189; Jan. 6; v. 270; p. 187.

Fairbank, N. K., Company, The, Chicago, Ill. "The glory of a woman is her skin." (For Toilet Soap.) No. 5,190; Jan. 6; v. 270; p. 187.

King Car Corporation of New York, New York, N. Y. "King '8' Limousan.'" (For Automobiles.) No. 5,191; Jan. 6; v. 270; p. 187.

Reynolds, R. J., Tobacco Company, Winston-Salem, N. C. "P. A. lets the cat out of the smoke-bag." (For Smoking-Tobacco.) No. 5,192; Jan. 6; v. 270; p. 187.

Sunbeam Chemical Company, Chicago, Ill. "Stylish Colors Everywhere 'Rit' ed with Rit." (For Dye-Soap.) No. 5,193; Jan. 6; v. 270; p. 187.

xvi

ALPHABETICAL LIST OF REGISTRANTS OF TRADE-MARKS.

(REGISTRATION APPLIED FOR.)

A/S Det Almindelige Handelskompagni, Copenhagen, Denmark. California hops. No. 122,238; Jan. 6; v. 270; p. 162.

Abrams, Saul D., Boston, Mass. Tea, coffee, cocoa, spices, &c. No. 120,514; Jan. 6; v. 270; p. 153.

Adams, J. D., & Company, Indianapolis, Ind. Road-graders. No. 122,416; Jan. 6; v. 270; p. 163.

Agra Company, Detroit, Mich. Soaps. No. 124,380; Jan. 6; v. 270; p. 174.

Albert-Jacobs Company, New York, N. Y. Job and delivery tags. No. 124,651; Jan. 6; v. 270; p. 175.

Allcock, S., & Co. Limited, Redditch, England. Sproatbooks and other fishhooks. No. 122,456; Jan. 6; v. 270; p. 163.

Allis-Chalmers Manufacturing Company, Milwaukee, Wis. Comminuting machinery. No. 119,620; Jan. 6; v. 270; p. 151.

Alpine Co., Inc., New York, N. Y. Ginger-ale, cream-soda, sarsaparilla, and other fruit-flavored non-alcoholic non-cereal beverages. No. 123,199; Jan. 6; v. 270; p. 169.

Alsteel Manufacturing Co., Battle Creek, Mich. Combination automobile-tool. No. 122,754; Jan. 6; v. 270; p. 165.

American Aniline Products, Inc., New York, N. Y. Dyes. No. 115,634; Jan. 6; v. 270; p. 143.

American Import Co., San Francisco, Calif. Ladies' and misses' garments. No. 118,102; Jan. 6; v. 270; p. 146.

American La France Fife Engine Co., Inc., Elmira, N. Y. Asbestos suits, helmets, hoods, gloves, mittens, &c. No. 114,966; Jan. 6; v. 270; p. 142.

American Non-Ferrous Metals Corporation, Chester, Pa. Bearing-metal. No. 122,005; Jan. 6; v. 270; p. 160.

American Optical Company, Southbridge, Mass. Ophthalmic lenses. No. 123,724; Jan. 6; v. 270; p. 172.

American Overgaiter Co., Baltimore, Md. Overgaiters. No. 121,734; Jan. 6; v. 270; p. 159.

American Pure Food Process Co., Baltimore, Md. Glass jars. No. 122,811; Jan. 6; v. 270; p. 166.

American Stamping Company, Elizabeth, N. J. Sheet metal used for toys, &c. No. 122,505; Jan. 6; v. 270; p. 164.

American Steel & Wire Company of New Jersey, Cleveland, Ohio. Oval fence-wire and wire fencing. No. 118,341; Jan. 6; v. 270; p. 147.

Apsley Rubber Company, Hudson, Mass. Canvas Outing-shoes. No. 123,531; Jan. 6; v. 270; p. 172.

Armstrong Cork Company, Pittsburgh, Pa. Composition soles and heels for boots and shoes. Nos. 118,977-8; Jan. 6; v. 270; p. 148.

Arctic Ice & Coal Co., Greensboro, N. C. Ice-cream and ices. No. 120,083; Jan. 6; v. 270; p. 152.

Aspegren & Co., New York, N. Y. Shortening and frying medium. No. 123,298; Jan. 6; v. 270; p. 170.

Auer & Twitchell, Inc., Dover, Del., and Philadelphia, Pa. Certain coated waterproof fiber table-covers. No. 114,061; Jan. 6; v. 270; p. 141.

Axelson Machine Co., Los Angeles, Calif. Lathes and metal-working grinders. No. 118,456; Jan. 6; v. 270; p. 147.

Baach, J., Co., Chicago, Ill. Women's one-piece underwear. No. 121,709; Jan. 6; v. 270; p. 158.

Baer Collapsible Rim Corporation, San Francisco, Calif. Collapsible rim. No. 122,156; Jan. 6; v. 270; p. 161.

Barva Heel & Tire Factory, Inc., Fort Wayne, Ind. Rubber heels. No. 123,332; Jan. 6; v. 270; p. 170.

Beaver Varnish Company, Buffalo, N. Y. Paste and ready-mixed paints and varnishes. No. 122,423; Jan. 6; v. 270; p. 163.

Bee Ess Knitting Mills, Inc., New York, N. Y. Sweaters, Silk, wool, and cotton. No. 121,857; Jan. 6; v. 270; p. 160.

Berbecker & Rowland Manufacturing Company, Waterville, Conn. Metallic articles of upholstering and cabinet hardware. No. 106,257; Jan. 6; v. 270; p. 138.

Blankinship, John S., Lynchburg, Va. Household tables and chairs, bedsteads, &c. No. 119,015; Jan. 6; v. 270; p. 149.

Bong, C. Harry, Chicago, Ill. Lotions for soothing and treating irritations of the skin. No. 116,517; Jan. 6; v. 270; p. 145.

Brandquist, Eric W., New York, N. Y. Spark-plugs for internal-combustion engines. No. 122,385; Jan. 6; v. 270; p. 163.

Brinton, Willard C., New York, N. Y. No. 119,593; Jan. 6; v. 270; p. 150.

Brown, Fred W., Columbus, Ohio. Monthly publication for advertising purposes. No. 122,330; Jan. 6; v. 270; p. 162.

Brown, Fred W., Columbus, Ohio. Monthly publication for advertising purposes. No. 124,067; Jan. 6; v. 270; p. 173.

Brun, Louis, Fils, Arre, France. Stockings and socks. No. 119,389; Jan. 6; v. 270; p. 149.

Brunswick-Balke-Collender Company, Wilmington, Del., and Chicago, Ill. Billiard and pocket-billiard balls. No. 123,201; Jan. 6; v. 270; p. 169.

Byrne, Joseph F., Omaha, Nebr. Hosiery for women. No. 116,324; Jan. 6; v. 270; p. 144.

Byron, Weston Co., Dalton, Mass. Machine-bookkeeping paper. No. 101,590; Jan. 6; v. 270; p. 137.

Bullen, Joseph W., Folcroft, Pa. Liquid compounds used as floor-oils. No. 122,327; Jan. 6; v. 270; p. 162.

California Wine Association, San Francisco, Calif. Grape-juice. No. 124,593; Jan. 6; v. 270; p. 174.

Caradine, James T., St. Louis, Mo. Waterproof coats and slickers. No. 121,748; Jan. 6; v. 270; p. 159.

Carson Petroleum Company, Chicago, Ill. Petroleum products. No. 116,644; Jan. 6; v. 270; p. 145.

Carteret Silk Company, Jersey City, N. J. Underwear, petticoats, and outer waists. No. 121,711; Jan. 6; v. 270; p. 158.

Celro-Kola Co., Portland, Oreg. Non-alcoholic beverage. No. 123,961; Jan. 6; v. 270; p. 173.

Charms Company, Newark, N. J. Candy and fruit tablets. No. 119,469; Jan. 6; v. 270; p. 150.

Chipman Knitting Mills, Easton, Pa. Hosiery. No. 108,121; Jan. 6; v. 270; p. 139.

Clark & MacKusick Company, Boston, Mass. Coffee. No. 113,118; Jan. 6; v. 270; p. 140.

Class Journal Corporation, Seattle, Wash. Monthly magazine. Nos. 121,564-5; Jan. 6; v. 270; p. 158.

Clayton Chemical Co., New York, N. Y. Preparation for the relief of inflammation and pain by cutaneous absorption. No. 123,020; Jan. 6; v. 270; p. 168.

Clode, E. J., New York, N. Y. Printed books published in series. No. 124,469; Jan. 6; v. 270; p. 174.

Cochran, H. K., Company, Little Rock, Ark. Grain-seed. No. 121,921; Jan. 6; v. 270; p. 160.

Cody, John P., Evansville, Ind. Caps and hats. No. 121,171; Jan. 6; v. 270; p. 156.

Cohn, Doris, New York, N. Y. Ladies' leather shoes. No. 116,023; Jan. 6; v. 270; p. 143.

Cohen, Goldman & Co. Inc., New York, N. Y. Men's and children's outer garments. No. 122,586; Jan. 6; v. 270; p. 164.

Columbia Fastener Company, Chicago, Ill. Snap-fasteners. No. 119,849; Jan. 6; v. 270; p. 152.

Columbia Fastener Company, Chicago, Ill. Snap-fasteners. No. 120,815; Jan. 6; v. 270; p. 154.

Commerce Publications Company Inc., New York, N. Y. Monthly magazines. No. 121,457; Jan. 6; v. 270; p. 157.

Commonwealth Steel Company, St. Louis, Mo. Railway-car truck-frames, locomotive-tender frames, &c. No. 122,073; Jan. 6; v. 270; p. 161.

Concrete-Cement Age Publishing Co., Detroit, Mich. Monthly magazine for building-supply dealers. No. 122,882; Jan. 6; v. 270; p. 166.

Conkey, G. E., Co., Cleveland, Ohio. Starting feed and meat, grain, and bone-mash. No. 119,400; Jan. 6; v. 270; p. 150.

Conkey, G. E., Co., Cleveland, Ohio. Starting feed for chicks. No. 119,399; Jan. 6; v. 270; p. 149.

Converse Rubber Shoe Co., Malden, Mass. Boots and shoes of rubber, canvas, or combination. No. 119,971; Jan. 6; v. 270; p. 152.

Corrasanti Chemical Co. Inc., Newark, N. J. Boiler compounds. No. 123,238; Jan. 6; v. 270; p. 170.

Cowden Manufacturing Co., St. Paul, Minn. Overalls. No. 121,294; Jan. 6; v. 270; p. 156.

Crane, John, Maywood, Ill. Packing. No. 119,735; Jan. 6; v. 270; p. 151.

Crucible Steel Company of America, Pittsburgh, Pa. Steel bars, rods, billets, blocks, forgings, &c. Nos. 122,292-3; Jan. 6; v. 270; p. 162.

Danville, Albert, Sacramento, Calif. Preparation for improving gasolene. No. 120,241; Jan. 6; v. 270; p. 152.

De Pew, Thomas H., Canton, Ohio. Phonographs and records. No. 123,923; Jan. 6; v. 270; p. 173.

Denver Powerine Company, Denver, Colo. Gasolene. No. 118,431; Jan. 6; v. 270; p. 147.

Derf Manufacturing Company, New York, N. Y. Spark-plugs. No. 119,796; Jan. 6; v. 270; p. 151.

Derryvale Linen Company, New York, N. Y. Linen, cotton, and mixed piece goods, towels, glass-cloth, &c. Nos. 122,975-6; Jan. 6; v. 270; p. 168.

xvii

Diehl, Edward, Nashville, Tenn. Non-alcoholic non-cereal maltless beverage and syrup for making same. No. 123,796; Jan. 6; v. 270; p. 173.

Divine, Dwight & Sons, Ellenville, N. Y. Pocket, pen, kitchen knives, &c. Nos. 119,501–2; Jan. 6; v. 270; p. 150.

Divine, Dwight & Sons, Ellenville, N. Y. Pocket, pen, kitchen knives, &c. No. 119,504; Jan. 6; v. 270; p. 150.

Draper Manufacturing Company, Port Huron, Mich. Hollow balanced balls of brass or other metal. No. 121,760; Jan. 6; v. 270; p. 159.

Du Pont, E. I., de Nemours & Company, Wilmington, Del. Lacquers. No. 120,413; Jan. 6; v. 270; p. 153.

Duplus Chemical Co., Los Angeles, Calif., and El Paso, Tex. Insecticide and germicide. No. 122,884; Jan. 6; v. 270; p. 167.

Eastern Fountain Co., Boston, Mass. Drinking-fountains and parts thereof for human use. No. 122,350; Jan. 6; v. 270; p. 163.

Elastowear Manufacturing Company, Cincinnati, Ohio. Girdles, brassières, hip-reducing corsets, &c. No. 118,755; Jan. 6; v. 270; p. 148.

Electric Controller & Manufacturing Company, Cleveland, Ohio. Electric apparatus, machines, and supplies. No. 123,632; Jan. 6; v. 270; p. 172.

Ely & Walker Dry Goods Co., St. Louis, Mo., and New York, N. Y. Hose-supporter. No. 120,303; Jan. 6; v. 270; p. 152.

Emerson Phonograph Company, Inc., New York, N. Y. Phonograph-records. No. 124,336; Jan. 6; v. 270; p. 174.

Emerson Shoe Company, Rockland, Mass. Leather boots and shoes. Nos. 121,462–4; Jan. 6; v. 270; pp. 157–8.

Enterprise Manufacturing Company, Atlanta, Ga. Middy-blouses and dresses for children, misses, and ladies. No. 122,980; Jan. 6; v. 270; p. 168.

Estelle Company, Chicago, Ill. Dresses. No. 121,097; Jan. 6; v. 270; p. 156.

Eye Brand Confectionery, Inc., Brooklyn, N. Y. Candies. No. 115,343; Jan. 6; v. 270; p. 142.

Faehndrich, William, New York, N. Y. Cheese. No. 122,828; Jan. 6; v. 270; p. 166.

Fairchild Company, Chicago, Ill. Semimonthly publication. No. 122,011; Jan. 6; v. 270; p. 160.

Faw, J. H., Inc., New York, N. Y. Electrical wire and fuses. No. 122,938; Jan. 6; v. 270; p. 167.

Feehan, Medord A., Haverhill, Mass. Men's, women's, and children's shoes, boots, and slippers. No. 118,756; Jan. 6; v. 270; p. 148.

Fleckenstein, C. G. Co., Muskegon, Mich. Leather soles and heels. No. 113,353; Jan. 6; v. 270; p. 140.

Franklin Simon & Co., Inc., New York, N. Y. Men's and boys' furnishings, undergarments, and clothing. No. 118,940; Jan. 6; v. 270; p. 148.

Freadrich, Joseph J., St. Louis, Mo. Leather belting. No. 122,427; Jan. 6; v. 270; p. 163.

Frieber, Benjamin, Chicago, Ill. Lamp-lenses. No. 116,173; Jan. 6; v. 270; p. 144.

Furry Fruit & Produce Co., Yakima, Wash. Fresh fruits. No. 122,164; Jan. 6; v. 270; p. 161.

Galbraith Milling Company, Mount Morris, N. Y. Wheat-flour. No. 117,874; Jan. 6; v. 270; p. 146.

Gensonite Welding Electrode Co., Philadelphia, Pa. Flux or covered electrodes. No. 122,883; Jan. 6; v. 270; p. 167.

George Borgfeldt & Co., New York, N. Y. Toilet powder. No. 123,102; Jan. 6; v. 270; p. 169.

Gesell, Frank A., Los Angeles, Calif. Bank-deposit account-books. No. 114,072; Jan. 6; v. 270; p. 141.

Gilbert, Frederick G., New Haven, Conn. Cigars, cigarettes, and tobacco. No. 122,166; Jan. 6; v. 270; p. 161.

Goetz, Isidor B., Milwaukee, Wis. Non-alcoholic beverages and syrups and ingredients for making same. No. 122,773; Jan. 6; v. 270; p. 165.

Grand Union Tea Co., Brooklyn, N. Y. Spaghetti and macaroni. No. 123,634; Jan. 6; v. 270; p. 172.

Graphite Products Limited, London, England. Paints, varnishes, &c. No. 120,608; Jan. 6; v. 270; p. 153.

Grossenbacker, John G., Apopka, Fla. Insecticides. No. 122,212; Jan. 6; v. 270; p. 162.

H.-B. Tempering Process Co., Clearbrook, Minn. Composition for tempering steel or other metals. No. 122,194; Jan. 6; v. 270; p. 162.

Haas, Baruch & Co., Los Angeles, Calif. Canned shrimp, salmon, oysters, and pepper sauce, honey, &c. No. 110,022; Jan. 6; v. 270; p. 139.

Hale Company, San Francisco, Calif. Canned fruits. No. 123,642; Jan. 6; v. 270; p. 172.

Haller Baking Company, Pittsburgh, Pa. Bread, cakes, and pastry. No. 123,054; Jan. 6; v. 270; p. 169.

Harrold Tool & Forge Co., Columbiana, Ohio. Tools. No. 115,403; Jan. 6; v. 270; p. 142.

Hartman Company, Chicago, Ill. Hog-waterers of the nature of tanks, serving as a water-supply. No. 120,421; Jan. 6; v. 270; p. 153.

Hassebroek Brothers, St. Peter, Ill. Patches for wheel-tire tubes. No. 121,717; Jan. 6; v. 270; p. 159.

Hastings, Henry M., San Francisco, Calif. Printed forms for estimates of printing-work. No. 115,590; Jan. 6; v. 270; p. 142.

Hathaway, C. F., & Sons, North Cambridge, Mass. Bread. No. 121,114; Jan. 6; v. 270; p. 156.

Hawaiian Pineapple Company, Limited, Iwilei, Honolulu, Hawaii. Canned pineapple. No. 122,892; Jan. 6; v. 270; p. 167.

Heller, L., & Son, Providence, R. I. Imitation-pearl necklaces. No. 119,802; Jan. 6; v. 270; p. 151.

Hensch Food Company, Cleveland, Ohio. Foods for infants, invalids, and convalescents. No. 124,400; Jan. 6; v. 270; p. 174.

Heroux, Frederick A., Oakland, Calif. Bread. No. 123,208; Jan. 6; v. 270; p. 169.

Hiram Walker & Sons Metal Products, Limited, Walkerville, Ontario, Canada. Heat-resisting castings. No. 113,169; Jan. 6; v. 270; p. 140.

Hollenbach, Charles, Chicago, Ill. Fresh sausage. No. 122,599; Jan. 6; v. 270; p. 164.

Hollinshed, Chas., Co., Inc., New York, N. Y. Soy-bean oil. No. 122,835; Jan. 6; v. 270; p. 166.

Howard Bros. Chemical Co., Buffalo, N. Y. Soap. No. 123,163; Jan. 6; v. 270; p. 169.

Ideal Roller Company, Chicago, Ill. Rollers for printing-presses, lithographing-presses, &c. No. 119,071; Jan. 6; v. 270; p. 149.

Import Drug Specialties Company, Cleveland, Ohio. Liquid shoe dressing and cleanser. No. 116,053; Jan. 6; v. 270; p. 143

International Button Co., Rochester, N. Y. Buttons. No. 120,920; Jan. 6; v. 270; p. 155.

International Duplex Coat Co. Inc., New York, N. Y. Reversible leather coat. No. 120,827; Jan. 6; v. 270; p. 154.

International Feature Service, Inc., New York, N. Y. Series of comic drawings or pictures. No. 122,214; Jan. 6; v. 270; p. 162.

International Feature Service, Inc., New York, N. Y. Series of comic drawings or pictures. No. 122,216; Jan. 6; v. 270; p. 162.

International Harvester Company, Chicago, Ill. Rope, cord, twine, and binder-twine. No. 121,627; Jan. 6; v. 270; p. 158.

International Merchants, Incorporated, San Francisco, Calif. Butter. No. 122,213; Jan. 6; v. 270; p. 162.

Jacobson, Harry, Co., Inc., New York, N. Y. Men's clothing. No. 116,264; Jan. 6; v. 270; p. 144.

Jensen, Frans G., Springfield, Mass. Candied fruits, nuts, and candy. No. 122,122; Jan. 6; v. 270; p. 161.

Johnson Bros. & Alexander, Chicago, Ill. Candies. No. 106,620; Jan. 6; v. 270; p. 139.

Joseph Dixon Crucible Company, Jersey City, N. J. Pencils. No. 124,595; Jan. 6; v. 270; p. 174.

Joseph Krieg-Fink Co. Inc., Jersey City, N. J. Non-intoxicating maltless beverage. No. 123,986; Jan. 6; v. 270; p. 173.

Kaelin, Henry, & Son, Brooklyn, N. Y. Fresh vegetables. No. 122,943; Jan. 6; v. 270; p. 167.

Kaut, Wm., Footwear Company, Carthage, Mo. Leather boots and shoes. Nos. 120,830–3; Jan. 6; v. 270; pp. 154–5.

Kaut, Wm., Footwear Company, Carthage, Mo. Boots and shoes made of leather. No. 119,656; Jan. 6; v. 270; p. 151.

Kaut, Wm., Footwear Company, Carthage, Mo. Leather boots and shoes. No. 121,472; Jan. 6; v. 270; p. 158.

Kaut, William, Footwear Company, Carthage, Mo. Leather boots, shoes, slippers, and sandals. No. 121,473; Jan. 6; v. 270; p. 158.

Kaut, Wm., Footwear Co., Carthage, Mo. Leather boots, shoes, slippers, and sandals. No. 122,540; Jan. 6; v. 270; p. 164.

Keasbey & Mattison Company, Ambler, Pa. Medicinal preparation for headaches and nervous diseases. No. 115,983; Jan. 6; v. 270; p. 143.

Keasbey & Mattison Company, Ambler, Pa. Medicinal remedy for colds and malaria. No. 115,985; Jan. 6; v. 270; p. 143.

Keasbey & Mattison Company, Ambler, Pa. Preparation for rheumatism and cystitis. No. 115,984; Jan. 6; v. 270; p. 143.

Kellogg, W. B., Co. Inc., New York, N. Y. Set and unset pearls and imitation pearls. No. 112,648; Jan. 6; v. 270; p. 140.

Kenosha Wheel & Axle Company, Kenosha, Wis. Cast-metal vehicle-wheels. No. 123,316; Jan. 6; v. 270; p. 170.

Kesner & Jerlaw, New York, N. Y. Phonographs. No. 123,546; Jan. 6; v. 270; p. 172.

Kohnstamm, H., & Co., New York, N. Y. Starch for laundry purposes and in treating textiles. No. 122,987; Jan. 6; v. 270; p. 168.

Koppel Industrial Car & Equipment Company, Koppel and Pittsburgh, Pa. Welded and riveted pipe, railway-spikes, &c. No. 120,485; Jan. 6; v. 270; p. 153.

La Monte, George, & Son, Nutley, N. J., and New York, N. Y. Safety-paper used for railway-tickets, &c. No. 107,963; Jan. 6; v. 270; p. 139.

Lake Reedy Packing Co., Frostproof, Fla. Fresh citrus fruits. No. 122,898; Jan. 6; v. 270; p. 167.

Lamborn & Co., New York, N. Y. Lubricating-oils. No. 123,487; Jan. 6; v. 270; p. 171.

Larus & Brother Company, Richmond, Va. Plug-tobacco. No. 119,561; Jan. 6; v. 270; p. 150.

Lawson & Company Incorporated, New York, N. Y. Jigs and vises on milling-machines, lathes, planers, grinders, &c. No. 116,418; Jan. 6; v. 270; p. 145.

Leopold, Solomon, and Eisendrath, Chicago, Ill. Men's and boys' suits, vests, trousers, and overcoats. No. 114,270; Jan. 6; v. 270; p. 141.

Lerner Waist Co., New York, N. Y. Underwear and other clothing. No. 119,835; Jan. 6; v. 270; p. 152.

Levy, Lewis, Philadelphia, Pa. Dresses. No. 122,778; Jan. 6; v. 270; p. 165.

Levy, B. H., Bro. & Co., Savannah, Ga. Men's suits and overcoats. No. 120,312; Jan. 6; v. 270; p. 153.

Levy, George C., New York, N. Y. Catamenial bandage. No. 121,149; Jan. 6; v. 270; p. 156.

Levy, Joseph, Boston, Mass. Time-stamps. No. 118,761; Jan. 6; v. 270; p. 148.

Lewis, Connors & Company, Chicago, Ill. Logarithmic-scale computing devices. No. 122,262; Jan. 6; v. 270; p. 163.

Limpert Bros. Inc., New York, N. Y. An extract having a maple flavor. No. 116,270; Jan. 6; v. 270; p. 144.

Linehan-Conover Company, Worcester, Mass. Corsets, corset-waists, and brassières. No. 113,454; Jan. 6; v. 270; p. 140.

Locke Shoe Co., Wheeling, W. Va. Leather boots and shoes. No. 122,017; Jan. 6; v. 270; p. 160.

Lockwood, John M., Jr., West Hoboken, N. J. Dolls. No. 122,489; Jan. 6; v. 270; p. 163.

Los Angeles Examiner, Los Angeles, Calif. Newspaper-sections. Nos. 118,267-8; Jan. 6; v. 270; pp. 146-7.

Los Angeles Examiner, Los Angeles, Calif. Newspaper-sections. No. 124,357; Jan. 6; v. 270; p. 174.

Lundborg Company, The, New York, N. Y. Perfume, toilet water, face - powder, toilet cream, and sachet. No. 120,572; Jan. 6; v. 270; p. 153.

Lynard, John, Owatonna, Minn. Eggs, poultry, and butter. No. 123,212; Jan. 6; v. 270; p. 170.

Mann, Alexander S., Providence, R. I. Liquid antiseptic. No. 121,249; Jan. 6; v. 270; p. 156.

Manufacturers Record Publishing Company, Baltimore, Md. A weekly magazine. No. 122,846; Jan. 6; v. 270; p. 166.

Marathon Shoe Co., Wausau, Wis. Shoes. No. 119,711; Jan. 6; v. 270; p. 151.

Mason, A. & Magenheimer Conf. Mfg. Co., Brooklyn, N. Y. Candies and chocolate. No. 115,993; Jan. 6; v. 270; p. 143.

Mayer, Oscar F., & Bro., Chicago, Ill. Fresh, dried, smoked, and canned pork, beef, &c. No. 116,099; Jan. 6; v. 270; p. 144.

McCormick & Co., Baltimore, Md. Lubricating, rust-preventing and machine oils. No. 114,056; Jan. 6; v. 270; p. 141.

Mentzer, John P., Chicago, Ill. Dry storage batteries. No. 113,491; Jan. 6; v. 270; p. 140.

Metz, H. A., Laboratories, Inc., New York, N. Y. Anesthetics. No. 123,214; Jan. 6; v. 270; p. 170.

Metz, Herman A., New York, N. Y. Dyestuffs and chemicals. No. 119,425; Jan. 6; v. 270; p. 150.

Meyer, John J., New York, N. Y. Cleaning compound. No 117,468; Jan. 6; v. 270; p. 146.

Meyer, Milton J. & Co. Inc., New York, N. Y. Leather shoes. No. 121,179; Jan. 6; v. 270; p. 156.

Miller, Stanley G., Chicago, Ill. Yearly interest-tables. No. 112,396; Jan. 6; v. 270; p. 139.

Millman, Abe, New York, N. Y. Infants' and children's dresses. No. 122,128; Jan. 6; v. 270; p. 161.

Milwaukee Talking Machine Manufacturing Co., Milwaukee, Wis. Phonographs and phonograph-cabinets. No. 121,118; Jan. 6; v. 270; p. 156.

N. & S. Engine Co., Seattle, Wash. Internal-combustion engines, &c. No. 122,494; Jan. 6; v. 270; p. 163.

Narragansett Bay Oyster Co., Providence, R. I. Fresh, dried, and canned oysters. Nos. 103,898-9; Jan. 6; v. 270; pp. 137-8.

Nash Engineering Co., South Norwalk, Conn. Relief and ball float valves for machinery. No. 121,406; Jan. 6; v. 270; p. 157.

National Aniline & Chemical Company Incorporated, New York, N. Y. Food-colors. No. 119,000; Jan. 6; v. 270; p. 148.

National Aniline & Chemical Company Incorporated, New York, N. Y. Food-colors. No. 119,004; Jan. 6; v. 270; p. 149.

National Aniline & Chemical Company Incorporated, New York, N. Y. Food-colors. No. 119,367; Jan. 6; v. 270; p. 149.

National Biscuit Company, Jersey City, N. J., and New York, N. Y. Biscuit. No. 124,148; Jan. 6; v. 270; p. 173.

National Brewers Academy Consulting Bureau, New York, N. Y. Compound used in the manufacture of beer or near beer. No. 119,810; Jan. 6; v. 270; p. 151.

National Enameling & Stamping Co., New York, N. Y. Tinware, galvanized and japanned ware. No. 121,012; Jan. 6; v. 270; p. 155.

National Fruit Flavor Co., New Orleans, La. Flavoring extracts for food. No. 121,777; Jan. 6; v. 270; p. 159.

National Grave Vault Company, Galion, Ohio. Grave-vaults. No. 124,147; Jan. 6; v. 270; p. 173.

National Mills, Spartanburg, S. C. Hosiery for men, women, and children. No. 118,323; Jan. 6; v. 270; p. 147.

National Poultry Co., Los Angeles, Calif. Dressed poultry. No. 117,569; Jan. 6; v. 270; p. 146.

Nebeling, Edward R., New York, N. Y. Alloyed platinum. No. 122,652; Jan. 6; v. 270; p. 164.

Newton Broom Co., Newton, Ill. Brooms. No. 120,768; Jan. 6; v. 270; p. 154.

Nowlin, A. S., & Co., Lynchburg, Va. Coal. No. 121,314; Jan. 6; v. 270; p. 156.

Nulomoline Company, The, New York, N. Y. Table-syrup. No. 120,577; Jan. 6; v. 270; p. 153.

Ochs & Frank, Baltimore, Md. Ladies' waists and dresses. No. 123,361; Jan. 6; v. 270; p. 171.

Omo Mfg. Co., Middletown, Conn. Sanitary belts, aprons, and gum-tissue for surgical purposes. Nos. 119,204-5; Jan. 6; v. 270; p. 149.

Ori-Ori Company, New York, N. Y. Hair dyes and shampoo. No. 121,409; Jan. 6; v. 270; p. 157.

Oritz y Palacios, Asunción, Fuencarral, Spain. Soaps. No. 100,464; Jan. 6; v. 270; p. 137.

Osmundson, Chris, Webster City, Iowa. Spades, shovels. No. 119,985; Jan. 6; v. 270; p. 152.

Oswald M'Cardell & Co., Manchester, England. Insecticides. Nos. 123,215-16; Jan. 6; v. 270; p. 170.

Overton, James H., Quincy, Ill. Waterproof coating for textile fabrics and leather. No. 122,184; Jan. 6; v. 270; p. 161.

Palnut Corporation, Buffalo, N. Y. Nut-locks. No. 122,951; Jan. 6; v. 270; p. 167.

Parisian Mfg. Company, Philadelphia, Pa. Hair-wavers. No. 123,363; Jan. 6; v. 270; p. 171.

Parsons Chemical Works, Grand Ledge, Mich. Medicated food for live stock. No. 115,576; Jan. 6; v. 270; p. 142.

Pearl City Fruit Co. Ltd., Honolulu, Hawaii. Pineapple-extract syrup. No. 122,912; Jan. 6; v. 270; p. 167.

Pearl City Fruit Co. Ltd., Honolulu, Hawaii. Pineapple jelly. No. 122,913; Jan. 6; v. 270; p. 167.

Pepsoline Company, Huntington, W. Va. Medicated oil for rheumatic pains, toothache, burns, &c. No. 118,945; Jan. 6; v. 270; p. 141.

Peters, Arnold B., San Francisco, Calif. Tooth-powder. No. 121,019; Jan. 6; v. 270; p. 155.

Plummer, A. Buckland, Chicago, Ill. Foot-pads in the nature of insoles for use in boots, shoes, slippers, &c. No. 120,222; Jan. 6; v. 270; p. 152.

Polson Rubber Co., Cleveland, Ohio. Rubber tires, inner tubes, rubber tubes, tube-patches, reliners, &c. No. 122,023; Jan. 6; v. 270; p. 160.

Porter, Robert W., Mobile, Ala. Toy furniture. No. 122,656; Jan. 6; v. 270; p. 165.

Radford, William A., Chicago, Ill. Monthly magazine. No. 122,733; Jan. 6; v. 270; p. 165.

Ready To Wear Publishing Company, New York, N. Y. Trade publication issued daily. No. 122,660; Jan. 6; v. 270; p. 165.

Regal Manufacturing Company, Knoxville, Tenn. Overalls. No. 116,933; Jan. 6; v. 270; p. 145.

Reid Bros., Inc., San Francisco, Calif., and Seattle, Wash. Measuring and scientific appliances. No. 120,930; Jan. 6; v. 270; p. 155.

Reizenstein, Emile, Waltham, Mass. Plastic composition for modeling. No. 123,714; Jan. 6; v. 270; p. 172.

Reliance Manufacturing Company, Chicago, Ill. Workshirts. No. 116,109; Jan. 6; v. 270; p. 144.

Reliance Wheel Co., Youngstown, Ohio. Pressed-steel disk wheels for automobiles and aeroplanes. No. 121,318; Jan. 6; v. 270; p. 157.

Remikore, Abraham, Sharon, Pa. Bread. No. 119,209; Jan. 6; v. 270; p. 149.

Rice & Hutchins, Incorporated, Boston, Mass. Boots, shoes, and slippers. No. 123,456; Jan. 6; v. 270; p. 171.

Richter, F. Ad. & Co. of New York, New York, N. Y. Liniment. No. 115,540; Jan. 6; v. 270; p. 142.

Richter, F. Ad. & Co. of New York, New York, N. Y. Liniment for rheumatism, neuralgia, lameness, and the like. No. 115,779; Jan. 6; v. 270; p. 143.

Ritter Hosiery Company, Fleetwood, Pa. Men's hosiery. No. 123,365; Jan. 6; v. 270; p. 171.

Riverside Boiler Works, Inc., Cambridgeport, Mass. Tanks and tanks for hot water. Nos. 123,755-6; Jan. 6; v. 270; pp. 172-3.

Rodenberg, M. S., Co., Providence, R. I. Neck-chains, watch-chains, and swivels for such chains. No. 120,676; Jan. 6; v. 270; p. 154.

Rohm & Haas Company, Philadelphia, Pa. Anhydrous sodium hydrosulfite. No. 123,039; Jan. 6; v. 270; p. 168.

Rohm & Haas Company, Philadelphia, Pa. Chemical used for tanning hides. No. 123,040; Jan. 6; v. 270; p. 168.

Rohm & Haas Company, Philadelphia, Pa. Sulfoxalate of sodium formaldehyde. No. 123,041; Jan. 6; v. 270; p. 168.

Roulston, Thos., Inc., Brooklyn, N. Y. Bread. No. 115,262; Jan. 6; v. 270; p. 142.

Rudin, Emil A., Toronto, Ontario, Canada. Package-binders and parts thereof. No. 120,431; Jan. 6; v. 270; p. 153.

Rueppel-Jones Importing Company, Inc., New York, N. Y. Sardines. No. 122,858; Jan. 6; v. 270; p. 166.

Safe-Cabinet Company, The, Marietta, Ohio. Document-files. No. 116,110; Jan. 6; v. 270; p. 144.

ALPHABETICAL LIST OF INVENTIONS

FOR WHICH

PATENTS WERE ISSUED ON THE 6TH DAY OF JANUARY, 1920.

Grate-bars. Means for locking. L. L. Close. No. 1,327,270; Jan. 6; v. 270; p. 73.
Grease-cup. S. A. Hough and S. Baader. No. 1,327,238; Jan. 6; v. 270; p. 67.
Grease-detaining device. G. A. Smith. No. 1,327,173; Jan. 6; v. 270; p. 55.
Gridiron. J. J. Seguler. No. 1,327,258; Jan. 6; v. 270; p. 71.
Grinder and shaker, Combined. W. A. Hammer. No. 1,327,385; Jan. 6; v. 270; p. 94.
Grinding-mill. S. J. and J. S. Mills. No. 1,327,347; Jan. 6; v. 270; p. 87.
Gromets, Apparatus for making. A. C. Pratt. No. 1,327,170; Jan. 6; v. 270; p. 54.
Gun, Machine-. A. T. Dawson and G. T. Buckham. No. 1,327,086; Jan. 6; v. 270; p. 39.
Gun, Air-. O. Seemüller. No. 1,327,064; Jan. 6; v. 270; p. 35.
Gun-carriage. E. F. Norelius. No. 1,327,603; Jan. 6; v. 270; p. 135.
Gun-carriages for the purpose of training the guns, Apparatus for shifting trail. E. Schneider. No. 1,326,975; Jan. 6; v. 270; p. 18.
Gun, Centrifugal. F. R. Barnes. No. 1,327,518; Jan. 6; v. 270; p. 119.
Guns, Controlling. J. B. Henderson. No. 1,327,204; Jan. 6; v. 270; p. 61.
Gun-mounting. A. T. Dawson and G. T. Buckham. No. 1,327,084; Jan. 6; v. 270; p. 39.
Gun-mounting. A. T. Dawson and G. T. Buckham. No. 1,327,085; Jan. 6; v. 270; p. 39.
Hairpins, Machine for counting and arranging. S. H. Goldberg. No. 1,326,925; Jan. 6; v. 270; p. 8.
Hammer, Drop-. W. A. Knapp. No. 1,327,331; Jan. 6; v. 270; p. 84.
Hamper construction. A. Walden. No. 1,327,362; Jan. 6; v. 270; p. 90.
Handkerchief. M. R. Quinn. No. 1,327,062; Jan. 6; v. 270; p. 35.
Hanger: See—
  Box-hanger.
  Brush-handle.
Handle: See—
Harrow. O. D. Lent. No. 1,327,337; Jan. 6; v. 270; p. 85.
Harrow, Wheeled. R. R. Dupler. No. 1,327,424; Jan. 6; v. 270; p. 101.
Harrows, Plowing attachment for. A. C. Stalter. No. 1,327,119; Jan. 6; v. 270; p. 45.
Head-covering and hair-comb, Combined. A. K. Dawson. No. 1,327,528; Jan. 6; v. 270; p. 121.
Headlight, Dirigible. F. Spong. No. 1,327,574; Jan. 6; v. 270; p. 130.
Headlight, No-glare. S. L. Lebby. No. 1,327,563; Jan. 6; v. 270; p. 128.
Heat-distributer. L. K. Belcher. No. 1,326,904; Jan. 6; v. 270; p. 4.
Heater: See—
  Radiator-heater.   Water-heater.
  Railway-switch heater.
Heater. L. H. Whitehorn. No. 1,327,508; Jan. 6; v. 270; p. 117.
Heating apparatus. A. R. Pritchard. No. 1,327,213; Jan. 6; v. 270; p. 63.
Heating system. J. E. MacDonald. No. 1,326,944; Jan. 6; v. 270; p. 12.
Heel-clamping device. M. F. Brogan. No. 1,327,020; Jan. 6; v. 270; p. 27.
Hemp-brake. R. Eades. No. 1,327,533; Jan. 6; v. 270; p. 122.
Hexanitrodiphenylamin, Making. J. Marshall. No. 1,326,947; Jan. 6; v. 270; p. 13.
Hinge. A. R. Hosier. No. 1,327,431; Jan. 6; v. 270; p. 102.
Hinge, Gravity-. A. S. Hughes. No. 1,327,045; Jan. 6; v. 270; p. 32.
Hinge, Spring-. J. M. Shields. No. 1,327,065; Jan. 6; v. 270; p. 35.
Hoisting and conveying machine. E. W. Taylor. No. 1,327,071; Jan. 6; v. 270; p. 36.
Homopolar machines, Cooling system for. R. V. Morse. No. 1,327,350; Jan. 6; v. 270; p. 87.
Honey, Apparatus for heating and ripening. H. A. Mitchell. No. 1,327,166; Jan. 6; v. 270; p. 54.
Hook: See—
  Lighting-fixture bowl-hook.
Hooks, Sewing-on garment-. J. Blasi. No. 1,327,191; Jan. 6; v. 270; p. 59.
Horseshoe. A. S. Crawford. No. 1,327,523; Jan. 6; v. 270; p. 120.
Horseshoe antislipping attachment. L. Schwoyer. No. 1,327,493; Jan. 6; v. 270; p. 114.
House: See—
  Sweet-potato-curing house.
Hydrant shut-off. W. N. King. No. 1,327,283; Jan. 6; v. 270; p. 75.
Hydraulic jack. D. E. Hennessy. No. 1,327,470; Jan. 6; v. 270; p. 109.
Hydraulic transmission. T. E. Brown. No. 1,327,080; Jan. 6; v. 270; p. 38.
Hydrocarbon compounds, Electrical apparatus for the electrochemical treatment of liquid. L. B. Cherry. No. 1,327,023; Jan. 6; v. 270; p. 27.
Hydrocarbon lights, Vaporizer for. A. G. Kaufman. No. 1,327,161; Jan. 6; v. 270; p. 53.

Hydrocarbon-motor. F. J. Druar. No. 1,327,148; Jan. 6; v. 270; p. 50.
Hydrocarbon-motor. H. D. Church. No. 1,327,147; Jan. 6; v. 270; p. 50.
Hydropower-heater. E. Kelley. No. 1,327,395; Jan. 6; v. 270; p. 96.
Ice-making apparatus. W. D. Willcox. No. 1,327,414; Jan. 6; v. 270; p. 99.
Ignition device. H. R. Van Deventer. No. 1,327,361; Jan. 6; v. 270; p. 89.
Ignition device. H. R. Van Deventer. No. 1,327,502; Jan. 6; v. 270; p. 116.
Ignition-device interrupter. C. T. Mason. No. 1,327,344; Jan. 6; v. 270; p. 86.
Ignition-generator. W. W. Dean. No. 1,327,375; Jan. 6; v. 270; p. 92.
Indicator: See—
  Direction-indicator.   Station-indicator.
  Street-indicator.
Ingots, Apparatus for manipulation of metal. E. W. Davies. No. 1,327,315; Jan. 6; v. 270; p. 81.
Internal-combustion engine. F. M. Guy. No. 1,327,202; Jan. 6; v. 270; p. 60.
Internal-combustion engine. L. Mayers. No. 1,327,345; Jan. 6; v. 270; p. 86.
Internal-combustion engine. S. B. Haessly. No. 1,327,384; Jan. 6; v. 270; p. 94.
Iron: See—
  Flat-iron.
Iron. Y. Harada. No. 1,326,928; Jan. 6; v. 270; p. 9.
Iron compounds, Manufacturing. R. S. Penniman, Jr., and N. M. Zoph. No. 1,327,061; Jan. 6; v. 270; p. 35.
Jack: See—
  Automobile-jack.   Hydraulic jack.
Jacket, Adjustable. R. S. Buch. No. 1,327,224; Jan. 6; v. 270; p. 65.
Jig. G. H. Elmore. No. 1,327,537; Jan. 6; v. 270; p. 128.
Joint: See—
  Pipe-joint.   Rail-joint.
Kerosene-burner. J. H. Kincaly. No. 1,327,048; Jan. 6; v. 270; p. 32.
Kettle, Vapor croup-. C. P. Hague. No. 1,327,550; Jan. 6; v. 270; p. 125.
Key-ring holder. J. A. Eichstedt. No. 1,327,534; Jan. 6; v. 270; p. 122.
Kitchen-fixture. Z. V. Matthews. No. 1,327,489; Jan. 6; v. 270; p. 113.
Knitting lace-work, Machine for. J. Eppler. No. 1,327,228; Jan. 6; v. 270; p. 66.
Knitting-machine. W. H. Swartz and O. B. Richards. No. 1,327,122; Jan. 6; v. 270; p. 46.
Label-holder. G. H. Taylor. No. 1,327,298; Jan. 6; v. 270; p. 78.
Labeling machine, Can-. A. P. Ekvall and H. Stake. No. 1,327,465; Jan. 6; v. 270; p. 108.
Lamp, Automobile safeguard-. K. Dombkowski. No. 1,326,918; Jan. 6; v. 270; p. 7.
Lamp-bracket. F. M. Jones. No. 1,327,479; Jan. 6; v. 270; p. 111.
Lamp, Electric pocket-. C. Boltshauser. No. 1,327,017; Jan. 6; v. 270; p. 26.
Lamp-locking construction. E. H. Freeman. No. 1,326,924; Jan. 6; v. 270; p. 8.
Lamp socket, Electric-. G. Snider. No. 1,307,496; Jan. 6; v. 270; p. 115.
Lasting machine, Staple-. M. Brock. No. 1,327,196; Jan. 6; v. 270; p. 59.
Lathe, Vertically-adjustable engine-. A. C. Booth. No. 1,327,016; Jan. 6; v. 270; p. 135.
Leaf-spring. C. Boles. No. 1,327,016; Jan. 6; v. 270; p. 26.
Lever, Watch-setting. W. W. Jordan. No. 1,327,391; Jan. 6; v. 270; p. 95.
Light: See—
  Electric light.   Pistol-light.
  Headlight.
Lighting-fixture-bowl hook. L. A. Hufschmidt. No. 1,327,598; Jan. 6; v. 270; p. 134.
Liquids, fluids, and oils, Conversion of. J. H. Adams. No. 1,327,263; Jan. 6; v. 270; p. 72.
Liquids, Means for cooling. J. Hutchinson. No. 1,327,560; Jan. 6; v. 270; p. 127.
Loading and unloading apparatus. A. S. Hecker. No. 1,327,324; Jan. 6; v. 270; p. 82.
Loading device. A. J. Larson. No. 1,327,436; Jan. 6; v. 270; p. 103.
Lock: See—
  Automobile-lock.   Permutation-lock.
  Nut-lock.   Sash-lock.
Lock-mounting plate A. F. Erickson. No. 1,327,426; Jan. 6; v. 270; p. 101.
Locks, Dial-indicator for combination-. H. G. Balthasar. No. 1,327,457; Jan. 6; v. 270; p. 107.
Locks, Recorder for registering. C. E. Larrabee. No. 1,327,334; Jan. 6; v. 270; p. 84.
Locomotive. W. C. Lawson. No. 1,327,243; Jan. 6; v. 270; p. 68.
Locomotives, Tool for facilitating the positioning of driving-shoes in driving-box bearings of. C. Guggenbuehler. No. 1,327,468; Jan. 6; v. 270; p. 109.
Loom feeler-motion. E. S. Stimpson. No. 1,327,069; Jan. 6; v. 270; p. 36.
Loom feeler-motion. E. S. Stimpson. No. 1,327,070; Jan. 6; v. 270; p. 36.

Pulp, Preparing. C. Bache-Wiig. No. 1,327,221; Jan. 6; v. 270; p. 65.
Pulp-screen. K. Wandel. No. 1,327,126; Jan. 6; v. 270; p. 46.
Pump. A. Dryen. No. 1,327,423; Jan. 6; v. 270; p. 101.
Pump attachment, Multiple-cylinder-. M. Sullivan. No. 1,327,449; Jan. 6; v. 270; p. 105.
Pump, Automatic. O. Berry. No. 1,327,371; Jan. 6; v. 270; p. 91.
Pump casing, Reinforced-. R. H. Aldrich. No. 1,327,512; Jan. 6; v. 270; p. 118.
Pump, Internal-combustion hydraulic. G. Griffith. No. 1,327,036; Jan. 6; v. 270; p. 30.
Pump, Liquid-. K. Dellgren. No. 1,327,272; Jan. 6; v. 270; p. 73.
Pump or compressor. A. E. L. Scanes. No. 1,327,294; Jan. 6; v. 270; p. 77.
Pump, Rotary water-. M. V. Andrews and S. W. Holman. No. 1,327,517; Jan. 6; v. 270; p. 119.
Puncture-tester. F. Overmyer. No. 1,327,251; Jan. 6; v. 270; p. 70.
Puzzle. F. L. Ince. No. 1,327,388; Jan. 6; v. 270; p. 95.
Quenching apparatus. C. G. Olson. No. 1,327,443; Jan. 6; v. 270; p. 104.
Radiator. F. W. Merritt. No. 1,327,165; Jan. 6; v. 270; p. 53.
Radiator-core. J. M. Fedders. No. 1,327,380; Jan. 6; v. 270; p. 93.
Radiator-heater, Electrical. W. Hurst. No. 1,327,279; Jan. 6; v. 270; p. 76.
Rail adjusting and gaging device. S. Morano. No. 1,326,953; Jan. 6; v. 270; p. 14.
Rail-joint. O. Freimark. No. 1,327,541; Jan. 6; v. 270; p. 124.
Railway block-signal system, Automatic electric. L. W. Kite. No. 1,327,329; Jan. 6; v. 270; p. 83.
Railway-link. L. W. Elsinger. No. 1,327,535; Jan. 6; v. 270; p. 122.
Railway-switch heater. W. T. Lawlor. No. 1,327,483; Jan. 6; v. 270; p. 112.
Railway-tracks, Understructure for supporting. E. F. L. Vagneux. No. 1,327,219; Jan. 6; v. 270; p. 64.
Razor, Safety-. J. D. Goodwin. No. 1,327,547; Jan. 6; v. 270; p. 125.
Razors, Honing device or holder for safety-. W. Summerbell. No. 1,327,498; Jan. 6; v. 270; p. 115.
Rectifier system. H. E. Burket. No. 1,327,521; Jan. 6; v. 270; p. 120.
Refrigerator. F. L. Hewitt. No. 1,327,473; Jan. 6; v. 270; p. 110.
Registering and recording mechanism. M. M. Goldberg. No. 1,327,153; Jan. 6; v. 270; p. 51.
Resilient wheel. G. Hughes. No. 1,327,096; Jan. 6; v. 270; p. 41.
Restraining device, Animal-. C. E. Cline. No. 1,327,374; Jan. 6; v. 270; p. 92.
Retorts, Machine for charging and discharging. J. G. W. Aldridge. No. 1,327,582; Jan. 6; v. 270; p. 131.
Rheostat. W. L. Bliss. No. 1,327,135; Jan. 6; v. 270; p. 48.
Ring: See—
    Finger-ring.
Rivets, Die for making double-ended. W. L. Curtis. No. 1,327,525; Jan. 6; v. 270; p. 121.
Road-making. C. J. Åberg. No. 1,327,131; Jan. 6; v. 270; p. 47.
Rock formations, Apparatus for use in sealing crevices in. G. W. Christians. No. 1,327,269; Jan. 6; v. 270; p. 73.
Rock formations, Sealing crevices in. G. W. Christians. No. 1,327,268; Jan. 6; v. 270; p. 73.
Rod: See—
    Sash-rod.
Rolling-pin and culinary holder, Combined. G. P. Cover. No. 1,327,461; Jan. 6; v. 270; p. 108.
Rotary engine. J. Theemling. No. 1,327,575; Jan. 6; v. 270; p. 130.
Rugs in dyeing same, Support for. W. E. Olson. No. 1,326,958; Jan. 6; v. 270; p. 15.
Sand-trap. P. Arbon. No. 1,327,583; Jan. 6; v. 270; p. 131.
Sash-fastener. J. H. Edwards. No. 1,327,594; Jan. 6; v. 270; p. 133.
Sash-lock. C. J. Kasper. No. 1,326,937; Jan. 6; v. 270; p. 11.
Sash-rod, Curtain. E. E. Moller. No. 1,326,951; Jan. 6; v. 270; p. 13.
Sawmill-knee-adjusting mechanism. J. Hill, Jr. No. 1,327,555; Jan. 6; v. 270; p. 126.
Scale, Attachment for dial-. C. M. Sweet. No. 1,327,450; Jan. 6; v. 270; p. 106.
Scale, Pendulum-. E. C. Pool. No. 1,326,963; Jan. 6; v. 270; p. 16.
Scale, Weighing-. M. B. Mills. No. 1,327,208; Jan. 6; v. 270; p. 62.
Score-keeping apparatus. E. Steigerwald, and F. L. H. Pfeil. No. 1,327,177; Jan. 6; v. 270; p. 56.
Scraper. C. Gottschalk. No. 1,327,155; Jan. 6; v. 270; p. 52.
Scraper. K. S. Chung. No. 1,327,522; Jan. 6; v. 270; p. 120.
Screen: See—
    Pulp-screen.
Sealing device Shaft-. E. T. Williams. No. 1,327,002; Jan. 6; v. 270; p. 28.

Seat: See—
    Water-closet seat.
Section-switch. H. W. Davis. No. 1,327,463; Jan. 6; v. 270; p. 108.
Self-opening gate. C. F. Sebring. No. 1,327,257; Jan. 6; v. 270; p. 71.
Separator: See—
    Grain-separator.
Sewer-structure invert-sections, Mold for. J. H. Zinn. No. 1,327,006; Jan. 6; v. 270; p. 24.
Sewers, Apparatus for removing sediment from catch-basins of. G. W. Otterson. No. 1,327,211; Jan. 6; v. 270; p. 62.
Sewing-machines, Crossthread-laying mechanism for. J. R. Moffatt. No. 1,327,348; Jan. 6; v. 270; p. 87.
Sewing-machine motor. F. J. Osius. No. 1,327,210; Jan. 6; v. 270; p. 62.
Sewing-machines, Thread-nipper-releasing device for. G. S. Gatchell. No. 1,327,232; Jan. 6; v. 270; p. 66.
Shaft-coupling, Flexible. B. E. Thomas. No. 1,326,993; Jan. 6; v. 270; p. 22.
Shank-stiffener. H. C. Egerton. No. 1,327,091; Jan. 6; v. 270; p. 40.
Sharpener, Pencil-. C. Cleveland. No. 1,327,459; Jan. 6; v. 270; p. 107.
Sharpening machine, Saw-. R. Asmondis. No. 1,327,012; Jan. 6; v. 270; p. 26.
Sheeted material, Wind-up device for. J. T. Brogden. No. 1,327,420; Jan. 6; v. 270; p. 100.
Sheet-feeding mechanism. W. C. Glass. No. 1,327,546; Jan. 6; v. 270; p. 124.
Sheet, Flexible reinforced transparent. C. F. Jenkins. No. 1,327,281; Jan. 6; v. 270; p. 75.
Sheet-metal-cutting machine. C. P. Buck. No. 1,327,082; Jan. 6; v. 270; p. 38.
Sheet-metal-elbow-forming machine. A. Dieckmann. No. 1,326,916; Jan. 6; v. 270; p. 6.
Sheets, Mechanism for controlling the feeding and printing of. B. F. Upham. No. 1,327,182; Jan. 6; v. 270; p. 57.
Shellac surrogate and producing same. J. R. Köhler. No. 1,327,332; Jan. 6; v. 270; p. 84.
Sherardizing apparatus. C. J. Kirk. No. 1,327,102; Jan. 6; v. 270; p. 42.
Shingle, Strip-. H. Abraham. No. 1,326,899; Jan. 6; v. 270; p. 5.
Ships, Cooling air in submarine and submersible. H. E. Yarrow. No. 1,327,509; Jan. 6; v. 270; p. 117.
Shirt. J. Hurwitz. No. 1,327,476; Jan. 6; v. 270; p. 111.
Short-circuiting mechanism. J. L. Tonge. No. 1,327,259; Jan. 6; v. 270; p. 71.
Shuttles, Machinery for truing loom-. J. Altmann. No. 1,327,515; Jan. 6; v. 270; p. 119.
Sight. J. L. Bumpas and P. Falcke. No. 1,327,141; Jan. 6; v. 270; p. 49.
Sign. E. O. Sterns. No. 1,326,985; Jan. 6; v. 270; p. 20.
Signal: See—
    Automobile-signal.   Direction-signal.
Signal and communicating with trains, Actuating. H. A. Thompson. No. 1,327,411; Jan. 6; v. 270; p. 98.
Signaling system. B. H. Peter. No. 1,327,570; Jan. 6; v. 270; p. 129.
Skate, Roller-. F. Gunnarson. No. 1,327,549; Jan. 6; v. 270; p. 125.
Skiving-machine. N. V. Dyer. No. 1,327,028; Jan. 6; v. 270; p. 28.
Smelting system, Hermetic unit. W. M. Johnson. No. 1,327,282; Jan. 6; v. 270; p. 75.
Snail and slug trap. R. S. Walker. No. 1,327,579; Jan. 6; v. 270; p. 131.
Soda-fountain apparatus. C. L. Bastian. No. 1,327,189; Jan. 6; v. 270; p. 58.
Solder, Making. J. Salm. No. 1,326,971; Jan. 6; v. 270; p. 18.
Sole-pressing machine. W. C. Stewart. No. 1,327,179; Jan. 6; v. 270; p. 56.
Sound-controller. W. A. Sommerhof. No. 1,327,118; Jan. 6; v. 270; p. 45.
Spark-plug. H. C. Garber. No. 1,327,382; Jan. 6; v. 270; p. 93.
Spark plug, Multiple-. J. L. Nilson and J. Prince. No. 1,327,057; Jan. 6; v. 270; p. 34.
Spindle, Electrically-driven. J. Hurtig. No. 1,327,160; Jan. 6; v. 270; p. 52.
Spray device, Adjustable shower-. G. H. Gregory. No. 1,327,428; Jan. 6; v. 270; p. 102.
Spring: See—
    Bed-spring.   Leaf-spring.
Spring suspension. G. E. Rigby. No. 1,327,063; Jan. 6; v. 270; p. 35.
Square, Line-. J. A. Carlson. No. 1,327,198; Jan. 6; v. 270; p. 60.
Stabilizer. A. J. Macy. No. 1,327,055; Jan. 6; v. 270; p. 33.
Stabilizing device. F. D. Blessmeyer. No. 1,327,586; Jan. 6; v. 270; p. 132.
Stall, Adjustable cattle-. S. L. Hanson. No. 1,327,386; Jan. 6; v. 270; p. 94.
Stammering, Device for the prevention of. F. J. Rogers. No. 1,327,407; Jan. 6; v. 270; p. 98.
Stamp or label affixer. W. F. Schweiger and W. J. Balkwill. No. 1,326,978; Jan. 6; v. 270; p. 19.
Stamping-machine. B. S. Lee. No. 1,327,050; Jan. 6; v. 270; p. 33.

ALPHABETICAL LIST OF TRADE-MARKS.

ALPHABETICAL LIST OF LABELS.

"Derryvale." (For Linen Piece Goods.) Derryvale Linen Company. No. 5,189; Jan. 6; v. 270; p. 187.
"Hays Gloves. (For Leather Gloves.) The Daniel Hays Company. No. 5,188; Jan. 6; v. 270; p. 187.
"King '8' 'Limoudan.'" (For Automobiles.) King Car Corporation of New York. No. 5,191; Jan. 6; v. 270; p. 187.
"P. A. lets the cat out of the smoke-bag." (For Smoking-Tobacco.) R. J. Reynolds Tobacco Company. No. 5,192; Jan. 6; v. 270; p. 187.

"Stylish Colors Everywhere 'Rit' ed with Rit." (For Dye-Soap.) Sunbeam Chemical Company. No. 5,193; Jan. 6; v. 270; p. 187.
"The glory of a woman is her skin." (For Toilet Soap.) The N. K. Fairbank Company. No. 5,190; Jan. 6; v. 270; p. 187.
"The Tyre to Tie To." (For Tires and Tubes.) Braender Rubber & Tire Co. No. 5,187; Jan. 6; v. 270; p. 187.

ALPHABETICAL LIST OF TRADE-MARK TITLES.

(REGISTRATION APPLIED FOR.)

Account-books, Bank-deposit. F. A. Gesell. No. 114,672; Jan. 6; v. 270; p. 141.
Anesthetics. H. A. Metz Laboratories. No. 123,214; Jan. 6; v. 270; p. 170.
Antiseptic, Liquid. A. S. Mann. No. 121,249; Jan. 6; v. 270; p. 156.
Asbestos suits, helmets, and hoods, rubber gloves, &c. American La France Fire Engine Co. No. 114,966; Jan. 6; v. 270; p. 142.
Automobile accessories. Joseph N. Smith & Company. No. 105,630; Jan. 6; v. 270; p. 139.
Automobiles. Vreeland Motor Co. No. 123,231; Jan. 6; v. 270; p. 170.
Bandage, Catamenial. G. C. Levy. No. 121,149; Jan. 6; v. 270; p. 156.
Batteries, Dry storage. J. P. Mentzer. No. 113,491; Jan. 6; v. 270; p. 140.
Bearing metal. American Non-Ferrous Metals Corporation. No. 122,005; Jan. 6; v. 270; p. 160.
Bearing metals, Antifriction. Union Smelting & Refining Co. No. 117,145; Jan. 6; v. 270; p. 145.
Beer or near beer, Compound used in the manufacture of. National Brewers Academy & Consulting Bureau. No. 119,810; Jan. 6; v. 270; p. 151.
Belting, Leather. J. J. Freadrich. No. 122,427; Jan. 6; v. 270; p. 163.
Belts, aprons, and gum tissue, Sanitary. Omo Mfg. Co. Nos. 119,204-5; Jan. 6; v. 270; p. 149.
Beverge, Non-alcoholic. Celro-Kola Co. No. 123,961; Jan. 6; v. 270; p. 173.
Beverage, Non-alcoholic. Joseph Krieg-Fink Co. No. 123,986; Jan. 6; v. 270; p. 173.
Beverage, Non-intoxicating. Southern Beverage Company. No. 118,493; Jan. 6; v. 270; p. 147.
Beverages and syrups and ingredients for making same, Non-alcoholic. I. B. Goetz. No. 122,773; Jan. 6; v. 270; p. 165.
Beverages, Non-alcoholic. W. Bachrach. No. 123,104; Jan. 6; v. 270; p. 169.
Beverages, Non-alcoholic, and syrup for making same. E. Diehl. No. 123,796; Jan. 6; v. 270; p. 173.
Billiard-balls. Brunswick-Balke-Collender Company. No. 123,001; Jan. 6; v. 270; p. 169.
Biscuit. National Biscuit Company. No. 124,148; Jan. 6; v. 270; p. 173.
Boiler compounds. Corrasanti Chemical Co. No. 123,238; Jan. 6; v. 270; p. 170.
Books published in series, Printed. E. J. Clode. No. 124,469; Jna. 6; v. 270; p. 174.
Boots and shoes. Converse Rubber Shoe Co. No. 119,971; Jan. 6; v. 270; p. 152.
Boots and shoes. Wm. Kaut Footwear Company. No. 119,656; Jan. 6; v. 270; p. 151.
Boots and shoes for misses and children. Wm. Kaut Footwear Company. Nos. 120,830-3; Jan. 6; v. 270; pp. 154-5.
Boots and shoes, Leather. Emerson Shoe Company. Nos. 121,462-4; Jan. 6; v. 270; p. 157.
Boots and shoes, Leather. Locke Shoe Co. No. 122,017; Jan. 6; v. 270; p. 160.
Boots and shoes, Leather. F. M. Schumacher. No. 119,777; Jan. 6; v. 270; p. 151.
Boots and shoes, Leather. Wm. Kaut Footwear Company. No. 121,472; Jan. 6; v. 270; p. 158.
Boots, shoes, and slippers. Rice & Hutchins. No. 123,456; Jan. 6; v. 270; p. 171.
Boots, shoes, slippers, and sandals, Leather. Wm. Kaut Footwear Company. No. 121,473; Jan. 6; v. 270; p. 158.
Boots, shoes, slippers, sandals, Leather. Wm. Kaut Footwear Co. No. 122,540; Jan. 6; v. 270; p. 164.
Bread. C. F. Hathaway & Sons. No. 121,114; Jan. 6; v. 270; p. 156.
Bread. F. A. Heroux. No. 123,208; Jan. 6; v. 270; p. 169.
Bread. A. Reznikove. No. 119,209; Jan. 6; v. 270; p. 149.
Bread. T. Roulston. No. 115,262; Jan. 6; v. 270; p. 142.
Bread, cakes, and pastry. Haller Baking Company. No. 123,054; Jan. 6; v. 270; p. 169.

Brooms. Newton Broom Co. No. 120,768; Jan. 6; v. 270; p. 154.
Brooms. White-Valentine Company. No. 122,868; Jan. 6; v. 270; p. 166.
Butter. International Merchants, Incorporated. No. 122,213; Jan. 6; v. 270; p. 162.
Buttons. International Button Co. No. 120,920; Jan. 6; v. 270; p. 155.
Candied fruits and nuts and candy. F. G. Jensen. No. 122,122; Jan. 6; v. 270; p. 161.
Candies. Eye Brand Confectionery. No. 115.343; Jan. 6; v. 270; p. 142.
Candies. Johnson Bros. & Alexander. No. 106,620; Jan. 6; v. 270; p. 139.
Candies. V. Vivaudou. No. 123,507; Jan. 6; v. 270; p. 171.
Candies and chocolate. Mason, Au & Magenheimer Conf. Mfg. Co. No. 115,993; Jan. 6; v. 270; p. 143.
Candy. Shutter-Johnson Candy Co. No. 123,944; Jan. 6; v. 270; p. 173.
Candy and fruit tablets. Charms Company. No. 119,469; Jan. 6; v. 270; p. 150.
Canned corn and peas. Waterloo Canning Association. No. 113,882; Jan. 6; v. 270; p. 141.
Canned fruits, vegetables, and fish. Hale Company. No. 123,642; Jan. 6; v. 270; p. 172.
Canned goods, rice, tea, &c. Tolerton & Warfield Co. No. 88,376; Jan. 6; v. 270; p. 137.
Canned pineapples. Hawaiian Pineapple Company. No. 122,892; Jan. 6; v. 270; p. 167.
Canned shrimp, salmon, oysters, and pepper sauce, honey, &c. Haas, Baruch & Co. No. 110,022; Jan. 6; v. 270; p. 139.
Caps and hats for men and children. J. P. Cody. No. 121,171; Jan. 6; v. 270; p. 156.
Car truck-frames, &c. Railway-. Commonwealth Steel Company. No. 122,073; Jan. 6; v. 270; p. 161.
Castings, Heat-resisting. Hiram Walker & Sons Metal Products. No. 113,169; Jan. 6; v. 270; p. 140.
Catsup, canned vegetables and fruits. Sterling Products Co. No. 113,636; Jan. 6; v. 270; p. 140.
Chains and swivels, Neck and watch. M. S. Rodenberg Co. No. 120,676; Jan. 6; v. 270; p. 154.
Cheese. W. Faehndrich. No. 122,828; Jan. 6; v. 270; p. 166.
Cigars, cigarettes, and tobacco. F. G. Gilbert. No. 122,166; Jan. 6; v. 270; p. 161.
Cigars, cigarettes, and tobacco. R. J. Seidenberg Co. No. 117,198; Jan. 6; v. 270; p. 145.
Cleaning compound. J. J. Meyer. No. 117,463; Jan. 6; v. 270; p. 146.
Closets, Chemical. Standard Steel Corp. No. 117,999; Jan. 6; v. 270; p. 146.
Clothing, Men's. H. Jacobson Co. No. 116,264; Jan. 6; v. 270; p. 144.
Clothing, Men's and boys'. F. Simon & Co. No. 118,940; Jan. 6; v. 270; p. 148.
Coal. A. S. Nowlin & Co. No. 121,314; Jan. 6; v. 270; p. 156.
Coats. P. Sangoff. No. 118,354; Jan. 6; v. 270; p. 147.
Coats, Reversible leather. International Duplex Coat Co. No. 120,827; Jan. 6; v. 270; p. 140.
Coffee. Clark & MacKusick Company. No. 113,118; Jan. 6; v. 270; p. 140.
Colors. G. Siegle Company. No. 113,388; Jan. 6; v. 270; p. 140.
Comminuting machinery, &c. Allis-Chalmers Manufacturing Company. No. 119,620; Jan. 6; v. 270; p. 151.
Compound and ointment of iodin and oil. William S. Merrill Company. No. 123,132; Jan. 6; v. 270; p. 169.
Computing device, Logarithmic-scale. Lewis, Connors & Company. No. 122,362; Jan. 6; v. 270; p. 163.
Corsets, corset-waists, brassières. Linehan-Conover Company. No. 113,454; Jan. 6; v. 270; p. 140.
Cosmetics. Usit Mfg. Co. of America. No. 117,360; Jan. 6; v. 270; p. 146.
Cutlery, razors, &c., Pocket-. Union Cutlery Co. No. 121,818; Jan. 6; v. 270; p. 160.
Dolls. J. M. Lockwood, Jr. No. 122,489; Jan. 6; v. 270; p. 163.

Drawings or pictures, Comic. International Feature Service. No. 122,214; Jan. 6; v. 270; p. 162.
Drawings or pictures, Comic. International Feature Service. No. 122,216; Jan. 6; v. 270; p. 162.
Dresses. Estelle Company. No. 121,097; Jan. 6; v. 270; p. 156.
Dresses. L. Levy. No. 122,778; Jan. 6; v. 270; p. 165.
Dresses, Infants' and children's. A. Millman. No. 122,128; Jan. 6; v. 270; p. 161.
Drinking-fountains and parts. Eastern Fountain Co. No. 122,350; Jan. 6; v. 270; p. 163.
Dyes. American Aniline Products. No. 115,634; Jan. 6; v. 270; p. 143.
Dyestuffs and chemicals. H. A. Metz. No. 119,425; Jan. 6; v. 270; p. 150.
Eggs, poultry, and butter. J. Lynard. No. 123,212; Jan. 6; v. 270; p. 170.
Electrical apparatus, machines, and supplies. Electric Controller & Manufacturing Company. No. 123,632; Jan. 6; v. 270; p. 172.
Electrical wire and fuses. J. H. Faw, Inc. No. 122,938; Jan. 6; v. 270; p. 167.
Electrodes. Gensonite Welding Electrode Co. No. 122,883; Jan. 6; v. 270; p. 167.
Engines and parts thereof, winches, and capstans. N. & S. Engine Co. No. 122,494; Jan. 6; v. 270; p. 163.
Feathers. Star Bedding Company. No. 122,504; Jan. 6; v. 270; p. 164.
Feed, Poultry. G. E. Conkey Co. Nos. 119,399–400; Jan. 6; v. 270; pp. 149–50.
Files, Document-. Safe-Cabinet Company. No. 116,110; Jan. 6; v. 270; p. 144.
Fire - extinguishing - powder compound. Select Products Sales Corporation. No. 122,502; Jan. 6; v. 270; p. 164.
Flavoring extracts. National Fruit Flavor Co. No. 121,777; Jan. 6; v. 270; p. 159.
Flavoring extracts. C. F. Sauer Co. No. 106,998; Jan. 6; v. 270; p. 139.
Flavoring extracts and syrups. Limpert Bros. No. 116,270; Jan. 6; v. 270; p. 144.
Floor-finish. B. L. Webb. No. 122,030; Jan. 6; v. 270; p. 160.
Flour, Wheat-. Galbraith Milling Company. No. 117,874; Jan. 6; v. 270; p. 146.
Food-colors. National Aniline & Chemical Company. No. 119,000; Jan. 6; v. 270; p. 148.
Food-colors. National Aniline & Chemical Company Inc. No. 119,004; Jan. 6; v. 270; p. 149.
Food-colors. National Aniline & Chemical Company. No. 119,367; Jan. 6; v. 270; p. 149.
Food for live stock, Medicated. Parsons Chemical Works. No. 115,576; Jan. 6; v. 270; p. 142.
Foot-pads. A. B. Plummer. No. 120,222; Jan. 6; v. 270; p. 152.
Foods. O. F. Mayer & Bros. No. 116,099; Jan. 6; v. 270; p. 144.
Foods, Infants', &c. Hensch Food Company. No. 124,400; Jan. 6; v. 270; p. 174.
Formaldehyde, sulfoxalate of sodium. Rohm & Haas Company. No. 123,041; Jan. 6; v. 270; p. 168.
Fruits, Fresh. Furry Fruit & Produce Co. No. 122,164; Jan. 6; v. 270; p. 161.
Fruits, Fresh citrus. Lake Reedy Packing Co. No. 122,898; Jan. 6; v. 270; p. 167.
Garments, Ladies' and misses'. American Import Co. No. 118,102; Jan. 6; v. 270; p. 146.
Garments, Men's and children's outer. Cohen, Goldman & Co. No. 122,586; Jan. 6; v. 270; p. 164.
Gasolene. Preparation for improving. A. Danville. No. 120,241; Jan. 6; v. 270; p. 152.
Gasolene. Denver Powerine Company. No. 118,431; Jan. 6; v. 270; p. 147.
Ginger-ale. R. M. Schlesinger. No. 124,018; Jan. 6; v. 270; p. 173.
Ginger-ale. Southwestern Coca-Cola Bottling Co. No. 124,627; Jan. 6; v. 270; p. 175.
Ginger-ale, cream-soda, sarsaparilla, &c. Alpine Co. No. 123,199; Jan. 6; v. 270; p. 169.
Girdles, brassières, hip-reducers, &c. Elastowear Manufacturing Company. No. 118,755; Jan. 6; v. 270; p. 148.
Glass jars. American Pure Food Process Co. No. 122,811; Jan. 6; v. 270; p. 166.
Glue. Simmons Hardware Company. No. 116,905; Jan. 6; v. 270; p. 145.
Grape-juice. California Wine Association. No. 124,593; Jan. 6; v. 270; p. 174.
Hair dyes and shampoo. Ori-Ori Company. No. 121,409; Jan. 6; v. 270; p. 157.
Hair-wavers. Parisian Mfg. Company. No. 123,363; Jan. 6; v. 270; p. 171.
Hats. S. Schiller. No. 121,816; Jan. 6; v. 270; p. 159.
Headlights and turbo-generators, Electric. Schroeder Headlight & Generator Co. No. 121,424; Jan. 6; v. 270; p. 157.
Hog-waterers. Hartman Company. No. 120,421; Jan. 6; v. 270; p. 153.
Hops, California. A/S Det Almindelige Handelskompagni. No. 122,238; Jan. 6; v. 270; p. 162.
Hose-supporter. Ely & Walker Dry Goods Co. No. 120,363; Jan. 6; v. 270; p. 152.
Hosiery. Chipman Knitting Mills. No. 108,121; Jan. 6; v. 270; p. 139.

Hosiery. National Mills. No. 118,323; Jan. 6; v. 270; p. 147.
Hosiery. A. Stieglitz & Co. No. 121,362; Jan. 6; v. 270; p. 157.
Hosiery for women. J. F. Byrne. No. 116,324; Jan. 6; v. 270; p. 144.
Hosiery, Men's. Ritter Hosiery Company. No. 123,365; Jan. 6; v. 270; p. 171.
Hydrosulfite, Anhydrous sodium. Rohm & Haas Company. No. 123,089; Jan. 6; v. 270; p. 168.
Ice-cream and ices. Arctic Ice & Coal Co. No. 120,083; Jan. 6; v. 270; p. 152.
Interest tables, Yearly-. S. G. Miller. No. 112,396; Jan. 6; v. 270; p. 139.
Insecticide and germicide. Dupuis Chemical Co. No. 122,884; Jan. 6; v. 270; p. 167.
Insecticides. J. G. Grossenbacher. No. 122,212; Jan. 6; v. 270; p. 162.
Insecticides. Oswald M'Cardell & Co. Nos. 123,215–6; Jan. 6; v. 270; p. 170.
Jelly, Pineapple. Pearl City Fruit Co. No. 122,913; Jan. 6; v. 270; p. 167.
Jigs, vises, lathes, planers, &c. Lawson & Company. No. 116,418; Jan. 6; v. 270; p. 145.
Knives. Dwight Divine & Sons. Nos. 119,501–2; Jan. 6; v. 270; p. 150.
Knives. Dwight Divine & Sons. No. 119,504; Jan. 6; v. 270; p. 150.
Lacquers. E. I. du Pont de Nemours & Company. No. 120,413; Jan. 6; v. 270; p. 153.
Lamp-lenses. B. Trieber. No. 116,173; Jan. 6; v. 270; p. 144.
Lathes and grinders. Axelson Machine Co. No. 118,456; Jan. 6; v. 270; p. 147.
Lenses, Auto-. Unique Auto Specialties Co. No. 122,066; Jan. 6; v. 270; p. 161.
Lenses, Ophthalmic. American Optical Company. No. 123,724; Jan. 6; v. 270; p. 172.
Linen and cotton piece goods, &c. Derrydale Linen Company. Nos. 122,975–6; Jan. 6; v. 270; p. 168.
Liniment. F. Ad. Richter & Co. of New York. No. 115,540; Jan. 6; v. 270; p. 142.
Liniment. F. Ad. Richter & Co. of New York. No. 115,779; Jan. 6; v. 270; p. 143.
Locks, Nut-. Painut Corporation. No. 122,951; Jan. 6; v. 270; p. 167.
Lotions, Skin-. C. H. Bong. No. 116,517; Jan. 6; v. 270; p. 145.
Magazine, Monthly. Class Journal Corporation. Nos. 121,564–5; Jan. 6; v. 270; p. 158.
Magazine, Monthly. Concrete-Cement Age Publishing Co. No. 122,882; Jan. 6; v. 270; p. 166.
Magazines, Monthly. Commerce Publications Company. No. 121,457; Jan. 6; v. 270; p. 157.
Magazine, Monthly. W. A. Radford. No. 122,733; Jan. 6; v. 270; v. 270; p. 165.
Magazine, Weekly. Manufacturers Record Publishing Company. No. 122,846; Jan. 6; v. 270; p. 166.
Marcel and water waver. Samstag & Hilder Bros. No. 123,459; Jan. 6; v. 270; p. 171.
Measuring and scientific appliances. Reid Bros. No. 120,936; Jan. 6; v. 270; p. 155.
Middy-blouses and dresses. Enterprise Manufacturing Company. No. 122,980; Jan. 6; v. 270; p. 168.
Necklaces, Imitation-pearl. L. Heller & Son. No. 119,802; Jan. 6; v. 270; p. 151.
Negligées. G. G. Thompson. No. 121,048; Jan. 6; v. 270; p. 155.
Newspaper-sections. Los Angeles Examiner. Nos. 118,287–8; Jan. 6; v. 270; p. 146–7.
Newspaper-sections. Los Angeles Examiner. No. 124,351; Jan. 6; v. 270; p. 174.
Oat and corn flakes, farina, rice, sweet chocolate, &c. Union Pacific Tea Co. No. 101,973; Jan. 6; v. 270; p. 137.
Oil, Medicated. Pepsotone Company. No. 113,945; Jan. 6; v. 270; p. 141.
Oil, Soy-bean. Chas. Hollinshed Co. No. 122,835; Jan. 6; v. 270; p. 166.
Oils, Floor-. J. W. Bullen. No. 122,327; Jan. 6; v. 270; p. 162.
Oils, greases, and waxes. Vacuum Oil Company. No. 121,495; Jan. 6; v. 270; p. 158.
Oils, greases, waxes, gasolene, &c. Vacuum Oil Company. No. 122,618; Jan. 6; v. 270; p. 164.
Oils, Lubricating-. Lamborn & Co. No. 123,487; Jan. 6; v. 270; p. 170.
Oils, Lubricating, &c. McCormick & Co. No. 114,056; Jan. 6; v. 270; p. 141.
Overalls. Cowden Manufacturing Co. No. 121,294; Jan. 6; v. 270; p. 156.
Overalls. Regal Manufacturing Company. No. 116,933; Jan. 6; v. 270; p. 145.
Overalls, jumpers, and work-shirts. Textile Products Manufacturing Company. No. 119,781; Jan. 6; v. 270; p. 151.
Overgaiters. American Overgaiter Co. No. 121,734; Jan. 6; v. 270; p. 159.
Oysters, Fresh, dried, and canned. Narragansett Bay Oyster Co. Nos. 103,808–9; Jan. 6; v. 270; pp. 137–8.
Paints, varnishes, &c., for ships' bottoms. Graphite Products Limited. No. 120,608; Jan. 6; v. 270; p. 153.

Paper, Machine-bookkeeping. Byron Weston Co. No. 101,590; Jan. 6; v. 270; p. 137.
Paper used for railroad-tickets, &c., Safety-. G. La Monte & Son. No. 107,963; Jan. 6; v. 270; p. 139.
Package-binders and parts thereof. E. A. Rudin. No. 120,431; Jan. 6; v. 270; p. 153.
Packing. J. Crane. No. 119,735; Jan. 6; v. 270; p. 151.
Pants, Infants'. Samstag & Hilder Bros. No. 123,460; Jan. 6; v. 270; p. 171.
Paper, Window-display. Lester P. Winchenbaugh Co. No. 121,328; Jan. 6; v. 270; p. 157.
Paper, Writing-. Whiting Paper Company. No. 116,938; Jan. 6; v. 270; p. 145.
Paste, paints, and varnishes. Beaver Varnish Company. No. 122,423; Jan. 6; v. 270; p. 163.
Pearls and imitation pearls. W. B. Kellogg Co. No. 112,648; Jan. 6; v. 270; p. 140.
Pencils. Joseph Dixon Crucible Company. No. 124,595; Jan. 6; v. 270; p. 174.
Perfume, toilet water, &c. Lundborg Company. No. 120,572; Jan. 6; v. 270; p. 153.
Petroleum products. Carson Petroleum Company. No. 116,644; Jan. 6; v. 270; p. 145.
Phonographs and cabinets. Milwaukee Talking Machine Manufacturing Co. No. 121,118; Jan. 6; v. 270; p. 156.
Phonograph-records. Emerson Phonograph Company. No. 124,336; Jan. 6; v. 270; p. 174.
Phonographs. Kesner & Jerlaw. No. 123,546; Jan. 6; v. 270; p. 172.
Phonographs and records. T. H. De Pew. No. 123,923; Jan. 6; v. 270; p. 173.
Pianos, piano-players, and organs. Story & Clark Piano Company. Nos. 124,629-30; Jan. 6; v. 270; p. 175.
Piston-rings. V. Plex Piston Ring Company. No. 122,796; Jan. 6; v. 270; p. 165.
Pipe, railway-spikes, &c., Welded and riveted. Koppel Industrial Car & Equipment Company. No. 120,485; Jan. 6; v. 270; p. 153.
Plastic composition for modeling. E. Reizenstein. No. 123,714; Jan. 6; v. 270; p. 172.
Platinum, Alloyed. E. R. Nebeling. No. 122,652; Jan. 6; v. 270; p. 164.
Poultry, Dressed. National Poultry Co. No. 117,569; Jan. 6; v. 270; p. 145.
Powder, Tooth-. A. B. Peters. No. 121,019; Jan. 6; v. 270; p. 155.
Preparation for headaches and nervous diseases. Keasbey & Mattison Company. No. 115,983; Jan. 6; v. 270; p. 143.
Preparation for malaria. I. Solomovitz. No. 121,026; Jan. 6; v. 270; p. 155.
Preparation for relief of inflammation and pain by cutaneous absorption. Clayton Chemical Co. No. 123,020; Jan. 6; v. 270; p. 168.
Preparation for rheumatism and cystitis. Keasbey & Mattison Company. No. 115,984; Jan. 6; v. 270; p. 143.
Preparation for skin diseases, Pharmaceutical. Sunbeam Chemical Company. No. 117,255; Jan. 6; v. 270; p. 145.
Printing-work, Printed forms for estimates of. H. M. Hastings. No. 115,590; Jan. 6; v. 270; p. 142.
Publication. Fairchild Company. No. 122,011; Jan. 6; v. 270; p. 160.
Publication, Advertising. F. W. Brown. No. 124,067; Jan. 6; v. 270; p. 173.
Publication, Annual. United Publishers Corporation. No. 123,592; Jan. 6; v. 270; p. 172.
Publication for advertising. F. W. Brown. No. 122,330; Jan. 6; v. 270; p. 163.
Publication, Trade. Ready To Wear Publishing Company. No. 122,660; Jan. 6; v. 270; p. 165.
Remedy, Eye. Wheeler Optical Company. No. 117,960; Jan. 6; v. 270; p. 146.
Remedy for colds and malaria. Keasbey & Mattison Company. No. 115,985; Jan. 6; v. 270; p. 143.
Rice. Stuttgart Rice Mill Company. No. 123,440½; Jan. 6; v. 270; p. 171.
Resins and volatile oils. Ungerer & Company. No. 123,146; Jan. 6; v. 270; p. 169.
Rice, pickles, and olives. Tolerton & Warfield Co. No. 105,724; Jan. 6; v. 270; p. 139.
Rim, Collapsible. Baer Collapsible Rim Corporation. No. 122,156; Jan. 6; v. 270; p. 156.
Road-graders. J. D. Adams & Company. No. 122,416; Jan. 6; v. 270; p. 163.
Rollers for printing-presses, &c. Ideal Roller Company. No. 119,071; Jan. 6; v. 270; p. 149.
Rope, cord, twine, and binder-twine. International Harvester Company. No. 121,627; Jan. 6; v. 270; p. 158.
Rubber heels. Barva Heel & Tire Factory. No. 123,332; Jan. 6; v. 270; p. 170.
Sardines. Rueppel-Jones Importing Company. No. 122,858; Jan. 6; v. 270; p. 166.
Sausage, Fresh. C. Hollenbach. No. 122,599; Jan. 6; v. 270; p. 164.
Saws. Simonds Manufacturing Company. No. 121,728; Jan. 6; v. 270; p. 159.
Saws. Simonds Manufacturing Company. No. 122,735; Jan. 6; v. 270; p. 166.
Seed, Grain. H. K. Cochran Company. No. 121,921; Jan. 6; v. 270; p. 160.

Sheet metal, Decorated. American Stamping Company. No. 122,505; Jan. 6; v. 270; p. 164.
Shirts, Work-. Reliance Manufacturing Company. No. 116,109; Jan. 6; v. 270; p. 144.
Shirts and underwear. Sanger Brothers. No. 119,682; Jan. 6; v. 270; p. 151.
Shoe-buckles, combs, &c., Metal. Trifari & Krussman. No. 114,722; Jan. 6; v. 270; p. 141.
Shoes, boots, and slippers. M. A. Feehan. No. 118,756; Jan. 6; v. 270; p. 148.
Shoes, Canvas outing-. Apsley Rubber Company. No. 123,531; Jan. 6; v. 270; p. 172.
Shoe dressing and cleanser. Import Drug Specialties Company. No. 116,053; Jan. 6; v. 270; p. 143.
Shoes, Ladies'. D. Cohen. No. 116,023; Jan. 6; v. 270; p. 143.
Shoes, Leather. Milton J. Meyer & Co. No. 121,179; Jan. 6; v. 270; p. 156.
Shoes, Leather, rubber, &c. Marathon Shoe Co. No. 119,711; Jan. 6; v. 270; p. 151.
Shortening and frying medium. Aspegren & Co. No. 123,298; Jan. 6; v. 270; p. 170.
Signals, Warning-. Stewart-Warner Speedometer Corporation. No. 98,375; Jan. 6; v. 270; p. 137.
Silverware-polish. United Drug Company. No. 117,958; Jan. 6; v. 270; p. 146.
Snap-fasteners. Columbia Fastener Company. No. 120,815; Jan. 6; v. 270; p. 154.
Snap-fasteners. Columbia Fastener Company. No. 119,849; Jan. 6; v. 270; p. 152.
Snap-fasteners. United Trimming Co. No. 121,161; Jan. 6; v. 270; p. 156.
Soap. Howard Bros. Chemical Co. No. 123,163; Jan. 6; v. 270; p. 169.
Soap. Washer Maid Company. No. 124,324; Jan. 6; v. 270; p. 174.
Soap, Liquid toilet. Sanitary Products Company. No. 117,143; Jan. 6; v. 270; p. 145.
Soaps. Agra Company. No. 124,380; Jan. 6; v. 270; p. 174.
Soaps. Asunción Oritz y Palacios. No. 100,464; Jan. 6; v. 270; p. 137.
Soles and heels. Boot and shoe. Armstrong Cork Company. Nos. 118,977-8; Jan. 6; v. 270; p. 148.
Soles and heels, Leather. C. G. Fleckenstein Co. No. 118,353; Jan. 6; v. 270; p. 140.
Spades, shovels. C. Osmundson. No. 119,985; Jan. 6; v. 270; p. 152.
Spaghetti and macaroni. Grand Union Tea Co. No. 123,634; Jan. 6; v. 270; p. 172.
Sparklers. Victory Sparkler Company. No. 122,740; Jan. 6; v. 270; p. 165.
Spark-plugs. Derf Manufacturing Company. No. 119,796; Jan. 6; v. 270; p. 151.
Spark-plugs. E. W. Brandquist. No. 122,385; Jan. 6; v. 270; p. 163.
Sprout-hooks, &c. S. Allcock & Co. No. 122,456; Jan. 6; v. 270; p. 163.
Stamps, Time-. J. Levy. No. 118,761; Jan. 6; v. 270; p. 148.
Starch. H. Kohnstamm & Co. No. 122,987; Jan 6; v. 270; p. 168.
Steel. Vanadium-Alloys Steel Co. No. 120,893; Jan. 6; v. 270; p. 155.
Steel, &c., Composition for tempering. H-B. Tempering Process Co. No. 122,194; Jan. 6; v. 270; p. 162.
Steel bars, rods, blocks, and forgings. Crucible Steel Company of America. Nos. 122,292-3; Jan. 6; v. 270; p. 162.
Stockings and socks. Louis Brun Fils. No. 119,389; Jan. 6; v. 270; p. 149.
Suits, coats, vests, &c., Men's and boys'. Leopold, Solomon and Eisendrath. No. 114,270; Jan. 6; v. 270; p. 141.
Suits and overcoats, Men's. B. H. Levy Bro. & Co. No. 120,312; Jan. 6; v. 270; p. 153.
Sweaters. Bee Ess Knitting Mills. No. 121,857; Jan. 6; v. 270; p. 160.
Syrup, Pineapple-extract. Pearl City Fruit Co. No. 122,912; Jan. 6; v. 270; p. 167.
Syrup, Table-. Nulomoline Company. No. 120,577; Jan. 6; v. 270; p. 153.
Tables, chairs, settees, desks, &c. J. S. Blankinship. No. 119,015; Jan. 6; v. 270; p. 149.
Tags, Job and delivery. Albert Jacobs Company. No. 124,651; Jan. 6; v. 270; p. 175.
Tanks. Riverside Boiler Works. Nos. 123,755-6; Jan. 6; v. 270; p. 172-3.
Tanning hides, Chemical for. Rohm & Haas Company. No. 123,040; Jan. 6; v. 270; p. 168.
Talking-machines and supplies. S. S. Schiff. No. 122,862; Jan. 6; v. 270; p. 166.
Tea, coffee, spices, &c. S. D. Abrams. No. 120,514; Jan. 6; v. 270; p. 153.
Tin, galvanized and japanned ware. National Enameling & Stamping Co. No. 121,012; Jan. 6; v. 270; p. 155.
Tire tubes. Patches for wheel-. Hassebrock Brothers. No. 121,717; Jan. 6; v. 270; p. 159.
Tires, Inner tubes for pneumatic. Spencer Carroll Company. No. 118,653; Jan. 6; v. 270; p. 148.
Tires, inner tubes, &c., Rubber. Polson Rubber Co. No. 122,023; Jan. 6; v. 270; p. 160.

(REGISTRATION APPLIED FOR.)

Tobacco, Plug-. Larus & Brother Company. No. 119,561; Jan. 6; v. 270; p. 150.

Toilet powder. George Borgfeldt & Co. No. 123,102; Jan. 6; v. 270; p. 169.

Tools. Harrold Tool & Forge Co. No. 115,403; Jan. 6; v. 270; p. 142.

Tool, shovel, and incline, Combination automobile. Alsteel Manufacturing Co. No. 122,754; Jan. 6; v. 270; p. 165.

Toy furniture. R. W. Porter. No. 122,656; Jan. 6; v. 270; p. 165.

Trucks and accessories, Electric. W. C. Brinton. No. 119,593; Jan. 6; v. 270; p. 150.

Trucks, Motor-. Winther Motor Truck Company. No. 114,490; Jan. 6; v. 270; p. 141.

Underwear, aprons, rubber coats, &c. Lerner Waist Co. No. 119,835; Jan. 6; v. 270; p. 152.

Underwear, petticoats, and waists. Carteret Silk Company. No. 121,711; Jan. 6; v. 270; p. 158.

Underwear, Women's. J. Baach Co. No. 121,709; Jan. 6; v. 270; p. 158.

Upholstery and cabinet hardware. Berbecker & Rowland Manufacturing Company. No. 106,257; Jan. 6; v. 270; p. 189.

Valves for machinery. Nash Engineering Co. No. 121,406; Jan. 6; v. 270; p. 157.

Valves, Metal for making. Draper Manufacturing Company. No. 121,760; Jan. 6; v. 270; p. 159.

Varnish preparation. Titanine, Inc. No. 115,682; Jan. 6; v. 270; p. 143.

Vaults, Grave-. National Grave Vault Company. No. 124,147; Jan. 6; v. 270; p. 173.

Vegetables, Fresh. Henry Kaelin & Son. No. 122,943; Jan. 6; v. 270; p. 167.

Veterinary medicine. J. D. Shields. No. 121,790; Jan. 6; v. 270; p. 159.

Waterproof fiber table-cover. Auer & Twitchell. No. 114,061; Jan. 6; v. 270; p. 141.

Waterproof coats and slickers. J. T. Caradine. No. 121,748; Jan. 6; v. 270; p. 159.

Wire and wire fencing, Fence-. American Steel & Wire Company of New Jersey. No. 118,341; Jan. 6; v. 270; p. 147.

Waists and dresses. Ochs & Frank. No. 123,361; Jan. 6; v. 270; p. 171.

Watch-wristlets. A. Simon. No. 118,484; Jan. 6; v. 270; p. 147.

Waterproofing-oils for leather. A. W. Ziegeniss. No. 121,916; Jan. 6; v. 270; p. 160.

Waterproof coating for textiles and leather. J. H. Overton. No. 122,184; Jan. 6; v. 270; p. 161.

Wheels, Automobile and aeroplane. Reliance Wheel Co. No. 121,318; Jan. 6; v. 270; p. 157.

Wheels, Cast-metal vehicle-. Kenosha Wheel & Axle Company. No. 123,316; Jan. 6; v. 270; p. 170.

Yarn, Wool knitting-. Sears, Roebuck and Co. No. 113,390; Jan. 6; v. 270; p. 140.

CLASSIFICATION OF PATENTS

ISSUED JANUARY 6, 1920.

NOTE.—First number=class, second number=subclass, third number=patent number.

2—	41: 1,327,476	33—	169: 1,327,114	64—	62: 1,327,003	89—	36: 1,327,326	116—	31: 1,327,605	152—	11: 1,327,371

2—
41: 1,327,476
54: 1,327,062
62: 1,326,915
73: 1,327,408
106: 1,327,528

4—
5: 1,327,262
12: 1,327,042
18: 1,327,275
26: 1,327,428
27: 1,327,295
39: 1,326,919

5—
4: 1,327,103
1,327,554
25: 1,327,231
43: 1,327,108
46: 1,327,178

8—
1: 1,327,260
2: 1,327,294
18: 1,327,200
96: 1,327,008
100: 1,327,007
138: 1,327,497

10—
89: 1,327,312
21: 1,327,179
125: 1,327,020

12—
2: 1,327,196
6: 1,327,533

13—
8: 1,327,110
25: 1,327,065
28: 1,326,929
37: 1,326,900
59: 1,327,146
60: R. 14,786

15—

16—
25: 1,327,065
104: 1,327,431
163: 1,327,045

17—
10: 1,326,905
73: 1,327,073

18—
6: 1,327,330
18: 1,327,307
45: 1,327,264
56: 1,326,991

20—
40.5: 1,327,321
52: 1,327,394
87: 1,327,025
31: 1,327,227
62: 1,327,583
69: 1,327,310
150: 1,327,556
162: 1,327,253

21—

22—
80: 1,326,936
112: 1,327,224

23—
10: 1,327,029
13: 1,327,326
22: 1,327,164
24: 1,326,947
1,326,973

24—
28: 1,327,396
3: 1,327,534
16: 1,327,601
73: 1,327,434
266: 1,327,078

25—
132: 1,327,481
121: 1,326,902
131.5: 1,327,081

27—
6: 1,327,442

28—
2: 1,327,170

29—
2: 1,327,336
84: 1,327,561
87.1: 1,327,015
96: 1,327,214

30—
3: 1,327,134
5: 1,327,388
12: 1,327,547

32—
10: 1,327,149

33—
26: 1,327,154
32: R. 14,788
57: 1,327,141
137: 1,327,198
163: 1,327,216

33—
169: 1,327,114

34—
12: 1,327,486
15: 1,326,909
19: 1,327,313
24: 1,327,314

35—
5: 1,327,262
12: 1,327,474
16: 1,327,306

36—
76: 1,327,091

37—
7: 1,327,047
14: 1,327,324
24: 1,327,418
33: 1,327,578
39: 1,327,335

39—
34: 1,327,257

40—
11: 1,327,298
13: 1,327,544
25: 1,327,010
59: 1,327,274
64: 1,327,552
91: 1,326,980
113: 1,327,317
125: 1,327,387
132: 1,326,985
145: 1,327,427

43—
19: 1,327,229
27: 1,327,230
1,327,579
26: 1,327,490
28: 1,327,040

44—
1: 1,327,175

45—
17: 1,327,242
37: 1,326,940

46—
4: 1,326,976
1,327,171
14: 1,327,360
21: 1,327,036
24: 1,327,072
25: 1,327,019
40: 1,327,168
104: 1,327,117
41: 1,327,388
51: 1,327,549
59: 1,326,954
1,327,464

48—
11: 1,327,001
104: 1,327,117

49—
56: 1,327,405

51—
11: 1,327,440
12: 1,326,913
16: 1,327,498

53—
20: 1,327,244
1: 1,326,942
3: 1,327,532
5: 1,327,258

55—
18: 1,327,080
19: 1,327,424
31: 1,327,337
82: 1,327,119

56—
68: 1,327,305

57—
9: 1,326,969
34: 1,327,059

58—
56: 1,327,051
66: 1,327,391
121: 1,327,226

59—
138: 1,327,392
78: 1,327,355
95: 1,327,013

60—
39: 1,327,031
54: 1,327,080
70: 1,327,908

61—
36: 1,327,268
1,327,269
66: 1,327,285
1,327,286

62—
90: 1,327,214
106: 1,327,414
122: 1,326,961
136: 1,327,560

63—
15: 1,326,978

64—
10: 1,327,301
22: 1,327,173
24: 1,327,136
1,327,429
39: 1,327,028
59: 1,327,169

64—
62: 1,327,003

65—
65: 1,327,437

66—
4: 1,327,217
22: 1,327,122
33: 1,327,228

67—
6: 1,327,585
50: 1,327,161
70: 1,327,048
98: 1,327,447

68—
9: 1,326,982
12: 1,326,911
26: 1,326,928
32: 1,327,526
1,327,527

69—
16: 1,327,028

70—
16: 1,327,426
18: 1,327,406
1,327,601
53: 1,327,140
56: 1,327,457
131: 1,327,432

72—
30: 1,327,384
46: 1,327,292
124: 1,327,446
138: 1,327,151

73—
51: 1,327,251
52: 1,326,957

74—
7: 1,327,276
1,327,302
1,327,303
1,327,304
1,327,501
13: 1,327,068
1,327,559
14: 1,327,192
26: 1,327,209
1,327,210
41: 1,327,107
46: 1,327,501
56: 1,327,250
58: 1,326,935
70: 1,327,046
81: 1,327,137
85: 1,327,147

75—
1: 1,326,971
1,327,988

76—
3: 1,327,012
101: 1,327,099
1,327,100
1,327,101

77—
73.5: 1,327,566

78—
30: 1,327,331

79—
3: 1,327,322

80—
20: 1,327,525
48: 1,327,315

81—
15: 1,326,907
19: 1,326,999
23: 1,326,993
66: 1,327,309
114: 1,327,524
119: 1,327,370
126: 1,327,595

82—
17: 1,327,187
28: 1,327,604

83—
8: 1,327,347
13: 1,327,385
27: 1,327,444
79: 1,327,537
82: 1,326,908

84—
44: 1,327,157
161: 1,327,342

85—
20: 1,326,910
51: 1,327,417

86—
87: 1,327,378

87—
19: 1,327,166

88—
14: 1,327,005
17: 1,326,997
18.7: 1,327,084

89—
20: 1,327,183
24: 1,327,204
1: 1,327,086
4: 1,327,087
10: 1,327,518

89—
36: 1,327,326
38: 1,327,084
1,327,085
40: 1,326,975

90—
58: 1,327,370

91—
14: 1,327,127
36: 1,327,420
43: 1,327,014
46: 1,326,979
49: 1,327,300
51: 1,327,299
59.1: 1,327,273
68: 1,327,197

92—
3: 1,327,590
33: 1,327,126
1,327,289

93—
59.1: 1,327,333

94—
44: 1,327,131

95—
1.1: 1,327,138

97—
18: 1,327,562
35: 1,327,212
1,327,413

98—
26: 1,327,130

99—
11: 1,327,113
1,327,112

100—
15: 1,327,308
19: 1,327,471
28: 1,327,472
47: 1,327,254
51: 1,327,069
292: 1,327,241

101—
351: 1,327,580

102—
2: 1,327,187
1,327,488
26: 1,327,372
1,327,545
75: 1,327,451
1,327,531

103—
29: 1,327,037
1,327,600
44: 1,327,517
61: 1,327,512
64: 1,327,583
76: 1,327,423
85: 1,327,272
91: 1,327,071
101: 1,327,249
1,327,290
151: 1,327,215
162: 1,326,949
235: 1,327,243
244: R. 14,785
354: 1,327,586
400: 1,327,367

106—
9: 1,327,448
24: 1,327,145
36.1: 1,327,569
40.1: 1,326,930

107—
15: 1,326,930
50: 1,327,461
67: 1,327,328

108—
5.6: 1,327,395
7: 1,326,899

110—
40: 1,327,399
44: 1,326,906

111—
21: 1,327,089
76: 1,327,353

112—
22: 1,327,237
100: 1,327,348
114: 1,327,232
254: 1,327,181
265: 1,327,191

113—
10: 1,327,098
116: 1,327,454

114—
16: 1,327,509
208: 1,327,201
222: 1,327,522

116—
1: 1,327,266
1,327,323
1,327,416
1,327,573
31: 1,327,027
1,327,128

116—
31: 1,327,605
44: 1,327,021

118—
11: 1,326,950

119—
27: 1,327,386
33: 1,327,104
88: 1,327,246
99: 1,327,374
157: 1,327,088

120—
15: 1,327,038
83: 1,327,236
85: 1,327,459

121—
14: 1,327,419
209: 1,327,188
485: 1,327,032

123—
3: 1,327,495
14: 1,327,575
25: 1,327,551
52: 1,327,311
59: 1,327,172
1,327,345
74: 1,327,462
80: 1,327,202
122: 1,327,384
149: 1,327,361
1,327,502
166: 1,327,284
178: 1,327,148

124—
10: 1,327,046

126—
9: 1,327,115
10: 1,327,203
176: 1,327,270
215: 1,326,904
256: 1,327,508
307: 1,327,357
2: 1,327,222
49: 1,327,466
137: 1,327,407
239: 1,327,167
269: 1,327,499
340: 1,327,577
38: 1,327,186

128—

129—

130—
4: 1,327,000
13: 1,327,297
19: 1,327,325
23: 1,327,193
52: 1,327,139
3: 1,327,357

131—

133—

134—
15: 1,327,239
26: 1,326,917
1,327,332

135—
59: 1,327,061
46: 1,326,931

137—
68: 1,327,283
73: 1,326,988
1,327,195

138—
93: 1,327,000
33: 1,327,470
1,327,070

140—
105: 1,327,467

141—
11: 1,327,039
143—
114: 1,327,555
163: 1,327,054

144—
1: 1,327,390
29: 1,327,018
114: 1,327,515

145—
47: 1,327,155
121: 1,327,049

146—
6: 1,327,083
7: 1,327,316
26: 1,327,346
6: 1,327,400
1,327,401

149—
5: 1,327,105

151—
2: 1,327,373
25: 1,326,992
47: 1,327,152
53: 1,327,435

152—
2: 1,327,369
8: 1,327,478

152—
11: 1,327,371
14: 1,327,538
18: 1,327,503
21: 1,327,180
31: 1,327,096

153—
32: 1,327,343
37: 1,326,981
69.5: 1,326,916
80.5: 1,327,491

154—
31: 1,327,158
53: 1,327,281

155—
18: 1,327,475
23: 1,326,943
45: 1,326,921

156—
16: 1,327,363
1,327,364
19: 1,326,951
23: 1,327,460
26: 1,327,150

158—
27: 1,326,941
11: 1,327,092
28: 1,327,256
77: 1,327,571
78: 1,326,996

160—
1: 1,327,036

162—
1: 1,327,404
8: 1,326,925
68: 1,326,986
71: 1,327,082

166—
10: 1,327,077

167—
3: 1,327,550
13: 1,327,493
35: 1,327,523
20: 1,326,922

169—
31: 1,326,927
169: 1,327,066

170—

171—
209: 1,327,160

212—
1,327,349
284: 1,327,508
225: R. 14,787
252: 1,327,371
1,327,180

172—
152: 1,327,421

173—
239: 1,327,129
314: 1,326,962
356: 1,326,924
358: 1,327,494

175—
183: 1,327,341

178—
345: 1,327,340
354: 1,326,972
364: 1,327,521

176—
103: 1,327,280

177—
7: 1,327,124
100.1: 1,326,955

178—
20: 1,326,994
88: 1,327,352

179—
81: 1,327,412
90: 1,327,500
170: 1,327,185

180—
14: 1,327,376
17: 1,327,206
49: 1,327,485
64: 1,326,960
80: 1,327,511

181—
21: 1,327,118

182—
9: 1,327,278
12: 1,327,184
13: 1,327,287
37: 1,327,494

184—
48: 1,326,901
6: 1,327,565
21: 1,327,043
45: 1,327,238
47: 1,327,513

185—
17: 1,326,984
76: 1,327,441
39: 1,327,463
90: 1,327,090
7: 1,327,506
8: 1,327,053
1,327,436
14: 1,327,469
22: 1,327,296
63: 1,327,058

187—

180—

191—

192—

193—
1: 1,326,903

194—

xxxvii

CLASSIFICATION OF PATENTS.

THE
OFFICIAL GAZETTE

OF THE

United States Patent Office.

Vol. 270— No. 2. **TUESDAY, JANUARY 13, 1920.** Price—$5 per year.

The OFFICIAL GAZETTE is mailed under the direction of the Superintendent of Documents, Government Printing Office, to whom all subscriptions should be made payable and all communications respecting the Gazette should be addressed. Issued weekly. Subscriptions, $5.00 per annum; single numbers, 10 cents each.

Printed copies of patents are furnished by the Patent Office at 10 cents each. For the latter, address the Commissioner of Patents, Washington, D. C.

CONTENTS.

Issue of January 13, 1920.

It is much more fun to watch your money grow than to watch it go. Buy W. S. S.

Interference Notices.

DEPARTMENT OF THE INTERIOR,
UNITED STATES PATENT OFFICE,
Washington, D. C., January 5, 1920.

Nicholas B. Bartz, his assigns or legal representatives, take notice:

An interference having been declared by this Office between the application of Griffith Alverson Co., care of Campholatum Co., Mason City, Iowa, for registration of a trade-mark and trade-mark registered October 8, 1912, No. 88,611, to Nicholas B. Bartz, 84 Adams street, Chicago, Ill., and a notice of such declaration sent by registered mail to said Nicholas B. Bartz at the said address having been returned by the post-office undeliverable, notice is hereby given that unless said Nicholas B. Bartz, his assigns or legal representatives, shall enter an appearance therein within thirty days from the first publication of this order the interference will be proceeded with as in case of default.

This notice will be published in the OFFICIAL GAZETTE for three consecutive weeks.

M. H. COULSTON,
Assistant Commissioner.

DEPARTMENT OF THE INTERIOR,
UNITED STATES PATENT OFFICE,
Washington, D. C., January 5, 1920.

Moki Herb Remedy Company, its assigns or legal representatives, take notice:

An interference having been declared by this Office between the application of Edwin R. Mohler, No. 900 Penn street, Reading, Pa., for registration of a trade-mark and trade-mark registered November 1, 1892; No. 21,922, to Moki Herb Remedy Company, Tempe, Ariz., and a notice of such declaration sent by registered mail to said Moki Herb Remedy Company at the said address having been returned by the post-office undeliverable, notice is hereby given that unless said Moki Herb Remedy Company, its assigns or legal representatives, shall enter an appearance therein within thirty days from the first publication of this order the interference will be proceeded with as in case of default.

This notice will be published in the OFFICIAL GAZETTE for three consecutive weeks.

M. H. COULSTON,
Assistant Commissioner.

DEPARTMENT OF THE INTERIOR,
UNITED STATES PATENT OFFICE,
Washington, D. C., January 9, 1920.

Murphy Wall Bed Co. of California, its assigns or legal representatives, take notice:

An interference having been declared by this Office between the application of Murphy Wall Bed Company, of 422 Crocker Building, San Francisco, Calif., for registration of a trade-mark and trade-mark registered December 23, 1913, No. 94,655, to Murphy Wall Bed Co. of California, of 809–10–11 Longacre Building, New York, N. Y., and a notice of such declaration sent by registered mail to said Murphy Wall Bed Co. of California at the said address having been returned by the post-office undeliverable, notice is hereby given that unless said Murphy Wall Bed Co. of California, its assigns or legal representatives, shall enter an appearance therein within thirty days from the first publication of this order the interference will be proceeded with as in case of default.

This notice will be published in the OFFICIAL GAZETTE for three consecutive weeks.

R. F. WHITEHEAD,
First Assistant Commissioner.

Adverse Decisions in Interference.

PATENT No. 1,307,345.

On December 12, 1919, a decision was rendered that Frank E. Button was not the first inventor of the subject-matter covered by claim 8 of his Patent No. 1,307,345, subject, "Vehicle-control system," and no appeal having been taken within the time allowed such decision has become final.

PATENT No. 1,245,501.

On December 11, 1919, a decision was rendered that Henry L. Pitman was not the first inventor of the subject-matter covered by claim 28 of his Patent No. 1,245,501, subject, "Calculating-machines," and no appeal having been taken within the time allowed such decision has become final.

Rule 72, as Amended April 17, 1919.

RULE 72. After the completion of the application the Office will not return the specification for any purpose whatever. If applicants have not preserved copies of the papers which they wish to amend, the Office will furnish them on the usual terms.

The drawing may be withdrawn only for such corrections as cannot be made by the Office; but a drawing cannot be withdrawn unless a photographic copy has been filed and accepted by the Examiner as a part of the application. Permissible changes in the construction shown in any drawing may be made only by the Office and after an approved photographic copy has been filed. Sketches filed to show proposed changes in construction must be in permanent ink. (See Rule 80.) Substitute drawings will not be admitted in any case unless required by the Office.

APPLICATIONS UNDER EXAMINATION.

Condition at Close of Business January 9, 1920.

Room No.	Divisions and subjects of invention.	Oldest new application and oldest action by applicant awaiting office action. New.	Amended.	No. of applications awaiting action.
314	1. Closure Operators; Fences; Gates; Harrows and Diggers; Plows; Planting; Scattering Unloaders; Trees, Plants, and Flowers.	Oct. 15	Sept. 8	401
128	2. Bee Culture; Curtains, Shades, and Screens; Dairy; Medicines; Pneumatics; Preserving; Presses; Tents, Canopies, Umbrellas, and Canes; Tobacco.	June 3	July 11	919
175	3. Electric Heating and Rheostats; Electrochemistry; Heating; Metal-Founding; Metallurgical Apparatus; Metallurgy; Metal Treatment; Plastic Metal Working.	Sept. 11	Sept. 3	337
234	4. Conveyers; Elevators; Excavating; Handling—Hand and Hoist-Line Implements; Hoisting; Material or Article Handling; Pneumatic Despatch; Pushing and Pulling Implements; Railway Mail Delivery; Store-Service; Traversing Hoists.	June 21	Nov. 5	754
167	5. Book-Making; Books, Strips and Leaves; Harvesters; Jewelry; Manifolding; Music; Printed Matter; Tying Cords or Strands.	Aug. 17	Aug. 26	233
318	6. Bleaching and Dyeing; Chemicals; Explosives; Fertilizers; Liquid Coating Compositions; Plastic Compositions; Substance Preparation.	Aug. 13	Nov. 4	485
312	7. Games and Toys; Optics; Photography; Velocipedes	Oct. 2	Nov. 12	565
131	8. Beds; Chairs and Seats; Flexible-Sheet Securing Devices; Furniture; Kitchen and Table Articles; Store Furniture; Supports.	Sept. 29	Oct. 9	396
221	9. Air and Gas Pumps; Hydraulic Motors; Injectors and Ejectors; Motors, Fluid; Motors, Fluid-Current; Pumps.	Sept. 8	Oct. 1	244
235	10. Carriages and Wagons; Land-Vehicles; Land-Vehicles—Bodies and Tops; Land-Vehicles—Dumping; Motor Vehicles.	July 24	Sept. 29	952
151	11. Boot and Shoe Making; Boots, Shoes, and Leggings; Button, Eyelet, and Rivet Setting; Harness; Leather Manufactures; Nailing and Stapling; Spring Devices; Whips and Whip Apparatus.	July 11	July 21	501
222	12. Machine Elements	June 14	Oct. 1	1,009
329	13. Bolt, Nail, Nut, Rivet, and Screw Making; Button Making; Chain, Staple, and Horseshoe Making; Driven, Headed, and Screw-Threaded Fastenings; Gear Cutting, Milling, and Planing; Metal Drawing; Metal Forging and Welding; Metal Rolling; Metal Tools and Implements, Making; Metal Working; Needle and Pin Making; Turning.	June 24	Oct. 22	958
323	14. Compound Tools; Cutting and Punching Sheets and Bars; Farriery; Metal-Bending; Sheet-Metal Ware, Making; Tools; Wire Fabrics and Structure; Wire-Working.	July 2	Oct. 24	417
308	15. Bread, Pastry, and Confection Making; Coating; Fuel; Glass; Laminated Fabrics and Analogous Manufactures; Paper-Making and Fiber Liberation; Plastic Block and Earthenware Apparatus; Plastics.	June 12	Oct. 9	888
111	16. Radiant Energy; Telegraphy; Telephony	June 12	July 7	857
307	17. Label Pasting and Paper Hanging; Nut and Bolt Locks; Ornamentation; Paper Manufactures; Printing; Type Casting; Sheet Material Associating or Folding; Sheet Feeding or Delivering; Type Setting.	Sept. 22	Nov. 13	237
229	18. Fluid-Pressure Regulators; Liquid Heaters and Vaporizers; Motors, Expansible Chamber Type; Power Plants; Speed Responsive Devices; Steam and Vacuum Pumps.	Aug. 4	Oct. 25	672
236	19. Automatic Temperature and Humidity Regulation; Furnaces; Heating Systems; Stoves and Furnaces; Domestic Cooking Vessels; Thermostats and Humidostats.	June 16	Aug. 1	562
179	20. Artificial Body Members; Builders' Hardware; Closure-Fasteners; Cutlery; Dentistry; Locks and Latches; Safes; Undertaking.	Oct. 13	Sept. 18	644
212	21. Brakes and Gins; Carding; Cloth-Finishing; Continuous-Strip Feeding; Cordage; Felt and Fur; Knitting and Netting; Silk; Spinning; Weaving; Winding and Reeling.	June 23	Oct. 13	359
249	22. Aeronautics; Firearms; Ordnance	Sept. 8	Oct. 23	299
217	23. Acoustics; Coin-Handling; Horology; Recorders; Registers; Sound Recording and Reproducing; Time-Controlling Mechanism.	July 11	July 16	588
144	24. Apparel; Apparel Apparatus; Garment Supporters; Sewing-Machines.	June 7	Oct. 13	608
315	25. Beating; Butchering; Centrifugal Bowl Separators; Mills; Threshing; Vegetable Cutters and Crushers; Gas Separation.	Nov. 24	Nov. 20	209
105	26. Electricity, Generation; Motive Power; Prime Mover Dynamo Plants	Apr. 30	July 16	748
214	27. Brushing and Scrubbing; Grinding and Polishing; Laundry; Washing Apparatus	Sept. 2	Sept. 26	500
225	28. Internal-Combustion Engines	Sept. 2	Oct. 1	585
147	29. Boring and Drilling; Chucks or Sockets; Coopering; Rod Joints or Couplings; Wheelwright-Machines; Wood-Sawing; Wood-Turning; Woodworking; Woodworking Tools.	Apr. 1	Aug. 1	623
152	30. Illuminating-Burners; Illumination; Liquid and Gaseous Fuel Burners; Type-Writing Machines	July 9	Sept. 25	859
172	31. Alcohol; Ammonia, Water, and Wood Distillation; Charcoal and Coke; Gas, Heating and Illuminating; Hides, Skins, and Leather; Hydraulic Cement and Lime; Mineral Oils; Oils, Fats, and Glue; Sugar and Salt.	June 26	July 3	838
278	32. Gas and Liquid Contact Apparatus; Heat Exchange; Refrigeration	June 7	Nov. 3	869
70	33. Bridges; Hydraulic and Earth Engineering; Masonry and Concrete Structures; Metallic Building Structures; Roads and Pavements; Roofs.	Aug. 11	Oct. 10	352
304	34. Railways; Railway Rolling Stock; Railway Switches and Signals; Railways, Surface Track; Railway Wheels and Axles; Track-Sanders; Vehicle-Fenders.	Nov. 6	Dec. 5	222
57	35. Buckles, Buttons, Clasps, Etc.; Card, Picture, and Sign Exhibiting; Signals and Indicators; Toilet	Nov. 10	Dec. 1	372
204	36. Automatic Weighers; Driers; Geometrical Instruments; Measuring Instruments; Force Measuring	Oct. 4	Sept. 20	901
107	37. Electric Lamps; Electricity, Circuit Makers and Breakers; Electricity, General Applications	July 11	July 19	962
378	38. Animal Husbandry; Earth Boring; Fishing and Trapping; Mining, Quarrying, and Ice-Harvesting; Stationery; Stone-Working; Wells.	Nov. 12	Nov. 18	283
220	39. Fluid Sprinkling, Spraying, and Diffusing; Joint Packings; Multiple Valves; Packed Shaft or Rod Joints; Pipe Joints or Couplings; Valved Pipe Joints or Couplings; Valves; Water Distribution.	Apr. 7	June 20	900
273	40. Baggage; Bottles and Jars; Check-Controlled Apparatus; Cloth, Leather, and Rubber Receptacles; Deposit and Collection Receptacles; Metallic Receptacles; Package and Article Carriers; Paper Receptacles; Special Receptacles and Packages; Wooden Receptacles.	July 7	Oct. 25	545
125	41. Resilient Tires and Wheels	July 18	Oct. 20	758
114	42. Electricity, Conductors; Electricity-Transmission to Vehicles; Electricity, Conduits; Electric Signaling.	July 14	Aug. 5	734
382	43. Baths and Closets; Dispensing; Dispensing Beverages; Electricity, Medical and Surgical; Fire-Extinguishers; Sewerage; Surgery, Water Purification.	Sept. 30	Nov. 17	427
253	44. Air-Guns, Catapults, and Targets; Ammunition and Explosive Devices; Ammunition and Explosive Charge Making; Boats and Buoys; Filling and Closing Portable Receptacles; Marine Propulsion; Railway Draft Appliances; Ships.	July 2	Oct. 20	299
379	45. Clutches; Journal-Boxes, Pulleys, and Shafting; Lubrication; Motors	May 5	Oct. 4	755
382	46. Educational Appliances; Fire-Escapes; Ladders; Paper Files and Binders; Railway-Brakes; Wooden Buildings.	June 7	Oct. 22	544

Oldest new case, Apr. 1; oldest amended, June 20.
Total number of applications awaiting action 27,173

163	TRADE-MARKS, DESIGNS, LABELS AND PRINTS:			
	Trade-Marks	Oct. 2	Dec. 3	2,506
	Designs	Sept. 1	Sept. 18	1,151
	Labels and Prints	Sept. 22	Oct. 20	633

PATENTS

GRANTED JANUARY 13, 1920.

1,327,606. FINGER-RING. SAMUEL BACHARACH, Philadelphia, Pa. Filed May 31, 1919. Serial No. 301,114. 3 Claims. (Cl. 63—15.)

1. A finger ring, comprising an annular coupling member provided externally with a pair of annular flanges, and a pair of separate annular members each mounted revolubly upon said annular coupling member and provided with a groove into which loosely fits one of said flanges, said second mentioned annular members each having a finish suitable for a finger ring.

1,327,607. DUAL-TIRED WHEEL. ERLE KING BAKER, Chicago, Ill., assignor to Baker Wheel & Rim Company, Chicago, Ill., a Corporation of Illinois. Filed Feb. 11, 1918. Serial No. 216,442. 5 Claims. (Cl. 21—69.)

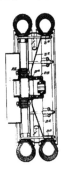

1. The herein described improvement comprising a dual wheel attachment composed of a rim separating and bridging ring, in combination with a complementary-rim carrying-ring partly telescoped upon the first mentioned ring, and means associated with said rim-carrying ring and adapted to rigidly secure the two rings together and to the fixed rim of a primary wheel.

1,327,608. MIRROR - HOLDER. ELMER BARNARD, Cleburne, Tex. Filed Apr. 26, 1919. Serial No. 292,847. 1 Claim. (Cl. 45—97.)

In a mirror holder, a clamp, an arm pivotally connected to the clamp, means for holding the arm at different positions of adjustment with respect to the clamp, an arm pivotally connected to the first mentioned arm, means for holding the said arms at different positions of adjust-

ment with relation to each other, a hollow arm pivotally connected to the second mentioned arm, means for holding the said arms in different positions of adjustment, a post in the outer end of the last mentioned arm, the said post terminating in a pintle projecting beyond the end of said arm, means for holding the post in the arm, a spring encir-

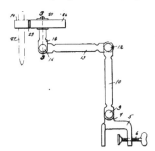

cling the pintle, and having ends extending therefrom, clamping members each having a side fulcrumed on the spring, the extensions of the spring each extending along the side of one of the clamping members and embracing its edge, the said clamping members terminating in jaws to embrace and frictionally support the handle of a mirror.

1,327,609. DRYING - TUMBLER. WILLIAM BARTHOLOMEW, Chicago, Ill., assignor to Troy Laundry Machinery Company, Ltd., Chicago, Ill., a Corporation of New York Filed Mar. 31, 1919. Serial No. 286,834. 8 Claims. (Cl. 34—5.)

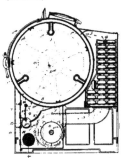

1. In combination with a drying tumbler having an air circulating blower which repeatedly forces a body of air through the drier, a delinting chamber having a screened communication with the blower, and having a lint discharge port, means for transferring lint from the screen to the lint discharge port, and means whereby the blower delivers to the delinting chamber air in excess of that which it draws through the screen of the delinting chamber and thereby sets up a lint discharging current through said port.

1,327,610. CLASS RECORD-BOOK. MILTON O. BILLOW, Harrisburg, Pa. Filed Feb. 11, 1919. Serial No. 276,380. 2 Claims. (Cl. 283—63.)

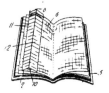

1. The combination with a book including a number of leaflets, of a plurality of sheets the same size as said leaflets and arranged at spaced intervals in the book, each of said sheets having one of their ends extended beyond one common free edge of said leaflets and said extension being folded longitudinally to form a pair of sections outwardly foldable to overlap one or more of said leaflets.

1,327,611. SUCKER-ROD ATTACHMENT TO PREVENT SANDING UP OF WELL-PUMPS. ROBERT LEE BURNS and FRED FREAMOND WINGER, Taft, Calif., assignors to Standard Oil Company, San Francisco, Calif., a Corporation of California. Filed Mar. 10, 1919. Serial No. 281,733. 2 Claims. (Cl. 287—58.)

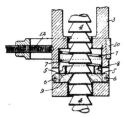

1. A sucker-rod attachment for the described purpose comprising a stock adapted for suspension from a source of reciprocative motion, said stock having a tubular split foot; a pawl pivoted and housed within said foot; a ratchet bar adapted for connection with the sucker-rod, said bar being fitted through said foot for relative linear movement therein, the ratchet teeth of said bar positively engaging the pawl on the upward stroke of the stock and slipping it in the reverse direction; and a regulatable clamp embracing said foot, whereby the ratchet bar may be adjusted therein.

1,327,612. SELF-FEEDER FOR FLOCK-CUTTERS. CHARLES B. COX, Jr., Stafford Springs, Conn. Filed July 18, 1919. Serial No. 311,764. 7 Claims. (Cl. 13- -22.)

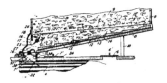

3. An attachment for a flock cutter comprising a casing or hopper to receive the material to be reduced and having a delivery passageway, said passageway being formed with a curved wall, a rotating member in the passageway, and provided with pins, that are curved oppositely to the direction of rotation, fixed pins coöperating with the curved pins for preventing the material which is to be reduced from collecting on the curved pins and for causing the material to be discharged forcibly into the machine.

1,327,613. IRONING-MACHINE. ALVA J. FISHER, Evanston, Ill., assignor to Hurley Machine Company, Chicago, Ill., a Corporation of Illinois. Original application filed Oct. 15, 1914, Serial No. 866,773. Divided and this application filed Oct. 4, 1915. Serial No. 53,904. 4 Claims. (Cl. 68—9.)

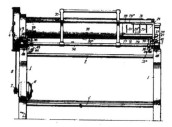

1. In an ironing machine, the combination, with a roll, of a hollow shoe having a body corresponding substantially with the curvature of the roll, and having outlets at its upper portion, means for heating the shoe, and a sheet of non-corrodible material affixed to said body to form the ironing surface thereof, one end of the sheet being arranged above said outlets to act as a deflector.

3. In an ironing machine, the combination of a roll, a hollow heated shoe coöperating therewith pivoted at its lower portion, a handle and yielding connections between the handle and shoe for holding the latter in operating position with a yielding pressure, comprising a rock shaft to which the handle is connected, a crank arm thereon, and a spring pressed rod pivotally connected with the crank arm and the shoe, and also adjustable means for limiting both extreme movements of the handle and its said connections.

1,327,614. TORPEDO-LAUNCHING APPARATUS. HUGO E. GRIESHABER, New London, Conn., assignor to Electric Boat Company, a Corporation of New Jersey. Filed July 30, 1917. Serial No. 183,427. 36 Claims. (Cl. 114—238.)

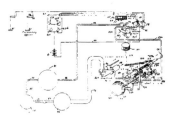

1. In a torpedo launching apparatus, the combination of a tube, a breech-door, a muzzle-door, a rotatable member for opening and closing the muzzle-door, a locking device for said member, a locking device for the breech-door, means operated by opening the muzzle-door for actuating the locking device for the breech-door to lock that door, and means operated by opening the breech-door for actuating the locking device for said member to lock said member against rotation, substantially as described.

1,327,615. ELECTRIC SWITCH. MONROE GUETT, Hartford, Conn., assignor to The Hart & Hegeman Manufacturing Company, Hartford, Conn., a Corporation of Connecticut. Filed May 28, 1918. Serial No. 236,978. 10 Claims. (Cl. 200—166.)

1. A contact for electric switches, comprising a main portion, arms extending from the main portion, a flexible connection between the arms, a terminal, and a flexible piece connecting the terminal and the flexible connection.

1,327,616. STEERING-GEAR. JOSEPH L. HOFER, Bridgewater, S. D. Filed May 23, 1919. Serial No. 299,111. 4 Claims. (Cl. 74—79.)

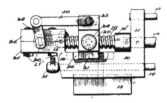

1. A steering gear including a bearing block having spaced arms, a screw journaled between said arms, one of the arms being formed with mating bearing plates, a rocker shaft journaled between said mating plates, a steering crank carried by said shaft, a nut carried by the screw and slidably engaged with the block whereby the nut will be reciprocated by rotation of the screw, and an operative connection between the nut and shaft whereby the shaft will be oscillated by the nut.

1,327,617. TRACTOR-HITCH. MIKE HOLCZER, Norfolk, Va. Filed Sept. 15, 1919. Serial No. 323,898. 3 Claims. (Cl. 213—67.)

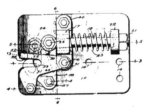

1. In a tractor hitch the combination with a coupling member embodying a removable coupling pin of a base plate adapted for attachment to the tractor having a slot formed therein extending through one side thereof, a hook plate pivotally mounted upon said base and normally coacting with said slot to form an aperture to receive said pin. said hook plate being adapted under certain conditions to shift to allow said coupling pin to be withdrawn from said plate through said slot, and means adapted to hold said hook plate in normal position and return said hook plate to normal position after it has been shifted to release said pin.

1,327,618. DISPLAY-EASEL FOR TAILORS AND THE LIKE. RICHARD C. KAISER, New Rochelle, N. Y., assignor to Detmer Woolen Company, New York, N. Y., a Corporation of New York. Filed Feb. 27, 1919. Serial No. 279,566. 2 Claims. (Cl. 35—17.)

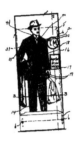

1. In combination, a front easel member having openings to imitate the outlines of the trousers of a man and having openings above said trousers openings to imitate the body, sleeve, lapel and collar portions of the coat of a man, the outlines of said collar and lapel portions being separated by a triangular strip upon which the imitation of a collar and tie are imprinted and above which is imprinted the representation of a man's head and means bearing the representation of a sheet of fabric conforming to the openings in the said easel member, so that when the said means is held behind the said easel member it accurately covers the said openings with the representation of the said fabric, and an imitation of a human being wearing a suit of clothes is secured, and means contacting with said representation means to keep the same in close contact with the adjacent face of the said easel member.

1,327,619. FIELD-MAGNET FRAME. CARL G. KOPPITZ, Greensburg, Pa., assignor to Railway and Industrial Engineering Company, Greensburg, Pa., a Corporation of Pennsylvania. Filed July 14, 1917. Serial No. 180,644. 2 Claims. (Cl. 171—252.)

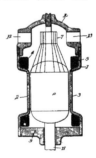

2. A field magnet frame consisting of pressed tubing having portions depressed into shape to fit an armature and form polar projections.

1,327,620. SOLDERING COMPOSITION. FRED E. LAMPE, Newark, N. J. Filed Nov. 10, 1919. Serial No. 336,882. 2 Claims. (Cl. 148—25.)

1. The herein described composition for soldering which comprises powdered solder, resin and salammoniac, light and dark petroleum and ceresin wax.

1,327,621. LEAF-TURNER. KNUT OLOF WILLIAM LINDQUIST, Chicago, Ill. Filed Jan. 19, 1917. Serial No. 143,315. 2 Claims. (Cl. 84—17.)

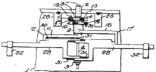

1. In a leaf turner, a frame, spaced frame-fingers carried by said frame, a stationary shaft carried by said frame, superimposed rotary toothed disks loose upon said shaft, arms carried by said disks and arranged to swing one above the other with said disks, heels for said arms, a reciprocating rack bar slidable against said frame-fingers for alternate actuating engagement with said disks, guard bars carried by said rack bar for engagement with said disks when said disks are not operatively engaged by said rack bar, fingers pivotally connected to the aforesaid shaft and radiating therefrom, stepped shoulders formed upon said fingers and engaging the aforesaid heels, and spacers carried by said fingers.

1,327,622. CALLING MECHANISM FOR TELEPHONE-EXCHANGES. FRANK A. LUNDQUIST, Chicago, Ill., assignor to Casper L. Redfield, trustee, Chicago, Ill. Filed Mar. 11, 1918. Serial No. 221,598. 12 Claims. (Cl. 179—90.)

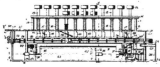

1. In a calling mechanism, a series of keys representing different numbers, a pneumatic device associated with said keys, a source of air pressure for operating the pneumatic device, means by which upon depressing a key having thereon any particular number the pneumatic device will set the mechanism for a number of electrical impulses which correspond to the number on the depressed key, means for releasing the pneumatic device so that the mechanism may return to normal position, and automatically operating means for releasing the depressed key upon the completion of such return movement.

1,327,623. DUMP-CAR. THOMAS R. McKNIGHT, Aurora, Ill., assignor to Western Wheeled Scraper Company, Aurora, Ill., a Corporation of Illinois. Filed Mar. 19, 1917. Serial No. 155,839. 17 Claims. (Cl. 105—271.)

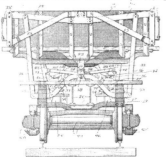

1. A dump-car comprising a suitable support, a car bed mounted upon said support and adapted to tilt to discharge its load, a laterally-movable member for normally holding the car bed in operative position, and an adjustable guide carried by the car bed for moving said laterally-movable member.

1,327,624. LOOSE-LEAF BINDER. FRED L. MANNY, Benton Harbor, Mich., assignor to Baker-Vawter Company, Benton Harbor, Mich., a Corporation of Michigan. Filed Feb. 11, 1918. Serial No. 216,623. 7 Claims. (Cl. 129—1.)

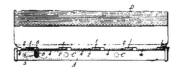

2. In a binder structure having covers and a pair of opposite side bars, means for hinging a cover to one side bar including a series of pivots carried by one of said last-mentioned two members, a series of bearings carried by the other member, said pivots and bearings being arranged to be disengaged by relative movement in an axial direction, a detent arranged to prevent such relative axial movement when the pivots and bearings are in engaged position, and means for shifting said detent to inoperative position.

1,327,625. GARMENT. HARRY A. MARIL, Minneapolis, Minn. Filed Sept. 8, 1919. Serial No. 322,381. 3 Claims. (Cl. 2—144.)

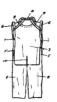

2. A garment of the class described, consisting of a front apron portion, legs extending downwardly from said apron portion and being cut out in their upper rear parts at a point substantially below the clotch, shoulder loop straps secured at upper side positions to said apron portion, a neck strap secured at the upper end of said apron portion, diagonal back straps connecting said shoulder and neck straps.

1,327,626. RIM, TIRE, AND WHEEL CARRIER FOR AUTOMOBILES. CHARLES E. MOORE, Terre Haute, Ind. Filed Aug. 6, 1919. Serial No. 315,696. 5 Claims. (Cl. 224—29.)

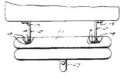

1. In a combination wheel and tire carrier, the combination with a pair of annular members concentrically arranged and provided with adjacent annular recesses adapted for the reception of the clencher flanges of a tire, which may be supported between the members, of

web members supporting the annular members, brackets connected to one of the web members and secured to the automobile, means for clamping the webs together, a spindle carried by one of the webs and having means to be engaged by the hub of a wheel to be carried, and means on the spindle to hold the hub of the wheel in place.

1,327,627. PAPER-MATCH MACHINE. JOHN MOSCINI, Brooklyn, N. Y. Filed Dec. 19, 1918, Serial No. 267,476. Renewed Oct. 7, 1919. Serial No. 329,083. 7 Claims. (Cl. 144—51.)

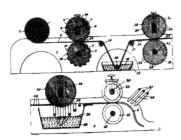

1. In a machine of the character described, the combination with means for cutting a strip of material into transversely arranged intermeshing fingers alternate ones of which are joined to opposite uncut margins of the strip, of means for bending down the free end of said fingers for receiving coatings of striking substance while the uncut margins of the strip travel in a horizontal plane, and means for finally cutting said fingers from the margins of the strip to produce finished individual matches.

1,327,628. SHELVING. JOHN B. O'CONNOR, Aurora, Ill., assignor to Lyon Metallic Manufacturing Company, Aurora, Ill., a Corporation of Illinois. Filed Nov. 11, 1918. Serial No. 262,048. 9 Claims. (Cl. 211—27.)

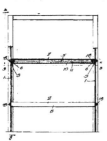

1. In sectional shelving, the combination with the upright partitions, of a sheet metal shelf having a metallic reinforcing member extending entirely along one edge of the shelf and bent at the corners of the shelf to extend part way along the ends of the shelf, the edge of the shelf being bent to engage the reinforcing member to hold the parts together.

1,327,629. TACHOMETER. VLADIMIR OLHOVSKY, New York, N. Y., assignor to Ernst J. Ohnell, Brooklyn, N. Y. Filed May 31, 1918. Serial No. 237,618. 1 Claim. (Cl. 264—20.)

A measuring instrument comprising a frame, a rotative shaft journaled therein, two pairs of arms pivotally

carried by said shaft and projecting on opposite sides of their axes, one pair of arms being between the other pair of arms, weights between each pair of arms at opposite ends thereof, bushings between the outer arms and the corresponding weights, means securing said arms and

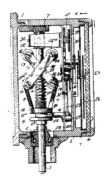

bushings to said weights, bushings on the outside of the inner pair of arms, means securing said bushings to said arms and weights whereby said parts are equally balanced on opposite sides of the shaft and pivot, and spring means connecting said arms with said shaft.

1,327,630. SCOURING APPARATUS WITH SAND-THROW. GASTON CHARLES ORY, Paris, France. Filed Aug. 19, 1919. Serial No. 318,613. 1 Claim. (Cl. 98—27.)

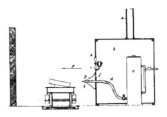

A device protecting the workman in the scouring operation by means of sand throw, characterized by a cabin for the workman located in or near the working room, a sand-throwing nozzle passing through the wall of the cabin, mounting means for the nozzle, said mounting means enabling the nozzle to be directed in any desired direction and also preventing the passage of dust into the cabin from the working room, and means to suck air from the cabin and blow the same into the working room.

1,327,631. MANUFACTURE OF A CLEANSING MATERIAL. GEORGES AUGUSTE PAULIN, Asnières, France. Filed July 12, 1918. Serial No. 244,568. 3 Claims. (Cl. 87—5.)

2. A cleansing material comprising so-called caseinates and saponified resin, being intimately mixed together, the product being soluble in cold water and in boiling alcohol.

1,327,632. FLEXIBLE PIPE. JOHN HENRY PHILLIPS, Jr., Jackson, Mich. Filed Apr. 26, 1918. Serial No. 230,862. 6 Claims. (Cl. 285—9.)

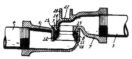

1. In a flexible pipe, the combination of a female joint member having a laterally facing socket with an annular gasket seat therein, a male joint member having a laterally projecting nipple rotatable within said socket and a retaining yoke seat on its rear side disposed axially relative to said nipple, a conical gasket disposed on said gasket seat within said socket with its smaller end outward, a nipple bearing ring beveled on its outer side disposed on said gasket to engage the end of said nipple, and a retaining yoke, one arm of which is rotatably mounted on said female coupling member, so that its other arm may be swung into said yoke seat on the male coupling member and engage the same axially of said nipple, the supporting arm of said retaining yoke being threaded and provided with an adjusting nut.

1,327,633. MECHANISM FOR DISENGAGING AND ENGAGING THE MAIN GOVERNORS IN STEAM HOISTING-ENGINES. EUGÈNE SCHNEIDER, Paris, France, assignor to Schneider & Cie., Paris, France, a Limited Joint-Stock Company of France. Filed Dec. 24, 1917. Serial No. 208,714. 4 Claims. (Cl. 264—3.)

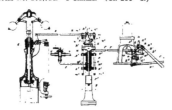

1. In apparatus for disconnecting an engine governor, while running, from its valve gear, the combination of link members adapted to connect said governor and valve gear, and means independent of the governor acting in one direction to disconnect the governor from said valve gear and to restore the valve gear to a predetermined position and acting in the opposite direction to connect said link members.

1,327,634. ADJUSTABLE BULKHEAD FOR FREIGHT-CARS. SAMUEL BOYKIN SHORT, Humboldt, Tenn. Filed June 20, 1919. Serial No. 305,620. 3 Claims. (Cl. 105—376.)

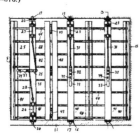

1. A bulkhead as characterized, comprising a main section and a door section in hinged relation thereto, said sections each comprising spaced intersecting members, certain of the members of the main section having projections adapted to be engaged with the floor of a car, and with locking elements adapted to be projected into engagement with the roof of the car, and said door section having locking elements adapted to be projected into engagement with both the floor and the roof.

1,327,635. WHEEL-MILL. EDWIN E. SLICK, Westmont borough, Pa. Filed Dec. 26, 1916. Serial No. 138,741. 1 Claim. (Cl. 80—16.)

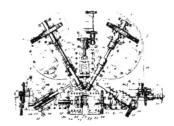

In a wheel mill, a web roll and a prime mover for driving the same, both mounted on a movable base, whereby said web roll may be projected to its work.

1,327,636. BOLTING - MACHINE. SIMON SNYDER and LLOYD CALVIN WINEGARDNER, Muncy, Pa. Filed Feb. 21, 1917. Serial No. 150,057. 7 Claims. (Cl. 83—38.)

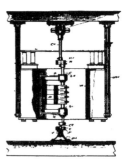

1. In combination, a sieve structure freely suspended for gyration, a sectional driving shaft having a driven section journaled in bearings within said structure and a driving section journaled in a universal bearing secured to a fixed support, and means for connecting the adjacent ends of said shaft sections so as to permit a swinging movement of said driving section and relative movement of both sections in the direction of their length, said means comprising a coupling member on one shaft section having projections thereon protruding into interengaging means on an adjacent coupling member on the other shaft section, whereby the two members are caused to rotate together while permitting a rocking and sliding movement of one member within or upon the other.

1,327,637. HAY GATHERER AND STACKER. WILLIAM I. SONNER, Blaine, Idaho. Filed Mar. 6, 1918. Serial No. 220,788. 6 Claims. (Cl. 214—105.)
1. In a hay gatherer and stacker, a wheeled vehicle provided with a rake pivotally mounted thereon inde-

pendently of its wheels, and means on the vehicle controllable by the operator for adjusting said rake with re-

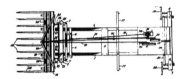

lation to said vehicle so as to accumulate a load and upon release to permit the rake to incline downwardly so as to discharge the load.

1,327,638. LOOPING-MACHINE. WILLIAM JAMES STEERE, Rockwood, Tenn. Filed Sept. 21, 1918. Serial No. 255,157. 5 Claims. (Cl. 112—252.)

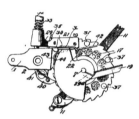

1. In a device of the class described, the combination with a bracket, a shaft mounted upon said bracket, of a guard plate fixedly secured to said shaft, a guiding blade attached to said guard blade, a brush interposed between the bracket and guiding plate and mounted upon said shaft, means for rotating said brush, a cutter device carried by said bracket, and means on said cutter device and coöperating with said brush for operating the cutter device as said brush is moved with respect to said guard plate.

1,327,639. ROLL-POLISHER. GEORGE B. STEVENS, Granite City, Ill. Filed Apr. 20, 1918. Serial No. 229,873. 5 Claims. (Cl. 51—4.)

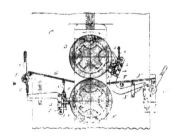

1. In combination with mill housings forming spreading supports, of a roll polisher comprising an emery-carrying bar, and swing hangers pivotally connecting the ends of said bar and supporting housings, and oscillatable lengthwise of the bar, and maintaining engagement during the spreading action, substantially as described.

1,327,640. ELECTRIC SWITCH. CLARENCE C. STIRLING, Hartford, Conn., assignor to The Hart & Hegeman Manufacturing Company, Hartford, Conn., a Corporation of Connecticut. Filed Aug. 14, 1918. Serial No. 249,758. 10 Claims. (Cl. 200—72.)

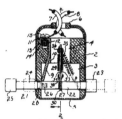

1. A switch comprising an actuator having insulating and conducting portions, a movable switching member having a dislodgable connection with the actuator, the actuator on its movement carrying the switching member therewith, a fixed part against which the switching member is abutted on the movement of the actuator, the latter having a further movement beyond the point at which the switching member engages the fixed part, and spring means conditioned by the actuator on each of its movements for shifting the switching member when it is freed from the actuator on said opposite movements into alternate engagement with the insulating and conducting portions of the actuator.

1,327,641. MACHINE FOR FORMING METAL TUBES. FRANK H. STOLP, Geneva, N. Y. Filed May 12, 1917. Serial No. 168,260. Renewed June 18, 1918. Serial No. 240,687. 12 Claims. (Cl. 113—33.)

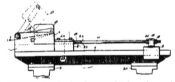

1. In a machine for forming metal tubes, the combination of a forming die, a plunger adapted to force a sheet metal blank into said forming die, a mandrel passing through said die and being adapted to carry with it the sheet metal blank forced into said forming die, a series of folding dies in line with said forming die, said mandrel being adapted to force the sheet metal blank from said forming die into said folding dies.

1,327,642. ELECTRIC REGULATOR. LEONARD SYKES, Fort Wayne, Ind. Filed Jan. 18, 1918. Serial No. 212,505. 5 Claims. (Cl. 219—49.)

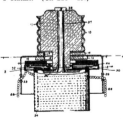

1. In an electric regulator the combination of a metallic member, a resistance coil wound thereon and connected

at one end to the member, a contact adapted to be rolled bodily across a portion of the resistance coil, a metallic revolubly mounted member engaging the contact and adapted to coöperate with the metallic member for causing the contact to roll in a radial direction across the resistance coil, and means engaging the revolubly mounted metallic member adapted to force the same toward the first named metallic member.

1,327,643. COMBINED STEERING AND HANDLING SYSTEM FOR TOW-BOATS AND THEIR VESSELS. THOMAS R. TARN, Brooklyn, N. Y. Filed Apr. 15, 1919. Serial No. 290,198. 4 Claims. (Cl. 114—163.)

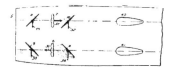

1. In a control system for tow boats, the combination with a tow boat, and a plurality of propelling screws therefor, of a plurality of pairs of rudders, one member of each pair of rudders located aft of one of the propellers, and means for independently operating each pair of rudders.

1,327,644. HOPPER FOR FILLING CARTONS WITH RAISINS AND SIMILAR ARTICLES OF MERCHANDISE. HARRY HOMER TAYLOR, Fresno, Calif. Filed Feb. 3, 1919. Serial No. 274,784. 2 Claims. (Cl. 249—65.)

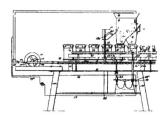

1. In a device of the character described the combination of a track adapted to have a plurality of cartons arranged thereon, a generator, a solenoid, a weighing scales, a wire circuit connecting the generator, the solenoid and the scales, and arranged so that when the platform of the scales is depressed the electrical circuit will be completed and the solenoid will be energized, and when the platform resumes its normal position the circuit will be broken and the solenoid will be idle, means connected with the solenoid adapted to move the cartons a predetermined space forward at each impulse of the solenoid, together with a hopper having duplicate outlet openings in line with, and directly over said track, and spaced apart, an inverted V partition between the openings, one of said openings being directly over the scales platform, two wings within the hopper arranged to regulate the size of said openings, and means for automatically moving said wings synchronously with the movement of the cartons so that when a predetermined weight is placed in a carton on the scales, the outlet opening directly above said carton is closed and as the carton moves forward under said openings the wings limit the size of the openings so that the openings are at all times directly over a carton being filled until it contains a predetermined weight, substantially as described.

1,327,645. SNOW - REMOVAL APPARATUS. DOUGLAS K. WARNER, New Haven, Conn. Filed Apr. 9, 1915. Serial No. 20,215. 7 Claims. (Cl. 37—62.)

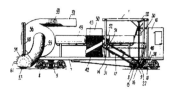

5. The combination with a snow removal apparatus of a vehicle operating parallel to said apparatus and forming a receiver for the snow removed by said apparatus, and means for changing the relative positions of the removal apparatus and the receiving vehicle, whereby the snow delivered from said removal apparatus will be equally distributed on the receiving vehicle.

1,327,646. SHOULDER - STRAP - SEWING MACHINE. JOHN P. WEIS, Nyack, N. Y., assignor, by mesne assignments, to Metropolitan Sewing Machine Corporation, Dover, Del., a Corporation of Delaware. Filed Aug. 6, 1917. Serial No. 184,567. 97 Claims. (Cl. 112—100.)

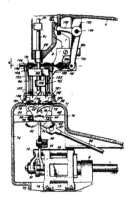

1. In a sewing machine, the combination of stitching mechanism comprising two sets of needles, looper mechanism coöperating with the needles, a single thread carrying finger coöperating with each set of needles, and means for supporting said finger whereby it may swing about a vertical axis located at the center of a set of needles so that it is movable in a circular path practically around the path of the needles.

1,327,647. COMBINED LOOPER AND FEEDING MECHANISM FOR SEWING-MACHINES. JOHN P. WEIS, Nyack, N. Y., assignor to Metropolitan Sewing Machine Corporation, Nyack, N. Y., a Corporation of Delaware. Filed Dec. 21, 1917, Serial No. 208,216. Renewed Oct. 28, 1919. Serial No. 334,096. 55 Claims. (Cl. 112—208.)

16. A combined feed and looper mechanism comprising a feed carrier having spaced supporting portions, feed dogs carried by said spaced supporting portions, means for imparting a four-motion movement to said carrier, looper mechanism partly located within the space of said

carrier, adjustable means for imparting a differential movement to one of said feed dogs and adjustable during

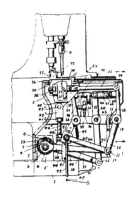

the operation of the feed mechanism, and means for adjusting the carrier and its feed dogs.

1,327,648. STROP-DRESSING. LAURENCE G. WESSON, Cleveland, and ZAY JEFFRIES, East Cleveland, Ohio. Filed Dec. 1, 1916. Serial No. 134,380. 3 Claims. (Cl. 51—1.)

1. An abrasive strop dressing consisting of a relatively permanent emulsion of levigated alumina, soap and water.

1,327,649. STORAGE - BATTERY JAR. THEODORE A. WILLARD, East Cleveland, Ohio, assignor to Willard Storage Battery Company, Cleveland, Ohio, a Corporation of West Virginia. Filed Aug. 27, 1917. Serial No. 188,297. 2 Claims. (Cl. 204—29.)

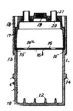

1. A storage battery adapted particularly for aeroplane use and comprising a jar adapted to be supported independently of an outer casing, said jar comprising a one-piece body with lateral walls and dividing partitions forming a container for a number of cells, said jar body having on the lateral walls thereof means adapted to accommodate clamping means by which the jar may be rigidly supported.

1,327,650. STORAGE BATTERY ADAPTED PARTICULARLY FOR AEROPLANES. THEODORE A. WILLARD, East Cleveland, Ohio, assignor to Willard Storage Battery Company, Cleveland, Ohio, a Corporation of West Virginia. Filed Aug 27, 1917. Serial No. 188,298. 5 Claims. (Cl. 204—29.)

2. A storage battery comprising a container having a lower chamber containing battery plates and an elec-

trolyte, and an upper chamber, said upper chamber comprising a diaphragm extending across the container above

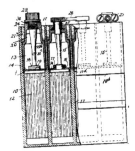

the plates, and a cover having an integral skirt extending down in the container to the diaphragm.

1,327,651. HYDRAULIC DREDGING APPARATUS. LESLIE W. BEAVEN, Chicago, Ill. Filed Dec. 14, 1918. Serial No. 266,758. 7 Claims. (Cl. 37—9.)

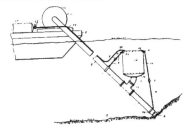

1. In hydraulic dredging apparatus means for controlling the intake thereof comprising a mobile intake pipe, a float chamber secured thereto and having communication therewith and having sufficient buoyancy to carry the weight of said pipe.

1,327,652. DIE AND METHOD OF JOINING ITS ENDS. ALBERT R. BRADEN, Beverly, Mass., assignor to United Shoe Machinery Corporation, Paterson, N. J., a Corporation of New Jersey. Filed Apr. 11, 1918. Serial No. 228,008. 17 Claims. (Cl. 76—107.)

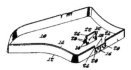

1. A die formed with a cutting edge and having adjacent ends, a member extending over the opposite walls of the die at each side of the juncture between the ends and continuing the cutting edge, and means for securing the member to the die.

1,327,653. DRAFT-CHECKING DEVICE. AUGUST W. CORDES, New York, N. Y. Filed May 14, 1915. Serial No. 27,977. 1 Claim. (Cl. 20—11.)

The combination of a unit having a pocket formed therein, said pocket having a relatively enlarged inner end portion, a pliable lining in surface engagement with the walls of said pocket and conforming to the shape thereof, a second unit contiguous to the first member and provided with a groove, a sealing member bridging the joint between said units and extending into said pocket between and in surface engagement with the lining therein, the inner edge of said member being located

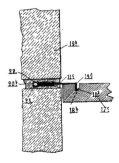

within the enlarged portion of said pocket, an edge member extending from said sealing member into said groove in engagement with one wall thereof and a flange extending at an inclination from said edge member into engagement with the opposite wall of said groove whereby a withdrawal of said edge member from said groove is resisted.

1,327,654. FERTILIZER - DISTRIBUTER. CALVIN R. DAVIS, Rockford, Ill., assignor to Emerson-Brantingham Company, Rockford, Ill., a Corporation of Illinois. Filed Apr. 11, 1916. Serial No. 90,482. 10 Claims. (Cl. 280—103.)

1. In a vehicle, the combination of channel shaped side sills, the front ends of which are arched upwardly and terminate in upright portions that extend below the plane of the sills, a reinforcing element for each sill shaped to fit within the channel walls thereof extending through the arched portion to the lower end of said upright portion and thence turned inwardly, a cross-bar secured to the inturned ends of said reinforcing elements, and a dirigible supporting wheel pivotally mounted on an upright axis on each of said upright sill portions.

1,327,655. PROJECTILE. KENNEDY DOUGAN, Minneapolis, Minn. Filed Apr. 27, 1918. Serial No. 232,090. 4 Claims. (Cl. 102—26.)

1. A projectile so formed as to be rotated on its longitudinal axis by contact with the air in its passage therethrough, and means carried by said projectile for governing its angular velocity during its flight.

1,327,656. HEADSTOCK-BRAKE. HARCOURT C. DRAKE and AUGUST SLAGENHAUF, Brooklyn, N. Y. Filed Mar. 5, 1919. Serial No. 280,849. 7 Claims. (Cl. 74—18.)

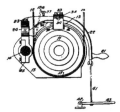

3. In a head-stock brake, the combination, a revolving head-stock driven by a belt, an arm pivotally secured adjacent to said head-stock to swing in a vertical and in a horizontal direction and extended transversely to the axis of said head-stock, a brake shoe secured to said arm and arranged to engage said head stock when the arm is moved about either its horizontal or vertical pivot.

1,327,657. SKEIN-DYEING MACHINE. HOWARD M. DUDLEY, Philadelphia, Pa. Filed Aug. 22, 1917. Serial No. 187,531. 5 Claims. (Cl. 8—18.)

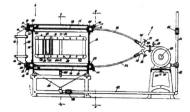

1. In a fiber treating device, in combination, a dyeing chamber, a removable frame adapted to carry fiber skeins within the dyeing chamber, a series of foraminous pipes below the frame, means whereby a liquid may be removed from the dyeing chamber above the frame, a removable top carrying a series of foraminous pipes whereby a liquid may be removed from the dyeing chamber below the frame, and means for forcing a liquid through either series of pipes and the dyeing chamber.

1,327,658. DYEING-MACHINE. HOWARD M. DUDLEY, Philadelphia, Pa. Filed Nov. 13, 1917. Serial No. 201,760. 12 Claims. (Cl. 8—18.)

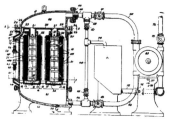

1. In a dyeing machine, in combination, a receptacle, a series of cores within the receptacle, each core carrying extended arm supporting a series of annular members, a series of foraminous spindles slidable over the annular

members and capable of having fiber wound thereon, means whereby a liquid may be passed transversely through the spindles and through the fiber and means for compressing the fiber upon the spindles.

1,327,659. FABRIC-TREATING DEVICE. HOWARD M. DUDLEY, Philadelphia, Pa. Filed Dec. 20, 1917. Serial No. 208,045. 9 Claims. (Cl. 8—17.)

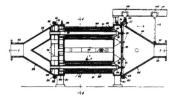

1. In a dyeing machine, in combination, a series of fabric chambers, a foraminous core capable of having a fabric wound thereon, a foraminous cover capable of abutment upon the exterior of the fabric, means for closing all of the openings of the core except those adjacent to the fabric, a carrier for the wound core capable of insertion within a fabric chamber, means whereby a liquid may pass inwardly through the wound fabric, means whereby a liquid may pass outwardly through the wound fabric and means for passing a liquid in either direction through the device.

1,327,660. DYEING-MACHINE. HOWARD M. DUDLEY, Philadelphia, Pa. Filed Dec. 24, 1917. Serial No. 208,549. 3 Claims. (Cl. 8—18.)

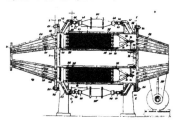

1. In a dyeing machine, in combination, a body, a series of fiber chambers within the body, a foraminous end in each fiber chamber, a foraminous plate slidable within each chamber, means for removing the foraminous plate with respect to the foraminous end, maintaining it in such position and compressing fiber between the end and the plate, a liquid chamber at each end of the fiber chambers, inwardly diverging member within each liquid chamber for diverging a liquid passed therethrough and means for passing a liquid in opposite directions through the device.

2. In a dyeing machine, in combination, a body, a series of fiber chambers within the body, a foraminous end having inwardly extended members in each fiber chamber, a foraminous plate having inwardly extended members slidable within each chamber, means for moving the foraminous plate with respect to the foraminous end, maintaining it in such position and compressing fiber between the end and the plate, a liquid chamber at each end of the fiber chambers, inwardly diverging members within each liquid chamber for diverging a liquid passed therethrough and means for passing a liquid in opposite directions through the device.

3. In a dyeing machine, in combination, a body, a series of fiber chambers within the body, a foraminous end in each fiber chamber, a foraminous plate slidable within each

chamber, means for moving the foraminous plate with respect to the foraminous end, maintaining it in such position and compressing fiber between the end and the plate, a liquid chamber at each end of the fiber chambers, a series of inwardly diverging tubes within each liquid chamber and means for continuously passing a liquid in opposite directions through the tubes, the foraminous members and fiber within the fiber chambers.

1,327,661. DYEING DEVICE. HOWARD M. DUDLEY, Philadelphia, Pa. Filed Jan. 7, 1918. Serial No. 210,619. 8 Claims. (Cl. 8—17.)

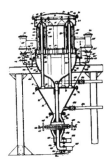

1. In a fabric treating device, in combination, a series of fabric chambers with imperforate side walls, a series of hollow foraminous fabric reels capable of placement within the fabric chamber and hollow reel, a liquid chamber connected to the lower ends of the hollow reels, a liquid chamber connected to the lower ends of the fabric chambers and means for passing a liquid in opposite directions through the device and fabric wound upon the reels.

1,327,662. DYEING-MACHINE. HOWARD M. DUDLEY, Philadelphia, Pa. Filed Jan. 26, 1918. Serial No. 213,893. 17 Claims. (Cl. 8—18.)

1. In a dyeing machine, in combination, a series of fiber chambers, a foraminous spindle capable of having fiber wound thereon within each fiber chamber, means for forcing a liquid through the series of spindles and fiber wound thereon and means for drawing a liquid in a reverse direction through the series of spindles and fiber wound thereon.

1,327,663. FIBER-TREATING MACHINE. HOWARD M. DUDLEY, Philadelphia, Pa. Filed Mar. 13, 1918. Serial No. 222,092. 8 Claims. (Cl. 8—18.)

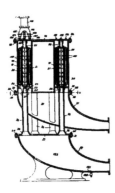

1. In a fiber treating machine, in combination, a receptacle, a series of removable hollow foraminous spindles capable of having fiber placed thereon within the receptacle, means for closing one end of the spindles, means for compressing the fiber in the direction of the axes of the spindles, means for compressing the fiber at right angles to the axes of the spindles, means for passing a liquid into the interiors of the spindles and outwardly therefrom through fiber placed thereon and means for passing a liquid from the receptacle into the interiors of the spindles through fiber placed thereon.

1,327,664. SAMPLE-AFFIXING MACHINE. WILLIAM P. DUN LANY, Chicago, Ill., assignor to Sears, Roebuck and Company, Chicago, Ill., a Corporation of New York. Filed Jan. 7, 1916. Serial No. 70,719. 71 Claims. (Cl. 216—14.)

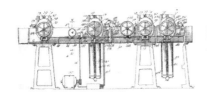

8. A machine for affixing samples to sheets having, in combination, a flat support for a sheet, means for supporting a sample, a reciprocatory support, a device movable on said support and arranged to pick up a sample and apply it to the flat surface of the sheet, and means for reciprocating said support, said device being adapted to be actuated solely by engagement with the sample and the sheet.

1,327,665. MACHINE FOR AFFIXING SAMPLES TO SHEETS. WILLIAM P. DUN LANY, Chicago, Ill., assignor to Sears, Roebuck and Company, Chicago, Ill., a Corporation of New York. Filed July 14, 1916. Serial No. 109,411. 61 Claims. (Cl. 216—14.)

42. A sample machine having, in combination, a track, means for applying an adhesive substance to a sheet, a rotatable drum supported to travel on said track and having devices arranged to apply a sample to the adhesive

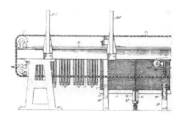

substance on the sheet, and means for causing the drum to travel.

1,327,666. PROCESS OF MANUFACTURING SULFITE FIBER AND RECOVERING SULFUR DIOXID. JAMES P. V. FAGAN, HERBERT G. SPEAR, and ROBERT B. WOLF, Berlin, N. H.; said Fagan and said Spear assignors of their right to Brown Company, Berlin, N. H., a Corporation of Maine. Filed Apr. 30, 1918. Serial No. 231,622. 12 Claims. (Cl. 92—11.)

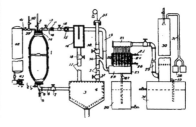

1. The herein described process of recovering sulfur dioxid and in the manufacture of sulfite pulp, which consists in blowing into a condenser from the top of the digester, at or during the last portion of the cooking operation, those vapors and gases which are usually blown with the digester contents into the blow pit, and separating and recovering sulfur dioxid from such vapors and gases.

1,327,667. METAL-SEPARATOR. AMBROSE D. FISH, Portland, Oreg. Filed Apr. 10, 1916. Serial No. 90,229. 4 Claims. (Cl. 83—67.)

1. A metal separator, comprising in combination, a container, a metallic solution in said container, means for feeding metal-containing matter in pulverized condition into said metallic solution, means for moving said metal-containing matter through said metallic solution at varying depths, an inverted cover over said container having its lower edges submerged in said metallic solution, whereby to seal the same, and means for heating said metallic solution, substantially as described.

1,327,668. APPARATUS FOR TREATING SKINS, FABRIC, TOBACCO, AND THE LIKE. JAMES U. FLANAGAN, Wilmington, Del., assignor of three-fourths to F. F. Slocomb & Co., Incorporated, Wilmington, Del., a Corporation of Delaware. Filed May 21, 1914. Serial No. 839,951. 5 Claims. (Cl. 34—19.)

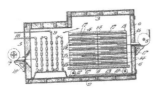

1. An apparatus for treating glaze-coated skins, comprising an inclosure, means at one end of said inclosure for introducing a blast, transportation means adapted to enter said inclosure, and trays supported upon said transportation means and having spaces between them, each of said trays carrying a skin stretched thereon.

1,327,669. ALARM MECHANISM FOR CLOCKS. MATTIE A. GAGE, New York, N. Y. Filed Mar. 23, 1915. Serial No. 16,363. 9 Claims. (Cl. 58—16.)

7. In an alarm clock, a main dial, hands for indicating the hours and minutes on said dial, a clock train for controlling the movement of said hands, an alarm hand having a let off position, a spindle upon which said hand is carried extending through said clock and controllable from the rear thereof for setting said hand, a pinion on said spindle driven from said clock train and normally disengaged from said spindle, and means operated in the setting of said hand to cause said pinion and spindle to rotate together to the let off position of said alarm hand.

1,327,670. LIQUID JACKING APPARATUS FOR MOTOR-VEHICLES. EDMUND GRAHAM and GEORGE BOWMAN, Belfast, Ireland. Filed June 17, 1918. Serial No. 240,509. 7 Claims. (Cl. 138—9.)

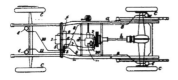

1. Liquid jacking apparatus for motor vehicles comprising, in combination, a liquid receptacle on the vehicle, a pump in communication with said receptacle, means whereby the pump can be driven from the change speed gear of the vehicle by means of intermediate gear which can be thrown into action by means of a pedal operated lever, a distributer on the vehicle and in communication with said pump, and a plurality of liquid jacks in communication with said distributer, the distributer being constructed and arranged to permit liquid from the pump to be distributed to any one or all of the jacks as desired.

1,327,671. TRAFFIC-SIGNAL FOR AUTOS. HARRY J. HANKEE, Minneapolis, Minn. Filed Mar. 14, 1919. Serial No. 282,613. 10 Claims. (Cl. 175—337.)

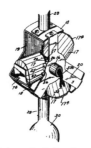

1. In an electro-mechanical motion device, the combination with a magnet radiating from the axis of its support, an armature also radiating from the axis of support, said magnet and armature having outer end and axial poles coöperating to produce relative oscillatory and lateral movements when said magnet is energized, the oscillatory member being normally held against but adapted to be free for oscillation by said lateral movement.

1,327,672. BUTTON-INSPECTING MACHINE. HERBERT HASTINGS, Rochester, N. Y., assignor to German-American Button Co., Rochester, N. Y., a Corporation of New York. Filed May 28, 1917. Serial No. 171,578. 19 Claims. (Cl. 193—24.)

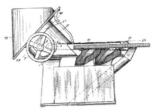

1. In a machine for feeding buttons the combination of a revolving disk adapted to feed buttons, said disk having a ring of openings therein each capable of receiving and carrying a button, means operating automatically and intermittently to open a group of said pockets and permit the buttons therein to drop therefrom.

1,327,673. PIPE-HOLDER. JAMES HECKMAN, Clarendon, Tex. Filed July 7, 1919. Serial No. 308,992. 2 Claims. (Cl. 24—248.)

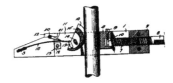

2. In a pipepuller, the combination of a frame, a pipe-engaging jaw slidably mounted in the frame, a threaded bolt mounted in the frame and connected to said jaw for adjusting same, an opposed cam having a V-shaped pipe-engaging face, a link connected to the cam, a spring con-

nected to the link and mounted at the end of the frame, and means for adjustably exerting pressure on the spring to control the action of the cam substantially as shown.

1,327,674. DENTURE. CHARLOTTE HINCHEY, Buffalo, N. Y. Filed Oct. 10, 1919. Serial No. 329,772. 4 Claims. (Cl. 32—4.)

1. A denture comprising an upper plate adapted to support teeth and provided on its upper front part with a projection which is adapted to engage with a cavity in the front part of the roof of the mouth.

1,327,675. VALVE MECHANISM. JOHN C. HORNUNG, Chicago, Ill. Filed Oct. 10, 1918. Serial No. 257,610. 3 Claims. (Cl. 236—80.)

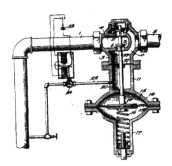

1. The combination with communicating fluid conducting inlet and control chambers having inlet and outlet pipes respectively communicating therewith ; of a balanced valve structure governing the communication between said chambers, an actuating element for imparting closing movement to the balanced valve structure and operated by pressure of fluid delivered to the control chamber, a temperature controlled means for effecting delivery of additional incoming fluid into the control chamber independent of the inlet chamber and between the outlet pipe and the actuating element of the valve structure.

1,327,676. CIRCULAR LOOM. JOSEPH A. KENNEDY, Pawtucket, R. I., assignor to Chernack Manufacturing Company, Providence, R. I., a Corporation of Rhode Island. Filed Feb. 2, 1916. Serial No. 75,865. 14 Claims. (Cl. 139—7.)

1. In a circular loom the combination with a plurality of parallel guides arranged concentrically about an axis, sliding heddles mounted between and in engagement with said guides, cylindrical cams concentrically arranged with an annular space between them for operating said heddles, the heddles and the ends of said slides extending into

such annular space, and a ring engaged with the inner ends of said guides, said ring having notches or recesses

into which the ends of said guides pass, and by which such ends are restrained from deflection.

1,327,677. METHOD OF AND MACHINE FOR PRODUCING INTERNALLY COATED OR LINED WOVEN TUBES. JOSEPH A. KENNEDY, Pawtucket, R. I., assignor to Chernack Manufacturing Company, Pawtucket, R. I., a Corporation of Rhode Island. Filed Apr. 1, 1916. Serial No. 88,241. 17 Claims. (Cl. 154—6.)

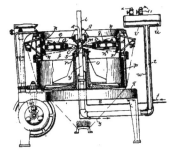

1. An apparatus for producing internally coated or lined tubes, comprising a collection of instrumentalities adapted and operable to interweave the elements of a tube, and means for conducting a plastic composition into the newly formed tube, said means being constructed to spread such composition against the inner surface, and excluding it from the outer surface, of the tube.

1,327,678. APPORTIONING DEVICE. ARNOLD LARSEN, Cleveland, Ohio, assignor to The Wm. Gent Vending Machine Company, Cleveland, Ohio, a Corporation of Ohio. Filed Aug. 17, 1916. Serial No. 115,533. 5 Claims. (Cl. 194—1.)

5. A device of the character set forth comprising a body portion having a through passageway, a partition dividing said passageway into a main chute and a branch chute, the body portion having an inlet passage, a movable member bisecting the main chute, a second member which normally hangs vertically and has a cam portion reposing within the branch chute so that an object passing through the branch chute will engage said cam portion and swing the

second member laterally from its normal vertical position, and interengaging connections between said members

whereby such movement of the last mentioned member will positively withdraw the former member from the main chute.

1,327,679. DIVING APPARATUS. BENJAMIN F. LEAVITT, Toledo, Ohio, assignor to The Leavitt Diving Armor Company, Toledo, Ohio, a Corporation of Ohio. Filed Jan. 15, 1917. Serial No. 142,438. 7 Claims. (Cl. 61—71.)

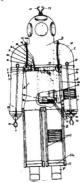

1. In a diving apparatus, the combination with an arm section, of a member swively carried by said section at the free end thereof and constituting a closure for the section, a pair of rock shafts carried by said member, gripping members respectively carried by said rock shafts exteriorly to the arm section, and handles carried by said rock shafts within the arm section.

1,327,680. TRUNK-HARNESS. BERNARD LEAHY, Bridgeport, Conn. Filed May 18, 1918. Serial No. 235,278. 2 Claims. (Cl. 224—49.)

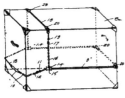

1. A trunk harness including a strap extending around the sides and ends of a trunk, a handle connected to said

270 O. G.—15

strap, collars slidably arranged on said strap, a second strap connected at one end to one of said collars, a hook connected to the opposite end of the second strap, and a chain connected to the other collar and adapted for connection with said hook.

1,327,681. PRESSED - STEEL TRANSMISSION - CASE. AUGUST H. LEIPERT, Brooklyn, N. Y., assignor to International Motor Company, New York, N. Y., a Corporation of Delaware. Filed Apr. 23, 1919. Serial No. 292,065. 1 Claim. (Cl. 74—56.)

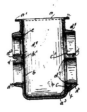

A pressed sheet metal case having openings in its walls for shafts and integral drop-forgings welded to the walls and formed with bearing members for the shafts, each such forging being provided with a shoulder at one of the bearings to seat in one of the openings, the forging at the other bearing being plane to rest against the outer wall of the case.

1,327,682. SWITCHBOARD FOR CHARGING STORAGE BATTERIES. CLARENCE E. OGDEN, Cincinnati, Ohio. Filed Sept. 9, 1918. Serial No. 253,167. 3 Claims. (Cl. 171—314.)

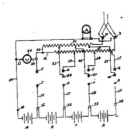

1. A switchboard for charging storage batteries, comprising a line circuit, resistance arranged to be introduced into said circuit, connections for a plurality of storage batteries, a contact on said board for each number of batteries to be charged within the capacity of the line circuit, said contacts being permanently connected with said resistance at points adapted to the charging of the correlated number of batteries automatically to introduce when either is closed the required resistance for the charging of its number of batteries, and means for closing the circuit through any one of said contacts, whereby the correlated number of batteries may be charged.

1,327,683. WOVEN PILE FABRIC. FREDERICK OTT, Norristown, Pa., assignor to A. T. Baker & Company, Manayunk, Pa., a Firm. Filed Dec. 7, 1917. Serial No. 205,938. 27 Claims. (Cl. 139—71.)

1. A double woven pile fabric comprising opposite backing textures, each including ground weft threads and

ground warp threads, and pile warp threads connecting said backing textures in spaced relation ; said pile threads arranged in a pattern comprising twelve pile threads, repeated transversely with respect to the fabric, and including three series, each including two pairs of pile threads shedded alike, but unlike the adjoining series ; said pile threads divided in groups of four, transversely with respect to the fabric, by said warp ground threads,

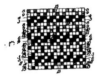

disposed in pairs between said pile thread pairs which are shedded alike : each such group of four including two pairs of pile threads which are shedded unlike ; all of said warp threads shedded. in a reclining twill in said backing textures and presenting a corresponding twill in the respective facings formed by cutting said fabric between said backing textures ; and said ground warp threads being shedded two up and one down with reference to said backings.

1,327,684. WOVEN PILE FABRIC. FREDERICK OTT, Norristown, Pa., assignor to A. T. Baker & Company, Manayunk, Pa., a Firm. Original application filed Dec. 7, 1917, Serial No. 205,938. Divided and this application filed May 10, 1918. Serial No. 233,626. 11 Claims. (Cl. 139—71.)

1. A double woven pile fabric comprising opposite backing textures, each including ground weft threads and ground warp threads, and pile warp threads connecting said backing textures in spaced relation ; said pile threads arranged in a pattern comprising twelve pile threads, repeated transversely with respect to the fabric, and including three series, each including two pairs of pile threads shedded alike, but unlike the adjoining series ; said pile threads divided in groups of two, transversely with respect to the fabric, by said warp ground threads, disposed singly, and alternately, between said pile thread pairs which are shedded alike, and between those which are shedded unlike ; all of said warp threads shedded in a reclining twill in said backing textures and presenting a corresponding twill in the respective facings formed by cutting said fabric between said backing textures ; and said ground warp threads being shedded two up and one down with reference to said backings.

1,327,685. LIFTING-JACK. GEORGE H. PAGE, Richmond, Mo. Filed Feb. 21, 1916. Serial No. 79,589. 5 Claims. (Cl. 254—130.)
1. A lifting jack comprising a standard provided with a vertically arranged series of shoulders and a corresponding series of notches at the rear of said shoulders, a lift-

ing lever provided with a pivot bolt adapted to be supported on any one of said shoulders, and a keeper mem-

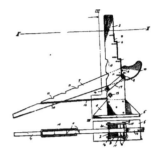

ber carried pivotally by said bolt and coöperating with said notches for retaining said bolt in shouldered position.

1,327,686. LIQUID - MEASURING DEVICE. WILLIAM ROSE, Chicago, Ill. Filed July 7, 1919. Serial No. 309,184. 4 Claims. (Cl. 221—95.)

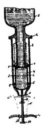

1. A dispenser for inverted bottles comprising a tube open at its upper end to receive a bottle neck and having a tapering, open, lower end, a cup slidable in the tube and resting normally on the inner surface of the tapering lower end of the tube to normally close the lower end of the tube, the upper end of the cup surrounding the lower end of the bottle neck in spaced relation to the latter, means to guide the cup in the tube, and a rod connected to the cup and projecting through the lower end of the tube for manipulation to slide the cup in the tube.

1,327,687. PRIMING AND TESTING CUP. OSCAR A. SMITH, Cleveland, Ohio. Filed Nov. 8, 1917. Serial No. 200,869. 10 Claims. (Cl. 123—187.5.)

1. A priming and testing cup comprising a body having a valve seat and a passageway communicating therewith, a cup at the outer end of said passageway, and a valve adapted to engage said seat and having a stem extending axially through the passageway and also through the cup, the mouth of said cup being located entirely at one side of said stem.

1,327,688. AZO DYES AND PROCESS OF MAKING SAME. RICHARD TAGGESELL, Buffalo, N. Y., assignor to National Aniline & Chemical Company, Inc., New York, N. Y., a Corporation of New York. Filed Sept. 6, 1919. Serial No. 322,138. 3 Claims. (Cl. 8—1.)

1. The method of producing new azo dyestuffs, which comprises combining one molecule of tetrazotized meta-toluenediamin sulfonic acid. $CH_3 : NH_2 : SO_3H, 1 : 2 : 6 : 4$, with one molecule of a meta toluenediamin sulfonic acid, and combining the resulting intermediate product with a suitable unsulfonated compound, substantially as described.

1,327,689. CHAPLET. GEORGE L. WAITT, Buffalo, N. Y. Filed June 14, 1919. Serial No. 304,350. 4 Claims. (Cl. 22—184.)

1. A chaplet, comprising a strut and heads arranged at opposite ends of said strut, said strut consisting of two plies which engage each other and are connected with each other at one pair of corresponding longitudinal edges while the opposite longitudinal edges thereof are disconnected, and each of said heads consisting of two plates arranged flush and connected at their opposing inner edges with one pair of transverse edges of said strut plies.

1,327,690. CLOTHES-WRINGER. JAMES J. WOOD, Fort Wayne, Ind., assignor to Nell C. Hurley, Chicago, Ill. Filed July 25, 1918. Serial No. 246,646. 6 Claims. (Cl. 68—32.)

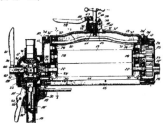

1. In a clothes wringer, a frame having a bridge, a roll relatively fixed in said frame, a roll relatively movable in said frame, a single spring for acting on both ends of the last said roll to press it toward the other, a tension screw for said spring, a nut for said screw through which it is screwed to tension the spring, a housing carried by the frame in which said screw and nut are arranged to move axially, and a latch carried by said frame engaging said nut so as to prevent rotation and vertical displacement thereof, said latch movable to free the nut for vertical displacement.

1,327,691. APPARATUS FOR SEPARATING OIL AND GAS DIRECT FROM WELLS. ALBERT M. BALLARD, Drumright, Okla., assignor to Sun Company, Philadelphia, Pa., a Corporation of New Jersey. Filed Mar. 12, 1919. Serial No. 282,141. 1 Claim. (Cl. 137—103.)

In an oil and gas separator, the combination with a tank having a gas outlet arranged at a relatively high elevation and an oil outlet arranged at a relatively low elevation, of a float in the tank, an oil and gas inlet pipe opening into the tank, a valve controlling the gas outlet, connections between the float and the gas outlet valve adapted to close the latter as the level of the oil rises and lifts the float, a valve controlling the oil outlet, a rod extending vertically through the float along which the

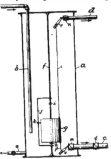

float is vertically guided, another vertically extending guide rod outside the float, and means on the float slidably engaging the second guide rod and thereby holding the float from rotating on the first guide rod.

1,327,692. PROCESS OF CURING TOBACCO. ERNEST G. BEINHART, Washington, D. C. Filed May 8, 1919. Serial No. 295,726. 3 Claims. (Cl. 131—6.) (Filed under the act of Mar. 3, 1883, 22 Stat. L., 625.)

1. The process of curing tobacco by subjecting the leaf harvested separately or harvested upon the stalk or part of the stalk to the action of air possessing a temperature of about 105 F. and a drying action of a humidity preferably about 60% relative humidity to lower the moisture content of the green leaf and establish a film of dead chlorophyll cells in the leaf surface to form a green overcast, thence subjecting the leaf to air possessing a temperature of 90° F. or thereabout, and a relative humidity of 95%, or thereabout, for forty-eight hours more or less, to bring the leaf color to yellow-mottle or yellow wash stage, then raising the temperature of the air to about 105° F. and lowering the humidity of the air to 72% relative humidity, or thereabout, maintaining this condition for forty-eight to seventy-two hours on the leaves primed or picked (from the lower part of the plant, and leaves picked from the upper part of the plant), or until the color of the leaf has passed from the yellow-mottle or yellow wash stage into the brown stage, the whole surface of the leaf and veins assuming the characteristic color, texture, grain conglomeration, body and quality of well cured tobacco.

1,327,693. THERMOS-TANK AND VALVE THEREFOR. JAMES O. BEWAN, Roanoke, Ala. Filed Feb. 15, 1919. Serial No. 277,249. 2 Claims. (Cl. 137—21.)

1. The combination with a thermos tank having a common supply and discharge pipe at its lower end, of an air

pipe arranged at the upper end of the tank, said pipe having a lateral air vent and a perforated end cap, a cage arranged in the pipe between the lateral vent and the end cap, a ball valve therein regulating flow of air from the tank through said cage and cap, and a spring flap valve adapted to normally close the lateral opening against admission of air to the tank.

1,327,694. HASP-STAPLE. HAROLD BLYE, Grand Rapids, Mich., assignor to National Brass Company, Grand Rapids, Mich., a Corporation of Michigan. Filed Dec. 18, 1918. Serial No. 267,345. 2 Claims. (Cl. 292—340.)

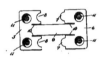

2. A hasp staple comprising a relatively narrow loop of sheet metal, a base section integrally connected to each end of the loop, one of said sections having a plurality of projections at its inner edge, and the other having a plurality of depressions in its inner edge to receive said projections and thereby keep the base sections in alinement.

1,327,695. LATCH SET. HAROLD BLYE, Grand Rapids, Mich., assignor to National Brass Company, Grand Rapids, Mich., a Corporation of Michigan. Filed Jan. 13, 1919. Serial No. 270,935. 6 Claims. (Cl. 292—337.)

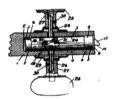

1. In a device of the character described, a face plate having an opening therethrough, a sleeve attached to the rear side of the plate and provided with a bayonet slot therein, a cap similarly provided with a bayonet slot therein, a cylindrical housing formed of two semi-cylindrical parts disposed between the cap and sleeve and inserted at their ends into the cap and sleeve, pins on said housing parts located in the slots, a latch bolt projecting partially through the opening in said face plate, means to retract the bolt into the housing, and spring means normally forcing the bolt partially out of the housing, substantially as described.

1,327,696. STRIPPING MECHANISM FOR CARDING-MACHINES. ARTHUR G. BOOZER, Providence, R. I., assignor of one-half to George Hill, Tucapau, S. C. Filed Apr. 12, 1918. Serial No. 228,263. 9 Claims. (Cl. 19—15.)

8. In stripping mechanism for card clothing of carding machines, a plurality of suction nozzles maintained to extend across the clothing to be stripped, pipes for each of the nozzles, a conduit that communicates with each of the pipes and with means for producing a partial vacuum therein, hinged valves associated with each of the pipes between the nozzles and the conduit the valves

---

having arms to which springs are attached for moving the arms toward valve actuating means, and valve actuating means comprising a driven shaft having thereon a plu-

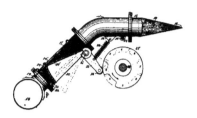

rality of disks with peripheral recesses which are positioned to that adjacent valves will not be successively actuated.

1,327,697. CRUCIBLE-MOUTHPIECE FOR LINOTYPE-MACHINES. WILLIAM E. BORST and CLARENCE C. GILLEO, Grand Rapids, Mich. Filed Apr. 1, 1919. Serial No. 286,753. 4 Claims. (Cl. 22—70.)

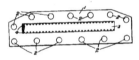

1. A mouthpiece for crucibles of linotype machines comprising a plate adapted for attachment at the mouth of a crucible and provided with upper and lower rows of openings therethrough, said rows of openings being located horizontally and the openings in a row being spaced short distances from each other.

1,327,698. MACHINE FOR FILLING FEED-BELTS FOR MACHINE-GUNS. JOHN M. BROWNING, Ogden, Utah. Filed Sept. 9, 1919. Serial No. 322,686. 2 Claims. (Cl. 86—48.)

1. In a machine for filling the pockets of cartridge feed-belts, the combination of fluted belt holding and feeding wheels, means to rotate said wheels step by step, a reciprocating slide to insert the cartridges in the pockets, and a spring stop attached above said slide to yield upward out of the path of said slide, and to regulate the position of the belt and the cartridges therein between said fluted wheels.

1,327,699. MIXER FOR GASEOUS FUEL. ERNEST CAMP, San Diego, Calif. Filed June 26, 1918. Serial No. 241,939. 4 Claims. (Cl. 48—180.)

4. The method of mixing fluent materials, which consists in directing the materials through a conduit in a

plurality of streams and in spirals which are of relatively different lengths so that the said streams will intersect

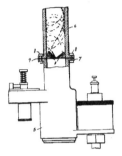

each other at spaced points during their passage through the conduit.

1,327,700.   ATTACHMENT FOR GRAIN OR GRIST MILLS. WILFRED P. CARSON, Greensboro, N. C. Filed Mar. 24, 1919. Serial No. 284,611. 6 Claims. (Cl. 130—15.)

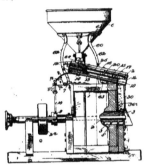

3. A grain feed shoe or box having a bottom floor to receive the screenings and a discharge therefor, an upper coarse screen and a lower fine screen in said box, means providing a grain passage from the fine screen and a grain outlet therefor from the shoe, and means providing opposite lateral outlets for the screenings from said coarse screen, and vertical passages from said outlets leading to said floor and arranged beyond the side edges of said screens.

1,327,701.   WATCH-HOLDER. BENJAMIN F. CHRIST, Idagrove, Iowa. Filed May 21, 1919. Serial No. 298,593. 1 Claim. (Cl. 24—3.)

A device of the character specified comprising a plate shaped to fit the back of a watch and having means on one face for grasping the edge and stem of the watch, to hold it to the holder, said holder having a clasp for en-

gaging the pocket to hold the holder in the pocket, the clasp comprising a radial extension from the plate bent back over upon the rear face of the plate to lie close thereto in spaced relation, the holding means comprising lugs engaging the edge of the case at the opposite side from the extension, and a tongue spaced from the extension for engaging the stem of the watch between the same and the extension.

1,327,702.   ADJUSTABLE-SOCKET RATCHET-WRENCH. OHIO C. BARBER CLARK, Akron, Ohio. Filed Aug. 9, 1919. Serial No. 316,430. 2 Claims. (Cl. 81—112.)

1. In a ratchet wrench, a socket formed as a body having one end formed as an open shell provided at diametrically opposite points with longitudinal slots, a disk member slidable within said shell and provided with recesses diverging toward the open end of said shell, jaw members disposed within said shell and fitting within said recesses, and a transverse pin extending through said disk member, said jaws, and said slots.

1,327,703.   CARBURETER. CHARLES HENRI CLAUDEL, Levallois-Perret, France. Filed Jan. 26, 1914, Serial No. 814,403. Renewed Oct. 21, 1919. Serial No. 332,330. 17 Claims. (Cl. 261—62.)

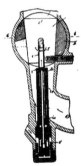

1. The combination in a carbureter of a rotatable valve having an opening therein constituting a mixing chamber, a fuel injection device extending into and located within said opening in said valve and means carried by the valve for preventing the expansion of the air in the mixing chamber in certain positions of the valve.

1,327,704.   MILK-PAIL. RINEHOLDT H. DAMITZ, Kennedy, Minn. Substitute for application Serial No. 179,264, filed July 7, 1917. This application filed June 17; 1919. Serial No. 304,952. 1 Claim. (Cl. 31—14.)

A milk pail including a receptacle, a cover for the receptacle including a basin-shaped upper wall having a central opening, the wall of the opening being extended downwardly to form a flange, a screen mounted in the opening, a ring engaged in said flange, depending divergent arms carried by the said ring, inwardly directed

lugs carried by the lower portions of the arms, and a gravity disk disposed between the arms.

1,327,705. VAGINAL DOUCHE AND MEDICATOR. CYRUS W. DE LONG, Gainesville, Fla. Filed July 11, 1919. Serial No. 310,179. 3 Claims. (Cl. 128—241.)

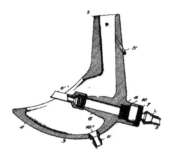

1. In a device of the character described, a hollow member having an enlarged central basin-forming portion and a narrowed forward end, a handle-forming hollow cylindrically shaped rear end, projecting upward from and communicating with the rear of the basin, and means for conducting fluid to and from said device.

1,327,706. COLLAPSIBLE FOOTREST. EDGARD C. DE SMET, St. Cloud, Minn., assignor to Samuel C. Pandolfo, St. Cloud, Minn. Filed Apr. 7, 1919. Serial No. 288,129. 8 Claims. (Cl. 155—9.)

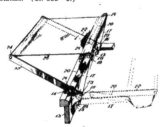

6. A foot-rest of the class described, comprising, in combination with a supporting frame, a frame element pivotally secured at its lower ends to said supporting frame, while the upper or free end is secured together by a transversely disposed portion, a second frame element, of greater length than the first mentioned element, pivotally secured at its lower end to said supporting frame at points disposed in a vertical plane rearward of the pivotal points of the first mentioned element, the outer or free ends of said second element being secured together by means of a transversely disposed portion, flexible material secured to the transversely disposed portions of both elements so as to form a top, and a member or link on each side of the foot rest, one end of each link being pivotally secured to the first-mentioned element, while the other end of each link is pivotally secured to the second mentioned element at a point forward of the pivotal connections of said second mentioned element on the supporting frame and forward of the pivotal connections of said links with the first mentioned element when the foot-rest is in "set-up" position.

1,327,707. FABRIC FOR AIRCRAFT AND PROCESS OF MAKING SAME. NEVILLE ALEXANDER THOMAS NIX FEARY, Peterborough, England. Filed Apr. 21, 1919. Serial No. 291,583. 9 Claims. (Cl. 154—46.)

2. A fabric for the purposes set forth comprising cork, impregnated with oil, oil varnish or the like under pressure.

1,327,708. STRAINER FOR WATER-SUPPLY PIPES OF LOCOMOTIVES. JOSEPH GUY, Humbermouth, Newfoundland. Filed Aug. 16, 1918. Serial No. 250,156. 2 Claims. (Cl. 210—16.)

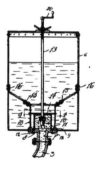

1. In combination with a locomotive water supply tank having an outlet connection communicating with its bottom and in the mouth of which is formed a valve seat, of a circular strainer in the tank engaged over said outlet connection and having a perforated top portion, a thrust bar arranged in and secured to the side walls of the tank, vertical stay rods adjacent the strainer and connected at their upper ends to said thrust bar, said rods having a connection with the strainer to prevent movement of the same with relation to the outlet connection, a rotatable valve stem extending through the top of said tank, a valve connected to the lower end of the stem adapted to engage in the seat in the outlet connection, and means connected to the upper end of the stem to facilitate rotation thereof.

1,327,709. AUTOMATICALLY-THREADING SHUTTLE. HUDSON W. HAKES, Millbury, Mass. Filed Apr. 4, 1919. Serial No. 287,478. 9 Claims. (Cl. 139—46.)
1. An automatically threading device for a loom shuttle having a single longitudinal thread passage, an inclined deflecting flange extending over the thread passage at one end thereof, and a second oppositely inclined de-

flecting flange extending over the thread passage at its opposite end, with said deflecting flanges spaced apart

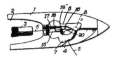

to provide a clear space between the transverse edges of said flanges.

1,327,710. METHOD OF MAKING ANCHOR-BLOCKS. GEORGE P. HEMSTREET, Hastings-upon-Hudson, N. Y., assignor to The International Pavement Company, Hartford, Conn., a Corporation of Connecticut. Original application filed July 15, 1916, Serial No. 109,428. Divided and this application filed Sept. 11, 1919. Serial No. 323,100.   4 Claims.   (Cl. 25—84.)

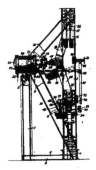

1. The improvement in the art of making anchor paving blocks which comprises affixing an anchor member thereto while the block is in semi-plastic condition and simultaneously applying pressure to the sides of the block.

1,327,711. SUPPORT FOR GRATINGS. WALTER E. IRVING, Glenbrook, Conn. Filed July 3, 1919. Serial No. 308,540   6 Claims.   (Cl. 189—84.)

1. A support for gratings comprising in combination an anchorage, a plurality of horizontally projecting members mounted on said anchorage and a horizontal bar fastened to said projecting members offset from the anchorage and having its upper edge adapted to serve as a support for the ends of the bars of a superposed grating.

1,327,712. DISPENSING - MACHINE. OTTO JAEGER, Elkins Park, Pa., assignor to Harry S. Kelsey, Boston, Mass. Filed June 26, 1919. Serial No. 306,787. 10 Claims.   (Cl. 211—8.)

5. In a dispensing machine and in combination, a casing having a plurality of storing compartments, a movable door closing said compartments and tending to move in a direction to open them successively, an escapement device for controlling the movement of the door in said direction and comprising two racks carried by the door

and a coöperating lever, said door and racks tending to move said lever back and forth from one rack to the other in alternate succession, and said lever permitting the door to move to open one compartment each time the lever is permitted to move back and forth, a hook op-

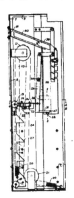

eratively connected to the lever, and a latch adapted to be engaged by said hook to lock the lever against movement by one rack when it is moved by the other rack to a predetermined position, said latch being operative to release the lever.

1,327,713. CIRCULAR-SAW SUPPORT. GEORGE O. JOYNER and GUS J. WHITE, Little Rock, Ark. Filed Apr. 18, 1919. Serial No. 290,983.   7 Claims.   (Cl. 76—26.)

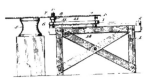

1. In a saw support of the character described, the combination with a horizontally movable carriage, of means thereon for supporting the central portion of a circular saw, and means for automatically moving said central portion of the saw vertically during the horizontal movement of the carriage.

1,327,714. PROCESS FOR PRODUCING CHLOROPICRIN. ROBERT J. KING, Stamford, Conn. Filed Nov. 26, 1917. Serial No. 204,045.   3 Claims.   (Cl. 23—24.)

1. In a process for producing chloropicrin, forming an admixture of bleaching powder with water and adding a solution of calcium picrate thereto.

1,327,715. CUTTING DEVICE. WILLIAM J. LEIGHTY, Chicago, Ill. Filed June 5, 1918. Serial No. 238,355. 18 Claims.   (Cl. 266—23.)

14. A device of the class described, comprising a frame portion, a pair of rotative members carried by said frame-portion with one member eccentrically mounted in the other, means whereby the outer member is held against rotation, a driving gear secured to the eccentrically mounted member, means intermediate of the driving gear and the outer member whereby said first means are forced out of holding relation with the outer member and the latter caused to rotate with the gear, means for deter-

mining the position of the eccentrically mounted member and driving gear relative to the outer member, and blow-

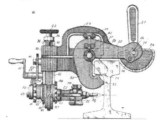

pipe carrying means secured to the eccentrically mounted member.

1,327,716. HORSESHOE. ANTHONY J. McCORMACK, New Haven, Conn., assignor to The Mac-Rim Company, New Haven, Conn., a Corporation of Connecticut. Filed Aug. 9, 1919. Serial No. 316,341. 4 Claims. (Cl. 168—13.)

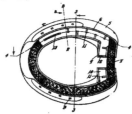

1. A horseshoe comprising a base having a channel in the bottom thereof, narrow rests rising from the bottom of said channel to penetrate a cushion, said rests being spaced a substantial distance apart to permit the cushion to sink into the spaces between the rests, a cushion seated against said rests, and means outside of said channel for securing a shoe to a hoof.

1,327,717. RESILIENT TIRE-CUSHION. EDWARD Mc-DOWELL, Atlanta, Ga. Filed June 4, 1918. Serial No. 238,171. 1 Claim. (Cl. 152—5.)

An inner cushion for tire casings, consisting of a rope-like core interfitting the casing and comprising a plurality of twisted strands, each strand including a plurality of twisted plaits, and each plait consisting of a number of plaited flat strips of waste rubber.

1,327,718. PNEUMATIC-DESPATCH-TUBE APPA-RATUS. JAMES G. MACLAREN, Mamaroneck, N. Y. Filed Aug. 25, 1917. Serial No. 188,186. 12 Claims. (Cl. 243—14.)
1. A pneumatic carrier system comprising, in combination, a transmission tube, an entrance gate for said tube,

air current creating means, timing means controlling said gate and pressure-responsive means subject to control by pressure conditions due to a carrier in transit to control

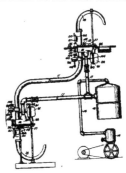

the operation of said timing means, whereby said gate may be maintained in carrier-transmitting position, irre-spective of the time required for the transmission of the carrier.

1,327,719. LOCK COLLAR-BUTTON. REID J. Mc-CREDIE, Buffalo, N. Y. Filed Nov. 22, 1918. Serial No. 263,712. 3 Claims. (Cl. 24—104.)

3. A collar button comprising a collar engaging ele-ment and an anchoring element, the collar engaging ele-ment having a base provided with a slot and a standard extending from the base adjacent the slot, the anchoring element having a base and a tongue extending from the base and adapted to pass through the buttonhole of a collar band and through the slot of the base of said collar engaging element, said tongue and standard having corrugations and means carried by the collar engaging element for releasably holding the tongue and standard corrugations in interfitting relation.

1,327,720. PUNCHING-MACHINE. PATRICK MASTER-SON, South Porcupine, Ontario, Canada. Filed July 23, 1918. Serial No. 246,340. 8 Claims. (Cl. 76—5.)

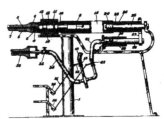

1. In a punching machine, a dolly provided with a center punch and a forked guide, extending from the face of the dolly substantially parallel to the punch and to one side thereof.

1,327,721. METHOD OF MANUFACTURING FIBROUS CEMENT PRODUCTS. RICHARD V. MATTISON, Jr., Upper Dublin township, Montgomery county, Pa. Filed Feb. 12, 1919. Serial No. 276,679. 6 Claims. (Cl. 25—42.)

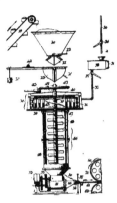

1. The continuous process of manufacturing fibrous cement products which consists of combining cement, fiber and water, thoroughly mixing the same to produce a homogeneous mass, feeding the same continuously through the die of an auger mill, cutting the extruded mass into desired lengths and subjecting them to treatment for removal of water, and allowing the material of the product to set.

1,327,722. MATRIX FOR SOUND-RECORDS. FRED G. MAYER, Richmond, Ind., assignor to The Starr Piano Company, Richmond, Ind., a Corporation of Indiana. Filed July 2, 1919. Serial No. 308,197. 2 Claims. (Cl. 18—5.3.)

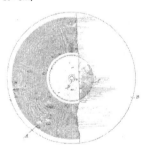

2. A matrix for phonographic sound records comprising a matrix sheet, a backing to which said sheet is secured, and a thin metal disk with tapered edges intermediate the central portion of the matrix sheet and the backing.

1,327,723. TOY POPGUN. ZACARIAH M. MIDYETT, Jackson, Tenn. Filed Apr. 25, 1918. Serial No. 230,717. 2 Claims. (Cl. 46—46.)

1. In combination with a pop gun, a cork or other missile adapted to fit in the muzzle thereof, a hollow guard member adapted to slip over the muzzle of the gun and

the cork and receive the latter when the gun is "fired" and a coil or helical spring working in the guard member and connected at one end with the cork, said spring

adapted to automatically return the cork into normal or "firing" position by its recoil action after the same is "fired" or discharged.

1,327,724. COTTON-SEED LINTER. ROBERT E. MONTGOMERY, Lawton, Okla. Filed Feb. 18, 1916. Serial No. 79,150. 3 Claims. (Cl. 13—17.)

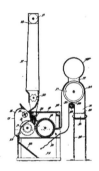

1. In a cotton seed linting mechanism, the combination with means for removing the fine particles of lint from previously ginned seed, of means for causing an air current to separate the fine lint from the motes and trash and to carry said lint in suspension, a rotary condenser through which said current passes adapted to collect on its surface said fine particles but to permit the air and dust to pass through, means for removing said dust laden air, a doffing roller adapted to brush from said rotary condenser the lint collected thereon, and a belt conveyer in position to receive the lint brushed off by said doffing roller.

1,327,725. CAROUSEL. CHARLES E. MORRIS, Leavenworth, Kans., assignor to Charles W. Parker, Leavenworth, Kans. Filed Mar. 15, 1917. Serial No. 154,918. 6 Claims. (Cl. 46—27.)

1. In a carousel, a crank shaft having a crank, a horse rod, and an inverted U-shaped box member pivotally mounted on said crank and having each arm provided on its inner side with a recess having at its lower end a seat and having a groove in one edge communicating with

said recess, the grooves in said arms being in like edges, the upper end of the horse rod having a T-shaped head insertible between said arms, the arms of the T being insertible respectively through said grooves into said recesses, and adapted, when the horse rod is swung to the vertical position, to respectively rest upon said seats.

1,327,726. COMPOSITION FOR PAVING AND OTHER PURPOSES. Samuel R. Murray, Indianapolis, Ind. Filed Apr. 1, 1918. Serial No. 225,896. 6 Claims. (Cl. 106—31.)

6. The process of producing a composition which consists in pulverizing earthy materials, heating the pulverized material, mixing therewith sufficient bituminous cement to lightly coat the particles, cooling the mixture, repulverizing the mixture, heating the pulverized mixture and mixing therewith a further quantity of bituminous cement.

1,327,727. BOILER - SETTING. Lester Nevers and Frank Whitbeck, Grand Rapids, Mich. Filed Apr. 5, 1917. Serial No. 160,062. 5 Claims. (Cl. 110—60.)

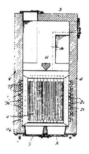

5. In combination with a boiler, a setting therefor forming a fire place under the boiler, said fire place being provided with an outlet, a grate in the fire place, an upright post located centrally at the back of the fire place and dividing the outlet thereof into two separate passages, said post being provided at its front portion with forwardly converging side faces, fire doors located at the front of the fire place on opposite sides of the middle of the front to enable the sides of the fire place to be alternately supplied with fuel, an air inlet flue located in the rear of the grate and having branches extending to the sides of the setting and forwardly along the sides of the fire place below the plane of the said grate and provided with upwardly extending outlets communicating with the fire place above the grate and arranged at spaced points, steam pipes located in the said branches and below the plane of the grate and having branch pipes extending upwardly in the said outlets and arranged to discharge into the fire place and draw heated air from the flue into the said fire place, the said steam outlets on each side of the fire place being adapted to force the smoke and gases from one side of the fire place to the opposite side thereof.

1,327,728. MACHINE FOR MAKING COIL-SPRINGS. Arthur McKeyes Parker, Georgetown, S. C. Filed June 12, 1919. Serial No. 303,573. 5 Claims. (Cl. 153—67.)

4. A device of the character specified, comprising a suitable supporting plate having a series of means for engagement by wire winding spindles of various size, a bar for pressing the wire into contact with the plate as it is wound on the spindle, a lever for laying the coils

---

on the spindle, said lever being normally spring pressed intermediate its ends toward the support, means for holding the end of the lever remote from the spindle to the

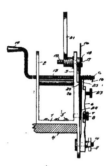

plate, and means in connection with the lever and engaging the plate for pressing the operative end of the said lever away from the bar.

1,327,729. FOUNTAIN-PEN. Benjamin S. Paschall, New York, N. Y. Filed Apr. 2, 1919. Serial No. 286,912. 6 Claims. (Cl. 120—50.)

1. In combination, a fountain pen, and means for retaining in the pen ink fed by the expansion of a gaseous body within the pen, comprising a reversely bent tube having an enlarged chamber therein.

1,327,730. RADIATOR - SHIELD. George W. Payne, Kansas City, Mo. Filed Sept. 16, 1918. Serial No. 254,190. 1 Claim. (Cl. 257—132.)

In a radiator shield for automobiles, the combination with a radiator having cellular filling, of arms hingedly suspended from the cellular filling, a trough-shaped member supportingly engaged by said arms, a spring actuated shade roller mounted in said trough-shaped member and provided with an extensible shield, a stub shaft revolubly mounted on the radiator and provided outwardly of the radiator with a drum having a cable attached to the shield and inwardly of the radiator with a pinion, a revolubly mounted shaft having a gear wheel in engagement with the pinion on said stub shaft, and means for turning said list mentioned shaft.

1,327,731. PNEUMATIC MOTOR FOR PIANO-PLAYERS. CLAUS E. PETERSON, Worcester, Mass., assignor to Iverson Piano Player Company, Boston, Mass., a Corporation of Massachusetts. Filed May 15, 1918. Serial No. 234,702. 2 Claims. (Cl. 230—36.)

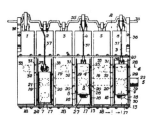

1. In an apparatus of the class described, in combination, a raceway for a valve, a reciprocating valve, pins projecting from the opposite sides of the valve near its ends, and a pair of elongated staples extending the length of the raceway and passing over said pins.

1,327,732. HEADLIGHT. TRUMAN W. POST, Brooklyn, N. Y., assignor to Electric Auto-Lite Corporation, Toledo, Ohio, a Corporation of Delaware. Filed Mar. 3, 1916. Serial No. 81,789. 3 Claims. (Cl. 240—7.)

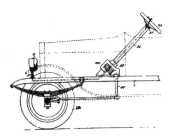

3. In an automotive vehicle the combination of a headlight including a plurality of lamps, one of said lamps being adapted to project light rays forwardly; another of said lamps being adapted to project light rays forwardly and downwardly; and two other of said lamps being arranged to project light rays laterally; separate circuits for each of said lamps, a manually operable switch for closing either or both of the circuits of said two first mentioned lamps and means controlled by the steering mechanism of said vehicle for closing the circuits of said last two mentioned lamps.

1,327,733. ADJUSTABLE ILLUMINATING - FIXTURE. WARREN W. POTTS, Elkhart, Ind. Filed Apr. 28, 1919. Serial No. 293,206. 3 Claims. (Cl. 240—67.)

1. An adjustable hanger for electric illuminating fixtures, comprising a fixed center post. a casing surrounding said post adapted to telescope therewith, providing a support for the electric fixture, a pair of conductor rods mounted adjacent said post, a pair of tubes in said casing receiving said conductor rods and adapted to telescope therewith, said tubes being insulated from said casing and providing a circuit completing means from the conductor rods to the electric fixture, said central post having an

elongated notched portion along one of its sides, and a dogging device carried by said casing adapted to selectively

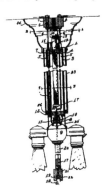

engage said notches, whereby the electric fixture may be vertically adjusted.

1,327,734. WATERING DEVICE FOR STOCK. HUGO C. RASSMANN, Beaver Dam, Wis. Filed Mar. 7, 1918. Serial No. 221,016. 4 Claims. (Cl. 119—80.)

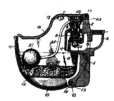

1. In a watering device, the combination with a support, of a structure pivotally attached thereto and comprising a bowl and a receptacle communicating with each other, a valved fount, a float lever pivotally mounted in and carried by said receptacle, said float lever being operatively associated with the valve of the valved fount, and a cover for said receptacle pivoted to said support and having a part coöperative with a part on the receptacle to form a latch device.

1,327,735. SUPPORTING AND ALINING MEANS FOR STANCHIONS. HUGO C. RASSMANN, Beaver Dam, Wis., assignor to F. Rassmann Manufacturing Company, Beaver Dam, Wis. Filed Apr. 23, 1919. Serial No. 292,059. 10 Claims. (Cl. 119—147.)

1. In supporting means for stanchions, the combination with an elongated hollow bracket having a plurality of sockets therein and having an elongated slot, and a connecting device for a stanchion entering said bracket and having a head to be mounted in any one of said sockets, of a movable locking device disposed in said bracket and adapted to be disposed over the head of said connecting device to prevent displacement of the latter from the socket in which it may be disposed.

1,327,736. PROCESS OF PRODUCING CARBID. JAMES HENRY REID, Newark, N. J., assignor to International Nitrogen Company, a Corporation of Delaware. Filed Mar. 15, 1913. Serial No. 754,461. 15 Claims. (Cl. 204—62.)

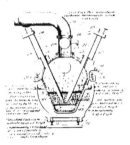

1. The process of producing carbid which consists in coking suitable proportions of a metal oxid and organic material capable of yielding a definite percentage of fixed carbon such that after coking they are in proper proportion to produce carbid and passing an electric current through the coked mass to form carbid.

1,327,737. PROCESS OF PROCURING AND SECURING PRODUCTS FROM CARBOHYDRATES. JAMES HENRY REID, Newark, N. J., assignor, by mesne assignments, to International Nitrogen Co., a Corporation of Delaware. Filed Jan. 13, 1914. Serial No. 811,851. 18 Claims. (Cl. 204—62.)

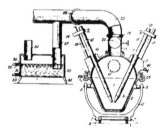

1. The process of making fluid hydrocarbon, which comprises exposing a carbohydrate, while associated with a metal oxy-compound, to successive stages of heat induced therein by resistance therethrough of increments thereof to a current of electricity so varying in character as to successively yield products of progressively increasing carbon content, subjecting the carbohydrate and metal oxy-compound to selective electrical action until each desired product is produced and evolved, and finally securing such products by condensation.

1,327,738. MEANS ACTUATED BY ALTERNATING ELECTRIC CURRENT FOR CONTROLLING OR OPERATING ELECTRIC FURNACES OR OTHER MECHANISMS. JAMES HENRY REID, Newark, N. J., assignor, by mesne assignments, to International Nitrogen Co., a Corporation of Delaware. Filed Dec. 19, 1914. Serial No. 878,071. 12 Claims. (Cl. 204—64.)

1. An apparatus for making and securing products electrically, which comprises the combination of a receptacle, electrodes therein, means for bringing the electrodes and receptacle into an electrical circuit, means including an armature of non-magnetic nature adapted to be acted upon by an alternating current for repelling the same, temperature-governed means for regulating the movement of said armature, said armature controlling the operative

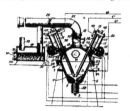

distance of the electrodes when in use, and means for reversing the movement of the electrodes while communicating with the controlling member.

1,327,739. METHOD OF BUILDING CONCRETE SHIPS. ALFRED RICHLEY, Cleveland, Ohio, assignor of one-half to William C. Cone, Toronto, Ontario, Canada. Original application filed May 23, 1918, Serial No. 236,126. Divided and this application filed May 31, 1919. Serial No. 300,918. 3 Claims. (Cl. 25—130.)

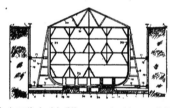

1. A method of building concrete ships, consisting in molding the hull within a dry dock, then coincidently filling the dry dock and hull with water while the hull is supported by the molds to effect the curing of the concrete, then pumping out the water and removing the molds.

1,327,740. FLUE-CLEANER. THOMAS J. ROSSELL, New Smyrna, Fla. Filed Apr. 5, 1919. Serial No. 287,792. 3 Claims. (Cl. 83—64.)

1. In a flue cleaner having an unobstructed fluid passage therethrough from one end to the other, the combination with a pair of elbow parts reversely disposed, of a relatively rigid conduit section connected to one of the parts and terminating at one end in a flexible conduit section having coupling means at the end thereof, means carried by the rigid section for controlling said fluid through said passage, a flue cleaning tube carried by the other part, and having scraping means at the terminal end thereof, and means for uniting the two parts universally, whereby the tube may swing in various directions and under the rigid section.

1,327,741. MEANS FOR FASTENING PLASTER-BOARDS AND THE LIKE. CLEO G. SHUMAN, Chicago, Ill., assignor to Gyp Steel Products Company, Chicago, Ill., a Corporation of Missouri. Filed Sept. 9, 1918. Serial No. 253,191. 7 Claims. (Cl. 72—118.)

7. As an article of manufacture, a rectangular blank of sheet metal provided with a plurality of slits extend-

ing from opposite ends thereof for a predetermined distance to provide a plurality of separated portions, of equal number, at both ends of the blank, the intermediate slits at one end of the blank being of less length than the adjacent slits in said end, while the slits in the other end of the blank are all substantially of equal length, and providing said blank with a slot extending from one of said

ends of the blank to a greater distance than the slits in said end, to adapt the blank to be forced edgewise on to the studding of a wall or partition so as to extend substantially equal distances beyond opposite sides of the studding and provide an equal number of slit portions on both sides of the studding adapted to fasten parallelly arranged plaster-boards on each side of the studding.

1,327,742. TIRE-CARRIER FOR AUTOMOBILES. CHARLES CLAIR STEEL and THOMAS H. LYNN, Williamsport, Pa. Filed Mar. 7, 1919. Serial No. 281,206. 5 Claims. (Cl. 224—29.)

1. In a tire carrier, the combination of a ring forming a continuous seat for a tire rim, two oppositely disposed fixed lugs projecting outwardly beyond the periphery of the ring for engagement with one edge or side of the rim, a centrally disposed brace for the ring, pivoted links located within the ring and each provided with an outwardly projecting lug, the lugs on the links adapted to engage the other edge or side of the tire, and lever mechanism connecting the two links for holding them in locking position and for moving them into and out of locking position.

1,327,743. PROCESS FOR MAKING POWDERED OR GRANULATED ALUMINUM. LEWIS B. TEBBETTS, 2d, St. Louis, Mo. Filed Dec. 4, 1917. Serial No. 205,359. 4 Claims. (Cl. 75—197.)
3. The process of pulverizing metallic aluminum, which consists in heating the metal to a temperature above the melting point of the aluminum, agitating the aluminum while in a heated condition, and reducing the temperature until the metal is solidified.

1,327,744. ATOMIZER FOR LIQUID-FUEL ENGINES. EUGÈNE HENRI TARTRAIS, Maisons-Laffitte, France. Filed Nov. 21, 1918. Serial No. 263,581. 3 Claims. (Cl. 123—32.)
1. A liquid atomizer for engines working under injection of liquid fuel comprising, in combination: a valve body to be secured onto the engine,—a knife shaped valve seat formed by the inner end of the valve body, a valve with a flat bearing face having a sharpened edge, a valve rod fitting without play into the valve body, passages pro-

vided on said rod in order to allow the liquid to pass along the same, a return spring tending to hold the valve against its seat and a joint connecting the outer end of

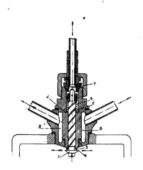

the valve to the passage or pipe carrying the injected liquid,—substantially as described and for the purpose specified.

1,327,745. CURRENT-MOTOR. WILBER H. THARP, Lewiston, Idaho. Filed July 20, 1914, Serial No. 852,122. Renewed Oct. 24, 1919. Serial No. 333,059. 4 Claims. (Cl. 170—117.)

1. In a current motor, an inclined guideway having upwardly projecting lateral flanges, a base having runners guided between said flanges, a shaft extending at right angles to the guideway, radially directed arms carried upon the shaft and extending parallel to the base and blades hinged to the ends of said shaft for vertical adjustment into angular relation to the corresponding arm, and means whereby the blades may be held in angularly adjusted relation, said blades being mounted for swinging movement transversely of the arms.

1,327,746. VEHICLE SPRING SUSPENSION. ROLLAND S. TROTT, Denver, Colo. Filed Sept. 17, 1913, Serial No. 790,337. Renewed Feb. 19, 1919. Serial No. 278,061. 18 Claims. (Cl. 267—52.)

1. In a vehicle, a horizontally movable axle, springs, and a cross-shaft connected with the springs to equalize the horizontal movement of the two ends of the axle.
13. The combination with a frame and axle, of a shaft journaled on the frame, links secured to said shaft, load-springs secured to the axles and connected with said links supporting said load-springs, and all of said parts

so arranged that the axle has free movement in a direction longitudinal of the frame, and all lateral or twisting movement is precluded.

18. The combination with a vehicle frame and axle, of a shaft connected across the frame, load springs secured to the axles, links secured on said shaft and pivotally connected with said load springs at one end thereof, links connecting the opposite ends of the springs to have swinging movement with the frame all of said parts arranged to permit movement of the axle in a direction of the longitudinal extent of the frame and to preclude twisting movement, springs positioned to resiliently oppose said movement of the axle and to restore the axle to its normal position.

1,327,747. FIRECRACKER-GUN. MORRELL J. UFFORD, Kansas, Ill. Filed June 5, 1919. Serial No. 301,956. 10 Claims. (Cl. 42—55.)

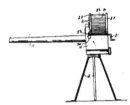

1. A fire cracker gun of the character described comprising a body having a firing chamber, a hopper conveying the fire crackers to an opening in the body, and igniting means mounted on the body, means for carrying the fire crackers one by one from the discharge end of the hopper into the firing chamber, and passing the fuse of the fire crackers through the igniting means.

1,327,748. SHELVING-SUPPORT. ANTHONY VANDERVELD, Grand Rapids, Mich., assignor to Grand Rapids Show Case Co., Grand Rapids, Mich., a Corporation of Michigan. Filed July 2, 1917. Serial No. 178,190. 5 Claims. (Cl. 45—54.)

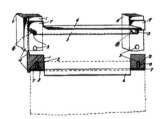

1. In combination, front and rear supporting standards each provided with a plurality of openings in a side thereof in vertical alinement, and a shelf support adjustably and detachably connected with said standards comprising a flat bar of metal, a ledge cut from the upper portion of the bar and turned substantially horizontal, said ledge being of a length substantially equal to the distance between the standards whereby a portion is left at each end of the bar above the ledge to lie against said standards, and lugs cut at each end of the bar adjacent the lower edges thereof, and turned to enter the openings in the standards.

1,327,749. TACK-HOLDER. JOHN W. WHIPP, Wade, Okla. Filed Apr. 14, 1919. Serial No. 289,874. 4 Claims. (Cl. 248—3.)

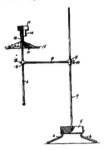

3. In a device of the character described, the combination of a conical disk having a peripheral upturned flange, means for supporting said disk, and a tack distributing means supported above said disk.

1,327,750. VEHICLE - SPRING. FRANKLYN J. WOLFF, Chicago, Ill., assignor of one-half to Harold W. Wolff, Chicago, Ill. Filed Apr. 1, 1916. Serial No. 88,239. 5 Claims. (Cl. 267—34.)

1. A vehicle spring comprising a plurality of superimposed leaves having projections, clips disposed alongside said leaves and embracing said projections and adapted for attachment to a vehicle axle, and a plate passing through said clips and extending above the leaves and having its ends formed to prevent separation of the clips and releasing of the leaves.

1,327,751. FISHING ROD AND REEL. JOHN L. BECK, Newark, N. J. Filed June 10, 1919. Serial No. 303,204. 10 Claims. (Cl. 43—36.)

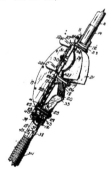

1. A fishing rod having a reel thereon, a handle for the rod, a manually operated means independent of the handle for positively operating the reel, means for con-

necting and disconnecting said operating means, the handle having a limited movement for controlling said connecting and disconnecting means.

1,327,752. COMBINATION-MACHINE FOR MAKING PHOTOPRINTS ON PRINTING-PLATES BY DIRECT CONTACT OR PROJECTION PRINTING. HERMAN C. BOEDICKER, Minneapolis, Minn. Filed Feb. 23, 1917. Serial No. 150,613. 9 Claims. (Cl. 88—24.)

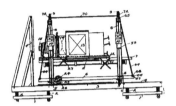

1. In a combination machine for making photo prints on printing plates, the combination of a base, vibration absorbing means supporting said base, a plate supported on said base and having means of adjustment longitudinally, vertically, and transversely thereof, a lamp, a hood, a condenser, a negative holder, a bellows, and a lens slidably mounted in said plate, said negative holder having means of engagement on one side thereof with said bellows, or said hood.

1,327,753. ENGINE-STARTER. WILLIAM E. BURROWS and WILLIAM A. SPANGLER, St. Joseph, Mo. Filed June 10, 1919. Serial No. 303,096. 5 Claims. (Cl. 60—18.)

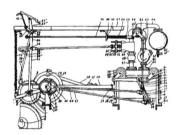

1. A rotatably mounted engine shaft; a drive gear secured on said shaft; a rotatably mounted starter shaft; mounting means in which said starter shaft is mounted; an engine starter whereby said starter shaft is rotated; a gear carried oscillatably mounted on said mounting means; a pinion secured on said starter shaft; an intermediate gear rotatably mounted in said gear carrier said intermediate gear being in engagement with said pinion; a spring for lifting the free end portion of said gear carrier; buck knee lowering means connected with said gear carrier whereby said spring is overcome and the free end portion of said gear carrier is manually lowered; yieldable holding means whereby said carrier is yieldably held in its lowered position; a pedal mounted on the upper end of said lowering means whereby the latter is manually operated for lowering said gear carrier; and buck knee moving means whereby the central portions of said buck knees are automatically moved for releasing said lowering means.

1,327,754. DOOR-HOLDER. CHARLES W. CADE, Bellevue, Pa., assignor to McKinney Manufacturing Company, Pittsburgh, Pa., a Corporation of Pennsylvania. Filed May 4, 1918. Serial No. 232,437. 2 Claims. (Cl. 292—265.)

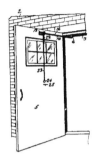

1. A door holder, comprising a rod mounted to swing horizontally on the door frame, a bracket on the door forming a guide for said rod, said rod having notches formed on its upper portion, its lower portion resting normally on the lower face of said guide, whereby said door may be opened normally to its fullest extent without interference due to said notches, and means for raising said rod and holding same in raised position with one of said notches in engagement with the upper face of said bracket.

1,327,755. DRAWER OR SHELF LINING. IDA SHERMAN COWLES, Waverly, Pa. Filed Mar. 15, 1918. Serial No. 222,600. 3 Claims. (Cl. 217—3.)

1. An adjustable lining for drawers or shelves composed of four rectangular sections which are counterparts in size, the first of which may have a plain underface and the second of which is provided with a strip of adhesive material along the inner longitudinal edge of its underface, the third with a strip of adhesive material along the inner transverse edge of its underface and the fourth with strips of adhesive material along both the inner longitudinal and inner transverse edges of its underface.

1,327,756. HOSIERY-DYEING MACHINE. HOWARD M. DUDLEY, Philadelphia, Pa. Filed June 22, 1918. Serial No. 241,314. 4 Claims. (Cl. 8—18.)

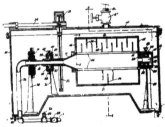

1. In a dyeing machine, in combination, a dyeing receptacle, two end plates connected by a series of spaced bars revoluble within the receptacle, a series of formiunous plates extending outwardly from the series of

bars and abutting upon the end plates, removable foraminous covers connecting the outer extremities of the outwardly extended plates forming a series of fabric chambers with the end plates, the series of bars and the outwardly extended plates, a series of bars extending into the fabric chambers from the series of spaced bars, a series of bars extending into the fabric chambers from the covers, means for revolving the series of fabric chambers, means for forcing a liquid through the fabric chambers and means for maintaining the fabric chambers beneath the liquid during its passage therethrough.

1,327,757. RUBBER TOOTHBRUSH. WILLIAM J. EGGERS, Brooklyn, N. Y. Filed Aug. 10, 1916. Serial No. 114,102. 1 Claim. (Cl. 15—52.)

A rubber tooth brush comprising an integral rubber handle, a unitary brush portion formed of bristles of rubber molded integral with a base vulcanized to the handle, part of said bristles being provided with channels extending through the base, a hollow metallic stiffening piece embedded in the handle extending beneath the base and communicating with the channels therein.

1,327,758. REFRACTORY MATERIAL. EDWARD D. FROHMAN, Pittsburgh, Pa. Filed Apr. 26, 1919. Serial No. 292,827. 3 Claims. (Cl. 106—10.)
1. A refractory material consisting of a mixture of finely divided dry fire clay, silicious material and sulfite pitch.

1,327,759. DEMOUNTABLE WHEEL-RIM. ABNER E. HENRY, Greensburg, Pa. Filed Apr. 21, 1919. Serial No. 291,511. 9 Claims. (Cl. 152—21.)

1. The combination, with the adjoining ends of a pair of rim sections, of a hinge having its leaves connected to the rim sections, the hinge rolls of the hinge being intermediate the adjoining ends of the rim sections, thereby hingedly uniting the rim sections, the intermediate parts of the hinge rolls being cut away, a sheet metal reinforcing bridging plate engaging the intermediate cut-away portion of the hinged rolls and being countersunk in the adjacent end portions of the rim sections, so as to reinforce the hinge, and means whereby one end of the plate may be secured to one of the leaves of the hinge.

1,327,760. BEET-TOPPER. ROBERT J. JOHNSON, Logan, Utah. Filed May 10, 1919. Serial No. 296,121. 14 Claims. (Cl. 55—107.)
1. The combination with a frame, of a carrier, means for mounting the carrier on the frame whereby it may move toward the beet tops, said carrier comprising angle plates, means for connecting the angle plates, whereby their vertical flanges may be spaced, a beet top splitting member in said space, and provided with slots, depth guides carried by the splitting member, means passing through said slots for connecting the depth guides to the splitting member, and a beet topping member carried by the rear of the splitting member and at right angles thereto.

---

13. The combination with a frame, of a carrier comprising angle plates, means for connecting the angle plates, whereby their vertical flanges may be spaced, a beet top splitting member in said space, means for swingingly

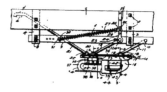

mounting said carrier on the frame, and a thrust and pull rod pivotally connected to the carrier and having detachable connection with the frame to prevent the carrier from moving too far forwardly and downwardly.

1,327,761. LINGERIE-CLASP. ABRAHAM KESTENMAN, Providence, R. I., assignor to Kestenman Bros. Mfg. Company, Providence, R. I., a Firm composed of Abraham Kestenman and Charles H. Kestenman. Filed Aug. 5, 1918. Serial No. 248,244. 4 Claims. (Cl. 24—259.)

2. In a lingerie-clasp for ladies' garments, the combination of two opposite jaw-members hinged together at one end, with the outer free end of the upper member formed with a hook adapted to snap over a loop on the corresponding end of the lower member, said loop being extended inwardly toward the hinge in a bowed spring formed integral with and overlying the lower member, the end of said spring opposite from the loop being reduced in width and joined to the lower member by lugs extending up across its opposite sides.

1,327,762. PENCIL-HOLDER. ERIC S. KINTSEL, Raton, N. Mex. Filed Feb. 13, 1919. Serial No. 276,805. 2 Claims. (Cl. 24—12.)

1. A point-protecting pencil holder comprising a relatively long and narrow frame formed with a ring at one end and with a guide element extending from the ring to the other end of the frame, a pencil engaging jaw

secured to said other end of the frame and extending therefrom through said ring, a tubular element formed with a constricted interior surface of a size and shape to fit around the converging part of a pencil inwardly of its projecting lead part and to leave a clear space around the latter, means movably securing said tubular element to said guide element for adjustment along the latter to compensate for varying lengths of pencils to be held thereby, and means to attach said frame to a support.

1,327,763. FUEL-OIL BURNER. CZESLAW KORZENIEW-SKI and STEPHEN CHOJNACKI, Cleveland, Ohio. Filed Sept. 7, 1918, Serial No. 253,044. Renewed Aug. 18, 1919. Serial No. 318,316. 2 Claims. (Cl. 158—65.)

2. The combination of a burner comprising a hollow head having a cap thereon with a chamber under the cap, a mixing tube leading to said chamber, a lateral burner located beside the mixing tube and communicating with said chamber, and a retort tube overlying the burner cap and extending downwardly beside the lateral burner and provided with an extension having a jet orifice directed toward said mixing tube.

1,327,764. FUEL-FEEDING APPARATUS. ANDREW LANE, Pittsburgh, Pa. Filed Feb. 24, 1919. Serial No. 278,967. 8 Claims. (Cl. 110—45.)

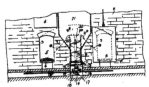

1. In fuel feeding apparatus for furnaces, the combination with a pair of grates, of a deflector between and elevated above the grates and independent thereof, and having a fuel passage formed therein, and means for delivering fuel from the upper end of said passage onto said deflector.

1,327,765. APPARATUS FOR BURNING SOLID FUEL. ANDREW LANZ, Pittsburgh, Pa. Filed Feb. 24, 1919. Serial No. 278,968. 5 Claims. (Cl. 110—36.)

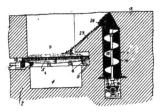

1. In solid fuel burning apparatus, the combination of a rotary grate, means for rotating same, a downwardly inclined deflector arranged to overhang an arc of the grate, and means for delivering the fuel to said deflector.

1,327,766. WRINGER. GEORGE W. LEWIS, Grinnell, Iowa, assignor to Lovell Manufacturing Company, Erie, Pa., a Corporation of Pennsylvania. Filed Sept. 21, 1916. Serial No. 121,379. 8 Claims. (Cl. 68—32.)

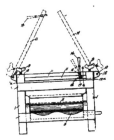

1. In a wringer, the combination of wringer rolls; a spring exerting pressure on the rolls; a frame in which the rolls are mounted comprising a screw exerting pressure on the spring; a cross bar in which the screw is mounted, said cross bar being pivotally secured at its ends to the frame and composed of parts separable intermediate the ends of the bar to release the springs; and detachable means normally holding the parts against separation.

1,327,767. VARIABLE-SPEED CLUTCH. FISHER H. LIPPINCOTT, Philadelphia, Pa. Filed Feb. 28, 1918. Serial No. 219,673. 8 Claims. (Cl. 192—11.)

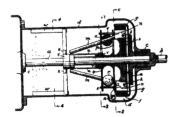

8. In a variable speed drive, the combination with a driving shaft and a driven shaft, of a friction drum turning with the driven shaft, a friction shoe turning with the driving shaft and movable radially thereof, a spring tending to retract the shoe from the drum, centrifugally acting means tending to move the shoe into driving relation with the drum, and manually controlled means to vary the power of the centrifugally acting means and thereby vary the degree of frictional engagement between the drum and shoe.

1,327,768. CLAMP FOR PLUMBERS' FORCE-PUMPS. ALBERT H. LOWE, Maplewood, Mo., assignor of one-half to Ross R. Maxwell, St. Louis, Mo. Filed Nov. 22, 1917. Serial No. 203,309. 6 Claims. (Cl. 4—1.)

1. The combination of a handle, a force cup having a flexible tubular extension, and a clamping member having

drawing means, said handle adapted to be engaged in said tubular extension, and secured to said tubular extension by said clamping member, and means provided by said clamping member comprising a pair of shoulders for engagement with the end of said tubular extension for preventing said handle from being driven through the end of said tubular extension.

1,327,769. APPARATUS FOR PREPARATION OF INERT GASES. EDOUARD ELIE MOLAS, Paris, France. Filed July 2, 1918. Serial No. 243,085. 3 Claims. (Cl. 60—29.)

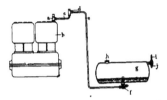

1. In combination with an internal combustion engine, an apparatus for preparing an inert gas from the burnt gases of said engine comprising a pipe, an adjustable intake valve connecting said pipe with the explosion chamber of said engine, a check valve inserted in said pipe and adapted to be actuated by the force of the explosion, said check valve being unaffected by the compression pressure in the engine, a storage tank containing a liquid having a basic character, and a cock connecting said pipe with said receptacle and adapted to discharge the gases beneath the level of the liquid in said tank.

1,327,770. ROOF-EDGING. JOSEPH C. NORTON, Cleveland, Ohio. Filed Mar. 26, 1919. Serial No. 285,347. 4 Claims. (Cl. 108—26.)

1. A roof-edging comprising the combination with a body portion of metal having two angularly related legs and bent to form a gravel-stop adjacent to the junction of such legs; of a strip of fabric covering the inner faces of said legs and extending between the fold of such gravel-stop.

1,327,771. DISPLAY AND VENDING DEVICE. CARLTON N. OGDEN, Houston, Tex. Filed May 5, 1919. Serial No. 294,824. 2 Claims. (Cl. 211—20.)

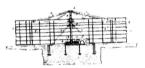

2. A device of the character described, including annular shelves, spaced apart, one above the other, and

fixed to a concentric vertical shaft and providing a clear space within the ring of shelving, an opening through the shelves to permit access to said space, a closure for said opening, and means for rotating said shaft and shelving.

1,327,772. BOOT OR SHOE. LOUIS PAGEAU, Montreal, Quebec, Canada. Filed Jan. 16, 1919. Serial No. 271,398. 1 Claim. (Cl. 36—3.)

A ventilated boot or shoe comprising a heel formed with a central, longitudinal recess which opens through its upper face, and with a plurality of lateral slots or holes communicating at their inner ends with said recess, a sole formed with a single, longitudinal opening which extends forwardly beyond the heel and the rear portion of which registers with the recess in said heel, and a strip of netting entirely covering the sole opening; substantially as described.

1,327,773. TRACTOR ATTACHMENT FOR AUTOMOBILES. WALTER C. PHILLIPS, Chicago, Ill., assignor to Guaranteed Tractors, Inc., Chicago, Ill., a Corporation of Illinois. Substitute for application Serial No. 197,822, filed Oct. 22, 1917. This application filed Apr. 5, 1919. Serial No. 287,738. 9 Claims. (Cl. 180—16.)

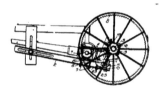

1. In a device for transforming an automobile into a tractor, the combination with a sub-frame, of means for attaching the sub-frame to the rear axle housing of the automobile, a standard at the rear of said sub-frame, a tractor axle clamp carried on said standard, and means the actuation of which positively moves said clamp vertically properly to adjust the tractor axle with respect to said sub-frame.

1,327,774. ELECTRIC WATER - HEATER. ALBERT EULGÉRE PLANTE, Montreal, Quebec, Canada, assignor of one-half to Benjamin Drolet, Montreal, Quebec, Canada. Filed June 2, 1919. Serial No. 301,350. 1 Claim. (Cl. 219—40.)

In an electric water heater, the combination of a vertical casing; upper and lower reversely-arranged, cup-shaped heads fitted on the corresponding ends of the casing and formed, respectively, with an outlet and an inlet for the water; a disk of insulating material seated in each head and co-acting with the same to define a water chamber in the head, each disk being provided on its outer face with a pair of spaced, concentric annular channels, and with a projecting, annular rib between said channels having a plurality of slots formed vertically through it; interfitted inner and outer tubular electrodes having their opposite ends fitting in the inner and outer channels in said disks and defining an elongated tubular water chamber between them, said slots providing communication between the two first-named chambers and the last-named chamber to permit the passage of the water through the

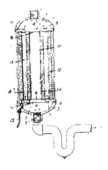

heater; and means for supplying current to said electrodes to heat the water during its passage.

1,327,775. BLOCKS. Benjamin N. Platt, Chicago, Ill. Filed June 17, 1918. Serial No. 240,289. 3 Claims. (Cl. 35—1.)

1. In a device of the class described, in combination, a plurality of blocks having individual characters thereon, said blocks having grooves in the corresponding edges thereof, standards coöperating with said grooves for supporting said blocks in selected arrangement, and means coöperating only with the bottoms of the blocks whereby said blocks may be arranged in tiers either in the same vertical plane or in a plurality of vertical planes.

1,327,776. TALKING-MACHINE. François Joseph Antonio Pratte, Montreal, Quebec, Canada, assignor to Alphonsine P. Pratte, Montreal, Quebec, Canada. Filed Jan. 16, 1919. Serial No. 271,470. 2 Claims. (Cl. 274— 2.)

1. In a talking machine, the combination of a tone arm; a plurality of amplifiers; and a controlling device intermediate the amplifiers and the tone arm and comprising a casing having a separate port in constant communication with each amplifier and with the tone arm, and a member movable within the casing having a passage individual to each amplifier and adapted to register with the corresponding amplifier port in the casing, all of said passages being registrable with the tone arm port in said casing, whereby said member may be moved into position to connect any selected amplifier with the tone arm.

1,327,777. CIRCUIT-INTERRUPTER. Karl C. Randall, Edgewood Park, Pa., assignor to Westinghouse Electric & Manufacturing Company, a Corporation of Pennsylvania. Filed Nov. 19, 1917. Serial No. 202,735. 7 Claims. (Cl. 175—294.)

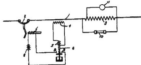

1. In an electric circuit, the combination with a circuit interrupter and an overload tripping device therefor, of a current-limiting device connected in circuit with the interrupter, and means for causing the current-limiting device to limit the current through the interrupter only when the load traversing the circuit exceeds the value for which the interrupter is intended.

1,327,778. COMBINED PACKAGE AND TRASH RECEPTACLE. Harry Reichman and Arthur R. Spangenberg, Cincinnati, Ohio. Filed July 15, 1918. Serial No. 244,912. 1 Claim. (Cl. 220—1.)

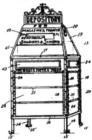

A combined trash and package receptacle having its outer walls adapted to the display of advertising matter thereon, said walls having edge plates spaced therefrom and containing grooves facing the outer surfaces of the walls, strips extending from one edge plate across the adjacent wall surface to the coöperating edge plate and reciprocally mounted in the spaces between the plates and their coöperating wall surface, and springs on the strips adapted to occupy the grooves of the plates to retain the strips in adjusted positions on advertising cards located on the wall surface.

1,327,779. OIL-BAFFLE FOR AUTOMOBILE-ENGINES. George A. Rendahl, Denver, Colo., assignor to Donald P. Hogan. Denver, Colo. Filed June 2, 1919. Serial No. 301,180. 10 Claims. (Cl. 184—11.)

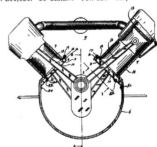

2. The combination with an internal combustion engine or motor of the V-type, of baffle plates detachably applied

to the engine block or frame between the inner extremities of the cylinders and the chamber of the crank case, the plates having attaching flanges offset toward the cylinder whereby the plates are offset inwardly from the cylinders.

1,327,780. COUNTER - FLANGING MACHINE. JEAN HENRY SCHARFFENBERG, Lynn, Mass., assignor to John Hammond Stewart, Lynn, Mass. Filed Apr. 14, 1916, Serial No. 91,067. Renewed May 26, 1919. Serial No. 299,895. 10 Claims. (Cl. 12—66.)

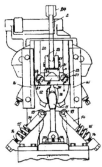

1. A counter flanging machine comprising complemental molding and gripping members adapted to hold a counter blank in molded form with its flange edge projecting, a traveler movable over such projecting edge, and a flange turner carried by said traveler and being freely movable with relation thereto in one direction, but rigidly restrained from relative motion in the opposite direction.

1,327,781. PROCESS OF EXTRACTING POTASSIUM FROM POTASH - BEARING SILICATE MINERALS. SAMUEL R. SCHOLES, Beaver, and RALPH F. BRENNER, Rochester, Pa., assignors to J. Howard Fry, Rochester, Pa. Filed May 10, 1917. Serial No. 167,694. 3 Claims. (Cl. 23—22.)

1. The process of extracting a potassium carbonate from a potassium bearing silicate which consists in finely dividing said silicate; adding a quantity of potassium carbonate sufficient to supply one equivalent of potassium oxid to each two equivalents of silicon dioxid present; melting the mixture thus produced to a glasslike mass; finely subdividing said glasslike mass; subjecting the finely divided glass like material thus obtained to the action of water while passing a gas containing carbon dioxid through the mixture; and continuing the latter operation until substantially the desired percentage of potassium carbonate has been dissolved out, substantially as described.

1,327,782. PROCESS OF OBTAINING COMBINED POTASSIUM FROM MINERALS. SAMUEL R. SCHOLES, Beaver, Pa., assignor to H. C. Fry Glass Company, Rochester, Pa., a Corporation of Pennsylvania. Filed Aug. 20, 1917. Serial No. 187,211. 5 Claims. (Cl. 23—22.)

1. The process of obtaining from the rock operated upon sufficient combined potassium to start a process of extracting said potassium from potassium bearing silicates, which consists in finely dividing said silicates; adding a sufficient quantity of a suitable sodium compound to the mass thus produced to form substantially one equivalent of sodium oxid for each two equivalents of silicon dioxid present; fusing the mixture thus produced; finely dividing the fused mixture; boiling the fused mixture in water while subjecting the same to the action of carbon dioxid;

continuing the treatment with carbon dioxid until a substantial portion of the combined potassium present has been dissolved from the rock material; recovering said potassium mixed with the combined sodium originally added; taking from the last named mixture a substantial portion of its combined sodium and potassium; returning the remaining portion of said combined sodium and potassium to a new cycle; and repeating said procedure until an amount of combined sodium equal to that originally added to the rock has been removed from the process, substantially as described.

1,327,783. AIR-PUMP. STEPHEN G. SKINNER, Chicago, Ill. Filed June 28, 1919. Serial No. 307,331. 5 Claims. (Cl. 230—27.)

5. An air pump comprising a cylinder, a piston adapted to be reciprocated in said cylinder, a base in which the lower end of said cylinder is secured, a bore in said base on one side of said cylinder, a foot piece in the form of a U-shaped bail of spring metal, having inturned ends engaging in said transverse bore, together with upper and lower horizontal shoulders formed on the sides of said base, providing between them a depression into which the legs of said U-shaped bail member snap when the bail is moved into a plane parallel with the bottom of the base.

1,327,784. SYSTEM OF CONTROL. GERALD F. SMITH, Braddock township, Allegheny county, Pa., assignor to Westinghouse Electric & Manufacturing Company, a Corporation of Pennsylvania. Filed Sept. 1, 1917. Serial No. 189,340. 9 Claims. (Cl. 172—179.)

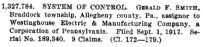

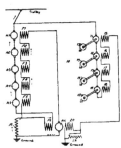

1. In a system of control, the combination with a supply circuit and a plurality of dynamo-electric machines severally having armatures and field windings, of a mechanical load, means for connecting one of said machines to excite the other field windings, and means responsive to the value of said mechanical load for cooperating to regulate the excitation of said exciting machine.

1,327,785. BURGLAR-ALARM. PETER H. SPETHMANN, New Effington, S. D. Filed Mar. 15, 1918. Serial No. 222,531. 2 Claims. (Cl. 116—44.)

2. In combination with a movable member, a rod supported for sliding movement and contacting with the

movable member to hold the same against movement, a spring engaged with the rod for urging the rod into contact with the movable member, a loop member carried by the rod and provided with a slot in the wall thereof, and

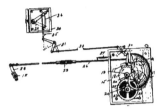

a rocking member disposed through the loop member and provided with a part extending within the slot, said slot permitting the rocking member to have partial movement independently of the loop member.

1,327,786. MEDICAL APPLIANCE. CHARLES H. STEPHAN, Springfield, Ohio. Filed Apr. 15, 1918. Serial No. 228,540. 4 Claims. (Cl. 174—89.)

1. A medical appliance comprising a hollow tubular portion, a hollow head fast thereto, a rubber cap covering said tubular portion and said head, a handle portion fast to the tubular portion and between which and the tubular portion the cap is held, and a handle having an extension passing through the handle portion, the tubular portion and the head, said handle being constructed to be screwed to said handle portion.

1,327,787. MOTOR-CONTROLLER. WILLIAM C. STEVENS, Milwaukee, Wis., assignor to The Cutler-Hammer Mfg. Co., Milwaukee, Wis., a Corporation of Wisconsin. Filed Sept. 6, 1917. Serial No. 189,937. 14 Claims. (Cl. 172—288.)

7. In combination, a motor, a main switch, an accelerating switch biased to accelerating position and electromagnetic means to move the latter switch away from accelerating position and the former switch to circuit closing position and then release said latter switch but subject to delay under given motor conditions.

1,327,788. FEELER MECHANISM FOR LOOMS. EDWARD S. STIMPSON, Hopedale, Mass., assignor to Draper Corporation, Hopedale, Mass., a Corporation of Maine. Filed May 31, 1919. Serial No. 300,952. 7 Claims. (Cl. 139—85.)

7. A feeler mechanism for looms having a side slipping feeler with a weft feeling tip, in combination with an auxiliary feeling finger mounted on the feeler forward of the weft feeler tip, said auxiliary feeling finger being adapted to be encountered by and slip laterally upon a smooth

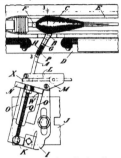

surface due to the impact thereof when the weft feeling tip does not make restraining contact with the weft.

1,327,789. SYSTEM OF CONTROL. NORMAN W. STORER, Pittsburgh, Pa., assignor to Westinghouse Electric & Manufacturing Company, a Corporation of Pennsylvania. Filed July 3, 1917. Serial No. 178,546. 10 Claims. (Cl. 172—179.)

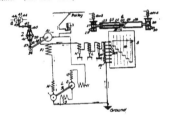

2. In a system of vehicle control, the combination with a dynamo-electric machine and a mechanical braking system, of means for electrically braking said machine, and means for automatically effecting the application of said braking system under predetermined high-speed conditions and releasing said application upon a predetermined decrease of speed.

1,327,790. IGNITION SYSTEM. HORACE V. S. TAYLOR, Pittsburgh, Pa., assignor to Westinghouse Electric and Manufacturing Company, a Corporation of Pennsylvania. Filed Jan. 5, 1916. Serial No. 70,421. 7 Claims. (Cl. 123—148.)

1. In an electrical system, the combination with a circuit comprising a battery and a switch, of means com-

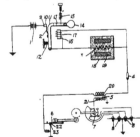

prising an electromagnet having a winding permanently in circuit with said switch for effecting the opening of said switch and permanently opening said switch when current traverses said circuit continuously for a predetermined period.

1,327,791. UNIVERSAL JOINT. WILLIAM H. THIEMER, Cleveland, Ohio, assignor to The Peters Machine and Manufacturing Company, Cleveland, Ohio, a Corporation of Ohio. Filed May 9, 1919. Serial No. 295,814. 5 Claims. (Cl. 64—102.)

1. In a universal joint, the combination of a hub having at each end thereof a seat for the stud of a bearing block, each seat comprising a member rigid with the hub and a member detachably connected to the former member, the said members when connected providing a bore for such stud, each member having a pair of spaced seats separated by an interposed shoulder, and means for connecting said members.

1,327,792. SPOT-WELDING APPARATUS. FRANK THORNTON, Jr., Mansfield, Ohio, assignor to Westinghouse Electric & Manufacturing Company, a Corporation of Pennsylvania. Filed Apr. 18, 1919. Serial No. 290,941. 5 Claims. (Cl. 219—4.)

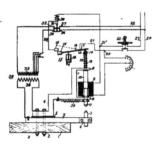

1. A spot-welding apparatus comprising a plurality of electrode members, electro-magnetic means for forcing the members into engagement with interposed work, and an automatically actuated circuit-closer for closing a heating circuit including the electrode members.

1,327,793. AUTOMOBILE PUMP ATTACHMENT. WALTER D. VOOTS, Waunakee, Wis. Filed Dec. 2, 1918. Serial No. 265,034. 1 Claim. (Cl. 74—5.)

In a pump attachment of the character specified, the combination of a hub cap having longitudinal seats at opposite sides, an arm having jaws projecting laterally therefrom and embracing the sides of the hub cap and

fitted in the seats thereof, and means for securing said jaws to the hub cap in the required adjusted position.

1,327,794. TIRE. FRANK L. WADHAM, Detroit, Mich. Filed Oct. 15, 1917. Serial No. 196,628. 1 Claim. (Cl. 152—5.)

The combination of an outer tire casing, sections of hose and tubing of equal length and of diameters to telescope one another and provide a concentric arrangement of said hose and tubing in said outer tire casing with a bore centrally of said hose and tubing having a diameter less than a radial thickness of the assembled hose and tubing, and the sections of said hose and tubing having the joints thereof in staggered relation, and a core in the bore of said hose and tubing made of a single length of tubing slitted throughout its length and spirally wound so as to practically fill the bore.

1,327,795. SYSTEM OF CONTROL. CHARLES C. WHITTAKER, Wilkinsburg, Pa., assignor to Westinghouse Electric & Manufacturing Company, a Corporation of Pennsylvania. Filed June 19, 1917. Serial No. 175,594. 11 Claims. (Cl. 171—225.)

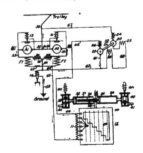

1. In a system of control, the combination with a plurality of dynamo-electric machines associated with a common load, of single means for simultaneously regulating the operation thereof, means dependent upon a material departure in the speed of either machine from normal for actuating said single regulating means to weaken the machine excitation, whereby further speed departures under the existing operating conditions are prevented.

1,327,796. STOVE. JAMES R. WOTHERSPOON, Philadelphia, Pa., and FRANK E. COATSWORTH, Lincoln, Nebr. Filed Dec. 5, 1916. Serial No. 135,128. 2 Claims. (Cl. 236—16.)

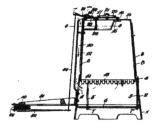

1. A stove provided with a passageway, one end of said passageway being situated adjacent to the top of the stove and the other end of the said passageway communicating with the interior of the lower portion of the stove and the said stove being provided with a check draft opening in its top, said opening being situated adjacent to the open end of said passageway adjacent the top of the stove, covers for opening and closing the check draft opening and the said passageway, said covers being rigidly connected with each other and the said covers being provided with pivot lugs upon the opposite edges thereof, supporting seats for said pivot lugs, retaining means for retaining the said pivot lugs in their seats and automatically acting means for actuating the said covers to alternately open and close the said passageway and said opening, substantially as described.

1,327,797. RADIATOR. CLARENCE S. ANDERSON, Lake Geneva, Wis. Filed May 9, 1918. Serial No. 233,521. 1 Claim. (Cl. 257—129.)

A radiator tube, comprising closely related companion strips, each strip having portions at regular intervals bent outwardly to form hollow ribs which project laterally at a right angle and which incline in the direction of the width of the strip and tube, the ribs on one side of the tube inclining in an opposite direction to the ribs on the other side of the tube, and closing strips secured between and connecting the edges of the tube strips, each closing strip being doubled upon itself and having parts of the folded portions cut and bent laterally in opposite directions to close the ends of the hollow ribs.

1,327,798. BELT-FASTENER. FRIDOLF F. BACKSTROM, Chicago, Ill., assignor to Western Felt Works, Chicago, Ill., a Corporation of West Virginia. Filed July 1, 1919. Serial No. 308,029. 2 Claims. (Cl. 24—33.)

1. A belt-fastener comprising an arcuate central portion adapted to overlie the meeting ends of a belt and provided with means flanking said meeting ends for permanent attachment to the belt, end portions hingedly and removably secured to said central portion, and means for securing said end portions to the belt.

1,327,799. WORK-HOLDER FOR METAL-WORKING MACHINES. HERBERT G. BEEDE, Pawtucket, R. I. Filed Mar. 9, 1918. Serial No. 221,424. 7 Claims (Cl. 90—60.)

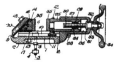

1. A vise adapted to be used as a flat vise or V-vise comprising a base, jaw-moving means, a movable jaw adapted to be moved by said means suitably guided on the base, and a fixed jaw member opposing the movable jaw member and provided with a plurality of faces for attachment exchangeably to said base, whereby to present a vertical or a sloping face toward said movable jaw member, and means adapted to attach said fixed jaw member to said base in any of said positions.

1,327,800. COMPENSATING - PYROMETER SYSTEM AND APPARATUS. HENRY EARL BEIGHLEE, Cleveland, Ohio, assignor, by mesne assignments, to The Cleveland Instrument Company, Cleveland, Ohio, a Corporation of Ohio. Filed May 10, 1912. Serial No. 696,521. 16 Claims. (Cl. 73—32.)

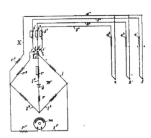

1. In apparatus of the class described, the combination with a thermo-electric couple, of an associated conductive member having a high temperature coefficient, a source of current controllable thereby, and an electrical measuring instrument adapted to be connected in circuit therewith, substantially as set forth.

1,327,801. SCRAPER-RING FOR SCRAPING OIL FROM CYLINDERS, PISTON-RODS, OR THE LIKE. HANS HENRIK BLACHE, Copenhagen, Denmark. Filed Sept. 6, 1918. Serial No. 252,982. 2 Claims. (Cl. 286—18.)

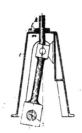

2. A scraper ring split radially to form a plurality of sections, and an annular spring encircling said ring and bearing against the outer face thereof so as to force said sections radially inward; said scraper ring having a portion of the face that confronts the surface to be scraped cut away to form a closed, circumferential recess, the bottom wall of which is substantially coaxial with the ring and the inner wall of which is substantially perpendicular to said bottom wall and is disposed near the median plane of the ring; the portion of the said recessed face of the ring above said inner wall having a gradually decreasing diameter from its inner to its outer edge, thereby producing a sharpened scraping step or shoulder which extends entirely around the ring; said spring being so located with relation to said scraping shoulder as to press the edge thereof against the surface to be scraped.

1,327,802. METHOD AND APPARATUS FOR THE MANUFACTURE OF TIRES. JOSEPH A. BOWERMAN, Chicopee Falls, Mass., assignor to The Fiske Rubber Company, Chicopee Falls, Mass., a Corporation of Massachusetts. Filed Apr. 9, 1919. Serial No. 288,820. 5 Claims. (Cl. 154—14.)

1. A spacing member for making tires having a spheroidal depression in one surface thereof.

1,327,803. PUMP-THAWING MEANS. FRANK C. BROKISH, Dodgeville, Wis. Filed Apr. 15, 1918. Serial No. 228,719. 1 Claim. (Cl. 137—72.)

In a pump, the combination with the barrel, and the piston rod rising through it to the operating mechanism; of a cylindrical casing appreciably larger than the barrel and having an internal partition through which the upper end of such barrel is screwed, the casing having a spout, and an opening in its wall immediately below the parti-

tion, a plate curved to fit against the casing and of a size to close over its opening, and an arm rising from the

plate and pivoted to said casing so as to allow the plate to be moved to expose said opening.

1,327,804. ELECTRICAL COMB. JAMES M. BROOKS, Washington, D. C. Filed Aug. 25, 1919. Serial No. 319,530. 6 Claims. (Cl. 219—21.)

3. A comb comprising a hollow body substantially flat and open at one side and curved at its opposite side, said sides converging toward the front of the body, the back of said body extending on an arc of curvature continuous with the curved side of the body and forming therewith an ironing surface, teeth projecting from the front of the body, electrical heating means within the hollow body, and a substantially flat plate detachably secured to and closing the open side of the body.

1,327,805. AUTOMATIC TELEPHONE - EXCHANGE. ALBERT M. BULLARD, New York, N. Y., assignor, by mesne assignments, to Western Electric Company, Incorporated, a Corporation of New York. Filed Mar. 12, 1906. Serial No. 305,548. 30 Claims. (Cl. 179—18.)

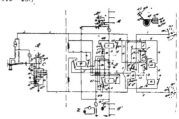

1. In an automatic telephone exchange, the combination with a number of telephone lines extending from substations to a central office, of hundreds selectors at the central office, each having contacts representing the

hundreds digits terminals of said lines, a distributer for each line at the central office adapted to select an idle hundreds selector, means at the calling station for operating said selector to connect said line with the hundreds digit terminal of the called line, a number of groups of tens-and-units selectors, the selectors of each group having contacts representing the tens-and-units digits associated with a given hundreds digit, a finder associated with said hundreds selector adapted to connect said hundreds digit terminal with an idle tens-and-units selector having its associated tens-and-units digit terminals thereon, means for operating said distributer and finder, and means at the calling station for operating said idle tens-and-units selector to complete the connection of the calling line with the desired line.

1,327,806. DEPOSITING-MACHINE. CLAUDE W. BUNDE, Chicago, Ill., assignor to National Candy Company, Chicago, Ill., a Corporation of New Jersey. Filed May 17, 1919. Serial No. 297,726. 14 Claims. (Cl. 107—17.)

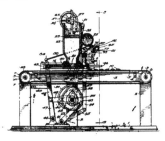

4. A depositing machine having a mold provided with an orifice open top and bottom, an ejector adapted to descend into the filled mold for discharging the work piece therefrom, and a duct leading down through the ejector and adapted to supply a lubricating fluid to the acting surface of the ejector approximately concentrically therewith.

1,327,807. TOOTHBRUSH. PAUL B. BURLEIGH, Omaha, Nebr. Filed Oct. 26, 1918. Serial No. 259,820. 3 Claims. (Cl. 15—39.)

1. The combination with a pliable tooth brush head, provided with brush bristles and having a portion extending at an obtuse angle to the rear portion of the head, of resilient means embedded in the head and corresponding in shape thereto and tapering correspondingly with the portion that extends at an obtuse angle, thereby affording resiliency for said portion, whereby said portion may yield when urging the bristles toward their work, a handle for the head, and means for uniting the head and the handle, said means being so positioned with relation to the rear portion of the embedded means, as to insure strength and rigidity at the point of connection of the uniting means and the head.

1,327,808. HINGE FOR TRESTLES AND THE LIKE. ROBERT G. CHESHIRE, Birmingham, England. Filed June 5, 1918. Serial No. 238,375. 3 Claims. (Cl. 228—68.)
1. A hinge for trestles and the like comprising two members of substantially the same configuration having

overlapping broad cheek portions and partially overlapping integral arm portions, a hinge pivot connecting

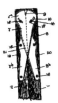

said members, an arcuate slot in each of said members, and a pin projecting from each of said members from opposite directions into the arcuate slot of the other member.

1,327,809. BOTTLE-CLOSURE. AUGUSTE DACCORD, New York, N. Y. Filed Mar. 28, 1918. Serial No. 225,227. 1 Claim. (Cl. 215—14.)

The combination with a bottle or similar vessel having a relatively wide neck, a proportionately large mouth, and an internal abutment therebetween, of a slightly conical convexo-concave disk adapted to be seated at its outer edge upon said abutment and forms a tight closure thereon with its apex below the top of the bottle or vessel, said disk admitting of inversion by pressure upon its said apex, being thereby disengaged from its seat on the abutment and positioned for ejection from the bottle or vessel by a thrust in a substantially lateral direction.

1,327,810. SELF-PROPELLING AERIAL BOMB. ARCHIE DI GRAZIA and RAY BIAGINI, Charleroi, Pa. Filed June 3, 1918. Serial No. 237,874. 6 Claims. (Cl. 244—1.)

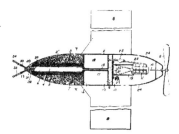

1. An aerial bomb consisting of an inclosing shell having a main explosive charge, a primer, and a barbed firing pin therefor at one end, and a propeller, an engine geared therewith, and an engine impairing explosive charge at the other end, and a time fuse for said explosive charge.

1,327,811. STABILIZER. GEORGE W. DUNHAM, Detroit, Mich., assignor to Graham Brothers, Evansville, Ind., a Corporation of Indiana. Filed Mar. 8, 1916. Serial No. 82,994. 3 Claims. (Cl. 180—70.)

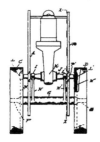

1. The combination with drive wheels, of a frame, an axle housing, a jack-shaft extending transversely of said frame and having means at its opposite ends for driving said wheels, means upon said frame for tying said jack-shaft thereto, and a stabilizer comprising rigid arms fixed to said axle housing, said arms having bearings fixed in relation to the jack-shaft.

1,327,812. SECTIONAL SHOE FOR THE RUNNER-VANES OF CENTRIFUGAL PUMPS. ALFRED H. EXTON, Chicago Heights, Ill., assignor to American Manganese Steel Company, Augusta, Me., a Corporation of Maine. Filed June 6, 1919. Serial No. 302,118. 5 Claims. (Cl. 253—194.)

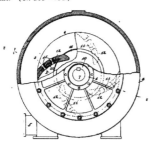

1. A wearing shoe for a centrifugal pump runner vane, comprising a plurality of longitudinally curved coplanar sections and means whereby said sections may be removably secured to said vane.

1,327,813. DEVICE FOR IGNITING GAS-JETS. MARTIN FISCHER, Zurich, Switzerland. Filed July 26, 1919. Serial No. 313,608. 4 Claims. (Cl. 67—6.1.)

1. A device for igniting a jet of gas comprising in combination a handle a shaft rotatably mounted on said handle a serrated disk loosely mounted on the shaft, a piece of pyrophorous metal, a spring pressing said piece against said disk, a spring loosely surrounding said rotatable shaft one end thereof being attached to the said disk, a second spring, one end of said second spring being fixed to said rotatable shaft and the other end on the handle, an arm fixed to said rotatable shaft running across the handle substantially as described.

1,327,814. METHOD OF AND APPARATUS FOR SPOT-WELDING. CHARLES LE G. FORTESCUE, Pittsburgh, Pa., assignor to Westinghouse Electric and Manufacturing Company, a Corporation of Pennsylvania. Filed Mar. 7, 1919. Serial No. 281,168. 10 Claims. (Cl. 219—10.)

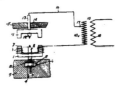

1. An electro-percussive welder comprising a plurality of electrode members and means tending to automatically force the members into engagement.

1,327,815. VENEER-PRESS. HARRY GRANT FRANCIS, Rushville, Ind. Filed Oct. 22, 1918. Serial No. 259,291. 1 Claim. (Cl. 144—281.)

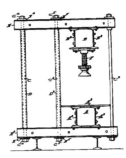

Two or more veneer presses adapted to either conjoint or individual use, each comprising a base, a head frame, and two sets of combined columns and ties capable of sustaining both compression and tension strains arranged on one side of the longitudinal center line of the base and supporting the head frame in cantaliver fashion, pressure means carried by the cantaliver portion of the head frame and tension ties connecting the ends of the cantaliver portion to the base, but removable so that if two presses be placed end to end there will be no obstruction to the moving of long work laterally beneath the pressure devices.

1,327,816. REPEATING DEVICE FOR TALKING-MACHINES. ALEXANDER FRASER, Renfrew, Ontario, Canada. Filed Oct. 28, 1918. Serial No. 259,991. 4 Claims. (Cl. 274—15.)

1. In a talking machine and in combination, a shaft, a swinging pivoted tone arm, a pivoted lever, feeding mechanism between the lever and the shaft from which the lever is adapted to be disengaged, a crank carried on the shaft, a pin thereon, a lever 42 adapted to be engaged by the pin, a tappet member carried by the tone arm carry-

ing lever adapted to engage the free end of the last mentioned lever and carrying the same laterally into position to be engaged by the tappet pin, means for connecting the

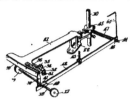

opposite end of the lever to the tone arm, and means whereby the swing of the lever when engaged by the tappet pin is caused to raise the tone arm carrying lever.

1,327,817. IMPACT - MACHINE. WERNER GERHARD, Chicago, Ill. Filed Aug. 14, 1917. Serial No. 186,141. 16 Claims. (Cl. 78—28.)

1. A device of the class described comprising an impact member ; and means for imparting initial operative motion to said member in the direction of the impact and then releasing it to complete its operative stroke, substantially as described.

1,327,818. SIGNALING DEVICE. IRVIN W. GRUHL, Los Angeles, Calif. Filed Feb. 11, 1918. Serial No. 216,625. 4 Claims. (Cl. 177—329.)

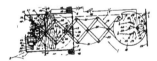

1. In combination, a motor car provided with a recess at each side of the body thereof, a lever frame adapted to fold into said recess, pairs of electro-magnets mounted within said recess, armatures operatably positioned between the magnets of said pairs and connected with the two terminal levers of the frame, said magnets being adapted to attract the armatures to thus extend and retract the frame.

1,327,819. SYSTEM OF CONTROL. RUDOLF E. HELLMUND, Pittsburgh, Pa., assignor to Westinghouse Electric and Manufacturing Company, a Corporation of Pennsylvania. Filed Dec. 29, 1915. Serial No. 69,187. 17 Claims. (Cl. 171—312.)
1. In a system of control, the combination with a supply circuit, of a plurality of dynamo-electric machines

severally having armatures and field-magnet windings, means for connecting said armatures to intermediate

points of the respective field windings and for connecting a plurality of sets of corresponding points in said field windings.

1,327,820. DYNAMO-ELECTRIC MACHINE. RUDOLF E. HELLMUND, Pittsburgh, Pa., assignor to Westinghouse Electric and Manufacturing Company, a Corporation of Pennsylvania. Filed Jan. 10, 1916. Serial No. 71,199. 3 Claims. (Cl. 171—228.)

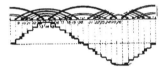

1. A stator member for a dynamo-electric machine of the compensated commutator type provided with a plurality of slots the spacing of which is materially less in each commutating zone than midway between the zones, and distributed exciting and cross-field windings in said slots, some of the cross-field-winding conductors in each commutating zone being located in slots between slots containing exciting-field-winding conductors.

1,327,821. DYNAMO-ELECTRIC MACHINE. RUDOLF E. HELLMUND, Swissvale, Pa., assignor to Westinghouse Electric & Manufacturing Company, a Corporation of Pennsylvania. Filed Dec. 14, 1916. Serial No. 136,893. 9 Claims. (Cl. 171—252.)

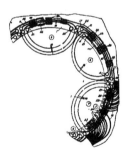

1. In a dynamo-electric machine, the combination with a core, of a winding for said core comprising a plurality of coil groups, a plurality of strap connectors for said groups disposed on one side of said core, each connector being mechanically connected to three coils for rigidly grouping the coils together, and leads for said winding disposed upon the opposite side of said core.

1,327,822. SYSTEM OF CONTROL. RUDOLF E. HELL-MUND, Swissvale, Pa., assignor to Westinghouse Electric and Manufacturing Company, a Corporation of Pennsylvania. Filed Jan. 16, 1917. Serial No. 142,644. 16 Claims. (Cl. 172—179.)

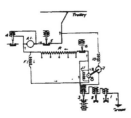

1. In a system of control, the combination with an electrical-braking dynamo-electric machine, of an additional braking system, and means dependent upon a relatively high value of regenerated current for rendering said braking system operative.

1,327,823. SYSTEM OF CONTROL. RUDOLF E. HELL-MUND, Swissvale, Pa., assignor to Westinghouse Electric and Manufacturing Company, a Corporation of Pennsylvania. Filed Jan. 16, 1917. Serial No. 142,645. 17 Claims. (Cl. 188—4.)

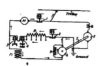

1. In a system of vehicle control, the combination with an electrically braking dynamo-electric machine, of other braking means, control means for adjusting the initial braking effect of said braking means during vehicle operation, means for rendering said braking means operative under predetermined conditions, and means for subsequently causing the cessation of the electrical braking action.

1,327,824. SHEET, BLANKET, OR THE LIKE. NELLIE GARDNER HOLLAND, Boston, Mass. Filed Dec. 12, 1918. Serial No. 266,476. 3 Claims. (Cl. 5—8.)

1. A sheet, blanket or the like having in either end a folded portion formed of an end portion of the sheet folded over transversely on itself and adapted to be maintained in the same flat, parallel plane as the body of the said sheet and when in its inoperative position in contact therewith throughout its entire length, the folded portion thus formed being adapted to be held in position by securing its sides to the body portion, and free lateral portions extending from and the entire length of the sides of the said sheet.

1,327,825. CIRCUIT - INTERRUPTER. FREDERICK B. HOLT, Antrobus, near Northwich, England, assignor to Westinghouse Electric and Manufacturing Company, a Corporation of Pennsylvania. Filed Feb. 21, 1916. Serial No. 79,567. 8 Claims. (Cl. 200—166.)

1. In a circuit interrupter, the combination with a movable contact member, of a coöperating stationary contact-terminal member of substantially U-shape having a laterally-extended base contact portion.

1,327,826. APPARATUS FOR MAKING STRAND FABRIC. WILLIAM JAMESON, Springfield, Mass., assignor to The Fiske Rubber Company, Chicopee Falls, Mass., a Corporation of Massachusetts. Filed Dec. 28, 1918. Serial No. 268,633. 4 Claims. (Cl. 154—1.)

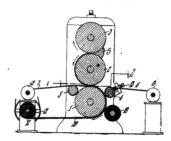

1. In an apparatus of the character indicated, in combination, a series of coöperating rolls, certain of said rolls being arranged to produce a sheet and certain of said rolls being arranged to receive and pass said sheet therebetween, means to feed a series of strands between one of said latter named rolls and said sheet, means to feed a second series of strands to the other side of said sheet in staggered relation to the first named strands, and means to vary the pressure between said sheet-producing rolls; substantially as described.

1,327,827. FLEXIBLE DRAFT CONNECTION. PEYTON R. JANNEY, Detroit, Mich. Filed May 25, 1918. Serial No. 236,504. 10 Claims. (Cl. 213—67.)

5. A draft appliance comprising a retaining member, a slidable member held by said retaining member, a connecting rod fixedly carried by said slidable member, a spheroidal bearing member carried by said connecting rod, a draw bar loosely carried by said connecting rod and engaging said bearing member, and means carried by said retaining member for limiting the forward movement of said slidable member.

1,327,828. CULTIVATOR. PEYTON R. JANNEY, Detroit, Mich. Filed Mar. 1, 1917, Serial No. 151,805. Renewed Sept. 16, 1919. Serial No. 324,222. 5 Claims. (Cl. 97—67.)

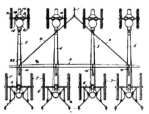

1. The combination with a common draw bar of a plurality of wheeled implement units, a forwardly extending tongue for each unit, a wheeled steering structure swivelly mounted near the forward end of each tongue, control means for steering each of said wheeled steering structures, and a coupling member connected to said tongue at a point to the rear of said wheeled steering structure and connected to said draw bar and adapted to permit movement of said tongue relative to said draw bar.

1,327,829. DETACHABLE STEERING DEVICE. PEYTON R. JANNEY, Detroit, Mich. Filed Oct. 20, 1917, Serial No. 197,603. Renewed Oct. 7, 1919. Serial No. 329,082. 8 Claims. (Cl. 280—97.)

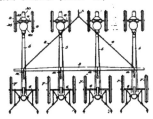

1. The combination with a wheeled implement and a tongue therefor, of a support and control for the forward end of the tongue comprising a wheeled structure, means for swively mounting said structure upon the tongue, a gear carried by said structure, a pinion engaging said gear, a control sheave coöperating with said pinion, and a flexible connection upon said control sheave and extending rearwardly to the operator upon the implement.

1,327,830. MACHINE FOR GRINDING EDGES OF GLASSWARE. ALBERT BREAKENRIDGE KNIGHT, Fairmont, W. Va. Filed Apr. 9, 1919. Serial No. 288,680. 5 Claims. (Cl. 51—11.)

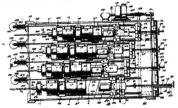

1. In apparatus for grinding glassware, a support, means connected therewith for holding and rotating a grinding element, a carriage connected with the support for movement toward and away from the grinding element, a chuck connected with the carriage, a pivoted lever, means effecting a loose connection between the pivoted lever and the carriage, means including a weight to move the carriage toward the grinding element, a cam to engage the pivoted lever, a lock rod connected with the carriage and provided with a stop shoulder, and a latch adapted to be shifted to a position in the path of travel of the stop shoulder.

1,327,831. DRAIN CUT-OFF. LENARD LITTLE, Gainesville, Ga. Filed Jan. 25, 1919. Serial No. 273,130. 3 Claims. (Cl. 137—79.)

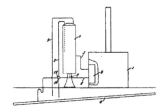

3. In a device of the class described, a heater; a tank; a connection between the heater and the tank; an outlet for the heater having a branch leading to the tank; an inlet for the tank; a valve casing common to the outlet and the inlet; and a valve journaled in the casing, the valve having a main port and an auxiliary port communicating with the main port, the auxiliary port communicating with the upper part of the inlet when the main port forms part of the outlet, the valve being rotatable to a position in which the main port forms part of the inlet and the auxiliary port is closed by a portion of the casing, or to a position in which the main port forms part of the inlet and the auxiliary port communicates with the outlet in the direction of the tank.

1,327,832. GEARING FOR ELECTRICAL MEASURING INSTRUMENTS. BERT G. LA BAR, Turtle Creek, Pa., assignor to Westinghouse Electric and Manufacturing Company, a Corporation of Pennsylvania. Filed Aug. 9, 1916. Serial No. 113,904. 6 Claims. (Cl. 74—58.)

1. In a two-speed gear device, the combination with a driving member and two driven members, of an oscillatory member, a worm screw mounted on the said oscillatory member and adapted to engage the said driven members, and a loosely mounted worm screw on the said oscillatory member operatively connected to the driving member and adapted to be resiliently held in a central position.

1,327,833. AIR - PUMP. JOSEPH LAFRANCE, Montreal, Quebec, Canada, assignor of one-half to Alexandre Chagnon, Montreal, Quebec, Canada. Filed Mar. 1, 1919. Serial No. 280,184. 3 Claims. (Cl. 230—27.)

1. An air pump comprising a frame, two cylinders disposed in longitudinal relation to one another secured to

said frame, a piston in each of said cylinders, a piston rod connecting said pistons, said piston rod having an air passage therethrough, an air tube connected to said piston

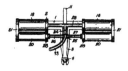

rod, a lever for operating said piston rod, and means on said frame whereby the pump may be rigidly secured to any convenient part of an automobile or the like; substantially as described.

1,327,834. SHEAF-LOADER. LESLIE R. LONG, Tipton, Iowa. Filed Dec. 28, 1917. Serial No. 209,253. 26 Claims. (Cl. 214—80.)

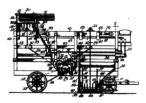

1. In a device of the class described, the combination of a pair of bundle receiving and discharging arms secured to and operable by the movement of a vehicle, each of said arms having means for raising said arms, the means of one arm being coöperatively connected with the means of the other arm to control the lowering of one of the arms when the other is raised and means permitting one arm to be raised and lowered independently of the other.

1,327,835. APPARATUS FOR TREATMENT OF OIL EMULSIONS. CHARLES W. McKIBBEN, Houston, Tex. Filed Dec. 18, 1918. Serial No. 267,287. 3 Claims. (Cl. 196—1.)

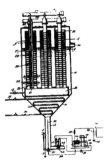

2. A device of the character described comprising a tank; two concentric vertically disposed pipes in the tank; a series of spaced apart disks between the pipes, alternate disks having openings near their axes and the intermediate disks having openings near their peripheries to provide a tortuous path for an emulsion through the outer vertical pipe to precipitate the water; and a con-

nection between the inner pipe and a suitable source of heat to raise the temperature of the liquid while passing through the outer pipe.

1,327,836. NUT-LOCKING DEVICE. ROBERT L. MARTIN, Thomas, W. Va. Filed Sept. 27, 1919. Serial No. 326,804. 3 Claims. (Cl. 151—18.)

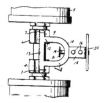

1. A locking device for a peripherally grooved nut comprising a resilient, U-shaped member having its free ends engaged with the peripherally grooved nut, and means carried by said U-shaped member for disengaging said ends from the nut.

1,327,837. ELECTRICAL INDICATOR. FREDERICK A. MUSCHENHEIM and FREDERICK W. BLASDALE, New York, N. Y. Filed Jan. 12, 1918. Serial No. 211,502. 8 Claims. (Cl. 177—339.)

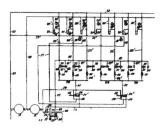

1. In a signaling system, a source of electricity, a plurality of circuits connected therewith, and having a portion in common, each of the separate portions of said circuits containing a gap, and the common portion also containing a gap and including a relay, individual signals controlled by the separate portions of said circuits, a circuit connected with said source of electricity and including a gap controlled by said relay, a group signal controlled by the last named circuit, a permanently operating circuit-closer for periodically opening and closing the gap in the common portion of the first named circuits, and another circuit-closer under the operator's control, for closing the gap in one of the separate portions of said circuits and causing the operation of the corresponding individual signal.

1,327,838. TESTING DEVICE FOR DETERMINING THE VISCOSITY OF RUBBER. RALPH B. NAYLOR, Springfield, Mass., assignor to The Fisk Rubber Company, Chicopee Falls, Mass., a Corporation of Massachusetts. Filed Feb. 5, 1919. Serial No. 275,154. 6 Claims. (Cl. 265—11.)

1. In a testing device of the class described, opposing gripping members for holding a test piece of rubber, and adapted for relative rotation about an axis perpendicular to the general plane of their gripping surfaces, means for

causing a known pressure between the members, means for causing a known torsion between the members, and means

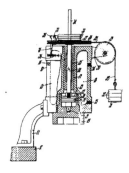

for indicating the resulting amount of relative rotation between the members.

1,327,839. LAST - THIMBLE. WILLIAM H. NEEDHAM, Worcester, Mass., assignor to Boston Pressed Metal Co., Worcester, Mass., a Corporation of Maine. Filed Jan. 21, 1919. Serial No. 272,346. 4 Claims. (Cl. 12—139.)

2. A last thimble having a cylindrical casing with a thickened end portion, said end portion being concaved to form an inwardly arched bottom for said thimble.

1,327,840. MUSIC-TYPEWRITER. CHARLES NORTHER, Turin, Italy, assignor to Charles Noerther & Cie., Turin, Italy. Filed May 17, 1916. Serial No. 98,043. 2 Claims. (Cl. 197—8.)

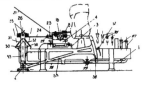

1. The combination with a typewriter having a movable carriage mounted thereupon, an auxiliary platen holding carriage slidably mounted upon said movable carriage, a pair of swinging arms, inclined walls carried by said arms, levers adapted to engage said walls for swinging said arms and means for connecting said arms to said auxiliary carriage substantially as and for the purpose specified.

1,327,841. TIRE-VULCANIZING DEVICE. FRED BROWN PFEIFFER, Akron, Ohio. Filed May 9, 1918. Serial No. 233,496. 1 Claim. (Cl. 18—38.)

In a device of the class described, an annular mold, a flexible hollow annular casing disposed within the mold, the casing being trough-shaped in cross section to receive a tire, and being made partly of metal to conduct

heat; means for supplying a fluid under pressure to the interior of the casing, and means for heating the fluid prior to its introduction into the casing.

1,327,842. HARD-CENTER CROSSING-FROG. CHARLES A. PSILANDER, Easton, Pa., assignor to William Wharton, Jr., & Co., Easton, Pa., a Corporation of Pennsylvania. Filed Sept. 3, 1919. Serial No. 321,405. 5 Claims. (Cl. 246—460.)

1. In a track structure, a center having a driving fit, and means for ejecting it with fluid pressure.

1,327,843. REINFORCED TREAD FOR SPRING-WHEELS. STEVE PYTLEWSKI, Minneapolis, Minn. Filed Apr. 11, 1919. Serial No. 289,353. 5 Claims. (Cl. 152—8.)

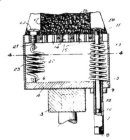

5. In a tire, the combination with a rigid annular rim, and a flexible tread, of a metallic mat disposed on the inner side of said tread, securing elements having enlarged heads extending through said tread, plungers extending through the mat engaged with said tread, said plungers being movably mounted in said securing elements, springs surrounding said plungers and yieldably holding said mat and said rim in spaced relation, and coiled retractile springs for limiting the outward movement of said mat and tread relative to the rim.

1,327,844. CONNECTOR-CLIP. GEORGE A. SCHAEFER, Chicago, Ill. Filed Feb. 11, 1918. Serial No. 216,595. 6 Claims. (Cl. 200—166.)

3. A connector clip comprising in combination, a one piece jaw of strip metal, said jaw having end portions conformed to engage an electrical conductor between them and a flat middle portion in a plane substantially at right angles to the planes of said end portions to engage a support, a strip of insulating material extending

substantially from end to end of said jaw along the outer surface thereof, and a flat spring of substantially the

conformation of and engaging the outer surface thereof for holding the end portions of said jaw in their conductor engaging position.

1,327,845. GIN. EDWARD R. TISCHER, Houston, Tex., assignor of forty-five per cent. to Gus Emmert, Houston, Tex. Filed May 5, 1919. Serial No. 294,803. 5 Claims. (Cl. 13—7.)

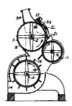

4. A gin for seed cotton, and the like including a casing, a gin roller rotatably mounted therein, whose periphery is provided with rows of friction plugs, a fluffing roller arranged adjacent said ginning roller, means for imparting rotation to said rollers in opposite directions, said means bing adapted to rotate the fluffing roller at a higher rate of speed than the ginning roller, a hopper through which the material to be ginned is delivered to the ginning roller, a shoe provided with a stripping edge adjacent the ginning roller and arranged between the hopper and the fluffing roller, said shoe coöperating with the friction plugs of said ginning roller, and arresting the seed, but permitting the passage of the lint between it and said roller to the fluffing roller, and a stripping roller provided with radiating beaters arranged to coöperate with said edge whereby the seed are extracted from the fiber.

1,327,846. BOILER-PATCH. EVANDER TODD, Winn, Ala. Filed Sept. 16, 1919. Serial No. 324,173. 6 Claims. (Cl. 137—99.)

1. A boiler patch comprising a plurality of bolts having angular extension heads to fit the inner faces of the boiler to be patched, and a plug shaped to be inserted between and to close the space between the bolts.

1,327,847. GOVERNOR FOR INTERNAL-COMBUSTION ENGINES. WILFRED F. VALLIER, Pontiac, Mich. Filed Sept. 24, 1917. Serial No. 192,974. 2 Claims. (Cl. 137—152.)

1. A governor for internal combustion engines comprising a fuel passage having a cylindrical intermediate portion and increased gradually in diameter from said portion toward its inlet end, the outlet end of said passage being enlarged to provide a mixing chamber, a fixed central barrier in said chamber around which the fuel passes, a spring-resisted valve sleeve in sliding contact

with the wall of said cylindrical intermediate portion of the passage and movable into said chamber for coaction with said barrier, a stem on said sleeve, and a suction operated disk fixedly mounted on said stem and positioned in said gradually increasing portion end of the fuel passage.

1,327,848. CARD-INDEX. GEORGE WOODHOUSE, Butte, Mont. Filed Sept. 20, 1918. Serial No. 254,945. 8 Claims. (Cl. 129—16.)

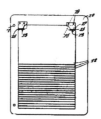

2. In a device of the class described, the combination of a support, loops carried upon said support, a card having tongues formed thereon, said tongues being carried by said loops, thus causing the card to be movably supported.

1,327,849. VEHICLE-WHEEL. JOHN ZIELISKO, Sniatyn, Alberta, Canada. Filed Oct. 5, 1918. Serial No. 256,976. 1 Claim. (Cl. 295—9.)

In a vehicle wheel adapted to be used upon a railway track or upon a level surface, the combination with the axle of said vehicle and the wheels thereof, said wheels each comprising a hub, rim and treads, of a collar rotatably mounted on the hub of said wheel, an annular bearing having one of its elements formed in said collar and the other element secured to the axle, frictional means for maintaining said collar when in an adjusted position, a rigid ring formed from a flat annular plate firmly secured to one side of the rim of said wheel, a plurality of segmental plates having arcuate edges pivoted at one of their corners to said fixed ring so as to swing thereon, said plates being adapted to extend beyond the tread of said vehicle wheel or be retracted so as to present a lesser diameter, and rods pivotally secured to said plates at one end and to said collar at the other end, whereby the action of said plates may be controlled.

1,327,850. FAUCET. FREDRICK ZIEMER, Freeport, N. Y. Filed Oct. 17, 1917. Serial No. 197,073. 1 Claim. (Cl. 277—57.)

The combination with a joint having opposed inlets and an intermediate screw threaded seat, and a threaded stem projecting from the joint and between the inlets, said stem being opposite the seat, of a faucet divided longitudinally to form separate passages, said faucet having a single discharge spout, separate valves for controlling communication between said spout and the respective passages, said faucet having an exteriorly threaded cylindrical portion engaging the stem and closed at its rear end, there being opposed ports in the cylindrical portions, said closed end engaging the seat in the joint, and establishing communication between the passages and the respective inlets of the joint.

1,327,851. MANUFACTURE OF BOOT AND SHOE HEELS. RICHARD S. AYRES, Brookline, Mass. Filed Oct. 18, 1916. Serial No. 126,425. 3 Claims. (Cl. 18—55.)

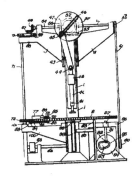

1. The process of making integral molded boot or shoe heels which consists first in preparing a mass of fibrous pulp material, then separating from said mass a predetermined amount, suitable for subsequent compression into the sized and shaped heel to be produced, giving to said predetermined mass a preliminary compressing and shaping, then drying said heel blank by removal of substantially all moisture therefrom, and finally molding, compressing and solidifying said heel blank into the desired finished shape and size.

270 O. G.—17

1,327,852. METHOD OF MANUFACTURING SECURING DEVICES. WILLIAM W. BLAKELY, Detroit, Mich. Filed Jan. 26, 1918. Serial No. 213,968. 4 Claims. (Cl. 140—2.)

1. The method of forming padded securing devices which comprises positioning padding material between wire portions, twisting the wire portions to interlock the padding material and fashioning the ends of the wires to form securing portions.

1,327,853. HORSESHOE-CALK. RANDOLPH BLOOM, Germantown, N. Y. Filed Nov. 19, 1917. Serial No. 202,834. 1 Claim. (Cl. 59—09.)

A horseshoe calk including a body portion of a rectangular configuration having attaching means upon its upper surface, and a plurality of spaced pairs of longitudinally alined surface engaging elements upon the lower surface of said body portion, said surface engaging elements forming prolongations of the side and end walls of said body portion.

1,327,854. GOLD-SAVING DEVICE. WILLIAM D. BLUDWORTH, Fairoaks, Calif. Filed May 15, 1919. Serial No. 297,231. 2 Claims. (Cl. 83—88.)

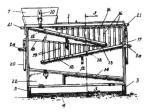

1. A gold saving device comprising a box mounted for transverse oscillatory movement, a hopper thereon, a plurality of oppositely slanting flat rifled sluices in the box positioned lengthwise thereof, one under the other, and the uppermost being adapted to communicate with the hopper, a rod pivotally mounted lengthwise of and above each sluice, and a row of spaced pivoted fingers on each rod running lengthwise of and terminating just above the floors of the sluices, such rods and fingers being adapted for oscillation in the reverse direction from the oscillation of the box.

1,327,855. RECORD-CARD. NORMAN B. BEALY, Butte, Mont. Filed Mar. 29, 1919. Serial No. 286,045. 6 Claims. (Cl. 283—51.)
1. A record card of the character described, having pictorial representations thereon of predetermined operations to be performed, reference characters for the re-

spective pictorial representations, and defined spaces on the card having designating reference characters cor-

responding to those of the pictorial representations and adapted to receive records of the corresponding operations as actually performed.

1,327,856. SPLICING-THIMBLE. MICHAEL J. BRAY, Upland, Pa. Filed Sept. 23, 1919. Serial No. 325,812. 2 Claims. (Cl. 114—225.)

1. A splicing thimble including a hollow shell pointed at one end and split for a portion of its length to define coacting jaws fitting one within the other and movable into binding engagement with a cable received within the shell.

1,327,857. MEANS FOR LIFTING BURNER-DRUMS. JOHN S. BRENNAN, Milwaukee, Wis. Filed July 7, 1919. Serial No. 309,091. 7 Claims. (Cl. 158—90.)

1. In a burner of the class described, a supply pipe member, a burner head disposed above the supply pipe member and connected therewith for vertical movement, the axis of said burner head being disposed at one side of the supply pipe member, a bracket mounted on the supply pipe member, means carried by said bracket for vertically moving the burner head, an arm projecting from said bracket in the direction of the axis of the burner head, a vertical rod having slidable bearing in said bracket arm and in the burner head, a lever in-

termediately pivoted to the bracket, a link pivoted to the lever and said rod and a burner drum normally seat-

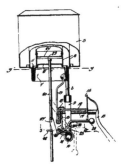

ing on the burner head and engageable by the upper end of the rod to lift said drum.

1,327,858. WICK. JOHN S. BRENNAN, Milwaukee, Wis. Filed Aug. 18, 1919. Serial No. 318,121. 5 Claims. (Cl. 67—69.)

1. An improved wick comprising a woven asbestos strip having its longitudinal edges selvaged, said strip being shaped to form a ring with its non-selvaged edges adjacent and parallel, and means for preventing said non-selvaged edges from unraveling.

1,327,859. EXPLOSIVE. LEON O. BRYAN and WENDELL R. SWINT, Wilmington, Del., assignors to E. I. du Pont de Nemours & Company, Wilmington, Del., a Corporation of Delaware. Filed Mar. 18, 1919. Serial No. 283,398. 15 Claims. (Cl. 52—3.)

1. An explosive containing as the main explosive trinitrotoluol, nitroglycerin, and a non-explosive inorganic oxygen-carrying salt.

1,327,860. AUTOMATIC RAILWAY-GATE. WADE L. CASSIDY, Hamlet, N. C. Filed Aug. 2, 1919. Serial No. 315,007. 3 Claims. (Cl. 89—18.)

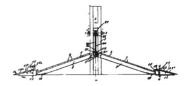

1. In an automatic gate, spaced supporting bars, platforms having their forward ends connected, pivoted gate-sections supported by the supporting bars, means for connecting the gate sections and forward ends of the platforms, guide ways for guiding the rear ends of the platforms, and a relatively wide board guiding the upper portions of the rear ends of the platforms.

1,327,861. GAS-PRODUCER. WILLIAM CLIMIE, Ayr, Scotland. Filed Feb. 25, 1919. Serial No. 279,163. 5 Claims. (Cl. 48—85.2.)

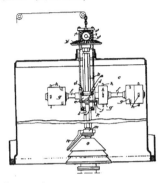

1. A gas producer comprising a casing, a fuel rake arranged therein, a device for imparting a traveling movement to said rake over the surface of the fuel, and toothed crushing rolls carried by the rake structure, said rolls tending to maintain the rake at the top surface of the fuel and to crush the crust thereof.

1,327,862. SULFITE-WASTE-LIQUOR PREPARATION AND PROCESS OF MAKING THE SAME. FRANK E. COOMBS, San Francisco, Calif. Filed Sept. 12, 1919. Serial No. 323,390. 5 Claims. (Cl. 8—6.)
1. As a new material sulfite liquor having its organic constituents reduced.

1,327,863. GRAIN-DRIER. HUBERT C. ELLIS, Evanston, Ill., assignor to Ellis Drier & Elevator Company, Chicago, Ill., a Corporation of Wisconsin. Filed Jan. 2, 1919. Serial No. 269,365. 8 Claims. (Cl. 257—80.)

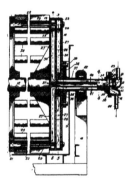

2. In a drier, the combination with a stationary trough or receptacle, of a series of heater pipes, a rotatable head to which the pipes are connected comprising an annular portion, a hub and connecting arms, said annular portion, spokes and hub having supply and outlet ducts therein, a trunnion rotatable with the head and having supply and outlet ducts therein communicating respectively with supply and outlet ducts in the hub, and means for supplying heating fluid to the supply duct in said trunnion.

1,327,864. PORTABLE CARRIAGE FOR CHILDREN. JOHN HERBERT EVERINGHAM, Manchester, England. Filed Aug. 28, 1919. Serial No. 320,443. 3 Claims. (Cl. 280—60.)

1. In a go-cart for children, an axle having relatively small wheels thereon, a base or frame secured to said axle, an upright member rigidly secured to the front edge of the base or frame, a small seat, with back and arms, hinge-wise connected along one edge to the top of the upright member, springs positioned between the other edge of the seat and the base to receive the weight in compression, a depending cross rail secured to the underside of the base at the front to form a foot-rest and prevent forward tilting, a pendant leg secured to the underside of the base at the rear to prevent rearward tilting ,and a holding handle pivotally connected to the upright member at the center, substantially as herein set forth.

1,327,865. POCKET-MIRROR. SAMUEL FLAXBAUM, New York, N. Y. Filed Apr. 17, 1919. Serial No. 290,818. 2 Claims. (Cl. 45—18.)

1. A mirror comprising a frame formed of a core member arranged upon the border and surrounding the edge of the mirror, and a fabric looped about the member with its margin and the inner portion of the fabric connected to the back of the mirror.

1,327,866. FOLDABLE BATHTUB. CURT W. HAGSTROM, Wilmette, Ill. Filed Feb. 20, 1918. Serial No. 218,183. 3 Claims. (Cl. 4—27.)

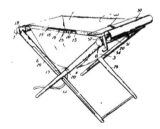

1. In a foldable tub, the combination of a fabric, a pair of rods supporting the transverse edges of the fabric, legs extending from each rod, plates mounted on the legs extending from one of these rods, said plates being provided with a slot, and the legs being provided with a circular recess in the rear of the slot, the legs extending from the other transverse supporting rod being provided with

a pin having a head with flattened portions adapted for insertion through said slot into the circular recess in the other legs.

1,327,867. TRACTION-LUG. JOHN S. HENSEL, Stevens Point, Wis. Filed Apr. 25, 1919. Serial No. 292,700. 3 Claims. (Cl. 21—215.)

2. The combination with a wheel rim having a notch in each edge and an opening intermediate said notches, of a traction device comprising a ground engaging member positioned substantially transversely of the rim, a lug on each end portion of the member and disposed in said notches, an arm extended from the intermediate portion of the member and disposed through said opening, and means for detachable engagement with said arm to hold the member engaged with the rim.

1,327,868. PUMP. HERMAN AUGUST HERPST, Norway, Mich. Filed Oct. 21, 1919. Serial No. 332,164. 3 Claims. (Cl. 103—8.)

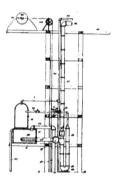

3. A water lift for mines comprising a water tank at different levels in the mine, an upright water pipe communicating tank of the lower level and leading to a point adjacent the bottom of the mine, a looped water pipe communicating with the tank of the upper level and exhausting to atmosphere, a looped pipe emptying into the tank of the upper level and adapted to receive water from the tank of the lower level, a main compressed air pipe leading substantially to the lower level of the mine, a pipe leading from said air pipe downwardly through said upright water pipe opening adjacent the lower open end thereof, an air reservoir adjacent each tank, a branch pipe from said main air pipe to each of said reservoirs, an outlet pipe from each end of the adjacently positioned water pipe loops, valves in said outlet pipes adapted to open between said air pipes and said loops and also to exhaust said loops to atmosphere, operating levers for said valves, a pull-cord attached to corresponding ends of said levers, a crank to which the free end of said cord is attached adapted for alternately pulling and releasing said cord and adjustable weights upon the other ends of said levers adapted to automatically return the levers to substantially vertical positions with the valves open to atmosphere.

1,327,869. AEROPLANE. EDWARD BERNARD JAEGER and EUGENE H. HELLER, Chicago, Ill., assignors to The Hill Pump Valve Company, Chicago, Ill., a Corporation of Illinois. Filed Jan. 9, 1918. Serial No. 211,093. 4 Claims. (Cl. 237—12.3.)

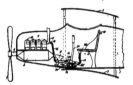

1. In an aeroplane, in combination with the combustion motor and the exhaust therefor, a plurality of hollow levers, means for conducting the exhaust gases through said levers, and a by-pass for disconnecting one of said levers from said conducting means.

1,327,870. RADIATOR FOR STEAM AND WATER. JENS LANGE, Hellerup, Denmark, assignor to Dansk Varmekedel Syndikat System Lange, Fabrikant-Firma, Copenhagen, Denmark, a Corporation of Denmark. Filed Apr. 28, 1916. Serial No. 94,132. 2 Claims. (Cl. 257—151.)

1. In combination with the elements of a radiator, superposed separable heat-absorbing blocks fitting in the spaces between said elements and provided with laterally extending parts adapted to meet in front of the said elements and to present a continuous front of the radiator.

1,327,871. DRAFT APPLIANCE. VICTOR NATANIEL LUNDSTROM, Clarissa, Minn. Filed July 14, 1919. Serial No. 310,853. 1 Claim. (Cl. 21—78.)

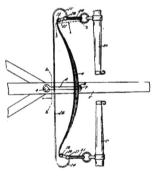

A double tree consisting of a leaf spring, an eye bolt fixed to the middle portion of the spring and adapted to be secured to a vehicle to be drawn, a cross bar slidably mounted upon said eye bolt and having forwardly curved extensions at its ends, link connections between the ends of the leaf spring and the respective end extensions of the cross bar, clevises pivotally mounted upon said cross bar extensions.

1,327,872. FOUNTAIN-HUMIDOR-BOX-LID SUPPORT. WILLIAM A. McANENY and DANIEL T. MAY, Denver, Colo., assignors to The McMurtry Manufacturing Company, Denver, Colo., a Corporation of Colorado. Filed July 3, 1916. Serial No. 107,291. 2 Claims. (Cl. 217—58.)

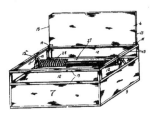

1. A display device comprising an inverted box-like member adapted to fit the top of a box whose contents are to be displayed and open to communicate with the interior of the box, the side and top walls of the member being transparent, and means positioned on opposite sides of the member and within the member to support a humidor above the top edges of the box and within the limits of the member whereby the humidor requires none of the space of the box.

1,327,873. METHOD OF UTILIZING SPANISH MOSS. MARK W. MARSDEN. Philadelphia, Pa. Filed July 18, 1918. Serial No. 245,576. 2 Claims. (Cl. 92—3.)

1. That improvement in the method of treating Spanish moss, which consists in dissolving and removing the extractive, subjecting the residue of the stock to boiling in a solution of soap and glycerin, and finally washing and drying the product.

1,327,874. CHIPPER'S GUIDE-MARKER. CHARLEY B. MATHEWS, Andalusia, Ala. Filed Aug. 14, 1919. Serial No. 317,592. 2 Claims. (Cl. 33—42.)

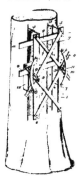

1. A guide marker, comprising longitudinal members having openings, scoring blades mounted on said longitudinal members, lateral guides secured to one longitudinal member and slidable on the other, said guides passing through said openings, and means permitting the adjustment of said longitudinal members with respect to each other.

1,327,875. VALVE-GRINDING MACHINE. ALBERT C. MORK, Minneapolis, Minn. Filed July 12, 1919. Serial No. 310,408. 5 Claims. (Cl. 51—4.)

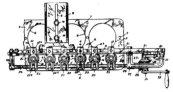

1. A valve grinding machine comprising a supporting bar having means for attaching the same to a cylinder casting, supporting heads adjustable on said supporting bar, valve engaging grinder stems mounted in said head for rotary and vertical movements, springs yieldingly forcing said grinder stems downward, gears rotatable with the said stems, a rack bar slidably mounted in respect to said supporting bar and engaging the several gears, a cam shaft supported from said bar and extending along the several heads, cams rotatable with, but slidable on said cam shaft, and non-rotary cam engaged devices movable vertically with the several grinder stems, said head having webs that embrace the respective cams and cause the same to move, therewith along said cam shaft.

1,327,876. HOISTING DEVICE. AXEL L. NYBLAD, Newport, England. Filed June 10, 1919. Serial No. 303,130. 4 Claims. (Cl. 254—190.)

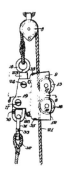

1. A device of the character described including a casing having two sides spaced apart; a guard located between said sides within the width of said casing and together with one end and the sides of said casing providing a channel through which a rope can pass; a yoke; a bolt connecting the ends of said yoke to the sides of said casing at a position between said guard and the opposite end of the casing; and an eyelet having its shank pivotally connected to the portion of said yoke between its ends; substantially as described.

1,327,877. RADIATOR - SHIELD. CHARLES H. PARMELEE, Seattle, Wash., assignor, by mesne assignments, to Pacific Radiator Shield Co., Seattle, Wash., a Corporation. Filed Apr. 2, 1918. Serial No. 226,309. 2 Claims. (Cl. 237—79.)

2. A radiator shield including a shield member having top and back walls, forwardly extending horizontal clamping hooks having shanks adjustably connected to said back wall and having their free hooked ends horizontally arranged to engage the end sections of a radiator to fasten the shield member to the radiator, and sheet metal sup-

porting brackets rigidly secured to and depending from said top wall, said brackets having their free ends resting

transversely upon the top of the radiator sections, substantially as described.

1,327,878. EXTENSION-TABLE. ETHEL D. PARROTT, Los Angeles, Calif. Filed July 21, 1919. Serial No. 312,246. 3 Claims. (Cl. 45—9.)

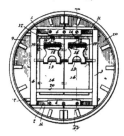

1. An extension table comprising a frame, main leaves slidable thereon, a sectional extension leaf hingedly united, and a strut member slidably journaled on the frame in a direction lengthwise of the table for edgewise adjustment of said leaf and hinged to one of the extension leaf sections.

1,327,879. VENTILATOR AND VENTILATING SYSTEM. ALLAN K. PRUDEN, St. Paul, Minn. Filed May 16, 1918. Serial No. 235,216. 2 Claims. (Cl. 98—2.)

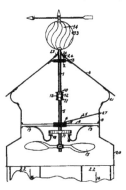

2. In a ventilator, the combination of a hood, a cap supported by said hood, but spaced therefrom, a wind motor, a shaft driven by said wind motor, a blower fan, a shaft for said blower fan, said shafts being mounted for the same axis of rotation, a slidable joint connecting said shafts, means carried by said wind motor shaft for driving said fan shaft, resilient means connecting said two shafts, said blower fan shaft being so mounted that when rotating a downward pressure will be exerted thereby against said resilient connecting means, a friction disk carried by said fan shaft, a drag associated with said friction disk, said friction disk impinging on said drag when the thrust of wind fan overbalances said resilient means a pre-determined amount.

1,327,880. CLUTCH. JOHN R. ROGERS, Brooklyn, N. Y. Filed Mar. 11, 1914. Serial No. 823,849. 5 Claims. (Cl. 192—1.)

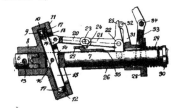

1. In a clutch, a driving shaft, a driven shaft, a clutch member on each of said shafts, one of said clutch members being inclined relatively to its shaft and the other clutch member pivotally mounted on its shaft and means for bringing said clutch members into coöperation with each other.

1,327,881. TOOL OR CUTTER HEAD. CARL H. ROTH, Newark, N. J. Filed Nov. 8, 1918. Serial No. 261,601. 1 Claim. (Cl. 90—53.)

In a tool or cutter-head for planers or shapers, in combination with the slider, a tool-box comprising a main plate and forwardly extending wall-members having a receiving space between them, said wall-members being provided at the upper marginal edge-portions near said main plate with a rod extending across said space, and said wall-members being further provided at the lower portions of the front marginal edge-portions with another rod, a cutter-holder provided at its upper edge with an eye for oscillatorily mounting said holder upon said first-mentioned rod, and a second cutter-holder provided with a centrally disposed eye for oscillatorily mounting said last-mentioned cutter-holder upon said second-mentioned rod, said first-mentioned cutter-holder during the movement of the machine-table or bed in one direction bearing against said main plate, and a cross-bar connected at its ends with the upper marginal portions of said wall-members and extending across the receiving space between said wall-members, and with which cross-bar the upper end-portion of said second-mentioned cutter-holder is adapted to be brought into fixed engagement during the movement of the machine-table or bed in the opposite direction, and means connected with each cutter-holder for securing a cutter-tool to each holder.

1,327,882. CROSSOVER. THOMAS J. SCANLAN, Montreal, Quebec, Canada. Filed Sept. 9, 1918. Serial No. 253,147. 10 Claims. (Cl. 246—387.)

9. In a device of the class described, the combination with a supporting plate provided with a stop opening, a

pair of fixed stops disposed on opposite sides of said opening, a movable stop adapted to extend through said open-

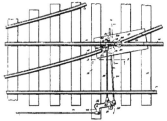

ing to hold a shiftable rail section between the same and either one of said fixed stops and a cam control for said movable stop.

1,327,883. INTERCHANGEABLE VEHICLE. WILLIAM M. SCHLUER, Orange, N. J. Filed Apr. 17, 1918. Serial No. 229,034. 18 Claims. (Cl. 296—26.)

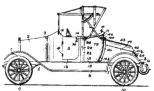

1. In a vehicle of the character set forth, the chassis of the vehicle, a main body, longitudinally extending runways located at the sides of said body, a front seat mounted upon said body, means for pivotally connecting the lower front edge-portions of said seat to said body, a rear seat, supporting means extending from said rear seat and movably disposed with relation to said runways, said rear seat being adapted to be moved beneath the front seat, so that the back and side-members of the rear seat can be made to embrace the corresponding members of said front seat, and means connected with said supporting means for tilting said rear seat to permit of the movement of said rear seat upon said runways.

1,327,884. HAND-PAINTED RAG DOLL. LITA SHINN and BESSIE SHINN, Muskogee, Okla. Filed May 31, 1916. Serial No. 100,995. 4 Claims. (Cl. 46—40.)

4. In a walking doll comprising a body, a tuck stitched horizontally across the lower front portion of the body approximately one inch from the lower edge and legs sewed firmly to the tuck.

1,327,885. APPARATUS FOR SAVING METALLIC VALUES. LINCOLN C. STOCKTON and CHARLES F. GODDARD, Denver, Colo., assignors, by direct and mesne assignments, to The Metal Separation Company, Denver, Colo., a Corporation of Colorado. Filed Mar. 18, 1918. Serial No. 223,014. 7 Claims. (Cl. 83—82.)

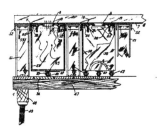

1. Concentrating apparatus, comprising a sluice having an opening in the bottom thereof, a readily removable tank positioned below said opening, means on the under side of said sluice to discharge water into said tank, and means to seal said tank against said under side of the sluice.

1,327,886. COLLAPSIBLE BED. FRANK M. STOLL, Denver, Colo. Filed Feb. 24, 1919. Serial No. 278,973. 8 Claims. (Cl. 5—72.)

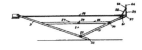

7. A device of the class described, comprising an end member, side bars, the said side bars adapted to be downwardly inclined from said end member, means on said side bars adapted to lock the latter to said end member when said side bars are downwardly inclined, and said side bars being adaptable for disconnection with the end member when elevated.

1,327,887. TENT-BED. FRANK M. STOLL, Denver, Colo. Filed Mar. 10, 1919. Serial No. 281,824. 4 Claims. (Cl. 5—72.)

1. In a tent bed, the combination with a bed, composed of two side rails and the foot rails, of a tent adapted to be supported over said bed and having a roof inclined downwardly in direction of the foot rail of the bed, a bar extending parallel with the foot rail of the bed, arms secured to the opposite extremities of the said bar, the foot rail of the bed having apertured ears secured thereto, the free extremities of said arms having buttons thereon adapted to be received in the apertures of said ears thereby pivoting said arms, said arms adapted to be moved on their pivots to elevate said bar and cause the same to engage with the roof of said tent and elevate the latter.

1,327,888. PACKING DEVICE. George Sykes, Penryn, Calif., assignor to Sykes Standard Fruit Wrap Company, Penryn, Calif., a Corporation of California. Filed Oct. 8, 1917. Serial No. 195,388. 3 Claims. (Cl. 217—26.)

1. A separator for use in packing fruit, comprising a sheet of conformable material having a plurality of slitted depressions therein adapted to be placed between two layers of fruit to separate and partially wrap the pieces of fruit.

1,327,889. CONCRETE STRUCTURE. William M. Thomas, Los Angeles, Calif. Filed Nov. 22, 1915. Serial No. 62,689. 11 Claims. (Cl. 72—56.)

1. In combination, preformed arch members having a portion of their extrados forming a portion of a deck floor, transverse supports extending up from the arch members, and another preformed portion of the floor mounted partly on said arch members and partly on the transverse supports, the spandrels and the spaces between transversely adjacent arch members being open.

1,327,890. ANIMAL-TRAP. Myron A. Twitchell, Elk Point, S. D. Filed Aug. 18, 1917. Serial No. 186,841. 1 Claim. (Cl. 43—21.)

An animal trap comprising a base, a U-shaped jaw pivoted thereon to swing toward and from the base to accordingly close and open, yieldable means to force the jaw closed, a trigger plate pivoted between its ends to the base and in front of the jaw, means engageable with the trigger in the rear of its pivot to prevent depression of the trigger below a predetermined point, the trigger being adapted to be baited in front of its pivot, and of such size that the animal for which the trap is intended cannot reach the bait without stepping on said plate, and a latch-plate pivoted between its upper and lower ends to and between the arms of the jaw, and releasably engageable at its lower edge with the trigger slightly in the rear of the trigger pivot, the latch-plate being adapted to be placed in such engagement by opening the jaw and forcing the upper end of the latch-plate forwardly.

1,327,891. ENGINE-HOOD AND RADIATOR COVER. Ralph H. Upson, Akron, Ohio, assignor to The Goodyear Tire & Rubber Company, Akron, Ohio, a Corporation of Ohio. Filed July 20, 1918. Serial No. 245,941. 5 Claims. (Cl. 74—56.)

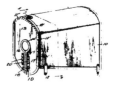

1. An engine cover comprising a body portion, means for attaching the body portion in applied position over the hood of the engine, a front wall portion attached to the body portion and provided with an opening to accommodate the shaft of the engine, said front wall being slit from said opening to its lower edge producing two depending flaps, means for detachably connecting said flaps, and stiffening elements located on opposite sides of the slit for holding the flaps flat against the radiator.

1,327,892. TIP-FASTENER FOR SHOE-LACES. Ephraim Viertels, New York, N. Y. Filed Aug. 23, 1918. Serial No. 251,084. 4 Claims. (Cl. 81—15.)

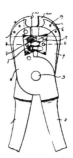

1. In a device for tipping shoelaces, die supports, dies secured to the said die supports, the said dies being composed of a series of spaced sheet metal laminations, means for connecting the said laminations to said supports, so that a lamination connected to one support is directly opposite an opposite lamination connected to the other support, and means for increasing and decreasing the distance between said dies, the opposed surfaces of said dies being adapted to close a metal blank on the end of a shoelace and clamp it to the said end thereof.

1,327,893. GAS-GENERATOR. Thomas Roland Wollaston, Manchester, England. Filed Jan. 19, 1918. Serial No. 212,649. 1 Claim. (Cl. 48—86.)

In a gas producer, vertical retorts situated above and in continuous communication with said producer, fuel supply means for said retorts, said retorts forming outlets for the gas generated in said producer whereby the fuel supplied to said retorts is coked, gas outlets from said retorts and a plurality of fuel distributing and variable interstice-producing means within said retorts and

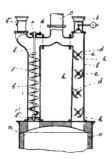

at different heights therein whereby the velocity of gas through the retort is controlled, substantially as herein set forth.

1,327,894. FREIGHT-CAR. VALENTY WROCLAWSKI, Chicago, Ill. Filed Aug. 18, 1919. Serial No. 318,162. 5 Claims. (Cl. 105—374.)

1. A car of the class described, comprising end walls rigidly secured to the bottom and sides of the car, supplemental end walls slidably mounted inwardly from said rigid end walls, and yielding shock-absorbing means located intermediate said supplemental end walls at the top and bottom of said car and normally urging said shiftable end walls toward each other and permitting a limited movement toward the respective rigid end walls.

1,327,895. ANTIFRICTION DEVICE. SERGE APOSTOLOFF, New York, N. Y. Filed May 21, 1918. Serial No. 235,884. 3 Claims. (Cl. 74—108.)

1. A bearing for movable surfaces comprising a pair of contacting members, the opposing faces of which are provided with grooves, the grooves of said members being arranged closely together to cause their intervening walls to terminate at their tops in substantially linear edges, the grooves of one member running crosswise to those of the other member.

1,327,896. HEATER. GEORGE W. BALOGH, Buffalo, N. Y. Filed May 28, 1918. Serial No. 237,011. 1 Claim. (Cl. 257—165.)

In a heater comprising a plurality of rectangular casings, brackets at the upper and lower corners of said casings,

tubular supports engaged in said brackets for securing said casings one above the other, two vertical partition plates in each of said casings and horizontal partition plates forming with said vertical plates six compartments in each of said casings, a tubular flue extending through

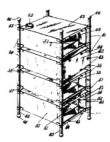

said compartments and adapted to be connected at its lower end to a heat supply pipe and at its upper end to a discharge pipe, and knobs at the lower ends of said tubular supports, substantially as described and for the purpose set forth.

1,327,897. GUN. ARTHUR S. BALDWIN, Baltimore, Md. Filed Feb. 12, 1917. Serial No. 148,017. 2 Claims. (Cl. 42—3.)

1. In a gun the combination with the gun-barrel, of breech mechanism, a sleeve slidable on the gun barrel; a plurality of arms, each having a rear end attached to the sleeve and projecting forwardly in front of the barrel and said arms diverging as they extend forward; a plurality of disks supported by the diverging arms one in front of the other,—said sleeve, diverging arms and disks all being movable with respect to the barrel, and means for connecting the sleeve with the breech mechanism.

1,327,898. ADVERTISING-CLOCK. JOHN U. BARR, New York, N. Y. Filed May 10, 1916. Serial No. 96,513. 6 Claims. (Cl. 88—27.)

2. In a device of the class described, the combination of a member provided with a light aperture, movable members mounted in said light aperture and designed to be disposed in line with the light from a projector, a carriage mounted for rotary movement and provided with slide openings adapted to be framed in said light aperture, an actuating shaft operatively connected to the carriage to rotate the same, a gear train connecting said movable members and shaft, an electric circuit including a source of electric energy, an electromagnet, a circuit closer for

periodically completing the circuit through the electromagnet and a driving connection between said electromagnet and said shaft whereby the movable members and the carriage are both actuated with a step-by-step motion on each actuation of the electromagnet.

1,327,899. BONNET FOR RAILWAY-SIGNAL FUSEE-CAPS AND METHOD OF MAKING IT. HARVEY O. BEMISDERFER, Fostoria, Ohio, assignor to Central Railway Signal Company, Pittsburgh, Pa., a Corporation of New Jersey. Filed Jan. 2, 1919. Serial No. 269.304. 10 Claims. (Cl. 102—20.)

1. A railway signal fusee cap bonnet comprising a strip of paper having its center extending across the closed end of the cap, its ends bent downward along the sides of and cemented to the side of the cap and a tearing member extending between the bonnet and the closed end of the cap in a direction transverse the strip and having an exposed end whereby the bonnet is free from folds over the end of the cap.

1,327,900. BEVERAGE-MIXER. MATHEW BLACK, Brooklyn, N. Y. Filed May 3, 1919. Serial No. 294,492. 2 Claims. (Cl. 259—135.)

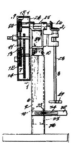

1. In beverage mixers and similar articles, a standard consisting of a fixed tubular support, a post extensibly sliding therein, a bracket mounted on the upper end of said post, an agitator and agitator shaft on said bracket at one side of said support, and a casing mounted on said bracket and containing means for driving said shaft and arranged on the opposite side of said support to act as a counterbalance to said shaft.

1,327,901. MACHINE OR APPARATUS FOR BREAKING UP OR PULVERIZING CAUSTIC SODA AND THE LIKE. WILLIAM BLACKER, Stalybridge, England. Filed Jan. 4, 1919. Serial No. 269,584. 3 Claims. (Cl. 259—83.)

1. In a machine of the class described, the combination with a frame, a swingable arm adapted to travel back and forth in said frame, and means for swinging said arm during its travel, of a rotatable drum mounted on said frame in position to be struck by said swingable arm, means for rotating said drum, and means for transmitting motion from said arm-swinging means to said drum-rotating means and comprising a bell-crank lever pivoted on said frame and having one arm thereof pivotally connected with the arm-swinging means, an arm connected with said drum rotating means, and a pivotal connection between said arm and said bell-crank lever.

1,327,902. CONCENTRATOR. HENRY BOLTHOFF, Denver, Colo. Filed Mar. 18, 1918. Serial No. 223,052. 10 Claims. (Cl. 83—88.)

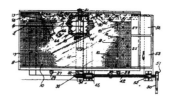

1. The combination in a concentrator, of a table longitudinally inclined from the head toward the tail thereof and movably mounted, the table having its top covered with coarse mesh material of a size and character to provide classifying cells, said cellular surface being substantially unobstructed, means for delivering the material to be treated, in the form of pulp, to the head of the table, means for delivering wash water to the head of the table, and means for imparting movement to the table of a character having tendency to cause the material thereon to travel toward one of its longitudinal edges.

1,327,903. SEPARATOR. FREDERICK A. BRUNS, Blaine, Wash. Filed May 27, 1919. Serial No. 300,213. 5 Claims. (Cl. 83—82.)

1. A separator of the class described comprising a perforated block having trough like channels on the top side

thereof; an agitator reciprocable on the top of said block; means for delivering material on to said block;

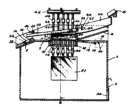

and means for directing a jet of water upwardly through each of the perforations in said block.

1,327,904. PROCESS OF TREATING FABRIC. WIL-LIAM C. CARTER, Radnor, Ohio, assignor to The Good-year Tire & Rubber Company, Akron, Ohio, a Corpora-tion of Ohio. Filed Oct. 19, 1916. Serial No. 126,558. 4 Claims. (Cl. 91—70.)

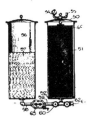

4. The process of impregnating yarn or fabric with a lubricant, which consists in bathing the yarn 'or fabric in a hot vapor, and then bringing a relatively cold body of a liquid carrier, containing the lubricant in suspension, into contact with the yarn or fabric, whereby the vacuum formed by condensation of the vapor, causes impregna-tion of the yarn or fabric.

1,327,905. LIFTING APPARATUS FOR MOTOR ROAD-VEHICLES AND THE LIKE. FEED COULTAS, Brad-ford, and ARTHUR PICK, Eldwick, Bingley,. England. Filed Sept. 18, 1918. Serial No. 254,562. 1 Claim. (Cl. 254—86.)

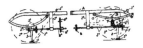

In combination, a spring supported vehicle chassis, brackets secured to and depending from said chassis, stir-rups carried by said brackets and encircling the axles of the vehicle, springs interposed between said stirrups and axles, and vehicle elevating means carried by said brackets.

1,327,906. APPARATUS FOR RECOVERING GASO-LENE FROM NATURAL GASES. ANDREW B. CROSS, Denver, Colo. Filed Mar. 5, 1918. Serial No. 220,502. 1 Claim. (Cl. 62—122.)

In an apparatus of the character described, a cylindri-cal receiver, a jacket surrounding the said receiver and spaced from the same, and caps on the ends of said jacket

having packing boxes through which the ends of said receiver pass, a pipe on one end of the receiver adapted to connect with a gas supply, a pressure regulator, a pipe connecting the opposite end of the receiver with the inlet of said pressure regulator, a pipe connecting the outlet

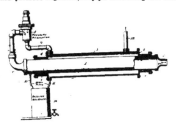

of the regulator with the jacket at one end thereof, an outlet pipe extending from the opposite end portion of the jacket, a tank, a drain pipe connecting the jacket and tank, and a drain pipe extending from the receiver adja-cent its outlet end, and connecting with the said tank.

1,327,907. GAME-BOARD. ALFRED C. CURRIE, St. John, New Brunswick, Canada. Filed Jan. 25, 1919. Serial No. 273,089. 5 Claims. (Cl. 46—21.)

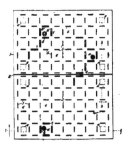

1. A game board provided with longitudinal and cross-wise rows of elongated slots or seats, and playing devices or gates each having a tongue adapted to any one of the slots or seats, the playing device and the tongue being elongated similarly to the slots, with the playing de-vices longer than the tongues or slots, whereby the play-ing devices may be so placed on the board as to form inclosures.

1,327,908. TYPEWRITING-MACHINE. WALTER FEN-TON, Manchester, England, assignor to Underwood Typewriter Company, New York, N. Y., a Corporation of Delaware. Filed Sept. 19, 1917. Serial No. 192,052. 51 Claims. (Cl. 197—60.)

1. In a typewriting machine, the combination of a carriage, two feed rollers connected thereto for a main work-sheet, two platens also connected to said carriage and means for rotating one of said platens; and a frame extending on each side of the typewriter; said platens and said carriage capable of sliding independently and horizontally along the extended frame to the right and left; all substantially as and for the purposes herein set forth.

1,327,909. SAFETY - HANGER FOR BRAKE - BEAMS. JOHN C. HANKS, Russell, Ky. Filed Aug. 9, 1919. Serial No. 316,334. 1 Claim. (Cl. 188—70.)

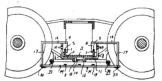

A safety hanger for brake beams comprising a pair of blocks positioned adjacent each end of a spring plank in spaced relation to each other, arms secured at one of their ends to said blocks and projecting outwardly therefrom, said arms being bent at their intermediate portions to provide downwardly extending arms, a tenon on the ends of said downwardly extending arms, and a frame provided with mortises in its ends for detachably connecting the frame to said arms.

1,327,910. TIRE-MAKING MACHINE. WILLIAM B. HARSEL, Akron, Ohio, assignor to The Goodyear Tire & Rubber Company, Akron, Ohio, a Corporation of Ohio. Filed July 20, 1918. Serial No. 245,864. 23 Claims. (Cl. 154—10.)

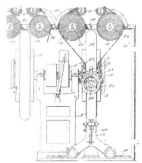

1. A strip-applying structure including a tire-forming core, a carriage movable in relation thereto, a guide-sustaining support carried by and movable with the carriage, and a strip-guiding element on the support and positionable thereby opposite a side of the core for applying a strip of material flatwise thereto.

1,327,911. LACING - HOOK - SETTING MACHINE. ARTHUR R. HAVENER, Waltham, Mass., assignor to American Lacing Hook Co., a Corporation of New Jersey. Filed Feb. 1, 1917. Serial No. 146,005. 54 Claims. (Cl. 218—17.)

1. A lacing hook setting machine having, in combination, means for setting a lacing hook in the upper of a boot or shoe and in a reinforcing strip therefor and means for automatically partially severing a portion of said strip therefrom after said lacing hook has been set.

11. A lacing hook setting machine having, in combination, means for imparting an initial feeding movement to a reinforcing strip, means for setting a series of lacing hooks in the upper of a boot or shoe and in said reinforcing strip, said setting means embodying a punch adapted to pierce a hole in said upper and reinforcing strip, mechanism adapted to move said punch laterally thereof to feed said upper and reinforcing strip and means for severing from said strip the portion which has been attached to said upper by said hooks.

16. A lacing hook setting machine having, in combination, means for setting a lacing hook in the upper of a boot or shoe and in a reinforcing strip therefor, a primary cutter adapted to move vertically to contact with said reinforcing strip, a secondary cutter adapted to coact with said primary cutter, mechanism adapted to feed said strip of reinforcing material between said cutters, means to impart a vertical reciprocatory motion to said secondary cutter and mechanism adapted to move said secondary cutter transversely of said primary cutter, whereby a portion of said reinforcing strip may be partly severed therefrom or entirely severed therefrom.

1,327,912. TIRE-TREAD FOR PNEUMATIC-TIRE CASINGS AND METHOD OF MAKING AND ATTACHING THE SAME. OLIVER J. HOBSON, Chicago, Ill., assignor of one-half to Otto Q. Beckworth, Chicago, Ill. Filed Apr. 14, 1919. Serial No. 289,891. 6 Claims. (Cl. 154—14.)

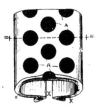

1. Insets respectively consisting of a plurality of layers of textile material embedded in rubber adapted, when vulcanized, to be tenaciously elastic, in combination with a strip of rubber also adapted, when vulcanized, to be tenaciously elastic, and an additional strip of rubber compound adapted, when vulcanized, to be firm and resilient, said additional strip provided with holes and said insets in said holes and fitting closely to the walls thereof, said additional strip adapted to be vulcanized to said first named strip, and said first named strip adapted to be vulcanized to the rubber of said insets and, when applied thereto, to the adjacent face of a tire casing.

1,327,913. ROTARY BORING-DRILL. HOWARD R. HUGHES, Houston, Tex. Filed May 19, 1919. Serial No. 297,979. 3 Claims. (Cl. 255—71.)

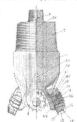

1. In a rotary boring drill, a head, two sets of cylindrical cross roller cutters so positioned as to drill a hole with a

conical shaped bottom, two side cutters mounted on pins projecting outwardly from the sides of the head, said cutters being retained in position by frusto-conical shaped bushings threaded on pins integral with said head, and locking means to hold said bushings on said pins.

1,327,914. PUMP-PISTON. GRANVILLE A. HUMASON, Houston, Tex. Filed Oct. 11, 1919. Serial No. 330,058. 8 Claims. (Cl. 103—63.)

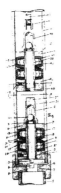

2. In a pump, a working barrel, a piston reciprocable therein, nuts at the upper and lower ends of said piston, expansion means between said nuts, said expansion means comprising a series of cups having their outer ends bearing against said working barrel and their concave faces toward each other, resilient disks between said cups, said disks having their outer edges bearing against the outer edges of said cups, whereby the tightening of one of said nuts will force the cups outwardly against said working barrel.

1,327,915. BOOK-TRIMMER. EDWARD R. KAST, Pearl River, N. Y., assignor to Kast Insetting and Gathering Machine Company, New York, N. Y., a Corporation of Delaware. Filed Dec. 24, 1917. Serial No. 208,658. 32 Claims. (Cl. 164—49.)

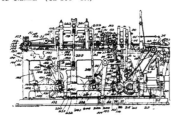

1. In combination, a saddle on which books are assembled and bound, means for elevating the books from said saddle and closing the same, and means for trimming the edges of each book as it is delivered, said trimming mechanism operating in time relation with said mechanism for delivering the books from the saddle.

1,327,916. DOOR - LATCH. WILLIAM M. KATZBERG, Hastings, Nebr. Filed May 1, 1918. Serial No. 231,882. 2 Claims. (Cl. 70—45.)
1. A door latch including a rod extending through a door and having one end portion bent to provide a rec-

tangular looped handle and having its opposite end portion arranged on the opposite side of the door and curved longitudinally to provide a combined handle and locking

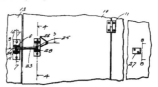

member, a plate secured to one side of the door and receiving the inner portion of said rectangular loop, and a keeper adapted to be engaged by said combined handle and locking member.

1,327,917. CONCRETE-MIXER. GEORGE E. KELLAR, Covina, Calif., assignor to Kellar-Thomason Company, a Corporation of California. Filed July 20, 1914. Serial No. 851,875. 1 Claim. (Cl. 220—1.)

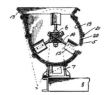

In a machine of the character referred to, a container having an outer wall and an inner lining, and a co-extensive, separating sheet of paper between said outer wall and said lining, whereby to prevent said walls from rusting together and rendering their separation difficult.

1,327,918. KNITTING-NEEDLE. HENRIETTA L. KELSEY, Philadelphia, Pa. Filed Mar. 19, 1918. Serial No. 223,284. 2 Claims. (Cl. 240—1.)

1. A needle for the uses set forth, having in the region of its pointed end luminous material protected against wear by overlying transparent material.

1,327,919. ROLL-POLISHER. FREDERICK S. KLUG and CHARLES E. FREELAND, Wheeling, W. Va. Filed Apr. 8, 1919. Serial No. 288,467. 5 Claims. (Cl. 80—1.)
5. In a roll polisher, a holder having a threaded eye and provided with a shouldered seat for the reception of a polishing block, means for clamping said block upon said seat, anti-friction rollers carried on the back of said

holder, a member resting against said rollers and adapted to be traversed by the latter during travel of said holder,

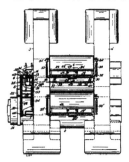

and means whereby the pressure of said member upon said holder through said rollers may be adjusted for regulating the pressure of the block upon the roll.

1,327,920. FURNITURE-CASTER. STANISLAW KOZIK, Indian Head, Md. Filed Apr. 22, 1919. Serial No. 291,838. 1 Claim. (Cl. 16—151.)

A ball bearing caster comprising a casing having a socket at its upper end and having superposed ball receiving chambers, balls in said chambers, the ball in the upper chamber being engaged by the walls of the chamber above and below the transverse median line of the ball, a ball bearing cage in the inner wall of the lower chamber, and anti-friction bearing balls in said cage engaging the ball in the lower chamber on substantially the horizontal median line thereof, the lower end of the lower casing being curved coincident to the upper portion thereof to prevent the escape of the lower ball.

1,327,921. PLOW CONSTRUCTION (DETACHABLE SHARE.) WILLIAM H. LEE, Syracuse, N. Y., assignor to Syracuse Chilled Plow Company, Syracuse, N. Y., a Corporation of New York. Filed Mar. 23, 1918. Serial No. 224,252. 4 Claims. (Cl. 97—18.)

1. In a plow, a frog having a lengthwise undercut beveled surface on the angular side thereof toward the land side of the plow, said surface extending forwardly and rearwardly in a general direction parallel to the face of the frog, and a share detachably mounted on the upper face of the frog and having a gunnel flange arranged to lap said angular side of the frog, the gunnel flange having a projecting upwardly facing inclined plane surface complemental to said bevel surface and arranged to engage the same and draw the share onto the face of the frog when the frog and share are assembled, substantially as and for the purpose set forth.

1,327,922. DRAFTSMAN'S FOUNTAIN RULING-PEN. EVERETT R. MORELAND, Carrollton, Mo. Filed Jan. 12, 1918. Serial No. 211,573. 2 Claims. (Cl. 120—43.)

1. A fountain ruling pen comprising nibs, a feed tube disposed between said nibs and having its outer ends thereof forked to provide arms thereby presenting feed openings to the inner side of the nibs, a stem extending through said tube, and outwardly diverging tapering fingers extending from said stem and disposed between said arms and adapted for contact with the inner sides of the nibs.

1,327,923. EDGE-LINING MACHINE. FRANK A. PHILLIPS, Northfield, Vt., assignor to Phillips & Slack, Inc., Northfield, Vt., a Corporation of Vermont. Filed Sept. 9, 1918. Serial No. 253,152. 9 Claims. (Cl. 125—18.)

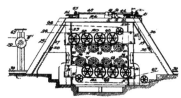

3. An edge lining machine having, in combination, upper and lower sets of grinding wheels disposed in a single plane and engaging opposite faces of the work, and means to vary both the vertical position and the relative inclination of each set of wheels.

5. An edge lining machine comprising upper and lower sets of grinding wheels, and means to feed stock between said wheels, said wheels engaging said stock in successive pairs, and each pair being of less thickness than the preceding pair.

8. An edge lining machine having, in combination, a plurality of wheels, a separate driving shaft for each wheel, a separate set of bearings for each shaft, and means to independently adjust each shaft and its associated set of bearings axially, whereby the axial position of each shaft and wheel may be separately determined.

1,327,924. GRASS-MOWING MACHINE. JOSEPH A. ROSEMAN, Glenview, Ill. Filed July 8, 1918. Serial No. 243,773. 2 Claims. (Cl. 56—7.)

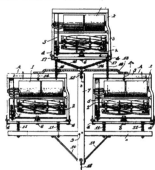

1. A mowing machine composed of several units, each unit having a cutting element, a heavy roller in the rear

of said cutting element holding said element securely on the ground, a frame surrounding said roller and cutting element, and means for flexibly securing said frames to one another.

1,327,925. CHAIN. EBERHARD SCHNEIDER, New York, N. Y.; Stanislawa Schneider administratrix of said Eberhard Schneider, deceased. Filed May 11, 1918. Serial No. 233,827. 5 Claims. (Cl. 74—31.)

1. A chain, comprising: a series of hollow spherical members having a central solid portion, and polar cavities terminating in apertures; and suitable link members, the stems thereof passing through said apertures and having integral heads fitting within said polar cavities.

5. The combination with a chain composed of a plurality of spherical members flexibly united; of a wheel composed of plate members having circumferential depressions coöperating to form suitable cups to receive said spherical members, the one plate being centrally extended to provide a tubular hub, and the other centrally extended to provide a sleeve fitting over said hub, and means to unite said plates.

1,327,926. AIR COLLECTING AND DELIVERING APPARATUS. WILLIAM D. SCOTT, Martins Ferry, Ohio. Filed Jan. 9, 1919. Serial No. 270,274. 3 Claims. (Cl. 230—11.)

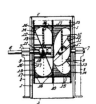

1. An air collecting and delivering apparatus comprising a casing having an air-intake opening in each of its opposite sides and a discharge opening in the front wall thereof, and a rotor mounted within said casing, said rotor comprising a shaft, a pair of fans mounted on said shaft, each fan consisting of a plurality of approximately semicircular blades disposed in upright radial positions with their chord-like edges diagonally crossing said shaft, a disk-like wall interposed between said fans and having the inner ends of said fan blades attached thereto, the blades of the opposite fans being reversely arranged so that each fan acts to draw air inward through the adjacent intake opening, a ring connecting the extreme outer ends of the blades of each fan, and transverse auxiliary blades interposed between each ring and the adjacent side of said disk-like wall.

1,327,927. VARIABLE GAS-PORT FOR GAS-ENGINES. CHARLES H. SHEASLEY, Franklin, Pa. Filed Aug. 31, 1916. Serial No. 117,927. 5 Claims. (Cl. 123—104.)
1. In a gas engine, in combination, a cylinder having a

gas port, a gas-supply duct leading to said port, a governor of the throttling type arranged to control the supply of

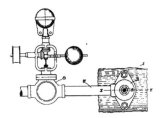

gas passing through said duct, and a manually adjustable means arranged to vary the effective area of said port.

1,327,928. OIL WATER-COLOR PAINT. EDITH L. SNYDER, Johnstown, Pa. Filed Aug. 10, 1917. Serial No. 185,541. 5 Claims. (Cl. 134—50.)
5. Oil water color paint containing in approximately the proportions indicated by the amounts stated: coloring matter one pound; glycerin four to ten ounces; white of egg two ounces; linseed oil four ounces; thin drying oil four ounces; copal varnish four ounces, and liquid glue four ounces.

1,327,929. COMBINED EGG-SEPARATOR AND JUICE-EXTRACTOR. PAUL TRIPKE, Jersey City, N. J. Filed Feb. 16, 1916. Serial No. 78,692. 7 Claims. (Cl. 65—12.)

1. A new article of manufacture, a base integrally formed into a dish or bowl having a central raised portion and a projecting or extending lipped portion, orifices, at intervals encircling said raised portion and piercing said base, said dish with said lipped portion adapted to hold the contents of an egg, said lipped portion to retain the yolk and said orifices to discharge the white.

1,327,930. ABDOMINAL SUPPORT. SHELDON VOORHEES, Syracuse, N. Y. Filed Aug. 4, 1917. Serial No 184,393. 3 Claims. (Cl. 128—167.)

1. An abdominal support including a single rigid sacro iliac plate, a single abdominal plate, each plate being

relatively narrow and elongated in a horizontal direction and adapted to bear at its central portion on the sacro iliac or abdominal region, of the body and having its ends arranged to come near the lateral limits of the body, and straps connecting the ends of the plates, said plates and straps forming substantially an inclined annulus adapted to support the abdomen from the hips without constricting the waist of the wearer, substantially as and for the purpose described.

1,327,931. REPRODUCING MANUSCRIPT, TYPEWRITTEN OR PRINTED MATTER, DRAWINGS, PHOTOGRAPHS, OR THE LIKE. SYDNEY JAMES WATERS, Esher, England. Filed Nov. 9, 1918. Serial No. 261,908. 4 Claims. (Cl. 41—38.5.)

1. The method of obtaining a stencil for the reproduction of manuscript, typewritten or printed matter, drawings, photographs or the like, which consists in exposing the matter to be reproduced (or a photographic negative taken therefrom) in front of a thin sensitized film having a suitable backing subsequently transferring the exposed film to a temporary support and removing the backing, then developing the film while adhering to the temporary support, thereupon transferring the film to a final backing of fine texture and finally stripping the temporary support from the film, leaving the latter adhering to the final backing, substantially as hereinbefore set forth.

1,327,932. PARACHUTE. CLYDE L. WELSH, Pittsburgh, Pa. Filed Apr. 17, 1919. Serial No. 290,855. 13 Claims. (Cl. 244—21.)

1. A parachute comprising a flexible dome, a rim, a plurality of reels mounted thereon, and flexible members connecting the said dome to the reels.

1,327,933. COATING MATERIAL. JAMES HOWARD YOUNG, Pittsburgh, Pa., assignor to Aspromet Company, Pittsburgh, Pa., a Corporation of Pennsylvania. Filed Sept. 11, 1918. Serial No. 253,513. 5 Claims. (Cl. 134—79.)

4. A coating material comprising viscose and a soluble soapy material incorporated therewith in sufficient volume to form a mixture of relatively lower surface tension than the viscose itself, and which is capable of spreading evenly over and firmly adhering to a sticky surface.

1,327,934. TOOL-HOLDER. FREDERICK TEMPLE ALCOCK, Kamloops, British Columbia, Canada. Filed June 7, 1919. Serial No. 302,377. 2 Claims. (Cl. 77—73.)

1. In combination with a holder for stocks and dies, of means connected with the holder for supporting a reamer in position to engage and ream the end of a pipe as the last of the threads are cut by the dies, said means comprising a sleeve shaped internally to fit the shank of the reamer and divided longitudinally into sections, and means

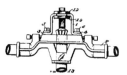

for adjustably connecting the sleeve to the holder, said means comprising a substantially U-shaped bracket having means for connecting the same to the holder, and lock nuts on opposite sides of the bracket.

1,327,935. CLUTCH-COUPLING FOR THE TRANSMISSION OF POWER BY SHAFTING. FRANCIS HERBERT ALEXANDER, Jesmond, Newcastle-upon-Tyne, England. Filed Jan. 6, 1919. Serial No. 269,866. 6 Claims. (Cl. 192—1.)

1. A clutch coupling of the type referred to comprising a member having a channel, a member carrying a dog adapted to co-act with this channel to compress air therein during relative rotation of said members, and means for inserting the dog into and withdrawing it from the channel.

1,327,936. CARD-INDEX. STANLEY ANTHONY, Boston, Mass., assignor to Acme Card System Company, Chicago, Ill., a Corporation of South Dakota. Filed Oct. 22, 1913, Serial No. 796,724. Renewed June 15, 1917. Serial No. 175,043. 23 Claims. (Cl. 129—16.)

13. In a card system, a sheet, and a support therefor to which the sheet is hinged, comprising a bar of resilient metal having a spacer at each end.

1,327,937. METALLIC SMOKEHOUSE. BART BILDERBACK, Rockville, Ind. Filed Sept. 6, 1919. Serial No. 322,178. 3 Claims. (Cl. 99—2.)

1. In a metallic smoke-house, a housing or cabinet consisting of all metallic walls, top and bottom; a pair of metallic inner-walls, spaced from the side walls and curved inwardly at the lower ends, toward each other, a flue-like space between the corresponding inner and outer walls, a multiplicity of vents formed in the inner-walls, a series of cleats mounted in pairs upon the inner walls, a slot-like drain formed between the lower edges

of the inner walls, a shield mounted above the slot-like drain, a fire box formed in the lower part of the housing and floored with fire brick, a meat-curing chamber formed between the inner walls, suitable doors adapted

to close the upper or meat curing chamber and the fire-box, and a suitable smoke-pipe located in the top of the housing, all substantially as described and shown and for the purposes set forth.

1,327,938. ARTIFICIAL ARM. ESLIE R. BIRCHARD, Toronto, Ontario, Canada, assignor to The Department of Soldiers Civil Re-Establishment, Invalided Soldiers' Commission of the Dominion of Canada. Filed June 25, 1919. Serial No. 306,708. 3 Claims. (Cl. 3—12.)

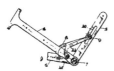

1. An artificial arm in which the operating connections between the bucket and the forearm member comprise a part mounted to slide longitudinally of the upper arm sheath; a link pivotally connected with the sliding part and with the bucket member; and a link pivotally connected with the sliding part and the forearm member, the distance between the pivot-point of the bucket link to the bucket and the pivot-point of the bucket to the upper arm sheath being greater than the distance between the pivot-point of the forearm link to the forearm member and the pivot-point of the forearm to the sheath.

1,327,939. STEAM-TRAP. JOSEPH F. BRIGHTMAN, Syracuse, N. Y. Filed Apr. 6, 1917. Serial No. 160.165. 4 Claims. (Cl. 137—101.)

1. In a steam trap, the combination of a container having alined inlet and outlet passages at its upper and lower ends, valves controlling said passages having stems extending toward each other, actuating means for

270 O. G.—18

the valves comprising an axially movable rod alined and coacting with the stems, a support located in the container adjacent the rod, and means carried by the support and within the container for actuating the rod, said means comprising a float and mechanical connections between the float and the rod, substantially as and for the purpose described.

1,327,940. AIR-CUSHION FOR PUMP-OPERATING MECHANISM. BRYNTE BRYNTESON, Odebolt, Iowa. Original application filed June 8, 1918, Serial No. 238,985. Divided and this application filed Mar. 5, 1919. Serial No. 280,856. 4 Claims. (Cl. 74—48.)

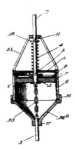

1. The combination of a reciprocating member composed of upper and lower sections, a flexible connection between the sections to permit limited independent movement thereof and cushioning means comprising a cylinder mounted on one of the sections and a piston operating in the cylinder and carried by the other section of the reciprocatory member.

1,327,941. CABINET-COUCH. HARRIETTE M. CAMP, Boston, Mass. Filed Apr. 11, 1918. Serial No. 227,984. 1 Claim. (Cl. 155—20.)

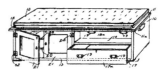

A cabinet-couch consisting in a cabinet box having a solid top completely covering the same and adapted to protect the contents of the box, a resilient bed structure applied to said top and extending the length thereof, the interior of said cabinet being divided transversely into storage spaces, drawers operable in certain of said storage spaces at one end of said box and slidable from either side of the cabinet, and when closed rendering the cabinet tight and protective of its contents, and doors at each side of said cabinet closing the storage space in the other end of said box, the arrangement of said drawers and doors permitting access to the storage space of said box from either side theerof at will.

1,327,942. MECHANICAL STARTER. THOMAS C. CHRISTIE, Lebanon, and ELMER A. EDMON, Dayton, Ohio. Filed July 24, 1917. Serial No. 182,559. 7 Claims. (Cl. 74—54.)

1. In a starting device for explosive engines, the combination with the shaft to be rotated of a ratchet wheel mounted upon the shaft, an actuating member mounted

co-axially with the ratchet wheel, a pawl carried by the actuating member and adapted to be intermittently engaged with the ratchet wheel to turn the same in unison with the actuator, a reciprocatory operating link

for the actuator, and an operating arm for the pawl moving in a path intersecting that of the operating link as the actuator approaches the limit of its retrograde or idle stroke whereby the interengagement of the link and arm will disengage the pawl from the ratchet wheel.

1,327,943. ARTICLE-STAND. MAX COHEN, Revere, Mass. Filed Dec. 8, 1917. Serial No. 206,133. 2 Claims. (Cl. 15—2.)

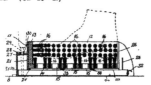

1. As a new article of manufacture, an article stand of a unit construction, comprising a frame provided with parallel side walls and one end wall, the other end being open; the lower portion of the side walls forming a drawer-way, means within the frame for supporting a brush above the drawer-way and permitting communication to the latter, and a partition wall spaced from the end wall and terminating above the drawer-way, said end wall and said partition being connected by a perforated top member.

1,327,944. SYSTEM FOR SEPARATING FLUID SUBSTANCES. ARTHUR STOCKDALE COSLER, New York, N. Y. Filed Oct. 5, 1918. Serial No. 257,023. 7 Claims. (Cl. 210—5.)

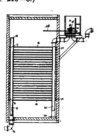

1. In a system for separating fluid substances, inclined shelves suitably inclosed and supported and adapted to spread the fluid and cause the elevation of the lighter element at the upper ends of the inclinations, a tubular

inlet member having discharge openings between said shelves respectively; and a tubular outlet member having inlets flush with the surfaces of the shelves and adapted to relieve the liquid of some of the heavier elements.

1,327,945. SPOT-LIGHT-MOUNTING DEVICE. WALTER P. COUSINO, Curtice, Ohio. Filed Feb. 14, 1919. Serial No. 277,032. 6 Claims. (Cl. 240—61.)

2. A spotlight mounting device comprising a fixed guide, a tubular relatively rockable bracket carrying member frictionally held in said guide, a reciprocable bar in said tubular member, and a rotatable spot-light holder mounted in the bracket rotatable by the bar and rockable with the member.

1,327,946. EGG-BOX. JOSEPH LEOPOLD COYLE, Vancouver, British Columbia, Canada, assignor of one-fourth to Frederick Dundas Todd, Victoria, British Columbia, Canada. Filed June 29, 1918, Serial No. 242,615. Renewed Nov. 26, 1919. Serial No. 340,798. 9 Claims. (Cl. 229—29.)

1. An egg box comprising a foldable blank forming the body of the box, and partitions individually removably mounted on the body blank foldable longitudinally within the box, and unfolding automatically when the body is extended, substantially as described.

1,327,947. SYSTEM OF BONDING RAILS. LAWRENCE P. CRECELIUS, Cleveland, Ohio, assignor to The Electric Railway Improvement Company, Cleveland, Ohio, a Corporation of Ohio. Filed Apr. 10, 1914. Serial No. 830,858. 2 Claims. (Cl. 173—278.)

1. In a system of bonding rails, in combination with a pair of adjoining rails, flat bond plates of good conducting material intimately attached to the rails, and a complete bond comprising a conductor with terminal sleeves, the latter having flat contact portions of considerable area lying flat against and secured to the outer faces of the bond plates.

1,327,948. PICNIC AND OTHER FOOD-HOLDER. ERNEST AUGUSTUS DENNIS, Glenroy, New Zealand. Filed Aug. 11, 1919. Serial No. 316,818. 1 Claim. (Cl. 220—20.)

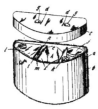

A cruet for picnic, camping and like purposes comprising a substantially D-shaped receptacle, partitions transversely of the receptacle dividing the same into compartments for receptacles, a D-shaped receptacle in a similarly shaped compartment at one end of the first mentioned receptacle, means bearing against the side of the second mentioned D-shaped receptacle for holding it in position and a cover for the first mentioned receptacle.

1,327,949. HOLDER FOR PHONOGRAPHIC DISK RECORDS. OTTO CULLMAN, Chicago, Ill. Filed Apr. 7, 1919. Serial No. 288,213. 5 Claims. (Cl. 211—16.)

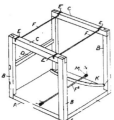

1. In a holder for phonographic disk records, a frame, partitions, means to hold said partitions in spaced relation and supported by said frame, in combination with levers pivotally mounted between said partitions, and means to yieldingly hold said partitions and levers in close relation.

1,327,950. GEARING FOR EGG-BEATERS, CREAM-WHIPPERS, AND THE LIKE. WILLIAM H. GEIGER, Oakland, Calif. Filed Apr. 18, 1918. Serial No. 229,292. 4 Claims. (Cl. 74—7.)

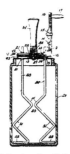

1. In gearing of the class described a base consisting of parallel spaced plates, gears mounted between the plates and having bearing bosses arranged in bearings thereof

and provided with bores of angular cross section, an intermediate transmission gear having its spindle engaged with the plates and projected above the upper plate to form a threaded extension, a grip handle directly connected with the threaded extension of said spindle, rotary elements having shanks or stems of angular cross section fitted in the bores of the bearing bosses of said gears, and means for communicating rotary motion to the train of gears.

1,327,951. CUT-OUT RELAY. NELSON R. HAAS, Dayton, Ohio, assignor to The Dayton Engineering Laboratories Company, a Corporation of Ohio. Filed Feb. 4, 1918. Serial No. 215,305. 8 Claims. (Cl. 200—87.)

1. In a device of the kind described, the combination with coöperating contacts for completing an electric circuit, one of the contact elements being flexible; of provisions normally maintaining the contacts apart; electromagnetic means causing the contacts to come together under pressure; and a member actuated by the electromagnetic means, coöperating with the flexible contact for causing an abrupt change in the bending operation of the flexible contact during the operation of electro-magnetic means.

1,327,952. TRANSPORT SYSTEM FOR POSTAGE AND OTHER GOODS. HANS KNUDSEN HALLER, Copenhagen, Denmark. Filed June 25, 1918. Serial No. 241,850. 13 Claims. (Cl. 214—38.)

1. In combination a conveyer, means for automatically giving it a back and forth movement, stationary shelves to contain articles, automatically self adjusting scrapers on the conveyer which sweep articles from the stationary shelves onto the conveyer and scrapers arranged at fixed points and automatically adjusted by the moving conveyer to sweep the articles from the conveyer, substantially as described.

1,327,953. WATER-MOTOR. JOHN R. HAMILTON, Yonkers, N. Y., assignor to Automatic Sprinkler Company of America, New York, N. Y., a Corporation of New York. Filed Aug. 6, 1918. Serial No. 248,506. 8 Claims. (Cl. 253—136.)

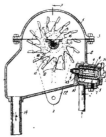

1. In water motors adapted for alarm gongs, a sectional motor casing, a motor wheel and connected motor shaft

supported in bearings in the lower section of said motor casing, said casing having a removable top section above said bearings, a nozzle chamber formed adjacent the bottom of said casing, a nozzle projecting through the wall of said chamber to coöperate with said wheel, a tubular screen in said chamber coöperating with the inlet end of said nozzle, a supply pipe connected to said chamber at the side of said chamber and screen, a deflecting shield located between said screen and said supply pipe to deflect dirt, etc., to the bottom of said nozzle chamber, and a removable plug in the bottom of said nozzle chamber.

1,327,954. SHUTTLE. JOHN B. HANCQ, Jamestown, N. Y. Filed May 16, 1919. Serial No. 297,585. 5 Claims. (Cl. 139—27.)

1. A spindle shuttle comprising a wooden shell having a lengthwise opening therein for the spindle, a metallic housing removably attached in one end of said lengthwise opening in said shell and having squared openings in the opposite sides thereof, a spindle butt socket fitting within said metallic housing, and a pivot pin for said spindle butt socket having squared ends receivable in said squared openings in the opposite sides of said removable housing to hold said spindle in line.

1,327,955. AUTOMATIC PHONOGRAPH-STOP. ADAM C. HENDRICKS, Martinsburg, W. Va. Filed June 12, 1919. Serial No. 303,589. 16 Claims. (Cl. 74—46.)

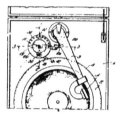

14. In a graphophone stop for disk instruments, a base adapted for attachment to the instrument cabinet adjacent the record carrying table, said base having in its upper side a recess, a fixed post rising from said base within said recess, a brake actuator pivotally mounted on said post and resting on said base, an adjustable brake carrying arm extending from said brake actuator for stopping the aforesaid table, said actuator having an upstanding annular flange spaced around said post and provided with notches in its upper edge, a sliding arm received in said notches and having a slot through which said post passes, the outer end of said arm forming a track and having a notch at the inner end of said track, a shoe adapted for mounting on the tone arm of the instrument to normally travel along said track and prevent operation of said actuator until said shoe reaches said notch, a spring confined in the recess of said base for then operating said brake actuator to apply the brake, a hand wheel rotatably mounted on the upper end of said post and obscuring said base and actuator from view, and coacting means on said sliding arm and said hand wheel for adjusting the former from the latter to vary the relation of said shoe and notch.

1,327,956. DRAWING-TABLE. EMILE RAYMOND KOECHLIN, Amsterdam, Netherlands, assignor to Naamlooze Vennootschap Weduwe J. Ahrend & Zoons Industrie- en Handelsvereeniging, Amsterdam, Netherlands, a Company of the Netherlands. Filed Oct. 5, 1918. Serial No. 257,038. 2 Claims. (Cl. 45—131.)

1. In a drawing table, including a movable drawing board and a support, guiding means adapted to permit said board being displaced into positions parallel with each other, said means comprising an articulated quadrilateral pivoted both to said table and said support, the sum of the lengths of two adjacent sides of said quadrilateral being slightly greater than that of the other two sides.

1,327,957. COMBINED MAIL-BOX AND DOOR-BELL. JAMES A. McDONALD, Fort Worth, Tex. Filed July 9, 1918. Serial No. 244,055. 1 Claim. (Cl. 232—19.)

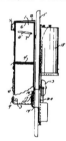

A combined mail box and door bell comprising a box provided with a stationary mail holding member having a top, a bottom, and sides and having a mail receiving slot in said top, a movable box member hingedly connected to said stationary member and movable far enough to expose said slot and forming a cover for said stationary member and provided with a door and a lock therefor, springs attached to said box member and holding the movable member yieldingly closed, said stationary member having slots in the sides thereof and said movable member having lugs rigid therewith and projecting in and movable in said slots but preventing the inner edge of said movable member from being drawn to the outer edge of said stationary member, and a signaling device to be automatically actuated by the moving of said movable member.

1,327,958. VEHICLE-SPRING. MICHAEL M. MCINTYRE, Cleveland, Ohio, assignor, by mesne assignments, to The Standard Parts Company, Cleveland, Ohio, a Corporation of Ohio. Filed Mar. 4, 1915. Serial No. 12,141. 2 Claims. (Cl. 267—27.)
1. The combination, with a flat plate spring, of a spring having a scroll and extending about the end of the first mentioned spring, shackle links connected to the end of the scroll and extending on opposite sides of the eye of

the first mentioned spring, a compression spring bearing against the eye of the first spring and located within the

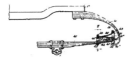

shackle links, and connections whereby the shackle will engage the eye of the first spring when the compression spring has been compressed to a predetermined extent.

1,327,959. GARMENT-SUPPORTER. JAMES W. MAC-BOYLE, Chicago, Ill. Filed June 24, 1919. Serial No. 306,358. 2 Claims. (Cl. 24—245.)

1. In a garment supporter, the combination with a strip of fabric having a loop formed near one end thereof and a pocket at said end, of a rigid catch member depending from the loop and having an elongated eye therein, and a plain oblong rigid stiffening member sewed in said pocket so that it forms a fabric-covered button at the end of the supporter which in use passes completely through the eye of the rigid catch member to coöperate therewith, substantially as and for the purpose described.

1,327,960. OCCUPANT-OPERATED VEHICLE AND STEERING APPARATUS. DANIEL W. MOODY, Chicago, Ill. Filed Jan. 13, 1919. Serial No. 270,780. 6 Claims. Cl. 208—114.)

1. A vehicle steering device comprising a substantially upright transverse arch supported upon the vehicle to be steered ; a pivot support consisting of a member which is relatively extended in a fore-and-aft direction depending rigidly from the crown of the arch, and a steering element carrier which is relatively extended transversely to said direction, pivoted vertically to said depending support.

1,327,961. CURTAIN-SUPPORT. FRANK A. PETERS, Chicago, Ill. Filed May 12, 1919. Serial No. 296,421. 8 Claims. (Cl. 156—22.)

1. A device of the kind described comprising a vertical longitudinally movable member, a horizontal member secured to the upper end thereof and adapted to support a curtain, fixed and vertically movable guiding means for said member, and means for holding the vertical member in adjusted position longitudinally.

3. A device of the kind described comprising a frame, a horizontal member pivotally connected at one end to one side of the frame adapted to support a curtain, and a catch for releasably securing the other end of said member to the other side of the frame.

4. A device of the kind described comprising a movable vertical member, a horizontal member carried thereby and adapted to support a curtain, and means for guiding the upper end of the vertical member irrespective of its vertical position.

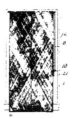

7. A device of the kind described comprising a frame, a vertical member, a horizontal member carried thereby and adapted to support a curtain, means for moving the vertical member longitudinally relatively to the frame, guiding means secured to the frame for supporting such member during such movement, and means for releasably clamping the vertical member in position.

8. A device of the kind described comprising a movable vertical member, a horizontal member adapted to support a curtain secured thereto, a fixed vertical guiding member, and connecting means slidably but not rotatably engaging the guiding member and rotatably engaging the movable vertical member but not slidable thereon.

1,327,962. DRUM-FILTER WIRING. EDSON S. PETTIS, Mill Valley, Calif. Filed Mar. 5, 1919. Serial No. 280,763. 5 Claims. (Cl. 210—14.)

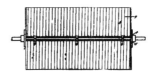

1. In combination with a filtering drum, a filtering medium surrounding the drum, a pair of cross bars, a wire covering for the filtering medium secured at each end to the cross bars, and means for securing the cross bars to the drum.

1,327,963. SIDE-SEAL CLOSURE. GEORGE RAMSEY, Brooklyn, N. Y., assignor to Anchor Cap & Closure Corporation, Brooklyn, N. Y., a Corporation of New York. Filed May 15, 1917. Serial No. 168,801. 9 Claims. (Cl. 215—81.)

1. A closure for glass receptacles and the like comprising a top portion, a skirt depending from said top portion, a groove on the exterior of said skirt to form a bead on the interior of said skirt, and transverse corrugations extending across said groove and terminating short of the margin of the skirt and providing friction members on the interior of said skirt adapted to contact with and engage the side wall of a suitable receptacle to frictionally maintain said cap in position upon such receptacle.

1,327,964. LUG-STRAP HOLDER. FREDERICK B. RAND, Sanford, Me. Filed Oct. 6, 1919. Serial No. 328,826. 3 Claims. (Cl. 139—48.)

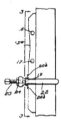

1. A lug strap holder, comprising a stick adapted to be clamped to the back of a picker staff, said stick having spaced apart pins fixed transversely therethrough to hold between them the lug strap, and a yoke equipped for clamping said stick to the picker staff.

1,327,965. PACKING OR GASKET CONSTRUCTION. MAX ROTTER, St. Louis, Mo., assignor to Busch-Sulzer Bros.-Diesel Engine Company, St. Louis, Mo., a Corporation of Missouri. Filed Apr. 14, 1917. Serial No. 161,966. 8 Claims. (Cl. 220—81.)

1. A gasket construction comprising the combination with the gasketed members provided with complementary bolt holes, one of said members being provided with main gasket groove sections between adjacent bolt holes and branch grooves surrounding each such bolt hole and joining the main groove sections, of a strip gasket disposed in said main groove sections and said branch grooves.

8. A gasket construction comprising in combination with the two gasketed members and bolts passing through said members for clamping the same together, a strip gasket between said members, said strip being parted adjacent each bolt and a part thereof being fitted at each side of each bolt.

1,327,966. CAN-CLOSING MACHINE. FRANK RUDOLPHI, New York, N. Y., assignor to American Can Company, a Corporation of New Jersey. Filed Dec. 1, 1915. Serial No. 64,473. 14 Claims. (Cl. 113—24.)

1. In a can closing machine, a seaming head having, in combination: a plurality of seaming rolls; means for independently adjusting said rolls to any position within limits; and means independent of said adjusting means for moving one of said rolls together with its adjusting means into inoperative position while on the seaming head, leaving the other roll adjusted for a seaming operation, and for restoring the inoperative roll to its adjusted position by the reversal of such throwing-out movement.

1,327,967. CAP FOR BOTTLES OR JARS. ROBERT A. RUSSELL, New York, N. Y., assignor, by direct and mesne assignments,. of one-third to Paragon Metal Cap Company, Inc., Brooklyn, N. Y., a Corporation of New York, one-third to Martin King, New York, N. Y., and one-third to Leslie R. N. Carvalho, Brooklyn, N. Y. Filed Apr. 2, 1915. Serial No. 18,706. 3 Claims. (Cl. 215—13.)

1. A lacquered sheet metal cap for bottles or jars comprising a body portion cut from sheet metal lacquered on both surfaces thereof throughout, said body portion being bent into cylindrical form and having the meeting edges thereof joined by an interfolded seam which conceals and covers the exposed raw edges of the metal formed in cutting the body portion, and a top for closing the end of said body portion, said top being cut from a sheet of metal lacquered on both sides thereof throughout, said top being joined to the body portion by an interfolded seam which conceals and covers the exposed raw upper edge of the metal of the body portion and the exposed raw edge of the metal of the top formed in cutting the top.

1,327,968. AIR-BRAKE-CONTROLLING MECHANISM. THOMAS W. SCOTT, Baltimore, Md., assignor to The American Train Control Co., Baltimore, Md., a Corporation of Maryland. Filed Dec. 17, 1915, Serial No. 67,374. Renewed Nov. 12, 1919. Serial No. 337,621. 2 Claims. (Cl. 246—180.)

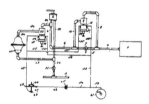

1. In an air-brake controlling mechanism the combination with an air brake apparatus including a reservoir, a train line and an engineer's valve, of connections for supplying air from the reservoir to the train line only through the engineer's valve; one electro-pneumatic means entirely separate and independent of all the devices of the engineer's valve for effecting an automatic application of the brakes, and a second electro-pneumatic means for cutting off the supply of all air to the train line to prevent a release of the brakes by the engineer.

1,327,969. CHANGE-MAKING MACHINE. EDWARD C. SIQUEIRA, ·Oakland, Calif. Filed Mar. 8, 1917. Serial No. 153,524. 3 Claims. (Cl. 133—4.)

1. A device of the character described comprising two tubes for coins of lowest denomination, two for the first multiple thereof, and one each for the higher multiples thereof, sliding plates positioned under said tubes and having openings adapted to register with said tubes and withdraw therefrom one coin at a time, depending arms formed in said plates, pivotally mounted members adapted

to coöperate with said arms and move said plates, means for operating said members, lugs formed on the pivotal

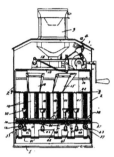

members corresponding to the higher multiples adapted to overlap the members of lower multiples but not the members corresponding to the lowest denomination.

1,327,970. MOUTHPIECE FOR MUSICAL INSTRUMENTS. FORTUNATO SORDILLO, Boston, Mass. Filed Jan. 18, 1919, Serial No. 271,906. Renewed Nov. 17, 1919. Serial No. 338,531. 3 Claims. (Cl. 84—79.)

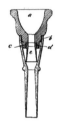

1. In a musical instrument in combination a substantially cup shaped open-ended mouth piece, an apertured bottom part on said mouth piece, a separable tubular throat piece, detachably secured to the apertured bottom part of said mouth piece, an outer tube surrounding said throat piece and disconnected therefrom and detachably secured to the outer side of said mouth piece.

1,327,971. POTATO - SEED PLANTER. WILLIAM R. TOWNE, San Francisco, Calif. Filed Sept. 16, 1918. Serial No. 254,858. 15 Claims. (Cl. 221—127.)

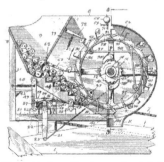

1. The combination with a hopper, of a chute leading from the hopper, a series of carriers mounted within the hopper and arranged to carry seed potatoes from the hopper, means for moving the carrier containing a seed potato nearest the chute to a point directly over the chute at regular intervals; and means for actuating the carrier to release the seed therefrom into the chute.

1,327,972. HAT-SEWING MACHINE. JAMES WHITELAW, St. Louis, Mo. Filed Jan. 21, 1916. Serial No. 73,283. 22 Claims. (Cl. 112—12.)

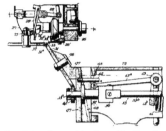

1. In a hat sewing machine the combination of a frame having upper and lower arms, a slide member mounted on the lower arm for generally vertical displacement, a work-supporting feed-member carried by said slide member and a brim table also carried by said slide member, both movable therewith up toward and down from the parts carried by the upper arm, complemental presser means and stitch forming means, said presser and stitch forming means carried by the upper arm.

7. In a hat sewing machine, a bevel-gear formed feed wheel having peripheral work feeding teeth, and a driving means coöperating with said teeth to rotate the wheel.

18. In a hat sewing machine, the combination of an upright depressible feed wheel adapted to enter the angle of the hat crown and brim, a coöperating horizontal presser wheel adapted to press against the inside edge of the crown, and laterally yielding means normally maintaining the presser wheel in position to coöperate with the feed wheel.

1,327,973. AUTOMATIC AIR-BRUSH MACHINE FOR COATING LAMPS, &c. CLAUDE E. ALLEN, Kenosha, Wis., assignor to C. M. Hall Lamp Company, Detroit, Mich., a Corporation of Michigan. Filed July 25, 1917. Serial No. 182,629. 5 Claims. (Cl. 91—45.)

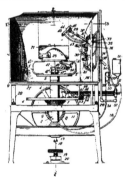

1. In a machine of the character described, the combination of a suitable main frame, a rotatable article-support and means for rotating the same, a plurality of standards arranged in proximity to said article-support, a jointed and adjustable arm mounted upon each standard, air

brushes carried by the several arms, a flexible supply pipe leading to each air brush, a valve controlling each supply pipe, a valve rod operatively connected with each valve, a rotatable cam support and circumferentially adjustable cams carried by said cam-support and adapted to co-operate with said valve rods to automatically open and close the valves at pre-determined intervals.

1,327,974. TREATING MANGANESE-SILVER ORES. LESLIE W. AUSTIN, San Jose, Calif. Filed Apr. 14, 1919. Serial No. 289,939. 3 Claims. (Cl. 75—18.)

3. The process of treating manganese silver-ores which consists in preliminarily treating said ore with pyrite in the presence of sulfuric acid, and then recovering the values by suitable methods.

1,327,975. PROPULSION OF AIR AND OTHER GASES OR FLUIDS. HERTHA AYRTON, Hyde Park, London, England. Filed May' 26, 1916. Serial No. 100,010. 9 Claims. (Cl. 230— 33.)

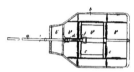

2. A method of propelling fluids to a relatively considerable distance consisting in the production of successive blasts by the beating action against a surface of a jointed fan of suitable construction capable of adapting itself to the shape of the surface against which it is struck, the beating action being characterized in that the portion of the fan next to the handle is caused to strike the surface first, this preliminary impact being followed by a rapid beating movement of the remaining portion of the fan against the surface, the effect being that each blast forms a vortex the upper surface of which revolves in a direction toward the source of propagation while the whole vortex moves rapidly away from that source, the blast being timed so that the vortex produced by one blast may overtake and merge with another at a distance from the source of propagation, the combined vortices forming one vortex of great force moving in the line of propagation.

1,327,976. PRESSING-MACHINE. DANA H. BENJAMIN, Cleveland Heights, Ohio, assignor to The American Laundry Machinery Company, Cincinnati, Ohio, a Corporation of Ohio. Filed Mar. 12, 1917. Serial No. 154,211. 3 Claims. (Cl. 68—9.)

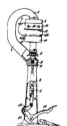

1. A sleeve sticker, comprising relatively movable pressing members having coöperating pressing surfaces, and a sleeve guiding member provided with a narrow slot lying opposite the space between said pressing members, said slot being open at one end and closed at the other to form a sleeve locating abutment.

1,327,977. PHONOGRAPH-CABINET. WESLEY H. BENNINGTON, Cleveland, Ohio. Filed Jan. 13, 1919. Serial No. 270,805. 2 Claims. (Cl. 45—52.)

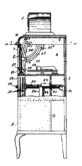

1. A phonograph cabinet including an instrument compartment, an oscillating temporary record support below the instrument compartment, and a record storage compartment below said temporary support, the instrument compartment being provided with a door in the front wall thereof, a pair of trunnions mounted on said door in juxtaposition to the lateral edges thereof and in the same transverse plane, vertical grooves in the side walls of the compartment, in which said trunnions travel, a second pair of trunnions mounted on the door in a transverse plane back of the first named trunnions, and segmental grooves in the side walls of the compartment, in which the last named trunnions travel.

1,327,978. COVER-SUPPORT. BURR B. BLOOD, Chicago, Ill., assignor of one-half to George Heidman and one-half to Norman A. Street, Chicago, Ill. Filed May 5, 1919. Serial No. 294,883. 5 Claims. (Cl. 217—60.)

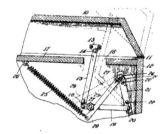

1. A cover support, comprising a link or arm, one end whereof is adapted to be pivotally secured to a cover or lid and depend therefrom, a second arm or link having one end pivotally secured to the lower end of the first arm or link, while the other end of the second arm or link has a fixed pivotal point, the pivotal points of the arms or links being such as to permit vertical movement of said arms or links, a third arm or link, one end whereof has a fixed pivotal point in a plane above the fixed pivotal point of said second arm or link, while the free end of said third arm or link is normally disposed in a plane below the normal plane of said second arm or link, a retracting spring, one end whereof is secured to the free end of said third arm or link while the other end of said spring is fixedly secured to the cabinet, and means intermediate of the second and third arms or links whereby the retracting action of the spring on the free end of the third arm or link is imparted to the second arm or link.

1,327,979. LOCK FOR AUTOMOBILES. Edwin C. Boehmig, Hammond, Ind. Filed Mar. 27, 1919. Serial No. 285,688. 2 Claims. (Cl. 70—126.)

1. In a device of the character described the combination with the clutch and brake pedals of an automobile of a lock having a key controlled bolt, means for securing the same rigidly to one of said pedals and an element carried by the other of said pedals into the path of movement of which said bolt may be projected, to thereby hold the clutch in disengaged position.

1,327,980. HAIR - DRESSING DEVICE. Hugo Brinkhaus, Brooklyn, N. Y. Filed Mar. 17, 1917. Serial No. 155,432. 11 Claims. (Cl. 132—19.)

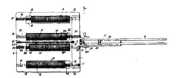

3. A hair dressing device comprising a heat-applying member, wave-producing devices movable in parallel planes of movement toward and away from said heat-applying member, said wave-producing devices also having wave-producing movement in parallel planes substantially at right angles to the direction of their movement toward and away from said heat-applying member, means for imparting said wave-producing movement to said devices operated by the movement of these devices toward and away from said heat-applying member, and manually operated means including a parallel motion for moving said wave-producing devices in parallel planes of movement toward or away from said heat-applying member.

1,327,981. BEAM-CLAMP. George H. Bruns, New York, N. Y. Filed Sept. 5, 1919. Serial No. 321,940. 6 Claims. (Cl. 248—32.)

1. A beam clamp of the class described comprising a pair of members, each of said members including a plate which is adapted to be disposed against and transversely to the beam, each of said members having a portion thereof extending over the side of the beam opposite to that against which its plate is located and being bent angularly to said plate, and said portions gripping said beam and firmly securing said members to the beam when the members are secured to each other.

1,327,982. IMPLEMENT-HOLDER FOR COOKING UTENSILS. John A. Burns, West Haven, Conn., assignor of one-half to Christian Ginter, Jr., New Haven, Conn. Filed Sept. 4, 1919. Serial No. 321,671. 1 Claim. (Cl. 65—65.)

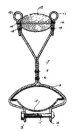

As a new article of manufacture, an implement-holder for application to the handles of cooking utensils, the said holder comprising two complementary strips of spring metal fastened together midway of their ends to form a rigid stem, having their lower ends bent outwardly and inwardly to form a handle-clip and their extremities perforated for the reception of a clamping-bolt, and the upper ends of the said strips being bent divergently to form yielding gripping-arms for the reception of the handle of a cooking implement between them, the extremities of the upper ends of the strips being folded upon themselves for the production of handle-retaining ribs which grip the handle and hold it against deflection with respect to the device.

1,327,983. VENEER SLICING AND SCORING MACHINE. Robert W. Burrows, Petaluma, Calif., assignor of one-half to Hobbs Wall & Co., San Francisco, Calif., a Corporation of California. Filed Dec. 3, 1918. Serial No. 265,085. 8 Claims. (Cl. 144—42.)

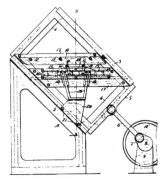

1. In a machine of the type set forth, a slicing knife, means to operate the knife, scoring means, and means to actuate the scoring means simultaneously with the knife so as to cause same to move diagonally in the plane in which the knife moves and to score a face of the material during slicing of the latter.

1,327,984. VALVE. Robert E. Campbell, Berkeley, Calif. Filed Mar. 27, 1918. Serial No. 225,106. 6 Claims. (Cl. 251—113.)

1. A valve comprising a casing having a central, longitudinal passage extending therethrough, one end of said

passage being enlarged, a member having a central passage formed therein adapted to be received in the enlarged portion of the casing passage, a valve seat on the inner end of said member, a spherical valve within the casing adapted to engage said seat, said valve having a central passage

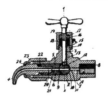

formed therein, means for turning the valve to bring the central passage into and out of register with the passages formed in the casing and in the insertible member, a removable spout on the casing, a resilient packing member interposed between the spout and the insertible member, and means for securing the spout on the casing.

1,327,985. AMMONIUM - PERCHLORATE EXPLOSIVE. Oscar Birger Carlson, Månsbo, Avesta, Sweden, assignor to Aktiebolaget Carlit, Stockholm, Sweden, a Corporation of Sweden. Filed Sept. 25, 1917. Serial No. 193,092. 2 Claims. (Cl. 52—1.)

1. Ammonium perchlorate explosive, characterized by the ammonium perchlorate used having a percentage of a chlorate, between 0.005 and 1% by weight.

1,327,986. ELECTRIC HEATER. Charles E. Clark and Archie G. Dowell, San Francisco, Calif.; said Dowell assignor to said Clark. Filed Feb. 26, 1919. Serial No. 279,267. 8 Claims. (Cl. 219—34.)

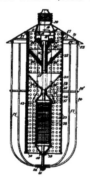

1. A cylindrical vertically suspended heater, comprising an electric plug and divergent surrounding canopy, a dielectric member suspended from the plug, conducting wires extending from the plug through the dielectric member, a suspended heating coil with which the wires are connected, and a foraminous cylindrical casing surrounding the heating coil.

1,327,987. PROCESS FOR CASTING STEEL INGOTS. Ray G. Coates, Pasadena, Calif., assignor, by direct and mesne assignments, to Valley Mould and Iron Corporation, New York, N. Y., a Corporation of New York. Filed Aug. 20, 1917. Serial No. 187,166. 13 Claims. (Cl. 22—216.)

2. The process of forming steel ingots which process comprises pouring the steel into shallow molds; then controlling the temperature of the poured steel by radiant heat whereby the isothermal zone of fusion measured at a mid transverse cross-section of the mass gradually ad-

vances inwardly and upwardly from coincidence with the surfaces of the mold to coincidence with the top surface of the steel mass.

1,327,988. DRAFT ATTACHMENT FOR STOVES. James H. Dean, Chicago, Ill., assignor to Cole Manufacturing Company, Chicago, Ill., a Corporation. Filed Aug. 30, 1919. Serial No. 320,845. 6 Claims. (Cl. 126—77.)

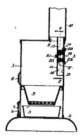

2. In a draft attachment for stoves, the combination of a stove casing, a vertically disposed, open-ended flue casing arranged on one side of said stove casing, and a shiftable valve member dividing said casing into upper and lower flue portions adapted to deliver air to the smoke pipe or to the combustion chamber at a point above the fire, said valve member being arranged to control the admission of air to one or the other of said flue portions, substantially as described.

1,327,989. GAS - METERING APPARATUS. Louis A. Ferguson, Evanston, and Harold S. Sines, Oak Park, Ill.; said Sines assignor to said Ferguson. Substitute for application Serial No. 872,713, filed Nov. 18, 1914. This application filed Jan. 24, 1917. Serial No. 144,123. 2 Claims. (Cl. 234—34.5.)

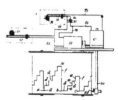

1. Mechanism for measuring and integrating the consumption of gas comprising a gas meter, a recording device adapted to indicate the greatest amount of gas integrated by the gas meter during any one of a number of intervals of time, electromagnetic mechanism for operating said recording device, a circuit for said electromagnetic mechanism, quickly acting contacts included in said circuit, a shaft driven from the integrating train of the gas meter,

a cam for operating said contacts loosely mounted on said shaft, a spring interposed between the shaft and cam, means normally preventing said cam from moving under the action of said spring and means for permitting the spring to actuate the cam when a predetermined amount of gas has been measured and integrated by the gas meter.

1,327,990. STORAGE APPARATUS FOR LIQUIDS. CHARLES L. FRENCH, Cambridge, Mass. Filed Nov. 18, 1916. Serial No. 132,193. 6 Claims. (Cl. 221—103.)

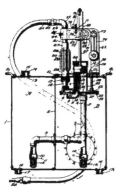

1. An apparatus for storing and delivering lubricating oils and the like having, in combination, a pump; a plurality of reservoirs for holding oils or the like of different kinds; supply conduits connecting said pump with the reservoirs; delivery conduits connected with said pump, and means for selectively controlling said supply and delivery conduits.

1,327,991. WRENCH. FRANK A. GATEWOOD, Sylvan Grove, Kans. Filed Aug. 6, 1919. Serial No. 315,722. 1 Claim. (Cl. 81—57.)

A wrench comprising a pair of side plates provided with notches in their side edges adjacent one end, a train of gearing mounted between the side plates, extensions projecting axially from the end members of the gearing to be engaged by a turning tool or by a nut-engaging socket, a locking handle having a foot portion adapted to fit between the side plates and constructed to engage and lock the adjacent gear, and studs on the opposite sides of said foot portion of the locking handle to engage the notches in the edges of the side plates.

1,327,992. BINDER. GEORGE G. H. FRITZSCHE, Brooklyn, N. Y. Filed Sept. 11, 1917. Serial No. 190,759. 3 Claims. (Cl. 129—40.)

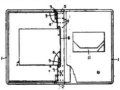

2. A folded pamphlet binder comprising cover boards a back, a reinforcing strip for said back secured to the inside edges of said cover boards in close proximity to the back and having series of holes therein, and retaining means for the pamphlet, each of said means having a prong arranged to enter one of said holes and rest between the back and strip, and an elongated loop adapted to yieldingly engage the pamphlet along its vertical central fold to hold it securely against the reinforcing strip throughout its length.

1,327,993. ALARM DEVICE FOR AUTOMOBILES. ALBERT A. GOLDBLATT, Brooklyn, N. Y. Filed Feb. 19, 1919. Serial No. 278,036. 7 Claims. (Cl. 116—1.)

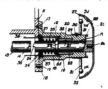

1. In a signal device of the class described, a stationary sleeve member, a shaft rotatably mounted in said sleeve member and protruding through one end thereof, a sound producing member mounted on the protruding end of the shaft and adapted to rotate therewith, means involving a tensional device for holding said shaft and sound producing member in a predetermined position relative to said sleeve member, and hammer devices mounted on said sleeve member and adapted to operate in connection with said sound producing member.

1,327,994. MECHANISM FOR SEAMING ENDS TO CAN-BODIES. JAMES A. GRAY, San Francisco, Calif., assignor to American Can Company, San Francisco, Calif., a Corporation of New Jersey. Filed Oct. 18, 1915. Serial No. 56,456. 22 Claims. (Cl. 113—23.)

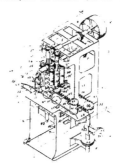

1. An apparatus for the described purpose, the same comprising alined vertically disposed members for receiv-

ing and clamping therebetween a can body with an end cover loosely applied thereto, means for imparting rotation to one of said members, devices for intermittently moving the opposing member toward and from the rotary member, a plurality of continuously rotatable seaming roll power spindles, rotatable seaming rolls eccentrically mounted thereon with respect to the axis of the same and associated with the rotary members, said spindles being adapted for moving said rolls into and out of engagement with the flange of a can end cover of a can while held clamped between the mentioned vertically alined members, and devices for adjusting the position of said rolls relative to each other to adapt the same for the seaming of end covers to can bodies of varying diameter.

1,327,995. REVERSING MECHANISM FOR INTERNAL-COMBUSTION ENGINES. GEORGE WILFRID ACLAND GREEN, OSWALD WANS, and FREDERICK HOWARD LIVENS, Lincoln, England, assignors to Ruston and Hornsby, Limited, Lincoln, England. Filed Sept. 27, 1919. Serial No. 326,938. 21 Claims. (Cl. 123—41.)

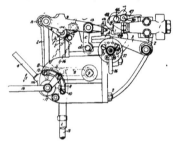

1. In a two-stroke internal combustion engine, a fuel injection pump, an inertia tappet actuating the pump, an eccentric actuating the inertia tappet, a connection between the eccentric and the inertia tappet, a joint in the connection, means for altering the path of the joint pin, and means for actuating the eccentric.

1,327,996. SPEAKING - PIPE. WILLIAM E. HASKELL, Brattleboro, Vt., assignor to Estey Organ Company, Brattleboro, Vt., a Corporation of Vermont. Filed June 17, 1919. Serial No. 304,817. 8 Claims. (Cl. 84—22.)

8. An open speaking labial pipe of greater cross section at its top than at its bottom having a mouth and a bottom which curves upwardly from the lower lip of the mouth toward the back of the pipe.

1,327,997. CORNSTALK-CUTTER. FREDRICH G. HEINECKE, Gaylord, Minn. Filed Oct. 1, 1919. Serial No. 327,700. 2 Claims. (Cl. 56—63.)

1. The combination, with a corn binding machine, of a blade for cutting the stumps of the corn stalks, said blade being secured at the front end of the said machine and having a straight main portion arranged in a position inclined to the horizontal and disposed diagonally of the line of draft and having a curved portion which projects laterally of it at its rear part, said main and curved portions having a cutting edge at their lower side which operates to slice through and cut off the projecting stumps of the corn stalks.

1,327,998. TARGET. AUGUST HENIGMAN, Bokoshe. Okla. Filed June 13, 1918. Serial No. 239,802. 5 Claims. (Cl. 124—15.)

1. In a target, the combination with a figure having an opening therethrough, a display member movably connected with said figure, and yielding means tending normally to move said member into display position; of a target proper having a stem passing to the rear through said opening in the figure, a lever pivoted between its ends in a support behind the figure, connections between one arm of the lever and the stem of the target, and a catch for the display member engaged by the other arm of the lever, and adapted to be released by impact on said target.

1,327,999. REGULATOR FOR ENGINES. WILLIAM WASHINGTON HILL, Sarona, Wis. Filed Apr. 10, 1919. Serial No. 289,109. 1 Claim. (Cl. 137—68.)

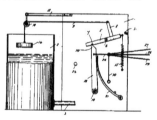

In an engine regulating device, a pivoted actuating lever operatively connected with the engine, an actuating spring for moving the said lever pivotally in one direction, a pivoted catch having a notch at one end which normally engages with the said lever and prevents it from being moved by the actuating spring, said catch having a projecting arm at its other end portion, a tank for liquid, a float adapted to be raised by the liquid in the tank, a guide sheave, a flexible connection passing over the guide sheave and connected to the said arm at one end and to the float at the other end, and a catch spring which operates the catch and releases the actuating lever when the float is raised by the liquid in the tank.

1,328,000. COMBINATION IRONING-TABLE. CHARLES G. JONES, Asheville, N. C. Filed Aug. 22, 1918. Serial No. 250,918. 3 Claims. (Cl. 45—47.)

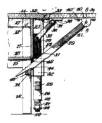

1. In furniture, a table top, a pivoted extension for the top, slidable legs, a connecting rod for said legs, a pitman pivoted on said rod and to said extension, a prop pivoted to said extension, and abutment means for the prop.

1,328,001. PERFORATED UTENSIL-COVER. CLARENCE WM. KINSMAN, New York, N. Y., assignor of two-thirds to Hermon H. Kinsman, New York, N. Y. Filed Apr. 8, 1919. Serial No. 288,445. 3 Claims. (Cl. 53—8.)

1. In a device of the class described, the combination of an apertured cover, a shutter, resilient means for yieldably holding said shutter in binding engagement with said cover and means for depressing the resilient means to relieve the shutter from its binding engagement to allow the shutter to be moved to open or close the apertures in said cover.

1,328,002. RAIL-SUPPORT. JOHN KROPACZ, Calgary, Alberta, Canada, assignor of one-third to Joseph Jakubecz, Calgary, Alberta, Canada. Filed Apr. 14, 1919. Serial No. 289,800. 6 Claims. (Cl. 238—26.)

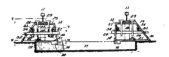

6. A device of the class described comprising hollow members, interlocking connections between adjacent ends, locking members connecting the ends together, the bottom walls of said members having openings formed therein spaced inwardly of the adjacent side walls to permit access to said locking means during the assembling of said members.

1,328,003. RAILWAY - SWITCH. DAVID L. LANDERS, Estill, S. C. Filed Oct. 17, 1916. Serial No. 126,168. 1 Claim. (Cl. 246—384.)

A railway switch attachment comprising an elongated rod having a rearwardly turned end, a branch portion

leading from said rod intermediate the ends thereof, said branch and said rearwardly turned end extending in the same direction, whereby said branch and said rearwardly

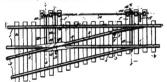

turned end may be connected to a pair of switch points to uniformly close the switch points when the rod is shifted in one direction to hold the switch points against accidental shifting.

1,328,004. SCREW-PROPELLER. HENRY LEITNER, Westminster, London, England. Filed Mar. 25, 1919. Serial No. 285,050. 4 Claims. (Cl. 170—159.)

1. A screw propeller comprising a sheet metal sheath and a hub across which the said sheath extends, the said hub having end plates formed with under-cut recesses, the walls of which grip the said sheet metal sheath, substantially as described.

1,328,005. SCREW-PROPELLER. HENRY LEITNER, Westminster, London, England. Filed Mar. 25, 1919. Serial No. 285,051. 3 Claims. (Cl. 170—159.)

1. A screw propeller comprising hollow blades formed of a sheet metal sheath having gaps adjacent the hub in combination with a hub composed of a central tube and end plates having horns forming power transmitting filling pieces for the gaps in the sheath adjacent to the hub, substantially as hereinbefore described.

1,328,006. METHOD OF MAKING PNEUMATIC TIRES. NELSON W. McLEOD, St. Louis, Mo. Filed Sept. 18, 1916. Serial No. 120,685. 15 Claims. (Cl. 154—14.)

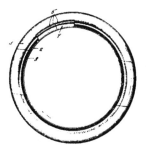

1. The method of making annular cord tire skeletons which comprises winding cord onto cord holding elements to form a cord web having marginal loops at said elements, inserting circular cord retaining members into the marginal loops, and releasing said loops from said cord holding elements.

1,328,007. INDICATING DEVICE. HOMER MANNON, HERMAN M. BROWN, and ROBERT G. PERKINS, Huntington, W. Va. Filed June 16, 1919. Serial No. 304,616. 2 Claims. (Cl. 33—148.)

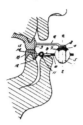

1. In a device of the class described, a support; a graduated carrier mounted to rock in the support; a graduated indicating member slidable in the carrier; attaching means assembled with the support; and attaching means assembled with the indicating member.

1,328,008. PROCESS FOR CAUSING OYSTERS TO PRODUCE PEARLS. KOKICHI MIKIMOTO, Tokyo, Japan. Filed July 23, 1919. Serial No. 312,855. 4 Claims. (Cl. 119—4.)

1. A process for causing oysters to produce pearls which consists in first enveloping a stimulus in the mantle-parenchyma of the living mollusk, sealing the mouth of the bag with a cord, detaching the bagged stimulus from the mollusk and introducing it through the cut made in that portion of the shell-secreting epidermis of the mother oyster into the subcutaneous tissue portion thereof, withdrawing the said cord, causing the excitation so as to retain the said stimulus in rest, substantially as set forth.

1,328,009. VALVE. WILLIAM GRANT MORRIS, Cairo, Egypt. Filed Sept. 5, 1918. Serial No. 252,676. 10 Claims. (Cl. 137—68.)

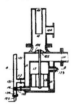

4. A mechanism for regulating the flow of fluids, comprising three chambers, a fluid supply to the first chamber, fluid outlets from the first and second chambers, a passage between the first and second chambers, means for regulating the flow through said passage controlled by the liquid level in the third chamber, means for controlling the fluid supply to the first chamber which also controls the supply and discharge of the third chamber, and additional means for regulating the rate of discharge from said third chamber.

1,328,010. PUMP. SWAN NELSON, Winnifred, Alberta, Canada. Filed Aug. 26, 1918. Serial No. 251,574. 2 Claims. (Cl. 253—179.)

1. A pump of the class described, comprising a vertically disposed tube, supporting means therefor, coacting with the upper portion of the tube, the opposite ends of the

tube being closed, the lower end portion of the tube being provided in its side walls with circumferentially spaced openings, and a shield overlying each of said openings, said shield having its lower and side marginal portions in contact with the casing below and at opposite sides of entrance opening, the upper marginal portion of the

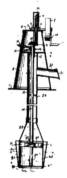

shield terminating above the opening, said shield being inwardly supported toward the tube from its upper edge to its lower edge and a water lifting means arranged within the tube above but in close proximity to the openings, the upper portion of the tube being provided with a discharge opening.

1,328,011. ENVELOP-MACHINE. ABRAHAM NOVICK, New York, N. Y., assignor, by mesne assignments, to United States Envelope Company, Springfield, Mass., a Corporation of Maine. Filed Feb. 10, 1915. Serial No. 7,268. 17 Claims. (Cl. 93—61.)

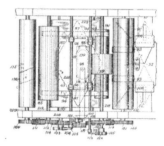

1. In an envelop machine, the combination of means for continuously advancing a web of paper, means for cutting an apertured window envelop blank from said web during the continuous advancement of said web, means for continuously advancing the blank for further operation thereon, means for stopping and squaring the position of said blank, means for applying a patch to the aperture of said blank while said blank is at rest, means for holding said blank at rest until said patch has been applied and rolls for continuously forwarding said blank after the patch has been applied.

11. In an envelop machine, the combination of means for advancing a web paper, means for making blank shaping window and severing cuts in said web during the continuous advancement of said web for forming window blanks, chip grippers for removing the chips from said web, means for continuously advancing a blank for further action thereon, means for gumming around the

window of said blank, oscillatory stops for stopping and alining said blank, an oscillatory presser foot for alternately holding said blank at rest and releasing said blank, reciprocating means for applying a patch to said blank while said blank is at rest, rolls for forwarding the blank after the patch has been applied, and means for gumming the bottom flap of said blank during the last named forwarding.

1,328,012. WARMING AND VENTILATING GAS-STOVE. PERCY JOHN OGLE, London, England, assignor to Ventiheta Limited. Filed July 7, 1919. Serial No. 309,104. 3 Claims. (Cl. 126—90.)

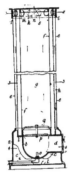

1. A gas stove comprising a base having an open top and housing an imperforate inverted bell-shaped burner chamber having an open top and provided below the top with a horizontal shelf, a burner tube extending through the wall of the burner chamber for supplying a mixture of air and gas thereto, a pipe communicating with the tube for conveying a mixture of air and gas to the same, an air chamber arranged between the burner chamber and the wall of said base, means for admitting air to said air chamber, an imperforate inner vertical tubular casing resting on said shelf and inclosing the top portion of said burner chamber, an outer vertical tubular casing surrounding the inner casing and spaced therefrom to provide an annular air passage, the lower end of the outer casing engaging the upper end of the base and the lower end of the air passage communicating with the air chamber, and a top for said casings.

1,328,013. EXCAVATING-SHOVEL. JOHN W. PAGE, Chicago, Ill. Filed Mar. 17, 1919. Serial No. 283,031. 7 Claims. (Cl. 87—54.)

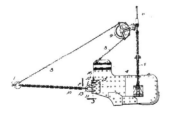

1. An excavating shovel, having side walls, a plate re-curved upon itself to form a vertical loop shaped opening and embracing the forward edge of a side wall and attached thereto, a vertical pin and in the loop and a clevis pivoted upon the pin and adapted to receive a hauling line.

1,328,014. MEANS FOR SALVAGING SUBMERGED VESSELS. FRANK G. PHILLIPS, Vancouver, British Columbia, Canada. Filed Oct. 31, 1919. Serial No. 334,705. 5 Claims. (Cl. 114—51.)

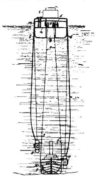

1. A salvaging vessel, comprising a hull having a chamber along the middle line which is open along the bottom to the sea and is closed above the water, weight lifting devices disposed along each side of the compartment and wire ropes from opposed lifting devices, which ropes are connected together to form loops that may be successively passed under the hull of a submerged vessel.

1,328,015. LUBRICATING MECHANISM. HARRY RALPH RICARDO, London, England. Filed Aug. 6, 1918. Serial No. 248,596. 10 Claims. (Cl. 184—6.)

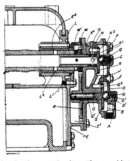

8. In lubricating mechanism the combination of a chamber having on one wall a flat surface in which is a port, a second chamber having on one wall a flat surface in which is a port, means for supplying lubricant under pressure to the first chamber, a passage leading from the port in the first chamber into the second chamber, a disk in which is an opening constituting a valve and rotatably mounted against the flat surface in the first chamber so as to control the opening of the port, a passage leading from the port in the second chamber to the parts to be lubricated, a second disk in which is an opening constituting a valve and rotatably mounted against the flat surface in the second chamber so as to control the opening of the port therein, and means for rotating both valves in such relation to each other that synchronism in the opening of the ports by the valves which respectively control them will only occur and a through passage for the flow of lubricant from the first chamber be provided intermittently and at predetermined intervals as set forth.

1,328,016. GENERATOR. WILLIAM P. RUDKIN, Oklahoma, Okla. Filed Nov. 21, 1918. Serial No. 263,496. 4 Claims. (Cl. 48—41.)

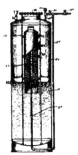

1. A generator of the class described comprising a closed liquid holding reservoir having a pressure chamber at the upper portion thereof, a container for holding gas generating material movably mounted for movement in the chamber and means establishing communication between the pressure chamber and the conwtainer whereby to convey the gas between the chamber and the container, said container being shiftable into and out of the liquid in the reservoir under the control of the pressure in the pressure chamber.

1,328,017. LUBRICATED FAN-MOUNTING. SAMUEL N. SENNA, Holyoke, Mass., assignor to B. F. Perkins & Son, Inc., Holyoke, Mass., a Corporation of Massachusetts. Filed Mar. 8, 1919. Serial No. 281,485. 3 Claims. (Cl. 64—49.)

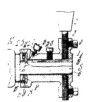

3. In a fan mounting, in combination, a motor presenting a projecting shaft and a stationary abutment adjacent the inner end of the projecting portion of said shaft, said shaft being provided with a keyway extending therealong and having a portion adjacent said inner end, a fan presenting a hub mounted upon said shaft and formed at its inner end to provide a bearing-receiving recess, said hub having a keyway therealong and having a portion adjacent said recess, a plate-thrust bearing received in said recess engaging said abutment with its rear plate and the bottom of said recess with its forward plate, a key received in, and of less length than, said keyways and located to leave the portions of such keyways adjacent said recess and bearing unoccupied, said hub also being provided with a lubricant duct communicating from the exterior of said hub with the said unoccupied portions, whereby lubricant may be fed to said bearing through said duct and keyways.

1,328,018. PICKER-CHECK. ISAAC SNOW, Lawrence, Mass. Filed May 16, 1919. Serial No. 297,454. 4 Claims. (Cl. 139—22.)

2. In a picker check, a stationary support provided with a guide, a picker loop having a side portion of inflexible material which is slidable longitudinally in the guide, a brake supported by the guide and bearing

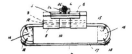

on the said side portion of the picker loop, and a spring for regulating the pressure of the brake.

1,328,019. LABEL FOR BALE-TIES. THOMAS H. STEWART, Atlanta, Ga., assignor to American Can Company, New York, N. Y., a Corporation of New Jersey. Filed Apr. 5, 1915. Serial No. 19,177. 1 Claim. (Co. 40—20.)

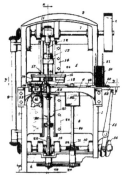

A tie label of bendable sheet metal, comprising a flat front label plate and rear off-set ends, said ends being connected with the front plate by integral parts 6 inclined away from each other from the front plate and toward the ends of the label, said inclined parts being perforated for the reception of a tie, and the passage for the tie from one perforation to the other being open and direct for the reception of a straight portion of a bale tie, the said label being bendable at the angles where the said integral parts join the front plate and the off-set ends to thereby extend the label longitudinally and flatten the same under the baling pressure.

1,328,020. APPARATUS FOR CUTTING AND APPLYING RING-LINERS TO THE FLANGES OF CAN ENDS. CLARENCE M. SYMONDS, San Anselmo, Calif., assignor to American Can Company, San Francisco, Calif., a Corporation of New Jersey. Filed Jan. 29, 1916. Serial No. 75,038. 12 Claims. (Cl. 113—80.)

1. In a machine for cutting ring liners from a web and applying the same to the flanges of can ends, the same comprising associated instrumentalities for cutting a blank from a web and from said blank cutting a ring liner, horizontally rotating means having shouldered openings for conveying the ring liner to an assembling station, devices for positioning a can end in axial alinement with the ring liner, and means for applying the ring liner to the flange of the alined can end.

1,328,021. GUN FOR DISCHARGING BOMBS, SHELLS, AND OTHER PROJECTILES. TOM THORNYCROFT and JOHN EDWARD THORNYCROFT, Westminster, England. Filed Sept. 11, 1919. Serial No. 323,214. 11 Claims. (Cl. 89—1.)

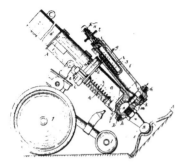

1. A gun for throwing bombs, shells and the like, comprising a gun barrel, a separate gas receiver normally in direct and free communication with the rear end of the gun barrel through a short passage of less cross sectional area than that of the receiver or gun barrel, means for connecting said gas receiver to said gun barrel, a charge container carried by the gas receiver and the wall of which has a gas outlet of restricted cross sectional area in communication with the gas receiver, as and for the purpose set forth, firing means for igniting a charge of propellant within said gas container and means for supporting said gun in position for use.

1,328,022. CLUTCH. JAMES A. WATSON, Silver Spring, Md. Filed Dec. 14, 1918. Serial No. 266,753. 9 Claims. (Cl. 192—10.)

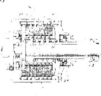

7. In a multiple disk clutch, two rotating members, and two series of disks interlocked with the members respectively, the interlocking means for one set of disks being constructed to permit said disks to have different rotary movements relatively to the member to which they are interlocked when all of the disks are in normal driving relation, for the purpose set forth.

1,328,023. THREAD-CONTROLLING MEANS FOR SEWING-MACHINES. JOHN P. WEIS, Nyack, N. Y., assignor to Metropolitan Sewing Machine Corporation, a Corporation of Delaware. Filed Sept. 25, 1918. Serial No. 255,665. 47 Claims. (Cl. 112—241.)

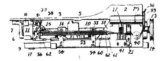

1. In a sewing machine the combination of thread controlling means comprising nipper mechanism, take-up

270 O. G.—19

mechanism and a plurality of independent tubes through which the thread passes, one thread to each tube whereby the threads are maintained separated one from another.

1,328,024. SAFETY - RAZOR. EDWARD R. WHARTON, Medford, Mass., assignor to Gillette Safety Razor Company, Boston, Mass., a Corporation of Massachusetts. Filed Feb. 3, 1917. Serial No. 146,497. 10 Claims. (Cl. 30—12.)

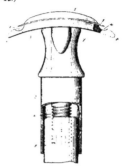

1. A safety razor comprising a transversely-flexible blade having a longitudinal cutting edge, in combination with a blade holder having a guard, a channel located behind the guard, means for positioning the blade with its cutting edge extending lengthwise over the channel, and means for adjustably flexing the blade transversely.

1,328,025. MACHINE FOR FORMING AND CUTTING DOUGHNUTS AND OTHER CAKES. CHARLES M. WHEELER, Bellingham, Wash. Filed July 26, 1917. Serial No. 182,932. 2 Claims. (Cl. 107—27.)

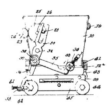

1. In a dough cutter, a hopper, feed rollers journaled therein, dies arranged in the lower portion thereof, a base for the hopper, a reciprocating cutter frame, superposed tracks carried by the sides of the base, inclined portions constituting continuations on the lower track, switches, means for returning the switches to their normal position, guides in operative relation to each upper track section adapted to be dislodged by the movement of the cutter frame so as to permit the frame to return to the lower tracks.

2. In a dough cutter, a hopper, feed rollers journaled therein, means for intermittently rotating the feed rollers, a base for the hopper, a reciprocating cutter frame, superposed tracks mounted on the sides of the base, extensions on the cutter frame engaging said tracks, an inclined portion on each lower track, switches for said upper track section, guide members having downwardly extending shoulders engaged by the cutter frame when moved in a backward direction, whereby the frame is arrested and forced to the lower track, and means carried by the hopper for reciprocating the cutter frame.

1,328,026. SNOWPLOW. Joseph Wojtasiewicz, Chadwicks, N. Y. Filed May 16, 1919. Serial No. 297,543. 4 Claims. (Cl. 37—68.)

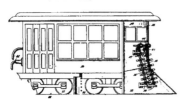

1. A snow plow comprising a car with a pointed forward end, pairs of inclined shafts journaled upon the opposite sides of said forward end, snow cutters upon said shafts, a transverse power shaft within the forward portion of the car, operative connections between said power shaft and cutter shafts whereby the cutter shafts upon the opposite sides of the car are adapted for simultaneous operation in opposite directions, and air blasting nozzles alined with the snow cutters for removing snow therefrom during operation.

1,328,027. DRY BATTERY. Sakizo Yai, Tokyo, Japan. Filed Jan. 30, 1919. Serial No. 274,070. 1 Claim. (Cl. 204—29.)

In a dry battery, a container, a mix therein, and a seal for the container, said seal having a circumferential flange extending therebeyond, and the wall of said container being bent to bear against the under and peripheral side of the said flange and also against the upper side thereof and to partially overlap the same.

1,328,028. ENVELOP. William W. L. Ahana, Honolulu, Hawaii. Filed Jan. 3, 1919. Serial No. 269,431. 1 Claim. (Cl. 229—86.)

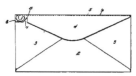

An envelop comprising a body having the usual inturend flaps constituting the back of the body, one of said flaps near its extremity and the line of fold thereof being cut from its edge inwardly to a point near the line of fold to form a tab integral with and removable from the said flap, a cord within the body and extending along the line fold of the said cut flap, and the end of said cord being glued to the underface of the said tab.

1,328,029. SASH-FASTENER. Lemuel O. Anderson, Miami, Fla., assignor of one-half to Franklin P. Armstrong, Miami, Fla. Filed May 19, 1919. Serial No. 298,153. 1 Claim. (Cl. 292—75.)
A sash fastener comprising a face plate having means of anchoring the same and having a central slot, a tubular

casing having both ends open and having one end provided with outturned apertured ears detachably connected to the plate, said casing having its inner end bent inwardly to form a shoulder, an apertured disk abutting said shoulder, a hollow tubular plunger snugly fitting within the casing having an inner end wall and open at its outer end, said

plunger having integral bearings extending from the edge thereof at diametrically opposite points, a roller journaled therein and projecting through the slot and an expansible spring in the casing between the end wall of the plunger and the disk and tending to force the roller to a projecting position.

1,328,030. PRESSED CORRUGATED SHEET-METAL ANNEALING-BOX. George P. Bard, Youngstown, Ohio. Filed May 10, 1919. Serial No. 296,139. 4 Claims. (Cl. 263—49.)

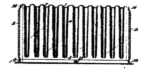

1. An improved annealing box composed essentially of an inverted U-shaped body-portion having transversely arranged corrugations with their ends stopping above the lower edge of the U-shaped portion, separate end pieces with inwardly curved sides and ends to fit the outer portions of the outer corrugations of the main body portion, thus forming engaging welded surfaces and having straight lower edges and a surrounding L-shaped combined strengthening and base piece fitting the straight lower edges of the ends and main body portion and welded thereto.

1,328,031. STAMP-CANCELER AND FOUNTAIN-BRUSH. John S. Britz, Port Huron, Mich. Filed Apr. 10, 1919. Serial No. 289,024. 4 Claims. (Cl. 101—371.)

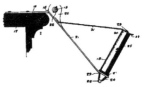

4. A device of the character described comprising a supporting arm having an apertured outer end, a spring on the inner part of the arm extending divergently therefrom into line with the aperture and having its extremity bent outwardly, a longitudinal slot formed in the outer end of the spring, a reservoir element having a nozzle adapted to be inserted partly through the aperture of the arm, ink applying means carried by the nozzle, the base of the reservoir having means to engage in said slot to

hold the reservoir in a predetermined relation to the spring, said spring having recesses in its underside beside the slot, and lugs at opposite sides of the base of the reservoir adapted to engage in said recesses.

1,328,032. INCUBATOR. STANLEY C. CALOW, Calgary, Alberta, Canada, assignor of one-half to Samuel Bennett, Calgary, Alberta, Canada. Filed June 1, 1918. Serial No. 237,768. 1 Claim. (Cl. 119—37.)

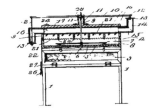

The combination of a casing containing an egg chamber, and a heating chamber above the egg chamber, a ventilating chamber within the casing immediately below the top thereof and above the heating chamber, a heating unit housed within the heating chamber and disposed immediately below the ventilating chamber, said ventilating chamber being provided with a plurality of transverse slots in its under side and having its ends projecting through and beyond the ends of the casing, one of said ends being turned up and the other being turned down, a rocker mounted on top of the casing, dampers carried by the ends of said rocker and normally closing the respectively adjacent ends of the ventilating chamber, a thermostatic plate mounted within the heating chamber, and a connecting rod secured to and extending between the thermostatic plate and the rocker.

1,328,033. ENGINE. GEORGE L. CHASE, Seattle, Wash. Filed Feb. 17, 1919. Serial No. 277,673. 2 Claims. (Cl. 121—60.)

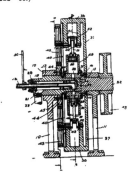

2. An engine comprising a fixed tubular shank having oppositely disposed ports extending through the walls thereof, said ports each communicating with a groove on the periphery of said shank that extends around said shank to a point adjacent the opposite port, a valve member adapted to fit snugly within said hollow shank, an inlet pipe connected with said valve member and having a passageway therethrough to one of said ports in said shank said inlet pipe being smaller than the passageway in said

hollow shank and said valve affording an unobstructed outlet for exhaust, and a cylinder base mounted for rotation on said shank and having ports that register with the ports and grooves in said shank.

1,328,034. MEANS FOR SCALPING OR OVERHAULING METAL. JAMES ROBERT COE, Waterbury, Conn., assignor to The American Brass Company, Waterbury, Conn., a Corporation of Connecticut. Filed Dec. 30, 1918. Serial No. 268,882. 5 Claims. (Cl. 29—81.)

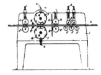

1. In a means for overhauling metal plates, the combination of a cutter head drum, a plurality of cutting members mounted therein and movable relatively thereto under the influence of centrifugal force in planes transverse to the axis of said drum, each of said members having a curved edge held adjacent to the periphery of said drum and a plurality of cutting teeth on said curved edge.

1,328,035. CARD-RECEPTACLE. WILLIAM C. CUTLER, North Glendale, Calif. Filed Dec. 11, 1918. Serial No. 266,324. 8 Claims. (Cl. 206—40.)

1. In a card case, a casing comprising a top having a rectangular recess along about the middle of the top and a slot within the recess, two sides projecting downwardly from the top having each a flange along the lower edge projecting inwardly practically parallel to the top, an end plate projecting down from the top at the rear end of the top to a point spaced from the lower flanges of the side plates at about the distance of the thickness of the bottom plate to be inserted between the lower edge of the rear end and the side flanges, and a front plate extending downwardly from the top at the front end of the case having a slot along the upper edge below the top.

1,328,036. STOCK-WATERING APPARATUS. HERBERT H. DREW, Edgerton, Wis. Filed Jan. 16, 1919. Serial No. 271,421. 3 Claims. (Cl. 119—74.)

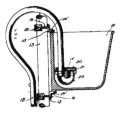

1. A stock watering apparatus including a support, a cup mounted on said support to swing on a vertical axis, a constant level source of water supply, a siphon pipe connected with said source of water supply and extended rearwardly of the cup to a point thereabove and having

its discharge end portion bent forwardly depending into the cup adjacent and inwardly of the pivotal axis of the cup, said supply pipe being spaced from the wall of the cup to permit free swinging movement of the cup on said vertical axis thereof.

1,328,037. FLEXIBLE LADDER. WILLIAM F. EARLY, Marion, N. C. Filed Apr. 5, 1919. Serial No. 287,751. 2 Claims. (Cl. 228—40.)

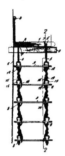

1. In a flexible ladder, a suspending member, treads mounted upon the suspending member and a cord or rope intertwined about the suspending member between the treads and engaging the treads in the rear and having portions immediately above the treads looped about the suspending member and the parts of the rope engaging the treads.

1,328,038. CORNET, TRUMPET, AND THE LIKE. GUSTAV A. ENDERS, Boston, Mass. Filed Aug. 6, 1917. Serial No. 184,738. 2 Claims. (Cl. 84—8.)

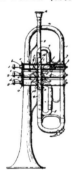

2. A wind instrument having three valves and their valve slides, a mouth-piece tube leading to the first valve, a bell portion, and a pipe or duct leading from the valves to the bell portion, said pipe or duct being straight for a considerable distance in advance of and beyond the valves and being situated in line with the inner end of the mouth-piece tube, each valve comprising a cylindrical valve casing having oppositely-situated ports and a spring-pressed plunger operable in said valve casing and provided with a transverse port which is alined with the oppositely-situated ports when the plunger is elevated, the oppositely-situated ports of all the casings being in line with each other and the ports of adjacent casings being connected by straight connections whereby when the plungers are elevated a straight passage of uniform diameter is provided

from a substantial portion of the mouthpiece tube through the valves and to a considerable distance beyond the valves, all of the plungers having the same relative arrangement of ports whereby the plungers are interchangeable and each plunger can be used equally well in any valve casing.

1,328,039. MACHINE FOR CUTTING OFF CONDENSER-TUBES. EUGENE FRANCIS ESSNER, San Francisco, Calif., assignor to Bethlehem Shipbuilding Corporation, Ltd., Bethlehem, Pa., a Corporation of Delaware. Filed Dec. 31, 1918. Serial No. 269,137. 14 Claims. (Cl. 29—69.)

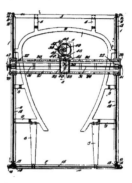

1. In a device of the character stated, a laterally movable carriage, a motor mounted in said carriage, a motor shaft having a gear thereon, a saw arbor, having a pinion thereon in mesh with said gear, a circular saw secured to the forward end of said arbor and having its front surface unobstructed for the purpose specified, and means to feed said motor and saw as a unit in a direction at substantially right angles to the line of movement of said carriage.

1,328,040. AEROCRUISER. THOMAS M. FINLEY, Oran, Mo. Filed June 29, 1917. Serial No. 177,816. 14 Claims. (Cl. 244—6.)

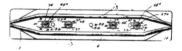

1. An airship of the class described including a body provided at the bottom with a longitudinal trough, and having vertical openings extending through the body and arranged at intervals and terminating at their lower ends at the trough, propellers operating in the trough, cars located between the vertical openings and suspended from the body, lifting propellers operating in the said vertical openings, means carried by the cars for actuating the propellers, and gearing for connecting the propellers with the actuating means.

1,328,041. ELECTRIC RELAY AND THE LIKE. KUNO FISCHER, Berlin-Charlottenburg, Germany, assignor to Siemens-Schuckert Werke, G. M. B. H., Berlin, Germany, a Corporation of Germany. Filed Aug. 15, 1913, Serial No. 784,948. Renewed June 10, 1919. Serial No. 303,254. 3 Claims. (Cl. 250—27.)

1. A circuit closing relay comprising a gas tube containing electrodes spaced a suitable distance apart and having corresponding outside terminals, a control circuit connected thereto comprising a source of current and controlling

means adapted to be actuated from said current source, said control circuit being normally interrupted by the spacing of said electrodes, and a circuit adapted to produce

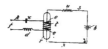

high frequency oscillations and having a coil surrounding said tube for ionizing the gas therein through said oscillations to close said control circuit at said electrode gap.

1,328,042. CARBURETER. WILLIAM S. GUTHRIE, Terrell, Tex. Filed Jan. 26, 1917. Serial No. 144,648. 6 Claims. (Cl. 261—19.)

1. A carbureter comprising a body having a carbureting passage provided with an oscillating throttle valve, means for supplying fuel and air to said passage, an auxiliary air passage independent of the fuel supply arranged so it discharges the greatest volume of air to the carbureting passage at a point beyond the air intake side of the throttle when the latter is partly closed and arranged so that the throttle valve in closing passes between the outlet of the auxiliary air passage and the engine.

1,328,043. ROLLER FOR PARTITIONS AND DOORS. THOMAS A. HILL, Brooklyn, N. Y., assignor, by mesne assignments, to The J. G. Wilson Corporation, a Corporation of Virginia. Filed Apr. 29, 1914. Serial No. 835,186. 3 Claims. (Cl. 16—7.)

1. In a roller bearing of the class described a vertically adjustable standard provided with a roller bearing at the bottom, said standard terminating at the top with sides sloping in opposite directions, a fixed portion of said bearing above said standard, slide members adapted to ride between said fixed portion and said sloping sides, said slide members being internally threaded, a pin threaded oppositely at opposite ends engaging the internal threads of said slide members and adapted when turned to force said slide members together or apart thereby controlling the vertical adjustment of said standard.

1,328,044. HYDROCARBON-FILTER. HENRY A. HILLS, Grand Rapids, Mich. Filed July 28, 1916. Serial No. 111,907. 12 Claims. (Cl. 210—16.)

1. In a filtering device, the combination of a casing, having an inlet and an outlet, a plurality of filtering elements intermediate of the inlet and outlet dividing the casing into successive compartments and a plurality of recep-

tacles connected at the bottoms of said compartments and provided with transparent walls and a valved drainage outlet from each receptacle.

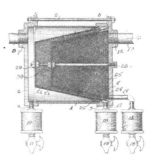

2. In a filtering device the combination of a casing, having an inlet and an outlet, a plurality of frusto-conical filtering elements nested one within the other in horizontal series so as to divide the casing into a plurality of successive compartments intermediate of the inlet and the outlet, a plurality of receptacles connected at the bottoms of said compartments, said receptacles being provided with transparent walls for viewing the contents of the receptacle and a draw-off valve for each receptacle.

3. A device of the class described comprising a drum, a pair of frusto-conical filtering elements disposed therein and mounted on one end thereof, a rod extending axially through the elements, means rigidly securing each element to the rod, an inlet and an outlet for said drum, the one disposed to introduce fluid into the drum for passage through said filtering elements and the other disposed to receive the filtrate therefrom, and detachable independent means on which said respective filtering elements are mounted permitting ready removal thereof one from another.

1,328,045. MULTISTAGE ADJUSTABLE FILTERING APPARATUS. HENRY A. HILLS, Grand Rapids, Mich. Filed May 7, 1917. Serial No. 167,014. 3 Claims. (Cl. 210—18.)

1. In a filtering apparatus the combination of a plurality of receptacles, a bed of filtering material in each receptacle, connections for passing the fluid to be filtered successively and upwardly through the filtering material in each receptacle, and means for interrupting communication of fluid to any one of said receptacles and for conducting the fluid from the receptacle preceding to the receptacle succeeding such receptacle.

1,328,046. UNITARY MULTISTAGE FILTER APPARATUS. HENRY A. HILLS, Grand Rapids, Mich. Filed May 7, 1917. Serial No. 167,015. 3 Claims. (Cl. 210—18.)

1. A filter apparatus of the class described comprising a unitary casing, a plurality of filter compartments therein, each provided with heating means at the bottom thereof, piping connections for passing the fluid to be filtered successively through each compartment and upwardly in each compartment so as to first heat and then filter the

fluid therein, and means for interrupting communication of the fluid to be filtered with any one of said compart-

ments and for conveying the fluid directly from the compartment preceding to the compartment succeeding such compartment.

1,328,047. PROCESS FOR THE EXTRACTION OF FATTY AND OILY MATTERS FROM WET SLUDGES. LEO D. JONES, Philadelphia, Pa., assignor to The Sharpless Specialty Company, West Chester, Pa., a Corporation of Pennsylvania. Filed Dec. 11, 1918. Serial No. 266,299. 5 Claims. (Cl. 87—6.)

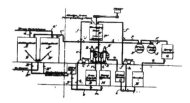

1. In the extraction of fatty, oily and like matters from wet sludge, the process which consists in treating said sludge with means for dissolving the matter to be extracted and floating the undissolved material on the aqueous solution, centrifugating the product so as to separate the solution of said matter from the aqueous solution and from the undissolved matter, and floating off said undissolved material.

1,328,048. TRAILER - VEHICLE. JACOB KNAPP, Cincinnati, Ohio, assignor to The Sechler & Company, Cincinnati, Ohio, a Corporation of Ohio. Filed July 27, 1917. Serial No. 183,069. 4 Claims. (Cl. 280—33.5.)

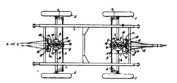

3. In a device of the character described, the combination with a steering connecting rod and a drawbar, of a fifth wheel plate comprising in part a pair of opposed extending ears, each having therein vertical pivoting means, and a locking means for the pivot, one of said ears being for connection with the connecting rod and the other of said ears being for connection with a drawbar.

1,328,049. VISE ATTACHMENT. FRANCESCO LANZETTA, Brooklyn, N. Y. Filed Feb. 15, 1919. Serial No. 277,125. 2 Claims. (Cl. 81—42.)

1. In a device of the class described, a vise embodying fixed and movable jaws, means for shifting the movable jaw toward and away from the fixed jaw, and means for maintaining the jaws vertically parallel during the clamping of an article therebetween, in combination with a rack, one end of which is secured to one of the lateral ends of

the movable jaw, rack guiding means associated with the corresponding end of the fixed jaw, and a latch associated with the fixed jaw, and positioned for engagement with the rack to lock said rack against longitudinal movement

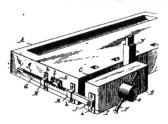

for the purpose of maintaining the end of the movable jaw to which the rack is attached in spaced relation to the corresponding end of the fixed jaw, when an article is clamped between the opposite lateral halves of said jaws.

1,328,050. MATRIX MOLDING DEVICE. ANDREW E. MARKWELL, Fort Worth, Tex., assignor of one-half to S. C. Evans, Fort Worth, Tex. Filed Mar. 6, 1919. Serial No. 280,998. 6 Claims. (Cl. 199—63.)

1. A matrix molding device for forming slots in a slug comprising a matrix having a vertical groove in the side thereof and a former having its operating end thick enough for normally filling said groove and movable therein and provided with a curved groove in its outer face near said operating end for forming a rib on one of the vertical walls of said slot.

1,328,051. MERCURY - COOLING SYSTEM. THOMAS MIDGLEY, Jr., Dayton, Ohio, assignor to The Dayton Engineering Laboratories Company, a Corporation of Ohio. Filed Jan. 12, 1918. Serial No. 211,694. 9 Claims. (Cl. 123—169.)

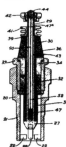

1. In a device of the character described, the combination with an element to be cooled provided with a cooling chamber; of a fluid cooling medium in the chamber; and means located in the chamber providing for the passage of the fluid cooling medium throughout the entire length of the chamber.

1,328,052. WHEEL. SAMUEL E. MORRAL, Morral, Ohio.
Filed Feb. 15, 1917. Serial No. 148,738. 3 Claims.
(Cl. 21—69.)

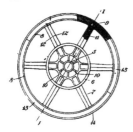

1. A wheel having its hub, spokes and rim with centrally located felly-penetrating spurs thereon cast in one
piece.

1,328,053. STAYBOLT STRUCTURE. JOHN MUNHALL,
Pittsburgh, Pa. Filed Jan. 29, 1919. Serial No.
273,721. 4 Claims. (Cl. 85—1.5.)

1. In a stay-bolt construction, the combination with a
bolt having a rounded head, a sleeve internally smooth
and of smaller size toward its inner end than toward its
outer end, and a bushing externally smooth and in shape
conforming to the internal shape of the sleeve and provided at its outer end with a seat for the bolt head.

1,328,054. PNEUMATIC TIRE. HERBERT NICHOLSON,
Chicago, Ill. Filed Oct. 6, 1916, Serial No. 124,015.
Renewed June 16, 1919. Serial No. 304,738. 1 Claim.
(Cl. 152—17.)

A tire comprising annular tread portions located in the
crown of the tire; each tread portion having a pair of
circular and laterally disposed anchor plates embedded
wholly within said crown and honged by their outer corners to the inner corners of the tread portions and a pair
of circular and laterally disposed sheaths of U-shape in
cross-section and also embedded wholly within said crown
and receiving the anchor plates.

1,328,055. ELECTRIC FAN. EMIL PHILLIPSON, New
York, N. Y., assignor to Plant & Company, New York,
N. Y., a Firm. Filed May 21, 1919. Serial No. 298,614.
8 Claims. (Cl. 230—1.)

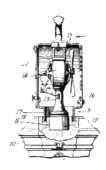

1. An apparatus of the character described comprising
an electric fan consisting of a base and a portion movable
relatively thereto, and a perforated housing secured to
said movable portion and inclosing said electric fan, substantially as specified.

1,328,056. APPARATUS FOR REPAIRING MOVING-
PICTURE FILMS. MAURICE S. ROSENFELD, New York,
N. Y., assignor, by mesne assignments, to Jacob
Schechter, New York, N. Y. Filed May 24, 1915, Serial
No. 30,222. Renewed Sept. 18, 1918. Serial No.
254,673. 9 Claims. (Cl. 154—42.)

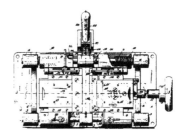

1. A device of the character described, having means
for holding a film in position, means for cutting a portion
from the film, a scraper, means for moving the ends of the
film relatively to the scraper for scraping the end of the
film, means for moving the ends of the film toward each
other to cause the ends of the film to overlap, and means
for holding the overlapped portions in contact.

1,328,057. MOUTHPIECE FOR BREATHING APPA-
RATUS. JOHN T. RYAN, Pittsburgh, Pa., assignor to
The Mine Safety Appliance Company, a Corporation of
Pennsylvania. Filed May 15, 1919. Serial No. 297,249.
3 Claims. (Cl. 128—147.)
1. A mouthpiece for breathing apparatus comprising a
body, a chamber depending therefrom and provided with

a discharge orifice, a passage connecting the body with said chamber, a non-return check valve in said passage,

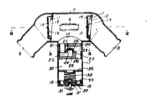

and a hand opening automatically closing relief valve controlling the discharge orifice from the chamber.

1,328,058. REGENERATOR FOR BREATHING APPARATUS. JOHN T. RYAN, Pittsburgh, Pa., assignor to Mine Safety Appliance Company, Pittsburgh, Pa., a Corporation of Pennsylvania. Filed May 31, 1919. Serial No. 300,857. 3 Claims. (Cl. 128—191.)

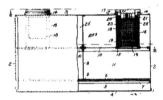

1. A regenerator for breathing apparatus comprising a casing, a partition extending from its top nearly to its bottom and dividing the same into two compartments, a horizontal perforated partition located at the lower end of the vertical partition and secured to the side walls of the casing, a pair of perforated horizontal partitions above the first named perforated partition and dividing each compartment into two chambers, and the chambers between the upper and lower perforated partitions being adapted to receive a granular regenerating agent, an orifice in the top of the casing above each of the compartments, orifices in the upper horizontal perforated partitions in line with the orifices in the top, tubular perforated members extending from the top wall of the casing to the upper horizontal perforated partitions and surrounding said orifices, and means to connect the inhalation and exhalation tubes to the top orifices.

1,328,059. RESONATOR. ARTHUR W. SCHREINER, Brooklyn, N. Y., assignor to Standard Scientific Company, New York, N. Y., a Corporation of New York. Filed Dec. 12, 1917. Serial No. 206,722. 1 Claim. (Cl. 181—0.5.)

In an acoustically tuned resonator, a body portion of suitable volume, having a receiving end, and a diagonally cut emitting end, adjoined thereto, substantially as described.

1,328,060. BOTTLE-CLOSURE. WULF SILVERMAN, New York, N. Y. Filed May 22, 1917. Serial No. 170,120. 3 Claims. (Cl. 215—55.)

1. A bottle closure comprising a collar having a continuous cylindrical inner wall, a shell for holding the collar and for affixing said collar to a bottle, a tube slidably and rotatably fitted within the collar and forming a tight joint with the wall thereof, said tube being closed at the bottom and having a flange at its lower end extending over and adapted to be seated on the lower end of said collar, said tube being provided with perforations so disposed that they are within and closed by said wall of the collar when the tube is raised but below the lower end of the collar when the tube is moved downwardly to remove its flange from its seat on the end of the collar, a flange at the upper end of said shell constructed with a cut arranged to receive and guide a rib on the tube, and a longitudinal rib projecting from the tube terminating above the shell flange when the tube is raised to a position with its flange seated on the lower end of the collar, said shell flange being inclined upwardly from its cut to form a cam for the lower end of said rib, whereby the tube flange may be forced onto said lower end of the collar.

1,328,061. ROTARY PUMP. KARL D. SMITH, Battle Creek, Mich., and BERNARD SAMELSON, New York, N. Y., assignors to Union Steam Pump Company, Battle Creek, Mich. Filed June 2, 1919. Serial No. 301,363. 4 Claims. (Cl. 103—43.)

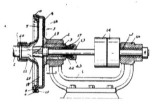

1. In a rotary pump, the combination of a supporting frame, a casing comprising an inner member having a tangentially disposed outlet and a hub-like projection mounted on said frame, and an outer member detachably mounted upon the inner, said outer portion being provided with an axially disposed inwardly flared inlet extension, a rotor shaft having a bearing in the said hub portion of said inner member, and a single pair of oppositely disposed flat rotor blades provided with a hub mounted on said shaft to project into said inlet extension, the blades being widened at their inner ends to the outer end of the hub.

1,328,062. SELECTIVE SPEED-TRANSMISSION MECHANISM. ALEXANDER STEWART, Clintonville, Wis. Filed Apr. 25, 1919. Serial No. 292,553. 7 Claims. (Cl. 74—59.)

1. In a transmission mechanism, a housing, a primary shaft extended thereinto, a secondary shaft extended through the housing parallel to the primary shaft, a counter shaft in the housing and parallel to the other two shafts, the primary and counter shafts being positioned

in planes extending substantially at right angles from the axis of the secondary shaft, a worm and worm gear

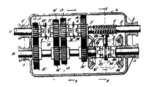

connected between the primary and counter shafts, and selective speed transmission mechanism between the counter and secondary shafts.

1,328,063. WEEDER. JUSTIN M. ST. JOHN, Cedar Rapids, Iowa. Filed June 21, 1917. Serial No. 175,990. 6 Claims. (Cl. 55—65.)

1. A weeder, comprising a head, a series of prongs mounted loosely therein, a foot-plate coöperating with the prongs and head to converge the points of the prongs as they are projected through said plate, and a guide for said foot-plate.

1,328,064. FASTENING DEVICE. ANTHONY VASSELLI, Newark, N. J., assignor, by mesne assignments, to Harriman National Bank of the City of New York. Filed Feb. 9, 1918. Serial No. 216,340. 2 Claims. (Cl. 74—8.)

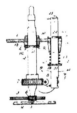

1. In a motor for talking machines and the like, a motor frame, a brake shaft rotatably mounted in and projecting above said frame and provided with a circumferential groove near its upper end adjacent to the upper side of said frame, a slotted disk fitted in said groove, a flange washer fitted upon said shaft and located between said disk and the upper side of said frame and its flange encircling said disk to hold said disk in place, a circumferential groove in said shaft below said frame, a slotted disk fitted in said groove, a flanged washer fitted upon

the shaft above and adapted to engage the upper side of said disk and its flange encircling said disk, and a coiled spring mounted upon said shaft between the underside of the frame and the lower washer and disk and serving to hold the washers in engagement with the slotted disks upon both sides of the frame.

1,328,065. SHAFT FOR TALKING-MACHINES. ANTHONY VASSELLI, Newark, N. J., assignor, by mesne assignments, to Harriman National Bank of the City of New York. Filed July 3, 1918. Serial No. 243,217. 4 Claims. (Cl. 64—89.)

1. In a turn table shaft for talking machines having thereon means for driving the governor and means for driving the turn table, the turn table driving means having a lost motion connection with the shaft.

1,328,066. LEVEL-WINDER. ANTHONY VASSELLI, Newark, N. J., assignor, by mesne assignments, to Harriman National Bank of the City of New York. Filed Mar. 10, 1919. Serial No. 281,775. 4 Claims. (Cl. 242—84.4.)

1. A device of the character described, comprising a spool, a crank for rotating the spool, a support carried by the device, oppositely disposed cams carried by the support, a cam carried by the crank, a tail carried by the support and engaging the crank cam, a member loosely carried by the support and disposed between the cams carried thereby, and a guide for the member.

1,328,067. WHEEL CONSTRUCTION. WILLIAM R. WILSON, Terre Haute, Ind. Filed Feb. 8, 1919. Serial No. 275,706. 8 Claims. (Cl. 21—69.)

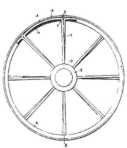

1. A wheel construction, including a hub, a pair of flanges surrounding said hub and spaced from each

other, the outer faces of said flanges being inclined outwardly to form overhanging edges, a plurality of substantially U shaped spokes having their ends resting against the overhanging faces of said flanges, locking plates having radial sockets therein for receiving the inner ends of said spokes, means for locking said plates in engagement with the hub and against the inclined faces of said flanges, and shoulders at the inner ends of said sockets upon which the ends of the spokes rest.

1,328,068. ELECTRICALLY-HEATED HUMIDIFIER. DANIEL H. YOUNG, Manchester, Iowa. Filed May 22, 1919. Serial No. 298,986. 7 Claims. (Cl. 219—38.)

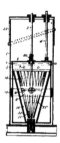

7. In a device of the character described, a boiler, a hollow body positioned therein to isolate therebetween an inclosed air-space, a hollow electrode lining the said hollow body and being of a relatively high electrical resistance, and another electrode positioned within, spaced and insulated from the first-mentioned hollow electrode and of a relatively lower electrical resistance.

1,328,069. ELECTROTHERMOGENIC DEVICE FOR HUMIDIFIERS. DANIEL H. YOUNG, Manchester, Iowa. Filed May 22, 1919. Serial No. 298,987. 6 Claims. (Cl. 219—38.)

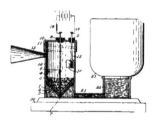

1. In a device of the character described, the combination with a boiler formed of electrically-conductive material, of a conductor mounted within said boiler and in movable contact therewith, another conductor mounted within said boiler insulated therefrom and carrying a hollow conical electrode, and a pair of hollow conical electrode-members positioned and spaced from opposite inner and outer walls of the first-mentioned electrode concentrically, supported on and insulated from the second-mentioned conductor and in movable contact with the inner wall of said boiler.

1,328,070. RAILWAY SIGNALING. JOHN V. YOUNG, Reading, Mass.; Ida A. Young, administratrix of said John V. Young, deceased, assignor to The Union Switch & Signal Company, Swissvale, Pa., a Corporation of Pennsylvania. Filed Apr. 4, 1918. Serial No. 226,565. 18 Claims. (Cl. 246—110.)

12. In combination, a slow-acting device, a lever for setting said slow-acting device into operation, and a tonnage signal controlled by said slow-acting device.

1,328,071. ROLLING MILITARY KITCHEN. FRANK G. BALDWIN, Cincinnati, Ohio, assignor to The Sechler & Company, Cincinnati, Ohio, a Corporation of Ohio. Filed Apr. 19, 1917. Serial No. 163,292. 2 Claims. (Cl. 126—276.)

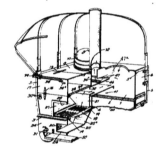

1. In a rolling military kitchen, the combination of a substantially rectangular frame and shell, with the interior of the shell at the rear divided into a fire box, two water compartments and a cooker above the fire box and the interior of the shell at the front divided into a single oven transverse the shell, a plurality of supports for vessels for cooking, a flue for the escape of products of combustion, and a baffle to cause the products of combustion to travel over the top of the oven before reaching the cooking vessels.

1,328,072. ELECTRICAL CIRCUIT-CONTROLLER. FERDINAND BECHOFF, New York, N. Y. Filed Feb. 1, 1918. Serial No. 214,979. 9 Claims. (Cl. 200—50.)

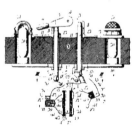

1. In a device of the character specified, the combination of pivoted contact levers carrying bridging contacts

at their free ends, stationary contacts in pairs positioned so as to be bridged by the bridging contacts, and interlocking surfaces on the contact levers by which the simultaneous bridging of more than one pair of contacts is prevented.

1,328,073. INDICATOR FOR CONTROLLING SWITCHES. FERDINAND BECHOFF, New York, N. Y. Filed Feb. 1, 1918. Serial No. 214,980. 8 Claims. (Cl. 116—81.)

1. In a device of the character described, the combination of a control lever; actuating members selectively operable by said control lever; an indicator, the action of which is dependent upon the alternate throwing of the control lever; and means for preventing the action of said indicator until the selected actuating member has been moved to its full extent.

1,328,074. KEY-LOCK. EDWARD O. BENNETT, Oakland, Calif., assignor of fifty per cent. to Hepburn Ruhl, San Francisco, Calif., and Chicago, Ill. Filed Apr. 17, 1918. Serial No. 229,192. 5 Claims. (Cl. 70—46.)

2. A lock including a casing; a cylinder revoluble in said casing and having a longitudinal keyhole; independently movable tumblers transversely slidable on opposite sides of said keyhole and having lugs extending into said keyhole; and a key to fill and fit the key-hole in said cylinder and having deviating grooves in the sides to engage said lugs.

1,328,075. OIL-BURNING FURNACE. ALBERT J. BOEBNER, Chicago, Ill. Filed May 27, 1919. Serial No. 300,101. 9 Claims. (Cl. 158—1.)

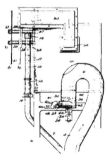

1. In a furnace of the character set forth, the combination of an air supply conduit, a fuel supply pipe extending parallel with the air supply conduit and exterior thereto, valves housed in and extending across the conduit and the pipe respectively and disposed in axial alinement, connections between said valves whereby they will be simultaneously operated, and means connected with one of the valves for adjusting the same.

1,328,076. PENCIL ATTACHMENT. HANS W. BORGLIN, Streator, Ill. Filed Mar. 6, 1919. Serial No. 280,966. 1 Claim. (Cl. 24—11.)

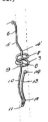

A loss preventing attachment for pencils, consisting of a single piece of elastic wire constructed and arranged substantially in the following manner, viz. the loop 7 provided at its upper end, from said loop the wire is continued downwardly then inwardly at an angle to the point 4, then downwardly a slight distance, then the pencil encircling bands 2 and 3 are produced, the wire is then continued downwardly a slight distance to bear on the pencil, then downwardly and outwardly to 10, then downwardly and inwardly, then the wire is bent upon itself at 11 and then continued upwardly and inwardly at an angle to 12 then upwardly and outwardly to 13 and finally upwardly and inwardly to 14, substantially as and for the purpose set forth.

1,328,077. METHOD OF AND APPARATUS FOR FORMING RIFLED BORES IN METAL. LEWIS E. BOYER, Easton, Pa., assignor to Ingersoll-Rand Company, Jersey City, N. J., a Corporation of New Jersey. Filed Oct. 31, 1916. Serial No. 128,647. 19 Claims. (Cl. 90—28.1.)

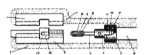

1. The method of imparting a rifled conformation to a single-ended bore forming the interior of a metal article by forging which consists in forcing a rifling member thereinto but not beyond the same and withdrawing the rifling member therefrom through the same end by a quick reciprocatory movement, whereby the contour of the wall of the bore formed in the article will correspond with that of the rifling member.

9. An apparatus for imparting a rifled conformation to the wall of an end-inclosed bore in a metal article by forging comprising article supporting means and means to force a rifling member into but not beyond the article and to withdraw the rifling member through the same end by a quick reciprocatory movement, the resultant contour of the interior corresponding with the rifling member.

1,328,078. GAUNTLET - GLOVE. WILLIAM A. COOK, Westfield, Mass. Filed Jan. 8, 1919. Serial No. 270,155. 1 Claim. (Cl. 2—9.)

As an improved article of manufacture, a gauntlet glove having a slit in the front portion thereof, such slit extending through the wrist portion into the palm portion to a point transversely adjacent to the base of the thumb-stall, and the part of such slit that is in said palm portion and transversely adjacent to said thumb-stall being widened, fastening means for the edge portions of the slit which are adjacent to said gauntlet, a gusset so ar-

ranged that it can be extended across or folded to one side away from said slit, said gusset being attached along one edge to said wrist and palm portions adjacent to one edge of said slit and above the gauntlet, said gauntlet having therein a slit which is in line with said first-named slit, and a gore attached to said gauntlet and covering the slit therein.

1,328,079. PROCESS OF MASHING. Charles B. Davis, New York, N. Y. Filed Jan. 29, 1915. Serial No. 5,161. 2 Claims. (Cl. 195—32.)

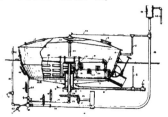

1. The process of heating mash or the like enzymatic mass, which consists in subjecting the same to the indirect heating action of hot water by bringing the water gradually up from the initial temperature of the mash to the desired temperature and applying the water, so gradually heated, to the mash indirectly and throughout the mass thereof, so that the mash will be gradually and uniformly heated throughout, and maintaining the heating water in a closed circuit.

1,328,080. PAINT AND VARNISH REMOVER. Carleton Ellis, Montclair, N. J. Filed Dec. 4, 1917. Serial No. 205,335. 4 Claims. (Cl. 87—5.)
1. A paint and varnish remover consisting of phenol, finish solvent material, glycerin, wax and moisture.

1,328,081. MACHINE FOR APPLYING PAINT TO EMBOSSED DESIGNS. John Engel, Green Bay, Wis. Filed July 29, 1918. Serial No. 247,216. 2 Claims. (Cl. 91—51.)
1. In a machine of the character specified, a plurality of rollers, means for adjusting said rollers in vertical di-

rection, means for supplying said rollers with paint, a plurality of plates having an end portion adapted to engage said rollers for evenly distributing paint on the sur-

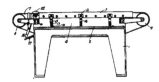

face of the rollers, means for adjusting the engagement of said plates with said rollers, and a plurality of belts adapted to carry the work in successive contact with said rollers.

1,328,082. PROCESS FOR THE PRODUCTION OF SYNTHETIC AMMONIA FROM THE AIR OR NITROGEN. Robert F. Gardiner, Clarendon, Va. Filed Jan. 13, 1919. Serial No. 270,969. 1 Claim. (Cl. 23—21.) (Filed under the act of Mar. 3, 1883, 22 Stat. L., 625.)
The process of producing synthetic ammonia consisting in bringing air into contact with an alkaline solution containing a metal from which nascent hydrogen is being evolved.

1,328,083. SPEED-TRANSFORMER. Maximilian M. Goldberg, Dayton, Ohio. Filed Nov. 4, 1915. Serial No. 59,643. 34 Claims. (Cl. 290—23.)

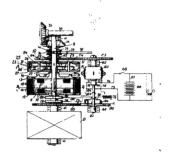

1. In a speed transformer, the combination with a rotatable armature and a bodily rotatable magnetic field adapted to act upon each other so as to reduce their relative speed, of a driven member, means for rotating the field at a constant speed, a gear fast to the armature, a gear fast to the field, a device adapted to be connected to the driven member, and two gears carried by said device and meshing with the gears fast to the armature and the field, the intermeshing gears being of such a ratio that a small change in the speed of the armature effects a large change in the speed of the driven member and the relative speed between the field and the armature is less than that between the field and the driven element except when both relative speeds become zero.

1,328,084. LINER FOR CENTRIFUGAL CREAM-SEPA-RATORS. CHARLES H. HACKETT, Waterloo, Iowa, assignor to Wilbur W. Marsh, Waterloo, Iowa. Filed Sept. 5, 1919. Serial No. 321,785. 3 Claims. (Cl. 233—43.)

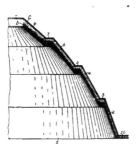

1. A liner for centrifugal liquid separators, comprising superimposed spaced separating devices, each device being formed of a plurality of stepped concentric frusta.

1,328,085. TOOL FOR MAKING HOLES NON-CIRCULAR. ERIK EDWARD HOLLANDER, Newark, N. J. Filed May 3, 1918. Serial No. 232,292. 11 Claims. (Cl. 90—33.)

1. In a tool of the character described, the combination of a cutter member adapted to reciprocate longitudinally and having a hollow end with a cutting arm in its wall whose extremity can spread radially outward, spreading means in said hollow end, and means at the outside of the cutter member for holding said cutting arm against lateral movement.

1,328,086. APPAREL-CORSET. DANIEL KOPS, New York, N. Y. Filed Nov. 1, 1919. Serial No. 335,023. 2 Claims. (Cl. 2—73.)

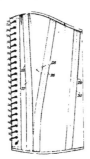

1. In an apparel corset, a plurality of stays extending from the upper edge of the garment at the rear thereof and converging downwardly to approximately the lower edge of the garment to produce a flattening effect and provide a support at the small of the back of the wearer.

1,328,087. RATCHET SOCKET-WRENCH. CHARLES C. LE CHOT, Akron, Ohio. Filed Feb. 13, 1919. Serial No. 276,878. 4 Claims. (Cl. 81—53.)

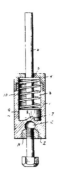

1. A wrench of the class described comprising a socket member provided with a compartment, an operating shank extending within the compartment, said shank and a wall of the chamber being provided with a ratchet interlock and yieldable means for normally maintaining said interlock.

1,328,088. INFLATING DEVICE FOR PNEUMATIC APPARATUS. WILLIAM D. LUTZ, Allendale, N. J. Filed Oct. 19, 1915. Serial No. 56,815. 5 Claims. (Cl. 60—44.)

1. An apparatus for confining gas under pressure, comprising a cylinder, a plug having a screw threaded connection with one end of the cylinder, said plug having a cylindrical bore extending therethrough to receive a cartridge, the plug being extended within said cylinder to incase the cartridge substantially throughout its length, and a second plug having a threaded connection with the first plug for closing it and retaining the cartridge therein.

1,328,089. VAPOR-PRIMER FOR AUTOMOBILES. THOMAS J. MCCARTHY, Newark, N. J. Filed Feb. 14, 1919. Serial No. 277,076. 5 Claims. (Cl. 123—180.)

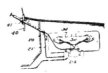

1. The method of priming an internal combustion engine with an explosive mixture, which comprises the creation of a sub-atmospheric pressure in a confined space or chamber, causing converging streams of air and liquid fuel to impact therein in predetermined proportions to thereby form a vaporized gaseous explosive mixture, com-

pressing the vapor in said chamber, introducing said vapor mixture under pressure into the intake of the engine and conveying the mixture into the engine cylinders where it may be subjected to the action of electric sparks.

1,328,090. PROCESS FOR MACERATING CRUSHED SUGAR-CANE. CHARLES McNEIL, Glasgow, Scotland. Filed Apr. 22, 1918. Serial No. 230,075. 3 Claims. (Cl. 100—47.)

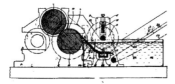

1. Macerating apparatus for sugar cane, comprising a pressure roll, a pressure plate between which and said roll the cane is passed, and means for introducing liquid under pressure through said plate into contact with the compressed cane, for the purpose described.

1,328,091. EGG - CANDLER. FLORENCE C. MAHAFFEY, Toledo, Ohio. Filed Aug. 18, 1919. Serial No. 318,160. 2 Claims. (Cl. 99—6.)

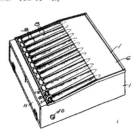

1. In an egg candler, a frame, a row of lamps located in one end of the frame, a horizontal platform located on the frame, a plurality of egg-shaped openings located above the lamps, a corrugated surface having inclined corrugations located intermediate the platform and the openings for directing the eggs from the platform to the openings.

1,328,092. PISTON-PUSH-ROD HOLDER. PETER MALTRY and WINFIELD T. HECKLER, Blue Island, Ill. Filed Nov. 27, 1918. Serial No. 264,428. 2 Claims. (Cl. 188—24.)

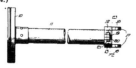

1. In an air brake, the combination of a piston, a push rod, and a thrust transmitting connector for said rod; said connector having a socket which receives the rod and terminates in a shoulder against which the end of the rod seats, and having ears adapted to receive the pintle of a brake lever; said connector being divided diametrically in a plane intermediate of its pintle ears into two sep-

arable members and provided with clamping bolts for drawing together said members in the direction to resist separation of the ears; said push rod and socket members having registering recesses and key-lugs located in alinement with the pintle ears and pressed into inter-engagement by the clamping action of the bolts.

1,328,093. AUTOMOBILE OR MOTORCYCLE HORN. RAY H. MANSON, Elyria, Ohio, assignor to The Garford Manufacturing Company, Elyria, Ohio, a Corporation of Ohio. Filed Oct. 23, 1913. Serial No. 796,758. 7 Claims. (Cl. 116—1.)

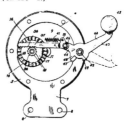

1. In an automobile horn, the combination of a frame, a vibratile diaphragm in said frame, bearings in said frame, a shaft in said bearings, a rotary cam wheel mounted on said shaft to rotate therewith, means through which the cam wheel operates the diaphragm when the cam wheel is rotated, mechanical means for operating the cam wheel including two members, one of which is mounted on the shaft and the other of which is a reciprocating rack mounted in said frame, each of said members having teeth thereon, said teeth having a greater pitch on one side than on the other, the sides of the teeth which have the greatest pitch adapted to engage each other, and the sides of the teeth having the least pitch adapted to pass freely over each other.

1,328,094. VENTILATOR. HARVEY F. MARANVILLE, Akron, Ohio. Filed May 25, 1916, Serial No. 99,722. Renewed Oct. 6, 1919. Serial No. 328,925. 2 Claims. (Cl. 98—3.)

2. A rotary cowl for ventilators comprising a pair of upright side walls and a top member, said side walls terminating at open inlet and outlet mouths arranged at opposite sides of said cowl and being tapered inwardly toward said inlet mouth beginning at a point substantially abreast of the pivot axis, both inlet and outlet mouths being formed with flaring lips, and a concave shield depending from said top member within said inlet mouth, said shield having its convex face turned toward said mouth and having its free edges extending to points substantially abreast of the pivot axis and spaced from said side walls to define narrow passageways.

1,328,095. ROTARY SHAFT AND COUPLING FOR ELECTRIC DENTAL ENGINES. ALFRED P. MERRILL, San Diego, Calif. Filed July 7, 1919. Serial No. 309,018. 4 Claims. (Cl. 64—89.)

2. In a device of the class described, the combination of a motor casing provided with an extended external thread-

ed shaft support, a shaft having its opposite ends extending beyond said extended portion, a flexible shaft detachably connected to one end of said shaft, a handle secured to the other end of said shaft for manually controlling the

revolution of said shaft, a sleeve surrounding said flexible shaft and formed with an opening adapted to register with an opening in said flexible shaft to facilitate the manual control of the revolution of said flexible shaft.

1,328,096. APPARATUS FOR EXTRACTING LYE FROM WOOD-ASHES. WILLIAM P. D. MOROSS and JOHN C. COSTELLO, Chattanooga, Tenn. Filed Aug. 2, 1917. Serial No. 184,107. 2 Claims. (Cl. 23—3.)

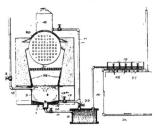

1. Apparatus for leaching wood ashes, comprising a tray or receptacle to receive the ashes, means for supplying water to the ashes within the receptacle, a closure for the top of the receptacle, serving as a deflector for the material agitated within the receptacle, means for introducing steam in a series of jets into the receptacle to stir or agitate the ashes and subject them to the heating and dissolving action of the steam, and means for withdrawing the liquor which drains to the bottom of the receptacle.

2. Apparatus for leaching wood ashes, comprising a tray or receptacle to receive the ashes, said tray having a depending trough or gutter and the bottom sloping from the sides thereinto, a cover or lid which may be opened or closed and when closed serving as a deflector for the material agitated within the receptacle, a steam conduit extending longitudinally above said gutter and provided with a plurality of openings for the escape of steam, a drain or trap connected to said trough, and a conduit connected to said drain.

1,328,097. TRAFFIC-SIGNAL. JESSE R. NAYLOR, Sacramento. Calif. Filed Apr. 18, 1918. Serial No. 229,307. 5 Claims. (Cl. 116—31.)

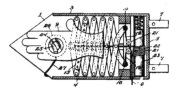

1. In a traffic signal, the combination of a bracket having a vertically elongated guide way, means for securing

said bracket to a part of a motor vehicle, a signaling member, an extensible signal supporting arm consisting of a lazy-tong structure, projections on both the inner extremities of the lazy-tong structure working in said guide way, an actuated spring-flexible member having its free end attached to the signaling member to retract the same, and a flexible signal projecting connection attached to the inner extremities of the lazy-tong structure.

1,328,098. VALVE. JOHN M. PALMER, Chicago, Ill. Filed Oct. 16, 1916. Serial No. 125,784. 13 Claims. (Cl. 251—70.)

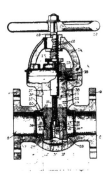

1. In a valve, a body, a gate reciprocating in said body, a stem threaded in said body and threaded in said gate, said threads being in opposite directions and a wedging member on said stem for spreading said gate, the threads on said stem being out of engagement with the threads in said body when the spreading action takes place.

1,328,099. CONVEYER. BERTRAND A. PARKES, Philadelphia, Pa., assignor to The Philadelphia Drying Machinery Company, Philadelphia, Pa., a Corporation of Pennsylvania. Filed Oct. 8, 1917. Serial No. 195,226. 6 Claims. (Cl. 193—2.)

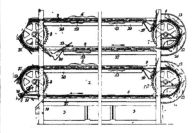

1. A conveyer comprising a horizontally arranged endless series of traveling sections each having a single material carrying surface, means for inverting said sections as they approach the end of their upper horizontal travel, said sections being reinverted as they pass into their lower horizontal travel whereby said material is transferred from the upper inverted sections traveling in one direction to the lower reinverted sections returning to complete the circuit of traverse.

1,328,100. DIRIGIBLE-EYE STRUCTURE FOR DOLLS. JOHN C. POORE, Boston, Mass. Filed June 17, 1919. Serial No. 304,779. 5 Claims. (Cl. 46—40.)

1. A dirigible eye structure for dolls, comprising a holder attachable to the interior of a doll head, a pair of fixed universal joint members attached to said holder, a pair of eyes having universal joint members coöperating with said fixed members, and supported in operative relation to eye openings in the head, and manually operable controlling mechanism carried by the holder and organized to universally swing the eyes in unison, said mechanism including a lever fulcrumed to swing universally on the holder and having an arm movable in an opening in the head, and connections between said lever and the eyes.

1,328,101. LIQUID - MEASURING PUMP. CHARLES F. PRESSLER, Fort Wayne, Ind. Filed Aug. 9, 1917. Serial No. 185,279. 8 Claims. (Cl. 221—101.)

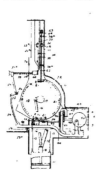

1. The combination with a pump mechanism, of a pivotally supported driving mechanism adapted to be connected to the pump mechanism, means to cause the two mechanisms to engage, means to lock said mechanisms in engagement, means having an operative connection to one of said mechanisms for automatically releasing the engagement of said mechanisms, and means to control the operation of the driving mechanism.

1,328,102. AIR CONTROL FOR INTERNAL-COMBUSTION ENGINES. JOSEPH PERCY REMINGTON, Philadelphia, Pa., assignor to Remington Manufacturing Company, Philadelphia, Pa., a Corporation of Pennsylvania. Filed May 3, 1917. Serial No. 166,133. 9 Claims. (Cl. 48—180.)

9. In an apparatus for supplying an explosive mixture to an engine, the combination of a carbureter, a throttle valve therefor, an auxiliary air inlet, a valve for said auxiliary air inlet, means for holding said valve closed against the suction of the engine, hand-controlled mechanism for operating the throttle and pedal-controlled mechanism

connected to the auxiliary air inlet valve for positively operating the same, and devices actuated by the auxiliary

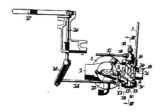

air inlet valve mechanism for opening the throttle for supplying a relatively lean mixture in varying quantities for fast running.

1,328,103. SEWER-TRAP. JOHN W. RIPPLE, Baltimore, Md. Filed Feb. 18, 1919. Serial No. 277,717. 2 Claims. (Cl. 182—14.)

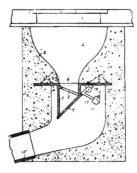

1. The combination with a sewer of a metal plate having an opening therein, a lip around the edge of said opening and projecting from said plate, an inclined flange on the inner surface and which decreases in size toward its lower end of the incline, and a valve pivoted to said plate and adapted to close said opening.

1,328,104. POURING-SPOUT FOR CANS. FRED T. SERVIS, Ontario, N. Y. Filed Feb. 28, 1919. Serial No. 279,725. 2 Claims. (Cl. 221—23.)

1. As a new article of manufacture, a device of the kind described comprising a spout portion, a conically shaped threaded portion connecting with the spout-portion, the threaded portion having means for causing it to enter the material of a can, and a member secured jointly by the spout portion and the threaded portion, the said member being adapted for covering or uncovering an air hole made in the can beside the device.

1,328,105. AUXILIARY AUTOMOBILE-SEAT. CHARLES M. SMITH, Bellingham, Wash. Filed Sept. 27, 1917. Serial No. 193,497. 1 Claim. (Cl. 21—43.)

The combination with a seat including a horizontal support having an upwardly directed bead at a longitudinal edge, and a cushion upon the support, of a supplemental and removable seat including a flat bar having one end portion disposed between the cushion and support and provided with laterally directed sustaining arms and having its opposite end portion extending beyond the bead of the support and provided with a body receiving seat member, the bar having an upwardly directed bend intermediate of said end portions in which the bead is snugly and removably received, the bar being otherwise in a single plane.

1,328,106. LOCK. BEN M. STONE, Chicago, Ill. Filed June 8, 1918. Serial No. 238,875. 8 Claims. (Cl. 70—115.)

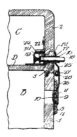

2. A support, a plate on the face of said support, a key-hole lock attached to said support, an integral leaf on and projecting at right angles to the longitudinal axis of said plate and provided with a hinge or pintle pin, the axis of the pin being parallel with the longitudinal axis of the plate, a hasp member hingedly secured to said leaf by said pin, a second key-hole lock, a support therefor, said lock being adapted for operative engagement with said hasp member, a keeper member adapted for operative engagement with the first mentioned lock, and a support for said keeper member.

1,328,107. EXPANSION-JOINT STRIP. SWINTON B. WARING, Wallingford, Pa., assignor to The Waring-Underwood Company, Philadelphia, Pa., a Corporation of Pennsylvania. Filed Apr. 26, 1913. Serial No. 763,807. 3 Claims. (Cl. 94—18.)

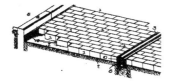

1. A preformed strip for use as an expansion joint filler in the construction of street paving comprising an elongated strip of asphalt having a reinforcement of paper.

270 O. G.—20

1,328,108. SEWING-MACHINE. JOHN P. WEIS, Nyack, N. Y., assignor to Metropolitan Sewing Machine Corporation, a Corporation of Delaware. Filed July 20, 1918. Serial No. 245,823. 26 Claims. (Cl. 112—100.)

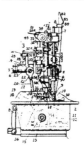

1. The combination of a work support, a presser foot, a presser bar carrying said foot, a feeding mechanism, a needle bar, a pair of needles carried by said needle bar and arranged in a plane at right angles to the line of feed, a thread guide disposed at one side of the needles and slightly in the rear of the plane of the needles, a thread hook movable across the line of feed to engage a cross thread extending through said thread guide and back across the line of feed for forming a loop in the cross thread, said hook and thread guide being so disposed relatively to the needles as to position the loop in the cross thread for the entrance only of the needle farthest removed from the thread guide, means surrounding the needle bar for supporting said thread hook, and means for operating said supporting means.

17. In a sewing machine, the combination of stitching mechanism comprising a needle bar carrying a pair of needles, looper mechanism coöperating with the needles, a spirally formed cross thread carrying finger coöperating with the needles, and take up means for taking up the thread of one needle to a greater extent than that of the other.

1,328,109. LOCK FOR ELECTRIC SWITCHES. ROBERT G. WHITLOCK, Los Angeles, Calif. Filed Dec. 29, 1916. Serial No. 139,443. 4 Claims. (Cl. 70—122.)

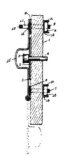

1. The combination of a board, a switch operating means thereon, a pair of plates on the outer-face of said board disposed on opposite sides of said switch operating means, fastening means extending through and engaging said plates and passing through said board, from the front thereof, means on the back of said board for holding said fastening means against removal releasable from the front of said plates, a cover leaf hinged on one of the plates, and a keeper on the other plate, said

cover leaf adapted to extend over the switch operating means and to be engaged by said keeper and when so engaged to cover the plate fastening means against detachment.

1,328,110. BASE-LOCK FOR RECIPROCATING ENGINES. George Wilson, Algona, Iowa. Filed Apr. 3, 1919. Serial No. 287,264. 17 Claims. (Cl. 105—107.)

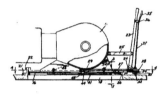

1. The combination with the platform and wheels of a car, of a sub-base having a three-point support from said platform, a reciprocating engine adjustably mounted on the sub-base, and a transmission mechanism for driving certain of said wheels from the engine.

1,328,111. RATCHET-BRACE. Evert Asche, Clara City, Minn. Filed June 27, 1918. Serial No. 242,288. 8 Claims. (Cl. 77—7.)

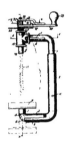

1. A bracket of the character described comprising a substantially U-shaped body formed with a foot at one end, a rotatable fitting at the opposite end and in alinement with said foot, means for locking said fitting in a plurality of adjusted positions, a tool receiving member having a shank or rod extending through the fitting, means for rotating said rod, and an adjusting member threaded into the fitting, said adjusting member having an annular flange whereby same may be moved at any point around the fitting for adjusting said tool receiving member toward and from said foot.

1,328,112. DRAWER ATTACHMENT. Giovanni Barchi, New York, N. Y. Filed June 13, 1919. Serial No. 303,885. 1 Claim. (Cl. 45—77.)

An article of manufacture comprising a strip of material bent upon itself at one end, said bent end having a depression or socket therein and a perforation formed in the strip and registering with the depression or socket and an anti-friction ball positioned within said depression or socket and projecting through said perforation.

1,328,113. RAIL-JOINT. Ben M. Bates, Baltimore, Md. Filed May 27, 1919. Serial No. 300,054. 1 Claim. (Cl. 238—46.)

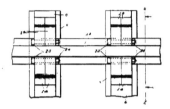

In a supporting means for railway rails, a tie comprising an I beam the base flange of which being of a greater width than the head flange thereof, said last mentioned flange having spaced notches entering from the edges thereof and terminating at the sides of the connecting web for the head and base flanges, the portion of the tie between the notches providing a seat on which a rail rests, blocks arranged in co-acting pairs having inner nose portions which contact with the opposite sides of the rails, said blocks having their outer faces provided with depending necks which enter the notches, foot plates formed on the ends of the necks and extending longitudinally in opposite directions therefrom and underlying the head flange of the tie, said necks and foot portions terminating inward of the inner faces of the blocks to permit of the same contacting with the webs of the ties and the inner faces of the co-acting blocks contacting, and removable securing means for the co-acting pairs of blocks.

1,328,114. FLYTRAP. Alois Bayer and August Klingele, Lorain, Ohio. Filed Mar. 15, 1919. Serial No. 282,814. 3 Claims. (Cl. 43—1.)

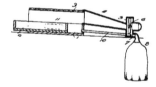

1. A trap comprising a housing, a bait holder in the housing, and common means for withdrawing flies from the housing and supplying an air blast to the housing behind the bait container.

1,328,115. JACK-BASE. Henry I. Benedict, New Orleans, La. Filed Dec. 7, 1918. Serial No. 265,780. 3 Claims. (Cl. 254—1.)

1. A lifting jack comprising a base formed with a tubular body having an internal flange, said flange having a recess or opening, a barrel vertically movable in the base formed with a plurality of lugs spaced apart axially of the barrel proportioned to pass through said recess

in said flange for engaging any lug with the top of the base by relative turning of the base and barrel, a lifting

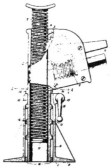

element telescopically fitting in the barrel, and means for operating said lifting element.

1,328,116. FURNACE. HENRY BENTON, Elizabeth, N. J. Filed Mar. 6, 1919. Serial No. 280,965. 5 Claims. (Cl. 110—24.)

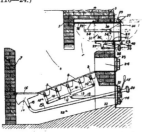

1. In a device of the character described, the combination of a dumping plate, an inner door disposed adjacent said dumping plate and mounted to swing, an outer door disposed adjacent said dumping plate and likewise mounted to swing, connections from said inner door to said outer door for enabling said inner door to be actuated by movements of said outer door, and mechanism controllable at the will of the operator for actuating said dumping plate.

1,328,117. ANIMAL-EXTERMINATOR. JOSEPH T. BERTHELOTE, Havre, Mont. Filed Sept. 28, 1918. Serial No. 256,039. 3 Claims. (Cl. 43—5.)

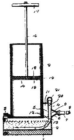

1. A device of the character described comprising a casing constituting a reservoir for a volatile liquid, a

wick guide at one side of said casing, the said side of said casing forming a portion of the wick guide and being provided with an opening surrounded by an outwardly extending nipple, a flexible conducting member engaged upon said nipple, a wire screen covering said opening, and means for directing a blast of air through said wick at said opening.

1,328,118. TUNNELING - MACHINE. INGEBRET BÖHN, Sörumsanden, Norway. Filed Dec. 4, 1917. Serial No. 205,369. 6 Claims. (Cl. 262—6.)

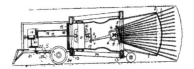

1. In a tunneling machine, a plurality of reciprocating cutter bars, a guide for the latter, a centrally pivoted oscillatory disk, universal connections between the cutters and disk, and means to impart an oscillatory movement to the latter, whereby the cutter bars are reciprocated.

1,328,119. MIXER. LOUIS MARSHALL BRAYMAN, Westville, N. H. Filed Feb. 27, 1919. Serial No. 279,660. 2 Claims. (Cl. 259—81.)

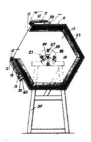

1. A mixer comprising a barrel of polygonal cross-section, having flat side walls, and end walls at right angles with said side walls, said barrel being mounted to rotate around a longitudinal axis, means for rotating said barrel, and members of substantial thickness located within said barrel and each secured permanently to an end wall and to a side wall of said barrel, and presenting a surface at an angle with the end wall and the side wall, whereby material in said barrel, when the mixer is in operation, is directed away from the ends thereof, the adjacent ends of said members being matched and contiguous.

1,328,120. COMBINATION COMB AND BRUSH. GRACE L. BRICKER. Anderson, Ind. Filed June 30, 1916. Serial No. 106,851. 1 Claim. (Cl. 132—35.)

In a device of the character described, a back substantially triangular in cross section and having a handle, said back and handle being formed from two triangularly shaped sections, said sections having one of their surfaces adjacent their apex edge rabbeted, the rabbets adapted to register with each other when the sections are brought together, thereby forming a recess for the reception of a comb, one face of each section being at an acute angle to the comb and provided with bristles, rivets extending transversely through the sections from the acute faces thereof and at right angles to the comb, and a pin passing through the sections and being centrally arched so that the end portions extend at right angles to the bristle carrying faces of the sections at a point below the ends of the transversely disposed pins.

1,328,121. SOIL-WORKING IMPLEMENT. BENJAMIN R. BROWN, Kinsley, Kans. Filed Nov. 8, 1918. Serial No. 261,675. 2 Claims. (Cl. 55—39.)

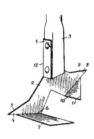

1. In a hoe, a handle, a main hoe blade having a lateral extension at right-angles thereto, said lateral extension having a lower point projecting below and lying substantially in the plane of said main blade and adapted for making a lateral vertical cut in the soil prior to the entry into the soil of the main blade, whereby the cut of the latter is made easier.

1,328,122. SAFETY-COMPARTMENT FOR SHIPS. YOUNG K. BUELL, New York, N. Y. Filed Apr. 14, 1917, Serial No. 162,027. Renewed July 10, 1919. Serial No. 309,969. 6 Claims. (Cl. 114—68.)

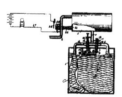

1. A ship having compartments, a bag in each compartment, means for supplying air to the bags, and means for each bag and operated automatically by its respective bag to cut off the supply thereto when such bag is fully inflated.

1,328,123. FASTENING DEVICE FOR CARDS, CALENDARS, &c. JAMES P. BURKE, Struthers, Ohio. Filed Apr. 10, 1919. Serial No. 288,980. 6 Claims. (Cl. 40—11.)

1. The herein described card fastening device comprising a body of flexible material, means to secure a card to the body, a finger piece integral with the body and bendable from the plane of the body in a position

at an angle thereto, and a wall engaging member integral with the finger piece and movable therewith with respect to the body.

1,328,124. AGRICULTURAL IMPLEMENT. HERBERT V. CALKINS, Longmont, Colo. Filed Aug. 28, 1918. Serial No. 251,783. 4 Claims. (Cl. 55—38.)

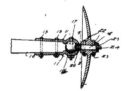

1. A tool of the class described comprising a handle, a pair of clips secured to the forward portion of the handle and having their forward end portions shaped to form a socket, a shaft having a ball head arranged within said socket, a pivot element extending through the portions of the clips forming the socket and through said ball head, and a ground working blade carried by said shaft and adapted to be positioned about said pivot element.

1,328,125. MEANS FOR SUPPORTING LAMPS. EUGENE GEORGE CAMELINAT, Birmingham, England. Filed Mar. 17, 1919. Serial No. 283,266. 3 Claims. (Cl. 240—57.)

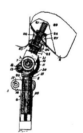

1. A lamp bracket for vehicles and the like comprising a stem for attaching to the lamp, a pillar, a knuckle joint comprising fork and tongue members between the lower end of the stem and the upper end of the pillar, the opposite plain faces of the tongue member having recesses, friction washers having both faces serrated located in said recesses in the tongue member and engaging the plain faces of the fork member, means for locking the joint in different angular positions, a split socket receiving the pillar, and means for contracting the socket around the pillar to fix the latter in different angular positions within the socket.

1,328,126. ELECTRIC CONTROLLER. THEODORE THOMAS CATER, Aurora, Mo. Filed Feb. 15, 1919. Serial No. 277,219. 6 Claims. (Cl. 219—19.)

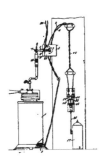

1. An electric controlling and regulating device comprising the combination with an operating instrumentality and a moving part operably connected to said instrumentality, of rocking means engageable with said moving part, a series of electric contacts selectively engageable with said rocking means, an electric circuit connected to said contacts, a switch in said circuit, tripping means engageable with said switch, a time piece operably connected to said tripping means, and spring means for operating said rocking means in conjunction with said contacts at a predetermined time.

1,328,127. CRANKING MECHANISM FOR EXPLOSIVE-ENGINES. ERVIN N. CESAR, Ponca City, Okla. Filed Apr. 12, 1919. Serial No. 289,624. 4 Claims. (Cl. 123—185.)

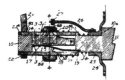

1. In a cranking device for explosive engines, the combination with an engine shaft, of a slidably and rotatably mounted cranking shaft, clutch means for periodically coupling said shafts, a cranking sleeve rotatably mounted on said cranking shaft, a spring actuated latch carried by said shaft and the said shaft and sleeve locked together against rotary movement, a tripping wheel mounted on said sleeve and adapted to have a certain rotary movement thereon, a stationarily held pawl engaging said tripping wheel against rotation in one direction upon reverse rotation of the cranking shaft, and cam means within the tripping wheel adapted to withdraw the aforesaid latch from the cranking sleeve and permit reverse rotation of the cranking shaft within the crank sleeve.

1,328,128. GAGE FOR HEADING AND FORGING MACHINES. WILLIAM L. CLOUSE, Tiffin, Ohio, assignor to The National Machinery Co., Tiffin, Ohio. Filed Oct. 7, 1918. Serial No. 257,195. 2 Claims. (Cl. 10—16.)
1. The combination with the gripping dies and heading dies of a bolt heading and forging machine, of a gage

shaft parallel with the path of movement of the heading die, bearings for the shaft, a gage finger extending from

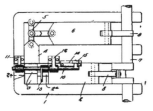

the shaft and between the bearings and movable into and out of position between the heading die and the gripping dies, and means for operating the shaft.

1,328,129. HEADLIGHT-DIMMER. THOMAS CONNELL and CARL T. STACH, Iowa City, Iowa. Filed Jan. 31, 1917. Serial No. 145,631. 2 Claims. (Cl. 240—45.)

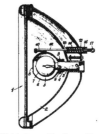

1. In a headlight, in combination with the lamp and its socket, a pair of shields having a hinged connection with said socket and adapted to close over the light, and formed to emit a ray of light when in closed position, and means for operating said shields comprising links connected thereto and to each other and a spring actuated rod common to said links.

1,328,130. TRUCK-BODY. FLOYD A. CRANDALL, Flint, Mich. Filed Feb. 6, 1919. Serial No. 275,332. 11 Claims. (Cl. 296—14.)

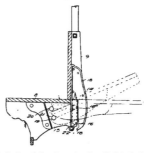

2. A device of the character described including a floor supporting beam, vertically alined lugs carried by said beam, an adjustable supporting arm, and bifurcations carried by the arm each provided with a groove having an open end receiving the vertically alined lugs and retaining the arm in vertical position.

1,328,131. DENTAL INSTRUMENT. FRANK BROUGH-
TON DAVIS, Erie, Pa. Filed May 23, 1917. Serial No.
170,510. 9 Claims. (Cl. 32—10.)

9. In a dental tool of the character described the combination of a bearing member; a block slidingly mounted
on the bearing member; a tool actuating member pivotally
mounted on the block; a pivoted handle for actuating the
tool actuating member; and means for adjusting the tool
actuating member and handle relatively to each other
to vary the movement of the tool with a given movement
of the handle.

1,328,132. VENTILATED GRAIN-STOREHOUSE. LIZ-
ZIE H. DICKELMAN, Forest, Ohio. Filed Feb. 14, 1917.
Serial No. 148,667. 7 Claims. (Cl. 98—26.)

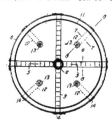

5. A ventilated grain store house comprising a central
perforated air shaft, laterally extending air tubes communicating with the interior of said air shaft at the bottom thereof, a base, said laterally extending tubes and
the lower part of said air shaft being secured to said base,
a roof secured to said central air shaft, walls carried by
said base and joining said roof, a plurality of auxiliary
air conduits, each of said air conduits communicating at
one end with the outer atmosphere and at the opposite
end with the interior of the store house between the central air shaft and the walls, and a removable perforated
thimble disposed in the end of the auxiliary conduit which
communicates with the interior of the grain store house,
the upper surface of the thimble being flush with the
upper surface of the base, and removably heating means
disposed in the auxiliary conduit underneath said perforated thimble.

1,328,133. AIR-PRESSURE LIQUID-TRANSFER DE-
VICE. HARRY G. DIFFENBAUGH, Salt Lake City, Utah.
Filed May 8, 1919. Serial No. 295,809. 4 Claims. (Cl.
221—77.)

1. Apparatus of the character described, adapted to be
used with containers for liquids having a head with a
filling hole provided in said head, comprising a main frame
mounted over the container, and provided with an arm
projecting above said filling hole, a delivery pipe passing
downwardly through said arm and through said filling

hole and terminating at its lower end above the inner face
of the bottom of the container, the upper end of said pipe
being normally closed by a suitable valve, means for forming a tight joint between said frame and said container

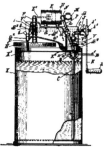

over the space surrounding said pipe, an air compressor
carried by said frame, means for driving said air compressor, and an air pressure pipe leading from said air compressor to the space between said delivery pipe and the
walls of said filling hole, substantially as described.

1,328,134. TOY FLYING-MACHINE. MAX A. DOELCK-
NER, Louisville, Ky. Filed Aug. 25, 1919. Serial No.
319,590. 2 Claims. (Cl. 46—14.)

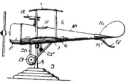

2. A toy flying machine having an upper plane stamped
from a single sheet of metal and provided with spaced
seats stamped therein, a lower plane similarly made and
provided with a transverse concavity stamped centrally
thereof, posts soldered at their ends within the seats of
the upper and lower planes, a body of conical form made
of a single piece of sheet metal lapped at the joint, said
body fitting and soldered in said transverse concavity,
a horizontal body fin of double form having a longitudinal
concavity fitting over and soldered to the pointed end of
said body, a vertical tail fin attached centrally to said horizontal fin, a motor fitting in the larger end of said body,
and a cap piece for said open end spun from a single piece
of sheet metal.

1,328,135. SIGNAL AND GUIDE LIGHT. HUGH HARRY
DONER, New York, N. Y. Filed Mar. 27, 1919. Serial
No. 285,663. 3 Claims. (Cl. 40—130.)

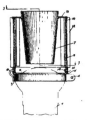

1. The combination with a portable lamp, of a hood
removably secured on the end of the lamp, said hood hav-

ing signals in its sides, a cone secured in the hood and projecting beyond the outer end of the hood, said cone causing a division of the light so that a portion thereof shines through the cone, and a portion is directed to illuminate the signals.

1,328,136. SHADE AND CURTAIN HANGER. DAVID JOSEPH DORSEY, Baton Rouge, La. Filed June 17, 1919. Serial No. 304,768. 1 Claim. (Cl. 156—27.)

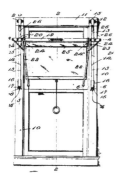

A shade and curtain hanger including vertical parallel bars having notches in their outer vertical edges, socket members carried by the upper portion of the window frame, the upper ends of said bars being formed for engagement in said socket members, bifurcated brackets on the lower portion of the window frame, the lower ends of the bars being threaded and removably engageable in said bifurcations, clamping nuts on said threaded ends for engagement with said bifurcations, a transverse member disposed between said bars, bar engaging rollers on the said transverse member, shade supporting means on the member, and movable spring urged levers carried by the transverse member and having means for engagement within the notches to hold the said member at different elevations on said bars.

1,328,137. DUMPING-WAGON. ARTHUR NATHAN DOUD, Winthrop, N. Y. Filed Sept. 24, 1918. Serial No. 255,471. 17 Claims. (Cl. 298—17.)

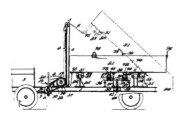

17. A dumping wagon, the combination with a chassis, of a body having members loosely resting in upwardly open sockets and held in the same by gravity, and means rocking the body in the sockets for dumping the body to either side and the rear, whereby the body can be lifted bodily from the chassis without removing or operating any mechanical element.

1,328,188. RAILWAY-BRAKE APPLIANCE. JAMES F. DRINKWATER, Willard, Ohio. Filed Oct. 30, 1918. Serial No. 260,356. 5 Claims. (Cl. 188—58.)

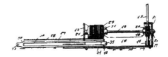

1. An apparatus of the character described comprising a base ; a horizontally disposed shaft carried thereby ; a gear carried by said shaft ; a brake staff having one end thereof journaled in said base ; a gear carried by said staff and meshing with the gear carried by said shaft ; a rack bar slidably carried by said base ; a worm gear carried by said shaft and meshing with said rack bar ; an elongated loop arranged parallel with the rack bar and having connection with a brake mechanism ; and an arm extending from said rack bar and having sliding connection with said loop, said rack bar being adapted to be operated by the rotation of said brake staff.

1,328,139. HYDRAULIC WATER-FORCING APPARATUS. WILLIAM SAINT GEORGE ELLIOTT, Jr., New York, N. Y. Filed June 17, 1919. Serial No. 304,822. 15 Claims. (Cl. 162—1.)

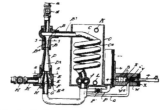

1. The herein described method of forcing water or liquids under high pressure ; consisting in confining the liquid in a closed circuit ; injecting a gaseous fluid such as steam into such circuit to exert pressure upon the liquid in such circuit ; and withdrawing surplus liquid at a predetermined pressure.

7. A high pressure liquid forcing apparatus ; including a closed circuit for liquid, an injector connected with the circuit for introducing steam therein and forcing the liquid to circulate, means for cooling the liquid in one part of the circuit, and an outlet for surplus liquid in the circuit.

1,328,140. OPERATING-TABLE. LORENZ ERTL, Ivanhoe, Minn. Filed July 28, 1919. Serial No. 313,677. 2 Claims. (Cl. 119—103.)

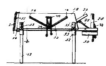

1. In a device of the class described, a top, legs for supporting the top, side boards hingedly mounted, a front board, flexible devices retaining the side boards in an adjusted position, an adjustably mounted elevating device connected with the top intermediate of the ends thereof, means carried by the side boards for limiting the outward movement thereof and devices positioned to be engaged by said means and constituting leg supports.

1,328,141. INTERNAL-COMBUSTION ENGINE. ROBERT L. FOLKS, Waycross, Ga. Filed Jan. 3, 1917. Serial No. 140,409. 2 Claims. (Cl. 123—65.)

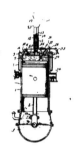

1. In a two cycle engine, a cylinder, a main crank shaft, a main piston coupled by a connecting rod to said crank shaft and adapted to overrun the inlet and exhaust ports of the cylinder, said cylinder having a spider-like head with constantly open orifices, an auxiliary piston in said cylinder having a rigidly attached piston rod guided by said cylinder head, a rotary cam coöperating with said piston rod to move the auxiliary piston toward the main piston, means for moving the latter away from the main piston with a relatively quick action, driving means between said crank shaft and rotary cam, an ignition element carried by the auxiliary piston and adapted to pass through the spider-like cylinder head, and an ignition member pivotally supported by the cylinder head and adapted to contact with the first named ignition element.

1,328,142. FUEL-SUPPLY MECHANISM FOR INTERNAL-COMBUSTION ENGINES. STEPHEN IVAN FEKETE, Detroit, Mich., assignor, by mesne assignments, to Essex Motors, Detroit, Mich., a Corporation of Michigan. Filed July 11, 1917. Serial No. 180,022. 10 Claims. (Cl. 123—31.)

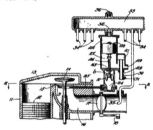

1. The fuel supply mechanism for an internal combustion engine which comprises a fuel pit, means for supplying fuel to the fuel pit in a continuous flow while the engine is running means for injecting into the engine the fuel which has accumulated in the fuel pit between successive strokes of the engine, and regulating means responsive to variations in pressure in the air intake of the engine to vary the flow of fuel to the fuel pit.

1,328,143. KITE-FRAME OR LIKE STRUCTURE. STERLING P. FERGUSSON, Washington, D. C. Filed Oct. 19, 1917. Serial No. 197,501. 4 Claims. (Cl. 244—23.)

1. A kite or like structure, having a frame built up of a plurality of longitudinal members extending from end to end of the structure, a plurality of transverse members extending from side to side of the structure, connectors at the crossing points of the longitudinal and transverse members, the intermediate connectors having through openings for said members while the end connectors are

provided with sockets having end closures to form abutments for the members, vertical strut members, sockets in said connectors for the vertical members, and diagonally disposed tension members connected to adjacent connectors, substantially as described.

1,328,144. AUTOMATIC MACHINE. MARK E. FERNALD, Saugus, Mass. Filed Aug. 16, 1913, Serial No. 785,079. Renewed Mar. 11, 1918. Serial No. 221,866. 7 Claims. (Cl. 33—180.)

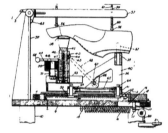

1. The method of positioning work having lateral reverse curves thereon relatively to the operating tools of an automatic machine in which the relative traverse of the work and tools is controlled by a leader having lateral reverse curves corresponding in direction and extent to the curves of the work, said method consisting in marking the work and then bringing the corresponding curves of the marked work and leader into alinement by registering the marks on the work with pointers having the same relation to the leader as the marks have to the work, substantially as described.

1,328,145. STOP MECHANISM. EDWARD E. FOSTER, Beverly, Mass., assignor to C. C. Blake, Incorporated, Boston, Mass., a Corporation of New York. Filed Nov. 13, 1915. Serial No. 61,396. 7 Claims. (Cl. 74—46.)

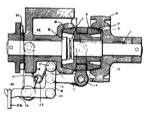

1. A stop mechanism, having, in combination, a driving pulley, a brake, a clutch member arranged to alternately

engage the pulley and brake, a spring for moving the clutch member into engagement with the pulley, and mechanism for positively moving the clutch member into engagement with the brake comprising a cam and connections between the cam and the clutch member including a toggle, one arm of which is inverted, substantially as described.

1,328,146. MATRIX FOR TYPOGRAPHICAL MA-CHINES. HERMAN R. FREUND, Brooklyn, N. Y., assignor to Intertype Corporation, Brooklyn, N. Y., a Corporation of New York. Filed Nov. 3, 1919. Serial No. 335,305. 3 Claims. (Cl. 199—64.)

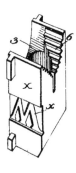

1. A relatively thick matrix adapted for use in typographical machines of the type embodying a distributer rail along which circulating matrices are adapted to travel, said matrix having distributer teeth of different lengths measured in the direction of the thickness of the matrix, the longer teeth intersecting a plane passing vertically through the center of weight of the matrix.

1,328,147. SPARK-PLUG. JOHN E. GENN, Chicago, Ill., assignor to Stewart-Warner Speedometer Corporation, Chicago, Ill., a Corporation of Virginia. Filed Aug. 15 1918. Serial No. 249,939. 6 Claims. (Cl. 123—169.)

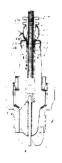

1. In a spark plug, an insulating member having a longitudinally corrugated bore, a conductor disposed therein and secured by cement filling the space between the surface of such conductor and the corrugated wall of the insulator.

1,328,148. FISH-SCALER. IONA GRAYSON, Tulsa, Okla. Filed Mar. 31, 1919. Serial No. 286,304. 8 Claims. (Cl. 17—10.)

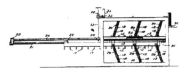

1. A fish scaler comprising outwardly curved scaling bars, suitably spaced apart, inwardly extending teeth carried thereby, a pusher bar operating between the scaling bars to move the fish in contact with the teeth and means for yieldingly holding the scaling bars in position.

1,328,149. AUTOMATIC VOLTAGE CONTROL. WILLIAM S. HARLEY, Milwaukee, Wis., assignor to Harley-Davidson Motor Co., Milwaukee, Wis. Filed Sept. 19, 1917. Serial No. 192,118. 2 Claims. (Cl. 123—149.)

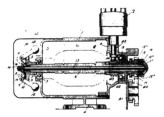

1. An apparatus of the class described comprising, in combination, a hollow armature shaft, a rod slidably disposed in said shaft, a governor on one end of said rod, a clutch on the other end of said rod, a sleeve loosely mounted on said shaft adjacent said clutch, a rotatable device connected with the sleeve, and means for rotating the sleeve.

1,328,150. COMBINED INTAKE AND EXHAUST MANIFOLD. WILLIAM S. HARLEY, Milwaukee, Wis., assignor to Harley-Davidson Motor Company, Milwaukee, Wis. Filed Feb. 19, 1918. Serial No. 218,079. 1 Claim. (Cl. 257—241.)

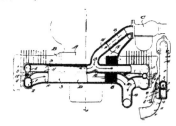

In a device of the class described, a combined exhaust and intake manifold comprising a one piece cast elongated main casing, each end of the casing having a pair of spaced openings, a longitudinally disposed wall extending from end to end of the casing between the openings to form a pair of pipe-like compartments each having a hole at each end, a laterally extending two compartment supplemental casing having its walls formed integrally with the wall of the first mentioned main casing, one end of one of the compartments of the laterally extending casing being in communication with one of the compartments of the main chamber, the other end of said compartment of the laterally extending casing being open, a passageway from the other compartment of the laterally extending casing to the other compartment of the main casing, and an outlet from the last named compartment of the main casing.

1,328,151. RADIATOR. Austin H. Hart, Bronxville, N. Y., assignor to Deposited Metal Products Company, a Corporation of New Jersey. Filed Jan. 25, 1918. Serial No. 213,699. 1 Claim. (Cl. 257—129.)

A radiator for automobiles and the like comprising a plurality of tubes having spaced communicating alined water chambers of substantial pear shape in horizontal section and tapered from front to rear, the chambers of one tube being staggered with respect to the chambers of the adjacent tubes.

1,328,152. COLLAPSIBLE STEAM-CHEST AND OVEN. Earl W. Howe, Norfolk, Va. Filed Oct. 3, 1919. Serial No. 328,198. 1 Claim. (Cl. 126—275.)

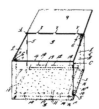

A collapsible cooking receptacle comprising a rectangular body member, said body member comprising front, rear and end walls, the adjacent ends of said walls being hingedly connected to each other, said hinged connections at two points diametrically opposite each other being set in thereby forming means for spacing the walls from each other, when collapsed, a bottom hingedly connected to the rear wall at a point spaced from the lower edge thereof, the free end of the bottom being provided with a hinged flange, a channel carried by the front wall for the reception of the hinged flange, said hinged connection of the bottom and its hinged flange allowing said bottom to be folded upwardly so as to nest between the collapsed sides of the body member, and a cover hingedly connected to the upper end of the rear wall whereby said receptacle may be closed as desired.

1,328,153. AUTOMOBILE-LAMP. William A. Irwin, New York, N. Y., and Leo Frederick Jackson, Taunton, Mass. Filed June 11, 1919. Serial No. 303,311. 2 Claims. (Cl. 240—45.)
2. The combination with a lamp casing and a source of light therein, of a hood serving as a dimming device in advance of the casing and in the beam of light projected forward therefrom, means extending between the casing

and the hood and spanning the space between them serving to fix the hood in rigid position, and transparent shell

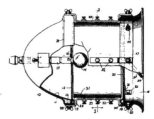

means filling the space between the casing and the hood and serving to allow free emission of light laterally through the space between the casing and the hood.

1,328,154. CUSHION-HEEL. Benjamin Jackerson, Brooklyn, N. Y. Filed Apr. 14, 1919. Serial No. 289,786. 3 Claims. (Cl. 36—36.)

1. A device of the character described comprising a metallic heel member having an integral marginal flange provided with an annularly disposed curved face, a pneumatic element positioned within the metallic member, and a protecting element retained in place between said pneumatic element and the inner edge of said marginal flange.

1,328,155. RAIL-JOINT. Joseph J. Jezik, East Bernard, Tex., assignor of one-half to Frank F. Kretek, East Bernard, Tex. Filed July 23, 1919. Serial No. 312,797. 5 Claims. (Cl. 238—250.)

1. A rail joint including a pair of coacting fish plates having pairs of elongated and cylindrical openings therein, L-shaped lugs carried adjacent the cylindrical openings and adapted to extend through the elongated openings of the coacting fish plates, and means to retain said lugs within said elongated openings.

1,328,156. WHEELED RAKE. Thomas J. Kincaid, Wills, Wis. Filed May 28, 1919. Serial No. 300,251. 2 Claims. (Cl. 55—19.)

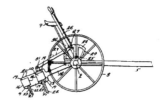

1. A wheeled rake comprising a body member, an axle carried by said body member, wheels rotatably mounted on

the ends of said axle, a rake disposed to the rear of said body member, said rake comprising a pair of toothed bars secured together, connecting bars having one of their ends bifurcated and adapted to receive the forward rake bar, said forward rake bar being secured in said bifurcation, the other ends of the connecting bars being pivotally secured to the axle, said connecting bars and toothed rake bars being in radial position to said axle and means carried by the body member and connected to the forward toothed bar whereby the rake as a whole may be raised or lowered as desired.

1,328,157. SNOWPLOW. JOHN KORHONEN. Englewood, N. J. Filed June 10, 1919. Serial No. 303,111. 1 Claim. (Cl. 37—57.)

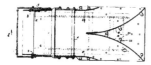

A snow plow comprising a tractor, a plow structure mounted on the tractor formed with a flat bottom extending from the front to the rear of the tractor, said body having a number of openings therein adjacent the rear, a plurality of deflecting members arranged at the rear formed with ears, and a bolt extending through each of the ears and certain of said openings for clamping the deflecting members in position, said bolts and said deflecting members being shiftable so that the bolts will occupy different openings as desired according to the position desired for the deflectors.

1,328,158. TYPEWRITING-MACHINE. NICOLAS KOUSNETZOFF and EUGENE M. KOUZMIN, New York, N. Y. Filed Mar. 22, 1919. Serial No. 284,273. 5 Claims. (Cl. 197—46.)

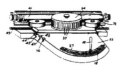

1. In a typewriting machine, a type character holder comprising a wheel, a vertical support around which the wheel may be rotated, said wheel having a plurality of parallel slots in its periphery, a series of flexible strips located in said slots and held detachably in the wheel, and a plurality of type characters carried at uniform levels on and by said strips.

1,328,159. SAW-FILING DEVICE. WILLIAM H. KRAMER, Newcastle, Ind. Filed May 31, 1918. Serial No. 237,424. 5 Claims. (Cl. 76—36.)

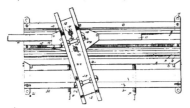

1. In a saw filing device, a frame, clamping means on said frame, file guiding means slidable on the frame, and adjustable flexible strips secured to the opposite side portions of the frame whereby to permit gaging of the file guiding means.

1,328,160. EXTERNAL - EXPLOSION ENGINE. WILLIAM EDWARD LAWN, Rochester, N. Y. Filed Nov. 23, 1917. Serial No. 203,607. 2 Claims. (Cl. 60—44.)

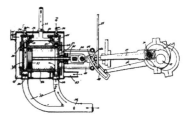

1. In an engine of the character set forth, the combination of a cylinder, a pair of inlet valves at the opposite ends of the cylinder, means to cause the alternate opening and closing of the inlet valves, a pair of exhaust valves at the ends of the cylinder, means to cause the alternate opening and closing of the exhaust valves, the inlet and exhaust valves at each end of the cylinder being alternately openend and closed, a piston reciprocating in the cylinder, a pair of combustion chambers external to the cylinder and between which and the cylinder the inlet valves are located, ignition devices in the several combustion chambers, and means to deliver fuel mixtures into the combustion chamber in alternation under high pressure, substantially as set forth.

1,328,161. WATER-HEATER. NATHAN OREN LYNN, Mendon, Mich. Filed Nov. 17, 1917. Serial No. 202,561. 4 Claims. (Cl. 126—260.)

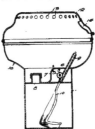

4. A heater including a fuel reservoir, a collar arranged about the upper portion of said reservoir, a cover for the reservoir having a filling and a wick receiving opening therein, said wick receiving opening being obliquely disposed, an oblique wick guiding tube arranged adjacent the wick receiving opening extending upwardly into the collar to a point in proximity to one side thereof to effect the indirect transmission of heat to an article arranged on the heater, and a shield having the upper portion thereof constricted and formed with a central openin detachably engaged with said collar for receiving and supporting an article to be heated.

1,328,162. BRUSH-HOLDER. CHARLES E. HECHT, Irvington, N. J., assignor to Hanlon & Goodman Co., New York, N. Y., a Corporation of New York. Filed June 13, 1919. Serial No. 303,833. 4 Claims. (Cl. 248—50.)
1. In a brush, the combination of a head having a recess in its upper surface, a metal socket piece mounted

in said recess and having a lip portion bent to extend along an edge surface of said head, said socket piece having pivot means therein, and a resilient hooked member bent into loop form, loosely pivoted on said

pivot means, the hook thereof being adapted to be forced over the lower edge of said lip portion, when the main portion of said hooked member is compressed within said socket piece.

1,328,163. CLOTHES-BASKET CARRIER. FRANK L. HUMPHREY, Enid, Okla. Filed Apr. 8, 1919. Serial No. 288,488. 1 Claim. (Cl. 105—150.)

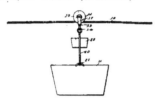

A carrier comprising a line supported pulley, an apertured link comprising spaced ears for pivotally receiving the pulley, rods having one of their ends pivotally secured to the outer ends of the body portion of the link, means carried by the ends of the rods for engagement with a clothes receptacle and a relatively short hook pivotally secured to the body portion of the link between the rods for detachable engagement with a clothes pin receptacle.

1,328,164. BRUSH ESPECIALLY ADAPTED FOR CLEANING STOVEPIPES. JOHN JOKISCH, Detroit, Mich. Filed Nov. 20, 1918. Serial No. 263,395. 1 Claim. (Cl. 15—41.)

In a brush for the purpose set forth, a handle comprising a plurality of hinged sections, bolt members carried by certain of the sections and co-acting with the adjacent sections for retaining said sections in alinement, a brush comprising two semicylindrical plates having their straight edges hingedly connected to the outer section of the handle and their outer peripheries provided with bristles, means on said outer handle section for supporting the brush plates when the latter are in alinement, an angularly disposed cutter member on said outer section of the brush, flexible means connected with the plate, guide means therefor, one of said flexible means designed, when a pull is exerted thereon to swing and retain the brush sections in operative position and the other of said flexible elements designed when a pull is exerted thereon to swing said sections toward each other and collapse the brush.

1,328,165. PUMP. LESLIE R. KIEHL, Raton, N. Mex. Filed July 18, 1919. Serial No. 311,700. 2 Claims. (Cl. 103—61.)

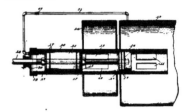

2. The combination with a steam boiler, of a pump including a pump cylinder having steam and water inlet ports therein, said ports being spaced apart, the steam ports establishing communication between the interior of the boiler and the pump cylinder, a water supply communicating with the pump cylinder and water inlet ports, a piston operating within the cylinder and comprising spaced heads to provide a water space therebetween and a steam equalizing pipe establishing communication between the boiler and one end of the cylinder.

1,328,166. AMUSEMENT DEVICE, (SKATING-CAR.) ERNEST KOHLER, Denver, Colo., assignor to The United Mines and Manufacturing Company, a Corporation of Arizona. Filed Aug. 28, 1919. Serial No. 320,394. 11 Claims. (Cl. 104—59.)

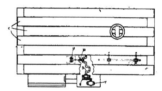

1. In an amusement apparatus, a supporting floor or platform comprising sections having independent movement with respect to each other in a horizontal plane; and a carriage for passengers constructed and arranged to be moved by relatively movable sections of the platform while resting on the same.

1,328,167. SAMPLE-CARRIER. JOSEPH N. KORY, Denver, Colo. Filed Mar. 25, 1919. Serial No. 284,952. 2 Claims. (Cl. 211—34.)

1. A sample tray comprising a backing plate having side flanges and a flange at one end, a transparent cover plate sitting upon the backing plate and engaged by said flanges, a scale card between the backing plate and cover plate, a carrier pad between the scale card and cover plate, and a fastener element engaging the cover plate to hold the cover plate in position.

1,328,168. GATE. ARTHUR W. KROON, Glenellyn, Ill. Filed Apr. 19, 1917, Serial No. 163,172. Renewed Nov. 13, 1919. Serial No. 337,886. 1 Claim. (Cl. 39—87.)

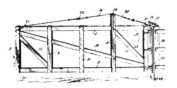

The combination with a gate and a post to which it is hinged, of a strut rising from the top of the gate intermediate its ends, tensioning members connected to the strut and extending in opposite directions therefrom, one of said members being anchored to the forward end of the gate, a bracket member supported by the post, a pivot pin carried by the bracket member independent of and in alinement with the axis of the gate hinge, and a hinge member mounted on the pivot pin to turn thereon, to which member the other tensioning member is connected.

1,328,169. COMBINATION DESK AND CHAIR. ROBERT LEE LEATHERMAN and FRANK PFROGNER, Mount Pleasant, Pa. Filed Apr. 22, 1918. Serial No. 230,078. 1 Claim. (Cl. 155—34.)

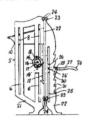

In a device of the character described, and in combination, a main supporting standard having parallel spaced slots, a shaft held to said standard, a gear on said shaft, a ratchet on said shaft, a pawl secured to said standard in contact with said ratchet, a desk having extending cleats arranged to slide in said spaced slots, a rack bar extending from said desk and meshing with said gear, an auxiliary standard, and a back secured to said desk having its ends projecting and clamped between said standards, whereby said desk is held in adjusted position.

1,328,170. SPLICE-BAR. WILLIAM LEE, New Bedford, Mass. Filed Aug. 4, 1919. Serial No. 315,219. 4 Claims. (Cl. 238—180.)

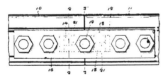

1. Splice bars for railway rails provided upon their inner faces with beveled spaced overlapping jack wedge elements and means for locking said elements in their adjusted relation.

1,328,171. CLOD-CRUSHER AND PACKER. NICHOLAS P. LEHR, Fremont, Ohio. Filed June 16, 1919. Serial No. 304,523. 6 Claims. (Cl. 55—77.)

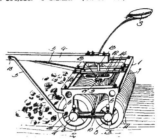

2. An implement of the class described comprising a frame, front and rear rollers carried by said frame, a longitudinal guide carried by said frame, a tongue whose rear end is slidable along said guide and pivotal with respect thereto, and draft means between said tongue and frame, extending upwardly from the sides of the frame to the tongue.

1,328,172. SPRING-FAN. ANNA LIND, Bridgeport, Conn. Filed Sept. 21, 1918. Serial No. 255,115. 3 Claims. (Cl. 74—45.)

1. In a gear driven rotary fan, a rotary disk having operative connection with the drive gears, a pair of weighted arms pivoted upon said disk and provided adjacent their inner ends with cam surfaces, a pair of spring shoes secured upon said disk at one end and having their other ends engaged by said cam surfaces, a split spring band disposed in concentric relation to said disk in position for engagement by said shoes, means for centering said ring with respect to the disk, and means for varying the diameter of said band.

1,328,173. VEHICLE-ALARM. JAMES W. McGOWAN, Omaha, Nebr. Filed Sept. 30, 1918. Serial No. 256,346. 14 Claims. . (Cl. 116—1.)

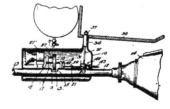

6. The combination with a vehicle having a part moving with each movement of the vehicle, of a mechanically operated alarm, and means for operating said alarm comprising, a rotatable member, means for driving said ro-

tatable member from said moving part, means for operating said mechanical alarm driven by said rotatable member comprising a shaft connected to said alarm and means carried by said rotatable member for rotating said shaft and private means for rendering said alarm inoperative.

1,328,174. ASH-SIFTER. THOMAS JOHN MacIVOR, London, Ontario, Canada. Filed Feb. 10, 1919. Serial No. 276,137. 4 Claims. (Cl. 83—60.)

1. An ash sifter adapted to receive bodily the ash pan of a furnace, stove, or the like, said sifter being bodily turnable through an angle to invert the ash pan, a receiving chamber in said sifter for the ashes to be sifted and adapted to receive said ashes by the inverting of the ash pan and a sifter bottom in said chamber, said sifter presenting a rounded external surface permitting of the bodily rocking of the sifter on a floor or like support to effect the sifting operation.

1,328,175. UMBRELLA. CHARLES W. MARTIN, Brooklyn, N. Y. Filed Nov. 7, 1918. Serial No. 261,503. 1 Claim. (Cl. 135—29.)

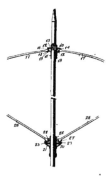

An umbrella structure embodying a runner having a plurality of spaced pairs of ears, stretchers having their inner ends extending between said ears, a flange extending laterally from the runner, a second flange surrounding the periphery of the first mentioned flange and disposed at right angles thereto to provide pockets for the ends of the stretchers, a retainer connecting the stretchers and ears, in combination with a notch and a stick operatively associated with said runner and notch, as and for the purpose set forth.

1,328,176. SURGICAL APPLIANCE FOR WOMEN. JOSEPH J. MARTINKA, Newark, N. J. Filed Sept. 13, 1919. Serial No. 323,455. 2 Claims. (Cl. 128—138.)

2. A device for preventing bed wetting by a woman or female child, comprising resilient jaws of plate-like form, means connecting the rear portions of said jaws together

in opposed relation, resilient means for holding the forward portions of the jaws under yielding pressure against

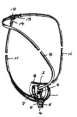

labia, and means connecting the jaws and adjustable to subject the same to positive pressure.

1,328,177. SANITARY SOAP - HOLDER. FRANCESCO MARTUCCI, Jersey City, N. J. Filed June 17, 1919. Serial No. 304,867. 3 Claims. (Cl. 45—136.)

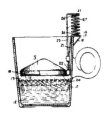

1. The herein described soap holder comprising a bracket having means for engagement over the rim of the mug while the bracket projects downward within the mug, a soap tray guided slidably along the bracket, and a spring acting between the bracket and the soap carrier tending to hold the soap carrier elevated.

1,328,178. DICTIONARY. SAMUEL MAYER, New York, N. Y. Filed Oct. 7, 1919. Serial No. 329,171. 6 Claims. (Cl. 40—86.)

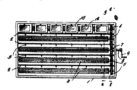

1. A dictionary comprising a cabinet, a grooved roller rotatably mounted in the cabinet, a vertically adjustable box mounted in the cabinet, an adjustable web secured in the box, and means carried by the box and engaging the grooved roller for operating the web.

1,328,179. ROLLER-BEARING. ERLING MEIER, Christiania, Norway. Filed June 16, 1919. Serial No. 304,550. 3 Claims. (Cl. 64—39.)

1. In a roller bearing an outside and an inside bearing ring provided with annular grooves for taking up the axial

pressure, rollers provided with heads or end flanges corresponding to the grooves of the bearing rings, said rollers being placed alternately with their heads in oppo-

site directions and axial grooves or notches leading from the side faces of the bearing rings for introducing the rollers in the same.

1,328,180. CARBURETER. Gaspare Mezzatesta, Hampton, Va. Filed May 6, 1918. Serial No. 232,800. 2 Claims. (Cl. 261—41.)

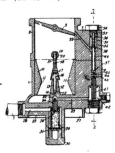

1. A carbureter comprising a casing having a skirt, and a bar extending transversely of the skirt, said bar having a fuel inlet and a feed chamber and provided with a main jet extending into the casing and with a downwardly extending tubular projection into which the inlet opens, an auxiliary jet opening into the feed chamber and tubular projection, a filtering device secured to the auxiliary jet and extending into the tubular projection, a closure for the tubular projection, a spring pressed bell in the casing above the main jet and carrying a needle valve working in said jet, and a butterfly valve in the casing.

1,328,181. SWING-CHAIR. Norman H. Miller, Meadville, Pa. Filed May 18, 1918. Serial No. 235,274. 1 Claim. (Cl. 155—35.)

In a collapsible swing chair, comprising a seat section and a back section, said sections being hingedly connected to each other, end sections hingedly connected to the ends of the back section, the inner edges of the lower rails of the end sections being provided with rabbets thereby forming a ledge at the lower ends of said rails for supporting the ends of the seat section, the under faces of

the lower rails of the end sections being provided with plates having upwardly extending right angled arms spaced from the ledges of said rails and adapted to receive between the ledges and the upwardly extending right angled arms lugs carried by the under face of the seat section at the ends thereof, recesses in the lower rail of the back section for the reception of the upstanding right angled arms when the sections are folded upon themselves and slidable pins carried by the inner face of the lower rails of the back section and adapted to be forced over the notches therein for preventing the right angled upstanding arms of the plates carried by the end pieces from coming out of said notches thereby securely holding the chair in collapsed condition.

1,328,182. PISTON. William James Miller, Goose Creek, Tex. Filed June 28, 1919. Serial No. 307,302. 1 Claim. (Cl. 103—63.)

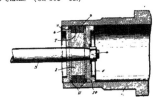

A follower head having an annular recess in its walls, packing material located in said recess, a plate secured to said head and having an annular recess therein and a ring removably engaging said recess.

1,328,183. SMOKER. Francis Mlekush, Rankin, Pa. Filed July 25, 1919. Serial No. 313,165. 3 Claims. (Cl. 99—2.)

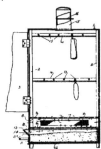

1. In a device of the character described, a casing, a pan fitting into the lower portion of said casing and adapted to contain fuel for generating smoke, said pan being provided with an air inlet opening for admitting air into pan across the top of the fuel, means for admitting air to the casing above the pan, and means for retarding upward flow of the smoke and for causing mixing of this smoke with the air for cooling the smoke prior to its entry into the body of the casing.

1,328,184. SELF-MEASURING DISPENSING VESSEL. Warren Moore, Ladysmith, Wis. Filed Feb. 24, 1917, Serial No. 150,846. Renewed Sept. 29, 1919. Serial No. 327,194 3 Claims. (Cl. 221—98.)

1. In a device of the kind described, a bowl, a cap therefor, a depending measuring casing carried by the cap, and

an oblique interior rib carried by the bowl and adapted to direct the contents of the bowl to said casing.

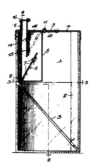

3. In a device of the kind described, a bowl, a cap, a slide movable on the inner face of the cap and operable from the exterior of the cap, a depending casing carried by the cap, a spout, a hinged lid carried by the spout, a removable, obliquely arranged partition in the lower portion of the casing, and an extensible partition in the upper portion, said last mentioned partition having one end pivotally connected to the casing and the other to the slide.

1,328,185. STORE-CASE. WILLIAM B. MORTON, Beatrice, Nebr. Filed July 19, 1919. Serial No. 312,020. 2 Claims. (Cl. 211—9.)

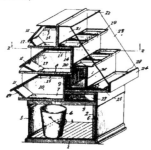

2. An improved store case including a base forming a storage space, a number of longitudinally extending partitions dividing the case lengthwise, a series of shelves in front of said partitions adapted to receive trays containing various commodities on display, one of said trays adapted to receive and hold a refrigerant, dead air spaces formed in the base beneath certain of said trays, transparent walls inclosing said shelves, upper and lower walls at the upper and lower ends of said longitudinally extending partitions, vertical transverse division plates extending between said upper and lower walls and said partitions and adapted to divide the rear portion of the case into a number of selling bins, and disappearing doors for the bins accessible from the rear of the case, substantially as described.

1,328,186. LOCK. EDWARD H. NIED, Akron, Ohio. Filed June 28, 1919. Serial No. 307,441. 1 Claim. (Cl. 70—129.)

In combination with the steering column and the steering wheel connected to the steering post of an automobile, of means for locking the steering wheel against turning on the column, comprising a plate secured to the column

below the wheel, an outstanding arm on said plate, a link pivotally connected to said arm, jaws pivotally connected to the link, each of said jaws having its outer end extended inwardly toward each other and reduced to provide

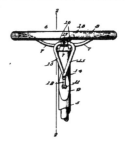

tongues which are adapted to lap when the jaws are brought together, said tongues having openings therethrough, the said jaws designed to receive one of the spokes of the steering wheel, and a locking device designed to be received in the openings of the jaws.

1,328,187. DEVICE FOR INDICATING MAGNETIC POLARITY. HENRY D. OAKLEY, Syracuse, N. Y. Filed July 6, 1918. Serial No. 243,538. 4 Claims. (Cl. 175—183.)

1. In a device of the class described, a tubular member containing liquid, means for mounting said member, a bar magnet inclosed within the tubular member, and a jacket for the magnet comprising a body of buoyant material.

1,328,188. CARBON-PAPER AND INK COMPOSITION THEREFOR. HYDESABURO OHASHI, New York, N. Y.; Marie V. Ohashi administratrix of said Hydesaburo Ohashi, deceased. Filed Dec. 5, 1916. Serial No. 135,198. 6 Claims. (Cl. 134—31.)

1. An ink including the reaction products of a water-soluble anilin dye, calcium chlorid, an emulsifying agent and an emulsifiable substance.

5. Carbon paper comprising paper treated with ink including a water-soluble anilin dye, calcium chlorid, an alkali and an emulsifiable material.

1,328,189. COMBINATION PHONOGRAPH AND MOVING-PICTURE MACHINE. JOHN F. OSBORN, Ludington, Mich. Filed May 28, 1918. Serial No. 237,042. 8 Claims. (Cl. 88—16.2.)

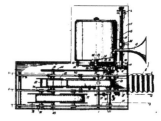

1. In combination with a moving picture machine, a phonographic attachment, a driving means carried by said

moving picture machine and coöperating with said phonographic attachment, said phonographic attachment comprising a record supporting mandrel, a supporting bracket therefor, and means carried by said supporting bracket and engaging said mandrel for bodily moving the same laterally and shifting the same out of engagement with the said driving means.

1,328,190. AUTOMATIC STUFFING-BOX. ALBERT C. PAULSMEIER, Alameda, Calif., assignor to Byron Jackson Iron Works, Inc., San Francisco, Calif., a Corporation Filed May 22, 1919. Serial No. 298,965. 6 Claims. (Cl. 253—199.)

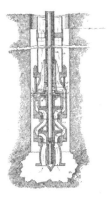

1. The combination with the driving shaft of a pump and the tubing inclosing the same, of means operated by the pump for expelling any leakage water which may enter the shaft tubing during the operation of the pump.

1,328,191. GARDEN - TOOL. ELDON L. PETERSON, Tacoma, Wash. Filed Apr. 22, 1919. Serial No. 291,794. 1 Claim. (Cl. 287—17.)

In combination with a handle member having a shank provided with a slotted head formed with bosses on the outer side thereof and having both of its faces provided with radially disposed ribs and its inner face formed with a central socket, a member having a shank provided with a round head, the face of which being ribbed to co-engage with the ribs on the head of the shank when the same is received in the slotted head thereof, a second member having a shank which terminates in a widened and bifurcated head, the said head having sockets therein and having ribs outward of the sockets, said sockets designed to engage with the bosses on the outer face of the head of the shank of the handle and of the ribs of the head on the said second member co-engaging with the ribs on the inner face of the head of the shank of the handle, and means passing centrally through the co-engaging heads of the handle shank and the members for adjustably connecting the members to the shank of the handle and to each other.

270 O. G.—21

1,328,192. EXHIBITING DEVICE. SIMON PFLASTER, New York, N. Y. Filed June 7, 1919. Serial No. 302,396. 7 Claims. (Cl. 88—27.)

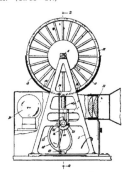

1. An exhibiting device of the character described, comprising a rotatable carrier provided with means for holding a plurality of slides which may move therefrom under the action of gravity when in the proper position, a pair of guides for said slides arranged beneath said carrier for receiving the slides successively under the action of gravity, a pair of cams formed with projections, said cams when moved acting to raise a slide in said guides and force the same back into said carrier while the projections act to move the carrier a sufficient distance whereby the next slide may fall by gravity into said guides, means for moving said cams intermittently, and a projecting device for projecting the slide in said guides.

1,328,193. SPRING-HOOK. EUGENE PILON, Farmpoint, Ontario, Canada. Filed July 29, 1919. Serial No. 314,110. 2 Claims. (Cl. 24—242.)

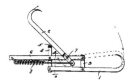

2. A spring hook, comprising a fixed member, bars perpendicular to the fixed member, the rear bar projecting from the fixed member to a greater extent than the forward bar and having a lateral extension at its outer end forming a stop, a bar paralleling the fixed member and connected to the laterally disposed bars and having a rear extension, a second member pivoted to the bar paralleling the fixed member at a point between the laterally extending bars and a contractile helical spring connecting the rear end of the pivoted member with the rear end of the bar paralleling the fixed member.

1,328,194. SEMAPHORE-SIGNAL. AUGUST V. POLLMILLER, Marceline, Mo. Filed Oct. 10, 1919. Serial No. 329,739. 1 Claim. (Cl. 246—479.)

A background for semaphore signals comprising a semicircular plate having its central point in registration with the pivotal point of the semaphore arm, said plate being painted a contrasting color to the semaphore arm, rivets passing through the semaphore standard and the background plate for securing the background plate in the same vertical plane as the semaphore arm, U-bolts arching the upper end of the standard and having their ends passing through the background plate, and nuts threaded on the ends of the U-bolts whereby the background plate

may be secured in such a manner as to prevent the splitting of the upper end of the standard under wind pressure on the background plate.

1,328,195. JOURNAL-BUSHING. SALMON W. PUTNAM, 3d, Rochester, N. Y., assignor to Arthur H. Ingle, Rochester, N. Y. Filed Nov. 25, 1918. Serial No. 264,075. 4 Claims. (Cl. 279—55.)

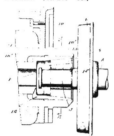

1. The combination with a driving sleeve comprising a tapered socket, and a journal holding chuck adapted to be fitted therein and equipped with a bushing, said chuck comprising an externally tapered ring cage having spaced apart grooves in the interior thereof lying in radial planes with the bottoms thereof oblique with reference to the axis of the cage, and removable insert jaws fitted in said grooves and adapted to center and clamp an axle journal between them.

1,328,196. AUTOMATIC CUTTING-OFF DEVICE FOR THREAD-WINDERS. NAPOLEON RAIL, Lowell, Mass. Filed Mar. 15, 1919. Serial No. 282,976. 7 Claims. (Cl. 242—19.)

6. The combination in a winding machine having a revoluble tube, and a plate adapted to move away from the tube as thread is wound thereon, of cutters so pivoted that when advanced they will cut such tube, together with connecting means between such plate and cutters whereby as the plate recedes the cutters advance.

1,328,197. VALVE-GRINDER. HARRY M. RAND, Westville, N. J. Filed June 3, 1919. Serial No. 301,400. 4 Claims. (Cl. 81—1.)

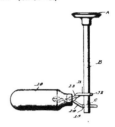

1. A valve grinding tool comprising a handle, a pair of spring arms extending from one end of said handle and adapted for resilient gripping engagement upon the stem of a valve, and a member extending from the same end of the handle in spaced relation to said clamping arms and adapted for insertion within the valve spring pinhole in the stem.

1,328,198. BURNER-MOUNTING. WILLIAM R. RAY, San Francisco, Calif. Filed July 31, 1919. Serial No. 314,577. 7 Claims. (Cl. 158—2.)

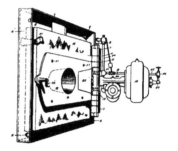

1. A burner mounting comprising a furnace front plate, a door hingedly secured to said plate having a central opening formed therein, a burner also supported on the same hinge mounting adapted to be swung to or from the central opening in the door, and means on the interior side of the door for supporting a refractory lining.

1,328,199. CHARGE - FORMING DEVICE. FLOYD D. RECTOR and WILLIAM Q. RECTOR, Louisville, Ky. Filed June 15, 1916. Serial No. 103,794. 5 Claims. (Cl. 48—180.)

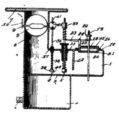

1. In a charge forming device, a body having gas and air inlet openings and an outlet opening therein, gas and

air chambers in said body, a mixing chamber in the body communicating with. the gas and air chambers and the outlet opening, means in the mixing chamber for regulating communication between the same and the gas chamber, adjustable spring means engaged with said regulating means for yieldably seating the same, a suction controlled valve arranged in the air inlet opening and connected to the adjustable spring means of said regulating means, a cut off in the outlet opening, and other means in the mixing chamber for regulating communication between the same and the gas chamber, said other regulating means being connected with the cut-off and operable thereby at predetermined periods.

1,328,200. CAR-ROOF CONSTRUCTION. NATHANIEL S. REEDER, New York, N. Y., assignor to Pressed Steel Car Company, Pittsburgh, Pa., a Corporation of New Jersey. Filed Dec. 19, 1916. Serial No. 137,770. 12 Claims. (Cl. 108—5.6.)

1. A roof carline having a laterally extending flange, said flange being biburcated, and one of the resultant portions bent downwardly.

1,328,201. FASTENING DEVICE. EMIL RENDANO, Brooklyn, N. Y., assignor of one-half to Emil Rendano and Nicholas Rendano, New York, N. Y., and one-half to Philip J. Forbes, Brooklyn, N. Y. Filed May 8, 1919. Serial No. 295,629. 1 Claim. (Cl. 72—118.)

As an article of manufacture, a fastening device for fastening wall boards to a support, comprising a plate provided with oppositely disposed struck-up clenching prongs extending approximately at a right angle from the face of the plate and having angular points bent slightly toward each other, said oppositely disposed prongs being in non-alinement lengthwise of said prongs and so positioned that their points overlap when the prongs are in the plane of said plate.

1,328,202. PROCESSING APPARATUS FOR CANNED PRODUCTS. ALAN C. RICHARDSON, Silver Spring, Md. Filed Aug. 27, 1919. Serial No. 320,269. 5 Claims. (Cl. 126—272.)

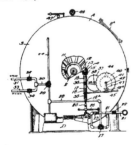

1. In a processing apparatus, a retort, means for agitating cans therein and for maintaining a temperature in the retort above the normal processing temperature at the commencement of the processing operation, and means for automatically reducing the temperature in the retort to the normal processing temperature after a predetermined lapse of time.

1,328,203. HYPODERMIC SYRINGE. RICHARD HENRI RIETHMÜLLER, Montclair, N. J., assignor to Herman A. Metz, New York, N. Y. Filed Apr. 29, 1919. Serial No. 293,411. 4 Claims. (Cl. 128—218.)

1. In a hypodermic syringe, a metallic casing provided with a lengthwise cut-out portion provided along one wall with a graduation, a needle detachably mounted in one end of the said casing, a barrel held in the said casing and visible through the said cut-out portion, the said graduation indicating the cubic contents of the said barrel, a gland screwing in the said casing against the said barrel to hold the latter in place in the casing, a plunger slidably fitted in the said barrel and provided with a plunger rod extending through the said gland, the outer end of the said plunger rod being provided with a handle, and a fingerpiece held on the said gland and having a limited turning motion thereon.

1,328,204. MIXING DEVICE. CROCKER H. SANFORD, Baltimore, Md., assignor, by direct and mesne assignments, to The Old Dominion Specialty Co., Inc., Baltimore, Md., a Corporation of Maryland. Filed July 19, 1918. Serial No. 245,710. 3 Claims. (Cl. 261—75.)

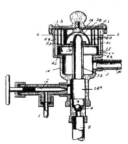

1. A fluid mixing device, comprising a casing having a chamber in which are inlet orifices for fluids and also having an outlet orifice, and also having intermediate said chamber and the outlet orifice a nozzle, a baffle opposed to the eduction orifice of the nozzle and to a wall around the nozzle, and spaced walls grouped about the baffle and having minute passages at staggered points, whereby the fluids are reduced to films and jets and are battered against imperforate portions of some of the walls.

1,328,205. BOTTLE-CLOSURE. FREDERICK W. SCHIL-
LING, Louisville, Ohio. Filed Jan. 5, 1917. Serial
No. 140,779. 1 Claim. (Cl. 215—9.)

The combination with a bottle neck having a mouth
provided with an external convexed rim and also formed
with an annular recess internally of said mouth, of a
cap comprising a circular disk having struck therefrom
concentrically of the same a hollow rib providing spaced
circular walls disposed inwardly relative to the marginal
edge of the said disk, the outermost annular wall being
adapted for frictional engagement in the recess in said
mouth, the portion of the disk concentrically of the hollow
rib being flat and contacting throughout with the edge
of the mouth, resilient strips formed at diameterically
opposite points on the disk at the peripheral edge thereof
and outwardly bowed to conform to the convexed rim
for engagement over the same, and downwardly divergent
tips formed on said strips to provide finger pieces.

1,328,206. BLANKET - FASTENER. WILLIAM A.
SCHLEICHER, Cleveland, Ohio. Filed Aug. 26, 1919.
Serial No. 319,961. 6 Claims. (Cl. 24—225.)

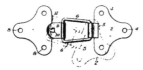

1. A flexible fastener, comprising a plurality of plates,
a link pivotally carried by one of said plates, a hook
carried by the other of such plates for receiving said
link, and means on such last mentioned plate adapted
to coöperate with said link during the engagement and
disengagement thereof with the hook, substantially as described.

1,328,207. TROUGH. CHRIST SCHMIDT, Everett, Wash.
Filed Mar. 15, 1919. Serial No. 282,906. 2 Claims.
(Cl. 119—75.)

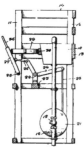

1. The combination with a watering trough having a
water supply pipe and a discharge pipe arranged in
parallelism, of a valve in each of said pipes, said valves
being disposed in alinement, a shaft connecting the valve
stems, so that when one valve is closed the other valve
will be open, a horizontally pivoted upwardly and outwardly inclined member spaced from the trough, a
spring interposed between said member and trough and
means connecting said member and said shaft, whereby, when the member is rocked upon its pivot toward
the trough the valve in the supply pipe will be opened
and the valve in the discharge pipe closed and when
said member is rocked in the opposite direction the
valves will be returned to normal position.

1,328,208. REAMER. EDWARD P. SCHONK, Wilkes-
Barre, Pa. Filed Oct. 16, 1918. Serial No. 258,770.
2 Claims. (Cl. 77—73.)

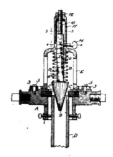

1. The combination with a die-stock, of a reaming attachment comprising a yoked bearing member connectible
to the die-stock and a reaming tool, slidably mounted
therein, said tool having a square stem portion and a
threaded stem portion, and a handle engaging said
threaded portion and forming means for withdrawing the
reaming tool to a disengaging position, one end of said
handle having a bore adapted to receive said square stem
portion and means for locking the tool in disengaging
position to permit the apparatus to be removed from the
work while the reaming tool is removed from contact
therewith.

1,328,209. LUBRICATOR. SAMUEL J. SHARP, Wheeling,
W. Va., assignor to J. L. Stifel & Sons, Wheeling, W. Va.,
a Firm. Filed May 22, 1919. Serial No. 298,871. 9
Claims. (Cl. 64—24.)

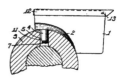

8. A lubricator for journal bearings, comprising a
lubricant container having its under side shaped to conform to the exterior of the bearing, adapting it for resting
directly upon the latter, a stem depending vertically from
the under side of said container and adapted to seat within
the oiler-hole of the bearing for anchoring said container
with respect to said bearing, said stem having a passage
leading therethrough from the interior of said container,
a wick disposed within said container and having an end
fitted within said passage, and a partition wall located
adjacent to and rearward of the position occupied by said
passage whereby the lubricant is prevented from flowing
to a point whence it may drain directly through said
passage.

1,328,210. APPARATUS FOR EXTRACTING MINERALS FROM ORES. GEORGE M. SHIRES, Houston, Tex. Filed Nov. 29, 1918. Serial No. 264,705. 6 Claims. (Cl. 23—3.)

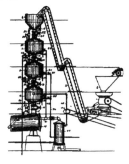

1. An apparatus for extracting sulfur from ore, including a plurality of heater drums connected together, and arranged one above the other, means for delivering ore thereto, means for introducing a heating fluid into said drums, and a separator arranged to receive the heated ore delivered from the drums, and provided with means to separate the refuse from the mineral therein.

1,328,211. FLYING-MACHINE. IRA L. SLOAN, North Yakima, Wash. Filed Dec. 28, 1917. Serial No. 209,315. 1 Claim. (Cl. 244—15.)

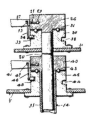

In a flying machine, a vertical shaft, a cylindrical head carried thereby and having radially arranged cylindrical recesses and ball shaped recesses at the inner ends of the cylindrical recesses, a plurality of blades, cylindrical pivot pins carried by the inner ends of the blades and extending into said radially arranged cylindrical recesses, said pivot pins being provided with enlarged ball shaped heads arranged within said ball shaped recesses, a relatively stationary cam surrounding the shaft and having a circumferential cam slot, arms connected to said blades and having collars mounted in said cam slot whereby the pitch of the blades is varied during rotation, the opposed sides of said head and said cam being provided with annular grooves, and ball-bearings mounted in said annular grooves.

1,328,212. GIN-SAW CLEANER, TOOTH STRAIGHTENER AND SHARPENER. WILLIAM D. STANIFER, Chickasha, Okla. Filed Oct. 18, 1919. Serial No. 331,560. 3 Claims. (Cl. 13—15.)
1. In a gin saw, cleaning device, a frame including a body portion, upwardly extending flanges formed on the body portion, a rod disposed within the frame, a plurality of cleaning elements supported on the rod, resilient means between the cleaning elements, for restricting lateral movement thereof with relation to the frame, threaded adjusting means operating through the side flanges of the frame and engaging the inner ends of the

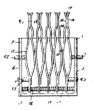

cleaning elements for adjusting the same, and threaded adjusting members extending through the side flanges of the frame and contacting with the outer cleaning elements intermediate their lengths for causing a lateral adjustment of the outer ends thereof.

1,328,213. CENTERING DEVICE. KARL ROBERT STARKENBERG, Andover, Mass., assignor to John J. Petroske, Methuen, Mass. Filed Apr. 27, 1918. Serial No. 231,226. 1 Claim. (Cl. 33—191.)

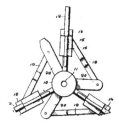

In a device of the class described, a hub member provided with a central aperture, a pin slidable therein, radial arms mounted in the hub member, the angle between the arms being approximately 120 degrees, jaws slidable on the arms, an operating member comprising a hub element through which the pin passes and on which said pin is mounted and arms radiating from the hub last named, and means pivotally connecting each of the arms last mentioned with one of the jaws.

1,328,214. STEEL-GRAIN-CAR DOOR. GEORGE TOWNILL and PETER TOWNILL, Plainfield, Ill. Filed May 9, 1918. Serial No. 233,427. 1 Claim. (Cl. 189—46.)

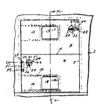

In a grain car door, formed in two sections, said sections being superimposed and adapted to be moved horizontally in opposite directions, a flanged runway to one side of the door opening for the reception of the upper section and a flanged abutment at the opposite side of the door opening as limiting means for said upper section a flanged runway at the opposite side of the door opening for the reception of the lower section of the door after the upper section has been moved into its runway, a flanged abutment at the opposite side of the runway for the lower section, said flanged abutments preventing and maintaining the sections in super-imposed engagement with each other, and a pliable joint closure between the engaging edges of the superimposed sections, said pliable joint closure comprising a strip of material riveted adjacent the lower edge of the upper section and spaced therefrom so that when the upper section is moved into its runway the lower flanged member of the runway will pass under said joint closure, said joint closure forming means for preventing fine material or grain from passing between the sections.

1,328,215. LEVER - FILLER FOR FOUNTAIN - PENS. DE WITT C. VAN VALER, New York, N. Y., assignor of one-half to Hobart W. Geyer, New York, N. Y. Filed Dec. 21, 1918. Serial No. 267,812. 6 Claims. (Cl. 120—46.)

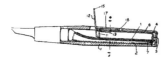

1. The combination with a fountain pen barrel having a slot therein and a compressible sack in said barrel, a compressing device for said sack consisting of a presser bar having an opening at one end, a lever located within said slot for depressing said bar, and a supporting element arranged in said barrel and extending longitudinally thereof having a substantially hook-shaped end fitting into the opening in said presser bar for guiding the bar, and means for pivotally connecting said lever with said supporting element.

1,328,216. BRAIDING-MACHINE. ERWIN WALTER, Mellingen, Switzerland. Filed Aug. 7, 1918. Serial No. 248,787. 2 Claims. (Cl. 28—4.)

1. In a braiding machine, in combination with a guide plate and bobbin spindles traveled therein, a plurality of studs rigidly secured in said guide plate, driver units revolubly mounted on said studs and adapted to coact with said spindles, each said driver unit comprising a sleeve freely rotatable on one of said studs, a set of disks rigidly secured on said sleeve, one disk thereof provided with peripheral notches for coöperation with said spindles, a second disk presenting coinciding peripheral notches and gear teeth between each two notches, and the third disk serving to make the thickness of the assembled set of disks equal to the extent of the coöperating portion of said spindles, the notch-interrupted gears of the several driver units all being in mutual engagement, and means in connection with one of said drivers adapted to be operated by the main machine drive.

1,328,217. DIFFERENTIAL. LEIGH WATKINS, Oakland, Calif. Filed Oct. 10, 1918. Serial No. 257,634. 5 Claims. (Cl. 74—7.)

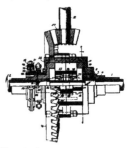

4. A differential for motor driven vehicles comprising a pair of power sleeves having annular flanges forming ring members, a straddling member straddling each of said ring members acting as a clutch, a swinging member having contact springs straddling part of each of said clutches for swinging the clutches to a clutched or unclutched position, means for actuating said swinging members, and means for connecting said clutches to said power member.

1,328,218. DOUBLE-ACTING-PUMP-OPERATING MECHANISM. PAUL J. WILSON, Grimes, Iowa. Filed Oct. 8, 1919. Serial No. 329,269. 3 Claims. (Cl. 103—82.)

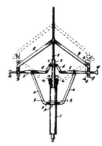

3. In a double acting pump embodying a mast and two pump rods, oppositely disposed arms having their lower ends bent laterally to form clamp elements which embrace and secure the arms to the mast, oppositely disposed levers pivoted intermediate of their ends to the arms, links connecting the inner ends of the levers to one of the pump rods, oppositely disposed arms secured to the other pump rod and terminating in forks which receive the outer ends of the said levers and a pair of rollers mounted in each fork to receive the outer ends of the coöperating lever.

1,328,219. ROTARY PRINTING-MACHINE. CARL WINKLER, Berne, Switzerland. Filed Feb. 14, 1917. Serial No. 148,694. 7 Claims. (Cl. 270—17.)

1. In a rotary printing machine, the combination of means for cutting sheets of paper, an impression cylinder

having sheet-gripping means, means for receiving the cut sheets and introducing them to the impression cylinder, a plate cylinder, a reversing cylinder for turning the sheets for printing said sheets on both sides, and a leading out cylinder coöperating with the impression cylinder, the leading out cylinder having means for gripping a sheet and removing it from the impression cylinder.

1,328,220. DRIVING-GEAR FOR PRINTING-MA-CHINES. CARL WINKLER, Berne, Switzerland. Filed Sept. 9, 1918. Serial No. 253,312. 6 Claims. (Cl. 74—59.)

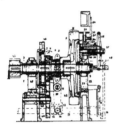

1. A driving gear for printing machines, which comprises in combination a shaft, a clutch element fastened to said shaft, a free wheel fastened to said shaft at some distance from said clutch element, a second clutch element mounted on the boss of said free wheel, a third driving clutch part mounted to slide on said shaft and adapted to be brought in and out of connection with said first clutch element, a fourth driving clutch element fastened to said third driving clutch element and adapted to be brought in and out of engagement with said second clutch element, a device common to both said third and fourth driving clutch elements to move same longitudinally on said shaft into engagement with the first or second clutch elements or into an intermediate position, and speed reducing spur wheel gearing adapted to be driven by said second clutch element, substantially as, and for the purpose set forth.

1,328,221. FILTER. EDWARD ZAHM, Buffalo, N. Y., assignor to Zahm Manufacturing Company, Buffalo, N. Y., a Corporation of New York. Filed May 25, 1917. Serial No. 170,899. 4 Claims. (Cl. 210—11.)

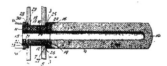

1. A filter comprising a filter tube having a body and a neck constructed integrally of porous material and having the neck portion thereof saturated with a strengthening material.

1,328,222. POWER - DRIVEN - IMPLEMENT FRAME. IRA ARMSTRONG, Merkel, Tex., assignor, by direct and mesne assignments, to Dixieland Motor Truck Company, Bowie county, Tex. Filed May 21, 1918. Serial No. 235,815. 3 Claims. (Cl. 111—52.)
1. In a machine of the character described a main frame having side extensions, subframes positioned beneath the side extensions, vertical bearing housings carried by the sub-frames, standards slidably passing through the housings, yokes carried by the standards, earth opening means

connected with the standards and yokes, hoppers carried by the sub-frames and having spouts extending in operative relation to the earth opening means, and adjusting means

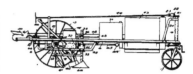

carried by the sub-frames and connected with the standards for vertically adjusting the same and releasably holding the earth opening means in adjusted position with respect to the ground.

1,328,223. NIGHT-WATCHMAN'S CHECKING APPARATUS. FRANCIS AUBRY-SCHALTENBRANDT, La Chaux-de-Fonds, Switzerland. Filed Mar. 17, 1919. Serial No. 283,213. 3 Claims. (Cl. 234—39.)

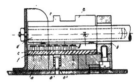

2. A marking attachment with which is adapted to be used as a set of operating keys each of which is provided with a differently positioned lug on the shank including a plate adapted to be mounted in slidable spaced relation to a support and having a plurality of vertical passages extending therethrough, a plurality of depressible punches slidably mounted and resiliently supported in the passages and having their lower ends positioned above the under surface of the plate, key bearing members retained transversely above the plate and positioned over the upper ends of the punches, an upright secured to one end of the plate and provided with a key hole and key receiving barrel supported above the plate and extending laterally therefrom so as to lie in spaced relation above the plate and extend through the key hole.

1,328,224. RECEPTACLE. REUBEN B. BENJAMIN, Chicago, Ill., assignor to Benjamin Electric Manufacturing Company, Chicago, Ill., a Corporation of Illinois. Filed Apr. 1, 1915. Serial No. 18,454. 4 Claims. (Cl. 173—331.)

1. In a device of the character described, a receptacle constructed to receive a device, which device has a center contact and a shell contact, said receptacle comprising a shell contact for engaging said first named shell contact and a movable protector which in a first position makes the electrically charged parts difficult of access and in a second position makes said parts accessible, said shell contact being substantially cylindrical and said protector being cylindrical and guided by said shell.

1,328,225. BURNER FOR GAS-FURNACES. WILLIAM P. BOYLE, Springfield, Mass. Filed Oct. 30, 1918. Serial No. 260,372. 3 Claims. (Cl. 158—110.)

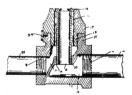

1. A gas burner consisting of a body having seperate inlets and a partition dividing the body into independent chambers, a tube connected with the partition and in communication with one of the chambers and one of the inlets, said tube having an externally and internally beveled mouth, a collar threaded on the body around the tube and spaced therefrom and provided with a deflecting mouth disposed adjacent the mouth of the tube, and means for locking the collar in adjusted position.

1,328,226. MACHINE FOR CUTTING UP MEAT AND OTHER SUBSTANCES. WILLIAM MARTIN BURKE, London, England. Filed Dec. 4, 1919. Serial No. 342,402. 2 Claims. (Cl. 17—19.)

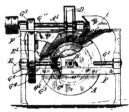

1. In a machine for cutting up meat and other substances, the combination with a feed-hopper of a drum mounted to rotate about a horizontal axis and having a peripheral channel into which the feed-hopper delivers, and a cutting-device placed at the top of the drum on the delivery-side of the feed-hopper and operating in the channel, the cutting-edges of which device move approximately transversely to the direction of the channel.

1,328,227. VARIABLE-PRESSURE ACETYLENE-GENERATOR. AUGUSTINE DAVIS, New York, N. Y., assignor to Davis-Bournonville Company, New York, N. Y., a Corporation of New York. Filed Nov. 19, 1918. Serial No. 263,143. 5 Claims. (Cl. 48—52.)

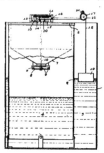

1. An acetylene generator of the kind wherein carbid is dropped into the water, comprising carbid feed means,

inclosures forming a gas chamber and two water chambers, the water chambers communicating at the bottom and one being exposed to the pressure of the gas chamber and the other constituting a displacement chamber open to the pressure of the atmosphere, a float capable of operating in a vertical range of positions in one of the chambers, and mechanical operative connections between the float and the carbid feed means including a setting device for causing the generator to operate at higher or lower pressures at will.

1,328,228. TOOL FOR LIFTING VALVE - SPRINGS. ARTHUR O. FEILBACH, North Milwaukee, Wis. Filed Jan. 27, 1919. Serial No. 273,372. 3 Claims. (Cl. 29—87.1.)

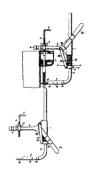

1. A tool of the class described comprising a head, an extension thereon, a screw-threaded rod carried by said extension, a spring engaging member consisting of a rod slidingly carried by the head and having a bent end, means adjustable on said end for engaging the spring, a lever pivoted to the head and means connecting said lever with said rod.

1,328,229. ELECTRIC HEATING UNIT. FRANK W. HEWITT, Arlington, Mass., assignor to Simplex Electric Heating Company, Cambridge, Mass., a Corporation of Massachusetts. Filed May 13, 1918. Serial No. 234,068. 1 Claim. (Cl. 219—46.)

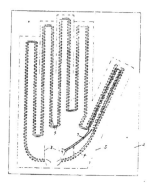

An electric heating unit, comprising a support of flexible sheet material of greater length than width, a naked electric conductor bent back and forth to form a plurality of parallelly arranged portions transversely of the length of the support, the length of each portion of the conductor being short as compared with the distance between portions, a plurality of rows of stitching arranged parallel to each other and extending along the length of the support, said rows of stitching engaging the support and embracing said electric conductor at the junction of the bent portions and the straight portions to securely mount said electric conductor on the support and leave the straight parallel portions free, whereby the parallelly arranged straight portions are held out of engagement with each other and the flexibility of the unit increased.

1,328,230. MACHINE-GUN. JAMES S. JOHNSTON, Utica, N. Y. Filed Mar. 13, 1915. Serial No. 14,226. 2 Claims. (Cl. 89—12.)

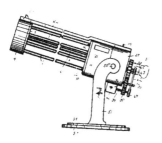

1. In a machine gun, barrels for the projection of bullets, cylindrical feeding drums having chambers for the reception of cartridges, holes in said drums for cooling purposes, gears for revolving said barrels and feeding drums, firing pins actuated by ratchets and springs for discharging said cartridges, whereby the bullets thereof will be projected through certain of said barrels simultaneously, mechanical means for cooling said gun, and a revoluble dial for mounting the same.

1,328,231. BEET - HARVESTER. MATSUNOSUKE KANZAKI, Salt Lake City, Utah. Filed Mar. 15, 1919. Serial No. 282,956. 3 Claims. (Cl. 55—9.)

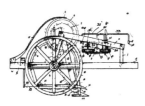

2. In a beet harvester the combination with ground wheels, of a U-shaped axle in said wheels ; a frame carried on said axle ; a sprocket wheel journaled on said axle ; another sprocket wheel mounted between vertical braces and adapted to engage in the ground ; a sprocket chain operable over said sprocket wheels ; laterally projecting pins secured in the alternate links of said chain ; a horizontal shaft mounted on the forward portion of said frame ; means to impart the motion of one of said ground wheels to said shaft ; a worm on said shaft ; worm gears engaged by said worm ; a topping knife adapted to be rotated by one of said worm gears ; a foliage shifter adapted to be

moved on its axis by the other one of said worm gears ; means to engage said knife and said foliage shifter with their respective worm gears and a lever release to disengage said knife and said foliage shifter from said worm gears.

1,328,232. AIR-PUMP. JOSEPH KEAN, Des Moines, Iowa ; Ida Kean administratrix of said Joseph Kean, deceased. Filed Feb. 14, 1916. Serial No. 78,088. 2 Claims. (Cl. 230—27.)

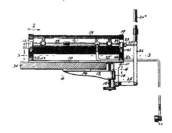

1. An air pump comprising a base plate, means for mounting said plate, a bracket depending from one end portion of said plate, caps formed with legs fixed to said plate, a cylinder connecting said caps and arranged parallel with said plate, an air pipe communicating with said cylinder, a hose communicating with said air pipe and extending beneath the cylinder and outwardly between a pair of said legs, a piston in said cylinder, a rod attached to said piston and extending through one of said caps, and a lever fulcrumed on said bracket and pivoted to said rod.

1,328,233. ROAD-GRADER. JOHN R. KEY, Leavenworth, Kans. Filed Aug. 15, 1917. Serial No. 186,409. 2 Claims. (Cl. 37—49.)

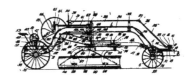

1. In a grading machine, a wheel frame, a supporting frame below the wheel frame, a ring journaled on the supporting frame, a scraper blade adjustably supported from and around the ring, a vertical shaft geared to said ring, a worm wheel journaled on said shaft, a worm engaging said wheel, a clutch yieldingly clutched to said worm wheel to lock the same to the shaft, and manually operable means for disengaging said clutch from said wheel.

1,328,234. SAND-PROTECTING DEVICE FOR TURBINE-PUMPS. FERDINAND W. KROGH, San Francisco, Calif. Filed Feb. 12, 1914. Serial No. 818,240. 1 Claim. (Cl. 64—22.)

In combination with the rotary shaft and its stationary bearing of a deep well pump, a double ended bushing for said bearing, provided at its ends with projecting annular depressed necks, means for oiling said bearing, sand devices fixed on said shaft provided with sleeves telescoping said depressed necks forming running joints therewith and chambers at the end thereof, a packing in said chambers

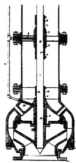

at the end of said necks adapted to form seals and prevent thereby the water from running into the bearing and the oil therefrom.

1,328,235. AIR - VALVE ATTACHMENT FOR CARBURETERS. HARRY L. LANE, Venice, Calif. Filed Apr. 2, 1918. Serial No. 226,308. 4 Claims. (Cl. 277—45.)

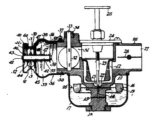

1. An air valve attachment for carbureters comprising a cylindrical valve body having a restricted portion at one end, a rod rigidly mounted in said body, a sleeve slidably mounted on said rod, a valve member secured to said sleeve consisting of a flat circular plate of smaller diameter than the inside of the restricted portion, said plate having openings therein, means for elastically holding said valve member within the restricted portion of the valve body, a follower plate mounted on said sleeve extending partially over the openings in said valve member, and means on said sleeve for elastically holding said follower plate against said valve member.

1,328,236. METAL - MELTING FURNACE. GARNET W. MCKEE, Rockford, Ill. Filed Nov. 12, 1917. Serial No. 201,541. 7 Claims. (Cl. 22—57.)

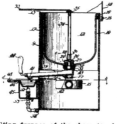

1. A melting furnace of the character described, comprising a melting pot, a member passing through the bot-

tom thereof rigidly secured thereto and having a valve controlled passage through which metal may be delivered from the pot, a spigot-carrying member pivotally mounted on the first named member, and a spigot detachably mounted on said pivot member and adapted to receive metal from said passage and to be swung laterally at its free end to deliver the metal at laterally spaced points.

1,328,237. METHOD OF SWEEPING STREETS. HENRY K. POTTER, Somerville, Mass. Filed Oct. 17, 1916. Serial No. 126,440. 10 Claims. (Cl. 15—17.)

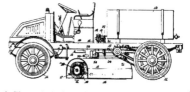

1. The method of cleaning pavements which consists in raising the dust on said pavements and directing the particles of dust into the path of downwardly projected small globules of oil.

1,328,238. AEROPLANE PLEASURE - RAILWAY. FRANKLIN M. WILLIAMS, New York, N. Y., assignor to Aeroplane Railway Patents Corporation, New York, N. Y., a Corporation of New York. Filed Aug. 6, 1919. Serial No. 315,688. 6 Claims. (Cl. 104—23.)

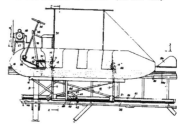

2. In a pleasure railway, the combination with a monorail and an elevated structure supporting said rail, of a carrier in the form of an aeroplane and comprising two portions arranged upon opposite sides of and depending below said rail.

1,328,239. COOKER. WILLIAM J. SCHAEFER, Ontario, Calif. Filed Aug. 10, 1916, Serial No. 114,168. Renewed May 29, 1918. Serial No. 237,372. 6 Claims. (Cl. 126—272.)

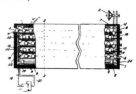

1. In a cooker, a casing, means for feeding articles therethrough, pipe means extending within said casing and provided with steam supply connections, a steam trap connected to receive water condensed in said pipe means, and perforated pipe means connected to receive the discharge from said trap and adapted to discharge same over the articles within the casing.

1,328,240. DUMPING MECHANISM FOR TRUCKS AND THE LIKE. August C. Settlage, New Bremen, Ohio. Filed Sept. 13, 1918. Serial No. 253,941. 3 Claims. (Cl. 298—19.)

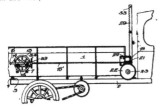

1. In a dumping mechanism for trucks, the combination with the main frame, of a body pivoted thereto at the rear end, a power shaft journaled in suitable bearings and carried by the body and extending from near the rear to the front, and provided at its forward end with a worm and at its rear end with a gear wheel, a gear wheel mounted in a suitable frame carried by the body at the rear thereof and in mesh with the gear wheel on the power shaft, whereby the power shaft is rotated, a worm wheel mounted on the forward part of the body and in mesh with the worm, a rack pivoted to the main frame in front of the body, a transverse shaft carried by the body and having pinions thereon in mesh with the rack on the frame, whereby when power is applied to the power shaft, the pinions will be caused to travel on the rack to raise the body.

1,328,241. VARIABLE - PITCH PROPELLER. Horace Eugene Weaver, Bryan, Ohio. Filed Aug. 14, 1918. Serial No. 249,807. 4 Claims. (Cl. 170—163.)

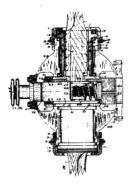

1. In a variable pitch propeller, a plurality of blades, a weighted member associated with each blade, means for inter-connecting the weighted member with its associated blade for right or left hand engine rotation or for a tractor or push propeller.

4. In a variable pitch propeller, a hub, a pair of blades, a pair of plates connected to the blades and located in the hub and having weighted segments located on opposite sides of the axis of the hubs and in parallel relation to each other, a yoke located between the plates, links connected to the arms of the yokes and the plates, the link connecting each plate being located on the side of the axis of the hub opposite to that on which the weight of that plate is located, a spring member for yieldingly resisting the movement of the yoke by the centrifugal action of the weighted portions of the plates.

1,328,242. MACHINE FOR GRINDING THE EDGES OF GLASS PLATES. Henry G. Farley, Portland, Me. Filed Sept. 11, 1915, Serial No. 50,139. Renewed Apr. 25, 1917. Serial No. 164,533. 1 Claim. (Cl. 51—11.)

In a machine for grinding the edges of glass plates, the combination of a conical grinding wheel having one portion of its conical surface in an upright position, a supporting table on which the plate rests adjacent to the wheel and at right angles to the upright portion of the same, the said table being narrower than the plate whereby the rear portion of the plate may be grasped by the hands of the operator to manipulate the same, said table being hingedly mounted in front of the grinding wheel, whereby the plate may be tilted.

1,328,243. EXTENSION - TABLE. Elmer A. Hensal, Panora, Iowa. Filed July 26, 1919. Serial No. 313,637. 9 Claims. (Cl. 45—9.)

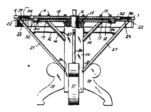

1. In a device of the class described, a post supported on legs, a fixed table mounted thereon, a rotary table mounted on said fixed table, outwardly and upwardly extending brackets detachably fixed to said post, means on the free end of said brackets for receiving an annular ring, a hinged member extending from the upper end of said post and secured to the upper end of said brackets for limiting the outward movement of said brackets and means for fixing a sectional table to said fixed table whereby said sectional table will rest upon said annular ring.

1,328,244. SPRING - SPOKE WHEEL. Adelbert F. Kelly, Spokane, Wash. Filed Feb. 18, 1918. Serial No. 217,801. 6 Claims. (Cl. 152—50.)

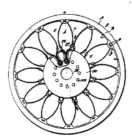

4. In a spring spoke wheel, a hub structure having a plurality of sets of spring spoke seating shoulders and each

set of shoulders being convexly curved and the shoulders of each set diverging from each other radially outward of the wheel from the longitudinal axis of the spoke therefor, and a bowed spring spoke for each set of shoulders and each spoke having concavely curved shoulder abutment portions converging radially inward of the wheel and toward the longitudinal axis of the spoke and in such relation to said shoulders as to seat on the latter in varying degrees or extents of area contact dependent upon the extent of stress imposed.

1,328,245. SIGNAL, INDICATOR, AND RECORDER. FREDERICK LIEBLER, New York, N. Y. Filed Aug. 5, 1913. Serial No. 783,019. 7 Claims. (Cl. 177—339.)

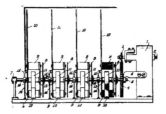

2. An indicator or recorder, comprising a magnet bearing signal member, a transversely movable armature, means for moving said armature, and means for bringing the magnetic member in magnetic co-action with the moving armature, the magnet and the armature being located on a shaft with such relation to each other that their bearings will not approach or recede from each other during process of operation.

1,328,246. HEATER. WHITING P. MERRY, Sharpsville, Pa. Filed Mar. 15, 1919. Serial No. 282,806. 6 Claims. (Cl. 126—70.)

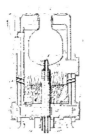

1. In a heater, the combination with an inner casing provided with a fire box and an ash pit below, of a hot air chamber in the upper part of the casing and spaced from its wall, means passing centrally upwardly through the heater for conducting cold air into said chamber to be heated, a double wall outer casing in surrounding relation to the inner casing, an air space between the inner wall and the inner casing, and a smoke flue connected to the upper part of the inner casing, an annular air space between the double wall outer casing and the inner casing and in communication with the first air space, the upper end of the inner wall of the outer casing having damper controlled openings, for the passage of the air, which becomes heated in the first air space, into the room.

1,328,247. ELECTRIC-CLOCK SYSTEM. ARTHUR F. POOLE, Chicago, Ill. Filed Sept. 10, 1917. Serial No. 190,587. 12 Claims. (Cl. 58—26.)

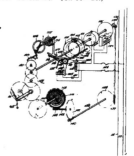

1. The combination with a spring-actuated member, of a source of commercial alternating-current, means actuated in synchronism with the alternating current, and means whereby the spring-actuated member is caused to operate in synchronism with the said synchronously actuated means.

1,328,248. MATTRESS. WILLIAM L. HAWN, Kansas City, Mo., assignor of one-half to Arch Kavanagh, Kansas City, Mo. Filed Oct. 2, 1919. Serial No. 328,017. 2 Claims. (Cl. 5—13.)

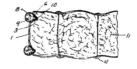

1. The method of forming mattresses which consists in folding back the edges of a sheet of material to form laps spaced apart, stitching the laps together inside the edges thereof, introducing a filling material in the space between the laps, securing the edges of the laps together to form a welt, forming a bag, and introducing the filling material into the bag.

1,328,249. SHOE-HEEL AND METHOD OF PRODUCING THE SAME. LARS JÖRGEN HENRIKSEN, Küflinge, Sweden. Filed Sept. 7, 1916. Serial No. 118,796. 5 Claims. (Cl. 36—34.)

1. The method of producing heels from lifts built up from small pieces of leather, consisting in forming the edges of the pieces in such manner that the cross section of each edge obtains the shape of a hook adapted positively to engage the hook of a contiguous piece, substantially as and for the purpose set forth.

1,328,250. COMBINATION - TOOL. HENRY B. KEIPER, Lancaster, Pa. Filed Aug. 6, 1919. Serial No. 315,653. 6 Claims. (Cl. 29—32.)
1. A convertible blower and combination tool, comprising a supporting frame having tool-carrying means and a

rotary blower casing mounted thereon, said means including a tool-driving shaft, and said casing having a rotary blower journaled therein, a gear casing adapted for attachment to either said blower casing or said tool-carrying

means with a gear therein in mesh with a gear on the blower shaft or on the tool driving shaft, for driving alternately said blower or other device by the same driving mechanism.

1,328,251. CLIMBING DEVICE. JOHN C. POETZ, Wenatchee, Wash. Substitute for application Serial No. 96,540, filed May 10, 1916. This application filed May 31, 1918. Serial No. 237,672. 4 Claims. (Cl. 227—8.)

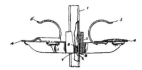

4. In combination with a rod of H-section, of foot supporting means including a pair of channel blocks straddling the opposite flanges of the rod. each block having a pair of opposing lugs extending inwardly from its lower edge and across the inner face of the supporting flange toward the web of the rod, outwardly extending brackets secured to the lower portions of the blocks, foot rests secured to the brackets, and means located on the inner side of each foot rest beneath which the foot is engageable.

1,328,252. OPERATING MECHANISM FOR WHISTLES. DUANE P. FULLER, Carlisle, Wash. Filed Apr. 9, 1919. Serial No. 288,697. 2 Claims. (Cl. 74—5.)

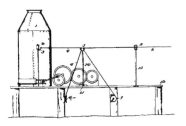

1. Means for transmitting motion comprising a pivoted post, a cord fastened at one end and having a sliding coöperation with the post, the other end of the cord extending away from said post, and an operating cord having a fixed terminal and an operating terminal, said operating cord having sliding connection with the post between its terminals.

REISSUES.

14,789. FLUID-PUMP. CHARLES A. ANDERSON, Chicago, Ill., assignor, by direct and mesne assignments, to G. E. Sundstrom, Chicago, Ill. Filed June 14, 1919. Serial No. 304,357. Original No. 1,267,040, dated May 21, 1918, Serial No. 54,294, filed Oct. 6, 1915. 11 Claims. (Cl. 230—34.)

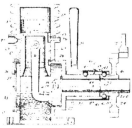

1. In a fluid pump, the combination of a cylinder, a piston, a crank shaft, connections therebetween for effecting reciprocation and oscillation of the piston, inlet and outlet ports for said cylinder, air passageways in said piston for coöperating with the ports to regulate the flow of the fluid, a crank case below said piston, fluid passageways serving to transfer compressed air from the crank case to the cylinder after preliminary compression in the crank case, a fluid vent in said crank case, and a piston channel connecting with the vent to open the crank case to the outside on a predetermined outward movement of the piston.

3. In a fluid pump, the combination of a cylinder, a piston, a crank shaft, a connection between said piston and crank shaft adapted upon rotation of the crank shaft to effect combined longitudinal reciprocation and rotary oscillation of said piston, air inlet and outlet ports for said cylinder and air passageways cut in said piston for coöperating with said ports to control the inflow and outflow of air, a closed crank case whereby air will be compressed in said case during in-stroke of the piston, means connecting said crank case with the cylinder at the end of the in-stroke of the piston whereby air compressed in the crank case may flow into the cylinder, the air in said crank case being expanded during out-stroke of the piston, an atmosphere vent hole for said crank case, said vent hole being closed during the greater part of the movement of said piston, and a channel cut in said piston for coöperating with said vent hole after a period of outward movement of said piston to connect the crank case with atmosphere.

8. In a device of the class described, the combination of a casing comprising a crank case chamber and a cylinder chamber, a piston therebetween, means in the crank case connected with the piston for simultaneously reciprocating and oscillating the piston, a port controlled by the piston so as to temporarily open when the piston is projected outwardly in the cylinder and admit a charge to the crank case and close as the piston begins moving inwardly toward the crank case, so as to compress the charge in the crank case, an inlet port controlled by the piston and adapted to open as the piston moves inwardly toward the crank case and admit a charge into the cylinder chamber and close thereafter to permit compression of the charge in the cylinder chamber, a by-pass controlled by the piston so as to transfer the compressed charge in the crank case chamber to the cylinder chamber after the closing of the inlet port to the cylinder cham-

ber and previous to the operation of the piston for compressing the charge in the cylinder chamber, and an exhaust port controlled by the piston for exhausting the combined charge from the cylinder chamber during compression.

14,790. CARBURETER. FREDERICK O. BALL, Detroit, Mich., assignor, by direct and mesne assignments, to Ball & Ball Carburetor Company, Detroit, Mich., a Corporation of Michigan. Filed May 26, 1919. Serial No. 299,965. Original No. 1,243,480, dated Oct. 16, 1917, Serial No. 117,607, filed Aug. 30, 1916. 10 Claims. (Cl. 261—41.)

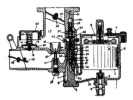

5. In a carbureter, the combination of a suction passage; means for delivering air and fuel to said passage; an auxiliary passage to which air is delivered leading to the suction passage, a throttle valve in the suction passage; a valve mechanism controlling the flow of air through the auxiliary passage, said valve mechanism being adapted to cut off the flow of air through the auxiliary passage; and devices actuated by fluctuations in the degree of vacuum at the discharge side of the throttle controlling said valve mechanism and enriching the mixture with a decrease in said vacuum.

14,791. PIPE-WRENCH. BEN WATTS, Jarbidge, Nev., assignor of forty-nine per cent. to Warren P. Godfrey, Jarbidge, Nev. Filed Oct. 9, 1919. Serial No. 329,613. Original No. 1,275,384, dated Aug. 13, 1918, Serial No. 230,510, filed Apr. 24, 1918. 12 Claims. (Cl. 81—134.)

1. A pipe wrench comprising a shank having a fixed jaw at one end, a guide loop pivotally engaged with the shank adjacent the jaw and extending laterally therefrom, a second shank disposed through the guide loop and overlapping an edge face of the first named shank, said second-named shank being provided with a jaw overlying the fixed jaw, a member pivotally engaged with the free end portion of the second shank and extending across the first-named shank, dogs pivotally engaged with said member and coacting with the opposite edge faces of the shank, each of said dogs being substantially semi-circular in form and having its straight face engageable with the edge face of the first-named shank, one of said dogs and the coacting edge face of the first-named shank being provided with teeth adapted to interlock, a pin carried by the member and overlying the toothed face of the first-named shank and rearwardly of the dog coacting with said face, and a flat spring carried by the second-named shank and contacting with the pin carried by the member for normally maintaining the straight faces of the dogs in contact with the coacting edge faces of the first-named shank.

The following trade-marks are published in compliance˜with˜section 6 of the act of February 20, 1905, as amended March 2, 1907. Notice of opposition must be filed within thirty days of this publication.

■■Marks applied for "under the ten-year proviso" are registrable under the provision in clause (b) of section 5 of said act as amended February 18, 1911.

As provided by section 14 of said act, a fee of ten dollars must accompany each notice of opposition.

Ser. No. 97,178. (CLASS 23. CUTLERY, MACHINERY, AND TOOLS, AND PARTS THEREOF.) JOHN BRAUN & SONS, Philadelphia, Pa., assignors to Pennsylvania Lawn Mower Works, Philadelphia, Pa., a Corporation of Pennsylvania. Filed July 29, 1916. Under ten-year proviso.

NEW DEPARTURE

Particular description of goods.—Lawn-Mowers.
Claims use since September, 1892.

Ser. No. 104,702. (CLASS 4. ABRASIVE, DETERGENT, AND POLISHING MATERIALS.) THE MOTOR-CAR SUPPLIES MANUFACTURING COMPANY, Denver, Colo. Filed June 26, 1917.

RENEW-O

Particular description of goods.—A Dressing for Fabrics, Leather, and Leather Imitations.
Claims use since or about the 1st of September, 1916.

Ser. No. 106,927. (CLASS 6. CHEMICALS, MEDICINES, AND PHARMACEUTICAL PREPARATIONS.) JOSEPH ROBERT, Paris, France. Filed Oct. 24, 1917.

STANNOXYL

Particular description of goods—Medicinal Preparations—Namely, Preparations for the Treatment of Staphylococique Maladies and for Eruptions Caused by the Same.
Claims use since the 31st of May, 1917.

Ser. No. 108,831. (CLASS 6. CHEMICALS, MEDICINES, AND PHARMACEUTICAL PREPARATIONS.) THE LORENZ COMPANY, Everett, Mass., assignor to Mihalovitch Brothers Company, Cincinnati, Ohio, a Corporation of Ohio. Filed Feb. 5, 1918. Under ten-year proviso.

LORENZ

Particular description of goods.—Perfumes, Tooth-Powder, Toilet Powders, Toilet Waters, Toilet Creams and Lotions, and Hair-Tonic.
Claims use since 1864.

Ser. No. 109,181. (CLASS 13. HARDWARE AND PLUMBING AND STEAM-FITTING SUPPLIES.) THE TOLEDO COOKER COMPANY, Toledo, Ohio. Filed Feb. 23, 1918.

CONSERVO

Particular description of goods.—Steam-Cookers.
Claims use since Feb. 8, 1918.

Ser. No. 111,500. (CLASS 39. CLOTHING.) JAMES HARBERT, Polson, Mont. Filed June 8, 1918.

CRAVA-DUSTA

Particular description of goods.—Raincoats of Rubberized and Otherwise Waterproofed Material.
Claims use since Oct. 1, 1917.

Ser. No. 113,440. (CLASS 39. CLOTHING.) THE SPARTAN MANUFACTURING COMPANY, Dayton, Ohio. Filed Sept. 26, 1918.

Particular description of goods.—Shop-Aprons, Overalls, Jackets, and Utility-Suits.
Claims use since about Jan. 1, 1916.

Ser. No. 113,635. (CLASS 39. CLOTHING.) CARRIE R. SCHMICK, Beach Cliff, Rocky River, Ohio. Filed Oct. 9, 1918.

"THE MOLLIE'S"

Particular description of goods.—One-Piece Dresses and Aprons.
Claims use since about Sept. 24, 1918.

Ser. No. 113,852. (CLASS 42. KNITTED, NETTED, AND TEXTILE FABRICS.) TRAUB, LEWIS & CO., New York, N. Y. Filed Oct. 22, 1918.

No claim being made to the words " New and Different." apart from the mark as shown in the drawing.
Particular description of goods.—Veilings and Nettings in the Piece.
Claims use since March, 1917.

Ser. No. 114,392. (CLASS 22. GAMES, TOYS, AND SPORTING GOODS.) THOMAS RUSSEL BALDWIN, Chicago, Ill. Filed Nov. 27, 1918.

Pego

Particular description of goods.—A Game Apparatus Consisting of a Board and Game-Pieces Used in Connection Therewith.
Claims use since Oct. 5, 1918.

Ser. No. 115,457. (CLASS 6. CHEMICALS, MEDICINES, AND PHARMACEUTICAL PREPARATIONS.) W. R. HOLLINGSHEAD COMPANY, Binghamton, N. Y. Filed Jan. 27, 1919.

BINGO

Our trade-mark consists of the arbitrarily-selected word " Bingo."
Particular description of goods.—An Egg-Substitute Powder.
Claims use since Oct. 1, 1918.

Ser. No. 115,556. (CLASS 43. THREAD AND YARN.) HOWARD F. SALISBURY, Providence, R. I. Filed Jan. 31, 1919.

SILVERWOOL

Particular description of goods.—Yarn.
Claims use since Jan. 10, 1919.

Ser. No. 115,631. (CLASS 39. CLOTHING.) GEORGE SPENCER & CO., Lutterworth, England. Filed Feb. 4, 1919.

Particular description of goods.—Blouses, Aprons, Bodices, Bonnets, Outer Coats, Cloaks, Undercoats, Caps, Pelisses, Bloomers, Knickers, Capes, Jerseys, Singlets, Jackets, Dresses, Dress-Shirts, Negligée Shirts, Work-Shirts, Muffs, Undershirts, Vests, Union-Garments, Mittens, Gloves, Underdrawers, Hosiery, Petticoats, Waistcoats, Dress-Skirts, Underskirts, Cardigan Jackets, Combination Shirt and Pants.
Claims use since Sept. 12, 1918.

Ser. No. 116,129. (CLASS 46. FOODS AND INGREDIENTS OF FOODS.) W. H. DYER COMPANY, Evansville, Ind. Filed Feb. 25, 1919.

TRIPLE A.A.A.

Particular description of goods.—Canned Pork and Beans, Canned Corned-Beef Hash, Canned Tongue, Canned Sausage, Canned Ox-Tongue, Canned Deviled Meats, Canned Hamburger Steak, Canned Potted Meats, Canned Roast Beef, Canned Veal-Loaf, Canned Selected Tripe, Canned Sausage-Meat, Canned Cooked Corned Beef, Canned Chilli Sauce, Canned Tomato Catsup, and Canned Orange Marmalade.
Claims use since January, 1918.

Ser. No. 116,302. (CLASS 23. CUTLERY, MACHINERY, AND TOOLS, AND PARTS THEREOF.) HUTH & CO., New York, N. Y. Filed Mar. 5, 1919.

Particular description of goods.—Cutlery—Namely, Machetes or Cane-Knives.
Claims use since November, 1918.

Ser. No. 116,593. (CLASS 6. CHEMICALS, MEDICINES, AND PHARMACEUTICAL PREPARATIONS.) WESTERN L. CAPELL, Omaha, Nebr. Filed Mar. 15, 1919.

MERCARODIN

Particular description of goods.—A Medical Compound for the Treatment of Syphilis.
Claims use since July, 1916.

Ser. No. 116,881. (CLASS 22. GAMES, TOYS, AND SPORTING GOODS.) WILLIAM FULD, Baltimore, Md. Filed Mar. 25, 1919.

Particular description of goods.—A Game Known as a Talking-Board.
Claims use since Feb. 1, 1892.

Ser. No. 117,048. (CLASS 42. KNITTED, NETTED, AND TEXTILE FABRICS.) ARSENIO JOSE FROES & COMPANY, INC., New York, N. Y. Filed Mar. 31, 1919.

Particular description of goods.—Table-Covers, Napkins, Table and Bureau Scarfs, and Handkerchiefs.
Claims use since Mar. 1, 1919.

Ser. No. 117,132. (CLASS 46. FOODS AND INGREDIENTS OF FOODS.) WILLIAM BEATTY, JR. AND CO., Philadelphia, Pa. Filed Apr. 3, 1919.

No claim is made for the word "Kisses" apart from the other features of the mark.
Particular description of goods.—Candy.
Claims use since Mar. 22, 1919.

Ser. No. 117,421. (CLASS 8. SMOKERS' ARTICLES, NOT INCLUDING TOBACCO PRODUCTS.) SOCIETE ANONYME LA BRUYERE, Paris and St. Claude, France. Filed Apr. 12, 1919.

OXFORD

Particular description of goods.—Tobacco-Pipes.
Claims use since Oct. 10, 1915.

Ser. No. 117,780. (CLASS 39. CLOTHING.) ABE M. MENDELSON, New York, N. Y. Filed Apr. 23, 1919.

Particular description of goods.—Knitted Sweaters.
Claims use since Oct. 1, 1917.

Ser. No. 118,145. (CLASS 43. THREAD AND YARN.) MARSHALL FIELD & COMPANY, Chicago, Ill. Filed May 5, 1919.

Sunlight

The word "Sunlight."
Particular description of goods.—Yarn.
Claims use since on or about 1898.

Ser. No. 118,246. (CLASS 22. GAMES, TOYS, AND SPORTING GOODS.) HOLLISTER M. J. RUCH, Syracuse, N. Y. Filed May 7, 1919.

Particular description of goods.—A Card Game.
Claims use since Apr. 29, 1919.

Ser. No. 118,302. (CLASS 4. ABRASIVE, DETERGENT, AND POLISHING MATERIALS.) GEO. M. DAVID, Barre, Vt. Filed May 9, 1919.

DA-VID-SKO

Particular description of goods.—Laundry-Tablets.
Claims use since Dec. 1, 1918.

Ser. No. 118,410. (CLASS 6. CHEMICALS, MEDICINES, AND PHARMACEUTICAL PREPARATIONS.) VICTORIA THOMPSON, Jacksonville, Fla. Filed May 12, 1919.

S. T. S.
GETS YOU

Particular description of goods.—A Preparation for Destroying Boll-Weevils and other Insects.
Claims use since Sept. 5, 1917.

Ser. No. 118,463. (CLASS 46. FOODS AND INGREDI-
ENTS OF FOODS.) THE BORDEN COMPANY, Jersey
City, N. J., and New York, N. Y. Filed May 14, 1919.
Under ten-year proviso.

Particular description of goods.—Condensed Milk, Evap-
orated Milk, Homogenized Milk, Dried Milk, Malted Milk,
Mixtures of Vegetable Oil with Constituents of Milk, Con-
densed Coffee, Mixtures of Coffee with Milk and Sugar,
Cocoa, Caramels, and Chocolate, Including Milk-Chocolate.
Claims use since the year 1893.

Ser. No. 118,903. (CLASS 46. FOODS AND INGREDI-
ENTS OF FOODS.) THE WILLIAM DAVIES COMPANY,
LIMITED, Chicago, Ill. Filed May 26, 1919.

Particular description of goods.—Bacon, Hams, Pure
Lard, Canned Beef, Sausage, Ox-Tongues, Lunch-Tongues,
and Pork and Beans.
Claims use since Mar. 1, 1919.

Ser. No. 119,728. (CLASS 26. MEASURING AND SCI-
ENTIFIC APPLIANCES.) AMERICAN BUREAU OF EN-
GINEERING, INC., Chicago, Ill. Filed June 18, 1919.

Particular description of goods.—Voltmeters, Cadmium
Leads for Testing Purposes, Armature-Testers, Combina-
tion Voltmeters and Ammeters.
Claims use since June 22, 1915.

Ser. No. 120,095. (CLASS 39. CLOTHING.) THE C.
AND E. SHOE COMPANY, Columbus, Ohio. Filed June 30,
1919.

The trade-mark consists in the fanciful display of the
word "Shukraft," no claim being made to the representation of the shoe and the syllable "Shu" apart from the
showing in the mark. The lining employed in the elliptical figure is for purposes of shading only.
Particular description of goods.—Leather Shoes for
Women's, Misses', and Children's Footwear.
Claims use since June 1, 1919.

Ser. No. 120,253. (CLASS 4. ABRASIVE, DETERGENT,
AND POLISHING MATERIALS.) NORMAN S. MCIN-
TOSH, Detroit, Mich. Filed July 3, 1919.

ACE

Particular description of goods. — A Cleaning Compound, a Preparation for Removing Carbon, Acid, Grease,
and Dirt from the Hands.
Claims use since the 1st day of June, 1919.

Ser. No. 120,354. (CLASS 6. CHEMICALS, MEDI-
CINES, AND PHARMACEUTICAL PREPARATIONS.)
PHOENIX DRUG COMPANY, New York, N. Y. Filed July
8, 1919.

OLA

Particular description of goods.—Nail-Polish.
Claims use since June 4, 1919.

Ser. No. 120,440. (CLASS 4. ABRASIVE, DETERGENT,
AND POLISHING MATERIALS.) SOCIETÀ INDUSTRIE
CHIMICHE ITTIOLO, Naples, Italy. Filed July 10, 1919.

Consisting in the word "Tiosapol."
Particular description of goods. — Soaps for Hygienic
and Medical Purposes.
Claims use since the 2d of January, 1919.

Ser. No. 120,526. (CLASS 19. VEHICLES, NOT IN-
CLUDING ENGINES.) ELGIN MOTOR CAR CORPORA-
TION, Argo, Ill. Filed July 14, 1919.

No claim is made to the exclusive use of the words
"Elgin" or "Six" except in association with the balance
of the mark.
Particular description of goods. — Motor - Vehicles—
Namely, Automobiles and Motor-Trucks.
Claims use since September, 1917.

Ser. No. 120,615. (CLASS 39. CLOTHING.) MILLER
BROS., Galveston, Tex. Filed July 16, 1919.

Particular description of goods. — Men's, Boys', and
Children's Clothing—Namely, Coats, Vests, Trousers,
Jumpers, Overalls, Shirts, and Palm Beach Suits.
Claims use since September, 1907.

Ser. No. 120,647. (CLASS 42. KNITTED, NETTED, AND TEXTILE FABRICS.) JORDAN MARSH COMPANY, Boston, Mass. Filed July 17, 1919.

Particular description of goods.—Handkerchiefs.
Claims use since July 1, 1919.

Ser. No. 120,741. (CLASS 4. ABRASIVE, DETERGENT, AND POLISHING MATERIALS.) GEORGE W. BAKER, Dallas, Tex. Filed July 21, 1919.

Particular description of goods.—Waterproof Dressing for Leather, Leather Substitutes, and Like Fabric.
Claims use since about Dec. 1, 1918.

Ser. No. 120,746. (CLASS 42. KNITTED, NETTED, AND TEXTILE FABRICS.) FULD, TRAUBE & CO., INC., New York, N. Y. Filed July 21, 1919.

DUPLEX

Particular description of goods.—Veils, Malines, Hair-Nets, and Chiffons.
Claims use since Jan. 15, 1917.

Ser. No. 120,809. (CLASS 42. KNITTED, NETTED, AND TEXTILE FABRICS.) ALCO TEXTILE PRODUCTS CO. INC., Albany, N. Y. Filed July 23, 1919.

Particular description of goods.—Handkerchiefs.
Claims use since about July 22, 1918.

Ser. No. 121,001. (CLASS 23. CUTLERY, MACHINERY, AND TOOLS, AND PARTS THEREOF.) METALWOOD MANUFACTURING CO., Detroit, Mich. Filed July 28, 1919.

METALWOOD

Particular description of goods.—Hydraulic Machinery and Equipment Consisting of Presses, Shock-Alleviators, Pumps, Accumulators, Hydraulic Stop and Check Valves, L's, T's, Crosses, Unions, Couplings, Nipples, Bushings for Hydraulic Machinery, and Hydraulic Tubing.
Claims use since May, 1918.

Ser. No. 121,190. (CLASS 40. FANCY GOODS, FURNISHINGS, AND NOTIONS.) WALDES & CO., Prague, Bohemia. Filed Aug. 1, 1919.

Particular description of goods.—Placket-Fasteners, Glove-Fasteners, Hand Sewing-Needles, Knitting-Needles, Crochet-Needles, Safety-Pins, Hairpins, Hatpins Not Made of Precious Metal, Hooks and Eyes, Buttons Not Made of Precious Metal, Buckles for Personal Wear Not Made of Precious Metal, Thimbles, Straight Solid-Headed Pins for Personal Use, Coat-Hangers Adapted to be Attached to Garments, Clasps for Personal Wear Not Made of Precious Metal, Button-Tapes, and Collar-Buttons and Cuff-Buttons Not Made of Precious Metal.
Claims use since February, 1912.

Ser. No. 121,302. (CLASS 4. ABRASIVE, DETERGENT, AND POLISHING MATERIALS.) ALBERT HINKLEY, Newark, N. J. Filed Aug. 6, 1919.

No claim being made to the exclusive use of the word "Hipolish" apart from the mark as shown in the drawing.
Particular description of goods.—Stove-Polish.
Claims use since May 2, 1919.

Ser. No. 121,341. (CLASS 7. CORDAGE.) THE HOOVEN & ALLISON COMPANY, Xenia, Ohio. Filed Aug. 7, 1919.

UTILEX.

Particular description of goods.—Fiber Ropes and Twines.
Claims use since Mar. 25, 1919.

Ser. No. 121,342. (CLASS 7. CORDAGE.) THE HOOVEN & ALLISON COMPANY, Xenia, Ohio. Filed Aug. 7, 1919.

SUPREX

Particular description of goods.—Fiber Ropes and Twines.
Claims use since June 2, 1919.

Ser. No. 121,343. (CLASS 7. CORDAGE.) THE HOOVEN & ALLISON COMPANY, Xenia, Ohio. Filed Aug. 7, 1919.

STANEX

Particular description of goods.—Fiber Ropes and Twines.
Claims use since June 2, 1919.

Ser. No. 121,477. (CLASS 42. KNITTED, NETTED, AND TEXTILE FABRICS.) LORTEX COMPANY, New York, N. Y. Filed Aug. 9, 1919.

The lining on the mark is intended for shading and not for color.
Particular description of goods.—Cotton Piece Goods, Linen Piece Goods, Wool and Cotton Fabrics in the Piece, Wool Goods in the Piece, Silk and Cotton Piece Goods, Silk Goods in the Piece, Fiber Piece Goods, and Silk and Wool Fabrics in the Piece.
Claims use since May 14, 1912.

Ser. No. 121,517. (CLASS 24. LAUNDRY APPLIANCES AND MACHINES.) BROKAW-EDEN MANUFACTURING COMPANY, Alton, Ill. Filed Aug. 11, 1919.

The Eden

Particular description of goods.—Laundry Appliances and Machines—Namely, Laundry and Clothes Washing Machines, Wringers, Ironers.
Claims use since February, 1912.

Ser. No. 121,596. (CLASS 29. BROOMS, BRUSHES, AND DUSTERS.) MICHAEL MARCUS, New York, N. Y. Filed Aug. 12, 1919.

MARCO

Particular description of goods.—Brooms, Shaving-Brushes, Paint-Brushes, Clothing-Brushes, Dust-Brushes, Paper-Hangers' Brushes, and Sweeping-Brushes and Tooth-Brushes.
Claims use since May 1, 1919.

Ser. No. 121,598. (CLASS 38. PRINTS AND PUBLICA-TIONS.) THE NEW YORK TIMES COMPANY, New York, N. Y. Filed Aug. 12, 1919.

Wide World

Particular description of goods.—Photographs and Re-prints Thereof.
Claims use since July 1, 1919.

Ser. No. 121,599. (CLASS 38. PRINTS AND PUBLICA-TIONS.) THE NEW YORK TIMES COMPANY, New York, N. Y. Filed Aug. 12, 1919.

Times Wide World

Particular description of goods.—Photographs and Re-prints Thereof.
Claims use since Apr. 1, 1919.

Ser. No. 121,694. (CLASS 4. ABRASIVE, DETERGENT, AND POLISHING MATERIALS.) LAUNDRY SUPPLIES CORPORATION, Richmond, Va. Filed Aug. 15, 1919.

Consisting of the word "Sour-Rite," as shown in the accompanying drawing. Applicant hereby disclaims any right to the use of the word "Sour" as a trade-mark apart from the mark shown on the drawing.
Particular description of goods.—A Preparation Used for Cleansing Purposes.
Claims use since May 15, 1919.

Ser. No. 121,780. (CLASS 4. ABRASIVE, DETERGENT, AND POLISHING MATERIALS.) PEET BROS. MANU-FACTURING COMPANY, Kansas City, Kans. Filed Aug. 18, 1919. Under ten-year proviso.

Particular description of goods.—Soap.
Claims use since 1894.

Ser. No. 121,793. (CLASS 23. CUTLERY, MACHINERY, AND TOOLS, AND PARTS THEREOF.) SIMONDS MANUFACTURING CO., Fitchburg, Mass. Filed Aug. 18, 1919.

No registration rights are claimed for the word "Saw" apart from the mark shown in the drawing.
Particular description of goods.—Saws.
Claims use since Aug. 1, 1919.

Ser. No. 121,833. (CLASS 40. FANCY GOODS, FUR-NISHINGS, AND NOTIONS.) FULFORD M'F'G CO., Providence, R. I. Filed Aug. 20, 1919.

The lining shown in the drawing is to express a shading as a background to the letters.
Particular description of goods.—Snap-Fasteners.
Claims use since Feb. 1, 1919.

Ser. No. 121,869. (CLASS 46. FOODS AND INGREDI-ENTS OF FOODS.) LOOSE-WILES BISCUIT COMPANY, New York, N. Y. Filed Aug. 21, 1919.

Particular description of goods.—Cakes, Wafers, and Crackers or Biscuits.
Claims use since Jan. 1, 1906.

Ser. No. 121,880. (CLASS 4. ABRASIVE, DETERGENT, AND POLISHING MATERIALS.) TEXAS OIL, GAS & MINERAL PRODUCTS COMPANY, Houston, Tex. Filed Aug. 21, 1919.

Particular description of goods.—A Liquid Polish for Polishing Metals, Glass.
Claims use since about the 15th day of July, 1919.

Ser. No. 121,941. (CLASS 46. FOODS AND INGREDI-ENTS OF FOODS.) LOOSE WILES BISCUIT COMPANY, New York, N. Y. Filed Aug. 23, 1919.

No claim being made to the pictorial representation of the goods shown on the drawing.
Particular description of goods.—Cakes, Wafers, and Crackers or Biscuits.
Claims use since Jan. 1, 1906.

Ser. No. 122,022. (CLASS 46. FOODS AND INGREDI-ENTS OF FOODS.) DAVID NEUMAN, Wilkes-Barre, Pa. Filed Aug. 26, 1919.

No claim being made to the words "Adwater," "Then Serve," and "Products" apart from the mark shown by the drawing.
Particular description of goods.—Chocolate, Cocoa, and Powdered Milk.
Claims use since July 29, 1919.

Ser. No. 122,114. (CLASS 46. FOODS AND INGREDI-ENTS OF FOODS.) MARK M. DIFFENBACHER, San Francisco, Calif. Filed Aug. 29, 1919.

No claim being made to the words "Wricley," "Origi-nal," or "Spearmint Candy," either occurrence, nor to the slogans "The arrow points to quality" and "The flavor hits the mark" apart from the mark shown.
Particular description of goods.—Spearmint Candy.
Claims use since Jan. 1, 1919.

Ser. No. 122,302. (CLASS 39. CLOTHING.) HOB MANUFACTURING CO., New York, N. Y. Filed Sept. 4, 1919.

Particular description of goods.—Infants' Caps, Sacks, and Booties of Knitted Material, Baby-Shoes, Baby-Caps, Bibs, Baby-Pants, Rubber Diapers, Infants' Sacks, and In-fants' Flannels.
Claims use since November, 1913.

Ser. No. 122,444. (CLASS 32. FURNITURE AND UP-HOLSTERY.) THE PERFECTION MATTRESS & SPRING Co., Birmingham, Ala. Filed Sept. 8, 1919.

The right to the exclusive use of a label colored red is disclaimed.
Particular description of goods.—Mattresses.
Claims use since October, 1907.

Ser. No. 122,528. (CLASS 6. CHEMICALS, MEDI-CINES, AND PHARMACEUTICAL PREPARATIONS.) ESSEX ANILINE WORKS INC., Boston, Mass. Filed Sept. 10, 1919.

Particular description of goods.—Dyestuffs.
Claims use since Nov. 1, 1918.

Ser. No. 122,557. (CLASS 4. ABRASIVE, DETERGENT, AND POLISHING MATERIALS.) S. & P. MANUFAC-TURING CO. INC., New York, N. Y. Filed Sept. 10, 1919.

The lining appearing in the drawing is intended to in-dicate shading only.
Particular description of goods.—Valve-Grinding Com-pounds.
Claims use since about Apr. 1, 1919.

Ser. No. 122,603. (CLASS 46. FOODS AND INGREDI-ENTS OF FOODS.) MARGUERITE C. McKENNA, New York, N. Y. Filed Sept. 12, 1919.

CINNIMO

Particular description of goods. — A Combination of Sugar and Cinnamon for Griddle-Cake and Waffle Sea-soning.
Claims use since Aug. 2, 1919.

Ser. No. 122,610. (CLASS 4. ABRASIVE, DETERGENT, AND POLISHING MATERIALS.) PEERLESS MINERAL PRODUCTS Co., INC., New York, N. Y. Filed Sept. 12, 1919.

DETERGRITE

Consisting of the word "Detergrite."
Particular description of goods.—Soap.
Claims use since July 31, 1919.

Ser. No. 122,620. (CLASS 42. KNITTED, NETTED, AND TEXTILE FABRICS.) WERTHEIMER BROS., New York, N. Y. Filed Sept. 12, 1919.

Particular description of goods.—Silk and Velvet Rib-bon.
Claims use since Jan. 1, 1915.

Ser. No. 122,791. (CLASS 4. ABRASIVE, DETERGENT, AND POLISHING MATERIALS.) GEORGE W. REIN-HARDT Co., Boston, Mass. Filed Sept. 16, 1919.

CLEVO-CLEAN

Particular description of goods.—A Compound for Use in Cleaning Fabrics, Glass, Marble, Crockery, Metals, and Enameled or Painted Surfaces.
Claims use since January, 1919.

Ser. No. 122,792. (CLASS 6. CHEMICALS, MEDI-CINES, AND PHARMACEUTICAL PREPARATIONS.) A. SIMONSON, New York, N. Y. Filed Sept. 16, 1919. Under ten-year proviso.

A. Simonson

Particular description of goods. — Cold-Cream, Com-plexion-Cream, Complexion-Balm, Massage-Cream; Skin-Invigorator, (a Skin-Massaging Preparation;) Almond Cream, Menthol Lotion, Toilet Water, Face-Bleach; Face-Powder, (in Powder, Cake, and Liquid Forms;) Rouge, (in Cake, Liquid, Powder, and Cream Forms;) Freckle-Lotion, Cuticle-Cream; Liquid Soap, (a Manicuring Prepa-ration for Softening the Cuticle and Nail and Containing other Ingredients Besides Soap;) Nail-Bleach, Nail-Clean-ser; Nail-Polish, (in Cream, Cake, and Liquid Forms;) Antiseptic, Egg Shampoo, Tar Shampoo, Pine Shampoo, Henna Shampoo, Dry-Shampoo Powder; Castile Shampoo, (a Shampoo Preparation Containing other Ingredients Be-sides Castile-Soap;) Shampooing-Cream, Hair-Dressing, Brilliantine, Hair-Darkener, Hair-Fixative, Tonic for Dry Hair, Tonic for Oily Hair, Quinin Tonic, Rum and Quinin Tonic, Hair-Whitener, Dandruff-Salve, Scalp-Balm; Hair-Curler, (a Hair-Curling Preparation;) Hair-Lightener, Hair-Colorings, Hair-Dyes; Hair-Removers, (in Liquid, Powder, and Cake Form;) Foot-Powder, and Foot-Lotion.
Claims use since 1892.

Ser. No. 122,799. (CLASS 6. CHEMICALS, MEDI-CINES, AND PHARMACEUTICAL PREPARATIONS.) FREDERICK H. YOUNG, Toledo, Ohio. Filed Sept. 16, 1919. Under ten-year proviso.

Particular description of goods.—Toilet Cream, Face-Powder, Talcum Powder, and Tooth-Powder.
Claims use since Feb. 15, 1893.

Ser. No. 122,800. (CLASS 6. CHEMICALS, MEDI-CINES, AND PHARMACEUTICAL PREPARATIONS.) FREDERICK H. YOUNG, Toledo, Ohio. Filed Sept. 16, 1919. Under ten-year proviso.

Particular description of goods.—Toilet Creams. Face-Powder, Talcum Powder, and Tooth-Powder.
Claims use since April, 1894.

Ser. No. 122,833. (CLASS 46. FOODS AND INGREDI-ENTS OF FOODS.) FRANCIS N. GIAVI, New York, N. Y. Filed Sept. 18, 1919.

Particular description of goods.—Olive-Oil.
Claims use since March, 1919.

Ser. No. 122,847. (CLASS 42. KNITTED, NETTED, AND TEXTILE FABRICS.) NAUMKEAG STEAM COT-TON CO., Salem, Mass. Filed Sept. 18, 1919.

NAUMKEAG

Particular description of goods.—Sheets, Pillow-Cases, and Bolster-Cases.
Claims use since 1896.

Ser. No. 122,855. (CLASS 46. FOODS AND INGREDI-ENTS OF FOODS.) AUGUST V. PETERSON, Portland, Oreg. Filed Sept. 18, 1919.

RYTAK

Particular description of goods.—Hardtack.
Claims use since Aug. 1, 1919.

Ser. No. 122,905. (CLASS 42. KNITTED, NETTED, AND TEXTILE FABRICS.) NAUMKEAG STEAM COTTON CO., Salem, Mass. Filed Sept. 19, 1919.

Particular description of goods.—Sheets and Pillow-Cases.
Claims use since 1910.

Ser. No. 122,906. (CLASS 42. KNITTED, NETTED, AND TEXTILE FABRICS.) NAUMKEAG STEAM COTTON CO., Salem, Mass. Filed Sept. 19, 1919.

Particular description of goods.—Cotton Piece Goods.
Claims use since 1878.

Ser. No. 122,925. (CLASS 6. CHEMICALS, MEDI-CINES, AND PHARMACEUTICAL PREPARATIONS.) VALENTIN, ORD & Co., LIMITED, Hayes, England. Filed Sept. 19, 1919.

OSMOS

Particular description of goods.—Artificial Mineral Water for Use as Aperient.
Claims use since Dec. 2, 1918.

Ser. No. 122,946. (CLASS 12. CONSTRUCTION MA-TERIALS.) NEW ENGLAND FELT ROOFING WORKS, Boston, Mass. Filed Sept. 20, 1919.

Particular description of goods.—Roofing Products—viz., Pitch, Felt, Cement, Sheathing, and Waterproof Paper.
Claims use since July 1, 1915.

Ser. No. 122,993. (CLASS 42. KNITTED, NETTED, AND TEXTILE FABRICS.) McLANE SILK COMPANY, Turners Falls, Mass. Filed Sept. 22, 1919.

Said trade-mark consists of the word "Beaver" repeated at intervals along the selvage edge of the fabric and a series of parallel short lines arranged at an acute angle to the edge of the fabric to resemble a rope and extending along the selvage edge of the fabric between each of said words "Beaver" and the next succeeding word, no claim being made to the exclusive right to the use of the representation of the material upon which the mark is produced apart from the mark shown in the drawing.

Particular description of goods.—Silk and Satin Piece Goods.

Claims use since Aug. 1, 1919.

Ser. No. 122,998. (CLASS 42. KNITTED, NETTED, AND TEXTILE FABRICS.) RICE-STIX DRY GOODS COMPANY, St. Louis, Mo. Filed Sept. 22, 1919.

No claim being made to the word "Dril" apart from the words "La Luna."

Particular description of goods.—Cotton Drills in the Piece.

Claims use since Sept. 10, 1919.

Ser. No. 123,010. (CLASS 6. CHEMICALS, MEDICINES, AND PHARMACEUTICAL PREPARATIONS.) PAUL C. ZIESCHANG, Columbus, Ohio. Filed Sept. 22, 1919.

The letters "P C" being in red.

Particular description of goods.—A Liquid Medicine in the Nature of a Tonic for the Treatment of the Nerves and Also for the Digestive System.

Claims use since Aug. 15, 1919.

Ser. No. 123,043. (CLASS 4. ABRASIVE, DETERGENT, AND POLISHING MATERIALS.) THE SCHOFIELD OIL CO., INC., New York, N. Y. Filed Sept. 23, 1919.

Particular description of goods.—Soap.

Claims use since July 15, 1919.

Ser. No. 123,099. (CLASS 46. FOODS AND INGREDIENTS OF FOODS.) ALASKA BAKONIZED FISH CO., Juneau, Territory of Alaska. Filed Sept. 25, 1919.

BaKONIZED

Particular description of goods.—Canned Fish.

Claims use since the 1st day of August, 1919.

Ser. No. 123,133. (CLASS 42. KNITTED, NETTED, AND TEXTILE FABRICS.) NAUMKEAG STEAM COTTON CO., Salem, Mass. Filed Sept. 25, 1919.

Particular description of goods.—Pillow-Cases.

Claims use since 1912.

Ser. No. 123,187. (CLASS 6. CHEMICALS, MEDICINES, AND PHARMACEUTICAL PREPARATIONS.) UNITED LABORATORIES, INC., St. Louis, Mo. Filed Sept. 26, 1919.

BROMO-PATICA

The word "Bromo" is disclaimed except as a part of the composite mark shown.

Particular description of goods.—Remedies for Headache, Insomnia, Neuralgia, Nervous Dyspepsia, Constipation, and Seasickness.

Claims use since the 9th of August, 1919.

Ser. No. 123,309. (CLASS 6. CHEMICALS, MEDICINES, AND PHARMACEUTICAL PREPARATIONS.) DENNEY & DENNEY, Philadelphia, Pa. Filed Oct. 1, 1919.

MYANA

Particular description of goods.—Perfumes, Toilet Waters, Face-Powders, Talcum Powders, Brilliantines, Sachet-Powders, and Rouges.

Claims use since January, 1918.

Ser. No. 123,451.   (CLASS 42.   KNITTED, NETTED, AND TEXTILE FABRICS.)   PACIFIC MILLS, Lawrence and Boston, Mass.   Filed Oct. 4, 1919.

Particular description of goods.—Cotton Piece and Cotton Dress Goods.
Claims use since Sept. 22. 1919.

Ser. No. 123,478.   (CLASS 42.   KNITTED, NETTED, AND TEXTILE FABRICS.)   FEARING, WHITON & CO., INC., Boston, Mass.   Filed Oct. 6, 1919.

No claim is made for the use of the word " Fabrics " in said trade-mark apart from the word " Fearton."
Particular description of goods.—Cotton Goods—Namely, Cotton Sheeting.
Claims use since July 1, 1919.

Ser. No. 123,542.   (CLASS 42.   KNITTED, NETTED, AND TEXTILE FABRICS.)   HAAS BROTHERS FABRICS' CORPORATION, New York, N. Y.   Filed Oct. 8, 1919.

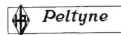

Particular description of goods.—Piece Goods Composed of a Worsted Warp and a Cashmere Filled Cloth.
Claims use since Sept. 15, 1919.

Ser. No. 123,544.   (CLASS 42.   KNITTED, NETTED, AND TEXTILE FABRICS.)   HAAS BROTHERS FABRICS' CORPORATION, New York, N. Y.   Filed Oct. 8, 1919.

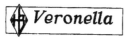

Particular description of goods.—Piece Goods Composed of a Silk Warp and a Worsted Filled Cloth.
Claims use since Sept. 15, 1919.

Ser. No. 123,653.   (CLASS 39.   CLOTHING.)   MANDEL & COHEN, New York, N. Y.   Filed Oct. 10, 1919.

The picture being fanciful.
Particular description of goods.—Hosiery for Boys and Girls.
Claims use since May 1, 1919.

Ser. No. 123,668.   (CLASS 39.   CLOTHING.)   SLATEDALE KNITTING MILLS, Harrisburg, Pa.   Filed Oct. 10, 1919.

The picture being fanciful.
Particular description of goods.—Hose for Men, Women, and Children.
Claims use since Sept. 15, 1919.

Ser. No. 123,669.   (CLASS 39.   CLOTHING.)   SLATEDALE KNITTING MILLS, Harrisburg, Pa.   Filed Oct. 10, 1919.

Particular description of goods.—Hose for Men, Women, and Children.
Claims use since Sept. 15, 1919.

Ser. No. 123,670.   (CLASS 39.   CLOTHING.)   SLATEDALE KNITTING MILLS, Harrisburg, Pa.   Filed Oct. 10, 1919.

Particular description of goods.—Hose for Men, Women, and Children.
Claims use since Sept. 15, 1919.

Ser. No. 123,734. (CLASS 39. CLOTHING.) GOODWEAR HOSIERY CO., Kenosha, Wis. Filed Oct. 13, 1919.

No claim being made for the words "Good Wear" apart from the mark shown.
Particular description of goods.—Hosiery.
Claims use since Oct. 6, 1919.

Ser. No. 123,759. (CLASS 42. KNITTED, NETTED, AND TEXTILE FABRICS.) EDWIN K. RHOADS, Philadelphia, Pa. Filed Oct. 13, 1919.

RHODESSA

Consists of the word "Rhodessa."
Particular description of goods.—Bedspreads; Sheets; Pillow-Cases, and Sheeting.
Claims use on bedspreads since about July 11, 1919, and on sheets, pillow-cases, and sheeting since about July 23, 1919.

Ser. No. 123,978. (CLASS 23. CUTLERY, MACHINERY, AND TOOLS, AND PARTS THEREOF.) THE GRAY TRACTOR COMPANY INC., Minneapolis, Minn. Filed Oct. 20, 1919.

Particular description of goods.—Farm-Tractors.
Claims use since Oct. 8, 1918.

Ser. No. 124,115. (CLASS 42. KNITTED, NETTED, AND TEXTILE FABRICS.) CHAS. KOHLMAN CO. INC., New York, N. Y. Filed Oct. 23, 1919.

Bloom of the South

Consisting of the words "Bloom of the South."
Particular description of goods.—Cotton Piece Goods.
Claims use since Nov. 4, 1918.

Ser. No. 124,132. (CLASS 38. PRINTS AND PUBLICATIONS.) EDUARD BLUM, Chicago, Ill. Filed Oct. 24, 1919.

LUMINOUS

Particular description of goods.—Portrait-Photographs.
Claims use since about the 9th day of December, 1913.

Ser. No. 124,221. (CLASS 23. CUTLERY, MACHINERY, AND TOOLS, AND PARTS THEREOF.) MAYHEW STEEL PRODUCTS INC., New York, N. Y. Filed Oct. 27, 1919.

PERPETUO

Consisting of the word "Perpetuo."
Particular description of goods.—Mechanics' Hand-Tools—viz., Screw-Drivers.
Claims use since Oct. 16, 1919.

Ser. No. 124,613. (CLASS 46. FOODS AND INGREDIENTS OF FOODS.) LAWRENCE CANNING CO., Rockland, Me. Filed Nov. 6, 1919.

Grobig

Particular description of goods.—Poultry and Stock Feeds and Fish-Meal.
Claims use since Sept. 10, 1916.

Ser. No. 124,742. (CLASS 40. FANCY GOODS, FURNISHINGS, AND NOTIONS.) THE WARNER BROS. CO., Bridgeport, Conn. Filed Nov. 10, 1919.

SPORT

Particular description of goods.—Hose-Supporters.
Claims use since Oct. 20, 1919.

Ser. No. 124,771. (CLASS 12. CONSTRUCTION MATERIALS.) A. B. WAINWRIGHT COMPANY, Philadelphia, Pa. Filed Nov. 11, 1919.

Particular description of goods.—Prepared Roofings.
Claims use since July 3, 1919.

Ser. No. 124,779. (CLASS 46. FOODS AND INGREDIENTS OF FOODS.) AUSTIN, NICHOLS & COMPANY, INCORPORATED, Brooklyn and New York, N. Y. Filed Nov. 12, 1919.

Particular description of goods.—Shelled Almonds, Brussels Sprouts, Burgerks, Creamery-Butter; Cream Cereal, a Wheat Breakfast Food; Breakfast-Cocoa, Instant Coffee, Coffee, Cranberries, Horse-Radish, Cranberry Jelly; Maphon, a Compound of Maple-Syrup and Strained Honey; Marshmallow Crème, Mayonnaise, Evaporated Milk, Molasses, Nutja, Rolled Oats, Peanuts, Refiners' Syrup.
Claims use since Apr. 30, 1890.

TRADE-MARK REGISTRATIONS GRANTED

JANUARY 13, 1920.

128,587. CANNED SALMON. Aberdeen Packing Co., Aberdeen, Wash.
Filed July 1, 1919. Serial No. 120,146. PUBLISHED SEPTEMBER 23, 1919.

128,588. MEAT PATTIES. Acme Packing Co., Chicago, Ill.
Filed July 21, 1919. Serial No. 120,735. PUBLISHED SEPTEMBER 23, 1919.

128,589. NECKTIES. Adrian Neckwear Co., Portland, Oreg.
Filed April 25, 1919. Serial No. 117,827. PUBLISHED SEPTEMBER 30, 1919.

128,590. CALCIUM CARBID. Air Reduction Company, Incorporated, New York, N. Y.
Filed July 3, 1919. Serial No. 120,235. PUBLISHED SEPTEMBER 30, 1919.

128,591. OLIVE-OIL. John A. Alban & Co., Inc., New York, N. Y.
Filed June 26, 1919. Serial No. 119,968. PUBLISHED SEPTEMBER 23, 1919.

128,592. BLOTTING-PAPER. The Albemarle Paper Mfg. Co., Richmond, Va.
Filed May 16, 1919. Serial No. 118,536. PUBLISHED OCTOBER 7, 1919.

128,593. SPECIALLY-PREPARED PEPTONE FOR BACTERIOLOGICAL USE. Allen & Hanburys, Ltd., London, England.
Filed May 28, 1919. Serial No. 118,979. PUBLISHED OCTOBER 7, 1919.

128.594. CERTAIN NAMED CONSTRUCTION MATERIALS. American Abrasive Metals Co., New York, N. Y.
Filed May 13, 1919. Serial No. 118,413. PUBLISHED SEPTEMBER 23, 1919.

128,595. COFFEE, CERTAIN NAMED CANNED FOODS AND FLAVORING EXTRACT. American Factories, Limited, Honolulu, Territory of Hawaii.
Filed June 10, 1919. Serial No. 119,379. PUBLISHED SEPTEMBER 23, 1919.

128,596. CERTAIN NAMED CANNED FOODS AND BUTTER. American Factories, Limited, Honolulu, Territory of Hawaii.
Filed June 10, 1919. Serial No. 119,381. PUBLISHED SEPTEMBER 23, 1919.

128,597. SOCKET - WRENCHES. American Grinder Manufacturing Company, Milwaukee, Wis.
Filed June 17, 1919. Serial No. 119,694. PUBLISHED SEPTEMBER 16, 1919.

128,598. HAIR - DRESSING PREPARATION. American Laboratories Incorporated, Richmond, Va.
Filed May 28, 1919. Serial No. 118,976. PUBLISHED SEPTEMBER 30, 1919.

128,599. ANTISEPTIC, DISINFECTANT, DEODORANT, AND PROPHYLACTIC FOR INTERNAL AND EXTERNAL USE. American Laboratories Incorporated, Richmond, Va.
Filed June 2, 1919. Serial No. 119,097. PUBLISHED OCTOBER 7, 1919.

128,600. FOOD - FLAVORING EXTRACTS. American Laboratories Incorporated, Richmond, Va.
Filed July 12, 1919. Serial No. 120,471. PUBLISHED SEPTEMBER 23, 1919.

128,601. LEAD - PENCILS. American Lead Pencil Company, New York, N. Y.
Filed May 20, 1919. Serial No. 118,725. PUBLISHED SEPTEMBER 23, 1919.

128,602. WHITE ARSENIC. The American Metal Company, Limited, New York, N. Y.
Filed July 3, 1919. Serial No. 120,236. PUBLISHED SEPTEMBER 30, 1919.

128,603. MUSTARD. American Mustard Co. Inc., New York, N. Y.
Filed July 15, 1919. Serial No. 120,564. PUBLISHED SEPTEMBER 30, 1919.

128,604. PRINTING AND WRITING PAPER. American Writing Paper Company, Holyoke, Mass.
Filed July 18, 1919. Serial No. 120,658. PUBLISHED SEPTEMBER 30, 1919.

128,605. COTTON PIECE GOODS. Amory, Browne & Co., New York, N. Y.
Filed June 13, 1919. Serial No. 119,547. PUBLISHED SEPTEMBER 23, 1919.

128,606. CANNED SALMON. A. O. Andersen & Co., Portland, Oreg.
Filed July 1, 1919. Serial No. 120,148. PUBLISHED SEPTEMBER 23, 1919.

128,607. CANNED SALMON. A. O. Andersen & Company, Portland, Oreg.
Filed July 1, 1919. Serial No. 120,149. PUBLISHED SEPTEMBER 23, 1919.

128,608. CANNED SALMON. A. O. Andersen & Co., Portland, Oreg.
Filed July 1, 1919. Serial No. 120,150. PUBLISHED SEPTEMBER 23, 1919.

128,609. INSECTICIDES AND FUNGICIDES. A. B. Ansbacher & Company, Inc., New York, N. Y.
Filed July 21, 1919. Serial No. 120,738. PUBLISHED OCTOBER 7, 1919.

128,610. CANVAS AND CLOTH-TOP SHOES, OUTING-SHOES, AND RUBBER FOOTWEAR. Apsley Rubber Company, Hudson, Mass.
Filed July 21, 1919. Serial No. 120,732. PUBLISHED OCTOBER 7, 1919.

128,611. CANVAS AND CLOTH-TOP SHOES, OUTING-SHOES, AND RUBBER FOOTWEAR. Apsley Rubber Company, Hudson, Mass.
Filed July 21, 1919. Serial No. 120,734. PUBLISHED OCTOBER 7, 1919.

128,612. BOTTLE AND PRESCRIPTION CORKS OF ALL KINDS. Armstrong Cork Company, Pittsburgh, Pa.
Filed July 5, 1919. Serial No. 120,273. PUBLISHED SEPTEMBER 23, 1919.

128,613. SPARK-PLUGS. Joseph René Ayotte, Chicago, Ill.
Filed May 31, 1919. Serial No. 119,060. PUBLISHED SEPTEMBER 30, 1919.

128,614. ANTISEPTIC FLUID FOR CLEANSING AND WHITENING THE TEETH. Leopold Bahr, Brooklyn, N. Y.
Filed June 12, 1919. Serial No. 119,497. PUBLISHED SEPTEMBER 30, 1919.

128,615. WORK-SHIRTS. Baltimore Bargain House, Baltimore and Cumberland, Md.
Filed June 12, 1919. Serial No. 119,495. PUBLISHED SEPTEMBER 30, 1919.

128,616. TOILET CREAMS, ASTRINGENT CREAMS, FACE-BLEACH CREAMS, AND FACE-POWDERS. BESSIE L. BARBER, Los Angeles, Calif. Filed June 24, 1919. Serial No. 119,881. PUBLISHED SEPTEMBER 30, 1919.

128,617. LINEN THREAD. THE BARBOUR BROTHERS Co., Paterson, N. J. Filed May 23, 1919. Serial No. 118,823. PUBLISHED SEPTEMBER 16, 1919.

128,618. ANTISEPTIC LIQUID. F. E. BARR & COMPANY, Chicago, Ill. Filed July 23, 1919. Serial No. 120,812. PUBLISHED SEPTEMBER 23, 1919.

128,619. RADIATOR-SEAL, A SO-CALLED ANTILEAK COMPOUND FOR RADIATORS. THE BEAR-CAT PRODUCTS Co., INC., Oklahoma, Okla. Filed June 16, 1919. Serial No. 119,627. PUBLISHED SEPTEMBER 23, 1919.

128,620. ISOLATED ELECTRIC-LIGHTING PLANTS. BEAUDETTE & GRAHAM ENGINEERING Co., Boston, Mass. Filed February 19, 1919. Serial No. 115,970. PUBLISHED APRIL 22, 1919.

128,621. GINGER-ALE. BEECH-NUT PACKING COMPANY, Canajoharie, N. Y. Filed July 16, 1919. Serial No. 120,595. PUBLISHED OCTOBER 7, 1919.

128,622. SINGLE AND COMPOUND AUTOMOBILE AIR-PUMPS AND OIL-PUMPS AND GREASE-GUNS. THE BELL PUMP & MANUFACTURING Co., Detroit, Mich. Filed June 16, 1919. Serial No. 119,628. PUBLISHED SEPTEMBER 16, 1919.

128,623. COTTON PIECE GOODS AND MOHAIR PIECE GOODS AND MIXTURES OF THE SAME. JOSEPH BENN & SONS INC., Greystone, R. I., and New York, N. Y. Filed June 28, 1919. Serial No. 120,033. PUBLISHED SEPTEMBER 30, 1919.

128,624. LAXATIVE MEDICINE. NINA B. BENSON, Memphis, Tenn. Filed June 7, 1919. Serial No. 119,288. PUBLISHED OCTOBER 14, 1919.

128,625. HAIR-TONIC FOR THE REMOVAL OF ALL HAIR AND SCALP TROUBLES. JOSEPH B. BERIAULT, Seattle, Wash. Filed June 10, 1919. Serial No. 119,396. PUBLISHED SEPTEMBER 23, 1919.

128,626. CREAM OR SALVE FOR CONGESTION AND INFLAMMATION, APPLIED LOCALLY. JOSEPH BERRY, Binghamton, N. Y. Filed July 10, 1919. Serial No. 120,404. PUBLISHED SEPTEMBER 23, 1919.

128,627. FUEL CONTROL FOR INTERNAL-COMBUSTION ENGINES. BERRY & LEWIS, New York, N. Y. Filed June 22, 1918. Serial No. 111,742. PUBLISHED SEPTEMBER 30, 1919.

128,628. HEALING COMPOUNDS OF AN ANTISEPTIC NATURE. DAVID ALEXANDER BICKELL, Lethbridge, Alberta, Canada, assignor to San-tro-pas Manufacturing Company, Limited, Lethbridge, Alberta, Canada. Filed November 23, 1918. Serial No. 114,311. PUBLISHED SEPTEMBER 23, 1919.

128,629. CONFECTIONERY — NAMELY, CANDY KISSES. BINGHAMTON CANDY Co., Binghamton, N. Y. Filed June 28, 1919. Serial No. 120,029. PUBLISHED OCTOBER 7, 1919.

128,630. VALVES FOR INTERNAL-COMBUSTION ENGINES. BIRRELL SILENT MOTOR Co. INC., Chicago, Ill. Filed June 20, 1919. Serial No. 119,793. PUBLISHED SEPTEMBER 30, 1919.

128,631. COMPOUND GROUND FEED FOR RABBITS AND SIMILAR ANIMALS. BLATCHFORD CALF MEAL COMPANY, Waukegan, Ill. Filed April 17, 1919. Serial No. 117,556. PUBLISHED SEPTEMBER 30, 1919.

128,632. CERTAIN NAMED FEEDS FOR ANIMALS AND POULTRY. BLATCHFORD CALF MEAL COMPANY, Waukegan, Ill. Filed July 17, 1919. Serial No. 120,633. PUBLISHED OCTOBER 14, 1919.

128,633. MEN'S NECKTIES AND FOUR-IN-HAND SCARFS. BLOCK & DREXLER, New York, N. Y.; said Drexler assignor to said Block. Filed March 31, 1919. Serial No. 117,033. PUBLISHED OCTOBER 7, 1919.

128,634. THROWN SILK. ABRAM BLOOM Co., INC., Paterson, N. J. Filed April 7, 1919. Serial No. 117,217. PUBLISHED SEPTEMBER 16, 1919.

128,635. CANDY. BODINSON-TERRELL CANDY Co., Chicago, Ill. Filed June 25, 1919. Serial No. 119,931. PUBLISHED SEPTEMBER 23, 1919.

128,636. TOILET WATER. THE BONHEUR Co. INC., Syracuse, N. Y. Filed August 12, 1919. Serial No. 121,562. PUBLISHED OCTOBER 7, 1919.

128,637. NON-ALCOHOLIC NON-CEREAL MALTLESS BEVERAGES SOLD AS SOFT DRINKS — VIZ., GINGER-BEER. THE BOOTH & PLATT Co., Bridgeport, Conn. Filed May 28, 1919. Serial No. 118,984. PUBLISHED OCTOBER 7, 1919.

128,638. SPARK-PLUGS. OTHO DALE BOWERS, Richmond, Ind. Filed April 28, 1919. Serial No. 117,919. PUBLISHED SEPTEMBER 16, 1919.

128,639. MEDICINAL PREPARATION FOR THE TREATMENT OF CATARRH AND OTHER DISEASES OF THE RESPIRATORY ORGANS. WILLIS C. BRADLEY, Marshfield, Oreg. Filed March 31, 1919. Serial No. 117,032. PUBLISHED OCTOBER 7, 1919.

128,640. GERMICIDE. BRADLEY & VROOMAN COMPANY, Chicago, Ill. Filed May 19, 1919. Serial No. 118,644. PUBLISHED SEPTEMBER 30, 1919.

128,641. LADIES' PETTICOATS. J. BRENER Co., Boston, Mass. Filed April 9, 1919. Serial No. 117,291. PUBLISHED OCTOBER 7, 1919.

128,642. HATS FOR MEN. BRIGHAM-HOPKINS COMPANY, Baltimore, Md. Filed June 17, 1919. Serial No. 119,696. PUBLISHED OCTOBER 7, 1919.

128,643. ROUGE. GEORGIE M. BROHARD, Philadelphia, Pa. Filed July 11, 1919. Serial No. 120,443. PUBLISHED OCTOBER 7, 1919.

128,644. WOMEN'S DRESS-SHIELDS. BROOKLYN SHIELD & RUBBER Co., Brooklyn, N. Y. Filed February 28, 1919. Serial No. 116,200. PUBLISHED SEPTEMBER 16, 1919.

128,645. STEEL FORGINGS AND STEEL CASTINGS. HARRY CADWALLADER, Jr., Philadelphia, Pa. Filed June 7, 1919. Serial No. 119,292. PUBLISHED SEPTEMBER 30, 1919.

128,646. VINEGAR. CASCADE CIDER COMPANY, Springville, N. Y. Filed June 30, 1919. Serial No. 120,093. PUBLISHED SEPTEMBER 23, 1919.

128,647. CHEMICALS FOR USE IN THE MANUFAC-
TURE OF LEATHER. CATARACT CHEMICAL COM-
PANY, INC., Buffalo, N. Y.
Filed March 31, 1919. Serial No. 117,035. PUBLISHED
OCTOBER 7, 1919.

128,648. MEN'S OUTER SHIRTS, PAJAMAS, KNIT
AND WOVEN UNDERWEAR, COLLARS, NECK-
TIES, AND HOSIERY. CHAIN SHIRT SHOPS, INC.,
New York, N. Y.
Filed May 12, 1919. Serial No. 118,374. PUBLISHED
OCTOBER 7, 1919.

128,649. MEDICINES FOR FEMALE DISEASES. CHAT-
TANOOGA MEDICINE CO., Chattanooga, Tenn.
Filed July 1, 1919. Serial No. 120,151. PUBLISHED
SEPTEMBER 30, 1919.

128,650. SHINGLES. CHINOOK LUMBER & SHINGLE CO.,
Seattle, Wash.
Filed June 6, 1917. Serial No. 104,352. PUBLISHED
SEPTEMBER 16, 1919.

128,651. CANNED SALMON, CANNED PEACHES, AND
CANNED TOMATOES. CHRISTENSON, HANIFY &
WEATHERWAX, San Franciso, Calif.
Filed July 19, 1919. Serial No. 120,694. PUBLISHED
SEPTEMBER 30, 1919.

128,652. CANNED PEARS, CANNED SALMON, AND
CANNED TOMATOES. CHRISTENSON, HANIFY &
WEATHERWAX, San Francisco, Calif.
Filed July 19, 1919. Serial No. 120,696. PUBLISHED
SEPTEMBER 23, 1919.

128,653. ICE-CREAM, BUTTER, SWEET MILK, FRESH
CREAM, FRESH BUTTERMILK, AND EGGS. CITY
CONSUMERS CO., Paducah, Ky.
Filed June 10, 1919. Serial No. 119,403. PUBLISHED
OCTOBER 7, 1919.

128,654. PREPARATION FOR THE AMELIORATION
OF PYORRHEA ALVEOLARIS, GINGIVITIS, AND
BLEEDING OR RECEDING GUMS. CHARLES S.
COHEN, Newark, N. J.
Filed June 22, 1917. Serial No. 104,608. PUBLISHED
FEBRUARY 11, 1919.

128,655. WHEAT-FLOUR. THE COLORADO MILLING &
ELEVATOR CO., Denver, Colo., and Weiser, Idaho.
Filed July 28, 1919. Serial No. 120,985. PUBLISHED
SEPTEMBER 30, 1919.

128,656. SPECIAL PACK, GRADE, AND QUALITY OF
DRESSED POULTRY, BUTTER, AND EGGS. Co-
LUMBIA PRODUCE COMPANY, Columbia, Nashville, Wa-
verly, McEwen, Dickson, Loretto, Lawrenceburg, Fay-
etteville, Petersburg, Chapel Hill, and Lewisburg,
Tenn.
Filed June 23, 1919. Serial No. 119,847. PUBLISHED
OCTOBER 7, 1919.

128,657. HOT-AIR FURNACES. COMMUNITY FURNACE
COMPANY, Covington, Ky.
Filed July 5, 1919. Serial No. 120,276. PUBLISHED
SEPTEMBER 23, 1919.

128,658. HYPOPHOSPHITES COMPOUND IN TABLET
FORM. CONTINENTAL DRUG CORPORATION, St. Louis,
Mo.
Filed July 11, 1919. Serial No. 120,449. PUBLISHED
SEPTEMBER 23, 1919.

128,659. CERTAIN NAMED MEN'S AND BOYS' GAR-
MENTS FOR UNDER AND OUTER WEAR. COOPER,
COATE & CASEY DRY GOODS CO., Los Angeles, Calif.,
and New York, N. Y.
Filed May 16, 1919. Serial No. 118,539. PUBLISHED
SEPTEMBER 16, 1919.

128,660. HYDRAULIC AND CENTRIFUGAL PUMPS
AND TURBINES. COPPUS ENGINEERING AND EQUIP-
MENT COMPANY, Worcester, Mass.
Filed December 4, 1916. Serial No. 99,700. PUB-
LISHED SEPTEMBER 30, 1919.

128,661. CANDY. CLARENCE A. CRANE, Cleveland, Ohio.
Filed August 9, 1919. Serial No. 121,447. PUBLISHED
OCTOBER 7, 1919.

128,662. DRIED PARTS OF EPHEDRA-PLANT FOR
MAKING TEA FOR TREATING CERTAIN DIS-
EASES, AND BLOOD-PURIFIER. JAMES J. CRAW-
FORD, Los Angeles, Calif.
Filed June 9, 1919. Serial No. 119,337. PUBLISHED
SEPTEMBER 30, 1919.

128,663. COFFEE. CRESCENT COFFEE MILLS, INC., New
Orleans, La.
Filed July 1, 1919. Serial No. 120,153. PUBLISHED
SEPTEMBER 23, 1919.

128,664. COFFEE. CRESCENT COFFEE MILLS, INC., New
Orleans, La.
Filed July 1, 1919. Serial No. 120,154. PUBLISHED
SEPTEMBER 23, 1919.

128,665. TEA. CRESCENT COFFEE MILLS, INC., New Or-
leans, La.
Filed July 1, 1919. Serial No. 120,156. PUBLISHED
SEPTEMBER 23, 1919.

128,666. REMEDY FOR CUTS, BRUISES, BURNS,
SPRAINS, AND OTHER WOUNDS. CREOTINA CHEM-
ICAL COMPANY, St. Louis, Mo.
Filed April 14, 1919. Serial No. 117,440. PUBLISHED
SEPTEMBER 23, 1919.

128,667. COFFEE. CRESCENT COFFEE MILLS, INC., New
Orleans, La.
Filed July 1, 1919. Serial No. 120,157. PUBLISHED
SEPTEMBER 30, 1919.

128,668. PERFUMES. ALBERTO CRUSELLAS, Habana,
Cuba.
Filed July 24, 1919. Serial No. 120,866. PUBLISHED
SEPTEMBER 23, 1919.

128,669. COMPOUND FOR STOPPING LEAKS, ELIMI-
NATING RUST, PREVENTING CORROSION AND
FORMATION OF SCALE. MAX DANNENHIRSCH,
Philadelphia, Pa.
Filed July 10, 1919. Serial No. 120,408. PUBLISHED
SEPTEMBER 23, 1919.

128,670. CERTAIN NAMED METALS AND METAL
CASTINGS AND FORGINGS. ARTHUR C. DAVIDSON,
New York, N. Y.
Filed August 13, 1919. Serial No. 121,619. PUBLISHED
OCTOBER 7, 1919.

128,671. PNEUMATIC PUMPS. THE DE LAVAL SEPARA-
TOR COMPANY, New York, N. Y.
Filed May 17, 1919. Serial No. 118,594. PUBLISHED
SEPTEMBER 30, 1919.

128,672. INSECTICIDES. WILLIAM DAMASKE, Seattle,
Wash.
Filed May 29, 1919. Serial No. 119,031. PUBLISHED
SEPTEMBER 30, 1919.

128,673. MEDICINAL BALM FOR FOOT TROUBLES,
SKIN DISEASE, COLD IN HEAD, INSECT-BITES,
PILES, AND INFLAMMATION. ALLAN J. DASH,
Olean, N. Y.
Filed July 2, 1919. Serial No. 120,204. PUBLISHED
SEPTEMBER 30, 1919.

128,674. BUNSEN BURNERS. DETROIT HEATING &
LIGHTING COMPANY, Detroit, Mich.
Filed July 3, 1919. Serial No. 120,240. PUBLISHED
SEPTEMBER 23, 1919.

128,675. MEDICINES FOR CERTAIN NAMED AFFEC-
TIONS. DICKINSON DRUG CO., Los Angeles, Calif.
Filed June 10, 1919. Serial No. 119,402. PUBLISHED
OCTOBER 7, 1919.

128,676. WHEAT-FLOUR. H. DITTLINGER ROLLER MILLS
COMPANY, New Braunfels, Tex.
Filed May 5, 1919. Serial No. 118,138. PUBLISHED
OCTOBER 14, 1919.

128,677. EYE - WASH. FELIX IGNATIUS DROBINSKI,
Brooklyn, N. Y.
Filed July 23, 1919. Serial No. 120,820. PUBLISHED
SEPTEMBER 23, 1919.

128,678. DYES. DUGAS - HUNDLEY CORPORATION, New York, N. Y.
Filed July 26, 1919. Serial No. 120,953. PUBLISHED SEPTEMBER 23, 1919.

128,679. SALT BRICK. EDGERTON SALT BRICK COMPANY, Goldsboro, N. C., and Atlanta, Ga.
Filed July 17, 1919. Serial No. 120,636. PUBLISHED OCTOBER 7, 1919.

128,680. PICKLING COMPOUND FOR CURING MEATS. H. EHRLICH & SONS MFG. CO., St. Joseph, Mo.
Filed July 14, 1919. Serial No. 120,525. PUBLISHED SEPTEMBER 30, 1919.

128,681. ELECTRIC HEATERS, ELECTRIC COOKERS, ELECTRIC SWITCHES, ELECTRIC CIGAR-LIGHTERS, AND ELECTRIC CONNECTOR-PLUGS. THE ELECTRIC & ORDNANCE ACCESSORIES COMPANY LIMITED, Birmingham, England.
Filed May 20, 1919. Serial No. 118,728. PUBLISHED SEPTEMBER 30, 1919.

128,682. WINDOW-SCREENS. EMPIRE ROLLING SCREEN CO. INC., Rochester, N. Y.
Filed February 8, 1918. Serial No. 108,883. PUBLISHED SEPTEMBER 30, 1919.

128,683. CERTAIN NAMED STATIONERY AND PAPER. ENLOW CO. INC., New York, N. Y.
Filed March 31, 1919. Serial No. 117,042. PUBLISHED OCTOBER 7, 1919.

128,684. BREAD. ENTIRE WHEAT BREAD COMPANY, St. Louis, Mo.
Filed August 4, 1919. Serial No. 121,241. PUBLISHED OCTOBER 7, 1919.

128,685. HAIR-TONIC. FRANK EPPOLITO, Chicago, Ill.
Filed July 1, 1919. Serial No. 120,162. PUBLISHED SEPTEMBER 23, 1919.

128,686. BOND - PAPER, CORRESPONDENCE, NON-CARBONIZED TYPEWRITER, AND NON-CARBONIZED MANIFOLD PAPERS AND ONION-SKIN PAPERS. ESLEECK MANUFACTURING CO., Turners Falls, Mass.
Filed April 2, 1919. Serial No. 117,110. PUBLISHED SEPTEMBER 23, 1919.

128,687. BOND-PAPER, CORRESPONDENCE, NON-CARBONIZED TYPEWRITER PAPER, AND MANIFOLD WRITING - PAPERS AND ONION - SKIN PAPERS. ESLEECK MANUFACTURING CO., Turners Falls, Mass.
Filed April 2, 1919. Serial No. 117,112. PUBLISHED OCTOBER 7, 1919.

128,688. CERTAIN NAMED DYES. ESSEX CHEMICAL WORKS, INC., Belleville, N. J.
Filed June 28, 1919. Serial No. 120,049. PUBLISHED SEPTEMBER 16, 1919.

128,689. CERTAIN NAMED ABRASIVE, DETERGENT, AND POLISHING MATERIALS. THE ESSEX LABORATORIES INC., Newark, N. J.
Filed July 8, 1919. Serial No. 120,341. PUBLISHED SEPTEMBER 30, 1919.

128,690. CHILDREN'S PLAY-SUITS, MEN'S OVERALLS AND OVERSHIRTS. EVERWEAR MFG. CO., San Francisco, Calif.
Filed March 13, 1919. Serial No. 116,535. PUBLISHED SEPTEMBER 23, 1919.

128,691. SPARK-PLUGS. EXPRESS SPARK PLUG CORPORATION, Washington, D. C.
Filed June 10, 1919. Serial No. 119,410. PUBLISHED SEPTEMBER 9, 1919.

128,692. LEATHER. FEBECO LEATHER CORPORATION, Wilmington, Del., and New York, N. Y.
Filed July 9, 1919. Serial No. 120,377. PUBLISHED SEPTEMBER 23, 1919.

128,693. SNAP-FASTENERS AND PLACKET-FASTENERS. FEDERAL SNAP FASTENER CORPORATION, New York, N. Y.
Filed June 14, 1919. Serial No. 119,598. PUBLISHED SEPTEMBER 16, 1919.

128,694. MEDICINE FOR SCARS, FROST - BITES, CROUP, TOOTHACHE, BRONCHIAL COLDS, AND SPRAINS OR MUSCULAR PAIN. LEE FISHER, Mount Sterling, Ky.
Filed June 12, 1919. Serial No. 119,509. PUBLISHED SEPTEMBER 16, 1919.

128,695. HOSIERY FOR MEN, WOMEN, AND CHILDREN. ROBERT J. FISHER, Athens, Tenn.
Filed June 6, 1919. Serial No. 119,266. PUBLISHED SEPTEMBER 16, 1919.

128,696. PREPARATION FOR CERTAIN NAMED DISEASES. ANNIE T. FLOREIN, Cincinnati, Ohio.
Filed July 3, 1919. Serial No. 120,245. PUBLISHED OCTOBER 7, 1919.

128,697. MEDICINES FOR CERTAIN NAMED DISEASES AND AFFECTIONS. FOLEY & COMPANY, Chicago, Ill.
Filed June 27, 1919. Serial No. 120,002. PUBLISHED OCTOBER 7, 1919.

128,698. UNFINISHED AND MACHINED IRON AND STEEL FORGINGS. THE FORGED PRODUCTS CO., Chicago, Ill.
Filed June 7, 1919. Serial No. 119,298. PUBLISHED SEPTEMBER 16, 1919.

128,699. HAIR-TONICS. FRANK L. FRANCIS, Newark, N. J.
Filed June 12, 1919. Serial No. 119,507. PUBLISHED OCTOBER 7, 1919.

128,700. WOMEN'S LEATHER SHOES, FABRIC SHOES, AND SHOES CONSISTING OF PART LEATHER AND PART FABRIC. FREDERICK & NELSON, Seattle, Wash.
Filed April 29, 1919. Serial No. 117,973. PUBLISHED SEPTEMBER 30, 1919.

128,701. GINGER-ALE. FRENCH VALLEY SPRINGS INCORPORATED, Meadville, Pa.
Filed July 17, 1919. Serial No. 120,639. PUBLISHED OCTOBER 7, 1919.

128,702. CANDY. JOS. B. FUNKE COMPANY, La Crosse, Wis.
Filed June 6, 1919. Serial No. 119,265. PUBLISHED OCTOBER 7, 1919.

128,703. MEDICINAL PREPARATION FOR VENEREAL DISEASES. JOHN B. FUQUA, Altus, Okla.
Filed June 8, 1918. Serial No. 111,430. PUBLISHED SEPTEMBER 30, 1919.

128,704. DRESS-SHIELDS. ELLA N. GAILLARD, New York, N. Y., and Washington, D. C.
Filed June 27, 1919. Serial No. 120,004. PUBLISHED SEPTEMBER 23, 1919.

128,705. CONDENSED MILK. GALETON DAIRY PRODUCTS CO., Galeton, Pa.
Filed July 2, 1919. Serial No. 120,205. PUBLISHED SEPTEMBER 23, 1919.

128,706. CORN CURE. EVE GARTENLAUB, New York, N. Y.
Filed June 19, 1919. Serial No. 119,768. PUBLISHED OCTOBER 7, 1919.

128,707. FUR-DYES. THE GASKILL CHEMICAL CORPORATION, Brooklyn, N. Y.
Filed July 8, 1919. Serial No. 120,346. PUBLISHED SEPTEMBER 30, 1919.

128,708. ACETYLENE GAS. THE GAS PRODUCTS CO., Columbus, Ohio.
Filed July 19, 1919. Serial No. 120,703. PUBLISHED SEPTEMBER 23, 1919.

128,709. HOME-MADE CANDIES AND CHOCOLATES. WILLIAM HENRY GATES, Norfolk, Va.
Filed June 9, 1919. Serial No. 119,344½. PUBLISHED SEPTEMBER 30, 1919.

128,710. CERTAIN NAMED ELECTRICAL APPARATUS, MACHINES, AND SUPPLIES. GENERAL MOTORS CORPORATION, Detroit, Mich.
Filed June 30, 1919. Serial No. 120,107. PUBLISHED SEPTEMBER 30, 1919.

128,711. INSECTICIDES, DISINFECTANTS, AND DEODORIZERS. Charles M. Gerhold, Philadelphia, Pa.
Filed August 8, 1919. Serial No. 121,388. PUBLISHED OCTOBER 14, 1919.

128,712. ELECTRICALLY-HEATED VESSELS FOR HEATING BEVERAGES. H. B. Gibson Co., Inc., New York, N. Y.
Filed October 15, 1918. Serial No. 113,745. PUBLISHED SEPTEMBER 30, 1919.

128,713. EFFERVESCENT SALT COMBINED WITH FRUIT DERIVATIVES. Golden Seal Laboratories, Inc., Parkersburg, W. Va.
Filed July 7, 1919. Serial No. 120,307. PUBLISHED SEPTEMBER 23, 1919.

128,714. EGGS. Goodman & Beer Company, Inc., New Orleans, La.
Filed July 9, 1919. Serial No. 120,380. PUBLISHED OCTOBER 14, 1919.

128,715. BOOTS AND SHOES OF LEATHER, FABRIC, AND CANVAS FOR MEN, WOMEN, AND CHILDREN. W. R. Grace & Co., New York, N. Y.
Filed June 5, 1919. Serial No. 119,235. PUBLISHED SEPTEMBER 23, 1919.

128,716. DYES. W. R. Grace & Company, New York, N. Y., and San Francisco, Calif.
Filed August 11, 1919. Serial No. 121,528. PUBLISHED SEPTEMBER 30, 1919.

128,717. HAIR-DRESSINGS, SHAMPOO, AND HAIR-GLOSS. S. & M. Greene, Brooklyn, N. Y.
Filed August 1, 1919. Serial No. 121,175. PUBLISHED SEPTEMBER 30, 1919.

128,718. DRESS-SKIRTS. Grewen Fabric Co. Inc., Johnstown, N. Y.
Filed June 23, 1919. Serial No. 119,854. PUBLISHED SEPTEMBER 30, 1919.

128,719. MEN'S, BOYS', AND YOUTHS' LEATHER SHOES. W. H. Griffin Company, Manchester, N. H.
Filed June 3, 1919. Serial No. 119,157. PUBLISHED SEPTEMBER 9, 1919.

128,720. WEEDING-TROWELS. William I. Hare, New York, N. Y.
Filed May 1, 1919. Serial No. 118,053. PUBLISHED AUGUST 5, 1919.

128,721. WOMEN'S, MISSES', AND JUNIORS' SUITS, COATS, SKIRTS, AND DRESSES. Levy Harrison, Philadelphia, Pa.
Filed July 11, 1919. Serial No. 120,458. PUBLISHED OCTOBER 7, 1919.

128,722. MOTION-PICTURE FILMS. Charles S. Hart Film Company, New York, N. Y.
Filed June 4, 1919. Serial No. 119,193. PUBLISHED OCTOBER 7, 1919.

128,723. CEREAL NON-INTOXICATING MALT BEVERAGE. Harvard Company, Lowell, Mass.
Filed May 24, 1919. Serial No. 118,884. PUBLISHED OCTOBER 7, 1919.

128,724. GINGER-ALE, A NON-ALCOHOLIC CARBONATED BEVERAGE, MALTLESS, NOT OF A CEREAL NATURE. Harvard Brewing Company, (now by change of name Harvard Company,) Lowell, Mass.
Filed October 17, 1918. Serial No. 113,775. PUBLISHED OCTOBER 7, 1919.

128,725. LIVE HOGS. Fred H. Hassler, Manning, Iowa.
Filed February 26, 1919. Serial No. 116,158. PUBLISHED SEPTEMBER 23, 1919.

128,726. INSECTICIDES, GERMICIDES FOR OTHER USES THAN ON THE HUMAN BODY, DEODORIZERS, DISINFECTANTS. Haynes Chemical Corporation, Richmond, Va.
Filed June 30, 1919. Serial No. 120,109. PUBLISHED SEPTEMBER 23, 1919.

270 O. G.—23

128,727. BREAD AND CAKE. The Health Food Baking Co. Inc., Newport News, Va.
Filed June 4, 1919. Serial No. 119,195. PUBLISHED SEPTEMBER 30, 1919.

128,728. CERTAIN NAMED PIECES OF FURNITURE. Heywood Brothers and Wakefield Company, Gardner, Mass.
Filed July 12, 1918. Serial No. 112,086. PUBLISHED OCTOBER 7, 1919.

128,729. UNDERWEAR FOR MEN, WOMEN, AND CHILDREN. High Rock Knitting Company, Philmont, N. Y.
Filed May 15, 1919. Serial No. 118,516. PUBLISHED SEPTEMBER 2, 1919.

128,730. MARSHMALLOW CRÊME, MARSHMALLOW POWDER AND LEMON, VANILLA, ORANGE, STRAWBERRY, AND RASPBERRY FLAVORING EXTRACTS. The Hipolite Company, St. Louis, Mo.
Filed June 12, 1919. Serial No. 119,517. PUBLISHED OCTOBER 14, 1919.

128,731. TOILET-PAPER, PAPER TOWELING, AND PAPER NAPKINS. The John Hoberg Co., Green Bay, Wis.
Filed May 12, 1919. Serial No. 118,384. PUBLISHED OCTOBER 7, 1919.

128,732. CANDIES. Hoehle & Johnson Inc., Boston, Mass.
Filed July 10, 1919. Serial No. 120,420. PUBLISHED SEPTEMBER 23, 1919.

128,733. SHOE-LACES. Holyoke Braiding Company, Holyoke, Mass.
Filed February 14, 1919. Serial No. 115,855. PUBLISHED SEPTEMBER 16, 1919.

128,734. SHOE-LACES. Holyoke Braiding Company, Holyoke, Mass.
Filed February 14, 1919. Serial No. 115,856. PUBLISHED SEPTEMBER 16, 1919.

128,735. MEDICINE FOR RHEUMATISM, NEURITIS, LUMBAGO, AND ALL RHEUMATIC PAINS. Hoover Medicine Co., Des Moines, Iowa.
Filed May 31, 1919. Serial No. 119,070. PUBLISHED OCTOBER 7, 1919.

128,736. WORK-SHIRTS. Joseph Horowitz & Sons, Inc., New York, N. Y.
Filed June 28, 1919. Serial No. 120,055. PUBLISHED SEPTEMBER 30, 1919.

128,737. ALLOYS CONTAINING NICKEL AND ALUMINUM. Hoskins Manufacturing Company, Detroit, Mich.
Filed December 26, 1917. Serial No. 108,150. PUBLISHED SEPTEMBER 30, 1919.

128,738. ALLOYS CONTAINING NICKEL AND COPPER. Hoskins Manufacturing Company, Detroit, Mich.
Filed December 26, 1917. Serial No. 108,151. PUBLISHED SEPTEMBER 30, 1919.

128,739. COCOANUT-OIL. India Refining Company, Philadelphia, Pa.
Filed July 31, 1919. Serial No. 121,145. PUBLISHED OCTOBER 7, 1919.

128,740. FLAVORING LIQUID OR EXTRACT FOR FOODS. The W. K. Jahn Co., Brooklyn, N. Y.
Filed June 21, 1919. Serial No. 119,831. PUBLISHED SEPTEMBER 23, 1919.

128,741. WHEAT-FLOUR. Jensen & Sons Milling & Grain Co., Nelson, Nebr.
Filed June 17, 1918. Serial No. 111,616. PUBLISHED SEPTEMBER 30, 1919.

128,742. MEDICINE FOR THE TREATMENT OF TUBERCULOSIS. Charles H. Johnson, Salem, Ohio.
Filed July 7, 1919. Serial No. 120,309. PUBLISHED SEPTEMBER 23, 1919.

128,743. PREPARATION FOR TREATING ACIDITY AND INFANT AILMENTS—TO WIT, STOMACH AND BOWEL TROUBLES. MEAD JOHNSON & Co., Evansville, Ind.
Filed May 19, 1919. Serial No. 118,694. PUBLISHED OCTOBER 7, 1919.

128,744. MEDICINES FOR INTERNAL USE AS A STOMACH COMPOUND. AVRAM JUSTER, New York, N. Y.
Filed May 9, 1919. Serial No. 118,310. PUBLISHED OCTOBER 7, 1919.

128,745. LEATHER SHOES FOR MEN, WOMEN, AND CHILDREN. CHARLES M. KAPLAN, Philadelphia, Pa.
Filed May 12, 1919. Serial No. 118,387. PUBLISHED SEPTEMBER 16, 1919.

128,746. COATINGS FOR CANDIES AND CAKES. KELLEY-CLARKE Co., Seattle, Wash.
Filed September 27, 1918. Serial No. 113,450. PUBLISHED OCTOBER 14, 1919.

128,747. CHILDREN'S DRESSES. KELLNER BROS., New York, N. Y.
Filed April 25, 1919. Serial No. 117,841. PUBLISHED JULY 8, 1919.

128,748. SALVE USED IN THE TREATMENT OF CERTAIN NAMED AILMENTS. EDWARD HENRY KETTLEMAN, Independence, Kans.
Filed June 28, 1919. Serial No. 120,057. PUBLISHED SEPTEMBER 23, 1919.

128,749. INSECTICIDE. THE KIL-TONE COMPANY, Vineland, N. J.
Filed March 29, 1919. Serial No. 117,015. PUBLISHED SEPTEMBER 23, 1919.

128,750. OINTMENT USED IN THE TREATMENT OF SKIN DISEASES AND PILES. JOSEPH S. KING, Chicago, Ill.
Filed July 14, 1919. Serial No. 120,539. PUBLISHED OCTOBER 14, 1919.

128,751. WRAPPING-PAPER. KIRCHHEIMER BROS. CO., Chicago, Ill.
Filed May 20, 1919. Serial No. 118,735. PUBLISHED SEPTEMBER 23, 1919.

128,752. CERTAIN NAMED MACHINERY. KOPPEL INDUSTRIAL CAR & EQUIPMENT COMPANY, Koppel and Pittsburgh, Pa.
Filed November 30, 1918. Serial No. 114,430. PUBLISHED SEPTEMBER 30, 1919.

128,753. STOCK FEED COMPOSED OF A MIXTURE OF CRUSHED OR COARSELY-GROUND GRAINS AND ALFALFA-MEAL. CHAS. A. KRAUSE MILLING Co., Greenfield, Wis.
Filed June 13, 1919. Serial No. 119,559. PUBLISHED OCTOBER 14, 1919.

128,754. STOMACH AND LIVER TABLETS. KRIEG WALLACE & MCQUAIDE, Charleston, W. Va.
Filed July 23, 1919. Serial No. 120,829. PUBLISHED SEPTEMBER 23, 1919.

128,755. CERTAIN NAMED CLOTHING FOR MEN AND BOYS. B. KUPPENHEIMER & Co., Chicago, Ill.
Filed May 7, 1919. Serial No. 118,231. PUBLISHED SEPTEMBER 23, 1919.

128,756. CANNING APPARATUS COMPRISING A DOMESTIC BOILER AND A FUEL-BURNING HEATER THEREFOR. KWICK-BATH MFG. CORPORATION, Wilson, N. C.
Filed June 4, 1918. Serial No. 111,364. PUBLISHED SEPTEMBER 30, 1919.

128,757. ELECTRICALLY-DRIVEN APPARATUS COMPRISING VACUUM-CLEANERS. LANDERS, FRARY & CLARK, New Britain, Conn.
Filed June 4, 1919. Serial No. 119,197. PUBLISHED SEPTEMBER 30, 1919.

128,758. CERTAIN NAMED CUTLERY, MACHINERY, AND TOOLS, AND PARTS THEREOF. LATTA-MARTIN PUMP Co., Hickory, N. C.
Filed April 5, 1919. Serial No. 117,189. PUBLISHED AUGUST 19, 1919.

128,759. CERTAIN NAMED CUTLERY, MACHINERY, AND TOOLS, AND PARTS THEREOF. LATTA-MARTIN PUMP Co., Hickory, N. C.
Filed April 5, 1919. Serial No. 117,190. PUBLISHED AUGUST 19, 1919.

128,760. CERTAIN NAMED CUTLERY, MACHINERY, AND TOOLS, AND PARTS THEREOF. LATTA-MARTIN PUMP Co., Hickory, N. C.
Filed April 5, 1919. Serial No. 117,191. PUBLISHED AUGUST 19, 1919.

128,761. REMEDY FOR CERTAIN NAMED AILMENTS. JOHN W. LATTY, St. Louis, Mo.
Filed June 25, 1919. Serial No. 119,951. PUBLISHED SEPTEMBER 16, 1919.

128,762. PREPARATIONS FOR CERTAIN NAMED DISEASES AND AFFECTIONS. ROBERT L. LAWLESS, Danville, Va.
Filed June 7, 1919. Serial No. 119,309. PUBLISHED SEPTEMBER 30, 1919.

128,763. KNITTED UNDERWEAR FOR WOMEN, MISSES, AND CHILDREN. LAWRENCE KNITTING COMPANY, Wilmington, Del., and Philadelphia, Pa.
Filed July 10, 1919. Serial No. 120,424. PUBLISHED OCTOBER 7, 1919.

128,764. ANTISEPTIC AND DISINFECTANT. LEHN & FINK, INC., New York, N. Y.
Filed July 11, 1919. Serial No. 120,464. PUBLISHED SEPTEMBER 30, 1919.

128,765. CERTAIN NAMED FOOTWEAR FOR WOMEN AND MISSES. THE LINDER SHOE Co., Carlisle, Pa.
Filed July 24, 1919. Serial No. 120,874. PUBLISHED OCTOBER 7, 1919.

128,766. TUBULAR TAGS USED ON INSULATED WIRES. MATTHEW H. LOUGHRIDGE, Bogota, N. J.
Filed July 1, 1918. Serial No. 111,904. PUBLISHED SEPTEMBER 16, 1919.

128,767. CORN-SOLVENT FOR THE REMOVAL OF CORNS, WARTS, CALLOUSES. THE LOUIS DRUG COMPANY, Bay City, Mich.
Filed June 19, 1919. Serial No. 119,771. PUBLISHED SEPTEMBER 30, 1919.

128,768. PHOTOGRAPHIC DEVELOPERS. LOWENSTEIN RADIO COMPANY, INC., Brooklyn, N. Y., and Newark and Elizabeth, N. J.
Filed July 24, 1919. Serial No. 120,873. PUBLISHED SEPTEMBER 23, 1919.

128,769. SPARK - PLUGS. LYONS IGNITION COMPANY, Paterson, N. J.
Filed June 18, 1919. Serial No. 119,741. PUBLISHED SEPTEMBER 9, 1919.

128,770. PRESERVATIVE PREPARATION FOR TREATING VEGETABLE FIBERS. LYSTER CHEMICAL COMPANY, Augusta, Me., and New York, N. Y.
Filed July 8, 1919. Serial No. 120,351. PUBLISHED OCTOBER 7, 1919.

128,771. SPRAY FOR ANIMALS, &c. LYSTER CHEMICAL COMPANY, Augusta, Me., and New York, N. Y.
Filed July 8, 1919. Serial No. 120,352. PUBLISHED SEPTEMBER 30, 1919.

128,772. CHOCOLATES. J. G. MCDONALD CHOCOLATE Co., Salt Lake City, Utah.
Filed August 4, 1919. Serial No. 121,248. PUBLISHED OCTOBER 7, 1919.

128,773. BOOTS AND SHOES OF LEATHER. OF FABRIC, AND OF THE COMBINATION OF LEATHER AND FABRIC. W. H. MCELWAIN COMPANY, Boston, Mass.
Filed July 23, 1919. Serial No. 120,840. PUBLISHED OCTOBER 7, 1919.

128,774. CANNED SALMON. EDWARD BURTON MC-GOVERN, Seattle, Wash.
Filed July 1, 1919. Serial No. 120,171. PUBLISHED SEPTEMBER 23, 1919.

128,775. VARIOUS MEDICINAL PREPARATIONS AND PRODUCTS. THE DR. J. H. MCLEAN MEDICINE CO., St. Louis, Mo.
Filed June 9, 1919. Serial No. 119,352. PUBLISHED SEPTEMBER 30, 1919.

128,776. CERTAIN MEDICINAL PREPARATION—NAMELY, PURGATIVE PILLS. THE DR. J. H. MCLEAN MEDICINE Co., St. Louis, Mo.
Filed June 26, 1919. Serial No. 119,982. PUBLISHED SEPTEMBER 23, 1919.

128,777. SUGAR. ROBERT M. MCMULLEN, New York, N. Y.
Filed August 9, 1919. Serial No. 121,479. PUBLISHED OCTOBER 7, 1919.

128,778. COUGH REMEDY AND RECONSTRUCTIVE TONIC. MACMORRIS DRUG CO., Newark, N. J.
Filed July 19, 1919. Serial No. 120,707. PUBLISHED OCTOBER 14, 1919.

128,779. CERTAIN NAMED CONSTRUCTION MATERIALS. MARINE DECKING & SUPPLY CO., Philadelphia and Easton, Pa.
Filed May 10, 1919. Serial No. 118,350. PUBLISHED SEPTEMBER 16, 1919.

128,780. OINTMENT FOR CERTAIN NAMED AILMENTS. WARREN MARSHALL, Kansas City, Kans.
Filed June 13, 1919. Serial No. 119,573. PUBLISHED SEPTEMBER 16, 1919.

128,781. FUR-BEARING SKINS. MARTIN-LASKIN COMPANY, Milwaukee, Wis.
Filed April 29, 1919. Serial No. 117,983. PUBLISHED SEPTEMBER 16, 1919.

128,782. LIP-ROUGE, FACE-POWDER, FACE-CREAM, ROUGE-CREAM, NAIL-POLISH, AND CHEMICAL FACIAL HAIR-REMOVER. BLANCHE M. MASON, Chicago, Ill.
Filed June 6, 1919. Serial No. 119,271. PUBLISHED SEPTEMBER 16, 1919.

128,783. RUBBER SOLES AND HEELS. MAYFLOWER RUBBER WORKS COMPANY, Braintree, Mass.
Filed April 22, 1919. Serial No. 117,730. PUBLISHED OCTOBER 7, 1919.

128,784. CERTAIN NAMED CHEMICALS, MEDICINES, AND PHARMACEUTICAL PREPARATIONS. THE WILLIAM S. MERRELL COMPANY, Cincinnati, Ohio.
Filed July 21, 1919. Serial No. 120,764. PUBLISHED SEPTEMBER 23, 1919.

128,785. ELECTRIC PANEL-BOARDS. METROPOLITAN ELECTRIC MFG. CO., Long Island City, N. Y.
Filed June 12, 1919. Serial No. 119,528. PUBLISHED SEPTEMBER 9, 1919.

128,786 WATER-GAGES, OIL-GAGES, AND CRANK-CASE OIL-LEVEL INDICATORS. MICHIGAN LUBRICATOR COMPANY, Detroit, Mich.
Filed June 6, 1919. Serial No. 119,274. PUBLISHED AUGUST 26, 1919.

128,787. WATER-GAGES, OIL-GAGES, AND CRANK-CASE OIL-LEVEL INDICATORS. MICHIGAN LUBRICATOR COMPANY, Detroit, Mich.
Filed June 6, 1919. Serial No. 119,276. PUBLISHED AUGUST 26, 1919.

128,788. CERTAIN NAMED WOMEN'S AND MISSES' GARMENTS FOR OUTER AND UNDER WEAR. J. A. MIGEL, INC., New York, N. Y.
Filed June 16, 1919. Serial No. 119,662. PUBLISHED SEPTEMBER 30, 1919.

128,789. CANDY. CHARLES N. MILLER CO., Boston, Mass.
Filed June 4, 1919. Serial No. 119,200. PUBLISHED SEPTEMBER 30, 1919.

128,790. CANDIES. CHARLES N. MILLER COMPANY, Boston, Mass.
Filed August 12, 1919. Serial No. 121,592. PUBLISHED OCTOBER 7, 1919.

128,791. WRITING - PAPER. MICHAEL MILTON, New York, N. Y.
Filed June 6, 1919. Serial No. 119,272. PUBLISHED SEPTEMBER 23, 1919.

128,792. PNEUMATIC WATER PUMPING AND SUPPLY SYSTEMS. MILWAUKEE AIR POWER PUMP COMPANY, Milwaukee, Wis.
Filed June 9, 1919. Serial No. 119,356. PUBLISHED SEPTEMBER 16, 1919.

128,793. HEATING AND VENTILATING APPARATUS COMPRISING A CABINET CONTAINING A RADIATOR AND CIRCULATING - FANS. MOLINE HEAT, Moline, Ill.
Filed April 26, 1919. Serial No. 117,888. PUBLISHED SEPTEMBER 16, 1919.

128,794. FUEL-IGNITION SUBSTANCE CONSISTING OF ROSIN, LARD-OIL, AND SAWDUST IN SOLIDIFIED FORM. OTTO MORGENTHAL, Dayton, Ohio.
Filed May 14, 1919. Serial No. 118,479. PUBLISHED SEPTEMBER 23, 1919.

128,795. BREAKFAST-BACON. JOHN MORRELL & COMPANY, Ottumwa, Iowa.
Filed June 16, 1919. Serial No. 119,660. PUBLISHED SEPTEMBER 23, 1919.

128,796. WOMEN'S DRESSES. MOSHONTZ BROS. & CO., Cleveland, Ohio.
Filed July 14, 1919. Serial No. 120,545. PUBLISHED OCTOBER 7, 1919.

128,797. PEANUT-OIL. MUSHER & COMPANY, INCORPORATED, New York, N. Y.; Baltimore, Md.; San Diego, Calif., and Washington, D. C.
Filed December 31, 1918. Serial No. 114,916. PUBLISHED SEPTEMBER 30, 1919.

128,798. SESAME-OIL. MUSHER & COMPANY, INCORPORATED, New York, N. Y.; Baltimore, Md., and Washington, D. C.
Filed February 26, 1919. Serial No. 116,163. PUBLISHED SEPTEMBER 30, 1919.

128,799. OINTMENTS FOR THE RELIEF OF BURNS, WARTS, BOILS, AND WOUNDS. Mrs. MARY NAPOLEON, Albuquerque, N. Mex.
Filed March 31, 1919. Serial No. 117,056. PUBLISHED SEPTEMBER 30, 1919.

128,800. POULTRY-POWDER, LICE-KILLER, PREPARATION FOR THE TREATMENT OF CHICKEN-CHOLERA AND ROUP. NATIONAL BLUE RIBBON REMEDY COMPANY, St. Louis, Mo.
Filed July 28, 1919. Serial No. 121,013. PUBLISHED SEPTEMBER 16, 1919.

128,801. ANTISKID-CHAINS. NATIONAL CHAIN COMPANY, New York, N. Y.
Filed June 7, 1919. Serial No. 119,313. PUBLISHED OCTOBER 7, 1919.

128,802. APPLE JAM. NATIONAL FRUIT PRODUCTS COMPANY, INC., Alexandria, Va.
Filed June 18, 1919. Serial No. 119,744. PUBLISHED SEPTEMBER 23, 1919.

128,803. MOLASSES, MINCE-MEAT, OLIVES, MUSTARD, PEANUT-BUTTER, PEPPER, CATSUP, TEA. GEO. R. NEWELL & CO., Minneapolis, Minn.
Filed July 14, 1919. Serial No. 120,549. PUBLISHED SEPTEMBER 30, 1919.

128,804. CERTAIN NAMED ELECTRICAL APPARATUS, MACHINES, AND SUPPLIES. NICHOLAS POWER COMPANY, INC., New York, N. Y.
Filed March 27, 1918. Serial No. 109,830. PUBLISHED SEPTEMBER 30, 1919.

128,805. ARC-LAMPS AND PARTS THEREOF. NICHOLAS POWER COMPANY, INC., New York, N. Y.
Filed March 27, 1918. Serial No. 109,831. PUBLISHED SEPTEMBER 23, 1919.

128,806. CORN-REMOVER COMPOUNDS. THE No-OUCH MFG. Co., Sioux Falls, S. D.
Filed July 14, 1919. Serial No. 120,547. PUBLISHED OCTOBER 7, 1919.

128,807. TABLETS CONTAINING OLIVE-OIL FOR USE AS A LAXATIVE. THE OLIVE TABLET COM-PANY, Columbus, Ohio.
Filed June 13, 1919. Serial No. 119,574. PUBLISHED SEPTEMBER 23, 1919.

128,808. HOSPITAL-SHEETING MADE OF A WATER-PROOF-TREATED FABRIC. THE OMO MFG. Co., Middletown, Conn.
Filed June 4, 1919. Serial No. 119,206. PUBLISHED SEPTEMBER 23, 1919.

128,809. HOSPITAL-SHEETING MADE OF A WATER-PROOF-TREATED FABRIC. THE OMO MFG. Co., Middletown, Conn.
Filed June 4, 1919. Serial No. 119,207. PUBLISHED SEPTEMBER 23, 1919.

128,810. GUM TISSUE. THE OMO MFG. Co., Middletown, Conn.
Filed July 23, 1919. Serial No. 120,843. PUBLISHED OCTOBER 21, 1919.

128,811. PRESERVED SALMON-EGGS. ALVIN F. OP-PELT, Elma, Wash.
Filed August 8, 1919. Serial No. 121,410. PUBLISHED OCTOBER 7, 1919.

128,812. ELECTRICAL INTENSIFIERS FOR INTEN-SIFYING THE SPARK DELIVERED BY SPARK-PLUGS. BITTS PACE, Ironton, Ala.
Filed June 10, 1919. Serial No. 119,386. PUBLISHED SEPTEMBER 30, 1919.

128,813. PEANUTS IN THEIR NATURAL STATE. PA-CIFIC EXPORT LUMBER Co., Portland, Oreg.
Filed May 23, 1919. Serial No. 118,836. PUBLISHED SEPTEMBER 30, 1919.

128,814. HAIR-TONIC. THE PARMOLINE Co., Richmond, Va.
Filed June 11, 1919. Serial No. 119,489. PUBLISHED SEPTEMBER 23, 1919.

128,815. CEREAL BREAKFAST FOOD. THE PATENT CEREALS COMPANY, Geneva and New York, N. Y.
Filed July 28, 1919. Serial No. 121,017. PUBLISHED SEPTEMBER 30, 1919.

128,816. KNITTED AND FLAT UNDERWEAR FOR MEN IN ONE AND TWO PIECE GARMENTS. SAMUEL W. PECK & Co., Brooklyn, N .Y.
Filed May 15, 1919. Serial No. 118,524. PUBLISHED SEPTEMBER 16, 1919.

128,817. FRESH CITRUS FRUITS—NAMELY, OR-ANGES, LEMONS, AND GRAPE-FRUIT; DECIDU-OUS FRUITS—NAMELY, CANTALOUPS. THOMAS H. PEPPERS, Los Angeles, Calif.
Filed July 1, 1919. Serial No. 120,179. PUBLISHED SEPTEMBER 23, 1919.

128,818. METAL CAPS FOR JARS OR BOTTLES. PHOENIX-HERMETIC Co., Chicago, Ill.
Filed May 14, 1919. Serial No. 118,481. PUBLISHED SEPTEMBER 23, 1919.

128,819. CITRUS FRUITS—VIZ., ORANGES AND GRAPE-FRUIT. POLK COUNTY CITRUS SUB-EX-CHANGE, Bartow, Fla.
Filed August 6, 1919. Serial No. 121,315. PUBLISHED OCTOBER 7, 1919.

128,820. LOCOMOTIVE AND MACHINERY AXLES. THE POLLAK STEEL COMPANY, Cincinnati, Ohio.
Filed June 20, 1919. Serial No. 119,811. PUBLISHED SEPTEMBER 16, 1919.

128,821. HOMINY FEED. POSTUM CEREAL COMPANY, Battle Creek, Mich.
Filed July 1, 1919. Serial No. 120,183. PUBLISHED SEPTEMBER 23, 1919.

128,822. SHOES FOR LADIES, MISSES, CHILDREN, AND INFANTS, MADE OF LEATHER. POWELL & CAMPBELL, New York, N. Y.
Filed June 16, 1919. Serial No. 119,668. PUBLISHED OCTOBER 7, 1919.

128,823. ECZEMA - OINTMENT. POWEROL CHEMICAL COMPANY, Pittsburgh, Pa.
Filed June 13, 1919. Serial No. 119,576. PUBLISHED SEPTEMBER 23, 1919.

128,824. LIQUID PUT UP IN CAPSULES TO BE TAKEN INTERNALLY FOR THE TREATMENT OF GONORRHEA. LAWRENCE TAYLOR PRICE, Richmond, Va.
Filed July 21, 1919. Serial No. 120,770. PUBLISHED SEPTEMBER 23, 1919.

128,825. MEN'S AND BOYS' OUTER SHIRTS AND PAJAMAS. PRIME SHIRT Co. INC., New York, N. Y.
Filed July 24, 1919. Serial No. 120,881. PUBLISHED OCTOBER 7, 1919.

128,826. NOVELTY PAPER COVERINGS FOR BOXES. PRODUCER'S PAPER COMPANY, St. Paul, Minn.
Filed May 31, 1919. Serial No. 119,082. PUBLISHED SEPTEMBER 23, 1919.

128,827. ANTISEPTIC GERMICIDE, STYPTIC, AND DEODORANT DRUG. PROPER ANTISEPTIC LABORA-TORY, Cincinnati, Ohio.
Filed June 13, 1919. Serial No. 119,575. PUBLISHED SEPTEMBER 23, 1919.

128,828. CERTAIN NAMED FOOD PRODUCTS IN TINS, GLASS, AND PACKAGES. PURITY CROSS, INC., West Orange, N. J.
Filed May 14, 1919. Serial No. 118,480. PUBLISHED OCTOBER 7, 1919.

128,829. WHEAT-FLOUR. QUAKER CITY FLOUR MILLS COMPANY, Philadelphia, Pa.
Filed July 28, 1919. Serial No. 120,847. PUBLISHED SEPTEMBER 30, 1919.

128,830. CHEMICAL SOLUTION TO CLEAN OUT RADIATORS AND BOILERS. RADA-SOLVT Co., Los Angeles, Calif.
Filed April 17, 1919. Serial No. 117,574. PUBLISHED SEPTEMBER 23, 1919.

128,831. WHEAT-FLOUR. RENO FLOUR MILLS COM-PANY, Hutchinson, Kans.
Filed June 16, 1919. Serial No. 119,675. PUBLISHED SEPTEMBER 23, 1919.

128,832. FROSTING OR MAT - FINISHING LIQUID FOR GLASS, CHINA, AND HARD SUBSTANCES. L. REUSCHE & Co., New York, N. Y.
Filed June 20, 1919. Serial No. 119,813. PUBLISHED SEPTEMBER 30, 1919.

128,833. PREPARATIONS FOR USE IN CERTAIN NAMED DISEASES. A. B. RICHARDS MEDICINE Co., INC., Sherman, Tex.
Filed June 4, 1919. Serial No. 119,210. PUBLISHED OCTOBER 7, 1919.

128,834. CERTAIN NAMED TONICS. F. AD. RICHTER & Co., New York, N. Y.
Filed July 16, 1919. Serial No. 120,622. PUBLISHED OCTOBER 14, 1919.

128,835. LINIMENT FOR CERTAIN NAMED DIS-EASES AND AILMENTS. HOWARD H. RICKER, Minneapolis, Minn.
Filed June 21, 1919. Serial No. 119,838. PUBLISHED SEPTEMBER 23, 1919.

128,836. NON - INTOXICATING MALT BEVERAGES HAVING LESS THAN ONE-HALF OF ONE PER CENT. OF ALCOHOL. GEO. RINGLER & Co., New York, N. Y.
Filed August 14, 1918. Serial No. 112,718. PUBLISHED SEPTEMBER 23, 1919.

128,837. VENTILATORS FOR ROOFS AND SKY-LIGHTS. ROHRMAN-COOPER COMPANY, Chicago, Ill.
Filed May 5, 1919. Serial No. 118,184. PUBLISHED SEPTEMBER 16, 1919.

128,838.   WHEAT-FLOUR.   JACOB ROSENSTEIN, New York, N. Y.
Filed July 28, 1919.   Serial No. 121,022.   PUBLISHED SEPTEMBER 30, 1919.

128,839.   CHEMICAL PREPARATION FOR EXTERMINATING RODENTS.   RODENT EXTERMINATOR LAB ORATORIES, Chicago, Ill.
Filed July 7, 1919.   Serial No. 120,317.   PUBLISHED OCTOBER 7, 1919.

128,840.   SOAP.   SABERTON MFG. CO., Tampa, Fla.
Filed July 15, 1919.   Serial No. 120,582.   PUBLISHED SEPTEMBER 30, 1919.

128,841.   MAGAZINE-PENCILS.   SALZ BROTHERS, New York, N. Y.
Filed May 29, 1919.   Serial No. 119,052.   PUBLISHED SEPTEMBER 23, 1919.

128,842.   FRESH ORANGES.   SANTIAGO ORANGE GROWERS ASSOCIATION, Orange, Calif.
Filed June 10, 1919.   Serial No. 119,447.   PUBLISHED SEPTEMBER 30, 1919.

128,843.   FOOD-FLAVORING EXTRACTS.   THE C. F. SAUER COMPANY, Richmond, Va.
Filed May 28, 1919.   Serial No. 119,008.   PUBLISHED SEPTEMBER 23, 1919.

128,844.   CLEANING PREPARATION FOR REMOVING TAR, GREASE, AND OILS FROM AUTOMOBILES AND VARNISHED SURFACES.   WILLIAM H. SCHAFFER, Cumberland, Md.
Filed February 1, 1918.   Serial No. 108,755.   PUBLISHED OCTOBER 21, 1919.

128,845.   SARSAPARILLA, GINGER-ALE, AND LEMON-SODA.   ADAM SCHEIDT BEVERAGE CO., Norristown, Pa.
Filed July 24, 1919.   Serial No. 120,885.   PUBLISHED OCTOBER 7, 1919.

128,846.   PREPARATION FOR USE ON HAIR AND SCALP.   HERMAN SCLAR, Philadelphia, Pa.
Filed July 23, 1919.   Serial No. 120,859.   PUBLISHED OCTOBER 7, 1919.

128,847.   REMEDY FOR CORNS, CALLOUSES, WARTS, AND BUNIONS.   HARRY SCHLESINGER, Brooklyn, N. Y.
Filed July 18, 1919.   Serial No. 120,678.   PUBLISHED OCTOBER 14, 1919.

128,848.   MOTION-PICTURE FILMS.   SCREEN LETTER BOX, INC., New York, N. Y.
Filed June 7, 1919.   Serial No. 119,318.   PUBLISHED OCTOBER 7, 1919.

128,849.   FLOSS FOR EMBROIDERY PURPOSES, AND COTTON FOR CROCHETING PURPOSES.   THE F. SCHULEMANN CO., New York, N. Y.
Filed June 13, 1919.   Serial No. 119,585.   PUBLISHED SEPTEMBER 23, 1919.

128,850.   MEDICINAL PREPARATION USED EXTERNALLY FOR CONGESTION, INFLAMMATION, BRONCHITIS, SPASMODIC CROUP, SORE THROAT, AND TONSILLITIS.   SENORET CHEMICAL COMPANY, St. Louis. Mo.
Filed August 2, 1919.   Serial No. 121,216.   PUBLISHED SEPTEMBER 30, 1919.

128,851.   OUTER GARMENTS FOR BOYS—VIZ., COATS, JACKETS, TROUSERS, AND KNICKERBOCKERS.   SHEAHAN, KOHN & CO., Chicago, Ill.
Filed April 24, 1919.   Serial No. 117,822.   PUBLISHED SEPTEMBER 30, 1919.

128,852.   CHARGED TABLE - WATER.   ABRAHAM D. SHEPARD, Chicago, Ill.
Filed July 10, 1919.   Serial No. 120,434.   PUBLISHED SEPTEMBER 30, 1919.

128,853.   INSECTICIDES.   THE SHILEY CHEMICAL CO., Missouri Valley, Iowa.
Filed July 18, 1919.   Serial No. 120,679.   PUBLISHED SEPTEMBER 23, 1919.

128,854.   FACE-ROUGE.   NANCYE LATTA SHIREMAN, Birmingham, Ala.
Filed July 5, 1919.   Serial No. 120,292.   PUBLISHED SEPTEMBER 30, 1919.

128,855.   WASH-BLUE.   SIRMON & ELTING, New York, N. Y.
Filed June 5, 1919.   Serial No. 119,254.   PUBLISHED SEPTEMBER 16, 1919.

128,856.   OINTMENT FOR SKIN DISEASES, SCALP ERUPTIONS, BURNS, CUTS, AND KINDRED AFFECTIONS.   THE SKIN REMEDIES COMPANY, Celina, Tex.
Filed June 30, 1919.   Serial No. 120,130.   PUBLISHED SEPTEMBER 23, 1919.

128,857.   PREPARATION FOR THE RELIEF OF CONSTIPATION AND INDIGESTION.   F. A. SLOAN, Albemarle, N. C.
Filed June 30, 1919.   Serial No. 120,133.   PUBLISHED SEPTEMBER 23, 1919.

128,858.   BEESWAX, STEARIC ACID, AND SPERMACETTI.   SMITH & NICHOLS, INCORPORATED, New York, N. Y., and Boston, Mass.
Filed May 27, 1918.   Serial No. 111,224.   PUBLISHED SEPTEMBER 30, 1919.

128,859.   CERTAIN NAMED MEDICINES FOR INTERNAL AND EXTERNAL USE.   MORRIS S. SOIFER, Philadelphia, Pa.
Filed July 30, 1919.   Serial No. 121,131.   PUBLISHED OCTOBER 14, 1919.

128,860.   HOG-CHOLERA MEDICINE.   DAVID SORENSEN, Fortuna, Calif.
Filed June 2, 1919.   Serial No. 119,134.   PUBLISHED OCTOBER 7, 1919.

128,861.   FRESH CITRUS FRUITS — NAMELY, ORANGES, LEMONS, AND GRAPE-FRUIT.   SOUTH LAKE APOPKA CITRUS GROWERS ASSN., Oakland and Tildenville, Fla.
Filed July 1, 1919.   Serial No. 120,193.   PUBLISHED SEPTEMBER 23, 1919.

128,862.   STOCK FEEDS.   SOUTHERN FEED COMPANY, INC., Newport News, Va.
Filed May 19, 1919.   Serial No. 118,708.   PUBLISHED OCTOBER 7, 1919.

128,863.   SPECTACLE AND EYEGLASS FRAMES AND MOUNTINGS AND PARTS THEREFOR.   THE STANDARD OPTICAL CO., Geneva, N. Y.
Filed May 19, 1919.   Serial No. 118,711.   PUBLISHED AUGUST 26, 1919.

128,864.   MEDICATED SOAP.   FREDERICK STEARNS & Co., Detroit, Mich.
Filed May 17, 1919.   Serial No. 118,612.   PUBLISHED OCTOBER 28, 1919.

128,865.   TALCUM POWDERS, PERFUMES, TOILET WATER, FACE-POWDERS, AND FACE-CREAMS.   FREDERICK STEARNS & Co., Detroit, Mich.
Filed June 9, 1919.   Serial No. 119,371.   PUBLISHED SEPTEMBER 30, 1919.

128,866.   STARCH PRODUCT TO BE USED AS AN INGREDIENT IN BAKING.   STEIN-HALL MANUFACTURING COMPANY, Wilmington, Del., and Chicago, Ill.
Filed July 25, 1919.   Serial No. 120,939.   PUBLISHED SEPTEMBER 30, 1919.

128,867.   CANNED PEACHES AND CANNED APRICOTS.   CHARLES STERN & SONS INC., Los Angeles, Calif.
Filed July 1, 1919.   Serial No. 120,187.   PUBLISHED SEPTEMBER 30, 1919.

128,868.   CANNED FRUITS—NAMELY, CANNED PEACHES AND CANNED APRICOTS.   CHARLES STERN & SONS INC., Los Angeles, Calif.
Filed July 1, 1919.   Serial No. 120,189.   PUBLISHED SEPTEMBER 30, 1919.

128,869. CANDIES—NAMELY, SOUR LEMON CANDIES, PITTED - FRUIT - JELLY CANDIES, AND WESTERN - BERRY - JELLY CANDIES. STEARNS-HOLLINSHEAD Co., Portland, Oreg.
Filed June 10, 1919. Serial No. 119,454. PUBLISHED SEPTEMBER 30, 1919.

128,870. PEANUT-OIL. STEELE WEDELES COMPANY, Chicago, Ill.
Filed June 10, 1919. Serial No. 119,445. PUBLISHED SEPTEMBER 23, 1919.

128,871. HAIR AND SCALP TONIC AND CLEANSERS. STERLING PRODUCTS, (INCORPORATED,) Wheeling, W. Va.
Filed July 7, 1919. Serial No. 120,319. PUBLISHED SEPTEMBER 30, 1919.

128,872. CANNED FRUITS—NAMELY, CANNED PEACHES, CANNED PEARS, AND CANNED APRICOTS. CHARLES STERN & SONS INC., Los Angeles, Calif.
Filed July 1, 1919. Serial No. 120,191. PUBLISHED SEPTEMBER 30, 1919.

128,873. CANNED FRUITS—NAMELY, CANNED PEARS, CANNED PEACHES, CANNED APRICOTS. CHARLES STERN & SONS INC., Los Angeles, Calif.
Filed July 1, 1919. Serial No. 120,192. PUBLISHED SEPTEMBER 30, 1919.

128,874. HOSIERY. CHAS. D. STONE & Co., Chicago, Ill.
Filed July 9, 1919. Serial No. 120,396. PUBLISHED OCTOBER 7, 1919.

128,875. MEDICINE USED FOR RELIEF OF INDIGESTION, PELLAGRA, RHEUMATISM, GENERAL DEBILITY, AND AS A SYSTEMIC TONIC. SULF-IRON MEDICINE COMPANY, Birmingham, Ala.
Filed December 14, 1918. Serial No. 114,651. PUBLISHED SEPTEMBER 16, 1919.

128,876. WOOL WASHING AND TREATING OILS. SUN COMPANY, Philadelphia, Pa.
Filed May 22, 1919. Serial No. 118,810. PUBLISHED SEPTEMBER 30, 1919.

128,877. CERTAIN NAMED MEASURING AND SCIENTIFIC APPLIANCES. CHARLES J. TAGLIABUE MFG. CO., Brooklyn, N. Y.
Filed September 18, 1918. Serial No. 113,227. PUBLISHED SEPTEMBER 30, 1919.

128,878. CERTAIN NAMED MEASURING AND SCIENTIFIC APPLIANCES. CHARLES J. TAGLIABUE MFG. CO., Brooklyn, N. Y.
Filed September 18, 1918. Serial No. 113,228. PUBLISHED SEPTEMBER 30, 1919.

128,879. MEDICINAL JELLY FOR SORE THROAT, PNEUMONIA, AND INFLUENZA. ILLES TOTH, Washington, D. C.
Filed July 22, 1919. Serial No. 120,805. PUBLISHED SEPTEMBER 23, 1919.

128,880. CERTAIN NAMED MALT BEVERAGES, EXTRACTS, AND LIQUORS. THE JOHN F. TROMMER EVERGREEN BREWERY, Brooklyn, N. Y.
Filed November 28, 1917. Serial No. 107,659. PUBLISHED OCTOBER 7, 1919.

128,881. LIQUID PREPARATION FOR USE AS A MOUTH-WASH AND NASAL DOUCHE. ERNEST A. TROTH, Philadelphia, Pa.
Filed August 8, 1919. Serial No. 121,426. PUBLISHED OCTOBER 14, 1919.

128,882. BABBITT METAL. UNITED AMERICAN METALS CORPORATION, Brooklyn, N. Y.
Filed June 24, 1919. Serial No. 119,923. PUBLISHED SEPTEMBER 9, 1919.

128,883. HOSIERY FOR MEN, WOMEN, AND CHILDREN. UNITED HOSIERY MILLS CORPORATION, East Chattanooga, Tenn.
Filed July 19, 1919. Serial No. 120,726. PUBLISHED OCTOBER 7, 1919.

128,884. HOSIERY FOR CHILDREN. UNITED HOSIERY MILLS CORPORATION, East Chattanooga, Tenn.
Filed July 19, 1919. Serial No. 120,727. PUBLISHED OCTOBER 7, 1919.

128,885. HOSIERY FOR MEN, WOMEN, AND CHILDREN. UNITED HOSIERY MILLS CORPORATION, East Chattanooga, Tenn.
Filed July 19, 1919. Serial No. 120,729. PUBLISHED OCTOBER 7, 1919.

128,886. CERTAIN NAMED CUTLERY, MACHINERY, AND TOOLS, AND PARTS THEREOF. UNITED SHOE MACHINERY CORPORATION, Paterson, N. J., and Boston, Mass.
Filed January 2, 1919. Serial No. 114,963. PUBLISHED SEPTEMBER 16, 1919.

128,887. MOVING-PICTURE FILMS. UNIVERSAL FILM MANUFACTURING COMPANY, INC., New York, N. Y.
Filed June 23, 1919. Serial No. 119,877. PUBLISHED AUGUST 26, 1919.

128,888. MOVING-PICTURE FILMS. UNIVERSAL FILM MANUFACTURING COMPANY INC., New York, N. Y.
Filed August 7, 1919. Serial No. 121,369. PUBLISHED OCTOBER 7, 1919.

128,889. OLEOMARGARIN. ED. S. VAIL BUTTERINE CO., Chicago, Ill.
Filed August 25, 1917. Serial No. 105,880. PUBLISHED SEPTEMBER 9, 1919.

128,890. WORSTED FINGERING-YARN. VANITY YARN COMPANY, Boston, Mass.
Filed July 8, 1919. Serial No. 120,359. PUBLISHED SEPTEMBER 23, 1919.

128,891. ADDING AND CALCULATING MACHINES. VICTOR ADDING MACHINE Co., Chicago, Ill.
Filed May 28, 1919. Serial No. 119,009. PUBLISHED AUGUST 26, 1919.

128,892. RUBBER OFFSET - BLANKETS. VULCAN PROOFING COMPANY, Brooklyn, N. Y.
Filed June 20, 1919. Serial No. 119,818. PUBLISHED SEPTEMBER 23, 1919.

128,893. THICK OILY PREPARATIONS FOR TREATING HAIR AND SCALP AND USED WHEN PRESSING WITH HOT IRONS. ELLA WALKER MANUFACTURING COMPANY, Sioux City, Iowa.
Filed April 21, 1919. Serial No. 117,714. PUBLISHED SEPTEMBER 16, 1919.

128,894. SKIN-BALM. E. WEBER & Co., Philadelphia, Pa.
Filed July 7, 1919. Serial No. 120,327. PUBLISHED OCTOBER 7, 1919.

128,895. WORSTED KNITTING-YARNS. WILLIAM J. WEIHENMAYER, Philadelphia, Pa.
Filed April 21, 1919. Serial No. 117,716. PUBLISHED SEPTEMBER 16, 1919.

128,896. CERTAIN NAMED GRAIN-HANDLING MACHINERY. WELLER MANUFACTURING COMPANY, Chicago, Ill.
Filed March 6, 1917. Serial No. 101,949. PUBLISHED SEPTEMBER 30, 1919.

128,897. CANNED SALMON. THE WESTERN FISHERIES COMPANY, Seattle, Wash.
Filed July 7, 1919. Serial No. 120,331. PUBLISHED SEPTEMBER 23, 1919.

128,898. CANNED SALMON. THE WESTERN FISHERIES COMPANY, Seattle, Wash.
Filed July 7, 1919. Serial No. 120,333. PUBLISHED SEPTEMBER 23, 1919.

128,899. FACE-CREAM, FACE-POWDER, AND TOILET WATERS. WESTERN HAIR GOODS COMPANY, Chicago, Ill.
Filed June 21, 1919. Serial No. 119,844. PUBLISHED SEPTEMBER 16, 1919.

128,900. ELECTRIC HEATERS. WESTINGHOUSE ELECTRIC & MANUFACTURING COMPANY, East Pittsburgh, Pa.
Filed March 4, 1919. Serial No. 116,294. PUBLISHED MAY 27, 1919.

128,901. CERTAIN NAMED FOODS AND INGREDI-
ENTS OF FOODS. WHITE STOKES CO. INC, Chi-
cago, Ill.
Filed April 12, 1919. Serial No. 117,425. PUBLISHED
SEPTEMBER 23, 1919.

128,902. COVER-PAPERS. LESTER P. WINCHENBAUGH
Co., Boston, Mass.
Filed May 23, 1919. Serial No. 118,865. PUBLISHED
SEPTEMBER 23, 1919.

128,903. MEDICINAL PREPARATION FOR THE
TREATMENT OF HOG DISEASES. WM. WOLTERS,
Winfred, S. D.
Filed July 2, 1919. Serial No. 120,229. PUBLISHED
SEPTEMBER 30, 1919.

128,904. CANDY. JOHN G. WOODWARD & Co., Council
Bluffs, Iowa.
Filed July 7, 1919. Serial No. 120,328. PUBLISHED
SEPTEMBER 30, 1919.

128,905. HOISTS AND TROLLEYS. WRIGHT MFG. CO.,
Lisbon, Ohio.
Filed June 4, 1919. Serial No. 119,222. PUBLISHED
SEPTEMBER 9, 1919.

128,906. HAIR-TONIC, HAIR-POMADE, HAIR-SHAM-
POO, HAIR-SHINE, AND WHITENING-CREAM.
GILES T. YOUNG, Philadelphia, Pa.
Filed July 8, 1919. Serial No. 120,361. PUBLISHED
SEPTEMBER 23, 1919.

128,907. DYES AND DYESTUFFS. J. S. YOUNG &
COMPANY, Hanover, Pa.
Filed July 18, 1919. Serial No. 120,686. PUBLISHED
SEPTEMBER 23, 1919.

128,908. COATED BOOK AND LABEL PAPER. THEO-
DORE S. YOUNGSMA, Chicago, Ill.
Filed May 19, 1919. Serial No. 118,722. PUBLISHED
OCTOBER 7, 1919.

128,909. PREPARATIONS FOR HEADACHES, COUGHS,
COLD IN THE HEAD, LA GRIPPE, FEVER, AND
NEURALGIA. LOUIS ZEH, San Francisco, Calif.
Filed July 28, 1919. Serial No. 121,035. PUBLISHED
SEPTEMBER 30, 1919.

128,910. HEALING-OINTMENT, THE OINTMENT BE-
ING APPLIED EXTERNALLY FOR THE RELIEF
OF INFLAMMATION, STIFFNESS, BRUISES, &c.
OTTO ZEMAN, Chicago, Ill.
Filed July 21, 1919. Serial No. 120,784. PUBLISHED
OCTOBER 7, 1919.

128,911. CERTAIN NAMED OUTER GARMENTS FOR
WOMEN, MISSES, JUNIORS, AND CHILDREN.
ZELENKO & MOSKOWITZ, New York, N. Y.
Filed April 25, 1919. Serial No. 117,857. PUBLISHED
OCTOBER 7, 1919.

128,912. CERTAIN NAMED MEDICINES AND PHAR-
MACEUTICAL PREPARATIONS. VINCENT FERRER
MILLER, San Antonio, Tex.
Filed June 19, 1919. Serial No. 119,772. PUBLISHED
SEPTEMBER 30, 1919.

TRADE-MARK REGISTRATIONS CANCELED.

32,805. AN ANTIRHEUMATIC. FARBENFABRIKEN OF EL-
BERFELD COMPANY, New York, N. Y.
Registered May 2, 1889. Canceled March 8, 1919.

DECISIONS

COMMISSIONER OF PATENTS

AND OF

UNITED STATES COURTS IN PATENT CASES.

DECISIONS OF THE U. S. COURTS.

U. S. Circuit Court of Appeals—Sixth Circuit.

D'ARCY SPRING CO. *et al. v.* MARSHALL VENTILATED
MATTRESS CO.

Decided January 7, 1919.

[259 Fed. Rep., 236.]

1. PATENTS—CONSTRUCTION—VALIDITY.

The Marshall patent, No. 685,160, for a mattress comprising a cover and a plurality of transversely-extending strips of material stitched at intervals to form pockets, etc., and spiral springs arranged in such pockets, *Held* valid, showing invention.

2. SAME—DESCRIPTION—SUFFICIENCY.

Though the patentee did not anticipate the use to which the patented article could be and was put, he is entitled to protection for such use where the adaptability was inherent in the structure shown and described in claims and specifications.

3. SAME—CLAIMS—LIMITATION.

Where a claim defines an element in terms of its form, material, location, or function, thereby apparently creating an express limitation, and the limitation pertains to the inventive step rather than to its environment and imports a substantial function which the patentee considered of importance, forms excluded cannot be considered covered by the patent under the doctrine of equivalency.

4. SAME—INSTRUCTION—LIMITATIONS.

The Marshall patent, No. 685,160, for a mattress comprising a cover and a plurality of transversely-extending strips of material stitched at intervals to form pockets, the pocket of one strip alternating with those of adjacent strip, and spiral springs arranged in such pockets, *Held* limited therein to that form of arrangement and not to be infringed by a mattress similarly constructed where the pockets were arranged with centers equidistant in right-angled directions, so that there was no nesting of the springs.

5. SAME—INFRINGEMENT—DAMAGES.

The president and general manager of a corporation which infringed a patent is not individually liable for damages and profits on infringement unless he inflicted the damages or received the profits otherwise than through the usual relations between officer and corporation.

6. SAME—INFRINGEMENT SUIT—DEFENDANT.

In a suit against a corporation for infringement of patent the president and general manager, in active control of the corporate affairs, may be made defendant, so that he may be personally bound and enjoined.

APPEAL from the District Court of the United States for the Southern Division of the Western District of Michigan; Clarence W. Sessions, judge.

Suit by the Marshall Ventilated Mattress Company against the D'Arcy Spring Company and others. From a decree for complainant, defendants appeal. Decree reversed, in order that new decree may be entered, modified according to the opinion.

Mr. Otis A. Earl for the appellants.

Mr. Taylor E. Brown for the appellee.

Before WARRINGTON, KNAPPEN, and DENISON, Circuit Judges.

DENISON, *Cir. J.:*

Patent No. 685,160 was issued October 22, 1901, to Marshall, and became the property of appellee, who was plaintiff below. It disclosed a mattress or other cushion having a suitable cover, and the resilient body of which was composed of a mass of vertical spiral springs; each spring being contained in a cylindrical pocket of fabric closed at the top and bottom, and several of the pockets being fastened together at their sides, so that they constituted a strip or row of pockets. This was accomplished by taking two strips of fabric of suitable width and imposing one upon the other, or by folding longitudinally upon itself a strip twice as wide, and then stitching transversely at intervals across this double strip. Thus a row of pockets was created, and, after the springs were inserted therein, the ends were closed by whatever further stitching might be necessary. The single claim is:

A mattress comprising a cover and a plurality of transversely extending strips of textile material arranged therein and stitched at intervals to form pockets having closed ends, the pockets of one strip alternating with those of the adjacent strip, and spiral springs arranged in said pockets, substantially as described.

The court below found validity and infringement, and the defendants bring this appeal.

(1, 2) We agree with the court below that the patent involves invention and should be sustained. A strip of fabric, thus transformed into a unitary series of pockets containing springs, was new, and it has proved to have large commercial utility. Perhaps this utility and extensive use have developed from a method of business not described in the patent or anticipated by the patentee, viz. selling the prepared spring-containing strip as raw material suitable to be made up into a mattress or cushion; but this adaptability was inherent in the structure shown and described, and the patentee's lack of complete prevision is not important. (*Goshen Co. v. Bissell Co.*, C. C. A. 6, 72 Fed., 67, 74; 19 C. C. A., 13.)

(3, 4) We cannot give to the presence in the claim of the element, "a cover," the limiting effect which defendants attribute to it. The mattress-cover

[Vol. 270. No. 2.]347

shown in the drawing represented only the familiar environment or field provided for the operation of the mass of covered springs which represented the substance of the invention; and any of the varieties of cover found in the defendants' structures (when finished as intended) must be considered within the inventor's meaning, when he referred to a "cover."

The difficult question is presented by the clause of the claim which reads, "the pockets of one strip alternating with those of the adjacent strip." Obviously, there are two ways in which these rows or strips of pockets may be assembled in order to make a quasi-unitary support for a cushion-top: They may be put together alined, with pocket-centers equidistant in both right-angled directions, or the second row may be moved longitudinally one-half the width of a pocket, and then each pocket will enter partially between two pockets of the first row. In the former case, the rows are wholly distinct from each other and are spaced in both directions the extreme width of the pocket; in the latter case, the pockets of one strip alternate with those of the adjacent strip and the strips have broken joints, or it may be said that the pockets are staggered and nested. The question is whether the finding of infringement should be confined to those structures which have the pockets thus staggered (defendants' first form), or whether those which have the pockets of the first class described (defendants' second form) are so fully the equivalent of the staggered style that they cannot escape. The trial court adopted the latter view.

The rule that an express limitation may not be disregarded and the rule that a form equivalent to a specified form also infringes often seem to come into conflict. There is no fixed formula by which this conflict can be settled, but it must be determined by finding the true meaning of "equivalency" in the case to be decided. In a very fair sense and as to most of the functions involved, it is immaterial whether strips of pockets are arranged in alternate or opposite mutual relation. Considering the scope of the actual invention and of claims which might well have been formulated, there would be little difficulty in finding in defendants' second form the necessary equivalency upon which to predicate infringement, if it were not for the expressly stated requirement about the relative positions of the strips. We assume, as hereafter stated, that this requirement was not inserted under such circumstances as to estop the patentee from asserting his present theory. It follows that the case is to be treated as one of voluntary and unnecessary limitation.

It seems worth while to review briefly some of the controlling or leading cases upon each side of the subject and upon which the parties, respectively, rely. In *Winans* v. *Denmead* (15 How., 341; 14 L. Ed., 717) a claim to the frustum of a cone was held to include as an equivalent the frustum of an octagonal pyramid. It is doubtful whether there was so much discrepancy between the letter of the claim and the defendant's form as has been thought,

since a cone is a pyramid with an infinite number of sides, or, as cited in the opinion, "a polygon of many sides would be equivalent to a circle;" but, passing by this feature of identity, it is clear that the difference was merely in form, and that, in operation and functions and effect, the two were identical. The difference in form did not stand for anything else, and a rule of equivalency so strict as to exclude from the monopoly one form and include the other would tend to raise doubt as to the existence of any patentable invention.

In *Metallic Co.* v. *Brown* (C. C. A. 8, 104 Fed., 345, 352; 43 C. C. A., 568) the claim called for an element located at the side of the horizontal roasting-chamber, but the rule of equivalency served to bring within this claim a structure in which this element was underneath the chamber. Here, also, it may be noted that there was not even a literal inconsistency, since the word "side" is often applied to the top and bottom sides as well as to the horizontal sides; but again there was no function whatever indicated by the location at the horizontal side as distinguished from the location underneath. There was no room to suppose that the inventor could have thought that the location be specified was material to his invention and thus no room to say that he intended to make it material. The conclusion was not to be escaped that the inventor used the term only because it was appropriate for the specific form which happened to be before him.

In *Bundy Co.* v. *Detroit Co.* (94 Fed., 524, 538; 36 C. C. A., 375) this court disregarded the superficial distinction between a key which is rotated and one which is pushed longitudinally. Here, again, there was nothing whatever new in the form or motion of the key; the inventor's forward step pertained to another feature of the mechanism and was to be operated equally well by either form of key. It was in effect held that the specific form of claim reference to an element which was not an inherent part of the new step, but only pertained to a working field therefor, would not be permitted to dominate except in the plainest case.

In *Schieble Co.* v. *Clark* (C. C. A. 6, 217 Fed., 760; 133 C. C. A., 490) the claim called for a driving-shaft in combination with two pairs of running wheels, and the defendant brought the driving-shaft into direct relation with one pair of running wheels only; but he had had the other two running wheels upon his structure, and all their functions with relation to the driving-shaft were performed by a pair of supplementary and otherwise unnecessary rollers. The case does not go as far as some of the others do in disregarding distinctions plausibly claimed.

In *Keystone Co.* v. *Phœnix Co.* (95 U. S., 274; 24 L. Ed., 344) the claim called for "wide and thin drilled eyebars * * * applied on edge." Defendant used round bars, flattened at the ends where eyes were drilled, and (apparently) placed on edge. Though the two forms were equivalent enough in a general way, yet since it appeared that the "wide and thin" form had thereby additional utility, the claim was limited to the form specified.

In *White* v. *Dunbar* (119 U. S., 47; 7 Sup. Ct., 72; 30 L. Ed., 303) the claim specified a lining of textile fabric; defendant used a lining of paper. The main object of the invention was accomplished just as well by the paper as by the cloth; but the court, in its often-cited "nose of wax" opinion, held that they were not equivalents. The principle seems to be that since cloth and paper are not always equivalent and since cloth has distinctive qualities which the patentee might have considered important, he would not be allowed to escape his express declaration that he claimed cloth only. This court has often applied the same rule.

A recent instance is found in *Arnold-Creager Co.* v. *Barkwill Co.*, (246 Fed., 441; 158 C. C. A., 505.) Here the claim provided that certain elements should be located on the end of the material-reservoir, while defendant located them upon the side. This court considered the change sufficient to escape infringement, even though, in a broad sense, there was equivalency. We thought that, by his specification, the inventor had indicated his intent that the elements should be upon the end and his belief that there was substantial and material advantage in having them so located; and we observed that to transfer these elements to the side would require considerable reorganization of the machine and would entirely do away with certain simplicities of construction and directness of action which the inventor had believed important. Under those circumstances, we thought we could not disregard the distinction which the patentee had adopted.

Two of our decisions are urged upon us—one by each party—as controlling; but wo do not so regard either, when applied to a case of voluntary limitation. *Vanmannen* v. *Leonard* (248 Fed., 939. 941; 161 C. C. A., 57) was a case of estoppel by proceedings in the Patent Office. Whether the patentee would have been held so closely to his specified form if his selection had been voluntary and casual, rather than as evidencing the ground upon which he distinguished the reference and secured his patent, need not be considered. The *Vrooman-Penhollow Case* (179 Fed., 296; 102 C. C. A., 484) is also rightly to be thought of as presenting the question of estoppel. The patent issued with a requirement that one named roller should be of "much smaller diameter" than another named roller, and the defendant had the two of the same size. This requirement was inserted after a certain reference had been made, but the court thought it did not in fact serve to distinguish from the reference, and that since it could not have been plausibly thought to import differentiation and since the reference was amply distinguished otherwise, and the difference in size had no function whatever, the patentee could not be charged with having represented the relative size of the rollers to be a patentable difference. It was therefore held

that there was no estoppel to prevent the patentee from afterward claiming that the two forms were equivalent. If it had appeared to the court that the "smaller diameter" was—or that the inventor probably thought it was—important to the full accomplishment of his theory of the machine, there would have been a different case presented.

From a review of these and other familiar cases, we think it is safe to deduce the proposition that where the claim defines an element in terms of its form, material, location or function, thereby apparently creating an express limitation, where that limitation pertains to the inventive step rather than to its mere environment, and where it imports a substantial function which the patentee considered of importance to his invention, the court cannot be permitted to say that other forms, which the inventor thus declared not equivalent to what he claimed as his invention, are nevertheless to be treated as equivalent, even though the court may conclude that his actual invention was of a scope which would have permitted the broader equivalency. Applying this rule, we find that placing the transverse rows of pockets in this alternate nested relation requires the rows to be set about one-fourth closer together than if alined, and therefore increases the cost of filling the required cushion-surface. Certainly this disadvantage would not have been specified, unless it was important. Its distinct utility lies in the fact that a large part of the space which would otherwise be unoccupied between the upper coils of the springs is filled with similar springs, so that the supporting-surface becomes considerably more unitary and the effect is correspondingly smoother and more uniform, and in the further fact that when the springs are thus placed in much closer contact, the pocket is more especially useful in preventing intermeshing of the springs, and in the further fact that when thus placed the spring-containing pockets mutually support each other in their upright position in distinctly-greater degree than if they did not have the close-fitting alternate relationship.

We think the conclusion must follow that the expressly-stated limitation cannot be overcome by applying the rule of equivalency, and that the patentee intended and understood his monopoly to be confined to a structure in which the springs had the alternate relationship which he specified. We are confirmed in this conclusion as to his intent by what occurred in the Patent Office. He urged upon the Examiner the presence of this limitation as a reason for distinguishing from a reference; the Examiner replied that the distinction did not import patentable novelty, and the subject-matter was thereafter dropped from discussion, yet the limitation was retained until the end; and Marshall, therefore, after the subject had come to his atten- tion, declared his belief that the distinction was important. Though there may not be much real difference between relying upon an existing claim detail to avoid a reference and inserting a new detail for the same purpose, yet it is the latter action which creates the ordinary estoppel, and we assume, without deciding, that the record does not show that technical estoppel which often has been developed in this class of cases.

Plaintiff urges that this limitation pertains not to a mechanical element but only to a matter of location, and, hence, that a more liberal rule of equivalency should be applied. We cannot see that it is doctrinally important whether the element said to be missing in defendants' structure is a mechanical element or any other kind of an element. The matter of location or mutual arrangement may be less often vital than the matter of presence of a mechanical part, but this will be because of the peculiar facts of the case and not because of any general rule. Plaintiff also urges that the claim is sufficiently met if the pockets are capable of alternation, even though not so assembled, and says that the pockets which are alined in defendants' cushion (second form), as marketed, will, with use, fall into nested position. If this result happens, it is incidental and accidental. Owing to the difference in top area occupied by the springs in the two methods, it is evident that any partial shifting from the alined to the nested position injures the cushion. This cannot be intended. Marshall's thought that the cushion-cover needed that more perfect support given by the nested, as compared with the alined, form is further shown by his later patent, issued on a copending application, in which he showed and claimed the alined form, provided with supplementary smaller springs, arranged to fill the openings between the larger ones.

The second form must be held to be non-infringing.

(5, 6) The individual defendant, D'Arcy, the president and general manager of the corporation, was held personally liable for accounting as well as for injunction. This is complained of here, although it is not entirely clear that the point was ever brought to the attention of the district judge. It is the rule in this circuit that such individual liability for damages and profits on infringement does not exist unless the officer inflicted the damages or received the profits otherwise than through the usual relations between officer and corporation. (*McSherry Co. v. Dowagiac Co.*, 160 Fed., 948, 965; 89 C. C. A., 26.) There is neither allegation nor proof of any extraordinary relation in this respect, and the accounting for profits and damages should not have been ordered against D'Arcy. As to the propriety of making such a managing and directing officer as D'Arcy a defendant in order that he may be personally bound and enjoined, we have already expressed our approval of the view in the first circuit, rather than that in the seventh. (*National Co. v. Leland*, C. C. A., 194 Fed., 502, 507, 511; 37 C. C. A., 372; *Cazier v. Mackie Co.*, C. C. A. 7, 138 Fed., 654; 71 C. C. A., 104; *Proudfit Co. v. Kalamazoo Co.*, C. C. A. 6, 230 Fed., 120, 140; 144 C. C. A., 418.) For this purpose and to this extent we consider D'Arcy an "active participant," within the exception specified in *Western Co. v. Northern*

Co., (C. C. A. 6, 135 Fed., 80, 89; 67 C. C. A., 553.) If so, he is liable for the costs of the defense which he actively directed. The exemption from costs which we sanctioned in *Ohmer Co. v. Ohmer* (238 Fed., 182, 194; 151 C. C. A., 258) had reference to the costs of this court on appeal.

An injunction is now immaterial, the patent having expired. The decree should be modified, by excepting therefrom articles like plaintiff's Exhibit 17 and by denying D'Arcy's liability to account; in other respects, it should be affirmed.

We do not undertake to consider the extent of damages involved in a cushion in which part of the strips were in alternate relation and part were not. That question has not been argued and cannot be considered as arising on this record.

The decree below is reversed, in order that a new decree may be entered, modified according to this opinion. Appellants will recover costs.

U. S. Circuit Court of Appeals—Seventh Circuit.

KNIGHT SODA FOUNTAIN CO. *v.* WALRUS MFG. CO.

Decided April 4, 1919.

[258 Fed. Rep., 929.]

1. PATENTS—VALIDITY AND INFRINGEMENT—COMBINED JAR AND DIPPER.

The Faries patent, No. 779,271, for a jar and dipper for serving crushed fruit, etc., claim 3 *Held* not infringed. Claims 4 and 5 *Held* invalid for indefiniteness in view of the prior art.

2. SAME—MEASURE OF INVENTION—DEFINITENESS OF CLAIMS.

A patent is sustained not for what the inventor may have done, in effect, but for what is pointed out clearly and distinctly in his claims. As much as is not so claimed belongs to the public.

APPEAL from the District Court of the United States for the Eastern Division of the Northern District of Illinois.

Suit in equity by the Walrus Manufacturing Company against the Knight Soda Fountain Company. Decree for complainant, and defendant appeals. Reversed.

Mr. Donald M. Carter for the appellant.
Mr. Harry Lea Dodson for the appellee.

Before BAKER, ALSCHULER, and EVANS, Circuit Judges.

EVANS, *Cir. J.*:

The patent to Faries, No. 779,271, relates to a jar and dipper for serving crushed fruit, etc. Claims 3, 4, and 5, held valid and infringed, read as follows:

3. The combination of a jar, a cover for the jar, a rod extending below the cover, a dipper on the lower end of the rod, with its dipping edge extended away therefrom, and a handle above the cover, rigidly connected with the rod and shaped to aid in lifting the dipper in a proper filling and emptying position.
4. The combination of a jar having a wide mouth, a cover for the mouth of the jar, a rod attached to the cover and extended downward therefrom, and a dipper on the lower end of the rod, inclined to the rod at such an angle that, when the rod is against a side of the mouth of the jar, the dipper may be made to assume an approximately horizontal position.
5. The combination of a jar having a wide mouth, a cover for the mouth of the jar, a rod attached to the cover and extended obliquely downward therefrom, and a dipper on the lower end of the rod, inclined to the rod at such an angle that the dipper may be made to assume an approximately horizontal position inside the jar.

(1) Unquestionably the patent is very narrow. Only the precise form of construction described in each claim is protected. No wide range of mechanical equivalents can be indulged in. So construing the claims of the patent, we conclude that claim 3 is not infringed, because neither the last-named element—

and a handle above the cover rigidly connected with the rod and shaped to aid in lifting the dipper in a proper filling and emptying position,

nor its mechanical equivalent, appears in the appellant's structures.

As to claims 4 and 5 an examination of the file-wrapper is instructive. As first presented, patentee sought a patent covering, among other claims:

The combination of a jar, a cover for the jar, a dipper adapted to be inserted into the jar, and a connection between the dipper and the cover.

Upon a division being ordered, and with several patent citations confronting him, applicant amended his specifications by inserting:

One object of the invention is to provide a jar and dipper so shaped and proportioned that the dipping edge of the dipper may be presented downward to receive a filling of the contents of the jar, and the dipper may be raised in an approximately horizontal position by placing the back of the dipper rod against a side of the mouth of the jar.

And also:

By making the bottom of the jar concave and shaping the ladle to conform in a general way to the concave surface, the entire contents of the jar may be readily removed.

Patentee struck from his specifications the language:

One object of the invention is to provide a jar with a combined cover and dipper so disposed that the cover will always be on when the dipper is in,

and—

Another object is to provide means for sustaining the jar in a vertical position, and still another object is to provide a readily attachable label plate to designate the contents of the jar.

Claims covering generally the combination of the jar, the cover, and the dipper, with the latter two connected, were withdrawn after the broadest claim heretofore quoted was rejected.

Novelty, if any exists in claim 4, resides in the combination by virtue of the last clause of the claim describing the angle formed by the attachment of the dipper to the lower end of the rod. In view of the use of the word "oblique" in claim 5, the word "downward" in claim 4 may well be construed as meaning perpendicular to the cover. It seems to us that the element—

and a dipper on the end of the rod inclined to the rod at such an angle that when the rod is against a side of the mouth of the jar the dipper may be made to assume an approximately horizontal position—

is so indefinite and vague as to necessitate rejection of this claim.

(2) A patent is the creature of the statute. The terms and conditions upon which the grant is made are fixed by the statute. Section 9432, Compiled Statutes, 1918, requires the inventor to set forth his claims in—

such full, clear, concise, and exact terms as to enable any person skilled in the art * * * to make, construct, compound, and use the same.

What is not claimed distinctly in the invention, the public possesses. A patent is sustained, not for what the inventor may have done in effect,

but what is pointed out clearly and distinctly in his open letter. (*White* v. *Dunbar*, 119 U. S., 47, 51; 7 Sup. Ct., 72; 30 L. Ed., 303; *McCarty* v. *Lehigh Valley R. Co.*, 160 U. S., 110, 116; 16 Sup. Ct., 240; 40 L. Ed., 358; *Proudfit Looseleaf Co.* v. *Kalamazoo Looseleaf Binder Co.*, 230 Fed., 120, 140; 144 C. C. A., 418; *Houser* v. *Starr*, 203 Fed., 264, 267; 121 C. C. A., 462; *National Cash Register Co.* v. *Gratigny*, 213 Fed., 463, 467; 130 C. C. A., 109; *Harder et al.* v. *United States Piling Co.*, 160 Fed., 463, 466; 87 C. C. A., 447; *Avery & Sons* v. *J. I. Case Plow Works*, 148 Fed., 214, 218; 78 C. C. A., 110.)

While we may give liberal construction to the language used to protect the inventor, we cannot rewrite the claim, or insert an element or modify an element in the combination upon which alone validity depends. Words that describe a result may, of course, be adjective in character, that is, modifying in meaning, yet they must be definite and understandable. In this claim the words last quoted describe an angle formed by the rod and the dipper. Just what angle may not necessarily be defined, provided it is ascertainable by placing the rod against the mouth of the jar and the dipper assume a horizontal position. Unfortunately for claims 4 and 5, almost any angle will meet this test, especially if the mouth of the jar be made wide enough and the position of the dipper at the bottom of the jar be changed.

Had applicant included in the combination a jar with a concave bottom, and the dipper so attached to the lower end of the rod that it would fit in the concave bottom of the jar (such as was contemplated by the amended specifications), and the other elements appeared, a different question would have been presented.

In claim 5 the rod extends obliquely downward and the dipper on the lower end of the rod is inclined at such an angle that it may be made to assume an approximately horizontal position inside the jar. Here again the angle formed by the attachment of the dipper to the rod may vary widely and the described results still be obtained, provided the mouth of the jar be relatively large or the operator change the position of the dipper.

Nor can we ignore the prior art, even though no exact anticipation appears therein. Wettstein, in his patent, No. 356,514, covered a combination quite similar in purpose and in construction. In his specifications he says:

My invention relates to a device for measuring and conveying liquids and small loose solid substances from one bowl or receptacle into another in any easy manner, and to provide a suitable covering for the same where required—such as cream or milk pitchers, sugar bowls, or other receptacles containing liquid or solid food—the object being to exclude impurities and also flies and other insects and vermin therefrom; another object of the device being that it is so constructed that, when the spoon or scoop is replaced into its proper receptacle, the cover is placed thereon at the same time, where said scoop is used in combination with the cover.

White secured a patent covering caps and spoons for mustard-bottles. His top and his spoon were attached. Necessarily the dipper and the rod constituting the spoon formed an angle, and whether the dipper was "approximately horizontal" would depend upon the position of the rod at its place of connection with the top. Likewise the width of the mouth of the container necessarily determined to a certain degree whether the dipper would assume a horizontal position.

As the preëmpted field excluded patentee from the claims by him first made, and later withdrawn after rejection by the Patent Office, and as his advance, as set forth in his claims, is represented by the use of jars with a wide mouth (the indefinite and uncertain angle formed by the attachment of the rod and the dipper adding nothing), we must hold claims 4 and 5 invalid.

The decree is reversed, with costs, with directions to dismiss the bill.

Adherence of the Polish Republic to the International Convention for the Protection of Industrial Property.

DEPARTMENT OF STATE,
Washington, D. C., November 20, 1919.

The honorable the Secretary of the Interior.

SIR: I have the honor to inclose herewith, for the information of the Commissioner of Patents, a copy of a note from the Swiss Minister at this capital, by which this Government is informed of the adherence of the Polish Republic to the Paris International Convention for the Protection of Industrial Property of March 20, 1883, as revised at Brussels on December 14, 1900, and at Washington on June 2, 1911.

I have the honor to be, sir, your obedient servant,

For the Secretary of State:

WILLIAM PHILLIPS,
Assistant Secretary.

Inclosure.

From the Minister of Switzerland, November 10, 1919.

LEGATION OF SWITZERLAND,
Washington, D. C., November 10, 1919.

Mr. SECRETARY OF STATE: By direction of my Government, I have the honor to inform you that by a note of June 24, 1919, complemented by another note dated September 23, 1919, the Government of the Polish Republic has notified the Swiss Federal Council of its decision to accede to the Paris International Convention of March 20, 1883, for the Protection of Industrial Property, as revised at Brussels on December 14, 1900, and at Washington on June 2, 1911, and to the additional act and protocols.

With respect to the repression of false indications of the merchandise, the competent Polish authorities are considering that question, which, once settled, will enable the Government of the Polish Republic to arrive at a decision as to its acceding to the Madrid Arrangement of April 14, 1891.

The same Government adds that as regards its quota in the expenses of the International Bureau the Polish Republic wishes to be put in the third class.

Under paragraph 3 of article 16 of the Revised Union Convention of Paris the accession of the Principal Convention will take effect one month after the sending of the notice to the other States of the Union by the Swiss Government.

I beg your excellency kindly to take note of that accession and take the opportunity to renew to you, Mr. Secretary of State, the assurance of my high consideration.

HANS SULZER,
Minister of Switzerland.

ALPHABETICAL LIST OF PATENTEES

TO WHOM

PATENTS WERE ISSUED ON THE 13TH DAY OF JANUARY, 1920.

NOTE.—Arranged in accordance with the first significant character or word of the name. (In accordance with city and telephone directory practice.)

Acme Card System Company. (See Anthony, Stanley, assignor.)

Aeroplane Railway Patents Corporation. (See Williams, Franklin M., assignor.)

Ahana, William W. L., Honolulu, Hawaii. Envelop. No. 1,328,028; Jan. 13; v. 270; p. 276.

Aktiebolaget Carlit. (See Carlson, Oscar B., assignor.)

Alcock, Frederick T., Kamloops, British Columbia, Canada. Tool-holder. No. 1,327,934; Jan. 13; v. 270; p. 258.

Alexander, Francis H., Jesmond, Newcastle - upon - Tyne, England. Clutch-coupling for transmission of power by shafting. No. 1,327,935; Jan. 13; v. 270; p. 258.

Allen, Claude E., Kenosha, Wis., assignor to C. M. Hall Lamp Company, Detroit, Mich. Automatic air-brush machine for coating lamps, &c. No. 1,327,973; Jan. 13; v. 270; p. 265.

American Brass Company. (See Coe, James R., assignor.)

American Can Company. (See Gray, James A., assignor.)

American Can Company. (See Rudolphi, Frank, assignor.)

American Can Company. (See Stewart, Thomas H., assignor.)

American Can Company. (See Symonds, Clarence M., assignor.)

American Lacing Hook Co. (See Havener, Arthur R., assignor.)

American Laundry Machinery Company, The. (See Benjamin, Dana H., assignor.)

American Manganese Steel Company. (See Exton, Alfred H., assignor.)

American Train Control Co., The. (See Scott, Thomas W., assignor.)

Anchor Cap & Closure Corporation. (See Ramsey, George, assignor.)

Anderson, Charles A., assignor to G. E. Sundstrom, Chicago, Ill. Fluid-pump. (Reissue.) No. 14,789; Jan. 13; v. 270; p. 319.

Anderson, Clarence S., Lake Geneva, Wis. Radiator. No. 1,327,797; Jan. 13; v. 270; p. 233.

Anderson, Lemuel O., assignor of one-half to F. P. Armstrong, Miami, Fla. Sash-fastener. No. 1,328,029; Jan. 13; v. 270; p. 276.

Anthony, Stanley, Boston, Mass., assignor to Acme Card System Company, Chicago, Ill. Card - index. No. 1,327,936; Jan. 13; v. 270; p. 258.

Apostoloff. Serge, New York, N. Y. Anti-friction device. No. 1,327,895; Jan. 13; v. 270; p. 251.

Armstrong, Franklin P. (See Anderson, Lemuel O., assignor.)

Armstrong, Ira, Merkel, assignor to Dixieland Motor Truck Company, Bowie county, Tex. Power-driven-implement frame. No. 1,328,222; Jan. 13; v. 270; p. 313.

Asche, Evert, Clara City, Minn. Ratchet - brace. No. 1,328,111; Jan. 13; v. 270; p. 292.

Aspromet Company. (See Young, James H., assignor.)

Aubry-Schaltenbrandt, Francis, La Chaux-de-Fonds, Switzerland. Night-watchman's checking apparatus. No. 1,328,223; Jan. 13; v. 270; p. 313.

Austin, Leslie W., San Jose, Calif. Treating manganese silver ores. No. 1,327,974; Jan. 13; v. 270; p. 266.

Automatic Sprinkler Company of America. (See Hamilton, John R., assignor.)

Ayres, Richard S., Brookline, Mass. Manufacture of boot and shoe heels. No. 1,327,851; Jan. 13; v. 270; p. 243.

Ayrton, Hertha, Hyde Park, London, England. Propulsion of air and other gases or fluids. No. 1,327,975; Jan. 13; v. 270; p. 266.

Bacharach, Samuel, Philadelphia, Pa. Finger-ring. No. 1,327,606; Jan. 13; v. 270; p. 197.

Backstrom, Fridolf F., assignor to Western Felt Works, Chicago, Ill. Belt-fastener. No. 1,327,798; Jan. 13; v. 270; p. 233.

Baker, A. T., & Company. (See Ott, Frederick, assignor.)

Baker, Erle K., assignor to Baker Wheel & Rim Company, Chicago, Ill. Dual-tired wheel. No. 1,327,607; Jan. 13; v. 270; p. 197.

Baker-Vawter Company. (See Manny, Fred L., assignor.)

Baker Wheel & Rim Company. (See Baker, Earle K., assignor.)

Baldwin, Frank G., assignor to The Sechler & Company, Cincinnati, Ohio. Rolling military kitchen. No. 1,328,071; Jan. 13; v. 270; p. 284.

Ball & Ball Carburetor Company. (See Ball, Frederick O., assignor.) (Reissue.)

Ball, Frederick O., assignor to Ball & Ball Carburetor Company, Detroit, Mich. Carbureter. (Reissue.) No. 14,790; Jan. 13; v. 270; p. 320.

Ballard, Albert M., Drumright, Okla., assignor to Sun Company, Philadelphia, Pa. Apparatus for separating oil and gas direct from wells. No. 1,327,691; Jan. 13; v. 270; p. 213.

Balogh, George W., Buffalo, N. Y. Heater. No. 1,327,896; Jan. 13; v. 270; p. 251.

Baldwin, Arthur S., Baltimore, Md. Gun. No. 1,327,897; Jan. 13; v. 270; p. 251.

Barchi, Giovanni, New York, N. Y. Drawer attachment. No. 1,328,112; Jan. 13; v. 270; p. 292.

Bard, George P., Youngstown, Ohio. Pressed corrugated sheet-metal annealing-box. No. 1,328,030; Jan. 13; v. 270; p. 276.

Barnard, Elmer, Cleburne, Tex. Mirror - holder. No. 1,327,608; Jan. 13; v. 270; p. 197.

Barr, John U., New York, N. Y. Advertising-clock. No. 1,327,898; Jan. 13; v. 270; p. 251.

Bartholomew, William, assignor to Troy Laundry Machinery Company, Ltd., Chicago, Ill. Drying-tumbler. No. 1,327,609; Jan. 13; v. 270; p. 197.

Bates, Ben M., Baltimore, Md. Rail-joint. No. 1,328,113; Jan. 13; v. 270; p. 292.

Bayer, Alois, and A. Klingele, Lorain, Ohio. Flytrap. No. 1,328,114; Jan. 13; v. 270; p. 292.

Beaven, Leslie W., Chicago, Ill. Hydraulic dredging apparatus. No. 1,327,651; Jan. 13; v. 270; p. 205.

Bechoff, Ferdinand. New York, N. Y. Electrical circuit-controller. No. 1,328,072; Jan. 13; v. 270; p. 284.

Bechoff, Ferdinand, New York, N. Y. Indicator for controlling switches. No. 1,328,073; Jan. 13; v. 270; p. 285.

Beck, John L., Newark, N. J. Fishing rod and reel. No. 1,327,751; Jan. 13; v. 270; p. 224.

Beckworth, Otto Q. (See Hobson, Oliver J., assignor.)

Beede, Herbert G., Pawtucket, R. I. Work-holder for metal-working machines. No. 1,327,799; Jan. 13; v. 270; p. 233.

Belghlee, Henry E., assignor, by mesne assignments, to The Cleveland Instrument Company, Cleveland, Ohio. Compensating pyrometer system and apparatus. No. 1,327,800; Jan. 13; v. 270; p. 233.

Beinhart, Ernest G., Washington, D. C. Curing tobacco. No. 1,327,692; Jan. 13; v. 270; p. 213.

Bemisderfer, Harvey O., Fostoria, Ohio, assignor to Central Railway Signal Company, Pittsburgh, Pa. Bonnet for railway - signal fusee - caps and making it. No. 1,327,899; Jan. 13; v. 270; p. 252.

Benedict, Henry I., New Orleans, La. Jack-base. No. 1,328,115; Jan. 13; v. 270; p. 292.

Benjamin, Dana H., Cleveland Heights, assignor to The American Laundry Machinery Company, Cincinnati, Ohio. Pressing-machine. No. 1,327,976; Jan. 13; v. 270; p. 266.

Benjamin Electric Manufacturing Company. (See Benjamin, Reuben B., assignor.)

Benjamin, Reuben B., assignor to Benjamin Electric Manufacturing Company, Chicago, Ill. Receptacle. No. 1,328,224; Jan. 13; v. 270; p. 313.

Bennett, Edward O., Oakland, Calif., assignor of fifty per cent to H. Ruhl, San Francisco, Calif., and Chicago, Ill. Key-lock. No. 1,328,074; Jan. 13; v. 270; p. 285.

Bennett, Samuel. (See Calow, Stanley C., assignor.)

Bennington, Wesley H., Cleveland, Ohio. Phonograph-cabinet. No. 1,327,977; Jan. 13; v. 270; p. 266.

Benton, Henry, Elizabeth, N. J. Furnace. No. 1,328,116; Jan. 13; v. 270; p. 293.

Berthelote, Joseph T., Havre, Mont. Animal-exterminator. No. 1,328,117; Jan. 13; v. 270; p. 293.

Bethlehem Shipbuilding Corporation, Ltd. (See Essner, Eugene F., assignor.)

Bewan, James O., Roanoke, Ala. Thermos-tank and valve therefor. No. 1,327,693; Jan. 13; v. 270; p. 213.

Biagini, Atto. (See Di Grazia and Biakini.)

Bilderback, Bart, Rockville, Ind. Metallic smokehouse. No. 1,327,937; Jan. 13; v. 270; p. 258.

Billow, Milton O. Harrisburg, Pa. Class record-book. No. 1,327,610; Jan. 13; v. 270; p. 198.

Birchard, Eslie R., Toronto, Ontario, Canada, assignor to The Department of Soldiers Civil Re-Establishment, Invalided Soldiers' Commission of The Dominion of Canada. Artificial arm. No. 1,327,938; Jan. 13; v. 270; p. 259.

Blache, Hans H., Copenhagen, Denmark. Scraper-ring for scraping oil from cylinders, piston-rods, or the like. No. 1,327,801; Jan. 13; v. 270; p. 234.

Black, Mathew, Brooklyn, N. Y. Beverage-mixer. No. 1,327,900; Jan. 13; v. 270; p. 252.

Blacker, William, Stalybridge, England. Machine or apparatus for breaking up or pulverizing caustic soda and the like. No. 1,327,901; Jan. 13; v. 270; p. 252.

Blake, C. C., Incorporated. (See Foster, Edward E., assignor.)

Blakely, William W., Detroit, Mich. Manufacturing securing devices. No. 1,327,852; Jan. 13; v. 270; p. 243.

Blasdale, Frederick W. (See Muschenheim and Blasdale.)

Blood, Burr B., assignor of one-half to G. Heldman and N. A. Street, Chicago, Ill. Cover-support. No. 1,327,978; Jan. 13; v. 270; p.266.

Bloum, Randolph, Germantown, N. Y. Horseshoe-calk. No. 1,327,853; Jan. 13; v. 270; p. 243.

Bludworth, William D., Fairoaks, Calif. Gold-saving device. No. 1,327,854; Jan. 13; v. 270; p. 243.

Blye, Harold, assignor to National Brass Company, Grand Rapids, Mich. Hasp-staple. No. 1,327,694; Jan. 13; v. 270; p. 214.

Blye, Harold, assignor to National Brass Company, Grand Rapids, Mich. Latch set. No. 1,327,695; Jan. 13; v. 270; p. 214.

Boedicker, Herman C., Minneapolis, Minn. Combination-machine for making photoprints on printing-plates by direct contact or projection printing. No. 1,327,752; Jan. 13; v. 270; p. 225.

Boehmig, Edwin C., Hammond, Ind. Lock for automobiles. No. 1,327,979; Jan. 13; v. 270; p. 267.

Böhn, Ingebret, Sörumsanden, Norway. Tunneling-machine. No. 1,328,118; Jan. 13; v. 270; p. 293.

Bolthoff, Henry, Denver, Colo. Concentrator. No. 1,327,902; Jan. 13; v. 270; p. 252.

Boozer, Arthur G., Providence, R. I., assignor of one-half to G. Hill, Tucapau, S. C. Stripping mechanism for carding-machines. No. 1,327,696; Jan. 13; v. 270; p. 214.

Borener, Albert J., Chicago, Ill. Oil-burning furnace. No. 1,328,075; Jan. 13; v. 270; p. 285.

Borglin, Hans W., Streator, Ill. Pencil attachment. No. 1,328,076; Jan. 13; v. 270; p. 285.

Borst, William E., and C. C. Gilleo, Grand Rapids, Mich. Crucible-mouthpiece for linotype-machines. No. 1,327,697; Jan. 13; v. 270; p. 214.

Boston Pressed Metal Co. (See Needham, William H., assignor.)

Bowman, George. (See Graham and Bowman.)

Bowerman, Joseph A., assignor to The Fiske Rubber Company, Chicopee Falls, Mass. Method and apparatus for manufacture of tires. No. 1,327,802; Jan. 13; v. 270; p. 234.

Boyer, Lewis B., Easton, Pa., assignor to Ingersoll-Rand Company, Jersey City, N. J. Method of and apparatus for forming rifled bores in metal. No. 1,328,077; Jan. 13; v. 270; p. 285.

Boyle, William P., Springfield, Mass. Burner for gas-furnaces. No. 1,328,225; Jan. 13; v. 270; p. 314.

Braden, Albert R., Beverly, Mass., assignor to United Shoe Machinery Corporation, Paterson, N. J. Die and joining its ends. No. 1,327,652; Jan. 13; v. 270; p. 205.

Braly, Norman B., Butte, Mont. Record-card. No. 1,327,855; Jan. 13; v. 270; p. 243.

Bray, Michael J., Upland, Pa. Splicing-thimble. No. 1,327,856; Jan. 13; v. 270; p. 244.

Brayman, Louis M., Westville, N. H. Mixer. No. 1,328,119; Jan. 13; v. 270; p. 293.

Brennan, John S., Milwaukee, Wis. Means for lifting burner-drums. No. 1,327,857; Jan. 13; v. 270; p. 244.

Brennan, John S., Milwaukee, Wis. Wick. No. 1,327,858; Jan. 13; v. 270; p. 244.

Brenner, Ralph F. (See Scholes and Brenner.)

Bricker, Grace L., Anderson, Ind. Combination comb and brush. No. 1,328,120; Jan. 13; v. 270; p. 293.

Brightman, Joseph F., Syracuse, N. Y. Steam-trap. No. 1,327,939; Jan. 13; v. 270; p. 259.

Brinkhaus, Hugo, Brooklyn, N. Y. Hair-dressing device. No. 1,327,980; Jan. 13; v. 270; p. 267.

Britz, John S., Port Huron, Mich. Stamp-canceler and fountain-brush. No. 1,328,031; Jan. 13; v. 270; p. 276.

Brokish, Frank C., Dodgeville, Wis. Pump-thawing means. No. 1,327,803; Jan. 13; v. 270; p. 234.

Brooks, James M., Washington, D. C. Electrical comb. No. 1,327,804; Jan. 13; v. 270; p. 234.

Brown, Benjamin R., Kinsley, Kans. Soil-working implement. No. 1,328,121; Jan. 13; v. 270; p. 294.

Brown Company. (See Fagan, Spear, and Wolf, assignors.)

Brown, Herman M. (See Mannon, Brown, and Perkins.)

Browning, John M., Ogden, Utah. Machine for filling feed-belts for machine-guns. No. 1,327,698; Jan. 13; v. 270; p. 214.

Bruns, Frederick A., Blaine, Wash. Separator. No. 1,327,903; Jan. 13; v. 270; p. 252.

Bruns, George F., New York, N. Y. Beam-clamp. No. 1,327,981; Jan. 13; v. 270; p. 267

Bryan, Leon O., and W. R. Swint, assignors to E. I. du Pont de Nemours & Company, Wilmington, Del. Explosive. No. 1,327,859; Jan. 13; v. 270; p. 244.

Brynteson, Brynte, Odebolt, Iowa. Air-cushion for pump-operating mechanism. No. 1,327,940; Jan. 13; v. 270; p. 259.

Buell, Young K., New York, N. Y. Safety-compartment for ships. No. 1,328,122; Jan. 13; v. 270; p. 294.

Bullard, Albert M., New York, N. Y., assignor, by mesne assignments, to Western Electric Company, Incorporated. Automatic telephone-exchange. No. 1,327,805; Jan. 13; v. 270; p. 284.

Bunde, Claude W., assignor to National Candy Company, Chicago, Ill. Depositing-machine. No. 1,327,806; Jan. 13; v. 270; p. 235.

Burke, James P., Struthers, Ohio. Fastening device for cards, calendars, &c. No. 1,328,123; Jan. 13; v. 270; p. 294.

Burke, William M., London, England. Machine for cutting up meat and other substances. No. 1,328,226; Jan. 13; v. 270; p. 314.

Burleigh, Paul B., Omaha, Nebr. Toothbrush. No. 1,327,807; Jan. 13; v. 270; p. 235.

Burns, John A., assignor of one-half to C. Ginter, Jr., New Haven, Conn. Implement-holder for cooking utensils. No. 1,327,982; Jan. 13; v. 270; p. 267.

Burns, Robert L., and F. F. Winger, Taft, assignors to Standard Oil Company, San Francisco, Calif. Sucker-rod attachment to prevent sanding up of well-pumps. No. 1,327,611; Jan. 13; v. 270; p. 198.

Burrows, Robert W., assignor to Hobbs Wall & Co., San Francisco, Calif. Veneer slicing and scoring machine. No. 1,327,983; Jan. 13; v. 270; p. 267.

Burrows, William E., and W. A. Spangler, St. Joseph, Mo. Engine-starter. No. 1,327,753; Jan. 13; v. 270; p. 225.

Busch-Sulzer Bros.-Diesel Engine Company. (See Rotter, Max, assignor.)

Byron Jackson Iron Works, Inc. (See Paulsmeier, Albert C., assignor.)

Cade, Charles W., Bellevue, assignor to McKinney Manufacturing Company, Pittsburgh, Pa. Door-holder. No. 1,327,754; Jan. 13; v. 270; p. 225.

Calkins, Herbert V., Longmont, Colo. Agricultural implement. No. 1,328,124; Jan. 13; v. 270; p. 294.

Calow, Stanley C., assignor of one-half to S. Bennett, Calgary, Alberta, Canada. Incubator. No. 1,328,032; Jan. 13; v. 270; p. 277.

Camelinat, Eugene G., Birmingham, England. Means for supporting lamps. No. 1,328,125; Jan. 13; v. 270; p. 294.

Camp, Ernest, San Diego, Calif. Mixer for gaseous fuel. No. 1,327,899; Jan. 13; v. 270; p. 214.

Camp, Harriette M., Boston, Mass. Cabinet-couch. No. 1,327,941; Jan. 13; v. 270; p. 259.

Campbell, Robert E., Berkeley, Calif. Valve. No. 1,327,984; Jan. 13; v. 270; p. 267.

Carlson, Oscar B., Mänsbo, Avesta, assignor to Aktiebolaget Carlit, Stockholm, Sweden. Ammonium perchlorate explosive. No. 1,327,985; Jan. 13; v. 270; p. 268.

Carson, Wilfred F., Greensboro, Calif. Attachment for grain or grist mills. No. 1,327,700; Jan. 13; v. 270; p. 215.

Carter, William C., Radnor, assignor to The Goodyear Tire & Rubber Company, Akron, Ohio. Treating fabric. No. 1,327,904; Jan. 13; v. 270; p. 253.

Carvalho, Leslie R. N., et al. (See Russell, Robert A., assignor.)

Cassidy, Wade L., Hamlet, N. C. Automatic railway-gate. No. 1,327,860; Jan. 13; v. 270; p. 244.

Cater, Theodore T., Aurora, Mo. Electric controller. No. 1,328,126; Jan. 13; v. 270; p. 295.

Central Railway Signal Company. (See Bemisderfer, Harvey O., assignor.)

Cesar, Ervin N., Ponca City, Okla. Cranking mechanism for explosive-engines. No. 1,328,127; Jan. 13; v. 270; p. 295.

Chagnon, Alexandre. (See Lafrance, Joseph, assignor.)

Chase, George L., Seattle, Wash. Engine. No. 1,328,033; Jan. 13; v. 270; p. 277.

Chernack Manufacturing Company. (See Kennedy, Joseph A., assignor.)

Cheshire, Robert G., Birmingham, England. Hinge for trestles and the like. No. 1,327,808; Jan. 13; v. 270; p 235.

Chojnacki, Stephen. (See Korzeniewski and Chojnacki.)

Christ, Benjamin F., Idagrove, Iowa. Watch-holder. No. 1,327,701; Jan. 13; v. 270; p. 215.

Christie, Thomas C., Lebanon, and E. A. Edmon, Dayton, Ohio. Mechanical starter. No. 1,327,942; Jan. 13; v. 270; p. 259.

Clark, Charles E., and A. G. Dowell, San Francisco, Calif.; said Dowell assignor to said Clark. Electric heater. No. 1,327,986; Jan. 13; v. 270; p. 268.

Clark, Ohio C. B., Akron, Ohio. Adjustable-socket ratchet-wrench. No. 1,327,702; Jan. 13; v. 270; p. 215.

Claudel, Charles H., Levallois-Perret, France. Carbureter. No. 1,327,703; Jan. 13; v. 270; p. 215.

Cleveland Instrument Company, The. (See Beighlee, Henry E., assignor.)

Climie, William, Ayr, Scotland. Gas - producer. No. 1,327,861; Jan. 13; v. 270; p. 245.

Clouse, William A., assignor to The National Machinery Co., Tiffin, Ohio. Gage for heading and forging machines. No. 1,328,128; Jan. 13; v. 270; p. 295.

Coates, Ray G., Pasadena, Calif., assignor to Valley Mould and Iron Corporation, New York, N. Y. Casting steel ingots. No. 1,327,987 ; Jan. 13 ; v. 270 ; p. 268.
Coatsworth, Frank E. (See Wotherspoon and Coatsworth.)
Coe, James R., assignor to The American Brass Company, Waterbury, Conn. Means for scalping or overhauling metal. No. 1,328,034 ; Jan. 13 ; v. 270 ; p. 277.
Cohen, Max, Revere, Mass. Article-stand. No. 1,327,943 ; Jan. 13 ; v. 270 ; p. 260.
Cole Manufacturing Company. (See Dean, James H., assignor.)
Cone, William C. (See Richley, Alfred, assignor.)
Connell, Thomas, and C. T. Stach, Iowa City, Iowa. Headlight-dimmer. No. 1,328,129 ; Jan. 13 ; v. 270 ; p. 295.
Cook, William A., Westfield, Mass. Gauntlet-glove. No. 1,328,078 ; Jan. 13 ; v. 270 ; p. 285.
Coombs, Frank E., San Francisco, Calif. Sulfite-waste-liquor preparation and making same. No. 1,327,862 ; Jan. 13 ; v. 270 ; p. 245.
Cordes, August W., New York, N. Y. Draft-checking device. No. 1,327,653 ; Jan. 13 ; v. 270 ; p. 205.
Cosler, Arthur S., New York, N. Y. System for separating fluid substances. No. 1,327,944 ; Jan. 13 ; v. 270 ; p. 260.
Costello, John C. (See Moross and Costello.)
Coultas, Fred, Bradford, and A. Pick, Eldwick, Bingley, England. Lifting apparatus for motor road-vehicles and the like. No. 1,327,905 ; Jan. 13 ; v. 270 ; p. 253.
Cousino, Walter P., Curtice, Ohio. Spot-light-mounting device. No. 1,327,945 ; Jan. 13 ; v. 270 ; p. 260.
Cowles, Ida S., Waverly, Pa. Drawer or shelf lining. No. 1,327,755 ; Jan. 13 ; v. 270 ; p. 225.
Cox, Charles B., Jr., Stafford Springs, Conn. Self-feeder for flock-cutters. No. 1,327,612 ; Jan. 13 ; v. 270 ; p. 198.
Coyle, Joseph L., Vancouver, British Columbia, assignor of one-fourth to F. D. Todd, Victoria, Canada. Egg-box. No. 1,327,946 ; Jan. 13 ; v. 270 ; p. 260.
Crandall, Floyd A., Flint, Mich. Truck-body. No. 1,328,130 ; Jan. 13 ; v. 270 ; p. 295.
Crecelius, Lawrence P., assignor to The Electric Railway Improvement Company, Cleveland, Ohio. System of bonding rails. No. 1,327,947 ; Jan. 13 ; v. 270 ; p. 260.
Cross, Andrew B., Denver, Colo. Apparatus for recovering gasoline from natural gases. No. 1,327,906 ; Jan. 13 ; v. 270 ; p. 253.
Culliman, Otto, Chicago, Ill. Holder for phonographic disk records. No. 1,327,949 ; Jan. 13 ; v. 270 ; p. 261.
Currie, Alfred C., St. John, New Brunswick, Canada. Game-board. No. 1,327,907 ; Jan. 13 ; v. 270 ; p. 253.
Cutler-Hammer Mfg. Co., The. (See Stevens, William C., assignor.)
Cutler, William C., North Glendale, Calif. Card-receptacle. No. 1,328,035 ; Jan. 13 ; v. 270 ; p. 277.
Daccord, Auguste, New York, N. Y. Bottle-closure. No. 1,327,809 ; Jan. 13 ; v. 270 ; p. 235.
Damitz, Rineholdt H., Kennedy, Minn. Milk-pail. No. 1,327,704 ; Jan. 13 ; v. 270 ; p. 215.
Dansk Varmekedel Syndikat System Lange Fabrikant-Firma. (See Lange, Jens, assignor.)
Davis, Augustine, assignor to Davis-Bournonville Company, New York, N. Y. Variable-pressure acetylene-generator. No. 1,328,227 ; Jan. 13 ; v. 270 ; p. 314.
Davis-Bournonville Company. (See Davis, Augustine, assignor.)
Davis, Calvin R., assignor to Emerson & Brantingham Company, Rockford, Ill. Fertilizer-distributer. No. 1,327,654 ; Jan. 13 ; v. 270 ; p. 206.
Davis, Charles B., New York, N. Y. Mashing. No. 1,328,079 ; Jan. 13 ; v. 270 ; p. 286.
Davis, Frank B., Erie, Pa. Dental instrument. No. 1,328,131 ; Jan. 13 ; v. 270 ; p. 296.
Dayton Engineering Laboratories Company, The. (See Haas, Nelson R., assignor.)
Dayton Engineering Laboratories Company, The. (See Midgley, Thomas, Jr., assignor.)
Dean, James H., assignor to Cole Manufacturing Company, Chicago, Ill. Draft attachment for stoves. No. 1,327,988 ; Jan. 13 ; v. 270 ; p. 268.
De Long, Cyrus W., Gainesville, Fla. Vaginal douche and medicator. No. 1,327,705 ; Jan. 13 ; v. 270 ; p. 216.
Dennis, Ernest A., Glenroy, New Zealand. Picnic and other food-holder. No. 1,327,948 ; Jan. 13 ; v. 270 ; p. 261.
Department of Soldiers Civil Re-Establishment, Invalided Soldiers' Commission, The. (See Birchard, Eslie R., assignor.)
Deposited Metal Products Company. (See Hart, Austin H., assignor.)
De Smet, Edgard C., assignor to S. C. Pandolfo, St. Cloud, Minn. Collapsible footrest. No. 1,327,706 ; Jan. 13 ; v. 270 ; p. 216.
Detmer Woolen Company. (See Kaiser, Richard C., assignor.)
Dickelman, Lizzie H., Forest, Ohio. Ventilated grain-storehouse. No. 1,328,132 ; Jan. 13 ; v. 270 ; p. 296.
Diffenbaugh, Harry G., Salt Lake City, Utah. Air-pressure liquid-transfer device. No. 1,328,133 ; Jan. 13 ; v. 270 ; p. 296.
Di Grazia, Archie, and R. Biagini, Charleroi, Pa. Self-propelling aerial bomb. No. 1,327,810 ; Jan. 13 ; v. 270 ; p. 235.

270 O. G.—23a

Dixieland Motor Truck Company. (See Armstrong, Ira, assignor.)
Doelckner, Max A., Louisville, Ky. Toy flying-machine. No. 1,328,134 ; Jan. 13 ; v. 270 ; p. 296.
Doner, Hugh H., New York, N. Y. Signal and guide light. No. 1,328,135 ; Jan. 13 ; v. 270 ; p. 296.
Dorsey, David J., Baton Rouge, La. Shade and curtain hanger. No. 1,328,136 ; Jan. 13 ; v. 270 ; p. 297.
Doud, Arthur N., Winthrop, N. Y. Dumping-wagon. No. 1,328,137 ; Jan. 13 ; v. 270 ; p. 297.
Dougan, Kennedy, Minneapolis, Minn. Projectile. No. 1,327,655 ; Jan. 13 ; v. 270 ; p. 206.
Dowell, Archie G. (See Clark, Charles E., assignor.)
Drake, Harcourt C., and A. Slagenhauf, Brooklyn, N. Y. Headstock-brake. No. 1,327,656 ; Jan. 13 ; v. 270 ; p. 206.
Draper Corporation. (See Stimpson, Edward S., assignor.)
Drew, Herbert H., Edgerton, Wis. Stock-watering apparatus No. 1,328,036 ; Jan. 13 ; v. 270 ; p. 277.
Drinkwater, James F., Willard, Ohio. Railway-brake appliance. No. 1,328,138 ; Jan. 13 ; v. 270 ; p. 297.
Drolet, Benjamin. (See Plante, Albert E., assignor.)
Dudley, Howard M., Philadelphia, Pa. Hosiery-dyeing machine. No. 1,327,756 ; Jan. 13 ; v. 270 ; p. 225.
Dudley, Howard M., Philadelphia, Pa. Skein-dyeing machine. No. 1,327,657 ; Jan. 13 ; v. 270 ; p. 206.
Dudley, Howard M., Philadelphia, Pa. Dyeing-machine. No. 1,327,658 ; Jan. 13 ; v. 270 ; p. 206.
Dudley, Howard M., Philadelphia, Pa. Fabric-treating device. No. 1,327,659 ; Jan. 13 ; v. 270 ; p. 207.
Dudley, Howard M., Philadelphia, Pa. Dyeing-machine. No 1,327,660 ; Jan. 13 ; v. 270 ; p. 207.
Dudley, Howard M., Philadelphia, Pa. Dyeing device. No. 1,327,661 ; Jan. 13 ; v. 270 ; p. 207.
Dudley, Howard M., Philadelphia, Pa. Dyeing-machine. No. 1,327,662 ; Jan. 13 ; v. 270 ; p. 207.
Dudley, Howard M., Philadelphia, Pa. Fiber-treating machine. No. 1,327,663 ; Jan. 13 ; v. 270 ; p. 208.
Dunham, George W., Detroit, Mich., assignor to Graham Brothers, Evansville, Ind. Stabilizer. No. 1,327,811 ; Jan. 13 ; v. 270 ; p. 236.
Dun Lany, William P., assignor to Sears, Roebuck and Company, Chicago, Ill. Sample-affixing machine. No. 1,327,664 ; Jan. 13 ; v. 270 ; p. 208.
Dun Lany, William P., assignor to Sears, Roebuck and Company, Chicago, Ill. Machine for affixing samples to sheets. No. 1,327,665 ; Jan. 13 ; v. 270 ; p. 208.
Du Pont, E., de Nemours & Company. (See Bryan and Swint, assignors.)
Early, William F., Marion, N. C. Flexible ladder. No. 1,328,037 ; Jan. 13 ; v. 270 ; p. 278.
Edmon, Elmer A. (See Christie and Edmon.)
Eggers, William J., Brooklyn, N. Y. Rubber toothbrush. No. 1,327,757 ; Jan. 13 ; v. 270 ; p. 226.
Electric Auto-Lite Corporation. (See Post, Truman W., assignor.)
Electric Boat Company. (See Grieshaber, Hugo E., assignor.)
Electric Railway Improvement Company, The. (See Crecelius, Lawrence P., assignor.)
Elliott, William S., Jr., New York, N. Y. Hydraulic water-forcing apparatus. No. 1,328,139 ; Jan. 13 ; v. 270 ; p. 297.
Ellis, Carleton, Montclair, N. J. Paint and varnish remover. No. 1,328,080 ; Jan. 13 ; v. 270 ; p. 286.
Ellis Drier & Elevator Company. (See Ellis, Hubert C., assignor.)
Ellis, Hubert C., Evanston, assignor to Ellis Drier & Elevator Company, Chicago, Ill. Grain-drier. No. 1,327,863 ; Jan. 13 ; v. 270 ; p. 245.
Emerson & Brantingham Company. (See Davis, Calvin R., assignor.)
Emmert, Gus. (See Tischer, Edward R., assignor.)
Enders, Gustav A., Boston, Mass. Cornet, trumpet, and the like. No. 1,328,038 ; Jan. 13 ; v. 270 ; p. 278.
Engel, John, Green Bay, Wis. Machine for applying paint to embossed designs. No. 1,328,081 ; Jan. 13 ; v. 270 ; p. 286.
Ertl, Lorenz, Ivanhoe, Minn. Operating-table. No. 1,328,140 ; Jan. 13 ; v. 270 ; p. 297.
Essex Motors. (See Fekete, Stephen I., assignor.)
Essner, Eugene F., San Francisco, Calif., assignor to Bethlehem Shipbuilding Corporation, Ltd., Bethlehem, Pa. Machine for cutting off condenser-tubes. No. 1,328,039 ; Jan. 13 ; v. 270 ; p. 278.
Estey Organ Company. (See Haskell, William E., assignor.)
Evans, S. C. (See Markwell, Andrew E., assignor.)
Everingham, John H., Manchester, England. Portable carriage for children. No. 1,327,864 ; Jan. 13 ; v. 270 ; p. 245.
Exton, Alfred H., Chicago Heights, Ill., assignor to American Manganese Steel Company, Augusta, Me. Sectional shoe for the runner-vanes of centrifugal pumps. No. 1,327,812 ; Jan. 13 ; v. 270 ; p. 236.
Fagan, James P. Y., H. G. Spear, and R. B. Wolf ; said Fagan and said Spear assignors to Brown Company, Berlin, N. H. Manufacturing sulfite fiber and recovering sulfur dioxid. No. 1,327,666 ; Jan. 13 ; v. 270 ; p. 208.
Farley, Henry G., Portland, Me. Machine for grinding the edges of glass plates. No. 1,328,242 ; Jan. 13 ; v. 270 ; p. 317.

Feary, Neville A. T. N., Peterborough, England. Fabric for aircraft and making same. No. 1,327,707; Jan. 13; v. 270; p. 216.

Fellbach, Arthur O., North Milwaukee, Wis. Tool for lifting valve-springs. No. 1,328,228; Jan. 13; v. 270; p. 314.

Fekete, Stephen I., assignor, by mesne assignments, to Essex Motors, Detroit, Mich. Fuel-supply mechanism for internal-combustion engines. No. 1,328,142; Jan. 13; v. 270; p. 298.

Fenton, Walter, Manchester, England, assignor to Underwood Typewriter Company, New York, N. Y. Typewriting-machine. No. 1,327,908; Jan. 13; v. 270; p. 253.

Ferguson, Louis A., Evanston, and H. S. Sines, Oak Park, Ill.; said Sines assignor to said Ferguson. Gas-metering apparatus. No. 1,327,989; Jan. 13; v. 270; p. 268.

Fergusson, Sterling P., Washington, D. C. Kite-frame or like structure. No. 1,328,143; Jan. 13; v. 270; p. 298.

Fernald, Mark E., Saugus, Mass. Automatic machine. No. 1,328,144; Jan. 13; v. 270; p. 298.

Finley, Thomas M., Oran, Mo. Aerocruiser. No. 1,328,040; Jan. 13; v. 270; p. 278.

Fischer, Kuno, Berlin-Charlottenburg, assignor to Siemens Schuckert Werke, G. m. b. H., Berlin, Germany. Electric relay and the like. No. 1,328,041; Jan. 13; v. 270; p. 278.

Fischer, Martin, Zurich, Switzerland. Device for igniting gas-jets. No. 1,327,813; Jan. 13; v. 270; p. 236.

Fish, Ambrose D., Portland, Oreg. Metal-separator. No. 1,327,667; Jan. 13; v. 270; p. 208.

Fisher, Alva J., Evanston, assignor to Hurley Machine Company, Chicago, Ill. Ironing-machine. No. 1,327,613; Jan. 13; v. 270; p. 198.

Fisk Rubber Company, The. (See Naylor, Ralph B., assignor.)

Fiske Rubber Company, The. (See Bowerman, Joseph A., assignor.)

Fiske Rubber Company, The. (See Jameson, William, assignor.)

Flanagan, James U., assignor of three-fourths to F. F. Slocomb & Co., Incorporated, Wilmington, Del. Apparatus for treating skins, fabric, tobacco, and the like. No. 1,327,668; Jan. 13; v. 270; p. 209.

Flaxbaum, Samuel, New York, N. Y. Pocket-mirror. No. 1,327,865; Jan. 13; v. 270; p. 245.

Folks, Robert L., Waycross, Ga. Internal-combustion engine. No. 1,328,141; Jan. 13; v. 270; p. 298.

Forbes, Philip J., et al. (See Rendano, Emil, assignor.)

Fortescue, Charles L., Pittsburgh, Pa., assignor to Westinghouse Electric and Manufacturing Company. Method of and apparatus for spot-welding. No. 1,327,814; Jan. 13; v. 270; p. 236.

Foster, Edward E., Beverly, assignor to C. C. Blake, Incorporated, Boston, Mass. Stop mechanism. No. 1,328,145; Jan. 13; v. 270; p. 298.

Francis, Harry G., Rushville, Ind. Veneer - press. No. 1,327,815; Jan. 13; v. 270; p. 236.

Fraser, Alexander, Renfrew, Ontario, Canada. Repeating device for talking-machines. No. 1,327,816; Jan. 13; v. 270; p. 236.

Freeland, Charles E. (See Klug and Freeland.)

French, Charles L., Cambridge, Mass. Storage apparatus for liquids. No. 1,327,990; Jan. 13; v. 270; p. 269.

Freund, Herman R., assignor to Intertype Corporation, Brooklyn, N. Y. Matrix for typographical machines. No. 1,328,146; Jan. 13; v. 270; p. 299.

Fritzsche, George G. H., Brooklyn, N. Y. Binder. No. 1,327,992; Jan. 13; v. 270; p. 269.

Frohman, Edward D., Pittsburgh, Pa. Refractory material. No. 1,327,758; Jan. 13; v. 270; p. 226.

Fry, H. C., Glass Company. (See Scholes, Samuel R., assignor.)

Fry, J. Howard. (See Scholes and Brenner, assignors.)

Fuller, Dunne P., Carlisle, Wash. Operating mechanism for whistles. No. 1,328,252; Jan. 13; v. 270; p. 319.

Gage, Mattie A., New York, N. Y. Alarm mechanism for clocks. No. 1,327,669; Jan. 13; v. 270; p. 209.

Gardiner, Robert F., Clarendon, Va. Production of synthetic ammonia from the air or nitrogen. No. 1,328,082; Jan. 13; v. 270; p. 286.

Garford Manufacturing Company, The. (See Manson, Ray H., assignor.)

Gatewood, Frank A., Sylvan Grove, Kans. Wrench. No. 1,327,991; Jan. 13; v. 270; p. 269.

Geiger, William H., Oakland, Calif. Gearing for egg-beaters, cream-whippers, and the like. No. 1,327,950; Jan. 13; v. 270; p. 261.

Genn, John E., assignor to Stewart-Warner Speedometer Corporation, Chicago, Ill. Spark-plug. No. 1,328,147; Jan. 13; v. 270; p. 299.

Gent, Wm., Vending Machine Company, The. (See Larsen, Arnold, assignor.)

Gerhard, Werner, Chicago, Ill. Impact-machine. No. 1,327,817; Jan. 13; v. 270; p. 237.

German-American Button Co. (See Hastings, Herbert, assignor.)

Geyer, Hobart W. (See Van Valer, De Witt C., assignor.)

Gilleo, Clarence C. (See Borst and Gilleo.)

Gillette Safety Razor Company. (See Wharton, Edward R., assignor.)

Ginter, Christian, Jr. (See Burns, John A., assignor.)

Goddard, Charles F. (See Stockton and Goddard.)

Godfrey, Warren P. (See Watts, Ben, assignor.) (Reissue.)

Goldberg, Maximilian M., Dayton, Ohio. Speed-transformer. No. 1,328,083; Jan. 13; v. 270; p. 286.

Goldblatt, Albert A., Brooklyn, N. Y. Alarm device for automobiles. No. 1,327,993; Jan. 13; v. 270; p. 269.

Goodyear Tire & Rubber Company, The. (See Carter, William C., assignor.)

Goodyear Tire & Rubber Company, The. (See Harsel, William B., assignor.)

Goodyear Tire & Rubber Company, The. (See Upson, Ralph H., assignor.)

Graham Brothers. (See Dunham, George W., assignor.)

Graham, Edmund, and G. Bowman, Belfast, Ireland. Liquid jacking apparatus for motor-vehicles. No. 1,327,670; Jan. 13; v. 270; p. 209.

Grand Rapids Show Case Co. (See Vanderveld, Anthony, assignor.)

Gray, James A., assignor to American Can Company, San Francisco, Calif. Mechanism for seaming ends to can-bodies. No. 1,327,994; Jan. 13; v. 270; p. 269.

Grayson, Iona, Tulsa, Okla. Fish-scaler. No. 1,328,148; Jan. 13; v. 270; p. 299.

Green, George W. A., O. Wans, and F. H. Livens, assignors to Ruston and Hornsby, Limited, Lincoln, England. Reversing mechanism for internal-combustion engines. No. 1,327,995; Jan. 13; v. 270; p. 270.

Grieshaber, Hugo E., New London, Conn., assignor to Electric Boat Company. Torpedo-launching apparatus. No. 1,327,614; Jan. 13; v. 270; p. 198.

Gruhl, Irvin W., Los Angeles, Calif. Signaling device. No. 1,327,818; Jan. 13; v. 270; p. 287.

Guaranteed Tractors. (See Phillips, Walter C., assignor.)

Guett, Monroe, assignor to The Hart & Hegeman Manufacturing Company, Hartford, Conn. Electric switch. No. 1,327,615; Jan. 13; v. 270; p. 199.

Guthrie, William S., Terrell, Tex. Carbureter. No. 1,328,042; Jan. 13; v. 270; p. 279.

Guy, Joseph, Humbermouth, Newfoundland. Strainer for water-supply pipes of locomotives. No. 1,327,708; Jan. 13; v. 270; p. 216.

Gyp Steel Products Company. (See Shuman, Cleo G., assignor.)

Hass, Nelson R., Dayton, Ohio, assignor to the Dayton Engineering Laboratories Company. Cut-out relay. No. 1,327,951; Jan. 13; v. 270; p. 261.

Hackett, Charles H., assignor to W. W. Marsh, Waterloo, Iowa. Liner for centrifugal cream-separators. No. 1,328,084; Jan. 13; v. 270; p. 287.

Hagstrom, Curt W., Wilmette, Ill. Foldable bathtub. No. 1,327,866; Jan. 13; v. 270; p. 245.

Hakes, Hudson W., Millbury, Mass. Automatically-threading shuttle. No. 1,327,709; Jan. 13; v. 270; p. 216.

Hall, C. M., Lamp Company. (See Allen, Claude E., assignor.)

Haller, Hans K., Copenhagen, Denmark. Transport system for postage and other goods. No. 1,327,952; Jan. 13; v. 270; p. 261.

Hamilton, John R., Yonkers, assignor to Automatic Sprinkler Company of America, New York, N. Y. Water-motor. No. 1,327,953; Jan. 13; v. 270; p. 261.

Hancq, John B., Jamestown, N. Y. Shuttle. No. 1,327,954; Jan. 13; v. 270; p. 262.

Hankee, Harry J., Minneapolis, Minn. Traffic-signal for autos. No. 1,327,671; Jan. 13; v. 270; p. 209.

Hanks, John C., Russell, Ky. Safety-hanger for brake-beams. No. 1,327,909; Jan. 13; v. 270; p. 254.

Hanlon & Goodman Co. (See Hecht, Charles E., assignor.)

Harley-Davidson Motor Co. (See Harley, William S., assignor.)

Harley, William S., assignor to Harley-Davidson Motor Co., Milwaukee, Wis. Automatic voltage control. No. 1,328,149; Jan. 13; v. 270; p. 299.

Harley, William S., assignor to Harley-Davidson Motor Company, Milwaukee, Wis. Combined intake and exhaust manifold. No. 1,328,150; Jan. 13; v. 270; p. 299.

Harriman National Bank of the City of New York. (See Vasselli, Anthony, assignor.)

Harsel, William B., assignor to The Goodyear Tire & Rubber Company, Akron, Ohio. Tire-making machine. No. 1,327,910; Jan. 13; v. 270; p. 254.

Hart & Hegeman Manufacturing Company, The. (See Guett, Monroe, assignor.)

Hart & Hegeman Manufacturing Company, The. (See Stirling, Clarence C., assignor.)

Hart, Austin H., Bronxville, N. Y., assignor to Deposited Metal Products Company. Radiator. No. 1,328,151; Jan. 13; v. 270; p. 300.

Haskell, William E., assignor to Estey Organ Company, Brattleboro, Vt. Speaking-pipe. No. 1,327,996; Jan. 13; v. 270; p. 270.

Hastings, Herbert, assignor to German-American Button Co., Rochester, N. Y. Button-inspecting machine. No. 1,327,672; Jan. 13; v. 270; p. 209.

Havener, Arthur R., Waltham, Mass., assignor to American Lacing Hook Co. Lacing-hook-setting machine. No. 1,327,911; Jan. 13; v. 270; p. 254.

Hawn, William L., assignor of one-half to A. Kavanagh, Kansas City, Mo. Mattress. No. 1,328,248; Jan. 13; v. 270; p. 318.

Hecht, Charles E., Irvington, N. J., assignor to Hanlon & Goodman Co., New York, N. Y. Brush-holder. No. 1,328,162; Jan. 13; v. 270; p. 301.

Heckler, Winfield T. (See Maltry and Heckler.)

Heckman, James, Clarendon, Tex. Pipe-holder. No. 1,327,673; Jan. 13; v. 270; p. 209.
Heldman, George, et al. (See Blood, Burr B., assignor.)
Heinecke, Fredrich G., Gaylord. Minn. Cornstalk-cutter. No. 1,327,997; Jan. 13; v. 270; p. 270.
Heller, Eugene H. (See Jaeger and Heller.)
Hellmund, Rudolf E., Pittsburgh, Pa., assignor to Westinghouse Electric and Manufacturing Company. System of control. No. 1,327,819; Jan. 13; v. 270; p. 237.
Hellmund, Rudolf E., Pittsburgh, Pa., assignor to Westinghouse Electric and Manufacturing Company. Dynamo-electric machine. No. 1,327,820; Jan. 13; v. 270; p. 237.
Hellmund, Rudolf E., Swissvale, Pa., assignor to Westinghouse Electric & Manufacturing Company. Dynamo-electric machine. No. 1,327,821; Jan. 13; v. 270; p. 237.
Hellmund, Rudolf E., Swissvale, Pa., assignor to Westinghouse Electric and Manufacturing Company. System of control. No. 1,327,822; Jan. 13; v. 270; p. 238.
Hellmund, Rudolf E., Swissvale, Pa., assignor to Westinghouse Electric and Manufacturing Company. System of control. No. 1,327,823; Jan. 13; v. 270; p. 238.
Hemstreet, George P., Hastings-upon-Hudson, N. Y., assignor to The International Pavement Company, Hartford, Conn. Making anchor-blocks. No. 1,327,710; Jan. 13; v. 270; p. 217.
Hendricks, Adam C., Martinsburg, W. Va. Automatic phonograph-stop. No. 1,327,955; Jan. 13; v. 270; p. 262.
Henigman, August. Bokoshe, Okla. Target. No. 1,327,998; Jan. 13; v. 270; p. 270.
Henriksen, Lars J., Käflinge, Sweden. Shoe-heel and producing same. No. 1,328,249; Jan. 13; v. 270; p. 318.
Henry, Abner E., Greensburg, Pa. Demountable wheel-rim. No. 1,327,759; Jan. 13; v. 270; p. 226.
Hensal, Elmer A., Panora, Iowa. Extension-table. No. 1,328,243; Jan. 13; v. 270; p. 317.
Hensel, John S., Stevens Point, Wis. Traction-lug. No. 1,327,867; Jan. 13; v. 270; p. 246.
Herpst, Herman A., Norway, Mich. Pump. No. 1,327,868; Jan. 13; v. 270; p. 246.
Hewitt, Frank W., Arlington, assignor to Simplex Electric Heating Company, Cambridge, Mass. Electric heating unit. No. 1,328,229; Jan. 13; v. 270; p. 314.
Hill, George. (See Boozer, Arthur G., assignor.)
Hill Pump Valve Company, The. (See Jaeger and Heller, assignors.)
Hill, Thomas A., Brooklyn, N. Y., assignor, by mesne assignments, to The J. G. Wilson Corporation. Roller for partitions and doors. No. 1,328,043; Jan. 13; v. 270; p. 279.
Hill, William W., Sarona, Wis. Regulator for engines. No. 1,327,999; Jan. 13; v. 270; p. 270.
Hills, Henry A., Grand Rapids, Mich. Hydrocarbon-filter. No. 1,328,044; Jan. 13; v. 270; p. 279.
Hills, Henry A., Grand Rapids, Mich. Multistage adjustable filtering apparatus. No. 1,328,045; Jan. 13; v. 270; p. 279.
Hills, Henry A., Grand Rapids, Mich. Unitary multistage filter apparatus. No. 1,328,046; Jan. 13; v. 270; p. 279.
Hinchey, Charlotte. Buffalo, N. Y. Denture. No. 1,327,674; Jan. 13; v. 270; p. 210.
Hobbs Wall & Co. (See Burrows, Robert W., assignor.)
Hobson, Oliver J., assignor of one-half to O. Q. Beckworth, Chicago, Ill. Tire-tread for pneumatic-tire casings and making and attaching same. No. 1,327,912; Jan. 13; v. 270; p. 254.
Hofer, Joseph L., Bridgewater, S. D. Steering-gear. No. 1,327,616; Jan. 13; v. 270; p. 199.
Hogan, Donald P. (See Rendahl, George A., assignor.)
Holczer, Mike, Norfolk, Va. Tractor-hitch. No. 1,327,617; Jan. 13; v. 270; p. 199.
Holland, Nellie G., Boston, Mass. Sheet, blanket, or the like. No. 1,327,824; Jan. 13; v. 270; p. 238.
Hollander, Erik E., Newark, N. J. Tool for making holes non-circular. No. 1,328,085; Jan. 13; v. 270; p. 287.
Holt, Frederick B., Antrobus. near Northwich, England, assignor to Westinghouse Electric and Manufacturing Company. Circuit-interrupter. No. 1,327,825; Jan. 13; v. 270; p. 238.
Horning, John C., Chicago, Ill. Valve mechanism. No. 1,327,675; Jan. 13; v. 270; p. 210.
Howe, Earl W., Norfolk, Va. Collapsible steam-chest and oven. No. 1,328,152; Jan. 13; v. 270; p. 300.
Hughes, Howard R., Houston, Tex. Rotary boring-drill. No. 1,327,913; Jan. 13; v. 270; p. 254.
Humason, Granville A., Houston, Tex. Pump-piston. No. 1,327,914; Jan. 13; v. 270; p. 255.
Humphrey, Frank L., Enid. Okla. Clothes-basket carrier. No. 1,328,163; Jan. 13; v. 270; p. 302.
Hurley Machine Company. (See Fisher, Alva J., assignor.)
Hurley, Neil C. (See Wood, James J., assignor.)
Ingersoll-Rand Company. (See Boyer, Lewis E., assignor.)
Ingle, Arthur H. (See Putnam, Salmon W., 3d, assignor.)
International Motor Company. (See Leipert, August H., assignor.)
International Nitrogen Company. (See Reid, James H., assignor.)
International Pavement Company, The. (See Hemstreet, George P., assignor.)

Intertype Corporation. (See Freund, Herman R., assignor.)
Irving, Walter E., Glenbrook. Conn. Support for gratings. No. 1,327,711; Jan. 13; v. 270; p. 217.
Irwin, William A., New York, N. Y., and L. F. Jackson. Taunton. Mass. Automobile-lamp. No. 1,328,153; Jan. 13; v. 270; p. 300.
Iverson Piano Player Company. (See Peterson, Claus E., assignor.)
Jackerson, Benjamin, Brooklyn, N. Y. Cushion-heel. No. 1,328,154; Jan. 13; v. 270; p. 300.
Jackson, Leo F. (See Irwin and Jackson.)
Jaeger, Edward B., and E. H. Heller, assignors to The Hill Pump Valve Company. Chicago, Ill. Aeroplane. No. 1,327,869; Jan. 13; v. 270; p. 246.
Jaeger, Otto, Elkins Park, Pa., assignor to H. S. Kelsey, Boston, Mass. Dispensing-machine. No. 1,327,712; Jan. 13; v. 270; p. 217.
Jakubecz, Joseph. (See Kropacz, John, assignor.)
Jameson, William, Springfield, assignor to The Fiske Rubber Company, Chicopee Falls, Mass. Apparatus for making strand fabric. No. 1,327,826; Jan. 13; v. 270; p. 238.
Janney, Peyton R., Detroit, Mich. Flexible draft connection. No. 1,327,827; Jan. 13; v. 270; p. 238.
Janney. Peyton R., Detroit, Mich. Cultivator. No. 1,327,828; Jan. 13; v. 270; p. 239.
Janney, Peyton R., Detroit, Mich. Detachable steering device. No. 1,327,829; Jan. 13; v. 270; p. 239.
Jeffries, Zay. (See Wesson and Jeffries.)
Jezik, Joseph J., assignor of one-half to F. F. Kretek, East Bernard, Tex. Rail-joint. No. 1,328,155; Jan. 13; v. 270; p. 300.
Johnson, Robert J., Logan, Utah. Beet-topper. No. 1,327,760; Jan. 13; v. 270; p. 226.
Johnson, James S., Utica, N. Y. Machine-gun. No. 1,328,230; Jan. 13; v. 270; p. 315.
Jokisch, John. Detroit, Mich. Brush especially adapted for cleaning stovepipes. No. 1,328,164; Jan. 13; v. 270; p. 300.
Jones, Charles G., Asheville ,N. C. Combination ironing-table. No. 1,328,000; Jan. 13; v. 270; p. 271.
Jones, Leo D., Philadelphia, assignor to The Sharpless Specialty Company, West Chester, Pa. Extraction of fatty and oily matters from wet sludges. No. 1,328,047; Jan. 13; v. 270; p. 280.
Joyner, George O., and G. J. White, Little Rock, Ark. Circular-saw support. No. 1,327,713; Jan. 13; v. 270; p. 217.
Kaiser, Richard C., New Rochelle, assignor to Detmer Woolen Company, New York, N. Y. Display-easel for tailors and the like. No. 1,327,618; Jan. 13; v. 270; p. 199.
Kanzaki, Matsunosuke, Salt Lake City. Utah. Beet-harvester. No. 1,328,231; Jan. 13; v. 270; p. 315.
Kast, Edward R., Pearl River, assignor to Kast Insetting and Gathering Machine Company, New York, N. Y. Book-trimmer. No. 1,327,915; Jan. 13; v. 270; p. 255.
Kast Insetting and Gathering Machine Company. (See Kast, Edward R., assignor.)
Katzberg, William M., Hastings, Nebr. Door-latch. No. 1,327,916; Jan. 13; v. 270; p. 255.
Kavanagh, Arch. (See Hawn, William L., assignor.)
Kean, Ida, administratrix. (See Kean, Joseph.)
Kean, Joseph, deceased. Des Moines, Iowa; I. Kean. administratrix. Air-pump. No. 1,328,232; Jan. 13; v. 270; p. 315.
Keiper, Henry B., Lancaster, Pa. Combination-tool. No. 1,328,250; Jan. 13; v. 270; p. 318.
Kellar, George E., Covina, Calif., assignor to Kellar-Thomason Company. Concrete-mixer. No. 1,327,917; Jan. 13; v. 270; p. 255.
Kellar-Thomason Company. (See Kellar, George E., assignor.)
Kelly, Adelbert F., Spokane, Wash. Spring-spoke wheel. No. 1,328,244; Jan. 13; v. 270; p. 317.
Kelsey, Harry S. (See Jaeger, Otto, assignor.)
Kelsey, Henrietta L., Philadelphia, Pa. Knitting-needle. No. 1,327,918; Jan. 13; v. 270; p. 255.
Kennedy, Joseph A., Pawtucket, assignor to Chernack Manufacturing Company. Providence, R. I. Circular loom. No. 1,327,676; Jan. 13; v. 270; p. 210.
Kennedy, Joseph A., assignor to Chernack Manufacturing Company, Pawtucket, R. I. Method of and machine for producing internally coated or lined woven tubes. No. 1,327,677; Jan. 13; v. 270; p. 210.
Kestenman, Abraham, assignor to Kestenman Bros. Mfg. Company, Providence, R. I. Lingerie - clasp. No. 1,327,761; Jan. 13; v. 270; p. 226.
Kestenman Bros. Mfg. Company. (See Kestenman, Abraham, assignor.)
Key, John R., Leavenworth, Kans. Road-grader. No. 1,328,233; Jan. 13; v. 270; p. 315.
Kiehl, Leslie R., Raton, N. Mex. Pump. No. 1,328,165; Jan. 13; v. 270; p. 302.
Kincaid, Thomas J., Wills, Wis. Wheeled rake. No. 1,328,156; Jan. 13; v. 270; p. 300.
King, Martin, et al. (See Russell, Robert A., assignor.)
King, Robert J., Stamford, Conn. Producing chloropicrin. No. 1,327,714; Jan. 13; v. 270; p. 217.
Kinsman, Clarence W., assignor of two-thirds to H. H. Kinsman, New York, N. Y. Perforated utensil-cover. No. 1,328,001; Jan. 13; v. 270; p. 271.
Kinsman, Hermon H. (See Kinsman, Clarence W., assignor.)

Kintsel, Eric S., Raton, N. Mex. Pencil - holder. No. 1,327,762 ; Jan. 13 ; v. 270 ; p. 226.
Klingele, August. (See Bayer and Klingele.)
Klug, Frederick S., and C. E. Freeland, Wheeling, W. Va. Roll-polisher. No. 1,327,919 ; Jan. 13 ; v. 270 ; p. 255.
Knapp, Jacob, assignor to The Sechler & Company, Cincinnati, Ohio. Trailer-vehicle. No. 1,328,048 ; Jan. 13 ; v. 270 ; p. 280.
Knight, Albert B., Fairmont, W. Va. Machine for grinding edges of glassware. No. 1,327,830 ; Jan. 13 ; v. 270 ; p. 239.
Koechlin, Emile R., assignor to Naamlooze Vennootschap Weduwe J. Ahrend & Zoons Industrie- en Handelsvereeniging, Amsterdam, Netherlands. Drawing-table. No. 1,327,956 ; Jan. 13 ; v. 270 ; p. 262.
Kohler, Ernest, Denver, Colo., assignor to The United Mines and Manufacturing Company. Amusement device, (skating-car.) No. 1,328,166 ; Jan. 13 ; v. 270 ; p. 302.
Kouzmin, Eugene M. (See Kousnetzoff and Kouzmin.)
Koppitz, Carl G., assignor to Railway and Industrial Engineering Company, Greensburg, Pa. Field - magnet frame. No. 1,327,619 ; Jan. 13 ; v. 270 ; p. 199.
Kops, Daniel, New York, N. Y. Apparel - corset. No. 1,328,086 ; Jan. 13 ; v. 270 ; p. 287.
Korhonen, John, Englewood, N. J. Snowplow. No. 1,328,157 ; Jan. 13 ; v. 270 ; p. 301.
Kory, Joseph N., Denver, Colo. Sample - carrier. No. 1,328,167 ; Jan. 13 ; v. 270 ; p. 302.
Korzeniewski, Czeslaw, and S. Chojnacki, Cleveland, Ohio. Fuel-oil burner. No. 1,327,768 ; Jan. 13 ; v. 270 ; p. 227.
Kozik, Stanislaw, Indian Head, Md. Furniture-caster. No. 1,327,920 ; Jan. 13 ; v. 270 ; p. 256.
Kousnetzoff, Nicholas, and E. M. Kouzmin, New York, N. Y. Typewriting-machine. No. 1,328,158 ; Jan. 13 ; v. 270 ; p. 301.
Kramer, William H., Newcastle, Ind. Saw-filing device. No. 1,328,159 ; Jan. 13 ; v. 270 ; p. 301.
Kretek, Frank F. (See Jezik, Joseph J., assignor.)
Kroon, Arthur W., Glenellyn, Ill. Gate. No. 1,328,168 ; Jan. 13 ; v. 270 ; p. 303.
Kropacz, John, assignor of one-third to J. Jakubecz, Calgary, Alberta, Canada. Rail-support. No. 1,328,002 ; Jan. 13 ; v. 270 ; p. 271.
Krogh, Ferdinand W., San Francisco, Calif. Sand-protecting device for turbine-pumps. No. 1,328,234 ; Jan. 13 ; v. 270 ; p. 315.
La Bar, Bert G., Turtle Creek, Pa., assignor to Westinghouse Electric and Manufacturing Company. Gearing for electrical measuring instruments. No. 1,327,832 ; Jan. 13 ; v. 270 ; p. 239.
Lafrance, Joseph, assignor of one-half to A. Chagnon, Montreal, Quebec, Canada. Air-pump. No. 1,327,883 ; Jan. 13 ; v. 270 ; p. 239.
Lampe, Fred E., Newark, N. J. Soldering composition. No. 1,327,620 ; Jan. 13 ; v. 270 ; p. 199.
Landers, David L., Estill, S. C. Railway-switch. No. 1,328,003 ; Jan. 13 ; v. 270 ; p. 271.
Lane, Harry L., Venice, Calif. Air-valve attachment for carbureters. No. 1,328,235 ; Jan. 13 ; v. 270 ; p. 316.
Lange, Jens, Hellerup, Denmark, assignor to Dansk Varmekedel Syndikat System Lange, Fabrikant-Firma, Copenhagen, Denmark. Radiator for steam and water. No. 1,327,870 ; Jan. 13 ; v. 270 ; p. 246.
Lanz, Andrew, Pittsburgh, Pa. Fuel-feeding apparatus. No. 1,327,764 ; Jan. 13 ; v. 270 ; p. 227.
Lanz, Andrew, Pittsburgh, Pa. Apparatus for burning solid fuel. No. 1,327,765 ; Jan. 13 ; v. 270 ; p. 227.
Lanzetta, Francesco, Brooklyn, N. Y. Vise attachment. No. 1,328,049 ; Jan. 13 ; v. 270 ; p. 280.
Larsen, Arnold, assignor to The Wm. Gent Vending Machine Company, Cleveland, Ohio. Apportioning device. No. 1,327,676 ; Jan. 13 ; v. 270 ; p. 210.
Lawn, William E., Rochester, N. Y. External-explosion engine. No. 1,328,160 ; Jan. 13 ; v. 270 ; p. 301.
Leavitt, Benjamin F., assignor to The Leavitt Diving Armor Company, Toledo, Ohio. Diving apparatus. No. 1,327,679 ; Jan. 13 ; v. 270 ; p. 211.
Leahy, Bernard, Bridgeport, Conn. Trunk-harness. No. 1,327,680 ; Jan. 13 ; v. 270 ; p. 211.
Leatherman, Robert L., and F. Pfrogner, Mount Pleasant, Pa. Combination desk and chair. No. 1,328,169 ; Jan. 13 ; v. 270 ; p. 303.
Leavitt Diving Armor Company, The. (See Leavitt, Benjamin F., assignor.)
Le Chot, Charles C., Akron, Ohio. Ratchet socket-wrench. No. 1,328,087 ; Jan. 13 ; v. 270 ; p. 287.
Lee, William, New Bedford, Mass. Splice-bar. No. 1,328,170 ; Jan. 13 ; v. 270 ; p. 303.
Lee, William H., assignor to Syracuse Chilled Plow Company, Syracuse, N. Y. Plow construction (detachable share.) No. 1,327,921 ; Jan. 13 ; v. 270 ; p. 256.
Lehr, Nicholas P., Fremont, Ohio. Clod crusher and packer. No. 1,328,171 ; Jan. 13 ; v. 270 ; p. 303.
Leighty, William J., Chicago, Ill. Cutting device. No. 1,327,871 ; Jan. 13 ; v. 270 ; p. 217.
Leipert, August H., Brooklyn, assignor to International Motor Company, New York, N. Y. Pressed-steel transmission-case. No. 1,327,681 ; Jan. 13 ; v. 270 ; p. 211.
Leitner, Henry, Westminster, London, England. Screw-propeller. No. 1,328,004 ; Jan. 13 ; v. 270 ; p. 271.
Leitner, Henry, Westminster, London, England. Screw-propeller. No. 1,328,005 ; Jan. 13 ; v. 270 ; p. 271.

Lewis, George W., Grinnell, Iowa, assignor to Lovell Manufacturing Company, Erie, Pa. Wringer. No. 1,327,766 ; Jan. 13 ; v. 270 ; p. 227.
Liebler, Frederick, New York, N. Y. Signal, indicator, and recorder. No. 1,328,245 ; Jan. 13 ; v. 270 ; p. 318.
Lind, Anna, Bridgeport, Conn. Spring-fan. No. 1,328,172 ; Jan. 13 ; v. 270 ; p. 303.
Lindquist, Knut O. W., Chicago, Ill. Leaf-turner. No. 1,327,621 ; Jan. 13 ; v. 270 ; p. 200.
Lippincott, Fisher H., Philadelphia, Pa. Variable-speed clutch. No. 1,327,767 ; Jan. 13 ; v. 270 ; p. 227.
Little, Lenard, Gainesville, Ga. Drain cut-off. No. 1,327,831 ; Jan. 13 ; v. 270 ; p. 239.
Livens, Frederick H. (See Green, Wans, and Livens.)
Long, Leslie R., Tipton, Iowa. Sheaf-loader. No. 1,327,834 ; Jan. 13 ; v. 270 ; p. 240.
Lovell Manufacturing Company. (See Lewis, George W., assignor.)
Lowe, Albert H., Maplewood, assignor of one-half to R. R. Maxwell, St. Louis, Mo. Clamp for plumbers' force-pumps. No. 1,327,768 ; Jan. 13 ; v. 270 ; p. 227.
Lundquist, Frank A., assignor to C. L. Redfield, trustee, Chicago, Ill. Calling mechanism for telephone-exchanges. No. 1,327,622 ; Jan. 13 ; v. 270 ; p. 200.
Lundstrom, Victor N., Clarissa, Minn. Draft appliance. No. 1,327,871 ; Jan. 13 ; v. 270 ; p. 246.
Lutz, William D., Allendale, N. J. Inflating device for pneumatic apparatus. No. 1,328,088 ; Jan. 13 ; v. 270 ; p. 287.
Lynn, Nathan O., Mendon, Mich. Water-heater. No. 1,328,161 ; Jan. 13 ; v. 270 ; p. 301.
Lynn, Thomas H. (See Steel and Lynn.)
Lyon Metallic Manufacturing Company. (See O'Connor, John B., assignor.)
McAneny, William A., and D. T. May, assignors to The McMurtry Manufacturing Company, Denver, Colo. Fountain-humidor-box-lid support. No. 1,327,872 ; Jan. 13 ; v. 270 ; p. 247.
McCarthy, Thomas J., Newark, N. J. Vapor-primer for automobiles. No. 1,328,089 ; Jan. 13 ; v. 270 ; p. 287.
McCormack, Anthony J., assignor to The Mac-Rim Company, New Haven, Conn. Horseshoe. No. 1,327,716 ; Jan. 13 ; v. 270 ; p. 218.
McCredie, Reid J., Buffalo, N. Y. Lock collar-button. No. 1,327,719 ; Jan. 13 ; v. 270 ; p. 218.
McDonald, James A., Fort Worth, Tex. Combined mail-box and door-bell. No. 1,327,957 ; Jan. 13 ; v. 270 ; p. 262.
McDowell, Edward, Atlanta, Ga. Resilient tire-cushion. No. 1,327,717 ; Jan. 13 ; v. 270 ; p. 218.
McGowan, James W., Omaha, Nebr. Vehicle-alarm. No. 1,328,173 ; Jan. 13 ; v. 270 ; p. 303.
McIntyre, Michael M., assignor, by mesne assignments, to The Standard Parts Company, Cleveland, Ohio. Vehicle-spring. No. 1,327,958 ; Jan. 13 ; v. 270 ; p. 262.
McKee, Garnet W., Rockford, Ill. Metal-melting furnace. No. 1,328,236 ; Jan. 13 ; v. 270 ; p. 316.
McKibben, Charles W., Houston, Tex. Apparatus for treatment of oil emulsions. No. 1,327,835 ; Jan. 13 ; v. 270 ; p. 240.
McKinney Manufacturing Company. (See Cade, Charles W., assignor.)
McKnight, Thomas R., assignor to Western Wheeled Scraper Company, Aurora, Ill. Dump-car. No. 1,327,623 ; Jan. 13 ; v. 270 ; p. 200.
McLeod, Nelson W., St. Louis, Mo. Making pneumatic tires. No. 1,328,006 ; Jan. 13 ; v. 270 ; p. 271.
McMurtry Manufacturing Company, The. (See McAneny and May, assignors.)
McNeil, Charles. Glasgow, Scotland. Macerating crushed sugar-cane. No. 1,328,090 ; Jan. 13 ; v. 270 ; p. 288.
MacBoyle, James W., Chicago, Ill. Garment-supporter. No. 1,327,959 ; Jan. 13 ; v. 270 ; p. 263.
Macivor, Thomas J., London, Ontario, Canada. Ash-sifter. No. 1,328,174 ; Jan. 13 ; v. 270 ; p. 304.
Macnern, James G., Mamaroneck, N. Y. Pneumatic-despatch-tube apparatus. No. 1,327,718 ; Jan. 13 ; v. 270 ; p. 218.
Mac-Rim Company, The. (See McCormack, Anthony J., assignor.)
Mahaffey, Florence C., Toledo, Ohio. Egg-candler. No. 1,328,091 ; Jan. 13 ; v. 270 ; p. 288.
Maitry, Peter, and W. T. Heckler, Blue Island, Ill. Piston-push-rod holder. No. 1,328,092 ; Jan. 13 ; v. 270 ; p. 288.
Mannon, Homer, H. M. Brown, and R. G. Perkins, Huntington, W. Va. Indicating device. No. 1,328,007 ; Jan. 13 ; v. 270 ; p. 272.
Manny, Fred L., assignor to Baker-Vawter Company, Benton Harbor, Mich. Loose-leaf binder. No. 1,327,624 ; Jan. 13 ; v. 270 ; p. 200.
Manson, Ray H., assignor to The Garford Manufacturing Company, Elyria, Ohio. Automobile or motorcycle horn. No. 1,328,093 ; Jan. 13 ; v. 270 ; p. 288.
Maranville, Harvey F., Akron, Ohio. Ventilator. No. 1,328,094 ; Jan. 13 ; v. 270 ; p. 288.
Marti, Harry A., Minneapolis, Minn. Garment. No. 1,327,625 ; Jan. 13 ; v. 270 ; p. 200.
Markwell, Andrew E., assignor of one-half to S. C. Evans, Fort Worth, Tex. Matrix molding device. No. 1,328,050 ; Jan. 13 ; v. 270 ; p. 280.
Marsden, Mark W., Philadelphia, Pa. Utilizing Spanish moss. No. 1,327,873 ; Jan. 13 ; v. 270 ; p. 247.
Marsh, Wilbur W. (See Hackett, Charles H., assignor.)

Martin, Charles W., Brooklyn, N. Y. Umbrella. No. 1,328,175; Jan. 13; v. 270; p. 304.
Martin, Robert L., Thomas, W. Va. Nut-locking device. No. 1,327,836; Jan. 13; v. 270; p. 240.
Martinka, Joseph J., Newark, N. J. Surgical appliance for women. No. 1,328,176; Jan. 13; v. 270; p. 304.
Martucci, Francesco, Jersey City, N. J. Sanitary soap-holder. No. 1,328,177; Jan. 13; v. 270; p. 304.
Masterson, Patrick, South Porcupine, Ontario, Canada. Punching-machine. No. 1,327,720; Jan. 13; v. 270; p. 218.
Mathews, Charley B., Andalusia, Ala. Chipper's guide-marker. No. 1,327,874; Jan. 13; v. 270; p. 247.
Mattison, Richard V., Jr., Upper Dublin township, Montgomery county, Pa. Manufacturing fibrous cement products. No. 1,327,721; Jan. 13; v. 270; p. 219.
Maxwell, Ross R. (See Lowe, Albert H., assignor.)
May, Daniel T. (See McAneny and May.)
Mayer, Fred G., assignor to The Starr Piano Company, Richmond. Ind. Matrix for sound-records. No. 1,327,722; Jan. 13; v. 270; p. 219.
Mayer, Samuel, New York, N. Y. Dictionary. No. 1,328,178; Jan. 13; v. 270; p. 304.
Meier, Erling, Christiania, Norway. Roller-bearing. No. 1,328,179; Jan. 13; v. 270; p. 304.
Merrill, Alfred P., San Diego, Calif. Rotary shaft and coupling for electric dental engines. No. 1,328,095; Jan. 13; v. 270; p. 288.
Merry, Whiting P., Sharpsville, Pa. Heater. No. 1,328,246; Jan. 13; v. 270; p. 318.
Metal Separation Company, The. (See Stockton and Goddard, assignors.)
Metropolitan Sewing Machine Corporation. (See Weis, John P., assignor.)
Metz, Herman A. (See Riethmüller, Richard H., assignor.)
Mezzatesta, Gaspare, Hampton, Va. Carbureter. No. 1,328,180; Jan. 13; v. 270; p. 305.
Midgley, Thomas, Jr., Dayton, Ohio, assignor to The Dayton Engineering Laboratories Company. Mercury-cooling system. No. 1,328,051; Jan. 13; v. 270; p. 280.
Midyett, Zacariah M., Jackson, Tenn. Toy popgun. No. 1,327,723; Jan. 13; v. 270; p. 219.
Mikimoto, Kokichi, Tokyo, Japan. Causing oysters to produce pearls. No. 1,328,008; Jan. 13; v. 270; p. 272.
Miller, Norman H., Meadville, Pa. Swing-chair. No. 1,328,181; Jan. 13; v. 270; p. 305.
Miller, William J., Goose Creek, Tex. Piston. No. 1,328,182; Jan. 13; v. 270; p. 305.
Mine Safety Appliance Company, The. (See Ryan, John T., assignor.)
Miekush, Francis, Rankin, Pa. Smoker. No. 1,328,183; Jan. 13; v. 270; p. 305.
Molas, Edouard E., Paris, France. Apparatus for preparation of inert gases. No. 1,327,769; Jan. 13; v. 270; p. 228.
Montgomery, Robert E., Lawton, Okla. Cotton-seed linter. No. 1,327,724; Jan. 13; v. 270; p. 219.
Moody, Daniel W., Chicago, Ill. Occupant-operated vehicle and steering apparatus. No. 1,327,960; Jan. 13; v. 270; p. 263.
Moore, Charles E., Terre Haute, Ind. Rim, tire, and wheel carrier for automobiles. No. 1,327,626; Jan. 13; v. 270; p. 200.
Moore, Warren, Ladysmith, Wis. Self-measuring dispensing vessel. No. 1,328,184; Jan. 13; v. 270; p. 305.
Moreland, Everett R., Carrollton, Mo. Draftsman's fountain ruling-pen. No. 1,327,922; Jan. 13; v. 270; p. 256.
Mork, Albert C., Minneapolis, Minn. Valve-grinding machine. No. 1,327,875; Jan. 13; v. 270; p. 247.
Moross, William P. D., and J. C. Costello, Chattanooga, Tenn. Apparatus for extracting lye from wood-ashes. No. 1,328,096; Jan. 13; v. 270; p. 289.
Morral, Samuel E., Morral. Ohio. Wheel. No. 1,328,052; Jan. 13; v. 270; p. 281.
Morris, Charles E., assignor to C. W. Parker, Leavenworth, Kans. Carousel. No. 1,327,725; Jan. 13; v. 270; p. 219.
Morris, William G., Cairo, Egypt. Valve. No. 1,328,009; Jan. 13; v. 270; p. 272.
Morton, William B., Beatrice. Nebr. Store-case. No. 1,328,185; Jan. 13; v. 270; p. 306.
Moscini, John, Brooklyn, N. Y. Paper-match machine. No. 1,327,627; Jan. 13; v. 270; p. 201.
Munhall, John, Pittsburgh, Pa. Staybolt structure. No. 1,328,053; Jan. 13; v. 270; p. 281.
Murray, Samuel R., Indianapolis, Ind. Composition for paving and other purposes. No. 1,327,726; Jan. 13; v. 270; p. 220.
Muschenheim, Frederick A., and F. W. Blasdale, New York, N. Y. Electrical machine. No. 1,327,837; Jan. 13; v. 270; p. 240.
Naamlooze Vennootschap Weduwe J. Ahrend & Zoons Industries- en Handelsvereeniging. (See Koechlin, Emile R., assignor.)
National Aniline & Chemical Company. (See Taggesell, Richard, assignor.)
National Brass Company. (See Bye, Harold, assignor.)
National Candy Company. (See Bunde, Claude W., assignor.)
National Machinery Co., The. (See Clouse, William L., assignor.)
Naylor, Jesse R., Sacramento, Calif. Traffic-signal. No. 1,328,097; Jan. 13; v. 270; p. 289.

Naylor, Ralph B., Springfield, assignor to The Fisk Rubber Company, Chicopee Falls, Mass. Testing device for determining the viscosity of rubber. No. 1,327,838; Jan. 13; v. 270; p. 240.
Needham, William H., assignor to Boston Pressed Metal Co., Worcester, Mass. Last-thimble. No. 1,327,839; Jan. 13; v. 270; p. 241.
Nelson, Swan, Winnifred. Alberta, Canada. Pump. No. 1,328,010; Jan. 13; v. 270; p. 272.
Nevers, Lester, and F. Whitbeck, Grand Rapids, Mich. Boiler-setting. No. 1,327,727; Jan. 13; v. 270; p. 220.
Nicholson, Herbert, Chicago, Ill. Pneumatic tire. No. 1,328,054; Jan. 13; v. 270; p. 281.
Nied, Edward H., Akron, Ohio. Lock. No. 1,328,186; Jan. 13; v. 270; p. 306.
Noerther, Charles, & Cie. (See Nörther, Charles, assignor.)
Nörther, Charles, assignor to Charles Noerther & Cie., Turin, Italy. Music-typewriter. No. 1,327,840; Jan. 13; v. 270; p. 241.
Norton, Joseph C., Cleveland, Ohio. Roof-edging. No. 1,327,770; Jan. 13; v. 270; p. 228.
Novick, Abraham, New York, N. Y., assignor, by mesne assignments, to United States Envelope Company, Springfield, Mass. Envelop-machine. No. 1,328,011; Jan. 13; v. 270; p. 272.
Nyblad, Axel L., Newport, England. Hoisting device. No. 1,327,876; Jan. 13; v. 270; p. 247.
Oakley, Henry D., Syracuse, N. Y. Device for indicating magnetic polarity. No. 1,328,187; Jan. 13; v. 270; p. 306.
O'Connor, John B., assignor to Lyon Metallic Manufacturing Company. Aurora, Ill. Shelving. No. 1,327,628; Jan. 13; v. 270; p. 201.
Ogden, Carlton N., Houston, Tex. Display and vending device. No. 1,327,771; Jan. 13; v. 270; p. 228.
Ogden, Clarence E., Cincinnati, Ohio. Switchboard for charging storage batteries. No. 1,327,682; Jan. 13; v. 270; p. 211.
Ogle, Percy J., London, England, assignor to Ventiheta Limited. Warming and ventilating gas-stove. No. 1,328,012; Jan. 13; v. 270; p. 273.
Ohashi, Hydesaburo, deceased, New York, N. Y.; M. V. Ohashi, administratrix. Carbon-paper and ink composition therefor. No. 1,328,188; Jan. 13; v. 270; p. 306.
Ohnell, Ernst J. (See Olhovsky, Vladimir, assignor.)
Old Dominion Specialty Co., The. (See Sanford, Crocker H., assignor.)
Ohashi, Marie V., administratrix. (See Ohashi, Hydesaburo.)
Olhovsky, Vladimir, New York, assignor to E. J. Ohnell, Brooklyn, N. Y. Tachometer. No. 1,327,629; Jan. 13; v. 270; p. 201.
Ory, Gaston C., Paris, France. Scouring apparatus with sand-throw. No. 1,327,630; Jan. 13; v. 270; p. 201.
Osborn, John F., Ludington, Mich. Combination phonograph and moving-picture machine. No. 1,328,189; Jan. 13; v. 270; p. 306.
Ott, Frederick, Norristown, assignor to A. T. Baker & Company, Manayunk, Pa. Woven pile fabric. No. 1,327,683; Jan. 13; v. 270; p. 211.
Ott, Frederick, Norristown, assignor to A. T. Baker & Company, Manayunk, Pa. Woven pile fabric. No. 1,327,684; Jan. 13; v. 270; p. 212.
Pacific Radiator Shield Co. (See Parmelee, Charles H., assignor.)
Page, George H., Richmond, Mo. Lifting-jack. No. 1,327,685; Jan. 13; v. 270; p. 212.
Page, John W., Chicago, Ill. Excavating-shovel. No. 1,328,013; Jan. 13; v. 270; p. 273.
Pageau, Louis, Montreal, Quebec, Canada. Boot or shoe. No. 1,327,772; Jan. 13; v. 270; p. 289.
Palmer, John M., Chicago, Ill. Valve. No. 1,328,098; Jan. 13; v. 270; p. 289.
Pandolfo, Samuel C. (See De Smet, Edgard C., assignor.)
Paragon Metal Cap Company et al. (See Russell, Robert A., assignor.)
Parker, Arthur M., Georgetown, S. C. Machine for making coil-springs. No. 1,327,728; Jan. 13; v. 270; p. 220.
Parker, Charles W. (See Morris, Charles E., assignor.)
Parkes, Bertrand A., assignor to The Philadelphia Drying Machinery Company, Philadelphia, Pa. Conveyer. No. 1,328,099; Jan. 13; v. 270; p. 289.
Parmelee, Charles H., assignor, by mesne assignments, to Pacific Radiator Shield Co., Seattle, Wash. Radiator-shield. No. 1,327,877; Jan. 13; v. 270; p. 247.
Parrott, Ethel D., Los Angeles, Calif. Extension-table. No. 1,327,878; Jan. 13; v. 270; p. 248.
Paschall, Benjamin S., New York, N. Y. Fountain-pen. No 1,327,729; Jan. 13; v. 270; p. 220.
Paulin, Georges A., Asnières, France. Manufacture of cleansing material. No. 1,327,631; Jan. 13; v. 270; p. 201.
Paulsmeier, Albert C., Alameda, assignor to Byron Jackson Iron Works, Inc., San Francisco, Calif. Automatic stuffing-box. No. 1,328,190; Jan. 13; v. 270; p. 307.
Payne, George W., Kansas City, Mo. Radiator-shield. No. 1,327,730; Jan. 13; v. 270; p. 220.
Perkins, R. F., & Son. (See Senna, Samuel N., assignor.)
Perkins, Rowland F. (See Mannon, Brown, and Perkins.)
Peters, Frank A., Chicago, Ill. Curtain-support. No. 1,327,961; Jan. 13; v. 270; p. 263.
Peters Machine and Manufacturing Company, The. (See Thiemer, William H., assignor.)

Peterson, Claus E., Worcester, assignor to Iverson Piano Player Company, Boston, Mass. Pneumatic motor for piano-players. No. 1,327,731 ; Jan. 13 ; v. 270 ; p. 221.

Peterson, Eldon L., Tacoma, Wash. Garden-tool. No. 1,328,191 ; Jan. 13 ; v. 270 ; p. 307.

Petroske, John J. (See Starkenberg, Karl R., assignor.)

Pettis, Edson S., Mill Valley, Calif. Drum-filter wiring. No. 1,327,962 ; Jan. 13 ; v. 270 ; p. 263.

Pfeifer, Fred B., Akron, Ohio. Tire-vulcanizing device. No. 1,327,841 ; Jan. 13 ; v. 270 ; p. 241.

Pflaster, Simon, New York, N. Y. Exhibiting device. No. 1,328,192 ; Jan. 13 ; v. 270 ; p. 307.

Pfrogner, Frank. (See Leatherman and Pfrogner.)

Philadelphia Drying Machinery Company, The. (See Parkes, Bertrand A., assignor.)

Phillips & Slack, Inc. (See Phillips, Frank A., assignor.)

Phillips, Frank A., assignor to Phillips & Slack, Inc., Northfield, Vt. Edge-lining machine. No. 1,327,923 ; Jan. 13 ; v. 270 ; p. 256.

Phillips, Frank G., Vancouver, British Columbia, Canada. Means for salvaging submerged vessels. No. 1,328,014 ; Jan. 13 ; v. 270 ; p. 273.

Phillips, John H., Jr., Jackson, Mich. Flexible pipe. No. 1,327,632 ; Jan. 13 ; v. 270 ; p. 202.

Phillips, Walter C., assignor to Guaranteed Tractors, Inc., Chicago, Ill. Tractor attachment for automobiles. No. 1,327,773 ; Jan. 13 ; v. 270 ; p. 228.

Phillipson, Emil, assignor to Plant & Company, New York, N. Y. Electric fan. No. 1,328,055 ; Jan. 13 ; v. 270 ; p. 281.

Pick, Arthur. (See Coultas and Pick.)

Pilon, Eugene, Farmpoint, Ontario, Canada. Spring-hook. No. 1,328,193 ; Jan. 13 ; v. 270 ; p. 307.

Plant & Company. (See Phillipson, Emil, assignor.)

Plante, Albert E., assignor of one-half to B. Drolet, Montreal, Quebec, Canada. Electric water-heater. No. 1,327,774 ; Jan. 13 ; v. 270 ; p. 228.

Platt, Benjamin N., Chicago, Ill. Block. No. 1,327,775 ; Jan. 13 ; v. 270 ; p. 229.

Poetz, John C., Wenatchee, Wash. Climbing device. No. 1,328,251 ; Jan. 13 ; v. 270 ; p. 319.

Pollmiller, August V., Marceline, Mo. Semaphore-signal. No. 1,328,194 ; Jan. 13 ; v. 270 ; p. 307.

Poole, Arthur F., Chicago, Ill. Electric-clock system. No. 1,328,247 ; Jan. 13 ; v. 270 ; p. 318.

Poore, John C., Boston, Mass. Dirigible-eye structure for dolls. No. 1,328,100 ; Jan. 13 ; v. 270 ; p. 290.

Post, Truman W., Brooklyn, N. Y., assignor to Electric Auto-Lite Corporation, Toledo, Ohio. Headlight. No. 1,327,732 ; Jan. 13 ; v. 270 ; p. 221.

Potter, Henry K., Somerville, Mass. Sweeping streets. No. 1,328,237 ; Jan. 13 ; v. 270 ; p. 316.

Potts, Warren W., Elkhart, Ind. Adjustable illuminating-fixture. No. 1,327,733 ; Jan. 13 ; v. 270 ; p. 221.

Pratte, François J. A., assignor to A. P. Pratte, Montreal, Quebec, Canada. Talking-machine. No. 1,327,776 ; Jan. 13 ; v. 270 ; p. 229.

Pressed Steel Car Company. (See Reeder, Nathaniel S., assignor.)

Pratte, Alphonsine P. (See Pratte, François J. A., assignor.)

Pressler, Charles F., Fort Wayne, Ind. Liquid-measuring pump. No. 1,328,101 ; Jan. 13 ; v. 270 ; p. 290.

Pruden, Allan K., St. Paul, Minn. Ventilator and ventilating system. No. 1,327,879 ; Jan. 13 ; v. 270 ; p. 248.

Psilander, Charles A., assignor to William Wharton, Jr. & Co., Easton, Pa. Hard-center crossing-frog. No. 1,327,842 ; Jan. 13 ; v. 270 ; p. 241.

Putnam, Salmon W., 3d, assignor to A. H. Ingle, Rochester, N. Y. Journal-bushing. No. 1,328,195 ; Jan. 13 ; v. 270 ; p. 308.

Pytlewski, Steve, Minneapolis, Minn. Reinforced tread for spring-wheels. No. 1,327,843 ; Jan. 13 ; v. 270 ; p. 241.

Rail, Napoleon, Lowell, Mass. Automatic cutting-off device for thread-winders. No. 1,328,196 ; Jan. 13 ; v. 270 ; p. 308.

Railway and Industrial Engineering Company. (See Koppitz, Carl G., assignor.)

Ramsey, George, assignor to Anchor Cap & Closure Corporation, Brooklyn, N. Y. Side-seal closure. No. 1,327,963 ; Jan. 13 ; v. 270 ; p. 263.

Rand, Frederick B., Sanford, Me. Lug-strap holder. No. 1,327,964 ; Jan. 13 ; v. 270 ; p. 264.

Rand, Harry M., Westville, N. J. Valve-grinder. No. 1,328,197 ; Jan. 13 ; v. 270 ; p. 308.

Randall, Karl C., Edgewood Park, Pa., assignor to Westinghouse Electric & Manufacturing Company. Circuit-interrupter. No. 1,327,777 ; Jan. 13 ; v. 270 ; p. 229.

Rassmann, F., Manufacturing Company. (See Rassmann, Hugo C., assignor.)

Rassmann, Hugo C., Beaver Dam, Wis. Watering device for stock. No. 1,327,734 ; Jan. 13 ; v. 270 ; p. 221.

Rassmann, Hugo C., assignor to F. Rassmann Manufacturing Company, Beaver Dam, Wis. Supporting and mining means for stanchions. No. 1,327,735 ; Jan. 13 ; v. 270 ; p. 221.

Ray, William R., San Francisco, Calif. Burner-mounting. No. 1,328,198 ; Jan. 13 ; v. 270 ; p. 308.

Rector, Floyd D. and W. Q., Louisville, Ky. Charge-forming device. No. 1,328,199 ; Jan. 13 ; v. 270 ; p. 308.

Rector, William Q. (See Rector, Floyd D. and W. Q.)

Redfield, Casper L., trustee. (See Lundquist, Frank A., assignor.)

Reeder, Nathaniel S., New York, N. Y., assignor to Pressed Steel Car Company, Pittsburgh, Pa. Car-roof construction. No. 1,328,200 ; Jan. 13 ; v. 270 ; p. 309.

Reichman, Harry, and A. R. Spangenberg, Cincinnati, Ohio. Combined package and trash receptacle. No. 1,327,778 ; Jan. 13 ; v. 270 ; p. 229.

Reid, James H., Newark, N. J., assignor to International Nitrogen Company. Producing carbid. No. 1,327,736 ; Jan. 13 ; v. 270 ; p. 232.

Reid, James H., Newark, N. J., assignor, by mesne assignments, to International Nitrogen Co. Procuring and securing products from carbohydrates. No. 1,327,737 ; Jan. 13 ; v. 270 ; p. 222.

Reid, James H., Newark, N. J., assignor, by mesne assignments, to International Nitrogen Co. Means actuated by alternating electric current for controlling or operating electric furnaces or other mechanisms. No. 1,327,738 ; Jan. 13 ; v. 270 ; p. 222.

Remington, Joseph P., assignor to Remington Manufacturing Company, Philadelphia, Pa. Air control for internal-combustion engines. No. 1,328,102 ; Jan. 13 ; v. 270 ; p. 290.

Remington Manufacturing Company. (See Remington, Joseph P., assignor.)

Rendahl, George A., assignor to D. P. Hogan, Denver, Colo. Oil-baffle for automobile-engines. No. 1,327,779 ; Jan. 13 ; v. 270 ; p. 229.

Rendano, Emil, Brooklyn, assignor of one-half to E. Rendano and N. Rendano, New York, and one-half to P. J. Forbes, Brooklyn, N. Y. Fastening device. No. 1,328,201 ; Jan. 13 ; v. 270 ; p. 273.

Rendano, Nicholas, et al. (See Rendano, Emil, assignor.)

Ricardo, Harry R., London, England. Lubricating mechanism. No. 1,328,015 ; Jan. 13 ; v. 270 ; p. 273.

Richardson, Alan C., Silver Spring, Md. Processing apparatus for canned products. No. 1,328,202 ; Jan. 13 ; v. 270 ; p. 309.

Richley, Alfred, Cleveland, Ohio, assignor of one-half to W. C. Cone, Toronto, Ontario, Canada. Building concrete ships. No. 1,327,739 ; Jan. 13 ; v. 270 ; p. 222.

Riehmiller, Richard H., Montclair, N. J., assignor to H. A. Metz, New York, N. Y. Hypodermic syringe. No. 1,328,203 ; Jan. 13 ; v. 270 ; p. 309.

Ripple, John W., Baltimore, Md. Sewer-trap. No. 1,328,103 ; Jan. 13 ; v. 270 ; p. 290.

Rogers, John R., Brooklyn, N. Y. Clutch. No. 1,327,880 ; Jan. 13 ; v. 270 ; p. 248.

Rose, William, Chicago, Ill. Liquid-measuring device. No. 1,327,686 ; Jan. 13 ; v. 270 ; p. 212.

Roseman, Joseph A., Glenview, Ill. Grass-mowing machine. No. 1,327,924 ; Jan. 13 ; v. 270 ; p. 256.

Rosenfeld, Maurice S., assignor by mesne assignments, to J. Schechter, New York, N. Y. Apparatus for repairing moving-picture films. No. 1,328,056 ; Jan. 13 ; v. 270 ; p. 281.

Rossell, Thomas J, New Smyrna, Fla. Flue-cleaner. No. 1,327,740 ; Jan. 13 ; v. 270 ; p. 222.

Roth, Carl H., Newark, N. J. Tool or cutter head. No. 1,327,881 ; Jan. 13 ; v. 270 ; p. 248.

Rotter, Max, assignor to Busch-Sulzer Bros.-Diesel Engine Company, St. Louis, Mo. Packing or gasket construction. No. 1,327,965 ; Jan. 13 ; v. 270 ; p. 264.

Rudkin, William P., Oklahoma, Okla. Generator. No. 1,328,016 ; Jan. 13 ; v. 270 ; p. 274.

Rudolphi, Frank, New York, N. Y., assignor to American Can Company. Can-closing machine. No. 1,327,966 ; Jan. 13 ; v. 270 ; p. 264.

Ruhl, Hepburn. (See Bennett, Edward O., assignor.)

Russell, Robert A., New York, assignor of one-third to Paragon Metal Cap Company, Inc., Brooklyn, one-third to M. King, New York, and one-third to L. R. N. Carvalho, Brooklyn, N. Y. Cap for bottles or jars. No. 1,327,967 ; Jan. 13 ; v. 270 ; p. 264.

Ruston and Hornsby. (See Green, Wans, and Livens, assignors.)

Ryan, John T., Pittsburgh, Pa., assignor to The Mine Safety Appliance Company. Mouthpiece for breathing apparatus. No. 1,328,057 ; Jan. 13 ; v. 270 ; p. 281.

Ryan, John T., assignor to Mine Safety Appliance Company, Pittsburgh, Pa. Regenerator for breathing apparatus. No. 1,328,058 ; Jan. 13 ; v. 270 ; p. 282.

Samelson, Bernard. (See Smith and Samelson.)

Sanford, Crocker H., assignor to The Old Dominion Specialty Co., Inc., Baltimore, Md. Mixing device. No. 1,328,204 ; Jan. 13 ; v. 270 ; p. 309.

Sanders, Thomas J., Montreal, Quebec, Canada. Cross-over. No. 1,327,882 ; Jan. 13 ; v. 270 ; p. 248.

Schaefer, George A., Chicago, Ill. Connector-clip. No. 1,327,844 ; Jan. 13 ; v. 270 ; p. 241.

Schaefer, William J., Ontario, Calif. Cooker. No. 1,328,239 ; Jan. 13 ; v. 270 ; p. 316.

Scharffenberg, Jean H., assignor to J. H. Stewart, Lynn, Mass. Counter-lasting machine. No. 1,327,780 ; Jan. 13 ; v. 270 ; p. 230.

Schechter, Jacob. (See Rosenfeld, Maurice S., assignor.)

Schilling, Frederick W., Louisville, Ohio. Bottle-closure. No. 1,328,205 ; Jan. 13 ; v. 270 ; p. 310.

Schleicher, William A., Cleveland, Ohio. Blanket-fastener. No. 1,328,206 ; Jan. 13 ; v. 270 ; p. 310.

Schluer, William M., Orange, N. J. Interchangeable vehicle. No. 1,327,883 ; Jan. 13 ; v. 270 ; p. 249.

Schmidt, Christ, Everett, Wash. Trough. No. 1,328,207; Jan. 13; v. 270; p. 310.

Schneider & Cie. (See Schneider, Eugène, assignor.)

Schneider, Eberhard. deceased, New York, N. Y.; S. Schneider, administratrix. Chain. No. 1,327,925; Jan. 13; v. 270; p. 257.

Schneider, Eugène. assignor to Schneider & Cie., Paris, France. Mechanism for disengaging and engaging the main governors in steam hoisting-engines. No. 1,327,633; Jan. 13; v. 270; p. 202.

Schneider, Stanislawa, administratrix. (See Schneider, Eberhard.)

Scholes, Samuel R., Beaver, and R. F. Brenner, assignors to J. Howard Fry, Rochester, Pa. Extracting potassium from potash-bearing silicate minerals. No. 1,327,781; Jan. 13; v. 270; p. 230.

Scholes, Samuel R., Beaver, assignor to H. C. Fry Glass Company, Rochester, Pa. Obtaining combined potassium from minerals. No. 1,327,782; Jan. 13; v. 270; p. 230.

Schonk, Edward P., Wilkes-Barre, Pa. Reamer. No. 1,328,208; Jan. 13; v. 270; p. 310.

Scott, Thomas W., assignor to The American Train Control Co., Baltimore. Md. Air-brake-controlling mechanism. No. 1,327,968; Jan. 13; v. 270; p. 264.

Scott, William D., Martins Ferry, Ohio. Air collecting and delivering apparatus. No. 1,327,926; Jan. 13; v. 270; p. 257.

Schreiner, Arthur W., Brooklyn, assignor to Standard Scientific Company, New York, N. Y. Resonator. No. 1,328,059; Jan. 13; v. 270; p. 282.

Sears, Roebuck and Company. (See Dun Lany, William P., assignor.)

Sechler & Company, The. (See Baldwin, Frank G., assignor.)

Sechler & Company, The. (See Knapp, Jacob, assignor.)

Senna, Samuel N., assignor to B. F. Perkins & Son, Inc., Holyoke, Mass. Lubricated fan-mounting. No. 1,328,017; Jan. 13; v. 270; p. 274.

Servis. Fred T., Ontario, N. Y. Pouring-spout for cans. No. 1,328,104; Jan. 13; v. 270; p. 290.

Settlage, August C., New Bremen, Ohio. Dumping mechanism for trucks and the like. No. 1,328,240; Jan. 13; v. 270; p. 317.

Sharp, Samuel J. assignor to J. L. Stifel & Sons, Wheeling, W. Va. Lubricator. No. 1,328,209; Jan. 13; v. 270; p. 310.

Sharpless Specialty Company, The. (See Jones, Leo D., assignor.)

Sheasley, Charles H., Franklin, Pa. Variable gas-port for gas-engines. No. 1,327,927; Jan. 13; v. 270; p. 257.

Shinn, Bessie. (See Shinn, Lita and B.)

Shinn. Lita and B., Muskogee, Okla. Hand-painted rag doll. No. 1,327,884; Jan. 13; v. 270; p. 249.

Shires, George M., Houston, Tex. Apparatus for extracting minerals from ores. No. 1,328,210; Jan. 13; v. 270; p. 311.

Short, Samuel B., Humboldt, Tenn. Adjustable bulkhead for freight-cars. No. 1,327,634; Jan. 13; v. 270; p. 202.

Shuman. Cleo G., assignor to Gyp Steel Products Company, Chicago, Ill. Means for fastening plaster-boards and the like. No. 1,327,741; Jan. 13; v. 270; p. 222.

Siemens, Schuckert Werke, G. m. b. H. (See Fischer, Kuno, assignor.)

Silverman, Wulf, New York, N. Y. Bottle-closure. No. 1,328,060; Jan. 13; v. 270; p. 282.

Sines, Harold S. (See Ferguson, Louis A., assignor.)

Simplex Electric Heating Company. (See Hewitt, Frank W., assignor.)

Siqueira, Edward C., Oakland, Calif. Change-making machine. No. 1,328,969; Jan. 13; v. 270; p. 264.

Skinner, Stephen G., Chicago, Ill. Air-pump. No. 1,327,783; Jan. 13; v. 270; p. 230.

Slagenhauf, August. (See Drake and Slagenhauf.)

Slick. Edwin E., Westmont Borough, Pa. Wheel-mill. No. 1,327,635; Jan. 13; v. 270; p. 202.

Sloan, Ira L., North Yakima, Wash. Flying-machine. No. 1,328,211; Jan. 13; v. 270; p. 311.

Slocomb. F. F. & Co. (See Flanagan, James U., assignor.)

Smith. Charles M., Bellingham, Wash. Auxiliary automobile-seat. No. 1,328,105; Jan. 13; v. 270; p. 291.

Smith, Gerald F., Braddock township, Allegheny county, Pa. assignor to Westinghouse Electric & Manufacturing Company. System of control. No. 1,327,784; Jan. 13; v. 270; p. 230.

Smith, Karl D., Battle Creek. Mich., and B. Samelson, New York, N. Y., assignors to Union Steam Pump Company, Battle Creek, Mich. Rotary pump. No. 1,328,061; Jan. 13; v. 270; p. 282.

Smith, Oscar A., Cleveland, Ohio. Priming and testing cup. No. 1,327,687; Jan. 13; v. 270; p. 212.

Snow. Isaac. Lawrence. Mass. Picker-check. No. 1,328,018; Jan. 13; v. 270; p. 274.

Snyder, Edith L., Johnstown, Pa. Oil water-color paint. No. 1,327,928; Jan. 13; v. 270; p. 257.

Snyder, Simon, and L. C. Winegardner, Muncy, Pa. Bolting-machine. No. 1,327,636; Jan. 13; v. 270; p. 202.

Sonner, William I., Blaine. Idaho. Hay gatherer and stacker. No. 1,327,637; Jan. 13; v. 270; p. 202.

Sordillo, Fortunato. Boston, Mass. Mouthpiece for musical instruments. No. 1,327,970; Jan. 13; v. 270; p. 265.

Spangenberg, Arthur R. (See Reichman and Spangenberg.)

Spangler, William A. (See Burrows and Spangler.)

Spear, Herbert G. (See Fagan, Spear and Wolf.)

Spethmann, Peter H., New Effington, S. D. Burglar-alarm. No. 1,327,785; Jan. 13; v. 270; p. 230.

Stach, Carl T. (See Connell and Stach.)

Standard Oil Company. (See Burns and Winger, assignors.)

Standard Parts Company, The. (See McIntyre, Michael M., assignor.)

Standard Scientific Company. (See Schreiner, Arthur W., assignor.)

Stanifer, William D., Chickasha, Okla. Gin-saw cleaner, tooth straightener and sharpener. No. 1,328,212; Jan. 13; v. 270; p. 311.

Starkenberg, Karl R., Andover, assignor to J. J. Petroske, Methuen, Mass. Centering device. No. 1,328,213; Jan. 13; v. 270; p. 311.

Starr Piano Company, The. (See Mayer, Fred G., assignor.)

Steel, Charles C. and T. H. Lynn, Williamsport, Pa. Tire-carrier for automobiles. No. 1,327,742; Jan. 13; v. 270; p. 222.

Steere, William J., Rockwood, Tenn. Looping-machine. No. 1,327,638; Jan. 13; v. 270; p. 203.

Stephan, Charles H., Springfield, Ohio. Medical appliance. No. 1,327,786; Jan. 13; v. 270; p. 231.

Stevens, George B., Granite City, Ill. Roll-polisher. No. 1,327,639; Jan. 13; v. 270; p. 203.

Stevens, William C., assignor to The Cutler-Hammer Mfg. Co., Milwaukee, Wis. Motor-controller. No. 1,327,787; Jan. 13; v. 270; p. 231.

Stewart, Alexander, Clintonville, Wis. Selective speed-transmission mechanism. No. 1,328,062; Jan. 13; v. 270; p. 282.

Stewart, John H. (See Scharffenberg, Jean H., assignor.)

Stewart. Thomas H., Atlanta, Ga., assignor to American Can Company, New York, N. Y. Label for bale-ties. No. 1,328,019; Jan. 13; v. 270; p. 274.

Stewart-Warner Speedometer Corporation. (See Genn, John E., assignor.)

Stifel, J. L., & Sons. (See Sharp, Samuel J., assignor.)

Stimpson, Edward S., assignor to Draper Corporation, Hopedale, Mass. Feeler mechanism for looms. No. 1,327,788; Jan. 13; v. 270; p. 231.

Stirling, Clarence C., assignor to The Hart & Hegeman Manufacturing Company, Hartford. Conn. Electric switch. No 1,327,640; Jan. 13; v. 270; p. 203.

St. John, Justin M., Cedar Rapids, Iowa. Weeder. No. 1,328,063; Jan. 13; v. 270; p. 283.

Stockton, Lincoln C., and C. F. Goddard, assignors to The Metal Separation Company, Denver, Colo. Apparatus for saving metallic values. No. 1,327,885; Jan. 13; v. 270; p. 249.

Stoll, Frank M., Denver. Colo. Collapsible bed. No. 1,327,886; Jan. 13; v. 270; p. 249.

Stoll, Frank M., Denver. Colo. Tent-bed. No. 1,327,887; Jan. 13; v. 270; p. 249.

Stolp, Frank H., Geneva, N. Y. Machine for forming metal tubes. No. 1,327,461; Jan. 13; v. 270; p. 203.

Stone, Ben M., Chicago, Ill. Lock. No. 1,328,106; Jan. 13; v. 270; p. 291.

Storer, Norman W., Pittsburgh, Pa., assignor to Westinghouse Electric & Manufacturing Company. System of control. No. 1,327,789; Jan. 13; v. 270; p. 231.

Street, Norman A., et al. (See Blood, Burr B., assignor.)

Sun Company. (See Ballard, Albert M., assignor.)

Sundstrom, G. E. (See Anderson, Charles A., assignor.) (Reissue.)

Swint, Wendell R. (See Bryan and Swint.)

Sykes, George, assignor to Sykes Standard Fruit Wrap Company, Penryn, Calif. Packing device. No. 1,327,888; Jan. 13; v. 270; p. 250.

Sykes, Leonard, Fort Wayne. Ind. Electric regulator. No. 1,327,642; Jan. 13; v. 270; p. 208.

Sykes Standard Fruit Wrap Company. (See Sykes, George, assignor.)

Symonds, Clarence M., San Anselmo, assignor to American Can Company, San Francisco, Calif. Apparatus for cutting and applying ring-liners to the flanges of can ends. No. 1,328,020; Jan. 13; v. 270; p. 274.

Syracuse Chilled Plow Company. (See Lee, William H., assignor.)

Taggesell. Richard, Buffalo, assignor to National Aniline & Chemical Company. Inc., New York, N. Y. Azo dyes and making same. No. 1,327,688; Jan. 13; v. 270; p. 213.

Tarn, Thomas R., Brooklyn, N. Y. Combined steering and handling system for tow-boats and their vessels. No. 1,327,643; Jan. 13; v. 270; p. 204.

Tartrais, Eugène H., Maisons-Laffitte, France. Atomizer for liquid-fuel engines. No. 1,327,744; Jan. 13; v. 270; p. 223.

Taylor, Harry H. Fresno. Calif. Hopper for filling cartons with raisins and similar articles of merchandise. No. 1,327,644; Jan. 13; v. 270; p. 204.

Taylor, Horace V. S., Pittsburgh, Pa., assignor to Westinghouse Electric and Manufacturing Company. Ignition system. No. 1,327,790; Jan. 13; v. 270; p. 231.

Tebbetts, Lewis B., 2d, St. Louis, Mo. Making powdered or granulated aluminum. No. 1,327,743; Jan. 13; v. 270; p. 228.

Wolff, Franklyn J., assignor of one-half to H. W. Wolff, Chicago, Ill. Vehicle-spring. No. 1,327,750; Jan. 13; v. 270; p. 224.

Wolff, Harold W. (See Wolff, Franklyn J., assignor.)

Wollaston, Thomas R., Manchester, England. Gas-generator. No. 1,327,893; Jan. 13; v. 270; p. 250.

Wood, James J., Fort Wayne, Ind., assignor to N. C. Hurley, Chicago, Ill. Clothes-wringer. No. 1,327,690; Jan. 13; v. 270; p. 213.

Woodhouse, George. Butte, Mont. Card-index. No. 1,327,848; Jan. 13; v. 270; p. 242.

Wotherspoon, James R., Philadelphia, Pa., and F. E. Coatsworth, Lincoln, Nebr. Stove. No. 1,327,796; Jan. 13; v. 270; p. 233.

Wroclawski, Valenty, Chicago, Ill. Freight-car. No. 1,327,894; Jan. 13; v. 270; p. 251.

Yai, Sakizo, Tokyo, Japan. Dry battery. No. 1,328,027; Jan. 13; v. 270; p. 276.

Young, Daniel H., Manchester, Iowa. Electrically-heated humidifier. No. 1,328,068; Jan. 13; v. 270; p. 284.

Young, Daniel H., Manchester, Iowa. Electrothermogenic device for humidifiers. No. 1,328,069; Jan. 13; v. 270; p. 284.

Young, Ida A., administratrix. (See Young, John V.)

Young, James H., assignor to Aspromet Company, Pittsburgh, Pa. Coating material. No. 1,327,933; Jan. 13; v. 270; p. 258.

Young, John V., deceased, Reading, Mass.; I. A. Young, administratrix, assignor to The Union Switch & Signal Company, Swissvale, Pa. Railway signaling. No. 1,326,070; Jan. 13; v. 270; p. 284.

Zahm, Edward, assignor to Zahm Manufacturing Company, Buffalo, N. Y. Filter. No. 1,328,221; Jan. 13; v. 270; p. 313.

Zahm Manufacturing Company. (See Zahm, Edward, assignor.)

Zielisko, John, Sniatyn, Alberta, Canada. Vehicle-wheel. No 1,327,849; Jan. 13; v. 270; p. 242.

Ziemer, Frederick, Freeport, N. Y. Faucet. No. 1,327,850; Jan. 13; v. 270; p. 243.

ALPHABETICAL LIST OF REGISTRANTS OF TRADE-MARKS.

Aberdeen Packing Co., Aberdeen, Wash. Canned salmon. No. 128,587; Jan. 13; v. 270; p. 335.

Acme Packing Co., Chicago, Ill. Meat patties. No. 128,588; Jan. 13; v. 270; p. 335.

Adrian Neckwear Co., Portland, Oreg. Neckties. No. 128,589; Jan. 13; v. 270; p. 335.

Air Reduction Company, Incorporated, New York, N. Y. Calcium carbid. No. 128,590; Jan. 13; v. 270; p. 335.

Alban, John A., & Co., Inc., New York. N. Y. Olive-oil. No. 128,591; Jan. 13; v. 270; p. 335.

Albemarle Paper Mfg. Co., Richmond, Va. Blotting-paper. No. 128,592; Jan. 13; v. 270; p. 335.

Allen & Hanburys, Ltd., London, England. Pepton for bacteriological use. No. 128,593; Jan. 13; v. 270; p. 335.

American Abrasive Metals Co., New York, N. Y. Treads and panels for stairways, floors, &c. No. 128,594; Jan. 13; v. 270; p. 335.

American Factories, Limited, Honolulu, Hawaii. Canned salmon and vegetables, &c. No. 128,596; Jan. 13; v. 270; p. 335.

American Factories, Limited, Honolulu, Hawaii. Coffee, canned fruits, lemons. No. 128,595; Jan. 13; v. 270; p. 335.

American Grinder Manufacturing Company, Milwaukee, Wis. Socket-wrenches. No. 128,597; Jan. 13; v. 270; p. 335.

American Laboratories Incorporated, Richmond. Va. Antiseptic, disinfectant, &c. No. 128,599; Jan. 13; v. 270; p. 335.

American Laboratories Incorporated, Richmond, Va. Food-flavoring extracts. No. 128,600; Jan. 13; v. 270; p. 335.

American Laboratories Incorporated, Richmond, Va. Hair-dressing preparation. No. 128,598; Jan. 13; v. 270; p. 335.

American Lead Pencil Company, New York, N. Y. Lead-pencils. No. 128,601; Jan. 13; v. 270; p. 335.

American Metal Company, Limited, The, New York, N. Y. White arsenic. No. 128,602; Jan. 13; v. 270; p. 335.

American Mustard Co. Inc., New York, N. Y. Mustard. No. 128,603; Jan. 13; v. 270; p. 335.

American Writing Paper Co., Holyoke, Mass. Printing and writing paper. No. 128,604; Jan. 13; v. 270; p. 335.

Amory, Browne & Co., New York, N. Y. Cotton piece goods. No. 128,605; Jan. 13; v. 270; p. 335.

Andersen, A. O , & Co., Portland. Oreg. Canned salmon. Nos. 128,606–8; Jan. 13; v. 270; p. 335.

Ansbacher, A. B., & Company, Inc., New York, N. Y. Insecticides and fungicides. No. 128,609; Jan. 13; v. 270; p. 335.

Apsley Rubber Company, Hudson, Mass. Shoes and rubber footwear. Nos. 128,610–11; Jan. 13; v. 270; p. 335.

Armstrong Cork Company, Pittsburgh, Pa. Corks. No. 128,612; Jan. 13; v. 270; p. 335.

Ayotte, Joseph R., Chicago, Ill. Spark-plug. No. 128,613; Jan. 13; v. 270; p. 335.

Bahr, Leopold, Brooklyn, N.Y. Antiseptic for cleansing the teeth. No. 128,614; Jan. 13; v. 270; p. 335.

Baltimore Bargain House, Baltimore and Cumberland, Md. Work-shirts. No. 128,615; Jan. 13; v. 270; p. 335.

Barber, Bessie L., Los Angeles, Calif. Toilet creams, face-bleach, &c. No. 128,616; Jan. 13; v. 270; p. 336.

Barbour Brothers Co., Paterson, N. J. Linen thread. No. 128,617; Jan. 13; v. 270; p. 336.

Barr, F. E. & Company, Chicago, Ill. Antiseptic liquid. No. 128,618; Jan. 13; v. 270; p. 336.

Bear-Cat Products Co., Inc., The, Oklahoma, Okla. Radiator-seal. No. 128,619; Jan. 13; v. 270; p. 336.

Beaudette & Graham Engineering Co., Boston, Mass. Electric-lighting plants. No. 128,620; Jan. 13; v. 270; p. 336.

Beech-Nut Packing Corporation, Canajoharie, N. Y. Ginger-ale. No. 128,621; Jan. 13; v. 270; p. 336.

Bell Pump & Manufacturing Co., Detroit, Mich. Automobile air pumps and oil-pumps and grease-cups. No. 128,622; Jan 13; v. 270; p. 336.

Benn, Joseph, & Sons Inc., Greystone, R. I., and New York, N. Y. Cotton and mohair piece goods, &c. No. 128,623; Jan. 13; v. 270; p. 336.

Benson, Nina B., Memphis, Tenn. Laxative medicine. No. 128,624; Jan. 13; v. 270; p. 336.

Berlault, Joseph B., Seattle, Wash. Hair-tonic. No. 128,625; Jan. 13; v. 270; p. 336.

Berry & Lewis, New York, N. Y. Fuel control for internal-combustion engines. No. 128,627; Jan. 13; v. 270; p. 336.

Berry. Joseph, Binghamton, N. Y. Cream or salve for congestion and inflammation. No. 128,626; Jan. 13; v. 270; p. 336.

Bickell, David A., assignor to San-tro-pas Manufacturing Company, Limited, Lethbridge, Alberta, Canada. Healing compounds. No. 128,628; Jan. 13; v. 270; p. 336.

Binghamton Candy Co., Binghamton, N. Y. Confectionery. No. 128,629; Jan. 13; v. 270; p. 336.

Birrell Silent Motor Co. Inc., Chicago, Ill. Valves for internal-combustion engines. No. 128,630; Jan. 13; v. 270; p. 336.

Blatchford Calf Meal Company, Waukegan, Ill. Compound ground feed for rabbits, &c. No. 128,631; Jan. 13; v. 270; p. 336.

Blatchford Calf Meal Company, Waukegan, Ill. Feeds for animals and poultry. No. 128,632; Jan. 13; v. 270; p. 336.

Block & Drexler, New York, N. Y.; said Drexler assignor to said Block. Men's neckties and scarfs. No. 128,633; Jan. 13; v. 270; p. 336.

Bloom, Abram, Co., Inc., Paterson, N. J. Thrown silk. No. 128,634; Jan. 13; v. 270; p. 336.

Bodinson-Terrell Candy Co., Chicago, Ill. Candy. No. 128,635; Jan. 13; v. 270; p. 336.

Bonhour Co. Inc., Syracuse, N. Y. Toilet water. No. 128,636; Jan. 13; v. 270; p. 336.

Booth & Platt Co., Bridgeport, Conn. Ginger-beer. No. 128,637; Jan. 13; v. 270; p. 336.

Bowers, Otho D., Richmond, Ind. Spark-plugs. No. 128,638; Jan. 13; v. 270; p. 336.

Bradley & Vrooman Company, Chicago, Ill. Germicide. No. 128,640; Jan. 13; v. 270; p. 336.

Bradley, Willis C., Marshfield, Oreg. Medicinal preparation for the treatment of catarrh, &c. No. 128,639; Jan. 13; v. 270; p. 336.

Brener, J., Co., Boston, Mass. Ladies' petticoats. No. 128,641; Jan. 13; v. 270; p. 336.

Brigham-Hopkins Company, Baltimore, Md. Men's hats. No. 128,648; Jan. 13; v. 270; p. 336.

Brohard. George M., Philadelphia, Pa. Rouge. No. 128,643; Jan. 13; v. 270; p. 336.

Brooklyn, Shield & Rubber Co., Brooklyn, N. Y. Women's dress-shields. No. 128,644; Jan. 13; v. 270; p. 336.

Cadwallader, Harry, Jr., Philadelphia, Pa. Steel forgings and castings. No. 128,645; Jan. 13; v. 270; p. 336.

Cascade Cider Company, Springville. N. Y. Vinegar. No. 128,646; Jan. 13; v. 270; p. 336.

Cataract Chemical Company, Inc., Buffalo, N. Y. Chemicals for use in the manufacture of leather. No. 128,647; Jan. 13; v. 270; p. 337.

Chain Shirt Shops, Inc., New York, N. Y. Men's shirts, underwear, &c. No. 128,648; Jan. 13; v. 270; p. 337.

Chattanooga Medicine Co., Chattanooga, Tenn. Medicine for female diseases. No. 128,649; Jan. 13; v. 270; p. 337.

Chinook Lumber & Shingle Co., Seattle, Wash. Shingles. No. 128,650; Jan. 13; v. 270; p. 337.

Christenson, Hanify & Weatherwax, San Francisco, Calif. Canned pears, salmon, and tomatoes. No. 128,652; Jan. 13; v. 270; p. 337.

Christenson, Hanify & Weatherwax, San Francisco. Calif. Canned salmon, peaches, and tomatoes. No. 128,651; Jan. 13; v. 270; p. 337.

City Consumers Co., Paducah, Ky. Ice-cream, butter, milk, &c. No. 128,653; Jan. 13; v. 270; p. 337.
Cohen, Charles S., Newark, N. J. Preparation for the amelioration of pyorrhea, &c. No. 128,654; Jan. 13; v. 270; p. 337.
Colorado Milling & Elevator Co., Denver, Colo., and Weiser, Idaho. Wheat-flour. No. 128,655; Jan. 13; v. 270; p. 337.
Columbia Produce Company, Columbia, Nashville, Waverly, McEwen, Dickson, Loretto, Lawrenceburg, Fayetteville, Petersburg, Chapel Hill, and Lewisburg, Tenn. Dressed poultry, butter, eggs. No. 128,856; Jan. 13; v. 270; p. 337.
Community Furnace Company, Covington, Ky. Hot-air furnaces. No. 128,657; Jan. 13; v. 270; p. 337.
Continental Drug Corporation, St. Louis, Mo. Hypophosphites compound and a non-alcoholic tonic. No. 128,658; Jan. 13; v. 270; p. 337.
Cooper, Coate & Casey Dry Goods Co., Los Angeles, Calif., and New York, N. Y. Garments. No. 128,659; Jan. 13; v. 270; p. 337.
Coppus Engineering and Equipment Company., Worcester, Mass. Hydraulic and centrifugal pumps and turbines. No. 128,660; Jan. 13; v. 270; p. 337.
Crane, Clarence A., Cleveland, Ohio. Candy. No. 128,661; Jan. 13; v. 270; p. 337.
Crawford, James J., Los Angeles, Calif. Dried parts of ephedra-plant. No. 128,662; Jan. 13; v. 270; p. 337.
Crescent Coffee Mills, Inc., New Orleans, La. Coffee. Nos. 128,663-4; Jan. 13; v. 270; p. 337.
Crescent Coffee Mills, Inc., New Orleans, La. Coffee. No. 128,667; Jan. 13; v. 270; p. 337.
Crescent Coffee Mills, Inc., New Orleans, La. Tea. No. 128,665; Jan. 13; v. 270; p. 337.
Creotina Chemical Company, St. Louis, Mo. Remedy for cuts, bruises, burns, sprains, &c. No. 128,666; Jan. 13; v. 270; p. 337.
Crusellas, Alberto, Habana, Cuba. Perfumes. No. 128,668; Jan. 13; v. 270; p. 337.
Damaske, William, Seattle, Wash. Insecticides. No. 128,672; Jan. 13; v. 270; p. 337.
Dannenhirsch, Max, Philadelphia, Pa. Compound for stopping leaks in radiators, boilers, &c. No. 128,669; Jan. 13; v. 270; p. 337.
Dasb, Allan J., Olean, N. Y. Medicinal balm for inflammations. No. 128,673; Jan. 13; v. 270; p. 337.
Davidson, Arthur C., New York, N. Y. Steel. No. 128,670; Jan. 13; v. 270; p. 337.
De Laval Separator Company, New York, N. Y. Pneumatic pumps. No. 128,671; Jan. 13; v. 270; p. 337.
Detroit Heating & Lighting Company, Detroit, Mich. Bunsen burners. No. 128,674; Jan. 13; v. 270; p. 337.
Dickinson Drug Co., Los Angeles, Calif. Tonic, powders, ointment, and cream. No. 128,675; Jan. 13; v. 270; p. 337.
Dittlinger, H., Roller Mills Company, New Braunfels, Tex. Wheat-flour. No. 128,676; Jan. 13; v. 270; p. 337.
Drobinski, Felix I., Brooklyn, N. Y. Eye-wash. No. 128,677; Jan. 13; v. 270; p. 337.
Dugas-Hundley Corporation, New York, N. Y. Dyes. No. 128,678; Jan. 13; v. 270; p. 338.
Edgerton Salt Brick Company, Goldsboro, N. C., and Atlanta, Ga. Salt brick. No. 128,679; Jan. 13; v. 270; p. 338.
Ehrlich, H. & Sons Mfg. Co., St. Joseph, Mo. Pickling compound for meats. No. 128,680; Jan. 13; v. 270; p. 338.
Electric & Ordnance Accessories Company Limited, Birmingham, England. Electric heaters, cookers, &c. No. 128,681; Jan. 13; v. 270; p. 338.
Empire Rolling Screen Co., Inc., Rochester, N. Y. Window-screens. No. 128,682; Jan. 13; v. 270; p. 338.
Enlow Co., Inc., New York, N. Y. Stationery. No. 128,683; Jan. 13; v. 270; p. 338.
Entire Wheat Bread Company, St. Louis, Mo. Bread. No. 128,684; Jan. 13; v. 270; p. 338.
Eppolito, Frank, Chicago, Ill. Hair-tonic. No. 128,685; Jan. 13; v. 270; p. 338.
Eslseck Manufacturing Co., Turners Falls, Mass. Bond, &c., paper. No. 128,687; Jan. 13; v. 270; p. 338.
Eslseck Manufacturing Co., Turners Falls, Mass. Bond-paper, non-carbonized type-writer and manifold papers, &c. No. 128,686; Jan. 13; v. 270; p. 338.
Essex Chemical Works, Inc., Belleville, N. J. Fur black, &c., dyes. No. 128,688; Jan. 13; v. 270; p. 338.
Essex Laboratories Inc., Newark, N. J. Cleaning compound. No. 128,689; Jan. 13; v. 270; p. 338.
Everwear Mfg. Co., San Francisco, Calif. Children's play-suits, men's overalls and overshirts. No. 128,690; Jan. 13; v. 270; p. 338.
Express Spark Plug Corporation, Washington, D. C. Spark-plugs. No. 128,691; Jan. 13; v. 270; p. 338.
Febeco Leather Corporation, Wilmington, Del., and New York, N. Y. Leather. No. 128,692; Jan. 13; v. 270; p. 338.
Federal Snap Fastener Corporation, New York, N. Y. Snap and placket fasteners. No. 128,693; Jan. 13; v. 270; p. 338.
Fisher, Lee, Mount Sterling, Ky. Medicine for scars, croup, &c. No. 128,694; Jan. 13; v. 270; p. 338.
Fisher, Robert J., Athens, Tenn. Hosiery. No. 128,695; Jan. 13; v. 270; p. 338.
Florein, Annie T., Cincinnati, Ohio. Preparation for treatment of female irregularities, &c. No. 128,696; Jan. 13; v. 270; p. 338.

Foley & Company, Chicago, Ill. Medicines, salves, &c. No. 128,697; Jan. 13; v. 270; p. 338.
Forged Products Co., Chicago, Ill. Unfinished and machined iron and steel forgings. No. 128,698; Jan. 13; v. 270; p. 338.
Francis, Frank L., Newark, N. J. Hair-tonics. No. 128,699; Jan. 13; v. 270; p. 338.
Frederick & Nelson, Seattle, Wash. Women's shoes. No. 128,700; Jan. 13; v. 270; p. 338.
French Valley Springs, Incorporated, Meadville, Pa. Ginger-ale. No. 128,701; Jan. 13; v. 270; p. 338.
Funke, Jos. B., Company, La Crosse, Wis. Candy. No. 128,702; Jan. 13; v. 270; p. 338.
Fuqua, John B., Altus, Okla. Medicinal preparation for venereal diseases. No. 128,703; Jan. 13; v. 270; p. 338.
Gaillard, Ella M., New York, N. Y., and Washington, D. C. Dress-shields. No. 128,704; Jan. 13; v. 270; p. 338.
Galeton Dairy Products Co., Galeton, Pa. Condensed milk. No. 128,705; Jan. 13; v. 270; p. 338.
Gartenlaub, Eve, New York, N. Y. Corn cure. No. 128,706; Jan. 13; v. 270; p. 338.
Gaskill Chemical Corporation, Brooklyn, N. Y. Fur-dyes. No. 128,707; Jan. 13; v. 270; p. 338.
Gas Products Co., Columbus, Ohio. Acetylene gas. No. 128,708; Jan. 13; v. 270; p. 338.
Gates, William H., Norfolk, Va. Home-made candies and chocolates. No. 128,709; Jan. 13; v. 270; p. 338.
General Motors Corporation, Detroit, Mich. Electricity-generating units. No. 128,710; Jan. 13; v. 270; p. 338.
Gerhold, Charles M., Philadelphia, Pa. Insecticides, disinfectants, and deodorizers. No. 128,711; Jan. 13; v. 270; p. 339.
Gibson, Il. B., Co., Inc., New York, N. Y. Vessels for heating beverages. No. 128,712; Jan. 13; v. 270; p. 339.
Golden Seal Laboratories, Inc., Parkensburg, W. Va. Effervescent salt combined with fruit derivatives. No. 128,713; Jan. 13; v. 270; p. 339.
Goodman & Beer Company, Inc., New Orleans, La. Eggs. No. 128,714; Jan. 13; v. 270; p. 339.
Grace, W. R., & Co., New York, N. Y. Boots and shoes. No. 127,715; Jan. 13; v. 270; p. 339.
Grace, W. R., & Co., New York, N. Y., and San Francisco, Calif. Dyes. No. 128,716; Jan. 13; v. 270; p. 339.
Greene, S. & M., Brooklyn, N. Y. Hair dressings and gloss, shampoo. No. 128,717; Jan. 13; v. 270; p. 339.
Grewen Fabric Co., Inc., Johnstown, N. Y. Dress-skirts. No. 128,718; Jan. 13; v. 270; p. 339.
Griffin, W. H., Company, Manchester, N. H. Men's, boys', and youths' leather shoes. No. 128,719; Jan. 13; v. 270; p. 339.
Hare, William I., New York, N. Y. Weeding-trowels. No. 128,720; Jan. 13; v. 270; p. 339.
Harrison, Levy, Philadelphia, Pa. Suits, coats, skirts, dresses. No. 128,721; Jan. 13; v. 270; p. 339.
Hart, Charles S., Film Company, New York, N. Y. Motion-picture films. No. 128,722; Jan. 13; v. 270; p. 339.
Harvard Brewing Co., (now by change of name Harvard Company.) Lowell, Mass. Ginger-ale. No. 128,724; Jan. 13; v. 270; p. 339.
Harvard Company. (See Harvard Brewing Co.)
Harvard Company, Lowell, Mass. Cereal non-intoxicating malt beverage. No. 128,723; Jan. 13; v. 270; p. 339.
Hussler, Fred H., Manning, Iowa. Live hogs. No. 128,725; Jan. 13; v. 270; p. 339.
Haynes Chemical Corporation, Richmond, Va. Insecticides, deodorizers, &c. No. 128,726; Jan. 13; v. 270; p. 339.
Health Food Baking Co., Inc., Newport News, Va. Bread and cake. No. 128,727; Jan. 13; v. 270; p. 339.
Heywood Brothers and Wakefield Company, Gardner, Mass. Furniture. No. 128,728; Jan. 13; v. 270; p. 339.
High Rock Knitting Company, Philmont, N. Y. Underwear. No. 128,729; Jan. 13; v. 270; p. 339.
Hipolite Company, St. Louis, Mo. Marshmallow powder and lemon, &c., flavoring extracts. No. 128,730; Jan. 13; v. 270; p. 339.
Hoberg, John, Co., Green Bay, Wis. Toilet paper, &c. No. 128,731; Jan. 13; p. 270; p. 339.
Hoebie & Johnson, Inc., Boston, Mass. Candies. No. 128,732; Jan. 13; v. 270; p. 339.
Holyoke Braiding Company, Holyoke, Mass. Shoe-laces. Nos. 128,733-4; Jan. 13; v. 270; p. 339.
Hoover Medicine Co., Des Moines, Iowa. Remedy for rheumatism, neuritis, &c. No. 128,735; Jan. 13; v. 270; p. 339.
Horowitz, Joseph, & Sons, Inc., New York, N. Y. Workshirts. No. 128,736; Jan. 13; v. 270; p. 339.
Hoskins Manufacturing Company, Detroit, Mich. Alloys containing nickel and aluminum. Nos. 128,737-8; Jan. 13; v. 270; p. 339.
India Refining Company, Philadelphia, Pa. Coconnut-oil. No. 128,739; Jan. 13; v. 270; p. 339.
Jahn, W. K., Co., Brooklyn, N. Y. Flavoring for foods. No. 128,740; Jan. 13; v. 270; p. 339.
Jensen & Sons Milling & Grain Co., Nelson, Nebr. Wheat-flour. No. 128,741; Jan. 13; v. 270; p. 339.
Johnson, Charles H., Salem, Ohio. Medicine for tuberculosis. No. 128,742; Jan. 13; v. 270; p. 339.
Johnson, Mead, & Co., Evansville, Ind. Preparation for treating acidity and infant ailments. No. 128,743; Jan. 13; v. 270; p. 340.

Juster, Avram, New York, N. Y. Medicines for use as a stomach compound. No. 128,744; Jan. 13; v. 270; p. 340.

Kaplan, Charles M., Philadelphia, Pa. Leather shoes. No. 128,745; Jan. 13; v. 270; p. 340.

Kelley-Clarke Co., Seattle, Wash. Coatings for candies and cake. No. 128,746; Jan. 13; v. 270; p. 340.

Kellner Bros., New York, N. Y. Children's dresses. No. 128,747; Jan. 13; v. 270; p. 340.

Kettleman, Edward H., Independence, Kans. Salve. No. 128,748; Jan. 13; v. 270; p. 340.

Kil-Tone Company, Vineland, N. J. Insecticide. No. 128,749; Jan. 13; v. 270; p. 340.

King, Joseph S., Chicago, Ill. Ointment for treatment of skin diseases and piles. No. 128,750; Jan. 13; v. 270; p. 340.

Kirchheimer Bros. Co., Chicago, Ill. Wrapping-paper. No. 128,751; Jan. 13; v. 270; p. 340.

Koppel Industrial Car & Equipment Company, Koppel and Pittsburgh, Pa. Steam-locomotives, bucket excavators, &c. No. 128,752; Jan. 13; v. 270; p. 340.

Krause, Chas. A., Milling Co., Greenfield, Wis. Stock feed. No. 128,753; Jan. 13; v. 270; p. 340.

Krieg Wallace & McQuaide, Charleston, W. Va. Stomach and liver tablets. No. 128,754; Jan. 13; v. 270; p. 340.

Kuppenheimer, B., & Co., Chicago, Ill. Men's and boys' suits, overcoats, &c. No. 128,755; Jan. 13; v. 270; p. 340.

Kwick-Bath Mfg. Corporation. Wilson, N. C. Canning apparatus. No. 128,756; Jan. 13; v. 270; p. 340.

Landers, Frary & Clark, New Britain, Conn. Electrically-driven apparatus. No. 128,757; Jan. 13; v. 270; p. 340.

Latta-Martin Pump Co., Hickory, N. C. Certain named cutlery, machinery, and tools, and parts thereof. Nos. 128,758-60; Jan. 13; v. 270; p. 340.

Latty, John W., St. Louis, Mo. Remedy for cuts, burns, &c. No. 128,761; Jan. 13; v. 270; p. 540.

Lawless, Robert L., Danville, Va. Preparation for treatment of cancers, tumors, &c. No. 128,762; Jan. 13; v. 270; p. 340.

Lawrence Knitting Company, Wilmington, Del., and Philadelphia, Pa. Knitted underwear. No. 128,763; Jan. 13; v. 270; p. 340.

Lehn & Fink, Inc., New York, N. Y. Antiseptic and disinfectant. No. 128,764; Jan. 13; v. 270; p. 340.

Lindner Shoe Co., Carlisle, Pa. Boots, shoes, &c. No. 128,765; Jan. 13; v. 270; p. 340.

Longbridge, Matthew H., Bogota, N. J. Tubular tags used on insulated wires. No. 128,766; Jan. 13; v. 270; p. 340.

Louis Drug Co., The, Bay City, Mich. Solvent for removal of corns, &c. No. 128,767; Jan. 13; v. 270; p. 340.

Lowenstein Radio Company, Inc., Brooklyn, N. Y., and Newark and Elizabeth, N. J. Photographic developers. No. 128,768; Jan. 13; v. 270; p. 340.

Lyons Ignition Company, Paterson, N. J. Spark-plugs. No. 128,769; Jan. 13; v. 270; p. 340.

Lyster Chemical Company, Augusta, Me. and New York, N. Y. Preservative preparation for vegetable fibers. No. 128,770; Jan. 13; v. 270; p. 340.

Lyster Chemical Company, Agusta, Me. and New York, N. Y. Spray for animals. No. 128,771; Jan. 13; v. 270; p. 340.

McDonald, J. G., Chocolate Co., Salt Lake City Utah. Chocolates. No. 128,772; Jan. 13; v. 270; p. 340

McElwain, W. H., Company, Boston, Mass. Boots and shoes. No. 128,773; Jan. 13; v. 270; p. 340.

McGovern, Edward B., Seattle, Wash. Canned salmon. No. 128,774; Jan. 18; v. 270; p. 341.

McLean, Dr. J. H., Medicine Co., St. Louis, Mo. Medical preparations and products. No. 128,775; Jan. 13; v. 270; p. 341.

McLean, Dr. J. H., Medicine Co., St. Louis, Mo. Purgative pills. No. 128,776; Jan. 13; v. 270; p. 341.

McMullen, Robert M., New York, N. Y. Sugar. No. 128,777; Jan. 13; v. 270; p. 341.

MacMorris Drug Co., Newark, N. J. Cough remedy and reconstructive tonic. No. 128,778; Jan. 13; v. 270; p. 341.

Marine Decking & Supply Co., Philadelphia and Eastern, Pa. Construction materials. No. 128,779; Jan. 13; v. 270; p. 341.

Marshall, Warren, Kansas City, Kans. Ointment for burns, cuts, &c. No. 128,780; Jan. 13; v. 270; p. 341.

Martin-Laskin Company, Milwaukee, Wis. Fur-bearing skins. No. 128,781; Jan. 13; v. 270; p. 341.

Mason, Blanche M., Chicago, Ill. Lip-rouge, face-powder, &c. No. 128,782; Jan. 13; v. 270; p. 341.

Mayflower Rubber Works Company, Braintree, Mass. Rubber soles and heels. No. 128,783; Jan. 13; v 270; p. 341.

Merrell, William S., Company, Cincinnati, Ohio. Concentrated form of Echinacea angustifolia. No. 128,784; Jan. 13; v. 270; p. 341.

Metropolitan Electric Mfg. Co., Long Island City, N. Y. Electric panel-boards. No. 128,785; Jan. 13; v. 270; p. 341.

Michigan Lubricator Company, Detroit, Mich. Water-gages, &c. Nos. 128,786-7; Jan. 13; v. 270; p. 341.

Migel, J. A., Inc., New York N. Y. Women's and misses' garments. No. 128,788; Jan. 13; v. 270; p. 341.

Miller, Charles N., Company, Boston, Mass. Candies. No. 128,790; Jan. 13; v. 270; p. 341.

Miller, Charles N., Co., Boston, Mass. Candy. No. 128,789; Jan. 13; v. 270; p. 341.

Miller, Vincent F., San Antonio, Tex. Cordial, skin-cream, &c. No. 128,912; Jan. 13; v. 270; p. 345.

Milton, Michael, New York, N. Y. Writing-paper. No. 128,791; Jan. 13; v. 270; p. 341.

Milwaukee Air Power Pump Company, Milwaukee, Wis. Pneumatic water pumping and supply systems. No. 128,792; Jan. 13; v. 270; p. 341.

Moline Heat, Moline, Ill. Heating and ventilating apparatus. No. 128,793; Jan. 13; v. 270; p. 341.

Morgenthal, Otto, Dayton, Ohio. Fuel-ignition substance. No. 128,794; Jan. 13; v. 270; p. 341.

Morrell, John, & Company, Ottumwa, Iowa. Breakfast-bacon. No. 128,795; Jan. 13; v. 270; p. 341.

Moshontz Bros. & Co., Cleveland, Ohio. Women's dresses. No. 128,796; Jan. 13; v. 270; p. 341.

Musher & Company Incorporated, New York, N. Y.; Baltimore, Md.; San Diego, Calif., and Washington, D. C. Peanut-oil. No. 128,797; Jan. 13; v. 270; p. 341.

Musher & Company Inc., New York, N. Y. Sesame-oil. No. 128,798; Jan. 13; v. 270; p. 341.

Napoleon, Mrs. Mary, Albuquerque, N. Mex. Ointments for burns, warts, &c. No. 128,799; Jan. 13; v. 270; p. 341.

National Blue Ribbon Remedy Company, St. Louis, Mo. Poultry-powder, lice-killer, preparation for treatment of chicken-cholera and roup. No. 128,800; Jan. 13; v. 270; p. 341.

National Chain Company, New York, N. Y. Antiskid-chains. No. 128,801; Jan. 13; v. 270; p. 341.

National Fruit Products Company, Inc., Alexandria, Va. Apple jam. No. 128,802; Jan. 13; v. 270; p. 341.

Newell, George R., & Co., Minneapolis, Minn. Molasses, olives, &c. No. 128,803; Jan. 13; v. 270; p. 341.

Nicholas Power Company, Inc., New York, N. Y. Arc-lamps and parts. No. 128,805; Jan. 13; v. 270; p. 341.

Nicholas Power Company, Inc., New York, N. Y. Electric-light-projecting equipment for motion-picture machines, &c. No. 128,804; Jan. 13; v. 270; p. 341.

No-Ouch Mfg. Co., Sioux Falls, S. D. Corn-remover compounds. No. 128,806; Jan. 13; v. 270; p. 342.

Olive Tablet Company, Columbus, Ohio. Olive-oil tablets. No. 128,807; Jan. 13; v. 270; p. 342.

Omo Mfg. Co., Middletown, Conn. Gum tissue. No. 128,810; Jan. 13; v. 270; p. 341.

Omo Mfg. Co., Middletown, Conn. Hospital-sheeting. Nos. 128,808-9; Jan. 13; v. 270; p. 342.

Oppelt, Alvin F., Elma, Wash. Preserved salmon-eggs. No. 128,811; Jan. 13; v. 270; p. 342.

Pace, Bitts, Ironton, Ala. Electrical intensifiers. No. 128,812; Jan. 13; v. 270; p. 342.

Pacific Export Lumber Co., Portland, Oreg. Peanuts. No. 128,813; Jan. 13; v. 270; p. 342.

Parmoline Co., Richmond, Va. Hair-tonic. No. 128,814; Jan. 13; v. 270; p. 342.

Patent Cereals Co., Geneva and New York, N. Y. Cereal breakfast food. No. 128,815; Jan. 13; v. 270; p. 342.

Peck, Samuel W., & Co., Brooklyn, N. Y. Knitted and flat underwear for men. No. 128,816; Jan. 13; v. 270; p. 342.

Peppers, Thomas H., Los Angeles, Calif. Fresh citrus and deciduous fruits. No. 128,817; Jan. 13; v. 270; p. 342.

Phoenix-Hermetic Co., Chicago, Ill. Metal caps for jars or bottles. No. 128,818; Jan. 13; v. 270; p. 342.

Polk County Citrus Sub-Exchange, Bartow, Fla. Citrus fruits. No. 128,819; Jan. 13; v. 270; p. 342.

Pollak Steel Company, Cincinnati, Ohio. Locomotive and machinery axles. No. 128,820; Jan. 13; v. 270; p. 342.

Postum Cereal Company, Battle Creek, Mich. Hominy feed. No. 128,821; Jan. 13; v. 270; p. 342.

Powell & Campbell, New York, N. Y. Shoes. No. 128,822; Jan. 13; v. 270; p. 342.

Powerol Chemical Company, Pittsburgh, Pa. Eczema-ointment. No. 128,823; Jan. 13; v. 270; p. 342.

Price, Lawrence T., Richmond Va. Liquid for the treatment of gonorrhea. No. 128,824; Jan. 13; v. 270; p. 342.

Prime Shirt Co., Inc., New York, N. Y. Outer shirts and pajamas. No. 128,825; Jan. 13; v. 270; p. 342.

Producer's Paper Company, St. Paul, Minn. Novelty paper coverings for boxes. No. 128,826; Jan. 13; v. 270; p. 342.

Proper Antiseptic Laboratory, Cincinnati, Ohio. Antiseptic, germicide, &c. No. 128,827; Jan. 13; v. 270; p. 342.

Purity Cross, Inc., West Orange, N. J. Food products in tins, &c. No. 128,828; Jan. 13; v. 270; p. 342.

Quaker City Flour Mills Co., Philadelphia Pa. Wheat-flour. No 128,829; Jan. 13; v. 270; p. 342.

Rada-Solvt Co., Los Angeles, Calif. Chemical solution to clean out radiators and boilers. No. 128,830; Jan. 13; v. 270; p. 342.

Reno Flour Mills Company, Hutchinson, Kans. Wheat-flour. No. 128,831; Jan. 13; v. 270; p. 342.

Reusche, L., & Company, New York, N. Y. Finishing for glass, china, &c. No. 128,832; Jan. 13; v. 270; p. 342.

Richards, A. B., Medicine Co. Inc., Sherman. Tex. Salve and liniment. No. 128,833; Jan. 13; v. 270; p. 342.

Richter, F. Ad., & Co., New York, N. Y. Tonics. No. 128,834; Jan. 13; v. 270; p. 342.

Ricker, Howard H., Minneapolis, Minn. Liniment. No. 128,835; Jan. 13; v. 270; p. 342.

Ringler, Geo., & Co., New York, N. Y. Non-intoxicating beverages. No. 128,836; Jan. 13; v. 270; p. 342.

Rohrman-Cooper Company, Chicago, Ill. Ventilators for roofs and skylights. No. 128,837; Jan. 13; v. 270; p. 342.

Rosenstein, J., New York, N. Y. Wheat-flour. No. 128,838; Jan, 13; v. 270; p. 343.

Rodent Exterminator Laboratories, Chicago, Ill. Preparation for exterminating rodents. No. 128,839; Jan. 13; v. 270; p. 343.

Saberton Mfg. Co., Tampa, Fla. Soap. No. 128,840; Jan. 13; v. 270; p. 343.

Salz Brothers, New York, N. Y. Magazine-pencils. No. 128,841; Jan. 13; v. 270; p. 343.

Santiago Orange Growers Association, Orange, Calif. Fresh oranges. No. 128,842; Jan. 13; v. 270; p. 343.

San-tro-pas Manufacturing Company, Limited. (See Bickell, David A., assignor.)

Sauer, C. F., Co., Richmond, Va. Food-flavoring extracts. No. 128,843; Jan. 13; v. 270; p. 343.

Schaffer, William H., Cumberland, Md. Cleaning preparation for removing tar, &c., from automobiles, &c. No. 128,844; Jan. 13; v. 270; p. 343.

Scheidt, Adam, Beverage Co., Norristown, Pa. Sarsaparilla, ginger-ale, lemon-soda. No. 128,845; Jan. 13; v. 270; p. 343.

Schlar, Herman, Philadelphia, Pa. Hair and scalp preparation. No. 128,846; Jan. 13; v. 270; p. 343.

Schlesinger, Harry, Brooklyn, N. Y. Remedy for corns, warts, &c. No. 128,847; Jan. 13; v. 270; p. 343.

Schulemann, F., Co., New York, N. Y. Floss for embroidery and cotton for crocheting. No. 128,849; Jan. 13; v. 270; p. 343.

Screen Letter Box, Inc., New York, N. Y. Motion-picture films. No. 128,848; Jan. 13; v. 270; p. 343.

Senoret Chemical Co., St. Louis, Mo. Medicinal preparation useful as external treatment for congestion, &c. No. 128,850; Jan. 13; v. 270; p. 343.

Sheahan, Kohn & Co., Chicago, Ill. Outer garments for boys. No. 128,851; Jan. 13; v. 270; p. 343.

Shepard, Abraham D., Chicago, Ill. Charged table-water. No. 128,852; Jan. 13; v. 270; p. 343.

Shiley Chemical Co., Missouri Valley, Iowa. Insecticide. No. 128,853; Jan. 13; v. 270; p. 343.

Shireman, Nancye L., Birmingham, Ala. Face-rouge. No. 128,854; Jan. 13; v. 270; p. 343.

Siemon & Elting, New York, N. Y. Wash-blue. No. 128,855; Jan. 13; v. 270; p. 343.

Skin Remedies Company, Celina, Tex. Ointment for skin diseases, &c. No. 128,856; Jan. 13; v. 270; p. 343.

Sloan, F. A., Albemarle, N. C. Preparation for relief of constipation and indigestion. No. 128,857; Jan. 13; v. 270; p. 343.

Smith & Nichols, Incorporated, New York, N. Y. Beeswax, stearic acid, spermaceti. No. 128,858; Jan. 13; v. 270; p. 343.

Solfer, Morris S., Philadelphia, Pa. Headache-pills, blood, liver, and stomach tablets, &c. No. 128,859; Jan. 13; v. 270; p. 343.

Sorenson, David, Fortuna, Calif. Hog-cholera medicine. No. 128,860; Jan. 13; v. 270; p. 343.

South Lake Apopka Citrus Growers Assn., Oakland and Tildenville, Fla. Fresh citrus fruits. No. 128,861; Jan. 13; v. 270; p. 343.

Southern Feed Company, Inc., Newport News, Va. Stock feeds. No. 128,862; Jan. 13; v. 270; p. 343.

Standard Optical Co., Geneva, N. Y. Spectacle and eyeglass frames, &c. No. 128,863; Jan. 13; v. 270; p. 343.

Stearns, Frederick, & Co., Detroit, Mich. Medicated soap. No. 128,864; Jan. 13; v. 270; p. 343.

Stearns, Frederick, & Co., Detroit, Mich. Talcum powders, perfumes, &c. No. 128,865; Jan. 13; v. 270; p. 343.

Stearns-Hollingshead Co., Portland, Oreg. Candies of all kinds. No. 128,869; Jan. 13; v. 270; p. 344.

Steele Wedeles Company, Chicago, Ill. Peanut-oil. No. 128,870; Jan. 13; v. 270; p. 344.

Stein-Hall Manufacturing Co., Wilmington, Del., and Chicago, Ill. Starch product used in baking. No. 128,866; Jan. 13; v. 270; p. 344.

Sterling Products, (Incorporated,) Wheeling, W. Va. Hair and scalp tonic. No. 128,871; Jan. 13; v. 270; p. 344.

Stern, Charles, Sons Inc., Los Angeles, Calif. Canned fruits. Nos. 128,872-3; Jan. 13; v. 270; p. 344.

Stern, Charles, & Sons Inc., Los Angeles, Calif. Canned peaches and canned apricots. Nos. 128,867-8; Jan. 13; v. 270; p. 343.

Stone, Chas. D., & Co., Chicago, Ill. Hosiery. No. 128,874; Jan. 13; v. 270; p. 344.

Sulfron Medicine Company, Birmingham, Ala. Medicine for indigestion, pellagra, &c. No. 128,875; Jan. 13; v. 270; p. 344.

Sun Company, Philadelphia, Pa. Wool washing and treating oils. No. 128,876; Jan. 13; v. 270; p. 344.

Tagliabue, C. J., Mfg. Co., Brooklyn, N. Y. Thermometers, gages, &c. Nos. 128,877-8; Jan. 13; v. 270; p. 344.

Toth, Illes, Washington, D. C. Medicinal jelly for sore throat, &c. No. 128,879; Jan. 13; v. 270; p. 344.

Trommer, John F., Evergreen Brewery, Brooklyn, N. Y. Non-alcoholic malt beverage. No. 128,880; Jan. 13; v. 270; p. 344.

Troth, Ernest A., Philadelphia, Pa. Liquid preparation for use as a mouth-wash and nasal douche. No. 128,881; Jan. 13; v. 270; p. 344.

United American Metals Corporation, Brooklyn, N. Y. Babbitt metal. No. 128,882; Jan. 13; v. 270; p. 344.

United Hosiery Mills Corporation, East Chattanooga, Tenn. Hosiery. Nos. 128,883-5; Jan. 13; v. 270; p. 344.

United Shoe Machinery Company, Paterson, N. J., and Boston, Mass. Hand shoe-knives and knives and groovers for shoe machinery. No. 128,886; Jan. 13; v. 270; p. 344.

Universal Film Manufacturing Company, Inc., New York, N. Y. Moving-picture films. Nos. 128,887-8; Jan. 13; v. 270; p. 344.

Vail, Ed. S., Butterine Co., Chicago, Ill. Oleomargarin. No. 128,889; Jan. 13; v. 270; p. 344.

Vanity Yarn Company, Boston, Mass. Worsted fingering-yarn. No. 128,890; Jan. 13; v. 270; p. 344.

Victor Adding Machine Co., Chicago, Ill. Adding and calculating machines. No. 128,891; Jan. 13; v. 270; p. 344.

Vulcan Proofing Company, Brooklyn, N. Y. Rubber off-set-blankets. No. 128,892; Jan. 13; v. 270; p. 344.

Walker, Ella, Manufacturing Company, Sioux City, Iowa. Hair and scalp preparation. No. 128,893; Jan. 13; v. 270; p. 344.

Weber, E., & Co., Philadelphia, Pa. Skin-balm. No. 128,894; Jan. 13; v. 270; p. 344.

Weihenmayer, William J., Philadelphia, Pa. Worsted knitting-yarns. No. 128,895; Jan. 13; v. 270; p. 344.

Weller Manufacturing Company, Chicago, Ill. Grain-handling machinery. No. 128,896; Jan. 13; v. 270; p. 344.

Western Fisheries Company, Seattle, Wash. Canned salmon. Nos. 128,897-8; Jan. 13; v. 270; p. 344.

Western Hair Goods Company, Chicago, Ill. Face cream and powder, toilet waters. No. 128,899; Jan. 13; v. 270; p. 344.

Westinghouse Electric & Manufacturing Company, East Pittsburgh, Pa. Electric heaters. No. 128,900; Jan. 13; v. 270; p. 344.

White Stokes Co. Inc., Chicago, Ill. Marshmallow inner layers or filling, toppings for cakes, &c. No. 128,901; Jan. 13; v. 270; p. 345.

Winchenbaugh, Lester P., Co., Boston, Mass. Cover-papers. No. 128,902; Jan. 13; v. 270; p. 345.

Wolters, Wm., Winfield, S. D. Medicinal preparation. No. 128,903; Jan. 13; v. 270; p. 345.

Woodward, John G., & Co., Council Bluffs, Iowa. Candy. No. 128,904; Jan. 13; v. 270; p. 345.

Wright Mfg. Co., Lisbon, Ohio. Hoists and trolleys. No. 128,905; Jan. 13; v. 270; p. 345.

Young, J. S., & Company, Hanover, Pa. Dyes and dyestuffs. No. 128,907; Jan. 13; v. 270; p. 345.

Young, Giles T., Philadelphia, Pa. Hair tonic and pomade, &c. No. 128,906; Jan. 13; v. 270; p. 345.

Youngsma, Theodore S., Chicago, Ill. Coated book and label paper. No. 128,908; Jan. 13; v. 270; p. 345.

Zeh, L., San Francisco, Calif. Preparations for coughs, colds, neuralgia, &c. No. 128,909; Jan. 13; v. 270; p. 345.

Zeman, Otto, Chicago, Ill. Healing-ointment. No. 128,910; Jan. 13; v. 270; p. 345.

Zelenko & Moskowitz, New York, N. Y. Clothing. No. 128,911; Jan. 13; v. 270; p. 345.

ALPHABETICAL LIST OF REGISTRANTS OF TRADE-MARKS.

(REGISTRATION APPLIED FOR.)

Alaska Bakonized Fish Co., Juneau, Alaska. Canned fish. No. 123,099; Jan. 13; v. 270; p. 330.
Alco Textile Products Co. Inc., Albany, N. Y. Handkerchiefs. No. 120,809; Jan. 13; v. 270; p. 325.
American Bureau of Engineering, Inc., Chicago, Ill. Voltmeters, armature-testers, &c. No. 119,728; Jan. 13; v. 270; p. 324.
Austin, Nichols & Company Incorporated, Brooklyn and New York, N. Y. Shelled almonds, brussels sprouts, &c. No. 124,779; Jan. 13; v. 270; p. 332.
Baker, George W., Dallas, Tex. Waterproof dressing for leather, &c. No. 120,741; Jan. 13; v. 270; p. 325.
Baldwin, Thomas R., Chicago, Ill. Game apparatus. No. 114,392; Jan. 13; v. 270; p. 322.
Beatty, William, Jr. and Co., Philadelphia, Pa. Candy. No. 117,132; Jan. 13; v. 270; p. 323.
Blum, Eduard, Chicago, Ill. Portrait-photographs. No. 124,132; Jan. 13; v. 270; p. 332.
Borden Company, Jersey City, N. J., and New York, N. Y. Condensed, evaporated, homogenized, dried, and malted milk, &c. No. 118,463; Jan. 13; v. 270; p. 324.
Braun, John, & Sons, assignors to Pennsylvania Lawn Mower Works, Philadelphia, Pa. Lawn-mowers. No. 97,178; Jan. 13; v. 270; p. 321.
Brokaw-Eden Manufacturing Comany, Alton, Ill. Laundry appliances and machines. No. 121,517; Jan. 13; v. 270; p. 326.
C. and E. Shoe Company, Columbus, Ohio. Leather shoes for women, misses, and children. No. 120,095; Jan. 13; v. 270; p. 324.
Capell, Western L., Omaha, Nebr. Medical compound for supplies. No. 116,593; Jan. 13; v. 270; p. 322.
David, Geo. M., Barre, Vt. Laundry-tablets. No. 118,802; Jan. 13; v. 270; p. 323.
Davies, William, Company, Limited, Chicago, Ill. Bacon, hams, lard, &c. No. 118,903; Jan. 13; v. 270; p. 324.
Denney & Denney, Philadelphia, Pa. Perfumes, toilet waters, face-powders, &c. No. 123,309; Jan. 13; v. 270; p. 330.
Diffenbacher, Mark M., San Francisco, Calif. Spearmint candy. No. 122,114; Jan. 13; v. 270; p. 327.
Dyer, W. H., Company, Evansville, Ind. Canned foods. No. 116,129; Jan. 13; v. 270; p. 322.
Elgin Motor Car Corporation, Argo, Ill. Motor-vehicles. No. 120,526; Jan. 13; v. 270; p. 324.
Essex Aniline Works, Inc., Boston, Mass. Dyestuffs. No. 122,528; Jan. 13; v. 270; p. 328.
Fearing, Whiton & Co., Inc., Boston. Mass. Cotton sheeting. No. 123,478; Jan. 13; v. 270; p. 331.
Froes, Arsenio Jose. & Company, Inc., New York, N. Y. Table covers, napkins, table and bureau scarfs, handkerchiefs. No. 117,048; Jan. 13; v. 270; p. 323.
Fuld, Traube & Co., New York, N. Y. Veils, malines, hair-nets, chiffons. No. 120,746; Jan. 13; v. 270; p. 325.
Fuld, William, Baltimore, Md. Game known as a talking-board. No. 116,881; Jan. 13; v. 270; p. 323.
Fulford Mfg Co., Providence, R. I. Snap-fasteners. No. 121,833; Jan. 13; v. 270; p. 327.
Giavi, Francis N., New York, N. Y. Olive-oil. No. 122,833; Jan. 13; v. 270; p. 329.
Goodwear Hosiery Co., Kenosha, Wis. Hosiery. No. 123,784; Jan. 13; v. 270; p. 332.
Gray Tractor Company, Inc., Minneapolis, Minn. Farm-tractors. No. 123,978; Jan. 13; v. 270; p. 332.
Guinzburg, Edwin A., New York, N. Y. Shoe-tongue pads. No. 124,896; Jan. 13; v. 270; p. 333.
Haas Brothers Fabrics' Corporation, New York, N. Y. Piece goods. No. 123,542; Jan. 13; v. 270; p. 331.
Hans Brothers Fabrics' Corporation, New York, N. Y. Piece goods. No. 123,544; Jan. 13; v. 270; p. 331.
Hammondsport Products Co. Inc., Hammondsport, N. Y. Grape-juice. No. 124,937; Jan. 13; v. 270; p. 333.
Harbert, James, Polson, Mont. Raincoats. No. 111,500; Jan. 13; v. 270; p. 321.
Hezel Milling Company, East St. Louis, Ill. Self-rising wheat-flour. No. 124,793; Jan. 13; v. 270; p. 333.
Hinsley, Albert, Newark, N. J. Stove-polish. No. 121,802; Jan. 13; v. 270; p. 325.
Hob Manufacturing Co., New York, N. Y. Infants' caps, sacks, and booties, baby-shoes, &c. No. 122,302; Jan. 13; v. 270; p. 327.
Hollingshead, W. R., Company, Binghamton, N. Y. Egg-substitute powder. No. 115,457; Jan. 13; v. 270; p. 322.
Hooven & Allison Company, Xenia, Ohio. Fiber ropes and twines. Nos. 121,341-3; Jan. 13; v. 270; pp. 325-6.

Huth & Co., New York, N. Y. Cutlery. No. 116,302; Jan. 13; v. 270; p. 322.
Jordan Marsh Company, Boston, Mass. Handkerchiefs. No. 120,647; Jan. 13; v. 270; p. 325.
Kohlman, Chas., Co., Inc., New York, N. Y. Cotton piece goods. No. 124,115; Jan. 13; v. 270; p. 332.
Laundry Supplies Corporation, Richmond, Va. Preparation for cleansing purposes. No. 121,694; Jan. 13; v. 270; p. 326.
Lawrence Canning Co., Rockland, Me. Poultry and stock feeds, fish-meal. No. 124,613; Jan. 13; v. 270; p. 332.
Loose-Wiles Biscuit Company, New York, N. Y. Cakes, wafers, crackers. No. 121,869; Jan. 13; v. 270; p. 327.
Loose-Wiles Biscuit Company, New York, N. Y. Cakes, wafers, crackers. No. 121,941; Jan. 13; v. 270; p. 327.
Lorenz Company, Everett, Mass., assignor to Mihalovitch Brothers Company, Cincinnati, Ohio. Perfumes, tooth and toilet powders, &c. No. 108,831; Jan. 13; v. 270; p. 321.
Lortex Company, New York, N. Y. Cotton, linen, &c., piece goods. No. 121,477; Jan. 13; v. 270; p. 326.
Mandel & Cohen, New York, N. Y. Hosiery for boys and girls. No. 123,653; Jan. 13; v. 270; p. 331.
Marcus, Michael, New York, N. Y. Brooms and brushes. No. 121,596; Jan. 13; v. 270; p. 326.
Marshall Field & Company, Chicago, Ill. Yarn. No. 118,145; Jan. 13; v. 270; p. 323.
Marshall Field & Company, Chicago, Ill. Pins, safety-pins, snap-fasteners, &c. No. 125,225; Jan. 13; v. 270; p. 333.
Mayhew Steel Products Inc., New York, N. Y. Mechanics' hand-tools. No. 124,221; Jan. 13; v. 270; p. 332.
McIntosh, Norman S., Detroit, Mich. Cleaning compound for the hands. No. 120,253; Jan. 13; v. 270; p. 324.
McKenna, Marguerite C., New York, N. Y. Combination of sugar and cinnamon. No. 122,603; Jan. 13; v. 270; p. 328.
McLane Silk Company, Turners Falls, Mass. Silk and satin piece goods. No. 122,993; Jan. 13; v. 270; p. 330.
Mendelson, Abe M., New York, N. Y. Knitted sweaters. No. 117,780; Jan. 13; v. 270; p. 323.
Metalwood Manufacturing Co., Detroit, Mich. Hydraulic machinery and equipment. No. 121,001; Jan. 13; v. 270; p. 325.
Mihalovitch Brothers Company. (See Lorenz Company, assignor.)
Miller Bros., Galveston, Tex. Men's, boys', and children's clothing. No. 120,615; Jan. 13; v. 270; p. 324.
Motor-Car Supplies Manufacturing Company, Denver, Colo. Dressing for fabrics and leather. No. 104,702; Jan. 13; v. 270; p. 321.
Naumkeag Steam Cotton Co., Salem, Mass. Cotton piece goods. No. 122,906; Jan. 13; v. 270; p. 329.
Naumkeag Steam Cotton Co., Salem, Mass. Pillow-cases. No. 123,133; Jan. 13; v. 270; p. 330.
Naumkeag Steam Cotton Co., Salem, Mass. Sheets and pillow-cases. No. 122,905; Jan. 13; v. 270; p. 329.
Naumkeag Steam Cotton Co., Salem, Mass. Sheets, pillow and bolster cases. No. 122,847; Jan. 13; v. 270; p. 329.
Neuman, David, Wilkes-Barre, Pa. Chocolate, cocoa, and powdered milk. No. 122,022; Jan. 13; v. 270; p. 327.
New England Felt Roofing Works, Boston, Mass. Roofing products. No. 122,946; Jan. 13; v. 270; p. 329.
New York Times Company, New York, N. Y. Photographs and reprints thereof. Nos. 121,598-9; Jan. 13; v. 270; p. 326.
Pacific Mills, Lawrence and Boston, Mass. Cotton piece and cotton dress goods. No. 123,451; Jan. 13; v. 270; p. 331.
Peerless Mineral Products Co., Inc., New York, N. Y. Soap. No. 122,610; Jan. 13; v. 270; p. 328.
Peet Bros. Manufacturing Company, Kansas City, Kans. Soap. No. 121,760; Jan. 13; v. 270; p. 326.
Pennsylvania Lawn Mower Works. (See Braun, John, & Sons, assignors.)
Perfection Mattress & Spring Company, Birmingham, Ala. Mattresses. No. 122,444; Jan. 13; v. 270; p. 328.
Peterson, August V., Portland, Oreg. Hardtack. No. 122,853; Jan. 13; v. 270; p. 329.
Phoenix Drug Company, New York, N. Y. Nail-polish. No. 120,354; Jan. 13; v. 270; p. 324.
Reinhardt, George W., Co., Boston, Mass. Compound for cleaning fabrics, glass, &c. No. 122,791; Jan. 13; v. 270; p. 328.

Rhoades, Edwin K., Philadelphia, Pa. Bedspreads, sheets, pillow-cases, sheeting. No. 123,759; Jan. 13; v. 270; p. 332.

Rice-Stix Dry Goods Company, St. Louis, Mo. Cotton drills in the piece. No. 122,998; Jan. 13; v. 270; p. 330.

Robert, Joseph, Paris. France. Medicinal preparations. No. 106,927; Jan. 13; v. 270; p. 321.

Ruch, Hollister M. J., Syracuse, N. Y. Card game. No. 118,246; Jan. 13; v. 270; p. 323.

S. & P. Manufacturing Co. Inc., New York, N. Y. Valve-grinding compounds. No. 122,557; Jan. 13; v. 270; p. 328.

Safepack Mills, Boston, Mass. Composition roofing in rolls and composition roofing-shingles. Nos. 125,024–5; Jan. 13; v. 270; p. 333.

Salisbury, Howard F., Providence, R. I. Yarn. No. 115,556; Jan. 13; v. 270; p. 322.

Schmick, Carrie R., Beach Cliff, Rocky River, Ohio. One-piece dresses and aprons. No. 113,635; Jan. 13; v. 270; p. 321.

Schofield Oil Co., Inc., New York, N. Y. Soap. No. 123,043; Jan. 13; v. 270; p. 330.

Simonds Manufacturing Co., Fitchburg, Mass. Saws. No. 121,793; Jan. 13; v. 270; p. 326.

Simonson, A., New York, N. Y. Cold-cream, toilet water, &c. No. 122,792; Jan. 13; v. 270; p. 328.

Slatedale Knitting Mills, Harrisburg, Pa. Hose for men, women, and children. Nos. 123,668–70; Jan. 13; v. 270; p. 331.

Società Industrie Chimiche Ittiolo, Naples, Italy. Soaps for hygienic and medical purposes. No. 120,440; Jan. 13; v. 270; p. 324.

Societe Anonyme La Bruyere, Paris and St. Claude, France. Tobacco-pipes. No. 117,421; Jan. 13; v. 270; p. 323.

Spartan Manufacturing Company, Dayton, Ohio. Shop-aprons, overalls, jackets, utility-suits. No. 113,440; Jan. 13; v. 270; p. 321.

Spencer, George, & Co., Lutterworth, England. Blouses, aprons, cloaks, caps, &c. No. 115,631; Jan. 13; v. 270; p. 322.

Texas Oil, Gas & Mineral Products Company, Houston, Tex. Liquid polish for polishing metals and glass. No. 121,880; Jan. 13; v. 270; p. 327.

Thompson, Victoria, Jacksonville, Fla. Preparation for destroying boll-weevils, &c. No. 118,410; Jan. 13; v. 270; p. 323.

Toledo Cooker Company, Toledo, Ohio. Steam-cookers. No. 109,181; Jan. 13; v. 270; p. 321.

Traub, Lewis & Co., New York, N. Y. Veilings and net-tings in the piece. No. 113,852; Jan. 13; v. 270; p. 322.

United Laboratories, Inc., St. Louis, Mo. Remedies for headache, insomnia, constipation, &c. No. 123,187; Jan. 13; v. 270; p. 330.

Valentin, Ord & Co., Limited, Hayes, England. Artificial mineral water. No. 122,925; Jan. 13; v. 270; p. 329.

Wainwright, A. B., Company, Philadelphia, Pa. Prepared roofings. No. 124,771; Jan. 13; v. 270; p. 332.

Waldes & Co., Prague, Bohemia. Placket and glove fasten-ers, needles, buttons, &c. No. 121,190; Jan. 13; v. 270; p. 325.

Warner Bros. Co., Bridgeport, Conn. Hose-supporters. No. 124,742; Jan. 13; v. 270; p. 332.

Wertheimer Bros., New York, N. Y. Silk and velvet ribbon. No. 122,620; Jan. 13; v. 270; p. 328.

Young, Frederick H., Toledo, Ohio. Toilet creams, face, talcum, and tooth powders. Nos. 122,799–800; Jan. 13; v. 270; p. 329.

Zieschang, Paul C., Columbus, Ohio. Medicine for the nerves and digestive system. No. 123,010; Jan. 13; v. 270; p. 330.

ALPHABETICAL LIST OF INVENTIONS

FOR WHICH

PATENTS WERE ISSUED ON THE 13TH DAY OF JANUARY, 1920.

Abdominal support. S. Voorhees. No. 1,327,930; Jan. 13; v. 270; p. 257.

Acetylene-generator. Variable-pressure. A. Davis. No. 1,328,227; Jan. 13; v. 270; p. 314.

Aerial bomb, Self-propelling. A. Di Grazia and E. Biagini. No. 1,327,810; Jan. 13; v. 270; p. 235.

Aerocruiser. T. M. Finley. No. 1,328,040; Jan. 13; v. 270; p. 278.

Aeroplane. E. B. Jaeger and E. H. Heller. No. 1,327,869; Jan. 13; v. 270; p. 246.

Aeroplanes, Storage battery adapted particularly for. T. A. Willard. No. 1,327,650; Jan. 13; v. 270; p. 205.

Agricultural implement. H. V. Calkins. No. 1,328,124; Jan. 13; v. 270; p. 294.

Air and other gases or fluids, Propulsion of. H. Ayrton. No. 1,327,975; Jan. 13; v. 270; p. 266.

Air-brake-controlling mechanism. T. W. Scott. No. 1,327,968; Jan. 13; v. 270; p. 264.

Air collecting and delivering apparatus. W. D. Scott. No. 1,327,926; Jan. 13; v. 270; p. 257.

Aircraft and making the same. Fabric for N. A. T. N. Feary. No. 1,327,707; Jan. 13; v. 270; p. 216.

Air-pressure liquid-transfer device. H. G. Diffenbaugh. No. 1,328,133; Jan. 13; v. 270; p. 296.

Alarm : See—
Burglar-alarm.   Vehicle-alarm.

Aluminum, Making powdered or granulated. L. B. Tebbetts, 2d. No. 1,327,743; Jan. 13; v. 270; p. 223.

Ammonia from the air or nitrogen, Production of synthetic. R. F. Gardiner. No. 1,328,082; Jan. 13; v. 270; p. 286.

Amusement device. E. Kohler. No. 1,328,166; Jan. 13; v. 270; p. 302.

Animal-trap. M. A. Twitchell. No. 1,327,890; Jan. 13; v. 270; p. 250.

Annealing-box, Pressed corrugated sheet-metal. G. P. Bard. No. 1,328,030; Jan. 13; v. 270; p. 276.

Antifriction device. S. Apostoloff. No. 1,327,895; Jan. 13; v. 270; p. 251.

Apportioning device. A. Larsen. No. 1,327,678; Jan. 13; v. 270; p. 210.

Arm, Artificial. E. R. Birchard. No. 1,327,938; Jan. 13; v. 270; p. 259.

Article-stand. M. Cohen. No. 1,327,943; Jan. 13; v. 270; p. 260.

Ash-sifter. T. J. MacIvor. No. 1,328,174; Jan. 13; v. 270; p. 304.

Auto traffic-signal. H. J. Hankee. No. 1,327,671; Jan. 13; v. 270; p. 209.

Automatic machine. M. E. Fernald. No. 1,328,144; Jan. 13; v. 270; p. 298.

Automobile alarm device. A. A. Goldblatt. No. 1,327,993; Jan. 13; v. 270; p. 269.

Automobile-lock. E. C. Boehmig. No. 1,327,979; Jan. 13; v. 270; p. 267.

Automobile-seat, Auxiliary. C. M. Smith. No. 1,328,105; Jan. 13; v. 270; p. 291.

Automobile-tire carrier. C. C. Steel and T. H. Lynn. No. 1,327,742; Jan. 13; v. 270; p. 223.

Automobile tractor attachment. W. C. Phillips. No. 1,327,773; Jan. 13; v. 270; p. 228.

Automobiles, Rim, tire, and wheel carrier for C. E. Moore. No. 1,327,626; Jan. 13; v. 270; p. 200.

Automobiles, Vapor-primer for. T. J. McCarthy. No. 1,328,089; Jan. 13; v. 270; p. 287.

Bar : See—
Splice-bar.

Bathtub, Foldable. C. W. Hagstrom. No. 1,327,866; Jan. 13; v. 270; p. 245.

Batteries, Switchboard for charging storage. C. E. Ogden. No. 1,327,682; Jan. 13; v. 270; p. 211.

Battery : See—
Dry battery.

Beam-clamp. G. H. Bruns. No. 1,327,981; Jan. 13; v. 270; p. 267.

Bearing, Roller-. E. Meier. No. 1,328,179; Jan. 13; v. 270; p. 304.

Bed, Collapsible. F. M. Stoll. No. 1,327,886; Jan. 13; v. 270; p. 249.

Bed, Tent-. F. M. Stoll. No. 1,327,887; Jan. 13; v. 270; p. 249.

Beet-topper. R. J. Johnson. No. 1,327,760; Jan. 13; v. 270; p. 226.

Belt-fastener. F. F. Backstrom. No. 1,327,798; Jan. 13; v. 270; p. 233.

Binder. G. G. H. Fritzsche. No. 1,327,992; Jan. 13; v. 270; p. 269.

Beverage-mixer. M. Black. No. 1,327,900; Jan. 13; v. 270; p. 252.

Blanket-fastener. W. A. Schleicher. No. 1,328,206; Jan. 13; v. 270; p. 310.

Block. B. N. Platt. No. 1,327,775; Jan. 13; v. 270; p. 229.

Blocks, Making anchor-. G. P. Hemstreet. No. 1,327,710; Jan. 13; v. 270; p. 217.

Board : See—
Game-board.

Boards, Means for fastening plaster-. C. G. Shuman. No. 1,327,741; Jan. 13; v. 270; p. 222.

Boiler-patch. E. Todd. No. 1,327,846; Jan. 13; v. 270; p. 242.

Boiler-setting. L. Nevers and F. Whitbeck. No. 1,327,727; Jan. 13; v. 270; p. 220.

Bolting-machine. S. Snyder and L. C. Winegardner. No. 1,327,636; Jan. 13; v. 270; p. 202.

Bonnet for railway-signal fusee-caps and making it. H. O. Bemisderfer. No. 1,327,899; Jan. 13; v. 270; p. 252.

Book, Class-record. M. O. Billow. No. 1,327,610; Jan. 13; v. 270; p. 198.

Book-trimmer. E. R. Kast. No. 1,327,915; Jan. 13; v. 270; p. 255.

Boot or shoe. L. Pageau. No. 1,327,772; Jan. 13; v. 270; p. 228.

Boring drill, Rotary. H. R. Hughes. No. 1,327,913; Jan. 13; v. 270; p. 254.

Bottle-closure. A. Daccord. No. 1,327,809; Jan. 13; v. 270; p. 235.

Bottle-closure. F. W. Schilling. No. 1,328,205; Jan. 13; v. 270; p. 310.

Bottle-closure. W. Silverman. No. 1,328,060; Jan. 13; v. 270; p. 282.

Box : See—
Annealing-box.   Stuffing-box.
Egg-box.

Brace : See—
Ratchet-brace.

Braiding-machine. E. Walter. No. 1,328,216; Jan. 13; v. 270; p. 312.

Brake : See—
Headstock-brake.

Breathing apparatus, Mouthpiece for. J. T. Ryan. No. 1,328,057; Jan. 13; v. 270; p. 281.

Breathing apparatus, Regenerator for. J. T. Ryan. No. 1,328,058; Jan. 13; v. 270; p. 282.

Brush-holder. C. E. Hecht. No. 1,328,162; Jan. 13; v. 270; p. 301.

Burglar-alarm. P. H. Spethmann. No. 1,327,785; Jan. 13; v. 270; p. 230.

Burner : See—
Fuel-oil-burner.   Furnace-burner.

Burner-mounting. W. R. Ray. No. 1,328,198; Jan. 13; v. 270; p. 308.

Bushing, Journal-. S. W. Putnam. No. 1,328,195; Jan. 13; v. 270; p. 308.

Button-inspecting machine. H. Hastings. No. 1,327,672; Jan. 13; v. 270; p. 209.

Button, Lock collar-. R. J. McCredie. No. 1,327,719; Jan. 13; v. 270; p. 218.

Cabinet, Phonograph-. W. H. Bennington. No. 1,327,977; Jan. 13; v. 270; p. 266.

Can-bodies, Mechanism for seaming ends to. J. A. Gray. No. 1,327,994; Jan. 13; v. 270; p. 269.

Can-closing machine. F. Rudolphi. No. 1,327,966; Jan. 13; v. 270; p. 264.

Can ends, Apparatus for cutting and applying ring-liners to the flanges of. C. M. Symonds. No. 1,328,020; Jan. 13; v. 270; p. 274.

Canned products, Processing apparatus for. A. C. Richardson. No. 1,328,202; Jan. 13; v. 270; p. 309.

Cans, Pouring-spout for. F. T. Servis. No. 1,328,104; Jan. 13; v. 270; p. 290.

Cap, Bottle or jar. R. A. Russell. No. 1,327,967; Jan. 13; v. 270; p. 264.

Car door, Steel grain-. G. and P. Townill. No. 1,328,214; Jan. 13; v. 270; p. 311.

Car, Dump-. T. R. McKnight. No. 1,327,623; Jan. 13; v. 270; p. 200.

Car, Freight-. V. Wroclawski. No. 1,327,894; Jan. 13; v. 270; p. 251.

Car-roof construction. N. S. Reeder. No. 1,328,200; Jan. 13; v. 270; p. 309.

Cars, Adjustable bulkhead for freight-. S. B. Short. No. 1,327,634; Jan. 13; v. 270; p. 202.

Carbid, Producing. J. H. Reid. No. 1,327,736; Jan. 13; v. 270; p. 222.

ALPHABETICAL LIST OF TRADE-MARKS.

Medicine, Laxative. N. B. Benson. No. 128,624; Jan. 13; v. 270; p. 336.
Medicines for female diseases. Chattanooga Medicine Co. No. 128,640; Jan. 13; v. 270; p. 337.
Medicines for use as a stomach compound. A. Juster. No. 128,744; Jan. 13; v. 270; p. 340.
Medicines, salves, &c. Foley & Company. No. 128,697; Jan. 13; v. 270; p. 338.
Milk, Condensed. Galeton Dairy Products Co. No. 128,705; Jan. 13; v. 270; p. 338.
Molasses, olives, &c. Geo. R. Newell & Co. No. 128,803; Jan. 13; v. 270; p. 341.
Mouth-wash and nasal douche. E. A. Troth. No. 128,881; Jan. 13; v. 270; p. 344.
Mustard. American Mustard Co. No. 128,603; Jan. 13; v. 270; p. 335.
Neckties. Adrian Neckwear Co. No. 128,589; Jan. 13; v. 270; p. 335.
Neckties and scarfs, Men's. Block & Drexler. No. 128,633; Jan. 13; v. 270; p. 336.
Oil, Coroanut-. India Refining Company. No. 128,739; Jan. 13; v. 270; p. 339.
Oil, Olive-. John A. Alban & Co. No. 128,891; Jan. 13; v. 270; p. 335.
Oil, Peanut-. Steele Wedeles Company. No. 128,870; Jan. 13; v. 270; p. 344.
Oil, Sesame-. Musher & Company. No. 128,798; Jan. 13; v. 270; p. 341.
Oil tablets, Olive-. Olive Tablet Company. No. 128,807; Jan. 13; v. 270; p. 342.
Oils, Wool washing and treating. Sun Company. No. 128,876; Jan. 13; v. 270; p. 341.
Ointment. Skin Remedies Company. No. 128,856; Jan. 13; v. 270; p. 343.
Ointment, Eczema-. Powerol Chemical Company. No. 128,832; Jan. 13; v. 270; p. 342.
Ointment for burns, cuts, &c. W. Marshall. No. 128,780; Jan. 13; v. 270; p. 341.
Ointment for treatment of skin diseases and piles. J. S. King. No. 128,750; Jan. 13; v. 270; p. 340.
Ointment, Healing-. O. Zeman. No. 128,910; Jan. 13; v. 270; p. 345.
Ointments for burns, &c. Mrs. M. Napoleon. No. 128,799; Jan. 13; v. 270; p. 341.
Oleomargarin. Ed S. Vail Butterine Co. No. 128,889; Jan. 13; v. 270; p. 344.
Oranges, Fresh. Santiago Orange Growers Association. No. 128,842; Jan. 13; v. 270; p. 343.
Paper. American Writing Paper Company. No. 128,604; Jan. 13; v. 270; p. 335.
Paper. Esbeck Manufacturing Co. No. 128,687; Jan. 13; v. 270; p. 338.
Paper, Blotting-. Albemarle Paper Mfg. Co. No. 128,592; Jan. 13; v. 270; p. 335.
Paper, Coated book and label. T. S. Youngsma. No. 128,908; Jan. 13; v. 270; p. 345.
Paper covering for boxes. Producer's Paper Company. No. 128,826; Jan. 13; v. 270; p. 342.
Paper, paper toweling and napkins, Toilet-. John Hoberg Co. No. 128,731; Jan. 13; v. 270; p. 339.
Paper, Wrapping-. Kirchhelmer Bros. Co. No. 128,751; Jan. 13; v. 270; p. 340.
Paper, Writing-. M. Milton. No. 128,791; Jan. 13; v. 270; p. 341.
Papers, Cover-. Lester P. Winchenbaugh Co. No. 128,902; Jan. 13; v. 270; p. 345.
Peanut-oil. Musher & Company. No. 128,797; Jan. 13; v. 270; p. 341.
Peanuts. Pacific Export Lumber Co. No. 128,813; Jan. 13; v. 270; p. 342.
Pencils, Lead-. American Lead Pencil Company. No. 128,601; Jan. 13; v. 270; p. 335.
Pencils, Magazine-. Salz Brothers. No. 128,841; Jan. 13; v. 270; p. 343.
Peptone. Allen & Hanburys. No. 128,593; Jan. 13; v. 270; p. 335.
Perfumes. A. Crusellas. No. 128,668; Jan. 13; v. 270; p. 337.
Petticoats. J. Brener Co. No. 128,641; Jan. 13; v. 270; p. 336.
Photographic developers. Lowenstein Radio Company. No. 128,768; Jan. 13; v. 270; p. 340.
Pickling compound for curing meats. H. Ehrlich & Sons Mfg. Co. No. 128,680; Jan. 13; v. 270; p. 338.
Picture-films. C. S. Hart Film Company. No. 128,722; Jan. 13; v. 270; p. 339.
Picture-films. Universal Film Manufacturing Company. No. 128,888; Jan. 13; v. 270; p. 344.
Picture films, Motion-. Screen Letter Box. No. 128,848; Jan. 13; v. 270; p. 343.
Picture machines, &c., Projecting equipment for motion-. Nicholas Power Company. No. 128,804; Jan. 13; v. 270; p. 341.
Pills, tablets, balsam, &c. M. S. Soifer. No. 128,859; Jan. 13; v. 270; p. 343.
Play-suits, men's overalls and overshirts. Everwear Mfg. Co. No. 128,690; Jan. 13; v. 270; p. 338.
Poultry, butter, &c. Columbia Produce Co. No. 128,856; Jan. 13; v .270; p. 337.
Poultry-powder, &c. National Blue Ribbon Remedy Company. No. 128,800; Jan. 13; v. 270; p. 341.
Powders, perfumes, &c., Talcum. Frederick Stearns & Co. No. 128,865; Jan. 13; v. 270; p. 343.
Preparation for the amelioration of pyorrhea, &c. C. S. Cohen. No. 128,654; Jan. 13; v. 270; p. 337.

Preparation for the relief of constipation and indigestion. F. A. Sloan. No. 128,857; Jan. 13; v. 270; p. 343.
Preparation for the treatment of menstrual irregularities, &c. A. T. Florein. No. 128,696; Jan. 13; v. 270; p. 338.
Preparation for treating acidity and infant ailments. Mead, Johnson & Co. No. 128,743; Jan. 16; v. 270; p. 340.
Preparation for the treatment of cancers, &c. R. L. Lawless. No. 128,762; Jan. 13; v. 270; p. 340.
Preparations for headaches, coughs, &c. L. Zeh. No. 128,909; Jan. 13; v. 270; p. 345.
Preservative for vegetable fibers. Lyster Chemical Company. No. 128,770; Jan. 13; v. 270; p. 340.
Pumping systems, &c. Latta-Martin Pump Co. Nos. 128,758–60; Jan. 13; v. 270; p. 340.
Pumps and grease-guns, Automobile air and oil. Bell Pump & Manufacturing Co. No. 128,622; Jan. 13; v. 270; p. 336.
Pumps and turbines. Coppus Engineering and Equipment Company. No. 128,660; Jan. 13; v. 270; p. 337.
Pumps, Pneumatic. De Laval Separator Company. No. 128,671; Jan. 13; v. 270; p. 337.
Radiator-seal. Bear-Cat Products Co. No. 128,619; Jan. 13; v. 270; p. 336.
Radiators and boilers, Solution to clean out. Rada-Solvt Co. No. 128,830; Jan. 13; v. 270; p. 342.
Radiators, boilers, &c., Compound for stopping leaks in. M. Dannenhirsch. No. 128,669; Jan. 13; v. 270; p. 337.
Remedy for cuts, burns, &c. Creotina Chemical Company. No. 128,666; Jan. 13; v. 270; p. 337.
Remedy for cuts, burns, &c. J. W. Latty. No. 128,761; Jan. 13; v. 270; p. 340.
Remedy for corns, warts, &c. H. Schlesinger. No. 128,847; Jan. 13; v. 270; p. 343.
Rodent-exterminating preparation. Rodent Exterminator Laboratories. No. 128,839; Jan. 13; v. 270; p. 343.
Rouge. G. M. Brohard. No. 128,643; Jan. 13; v. 270; p. 336.
Rouge, Face-. N. L. Shireman. No. 128,854; Jan. 13; v. 270; p. 343.
Rouge, face-powder, &c., Lip-. B. M. Mason. No. 128,782; Jan. 13; v. 270; p. 341.
Rubber offset-blankets. Vulcan Proofing Company. No. 128,892; Jan. 13; v. 270; p. 344.
Rubber soles and heels. Mayflower Rubber Works Company. No. 128,783; Jan. 13; v. 270; p. 341.
Salmon-eggs, Preserved. A. F. Oppelt. No. 128,811; Jan. 13; v. 270; p. 342.
Salt brick. Edgerton Salt Brick Company. No. 128,679; Jan. 13; v. 270; p. 338.
Sarsaparilla, ginger-ale, lemon-soda. Adam Scheidt Beverage Co. No. 128,845; Jan. 13; v. 270; p. 343.
Salve. E. H. Kettleman. No. 128,748; Jan. 13; v. 270; p. 340.
Salve and liniment. A. B. Richards Medicine Co. No. 128,833; Jan. 13; v. 270; p. 342.
Sheeting, Hospital-. Omo Mfg. Co. Nos. 128,808–9; Jan. 13; v. 270; p. 342.
Shingles. Chinook Lumber & Shingle Co. No. 128,650; Jan. 13; v. 270; p. 337.
Shirts and pajamas. Prime Shirt Co. No. 128,825; Jan. 13; v. 270; p. 342.
Shirts, underwear, &c., Men's. Chain Shirt Shops. No. 128,648; Jan. 13; v. 270; p. 337.
Shirts, Work-. Baltimore Bargain House. No. 128,615; Jan. 13; v. 270; p. 335.
Shirts, Work-. Joseph Horowitz & Sons. No. 128,736; Jan. 13; v. 270; p. 339.
Shoes. Powell & Campbell. No. 128,822; Jan. 13; v. 270; p. 342.
Shoes and rubber footwear. Apsley Rubber Company, Nos. 128,610–11; Jan. 13; v. 270; p. 335.
Shoes, Leather. Frederick & Nelson. No. 128,700; Jan. 13; v. 270; p. 338.
Shoes, Leather. C. M. Kaplan. No. 128,745; Jan. 13; v. 270; p. 340.
Shoes, Men's, boys', and youths'. W. H. Griffin Company. No. 128,719; Jan. 13; v. 270; p. 339.
Silk, Thrown. Abram Bloom Co. No. 128,634; Jan. 13; v. 270; p. 336.
Skins, Fur-bearing. Martin-Laskin Company. No. 128,781; Jan. 13; v. 270; p. 341.
Skirts, Dress-. Grewen Fabric Co. No. 128,718; Jan. 13; v. 270; p. 339.
Snap and placket fasteners. Federal Snap Fastener Corporation. No. 128,693; Jan. 13; v. 270; p. 338.
Soap, Saberton Mfg. Co. No. 128,840; Jan. 13; v. 270; p. 343.
Soap, Medicated. Frederick Stearns & Co. No. 128,864; Jan. 13; v. 270; p. 343.
Spark-plugs. J. R. Ayotte. No. 128,613; Jan. 13; v. 270; p. 335.
Spark-plugs. O. D. Bowers. No. 128,688; Jan. 13; v. 270; p. 336.
Spark-plugs. Express Spark Plug Corporation. No. 128,691; Jan. 13; v. 270; p. 338.
Spark-plugs. Lyons Ignition Company. No. 128,769; Jan. 13; v. 270; p. 340.
Spectacle and eyeglass frames, &c. Standard Optical Co. No. 128,863; Jan. 13; v. 270; p. 343.
Spray for animals. Lyster Chemical Company. No. 128,771; Jan. 13; v. 270; p. 340.
Stairway treads and panels, floors, &c. American Abrasive Metals Co. No. 128,594; Jan. 13; v. 270; p. 335.

Starch product. Stein-Hall Manufacturing Company. No. 128,866; Jan. 13; v. 270; p. 343.
Stationery. Enlow Co. No. 128,683; Jan. 13; v. 270; p. 338.
Steel. A. C. Davidson. No. 128,670; Jan. 13; v. 270; p. 337.
Sugar. R. M. McMullen. No. 128,777: Jan. 13; v. 270; p. 341.
Suits, coats, skirts, dresses. L. Harrison. No. 128,721; Jan. 13; v. 270; p. 339.
Tablets, Stomach and liver. Krieg Wallace & McQuaide. No. 128,754; Jan. 13; v. 270; p. 340.
Tags used on insulated wires, Tubular. M. H. Loughridge. No. 128,766; Jan. 13; v. 270; p. 340.
Tea. Crescent Coffee Mills. No. 128,665; Jan. 13; v. 270; p. 337.
Teeth, Antiseptic fluid for. L. Bahr. No. 128,614; Jan. 13; v. 270; p. 335.
Thermometers. C. J. Tagliabue Mfg. Co. Nos. 128,877-8; Jan. 13; v. 270; p. 344.
Thread, Linen. Barbour Brothers Co. No. 128,617, Jan. 13; v. 270; p. 336.
Toilet water. Bonheur Co. No. 128,636; Jan. 13; v. 270; p. 336.
Tonic, powders, ointment, and cream. Dickinson Drug Co. No. 128,675; Jan. 13; v. 270; p. 337.
Tonics. F. Ad. Richter & Co. No. 128,834; Jan. 13; v. 270; p. 342.

Treatment of gonorrhea, Liquid for the. L. T. Price. No. 128,824; Jan. 13; v. 270; p. 342.
Trowels, Weeding-. W. I. Hare. No. 128,720; Jan. 13; v. 270; p. 339.
Underwear. High Rock Knitting Company. No. 128,729; Jan. 13; v. 270; p. 339.
Underwear for men. Samuel W. Peck & Co. No. 128,816; Jan. 13; v. 270; p. 342.
Valves for internal-combustion engines. Birrell Silent Motor Co. No. 128,630; Jan. 13; v. 270; p. 336.
Ventilators for roofs and skylights. Rohrman-Cooper Company. No. 128,837; Jan. 13; v. 270; p. 342.
Vessels for heating beverages. H. B. Gibson Co. No. 128,712; Jan. 13; v. 270; p. 339.
Vinegar. Cascade Cider Company. No. 128,646; Jan. 13; v. 270; p. 336.
Water, Charged table-. A. D. Shepard. No. 128,852; Jan. 13; v. 270; p. 343.
Water pumping and supply systems, Pneumatic. Milwaukee Air Power Pump Company. No. 128,792; Jan. 13; v. 270; p. 341.
Window-screens. Empire Rolling Screen Co. No. 128,682; Jan. 13; v. 270; p. 338.
Wrenches, Socket-. American Grinder Manufacturing Company. No. 128,597; Jan. 13; v. 270; p. 335.
Yarn, Worsted fingering-. Vanity Yarn Company. No. 128,890; Jan. 13; v. 270; p. 344.
Yarns, Worsted knitting-. W. J. Weihenmayer. No. 128,895; Jan. 13; v. 270; p. 344.

ALPHABETICAL LIST OF TRADE-MARK TITLES.

(REGISTRATION APPLIED FOR.)

Almonds, brussels sprouts, &c., Shelled. Austin, Nichols & Company. No. 124,779; Jan. 13; v. 270; p. 332.
Aprons, overalls, &c., Shop-. Spartan Manufacturing Company. No. 113,440; Jan. 13; v. 270; p. 321.
Bacon, hams, lard, &c. William Davies Company. No 118,903; Jan. 13; v. 270; p. 324.
Bedspreads, sheets, &c. E. K. Rhoads. No. 123,759; Jan. 13; v. 270; p. 332.
Blouses, aprons, bodices. &c. George Spencer & Co. No. 115,631; Jan. 13; v. 270; p. 322.
Brooms and brushes. M. Marcus. No. 121,596; Jan. 13; v. 270; p. 326.
Cakes, wafers, crackers. Loose-Wiles Biscuit Company. No. 121,869; Jan. 13; v. 270; p. 327.
Cakes, wafers, crackers. Loose Wiles Biscuit Company. No. 121,941; Jan. 13; v. 270; p. 327.
Candy. William Beatty, Jr. and Co. No. 117,132; Jan. 13; v. 270; p. 323.
Candy, Spearmint. M. M. Diffenbacher. No. 122,114; Jan. 13; v. 270; p. 327.
Canned fish. Alaska Bakonized Fish Co. No. 123,099; Jan. 13, v. 270; p. 330.
Canned foods. W. H. Dyer Company. No. 116,129; Jan. 13; v. 270; p. 322.
Caps, sacks, and booties, &c. Infants'. Hob Manufacturing Co. No. 122,302; Jan. 13; v. 270; p. 327.
Chocolate, cocoa, Powdered milk-. D. Neuman. No. 122,022; Jan. 13; v. 270; p. 327.
Cleaning compound for fabrics, glass, &c. G. W. Reinhardt Co. No. 122,791; Jan. 13; v. 270; p. 328.
Cleaning compound for removing carbon, &c., from the hands. N. S. McIntosh. No. 120,253; Jan. 13; v. 270; p. 324.
Cleansing preparation. Laundry Supplies Corporation. No. 121,694; Jan. 13; v. 270; p. 326.
Clothing. Miller Bros. No. 120,615; Jan. 13; v. 270; p. 324.
Cookers, Steam-. Toledo Cooker Company. No. 109,181; Jan. 13; v. 270; p. 321.
Cotton goods. Fearing, Whiton & Co. No. 123,478; Jan. 13; v. 270; p. 331.
Cotton, linen, &c., piece goods. Lortex Company. No. 121,477; Jan. 13; v. 270; p. 326.
Cotton piece and dress goods. Pacific Mills. No. 123,451; Jan. 13; v. 270; p. 331.
Cotton piece goods. Chas. Kohlman Co.· No. 124,115; Jan. 13; v. 270; p. 332.
Cotton piece goods. Naumkeag Steam Cotton Co. No. 122,906; Jan. 13; v. 270; p. 329.
Creams and powders, Toilet. F. H. Young. Nos. 122,799-800; Jan. 13; v. 270; p. 329.
Creams, rouge, &c., Cold and complexion. A. Simonson. No. 122,792; Jan. 13; v. 270; p. 328.
Cutlery. Huth & Co. No. 116,302; Jan. 13; v. 270; p. 322.
Dresses and aprons, One-piece. C. R. Schmick. No. 113,035; Jan. 13; v. 270; p. 321.
Dressing for fabrics and leather. Motor Car Supplies Manufacturing Company. No. 104,702; Jan. 13; v. 270; p. 321.
Drills in the piece, Cotton. Rice Stix Dry Goods Company. No. 122,998; Jan. 13; v. 270; p. 330.
Dyestuffs. Essex Aniline Works. No. 122,528; Jan. 13; v. 270; p. 328.
Flour, Self-rising wheat-. Hezel Milling Company. No. 124,793; Jan. 13; v. 270; p. 333.
Egg-substitute powder. W. R. Hollingshead Company. No. 115,457; Jan. 13; v. 270; p. 322.

Farm-tractors. Gray Tractor Company. No. 123,978; Jan. 13; v. 270; p. 332.
Feeds and fish-meal, Poultry and stock. Lawrence Canning Co. No. 124,613; Jan. 13; v. 270; p. 332.
Game. W. Fuld. No. 116,881; Jan. 13; v. 270; p. 323.
Game apparatus. T. R. Baldwin. No. 114,392; Jan. 13; v. 270; p. 322.
Game, Card. H. M. J. Ruch. No. 118,246; Jan. 13; v. 270; p. 323.
Grape-juice. Hammondsport Products Co. No. 124,937; Jan. 13; v. 270; p. 333.
Handkerchiefs. Alco Textile Products Co. No. 120,809; Jan. 13; v. 270; p. 325.
Handkerchiefs. Jordan Marsh Company. No. 120,647; Jan. 13; v. 270; p. 325.
Hardtack. A. V. Peterson. No. 122,853; Jan. 13; v. 270; p. 329.
Hose. Slatedale Knitting Mills. Nos. 123,688-70; Jan. 13; v. 270; p. 331.
Hose-supporters. Warner Bros. No. 124,742; Jan. 13; v. 270; p. 332.
Hosiery. Goodwear Hosiery Co. No. 123,784; Jan. 13; v. 270; p. 332.
Hosiery for boys and girls. Mandel & Cohen. No. 123,653; Jan. 13; v. 270; p. 331.
Hydraulic machinery and equipment. Metalwood Manufacturing Co. No. 121,001; Jan. 13; v. 270; p. 325; Knitted sweaters. A. M. Mendelson. No. 117,780; Jan. 13; v. 270; p. 323.
Laundry appliances and machines. Brokaw-Eden Manufacturing Company. No. 121,517; Jan. 13; v. 270; p. 326.
Laundry-tablets. G. M. David. No. 118,302; Jan. 13; v. 270; p. 323.
Mattresses. Perfection Mattress & Spring Co. No. 122,444; Jan. 13; v. 270; p. 328.
Medicinal preparations. J. Robert. No. 106,927; Jan. 13; v. 270; p. 321.
Medical compound for syphilis. W. L. Capell. No. 116,593; Jan. 13; v. 270; p. 322.
Medicine, Tonic. E. C. Zieschang. No. 123,010; Jan. 13; v. 270; p. 330.
Metal and glass polish. Texas Oil, Gas & Mineral Products Company. No. 121,880; Jan. 13; v. 270; p. 327.
Milk, &c., Condensed, evaporated, homogenized, dried, and malted. Borden Company. No. 118,463; Jan. 13; v. 270; p. 323.
Mowers, Lawn-. John Braun & Sons. No. 97,178; Jan. 13; v. 270; p. 321.
Nail-polish. Phoenix Drug Company. No. 120,854; Jan. 13; v. 270; p. 324.
Oil, Olive-. F. N. Giavi. No. 122,833; Jan. 13; v. 270; p. 329.
Perfumes, toilet waters, powders, &c. Denney & Denney. No. 123,309; Jan. 13; v. 270; p. 330.
Perfumes, tooth and toilet powders, &c. Lorenz Company. No. 108,831; Jan. 13; v. 270; p. 321.
Photographs and reprints thereof. New York Times Company. Nos. 121,598-9; Jan. 13; v. 270; p. 326.
Photographs, Portrait-. E. Blum. No. 124,132; Jan. 13; v. 270; p. 332.
Piece goods. Haas Brothers Fabrics' Corporation. No. 123,542; Jan. 13; v. 270; p. 331.
Pillow-cases. Naumkeag Steam Cotton Co. No. 123,133; Jan. 13; v. 270; p. 330.
Pins, snap-fasteners, &c. Marshall Field & Company. No. 125,225; Jan. 13; v. 270; p. 333.

Pipes, Tobacco-. Societe Anonyme La Bruyere. No. 117,421; Jan. 13; v. 270; p. 323.

Placket and glove fasteners, hairpins, &c. Waldes & Co. No. 121,190; Jan. 13; v. 270; p. 325.

Preparation for destroying boll-weevils, &c. V. Thompson. No. 118,410; Jan. 13; v. 270; p. 323.

Raincoats. J. Harbert. No. 111,500; Jan. 13; v. 270; p. 321.

Remedies for headache, insomnia, &c. United Laboratories. No. 123,187; Jan. 13; v. 270; p. 330.

Ribbon, Silk and velvet. Werthelmer Bros. No. 122,620; Jan. 13; v. 270; p. 328.

Roofing and shingles. Safepack Mills. Nos. 125,024–5; Jan. 13; v. 270; p. 333.

Roofings, Prepared. A. B. Wainwright Company. No. 124,771; Jan. 13; v. 270; p. 332.

Roofing products. New England Felt Roofing Works. No. 122,946; Jan. 13; v. 270; p. 329.

Ropes and twines, Fiber. Hooven & Allison Company. Nos. 121,341–3; Jan. 13; v. 270; pp. 325–6.

Saws. Simonds Manufacturing Co. No. 121,793; Jan. 13; v. 270; p. 326.

Sheets and pillowcases. Naumkeag Steam Cotton Co. No. 122,905; Jan. 13; v. 270; p. 329.

Sheets, pillow and bolster cases. Naumkeag Steam Cotton Co. No. 122,847; Jan. 13; v. 270; p. 329.

Shoe-tongue pads. E. A. Guinzburg. No. 124,896; Jan. 13; v. 270; p. 333.

Shoes for women, misses, and children, Leather. C. and E. Shoe Company. No. 120,095; Jan. 13; v. 270; p. 324.

Silk and satin piece goods. McLane Silk Company. No. 122,993; Jan. 13; v. 270; p. 330.

Snap-fasteners. Fulford Mfg. Co. No. 121,833; Jan. 13; v. 270; p. 327.

Soap. Peet Bros. Manufacturing Company. No. 121,780; Jan. 13; v. 270; p. 326.

Soap. Peerless Mineral Products Co. No. 122,610; Jan. 13; v. 270; p. 328.

Soap. Schofield Oil Co. No. 123,043; Jan. 13; v. 270; p. 330.

Soaps for hygienic and medical purposes. Società Industrie Chimiche Ittiolo. No. 120,440; Jan 13; v. 270; p. 324.

Stove-polish. A. Honkley. No. 121,302; Jan. 13; v. 270; p. 325.

Sugar and cinnamon combination. M. C. McKenna. No. 122,603; Jan. 13; v. 270; p. 328.

Table covers, napkins, &c. Arsenio Jose Froes & Company. No. 117,048; Jan. 13; v. 270; p. 323.

Tools, Mechanics' hand-. Mayhew Steel Products. No. 124,221; Jan. 13; v. 270; p. 332.

Valve-grinding compounds. S. & P. Manufacturing Co. No. 122,557; Jan. 13; v. 270; p. 328.

Vehicles, Motor-. Elgin Motor Car Corporation. No. 120,526; Jan. 13; v. 270; p. 324.

Veilings and nettings. Traub, Lewis & Co. No. 113,852; Jan. 13; v. 270; p. 322.

Veils, malines, hair-nets, chiffons. Fuld, Traube & Co. No. 120,746; Jan. 13; v. 270; p. 325.

Voltmeters, armature-testers, &c. American Bureau of Engineering. No. 119,728; Jan. 13; v. 270; p. 324.

Water, Artificial mineral. Valentin, Ord & Co. No. 122,925; Jan. 13; v. 270; p. 329.

Waterproof dressing for leather, &c. G. W. Baker. No. 120,741; Jan. 13; v. 270; p. 325.

Yarn. Marshall Field & Company. No. 118,145; Jan. 13; v. 270; p. 323.

Yarn. H. F. Salisbury. No. 115,556; Jan. 13; v. 270; p. 322.

CLASSIFICATION OF PATENTS

ISSUED JANUARY 13, 1920.

NOTE.—First number=class, second number=subclass, third number=patent number.

Column 1

2— 9: 1,328,078
73: 1,328,086
144: 1,327,625
3— 12: 1,327,938
4— 1: 1,327,768
27: 1,327,866
5— 3: 1,327,824
13: 1,328,248
72: 1,327,886
1,327,887
8— 1: 1,327,688
6: 1,327,862
17: 1,327,659
1,327,661
18: 1,327,657
1,327,658
1,327,650
1,327,662
1,327,663
1,327,756
10— 16: 1,328,128
12— 66: 1,327,780
139: 1,327,839
13— 7: 1,327,845
15: 1,328,212
17: 1,327,724
22: 1,327,612
15— 2: 1,327,943
17: 1,328,237
39: 1,327,807
41: 1,328,164
52: 1,327,757
16— 7: 1,328,043
151: 1,327,920
17— 10: 1,328,148
19: 1,328,226
18— 5.3: 1,327,722
38: 1,327,841
55: 1,327,851
19— 15: 1,327,696
20— 11: 1,327,653
21— 43: 1,328,105
69: 1,327,607
1,328,052
1,328,067
78: 1,327,871
215: 1,327,867
22— 57: 1,328,236
70: 1,327,697
184: 1,327,689
216: 1,327,987
23— 3: 1,328,096
1,328,210
21: 1,328,082
22: 1,327,781
1,327,782
24: 1,327,714
24— 3: 1,327,704
11: 1,328,076
12: 1,327,772
33: 1,327,798
104: 1,327,719
225: 1,328,205
242: 1,328,193
245: 1,327,959
248: 1,327,613
259: 1,327,761
25— 42: 1,327,721
84: 1,327,710
130: 1,327,739
28— 4: 1,328,216
29— 32: 1,328,250
69: 1,328,039
81: 1,328,034
87.1: 1,328,028
30— 12: 1,328,024
31— 14: 1,327,704
32— 4: 1,327,674
10: 1,328,131
33— 42: 1,327,874
148: 1,328,007
180: 1,328,144
191: 1,328,213
34— 5: 1,327,609
19: 1,327,668
35— 1: 1,327,775
17: 1,327,618

Column 2

36— 3: 1,327,772
31: 1,328,249
36: 1,328,154
37— 9: 1,327,651
49: 1,328,2 3
54: 1,328,013
57: 1,328,137
62: 1,327,645
63: 1,328,026
39— 18: 1,327,860
87: 1,328,168
40— 11: 1,328,123
20: 1,328,019
86: 1,328,178
130: 1,328,135
41— 38.5: 1,327,931
42— 3: 1,327,897
55: 1,327,747
43— 1: 1,328,114
5: 1,328,117
21: 1,327,890
36: 1,327,751
45— 9: 1,327,878
1,328,243
18: 1,327,865
47: 1,328,000
52: 1,327,977
54: 1,327,748
77: 1,328,112
97: 1,327,608
131: 1,327,956
136: 1,328,177
46— 14: 1,328,134
21: 1,327,907
27: 1,327,725
40: 1,327,884
1,328,100
46: 1,327,723
48— 41: 1,328,016
52: 1,328,227
85.2: 1,327,861
86: 1,327,893
180: 1,327,699
1,328,102
1,328,199
51— 1: 1,327,648
4: 1,327,639
1,327,875
11: 1,327,830
1,328,242
52— 1: 1,327,985
3: 1,327,859
53— 8: 1,328,001
55— 9: 1,328,231
19: 1,328,156
38: 1,328,124
39: 1,328,121
65: 1,328,063
77: 1,328,171
107: 1,327,760
58— 7: 1,327,924
63: 1,327,997
15: 1,328,247
26: 1,328,247
59— 69: 1,328,253
60— 18: 1,327,753
29: 1,327,769
44: 1,328,088
1,328,160
61— 71: 1,327,679
62— 122: 1,327,906
63— 15: 1,327,606
64— 22: 1,328,234
24: 1,328,209
39: 1,328,138
49: 1,328,017
89: 1,318,065
1,328,095
102: 1,327,791
65— 12: 1,327,929
63: 1,327,982
67— 6.1: 1,327,813
69: 1,327,858
68— 9: 1,327,613
1,327,976
32: 1,327,690
1,327,766

Column 3

70— 45: 1,327,916
46: 1,328,071
115: 1,328,106
122: 1,328,109
126: 1,327,979
129: 1,328,186
72— 56: 1,327,889
118: 1,327,741
1,328,201
73— 32: 1,327,800
74— 5: 1,327,793
1,328,252
7: 1,327,950
8: 1,328,064
13: 1,327,656
31: 1,327,925
45: 1,328,172
46: 1,327,955
1,328,145
48: 1,327,940
54: 1,327,942
56: 1,327,681
1,327,891
58: 1,327,832
59: 1,328,062
1,328,220
79: 1,327,616
108: 1,327,895
75— 18: 1,327,971
197: 1,327,713
76— 5: 1,327,720
26: 1,327,713
36: 1,328,159
107: 1,327,652
77— 7: 1,328,111
73: 1,327,934
1,328,208
78— 28: 1,327,817
80— 1: 1,327,919
16: 1,327,635
81— 1: 1,328,197
15: 1,327,892
42: 1,328,049
53: 1,328,087
57: 1,327,991
112: 1,327,702
134: R.14,791
83— 38: 1,327,636
60: 1,328,174
64: 1,327,740
67: 1,327,667
82: 1,327,885
1,327,903
88: 1,327,834
1,327,902
84— 28: 1,328,038
17: 1,327,621
22: 1,327,996
79: 1,327,970
85— 1.5: 1,328,053
86— 48: 1,327,698
87— 5: 1,327,631
1,328,080
6: 1,328,047
88— 16.2: 1,328,189
24: 1,327,732
27: 1,327,808
1,328,192
89— 1: 1,328,021
12: 1,328,230
90— 28.1: 1,327,828
33: 1,328,085
53: 1,327,881
60: 1,327,799
91— 45: 1,327,973
51: 1,328,081
70: 1,327,904
92— 3: 1,327,873
93— 11: 1,327,666
61: 1,328,011
94— 18: 1,328,107
97— 18: 1,327,921
67: 1,327,828
98— 3: 1,327,879
3: 1,328,094
26: 1,328,132

Column 4

98— 27: 1,327,630
99— 2: 1,327,937
1,328,183
6: 1,328,091
100— 47: 1,328,090
101— 371: 1,328,031
102— 20: 1,327,899
26: 1,327,655
103— 8: 1,327,868
43: 1,328,061
61: 1,328,165
63: 1,327,914
1,328,182
82: 1,328,218
104— 23: 1,328,233
59: 1,328,166
105— 107: 1,328,110
150: 1,328,163
271: 1,327,623
374: 1,327,894
376: 1,327,634
106— 10: 1,327,758
31: 1,327,726
107— 17: 1,327,806
27: 1,328,025
108— 5.6: 1,328,200
26: 1,327,770
110— 24: 1,328,116
36: 1,327,765
45: 1,327,764
60: 1,327,727
111— 52: 1,328,222
12: 1,327,972
112— 100: 1,327,646
208: 1,327,647
241: 1,328,023
232: 1,327,638
113— 23: 1,327,994
24: 1,327,966
33: 1,327,641
51: 1,328,014
68: 1,328,122
163: 1,327,643
225: 1,327,856
238: 1,327,614
116— 1: 1,327,993
31: 1,328,073
44: 1,327,785
119— 4: 1,328,008
37: 1,328,032
74: 1,328,036
75: 1,328,207
80: 1,327,734
103: 1,328,140
147: 1,327,735
120— 43: 1,327,922
46: 1,328,215
50: 1,327,729
121— 60: 1,328,033
123— 31: 1,328,142
32: 1,327,744
41: 1,327,995
65: 1,328,141
104: 1,327,927
148: 1,327,790
149: 1,328,149
169: 1,328,051
180: 1,328,089
183: 1,328,127
187.5: 1,327,687
124— 15: 1,327,998
125— 13: 1,327,923
126— 70: 1,328,246
77: 1,327,888
90: 1,328,012
260: 1,328,161
272: 1,328,202
275: 1,328,152
276: 1,328,071
128— 138: 1,328,176

Column 5

128— 147: 1,328,057
167: 1,327,930
191: 1,328,058
218: 1,328,203
241: 1,327,705
129— 1: 1,327,624
16: 1,327,848
1,327,936
40: 1,327,992
130— 15: 1,327,700
131— 6: 1,327,692
132— 19: 1,327,980
35: 1,328,120
133— 4: 1,327,969
31: 1,328,188
50: 1,327,928
79: 1,327,933
135— 29: 1,328,175
137— 21: 1,327,693
68: 1,327,999
1,328,009
10: 1,327,831
99: 1,327,846
101: 1,327,939
103: 1,327,691
152: 1,327,847
138— 9: 1,327,670
139— 7: 1,327,676
22: 1,328,018
27: 1,327,954
46: 1,327,709
48: 1,327,964
71: 1,328,683
1,327,684
85: 1,327,788
140— 2: 1,327,832
144— 42: 1,327,983
51: 1,327,627
281: 1,327,815
148— 25: 1,327,620
151— 18: 1,327,836
152— 5: 1,327,717
1,327,794
8: 1,327,843
17: 1,328,054
21: 1,327,759
50: 1,328,244
67: 1,327,728
153— 1: 1,327,826
154— 6: 1,327,677
10: 1,327,910
14: 1,327,802
1,327,912
1,328,006
42: 1,328,056
46: 1,327,707
155— 9: 1,327,706
20: 1,327,941
24: 1,328,169
35: 1,328,181
156— 22: 1,327,961
27: 1,328,136
158— 1: 1,328,075
2: 1,328,198
65: 1,327,763
75: 1,327,837
110: 1,328,225
162— 1: 1,328,139
164— 49: 1,327,915
168— 13: 1,327,716
170— 117: 1,327,745
1,328,004
1,328,000
163: 1,328,241
171— 225: 1,327,795
228: 1,327,820
252: 1,327,610
1,327,821
312: 1,327,819
172— 179: 1,327,784
1,327,789
1,327,922
1,328,239
288: 1,327,787
173— 72: 1,327,803
278: 1,327,947
331: 1,328,224

Column 6

174— 89: 1,327,786
175— 183: 1,328,187
294: 1,327,777
337: 1,327,671
329: 1,327,818
339: 1,327,837
1,328,245
177— 18: 1,327,805
179— 90: 1,327,622
16: 1,327,773
180— 70: 1,327,811
0.5: 1,328,059
181— 14: 1,328,103
182— 6: 1,328,015
184— 11: 1,327,779
188— 4: 1,327,823
24: 1,328,092
58: 1,328,138
70: 1,327,909
189— 46: 1,328,214
84: 1,327,711
192— 1: 1,327,880
1,327,805
10: 1,328,022
11: 1,327,767
193— 2: 1,328,099
24: 1,327,672
194— 1: 1,327,678
195— 32: 1,328,079
196— 1: 1,327,835
197— 8: 1,327,840
46: 1,328,158
60: 1,327,908
63: 1,328,050
199— 64: 1,328,146
200— 50: 1,328,072
72: 1,327,640
87: 1,327,951
166: 1,327,615
1,327,825
1,327,844
204— 29: 1,327,649
1,327,650
1,328,027
62: 1,327,736
64: 1,327,738
206— 40: 1,328,035
208— 114: 1,327,960
210— 5: 1,327,944
11: 1,328,221
14: 1,327,962
16: 1,327,708
1,328,044
18: 1,328,045
1,328,046
211— 8: 1,327,712
9: 1,328,185
16: 1,327,949
20: 1,327,771
27: 1,327,628
34: 1,328,167
67: 1,327,617
1,327,827
213— 2: 1,327,198
214— 38: 1,327,952
80: 1,327,834
105: 1,327,637
215— 9: 1,328,205
13: 1,327,967
14: 1,327,809
55: 1,328,060
81: 1,327,963
216— 14: 1,327,664
1,327,665
217— 57: 1,327,911
218— 17: 1,327,888
26: 1,327,888
58: 1,327,872
60: 1,327,978
219— 7: 1,327,792
10: 1,327,814
19: 1,328,126
21: 1,327,804
34: 1,327,988
38: 1,328,068
1,328,060
40: 1,327,774

219— 46: 1,328,229	230— 1: 1,328,055	240— 1: 1,327,918	248— 32: 1,327,981	259— 81: 1,328,119	279— 55: 1,328,195
49: 1,327,642	11: 1,327,926	7: 1,327,732	50: 1,328,162	83: 1,327,901	280— 33.5: 1,328,048
220— 1: 1,327,778	27: 1,327,783	45: 1,328,129	249— 65: 1,327,644	135: 1,327,900	60: 1,327,864
1,327,917	1,327,833	1,328,153	250— 27: 1,326,041	261— 19: 1,328,042	97: 1,327,829
20: 1,327,948	1,328,232	57: 1,328,125	251— 70: 1,328,098	41: R.14,790	103: 1,327,654
81: 1,327,965	33: 1,327,975	51: 1,327,945	113: 1,327,984	1,328,180	283— 51: 1,327,855
221— 23: 1,328,104	34: R.14,789	67: 1,327,733	253— 136: 1,327,953	62: 1,327,703	63: 1,327,610
77: 1,328,133	36: 1,327,731	242— 19: 1,328,196	179: 1,328,010	75: 1,328,204	285— 9: 1,327,632
95: 1,327,686	232— 19: 1,327,957	84.4: 1,328,066	194: 1,327,812	262— 6: 1,328,118	286— 18: 1,327,801
98: 1,328,184	233— 43: 1,328,084	243— 14: 1,327,718	190: 1,328,190	263— 49: 1,328,030	287— 17: 1,328,191
101: 1,328,101	234— 34.5: 1,327,989	244— 1: 1,327,810	254— 1: 1,328,115	264— 3: 1,327,633	58: 1,327,611
103: 1,327,990	39: 1,328,223	6: 1,328,040	86: 1,327,905	20: 1,327,629	290— 23: 1,328,083
127: 1,327,971	236— 16: 1,327,796	15: 1,328,211	130: 1,327,685	265— 11: 1,327,838	292— 75: 1,328,029
224— 29: 1,327,626	80: 1,327,675	21: 1,327,932	190: 1,327,876	266— 23: 1,327,715	265: 1,327,754
1,327,742	237— 12.3: 1,327,869	23: 1,328,143	255— 71: 1,327,913	267— 27: 1,327,958	337: 1,327,695
49: 1,327,680	79: 1,327,877	246— 110: 1,328,070	257— 80: 1,327,863	34: 1,327,750	340: 1,327,694
227— 81: 1,328,251	238— 26: 1,328,002	180: 1,327,968	129: 1,327,797	270— 52: 1,327,746	295— 9: 1,327,849
228— 40: 1,328,037	46: 1,328,113	384: 1,328,003	1,328,151	17: 1,328,219	296— 14: 1,328,130
68: 1,327,808	180: 1,328,170	387: 1,327,882	132: 1,327,730	274— 2: 1,327,776	26: 1,327,883
229— 29: 1,327,946	250: 1,328,155	460: 1,327,842	151: 1,327,870	15: 1,327,816	298— 17: 1,328,137
86: 1,328,028		479: 1,328,194	165: 1,327,896	277— 45: 1,328,235	19: 1,328,240
		248— 3: 1,327,749	241: 1,328,150	57: 1,327,850	

Patents Nos. 1,328,253 to 1,328,801.

THE
OFFICIAL GAZETTE

OF THE

𝔘nited 𝔖tates 𝔓atent 𝔒ffice.

Vol. 270—No. 3.   TUESDAY, JANUARY 20, 1920.   Price—$5 per year.

The OFFICIAL GAZETTE is mailed under the direction of the Superintendent of Documents, Government Printing Office, to whom all subscriptions should be made payable and all communications respecting the Gazette should be addressed. Issued weekly. Subscriptions, $5.00 per annum; single numbers, 10 cents each.

Printed copies of patents are furnished by the Patent Office at 10 cents each. For the latter, address the Commissioner of Patents, Washington, D. C.

CONTENTS.

Issue of January 20, 1920.

Patents	549—No. 1,328,253 to No. 1,328,801, inclusive.
Designs	4—No. 54,359 to No. 54,362, inclusive.
Trade-Marks	197—No. 128,913 to No. 129,109, inclusive.
Reissues	2—No. 14,792 to No. 14,793, inclusive.

Total 752

To make your future rosy, use W. S. S. paint.

Interference Notices.

DEPARTMENT OF THE INTERIOR,
UNITED STATES PATENT OFFICE,
Washington, D. C., January 5, 1920.
Nicholas B. Bartz, his assigns or legal representatives, take notice:
An interference having been declared by this Office between the application of Griffith Alverson Co., care of Campholatum Co., Mason City, Iowa, for registration of a trade-mark and trade-mark registered October 8, 1912, No. 88,611, to Nicholas B. Bartz, 84 Adams street, Chicago, Ill., and a notice of such declaration sent by registered mail to said Nicholas B. Bartz at the said address having been returned by the post-office undeliverable, notice is hereby given that unless said Nicholas B. Bartz, his assigns or legal representatives, shall enter an appearance therein within thirty days from the first publication of this order the interference will be proceeded with as in case of default.
This notice will be published in the OFFICIAL GAZETTE for three consecutive weeks.
M. H. COULSTON,
Assistant Commissioner.

DEPARTMENT OF THE INTERIOR,
UNITED STATES PATENT OFFICE,
Washington, D. C., January 5, 1920.
Moki Herb Remedy Company, its assigns or legal representatives, take notice:
An interference having been declared by this Office between the application of Edwin R. Mohler. No. 900 Penn street, Reading, Pa., for registration of a trade-mark and trade-mark registered November 1, 1892, No. 21,922, to Moki Herb Remedy Company, Tempe, Ariz., and a notice of such declaration sent by registered mail to said Moki Herb Remedy Company at the said address having been returned by the post-office undeliverable, notice is hereby given that unless said Moki Herb Remedy Company, its assigns or legal representatives, shall enter an appearance therein within thirty days from the first publication of

this order the interference will be proceeded with as in case of default.
This notice will be published in the OFFICIAL GAZETTE for three consecutive weeks.
M. H. COULSTON,
Assistant Commissioner.

DEPARTMENT OF THE INTERIOR,
UNITED STATES PATENT OFFICE,
Washington, D. C., January 9, 1920.
Murphy Wall Bed Co. of California, its assigns or legal representatives, take notice:
An interference having been declared by this Office between the application of Murphy Wall Bed Company, of 422 Crocker Building, San Francisco, Calif., for registration of a trade-mark and trade-mark registered December 23, 1913, No. 94,655, to Murphy Wall Bed Co. of California, of 809–10–11 Longacre Building, New York, N. Y., and a notice of such declaration sent by registered mail to said Murphy Wall Bed Co. of California at the said address having been returned by the post-office undeliverable, notice is hereby given that unless said Murphy Wall Bed Co. of California, its assigns or legal representatives, shall enter an appearance therein within thirty days from the first publication of this order the interference will be proceeded with as in case of default.
This notice will be published in the OFFICIAL GAZETTE for three consecutive weeks.
R. F. WHITEHEAD,
First Assistant Commissioner.

DEPARTMENT OF THE INTERIOR,
UNITED STATES PATENT OFFICE,
Washington, D. C., January 9, 1920.
George T. Robie, his assigns or legal representatives, take notice:
An interference having been declared by this Office between the application of Boston Belting Corporation, of 80 Elmwood street, Boston, Mass., for registration of a trade-mark and trade-mark registered March 21, 1899, No. 32,628, to George T. Robie, of 88 and 90 Lake street, Chicago, Ill., and a notice of such declaration sent by registered mail to said George T. Robie at the said address having been returned by the post-office undeliverable, notice is hereby given that unless said George T. Robie, his assigns or legal representatives, shall enter an appearance therein within thirty days from the first publication of this order the interference will be proceeded with as in case of default.
This notice will be published in the OFFICIAL GAZETTE for three consecutive weeks.
R. F. WHITEHEAD,
First Assistant Commissioner.

DEPARTMENT OF THE INTERIOR,
UNITED STATES PATENT OFFICE,
Washington, D. C., January 13, 1920.
Dodge & Starkel, their assigns or legal representatives, take notice:
An interference having been declared by this Office between the application of the Globe Canning Co., Eastport and North Lubec, Me., for registration of a trade-mark and trade-mark registered March 10, 1908, No. 68,135, to Dodge & Starkel, 42 River street, Chicago, Ill., and a notice of such declaration sent by registered mail to said Dodge & Starkel at the said address having been returned by the post-office undeliverable, notice is hereby given that unless said Dodge & Starkel, their assigns or legal representatives, shall enter an appearance therein within thirty days from the first publication of this order the interference will be proceeded with as in case of default.
This notice will be published in the OFFICIAL GAZETTE for three consecutive weeks.
R. F. WHITEHEAD,
First Assistant Commissioner.

APPLICATIONS UNDER EXAMINATION.

Condition at Close of Business January 16, 1920.

Room No.	Divisions and subjects of invention.	New.	Amended.	No. of applications awaiting action.
311	1. Closure Operators; Fences; Gates; Harrows and Diggers; Plows; Planting; Scattering Unloaders; Trees, Plants, and Flowers.	Oct. 21	Sept. 13	396
128	2. Bee Culture; Curtains, Shades, and Screens; Dairy; Medicines; Pneumatics; Preserving; Presses; Tents, Canopies, Umbrellas, and Canes; Tobacco.	July 2	July 26	917
175	3. Electric Heating and Rheostats; Electrochemistry; Heating; Metal-Founding; Metallurgical Apparatus; Metallurgy; Metal Treatment; Plastic Metal Working.	Sept. 11	Sept. 3	308
231	4. Conveyers; Elevators; Excavating; Handling—Hand and Hoist-Line Implements; Hoisting; Material or Article Handling; Pneumatic Despatch; Pushing and Pulling Implements; Railway Mail Delivery; Store-Service; Traversing Hoists.	June 21	Nov. 12	742
167	5. Book-Making; Books, Strips and Leaves; Harvesters; Jewelry; Manifolding; Music; Printed Matter; Tying Cords or Strands.	Aug. 19	Oct. 27	232
318	6. Bleaching and Dyeing; Chemicals; Explosives; Fertilizers; Liquid Coating Compositions; Plastic Compositions; Substance Preparation.	Sept. 15	Nov. 4	485
312	7. Games and Toys; Optics; Photography; Velocipedes.	Oct. 3	Nov. 19	557
131	8. Beds; Chairs and Seats; Flexible-Sheet Securing Devices; Furniture; Kitchen and Table Articles; Store Furniture; Supports.	Oct. 13	Oct. 17	383
221	9. Air and Gas Pumps; Hydraulic Motors; Injectors and Ejectors; Motors, Fluid; Motors, Fluid-Current; Pumps.	Sept. 8	Nov. 4	245
235	10. Carriages and Wagons; Land-Vehicles; Land-Vehicles—Bodies and Tops; Land-Vehicles—Dumping; Motor Vehicles.	Aug. 19	Sept. 30	984
151	11. Boot and Shoe Making; Boots, Shoes, and Leggings; Button, Eyelet, and Rivet Setting; Harness; Leather Manufactures; Nailing and Stapling; Spring Devices; Whips and Whip Apparatus.	July 19	Oct. 31	471
222	12. Machine Elements.	June 14	Oct. 6	1,021
329	13. Bolt, Nail, Nut, Rivet, and Screw Making; Button Making; Chain, Staple, and Horseshoe Making; Driven, Headed, and Screw-Threaded Fastenings; Gear Cutting, Milling, and Planing; Metal Drawing; Metal Forging and Welding; Metal Rolling; Metal Tools and Implements, Making; Metal Working; Needle and Pin Making; Turning.	June 25	Oct. 22	946
323	14. Compound Tools; Cutting and Punching Sheets and Bars; Farriery; Metal-Bending; Sheet-Metal Ware, Making; Tools; Wire Fabrics and Structure; Wire-Working.	July 2	Oct. 24	443
308	15. Bread, Pastry, and Confection Making; Coating; Fuel; Glass; Laminated Fabrics and Analogous Manufactures; Paper-Making and Fiber Liberation; Plastic Block and Earthenware Apparatus; Plastics.	June 19	Oct. 21	932
111	16. Radiant Energy; Telegraphy; Telephony.	June 30	July 23	856
307	17. Label Pasting and Paper Hanging; Nut and Bolt Locks; Ornamentation; Paper Manufactures; Printing; Type Casting; Sheet Material Associating or Folding; Sheet Feeding or Delivering; Type Setting.	Sept. 22	Nov. 14	237
229	18. Fluid-Pressure Regulators; Liquid Heaters and Vaporizers; Motors, Expansible Chamber Type; Power Plants; Speed Responsive Devices; Steam and Vacuum Pumps.	Aug. 4	Oct. 29	690
236	19. Automatic Temperature and Humidity Regulation; Furnaces; Heating Systems; Stoves and Furnaces; Domestic Cooking Vessels; Thermostats and Humidostats.	July 1	Aug. 1	551
179	20. Artificial Body Members; Builders' Hardware; Closure-Fasteners; Cutlery; Dentistry; Locks and Latches; Safes; Undertaking.	Oct. 15	Sept. 20	665
212	21. Brakes and Gins; Carding; Cloth-Finishing; Continuous-Strip Feeding; Cordage; Felt and Fur; Knitting and Netting; Silk; Spinning; Weaving; Winding and Reeling.	July 3	Oct. 13	357
249	22. Aeronautics; Firearms; Ordnance.	Sept. 10	Nov. 10	294
217	23. Acoustics; Coin-Handling; Horology; Recorders; Registers; Sound Recording and Reproducing; Time-Controlling Mechanism.	July 9	Oct. 22	600
141	24. Apparel; Apparel Apparatus; Garment Supporters; Sewing-Machines.	June 10	Nov. 1	607
315	25. Agitating; Butchering; Centrifugal Bowl Separators; Mills; Threshing; Vegetable Cutters and Crushers; Gas Separation.	Nov. 24	Nov. 20	194
105	26. Electricity, Generation; Motive Power; Prime Mover Dynamo Plants.	May 3	Aug. 14	744
214	27. Brushing and Scrubbing; Grinding and Polishing; Laundry; Washing Apparatus.	Sept. 16	Sept. 26	509
223	28. Internal-Combustion Engines.	Sept. 2	Oct. 17	579
117	29. Boring and Drilling; Chucks or Sockets; Coopering; Rod Joints or Couplings; Wheelwright-Machines; Wood-Sawing; Wood-Turning; Woodworking; Woodworking Tools.	Apr. 15	Aug. 1	604
· 152	30. Illuminating-Burners; Illumination; Liquid and Gaseous Fuel Burners; Type-Writing Machines.	July 9	Oct. 2	862
172	31. Alcohol; Ammonia, Water, and Wood Distillation; Charcoal and Coke; Gas, Heating and Illuminating; Hides, Skins, and Leather; Hydraulic Cement and Lime; Mineral Oils; Oils, Fats, and Glue; Sugar and Salt.	July 7	July 3	850
278	32. Gas and Liquid Contact Apparatus; Heat Exchange; Refrigeration.	June 11	Nov. 3	912
70	33. Bridges; Hydraulic and Earth Engineering; Masonry and Concrete Structures; Metallic Building Structures; Roads and Pavements; Roofs.	Aug. 11	Oct. 31	370
301	34. Railways; Railway Rolling Stock; Railway Switches and Signals; Railways, Surface Track; Railway Wheels and Axles; Track-Sanders; Vehicle-Fenders.	Nov. 14	Dec. 18	233
57	35. Buckles, Buttons, Clasps, Etc.; Card, Picture, and Sign Exhibiting; Signals and Indicators; Toilet.	Nov. 26	Dec. 5	403
204	36. Automatic Weighers; Driers; Geometrical Instruments; Measuring Instruments; Force Measuring.	Oct. 7	Sept. 20	899
107	37. Electric Lamps; Electricity, Circuit Makers and Breakers; Electricity, General Applications.	July 11	July 15	991
378	38. Animal Husbandry; Earth Boring; Fishing and Trapping; Mining, Quarrying, and Ice-Harvesting; Stationery; Stone-Working; Wells.	Nov. 12	Nov. 18	308
220	39. Fluid Sprinkling, Spraying, and Diffusing; Joint Packings; Multiple Valves; Packed Shaft or Rod Joints; Pipe Joints or Couplings; Valved Pipe Joints or Couplings; Valves; Water Distribution.	Apr. 7	July 1	999
273	40. Baggage; Bottles and Jars; Check-Controlled Apparatus; Cloth, Leather, and Rubber Receptacles; Deposit and Collection Receptacles; Metallic Receptacles; Package and Article Carriers; Paper Receptacles; Special-Receptacles and Packages; Wooden Receptacles.	July 7	Oct. 25	543
125	41. Resilient Tires and Wheels.	July 18	Oct. 30	778
114	42. Electricity, Conductors; Electricity-Transmission to Vehicles; Electricity, Conduits; Electric Signaling.	July 16	Aug. 14	738
382	43. Baths and Closets; Dispensing; Dispensing Beverages; Electricity, Medical and Surgical; Fire-Extinguishers; Sewerage; Surgery; Water Purification.	Sept. 6	Nov. 17	419
253	44. Air-Guns, Catapults, and Targets; Ammunition and Explosive Devices; Ammunition and Explosive Charge Making; Boats and Buoys; Filling and Closing Portable Receptacles; Marine Propulsion; Railway Draft Appliances; Ships.	July 2	Oct. 23	316
379	45. Clutches; Journal-Boxes, Pulleys, and Shafting; Lubrication; Motors.	Aug. 4	Oct. 25	776
332	46. Educational Appliances; Fire-Escapes; Ladders; Paper Files and Binders; Railway-Brakes; Wooden Buildings.	June 11	Nov. 1	537

Oldest new case, Apr. 7; oldest amended, July 1.
Total number of applications awaiting action.. 27,438

Room No.	Divisions and subjects of invention.	New.	Amended.	No.
163	TRADE-MARKS, DESIGNS, LABELS AND PRINTS:			
	Trade-Marks.	Oct. 4	Dec. 3	2,465
	Designs.	Sept. 2	Sept. 18	1,204
	Labels and Prints.	Nov. 17	Oct. 20	483

PATENTS

1,328,253. PRINTING - PRESS. REED ADAMS, Lapeer, Mich. Filed Apr. 7, 1916. Serial No. 89,519. 3 Claims. (Cl. 74—46.)

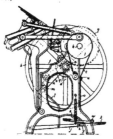

1. The combination with a printing press having form-bearing parts, a mechanism of small inertia adapted to actuate one of said parts and located mechanically adjacent thereto, a brake adapted to act on said actuating mechanism, a driving mechanism for said press, and means for disconnecting said driving mechanism from said form-actuating mechanism and applying the brake to the latter and for connecting said driving mechanism therewith and releasing said brake.

1,328,254. DOLL. STELLA ADLER, St. Louis, Mo. Filed Mar. 13, 1919. Serial No. 282,260. 3 Claims. (Cl. 46—40.)

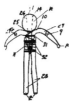

1. A process for making dolls, same including the cutting of lengths of wire as cores for the head and neck, arms, legs and feet, the leg wires being cut long enough to extend up to the shoulders and thus helping fill out, and form the body; then bending the ends of the leg wires outwardly to form the feet; then wrapping said leg wires spirally with strip paper to fill out the body, legs and feet; then rolling two tufts of paper and binding a tuft at the back of each foot to form the heel; then wrapping the arm elements likewise spirally with strip paper to fill out the arms; then bending same to form the hands, elbows and shoulders and so as to leave depending shoulder joints as means of attachment to the legs; then bending the head and neck wire to form a head core with depending neck core; then filling out the head core with cotton to form the rounded head; then wrapping the head and neck core with paper to form the face and neck; then binding the head and neck element to the two depending shoulder joints so that the arms will stand out in opposite directions, with the hands turned forwardly; then placing the

two leg elements one on either side of the depending shoulder joints with the upper ends thereof positioned beneath the shoulders and with the feet turned forwardly; then binding the leg elements to the head, neck and arm elements to form the body.

1,328,255. FAN. PER AUGUST ANDERSON, New York, N. Y. Filed May 17, 1919. Serial No. 297,770. 3 Claims. (Cl. 230—1.)

1. In an automatic fan, a support, electro-magnets carried thereby in opposed, spaced relation, an armature member having its one end pivotally connected to said support and depending between said magnets and pivotally oscillated thereby, switching means, including members carried directly by said armature member and partaking of the movements thereof whereby the circuits controlling said magnets are closed and broken and a fan member pivotally mounted on said support independently of said armature member and operatively connected with the latter so as to be pivotally vibrated thereby.

1,328,256. MULTIPLE - BLADE TYPE-MOLD. JOHN SELLERS BANCROFT and AMOS L. KNIGHT, Philadelphia, Pa., assignors to Lanston Monotype Machine Company, Philadelphia, Pa., a Corporation of Virginia. Filed June 7, 1918. Serial No. 238,731. 19 Claims. (Cl. 199—84.)

1. A type mold comprising two type blocks each forming a side wall of the mold cavity, one of said type blocks having a portion adjacent the mold cavity reduced in height, whereby a mold cavity shaped to produce overhang type is formed, a mold blade slidable between said blocks and a supplemental mold blade adapted to be moved in unison with the said mold blade to exert an ejecting

action on the overhang portion of the type cast, said supplemental blade being slidable upon said reduced portion of said block.

1,328,257. TYPOGRAPHIC COMPOSING - MACHINE. JOHN SELLERS BANCROFT and MAURITZ C. INDAHL, Philadelphia, Pa., assignors to Lanston Monotype Machine Company, Philadelphia, Pa., a Corporation of Virginia. Filed Sept. 6, 1918. Serial No. 252,929. 10 Claims. (Cl. 199—77.)

1. In a typographic composing machine, a mold, a matrix carrier, and matrices movable toward and from the mold to seat a desired matrix on the mold, means for centering and seating a matrix on the mold with a relatively light yielding pressure, and means for applying a relatively heavy clamping pressure to the matrix after it is seated on the mold.

1,328,258. PROCESS FOR THE CONTINUOUS PRODUCTION OF ETHER. EMILE AUGUSTIN BARBET, Paris, France, assignor to E. Barbet & Fils & Cie., Paris, France. Filed May 5, 1916. Serial No. 95,613. 6 Claims. (Cl. 23—24.)

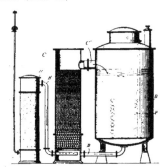

1. The process for the continuous production of ether by the dehydration of alcohol by means of sulfuric acid and in a closed cycle, which comprises bringing together ethyl alcohol and sulfuric acid; maintaining the acid and alcohol in contact until the alcohol is entirely absorbed by the acid and ethyl sulfuric acid is thereby formed; immediately and separately subjecting the ethyl sulfuric acid to the action of heat in order to effect partial decomposition of the ethyl sulfuric acid and to set free either; bringing the acid incompletely freed from either into contact with a further quantity of ethyl alcohol, thus completing the cycle, and varying the composition of the reaction mass throughout this cyclic process only by causing the necessary chemical and physical changes to take place in the process and by introducing further quantities of alcohol into the system.

1,328,259. COOLING-PLATE FOR CONTINUOUS-RECTIFICATION APPARATUS. EMILE AUGUSTIN BARBET, Paris, France. Filed Mar. 26, 1917. Serial No. 157,578. 2 Claims. (Cl. 195—13.)
1. A cooling plate structure for rectifying columns comprising a dished bottom plate, an upstanding chimney arranged therein, a hood surrounding the said chimney, a substantially horizontal perforated diaphragm surmounting the said dished plate for causing the vapors passing through the liquid on the diaphragm to be broken up into

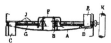

small bubbles and a cooling coil associated with the said device, such cooling coil being located below the normal liquid level of the reflux liquid supported on said perforated diaphragm, the perforations in said diaphragm being located only close to the said cooling coil.

1,328,260. TRACKING DEVICE. JAMES W. BARNES, New York, N. Y., assignor to Estey Piano Co., New York, N. Y. Filed Jan. 13, 1916. Serial No. 71,900. 20 Claims. (Cl. 84—161.)

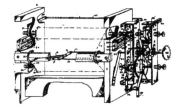

1. In mechanism of the character described, in combination, delivery and take-up spools, supporting means whereby said spools are free to swing endwise in unison, a fixed tracker bar, and means to act on a music sheet for guiding the same in proper registry with said tracker bar during its travel thereover.

1,328,261. MACHINE WITH ROTARY AND SELF-CONTROLLING CYLINDERS. WILHELM ALBERT CARL BLANKENBURG, Amsterdam, Netherlands. Filed July 2, 1914. Serial No. 848,626. 7 Claims. (Cl. 123—43.)

1. In a combustion engine of the class described, a revolving and self-controlling cylinder having one end closed with its interior hemispherically vaulted with a central circular opening and provided with a restricted tube-shaped collar having its outer surface formed with a valve-face and one or more ports opening upon said valve-face, a valve-seat having a plug-like projection fitting said circular opening of the cylinder end and serving to complete the head of said cylinder.

1,328,262. COVER FOR FLOOR-SUMPS. EDWARD W. N. BOOSEY, Detroit, Mich. Filed Mar. 1, 1919. Serial No. 280,153. 8 Claims. (Cl. 210—5.)
1. A cover for sumps consisting of a base member having flanged apertures adjacent one side for calking of a

pipe member thereto and an integral tubular portion positioned eccentrically of the cover and opening therethrough.

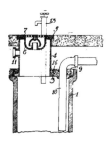

the said tubular portion being adapted to receive an apertured cover, and a trap reservoir therebeneath.

1,328,263. MACHINE FOR ASSORTING AND COUNTING PAPER MONEY. JOHN P. BUCKLEY and ALLAN E. LARD, Washington, D. C. Filed July 12, 1916, Serial No. 108,919. Renewed June 5, 1919. Serial No. 301,998. 33 Claims. (Cl. 235—92.)

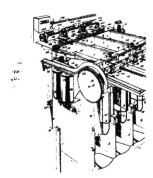

1. In a machine for counting paper money, the combination of feeding means adapted to feed bills; means controlled by said feeding means to arrest said feeding means when more than a single bill is introduced thereto at the same time; and a register associated with and controlled by said feeding means and operable only when a single bill is passed by said feeding means.

1,328,264. PRESS FOR MOUNTING SOUND-MATRICES. CHARLES F. BURROUGHS, East Orange, N. J., assignor to Composition Machinery Corporation, Newark, N. J., a Corporation of New Jersey. Filed June 15, 1918, Serial No. 240,188. Renewed Oct. 3, 1919. Serial No. 328,332. 12 Claims. (Cl. 29—89.)

1. The means for mounting a thin matrix upon a bed-piece having a clamping-ring upon its margin to engage the edge of the matrix such means consisting of a head and force movable in relation to one another with means for pressing them forcibly together and the head provided with an annular seat to receive the clamping-ring, and

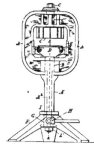

the force being fitted to press upon the bed-piece opposite to the said ring.

1,328,265. INTERNAL-COMBUSTION ENGINE. HUBERT CAUNT, East Calgary, Alberta, Canada. Filed Feb. 24, 1919. Serial No. 278,886. 2 Claims. (Cl. 123—76.)

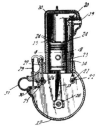

1. In an internal combustion engine having a plurality of cylinders, each of said cylinders being provided with a plurality of scavenging ducts communicating the crank case of the engine with the cylinders thereof, a manifold arranged upon said crank case, said manifold being adapted to communicate with said crank case, a plurality of intermittently actuated valves adapted to sever communication between said crank case and manifold, said valves corresponding in number to the number of the cylinders of the engine, and means for retaining said valves open during the intake and compression strokes of the pistons to permit the entrance of air from said manifold to the crank case, said means being adapted to close said valves at the beginning of the working stroke whereby the air drawn into the crank case is compressed and injected into the cylinders of the engine through the scavenging ports at the completion of the working stroke of the piston.

1,328,266. APPARATUS AND PROCESS FOR PRODUCING MOTION-PICTURES. HAROLD GLOY CHRISTENSEN, New York, N. Y. Filed July 19, 1919. Serial No. 312,072. 8 Claims. (Cl. 88—16.)

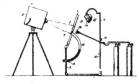

1. The process of producing motion pictures consisting of distorting a visible photographic image contained in a

photographic plate by projecting heat from a lighted gasolene torch against said plate, and taking a motion picture
of said image while undergoing distortion.

1,328,267. FELT PAPER. CLARENCE P. COWAN, Pont
Rouge, Quebec, Canada, assignor to Charles S. Bird,
Walpole, Mass. Filed July 16, 1918. Serial No. 245,228.
5 Claims. (Cl. 154—51.)
1. Felt stock, composed of a mixture of disintegrated
peat moss, rags and paper.

1,328,268. METHOD OF AND APPARATUS FOR DRAW-
ING CONTINUOUS SHEETS OF GLASS. JOSEPH P.
CROWLEY, Toledo, Ohio, assignor to The Libbey-Owens
Sheet Glass Company, Charleston, W. Va., a Corpora-
tion of Ohio. Filed Mar. 15, 1917. Serial No. 155,001.
19 Claims. (Cl. 49—17.)

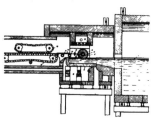

2. An apparatus for forming a continuous sheet of
glass, comprising a receptacle for molten glass, a rotating
roll partly immersed in the glass, and means to draw the
glass in a sheet from the roll in a direction normal
thereto.
6. The method of drawing a continuous sheet of glass,
which consists in causing a surface to move upward from
a mass of molten glass and carry glass upward therewith,
and drawing glass laterally from a drawing point at said
surface above the level of said mass while a portion of
the glass is carried upward with said surface beyond the
drawing point and away from the upper face of the sheet.

1,328,269. SIGNAL SYSTEM FOR CONTROLLING
STREET TRAFFIC. BENJAMIN W. DAVIS, Chicago,
Ill. Filed Oct. 30, 1914. Serial No. 869,446. 5 Claims.
(Cl. 177—339.)

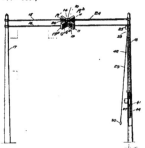

1. In a signal system for controlling street traffic, a
signal member comprising distinctive signal elements, an
electric circuit for illuminating said signal elements, said
circuit comprising an extensible cable, and a switch member carried by said cable.

1,328,270. STEAM - EJECTOR. MAURICE DELAPORTE,
Paris, France. Filed Sept. 7, 1917. Serial No. 190,119.
6 Claims. (Cl. 230—13.)

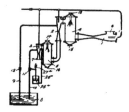

1. An apparatus for extracting gases from a receptacle,
comprising in combination with a first and a second steam
ejector arranged in series with each other and an intermediate auxiliary condenser, means for introducing liquid
to the mass of gas delivered to the second ejector, the
inlet of said means for introducing the liquid to the mass
of gas being located at a point where the gases extracted
from the receptacle have already been subjected to a
certain amount of compression.

1,328,271. OIL-CUP HOLDER. WILLIAM R. DUTEMPLE,
Auburn, R. I. Filed Dec. 1, 1919. Serial No. 341,668.
3 Claims. (Cl. 248—20.)

2. In an oil cup holder, the combination of a base
plate, a back plate disposed at right angles thereto, horizontally disposed supports upon the back plate overhanging the base plate, a pintle in the supports, a yoke comprising a cross piece and parallel flat arms pivotally
mounted at their rear ends on the pintle and provided
with longitudinally curved portions, and a helical spring
attached to one of the arms adjacent the pintle and to
the base beneath the supports.

1,328,272. AIR-HEATER. CLARENCE E. FEAZEL, Columbus, Ohio. Filed Dec. 13, 1917. Serial No. 206,996.
1 Claim. (Cl. 257—241.)

An air heating attachment for internal combustion
engines comprising an elongated cylinder having air intake openings at one end thereof, a second cylinder located concentrically within the former and having air intake openings at the opposite end thereof, a cap closure
common to both cylinders for each end of the assemblage,
said cylinders being of a size to form an annular chamber
between them, an open ended pipe extending into said
second named cylinder through one of said cap closures a
substantial distance beyond the openings in the latter,
said pipe being also of a size to form a second annular
chamber in communication with said first named chamber

to form a tortuous passageway, and a valve structure in said pipe for governing the amount of air passing therethrough.

·1,328,273. GLASS-MOLDING APPARATUS. ENOCH T. FERNGREN, Kansas City, Mo. Filed Mar. 11, 1912. Serial No. 682,895. 37 Claims. (Cl. 49—5.)

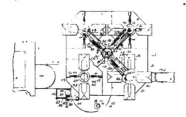

1. The combination with a glass furnace, of a conduit communicating with said furnace below its fluid level and having an upwardly facing delivery port positioned for discharging molten glass under hydrostatic pressure therefrom, a movable glass receptacle adapted to continuously receive and remove molten glass as it issues from said delivery port, whereby a continuous discharge of molten glass under hydrostatic pressure is diverted and moved transversely from said port, and means for operating said receptacle.

3. In a glass feeding apparatus, a glass furnace, a conduit communicating with said furnace, and for conveying glass therefrom, said conduit being provided with a discharge port for the issuance of glass therefrom, a device forming a confining continuation to said port, means on said device forming a series of pockets, adapted by movement thereof to continuously receive sever and divert molten glass issuing from said port, while traversing the same and means for operating said device.

5. In a glass feeding apparatus, the combination with a neck and blank mold having an intake port in the bottom thereof, of a glass reservoir, a conduit connected with said reservoir for conveying molten glass therefrom, said conduit having a discharge port adapted by registration with said intake port to pass molten glass through said ports and an element covering said discharge port adapted to retard and to continuously divert, transversely, the passage of molten glass from said discharge port, by its movement across said discharge port, prior to feeding said mold and means for operating said element.

7. In a glass feeding apparatus, a glass furnace, a conduit communicating with said furnace for carrying glass therefrom, said conduit being provided with a discharge port, a device forming a closed extension to said port and adapted to continuously remove glass from said port, and to divert the glass alternately in one, then the other of two directions and means for operating said device.

1,328,274. VALVE. WILLS M. FLEMING, Holyoke, Mass., assignor, by mesne assignments, to Worthington Pump and Machinery Corporation, New York, N. Y., a Corporation of Virginia. Filed Nov. 5, 1914. Serial No. 870,425. 2 Claims. (Cl. 103—75.)

1. The combination, with a cylinder, a piston, and a valve chest at one side of the cylinder having walls forming an inlet chamber, an outlet chamber and a clearance space between them, said clearance space being in direct communication with the cylinder by an open passage, of an inlet valve in the wall between the inlet chamber and the clearance chamber, a tension spring connected to the inlet valve, an adjustable plug in the outer wall of the valve chest, a shackle-bolt extending through said plug and freely rotatable therein and engaging the tension

spring, a nut on said bolt outside the plug for locking the bolt in fixed position, an outlet valve in the wall between the outlet chamber and the clearance chamber, and means for pressing said outlet valve to its seat.

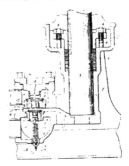

1,328,275. CINEMATOGRAPHIC TARGET. HUBERT F. FRANKLIN, Brooklyn, N. Y., assignor, by mesne assignments, to Animated Target Company, Inc., New York, N. Y., a Corporation of New York. Filed July 27, 1916. Serial No. 111,357. 10 Claims. (Cl. 124—15.)

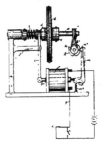

1. A cinematograph target embodying therein a controlling mechanism for a projector including therein a switch adapted to be automatically actuated to control an electric circuit substantially simultaneously with the discharge of a firearm, means whereby the transmission of power to the film feeding mechanism of the projector is controlled, means included in said circuit adapted to actuate said first named means and automatically acting means whereby the actuation of said switch mechanism is made inoperative as to said first named means except when a full picture is exposed to the sight opening of the projector.

1,328,276. METHOD OF FORGING CYLINDERS OF ENGINES AND SIMILAR STRUCTURES. ERNEST FUCHS, Paris, France, assignor to Louis Renault, Billancourt, France. Filed Oct. 16, 1918. Serial No. 258,377. 1 Claim. (Cl. 29—148.)

The method of forging cylinders of engines or similar structures, which consists in forging a rough model, machining the base and the external walls thereof, raising the head of the cylinder to the required temperature and forging the head into the necessary shape.

1,328,277. TANK-REGULATOR. WESTON M. FULTON, Knoxville, Tenn., assignor to The Fulton Company, Knoxville, Tenn., a Corporation of Maine. Filed June 26, 1914. Serial No. 847,486. 6 Claims. (Cl. 236—18.)

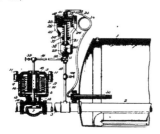

1. In a device of the character described, a hot-water tank provided with a conduit for supplying a heating medium thereto, a valve in said conduit, a by-pass for conveying heating medium around said valve, an extensible and contractible wall connected to said valve and provided with a vent constituting a means of communication between said conduit and said by-pass, a pilot valve in said by-pass, an extensible and collapsible vessel having a movable end wall connected to said pilot valve, and a thermosensitive bulb in communication with said vessel and subjected to the temperature of the water in said tank.

1,328,278. EXTRACTION OF OIL FROM VEGETABLE FRUITS. NORMAN ALEXANDER GAVIN, Kinshasha, Belgian Kongo; Mary Macdonald Gavin, executrix of said Norman Alexander Gavin, deceased, assignor to Lever Brothers Limited, Port Sunlight, England. Filed Mar. 3, 1917. Serial No. 152,347. 2 Claims. (Cl. 87—6.)

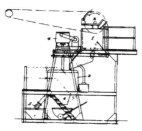

1. A process of extraction of oil from the pericarp of palm oil and the like nuts consisting in cooking the nuts, passing them into a centrifugal to be subjected to centrifugal force, breaking the resultant mass, screening the mat of fiber and nuts so formed, and then pressing the fiber.

1,328,279. DIE-HOLDER. JOSEPH GRAUER, Brooklyn, N. Y. Filed Nov. 6, 1917. Serial No. 200,490. 2 Claims. (Cl. 10—123.)
1. In a die holder, a housing provided with a recess at one end and leverage means at the other, a die adapted

to be securely held in said recess, a guide, a guide holder provided with means for holding said guide, said guide

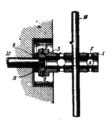

holder being also provided with jaws adapted to fit over said die and means for securing the said guide holder and accompanying guide in position over the said die.

1,328,280. BOTTLE - CLOSURE. CHARLES HAMMER, Queens, N. Y., assignor to American Metal Cap Company, Brooklyn, N. Y., a Corporation of New York. Filed June 21, 1918. Serial No. 241,111. 9 Claims. (Cl. 215—13.)

1. A closure comprising a body formed of a metal strip bent into the form of a cylinder with the ends secured together, such securing means comprising one end of the strip being provided with a tongue which is bent back toward one face to form a channel, the other strip end being provided with a projection which is doubled back against the strip on the opposite face from said tongue bend at the other end, the strip also having corner portions adjacent the ends of said doubled projection that are each bent down on a line oblique to such end to form open channels on the same face of the strip as the doubled projection, the said tongue end portions being caused to enter beneath said bent corner portions respectively, said end portions being pressed together to form an interlocking flat side joint.

1,328,281. BROACHING-MACHINE. HENRY L. HANSON, Worcester, Mass. Filed Apr. 10, 1919. Serial No. 288,987. 6 Claims. (Cl. 90—33.)

1. In a broaching machine, the combination with a horizontal frame open at the top, and a horizontally reciprocatory slide, of means whereby a broach can be attached to, and detached from the slide by a vertical motion through said open top, said means comprising a vertical T-shaped slot.

1,328,282. COMPOSITION FOR COATING NEW IRON AND STEEL. ALBERT C. HOLZAPFEL and PAUL WALTHER, New York, N. Y. Filed Nov. 13, 1918. Serial No. 262,369. 2 Claims. (Cl. 134—51.)
2. A bituminous varnish or solution for coating iron and steel, comprising approximately 12 parts by weight of stearin pitch, 20 parts by weight of asphaltum, and 68 parts by weight of tar oil.

1,328,283. AUTOMOBILE-BUMPER. EMANUEL W. KAISER, Newark, N. J. Filed July 19, 1919. Serial No. 312,040. 10 Claims. (Cl. 293—55.)

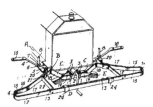

5. A vehicle fender, including an impact-receiving member extending transversely of the vehicle chassis and wheels and spaced therefrom, said impact-receiving member having a bearing foot which has an extended and direct bearing against the vehicle chassis, and fastening means arranged at each end of said foot beyond its bearing surface for supporting the fender on the vehicle.

1,328,284. WINDOW-LATCH. DAVID D. LEWIS, Detroit, Mich. Filed Oct. 19, 1916. Serial No. 126,476. 2 Claims. (Cl. 292—52.)

2. In sash lock construction, the combination with a corrugated strip adapted to be secured to a window casing adjacent the sash, of a base plate adapted to be secured to the sash adjacent the strip, a pair of pivot studs disposed on the base plate adjacent the corrugated strip, a pair of oppositely disposed dogs each pivoted on a stud and each having an end adapted to engage a recess of the strip, said dogs being operative to lock the sash against movement in the direction of extension of the dog, a yoke pivot stud secured on the base plate, said dog and yoke studs being relatively positioned at points corresponding to the apices of a triangle, a sheet metal crescent shaped yoke pivoted between its ends on the yoke stud, an operating arm extending from the yoke adjacent the yoke studs and having a thumb piece formed on the end portion thereof, lateral projections on each dog, inturned end portions on the yoke and engaging the projections of the adjacent dog, and a crescent shaped spring secured on the yoke stud with the end portions thereof yieldingly forcing the dogs into engagement with the corrugated strip.

1,328,285. STEAM-TURBINE BLOWER. WILLIAM MC-CLAVE, Scranton, Pa., assignor to McClave-Brooks Company, Scranton, Pa., a Corporation of Pennsylvania. Filed Sept. 25, 1917. Serial No. 193,167. 6 Claims. (Cl. 230—11.)

1. In a steam turbine blower, the combination with a rotor, an impeller spaced therefrom and a shaft common

to the rotor and impeller, of a rotor housing and air ducts leading through the walls of said housing in proximity to

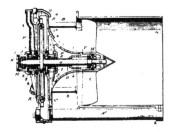

the shaft and discharging into the intake for the impeller whereby cooling air will be drawn through said ducts.

1,328,286. STEAM-TURBINE BLOWER. WILLIAM MC-CLAVE, Scranton, Pa., assignor to McClave-Brooks Company, Scranton, Pa., a Corporation of Pennsylvania. Filed Aug. 24, 1918. Serial No. 251,308. 5 Claims. (Cl. 286—8.)

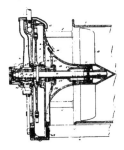

5. A steam chamber, a high speed shaft passing therethrough and having a journal bearing on one side of said chamber and spaced therefrom, a cooling duct between the chamber and said bearing, means for causing a circulation of air through said duct, a pair of leakage arresters in said duct, each encircling the shaft but exposing the shaft to the cooling air between them, and means for maintaining the arresters in sealing relation with opposite walls of the duct and spaced apart, thereby providing space to permit the shaft to divert the escaped steam from the bearing by centrifugal action.

1,328,287. EYE-PROTECTOR. ROBERT MALCOM, Chicago, Ill. Filed Dec. 23, 1918. Serial No. 267,909. 5 Claims. (Cl. 2—149.)

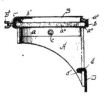

1. An eye protector, comprising a pair of eye cups, one end of which is circular and the other elongated on

a line diagonal to the axis thereof, a lens retaining ring secured in one end of each eye cup and held in position by frictional engagement therewith, said ring being provided with an outwardly extending shoulder abutting against the end of the eye cup, and means for holding the lens in each of said rings.

1,328,288. SPINTHEROMETER FOR RADIOTELEGRAPHIC PLANTS. ALGERI MARINO, Venice, Italy. Filed Dec. 20, 1917. Serial No. 208,057. 12 Claims. (Cl. 250—38.)

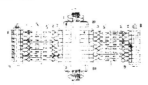

1. A spintherometer comprising a series of superposed plates, a thick portion in each plate, a thin portion adjacent to the thick portion, said thin portion being formed with holes, ribs on said thin portion to form electrodes, the electrodes being of the same thickness as the thick portion, another thick portion at the opposite end of said thin portion, insulating setting pieces between the thick portions of the two adjacent plates to hold the corresponding electrodes at proper distance, means in said thick portions for assembling the plates and means for inserting the electrodes in a circuit.

1,328,289. PISTON-RING. CHARLES W. MOORE, Indianapolis, Ind. Filed Feb. 12, 1919. Serial No. 276,456. 2 Claims. (Cl. 121—108.)

1. A piston ring comprising a pair of annular members each having an angularly extending boss at one end edge and an angularly extending recess diametrically opposite thereto in the same edge, the members being disposed in end contact with the boss of each member in the recess of the other, each member having a cut from end to end opening through its boss.

1,328,290. CONNECTOR FOR ARMORED CONDUCTORS. DONALD C. OVERBAGH, Chicago, Ill. Filed Oct. 31, 1918. Serial No. 260,422. 3 Claims. (Cl. 285—26.)

2. A connector for armored conductors forming a fitting and formed of a hollow member having a portion at which the connector is adapted to connect with the opening of an outlet-box and a portion for receiving the ends of a plurality of armor-portions of conductors, opening into said first-named portion, and means for securing said armor portions in place.

1,328,291. METHOD OF AND APPARATUS FOR PRODUCING PHOTOGRAPHS AND PROJECTING THE SAME IN NATURAL COLORS. EDWARD C. S. PARKER, U. S. Navy. Filed May 9, 1919. Serial No. 296,008. 6 Claims. (Cl. 88—16.4.)

1. The method of producing moving pictures which comprises forming a plurality of similarly deformed pictures of the object upon the film and then simultaneously projecting said deformed pictures to reconstruct the projection in normal proportions.

1,328,292. PHOTOGRAPHIC APPARATUS. EDWARD C. S. PARKER, U. S. Navy. Filed May 9, 1919. Serial No. 296,009. 6 Claims. (Cl. 88—1.)

1. A photographic apparatus, comprising two cylindrical lenses disposed with the axes of their curved surfaces relatively perpendicular, means for dividing the light pencil proceeding from the object through said lenses into a plurality of pencils, a sensitized transparent slide receiving the images produced by said pencils, and light filters respectively of different colors interposed between said dividing means and said slide.

1,328,293. PHOTOGRAPHIC APPARATUS. EDWARD C. S. PARKER, U. S. Navy. Filed May 9, 1919. Serial No. 296,010. 2 Claims. (Cl. 88—1.)

1. Means for dividing a pencil of light rays into a plurality of separate pencils and for causing a plurality of

separate pencils to coalesce into a single pencil comprising a cylindrical converging lens, and two cylindrical converging lenses each of a width equal to one half of the width of said first-named lens and each overlapping a half section of said first-named lens, the axes of the cylin-

drical surfaces of all of said lenses being parallel : whereby a pencil of light when traversing said lenses in one direction is divided into a plurality of separate pencils and whereby separate pencils traversing said lenses in the opposite direction are caused to coalesce to form a single pencil.

1,328,294. PHOTOGRAPHIC APPARATUS. Edward C. S. Parker, U. S. Navy. Filed May 9, 1919. Serial No. 296,011. 2 Claims. (Cl. 88—1.)

1. A photographic apparatus, comprising a converging cylindrical lens, a plurality of converging cylindrical lenses disposed edge to edge with their central longitudinal axes in the same plane and the axes of their curved surfaces parallel and relatively perpendicular to the axes of the curved surfaces of said first-named lens and receiving light rays traversing said first-named lens, whereby said light rays are divided into a plurality of separate groups of rays, and a sensitized slide receiving the images formed by said plurality of lenses.

1,328,295. PEANUT-PICKING MACHINE. Theophilus I. Phelps, Lewiston, N. C. Filed Aug. 4, 1913, Serial No. 782,908. Renewed Nov. 29, 1919. Serial No. 341,468. 1 Claim. (Cl. 130—30.)
In a peanut picking machine comprising a frame, a stemming trough, vertical vibrating arms pivoted intermediate their ends upon said frame, a bar passing under said stemming trough and connected to the lower ends of said vibrating arms, a second set of arms supporting the outer end of said stemming trough, horizontally extending

links slidably mounted upon said frame and connected intermediate their ends to said vibrating links, operating arms pivotally mounted upon said frame and engaging the rear ends of said horizontally extending links, a receiving trough, links supporting the rear end of said receiving trough, a rod extending across and under the bottom of

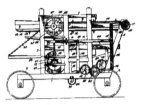

said receiving trough near the outer end thereof and connected to the outer ends of said horizontal links for connecting said links to said receiving trough and bracing said receiving trough, and crank means connected with one of said operating arms for swinging said operating arms.

1,328,296. COMBUSTION OF FUEL. Charles H. Ridderstedt, Pittsburgh, Pa. Filed Nov. 19, 1918. Serial No. 263,115. 3 Claims. (Cl. 110—28.)

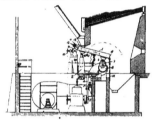

1. Improvements in the combustion of fuel comprising the combination of a jigger impervious to the passage of solid ingredients of the fuel bed, means for supplying air through the jigger for supporting combustion, and cam jigger mechanism for rapidly jigging the jigger to bounce the solid ingredients of the fuel bed, substantially as described.

1,328,297. ANTISKID DEVICE. James Edgar Rogers, Danbury, Conn., assignor of one-third to Paul U. Sunderland, Danbury, Conn. Filed Mar. 15, 1919. Serial No. 282,942. 4 Claims. (Cl. 152—14.)

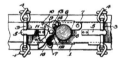

1. An antiskid attachment for wheels comprising a body plate adapted to seat on the wheel felly and formed with a central lateral recess to receive a spoke, a gate pivoted to the body on one side of the recess to swing across the latter, a pin on the free end of the gate, a catch lever pivoted between its ends on the body and having a hooked terminal to engage over the pin, a latch pin slidable through the body and into the path of the opposite end of the catch lever for holding it operative, a leaf spring secured to the bottom side of the plate in a guiding groove formed therein and serving to hold the latch pin operative, and antiskid means carried by the body.

1,328,298. ANTISKID DEVICE. JAMES EDGAR ROGERS, Danbury, Conn., assignor of one-third to Paul U. Sunderland, Danbury, Conn. Filed Mar. 31, 1919. Serial No. 286,421. 2 Claims. (Cl. 152—14.)

1. In an anti-skid device, a relatively solid and substantial U-shaped member formed to embrace the wheel felly, a relatively thin and wide independent spring arm having one end engaged with the outer side face of one of the arms of the U-member, means to secure said end of the spring arm to said arm of the U-member, the opposite end of said spring arm being free and projecting beyond said arm of the U-member, said free end of the spring arm being shaped to engage over the tire rim and with a side of the tire and having its terminal extending outwardly to form a finger grip or the like, and a tread member connected to the U-member and disposed in part over the spring arm and terminal of the latter.

1,328,299. PROCESS OF GRINDING CALCIUM CARBONATE AND PRODUCT THEREOF. JOHN H. RYAN, Chicago, Ill., assignor to Duncan R. Seaman, Chicago, Ill. Filed Mar. 24, 1919. Serial No. 284,602. 3 Claims. (Cl. 83—9.)

1. A process of reducing calcium carbonate previously crushed or in a relatively fine condition to amorphous powder consisting in mixing the material in batches with sufficient amount of water to cause in effect an emulsifying action between the water and the very fine substantially amorphous particles contained in the calcium carbonate to form a plastic mass of the batch, hold the coarser particles in suspension throughout said plastic mass and simultaneously subjecting them to a grinding action to rapidly reduce all of said coarse particles to an impalpable powder.

1,328,300. PENCIL. WILLIAM M. SAUNDERS, Waterbury, Conn., assignor to The Hoge Manufacturing Company, New York, N. Y., a Corporation of New York. Filed Oct. 16, 1919. Serial No. 331,019. 6 Claims. (Cl. 120—18.)

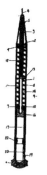

1. In a pencil, the combination of a barrel, a follower-carrier rotatably mounted therein, a follower for said

carrier, a helical spring surrounding said carrier and rotatable relatively to said carrier and barrel, said follower engaging said spring, and fixed means within said barrel normally engaged by the ends of said spring so as to hold said spring from turning, said ends being movable by said follower axially of said pencil relatively to said fixed means so as to disengage the same.

1,328,301. BREAD-BOARD. LEMUEL W. SERRELL, New York, N. Y. Filed June 13, 1918. Serial No. 239,719. 7 Claims. (Cl. 146—12.)

1. A bread-board comprising a base provided in its upper surface with two spaced parallel grooves, a hinge-plate within each groove pivotally connected at one end to the base, and a knife-guide secured at its ends to said hinge-plates.

1,328,302. COVER-FASTENER FOR BOXES. CARL L. SHELTON, Greenfield, Tenn., assignor of one-half to Vermont Box Company, Bristol, Vt. Filed Aug. 12, 1919. Serial No. 316,946. 3 Claims. (Cl. 217—62.)

1. The combination with a box having a cover, of a length of longitudinally curved spring metal traversing said cover and said box, and anchoring devices associated with said length of spring metal, said cover and said box being provided with transverse grooves adapted for registration for receiving said length of longitudinally curved spring metal, whereby the cover may be securely retained in closed position.

1,328,303. LOCOMOTIVE-BOILER. WILLIAM SHINN, Grandin, Mo., assignor of one-half to Charles Shinn, Grandin, Mo. Filed Mar. 1, 1919. Serial No. 279,978. 2 Claims. (Cl. 122—65.)

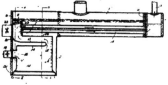

1. In a steam boiler, a water chamber, a fire-box disposed below the rear end of the water chamber, the rear portion of the bottom wall of the water chamber terminating short of its side walls, inner side walls extending from the bottom of the water chamber to the bottom of

the fire-box and spaced from the side walls of the water chamber and secured to the same at the lower ends thereof, spaced inner and outer walls extending from the bottom of the water chamber and constituting the front wall of the fire-box and secured together at their lower ends, and spaced crown sheets extending across the fire-box below the water chamber and spaced from the inner front wall of the fire-box and forming a water compartment in communication with the spaces between the inner and outer side walls.

1,328,304. FIRELESS COOKER. JOHN L. SNIDER, Denton, N. C., assignor to Royal Metalware Manufacturing Co., Denton, N. C., a Corporation of North Carolina. Filed June 12, 1919. Serial No. 303,619. 3 Claims. (Cl. 53—11.)

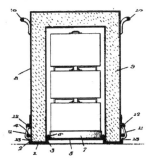

1. A device of the character described embodying a base, a hood, said base having a trough to receive the lower end of the hood and provided with outer and inner walls, and also having a raised pan within the trough having its rim integral with and its bottom depressed from the inner wall of the trough for supporting a radiator, and latches carried by the hood, said outer wall having a bead and portions below the bead for the engagement of the latches.

1,328,305. PHOTOGRAPHIC DEVELOPING-MACHINE. SAMUEL J. SUSSMAN, Brooklyn, N. Y. Filed July 30, 1918. Serial No. 247,442. 8 Claims. (Cl. 95—89.)

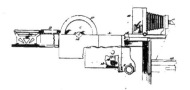

1. In a photographic developing machine, a tank, a pair of arms pivotally mounted therein, means on the arms to engage a print, means for rotating the arms to immerse the print, and means for returning the arms to normal position.

1,328,306. LIFTING-JACK. WALTER B. TEMPLETON, Chicago, Ill. Filed Jan. 17, 1918. Serial No. 212,165. 5 Claims. (Cl. 254—110.)

1. In a lifting jack, the combination of a casing, a ratchet bar sliding therein, an operating lever fulcrumed in said casing and carrying articulated to it on opposite sides of its fulcrum a pair of alternately acting pawls, a pawl-actuating link comprising two link members interconnected to slide endwise upon each other, and having

resilient means operatively connected with said members and acting upon each, an articulated connection between one of said link members and one of said pawls, guiding means attached to the second one of said pawls, guide-engaging means carried by the second one of said link members, coöperating with said articulated connection and said guiding means, to urge one of said pawls toward

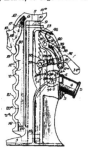

and the other away from said ratchet bar and to also cause said resilient means to urge both said pawls into operative engagement with said ratchet bar when said guide-engaging means is moved to one end of said guiding means, and to cause all said urgings to be reversed in direction when said guide-engaging means is moved to the opposite end of said guiding means, and manually operated means for changing the position of said guide-engaging means along said guiding means.

1,328,307. CARTRIDGE. FRANK M. THOMAS, Catskill, N. Y. Filed Jan. 31, 1918. Serial No. 214,674. 9 Claims. (Cl. 102—21.)

5. An incendiary projectile including a foraminous casing, and a combustible material within said casing and immersed in a liquid, said combustible material adapted to be ignited upon contact with air.

1,328,308. OILING HOPPERS. FRANK H. VAN HOUTEN, Jr., Beacon, N. Y., assignor to Dutchess Tool Company, New York, N. Y., a Corporation of New York. Filed Sept. 14, 1918. Serial No. 254,148. 9 Claims. (Cl. 107—15.)

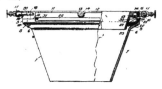

1. A trough for a dough divider hopper having a reservoir for liquid, a spillway, and means for leveling the trough.

1,328,309. ELECTRIC INTERLOCK FOR COUNTER-BALANCED ELEVATOR-DOORS. BENJAMIN WEXLER, Brooklyn, N. Y., assignor to The Peelle Company, Brooklyn, N. Y., a Corporation of New York. Filed Aug. 24, 1917. Serial No. 187,952. 4 Claims. (Cl. 187—31.)

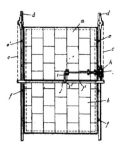

1. An electric interlock for counterbalanced elevator doors embodying therein a plurality of vertically sliding counterbalanced door sections having movement in opposite directions and in the same vertical plane, an electrical switch mechanism mounted in an elevator shaft adjacent and at one side of a door opening closed by, and adjacent the meeting line of said door sections, a latch member carried by one of said sections intermediate the sides thereof and adapted to enter a keeper upon the other door section, and a laterally reciprocatory plunger operatively connected with said latch member and adapted to actuate said switch mechanism when the doors are in a predetermined position, whereby the actuation of said switch is permitted only when said latch member is operative to lock said door sections in the closed position.

2. An electric interlock for counter-balanced elevator doors embodying therein a plurality of vertically sliding counter-balanced door sections having movement in opposite directions and in the same vertical plane, an electrical switch mechanism mounted in an elevator shaft adjacent and at one side of a door opening closed by, and adjacent the meeting line of said door sections, a laterally reciprocatory plunger carried by one of said sections adapted to actuate said switch mechanism when the doors are in a predetermined position, a latch member carried by and movable with said plunger and adapted to enter a keeper upon the other door section, whereby the actuation of said switch by said plunger is permitted only when said latch member is operative to lock said door sections in the closed position.

3. An electric interlock for counter-balanced elevator doors embodying therein a plurality of vertically sliding counterbalanced door sections having movement in opposite directions and in the same vertical plane, an electrical switch mechanism mounted in an elevator shaft adjacent and at one side of a door opening closed by, and adjacent the meeting line of said door sections, a laterally reciprocatory plunger carried by one of said sections and adapted to actuate said switch mechanism when the doors are in a predetermined position, a latch member having a beveled hook on the lower end thereof carried by and extending at substantially right angles to said plunger and adapted to enter a keeper upon the other door section, whereby the actuation of said switch by said plunger is permitted only when said latch member is operative to lock said door section in the closed position.

4. An electric interlock for counterbalanced elevator doors embodying therein a casing mounted in an elevator shaft adjacent and at one side of the door opening and having a beveled extension presenting toward said door opening and an opening below said extension, an electrical make and break mechanism embodying therein a pivoted arm projecting across and adapted to normally have movement toward said opening in said casing, a plurality of vertically sliding counterbalanced door sections adapted to have movement toward and from each other, a horizontally slidable plunger mounted upon one of said sections, a spring acting to normally thrust said plunger toward said casing, said plunger being adapted to engage said arm through said opening when the doors are in a predetermined position, and a latch member having a beveled hook on the lower end thereof carried by and extending at substantially right angles to said plunger and adapted to enter a keeper upon the other door section whereby the actuation of said switch by said plunger is permitted only when said latch member is operative to lock said door sections in the closed position.

1,328,310. ASPHALTIC PAVEMENT AND FOUNDATION FOR PAVEMENTS. HARRY PARSONS WILLIS, Waterford, N. Y., assignor to Willite Road Construction Company of America, New York, N. Y., a Corporation of Maine. Original application filed Dec. 7, 1914, Serial No. 875,767. Divided and this application filed July 10, 1916. Serial No. 108,423. 6 Claims. (Cl. 94—4.)

1. A road pavement having compression and tensile values relatively proportioned to provide characteristics of stability, resiliency and elasticity operative to resist deterioration of the foundation course of the pavement in the presence of traffic load strains thereon by distributing such strains laterally of the direction of strain application, and by maintaining such characteristics in the presence of weather conditions, said pavement having a foundation course consisting of a filler including finely divided earthy material of any kind, a mineral asphaltic binder and a mineral salt mixed with the binder and having the characteristic of tempering the binder, said filler, binder and tempering agent being admixed in the presence of heat to produce a mixture of which the filler constitutes approximately 80% of the mass, the said mass when compacted producing a substantially voidless homogeneous course having the said characteristics of stability, resiliency and elasticity.

1,328,311. METHOD OF OPERATING FLAMING-ARC LIGHTS FOR PROJECTORS. PRESTON R. BASSETT, Brooklyn, N. Y., assignor to Elmer A. Sperry, Brooklyn, N. Y. Filed Dec. 18, 1916. Serial No. 187,743. 6 Claims. (Cl. 176—51.)

1. The method of operating electrodes for projectors at moderate amperage in which the positive electrode is provided with a core containing light emitting admixtures which consists in causing such a spindling of said electrode that the crater face operates at an abnormal current density and in positioning the negative electrode at such an angle to the positive that the negative flame sweeps past said crater face without enveloping the electrode back of said face.

2. The method of operating electrodes for projectors at moderate amperage and voltage in which the positive electrode is provided with a core containing light emitting

admixtures which consist in causing such a spindling of said electrode that the crater face operates at an abnormal current density and in positioning the two electrodes at such an angle to one another that the negative flame touches the positive electrode only at said crater face.

3. The method of operating flaming arc electrodes at an amperage insufficient to produce a negative tongue, which consist in positioning the negative electrode at such an angle as to produce a substantially vertical arc flame and in so positioning the positive electrode that the crater face only touches the flame.

4. The method of operating flaming arc electrodes at moderate amperage and voltage which consists in positioning the electrodes at an angle to one another so that the negative flame sweeps past the positive electrode tip and touches said tip before said flame reaches its broadest portion.

5. The method of operating electrodes for projectors at moderate amperage in which the positive electrode is provided with a core containing light emitting admixture, which consists in operating said electrodes at sufficient current density to cause such a spindling of the electrode that substantially only the core is exposed at the arcing end, and in confining the crater to the exposed core **face by positioning the two electrodes at such an angle** so that the negative flame sweeps past the positive tip without enveloping it.

1,328,312. HARNESS-HANGER. ALBERT M. BEAN, Colville, Wash. Filed Jan. 20, 1919. Serial No. 272,039. 3 Claims. (Cl. 54—84.)

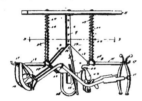

1. A harness hanger comprising an over-head support having a guide member, a combined guide and latch frame slidably fitted upon the guide member, arms mounted in the frame and extending outwardly therefrom in a horizontal plane in alinement with each other and having forked ends, telescoping guide members carried by the support and the arms, and means carried by the frame for engaging the first named guide member to lock the frame in adjusted position.

1,328,313. MARINE-MOTOR ATTACHMENT. RALPH W. BORCHERT, St. Louis, Mo. Filed June 2, 1919. Serial No. 301,193. 10 Claims. (Cl. 115—17.)

1. A device of the character described, comprising a bracket, a motor pivotally supported by said bracket, a switch for controlling the operation of the motor, a propeller supported and driven by the motor, means for supporting the motor and thereby the propeller in different adjustments upon the pivot, and means in connection with the pivot to prevent said switch from opening in one position of the motor and propeller and to permit said switch to open in another position of the motor and propeller.

1,328,314. METHOD OF WORKING UPPERS OVER LASTS. MATTHIAS BROCK, Boston, Mass., assignor, by mesne assignments, to United Shoe Machinery Corporation, Paterson, N. J., a Corporation of New Jersey. Filed July 30, 1917. Serial No. 183,501. 5 Claims. (Cl. 12—145.)

1. That improvement in methods of lasting shoes which consists in supporting a last with a sole and upper assembled thereon, wiping in the upper over the sole bottom while maintaining the upper out of direct contact with the sole and substantially in the plane of the sole, and then bringing the upper into lasted position against the sole margin.

1,328,315. BRAKE-HANGER. THOMAS L. BURTON, St. Louis, Mo., assignor to The American Brake Company, St. Louis, Mo., a Corporation of Missouri. Filed June 12, 1918. Serial No. 239,509. 3 Claims. (Cl. 188—70.)

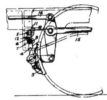

1. In a brake device, the combination of a brake hanger pivotally attached to the truck frame, a brake shoe pivotally connected to said hanger, a bracket member also mounted on the frame and having a yielding frictional connection with the hanger, a stop for limiting the release movement of said bracket member, and another stop for limiting the forward movement of said bracket member in application.

1,328,316. LUGGAGE-CARRIER. WILLIAM WALLACE CAMERON, La Crosse, Wis., assignor of one-half to Harry J. Hirshheimer, La Crosse, Wis. Filed Sept. 25, 1917. Serial No. 193,074. 4 Claims. (Cl. 224—29.)

1. In a collapsible luggage carrier, the combination of a longitudinal bar, supports for the bar comprising horizontal shafts having right angled arms thereon, pivoted connections between the bar and the supports, means for pivoting the shafts to a platform, said supports being adapted to swing the bar to a position above the level of the platform and downward to rest upon the shafts, a stop on the bar adapted to contact an arm to limit the movement thereof with respect to the arms when in its upper position, and means connected with one of the shafts for holding the carrier in its alternative position.

1,328,317. PULP BOTTLE. EDWARD E. CLAUSSEN, Hartford, Conn. Filed July 18, 1918. Serial No. 245,525. 4 Claims. (Cl. 229—4.)

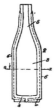

1. A pulp bottle having two halves, each provided with a marginal bead, the marginal beads being compressed together.

1,328,318. LOOSE-LEAF COVER AND COPY-HOLDER. SHERWIN CODY, Chicago, Ill. Filed Apr. 25, 1918. Serial No. 230,642. 2 Claims. (Cl. 120—128.)

2. A book cover and copy holder comprising a pair of cover members, a flexible connection between adjacent ends of said members, a book holding cord forming a loop to embrace said flexible connection, the free edge of one cover member having a pair of spaced openings therein, the free edge of the other member having a slot formed at the corresponding edge and extending inwardly from the edge thereof, and an endless cord passing through the spaced openings in one cover member with the free looped end knotted at spaced intervals and selectively positioned in the other cover member slot whereby the cover members are held in upright inclined formation.

1,328,319. AUTOMATIC WEIGHING-SCALE. SAMUEL G. CRANE, Toledo, Ohio, assignor to Toledo Scale Company, Toledo, Ohio, a Corporation of Ohio. Filed Mar. 4, 1915. Serial No. 11,965. 18 Claims. (Cl. 265—56.)

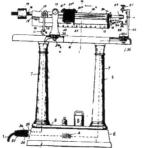

1. In an automatic electric scale, a beam formed of magnetic material of varying cross-sectional area, a poise having a solenoid coil embracing the beam and movable relatively to the beam when energized, and means for energizing said solenoid coil.

1,328,320. ELECTRIC AUTOMATIC SCALE. SAMUEL G. CRANE, Toledo, Ohio, assignor to Toledo Scale Company, Toledo, Ohio, a Corporation of Ohio. Filed Mar. 4, 1915. Serial No. 11,967. 32 Claims. (Cl. 265—56.)

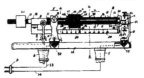

1. In a scale, a goods-receiver, a scale beam comprising a series of coils of wire, connections between the scale beam and goods-receiver and a poise movable over said coils by the inductive force exerted by the coils.

2. In a scale, a goods-receiver, a scale beam comprising a series of coils of wire, insulating strips spacing said coils from each other, connections between the scale beam and goods-receiver, means for energizing said coils, and a poise automatically movable relatively to said coils by the inductive force exerted by the coils.

3. In a scale, a goods-receiver, a scale beam comprising a series of solenoid coils arranged adjacent each other, insulating spacers between said coils, connections between the scale beam and goods-receiver, means for energizing said coils, and a poise coöperating with said coils by the inductive force exerted by the coils.

4. In a scale, a goods-receiver, a scale beam comprising a series of solenoid coils arranged adjacent each other, insulating spacers between said coils, connections between the scale beam and goods-receiver, and a poise automatically movable relatively to and coöperating with said coils by the inductive force exerted by the coils.

5. In a scale, a goods-receiver, a scale beam comprising a series of electric mechanisms arranged adjacent each other, insulating spacers between said mechanisms, connections between the scale beam and goods receiver, means for energizing said mechanisms, and a poise including an electric mechanism movable relatively to and coöperating with said beam mechanisms by the inductive force exerted by the beam mechanisms.

1,328,321. ELECTRIC SYSTEM. JOHN L. CREVELING, White Plains, N. Y., assignor to Gould Coupler Company, a Corporation of New York. Filed Apr. 4, 1916. Serial No. 88,801. 24 Claims. (Cl. 171—313.)

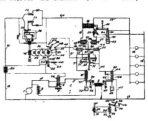

1. The combination with a source of electrical potential difference, a storage battery circuit and a translation circuit, of means for connecting the source under certain conditions with the battery circuit to impress the voltage of the source thereupon and under other conditions with the translation circuit to impress the voltage of the source thereupon and affecting the source.

7. The combination with a source of electrical potential difference, a storage battery circuit and a transla-

tion circuit, of means for connecting the source with the battery circuit and with the translation circuit and means for determining which of said connections shall be made and affecting the source depending upon the amount of current supplied to the battery.

21. The combination with a source of electrical potential difference, a storage battery, a battery circuit, translating devices and a translating circuit, of a regulator between the battery circuit and the translating circuit, and automatic means for affecting the connection of the source with the battery circuit and the translating circuit responsive to conditions of the storage battery and suppressing the output of the source while affecting its circuit connections.

1,328,322. METHOD OF MAKING SHOES. JOSEPH FAUSSE, Brockton, Mass., assignor to United Shoe Machinery Corporation, Paterson, N. J., a Corporation of New Jersey. Filed Aug. 3, 1918. Serial No. 248,128. 10 Claims. (Cl. 12—142.)

1. That improvement in methods of making stitchdown shoes which consists in cutting an upper with fullness at the rear lower corners of the vamp, backseaming said upper to produce excess length at the lower edge thereof around the heel, centering the backseam on a molded heel stiffener having an outturned flange, drawing the upper snug in the crease between the flange and body of the stiffener, and sewing the stiffener along its upper edge to the upper.

9. That improvement in methods of making shoes which consists in centering the heel stiffener and an upper at the backseam of the upper and while maintaining the parts in that position straightening the upper over the stiffener to one wing end of the stiffener and fastening the upper to that wing end, and thereafter similarly straightening the upper to the other wing end and fastening the upper to that wing end.

1,328,323. RADIATOR-CORE. JOHN M. FEDDERS, Buffalo, N. Y., assignor to Fedders Manufacturing Company, Inc., Buffalo. N. Y., a Corporation of New York. Filed Apr. 5, 1916. Serial No. 89,090. 1 Claim. (Cl. 257—130.)

A radiator core comprising a plurality of water tubes and a plurality of radiating fins arranged between the several water tubes, each of said tubes being constructed of two corrugated strips of metal and each of said fins being constructed of a single corrugated strip of metal, and each of said fin strips being provided on its opposite sides with centering loops which are of substantially the same form in cross section as the corrugations of the water tubes and fin strips and project laterally from the concave faces of its corrugations and engage with the concave faces of the corrugations of adjacent strips and each centering loop being provided with a stiffening bead extending lengthwise of the respective loop.

270 O. G.—25

1,328,324. REFRIGERATOR CONSTRUCTION. HERBERT J. GWYER, Yonkers, N. Y. Filed June 10, 1919. Serial No. 303,197. 8 Claims. (Cl. 45—71.)

8. In a cabinet construction, the combination of corner posts, side panels having interlocking engagement with said corner posts, top and bottom framing pieces interengaged with the ends of the corner posts and side panels and arranged to hold said parts in close fitting engagement and means for drawing the top and bottom framing pieces into place.

1,328,325. DRILL. ARTHUR L. HAWKESWORTH, Butte, Mont. Filed Mar. 21, 1919. Serial No. 283,952. 4 Claims. (Cl. 287—29.)

1. In combination with a drill bar or shank, a bit movable across the axis of the shank, a transverse dovetail tongue tapering in a given direction and bounding dove-tail grooves tapering in the opposite direction formed on one of the members, a corresponding dove-tail tapering groove and bounding tongues on the opposite member interlocking with the formations of the first member, the transverse engaging surfaces between the members being inclined to the axis of the shank.

1,328,326. ELECTRIC CIRCUIT. PETER COOPER HEWITT, Ringwood Manor, N. J. Filed June 25, 1913, Serial No. 775,632. Renewed June 10, 1919. Serial No. 303,251. 15 Claims. (Cl. 178—44.)

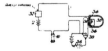

1. The combination of a device having a variable resistance, magnetic means external thereto for increasing its resistance and means for utilizing this increased resistance by diminishing the effect of the external means in inverse ratio to the current flow through the resistance.

1,328,327. ELECTRIC CIRCUIT. PETER COOPER HEWITT, Ringwood Manor, N. J. Continuation in part of application Serial No. 775,632, filed June 25, 1913. This application filed Jan. 30, 1917, Serial No. 145,378. Renewed Oct. 16, 1919. Serial No. 331,244. 10 Claims. (Cl. 179—171.)

1. In an electrical system, a gas or vapor electric device, means for passing current through the same, and means for affecting the device by electro-static force and for causing the said force to be diminished by an increased current flow through said device.

1,328,328. BOX. RICHARD G. INWOOD, South Bend, Ind., assignor to Wirebounds Patents Company, Kittery, Me., a Corporation of Maine. Filed Aug. 5, 1914. Serial No. 855,282. 14 Claims. (Cl. 217—12.)

1. A box comprising, in combination, two cleats substantially closing the ends of the box ; material for sides of the box the cleats being attached to the face of said material ; and binding means encircling the box substantially parallel to the ends thereof.

1,328,329. ACETYLENE-TORCH. CARL JOHNSON, Chicago, Ill. Filed Aug. 4, 1916. Serial No. 113,166. 7 Claims. (Cl. 158—27.4.)

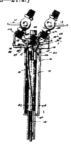

2. In a device of the class described, a head, an oxygen pipe and an acetylene pipe connected to said head, one of said pipes being located within the other, said head having chambers therein and ducts leading from each of said chambers to one of said pipes, a normally open, gravity-actuated valve in one of said ducts, and a burner operatively connected to the other ends of said pipes.

1,328,330. TIRE-HEATER. FRANK G. KNOFLICEK, Silvis, Ill. Filed Nov. 28, 1917, Serial No. 204,478. Renewed June 9, 1919. Serial No. 303,002. 14 Claims. (Cl. 263—5.)

1. An apparatus of the class described comprising co-acting tubular burner members in spaced relation, con-

nected at the ends, and provided with lateral orifices, combined tubular supply and vaporizing members respectively engaged longitudinally with the burner members and

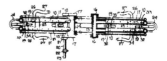

communicating therewith at one end, clip devices uniting said burner members, and means for supplying hydrocarbon to the vaporizing members.

1,328,331. LAMP-SHADE HOLDER. MAX KOSSMANN, Brooklyn, N. Y. Filed June 3, 1919. Serial No. 301,542. 4 Claims. (Cl. 240—108.)

1. In a bulb holder, a strip of suitable wire bent to form a rectangular frame, the side members of the frame being formed, intermediate the ends, into a substantially circular loop to form elbows at the point of connection of said loops and the straight portions of the side members, each loop being bent at its upper portion at an angle relative to the remainder of the loop to form shoulders or supports, to engage the rounded end of a bulb.

1,328,332. BED FOR GAME-TABLES AND METHOD OF MAKING SAME. PAUL S. LIETZ, Chicago, Ill., assignor to The Brunswick-Balke-Collender Company, Chicago, Ill., a Corporation of Delaware. Filed Sept. 4, 1917. Serial No. 189,660. 10 Claims. (Cl. 46—12.)

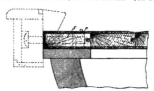

1. A bed for game tables comprising a core substantially co-extensive in area with the area of the bed, and a shell completely inclosing said core and consisting of a hard, dense moisture proof composition.

1,328,333. SHOE. WILLIAM L. MANN, Georgetown, Tex. Filed Aug. 6, 1919. Serial No. 315,624. 3 Claims. (Cl. 36—50.)

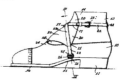

1. A shoe comprising a sole, an upper attached to said sole, means for adjustably engaging a strap attached to the

shoe on each side of the upper, an inner flap extending from one side of the forward portion of the upper and so constructed and arranged as to be adapted to form the inner section of the instep portion of the shoe, an outer flap extending forwardly from the opposite side of the upper from that of the inner flap and constructed and arranged to be superimposed over the inner flap and form the outer portion of the shoe instep, a strap having one of its ends connected to the free end of the inner flap and adapted to adjustably engage the means on the shoe nearest to the inner flap and extend upwardly over the instep of the shoe, and a second strap having one of its ends connected to the free end of the outer flap and adapted to pass downwardly and adjustably engage the other means on the opposite side of the shoe and upwardly over the instep and around the back of the shoe to be engaged by the free end of the strap connected with the inner flap.

1,328,334. PROJECTILE. CHARLES NEWTON, Buffalo, N. Y., assignor to Frank N. Stone, Cleveland, Ohio. Filed Aug. 24, 1915. Serial No 47,138. 6 Claims. (Cl. 102—28.)

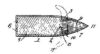

1. A projectile comprising rear jacket and core sections, and front jacket and core sections connected with said rear jacket and core sections by an interlocking joint which is enlarged rearwardly.

1,328,335. TRACTOR. NILS NILSON and LEONARD NILSON, Wayzata, Minn. Original application filed June 5, 1911, Serial No. 631,493. Renewed June 17, 1915, Serial No. 34,741. Divided and this application filed Nov. 12, 1915. Serial No. 61,117. 3 Claims. (Cl 213—67.)

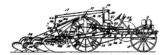

1. The combination, with a frame having forward guiding means and a rear traction wheel, of a draft-attaching means secured to said frame and extending above the axis of said wheel, and a draft means connected with the upper portion of said draft-attaching means, whereby the pull of said draft means upon said attaching means will increase the traction of said wheel and a beam having a non-draft guiding connection with said frame and a connection with said draft means in the rear of said guiding connection.

1,328,336. ARTIFICIALLY - COOLED HIGH-FREQUENCY COIL. EDWIN F. NORTHRUP, Princeton, N. J., assignor to The Ajax Metal Company, Philadelphia, Pa., a Corporation of Pennsylvania. Filed Apr. 18, 1919. Serial No. 291,161. 14 Claims. (Cl. 204—64.)
1. An artificially - cooled inductor furnace coil for electric inductive heating purposes, in combination with a source of high frequency current.
14. The process of melting materials requiring a high temperature, which consists in inclosing the materials within a conductor in inductive relation thereto, artificially cooling the conductor to reduce its resistance, im-

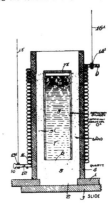

prove its insulation and permit closer coupling, and passing a high frequency electric current through the conductor.

1,328,337. MEANS FOR AUTOMATICALLY CUTTING OFF THE FEED-MOTION OF MACHINE-TOOLS. NILS JOSEF OLSSON, Gottenborg, Sweden, assignor to Aktiebolaget Svenska Kullagerfabriken, Gottenborg, Sweden, a Corporation of Sweden. Filed Aug. 1, 1918. Serial No. 247,784. 3 Claims. (Cl. 51—4.)

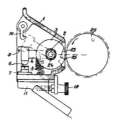

1. In machine tools an arrangement for automatically cutting off the feed motion of the machine when the work has reached its desired ultimate size, comprising a pivotally mounted lever, a shaft carrying said lever, said lever consisting of two parts adjustably connected with each other one of said parts being formed as a disk the center of which coincides with the center of said shaft. said disk being so arranged and formed as to be locked by the work during the operation thereof and be released for initiating the said cutting off action when the work reaches its desired ultimate size.

1,328,338. ELECTRIC SNAP - SWITCH. FRANK H. QUADE, Jr., Fresno, Calif., assignor to Lisenby Manufacturing Company, Fresno, Calif., a Corporation. Filed June 10, 1919. Serial No. 303,078. 2 Claims. (Cl. 200—67.)
1. An electric snap-switch comprising a non-conducting base, a pair of spaced binding posts mounted thereon and connected to pins projecting therethrough, a contact strip turnably mounted on one of the pins, and adapted to have one edge thereof abut against the other pin, an arm turna-

bly mounted on a bearing provided in the base and having a pin thereon adapted to constantly engage the sides of a longitudinal slot provided in the contact strip, the arm being adapted for limited movement on its bearing, a pull rod positioned substantially at right angles to the

arm and the bearing thereof, and means whereby a sliding movement of the rod in either direction will cause a sudden movement of the arm in the same direction about its pivotal point only after a predetermined travel of the arm, thereby causing the contact strip to make or break connection with the contact pin.

1,328,339. FLOOR-CLEANING MACHINE. WILLIAM A. ROWE, Eau Claire, Wis. Filed June 3, 1918. Serial No. 237,943. 17 Claims. (Cl. 15—14.)

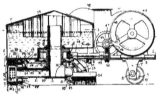

12. In a floor cleaning machine, a water receiving tank, a rotatably mounted conduit discharging at one of its ends into said tank and having a plurality of radially disposed branch conduits at its other end, means for rotating said conduit, independently rotatable floor engaging wipers mounted on the outer ends of the branch conduits, and means for creating an induced aid draft through the conduits to convey the water from the wipers to said tank.

1,328,340. MOTOR-DRIVEN COMPRESSOR. LAWRENCE D. SAUNDERS, Wilkinsburg, Pa., assignor to The Westinghouse Air Brake Company, Wilmerding, Pa., a Corporation of Pennsylvania. Filed Oct. 6, 1914. Serial No. 865,302. 3 Claims. (Cl. 230—27.)

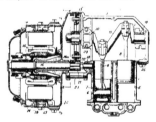

1. In a motor driven compressor, the combination of a closed crank casing, horizontal cylinders connected therewith, a crank shaft mounted in bearings within the crank chamber, pistons connected with the cranks, a gear located on one end of the crank shaft within the casing, a motor casing at the side of the compressor casing, its rear housing being formed integral with the side wall of the crank casing, and containing an elongated bearing at the cylinder side of the crank shaft and in the same hori-

zontal plane therewith, an armature shaft mounted in said bearing and extending into the compressor casing, an armature on said shaft outside of said elongated bearing, a pinion carried by the armature shaft within the compressor casing and meshing with the gear on the crank shaft, and another bearing for the inner end of the armature shaft supported on the cylinder wall within the casing.

1,328,341. MANUALLY - OPERATED SLACK - ADJUSTER. FRANCIS E. SCHWENTLER, St. Louis, Mo., assignor to The American Brake Company, St. Louis, Mo., a Corporation of Missouri. Filed Sept. 30, 1916. Serial No. 122,994. 4 Claims. (Cl. 188—49.)

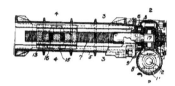

1. In a slack adjuster, the combination of a casing having a hub portion at one end, a screw rotatably mounted in said casing and having a bearing in the hub portion, a gear housing secured to the hub portion of the casing, a gear wheel fixed on said screw and fitted between the hub portion of the casing and the outer wall of the gear housing for preventing longitudinal movement of the screw, and means for operating said gear wheel.

1,328,342. PRODUCTION OF AMMONIUM SULFATE. WILLIAM A. SLOSS, Toledo, Ohio. Filed May 22, 1919. Serial No. 298,947. 8 Claims. (Cl. 23—21.)
2. The process of purifying ammonium sulfate which comprises heating commercial ammonium sulfate to a temperature above that at which pyridin becomes volatile, and treating the same with ammonia while said temperature is maintained.

1,328,343. VEHICLE. PHILESTER SMITH, Rochester, N. Y. Filed Apr. 18, 1919. Serial No. 291,164. 5 Claims. (Cl. 208—165.)

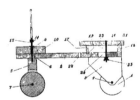

1. In a vehicle having a steering post, a handle formed from a single piece of material bent to provide a loop, and two parallel portions, the parallel portions being pivoted to the steering post below the upper end of the latter and on opposite sides thereof, and a sleeve mounted on said parallel portions of the handle and adapted to move to coöperate with the upper end of the post to prevent the pivoting of the handle on the post.

1,328,344. TOY. ABRAHAM M. SMOLENS, New York, N. Y. Filed Apr. 7, 1919. Serial No. 288,033. 5 Claims. (Cl. 124—15.)
1. In a toy, a figure, a base therefor, coil springs connecting the figure and base, a pad to connect one end of

each spring to said figure, a second pad to secure the other end of each spring to the base, and a wood pin

passing through said springs and secured to the last named pad.

1,328,345. BURIAL-CASKET ATTACHMENT. FRANK P. J. SPARMAKER, Audubon, N. J. Filed Apr. 30, 1919. Serial No. 293,687. 3 Claims. (Cl. 292—76.)

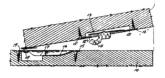

2. In an attachment of the character stated separable elements consisting of a receptacle and a cover, a spring pressed hook-like detent carried by one of said elements and a socket, having a slotted portion, provided with a rounded protuberance in alinement with but located beyond said slotted portion carried by the other of said elements said socket having an inclined groove leading toward said slotted portion.

1,328,346. FRICTION - GEARING FOR MOTOR - VEHICLES. HAROLD E. STONEBRAKER, Brooklyn, N. Y. Filed Nov. 29, 1918. Serial No. 264,619. 10 Claims. (Cl. 180—70.)

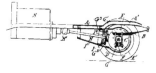

1. In a vehicle, the combination with frictionally engaging driving and driven members, of means controlled by the speed of the vehicle for pressing said frictional members together.

1,328,347. DIE. WILLIAM G. TROHON, Danvers, Mass., assignor to United Shoe Machinery Corporation, Paterson, N. J., a Corporation of New Jersey. Filed June 26, 1918. Serial No. 242,011. 39 Claims. (Cl. 164—29.)

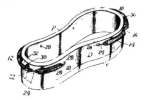

1. A die provided with a guard including a resilient member attached to the die.

1,328,348. DOWNSPOUT CUT-OFF. ERNST W. VOGT, Silverton, Ohio. Filed June 16, 1916. Serial No. 104,001. 2 Claims. (Cl. 137—9.)

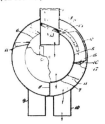

2. A means for controlling the flow of water in a downspout cutoff comprising a rotary drum having a chamber disposed along its periphery, said chamber being open at the top and closed at the bottom by two interspaced members having central bleed holes therein, and a ball intermediate said members, a ledge-forming member to trap a small quantity of water comprising a ring-shaped member to fit an inlet pipe, having a beveled edge adapted to form a channel in coöperation with such pipe, and a pipe leading from such channel to the chamber, said pipe being disposed in an arc to conform to the shape of the drum.

1,328,349. DEVICE FOR TESTING CORRUGATED PAPER-BOARD AND CORRUGATED-PAPER-BOARD BOXES. JOHN W. WEBB, Chicago, Ill., assignor, by mesne assignments, to Webb Tester Incorporated, Chicago, Ill., a Corporation of Delaware. Filed Oct. 10, 1918. Serial No. 257,563. 8 Claims. (Cl. 265—12.)

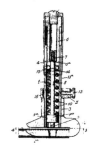

1. A testing device of the character described and comprising a shank, an orificed finger secured to said shank adjacent one end thereof and arranged at right angles thereto, a plunger member slidingly mounted in said shank and equipped with a plunger point in alinement with the orifice in said finger, a coiled spring arranged to bear at one end against said plunger member, and a manually operable member arranged to coöperate with the other end of said spring to yieldingly force said plunger member toward said finger, said shank and said manually operable member being one or the other marked with a graduated scale to indicate their relative movement.

1,328,350. CRANK - SHAFT. ROBERT A. WEINHARDT, Chicago, Ill., assignor, by mesne assignments, to Continental Motors Corporation, Detroit, Mich., a Corporation of Virginia. Filed June 28, 1916. Serial No. 106,382. 5 Claims. (Cl. 74—5.)

4. In a crank shaft having journal portions disposed at intervals connected by single and double throw crank

arms, counterbalance weights secured in angular relation to the several crank arms at points adjacent the several journal portions, the pair of counterbalance weights be-

tween each pair of journals being adapted to maintain a substantially perfect balance with the crank arms between said journals.

1,328,351. MOLD FOR MOLDING ARTIFICIAL TEETH. GEORGE H. WHITELEY, Jr., York, Pa., assignor to The Dentists' Supply Company, a Corporation of New York. Filed Sept. 11, 1913. Serial No. 789,243. 2 Claims. (Cl. 18—42.)

1. A mold device of general rectangular shape for the manufacture of artificial teeth, which consists of a two-part mold having contacting portions, each mold part having a plurality of recesses bounded by relatively sharp contacting parts which in the assembled mold parts provide a plurality of inclosed hollow spaces conforming to the shape of the artificial teeth to be molded, each of said mold parts having its surface consisting of a continuous irregular layer of electrically deposited metal forming the surface of the mold including the recesses and the contacting parts so that the surface is devoid of joints, and said thin electrolytically formed layer backed with a deep mass of resistant material for holding the continuous thin surface layer against distortion, said backing mass being a great many times the thickness of the electrolytically deposited layer and entirely covered on the molding surface by the electrically deposited layer.

1,328,352. MOTION-PICTURE APPARATUS AND MOTION-PICTURE FILM THEREFOR. HAROLD WORKMAN, Glasgow, Scotland. Filed May 8, 1916. Serial No. 96,191. 7 Claims. (Cl. 88—16.4.)

1. Projecting apparatus capable of showing either a color record cinematograph film of the class described or a standard film as herein defined, such color film being formed so as to run on standard sprocket rims, and so as to have a plurality of rows of perforations true to gage to drive it, the projector having feed and take up sprocket wheels comprising standard sprocket rims, and an intermittent movement comprising that suited for standard film, a wide multiple gate-apertured film track, a corresponding number of lenses, means for illuminating, and distributing and directing the light through such gate apertures and such lenses, means for cutting off the light during the period of motion of the film, means for adjusting the illumination for that one of the gate apertures which corresponds to the standard sprocket rims, means for closing the remaining gate aperture or apertures, and means for retaining the standard film in its track.

1,328,353. FAN. FRED W. WUERTH, Cincinnati, Ohio. Filed June 23, 1919. Serial No. 306,018. 4 Claims. (Cl. 230—7.)

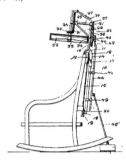

1. A rocking chair attachment including a frame, said frame embodying a member having a plurality of branches, certain of said branches embracing the upper edge of the back of the chair, the other of said branches being hollow, a second member embracing the lower edge of the back of the chair and slidably fitted in the last mentioned branch whereby the frame can be adjusted to chairs of different sizes, and means for holding said members fixed relatively, a fan carried by the first mentioned member of the frame, and means for operating the fan upon rocking movements of the chair.

1,328,354. APPARATUS FOR FEEDING LIQUID FUEL TO CARBURETERS. CHARLES H. ANDERSON, Lexington, Ky. Filed Jan. 17, 1919. Serial No. 271,649. 4 Claims. (Cl. 158—36.)

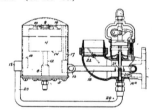

1. In a vacuum feed for internal combustion engines, the combination of a fuel tank having a pipe connection above and a pipe connection below the normal fuel level in the tank, with the suction pipe of the engine and at the same side of the throttle valve in the suction pipe, whereby the vacuum in the two pipe connections with the suction pipe will be balanced, a spray nozzle in the suction pipe and connected with the fuel pipe leading from below the fuel level in the tank, and means actuated by the suction for controlling the supply of fuel to the suction pipe through the spray nozzle.

1,328,355. LOCKING MECHANISM FOR VAULT-DOORS. FRANKLIN E. ARNDT, Galion, Ohio, assignor to David C. Boyd, Galion, Ohio. Filed June 14, 1919. Serial No. 304,291. 13 Claims. (Cl. 292—6.)

13. In a vault, a body open at one end and having an inwardly extending flange at this end, a vault door disposed against the outer face of said flange, a plurality of locking members mounted upon the inner face of the door for longitudinal movement and for movement in a plane at right angles to the door, members having cross

bars mounted upon the inner face of the door adjacent its margins and beneath which cross bars the locking members operate, means yieldingly urging the locking members against the cross bars, and manually operable means movable in one direction to shift said locking members outward to engage over the inner face of the flange on the vault door and successively shift the inner ends of

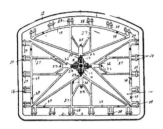

the locking members away from the door to cause the extremities of the locking members to bear against said flange and urge the door toward the flange, said manually operable means being movable in an opposite direction independently of the locking members, whereby to prevent a retraction of the locking members upon a retraction of the actuating means.

1,328,356. REPEATING RIFLE. JAMES W. BALLARD, Fairfax, Va. Filed July 14, 1917. Serial No. 180,614. 4 Claims. (Cl. 89—33.)

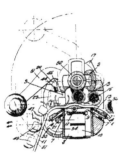

1. In a rifle, the combination of magazine-feeding mechanism, and belt-feeding mechanism adapted to be operated when said magazine-feeding mechanism is in inoperative position, of means for locking the magazine-feeding mechanism in inoperative position to permit the operation of said belt-feeding mechanism.

1,328,357. METHOD OF AND MEANS FOR SEALING STORAGE - BATTERY CONNECTORS AND POSTS. FRED W. BARHOFF, Hartford, Conn., assignor to The Hartford Storage Battery Manufacturing Company, Hartford, Conn., a Corporation of Connecticut. Filed Apr. 7, 1919. Serial No. 288,096. 3 Claims. (Cl. 204—29.)

2. In a storage battery, the combination of chambered terminal posts, a connector having conductor terminals

extending into and making contact with the walls of the chambers in the posts, and pliable metallic bands

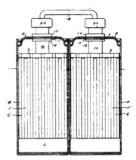

folded about outwardly extending parts of the posts and conductors and rigidly securing them together.

1,328,358. MEANS FOR SEALING STORAGE-BATTERY COVERS IN CELLS. FRED W. BARHOFF, Hartford, Conn., assignor to The Hartford Storage Battery Manufacturing Company, Hartford, Conn., a Corporation of Connecticut. Filed Apr. 7, 1919. Serial No. 288,097. 5 Claims. (Cl. 204—29.)

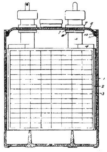

3. The combination with a storage battery jar of a cover fitting the jar, said cover having a groove in its outer edge, a flexible packing arranged in said groove, and means whereby fluid may be forced back of said packing for expanding the packing in the groove against the inner wall of the jar.

1,328,359. METHOD OF AND MEANS FOR SEALING TERMINAL POSTS IN STORAGE-BATTERY COVERS. FRED W. BARHOFF, Hartford, Conn., assignor to The Hartford Storage Battery Manufacturing Company, Hartford, Conn., a Corporation of Connecticut. Filed Apr. 7, 1919. Serial No. 288,098. 4 Claims. (Cl. 204—29.)

1. The method of sealing terminal posts in the covers of storage battery cells which consists in contracting

metallic rings into openings in the posts above the covers and simultaneously forcing the covers down upon parts of the posts below the covers.

4. Means for sealing terminal posts in storage battery covers which comprises a post with a shoulder and a wedge-shaped groove above the shoulder, and a split ring of pliable metal adapted to be compressed into and expanded from said groove.

1,328,360. GLASS-WASHING APPARATUS. NEAL M. BEEDE, Boston, Mass., assignor of one-half to Albert R. Brewster, Boston, Mass. Filed Sept. 14, 1917. Serial No. 191,472. 4 Claims. (Cl. 141—7.)

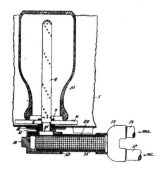

4. An apparatus for washing glassware including a support for a glass article, means for projecting a liquid upon said article, a casing having a mixing chamber for liquid passing to said projecting means, a hot and cold water supply communicating with said mixing chamber, and a medium distributed throughout said chamber to receive a liquid delivered thereto whereby one extreme in temperature of said liquid is employed to prevent a sudden change to an opposite extreme.

1,328,361. LAUNDRY-WRINGER. HARLOW H. BELDING, West Chicago, Ill. Filed Feb. 17, 1919. Serial No. 277,462. 4 Claims. (Cl. 68—32.)

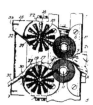

3. In combination with a wringer having a pair of compression rollers; a pair of rotatable brushes in a vertical plane, each brush in contact with its respective roller and means to drive each roller and its brush in the same direction.

1,328,362. DEVICE FOR REMOVING VALVES AND THEIR SEATS OR CAGES. PEARL BORDEAUX, Mount Desert, Me. Filed Jan. 27, 1919. Serial No. 273,359. 2 Claims. (Cl. 29—88.2.)

1. A device of the character described comprising a disk shaped body having a threaded opening through

same from one surface to the other so that it may be used either side down and a tubular extractor threaded externally to engage the the threads in said body, the

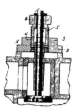

said extractor having a bore of two diameters, the larger of which is adapted to receive the sleeve on the valve cage and the smaller one, the valve stem.

1,328,363. HARROW. JAMES W. BOWMAN, Morley, Mo. Filed Sept. 21, 1918. Serial No. 255,095. 1 Claim. (Cl. 55—11.)

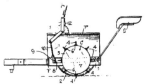

A harrow comprising a portable frame substantially rectangular in form, arms pivotally engaged with the ends of the frame adjacent the rear side of the frame for swinging movement in a vertical plane, a cylinder comprising heads having trunnions rotatably engaged with the arms, bars connecting the peripheral portions of the heads and circumferentially spaced, ground working teeth carried by bars and substantially radiating from the cylinder, a platform carried by the frame and overlying the cylinder, a member connecting the forward end portions of the arms, a lever supported for rocking movement by the platform and extending therebelow, and an operative connection between the lower portion of the lever and the member connecting the forward end portions of the arms, whereby the cylinder may be raised or lowered by the lever.

1,328,364. SUPERHEATER-HEADER. BENJAMIN BROIDO, New York, N. Y., assignor to Locomotive Superheater Company, New York, N. Y., a Corporation of Delaware. Filed Nov. 25, 1918 Serial No. 264,058. 6 Claims. (Cl. 122—462.)

1. In apparatus of the class described, the combination of a header having a plurality of openings through its wall; pipe ends corresponding in number to the openings; a bar parallel and adjacent to the header and with a like number of correspondingly spaced holes extending between two of its faces, said bar being secured to the header so that the holes in one of the faces communicate with the openings through the header wall; and clamping means holding a pipe end against each hole in the second face of the bar, said clamping means engaging the pipes and the bar.

1,328,365. WATER - TUBE-BOILER SUPERHEATER. BENJAMIN BROIDO, New York, N. Y., assignor to Locomotive Superheater Company, New York, N. Y., a Corporation of Delaware. Filed June 20, 1919. Serial No. 305,520. 4 Claims. (Cl. 122—473.)

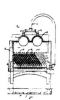

1. In a boiler, the combination of two parallel water legs; water tubes connecting them and arranged in spaced rows; a pair of parallel superheater headers adjacent to one of the water legs and arranged transversely to the water tubes; a sub-header secured to one of the headers and extending into the space between two rows of water tubes and adjacent to the water legs; a second sub-header secured to the other header and extending into the space on the side of the first away from the water leg and not as far as the first; both sub-headers being of a diameter substantially equal to the space between the rows of tubes; and a plurality of tubular superheater elements attached to the pair of sub-headers and extending into the space between the water tubes, the elements being of materially smaller diameter than the space.

1,328,366. FLEXIBLE COUPLING. ELLIS E. BROWN, Reading, Pa. Filed July 21, 1919. Serial No. 312,410. 6 Claims. (Cl. 64—96.)

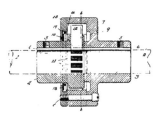

1. In a flexible coupling, the combination of a driving and a driven member, one of which is formed with a plurality of pockets, and the other with a plurality of spring members adapted for engagement in said pockets, one member having an oil reservoir therein, and a closure cap for the reservoir, said cap having a spring backed closure gasket located therein.

1,328,367. DEVICE FOR MAKING MULTICOLORED TILES AND THE LIKE. ANTONIO COTOLI, Habana, Cuba. Filed Jan. 2, 1919. Serial No. 269,180. 2 Claims. (Cl. 25—123.)

1. In a device of the character described, the combination with a mold having a plurality of compartments of varying design, of a plate provided with a plurality of circular openings uniformly distributed over a predetermined area of said plate, nozzles projecting selectively through certain of said openings into some of said compartments, said nozzles having mouth pieces of different shape at one

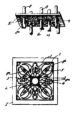

end and having circular cross-section at the other end, and paint supply tubes attached to said circular end portions.

1,328,368. METHOD OF AND MEANS FOR DISTRIBUTING PIGMENTS. ANTONIO COTOLI, Habana. Cuba. Filed Jan. 13, 1919. Serial No. 270,849. 4 Claims. (Cl. 101—115.)

1. The method of coloring a stationarily arranged surface to reproduce a design thereon, including the step of spreading a plurality of powdered pigments over a like number of plates spaced from said surface, each plate having perforations the outlines of which correspond to the design, and subjecting the surface to further treatment.

1,328,369. AIRSHIP. QUIRINO V. DISTEFANO, Waterbury, Conn. Filed Dec. 19, 1917. Serial No. 207,951. 4 Claims. (Cl. 244—25.)

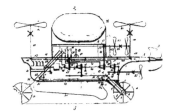

2. A machine of the class described having a body, lifting propellers carried by the body and having shafts extending into the body, a longitudinal shaft within the body, means to drive the shafts of the propellers from said longitudinal shaft, an engine, a shaft driven by said engine, means to drive the longitudinal shaft from the engine shaft, upper and lower driving propellers having horizontal shafts, means to drive the horizontal shaft from the engine shaft, a third horizontal shaft being supported by the base of the body and driven from the engine shaft, an inclined casing extending from the body, an inclined shaft in said casing, driving connections between the inclined shaft and the horizontal shaft mounted on the base of the body for driving said inclined shaft, traction means carried by said inclined casing and driven by said inclined shaft, and controlling means for the propellers and their driving connections.

1,328,370. LEVELING DEVICE FOR THRESHING-MACHINES, &c. ABRAHAM L. DUTTON, Otis, Colo. Filed Apr. 10, 1919. Serial No. 289,039. 1 Claim. (Cl. 33—215.)

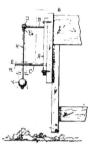

A device for plumbing objects, consisting of a block to be attached to the object to be plumbed, two rods fastened to said block parallel to each other and spaced apart, the upper of the two rods having an eye which is in a vertical plane, the lower rod having an enlarged eye in a horizontal plane directly underneath the eye in the upper rod, a pendulum bent to form an eye at its upper end and interlock with the eye in the upper rod, and having a swinging movement in the eye of the lower rod.

1,328,371. RECORD-SURFACING AND THE PRODUCTION THEREOF. VICTOR H. EMERSON, New York, N. Y., and ALEXANDER N. PIERMAN, Newark, N. J., assignors to Emerson Phonograph Company, Inc., New York, N. Y., a Corporation of New York. Filed Jan. 4, 1919. Serial No. 269,663. 8 Claims. (Cl. 18—48.3.)

1. The process of preparing a record-surface, which consists of applying to a fabric a liquid menstruum containing record-material and linseed oil, and drying the same thoroughly and until all the volatile content has passed off completely.

1,328,372. ICE-CUTTING MACHINE. ERNEST H. FRANKAMP, Republic, Kans. Filed Aug. 1, 1918. Serial No. 247,832. 2 Claims. (Cl. 262—20.)

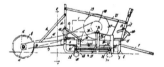

1. In an ice cutting machine, a main frame, a cutter frame, pivoted to an end of the main frame, a guide frame pivoted to a side of the main frame, an operating lever, and connecting means between the operating lever and the cutter and guide frames for effecting simultaneous movement of the cutter and guide frames.

1,328,373. AIR-HOSE COUPLING. CHINTO A. GARZONI, De Lancey, Pa. Filed Nov. 12, 1918. Serial No. 262,211. 6 Claims. (Cl. 284—12.)

1. In the combination, a pair of coupling members, a coupling head carried by each member, and having an air passage therethrough, a normally closed valve in said head, a pair of jaws carried by each head, one jaw having an opening therein, said jaw being further provided with a threaded recess communicating with said opening, the

co-acting jaw having a threaded opening, a packing nut threaded into said threaded recess and threaded opening in the jaws for detachably connecting the jaws of each

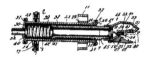

head, and a valve stem passing through the opening in the jaw and through the threaded recess and through said packing nut.

1,328,374. ELECTRICAL SYSTEM. HAYNER H. GORDON, Washington, D. C. Filed Dec. 4, 1916. Serial No. 134,918. 17 Claims. (Cl. 123—148.)

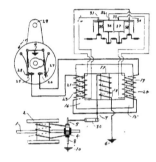

1. In an ignition system the method of producing an ignition current which consists of controlling the direction of flow of magnetic flux in a multiple magnetic circuit transformer.

1,328,375. PLANTER ATTACHMENT. GEORGE D. GRIFFICE, Big Spring, Tex. Filed Dec. 31, 1918. Serial No. 269,039. 9 Claims. (Cl. 111—83.)

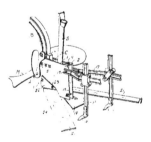

1. In combination with a ground working member, an attachment arranged rearwardly thereof and including a member provided with a seed receiving chamber discharging at the lower portion of the member, a ground working member carried by said first named member and extending below said first named member, and a presser foot carried by the first named member rearwardly of the compartment.

1,328,376. CABLE - CLAMP. WILLIAM J. HISS, New York, N. Y., assignor to Diamond Expansion Bolt Company, New York, N. Y., a Corporation of New York. Filed Feb. 14, 1919. Serial No. 277,002. 4 Claims. (Cl. 248—36.)

1. An article of manufacture comprising a cable clamp having an integral hook, base, and flap bent back on the base said flap being provided with one or more wings bent at an angle to the flap and adapted to reinforce the junction of the hook and base portions of the clip.

1,328,377. CABLE-CLAMP. WILLIAM J. HISS, New York, N. Y., assignor to Diamond Expansion Bolt Company, New York, N. Y., a Corporation of New York Filed Feb. 14, 1919. Serial No. 277,003. 4 Claims. (Cl. 248—36.)

1. An article of manufacture comprising a sheet metal cable clamp, having a hook portion, a base, a flap bent back on the base and having an arm adapted to be sprung under the hook portion and form a saddle and support for said hook portion.

1,328,378. MICROMETER AND GAGE ATTACHMENT. FRANK MAURICE JOHNSON, Denver, Colo. Filed Oct. 11, 1917. Serial No. 195,999. 2 Claims. (Cl. 33—147.)

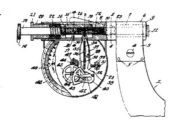

1. A micrometer attachment, comprising a movable anvil, a tubular member, an element sliding in the tubular member and actuated by movement of the anvil, resilient means for holding the sliding element in normal position, a lever secured to the sliding element, an adjustable fulcrum for the lever, and means controlled by the lever for indicating the movement of the anvil.

1,328,379. MECHANICAL MOVEMENT. JOSEPH R. JOHNSON, Louisville, Ky. Filed May 29, 1919. Serial No. 300,536. 2 Claims. (Cl. 74—14.)

1. A mechanism for imparting a vibratory motion to a body, said mechanism comprising a reciprocatory impact member, a support for said member, said support having end portions between which the impact member works, and a revoluble member for operating the impact member to deliver blows alternately to the aforesaid end portions of the support, the impact member having a recess in which the revoluble member revolves, said recess having diametrically opposite cam walls.

1,328,380. REFRACTORY LINING. WILBUR G. LAIRD, New York, N. Y., assignor to Henry L. Doherty, New York, N. Y. Filed July 5, 1918. Serial No. 243,387. 8 Claims. (Cl. 266—43.)

1. A refractory lining comprising a heat resistant backing and a non-fluxing refractory facing secured to said backing consisting of refractory locking blocks embedded in said backing and thin refractory plates held by said blocks.

1,328,381. SEMAPHORE-SIGNAL-OPERATING MECHANISM. JOHN C. LINDNER, Rochester, N. Y., assignor to General Railway Signal Company, Gates, N. Y., a Corporation of New York. Filed Nov. 26, 1917. Serial No. 203,973. 12 Claims. (Cl. 246—223.)

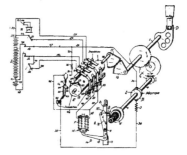

4. In a semaphore signal operating mechanism comprising an operating motor and a hold clear magnet, the combination with a circuit including the source of energy for supplying current to the operating motor, of a second circuit including a separate source of energy for supplying current to the hold clear magnet, and means operated automatically in accordance with the movement of the semaphore blade for establishing said circuits successively.

1,328,382. MOTION-PICTURE-FILM-FEED MECHANISM. FREDERICK R. LOCKHART and HARRY J. ORD, Toronto, Ontario, Canada, assignors to Frank M. Beesley, Toronto, Ontario, Canada. Filed July 19, 1916, Serial No. 110,077. Renewed July 15, 1918. Serial No. 245,075. 5 Claims. (Cl. 88—18.6.)

1. In a motion picture film feed mechanism a pair of shafts, a sprocket carried by one of said shafts, a film

engaged by said sprocket and moved thereby, a rocker arm sleeved on said shaft, a cam carried by the other

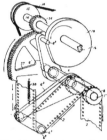

of said shafts and adapted to operate said rocker arm to intermittently depress said film.

1,328,383. WIND-SHIELD. MARGERY E. N. LUDLOW, Haverford, Pa. Filed Mar. 14, 1917. Serial No. 154,789. 1 Claim. (Cl. 21—148.)

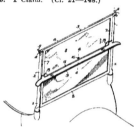

The combination of a wind shield having a pivoted upper section, the upper section consisting of a frame having side members; a sheet of glass located in the side members made in one piece and having pockets at each end to receive the side members and flanged to receive the lower edge of the glass; and a trough section extending the full width of the wind shield structure and beyond the same so as to carry the water away from the wind shield.

1,328,384. WEIGHT-MOTOR. EDWARD A. McLEOD and MICHAEL F. QUIRK, Springfield, Ohio, assignors of one-sixth to Isaac Evans and one-sixth to Anna J. McLeod, Springfield, Ohio. Filed Nov. 21, 1918. Serial No. 263,463. 28 Claims. (Cl. 185—5.)

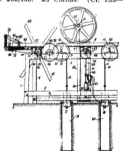

18. In a weight motor, the combination, with an inertia wheel, a device operable thereby, a track upon

which said wheel moves, a plurality of stationary rotatable drums each having a weight suspended therefrom, and elements coöperating with the inertia wheel and each of said drums, respectively, and operable to release said drums and said weights, whereby said elements are actuated alternately to cause said wheel to move back and forth on said track and impart reciprocal operative movement to said device.

1,328,385. COTTON - PICKER. CONRAD SANDIG MATTHIESSEN, Philadelphia, Pa., assignor of one-tenth to Charles J. Hepburn and one-fifth to William M. Longstreth, Philadelphia, Pa., and one-tenth to Ward F. Sprenkel, New York, N. Y. Filed Oct. 1, 1918. Serial No. 256,407. 5 Claims. (Cl. 56—31.)

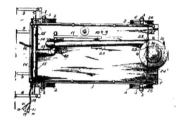

4. In a cotton picker, the combination of a platform mounted on wheels each of the latter adapted to swivel on a vertical axis, an independent draft attachment connected with each front wheel, connections between the rear wheels whereby they are shifted simultaneously, pneumatic devices carried on the platform and flexible picker tubes connected with said pneumatic devices.

5. In a cotton picker, the combination of a vehicle having a suction apparatus thereon, a flexible tube connected with said apparatus, a nozzle at the end of the flexible tube, levers carried by the tube and having jaws adapted to be moved across the open end of the nozzle to engage the cotton, and a spring for yieldingly holding the jaws normally separated, the said nozzle adapted to be carried by the hand and the levers manipulated by manual pressure directly applied to the same.

1,328,386. NOZZLE FOR PNEUMATIC COTTON-PICKERS. CONRAD S. MATTHIESSEN, Philadelphia, Pa. Filed Aug. 2, 1919. Serial No. 314,972. 4 Claims. (Cl. 56—32.)

1. In a cotton picker, the combination of a suction nozzle, levers at one side thereof, each lever having a jaw located in advance of the open end of the nozzle, one of said jaws being fixed and the other movable, and a spring for holding the levers and the jaws normally separated.

1,328,387. SAFETY INDICATOR AND ALARM. YNOCENTE J. MOLINA, Douglas, Ariz. Filed Jan. 21, 1919. Serial No. 272,366. 3 Claims. (Cl. 116—31.)

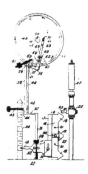

1. In an apparatus of the class described, the combination with a cylinder provided with a piston rod, a signal provided with a valve having a stem positioned contiguous to said piston rod, a bracket secured to said bracket, said bracket provided with a socket, a vertically slidable plate supported in said socket of the bracket, means for fastening said plate in an adjusted position upon said bracket, and said plate provided with a cam projection adapted to operate said stem of the valve for actuating the signal.

1,328,388. AUXILIARY OILING SYSTEM FOR FORD CARS. ALFRED MOTZER, Meriden, Conn., assignor to The Hobson & Motzer Co., Meriden, Conn., a Firm composed of Harry C. Hobson and Alfred Motzer. Filed May 13, 1919. Serial No. 296,875. 1 Claim. (Cl. 184—55.)

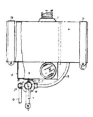

In a gravity auxiliary oiling system for Ford cars, the combination with a reservoir, of mounting means therefor, of a feed-chamber suspended from the said reservoir and of smaller capacity than the same, an oil-level indicator mounted in the said feed-chamber for indicating the amount of oil therein at any given time, a valve-casing suspended from the said feed-chamber, a lead-pipe from the reservoir to the said valve-casing, a feed-pipe leading from the said casing to the engine, and a two-way valve mounted in the said casing and provided with passages, whereby in its open position the valve permits the feed-chamber to be filled by gravity from the reservoir and in its closed position shuts the chamber off from the reservoir and permits the oil in the chamber to be fed by gravity into the feed-pipe and thence into the engine.

1,328,389. ALLIGATOR-WRENCH. HARRY G. NORWOOD, Baltimore, Md., assignor, by mesne assignments, to Napoleon B. Lobe and S. Burns Ratcliffe, Baltimore, Md., trading as N. B. Lobe & Co., Baltimore, Md. Filed Nov. 29, 1918. Serial No. 264,550. 5 Claims. (Cl. 81—92.)

3. An alligator wrench comprising a handle formed integrally with a pair of jaws having facing edges mutually inclined and each of said edges being provided with teeth, a slot in said handle dividing said handle into two limbs and means for varying the forces opposed by said limbs to the mutual movement of said jaws.

1,328,390. GAME. ADAM NUGENT, Nutley, N. J. Filed Aug. 2, 1919. Serial No. 314,892. 2 Claims. (Cl. 46—63.)

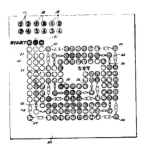

1. In a game of the class described, the combination with a rectangular board, having a level upper surface, a plurality of colored circles marked on said board, said circles being arranged in rows of different colors, the rows being arranged in three horizontal and four transverse rows, circles indicating the starting of each of said rows, fillers arranged at the corners between the outer and intermediate rows, numbered checkers in groups of four disposable on said colored circles, and a manually operable indicator by which the movement of said checkers is controlled.

1,328,391. VEHICLE-BODY. JACQUES M. PERLMAN, New York, N. Y. Filed Feb. 28, 1919. Serial No. 279,680. 8 Claims. (Cl. 296—108.)

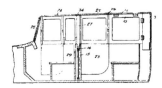

4. A vehicle body provided with means of converting it into different styles including a transverse extension adapted to be elevated at the rear of the driver's seat and a top member carried thereby and adapted to be extended therefrom forward over the driver's seat or rearward over the rear compartment.

1,328,392. GRID-PLATE FOR STORAGE BATTERIES. PAUL B. RABE, Chicago, Ill., assignor to O. K. Giant Battery Co., Gary, Ind., a Corporation of Delaware. Filed Apr. 30, 1919. Serial No. 293,603. 1 Claim. (Cl. 204—29.)

A grid plate for storage batteries comprising in combination with a pair of longitudinal bars, a plurality of transverse bars extending between the longitudinal bars, said transverse bars being disposed in parallel rows, the transverse bars in said parallel rows being located in staggered relation to each other, each of said transverse bars being provided on its inner surface with a web of less cross-section than the said transverse bars, said webs projecting inwardly into the space between the parallel rows of said transverse bars substantially as and for the purpose set forth.

1,328,393. STORAGE BATTERY. PAUL B. RABE, Chicago, Ill., assignor to O. K. Giant Battery Co., Gary, Ind., a Corporation of Delaware. Filed Apr. 30, 1919. Serial No. 293,604. 4 Claims. (Cl. 204—29.)

3. A storage cell comprising in combination with a suitable receptacle, an electrolyte therein, a hollow rod supported in said receptacle and having its interior open to the atmosphere, a plurality of grid plates supported by said rod, and apertures in said rod affording communication between the rod interior and the electrolyte.

1,328,394. STORAGE BATTERY. PAUL B. RABE, Chicago, Ill., assignor to O. K. Giant Battery Co., Gary, Ind., a Corporation of Delaware. Filed Apr. 30, 1919. Serial No. 293,606. 5 Claims. (Cl. 204—29.)

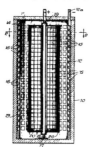

3. A storage battery cell comprising in combination with a cell receptacle, grid plates of one polarity supported within said receptacle, a rod of low-fusing metal vertically disposed in said receptacle, a plurality of longitudinal slots in said rod, a plurality of vertically disposed grid plates each having one of its lateral edges fitted in one of said slots and secured therein by being

"burned" to said rod, said last mentioned grid plates radiating from said rod, said last mentioned grid plates being of different polarity than the grid plates first mentioned.

1,328,395. CONVEYING AND STEAM AND WATER BLEACHING APPARATUS FOR DEHYDRATING PLANTS. ROBERT REA and FRANK W. WATERS, Portland, Oreg. Filed Nov. 29, 1918. Serial No. 264,706. 4 Claims. (Cl. 99—2.)

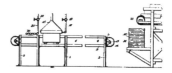

1. In an apparatus of the character described, the combination of an endless chain conveyer, provided with angle-iron frames arranged to receive screen bottomed sliced product holding frames, and convey them along its top surface and discharge them at its end, with a hood surrounding the upper part of said conveyer and a row of steam distributing perforated pipes arranged above and also a row of steam distributing perforated pipes arranged below the upper part of said endless conveyer, and means for driving said conveyer.

1,328,396. FRUIT, VEGETABLE, AND OTHER FOOD DEHYDRATING FURNACE AND ITS COÖPERATING APPARATUS. ROBERT REA and FRANK W. WATERS, Portland, Oreg. Filed Nov. 29, 1918. Serial No. 264,707. 9 Claims. (Cl. 34—46.)

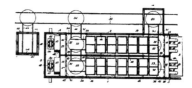

1. A fruit and other food dehydrating drier, adapted to receive car load lots of product to be dried, said drier being provided with car inclosing means, and suitable car supporting entrance and exit tracks and switches, and downwardly inclined car forwarding tracks in said drier, means for heating said drier, means, including adjustable shutters, for regulating the heat in said drier, means including a bleaching apparatus in said drier arranged to apply a bleaching treatment to said car loads of fruit and vegetable products, means including suction fans, for exhausting the hot air as desired, from said drier, and means, including an auxiliary dry air heating chamber, arranged to give a dry air treatment to the car loads of products after being dehydrated in said drier.

1,328,397. STEAM BLEACHING APPARATUS. ROBERT REA and FRANK W. WATERS, Portland, Oreg. Filed Nov. 29, 1918. Serial No. 264,708. 5 Claims. (Cl. 99—2.)

1. A steam bleaching apparatus for a food drier, comprising a counterbalanced perforated pipe frame arranged and adapted to be moved in said drier into a position of use at predetermined times to give a steam

bleaching treatment to the product to be dried within said drier, and means including a hose for connecting said

perforated pipe frame to a supply of steam, and a valve arranged to control the steam flowing to and through said frame.

1,328,398. HEAT-REGULATING ADJUSTABLE-SHUTTER MECHANISM FOR FOOD-DEHYDRATING PLANTS. ROBERT REA and FRANK W. WATERS, Portland, Oreg. Filed Nov. 29, 1918. Serial No. 264,709. 3 Claims. (Cl. 34—39.)

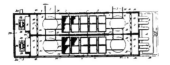

1. In a heating medium regulating adjustable shutter mechanism for fruit and vegetable dehydrating driers containing two food drying chambers, the combination of a pair of independent positioned partitions comprising fixed members and pivotally swinging shutters between said fixed members, said shutters being arranged in independent groups of several shutters each, and means including a fastening device comprising the semi-circular plate, and a wire partly secured to each group of shutters, and to a fixed part of said partitions for securing each group of shutters in predetermined parts of this open or closed position, with a food product dehydrating drier comprising the box shaped structure containing entrance and exit passageways, and the chambers provided with car tracks and arranged to receive car loads of product to be dried; said shutter partitions being placed across the opposite ends of said drier directly in front of and facing the opposite ends of said chambers; the independent groups of shutters in each vertical row of shutters being arranged and adapted to regulate the flow of the heating medium into and through said chambers.

1,328,399. NUT-LOCK. FREDERICK REDDY, Ottawa, Ontario, Canada. Filed May 17, 1919. Serial No. 297,797. 1 Claim. (Cl. 151—28.)

A nut lock comprising a bolt having a longitudinal groove, a nut to fit the same and having its outer face

formed with a circular recess disposed eccentric relative to the center of the bolt and the outer end of said recess further enlarged and concaved, a circular washer to fit the recess and having a circular opening eccentrically located therein to receive the bolt, a tongue formed on said washer extending into the opening thereof to seat in the groove of the bolt, and a ring formed with lateral terminals whereby the ring may be contracted, inserted in the recess and subsequently permitted to expand to seat in the concaved portion of said recess to secure the washer against dislodgment.

1,328,400. EXTENSION-PEDAL. HENRY C. REICH, New York, N. Y. Filed Oct. 10, 1917, Serial No. 195,779. Renewed Nov. 5, 1919. Serial No. 335,908. 1 Claim. (Cl. 74—81.)

In combination, an extension attachment for pedals having a standard consisting of two elements relatively movable in a longitudinal direction, one of said elements consisting of a single member fitting between parallel members of the other element, said other element being connected to a base plate provided with integral clips and a rocking slidable clip for attachment to the pedal, said base plate having a slot, a clamping bolt with a wing nut extending through said slot for purposes of adjusting said clip, and a foot plate mounted pivotally on the upper end of the aforesaid standard.

1,328,401. NUT-LOCK. WILLIAM G. SAVIDGE, Northumberland, Pa. Filed Oct. 2, 1915. Serial No. 53,811. Renewed Apr. 30, 1919. Serial No. 293,811. 2 Claims. (Cl. 151—19.)

2. A nut lock including a main nut having an annular groove in the outer face thereof, the inner wall of said groove having a plurality of slits extending throughout the entire length of the bore of the nut and defining a plurality of fingers, said fingers being tapered outwardly from the object-engaging face of the nut, an annular locking element engaged in said groove having an inclined inner surface engaged with said fingers, means independent of said nut and said locking element for moving the latter into said groove and compressing said fingers, and teeth formed on the outer face of the locking element engaging and securing said means.

1,328,402. SPRING-MOTOR. CHARLES SCHIFFL, Montclair, N. J. Original application filed Feb. 28, 1917, Serial No. 151,420. Divided and this application filed Oct. 24, 1917. Serial No. 198,198. 9 Claims. (Cl. 185—9.)

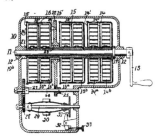

3. In a spring motor, a plurality of spring barrels, a pairs of power springs in each barrel, a partition between the springs in the pair, the springs in each barrel being arranged to act in parallel, and the barrels being arranged to act one upon another in series.

1,328,403. ELECTRICITY-DISPELLING DEVICE FOR PAPER-PRINTING APPARATUS. LLOYD D. SHAW, Higgins, Tex. Filed Apr. 26, 1919. Serial No. 292,931. 2 Claims. (Cl. 175—264.)

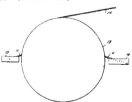

1. In an electricity dispelling device for paper treating apparatus, a receptacle for containing the fluid, a discharge brush comprising a body portion of relatively rigid material and an absorbent material thereon, said absorbent material being adapted to carry water by capillary attraction, the said brush being supported on the bottom and the edge of one side of the said receptacle and projecting diagonally therefrom.

1,328,404. AUTOMOBILE-SIGNAL. WILLIAM SKARNULIS, New Britain, Conn. Filed July 16, 1919. Serial No. 311,149. 1 Claim. (Cl. 116—31.)

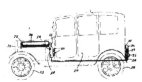

In an automobile signal actuating mechanism of the character described, the combination with a casing secured to the front of a vehicle, of a plurality of signal plates within said casing, bell-crank levers to the long arms of which said plates are slidably engaged, angular elements to which the front arms of said levers are connected by a pin and slot connection, pairwise arranged cylinders within the casing adapted to receive one arm of said angular elements constituting a piston adapted to work in said cylinder and supply pipes for supplying exhaust gases to said cylinders and pistons, springs for normally holding the signal plates in their elevated position of rest, springs for normally holding the pistons in their advanced positions and means for controlling the supply of the exhaust gases.

1,328,405. RAILWAY-RAIL. EDWARD V. SOURBIER and MICHAEL MADDEN, Harrisburg, Pa. Filed Mar. 15, 1919. Serial No. 282,792. 2 Claims. (Cl. 238—319.)

1. A railway rail including the usual tread, web and base flange, a rib depending from the base flange and extending longitudinally of the rail and spaced apart retaining members arranged in pairs and depending from the base flange.

1,328,406. SUPPORTER. ALBERT T. VAN ALSTYN, Grand Rapids, Mich. Filed May 15, 1916. Serial No. 97,559. 9 Claims. (Cl. 241—8.)

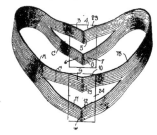

1. A supporter comprising an encircling member having spaced circumferentially extending slits forming front and rear dips, and means separating the slitted portions intermediate their lengths to hold said parts in dipped relation when in use in order to conform to the configuration of the body encircled.

1,328,407. MACHINE FOR EMBOSSING WITHOUT DIES. FREDERICK A. VIRKUS, La Grange, Ill., assignor to Wood, Nathan & Virkus Company, New York, N. Y., a Corporation of Virginia. Filed Jan. 19, 1914, Serial No. 812,964. Renewed June 10, 1919. Serial No. 303,256. 9 Claims. (Cl. 91—59.)

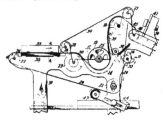

1. In a machine for embossing without dies, the combination with a carrier for printed sheets or the like, of a

receptacle for powdered material, means coöperating with said carrier for forcing the sheets under the surface of the powdered material in said receptacle and moving the sheets out of the same, and means for jarring the sheets after they come out of the powdered material to remove the surplus powdered material therefrom.

4. In a machine of the character described, the combination of an endless apron for receiving printed sheets or the like, a receptacle for powdered material, a pair of idler disks mounted in position to extend down into said receptacle near the edges of said apron and cause the apron to move down into said receptacle, and a pair of spring belts passing in contact with the carrier apron while in said receptacle.

6. In a machine of the character described, the combination of a platform, a side gage thereon, an endless rubber apron passing over said platform adjacent to said side gage, a pair of wire belts movable along in contact with said rubber apron, one of said wire belts being located adjacent to said side gage and the other being adjustable toward and from the same, and means for applying powdered material to the sheets on the rubber apron.

1,328,408. FILM-END FASTENER FOR MOTION-PIC-TURE-FILM REELS. MOSES F. WALKER, Cadiz, Ohio. Continuation of application Serial No. 222,436, filed Mar. 14, 1918. This application filed Sept. 25, 1918. Serial No. 255,717. 5 Claims. (Cl. 242—74.)

1. The combination with a film reel having a hollow hub provided with a relatively wide transverse opening, of a leaf spring forming substantially a continuation of the hub surface to support the film and expanded within the hub and bearing against the inner side thereof, and constituting means for binding the end of a film strip inserted through said opening.

1,328,409. CYLINDER-FORMING MACHINE. HOWARD L. WEED, Detroit, Mich. Filed May 11, 1917. Serial No. 167,994. 7 Claims. (Cl. 77—1.)

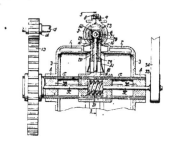

1. Means for forming a cylindrical surface having a circular axis comprising a hollow shaft and means to continuously rotate it in one direction, a second shaft within the hollow shaft and means to continuously rotate it in one direction, an arm secured to the hollow shaft, a cutting tool and a shaft therefor journaled in the outer

270 O. G.—26

end of said arm in a plane at substantially right angles to the axis of the hollow shaft, and means to drive the cutting tool from said second shaft.

1,328,410. ROTARY ENGINE. HOWARD L. WEED, Detroit, Mich. Original application filed Sept. 7, 1915, Serial No. 49,153. Divided and this application filed July 29, 1918. Serial No. 247,176. 9 Claims. (Cl. 123—11.)

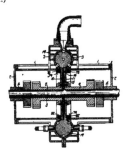

1. A rotary engine comprising a casing that includes a cylinder, an engine shaft mounted in the casing, rotors comprising disks concentric with and loose upon the engine shaft, pistons traveling in the cylinder, said pistons being rigid with the corresponding rotor-disks, a disk loose upon the engine shaft under all conditions and interposed between the rotor-disks, said rotor-disks being arranged to closely engage the last mentioned disk to insure a tight seal for the cylinder, and means for transmitting motion from the rotors to the engine shaft.

1,328,411. CRIMPING-MACHINE. ALBERT J. BATES, Jr., Chicago, Ill., assignor, by mesne assignments, to David S. Gardner, Chicago, Ill. Filed May 11, 1917. Serial No. 167,889. 7 Claims. (Cl. 270—61.)

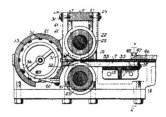

1. In a machine of the character described, the combination of a pair of coöperating crimping elements, a movable fixing or setting device in rear of the crimping elements containing spaced pockets to receive the sheets after the latter have been operated upon by the crimping elements, means for heating said fixing or setting device, and a feed device operating to advance each sheet between said crimping elements and later compress and force the same into a pocket of the fixing or setting device.

1,328,412. PHONOGRAPH-RESONATOR. WILLIAM C. BECKWITH, Urbana, Ill. Filed Jan. 15, 1917. Serial No. 142,353. 10 Claims. (Cl. 181—27.)

1. A device for transmitting reproduced sounds comprising in combination a horn generally rectangular in cross-section, having straight line sides, and provided

with top and bottom sound boards substantially parallel for a portion of their length, merging into oppositely

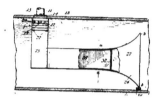

curved surfaces terminating at the end of the horn, and means for connecting said horn with the tone arm of a phonograph.

1,328,413. PARACHUTE. HAROLD BLACKBURN, Doncaster, England. Filed Aug. 13, 1919. Serial No. 317,109. 7 Claims. (Cl. 244—21.)

1. In a parachute the combination of an umbrella part, a load-carrying hook, rigging cords at one end attached to the umbrella part, and at the other end to said hook, a frame around which the rigging cords are spaced and secured intermediate of their ends, a platform of netting stretched across said frame, a skirt of flexible material secured to and extending upwardly of said frame externally of the rigging ropes, and means for drawing together the free edges of the skirt, substantially as set forth.

1,328,414. METHOD OF MAKING PISTON - RINGS. GEORGE H. BLETTNER, Chicago, Ill. Filed May 5, 1917. Serial No. 166,551. 8 Claims. (Cl. 29—156.1.)

1. The method of making piston rings which consists in forming the rings from a pattern having the non-circular contour of an inherently expanded split ring which has been shaped in the required form while contracted.

1,328,415. VEHICLE-BODY BRACE. ALBERT O. BUCKIUS, Jr., Chicago, Ill., assignor to Chicago Manufacturing and Distributing Co., a Corporation of Illinois. Filed May 5, 1919. Serial No. 294,683. 2 Claims. (Cl. 280—163.)

2. In a vehicle body brace, in combination, a transverse supporting bar, a suspending member therefor having a threaded stem, a split clamp having an integral tubular hub portion at one side of the same running on the bar, the clamp opening extending into the walls of its hub portion and the threaded stem of the suspending member being extended through the bore of the clamp hub, and clamping nuts running on the stem of the said suspending member at opposite sides of the clamp hub.

1,328,416. PROCESS OF OBTAINING POTASSIUM SALTS FROM LIQUIDS CONTAINING THE SAME. GEORGE B. BURNHAM, Berkeley, Calif. Filed Sept. 18, 1916. Serial No. 120,602. 5 Claims. (Cl. 28—22.)

1. The process of recovering potassium chlorid from solutions containing sodium, potassium, sulfate and chlorid ions, which consists in evaporating the solution to approximate saturation with potassium sodium sulfate, cooling the solution to below 4.4° C. to saturation with potassium chlorid whereby other salts are crystallized out, removing the solution from the deposited salts, evaporating the solution about 4.4° C. to saturation with potassium sodium sulfate, evaporating the solution to deposit some of the potassium sodium sulfate, cooling the solution to approximate saturation with potassium chlorid, removing the solution from the deposited salts, and further cooling the solution to crystallize out potassium chlorid.

1,328,417. PROCESS OF OBTAINING POTASSIUM SALTS FROM SALINE WATERS. GEORGE B. BURNHAM, Berkeley, Calif. Filed July 1, 1918. Serial No. 242,738. 5 Claims. (Cl. 23—22.)

1. The process of recovering potassium salts from liquors containing sodium, potassium, chlorid, sulfate and carbonate ions, which consists in evaporating the liquor to crystallize out hanksite, removing the liquor from the deposited crystals, evaporating the removed liquor to crystallize out potassium sodium sulfate, removing the liquor from the deposited crystals, evaporating the liquor to crystallize out potassium sodium sulfate and a carbonate salt, removing the liquor from the deposited crystals and cooling the liquor to crystallize out potassium chlorid.

1,328,418. PROCESS OF RECOVERING POTASSIUM SODIUM SULFATE AND OTHER POTASSIUM SALTS FROM SALINE WATERS. GEORGE B. BURNHAM, Berkeley, Calif. Filed July 1, 1918. Serial No. 242,956. 7 Claims. (Cl. 23—22.)

1. The process of recovering potassium and sodium salts from liquor containing potassium, sodium, chlorid and sulfate ions, which consists in cooling the liquor to crystallize out Glauber salts, separating the liquor from the deposited crystals, evaporating the liquor at a higher temperature to crystallize out sodium chlorid, separating the liquor from the deposited crystals and further evaporating the liquor to crystallize out sodium chlorid and potassium sodium sulfate.

1,328,419. HEATER. HARLEY S. BUSBY, Washington, Iowa, assignor to Western Hog Oiler Co., Inc., Washington, Iowa, a Corporation of Iowa. Filed Oct. 11, 1916. Serial No. 124,941. 1 Claim. (Cl. 158—91.)

In a heater, a base, a fuel oil burner mounted in said base, said burner consisting of a plate having laterally

disposed air openings, a fuel-pipe passing through the
central portion of said plate, and having a reduced tip
so that the walls are sufficiently thin so as to become
heated to a degree sufficient to vaporize the fuel emerging
therefrom, an arch-shaped air pipe mounted on said plate

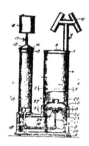

having terminal openings engaging with said laterally
disposed openings and having a central circular opening
adjacent the upper end of said fuel pipe, said air pipe
being also provided with a cylindrical dome-shaped portion immediately above said fuel-pipe.

1,328,420. SEPARATOR. Rufus N. Chamberlain, Chicago, Ill. Filed Sept. 12, 1918. Serial No. 253,807.
20 Claims. (Cl. 204—29.)
8. A fibrous separator for storage batteries having
structural characteristics of wood and a thin film of un-
vulcanized rubber disposed upon the surface of the inner
fibers throughout but not filling the pores.

1,328,421. AEROPLANE. John L. Cochennet, Chicago,
Ill. Filed Apr. 14, 1917. Serial No. 162,086. 6 Claims.
(Cl. 244—12.)

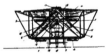

6. An aeroplane including, in combination, a single
horizontal plane, oblique lower planes forming a juncture
with the top plane intermediate its ends, and propelling
mechanism located beneath the top plane, substantially
as described.

1,328,422. COMBINED SELF-LOCKING CLIP AND
SHIELD. Edward Coulson, Lake Forest, Ill. Filed
Apr. 3, 1919. Serial No. 287,122. 4 Claims. (Cl.
132—19.)

3. In combination with the heating tube of a hair
waving appliance, a clip and scalp protector comprising
a pair of thin curved strips hinged together at one pair
of extremities and provided at their other extremities

with co-engaging means whereby the clip may be clamped
around the end of the tube adjacent the scalp to seal
the tube and protect the scalp from the heat applied to
the hair during the waving operation.

1,328,423. WIRE-BINDING TOOL. Llewellyn Davies,
Sisson, Calif. Filed Apr. 1, 1918. Serial No. 225,911.
7 Claims. (Cl. 140—121.)

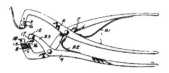

6. A wire binding tool comprising a pair of pivoted
levers, a jaw on one end of one of said levers, said jaw
having an opening on the rear face thereof adapted to
receive and hold a wire end, a jaw on the other lever
arranged opposite to and adapted to coöperate with the
first jaw and means coöperating with the last named jaw
for clamping a wire thereto.

1,328,424. BELT-FASTENER-SETTING MACHINE.
James K. Diamond, Grand Rapids, Mich., assignor to
Clipper Belt Lacer Company, Grand Rapids, Mich. Filed
Sept. 10, 1919. Serial No. 322,836. 7 Claims. (Cl.
1—50.)

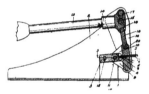

1. In a machine for setting belt fasteners, the combination of a frame comprising a pair of side members, a
fastener holder disposed between said side members to
face forwardly and having spaced fastener receiving
grooves in its face, a locking pin insertible through said
holder transversely of said grooves and adapted to be
inserted and removed through one of the side members,
coacting jaws having rearwardly projecting arms at their
ends, a pivot therefor constituting a supporting member
for said holder, said holder being recessed at its ends to
receive said arms, an actuating lever pivotally mounted
between said side members above said jaws, links connected to the ends of the lower jaw and eccentrically connected to said lever, and a link connecting the upper
jaw to said lever, the pivots connecting said link to said
lever and said jaw being disposed relative to the lever
pivot so that a toggle action is secured in closing the jaw,
said machine being adapted to rest on the end of the
frame to facilitate the introduction of the fastener.

1,328,425. PARACHUTE. Charles Hugh Duffy, Chevy
Chase, Md. Filed Oct. 10, 1918. Serial No. 257,647.
11 Claims. (Cl. 244—21.)
1. A parachute including a parachute-body of suitable
fabric, rigging ropes of suitable flexible material, and

means permanently attached to the parachute-body to receive that portion of the said rigging-ropes extending from

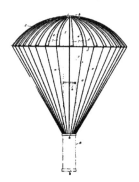

the parachute body to protect the ropes against twisting
and tangling.

1,328,426. BELT-FASTENER. GEORGES FLURY, Bienne,
Switzerland. Filed Apr. 18, 1918. Serial No. 229,293.
2 Claims. (Cl. 24—35.)

2. A fastener for connecting together the ends of belting,
constituted by an H-shaped member adapted to lie in
contact with one face of the belt and the side elements
of which are each provided with a single line of downwardly projecting claws while the central cross-member
operates as a tie bar when the claws on the two side
elements enter respectively the two ends of the belting
to be joined.

1,328,427. ELECTRICAL THERMOSTAT. ALBERT GOLD-
STEIN, New York, N. Y., assignor to Simon B. Hess,
New York, N. Y. Original application filed Nov. 18,
1914, Serial No. 872,680. Divided and this application
filed Oct. 9, 1915. Serial No. 55,100. 2 Claims. (Cl.
200—140.)

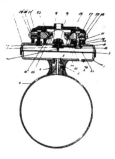

1. An electrical thermostat comprising a case, a
diaphragm in said case dividing the space therein into

two chambers, a contact piece in proximity to the
diaphragm in one of said chambers, the contained air in
said chamber being freely open to the atmosphere, an
expansion chamber connected to the other of said two
chambers, and an adjustable vent, the adjustment of
said vent being secured by the manipulation of a screw
joint by means of which the expansion chamber is attached to said other chamber.

2. In a thermostatic device, a diaphragm case, an expansion chamber, and an adjustable vent, the adjustment
of said vent being secured by the manipulation of a screw
joint by means of which the expansion chamber is attached to the diaphragm case.

1,328,428. SOCKET - WRENCH. DAVID F. GRAHAM,
Coudersport, Pa., assignor to The Graham Roller Bear-
ing Company, Coudersport, Pa. Filed May 8, 1919.
Serial No. 295,572. 5 claims. (Cl. 81—121.)

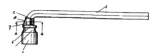

5. In a socket wrench, the combination with a handle,
of a socket member engageable with said handle, a removable socket retaining clip having sliding engagement
with said handle above the socket member and provided
with a spring socket engaging member.

**1,328,429. ARM-BINDER AND ELEVATING CONTROL-
SHAFT LOCK.** JAMES CLYDE HALDEMAN, Salem, Ohio,
assignor to The Silver Manufacturing Company, Salem,
Ohio, a Corporation of Ohio. Filed May 2, 1919.
Serial No. 294,186. 7 Claims. (Cl. 77—28.)

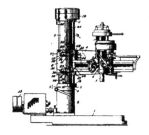

1. In a drilling machine, a column, an arm slidably
mounted thereon, means for vertically moving the arm,
a control shaft controlling the arm moving means, a
clamp screw for clamping the arm upon the column and
a clamping plate upon the clamping screw for simultaneously clamping the control shaft against movement.

1,328,430. BORING AND SLOTTING TOOL. HOSEA
HATHAWAY, Brookline, Mass. Filed Nov. 5, 1918.
Serial No. 261,248. 1 Claim. (Cl. 144—240.)

An elongated boring and slotting tool of substantially
cylindrical form, having longitudinal grooves oblique
to the axis of the tool and separated by independent
peripheral portions which are backed off and eccentric to
the axis of the tool, so that each peripheral portion has
a higher and a lower longitudinal edge, the outer ends
of said grooves intersecting the end of the tool and forming cutting edges adapted to bore a round hole, the longitudinal edges of said grooves interesecting the said

peripheral portions and forming cutting angles at the higher edges thereof, said cutting angles being subdivided by notches formed in said peripheral portions, into rows of spaced apart hole-elongating teeth, which are oblique

to the axis of the tool, and have cutting edges equidistant from the axis of the tool and backs eccentric to said axis, the hole-elongating teeth of each row being staggered relatively to the teeth of the other row, so that the hole-elongating duty is divided between the rows of teeth.

1,328,431. MACHINE FOR PERFORATING, SLITTING, AND REWINDING PAPER. DAVID W. HUDSON, Green Bay, Wis., assignor to Hudson-Sharp Machine Company, Green Bay, Wis., a Corporation of Wisconsin. Filed May 8, 1916. Serial No. 96,219. 5 Claims. (Cl. 164—65.)

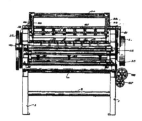

1. In a machine of the character described, a support for a roll of paper, means for supporting and rotating a series of rewinding cores whereon the paper is rewound on smaller rolls, means for placing a second series of cores in proper position, an angle plate extending the full width of the paper, arms on said angle plate, sleeves surrounding said arms, means for limiting the movement of said arms in said sleeves, a spring interposed between said arms and said sleeves, and means for raising and lowering said sleeves, substantially as described.

1,328,432. SEPARABLE BUTTON. HERBERT IVERSEN, Chicago, Ill. Filed Aug. 22, 1918. Serial No. 250,919. 6 Claims. (Cl. 24—104.)

1. A separable button comprising a button head and a base plate to which said button head is secured, an L-shaped metal pin being secured to said base plate, and a locking disk coöperating with said pin and arranged to clamp an interposed fabric against said base plate.

1,328,433. MOLDING APPARATUS. JOHN LOUIS JOHNSON, Chicago, Ill. Filed June 20, 1919. Serial No. 305,457. 12 Claims. (Cl. 22—48.)

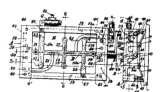

1. In an apparatus of the nature described, the combination, of a portable housing, a pattern plate in said housing, means for supporting said pattern plate in said housing, means for imparting horizontal movement to said pattern plate, and means for adjustably limiting the horizontal movement of said pattern plate.

1,328,434. SHIP-SALVAGING. CHARLES O. KNUDSEN, Brooklyn, N. Y. Filed Apr. 21, 1919. Serial No. 291,493. 9 Claims. (Cl. 114—51.)

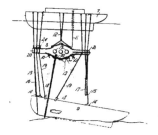

1. In ship salvaging apparatus, the combination with a salvaging vessel provided with wreck-lifting slings, of a submarine in communication with said salvaging vessel and provided with means engaging said slings for assisting in the placing of said slings about the submerged wreck.

1,328,435. YARN-DYER. ALBERT KRASA, Chicago, Ill. Filed Sept. 25, 1919. Serial No. 326,161. 11 Claims. (Cl. 8—19.)

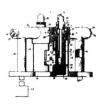

1. In a yarn dyer, in combination, a dye wick, and means operating under a uniform head to feed dye to said wick.

1,328,436. METHOD OF FORMING PISTON-RINGS. ALBERT J. II. KUHSIEK, Richmond Hill, N. Y. Filed Dec. 9, 1918. Serial No. 265,845. 3 Claims. (Cl. 29—156.1.)

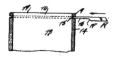

1. The method of forming piston-rings, consisting in first preparing a blank of relatively soft steel, then drawing the blank into the form of a shell or cup, then cutting the wall of the shell into rings, and then splitting the rings.

1,328,437. POWER SHIFT MECHANISM. LINCOLN A. LANG, Chicago, Ill., assignor to The Northern Trust Company, Chicago, Ill., a Corporation of Illinois, trustee. Filed May 17, 1917. Serial No. 169,217. 9 Claims. (Cl. 121—41.)

1. In a device of the class described, the combination of a pilot member, a cylinder, a piston for said cylinder, a source of motive fluid for moving said piston, valve mechanism for controlling said motive fluid, spring means normally tending to prevent movement of said valve mechanism, and a controlling connection between said pilot member and said valve mechanism, the arrangement being such that resistance preventing actuation of the valve mechanism is sufficient to cause movement of the pilot member without operating said valve mechanism when the piston is moved by external forces.

1,328,438. WELL-SCREEN. MAHLON E. LAYNE, Memphis, Tenn. Filed Apr. 9, 1917. Serial No. 160,588. 2 Claims. (Cl. 166—8.)

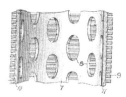

1. In a well screen, the combination of a supporting frame, a helical groove formed thereon and a helix of screening wire wound thereon, said wire having a flat base contacting with the surface of the supporting frame and having a projection extending into the groove.

1,328,439. BRASSIÈRE. GOLDSTONE D. LEONARD, New York, N. Y. Filed Apr. 3, 1919. Serial No. 287,295. 1 Claim. (Cl. 2—98.)

A brassière composed of two side sections, the rear edges of which are slanting in opposite directions so that the adjoining rear parts of said sections will overlap one another throughout their entire length, said sections being permanently joined to one another only at the adjoining upper ends of their rear edges, fastening means along the front edges of said sections and a ribbon fastened to

the lower end of the rear edge of each section, said ribbons being adapted to be passed around the waist line of the wearer and to be tied in front for the adjustment of the brassière in width.

1,328,440. DIFFERENTIAL MECHANISM. FRANK M. LEWIS, Chicago, Ill. Filed June 4, 1914. Serial No. 842,825. 2 Claims. (Cl. 74—7.)

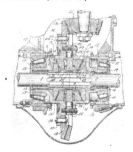

1. In a differential mechanism, in combination, a pair of alined axle sections, a driving member having a hub encircling the meeting ends of said axle sections and major clutch teeth on both sides, shiftable clutch members mounted on the opposite end portions of said hub and having major clutch teeth on one side in mesh with the teeth of the driving member, each shiftable clutch member having minor clutch teeth on one side thereof, means carried by the respective shiftable clutch members to permit and to limit relative rotative movement of the shiftable clutch members and to allow said members to move toward and from the driving member, and driven members keyed to said axle sections and each formed with minor clutch teeth on one side for operative engagement with the minor clutch teeth of the respective shiftable clutch members.

1,328,441. LENS-MOUNTING. LOUIS LINK, New York, N. Y. Filed May 12, 1919. Serial No. 296,507. 4 Claims. (Cl. 88—39.)

1. A lens mounting embodying a split ring, in the inner periphery of which is a channel forming a seat for a lens,

-a tongue rigid with one end of the split ring and adapted to overlie the outer surface of the other end of said ring, and a handle portion, associated with the end of the split ring which the tongue overlies, and embodying means adapted to engage the tongue and force it into tight engagement with the portion of the ring which it overlies for the purpose of normally locking the ring against spreading, said handle portion being retractable to release the tongue from engagement with the portion of the ring which it overlies to allow of the removal of the lens.

1,328,442.   BAGGAGE-CAR-SIDE-DOOR HANGER. David McBride, Wilmington, Del.   Filed June 13, 1919. Serial No. 303,858.   1 Claim.   (Cl. 16—7.)

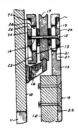

The combination with a car side having a door opening and a track positioned over said opening; of a hanger comprising spaced portions provided with vertical slots and horizontal parallel notches at either side thereof inset to provide side shoulders; a door secured to the hanger, a bolt engaged through the slots, a plate provided with similar notches and disposed on the bolt to engage the notches of one portion of the hanger, a sheave on the bolt to engage the track for movably supporting the door, and a second plate between the shoulders of the other hanger portion and threadedly receiving the bolt therein, said second plate having notches coöperating with the notched surface of the last-named hanger portion, as and for the purpose specified.

1,328,443.   NUT-LOCK. Henry L. Marburger, Baltimore, and Louis H. Berg, Baltimore county, Md.   Filed Dec. 30, 1918.   Serial No. 268,786.   1 Claim.   (Cl. 151—28.)

The combination with a threaded bolt, of a nut screwed on said bolt, a flat portion on the threaded end of said bolt, a nut lock having a body portion provided with a flat sided hole to fit the threaded end of said bolt and the flat portion of said bolt whereby said nut lock is prevented from turning, spring portions and holding fingers on said nut lock, grooves in said nut for the reception of said fingers, said spring portions being out of contact with said nut from said body portion to said holding fingers, and a flat-sided hollow cylindrical neck formed integrally with said body portion and embracing said end of said bolt.

1,328,444.   SCHOOL-DESK. Anna Martin, Cincinnati, Ohio.   Filed Mar. 21, 1917.   Serial No. 156,271.   1 Claim.   (Cl. 45—6.)

In a school desk the combination of a frame comprising substantially vertical back supports and compartment supports at an angle to the back supports, said back and compartment supports having inclined ways formed upon their interior, a back secured to the back supports, a compartment secured upon the compartment supports,

and a partition mounted in the ways and forming with the bottom of the compartment and the back a V-shaped open-ended receptacle adapted to hold equipment for special branches of the scholar's course.

1,328,445.   APPARATUS FOR FLUSHING URINALS Dudley Newton, Berkeley, Calif.   Filed Sept. 6, 1918. Serial No. 252,925.   5 Claims.   (Cl. 4—18.)

4. The combination of a flushing tank, an air container therein having a closed top and an open bottom communicating with the remainder of the tank, means for maintaining a normal level of water therein, a conduit leading from the air container, a trap to which said conduit leads, a receptacle for receiving liquids, a siphon communicating with the receptacle, and a second conduit communicating between the trap and the siphon.

1,328,446.   PROCESS AND APPARATUS FOR ATOMIZING MATERIALS IN A MELTED STATE. Eugène Odam, Paris, France.   Filed Jan. 2, 1919.   Serial No. 269,388.   4 Claims.   (Cl. 83—91.)

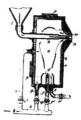

1. A process for the pulverization of molten materials, previously brought to the molten state, comprising pro-

ducing a jet of gases produced by the combustion under pressure of a fuel and introducing the molten material into said jet, said jet being concentric and parallel to the flow of said molten material into said jet, said molten material being pulverized by the sudden expansion of said gases in the air.

1,328,447. CONDIMENT - STOPPER. ELI J. PALMER, Chicago, Ill. Filed Feb. 4, 1918. Serial No. 215,301. 2 Claims. (Cl. 65—57.)

1. The combination with a container, of a cap removably engaged thereon having apertures therein, a sleeve secured therein having a passage therethrough a portion of which is of enlarged diameter, a weighted top movably disposed on said top, pins thereon adapted to normally engage in said apertures to keep the same clean, a tapered stem having a groove therein secured on said top adapted to slidably engage through the passaged sleeve to afford a guide for said top, said tapered stem projects through the enlarged passage of said sleeve affording a construction whereby packing of condiment around said stem is obviated, a guide pin on said top longer than said cleaning pins adapted to engage in one of said apertures to insure registration of said cleaning pins with the remaining apertures, and a spring clip removably engaged in said groove adapted to engage said sleeve to limit the outward movement of said weighted top.

1,328,448. AUTOMATIC RATCHET. CHESTER R. PIEPER, La Crosse, Wis., assignor to The Gund Manufacturing Company, La Crosse, Wis., a Corporation of Wisconsin. Filed Jan. 28, 1918. Serial No. 214,233. 2 Claims. (Cl. 248—6.)

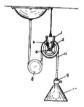

1. In an automatic ratchet for lamp cords and the like, the combination with a free running lamp cord having a lamp suspended at one end thereof, and a counterweight in a loop thereof, of a pulley positioned intermediate of said loop and said lamp, said pulley comprising in combination a support, a pulley wheel having a surface normally positioned in an angle to the vertical, and having an aperture in said surface, means carried by said pulley wheel support for allowing the rotation of said pulley wheel in one direction and to prevent the slow rotation of said pulley wheel in the opposite direction, but allowing the quick rotation of said pulley wheel in said last named direction.

1,328,449. UNIVERSAL JOINT. FRED H. REAM, Kansas City, Mo. Filed May 17, 1919. Serial No. 297,928. 1 Claim. (Cl. 64—91.)

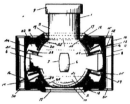

In a universal joint, the combination of a cored mobile member having a spherical body portion provided circumferentially with a series of radially projecting cogs having convexed sides and concentrically formed ends, and a halved annular housing member confining said mobile member, said housing member comprising two interlocking annular half sections divided in a plane oblique to the axis of the joint and provided in their outer sides with annular concentrically formed thrust bearings engaging opposite sides of the spherical body of the mobile member and a series of revoluble cone-shaped rollers imposed between the cogs of the spherical body of the mobile member and having their inner ends formed concentrically with the spherical body and bearing thereon.

1,328,450. CONTACT DEVICE. GUSTAVE B. REISBACH, Milwaukee, Wis., assignor to The Cutler-Hammer Mfg. Co., Milwaukee, Wis., a Corporation of Wisconsin. Filed Mar. 16, 1916. Serial No. 84,695. 11 Claims. (Cl. 200—166.)

1. A contact device comprising a contact shoe, a holder therefor, said shoe and holder having engaging parts to restrain lateral play of the former while permitting perpendicular play thereof, and resilient means opposing the latter play of said shoe, said shoe and said holder being adapted for relative positioning against the action of said resilient means to free certain of said engaging parts for permitting removal of said shoe from said holder.

1,328,451. SHAFT - BEARING CONSTRUCTION FOR WARPERS. ALONZO E. RHOADES, Hopedale, Mass., assignor to Draper Corporation, Hopedale, Mass., a Corporation of Maine. Filed May 29, 1919. Serial No. 300,562. 2 Claims. (Cl. 64—10.)

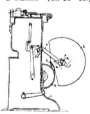

1. A shaft bearing construction comprising a bearing member having a cylindrical seat, a bearing sleeve fitting

said seat and the shaft, both said member and said sleeve having lateral openings of a width as great as the shaft diameter whereby when the said openings are in radial alinement the shaft may be passed therethrough into bearing position in the sleeve, an arm connected to and extended radially from the sleeve, a plate detachably secured to the end face of the bearing member having a sector shaped recess to receive said arm and to permit same to be rotarily adjusted therein with respect to the bearing member to bring the openings in said member and said sleeve in alinement and thus prevent the removal of the shaft, the detachability of said plate being adapted to permit the removal and replacement of the sleeve.

1,328,452. FILLING-REPLENISHING LOOM. ALONZO E. RHOADES, Hopedale, Mass., assignor to Draper Corporation, Hopedale. Mass., a Corporation of Maine. Filed July 28, 1919. Serial No. 313,951. 18 Claims. (Cl. 139—85.)

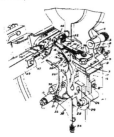

18. In a filling replenishing loom, a shuttle feeler, means for moving it rearwardly on call for replenishment of filling, a stop that engages the shuttle feeler and stops it in an intermediate position, and a trip for disengaging the stop from the shuttle feeler.

1,328,453. AUTOMATIC SPARK-CONTROLLING DEVICE. DANIEL ROESCH, Chicago, Ill. Filed July 17, 1915. Serial No. 40,355. 36 Claims. (Cl. 123—117.)

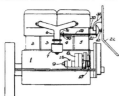

1. In a device of the class described, the combination with an engine and means for automatically timing the ignition of said engine according to changes in speed, of mechanisms connected to time the ignition of the engine independently or coincident with said means, comprising a fluid pressure operated element, communication means between said element and the manifold of said engine, and an adjustable device projecting into the interior of said manifold and adjustable into different positions therein to utilize the different effects of pressure and flow therein, said device connected and communicating with said last mentioned means.

1,328,454. ELECTRIC SIGNALING DEVICE. RALPH R. ROOT, Cleveland, Ohio. Filed Feb. 8, 1915. Serial No. 6,683. 3 Claims. (Cl. 177—7.)

2. In a signaling device, the combination of a supporting means, a diaphragm carried by the supporting

---

means, an electromagnet carried by the supporting means, an armature, means for transmitting the vibration of the armature to the diaphragm, a make and break de-

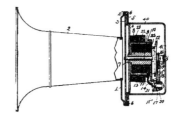

vice, a yoke carried by the supporting means, a cover incasing the operating parts of the device said cover being secured to the yoke.

1,328,455. BOTTLE CAP. LEVI M. ROSENTHAL, New York, N. Y., assignor to Samuel Rosenthal. New York, N. Y. Filed Apr. 4, 1916. Serial No. 88,771. 3 Claims. (Cl. 215—10.)

1. A bottle cap provided with an inner packing disk and having side walls, a central boss having an axis perpendicular to said packing disk, an intermediate annular portion connecting the said side walls and the said boss, the said intermediate annular portion being wider than the walls of the neck of the bottle to which the cap is to be applied, the top of the said boss being at substantially the same level as the top of the said side walls, the said intermediate annular portion having a shape out of conformity with the shape of the said packing disk, the said intermediate annular portion being substantially uniformly bendable, said intermediate annular portion being capable of being uniformly bent so as to raise said boss when the said side walls are fastened to the neck of the bottle, so that the top of the said boss is then raised with respect to the top of the said walls.

1,328,456. PROCESS AND APPARATUS FOR ORE SEPARATION. JAMES D. ROSS, Seattle, Wash. Filed July 27, 1916. Serial No. 111,604. 2 Claims. (Cl. 83—85.)

2. The herein described method of treating ore consisting in precipitating downwardly in an oblique path a downwardly oblique continuous stream of ore, sub-

jecting such continuous stream to successive jets of mixed air and water directed angularly into the ore pulp during the progress through such oblique path, and in removing portions of the ore by flotation at intervals between the successive jets of mixed air and water.

1,328,457. OVERLOAD DEVICE. ARTHUR R. SANBORN, Schenectady, N. Y., assignor to General Electric Company, a Corporation of New York. Filed Oct. 26, 1916. Serial No. 127,806. 12 Claims. (Cl. 175—294.)

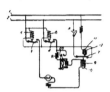

1. The combination with a circuit controlling electromagnetically actuated contactor, of means for opening the contactor and maintaining it open upon the occurrence of an overload, comprising a mechanically opened overload switch magnetically held in its open position by a normally deënergized magnet which is energized when the overload occurs through a circuit including the overload switch.

1,328,458. BUCKET. LOUIS SCHIEK and WILLIAM SCHIEK, Chicago, Ill. Filed Aug. 10, 1917. Serial No. 185,623. 3 Claims. (Cl. 280—61.)

1. A 'bucket having a band secured to and extending below the bottom thereof, a bead on said band, a wheeled base extending within said band and engaging said bead, and spring controlled latch rods having locking ends extending beyond said base and engaging said bead.

1,328,459. INSTRUMENT FOR PRODUCING INTRAOSSEOUS ANESTHESIA. ARTHUR E. SMITH, Chicago, Ill. Filed Oct. 18, 1918. Serial No. 258,706. 6 Claims. (Cl. 128—305.)

2. In combination, the following coöperative instruments, a double bladed lancet adapted to make an incision in the tissue and to separate the same and a drill guide of such size as to fit between the blades thereof.

1,328,460. AUTOMATIC CIRCUIT-BREAKER. RAYMOND D. SMITH, Arlington, Mass. Filed Sept. 7, 1916, Serial No. 118,908. Renewed Apr. 10, 1919. Serial No. 289,135. 17 Claims. (Cl. 200—116.)
1. An automatic circuit-breaker embodying in combination with means for making an breaking a circuit; a manually operable actuating member arranged to be movable relative to said means and adapted when so

moved to energize tensioning means tending to break the circuit; a detent device, with a controlling thermostat therefor, normally arranged and positioned to latch and hold said first means in a position to close the circuit against the opening action of said tension-

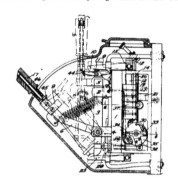

ing means; and a normally inactive heating unit operatively related to the said thermostat and operably related to said member whereby the said thermostat may be thermally energized to cause a release of said means from restraint by said detent device.

1,328,461. OBSERVATION-TOWER. JOSEPH B. STRAUSS, Chicago, Ill. Filed Dec. 28, 1914. Serial No. 879,319. 6 Claims. (Cl. 189—15.)

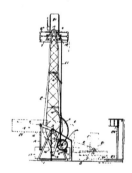

1. An observation tower comprising a support, a tower arm pivotally connected therewith, said tower arm made up of a plurality of sections adapted to be moved relatively to lengthen and shorten the tower, a carrying device pivotally connected with the outer end of said tower, and means for holding the said carrying device so that the base thereof will be substantially horizontal in all the various positions of the arm comprising an adjustable connection extending between said carrying device and a fixed part on said support, and means for simultaneously moving the sections of the tower relatively and adjusting said connection to lengthen or shorten the tower.

2. An observation device comprising a support, a tower arm made up of a plurality of sections adapted to be moved relatively to lengthen or shorten the tower, the lower section of said tower being rotatably mounted upon said support, a carrying device pivotally connected

to the upper section of said tower by two pivotal connections, one on each side thereof, an adjustable connecting device connecting said carrying device to the fixed part near the bottom of the tower, and which holds said carrying device substantially horizontal during all the various positions of the tower, mechanism for moving the sections of the tower relatively to lengthen or shorten the tower, and means for automatically adjusting said connecting device to compensate for the lengthening and shortening of said tower.

3. An observation device comprising a tower, having two sections, a support to which one section is pivotally connected, each of said sections having a plurality of metal angular pieces, one at each corner thereof, connecting pieces connecting the angular pieces of each section together to form the sections, the angular pieces of one section overlapping the angular pieces of the adjacent section to form sliding connection, and means for sliding the angular pieces of one section along the angular pieces of the adjacent section, to lengthen or shorten the tower.

4. An observation device comprising a support, a tower arm rotatably mounted on said support, and having two sections adapted to be moved relatively to lengthen and shorten the tower arm, a carrying device movably connected to the upper section of the tower arm, a controlling arm for keeping the carrying device in a substantially horizontal position during all the various positions of the tower arm, said controlling arm having two relatively movable sections one connected with the carrying device and the other connected with a fixed part near the bottom of the other arm, tooth racks associated with the upper section of said tower arm and said means for simultaneously driving said pinions so as to simultaneously move relatively the sections of said tower arm and the sections of said controlling arm to vary the height of said controlling device.

5. An observation tower comprising a tower arm, a portable device upon which said tower arm is pivotally mounted, a carrying device pivotally connected with the outer end of said tower arm, a controlling arm pivotally connected with said carrying device and said portable device, the tower arm and controlling arm being made in sections, and means for moving said sections relatively so as to shorten and lengthen the tower arm.

1,328,462. COMBINED FOLDING CHAIR AND TABLE. IGNACY STYNKOWIC, East Hammond, Ind. Filed May 7, 1919. Serial No. 295,405. 3 Claims. (Cl. 45—31.)

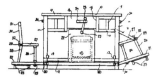

1. In a device of the class described, the combination with a table having four legs, of platforms hingedly engaged upon each side of said table, supports for said platforms, chairs arranged upon said platforms, said chairs each having a single pivoted front leg and a pair of rigid rear legs, and means for holding said chairs and platforms when in a folded position below the said table top.

1,328,463. SPARK-PLUG FOR INTERNAL-COMBUSTION ENGINES. WALTER EVERETT TAFT, Providence, R. I., assignor to The Associate Company, Boston, Mass., a Corporation of Massachusetts. Filed Mar. 6, 1917. Serial No. 152,863. 2 Claims. (Cl. 123—169.)

1. In a spark plug, comprising a pair of electrodes for coöperating one with the other, one of the said electrodes being in the form of a straight wire, and axially positioned in the spark plug structure, the other

of the said electrodes consisting of a washer-like structure having an opening through which the said wire extends, the walls of the said opening opposed to the said wire being in spaced relation to the said wire, the said walls being in the form of a plurality of inwardly

projecting annular ribs having a V-shaped cross-section, the adjacent ribs being separated by a recess of appreciable width and depth, and the said washer-like structure being composed of a plurality of washers each of which has a hole with beveled side walls.

1,328,464. FILM-TREATING APPARATUS. FREDRICK B. THOMPSON, Chicago, Ill. Filed Aug. 16, 1915. Serial No. 45,846. 9 Claims. (Cl. 193—2.)

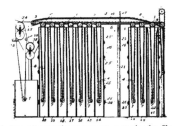

1. In a film treating apparatus, a carrier for film tape consisting of a sprocket chain comprising articulate side portions comprising alternate links of different depth, and cross-bars connecting the links of greater depth on opposite sides of the chain with each other and affording a foraminous support for the film tape, the pivotal connections between the links of said articulate side portions being loosely made to permit free relative pivotal movement of said links and permitting lateral distortion of the structure, whereby the same may be twisted to form a helix.

1,328,465. SYSTEM OF POWER TRANSMISSION. ROBERT TREAT, Schenectady, N. Y., assignor to General Electric Company, a Corporation of New York Filed Mar. 4, 1918. Serial No. 220,268. 7 Claims. (Cl. 172—120.)

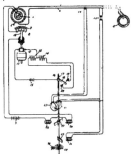

1. The combination with a synchronous dynamo-electric machine, of a source of alternating current for

driving the same, means for exciting said machine, and means responsive both to the alternating current power and the alternating current voltage supplied to said machine for varying the excitation thereof.

1,328,466. CIGAR-LIGHTER. TYCHO VAN ALLER, Schenectady, N. Y., assignor to General Electric Company, a Corporation of New York. Filed Oct. 19, 1917. Serial No. 197,417. 5 Claims. (Cl. 219—32.)

1. An electric heating device comprising the combination with a pair of similarly formed insulating slabs, of a U-shaped member embedded in the face of one slab, screws entering said U-shaped member for securing said slabs together, two conducting strips fastened to the inner face of one of said slabs and adapted for connection with a source of electric current, a heating unit placed over said U-shaped members, said unit having conducting pins thrust into frictional engagement with said conducting strips and a perforated cap supported by said U-shaped member.

1,328,467. UNIVERSAL MOTOR. ALFRED F. WELCH, Fort Wayne, Ind., assignor to General Electric Company, a Corporation of New York. Filed Jan. 4, 1918. Serial No. 210,259. 4 Claims. (Cl. 172—276.)

1. A commutator motor designed for operation on either alternating or direct currents comprising an armature winding and a field winding connected in series therewith, the number of ampere turns in said field winding being equal to the square root of $C^2 + E^2$, where C is the number of compensating ampere turns necessary for substantially neutralizing the reaction of the armature winding and E is the number of exciting ampere turns necessary for giving efficient and satisfactory operation as a universal motor, the axis of said field winding being displaced from the axis of said armature winding by an angle whose cosine is

$$\frac{C}{\sqrt{C^2+E^2}}$$

1,328,468. FURNACE FOR OIL-CRACKING STILLS. FRANK E. WELLMAN, Kansas City, Kans., assignor to The Kansas City Gasoline Company, Kansas City, Kans., a Corporation of Kansas. Filed Jan. 19, 1917. Serial No. 143,357. 8 Claims. (Cl. 263—9.)

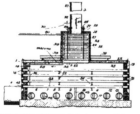

1. A furnace for cracking retorts comprising a heating chamber, a source of heat therefor, a plurality of ducts leading from said source to different points within said chamber, a damper for each of said ducts, operating means common to a plurality of said dampers and means for separately adjusting the position of each damper in relation to the common operating means.

1,328,469. SCREW-GRINDING MACHINE. WILLIAM WENDTLAND, New York, N. Y. Filed Sept. 19, 1918. Serial No. 254,725. 3 Claims. (Cl. 51—4.)

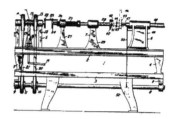

1. In a machine of the class described, a bed with a head stock, a tail stock, and master screw supports, a master screw mounted in said supports, a center for a blank secured to said master screw, another center to receive one end of the blank mounted in a spindle of the tail stock, means for mounting the spindle so that it can slide in the tail stock and means for causing the center of the spindle of the tail stock to properly engage the blank at all times regardless of the position in which the blank places the spindle through the action of the master screw.

1,328,470. GARMENT-RETAINER FOR TRUNKS. GEORGE HENRY WHEARY, Racine, Wis. Filed June 7, 1915. Serial No. 32,508. 5 Claims. (Cl. 190—36.)

1. The combination with a trunk provided with garment hangers, of a garment retainer therefor, comprising flexible members connected at their upper end portions to the trunk and extending over and downwardly in front of the hangers, a transverse spacing bar to which the lower ends of the flexible members are connected in spaced relation, a strap connected at one end to the spacing bar, and a member to which the opposite end of the strap is connected.

1,328,471. WOOD-SPLITTING MACHINE. HORACE M. YOUNG, Niagara Falls, N. Y. Filed Sept. 16, 1918. Serial No. 254,182. 30 Claims. (Cl. 144—193.)

1. In a wood splitting machine, a support, a wood splitting element in operative relation to said support, means for feeding wood to said wood splitting element, and means for gaging the wood to size to separate the split pieces larger than a given size from the pieces of or smaller than the given size.

10. A portable wood splitting machine comprising a reach or bed, axles to which said reach or bed is secured, wheels on said axles, splitting disks above said reach or bed, means for feeding wood to the successive splitting disks, a trough beneath said bed adapted to be elevated when transporting said machine, and means for holding said trough in elevated position.

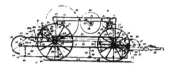

18. In combination, in a wood splitting machine, means for splitting wood, means for separating wood according to sizes after being split, and means for automatically returning pieces larger than a predetermined size to the feeding end of said machine.

1,328,472. ENVELOP-CLASPING MACHINE. HARRY F. AFFELDER, Cleveland, Ohio. Filed May 11, 1917. Serial No. 167,879. 14 Claims. (Cl. 93—61.)

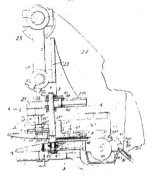

1. In a machine of the character described, a bed or frame having supporting means for two different portions of an envelop, means for feeding through the machine adjacent the supporting means two strips of material with plain, substantially parallel edges one for forming clasps and the other reinforcing tabs, coöperating punches and dies for making a clasp from one strip and applying the same to one portion of the envelop and in the same operation for forming a tab from the other strip and applying it to another portion of the envelop, and means for operating the feeding means for the two strips and the clasp and tab forming and applying members in predetermined relationship.

1,328,473. MEANS FOR CONTROLLING ALTERNATING CURRENTS. ERNST F. W. ALEXANDERSON, Schenectady, N. Y., assignor to General Electric Company, a Corporation of New York. Filed Apr. 20, 1918. Serial No. 229,686. 7 Claims. (Cl. 171—119.)

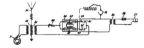

1. Means for controlling the flow of high frequency currents comprising two magnetic cores and a winding

---

on each core, means for causing the high frequency current to be controlled to flow through the two windings in parallel and means for causing a controlling current to flow through the two windings in series.

1,328,474. PUMP. JOHN ASTROM, Fort Wayne, Ind., assignor to Fort Wayne Engineering & Manufacturing Co., Fort Wayne, Ind. Filed Nov. 11, 1919. Serial No. 337,274. 3 Claims. (Cl. 103—75.)

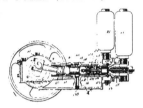

1. A pump structure comprising a crank casing, an inclosed cross-head guideway and a pump cylinder all formed in a single casting, valve mechanism at the outer end of the cylinder, a cross-head in said guideway, a crank in the crank casing connected with said cross-head, a piston plunger connected with the cross-head and extending into the pump cylinder, packing on said plunger in the pump cylinder, and an annular inclosed chamber surrounding the piston plunger between the cross-head guideway and pump cylinder.

1,328,475. FIREARM. ALBERT MAURICE AUBERT, Billancourt, France. Filed July 3, 1917. Serial No. 178,505. 4 Claims. (Cl. 42—4.)

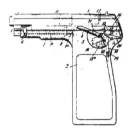

1. In an automatic fire arm, the combination with the frame and the breech slide thereon, said slide having two notches; of an arcuate shaped trigger pivoted in the frame, a trigger lever thereon projecting at the side thereof for operation by the thumb, said arcuate trigger having a nose for engaging said notches.

1,328,476. COPY-HOLDER. WILLIAM H. AVERILL, Boston, Mass., assignor to Owl Supply Company, Boston, Mass., a Corporation of Massachusetts. Filed June 15, 1915. Serial No. 34,157. 8 Claims. (Cl. 120—28.)

1. A copy-holder comprising a base formed to bestride a horizontal member of a typewriter frame, and composed of outer and inner ears and a connecting neck, said outer ear being provided with means for clamping the base to the frame member, and with a vertical socket, the upper end of which terminates approximately in the plane of the upper edge of said outer ear, a short stud shaped to removably engage said socket and adapted to turn on a vertical axis in said socket, a supporting arm, one end of said arm and the upper end of said stud having complemental frictional hinge members located contiguous to the outer end of said socket, a horizontal pintle connect-

ing said hinge members and provided with means for regulating the frictional engagement thereof to maintain the arm either vertically in alinement with the stud or at various inclinations thereto, and copy-engaging means

carried by said arm at the other end thereof, the copy engaged by said means being adjustable by rotative movement of the stud in the socket, and by swinging movements of the arm on the stud.

1,328,477. TIME-RETARDED CUT-OFF SWITCH. MALCOLM H. BAKER, Braintree, Mass.; Marie H. Baker, administratrix of said Malcolm H. Baker, deceased, assignor to Kenneth W. Crosby, trustee, Boston, Mass. Filed Mar. 29, 1915, Serial No. 17,805. Renewed Apr. 14, 1919. Serial No. 290,081. 37 Claims. (Cl. 200—122.)

1. The combination of an electric switch, an electric load connected to be governed thereby; an auxiliary circuit connected in shunt to said load; an automatic circuit breaker arranged in said circuit for opening said switch and having a time limit,—the current through said auxiliary circuit producing mechanical energy for releasing the circuit breaker; and means automatically to deënergize said auxiliary circuit when said switch is opened by said circuit breaker.

1,328,478. THERMODYNAMICALLY-CONTROLLED SOCKET-SWITCH FOR ELECTRIC LIGHTS. MALCOLM H. BAKER, Braintree, Mass.; Marie H. Baker, administratrix of said Malcolm H. Baker, deceased, assignor to Kenneth W. Crosby, trustee, Boston, Mass. Filed Sept. 24, 1915, Serial No. 52,401. Renewed Apr. 14, 1919. Serial No. 290,082. 10 Claims. (Cl. 200—122.)

1. In an electric lamp switch, in combination; a circuit path through the switch to one terminal of the

lamp; a continued path through the switch from the other terminal of the lamp; a pair of contacting members in series with the said circuit path, one of said members being resiliently mounted to tend normally to separate from the other member; a resistance in series with said contacting members between said resiliently mounted member and the related lamp terminal; manually controlled means adapted to position and to maintain said resiliently mounted member in contact with said other member; a detent and controlling thermostat therefor positioned, when deënergized, and by engagement with said resiliently mounted member to maintain said contact after said manually controlled means are withdrawn, and adapted, when energized to release said resiliently mounted member for circuit breaking movement thereof; and a shunt circuit around said resistance and including said manually controlled means,—whereby when said latter means are withdrawn from engagement with said resiliently mounted member, said resistance is thereby placed solely in series with the lamp circuit and rendered operative to energize the thermostat.

1,328,479. THERMODYNAMICALLY-CONTROLLED SOCKET-SWITCH FOR ELECTRIC LIGHTS. MALCOLM H. BAKER, Braintree, Mass.; Marie H. Baker, administratrix of said Malcolm H. Baker, deceased, assignor to Kenneth W. Crosby, trustee, Boston, Mass. Filed Sept. 28, 1915, Serial No. 53,052. Renewed Apr. 14, 1919. Serial No. 290,083. 8 Claims. (Cl. 200—122.)

1. In an electric lamp socket switch, in combination; a current path through the switch to one terminal of the lamp; a return current path through the switch from the other terminal of the lamp; a pair of coöperative contact members in series with said first path, one of said members being resiliently mounted normally to separate from the other member; a flexing, resilient thermostat positioned when normally cool to prevent contact breaking movement of said resiliently mounted member relative to said other member; a resistance winding carried by said thermostat for heating the same; a shunt circuit across the lamp terminals and containing said resistance winding; an auxiliary contact device adapted normally to close said shunt circuit; and manual control means adapted by engagement with said resiliently mounted member to move the latter into contact with said other member and simultaneously to actuate said device for opening said shunt circuit, and further arranged when withdrawn from engagement with said resiliently mounted member, to permit said auxiliary contact device to close the said shunt circuit,—thereby to energize said thermostat for permitting circuit-breaking movement of said resiliently mounted member after a predetermined time.

1,328,480. THERMODYNAMICALLY-CONTROLLED PENDENT SWITCH FOR ELECTRIC CIRCUITS. MALCOLM H. BAKER, Braintree, Mass.; Marie H. Baker, administratrix of said Malcolm H. Baker, deceased, assignor to Kenneth W. Crosby, trustee, Boston, Mass. Filed Oct. 21, 1915, Serial No. 57,104. Renewed Apr. 14, 1919. Serial No. 290,085. 6 Claims. (Cl. 200—122.)

1. In an electric switch, the combination with main circuit controlling contacts adapted normally to open, and thermostatic control means arranged to be electrothermally operated for governing the opening of said

contacts, of a manually operable control rod arranged for longitudinal, reciprocative movement between switch-closing and switch-opening positions thereof, mechanism arranged to be operated by said rod for closing said contacts, detent means arranged yieldingly to hold said rod in the said two positions thereof, and a circuit controlling device connected electrically to govern said means

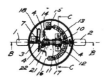

and positioned to be operated by said rod;—whereby in the switch closing position of said rod, said means are deënergized and thereby positioned to prevent opening of said contacts when said rod is moved to its said switch-opening position, and whereby movement of said rod to its said latter position energizes said means for permitting the opening of said contacts after a predetermined time.

1,328,481. FLUSH PUSH-BUTTON SWITCH FOR ELECTRIC CIRCUITS. MALCOLM H. BAKER, Braintree, Mass.; Marie H. Baker, administratrix of said Malcolm H. Baker, deceased, assignor to Kenneth W. Crosby, trustee, Boston, Mass. Filed Nov. 8, 1915, Serial No. 60,457. Renewed Apr. 14, 1919. Serial No. 290,087. 6 Claims. (Cl. 200—122.)

1. In an electric circuit switch having a pivoted contact member arranged for rocking movement and manual controlling means to cause rocking of the same to close and to open the switch, in combination automatic switch opening mechanism comprising a detent and controlling thermostat therefor positioned when the said thermostat is thermally deënergized to prevent the switch opening movement of said rocking member, rocking driving means for said member and having a resilient connection therewith, a detent device to hold said driving means when moved to a position to put a switch opening tension on said member, a normally inoperative electric heater for the thermostat, and means, controlled by said driving means in said last mentioned position theerof, and adapted to establish said heater in operable relation to the switch controlled circuit.

1,328,482. THERMODYNAMICALLY - CONTROLLED ELECTRIC SWITCH. MALCOLM H. BAKER, Braintree, Mass.; Marie H. Baker, administratrix of said Malcolm H. Baker, deceased, assignor to Kenneth W. Crosby, trustee, Boston, Mass. Filed Nov. 8, 1915, Serial No. 60,458. Renewed Apr. 14, 1919. Serial No. 290,088. 7 Claims. (Cl. 200—122.)
1. An electric circuit switch embodying in combination; a yielding contact member; a coöperative contact element comprising a thermo-dynamically impelled conductor adapted upon suitable thermal change to break contact with said member; a heating resistance for said element; a manually controllable device operatively re-

lated to said element whereby said element may be placed and normally maintained in contact with said member; auxiliary circuit-controlling means operably re-

lated to said device for governing said heating resistance, whereby the latter is energized at one position of said device and deënergized at another position thereof.

1,328,483. SHAKING-TABLE. ALONZO LINTON BAUSMAN, Chicopee, Mass., assignor to National Equipment Company, Springfield, Mass., a Corporation of Massachusetts. Filed Mar. 8, 1919. Serial No. 281,514. 3 Claims. (Cl. 107—8.)

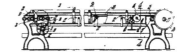

1. A shaking table, comprising, a flexible carrier having downwardly extending projections thereon, a support for the carrier provided with upwardly extending projections, means to move the carrier over its support to cause the projections thereon to ride over the projections on the support, and means for varying the engagement between the projections on the carrier and the projections on the support.

1,328,484. EXPLOSIVE-ENGINE. ASHLEY C. BENNETT, Minneapolis, Minn. Filed Apr. 8, 1915. Serial No. 19,862. 2 Claims. (Cl. 123—44.)

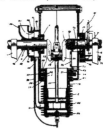

1. A rotary explosive engine comprising a fixed crank shaft and a plurality of cylinders rotatable about said crank shaft, a sleeve for each cylinder, a piston operating in each sleeve, said cylinders and sleeves being provided with coöperating ports whereby rotation of the sleeves will control the admission and exhaust of each cylinder, a spiral gear on the crankshaft, a shaft having operative connection with each sleeve, each of said shafts having a spiral gear meshing with the spiral gear on the crank shaft whereby rotation of the shafts with the cylinders will rotate the sleeves, and means to slide the crankshaft spiral gear for simultaneously varying the relation of the cylinder ports and sleeve ports in each cylinder to advance or retard the point of beginning of admission and exhaust as may be desired.

1,328,485. EXPLOSION - ARRESTER. EDWARD R. BERRY, Malden, Mass., assignor to General Electric Company, a Corporation of New York. Filed Jan. 31, 1918. Serial No. 214,760. 6 Claims. (Cl. 48—192.)

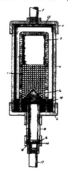

1. A device for extinguishing the backfiring in gas burning apparatus, comprising a receptacle having an inlet and an outlet adapted to be connected in a gas supply conduit, a porous diaphragm of retractory material inclosing a part of the space within said receptacle in the path of the gas flow, a quantity of easily fusible material within said inclosed space and means for retaining said material when fused to cut off the flow of gas.

1,328,486. MIXING APPARATUS FOR GRANULAR, POWDERED, OR THE LIKE MATERIAL. WILLIAM STAETTELL HUMPHREYS BEVIN and JOHN STANLEY RAWSTHORNE, Liverpool, England. Filed June 26, 1917. Serial No. 176,984. 1 Claim. (Cl. 83—73.)

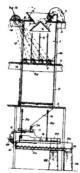

In an apparatus for intimately admixing granular or powdered material, in combination, an upper receptacle divided into a plurality of compartments, a lower receptacle divided into a plurality of compartments, the compartments of said lower receptacle being arranged transversely of the compartments in the upper receptacle, a separate floor pivoted in each of said upper and lower compartments, and means for tilting said floors upon their pivots, for the purpose set forth.

1,328,487. MINE LOADING-MACHINE. FRANK BILLINGS, Cleveland, Ohio. Filed Sept. 6, 1912. Serial No. 718,883. 7 Claims. (Cl. 37—14.)

1. In a loading machine, the combination of a ram, a pair of jaws at the outer end thereof having bottom and side walls and movable in an approximate horizontal plane toward and away from each other, scraper members with respect to which the jaws are movable, the

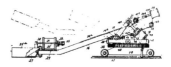

bottom and end edges of the scrapers extending adjacent the said walls of the jaws and maintaining such relationship during the opening movement of the jaws and means for moving the jaws.

1,328,488. DUST-CAP AND ATTACHING MEANS THEREFOR. JUNIUS A. BOWDEN, Los Angeles, Calif. Filed Mar. 22, 1919. Serial No. 284,415. 8 Claims. Cl. 152—12.)

1. As means of holding a dust cap detachably connected to a nut, a metal band formed with a series of spring tongues integral therewith, said band adapted to be secured to said nut, said tongues formed to flare outwardly of said band and flattened at the juncture of the tongues where the tongues join the band, said cap adapted to detachably coengage said band.

1,328,489. RAILROAD WAY CONSTRUCTION AND MAINTENANCE CAR. ROBERT E. BRESSLER, Hammond, Ind., assignor to O. F. Jordan Company, East Chicago, Ind., a Corporation of Indiana. Filed Sept. 3, 1918. Serial No. 252,398. 10 Claims. (Cl. 37—58.)

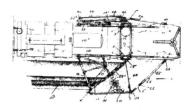

1. The improvements herein described comprising a car, in combination with a side wing having its inner end pivoted thereto, a material carrying wing having its rear end pivoted to the side wing, means for swinging the side wing, and combined means for bracing the forward end of the material carrying wing and for causing it to swing when the swinging movement is imparted to the side wing.

1,328,490. GOVERNOR TO CONTROL ELECTRIC TERMINALS. ANDREW J. BROOKINS, Chicago, Ill. Filed Dec. 9. 1918. Serial No. 265,868. 6 Claims. (Cl. 200—80.)

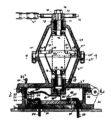

1. In a governor, an axially movable and rotatably mounted member, ball members, and means connected thereto to convert the movement of said ball members, by centrifugal force, to axial movement of said rotatably mounted member, said ball members comprising a plurality of elements in spaced relation and balls interposed between said elements, in combination with a track positioned in the path of movement of one of said plurality of elements to limit upon a pre-determined movement thereof by centrifugal force the outward travel, of said ball members.

1,328,491. BRAKE. FRANK M. CAMPBELL, South Bend, Wash. Filed Sept. 13, 1918. Serial No. 253,879. 2 Claims. (Cl. 188—3.)

2 A pneumatic vehicle brake comprising a member fixed relative to the vehicle and having a central hub surrounding the axle next to a wheel, said hub having external, axially extending ribs and peripheral recesses for the reception of packing rings, said fixed member also having an outwardly spaced cylindrical flange also provided with packing-ring-receiving grooves, packing rings in each set of grooves, a braking disk having two cylindrical flanges fitting each upon its respective packing rings, the inner of said flanges having axially extending ribs meshing with the ribs of the fixed member, rods connecting both said members, springs surrounding said rods and acting to draw said members together, and means for supplying air under pressure to the space between said two members.

1,328,492. WORK-HOLDING CRADLE FOR SPIKE-HOLE-PLUG MACHINES. FRANK V. CARMAN, Oakland, Calif. Filed Oct. 27, 1919. Serial No. 333,785. 9 Claims. (Cl. 144—12.)
1. A work-holding-cradle comprising a carriage; a cradle-body mounted on the carriage for axial rotation;

means for locking the body at the limits of a quarter revolution; a movable follower in the body for feeding

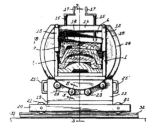

the work forward; and means at the forward end of the cradle body for clamping the work.

1,328,493. HAND-BRAKE-OPERATING MECHANISM. JAMES A. CARNEY, Aurora, Ill. Filed June 4, 1914. Serial No. 843,004. 12 Claims. (Cl. 74—16.)

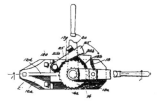

1. In a device of the class described, a bracket adapted to be attached to a car wall and having an offset bearing portion, a drum rotatably mounted in said bearing portion and extending therefrom toward said car wall, a shaft extending through said drum, a ratchet carried by said drum, a lever mounted on said shaft, a gravity actuated pawl pivoted on said lever normally to engage said ratchet, whereby said ratchet will be rotated upon proper movement of the lever, and a gravity actuated detent to prevent reverse rotation of the ratchet.

1,328,494. BRAKE-OPERATING MECHANISM. JAMES A. CARNEY, Aurora, Ill. Filed Aug. 31, 1914. Serial No. 859,390. 12 Claims. (Cl. 188—57.)

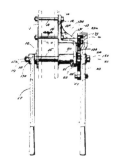

1. In a device of the class described, a bracket member adapted to be attached to a car wall, a shaft supported by said bracket member, a drum rotatably mounted on said shaft, a ratchet wheel carried by said drum, a

lever mounted on said shaft adjacent said ratchet wheel and normally depending therefrom, a pawl pivoted on said lever and actuated by gravity to engage normally said ratchet wheel whereby rotation of said lever in one direction will rotate said ratchet wheel, a detent member to prevent reverse rotation of said ratchet wheel, and means carried by said lever independently of said pawl to disengage said detent upon abnormal throw of said lever.

1,328,495. X-RAY APPARATUS. WILLIAM D. COOLIDGE, Schenectady, N. Y., assignor to General Electric Company, a Corporation of New York. Filed July 15, 1918. Serial No. 245,054. 9 Claims. (Cl. 250—34.)

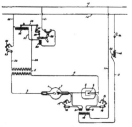

1. An X-ray system comprising the combination of an X-ray tube, a current limiting device in circuit with said tube, means for varying the X-ray output of said tube and automatic means for simultaneously changing the setting of said current-limiting device.

1,328,496. PNEUMATIC SHOCK-ABSORBER. CHARLES H. COX, Los Angeles, Calif. Filed Aug. 22, 1918. Serial 251,027. 8 Claims. (Cl. 267—50.)

1. A pneumatic shock absorber comprising a rigid casing adaptable to anchorage; a pair of globular formed inflated and deformable, semi-flexible unionized air cushions attached to said casing, one at each end thereof; and a yieldingly supported duplex plunger having convex ends slidably mounted within said casing and in engagement with said cushions.

1,328,497. TURBINE INSTALLATION FOR SHIPS. EDGAR D. DICKINSON, Schenectady, N. Y., assignor to General Electric Company, a Corporation of New York. Filed June 14, 1918. Serial No. 239,931. 14 Claims. (Cl. 60—70.)

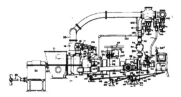

1. In combination, a main turbine, a cruising turbine, electrical clutch mechanism for connecting them together,

a switch for said clutch mechanism, controlling levers for said turbines, interloking mechanism for said levers, and means associated with said levers for controlling said switch.

1,328,498. NURLING-TOOL. ALEXANDER DJIDICS, New York, N. Y. Filed Feb. 10, 1919. Serial No. 276,152. 7 Claims. (Cl. 80—5.1.)

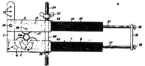

1. In a nurling tool, the combination with a pair of jaws carrying coöperating nurling wheels, of handles on said jaws adapted to be grasped together in the hand of the operator for the purpose specified, and means for yieldingly connecting said jaws together.

1,328,499. OIL-ENGINE. LOUIS K. DOBLLING, New Rochelle, N. Y., assignor to De La Vergne Machine Company, New York, N. Y., a Corporation of New York. Filed Dec. 10, 1915. Serial No. 66,064. 12 Claims. (Cl. 123—32.)

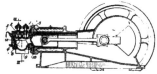

1. An oil engine having a combustion chamber supplied with oil and air only and provided with a spray injector delivering a mechanical oil spray thereto, inlet and exhaust valves disposed in the wall of said chamber in successive positions along the direction of the spray from said injector, a hot plate igniter forming the wall of the chamber opposite said valves and in position to intercept the said spray, in combination with a piston and cylinder communicating with the combustion chamber, and a valve-controlling system coördinated with the aforesaid parts whereby air is compressed in said chamber and the fuel is injected into same at or about compression dead center.

1,328,500. SCAFFOLD. WILLIAM M. DONALDSON, Portland, Oreg. Filed Mar. 22, 1918. Serial No. 224,033. 2 Claims. (Cl. 20—81.6.)

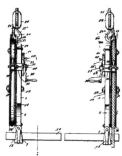

1. In a scaffold, the combination of a pair of hoists including frames, means carried by said hoists for raising

and lowering the same, each frame provided with stirrups, a stirrup plate carried by said stirrups, a bar provided with right and left handed threaded portions, mounted upon said frame contiguous to said stirrups, jaws upon said right and left handed threaded portions, means formed upon said jaws and said stirrup plate for slidably retaining the same together, and means for rotating said bar for causing said jaws to move relative to each other.

1,328,501. CONTROL OF ELECTRIC MOTORS. JOHN EATON, Schenectady, N. Y., assignor to General Electric Company, a Corporation of New York. Filed Dec. 8, 1916. Serial No. 135,892. 21 Claims. (Cl. 172—288.)

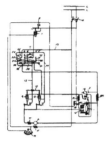

1. Means for controlling an electric motor, comprising a main reversing controller having contacts carrying the motor current, an electromagnetic switch for the motor circuit having an operating winding controlled by said contacts, and connections whereby throwing the controller to the reverse position causes the winding of said switch to be energized in accordance with the speed of the motor.

1,328,502. BRAKE. HERMAN C. EICHMEIER, St. Maries, Idaho. Filed Mar. 10, 1919. Serial No. 281,785. 3 Claims. (Cl. 74—13.)

2. In a brake device of the character described, the combination with a drive shaft, of a disk secured thereto for rotation therewith and having teeth, a relatively stationary member disposed upon one side of the disk, guide elements carried by said member, a second disk slidable upon the guide elements and having teeth to engage with the first named teeth, yielding means to move the second disk toward the first named disk, means serving to normally retain the second disk spaced from the first disk, and automatically operated upon the rotation of the first named disk in a reverse direction for releasing the second disk so that it is free to move toward the first disk, and separate means to move the second disk away from the first disk.

1,328,503. APPLE CUTTER AND CORER. SIVERT A. ERDAHL, Madison, Minn. Filed Aug. 6, 1919. Serial No. 315,665. 2 Claims. (Cl. 146—6.)

1. An implement of the class described comprising a base, a lever pivoted on the base and having an arched

portion with a hand grip at its extreme end, said arched portion having perforations in its lower extremities and

at its upper portion and cutting members having apertured portions adapted for removable attachment through the perforations.

1,328,504. GARMENT-SUPPORTER. JOHN ETZEL, East Pittsburgh, Pa. Filed Aug. 27, 1917. Serial No. 188,369. 1 Claim. (Cl. 24—261.)

In a garment supporter, a clasp formed with one closed end, the sides of said clasp being crossed and terminating in oppositely disposed regularly curved extremities, said sides being formed with oppositely disposed humps between the closed end and the point at which they are crossed, said sides, further, being formed with offset portions between said humps and the said curved extremities, said offset portions being disposed in opposite directions whereby the tips of the curved extremities are caused to lie one above the other.

1,328,505. PROCESS OF DRYING LUMBER. FREDERICK K. FISH, Jr., New York, N. Y., assignor to Lumber Tie and Timber Vulcanizing Company, New York, N. Y. Filed Sept. 20, 1916, Serial No. 121,187. Renewed Nov. 9, 1918. Serial No. 261,938. 92 Claims. (Cl. 99—123.)

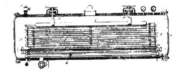

1. The process of treating wood comprising subjecting the wood to superheated water until its water soluble constituents are dissolved and with its sap water largely removed and the wood thoroughly sterilized throughout, and arresting the treatment before any deterioration of the wood occurs, to produce a wood resistant to decay and with its strength and elastic properties unimpaired.

8. The process of treating wood comprising submerging the wood in a fixed body of water under pressure and with heat to extract water-soluble constituents and sap water from the wood and melt the resins therein, removing the water, and subsequently subjecting the wood to a temperature sufficient to induce evaporation of the moisture in the wood and prevent hardening of the resins and cause the resins to permeate the individual fibers of the wood.

10. The process of treating wood by subjecting it to a deposition of tanning collodial substances on the surface

portions of the wood thereby tanning the same while removing the major portion of the water soluble constituents.

11. The herein described process which comprises treating the wood to remove the major portion of the water soluble constituents and sap water therefrom, and expand the fibers thereof, then drying the wood to remove the major portion of the moisture in the wood, the tanning colloids removed from the wood and retained in the water being deposited on the fibers of the wood to thereby tan the same.

1,328,506. STERILIZED WOOD. FREDERICK K. FISH, Jr., New York, N. Y., assignor to Lumber Tie and Timber Vulcanizing Company, New York, N. Y. Filed Sept. 27, 1916, Serial No. 122,415. Renewed Apr. 18, 1919. Serial No. 291,171. 21 Claims. (Cl. 99—12.)

1. As a new article of manufacture, wood having its gummy sap matters removed therefrom and its natural preservatives disseminated throughout the wood structure.

10. As a new article of manufacture, a sterilized wood having a portion of its soluble part of its sap removed and the preservative part of the sap, or as much of it as has not been converted into soluble constituents retained and set therein, and its individual fibers permeated by its resins.

17. A tanned wood having soluble gums and sap water removed therefrom, and its colloids retained and adsorbed on the fibers of the wood.

1,328,507. PROCESS OF DRYING LUMBER. FREDERICK K. FISH, Jr., New York, N. Y. Filed Jan. 18, 1918, Serial No. 212,467. Renewed Aug. 13, 1919. Serial No. 317,392. 49 Claims. (Cl. 34—24.)

1. The process of treating wood which comprises applying to wood water in a superheated condition, then submerging the wood therewith, and permeating the wood throughout and arresting the treatment and removing the water before any substantial destruction of the fibers occurs to remove the major portion of the fermentable substances.

12. The process of treating wood which comprises preheating wood applying to and surrounding the wood with superheated water, which has been similarly used, removing the superheated water and subsequently subjecting the wood to a temperature sufficient to induce evaporation of the moisture in the wood and prevent hardening of the resins thereby causing the resins to permeate the fibers of the wood.

13. The process of treating wood comprising subjecting the wood to the action of a vacuum to remove the air therefrom, then submerging the wood in fluid under pressure to dissolve and extract the soluble gums and sap, subsequently drying the wood, and thereafter conditioning the wood.

1,328,508. TIPPING HAND-TOOL. MARCUS FRIED, Lawrence, Mass. Filed July 20, 1918. Serial No. 245,886. 5 Claims. (Cl. 81—15.)

1. A tool of the character described having pivotally connected arms, male and female dies normally sepa-

rated and yieldingly carried by said arms to compensate for the arcs of movement of said arms, and means for insuring accurate interengagement of the dies when brought together.

1,328,509. METHOD OF FORMING RINGS FROM SOLID BARS. JOSEPH A. GANSTER, Philadelphia, Pa. Filed June 21, 1917. Serial No. 176,001. 6 Claims. (Cl. 29—156.)

1. The method of forming rings from solid bars, which consists in rotating a bar, applying a forming mandrel axially to the end of the bar to displace the material thereof and form a recess therein, removing the mandrel from the recess, subjecting the wall of the recess to radial pressure to size the same, and severing a section of the recessed portion of the bar to form a ring.

1,328,510. INSULATED HANDLE FOR ALUMINIUM SAUCEPANS. FRANCIS WILLIAM GOWER, HUGH JAMES OWEN, and ERNEST COX, Birmingham, England. Filed Apr. 15, 1919. Serial No. 290,313. 3 Claims. (Cl. 16—169.)

1. A culinary vessel comprising a cast body part, with an integral tubular boss, a tubular handle with an outer free end, a tubular connecting piece upon opposite ends of which the boss and the handle are cast and a metallic washer interposed between the inner end of the handle part and the boss, the handle and connecting piece being formed with interlocking means by which an unobstructed air space is provided in the handle and connecting piece.

1,328,511. SUSPENDED ARCH FOR BOILERS AND THE LIKE. WALTER E. GEHRING, Milwaukee, Wis. Filed May 12, 1919. Serial No. 296,446. 5 Claims. (Cl. 263—46.)

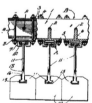

1. A structure of the class described comprising a support including a longitudinally extending member, a

[by the member and slidable
:h of said handers having a
number of blocks, each having
opening through opposite sides
alined, each of said blocks be-
respective hanger by sliding the
over out of the slot of the former
he same until said hanger is out
of the sides of the block.

plurality of hang
longitudinally
block holder-
a holder
thereof,
ing der

BEARING. KARL H. HANSEN, Se-
wagner, by mesne assignments, to Kop-
r and Equipment Company, Pittsburgh,
.u. of Pennsylvania. Filed Nov. 3, 1917.
62 1 Claim. (Cl. 105—224.)

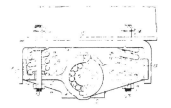

In an axle-bearing or journal-box, the combination of
a box having extensions forming spring-seats, an inverted U-shaped pedestal-strap, bolts carried by the car-
frame and supporting said box and said strap, and
springs surrounding said bolts and interposed between
said strap and said spring seats.

1,328,513. SYSTEM OF CONTROL. RUDOLF E. HELL-
MUND, Swissvale, Pa., assignor to Westinghouse Electric and Manufacturing Company, a Corporation of Pennsylvania. Filed Mar. 14, 1917. Serial No. 154,864. 19
Claims. (Cl. 172—179.)

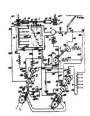

1. In a system of regenerative control, the combination with a supply circuit and a momentum-driven
dynamo-electric machine, of independent means for inherently imparting a predetermined compound characteristic to said machine, and means coöperating with
said independent means for automatically adjusting
the machine speed.

1,328,514. SYSTEM OF CONTROL. RUDOLF E. HELL-
MUND, Swissvale, Pa., assignor to Westinghouse Electric & Manufacturing Company, a Corporation of Pennsylvania. Filed May 26, 1917. Serial No. 171,166. 24
Claims. (Cl. 172—179.)
1. In a system of control, the combination with a
dynamo-electric machine, of means for regulating the

machine speed while normal load conditions prevail,
and other means for automatically controlling the load

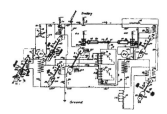

conditions of the machine to prevent abnormal electrical
conditions in said machine while it remains connected for
operation.

1,328,515. SYSTEM OF CONTROL. RUDOLF E. HELL-
MUND, Swissvale, Pa., assignor to Westinghouse Electric & Manufacturing Company, a Corporation of
Pennsylvania. Filed Aug. 7, 1917. Serial No. 184,797.
19 Claims. (Cl. 172—179.)

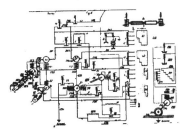

1. In a system of control, the combination with a
dynamo-electric machine having an armature and a field
winding, of means for varying the field-winding excitation
to automatically maintain a substantially constant machine speed, means for manually determining said constant speed, and means for directly modifying certain
portions of the machine circuits to prevent predetermined abnormal electrical conditions of the machine.

1,328,516. CIGAR-LIGHTER. MAURICE A. HEMSING,
Davenport, Iowa, assignor to Davenport Manufacturing
Company, Davenport, Iowa. Filed June 24, 1918.
Serial No. 241,497. 4 Claims. (Cl. 175—296.)

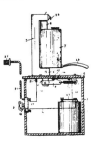

2. In combination with a suitably mounted standard,
provided at its upper end with an electric terminal, and

a lamp rockingly mounted and provided with a wick-tube in proximity to said terminal; a spring-controlled bar operatively connected with said lamp and provided with a circuit-closing member; a wire terminal supported in the path of said circuit-closing member; and means for imparting a supply of electrical energy to said terminals and being operable by a key removable therefrom.

1,328,517. POWER-TRANSMISSION MACHINE. WILLIAM S. HOLDAWAY, Jr., Salt Lake City, Utah. Filed Jan. 20, 1919. Serial No. 272,213. 7 Claims. (Cl. 74—84.)

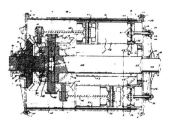

1. A power transmitting mechanism comprising alined shafts; a fluid casing receiving said shafts from opposite ends and secured on and rotatable with one of said shafts; a plurality of piston cylinders fixed to and spaced annularly in said casing having ports cut in their side walls; a piston operable in each of said cylinders; a bevel pinion secured on and rotatable with one of said shafts; bevel gears journaled on the other of said shafts the teeth of which gears mesh with the teeth of said bevel pinion; wrist pins in said bevel gears; rods connecting said wrist and said pistons; a valve in each of said piston cylinders to open and close said ports; a collar carried on one of said shafts; and a stem connecting each one of said valves with said collar.

1,328,518. CULTIVATOR-FENDER. CHARLES B. HOOK, Muncie, Ind. Filed Apr. 2, 1919. Serial No. 286,879. 4 Claims. (Cl. 97—13.)

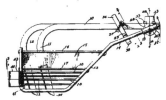

1. The combination with a cultivator beam, of a hollow casting the interior chamber of which opens through one side of the casting, a tubular member having a lateral extension held in the interior chamber for free rotation at all times, and a fender including a stem portion adjustably mounted in the tubular member.

1,328,519. REACTANCE-SHUNT FOR COMMUTATOR-MACHINES. JOHN I. HULL, Schenectady, N. Y., assignor to General Electric Company, a Corporation of New York. Filed July 18, 1916. Serial No. 109,990. 6 Claims. (Cl. 172—274.)

1. In combination, a commutator machine, an exciting winding therefor connected in shunt to the terminals of

said machine, and means connected ... citing winding for preventing low fre ... of said machine.

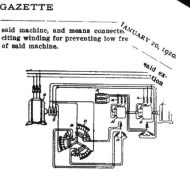

5. In combination, an induction motor, a commutator regulating machine concatenated therewith, a commutator exciter for said regulating machine, exciting windings for said regulating machine connected between the secondary terminals of said motor and the terminals of said exciter, an exciting winding for said exciter connected in shunt to the secondary terminals of said motor, and means for preventing low frequency self excitation of said exciter especially when the speed of said motor is near synchronism.

1,328,520. ALTERNATING-CURRENT DYNAMO-ELECTRIC MACHINE ADAPTED FOR SYNCHRONOUS WORKING. LOUIS JOHN HUNT, Sandycroft, Wales. Filed Feb. 10, 1919. Serial No. 276,001. 3 Claims. (Cl. 172—274.)

1. The combination with an alternating current dynamo electric machine having windings on its rotor portion adapted to operate with two different pole numbers either separately or in cassade, and windings on its stator portion adapted to operate both with alternating currents and with a direct current for synchronous working purposes, of two sets of slip rings connected to separate points in the rotor winding, the one set for the one pole number and the other set for the other pole number, a plurality of starting resistances corresponding in number to the number of slip rings in each set, connections from the one set of slip rings to such resistances, means for connecting the slip rings of the other set severally to such resistances, means for connecting the one set of slip rings in star through resistances, and means for open circuiting the other set of slip rings.

1,328,521. ROAD-SWEEPING MACHINE. JOHN WILLIAM JEMMISON, Huddersfield, England, assignor to Clayton & Company (Huddersfield) Limited, Huddersfield, England, a Corporation of Great Britain. Filed June 10, 1919. Serial No. 303,039. 3 Claims. (Cl. 15—17.)

1. In a road sweeping machine, a receptacle for the sweepings, communicating brush chambers arranged one above another, the top chamber having an outlet into the said receptacle, brushes arranged in the said cham-

bers, and means for revolving one brush in one direction and the other brush in the reverse direction to raise

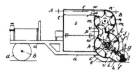

the dust through the said chambers and discharge it into the said receptacle.

1,328,522. OIL-REFINING APPARATUS. ALBERT R. JONES, Independence, Kans. Filed Oct. 9, 1916. Serial No. 124,668. 1 Claim. (Cl. 196—3.)

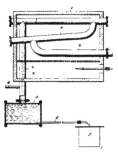

In apparatus for the treatment of mineral oils, a pipe still having convolutions or sections approximating a horizontal position, a furnace containing said convolutions, and a vertical primary pipe section passing upwardly through the furnace, exposed to heat therein throughout a sufficient portion of its length to effect cracking of oil contained therein, and connected at its upper end to an upper pipe or section of the still, and near its lower end to a feed pipe of reduced diameter, with a trap for carbon particles connected below the feed pipe.

1,328,523. OVERHEAD TRACK. BURTON S. JORDAN, Ottawa, Ill., assignor to J. E. Porter Company, Ottawa, Ill., a Corporation of Illinois. Filed Oct. 23, 1919. Serial No. 332,598. 6 Claims. (Cl. 104—109.)

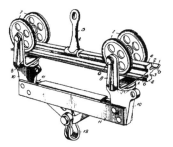

1. In combination with a plurality of oppositely disposed wheels connected together, a track member for supporting said wheels and having a substantially flat,

---

horizontally arranged flange for each wheel, the latter and the flange therefor having coacting means inside of the outer edge of said flange for holding the wheel from lateral displacement on said flange in either direction.

1,328,524. CORRUGATED-PAPER-BOARD BOX. CLYDE S. KNAPP, Chicago, Ill., assignor to Sefton Manufacturing Corporation, Chicago, Ill., a Corporation of New York. Filed July 29, 1918. Serial No. 247,102. 3 Claims. (Cl. 229—15.)

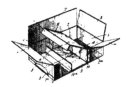

1. A rectangular box of the character described and comprising a box proper provided at top and bottom on two opposite sides with meeting outer closure flaps and on the other two sides with inner closure flaps extending toward each other and leaving an intermediate gap, and a partition structure comprising a vertical wall provided with connected top and bottom members arranged to fill the gap between said inner closure flaps.

1,328,525. ALTERNATING - CURRENT MOTOR. WILLEM C. KORTHALS-ALTES, Schenectady, N. Y., assignor to General Electric Company, a Corporation of New York. Filed Feb. 14, 1918. Serial No. 217,167. 10 Claims. (Cl. 172—280.)

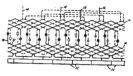

1. An alternating current motor, comprising a stator having a secondary winding, a slotted rotor having a primary winding, and a regulating winding in conducting relation with said secondary winding; said primary and regulating windings being arranged in the rotor slots to form a mechanically single two-layer balanced winding.

1,328,526. PLUNGER-GUIDE CONSTRUCTION. WILLIAM P. KRAUSE, Chicago, Ill., assignor to Mumford Molding Machine Company, Chicago, Ill., a Corporation of New Jersey. Filed June 26, 1916. Serial No. 105,997. 7 Claims. (Cl. 74—86.)

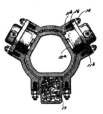

2. In combination with a cylinder having a reciprocable plunger therein, separately adjusting guiding members lying against said plunger, and lubricating means carried by each of said guiding members.

1,328,527. MOLDING-MACHINE. WILLIAM P. KRAUSE, Chicago, Ill., assignor to Mumford Molding Machine Company, Jersey City, N. J., a Corporation of New Jersey. Filed Mar. 29, 1917. Serial No. 158,413. 2 Claims. (Cl. 121—14.)

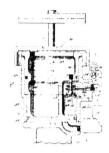

2. A machine of the class described comprising a cylinder having a large and a small portion, a plunger having a large and a small portion reciprocably mounted in the similar portions of said cylinder, means to admit operating fluid beneath the larger portion of said plunger for jolting, means to admit operating fluid beneath the smaller portion of said plunger for squeezing, said plunger being recessed, and valve-controlling mechanism coacting with said plunger to effect the jolting thereof, said mechanism projecting into said plunger recess.

1,328,528. SOAP - HOLDER. FRANK LEACH, Detroit, Mich. Filed Mar. 1, 1919. Serial No. 280,031. 1 Claim. (Cl. 45—28.)

In a device of the class described, a relatively long, narrow, bar having a fixed laterally directed arm at one end, said bar having a longitudinal slot therein, a movable arm parallelizing the aforesaid arm and having working fit in said slot of the bar, the inner end of the second-mentioned arm having a screw-threaded socket therein, a thumb screw projecting through said slot and working in said socket to clamp said movable arm at various adjusted positions on the bar, the opposed faces of said arms being serrated throughout their entire lengths so as to provide relatively long, narrow spaced teeth to bite into the soap and thereby hold the soap against twisting or displacement laterally of said bar and to maintain the soap clamped between the arms in contact with said serrations until the soap is used down to the plane of the bar, and an attaching means carried by the bar.

1,328,529. AIR-PUMP. CHARLES G. LILLOS, Minneapolis, Minn. Filed Jan. 2, 1919. Serial No. 269,230. 3 Claims. (Cl. 230—27.)

1. In an air pump comprising two pairs of spaced vertical cylinders connected together by a top plate and having conduits for delivering compressed air, a reciprocatory piston rod for each cylinder extending beyond the top thereof, a foot tread for each pair of cylinders secured to the top of the piston rods and bridging the space between the cylinders, a guide member on each pair of cylinders adapted to slide vertically in the space between them, a rotatable pulley for each tread mounted on the under side of the top plate between the cylinders, a cable connecting said guides and running over said pulleys to roll thereon, and adapted to raise either of said guides when the other is moved downwardly, and rod connections for each tread to rigidly connect the latter with the guide between its respective cylinders.

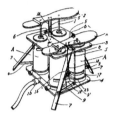

1,328,530. METHOD OF SEALING GLASS BULBS. ALBERT J. LOEPSINGER, Providence, R. I., assignor to General Fire Extinguisher Company, New York, N. Y., a Corporation of New York. Original application filed July 3, 1912, Serial No. 707,471. Divided and this application filed Mar. 11, 1916. Serial No. 83,681. 2 Claims. (Cl. 49—77.)

1. The method of sealing glass bulbs containing a gas in solution which consists in placing the bulb in a receptacle containing a conducting material and then fusing said bulb.

1,328,531. TRIMMING - MACHINE. THOMAS LUND, Beverly, Mass., assignor to United Shoe Machinery Corporation, Paterson, N. J., a Corporation of New Jersey. Filed May 4, 1918. Serial No. 232,500. 10 Claims. (Cl. 12—88.)

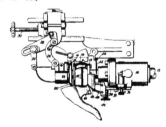

2. In a machine of the class described, a cutter, and a segmental toplift guard supported so as to be radially adjustable relatively to the cutter and movable about an axis by friction between the guard and the shoe whereby frictional drag on the shoe is avoided as the shoe is turned to trim the heel progressively.

1,328,532. STAYBOLT. ROBERT J. McKAY, Pittsburgh, Pa. Filed May 5, 1915. Serial No. 26,129. 1 Claim. (Cl. 85—1.5.)

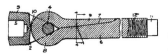

A stay-bolt comprising an eye-head and a shank having inter-locking loops, and a projection on said eye-head projecting into the loop portion of said eye-head and engaging the looped end of said shank.

1,328,533. RAILWAY-TIE PLATE AND RAIL-FASTENING AND ANTICREEPER. EMERY M. McVICKER, Milwaukee, Wis. Filed Jan. 13, 1919. Serial No. 270,898. 9 Claims. (Cl. 238—304.)

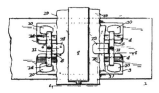

1. A tie plate with a groove, the edges of the groove forming a shoulder for the base flange of the rail and a removable rail fastening fitting into the groove with the inner end overlapping the rail flange and the outer end fitting into notches in the tie plate holding the rail fastening and the rail in position, and means for fastening the rail flange on the other side.

1,328,534. ADDRESS-MATCHER. WALTER J. MAGUIRE, Portland, Oreg. Filed Mar. 3, 1919. Serial No. 280,316. 5 Claims. (Cl. 101—50.)

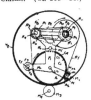

2. The combination of a mimeograph machine and an address matching device having an address bearing tape, a perforated cylinder for driving said tape, an inking pad covering the driving surface of said cylinder, a star wheel for actuating said cylinder intermittently, reels for carrying said tape and a means for compensating changes in the reel diameters.

1,328,535. MACHINE FOR DRESSING SILK. ARTHUR MELLOR, Brighouse, England. Filed Aug. 26, 1919. Serial No. 320,036. 3 Claims. (Cl. 19—6.)

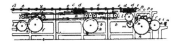

1. In a dressing machine, an endless traveling comb for operating on tufts of silk, a rotary stripping brush ar-

ranged below the return stretch of the said comb and operating to remove the combings from it, and means for diverting the said return stretch from a straight path where it passes over the said brush and thereby increasing the area of contact between the brush and the comb.

1,328,536. BOTTLE OR JAR CLOSURE DEVICE. HARLAN MOORE, New York, N. Y. Filed July 15, 1918. Serial No. 244,920. 6 Claims. (Cl. 215—14.)

1. As an article of manufacture, a receptacle closure comprising a disk substantially circular in form having a smooth periphery and an incision in each of its top and bottom sides, said incisions extending only through a section of the thickness of the disk and not registering with each other, the top and bottom sections of the disk between the top and bottom incisions being separable, whereby after the closure has been placed in the mouth of a receptacle and the edge of the top incision is lifted or bent up, the air is permitted to enter into the receptacle through the passage formed between the separated top and bottom sections and bottom incision and at the same time a projecting tab is formed with which to remove said closure from the receptacle.

1,328,537. HOE WITH KNIFE ATTACHMENT. DAVID NEUMAN, Albany, Ga. Filed Oct. 2, 1919. Serial No. 327,853. 1 Claim. (Cl. 55—39.)

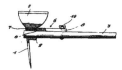

A garden implement comprising a hoe or like tool having an eye formed with a rearwardly tapered handle opening, a handle received in said opening, said eye having a forwardly tapered dovetail groove in its upper outer face, a second tool having a forwardly tapered dovetail back received in said groove and having a rearwardly extending shank thicker than the depth of said groove, the front end of said thicker portion forming a shoulder abutting the rear end of said eye to prevent rearward movement of the hoe on its handle.

1,328,538. CONFORMATOR. CHARLES A. NEWBERG and EDWARD I. WEISBERGER, Brooklyn, N. Y. Filed Jan. 13, 1919. Serial No. 270,907. 4 Claims. (Cl. 33—166.)

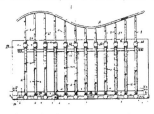

1. A device of the class described comprising a base, a bar supported by said base for rotary movements, a multiplicity of members engaged with said bar and being capable of adjustment one independently of the other longi-

tudinally of the bar, said members being in parallelism, arms slidably engaged with said members and movable longitudinally thereof, said arms extending beyond the members, a flexible spline with which the extended portions of the arms are slidably engaged, and means for locking each of the arms against movement longitudinally of the member.

1,328,539. TIRE-PROTECTOR. WALDO E. NILES, North Abington, Mass. Filed Nov. 14, 1917. Serial No. 201,928. 2 Claims. (Cl. 152—16.)

1. In a tire protector, the combination of a flexible annular body position, metallic strips secured to the body portion and projecting laterally from the same, a covering for each strip projecting beyond the free end of the same and forming a flexible tongue adapted to be secured against the bead of a tire for holding the protector in place.

1,328,540. WASTE-HEAT RADIATOR. JAMES E. NUTE, Portland, Me. Filed Feb. 16, 1917. Serial No. 149,139. 3 Claims. (Cl. 257—167.)

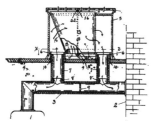

1. In a device of the character described, the combination with a heater and smoke funnel having a partition therein, of an air tight radiator having intake and exit openings in the bottom thereof connected with said funnel, one on each side of said partition, a removable air chamber mounted in said radiator between said openings and open at the top and bottom and means for locking the air chamber to the radiator.

1,328,541. PROCESS OF IMPREGNATING FIBROUS MATERIALS. JOHN F. PALMER, St. Joseph, Mich. Filed Apr. 17, 1917. Serial No. 162,662. 3 Claims. (Cl. 91—68.)

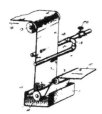

1. The process of frictioning a fibrous material which consists in subjecting said material to a coating of rub-

ber in solution and then driving the rubber substance into and through said material by means of a concentrated current of air under pressure.

1,328,542. SHOW-CASE. WILLARD PEERENBOOM, Appleton, Wis. Filed June 17, 1919. Serial No. 304,835. 1 Claim. (Cl. 211—25.)

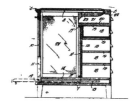

A showcase comprising corner posts, rails connecting the upper ends of the posts, a top pane carried by said rails and covering the entire top of the case, a bottom carried by the lower portions of the corner posts, a longitudinal partition in the case rising from said bottom and having its upper edge spaced from the top pane, a bank of drawers disposed in the case rearwardly of said partition, a top drawer slidable in the case above said bank of drawers and above the upper edge of the partition, said drawer having its inner portion open to form an angular continuation of display space afforded in the case forwardly of the partition, a door for closing the front of the case, and a sliding pivotal support for said door at the bottom of the case, whereby the rear of the door may be swung downwardly and outwardly and then slid rearwardly to dispose its inner portion under the bank of drawers.

1,328,543. CABLE-CLAMP. HENRY W. PLEISTER, Westfield, N. J., assignor to Henry B. Newhall, Jr., executor of Henry B. Newhall, deceased. Filed Feb. 25, 1919. Serial No. 279,133. 2 Claims. (Cl. 248—86.)

1. The combination in a cable clamp of a one piece cable clamp formed from sheet metal having a hook portion, a base, a bracket member bent back on the base and two shelves or brackets bent up from the bracket member having their free ends touching each other and extending well out on the curved portion of the hook member, thereby forming substantially an inverted V.

1,328,544. OIL-DEFLECTOR FOR ENGINE-CYLINDERS. ALLEN H. PLUMMER and CHARLES P. MULLEN, Conshohocken, Pa. Filed Apr. 2, 1919. Serial No. 286,896. 5 Claims. (Cl. 123—191.)
1. The combination with an internal combustion engine cylinder, a piston in said cylinder, and a spark plug in the cylinder head; of an inwardly projecting

flange extending continuously around the cylinder at its juncture with the cylinder head, said flange being arched

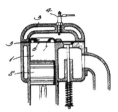

in transverse section to deflect all oil thrown off by the piston away from said spark plug.

1,328,545. KNITTED GARMENT. DENNIS C. O'SHEA, Chicago, Ill. Filed May 29, 1917. Serial No. 171,661. 3 Claims. (Cl. 2—94.)

1. In a garment, a sleeve carrying an extension at its lower end of a length sufficient to reach the knuckles of the wearer, said extension having a slit extending inwardly on its palm side to a sufficient depth to reach approximately to the wrist of the wearer, and means carried by the outer edge of said sleeve extension for securing the latter to the fingers of the wearer, whereby the said extension forms an open palm mitten covering the back of the wearer's hand.

1,328,546. ELECTRIC FUEL-HEATER. LUDWIG REICHOLD, Pittsfield, Mass., assignor to General Electric Company, a Corporation of New York. Filed July 30, 1919. Serial No. 314,379. 7 Claims. (Cl. 219—88.)

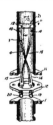

5. The combination with an internal combustion engine provided with an intake pipe of an electric heater in said intake pipe comprising a flat resistance element the middle portion of which is folded at two points, with the two legs or prongs twisted and its ends connected to the circuit terminals.

1,328,547. TOOL FOR CUTTING TIRE-TREADS. JAMES E. SHAW, Trinidad, Colo. Filed Apr. 16, 1919. Serial No. 290,591. 1 Claim. (Cl. 164—80.)

A tire tread cutting tool, comprising a blade body, which has a wide portion at one end, and is provided with an inclined dull bearing edge substantially approximating the length of the blade, and adapted to ride upon the tread surface of the tire, the outer end of the blade having a hook portion provided with a cutting edge extending at a slight acute angle to the dull inclined bearing edge, said cutting edge terminating in a pointed part, said wide portion at one end of the blade body having a wide substantially gradual curved belly part constituting a fulcruming bearing adapted to fulcrum upon the tread surface of the tire when the blade is

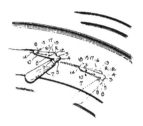

tilted, and a handle projecting at right angles to the back edge of the blade body in a position closely approximating the fulcruming bearing, whereby said handle may be employed for tilting the blade body on the fulcruming bearing, to regulate the depth of the cut to be made by the cutting edge, said fulcruming bearing or belly part protruding laterally beyond the point of the cutting edge, in order to facilitate the regulating of the depth of the cut made by said cutting edge, when the handle is manipulated.

1,328,548. PAPER-KNIFE. JUHANI LEOPOLD SOISALON-SOININEN, Boxbacka, Finland. Filed Feb. 6, 1919. Serial No. 275,452. 2 Claims. (Cl. 120—1.)

1. A paper knife made of steel wire, one end thereof being bent to form a loop, the other end thereof being flattened along half the length of the wire, said loop serving as a handle, said flattened end serving as a blade, and said loop being so spaced from the body of the knife that the leaves of a book may be inserted between the loop and the said body, whereby the knife is adapted for cutting the leaves of a book.

1,328,549. TORPEDO-GUARD. OLIVER H. THOMPSON, Brookings, S. D. Filed Sept. 27, 1918. Serial No. 255,921. 2 Claims. (Cl. 114—240.)

2. In a device of the class described, a guard unit including a member having an outer concave surface, a second unit similarly formed and having its end over-

lapping the unit first named, vertically movable brackets for mounting the units and permitting swinging move-

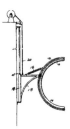

ment of said units, and springs normally retaining the units in position.

1,328,550. VOTING-MACHINE. Lewis John Timpany, Taco Taco, Cuba. Filed May 1, 1917. Serial No. 165,751. 9 Claims. (Cl. 235—50.)

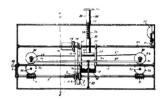

1. A voting machine, including an impression device having an actuating key, an impression receiving element, mechanism for feeding said element under said impression device, means for rendering said feeding means inoperative after said receiving element has been fed a predetermined distance, and means connected with said impression device and operable by the actuation of said device to throw said feeding means into operative position.

1,328,551. MEANS FOR SEPARATING SMALL FROM LARGE FISH. Peter Wallace, Vancouver, British Columbia, Canada. Filed Mar. 21, 1919. Serial No. 284,117. 3 Claims. (Cl. 17—10.)

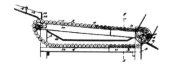

1. A means for separating under-sized fish from those of full size, said means comprising an endless conveyer of transverse rollers rotatably mounted at the required distance apart between side chains to provide parallel interspaces between them, said rollers traveling along track bars to rotate the rollers, means for delivering the fish and arranging them with their length parallel to the rollers, means for receiving the undersized fish that pass through between the rollers, and means for receiving the full sized fish at the other end of the conveyer.

1,328,552. APPARATUS FOR MAKING SULFURIC ACID. Harry V. Welch, Los Angeles, Calif., assignor to International Precipitation Company, Los Angeles, Calif., a Corporation of California. Filed Oct. 1, 1918. Serial No. 256,379. 7 Claims. (Cl. 204—8.)

4. In a chamber acid plant an electrical precipitator having its inlet and outlet connected to said chamber so as to circulate the gases in a local circulation through said chamber and to remove sulfuric acid mist from such gases, said electrical precipitator being provided with means for maintaining a descending film of dilute acid in contact with the gases passing therethrough.

1,328,553. MINER'S LAMP. Alonzo D. Zimmerman, Superior, Colo. Filed Mar. 26, 1919. Serial No 285,394. 4 Claims. (Cl. 48—4.)

1. In a miner's lamp, the combination with a casing having upper and lower chambers, the former being in superimposed relation to the latter, of a partition wall between the two chambers and provided with a central opening, a water conducting tube extending from the water chamber of the lamp through said opening and into the lower chamber, a scraper mounted in the lower chamber and engaging the water conducting tube, whereby the scraper is maintained concentrically in the lower chamber, a closure for the lower chamber, and means carried by the closure engaging said scraper, for imparting motion thereto when the closure is rotated.

1,328,554. SAW GAGING AND SETTING TOOL. Bernard J. Barger, El Paso, Tex. Filed May 1, 1919. Serial No. 293,925. 6 Claims. (Cl. 76—46.)

1. In a tool of the class described, a shank provided at one end with a forked head having a throat extending through both of its furcations to receive a saw blade, a saw clamping device carried by said head, a bar carried by and slidable longitudinally of said shank, saw gaging

means on one end of said bar, and saw setting means on the other end thereof, said bar being reversible for positioning either of said means between the furcations of said forked head.

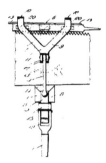

1,328,555. CONSTRUCTION OF REINFORCED-CONCRETE FLOORS. HORATIO LEONARD BARRACLOUGH, London, England. Filed July 17, 1919. Serial No. 311,674. 2 Claims. (Cl. 72—66.)

1. A reinforced concrete floor comprising a plurality of previously cast reinforced concrete inverted T-shaped girders or beams, having the tops of their webs provided toward the center of the longitudinal extent of the girder or beams with small flanges of increasing width toward the said center and tapering off to nothing at each end of the beam, said girders being laid close against each other on supports, and a filling of concrete cast in situ between them.

1,328,556. COATING COMPOSITION FOR KITCHEN UTENSILS. FLORA W. BLOCH, Milwaukee, Wis. Filed Sept. 19, 1918. Serial No. 254,868. Renewed Dec. 12, 1919. Serial No. 344,468. 2 Claims. (Cl. 99—11.)

2. A composition for coating cooking vessels, comprising a mixture of bees wax and vegetable oil in substantially equal proportions.

1,328,557. TOY CAR. OTTO M. BRAUER, Gothenburg, Nebr. Filed Feb. 3, 1919. Serial No. 274,728. 3 Claims. (Cl. 208—165.)
1. In a toy car, the combination of a platform, a wheeled support for the rear end of the platform, a steering head pivotally attached to the under side of the platform adjacent the front end thereof and comprising cheeks and a longitudinal beam secured between said cheeks and receiving the pivot for the steering head, standards at the front ends of said cheeks in advance of the front end

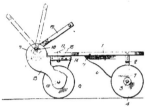

of the platform, a steering wheel mounted between the lower portions of said cheeks in the vertical plane of the pivot, and a handle pivoted between the said standards for movement in a vertical plane.

1,328,558. LID FOR SAUCEPANS AND THE LIKE. SAMUEL A. BROOKS, Elmwood Place, Ohio, assignor of one-half to James M. Shay, Cincinnati, Ohio, and one-half to Alfred W. Miller, Elmwood Place, Ohio. Filed Nov. 19, 1915, Serial No. 62,269. Renewed Nov. 4, 1919. Serial No. 335,747. 2 Claims. (Cl. 53—8.)

1. The combination with a pan having a peripheral bead around the opening thereof, of a lid for said pan having a body portion to cover the opening of the said pan, and a flange depending from said body portion and inturned so as to engage around said bead, said inturned portion extending slightly more than half way and less than the entire way around said body portion.
2. The combination with a pan having a peripheral bead around the opening thereof, of a lid for said pan having a body portion to cover the opening of the said pan, and a flange depending from said body portion and inturned so as to engage around said bead, said inturned portion extending slightly more than half way and less than the entire way around said body portion, said body portion having a foraminated section therein on the side opposite the inturned flange.

1,328,559. BURGLAR-ALARM. ERNEST EMIL BROWN, Decatur, Ill. Filed Mar. 8, 1919. Serial No. 281,324. 1 Claim. (Cl. 116—42.)

A burglar alarm adapted for use in connection with a hinged door and including an elongated support having its lower end extended outwardly and apertured for forming a guide lug, a second guide lug secured to the intermediate portion of said elongated support, a plunger slidably extended through said guide lugs and having its lower end portion extended angularly for providing a manipulating element, a disk washer secured to the intermediate portion of said plunger, a coil spring confined between said disk washer and the first named guide lug, said plunger being provided with a transverse opening, a releasing pin extended through said transverse opening and engaged with the underside of the first named lug, a flexible element connected to said releasing pin and to said hinged door, said plunger being rotatably extended through said guide lugs, whereby when said door is swung to an open position the plunger will be partly rotated for retaining said releasing pin in alinement with said flexible element, and a signal associated with said plunger.

1,328,560. SUPPLY MEANS FOR AIRCRAFT. GODFREY L. CABOT, Boston, Mass. Filed Feb. 28, 1919. Serial No. 279,746. 12 Claims. (Cl. 258—1.)

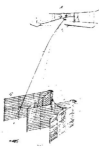

1. In an aircraft supply means, spaced cable-engaging members, a cable depending from the aircraft for picking up either cable engaging member, means for guiding the cable to one or the other of said cable-engaging members according to the relative position of the aircraft, a burden carrier, and connecting means between said cable-engaging members and said burden carrier including means for freeing one cable-engaging member when the other member is raised by said cable.

1,328,561. LOOSE-LEAF BINDER. JOSEPH CARNEY, Newark, N. J., assignor to Paragon Binder Corporation, Newark, N. J., a Corporation of New York. Filed Mar. 21, 1918. Serial No. 223,824. 3 Claims. (Cl. 129—23.)

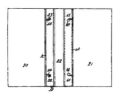

1. In a loose leaf binder the combination of a pair of book covers, a pair of post members extending from each cover, one pair of post members each having an opening near its foot and the other pair each having an opening near its outer end, the post members spaced so that one pair will lie adjacent to the other pair when the binder is closed and a locking slide coacting with said openings to lock said post members together when the binder is in its closed position.

1,328,562. ELECTRIC SWITCH. JOHN F. CAVANAGH, Meriden, Conn., assignor to The Connecticut Telephone & Electric Company, Inc., Meriden, Conn., a Corporation of Connecticut. Filed Aug. 15, 1918. Serial No. 250,019. 2 Claims. (Cl. 200—159.)

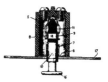

1. In a device of the character described, a base, a face plate attached to one end of said base and having a guide aperture for a plug, spring contacts mounted in said base in spaced relation to each other, terminals for said spring contacts, a plug for insertion in said aperture and guided thereby, said plug having an insulating portion near one end, said portion having an annular depression, a portion of conducting material mounted on said insulating portion between the ends of the latter and having an annular depression, said plug being of such conformation that it may be entirely withdrawn from said guide aperture, and said plug being releasably held in the off or the on position by means of the spring contacts engaging in said annular depressions.

1,328,563. LOOM-REED CLEANING AND POLISHING MACHINE. EDGAR F. HATHAWAY, Dorchester, Mass. Filed June 20, 1918. Serial No. 241,021. 49 Claims. (Cl. 51—5.)

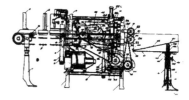

1. Mechanism for cleaning loom reeds having spaced dents, comprising a support for a plurality of assembled loom reeds, cleaning means for the dents of the reeds and for removing foreign matter from between said dents, and means for effecting the movement of said loom reeds from said support to said cleaning means.

1,328,564. RESILIENT HEEL OR HEEL-LIFT, RAYMOND I. HILL, Elyria, Ohio, assignor, by direct and mesne assignments, to The Hill Rubber Heel Company, Elyria, Ohio, a Corporation of Ohio. Filed Sept. 26, 1917. Serial 193,233. 4 Claims. (Cl. 36—35.)

1. A resilient heel or heel section having a concave attaching face which is provided with upstanding yieldable intersecting webs substantially normal to the tread

face, the webbed portion being substantially centrally and symmetrically disposed with reference to the margin of the heel.

1,328,565. DRAFT - CONTROLLER FOR SMOKE - CON-DUITS. LAWRENCE W. HOWARD, Manchester, N. H. Filed Oct. 7, 1918. Serial No. 257,193. 2 Claims. (Cl. 126—292.)

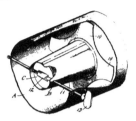

1. A draft and smoke controller comprising in combination with a smoke conduit a restricting tapering member coaxial with the conduit, a plate extending outwardly from the base of the conical member perpendicular to its axis, smoke passages cut from the periphery of the plate forming resilient fingers bearing against the interior of the conduit, and means positioned within the conical member for further restricting the passage therethrough.

1,328,566. CALIPERS. GEORGE H. JOHNSTON, Apollo, Pa. Filed Jan. 15, 1919. Serial No. 271,262. 8 Claims. (Cl. 33—153.)

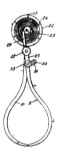

1. A caliper including swingingly connected legs, adjusting means rotatably mounted upon one of the legs and provided with a cam groove, and a rock arm pivoted at a point intermediate of its ends and operatively connected at one end portion with the other of the legs, the other end of the lever engaging in said groove whereby the latter leg may be adjustably positioned with respect to the first leg.

1,328,567. APPARATUS FOR INJECTING FLUIDS AND SEMISOLIDS. EDMUND VAUGHAN JONES, Rock Ferry, England. Filed July 23, 1919. Serial No. 312,868. 5 Claims. (Cl. 221—79.)

1. In apparatus for injecting fluids and semi-solids, the combination of a tubular casing having an outlet at one end and being open at the other, a ram provided with a piston head fitting the casing and a screw-threaded shank, a two part nut the parts of which are hinged together and

the bore of which when closed fits the said shank and the body of which when closed fits into the open end of

the casing, and attachment means formed on the two part nut and on the casing for retaining the nut in position in the casing; substantially as described.

1,328,568. SALT AND PEPPER SHAKER. CHARLES JORGENSEN, New Orleans, La. Filed Oct. 1, 1919. Serial No. 327,614. 3 Claims. (Cl. 65—45.)

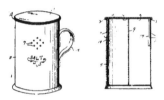

1. A salt and pepper shaker comprising a casing having a plurality of openings in its sides, a vertical partition in said casing, a helical movable operating cover for the top of said casing, and shutter plates carried by and helically movable with the cover over openings.

1,328,569. IMPACT DEVICE. OLLYN A. LAYNE, Los Angeles, Calif. Filed June 25, 1918. Serial No. 241,750. 3 Claims. (Cl. 166—20.)

1. A device of the character described, comprising in combination a vertical stem, a plurality of downwardly

flaring hollow cones spaced apart vertically on the stem and adapted to substantially fit inside a well casing, and means to strike a downward blow on the cones to deliver an impact to fluid below the cones in the casing.

1,328,570. MECHANISM FOR AND PROCESS OF CONSTRUCTING CHENILLE. CHARLES LEA, Boston, Mass., assignor, by mesne assignments, to McCleary, Wallin and Crouse, Amsterdam, N. Y., a Corporation of New York. Filed Nov. 2, 1916. Serial No. 129,072. 30 Claims. (Cl. 139—40.)

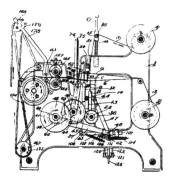

1. That process of forming chenille comprising interweaving warp and weft threads while maintaining said warp threads under continuous tension, continuously severing the resulting fabric into chenille strips, and forming under the influence of moisture the resulting strips during and continuously with the weaving process and while under said continuous tension.

1,328,571. GYROSCOPIC STEERING MECHANISM OF AUTOMOBILE TORPEDOES. EDGAR LEES, Weymouth, England, assignor to The Whitehead Torpedo Works (Weymouth) Limited, Weymouth, England. Filed Sept. 4, 1918. Serial No. 252,642. 15 Claims. (Cl. 114—24.)

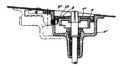

1. In the gyroscopic steering mechanism of automobile torpedoes, the combination with adjustable gear for causing the torpedo, after it has been launched or ejected, to become turned through a predetermined angle with respect to the direction in which it was launched or ejected, of a device which is adjustable independently of the adjustment of said gear for determining and visibly indicating the direction in which the turn will take place.

1,328,572. PNEUMATIC-TIRE PRESSURE-GAGE. KENNETH F. LEES, New Haven, Conn. Filed Jan. 28, 1919. Serial No. 273,615. 8 Claims. (Cl. 73—111.)

1. In a tire pressure gage, the combination with a casing provided with means for attachment to a tire and with means whereby communication may be established between the interior of said casing and the interior of said tire, of a movable member within said casing and subjected to the pressure in the tire when such communi-

cation is established, means coöperating with said member for preventing pressure indicating movement thereof under pressures below a predetermined amount and for

permitting such movement thereof when said amount is exceeded, and means operated by said member for indicating movement thereof.

1,328,573. GREASE-CUP. WILMAR F. LENT, New Haven, Conn., assignor to The Greist Manufacturing Company, a Corporation of Connecticut. Filed Mar. 1, 1919. Serial No. 280,034. 4 Claims. (Cl. 184—38.)

2. In a grease cup, the combination with a receptacle or holder, of a follower fitting said receptacle or holder and provided with a screw threaded shank or stem having relieved or cut-away portions, of means coöperating with said screw-threaded shank whereby said follower may be caused to travel by a screw adjustment in said receptacle or holder, or whereby said shank or stem may be disengaged so that said follower may be moved manually quickly in said receptacle or holder, said means comprising two nuts, one fixed and the other adjustable, said nuts having relieved or cutaway internal threaded portions which may be brought into or out of register with each other, and a stop for limiting the turning movement of said adjustable nut.

1,328,574. METALLIC-RAILROAD-CROSSTIE. JOSEPH LEVENTRY, Johnstown, Pa. Filed Mar. 20, 1919. Serial No. 283,710. 6 Claims. (Cl. 238—38.)

3. A railroad cross tie including coacting sections each provided with an upstanding flange having spaced recesses formed therein and adapted to register when the sections are assembled to form seats for the reception of rails, the flange of each tie section being provided with a laterally curved lug adapted to enter a recess in the flange of the mating section, and means extending through the flanges for uniting said sections.

1,328,575. METHOD FOR SYNTHETIC PRODUCTION OF CYANIDS AND NITRIDS. AXEL RUDOLF LIND-BLAD, Stockholm, Sweden. Filed Oct. 18, 1918. Serial No. 258,739. 2 Claims. (Cl. 204—31.)

1. A process for producing nitrids and cyanids, which consists in charging the raw materials into an electric furnace and subjecting them to heat by the action of an electric current, and during such heating sucking nitrogenous gases through the charge contained in the furnace from a higher to a lower level, whereby the gases and other materials of the charge pass through the furnace in the same direction.

1,328,576. AGITATING DEVICE. WILLIAM LINDSAY, Chicago, Ill. Filed Oct. 21, 1918. Serial No. 259,100. 9 Claims. (Cl. 259—72.)

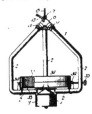

1. An agitating device in which is combined a freely supported movable structure, and an electric motor mounted thereon, said motor having a rotary unbalanced field.

1,328,577. WINDOW - SCREEN. JEFFERSON F. MC-GEORGE, Marshall, Tex. Filed Nov. 19, 1919. Serial No. 339,060. 3 Claims. (Cl. 156—37.)

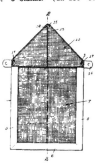

3. A window screen including a frame, said frame including spaced upper bars, a wire mesh supported on the frame, said wire mesh extending beyond the upper end of the frame to provide upper sections, said upper sections adapted to be folded over each other, means for securing a portion of the section to one of the space bars, and means for securing the upper sections of the edges together to provide an exit.

270 O. G.—28

1,328,578. GAS-VALVE. SETH G. MALBY, Derby, Conn., assignor to Ansonia Manufacturing Company, Ansonia, Conn., a Corporation of Connecticut. Filed Sept. 18, 1919. Serial No. 324,384. 5 Claims. (Cl. 251—48.)

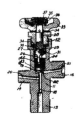

2. A device of the character described comprising a chamber, a threaded plug adapted to close said chamber and provided with a slot, a key engaging said slot and provided with a circular head, a valve stem having a socket which receives said head, and a soft metal pin passing through the walls of the socket and the head of the key.

1,328,579. CURTAIN-BRACKET. MICHAEL J. MANAHAN, Indianapolis, Ind., assignor of one-third to Elmer H. Remick, Indianapolis, Ind. Filed June 30, 1919. Serial No. 307,552. 2 Claims. (Cl. 156—24.)

1. A shade roller bracket having relatively movable clamping elements provided with bearing feet for contact respectively with opposite edge surface of a window casing member, means for effecting the relative adjustment of said elements including a bolt joined to one of them and engaged with the other, and a nut threaded upon the bolt for contact with the second named element, and a shade roller socket arm threaded upon said bolt and having a bearing foot for contact with the front surface of the window casing member.

2. A shade roller bracket having relatively movable clamping elements provided with bearing feet for contact with opposite edge surfaces of a window casing member, one of said elements having a face plate supporting a pole socket arm, and the other element having ears for contact with the front surface of the window casing member, adjusting means connecting the said elements and consisting of a bolt and nut of which the former extends perpendicularly to the planes of said bearing feet, and a shade roller socket arm threaded upon the bolt between the planes of the bearing feet and provided at its rear end with a foot for contact with the front surface of the casing member.

1,328,580. CIRCULAR-KNITTING MACHINE. MAX C. MILLER, Providence, R. I., assignor to Jenckes Knitting Machine Company, Pawtucket, R. I., a Corporation of Rhode Island. Filed July 14, 1913. Serial No. 779,040. 19 Claims. (Cl. 66—24.)

19. The mode herein described of producing upon the needles of a knitting machine a closed toe upon the foot web of a stocking, said mode consisting in first engaging loops of the starting course of a toe pocket, then carrying said loops backwardly out of range of the needles upon which the toe pocket is afterward produced by reciprocating knitting, and retaining them in such

position during the formation of the toe pocket, then applying said loops to the hitherto inactive needles of the

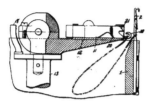

machine, and then knitting the foot web upon all of the needles.

1,328,581. CANDLE - SOCKET. HARRY J. MORBY, Syracuse, N. Y., assignor to Pass & Seymour, Inc., Solvay, N. Y., a Corporation of New York. Filed Feb. 27, 1918. Serial No. 219,419. 4 Claims. (Cl. 173—362.)

1. In a device of the character described, the combination with a lamp base having lamp and wire terminals, of a support for the lamp base, and for a candle shell or casing comprising a sleeve in axial alinement with the base spaced therefrom, a disk mounted on the sleeve, means integral with the disk for supporting and centering the candle shell thereon, and a post integral with and extending upward from the disk and having its upper end portion parallel with the disk, said lamp base being secured to said latter portion.

1,328,582. MEANS FOR FORMING RECESSES IN SAND MOLDS. ABRAM C. MOTT, Jr., and LEWIS KINSLEY, Philadelphia, Pa., assignors to Abram Cox Stove Company, Philadelphia, Pa., a Corporation of Pennsylvania. Filed Oct. 14, 1918. Serial No. 257,974. 5 Claims. (Cl. 22—19.)

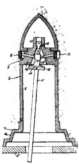

3. The combination of a body portion having an annular recess therein; a ring mounted in the body portion;

a central socket in the body portion; a rod having a ball at one end adapted to the socket, said body portion having radial passages; and rods mounted in the radial passages bearing against the ring so that when the rod is moved out of the center the ring will be projected beyond the walls of the pattern.

1,328,583. BARN-DOOR HINGE. WILLIAM J. NIVA, Minneapolis, Minn. Filed June 7, 1919. Serial No. 302,591. 1 Claim. (Cl. 16—106.)

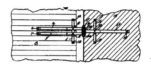

A barn door hinge comprising in combination a pair of yokes, one of said yokes having a strap riveted thereto, the other of said yokes having two straps riveted thereto, the adjoining ends of said straps being formed into a hinge joint.

1,328,584. DOOR-OPERATING MECHANISM. ALBERT S. NOONAN, Philadelphia, Pa., assignor to Foss-Hughes Company, Philadelphia, Pa., a Corporation of Pennsylvania. Filed June 15, 1918. Serial No. 240,233. 2 Claims. (Cl. 268—9.)

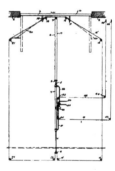

1. The combination of a pair of doors; a cylinder mounted adjacent said doors and having its longitudinal axis extending at right angles to the plane of the doors when said doors are closed; a piston for the cylinder; a piston rod connected to the piston and extending through both ends of the cylinder; flexible connections between one end of the rod and the doors for closing the latter and other flexible connections between the other end of said rod and the doors for opening the doors; guide pulleys for said connections; and a valve for controlling the admission and exhaust of motive fluid for the cylinder.

1,328,585. AUTOMATIC LOOM. JONAS NORTHROP, Hopedale, Mass., assignor to Hopedale Manufacturing Company, Milford, Mass., a Corporation of Massachusetts. Filed Sept. 14, 1917. Serial No. 191,403. 8 Claims. (Cl. 139—85.)

1. A loom having, in combination, a weft replenishing mechanism, a lay having a shuttle box at its replenishing end including a top plate and a front wall, and an in-

coming filling end support secured at its forward end to a fixed part of the loom, the rear free end of the support

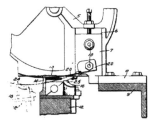

resting lightly on either the top plate or the front wall of the shuttle box during the backward and forward movements of the lay.

1,328,586. BRASSIÈRE. Bertha C. Olson, New York, N. Y. Filed Jan. 30, 1919. Serial No. 273,951. 3 Claims. (Cl. 2—73.)

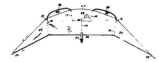

3. A brassière of the class described comprising a central body portion and oppositely directed end portions extending from the central body portion at an angle thereto, said body portion and end portions being composed of two thicknesses of fabric, the main body portion being provided centrally of the bottom edge thereof with a dart and other darts formed in the opposite side edge of the body portion on opposite sides of said central dart and at a predetermined distance therefrom.

1,328,587. COLLAPSIBLE BARREL. Samuel R. Port, Martinsville, Ind. Filed June 4, 1919. Serial No. 301,633. 1 Claim. (Cl. 217—44.)

A collapsible barrel including flexible strips, parallel staves secured thereto having transverse grooves in which the strips are seated, means for detachably connecting together the ends of each strip to hold the staves in tubular form, the ends of certain of the staves being cut away to form recesses, heads insertible into the ends of the space surrounded by the staves, crossed strips secured to the head and seated within the recesses and having longitudinal grooves, fastening wires extending longitudinally along the strips upon the heads and within the grooves and projecting beyond the ends thereof, and means upon certain of the staves for engagement by said wires to fasten the heads between the staves.

1,328,588. POWER TRANSMISSION. Thomas Paul Reddin, Bridgeport, Conn. Filed Mar. 25, 1919. Serial No. 284,894. 3 Claims. (Cl. 74—34.)

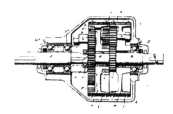

1. A power transmission comprising driving and driven shafts, a plurality of drums loose in relation to the said shafts, a driving gear fixed to the driving shaft, a head or bracket fixed to the driven shaft, gears carried by one of the drums and driven by the driving gear, a gear carried by the remaining drum which meshes with the last named gears, another gear carried by the remaining drum, gears carried by the head or bracket meshing with the gear last named, a gear carried by the driving shaft meshing with the gears last named, and means for holding either of said drums against rotation.

1,328,589. OVEN-BURNER FOR GAS-RANGES. Clarence V. Roberts, Philadelphia, Pa., assignor to Roberts & Mander Stove Company, Philadelphia, Pa., a Corporation of Pennsylvania. Filed Oct. 20, 1917. Serial No. 197,569. 1 Claim. (Cl. 158—105.)

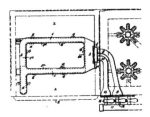

The combination in a gas range, of an oven; a gas burner made in a single casting and having two longitudinal sections perforated for the escape of gas and two end sections, also perforated; a partition in one of the end sections; an igniting portion forming a continuation of the other end section and having a partition therein, said igniting portion also being perforated, the parts being so arranged that the gas escaping from one, or both, of the burners, can be ignited, or the gas escaping from one burner can be ignited from the flame of the other burner.

1,328,590. CARBURETER FOR INTERNAL-COMBUSTION ENGINES. Frederick Henry Royce, Derby, England, assignor to Rolls-Royce Limited, Derby, England. Filed Feb. 18, 1918. Serial No. 217,906. 6 Claims. (Cl. 137—139.)

1. In a carbureter for internal combustion engines, the combination with a float tank and jet; of a fuel valve; a chamber containing a valve seat and communicating with the tank and jet; a valve spindle disposed within the chamber and protruding beyond the same; a stop mounted on the protruding end of the valve spindle; a nut threaded on said spindle end above said stop and having its under

face contacting with the same and its outer face flush with the end face of the spindle; and adjusting means for the valve comprising a member on which the stop normally rests, said nut having a definite, predetermined

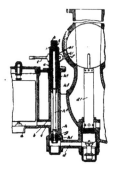

thickness which enables it to act as a gage to determine the normal or initial distance which the valve shall be set from its seat when the parts of the engine are being reassembled, without experimental running of the engine; substantially as described.

1,328,591. STUB-END BEARING FOR LOCOMOTIVE-RODS. KENNETH RUSHTON, Philadelphia, Pa., assignor to The Baldwin Locomotive Works, Philadelphia, Pa., a Corporation of Pennsylvania. Filed May 12, 1919. Serial No. 296,582. 2 Claims. (Cl. 64—10.)

1. The combination in a stub end bearing for locomotive rods, of a wheel; a crank pin projecting therefrom; a flanged plate secured to the outer end of the pin; a rod having a bearing at its end, the width of the bearing being less than the length of the projecting portion of the crank pin so as to leave a clear space between the bearing and the plate, the flange of the plate extending over the bearing so as to inclose the space between the plate and the bearing.

1,328,592. RAILWAY-TRUCK. KENNETH RUSHTON, Philadelphia, Pa., assignor to The Baldwin Locomotive Works, Philadelphia, Pa., a Corporation of Pennsylvania. Filed Nov. 6, 1919. Serial No. 335,988. 5 Claims. (Cl. 105—190.)

1. The combination in a railway truck, of a frame; transoms; links; main springs suspended from the transoms by the links; a bolster; a lever at each side of the

truck, each lever having its fulcrum on the bolster and resting upon the upper end of the main spring; and supplemental springs located between the bolster and each lever.

1,328,593. STEAM-ACCUMULATOR. JOHANNES KARL RUTHS, Djursholm, Sweden, assignor to Aktiebolaget Vaporackumulator, Stockholm, Sweden. Filed May 21, 1918. Serial No. 235,892. 2 Claims. (Cl. 60—94.)

1. In combination with steam-piping a steam accumulator in parallel with said steam-piping and provided with independent charging and discharging conduits, a non-return valve in the discharging conduit and a non-return valve in the charging conduit.

1,328,594. BRAKE-SHOE. FITZ WILLIAM SARGENT, Mahwah, N. J., assignor to The American Brake Shoe and Foundry Company, Wilmington, Del., a Corporation of Delaware. Filed July 8, 1919. Serial No. 309,345. 14 Claims. (Cl. 188—82.)

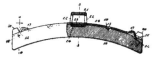

1. A brake-shoe comprising a body portion provided with a longitudinally extending groove on the rear face thereof and a plurality of pockets; a back fitting within said groove, and means formed in said back and adapted to be forced into said pockets to thereby retain the shoe and back in their said positions.

1,328,595. BRAKE-SHOE. FITZ WILLIAM SARGENT, Mahwah, N. J., assignor to The American Brake Shoe and Foundry Company, Wilmington, Del., a Corporation of Delaware. Filed July 8, 1919. Serial No. 309,346. 7 Claims. (Cl. 188—82.)

1. A brake shoe comprising a body portion provided with a longitudinally extending groove on the rear face thereof, said groove provided with dove-tailed side walls, said body portion provided with a plurality of pockets near its opposite ends, a reinforcing back fitting within said groove and within said dove-tailed side walls, said back being bent midway of its ends to form a retaining lug, and said back having tongues near its opposite ends and adapted to be forced into the said pockets to thereby retain the body portion from longitudinal movement with regard to the back.

1,328,596. BRAKE-SHOE. FITZ WILLIAM SARGENT, Mahwah, N. J., assignor to The American Brake Shoe and Foundry Company, Wilmington, Del., a Corporation of Delaware. Filed July 8, 1919. Serial No. 309,347. 4 Claims. (Cl. 188—82.)

2. A brake shoe comprising a cast metal body, a reinforcing back embedded therein and provided with an out-

wardly looped integral lug, and a transverse lug-reinforcing strip with the ends thereof embedded in the body

metal of the shoe and the central portion projecting across the top of the looped lug of the back.

1,328,597. ELECTRICAL VACUUM APPARATUS. MORITZ SCHENKEL, Charlottenburg, near Berlin, Germany, assignor to Siemens-Schuckert-Werke, G. M. B. H., Berlin, Germany, a Corporation of Germany. Filed Sept. 6, 1916. Serial No. 118,697. 7 Claims. (Cl. 175—354.)

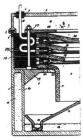

5. In electric vacuum apparatus the combination of an evacuated receptacle, an annular chamber, at least one electrode separating said receptacle from said chamber and means within said chamber for barring the way to the heat developed within said electrodes.

1,328,598. SURGICAL SPLINT. FREDERICK W. SCHILLING, Louisville, Ohio. Filed Nov. 11, 1915. Serial No. 60,908. 3 Claims. (Cl. 128—87.)

3. A surgical splint comprising a body portion adapted to fit the forearm, a flat portion adapted to fit the palm of the hand and provided with sockets, a hand grip adapted to be secured to said flat portion and buttons carried by said hand grip and adapted to engage the sockets in said flat portion.

1,328,599. WIRE-STRETCHER. MELVIN SEVERSON, Galesville, Wis. Filed June 4, 1919. Serial No. 301,630. 4 Claims. (Cl. 254—72.)

1. A fence' wire stretcher having a staff for terminal bearing contact with an intermediate fence post and lat-

eral bearing toward an adjacent post, a gage bar disposed adjacent to the second-named post and provided with spaced seats for the respective reception of said staff, tensioning devices carried by the staff and including a follower for movement longitudinally thereof, and connections with said follower including means for engaging a fence runner.

1,328,600. BALL-CRANK CONNECTION. WALTER S. SMITH, Brooklyn, N. Y. Filed June 30, 1919. Serial No. 307,546. 4 Claims. (Cl. 74—17.)

1. A ball crank joint, comprising a ball member and a metallic socket member having the grain of the metal substantially parallel to its bearing face.

1,328,601. SPRING SHOCK-ABSORBER. FREDERICK L. SPRING, Indianapolis, Ind. Filed Apr. 19, 1918. Serial No. 229,487. 1 Claim. (Cl. 267—27.)

The combination with the axles of a vehicle, brackets carried thereby, and body springs, of shackle blocks having bifurcated ends for engagement with said brackets, shock absorbing springs, comprising a plurality of leaves, ears on said shackle blocks, straps extending over said shock absorbing springs in alinement with said ears, bolts extending through said ears, and the ends of the straps and at the edges of said shock absorbing springs, links pivotally connecting the ends of the body springs and the shackle blocks, shoulders for limiting the swinging movement of said links, and means to hold the inner ends of the shock absorbing springs in alinement with the body springs.

1,328,602. ELEVATOR. BUFORD J. STEEN, Goose Creek, Tex. Filed Feb. 24, 1919. Serial No. 278,802. 1 Claim. (Cl. 24—249.)

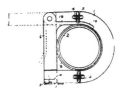

An elevator, including an arcuate member, conforming in contour to and adapted to be fitted around a pipe, a securing arm pivoted at one end to one end of said member, the other end of said member and arm being formed to interengage providing means whereby the arm may be locked in position to hold said arcuate member, against detachment from the pipe, and an actuating finger carried by said arm, and adapted to be actuated by the pipe, when the elevator is applied thereto to swing the arm into interlocking engagement with said member, and to hold said arm in locked position when the elevator is secured to the pipe.

1,328,603. MACHINE FOR GRAINING LITHOGRAPHIC CYLINDERS. CHARLES P. STIRLING, Somerville, N. J., assignor to Cott-a-lap Co., Somerville, N. J., a Corporation of New Jersey. Filed Apr. 29, 1919. Serial No. 293,513. 3 Claims. (Cl. 51—4.)

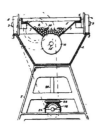

1. The combination of a bed; means for supporting a cylinder in the bed; a hopper arranged to reciprocate above the bed, said hopper being open at the center to receive a portion of the cylinder; means for rotating the cylinder; and means for reciprocating the hopper, said hopper being adapted to receive balls and granular material for graining the cylinder.

1,328,604. FILING DEVICE. SILAS EDGAR TROUT, Philadelphia, Pa. Filed June 21, 1917. Serial No. 176,048. 8 Claims. (Cl. 129—16.)

6. A filing device comprising sections joined to form a receptacle, certain of said sections carrying portions extended inwardly in spaced relation to the sides to constitute retainers for spacer elements.

1,328,605. DEMOUNTABLE SPLIT RIM. JAMES H. WAGENHORST, Akron, Ohio, assignor to The B. F. Goodrich Company, New York, N. Y., a Corporation of New York. Filed Oct. 4, 1915. Serial No. 53,974. 9 Claims. (Cl. 152—21.)

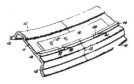

3. A demountable tire-carrying rim transversely split and having a locking shoulder near one rim end, and a locking plate rigidly mounted on the other rim end and overlapping the joint, said plate having hooked engagement with said shoulder by relative lateral movement of the rim ends to prevent circumferential separation of the latter.

1,328,606. ELECTRIC-SWITCH BOX. FRED G. WHITE, Kansas City, Mo., assignor of one-half to Eugene W. Engle, Kansas City, Mo. Filed Oct. 23, 1917. Serial No. 198,076. 5 Claims. (Cl. 200—50.)

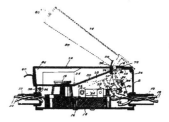

2. A lock box for electric switches, comprising a box having a movable cover, a movable switch element contained within said box, a swinging segment having a notched portion for engaging the switch element, and a connection between said segment and cover whereby said segment is actuated by the movement of the cover to open and close said switch element.

1,328,607. ELECTRIC HEADLIGHT. OVERTON WINSTON, Minneapolis, Minn. Filed June 28, 1916. Serial No. 106,373. 2 Claims. (Cl. 240—48.6.)

1. The combination with a concave reflector, of a light bulb within said reflector having two filaments, one in the axis of said reflector and one above the axis of said reflector, said bulb having a light dimming surface, the lower margin of which is in the horizontal plane of said vertically offset filament and the upper margin of which is on the line intersected by lines radiating from said offset filament and intersecting the upper marginal portion of said reflector.

1,328,608. HOT-WATER BOILER. WILLIAM J. WOODWARD, Leetonia, Ohio. Filed Jan. 10, 1919. Serial No. 270,533. 2 Claims. (Cl. 122—32.)

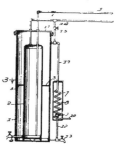

1. In a device of the kind set forth, a pair of boilers comprising an outer boiler and an inner boiler, means

for connecting the inner boiler to a pressure main, a water heater, connections between the water heater and the upper and lower ends of the outer boiler whereby a circulation may be set up in the latter, a valve controlled connection between said means and said connections. and drains for both boilers.

1,328,609. LIFTING-JACK. PHILIP ZAUGG, Blue Creek township, Adams county, Ind. Filed June 9, 1919. Serial No. 302.935. 3 Claims. (Cl. 254—123.)

1. In a lifting jack, a standard having a journal-bearing disposed at its top and formed integrally therewith. a lever formed of a single length of rod and comprising journals, a supporting element and a manipulative arm, said supporting element being disposed between said journals, one of said journals being seated in said bearing, a concave seat being provided in said standard for the other of said journals, and a removable bearing member to retain said other journal in said concave seat, said standard being coöperative with said arm for stopping and holding said supporting element

---

1,328,610 METHOD OF AND MEANS FOR CONTROLLING HIGH - FREQUENCY ALTERNATING CURRENTS. ERNST F. W. ALEXANDERSON, Schenectady, N. Y., assignor to General Electric Company, a Corporation of New York. Filed Jan. 21, 1916. Serial No. 73.443. 29 Claims (Cl. 250—19.)

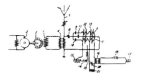

8 The combination in a wireless signaling system of an antenna, a source of high frequency alternating current connected to said antenna, an electromagetic device comprising windings included in shunt to each other in a circuit with said high frequency source and a condenser in series with said windings to neutralize part of the voltage of said windings.

1,328,611. STOKER. MAXWELL ALPERN, Philadelphia, Pa., assignor to American Engineering Company, Philadelphia, Pa., a Corporation of Pennsylvania. Filed Feb. 25, 1914. Serial No. 820,903. 15 Claims. (Cl. 110—44.)

1. In an underfeed stoker, the combination of downwardly inclined series of twyers ; a retort between said twyers and having a relatively fixed bottom ; a wind box ; a downwardly inclined reciprocable grate mounted below said retort ; plates associated with said grate to form a casing connected to receive air under pressure

from the wind box ; with means wholly outside and independent of the retort for reciprocating said grate in-

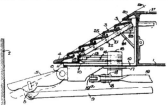

cluding a member connected to a source of power and means extending into said casing connecting said member to the grate.

1,328,612. CONNECTOR ROBERT A. BECKER, Poughkeepsie, N. Y., assignor of one-half to Charles Tremain, Poughkeepsie. N. Y. Filed Aug. 8, 1917. Serial No. 185,006. 2 Claims. (Cl. 287—116.)

1. A connector. comprising a centrally apertured radially unyielding member provided externally with wrench-gripping surfaces between screw-threaded portions and at its ends tapered outwardly, each of said tapered portions only being provided with a longitudinally extending slot terminating inwardly in a slot directed transversely and circumferentially in opposite directions from said first slot, to form radially yieldable portions, and internally threaded conically bored caps adapted to engage said threaded surfaces and operative thereby. to contract the tapered portions of said member.

1,328,613. INDICATING DEVICE FOR VOTING-MACHINES. BORNETT L. BOBROFF, Milwaukee, Wis., assignor, by mesne assignments, to Edward Dillmann and Henry J. Turck, trustees. Milwaukee. Wis. Filed July 23, 1917. Serial No. 182,163. 4 Claims. (Cl. 40—70.)

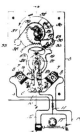

4. In a device of the class described, a carrying plate having a sight opening therein, a shaft supported by the plate, an indicating disk rotatable on the shaft and having symbols thereon adapted to register with the sight opening, an operating member revoluble on the shaft, a releasable connection between the member and the disk, means for rotating the member in one direction to revolve the disk in one direction whereby to successively bring the symbols on the latter into registration with the sight opening, means connected with said disk to hold the same in one of its indicating positions, said operating member being movable in a reverse direction without actuating said disk, and means carried by the operating member for releasing the last mentioned means when said member is rotated in a reverse direction.

1,828,614. PROCESS OF RECOVERING BORAX FROM SALINE WATERS. GEORGE B. BURNHAM, Borosolvay, Calif. Filed June 30, 1919. Serial No. 307,750. 6 Claims. (Cl. 23—13.)

1. The process of recovering borax from liquors containing sodium sulfate, carbonate and borate, which consists in cooling the liquor to crystallize out sodium sulfate and sodium carbonate, removing the cold liquor from the deposited crystals and maintaining the liquor cold, whereby borax crystals are deposited.

1,828,615. PILING-MACHINE. HORACE J. CARTER and CHARLES TAYLOR, Wilmington, Del. Filed June 19, 1919. Serial No. 305,423. 8 Claims. (Cl. 8—19.)

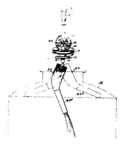

1. In a fabric piler the combination with a keir having a bottle mouth, of a rotatable member arranged thereabove, a chute pivotally connected to said rotatable member, means for rotating said rotatable member and means for oscillating said chute.

1,828,616. AUTO-FUEL-SUPPLY LOCK. JOHN R. CASSINGHAM and WALTER W. AYRES, Oklahoma, Okla., assignors of one-half to Henry W. Morrison and John W. Morrison, Oklahoma, Okla. Filed Mar. 8, 1918. Serial No. 221,253. 3 Claims. (Cl. 251—6.)

1. A device of the character described including in combination a fuel supply pipe of a motor vehicle, a main casing having nipples mounted in the opposite end walls and in communication with the supply pipe, a valve casing mounted in the main casing and in communication with the inner ends of the nipples and provided with a valve seat, a valve head disposed within the valve casing, a stem connected to the head and adjustable within the casing and having the upper end squared, a permutation lock within the casing and embodying a lock casing, a retractile bolt operably mounted therein and provided on its outer edge with a recess for removably embracing the squared portion of the valve stem, a dial casing connected to the lock casing, an operating nipple mounted in the lock casing for operating the bolt for releasing the stem, and a key insertible in the main casing for engagement with the squared end of the stem for adjusting the stem subsequent to the actuation of the operating knob.

1,828,617. BUCKLE. FREDERICK COCKER, Derby, Conn., assignor to Robert N. Bassett Company, Incorporated, Shelton, Conn., a Corporation of Connecticut. Filed Oct. 30, 1918. Serial No. 260,386. 5 Claims. (Cl. 24—191.)

1. A sheet metal lever buckle of the class wherein laterally projecting trunnions on one member are seated in apertured side ears on the other member characterized in that one of said ears is provided with a guideway which extends from the outer edge of the ear into its aperture and through which one of the trunnions may be passed during the process of assembling the buckle.

1,828,618. MACHINE FOR SPREADING FERTILIZER. WILLARD J. COOK, Stoughton, Wis., assignor to Moline Plow Company, a Corporation of Illinois. Filed July 11, 1919. Serial No. 310,116. 4 Claims. (Cl. 275—5.)

1. In a straw spreader, the combination of a wagon body to hold the straw, upper and lower beaters at the rear end of the body, means sustained by the wagon body for feeding the body of straw rearwardly to the action of the beaters, a spreading device sustained by the body in rear of the lower beater in position to receive the material from the beaters, and a hood sustained by the body and provided with a rear wall extending in rear of the upper beater in position to direct the material from the two beaters to the spreading device and having side walls connected with the rear wall and extending at the ends of the upper beater.

1,828,619. AUTOMOBILE-LOCK. WILLIAM H. DAMON, Los Angeles, Calif. Filed Feb. 8, 1919. Serial No. 275,888. 3 Claims. (Cl. 70—90.)

3. An automobile lock comprising a member adapted to be clamped to an axle and having a slot and a second member adapted to be clamped to a steering knuckle arm and formed of two pieces of heavy sheet metal stamped and pressed into shape, one piece having a half bearing formed crosswise at one end, and the other piece having a

mating half bearing, said half bearings being adapted to fit the steering knuckle arm and there being interlocking hooks extending one way from the half bearings, and the pieces fitting together at the opposite sides of the half bearings from the hooks, and there being rivets securing the pieces together and there being a perforation through the outer ends of the pieces; so that the second member will pass through the slot in the first member and so that a lock may be applied through the perforation in the second member.

1,328,620. SOUNDING-CHAMBER FOR THERMIC TELEPHONES AND OTHER APPARATUS. PIETER DE LANGE and ROBERT AERNOUT BARON VAN LYNDEN, Utrecht, Netherlands, assignors, by mesne assignments, to American Thermophone Company, Boston, Mass., a Corporation of Massachusetts. Filed Nov. 4, 1915. Serial No. 59,618. 13 Claims. (Cl. 179—182.)

3. In a sounding chamber for sound producers or receivers of any kind, intended to be introduced into the auditory passage of the human ear, a base having a curved end, and an auxiliary body forming a one-sided bulge movable transversely along said curved end of the base.

1,328,621. HOLDER FOR BED-COVERS. WILLIAM L. DENNISON, Columbus, Ohio. Filed May 15, 1918. Serial No. 234,631. 1 Claim. (Cl. 24—84.)

A new article of manufacture comprising a clasp, a flexible member, an oval link connecting one end of the flexible member to the clasp, and an attaching device carried at the free end of the flexible member, said attaching device consisting of a transverse portion and a hook member formed at each end thereof, the two hook members being right angularly disposed with reference to the said transverse portion and having their free legs diverging, whereby the attaching device may be made to engage a wire mattress or to engage the said link in the manner and for the purpose herein specified.

1,328,622. ELECTRIC SWITCH. OSCAR P. ERHARDT, West Haven, Conn., assignor to The A. C. Gilbert Company, New Haven, Conn., a Corporation of Connecticut. Filed Aug. 2, 1917. Serial No. 184,069. 10 Claims. (Cl. 200—154.)

1. In an electric switch, a contact plate, a spring pressed contact member normally in contact with said

plate, and a controlling member of insulating material adapted to be interposed between said plate and said con-

tact member to separate the same, said controlling member constructed to form insulated supporting means for said plate.

1,328,623. FABRIC. DAVID FREDERICK FRY and CHARLES ROBERT WHITTON, Northampton, England. Filed Feb. 15, 1919. Serial No. 277,222. 5 Claims. (Cl. 154—46.)

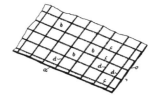

1. As a new article of manufacture, a two ply sheet material comprising, a layer of a textile character in sheet form constituting a foundation, and a layer consisting of an aggregation of leather sections secured to the foundation by rows of stitches, the edges of said leather sections overlapping each other.

1,328,624. DILATOR. FRANK B. GRAHAM, Kansas City, Mo. Filed Aug. 13, 1917. Serial No. 185,937. 2 Claims. (Cl. 128—345.)

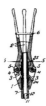

1. A dilator of the kind described having a head, dilating means carried by said head, a longitudinal expanding member having screw-threaded and detachable connection with said head and adapted when turned axially in one direction to expand said dilating means, and releasable means for holding the dilating means expanded, when the expanding member has been removed.

1,328,625. REFRIGERATOR. JAMES E. HAWKINS, Glendale, Calif. Filed Aug. 8, 1919. Serial No. 316,113. 5 Claims. (Cl. 45—71.)

1. A refrigerator comprising a frame, a porous covering over the frame and resting on the top thereof, said covering having depending side curtains, and an inverted

water receptacle having its mouth lowermost and its edge resting on said covering on the top of the frame in order

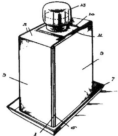

that the water is compelled to seep under the lower edge of the receptacle.

1,328,626. TYPEWRITING - MACHINE. WILLIAM F. HELMOND, Hartford, Conn., assignor to Underwood Typewriter Company, New York, N. Y., a Corporation of Delaware. Filed Apr. 30, 1919. Serial No. 293,837. 6 Claims. (Cl. 197—33.)

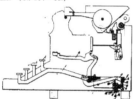

1. In a typewriting machine, the combination with key-levers and a rod on which they are journaled, of a plate adapted to hold said key-levers to their bearing upon the rod, a mounting for said rod, returning springs for said key-levers held in position upon said mounting, screws adapted to bear against said springs and to be adjusted to vary the position of the springs, and an extension of said plate adapted to bear against flat surfaces upon said screws to hold the screws against turning.

1,328,627. CHUCK. HENRY S. HUBBELL, Ashburnham, Mass., assignor to T. R. Almond Manufacturing Company, Ashburnham, Mass., a Corporation of New York. Filed Mar. 13, 1916. Serial No. 83,743. 1 Claim. (Cl. 279—71.)

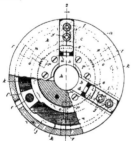

In a lathe chuck, a body comprising a forward member having radial slots, an annular outer integral wall and an integral inner boss projecting rearwardly from said forward member to form a relatively deep annular rear recess, said forward member, outer wall and inner boss

constituting a single metal unit, individually adjustable, jaws movably mounted in said radial slots and occupying an initial stationary position predetermined by the element to be gripped, a scroll rotatably mounted in said recess in surface engagement with the inner face of said forward member, said scroll being provided with a plurality of duplicate cam grooves communicating with each other and extending continuously circumferentially thereof and being slightly eccentric to said scroll, individual devices whereby each jaw is operatively connected with a coöperating cam groove, means to hold the scroll in place within the chuck body and means for rotating said scroll whereby said cam grooves impart a final tightening movement in one direction to said jaws from said initial position and a simple loosening movement in the opposite direction.

1,328,628. FASTENER. WILLIAM WILMOT JILLARD, Philadelphia, Pa. Filed Mar. 14, 1919. Serial No. 282,650. 3 Claims. (Cl. 24—226.)

1. A garment fastener comprising a substantially crescentic, flat head, a shank extending from the concave edge of said head, the outer extremity of said shank being disposed to one side of the short axis of the head and lying substantially opposite one of the projecting tips of said crescentic head, and means at said outer extremity of the shank for securing the fastener to a garment.

1,328,629. WHEEL-ATTACHED SLED-RUNNER. JOHN JOHNSON, New York, N. Y. Filed Mar. 6, 1918. Serial No. 220,714. 2 Claims. (Cl. 280—13.)

2. In a converted vehicle of the class described, runners adapted to be detachably connected with the wheels of said vehicle, a plurality of yoke-shaped clamp devices for connecting said runners with said wheels, a hook-shaped device secured to one of said clamp devices on each wheel, a bar adapted to be detachably connected with said last named clamp devices on the front wheels of the vehicle, loops or eyes mounted on the end portions of said bar and adapted to receive said hook-shaped devices, a casing secured to said bar and a whiffletree pivoted to the top of said casing and with which the harness traces are detachably connected.

1,328,630. FLOATING HEATER. SAMUEL M. KASS, Philadelphia, Pa. Filed Jan. 16, 1919. Serial No. 271,347. 3 Claims. (Cl. 126—360.)

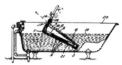

1. A heater comprising a chamber weighted at one end and adapted to float in an inclined position in a liquid to be heated, and a heating means in said chamber adapted to convey its heat to the liquid through the chamber.

1,328,631. CONTROLLING MEANS FOR ELECTRIC MOTORS. LEONARD KEBLER, Bronxville, N. Y., assignor to Ward Leonard Electric Co., a Corporation of New York. Filed Feb. 3, 1917. Serial No. 146,502. 19 Claims. (Cl. 172—179.)

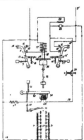

1. In combination, a circuit breaker, a rheostat, biased means to open the circuit breaker, means to hold said circuit breaker closed, and mechanism operatively associated with the rheostat to make said holding means effective when the rheostat is at one extreme of its adjustment.

1,328,632. TIRE. FRANKLIN W. KREMER, Rutherford, N. J. Filed Aug. 6, 1915, Serial No. 43,973. Renewed Nov. 17, 1919. Serial No. 338,528. 4 Claims. (Cl. 152—6.)

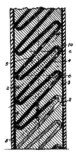

1. A tire having associated therewith a spring comprising zig zag sections, said sections making angles with one another such that the bisectors of said angles all extend across the median line of the spring in a diagonal direction.

1,328,633. ELEVATOR ATTACHMENT. ARNOLD A. KUEHLHORN, Chicago, Ill. Filed Aug. 5, 1918. Serial No. 248,475. 1 Claim. (Cl. 20—19.)

A device of the character described comprising a sill plate pivoted intermediate its width to the elevator door or gate, angularly disposed guide members at each floor of the building, said guide members having spaced parallel straight side walls or flanges, and rollers attached to and projecting laterally from said sill plate for engaging between said flanges whereby the sill is moved to horizontal position to bridge the space between the elevator floor and respective floors of the building when the elevator gates are open, said sill plate adapted to rock on its pivot to vertical position by force of gravity when the elevator gates are being closed.

1,328,634. PIANO-LIFTING TRUCK. FRANK D. LEA, Findlay, Ohio. Filed Apr. 2, 1919. Serial No. 287,021. 3 Claims. (Cl. 280—44.)

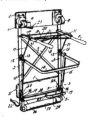

1. In a lifting truck of the class described, the combination with a frame comprising side and end bars, of lifting means for said frame consisting of lifting slides mounted on the side bars of the frame, a roller supported by the lower ends of said lifting slides and instrumentalities for effecting a relative movement of the lifting slides and the frame including a lever bail having the sides thereof pivoted at their inner extremities to the side bars of the frame, links pivotally connected with the sides of the lever bail intermediate the ends of said bail, connections between the links and the lifting slides, means for positively connecting the lifting slides with the side bars comprising a cross plate attached to said lifting slides, and connecting and guiding brackets also secured to said lifting slides and engaging with the side bars of the truck frame for sliding action relatively thereto, the lower end bar of the truck frame being cut away at one side to form clearance recesses permitting the relative movement of the guide brackets and side bars aforesaid.

1,328,635. CLUTCH AND BRAKE CONTROL MECHANISM. ERICH H. LICHTENBERG, Milwaukee, Wis., assignor to Koehring Machine Company, Milwaukee, Wis. Filed Sept. 18, 1916. Serial No. 120,744. 12 Claims. (Cl. 74—46.)

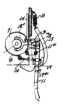

1. In control mechanism of the class described, the combination, of a driving member, control means therefor comprising a clutch for connecting said driving member with the work, a brake governing the action of said driving member, a main control member, operating connections intermediate said control member and the brake and clutch, and a spring so connected with said main control member as to automatically act thereon to hold it in its brake applying or clutch controlling positions.

1,328,636. PROCESS FOR THE DIRECT PRODUCTION OF REFINED IRON AND REFINED STEEL FROM TITANIFEROUS IRON ORES. JOHANNES JACOBUS LOKE and WILLEM ALEXANDER LOKE, The Hague, Netherlands. Filed Sept. 29, 1916. Serial No. 122,920½. 6 Claims. (Cl. 75—14.)

1. The process for the production of an iron product that consists in the passing of reducing gases through a molten mass of iron-oxid, protected from air, and titanium compounds at a temperature that will reduce the titanium compounds.

1,328,637. HOG-SCRAPER. CARL F. NAYER, Chicago, Ill., assignor to Packers Machinery & Equipment Company, Chicago, Ill. Filed Oct. 31, 1918. Serial No. 260,447. 18 Claims. (Cl. 17—11.)

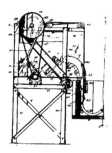

1. In a dehairing machine of the character described, a plurality of dehairing devices each operating upon the carcass in a circular path and an inclined conveyer, said dehairing devices and conveyer being mounted in a manner to support said carcass between them during the dehairing operation.

1,328,638. COTTON-CHOPPER. JAMES D. OGDEN, Crawford, Tex. Filed Apr. 15, 1919. Serial No. 290,195. 3 Claims. (Cl. 97—48.)

2. A cotton chopper, comprising a main frame including longitudinal and transverse beams and depending standards at the ends of the transverse beam, cutting and thinning mechanisms connected to the said depending standards, a rod journaled forwardly of the standards and having off-standing arms connected to the thinning mechanism, a second rod journaled in the rear of the depending standards and connected to the cutting mechanism and operating levers for the respective rods.

1,328,639. WHISTLE. FRANK PARIZEK, Chicago, Ill. Filed Feb. 14, 1919. Serial No. 276,901. 7 Claims. (Cl. 116—1.)

1. A signaling device of the character described comprising a sound box and a valve compartment integral therewith, a nipple attached to the valve compartment and

having one of its ends adapted to fit the pet-cock opening of an engine, the valve mechanism in said compartment

comprising two oppositely acting valves, and means carried by said valve compartment for operating said valve mechanism, said nipple forming a seat for one of said valves.

1,328,640. TURBINE-BLADE ATTACHMENT. CHARLES ALGERNON PARSONS, STANLEY SMITH COOK, and ANDREW PHILP BENNETT, Newcastle-upon-Tyne, England; said Cook and said Bennett assignors to said Parsons. Filed Feb. 4, 1919. Serial No. 274,942. 9 Claims. (Cl. 253—77.)

1. In a turbine a blade carrier having a groove, blades and packing pieces located in the groove, a recess in a wall of the groove which is circumferentially longer than a packing piece or pieces and so related to the blades and packing pieces that when they are inserted in the groove the recess spans a packing piece or pieces and its ends lie opposite other packing pieces, a locking piece located in the recess and spanning a packing piece or pieces, the ends of said locking piece overlapping the other packing pieces, interengaging projections on the walls of the groove, the packing pieces and locking piece, whereby the overlapped packing pieces positively lock the locking piece, and the locking piece positively locks the spanned packing piece or pieces, and means for holding the locking piece in the recess.

1,328,641. SHOCK-ABSORBER. LILBURN HOWARD VAN BRIGGLE, Indianapolis, Ind. Filed Oct. 25, 1919. Serial No. 333,389. 4 Claims. (Cl. 267—9.)

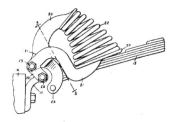

4. A shock absorber for supporting the ends of the main spring of an automobile on a perch of the automobile, including a member extending substantially parallel with the main spring and with the inner end thereof supported

by the main spring and with the outer end of said member extending to a point above the perch and tongues extending downward and at the lower end of said extension fulcrumed on said perch, a shock absorber lever fulcrumed substantially between its ends to the outermost part of said member and above the perch and having a lower end that is in pivotal connection with the end of said main spring, a spiral spring supported by the inner end of said member and supporting the upper inner end of said lever, the parts being arranged so that a downward movement of the main spring will cause said member which carries said lever and auxiliary spring to turn correspondingly on its fulcrum in the perch and cause the upper end of said lever to move inward as its lower end is forced outward by the main spring.

1,328,642. DUST-SEPARATOR. CHARLES A. XARDELL, Utica, N. Y. Filed Mar. 13, 1919. Serial No. 282,305. 6 Claims. (Cl. 183—103.)

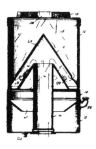

1. A dust separator consisting of upper and lower removably attached casing parts, said upper casing part being provided with means for attachment in any desired position, and the said lower casing part having a centrally disposed air ingress tube extending up into the chamber of the said upper casing part and carrying at its top a truncated cone, said upper casing part having mounted therein a second cone placed above said truncated cone to afford a dust separating chamber, said second cone being provided with air escape openings.

1,328,643. TRACTION-BELT. RICHARD L. ARNDT, San Francisco, Calif., assignor to Union Tractor Company, San Francisco, Calif., a Corporation of California. Filed May 1, 1919. Serial No. 294,014. 5 Claims. (Cl. 21—150.)

1. A traction belt comprising a series of link plates; gudgeon pins on said plates; sleeves on said plates having internal lugs engaging said pins.

1,328,644. EYEGLASS-CASE. JOHN M. BRADLEY and CHARLES F. PIKE, Philadelphia, Pa., assignors to The Safety Eyeglass Company, Wilmington, Del., a Corporation of Delaware. Filed Apr. 13, 1918. Serial No. 228,452. 1 Claim. (Cl. 24—3.)
An eyeglass case comprising a vertical body or support consisting of a thin strip of elastic sheet material

having its upper end bent rearward forming an elastic hook to engage in a pocket or other opening in a garment, and also provided with integral lateral supports having their ends bent forward forming hooks to prevent lateral

movement of the glasses when supported on the body, the lower end of the body being formed as a disk having means for securing a reel, comprising radial fingers bent to clasp the casing of the reel.

1,328,645. EYEGLASS-CASE. JOHN M. BRADLEY and CHARLES F. PIKE, Philadelphia, Pa., assignors to The Safety Eyeglass Company, Wilmington, Del., a Corporation of Delaware. Filed Apr. 13, 1918. Serial No. 228,453. 1 Claim. (Cl. 24—13.)

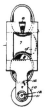

An eyeglass case comprising a body or support consisting of a skeleton sheet of suitable material provided with a curved hook of elastic material to engage in a pocket or other opening in a garment, and carrying at its lower end a reel having a chain for attachment to the eyeglasses, a suitable support being provided to prevent lateral displacement, comprising a sheet of material at substantially a right angle to the body having a slot parallel with and at a short distance from the body.

1,328,646. EYEGLASS-CASE. JOHN M. BRADLEY and CHARLES F. PIKE, Philadelphia, Pa., assignors to The Safety Eyeglass Company, Wilmington, Del., a Corporation of Delaware. Filed Apr. 13, 1918. Serial No. 228,454. 2 Claims. (Cl. 24—13.)

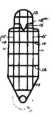

2. An eyeglass case composed of a single piece of wire bent to form side wires, a hook, lateral supports, and fingers to embrace and hold a reel.

1,328,047. COMBINATION-FLUE. REINHOLD ADOLPH CARL, Elgin, Tex. Filed Mar. 13, 1917. Serial No. 154,638. 1 Claim. (Cl. 98—30.)

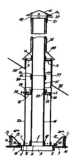

In a device of the class described, a flue having an outstanding flange at its upper end; a lower ventilating sleeve surrounding the lower end of the flue and open at its upper end; an upper sleeve surrounding the upper end of the flue and provided at its lower end with an apron spaced from the upper end of the lower sleeve and extended outwardly beyond the periphery of the same; a cap carried by the upper end of the upper sleeve and located above the upper end of the flue; and an inwardly projecting flange on the upper sleeve, said flange coöperating with the flange of the flue to support the upper sleeve and to space the apron from the upper end of the lower sleeve, the flange on the flue coöperating with the upper sleeve to space the same transversely from the upper end of the flue and to define an air chamber about the upper end of the flue, the chamber being adapted to receive heated air from the lower sleeve, by way of the apron, and to confine the heated air about the upper end of the flue, thereby increasing the upward flow of the products of combustion through the flue and increasing the upward flow through the lower ventilating sleeve.

1,328,648. PUMP-PIPE LIFTER. GEORGE P. DAVIS, McIntosh, N. Mex. Filed Feb. 19, 1917. Serial No. 149,578. 1 Claim. (Cl. 24—249.)

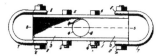

A pipe lifter comprising a pair of spaced parallel side rails, a bolt passing through each of the opposite ends of the rails, a rectangular block shaped gripping member pivotally mounted upon each bolt and adapted to swing vertically between said side rails, said gripping members having their free inner ends abutting only when the members are in a horizontal position and each being provided with a transverse semi-circular cut out portion to surround a pipe, and bolts passing through the side rails to be arranged beneath the free inner ends of said gripping members to form stops whereby the gripping members are normally held in the same horizontal plane with their free ends abutting.

1,328,649. ANTIFREEZING APPLIANCE FOR WATER-PIPES. THOMAS A. DAVIS, San Antonio, Tex. Filed June 7, 1918, Serial No. 238,681. Renewed June 20, 1919. Serial No. 305,703. 8 Claims. (Cl. 137—35.)
5. In an anti-freezing appliance for water pipes, a casing, a partition dividing the casing into upper and

lower chambers and having water ducts connecting the chambers, an induction valve chamber below the lower chamber and connected with an induction pipe, an eduction pipe connected with the lower chamber, a check valve loosely contained in the valve chamber and having

a stem projecting into the lower chamber, a displaceable cover attached to the casing, an abutment held by the cover for the valve stem to maintain the valve in open position under induction water pressure pending the displacement of the cover.

1,328,650. COMBINATION BATH-SPRAY. JEROME J. DONOVAN, Oakland, Calif. Filed May 19, 1916. Serial No. 98,663. 3 Claims. (Cl. 285—197.)

1. A device of the character described comprising a tubular coupling member having external threads shaped to engage complemental threads of a faucet, and a cap having internal threads engaging the threads of the coupling member.

1,328,651. CALIPERS. ROBERT EAMES, Detroit, Mich. Filed June 13, 1919. Serial No. 303,882. 1 Claim. (Cl. 33—148.)

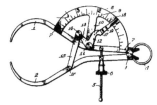

An instrument comprising adjustable legs, a bell crank pivotally supported relative to one of said legs and terminating in a pointer movable over said leg and a link connecting the short arm of said bell crank to the other leg so as to move said bell crank when said legs are adjusted relative to each other.

1,328,652. POT-LID. LILLIE EHLERS, Stickney, S. D. Filed June 7, 1918. Serial No. 238,697. 2 Claims. (Cl. 53—8.)

1. A lid for vessels comprising a reticulated body, a peripheral reinforcement therefor, said body having a cen-

tral opening, a reinforcing band surrounding the same and secured to the body, said band being of a size to receive therethrough the handle of a spoon.

1,328,653. SAFETY-VALVE FOR PRESSURE-COOKERS. WALTON C. FERRIS, Lincoln, Nebr., assignor to National Manufacturing Company, Lincoln, Nebr. Filed Apr. 5, 1919. Serial No. 287,749. 5 Claims. (Cl. 137—53.)

1. In a device of the character described, a bowl having a valve seat passage adapted to communicate with the cooker chamber, a cap fitted over the bowl and having a valve stem guide, a valve mounted with its stem in the said guide and adapted to close said valve seat passage, and a tension device connecting said valve with the said cap, said bowl having provision for the escape of steam, when the valve seat passage is open, means for holding said cap on said bowl in different positions, whereby to increase or diminish the effect of said tension device according to the position of the said cap.

1,328,654. AUTOMOBILE DEVICE. GEORGE H. FILKINS, Watervliet, N. Y., assignor of one-half to John F. Murray, Troy, N. Y. Filed July 16, 1917. Serial No. 180,919. 3 Claims. (Cl. 280—33.5.)

3. A coupling device including a central clamp member and auxiliary clamps positioned respectively to the right and left of said central clamp, one of said auxiliary clamps being adapted to embrace the steering rod of a vehicle, while the other clamp is attachable to the rear axle of a preceding vehicle, connecting rods carried by each of said auxiliary clamps for coupling engagement with said central clamp, and swiveled bearings carried by said central clamp and engaging said connecting rods to provide pivot means whereby said auxiliary clamps may be adjusted relatively to said central clamp.

1,328,655. PROCESS OF DRYING LUMBER. FREDERICK K. FISH, Jr., New York, N. Y. Filed Apr. 23, 1919. Serial No. 292,053. 8 Claims. (Cl. 99—12.)

1. The process of drying lumber, which consists in subjecting the lumber to a body of live steam under pressure, while simultaneously applying dry heat, then subjecting the lumber to a body of dry heat while periodically removing the accumulating moisture from around the lumber.

1,328,656. SAPLESS COMPOSITE WOOD. FREDERICK K. FISH, Jr., New York, N. Y. Filed Apr. 30, 1919. Serial No. 293,861. 10 Claims. (Cl. 99—12.)

8. As a new article of manufacture, a wood having its gummy sap matters removed therefrom and its individual fibers permanently enlarged by the permeation thereof of the natural preservatives of the wood combined with a foreign preservative, the preservatives replacing the gummy sap matter.

1,328,657. PROCESS FOR TREATING AND DRYING WOOD. FREDERICK K. FISH, Jr., New York, N. Y. Filed Nov. 21, 1919. Serial No. 339,616. 58 Claims. (Cl. 99—12.)

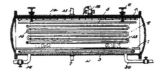

1. The process of treating wood comprising sweating the wood to soften and heat it, then subjecting it to a vacuum, then to steam to raise the temperature of the wood, then to vacuum, then to heated water to dissolve and remove water soluble constituents, removing the water and thereafter drying the wood.

1,328,658. PROCESS OF DRYING LUMBER. FREDERICK K. FISH, Jr., New York, N. Y., assignor to Lumber Tie & Timber Vulcanizing Company, New York, N. Y. Filed Mar. 22, 1917, Serial No. 156,542. Renewed Dec. 13, 1919. Serial No. 344,749. 8 Claims. (Cl. 99—12.)

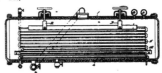

1. The process of extracting the fluid content of wood and substances contained therein, which consists in associating with the wood a heat radiating medium; then sweating the wood; then subjecting the wood to a body of steam under pressure; then creating around the wood a partial vacuum; then submerging the wood in superheated water; then again creating a vacuum around the wood; then subjecting the wood to dry heat of high temperature; then subjecting the wood to a moderately heated, moist atmosphere.

2. The process of extracting the fluid content of wood and substances contained therein by subjecting the wood to steam under pressure; then submerging the wood in super-heated water alternated with a vacuum; then setting the resin in the wood by dry heat without pressure; finally cooling the wood in the presence of a moderately heated, moist atmosphere.

8. The process of extracting the fluid content of wood, which consists in first sweating the wood; then subjecting it to a body of steam at a high temperature and under pressure; then immersing the wood in super-heated water under pressure; then creating around the wood a vacuum and simultaneously and gradually reducing the temperature until sufficient evaporation has taken place from the center of the wood to expel the fluid content thereof; then subjecting to dry heat of high temperature until the resins have thoroughly permeated the cellular structure thereof; finally harmonizing the internal temperature of the wood and a moderately heated atmosphere surrounding the wood.

1,328,659. PROCESS OF DRYING LUMBER. FREDER-
ICK K. FISH, Jr., New York, N. Y., assignor to Lumber
Tie and Timber Vulcanizing Company, New York, N. Y.
Filed Mar. 8, 1917, Serial No. 153,488. Renewed Dec.
13, 1919. Serial No. 344,750. 4 Claims. (Cl. 99—12.)

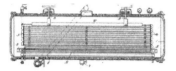

3. The process of drying wood, which consists in subjecting the wood to a moderately heated, moist atmosphere
without pressure ; then to a body of steam at substantially
the dew point thereof until its pores are opened up and
its gummy sap matters dissolved ; then gradually reducing
the pressure to below atmospheric pressure ; finally drying at atmospheric pressure and without heat.

1,328,660. PROCESS OF DRYING LUMBER. FREDER-
ICK K. FISH, Jr., New York, N. Y., assignor to Lumber
Tie and Timber Vulcanizing Company, New York, N. Y.
Filed Mar. 8, 1917, Serial No. 153,489. Renewed Dec.
13, 1919. Serial No. 344,751. 4 Claims. (Cl. 99—12.)

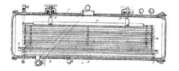

4. The process of drying wood, which consists in subjecting the wood to a body of live steam under pressure ;
then withdrawing moisture therefrom while decreasing
the pressure ; finally drying in a body of moderately
heated, moist atmosphere at atmospheric pressure and
harmonizing the temperature of the interior of the wood
with the surrounding atmosphere.

1,328,661. PROCESS OF DRYING LUMBER. FREDER-
ICK K. FISH, Jr., New York, N. Y., assignor to Lumber
Tie & Timber Vulcanizing Company, New York, N. Y.
Filed Mar. 22, 1917, Serial No. 156,541. Renewed Dec.
13, 1919. Serial No. 344,752. 6 Claims. (Cl. 99—12.)

2. The process of extracting the fluid content of wood
and substances contained therein, consisting of associating the wood with a heat absorbent ; then subjecting
the whole to a sweating ; then surrounding the whole
with a body of steam ; then submerging it in super-heated
water until its structure is softened, its pores opened up
and its gummy sap matters dissolved ; then removing
the super-heated water from the presence of the wood ;
then surrounding it with a body of dry heat ; finally subjecting it to a moderately heated, moist atmosphere after
sufficient vaporization of its fluid content and substances
contained therein has taken place.

6. The process of extracting the fluid content and substances contained therein from wood, which consists in
co-mingling with the wood a medium which more readily
absorbs and radiates heat ; then subjecting the whole to
a sweating process at a moderate temperature ; then subjecting it to the action of saturated steam in a hermeti-
cally closed sterilizer under pressure and at a temperature equal to the boiling point of the fluid content which
it is desired to extract therefrom ; then reducing the pressure and temperature of the steam ; then submerging
the wood in super-heated water until its structure is
softened, its pores opened up and its gummy sap matter
dissolved ; then removing the super heated water from
the presence of the wood ; then subjecting the wood to a
body of dry heat ; finally cooling in the presence of a
moderately heated, moist atmosphere.

1,328,662. PROCESS OF DRYING LUMBER. FREDER-
ICK K. FISH, Jr., New York, N. Y. Filed Dec. 17, 1919.
Serial No. 345,601. 5 Claims. (Cl. 99—12.)

3. The process of drying wood, which consists in placing the wood in a sweat chamber, creating in said chamber a moderately heated, moist atmosphere ; then placing
the wood in a sterilizer and producing therein a body
of steam under pressure then placing the wood in an
equalizing chamber and subjecting it to dry heat ; finally
placing it in a cooling chamber and creating therein a
moderately heated, moist atmosphere.

1,328,663. WHEEL-PULLER. GEORGE E. FRISZ and
JAMES D. WILTSHIRE, Indianapolis, Ind. Filed July
1, 1918. Serial No. 242,799. 10 Claims. (Cl. 29—85.)

1. A universal puller device of the class described
comprising a body, a pressure producing member mounted
thereupon for effecting removal operation, and interchangeable wheel part engaging members adapted to be
engaged with different parts of the hub or member to be
removed.

1,328,664. DISPENSING - CABINET. JOHN FRITSCHE,
Philadelphia, Pa. Filed Feb. 5, 1917. Serial No. 146,683.
12 Claims. (Cl. 45—82.)
2. An article dispensing device, comprising a casing
having a plurality of compartments, a guide leading from
one compartment and extending into the other compart-

ment, a door controlling access to one of said compartments and including a slot registering with said guide,

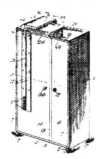

article holders superimposed in said slot adapted to engage said guide and having grasping portions extending exterior of the casing.

1,328,665. SHOE. JOSEPH T. B. GILLENWATERS, Cave City, Ky. Filed Dec. 30, 1918. Serial No. 268,878. 3 Claims. (Cl. 36—1.)

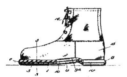

1. In a shoe, the combination of a braided fabric strip coiled to form a shoe sole, an upper having its lower edge extending between the outermost coil of said sole and the coil next thereto, metal reinforcing plates provided with upturned perforated edges extending across portions of the outer surface of said sole, and stitching extending through said perforations transversely across said sole for connecting the upper, the coils of said sole and the metal reinforcing plate together.

1,328,666. METALLURGICAL PROCESS. WILLIAM E. GREENAWALT, Denver, Colo. Filed Aug. 5, 1918. Serial No. 248,471. 14 Claims. (Cl. 204—15.)

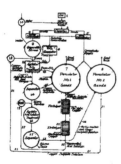

1. A metallurgical process which consists in treating ores of copper with sulfurous acid in the presence of a

270 O. G.—29

solution of copper sulfate to extract a portion of the copper, electrolyzing the resulting solution containing the copper as sulfate and sulfite to deposit the copper and regenerate sulfuric acid, and then applying the regenerated sulfuric acid solution to the ore to extract the remainder of the extractable copper.

1,328,667. SHOE-SHINING STAND. NELSON J. GREENISON, New York, N. Y. Filed May 21, 1919. Serial No. 298,599. 1 Claim. (Cl. 15—58.)

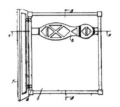

In a shoe-shining stand, a suitable receptacle, a pair of studs arranged in spaced relation to each other on each side of said receptacle, a foot-supporting stand, and depending legs formed integral with said foot-supporting stand, each of said legs having a straight slot projecting inwardly of the body portion from the free end thereof and adapted to receive one of each pair of the afore-mentioned studs, means for closing the lower end of each of said slots, means extending transversely of each of said slots near its upper end and coacting with its respective stud to prevent vertical movement of said legs, and a curved slot projecting inwardly of the body portion from the side edge thereof and adapted to receive the other stud of each pair to prevent movement of the legs of the foot-supporting stand about the first-mentioned studs, substantially as described.

1,328,668. CORN-HARVESTER. CLINTON A. HAGADONE, Western Springs, Ill., assignor, by mesne assignments, to International Harvester Company, a Corporation of New Jersey. Filed July 10, 1916. Serial No. 108,240. 1 Claim. (Cl. 56—129.)

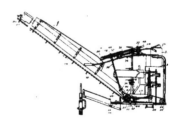

In a harvester, binding mechanism, an elevator having a movable element, a shaft through which motion is transmitted to the movable element of said elevator, a second shaft operatively connected to said first mentioned shaft, a sprocket wheel mounted on said second shaft, a second sprocket wheel supported adjacent said binding mechanism, and a chain driven from said first-named sprocket wheel and extending around the second-named sprocket wheel, said chain being located in the path of the bundles discharged from said binding mechanism and operating to positively withdraw the bundles from said binding mechanism, and feed said bundles to the elevator.

1,328,669. OPTICAL TRIAL-FRAME HOLDER. FRED-
ERICK H. HARM, St. Paul, Minn. Filed Apr. 18, 1919.
Serial No. 291,134. 2 Claims. (Cl. 88—20.)

1. In a device of the kind described, a skeleton hood
adapted to be adjusted upon a person's head and having
at the front a bracket, a vertically disposed link pivotally
clamped with its upper end to the bracket, a horizontally
disposed arm pivotally clamped with the front end to the
lower end of the link, a vertical rod slidably secured in
the rearward end of the horizontal arm, and a horizontal
bar operatively connected with the vertical rod, and a
pair of trial frames mounted on said horizontal bar.

1,328,670. FINAL ADJUSTING DEVICE FOR MA-
CHINE-TOOLS. ERNEST C. HEAD, Van Wert, Ohio, assignor to Colburn Machine Tool Company, Franklin,
Pa., a Corporation of Pennsylvania. Filed Nov. 10,
1917. Serial No. 201,242. 16 Claims. (Cl. 74—7.)

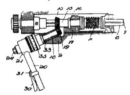

1. A manually-operated adjusting device for machine-
tools comprising, in combination with a rotatable feed
element and the saddle, a gear mounted on said feed
element and adapted to rotate the same, means to cause
said gear to travel with said saddle, a pinion carried by
said saddle in mesh with said gear, a shaft operable to
rotate said pinion, and manually-operated means to rotate said shaft.

1,328,671. SHEAR-TRIMMER. JOHN M. HILLIARD,
Waco, Tex., assignor of one-half to C. W. Lott, Waco,
Tex. Filed June 11, 1919. Serial No. 303,386. 5
Claims. (Cl. 164—43.)

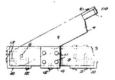

1. In a shear trimmer, a base, end metal face plates
on the base, a blade arranged in front of the base in
spaced relation thereto and having right angular ends
disposed in spaced relation to the respective end face
plates of the base, substantially L-shape brackets secured to the bottom of the base and receiving the lower

edges of the blade and the arms thereof, and a movable
cutter embodying a blade receivable between the front
of the base and the first named blade and having end
arms pivoted to the base and movable in the space between the face plates of the base and the ends of the
first named blade, said blade of the movable cutter having
a substantially right angular flange which overlies the
first named blade.

1,328,672. BUCKET-CLOSURE. ISAAC HIRSOHN, New
York, N. Y. Filed Mar. 29, 1917. Serial No. 158,196.
7 Claims. (Cl. 220—56.)

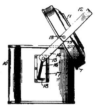

1. In a bucket closure, the combination of bucket
having slots at its sides, a lid, a bail pivoted at the
sides of the lid, and means connected with the bail and
working in the slots to release the said lid and bail when
the latter is tipped.

1,328,673. GLASS-DRAWING APPARATUS. HALBERT
K. HITCHCOCK, Pittsburgh, Pa., assignor to Pittsburgh
Plate Glass Company, a Corporation of Pennsylvania.
Filed Oct. 8, 1917. Serial No. 195,437. 6 Claims. (Cl.
49—17.1.)

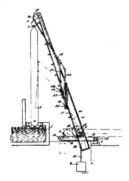

1. In combination in apparatus for drawing glass
articles from a bath of molten glass, a tilting take-down
frame pivoted at its lower end adjacent the bath of glass,
a bait and means for moving it vertically carried by the
frame, an air supply, and a system of jointed pipes connected thereto and to the bait carried by the frame and
so arranged that the end connected to the bait is caused
to move substantially vertically with the bait throughout the drawing movement thereof.

1,328,674. STOOKER. FREDERICK KOHLRUSS, Balgonie,
Saskatchewan, Canada. Filed July 22, 1918. Serial
No. 246,113. 8 Claims. (Cl. 56—417.)
1. In a stooker, the combination with the main frame
and shock former comprising a semi-cylindrical lower
portion and arc-shape flaps forming the upper portion,
of means for carrying the shock former upon the main

frame and adapted to be swung to carry the former toward an upended position, levers pivoted upon the lower portion of the former, a link connection between

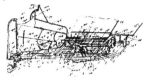

out end of each lever and the corresponding former flap, and means drawing upon the opposite end of each lever as the former is carried upward to turn the levers upon their pivot to close the flaps.

1,328,675.   APPAREL-CORSET.   DANIEL KOPS, New York, N. Y.   Filed Nov. 1, 1919.   Serial No. 335,022. 5 Claims.   (Cl. 2—73.)

1. In an apparel corset, a front steel section, and a strap member secured along one edge to the said front steel section and extending from a point adjacent the lower end thereof so as to overlie the groin section of the body to approximately the waist line of the garment, and at the opposite side thereof to the body of the garment adjacent the hip section thereof so that when the garment is adjusted to position there is exerted an upward pull in the lower portion of the strap against the lower portion of the front steel section to exert an upward pressure against the underlying portion of the body of the wearer and there is also exerted a downward pull in the upper portion of the strap from the waist line section of the garment to maintain the same in position and thereby support the underlying portion of the abdomen of the wearer.

1,328,676.   TIRE-CORE.   EMIL A. KRANNICH, Columbiana, Ohio, assignor of one-half to Louis A. Andregg, Mansfield, Ohio.   Filed Nov. 30, 1917.   Serial No. 204,536. 19 Claims.   (Cl. 18—45.)

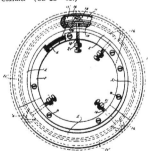

1. The herein described method consisting in building up a tire with a portion thereof flattened, and finally stretching and rounding said flattened portion into completed tire form by direct acting uniform pressure sections.

1,328,677.   ADJUSTABLE BRACKET FOR MIRRORS AND OTHER OBJECTS.   WILLIAM LA HODNY, Buffalo, N. Y.   Filed Aug. 27, 1917.   Serial No. 188,275.   2 Claims. (Cl. 45—97.)

1. An adjustable supporting bracket comprising inner, outer and intermediate arm sections consisting of relatively thin wide metal plates arranged vertically on edge, transversely horizontal pivots connecting said sections and permitting the sections to be adjusted vertically to different angular relations, a supporting member to which said inner section is connected by a vertical pivot to swing laterally, a yoke connected by a vertical pivot to said outer section to swing laterally, and a member adapted to be fixed to an object and swiveled to said yoke by a horizontal pivot perpendicular to said member and to said yoke pivot to permit said object to turn about a horizontal axis and swing to a position close beside said arm sections.

1,328,678.   CABLE-PULLING DEVICE.   THOMAS D. LEMIEUX. Lakewood, Ohio.   Filed Aug. 29, 1919. Serial No. 320,559.   6 Claims.   (Cl. 254—177.)

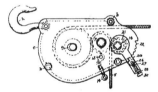

1. A cable pulling device comprising a casing and a series of gear sheaves of different sizes in tandem therein, the middle of said sheaves being on fixed bearings and the outer sheaves having shifting bearings in respect to said inner sheave.

1,328,679.   FAN OR BLOWER.   GEORGE S. LEONARD, Minneapolis, Minn., assignor to Huntley Manufacturing Company, of Silver Creek.   Filed May 3, 1917.   Serial No. 166,204.   12 Claims.   (Cl. 230—11.)

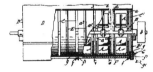

6. In a fan, the combination of a plurality of sets of fan blades, a series of compartments in which said blades are arranged, air inlet passages at both sides of each of said compartments, an air inlet housing which incloses one end and both sides of said series of compartments and with which each of said air passages communicates and through which the air supplied to said

fan blades passes, said air inlet housing gradually increasing in size toward one side thereof and having an air inlet opening at the largest portion of said side and extending in a direction substantially parallel with the axis of said fan, and a slide which is adjustable to regulate the size of said opening and which is movable in a direction substantially parallel with the axis of said fan.

1,328,680. APPARATUS FOR THE RECOVERY OF GASOLENE FROM CASING-HEAD GAS IN OIL-WELLS. WALTER R. McGINNIS, St. Louis, Mo., assignor to Pilsbry-Becker Engineering & Supply Company, St. Louis, Mo., a Corporation of Missouri. Filed May 14, 1917. Serial No. 168,436. 1 Claim. (Cl. 196—25.)

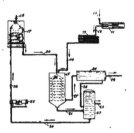

The apparatus for recovering gasolene from casing-head gas comprising a compressor; a cooling coil connected to said compressor; a converter fed from said cooling coil; a liquid-cooler; a refrigerating coil mounted in said liquid-cooler; a conduit connecting the liquid-cooler with said converter; a primary separator and a secondary separator connected to said converter and to each other; means for drawing off free gas and gasolene from said separators; and means for returning the liquid from said separators to the liquid-cooler.

1,328,681. AUTOMOBILE STEERING ATTACHMENT. DUNCAN MACDONALD, West Homestead, Pa. Filed Oct. 8, 1917. Serial No. 195,281. 3 Claims. (Cl. 280—94.)

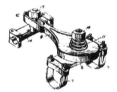

3. In an automobile steering apparatus, a head fixed to the automobile axle, an arm rotatably mounted on said head and secured to the steering tie rod, spaced recesses in the top of said head, similarly spaced projections in the bottom of said arm, said projections adapted to fit within said recesses when the automobile is moving in a straight line and to be disassociated therefrom when the steering rod is moved to substantially deflect the forward wheels from a straight line.

1,328,682. HOT-WATER HEATER. FREDERICK WILLIAM MAGEE, London, Ontario, Canada, assignor of one-half to Thomas William Baker, London, Ontario, Canada. Filed Mar. 30, 1918. Serial No. 225,793. 14 Claims. (Cl. 126—359.)

2. An instantaneous heater comprising a cylindrical casing, a dished head at the upper end of the casing into which the water supply is discharged, a multiplicity of nipple tubes carried by and arranged evenly throughout

the whole surface of the head and passing through the bottom of the dished head and projecting above and

below such surface and having perforations in the upwardly projecting portion in proximity to the head.

1,328,683. CAR-UNDERFRAME. WILLIAM N. OEHM, Michigan City, Ind. Filed Feb. 21, 1919. Serial No. 278,434. 6 Claims. (Cl. 105—414.)

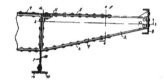

1. A car frame comprising center sills, bolsters, cross bearers and cover plates, the thickness of the metal of all of said members so graduated as to provide increased thickness where greatest stress and greatest corrosion normally occur.

1,328,684. CAR-END SHEET. WILLIAM N. OEHM, Michigan City, Ind. Filed Feb. 21, 1919. Serial No. 278,436. 6 Claims. (Cl. 105—406.)

1. A car end comprising an integral plate formed with the thickness of the material of which it is composed diminishing by uniform gradation from its center to its ends.

1,328,685. INTERNAL-COMBUSTION ENGINE. ELIAS H. PALMER, Ladson, S. C. Filed Apr. 28, 1917. Serial No. 165,302. 1 Claim. (Cl. 60—15.)

In an internal combustion engine the combination of a power cylinder and a compressing cylinder arranged end to end in spaced relation to each other, and each having heads at both ends, a frame rigidly connecting said cylinders, reciprocatory pistons working in said cylinders, a connecting rod common to both pistons and having a fixed connection therewith, a bypass connecting said cylinders, means for preventing return flow through said bypass while permitting a free flow from the power cylinder to the compressing cylinder, the last named cylinder having an exhaust port, a charging cylinder in communication with the power cylinder, a cross head having a fixed connection with and carried by said piston

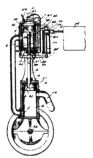

rod, a piston rod for said charging piston having a normally fixed but adjustable connection with said cross head and means for adjusting the last named piston rod relative to said cross head for varying the limits of movement of the charging piston relatively to the limits of movement of the power piston.

1,328,686. SUPPORT FOR FURNACE-POKERS, &c. JOSEPH PAVLIK, New York, N. Y. Filed July 29, 1919. Serial No. 314,040. 9 Claims. (Cl. 126—173.)

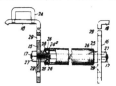

1. A poker rest for fire-openings comprising a pair of arms and a tie rod having a supporting roller thereon, said tie rod mounted for adjustment and connectible to said side arms at different heights.

1,328,687. INSULATOR-SUPPORT. BENTLEY A. PLIMPTON, Victor, N. Y. Filed Oct. 31, 1917. Serial No. 199,579. 3 Claims. (Cl. 173—321.)

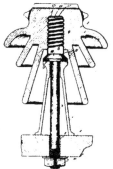

1. The combination with a threaded insulator thimble, of a pin having an integral threaded thimble portion at its upper end, a rigid collar on the pin beneath the thimble portion and having an upper surface against which the outer end of the thimble engages, a hollow truss member abutting the underside of the collar out of contact with the thimble and on which the collar rests and through which the body portion of the pin extends, a support for the truss member, and retaining means attached to the pin on the under side of the support.

1,328,688. SHAFT-CLAMP. FRANK J. POND, Tulsa, Okla. Filed Mar. 26, 1919. Serial No. 285,190. 3 Claims. (Cl. 64—98.)

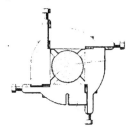

1. A means for coupling a wheel or reel to a shaft comprising a series of bars, each having at one end a slot and at the other a head adapted to pass through the slot of an adjacent bar, a set screw threaded through the slot of each bar for engaging the adjacent bar whose head is engaged with the slot for clamping the bars on the shaft, each bar having a recess on the face adjacent to the shaft, and a braking shoe in each recess and detachably connected with the bar.

1,328,689. ADJUSTABLE BLANK-HOLDER FOR PATTERN-GRADING AND OTHER MACHINES. ALBERT F. PRESTON, Boston, Mass. Filed Feb. 9, 1917. Serial No. 147,708. 15 Claims. (Cl. 33—23.)

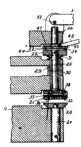

1. In a machine for outlining from a blank an article similar to a model, a holder for the blank and model, complemental clamps for holding the model, complemental clamps for holding the blank, both sets of clamps being mounted on said holder rotatably and in alinement to rotate about the same axis, and means for shifting one of said clamps transversely of said axis.

1,328,690. SACK - HOLDER. ALBERT LOUIS RENFRO, Bakersfield, Calif., assignor of one-half to William K. Lee, Bakersfield, Calif. Filed Sept. 25, 1919. Serial No. 326,149. 1 Claim. (Cl. 83—26.)

A bag holder of the character specified, comprising an open substantially rectangular frame adapted to be secured thereto a discharge spout, a yoke consisting of a body and arms extending laterally from the body, the arms being slidably connected with the side members of the frame near the end members thereof, hooks supported by the body of the yoke and by that side member of the

frame remote from the said body, and means on the free ends of the yoke arms to limit the movement of the yoke body away from the frame.

1,328,691. STEERING-WHEEL LOCK FOR MOTOR-VEHICLES. CHARLES H. RESCH, Youngstown, Ohio. Filed Oct. 13, 1919. Serial No. 330,222. 7 Claims. (Cl. 70—129.)

1. In a steering wheel lock, a steering post, a hand wheel on the upper end of said post, a column surrounding the post and having the upper end thereof circumferentially enlarged, a collar fast on said post at the upper end of the column and having the inner surface thereof channeled and the lower wall of the channel formed with a slot, said column being formed with an offset immediately below the slotted portion of said collar, the offset being formed with a vertical way adapted to register with the slot in said collar, a bolt slidably mounted in said way and having the upper end thereof formed with a nose normally disposed within said channel and adapted to be moved into said slot and the upper portion of the way to form a rigid connection between the collar and column whereby the post will be held against turning movement.

1,328,692. HEADLIGHT. FRANÇOIS RICHARD, Cleveland, Ohio, assignor to The Richard Auto Mfg. Company, Cleveland, Ohio. Filed Apr. 12, 1917. Serial No. 161,531. 2 Claims. (Cl. 240—7.)

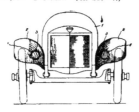

2. In combination, an automobile front fender having a forward end surface curved both downwardly and inwardly, said inwardly disposed portion also receding and provided with an opening, glass fitted in said opening so that its inward portion slopes in a rearward direction whereby such glass becomes correspondingly more nearly inconspicuous, and means for projecting light forwardly through said glass.

1,328,693. FENCE - WIRE FASTENER. WILLIAM F. ROBERTSON, Malta, Mont. Filed Mar. 6, 1919. Serial No. 281,019. 3 Claims. (Cl. 256—56.)

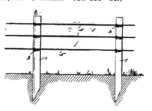

1. A fence post provided with a plurality of openings in its length, a retaining member at one side of the post and having a corresponding number of wire engaging elements extending through the openings thereof, and wedging means mounted on the said member and engaging the post to adjust the member laterally and cause the wire engaging elements thereof to clamp the wires against the post.

1,328,694. SOLDER FOR ALUMINUM. JULIAN SEGURA, New York, N. Y. Filed Oct. 21, 1919. Serial No. 332,321. 2 Claims. (Cl. 75—1.)

1. A solder for aluminum composed of lead ranging from 75 to 95 parts; tin ranging from 185 to 205 parts; zinc ranging from 185 to 205 parts; antimony ranging from 5 to 20 parts and white metal ranging from 5 to 25 parts (the composition of the white metal ranging from 80 to 90% tin, 5 to 15% antimony, and 3 to 10% copper).

1,328,695. RAIL JOINT AND FASTENER. JOHN SINKOVICH, Youngstown, Ohio. Filed July 29, 1919. Serial No. 314,096. 3 Claims. (Cl. 238—298.)

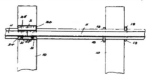

3. A rail chair comprising a base plate, a depending portion centrally carried thereby, an integral flange formed at one side of the base plate, a plate hinged to the other edge of the base plate, and rail engaging bolts carried by the free edge of the last named plate.

1,328,696. FISHING-REEL. JOSEPH I. SMITH, The Dalles, Oreg. Filed May 10, 1918. Serial No. 233,676. 1 Claim. (Cl. 242—84.1.)

A device of the character specified, comprising a substantially cylindrical casing, a reel in the said casing, said reel comprising a shaft provided at each end with a head, one end of the shaft being recessed, a journal pin engaging the said end and provided with a brake disk for coöperating with the head, a cup shaped casing connected with the outer end of the journal pin and inclosing the brake disk, and means for rotating the reel, said means comprising a pinion on the journal pin, a stub shaft journaled in the cup shaped casing and provided at its inner end with a pinion meshing with the pinion of the journal pin, and a handle hinged to the outer end of the stub shaft adapted to fold in either direction, the cup shaped casing having an opening for receiving the grip of the handle, and means for regulating the tension of the brake disk.

1,328,697. QUACK-GRASS DESTROYER. WALTER F. A. STRDY, Neenah, Wis. Filed Aug. 27, 1918. Serial No. 251,623. 6 Claims. (Cl. 55—134.)

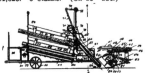

1. A quack grass destroyer having a plow, a reciprocatory longitudinally barred riddle of which the elements are spaced to provide intervals, means for conveying the quack grass from the plow to said riddle, an apron located beneath the riddle for receiving dirt detached from the quack grass roots and independent receptacles for said quack grass and dirt.

1,328,698. BALE-TIE BUCKLE. JAMES T. A. TODD, Fort Worth, Tex. Filed Mar. 20, 1918. Serial No. 223,490. 2 Claims. (Cl. 24—23.)

2. The combination of bale tie and a bale tie buckle having a body provided with a loop-engaging member at one end, one end of said tie being looped thereon, a friction bar at the other end of said body, a pressing member intermediate the ends of said body and disposed inwardly out of the plane of said body and parallel thereto and cooperating with said friction bar for gripping the other end of said tie and serving to press the free end of the tie against the bale, and flanges projected inwardly from said body for holding the free end of said tie against the bale and preventing the end of the tie from projecting outwardly.

1,328,699. SELF-SHARPENING ADJUSTABLE PACKER-HEAD PLATE FOR TILE-MACHINES. JOSEPH VOGT, Richmond, Minn. Filed June 28, 1919. Serial No. 307,274. 10 Claims. (Cl. 25—36.)

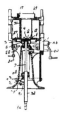

1. In a movable spindle packer head for cement tile machines, the combination with a packer head having a top wall, of means secured at spaced intervals to the top wall near the margin thereof, for renewing the packer spindle head

1,328,700. SHOCK-ABSORBER. JOSEPH F. WAGONER, Danville, Ill. Filed Dec. 7, 1917. Serial No. 206,036. 1 Claim. (Cl. 42—74.)

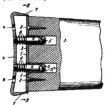

A shock absorber for gun stocks comprising a plate secured upon the end of a gun stock and provided with holes, sleeve members secured within said holes, the gun stock being provided with recesses receiving and of considerably greater lenth than said sleeve members, a shoulder engaging plate having a peripheral flange slidably engaging the periphery of the gun stock at the end thereof, pins extending from said shoulder engaging plate and slidable through said sleeves, a spring surrounding each pin and interposed between said plates, an adjusting nut threaded on each pin and enaging the inner end of the sleeve member whereby to regulate the tension of the spring and a lock nut engaged upon each pin and engaging said first named nut.

1,328,701. LACING-STUD-SETTING MACHINE. EDWARD E. WAKEFIELD, Providence, R. I., assignor to Tubular-Rivet & Stud Company, Providence, R. I., a Corporation of Massachusetts. Filed Sept. 19, 1917. Serial No. 192,043. 3 Claims. (Cl. 218—17.)

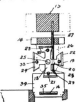

3. In a lacing stud setting machine, feeding means for simultaneously advancing the work and a reinforcing strip step by step to receive a stud through both, a pivotally mounted rotatable cutter having blades of different widths for partially severing the strip at intervals, a spring pawl for rotating said blades to present a fresh one after each cutting operation and finally presenting a wide blade for completely severing the strip after a predetermined number of partially severing operations.

1,328,702. COOKING UTENSIL. LLOYD VALENTINE WINTER, Juneau, Alaska. Filed July 15, 1919. Serial No. 310,954. 5 Claims. (Cl. 53—5.)

1. A cooking utensil comprising a base section provided with a support and having an open top and bottom, said section being adapted to be placed over a stove in open communication with the combustion chamber thereof, cooking means having its main portion exposed to the heat of combustion and having a marginal flange mounted on the support of the base section, said marginal flange being provided with vents spaced from the portion of

the flange resting on the support of said base section to allow passage of fumes downwardly therethrough and through the base section into the stove, and a cover section resting upon the upper face of the portion of said flange resting on the support of said base section, the inner surface of said cover section being adapted to cool the fumes and constrain them to flow downwardly through said vents.

1,328,703. MATCH-BOX. LOUIS YODY, Sharpsville, Pa. Filed Mar. 29, 1919. Serial No. 285,946. 2 Claims. (Cl. 206—21.)

1. A match box having a delivery opening therein, a partition dividing the box into two chambers, one chamber having a slot in its wall and an inclined bottom to permit the matches to pass from one chamber to the other, a lifting device consisting of a stem passing through the box and a tubular member having a slot therein for receiving the matches passing through said slot, spring means for the receiving device to bring the tubular member opposite the delivery opening, means for holding the delivery device in its lowest position and a spring plunger in said tubular member.

1,328,704. RECEPTACLE-SPOUT. JAMES YOUNGBERG, Alameda, Calif., assignor to William Cluff Company, San Francisco, Calif., a Corporation of California. Filed May 7, 1918. Serial No. 233,168. 1 Claim. (Cl. 221—11.)

A receptacle for discharging granular materials comprising a slotted spout having sector shaped members formed to lie in two planes one of which has a flange at right angles thereto, and a receptacle provided with an opening to receive the spout and with a tongue to pass through the slot, said tongue being bent down on the spout to hold it in place, and one member of the spout extending into a narrow slot to prevent lateral movement thereof.

1,328,705. HOLDER ATTACHMENT FOR LADDERS. HENRY ALPEN, Hempstead, N. Y. Filed Nov. 23, 1918. Serial No. 263,847. 3 Claims. (Cl. 20—85.)

1. A device of the class described comprising separable jaws, an expansible resilient ring having overlapped portions and lateral ends, said ends being secured to the jaws, one of said overlapped portions having an eye formed therein through which the other of said portions is slidably engaged and a receptacle supporting basket removably engaged with the ring and disposed in position to support a receptacle disposed within the ring.

1,328,706. ADJUSTABLE AND KNOCKDOWN WINDOW-SEAT. EDWARD ANDERSON, Brooklyn, N. Y. Filed June 5, 1919. Serial No. 302,004. 2 Claims. (Cl. 20—87.)

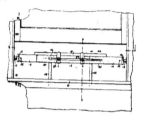

1. An adjustable and knockdown window seat, comprising a crossbar made in adjustable sections and extending across the winddow above the sill thereof, means for detachably fastening the outer ends of the sections of the crossbar to a window frame, a platform provided with bearings slidably engaging the said crossbar, clamping bolts held on the said bearings and engaging the said sections to fasten the platform in position on the crossbar and to fasten the sections of the crossbar together, transverse guideways on the under side of the platform, and seat supports slidably and detachably engaging the said guideways and adapted to rest on the window sill.

1,328,707. [WITHDRAWN.]

1,328,708. HORSESHOE. EUGENE HENRY BLONDEAU, Marquette, Mich. Filed Apr. 11, 1919. Serial No. 289,362. 1 Claim. (Cl. 168—18.)

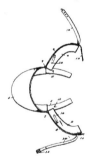

In a removable horseshoe, a horseshoe proper having orifices in the side portions thereof; a boot, including a toe portion and side portions which are hingedly secured to the ends of the toe portion, said boot having its lower edge flanged inwardly and the flange of the toe portion overlying and secured to the toe portion of the horseshoe, the flanges of the side portions of the shoe having depending spring lugs passing therethrough which are designed to enter the orifices of the shoe when the side portions of the boot are swung thereover, and securing means for said side portions of the boot.

1,328,709. MANURE-SPREADER. EDWARD W. BURGESS, Chicago, Ill., assignor, by mesne assignments, to International Harvester Company, a Corporation of New Jersey. Filed Feb. 8, 1916. Serial No. 77,023. 3 Claims. (Cl. 275—1.)

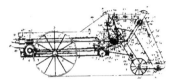

1. In combination, a source of power, a manure spreader having carrying wheels and an endless apron, operative connections between said source of power and said apron, including gearing normally adapted for driving said apron in a rearward direction, means for disconnecting said apron drive from said source of power, an endless belt manure loader attachment detachably carried by said spreader at the rear thereof, operative connections between said source of power and said loader for driving the outer run of said loader upwardly and forwardly, and operative connection between said loader and said apron drive gearing for driving said apron in a forward direction when said apron drive gearing is disconnected from its power source.

1,328,710. STEERING MECHANISM FOR TRACTION-ENGINES. EDWARD W. BURGESS, Chicago, Ill., assignor, by mesne assignments, to International Harvester Company, a Corporation of New Jersey. Filed Aug. 19, 1916, Serial No. 115,854. Renewed Sept. 24, 1917. Serial No. 193,033. 16 Claims. (Cl. 97—81.)

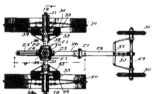

1. In a tractor steering mechanism, a pivoted steering axle, a ground contacting guide arm pivotally connected with the axle at a point behind the steering axle, and means actuated by relative movement of the axle and arm for returning them to normal position.

1,328,711. GAME DEVICE. CHARLES BOWNE CARR, New York, N. Y. Filed Oct. 9, 1918. Serial No. 257,491. 3 Claims. (Cl. 46—63.)

1. A game comprising dice, cards, and a game board formed in two sections hingedly connected together, each of said sections having sides and end pieces forming a box-like structure, holders arranged within one of said sections adapted to hold playing accessories when not in use, said game-board having a playing surface formed on the top thereof comprising a plurality of concentrically arranged vari colored stripes, and extensions on said playing surface having sections therein adapted to contain playing cards.

1,328,712. METHOD OF MELTING BRASS AND SIMILAR SCRAP. WALTER R. CLARK, Bridgeport, Conn., assignor to Bridgeport Brass Company, Bridgeport, Conn., a Corporation of Connecticut. Filed May 6, 1918. Serial No. 232,753. 6 Claims. (Cl. 204—64.)

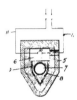

1. In the method of melting brass and similar scrap in an electric induction furnace having a secondary channel, the step of warming by extraneous means the upper surface of the charge only to such an extent as to prevent the chilling and incrustation of the same.

1,328,713. ELECTRIC FURNACE. WALTER R. CLARK, Bridgeport, Conn., assignor to Bridgeport Brass Company, Bridgeport, Conn., a Corporation of Connecticut. Original application filed May 6, 1918, Serial No. 232,753. Divided in part and this application filed May 31, 1918. Serial No. 237,562. 9 Claims. (Cl. 204—64.)

1. In combination with an electric furnace of the induction type having a molten secondary in communication with the lower part of the charge, an electric resistance element in the furnace chamber above the charge for preventing the chilling of the upper surface of the latter.

1,328,714. METHOD OF AND MEANS FOR MELTING BRASS AND SIMILAR SCRAP. WALTER R. CLARK, Bridgeport, Conn., assignor to Bridgeport Brass Company, Bridgeport, Conn., a Corporation of Connecticut. Filed June 13, 1918. Serial No. 239,742. 9 Claims. (Cl. 204—64.)

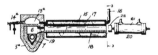

1. The method of melting brass and similar scrap, which comprises advancing the scrap slowly toward and into an electric furnace, and preheating the scrap during such slow advance.

1,328,715. COMBINED FOLDING SLED AND BABY-CARRIAGE ATTACHMENT. ADOLPH CLEIN, Chicago, Ill. Filed Jan. 27, 1919. Serial No. 273,257. 5 Claims. (Cl. 280—13.)

1. A combined child's sled and baby-carriage runner, comprising a sled having two angle-sectioned runners each having an outwardly directed web underhanging and directly supporting the pair of wheels at one side of the baby-carriage, two pairs of risers respectively secured to the opposed faces of the two runners but unsecured to the baby-carriage, foldable cross-bars connecting opposite risers on the two runners, and a sled seat carried jointly by the risers and the cross-bars and disposed under the vehicle, yielding means for detachably securing each of the said outwardly directed runner webs to the wheels supported thereby, and means carried by the said sled seat for maintaining the cross-bars unfolded and thereby coöperating with the said securing means in affording a rigid support for the vehicle.

1,328,716. THRUST-BEARING. LOUIS COATALEN and HERBERT CHAS. MACLEOD STEVENS, Wolverhampton, England. Filed July 16, 1919. Serial No. 311,284. 2 Claims. (Cl. 64—49.)

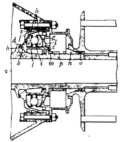

1. In thrust bearings, the combination comprising a shaft, a pair of collars on the shaft, a housing, and a pair of shoulders on the housing, a thrust ball ring located between the shoulders on the housing, a pair of divided rings mounted between the shaft collars for holding the ball ring in position and transmitting to it endwise pressures on the shaft, and means for securing the parts of the divided rings, substantially as described.

1,328,717. HOISTING-BLOCK. FRANK E. COATES, San Francisco, Calif., assignor of one-sixth to Chas. E. Beugler and one-sixth to C. H. Boardman, Oakland, Calif. Filed Jan. 29, 1919. Serial No. 273,696. 9 Claims. (Cl. 254—188.)

1. A hoisting block comprising spaced block plates, a sheave pin journaled in said plates, a sheave keyed to the pin, a second sheave loosely mounted on the pin and means for transversely shifting the last-named sheave and engaging it with the first-named sheave and the sheave pin.

1,328,718. MUSICAL-NOTATION INDICATOR. JOHANNA COHN, New York, N. Y. Filed Dec. 5, 1916. Serial No. 135,149. 4 Claims. (Cl. 84—48.)

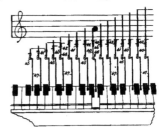

1. In a musical indicator, the combination with portable supporting means adapted to be located adjacent the keys of a musical instrument of pivoted indicators representing keys and their notes and adapted to be moved in and out of display, and means for displaying and associating the indicators with their respective keys synchronously with the operation of the latter.

1,328,719. TOY. PERRY M. CONDON, Albany, N. Y. Filed May 10, 1919. Serial No. 296,046. 3 Claims. (Cl. 208—165.)

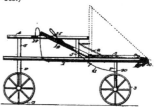

1. A device of the character specified comprising a wheel supported body, a seat at the rear of the body and elevated above the same, an arm hinged to the body at the front of the seat and adapted to swing down upon the body or upward into vertical position against the forward end of the seat, a spring normally pressing the arm upward, said arm being channel shaped and being adapted to receive a ball to be tossed to the occupant of the seat by the upward movement of the arm, means adjacent to the occupant of the seat for drawing the arm down, and a chute leading from the seat to the lower end of the arm and registering with the channel of the arm when the arm is lowered.

1,328,720. COMBINATION TERMINAL BLOCK AND LIGHTNING-ARRESTER. ROY CONNELL, Buffalo, N. Y. Filed June 20, 1919. Serial No. 305,604. 2 Claims. (Cl. 175—80.)

1. A combination terminal and lightning arrester, comprising an insulating base, a pair of binding posts mounted

thereon, collars surrounding said binding posts and lock nuts for clamping the collars in position, binding nuts on the posts, and a resistance block extending between and having its ends embracing the collars.

1,328,721. SPRAY-GUN. FREDERICK EDMUND CRUMMEY, San Jose, Calif., assignor to Bean Spray Pump Co., San Jose, Calif., a Corporation of California. Filed Nov. 26, 1918. Serial No. 264,264. 5 Claims. (Cl 299—117.)

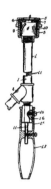

5. A spray-gun comprising a pipe provided with an inlet connection ; a valve head-shell at one end of the pipe ; an apertured cap on said head-shell ; a valve-seat sleeve removably fitted and held within the head-shell by the cap, said sleeve having in its wall a pair of oppositely disposed port slots disposed at an angle to the axis of the sleeve, and having also in its wall a pair of oppositely disposed port slots disposed at an angle opposite to the angle at which the first named pair is disposed, the inner ends of all the port slots communicating with the bore of the pipe and their outer ends communicating with the apertured cap, the outer ends of the first named pair of port slots lying nearer the cap than the outer ends of the second named pair of port-slots, said second named pair of port slots having a greater width than first named pair ; and a reciprocative valve within the sleeve to control the communication of the outer ends of both pairs of port slots with the apertured cap.

1,328,722. MILK-STERILIZING APPARATUS. FLOYD E. CRYDER, Chicago, Ill. Filed Oct. 3, 1918. Serial No. 256,722. 7 Claims. (Cl. 126—272.)

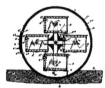

1. In a milk sterilizing apparatus, the combination with a casing, of means for heating the interior of the casing, cradles within said casing for containing the milk to be treated, means for revolubly supporting the cradles, and means for oscillating said cradles during their revolution.

1,328,723. ELECTRIC HEATER. JAMES M. CURLESS, Chicago, Ill., assignor to Benjamin Electric Manufacturing Company, Chicago, Ill., a Corporation of Illinois. Filed July 28, 1917. Serial No. 183,286. 5 Claims. (Cl. 219—44.)

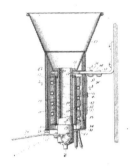

5. A heating device comprising a container for the material to be heated having an enlarged upper portion, a reduced intermediate portion, and a still further reduced lower portion, a plurality of spaced parallel posts extending alongside said reduced lower portion, a heating coil wound spirally around said posts, an outer casing surrounding said lower reduced portion and also surrounding said coil and posts and extending upwardly around said intermediate reduced portion, and a valve controlling the flow from the lower reduced portion.

1,328,724. TRANSMISSION-LOCK. HOWARD S. CURRIER, Detroit, Mich. Filed Feb. 28, 1919. Serial No. 279,699. 9 Claims. (Cl. 74—58.)

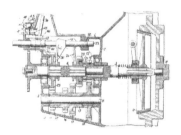

5. In combination with a transmission adapted for use in motor vehicles and including a driving shaft and a driven shaft, means for inter-connecting said shafts so that the latter turns oppositely to the former, a ratchet wheel driven in one direction when the shafts are so connected, a spring pressed pawl adapted to coöperate with said ratchet wheel to prevent movement in the opposite direction and arranged to snap down successively on the teeth of said wheel when the latter turns in the direction first stated, means for removing said pawl from the path of the wheel and for locking it in the last named position.

1,328,725. SLUG. EDWARD LUCIUS CUSHMAN, Miami, Fla. Filed Sept. 4, 1919. Serial No. 321,508. 3 Claims. (Cl. 101—396.)

1. A slug for linotype or intertype machines, having projections raised above the general level of the face of the slug where printing characters are omitted for the purpose specified.

1,328,726. APPARATUS FOR AND METHOD OF CLEARING SERVICE-PIPES. RICHARD LEE DEZENDORF, Richmond Hill, N. Y. Filed Feb. 28, 1918. Serial No. 219,628. 10 Claims. (Cl. 137—71.)

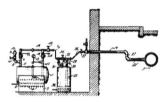

1. The process of clearing service pipes, which consists in injecting into the pipe to be cleared a wet charge and following the same by a hot dry charge.

1,328,727. COMBINED PENDULOUS TABLE AND CHAIRS. VASILY N. DMITRIEFF, New York, N. Y., assignor of forty per cent. to Rudolph Kliavin, Seattle, Wash. Filed July 1, 1919. Serial No. 307,951. 2 Claims. (Cl. 114—195.)

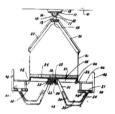

1. In a device of the class described, the combination with a rectangular table top, means for supporting said table top from a point thereabove, so that said table top is free to swing in any direction, a central beam carried below said table top, a plurality of forks engageable with said beam, means for clamping said forks in adjustment, arms formed with said forks, chairs adjustably engaged at the extreme ends of said arms, said arms constituting means for adjusting said chairs to or from said table top.

1,328,728. DEVICE FOR PACKING SILAGE. JOHN E. DOBSON and SAMUEL M. CROOKSHANK, Knoxville, Tenn. Filed Nov. 20, 1918. Serial No. 263,377. 5 Claims. (Cl. 100—56.)

1. In a device of the class described, a framework comprising a plurality of deflected elements, a shaft mounted transversely thereof, a roller mounted between diverging portions of the framework, a second shaft mounted trans-versely of the main portion of the framework, rollers carried by the second shaft and beyond the sides of the framework, the several rollers traveling in concentric paths, and means for effecting rotatable connection with an axial member about which the device is adapted to travel.

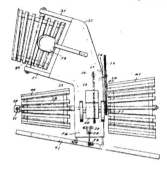

5. In a device of the class described, a framework comprising a plurality of elements extending parallel with reference to each other and then deflected to form a diverging portion of the framework, a shaft mounted transversely of the divergent portions, a roller mounted on the shaft, said shaft extending radially with reference to a vertical axial member about which the framework is movable in a circular path, a second shaft radiating from vertical axial member and mounted in the framework, and a plurality of rollers carried by the second shaft, the roller first named traveling in a circular path between the paths of travel of the other rollers.

1,328,729. ELECTRIC PERMUTATION-LOCK. GEORGE E. DOLAN and SIGWALD MILLER, San Francisco, Calif.; said Dolan assignor of one-half of his right to William T. Lloyd, San Francisco, Calif. Filed May 3, 1917. Serial No. 166,094. 7 Claims. (Cl. 200—43.)

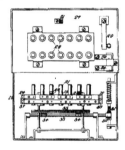

1. In an electric circuit control, a circuit, a series of depressible plugs movable to close the circuit, a member engageable with the plugs for restoring the latter to normal position after operation thereof, rotatable means to effect operation of said member, and depressible means to operate said rotatable means.

1,328,730. PLANTER. HARRY L. DOOLEY, Rock Island, Ill., assignor to Deere & Company, Moline, Ill., a Corporation of Illinois. Filed Mar. 24, 1910, Serial No. 551,232. Renewed June 10, 1919. Serial No. 303,253. 10 Claims. (Cl. 111—38.)

1. In a planter, the combination of a seeder shaft, driving connections adapted to intermittently connect the

seeder shaft to the axle to give the shaft repeated definite movements, a seed separating plate, a driving gear beneath the plate and connected to it, the gear having a plurality of concentric series of teeth, a plurality of pinions on the seeder shaft each permanently meshing with one of the said series of teeth, and a slidable key connected with the seeder shaft and adapted to engage any one of the pinions, the said pinions being provided with longitudinal keyways for receiving the key, the numbers and relative positions of the keyways being such that after each actuation of the shaft and of the pinions a keyway of each pinion is in alinement with the said key.

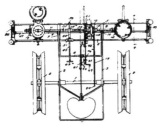

3. In a corn planter the combination of a seeder plate having uniformly spaced seed cells each taking a predetermined number of kernels, a series of sets of gear teeth arranged directly beneath and connected to the plate, a kernel receptacle below the plate situated to register with the last cell of each of several series of cells predetermined to be brought to it at each movement of the plate, a series of pinions permanently connected respectively with the teeth of the aforesaid several sets of gear teeth, said pinions having clutch parts whose members are multiples of the cells in the plate, a shaft for actuating all of the said driving pinions, a continuously moving prime driver, a tappet-actuated clutch for imparting power to the said shaft intermittingly through successive equal predetermined cycles, and supplemental power transmitting clutch parts adapted to connect the driven element of the tappet-actuated clutch alternately with the said pinions, substantially as set forth.

4. The combination in a planter, of two seed separating and depositing mechanisms, a transverse frame between the two mechanisms, means for adjustably connecting the two mechanisms to the frame whereby the distance between them may be varied, a two part operating shaft, one part for each of the said seed separating mechanisms, means for connecting the inner ends of the shaft parts, the said connecting means being adapted to permit the adjustment of the shaft parts relative to each other in accordance with the distance between the seed separating and depositing mechanisms, means slidably engaging the shaft for intermittently driving it through definite predetermined angles, change-speed gearing between each shaft part, and the corresponding seed separating and depositing mechanism, comprising a series of pinions loosely mounted on each shaft part and fixed against bodily movement with respect to the frame, means for moving the said shaft as a whole longitudinally, and means dependent on the longitudinal movement of the shaft for connecting thereto one or another of the pinions at each end.

9. In a corn planter, the combination of a frame, a seeder mechanism having a rotary single-kernel-cell plate adapted to travel at each of its movements over either of several distances which are multiples of a predetermined unit distance, three differently speeded drilling drivers for said plate each adapted to continuously rotate the plate, means for interrupting the action of all of the said drilling drivers, means for connecting either of said drivers to the plate either before or after such interruption without altering the driving relations thereof to the plate, and means brought into operation at will for throwing out of action the interrupting means, substantially as set forth.

1,328,731. DEMOUNTABLE RIM. CHESTER C. HARBRIDGE, Detroit, Mich. Filed July 3, 1916. Serial No. 107,226. 9 Claims. (Cl. 152—21.)

3. The combination with a wheel body comprising a band, of a demountable tire rim having plates secured to its inner periphery and adapted to seat upon the band, rim securing lugs, nuts for operating said lugs, and means for drawing the lugs to draw the rim and band together, said lugs and plates having interfitting edges.

1,328,732. INSULATOR-PIN. RHINEHART W. HARMS, Chicago, Ill., assignor to The R. Thomas and Sons Company, East Liverpool, Ohio, a Corporation of Ohio. Filed May 8, 1915. Serial No. 26,756. 7 Claims. (Cl. 173—321.)

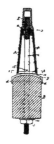

5. An insulator pin having a hollow standard with a tapped hole at its upper end, in combination with a securing bolt lying within the standard and having a threaded end screwed through said tapped hole and projecting beyond the upper end of the standard to enter the interiorly threaded thimble of a coöperating insulator, together with means for locking said standard and bolt against relative rotation after the insertion of the bolt, and a separable base plate on which said standard is mounted with limited freedom of rotation.

1,328,733. METHOD OF AND APPARATUS FOR SEPARATING LEAVES. JAMES B. HARRISS, Newark, N. J. Filed July 10, 1916. Serial No. 108,519. 29 Claims. (Cl. 131—60.)

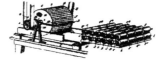

1. An apparatus for separating facially cohering tobacco leaves from a pack of such leaves, embodying means for advancing the pack bodily in an edgewise direction, and means operable upon the pack during such advancing movement for stripping leaves from the pack.

2. An apparatus for separating facially cohering tobacco leaves from a pack of such leaves, embodying means for advancing the pack bodily in an edgewise direction,

and means located adjacent the path of movement of the pack for engaging an advancing edge thereof and operable to cause a separation of the leaves of the pack.

9. In an apparatus for separating the leaves of a cohering pack of leaves, a traveling support for the leaves, suction means for causing a pack of the cohering leaves to adhere to the support, and means adapted in the travel of the support to remove a portion of the pack of leaves while the support continues its travel carrying with it the remainder of such pack.

1,328,734. METHOD AND APPARATUS FOR SEPARATING LEAVES FROM PACKAGES. JAMES B. HARRISS, Newark, N. J. Filed Apr. 12, 1917. Serial No. 161,541. 16 Claims. (Cl. 131—60.)

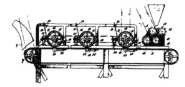

1. That improvement in the art of loosening and separating the facially cohering tobacco leaves from packs of such leaves, the steps which consist in causing the packs to move in a given travel path, and subjecting the packs while moving in said path to yielding pressure exerted on opposite faces thereof, whereby the packs are flexed and the leaf-layers loosened.

1,328,735. METHOD AND APPARATUS FOR SEPARATING LEAVES FROM PACKAGES. JAMES B. HARRISS, Newark, N. J. Filed Apr. 12, 1917. Serial No. 161,542. 17 Claims. (Cl. 131—60.)

1. The method of separating the leaves of a pack of superposed tobacco leaves wherein the leaves are facially but separably united, which consists in subjecting the pack to opposed pulling strains exerted from opposite faces thereof to cause a separation of pack leaf layers.

1,328,736. ELECTRICALLY-OPERATED TYPEWRITER. ERNEST HAUSBERG, Charles City, Iowa. Filed Mar. 11. 1916. Serial No. 83,567. 14 Claims. (Cl. 197—14.)

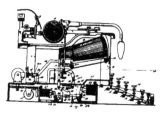

1. In an electrically operated typewriter having a series of substantially vertically arranged type bar operat-

ing levers, the combination of hooked levers pivoted to the lower ends of the type bar operating levers, a universal operating bar extended across the machine frame above the said hooked levers, to coöperate therewith, a series of selective electromagnets, means for energizing any of them, means operated by said selective magnets for elevating the free ends of said hooked levers to position for engaging the universal operating bar when a corresponding selective magnet is energized, a universal operating magnet, an armature therefor, and means operated by said armature for moving said universal operating bar so as to effect a movement of the selected type bar operating lever.

1,328,737. CLEANER. HOWARD EARL HOOVER, Chicago, Ill., assignor to The Hoover Suction Sweeper Company, New Berlin, Ohio, a Corporation of Ohio. Filed Oct. 8, 1917. Serial No. 195,231. 26 Claims. (Cl. 15—60.)

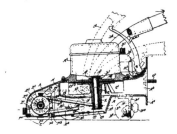

1. In a suction cleaner a hood in combination with a brush frame which it incloses and a brush adjustably mounted in said frame said frame pivotally mounted so that it can swing outside of the hood.

21. In a suction cleaner the combination with a suction cleaner hood of a series of fingers extending rearwardly from the front wall thereof, and shorter than the width of the opening and terminating near but out of contact with the rear wall of the hood, said fingers being of substantially uniform cross section lying within the hood and turned up at their inner ends.

1,328,738. STREET-CLEANER. JAMES L. HOPKINS, St. Louis, Mo. Filed Feb. 23, 1910. Serial No. 545,429. 16 Claims. (Cl. 299—36.)

13. In a street cleaner, the combination of a traveling frame, means carried thereby for flushing the street surface, and a second means carried by said frame to the rear of the first mentioned means for depositing a germicidal solution upon the street surface subsequent to the flushing operation.

1,328,739. ANTISKID DEVICE FOR MOTOR-PRO-PELLED VEHICLES. NEVIL MONROE HOPKINS, Washington, D. C. Filed Sept. 25, 1919. Serial No. 326,199. 9 Claims. (Cl. 291—23.)

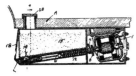

1. An anti-skid device comprising a charging chamber for receiving abrasive material, mechanism for forcibly ejecting said material, motor means for actuating said mechanism and a box-like casing for inclosing said parts in assembeld relation as a single compact structural unit.

1,328,740. CULTIVATOR. CHARLIE T. HUGGINS, Hemingway, S. C. Filed Oct. 7, 1919. Serial No. 328,970. 1 Claim. (Cl. 97—11.)

A cultivator ground treating element comprising a blade having a central, rearwardly directed stem bent upon itself with the initial free end portion overlying the rear face of the fixed end portion and its initial free extremity fastened to the rear of the point of the blade, said overlying portion of the stem being adapted to receive means for fastening it to a standard.

1,328,741. CAMERA. MICHAEL F. KENNEDY. Jr., Atlanta, Ga. Filed Mar. 3, 1919. Serial No. 280,205. 4 Claims. (Cl. 88—17.)

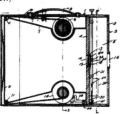

3. A camera including a dark room having film rollers with a film and a lens opening, a shutter for controlling the lens opening, an operating rod for actuating said shutter having a slot in its lower end, a dog adjustably mounted within said slot, a time controlled mechanism adapted to engage the dog when said dog is in one position for automatically operating the rod at predetermined times, said dog adapted to be moved to another position to permit the manual operation of the rod, and means controlled by said rod for winding a portion of the film from one roller to another after each operation of the shutter.

1,328,742. TAILSTOCK FOR BUTTON-BLANK-SAWING MACHINES. WILLIAM J. KOCH, La Crosse, Wis., assignor to Wisconsin Pearl Button Company, La Crosse county, Wis., a Corporation. Filed May 5, 1919. Serial No. 294,890. 10 Claims. (Cl. 79—16.)

1. In a tail stock for button blank sawing machines, the combination with a lower or base member having

vertical posts, of an upper member provided on its lower side with sockets mounted on said posts, means for adjusting the upper member vertically on the posts,

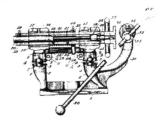

and means for securing the said member in its adjusted position, and a plunger mounted on said upper member to force the shell toward a tubular saw.

1,328,743. HEATER. WALTER R. LANUM, Savannah, Ga. Filed Mar. 2, 1918. Serial No. 219,961. 1 Claim. (Cl. 126—60.)

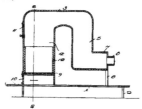

A heater consisting of a unitary structure forming a hollow U-shaped body having one vertical member extended horizontally from its lower end, a grate supported in the other vertical member of the body, a closure plate depending from the horizontally extended portion of the body, and opposed side plates hinged to the body and adapted to close the space between the vertically disposed members thereof.

1,328,744. PIPE-WRENCH. JOHN E. LENHOLT, Leete Island, Conn., assignor of one-half to Charles R. Tainter, Guilford, Conn. Filed Aug. 9, 1918. Serial No. 249,168. 5 Claims. (Cl. 81—65.)

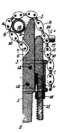

4. A chain pipe wrench comprising a handle member with a jaw at one end, a chain secured at one end directly to the handle member adjacent to the jaw, and a claw on the other side of the handle member for receiving and holding the other end portion of the chain, said chain comprising a series of alternate solid flat links and ring-shaped links, with the flat links arranged for edge engagement with the work.

1,328,745. ROTARY BAKING-OVEN. CHARLES O. LUCAS, Dayton, Ohio. Filed July 25, 1919. Serial No. 313,163. 1 Claim. (Cl. 107—59.)

In a rotary oven, the combination with a lower shell section, of an upper shell section between which and the lower section a substantial crevice is left to permit the escape of used heat from the upper section of the shell.

1,328,746. CATAMARAN. DANIEL MACIUK, Toronto, Ontario, Canada. Filed June 17, 1919. Serial No. 304,957. 2 Claims. (Cl. 9—3.)

1. In a catamaran, the combination with a pair of cylindrical floats having conical ends, bands surrounding said floats, connections extending between said bands whereby said floats are held in spaced parallel relation, a bolt adapted to be received between said floats, said bolt containing a cock pit, means for access thereto, and levers pivotally secured upon the sides of said boat at the front and rear thereof, engageable with the connections between said floats.

1,328,747. COTTON-SEED-WEIGHING APPARATUS. FRANK C. MATTERN, Great Neck, N. Y., assignor to Fairbanks Company, a Corporation of New York. Filed Apr. 26, 1917. Serial No. 164,611. 3 Claims. (Cl. 193—46.)

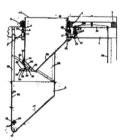

1. The combination with a hopper, and a gate closure hinged at its upper edge to one side of the lower end of said hopper, of a toggle link having one end thereof pivotally connected to said gate, a second toggle link having one end thereof pivotally connected to the other end of said first-mentioned toggle link, a rotatable operating shaft spaced from the said side wall of the hopper upon which the gate is hinged and rigidly connected to the said second-mentioned toggle link to force said toggle links into substantial alinement to close the gate, and fold the toggle links to swing the gate into an open position in substantial alinement with the wall of the hopper upon which said gate is hinged, and means for rotating said shaft.

1,328,748. CRATE FOR BOTTLES. JOHN FRANCIS MAURER, West New York, N. J. Filed Mar. 29, 1919. Serial No. 285,997. 5 Claims. (Cl. 217—22.)

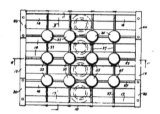

1. A crate or box for holding bottles, comprising a casing open at the top and provided at the bottom with spaced slats for the bottles to rest on, longitudinal partitions attached to the ends of the casing and resting on the said slats, transverse partition rods attached to the sides of the casing and extending transversely through the said partitions, spacing heads straddling the said partitions above the said transverse rods, and transverse head rods attached at their ends to the sides of the casing and extending through the said heads.

1,328,749. CAR FOR TUNNEL-KILNS. PAUL A. MEEHAN, New Castle, Pa., assignor to American Dressler Tunnel Kilns, Inc., New York, N. Y., a Corporation of New York. Filed Apr. 8, 1919. Serial No. 288,651. 3 Claims. (Cl. 106—180.)

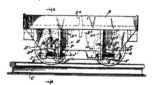

1. A car of the type specified, comprising in combination a plurality of supporting wheels, a separate axle for each of said wheels and a metallic car frame mounted on said wheels and formed with depending flanges arranged one at each side of each wheel and recessed to provide bearing seats open at their lower ends for and positively engaged by each of said axles.

1,328,750. APPARATUS FOR FEEDING PULVERIZED FUEL. PHILIP MEIDER, Jr., Pittsburgh, Pa. Filed June 23, 1919. Serial No. 306,110. 3 Claims. (Cl. 193—10.)

1. In apparatus for feeding pulverized fuel to furnaces, the combination of a main pipe for carrying the combined fuel and air, a comparatively short section of pipe communicating with said main pipe, a pipe sur-

rounding said last-named pipe and extending to the fuel burning device or furnace, and means for introducing

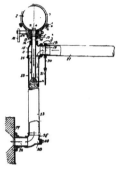

secondary air under pressure into said last-named pipe at a point above the outlet of said short section of pipe.

1,328,751. KNOCKDOWN BED-SPRING. GEORGE A. C. MONROE, Geneva, Ill. Filed Nov. 14, 1918. Serial No. 262,500. 1 Claim. (Cl. 5—64.)

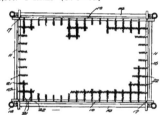

A bed spring support including frame members overlapping adjacent their ends and each extended in advance of the overlapping portions, said extensions each having a plurality of sockets in spaced relation adapted to be adjustably engaged with a sustaining element, and means for adjustably coupling the overlapping portions of the frame members.

1,328,752. GATE-VALVE. HERBERT A. MOODY, Turners Falls, Mass. Filed Nov. 7, 1918. Serial No. 261,482. 4 Claims. (Cl. 251—56.)

1. The combination with a sliding gate valve carrying wheels at the sides thereof, on which it travels, of means to shift the valve laterally with respect to the wheels, to vary the position of the valve with respect to its seat.

270 O. G.—30

1,328,753. BENCH. GLENN MORE, Jamestown, N. Y., assignor to Blackstone Manufacturing Company, Jamestown, N. Y., a Corporation of New York. Filed Mar. 17, 1919. Serial No. 283,021. 2 Claims. (Cl. 45—51.)

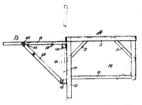

1. A shelf comprising, in combination with a support provided with a vertically extending member carrying a bracket adjacent the top, and a horizontal member, of a link pivoted to said vertical member below said bracket, and a frame pivotally secured to said link, the inner end of said frame, when in operative position, extending under said horizontal portion and the frame resting on said bracket, substantially as described.

1,328,754. REMOVABLE WRINGER MECHANISM. GLENN MORE, Jamestown, N. Y., assignor to Blackstone Manufacturing Company, Jamestown, N. Y., a Corporation of New York. Filed Mar. 17, 1919. Serial No. 283,023. 28 Claims. (Cl. 74—59.)

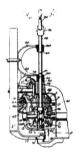

1. A fixed support, a rotatable driving shaft horizontally mounted thereon, a frame pivotally mounted on the fixed support and adapted to swing in a horizontal plane, a driven shaft horizontally mounted in said frame, means intermediate the shafts for communicating motion from the driving to the driven shaft, said means including mechanism for reversing the direction of motion of the driven shaft, and a handle disassociated from the frame and adapted to swing both in a vertical and a hroizontal path of movement for controlling the reversing mechanism.

1,328,755. MINING - MACHINE. EDMUND C. MORGAN, Chicago, Ill. Filed Feb. 10, 1913. Serial No. 747,250. 48 Claims. (Cl. 262—30.)

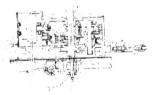

1. The combination with a mining machine, of feeding mechanism therefor comprising a rope drum and a rope

connected thereto, a freely detachable rope pulley guide
adapted to be hooked to various parts of the frame of
said mining machine, and power mechanism for operating
said feeding mechanism to effect longitudinal bodily movement of said mining machine when said rope passes
through said pulley guide and its free end is anchored at
a distance from said mining machine.

1,328,756.　PLOW.　CARL W. MOTT, Chicago, Ill., assignor, by mesne assignments, to International Harvester Company, a Corporation of New Jersey.　Filed
Sept. 3, 1914.　Serial No. 860,034.　7 Claims.　(Cl.
97—36.)

4. In a caster adapted to support a frame, a wheel, a
supporting member therefor having independent swinging
movement relative to said frame about a fixed vertical axis
and about a horizontal axis and means for limiting the
swing about both axes.

1,328,757.　OVERSHOE FOR TIRES.　BROOKS J. MULLI-
KIN, New York, N. Y.　Filed Mar. 1, 1919.　Serial No.
279,931.　1 Claim.　(Cl. 152—17.)

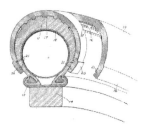

As an article of manufacture, an overshoe adapted to
fit exteriorly onto a tire and provided with a tread portion, the sides of the overshoe extending below the center
of the tire, the portion of said sides below the center of
the tire being thickened and provided with suction recesses adapted to hold the sides of the overshoe by suction on the sides of the tire, the said thickened sides being made of live rubber.

1,328,758.　SHOCK-ABSORBING CONTAINER.　OTTO S.
MUNTZ, Dubuque, Iowa.　Filed May 29, 1919.　Serial
No. 300,703.　4 Claims.　(Cl. 220—15.)

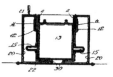

1. A shock absorbing container, comprising an outer
casing, an inner receptacle having projecting flanges and
resilient flange supporting means in the casing, said means
comprising a fluid under pressure.

1,328,759.　SHUTTER-ADJUSTING DEVICE.　LEONARD
COMBS PAGENHARDT, Westernport, Md.　Filed Aug. 13,
1919.　Serial No. 317,219.　11 Claims.　(Cl. 88—19.3.)

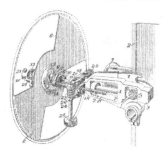

1. In combination with a revolving shutter shaft and a
shutter carried and revolved thereby; means on the shaft
by which the shutter is carried and by which adjustments
of the shutter in the plane of rotation are effected, means
for moving said carrying means along the axis of the
shaft and thereby effecting said shutter adjustments, and
means carried by the shaft in engagement with a portion
of the shutter for preventing axial movement of the
shutter.

1,328,760.　TOY WAGON.　SIMON G. PETTERSON and
BERTILL CARL PETTERSON, Pine Bluff, Ark.　Filed Feb.
15, 1919.　Serial No. 277,158.　4 Claims.　(Cl. 46—45.)

1. A wagon of the character specified, comprising a
wagon body, wheels for supporting the body, a crank
shaft having cranks and journaled at one end of the body
to which the wheels at the said end are secured, said
body having on the upper face thereof a plurality of
guideways, a slide movable in each guideway, a connection between each slide and a crank of the shaft, the
cranks being oppositely arranged to reciprocate the slides
in opposite directions, and figures supported by the
slides, said figures comprising representations, one of
said figures being connected to each slide.

1,328,761.　IRREVERSIBLE STEERING-GEAR.　LUCIUS
J. PHELPS, San Diego, Calif.　Filed Dec. 13, 1917.
Serial No. 206,952.　6 Claims.　(Cl. 74—39.)

2. In combination with a steering shaft; a fixed rack;
a plurality of pinions attached to the shaft and meshing
with the rack; a fixed member having an annular braking

surface; a brake-shoe having an exterior braking surface adapted to contact and coöperate with the annular surface aforesaid; a pinion secured to said brake-shoe and meshing with the aforementioned pinions; a pair of swinging wedge blocks interposed between the fixed braking surface and the shoe; a spring for each block acting to force the block into engagement with the fixed braking surface; an actuator extending inwardly between said blocks and adapted to rock one or the other thereof; and a steering-wheel connected to said actuator.

1,328,762. STEERING-GEAR ATTACHMENT. OSWALD S. PULLIAM, New York, N. Y. Filed Apr. 5, 1919. Serial No. 287,817. 1 Claim. (Cl. 116—31.)

The combination with the steering column of a motor vehicle, a post extending longitudinally through the column, a gear wheel carried by said post, a pair of spaced brackets carried by said steering column, a shaft rotatably mounted in said spaced brackets, a gear wheel carried by said shaft and projecting through an opening in the steering column into mesh with the gear carried by the steering post, a dial formed integral with one of said brackets, and a pointer carried by the free upper end of said shaft and movable over said dial, said pointer being adapted to be rotated by the steering post to indicate the position of the front wheels relative to the body of the motor vehicle.

1,328,763. TIRE-LATHE. SALMON W. PUTNAM, 3d, Rochester, N. Y., assignor to Arthur H. Ingle, Rochester, N. Y. Filed Oct. 7, 1918. Serial No. 257,154. 5 Claims. (Cl. 82—8.)

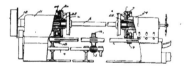

1. A tire lathe, comprising independent head and tail stock face plates spaced apart to receive between them a car axle with wheels thereon to be machined, a gear on each face plate, a countershaft journaled in the lathe bed and carrying pinions in mesh with said gears, a gear fast on said countershaft substantially midway between said pinions, a driving shaft parallel to said countershaft, and a pinion on said driving shaft in mesh with the gear on the countershaft.

1,328,764. GAGE FOR POSITIONING SHEET MATERIAL. AUSTIN D. RHODES, Waltham, Mass., assignor to American Lacing Hook Co., a Corporation of New Jersey. Filed July 29, 1918. Serial No. 247,116. 8 Claims. (Cl. 218—17.2.)

8. In combination, a work support, a presser foot and a gage pivotally mounted upon said presser foot and

adapted normally to project beneath the work contacting surface of said presser foot, a portion of the front edge of said gage being inclined downwardly and forwardly from the work contacting surface of said presser foot for

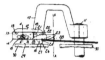

a portion of its length below said surface and then rearwardly and downwardly toward the work contacting surface of said work support and means to raise and lower said presser foot.

1,328,765. CONTROL MECHANISM FOR MIXING-MACHINES. JOHN F. ROBB, Washington, D. C., assignor to Koehring Machine Company, Milwaukee, Wis. Filed May 1, 1916. Serial No. 94,754. 23 Claims. (Cl. 83—73.)

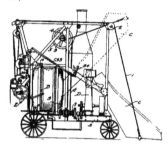

1. In combination, a mixing machine comprising a movable mixer, charging means for the mixer, means for indicating the speed of the mixer, and means for causing operation of the charging means governed by said speed indicating means.

1,328,766. SADIRON. NATHAN RUBENSTEIN, New York, N. Y. Filed June 11, 1919. Serial No. 303,403. 1 Claim. (Cl. 68—26.)

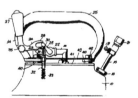

In a sad iron, the combination of an iron having an interior chamber and an L-shaped passage in its lower and front walls and outlets from the passage through the lower wall, means for circulating steam through the chamber, an exterior pipe adapted to pass the steam from the chamber to the passage, a cock in the pipe, a handle secured to the iron, a diaphragm between the handle and the iron, a bell-crank lever pivoted to the handle and having a knob on one end and adjacent the front end of said handle, and a fork on the other end of the bell crank lever and adapted to open the cock.

1,328,767. BOOK-COVER-MAKING MACHINE. JESSE SATENSTEIN, New York, N. Y. Filed Oct. 15, 1918. Serial No. 258,247. 3 Claims. (Cl. 11—2.)

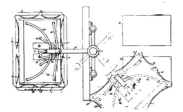

2. A book cover making machine having an integrally operated swinging arm and lifting palette for extracting fillers from one source of supply to deposit the same on a covering member; and a plurality of bowed spring members, the edges whereof extend outward from the edge of said palette to prevent the lift of the edges of said fillers while having a covering material placed thereover.

1,328,768. GREASE-DRUM. HARRY A. SEARLE, Council Bluffs, Iowa. Filed Feb. 4, 1919. Serial No. 274,919. 6 Claims. (Cl. 221—80.)

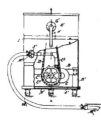

6. A container comprising a shell, a transverse member therein secured to the opposite walls above the bottom and transversely bracing said shell, and a pump suspended and supported solely by said member entirely out of contact with the bottom and walls of said shell.

1,328,769. SEALING - WAX APPLIER. CARROLL K. SPENCER, River Forest, Ill. Filed Jan. 16, 1919. Serial No. 271,345. 3 Claims. (Cl. 219—21.)

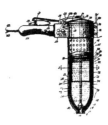

1. In a sealing wax applier, the combination with a foraminated outer shell apertured at its lower end, of a vertically positioned tube traversing the aperture of said outer shell, and exteriorly flanged at its inner end, an inner shell spaced from the outer shell and surrounding said tube below the flange thereof, and an annular foot threaded upon the lower end of said tube and exterting pressure through said outer and inner shells against the flange of the tube.

1,328,770. CAR-MOVER. FRANK F. STERNER, Harnedsville, Pa. Filed May 3, 1918. Serial No. 232,260. 1 Claim. (Cl. 254—35.)

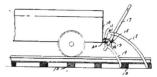

A car pusher including a yoke member having the extremities of its arms turned inwardly for biting engagement with the draft sill of the car, a bolt disposed vertically through the arms for forcing and holding the arms in such engagement with the sill, railway tie engaging arms, a block secured within the bight portion of the yoke and having a horizontal pivot member disposed therethrough, and a lever mounted for rocking movement on said pivot member and having the said arms pivotally connected thereto above and below the said pivot member, respectively.

1,328,771. HAIR - CURLER. IDA WHALEY STRAHAN, Montclair, N. J. Filed June 24, 1919. Serial No. 306,466. 6 Claims. (Cl. 132—19.)

5. A hair curler including a cap comprising a spiral spring, a covering adapted to envelop such spring, the hair of the user being applied to the outer surface of said covering, and means associated with the cap for forcing the hair into the groove.

1,328,772. HORN. GEORGE F. LONG, New York, N. Y., assignor to The G. Piel Company, Inc., Long Island City, N. Y., a Corporation of New York. Filed Apr. 25, 1912, Serial No. 693,222. Renewed June 13, 1919. Serial No. 304,085. 17 Claims. (Cl. 116—1.)

1. In an alarm or signal apparatus, a diaphragm, means for mechanically vibrating said diaphragm including a rotary disk, a series of projections mounted on said disk, operating means for said disk, and means for causing said disk to stop in a predetermined position after being operated by said operating means.

1,328,773. CHECKWRITER. LIBANUS M. TODD and ARTHUR C. LA MAY, Rochester N. Y., assignors, by mesne assignments, to Todd Protectograph Company, Rochester, N. Y., a Corporation of New York. Filed July 26, 1915. Serial No. 42,021. 19 Claims. (Cl. 197—6.2.)

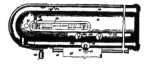

1. The combination of a printing couple comprising a rotatable type carrier and a platen, the members of said printing couple having a relative movement to bring various type forms on the carier, selectively, to a common position for coöperation with the platen, and having also a relative printing movement to impress the selected type forms upon the work; a fountain ink container; an inking device for applying ink to the type forms; and means for supplying ink from said fountain container to said inking device actuated automatically by the rotary movement of said type carrier.

1,328,774. ELECTRICAL ATTACHMENT-PLUG. WILLIAM C. TREGONING, Cleveland, Ohio, assignor, by mesne assignments, to Benjamin Electric Manufacturing Company, Chicago, Ill., a Corporation of Illinois. Filed Feb. 6, 1913, Serial No. 746,481. Renewed Feb. 10, 1919. Serial No. 276,244. 19 Claims. (Cl. 173—359.)

1. In an electrical attachment plug, a hand-hold member having a screw-shell contact, an insulating thimble, and a head having a metal connecting member, a center contact, and a terminal binding screw for said contact rotatably mounted within said hand-hold member, and a spring ring to secure said parts in fixed rotatable relation.

1,328,775. ADJUSTABLE CASTER. GEORGE F. VAN METER, Indianapolis, Ind. Filed Aug. 22, 1919. Serial No. 319,175. 3 Claims. (Cl. 16—164.)

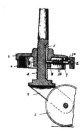

2. In a caster, the combination of a nut, outer and inner walls therein, an opening that registers with an opening in the inner wall and being provided in the outer wall, a pin entering the several openings in the walls, a spring abutting the pin and the several walls, and a shank having a channel arranged in the transverse height thereof whereby the nut will be retained is a specified position with respect to the shank.

1,328,776. VALVE-SPRING REMOVER. PEDER C. VANG, Omaha, Nebr. Filed Mar. 7, 1919. Serial No. 281,163. 2 Claims. (Cl. 29—87.1.)

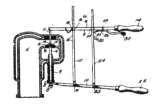

1. A valve spring release comprising a normally horizontal bar having at one of its ends a depending pin adapted to engage the upper face of a valve, a vertically adjustable bar adjustably secured to the horizontal bar, a rockable lever pivoted to the lower end of the vertically adjustable bar, one end of said rockable lever being adapted to engage under a valve spring, said horizontal bar and rockable lever being provided with handle members, a vertically disposed bar pivoted to the rockable lever and provided with ratchet teeth and detent means carried by the horizontal bar and coöperating with the ratchet teeth whereby the rockable lever will be held to any position to which it may be rocked.

1,328,777. UNWINDING DEVICE. JENNY ZERVUDACHI, née RODOCANACHI, Paris, France. Filed Oct. 1, 1919. Serial No. 327,720. 6 Claims. (Cl. 242—128.)

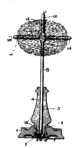

1. An unwinding device, comprising a tubular support, a vertical stem mounted to turn in the support and a removable transversely extending member carried by the stem adjacent its upper end.

1,328,778. JIG. JAMES B. BARBEE, Central City, and OTTO J. CROSS, Nederland, Colo. Filed June 25, 1918. Serial No. 241,818. 3 Claims. (Cl. 83—80.)
1. A pulsating jigger comprising a water tank having a transverse partition forming at one end of the tank a tailings chamber, a longitudinal partition of less depth than the vertical depth of the tank in the plane of the partition, a cover forming with the partition and the tank walls an air chamber, a jigging screen mounted in the tank along the other side of the partition and substantially

at the top thereof, and having a discharge projecting into the tailings chamber, the transverse partition apertured to provide for equalization of water level between the

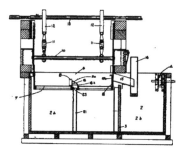

several chambers, the motions of the screen pulsating the water between the air chamber and its own compartment to facilitate the treatment of the pulp.

1,328,779. CUSHIONED WHEEL. GEORGE R. BARKER, Chicago, Ill. Filed June 8, 1917. Serial No. 173,656. 7 Claims. (Cl. 152—36.)

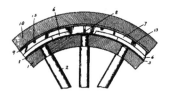

1. In a wheel having a plurality of cushioning elements consecutively disposed in annular formation between inner and outer members, an inner felly, and segmental rim elements secured independently of each other to the felly in substantially continuous annular formation; each rim element comprising a single-piece sheet metal plate formed to a U-shaped cross-section and straddling a portion of the felly and having its central portion folded upon itself to form a web extending radially outward of the felly, and a driving dog secured to the said plate and extending transversely of the web.

1,328,780. VALVE. GEORGE S. BARKER, Denver, Colo. Filed Aug. 10, 1918. Serial No. 249,288. 2 Claims. (Cl. 251—43.)

2. A valve comprising clamping members one of which is provided with a stem, the other clamping member detachably engaging the stem, the first mentioned clamping member having a valve seat, a valve having a stem received in the first mentioned stem and adapted to close against said seat, a retaining member detachably engaging within the first mentioned stem and adapted to detachably engage the second mentioned stem for operating the valve and adapted to be used as means for conducting air through the first mentioned stem when it is applied to the same in a position to hold the valve proper at an open position with relation to the seat.

1,328,781. BUNDLE-CARRIER FOR HARVESTERS. BERT R. BENJAMIN, Oak Park, Ill., assignor, by mesne assignments, to International Harvester Company, a Corporation of New Jersey. Filed Dec. 1, 1916. Serial No. 134,541. 22 Claims. (Cl. 56—480.)

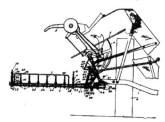

3. In combination, a frame, and a bundle carrier including a member pivotally supported intermediate its ends and movable about a plurality of independent pivots on said frame and bodily with respect to said frame.

1,328,782. FUSE-PLUG. REUBEN B. BENJAMIN, Chicago, Ill., assignor to Benjamin Electric Manufacturing Company, Chicago, Ill., a Corporation of Illinois. Filed Aug. 25, 1915. Serial No. 47,845. 19 Claims. (Cl. 200—125.)

1. A fuse plug comprising an insulating base, contacts supported thereby for engagement with the contacts of a receptacle, a plurality of fuses also supported thereby, and means for selectively placing said fuses in circuit with said contacts comprising a connector plug constructed to be inserted and withdrawn without removing the fuses from the receptacle, said connector plug being completely, readily and quickly detachable with respect to said insulating base by a pull on the plug.

1,328,783. ATTACHMENT-PLUG. REUBEN B. BENJAMIN, Chicago, Ill., assignor to Benjamin Electric Manufacturing Company, Chicago, Ill., a Corporation of Illinois. Filed Nov. 5, 1915. Serial No. 59,800. 7 Claims. (Cl. 173—359.)

6. An attachment plug, comprising shell and center contacts and wiring terminals therefor, said shell con-

tact being swiveled with respect to said wiring terminals, whereby the threaded shell may be screwed into the socket without twisting the conductors leading to said wiring terminals, and a flexible tubular extension handle secured to said threaded shell for screwing said threaded shell into the socket, said tubular handle surrounding the conductors leading to said wiring terminals and forming a passage therefor, and being rotatable about said conductors, whereby the conductors will not be twisted by said extension handle when the plug is screwed in.

1,328,784. BINDING-TERMINAL. REUBEN B. BENJAMIN and ERNST G. K. ANDERSON, Chicago, Ill., assignors to Benjamin Electric Manufacturing Company, Chicago, Ill., a Corporation of Illinois. Filed May 2, 1916. Serial No. 94,863. 4 Claims. (Cl. 173—259.)

1. A binding terminal comprising a member having a tapering passage therethrough, and two interengaging threaded members, one of said members being movable longitudinally in said passage, and slidable along one wall thereof, whereby said wall forms a backing for said member, and the other member being held from movement longitudinally of said passage, whereby relative rotation of said members will cause said movable member to move longitudinally in said passage; there being space between the wall of the tapering passage and the movable member to receive the end of a conductor, relative rotation of said two inter-engaging threaded members causing the conductor to be wedged between the longitudinally movable member and the wall of said tapering passage.

1,328,785. ELECTRICAL RECEPTACLE. REUBEN B. BENJAMIN, Chicago, Ill., assignor to Benjamin Electric Manufacturing Company, Chicago, Ill., a Corporation of Illinois. Filed Apr. 19, 1917. Serial No. 163,291. 28 Claims. (Cl. 240—81.)

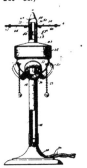

1. An electric stand lamp comprising an insulating base having upper and lower faces, a stand for supporting said base, a plurality of lamp receptacles supported underneath and by said base, binding terminals supported on the upper face of said base, and electrical connections from said binding terminals to the contacts of said receptacles extending through said base.

1,328,786. AUTOMOBILE - BUMPER. WILLIAM STEPHENSON BOOTH, Owosso, Mich. Filed June 5, 1919. Serial No. 302,012. 10 Claims. (Cl. 293—55.)

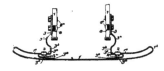

1. A bumper for automobiles and the like; comprising a main bar having a front portion extending across the wheel base and return bends at the ends of such front portion; and supporting members attached to the chassis of the vehicle; the front portions of the supporting members forming secondary shock absorbing means lying in rear of the front portion of the main bar and in advance of the return bend portions thereof and adapted to come into action when said front portion is unduly compressed or distorted.

1,328,787. STEEL BEARING FOR DISKS. HARRISON B. BOZARD, Hamilton, Ontario, Canada, assignor to International Harvester Company of Canada, Limited, a Corporation of Ontario. Filed Mar. 14, 1919. Serial No. 282,695. 5 Claims. (Cl. 64—26.)

1. In a disk drill, the combination with a support, of a pair of disks having bearing contact with said support, and a pair of housings having oil pockets therein extending below the inner points of bearing contact between said support and said disks.

1,328,788. AUTOMATIC IGNITER FOR ORCHARD-HEATERS. NELSON H. BRAY, San Francisco, Calif. Filed Mar. 4, 1918. Serial No. 220,150. 6 Claims. (Cl. 67—3.)

2. An igniter including a reservoir containing liquid; a sealed chamber containing a compound ignitible by said liquid; a tube having one end sealed by said liquid and

extending into said reservoir, whereby said liquid will be drawn into said chamber by volumetric contraction of the contents of said chamber.

1,328,789. RADIATOR. Patrick H. Cusick, Oregon, Wis. Filed July 16, 1918. Serial No. 245,250. 2 Claims. (Cl. 257—151.)

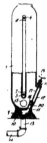

1. A radiator, comprising a plurality of connected end and intermediate sections, each end section having an enlarged, solid pedestal integral therewith and adapted to rest directly upon the floor, tie rods holding said sections together the base of one end section having extending through it a passage for the heating medium which opens at its lower end through the under face of said pedestal and communicates at its upper end with the circulation space within the said section, the lower portion of said passage being designed to receive the projecting end of a transmission pipe for the heating medium.

1,328,790. STEEL TRACK. Sanford Bowton Dickinson, Bath, N. Y. Filed Oct. 16, 1918. Serial No. 258,366. 3 Claims. (Cl. 238—26.)

1. A railway, comprising a series of supporting piers, having cushioning members embedded in their upper faces, transversely positioned standards having their base portions supported on the cushioning members, trusses secured on the standards, and rails secured on the trusses.

1,328,791. CORN-HARVESTER. Walter B. Gelatt, Seymour, Iowa. Filed Feb. 19, 1918. Serial No. 218,103. 1 Claim. (Cl. 56—16.)

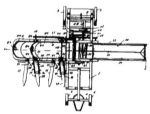

In a corn harvester, a portable frame, inner and outer pairs of forwardly directed stalk guiding members carried thereby, the members of each pair being spaced apart to pass on opposite sides of a row of stalks during advancement of the harvester, stalk cutting means associated with each pair of guiding members, a horizontal stalk conveyer disposed transversely of the frame adjacent the rearward ends of said pairs of stalk guiding members, means carried by each pair of guiding members for feeding cut stalks onto the upper run of the conveyer in substantial vertical position, ensilage cutting means positioned to receive stalks from the conveyer, an outer stalk receiving member positioned above the conveyer and positioned to receive stalks from the outer pair of said stalk guiding and cutting members, said stalk receiving member being transversely arched outwardly so as to urge the stalks toward the central portion of the upper run of the conveyer, and a similar inner receiving member positioned to receive stalks from the inner pair of stalk guiding members, said inner receiving member having its lower end positioned above the lower end of the outer receiving member so as to permit passage of stalks carried by the conveyer, the inner receiving member preventing interference with stalks discharged from said outer guiding members by stalks discharged from the inner guiding members and insuring that the stalks received from said inner guiding members will be deposited upon the conveyer during travel thereof with their butt ends in advance of the butt ends of the stalks received from the outer guiding members.

1,328,792. WINDING-MACHINE FOR THE MANUFACTURE OF HOLLOW INSULATING-CYLINDERS FOR ELECTROTECHNICAL PURPOSES. Emil Haefely, Basel, Switzerland. Filed Oct. 25, 1919. Serial No. 333,844. 2 Claims. (Cl. 93—81.)

1. A winding machine for the manufacture of hollow insulating cylinders for electro-technical purposes, from a band of fibrous material supplied with an agglutinant, comprising two heating cylinders, a rotary winding roller between them to wind the band upon it, a pressure cylinder to exert thereon the necessary pressure for the winding operation, means for adjusting the relative distance apart of the heating cylinders according to the size of the winding roller to be employed, vertical driving shafts, worms thereon, worm-wheels carried by the winding roller, and means for laterally engaging said worm-wheels into their respective worms, substantially as described.

1,328,793. CRANE. Arthur F. Hainsworth, Leeds, England. Filed Aug. 18, 1917. Serial No. 186,885. 3 Claims. (Cl. 212—8.)

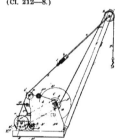

1. In a crane, the combination with a jib, of a jib drum, a hoisting drum having a disconnectible gearing

connection with said jib drum so that said drums may be simultaneously rotated, if desired, or so that said hoisting drum may rotate independently of said jib drum, a shaft on which said jib drum is mounted, and with which shaft said drum has a screw threaded connection, a friction piece splined to said shaft, and a ratchet wheel interposed between said drum and said friction piece.

1,328,794. METHOD AND APPARATUS FOR WEAVING TEXTILE FABRICS. EMANUEL INGHAM, San Diego, Calif. Filed Oct. 17, 1917. Serial No. 197,128. 25 Claims. (Cl. 139—7.)

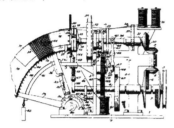

1. In a loom, the combination with a curved form, and means for supporting warp threads therearound, of a rigid annular needle constructed to lay weft threads around such form across the warp and disposed in a plane extending transversely of such warp.

1,328,795. AUXILIARY BUFFER FOR SHOCKERS. CLEMMA R. RANEY, Chicago, Ill., assignor, by mesne assignments, to International Harvester Company, a Corporation of New Jersey. Filed Dec. 19, 1917. Serial No. 207,863. 14 Claims. (Cl. 56—407.)

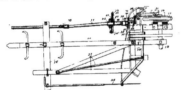

1. In a shocker, a frame, sheaf delivery means, means for operating said delivery means, and mechanism carried by and supported entirely on said frame for controlling said operating means, said controlling mechanism having means for taking up excessive strains on said controlling mechanism.

1,328,796. VALVE-CHEST. BURT R. VAN VALKENBURG, Oakland, Calif. Filed May 17, 1916. Serial No. 98,184. 6 Claims. (Cl. 84—156.)

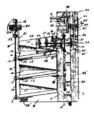

1. A valve chest of the character described comprising a carrier strip and a front strip secured together in spaced relation to provide a vacuum chamber between them, pneumatic carrier blocks attached to the external face of said carrier strip, pneumatics attached to the respective blocks, each block having the end which abuts the carrier strip provided with a recess communicating with a passage way leading to the atmosphere, said carrier strip having openings registering with said recesses to provide passage ways leading from said recesses to the vacuum chamber, secondary valves mounted to selectively place said recesses in communication either with the atmosphere or with the vacuum chamber, primary valves controlling the operation of the last mentioned valves, and means for operatively attaching said primary valves to said carrier strip in positions to be exposed by removal of said front strip.

1,328,797. MEANS FOR CONTROLLING ALTERNATING CURRENTS. ERNST F. W. ALEXANDERSON, Schenectady, N. Y., assignor to General Electric Company, a Corporation of New York. Filed Nov. 26, 1915. Serial No. 63,438. 10 Claims. (Cl. 171—119.)

5. Means for controlling the flow of high frequency current comprising an electromagnetic device having two cores both of which are traversed by a flux produced by the high frequency current and by a second flux produced by a controlling current, the circuit of the controlling current interlinking the two portions of the high frequency circuit in opposite directions and covering substantially the entire length of the high frequency magnetic circuit.

1,328,798. ELECTRIC SWITCH. KNUD KNUDSEN, Plainville, Conn., assignor to The Trumbull Electric Manufacturing Company, Plainville, Conn., a Corporation of Connecticut. Filed Nov. 11, 1918. Serial No. 262,039. 9 Claims. (Cl. 200—109.)

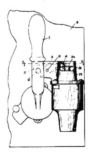

1. In an electric switch, the combination with the movable element of the switch mechanism, of a latch lever pivoted intermediate its ends and adapted to engage the movable switch element at one end to hold the same in a predetermined position, a trip lever pivoted on an axis substantially in line with the opposite end of the latch lever and adapted to engage said end of the latch lever to hold the same with the opposite end in holding engagement with the movable element of the switch mechanism, and means for actuating said trip lever to free the same

from holding engagement with the one end of the latch lever to thereby permit the latch lever to swing on its pivot so as to free the opposite end of said lever from holding engagement with the movable switch element.

1,328,799. PADDLE OR PLUNGER FOR MOLTEN GLASS. KARL E. PEILER, Hartford, Conn., assignor to Hartford-Fairmont Company, Canajoharie, N. Y., a Corporation of New York. Filed Mar. 27, 1917. Serial No. 157,634. 4 Claims. (Cl. 49—14.)

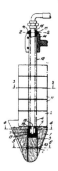

1. An implement for working molten glass, including a head of refractory material having a shouldered opening through it and having a flat surface at one side of the opening, a tubular reinforcement extending into one end of the opening, a tube fastened within the reinforcement for conveying cooling fluid, an enlarged cap threaded to the reinforcement and flatted on one side to engage the flatted surface of the head and bearing against the shoulder of the opening, and a refractory plug closing the other end of the opening.

1,328,800. SOIL-PULVERIZER. WILLIAM H. SHERROD, Seattle, Wash. Filed Nov. 6, 1918. Serial No. 261,418. 1 Claim. (Cl. 97—63.)

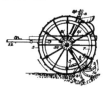

A soil stirring and cutting machine comprising a reel mounted to turn about its axis and having longitudinally extending blades placed tangentially, soil carrying blades placed radially and within the cutting blades.

1,328,801. DUST-CAP AND ATTACHING MEANS THEREFOR. JUNIUS A. BOWDEN, Los Angeles, Calif. Filed Feb. 21, 1919. Serial No. 278,454. 6 Claims. (Cl. 152—12.)

1. Means of protecting an air inlet stem of a tire, comprising a nut, a cap and spring means, said spring means in the form of a slotted band, said nut adapted to be

secured upon said stem, said spring means seated upon said nut and means adapted to prevent displacement of

the spring means therefrom, said cap adapted to detachably engage said spring means for the purpose described.

REISSUES.

14,792. BALL - BEARING FOR GRAVITY - CARRIERS. HERMAN J. BUCK, Ellwood City, Pa., assignor to Mathews Gravity Carrier Company, Ellwood City, Pa., a Corporation. Filed May 5, 1919. Serial No. 295,009. Original No. 1,238,880, dated Sept. 4, 1917, Serial No. 816,142, filed Feb. 3, 1914. 11 Claims. (Cl. 64—36.)

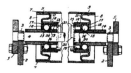

8. The combination, with an axle rod and a carrier roll having heads recessed around said rod, of anti-friction bearings, each constituting a self-contained unit comprising a sleeve longitudinally movable upon the rod and having a circumferential groove, a cage encircling said sleeve and seated in the recess of the roll head, and balls arranged between the sleeve and cage and seated in the groove in said sleeve.

14,793. FASTENER FOR HINGED STRUCTURES. ROY ALSTAN LIPPINCOTT and EDWARD FIELDER BILLSON, Melbourne, Victoria, Australia. Filed Sept. 22, 1919. Serial No. 325,556. Original No. 1,297,195, dated Mar. 11, 1919, Serial No. 256,411, filed Oct. 1, 1918. 2 Claims. (Cl. 268—15.)

1. Controlling means for swinging closures, comprising in combination a swinging closure and its casing, a rod pivoted to the closure, a casting pivotally mounted on the casing, said casting having a cylindrical body and an extension projecting therefrom, the casting having a rod receiving opening extending therethrough and a notch which communicates with the opening, an eye mounted in the extension and provided with a threaded stem, the eye being seated in the notch in the extension and adapted to engage the rod and the threaded stem passing through the extension, and a lock nut engaging the threaded extension.

DESIGNS.

54,359. EDGING. John G. Chapman, Port Washington, N. Y., assignor to Sanford Narrow Fabric Co., New York, N. Y., a Corporation of New York. Filed Aug. 2, 1919. Serial No. 315,026. Term of patent 3½ years.

The ornamental design for an edging, as shown.

54,360. EDGING. John G. Chapman, Port Washington, N. Y., assignor to Sanford Narrow Fabric Co., New York, N. Y., a Corporation of New York. Filed Aug. 2, 1919. Serial No. 315,027. Term of patent 14 years.

The ornamental design for an edging, as shown.

54,361. EDGING. John G. Chapman, Port Washington, N. Y., assignor to Sanford Narrow Fabric Co., New York, N. Y., a Corporation of New York. Filed Aug. 2, 1919. Serial No. 315,028. Term of patent 14 years.

The ornamental design for an edging, as shown.

54,362. SERVICE-EMBLEM. William Frederic Stevens, Chicago, Ill. Filed Dec. 16, 1918. Serial No. 267,062. Term of patent 3½ years.

The ornamental design for a service emblem as shown.

TRADE-MARKS

The following trade-marks are published in compliance with section 6 of the act of February 20, 1905, as amended March 2, 1907. Notice of opposition must be filed within thirty days of this publication.

Marks applied for "under the ten-year proviso" are registrable under the provision in clause (b) of section 5 of said act as amended February 18, 1911.

As provided by section 14 of said act, a fee of ten dollars must accompany each notice of opposition.

Ser. No. 100,004. (CLASS 39. CLOTHING.) CARSON, PIRIE, SCOTT & Co., Chicago, Ill., assignor to Carson Pirie Scott & Company, Chicago, Ill., a Corporation of Illinois. Filed Dec. 18, 1916.

Particular description of goods.—Overalls.
Claims use since about Apr. 5, 1916.

Ser. No. 101,569. (CLASS 50. MERCHANDISE NOT OTHERWISE CLASSIFIED.) THE HERKIMER FIBRE COMPANY, Herkimer, N. Y. Filed Feb. 21, 1917.

Particular description of goods.—Manufactured Leather-Board.
Claims use since the early part of 1908.

Ser. No. 102,607. (CLASS 19. VEHICLES, NOT IN-CLUDING ENGINES.) ABBOTT CORPORATION, Detroit, Mich. Filed Mar. 31, 1917.

Particular description of goods.—Automobile Pleasure-Cars, Automobile Business-Cars, and Motor-Trucks.
Claims use since January, 1910.

Ser. No. 105,482. (CLASS 46. FOODS AND INGREDI-ENTS OF FOODS.) MARRE & COMPANY, Buenos Aires, Argentina. Filed Aug. 4, 1917.

Particular description of goods.—Cheese and Butter.
Claims use since June 30, 1908.

Ser. No. 106,744. (CLASS 46. FOODS AND INGREDI-ENTS OF FOODS.) NINAVILLA FARM PRODUCTS Co., Blind Slough, Oreg. Filed Oct. 12, 1917.

Particular description of goods.—Fresh Vegetables.
Claims use since July 1, 1915.

Ser. No. 106,883. (CLASS 39. CLOTHING.) EDWIN B. NATHAN, New York, N. Y. Filed Oct. 20, 1917.

Particular description of goods.—Mufflers, Shawls, Sweaters, Helmets of Knit Fabric, Boots and Slippers of Knit Fabric, for Men, Women, and Children's Wear, Vests of Knit Fabric, and Gloves of Knit Fabric.
Claims use since about Apr. 1, 1917.

Ser. No. 108,835. (CLASS 6. CHEMICALS, MEDI-CINES, AND PHARMACEUTICAL PREPARATIONS.) THE LORENZ COMPANY, Everett, Mass. Filed Feb. 5, 1918.

MILITARY

Particular description of goods.—Tooth-Powder and Foot-Powder.
Claims use since 1908.

Ser. No. 109,812. (CLASS 46. FOODS AND INGREDI-ENTS OF FOODS.) NEBRASKA FOUNTAIN & SUPPLY Co., Omaha, Nebr. Filed Mar. 26, 1918.

Particular description of goods.—A Topping for Ice-Cream Sundaes and Hot Chocolate.
Claims use since Feb. 8, 1910.

Ser. No. 110,794. (CLASS 45. BEVERAGES, NON-ALCOHOLIC.) MANFRED WAHL, Philadelphia, Pa. Filed May 9, 1918.

Particular description of goods.—A Pure Culture or Ferment Employed in the Production of Cereal Beverages Which are Either Non-Alcoholic or Contain Not Over One-Half of One Per Cent. of Alcohol, by Volume.
Claims use since July 1, 1917.

Ser. No. 113,202. (CLASS 19. VEHICLES, NOT IN-CLUDING ENGINES.) VICTOR AIRCRAFT CORPORA-TION, Freeport, N. Y. Filed Sept. 16, 1918.

Particular description of goods.—Aeroplanes.
Claims use since the 31st day of July, 1918.

Ser. No. 114,528. (CLASS 42. KNITTED, NETTED, AND TEXTILE FABRICS.) CARSON, PIRIE, SCOTT & Co., Chicago, Ill., assignor to Carson Pirie Scott & Company, Chicago, Ill., a Corporation of Illinois. Filed Dec. 7, 1918.

The picture shown in the drawing is fanciful.
Particular description of goods.—Nainsooks, Muslins, and Longcloth and Cambrics.
Claims use since about May, 1918.

Ser. No. 116,680. (CLASS 9. EXPLOSIVES, FIRE-ARMS, EQUIPMENTS, AND PROJECTILES.) E. I. DU PONT DE NEMOURS & COMPANY, Wilmington, Del. Filed Mar. 18, 1919.

Particular description of goods.—A High Explosive of the Dynamite Type.
Claims use since Dec. 12, 1918.

Ser. No. 116,982. (CLASS 23. CUTLERY, MACHINERY, AND TOOLS, AND PARTS THEREOF.) WALLIS TRAC-TOR COMPANY, Racine, Wis. Filed Mar. 27, 1919.

WALLIS

Particular description of goods.—Tractors.
Claims use since January, 1913.

Ser. No. 116,992. (CLASS 42. KNITTED, NETTED, AND TEXTILE FABRICS.) LAMBORN & CO., New York, N. Y. Filed Mar. 28, 1919.

Particular description of goods.—Textile Fabrics—Namely, Cotton Piece Goods, Cotton Netting, Cotton Bunting, and Silk Piece Goods.
Claims use since April, 1918.

Ser. No. 117,011. (CLASS 39. CLOTHING. HIRSCH, FRIEDMAN Co., Chicago, Ill. Filed Mar. 29, 1919.

Particular description of goods.—Men's and Boys' Dress and Negligée Shirts and Also Men's and Boys' Silk, Cotton, and Woolen Underwear, Pajamas, and Night-Shirts.
Claims use since Mar. 26, 1919.

Ser. No. 117,125. (CLASS 37. PAPER AND STATIONERY.) RECORD CARD Co., New York, N. Y. Filed Apr. 2, 1919.

Particular description of goods.—Filing-Cards.
Claims use since Dec. 27, 1918.

Ser. No. 117,446. (CLASS 22. GAMES, TOYS, AND SPORTING GOODS.) GEORGE C. DUTTON, Boston, Mass. Filed Apr. 14, 1919.

No claim is made to the words "A New Idea in Toyland."
Particular description of goods.—Games. The Specific Nature of the Goods Consists of a Series of Toys, Such as Dolls or Animals, the Series of Dolls or of Animals Embodying a Plurality of Dolls or a Plurality of Animals Each Identical with the Others of the Same Series Except as to Size.
Claims use since Apr. 5, 1919.

Ser. No. 117,572. (CLASS 6. CHEMICALS, MEDICINES, AND PHARMACEUTICAL PREPARATIONS.) OTORINO MANUFACTURING COMPANY, New York, N. Y. Filed Apr. 17, 1919.

Particular description of goods.—A Medicine for the Diseased Mucous Membrane of the Nose, Throat, Mouth, and Ear.
Claims use since on or about the 26th day of March, 1919.

Ser. No. 117,966. (CLASS 1. RAW OR PARTLY-PREPARED MATERIALS.) BARNET LEATHER COMPANY, New York, N. Y. Filed Apr. 29, 1919.

No claim being made to the words "Made in U. S. A.," the words and numerals "Barnet Leather Co., Est. 1873, Chicago, Paris, New Orleans, New York, Boston, Tanneries, Little Falls, N. Y.," apart from the mark shown in the drawing.
Particular description of goods.—Patent-Leather and Finished Calfskins.
Claims use since May, 1903.

Ser. No. 118,232. (CLASS 46. FOODS AND INGREDIENTS OF FOODS.) DANIEL L. LEVINSON, Chicago, Ill. Filed May 7, 1919.

"APPELEINE"

Particular description of goods.—A Powdered Preparation for Making a Fruit Acid and Spice-Flavored Marmalade and Jam.
Claims use since Dec. 1, 1918.

Ser. No. 118,499. (CLASS 46. FOODS AND INGREDIENTS OF FOODS.) YORK PRETZEL BAKERY, York, Pa. Filed May 14, 1919.

"SUMGUD"

Particular description of goods.—Pretzels, Cakes, Crackers, and Biscuits.
Claims use since Apr. 14, 1919.

Ser. No. 118,559. (CLASS 6. CHEMICALS, MEDI-
CINES, AND PHARMACEUTICAL PREPARATIONS.)
JENNINGS MANUFACTURING COMPANY, Grand Rapids,
Mich. Filed May 16, 1919.

Particular description of goods.—Perfumery, Toilet
Water, Face-Powder, Face-Cream, and Talcum Powder.
Claims use since September, 1895.

Ser. No. 119,283. (CLASS 19. VEHICLES, NOT IN-
CLUDING ENGINES.) WARD MOTOR VEHICLE COM-
PANY, Mount Vernon, N. Y. Filed June 6, 1919.

No claim being made to the words " Ward Motor
Vehicle Co." apart from the mark shown in the drawing.
Particular description of goods.—Automobiles.
Claims use since the early part of 1911.

Ser. No. 119,693. (CLASS 12. CONSTRUCTION MA-
TERIALS.) THE ASPHALT MANUFACTURING COMPANY,
Lancaster, Ohio. Filed June 17, 1919.

·TAMCO

Particular description of goods.—Slate-Surfaced Roofings and Slate-Surface Shingles.
Claims use since April, 1918.

Ser. No. 119,871. (CLASS 6. CHEMICALS, MEDI-
CINES, AND PHARMACEUTICAL PREPARATIONS.)
THE SEYDEL MANUFACTURING COMPANY, Jersey City,
N. J. Filed June 23, 1919.

No claim being made to the words " Seydel Chemicals "
apart from the mark shown in the drawing.
Particular description of goods.—Ethyl Benzoate,
Methyl Benzoate, Benzyl Benzoate, Beta-Naphthol Ben-
zoate, Ammonium Benzoate, Lithium Benzoate, Mercury
Benzoate, and Benzyl Alcohol.
Claims use since Jan. 30, 1913.

Ser. No. 119,872. (CLASS 6. CHEMICALS, MEDI-
CINES, AND PHARMACEUTICAL PREPARATIONS.)
SEYDEL MANUFACTURING COMPANY, Jersey City, N. J.
Filed June 23, 1919.

No claim being made to the word " Trade-Mark."
Particular description of goods.—Sizing and Finishing
Compounds for Textile Fabrics and Threads.
Claims use since Jan. 30, 1905.

Ser. No. 119,974. (CLASS 22. GAMES, TOYS, AND
SPORTING GOODS.) THE A. C. GILBERT COMPANY,
New Haven, Conn. Filed June 26, 1919.

GILBERT

Particular description of goods.—Metal Building Toys,
Wooden Building Toys, Toy Blocks, Toy Sets Adapted
to the Construction or Assembly of Children's Express-
Wagons, Wheelbarrows, Go-Carts, Coasters, Gliders, and
the Like; Children's Sleds; Permanently-Assembled Ex-
press-Wagons, Wheelbarrows, Go-Carts, Coasters, Gliders,
and Similar Wheeled Vehicles for Actual Use by Children;
Spring-Operated Mechanical Toys, Electric-Motor-Driven
Mechanical Toys, Toy Wagons, Toy Carriages, Toy Air-
craft, Toy Industrial Machinery, Toy Boats, Toy Auto-
mobiles, Toy Tractors, Toy Tanks, Toy Engines, Toy
Railways, Toy Elevators, Toy Bridges, Toy Phonographs,
Toy Sewing-Machines, Toy Typewriters, Toy Guns, Toy
Gear-Boxes, Toy Chemistry Outfits, Toy Soldiering Out-
fits, Toy Nurses' Outfits, Toy Soldering Outfits, Toy
Clocks, Toy Watches, Toy Tools, Toy Musical Instruments,
Toy Playhouses, Toy Houses, Magic Sets and Apparatus,
Puzzle Sets and Apparatus, Card Games, Toy Figures,
Sounding Toys, Toy Joke Sets, Tops, Toy Rattles, Toy
Reins, Toy Bells, Hobby-Horses, Toy Money-Boxes and
Safes, Whirligigs, Wheeled Bell Toys, Toy Stoves, Toy
Washing-Machines, Toy Sadirons, Toy Culinary and Table
Articles, Toy Furniture, Toy Cycles, Toy Heaters, and
Toy Cameras.
Claims use since on or about July, 1913.

Ser. No. 120,070. (CLASS 45. BEVERAGES, NON-
ALCOHOLIC.) RAINIER PRODUCTS COMPANY, Seattle,
Wash. Filed June 28, 1919.

The lining on the drawing is for shading only.
Particular description of goods.—Birch-Beer, Root-
Beer, Sarsaparilla, Ginger-Ale, Soda-Water of Various
Flavors, and Cider.
Claims use since June 2, 1919.

Ser. No. 120,373. (CLASS 45. BEVERAGES, NON-ALCOHOLIC.) FRUIT VALLEY CORPORATION, Rochester, N. Y. Filed July 9, 1919.

Particular description of goods.—A Concentrated Syrup Consisting of Non-Alcoholic Non-Cereal Maltless Solutions Combined with Sugar Dissolved in Water and a Beverage Made from the Same by Adding Plain or Charged Water.

Claims use since Apr. 9, 1919.

Ser. No. 120,376. (CLASS 6. CHEMICALS, MEDICINES, AND PHARMACEUTICAL PREPARATIONS.) SHINZO FUKUHARA, Tokyo, Japan. Filed July 9, 1919.

No claim is made for use of the word " Shiseido," " Shimbashi," or " Tokyo " apart from the mark shown in the drawing, as " Shiseido " is the name of the proprietor's shop, while " Shimbashi " and " Tokyo " form a part of the address and are geographical.

Particular description of goods.—Perfumes, Incense Perfumes, Perfumed Waters, Perfumed Oils, Incenses, Toilet Powders, Toilet Waters, Toilet Creams, Face-Lotions, Face-Powders, Hair-Ointments, Soaps, Tooth-Powders, Tooth-Creams.

Claims use since the 1st day of November, 1917.

Ser. No. 120,416. (CLASS 45. BEVERAGES, NON-ALCOHOLIC.) OTTO EBERLIN, Hermann, Mo. Filed July 10, 1919. Under ten-year proviso.

Pear Champagne

Particular description of goods.—Non-Alcoholic Non-Cereal Maltless Carbonated Pear-Flavored Beverage Containing Less Than Half of One Per Cent. of Alcohol, by Volume, Sold as a Soft Drink.

Claims use since prior to Jan. 1, 1889.

Ser. No. 120,474. (CLASS 26. MEASURING AND SCIENTIFIC APPLIANCES.) THE BROWN INSTRUMENT COMPANY, Philadelphia, Pa. Filed July 12, 1919.

RESISTEAT

Particular description of goods.—Protecting-Tubes for Pyrometers.

Claims use since on or about Apr. 5, 1918.

270 O. G.—31

Ser. No. 120,947. (CLASS 39. CLOTHING.) ADWEAR PROCESS SOLE LEATHER MACHINE COMPANY, Philadelphia, Pa. Filed July 26, 1919.

No claim is made for the representations of the shoe-soles apart from their showing in the drawing. The Geneva cross of the mark is not used red and never will be used red as a part of said mark.

Particular description of goods.—Men's, Women's, and Children's Processed-Leather Shoe-Soles, Boot-Soles, Boots, and Shoes.

Claims use since May 20, 1919.

Ser. No. 120,997. (CLASS 39. CLOTHING.) THE KENNESAW HOSIERY COMPANY, Marietta, Ga. Filed July 28, 1919.

No claim is made for the word " Hose " apart from the mark shown in the drawing.

Particular description of goods.—Men's, Ladies', and Children's Hosiery.

Claims use since July 19, 1919.

Ser. No. 121,063. (CLASS 40. FANCY GOODS, FURNISHINGS, AND NOTIONS.) WALDES & Co., Prague, Bohemia. Filed July 29, 1919.

SNAPPYSNAPS

No exclusive right is claimed for the use of the word " Snaps " apart from its use in connection with the word " Snappy."

Particular description of goods.—Placket - Fasteners, Glove-Fasteners, Buttons Not Made of Precious Metal, Snap-Fasteners, and Clasps for Personal Wear Not Made of Precious Metal.

Claims use since December, 1915.

Ser. No. 121,230. (CLASS 39. CLOTHING.) BRAUER BROS. SHOE COMPANY, St. Louis, Mo. Filed Aug. 4, 1919.

BLUE JAY

Particular description of goods.—Shoes of Leather and of Cloth or Canvas.

Claims use since May 31, 1919.

Ser. No. 121,344. (CLASS 7. CORDAGE.) THE HOOVEN & ALLISON COMPANY, Xenia, Ohio. Filed Aug. 7, 1919.

PERFEX

Particular description of goods.—Fiber Ropes and Twines.
Claims use since June 12, 1919.

Ser. No. 121,509. (CLASS 1. RAW OR PARTLY-PRE-PARED MATERIALS.) N. WERTHEIMER & SONS, Ligonier, Ind. Filed Aug. 9, 1919.

Particular description of goods.—Field-Seeds.
Claims use since Sept. 10, 1914.

Ser. No. 121,559. (CLASS 40. FANCY GOODS, FURNISHINGS, AND NOTIONS.) WALDES & CO., Prague, Bohemia. Filed Aug. 11, 1919.

Particular description of goods.—Placket-Fasteners, Glove-Fasteners, Hand Sewing-Needles, Knitting-Needles, Crochet-Needles, Safety-Pins, Hairpins, Hatpins Not Made of Precious Metal, Hooks and Eyes, Buttons Not Made of Precious Metal, Buckles for Personal Wear Not Made of Precious Metal, Snap-Fasteners, Thimbles, Straight Solid-Headed Pins for Personal Use, Coat-Hangers Adapted to be Attached to Garments, Clasps for Personal Wear Not Made of Precious Metal, Button-Tapes, and Collar-Buttons and Cuff-Buttons Not Made of Precious Metal.
Claims use since Jan. 9, 1915.

Ser. No. 121,605. (CLASS 39. CLOTHING.) REVERE RUBBER COMPANY, Providence, R. I. Filed Aug. 12, 1919.

USKIDE

Particular description of goods.—Shoe-Soles at Present Made of Rubber and Fiber.
Claims use since about May 13, 1919.

Ser. No. 121,629. (CLASS 46. FOODS AND INGREDIENTS OF FOODS.) LAKE WALES CITRUS GROWERS ASSOCIATION, Lake Wales, Fla. Filed Aug. 13, 1919.

Particular description of goods.—Citrus Fruits—viz., Fresh Oranges and Grape-Fruit.
Claims use since Dec. 4, 1918.

Ser. No. 121,646. (CLASS 1. RAW OR PARTLY-PRE-PARED MATERIALS.) THE STANFORD SEED CO., INC., Binghamton, Buffalo, and Albany, N. Y. Filed Aug. 13, 1919.

Particular description of goods.—Seeds—Namely, Timothy, Clover, Alsike, Alfalfa, Redtop, Blue-Grasses, Rape, Vetches, Amber Cane, Peas, Beans, Millets, Popcorn, Grass-Seeds, Seed-Corn, and Seed-Grains.
Claims use since August, 1912.

Ser. No. 121,949. (CLASS 44. DENTAL, MEDICAL, AND SURGICAL APPLIANCES.) UNITED STATES RUBBER COMPANY, New Brunswick, N. J., and New York, N. Y. Filed Aug. 23, 1919.

USCO

Particular description of goods.—Dental Dam, Surgeons' Gloves, Light Acid-Gloves, Seamless Nipples, and Nipples for Use in Nursing Sheep.
Claims use since August, 1918.

Ser. No. 122,002. (CLASS 45. BEVERAGES, NON-ALCOHOLIC.) THORNTON MINERAL SPRINGS COMPANY, Thornton, Ill. Filed Aug. 25, 1919.

WHITE CROSS

Particular description of goods.—Non-Alcoholic Non-Cereal Maltless Beverages Sold as Soft Drinks and Syrups for Making the Same.
Claims use since October, 1917.

Ser. No. 122,367. (CLASS 39. CLOTHING.) SAMUEL ROSENBAUM & SONS COMPANY, Kalamazoo, Mich. Filed Sept. 5, 1919.

No claim being made to the word "Knickers" apart from the mark shown.
Particular description of goods.—Trousers.
Claims use since June 15, 1919.

Ser. No. 122,424. (CLASS 40. FANCY GOODS, FURNISHINGS, AND NOTIONS.) COLUMBIA FASTENER COMPANY, Chicago, Ill. Filed Sept. 8, 1919.

Particular description of goods.—Snap Dress-Fasteners.
Claims use since Aug. 25, 1919.

Ser. No. 122,707. (CLASS 7. CORDAGE.) KRENNING-SCHLAPP GROCER COMPANY, St. Louis, Mo. Filed Sept. 15, 1919.

Particular description of goods.—Clotheslines.
Claims use since on or about Jan. 1, 1904.

Ser. No. 122,779. (CLASS 46. FOODS AND INGREDIENTS OF FOODS.) L. P. LARSON JR. COMPANY, Chicago, Ill. Filed Sept. 16, 1919.

Particular description of goods.—A Confection Known as Mints.
Claims use since Aug. 1, 1919.

Ser. No. 122,826. (CLASS 39. CLOTHING.) DOUBLE SUCTION RUBBER HEEL & SOLE COMPANY, Baltimore, Md. Filed Sept. 18, 1919.

Particular description of goods.—Rubber Heels and Rubber Soles for Shoes.
Claims use since Sept. 10, 1919.

Ser. No. 122,873. (CLASS 7. CORDAGE.) AMERICAN TWINE CO., INC., New York, N. Y. Filed Sept. 18, 1919.

Particular description of goods.—Twine.
Claims use since July 21, 1919.

Ser. No. 122,889. (CLASS 39. CLOTHING.) GRIGGS-PAXTON SHOE CO. INC., Roanoke, Va. Filed Sept. 19, 1919.

The BLUE RIDGE Shoe

Without waiving any common-law right, applicant hereby disclaims the use of the words "The" and "Shoe" apart from the mark shown.
Particular description of goods.—Boots and Shoes of Leather, Leather and Fabric, and Rubber and Fabric.
Claims use since December, 1915.

Ser. No. 122,903. (CLASS 44. DENTAL, MEDICAL, AND SURGICAL APPLIANCES.) MCINTOSH BATTERY & OPTICAL CO., Chicago, Ill. Filed Sept. 19, 1919.

Particular description of goods. — An Electromedical Switchboard for Electric-Bath Use.
Claims use since June, 1919.

Ser. No. 122,940. (CLASS 6. CHEMICALS, MEDICINES, AND PHARMACEUTICAL PREPARATIONS.) WILLIAM R. FESSLER, Kansas City, Kans. Filed Sept. 20, 1919.

The picture shown is a likeness of George P. Fessler.
Particular description of goods.—A Pharmaceutical Preparation for the Treatment and Relief of Pain and Rheumatism.
Claims use since July 1, 1919.

Ser. No. 122,994. (CLASS 46. FOODS AND INGREDIENTS OF FOODS.) MOORE FOOD PRODUCTS COMPANY, Chicago, Ill. Filed Sept. 22, 1919.

The color blue being a feature of the mark. The cross-hatching on the drawing is intended to represent such color.
Particular description of goods.—A Special Food Product Commonly Classified as a Breakfast Food, Comprising a Combination of Cereals.
Claims use since Sept. 10, 1919.

Ser. No. 123,150. (CLASS 44. DENTAL, MEDICAL, AND SURGICAL APPLIANCES.) ALEXANDER A. ANZELL, New York, N. Y. Filed Sept. 26, 1919.

Particular description of goods.—Dental and Surgical Mirrors, Head-Mirrors, Laryngeal Mirrors, and Retinoscopes.
Claims use since Jan. 15, 1919.

Ser. No. 123,486. (CLASS 12. CONSTRUCTION MATERIALS.) LAMBORN & CO., New York, N. Y. Filed Oct. 6, 1919.

Particular description of goods.—Prepared Felt Roofing.
Claims use since April, 1918.

Ser. No. 123,520. (CLASS 19. VEHICLES, NOT INCLUDING ENGINES.) JOSÉ CUNILL DE FIGUEROLA, New York, N. Y. Filed Oct. 7, 1919.

Particular description of goods.—Automobiles and Motor-Trucks.
Claims use since September, 1916.

Ser. No. 123,800. (CLASS 39. CLOTHING.) JOHN M. GIVEN, INC., Pittsburgh, Pa.; Chicago, Ill., and New York, N. Y. Filed Oct. 15, 1919.

Toddler

Particular description of goods.—Children's Hosiery.
Claims use since Oct. 8, 1919.

Ser. No. 123,802. (CLASS 39. CLOTHING.) JOHN M. GIVEN, INC., Pittsburgh, Pa.; New York, N. Y., and Chicago, Ill. Filed Oct. 15, 1919.

Particular description of goods.—Hosiery.
Claims use since May 23, 1914.

Ser. No. 123,810. (CLASS 45. BEVERAGES, NON-ALCOHOLIC.) HORLACHER BREWING CO., Allentown, Pa. Filed Oct. 15, 1919.

Particular description of goods.—Non-Alcoholic Non-Cereal Maltless Beverages Sold as Soft Drinks and Syrups for Making the Same.
Claims use since May 5, 1916.

Ser. No. 123,871. (CLASS 39. CLOTHING.) THOMAS E. BROWN, Philadelphia, Pa. Filed Oct. 17, 1919.

Particular description of goods.—Hosiery.
Claims use since January, 1913.

Ser. No. 123,964. (CLASS 39. CLOTHING.) COOPER, COAT & CASEY DRY GOODS CO., Los Angeles, Calif., and New York, N. Y. Filed Oct. 20, 1919.

Particular description of goods.—Men's and Women's Night-Wear.
Claims use since Apr. 1, 1919.

Ser. No. 124,152. (CLASS 23. CUTLERY, MACHINERY, AND TOOLS. AND PARTS THEREOF.) SOUTHERN MOTOR MANUFACTURING ASSOCIATION, LTD., Houston, Tex. Filed Oct. 24, 1919.

Particular description of goods.—Tractors.
Claims use since June, 1918.

Ser. No. 124,260. (CLASS 1. RAW OR PARTLY-PRE-PARED MATERIALS.) CHEVAUX KID LEATHER CO., Boston, Mass. Filed Oct. 28, 1919.

No claim being made to the words " Chevaux Kid Leather Co." and " Boston, Mass." except in association with the mark shown in the drawing.
Particular description of goods.—Finished Leather.
Claims use since February, 1919.

Ser. No. 124,280. (CLASS 42. KNITTED, NETTED, AND TEXTILE FABRICS.) NASHUA MANUFG. COM-PANY, Nashua, N. H. Filed Oct. 28, 1919.

Consisting of the word " Wintumn."
Particular description of goods.—Cotton Blankets.
Claims use since Sept. 29, 1919.

Ser. No. 124,282. (CLASS 42. KNITTED, NETTED, AND TEXTILE FABRICS.) NASHUA MANUFG. COM-PANY, Nashua, N. H. Filed Oct. 28, 1919.

Consisting of the word " Barlan."
Particular description of goods.—Cotton Blankets.
Claims use since Sept. 29, 1919.

Ser. No. 124,290. (CLASS 46. FOODS AND INGREDI-ENTS OF FOODS.) M. J. WEINBERG & BRO., New York, N. Y. Filed Oct. 28, 1919.

MY
FAVORITE

Consisting of the words " My Favorite."
Particular description of goods.—Creamery-Butter and Eggs.
Claims use since Sept. 1, 1919.

Ser. No. 124,346. (CLASS 40. FANCY GOODS, FUR-NISHINGS, AND NOTIONS.) HEWES & POTTER, Bos-ton, Mass. Filed Oct. 30, 1919. Under ten-year proviso.

LONDON

Particular description of goods.—Garters.
Claims use since November, 1886.

Ser. No. 124,371. (CLASS 42. KNITTED, NETTED, AND TEXTILE FABRICS.) TURNER & WALLS, New York, N. Y. Filed Oct. 30, 1919.

SUNCHENE

Consisting of the word " Sunchene."
Particular description of goods.—Silk Piece Goods and Cotton Piece Goods and Combinations of the Same.
Claims use since Oct. 27, 1919.

Ser. No. 124,396. (CLASS 42. KNITTED, NETTED, AND TEXTILE FABRICS.) EMPIRE SILK COMPANY, Wilmington, Del., and New York, N. Y. Filed Oct. 31, 1919.

Brokette

Particular description of goods.—Silk Piece Goods.
Claims use since the 22d day of October, 1919.

Ser. No. 124,487. (CLASS 48. MALT BEVERAGES, EXTRACTS, AND LIQUORS.) MASSACHUSETTS BREWERIES COMPANY, Alexandria, Va., and Boston, Mass. Filed Nov. 3, 1918.

EMBRUCO

Particular description of goods.—Malt Beverages.
Claims use since Aug. 8, 1918.

Ser. No. 124,610. (CLASS 23. CUTLERY, MACHINERY, AND TOOLS, AND PARTS THEREOF.) LYNCHBURG FOUNDRY COMPANY, Lynchburg, Va. Filed Nov. 6, 1919.

Particular description of goods. — Plows and Parts Thereof.
Claims use since Oct. 15, 1919.

Ser. No. 124,625. (CLASS 23. CUTLERY, MACHINERY, AND TOOLS, AND PARTS THEREOF.) GEORGE C. SHELDON, Nehawka, Nebr. Filed Nov. 6, 1919.

Particular description of goods.—Concrete-Mixers.
Claims use since Aug. 4, 1919.

Ser. No. 124,626. (CLASS 46. FOODS AND INGREDIENTS OF FOODS.) SCHEER, GRANDI & CO., San Francisco, Calif. Filed Nov. 6, 1919.

Particular description of goods.—Butter.
Claims use since Sept. 8, 1919.

Ser. No. 124,846. (CLASS 46. FOODS AND INGREDIENTS OF FOODS.) BARBER & BENNETT, INC., Albany, N. Y. Filed Nov. 13, 1919.

FORT ORANGE

Particular description of goods.—Stock Feed, Horse Feed, Dairy Feed, Poultry Feed.
Claims use since 1916.

Ser. No. 125,014. (CLASS 19. VEHICLES, NOT INCLUDING ENGINES.) NOMA MOTOR CORPORATION, New York, N. Y. Filed Nov. 17, 1919.

Particular description of goods.—Automobiles and Automobile-Bodies.
Claims use since Feb. 1, 1919.

Ser. No. 125,029. (CLASS 43. THREAD AND YARN.) SEAMANS & COBB CO., Boston, Mass. Filed Nov. 17, 1919.

SEACO

The word " Seaco."
Particular description of goods. — Cotton Sewing-Threads.
Claims use since the latter part of 1911.

Ser. No. 125,043. (CLASS 7. CORDAGE.) AMERICAN MANUFACTURING COMPANY, Boston, Mass., and Brooklyn, N. Y. Filed Nov. 18, 1919.

BELLE
STAR

Particular description of goods. — Rope, Cord, and Twine Manufactured from Vegetable Fiber.
Claims use since Jan. 7, 1915.

Ser. No. 125,164. (CLASS 46. FOODS AND INGREDIENTS OF FOODS.) ELMER J. PHILLIPS, Wilkes-Barre, Pa. Filed Nov. 21, 1919.

KORRUGATED

Particular description of goods.—Potato Chips.
Claims use since the 18th day of June, A. D. 1919.

TRADE-MARK REGISTRATIONS GRANTED

JANUARY 20, 1920.

128,913. GAS-PRODUCER APPARATUS. AKERLUND & SEMMES, INC., New York, N. Y.
Filed March 15, 1919. Serial No. 116,588. PUBLISHED SEPTEMBER 23, 1919.

128,914. MEDICINE FOR COLDS, LA GRIPPE, PNEUMONIA, ASTHMA, TUBERCULOSIS, BRONCHIAL TROUBLES, AND RUN-DOWN CONDITIONS. ALFRED BROTHERS, Whitinsville, Mass.
Filed May 15, 1919. Serial No. 118,503. PUBLISHED SEPTEMBER 30, 1919.

128,915. LIQUID MEDICINE FOR THE TREATMENT OF COLDS, LA GRIPPE, INFLUENZA, COUGHS, AND RHEUMATISM. HENRY N. ALFORD, Atlanta, Ga.
Filed December 27, 1918. Serial No. 114.833. PUBLISHED OCTOBER 7, 1919.

128,916. WHEAT-FLOUR. AMERICAN FLOUR CORPORATION, New York, N. Y.
Filed August 9, 1919. Serial No. 121,437. PUBLISHED NOVEMBER 4, 1919.

128,917. HARMONICAS (THE REED INSTRUMENT PLAYED BY THE BREATH) OR MOUTH-ORGANS. AMERICAN HARMONICA & ACCORDION MANUFACTURING COMPANY, New York. N. Y.
Filed March 27, 1919. Serial No. 116,946. PUBLISHED OCTOBER 28, 1919.

128,918. PHARMACEUTICAL PREPARATION TO BE APPLIED EXTERNALLY FOR COLDS AND CONGESTIONS. AMERICAN LABORATORIES, Indianapolis, Ind.
Filed March 1, 1919. Serial No. 116,230. PUBLISHED SEPTEMBER 23, 1919.

128,919. COFFEE. AMERICAN STANDARD FOOD ASSN., Milwaukee, Wis.
Filed June 10, 1919. Serial No. 119,382. PUBLISHED OCTOBER 28, 1919.

128,920. CIGARETTES. THE AMERICAN TOBACCO COMPANY, New York, N. Y.
Filed June 10, 1919. Serial No. 119,377. PUBLISHED OCTOBER 14, 1919.

128,921. CIGARETTES AND SMOKING AND CHEWING TOBACCO. THE AMERICAN TOBACCO CO., New York, N. Y.
Filed June 30, 1919. Serial No. 120,085. PUBLISHED OCTOBER 28, 1919.

128,922. PLEASURE - AUTOMOBILES AND MOTOR-TRUCKS. APPERSON BROS. AUTOMOBILE Co., Kokomo, Ind.
Filed February 17, 1919. Serial No. 115,897. PUBLISHED SEPTEMBER 23, 1919.

128,923. GARMENT - SUPPORTS FORMED OF WEBBING AND WORN AS BELTS ENCIRCLING THE WAIST OF THE WEARER. LOUIS ARONS, Chicago, Ill.
Filed July 1, 1918. Serial No. 111,893. PUBLISHED SEPTEMBER 16, 1919.

128,924. OILED DUCK. ARMSTRONG CORK COMPANY, Pittsburgh and Lancaster, Pa.
Filed April 9, 1919. Serial No. 117,289. PUBLISHED SEPTEMBER 23, 1919.

128,925. MOTOR - TRUCKS AND PARTS THEREOF. ATTERBURY MOTOR CAR COMPANY, Buffalo, N. Y.
Filed January 2, 1919. Serial No. 114.940. PUBLISHED SEPTEMBER 23, 1919.

128,926. MILITARY AND SPORTING SHOULDER-RIFLES. AUTO-ORDNANCE CORPORATION, New York, N. Y.
Filed July 9, 1919. Serial No. 120,367. PUBLISHED OCTOBER 28, 1919.

128,927. FRESH PEACHES, CANNED APPLES, CANNED PEACHES, CANNED TOMATOES, AND CANNED BEANS. BACK CREEK VALLEY ORCHARD COMPANY, Hedgesville, W. Va.
Filed June 28, 1917. Serial No. 104,726. PUBLISHED OCTOBER 28, 1919.

128,928. WATERPROOF DRESSING FOR TEXTILE FABRICS AND THE LIKE. BAKER-OVERTON COMPANY, Dallas, Tex.
Filed April 21, 1919. Serial No. 117,916. PUBLISHED SEPTEMBER 2, 1919.

128,929. READY-MIXED PAINT. THE BARRETT COMPANY, New York, N. Y.
Filed June 16, 1919. Serial No. 119,630. PUBLISHED OCTOBER 7, 1919.

128,930. LOCKS. JOSEPH GEORGE BEDDOES, Birmingham, England.
Filed January 7, 1919. Serial No. 115,022. PUBLISHED OCTOBER 7, 1919.

128,931. CONDENSED MILK. THE BORDEN COMPANY, New York, N. Y.
Filed June 2, 1919. Serial No. 119,104. PUBLISHED OCTOBER 28, 1919.

128,932. CONDENSED MILK. THE BORDEN COMPANY, New York, N. Y.
Filed June 2, 1919. Serial No. 119,109. PUBLISHED OCTOBER 28, 1919.

128,933. CONFECTIONERY — NAMELY, CARAMELS. THE BORDEN COMPANY, New York, N. Y.
Filed June 2, 1919. Serial No. 119,106. PUBLISHED OCTOBER 28, 1919.

128,934. CONDENSED MILK. THE BORDEN COMPANY, New York, N. Y.
Filed June 2, 1919. Serial No. 119,112. PUBLISHED OCTOBER 28, 1919.

128,935. CONDENSED MILK. THE BORDEN COMPANY, New York, N. Y.
Filed June 2, 1919. Serial No. 119,115. PUBLISHED OCTOBER 28, 1919.

128,936. CONDENSED MILK. THE BORDEN COMPANY, New York, N. Y.
Filed June 2, 1919. Serial No. 119,113. PUBLISHED OCTOBER 28, 1919.

128,937. CONDENSED MILK. THE BORDEN COMPANY, New York, N. Y.
Filed June 2, 1919. Serial No. 119,102. PUBLISHED OCTOBER 28, 1919.

128,938. CONDENSED MILK. THE BORDEN COMPANY, New York, N. Y.
Filed June 2, 1919. Serial No. 119,110. PUBLISHED OCTOBER 28, 1919.

128,939. CONDENSED MILK. THE BORDEN COMPANY, New York, N. Y.
Filed June 2, 1919. Serial No. 119,114. PUBLISHED NOVEMBER 4, 1919.

128,940. CONDENSED MILK. THE BORDEN COMPANY, New York, N. Y.
Filed June 2, 1919. Serial No. 119,117. PUBLISHED OCTOBER 28, 1919.

128,941. CONDENSED MILK. THE BORDEN COMPANY, New York, N. Y.
Filed June 2, 1919. Serial No. 119,108. PUBLISHED OCTOBER 28, 1919.

128,942. CERTAIN NAMED FOODS AND INGREDI-ENTS OF FOOD. BORDEN'S FARM PRODUCTS COM-PANY, INC., Wassaic and New York, N. Y.
Filed June 5, 1919. Serial No. 119,227. PUBLISHED OCTOBER 28, 1919.

128,943. SAUCE FOR USE ON FISH, GAME, CHOPS, STEAKS, SOUPS, STEWS, GRAVIES, AND MEATS. W. P. BOWMAN, Leeds, England.
Filed April 19, 1919. Serial No. 117,611. PUBLISHED AUGUST 26, 1919.

128,944. FRESH CITRUS FRUITS—NAMELY, OR-ANGES, LEMONS, AND GRAPE-FRUIT. ALBERT SUMNER BRADFORD, Placentia, Calif.
Filed August 18. 1919. Serial No. 121,740. PUB-LISHED NOVEMBER 4, 1919.

128,945. GAMES OF JACK-STRAWS. MILTON BRAD-LEY COMPANY, Springfield, Mass.
Filed August 4, 1919. Serial No. 121,235. PUB-LISHED OCTOBER 28, 1919.

128,946. TABASCO-FLAVOR CATSUP. BROOKS TO-MATO PRODUCTS COMPANY, Collinsville, Ill.
Filed July 16, 1919. Serial No. 120,594. PUBLISHED OCTOBER 21, 1919.

128,947. DISINFECTANT. JOSEPH WARREN BULLEN, Folcroft, Pa.
Filed May 13, 1919. Serial No. 118,420. PUBLISHED OCTOBER 7, 1919.

128,948. DISINFECTANT. JOSEPH WARREN BULLEN, Folcroft, Pa.
Filed May 13, 1919. Serial No. 118,418. PUBLISHED OCTOBER 7, 1919.

128,949. WRITING-PAPER. BYRON WESTON CO., Dal-ton, Mass.
Filed January 18, 1917. Serial No. 100,693. PUB-LISHED OCTOBER 7, 1919.

128,950. CERTAIN NAMED CUTLERY, MACHINERY, AND TOOLS, AND PARTS THEREOF. HARRY CAD-WALLADER, Jr., Philadelphia, Pa.
Filed March 12, 1919. Serial No. 116,483. PUBLISHED SEPTEMBER 30, 1919.

128,951. CANNED VEGETABLES, FRUITS, FISH, PIMIENTOS, CHILLI, OLIVES, AND BERRIES, JELLIES, HONEY, AND DRIED FRUITS. CALI-FORNIA PACKING CORPORATION, San Francisco, Calif.
Filed April 24, 1918. Serial No. 110,406. PUBLISHED SEPTEMBER 23, 1919.

128,952. ANILIN COLORS AND COAL-TAR DYES. JOHN CAMPBELL & CO., New York, N. Y.
Filed November 27, 1918. Serial No. 114,393. PUB-LISHED SEPTEMBER 16, 1919.

128,953. CANDY. JACOBS CANDY COMPANY LTD., New Orleans, La.
Filed April 14, 1919. Serial No. 117,456. PUBLISHED SEPTEMBER 23, 1919.

128,954. SALVE FOR HEALING OF LACERATED, BRUISED, SORE, OR TENDER TISSUES OF HUMAN BODY. GEORGE T. CARNER, Fulton, N. Y.
Filed February 24, 1919. Serial No. 116,078. PUB-LISHED OCTOBER 7, 1919.

128,955. LINIMENT USED PRINCIPALLY FOR MUS-CULAR PAINS GENERALLY DESIGNATED AS RHEUMATISM, LUMBAGO, STRAINS, SORENESS, ACHES, &c. EDWARD R. CASTELLO, Chicago, Ill.
Filed March 17, 1919. Serial No. 116,647. PUBLISHED SEPTEMBER 23, 1919.

128,956. THERMOMETERS, BAROMETERS, AND RAIN-GAGES. THE CHANEY MANUFACTURING COM-PANY, Springfield, Ohio.
Filed January 3, 1919. Serial No. 114,968. PUB-LISHED AUGUST 26, 1919.

128,957. CERTAIN NAMED TOILET PREPARATIONS. RALPH CILUZZI, New York, N. Y.
Filed July 23, 1918. Serial No. 112,312. PUBLISHED OCTOBER 7, 1919.

128,958. VEILS. NATHAN B. COHEN, Scranton, Pa.
Filed January 15, 1919. Serial No. 115,198. PUB-LISHED SEPTEMBER 30, 1919.

128,959. ICE-CREAM CONES. CONSOLIDATED WAFER COMPANY, New York, N. Y., and Chicago, Ill.
Filed June 2, 1919. Serial No. 119,119. PUBLISHED OCTOBER 28, 1919.

128,960. HAM, BACON, SHOULDER, AND SUGAR-CURED PICNICS. CORN BELT PACKING COMPANY, Dubuque, Iowa.
Filed May 15, 1919. Serial No. 118,509. PUBLISHED NOVEMBER 4, 1919.

128,961. CLEANSER AND POLISH. IRWIN W. COX, Chicago, Ill.
Filed February 18, 1919. Serial No. 115,947. PUB-LISHED SEPTEMBER 30, 1919.

128,962. CERTAIN NAMED CUTLERY, MACHINERY, AND TOOLS, AND PARTS THEREOF. ALBERT THOMAS HENRY COWARD, Sheffield, England.
Filed March 7, 1919. Serial No. 116,360. PUBLISHED SEPTEMBER 30, 1919.

128,963. GOLF-CLUBS. THE CRAWFORD, MCGREGOR & CANBY COMPANY, Dayton, Ohio.
Filed February 26, 1919. Serial No. 116,146. PUB-LISHED OCTOBER 14, 1919.

128,964. CERTAIN NAMED FOODS AND INGREDI-ENTS OF FOOD. CRESCA COMPANY, New York, N. Y.
Filed April 23, 1919. Serial No. 117,773. PUBLISHED OCTOBER 21, 1919.

128,965. CERTAIN NAMED FOODS AND INGREDI-ENTS OF FOODS. THE WILLIAM DAVIES COMPANY, LIMITED, Chicago, Ill.
Filed December 7, 1918. Serial No. 114,531. PUB-LISHED SEPTEMBER 23, 1919.

128,966. BACON, HAMS, PURE LARD, CORNED BEEF, AND OTHER NAMED FOODS AND INGREDIENTS OF FOODS. THE WILLIAM DAVIES COMPANY, LIM-ITED, Chicago, Ill.
Filed April 28, 1919. Serial No. 117,930. PUBLISHED SEPTEMBER 23, 1919.

128,967. CERTAIN NAMED FOODS AND INGREDI-ENTS OF FOOD. THE WILLIAM DAVIES COMPANY, LIMITED, Chicago, Ill.
Filed December 7, 1918. Serial No. 114,532. PUB-LISHED SEPTEMBER 23, 1919.

128,968. WHEAT-FLOUR. H. DITTLINGER ROLLER MILLS COMPANY, New Braunfels, Tex.
Filed May 5, 1919. Serial No. 118,139. PUBLISHED OCTOBER 28, 1919.

128,969. CERTAIN NAMED LADIES' WEARING-AP-PAREL. DOUGLASS BARNES CORPORATION, New York, N. Y.
Filed March 6, 1919. Serial No. 116,329. PUBLISHED AUGUST 5, 1919.

128,970. GOVERNORS FOR ENGINES. THE DUPLEX ENGINE-GOVERNOR COMPANY, INC., Brooklyn, N. Y.
Filed February 14, 1919. Serial No. 115,854. PUB-LISHED SEPTEMBER 30, 1919.

128,971. COMBINATION PHONOGRAPH AND LAMP-STAND. ELECTRIC PHONOGRAPH CORPORATION, New York, N. Y.
Filed April 24, 1918. Serial No. 110,413. PUBLISHED OCTOBER 7, 1919.

128,972. FRESH MILK. THE ELECTROPURE DAIRY COM-PANY, Wilmington, Del., and Chicago. Ill.
Filed September 5, 1918. Serial No. 113,030. PUB-LISHED OCTOBER 28, 1919.

128,973. CERTAIN NAMED OUTER AND UNDER GARMENTS FOR MEN, WOMEN, AND CHILDREN. ELY & WALKER D. G. Co., St. Louis, Mo.
Filed September 27, 1918. Serial No. 113,444. PUBLISHED SEPTEMBER 30, 1919.

128,974. GINGER-ALE. EMMERLING PRODUCTS COMPANY, Johnstown, Pa.
Filed July 31, 1919. Serial No. 121,141. PUBLISHED OCTOBER 28, 1919.

128,975. SALVE FOR SWEATY FEET. FILLETIN & CHOCHKOFF COMPANY, Milwaukee, Wis.
Filed November 4, 1918. Serial No. 114,037. PUBLISHED SEPTEMBER 16, 1919.

128,976. WALLETS, BILL-FOLDS, AND THREE-FOLDS OF LEATHER. PHILIP FLORIN, New York, N. Y.
Filed July 26, 1919. Serial No. 120,957. PUBLISHED OCTOBER 28, 1919.

128,977. WRITING AND PRINTING BOND-PAPER, LEDGER-PAPER, WRITING-PAPER, AND MAILING - ENVELOPS. FOREST PAPER COMPANY, INC., New York, N. Y.
Filed December 7, 1918. Serial No. 114,535. PUBLISHED SEPTEMBER 23, 1919.

128,978. PHONOGRAPHS, MECHANICAL MOTORS FOR PHONOGRAPHS, TONE-ARMS. AND REPRODUCERS. FULTON BROS. MFG. Co., Waukegan, Ill.
Filed June 23, 1919. Serial No. 119,853. PUBLISHED OCTOBER 28, 1919.

128,979. DENTAL CASTING-MACHINES AND PARTS OF THE SAME. GARDNER BROS., Memphis, Tenn.
Filed March 17, 1919. Serial No. 116,652. PUBLISHED OCTOBER 7, 1919.

128,980. MONUMENTS AND TOMBSTONES. HERBERT MATTHEW GAULT, Baltimore, Md.
Filed April 22, 1919. Serial No. 117,724. PUBLISHED SEPTEMBER 23, 1919.

128,981. CERTAIN NAMED MACHINERY AND TOOLS AND PARTS THEREOF. GENERAL MOTORS CORPORATION, New York, N. Y., and Harrison, N. J.
Filed February 21, 1919. Serial No. 116,050. PUBLISHED SEPTEMBER 16, 1919

128,982. SALICYLIC OINTMENT. THEODORE GILMAN, Jr., New York, N. Y.
Filed May 6, 1919. Serial No. 118,207. PUBLISHED SEPTEMBER 30, 1919.

128,983. TALKING-MACHINES, VIOLINS, GUITARS, BANJOS. M A N D O L I N S , UKULELES, JEWS'-HARPS. MOUTH - HARMONICAS, ACCORDIONS, PICCOLOS, AND CORNETS. GIMBEL BROTHERS, NEW YORK, New York, N. Y.
Filed July 2, 1919. Serial No. 120,207. PUBLISHED OCTOBER 28, 1919.

128,984. CAMP-CHAIRS, STOOLS FOR HOME AND OFFICE USE, FOLDING CHAIRS, LIBRARY-STEPS, AND INVALID-CHAIRS. CHARLES GLANTZ, Arkville, N. Y.
Filed January 25, 1919. Serial No. 115,422. PUBLISHED OCTOBER 28, 1919.

128,985. CERTAIN NAMED FOODS AND INGREDIENTS OF FOOD. GLOBE GROCERY STORES, INC., Brooklyn, N. Y.
Filed July 8, 1919. Serial No. 120,345. PUBLISHED OCTOBER 28, 1919.

128,986. NON - ALCOHOLIC NON - INTOXICATING MALTLESS NON-CEREAL ORANGE BEVERAGE SOLD AS A SOFT DRINK. JOHN GRAF Co., Milwaukee, Wis.
Filed July 19, 1919. Serial No. 120,704. PUBLISHED OCTOBER 28, 1919.

128,987. CANNED VEGETABLES. GRAND RIVER CANNING COMPANY, Markesan, Wis.
Filed August 18,1916. Serial No. 97,435. PUBLISHED SEPTEMBER 23, 1919.

128,988. PREPARATION FOR THE TREATMENT OF CONSUMPTION AND TUBERCULOSIS. STANLEY & GRIFFIN. Lowell, Mass.
Filed March 22, 1919. Serial No. 116,824. PUBLISHED SEPTEMBER 2, 1919.

128,989. EVAPORATED MILK. G. BATCHELLER HALL Co., Seattle, Wash.
Filed June 22, 1918. Serial No. 111,745. PUBLISHED NOVEMBER 19, 1918.

128,990. GLOVES AND MITTENS. O. C. HANSEN MFG. Co., Milwaukee, Wis.
Filed November 19, 1918. Serial No. 114,240. PUBLISHED SEPTEMBER 23, 1919.

128,991. WHITE LEAD IN OIL, ZINC IN OIL, DRY RED LEAD, AND COLORS IN OIL. LOUIS H. C. HART, St. Louis, Mo.
Filed July 9, 1919. Serial No. 120,385. PUBLISHED OCTOBER 7, 1919.

128,992. WHITE LEAD IN OIL, ZINC IN OIL. DRY RED LEAD, AND COLORS IN OIL. LOUIS H. C. HART, St. Louis. Mo.
Filed June 12, 1919. Serial No. 119,516. PUBLISHED OCTOBER 7, 1919.

128,993. WHITE LEAD IN OIL, ZINC IN OIL, DRY RED LEAD, AND COLORS IN OIL. LOUIS H. C. HART, St. Louis, Mo.
Filed June 12, 1919. Serial No. 119,514. PUBLISHED OCTOBER 7, 1919.

128,994. WHITE LEAD IN OIL, ZINC IN OIL, DRY RED LEAD, AND COLORS IN OIL. L. H. C. HART, St. Louis, Mo.
Filed July 9, 1919. Serial No. 120,381. PUBLISHED OCTOBER 7, 1919.

128,995. WHITE LEAD IN OIL, ZINC IN OIL, DRY RED LEAD, AND COLORS IN OIL. LOUIS H. C. HART, St. Louis, Mo.
Filed June 12, 1919. Serial No. 119,515. PUBLISHED OCTOBER 7, 1919.

128,996. SHOE-COUNTERS MADE FROM LEATHER, LEATHER-BOARD, OR CANVAS. HARWOOD COUNTER COMPANY, Lynn, Mass.
Filed March 4, 1919. Serial No. 116,286. PUBLISHED OCTOBER 7, 1919.

128,997. ESSENTIAL OILS USED AS INGREDIENTS OF PHARMACEUTICAL PREPARATIONS. FREDERICK WILLIAM HEINE, New York, N. Y.
Filed September 13, 1918. Serial No. 113,159. PUBLISHED SEPTEMBER 23, 1919.

128,998. POLISH FOR FURNITURE, WOODWORK, HARDWOOD FLOORS, AND AUTOMOBILE-BODIES. OSCAR WALSH HENDRY, Toronto, Ontario, Canada.
Filed April 24, 1919. Serial No. 117,825. PUBLISHED OCTOBER 7, 1919.

128,999. MEDICINE FOR THE TREATMENT OF INDIGESTION. W. H. HERDMAN, Portland, Oreg.
Filed April 26, 1919. Serial No. 117,876. PUBLISHED SEPTEMBER 2, 1919.

129,000. CIGARS, CIGARETTES, AND SMOKING-TOBACCO. R. & J. HILL, LIMITED, London, England.
Filed July 2, 1919. Serial No. 120,210. PUBLISHED OCTOBER 28, 1919.

129,001. TOILET-PAPER, PAPER TOWELING, PAPER NAPKINS, AND TISSUE - PAPER. THE JOHN HOBERG Co., Green Bay, Wis.
Filed May 12, 1919. Serial No. 118,385. PUBLISHED SEPTEMBER 23, 1919.

129,002. WHEAT-FLOUR. HOLMES AND BARNES, LTD., Baton Rouge, La.
Filed December 14, 1918. Serial No. 114,644. PUBLISHED SEPTEMBER 30, 1919.

129,003. DAIRY PRODUCTS—NAMELY, BUTTER. WILLIAM LAWRENCE HOULTON, Uneedus, La.
Filed July 19, 1919. Serial No. 120,705. PUBLISHED NOVEMBER 4, 1919.

129,004. PIANOS AND PLAYER-PIANOS. R. S. HOWARD COMPANY, New York, N. Y.
Filed July 1, 1919. Serial No. 120,165. PUBLISHED OCTOBER 7, 1919.

129,005. WATERPROOF HANDBAGS AND PURSES. THEODORE HUTNIKOW, Brooklyn, N. Y.
Filed June 14, 1919. Serial No. 119,605. PUBLISHED OCTOBER 28, 1919.

129,006. COOKIES. ITEN BISCUIT CO., Clinton, Iowa, and Omaha, Nebr.
Filed May 19, 1919. Serial No. 118,675. PUBLISHED SEPTEMBER 30, 1919.

129,007. CERTAIN NAMED CROCKERY, EARTHENWARE, AND PORCELAIN. A/S. HERMAN A. KÄHLER, Næstved, Denmark.
Filed April 28, 1919. Serial No. 117,987. PUBLISHED OCTOBER 7, 1919.

129,008. SHEET-METAL-SHAPING MACHINES. GUSSIE M. KENNEDY, Los Angeles, Calif.
Filed March 27, 1919. Serial No. 116,968. PUBLISHED SEPTEMBER 30, 1919.

129,009. BARBERS' CHAIRS. KOKEN BARBERS' SUPPLY COMPANY, St. Louis, Mo.
Filed April 21, 1919. Serial No. 117,677. PUBLISHED OCTOBER 28, 1919.

129,010. WHEAT-FLOUR. MICHEL J. KOURI, New York, N. Y.
Filed August 9, 1919. Serial No. 121,474. PUBLISHED NOVEMBER 4, 1919.

129,011. CHEMICAL COMPOUND FOR CERTAIN NAMED PURPOSES. LOUIS W. KRAMER, Denver, Colo.
Filed April 23, 1918. Serial No. 110,398. PUBLISHED SEPTEMBER 16, 1919.

129,012. POULTRY FEED COMPOSED OF A MIXTURE OF GRAINS AND SEEDS AND KNOWN AS "SCRATCH FEED." CHAS. A. KRAUSE MILLING CO., Greenfield, Wis.
Filed February 6, 1918. Serial No. 108,848. PUBLISHED OCTOBER 21, 1919.

129,013. CERTAIN NAMED CHEMICALS, MEDICINES, AND PHARMACEUTICAL PREPARATIONS. KUHLMAN & CHAMBLISS CO., INC., Knoxville, Tenn.
Filed January 29, 1919. Serial No. 115,505. PUBLISHED SEPTEMBER 16, 1919.

129,014. CERTAIN NAMED FOODS. MANZABURO KUSHIRO, South Pasadena, Calif.
Filed May 6, 1919. Serial No. 118,211. PUBLISHED OCTOBER 28, 1919.

129,015. CERTAIN NAMED FOODS. THE H. T. LANGE COMPANY, Eau Claire, Wis.
Filed May 5, 1919. Serial No. 118,160. PUBLISHED SEPTEMBER 23, 1919.

129,016. NON-ALCOHOLIC NON-CEREAL MALTLESS SYRUPS OF COCOA AND SUGAR USED IN MAKING SOFT DRINKS. THE LAWDEN COMPANY, New York, N. Y.
Filed July 1, 1919. Serial No. 120,169. PUBLISHED NOVEMBER 4, 1919.

129,017. CERTAIN NAMED FOODS. FRANCIS H. LEGGETT & CO., New York, N. Y.
Filed October 26, 1917. Serial No. 106,973. PUBLISHED OCTOBER 28, 1919.

129,018. CERTAIN NAMED FOODS AND INGREDIENTS OF FOODS. WILLIAM J. LEMP, Sappington, Mo.
Filed May 5, 1919. Serial No. 118,158. PUBLISHED OCTOBER 7, 1919.

129,019. CANNED SARDINES. LUBEC SARDINE COMPANY, Lubec, Me.
Filed August 8, 1919. Serial No. 121,398. PUBLISHED NOVEMBER 4, 1919.

129,020. LIFTING-JACKS. McKIERNAN-TERRY DRILL COMPANY, Dover, N. J., and New York, N. Y.
Filed May 9, 1919. Serial No. 118,316. PUBLISHED SEPTEMBER 16, 1919.

129,021. INFANTS', CHILDREN'S, AND MISSES' HATS. R. H. MACY & CO., New York, N. Y.
Filed April 24, 1919. Serial No. 117,815. PUBLISHED OCTOBER 7, 1919.

129,022. SOAPS. MAGIC-KELLER SOAP WORKS, Louisville, Ky.
Filed May 12, 1919. Serial No. 118,396. PUBLISHED JULY 15, 1919.

129,023. CANNED FRUIT, COFFEES, TEAS, SPICES, CANNED VEGETABLES, AND RICE. ABRAHAM M. MALOUF, Salt Lake City, Utah.
Filed March 12, 1917. Serial No. 102,082. PUBLISHED SEPTEMBER 30, 1919.

129,024. TALKING-MACHINES, GRAFONOLAS, PHONOGRAPHS, GRAPHOPHONES, GRAMOPHONES, SOUND-REPRODUCING MACHINES, AND PARTS THEREFOR. MANDEL MFG. COMPANY, Chicago, Ill.
Filed May 3, 1919. Serial No. 118,117. PUBLISHED OCTOBER 28, 1919.

129,025. CANNED BEANS. MARSHALL CANNING COMPANY, Marshalltown, Iowa.
Filed March 13, 1919. Serial No. 116,548. PUBLISHED MAY 6, 1919.

129,026. COCOA-PALM SHAMPOO. HAROLD H. MATHER, Albany, N. Y.
Filed March 24, 1919. Serial No. 116,841. PUBLISHED OCTOBER 14, 1919.

129,027. SHORTENING COMPOUND CONSISTING OF A MIXTURE OF FATS AND OILS OF APPROXIMATELY A LARDLIKE CONSISTENCY. D. D. METCALF, Greenville, Ala.
Filed August 4, 1919. Serial No. 121,256. PUBLISHED NOVEMBER 4, 1919.

129,028. CHEWING-GUM. DAVID MILLHAUSER, New York, N. Y.
Filed July 31, 1919. Serial No. 121,151. PUBLISHED NOVEMBER 4, 1919.

129,029. CALCULATING AND ADDING MACHINES. MONROE CALCULATING MACHINE COMPANY, Orange, N. J.
Filed April 7, 1919. Serial No. 117,288. PUBLISHED AUGUST 5, 1919.

129,030. CERTAIN NAMED TABLE AND COOKING OILS AND SAUCES AND DRESSINGS. MUSHER & COMPANY, INCORPORATED, New York, N. Y.; Baltimore, Md.; San Diego, Calif., and Washington, D. C.
Filed May 9, 1919. Serial No. 118,319. PUBLISHED OCTOBER 28, 1919.

129,031. SWEATERS, BATHING-SUITS, UNDERWEAR, AND HOSIERY, ALL MADE OF KNITTED MATERIAL. NAVY KNITTING MILLS, INC., New York, N. Y.
Filed February 1, 1919. Serial No. 115,573. PUBLISHED JULY 29, 1919.

129,032. NON-ALCOHOLIC FRUIT-JUICES SOLD AS A SOFT DRINK. NORMANDIE COMPANY, Norfolk, Va.
Filed January 27, 1919. Serial No. 115,463. PUBLISHED OCTOBER 7, 1919.

129,033. NON-ALCOHOLIC FRUIT-JUICES SOLD AS A SOFT DRINK. NORMANDIE COMPANY, Norfolk, Va.
Filed January 27, 1919. Serial No. 115,464. PUBLISHED OCTOBER 7, 1919.

129,034. PASTE CEMENT IN THE NATURE OF AN ADHESIVE FOR USE IN RADIATORS FOR AUTOMOBILES AND MOTOR-VEHICLES AND RADIATORS FOR HEATING PURPOSES. THE NORTHWESTERN CHEMICAL CO., Marietta, Ohio.
Filed April 27, 1918. Serial No. 110,484. PUBLISHED OCTOBER 28, 1919.

129,035. CERTAIN NAMED ADHESIVES. THE NORTH-WESTERN CHEMICAL CO., Marietta, Ohio.
Filed April 27, 1918. Serial No. 110,491. PUBLISHED OCTOBER 28, 1919.

129,036. WHEAT-FLOUR. THE NORTHWESTERN CONSOLIDATED MILLING COMPANY, Minneapolis, Minn., and New York, N. Y.
Filed August 7, 1919. Serial No. 121,354. PUBLISHED NOVEMBER 4, 1919.

129,037. FERTILIZER MATERIALS. NITRATE AGENCIES COMPANY, New York, N. Y.
Filed July 7, 1919. Serial N°. 120,316. PUBLISHED OCTOBER 28, 1919.

129,038. WHEAT-FLOUR. OMAHA FLOUR MILLS CO., Omaha, Nebr.
Filed August 25, 1919. Serial No. 121,986. PUBLISHED NOVEMBER 4, 1919.

129,039. WHEAT-FLOUR. OMAHA FLOUR MILLS CO., Omaha, Nebr.
Filed August 25, 1919. Serial No. 121,987. PUBLISHED NOVEMBER 4, 1919.

129,040. WHEAT-FLOUR. OMAHA FLOUR MILLS CO., Omaha, Nebr.
Filed August 25, 1919. Serial No. 121,985. PUBLISHED NOVEMBER 4, 1919.

129,041. BICYCLES. CORNELIUS J. O'RIELY, Los Angeles, Calif.
Filed January 14, 1919. Serial No. 115,183. PUBLISHED SEPTEMBER 23, 1919.

129,042. CERTAIN NAMED ELECTRICAL APPARATUS, MACHINES, AND SUPPLIES. FRANK D. PARMENTER, Toronto, Ontario, Canada.
Filed September 26, 1918. Serial No. 113,431. PUBLISHED SEPTEMBER 30, 1919.

129,043. WRITING, PRINTING, BLOTTING, AND WRAPPING PAPERS. PARSONS & WHITTEMORE, INCORPORATED, New York, N. Y.
Filed July 20, 1918. Serial No. 112,237. PUBLISHED SEPTEMBER 23, 1919.

129,044. CEREAL BREAKFAST FOOD MADE FROM RICE. THE PATENT CEREALS COMPANY, Geneva and New York, N. Y.
Filed June 16, 1919. Serial No. 119,669. PUBLISHED OCTOBER 21, 1919.

129,045. MOUTH-HARMONICAS. THE PEERLESS MUSICAL INSTRUMENT MFG. CO., Meriden, Conn.
Filed May 27, 1919. Serial No. 118,971. PUBLISHED OCTOBER 28, 1919.

129,046. MANDOLINS, GUITARS, BANJOS, AND BANJO-MANDOLINS. PERLBERG & HALPIN, New York, N. Y.
Filed April 12, 1918. Serial No. 110,146. PUBLISHED OCTOBER 7, 1919.

129,047. REMEDY FOR NEURALGIA, SICK AND BILIOUS HEADACHE. ADELAIDE R. PERRY, Buffalo, N. Y.
Filed February 12, 1917. Serial No. 101,339. PUBLISHED SEPTEMBER 16, 1919.

129,048. COMPOUND FOR TREATING CERTAIN DISEASES OF ANIMALS AND USED EXTERNALLY BY HUMANS. WILLIAM PIDGEON, Beloit, Ohio.
Filed April 16, 1919. Serial No. 117,540. PUBLISHED SEPTEMBER 30, 1919.

129,049. MALT BEVERAGE COMMONLY KNOWN AS NEAR BEER. PITTSBURGH BREWING COMPANY, Pittsburgh, Pa.
Filed January 6, 1919. Serial No. 115,016. PUBLISHED OCTOBER 21, 1919.

129,050. BARS OF OPEN-HEARTH STEEL SOLD IN BULK. THE POLLAK STEEL COMPANY, Cincinnati, Ohio.
Filed April 24, 1919. Serial No. 117,816. PUBLISHED SEPTEMBER 30, 1919.

129,051. CIGARS. E. POPPER & CO. INC., New York, N. Y.
Filed December 19, 1918. Serial No. 114,718. PUBLISHED FEBRUARY 11, 1919.

129,052. WELDED STEEL AND IRON TUBING. PRESSED METAL RADIATOR COMPANY, Pittsburgh, Pa.
Filed April 28, 1919. Serial No. 117,947. PUBLISHED SEPTEMBER 30, 1919.

129,053. CLEANSING COMPOUNDS. JIMMY QUICK PRODUCTS CO., San Francisco, Calif.
Filed May 3, 1919. Serial No. 118,113. PUBLISHED OCTOBER 21, 1919.

129,054. WOMEN'S DRESSES, GOWNS, SKIRTS, COATS, AND CAPES. ISIDORE RABINOWITZ APPAREL CO. INC., New York, N. Y.
Filed April 7, 1919. Serial No. 117,250. PUBLISHED SEPTEMBER 16, 1919.

129,055. PHONOGRAPHS, PHONOGRAPH-RECORDS, AND PHONOGRAPH-NEEDLES. RAYMOND PHONOGRAPH CO. INC., Atlanta, Ga.
Filed January 18, 1919. Serial No. 115,295. PUBLISHED SEPTEMBER 30, 1919.

129,056. FURNITURE-POLISH. THE W. T. RAWLEIGH COMPANY, Freeport, Ill.
Filed April 22, 1919. Serial No. 117,742. PUBLISHED OCTOBER 7, 1919.

129,057. CIGARETTES. REED TOBACCO COMPANY, Richmond, Va.
Filed June 13, 1919. Serial No. 119,583. PUBLISHED OCTOBER 14, 1919.

129,058. CIGARETTES. REED TOBACCO COMPANY, Richmond, Va.
Filed June 13, 1919. Serial No. 119,580. PUBLISHED OCTOBER 14, 1919.

129,059. WHEAT-FLOUR. THE RED STAR MILLING COMPANY, Wichita, Kans.
Filed December 16, 1918. Serial No. 114,680. PUBLISHED OCTOBER 28, 1919.

129,060. CERTAIN NAMED DENTAL, MEDICAL, AND SURGICAL APPLIANCES. REID BROS., INC., San Francisco, Calif., and Seattle, Wash.
Filed September 30, 1918. Serial No. 113,500. PUBLISHED OCTOBER 14, 1919.

129,061. WOMEN'S AND CHILDREN'S KNITTED AND WOVEN UNDERWEAR. JOHN S. RICHMOND, Philadelphia, Pa.
Filed March 8, 1919. Serial No. 116,426. PUBLISHED JULY 8, 1919.

129,062. WHEAT-FLOUR. ROANOKE CITY MILLS, Roanoke, Va.
Filed July 25, 1919. Serial No. 120,927. PUBLISHED NOVEMBER 4, 1919.

129,063. TRUNKS. D. E. ROSE TRUNK COMPANY, Topeka, Kans.
Filed July 24, 1919. Serial No. 120,882. PUBLISHED OCTOBER 28, 1919.

129,064. BOOTS AND SHOES MADE OF CERTAIN NAMED MATERIALS. ROSMAN & LAVESON, Philadelphia, Pa.
Filed November 20, 1918. Serial No. 114,256. PUBLISHED SEPTEMBER 9, 1919.

129,065. NOTE-SHEETS FOR PLAYER-PIANOS AND THE LIKE. RYTHMODIK MUSIC CORPORATION, Belleville, N. J., and New York, N. Y.
Filed June 13, 1918. Serial No. 111,551. PUBLISHED SEPTEMBER 30, 1919.

129,066. DISINFECTANTS. FRANKLIN SANFORD, Cincinnati, Ohio.
Filed May 5, 1919. Serial No. 118,133. PUBLISHED OCTOBER 7, 1919.

129,067. PUZZLES. CHARLES A. SCHMITZ, Boston, Mass.
Filed July 23, 1919. Serial No. 120,852. PUBLISHED OCTOBER 14, 1919.

129,068. CALLOUS-REMOVING PREPARATIONS. SCOTCH-TONE COMPANY, Oklahoma, Okla. Filed November 14, 1918. Serial No. 114,172. PUBLISHED SEPTEMBER 23, 1919.

129,069. LARD COMPOUNDS COMPOSED OF COTTON-SEED OIL, BEEF-FAT, OLEO-STEARIN, AND PURE LARD. GEORGE SCHLUDERBERG, Highlandtown and Baltimore, Md. Filed April 8, 1916. Serial No. 94,264. PUBLISHED OCTOBER 28, 1919.

129,070. PREPARED ROOFING. SHAPLEIGH HARDWARE COMPANY, St. Louis, Mo. Filed April 12, 1919. Serial No. 117,422. PUBLISHED SEPTEMBER 23, 1919.

129,071. MEN'S AND BOYS' CLOTHING—NAMELY, OUTER SUITS, OVERCOATS, AND SPORT-COATS. SHIREK & HIRSCH, New York, N. Y. Filed April 22, 1919. Serial No. 117,751. PUBLISHED SEPTEMBER 16, 1919.

129,072. DOLLS. HERBERT OTTO SHULTS, Chicago, Ill. Filed December 5, 1918. Serial No. 114,503. PUBLISHED OCTOBER 28, 1919.

129,073. CANDIES, CHOCOLATES, AND CARAMELS. CHARLES SIEGEL, New York, N. Y., assignor to Victory Confectionery Co., New York, N. Y., a Corporation of New Jersey. Filed August 2, 1919. Serial No. 121,218. PUBLISHED NOVEMBER 4, 1919.

129,074. GAMES AND GAME-BOARDS OF A CHECKER OR CHESS LIKE VARIETY. EDWARD C. SIMCOX, Columbus, Ohio. Filed January 17, 1918. Serial No. 108,513. PUBLISHED OCTOBER 14, 1919.

129,075. SCALES FOR WEIGHING. SIMMONS HARDWARE COMPANY, St. Louis, Mo. Filed March 15, 1919. Serial No. 116,620. PUBLISHED SEPTEMBER 30, 1919.

129,076. CERTAIN NAMED MEASURING AND SCIENTIFIC APPLIANCES. SIMMONS HARDWARE COMPANY, St. Louis, Mo. Filed April 15, 1919. Serial No. 117,515. PUBLISHED SEPTEMBER 2, 1919.

129,077. HARNESS, RIDING-SADDLES, HORSE-COLLARS, SWINGLE AND DOUBLE TREES, NECK-YOKES. SIMMONS HARDWARE COMPANY, St. Louis, Mo. Filed May 14, 1919. Serial No. 118,489. PUBLISHED OCTOBER 7, 1919.

129,078. STOCK FEEDS AND POULTRY FEEDS. THE SIMMONS MILLING COMPANY, Cincinnati, Ohio. Filed August 18, 1919. Serial No. 121,794. PUBLISHED NOVEMBER 4, 1919.

129,079. BREAD, PIES, AND ICE-CREAM. PAUL F. SKINNER, Omaha, Nebr. Filed April 11, 1919. Serial No. 117,390. PUBLISHED OCTOBER 28, 1919.

129,080. CANNED APRICOTS, DRIED FRUITS—NAMELY, PRUNES—AND CANNED TOMATOES WITH PURÉE FROM TRIMMINGS. SMITH-FRANK PACKING CO., Sacramento, Calif. Filed August 8, 1919. Serial No. 121,422. PUBLISHED NOVEMBER 4, 1919.

129,081. CHEMICAL PREPARATION FOR PRESERVING EGGS. DAYTON D. SMITH, Philadelphia, Pa. Filed May 12, 1919. Serial No. 118,406. PUBLISHED SEPTEMBER 30, 1919.

129,082. CIGARS. HARRY H. SNOVEL, Van Wert, Ohio. Filed March 10, 1919. Serial No. 116,447. PUBLISHED OCTOBER 14, 1919.

129,083. CERTAIN NAMED NON-ALCOHOLIC BEVERAGES. SOUTHERN BEVERAGE COMPANY, Galveston, Tex. Filed May 14, 1919. Serial No. 118,492. PUBLISHED NOVEMBER 4, 1919.

129,084. ENAMEL PAINTS, VARNISH-STAINS, OIL-PAINTS, VARNISH - REMOVERS, FLOOR - LAC-QUERS. STANDARD COOPER-BELL CO., Chicago, Ill. Filed July 17, 1918. Serial No. 112,193. PUBLISHED OCTOBER 7, 1919.

129,085. DEXTRINIZED STARCH PRODUCT TO BE USED AS AN INGREDIENT IN BAKING. STEIN-HALL MANUFACTURING COMPANY, Wilmington, Del., and Chicago, Ill. Filed July 25, 1919. Serial No. 120,938. PUBLISHED NOVEMBER 4, 1919.

129,086. FLAVORING EXTRACTS FOR FOOD AND ROASTED COFFEE. STEINWENDER - STOFFREGEN COFFEE COMPANY, St. Louis, Mo. Filed September 23, 1918. Serial No. 113,321. PUBLISHED OCTOBER 28, 1919.

129,087. VARNISH FOR COLORING AND COATING THE SURFACE OF RUBBER TIRES. THE STERLING VARNISH COMPANY, Pittsburgh, Pa. Filed June 10, 1919. Serial No. 119,455. PUBLISHED OCTOBER 28, 1919.

129,088. WRITING AND PRINTING PAPER. STONE & ANDREW INC., Boston, Mass. Filed November 26, 1918. Serial No. 114,386. PUBLISHED OCTOBER 7, 1919.

129,089. RICE. STUTTGART RICE MILL COMPANY, Stuttgart, Ark. Filed July 12, 1919. Serial No. 120,498. PUBLISHED NOVEMBER 4, 1919.

129,090. RICE. STUTTGART RICE MILL COMPANY, Stuttgart, Ark. Filed June 27, 1919. Serial No. 120,014. PUBLISHED SEPTEMBER 30, 1919.

129,091. MEN'S AND WOMEN'S LEATHER BOOTS AND SHOES. E. E. TAYLOR COMPANY, Boston, Mass. Filed May 27, 1918. Serial No. 111,228. PUBLISHED JULY 22, 1919.

129,092. CHEWING - GUM. GEORGE W. TODD, Omaha, Nebr. Filed August 12, 1919. Serial No. 121,606. PUBLISHED NOVEMBER 4, 1919.

129,093. PREPARATION FOR THE TREATMENT OF CERTAIN NAMED DISEASES. LORENZA D. TRENT, Ironton, Ohio. Filed March 24. 1919. Serial No. 116,857. PUBLISHED SEPTEMBER 30, 1919.

129,094. SHOES MADE OF LEATHER. UNITED STATES RUBBER COMPANY, New Brunswick, N. J., and New York, N. Y. Filed July 6, 1919. Serial No. 111,973. PUBLISHED SEPTEMBER 30, 1919.

129,095. POWER DRAG-SAWS. R. M. WADE & CO., Portland, Oreg. Filed April 21, 1919. Serial No. 117,718. PUBLISHED SEPTEMBER 16, 1919.

129,096. CERTAIN NAMED FOODS AND INGREDIENTS OF FOOD. WALKER-MATTESON CO., Joliet, Ill. Filed March 8, 1919. Serial No. 116,432. PUBLISHED OCTOBER 7, 1919.

129,097. POLISHING AND CLEANSING COMPOUND FOR VARNISHED OR ENAMELED SURFACES REQUIRING A HIGH POLISH. FRANK B. WEBSTER, Los Angeles, Calif. Filed June 17, 1919. Serial No. 119,725. PUBLISHED OCTOBER 7, 1919.

129,098. ALL-STEEL ONE-LEVER SEVEN OR EIGHT FOOT BOLTED AND RIVETED ROAD-DRAGS. WESTERN BOILER PIPE COMPANY, Monmouth, Ill. Filed May 12, 1919. Serial No. 118,412. PUBLISHED SEPTEMBER 30, 1919.

129,099. AUTOMOBILES. THE WESTCOTT MOTOR CAR COMPANY, Springfield, Ohio. Filed April 21. 1919. Serial No. 117,719. PUBLISHED JUNE 24. 1919.

129,100. PLANCHETTE - BOARDS. THEODORE H. WHITE, Los Angeles, Calif.
Filed July 25, 1919. Serial No. 120,946. PUBLISHED OCTOBER 14, 1919.

129,101. ASPHALT SHINGLES, ROOFING - PAPERS, AND ROOFING-CEMENTS. WHITE STAR REFINING Co., Detroit, Mich.
Filed March 29, 1919. Serial No. 117,030. PUBLISHED SEPTEMBER 23, 1919.

129,102. COVERING USED TO COAT CANDY. H. O. WILBUR & SONS, INC., Philadelphia, Pa.
Filed June 16, 1919. Serial No. 119,687. PUBLISHED OCTOBER 21, 1919.

129,103. SCALP PREPARATION AND HAIR-GROWER. BETTIE WILLIAMS, New York, N. Y.
Filed April 23, 1919. Serial No. 117,789. PUBLISHED SEPTEMBER 9, 1919.

129,104. COUGH-DROPS. WILLIAMS CHOCOLATE Co., Scranton, Pa.
Filed March 20, 1919. Serial No. 116,755. PUBLISHED SEPTEMBER 16, 1919.

129,105. RIBBONS OF PILE FABRICS. A. WIMPF-HEIMER & BRO., INC., New York, N. Y.
Filed April 17, 1918. Serial No. 110,288. PUBLISHED NOVEMBER 12, 1918.

129,106. COTTON-SEED-OIL STEARIN. WYATT BROS., Chicago, Ill.
Filed July 24, 1919. Serial No. 120,894. PUBLISHED OCTOBER 21, 1919.

129,107. WRITING - TABLETS, WRITING - PAPERS, AND CORRESPONDENCE-ENVELOPS. THE WYNNE PAPER Co., New York, N. Y.
Filed March 22, 1918. Serial No. 109,734. PUBLISHED SEPTEMBER 23, 1919.

129,108. GLOBES, SHADES, AND REFLECTORS, ALL MADE OF GLASS. YOUNG & EGAN, INC., New York, N. Y.
Filed March 27, 1919. Serial No. 116,983. PUBLISHED SEPTEMBER 23, 1919.

129,109. CHILDREN'S AND BOYS' CLOTHES—NAMELY, SUITS, OVERCOATS, AND PANTS. ARMOR-CLAD BOY'S CLOTHES Co., New York, N. Y.
Filed September 12, 1918. Serial No. 113,136. PUBLISHED JULY 29, 1919.

DECISIONS

OF THE

COMMISSIONER OF PATENTS

AND OF

UNITED STATES COURTS IN PATENT CASES.

COMMISSIONER'S DECISIONS.

EX PARTE SMITH WHEEL, INC.

Decided December 19, 1919.

TRADE-MARKS—"EVERLASTING," FOR VEHICLE-WHEELS—
DESCRIPTIVE.

The word "Everlasting" *Held* descriptive, and
therefore not registrable as a trade-mark for vehicle-
wheels. This word expresses aptly the idea that applicant's wheels will last a very long time, and therefore cannot be monopolized.

ON APPEAL.

TRADE-MARK FOR CAST-METAL WHEELS.

Mr. Howard P. Denison for the applicant.

NEWTON, *Commissioner:*

This is an appeal from a decision of the Examiner
of Trade-Marks refusing to register "Everlasting"
in what may be termed the ordinary stencil letter-
ing, arranged in the arc of a circle, as a trade-mark
for vehicle-wheels, on the ground that the word is
descriptive, citing *Patterson-Allen Engineering Company,* (118 MS. Dec., 389,) where, in passing on the
same word as a trade-mark for valves, it was held
that "Everlasting" should be refused registration
in view of the *Standard Paint Co.* v. *Trinidad Asphalt Mfg. Co.,* (220 U. S., 446;) *in re Freund Bros.
& Co.,* (169 O. G., 206; 37 App. D. C., 109;) *in re
Seamless Rubber Co.,* (153 O. G., 547; 34 App. D. C.,
357;) *Florence Mfg. Co.* v. *J. C. Dowd & Co.,*
(178 Fed. Rep., 73;) *in re Central Consumers Co.,*
(140 O. G., 1211; 32 App. D. C., 523,) all of which
hold words similar in character to "Everlasting"
descriptive. Indeed, this same word "Everlasting"
had also been previously held descriptive in *Edw.
Reilly,* (114 MS. Dec., 330.)

Applicant contends that, inasmuch as "Everlasting" is apparently such an exaggeration as to
be absurd, the mark should be registered, since no
one would be misled and the word was not necessary
to describe any quality or property that others
might wish to describe, and cites *Holeproof Hosiery
Co.* v. *Wallach Bros.,* (172 Fed. Rep., 859,) holding
"Holeproof," for hosiery, a valid mark; *Aluminum
Cooking Utensil Co.* v. *National Aluminum Works,*
(226 Fed. Rep., 815,) upholding "Wearever," for
aluminum ware; *New York Mackintosh Co.* v. *Flam
et al.,* (198 Fed. Rep., 571,) upholding "Bestyette,"
for waterproof capes, etc.

It is undoubtedly true that applicant's wheels are
not technically or strictly speaking everlasting, and
no one would be led to believe that they were; but
"Everlasting" has another meaning—viz., continuing indefinitely (see *Webster's Collegiate Dic-*

tionary, 1902 edition)—and is the only single word
I know of that expresses the idea that applicant's
wheels last a very long time, and it is useful to
advertisers in describing this quality of continuing
indefinitely and cannot be monopolized.

The decision of the Examiner of Trade-Marks
must accordingly be affirmed.

DECISIONS OF THE U. S. COURTS.

U. S. Circuit Court of Appeals—Fourth Circuit.

BISIGHT CO. *et al.* v. ONEPIECE BIFOCAL LENS CO.

Decided January 20, 1919.

[259 Fed. Rep., 275.]

1. PATENTS—VALIDITY OF CLAIM—LIMITATION.
    A patent claim may be limited by reference to the
    specifications.

2. SAME—VALIDITY—BIFOCAL LENS.
    The Connor machine patent, No. 836,486, claim 1, for
    making bifocal lenses, as limited by its reference to the
    specifications, is not invalid because too broad.

3. SAME—INFRINGEMENT—MAKING BIFOCAL LENSES.
    The Connor machine patent, No. 836,486, claim 1, for
    making bifocal lenses, *Held* infringed.

4. SAME—VALIDITY—ANTICIPATION.
    The Connor machine patent, No. 836,486, claim 1, for
    producing bifocal lenses, is not anticipated by grinding-
    machines in remote arts, such as grinding buttons, since
    more than mechanical skill was required to apply the
    grinding process to lenses.

CROSS-APPEALS from the District Court of the
United States for the District of Maryland, at Baltimore; John C. Rose, judge.

Suit by the Onepiece Bifocal Lens Company
against the Bisight Company and Benjamin Mayer.
Decree for complainant, (246 Fed., 450,) and defendants appeal, with cross-appeal by complainant.
Decree modified.

Mr. Victor D. Borst (Mr. William M. Stockbridge
and *Mr. Cyrus N. Anderson* on the brief) for the appellants and cross-appellees.

Mr. V. H. Lockwood and *Mr. Edward Rector* for
the appellee and cross-appellant.

Before KNAPP and WOODS, Circuit Judges, and
McDOWELL, District Judge.

WOODS, *Cir. J.:*

Consideration of the claims, infringements, and
defenses set up in these appeals involve very fine
distinctions of the application of the patent law to
bifocal lenses. Study of the record and arguments
satisfies us that the district judge reached just conclusions as to most of the matters in controversy,
and no good end would be attained by a statement

of our reasons for approving his conclusions. (246 Fed., 450.)

(1, 2) We think, however, that the district court was in error in holding invalid claim 1 of the Connor machine patent, No. 836,486. That claim reads as follows:

Apparatus for producing bifocal lenses including a rotary holder for the lens crystal, and means for grinding two bifocal surfaces of different dioptrics simultaneously on one face thereof, substantially as set forth.

The district court held this claim invalid, because the rotary lens-holder is old in the art and the claim was too broad, in that it covered all apparatus which will make the product described, provided only that a rotary lens-holder forms a part of them. A claim may be limited by reference to the specifications in the application. (*Seymour* v. *Osborne*, 11 Wall., 516–547; 20 L. Ed., 33; *The Corn-Planter Patent*, 23 Wall., 181–218; 23 L. Ed., 161.) We think the broad claim is so limited in this instance by the words " substantially as set forth," referring to the specifications in the application which it is conceded describe the apparatus, and that the claim is therefore valid.

(3) We are of opinion, also, that the defendant has infringed. It is true that in Connor's specifications he describes—

a crystal holder member, and rotary grinding member co-operating therewith and having a spherically disposed grinding surface and an adjacent nonspherically disposed grinding surface,

and that Mayer's machine, which the defendants operate, has both surfaces spherical. Connor's apparatus being the first to accomplish the desired end, or at least an important generic invention, should not be so narrowly construed as to permit real infringement by a variation which, if substantial, is merely an inferior application of Connor's invention. (*Continental Paper Bag Co.* v. *Eastern Paper Bag Co.*, 210 U. S., 405; 28 Sup. Ct., 748; 52 L. Ed., 1122; *King Ax Co. et al.* v. *Hubbard*, 97 Fed., 795; 38 C. C. A., 423.)

(4) Connor's invention cannot be regarded anticipated by grinding-machines in a remote art. such as the grinding of buttons. Evidently something more than mechanical skill was required to apply the grinding process to lenses, even if it had been suggested by the apparatus for grinding buttons. (*Hobbs* v. *Beach*, 180 U. S., 383–392; 21 Sup. Ct., 409; 45 L. Ed., 586.) The decree of the district court, with this modification, protects the plaintiff in the exclusive use of all inventions covered by its patents, and meets fully the justice of the case. The decree of the district court is modified accordingly.

Modified.

U. S. Circuit Court of Appeals—Sixth Circuit.

DUNN WIRE-CUT LUG BRICK CO. *v.* TORONTO FIRE CLAY CO. *et al.*

Decided January 7, 1919; on motion to reopen May 6, 1919.

[259 Fed. Rep., 258.]

1. PATENTS—PRESUMPTION OF INVENTIVE NOVELTY FROM USE—ATTRIBUTION TO PRODUCT.

Though brick of a certain type, which have gone on the market and had a large sale, are the product of the

patentee's patented machine, which has been manufactured by him and sold to brickmakers, such credit and such presumption of inventive novelty as arise from public use should be given to the product—the bricks—and not to the machine.

2. SAME — VALIDITY — INVENTIVE CHARACTER — PAVING-BRICKS.

Dunn's patent, No. 918,980, for wire-cut paving-brick having wire-cut ribs on the side, *Held* valid because the concept had inventive character, as distinguished from mere skill.

3. SAME—NEW PRODUCT—VARIATIONS IN METHOD OF MAKING.

The inventor of a new and useful product or article of manufacture may have a patent covering it and giving a monopoly upon it regardless of great variations in the method of making.

4. SAME—METHOD AND PRODUCT—SEPARATE PATENTS.

In the ordinary and typical case the method of manufacture and the product manufactured are separable inventions supporting separate patents, one of which may be valid and the other not.

5. SAME—PRODUCT PATENT—INFRINGEMENT BY MANUFACTURING DEVICE.

Dunn's patent, No. 918,980, for wire-cut paving-brick having wire-cut ribs on the side, *Held* infringed by the product of defendant's manufacturing device.

6. SAME—INFRINGEMENT—WHAT CONSTITUTES.

As between plaintiff's earlier and defendant's later patent a finding that the earlier device, if later, would not have infringed the later patent is not helpful in deciding whether defendant's device infringes plaintiff's patent.

On motion to reopen.

7. SAME—LATE INTRODUCTION OF EVIDENCE—CONDITIONS OF PERMISSION.

In suit for infringement of patent where, after direction of the usual interlocutory decree on finding of infringement, defendants present foreign patents said to anticipate plaintiff's product and ask leave to apply to reopen the case and put them into the record on account of the public interest and the interest of the courts the proposed evidence will be permitted to be brought into the record on defendants' meeting additional expenses of another trial, their showing to excuse failure to put in the evidence in due time not being satisfactory.

APPEAL from the District Court of the United States for the Eastern Division of the Southern District of Ohio; John E. Sater, judge.

Suit in equity for infringement of patent by the Dunn Wire-Cut Lug Brick Company against the Toronto Fire Clay Company and others. From decree dismissing the bill, plaintiff appeals. Order entered that the district court have leave to reopen the case, etc.

Mr. J. C. Sturgeon and *Mr. S. H. Tolles* for the appellant.

Mr. David M. Gruber and *Mr. Joseph T. Harrison* for the appellees.

Before WARRINGTON, KNAPPEN, and DENISON, Circuit Judges.

DENISON, *Cir. J.*:

The company which had purchased the patent appeals from the decree dismissing its infringement bill brought against the Toronto Company and Nicholson, and based upon Patent No. 918,980, issued April 20, 1909, to Dunn, for paving-brick. The trial court overruled the defense of invalidity, but held that there was no infringement, and both of these subjects must be determined.

Brick were originally made by molding or pressing in individual dies or forms. The product was a molded brick or a pressed brick. It was found to be cheaper to squeeze the plastic clay through a die shaped like a cross-section of the finished brick and producing a continuous blank from which pieces could be cut or sliced off to form separate bricks. Because it came to be the more common practice to slice off these bricks from the blank by using a moving wire as the cutting edge (either one wire at a time or several in a gang), bricks of this class came to have the name "wire-cut bricks." Whether the cutting was done by wire or a knife or a saw was not important, because these methods are, in any broad sense, obviously equivalent. A cutting-wire works like the cutting edge of a knife, and the cutting edge of a knife, for this purpose, a wire; hence all such brick, whether sliced by wire or knife or saw, are, in the trade, universally called "wire-cut brick."

For paving, it is desirable that the brick should not fit close together, but should be spaced slightly apart, in order that waterproofing and adhesive material may fill the interstices and make a perfect bond. Accordingly, they were made with buttons, ribs, or slight projections of other forms upon one or both of the vertical faces of the two adjacent bricks. These were formed by suitable depressions in the dies in which the pressing was done; and, up to Dunn's time, all paving-brick with lugs or ribs had been re-pressed brick. Dunn observed, and seems to have been the first fully to understand, that, for the purpose of paving, the brick were injured by this re-pressing. The surface was too smooth, the corners were not sharp enough, and the texture or lamination was distorted; but the ordinary wire-cut brick were unsuitable for this purpose, because they had no spacing-ribs. It seems fairly to be inferred that, if the idea of putting ribs on wire-cut brick had occurred to any one, it had been rejected because of the difficulties or expense involved. In ordinary hand operation, to get this result would necessarily be slow, and operating upon such material would be likely to break away parts of the brick or ribs and produce defective brick.

In this situation, it occurred to Dunn that, by the same operation by which he cut off the brick from the blank by sweeping the cutting-wire across its face, he could leave ribs along the face, and he could accomplish this result by making the cutting edge irregular, instead of straight. In the form in which he developed his idea, he carried the wire on each side of his blank of clay in a slot which was straight most of the way, but included two semicircular offsets. The result was a brick, plane upon each side, excepting where crossed by two projecting ribs. He first applied for a patent upon the machine accomplishing these results, but, while that application was pending, filed also an application for a patent

270 O. G.—82   [Vol. 270.

upon the product of his machine. This is the patent in suit. The patent upon the machine was not issued until September 7, 1909. The first claim of the patent in suit is:

As an article of manufacture, a wire-cut brick having wire-cut ribs on the side thereof, substantially as set forth.

(1) Dunn's product has been very largely accepted as a better paving-brick than before existed. Although the brick of this type which have gone on the market and had this large and wide sale are the product of his patented machine, which has been manufactured by him and sold to brickmakers, yet such credit and such presumption of inventive novelty as arise from public use should be given to the product, and not to the machine. There would be no use for the machine, unless the product were desired. We therefore give some weight to this wide public use as bearing on the patent's validity.

(2) We think Dunn's concept had inventive character as distinguished from mere skill. The fact that this very simple product, which proved to be so useful, never had been developed during all the progress of the art, goes far to give it character. Re-pressing, with its cost and disadvantages, was avoided and a better brick was produced by simple means. We agree with the district judge in saying:

His brick is new and useful, and involved invention in no mean degree, and entitles him to the breadth of equivalency pertaining to an invention of that character—

and agree also with his summary quoted in the margin.[1]

Without regard to whether a patent upon a product may be wholly independent of any thought of the means by which it is produced, there can, in this case, be no such independence. Some degree of reference to the method of the production is carried into the claim by the words "wire-cut ribs." Where a process or a machine will produce only a specific product, and where a given product can be produced only by the specific process or machine, (if there are such cases; see *Macbeth Co.* v. *General Co.*, C. C. A. 6, 246 Fed., 695, 698; 158; C. C. A., 651,) it is difficult to see much lack of identity between the invented process or machine and the invented product, and such situations have given rise to some rather casual and seemingly *obiter* statements that process and product or machine and product constitute only one invention, (e. g.. *Downes* v. *Teter-Heany*, C. C. A. 3, 150 Fed., 122; 80 C. C. A., 76.) It is thought that every such case will be found to depend upon

<hr/>

[1] Dunn conceived and produced a wire-cut brick with wholly wire-cut lugs, thereby dispensing entirely with the re-pressing process and with the expenditure necessary to effect the same. The development of his concept involved much study and experimentation. He was hampered not merely by want of funds, but by the distrust, discouraging conduct, and opposition of brickmakers and engineers. However, by persistent energy and determination he overcame the obstacles encountered and eventually won recognition by practically demonstrating the commercially successful character of his brick and the mode of its production. The roughness of the sides of the brick, which at first provoked opposition, was found in actual experience to be advantageous, as the filler was thereby enabled more firmly to set and more securely to hold than is possible with the smoother surfaced brick. The demand for his brick, following the test of actual service, was such that the output rose from 2,233,000 in 1910, to 138,000,000 in 1915. In the same period he granted 33 licenses to manufacturers.

this—actual or supposed—necessary identity of the means and the result.[2]

(3, 4) Certain it is, in view of the weight of authority and the latest decisions, that the inventor of a new and useful product or article of manufacture may have a patent which covers it and gives a monopoly upon it regardless of great variations in the method of making (*Powder Co.* v. *Powder Wks.*, 98 U. S., 126, 136, 137; 25 L. Ed., 77; *Leeds Co.* v. *Victor Co.*, 213 U. S., 301, 318; 29 Sup. Ct., 495; 53 L. Ed., 805; *Durand* v. *Schulze.* C. C. A. 3, 61 Fed., 819, 821; 10 C. C. A., 97; *Maurer* v. *Dickerson*, C. C. A. 3, 113 Fed., 870, 874; 51 C. C. A., 494; *Lamb* v. *Lamb*, C. C. A. 6, 120 Fed., 267, 269; 56 C. C. A., 547; *Sanitas Co.* v. *Voigt*, C. C. A. 6., 139 Fed., 551, 552, 553; 71 C. C. A., 535; *Acme Co.* v. *Commercial Co.*, C. C. A. 6, 192 Fed., 321, 325, 326; 112 C. C. A., 573) and that in the ordinary and typical case, the method and the product are separable inventions, supporting separate patents, one of which may be valid and the other not, (*Rubber Co.* v. *Goodyear*, 76 U. S., 9 Wall., 788; 19 L. Ed., 566.) It is therefore the duty of the court to find, if it reasonably can, for a product patent some construction and scope which shall avoid, on the one hand, destroying its value—if not its validity—by confining it to the precise method of making which the patent has happened to show, and avoid, on the other hand, a construction so broad as to make it invalid because for an old product. As illustrated by the present case, if Dunn is confined to wire-cut brick with wire-cut lugs produced precisely as shown by him, the patent is commercially worthless because easily avoided; while, if it is construed to cover a wire-cut brick which, before burning, has had irregularities produced upon its face by any cutting or carving means whatever, it would be void because of common practice relating to all kinds of tile, brick and pottery.

The theory that this patent extends only to the output of the method shown in the machine patent is inconsistent with the action of the Patent Office. Dunn first claimed—

a wire-cut brick having wire-cut ribs on one side thereof formed complete during the operation of cutting the brick.

This was rejected as "claiming the article by the method of making it." The Patent Office recognized and applied the rule above stated. Dunn then substituted the claim allowed and issued.

[2] We find no authoritative decision lending more color of support to the idea that a patent for a product is to be confined to the result of the described process, than may be derived from some of the language in *Goodyear Co.* v. *Davis*, (102 U. S., 222, 224; 26 L. Ed., 149.) It was there said: "The invention is a product or manufacture made in a defined manner. It is not a product alone, separated from the process by which it is created." This conclusion was the result of an exhaustive study of the facts of the particular case, and was intended to refer to those facts. The claim was for "the plate of hard rubber or vulcanite, or its equivalent." The defendant did not use hard rubber or vulcanite, and the question was whether celluloid, an article unknown when the patent issued, was an equivalent. The case does not hold that if the defendant had employed a hard rubber plate he could have escaped because he manufactured this hard rubber by a process different from that described by Cummings. Nothing which was not made by the process of vulcanization could be the equivalent of the "hard rubber or vulcanite" of the claim. The process of vulcanization was imported into the claim by its very terms.

(5) The true scope of the claim can best be developed by tracing it from the form shown in the drawing to the form used by defendant. It is, doubtless, more economical to have the same stroke of the wire or cutter sever the brick from the blank and produce the ribs; but the claim cannot be so restricted without destroying the differentiation between the patent for the machine and the patent for the product. We think it clear that the patented product would be produced just the same if Dunn took a brick which had already been severed from the blank on both sides by some other wire-cutting machine, and passed that brick through his machine, using his wire cutter to completely reshape one entire side of that brick. The brick would be wire-cut, and the ribs would be wire-cut, although one face of the brick would have been treated twice instead of once. This would not be an unnatural treatment, if it was desired to have the ribs upon any face excepting the one produced by the cutting-wire. When we admit the equivalency between the cutting-knife and the cutting-wire, we see that this supposititious treatment is that which defendant Nicholson has adopted (and the Toronto Company uses). He first cuts his blank into separate brick by the usual wire-cutting process, then passes his severed brick along a feed-table and over a cutter which he calls a knife, the form of which is shown by 29, 30 in the following Figures 3 and 6 taken from the patent

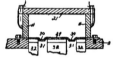

Fig. 3.

Fig. 6.

issued to him, No. 1,148,529 of August 3, 1915. This cutter or knife is the perfect equivalent for this purpose of a wire bent into the same form.

Defendant suggests no difference in operation excepting that he thinks such sharp corners could not be put on the ribs of a wire-cutter; and this is immaterial. We must infer that this knife wholly reshapes that surface of the brick and transforms a plane surface into a surface with ribs. It seems improbable that the blank of plastic material can travel forward over this knife, with the uncut portions or ribs depending into the depressions 30 of the cutter and with the necessary resulting distortion of the material, without filling these depressions and causing the entire ribs to be formed and shaped by the knife. If possibly this does not completely occur, yet it is certain that the sides of the ribs are thus formed and shaped, and that, at the most, only their extreme tops—a very small fraction of their whole surface—escapes this knife or wire-cutting origin, and these rib tops have already been "wire-cut." We are convinced that, in the true sense of the patent, in the sense necessary for its right construction, the ribs on defendants' brick are "wire-cut;" the extent to which they may fail to be so formed is comparatively negligible. Thus we see that the patent grant may fairly be construed to cover a method of production slightly variant from, but practically equivalent to, that described in the patent, and yet that its monopoly will leave untouched wire-cut brick with ribs produced by hand carving or by cutting out mere channels or by any method which is not, in substantial effect, the simultaneous creation of the plane surface and the ribs thereon by a cutting edge which sweeps through the body of the clay. Just where the dividing-line might be between that which thus infringes and that which would not, is not involved, and perhaps the question will never arise.

The defendants' product is the result of a two-step wire-cutting process; plaintiff's patent describes a one-step process for making his product; and it is said that for this reason infringement is avoided. We cannot find, either in the specification or claim or in the Patent Office action or in the history of the art, any reason for limiting the patent in accordance with this theory. We are convinced that to do so would not only be to disregard the basis of the existence of product patents as a class by themselves, but also would be to reissue this patent with the very claim which was rejected by the Patent Office and discarded by the applicant. The cases cited in support of restricting the patent to the one-step process are *Plummer* v. *Sargent*, (120 U. S., 442, 448, 449; 7 Sup. Ct., 640, 642; 30 L. Ed. 737;) *Royer* v. *Coupe*, (146 U. S., 524, 530, 531; 13 Sup. Ct., 166, 168, 169; 36 L. Ed., 1073;) *U. S. Glass Co.* v. *Atlas Glass Co.*, (C. C. A. 3, 90 Fed., 724; 33 C. C. A., 254.)

In our judgment, these cases do not support the argument. In the Plummer case, the patent was for a process of lacquering or japanning, consisting, according to the claim, of "the application of oil and heat, substantially as described." In order to sustain this patent against the defense of anticipation, it was necessary to limit the process rather closely to the succession of particular steps described in the specification, and it was held that, when the patent was so limited, defendant's process was not equivalent. In the Royer case there was also a patent for a process which was claimed as a—
treatment of the prepared rawhide in the manner and for the purposes set forth.

It was held that the process, in its broadest aspect, was old; that—
the only subject-matter of invention which the plaintiff could properly claim was the whole process described in his patent, comprising the different steps therein set forth;

and that—
in that view, it must be shown that the defendant used all the different steps of that process, or there could be no infringement.

Obviously, if the patentee's finished hide had been identified by some physical characteristics, and he had claimed an article of manufacture thus identified, there would have been a different question. In the Glass Co. case it appeared that the process patented was confined by the claim to a succession of specific steps, and that the defendant omitted two of these steps. The conclusion was inevitable that "identity of method cannot exist."

(6) It is also suggested that the device of the patent in suit, if it had been later than the patent issued to Nicholson, would not have infringed that patent, and, hence, that defendants' device does not infringe plaintiff's patent. *Electric Co.* v. *Pittsburgh Co.* (125 Fed., 926; 60 C. C. A., 636) is cited to support this transposition and modification of the familiar rule—"that which, if later, would infringe, will anticipate, if earlier." The case seems hardly to support the citation; the language used by Judge Coxe (125 Fed., 930; 60 C. C. A., 636) is only a method of saying that the two things were wholly foreign to each other. If we could lay out of view the fact that plaintiff's patent is for a product and Nicholson's later patent is for a machine, it would still be true that anticipation depends upon the nature and extent of the earlier disclosure while infringement depends upon the character of the grant as fixed by the claim. The later patent is necessarily relatively specific as compared to an earlier invention; and a finding whether the earlier device, if later, would have infringed the later patent, is not helpful in determining whether the device of the later patent infringes the earlier one. The two questions have no necessary relation to each other. We have had occasion to point out that in this situation equivalency is not mutual. (*General Co.* v. *Electric Co.*, 243 Fed., 188, 193, 1007; 156 C. C. A., 54, 664; *Curry* v. *Union Co.*, 230 Fed., 422, 429; 144 C. C. A., 564.)

Nor does the fact that Nicholson uses his hands, in transferring his brick from the first wire-cutting device to the second, control the question of infringement. It is true that in *Brown* v. *Davis* (116 U. S., 237, 249; 6 Sup. Ct., 379; 29 L. Ed., 659) the use of the human hand is relied upon as demonstrating non-infringement; but in that case one of the elements of the claim sued upon was a peculiar lever, and defendant dispensed with the lever and used his hand. This was the common case of omission of one of the elements of the claim.

There should be the usual injunction and accounting as to defendants' brick produced in the manner which we have described, and to permit the entry of such decree below, the existing decree should be set aside.

———

ON MOTION TO REOPEN.

PER CURIAM:

(7) By opinion filed January 7, 1919, we sustained the patent in suit and directed the usual interlocutory decree. The defendants now present three

German patents which are said to anticipate, and ask leave to apply to the court below to reopen the case and put these into the record. The showing to excuse the failure to find this evidence in due time is not satisfactory. It is not clear that, in the search made in preparation for the answer, any effort was made to examine foreign patents. A generally similar showing could be made in every case where there is a later discovery, and, if none but the parties were concerned, we should hesitate to grant the motion. (*Westinghouse Co.* v. *Stanley Co.*, C. C. A. 1, 138 Fed., 823; 71 C. C. A., 189; *Kissinger Co.* v. *Bradford Co.*, C. C. A. 6, 123 Fed., 91; 59 C. C. A., 221; *Novelty Co.* v. *Buser*, C. C. A. 6, 158 Fed., 83; 85 C .C. A., 413; 14 *Ann. Cas.*, 192.)

However, others than the parties are interested. At least one of the German patents is superficially pertinent enough so that the validity of the patent in suit would be likely to be litigated over again by the next alleged infringer, both in the trial and appellate courts. In the meantime, the public would be uncertain whether the industry was or was not subject to this burden. In the interest of the public concerned with the patent, and in the interest of the courts, we think the proposed evidence should be brought into this record, (*Firestone Co.* v. *Seiberling*, C. C. A. 6, 245 Fed., 937; 158 C. C. A., 225;) but the plaintiff ought not to suffer damage from what is not its fault. It will be put to the additional expense of another trial in the district court and perhaps another appeal, and a great part of this will be duplication which could have been avoided if the original defense had been more thorough. As a condition of allowing the belated defense to be now made, the defendants should meet this additional expense. The amount thereof is affected by so many uncertainties that it must be somewhat arbitrarily fixed. We apparently have the same opportunity as the trial court would have to make a reasonable estimate. We think $300 is certainly not too much to make the plaintiff good against the greater expense and delay which will result if the case is reopened and reheard upon the modified record, than there would have been if the entire defense had been originally presented.

The order will be that the district court have leave to reopen the case and admit the proposed evidence and such further proofs as may be offered by either party in relation thereto and thereupon again determine the issue in the case upon the record as thus supplemented—all upon condition that the defendant pay to plaintiff, within such time as the court below may fix, the sum of $300.

ADJUDICATED PATENTS.

(U. S. C. C. A. Pa.) The Collis patent, No. 1,204,945, for a process for simultaneously drying and finishing hosiery articles, *Held* invalid, as covering nothing more than the function of an apparatus, not patentable in view of the prior art. *Paramount Hosiery Form Drying Co.* v. *Moorhead Knitting Co.*, 260 Fed. Rep., 841.

ALPHABETICAL LIST OF PATENTEES

TO WHOM

PATENTS WERE ISSUED ON THE 20TH DAY OF JANUARY, 1920.

NOTE.—Arranged in accordance with the first significant character or word of the name. (In accordance with city and telephone directory practice.)

Abram Cox Stove Company. (See Mott and Kinsley, assignors.)

Adams, Reed, Lapeer, Mich. Printing-press. No. 1,328,253; Jan. 20; v. 270; p. 355.

Adler, Stella, St. Louis, Mo. Doll. No. 1,328,254; Jan. 20; v. 270; p. 255.

Affelder, Harry F., Cleveland, Ohio. Envelop-clasping machine. No. 1,328,472; Jan. 20; v. 270; p. 397.

Ajax Metal Company, The. (See Northrup, Edwin F., assignor.)

Aktiebolaget Svenska Kullagerfabriken. (See Olsson, Niles J., assignor.)

Aktiebolaget Vaporackumulator. (See Ruths, Johannes K., assignor.)

Alexanderson, Ernst F. W., Schenectady, N. Y., assignor to General Electric Company. Means for controlling alternating currents. No. 1,328,473; Jan. 20; v. 270; p. 397.

Alexanderson, Ernst F. W., Schenectady, N. Y., assignor to General Electric Company. Method of and means for controlling high-frequency alternating currents. No. 1,328,610; Jan. 20; v. 270; p. 423.

Alexanderson, Ernst F. W., Schenectady, N. Y., assignor to General Electric Company. Means for controlling alternating currents. No. 1,328,797; Jan. 20; v. 270; p. 457.

Almond, T. R., Manufacturing Company. (See Hubbell, Henry S., assignor.)

Alpen, Henry, Hempstead, N. Y. Holder attachment for ladders. No. 1,328,705; Jan. 20; v. 270; p. 440.

Alpern, Maxwell, assignor to American Engineering Company, Philadelphia, Pa. Stoker. No. 1,328,611; Jan. 20; v. 270; p. 423.

American Brake Company, The. (See Burton, Thomas L., assignor.)

American Brake Shoe and Foundry Company, The. (See Sargent, Fitz William, assignor.)

American Brake Company, The. (See Schwentler, Francis E., assignor.)

American Dressler Tunnell Kilns. (See Meehan, Paul A., assignor.)

American Engineering Company. (See Alpern, Maxwell, assignor.)

American Lacing Hook Co. (See Rhodes, Austin D., assignor.)

American Metal Cap Company. (See Hammer, Charles, assignor.)

American Thermophone Company. (See de Lange and van Lynden, assignors.)

Anderson, Charles H., Lexington, Ky. Apparatus for feeding liquid fuel to carbureters. No. 1,328,354; Jan. 20; v. 270; p. 374.

Anderson, Ernst G. K. (See Benjamin and Anderson.)

Anderson, Per A., New York, N. Y. Fan. No. 1,328,255; Jan. 20; v. 270; p 255.

Andregg, Louis A. (See Krannich, Emil A., assignor.)

Animated Target Company, Inc. (See Franklin, Hubert F., assignor.)

Anderson, Edward, Brooklyn, N. Y. Adjustable and knockdown window-seat. No. 1,328,706; Jan. 20; v. 270; p. 440.

Ansonia Manufacturing Company. (See Malby, Seth G., assignor.)

Arndt, Franklin E., assignor to D. C. Boyd, Galion, Ohio. Locking mechanism for vault-doors. No. 1,328,355; Jan. 20; v. 270; p. 374.

Arndt, Richard L., assignor to Union Tractor Company, San Francisco, Calif. Traction-belt. No. 1,328,643; Jan. 20; v. 270; p. 429.

Associate Company, The. (See Taft, Walter E., assignor.)

Astrom, John, assignor to Fort Wayne Engineering & Manufacturing Co., Fort Wayne, Ind. Pump. No. 1,328,474; Jan. 20; v. 270; p. 397.

Aubert, Albert M., Billancourt, France. Firearm. No. 1,328,475; Jan. 20; v. 270; p. 397.

Averill, William H., assignor to Owl Supply Company, Boston, Mass. Copy-holder. No. 1,328,476; Jan. 20; v. 270; p. 397.

Ayres, Walter W. (See Cassingham and Ayres.)

Baker, Malcolm H., deceased, Braintree; M. H. Baker, administratrix, assignor to K. W. Crosby, trustee, Boston, Mass. Time-retarded cut-off switch. No. 1,328,477; Jan. 20; v. 270; p. 398.

Baker, Malcolm H., deceased, Braintree; M. H. Baker, administratrix, assignor to K. W. Crosby, trustee, Boston, Mass. Thermodynamically - controlled socket-switch for electric lights. No. 1,328,478; Jan. 20; v. 270; p. 398.

Baker, Malcolm H., deceased, Braintree; M. H. Baker, administratrix, assignor to K. W. Crosby, trustee, Boston, Mass. Thermodynamically - controlled socket-switch for electric lights. No. 1,328,479; Jan. 20; v. 270; p. 398.

Baker, Malcolm H., deceased, Braintree; M. H. Baker, administratrix, assignor to K. W. Crosby, trustee, Boston, Mass. Thermodynamically - controlled pendent switch for electric circuits. No. 1,328,480; Jan. 20; v. 270; p. 398.

Baker, Malcolm H., deceased, Braintree; M. H. Baker, administratrix, assignor to K. W. Crosby, trustee, Boston, Mass. Flush push-button switch for electric circuits. No. 1,328,481; Jan. 20; v. 270; p. 399.

Baker, Malcolm H., deceased, Braintree; M. H. Baker, administratrix, assignor to K. W. Crosby, trustee, Boston, Mass. Thermodynamically - controlled electric switch. No. 1,328,482; Jan. 20; v. 270; p. 399.

Baker, Marie H., administratrix. (See Baker, Malcolm H.)

Baker, Thomas W. (See Magee, Frederick W., assignor.)

Baldwin Locomotive Works, The. (See Rushton, Kenneth, assignor.)

Ballard, James W., Fairfax, Va. Repeating rifle. No. 1,328,356; Jan. 20; v. 270; p. 375.

Bancroft, John S., and A. L. Knight, assignors to Lanston Monotype Machine Company, Philadelphia, Pa. Multiple-blade type-mold. No. 1,328,256; Jan. 20; v. 270; p. 355.

Bancroft, John S., and M. C. Indahl, assignors to Lanston Monotype Machine Company, Philadelphia, Pa. Typographic composing-machine. No. 1,328,257; Jan. 20; v. 270; p. 356.

Barbee, James B., Central City, and O. J. Cross, Nederland, Colo. Jig. No. 1,328,778; Jan. 20; v. 270; p. 453.

Barbet, E., & Fils & Cie. (See Barbet, Emile A., assignor.)

Barbet, Emile A., assignor to E. Barbet & Fils & Cie., Paris, France. Continuous production of ether. No. 1,328,258; Jan. 20; v. 270; p. 356.

Barbet, Emile A., Paris, France. Cooling-plate for continuous rectification apparatus. No. 1,328,259; Jan. 20; v. 270; p. 356.

Barger, Bernard J., El Paso, Tex. Saw gaging and setting tool. No. 1,328,554; Jan. 20; v. 270; p. 412.

Barhoff, Fred W., assignor to The Hartford Storage Battery Manufacturing Company, Hartford, Conn. Method of and means for sealing storage-battery connectors and posts. No. 1,328,357; Jan. 20; v. 270; p. 375.

Barhoff, Fred W., assignor to The Hartford Storage Battery Manufacturing Company, Hartford, Conn. Means for sealing storage-battery covers in cells. No. 1,328,358; Jan. 20; v. 270; p. 375.

Barhoff, Fred W., assignor to The Hartford Storage Battery Manufacturing Company, Hartford, Conn. Method of and means for sealing terminal posts in storage-battery covers. No. 1,328,359; Jan. 20; v. 270; p. 375.

Barker, George S., Chicago, Ill. Cushioned wheel. No. 1,328,779; Jan. 20; v. 270; p. 454.

Barker, George S., Denver, Colo. Valve. No. 1,328,780; Jan. 20; v. 270; p. 454.

Barnes, James W., assignor to Estey Piano Co., New York, N. Y. Tracking device. No. 1,328,260; Jan. 20; v. 270; p. 356.

Barraclough, Horatio I., London, England. Construction of reinforced-concrete floors. No. 1,328,555; Jan. 20; v. 270; p. 413.

Bassett, Preston R., assignor to E. A. Sperry, Brooklyn, N. Y. Operating flaming-arc lights for projectors. No. 1,328,311; Jan. 20; v. 270; p. 366.

Bassett, Robert N., Company. (See Cocker, Frederick, assignor.)

Bates, Albert J., Jr., assignor, by mesne assignments, to D. S. Gardner, Chicago, Ill. Crimping-machine. No. 1,328,411; Jan. 20; v. 270; p. 385.

Bausman, Alonzo L., Chicopee, assignor to National Equipment Company, Springfield, Mass. Shaking-table. No. 1,328,483; Jan. 20; v. 270; p. 399.

Bean, Albert M., Colville, Wash. Harness-hanger. No. 1,328,312; Jan. 20; v. 270; p. 367.

Bean Spray Pump Co. (See Crummey, Frederick E., assignor.)

Becker, Robert A., assignor of one-half to C. Tremain, Poughkeepsie, N. Y. Connector. No. 1,328,612; Jan. 20; v. 270; p. 423.

Beckwith, William C., Urbana, Ill. Phonograph-resonator. No. 1,328,412; Jan. 20; v. 270; p. 385.

Beede, Neal M., assignor to A. R. Brewster, Boston, Mass. Glass-washing apparatus. No. 1,328,360; Jan. 20; v. 270; p. 376.

Beesley, Frank M. (See Lockhart and Ord, assignors.)

Belding, Harlow H., West Chicago, Ill. Laundry-wringer. No. 1,328,361; Jan. 20; v. 270; p. 376.

Benjamin, Bert R., Oak Park, Ill., assignor, by mesne assignments, to International Harvester Company. Bundle-carrier for harvesters. No. 1,328,781; Jan. 20; v. 270; p. 454.

Benjamin Electric Manufacturing Company. (See Benjamin and Anderson, assignors.)

Benjamin Electric Manufacturing Company. (See Benjamin, Reuben B., assignor.)

Benjamin Electric Manufacturing Company. (See Curless, James M., assignor.)

Benjamin Electric Manufacturing Company. (See Tregonning, William C., assignor.)

Benjamin, Reuben B., assignor to Benjamin Electric Manufacturing Company, Chicago, Ill. Fuse-plug. No. 1,328,782; Jan. 20; v. 270; p. 454.

Benjamin, Reuben B., assignor to Benjamin Electric Manufacturing Company, Chicago, Ill. Attachment-plug. No. 1,328,783; Jan. 20; v. 270; p. 454.

Benjamin, Reuben B., and E. G. K. Anderson, assignors to Benjamin Electric Manufacturing Company, Chicago, Ill. Binding terminal. No. 1,328,784; Jan. 20; v. 270; p. 455.

Benjamin, Reuben B., assignor to Benjamin Electric Manufacturing Company, Chicago, Ill. Electrical receptacle. No. 1,328,785; Jan. 20; v. 270; p. 455.

Bennett, Andrew P. (See Parsons, Cook, and Bennett.)

Bennett, Ashley C., Minneapolis, Minn. Explosive-engine. No. 1,328,484; Jan. 20; v. 270; p. 399.

Berg, Louis H. (See Marburger and Berg.)

Berry, Edward R., Malden, Mass., assignor to General Electric Company. Explosion-arrester. No. 1,328,485; Jan. 20; v. 270; p. 400.

Beugler, Chas. E., et al. (See Coates, Frank E., assignor.)

Bevin, William S. H., and J. S. Rawsthorne, Liverpool, England. Mixing apparatus for granular, powdered, or like material. No. 1,328,486; Jan. 20; v. 270; p. 400.

Billings, Frank, Cleveland, Ohio. Mine-loading machine. No. 1,328,487; Jan. 20; v. 270; p. 400.

Billson, Edward F. (See Lippincott and Billson.) (Reissue.)

Bird, Charles S. (See Cowan, Clarence P., assignor.)

Blackburn, Harold, Doncaster, England. Parachute. No. 1,328,413; Jan. 20; v. 270; p. 386.

Blackstone Manufacturing Company. (See More, Glenn, assignor.)

Blankenburg, Wilhelm A. C., Amsterdam, Netherlands. Machine with rotary and self-controlling cylinders. No. 1,328,261; Jan. 20; v. 270; p. 356.

Blettner, George H., Chicago, Ill. Making piston-rings. No. 1,328,414; Jan. 20; v. 270; p. 386.

Bloch, Flora W., Milwaukee, Wis. Coating composition for kitchen utensils. No. 1,328,556; Jan. 20; v. 270; p. 413.

Blondeau, Eugene H., Marquette, Mich. Horseshoe. No. 1,328,708; Jan. 20; v. 270; p. 440.

Boardman, C. H., et al. (See Coates, Frank E., assignor.)

Bohroff, Bornett L., assignor, by mesne assignments, to B. Dillmann and H. J. Turck, trustees, Milwaukee, Wis. Indicating device for voting-machines. No. 1,328,613; Jan. 20; v. 270; p. 423.

Boosey, Edward W. N., Detroit, Mich. Cover for floor-sumps. No. 1,328,262; Jan. 20; v. 270; p. 356.

Booth, William S., Owosso, Mich. Automobile-bumper. No. 1,328,786; Jan. 20; v. 270; p. 455.

Borchert, Ralph W., St. Louis, Mo. Marine-motor attachment. No. 1,328,313; Jan. 20; v. 270; p. 367.

Bordeaux, Pearl, Mount Desert, Me. Device for removing valves and their seats or cages. No. 1,328,362; Jan. 20; v. 270; p. 376.

Bowden, Junius A., Los Angeles, Calif. Dust-cap and attaching means therefor. No. 1,328,801; Jan. 20; v. 270; p. 458.

Bowden, Junius A., Los Angeles, Calif. Dust-cap and attaching means therefor. No. 1,328,488; Jan. 20; v. 270; p. 400.

Bowman, James W., Morley, Mo. Harrow. No. 1,328,363; Jan. 20; v. 270; p. 376.

Boyd, David C. (See Arpdt, Franklin E., assignor.)

Bozard, Harrison B., Hamilton, Ontario, Canada, assignor to International Harvester Company of Canada, Limited. Steel bearing for disks. No. 1,328,787; Jan. 20; v. 270; p. 455.

Bradley, John M., and C. F. Pike, Philadelphia, Pa., assignors to The Safety Eyeglass Company, Wilmington, Del. Eyeglass-case. No. 1,328,644; Jan. 20; v. 270; p. 429.

Bradley, John M., and C. F. Pike, Philadelphia, Pa., assignors to The Safety Eyeglass Company, Wilmington, Del. Eyeglass-case. No. 1,328,645; Jan. 20; v. 270; p. 429.

Bradley, John M., and C. F. Pike, Philadelphia, Pa., assignors to The Safety Eyeglass Company, Wilmington, Del. Eyeglass-case. No. 1,328,646; Jan. 20; v. 270; p. 429.

Brauer, Otto M., Gothenburg, Nebr. Toy car. No. 1,328,557; Jan. 20; v. 270; p. 413.

Bray, Nelson H., San Francisco, Calif. Automatic igniter for orchard-heaters. No. 1,328,788; Jan. 20; v. 270; p. 455.

Bressler, Robert E., Hammond, assignor to O. F. Jordan Company, East Chicago, Ind. Railway way construction and maintenance car. No. 1,328,489; Jan. 20; v. 270; p. 400.

Brewster, Albert R. (See Beede, Neal M., assignor.)

Bridgeport Brass Company. (See Clark, Walter R., assignor.)

Brock, Matthias, Boston, Mass., assignor, by mesne assignments, to United Shoe Machinery Corporation, Paterson, N. J. Working uppers over lasts. No. 1,328,314; Jan. 20; v. 270; p. 367.

Broido, Benjamin, assignor to Locomotive Superheater Company, New York, N. Y. Superheater-header. No. 1,328,364; Jan. 20; v. 270; p. 376.

Broido, Benjamin, assignor to Locomotive Superheater Company, New York, N. Y. Water-tube-boiler superheater. No. 1,328,365; Jan. 20; v. 270; p. 377.

Brookins, Andrew J., Chicago, Ill. Governor to control electric terminals. No. 1,328,490; Jan. 20; v. 270; p. 401.

Brooks, Samuel A., Elmwood Place, assignor of one-half to J. M. Shay, Cincinnati, and one-half to A. W. Miller, Elmwood Place, Ohio. Lid for saucepans and the like. No. 1,328,558; Jan. 20; v. 270; p. 413.

Brown, Ellis R., Reading, Pa. Flexible coupling. No. 1,328,366; Jan. 20; v. 270; p. 377.

Brown, Ernest E., Decatur, Ill. Burglar-alarm. No. 1,328,559; Jan. 20; v. 270; p. 413.

Brunswick-Balke-Collender Company, The. (See Lietz, Paul S., assignor.)

Buck, Herman J., assignor to Mathews Gravity Carrier Company, Ellwood City, Pa. Ball-bearing for gravity-carriers. (Reissue.) No. 14,792; Jan. 20; v. 270; p. 458.

Buckius, Albert O., Jr., Chicago, Ill., assignor to Chicago Manufacturing and Distributing Co. Vehicle-body brace. No. 1,328,415; Jan. 20; v. 270; p. 386.

Buckley, John P., and A. E. Lard, Washington, D. C. Machine for assorting and counting paper money. No. 1,328,263; Jan. 20; v. 270; p. 357.

Burgess, Edward W., Chicago, Ill., assignor, by mesne assignments, to International Harvester Company. Manure-spreader. No. 1,328,709; Jan. 20; v. 270; p. 441.

Burgess, Edward W., Chicago, Ill., assignor, by mesne assignments, to International Harvester Company. Steering mechanism for traction-engines. No. 1,328,710; Jan. 20; v. 270; p. 441.

Burnham, George B., Berkeley, Calif. Obtaining potassium salts from liquids containing same. No. 1,328,416; Jan. 20; v. 270; p. 386.

Burnham, George B., Borosolvay, Calif. Recovering borax from saline waters. No. 1,328,614; Jan. 20; v. 270; p. 424.

Burnham, George B., Berkeley, Calif. Obtaining potassium salts from saline waters. No. 1,328,417; Jan. 20; v. 270; p. 386.

Burnham, George B., Berkeley, Calif. Recovering potassium sodium sulfate and other potassium salts from saline waters. No. 1,328,418; Jan. 20; v. 270; p. 386.

Burroughs, Charles F., East Orange, N. J., assignor to Composition Machinery Corporation, Newark, N. J. Press for mounting sound-matrices. No. 1,328,264; Jan. 20; v. 270; p. 357.

Burton, Thomas L., assignor to The American Brake Company, St. Louis, Mo. Brake-hanger. No. 1,328,315; Jan. 20; v. 270; p. 367.

Busby, Harley S., assignor to Western Hog Oiler Company, Inc., Washington, Iowa. Heater. No. 1,328,419; Jan. 20; v. 270; p. 386.

Cabot, Godfrey L., Boston, Mass. Supply means for aircraft. No. 1,328,560; Jan. 20; v. 270; p. 214.

Cameron, William W., assignor of one-half to H. J. Hirshheimer, La Crosse, Wis. Luggage - carrier. No. 1,328,316; Jan. 20; v. 270; p. 368.

Campbell, Frank M., South Bend, Wash. Brake. No. 1,328,491; Jan. 20; v. 270; p. 401.

Carl, Reinhold A., Elgin, Tex. Combination-flue. No. 1,328,647; Jan. 20; v. 270; p. 430.

Carman, Frank V., Oakland, Calif. Work-holding cradle for spike-hole-plug machine. No. 1,328,492; Jan. 20; v. 270; p. 401.

Carney, James A., Aurora, Ill. Hand-brake-operating mechanism. No. 1,328,493; Jan. 20; v. 270; p. 401.

Carney, James A., Aurora, Ill. Brake-operating mechanism. No. 1,328,494; Jan. 20; v. 270; p. 401.

Carney, Joseph, assignor to Paragon Binder Corporation, Newark, N. J. Loose-leaf binder. No. 1,328,561; Jan. 20; v. 270; p. 414.

Carr, Charles B., New York, N. Y. Game device. No. 1,328,711; Jan. 20; v. 270; p. 441.

Carter, Horace J., and C. Taylor, Wilmington, Del. Piling-machine. No. 1,328,615; Jan. 20; v. 270; p. 424.

Cassingham, John R., and W. W. Ayres, assignors of one-half to H. W. Morrison and J. W. Morrison, Oklahoma, Okla. Auto-fuel-supply lock. No. 1,328,616; Jan. 20; v. 270; p. 424.

Caunt, Hubert, East Calgary, Alberta, Canada. Internal-combustion engine. No. 1,328,265; Jan. 20; v. 270; p. 357.

Cavanagh, John F., assignor to The Connecticut Telephone & Electric Company, Inc., Meriden, Conn. Electric switch. No. 1,328,562; Jan. 20; v. 270; p. 414.

Chamberlain, Rufus N., Chicago, Ill. Separator. No. 1,328,420; Jan. 20; v. 270; p. 387.

Chicago Manufacturing and Distributing Co. (See Buckius, Albert O., Jr., assignor.)

Christensen, Harold G., New York, N. Y. Apparatus and process for producing motion-pictures. No. 1,328,266; Jan. 20; v. 270; p. 357.

Clark, Walter R., assignor to Bridgeport Brass Company, Bridgeport, Conn. Melting brass and similar scrap. No. 1,328,712; Jan. 20; v. 270; p. 441.

Clark, Walter R., assignor to Bridgeport Brass Company, Bridgeport, Conn. Electric furnace. No. 1,328,713; Jan. 20; v. 270; p. 441.

Clark, Walter R., assignor to Bridgeport Brass Company, Bridgeport, Conn. Method of and means for melting brass and similar scrap. No. 1,328,714; Jan. 20; v. 270; p. 441.

Claussen, Edward E., Hartford, Conn. Pulp-bottle. No. 1,328,317; Jan. 20; v. 270; p. 368.

Clayton & Company (Huddersfield) Limited. (See Jemmison, John W., assignor.)

Clein, Adolph, Chicago, Ill. Combined folding sled and baby-carriage attachment. No. 1,328,715; Jan. 20; v. 270; p. 442.

Clipper Belt Lacer Company. (See Diamond, James K., assignor.)

Cluff, William, Company. (See Youngberg, James, assignor.)

Coatalen, Louis, and H. C. M. Stevens, Wolverhampton, England. Thrust-bearing. No. 1,328,716; Jan. 20; v. 270; p. 442.

Coates, Frank E., San Francisco, assignor of one-sixth to C. E. Bengler and one-sixth to C. H. Boardman. Oakland, Calif. Hoisting-block. No. 1,328,717; Jan. 20; v. 270; p. 442.

Cochennet, John L., Chicago, Ill. Aeroplane. No. 1,328,421; Jan. 20; v. 270; p. 387.

Cocker, Frederick, Derby, Conn., assignor to Robert N. Bassett Company, Incorporated, Shelton, Conn. Buckle. No. 1,328,617; Jan. 20; v. 270; p. 424.

Cody, Sherwin, Chicago, Ill. Loose-leaf cover and copyholder. No. 1,328,318; Jan. 20; v. 270; p. 368.

Cohn, Johanna, New York, N. Y. Musical-notation indicator. No. 1,328,718; Jan. 20; v. 270; p. 442.

Colburn Machine Tool Company. (See Head, Ernest C., assignor.)

Composition Machinery Corporation. (See Burroughs, Charles F., assignor.)

Condon, Perry M., Albany, N. Y. Toy. No. 1,328,719; Jan. 20; v. 270; p. 442.

Connecticut Telephone & Electric Company, The. (See Cavanagh. John F., assignor.)

Connell, Roy, Buffalo. N. Y. Combination terminal block and lightning-arrester. No. 1,328,720; Jan. 20; v. 270; p. 442.

Continental Motors Corporation. (See Weinhardt. Robert A., assignor.)

Cook, Stanley S. (See Parsons, Cook, and Bennett.)

Cook, Willard J. Stoughton, Wis., assignor to Moline Plow Company. Machine for spreading fertilizer. No. 1,328,618; Jan. 20; v. 270; p. 424.

Coolidge, William D., Schenectady, N. Y., assignor to General Electric Company. X-ray apparatus. No. 1,328,495; Jan. 20; v. 270; p. 402.

Cotoli, Antonio, Habana. Cuba. Device for making multicolored tiles and the like. No. 1,328,367; Jan. 20; v. 270; p. 377.

Cotoli, Antonio, Habana, Cuba. Method of and means for distributing pigments. No. 1,328,368; Jan. 20; v. 270; p. 377.

Cott-a-lap Co. (See Stirling, Charles P., assignor.)

Coulson, Edward, Lake Forest, Ill. Combined self-locking clip and shield. No. 1,328,422; Jan. 20; v. 270; p. 387.

Cowan, Clarence E., Pont Rouge, Quebec, Canada, assignor to C. S. Bird. Walpole, Mass. Felt paper. No. 1,328,267; Jan. 20; v. 270; p. 358.

Cox, Charles H., Los Angeles, Calif. Pneumatic shock-absorber. No. 1,328,496; Jan. 20; v. 270; p. 402.

Cox, Ernest. (See Gower, Owen, and Cox.)

Crane, Samuel G., assignor to Toledo Scale Company. Toledo, Ohio. Automatic weighing-scale. No. 1,328,319; Jan. 20; v. 270; p. 368.

Crane, Samuel G., assignor to Toledo Scale Company. Toledo. Ohio. Electric automatic scale. No. 1,328,320; Jan. 20; v. 270; p. 368.

Creveling, John L., White Plains, N. Y., assignor to Gould Coupler Company. Electric system. No. 1,328,321; Jan. 20; v. 270; p. 368.

Crookshank, Samuel M. (See Dobson and Crookshank.)

Crosby, Kenneth W., trustee. (See Baker, Malcolm H., assignor.)

Cross, Otto J. (See Barbee and Cross.)

Crowley, Joseph P., Toledo, Ohio, assignor to The Libbey Owens Sheet Glass Company, Charleston, W. Va. Method of and apparatus for drawing continuous sheets of glass. No. 1,328,268; Jan. 20; v. 270; p. 358.

Crummey, Frederick E., assignor to Bean Spray Pump Co.. San Jose, Calif. Spray-gun. No. 1,328,721; Jan. 20; v. 270; p. 443.

Cryder, Floyd E., Chicago, Ill. Milk-sterilizing apparatus. No. 1,328,722; Jan. 20; v. 270; p. 443.

Curless, James M., assignor to Benjamin Electric Manufacturing Company, Chicago, Ill. Electric heater. No. 1,328,723; Jan. 20; v. 270; p. 443.

Currier, Howard S., Detroit, Mich. Transmission - lock. No. 1,328,724; Jan. 20; v. 270; p. 443.

Cushman, Edward L., Miami, Fla. Slug. No. 1,328,725; Jan. 20; v. 270; p. 444.

Cusick, Patrick H., Oregon, Wis. Radiator. No. 1,828,789; Jan 20; v. 270; p. 456.

Cutler-Hammer Mfg. Co. (See Reisbach, Gustave B., assignor.)

Damon, William H., Los Angeles, Calif. Automobile-lock. No. 1,328,619; Jan. 20; v. 270; p. 424.

Davenport Manufacturing Company. (See Hemsing, Maurice A., assignor.)

Davies, Llewellyn, Sisson, Calif. Wire-binding tool. No. 1,328,423; Jan. 20; v. 270; p. 387.

Davis, Benjamin W., Chicago, Ill. Signal system for controlling street traffic. No. 1,328,269; Jan. 20; v. 270; p. 358.

Davis, George P., McIntosh, N. Mex. Pump-pipe lifter. No. 1,328,648; Jan. 20; v. 270; p. 430.

Davis, Thomas A., San Antonio, Tex. Antifreezing appliance for water-pipes. No. 1,328,649; Jan. 20; v. 270; p. 430.

Deere & Company. (See Dooley, Harry L., assignor.)

De Lange, Pieter, and R. A. van Lynden, Utrecht, Netherlands, assignors, by mesne assignments, to American Thermophone Company, Boston, Mass. Sounding-chamber for thermic telephones and other apparatus. No. 1,328,620; Jan. 20; v. 270; p. 425.

Delaporte, Maurice, Paris, France. Steam-ejector. No. 1,328,270; Jan. 20; v. 270; p. 358.

De La Vergne Machine Company. (See Doelling, Louis K., assignor.)

Dennison, William L., Columbus, Ohio. Holder for bedcovers. No. 1,328,621; Jan. 20; v. 270; p. 425.

Dentists' Supply Company, The. (See Whiteley, George H., Jr., assignor.)

Dezendorf, Richard L., Richmond Hill. N. Y. Apparatus for and method of clearing service-pipes. No. 1,328,726; Jan. 20; v. 270; p. 444.

Diamond, James K., assignor to Clipper Belt Lacer Company, Grand Rapids, Mich. Belt-fastener-setting machine. No. 1,328,424; Jan. 20; v. 270; p. 387.

Diamond Expansion Bolt Company. (See Hiss, William J., assignor.)

Dickinson, Edgar D., Schenectady, N. Y., assignor to General Electric Company. Turbine installation for ships. No. 1,328,497; Jan. 20; v. 270; p. 402.

Dickinson, Sanford B., Bath, N. Y. Steel track. No. 1,328,790; Jan. 20; v. 270; p. 456.

Dillman, Edward, et al., trustees. (See Bobroff, Bornett L., assignor.)

Distefano. Quirino V., Waterbury, Conn. Airship. No. 1,328,369; Jan. 20; v. 270; p. 377.

Djidics, Alexander, New York, N. Y. Nurling-tool. No. 1,328,498; Jan. 20; v. 270; p. 402.

Dmitrieff, Vasily N., New York, N. Y., assignor of forty per cent. to R. Kliavin, Seattle, Wash. Combined pendulous table and chairs. No. 1,328,727; Jan. 20; v. 270; p. 444.

Dobson. John E., and S. M. Crookshank. Knoxville, Tenn. Device for packing silage. No. 1,328,728; Jan. 20; v. 270; p. 444.

Doelling, Louis K., New Rochelle, assignor to De La Vergne Machine Company, New York, N. Y. Oil-engine. No. 1,328,499; Jan. 20; v. 270; p. 402.

Doherty, Henry L. (See Laird, Wilbur G., assignor.)

Dolan, George E., and S. Miller; said Dolan assignor of one-half of his right to W. T. Lloyd, San Francisco, Calif. Electric permutation-lock. No. 1,328,729; Jan. 20; v. 270; p. 444.

Donaldson, William M., Portland, Oreg. Scaffold. No. 1,328,500; Jan. 20; v. 270; p. 402.

Donovan, Jerome J., Oakland, Calif. Combination bath-spray. No. 1,328,650; Jan. 20; v. 270; p. 430.

Dooley, Harry L., Rock Island, assignor to Deere & Company, Moline, Ill. Planter. No. 1,328,730; Jan. 20; v. 270; p. 444.

Draper Corporation. (See Rhoades, Alonzo E., assignor.)

Duffy, Charles H., Chevy Chase, Md. Parachute. No. 1,328,425; Jan. 20; v. 270; p. 387.

Dutchess Tool Company. (See Van Houten, Frank H., Jr., assignor.)

Dutemple, William R., Auburn, R. I. Oil-cup holder. No. 1,328,271; Jan. 20; v. 270; p. 358.

Dutton, Abraham L., Otis, Colo. Leveling device for threshing-machines, &c. No. 1,328,370; Jan. 20; v. 270; p. 378.

Eames, Robert, Detroit, Mich. Calipers. No. 1,328,651; Jan. 20; v. 270; p. 430.

Eaton, John. Schenectady, N. Y.; assignor to General Electric Company. Control of electric motors. No. 1,328,501; Jan. 20; v. 270; p. 403.

Ehlers, Ullin. Stickney. S. D. Pot-lid. No. 1,328,652; Jan. 20; v. 270; p. 430.

Eichmeyer, Herman C., St. Maries, Idaho. Brake. No. 1,328,502; Jan. 20; v. 270; p. 403.

Kohlruss, Frederick, Balgonie, Saskatchewan, Canada. Stooker. No. 1,328,674; Jan. 20; v. 270; p. 434.
Koppel Industrial Car and Equipment Company. (See Hansen, Karl H., assignor.)
Kops, Daniel. New York, N. Y. Apparel-corset. No. 1,328,675; Jan. 20; v. 270; p. 435.
Korthals-Altes, Willem C., Schenectady, N. Y., assignor to General Electric Company. Alternating-current motor. No, 1,328,525; Jan. 20; v. 270; p. 407.
Kossmann, Max, Brooklyn, N. Y. Lamp-shade holder. No. 1,328,331; Jan. 20; v. 270; p. 370.
Krannich, Emil A., Columbiana, Ohio, assignor of one-half to L. A. Andregg, Mansfield, Ohio. Tire-core. No. 1,328,676; Jan. 20; v. 270; p. 435.
Krasa, Albert, Chicago, Ill. Yarn-dyer. No. 1,328,435; Jan. 20; v. 270; p. 389.
Krause, William P., assignor to Mumford Molding Machine Company, Chicago, Ill. Plunger-guide construction. No. 1,328,526; Jan. 20; v. 270; p. 407.
Krause, William P., Chicago, Ill., assignor to Mumford Molding Machine Company, Jersey City, N. J. Molding-machine. No. 1,328,527; Jan. 20; v. 270; p. 408.
Kremer, Franklin W., Rutherford, N. J. Tire. No. 1,328,632; Jan. 20; v. 270; p. 427.
Kuchhorn, Arnold A., Chicago, Ill. Elevator attachment. No. 1,328,633; Jan. 20; v. 270; p. 427.
Kuhsiek, Albert J. H., Richmond, Hill, N. Y. Forming piston-rings No. 1,328,436; Jan. 20; v. 270; p. 390.
La Hodny, William, Buffalo, N. Y. Adjustable bracket for mirrors and other objects. No. 1,328,677; Jan. 20; v. 270; p. 435.
Laird, Wilbur G., assignor to H. L. Doherty, New York, N. Y. Refractory lining. No. 1,328,380; Jan. 20; v. 270; p. 379.
La May, Arthur C. (See Todd and La May.)
Lang, Lincoln A., assignor to The Northern Trust Company, Chicago, Ill. Power-shift mechanism. No. 1,328,437; Jan. 20; v. 270; p. 390.
Lanston Monotype Machine Company. (See Bancroft and Indahl, assignors.)
Lanston Monotype Machine Company. (See Bancroft and Knight, assignors.)
Lanum, Walter R., Savannah, Ga. Heater. No. 1,328,743; Jan. 20; v. 270; p. 447.
Lard, Allan E. (See Buckley and Lard.)
Layne, Mahlon E., Memphis, Tenn. Well-screen. No. 1,328,438; Jan. 20; v. 270; p. 390.
Layne, Ollyn A., Los Angeles, Calif. Impact device. No. 1,328,569; Jan. 20; v. 270; p. 415.
Lea, Charles, Boston, Mass., assignor, by mesne assignments, to McCleary, Wallin and Crouse, Amsterdam, N. Y. Mechanism for and process of constructing chenille. No. 1,328,570; Jan. 20; v. 270; p. 416.
Lea, Frank D., Findlay, Ohio. Piano-lifting truck. No. 1,328,434; Jan. 20; v. 270; p. 427.
Leach, Frank, Detroit, Mich. Soap-holder. No. 1,328,528; Jan. 20; v. 270; p. 408.
Lee, William K. (See Renfro, Albert L., assignor.)
Lenholt, John E., Lecte Island, assignor of one-half to C. R. Tainter, Guilford, Conn. Pipe-wrench. No. 1,328,744; Jan. 20; v. 270; p. 447.
Lees, Edgar, assignor to The Whitehead Torpedo Works (Weymouth) Limited, Weymouth, England. Gyroscopic steering mechanism of automobile-torpedoes. No. 1,328,571; Jan. 20; v. 270; p. 416.
Lees, Kenneth F., New Haven, Conn. Pneumatic-tire pressure-gage. No. 1,328,572; Jan. 20; v. 270; p. 416.
Lemieux, Thomas D., Lakewood, Ohio. Cable-pulling device. No. 1,328,678; Jan. 20; v. 270; p. 435.
Lent, Wilmar F., New Haven, Conn., assignor to The Greist Manufacturing Company. Grease-cup. No. 1,328,573; Jan. 20; v. 270; p. 416.
Leonard, George S., Minneapolis, Minn., assignor to Huntley Manufacturing Company. Silver Creek. Fan or blower. No. 1,328,679; Jan. 20; v. 270; p. 435.
Leonard, Goldstone D., New York, N. Y. Brassière. No. 1,328,439; Jan. 20; v. 270; p. 390.
Leventry, Joseph, Johnstown, Pa. Metallic railway crosstie. No. 1,328,574; Jan. 20; v. 270; p. 416.
Lever Brothers Limited. (See Gavin, Norman A., assignor.)
Lewis, David O., Detroit, Mich. Window-latch. No. 1,328,284; Jan. 20; v. 270; p. 361.
Lewis, Frank M., Chicago, Ill. Differential mechanism. No. 1,328,440; Jan. 20; v. 270; p. 390.
Libbey Owens Sheet Glass Company, The. (See Crowley, Joseph P., assignor.)
Lichtenberg, Erich H., assignor to Koehring Machine Company, Milwaukee, Wis. Clutch and brake control mechanism. No. 1,328,635; Jan. 20; v. 270; p. 427.
Lietz, Paul S., assignor to The Brunswick-Balke-Collender Company, Chicago, Ill. Bed for game-tables and making same. No. 1,328,332; Jan. 20; v. 270; p. 370.
Lillos, Charles G., Minneapolis, Minn. Air-pump. No. 1,328,529; Jan. 20; v. 270; p. 408.
Lindblad, Axel R., Stockholm, Sweden. Synthetic production of cyanids and nitrids. No. 1,328,575; Jan. 20; v. 270; p. 417.
Lindner, John C., Rochester, N. Y., assignor to General Railway Signal Company, Gates, N. Y. Semaphore-signal-operating mechanism. No. 1,328,381; Jan. 20; v. 270; p. 379.
Lindsay, William, Chicago, Ill. Agitating device. No. 1,328,576; Jan. 20; v. 270; p. 417.

Link, Louis, New York, N. Y. Lens-mounting. No. 1,328,441; Jan. 20; v. 270; p. 390.
Lippincott, Roy A., and E. F. Billson, Melbourne, Victoria, Australia. Fastener for hinged structures. (Reissue.) No. 14,793; Jan. 20; v. 270; p. 458.
Lisenby Manufacturing Company. (See Quade, Frank H., Jr., assignor.)
Lloyd, William T. (See Dolan and Miller, assignors.)
Lobe, N. B., & Co. (See Norwood, Harry G., assignor.)
Lockhart, Frederick R., and H. J. Ord, assignors to F. M. Beesley, Toronto, Ontario, Canada. Motion-picture-film-feed mechanism. No. 1,328,382; Jan. 20; v. 270; p. 379.
Locomotive Superheater Company. (See Broido, Benjamin, assignor.)
Loepsinger, Albert J., Providence, R. I., assignor to General Fire Extinguisher Company, New York, N. Y. Sealing glass bulbs. No. 1,328,530; Jan. 20; v. 270; p. 408.
Loke, Johannes J. and W. A., The Hague, Netherlands. Direct production of refined iron and refined steel from titaniferous iron ores. No. 1,328,636; Jan. 20; v. 270; p. 428.
Loke, Willem A. (See Loke, Johannes J. and W. A.)
Long, George F., New York, assignor to The G. Piel Company, Inc., Long Island City, N. Y. Horn. No. 1,328,772; Jan. 20; v. 270; p. 452.
Longstreth, William M., et al. (See Matthiessen, Conrad S., assignor.)
Lott, C. W. (See Hilliard, John M., assignor.)
Lucas, Charles O., Dayton, Ohio. Rotary baking-oven. No. 1,328,745; Jan. 20; v. 270; p. 448.
Ludlow, Margery E. N., Haverford, Pa. Wind-shield. No. 1, 328,383; Jan. 20; v. 270; p. 380.
Lumber Tie & Timber Vulcanizing Company. (See Fish, Frederick K., Jr., assignor.)
Lund, Thomas, Beverly, Mass., assignor to United Shoe Machinery Corporation, Paterson, N. J. Trimming-machine. No. 1,328,531; Jan. 20; v. 270; p. 408.
McBride, David, Wilmington, Del. Baggage-car-side-door hanger. No. 1,328,442; Jan. 20; v. 270; p. 391.
McClave-Brooks Company. (See McClave, William, assignor.)
McClave, William, assignor to McClave-Brooks Company, Scranton, Pa. Steam-turbine blower. No. 1,328,285; Jan. 20; v. 270; p. 361.
McClave, William, assignor to McClave-Brooks Company, Scranton, Pa. Steam-turbine blower. No. 1,328,286; Jan. 20; v. 270; p. 361.
McClary, Wallin and Crouse. (See Lea, Charles, assignor.)
McGeorge, Jefferson F., Marshall, Tex. Window-screen. No. 1,328,577; Jan. 20; v. 270; p. 417.
McGinnis, Walter R., assignor to Pilsbry-Becker Engineering & Supply Company, St. Louis, Mo. Apparatus for recovery of gasoline from casing-head gas in oil-wells. No. 1,328,680; Jan. 20; v. 270; p. 436.
McKay, Robert J., Pittsburgh, Pa. Staybolt. No. 1,328,532; Jan. 20; v. 270; p. 409.
McLeod, Anna J., et al. (See McLeod and Quirk, assignors.)
McLeod, Edward A., and M. F. Quirk, assignors of one-sixth to I. Evans and one-sixth to A. J. McLeod, Springfield, Ohio. Weight-motor. No. 1,328,384; Jan. 20; v. 270; p. 380.
McVicker, Emery M., Milwaukee, Wis. Railway tie-plate and rail fastening and anticreeper. No. 1,328,533; Jan. 20; v. 270; p. 409.
Macdonald, Duncan, West Homestead, Pa. Automobile-steering attachment. No. 1,328,681; Jan. 20; v. 270; p. 436.
Maciuk, Daniel, Toronto, Ontario, Canada. Catamaran. No. 1,328,746; Jan. 20; v. 270; p. 448.
Madden, Michael. (See Sourbier and Madden.)
Magee, Frederick W., assignor of one-half to T. W. Baker, London, Ontario, Canada. Hot-water heater. No. 1,328,682; Jan. 20; v. 270; p. 436.
Maguire, Walter J., Portland, Oreg. Address matcher. No. 1,328,534; Jan. 20; v. 270; p. 409.
Malby, Seth G., Derby, assignor to Ansonia Manufacturing Company, Ansonia, Conn. Gas-valve. No. 1,328,578; Jan. 20; v. 270; p. 417.
Malcom, Robert, Chicago, Ill. Eye - protector. No. 1,328,287; Jan. 20; v. 270; p. 361.
Manahan, Michael J., assignor of one-third to E H. Remick, Indianapolis, Ind. Curtain - bracket. No. 1,328,579; Jan. 20; v. 270; p. 417.
Mann, William L., Georgetown, Tex. Shoe. No. 1 328,333; Jan. 20; v. 270; p. 370.
Marburger, Henry L., Baltimore, and L. H. Berg, Baltimore county, Md. Nut-lock. No. 1,328,443; Jan. 20; v. 270; p. 391.
Marino, Algeri, Venice, Italy. Spintherometer for radiotelegraphic plants. No. 1,328,288; Jan. 20; v. 270; p. 362.
Martin, Anna, Cincinnati, Ohio. School-desk. No. 1,328,444; Jan. 20; v. 270; p. 391.
Mathews' Gravity Carrier Company. (See Buck, Herman J., assignor.) (Reissue.)
Mattern, Frank C., Great Neck, N. Y., assignor to Fairbanks Company. Cotton-seed-weighing apparatus. No. 1,328,747; Jan. 20; v. 270; p. 448.

Matthiessen, Conrad S., assignor of one-tenth to C. J. Hepburn, one-fifth to W. M. Longstreth, Philadelphia, Pa., and one-tenth to W. F. Sprenkel, New York, N. Y. Cotton-picker. No. 1,328,385 ; Jan. 20 ; v. 270 ; p. 380.

Matthiessen, Conrad S., Philadelphia, Pa. Nozzle for pneumatic cotton-pickers. No. 1,328,386 ; Jan. 20 ; v. 270 ; p. 380.

Maurer, John F., West New York, N. J. Crate for bottles. No. 1,328,748 ; Jan. 20 ; v. 270 ; p. 448.

Meehan, Paul A., New Castle, Pa., assignor to American Dressler Tunnel Kilns, Inc., New York, N. Y. Car for tunnel-kilns. No. 1,328,749 ; Jan. 20 ; v. 270 ; p. 448.

Melder, Philip, Jr., Pittsburgh, Pa. Apparatus for feeding pulverized fuel. No. 1,328,750 ; Jan. 20 ; v. 270 ; p. 448.

Mellor, Arthur, Brighouse, England. Machine for dressing silk. No. 1,328,535 ; Jan. 20 ; v. 270 ; p. 409.

Miller, Alfred W., et al. (See Brooks, Samuel A., assignor.)

Miller, Max C., Providence, assignor to Jenckes Knitting Machine Company, Pawtucket, R. I. Circular-knitting machine. No. 1,328,580 ; Jan. 20 ; v. 270 ; p. 417.

Miller, Sigwald. (See Dolan and Miller.)

Molina, Ynocente J., Douglas, Ariz. Safety indicator and alarm. No. 1,328,387 ; Jan. 20 ; v. 270 ; p. 381.

Moline Plow Company. (See Cook, Willard J., assignor.)

Monroe, George A. C., Geneva, Ill. Knockdown bedspring. No. 1,328,751 ; Jan. 20 ; v. 270 ; p. 449.

Moody, Herbert A., Turners Falls, Mass. Gate-valve. No. 1,328,752 ; Jan. 20 ; v. 270 ; p. 449.

Moore, Charles W., Indianapolis, Ind. Piston-ring. No. 1,328,289 ; Jan. 20 ; v. 270 ; p. 362.

Moore, Harlan. New York, N. Y. Bottle or jar closure device. No. 1,328,536 ; Jan. 20 ; v. 270 ; p. 409.

More, Glenn, assignor to Blackstone Manufacturing Company, Jamestown, N. Y. Bench. No. 1,328,753 ; Jan. 20 ; v. 270 ; p. 449.

More, Glenn, assignor to Blackstone Manufacturing Company, Jamestown, N. Y. Removable wringer mechanism. No. 1,328,754 ; Jan. 20 ; v. 270 ; p. 449.

Morey, Harry J., Syracuse, assignor to Pass & Seymour, Inc., Solvay, N. Y. Candle-socket. No. 1,328,581 ; Jan. 20 ; v. 270 ; p. 418.

Morgan, Edmund C., Chicago, Ill. Mining-machine. No. 1,328,755 ; Jan. 20 ; v. 270 ; p. 449.

Morrison, Henry W., et al. (See Cassingham and Ayres, assignors.)

Morrison, John W., et al. (See Cassingham and Ayres, assignors.)

Mott, Abram C., Jr., and L. Kinsley, assignors to Abram Cox Stove Company, Philadelphia, Pa. Means for forming recesses in sand molds. No. 1,328,582 ; Jan. 20 ; v. 270 ; p. 418.

Mott, Carl W., Chicago, Ill., assignor, by mesne assignments, to International Harvester Company. Plow. No. 1,328,756 ; Jan. 20 ; v. 270 ; p. 450.

Motzer, Alfred, assignor to The Hobson & Motzer Co., Meriden, Conn. Auxiliary oiling system for Ford cars. No. 1,328,388 ; Jan. 20 ; v. 270 ; p. 381.

Mullen, Charles P. (See Plummer and Mullen.)

Mullikin, Brooks J., New York, N. Y. Overshoe for tires. No. 1,328,757 ; Jan. 20 ; v. 270 ; p. 450.

Mumford Molding Machine Company. (See Krause, William P., assignor.)

Munts, Otto S., Dubuque, Iowa. Shock-absorbing container. No. 1,328,758 ; Jan. 20 ; v. 270 ; p. 450.

Murray, John F. (See Filkins, George H., assignor.)

National Equipment Company. (See Bausman, Alonzo L., assignor.)

National Manufacturing Company. (See Ferris, Walton C., assignor.)

Nayer, Carl F., assignor to Packer's Machinery & Equipment Company, Chicago, Ill. Hog-scraper. No. 1,328,637 ; Jan. 20 ; v. 270 ; p. 428.

Neuman, David, Albany, Ga. Hoe with knife attachment. No. 1,328,537 ; Jan. 20 ; v. 270 ; p. 409.

Newberg, Charles A., and E. I. Weisberger, Brooklyn, N. Y. Conformator. No. 1,328,538 ; Jan. 20 ; v. 270 ; p. 409.

Newhall, Henry B., Jr., executor. (See Pleister, Henry W., assignor.)

Newton, Charles, Buffalo, N. Y., assignor to F. N. Stone, Cleveland, Ohio. Projectile. No. 1,328,334 ; Jan. 20 ; v. 270 ; p. 371.

Newton, Dudley, Berkeley, Calif. Apparatus for flushing urinals. No. 1,328,445 ; Jan. 20 ; v. 270 ; p. 391.

Niles, Waldo E., North Abington, Mass. Tire-protector. No. 1,328,539 ; Jan. 20 ; v. 270 ; p. 410.

Nilson, Leonard. (See Nilson, Nils and L.)

Nilson, Nils and L. Wayzata, Minn. Tractor. No. 1,328,335 ; Jan. 20 ; v. 270 ; p. 371.

Niva, William J., Minneapolis, Minn. Barn-door hinge. No. 1,328,583 ; Jan. 20 ; v. 270 ; p. 418.

Noonan, James S., assignor to Foss-Hughes Company, Philadelphia, Pa. Door - operating mechanism. No. 1,328,584 ; Jan. 20 ; v. 270 ; p. 418.

Northern Trust Company, The. (See Lang, Lincoln A., assignor.)

Northrup, Edwin F., Princeton, N. J., assignor to The Ajax Metal Company, Philadelphia, Pa. Artificially-cooled high-frequency coil. No. 1,328,336 ; Jan. 20 ; v. 270 ; p. 371.

Northrop, Jonas, Hopedale, assignor to Hopedale Manufacturing Company, Milford, Mass. Automatic loom. No. 1,328,585 ; Jan. 20 ; v. 270 ; p. 418.

Norwood, Harry G., assignor, by mesne assignments, to N. B. Lobe & Co., Baltimore, Md. Alligator-wrench. No. 1,328,389 ; Jan. 20 ; v. 270 ; p. 381.

Nugent, Adam, Nutley, N. J. Game. No. 1,328,390 ; Jan. 20 ; v. 270 ; p. 381.

Nute, James E., Portland, Me. Waste-heat radiator. No. 1,328,540 ; Jan. 20 ; v. 270 ; p. 410.

Odam, Eugène, Paris, France. Process and apparatus for atomizing materials in a melted state. No. 1,328,446 ; Jan. 20 ; v. 270 ; p. 391.

Oehm, William N., Michigan City, Ind. Car-underframe. No. 1,328,683 ; Jan. 20 ; v. 270 ; p. 436.

Oehm, William N., Michigan City, Ind. Car-end sheet. No. 1,328,684 ; Jan. 20 ; v. 270 ; p. 436.

Ogden, James D., Crawford, Tex. Cotton-chopper. No. 1,328,638 ; Jan. 20 ; v. 270 ; p. 428.

O. K. Giant Battery Co. (See Rabe, Paul B., assignor.)

Olson, Bertha C., New York, N. Y. Brassière. No. 1,328,586 ; Jan. 20 ; v. 270 ; p. 419.

Olsson, Nils J., assignor to Aktiebolaget Svenska Kullagerfabriken, Gottenborg, Sweden. Means for automatically cutting off the feed - motion of machine - tools. No. 1,328,337 ; Jan. 20 ; v. 270 ; p. 371.

Ord, Harry J. (See Lockhart and Ord.)

O'Shea, Dennis C., Chicago, Ill. Knitted garment. No. 1,328,545 ; Jan. 20 ; v. 270 ; p. 411.

Overbagh, Donald C., Chicago, Ill. Connector for armored conductors. No. 1,328,290 ; Jan. 20 ; v. 270 ; p. 362.

Owen, Hugh J. (See Gower, Owen, and Cox.)

Owl Supply Company. (See Averill, William H., assignor.)

Packer's Machinery & Equipment Company. (See Nayer, Carl F., assignor.)

Pagenhardt, Leonard C., Westernport, Md. Shutter-adjusting device. No. 1,328,759 ; Jan. 20 ; v. 270 ; p. 450.

Palmer, Eli J., Chicago, Ill. Condiment - stopper. No. 1,328,447 ; Jan. 20 ; v. 270 ; p. 392.

Palmer, Elias H., Ladson, S. C. Internal-combustion engine. No. 1,328,685 ; Jan. 20 ; v. 270 ; p. 436.

Palmer, John F., St. Joseph, Mich. Impregnating fibrous materials. No. 1,328,541 ; Jan. 20 ; v. 270 ; p. 410.

Paragon Binder Corporation. (See Carney, Joseph, assignor.)

Parizek, Frank, Chicago, Ill. Whistle. No. 1,328,639 ; Jan. 20 ; v. 270 ; p. 428.

Parker, Edward C. S., U. S. Navy. Method of and apparatus for producing photographs and projecting the same in natural colors. No. 1,328,291 ; Jan. 20 ; v. 270 ; p. 362.

Parker, Edward C. S., U. S. Navy. Photographic apparatus. No. 1,328,292 ; Jan. 20 ; v. 270 ; p. 360.

Parker, Edward C. S., U. S. Navy. Photographic apparatus. No. 1,328,293 ; Jan. 20 ; v. 270 ; p. 362.

Parker, Edward C. S., U. S. Navy. Photographic apparatus. No. 1,328,294 ; Jan. 20 ; v. 270 ; p. 363.

Parsons, Charles A., S. S. Cook, and A. P. Bennett, Newcastle-upon-Tyne, England ; said Cook and said Bennett assignors to said Parsons. Turbine-blade attachment. No. 1,328,640 ; Jan. 20 ; v. 270 ; p. 428.

Pass & Seymour. (See Morey, Harry J., assignor.)

Pavlik, Joseph, New York, N. Y. Support for furnace-pokers, &c. No. 1,328,686 ; Jan. 20 ; v. 270 ; p. 437.

Peelle Company, The. (See Wexler, Benjamin, assignor.)

Peerenboom, Willard, Appleton, Wis. Show-case. No. 1,328,542 ; Jan. 20 ; v. 270 ; p. 410.

Peller, Karl E., Hartford, Conn., assignor to Hartford-Fairmont Company, Cannjoharie, N. Y. Paddle or plunger for molten glass. No. 1,328,799 ; Jan. 20 ; v. 270 ; p. 458.

Perlman, Jacques M., New York, N. Y. Vehicle-body. No. 1,328,391 ; Jan. 20 ; v. 270 ; p. 381.

Petterson, Bertill C. (See Petterson, Simon G. and B. C.)

Petterson, Simon G. and B. C., Pine Bluff, Ark. Toy wagon. No. 1,328,760 ; Jan. 20 ; v. 270 ; p. 450.

Phelps, Lucius J., San Diego, Calif. Irreversible steering-gear. No. 1,328,761 ; Jan. 20 ; v. 270 ; p. 450.

Phelps, Theophilus P., Lewiston, N. C. Peanut-picking machine. No. 1,328,295 ; Jan. 20 ; v. 270 ; p. 363.

Piel, G., Company, The. (See Long, George F., assignor.)

Pieper, Chester R., assignor to The Gund Manufacturing Company, La Crosse, Wis. Automatic ratchet. No. 1,328,448 ; Jan. 20 ; v. 270 ; p. 392.

Pierman, Alexander N. (See Emerson and Pierman.)

Pike, Charles F. (See Bradley and Pike.)

Pilsbry-Becker Engineering & Supply Company. (See McGinnis, Walter R., assignor.)

Pittsburgh Plate Glass Company. (See Hitchcock, Halbert K., assignor.)

Pleister, Henry W., Westfield, N. J., assignor to H. B. Newhall, Jr., executor. Cable-clamp. No. 1,328,543 ; Jan. 20 ; v. 270 ; p. 410.

Plimpton, Bentley A., Victor, N. Y. Insulator-support. No. 1,328,687 ; Jan. 20 ; v. 270 ; p. 437.

Plummer, Allen H., and C. P. Mullen, Conshohocken, Pa. Oil-deflector for engine-cylinders. No 1,328,544 ; Jan. 20 ; v. 270 ; p. 410.

Pond, Frank J., Tulsa, Okla. Shaft-clamp. No. 1,328,688 ; Jan. 20 ; v. 270 ; p. 437.

Port, Samuel R., Martinsville, Ind. Collapsible barrel. No. 1,328,587 ; Jan. 20 ; v. 270 ; p. 419.

Porter, J. E., Company. (See Jordan, Burton S., assignor.)

Preston, Albert F., Boston, Mass. Adjustable blank-holder for pattern-grading and other machines. No. 1,328,689 ; Jan. 20 ; v. 270 ; p. 437.

Smith, Raymond D., Arlington, Mass. Automatic circuit-breaker. No. 1,328,460; Jan. 20; v. 270; p. 394.

Smith, Philester, Rochester, N. Y. Vehicle. No. 1,328,343; Jan. 20; v. 270; p. 372.

Smolens, Abraham M., New York, N. Y. Toy. No. 1,328,344; Jan. 20; v. 270; p. 372.

Smith, Walter S., Brooklyn, N. Y. Ball-crank connection. No. 1,328,600; Jan. 20; v. 270; p. 421.

Snider, John L., assignor to Royal Metalware Manufacturing Co., Denton, N. C. Fireless cooker. No. 1,328,304; Jan. 20; v. 270; p. 365.

Soisalon-Soininen, Juhani L., Boxbacka, Finland. Paper-knife. No. 1,328,548; Jan. 20; v. 270; p. 411.

Sourbier, Edward V., and M. Madden, Harrisburg, Pa. Railway-rail. No. 1,328,405; Jan. 20; v. 270; p. 384.

Sparmaker, Frank P. J., Audubon, N. J. Burial-casket attachment. No. 1,328,345; Jan. 20; v. 270; p. 373.

Spencer, Carroll K., River Forest, Ill. Sealing-wax applier. No. 1,328,769; Jan. 20; v. 270; p. 452.

Sperry, Elmer A. (See Bassett, Preston R., assignor.)

Sprenkel, Ward F., et al. (See Matthiessen, Conrad S., assignor.)

Spring, Frederick L., Indianapolis, Ind. Spring shock-absorber. No. 1,328,601; Jan. 20; v. 270; p. 421.

Steen, Inford J., Goose Creek, Tex. Elevator. No. 1,328,602; Jan. 20; v. 270; p. 421.

Sterner, Frank F., Harnedsville, Pa. Car - mover. No. 1,328,770; Jan. 20; v. 270; p. 452.

Stevens, Herbert C. M. (See Coatalen and Stevens, assignors.)

Stirling, Charles P., assignor to Cott-a-lap Co., Somerville, N. J. Machine for graining lithographic cylinders. No. 1,328,603; Jan. 20; v. 270; p. 422.

Stone, Frank N. (See Newton, Charles, assignor.)

Stonebraker, Harold E., Brooklyn, N. Y. Friction-gearing for motor-vehicles. No. 1,328,346; Jan. 20; v. 270; p. 373.

Straban, Ida W., Montclair, N. J. Hair - curler. No. 1,328,771; Jan. 20; v. 270; p. 452.

Strauss, Joseph B., Chicago, Ill. Observation-tower. No. 1,328,461; Jan. 20; v. 270; p. 394.

Strey, Walter F. A., Neenah, Wis. Quack-grass destroyer. No. 1,328,697; Jan. 20; v. 270; p. 439.

Stynkowic, Ignacy, East Hammond, Ind. Combined folding chair and table. No. 1,328,462; Jan. 20; v. 270; p. 395.

Sunderland, Paul U. (See Rogers, James E., assignor.)

Sussman, Samuel J., Brooklyn, N. Y. Photographic developing-machine. No. 1,328,305; Jan. 20; v. 270; p. 365.

Taft, Walter E., Providence, R. I., assignor to The Associate Company, Boston, Mass. Spark-plug for internal-combustion engines. No. 1,328,463; Jan. 20; v. 270; p. 395.

Tainter, Charles R. (See Lenholt, John E., assignor.)

Taylor, Charles. (See Carter and Taylor.)

Templeton, Walter B., Chicago, Ill. Lifting-jack. No. 1,328,306; Jan. 20; v. 270; p. 365.

Thomas, Frank M., Catskill, N. Y. Cartridge. No. 1,328,307; Jan. 20; v. 270; p. 365.

Thomas, R., and Sons Company, The. (See Harms, Rhinehart W., assignor.)

Thompson, Fredrick B., Chicago, Ill. Film-treating apparatus. No. 1,328,464; Jan. 20; v. 270; p. 395.

Thompson, Oliver H., Brookings, S. D. Torpedo-guard. No. 1,328,549; Jan. 20; v. 270; p. 411.

Timpany, Lewis J., Taco Taco, Cuba. Voting-machine. No. 1,328,550; Jan. 20; v. 270; p. 412.

Todd, James T. A., Fort Worth, Tex. Bale-tie buckle. No. 1,328,698; Jan. 20; v. 270; p. 439.

Todd, Libanus M., and A. C. La May, assignors, by mesne assignments, to Todd Protectograph Company, Rochester, N. Y. Checkwriter. No. 1,328,773; Jan. 20; v. 270; p. 453.

Todd Protectograph Company. (See Todd and La May, assignors.)

Toledo Scale Company. (See Crane, Samuel G., assignor.)

Treat, Robert, Schenectady, N. Y., assignor to General Electric Company. System of power transmission. No. 1,328,465; Jan. 20; v. 270; p. 395.

Tregoning, William C., Cleveland, Ohio, assignor, by mesne assignments, to Benjamin Electric Manufacturing Company, Chicago, Ill. Electrical attachment - plug. No. 1,328,774; Jan. 20; v. 270; p. 453.

Tremain, Charles. (See Becker, Robert A., assignor.)

Trohon, William G., Danvers, Mass., assignor to United Shoe Machinery Corporation, Paterson, N. J. Die. No. 1,328,347; Jan. 20; v. 270; p. 373.

Trout, Silas E., Philadelphia, Pa. Filing device. No. 1,328,604; Jan. 20; v. 270; p. 422.

Trumbull Electric Manufacturing Company, The. (See Knudsen, Knud, assignor.)

Tubular-Rivet & Stud Company. (See Wakefield, Edward E., assignor.)

Turck, Henry J., et al., trustees. (See Bobroff, Bornett L., assignor.)

Underwood Typewriter Company. (See Helmond, William F., assignor.)

Union Tractor Company. (See Arndt, Richard L., assignor.)

United Shoe Machinery Corporation. (See Brock, Matthias, assignor.)

United Shoe Machinery Corporation. (See Fausse, Joseph, assignor.)

United Shoe Machinery Corporation. (See Lurd, Thomas, assignor.)

United Shoe Machinery Corporation. (See Trohon, William G., assignor.)

Van Aller, Tycho, Schenectady, N. Y., assignor to General Electric Company. Cigar-lighter. No. 1,328,466; Jan. 20; v. 270; p. 396.

Van Alstyn, Albert T., Grand Rapids, Mich. Supporter. No. 1,328,406; Jan. 20; v. 270; p. 384.

Van Briggle, Lilburn H., Indianapolis, Ind. Shock-absorber. No. 1,328,641; Jan. 20; v. 270; p. 428.

Van Houten, Frank H., Jr., Beacon, assignor to Dutchess Tool Company, New York, N. Y. Oiling hoppers. No. 1,328,308; Jan. 20; v. 270; p. 365.

Van Lynden, Robert A. (See de Lange and van Lynden.)

Van Meter, George F., Indianapolis, Ind. Adjustable caster. No. 1,328,775; Jan. 20; v. 270; p. 453.

Vang, Peder C., Omaha, Nebr. Valve-spring remover. No. 1,328,776; Jan. 20; v. 270; p. 453.

Van Valkenburg, Burt R., Oakland, Calif. Valve-chest. No. 1,328,796; Jan. 20; v. 270; p. 457.

Vermont Box Company. (See Shelton, Carl L., assignor.)

Virkus, Frederick A., La Grange, Ill., assignor to Wood, Nathan & Virkus Company, New York, N. Y. Machine for embossing without dies. No. 1,328,407; Jan. 20; v. 270; p. 384.

Vogt, Ernst W., Silverton, Ohio. Downspout cut-off. No. 1,328,348; Jan. 20; v. 270; p. 373.

Vogt, Joseph, Richmond, Minn. Self-sharpening adjustable packer-head plate for tile-machines. No. 1,328,699; Jan. 20; v. 270; p. 439.

Wagenhorst, James H., Akron, Ohio, assignor to The B. F. Goodrich Company, New York, N. Y. Demountable split rim. No. 1,328,605; Jan. 20; v. 270; p. 422.

Wagoner, Joseph B., Danville, Ill. Shock-absorber. No. 1,328,700; Jan. 20; v. 270; p. 439.

Wakefield, Edward E., assignor to Tubular-Rivet & Stud Company, Providence, R. I. Lacing-stud-setting machine. No. 1,328,701; Jan. 20; v. 270; p. 439.

Walker, Moses F., Cadiz, Ohio. Film-end fastener for motion-picture-film reels. No. 1,328,408; Jan. 20; v. 270; p. 385.

Wallace, Peter, Vancouver, British Columbia, Canada. Means for separating small from large fish. No. 1,328,551; Jan. 20; v. 270; p. 412.

Walther, Paul. (See Holzapfel and Walther.)

Ward Leonard Electric Co. (See Kebler, Leonard, assignor.)

Waters, Frank W. (See Rea and Waters.)

Webb, John W., assignor, by mesne assignments, to Webb Tester Incorporated, Chicago, Ill. Device for testing corrugated paper - board and corrugated - paper - board boxes. No. 1,328,349; Jan. 20; v. 270; p. 373.

Webb Tester Incorporated. (See Webb, John W., assignor.)

Weed, Howard L., Detroit, Mich. Cylinder-forming machine. No. 1,328,409; Jan. 20; v. 270; p. 385.

Weed, Howard L., Detroit, Mich. Rotary engine. No. 1,328,410; Jan. 20; v. 270; p. 385.

Weinhardt, Robert A., Chicago, Ill., assignor, by mesne assignments, to Continental Motors Corporation, Detroit, Mich. Crank-shaft. No. 1,328,350; Jan. 20; v. 270; p. 373.

Weisberger, Edward I. (See Newberg and Weisberger.)

Welch, Alfred F., Fort Wayne, Ind., assignor to General Electric Company. Universal motor. No. 1,328,467; Jan. 20; v. 270; p. 396.

Welch, Harry V., assignor to International Precipitation Company, Los Angeles, Calif. Apparatus for making sulfuric acid. No. 1,328,552; Jan. 20; v. 270; p. 412.

Wellman, Frank E., assignor to The Kansas City Gasoline Company, Kansas City, Kans. Furnace for oil-cracking stills. No. 1,328,468; Jan. 20; v. 270; p. 396.

Wendtland, William, New York, N. Y. Screw-grinding machine. No. 1,328,469; Jan. 20; v. 270; p. 396.

Western Hog Oiler Co. (See Busby, Harley S., assignor.)

Westinghouse Electric and Manufacturing Company. (See Hellmund, Rudolf E., assignor.)

Westinghouse Air Brake Company, The. (See Saunders, Lawrence D., assignor.)

Wexler, Benjamin, assignor to The Peelle Company, Brooklyn, N. Y. Electric interlock for counterbalanced elevator-doors. No. 1,328,309; Jan. 20; v. 270; p. 366.

Wheary, George H., Racine, Wis. Garment-retainer for trunks. No. 1,328,470; Jan. 20; v. 270; p. 396.

White, Fred G., assignor of one-half to E. W. Engle, Kansas City, Mo. Electric switch-box. No. 1,328,606; Jan. 20; v. 270; p. 422.

Whitehead Torpedo Works (Weymouth) Limited, The. (See Lees, Edgar, assignor.)

Whiteley, George H., Jr., York, Pa., assignor to The Dentists' Supply Company. Mold for molding artificial teeth. No. 1,328,351; Jan. 20; v. 270; p. 374.

Whitton, Charles R. (See Fry and Whitton.)

Willis, Harry F., Waterford, assignor to Willite Road Construction Company of America, New York, N. Y. Asphaltic pavement and foundation for pavements. No. 1,328,310; Jan. 20; v. 270; p. 366.

Willite Road Construction Company of America. (See Willis, Harry F., assignor.)

Wiltshire, James D. (See Frisz and Wiltshire.)

Winston, Overton, Minneapolis, Minn. Electric head-light. No. 1,328,607; Jan. 20; v. 270; p. 422.

Winter, Lloyd V., Juneau, Alaska. Cooking utensil. No. 1,328,702; Jan. 20; v. 270; p. 439.

Wirebounds Patents Company. (See Inwood, Richard G., assignor.)

Wisconsin Pearl Button Company. (See Koch, William J., assignor.)
Wood, Nathan & Virkus Company. (See Virkus, Frederick A., assignor.)
Woodward, William J., Leetonia, Ohio. Hot-water boiler. No. 1,328,608; Jan. 20; v. 270; p. 422.
Workman, Harold, Glasgow, Scotland. Motion-picture apparatus and motion-picture film therefor. No. 1,328,352; Jan. 20; v. 270; p. 374.
Worthington Pump and Machinery Corporation. (See Fleming, Wills M., assignor.)
Wuerth, Fred W., Cincinnati, Ohio. Fan. No. 1,328,353; Jan. 20; v. 270; p. 374.
Yody, Louis, Sharpsville, Pa. Match-box. No. 1,328,703; Jan. 20; v. 270; p. 440.

Young, Horace M., Niagara Falls, N. Y. Wood-splitting machine. No. 1,328,471; Jan. 20; v. 270; p. 396.
Youngberg, James, Alameda, assignor to William Cluff Company, San Francisco, Calif. Receptacle-spout. No. 1,328,704; Jan. 20; v. 270; p. 440.
Xardell, Charles A., Utica, N. Y. Dust-separator. No. 1,328,642; Jan. 20; v. 270; p. 429.
Zaugg, Philip, Blue Creek township, Adams county, Ind. Lifting-jack. No. 1,328,609; Jan. 20; v. 270; p. 423.
Zervudachi, Jenny, née Rodocanachi, Paris. France. Unwinding device. No. 1,328,777; Jan. 20; v. 270; p. 453.
Zimmerman, Alonzo D., Superior, Colo. Miner's lamp. No. 1,328,553; Jan. 20; v. 270; p. 412. .

ALPHABETICAL LIST OF PATENTEES OF DESIGNS.

Chapman, John G., Port Washington, assignor to Sanford Narrow Fabric Co., New York, N. Y. Edging. Nos. 54,359–61; Jan. 20; v. 270; p. 459.

Sanford Narrow Fabric Co. (See Chapman, John C., assignor.)
Stevens, William F., Chicago, Ill. Service-emblem. No. 54,362; Jan. 20; v. 270; p. 459.

ALPHABETICAL LIST OF REGISTRANTS OF TRADE-MARKS.

Akerlund & Semmes, Inc., New York, N. Y. Gas-producer apparatus. No. 128,913; Jan. 20; v. 270; p. 471.
Alford, Henry N., Atlanta, Ga. Medicine for colds, influenza, &c. No. 128,915; Jan. 20; v. 270; p. 471.
Alfred Brothers, Whittinsville, Mass. Medicine for colds, asthma, &c. No. 128,914; Jan. 20; v. 270; p. 471.
American Flour Corporation, New York, N. Y. Wheat-flour. No. 128,916; Jan. 20; v. 270; p. 471.
American Harmonica & Accordion Manufacturing Co., New York, N. Y. Harmonicas. No. 128,917; Jan. 20; v. 270; p. 471.
American Laboratories, Indianapolis, Ind. Pharmaceutical preparation for colds and congestions. No. 128,918; Jan. 20; v. 270; p. 471.
American Standard Food Assn., Milwaukee, Wis. Coffee. No. 128,919; Jan. 20; v. 270; p. 471.
American Tobacco Company, The, New York, N. Y. Cigarettes. No. 128,920; Jan. 20; v. 270; p. 471.
American Tobacco Co., New York, N. Y. Cigarettes and tobacco. No. 128,921; Jan. 20; v. 270; p. 471.
Apperson Bros. Automobile Co., Kokomo, Ind. Pleasure-automobiles and motor-trucks. No. 128,922; Jan. 20; v. 270; p. 471.
Armor-Clad Boy's Clothes Co., New York, N. Y. Children's and boys' clothes, suits, overcoats, and pants. No. 129,109; Jan. 20; v. 270; p. 477.
Armstrong Cork Company, Pittsburgh, Pa. Oiled duck. No. 128,924; Jan. 20; v. 270; p. 471.
Arons, Louis, Chicago, Ill. Garment-supports. No. 128,923; Jan. 20; v. 270; p. 471.
A/S. Herman A. Kähler, Næstved, Denmark. Crockery, earthenware, porcelain. No. 129,007; Jan. 20; v. 270; p. 474.
Atterbury Motor Car Company, Buffalo, N. Y. Motor-trucks and parts. No. 128,925; Jan. 20; v. 270; p. 471.
Auto-Ordnance Corporation, New York, N. Y. Shoulder-rifles. No. 128,926; Jan. 20; v. 270; p. 471.
Back Creek Valley Orchard Company, Hedgesville, W. Va. Fresh peaches, canned apples, peaches, tomatoes, and beans. No. 128,927; Jan. 20; v. 270; p. 471.
Baker-Overton Company, Dallas, Tex. Waterproof dressing for textiles, &c. No. 128,928; Jan. 20; v. 270; p. 471.
Barrett Company, New York, N. Y. Ready-mixed paint. No. 128,929; Jan. 20; v. 270; p. 471.
Beddoes, Joseph G., Birmingham, England. Locks. No. 128,930; Jan. 20; v. 270; p. 471.
Borden Company, The, New York, N. Y. Condensed milk. Nos. 128,931–2; Jan. 20; v. 270; p. 471.
Borden Company, The, New York, N. Y. Condensed milk. Nos. 128,934–41; Jan. 20; v. 270; p. 471–2.
Borden Company, The, New York, N. Y. Confectionery. No. 128,933; Jan. 20; v. 270; p. 471.
Borden's Farm Products Company, Inc., Wassaic and New York, N. Y. Foods and ingredients of food. No. 128,942; Jan. 20; v. 270; p. 472.
Bowman, W. P., Leeds, England. Sauce for fish, game, &c. No. 128,943; Jan. 20; v. 270; p. 472.
Bradford, Albert S., Placentia, Calif. Fresh citrus fruits. No. 128,944; Jan. 20; v. 270; p. 472.
Bradley, Milton, Company, Springfield, Miss. Games of jack-straws. No. 128,945; Jan. 20; v. 270; p. 472.
Brooks Tomato Products Company, Collinsville, Ill. Tabasco-flavor catsup. No. 128,946; Jan. 20; v. 270; p. 472.
Bullen, Joseph W., Folcroft, Pa. Disinfectant. Nos. 128,947–8; Jan. 20; v. 270; p. 472.

Byron Weston Co., Dalton, Mass. Writing-paper. No. 128,949; Jan. 20; v. 270; p. 472.
Cadwallader, Harry, Jr., Philadelphia. Pa. Cutlery, machinery, tools, and parts. No. 128,950; Jan. 20; v. 270; p. 472.
California Packing Corporation, San Francisco, Calif. Canned vegetables and fruits, &c. No. 128,951; Jan. 20; v. 270; p. 472.
Campbell, John, & Co., New York, N. Y. Anilin colors and coal-tar dyes. No. 128,952; Jan. 20; v. 270; p. 472.
Carner, George T., Fulton, N. Y. Salve. No. 128,954; Jan. 20; v. 270; p. 472.
Castello, Edward B., Chicago, Ill. Liniment. No. 128,955; Jan. 20; v. 270; p. 472.
Chaney Manufacturing Company, The, Springfield, Ohio. Thermometers, barometers, rain-gages. No. 128,956; Jan. 20; v. 270; p. 472.
Ciluzzi, Ralph, New York, N. Y. Perfumes, powders, &c. No. 128,957; Jan. 20; v. 270; p. 472.
Cohen, Nathan B., Scranton, Pa. Veils. No. 128,958; Jan. 20; v. 270; p. 472.
Consolidated Wafer Company, New York, N. Y., and Chicago, Ill. Ice-cream cones. No. 128,959; Jan. 20; v. 270; p. 472.
Corn Belt Packing Company, Dubuque, Iowa. Ham, bacon, &c. No. 128,960; Jan. 20; v. 270; p. 472.
Cox, Irwin W., Chicago, Ill. Cleanser and polish. No. 128,961; Jan. 20; v. 270; p. 472.
Coward, Albert T. H., Sheffield, England. Cutlery, machinery, and tools, and parts. No. 128,962; Jan. 20; v. 270; p. 472.
Crawford. McGregor & Canby Company, The, Dayton, Ohio. Golf-clubs. No. 128,963; Jan. 20; v. 270; p. 472.
Crescn Company, New York, N. Y. Foods. No. 128,964; Jan. 20; v. 270; p. 472.
Davies, William, Company, Chicago, Ill. Foods and ingredients of food. No. 128,965; Jan. 20; v. 270; p. 472.
Davies, William, Company, Limited, Chicago, Ill. Bacon, sausage, and canned lunch-tongue, &c. No. 128,966; Jan. 20; v. 270; p. 472.
Davies, William, Company, Limited, Chicago, Ill. Foods and ingredients of food. No. 128,967; Jan. 20; v. 270; p. 472.
Dittlinger, H., Roller Mills Company, New Braunfels. Tex. Wheat-flour. No. 128,968; Jan. 20; v. 270; p. 472.
Douglass Barnes Corporation, New York, N. Y. Ladies' sport-coats, sweaters, slip-ons, &c. No. 128,969; Jan. 20; v. 270; p. 472.
Duplex Engine-Governor Company, Inc., Brooklyn, N. Y. Governors for engines. No. 129,970; Jan. 20; v. 270; p. 472.
Electric Phonograph Corporation, New York, N. Y. Combination phonograph and lamp-stand. No. 128,971; Jan. 20; v. 270; p. 472.
Electropure Dairy Company, Wilmington, Del., and Chicago, Ill. Milk. No. 128,972; Jan. 20; v. 270; p. 472.
Ely & Walker D. G. Co., St. Louis, Mo. Hosiery, underwear, &c. No. 128,973; Jan. 20; v. 270; p. 473.
Emmerling Products Company, Johnstown, Pa. Ginger-ale. No. 128,974; Jan. 20; v. 270; p. 473.
Filletin & Chochkoff Company, Milwaukee, Wis. Salve for sweaty feet. No. 128,975; Jan. 20; v. 270; p. 473.
Florin. Philip, New York, N. Y. Wallets, bill-folds, and three-folds of leather. No. 128,976; Jan. 20; v. 270; p. 473.

Simcox, Edward C., Columbus, Ohio. Games and gameboards of a checker or chess like variety. No. 129,074; Jan. 20; v. 270; p. 476.

Simmons Hardware Company, St. Louis, Mo. Scales. No. 129,075; Jan. 20; v. 270; p. 476.

Simmons Hardware Company, St. Louis, Mo. Measuring and scientific appliances. No. 129,076; Jan. 20; v. 270; p. 476.

Simmons Hardware Company, St. Louis, Mo. Harness, riding-saddles, &c. No. 129,077; Jan. 20; v. 270; p. 476.

Simmons Milling Company, The, Cincinnati, Ohio. Stock and poultry feeds. No. 129,078; Jan. 20; v. 270; p. 476.

Skinner, Paul F., Omaha, Nebr. Bread, pies, ice-cream. No. 129,079; Jan. 20; v. 270; p. 476.

Smith-Frank Packing Co., Sacramento, Calif. Canned fruits and vegetables. No. 129,080; Jan. 20; v. 270; p. 476.

Smith, Dayton D., Philadelphia, Pa. Chemical preparation for preserving eggs. No. 129,081; Jan. 20; v. 270; p. 476.

Snovel, Harry H., Van Wert, Ohio. Cigars. No. 129,082; Jan. 20; v. 270; p. 476.

Southern Beverage Company, Galveston, Tex. Non-alcoholic beverages. No. 129,083; Jan. 20; v. 270; p. 476.

Standard Cooper-Bell Co., Chicago, Ill. Enamel and oil paints, stains, &c. No. 129,084; Jan. 20; v. 270; p. 476.

Stein-Hall Manufacturing Company, Wilmington, Del., and Chicago, Ill. Starch product for an ingredient in baking. No. 129,085; Jan. 20; v. 270; p. 476.

Steinwender-Stoffregen Coffee Company, St. Louis, Mo. Food-flavoring extracts, roasted coffee. No. 129,086; Jan. 20; v. 270; p. 476.

Sterling Varnish Company, Pittsburgh, Pa. Varnish for the surface of rubber tires. No. 129,087; Jan. 20; v. 270; p. 476.

Stone & Andrew Inc., Boston, Mass. Writing and printing paper. No. 129,088; Jan. 20; v. 270; p. 476.

Stuttgart Rice Mill Company, Stuttgart, Ark. Rice. Nos., 129,089-90; Jan. 20; v. 270; p. 476.

Taylor, E. E., Company, Boston, Mass. Leather boots and shoes. No. 129,091; Jan. 20; v. 270; p. 476.

Todd, George W., Omaha, Nebr. Chewing-gum. No. 129,092; Jan. 20; v. 270; p. 476.

Trent, Lorenzo D., Ironton, Ohio. Preparation for treatment of certain named diseases. No. 129,093; Jan. 20; v. 270; p. 476.

United States Rubber Company, New Brunswick, N. J., and New York, N. Y. Leather shoes. No. 129,094; Jan. 20; v. 270; p. 476.

Wade, R. M., & Co., Portland, Oreg. Power drag-saws. No. 129,095; Jan. 20; v. 270; p. 476.

Walker-Matteson Co., Joliet, Ill. Canned goods, mustard, catsup, &c. No. 129,096; Jan. 20; v. 270; p. 476.

Webster, Frank B., Los Angeles, Calif. Polishing and cleansing compound for automobiles, &c. No. 129,097; Jan. 20; v. 270; p. 476.

Western Boiler Pipe Company, Monmouth, Ill. Roaddrags. No. 129,098; Jan. 20; v. 270; p. 476.

Westcott Motor Car Company, Springfield, Ohio. Automobiles. No. 129,099; Jan. 20; v. 270; p. 476.

White, Theodore H., Los Angeles, Calif. Planchetteboards. No. 129,100; Jan. 20; v. 270; p. 477.

White Star Refining Co., Detroit, Mich. Asphalt shingles, roofing papers and cements. No. 129,101; Jan. 20; v. 270; p. 477.

Wilbur, H. O., & Sons, Inc., Philadelphia, Pa. Covering used to coat candy. No. 129,102; Jan. 20; v. 270; p. 477.

Williams, Bettie, New York, N. Y. Scalp preparation and hair-grower. No. 129,103; Jan. 20; v. 270; p. 477.

Williams Chocolate Co., Scranton, Pa. Cough-drops. No. 129,104; Jan. 20; v. 270; p. 477.

Wimpfheimer, A., & Bro. Inc., New York, N. Y. Ribbons of pile fabrics. No. 129,105; Jan. 20; v. 270; p. 477.

Wyatt Bros., Chicago, Ill. Cotton-seed-oil stearin. No. 129,106; Jan. 20; v. 270; p. 477.

Wynne Paper Co., New York, N. Y. Writing-tablets, &c. No. 129,107; Jan. 20; v. 270; p. 477.

Young & Egan, Inc., New York, N. Y. Globes, shades, and reflectors of glass. No. 129,108; Jan. 20; v. 270; p. 477.

ALPHABETICAL LIST OF REGISTRANTS OF TRADE-MARKS.
(REGISTRATION APPLIED FOR.)

Abbott Corporation, Detroit, Mich. Automobile pleasure and business cars and motor-trucks. No. 102,607; Jan. 20; v. 270; p. 461.

Adwear Process Sole Leather Machine Company, Philadelphia, Pa. Shoe and boot soles and boots and shoes of processed leather. No. 120,947; Jan. 20; v. 270; p. 465.

American Manufacturing Company, Boston, Mass., and Brooklyn, N. Y. Rope, cord, and twine of vegetable fiber. No. 125,043; Jan. 20; v. 270; p. 470.

American Twine Co., Inc., New York, N. Y. Twine. No. 122,873; Jan. 20; v. 270; p. 467.

Anzell, Alexander A., New York, N. Y. Dental, &c., mirrors, retinoscopes. No. 123,150; Jan. 20; v. 270; p. 468.

Asphalt Manufacturing Company, The, Lancaster, Ohio. Slate-surfaced roofings and shingles. No. 119,693; Jan. 20; v. 270; p. 464.

Barber & Bennett, Inc., Albany, N. Y. Stock, horse, dairy, and poultry feed. No. 124,846; Jan. 20; v. 270; p. 470.

Barnet Leather Company, New York, N. Y. Patent leather and finished calfskins. No. 117,966; Jan. 20; v. 270; p. 463.

Brauer Bros. Shoe Company, St. Louis, Mo. Shoes of leather, cloth, or canvas. No. 121,230; Jan. 20; v. 270; p. 465.

Brown Instrument Company, The, Philadelphia, Pa. Protecting-tubes for pyrometers. No. 120,474; Jan. 20; v. 270; p. 465.

Brown, Thomas E., Philadelphia, Pa. Hosiery. No. 123,871; Jan. 20; v. 270; p. 469.

Carson, Pirie, Scott & Co., assignor to Carson Pirie Scott & Company, Chicago, Ill. Nainsooks, muslins, longcloth, and cambrics. No. 114,528; Jan. 20; v. 270; p. 462.

Carson, Pirie, Scott & Co., assignor to Carson Pirie Scott & Company, Chicago, Ill. Overalls. No. 100,004; Jan. 20; v. 270; p. 461.

Chevaux Kid Leather Co., Boston, Mass. Finished leather. No. 124,260; Jan. 20; v. 270; p. 469.

Columbia Fastener Company, Chicago, Ill. Snap dressfasteners. No. 122,424; Jan. 20; v. 270; p. 467.

Cooper, Coate & Casey Dry Goods Co., Los Angeles, Calif., and New York, N. Y. Men's and women's night-wear. No. 123,964; Jan. 20; v. 270; p. 469.

Cunill de Figuerola, José, New York, N. Y. Automobiles and motor-trucks. No. 123,520; Jan. 20; v. 270; p. 468.

Double Suction Rubber Heel & Sole Company, Baltimore, Md. Rubber heels and soles for shoes. No. 122,826; Jan. 20; v. 270; p. 467.

Du Pont, E. I. de Nemours & Company, Wilmington, Del. High explosive of dynamite type. No. 116,680; Jan. 20; v. 270; p. 462.

Dutton, George C., Boston, Mass. Games. No. 117,446; Jan. 20; v. 270; p. 463.

Eberlin, Otto, Hermann, Mo. Non-alcoholic maltless pear-flavored beverage. No. 120,416; Jan. 20; v. 270; p. 465.

Empire Silk Company, Wilmington, Del., and New York, N. Y. Silk piece goods. No. 124,396; Jan. 20; v. 270; p. 469.

Fessler, William R., Kansas City, Kans. Pharmaceutical preparation. No. 122,940; Jan. 20; v. 270; p. 468.

Fruit Valley Corporation, Rochester, N. Y. Concentrated syrup and non-alcoholic beverage made from same. No. 120,373; Jan. 20; v. 270; p. 465.

Fukuhara, Shinzo, Tokyo, Japan. Perfumes, toilet waters, powders, creams, and lotions, &c. No. 120,376; Jan. 20; v. 270; p. 465.

Gilbert, A. C., Company, The, New Haven, Conn. Metal and wooden building toys, &c. No. 119,974; Jan. 20; v. 270; p. 464.

Griggs-Paxton Shoe Co. Inc., Roanoke, Va. Boots and shoes. No. 122,889; Jan. 20; v. 270; p. 467.

Herkimer Fibre Company, The, Herkimer, N. Y. Manufactured leather-board. No. 101,569; Jan. 20; v. 270; p. 461.

Hewes & Potter, Boston, Mass. Garters. No. 124,348; Jan. 20; v. 270; p. 469.

Hirsch, Freedman Co., Chicago, Ill. Men's and boys' dress and negligée shirts, underwear, &c. No. 117,011; Jan. 20; v. 270; p. 463.

Hooven & Allison Company, The, Xenia, Ohio. Fiber ropes and twines. No. 121,344; Jan. 20; v. 270; p. 466.

Horlacher Brewing Co., Allentown, Pa. Non-alcoholic beverages and syrups for making same. No. 123,810; Jan. 20; v. 270; p. 469.

Jennings Manufacturing Company, Grand Rapids, Mich. Perfumery, toilet water, face and talcum powder, and face cream. No. 118,559; Jan. 20; v. 270; p. 464.

John M. Given, Inc., Pittsburgh, Pa.; Chicago, Ill., and New York, N. Y. Children's hosiery. No. 123,800; Jan. 20; v. 270; p. 468.

John M. Given, Inc., Pittsburgh, Pa.; New York, N. Y. and Chicago, Ill. Hosiery. No. 123,802; Jan. 20; v. 270; p. 468.

Kennesaw Hosiery Company, The, Marietta, Ga. Men's, ladies', and children's hosiery. No. 120,997; Jan. 20; v. 270; p. 465.

Krenning-Schlapps Grocer Company, St. Louis, Mo. Clotheslines. No. 122,707; Jan. 20; v. 270; p. 467.

L. P. Larson, Jr., Company, Chicago, Ill. Confection. No. 122,779; Jan. 20; v. 270; p. 467.

Lake Wales Citrus Growers Association, Lake Wales, Fla. Citrus fruits. No. 121,629; Jan. 20; v. 270; p. 466.

Lamborn & Co., New York, N. Y. Prepared felt roofing. No. 123,486; Jan. 20; v. 270; p. 468.

Lamborn & Co., New York, N. Y. Textile fabrics—namely, netting and bunting and silk piece goods. No. 116,992; Jan. 20; v. 270; p. 463.

Levinson, Daniel L., Chicago, Ill. Powdered preparation for making a fruit acid, and spice-flavored marmalade and jam. No. 118,232; Jan. 20; v. 270; p. 463.

Lorenz Company, The, Everett, Mass. Tooth and foot powder. No. 105,835; Jan. 20; v. 270; p. 462.

Lynchburg Foundry Company, Lynchburg, Va. Plows and parts thereof. No. 124,610; Jan. 20; v. 270; p. 470.

McIntosh Battery & Optical Co., Chicago, Ill. Electro-medical switchboard for electric-bath use. No. 122,903; Jan. 20; v. 270; p. 467.

Marre & Company, Buenos Aires, Argentina. Cheese and butter. No. 105,482; Jan. 20; v. 270; p. 461.

Massachusetts Breweries Company, Alexandria, Va., and Boston, Mass. Malt beverages. No. 124,487; Jan. 20; v. 270; p. 470.

Moore Food Products Company, Chicago, Ill. Breakfast food. No. 122,994; Jan. 20; v. 270; p. 468.

Nashua Manufg. Company, Nashua, N. H. Cotton blankets. No. 124,280; Jan. 20; v. 270; p. 469.

Nashua Manufg. Company, Nashua, N. H. Cotton blankets. No. 124,282; Jan. 20; v. 270; p. 469.

Nathan, Edwin B., New York, N. Y. Mufflers, helmets, gloves, shawls, &c., of knit fabric. No. 106,883; Jan. 20; v. 270; p. 461.

Nebraska Fountain & Supply Co., Omaha, Nebr. Topping for ice-cream sundaes and hot chocolate. No. 109,812; Jan. 20; v. 270; p. 462.

Ninavilla Farm Products Co., Blind Slough, Oreg. Fresh vegetables. No. 106,744; Jan. 20; v. 270; p. 461.

Noma Motor Corporation, New York, N. Y. Automobiles and automobile-bodies. No. 125,014; Jan. 20; v. 270; p. 470.

Otorino Manufacturing Company, New York, N. Y. Medicine for the diseased mucous membrane of the nose, throat, mouth, and ear. No. 117,572; Jan. 20; v. 270; p. 463.

Phillips, Elmer J., Wilkes-Barre, Pa. Potato chips. No. 125,164; Jan. 20; v. 270; p. 470.

Rainier Products Company, Seattle, Wash. Birch and root beer, sarsaparilla, ginger-ale, and cider. No. 120,070; Jan. 20; v. 270; p. 464.

Record Card Co., New York, N. Y. Filing-cards. No. 117,125; Jan. 20; v. 270; p. 463.

Revere Rubber Company, Providence, R. I. Shoe-soles of rubber and fiber. No. 121,805; Jan. 20; v. 270; p. 466.

Rosenbaum, Samuel, & Sons Company, Kalamazoo, Mich. Trousers. No. 122,367; Jan. 20; v. 270; p. 467.

Scheer, Grandi & Co., San Francisco, Calif. Butter. No. 124,626; Jan. 20; v. 270; p. 470.

Seamans & Cobb Co., Boston, Mass. Cotton sewing-threads. No. 125,029; Jan. 20; v. 270; p. 470.

Seydel Manufacturing Company, Jersey City, N. J. Ethyl, methyl, benzyl, &c., benzoates and benzyl alcohol. No. 119,871; Jan. 20; v. 270; p. 464.

Seydel Manufacturing Company, Jersey City, N. J. Sizing and finishing compounds for textile fabrics and threads. No. 119,872; Jan. 20; v. 270; p. 464.

Sheldon, George C., Nehawka, Nebr. Concrete-mixer. No. 124,625; Jan. 20; v. 270; p. 470.

Southern Motor Manufacturing Association Ltd., Houston, Tex. Tractors. No. 124,152; Jan. 20; v. 270; p. 469.

Stanford Seed Co., Inc., The, Binghamton, Buffalo, and Albany, N. Y. Seeds. No. 121,646; Jan. 20; v. 270; p. 466.

Thornton Mineral Springs Company, Thornton, Ill. Non-alcoholic beverages and syrups for making same. No. 122,002; Jan. 20; v. 270; p. 466.

Turner & Walls, New York, N. Y. Silk and cotton piece goods and combinations of same. No. 124,371; Jan. 20; v. 270; p. 469.

United States Rubber Company, New Brunswick, N. J., and New York, N. Y. Dental dam, surgeons' gloves, seamless nipples, &c. No. 121,949; Jan. 20; v. 270; p. 466.

Victor Aircraft Corporation, Freeport, N. Y. Aeroplanes. No. 113,202; Jan. 20; v. 270; p. 462.

Wahl, Manfred, Philadelphia, Pa. Culture or ferment for the production of cereal beverages. No. 110,794; Jan. 20; v. 270; p. 462.

Waldes & Co., Prague, Bohemia. Placket and glove fasteners, knitting-needles, hat-pins, buttons, &c. No. 121,559; Jan. 20; v. 270; p. 466.

Waldes & Co., Prague, Bohemia. Placket, glove, and snap fasteners, buttons, clasps. No. 121,063; Jan. 20; v. 270; p. 465.

Wallis Tractor Company, Racine, Wis. Tractors. No. 116,982; Jan. 20; v. 270; p. 462.

Ward Motor Vehicle Company, Mount Vernon, N. Y. Automobiles. No. 119,283; Jan. 20; v. 270; p. 464.

Weinberg, M. J., & Bro., New York, N. Y. Creamery-butter and eggs. No. 124,290; Jan. 20; v. 270; p. 469.

Wertheimer, N., & Sons, Ligonier, Ind. Field-seeds. No. 121,509; Jan. 20; v. 270; p. 466.

York Pretzel Bakery, York, Pa. Pretzels, cakes, crackers, and biscuits. No. 118,499; Jan. 20; v. 270; p. 463.

ALPHABETICAL LIST OF INVENTIONS

FOR WHICH

PATENTS WERE ISSUED ON THE 20TH DAY OF JANUARY, 1920.

Acid, Apparatus for making sulfuric. H. V. Welch. No. 1,328,552 ; Jan. 20 ; v. 270 ; p. 412.

Address-matcher. W. J. Maguire. No. 1,328,534 ; Jan. 20 ; v. 270 ; p. 409.

Aeroplane. J. L. Cochennet. No. 1,328,421 ; Jan. 20 ; v. 270 ; p. 387.

Agitating device. W. Lindsay. No. 1,328,576 ; Jan. 20 ; v. 270 ; p. 417.

Aircraft, Supply means for. G. L. Cabot. No. 1,328,560 ; Jan. 20 ; v. 270 ; p. 414.

Air-heater. C. E. Feazel. No. 1,328,272 ; Jan. 20 ; v. 270 ; p. 358.

Airship. Q. V. Distefano. No. 1,328,369 ; Jan. 20 ; v. 270 ; p. 377.

Alarm : See—
  Burglar-alarm.

Alligator-wrench. H. G. Norwood. No. 1,328,389 ; Jan. 20 ; v. 270 ; p. 381.

Aluminum, Solder for. J. Segura. No. 1,328,694 ; Jan. 20 ; v. 270 ; p. 438.

Alternating-current motor. W. C. Korthals-Altes. No. 1,328,525 ; Jan. 20 ; v. 270 ; p. 407.

Ammonium sulfate, Production of. W. A. Sloss. No. 1,328,342 ; Jan. 20 ; v. 270 ; p. 372.

Anesthesia, Instrument for producing intra-osseous. A. E. Smith. No. 1,328,459 ; Jan. 20 ; v. 270 ; p. 394.

Antiskid device. J. E. Rogers. No. 1,328,297 ; Jan. 20 ; v. 270 ; p. 363.

Antiskid device. J. E. Rogers. No. 1,328,298 ; Jan. 20 ; v. 270 ; p. 364.

Apple cutter and corer. S. A. Erdahl. No. 1,328,503 ; Jan. 20 ; v. 270 ; p. 403.

Atomizing materials in a melted state, Process of and apparatus for. E. Odam. No. 1,328,446 ; Jan. 20 ; v. 270 ; p. 391.

Auto-fuel-supply lock. J. R. Cassingham and W. W. Ayres. No. 1,328,616 ; Jan. 20 ; v. 270 ; p. 424.

Automobile-bumper. E. W. Kaiser. No. 1,328,283 ; Jan. 20 ; v. 270 ; p. 361.

Automobile-bumper. W. S. Booth. No. 1,328,786 ; Jan. 20 ; v. 270 ; p. 455.

Automobile device. G. H. Filkins. No. 1,328,654 ; Jan. 20 ; v. 270 ; p. 431.

Automobile-lock. W. H. Damon. No. 1,328,619 ; Jan. 20 ; v. 270 ; p. 424.

Automobile-signal. W. Skarnulis. No. 1,328,404 ; Jan. 20 ; v. 270 ; p. 384.

Automobile steering attachment. D. Macdonald. No. 1,328,681 ; Jan. 20 ; v. 270 ; p. 436.

Ball-crank connection. W. S. Smith. No. 1,328,600 ; Jan. 20 ; v. 270 ; p. 421.

Barrel, Collapsible. S. R. Port. No. 1,328,587 ; Jan. 20 ; v. 270 ; p. 419.

Batteries, Grid-plate for storage. P. B. Rabe. No. 1,328,392 ; Jan. 20 ; v. 270 ; p. 382.

Battery : See—
  Storage battery.

Battery connectors and posts, Method of and means for sealing storage-. F. W. Barhoff. No. 1,328,357 ; Jan. 20 ; v. 270 ; p. 375.

Battery covers in cells, Means for sealing storage-. F. W. Barhoff. No. 1,328,358 ; Jan. 20 ; v. 270 ; p. 375.

Battery covers. Method of and means for sealing terminal posts in storage-. F. W. Barhoff. No. 1,328,359 ; Jan. 20 ; v. 270 ; p. 375.

Bearing, Axle-. K. H. Hansen. No. 1,328,512 ; Jan. 20 ; v. 270 ; p. 405.

Bearing for disks, Steel. H. B. Bozard. No. 1,328,787 ; Jan. 20 ; v. 270 ; p. 455.

Bearing for gravity-carriers, Ball-. H. J. Buck. (Reissue.) No. 14,792 ; Jan. 20 ; v. 270 ; p. 458.

Bearing, Thrust-. L. Coatalen and H. C. M. Stevens. No. 1,328,716 ; Jan. 20 ; v. 270 ; p. 442.

Bed-cover holder. W. L. Dennison. No. 1,328,621 ; Jan. 20 ; v. 270 ; p. 425.

Bed-spring, Knockdown. G. A. C. Monroe. No. 1,328,751 ; Jan. 20 ; v. 270 ; p. 449.

Belt-fastener. G. Flury. No. 1,328,426 ; Jan. 20 ; v. 270 ; p. 388.

Belt-fastener-setting machine. J. K. Diamond. No. 1,328,424 ; Jan. 20 ; v. 270 ; p. 387.

Belt, Traction-. R. L. Arndt. No. 1,328,643 ; Jan. 20 ; v. 270 ; p. 429.

Bench. G. B. More. No. 1,328,753 ; Jan. 20 ; v. 270 ; p. 459.

Binding-terminal. R. B. Benjamin and E. G. K. Anderson. No. 1,328,784 ; Jan. 20 ; v. 270 ; p. 455.

Bleaching apparatus, Steam. R. Rea and F. W. Waters. No. 1,328,397 ; Jan. 20 ; v. 270 ; p. 382.

Block : See—
  Hoisting-block.

Block and lightning-arrester, Combination terminal. R. Connell. No. 1,328,720 ; Jan. 20 ; v. 270 ; p. 442.

Blower, Steam-turbine. W. McClave. No. 1,328,285 ; Jan. 20 ; v. 270 ; p. 361.

Blower, Steam-turbine. W. McClave. No. 1,328,286 ; Jan. 20 ; v. 270 ; p. 361.

Board : See—
  Bread-board.

Boiler : See—
  Hot-water boiler.   Locomotive-boiler.

Boilers, &c., Suspended arch for. W. E. Gehring. No. 1,328,511 ; Jan. 20 ; v. 270 ; p. 404.

Bolt : See—
  Staybolt.

Book-cover-making machine. J. Satenstein. No. 1,328,767 ; Jan. 20 ; v. 270 ; p. 452.

Borax from saline waters, Recovering. G. B. Burnham. No. 1,328,614 ; Jan. 20 ; v. 270 ; p. 424.

Bottle-closure. C. Hammer. No. 1,328,280 ; Jan. 20 ; v. 270 ; p. 360.

Bottle or jar closure device. H. Moore. No. 1,328,536 ; Jan. 20 ; v. 270 ; p. 409.

Bottle, Pulp. E. E. Claussen. No. 1,328,317 ; Jan. 20 ; v. 270 ; p. 368.

Box : See—
  Match-box.   Switch-box.
  Paper-board box.

Box. R. G. Inwood. No. 1,328,328 ; Jan. 20 ; v. 270 ; p. 370.

Box-cover fastener. C. L. Shelton. No. 1,328,302 ; Jan. 20 ; v. 270 ; p. 364.

Brace : See—
  Vehicle-body brace.

Bracket : See—
  Curtain-bracket.   Mirror-bracket.

Brake. F. M. Campbell. No. 1,328,491 ; Jan. 20 ; v. 270 ; p. 401.

Brake. H. C. Eichmeier. No. 1,328,502 ; Jan. 20 ; v. 270 ; p. 403.

Brake-hanger. T. L. Burton. No. 1,328,315 ; Jan. 20 ; v. 270 ; p. 367.

Brake-operating mechanism. J. A. Carney. No. 1,328,494 ; Jan. 20 ; v. 270 ; p. 401.

Brake-operating mechanism, Hand-. J. A. Carney. No. 1,328,493 ; Jan. 20 ; v. 270 ; p. 401.

Brass and similar scrap, Melting. W. B. Clark. No. 1,328,712 ; Jan. 20 ; v. 270 ; p. 441.

Brass and similar scrap, Method and means for melting. W. R. Clark. No. 1,328,714 ; Jan. 20 ; v. 270 ; p. 441.

Brassiere. R. C. Olson. No. 1,328,586 ; Jan. 20 ; v. 270 ; p. 419.

Brassiere. G. D. Leonard. No. 1,328,439 ; Jan. 20 ; v. 270 ; p. 390.

Bread-board. L. W. Serrell. No. 1,328,301 ; Jan. 20 ; v. 270 ; p. 364.

Broaching-machine. H. L. Hanson. No. 1,328,281 ; Jan. 20 ; v. 270 ; p. 360.

Bucket. L. and W. Schiek. No. 1,328,458 ; Jan. 20 ; v. 270 ; p. 394.

Bucket-closure. I. Hirsohn. No. 1,328,672 ; Jan. 20 ; v. 270 ; p. 434.

Buckle. F. Cocker. No. 1,328,617 ; Jan. 20 ; v. 270 ; p. 424.

Buckle, Bale-tie. J. T. A. Todd. No. 1,328,698 ; Jan. 20 ; v. 270 ; p. 439.

Burglar-alarm. E. E. Brown. No. 1,328,559 ; Jan. 20 ; v. 270 ; p. 413.

Burner : See—
  Oven-burner.

Button, Separable. H. Iversen. No. 1,328,432 ; Jan. 20 ; v. 270 ; p. 389.

Cabinet, Dispensing-. J. Fritsche. No. 1,328,664 ; Jan. 20 ; v. 270 ; p. 432.

Cable-clamp. H. W. Pleister. No. 1,328,543 ; Jan. 20 ; v. 270 ; p. 410.

Cable-clamp. W. J. Hiss. No. 1,328,376 ; Jan. 20 ; v. 270 ; p. 379.

Cable-clamp. W. J. Hiss. No. 1,328,377 ; Jan. 20 ; v. 270 ; p. 379.

Cable-pulling device. T. D. Lemieux. No. 1,328,678 ; Jan. 20 ; v. 270 ; p. 435.

Calipers. G. H. Johnston. No. 1,328,566 ; Jan. 20 ; v. 270 ; p. 415.

Calipers. R. Eames. No. 1,328,651 ; Jan. 20 ; v. 270 ; p. 430.

Whistle. F. Parizek. No. 1,328,639; Jan. 20; v. 270; p. 428.
Winding-machine for the manufacture of hollow insulating cylinders for electrotechnical purposes. E. Haefely. No. 1,328,792; Jan. 20; v. 270; p. 456.
Window-screen. J. F. McGeorge. No. 1,328,577; Jan. 20; v. 270; p. 417.
Window-seat, Adjustable and knockdown. E. Anderson. No. 1,328,706; Jan. 20; v. 270; p. 440.
Wire fastener, Fence-. W. P. Robertson. No. 1,328,693; Jan. 20; v. 270; p. 438.
Wire-stretcher. M. Severson. No. 1,328,599; Jan. 20; v. 270; p. 421.
Wood, Sapless composite. F. K. Fish, Jr. No. 1,328,656; Jan. 20; v. 270; p. 431.

Wood-splitting machine. H. M. Young. No. 1,328,471; Jan. 20; v. 270; p. 396.
Wood, Sterilized. F. K. Fish, Jr. No. 1,328,506; Jan. 20; v. 270; p. 404.
Wood, Treating and drying. F. K. Fish, Jr. No. 1,328,657; Jan. 20; v. 270; p. 431.
Wrench: See—
  Alligator-wrench.   Socket-wrench.
  Pipe-wrench.
Wringer: See—
  Laundry-wringer.
Wringer mechanism, Removable. G. More. No. 1,328,754; Jan. 20; v. 270; p. 456.
X-ray apparatus. W. D. Coolidge. No. 1,328,495; Jan. 20; v. 270; p. 402.

ALPHABETICAL LIST OF DESIGNS.

Edging. J. G. Chapman. Nos. 54,359–61; Jan. 20; v. 270; p. 459.

Emblem. Service. W. F. Stevens. No. 54,362; Jan. 20; v. 270; p. 459.

ALPHABETICAL LIST OF TRADE-MARKS.

Adhesives. The Northwestern Chemical Co. No. 129,035; Jan. 20; v. 270; p. 475.
Asphalt shingles, roofing papers and cements. White Star Refining Co. No. 129,101; Jan. 20; v. 270; p. 477.
Automobiles. Westcott Motor Car Company. No. 129,099; Jan. 20; v. 270; p. 476.
Automobiles and motor-trucks. Apperson Bros. Automobile Co. No. 128,922; Jan. 20; v. 270; p. 471.
Bacon, hams, lard, &c. William Davies Company. No. 128,966; Jan. 20; v. 270; p. 472.
Beverage, Malt. Pittsburgh Brewing Company. No. 129,049; Jan. 20; v. 270; p. 475.
Beverages, Non-alcoholic. Southern Beverage Company. No. 129,083; Jan. 20; v. 270; p. 476.
Bicycles. C. J. O'Riely. No. 129,041; Jan. 20; v. 270; p. 475.
Boots and shoes, Leather. E. E. Taylor Company. No. 129,091; Jan. 20; v. 270; p. 476.
Boots, shoes, overshoes, hosiery. Rosman & Laveson. No. 129,064; Jan. 20; v. 270; p. 475.
Bread, pies, ice-cream. P. F. Skinner. No. 129,079; Jan. 20; v. 270; p. 476.
Butter. W. L. Houlton. No. 129,003; Jan. 20; v. 270; p. 473.
Butter, milk, hams, &c. W. J. Lemp. No. 129,018; Jan. 20; v. 270; p. 474.
Calculating and adding machines. Monroe Calculating Machine Company. No. 129,029; Jan. 20; v. 270; p. 474.
Callous-removing preparations. Scotch-Tone Company. No. 129,068; Jan. 20; v. 270; p. 476.
Candies, chocolates, and caramels. C. Siegel. No. 129,065; Jan. 20; v. 270; p. 476.
Candy. Jacobs Candy Company. No. 128,953; Jan. 20; v. 270; p. 472.
Candy. Covering used to coat. H. O. Wilbur & Sons. No. 129,102; Jan. 20; v. 270; p. 477.
Canned beans. Marshall Canning Company. No. 129,025; Jan. 20; v. 270; p. 474.
Canned foods, catsup, &c. Walker-Matteson Co. No. 129,096; Jan. 20; v. 270; p. 476.
Canned fruit, coffees, &c. A. M. Malouf. No. 129,023; Jan. 20; v. 270; p. 474.
Canned fruits and vegetables, tea, &c. H. T. Lange Company. No. 129,015; Jan. 20; v. 270; p. 474.
Canned fruits and vegetables. Smith-Frank Packing Co. No. 129,080; Jan. 20; v. 270; p. 476.
Canned sardines. Lubec Sardine Company. No. 129,019; Jan. 20; v. 270; p. 474.
Canned vegetables. Grand River Canning Co. No. 128,987; Jan. 20; v. 270; p. 473.
Canned vegetables and fruits, jellies, &c. California Packing Corporation. No. 128,951; Jan. 20; v. 270; p. 472.
Catsup. Brooks Tomato Products Company. No. 128,946; Jan. 20; v. 270; p. 472.
Cement, Paste. Northwestern Chemical Co. No. 129,034; Jan. 20; v. 270; p. 474.
Chairs, Barbers'. Koken Barbers' Supply Company. No. 129,009; Jan. 20; v. 270; p. 474.
Chairs, &c., Camp, folding, and invalid. C. Glantz. No. 128,984; Jan. 20; v. 270; p. 473.
Chemical compound. L. W. Kramer. No. 129,011; Jan. 20; v. 270; p. 474.
Chemicals, medicines, &c. Kuhlman & Chambliss Co. No. 129,013; Jan. 20; v. 270; p. 474.
Cigarettes. The American Tobacco Company. No. 128,920; Jan. 20; v. 270; p. 471.
Cigarettes. Reed Tobacco Company. Nos. 129,057–8; Jan. 20; v. 270; p. 475.

Cigarettes and tobacco. The American Tobacco Co. No. 128,921; Jan. 20; v. 270; p. 471.
Cigars. E. Popper & Co. No. 129,051; Jan. 20; v. 270; p. 475.
Cigars H. H. Snovel. No. 129,082; Jan. 20; v. 270; p. 476.
Cigars, cigarettes, smoking-tobacco. R. & J. Hill. No. 129,000; Jan. 20; v. 270; p. 473.
Clamps, &c., used with metal-working machinery. H. Cadwallader, Jr. No. 128,950; Jan. 30; v. 270; p. 472.
Cleanser and polish. I. W. Cox. No. 128,961; Jan. 20; v. 270; p. 472.
Cleansing compounds. Jimmy Quick Products Co. No. 129,053; Jan. 20; v. 270; p. 475.
Clothing, Men's and boys'. Shirek & Hirsch. No. 129,071; Jan. 20; v. 270; p. 476.
Coffee. American Standard Food Assn. No. 128,919; Jan. 20; v. 270; p. 471.
Colors and coal-tar dyes, Anilin. John Campbell & Co. No. 128,952; Jan. 20; v. 270; p. 472.
Compound, Shortening. D. D. Metcalf. No. 129,027; Jan. 20; v. 270; p. 474.
Confectionery. The Borden Company. No. 128,933; Jan. 20; v. 270; p. 471.
Cookies. Iten Biscuit Co. No. 129,006; Jan. 20; v. 270; p. 474.
Cough-drops. Williams Chocolate Co. No. 129,104; Jan. 20; v. 270; p. 477.
Crockery, earthenware, porcelain. A/S. Herman A. Kähler. No. 129,007; Jan. 20; v. 270; p. 474.
Dental casting-machines, &c. Gardner Bros. No. 128,979; Jan. 20; v. 270; p. 473.
Disinfectant. J. W. Bullen. Nos. 128,947–8; Jan. 20; v. 270; p. 472.
Disinfectants. F. Sanford. No. 129,066; Jan. 20; v. 270; p. 475.
Dolls. H. O. Shults. No. 129,072; Jan. 20; v. 270; p. 476.
Dresses, coats, &c., Women's. Isidore Rabinowitz Apparel Co. No. 129,054; Jan. 20; v. 270; p. 475.
Drinks, Soft. John Graf Co. No. 128,986; Jan. 20; v. 270; p. 473.
Duck, Oiled. Armstrong Cork Company. No. 128,924; Jan. 20; v. 270; p. 471.
Egg-preserving preparation. D. D. Smith. No. 129,081; Jan. 20; v. 270; p. 476.
Electric-light fixtures, Metal connections for. F. D. Parmenter. No. 129,042; Jan. 20; v. 270; p. 475.
Engine-governor. Duplex Engine-Governor Company. No. 128,970; Jan. 20; v. 270; p. 472.
Feed, Poultry. Chas. A. Krause Milling Co. No. 129,012; Jan. 20; v. 270; p. 474.
Feeds, Stock and poultry. Simmons Milling Company. No. 129,078; Jan. 20; v. 270; p. 475.
Fertilizer materials. Nitrate Agencies Company. No. 129,037; Jan. 20; v. 270; p. 475.
Fish, game, &c., Sauce for. W. P. Bowman. No. 128,943; Jan. 20; v. 270; p. 472.
Flavoring extracts, roasted coffee. Food-. Steinwender-Stoffregen Coffee Company. No. 129,086; Jan. 20; v. 270; p. 476.
Flour, Wheat-. American Flour Corporation. No. 128,916; Jan. 20; v. 270; p. 471.
Flour, Wheat-. H. Dittlinger Roller Mills Company. No. 128,968; Jan. 20; v. 270; p. 472.
Flour, Wheat-. Holmes and Barnes. No. 129,002; Jan. 20; v. 270; p. 473.
Flour, Wheat-. M. J. Kouri. No. 129,010; Jan. 20; v. 270; p. 474.

Talking-machines, grafonolas, &c. Mandel Mfg. Company. No 129,024 ; Jan 20 ; v. 270 ; p. 474.
Talking-machines, violins, harps, &c. Gimbel Brothers, New York. No. 128,983 ; Jan. 20 ; v. 270 ; p. 473.
Thermometers, barometers, rain-gages. The Chaney Manufacturing Company. No. 128,956 ; Jan. 20 ; v. 270 ; p. 472.
Tires, Varnish for rubber. Sterling Varnish Company. No. 129,087 ; Jan. 20 ; v. 270 ; p. 476.
Trucks and parts thereof, Motor-. Atterbury Motor Car Company. No. 128,925 ; Jan. 20 ; v. 270 ; p. 471.
Trunks. D. E. Rose Trunk Company. No. 129,063 ; Jan. 20 ; v. 270 ; p. 475.

Tubing. Pressed Metal Radiator Company. No. 129,052 ; Jan. 20 ; v 270 ; p. 475.
Veils. N. B. Cohen. No 128,958 ; Jan. 20 ; v. 270 ; p. 472.
Wallets, bill-folds, and three-folds, Leather-. P. Florin. No. 128,976 ; Jan. 20 ; v. 270 ; p. 473.
Waterproof dressing for textiles, &c. Baker Overton Company. No. 128,928 ; Jan. 20 ; v. 270 ; p. 471.
Waterproof hand-bags and purses. T. Hucnikow. No. 129,005 ; Jan. 20 ; v. 270 ; p. 474
Wearing-apparel for ladies. Douglass Barnes Corporation. No. 128,969 ; Jan. 20 ; v. 270 ; p. 472.

ALPHABETICAL LIST OF TRADE-MARK TITLES.

(REGISTRATION APPLIED FOR.)

Aeroplanes. Victor Aircraft Corporation. No. 113,202 ; Jan. 20 ; v. 270 ; p. 462.
Automobile-cars and motor-trucks. Abbott Corporation. No. 102,607 ; Jan. 20 ; v. 270 ; p. 461.
Automobiles. Ward Motor Vehicle Company. No. 119,283 ; Jan. 20 ; v. 270 ; p. 464.
Automobiles and automobile-bodies. Noma Motor Corporation. No. 125,014 ; Jan. 20 ; v. 270 ; p. 470.
Automobiles and motor-trucks. José Cunill de Figuerola. No. 123,520 ; Jan. 20 ; v. 270 ; p. 468.
Beer, sarsaparilla, &c., Birch and root. Rainier Products Company. No. 120,070 ; Jan. 20 ; v. 270 ; p. 464.
Benzoates and benzyl alcohol, Ethyl, methyl, &c. Seydel Manufacturing Company. No. 119,871 ; Jan. 20 ; v. 270 ; p. 464.
Beverage, Non-alcoholic. O. Eberlin. No. 120,416 ; Jan. 20 ; v. 270 ; p. 465.
Beverages and syrups. Horlacher Brewing Co. 'No. 123,810 ; Jan. 20 ; v. 270 ; p. 469.
Beverages and syrups for making same, Non-alcoholic. Thornton Mineral Springs Company. No. 122,002 ; Jan. 20 ; v. 270 ; p. 466.
Beverages, Culture or ferment employed in the production of cereal. M. Wahl. No. 110,794 ; Jan. 20 ; v. 270 ; p. 462.
Beverages, Malt. Massachusetts Breweries Company. No. 124,487 ; Jan. 20 ; v. 270 ; p. 470.
Blankets, Cotton. Nashua Manufg. Company. No. 124,280 ; Jan. 20 ; v. 270 ; p. 469.
Blankets, Cotton. Nashua Manufg. Company. No. 124,282 ; Jan. 20 ; v. 270 ; p. 469.
Boots and shoes. Griggs-Paxton Shoe Co. No. 122,889 ; Jan. 20 ; v. 270 ; p. 467.
Butter. Scheer, Grandi & Co. No. 124,626 ; Jan. 20 ; v. 270 ; p. 470.
Butter and eggs. M. J. Weinberg & Bro. No. 124,290 ; Jan. 20 ; v. 270 ; p. 469.
Cards, Filing-. Record Card Co. No. 117,125 ; Jan. 20 ; v. 270 ; p. 463.
Cheese and butter. Marre & Company. No. 105,482 ; Jan. 20 ; v. 270 ; p. 461.
Clothes-lines. Kreining-Schlapp Grocer Company. No. 122,707 ; Jan. 20 ; v. 270 ; p. 467.
Concrete-mixers. G. C. Sheldon. No. 124,625 ; Jan. 20 ; v. 270 ; p. 470.
Confection. L. P. Larson, Jr. Company. No. 122,779 ; Jan. 20 ; v. 270 ; p. 467.
Cotton sewing-threads. Seamans & Cobb Co. No. 125,029 ; Jan. 20 ; v. 270 ; p. 470.
Dental dam, surgeons' gloves, &c. United States Rubber Company. No. 121,949 ; Jan. 20 ; v. 270 ; p. 466
Electromedical switchboard for electric-bath use. McIntosh Battery & Optical Co. No. 122,903 ; Jan. 20 ; v. 270 ; p. 467.
Explosive of the dynamite type, High. E. I. du Pont de Nemours & Company. No. 116,680 ; Jan. 20 ; v. 270 ; p. 462.
Fabrics, Textile. Lamborn & Co. No. 116,992 ; Jan. 20 ; v. 270 ; p. 463.
Feeds, Stock, &c. Barber & Bennett. No. 124,846 ; Jan. 20 ; v. 270 ; p. 470.
Food product. Moore Food Products Company. No. 122,994 ; Jan. 20 ; v. 270 ; p. 468.
Fruits, Citrus. Lake Wales Citrus Growers Association. No. 121,629 ; Jan. 20 ; v. 270 ; p. 466.
Games G. C. Dutton. No. 117,446 ; Jan. 20 ; v. 270 ; p. 463.
Garters. Hewes & Potter. No. 124,346 ; Jan. 20 ; v. 270 ; p. 469.
Hosiery. T. E. Brown. No. 123,871 ; Jan. 20 ; v. 270 ; p. 469.
Hosiery. John M. Given, Inc. No. 123,802 ; Jan. 20 ; v. 270 ; p. 468.
Hosiery. Kennesaw Hosiery Company. No. 120,997 ; Jan. 20 ; v. 270 ; p. 465.

Hosiery, Children's. John M. Given, Inc. No. 123,800 ; Jan. 20 ; v. 270 ; p. 468.
Leather and finished calfskins, Patent-. Barnet Leather Company. No. 117,966 ; Jan. 20 ; v. 270 ; p. 463.
Leather-board, Manufactured. Herkimer Fibre Company. No. 101,509 ; Jan. 20 ; v. 270 ; p. 461.
Leather, Finished. Chevaux Kid Leather Co. No. 124,260 ; Jan. 20 ; v. 270 ; p. 469.
Medicine for the diseased mucous membrane of the nose, throat, mouth, and ear. Otorino Manufacturing Company. No. 117,572 ; Jan. 20 ; v. 270 ; p. 463.
Mirrors and retinoscopes, Dental, &c. A. A. Anzell. No. 123,150 ; Jan. 20 ; v. 270 ; p. 468.
Mufflers, sweaters, boots, vests, &c., of knit fabric. E. B. Nathan. No. 106,883 ; Jan. 20 ; v. 270 ; p. 461.
Nainsooks, muslins, longcloth, cambrics. Carson, Pirie, Scott & Co. No. 114,528 ; Jan. 20 ; v. 270 ; p. 462.
Night-wear. Cooper, Coate & Casey Dry Goods Co. No. 123,964 ; Jan. 20 ; v. 270 ; p. 469.
Overalls. Carson, Pirie, Scott & Co. No. 100,004 ; Jan. 20 ; v. 270 ; p. 461.
Perfumery, toilet water, &c. Jennings Manufacturing Company. No. 118,559 ; Jan. 20 ; v. 270 ; p. 464.
Perfumes, incenses, &c. S. Fukuhara. No. 120,376 ; Jan. 20 ; v. 270 ; p. 465.
Pharmaceutical preparation. W. R. Fessler. No. 122,040 ; Jan. 20 ; v. 270 ; p. 468.
Placket and glove fasteners, needles, buttons, &c. Waldes & Co. No. 121,539 ; Jan. 20 ; v. 270 ; p. 466.
Placket, glove, and snap fasteners, buttons, clasps. Waldes & Co. No. 121,063 ; Jan. 20 ; v. 270 ; p. 465.
Plows and parts therefor. Lynchburg Foundry Company. No. 124,610 ; Jan. 20 ; v. 270 ; p. 470.
Potato chips. E. J. Phillips. No. 125,164 ; Jan. 20 ; v. 270 ; p. 470.
Powders, Tooth and foot. Lorenz Company. No. 108,835 ; Jan. 20 ; v. 270 ; p. 462.
Preparation for making a fruit acid and spice-flavored marmalade and jam. D. L. Levinson. No. 118,232 ; Jan. 20 ; v. 270 ; p. 463.
Pretzels, cakes, crackers, biscuits. York Pretzel Bakery. No 118,499 ; Jan. 20 ; v. 270 ; p. 463.
Pyrometers, Protecting-tubes for. Brown Instrument Company. No 120,474 ; Jan. 20 ; v. 270 ; p. 465.
Roofing, Prepared felt. Lamborn & Co No. 123,486 ; Jan. 20 ; v. 270 ; p. 468.
Roofings and shingles, Slate-surfaced. Asphalt Manufacturing Company. No. 119,693 ; Jan. 20 ; v. 270 ; p. 464.
Rope, cord, twine. American Manufacturing Company. No. 125 043 ; Jan. 20 ; v. 270 ; p. 470.
Ropes and twines Fiber. Hooven & Allison Company. No. 121,344 ; Jan. 20 ; v. 270 ; p. 466
Rubber heels and soles for shoes. Double Suction Rubber Heel & Sole Company. No 122,826 ; Jan. 20 ; v. 270 ; p. 467.
Seeds. Stanford Seed Co. No. 121,646 ; Jan. 20 ; v. 270 ; p. 466
Seeds, Field-. N. Wertheimer & Sons. No. 121,509 ; Jan. 20 ; v. 270 ; p. 466.
Shirts, underwear, &c., Men's and boys'. Hirsch, Friedman Co. No. 117 011 ; Jan. 20 ; v 270 ; p. 463
Shoe-soles. Rubber and fiber. Revere Rubber Company. No. 121,605 ; Jan. 20 ; v. 270 ; p. 466.
Shoes, Leather &c. Brauer Bros. Shoe Company. No. 121,930 ; Jan. 20 ; v. 270 ; p. 465.
Silk and cotton piece goods and combinations of same. Turner & Walls. No. 124,371 ; Jan. 20 ; v. 270 ; p. 469.
Silk piece goods. Empire Silk Company. No. 124,896 ; Jan. 20 ; v. 270 ; p. 469.
Sizing and finishing compounds for textile fabrics and threads. Seydel Manufacturing Company. No. 119,872 ; Jan. 20 ; v. 270 ; p. 464.
Snap dress-fasteners. Columbia Fastener Company. No. 122,424 ; Jan. 20 ; v. 270 ; p. 467.

Soles, boots, and shoes. Adwear Process Sole Leather Machine Company. No. 120,947; Jan. 20; v. 270; p. 465.

Syrup and beverage made from the same, Concentrated. Fruit Valley Corporation. No. 120,373; Jan. 20; v. 270; p. 465.

Topping for ice-cream sundaes and hot chocolate. Nebraska Fountain & Supply Co. No. 109,812; Jan. 20; v. 270; p. 462.

Toys, toy blocks, &c., Building. A. C. Gilbert Company. No. 119,974; Jan. 20; v. 270; p. 464.

Tractors. Southern Motor Manufacturing Association. No. 124,152; Jan. 20; v. 270; p. 469.

Tractors. Wallis Tractor Company. No. 116,982; Jan. 20; v. 270; p. 462.

Trousers. Samuel Rosenbaum & Sons Company. No. 122,367; Jan. 20; v. 270; p. 467.

Twine. American Twine Co. No. 122,873; Jan. 20; v. 270; p. 467.

Vegetables, Fresh. Ninavilla Farm Products Co. No. 106,744; Jan. 20; v. 270; p. 461.

CLASSIFICATION OF PATENTS

ISSUED JANUARY 20, 1920

NOTE.—First number=class, second number=subclass, third number=patent number.

Column 1

```
1—   50: 1,328,424
2—   73: 1,328,675
     94: 1,328,545
     98: 1,328,439
    149: 1,328,287
    173: 1,328,586
4—   18: 1,328,445
5—   64: 1,328,751
8—   19: 1,328,615
9—    3: 1,328,746
10— 123: 1,328,279
11—   2: 1,328,767
12—  88: 1,328,531
    142: 1,328,322
    145: 1,328,314
15—  14: 1,328,339
     17: 1,328,521
     58: 1,328,667
     60: 1,328,737
16—   7: 1,328,442
    106: 1,328,583
    164: 1,328,775
    160: 1,328,510
17—  10: 1,328,551
     11: 1,328,637
18—  42: 1,328,351
     45: 1,328,676
   48.3: 1,328,371
19—   6: 1,328,535
20—  19: 1,328,633
   81.6: 1,328,500
     85: 1,328,705
     87: 1,328,706
21— 148: 1,328,383
    150: 1,328,643
22—  19: 1,328,582
     48: 1,328,433
23—  13: 1,328,614
     21: 1,328,342
     22: 1,328,416
         1,328,417
         1,328,418
     24: 1,328,258
24—   3: 1,328,644
     13: 1,328,545
         1,328,546
     23: 1,328,898
     35: 1,328,426
     84: 1,328,621
    104: 1,328,432
    191: 1,328,617
    226: 1,328,628
    249: 1,328,602
    261: 1,328,504
25—  36: 1,328,599
    123: 1,328,367
29—  85: 1,328,853
   87.1: 1,328,776
   88.2: 1,328,362
     89: 1,328,264
    148: 1,328,276
    156: 1,328,509
  156.1: 1,328,414
         1,328,436
33—  23: 1,328,487
    147: 1,328,378
    148: 1,328,551
    153: 1,328,566
    166: 1,328,533
    215: 1,328,370
34—  24: 1,328,507
     39: 1,328,398
     49: 1,328,396
36—   1: 1,328,665
     35: 1,328,564
     50: 1,328,333
37—  14: 1,328,487
     58: 1,328,489
40—  70: 1,328,613
42—   4: 1,328,475
     74: 1,328,700
45—   6: 1,328,444
     28: 1,328,528
     31: 1,328,462
     32: 1,328,664
     51: 1,328,753
     71: 1,328,324
         1,328,625
     97: 1,328,677
46—  12: 1,328,332
```

Column 2

```
46—  40: 1,328,254
     54: 1,328,760
     63: 1,328,390
         1,328,711
48—   4: 1,328,553
    192: 1,328,485
49—   5: 1,328,273
     14: 1,328,790
     17: 1,328,268
   17.1: 1,328,673
     77: 1,328,530
51—   4: 1,328,337
         1,328,469
      5: 1,328,563
53—   5: 1,328,702
      8: 1,328,558
         1,328,652
     11: 1,328,304
54—  84: 1,328,312
55—  11: 1,328,363
     39: 1,328,537
    134: 1,328,697
56—  16: 1,328,791
     31: 1,328,385
     32: 1,328,386
    120: 1,328,668
    407: 1,328,795
    417: 1,328,674
    480: 1,328,781
60—  15: 1,328,685
     70: 1,328,497
     94: 1,328,593
64—  10: 1,328,451
         1,328,591
     26: 1,328,787
     36: R.14,792
     49: 1,328,716
     91: 1,328,449
     96: 1,328,366
     98: 1,328,688
65—  45: 1,328,568
     57: 1,328,447
66—  24: 1,328,580
67—   3: 1,328,788
68—  26: 1,328,766
     32: 1,328,361
70—  90: 1,328,619
    129: 1,328,691
72—  66: 1,328,555
73— 111: 1,328,572
74—   5: 1,328,350
      7: 1,328,440
         1,328,670
     13: 1,328,502
     14: 1,328,372
     16: 1,328,493
     17: 1,328,600
     34: 1,328,517
         1,328,588
     39: 1,328,761
     46: 1,328,253
         1,328,635
     58: 1,328,724
     59: 1,328,754
     81: 1,328,400
     86: 1,328,526
75—   1: 1,328,694
     14: 1,328,636
76—  46: 1,328,554
77—   1: 1,328,409
     28: 1,328,429
79—  16: 1,328,742
80—  5.1: 1,328,498
81—  15: 1,328,508
     65: 1,328,744
     92: 1,328,389
    121: 1,328,428
82—   8: 1,328,763
83—   9: 1,328,299
     26: 1,328,692
     73: 1,328,486
         1,328,768
     80: 1,328,778
     85: 1,328,456
     91: 1,328,446
84—  48: 1,328,718
    156: 1,328,796
    161: 1,328,260
85—  1.5: 1,328,532
87—   6: 1,328,278
88—   1: 1,328,292
         1,328,293
```

Column 3

```
88—      1,328,294
     16: 1,328,266
   16.4: 1,328,291
         1,328,352
     17: 1,328,741
   18.6: 1,328,382
   19.3: 1,328,759
     20: 1,328,669
     39: 1,328,441
     48: 1,328,356
89—  33: 1,328,800
90—  33: 1,328,281
91—  59: 1,328,407
     68: 1,328,541
93—  61: 1,328,472
     81: 1,328,792
94—   4: 1,328,310
95—  89: 1,328,305
97—  11: 1,328,740
     13: 1,328,518
     36: 1,328,756
     48: 1,328,638
     63: 1,328,800
     81: 1,328,710
98—  30: 1,328,647
99—   2: 1,328,395
     11: 1,328,556
     12: 1,328,506
         1,328,655
         1,328,656
         1,328,657
         1,328,658
         1,328,659
         1,328,660
         1,328,661
         1,328,662
    123: 1,328,505
100—  56: 1,328,728
101—  50: 1,328,534
     115: 1,328,368
     396: 1,328,725
102—  21: 1,328,307
      28: 1,328,334
103—  75: 1,328,274
          1,328,474
104— 109: 1,328,523
105— 180: 1,328,749
     190: 1,328,592
     224: 1,328,612
     406: 1,328,684
     414: 1,328,683
107—   8: 1,328,483
      15: 1,328,308
110—  28: 1,328,296
      44: 1,328,611
111—  38: 1,328,730
114—  24: 1,328,571
      51: 1,328,434
     195: 1,328,727
     240: 1,328,549
115—  17: 1,328,313
116—   1: 1,328,639
          1,328,772
      31: 1,328,387
          1,328,404
      42: 1,328,762
119—  84: 1,328,256
120—   1: 1,328,548
      18: 1,328,300
     128: 1,328,318
121—   1: 1,328,527
      41: 1,328,437
     108: 1,328,289
122—   2: 1,328,608
      65: 1,328,303
123—  11: 1,328,364
     473: 1,328,365
      32: 1,328,410
      43: 1,328,261
      44: 1,328,484
      76: 1,328,265
     117: 1,328,453
     145: 1,328,374
     169: 1,328,463
     191: 1,328,544
124—  15: 1,328,275
          1,328,344
126—  60: 1,328,743
```

Column 4

```
126— 173: 1,328,686
     272: 1,328,722
     292: 1,328,565
     359: 1,328,682
     360: 1,328,630
128—} 87: 1,328,598
     305: 1,328,459
     345: 1,328,624
129—  16: 1,328,604
      23: 1,328,561
130—  30: 1,328,295
131—  60: 1,328,733
          1,328,734
132—  19: 1,328,735
          1,328,422
          1,328,771
134—  51: 1,328,282
137—   9: 1,328,348
      35: 1,328,649
      53: 1,328,653
      71: 1,328,726
     139: 1,328,590
139—   7: 1,328,794
      85: 1,328,452
          1,328,585
      40: 1,328,570
140— 121: 1,328,423
141—   7: 1,328,380
144—  12: 1,328,492
     193: 1,328,471
     240: 1,328,430
146—   6: 1,328,503
      12: 1,328,301
151—  19: 1,328,401
      28: 1,328,399
          1,328,443
152—   6: 1,328,632
      12: 1,328,488
      14: 1,328,297
      16: 1,328,539
      21: 1,328,608
          1,328,731
      36: 1,328,779
     117: 1,328,757
154—  46: 1,328,623
      51: 1,32,567
156—  24: 1,328,579
      37: 1,328,317
158— 27.4: 1,328,329
      36: 1,328,354
      91: 1,328,419
     105: 1,328,589
164—  29: 1,328,347
      43: 1,328,671
      63: 1,328,431
      80: 1,328,547
166—   8: 1,328,438
      20: 1,328,569
168—  18: 1,328,708
171—  19: 1,328,473
     313: 1,328,797
          1,328,321
172— 120: 1,328,465
     179: 1,328,513
          1,328,514
          1,328,515
          1,328,631
     274: 1,328,519
          1,328,520
     276: 1,328,467
     280: 1,328,525
     288: 1,328,501
173— 259: 1,328,784
     321: 1,328,687
     359: 1,328,732
          1,328,783
     362: 1,328,581
175—  30: 1,328,720
     264: 1,328,403
     294: 1,328,457
     296: 1,328,516
     354: 1,328,597
176—  51: 1,328,311
177—   7: 1,328,454
      39: 1,328,260
178—  44: 1,328,326
179— 171: 1,328,327
     182: 1,328,620
180—  70: 1,328,346
181—  27: 1,328,412
```

Column 5

```
183— 103: 1,328,642
184—  38: 1,328,573
      55: 1,328,388
185—   5: 1,328,384
       9: 1,328,402
187—  31: 1,328,309
188—   3: 1,328,491
      49: 1,328,341
      57: 1,328,494
      70: 1,328,315
      82: 1,328,594
          1,328,595
          1,328,596
189—  15: 1,328,461
190—  36: 1,328,470
193—   2: 1,328,464
      10: 1,328,750
      46: 1,328,747
195—  13: 1,328,259
196—   3: 1,328,522
197—  6.2: 1,328,773
      14: 1,328,736
      33: 1,328,626
      77: 1,328,257
199—  20: 1,328,729
200—  43: 1,328,729
      50: 1,328,606
      67: 1,328,338
      80: 1,328,490
     109: 1,328,798
     116: 1,328,460
     122: 1,328,477
          1,328,478
          1,328,479
          1,328,480
          1,328,481
          1,328,482
125—       1,328,782
     140: 1,328,427
     154: 1,328,622
     150: 1,328,562
     166: 1,328,450
204—   6: 1,328,552
      15: 1,328,666
      29: 1,328,357
          1,328,358
          1,328,359
          1,328,393
          1,328,394
          1,328,420
      31: 1,328,575
      64: 1,328,336
          1,328,712
          1,328,714
206—  21: 1,328,703
207—  22: 1,328,748
208— 165: 1,328,343
          1,328,557
          1,328,719
210—   5: 1,328,262
211—  25: 1,328,542
212—   8: 1,328,793
213—  67: 1,328,335
215—  10: 1,328,455
      13: 1,328,280
      14: 1,328,328
      44: 1,328,587
      62: 1,328,302
217—  17: 1,328,701
      21: 1,328,769
218—  32: 1,328,466
      38: 1,328,546
      44: 1,328,723
219—  15: 1,328,758
      56: 1,328,672
220—  11: 1,328,704
      79: 1,328,567
221—  80: 1,328,768
224—  29: 1,328,316
229—   4: 1,328,317
      15: 1,328,524
230—   7: 1,328,255
      11: 1,328,285
          1,328,679
      13: 1,328,270
      27: 1,328,340
          1,328,529
```

Column 6

```
235—  50: 1,328,550
      92: 1,328,263
236—  18: 1,328,277
238—  26: 1,328,790
      38: 1,328,574
     298: 1,328,695
     304: 1,328,533
     319: 1,328,405
240—   7: 1,328,692
    48.6: 1,328,607
      81: 1,328,785
     108: 1,328,331
     163: 1,328,415
241—   8: 1,328,406
242—  74: 1,328,408
    84.1: 1,328,696
     128: 1,328,777
244—  12: 1,328,421
      21: 1,328,413
          1,328,425
      25: 1,328,369
246— 223: 1,328,381
248—   6: 1,328,448
      20: 1,328,271
      36: 1,328,376
          1,328,543
250—  19: 1,328,610
      34: 1,328,495
      38: 1,328,288
251—   6: 1,328,616
      43: 1,328,780
      48: 1,328,578
      56: 1,328,752
      77: 1,328,640
253—  35: 1,328,770
254—  72: 1,328,599
     110: 1,328,306
     123: 1,328,609
     177: 1,328,678
     188: 1,328,717
255—  50: 1,328,707
256—  56: 1,328,693
257— 130: 1,328,323
     151: 1,328,789
     167: 1,328,540
     241: 1,328,272
258—   1: 1,328,560
260—  72: 1,328,576
262—  20: 1,328,372
      30: 1,328,755
263—   5: 1,328,330
       9: 1,328,488
      46: 1,328,511
265—  12: 1,328,349
      56: 1,328,319
          1,328,320
266—  43: 1,328,380
267—   9: 1,328,641
      27: 1,328,601
      50: 1,328,496
268—   9: 1,328,584
      15: R.14,793
270—  61: 1,328,411
275—   1: 1,328,709
       5: 1,328,618
279—  71: 1,328,627
280—  13: 1,328,629
          1,328,715
    33.5: 1,328,654
      44: 1,328,458
      61: 1,328,458
      94: 1,328,681
284—  12: 1,328,373
285—  26: 1,328,290
     197: 1,328,386
286—   8: 1,328,286
      29: 1,328,325
     116: 1,328,612
291—  23: 1,328,739
292—   6: 1,328,355
      52: 1,328,284
      76: 1,328,345
293—  55: 1,328,283
          1,328,786
296— 108: 1,328,391
299—  36: 1,328,738
     117: 1,328,721
```

Patents Nos. 1,328,802 to 1,329,351.

THE
OFFICIAL GAZETTE

OF THE

𝔘𝔫𝔦𝔱𝔢𝔡 𝔖𝔱𝔞𝔱𝔢𝔰 𝔓𝔞𝔱𝔢𝔫𝔱 𝔒𝔣𝔣𝔦𝔠𝔢.

Vol. 270—No. 4.   TUESDAY, JANUARY 27, 1920.   Price—$5 per year.

The OFFICIAL GAZETTE is mailed under the direction of the Superintendent of Documents, Government Printing Office, to whom all subscriptions should be made payable and all communications respecting the Gazette should be addressed. Issued weekly. Subscriptions, $5.00 per annum; single numbers, 10 cents each.

Printed copies of patents are furnished by the Patent Office at 10 cents each. For the latter, address the Commissioner of Patents, Washington, D. C.

CONTENTS

Issue of January 27, 1920.

Every time you buy a W, S. S. you drive another rivet into your ship of prosperity.

Adverse Decisions in Interference.

PATENT No. 1,215,310.

On December 26, 1919, a decision was rendered that William G. McCrea was not the first inventor of the subject-matter covered by claims 1, 2, 3, 4, 5, 6, 7, and 9 of his Patent No. 1,215,310, subject, "Fruit-juice-dispensing device," and no appeal having been taken within the time allowed such decision has become final.

PATENT No. 1,226,792.

On December 26, 1919, a decision was rendered that Alfred Mennick was not the first inventor of the subject-matter covered by claims 1, 2, 4, 6, and 7 of his Patent No. 1,226,792, subject, "Train-control system," and no appeal having been taken within the time allowed such decision has become final.

PATENT No. 1,292,338.

On December 27, 1919, a decision was rendered that Abraham J. Lobar was not the first inventor of the subject-matter covered by claims 1, 4, 6, and 8 of his Patent No. 1,292,338, subject, "Button," and no appeal having been taken within the time allowed such decision has become final.

PATENT No. 1,307,345.

On December 22, 1919, a decision was rendered that Frank E. Button was not the first inventor of the subject-matter covered by claims 9 and 10 of his Patent No. 1,307,345, subject, "Vehicle-control system," and no appeal having been taken within the time allowed such decision has become final.

ADJUDICATED PATENTS.

(U. S. C. C. A. N. Y.) The Danquard patent, No. 776,601, for a manually or mechanically operated piano, *Held* valid and infringed. *Auto Pneumatic Action Co.* v. *Otto Higel Co.*, 260 Fed. Rep., 950.

(U. S. C. C. A. Mass.) The Tufford patent, No. 1,177,833, for a mold for making rubber heels, *Held* valid and infringed. *I. T. S. Rubber Co.* v. *Panther Rubber Mfg. Co.*, 260 Fed. Rep., 934.

(U. S. D. C. Pa.) The Paige patent, No. 1,260,022, for mechanism for making bifocal lenses, *Held* not infringed. *Paige* v. *Brown*, 260 Fed. Rep., 955.

(U. S. C. C. A. Ohio.) The invention of the Tufford reissue patent, No. 14,049, for a rubber shoe-heel, *Held* sufficiently disclosed by the original specification, the application for reissue *Held* timely, and the patent not anticipated and valid; also infringed. *Fetzer & Spies Leather Co.* v. *I. T. S. Rubber Co.*, 260 Fed. Rep., 930.

(U. S. C. C. A. Ohio.) The Tufford reissue patent, No. 14,049, for a rubber shoe-heel, as to the new claims incorporated in the reissue, *Held* infringed on the showing made for a preliminary injunction, with the exception of claim 10. *U. S. Rubber Co.* v. *I. T. S. Rubber Co.*, 260 Fed. Rep., 947.

Correction of Drawings.

RULE 72. • • • • •

The drawing may be withdrawn only for such corrections as cannot be made by the Office; but a drawing cannot be withdrawn unless a photographic copy has been filed and accepted by the Examiner as a part of the application. Permissible changes in the construction shown in any drawing may be made only by the Office and after an approved photographic copy has been filed. Substitute drawings will not be admitted in any case unless required by the Office.

Cross-References in Cases Relating to Same Subject.

RULE 43. When an applicant files two or more applications relating to the same subject-matter of invention, all showing but only one claiming the same thing, the applications not claiming it must contain references to the application claiming it.

APPLICATIONS UNDER EXAMINATION.

Condition at Close of Business January 23, 1920.

Room No.	Divisions and subjects of invention.	Oldest new application and oldest action by applicant awaiting office action.		No. of applications awaiting action.
		New.	Amended.	
314	1. Closure Operators; Fences; Gates; Harrows and Diggers; Plows; Planting; Scattering Unloaders; Trees, Plants, and Flowers.	Nov. 4	Sept. 13	389
128	2. Bee Culture; Curtains, Shades, and Screens; Dairy; Medicines; Pneumatics; Preserving; Presses; Tents, Canopies, Umbrellas, and Canes; Tobacco.	July 7	July 26	950
175	3. Electric Heating and Rheostats; Electrochemistry; Heating; Metal-Founding; Metallurgical Apparatus; Metallurgy; Metal Treatment; Plastic Metal Working.	Sept. 3	Sept. 3	335
234	4. Conveyers; Elevators; Excavating; Handling—Hand and Hoist-Line Implements; Hoisting; Material or Article Handling; Pneumatic Despatch; Pushing and Pulling Implements; Railway Mail Delivery; Store-Service; Traversing Hoists.	June 24	Nov. 19	733
167	5. Book-Making; Books, Strips and Leaves; Harvesters; Jewelry; Manifolding; Music; Printed Matter; Tying Cords or Strands.	Aug. 19	Nov. 3	232
318	6. Bleaching and Dyeing; Chemicals; Explosives; Fertilizers; Liquid Coating Compositions; Plastic Compositions; Substance Preparation.	Sept. 16	Nov. 14	472
312	7. Games and Toys; Optics; Photography; Velocipedes	Oct. 22	Nov. 12	598
131	8. Beds; Chairs and Seats; Flexible-Sheet Securing Devices; Furniture; Kitchen and Table Articles; Store Furniture; Supports.	Oct. 13	Oct. 17	378
221	9. Air and Gas Pumps; Hydraulic Motors; Injectors and Ejectors; Motors, Fluid; Motors, Fluid-Current; Pumps.	Sept. 8	Nov. 12	260
235	10. Carriages and Wagons; Land-Vehicles; Land-Vehicles—Bodies and Tops; Land-Vehicles—Dumping; Motor Vehicles.	Aug. 4	Oct. 6	958
154	11. Boot and Shoe Making; Boots, Shoes, and Leggings; Button, Eyelet, and Rivet Setting; Harness; Leather Manufactures; Nailing and Stapling; Spring Devices; Whips and Whip Apparatus.	July 30	Nov. 12	461
222	12. Machine Elements	June 14	Oct. 6	1,045
329	13. Bolt, Nail, Nut, Rivet, and Screw Making; Button Making; Chain, Staple, and Horseshoe Making; Driven, Headed, and Screw-Threaded Fastenings; Gear Cutting, Milling, and Planing; Metal Drawing; Metal Forging and Welding; Metal Rolling; Metal Tools and Implements, Making; Metal Working; Needle and Pin Making; Turning.	June 26	Oct. 20	971
323	14. Compound Tools; Cutting and Punching Sheets and Bars; Farriery; Metal-Bending; Sheet-Metal Ware, Making; Tools; Wire Fabrics and Structure; Wire-Working.	July 2	Oct. 24	443
308	15. Bread, Pastry, and Confection Making; Coating; Fuel; Glass; Laminated Fabrics and Analogous Manufactures; Paper-Making and Fiber Liberation; Plastic Block and Earthenware Apparatus; Plastics.	July 5	Oct. 22	911
111	16. Radiant Energy; Telegraphy; Telephony	July 11	July 23	566
307	17. Label Pasting and Paper Hanging; Nut and Bolt Locks; Ornamentation; Paper Manufactures; Printing; Type Casting; Sheet Material Associating or Folding; Sheet Feeding or Delivering; Type Setting.	Sept. 25	Nov. 14	237
229	18. Fluid-Pressure Regulators; Liquid Heaters and Vaporizers; Motors, Expansible Chamber Type; Power Plants; Speed Responsive Devices; Steam and Vacuum Pumps.	Aug. 4	Oct. 29	682
236	19. Automatic Temperature and Humidity Regulation; Furnaces; Heating Systems; Stoves and Furnaces; Domestic Cooking Vessels; Thermostats and Humidostats.	July 5	Aug. 1	561
179	20. Artificial Body Members; Builders' Hardware; Closure-Fasteners; Cutlery; Dentistry; Locks and Latches; Safes; Undertaking.	Oct. 27	Sept. 23	663
212	21. Brakes and Gins; Carding; Cloth-Finishing; Continuous-Strip Feeding; Cordage; Felt and Fur; Knitting and Netting; Silk; Spinning; Weaving; Winding and Reeling.	Aug. 2	Oct. 13	344
249	22. Aeronautics; Firearms; Ordnance	Sept. 24	Nov. 20	284
217	23. Acoustics; Coin-Handling; Horology; Recorders; Registers; Sound Recording and Reproducing; Time-Controlling Mechanism.	Aug. 9	Oct. 22	590
144	24. Apparel; Apparel Apparatus; Garment Supporters; Sewing-Machines	June 14	Nov. 13	621
315	25. Agitating; Butchering; Centrifugal Bowl Separators; Mills; Threshing; Vegetable Cutters and Crushers; Gas Separation.	Dec. 4	Dec. 3	205
105	26. Electricity, Generation; Motive Power; Prime Mover Dynamo Plants	May 5	Aug. 14	752
214	27. Brushing and Scrubbing; Grinding and Polishing; Laundry; Washing Apparatus	Sept. 26	Sept. 26	496
225	28. Internal-Combustion Engines	Sept. 12	Oct. 21	586
147	29. Boring and Drilling; Chucks or Sockets; Coopering; Rod Joints or Couplings; Wheelwright-Machines; Wood-Sawing; Wood-Turning; Woodworking; Woodworking Tools.	May 7	Aug. 1	597
152	30. Illuminating-Burners; Illumination; Liquid and Gaseous Fuel Burners; Type-Writing Machines	July 9	Oct. 13	874
172	31. Alcohol; Ammonia, Water, and Wood Distillation; Charcoal and Coke; Gas, Heating and Illuminating; Hides, Skins, and Leather; Hydraulic Cement and Lime; Mineral Oils; Oils, Fats, and Glue; Sugar and Salt.	July 8	July 19	853
278	32. Gas and Liquid Contact Apparatus; Heat Exchange; Refrigeration	June 16	Nov. 4	942
70	33. Bridges; Hydraulic and Earth Engineering; Masonry and Concrete Structures; Metallic Building Structures; Roads and Pavements; Roofs.	Aug. 18	Oct. 29	358
304	34. Railways; Railway Rolling Stock; Railway Switches and Signals; Railways, Surface Track; Railway Wheels and Axles; Track-Sanders; Vehicle-Fenders.	Nov. 20	Nov. 15	201
57	35. Buckles, Buttons, Clasps, Etc.; Card, Picture, and Sign Exhibiting; Signals and Indicators; Toilet	Nov. 26	Dec. 8	403
204	36. Automatic Weighers; Driers; Geometrical Instruments; Measuring Instruments; Force Measuring	Sept. 29	Oct. 16	912
107	37. Electric Lamps; Electricity, Circuit Makers and Breakers; Electricity, General Applications	July 15	July 19	1,025
378	38. Animal Husbandry; Earth Boring; Fishing and Trapping; Mining, Quarrying, and Ice-Harvesting; Stationery; Stone-Working; Wells.	Nov. 12	Nov. 18	334
220	39. Fluid Sprinkling, Spraying, and Diffusing; Joint Packings; Multiple Valves; Packed Shaft or Rod Joints; Pipe Joints or Couplings; Valved Pipe Joints or Couplings; Valves; Water Distribution.	Apr. 8	July 1	933
273	40. Baggage; Bottles and Jars; Check-Controlled Apparatus; Cloth, Leather, and Rubber Receptacles; Deposit and Collection Receptacles; Metallic Receptacles; Package and Article Carriers; Paper Receptacles; Special Receptacles and Packages; Wooden Receptacles.	July 7	Oct. 25	553
125	41. Resilient Tires and Wheels	July 22	Oct. 30	775
114	42. Electricity, Conductors; Electricity-Transmission to Vehicles; Electricity, Conduits; Electric Signaling.	July 16	Aug. 14	742
382	43. Baths and Closets; Dispensing; Dispensing Beverages; Electricity, Medical and Surgical; Fire-Extinguishers; Sewerage; Surgery; Water Purification.	Sept. 6	Nov. 17	433
253	44. Air-Guns, Catapults, and Targets; Ammunition and Explosive Devices; Ammunition and Explosive Charge Making; Boats and Buoys; Filling and Closing Portable Receptacles; Marine Propulsion; Railway Draft Appliances; Ships.	July 9	Nov. 1	333
379	45. Clutches; Journal-Boxes, Pulleys, and Shafting; Lubrication; Motors	Aug. 25	Oct. 25	759
332	46. Educational Appliances; Fire-Escapes; Ladders; Paper Files and Binders; Railway-Brakes; Wooden Buildings.	June 16	Nov. 11	516

Oldest new case, Apr. 8; oldest amended, July 1.

Total number of applications awaiting action.. 27,556

163	TRADE-MARKS, DESIGNS, LABELS AND PRINTS:			
	Trade-Marks	Oct. 4	Dec. 8	2,435
	Designs	Sept. 3	Oct. 18	1,190
	Labels and Prints	Nov. 17	Dec. 2	484

PATENTS

1,328,802. TILTING BED. GIDEON ANDERSON, New York, N. Y., assignor to William West, New York, N. Y. Filed Dec. 13, 1917. Serial No. 206,899. 4 Claims. (Cl. 5—12.)

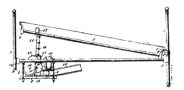

1. The combination with a pivoted bed spring frame, of means including a motor, for raising and lowering the same about its pivot, circuit breaking switches interpolated in the motor circuits, means advanced by the motor for selectively engaging said switches, and means for varying the positions of said switches with relation to the last mentioned means, whereby the period of energization of the motor may be varied.

1,328,803. PROCESS FOR MAKING BASIC STEEL IN OPEN-HEARTH STEEL-FURNACES. CHARLES HENRY FROST BAGLEY, Stockton-upon-Tees, England. Filed Sept. 19, 1918. Serial No. 254,750. 3 Claims. (Cl. 266—37.)

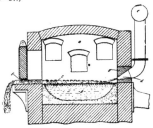

1. An improved process of manufacturing basic steel in fixed open hearth furnaces characterized in that the surface of metal is maintained somewhat below the lower edge of the slag holes, the slag is removed from time to time through a plurality of slag holes by means of a series of blasts of fluid acting only on a relatively small area of the surface of the metal and issuing from a plurality of twyers inclined at a suitable angle to the horizontal, and clear from close contact with the molten metal, after which further additions of lime and oxide are made which then act with great vigor and rapidity on the remaining impurities in the metal.

1,328,804. ATTACHMENT FOR ELECTRIC CONTROLLERS. ARVID R. ANDERSON, Columbus, Ohio, assignor to The Automatic Reclosing-Circuit Breaker Company, Columbus, Ohio, a Corporation of Ohio. Filed Jan. 20, 1917. Serial No. 143,492. 16 Claims. (Cl. 172—179.)

1. In combination with a controller for an electric circuit, means for opening the circuit at a remote point upon reverse movement of the controller handle in any position or upon failure of voltage, and means for closing

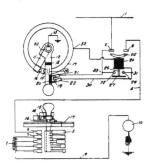

said circuit at such remote point, said last means being only operative when the controller is in "off" position.

1,328,805. DUMPING-BODY FOR AUTOMOBILE-TRUCKS, WAGONS, FREIGHT-CARS, AND OTHER VEHICLES. FRANK ANDERSON, Denver, and ALFRED WILD, Loveland, Colo. Filed Apr. 30, 1919. Serial No. 293,693. 7 Claims. (Cl. 298—13.)

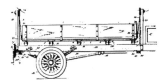

1. The combination with a chassis having channeled tracks thereon, of a body, having rollers which rest in said tracks, means for limiting the rolling movement of said body on said tracks, and means including gear operated drums for raising either side of said body into a dumping position, said means including flexible members wound upon said drums and arranged to be removably connected to the opposite corner portions of the opposite ends of said dumping body to be alternately changed from one corner to the opposite corner of the opposite ends of said dumping body; and means including a pawl and ratchet mechanism for locking said dumping body to said chassis; and a ring on said body to which said flexible connection, may be attached whereby the body may be drawn to its normal position on the chassis, and held against lateral movement.

1,328,806. CRUSHING-MACHINE. PETER C. ANDERSEN. Medford, Wis. Filed Apr. 12, 1919. Serial No. 289,684. 6 Claims. (Cl. 83—58.)

6. A crushing machine comprising a frame, a normally stationary crusher jaw mounted therein, a movable crusher jaw mounted therein and coöperating with said stationary jaw, said movable crusher jaw including a

plurality of superimposed oscillatory members, means swingingly supporting the outer ends of said members in the frame including link members having their ends pivotally connected to the frame and said oscillatory

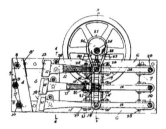

members, and means connected with the inner ends of said oscillatory members for supporting the same and imparting a reciprocal motion thereto to move said movable jaw toward and away from the stationary jaw.

1,328,807. SHIRT-BOSOM-IRONING MACHINE. FRITZ BALZER, Chicago, Ill., assignor to Troy Laundry Machinery Company, Ltd., Chicago, Ill., a Corporation of New York. Filed Sept. 9, 1916. Serial No. 119,198. 4 Claims. (Cl. 68—9.)

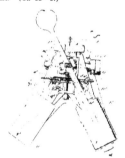

1. In a pressing machine, the combination with a plurality of stationary pressing members on which the articles to be pressed are placed, of a coöperating single ironing platen, a weighted arm pivoted intermediate its ends carrying said platen at one end thereof, said arm arranged to be swung horizontally and vertically whereby the platent may have successive coöperative engagement with said pressing members, said weighted arm tending normally to raise said platen from pressing engagement, and power actuated means effective for the several positions into which the army may be swung to aline with any one of the several presser members for moving said platen into pressing engagement with said pressing member.

1,328,808. STEERING MECHANISM FOR TRACTORS. JOHN B. BARTHOLOMEW, Peoria, Ill., assignor to Avery Company, Peoria, Ill., a Corporation of Illinois. Filed May 4, 1917. Serial No. 166,370. 4 Claims. (Cl. 97—81.)

1. The combination of the frame having the centrally positioned forwardly projecting element, the front dirigible truck wheels, the vertically tilting axle beam carrying said wheels and pivoted to the front end of the said frame element, the centrally arranged bearing support secured to the front end of said frame element and ex-

tended upward to horizontal planes remote therefrom, the centrally arranged power transmitting devices connected to the truck wheels for steering them, the steering

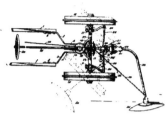

disk, the disk supporting arm pivoted to the said centrally arranged steering devices, and the centrally arranged means for lifting the steering disk.

1,328,809. DISCHARGING MECHANISM. ALBERT J. BATES, Chicago, Ill., assignor to Bates Expanded Steel Truss Co., Wilmington, Del., a Corporation of Delaware. Filed Jan. 10, 1916. Serial No. 71,220. 15 Claims. (Cl. 214—91.)

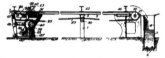

1. In an apparatus of the character described, the combination of a conveyer, means for advancing said conveyer, a plurality of separate alined shelves normally disposed above the plane of said conveyer and adapted to coöperatively support on elongated structural member, said shelves being mounted for bodily movement forward and then downward to deposit the member upon the conveyer, and means controllable at will to simultaneously move all of said shelves from their normal position to a position below the plane of said conveyer.

1,328,810. PIG-BROODER. ALBERT W. BEAMAN, Pittsboro, Ind. Filed Sept. 18, 1917. Serial No. 191,921. 5 Claims. (Cl. 119—16.)

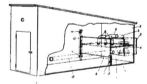

1. A pig brooder comprising a main chamber, an exterior adjacent heater, a brooding chamber within the main chamber and on a level with the same formed of a horizontal member, and a vertically adjustable guard having an opening along the floor level, and means for heating the brooding chamber to a higher degree than the main chamber.

1,328,811. MECHANISM FOR SYNCHRONIZING MACHINE-GUN FIRE. MARC BIRKIGT, Bois-Colombes, France. Filed May 31, 1917. Serial No. 172,097. 5 Claims. (Cl. 89—40.)

1. Mechanism for synchronizing the firing of machine guns relatively to the blades of a propeller of an aero-

plane revolving in front of the machine gun muzzle, embodying an operating motor, and a single rod mounted to freely oscillate about its axis and provided at one end

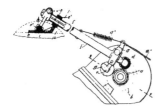

thereof with an operating arm to actuate the firing mechanism of the machine gun and at the other end with a lever disposed for actuation by the motor.

1,328,812. SHOCK-ABSORBER. JOHN R. BLAKE, Rolling Prairie, Ind. Filed Oct. 24, 1919. Serial No. 332,876. 4 Claims. (Cl. 267—27.)

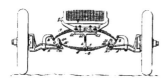

2. In a shock absorber of the character stated, the combination with the axle, the body and the main upwardly arched suspension spring pivotally connected at its ends to the axle and to whose arched portion the vehicle body is fixedly secured; of an auxiliary spring, means for sustaining the said auxiliary spring with its arched portion extended downwardly relatively to the axle and in advance of the said axle, the said means including shackle connections that connect with the opposite ends of the auxiliary spring, and a rigid connection that joins the centers of the upwardly and downwardly arched portions of the main and auxiliary springs, respectively.

1,328,813. HONEYCOMB - FOUNDATION MACHINE. HERBERT C. BLANCHARD, Medina, Ohio, assignor to The A. I. Root Company, Medina, Ohio, a Corporation. Filed Apr. 26, 1919. Serial No. 292,940. 2 Claims. (Cl. 6—11.)

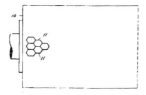

1. A foundation machine roll having hexagonal form dies, whose dimensions in the direction of revolution of the roll are less than those of a true hexagon of the same width on a line parallel with the roll axis.

1,328,814. LABEL-DETACHING DEVICE. CHARLES A. BOBST, Brooklyn, N. Y., assignor to National Binding Machine Company, New York, N. Y., a Corporation of New York. Filed Feb. 5, 1915, Serial No. 6,225. Renewed June 17, 1919. Serial No. 304,915. 3 Claims. (91—14.5.)

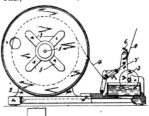

3. A label serving machine including in combination a support for a strip of tape, moistening means, and strip intercepting means comprising a member having a plurality of angularly disposed surfaces in cylindrical arrangement positioned to intercept the strip transversely, whereby individual labels may be separated from the strip along any transverse line of said angularly disposed surfaces.

1,328,815. COOLING-SYSTEM CONTROL. BLUFORD W. BROCKETT, Cleveland, Ohio. Filed Mar. 8, 1917. Serial No. 153,449. 6 Claims. (Cl. 123—174.)

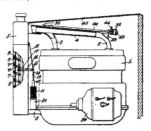

1. The combination of an internal combustion motor, a cooling system therefor including a radiator, means for interrupting the flow of air to said radiator, a source of electrical energy connected to a circuit when the motor is running, motor means under the control of said circuit for operating said interrupting means, and a device responsive to heat conditions of the motor for controlling said circuit.

1,328,816. SHOCK-ABSORBING HEEL. WILLIAM W. BROWN, Arkansas City, Ark. Filed Apr. 30, 1919. Serial No. 293,844. 2 Claims. (Cl. 36—38.)

1. A device of the class described, comprising a heel portion, an auxiliary section secured to said heel por-

tion, an inner casing provided with a horizontal flange, said flange secured between the auxiliary section and the heel portion against the heel portion, said auxiliary section being spaced at its outer edges from the inner casing, said auxiliary section being provided at its rear with a curved face contiguous to the inner face of the rear portion of the inner casing, a primary casing having its inner edge positioned within the inner casing, means movably securing the primary casing upon the inner section, and springs interposed between the auxiliary section and the primary casing, said inner edge of the primary casing being adapted to ride over the curved face at the rear of the auxiliary section and moved into engagement with the inner face of the rear portion of the inner casing, crowding the inner face of the primary casing against the front edge of the auxiliary section, whereby an auxiliary shock-absorbing action is accomplished in addition to the shock-absorbing action of said springs.

1,328,817. MOLD FOR ASBESTOS FLANGES. JOHN BUDINICH, Union Hill, N. J. Filed June 10, 1919. Serial No. 303,070. 2 Claims. (Cl. 25—118.)

2. A mold for asbestos flanges formed from a single band of metal bent into circular form and having its ends turned outward, a flange plate secured between the out-turned ends and the projecting into a ring formed by the band, a second flange plate secured to the inner face of the band opposite the outwardly turned ends thereof, said flange plates formed in their inner edges with notches.

1,328,818. PRACTICE-KEYBOARD. WALTER A. BUTLER, Troy, and ARTHUR V. COOPER, Amboy, N. Y. Filed May 8, 1919. Serial No. 295,650. 7 Claims. (Cl. 85—12.)

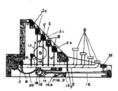

7. In a practice keyboard and in combination, a bank of keys; a correspondingly arranged bank of characters expressing values for the respective keys; a movable indicator for each of said characters; means for moving the several indicators by operation of the respective keys; and a stationary pointer for the respective characters normally covered and concealed by the corresponding indicator and exposed to view by the key-induced movement of said indicator.

1,328,819. MACHINE FOR SEPARATING WILD PEAS FROM WHEAT, &c. CLARENCE W. CARTER, Minneapolis, Minn. Filed Apr. 30, 1917. Serial No. 165,427. 11 Claims. (Cl. 130—18.)

4. A machine for separating wild peas from wheat, comprising a series of pans arranged in independent

groups, the pans of one group being mounted to receive the mixture of wheat and peas from the pans of the other group, the peas rolling down the surfaces of the pans for

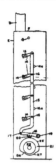

discharge therefrom while the wheat remains on the pans temporarily, and means for simultaneously tilting the pans of a group alternately with respect to the pans of the other group.

1,328,820. AIR-CIRCULATING SYSTEM FOR CARS. DANIEL CLARK, Edmonton, Alberta, Canada. Filed Mar. 29, 1918. Serial No. 225,498. 2 Claims. (Cl. 237—32.)

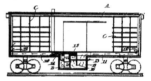

1. A car having a heating chamber, air conduits extending along the bottom of the car to opposite ends thereof, and serving for the passage of air to and from the heating chamber, said conduits being provided with suitable discharge ports at the end of the car, and racks on the interior walls of the car, forming air circulating spaces.

1,328,821. PANTOGRAPH EQUIPMENT FOR GROUPED EMBROIDERING-MACHINES. HERBERT CORRALL, Parkview, Helensburgh, Scotland, assignor to The Singer Manufacturing Company, a Corporation of New Jersey. Filed Feb. 14, 1917. Serial No. 148,504. 3 Claims. (Cl. 112—7.)

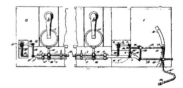

1. In a pantograph equipment for grouped embroidery machines, in combination, a laterally movable work-sustaining structure, a plurality of work-holders carried thereby, a plurality of rockers, a link connection between said rockers, independent link connections between said

structure and said rockers, and a parallelogram directly connected with and adapted to impart operative work-shifting movements to said structure by means of its direct connection and its indirect connections through said rockers with the structure, said parallelogram having means affording the sole adjustment for varying the amplitude of work-shifting movements in all directions derived from controlling movements of said parallelogram.

2. In a pantograph equipment for grouped embroidery machines, in combination, a work-sustaining structure, work-clamps carried thereby, means for supporting said structure for horizontal movement, rockers sustained independently of said structure, links connecting the rockers each with said structure independently of said supporting means, a link connecting together said rockers, and a parallelogram having a single connection with said structure independent of the connections of the structure with said rockers and provided with adjusting means for producing variations in the amplitude of movement effective through said connection with the structure.

3. In a pantograph equipment for grouped embroidery machines, in combination, a work-sustaining structure supported for horizontal movement, work-holders carried thereby, and a single horizontally disposed parallelogram connected with and adapted to impart to said structure work-shifting movements in all directions, said parallelogram comprising means affording the sole adjustment for varying the amplitude of movement of the structure under control of the parallelogram.

1,328,822. ADDING AND RECORDING MACHINE. JAMES L. DALTON and JOHN MAGNUS, Poplar Bluff, Mo., assignors to Dalton Adding Machine Company, St. Louis, Mo., a Corporation of Missouri. Filed May 15, 1909. Serial No. 496,285. 33 Claims. (Cl. 235—60.)

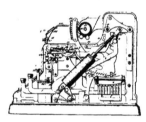

1. In an adding and recording machine, the combination of series of printing type, a normally retracted hammer for coöperating with the type of each series to print, means for releasing said hammers for printing operations, a selectively settable abutment for engaging and preventing varying numbers of said hammers from operating after they have been released, and a settable device for stopping movement of said abutment in any one of various selected positions.

1,328,823. HATBAND. JULES HENRI DE SIBOUR, Washington, D. C. Filed May 24, 1919. Serial No. 299,451. 2 Claims. (Cl. 2—109.)

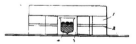

1. In a device of the class described, the combination of a band portion of suitable coloring to denote the branch of service, a suitable number of designating stripes thereon of appropriate color to indicate the period and place of service, and a bow provided with suitable service indicia.

1,328,824. VIOLIN-PEG. HARRY DORRELL, Peoria, Ill. Filed Apr. 14, 1919. Serial No. 289,958. 2 Claims. (Cl. 84—78.)

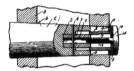

1. In combination, a violin head having a peg box having key ways therein, a tapered key supported in controlled frictional impingement of the key ways in the head, its outer end spaced from the outer wall of the peg box, a bearing member centered about the outlet of the keyway of the outside wall of the peg box, an extension member spaced from the end of the main body of the key and connected therewith and relatively adjustable to permit variable spacing, and adjusting means for effecting such relative spacing, whereby relative lengthwise spacing of the key and key extension may be had.

1,328,825. ALTERNATING-CURRENT RELAY. CHARLES VICKERY DRYSDALE, Dumbartonshire, Scotland. Filed Aug. 25, 1919. Serial No. 319,583. 12 Claims. (Cl. 200—91.)

1. In an alternating current relay working on the principle of tuning or resonance, the combination of a magnet, an oscillating contact-making needle disposed between the poles of said magnet, a coil surrounding said needle through which coil the alternating current passes, and means for varying the strength of the magnetic field in which the needle oscillates, for the purpose of tuning.

1,328,826. BABY-WALKER. JOHN A. EBERLE, St. Louis, Mo. Filed June 27, 1918. Serial No. 242,252. 1 Claim. (Cl. 155—45.)

A foldable baby walker comprising a base, a seat frame above said base, jointless seat supports pivoted to said base and having unrestrained pivotal connection with said seat frame, thereby permitting free downward movement of said jointless seat supports in opposite directions in

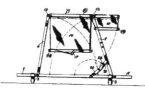

folding action, and means for holding said seat supports in elevated positions when the baby walker is unfolded.

1,328,827. BOTTLE-CAP REMOVER. JOSÉPH ECKERT, Dayton, Ohio. Filed Sept. 23, 1919. Serial No. 325,677. 2 Claims. (Cl. 65—47.)

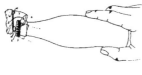

2. A new article of manufacture, comprising in a single structure; a bottle cap remover consisting of a base member having a fulcrum member and an outwardly extending arm provided at its free end with depending inwardly inclined lip members adapted to engage the closure cap of a bottle and to coöperate with said fulcrum member to remove said cap therefrom, said fulcrum member being positioned to engage the flat surface of said cap at substantially the center thereof.

1,328,828. CONDENSER. RAYMOND N. EHRHART, Edgewood Park, Pa., assignor to Westinghouse Electric & Manufacturing Company, a Corporation of Pennsylvania. Filed Oct. 8, 1917. Serial No. 195,316. 5 Claims. (Cl. 257—24.)

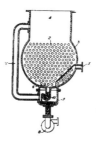

1. In a condenser, a shell having an inlet port formed therein, cooling elements inclosed by the shell, a hot well, a hydrostatic trap connecting the hot well with the shell through which condensate is drained to the hot well, and means for conducting fluids from the inlet port to the hot well for heating the condensate discharged from the trap.

1,328,829. TOY FERRIS WHEEL. JAMES J. FAIRBANKS, Gardner, Mass., assignor, by direct and mesne assignments, to The U. S. Toy & Novelties Mfg. Co., Templeton, Mass., a Corporation of Massachusetts. Filed June 16, 1919. Serial No. 304,369. 15 Claims. (Cl. 46—45.)

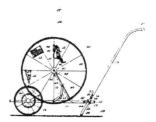

1. A trundling toy comprising a frame, ground wheels carried by one end thereof upon which the frame is supported, a relatively large wheel journaled above said frame and capable of bodily movement relatively thereto, a grooved wheel carried by the supporting wheels in frictional engagement with the larger wheel, and a handle adjustably carried by the other end of the frame.

1,328,830. CALENDAR. MITCHELL J. FRIEDMAN, Washington, D. C. Filed Dec. 26, 1918. Serial No. 268,337. 8 Claims. (Cl. 40—107.)

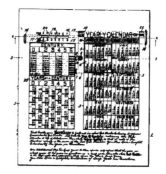

3. In a calendar of the class described, comprising a yearly tabulation of consecutively arranged dates for indicating the months in a common year, means for advancing the monthly tabulations of January and February, an opening adjacent the last tabulation in the month of February, a movable strip associated with said monthly tabulations and having printed thereon the numeral 29 and arranged to be shifted into register with the opening when the January and February tabulations are advanced to set the calendar to indicate a leap year.

1,328,831. KEY SYSTEM FOR CLARINETS. JAMES C. FLEMING, Denver, Colo. Filed May 14, 1919. Serial No. 296,990. 5 Claims. (Cl. 84—7.)

1. In a clarinet or like instrument, a body portion having tone openings, a key operated cover for each of the said openings, a rock shaft, each of the covers having an attached sleeve mounted on the rock shaft, a device that operates with the rock shaft and turns the said shaft in a direction for holding the covers to the tone holes in open position, connections between the shaft and the sleeves mounted on the rock shaft for turning all of the

sleeves to move their covers to the open position, and a thumb key for effecting rotation of the shaft and the

sleeves thereon to hold the covers attached to the said sleeves in their tone holes closing position.

1,328,832. BABY-CARRIER. THEODORE W. HANRATH, Chicago, Ill. Filed June 15, 1916. Serial No. 103,853. 2 Claims. (Cl. 224—6.)

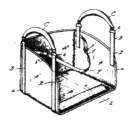

1. A collapsible baby carrier having a bottom, sides and back of flexible material with a transverse brace strip secured to the bottom at its front, handles at the top of said sides, and stay strips to which said handles are connected, one of said stay strips extending down said sides and around said bottom beneath said grace strip.

1,328,833. METHOD OF STAINING GLASS. JOHN W. HASBURG, Chicago, Ill. Filed June 18, 1919. Serial No. 305,158. 3 Claims. (Cl. 91—72.)

1. The process of decorating glass or ceramic ware which consists in applying a porous foundation coating to the surface to be decorated, then applying upon the coating a coloring material in a condition which permits it to penetrate said coating, and then burning or baking.

1,328,834. DRIVE FOR GRINDING-MILLS. ROBERT R. HOWELL, Minneapolis, Minn. Filed Mar. 28, 1919. Serial No. 285,806. 2 Claims. (Cl. 74—21.)

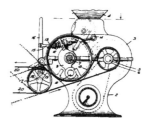

1. In a grinding mill the combination with driving pulleys of grinding rolls and a single belt for driving said pulleys, of an idler pulley arranged adjacent to one of said pulleys on the side thereof remote from the other driving pulley, the belt running from the source of power under the idler pulley and around the driving pulley remote from the idler thence back under an arc of the driving pulley adjacent the idler and over the idler to the source of power, the pull of the belt being away from the mill and in the direction of the source of power.

1,328,835. TURBINE. ALEXANDER T. KASLEY, Swissvale, Pa., assignor to Westinghouse Electric & Manufacturing Company, a Corporation of Pennsylvania. Original application filed July 5, 1913, Serial No. 777,432. Divided and this application filed Feb. 17, 1917. Serial No. 149,224. 8 Claims. (Cl. 253—65.)

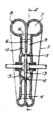

1. In a turbine, a casing longitudinally symmetrical about an intermediate partition wall, and a rotor wheel inclosed by the casing and operating in the plane of the partition wall.

1,328,836. CUTTER-BAR CONTROL FOR WEED-MOWERS. WALTER F. KASPER, Fairmont, Minn., assignor to Fairmont Gas Engine & Railway Motor Car Co., Fairmont, Minn., a Corporation. Filed Aug. 18, 1916. Serial No. 115,699. 5 Claims. (Cl. 56—232.)

1. The combination, with a railroad car platform, of a frame mounted transversely thereof and extending from side to side of said platform, bars pivoted at their inner ends on said platform and mounted for vertical oscillation, guide bars pivoted on the outer ends of said first named bars, cutter bars mounted in said guide bars and a suitable operating mechanism therefor, sheaves mounted on said transverse frame at intervals across said platform, flexible means having running connections with said sheaves and with said pivoted bars and said guide bars respectively, and levers mounted in pairs upon opposite sides of the middle portion of said platform and connected respectively to said flexible means, said levers of a pair being spaced a suitable distance apart for an oper-

ator to stand between them and movable forward and backward in the direction of travel of said car, whereby a workman can manipulate a lever with each hand and face the work ahead of the car, springs connected with said platform bars for normally resisting downward movement thereof, and means for equalizing the tension on said springs as said bars are lowered.

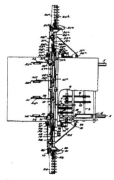

2. The combination, with a car, of a bar pivoted thereon, a cutter bar guide and shoe pivoted on said bar, levers mounted on said car and having flexible connections with said bar and shoe for tilting them, a sheave mounted on said car and provided with a cam surface, flexible means connecting said bar with said sheave, a spring normally tending to resist the downward pull of said flexible means, and a connection between said cam surface and said spring, the leverage of said cam increasing proportionately to the extension of said spring.

3. The combination, with a railroal car, of a bar pivotally supported in the frame of said car at one side thereof and projecting outwardly therefrom, a cutter guide bar carried by said shoe, an arm rigidly mounted on said shoe and projecting upwardly therefrom, means normally resisting downward movement of said pivoted bar and said cutter bar, a driving mechanism for said cutter bar, flexible means connected with said pivoted bar and having a running connection with said car, a spring connected with said flexible means, means for equalizing the tension on said spring as said bar is lowered, a pivoted bar having a flexible connection with said ratchet bar and operating levers mounted on the car and having flexible connections with said pivoted bar and with said pivoted arm, said operating levers being mounted for forward and backward movement on the car to allow a workman to face the work while the car is in motion.

4. The combination, with a railroad car, of a bar pivotally supported on the frame of said car at one side thereof and projecting outwardly therefrom, a shoe pivotally supported on the outer end of said bar, a cutter guide bar carried by said shoe, an arm rigidly mounted on said shoe and projecting upwardly therefrom, a helical spring connecting said arm with said car and normally resisting downward movement of said pivoted bar and said cutter bar, a driving mechanism for said cutter bar, a sheave mounted on said car, flexible means connected to said pivoted bar and passing over said sheave, a spring connected to said flexible means, a cam device in connection with said sheave for equalizing the tension on said spring as said bar is lowered, an upright pivoted bar near said car and having a flexible connection with said ratchet bar, and operating levers mounted on said car and having flexible connections with said pivoted bar and with said pivoted arm, said operating levers being mounted for forward and backward movement on the car to allow a workman to face the work while the car is in motion.

5. The combination, with a car, of a bar pivoted thereon, a cutter bar guide, a shoe pivoted on said bar, levers mounted on said car and having flexible connections with said bar and shoe for tilting them, a spring connected with said bar for normally resisting downward movement thereof, and means for equalizing the tension of said spring as said bar is lowered.

1,328,837. DUMP-BODY HOIST. WALTER C. KERN and WILLIAM YOUNG, Leavenworth, Kans. Filed July 3, 1919. Serial No. 308,640. 9 Claims. (Cl. 298—19.)

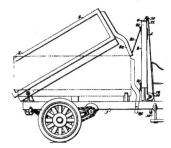

1. A dump body comprising a standard having guides, a carriage vertically movable on said guides, a pulley and cable mechanism for lowering said carriage, and a ratchet and pawl device for raising said carriage, said carriage being adapted to be connected with the dump body to raise and lower the same.

1,328,838. TUNING-FORK. WALTER I. KIRK, Chicago, Ill., assignor to Lyon & Healy, Chicago, Ill., a Corporation of Illinois. Filed Apr. 4, 1917. Serial No. 159,670. 7 Claims. (Cl. 84—43.)

1. A device of the class specified comprising a resonator, a supporting device mounted on the resonator and comprising separated standards or uprights, said resonator having an aperture between said standards, and a tuning fork mounted at the upper ends of said standards and extending downwardly therefrom so that the free ends of the prongs are adjacent said aperture.

1,328,839. TRACTOR. LEVI KRING, Westerville, Ohio. Filed Sept. 12, 1918. Serial No. 253,679. 1 Claim. (Cl. 180—53.)

A tractor comprising a frame, a power unit carried thereby, a shaft driven by said unit, a worm loosely mounted upon said shaft, a gear meshing with said worm, a drum rotated by said gear, traction mechanism co-operatively driven by said shaft, and controlling means

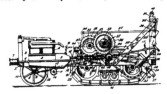

operable to impart motion from said shaft to said drum and traction mechanism in independent and alternate relation.

1,328,840. MACHINE FOR STAMPING WORKMEN'S INDIVIDUAL CARDS. Karl August Albert Lehmann, Biel, and Conrad Schindler, Pfäfers, Switzerland. Filed Nov. 27, 1917. Serial No. 204,185. 12 Claims. (Cl. 234—48.)

12. A machine for stamping workmen's individual cards comprising, a spring actuated member, means for locking the latter against the action of the spring, a card cutting mechanism operable by the movement of the spring actuated member, and means including the cutting mechanism to effect, on the insertion of a card into the machine, a releasing of the locking means.

1,328,841. STEEL OR IRON STRUCTURAL WORK. Thomas Royal Little, Liverpool, England. Filed Sept. 5, 1918. Serial No. 252,718. 1 Claim. (Cl. 114—79.)

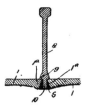

A steel ship or other steel structure comprising plating elements thickened at their edges, frame elements having landings on either side and a spigot portion adapted to extend between the adjacent thickened edges of the plating elements and welded connections between the plating elements and the frame elements where the thickened portions of the former abut against the spigot portions of the latter.

1,328,842. REGISTERING MECHANISM FOR FORM OR PLATE CYLINDERS OF MULTICOLOR-PRINTING MACHINES. Frank C. Marquardt, Brooklyn, N. Y., assignor to American Bank Note Company, New York, N. Y., a Corporation of New York. Filed May 18, 1918. Serial No. 235,330. 5 Claims. (Cl. 101—248.)
1. A registering mechanism for a form or plate cylinder for multicolor printing machines, embodying therein in

combination with a plate-carrying member and a member for applying power thereto, said members being capable of independent rotary movement about the same axis, of an adjusting mechanism for said plate-carrying member, comprising two studs carried by one of said members and

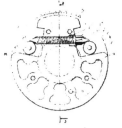

an adjustable screw threaded member carried by the other member and having conical ends engaging said studs, whereby power is applied to said plate-carrying member by said power member to rotate said members in unison, and said plate-carrying member may be turned independently of said power member.

1,328,843. AUTOMATIC LUBRICANT-SUPPLY SYSTEM FOR INTERNAL-COMBUSTION ENGINES. Stevie L. Martin, Snyder, Okla. Filed Apr. 23, 1918. Serial No. 230,305. Renewed June 24, 1919. Serial No. 306,464. 6 Claims. (Cl. 184—108.)

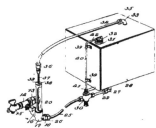

2. A supply system for internal combustion engines including a supply tank adapted for connection with an engine crank case, closure means for the tank, means for cutting off discharge from the tank, vent means for the tank adapted to automatically control the discharge of lubricant therefrom, and operating means for said cut off means adapted to permit release of said closure means only when the cut off means is closed.

1,328,844. CARBURETER. Louis H. Oberreich, Indianapolis, Ind. Filed Oct. 4, 1916. Serial No. 123,790. 7 Claims. (Cl. 123—131.)

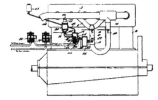

6. In combination, an internal combustion engine having main intake and exhaust passages, a branch connec-

tion from the exhaust passage to the intake passage for carrying part of the exhaust gases from the exhaust passage to the intake passage, and a fuel nozzle across which the exhaust gases traveling such branch connection are discharged to atomize the fuel, said branch connection being provided with an enlargement between said nozzle and the exhaust passage for dissipating any flames in the external passage before such flames reach the nozzle.

1,328,845. PROCESS FOR PRODUCING FLAKE GRAPHITE. SAMUEL W. OSGOOD, Chicago, Ill., assignor, by mesne assignments, to Nettie C. Kenner, Chicago, Ill. Filed Mar. 4, 1916. Serial No. 82,044. 29 Claims. (Cl. 252.)

1. The process of obtaining flake graphite consisting in subjecting kish to a rough-separating operation, thereby separating most of the graphite flakes from said kish, removing the iron particles from the resulting graphite flakes, removing the gritty material from the resulting graphite flakes, and grading the graphite flakes by air flotation.

1,328,846. SEED SPACING AND DROPPING MECHANISM FOR PLANTERS. JOHN E. PAULSON, Minneapolis, Minn. Filed June 23, 1919. Serial No. 306,221. 1 Claim. (Cl. 111—40.)

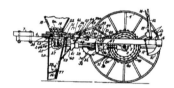

In a two-row planting machine having a frame and two ground wheels, two seed hoppers mounted on the frame, two dropping tubes one below each hopper, a seed feeding slide arranged to reciprocate in the bases of the hoppers, operative connection with a clutch in it between said slide and the ground wheels, a valve in the lower end of each dropping tube, a guided rod connected with each valve to open it, a spring acting on each rod to close its valve, a light rock-shaft journaled across the frame of the machine and provided with check-row forks and a spring for holding said forks in an upward position, two radial arms on the shaft arranged to engage each of them one of the valve rods to open the valves, a peg on the frame near each valve rod and a cam on each rod arranged to contact with the peg and disengage the rod from the radial arm shortly after the valve has been opened; a third rocker arm on said shaft, and means operated by said third arm for starting the clutch into action after each closing of the valves, and automatic means for disengaging the clutch again.

1,328,847. CALCULATING-MACHINE. ARTHUR PENTECOST, East Orange, N. J., assignor to Wales Adding Machine Company, Wilkes-Barre, Pa., a Corporation of Pennsylvania. Filed Nov. 7, 1916. Serial No. 129,927. 43 Claims. (Cl. 235—60.)

1. In a calculating machine, the combination with accumulating, and regular printing mechanisms, including printing hammers; of an auxiliary sign printing device, including a sign printing hammer; means to cock the sign printing hammer; a latch to retain the sign printing hammer in cocked position; means to trip the latch; and locking means operable independently of the regular printing hammers and displaceable preliminary to the registration of the first amount on the accumulating

mechanism, to prevent the release of the latch during idle strokes intervening between the clearing of the accumu-

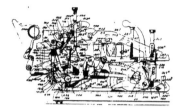

lating mechanism, and the introduction of the first amount into the machine.

1,328,848. PARACHUTE COMPRISING PNEUMATIC MEANS. ADALBERTO RAMAUGÉ, Buenos Aires, Argentina. Filed June 27, 1918. Serial No. 242,211. 2 Claims. (Cl. 244—21.)

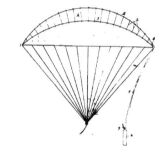

1. A parachute comprising two sheets of fabric connected together air-tight, means for introducing a buoyant inflating medium between the sheets at the lower and outer edges thereof to form a chamber when inflated, and a plurality of flexible tension cords to maintain, define, and limit the size and shape of the chamber when inflated.

1,328,849. GUN-CARRIAGE WITH ENDLESS TRACKS. EUGÈNE SCHNEIDER, Paris, France, assignor to Schneider & Cie., Paris, France, a Limited Joint-Stock Company of France. Filed Feb. 28, 1919. Serial No. 279,874. 11 Claims. (Cl. 89—40.)

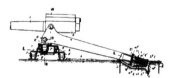

1. In a gun-mounting, a rectilinearly movable carriage, a trail, a constant pivotal anchorage for the tail of the trail, and a variable pivotal connection between the front end of the trail and the carriage to follow the travel of the trail front end as the trail changes its angularity around the constant pivotal anchorage during the rectilinear movement of the carriage.

1,328,850. FLYTRAP. JOHN W. SKELTON, Douglas, Ariz. Filed Aug. 6, 1919. Serial No. 315,713. 1 Claim. (Cl. 43—22.)

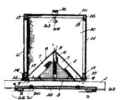

An insect trap comprising sills, a bait board disposed between the sills, a cage supported by and on the sills and provided with openings through its bottom adjacent its sides, a tapered block secured on the bottom of the cage and within the cage between the openings through the bottom, a post rising from said block, a tapered screen secured at its lower edges to the bottom of the cage and at the outer sides of the openings through the bottom and having its central portion supported by the said post, there being exit openings formed through said screen in the ridge thereof within the cage, and means for permitting the cage to be removed from over said screen.

1,328,851. PROCESS OF HEAT TREATMENT FOR CASTINGS. BURNS LYMAN SMITH, Syracuse, N. Y. Filed Jan. 12. 1917. Serial No. 142,103. 3 Claims. (Cl. 148—13.)

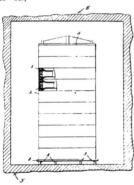

1. The herein described process of heat treatment for hollow spoke wheels having hollow fellies, the same consisting in arranging the wheels one above the other in a column with the edge of the felly of one wheel resting on the edge of the felly of the next lower wheel closing the top and bottom of the column and applying a gaseous heating medium direct to the peripheries of the wheels and gradually raising the temperature of the medium to a predetermined maximum temperature, maintaining such maximum temperature for a predetermined time, then gradually lowering the temperature, substantially as and for the purpose described.

1,328,852. APPARATUS FOR CASTING HOLLOW ONE-PIECE SPOKE-WHEELS. BURNS LYMAN SMITH, Syracuse, N. Y. Filed May 15, 1917. Serial No. 168,673. 10 Claims. (Cl. 22—130.)

1. A casting apparatus for casting hollow one piece spoke wheels, comprising complemental sections inclosing a mold cavity, cores supported in the cavity, each core comprising a spoke member, a hub section and rim section, each core having an internal passage extending lengthwise of the spoke member and into the hub section,

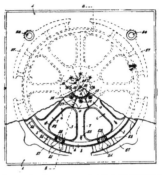

and also a closed passage extending lengthwise of the rim section, and intersecting the former passage, and an outlet vent communicating at its inner end with the first mentioned passage and at its outer end with the outer air, substantially as and for the purpose described.

1,328,853. STRAINER FOR VACUUM GASOLENE SYSTEMS. ARCHIE L. STEWARD, Chicago, Ill. Filed Mar. 31, 1919. Serial No. 286,425. 3 Claims. (Cl. 210—16.)

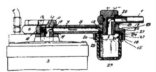

1. A strainer for gasolene vacuum tanks, comprising a hollow stem, one end of which is arranged to be supported directly on the vacuum tank in open communication with the interior thereof, and the other end of which is arranged for connection with the usual gasolene supply pipe for the vacuum tank, fittings having downwardly discharging gasolene passages therein, for removably securing said hollow stem to said vacuum tank and supply pipe, the discharge port of the gasolene passage of the fitting for the supply pipe being located below the inlet port to the passage in the hollow stem, a gasolene receptacle removably supported by said hollow stem, between the discharge port of the supply pipe and inlet port to the passage of the hollow stem, and a screen interposed between the discharge port of said fitting for the supply pipe and inlet port to the hollow stem.

1,328,854. RAILROAD-CROSSING SIGNAL. CARL W. F. STROBEL, Lima, Ohio. Filed Feb. 21, 1918. Serial No. 218,475. 4 Claims. (Cl. 246—126.)

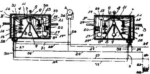

1. A railroad crossing signal including switch boxes adapted to be mounted upon the track on opposite sides

of the crossing, an electric signal for the crossing, an upright trip lever mounted within each switch box and projecting into the path of the rolling stock so as to be swung in either direction according to the direction in which the rolling stock is moving, an electric switch mounted within each box and arranged to be closed by the movement of the trip lever in one direction, circuits including the said switches and the electric signal, detents for locking the said switches in a closed position, electro-magnets mounted adjacent to the detents, a second electric switch mounted within each box and arranged to be closed by the movement of the trip lever in the opposite direction, and electric circuits including the said second switches of each box and the electro-magnet of the other box, whereby the detent of one box will be moved into inoperative position by the operation of the adjacent electro-magnet when the second switch of the other box is closed.

1,328,855. HYDROCARBON-MOTOR. ERNEST E. SWEET, Detroit, Mich., assignor to General Motors Company, Detroit, Mich., a Corporation of New Jersey. Filed Apr. 11, 1917. Serial No. 161,200. 7 Claims. (Cl. 123—174.)

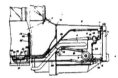

1. In an internal combustion engine, in combination, a cylinder jacket, a radiator, connections therebetween, a by-pass around said radiator, a valve mechanism for controlling said radiator and by-pass respectively, and a heater coil, one end of which is connected with the connection between the jacket and radiator between said valve mechanism and the radiator, and the other end with the other of the connections between said jacket and radiator.

1,328,856. GAS-FIRED WATER-HEATER OR STEAM-GENERATOR. WALTER MARTIN TAYLOR, London, England. Filed Sept. 3, 1918. Serial No. 252,431. 5 Claims. (Cl. 122—250.)

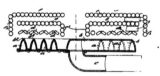

1. A water heater comprising in combination a gas burner consisting of a series of spiral tubes of successively increasing periphery and co-axially arranged in a horizontal plane to form a broken spiral, each tube being one convolution in length and provided along its crown with a line of openings, a central chamber arranged co-axially with the spiral tubes, a gas supply conduit communicating with the interior of the chamber, a plurality of radially disposed tubular arms connecting the central chamber and the spiral tubes, and a water coil consisting of a plurality of coiled pipe-units superposed one above the other, the lower-most pipe-unit being located above the gas burner and consisting of a single pipe spirally coiled and arranged to make two circuits in succession above each of the said spiral tubes thereby causing the water to circulate twice over each spiral tube and continuously in one direction from one end of the pipe to the other.

1,328,857. STANDPIPE. HARRY E. THOMPSON, Three Rivers, Mich., assignor to Fairbanks, Morse & Co., Chicago, Ill. Filed Mar. 11, 1919. Serial No. 281,921. 4 Claims. (Cl. 137—21.)

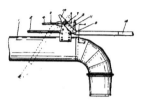

4. In a standpipe, the combination of a spout, a bracket mounted at the outer end of said spout, a valve actuating rod, a rocker member to which said rod is connected mounted on said bracket, and a pair of hand levers for said rocker member adapted to be swung downwardly astride the said spout.

1,328,858. RESILIENT HUB. JOHN TORRENT, Jr., Muskegon, Mich. Filed May 27, 1919. Serial No. 300,037. 1 Claim. (Cl. 152—44.)

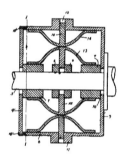

In a resilient hub, an axle, a housing embracing a portion of the axle, said housing and axle being relatively radially movable, spaced collars supported on the axle and providing a slot, bearings supported on the axle within the housing, bowed springs disposed adjacent the axle, and bowed springs disposed adjacent the inner wall of the housing, the bowed springs adjacent the axle contacting with the bearing members, the contacting springs being arranged in pairs, and means carried by the springs adjacent the axle for operating within the slot for preventing lateral movement of the central portions of the springs.

1,328,859. SACK AND THE LIKE. GUSTAF TROLLE-BONDE, Trolleholm, Sweden. Filed Mar. 28, 1919. Serial No. 285,914. 1 Claim. (Cl. 150—8.)

The combination with an annular frame provided at its top and bottom with outwardly extending flanges to form an annular channel to receive the folded upper end of a bag to which the frame is attached, the frame having an internal downwardly extended funnel provided at its small end with cross bars, and a flexible tubular element attached to the small end of the funnel and depending therefrom, whereby if a bag to which the frame is attached should tilt over the flexible tubular element will lie on the cross bars and prevent the contents of the bag spilling.

1,328,860. SHELF-TONGS. EDWARD J. WALSH, Jersey City, N. J. Filed May 29, 1918. Serial No. 237,270. 2 Claims. (Cl. 294—22.)

1. A shelf tong including a handle, a cross head carried thereby, a pair of levers pivoted intermediate their ends to said cross head and having their rear end portions diverging outwardly, a pair of arms pivoted to the rear end portions of said levers, an operating rod pivotally connecting said levers, an ear carried by said operating rod, and a coil spring connected to said ear and said cross head.

1,328,861. POULTRY - ROOST. JOHN E. WARRINGTON, Brooklyn, Ill. Filed June 23, 1919. Serial No. 305,959. 1 Claim. (Cl. 119—25.)

In a poultry roost, a plurality of horizontal supporting rails having socket-forming recesses in the top faces thereof, cups comprising stems having each a circumscribing recessed flange resting on the rails and provided with stems extending into the recesses, the upper ends of the stems being reduced to form shoulders and roost bars having sockets receiving said upper portions and engaging said shoulders.

1,328,862. SCREW-CLAMP. EVAN WATKINS, Cleveland, Ohio, assignor to The Columbian Hardware Company, Cleveland, Ohio, a Corporation of Ohio. Filed Feb. 26, 1919. Serial No. 279,282. 2 Claims. (Cl. 144—304.)

1. A clamp comprising a U-frame having a fixed jaw at one extremity, a rotatable tapped bushing mounted at the opposite extremity of said frame, a clamping screw rota-

table within the bushing positioned with its free end adapted to be actuated toward and away from the fixed

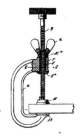

jaw, and means for independently actuating the screw and bushing, substantially as set forth.

1,328,863. LUGGAGE-CARRIER. FRANK T. WENTWORTH, Bloomfield, N. J. Filed Oct. 28, 1916, Serial No. 128,148. Renewed Dec. 8, 1919. Serial No. 343,424. 2 Claims. (Cl. 224—29.)

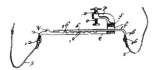

2. A luggage carrier embodying therein a base having a loop at one end thereof, and a rest on the under side thereof adjacent said loop, a bracket having an opening therethrough at the other end of said base, a clamp screw carried by said bracket and adapted to engage the under side of a running board, a slide adapted to pass through said opening in said bracket and having a loop at the outer end thereof, said base having a plurality of grooves upon the under side thereof and said slide having a tongue upon the upper side thereof adapted to enter different grooves upon said base, whereby the distance between said loops may be varied and the clamping action of said screw will hold said base and said slide in their adjusted position, and means coöperating with the loop in said base and in said slide respectively for holding articles of luggage upon the carrier.

1,328,864. APPARATUS FOR MAKING SHEET-GLASS. JAMES WHITTEMORE, Detroit, Mich., assignor to The Libbey-Owens Sheet Glass Company, Toledo, Ohio, a Corporation of Ohio. Filed May 16, 1918. Serial No. 234,867. 15 Claims. (Cl. 49—12.)

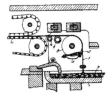

1. In apparatus for manipulating hot glass, the combination of means providing a glass engaging surface, means to supply moisture to said surface, and means to remove excess moisture from said surface by suction.

1,328,865. TRAIN-SIGNALING AND TRAIN-CONTROL SYSTEM. CHARLES H. WOODWARD, Bournemouth, England. Filed Oct. 18, 1915. Serial No. 56,649. 10 Claims. (Cl. 246—34.)

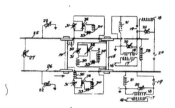

4. A system of electric train signaling or power control comprising, in combination with a track rail, means to include said rail as a part of a closed oscillatory circuit and a circuit carried by the train in contact with and tuned to resonate with the closed oscillatory rail circuit.

1,328,866. CREAM-SEPARATOR. GEORGE A. YEATTER, Monroe, Mich. Filed Nov. 15, 1916. Serial No. 131,493. 1 Claim. (Cl. 215—100.)

In a device of the character described, the combination of a flat disk-like closure said closure having its outer periphery bent inwardly and then downwardly and outwardly, thus, forming a curved supporting flange, the lower edge of which is offset inwardly from the outer portion of the disk like closure, a yieldable ring carried by said flange, the outer surface of the ring extending outwardly beyond said flange, whereby the closure may rest upon a milk bottle with the ring engaging the channeled portion of the milk bottle and the flange extending into the milk bottle, an integral conical neck rising from the central portion of said closure, a tapering stopper removably inserted into said neck, a tube carried by said stopper, an upright nipple secured to said closure and rising contiguous to said neck, a flexible tube for fitting over said nipple, whereby the tube will be gripped between said nipple and neck to be held against accidental displacement and a pumping means connected to the outer end of said tube.

1,328,867. SUBMARINE TOY. RENÉ EDOUARD DE WAELE, Paris, France. Filed Aug. 8, 1918. Serial No. 248,954. 14 Claims. (Cl. 46—37.)

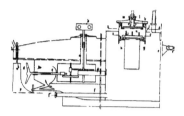

1. In a toy submarine boat, the combination of a propeller, and driving mechanism therefor; means for automatically effecting submergence of the boat; and means for automatically terminating the movement of the propeller during submergence.

1,328,868. SPARK-ARRESTER. BERT A. ASHBY, El Paso, Tex. Filed Feb. 21, 1919. Serial No. 278,417. 3 Claims. (Cl. 183—74.)

2. In a spark arrester the combination with a smoke flue, of a skeleton frame work adapted for insertion within the flue, a spring finger carried by said frame work and projecting normally obliquely downward in position to be compressed by the wall of the flue when the frame work is inserted therein, and screens carried by the frame work.

1,328,869. PACKET-HOLDER. BERT ASHBY, El Paso, Tex. Filed June 21, 1919. Serial No. 305,738. 4 Claims. (Cl. 24—18.)

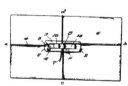

3. A package tie including a body, and a tongue connected to the body and having cord engaging means, the rear end portion of said tongue being extended down-

wardly for normally disposing said cord engaging means below the upper side of the body, the forward end portion of said tongue being normally disposed in the plane of the body for presenting a flat upper surface to the body.

1,328,870. TEMPO - CONTROL DEVICE. ANTON G. EILES, Cedar Rapids, Iowa, assignor of one-half to John H. Lee, Oak Park, Ill. Filed Aug. 19, 1916. Serial No. 115,804. 21 Claims. (Cl. 84—160.)

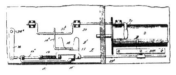

19. In means of the character set forth, the combination with a take-up roller, a pneumatic motor for actuating the same. and a valve controlling the speed of the motor, of a tempo rod parallel with said roller and comprising two slidable movably related sections, a tempo indicator carried by one of said sections, means for guiding said section and normally preventing movement thereof, means interposed between said sections and controlled by the music roll for automatically moving the other section, connections between said last-named section and said valve for transmitting motion to said valve, and manual shifting means whereby said rod-sections and said valve may be shifted to arbitrarily adjust the tempo.

1,328,871. DRAFTING DEVICE. LOUIS CHRISTOPHER HAHN, Cincinnati, Ohio. Filed Mar. 22, 1919. Serial No. 284,352. 2 Claims. (Cl. 33—1.)

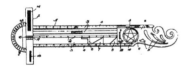

1. A drawing instrument, comprising an elongated plate having at one end a protractor segment, alined series of perforations extending along the plate at measured distances, one of said series coinciding with the axis of said protractor segment.

1,328,872. CORN-CLEANER. JAMES WALTON HARRIS, Turbeville, S. C. Filed July 11, 1918. Serial No. 244,411. 4 Claims. (Cl. 130—16.)

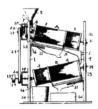

4. A grain cleaner including an inclined shaft, a rotary cylindrical screen carried thereby, a horizontal shaft, a universal joint connecting the horizontal shaft to the inclined shaft, a centrifugal fan casing mounted to dis-

270 O. G.—34

charge into the screen, a sleeve loose on the horizontal shaft, a centrifugal fan rigid with the sleeve and arranged within the casing, a counter-shaft geared to both the horizontal shaft and the sleeve, and means for applying power to the horizontal shaft.

1,328,873. DYNAMO - ELECTRIC STARTING, LIGHTING, AND IGNITION MECHANISM FOR AUTOMOBILES. JOHN ALLEN HEANY, Jersey City, N. J., assignor, by mesne assignments, to Industrial Research Corporation, a Corporation of Delaware. Original application filed Aug. 1, 1910, Serial No. 574,774. Divided and this application filed Nov. 3, 1917. Serial No. 200,092. 13 Claims. (Cl. 290—37.)

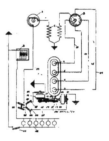

3. The combination with an engine, of a starting, lighting and ignition system therefor, comprising a storage battery; electrical transmitting devices, including a motor and motor dynamo, operatively connected to the engine; and circuits and switches connecting the motor and the storage battery with the electrical devices, the motor being rendered inoperative, and the motor dynamo functioning as a generator to charge said battery, when the engine starts up under its own power.

13. The method of operating a combination comprising an internal combustion engine, a storage battery, and a plurality of dynamo electric machines, which comprises concurrently supplying energy from the battery to operate all of said machines as motors to exert starting torque on the engine and then operating less than all of said machines as generators to charge the battery.

1,328,874. DECK-SASH SUPPORT. LEWIS N. HÉNAULT, Albany, N. Y. Filed Dec. 17, 1917. Serial No. 207,545. 1 Claim. (Cl. 16—142.)

In a deck sash support, the combination of a bracket including a pair of spaced parallel cross plates having alined openings, a bolt slidably engaging in said openings and provided with an enlarged journaled portion on one end adapted to enter the opening in one of said plates, a spring coiled about said bolt and connected thereto and arranged within the bracket for urging said journal into said opening, a locking member formed integrally with the bolt near the journaled end thereof, a second locking member rotatably mounted on said journaled end and adapted to be clamped between one of said bracket plates and said first named locking lever for returning the rotatable locking lever in various adjusted positions about the journal, a bracket formed upon the bracket plate remote from the bracket plate engaged by said journaled ends, a lever pivotally mounted upon said bracket and having one end bifurcated and slotted, a pin extending through said slot and through said bolt for connecting the lever and bolt to shift the bolt longitudinally upon shiftable movement of the lever.

7,828,875. SAFETY TREAD STRUCTURE. ARTHUR W. HERBERT, Youngstown, Ohio, assignor to The General Fireproofing Company, a Corporation of Ohio. Filed June 2, 1917. Serial No. 172,541. 3 Claims. (Cl. 20—79.)

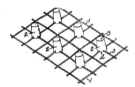

1. A safety tread structure including a carrier base consisting of a plurality of crossing wires, and relatively soft elongated friction studs having a straddling locked engagement at one end with said wires at their crossing points only.

1,328,876. MEASURING INSTRUMENT. ALFRED NILSSON HILL, Lund, Sweden. Filed Dec. 24, 1918. Serial No. 268,131. 2 Claims. (Cl. 73—110.)

1. A measuring instrument comprising a diaphragm, standards extending from the diaphragm, a rod connecting the standards, top and bottom bearings, a cylinder mounted in the bearings, said cylinder having two corresponding spiral slots through which the rod extends, and a pointer carried by the cylinder, whereby when the diaphragm pulsates the pointer will be circumferentially moved.

1,328,877. SHEET-FEEDING MECHANISM FOR PRINTING-PRESSES. ROBERT HOE, New York, N. Y. Filed June 26, 1913. Serial No. 775,837. 12 Claims. (Cl. 271—52.)

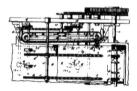

1. In a sheet feeding apparatus, the combination with a feed-board, of a cylinder carrying sheet stops and sheet seizing devices, means for removing the cylinder stops into position to hold the sheet while it is being taken by the sheet seizing devices and actuating the sheet seizing devices to take the sheet, sheet stops moving over the feed-board with the sheet and controlling the head of the sheet for transfer to the cylinder stops, sheet feeding means for advancing the sheet over the feed-board with its head controlled by the feed-board stops, and separate sheet feeding devices moving at a higher speed than the feed-board stops and cylinder and acting to press the sheet against the stops before and during the taking of the sheet by the cylinder.

2. In a sheet feeding apparatus, the combination with a feed-board, of a cylinder carrying sheet stops and sheet seizing devices, means for moving the cylinder stops into position to hold the sheet while it is being taken by the sheet seizing devices and actuating the sheet seizing devices to take the sheet, sheet stops carried by endless belts moving with the sheet over the feed-board and acting to control the head of the sheet for transfer to the cylinder stops and arranged to be raised and moved out of stopping position for transfer of the sheet to the cylinder stops, and sheet feeding means acting to press the head of the sheet against the feed-board stops and against the cylinder stops before and during the taking of the sheet by the cylinder.

3. The combination with a feed-board and sheet feeding means for advancing a sheet over the feed-board, of a friction device acting on the sheet and moving forward with the sheet and at an angle to the sheet to draw it sidewise for side registry, said device being constructed to slip on the sheet to permit the sheet to be held by a side stop.

4. The combination with a feed-board and sheet feeding means for advancing a sheet over the feed-board, of a friction device acting on the sheet at the side edge, an endless belt carrying said friction device and moving at an angle to the feed-board to draw the sheet sidewise by the frictional device, and a side stop carried by the belt and mounted to move parallel with the feed-board, said friction device being constructed to slip on the sheet to permit the sheet to be controlled by the side stop.

5. The combination with a feed-board and sheet feeding means for advancing a sheet over the feed-board, of a friction device acting on the sheet and moving forward with the sheet over the feed-board and at an angle to the sheet to draw it sidewise for side registry, said device being constructed to slip on the sheet to permit the sheet to be held by a side stop, a lever carrying said friction device, and a cam controlling said lever to move the friction devices transversely to the sheet to engage and release the sheet.

1,328,878. BED-SLAT. NATHAN KAPLAN, Covington, Ga. Filed Oct. 31, 1919. Serial No. 334,640. 1 Claim. (Cl. 5—25.)

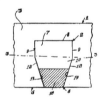

A bed rail having a seat in its inner surface, the seat extending part way through the rail horizontally and intersecting the lower edge of the rail to form an opening, the seat including an enlarged upper portion, and a reduced lower portion defined by side walls which converge downwardly and diverge horizontally; and a slat having an end extension defined by edge walls which diverge horizontally and converge downwardly to coöperate with the side walls of the lower portion of the seat in the bed rail, the thickness of the extension being less than the width of the opening, whereby the extension may be inserted edgewise through the opening, turned in the upper portion of the seat, and lowered into engagement with the side walls of the lower portion of the seat.

1,328,879. WATER-METER SPINDLE. EMIL M. KRUE-GER, Milwaukee, Wis., assignor to Badger Meter Manufacturing Company, Milwaukee, Wis., a Corporation of Wisconsin. Filed July 22, 1918. Serial No. 246,152. 2 Claims. (Cl. 64—79.)

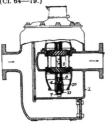

1. In a device of the described class, the combination with the wheel-supporting shaft, an adjustable cylindrical support, said support being provided with a pair of beads, and an elongated anti-friction bearing, said elongated bearing being provided with grooves for the reception of said beads.

2. In a device of the described class, the combination with the wheel-supporting shaft, an adjustable cylindrical support, said support being provided with a pair of beads, and an elongated anti-friction bearing, said elongated bearing being provided with grooves for the reception of said beads, and said cylindrical support being provided with a plurality of vertical ducts for the escape of refuse matter from said bearings.

1,328,880. MILKER-HEAD. MATTHEW LAMMERS, Sheboygan Falls, Wis. Filed June 11, 1918. Serial No. 239,387. 3 Claims. (Cl. 31—98.)

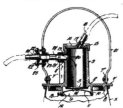

1. A milker head comprising a hollow shell having an inlet and a discharge orifice, a one-way valve for the inlet, a rotatably adjustable cover for the shell having an outlet, a flange extending laterally from the shell, an apron depending from the flange, a spring detachably connected to the apron, and a valve carried by the spring and adapted to close the discharge orifice.

1,328,881. CAN OR CONTAINER. WILLIS H. LAZARUS, St. Louis, Mo., assignor to S. Pfeiffer Manufacturing Company, St. Louis, Mo., a Corporation of Missouri. Filed Mar. 27, 1919. Serial No. 285,442. 3 Claims. (Cl. 221—27.)

1. In combination with a container, a tubular spout-containing chamber disposed within, and having communication with the interior of the container, the upper portion of the wall of the chamber having threads, and a tapering spout having an enlarged threaded extension at its lower end, the spout and its extension being adapted to loosely fit within and occupy the chamber when the container is not in use and being movable outwardly

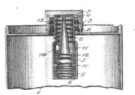

relatively to the container and chamber to provide a nozzle-outlet for the container when the container is in use, the spout, when in such latter position, having threaded supporting engagement at its said extension with the threaded upper portion of the wall of the chamber.

1,328,882. STEERING-WHEEL LOCK. JAMES W. MARKHAM, Armstrong, Ind. Filed Aug. 3, 1917. Serial No. 184,282. 1 Claim. (Cl. 70—129.)

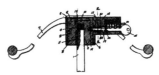

In combination with a steering shaft, a head keyed to said shaft, said head having a lateral opening, and an annular flange adjcent the bottom of the head, a steering wheel having a hub positioned on the head and engaging the flange, a lug integral with the hub, said lug having a threaded opening, adapted to register with the opening of the head, a bolt threaded throughout a portion of its length and positioned in the threaded opening of the lug, one end of said bolt adapted to move into the opening of the head for locking the head and hub together, said bolt having a squared recess, a key barrel having a reduced extension fitted in the squared recess, for rotating the bolt when the barrel is rotated, key mechanism for rotating the barrel, and means for forcing the hub into engagement with the flange.

1,328,883. FURNACE. LEWIS METESSER, New Orleans, La. Filed June 16, 1919. Serial No. 304,526. 17 Claims. (Cl. 110—44.)

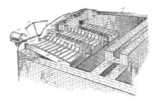

1. In a furnace and in combination with the fire-box thereof, a retort having a horizontally disposed bottom arranged longitudinally of the fire-box, the top of said retort inclining downwardly toward the rear end thereof, said bars arranged against the side walls of the fire-box

and having their forward ends secured to the fire front and wall thereof, the top of said side bars inclining rearwardly at the same angle of inclination as the tops of the retorts, lugs formed on the top of said bars, lugs formed on the upper face of said retort, and plates spanning the space between said retort and said side bars provided with notches adapted to receive the lugs formed on said side bars and the upper face of said retort.

1,328,884. SAFETY-POCKET FOR GARMENTS. CYRUS M. MILLER, Jr., St. Joseph, Mo., assignor to Wheeler & Motter Mercantile Company, St. Joseph, Mo., a Corporation of Missouri. Filed Sept. 23, 1918. Serial No. 255,285. 2 Claims. (Cl. 2—15.)

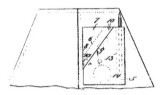

1. The combination with a garment, of a safety pocket consisting of a main member with an upper diagonally cut-away corner to form a pocket mouth edge which is free, the remaining edges of the pocket being firmly secured to the garment, and a triangular closing flap applied to and partially extending over the main member and having its one side and top edge secured to the main member and garment and its remaining inner edge loosely overlapping and parallel to the said mouth edge of the main member, the closing flap extending a considerable distance over the main member and wholly covering the mouth of the pocket formed by the latter.

1,328,885. RUFFLING MECHANISM FOR SEWING-MACHINES. JAMES R. MOFFATT, Chicago, Ill., assignor to Union Special Machine Company, Chicago, Ill., a Corporation of Illinois. Filed Dec. 2, 1916. Serial No. 134,658. 2 Claims. (Cl. 112—135.)

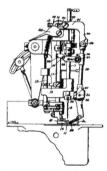

1. The combination of a stitch forming mechanism including a needle bar, a needle supported thereby, means for reciprocating the needle bar, a presser foot, a presser bar carrying said presser foot, a ruffling mechanism including a ruffling blade, a support on which said ruffling blade is pivotally mounted, means for yieldingly forcing said ruffling blade downwardly, means for oscillating said support, a bracket fixedly connected to the presser bar and pivotally supporting the upper end of said ruffling

blade support, means for raising the presser bar and the bracket connected thereto, and means for limiting the downward movement of the ruffling blade when said presser bar and bracket are lifted.

1,328,886. DIAPHRAGM CHECK-VALVE. SPENCER G. NEAL, New York, N. Y., assignor, by mesne assignments, to Automatic Straight Air Brake Company, Wilmington, Del., a Corporation of Delaware. Filed Dec. 26, 1916. Serial No. 138,754. 10 Claims. (Cl. 188—1.)

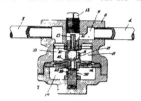

2. A diaphragm check value comprising a casing formed with an inlet chamber and a holding chamber, a movable abutment forming one wall of the holding chamber, means for permitting fluid from the inlet chamber to pass into the holding chamber, a supply chamber on the opposite side of the abutment from the holding chamber, a valve controlling communication between the supply chamber and the inlet chamber and actuated by the abutment, whereby when the superior pressure is in the holding chamber communication between the supply chamber and the inlet chamber will be closed and when the pressure in the holding chamber is reduced the pressure in the supply chamber will move the abutment and open communication between the supply chamber and the inlet chamber, and an apertured removable restriction plug to control the rate of flow between the supply chamber and the inlet chamber.

1,328,887. MOLDING APPARATUS. JOSEPH NITZGEN, New York, N. Y. Filed June 15, 1917. Serial No. 174,853. 3 Claims. (Cl. 18—5.)

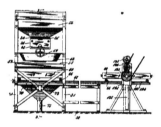

1. In a molding apparatus, a stationary track, a rotatable frame supported adjacent one end of the stationary track, a rotatable platform supported within the frame, molds adapted to be moved along the track and on to the rotatable platform, means for rotating the platform in one plane, means for rotating the frame in a plane opposite to the plane in which the platform is rotated, and means for delivering material to the mold.

1,328,888. PROCESS OF BREWING BEER AND LOW-ALCOHOLIC MALT BEVERAGES. CARL A. NOWAK, St. Louis, Mo. Filed Feb. 13, 1918. Serial No. 216,960. 2 Claims. (Cl. 195—1.)

2. The herein described process of brewing beer, which consists in adding ortho phosphoric acid to the wort in

the presence of the yeast for supplying a nutriment for the yeast and decomposing the carbonate contained in the wort, and subsequently adding to the wort of fermented beer meta phosphoric acid whereby the albumen contents of the beer is precipitated, and separating out the precipitate.

1,328,889. SEPARATOR FOR STEAM AND OIL. OLAF E. OLESON, Chicago, Ill., assignor to The Edward Valve & Manufacturing Co., Chicago, Ill., a Corporation of Illinois. Original application filed Aug. 24, 1914, Serial No. 858,186. Divided and this application filed Apr. 2, 1917. Serial No. 159,096. 14 Claims. (Cl. 183—111.)

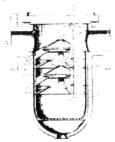

2. In a steam separator, the combination of a vertical casing having horizontal inlet and outlet openings, a plurality of separating units disposed in said casing and having outer walls within and separated from said casing, each of said units having a vertical wall at one side of its center within its outer wall, the vertical walls of the units together separating the upper portion of the casing into two parts and directing the steam from the inlet opening into the lowermost separating unit, the lowermost separating unit having a perforated bottom above the bottom of the casing to permit the passage of water into the bottom part of the casing below said perforated bottom.

1,328,890. AUTOMOBILE DUMP-BODY. CHARLES A. OMEN, Princeton, Ill. Filed May 29, 1918. Serial No. 237,210. 3 Claims. (Cl. 298—17.)

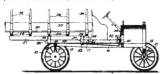

1. The combination with a truck-chassis frame provided with longitudinal members and with a rear cross-bar connected therewith, of a forward cross-bar mounted on intermediate portions of said longitudinal members, longitudinal sills mounted on said cross-bars, longitudinal beams resting on said sills and projecting rearwardly beyond the same, pivotal connection between the intermediate portions of said beams and the rear ends of said sills, means releasably locking the front end of said beams to said sills, and a load-receptacle wholly carried by said beams.

1,328,891. WORKBENCH FOR WATCHMAKERS AND JEWELERS. SISSAK K. OUZOUN-BOGHOSSIAN, Washington, D. C. Filed Nov. 4, 1918. Serial No. 261,021. 3 Claims. (Cl. 45—93.)

1. A collapsible and interchangeable workbench more particularly adapted for watchmakers' and jewelers' use

comprising a top-part A removably fitted on tops of two pedestal parts, said top part A comprising working surface D fitted with the railings E, a set of five drawers H fitted with the handles I, the opening J, swing door G with the handle I, and the apron drawer M sliding on the rail-

ings N, N, said pedestal parts having fixed pegs S, S, said top part A having slots to fit to said pegs S, S, said pedestals of said bench adapted to be used in combination in various styles of pedestals being exchanged, all substantially as set forth.

1,328,892. STARTER APPLICABLE TO MAGNETOS. HENRY PARKIN, Philadelphia, Pa., assignor of one-half to George G. Meeley, Philadelphia, Pa. Filed Jan. 2, 1919. Serial No. 269,387. 3 Claims. (Cl. 123—149.)

1. A starter applicable to magnetos comprising the combination of a driven member having a laterally projecting hub, a driving member revoluble on said hub, a spring driving connection between said members, said driven member having a notched portion, a laterally disposed bracket adapted to be secured to a face of the magneto, a latch arm pivoted to said bracket intermediate its, the latch arm's, ends, said latch arm being provided on its inner end with a biased nose adapted to engage said notch and at its opposite end with two spaced noses, and a spring post secured to said bracket and extending laterally outward therefrom to engage said last two noses.

1,328,893. FLEXIBLE COUPLING FOR PROPELLER-SHAFTS. ROBERT A. PATRICK, Freeport, N Y., assignor to Columbian Bronze Corporation, Freeport, N. Y., a Corporation of New York. Filed Apr. 20, 1917. Serial No. 163,325. 10 Claims. (Cl. 64—96.)

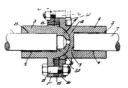

1. In a device of the class set forth, the combination of a pair of coupling members, rigid interlocking mem-

bers held to the coupling members having relative sliding and tilting movements in interlocked relation, and a flexible connecting and driving member interposed between the coupling members and positively held to the interlocking members.

1,328,894. GRINDING-MACHINE. ARTHUR E. PEARSON, Muskegon, Mich. Filed May 19, 1919. Serial No. 298,339. 2 Claims. (Cl. 51—4.)

1. In a grinding machine, a horizontally movable driven shaft having a driving pulley on one end and a driving gear on the other end, a driven shaft mounted each side of and parallel with the driving shaft and having gear wheels adapted to mesh with the gear wheel on the driving shaft, a link connecting the driving shaft with each of the driven shafts in such a manner that any backward or forward movement of the driving shaft will impart a like vertical movement to the driven shafts.

1,328,895. INDICATOR MECHANISM. OSCAR H. PIEPER and ALPHONSE F. PIEPER, Rochester, N. Y. Filed Dec. 27, 1915. Serial No. 68,895. 2 Claims. (Cl. 73—109.)

1. In an indicator mechanism, the combination of a supporting member having an opening therethrough, pressure indicator operating mechanism, a housing therefor, a plate having a transversely projecting annular flange, means for securing the housing and plate to opposite sides of the supporting member, an indicator scale supported within the flange on said plate, a threaded ring also supported on said plate, a crystal supported in said ring, a spacing ring bearing against the scale and the inner face of the crystal, and indicating means cooperating with said indicator scale and controlled by said operating mechanism.

1,328,896. PLOWING-MACHINE. CHASE C. REED, Toledo, Ohio, assignor to The R. & C. Engineering Company, Toledo, Ohio, a Corporation of Ohio. Filed Nov. 25, 1916, Serial No. 133,339. Renewed June 13, 1919. Serial No. 304,086. 14 Claims. (Cl. 97—72.)

2. In a plowing machine having a main frame and a motor mounted on said frame, a differential casing and

connected opposite shaft supports, said casing being pivotally mounted in said main frame on an axis running longitudinally of the machine, a cutter frame hinged on a transverse axis to said casing structure, a rotary cutter mounted in said frame, differential mechanism in said casing operatively connected with said motor and with the members of said divided shaft, and connections intermediate such members and said cutter for rotating the latter.

1,328,897. METHOD OF AND APPARATUS FOR DRYING MATERIAL. OTIS D. RICE, Winthrop, Mass. Filed Jan. 15, 1919. Serial No. 271,288. 5 Claims. (Cl. 34—19.)

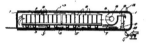

1. In a vacuum drying apparatus, the combination with a vacuum chamber to contain the material to be dried, of a fan situated within said chamber, means providing a closed circuit whereby the fan will operate to circulate a drying and heating medium continuously through said closed circuit and over the material to be dried, means to deliver heat to said circulating medium, and a suction apparatus connected to said chamber for removing part or all of the vapor caused by the evaporation of moisture in said material.

1,328,898. SCOURING SOAP CAKE, TO BE USED IN GENERAL SCOURING AND CLEANING PURPOSES. WILLIAM CORWIN RICKETTS, Dayton, Ohio. Filed Mar. 17, 1919. Serial No. 283,056. 3 Claims. (Cl. 87—5.)

1. A scouring soap cake, consisting of metal wool permeated with hard soap and formed into a cake, said cake having a solid body of said materials and a soft spongy scouring face which readily absorbs water and will conform to any surface applied thereto, as set forth.

1,328,899. LEVER-HOLDING MECHANISM FOR AUTOMOBILES. THOMAS J. RITTER, Jr., and BENJAMIN M. WARN, Lairdsville, Pa. Filed Apr. 18, 1919. Serial No. 291,002. 3 Claims. (Cl. 74—39.)

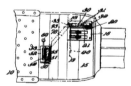

1. The combination of a floor plate having a slot, an automobile speed control lever playing in said slot, a swinging toothed member pivoted adjacent to said slot and adapted to swing in a plane substantially parallel with said plate into and out of engagement with said lever, a spring mechanism operative to yieldingly hold said toothed member normally in engagement with said lever, and means mounted independently of said toothed member for shifting it out of engagement with said lever.

1,328,900. NURSERY-SEAT. ANNIE K. ROWND, Rochester, N. Y. Filed June 16, 1919. Serial No. 304,530. 2 Claims. (Cl. 4—18.)

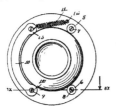

1. A nursery seat comprising an annular top, lugs projecting downwardly therefrom, and a swinging lever having a projection thereon, the lugs and projection and lever being adapted to engage the top of a bowl and fasten the seat thereto.

1,328,901. UMBRELLA. AMBROSE RYDER, New York, N. Y. Filed Oct. 10, 1917, Serial No. 195,686. Renewed May 27, 1919. Serial No. 300,182. 6 Claims. (Cl. 135—20.)

6. In an umbrella, the combination of ribs, trusses, a crown piece and covering, means coöperating with the ribs and trusses to hold the covering in open position, and a straight stick pivoted to said crown piece and acting as a rib for the covering, one of said trusses connecting the stick and said means and being of such limited length that when the covering is open the axis of the crown piece forms a relatively acute angle with the stick, whereby the covering is held in tilted position with respect to the stick, and the length of the ribs and covering on the side opposite the stick being greater than on the side toward the stick.

1,328,902. UMBRELLA. AMBROSE RYDER, New York, N. Y. Filed Aug. 7, 1919. Serial No. 315,897. 5 Claims. (Cl. 135—23.)

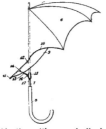

5. The combination with an umbrella having a stick depending adjacent one edge of the cover, of means to prevent flow of water from the cover onto the stick, said means comprising a cover extension secured to the ordinary cover and projecting outwardly over the stick when open.

1,328,903. CHENILLE SCARF. HARRY SANTORO, New York, N. Y. Filed Apr. 15, 1919. Serial No. 290,202. 3 Claims. (Cl. 139—9.)

2. The combination with strings of chenille, each string formed in parallel waves with the apex of each wave in alinement with the apex of its adjacent wave, and slightly overlapping the same, and a thread passing through the chenille waves to bind them in position, the said strip of chenille serving to prevent the thread from unravelling.

1,328,904. ATTACHMENT FOR COTTON-PICKERS. JOHN F. SCHENCK, Jr., Shelby, N. C. Filed Nov. 13, 1919. Serial No. 337,666. 4 Claims. (Cl. 19—8.)

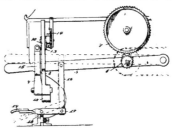

1. In a picker of the class specified, the combination with a hand lever carrying a driving pinion and mounted to have vertical movement, a gear for operating calender rolls, and a gravitating catch lever for the hand lever together with means for automatically releasing the catch lever when a lap is completed, of a foot pressure attachment connected to the said hand lever for raising the latter to cause the pinion thereof to engage said gear.

2. In a picker of the class specified, the combination with a gravitating lever carrying a driving pinion, a gear for operating calender rolls, a catch means for holding said lever elevated, and mechanism for automatically releasing the catch means and lever when a lap has been completed, of a foot lever connected to said gravitating lever for raising the latter and provided with a pressure plate and a connection relatively to said gravitating lever.

3. In a picker of the class specified, the combination with a gravitating lever carrying a driving pinion, a gear for operating calender rolls, catch means for holding said lever elevated, and mechanism for automatically releasing the catch means and lever when a lap has been completed, of foot operated means connected to said gravitating lever for raising the latter and effecting an engagement of the catch means therewith.

4. In a picker machine of the class specified, the combination with movable means carrying a driving pinion, a gear for operating calender rolls and disposed for engagement by said pinion, and mechanism for holding said movable means and pinion elevated to effect mesh of the pinion with the said gear and for releasing the movable means and pinion when a lap is completed and causing the latter to disengage from the gear, of foot operated means

connected to said movable means for raising the latter and engage the pinion with the gear to start the machine subsequent to removal of a lap.

1,328,905. RIVETING - MACHINE. ISAAC E. SEXTON, Boston, Mass. Filed Jan. 30, 1919. Serial No. 274,032. 3 Claims. (Cl. 78—49.)

1. A riveting machine for upsetting the shank of a previously headed rivet inserted in an annular article, the rivet head bearing on the convex outer surface and the shank projecting from the concave inner surface of the article, said machine comprising a mandrel having an anvil face, said mandrel and face being formed to occupy a portion of the interior of the annular article, a ram movable in a predetermined path toward and from the anvil face, and having an unobstructed end face, a work rest movable toward and from the anvil face and formed to bear on the inner surface of the article, and to permit the interposition of the rivet between the anvil face and the ram, and means whereby the work rest is normally held yieldingly in position to space the outer face of the article from the anvil face a distance substantially equal to the total length of the rivet, with the rivet head and the rivet shank bearing respectively on the outer surface of the article and on the anvil face, so that the ram in moving toward the anvil face, acts through the rivet head to force the rivet-containing portion of the article toward the anvil face, and at the same time to upset the rivet shank upon the inner surface of the article.

1,328,906. STEAM-JACKET FOR OIL-PUMPS. LEONARD C. STEFFERUD, Brandt, S. D. Filed Sept. 26, 1917. Serial No. 193,322. 2 Claims. (Cl. 184—104.)

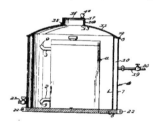

1. In a device as described, in combination, a steam jacket having a base portion, and an upstanding inner shell and an outer shell, the inner shell being higher than the outer shell, a concave top portion formed with an outwardly-extending flange adapted to rest upon the upper edge of the outer shell, a lubricating oil pump secured centrally upon said base-portion and having its sides spaced away from the inner shell and its top spaced away from said top portion, said top portion being provided with an opening, a cover adapted to close said opening, said opening giving access to said oil pump, a steam-conducting pipe connected to the outer shell, inlet and outlet pipes connected to said oil pump, the space between said shells constituting a steam chamber and the enveloping space around said oil pump providing a heated-air space, and means for controlling the supply of steam to the steam chamber.

1,328,907. FEELER-MOTION FOR LOOMS. EDWARD S. STIMPSON, Hopedale, Mass., assignor to Draper Corporation, Hopedale, Mass., a Corporation of Maine. Filed Aug. 8, 1917. Serial No. 185,156. 12 Claims. (Cl. 139—85.)

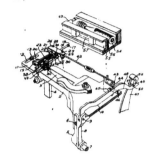

1. In a feeler motion for looms, the combination of the lay and shuttle-boxes, a filling feeler adapted to enter the shuttle and be moved frontwardly on a detecting beat, means with respect to which the feeler reciprocates on each detecting beat and positioned to act upon the side of the feeler as it moves frontwardly relative to said means to impart movement thereto longitudinally of the shuttle when the filling is substantially exhausted and adapted to be moved from its actuating position by the feeler as it moves frontwardly when a working supply of filling is present.

1,328,908. FEELER-MOTION FOR LOOMS. EDWARD S. STIMPSON, Hopedale, Mass., assignor to Draper Corporation, Hopedale, Mass., a Corporation of Maine. Filed Feb. 23, 1918. Serial No. 218,734. 4 Claims. (Cl. 139—85.)

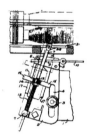

1. In a feeler motion for looms, the combination of a feeler member having a threaded rear portion, an end holder having a complemental threaded portion and a bifurcated end, and a filling engaging member secured between the bifurcated ends of the end holder.

1,328,909. MOTOR-CAR OF SMALL TYPE. SHINKICHI TAMURA, Kobe, and MASANORI WATANABE, Tokyo, Japan; said Watanabe assignor to said Tamura. Filed Aug. 1, 1918. Serial No. 247,882. 2 Claims. (Cl. 180—89.)

1. A device of the character described including, in combination, a supporting chasis, front and rear wheels connected thereto, an engine supported medially of the ends of the chasis, a body on the chasis and provided with an opening in the bottom for accommodating the head of the engine, a driver's seat arranged over the open-

ing in the body and having the lower edge of its rear portion hinged to the bottom. connecting means between

the front wheels and steering means forwardly of the driver's seat and the engine and directly connected with the front wheels.

1,328,910. ROAD-MAINTAINER. JAMES BOLTON, Council Bluffs, Iowa. Filed Oct. 4, 1919. Serial No. 328,447. 2 Claims. (Cl. 37—7.)

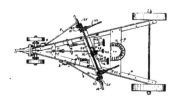

1. A road maintainer, comprising, in combination with a vehicle frame having a cross-plate provided with a hanger, a pair of draw-bars pivotally connected with the vehicle frame, a scraper-blade below the vehicle frame connected with the draw-bars, a pair of toothed sectors mounted upon the cross-plate adjacent to the ends thereof, hand-levers pivotally mounted on the sectors, a pair of flexible members each being connected with a hand-lever and the scraper-blade, a shaft journaled in the hanger and provided with grooved segments, flexible members connecting the grooved segments with the scraper-blade, a tilting-bar arranged to swing from the hanger, and a flexible member connecting the tilting-bar with one of the grooved segments of said shaft.

1,328,911. DIVERGENT SAW-TOOTH FASTENER. SPENCER C. CARY, Brooklyn, N. Y. Filed May 31. 1919. Serial No. 300,795. 3 Claims. (Cl. 85—11.)

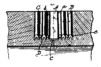

3. A divergent saw tooth fastener embodying a flat web the side edges of which are inclined and the penetrating edge of which is beveled to produce a straight cutting edge of appreciable length, and a plurality of corrugations at the respective sides of the web and parallel to the inclined edges thereof, said corrugations being provided with saw teeth the concave portions of which at the bases thereof are beveled, said cutting edge of the web being alined with cutting edges at the points of the teeth and said cutting edges of the web and the cutting edges at the points of the teeth lying in the medial plane of the fastener.

1,328,912. LABEL-MAKING MACHINE. MAX O. CLAUSS, New York, N. Y., assignor to H. E. Verran Company, a Corporation of New York. Filed May 20, 1918. Serial No. 235,594. 15 Claims. (Cl. 93—81.)

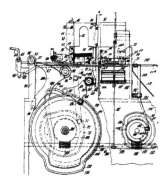

2. In a label making machine, a former bar, means for individually feeding labels to said bar, means for folding the sides of said label, means for folding said sides into superimposed position with respect to each other, means for applying paste to one of said sides prior to engagement therewith of said other side, means adapted to reciprocate said bar with an unformed label thereon from said feeding means to said folding and paste applying means; and means adapted to remove the formed labels from said bar.

1,328,913. SHOVEL OR SPADE PLOW. ISAAC COHEN, Schenectady, N. Y. Filed Dec. 12, 1917. Serial No. 206,811. 7 Claims. (Cl. 97—25.)

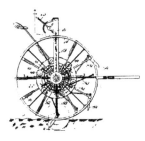

7. In apparatus of the character set forth, the combination with a frame, of wheels carrying the same, a rotatable drum mounted on the frame, means for rotating the drum from one of the wheels, radial arms pivoted on the drum, springs for yieldingly resisting the swinging movement of the arms, digging elements pivoted on the arms, gears journaled on the drum and having link connections with the digging elements, and fixed gear segments engaged by the gears upon the rotation of the drum.

1,328,914. ORDNANCE-SIGHTING APPARATUS. ARTHUR TREVOR DAWSON and GEORGE THOMAS BUCKHAM, Westminster, London, England, assignors to Vickers Limited, Westminster, London, England. Filed Nov. 11, 1918. Serial No. 262,087. 3 Claims. (Cl. 33—48.)
1. In sighting apparatus for ordnance having an independent line of sight, the combination with a member

moving with the gun during elevation, of a second member connected to the first member so as to be capable of being adjusted; when the axis of the gun trunnions is inclined to the horizontal, into a predetermined plane about an axis parallel to the axis of the gun, a sight carrier sup-

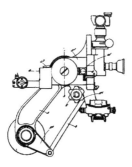

ported by said second member, a part moving with the gun during pointing only, and transverse guides and co-operating members between the sight carrier and said part, for varying the angular position of the sight line in the vertical plane during the adjustment of said second member.

1,328,915. LICENSE-HOLDER FOR MOTOR-VEHICLES. CHARLES H. FAWCETT, Independence, Iowa, assignor to Interstate Ever-License Company, Independence, Iowa. Filed Mar. 24, 1919. Serial No. 284,566. 9 Claims. (Cl. 40—10.)

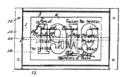

4. In a device of the character described, a closed hollow boxing having a transparent top, said boxing having inlet ports at its opposite ends, a slide having engaging means, and provided with a longitudinal slot extending nearly its entire length, a card removably mounted on said slide over said slot and releasably secured in said engaging means, supporting means within said boxing, said slide being movable through one of said inlet ports and supported upon said supporting means, a locking device within said boxing adapted to releasably lock said slide within the boxing, a knife adapted to pass through the other inlet port movable through the slot in said slide and having an edged extremity adapted to split said card apart, said knife being positioned to engage said slide locking means near the end of its cutting stroke to release said locking means from said slide.

1,328,916. SLICING-MACHINE. RAYMOND S. C. FOW, Philadelphia. Pa., assignor of seventy-nine one-hundredths to Rolland T. Frush and twenty-one one-hundredths to William Thompson, Philadelphia, Pa. Filed Mar. 19, 1919. Serial No. 283,498. 18 Claims. (Cl. 17—24.)

6. A slicing machine including a slicing knife; a carriage; and adjustable means for moving said carriage at various angles to the face of said knife to convey material, to be sliced, to the edge of said knife and then

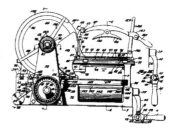

away from the face of said knife; substantially as described.

1,328,917. RAIL-CHAIR. GEORGE E. FREY, Steubenville, Ohio, assignor of one-half to R. E. Snider, Mingo Junction, Ohio. Filed Aug. 2, 1919. Serial No. 314,843. 6 Claims. (Cl. 238—272.)

1. A rail chair and clamp comprising a flat seat for a rail base, said seat having means whereby it may be attached to a trough-shaped crosstie, an integral wing extending laterally from each lateral edge of said seat, each of said wings having an opening therein, and a bar disposed in underlying relation to said seat and having terminals turned upward and inward into clamping relation to the opposite sides of the base of a rail mounted on said seat, said terminals being received in the openings in said wings.

1,328,918. METAL DOOR CONSTRUCTION. EDWARD FULDA, New York, N. Y. Filed Jan. 19, 1916. Serial No. 72,900. 4 Claims. (Cl. 189—46.)

1. In a metal door or panel made in sections, the combination substantially as described of an outer frame composed of a flanged metal bar constituting the outer edge of the complete door and a sheet metal facing constituting a side of the door or panel and fastened to the outer face of the flange of said bar with an edge of the sheet metal flush with the face of the portion of bar constituting the edge of the door and a counterpart frame of angle iron nested within the first and having a door side of sheet metal secured to the outer face of the flange thereof with an edge projecting to receive the edge of the bar constituting the edge of the door and within which it is nested.

1,328,919. METHOD OF UNITING VERTICAL PLATES BY ELECTRIC WELDING. EDWARD FULDA, New York, N. Y. Filed June 19, 1918. Serial No. 240,725. 10 Claims. (Cl. 219—10.)

1. The herein described improvement in forming a localized weld between the meeting vertical surfaces of super-

posed metal plates in vertical position, consisting in providing a heating and pressure localizing piece adapted to be supported on a surface of one of said plates independently of and prior to engagement by the welding dies,

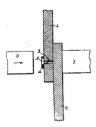

locating said piece in contact with the surface of a plate at the place of desired union and passing heating current through said piece and through both plates to effect a welding together of said plates over their engaged surfaces.

1,328,920. APPARATUS FOR INDICATING FUEL CONSUMPTION. BIRD M. GRAYBILL, Chicago, Ill., assignor to Stanley W. Cook, Brookline, Mass. Filed Dec. 30, 1915, Serial No. 69,313. Renewed June 11, 1919. Serial No. 303,528. 27 Claims. (Cl. 158—36.)

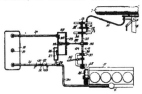

1. Method of continuously indicating the rate of fuel consumption of an internal combustion engine which consists in supplying to the engine an amount of fuel variable with the speed of the engine and at all times in excess of the maximum demands thereof, diverting the excess fuel over and above that utilized by the engine, and visibly indicating the rate of flow of the diverted fuel.

1,328,921. TOY-FURNITURE SET. DALE E. HOWE, Sioux Falls, S. D., assignor of one-half to J. M. Newton, Sioux Falls, S. D. Filed May 8, 1919. Serial No. 295,571. 7 Claims. (Cl. 46—35.)

1. A set of toy furniture cut from a solid rectangular block of material and including a pair of similar and

complemental chair members adapted to be nested in reverse positions with their seats fitting against each other and back of each chair extending along the front of the other chair, and a table member including a top and integral ends, the assembled chairs nesting snugly within the table.

1,328,922. CART-SADDLE. JAMES C. JARDINE, JAMES DICKIE, and GEORGE A. BOWNESS, Summerside, Prince Edward Island, Canada. Filed Jan. 8, 1919. Serial No. 270,131. 1 Claim. (Cl. 54—39.)

A saddle of the character described comprising a saddletree, a cantle section, a pommel section, a pair of pads, and means for detachably connecting said pads to said saddletree, said pads adapted to retain said cantle and pommel sections adjacent said saddletree substantially as and for the purpose specified.

1,328,923. DUMP-WAGON. JOSEPH H. JASPER, Philadelphia, Pa. Filed Mar. 26, 1919. Serial No. 285,223. 5 Claims. (Cl. 214—77.)

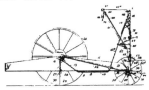

1. A wagon of the character described including a body portion; a frame having parts extending upwardly to provide a standard; guiding means on said standard; a block slidable on said guiding means whereby the block can be moved into various positions; a hoisting boom supported by said block; a hoisting cable connected to said boom; and means on said standard for moving said boom in various angular positions; substantially as described.

3. A wagon of the character described including a body portion; a frame including members extending longitudinally adjacent the sides of said body portion, and other members crossing under the bottom of said body portion and then extending upwardly to a position above said body portion, the longitudinal members extending beyond said upwardly extending portions of the first mentioned members and then extending upward and secured to said first mentioned members to provide a standard; and hoisting means supported by said standard; substantially as described.

1,328,924. RESILIENT RECOIL-PAD FOR GUN-STOCKS. LAWRENCE F. KENNEDY, St. Paul, Minn. Filed May 8, 1919. Serial No. 295,733. 2 Claims. (Cl. 42—74.)

2. A resilient recoil pad for gun stocks comprising a member of substantially rigid material, a member of

yielding material secured to said rigid member, a stud carried by said rigid member, said stud having an elongated head for coöperation with an elongated slot in the butt plate whereby said members may be attached and detached by turning the same through substantially ninety degrees, and an arm extending forwardly from said rigid member, said arm having a recess for engagement by a projection on the gun stock.

1,328,925. ROLLED CONDENSER FOR SPARKING APPARATUS. FRANZ KRATZ, Stuttgart, Germany, assignor to the Firm of Robert Bosch Aktiengesellschaft, Stuttgart, Germany. Filed Aug. 20, 1919. Serial No. 318,807. 2 Claims. (Cl. 250—41.)

1. A condenser comprising two cheeks with middle protuberances opposite to but apart from each other, and paper and tinfoil strips wound tightly onto the said proturberances so as to prevent the cheeks from separating.

1,328,926. FENCEPOST. MAURICE LACHMAN, New York, N. Y., assignor to Universal Electric Welding Company, New York, N. Y., a Corporation of New York. Filed June 10, 1916. Serial No. 102,838. 2 Claims. (Cl. 189—24.)

1. A metal post comprising T-shaped upright members, transverse plates intersecting said members at spaced intervals and having the web of said members seated in a recess thereof, the flanges of said members being removed at the intersection to expose the web and whereby the edge of the plate is brought into the same plane with the outer surface of the upright and a ridged button having the ridge thereof welded to the edge of the plate and the exposed web of the upright to lock the members together.

1,328,927. POLE OR POST. MAURICE LACHMAN, New York, N. Y., assignor to Universal Electric Welding Company, New York, N. Y., a Corporation of New York. Filed June 10, 1916. Serial No. 102,839. 2 Claims. (Cl. 189—24.)
2. A metal pole or post comprising T-shaped uprights, transverse plates intersecting said uprights and having recesses in which the webs of the uprights are disposed,

the flanges of said uprights seating against the edge of the plates and rivets integral with the plates and passing

through openings in the flanges of the uprights and headed against the outer surface thereof.

1,328,928. DUMPING DEVICE. WILLIAM F. LAWES, Bedford, N. H. Filed Sept. 7, 1918. Serial No. 253,042. 6 Claims. (Cl. 298—19.)

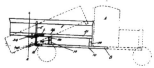

6. The combination with a vehicle frame, of a body medially pivoted thereon in such manner as to swing up and down, a substantially straight horizontal guideway carried by the body, and a dumping lever pivoted to the frame at a point in a line extending at a right angle from the forward part of said guideway, said lever having a handle and a part which engages the guideway.

1,328,929. TOY MACHINE-GUN. WALTER O. MCDANIEL, Indianapolis, Ind., assignor to The H-K Toy & Novelty Co., Indianapolis, Ind., a Corporation of Indiana. Filed June 12, 1918. Serial No. 239,617. 15 Claims. (Cl. 124—13.)

1. A toy machine gun having a gun stock provided with a journal, a magazine cylinder rotatably mounted on the journal, a hammer pivotally supported by the journal, and a trigger mounted in the gun stock to control the hammer.

1,328,930. MIRROR-MOUNTING. LOUIS J. STERN, Boston, Mass. Filed Nov. 6, 1919. Serial No. 336,150. 6 Claims. (Cl. 248—20.)

4. A mirror mounting including a clamping block, a bracket, a flexible strip adapted to be passed between said bracket and block and about a support, and means to clamp said bracket to said block with said strip therebetween.

1,328,931. GARTER. WILLIAM H. STEVENS, New York, N. Y. Filed July 17, 1917. Serial No. 180,990. 3 Claims. (Cl. 241—6.)

1. A combined side and leg garter comprising a short and a long length of material, a joint member pivotally connecting the lengths of material at one end thereof, respectively, an attaching member on the other end of the short length of material, and an attaching member on the other end of the long length of material and rotatably supported with relation thereto so that it may be turned end-for-end thereon, one end of the last named attaching member being provided with a part for engagement with a garment when the device is used as a side-garter, and the other end provided with a part for engagement with the joint member between the two lengths of material, when the device is used as a round-the-leg garter.

1,328,932. RAILROAD - CROSSING SIGNAL. CHARLES THERIOT, New Iberia, La., assignor of one-third to J. Wofford Sanders and one-third to Porteus R. Burke, New Iberia, La. Filed Feb. 25, 1919. Serial No. 279,058. 5 Claims. (Cl. 246—294.)

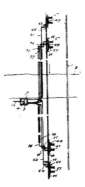

1. A railroad crossing signal comprising a supporting casing, a shaft journaled in said supporting casing, a signal carried by said shaft, a track mechanism for rotating the shaft in one direction to move the signal into signaling position upon the approach of a train, means locking the signal into signaling position, an automatic alarm adapted to be set in operation upon the signal moving into signaling position, a track mechanism adapted to be actuated by a train after passing the crossing to release the locking means, and means returning the signal to a non-signaling position.

1,328,933. RADIO RECEIVING APPARATUS. ROY E. THOMPSON, New York, N. Y. Filed Aug. 21, 1917. Serial No. 187,347. 12 Claims. (Cl. 250—20.)

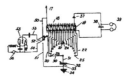

5. In radio receiving apparatus, the combination with a receiving antenna, of a circuit of utilization coupled thereto and constructed to have substantially no capacity effective in accumulating received energy therein, whereby uniform efficiency of reception is maintained over a range of various wave-lengths without adjustment of time period of the circuit of utilization.

1,328,934. DRIVING MECHANISM FOR OVERHEAD TRAVELING BRIDGE-CRANES. RAPHAEL W. VALLS, Kenton, Ohio, assignor to The Champion Engineering Company, Kenton, Ohio, a Corporation of Ohio. Filed May 26, 1919. Serial No. 299,750. 12 Claims. (Cl. 74—7.)

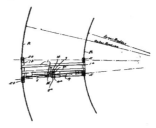

1. In combination with a traveling crane truck and its carrying wheels; two shafts respectively operatively connected with the carrying wheels at opposite ends of the truck; a driving shaft; gearing between the driving shaft and one of the wheel operating shafts; and gearing differing in ratio from the first gearing between the driven shaft and the other wheel operating shaft; whereby the wheels at opposite ends of the truck may be driven at the desired different peripheral speeds.

1,328,935. PAPER BOX. FRANK M. WADE, Wauwatosa, Wis., assignor to Milwaukee Paper Box Company, Milwaukee, Wis., a Corporation of Wisconsin. Filed Mar. 14, 1918. Serial No. 222,434. 2 Claims. (Cl. 229—39.)

1. A knock-down paper box, comprising a set of side, top and bottom walls permanently connected in an endless series, all of said walls being provided with end flaps adapted, when folded, to constitute the end walls of the box, the bottom flap having a transverse slit and comprising an inner member of the wall, the top flap being pro-

vided with a tongue adapted to interlock in said slit, and the other two flaps having their lower margins cut away to allow their extremities to fold upon each other between the interlocking flaps above said slit.

1,328,936. FLY-POISONING DEVICE. EDWARD L. WATSON, Dallas, S. D. Filed Apr. 19, 1919. Serial No. 291,283. 2 Claims. (Cl. 43—22.)

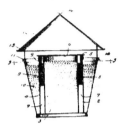

1. In a fly poisoning device, the combination of a container having a plurality of compartments arranged one within the other, the inner compartment containing lure to attract the flies and having a screened cover preventing their entrance to said compartment, an outer compartment accessible to the flies and containing poisoned bait, a roof releasably attached to the container and having its outer rim projecting substantially beyond the rim of the container to prevent the entrance of rain which would dilute the bait, and means for suspending said roof, substantially as and for the purposes described.

1,328,937. SANITARY MILK-CARRIER. BURT WILBUR, Syracuse, N. Y., assignor of one-half to George H. Jones, Syracuse, N. Y. Filed Apr. 8, 1916. Serial No. 89,911. 1 Claim. (Cl. 220—9.)

In combination with a milk carrier comprising an elongated paper tube gradually tapered from one end to its opposite end to form a bottle, the smaller end of which constitutes the top, an inverted cup-shaped paper bottom tightly fitted within the larger end of the tube and permanently secured thereto, a cup-shaped paper stopper tightly fitted in the smaller end of the tube, an outer metal tubular casing of substantially the same length and taper as the paper tube wedgingly fitted upon the exterior of said paper tube by downward sliding pressure, a metal bottom having an upwardly pressed central portion inserted within the inverted cup-shaped bottom of the paper tube and resting against the under side of said paper bottom, said metal bottom having an upturned marginal flange fitted upon the periphery of the adjacent lower end of the metal casing and detachably interlocked therewith, and a metal cap having a depressed central portion fitting within and against the bottom of the stopper and also provided with a marginal flange fitted upon the periphery of the upper end of the metal casing.

1,328,938. PROCESS OF PRODUCING ALKALI-METAL FERRICYANIDS AND THE LIKE. ROGER WILLIAMS, Providence, R. I., assignor to Nitrogen Products Company, Providence, R. I., a Corporation of Rhode Island. Filed Mar. 16, 1918. Serial No. 222,878. 9 Claims. (Cl. 23—13.)

1. The process of obtaining a water-soluble cyanid the base of which is in part at least composed of a heavy metal, which comprises converting a water-soluble cyanogen compound into said cyanid with formation, together with the product sought, of a water-soluble salt, said products and salt being intimately commingled, winning said product in solid form from the mixture of reaction products by extracting the salt from said mixture with an extracting agent which is substantially free from water and which is incapable of dissolving or entering into chemical combination with said cyanid at the temperature of the extracting operation, and separating said salt from said agent by heat treatment.

1,328,939. NUT-LOCK. WILLIAM P. ANDREW, Mount Pleasant, Pa. Filed Mar. 12, 1919. Serial No. 282,161. 2 Claims. (Cl. 151—8.)

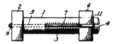

1. A nut and bolt lock comprising a bolt having a slot leading in from one end thereof and a bore leading from said slot to the other end of the slot, a locking member having arms extending from the slot around the nut and a stem entering the bore and means for fixing the locking member with relation to the bolt.

1,328,940. CASING-CUTTER. HARRY W. BEATTY, Oilfields, Calif. Filed Aug. 22, 1919. Serial No. 319,135. 3 Claims. (Cl. 81—195.)

2. A device of the character described comprising a sleeve, pivoted cutters mounted at the lower end of said sleeve, a stem mounted in said sleeve, a head carried by said stem, casing engaging means carried by the head and a cam surface upon the head with which the rear faces of the cutters engage and by which the cutters are projected outwardly upon relative movement of the parts longitudinally, the sleeve being capable of rotation with relation to the head and spring means tending to separate the sleeve and the head.

1,328,941. ADJUSTABLE DIAL FOR PRESSURE-GAGES AND LIKE DIAL INSTRUMENTS. GRIFFITH BREWER, London, England. Filed Oct. 31, 1918. Serial No. 260,570. 3 Claims. (Cl. 116—49.)

1. In pressure gages and the like dial instruments; an annular dial of sheet material of the requisite elasticity, having an internal periphery eccentric to an external periphery to constitute a face surface narrow at one part and increasing gradually in width in both directions from such narrower part to a point diametrically opposite to said narrower part, said dial being divided at its narrower part into adjacent ends said division leaving a small space between said adjacent ends, said dial being adapted to be inserted into an annular groove in a case by causing the adjacent ends of said dial to approach each other and the release of said adjacent ends and consequent expansion of said dial frictionally holding same in position.

1,328,942. DISH-WASHING DEVICE. JOHN T. CARTER, Jefferson City, Mo. Filed Aug. 13, 1918. Serial No. 249,734. 2 Claims. (Cl. 299—83.)

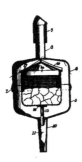

1. A device as characterized and comprising a two piece separable casing, one piece having a central aperture adapted for connection with a spigot, the other piece having a discharge tube in alinement with said central aperture, means within said discharge for imparting a whirling motion to a liquid passing therethrough, a reticulated soap container rotatably mounted on said means, a cone shaped imperforate cover for said soap container, and means carried on said cover for imparting a rotary motion to the container by a stream of water directed from the spigot to the apex of the cone-shaped cover.

1,328,943. CORD-BURNISHING DEVICE. CHAUNCEY C. CHAMBERLAIN, Ionia, Mich., assignor to Ypsilanti Reed Furniture Company, Ionia, Mich., a Corporation of Michigan. Filed May 24, 1919. Serial No. 299,641. 1 Claim. (Cl. 28—21.)
In a burnishing device of the character described, the combination of a head having diametrically extending slots at right angles to each other, separate pairs of jaws movable in said slots, those of each pair being spring pressed

toward each other, and means on the head for simultaneously opening all of the jaws simultaneously against the action of their closing means.

1,328,944. TRUSS. ALFRED L. COBB, Estes Park, Colo. Filed Sept. 30, 1919. Serial No. 327,489. 2 Claims. (Cl. 128—105.)

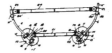

1. In a device of the kind described, a body portion including spaced arms, pads positioned on the lower end of each of the arms, spaced cleats positioned on one side of each of the pads, a bracket member disposed between the cleats, said cleats adapted to embrace a portion of each arm, said bracket members adapted to embrace the portions of the arms between the cleats, each of said bracket members having a head formed thereon, and a hook member having pivotal connection with the head for securing an adjusting strap to the pads.

1,328,945. COAT-COLLAR HOLDER. FRANCISCO CONCHA, Cuzco, Peru. Filed Dec. 2, 1918. Serial No. 265,089. 5 Claims. (Cl. 24—201.)

1. In a garment holder, the combination with a stud having a pendant shank; of a holder comprising a bar having means for attachment to the inside of the coat, fingers pivotally connected with and outstanding from said bar, and yielding means holding them normally end to end to retain said shank but permitting them to swing inward toward the bar.

1,328,946. CARBURETER-ADJUSTER. ROBERT M. DONALDSON and HARRY R. DONALDSON, Claysville, Pa. Filed Feb. 4, 1919. Serial No. 274,880. 2 Claims. (Cl. 137—139.)

1. In a motor vehicle, an operating means for permitting the needle valve of the carbureter to be operated from a

distance, said means comprising a pair of shafts arranged with their ends adjacent, the remote end of one shaft being connected with the valve to turn the same, the connection between the adjacent ends of the shafts comprising a pinion on one shaft, a lateral arm on the other and a rack bar pivoted to the arm and engaging the pinion.

1,328,947. LATHE-TOOL. GEORGE WILLIAM DOVER, Cranston, R. I. Filed May 16, 1919. Serial No. 297,499. 8 Claims. (Cl. 29—99.)

1. A lathe tool comprising a holding member having a transverse hole, a rotatable adjusting member in the transverse hole and having a bolt hole and a head in which is a groove, a bolt extending through the bolt hole and having a head in which is a groove corresponding to the groove in the head of the adjusting member, a cutting member in the grooves in the heads of the adjusting member and the bolt and means on the bolt engaging with the holding member for simultaneously clamping the cutting member between the head of the adjusting member and the head of the bolt and securing the adjusting member in the adjusted position.

1,328,948. SETTING FOR JEWELRY. GEORGE WILLIAM DOVER, Cranston, R. I. Filed June 11, 1919. Serial No. 303,460. 2 Claims. (Cl. 63—28.)

1. A setting for jewelry consisting of an elongated U-shaped body of sheet metal having a bottom and sides which terminate in thin lips, each side having an internal ledge adjacent the thin lips and in which, in oppositely disposed relation, are a series of angular recessed portions shaped to receive stones or the like, whereby a plurality or stones or the like may be secured in the setting by bending the thin lips over the stones or the like, in one operation.

1,328,949. SETTING FOR JEWELRY. GEORGE WILLIAM DOVER, Cranston, R. I. Filed June 30, 1919. Serial No. 307,573. 2 Claims. (Cl. 63—28.)

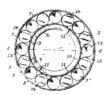

1. A setting for jewelry constructed to hold a central stone and a series of surrounding stones and having a thin annular outer lip, a thin annular parallel inner lip having a plurality of stone fastening members, said thin lips forming an annular trough in the bottom of which, in alternate positions, are a series of inverted cone-shaped depressions shaped to hold a stone and a series of round flat bottomed depressions shaped to hold a half pearl, whereby a central stone and the series of surrounding alternate stones and half pearls may be secured in the setting.

1,328,950. PAPER-BAG HOLDER. WILLIAM D. ELLIOT, Bigtimber, Mont. Filed July 30, 1919. Serial No. 314,186. 5 Claims. (Cl. 211—2.)

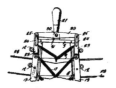

1. A paper bag holder, comprising a stand including a plurality of shelves for receiving the bags, a holder coöperating with each of the shelves to retain the bag in position thereon, a slide common to all of the holders upon the same side of the stand, a lever mounted upon the stand, a handle for operating the lever and a slotted link connection between the lever and slide.

1,328,951. AIR-VALVE. ANDREW FORSTER and JAMES HENRY BROWN, Cowes, Isle of Wight, England, assignors to J. Samuel White & Company, Limited, East Cowes, Isle of Wight, England. Filed July 15, 1918. Serial No. 245,019. 12 Claims. (Cl. 60—16.)

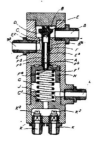

1. In a valve for controlling the flow of air to the fuel valves of an internal combustion engine of the Diesel type, the combination of a casing, a passage for compressed air formed through this casing, a valve seat in this passage, a valve spindle which can slide in the casing, a valve mounted on one end of this spindle and adapted to engage the seat in the air passage, a cylindrical chamber in the casing having a diameter greater than that of the valve face, a piston fitting and movable within the cylindrical chamber, means whereby the piston when moved in one direction by compressed air is caused to act on the valve and lift it off its seat, and means whereby the valve is caused to return to its seat when the piston is moved in the opposite direction as a result of reduction in the air pressure beneath it as set forth.

1,328,952. METHOD AND APPARATUS FOR TEACHING MANUSCRIPT FORM. ELVA R. GARFIELD, New York, N. Y. Filed Nov. 25, 1918. Serial No. 264,063. 8 Claims. (Cl. 35—12.)
1. That method of teaching manuscript or correspondence form and arrangement by means of blocks

which consists in taking a series of such blocks depicting the various manuscript elements which enter into the form and assembling them with other blocks, which

latter correspond to blank and marginal portions thereby producing a sheet wherein the representation of the various manuscript elements bear the proper relation to each other and to the sheet thus produced.

1,328,953. GRINDING-MACHINE. ORLANDO GARRISON, Dayton, Ohio. Filed June 4, 1917. Serial No. 172,717. 15 Claims. (Cl. 51—4.)

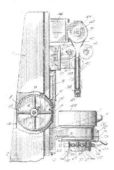

1. In a machine of the character described, an operating element and a work supporting table relatively movable in relation one with the other, a work engaging chuck revolubly mounted upon said table, a rotary index member adapted to be arrested in different positions of revoluble adjustment in relation with the table, said index member and said chuck being capable of independent rotation, and means for locking the chuck and index member against independent rotation.

1,328,954. HATPIN - GUARD. JOSHUA S. GRAHAM, Detroit, Mich. Filed Oct. 17, 1917. Serial No. 197,114. 1 Claim. (Cl. 24—155.)

A hat pin guard comprising an elongated hollow member thus forming an internal chamber, said member also

270 O. G.—35

being provided with a reduced longitudinally extending bore communicating with one end of said chamber, a plate like locking member having pins extending from opposite ends thereof and passing outwardly through said member to constitute a guide for said locking member, whereby the locking member may be shifted, said plate like locking member also having an opening therein which is wedge shaped at one end, one of said pins having a head on its outer end, a flat spring fixed within said first mentioned member and extending longitudinally of said chamber, said flat spring having a bifurcated end engaging about one of said pins to force the locking member in one direction to cause the opening thereof to slightly extend across the inner end of said bore, as and for the purposes set forth.

1,328,955. UNDERREAMER. FRANK A. HAUGH, Winfield, Kans. Filed Mar. 10, 1919. Serial No. 281,602. 8 Claims. (Cl. 255—75.)

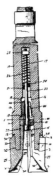

1. A reamer comprising a hollow body open at its lower end, a longitudinally movable hanger rod mounted within the body and having a head at this end, the head being formed with radially extending recesses, a spring urging the hanger rod upward, and a plurality of bits each having a shank extending up into the hollow body and insertible into a corresponding recess, the shanks having laterally projecting portions having rocking engagement with the head and being freely shiftable out of engagement with the head when the hanger rod is depressed to carry the shanks out of the hollow body.

1,328,956. INDEX OR FILE. ROBERT D. HAYES, New Haven, Conn., assignor to Index Visible, Incorporated, New Haven, Conn., a Corporation of New York. Filed July 31, 1917. Serial No. 183,769. 19 Claims. (Cl. 129—16.)

14. A record card for indexes or files, having a transparent strip applied to one face thereof and extending beyond one edge of the card to protect record matter at the rear of said card.

1,328,957. SHOE-PROTECTOR. ALBERT HENRY and GIL-
BERT V. B. FRICKE, Hoboken, N. J. Filed Feb. 28,
1919. Serial No. 279,687. 3 Claims. (Cl. 36—63.)

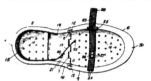

1. A protector shoe of the class described comprising
toe part and a heel part, said toe and heel parts being
movably connected to permit of the folding of one of
said parts upon the other, said parts being each provided with raised sides which extend around each of
said parts and the sides of said parts being overlapped
and interlocked where the separate parts of the shoe
are movably connected.

1,328,958. BELT OR GIRDLE SUPPORT. MARY
ETTIE HORSCHMANN, Springfield, Mo. Filed Mar. 29,
1919. Serial No. 286,040. 5 Claims. (Cl. 2—42.)

1. A belt or girdle having a support, secured at its
upper portion to the central rear portion of the belt or
girdle, and depending therefrom, said support having a
flexible body and stays secured across the said body and
projecting beyond the upper portion thereof, for connection with the belt or girdle.

1,328,959. WHEEL - LUBRICATOR. JOSEPH HUTCHIN-
SON and CLIFFORD C. HAMILTON, Gull Lake, Saskatchewan, Canada. Filed Mar. 21, 1919. Serial No. 283,970.
5 Claims. (Cl. 184—48.)

4. A lubricator including a grease cup and an adjustable
screw cap thereon, a tubular stem extending downwardly
from the cup, a forked saddle swiveled on the top of the
cup, and a yielding yoke controlling said cap, said yoke
comprising a cross bar seated in said saddle, a cross bar
slidably mounted on the tubular stem and resilient links
connecting the ends of the said cross bars.

1,328,960. RAILWAY-SIGNAL. LLOYD V. LEWIS, Edgewood borough, Pa., assignor to The Union Switch &
Signal Company, Swissvale. Pa., a Corporation of
Pennsylvania. Filed Aug. 2, 1918. Serial No. 248,064.
7 Claims. (Cl. 246—223.)

3. A signal comprising a semaphore biased to stop position, an arm operatively connected with said semaphore, a
movable chain provided with projections arranged to coact with said arm to move the semaphore to a proceed
position, a latch for holding said arm in the latter position, means including a magnet for connecting said arm
with said projections and for holding the arm on said
latch, a source of current, and means including a contact

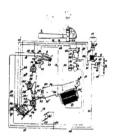

operated by said arm for connecting said entire source
with said magnet while the chain is moving the arm and
for disconnecting part of said source from said magnet
when the arm reaches the proceed position.

1,328,961. DOOR-SPRING. WILLIAM P. MARTIN, Nashua,
Iowa. Filed Oct. 8, 1919. Serial No. 329,294. 1
Claim. (Cl. 16—100.)

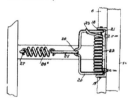

In a door closing device, a bracket including a pair of
opposed ears, adapted to be secured to a door casing, a
pintle mounted in the ears, a yoke having its ends embracing the pintle and having a central offset portion, a
coiled spring having one end thereof anchored to a door, a
connecting link connecting the spring and yoke, said link
having one of its ends positioned in the offset portion of
the yoke, and a coiled spring encircling the pintle and
having one of its ends connected to the yoke for exerting
pressure on the yoke.

1,328,962. LATHE. CHRISTEN OVERGAARD, Skovshoved,
near Copenhagen, Denmark. Filed Nov. 28, 1919.
Serial No. 341,231. 2 Claims. (Cl. 82—2.)

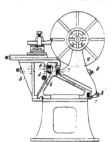

1. In a lathe, the combination with the head stock and
spindle, of a single guide bed having the form of a scalene-

triangle in cross-section, the apex of such triangle being directed upward and located to one side of a vertical plane passing through the spindle so as to provide a relatively large work-space between the latter and the bed; a tool rest mounted to slide along one of the inclined sides of the bed; and a tail stock and ·steady rest mounted to slide along the other inclined side of the bed, the tool rest being movable beyond the tail stock and the steady rest.

1,328,963. CONNECTION FOR MEMBERS OF AIR-CRAFT-FRAMES. Frederick Handley Page, London, England, assignor to Handley Page Limited, London, England. Filed Sept. 6, 1919. Serial No. 322,172. 3 Claims. (Cl. 244—31.)

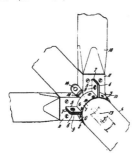

1. A framework for aircraft having members provided with clips, formed of sections with outstanding flanges attached to each other, split ended struts straddling the said flanges and seating against the clip, a wedge shaped block seated upon the clip between the ends of adjacent struts, and a bolt passing through the framework and through the wedge shaped block provided with means for the attachment of tension members thereto.

1,328,964. TOBACCO - EXTRACTOR. Harry J. Penn, Madison, N. C. Filed July 1, 1919. Serial No. 307,882. 2 Claims. (Cl. 131—59.)

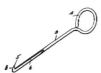

1. A device for extracting tobacco plugs from a container, comprising a shank provided with a laterally projecting hook the forward edge of the hook being sharpened to a cutting edge.

1,328,965. BALL SAFETY-CATCH FOR BROOCHES AND ARTICLES OF A SIMILAR NATURE. Erick Bernhard Peterson, Providence. R. I., assignor to George W. Dover, Incorporated, Providence, R. I., a Corporation of Rhode Island. Filed July 8, 1919. Serial No. 309,281. 1 Claim. (Cl. 24—156.)

A ball safety catch for brooches and the like comprising a hollow globular keeper having oppositely disposed radial pin-tongue openings, oppositely disposed radial slots and a raised closed base in the bottom of which is a groove forming practically a continuation of the radial slots, a solid spherical locking member in the hollow globular keeper and having a radial pin-tongue opening, coinciding with the radial pin-tongue opening in the keeper when the catch is open, and an annular rib in and guided by the

slots and groove in the keeper, the rib merging into an operating member which extends out through a slot in the keeper, and means for securing the locking member in the keeper, as shown and described.

1,328,966. ELECTROMAGNETIC BRAKE FOR MOTOR ROAD-VEHICLES. George Pollard, London, England, assignor to The Menco-Elma Syndicate Limited, London, England. Filed Oct. 14, 1918. Serial No. 258,088. 1 Claim. (Cl. 74—70.)

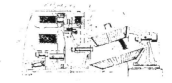

In a change-speed gear of the epicyclic type, the combination with a rotatable driving wheel, a rotatable member journaled coaxially with the latter and adapted to be rotated thereby, and a fixed annular electromagnet which is coaxial with the driving wheel and has lateral teeth, of a driven wheel which is journaled coaxially with said driving wheel and has an annular flange coaxial with the annular pole-face of said electromagnet, and a spring-controlled annular armature which is slidable on said flange in a direction parallel with the axis of the driving wheel, engages the flange to rotate therewith, engages the said member slidably in a direction parallel to said axis, is provided with teeth arranged to engage the former teeth, and has a cylindrical face that is arranged in close operative relation to the annular pole-face of the electromagnet in all positions of the armature, for the purpose specified.

1,328,967. ARROW. George Birkley Reaben, New York, N. Y. Filed Nov. 17, 1919. Serial No. 338,552. 1 Claim. (Cl. 102—26.)

An arrow having a chamber opening at the forward end, a whistle extending across said chamber, ports in the side walls of the arrow in rear of the whistle, a metal partition across the chamber in the rear of said ports, a firing plunger located within the inner chamber formed by said partition and movable when the arrow strikes end foremost against a torpedo in said chamber and on said partition for exploding the same, said arrow having an opening in its side wall adjacent the inner end of said partition to permit the placing of said torpedo.

1,328,968. MATCH-SAFE. Bertrom R. Russell, Sheridan, Nev. Filed Aug. 9, 1919. Serial No. 316,343. 1 Claim. (Cl. 206—20.)

In a match safe, the combination with a receptacle receiving section, of a match receiving receptacle slidably fitting the receptacle receiving section and provided with an enlarged outer end wall overlying the open end of the receptacle receiving section, the inner end wall of the match receiving receptacle having openings, spring tensioned members mounted upon the exterior of the upper wall of the receptacle receiving section and having right

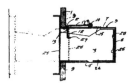

angle extending parts penetrating through the upper wall of the receptacle receiving section, said right angle extending parts of the members having laterally extending projections adapted to enter the openings of the inner end wall of the match receiving receptacle to limit the receptacle in an extended position and preventing the receptacle from being entirely withdrawn.

1,328,969. EMBROIDERING-MACHINE. HIPPOLYT SAURER, Arbon, Switzerland. Filed Aug. 7, 1918. Serial No. 248,704. 14 Claims. (Cl. 112—86.)

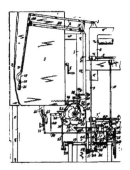

1. In an embroidering machine, the combination of an operating device for a special mechanism, a movable coupling between said device and said mechanism, a ratchet wheel and intermediate connections therefrom to shift said coupling, a pawl-carrying lever for coöperation with said ratchet wheel, an oscillating actuator and means under the control of the operator to effect operative engagement between said actuator and said pawl-carrying lever.

8. In an embroidering machine, the combination of a plurality of operating elements for a plurality of special mechanisms, a plurality of couplings between said elements and said mechanisms respectively, a plurality of levers engaged with said couplings, means to actuate said levers and a selecting device to engage one or another of said levers to hold it from operative movement.

1,328,970. FEED-TROUGH FOR PIGS AND OTHER ANIMALS. JOHN G. SHODRON, Fort Atkinson, Wis., assignor to James Manufacturing Company, Fort Atkinson, Wis., a Corporation of Wisconsin. Filed June 12, 1916. Serial No. 103,078. 2 Claims. (Cl. 119—63.)

1. A feed trough comprising end, side and bottom walls, having substantially flat downwardly converging side walls, and substantially flat downwardly converging bottom walls disposed in planes oblique to the side walls, and having a greater angle of convergence than the side walls, said bottom walls having a width allowing a

sufficient separation of the side walls to facilitate access of the head of an animal to the lowest portion of the trough along the meeting line of the bottom walls, whereby

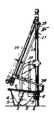

residual accumulations of liquid and resulting ice may be reduced to a minimum, and whereby the expansion of freezing liquid may be permitted along the broadly diverging bottom walls, without injury to the trough.

1,328,971. DESK-BASKET PAPER HOLDER AND CLIP. JOSEPH C. SOEMER, Newark, N. J. Filed Nov. 16, 1918. Serial No. 262,864. 6 Claims. (Cl. 129—1.)

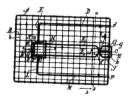

3. In a desk basket, the combination with a basket frame, of a paper holder frame pivotally attached to the basket frame and having a free end constructed to enter the basket, and a paper clip borne by the said free end of the paper holder frame.

1,328,972. ENGINE. NOAH S. STEIN, Bristol, Ind. Filed Feb. 2, 1918. Serial No. 215,143. 1 Claim. (Cl. 121—63.)

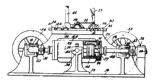

An engine including a bed plate formed with upstanding sides, spaced pairs of valve casings formed in each of the sides, each of said casings being provided with upper and lower ports, an intake valve in one casing of each pair and having upper and lower ports movable into and out of register with the corresponding ports in the casing of the valve, an outlet valve in the other casing of each pair and having upper and lower non-alining ports movable successively into register with the corresponding ports in its casing, gears connected to and revoluble with the respective valves, racks engaging the gears, means for moving the racks to rock the valves, cylinders mounted to rock at the respective sides of the bed plate about an axis extending between the spaced pairs of valve casings, a pair of ports in the side of the cylinder at each side of the axis and between and movable successively into register with the adjacent intake ports in the bed plate, and a pair of ports at each side of the axis of the cylinder and opening into the cylinder, said last named ports working between and being movable successively into register with the adjacent outlet ports in the bed plate, pistons in the cylinders and rods extending from the pistons.

1,328,973. SNOWPLOW. LAWRENCE H. STOWELL, Litchville, N. D. Filed Oct. 25, 1917. Serial No. 198,365. 1 Claim. (Cl. 37—62.)

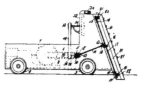

A snow plow, comprising a wheel supported body having its forward portion extending vertically and terminating in an elevated plaform, and having its front side inclined upwardly and rearwardly, an endless excavator mounted on the inclined face of the body and adapted to deliver the snow upon the elevated platform, a fan blower and nozzles connected with the fan blower and disposed to deliver blasts of air laterally across the platform to discharge the snow therefrom at the sides of the machine.

1,328,974. HYDRAULIC ENGINE. EARL A. THOMPSON, Gresham, Oreg. Filed Jan. 14, 1915, Serial No. 2,207. Renewed June 16, 1919. Serial No. 304,729. 20 Claims. (Cl. 103—67.)

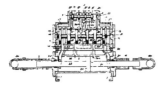

1. In a hydraulic engine, in combination, a main cylinder and a single operating piston therein, a main valve cylinder and main valve member therein, a pilot valve cylinder and pilot valve member therein, means controlled by said main valve member for directing a supply of operating fluid to the opposite ends of said main cylinder, means controlled by the movement of said pilot valve for directing a supply of operating fluid to the opposite ends of said main valve cylinder, and means controlled by the movements of said main operating piston and said main valve member for moving said pilot valve.

1,328,975. MANUFACTURE OF RAILWAY DRAFT-GEAR YOKES. HARRY T. ANDERSON, Butler, Pa., assignor to Harry Vissering & Company, Chicago, Ill., a Corporation of Illinois. Filed May 7, 1918. Serial No. 232,997. 7 Claims. (Cl. 29—167.)

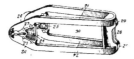

1. That improvement in the manufacture of railway draft gear yokes which consists in cutting a blank of metal longitudinally leaving the ends connected, spreading the longitudinal portions apart to form an opening between them and doubling and bending the blank to form a one-piece yoke having a pair of sides with openings therein.

1,328,976. DEVICE FOR TURNING SHEET-MUSIC. LEE S. ANDERSON, Detroit, Mich. Filed Sept. 15, 1919. Serial No. 323,690. 7 Claims. (Cl. 84—17.)

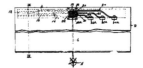

3. In a device for turning sheet music, a music rack provided with a longitudinal recess, a guide plate seated in said recess and adapted for longitudinal movement therein, means for operating such guide plate, a series of racks carried on the face of said guide plate longitudinally thereof, disposed in successive parallel planes, a series of pinions carried on the face of said music rack, each of said pinions adapted to engage a rack carried on the face of said guide plate, a radial arm carried by each of said pinions extended to overhang the sheet music, gripping fingers, one provided for each arm adapted to grip the sheets of sheet music to turn the same as the arm rotates about the axis of the pinion, means for limiting the rotation of said pinions.

1,328,977. FOLDABLE BED. HAROLD R. BASFORD, San Francisco, Calif. Filed Apr. 24, 1919. Serial No. 292,279. 2 Claims. (Cl. 5—5.)

1. A folding bed frame comprising in combination a pair of foldable side rails hinged together at their centers, a leg pivotally connected with each end of each pair of foldable side rails the leg having an abutment to prevent it from turning in one direction and which bears upon the top of the side rails, end rails connected with the tops of the legs and which rails contact at their ends with a projecting lug on the upper ends of the legs, and a bed fabric connecting the end rails.

1,328,978. WHEEL-INDICATOR. MILO D. BEACH, Litchfield, Conn. Filed May 2, 1919. Serial No. 294,318. 5 Claims. (Cl. 116—31.)

5. A steering indicator for vehicles comprising a turnable cam adapted for actuation by the steering mechanism of the vehicle, a spring actuated rocker coöperating with the cam, and an indicating device operated by the rocker which discloses the position of the steering wheels.

1,328,979. DOOR-OPENER. Benjamin Becker, St. Louis, Mo. Filed Apr. 4, 1919. Serial No. 287,448. 2 Claims. (Cl. 268—9.)

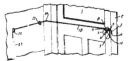

1. In a door opening device, a bracket having a curved face adapted to engage a door knob shank, said bracket having an opening to receive a retaining screw and a lever stop-arm at one side, a lever pivoted to said bracket and having a stop to coöperate with said stop-arm, the stop on said lever being provided with a recess, a spring projecting into said recess at one end and abutting the stop-arm on the bracket at the other end, and means connected to the free end of said lever for actuating the same.

1,328,980. CLOSURE AND TAP FOR TANKS, &c. Edward O. Benjamin, Newark, N. J. Filed June 15, 1918. Serial No. 240,113. 1 Claim. (Cl. 225—2.)

A liquid container discharge conduit formed with an internal taper screw thread, an enlarged outlet having an internal taper screw thread of greater cross section than said discharge conduit and a conical portion connecting the larger end of said conduit screw thread and the smaller end of said outlet screw thread, in combination with a closure and tap therefor comprising an imperforate taper plug adapted to fit said first mentioned screw thread and formed at its outer end for engagement by a wrench and a tap externally taper-threaded to fit said outlet screw thread and formed with a longitudinal passage of larger diameter than said conduit screw thread and with a lateral outlet, a water tight packing at the outer end of said passage, and a wrench extending through said passage and having a cylindrical portion for rotary and longitudinal sliding engagement with the water tight packing and provided at its inner end with a wrench head for a non-rotary engagement with the outer end of said plug whereby said plug may be withdrawn completely into said passage leaving an annular fluid escape passage around the same, said conical connecting portion serving to guide said plug to said conduit screw threads upon the return movement of said plug.

1,328,981. ELECTROLYTIC APPARATUS. Edward O. Benjamin, Newark, N. J. Filed June 24, 1918. Serial No. 241,510. 11 Claims. (Cl. 204—5.)

7. An electrode of the class described, comprising a plate of conducting material having its surface formed or provided with triangular pyramid frustums vertically alined so as to form upward channels between them and also oblique channels between the upward channels.

1,328,982. HACKSAW-BLADE. Bert L. Calkins, Detroit, Mich. Filed Aug. 30, 1919. Serial No. 320,847. 4 Claims. (Cl. 143—133.)

1. A saw blade having a series of relatively coarse teeth and associated therewith a series of teeth of substantially the same pitch but of lesser gullet opening than the first mentioned teeth.

1,328,983. FLEXIBLE SHAFTING. George H. Coates, Worcester, Mass. Filed Nov. 24, 1917. Serial No. 203,806. 7 Claims. (Cl. 64—30.)

1. A flexible shafting comprising series of alternating shaft sections and coupling sections, each coupling section comprising a series of attached plates having registering openings.

1,328,984. CONTROLLING DEVICE FOR COMPRESSORS. Rudolph Conrader, Erie, Pa. Filed Dec. 26, 1916. Serial No. 138,747. 7 Claims. (Cl. 230—24.)

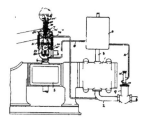

1. In a controlling device for compressors, the combination of a compressor governor comprising a valve, a speed sensitive element influencing the valve, and a fluid actuated pressure device influencing the valve, with a compressor intake, a relief device on the intake, a motor acting on said valve, and a connection between the intake and the motor whereby the governor is influenced in accordance with the operation of the relief device.

1,328,985. CLEAT. Charles D. Cook, Cranston, and Sidney S. Blaisdell, Providence, R. I. Filed Feb. 18, 1919. Serial No. 277,811. 4 Claims. (Cl. 114—218.)

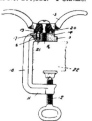

3. A new article of manufacture comprising a clamp, a cleat adjustably mounted on said clamp, and means for automatically locking the cleat in adjusted position by positioning the clamp on its support.

1,328,986. SELECTING SYSTEM. AMOS F. DIXON, Newark, N. J., assignor to Western Electric Company. Incorporated, New York, N. Y.. a Corporation of New York. Filed Aug. 1, 1917. Serial No. 183,892. 5 Claims. (Cl. 178—17.)

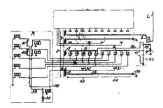

1. A selecting system comprising a distributing apparatus provided with a plurality of groups of switch contacts, a single group of selecting magnets common to said groups of contacts and arranged to be operated in various combinations for selection purposes, and means responsive to line current impulses for rendering said switch contacts successively effective to provide operating circuits for said selecting magnets.

1,328,987. FIBER-TREATING MACHINE. HOWARD M. DUDLEY, Philadelphia, Pa. Filed Dec. 4, 1918. Serial No. 265,212. 11 Claims. (Cl. 8—18.)

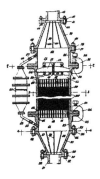

1. In a fiber treating machine, in combination, a fiber chamber, a removable foraminous bottom plate within the fiber chamber, means for supporting the bottom plate, a removable foraminous top plate within the fiber chamber, a spider follower abuttable upon the face of the top plate, means for moving the follower and top plate with respect to the bottom plate and means for forcing a liquid in reverse directions through the device.

1,328,988. WATERPROOF COMBINATION CIGARETTE, MATCH, AND COIN CASE. CARL J. ECKERT and PHILIP J. RICHMAN, Chicago, Ill. Filed Nov. 2, 1918. Serial No. 260,826. 2 Claims. (Cl. 150—8.)

1. A combination cigarette, match and coin case comprising a waterproof bag attached at one end to a threaded ring forming the only opening into the bag, and provided at the other end with a perforated lap; a flanged screwtop provided at its upper end with a perforated boss, threaded into the ring so as to form a closure for the opening into the bag, and forming a coin chamber opening into the interior of the bag; a suitable closure for such coin chamber; and a washer interposed between the

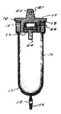

threaded ring and the flange of the screw-top; substantially as, and for the purpose described.

1,328,989. WATER-PUMPING SYSTEM. CHARLES P. EISENHAUER, Dayton, Ohio, assignor to The Burnett-Larsh Manufacturing Company, Dayton, Ohio, a Corporation of Ohio. Filed Aug. 7, 1919. Serial No. 315,839. 9 Claims. (Cl. 103—65.)

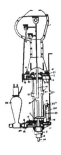

1. In a water system, the combination of a main chambered supporting base, and an auxiliary member similarly chambered, together with means for supporting said auxiliary member at a distant point from said main base portion, both the main base portion and auxiliary member having similarly formed points of attachment for associated operating parts.

1,328,990. IGNITION-SWITCH. VALÈRE A. FYNN, St. Louis, Mo., assignor to Wagner Electric Manufacturing Company, St. Louis, Mo., a Corporation of Missouri. Filed June 26, 1918. Serial No. 241,995. 6 Claims. (Cl. 123—165.)

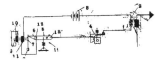

1. In apparatus of the class described, the combination with a primary ignition circuit comprising a source

of direct current E. M. F., a timer and an ignition switch, of means for causing said switch to open, and means responsive to pulsating current in the ignition circuit for rendering the said first named means inoperative.

1,328,991. HEEL FOR BOOTS AND SHOES. VITO B. GRECO, Waterloo, Iowa, assignor of one-half to William F. Baum, Waterloo, Iowa. Filed Apr. 28, 1919. Serial No. 293,335. 2 Claims. (Cl. 36—40.)

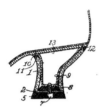

1. The combination with a heel having a bottom cavity, of a reinforced elastic lift therefor, comprising a resilient body having a diminished part received within said cavity, a rigid reinforcing body embedded within said lift with an exposed margin positioned between and in contact with the lift and the heel, to rigidly support the lower edge of the heel upon the marginal part of the lift.

1,328,992. HEADLIGHT. MELVIN G. HARLEY, South Bend, Ind. Filed July 2, 1917, Serial No. 178,251. Renewed June 30, 1919. Serial No. 307,780. 10 Claims. (Cl. 240—61.)

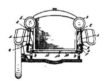

1. The combination with head lights, of means for rotatively supporting the lights, and means connecting the lights for simultaneously turning the same in the direction of each other.

1,328,993. SWITCH-BOX. DON H. HAYDEN, Cleveland, Ohio. Filed Dec. 18, 1918. Serial No. 267,226. 7 Claims. (Cl. 247—5.)

1. In a switch box, a wall bracket extending alongside the box, one of the parts having an opening and the other part having a looped or displaced part projecting through the opening, and a fastening pin extending parallel to the side of the box, through the looped portion, and holding the bracket in place.

1,328,994. APPARATUS FOR OPERATING ALARMS OR OTHER DEVICES. WILLIS K. HODGMAN, Taunton, Mass. Filed May 31, 1919. Serial No. 301,027. 4 Claims. (Cl. 169—23.)

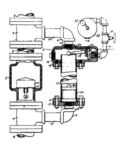

1. In an alarm apparatus, a water passage from a source of water supply under pressure to water distributing means, a check valve dividing said water passage into two sections and operable by a differential water pressure between said sections, a second water passage connecting said sections, a second check valve in said second water passage operable by a less differential water pressure than said first check valve, an alarm mechanism operable by a flow of water from said water passages, a third water passage connecting said second water passage and said alarm mechanism, a valve normally closing said third water passage, and means whereby said valve is opened by the completion of the prolonged movement of said second check valve when a predetermined differential water pressure exists between said sections.

1,328,995. CURTAIN-STRETCHER. ALFRED HOPKINS, Boston, Mass. Filed June 17, 1919. Serial No. 304,882. 4 Claims. (Cl. 45—24.)

1. A curtain stretcher comprising a rectangular portable frame composed of rigidly connected top, bottom and end members, provided with curtain-engaging means, a trolley track attached to the top member, a longitudinally slotted vertical cross-bar having curtain-engaging means, trolleys connected with the upper end of said bar adapted to run on said track, the lower end of the cross-bar being forked to bestride and slide upon the bottom frame-bar, a horizontal cross-bar having curtain-engaging means and slidable vertically in the slot of the vertical cross bar, coöperating locking members on the horizontal bar and on the frame-end members, whereby the horizontal bar may be locked to the frame in different positions, and means for raising and lowering the horizontal bar, said means including cords attached to opposite ends of the horizontal bar, and cord guides on the top frame-bar, said cords being operable from one end of the frame to move the horizontal bar vertically and maintain the latter in a horizontal position.

1,328,996. TRANSMITTER. WILLIAM G. HOUSKEEPER, Philadelphia, Pa., assignor to Western Electric Company, Incorporated, New York, N. Y., a Corporation of New York. Filed Mar. 25, 1918. Serial No. 224,309. 4 Claims. (Cl. 179—190.)

1. In a transmitter, a variable resistance element composed of selenium adapted to vary in resistance with variation in pressure.

1,328,997. SUPERHEAT-LIMITING DEVICE. DAVID S. JACOBUS, Jersey City, N. J., assignor to The Babcock & Wilcox Company, Bayonne, N. J., a Corporation of New Jersey. Filed Dec. 14, 1916. Serial No. 136,832. 10 Claims. (Cl. 236—32.)

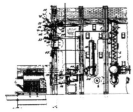

1. A system for the purpose described, comprising a superheater and its setting, an outlet pipe for the superheated steam, a thermostat in said pipe, and means controlled by said thermostat for admitting air into the setting when the temperature of the superheated steam flowing over the thermostat reaches a predetermined degree.

1,328,998. HIGH-HEAT-LEVEL EVAPORATOR SYSTEM. RUSSELL C. JONES, Garden City, N. Y., assignor to Griscom-Russell Company, a Corporation of Delaware. Filed Jan. 26, 1916, Serial No. 74,426. Renewed Nov. 4, 1919. Serial No. 335,748. 3 Claims. (Cl. 257—30.)

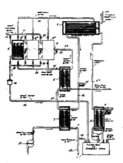

1. In apparatus of the class described; the combination of a primary feed water heater for the main boiler feed; a secondary feed water heater arranged for the passage of water from the primary heater to the boiler; an evaporator plant for furnishing distilled water, said evaporator plant being connected to said secondary feed water heater so that the vapors from the evaporator constitute the heating medium of the feed water heater and are condensed in said secondary feed water heater; connections between the secondary feed water heater and the evaporator feed water heater, whereby the condensed vapors from the secondary feed water heater constitute the heating medium for the evaporator feed water heater; and means for maintaining the temperature of condensation in the secondary feed water heater at a higher temperature than the feed water delivered to the main boilers.

1,328,999. WAGON-BODY. GEORGE F. KIME, Eldorado, Kans. Filed Feb. 16, 1918. Serial No. 217,542. 3 Claims. (Cl. 296—10.)

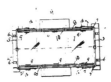

1. The combination in a wagon bed, of a bottom provided with hinged sides and rigid end pieces, said end pieces being provided with extensions adapted to fold parallel with said sides, and additional pieces pivotally connected upon the upper edge of the first mentioned side pieces, loop supports secured upon each rigid end piece, and end extensions adapted to be removably secured within said loop supports, substantially as described.

1,329,000. PAWL-AND-RATCHET MEANS. JULIUS W. KNOPP, Toledo, Ohio. Filed Apr. 9, 1919. Serial No. 288,679. 4 Claims. (Cl. 74—54.)

1. In combination, a ratchet-wheel, a member mounted for swinging movements concentric thereto, a pawl member carried by said member for normal engagement with said wheel, a catch carried by one of said members and normally movable to engage the other to retain the pawl out of engagement with said wheel, and means acting on the pawl when in one position of its movement to hold it released from the ratchet wheel and at the same time acting on the catch to hold it out of pawl engaging position.

1,329,001. TELEPHONE SYSTEM. ERIC R. LUNDIUS, Brooklyn, N. Y., assignor to Western Electric Company, Incorporated, New York, N. Y., a Corporation of New York. Filed Jan. 4, 1918. Serial No. 210,253. 11 Claims. (Cl. 179—84.)

1. A telephone system comprising a telephone line, a receiver connected therewith, a connecting circuit, a relay in the connecting circuit responsive to the connection thereof with the telephone line, a source of signaling current, a switching device for controlling the strength of the signaling current, a second relay whose energization is controlled by the response of the first relay for con-

necting the signaling current with the telephone line for causing the receiver to produce a warning signal,

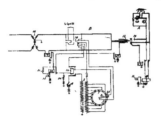

and a third relay controlled over the telephone line and deënergized by the opening thereof to cause the deënergization of the second relay.

1,329,002. CHECK-BOOK. BERNARD W. LYNCH, Wilmette, Ill. Filed Feb. 25, 1918. Serial No. 218,945. 2 Claims. (Cl. 283—58.)

1. In a check book or the like, the combination of a folding cover comprising a pair of leaves folding on a line of crease across the width of the cover, one of said leaves having corner plates in three of its corners for the accommodation of a bunch of disconnected checks, leaving the fourth corner of the checks free, a bank book comprising leaves secured together on a common line of folding and attached along said line of folding to one of the leaves of the folding cover, the pages of said leaves alternately displaying rulings for deposits and rulings for checks drawn, all of said rulings facing one edge of the holder when the pages are displayed, substantially as described.

1,329,003. WINDOW. BENJAMIN S. McCLELLAN, Chicago, Ill. Filed Jan. 17, 1913. Serial No. 742,567. 3 Claims. (Cl. 20—69.)

3. In a device of the class described a weather stop on a window frame, a member on the sash overlapping said stop, and resilient means secured to the sash and bearing against said stop to hold said member and stop in close relation.

1,329,004. TELEPHONE-EXCHANGE SYSTEM. HARRY W. MacDOUGALL, East Orange, N. J., assignor to Western Electric Company, Incorporated, New York, N. Y., a Corporation of New York. Filed June 4, 1917. Serial No. 172,672. 5 Claims. (Cl. 179—73.)

3. A telephone exchange system comprising a telephone line, a link circuit for connecting thereto, a source of

signaling current, a relay, means to energize said relay to connect said source of current to the line, additional means for directing said signaling current through the

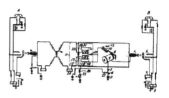

windings of said relay to maintain it energized, and a shunting circuit for said relay to disconnect said source of current from the line.

1,329,005. PROTRACTOR. JOHN NEUMAIER, Dayton, Ohio. Filed Feb. 28, 1919. Serial No. 279,825. 14 Claims. (Cl. 33—75.)

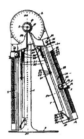

1. A protractor comprising a stationary arm, an index plate mounted on the end of said arm, a pair of swinging arms pivotally mounted on the end of said stationary arm and centrally of said index plate, locking means on each of said arms to lock said arms in any predetermined position indicated on said index plate.

1,329,006. CAR-BODY. WILLIAM N. OEHM, Michigan City, Ind. Filed Feb. 21, 1919. Serial No. 278,435. 9 Claims. (Cl. 105—406.)

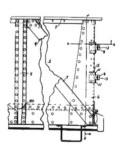

2. A car body comprising web plates, and stakes the metal of which each of said members is composed being thickest near its lower portion and decreasing in thickness toward its upper portion.

1,329,007. TRACK-SWITCH. JASON PAIGE, Chicago, Ill. Filed Oct. 30, 1919. Serial No. 334,394. 4 Claims. (Cl. 246—428.)

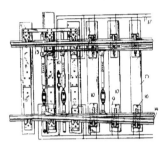

2. A special slide-plate for railroad track switches having electrical heating means integrally embedded therein.

1,329,008. SLACK-ADJUSTER. ARMAND H. PEYCKE, Chicago, Ill., assignor to American Steel Foundries, Chicago, Ill., a Corporation of New Jersey. Filed Dec. 15, 1917. Serial No. 207,305. 2 Claims. (Cl. 188—51.)

1. In brake mechanism, the combination of a fixed member, a brake lever having spaced walls, a threaded member carried by said brake lever between the spaced walls thereof, and a threaded member carried by said fixed member, said threaded members coöperating for varying slack conditions.

1,329,009. BRAKE MECHANISM. ARMAND H. PEYCKE, Chicago, Ill., assignor to American Steel Foundries, Chicago, Ill., a Corporation of New Jersey. Filed May 23, 1919. Serial No. 299,235. 2 Claims. (Cl. 188—24.)

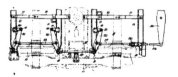

1. In brake mechanism, brake beams located on opposite sides of a bolster, brake levers operatively connected to said brake beams, and a direct connection over the bolster between said brake lever, said levers being inclined to avoid interference with a portion of said bolster.

1,329,010. BRAKE MECHANISM. ARMAND H. PEYCKE, Chicago, Ill., assignor to American Steel Foundries, Chicago, Ill., a Corporation of New Jersey. Filed Aug. 9, 1919. Serial No. 316,318. 5 Claims. (Cl. 188—24.)

1. In clasp brake mechanism, the combination of a brake beam, and a fulcrum bracket secured thereto extending toward the wheel having a slot for the reception of a release spring.

1,329,011. GUARD FOR POWER-PRESSES. JOHN EDWIN PHILLIPS, Birmingham, England. Filed Mar. 26, 1919. Serial No. 285,320. 9 Claims. (Cl. 74—46.)

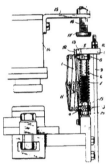

1. A guard for a power press comprising two collapsible and extensible frames mounted and adjustable to different angular positions upon a common vertical axis, and sliding actuating means for extending and collapsing the said frames.

1,329,012. MATCH-BOX. HUGO PICK, Chicago, Ill., assignor to Albert Pick & Company, Chicago, Ill., a Corporation of Illinois. Filed Aug. 9, 1916. Serial No. 113,845. 2 Claims. (Cl. 206—28.)

1. A match box comprising sides, ends and a top, the sides having converging portions with separable edges extending between the ends and normally spaced to hold the matches in the box, the ends and said converging portions being lapped and secured together.

1,329,013. SPARK-GAP ATTACHMENT FOR SPARK-PLUGS. HOMER C. POGUE, Chicago, Ill. Filed Feb. 19, 1919. Serial No. 277,970. 6 Claims. (Cl. 123—169.)
1. A spark gap attachment for spark plugs having an exposed threaded electrode comprising, in combination, a

a base member with a threaded opening by which it is adapted to be screwed on the exposed threaded electrode of the spark plug, an integral insulating top member hav-

ing a countersunk seat in its underface, and a binding screw passing through said top member with its head housed in said seat, substantially as described.

1,329,014. GEAR - SHIFT FOR CROSS - ACTUATORS. ARTHUR F. POOLE, Kenilworth, Ill., assignor to The Wahl Company, Wilmington, Del., a Corporation of Delaware. Filed July 8, 1918. Serial No. 243,995. 5 Claims. (Cl. 235—59.)

1. In a calculating machine, the combination of a totalizer, an actuator adapted to insert numerals therein *seriatim*, an automatic control for said actuator and a manual control for said actuator, said manual control being adapted to disconnect said actuator from said automatic control and bring said actuator into a predetermined condition.

1,329,015, TRAP AND DRAIN FOR RAILWAY-CARS. EDWARD POSSON, Chicago, Ill. Filed Oct. 14, 1916. Serial No. 125,699. 12 Claims. (Cl. 182—13.)

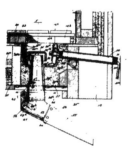

1. In a drain for a railway car, a receptacle mounted in the floor of the car, an angular conduit leading downwardly from said receptacle through said floor and outwardly toward the side of said car, a removable cap in said receptacle over the upper end of said conduit, and a removable plate in the wall of said conduit to permit removal of said cap from a position beneath said car.

1,329,016. VALVE. WILLIAM O. RENKIN, Oradell, N. J., assignor to Quigley Furnace Specialties Co., Inc., a Corporation of New York. Filed Jan. 31, 1918. Serial No. 214,730. 4 Claims. (Cl. 251—109.)

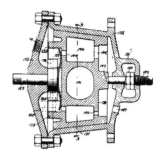

1. A valve having a circumferentially ported casing and a rotating radially perforated plug in combination, which plug is provided with air passages extending endwise through the plug and separate from any radial passages therethrough, and with openings in either end of the casing, whereby a current of fluid may be passed through casing and plug for the purpose of cleaning out matter accumulated in the casing.

1,329,017. VALVE-OPERATING MECHANISM. WILLIAM O. RENKIN, Oradell, N. J., assignor to Quigley Furnace Specialties Co., Inc., a Corporation of New York. Filed Nov. 22, 1918. Serial No. 263,694. 4 Claims. (Cl. 137—139.)

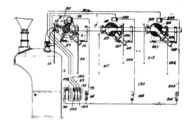

1. In a system for the distribution of fluid masses the combination, with a conduit, means for forcing fluid masses through said conduit, and a branch from said conduit located at a distance from the sending station, of a switch valve located at the branch point, means for turning said valve in one direction operable from a point near the branch point, and means for turning it in the other direction controllable from the sending station

---

1,329,018. APPARATUS FOR AUTOMATICALLY CONTROLLING FLOWING MATERIALS. WILLIAM O. RENKIN, Oradell, N. J., assignor to Quigley Furnace Specialties, Co., Inc., a Corporation of New York. Filed Dec. 17, 1918. Serial No. 267,114. 4 Claims. (Cl. 193—10.)

1. The combination, with a plurality of vertically movable spring supported containers, a conduit for supplying flowing materials to said containers, branches from said conduit to the various containers and means for alternately opening the branch to one container, closing the conduit beyond the branch, or closing the branch and opening the conduit, of a fluid pressure motor for operating said conduit and branch controlling means, a valve,

operated by the rise or fall of the container, directing the flow of fluid under pressure to said conduit and branch

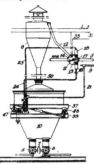

controlling means, and manually operated devices for modifying the pressure of said fluid on said means independently of the container's movement or position.

1,329,019. BUMPER-BRACKET HOLDER. PHILIP RIEDELE, Los Angeles, Calif. Filed Feb. 8, 1919, Serial No. 275,898. Renewed Nov. 22, 1919. Serial No. 339,932. 2 Claims. (Cl. 293—55.)

1 A bumper bracket holder comprising the combination with an S-shaped bracket having a segmental gripping plate at one end of a bumper bracket holder base, having a segmental upper face to fit the gripping plate and a practically flat lower face and laterally extending ears, the segmental upper face being longitudinally bifurcated to form a bolt slot, and a bolt inserted upwardly through the slot and through the gripping plate.

1,329,020. AUTOMATIC TIME - CONTROLLED TRIP MECHANISM. JOSEPH B. RODGER, Independence, Mo. Filed Feb. 4, 1919. Serial No. 275,274. 7 Claims. (Cl. 161—8.)

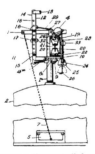

1. In combination, a time-controlled operative means, a movable catch, a suspended weight, means actuated by the first-named means to release the weight, means to be struck and operated by the weight after the same has acquired momentum, for tripping said catch, and means for returning the catch to normal position after it has been tripped.

1,329,021. SPRING-TIRE. ISAAC MORGAN SARTAIN, Tracy City, Tenn. Filed May 19, 1917. Serial No. 169,748. 1 Claim. (Cl. 152—8.)

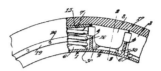

In a device of the class described, a rim including a base, side flanges, and partitions connecting the side flanges and forming compartments in the rim, the base having bosses extending into the compartments; a flexible tread made up of pivotally connected plates provided with bosses alined with the bosses of the base, the plates having inwardly projecting side wings received in the compartments, the outer surfaces of the wings coacting with the side flanges of the rim to prevent undue lateral movement, between the rim and the tread, the ends of the wings coöperating with the partitions to prevent undue circumferential creeping between the tread and the rim, the partitions having oppositely disposed radial ribs located between the side wings and helical compression springs located in the compartments, between the wings, the ends of the springs being engaged respectively, with the bosses of the base and the bosses of the plates to hold the springs out of engagement with the ribs, the side wings and the partitions.

1,329,022. RAILROAD-GATE. MICHAEL J. N. SCHNEIDER, Black River Falls, Wis. Filed Apr. 3, 1916. Serial No. 88,608. 1 Claim. (Cl. 39—1.)

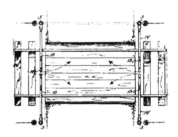

A gate structure including a journally mounted upright post, a horizontally extending fixed supporting bar projecting from the post at a point spaced from its lower end, means for revolving the post to swing said bar in a horizontal plane, relatively long connecting members depending upon the opposite ends of said bar, said connecting members being flexible in every direction, and a second bar carried by the ends of the flexible connecting members and normally spaced from and disposed substantially parallel to the supporting bar, said second bar being movable on the flexible connecting members laterally in every direction and parallel to the supporting bar, and also movable toward the latter bar to dispose either or both ends in contact therewith.

1,329,023. PRUNE - PITTING MACHINE. BARTON W. SCOTT, San Jose, Calif. Filed Oct. 9, 1919. Serial No. 329,450. 9 Claims. (Cl. 146—5.)

1. In a prune pitting machine, the combination of prune holder sections, spoon-shaped containers in said prune holder sections, a pitter adapted to pass longitudinally through said sections, said containers being open at the

top end and pivoted to swing upon their rear ends, and means for resiliently supporting the front ends of said con-

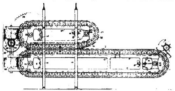

tainers, said prune holder sections being formed at the front ends with recesses to permit the pit to pass therethrough.

1,329,024. HEN'S NEST. WILLIAM M. SCOTT. Sullivan, Ill. Filed Oct. 3, 1918. Serial No. 256,693. 1 Claim. (Cl. 119—48.)

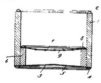

A hen's nest comprising a box-like main frame closed at the sides and open at the top; a foraminous bottom coöperating with the lower edge of the main frame and inclined laterally toward the main frame; a box-like auxiliary frame insertible into the top of the main frame and supported on the bottom, the auxiliary frame being closed at the sides and open at its lower end, the auxiliary frame fitting closely but slidably in the main frame and being of the same cross section from end to end, both externally and internally; a top carried by the upper edge of the auxiliary frame, the top being foraminous and comprising meshes of sufficient size to permit an egg to pass therethrough; and a strip secured to the lower edge of the main frame, the strip constituting a retainer for the bottom, enabling the bottom to withstand the weight of the auxiliary frame, the strip serving to space the bottom from the support whereon the nest is mounted, thereby to define an air chamber beneath the bottom.

1,329,025. GARMENT. IRWIN J. SMITH, Menands, N. Y. Filed Dec. 8, 1917. Serial No. 206,233. 5 Claims. (Cl. 2—144.)

4. An under garment having the body portion thereof made of knitted fibers of vegetable origin and the lower part of the limbs thereof made of knitted fibers of animal origin said portions being similar and of substantially the same weight.

1,329,026. POST. DANIEL H. SNYDER, Snyderville, Ohio. Filed June 10, 1918. Serial No. 239,114. 2 Claims. (Cl. 189—28.)

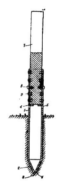

1, A post comprising an upper hollow metal portion extending above the ground and a lower hollow metal portion projecting into the ground, a wood post projecting into the upper portion of said metal post, a portion of the metal post at a point above the ground being projected inwardly to form a seat for the wood post and an aperture whereby air may communicate with the hollow portion of the post below the ground.

1,329,027. COIL FOR DYNAMO-ELECTRIC MACHINES. SIMON SPARROW, St. Louis, Mo., assignor to Wagner Electric Manufacturing Company, St. Louis, Mo., a Corporation of Missouri. Filed May 29, 1916. Serial No. 100,512. 3 Claims. (Cl. 171—206.)

2. In a dynamo electric machine the combination of a slotted structure, a winding therefor distributed in a number of concentric layers and comprising a plurality of inter-connected multi-turn coils, all the conductors which are extended into coil leads being located in adjacent layers.

1,329,028. LISTING AND ADDING MACHINE. GUSTAF DAVID SUNDSTRAND, Rockford, Ill., assignor to Rockford Milling Machine Company, Rockford, Ill., a Corporation of Illinois. Filed Mar. 11, 1912. Serial No. 682,971. 26 Claims. (Cl. 235—60.)

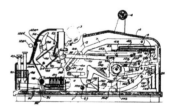

1. The combination of a plurality of pivoted type bars; a plurality of reciprocatory members, each having a cam slot therein; means on each type bar engaging the cam

slot in one of said members; means for controlling the movement of said members; and an adding wheel having a gear connection with each of said members.

1,329,029. TELEPHONE APPARATUS. JOHN S. TIMMONS, New York, N. Y. Filed Apr. 13, 1918. Serial No. 228,311. 12 Claims. (Cl. 179—156.)

1. In a telephone transmitter, a closed case sufficiently rigid not to be affected by air vibrations, combined with a microphone entirely inclosed within the case and having one electrode directly connected to the case, a diaphragm secured to the case and provided with the other electrode, said diaphragm free to vibrate independently of the case and having secured to it a part formed of sufficient weight to provide an effective inertia to produce a difference in phase vibrations of the two electrodes, and means for holding the case tightly to an operator so as to be vibrated bodily by muscular action caused by uttering articulate sounds.

1,329,030. PHONOGRAPHIC - RECORD CONTAINER. HYMAN UFFNER, Brooklyn, N. Y., assignor to Peerless Album Company, a Corporation of New York. Filed June 27, 1919. Serial No. 307,055. 3 Claims. (Cl. 129—20.)

1. A phonographic record container of the character designated, consisting essentially of a signature of maximum size provided with means embodying opposed supplementary supports whereby a record disk of less than maximum size may be supported above the bottom of the container and centralized with relation to the medial portion thereof, said supports being yielding to grasp the record, for the purpose described.

1,329,031. TRANSMITTER-SUPPORT. FRED D. WALDRON, Brooklyn, N. Y., assignor to Western Electric Company, Incorporated, New York, N. Y., a Corporation of New York. Filed Feb. 25, 1918. Serial No. 219,004. 4 Claims. (Cl. 179—157.)

1. In a transmitter support, a breast plate having a transmitter mounted thereon, means for suspending said breast plate in position, and a plate member having a resilient extension thereon coöperating with a strap member

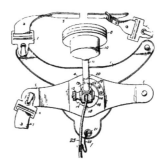

for holding said breast plate in a fixed position with respect to the user.

1,329,032. SHIPPING-CASE. HENRY J. WILLIAMS, Mobile, Ala. Filed Sept. 22, 1919. Serial No. 325,460. 4 Claims. (Cl. 217—12.)

1. A shipping case including opposed panels having cleats terminating flush with the edges of the panels, opposed panels having cleats provided with projecting ends lapping the ends of the cleats on the other panels, said projecting ends having their outer corners beveled, straps bent over the beveled ends of the cleats, draw nails extending through the straps and into the respective cleats engaged thereby to hold the straps taut and supplemental nails extending through the straps and into the cleats.

1,329,033. AEROPLANE-MOTOR. FRANK WOOD, Mount Comfort, Ind. Filed Dec. 11, 1917. Serial No. 206,646. 3 Claims. (Cl. 123—58.)

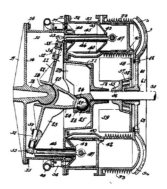

1. In a motor, a support, a plate mounted for gyration in the support, cylinders mounted on the support, pistons

in the cylinders, means for connecting the plate and cylinders, a shaft journaled in the support, a fan hub keyed to the shaft, said hub including a conical flange to provide a pocket, and having spaced apertures formed therein, vanes integral with the hub and adjacent the pocket, for drawing air through the apertures and pocket, said cylinders being arranged annularly about the fan.

1,329,034. CHAIN. RICHARD L. BINDER, Philadelphia, Pa. Filed July 11, 1919. Serial No. 310,169. 6 Claims. (Cl. 254—135.)

1. The combination with a shaft, of an anchor conforming to said shaft, a bolt passing through said shaft and the separated ends of said anchor, and a flexible tension member connected with an end of said anchor and adapted to be wound on said shaft.

1,329,035. TANK-HEATER. WALTER S. BRYSON, Turtle Lake, N. D. Filed May 11, 1918. Serial No. 233,881. 1 Claim. (Cl. 126—367.)

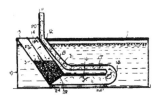

The combination with a tank, of a heater therefor comprising a downwardly inclined combustion chamber, a horizontal portion extending from the combustion chamber and having a width equal thereto and upwardly extended at its outer end, a rearwardly extending flue portion having the same width as the combustion chamber but spaced therefrom, and an upwardly and rearwardly extending flue portion gradually contracted toward its upper end and extended to a level with the upper end of the combustion chamber and engaging with the wall of the combustion chamber at this point but spaced from said wall for the remainder of its length, and a flue extending upward from said flue portion, the horizontal portion of the heater being spaced from the bottom of the tank, to thereby provide for a circulation of water entirely around the heater and through the space between the horizontal portions of the heater.

1,329,036. MACHINE FOR FORMING OR RENEWING AND SHARPENING THE TEETH OF GIN OR LINTER SAWS. ROBERT H. BUTTERS, Atlanta, Ga., assignor to The Butters-Camp Mfg. Co., a Corporation of Georgia. Filed Apr. 10, 1917. Serial No. 161,002. 72 Claims. (Cl. 76—40.)

1. In a machine for forming or renewing gin or linter saw teeth, a bevel cutter rotatable in a plane transverse to the plane of the saw and positioned to operate on

the stock of the saw at one side thereof whereby said cutter forms in the edge of the saw a notch having a face providing a tooth base and a laterally inclined opposing

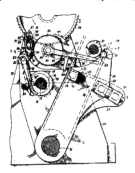

face, means for rotating the cutter and means for advancing the cutter relatively to the saw while operating thereon and in a path parallel to the plane of the saw.

1,329,037. POWER-CONVERTER. CLINTON C. BUTLER, Anoka, Minn. Filed July 1, 1919. Serial No. 307,912. 4 Claims. (Cl. 74—106.)

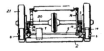

1. The combination with a motor-driven vehicle having an axle and a pair of driving wheels, of a frame, a shaft mounted for rotation thereon and having secured thereto a pair of friction wheels adapted to contact with said driving wheels for receiving motion therefrom, a pair of arms pivotally secured to said frame and adapted to engage said axle, a second shaft mounted for rotation on said frame, a pair of arms secured to said shaft, a connecting rod between each of said arms and each of said axle-engaging arms, and means for rotating said last mentioned shaft.

1,329,038. LUBRICATING SYSTEM FOR TRAVELING MOTORS. GLENN H. CURTISS, Hammondsport, N. Y., assignor, by mesne assignments, to Curtiss Aeroplane and Motor Corporation, Buffalo, N. Y., a Corporation of New York. Filed Dec. 11, 1914. Serial No. 876,716. 40 Claims. (Cl. 184—6.)

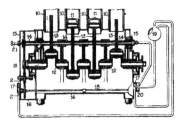

8. A lubricating system for aeronautical motors comprising a supply reservoir, a drainage receptacle arranged

to receive the oil draining from the lubricated parts, said drainage receptacle having communication with said supply reservoir through a plurality of outlets, a plurality of circulating pumps one for each of said outlets, scavenging said drainage receptacle and delivering the contents thereof to said supply reservoir, and an additional circulating pump feeding oil from said supply reservoir to the bearings of the motor.

1,329,039. MOUNTING FOR VEHICLE-TANKS. AUGUSTINE DAVIS, Jr., Covington, Ky., and ARTHUR L. BETTS, Cincinnati, Ohio; said Betts assignor to said Davis. Filed July 22, 1919. Serial No. 312,529. 11 Claims. (Cl. 280—5.)

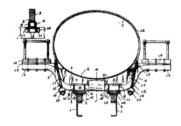

3. In a tank vehicle, the combination of a bolster, a tank cradled in the bolster, a pair of tank-straps the terminals of which pass at opposite sides of the bolster, the bolster projecting outward between the pairs of terminals, and anchorages for the terminals on the bolsters.

1,329,040. MANHOLE. AUGUSTINE DAVIS, Jr., Covington, Ky. Original application filed June 22, 1914, Serial No. 846,444. Divided and this application filed July 22, 1919. Serial No. 312,530. 2 Claims. (Cl. 220—39.)

1. A manhole construction comprising a flanged-out neck on a tank or shell, a manhole ring inserted into the neck, said ring having an outwardly projecting heavy threaded portion and an inner thin unthreaded portion lapping the edge of the neck, and an autogenous weld uniting the parts at this region.

1,329,041. PERMUTATION-LOCK. DAVID JOHN DAVIS, Haverfordwest, Wales. Filed Apr. 12, 1917. Serial No. 161,624. 1 Claim. (Cl. 70—55.)

A lock comprising a back plate provided with attaching means and having a central opening, said back plate

being also provided with a slot at one side of the opening between the same and the periphery of the back plate, a front plate of circular form having a slot in register with the slot of the back plate and provided with a central boss on its rear face bearing against the back plate and having a groove in alinement with the said slots, said boss being also provided with a shank projecting through the opening of the back plate and rigidly connecting the front and back plates which are spaced by the said boss, and a plurality of lock disks rotatably mounted one upon the other and upon the said boss between the front and back plates and provided with slots located within the peripheries of the lock disks and adapted to register with one another and with the slots of the front and back plates, said disks being exposed at the periphery of the front plate for manipulation, and a co-acting hasp member having a substantially hook-shaped portion movable through the said slots when the same are in register and lying in said groove and the slot of the back plate when in locked position.

1,329,042. LATHE. DONALD L. DERROM, Chicago, Ill. Filed May 20, 1918. Serial No. 235,600. 20 Claims. (Cl. 82—11.)

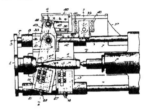

1. A lathe for turning an article having a conoidal surface and a cylindrical surface, having, in combination, means for supporting and rotating the work, a carriage movable longitudinally of the work, a tool on said carriage for turning the cylindrical portion of the work, a radius bar slidably and pivotally connected with the carriage, a tool on said bar for turning the conoidal portion of the work, a slide mounted on the carriage for movement longitudinally of the work, a slide mounted on the first mentioned slide for movement transversely of the work, the radius bar being pivoted to the second slide, and means for imparting a transverse movement to the second slide as the first slide is moved longitudinally.

1,329,043. INDICATING DEVICE FOR VEHICLES. CHARLES P. DIEMER, Sapulpa, Okla. Filed Apr. 9, 1917. Serial No. 160,736. 2 Claims. (Cl. 177—337.)

1. An indicating device for vehicles, comprising a casing, a tubular shaft rotatable in the casing and extending without the same, an arrow carried upon the shaft outwardly of the casing, illuminating means for the arrow, said arrow constituting a pointer to indicate direction of travel, and being normally disposed in a vertical position, a vertical arm fixed to the shaft, an armature ring carried by the arm within the casing and having a magnetic major upper portion and a non-magnetic minor lower portion, solenoids mounted at each side of the casing and

receiving the ring therethrough, said solenoids being disposed upon the lower portion of the magnetic part of the ring, the lower portion of the ring having a notch therein, an armature plate pivoted to the casing and having a projection normally held in the notch of the ring to prevent turning of the latter, and an electrical circuit including a source of energy and said solenoids, said circuit including a connection between the solenoids, means for closing the circuit through either solenoid and means for releasing the armature plate.

1,329,044. SCARECROW. ELVIN FARNAM, Los Angeles, Calif. Filed Apr. 8, 1919. Serial No. 288,490. **1** Claim. (Cl. 46—14.)

A scare-crow comprising a body member having a flat top, feathers mounted at their quill ends upon the flat top of the body member and extending outwardly, a plate adapted to cover and clamp down to the body member to hold the feathers and a pivot bearing in the plate adapted to ride upon a pivot extending upwardly through a hole in the body member so that the scare-crow will lie horizontally and flutter in the wind.

1,329,045. TOY. JOHAN FRIEDERICH FRANKE, Santa Ana, Calif. Filed July 25, 1919. Serial No. 313,321. 1 Claim. (Cl. 46—45.)

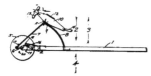

A toy comprising a handle having a bifurcated outer end, a shaft rotatably mounted across the points of the bifurcated end, the shaft terminating at one end in a crank, a tread wheel positively mounted upon the shaft within the bifurcated end, a spring blade fixed to the handle adjacent to the bifurcated end, a toy aeroplane mounted upon the free end of the spring blade and a pitman connecting the toy with the crank, and means mounted in operative relation to the tread wheel for simulating the whir of an aeroplane in action.

1,329,046. SPEED-INDICATOR. FLORINDA GARDNER, Salt Lake City, Utah. Filed Mar. 17, 1919. Serial No. 283,253. 4 Claims. (Cl. 116—65.)

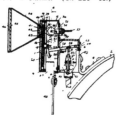

1. A speed indicator comprising the combination with a speedometer, of a magnifying glass mounted in front of the speedometer indication, and a screen mounted in front of the magnifying glass.

1,329,047. SLED-BRAKE. ARTHUR HAMMERSTROM, Deerfield, N. H. Filed Mar. 11, 1918. Serial No. 221,759. 1 Claim. (Cl. 21—46.)

In a sled brake, the combination with the runners of the sled, of a plate disposed transversely of the upper face of each runner and projecting from the sides thereof, said projecting ends of the plate having slots extending longitudinally of the runner, an inverted yoke having its arms disposed for vertical slidable movement in said slots and having the ends thereof oppositely beveled, a second yoke straddling the first yoke and having its ends secured to the runner, a bar extending transversely of the sled and having its ends engaging on the bight portions of the first yokes, springs between the plates and the bight portions of the first yoke for normally urging the said yokes upwardly, and means for engagement with the bar to depress the same and move the first yokes downwardly through the said slots.

1,329,048. CLEANER. HOWARD EARL HOOVER, Chicago, Ill., assignor to Hoover Suction Sweeper Company, New Berlin, Ohio, a Corporation of Ohio. Filed June 2, 1916. Serial No. 101,235. 15 Claims. (Cl. 15—60.)

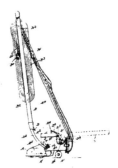

1. The combination with a handle bail and a case to which it is pivoted of a movable handle stop comprising a movable member adapted when in one position to confine the pivotal movement of the handle between predetermined limits and when in another position to leave the handle free to swing on its pivot and means for holding such stop in either of said positions.

1,329,049. TAMPER. CORWILL JACKSON, Kalamazoo, Mich. Filed May 23, 1919. Serial No. 299,262. 12 Claims. (Cl. 104—13.)

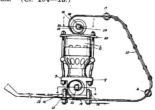

1. In a tamper, the combination of a shaft having an unbalancing weight mounted at its lower end, a driving

motor for said shaft, a casing provided with bearings for said shaft disposed at the lower end of the casing on opposite sides of said weight, a tamping bar clamped to the lower end of said casing transversely of said shaft, a yoke-like handle each arm of which comprises spaced spring members terminating in spring coils, and a pin disposed centrally at the upper end of said casing and laterally disposed pins on the sides at the lower end thereof to which the coils of said handle spring members are secured, said pins being resiliently mounted on said casing, all coacting for the purpose specified.

1,329,050. WEIGHT-MOTOR. CHARLES H. LOUDEN, Cascoe, Ark. Filed June 20, 1919. Serial No. 305,483. 1 Claim. (Cl. 74—45.)

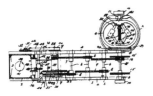

In a device of the kind described, a governor including a stationary disk, a shaft having one of its ends disposed centrally of the stationary disk, a yoke supported on the shaft, a disk carried by the yoke, and coöperating with the stationary disk, said yoke having a threaded head, a bushing adjustable within the threaded head and surrounding the shaft, a coiled spring having one of its ends connected to the shaft, the opposite end thereof contacting with the bushing, whereby the tension of the coiled spring is regulated and weight controlled means for moving the coiled spring longitudinally of the shaft, in one direction.

1,329,051. PORTABLE ELECTRIC LAMP. HANS K. LORENTZEN, New York, N. Y. Filed Mar. 17, 1916. Serial No. 84,817. 8 Claims. (Cl. 240—53.)

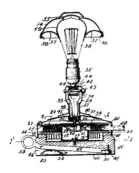

2. In combination, a lamp base having a depression in the top thereof, a horizontally disposed drum journaled in said depression and provided with spaced outstanding flanges at the upper end thereof forming a cord reel, a drum-winding spring seated in the depression below the outstanding flanges, contacts on the upper side of the reel, a lamp-supporting post mounted on the base above the reel and contacts on the lower end portion of said post engaging the contacts on the reel.

1,329,052. HEATER. STANISLAW J. LUKASZEWSKI. Detroit, Mich. Filed Feb. 23, 1916. Serial No 79,881. 3 Claims. (Cl. 158—1.)

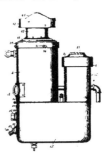

1. In a heater, the combination of a casing having a flat top, a shell mounted on one end of the casing, a burner within the casing, an air chamber mounted on the other end of the casing and provided with a perforated top, and means to retard the flow of air into said air chamber through the perforations in said top comprising a hood having a downwardly extending flange and a perforated top.

1,329,053. DETECTION-SIGNAL. SARGENT P. MARSH and ELMER E. MARSH, Cincinnati, Ohio. Filed Feb. 15, 1918. Serial No. 217,357. 33 Claims. (Cl. 116—1.)

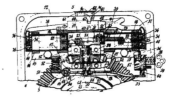

1. In a detection signal, in combination with a structure and an element movably supporting said structure whereby said element moves when the structure is moved, a sound-producing device, mechanism to mechanically operate said device, and an exclusively lock-controlled driving connection between said mechanism and said element.

1,329,054. RAILROAD - GATE. WILLIAM MAXWELL, Bloomington, Ill. Filed Apr. 28, 1919. Serial No. 293,130. 3 Claims. (Cl. 246—301.)

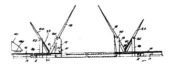

1. In a device of the class described, a standard; a gate mounted to swing thereon; a shaft supported for rocking movement and disposed transversely of the plane in which the gate swings; a spring latch on the shaft and coacting with the gate to hold the same closed, the latch being yieldable transversely of the plane in which the gate swings, to permit the gate to engage with the latch; car-carried means for rotating the shaft

to swing the latch approximately parallel to the plane in which the gate swings, thereby to disengage the latch from the gate; means for opening the gate; and car-actuated means for closing the gate.

1,329,055. PROCESS OF DIRECTLY AND COMPLETELY TRANSFORMING AND REDUCING IRON ORES INTO IRON, STEEL, OR CAST-IRON. GASPARD JAKOVA-MERTURI, Paris, France. Filed Oct. 16, 1917. Serial No. 196,870. 3 Claims. (Cl. 75—14.)

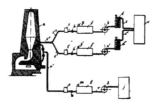

1. The herein-described process of treating iron ores in a blast furnace, which comprises the step of burning in the furnace containing the ore unmixed with fuel, a mixture of poor gas containing substantially 90% of carbonic oxid and 10% of hydrogen and rich gas containing substantially 50% of carbonic oxid and 50% of hydrogen supplied in suitable proportions, from separate gasogenes, and varying the relative proportions of the said poor and rich gases according to whether cast iron or steel is to be obtained.

1,329,056. WRAPPER. ROBERT H. MESTER, Webster Groves, Mo. Filed Aug. 8, 1919. Serial No. 316,196. 2 Claims. (Cl. 206—46.)

1. A wrapper for packages of gum and the like, comprising a sheet having transverse lines of partial separation near one end, spaced apart from each other and from the said end, the outermost of the said lines being at the end of the package when the wrapper is folded about the package, and the wrapper being notched at one edge at the ends of the lines.

1,329,057. ANTISLIPPING ATTACHMENT FOR GANG-PLANKS. EDWARD L. MILES, Stevens Point, Wis., assignor of one-half to Levi E. Genett, Stevens Point, Wis. Filed June 30, 1919. Serial No. 307,675. 1 Claim. (Cl. 57—18.)

The combination with a metal gang plank, of tubular members mounted on the corners of the gang plank, slidable pointed pins disposed in the tubular members, resilient means within the tubular members and engaging the tubular members and pins for normally urging the pins outwardly, and means for limiting the outward movement of the pins.

1,329,058. SHAMPOOING APPARATUS. ANTHONY NAINKA, Janesville, Wis. Filed Sept. 2, 1919. Serial No. 321,091. 3 Claims. (Cl. 4—2.)

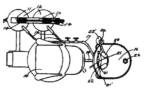

1. In a shampooing apparatus, a chair, a bowl mounted thereon and having its edge cut out to receive the person's neck, a head rest hingedly connected to the bowl and capable of being disposed over the bowl or to one side thereof, and a removable protector plate to be disposed in the forward end of the bowl.

1,329,059. HINGE. ALPHONSE M. NICKOL and CHARLES T. SCHEIN, Batesville, Ind. Filed Dec. 14, 1917. Serial No. 207,206. 1 Claim. (Cl. 16—106.)

A hinge adapted to fit in a cavity between two sections for pivotally connecting the sections comprising a pair of semi-circular (in cross section) plates pivoted together at their innermost ends, said plates adapted to lie in overlapped relation when in a closed position, and means for securing the hinge to the two sections.

1,329,060. ASSEMBLING-MACHINE FOR MATCHES AND SPLINTS. MICHAEL PARIDON, Barberton, Ohio, assignor to The Diamond Match Company, Chicago, Ill., a Corporation of Illinois. Filed Mar. 29, 1919. Serial No. 286,184. 5 Claims. (Cl. 144—191.)

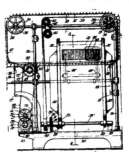

1. The combination of a trough, spring supporting elements therefor, and means for longitudinally reciprocating the trough, said elements being constructed and arranged to translate the longitudinal motion of the trough into a compound lateral and longitudinal motion gradually decreasing in action from the receiving to the discharging end of the trough.

1,329,061. ASSEMBLING - MACHINE FOR MATCHES AND SPLINTS. MICHAEL PARIDON, Barberton, Ohio, assignor to The Diamond Match Company, Chicago, Ill., a Corporation of Illinois. Filed May 19, 1919. Serial No. 298,053. 4 Claims. (Cl. 144—41.)

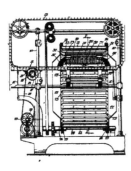

1. The combination with a trough, of two inclined splint-feeding structures extending downwardly to the respective sides of the trough and having parallel splint guiding channels, a distributing frame having two inclined portions leading to and overhanging the respective structures, means for agitating said trough and frame, and means for supplying splints to said frame.

1,329,062. TOY. PERCY PIERCE, Philadelphia, Pa. Filed Apr. 8, 1919. Serial No. 288,558. 3 Claims. (Cl. 244—12.)

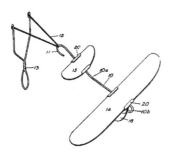

1. An aerial toy in the form of an aeroplane, comprising a body portion consisting of a flexible wire, planes having metal plates at the bottom thereof attached to said wire, the edges of said metal plates overlapping the upper faces of the planes at opposite sides thereof, and a keel secured below one of said planes.

1,329,063. TANK - HEATER. HIRAM S. THOMASSON, Minneapolis, Minn., assignor, by mesne assignments, of two-thirds to C. D. Enochs, trustee, Minneapolis, Minn. Filed Feb. 25, 1918. Serial No. 219,137. 5 Claims. (Cl. 126—360.)

2. In a tank heater the combination of a combustion chamber, a burner positioned in the lower portion thereof, means for supplying fuel to said burner, a downwardly extending pipe leading from the exterior of said combustion chamber to a point above and adjacent to said burner,

a horizontal outlet for the products of combustion leading from said combustion chamber to a smoke pipe, and a

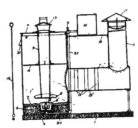

baffle plate in said combustion chamber positioned just above said outlet.

1,329,064. ANTISLIPPING ATTACHMENT FOR SHOES. ALEXANDER L. ULLRICH, Chicago, Ill. Filed Aug. 22, 1918, Serial No. 251,016. Renewed July 8, 1919. Serial No. 309,483. 4 Claims. (Cl. 36—62.)

1. A device of the class described comprising substantially parallel chains adapted to extend longitudinally from the bottom of a shoe sole, cross chains connecting said side chains, a laterally adjustable connector engaged with the ends of said parallel chains at the rear thereof and having means for engagement with a shoe sole, a similar connector uniting the front ends of said chains, and means for clamping said connectors to a shoe sole.

1,329,065. APPARATUS FOR DRAWING GLASS CYLINDERS. HUGO J. WALTER, Bradford, Pa., assignor to Consolidated Machine Company, Bradford, Pa. Filed Mar. 19, 1919. Serial No. 283,526. 5 Claims. (Cl. 49—17.1.)

1. In apparatus for drawing glass cylinders, wherein the bait is flexibly suspended from hoist cables, means located above the glass for engaging the bait carrying means just prior to the entry of the bait into the glass and for holding the bait against all lateral or swaying movement while entering and leaving the glass, the major part of the cylinder being drawn with the bait flexibly suspended.

1,329,066. VAPOR - BURNER. JOSEPH G. WIDHELM, Fremont, Nebr. Filed June 14, 1919. Serial No. 304,220. 2 Claims. (Cl. 158—64.)

1. In a device for the purpose set forth, the combination of a retort, a burner below the retort, a valve in the

burner having its stem depending below the same, an open-ended tubular vapor guard disposed between the burner

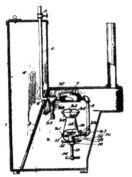

and the retort, a foot depending from the guard below the burner and engaging the valve stem, and means for securing said foot to the valve stem.

1,329,067. COTTON-PICKER. CLARK NOBLE WISNER, New Orleans, La., assignor to C. N. Wisner Cotton Picker Company, Incorporated, New Orleans, La. Filed Aug. 8, 1917. Serial No. 185,102. 6 Claims. (Cl. 56—32.)

2. In a picker head, the combination with a rotary cylinder, and heads thereon, of a pin carrier mounted to reciprocate transversely within said cylinder, and sets of pins secured to said reciprocating carrier and passing through the wall of the cylinder and adapted to project beyond the cylinder wall so as to be disposed substantially tangentially to the cylinder when projected.

1,329,068. UPHOLSTERY - SPRING CONSTRUCTION. LEONARD A. YOUNG, Detroit, Mich. Filed Sept. 25, 1919. Serial No. 326,413. 10 Claims. (Cl. 155—179.)

10. In a seat back structure, a main frame consisting of an upper S-section channel strip, a lower S-section

channel strip, transverse members, the end portions of which are secured in the corresponding grooves of the S-strips, a back spring structure consisting of body springs and inter-connecting members forming a unitary structure bodily mounted on the back frame, a stay member secured at the end portions in a groove of the upper S-strip and in a groove of a strip of the back spring structure, upholstery mounted on the body springs and overlying the stay member and a covering for the upholstery, the margins of which are secured in the grooves of the S-strips.

1,329,069. WRAPPING-MACHINE. HENRY R. BEVIER, Battle Creek, Mich., assignor to Johnson Automatic Sealer Co., Ltd., Battle Creek, Mich. Filed July 27, 1918. Serial No. 246,993. 3 Claims. (Cl. 93—2.)

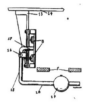

3. In a wrapping machine, the combination of a conveyer, sealing plates disposed in an opposed relation to act on the packages carried between them by the conveyer, said plates being pivotally mounted at their front ends, pivoted levers for urging the rear ends of said plates yieldingly inward, actuating weights adjustable on said levers, and heating means for said plates carried thereby.

1,329,070. TOILET-CABINET. EDMUND BRUDER, Chicago, Ill., assignor to Harold I. Koppelman, Wilmette, Ill. Filed Nov. 17, 1917. Serial No. 202,480. 2 Claims. (Cl. 45—119.)

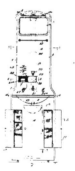

1. A toilet cabinet comprising, in combination, a base having a top wall with a central depression therein to form a wash basin, an upright hollow wall on said base rising upwardly from the rear edge of the basin, a pair of substantially flat water containers within said hollow wall, each having a valved outlet connected therewith and arranged to discharge into said basin, one of said containers terminating a substantial distance above said top wall of the base, a heating coil below the last-mentioned container and interposed in the connection leading from the lower end thereof to its valved inlet, and a heater also mounted within said wall directly below said coil and the container from which it leads, said base hav-

ing a central compartment therein directly beneath said basin adapted to receive a waste receptacle, and said basin having an outlet arranged to discharge into such receptacle.

1,329,071. SNAP-HOOK. BASIL M. CARROLL, Rising Star, Tex. Filed May 16, 1917. Serial No. 169.066. 1 Claim. (Cl. 24—234.)

A snap hook including a body equipped with a bill at one end and upstanding sides at the opposite end, the proximate terminals of said sides and the terminal of said bill being spaced, a keeper consisting of a strap having parallel sides which encompass the sides of said body and pivotally connect therewith, said strap spanning the space between the body, sides and the terminal of the bill of the hook, a spring interposed between the sides of the body and keeper, in advance of the pivotal axis of the latter, and exerting an upward pressure thereon to insure its snug engagement with said bill, said body being bulged inwardly to provide a constricted portion midway between the axis of the keeper and the free terminal of the hook bill to cause a wedging action against said keeper by rearward movement of an element carried in the bill, the said keeper falling short of the rear ends of the sides of said body so as to provide a recess for the insertion of an element beneath said keeper whereby the latter may be moved upwardly against the resistance of the spring for opening the bill of the hook.

1,329,072. PROCESS OF OBTAINING CALCIUM-FLUORID PRECIPITATE. WALLACE S. CHASE, Lakewood, Ohio, assignor, by mesne assignments, to National Carbon Company, Inc., a Corporation of New York. Filed Mar. 1, 1917. Serial No. 151,658. 5 Claims. (Cl. 23—13.)

1. The process of preparing insoluble fluorids of metals which consists in adding a concentrated solution of other compounds of said metals to a concentrated solution of hydrofluoric acid.

1,329,073. SWIMMING APPARATUS. SZILARD CZICZIRIGA, Coatesville, Pa. Filed Aug. 23, 1919 Serial No. 319,461. 2 Claims. (Cl. 9—21.)

1. In a swimming device, the combination with a belt, and means for securing said belt in position, of a pair of oppositely disposed inflatable floats, adjustable connections extending between said floats and said belt, means for holding said floats when in an adjusted position, valves for inflating said floats, a spring engaged with said belt, a pair of swinging gauntlets, and connections between each of said gauntlets and said spring, whereby said gauntlets are held against loss.

1,329,074. RESERVE DEVICE FOR FUEL-TANKS. JOHN FEHAN, Buffalo, N. Y. Filed June 2, 1919. Serial No. 301,206. 5 Claims. (Cl. 158—46.5.)

1. The combination with a fuel tank, of a fuel discharge chamber in said tank having a fuel inlet at a

point in close proximity to the tank bottom, a fuel outlet from said chamber at a point above said fuel inlet and

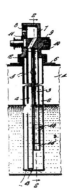

another fuel outlet from the bottom of the tank; together with valve means for controlling said outlets.

1,329,075. SIGHTING MEANS FOR FIREARMS, OPTICAL APPARATUS, AND THE LIKE. GERVASO FORNONZINI, Lanzada, Italy. Filed May 3, 1916. Serial No. 95,110. 3 Claims. (Cl. 33—52.)

1. A sight, comprising a metallic member having a hard, bright white-enameled portion, and a dull black portion, the two portions facing the sighter and being arranged in direct juxtaposition so as to present a marked contrast to each other, the black portion of said member being grooved to avoid reflection of light.

1,329,076. METHOD OF AND APPARATUS FOR TREATING OIL AND OBTAINING BY-PRODUCTS THEREFROM. EDWARD H. FROHNER, Youngstown, Ohio, assignor to Standard Oilcloth Co., New York, N. Y., a Corporation of Ohio. Filed Jan. 4. 1918. Serial No. 210,347. 2 Claims. (Cl. 87—12.)

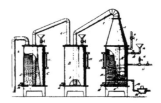

1. In a closed system, the method which consists in passing the gases, arising from the blowing of fatty oil, directly through a solvent to recover the oil contained in said gases, and then passing the gases freed of oil directly through an alkaline solution to remove the acrolein contained in said gases.

1,329,077. RENITENT RAILWAY - RAIL SUPPORT. ARTHUR R. FUGINA, Louisville, Ky. Filed Sept. 9, 1918. Serial No. 253,300. 1 Claim. (Cl. 238—302.)

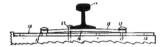

In a device as characterized, a base, an elongated curved elastic plate having slots extended in from the ends thereof, retaining means extended through said slots and secured to the base.

1,329,078. ADVERTISING DEVICE OR THE LIKE. PAUL W. FURSTENBERG, New York, N. Y. Filed Apr. 21, 1919. Serial No. 291,697. 6 Claims. (Cl. 40—152.)

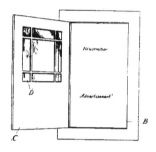

1. As a new article of manufacture, an advertising device having a body portion provided in one of its faces with a depression adapted to receive printed and pictorial matter, a flap pivotally associated with the body portion and normally occupying the depression therein, and a transparent panel forming a portion of said flap and through which only a part of the matter delineated on the depressed portion may be observed, said flap being pivotal into open position to allow of the viewing of such matter.

1,329,079. LEVER-CHOCKING DEVICE. OMER C. GOULET, Fall River, Mass., assignor to Delphine Goulet, Fall River, Mass. Filed Dec. 19, 1918, Serial No. 267,493. Renewed Nov. 15, 1919. Serial No. 338,327. 2 Claims. (Cl. 74—39.)

1. The combination of a machine frame having a substantially vertical surface, a support extending horizontally outward from said surface, a lever pivoted on said support and having one arm extending substantially parallel with said surface, and a chock pivoted to said arm for movement from and against said support, said chock being substantially disposed between said arm and surface when it is against said support and thus being effective to prevent movement of said lever toward said support.

1,329,080. COMBINED CARD-CONTAINER AND TABLE. FRANK GUNCHICK, Blanchard, Idaho. Filed Sept. 16, 1918. Serial No. 254,355. 1 Claim. (Cl. 190—12.)

In a suit case of the character described, interior longitudinal partitions formed at the lower portions of the sides, curved integral elements joining said partitions, the walls of said suit case and said partitions forming pockets, legs pivotally secured to the side walls of this case diminishing in width from their pivot point to their ends and adapted to be folded into said pocket, side by side, with their wider portions resting against the smaller ones, a covering having loose ends attached to the bottom of said case, and eyes on said loose ends adapted to be engaged by pins in said side walls, substantially as described and for the purpose set forth.

1,329,081. PROPELLER - DRIVE FOR AEROPLANES. ALBERT J. HARPMAN, Owatonna, Minn. Filed May 26, 1919. Serial No. 299,969. 2 Claims. (Cl. 170—150.)

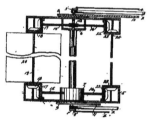

2. In a propeller drive for aeroplanes, the combination of a shaft, a propeller frame rotatably mounted on said shaft, an interrupted worm gear wheel keyed to said shaft, a jack shaft mounted in said frame at substantially right angles to said first named shaft, a star wheel keyed to said jack shaft and coöperating with said worm gear so as to give an interrupted rotary movement to said jack shaft as said frame is rotated around said first named shaft, a propeller vane journaled in said frame, means for rotating said propeller vane driven by said jack shaft, and means for rocking said first named shaft to change the angular position at which the interrupted motion of said jack shaft is controlled.

1,329,082. DRYING - MACHINE. DE WITT D. IRWIN, East Liverpool, Ohio, assignor of one-half to Edwin M. Knowles, East Liverpool, Ohio. Original application filed Apr. 14, 1919, Serial No. 289,881. Divided and this application filed July 21, 1919. Serial No. 312,444. 10 Claims. (Cl. 34—12.)

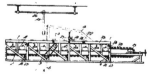

10. In a drying machine, an elongated casing having longitudinally spaced closable openings in its top and

similarly spaced closable openings in at least one vertical side, means for carrying the damp material to be dried through said tunnel, a housing resting on said casing and having an open bottom for communication with said openings, and means for generating a current of air through said housing and through said casing, said housing being movable longitudinally on said casing to different positions for communication with said openings at different distances from the end of the casing. whereby the clay may be subjected to the air current for the required length of time.

1,329,083. ELECTROMECHANICAL CHRONOMETER DRIVING MECHANISM. Cornelis Denis Joseph Jamin, Rotterdam, Netherlands. Filed Sept. 18, 1917. Serial No. 191,955. 4 Claims. (Cl. 58—28.)

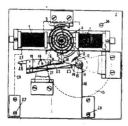

1. Chronometer driving mechanism, comprising a member movable alternately by electromagnetic force and by a constant mechanical force produced by the electromagnetic force ; and a balance for regulating the times of action of the two forces, said member transmitting to said balance the inertia set up in it by the mechanical force.

1,329,084. PORTABLE ELEVATOR. Homer Robert Kees and Elbert Franklin Thomas, Pampa, Tex. Filed Apr. 30, 1919. Serial No. 293,699. 4 Claims. (Cl. 214—46.)

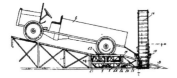

1. A device of the character specified, comprising a supporting frame having an inclined top for holding a truck in inclined position, a pair of wheels for supporting each rear wheel of the truck, shafts journaled in the frame at the low end, the corresponding wheels of the pairs being secured to the respective shafts, an elevator supported at the low end of the frame, and a driving connection between one of the shafts and the elevator, said connection comprising a shaft and a universal joint connection at each end of the shaft.

1,329,085. SLIDE FOR BUCKLES OR CLASPS. Rufus King, Plainville, Mass., assignor to Bugbee and Niles Company, North Attleboro. Mass., a Corporation of Massachusetts. Filed Mar. 25, 1918. Serial No. 224,404. 3 Claims. (Cl. 24—77.)

1. An improved buckle-slide for wrist straps and bands of webbing consisting of a substantially rectangular plate having opposite side-members connected by a central

cross-bar, and end-bars arranged in parallel spaced relation with the central cross-bar, both of said end-bars being cut away at the center to provide openings through

which the strap may be entered by doubling its edges together in the manner and for the purpose substantially as described.

1,329,086. METHOD OF RELEASING CUP-PASTRY FROM MOLDS. Roy G. Kratz, Omaha, Nebr., assignor to L. C. Sharp, Plattsmouth, Nebr. Filed July 22, 1918. Serial No. 246,269. 5 Claims. (Cl. 107—58.)

5. In the art of cup pastry molding and baking in which is employed split molds and cores ; the method of releasing the article from the split molds which consists in first opening one section of the mold while holding the article by a member internally and by the other mold section externally to prevent movement of the article in the direction of the opening mold section, then imparting movement to the member holding the article internally away from the said other mold section, thereby releasing the article from both mold sections and ejecting the same.

1,329,087. TYPEWRITER. Norbert Lallié, Nantes, France. Filed June 26, 1918. Serial No. 242,092. 1 Claim. (Cl. 197—6.1.)

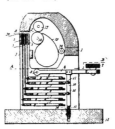

In a typewriter for Braille or analogous characters, superposed pivoted frames, operating keys and type-levers, a comb controlled by these levers, teeth provided on said comb acting on said frames, and points, for producing the Braille characters, operated by the frames.

1,329,088. PROCESS OF MAKING PRINTING-PLATES. Emil Leitner, Hoboken, N. J., assignor to Powers Photo Engraving Company, New York, N. Y., a Corporation of New York. Filed Feb. 10, 1914. Serial No. 817,914. 3 Claims. (Cl. 95—5.7.)

1. The process of deep etching a plate having a half tone design etched thereon in which the dots of the

design have the tone values of the original, which process consists in applying a protecting covering to both the top and the upper portions only of the sides of the dots formed by the first etch, and deep etching the low unprotected places between the dots, whereby the relative tone values of all parts of the plate are maintained by the prevention of the diminution in size of the dots during the deep etching.

2. The process of deep etching a plate having a half tone design etched thereon in which the dots of the design have the tone values of the original, which process consists in applying a covering consisting of a mixture of printers' ink and tar oil to both the top and the upper portions only of the sides of the dots formed by the first etch, dusting the plate with acid resist powder, and deep-etching the low unprotected places between the dots, whereby the relative tone values of all parts of the plate are maintained by the prevention of the diminution in size of the dots during the deep etching.

3. The process of deep etching a plate having a half tone design etched thereon in which the dots of the design have the tone values of the original, which process consists in applying a covering consisting of a mixture of printers' ink and tar oil to both the top and the upper portions only of the sides of the dots formed by the first etch, dusting the plate with asphaltum, heating the plate and deep etching the low unprotected planes between the dots, whereby the relative tone values of all parts of the plate are maintained by the prevention of the diminution in size of the dots during the deep etching.

1,329,089. BALL - HOLDER FOR BALL - BEARINGS. KONRAD WERNER LINDMAN, Stockholm, Sweden, assignor, by mesne assignments, to Nordiska Kullager Aktiebolaget, Gottenborg, Sweden, a Limited Company of Sweden. Filed Apr. 10, 1918. Serial No. 227,615. 4 Claims. (Cl. 64—50.)

1. In a ball bearing comprising outer and inner bearing rings and a row of balls between the rings, the combination of a ring between the bearing rings provided with curved notches into which the balls may be inserted axially of the bearing, and a ring member adapted to be detachably secured to the inner bearing ring and having an inner face provided with a groove conforming to the curvature of the balls and adapted to coöperate with the notched ring in holding the balls in place on the inner ring of the bearing.

1,329,090. STAMP-AFFIXING MACHINE. CARL LINDSTRÖM, Berlin, Germany. Filed May 9, 1913, Serial No. 766,039. Renewed June 18, 1919. Serial No. 305,181. 5 Claims. (Cl. 235—91.)

1. In a postal stamp affixing machine, having a register actuating means and a setting device therefor, whereby on the adjustment of said setting device, said actuating means will be made to register different number of stamps in accordance with said adjustment, said setting device comprising two revolving members coaxially positioned, and means for locking said revolving members together at different angular positions; one of said revolving members being provided with transverse pro-

jections; said actuating means comprising a muff axially displaceable on the other of said revolving members and cam surfaces on said muff for engaging with said transverse projections, whereby on the adjustment of said revolving members at different angular positions said projections coacting with said cam surfaces on said muff will displace the muff in axial direction.

1,329,091. AUTOMOBILE-ENGINE-STARTING MEANS. SAMUEL B. McHENRY, Bloomsburg, Pa. Filed Apr. 18, 1919. Serial No. 291,087. 9 Claims. (Cl. 185—41.)

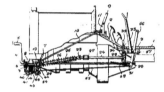

1. In automobile engine starting means, the combination of an endwise movable cranking member equipped with a spur gear, manual means for retracting said member, a spring-driven member having a spur gear for engagement with that of the cranking member, a shaft bearing a ratchet, a spring interposed between and connected with said shaft and the spring-driven member, a pawl for preventing retrograde rotation of the ratchet, a lever carrying a dog arranged to rotate the ratchet and place the spring under tension, locking means complementary to the first-named gear, and manual means for manipulating said locking means.

1,329,092. SHADE-ROLLER LOCK. WALTER C. MOORS, Owensboro, Ky., assignor of one-third to W. P. Pedley and one-third to Ernest Norris, Owensboro, Ky. Filed Nov. 4, 1919. Serial No. 335,632. 6 Claims. (Cl. 156—35.)

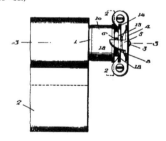

6. A roller lock comprising a pair of disks, one of which has means for attachment to the end of a roller, a dog pivoted between said disks to swing outwardly from

between them, a bracket for the roller having a lug extending at an angle across the edges of the disks, said dog having an abutment at the free end to contact with said lug, and a leaf spring secured between said disks and having its free end overlapping the outer portion of said dog and extending in the same general direction as the dog, said spring moving the dog inwardly and resisting the outward movement thereof, said disks and dog having portions to limit the inward and outward movement of the dog.

1,329,093. LOCOMOTIVE EXHAUST-NOZZLE. JOHN ANDREW ORMISTON, Calgary, Alberta, Canada, assignor of one-third to Arthur Green Slaght and one-third to William Patrick St. Charles, Toronto, Canada. Filed July 20, 1918. Serial No. 245,942. 1 Claim. (Cl. 102—4.)

In a locomotive, the combination with the exhaust pipe of a locomotive, of a nozzle tip secured to the upper end of the exhaust pipe and flaring outwardly, an inwardly extending annular flange at the upper end of the tip having a plurality of rows of orifices arranged therearound, the orifices of one row being staggered in relation to the orifices of the other row, and a conical member carried by the annular flange and depending downwardly into the tip.

1,329,094. PLASTIC COMPOSITION. FRANÇOIS RICHARD and FRANCIS M. BRADY, Cleveland, Ohio. Filed May 2, 1917. Serial No. 165,833. 3 Claims. (Cl. 106—21.)

1. The process of making an insulator which consists in mixing silica and carbon with lesser quantities of alumina and ferrous oxid with the addition of water and a binding substance, forming the mass, driving off the humidity by subjecting to a temperature around 100 Fahrenheit, gradually raising the temperature to 800 or 900 degrees Fahrenheit so as to burn out the carbon, thereafter rapidly increasing the heat applied until a contraction ensues, and finally raising the temperature sufficiently to incipiently fuse the ferrous oxid while leaving the silica mainly unfused.

1,329,095. MOLD FOR CONSTRUCTING HOLLOW WALLS OF CONCRETE. JOHN R. RICHARDSON, Madera, Calif. Filed May 5, 1919. Serial No. 294,795. 11 Claims. (Cl. 25—131.)

1. In a mold for molding in situ hollow walls having oppositely located and inward extending abutments with converging sides and truncated ends, a pair of similarly shaped supports which when associated provide means for forming the abutments and tie-bars for connecting the abutments which are maintained between the supports that constitute the abutment forming members.

1,329,096. GAS-BURNER. HARRY A. ROBINSON, Mansfield, Ohio, assignor to The Eclipse Stove Company, Mansfield, Ohio, a Corporation of Ohio. Filed Apr. 17, 1919. Serial No. 290,757. 3 Claims. (Cl. 158—116.)

1. A gas burner, comprising a burner head made up of inner and outer spaced shells conjointly forming an annular upwardly tapered gas chamber, said inner shell being provided with gas jet openings communicating with said upwardly tapered portion of said gas chamber, and said outer shell being provided with a bottom port opening within the inner periphery of the inner shell, fastening elements extending transversely and diagonally through the base portions of said inner and outer shells to clamp the same together, and a feed pipe communicating with said annular gas chamber.

1,329,097. SOAP-HOLDER. MORRIS RUBIN and WILLIAM LEVINE, New York, N. Y. Filed Oct. 17, 1919. Serial No. 331,351. 3 Claims. (Cl. 45—28.)

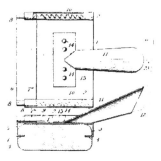

1. A device of the class described, comprising a plate having two of its edges rolled up to form guides, a jaw having guide members movable within said guides, springs within said guides with each of said springs having one of its ends connected to the guides, and its opposite end connected to the guide member, and a fixed abutment on the plate toward which the jaw is adapted to be drawn.

1,329,098. JACK. PAUL W. SCHIEMAN, Rockville Center, N. Y., assignor to The A. Dewes Company, New York, N. Y., a Corporation of New York. Filed May 24, 1917. Serial No. 170,589. 8 Claims. (Cl. 254—111.)

1. A jack comprising a casing, a base, a vertical toothed bar mounted in said casing to support the load, an actuating hand lever pivotally mounted at its inner portion between the sides of said casing, a pawl having a pin on its side and pivotally mounted on the inner end of said actuating lever and operable therefrom and adapted to engage said bar, and a second pawl pivotally mounted between said sides and adapted to engage said bar while the other or first pawl is disengaged operatively therefrom, said second pawl having a projecting arm combined with a cam-plate pivotally mounted adjacent to the side of said first pawl and having an upper portion to engage said arm and a lower angular portion containing an opening receiving said pin on said first pawl, and a spring engaging said cam-plate and acting to turn the upper portion of said plate outwardly against said arm of said

second pawl, said cam plate having an edge to ride against said arm when said plate is moved upwardly and withdraw said second pawl from said toothed bar and to recede from said arm when moved downwardly and thereby

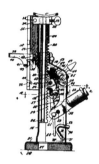

permit said second pawl to engage said bar and support the load until the first pawl is again moved upwardly and has engaged said bar, whereby on the oscillatory movement of the actuating lever the lifting-bar becomes lowered.

1,329,099. VALVE. IRA H. SPENCER, West Hartford, Conn., assignor to The Spencer Turbine Company, Hartford, Conn., a Corporation of Connecticut. Filed Oct. 21, 1918. Serial No. 259,106. 9 Claims. (Cl. 251—51.)

1. A valve case, a valve located in the case to control a fluid passage therein, a valve spindle, means to exert force on said spindle to move the valve in the case, a member to hold said spindle in one position, and means connected with said member to control its operation, said means being operable by pressure of fluid, the flow of which is controlled by said valve.

1,329,100. PROCESS FOR MAKING LINES AND WATER-MARKS ON PAPER AND APPARATUS THEREFOR. ONNI SUURSALMI, Jyväskylä, Finland, assignor to Kangas Pappersbruks Aktiebolag, Jyväskylä, Finland, a Company incorporated in Finland. Filed Aug. 13, 1919. Serial No. 317,278. 3 Claims. (Cl. 92—48.)

1. The process of making lines and water marks on paper during manufacture of the latter which consists in providing a series of apertures arranged in a manner corresponding to the desired lines or marks at predetermined points in the path to be traversed by the paper

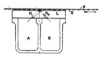

pulp during manufacture, and supplying a regulated flow of water to some and a regulated suction effect to others of the said apertures as the said paper pulp passes over them.

1,329,101. DUMPING-BODY FOR TRUCKS. CARL J. YOUNG, Seattle, Wash. Filed Apr. 15, 1919. Serial No. 290,196. 1 Claim. (Cl. 298—30.)

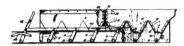

A dumping vehicle body comprising side and end walls and a bottom composed of spaced inverted V-shaped beams fixed at their ends to the side walls, transverse shafts mounted revolubly in the side walls beneath each of the openings between the said beams, segmental plates fixedly mounted on the shafts; the centers of curvature of the said plates being offset from the center of the shaft toward the side that the plates open, a stop fixed to a side wall to limit closing movement of the plates, crank arms secured to each shaft and a bar connecting said cranks whereby they may be moved to actuate the plates to and from closed position.

1,329,102. COMBINED RAKE AND HOE. JOZEF ZIP, Snow, N. D. Filed Mar. 4, 1919. Serial No. 280,534. 2 Claims. (Cl. 55—39.)

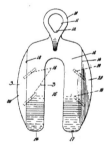

1. In an implement of the type described, the combination with a hub and an eye therethrough, said eye having an elliptical cross section, of a pair of supporting elements formed with said hub and extending in parallel relation therebelow, said supporting elements having sides converging outwardly, and having a straight outer surface, a pair of elongated oval members having sharp outer edges, and means connecting said oval members with the sides of said supporting elements.

1,329,103. SPRAYING APPARATUS. Cosmo Damiano Zipeto, Elmira, N. Y. Filed Apr. 18, 1919. Serial No. 290,970. 3 Claims. (Cl. 299—97.)

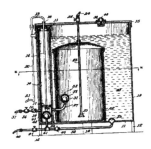

3. In combination with a fluid receiving tank, an air receptacle therein, a fluid pump within the tank comprising a cylinder spaced from the receptacle, a conduit communicating between the lower ends of said tank and cylinder, a normally closed automatic valve for said conduit in the cylinder, manually controlled air entrance means for said conduit, manually and automatically controlled fluid connections between said cylinder and receptacle and a valved outlet for the receptacle extending exteriorly of the tank.

1,329,104. BIRD-HOUSE. Hugo Ballin, New York, N. Y. Filed Jan. 30, 1917. Serial No. 145,343. 3 Claims. (Cl. 119—23.)

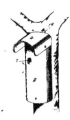

1. A collapsible bird house formed, in collapsed condition, of flat portions of flexible, weather-proof material adapted to be manually bent and connected together to form a completely erected bird house comprising a body portion having an entrance aperture, and adapted to be manually bent into tubular conformation; a floor portion fitting within said tubular body portion; a roof portion adapted to embrace the outer surfaces of said tubular body portion at opposite sides thereof and to close the upper end of said tubular body portion against the admission of rain and also to shed water coming in contact with said roof portion; means for detachably connecting the floor portion within the body portion; and means for detachably connecting the roof portion to the outside of the body portion at opposite sides thereof.

1,329,105. APPARATUS FOR WORKING GARBAGE AND REFUSE OF TOWNS. Giuseppe Beccari, Florence, Italy. Filed M..r. 21, 1916. Serial No. 85,567. 7 Claims. (Cl. 71—1.)

4. A manure and refuse fermentation apparatus comprising a building structure having a chamber therein for the reception of the material to be subjected to fermentation, and a radiator formed by a series of tubes disposed

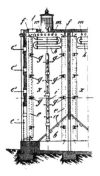

in the top part of the chamber and adapted to have comparatively cold fluid pass therethrough.

1,329,106. MEANS FOR CARRYING OUT SYSTEMS FOR SAVINGS-ACCOUNTS. John B. Bissinger, Jr., Lancaster, Pa. Filed July 3, 1919. Serial No. 308,346. 5 Claims. (Cl. 283—57.)

1. Means for carrying out a system of savings accounts comprising a check form having the body of a check and provided with a column containing the amount of the periodical payments, and a pass book form corresponding in size and shape with the check form and identified with the same and having a column corresponding with the said column of the check form and registering with the same when the two forms are arranged together one over the other, whereby both forms may be simultaneously and accurately punched, said forms being provided with identifying data.

1,329,107. HOISTING DEVICE. James P. O'Bryan, Hog Island, Pa. Filed June 14, 1919. Serial No. 304,248. 4 Claims. (Cl. 254—176.)

1. In a hoisting device, the combination with a casing, of a revoluble element journaled therein, said element comprising a pulley casting having an annular fulcruming bearing, a ring plate internally toothed and secured to one face of the pulley casting provided with a portion overlying the pulley casting, said portion having cavities or recesses, a plurality of cable actuated grips fulcrumed upon the bearing and having portions to enter the cavities or recesses of the overlying part of the ring plate to grip the cable against the ring plate, and means engaging the teeth of the ring plate for operating the element.

1,329,108. ENVELOP - FEEDER. FRANK J. BURKLEY, Omaha, Nebr. Filed July 3, 1919. Serial No. 308,367. 1 Claim. (Cl. 271—2.)

An envelop feeder for printing presses comprising a receptacle, said receptacle being formed in sections, each section being supported in such a manner that they may be adjusted in relation to each for the reception of different sizes of envelops, the forward ends of said sections having their bottoms cut away, a spring feed finger disposed between the bottoms of each section, a downwardly extending spring feed finger between the sections at their front ends, the ends of the feed fingers terminating adjacent each other, an inclined member disposed in the bottom of the receptacle, means for adjusting said inclined member for increasing or diminishing the inclination of the envelops and a gripper carried by said feed roller and so disposed as to enter the cut away portions of the bottoms of the sections to grasp an envelop flap and withdraw the envelop from the receptacle between the adjacent ends of the spring fingers.

1,329,109. FLUSHING-VALVE. ALEXANDER A. CARSON, Braintree, Mass. Filed June 29, 1915. Serial No. 37,017. 6 Claims. (Cl. 4—5.)

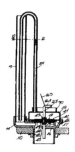

1. A flushing valve comprising a structure having a valve seat, and a cylinder thereabove and spaced therefrom and having an open lower end, a siphon having its uplimb communicating with the upper end of the cylinder, a piston movable in said cylinder in frictional engagement with the wall thereof and carrying a valve for coöperation with said valve seat, and means for temporarily sealing the cylinder above the piston against the entrance of air when the level of the water in the tank drops below the lower end of the cylinder.

1,329,110. AUTOMATIC SAMPLER. SEWARD E. COGSWELL, Central City, Nebr. Filed Sept. 19, 1918. Serial No. 254,753. 3 Claims. (Cl. 226—19.)

1. An escapement mechanism for an automatic sampler, a sliding container provided with staggered stop lugs, a swinging escapement bar pivoted at one end and provided

with a longitudinal slot, lugs carried by said bar at opposite sides of said slot, a crank arm disposed at one side of

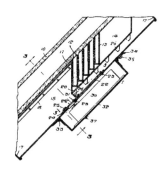

said bar and having a pin entering the said slot, and means for driving said crank arm.

1,329,111. SPOKE AND TIRE FOR AUTOMOBILE AND TRUCK WHEELS. AARON COLLIER, Petty, Tex. Filed Aug. 29, 1919. Serial No. 320,627. 1 Claim. (Cl. 152—50.)

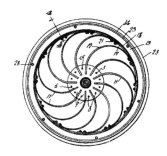

In a spring wheel construction, a felly, a removable inner section including a metallic band of a width equal to the width of the felly, said metallic band having an annular rib formed intermediate its width to provide lateral flanges, a hub, a plurality of curved spokes, secured to the hub, one extremity of each of the spokes being curved transversely of its length to conform to the curvature of the rib for securing the spokes against lateral displacement, and means extending through the felly band and spokes for securing the spokes and band to the felly.

1,329,112. HYGROMETER FOR REGULATING HUMIDIFYING AND HEATING SYSTEMS. STUART W. CRAMER and WILLIAM B. HODGE, Charlotte, N. C., assignors to Parks-Cramer Company, Fitchburg, Mass., a Corporation of Massachusetts. Filed Mar. 31, 1909. Serial No. 486,986. 11 Claims. (Cl. 236—44.)

1. In a humidity controlling device, a dry bulb member containing an expansible fluid and inclosed in a compartment, a wet bulb member containing an expansible fluid and inclosed in a compartment, an air passage into the dry bulb compartment, an air passage between said com-

partments, an air passage leading from said wet bulb compartment, and a valve operated by differences in the

able cap for said gear case provided with an internal gear, a locking member, and means to cause said locking

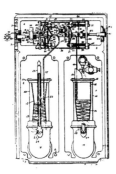

member to interlock with said gears to prevent the removal of said cap from said gear case.

expansion of the fluids contained in said wet and dry bulb members.

1,329,115. SPARK ARRESTER AND QUENCHER. EDGAR A. EVANS, Victoria, British Columbia, Canada. Filed Sept. 9, 1919. Serial No. 322,717. 7 Claims. (Cl. 183—10.)

1,329,113. MACHINE FOR THE SEPARATION OF GOLD, SILVER, AND PLATINUM FROM SAND. DANIEL DIVER, Calgary, Alberta, Canada. Filed May 10, 1916. Serial No. 96,555. 1 Claim. (Cl. 83—67.)

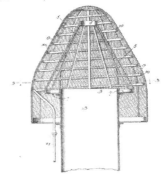

1. The combination with the upper end of a smokestack, of means for delivering a finely divided spray of water across the exit area of it.

1,329,116. LIFTING-JACK. JOHN FLANAGAN, Davenport, Iowa. Filed June 9, 1919. Serial No. 302,814. 1 Claim. (Cl. 254—131.)

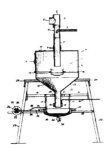

An amalgamator comprising in combination a cup, an amalgamating body therein having a substantially horizontal surface, a pipe adapted to discharge the sand or the like against the surface of said body, the lower end of the pipe being above the upper edge of the cup whereby a free space will be left through which the sand may be blown off and means for producing a fluid jet within the pipe adapted to assist in projecting the particles against the surface of the amalgamating body, a ring fitting around the edge of the cup having an inwardly turned flange adapted to prevent sand working between the amalgamating body and the cup.

1,329,114. AUTOMOBILE-LOCK. WILLIAM T. ESTBERG, Camden, N. J., assignor to Penn Pressed Metal Co., Camden, N. J., a Corporation of New Jersey. Filed May 23, 1919. Serial No. 299,151. 16 Claims. (Cl. 70—129.)

1. In an automobile locking mechanism, the combination with the gear case and its internal gear, of a remov-

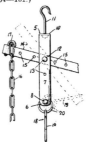

An article of the character described, the combination of a U-shaped hanger, a lever pivotally secured thereto, a hook loosely supporting said hanger, a flexible element carried by said lever, a rivet securing the free ends of the hanger together, a sleeve on said rivet, a ring on the sleeve, and a hook on said ring.

1,329,117. PRODUCTION OF BLACK UPON VEGETABLE TEXTILE FIBERS, SILK FIBERS, OR MIXTURES OF THE SAME. EMILE AUGUSTE FOURNEAUX, Manchester, England. Filed May 27, 1919. Serial No. 300,145. 3 Claims. (Cl. 8—5.)

1. An improved process for the production of prussiate anilin black upon vegetable textile fibers, silk fibers, or mixtures thereof characterized by the use of metaphosphate of anilin in the place of part, usually the greater part, of the anilin salt used in excess of the proportion required to convert the ferrocyanid into anilin hydroferrocyanid.

1,329,118. HARROW. ANTONI FRONCZAK, Wilkes-Barre, Pa. Filed Apr. 15, 1919. Serial No. 290,132. 1 Claim. (Cl. 55—80.)

In a harrow, the combination with a pair of foldable frames, a plurality of harrow teeth engaged in longitudinally disposed bars of said frames at spaced intervals therein, vertically mounted slidable rods in the corners of each of said frames, springs encircling said rod adapted to press them normally opposite to the teeth of said harrow, levers mounted adjacent to said rods, loops at the extremities of said bars engageable with said levers whereby said rods may be held in a depressed position, and wheels freely journaled in the lower portion of said rods adapted to be extended below said harrow teeth.

1,329,119. BABY-PANTS. MAUDE SINCLAIR GEORGE, St. Louis, Mo. Filed June 7, 1919. Serial No. 302,488. 3 Claims. (Cl. 2—131.)

1. A drawer-like diaper cover or protector comprising an outer cover of textile material and an independent inner waterproof lining coextensive with said cover, said cover and lining being folded transversely at their center to provide front and back flaps with an intermediate crotch portion, the end edges of said front and back flaps of said cover opposing to provide the waistband of the garment, means suspending said lining from the waistband portions of the front and back flaps of the cover, means closing opposing side edges of the front and back flaps of the cover and lining, thereby providing leg openings at the edges of the crotch portion, and means for adjusting the size of the leg openings of said lining only.

1,329,120. CONTROLLING MEANS FOR SAVING SYSTEMS COMBINED WITH INSURANCE PROTECTION. FRANK A. GESELL, Los Angeles, Calif. Filed Sept. 10, 1918. Serial No. 253,431. 5 Claims. (Cl. 283—59.)

1. A controlling device for a saving system comprising in combination a depositor sheet and a bank sheet, the said sheets having like identifying data, the said sheets having each a series of columns of which one is provided with periodical deposit numbers, another indicates the total deposits opposite the corresponding deposit numbers, another indicates withdrawal values opposite the corresponding total deposits, and credit means on the said bank sheet indicating a credit for each periodical deposit

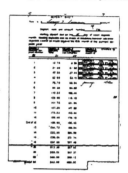

number and the said depositor sheet having means for receiving such credit means opposite the corresponding periodical deposit number.

1,329,121. HOSE-MENDER. FREDERICK HACHMANN, St. Louis, Mo., assignor of one-half to David M. Hutchinson, Ferguson, Mo. Filed Jan. 20, 1919. Serial No. 271,979. 1 Claim. (Cl. 285—77.)

A hose member comprising a coupling sleeve provided on each end with a shoulder and intermediate the end shoulders with an integral rib provided with a peripheral groove, a shell provided on each end with tongues mounted on said rib and secured thereto by forcing a portion of the metal into said groove.

1,329,122. THERMOSTAT. JOSEPH F. D. HOGE, New York, N. Y. Filed Sept. 18, 1916. Serial No. 120,642. 6 Claims. (Cl. 200—142.)

1. A thermostat comprising a detachable member, supporting means therefor, comprising a fusible connection, and a weight mass carried by such detachable member but heat insulated therefrom.

1,329,123. SNOWPLOW. CLAUDE C. HYDE, Otisville, N. Y. Filed Apr. 22, 1919. Serial No. 291,842. 2 Claims. (Cl. 37—57.)

1. A plow attachment for motor vehicles embodying brackets having means for attachment to the forward end of the vehicle, a pair of runners to be disposed in front of the wheels of the vehicle, wheel plows mounted on said

runners to deflect the snow toward opposite sides from in front of said wheels, means for connecting said runners and plows to said brackets for guiding said runners and plows for vertical motion, a V-shaped center plow having

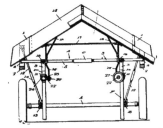

its ends extending in front of the wheel plows in overlapping relation, and means for supporting said center plow from said brackets for adjusting the center plow vertically in front of the wheel plows and supporting said center plow independent of the wheel plows.

1,329,124. CUSPIDOR. ERIC IVERSON, Omaha, Nebr. Filed July 19, 1919. Serial No. 311,967. 2 Claims. (Cl. 4—39.)

1. A cuspidor cover comprising a cylindrical member adapted to be disposed over a cuspidor, the upper end of said cylindrical member being open, pivoted members disposed in said opening and normally closing the same, said pivoted members being pivoted to each other and to the wall of the cylindrical member at diametrical points thereof, said pivoted members adjacent one of their pivotal points being provided with downwardly and outwardly extending integral arms, a coil spring connected to said arms and normally holding the pivoted members in closed positions in engagement with each other and lever means adapted to be actuated by the foot whereby the arms may be spread apart against the action of the coil spring between the downwardly and outwardly extending arms and the pivoted members moved away from each other thereby uncovering the opening in the cover.

1,329,125. MANUFACTURE OF ELECTRIC ACCUMULATORS. HENRY LEITNER, London, and WILLIAM HERBERT EXLEY, Pontefract, England. Filed Apr. 15, 1919. Serial No. 290,361. 2 Claims. (Cl. 204—29.)

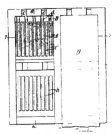

1. A mold for compressing active material into a support and around the lead members of an electric accu-

270 O. G.—37

mulator plate comprising a body provided on one side with a chamber adapted to receive an accumulator plate having oppositely extending supporting ribs with active material located between the same, a series of spaced ridges extending upwardly from the bottom of the chamber adapted to engage the active material on one side of the plate between the ribs on that side of the plate, and a cover for said body having downwardly extending spaced ridges adapted to engage the active material on the other side of the plate between the ribs on that side of the plate, the spaces between the ridges being unobstructed to permit the ridges to compress the active material, when the cover is moved toward the body, without being interfered with by the ribs of the plate.

1,329,126. ADJUSTABLE DUST-CAP FOR VALVE-STEMS. FRANK LEMING, Hingham, Mass. Filed Oct. 8, 1919. Serial No. 329,236. 2 Claims. (Cl. 152—12.)

1. A dust cap for valve stems comprising two semicylindrical shell members pivotally connected together at their outer ends and being adapted to be brought together to form a cylinder, said shell members being tapered forwardly on their exterior periphery at their base ends and being also tapped out on the inner periphery of said tapered portions, in combination with a separable sleeve member which is tapered on its inner periphery to fit loosely over the tapered exterior of the two shell members, said sleeve member being formed at its base ends with an interior annular groove, said shell members being formed with lateral projections which are adapted to engage in said groove when the members are assembled, and a spring connected with the interior of one of said shell members and having a free portion which engages the interior of the other of said shell members, normally spreading the two shell members slightly apart when the dust cap is detached from the valve stem, the two shell members being closed and the spring compressed by the action of the tapered sleeve when the cap is screwed onto a valve stem.

1,329,127. SEPARATION OF ORES. ALFRED ARTHUR LOCKWOOD, Merton Park, England. Filed Nov. 24, 1917. Serial No. 203,824. 4 Claims. (Cl. 83—85.)

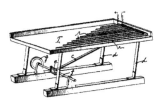

1. A process for separating ore tailings, concentrates and the like consisting in flowing a sheet of pulp containing material to be separated over a supporting surface, agitating and baffling the pulp during its passage over said surface and passing electric currents through the pulp between baffling elements and thereby evolving gas which adheres to and buoys certain of the components of the pulp relatively to other components, and collecting the components so buoyed.

1,329,128. TRAP. JOANNA VALLAT MCCAUGHAN, Long Beach, Miss. Filed May 15, 1919. Serial No. 297,217. 1 Claim. (Cl. 43—20.)

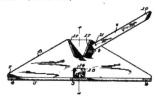

A trap of the character described comprising a pair of solid side walls of trapezoidal shape arranged in spaced parallel relation with the shorter of the parallel edges at the top, a bottom formed as a frame secured to the longer of the parallel edges of the side walls and including a central solid strip, said bottom also including wire screen stretched upon said frame, a wire screen wall connecting said side walls and secured to one of the inclined edges of each thereof, a wire screen covered frame pivoted between said side walls at the other inclined edges thereof, a bait holder secured upon the solid transverse strip of the bottom, and a pair of downwardly converging solid plates secured between said side walls at the upper edges thereof and defining an entrance opening.

1,329,129. APPARATUS FOR MAINTAINING PREDETERMINED PRESSURE CONDITIONS IN GAS-RETORTS. ARCHIBALD ALEXANDER MACINTOSH, St. Kilda, and WILLIAM HENRY HUNT, Melbourne, Victoria, Australia. Filed Apr. 2, 1917. Serial No. 159,283. 4 Claims. (Cl. 48—171.)

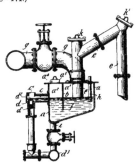

1. An apparatus of the class described, comprising a receptacle adapted to contain a liquid and having two compartments connecting adjacent the bottom of the receptacle, an intake pipe leading into and extending below the liquid level in the first compartment of the receptacle, an outlet pipe leading from the first compartment of the receptacle, and a device associated with the said receptacle and adapted to admit air to and permit the escape of liquid from the upper portion of the second compartment in the said receptacle, so that atmospheric pressure is maintained in both said compartments in the said receptacle.

1,329,130. APPARATUS FOR MAKING ORNAMENTAL PAPER. ERNST MAHLER, Neenah, Wis., assignor to Kimberly Clark Company, Neenah, Wis., a Corporation of Wisconsin. Filed Sept. 7, 1917. Serial No. 190,128. 3 Claims. (Cl. 92—40.)

3. In apparatus of the class described, the combination of a Fourdrinier wire, means for moving same in a straight line free from lateral shake while the paper is being formed on said wire, thereby causing formation of depressions and elevations in the paper web, a supply of liquid color under pressure, a supply of gaseous fluid under pressure, and a mixing nozzle communicating with said

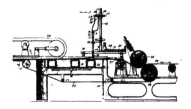

supplies of color and fluid for spraying the said color onto the upper surface of the wet plastic paper web moving with said wire, said spray being arranged to impinge upon the surface of said web at an acute angle to the horizontal.

1,329,131. LOCKING MEANS FOR JOINT-PINS, HINGE-PINS, COUPLING-PINS, AND THE LIKE. ERNEST MEPSTED, Pentonville, London, England. Filed Mar. 25, 1919. Serial No. 285,129. 5 Claims. (Cl. 85—5.)

1. The combination with a headed pin of the character set forth and a member in which the pin is inserted, of a fixed stud disposed in said member adjacent to the head of the pin, and a movable head adapted to engage the stud to detachably secure the pin in position.

1,829,132. ELECTRIC-ARC LAMP. FREDERICK W. MILLER, Los Angeles, Calif. Filed Mar. 8, 1919. Serial No. 281,476. 5 Claims. (Cl. 176—103.)

1. The combination in an arc lamp of a plurality of carbon feeder arms, and a rotatable plate having a spiral way with which said arms are engaged whereby rotation of said plate will move said arms to and from each other, so as to uniformly feed the carbons to a common point which determines the position of the arc.

1,329,133. CAN-OPENER. EUGENE O. MURMANN, Glendale, Calif. Filed Jan. 27, 1919. Serial No. 273,399. 3 Claims. (Cl. 30—3.)

3. A can opener comprising a fulcrum member provided with an angular extension, said extension being

provided at its forward end with a fulcrum, and a blade extending through the angle between said handle and extension with its penetrating tip covering said fulcrum.

1,329,134. ELONGATED CYLINDRICAL PROJECTILE-SHELL. THOMAS E. MURRAY, Jr., Brooklyn, N. Y. Filed Oct. 25, 1918. Serial No. 259,619 1 Claim. (Cl. 102—29.)

An elongated cylindrical projectile shell closed at one end and formed of two longitudinally divided sections struck up from sheet metal and electrically welded together at their meeting edges, and a cup-shaped booster tube concentric with said projectile shell and having the face of its end wall electrically welded to the face of the end wall of said shell.

1,329,135. METHOD OF ELECTRIC WELDING. THOMAS E. MURRAY, Jr., and JOSEPH B. MURRAY, Brooklyn, N. Y. Filed Jan. 15, 1919. Serial No. 271,209. 1 Claim. (Cl. 219—10.)

The method of making a metal housing for transmission gear, the said housing consisting of two tubular end portions and integral therewith a circular middle portion of greater diameter than said tubular portions, the said middle portion having in its opposite walls circular openings, which consists in forming from a metal blank a longitudinal half section of said housing consisting of two semi-tubular end portions and integral therewith a middle portion of arched form, the opening in said arch being semi-circular, placing a second and similar half section with the straight edges of its semi-tubular portions in registering contact with the straight edges of said first-named half section, and electrically welding together simultaneously the pairs of contacting edge surfaces of said semi-tubular portions.

1,329,136. METHOD OF ELECTRICAL WELDING. THOMAS E. MURRAY, Jr., and JOSEPH B. MURRAY, Brooklyn, N. Y. Filed May 21, 1919. Serial No. 298,749. 2 Claims. (Cl. 219—10.)

1. The method of electrical welding, which consists in subjecting the bodies to be united first to both the heating effect of the current and to pressure at the joint, and then interrupting said current and subjecting the heated metal to pressure only until a predetermined take-up of said metal at the joint is attained.

1,329,137. HAND-OPERATING ATTACHMENT FOR PUMPS. JOHN H. OLDHAM, Detroit, Mich., assignor to Blackmer Rotary Pump Co., Petoskey, Mich., a Corporation of Michigan. Filed Sept. 13, 1919. Serial No. 323,563. 3 Claims. (Cl. 103—62.)

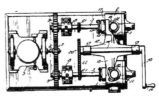

3. In a pumping unit, the combination of a plurality of pumps comprising rotative pump shafts arranged in parallel relation and discharge pipes communicating with said pumps, a prime mover, normally in driving connection with said pumps, a supporting frame having a manually operative crank shaft journaled therein and adapted to be removably clamped between said pipes, driving members carried by said pump shafts, and means for operatively connecting said crank shaft with either of said driving members to effect the operation of said pumps by said crank shaft.

1,329,138. DUST-COLLECTOR FOR BEATING-MACHINES. RALPH OLLEO, New York, N. Y., assignor to Frederick Osann Company, New York, N. Y., a Corporation of New York. Filed Sept. 4, 1918. Serial No. 252,511. 6 Claims. (Cl. 183—72.)

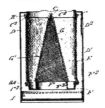

1. In apparatus of the class described, a conduit having a downwardly turned discharge end, a pervious tubular member formed of cloth secured to and depending from the discharge end of said conduit, a rigid annular member to which the lower end of the tubular member is attached, and a screen in the form of an inverted cup having its lower end secured to the said annular member, and forming a pocket with the annular member and the lower end of the tubular member.

1,329,139. FILING-CASE. JOHN CLINTON PARKER, Philadelphia, Pa., assignor to Lefax, Philadelphia, Pa., a Corporation of Pennsylvania. Filed Sept. 22, 1917. Serial No. 192,635. 3 Claims. (Cl. 45—2.)

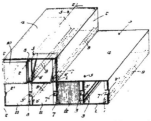

1. In a filing device, the combination with a case having a recessed wall and a recessed spacer adjacent thereto,

of a second case having a recessed wall in juxtaposed relation to said wall first named, the recesses of spacer and walls being in registration.

1,329,140. APPARATUS FOR CLOSING CONTAINERS BY PRESSURE. HENRI ALEXANDRE PERNOT, Paris, France, assignor to Compagnie Des Bouchages Hermetiques - Simplex, Paris, France, a Corporation of France. Filed May 21, 1919. Serial No. 298,782. 1 Claim. (Cl. 113—30.)

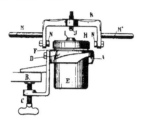

In a manually operated device for applying covers to cans adapted to be supported during closure by an enlargement of the body portion of the can, a can supporting collar for receiving said can, said collar having a seat on which the enlarged portion of the can is adapted to rest, and having diametrically oppositely disposed and equally spaced cam surfaces, a cover applying cap having a central bearing and means for applying clamping pressure to said cap comprising a yoke-shaped screw-clamp revolubly supported on said bearing and having anti-friction engagement with said cam surfaces.

1,329,141. TAP-ATTACHING THIMBLE. FRANK E. RICE, Detroit, Mich., assignor to American Tap Bush Co., Detroit, Mich., a Corporation of Michigan. Filed Oct. 26, 1918. Serial No. 259,887. 5 Claims. (Cl. 285—40.)

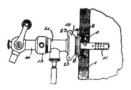

2. The combination with a tap, of attaching means therefor comprising a connector ring loosely but non-detachably mounted on the tap casing for restricted axial movement relative thereto and adapted to be detachably secured to a support and adjusting means having a threaded connection whereby the ring and tap casing are relatively adjustable and which said connection is permanently maintained throughout the said restricted axial movement.

1,329,142. LEVER-HOLDING MECHANISM FOR AUTOMOBILES. THOMAS J. RITTER, Jr., and BENJAMIN M. WARN, Lairdsville, Pa. Filed Aug. 6, 1919. Serial No. 315,610. 2 Claims. (Cl. 74—39.)

1. The combination of a floor plate having a slot, an automobile speed control lever playing in said slot, an oscillating locking plate pivoted adjacent to the rear end of said slot and provided with a shank extending outward and rearward on one side of its pivot and a convex seg-

ment projecting inward and forward on the other side of said pivot, said convex segment having a series of teeth on its arc-shaped edge adapted to engage said lever in neutral and forward positions, a spring connected with said

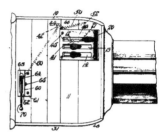

shank and adapted to yieldingly hold said toothed segment opposite said slot, and means mounted independently of said locking plate for shifting it out of engagement with said lever.

1,329,143. HUMIDIFIER. HARRY MIFFLETON ROGERS, Petersburg, Va. Filed May 31, 1919. Serial No. 300,898. 2 Claims. (Cl. 181—30.)

1. A pad for use in humidifiers having a head providing an enlarged evaporating surface, and a comparatively narrow stem, and comprising layers of flexible absorbent material, with a flexible metal inlay between said layers reinforcing same, substantially as described.

1,329,144. METHOD OF CONNECTING PLATES BY ELECTRICAL RIVETING. ALBERT B. RYPINSKI, Brooklyn, N. Y., assignor to Thomas E. Murray, New York, N. Y. Filed Aug. 26, 1919. Serial No. 319,917. 1 Claim. (Cl. 219—2.)

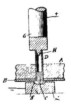

The method of uniting a metal plate to a non-metal plate, which consists in forming registering openings in both plates, inserting in said openings a tubular metal rivet with its head in contact with said metal plate and its shank protruding beyond said non-metal plate, placing said plates and rivet between electrodes, establishing current through said rivet to heat and soften the protruding portion of said shank, and compressing said portion while so softened to form a head in contact with said non-metal plate.

1,329,145. METALLIC BED-BOTTOM. Joseph Seelig, Lead, S. D. Filed Aug. 16, 1919. Serial No. 317,927. (Claims. (Cl. 5—40.)

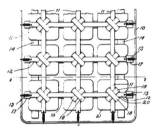

1. In a device of the class described, a lower frame, an upper frame having stays extending across the same, annular springs interposed between the two frames and secured to the lower frame, said springs being associated in nested pairs with the members of each pair angularly disposed to each other, an apertured locking plate for each pair of associated springs having the contacting sections of the nested springs protruding through the aperture in said plate, and a stay of the upper frame passing between the locking plate and the contacting sections of the springs protruding through the plate.

1,329,146. DUST-CAP VALVE. Horace G. Slater, Los Angeles, Calif. Filed Apr. 7, 1919. Serial No. 288,398. 3 Claims. (Cl. 152—12.)

1. In combination with the valve stem of a pneumatic tire having a check valve therein, a cap arranged to thread onto the stem, a circular shoulder formed on the inside of said cap, a head threaded into the upper end of the cap, a coiled spring in said cap, and a valve member on said shoulder engaged by said spring arranged to seat on the upper end of said valve and unseat the check valve in said valve stem.

1,329,147. LAMP-SHADE AND LIGHT-DIFFUSER. Ernest H. Strauss, Chicago, Ill. Filed June 18, 1917. Serial No. 175,473. 3 Claims. (Cl. 240—98.)

1. An oblong diffuser corrugated longitudinally and having the sides of the corrugations upon which the direct rays fall frosted so as to diffuse them, and the sides upon which reflected rays fall, clear so as to permit them to pass without absorption, the said frosted sides being approximately perpendicular to the general plane of the dif-

fuser so that the clear sides may be as wide as possible, and said diffuser being backed by a reflector of corresponding size and shape and, together with the reflector, inclosing the source of light, which is so disposed with reference to the corrugations as that no direct rays will pass through the clear sides thereof.

2. A combination of oblong diffusers corrugated longitudinally, and having the sides of the corrugations upon which direct rays fall frosted so as to diffuse them, and those upon which reflected rays fall, clear so as to pass them without absorption, the said diffusers being backed by reflectors of corresponding size and shape and, together with the reflectors, inclosing the sources of light, which are so disposed above the middle longitudinal lines of the diffusers as that no direct rays will fall upon the clear sides of their corrugations.

3. A combination of oblong diffusers corrugated longitudinally, and having the sides of the corrugations upon which direct rays fall frosted so as to diffuse them, and the sides upon which reflected rays fall, clear so as to permit them to pass without absorption, the said frosted sides being approximately perpendicular to the general plane of the diffusers so that the clear sides may be as wide as possible, and the diffusers being backed by reflectors of corresponding size and shape and, together with said reflectors, inclosing the sources of light, which are so disposed with reference to the corrugations that no direct rays will fall upon the clear sides thereof.

1,329,148. IODIN DUSTING-POWDER AND PROCESS FOR MAKING SAME. Nathan Sulzberger, New York, N. Y. Filed Oct. 14, 1915. Serial No. 55,756. 3 Claims. (Cl. 167—9.)

3. Process for making an antiseptic dusting-powder which comprises the impregnation of boracic acid with iodin by treating such boracic acid with a solution of iodin and evaporating the iodin solvent.

1,329,149. NAPKIN-FASTENER. Rosie Thamm, Berkeley, Calif. Filed June 8, 1918. Serial No. 238,936. 3 Claims. (Cl. 24—7.)

3. A napkin fastener including means for securing the fastener to the clothes, and a slotted member provided with a notch intermediate the ends of the slot of said slotted member.

1,329,150. METHOD OF AND APPARATUS FOR MEASURING THE HEIGHTS OF SUPERPOSED LIQUIDS OF VARYING SPECIFIC GRAVITIES. Raymond Gaudenz Thomas, Monticello, Iowa. Filed June 11, 1919. Serial No. 303,408. 5 Claims. (Cl. 78—54.)

4. Apparatus of the character described comprising a closed receptacle for containing a plurality of strata of

liquids of varying specific gravities under pressure therein, a stand pipe projecting down into said receptacle and provided with a gage glass portion at a distance above said receptacle, said portion including a reservoir chamber to receive a predetermined amount of the liquid forced from said receptacle into said stand pipe, an equalizing branch

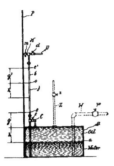

pipe connecting said stand pipe with the upper interior portion of said receptacle, a valve controlling said equalizing pipe, a pipe for conveying air pressure and opening into the top of said stand pipe, a valve for controlling said air pressure, and a vent cock for relieving said air pressure when desired, substantially as described.

1,329,151. AUTOMATIC LIQUID-WEIGHER. WALTER E. TURNER, Piqua, Ohio. Filed Mar. 17, 1919. Serial No. 283,052. 4 Claims. (Cl. 249—27.)

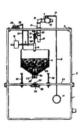

1. In a device of the type described, the combination with a vertically movable liquid receptacle, means for holding the latter in an elevated position until it is filled with liquid to a predetermined weight, a valve seat in the bottom of said receptacle, a valve normally in position on said seat to hold the liquid in said receptacle, a container to receive said liquid from said receptacle, a device adapted to engage the valve on the downward movement of the receptacle, to lift said valve from its seat to permit the receptacle to discharge its liquid into the container, and automatic means controlled by the liquid in the receptacle for holding said valve above its seat until all the liquid has been discharged from said receptacle.

1,329,152. STARTING MECHANISM FOR INTERNAL-COMBUSTION ENGINES. HORACE RUSS VAN VLECK, Montclair, N. J., assignor to The Motor-Compressor Company, a Corporation of Delaware. Filed Dec. 12, 1917. Serial No. 206,745. 9 Claims. (Cl. 123—148.)

1. The combination with an internal combustion engine having a magneto geared to the engine shaft so as to be driven thereby to supply ignition current during normal

operation of the engine, of a starting motor adapted to be connected to the engine shaft for rotating the engine shaft to start operation of the engine under its own power, and a starting magneto connected to and driven by the

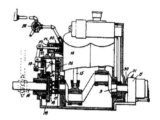

starting motor and arranged to supply ignition current to the engine during the starting operation when the engine shaft is driven by the starting motor; substantially as described.

1,329,153. REMOVABLE WELDED RAIL-ANCHOR. BENJAMIN WOLHAUPTER, New Rochelle, N. Y. Filed Oct. 28, 1918. Serial No. 259,989. 9 Claims. (Cl. 238—11.)

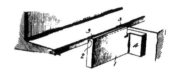

1. A rail anchor having a relatively-weak readily fracturable welded connection with the rail.

1,329,154. STALK-CUTTER ATTACHMENT. ARTHUR E. WYLIE, Axtell, Tex., assignor of one-half to J. G. Davis, Limestone county, Tex. Filed Apr. .7, 1919. Serial No. 288,189. 1 Claim. (Cl. 55—61.)

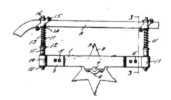

In a stalk cutter attachment for plows, the combination of a horizontal frame composed of two sections fastened together, a cutter mounted to revolve in the frame, arms extending forwardly and rearwardly from the ends of the frame, eyes at the outer ends of the arms, hangers having offset ends engaging in the eyes, clamp-collars for attachment to a plow beam, said clamp-collars slidably receiving the upper ends of the hangers, coiled springs supported on the hangers and engaging the clamp-collars, and means for supporting the hangers in the clamp-collars.

1,329,155. PLIERS. SOLOMON E. AARON, Boston, Mass. Filed Feb. 13, 1917, Serial No. 148,428. Renewed June 21, 1919. Serial No. 305,918. 3 Claims. (Cl. 81—9.5.)

1. In a tool of the class described, crossed pivoted levers having opposed pincer jaws at adjacent ends, and a pair of coacting splitting and stripping blades each secured to

the side of one of the levers and located between the ends of the jaws, the blades extending substantially perpendicu-

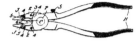

larly from the sides of the levers and having their operative edges in the planes of the respective pincer faces of the jaws.

1,329,156. MOUNTING AN AEROPLANE-PROPELLER AND CARRYING A GUN WHICH FIRES AXIALLY THROUGH THE PROPELLER. HERBERT AUSTIN, Bromsgrove, England. Filed Aug. 15, 1918. Serial No. 250,067. 6 Claims. (Cl. 244—25.)

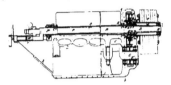

6. In an aeroplane, the combination of an engine, a gear wheel on the engine shaft from which the drive is given off, a tubular arm supported from one end only and having a backward extension which is rigidly carried by the engine case, a propeller and a gear wheel which are rotatably mounted on the said arm, the said last-mentioned wheel receiving the drive and transmitting it to the propeller, a gun of which the barrel enters the rear end of the tubular arm and a mounting which is fixed around such end and has rigid therewith a bar along which the gun is slidable during recoil, substantially as set forth.

1,329,157. SHUTTLE - GUARD FOR LOOMS. VARTAN KAVORK BADOIAN, Lawrence, Mass. Filed Jan. 30, 1917. Serial No. 145,394. 3 Claims. (Cl. 139—30.)

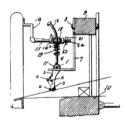

1. A shuttle guard for looms including a guard, means pivotally securing said guard to the hand rail of the loom, a guide rod secured to the loom frame, a sleeve slidable on said rod, means limiting the movement of said sleeve, and a curved rod secured to the guard and slidably connected to the sleeve for swinging the guard upwardly upon the lay of the loom swinging forwardly.

1,329,158. TREATMENT OF LIQUIDS TO EFFECT CRYSTALLIZATION THEREFROM WHILE THE LIQUID IS KEPT IN MOTION. BJARNE BAKKE, Christiania, Norway, assignor to Norsk Hydro-Elektrisk Kvaelstofaktieselskab, Christiania, Norway. Filed Sept. 29, 1919. Serial No. 327,304. 4 Claims. (Cl. 23—3.)

1. In the treatment of liquids to effect crystallization therefrom while the liquid is kept in motion in a revolving

tube the method which consists in maintaining the top part of the tube at a comparatively high temperature at

the same time as the bottom part of the tube is subjected to cooling.

,529,159. DIFFERENTIAL - MOTION MECHANISM. WILLIAM H. BROWN, Chicago, Ill. Filed May 31, 1917. Serial No. 171,884. 1 Claim. (Cl. 74—7.)

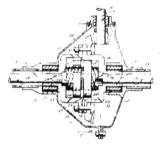

A differential motion mechanism, comprising a driving shaft, two separate driven shafts, a hollow casing rotatably mounted on said driven shafts and inclosing the opposed ends thereof and driven by said driving shaft, two collars located in said casing, one mounted on and rotative with each driven shaft, and two shift rings located in said casing, one for each collar and having screw-threaded engagement therewith, so that said shift rings may be moved toward and from each other, each ring being provided with radially projecting lugs for engaging longitudinal slots formed in the inner surface of said casing; the inner ends of said slots terminating in shoulders intermediate said shift rings and frictionally engaging the side faces thereof, when said shift rings have been moved into contact with said shoulders.

1,329,160. APPARATUS FOR TESTING GAS-LEAKAGE. GEORGE W. CHRISTIANS, Brooklyn, N. Y., assignor to Thomas E. Murray, New York, N. Y. Filed July 30, 1918. Serial No. 247,465. 2 Claims. (Cl. 73—51.)

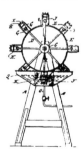

1. An apparatus for testing perviousness to gas leakage of a gas confining shell, comprising a rotary hub, tubular spokes thereon, supporting at their outer ends and con-

veying gas under pressure to the shells to be tested, a tank for containing liquid placed to receive each shell in turn during the rotation of said hub, and means for removably securing the shells in line with and upon the ends of said spokes; the said securing means comprising a circular band connecting said spokes, a pair of standards secured on said band on opposite sides of each of said spokes and securing said shell between them, and means supported by said standards for clamping said shells against the ends of said spokes.

1,329,161. WRENCH. Robert J. Colson, St. Louis, Mo. Filed Dec. 10, 1918. Serial No. 266,032. 2 Claims. (Cl. 81—179.)

1. In a wrench, a shank, a fixed jaw on one end thereof, and at right angles thereto, said jaw being provided with transversely disposed teeth, the shank being provided with a longitudinally disposed groove, a block arranged for sliding movement on the shank, a jaw pivotally connected to said block and adapted to move toward and away from the shank, a spring pressed member carried by said jaw and having its outer end arranged for sliding movement in the groove in the shank, and a dog located within the block and carried thereby, for engaging the teeth on the shank to lock said block against movement in one direction.

1,329,162. WATERPROOFING COMPOSITION. Daniel Jewett Davies, Pasadena, Calif. Filed May 8, 1918. Serial No. 233,359. 2 Claims. (Cl. 134—17.)

2. A waterproofing composition comprising one gallon neat's-foot oil, eight pounds rubber, one pound tallow, eight ounces beeswax, four ounces resin, and one ounce Burgundy pitch.

1,329,163. RAILWAY-RAIL-SECURING DEVICE. Earl Joseph Davis, Appleton, Wis. Filed Sept. 18, 1919. Serial No. 324,484. 2 Claims. (Cl. 238—295.)

1. A railway rail securing device comprising in combination with a spike having a beveled head adapted to engage the outer edge of the base portion of a railway rail a metallic plate carried by the spike and adapted to be interposed between the rail and tie, and means whereby the spike may be rotated.

1,329,164. DOUGH-MIXER. Walter Franklin Dehuff, Glen Rock, Pa. Filed June 2, 1919. Serial No. 301,172. 5 Claims. (Cl. 259—144.)

1. A dough mixer comprising a suitable support, a driving shaft journaled in the support, a beater, a bearing

sleeve mounted to oscillate on the driving shaft and carrying a casing in which the casing is mounted to rotate, a driving connection between the driving shaft

and the beater in the casing, means for rocking the sleeve, and a common controlling means for the driving shaft and for swinging the casing, and a bowl with which the beater coöperates.

1,329,165. PUMP-PACKING. John W. Drew, St. Louis, Mo., assignor to Moon Brothers Manufacturing Company, St. Louis, Mo., a Corporation of Missouri. Filed May 26, 1919. Serial No. 299,831. 3 Claims. (Cl. 230—27.)

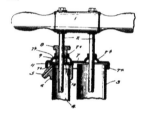

1. The combination of a pump cylinder having a casting secured to its upper end, said casting having threaded openings, a cap plate arranged above said casting and provided with registering openings, fastening means passing through said openings for securing the cap plate in position, a metal plate and leather gasket interposed between said cap plate and casting, a packing ring bearing upon said metal plate and surrounding the piston rod, and adjustable means in the cap plate for pressing the packing ring onto said metal plate.

1,329,166. APPARATUS FOR TREATING HANKS OF TEXTILE FABRICS WITH LIQUIDS. Wilhelm Dürsteler, Thalwil, Switzerland, assignor to Weidmann Dyeing Co., Ld., Thalwil, Switzerland. Filed July 10, 1919. Serial No. 309,919. 1 Claim. (Cl. 8—19.)

An apparatus for treating hanks of textile fabrics with liquids for the purpose of dyeing, bleaching, washing, weighting or the like, comprising a frame with two rows of horizontal carriers inserted in an upper and lower supporting structure on said frame and intended to receive at least one series of unstretched hanks, a casing in which the said frame is rotatably mounted about a horizontal axis, means for producing a circulation of the liquid in the said casing and means for rotating periodically the said frame about the said horizontal axis through an angle of 180° in order to effect a change of the hank parts in contact with the hank carriers and to render thus more uniform the action of the liquid on the textile fabrics.

1,329,167. RHEOSTAT. ROBERT W. EBELING, Oakland, Calif., assignor to R. W. Ebeling Company, Incorporated, a Corporation of California. Filed Sept. 18, 1917. Serial No. 191,951. 7 Claims. (Cl. 219—55.)

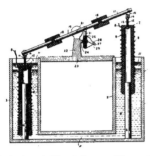

1. A circuit controlling device comprising a container, a conducting liquid therein, a resistance element positioned to be immersed within said liquid, an operating bar to which said resistance element is attached, and electomagnetic means for actuating said bar.

1,329,168. MULTIPLE - CIRCUIT - RESISTANCE CONTROL. ROBERT W. EBELING, Oakland, Calif., assignor to R. W Ebeling Company, Incorporated, a Corporation of California. Filed Sept. 18, 1917. Serial No. 191,953. 15 Claims. (Cl. 219—56.)

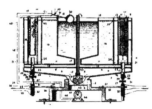

2. An improvement in means for controlling electrical resistances comprising a reservoir containing a conducting liquid, a resistance chamber, a valve communicating with said chamber, means for selectively operating said valve to place the chamber in communication with said reservoir or to drain the liquid from the chamber, and a resistance element within the chamber positioned to be submerged by said liquid.

1,329,169. FLUSH-VALVE. GEORGE W. FOSTER, New York, N. Y., assignor of one-half to George Mayer, New York, N. Y. Filed May 23, 1917. Serial No. 170,500. 1 Claim. (Cl. 137—21.)

In a flush valve, a threaded sleeve having its upper end beveled upwardly to form a valve seat, a cage comprising a threaded portion to embrace the threaded portion of the sleeve, parallel guide bars and a ring portion, a tube movable in the ring portion, a valve member comprising a sleeve to embrace the lower end of the tubular member, an annular enlargement formed on the valve

member having its ends beveled inwardly whereby either beveled end may be rested upon the valve seat by reversing the valve member, the guide bars engaging the

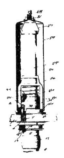

annular enlargement to guide the valve member to the seat, and a coiled spring embracing the tubular member and engaging the ring portion and the valve member to retain the latter seated.

1,329,170. MANUFACTURE OF FLOOR-COVERING. Jo FUNAHASHI, Kobe, Japan. Filed Dec. 11, 1915. Serial No. 66,345. 2 Claims. (Cl. 139—9.)

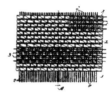

1. A fabric for floor covering or the like which comprises suitable warp threads and weft threads, certain of the warp threads being floated over several weft threads to produce pattern effects, in combination with binder filling threads equal in number to the weft threads and tying down the floating portions of the warp threads, each binder filling thread overlying a weft thread.

1,329,171. STRAINER FOR PUMPS. ROBERT S. GARRY and JEROME G. GARRY, Jenks, Okla. Filed July 3, 1919. Serial No. 308,460. 4 Claims. (Cl. 103—64.)

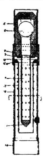

3. The combination with the working barrel of a pump and a coupling sleeve connected to the lower end thereof: of a depending strainer tube extending into and carried

by the coupling sleeve, an imperforate tube inside the strainer tube and supported thereby, said imperforate tube having a flared upper end engageable by the corresponding end of the strainer tube, and a strainer tube inside the imperforate tube and connected to the inlet of the working barrel.

1,329,172. SPOON. MARCUS GLUCK, New York, N. Y. Filed Apr. 8, 1919. Serial No. 288,623. 2 Claims. (Cl. 30—22.)

1. A spoon, including a tubular handle comprising a single sheet of material having its longitudinal edges overlapping and secured one to the other, and a bowl having its inner end secured to one of the ends of such handle and at the point of termination of the tube.

1,329,173. CONDUCTING - CORD HOLDER. HELEN A. GOLDTHWAITE, Saco, Me. Filed Dec. 10, 1918. Serial No. 266,164. 1 Claim. (Cl. 248—30.)

A conducting cord holder comprising a base having a clamping member formed thereon for engagement upon the edge of a shelf or table, a tubular upright rising from said base, a second tubular upright telescopically engaged within said first named upright, a cap member detachably and telescopically engaged within the upper end of said second named tubular member, a laterally and downwardly curved arm formed integrally upon the top of said cap member and terminating in an upwardly directed hook, a chain

having one endmost link engaged upon said hook, and a spring depending from said chain and having one end engaging within the other endmost link of said chain, the other end of said spring being formed as a hook adapted for detachable engagement with a conducting cord.

1,329,174. EXTRA-TIRE CARRIER. WALTER R. GREEN, Chicago, Ill. Filed Aug. 28, 1917. Serial No. 188,554. 5 Claims. (Cl. 224—29.)

1. A tire carrier of the class described for coöperation with a supported tire comprising curved means to fit over the upper portion of said supported tire on the upper tread surface thereof, diagonal braces depending from said means and another similarly curved means supported on the ends of said braces, and projecting outwardly from and lying against the lower portion of said tire to receive another tire seated therein.

1,329,175. GEAR-CUTTING ATTACHMENT. WILLIAM H. HACKLEMAN, Appleton, Wis. Filed Feb. 26, 1919. Serial No. 279,301. 1 Claim. (Cl. 90—1.)

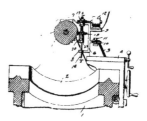

In an attachment of the character specified, a frame including offstanding portions projecting therefrom in the same direction, a shaft journaled in the offstanding portions of the frame and adapted to receive a cutter, a gear wheel provided with a collar which is mounted in one of the offstanding portions of the frame and lock nuts for securing the gear wheel to the shaft and holding the latter and gear wheel in proper position relatively to the frame.

1,329,176. LAWN-EDGE TRIMMER. HENRY HAUGEN, Stoughton, Wis. Filed July 7, 1917. Serial No. 179,165. 1 Claim. (Cl. 97—28.)

A lawn trimmer comprising a flat shovel-like portion having an extension formed at one side thereof and bent upwardly at substantially right angles thereto, said extension having its rear edge disposed at a rearward inclination, while the forward edge thereof is disposed perpendicular and sharpened to provide a cutting edge, the forward edge being cut into to provide a concaved notch to form a primary cutter, the lower portion of said extension being of a length corresponding to the length of the shovel where-

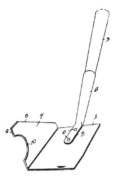

by to materially brace and strengthen the device and to provide means for packing the earth engaged thereby.

1,329,177. CONCRETE-FORM. John N. Heltzel, Warren, Ohio. Filed May 17, 1919. Serial No. 297,729. 11 Claims. (Cl. 25—118.)

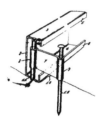

1. A device of the class described, comprising a side rail, a bracket pivotally secured thereto, and a stake slidable in said bracket.

1,329,178. OPERATING DEVICE FOR WINDOW-SASHES. William Patrick Hilley, Des Moines, Iowa. Filed Dec. 11, 1918. Serial No. 266,223. 15 Claims. (Cl. 268—4.)

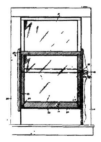

11. In a window, sashes, flexible supports for the sashes, a sliding and revoluble shaft, drums loosely mounted on

the shaft and upon which the flexible supports are wound, and a member fixedly secured to the shaft between the drums and having means for engaging the drums to cause them to turn therewith.

1,329,179. CENTRIFUGAL VALVE-CASTING MACHINE. Frederick Hilty, Waukegan, Ill., assignor to Laurence R. Wilder, Chicago, Ill. Filed Mar. 28, 1919. Serial No. 285,866. 9 Claims. (Cl. 22—65.)

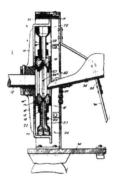

1. A centrifugal casting machine consisting of an annulus comprising a part channeled on its inner surface to receive the molten metal to be cast, a plurality of depressions on the outer periphery of said channeled member, sprues affording communication between said depressions and the inner channel, and a plurality of molds radiating from said annulus, each of said molds having one end thereof fitted into one of said depressions, means for supporting said molds, and means for rotating said annulus and parts carried thereby.

1,329,180. STORAGE-BATTERY SEPARATOR. Walter E. Holland and James M. Skinner, Philadelphia, Pa., assignors to Philadelphia Storage Battery Company, Philadelphia, Pa., a Corporation of Pennsylvania. Filed May 17, 1919. Serial No. 297,868. 8 Claims. (Cl. 204—29.)

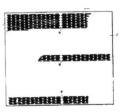

2. The combination in a storage battery cell of alternated positive and negative plates; wood separators between said plates respectively; with separators of insulating material having series of narrow elongated slots giving a porosity of at least 40% and mounted between certain of said plates and the adjacent wood separators.

1,329,181. STORAGE BATTERY AND METHOD OF PREPARING SAME. Walter E. Holland, Philadelphia, and Lawrence J. Pearson, Wyncote, Pa., assignors to Philadelphia Storage Battery Company, Philadelphia. Pa., a Corporation of Pennsylvania. Filed Sept. 5, 1919. Serial No. 321,875. 7 Claims. (Cl. 204—29.)

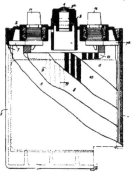

4. A storage battery consisting of a sealed container; a series of wet negative plates; a series of substantially dry positive plates; a series of wet wooden separators mounted between the positive and negative plates respectively.

1,329,182. VALVE-CAP. Edward E. Holt, Chicago, Ill., assignor to Holt Auto Devices Company, Chicago, Ill., a Corporation of Illinois. Filed Mar. 4, 1918. Serial No. 220,152. 2 Claims. (Cl. 152—12.)

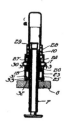

1. In a device of the class described, the combination with a corrugated valve stem having a longitudinally extending flattened surface, of a cylindrical member slidably mounted on the valve stem and having a flattened portion adapted to engage said surface, there being a plurality of openings in said cylindrical member, a split collar comprising sections encircling the cylindrical member and having a plurality of corrugation engaging extensions adapted to pass through said openings and engage the corrugations of the valve stem, a cam sleeve slidably mounted on the cylindrical member and adapted, when advanced, to force the sections of the split collar toward each other, a spring for advancing the cam sleeve, and a cylindrical closure surrounding the cam sleeve and spring and in engagement with the cam sleeve for the purpose of retracting the same against the force of the spring.

1,329,183. METHOD OF ASCERTAINING THE QUANTITY OF FAT IN MILK AND CREAM. Hans Marcussen Höyberg, Frederiksberg, near Copenhagen, Denmark. Filed Apr. 2, 1919. Serial No. 286,997. 2 Claims. (Cl. 23—3.)

1. Method of ascertaining the quantity of fat in milk and cream consisting in mixing 9.7 volumes of milk with 3.4 volumes of a solution of potassium sodium tartrate and sodium hydroxid in water and 0.6 volumes of isobutyl alcohol in a butyrometer glass, leaving the mixture for 15–20 minutes in a water-bath at a temperature of 60–70° C. and reading off the quantity of fat directly from the butyrometer glass.

1,329,184. DISPENSING - RECEPTACLE. Herbert B. Hyams, St. Paul, Minn. Filed Mar. 10, 1919. Serial No. 281,601. 2 Claims. (Cl. 221—23.)

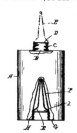

1. In a dispensing vessel the combination of a vessel body having an orifice, a delivery nozzle adapted to be detachably coupled to said receptacle over said orifice, and a pocket in a wall of said receptacle formed with a coupling element, said pocket being adapted to receive said nozzle when detached from said receptacle over said orifice and to detachably connect with said coupling.

1,329,185. TRACK LIFTER AND LINER. Haruo Kawashima, North Platte, Nebr. Filed Feb. 18, 1919. Serial No. 277,843. 11 Claims. (Cl. 254—43.)

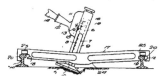

1. In combination a jack including a movable bar, a track engaging and lifting beam, and a pivotal connection between the beam and bar extending in angular relation to the direction of movement of the latter whereby the position of the bar with relation to the beam may be varied to cause pressure to be applied to the beam and effect movement of the track engaged with the beam laterally in either direction.

1,329,186. BROOM-HOLDER. Samuel C. Kindig, Baltimore, Md., assignor of one-half to William C. Ludwig, Baltimore, Md. Filed May 28, 1919. Serial No. 300,354. 1 Claim. (Cl. 24—257.)

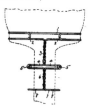

A broom holder formed with a rest at its upper end adapted to receive the straw end of the broom and having its ends apart to form an opening for the broom handle, a piece projecting downwardly from said rest and having two laterally projecting arms each having an opening in its outer end, and a clamp at the lower end of said downwardly projecting piece and having its extremities apart and extending around to form a guide for the broom handle.

1,329,187. LIGHT-SHADE. Charles D. Kline, Cleveland, Ohio. Filed Jan. 9, 1919. Serial No. 270,334. 1 Claim. (Cl. 240—108.)

A light shade having an opening in a side thereof, a lens disposed within the shade and pivoted thereto at a point below and adjacent the opening to swing downwardly out of the way, a catch above and adjacent the opening to engage the lens and retain it in operative position, and a cover exterior to the shade and pivoted thereto at one side of said opening.

1,329,188. AUTOMATIC CROSSING-GATE. Charles P. Knapp, Rochester, Ohio. Filed Nov. 10, 1917. Serial No. 201,333. 2 Claims. (Cl. 246—125.)

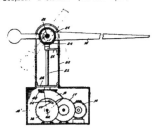

1. The combination with a gate, of normally open electric circuits, a motor included in said circuits, mechanism including gears operated by the motor for raising and lowering the gate, a reversing switch and a pin carried by the switch for engagement with the slot in one of said gears, whereby the switch will be automatically reversed at the end of each operation of the mechanism.

1,329,189. WIRE FENCE. Richard Knaur, Vienna, Austria, assignor to the Firm of Felten & Guilleaume Fabrik Elektrischer Kabel, Stahl- und Kupferwerke Aktiengesellschaft, Vienna, Austria. Filed Dec. 22, 1915. Serial No. 68,191. 2 Claims. (Cl. 245—8.)

1. A wire fence, comprising a plurality of zigzag members loosely secured together to form when extended

lozenge-shaped members, and flexible edge wires secured to the said members, whereby the fence can be folded with its members closed and the edge wires extending between the members thereof.

1,329,190. BELT. Takejiro Kusuda, Osaka, Japan. Filed Nov. 16, 1918. Serial No. 262,775. 2 Claims. (Cl. 74—63.)

1. A belt formed of a plurality of layers of flexible material secured together by rows of stitches, the number of rows of stitches at one side of said belt being greater than at the other side thereof.

1,329,191. FASTENING DEVICE. William H. Lucas, Claremore, Okla., assignor of one-half to H. H. Brown, Claremore, Okla. Filed Apr. 29, 1918. Serial No. 231,462. 1 Claim. (Cl. 287—1.)

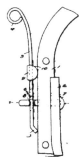

In a device of the class described, a supporting element, a supported element, a tie member extending through said elements, a resilient member associated with said supporting member and having its edges extending in parallel relation, means for detachably coupling said tie member to said resilient member, a strain applying device operating between said supporting member and resilient member and having guide ribs slidably engaging the parallel edges of the resilient member.

1,329,192. METHOD OF TESTING. Dunlap J. McAdam, Jr., Baltimore, Md., assignor to Tinius Olsen Testing Machine Company, Philadelphia, Pa., a Corporation of Pennsylvania. Filed May 18, 1916. Serial No. 98,349. 4 Claims. (Cl. 265—13.)

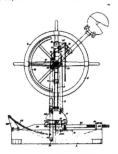

1. The method of testing which consists in rigidly mounting an elongated test piece with its ends overhang-

ing their support; thereafter simultaneously subjecting both of said ends to a suddenly applied shearing stress immediately adjacent such support; and noting the amount of said stress.

1,329,193. DISTRIBUTING SYSTEM. PAUL MACGAHAN, Pittsburgh, Pa., assignor to Westinghouse Electric and Manufacturing Company, a Corporation of Pennsylvania. Filed Dec. 10, 1914. Serial No. 876,461. 8 Claims. (Cl. 175—294.)

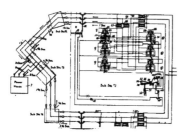

1. In a system of power distribution, the combination with a plurality of sub-stations, interconnectors to connect said sub-stations in a ring-type formation, and means for supplying power thereto, of disconnecting devices inserted in the interconnectors and on each side of the sub-stations, and means for operating said disconnecting devices which comprises an excess-current definite time-limit actuating means, the time elements of corresponding actuating means which are associated with various sub-stations varying from one another by equal time increments from one side of the power-supplying means around the system to the other side of the power-supplying means.

1,329,194. FRAME FOR SUITCASES. HYMAN MAKRUZIN, Philadelphia, Pa. Filed Jan. 6, 1919. Serial No. 269,741. 1 Claim. (Cl. 190—49.)

A frame of the character described consisting of longitudinally and transversely extending pieces of wood, the end portions of adjacent pieces abutting respectively at the corners of the frame, and corner brackets formed of longitudinally and transversely extending sockets of metal which are divided on their sides, and necks of angular form having their limbs connecting said sockets, said sockets being applied to the longitudinally and transversely extending pieces of wood and then having the limbs of the sockets clamped about the contiguous portions of said pieces and fastened by means of members punched in from the end portions of said sockets.

1,329,195. CATAMENIAL SACK. JOSEPH J. MARTINKA, Newark, N. J. Filed Sept. 13, 1919. Serial No. 323,454. 2 Claims. (Cl. 128—286.)
1. A catamenial sack comprising an open body provided with means for supporting therein a mass of absorbent

material, means for attaching the body to the wearer, and a bifurcated gasket of absorbent character removably

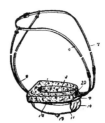

superimposed upon the body and having its ends detachably connected together.

1,329,196. TRACK-LEVEL. HISASHI MATOBA, Whitefish, Mont. Filed May 29, 1919. Serial No. 300,501. 2 Claims. (Cl. 33—145.)

1. A track level comprising a beam, a rail-engaging member near one end of said beam and having a part arranged to extend downwardly at the side of the rail, a frame at the other end of said beam, said beam and said frame having registering, vertical openings, a scale bar slidably mounted in said opening, a housing secured upon said frame, a keeper movably mounted in said housing and adapted to engage and hold said scale bar, and spring means for holding said keeper normally in operative position with respect to said scale bar.

1,329,197. TRACK GAGE AND LEVEL. HISASHI MATOBA, Whitefish, Mont. Filed May 29, 1919. Serial No. 300,503. 6 Claims. (Cl. 33—145.)

6. A track gage and level comprising in combination a beam, track-engaging members near the ends thereof, and each having a part adapted to engage the upper surface of the rail head and a part adapted to extend downwardly at the side of the railhead, and a spirit level carried by said beam, said spirit level being so disposed that its longitudinal axis is parallel to a line extending from the lower end of one of said downwardly extending parts of one of said track-engaging members to the under surface of said part adapted to engage the upper surface of the rail head of the other track-engaging member, and a level measuring element adjustably carried by said beam, near one end thereof.

1,329,198. RADIATOR. KONRAD MEIER, Winterthur, Switzerland. Filed Feb. 2, 1916. Serial No. 75,710. 5 Claims. (Cl. 257—151.)
5. A column radiator whose individual columns are oval in cross section with inverted ends, the more pointed in-

verted end forming a deeper groove than the opposite flatter inverted end, the deeper grooves forming convection channels open at the top and bottom, and the shallower

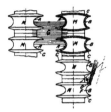

groove forming a radiation surface also open at the top and bottom, thereby obtaining a greater angle of direct radiation for the curved sides of the column.

1,329,199. SOAP-DISPENSING APPARATUS. CHARLES D. MYERS, Ware, Mass., assignor of one-half to Edward K. Lathrop, Springfield, Mass. Filed Apr. 6, 1918. Serial No. 227,039. 1 Claim. (Cl. 221—78.)

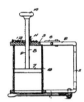

A device of the character described, comprising a substantially U-shaped supporting frame forming spaced parallel upper and lower rigid arms, the lower arm being formed with an opening, a cylinder forming a soap container open at opposite ends supported on the lower arm with its lower open end registering with the opening in said arm, a hinged extension on the upper arm for closing the upper open end of said container, a plunger working in the container and having a rack slidable through the extension, and means for locking the rack to hold the plunger in adjusted position in the container.

1,329,200. ATTACHMENT FOR MOTOR - VEHICLES. ALFRED NEWHOPE, Jacksonville, Fla. Filed Feb. 15, 1919. Serial No. 277,188. 2 Claims. (Cl. 152—14.)

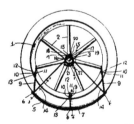

1. A traction surface increasing means for vehicle wheels, comprising a member of greater width than the tire of a wheel designed to be arranged on the outer surface of the tire, flexible means for securing the member to the rim of the wheel, and rigid supporting means between said member and the hub of the wheel.

1,329,201. JUMPING TOY. FRANCIS S. NEYD'HART, West Hoboken, N. J. Filed Jan. 31, 1919. Serial No. 274,351. 3 Claims. (Cl. 46—40.)

1. A figure toy comprising a body of sheet material and having eyes pressed outward from opposite sides of the head portion of the body to produce maximum strength or stiffness, and a spring member extending rearward from the posterior portion of the body and adapted to be put under tension through the rearward pressure of the body while the operator grasps the body at the eyes and presses rearward thereon while the tip of the tail is applied against a fixed object.

1,329,202. BED-SPRING. MAX NOVICK, New York, N. Y. Filed June 20, 1919. Serial No. 305,502. 3 Claims. (Cl. 5—8.)

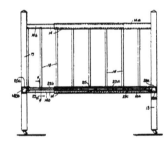

1. In a bedstead of the character set forth, the combination of head and foot pieces of variable length, each of said pieces comprising members having fixed spaced rods, and auxiliary rods parallel to the fixed rods and adjustable along the head and foot pieces to retain symmetry of spacing in all adjustments of said head and foot pieces.

1,329,203. HANDLE ATTACHMENT. ARTHUR PARRY, Port Orchard, Wash. Filed Oct. 23, 1919. Serial No. 332,628. 2 Claims. (Cl. 65—13.)

1. A handle attachment for cups and analogous receptacles comprising a handle provided at one end with a loop of approximately U-shape, a clip of substantially U-form adapted to receive the upper edge portion of the cup or receptacle, and having one member extending into the space between the members of the U-shaped loop of the handle, and a screw engaging the outer member of the clip and passing through one member of the U-shaped loop of the handle and engaging the other member of said loop.

1,329,204. ELECTRICAL WATER-HEATER. RALPH J. PATTERSON, Berlin, N. H. Filed Aug. 20, 1919. Serial No. 318,793. 9 Claims. (Cl. 219—39.)

9. In a water heater, a tubular casting provided with a flange having an upstanding rim, having internal and external screw-threads, a plurality of openings formed in said flange, tubular casings having their upper ends closed secured in said openings, heating units adapted for insertion in said casings, means for removably securing said heating units within said casings, a baffle plate secured to the upper ends of said casings, a hood provided with external screw-threads adapted to engage the screw-threads of said rim, an outlet opening for said hood, and a plurality of openings formed in said hood adjacent the lower end thereof.

1,329,205. METALLIC RAILWAY-TIE. WARREN C. PATTERSON, Tamaqua, Pa. Filed Sept. 26, 1919. Serial No. 326,446. 3 Claims. (Cl. 238—286.)

1. A metallic railway tie, comprising a top plate having integral, marginal flanges depending from its longitudinal edges and having openings formed therein adjacent to its ends, and open-top boxes secured beneath the openings upon the underside of the tie and comprising bottoms, end walls and side walls carrying outwardly extending flanges for attachment to the tie between the flanges thereof, said boxes being of greater depth than said flanges.

1,329,206. LICENSE-TAG BRACKET. CHARLES H. PEASE, Canaan, Conn. Filed Sept. 18, 1919. Serial No. 324,466. 1 Claim. (Cl. 40—125.6.)

The combination with an automobile having a dashboard, of a pair of brackets having straight portions positioned against the front faces of the dashboard, horizontal portions extending over the upper edge of the dashboard, said vertical and horizontal portions having perforations therein, securing devices in said perforations and projecting into the dashboard, said brackets having upwardly and rearwardly projecting portions positioned over the cowl of the automobile, and vertical portions at the upper ends of the brackets having perforations therein for the reception of securing devices connecting the license tag thereto.

1,329,207. DISPLAY-BASKET. THOMAS HILTON PEPPERS, Nashville, Ark. Filed Apr. 23, 1918. Serial No. 230,303. 3 Claims. (Cl. 40—7.)

1. A display case having a cover with simulations of its contents, and means for covering said box in shipment, said covering means rendering visible said simulations.

1,329,208. AIR-BAG. PETER POWELL, Boston, Mass., assignor of one-half to James Rosenfield, Boston, Mass. Filed Apr. 15, 1918. Serial No. 228,541. 15 Claims. (Cl. 18—45.)

8. In a device of the character described, the combination of an inner tube adapted to be filled with air under pressure, an outer casing arranged to confine the inner tube when inflated, the casing having an elongate opening in one side, and means comprising interfitting loops secured to the casing on opposite sides of the opening for closing the opening.

1,329,209. FOOT-OPERATED VALVE. PASQUALE A. RICCIO, Brooklyn, N. Y. Filed Aug. 30, 1919. Serial No. 320,836. 5 Claims. (Cl. 251—137.)

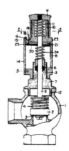

1. A device of the character described, comprising a lock casing, means for connecting the lock casing to a valve casing, a stem extending through the lock casing, a valve on the stem, a locking plate in the lock

casing having an opening receiving the stem, a spring exerting pressure on the plate causing it to frictionally engage the stem, and means outside of the casing for moving the plate to a position to release the stem.

1,329,210. AUTOMATIC AIR-RELEASE. HAROLD J RICKON, San Francisco, Calif., assignor of one-half to John A. Sandal, San Francisco, Calif. Filed Oct. 12, 1918. Serial No. 257,842. 1 Claim. (Cl. 21—69.)

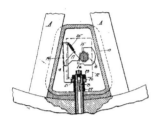

A device of the class described including a casing adapted to be secured to an automobile wheel adjacent to the tire valve, a door therefor, a lock for said door, means responsive to centrifugal force and disposed in said casing in position to engage the tire valve under centrifugal force due to the turning of the wheel for opening said valve, and means on the lock adapted, without unlocking the door, to be positioned by the lock to restrain said first means against operation.

1,329,211. NITROSTARCH EXPLOSIVE AND METHOD OF MANUFACTURING SAME. WALTER O. SNELLING and WILLIAM R. LAMS, Allentown, Pa., assignors, by mesne assignments, to Trojan Powder Company, New York, N. Y., a Corporation of New York. Filed June 22, 1918. Serial No. 241,354. 17 Claims. (Cl. 52—3.)
12. A nitro-starch explosive containing an organic stabilizing agent and a mineral oil.

1,329,212. METHOD OF MANUFACTURING NITRO-STARCH EXPLOSIVES. WALTER O. SNELLING and WILLIAM R. LAMS, Allentown, Pa., assignors to Trojan Powder Company, Allentown, Pa., a Corporation of New York. Original application filed June 22, 1918, Serial No. 241,354. Divided and this application filed Sept. 3, 1919. Serial No. 321,455. 5 Claims. (Cl. 52—3.)
1. The method of treating nitro-starch which consists in providing the nitro-starch particles with a minute film or coating of a heavy mineral oil and acting thereon with an organic stabilizing agent soluble in said mineral oil.

1,329,213. WHEEL. PAUL AUGUSTE TOURTIER, New Orleans, La. Filed Aug. 22, 1918. Serial No. 250,984. 6 Claims. (Cl. 152—81.)
2. A wheel having a hollow hub and a plurality of radial piston cylinders, a plurality of pistons working in said cylinders subject to air pressure within the hollow hub, a tread in a plurality of sections, each section carried by one of said pistons, each piston having an annular groove within its cylinder, and a pneumatic tube located in said groove and engaging the cylinder.
5. A wheel having a hollow hub forming an air chamber, piston cylinders extending radially from said hub and in communication with said chamber, pistons slidable in said cylinders and held against rotation, a tread in sections detachably connected to the pistons to move independently of one another with the pistons, each cylinder having opposing openings and each piston having opposing

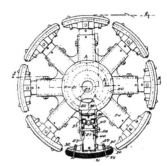

lengthwise slots, a bolt extending through the cylinder openings and through the slots of the piston, and bumpers carried by the piston at the ends of the slots.

1,329,214. FERMENTATION PROCESS FOR THE PRODUCTION OF ACETONE AND BUTYL ALCOHOL. CHARLES WEIZMANN and GEORGE ANTHONY HAMLYN, London, England. Filed Mar. 27, 1918. Serial No. 225,138. 5 Claims. (Cl. 23—24.)
1. A process of producing acetone and butyl alcohol consisting in submitting a sterilized starchy mash to the action of molds having a strong proteolytic action and fermenting the mash by bacteria of the amylobacter group.

1,329,215. RESILIENT TIRE. PETER J. WESTERGAARD, Reinbeck, Iowa. Filed July 3, 1919. Serial No. 308,606. 2 Claims. (Cl. 152—8.)

1. A resilient tire comprising a base band and side walls of stiff material, a resilient tread secured along its side edges thereto and springs supporting the central portion of said tread at intervals, each of said springs being of hollow T-shaped formation and embodying transversely opposite legs the end portions of which are brought into parallel relation to each other, a reinforcing body interposed between the resilient tread and said springs, and spring holding members projecting outwardly from the base band and engaging the said parallel end portions of the springs.
2. A resilient tire comprising a base band and side walls of stiff material, a resilient tread supported along its side edges thereto and springs supporting the central portion of said tread at intervals, each of said springs being of hollow T-shaped formation and embodying transversely opposite legs, the end portions of which are brought into parallel relation to each other, a reinforcing body interposed between the resilient tread and said springs, and spring holding members projecting outwardly from the base band and engaging the said parallel end portions of

the springs, the said parallel end portions of the springs being clamped together and the springs being maintained in spaced relation between said spring holding members.

1,329,216. MOTION-PICTURE APPARATUS. NORMAN T. WHITAKER, New York, N. Y. Filed Apr. 17, 1917. Serial No. 162,712. 15 Claims. (Cl. 40—53.)

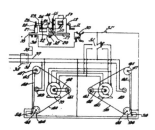

1. A changeable exhibitor comprising in combination a movable sheet provided with indicia, a motion picture projecting apparatus, and means connected to the sheet and motion picture projecting apparatus whereby the sheet will be intermittently moved.

1,329,217. LOCK-BEARING FOR THE COMPOSITION ROLLERS OF PRINTING-MACHINES. CARL WINKLER, Berne, Switzerland. Filed Sept. 9, 1918. Serial No. 253,313. 5 Claims. (Cl. 64—52.)

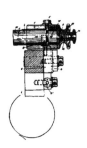

1. An improved bearing for the composition rollers of printing machines, comprising in combination a frame, a pin for pivoting said frame to the framework of the machine, a bolt adapted to be screwed into the framework of the machine, set-screws provided in said frame and adapted to bear against said bolt on opposite sides, and a head-piece adapted to slide in said frame and being so disposed that said pin is situated between said head-piece and said bolt substantially as set forth.

1,329,218. ACQUAINTANCE - PROMOTING MACHINE. CARL J. WITZORECK, Millvale, Pa. Filed June 13, 1918. Serial No. 239,905. 8 Claims. (Cl. 40—77.)

1. A machine of the class described comprising a cabinet having a view opening, a pocket drum mounted in the

cabinet, means for rotatably and axially moving the drum to bring any desired pocket in registry with the view opening, and a scene element disposed between the view open-

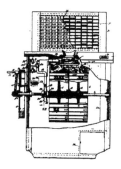

ing and drum and having a slot therein through which any desired pocket can be seen.

1,329,219. UMBRELLA. JOHN ALLESINA, Portland, Oreg. Filed June 16, 1919. Serial No. 304,424. 2 Claims. (Cl. 135—31.)

2. A device of the character described comprising a sliding sleeve provided on its periphery near its ends with rigid attaching means, resilient members provided with integral tongues adapted to be bent into engagement with the rigid attaching means to secure the resilient members in place on said sleeve, and right-angular ends integral with said resilient members.

1,329,220. STALK-CHOPPER. ADOLPH J. BARTZ, Crandall, Tex. Filed Oct. 5, 1917. Serial No. 194,894. 2 Claims. (Cl. 55—118.)

1. In a stalk cutting machine, spaced runners, a reciprocating cutter arranged between said runners, an endless conveyer communicating with the reciprocating cutter,

stalk crushing rolls adjacent the rear end of the conveyer, rotary chopping means communicating with the crushing

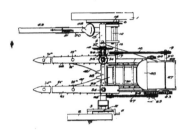

rolls and a hood surrounding said rolls and chopping means.

1,329,221. SEWING-MACHINE. JOSEPH BERGER, Utica, N. Y., assignor to Union Special Machine Company, Chicago, Ill., a Corporation of Illinois. Filed Dec. 2, 1914. Serial No. 875,109. 12 Claims. (Cl. 112—100.)

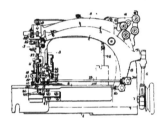

1. The combination of a work support, an overhanging arm, feeding mechanism, and stitch forming mechanism including a plurality of needles, a thread guiding member movable back and forth in a line substantially parallel with the line of feed, means mounted beneath the work support for supporting and operating said thread guiding member, a thread engaging hook having a shoulder adapted to engage the thread on the forward movement of the hook, means for moving said hook into engagement with the thread extending through said thread guiding member, and then across the line of feed and in front of the needles for forming and holding a loop in said thread for the needle farthest from said thread guiding member, and means carried by the overhanging arm for supporting the hook.

1,329,222. LAMP-BURNER. HENRY NORBERT BERNIER. Iroquois Falls, Ontario, Canada. assignor of one-half to Jules De Froy, Timmins, Canada. Filed Apr. 29, 1919. Serial No. 293,391. 3 Claims. (Cl. 67—79.)

1. In combination with a lamp burner, automatic extinguishing means comprising a pair of extinguisher members

disposed at opposite sides of the wick guide and each including an inverted trough-like body carried by a pivoted supporting member, a crank arm formed on each supporting member, a ring like guide-way in which said crank arms project, and balls disposed within said guide-way and normally inactive therein, tilting of the burner resulting in movement of either ball circumferentially of said guide-way to engage the associated crank arm for swinging the associated extinguisher member to dispose said trough-like body over the burning lamp wick.

1,329,223. EGG-TESTER. JAMES R. BLAKEMORE, Murfreesboro, Tenn., assignor to Green B. Sawyer, Murfreesboro, Tenn. Filed Apr. 8, 1919. Serial No. 288,576. 1 Claim. (Cl. 99—6.)

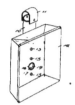

A device of the class described comprising a tubular member having a lateral opening and adapted to receive a light transmitting medium, a sight tube engaging in said opening and having an outwardly projecting annular bead bearing against the outer face of the tubular member, an annular member of yieldable material engaging in said bead, a holding member including a plate having an opening corresponding to the opening of the tubular member and bearing against the bead of the sight tube, and means for connecting the plate to the tubular member and compressing the plate against the bead and holding the sight tube and yieldable member in position.

1,329,224. FLUID-FUEL BURNER. DAVID HARTWELL BRAZIL, Montgomery, Ala. Filed Apr. 8, 1919. Serial No. 288,603. 10 Claims. (Cl. 158—65.)

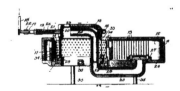

1. A fluid fuel burner comprising a housing having a plurality of gas egress ports, some of which are directed toward each other, a retort located above the housing and in position to receive flame from the inwardly directed egress ports and a conduit positioned within the housing adapted to receive gas from the retort and conduct it from a point above the housing downward centrally through said burner to and discharge it into the bottom of the housing.

1,329,225. VESSEL-RAISING APPARATUS. Matt Burke, Duluth, Minn. Filed Sept. 22, 1919. Serial No. 325,398. 6 Claims. (Cl. 114—51.)

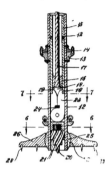

1. A cable attaching means for raising the sunken vessel, including a rotating boring tube, a drill removably connected thereto, and a cable secured to the drill head and extending longitudinally of the tube.

1,329,226. WIRE-STRAIGHTENING TOOL. Frank L. Cervenka, Granger, Tex. Filed July 17, 1918. Serial No. 245,320. 2 Claims. (Cl. 140—123.)

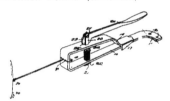

1. A wire straightening tool, comprising a lower jaw having a slot formed therein, an upper jaw having a reduced tongue extending through the slot to pivotally connect the upper jaw with the lower jaw and having side extensions serving as guiding means in respect to the lower jaw, the wire engaging faces of the jaws being provided with coöperating notches forming wire receiving openings when the jaws are in a closed position, a stem connecting said jaws, resilient means on the stem normally separating the jaws, a cam carried by the stem and having an operating lever adapted to move the same into engagement with one of said jaws for forcing said jaws together, and means for adjusting the tension of said spring on the stem.

1,329,227. RAIL-JOINT. John Clancy, Kenner, La. Filed Oct. 6, 1919. Serial No. 328,688. 1 Claim. (Cl. 238—262.)

The combination with the meeting ends of the rail, of connecting bars arranged at opposite sides of the rail, each bar having longitudinally extending ribs upon the inner face thereof and a longitudinally extended groove upon the outer face thereof, fastening bolts passed through said bars and through the alined ribs thereof, and said grooves adapted to receive the heads of the fastening elements to prevent turning of the bolts, nuts secured to the opposite free ends of the bolts and the said ribs coöperating with the web of the rail to prevent bending of the bolt.

1,329,228. MARINE PROPULSION. Timoteo Ruiz de Esparza, Calexico, Calif., assignor of two-fifths to Peter Barnes and one-tenth to Fred Defoy, Calexico, Calif. Filed Mar. 25, 1919. Serial No. 284,985. 2 Claims. (Cl. 115—28.)

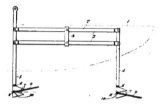

1. In vessel propelling means, the combination of movable carrying means, said means equipped with spaced abutments, and a propelling plane mounted to swing on the carrying means and movable between and adapted to bring up against the abutments.

1,329,229. LUBRICATOR. Michael L. Donovan, Omaha, Nebr. Filed Apr. 1, 1919. Serial No. 286,669. 3 Claims. (Cl. 221—47.)

1. In a grease gun, the combination of a reservoir, a conduit having a stepped upper end, a plate mounted on the conduit above the stepped upper end thereof, and means on the plate and reservoir for retaining the plate in proper position in said reservoir, and a filling cap arranged on the reservoir.

1,329,230. FIREARM CONTROL. Frank David Ely, Tientsin, China. Filed Apr. 14, 1917. Serial No. 162,215. 14 Claims. (Cl. 42—70.)

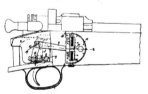

11. In combination with a fire arm firing control, a pendulum, a block for limiting the swinging movement

of the pendulum, a member controlling the firing of the arm from which the pendulum is suspended, said block normally preventing the movement of the pendulum toward the block, said block and pendulum having means adapted to register when said pendulum is in a substantially vertical position, and means controlling the position of the block, the registration of the means of the pendulum and block permitting the operation of the member controlling the firing of the fire arm.

1,329,231. VALVE. Isaiah G. Engle, Philadelphia, Pa. Filed Nov. 18, 1918. Serial No. 262,933. 5 Claims. (Cl. 251—159.)

1. A valve comprising a body portion, a threaded aperture extending thereinto, and a transversely extending aperture at one end and opening into said first aperture, said last-named aperture being adapted to receive means for locking in a given position a threaded member in said first aperture, and said means operating to permit the withdrawal of the threaded member from the threaded aperture without removing said means from said transverse aperture.

1,329,232. BITUMINOUS COMPOSITION. William Collins Erler, Terre Haute, Ind. Filed May 6, 1919. Serial No. 295,044. 2 Claims. (Cl. 106—31.)

1. A bituminous composition composed of the following ingredients in approximately the following proportions: asphalt, 12 parts; pitch, 6 parts; flour, 2 parts; and cement, 1 part.

1,329,233. ARC-WELDING SYSTEM. Otto H. Eschholz, Wilkinsburg, Pa., assignor to Westinghouse Electric & Manufacturing Company, a Corporation of Pennsylvania. Filed May 7, 1919. Serial No. 295,267. 9 Claims. (Cl. 219—15.)

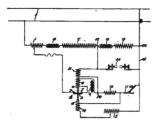

1. In an electric-arc welding system, the combination with a supply circuit, of means for reducing the supply voltage to a comparatively low value between the welding electrodes on open circuit, and means for limiting the welding current when an arc is drawn between electrodes.

1,329,234. POSITIONING-BUTTON. Franklin J. Evans, West Hazleton, Pa. Filed July 25, 1919. Serial No. 313,275. 5 Claims. (Cl. 33—169.)

5. A tool of the character specified, comprising a shank having a stem, a screw engaging an axial opening of the stem, a button mounted on the screw and movable laterally in every direction, a sleeve mounted on the stem and having an inner flange at its outer end, an expansible helical spring between the end of the stem and the inner

flange of the sleeve and a clamp nut mounted on the shank and coacting with the sleeve to secure the button in the adjusted position.

1,329,235. BOWLING-ALLEY. William L. Figenshu, Philadelphia, Pa., assignor of one-half to Oscar Heymann, Philadelphia, Pa. Filed May 29, 1919. Serial No. 300,016. 16 Claims. (Cl. 46—66.)

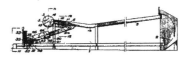

1. In a bowling alley, the combination with the going alley and a sectional return alley into which the balls pass from the bowling alley, of means in certain of said sections in the path of the balls, registering mechanism actuated by said means, a ball retainer into which the balls are finally discharged, and devices coöperating with said ball retainer to bring them into a position above the retainer accessible to the player.

1,329,236. WRAPPING MECHANISM FOR CANDY. Milford Berrian Ferguson and Edward Haas, Brooklyn, N. Y. Filed July 6, 1918. Serial No. 243,604. 17 Claims. (Cl. 93—2.)

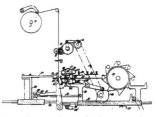

1. In a candy wrapping mechanism, means for presenting a candy with wrapping paper folded against part of the circumference thereof, a swinging tucker arm for bringing one end of the wrapping paper against the candy, and a pair of traveling belts for spinning the candy with the wrapping paper thereon whereby the wrapping paper is wrapped about the candy.

1,329,237. ELECTRIC PRECIPITATOR. Howard I. Frisbie, Anaconda, Mont. Filed Jan. 6, 1919. Serial No. 269,904. 3 Claims. (Cl. 183—7.)

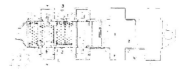

1. In an electric precipitator, a precipitating chamber having an inlet and an outlet and traversable by gases

between said inlet and outlet, suitable electrodes disposed across the chamber and forming collectively zones or fields of opposite polarity, the electrodes forming the zones of one polarity extending substantially the width of the precipitating chamber, the electrodes forming the zones of the opposite polarity being spaced a suitable distance form the walls of the chamber, and from the first mentioned electrodes to prevent short circuiting therewith, whereby a circuitous course is insured for the gases and a maximum precipitation results.

1,329,238. PISTON. ANDREW J. GOLATA and LOUIS L. ROBERTS, Detroit, Mich., assignors of one-tenth to William W. Carswell and one-tenth to Arthur L. Ellis, Detroit, Mich. Filed Nov. 9, 1917. Serial No. 201,047. 1 Claim. (Cl. 123—193.)

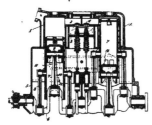

A piston for a two cycle engine comprising a cylindrical shell having the lower end thereof open and the upper end thereof closed and provided with piston ring grooves, that portion of said piston between said grooves provided with lateral openings in proximity to each other and lubricant holding chambers in the remaining portion between said grooves, said piston having exhaust openings intermediate the ends thereof, longitudinal and circumferentially disposed ribs on the outer wall of said shell providing lubricant holding pockets, with some of the pockets between the exhaust openings, and the entire outer surface of the piston forming a honeycomb or cellular wall, and diametrically opposed exterior bosses on said shell at the junction of some of said ribs affording connection for a pair of connecting rods.

1,329,239. TIRE - PEELING MACHINE. EDWARD P. HAFNER and JOHN T. ROBERTS, St. Louis, Mo. Filed July 12, 1919. Serial No. 310,381. 4 Claims. (Cl. 154—9.)

1. In a machine of the character described, a fixed support, two parallel rotatable members spaced apart, means for simultaneously imparting to said members rotations in opposite directions, and means for securing to said members the free ends of adhering layers of a sheet to be parted or peeled.

1,329,240. GRASS-ROPE REEL. CHARLES F. HAYS, Cottagegrove, Tenn. Filed Feb. 8, 1919. Serial No. 275,839. 6 Claims. (Cl. 242—77.)

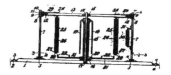

6. In a reel structure, the combination with a base, means for supporting a coil of rope upon the base, a plurality of rollers arranged on the outside of said coil, springs for forcing the rollers into contact with said coil, and means for supporting said rollers and springs in elevated relation to said base.

1,329,241. SHAFT-BEARING. RUDOLF E. HELLMUND, Swissvale, and BENJAMIN S. MOORE, Wilkinsburg, Pa., assignors to Westinghouse Electric and Manufacturing Company, a Corporation of Pennsylvania. Filed Feb. 19, 1917. Serial No. 149,480. 10 Claims. (Cl. 64—24.)

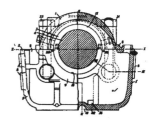

1. In a shaft bearing, the combination with a housing having an inner cylindrical surface provided with longitudinal grooves, of a divided bearing located within said housing, the lines of division of said bearing opening into said grooves.

2. In a shaft bearing, the combination with a housing having an inner cylindrical surface provided with longitudinal grooves, of a divided bearing located within said housing, the line of division of said bearing opening into said grooves, the walls of said grooves adjacent said bearing being shorter than the other walls.

3. A shaft bearing comprising a housing and a divided bearing located within said housing, the said housing being provided with oil-draining grooves along the split of said bearing and means for preventing oil from flowing out of the ends of said grooves.

4. A shaft bearing comprising a housing and a divided bearing located within said housing, the said housing being provided with oil-draining grooves along the split of said bearing, and the said bearing being provided with end flanges closing said grooves.

5. A shaft bearing comprising a housing member having an inner cylindrical surface and a bearing located therein, the said housing projecting beyond the end of said bearing and having an annular groove communicating with the outside of said housing by means of longitudinally extending grooves.

1,329,242. COIL-SUPPORTING DEVICE FOR DYNAMO-ELECTRIC MACHINES. RUDOLF E. HELLMUND, Swissvale, Pa., assignor to Westinghouse Electric and Manufacturing Company, a Corporation of Pennsylvania. Filed July 11, 1916. Serial No. 108,568. 6 Claims. (Cl. 171—252.)

4. In a dynamo-electric machine, the combination with a magnetizable core member provided with coils having

portions projecting beyond the ends thereof and inclined with respect thereto, of means for supporting the said projecting portions comprising coacting concentric annular

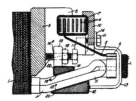

members and means for moving one of said annular members longitudinally with respect to the shaft to effect a clamping action on said projecting portions.

1,329,243. SYSTEM OF CONTROL. RUDOLF E. HELLMUND, Pittsburgh, Pa., assignor to Westinghouse Electric and Manufacturing Company, a Corporation of Pennsylvania. Filed Sept. 9, 1915. Serial No. 49,754. 12 Claims. (Cl. 172—274.)

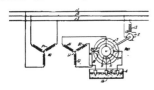

1. In a system of control, the combination with a polyphase induction motor having primary and secondary windings, of phase-advancing means connected in circuit with a portion only of the secondary phase windings, said phase-advancing means producing component E. M. F.'s in the remaining secondary phase windings.

1,329,244. WATER-MOTOR. IVERSON D. HUDGINS, Kirkwood, Ga., assignor of one-third to William Isaac Hobbs, Gainesville, Ga. Filed Apr. 21, 1919. Serial No. 291,549. 5 Claims. (Cl. 253—19.)

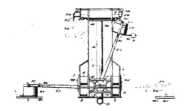

1. A motor including a supporting frame, a rock shaft journaled therein, angularly related arms supported upon the rock shaft, pivoted buckets carried by the arms, a tank provided with discharge pipes for conducting water to the buckets when the latter assume an elevated position, means for controlling the discharge water from the tank, counterbalance weights carried by the buckets, a pair of stationary keepers, and latch members carried by the buckets normally retained in engagement with the keepers by the action of the weights and adapted to be disengaged therefrom when the buckets are tilted on their pivotal axes by the counterbalancing effect of the liquid contents thereof.

1,329,245. SEWING - MACHINE. ROBERT R. HUGHES, Jr., New York, N. Y., assignor to Union Special Machine Company, Chicago, Ill., a Corporation of Illinois. Filed Mar. 19, 1915. Serial No. 15,448. 12 Claims. (Cl. 112—100.)

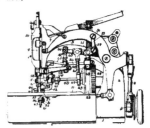

1. A sewing machine including in combination, spaced needles, means for laying a cross thread to be engaged alternately by said needles, means for guiding fabric sections in spaced relation to the respective needles, whereby said sections may be joined by said cross thread, and means for withdrawing said guiding means at the will of the operator.

1,329,246. ICE-CREAM-FREEZING PROCESS. ROBERT J. KIRKPATRICK, SEVERN M. SWORDLING, and WILFRID PAUL HEATH, Spokane, Wash. Filed Dec. 16, 1918. Serial No. 266,856. 2 Claims. (Cl. 99—8.)

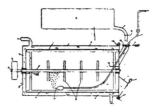

1. The process of making ice cream and other frozen foods, consisting in placing the food ingredients, in a liquid condition, in a refrigerating container, forcing a sterile inert gas into said container and thereby replacing the air therein, and agitating said ingredients while in said container and under pressure of said gas, to cause said gas to become incorporated and to commingle with said ingredients as they pass from a liquid to a solid or plastic condition.

2. The process of making ice cream and other frozen foods, consisting in placing the food ingredients, in a liquid condition, in a refrigerating container, forcing carbon dioxid gas into said container and thereby replacing the air therein and agitating said ingredients while in said container and under pressure of said gas, to cause said gas to become incorporated and to commingle with said ingredients as they pass from a liquid to a solid or plastic condition.

1,329,247. DYNAMO-ELECTRIC MACHINE. JAN ARTHUR KUYSER, Sale, England, assignor to Westinghouse Electric and Manufacturing Company, a Corporation of Pennsylvania. Filed Oct. 27, 1915. Serial No. 58,259. 8 Claims. (Cl. 171—252.)

1. A magnetizable core member for dynamo-electric machines provided with a plurality of intersecting longitudi-

nal and radial ventilating passages, certain of said longitudinal passages being continuous through certain of said

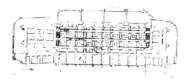

radial passages and communicating with others of said radial passages.

1,329,248. CLOSURE FOR MILK-BOTTLES. FRANCIS C. LARKIN, Rutherford, N. J. Filed June 30, 1919. Serial No. 307,670. 1 Claim. (Cl. 215—52.)

A bottle and closure therefor including a bottle neck having an internal shoulder forming a seat and internal threads on the mouth of the bottle, a transverse member in the mouth of the bottle in the plane of said shoulder and having a central apertured enlargement, a stem slidable vertically through said apertured enlargement, a head on the inner end of the stem, and a closure plug on the outer end of the stem formed to fit within the mouth of the bottle and rest on said shoulder, said closure being formed with external threads for coöperative engagement to hold the closure within the mouth of the bottle.

1,329,249. SHADE - ROLLER AND CURTAIN - POLE BRACKET. WILLIAM F. LEACH, Childress, Tex. Filed June 11, 1918. Serial No. 239,431. 3 Claims. (Cl. 156—24.)

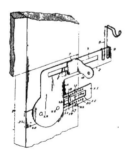

1. A device of the kind described comprising a body member having means for supporting a shade roller, a pair of clamping members pivotally connected with the body member, one of the clamping members having a fixed jaw, the other being provided with an arm in which

there is formed a longitudinal slot and in which there is formed further a series of holes both above and below the slot, and·an adjustable jaw carried by the said arm, the adjustable jaw having a tongue which passes through the slot and which is provided with a transverse portion lying against the arm on that face opposite which the jaw lies, the transverse portion having hooked ends for engagement one in any hole of either of the two series of holes, the jaw having hooked ends loosely engaging around the top and bottom edges of the arm.

1,329,250. TRAVELER'S CHECK. ALBERT LONSON, Callaway, Minn. Filed Aug. 30, 1917, Serial No. 188,963. Renewed Dec. 3, 1919. Serial No. 342,302. 2 Claims. (Cl. 283—6.)

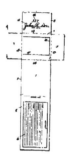

1. A traveler's check containing printed matter and blank spaces to be filled in to complete the check, said check having an extension lengthwise of the check and foldable and refoldable upon itself toward the body of the check, with flanking tabs on opposite sides for inclosing and ultimately sealing the folded and refolded portions, the first of the foldable portions of the extension in order of folding having a designated space adapted to receive identification means to be applied thereto by the person to whom the check is issued, and the second of the foldable portions in order having a tearable part of less area than said foldable portion, whereby the said identification means may be exposed to view, and the check also being adapted for the subsequent reception of identification means in close position to the first-named identification means in the completed check.

1,329,251. PILE-CUTTING MECHANISM. ALFRED F. McCOLLUM, Bloomsburg, Pa., assignor, by direct and mesne assignments, to The Magee Carpet Co., Bloomsburg, Pa., a Corporation of Pennsylvania. Filed Oct. 3, 1917. Serial No. 194,611. 11 Claims. (Cl. 139—23.)

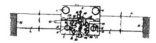

1. The combination in pile cutting mechanism of a carrier; a rotary multiblade knife thereon; a ratchet connected to said knife; a pawl for the ratchet; and means for reciprocating the cutter ‚with the ratchet to bring the latter intermittently into engagement with the pawl to cause rotation of the knife.

1,329,252. APPARATUS FOR MOISTENING CARBU-
RETED MIXTURES FOR GAS-ENGINES. WILLIAM
MILLARD, New York, N. Y., assignor to Carbon Destroyer
Corporation, New York, N. Y., a Corporation of New
York. Filed Nov. 21. 1917. Serial No. 203,290. 1
Claim. (Cl. 261—121.)

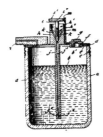

A unitary air-moistening device comprising a reservoir
adapted to contain liquid and air and having formed directly in and by one of its walls a passage intermediate
the lower portion of its interior and the atmosphere, a
valve applied directly to and carried by the said wall of
the reservoir and which controls the flow of air through
said passage into the lower portion of the reservoir, and
a conduit carried by one wall of the reservoir, in communication with the upper portion of the interior thereof,
and capable of direct connection to a conduit for carbureted air.

1,329,253. MACHINE FOR MAKING HOLLOW GLASS-
WARE. SIMON DOKK OLSEN, Leeds, England. Filed
Aug. 20, 1919. Serial No. 318,806. 6 Claims. (Cl.
49—9.)

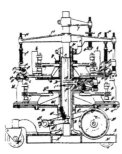

1. In a rotary table machine for making hollow glassware the combination of inverted and upright molds,
blowing mechanism coöperating therewith, devices for
transferring the work from the inverted to the upright
molds automatically, means for rotating the machine step
by step, and means for actuating the transfer device and
the blowing mechanism from one and the same moving
part of the machine by a common upward and downward
movement, substantially as described.

1,329,254. BOWLING GAME. FRED P. PURDY, Sharon.
Mass. Filed Feb. 24. 1919. Serial No. 278,576. 7
Claims. (Cl. 46—66.)
1. A bowling game comprising frames provided with
sets of pins thereon and having provision for supporting
the frames on the floor or ground with a bowling space

of any desired extent between them, deflectors for location back of said frames with a lateral inclination with
respect to said frames to guide and laterally deflect the
balls while still in transit to bowling stations adjacent
the ends of said frames, that the balls may be alternately

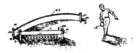

bowled by players standing at said stations, the frame
and deflector at one end of the bowling space being
separate from and independent of the frame and deflector
at the opposite end of said bowling space, and resetting
devices for the pins operable by the players when at said
stations.

1,329,255. AUTOMATIC PROTECTIVE GEAR FOR
ELECTRICAL SYSTEMS. MOSTYN ROSEBOURNE, Manchester, and FREDERICK ARTHUR COUSE, Urmston, England, assignors to Westinghouse Electric and Manufacturing Company, a Corporation of Pennsylvania
Filed Nov. 3, 1916. Serial No. 129,273. 6 Claims.
(Cl. 175—294.)

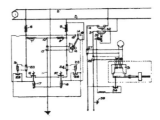

1. An electrical system of distribution comprising a
conductor connected to a neutral point thereof and to
ground, feeder conductors, a circuit interrupter inserted
therein, a differential relay controlled by the currents
traversing the feeder conductors and adapted to actuate
said circuit interrupter and means to operate said relay
when current traverses said conductor extending between the neutral point of the system and ground, whereby
the feeder conductors may be disconnected from circuit
by the operation of the circuit interrupter.

1,329,256. RADIATOR. ABRAM SHREIBMAN, Keokuk.
Iowa, assignor of one-third to J. L. Baldon and one-
third to J. E. Sellers, Elvaston, Ill. Filed Feb. 17,
1919. Serial No. 277,679. 1 Claim. (Cl. 257—129.)

A radiator for use in combination with an internal
combustion engine including an upper header, a water
inlet extending from said header, a semi-circular deflector

plate extending longitudinally of said header and being carried internally thereof, said deflector plate extending across the inner end of said water inlet and having open ends, thus deflecting the liquid passed thereinto from said inlet.

1,329,257. FOLDING IRONING - BOARD. ELLIS L. TERRY, Los Angeles, Calif. Filed Mar. 22, 1916, Serial No. 85,891. Renewed Sept. 29, 1919. Serial No. 327,154. 4 Claims. (Cl. 68—10.)

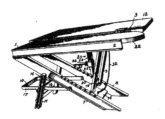

4. A collapsible support having side rails and cross-bars maintaining the side rails in opposed relation, primary swing legs hinged to one of said cross-bars, supplementary legs pivoted to the primary legs, a cross-bar connecting the supplementary legs, a notched brace engaging with the last-named cross-bar and having pivot connection with the primary legs, and hinged braces supporting the opposite end of the side rails, said braces engaging with corresponding notches in the primary legs whereby the side rails are maintained in a level position, a slidable bar transversely extensible from and sliding through the side rails, an auxiliary leg to support the slidable bar in extended position, means for varying the height of the auxiliary leg in accordance with the position of the supplementary legs, and adjustable connecting means between the supplementary legs and the auxiliary leg.

1,329,258. AUTOMATIC TRAIN-STOP. WILLIAM EDWARD WALSH, New Haven, Conn. Filed Dec. 26, 1918. Serial No. 260,333. 3 Claims. (Cl. 246—200.)

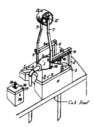

3. An automatic train stop comprising a valve, a plate on which the valve is mounted, posts connected with said plate, stops connected with the upper ends of said posts, lever arms operating said valve and arranged in the path of said stops, a roller mounted between the outer ends of said lever arms, means for locking the levers in the depressed position, and an inclined cam plate arranged to be swung into or out of the path of said roller.

1,329,259. CAN-END CLENCHER. IVAR F. WÄRME, Syracuse, N. Y., assignor to Continental Can Company, Incorporated, Syracuse, N. Y., a Corporation of New York. Filed July 18, 1916. Serial No. 109,971. 6 Claims. (Cl. 113—14.)

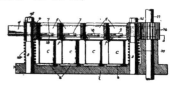

1. The combination of means for supporting a can, means for placing a can end on said can, and opposed clenching members movable bodily tangentially of the can end for engaging the curled edge of the can end and turning the same beneath the flange on the can body.

1,329,260. LABELING-MACHINE. JOHN L. WHITEHURST, Baltimore, Md., assignor, by mesne assignments, to John T. Whitehurst, Baltimore, Md. Filed Aug. 30, 1915. Serial No. 47,931. 4 Claims. (Cl. 216—44.)

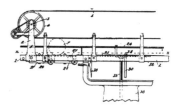

1. In a labeling machine, a bed, means to roll cans longitudinally of the bed from the entrance to the delivery end of the same, a table to hold a stack of labels, a pair of separated adhesive-applying devices situated at the entrance end of the bed, whereby a can in rolling over the said separated devices shall receive two applications of cement before reaching said table, and a removable depending stop bar adapted for use with short or half length labels.

1,329,261. FOLDING CHAIR. JACOB L. CELANE, New York, N. Y. Filed July 19, 1919. Serial No. 312,008. 6 Claims. (Cl. 155—8.)

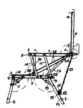

1. A folding chair comprising a plurality of frame members, a seat for one of said frame members, means connecting the two frame members including a plurality of link members to separate said frames and hold them in a parallel relation, an arm having one end thereof

pivoted to one of the frame members the other end thereof being adjustably positioned in the other frame member to hold the frames in a separated position, and legs pivotally secured to the lower frame.

1,329,262. CALCULATING-MACHINE. GEORGE C. CHASE, Providence, R. I. Filed Mar. 20, 1915. Serial No. 15,689. 54 Claims. (Cl. 235—82.)

1. A calculating machine having, in combination, a numeral-wheel and a gear for rotating said numeral-wheel, said gear being adapted to be rotated about its own axis and being also adapted to have its axis carried around the axis of the numeral-wheel without rotating said gear.

30. A calculating machine having, in combination, a series of numeral-wheels, a series of keys for actuating each of said numeral-wheels, a spring operating in connection with each of said numeral-wheels and tending to turn said numeral-wheel backward, means for normally holding each numeral-wheel against backward rotation under the action of said spring, means for releasing said holding means, and a stop for arresting each numeral-wheel when it has been brought to zero by the action of said spring.

1,329,263. GATE. LEON CHOUNARD, Vawn, Saskatchewan, Canada. Filed Mar. 8, 1918. Serial No. 221,187. 1 Claim. (Cl. 39—66.)

The combination with a slidably mounted gate, of an angularly movable shifter rod having an arm formed at one end and operatively connected with the gate at the other end, a double crank member consisting of two arms disposed at an angle to each other and mounted for rocking movement, the two arms having a common axis of movement, the double crank member being further provided with an angularly disposed arm, and a coupling connecting the last said arm with the arm of the shifter rod, the coupling being both angularly movable and longitudinally movable on both arms.

1,329,264. ROADWAY. WILLIAM V. T. CRAMER, Cincinnati, Ohio. Filed Oct. 11, 1919. Serial No. 330,116. 2 Claims. (Cl. 238—3.)

1. A removable roadway having two spaced tracks each comprising a plurality of strips laid relatively parallel and transversely of the road and spaced apart, and rigidly secured links connecting said strips to maintain them spaced apart, said links allowing the way to yield vertically while maintaining it as against lateral torsion.

1,329,265. TAPER-TURNING TOOL. MERRITT A. CULLING, Louisiana, Mo., assignor to Buffum Tool Company, Louisiana, Mo., a Corporation of Missouri. Filed Sept. 12, 1918. Serial No. 253,686. 8 Claims. (Cl. 82—35.)

1. A taper turning tool for screw machines, comprising a head, a cutter arranged on said head in such a manner that the cutting edge of same will act on the top side of the work, and means for enabling said cutter to be adjusted so as to raise and lower the cutting edge of same and also change the angular position of the cutting edge with relation to the axis of rotation of the work.

1,329,266. SEED-PAN. STEPHEN FAIRLY DAWKINS, Fayette, Miss. Filed July 15, 1919. Serial No. 310,895. 2 Claims. (Cl. 56—207.)

2. A seed pan of the character described, comprising a receptacle, a transverse rod secured in the sides of the receptacle at a point removed from its forward edge and at a distance above its bottom, a perforated cover for the receptacle having hinged mounting on said rod, and a series of guides secured to the bottom of the receptacle positioned longitudinally of the receptacle and located in advance of the hinged rod, said guides projecting above the forward end of the perforated cover and having their upper edges inclined downwardly from their rear to their forward ends.

1,329,267. COMMUTATOR-CYLINDER. JOHN S. DEAN, Wilkinsburg, Pa., assignor to Westinghouse Electric and Manufacturing Company, a Corporation of Pennsylvania. Filed Jan. 5, 1917. Serial No. 140,744. 5 Claims. (Cl. 171—321.)

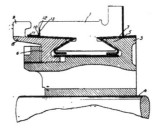

1. In a commutator cylinder, the combination with conducting and insulating segments, of a clamping ring therefor provided with a plurality of fan blades and an insulating member located intermediate said fan blades and said conducting segments, said fan blades overhanging said insulating member.

1,329,268. PIPE-CLIP AND METHOD OF FORMING SAME. LAWRENCE H. DICKELMANN and JOHN KUCHLER, Milwaukee, Wis. Filed Mar. 5, 1919. Serial No. 280,816. 3 Claims. (Cl. 113—116.)

1. A clip of the class described including a bowed body section, end sections extending from the ends of said body section and disposed in a common plane, and prongs extending from the outer portions of the end sections, the cross sectional areas of the prongs at their points of juncture with the end sections being less than other cross sectional areas of the prongs, the metal of said prongs being bent longitudinally to afford double thickness for the prongs.

1,329,269. LOCOMOTIVE TRANSMISSION SYSTEM. GEORGE M. EATON, Pittsburgh, Pa., assignor to Westinghouse Electric & Manufacturing Company, a Corporation of Pennsylvania. Filed Sept. 27, 1916. Serial No. 122,393. 18 Claims. (Cl. 105—49.)

1. In an electric vehicle, two axles having driving wheels mounted thereon, a jack shaft disposed between said axles and having a gear wheel mounted thereon, two yieldable driving connections meshing with said gear wheel, the driving connections being connected to said axles and the gear wheel on said jack shaft, and means for operating the gear wheel mounted on said jack shaft to operate the driving wheels.

1,329,270. SOLDERING AND MELTING APPARATUS. PERFECTO M. ELIAS and FELIX F. LLERA, Tucson, Ariz. Filed May 20, 1919. Serial No. 298,456. 1 Claim. (Cl. 158—27.5.)

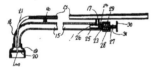

An apparatus for the purpose described, comprising a hydro-carbon container, means whereby the interior of said container may be connected with a source of fluid pressure supply, a blow-pipe connected with the interior of the container, a supplemental tube arranged in fixed relation to the blow-pipe and having a head and a foraminous diaphragm therein receiving the discharge end of the blow-pipe and also having a valve casing in its rear portion, a conduit section connecting intermediate points of the blow-pipe and valve casing, a valve arranged to be turned about its axis in said casing and having an angular bore and a flange, the latter to seat in the casing and also having a stem, a cap secured on the rear end of the valve casing and loosely receiving said stem, a spring surrounding the stem and interposed between the valve and said cap, a head sleeved on the stem in rear of said cap, and a pin through which the sleeve of the head is keyed to the stem; said pin being adapted to serve the additional function of a pointer.

1,329,271. METHOD OF MANUFACTURING PISTON-RINGS. STEPHEN D. HARTOG, St. Louis, Mo., assignor to S. D. Hartog Manufacturing Company, St. Louis, Mo., a Corporation. Filed Mar. 8, 1919. Serial No. 281,448. 3 Claims. (Cl. 29—150.1.)

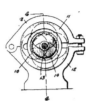

1. The herein described method of making piston packing rings which consists in forming a tubular metal body by casting, finishing the external peripheral surface of said body to bring the wall thereof to the requisite thickness, then cutting through the wall of said body to divide the same into a plurality of rings of uniform width, the direction of cut being outwardly from the interior of the body.

1,329,272. VANILLYL AMIN, VANILLYL ACYL AMID, AND PRODUCTION THEREOF. ELNATHAN K. NELSON, Takoma Park, Md. Filed Oct. 9, 1919. Serial No. 329,156. 2 Claims. (Cl. 23—24.) (Filed under the act of Mar. 3, 1883, 22 Stat. L., 625.)

1. The new derivative of vanillin described as vanillyl amin, which is a crystalline base melting at 131–133° C.

1,329,273. PROCESS FOR THE REMOVAL OF HYDRO-FLUORIC ACID FROM PHOSPHORIC ACID. WILLIAM H. ROSS, Washington, D. C. Filed July 26, 1919. Serial No. 313,645. 2 Claims. (Cl. 23—1.) (Filed under the act of Mar. 3, 1883, 22 Stat. L., 625.)

1. A process for the removal of hydrofluoric acid from concentrated phosphoric acid which consists in precipitating the fluorin by adding to the phosphoric acid calcium chlorid equivalent to the fluorin present.

1,329,274. DENTAL TOOL. PERRY R. SKINNER, Amsterdam, N. Y. Filed Feb. 6, 1919. Serial No. 275,306. 7 Claims. (Cl. 279—77.)

1. A device of the kind described comprising a handpiece having a tool socket, and means for locking and sustaining a tool consisting of a plurality of freely movable plates adapted to contact and be separated provided in their meeting edges with identations for receiving the shank of a tool.

1,329,275. MECHANICALLY - OPERATED HORN. GEORGE J. SEISS, Toledo, Ohio. Filed Mar. 11, 1918. Serial No. 221,602. 2 Claims. (Cl. 116—1.)

1. A horn body, a guide extending through the body transversely, said guide having a slot in one wall, an

actuator slidable in the guide and comprising a stamping of metal U-shaped in cross section having teeth on its

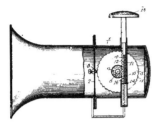

edges and a projection slidable in the slot of the guide, a diaphragm, and means for communicating the motion of the actuator to the diaphragm.

1,329,276. APPARATUS FOR ADDING TO THE OUT-PUT OF A MAIN POWER STATION, THE OUTPUT OF ONE OR MORE DISTANT SOURCES. SEVERN D. SPRONG, Brooklyn, N. Y. Filed Apr. 12, 1918. Serial No. 228,078. 11 Claims. (Cl. 290—4.)

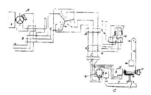

11. A main generating plant, an auxiliary generating plant distant from said main plant, a transmission line connecting said plants, means connected in and operating through said transmission line for causing said auxiliary plant to add its output through said transmission line to the output of said main plant, and a manually operable device at said main generating plant for controlling said operating means.

1,329,277. COMMUTATOR AND PROCESS OF PRODUC-ING THE SAME. CHARLES A VAN DUSEN, Toledo, Ohio, assignor, by mesne assignments, to The Toledo Standard Commutator Company, a Corporation of Ohio. Filed Feb. 12, 1919. Serial No. 276,461. 26 Claims. (Cl. 171—321.)

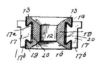

1. A cylindrical commutator comprising a group of seg-ments insulated from each other and provided with tange having projecting portions forming annular clamping surfaces with insulation overlying the same, and a one-piece holder comprising a cylindrical barrel provided at its ends with integral continuous inturned flanges perma-nently set in clamping position for holding the segments against axial and radial displacement, and solidly clamped against the insulated clamping surfaces thereof.

1,329,278. PROCESS AND APPARATUS FOR COOLING CAR-WHEELS. FREDERICK K. VIAL, Chicago, Ill., as-signor to Griffin Wheel Company, Chicago, Ill., a Cor-poration of Massachusetts. Filed Aug. 7, 1914. Serial No. 855,686. 18 Claims. (Cl. 263—44.)

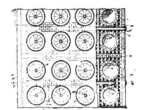

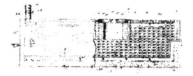

1. A structure formed with pits therein, said pits being surrounded by circulation spaces for a portion only of their depth.

1,329,279. AIR-REGULATING DEVICE FOR OIL-BURNERS. JOSEPH T. VOORHEIS, Philadelphia, Pa. Filed Oct. 9, 1919. Serial No. 329,573. 7 Claims. (Cl. 158—1.5.)

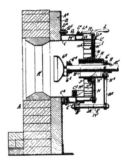

1. Air regulating means for oil burners consisting of a casing surrounding the burner, in combination with an end closing head for said casing, a series of air directing vanes secured to said head and extending from it so as to overlap the casing, and means for moving the head and attached vanes toward and away from the casing.

1,329,280. LIGHTING-FIXTURE. ALFRED A. WOHLAUER, New York, N. Y. Filed May 24, .1918. Serial No. 236,357. 3 Claims. (Cl. 240—115.)

1. A reflector and globe holder, comprising a ventilating cap, having a neck with threads formed thereon, a globe holder mounted in said neck, the lower portion of which is flanged outwardly forming a baffle plate of inverted

conoidal shape, terminating in a downwardly depending flange, a secondary enamel baffle plate which is fitted to

and coincides with the inverted conoidal flange, means mounted in said downwardly depending flange to hold a globe.

1,329,281. PUMP-BASE. FREDERICK W. ZINGSHEIM, Ferguson, Mo., assignor to Moon Brothers Manufacturing Company, St. Louis, Mo., a Corporation of Missouri. Filed May 26, 1919. Serial No. 299,767. 2 Claims. (Cl. 103—65.)

1. A pump base formed with flanged openings for the reception of the pump cylinders and having a reinforcing shoulder and a depending marginal flange, an intermediate plate formed with an opening for establishing communication between the openings in the top plate, a bottom plate having a reinforcing shoulder and an outwardly extending marginal flange, said top plate being folded under the flange or bottom plate.

1,329,282. CANDY-MAKING MACHINE. BENEDETTO E. ALLEGRETTI, Chicago, Ill. Filed June 20, 1919. Serial No. 305,665. 10 Claims. (Cl. 259—134.)

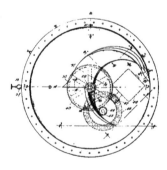

1. A candy machine comprising a saucer-shaped vessel; a stirring blade mounted for rotary movement in the vessel and adapted for automatic adjustment toward the vessel to take up wear between the bottom and side walls of the vessel and said stirring blade; and operative means connected with the blade.

1,329,283. THERMIONIC AMPLIFIER. HAROLD DE F. ARNOLD, Maplewood, N. J., assignor to Western Electric Company, Incorporated, New York, N. Y., a Corporation of New York. Continuation in part of application Serial No. 841,567, filed May 28, 1914, and application Serial No. 841,568, filed May 28, 1914, patented Mar. 2, 1915. This application filed July 30, 1918. Serial No. 247,422. 26 Claims. (Cl. 250—27.)

1. A thermionic discharge tube having a cathode, an anode and a controlling electrode, said anode being located in such close proximity to the cathode that the tube operates to produce energy amplification without substantial voltage amplification.

1,329,284. METHOD OF BLEACHING WOOD. ERNEST BATEMAN, Madison, Wis. Filed Sept. 8, 1919. Serial No. 322,580. 1 Claim. (Cl. 8—2.) (Filed under the act of Mar. 3, 1883, 22 Stat. L., 625.)

A method of bleaching wood which comprises applying thereto a solution of concentrated nitric acid combined with potassium chlorate.

1,329,285. TUBING CONSTRUCTION. ROY H. BROWNLEE, Pittsburgh, Pa. Filed Sept. 22, 1919. Serial No. 325,436. 10 Claims. (Cl. 137—75.)

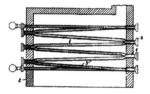

1. A tubing construction for a fire-heated furnace comprising a plurality of metallic heating tubes, adjacent tubes being set at an angle to each other; and metallic connecting tubes of greater diameter than the heating tubes arranged to project beyong the furnace wall and to the inner end of each of which the adjacent heating tubes are so welded that access may be had to the interior of both of said adjacent heating tubes from the exterior of the furnace through said connecting tube.

1,329,286. MUSIC-SHEET. ROMAINE CALLENDER, Philadelphia, Pa., assignor to The Aeolian Company, a Corporation of Connecticut. Filed Aug. 30, 1916. Serial No. 117,673. 5 Claims. (Cl. 84—162.)

1. A perforated music sheet for an automatic musical instrument having a straight line running lengthwise of the sheet provided with laterally extending distinguishing

points severally located at the beginnings of the component passages of the musical composition represented by the perforations in the music sheet, and interpretive directions located on the sheet in advance of the respective distinguishing points.

1,329,287. AUTOMATIC PARTY - LINE TELEPHONE SYSTEM. WILSON L. CAMPBELL, Chicago, Ill., assignor, by mesne assignments, to Automatic Electric Company, a Corporation of Illinois. Filed July 31, 1906, Serial No. 328,543. Renewed June 21, 1919. Serial No. 305,919. 22 Claims. (Cl. 179—17.)

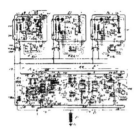

1. In a telephone exchange system, a telephone line, a pair of relays bridged across the said line, a private normal for said line, a bridge-cut-off relay, a private normal relay controlling the continuity of said private normal, and a circuit for energizing the last-mentioned two relays in series.

1,329,288. FEED - HOLDER. FRANCIS W. CARPENTER, Greenwich, Conn. Filed Oct. 11, 1919. Serial No. 330,069. 7 Claims. (Cl. 116—91.)

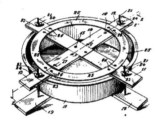

1. A feed holder for poultry comprising a receptacle, a two part frame member having one part extending above and the other below the receptacle, and clamping devices for securing the parts of the frame member to one another to fasten the receptacle in position between them.

1,329,289. DEMOUNTABLE RIM. DOUGLASS R. CARTER, Washington, D. C. Filed Apr. 10, 1919. Serial No. 289,095. 1 Claim. (Cl. 152—21.)

A demountable rim fastener consisting of a body portion or casing provided on its outer surface at one end

---

with a boss chamfered at an angle to form a cam surface flattened at its upper and lower extremities to form a bearing surface, a latching bolt inside the said casing, consisting of an enlarged end or head and a reduced part forming a stem which passes through the bottom of latch housing, a knurled knob or thumb-piece having its shank chamfered in a similar way as the boss on the latch housing and forming with the boss a male and female cam member, a helical spring around the stem of the latching bolt to retain the bolt the bolt in its locked position, a washer and cotterpin to hold the knob on the stem of the latching bolt and a flange on the bottom of the bolt housing to provide means for securing the said housing to the felly of the wheel.

1,329,290. ADJUSTABLE TRESTLE. JAMES M. CHAMPLIN, South Coventry, Conn. Filed May 7, 1919. Serial No. 295,352. 5 Claims. (Cl. 20—83.)

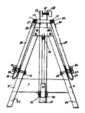

1. A trestle comprising a pair of legs, yokes connected with the upper ends of the legs, a vertical guideway mounted between said legs and supported thereby, a vertical movable support, means for adjustably connecting the said support with the guideway, a cross bar connected with the upper end of said support, stays pivotally connected with the ends of said cross bar, and means for adjustably connecting the lower ends of the said stays with said legs.

1,329,291. GAME OF SKILL. OTTO CHAPMAN, Mordialloc, Victoria, Australia. Filed Nov. 27, 1918. Serial No. 264,338. 2 Claims. (Cl. 46—59.)

1. In a game of skill of the kind set forth two rotatable winding drums arranged at some distance apart from each other, a single cord line one end of which is attached to one of said drums and the other end of which is attached to the other drum, and a runner attached to said cord.

1,329,292. REINFORCED HOLLOW BOARD. LOUIS CHRISTIN, Geneva, Switzerland. Filed May 3, 1918. Serial No. 232,897. 1 Claim. (Cl. 72—68.)

A section of molded rectangular plank comprising spaced parts connected at one side by a longitudinal rib and also connected by transverse ribs running at an angle to the longitudinal rib whereby there is formed an opening in the block bounded by the said ribs and extending from the said longitudinal rib to the opposite side of the plank, and a plurality of spaced reinforcing tubes extending longitudinally of the plank and connected to one another by wires running transversely through the members of the plank so that when in position, the reinforcing member is folded back upon itself like a cover on a book.

1,329,293. FURNACE-SLAGGING APPARATUS. EARL W. CLARK, Sharon, Pa. Filed Nov. 23, 1918. Serial No. 263,805. 19 Claims. (Cl. 214—32.)

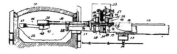

1. In an apparatus for slagging furnaces, supporting mechanism by which the apparatus may be moved about exteriorly of a furnace, conveying means for slagging material carried by said mechanism and adapted to be extended from the exterior to the interior of a furnace and including a distributing part adapted to be moved vertically with respect to a second part which supports it and which is adapted to be extended into the furnace.

1,329,294. SKIVING-MACHINE. EUGENE F. DAVENPORT, Melrose, Mass., assignor to United Shoe Machinery Corporation, Paterson, N. J., a Corporation of New Jersey. Filed Feb. 3, 1919. Serial No. 274,606. 9 Claims. (Cl. 69—9.5.)

1. A skiving machine comprising a tubular knife, a presser foot, a coöperating feed roll, and a yielding member positioned in advance of the presser foot and adapted to initiate the engagement of the work by the feed roll.

1,329,295. ROTARY CASTING. DIMITRI SENSAUD DE LAVAUD, New York, N. Y. Filed Mar. 3, 1919. Serial No. 280,452. 27 Claims. (Cl. 22—209.)

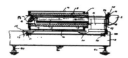

1. The process of casting an annular metallic article in a rotary mold on a substantially horizontal axis which consists in laying the metal in the mold in successively deposited spirally related subdivisions while guiding the flow of the metal adjacent to the mold to cause the metal to flow in a limited sheet sidewisely of the mold axis.

8. In a rotary casting machine, the combination of a rotary mold, a metal distributer adapted to project inside the mold and constructed and arranged for continuously discharging molten metal inside the mold, operating means for moving the distributer and mold relatively lengthwise to the mold, movable feeding means for delivering molten metal to the distributer adapted to be moved to control the rate of delivery of molten metal to the distributer, and

means controlled by the relative movement of either distributer or mold and operatively connected to the feeding means for moving the latter constantly to supply molten metal from the feeding means to the distributer in definite relation to the rate of discharge of molten metal by the distributer into the mold.

1,329,296. ROTARY CASTING. DIMITRI SENSAUD DE LAVAUD, New York, N. Y. Filed Apr. 21, 1919. Serial No. 291,662. 3 Claims. (Cl. 22—65.)

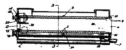

1. The method of cooling a metal mold in a rotary casting machine, which consists in providing a mold, supporting the mold only at points below its axis, rotating the mold as thus supported on a substantially horizontal axis, and providing a cooling fluid and confining and directing the fluid relative to a circumferential subdivision of the mold at any instant at a predetermined point relative to the axis of the mold during rotation of the mold, so that the fluid acts on successive circumferential subdivisions of the mold while other circumferential subdivisions of the mold are exposed to the atmosphere.

1,329,297. CHANGE-SPEED POWER-TRANSMITTING MECHANISM. TYRRELL H. DUNCOMBE, Romeo, Mich. Filed Oct. 9, 1918. Serial No. 257,441. 7 Claims. (Cl. 74—34.)

1. A change-speed power transmitting mechanism including a driving member, a driven member, means for transmitting motion at high speed from said driving to said driven member, means for transmitting motion from said driving to said driven member at low speeds, and a one way driving connection for said high speed connecting means, whereby the driven member is free to turn at a greater speed than the driving member when the high speed connection is effective and said driving and driven members are directly connected through said low speed connecting means when said low speed connecting means is effective.

1,329,298. LACING-MACHINE. HERBERT E. ENSLIN, Malden, Mass., assignor to United Shoe Machinery Corporation, Paterson, N. J., a Corporation of New Jersey. Filed Mar. 19, 1918. Serial No. 223,456. 8 Claims. (Cl. 112—5.)

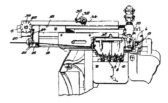

1. A machine for lacing shoe uppers, having, in combination, a reciprocating cord carrying needle, and mecha-

nism for applying tension to the cord during alternate reciprocations and relieving the tension during intermediate reciprocations of the needle.

1,329,299. POWER-WINDMILL. GEORGE D. FOSTER, North Yakima, Wash., assignor to Union Land & Power Company, North Yakima, Wash., a Corporation of Washington. Filed Aug. 17, 1916. Serial No. 115,434. 9 Claims. (Cl. 170—67.)

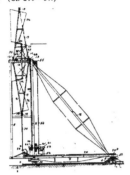

1. In a power windmill, the combination with a suitable frame, of a wheel mounted therein, a plurality of vanes carried thereby, and automatic reefing means for turning the vanes on their axes in unison and having yielding connections therewith to permit independent movement of the vanes with respect to one another.

1,329,300. BURNING FUEL. HENRY HICKS HURT, Yonkers, N. Y., assignor to Robeson Process Company, New York, N. Y., a Corporation of New Jersey. Filed May 11, 1918. Serial No. 233,925. 2 Claims. (Cl. 44—1.)

1. The process of firing fine fuel which comprises wetting down said fine fuel with a concentrated aqueous solution of organic matters and charging the wetted down material on a fire bed.

1,329,301. HAIR-DRYING COMB. ULRICH KORNSTEIN, New York, N. Y. Filed Mar. 20, 1919. Serial No. 283,900. 2 Claims. (Cl. 34—26.)

1. In a hair-drying comb, the combination with a comb having a hollow back, of a handle having a bore in which a portion of said hollow back is seated, a reinforcing bar in the bore of said handle, said bar projecting into said back a substantial distance beyond said handle, and fastening means passing through said handle, back and reinforcing bar.

1,329,302. TUBE-FRAME FOR LOOMS. CHARLES LEA, Boston, Mass., assignor to American Warp Drawing Machine Company, Boston, Mass., a Corporation of Maine. Filed Dec. 9, 1913, Serial No. 805,634. Renewed Mar. 11, 1918. Serial No. 221,864. 18 Claims. (Cl. 139—66.)

1. An Axminster tube-frame for the control of yarn for tuft weaving, embracing in combination a rigid longitudinal carrier-structure adapted to form a support for a

270 O. G.—39

---

yarn-supplying spool, and a series of tuft-tube members constructed to be assembled side by side on said carrier-structure in position to receive their appropriate yarn-ends from the spool, said tube members being structurally

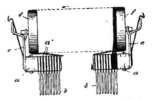

separate, and being mechanically engaged with the carrier-structure in operative relationship by a quick-detachable engagement with the carrier-structure whereby each tube member is properly positioned in relation to the yarn-spool while permitting rapid and easy replacement, substantially as described.

1,329,303. TUBE-FRAME. CHARLES LEA, Boston, Mass., assignor to American Warp Drawing Machine Company, Boston, Mass., a Corporation of Maine. Filed Dec. 9, 1913, Serial No. 805,633. Renewed Mar. 11, 1918. Serial No. 221,865. 14 Claims. (Cl. 139—66.)

1. An Axminster tube frame for the control of tuft yarns in weaving, embracing in its construction a rigid longitudinal carrier member adapted to form a support for the yarn-supplying spool, a cooperating tube-clamping member detachably secured to said carrier member in position to firmly clamp interposed portions of the tube-members against said carrier member, and a series of tube-members disposed in parallel arrangement transversely of said carrier member, said tube-members being formed at their rear or intake ends to be firmly but detachably engaged with said carrier member by said clamping member, substantially as described.

1,329,304. SINGLE RAILROAD-RAIL. ROYAL A. McCLURE and WILLIAM W. BOULTON, Seattle, Wash., assignors to Universal Elevated Railway Co., Seattle, Wash. Filed June 19, 1918. Serial No. 241,074. 3 Claims. (Cl. 104—118.)

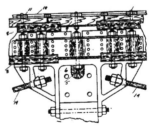

1. A railroad rail in combination with a structural base, a super-structural body mounted upon said base and

adapted to be rigidly attached thereto, a tread bar, a flexible member interposed between said tread bar and said super-structural body, and means attachable to said super-structural body having lateral projections on its outer ends for preventing displacement of said flexible member.

1,329,305. RAILROAD-RAIL. ROYAL A. McCLURE and WILLIAM W. BOULTON, Seattle, Wash., assignors to Universal Elevated Railway Co., Seattle, Wash. Filed June 19, 1918. Serial No. 241,075. 3 Claims. (Cl. 104—118.)

1. A railroad rail for single rail trucks comprising a steel tread, a concrete base adapted to form the body portion of said rail, flexible means interposed between said tread and said concrete base to impart resiliency to said rail.

1,329,306. RAILROAD-RAIL COUPLING. ROYAL A. McCLURE and WILLIAM W. BOULTON, Seattle, Wash., assignors to Universal Elevated Railway Co., Seattle, Wash. Filed June 19, 1918. Serial No. 241,077. 3 Claims. (Cl. 104—130.)

1. A railroad rail coupling in combination with a stationary and a movable rail, a longitudinally movable member centrally disposed within the end portion of one of said rails, centrally recessed means provided in the end portion of the other of said rails, whereby said member can be caused to engage said recessed means when said rails are brought into alinement.

1,329,307. TRAILER-WAGON. EMIL F. NORELIUS, Peoria, Ill., assignor to The Holt Manufacturing Company, Stockton, Calif., a Corporation of California. Filed Nov. 13, 1917. Serial No. 201,800. 10 Claims. (Cl. 21—150.)

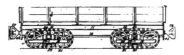

1. A running gear for trailer wagons embodying fixed front and rear axles, truck units pivotally mounted on vertical axes at the ends of the axles to turn laterally for steering, a connection between the front and rear truck units to cause them to angle in opposite directions when traveling a curved course, a draw bar pivotally mounted at the rear end of the wagon for coupling a similar vehicle in train therewith, and detachable means for rigidly connecting said draw bar with the fixed axle and detachable means for connecting said draw bar with the truck units for turning on its pivotal center in unison with said units and controlling the position of the latter.
3. In a vehicle, front and rear axle trees, a wagon bed carried thereby and connected to one of said axle trees centrally thereof on a fore and aft extending pivot and connected to the other axle tree at separated points thereon, whereby a three-point support is formed for the bed, and a running gear embodying members connected with the first mentioned axle tree at separated points and with the last-mentioned axle tree by a fore and aft extending pivot, whereby the running gear and body are pivotally connected with the axle trees at opposite ends of the vehicle.

1,329,308. CARBURETER. AUGUSTIN M. PRENTISS, Fort Caswell, N. C., assignor of one-half to Douglass E. Bulloch, Washington, D. C. Filed Feb. 19, 1916. Serial No. 79,379. 33 Claims. (Cl. 261—52.)

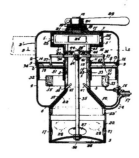

1. In a carbureter, a mixing chamber, a liquid fuel reservoir, means for maintaining liquid fuel therein at a substantially constant predetermined level, means for maintaining a positive pressure always greater than atmospheric upon said liquid fuel and means for varying the pressure upon said liquid fuel inversely as the pressure in the mixing chamber.

1,329,309. CARBURETER. AUGUSTIN M. PRENTISS, Rock Island, Ill., assignor of one-half to Douglass E. Bulloch, Washington, D. C. Filed Mar. 6, 1917. Serial No. 152,708. 48 Claims. (Cl. 261—16.)

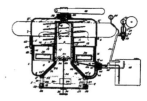

1. In a carbureter, a mixing chamber, an atomizing nozzle, an air supply and a liquid fuel supply thereto, and pressure means for regulating the liquid fuel supply so as to make said liquid fuel supply always bear a constant ratio to said air supply.

1,329,310. INFLATED GOLF-BALL AND PROCESS OF MAKING. FRED THOMAS ROBERTS, Cleveland, Ohio, assignor to The Aranar Company, Cleveland, Ohio, a Corporation of Ohio. Filed Aug. 16, 1917. Serial No. 186,476. 12 Claims. (Cl. 154—17.)
1. A golf ball comprising an inner core formed of joined parts containing highly compressed air and

vulcanized, a winding surrounding such core consisting of a large number of turns of an elastic band under tension, said core having a wall of sufficient thickness

relative to the volume of the cavity to retain the highly compressed fluid after the core has been vulcanized and before the winding is applied, and a casing fitting over said winding and forming the exterior of the ball.

1,329,311. METHOD OF MAKING BALLS. FRED THOMAS ROBERTS, Cleveland Heights, Ohio, assignor to The Aranar Company, Cleveland, Ohio, a Corporation of Ohio. Filed Jan. 7, 1918. Serial No. 210,655. 17 Claims. (Cl. 154—17.)

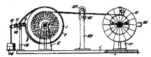

1. The process of making a golf ball, which consists in winding a resilient core with stretched rubber strands, previously treated with alternate mechanical stretchings and subsequent relaxations until the final tension exceeds the original elastic limit and then inclosing the same within a suitable cover.

1,329,312. MOLD FOR MAKING RUBBER ARTICLES. FRED THOMAS ROBERTS, Cleveland, Ohio. Filed June 24, 1918. Serial No. 241,469. 4 Claims. (Cl. 18—47.)

1. As a new article of manufacture, a mold for making rubber articles, said mold having at least a portion forming the molding surface made of an alloy composed of a large per cent. of aluminum and a comparatively small per cent. of magnesium.

1,329,313. BUFFER FOR DOORS. BENJAMIN H. SEABURY and JAMES C. OLLARD, Tacoma, Wash. Filed Mar. 6, 1918. Serial No. 220,855. 3 Claims. (Cl. 16—77.)

2. A buffer for cushioning the closing of automobile doors and for holding a door against its latch, said buffer including a casing having an opening and provided thereat with an inwardly extending guiding flange having its inner edge arranged to form a fulcrum, a hollow cap tapered outwardly and operating in the opening of the said casing and fulcrumed therein by the inner edge of the said flange to permit a universal lateral movement or play in addition to the inward and outward movement of the said member, said flange and tapered member co-acting to permit the lateral universal movement or play to increase with the inward movement of the said member, and a spring for urging the member outwardly.

1,329,314. SELF-PROPELLED VEHICLE. WILLIAM TURNBULL, Stockton, Calif., assignor to The Holt Manufacturing Company, Stockton, Calif., a Corporation of California. Filed Dec. 11, 1916. Serial No. 136,210. 8 Claims. (Cl. 180—9.)

1. In a self-propelled vehicle, the combination of an internal combustion engine, driving gears for the vehicle, a casing for said driving gears, means for conducting the exhaust gases from the engine to the gear casing whereby to expel dust and dirt therefrom, and means for preventing the gases from directly impinging upon said gears.

1,329,315. ELECTROLYTIC APPARATUS. VICTOR M. WEAVER, Harrisburg, Pa., assignor to Weaver Company, a Corporation of Wisconsin. Original application filed Aug. 22, 1914, Serial No. 858,001. Divided and application filed Jan. 11, 1915, Serial No. 286. Divided and this application filed July 9, 1915. Serial No. 38,858. 9 Claims. (Cl. 204—3.)

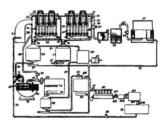

7. Apparatus for treating chlorid which comprises a closed chamber adapted to contain an electrolyte having a conducting interior bottom as one electrode and a conducting block depending from a sealed cover as the opposite electrode, and means for mechanically feeding non-gaseous material into said electrolyte at a definite and controllable rate of speed.

1,329,316. SELF-LAYING-TRACK VEHICLE. ELMER E. WICKERSHAM, Stockton, Calif., assignor to The Holt Manufacturing Company, Stockton, Calif., a Corporation of California. Filed May 26, 1917. Serial No. 171,173. 10 Claims. (Cl. 21—150.)

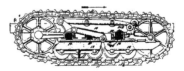

6. In a self-laying track vehicle, a main frame, a truck at each side thereof, an equalizer bar between the front

ends of opposite trucks to support the front of the main frame, and connections between the equalizer bar and the trucks to permit the latter to move bodily vertically independently of the equalizer bar.

1,329,317. SUBAQUEOUS TUNNEL. JOSEPH S. WILLIAMS, Riverton, N. J. Filed Dec. 8, 1906. Serial No. 346,892. 7 Claims. (Cl. 61—42.)

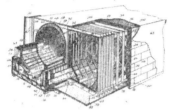

1. A tunnel construction comprising sections of trussed metal bridge framing, capable of independent construction and movement, the said sections being united at their ends to transmit vertical and longitudinal strains through a plurality of sections, and cementitious material embedding the framing when in place.

1,329,318. DRAFT-GEAR YOKE. HARRY T. ANDERSON, Crafton, Pa., assignor to Harry Vissering & Company, Chicago, Ill., a Corporation of Illinois. Filed Feb. 26, 1916, Serial No. 80,615. Renewed Apr. 24, 1919. Serial No. 292,422. 10 Claims. (Cl. 213—42.)

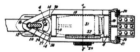

1. A draft gear yoke comprising an upper and a lower pair of draft members, the members of each of said pairs being joined at their rear ends and having the forward ends of both pairs lying on opposite sides of the coupler shank and united and formed for connection to said shank, and a column member uniting the rear ends of said pairs of draft members and arranged to lie behind the rear follower plate.

1,329,319. DRIVING MECHANISM FOR MOTOR-CARS. ARTHUR F. BAKER, Sedro Woolley, Wash., assignor to The Perfecto Gear Differential Co., Seattle, Wash., a Corporation. Filed Jan. 28, 1918. Serial No. 214,230. 8 Claims. (Cl. 74—99.)

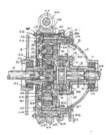

1. In a power transmission device in combination, two axles, a differential mechanism through which said axles

are driven, a planetary gear system to which the power is applied, and means for driving the differential through the intermediate gears of the planetary gear system.

1,329,320. SPARK-PLUG. HENRY WILSON CARPENTER, Key West, Fla., assignor, by direct and mesne assignments, to Philip Wilson. Filed May 17, 1918. Serial No. 285,079. 4 Claims. (Cl. 123—169.)

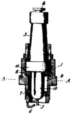

1. In a spark plug of the class described, the combination with a shell and a core therein, of a washer loosely mounted within the chamber surrounding the core, said washer narrowly restricting the entrance into the chamber and having sufficient of its surface exposed to the pressures in the combustion chamber of the engine to cause it to be freely moved in the plug chamber under the actuation of pressure of explosion, said washer being free to move under the action of equalization of pressure in the plug chamber and the combustion chamber following explosion.

1,329,321. VALVE OF INTERNAL-COMBUSTION ENGINES. ARTHUR THOMAS ELLIS, London, England, assignor of one-half to Harry Arthur Hands, London, England. Filed Aug. 8, 1919. Serial No. 316,251. 2 Claims. (Cl. 251—144.)

1. In combination with a valve stem having a threaded portion and an unthreaded, diametrically reduced portion between the threaded portion and the inner end of the stem, a spring-bearing collar screwed on said threaded portion and having a conical recess opposite said reduced portion of the stem, and a locking member having a conical portion to enter said conical recess, an opening to receive said reduced portion and also a slot leading from one side of said member to said opening to permit assembling and disassembling of said stem, collar and locking member.

1,329,322. MAKING POWDERED METALS AND REDUCED METALLIC COMPOUNDS. CARLETON ELLIS, Montclair, N. J. Filed Aug. 1, 1919. Serial No. 314,738. 21 Claims. (Cl. 23—28.)

2. The process of making a catalyzer which comprises heating a reducible nickel material in paraffin wax to the

cracking temperature of the latter whereby finely divided nickel material is obtained.

21. As a catalytic material, a reduced metal having an atomic weight between approximately 58.7 and 63.6, carried in a vehicle of cracked hydrocarbon which is essentially non-volatile at 300° C.

1,329,323. PROCESS OF MAKING CATALYTIC MATERIAL. CARLETON ELLIS, Montclair, N. J. Filed Jan. 31, 1919. Serial No. 274,357. 8 Claims. (Cl. 23—28.)

6. The process of making a catalyzer suitable for hardening oils which consists in heating catalytic raw material containing nickel united with an acid of the nitrogen oxid group in a strong reducing atmosphere and in introducing a quantity of a diluting agent during the initial stages of the heating in order to avoid sintering of the nickel compound.

1,329,324. GAS-MIXER. WILLIAM S. GRANGER, Duluth, Minn. Filed July 13, 1918. Serial No. 244,687. 1 Claim. (Cl. 48—180.)

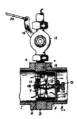

A gas mixer for a separable gas conduit for engines comprising a single-piece principal body member held intermediate of the separable portions of the conduit and forming a coöperative part thereof and having a tangentially disposed port therein, communicating with the outside atmosphere, a central cylindrical screw-threaded chamber within the principal body portion communicating with the port and having a plurality of holes in one end thereof, and a second cylindrical chamber screw-threaded externally and engageable within the chamber in the principal body portion but not closing the port therein, said second chamber having one head formed integral therewith and having a plurality of holes therein and a mixing wheel supported by and intermediate the heads.

1,329,325. PRINTING-MACHINE. GEORGE W. MASCORD, Barnes, London, England. Filed Apr. 4, 1918. Serial No. 226,760. 6 Claims. (Cl. 101—216.)

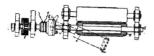

3. In printing machines, an impression cylinder, a printing cylinder, a spindle upon which said printing cylinder is mounted, a swiveling bearing upon which the said spindle is carried at one end, a magnetic clutch adjacent the said swiveling bearing, means adjacent the other end of the spindle for permitting the movement of the spindle away from the said impression cylinder and gear for causing the rotation of the said spindle, substantially as described.

1,329,326. DOOR-HANGER. LEVI L. PARSONS, New York, N. Y., assignor to Elevator Supply & Repair Company, a Corporation of Illinois. Filed Nov. 22, 1916. Serial No. 132,726. 6 Claims. (Cl. 16—90.)

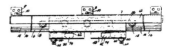

6. In apparatus of the class described, a roller carriage comprising a channel iron having spaced roller receiving openings stamped from the bottom of the channel, the stamped bottom material being bent outward to the two sides to form integral roller supporting ears upon the sides of said channel, rollers supported by said carriage with their axes substantially in the plane of the bottom of said channel, and sound deadening washers located between said rollers and the out-turned ears.

1,329,327. DOOR-HANGER. LEVI L. PARSONS, New York, N. Y., assignor to Elevator Supplies Company, Inc., a Corporation of Illinois. Filed Apr. 10, 1919. Serial No. 289,054. 3 Claims. (Cl. 16—90.)

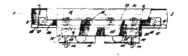

1. A door hanger comprising, in combination, a supporting frame of sheet metal having a track formed integral therewith by bending the metal in the form of an inverted U, rollers engaging the upper surface of said track, a hanger frame having a track member to ride upon said rollers, and guiding rollers carried by said hanger frame fitted into and guided by the under portions of said U-shaped track.

1,329,328. FEELER WITH CONCAVE TEETH. EDWARD S. STIMPSON, Hopedale, Mass., assignor to Draper Corporation, Hopedale, Mass., a Corporation of Maine. Filed July 18, 1918. Serial No. 245,563. 2 Claims. (Cl. 139—85.)

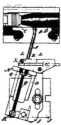

2. A laterally slipping feeler arm having a plurality of blunt rounded teeth each with a concave face.

1,329,329. UNION-SUIT. ANSELM STRAUB, Jr., Magnolia, N. J., assignor of one-half to William F. Tosney, Philadelphia, Pa. Filed May 10, 1919. Serial No. 296,116. 3 Claims. (Cl. 2—144.)

3. A union suit embodying two pieces of tubular web, one of said pieces of web constituting the leg member of

the garment and transversely centrally slit to **provide a** continuous edge which is united to the continuous edge at the bottom of the other of said pieces of web which constitutes the body member of the garment, the continuous

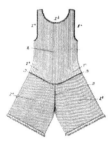

edge provided by the slit in said first named piece of web being greater in length than the continuous edge at the bottom of said last named piece of web, whereby said last named piece of web is stretched at its bottom portion when said continuous edges are united.

1,329,330. ELECTRIC FITTING. GEORGE B. THOMAS, Bridgeport, Conn., assignor to The Bryant Electric Company, Bridgeport, Conn., a Corporation of Connecticut. Filed Apr. 30, 1919. Serial No. 293,685. 9 Claims. (Cl. 240—78.)

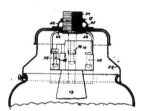

1. The combination with a socket carrier, of a lamp socket having longitudinally stepped seats, and means passing through the socket from its lamp-receiving end for securing said carrier and socket together on any of said seats, substantially as described.

1,329,331. CUSHION - TIRE. CYRUS SYLVESTOR WERT, Kendallville, Ind. Filed Apr. 25, 1918. Serial No. 230,726. 5 Claims. (Cl. 152—8.)

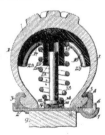

2. A tire, comprising a casing, a series of resilient sections extending in circumferential series around the casing and provided each with an integral inwardly projecting

tubular boss, sheathing means on the inside and outside of said boss, a spring supporting each section independently and fitting at the outer end around said boss, a ring, a spindle projecting from the ring through each spring and into the boss to form a guide, including a threaded portion secured in the ring; and locking means thereon for said spindle providing a base for said spring.

1,329,332. BOX. CHARLES H. BOMBARDIE, South Bend, Ind., assignor to Wirebounds Patents Company, Kittery, Me., a Corporation of Maine. Filed Feb. 20, 1917. Serial No. 149,924. 25 Claims. (Cl. 217—12.)

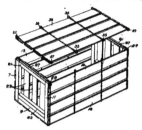

1. A box comprising relatively foldable side and bottom sections having coöperating reinforcing cleats, end sections having cleats corresponding to the fourth side of the box and constructed to interlock with the cleats of the side sections in a manner to prevent inward and outward displacement of said end sections, and readily manipulatable separable fastening means carried by said end sections and the side sections to hold the parts in open top box form.

1,329,333. BOX. CHARLES H. BOMBARDIE, South Bend, Ind., assignor to Wirebounds Patents Company, Kittery, Me., a Corporation of Maine. Filed Feb. 20, 1917. Serial No. 149,925. 8 Claims. (Cl. 217—12.)

1. A wirebound box comprising cleats outlining the ends of the box; side material for three sides of the box; the cleats corresponding to the fourth side being unattached to side material; a separate lid; and wire bindings extending around the cleats at the ends of the box; the portions of said bindings corresponding to the fourth side being separable and adapted for joinder with the remainder of said bindings either to secure the parts in open-top box form or to secure the lid.

1,329,334. BUMPER FOR AUTOMOBILES. CHARLES BOWEN, Fort Wayne, Ind., assignor of one-third to Fred Gaskins and one-third to Arthur G. Niebergall, Fort Wayne, Ind. Filed Nov. 8, 1919. Serial No. 336,614. 4 Claims. (Cl. 293—55.)

3. In a bumper for automobiles having a frame the sides of which recede from its end, a bumper proper com-

prised of a spring bar shaped with inwardly extending extremities ; a supporting bracket for each extremity of the bumper, having an outwardly extending arm secured

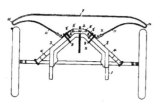

thereto, and a forwardly extending base adapted to fit against the corresponding receding side of the frame ; and a securing member for the base of each bracket.

1,329,335. METHOD OF AND APPARATUS FOR CONCENTRATING ORES. JOHN M. CALLOW, Salt Lake City, Utah, assignor, by mesne assignments, to Pneumatic Process Flotation Company, New York, N. Y., a Corporation of Delaware. Filed Apr. 1, 1914. Serial No. 828,805. 19 Claims. (Cl. 88—85.)

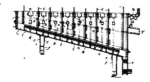

10. The herein described method for separating the metalliferous from the non-metalliferous ingredients of an ore mass, consisting in forming a pulp of said ore ingredients and water, causing the pulp to flow through a receptacle and form therein a pulp body of gradually increasing depth, delivering to the said pulp body at different horizontal planes bodies of air of different pressures, forming therewith bubbles, causing the bubbles to rise for varying distances through the pulp, adhere to and elevate the metalliferous particles, causing the metal-laden bubbles to flow laterally at approximately the top of the pulp, and collecting them and the concentrates thereby carried.

1,329,336. FLYING-BOAT HULL. GLENN H. CURTISS, Buffalo, N. Y., assignor to Curtiss Aeroplane and Motor Corporation, a Corporation of New York. Filed Oct. 13, 1916. Serial No. 125,425. 18 Claims. (Cl. 244—2.)

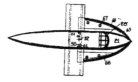

1. In a hull for flying boats, a hydroplaning bottom commencing at or near the bow end of the hull and terminating aft at a point distantly removed from the stern, a rearwardly facing step provided at the aft terminus of said bottom, and fins located at opposite sides of said bottom and directly opposite the resultant center of hydroplane lift to laterally augment the hydroplaning area thereof, a portion of each fin being detachable.

1,329,337. EXTENSION ANGLE-SQUARE. WILLIAM H. EGGLESTON, Grandville, Mich., assignor of one-half to David Ritzema, Grand Rapids, Mich. Filed Jan. 13, 1919. Serial No. 270,939. 4 Claims. (Cl. 33—98.)

1. In combination, an extension member comprising parts adjustable lengthwise of each other, means to secure the parts in fixed relation to each other in any position to which they may be adjusted, a member connected to each end of the extension member and having a squared opening therethrough, a bar of flat metal located under the end of each of said last mentioned members, a bolt extending through the bar and the said opening in each of said members, said bar being pivotally mounted on the bolt, and said bolt having a squared portion entering the said squared opening, and a binding nut threaded on to the bolt and adapted to bear against the upper side of each of the members at the ends of the extension member.

1,329,338. TOY. KATHERINE B. FULD, Baltimore, Md. Filed Aug. 21, 1919. Serial No. 318,855. 3 Claims. (Cl. 46—45.)

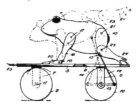

1. In a toy, in combination, a wheel supported platform, a body portion of a figure, a pair of foot members secured to said platform and having slots therein, a pair of fore leg members pivoted to the foot members in said slots and fast on the body portion, a pair of rear leg members pivoted to the body portion and free of said platform, said rear legs comprising an upper member on the body portion and a lower member pivoted to the upper member.

1,329,339. BUMPER. JOHN R. GAMMETER, Akron, Ohio, assignor to The B. F. Goodrich Company, New York, N. Y., a Corporation of New York. Filed Nov. 2, 1918. Serial No. 260,890. 4 Claims. (Cl. 4—18.)

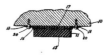

1. A bumper for closet seats and the like comprising a rubber cushion formed with a relatively wide and shallow longitudinal through aperture adjacent to and parallel with the base surface thereof, and a transversely-flat attaching plate having apertured portions at both ends and an offset middle portion occupying the aperture in said cushion.

1,329,340. REFRIGERATOR. HERBERT H. HILLMAN, Grand Haven, Mich., assignor to Challenge Refrigerator Company, Grand Haven, Mich., a Corporation of Michigan. Filed Aug. 19, 1918. Serial No. 250,448. 3 Claims. (Cl. 20—16.)

1. In a refrigerator wall; a body member having an inward projection which has an edge portion and an oppositely disposed second edge portion inclined inwardly and toward the first-mentioned edge portion to form an overhang; an inner member having a flange and a second flange inclined inwardly and toward the first-mentioned flange to form a hooked portion; the hooked portion being adapted to engage beneath the overhang and having a rocking movement on the overhang in the assembling of the two said members, and the inner member being adapted to be swung to bring the first-mentioned flange into tight engagement with the first-mentioned edge portion in the assembled position of the two members.

1,329,341. TENSION DEVICE FOR SPOOLING-MACHINES. FREDERICK JARRY, New Bedford, Mass. Filed Aug. 14, 1919. Serial No. 317,511. 6 Claims. (Cl. 242—155.)

1. In a tension device for spooling machines, a journal having a cut-out therein, an axle in the journal communicating with the cut-out, a braking shoe slidable in the cut-out and having a groove on its inner end receiving the axle and a groove on its outer end at right angles to the first named groove, an arm on the journal, a counterweighted lever pivoted to the arm and engaged in said groove of the outer end of the shoe, a thread engaging roller on the axle, and thread guiding members on opposite sides of the roller and located therebelow.

1,329,342. AEROPLANE CONSTRUCTION. HENRY KLECKLER, Buffalo, N. Y., assignor to Curtiss Aeroplane and Motor Corporation, a Corporation of New York. Filed Nov. 16, 1917. Serial No. 202,401. 14 Claims. (Cl. 244—14.)

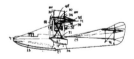

3. In an aircraft, supporting surfaces, a motor unit mounted intermediate the supporting surfaces, engine bed beams for supporting the motor unit, a tank mounted to the rear of the motor, the shape of the tank being such

that it provides in effect a substantially streamline prolongation of the motor, means for supporting the tank in its elevated position behind the motor, and a connection between the tank and motor.

1,329,343. COMBINED GASKET AND OIL-GASIFIER. ERNEST RABA, Valley, Okla. Filed July 11, 1919. Serial No. 310,198. 3 Claims. (Cl. 123—33.)

1. In an explosion engine a cylinder body and a removable head adapted to form a combustion chamber therefor, the cylinder body having an intake port formed therein opening into the combustion chamber, means for supplying oil and air to the intake port, and a gasifying device comprising a plate of metal arranged to serve as a gasket between the cylinder body and the removable head having the portion thereof over the intake port dished and perforated to permit the oil and air to pass through it into the combustion chamber.

1,329,344. POULTRY-CRATE. DIEDRICH H. SPRECKELS, Dexter, Minn. Filed Mar. 27, 1918. Serial No. 225,059. 1 Claim. (Cl. 217—64.)

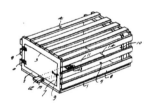

A crate including a body having end openings and doors for closing the same, a partition member fitting snugly within said body and slidable longitudinally thereof, and an adjusting member secured at one end to the partition member and slidable through one end of said body, said adjusting member comprising two sections hingedly secured together at their adjacent ends and each approximately one-half as long as the body whereby the partition member may be moved in either direction for substantially the full interior length of the body and, by withdrawing the adjusting member for one-half of its length and turning the outer portion thereof upwardly against the adjacent end of the body, the partition member may be secured in adjustment at the central portion of the body so as to divide the same into two separate compartments.

1,329,345. ELECTRIC PRIMER. WILLIAM M. UPP, Kansas City, Mo., assignor of one-half to Ernest Rumsey, Kansas City, Mo. Filed Jan. 31, 1919. Serial No. 274,290. 3 Claims. (Cl. 123—180.)

1. A priming device for internal combustion engines, comprising a fuel supply chamber having an ingress port and an egress port, a valve stem within said chamber

having a central inlet orifice extending through one end, valves on the stem to alternately open and close the re-

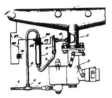

spective ports, a heater casing in communication with said chamber, and means for connecting the chamber to the manifold of an engine.

1,329,846. CARTRIDGE - BELT. EDWIN B. STIMPSON, Brooklyn, N. Y. Filed May 24, 1918. Serial No. 236,267. 2 Claims. (Cl. 89—35.)

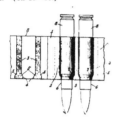

1. A cartridge belt comprising: layers of longitudinally reinforced paper placed in face to face relation, and spacing members inserted between said layers at intervals to form cartridge holding loops, said layers being attached to opposite sides of said spacing members.

1,329,347. [WITHDRAWN.]

1,329,348. REFRIGERATING APPARATUS. EDMUND J. COPELAND, Detroit, Mich., assignor to Kelvinator Corporation. Wilmington, Del., a Corporation of Delaware. Filed Jan. 31, 1918. Serial No. 214,605. 16 Claims. (Cl. 230—27.)

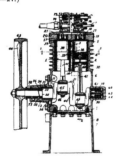

1. A compressor for refrigerating apparatus compris-

ing relatively movable elements one of which is composed of a non-ferrous, porous metal having a solid lubricant disseminated therein.

1,329,349 [WITHDRAWN.]

1,329,350. MEANS AND METHOD OF REGULATING AUTOMATIC MECHANICAL REFRIGERATORS. FRED. J. HEIDEMAN and JOSEPH N. HADJISKY, Detroit, Mich., assignors to Kelvinator Corporation, Wilmington, Del., a Corporation of Delaware. Filed Jan. 14, 1918. Serial No. 211.751. 10 Claims. (Cl. 62—4.)

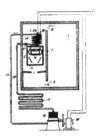

1. The method of automatically refrigerating a storage space mechanically which consists in admitting a volatile liquid to the initial turns of a refrigerant expansion coil, guiding the convection currents induced thereby so as to direct them first into contact with the terminal turns of said coil and controlling the admission of refrigerant according to the temperature existing in the region adjacent to said terminal turns.

1,329,351. PRESSURE-OPERATED REGULATING APPARATUS. FRED J. HEIDEMAN and JOSEPH N. HADJISKY, Detroit, Mich., assignors to Kelvinator Corporation, Wilmington, Del., a Corporation of Delaware. Filed Jan. 14, 1918. Serial No. 211,752. 15 Claims (Cl. 297—S.)

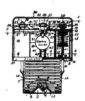

1. In a device of the character described, the combination, with an extensible metallic vessel, of a supporting plate covering one end of said vessel, a controlling device carried by the side of said plate opposite to said vessel, a longitudinally movable member traversing said plate and operatively connected to the opposite end of said vessel, and movement multiplying means operatively connecting said member to said device.

REISSUES.

14,794. METHOD OF AND APPARATUS FOR DRAW-
ING SHEET-GLASS. IRVING W. COLBURN, deceased,
Toledo, Ohio, by The Libbey-Owens Sheet Glass Company,
Toledo, Ohio, a Corporation of Ohio, assignee. Filed
Nov. 29, 1919. Serial No. 341,533. Original applica-
tion filed Jan. 29, 1908, Serial No. 413,296. Renewed
Mar. 26, 1912, Serial No. 686,460. Original No.
1,160,692, dated Nov. 16, 1915. 25 Claims. (Cl.
49—17.)

6. The method of drawing continuous molten glass,
drawing a sheet of glass from said mass of molten glass,
of causing the edge portions of said sheet to be formed
from said areas, and in tempering said areas independently
of the surrounding mass.

25. In an apparatus for drawing sheet glass from a receptacle containing molten glass having two several areas
of a relatively lower degree of temperature than the
main body of the molten mass, the combination of means
for drawing the sheet of glass from said receptacle said
means comprising edge-drawing rolls located above and
in close proximity to the molten mass at the edges of
the sheet and above said areas, and means for drawing
the central portion of the sheet separate and independent
from the edge-drawing rolls, and devices for cooling the
edge-drawing rolls.

14,795. CONCRETE-MIXER. MICHAEL GILSON and JOHN
P. GILSON, Fredonia, Wis. Filed Aug. 13, 1919. Serial
No. 317,890. Original No. 1,237,028, dated Aug. 14,
1917, Serial No. 146,682, filed Feb. 5, 1917. 5 Claims.
(Cl. 83—73.)

1. A mixer comprising a support, a mixing drum
rotatably and tiltably mounted on said support, said drum
being selectively movable to either loading or dumping position, means connected with the drum for rotating the
same in one direction when in loading position to mix
the contents and in the reverse direction when in dumping
position to aid in expelling the mixed contents, and means

operable at will for moving the drum from loading to
dumping position and vice versa and simultaneously disengaging the same from said rotating means.

14,796. STAYBOLT. ROBERT S. MENNIE, Chicago, Ill.,
assignor to Flannery Bolt Company, Pittsburgh, Pa.
Filed Sept. 24, 1919. Serial No. 326,095. Original
application filed May 18, 1914, Serial No. 839,314.
Renewed Mar. 22, 1918, Serial No. 224,077. Original
No. 1,288,955, dated Dec. 24, 1918. 16 Claims. (Cl.
85—1.5.)

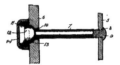

1. In a stay bolt connection, the combination with an
outer and inner boiler sheet, of a stay bolt secured to the
inner sheet and connected to the outer sheet by a universal joint, and a cap inclosing the outer end of the stay
bolt and welded to the outer sheet, whereby the pressure
within said cap results in a tensile stress on the welded
joint with substantially no bending stress.

2. In a stay bolt construction, the combination with a
boiler wall having an opening therein, of a cap having a
continuous edge abutting against said wall, surrounding
said opening and welded to said wall whereby the pressure
within said cap results in a tensile stress on the welded
joint with substantially no bending stress.

3. In a stay bolt connection for a boiler, the combination of a boiler plate having a depressed seat for the
head of the stay bolt and a bolt opening at the bottom
of the depression, a housing welded to the plate around
the depression, and a screw cap for closing said housing.

4. In a stay bolt connection for a boiler, the combination of a boiler plate having a depressed seat for the
head of the stay bolt, and a bolt opening at the bottom of
the depression, a sleeve welded to said plate around the
depressed seat, and a screw cap closing the outer end of
the sleeve.

5. In a stay bolt connection for a boiler, the combination of a boiler plate having a depressed seat for the head
of the stay bolt, and a bolt opening at the bottom of the
depression, a housing welded to said plate around the
depression and open for the passage of the bolt, a bolt,
the head of which is seated in said depression, and a
screw cap closing the opening in the housing.

6. In a stay bolt construction, the combination with
an outer and an inner boiler sheet, of a stay bolt secured
to the inner sheet and connected to the outer sheet by a
universal joint and a closure inclosing the outer end of
the stay bolt and secured to the outer sheet solely by a
welded joint, whereby the pressure within said cap results
in a tensile stress on the welded joint with substantially
no bending stress.

7. The combination with an outer and an inner sheet,
of a stay bolt passing through alined openings in said
sheets, said stay bolt having an enlarged head which,
with the walls of the adjacent opening, forms a ball and
socket joint, the opening in said outer sheet being only
slightly larger than said stay bolt to permit a limited
movement of the latter, without weakening the adjacent
wall, and a cap inclosing said head and welded to said
outer sheet whereby the pressure within said cap results
in a tensile stress on the welded joint with substantially
no bending stress.

8. In a stay bolt construction, the combination with a
boiler wall having an opening therein, of a cap having
a continuous wall in contact with said boiler wall, surrounding said opening and welded to said boiler wall
whereby the pressure within said cap results in a tensile
stress on the welded joint with substantially no bending
stress, and a stay bolt passing through said opening with

its head seated within the inclosure formed by said cap and said boiler wall.

9. In a device of the class described, a boiler wall having an opening therein, a member having a continuous wall around said opening and welded to said boiler wall, said member having a screw-threaded opening in aline-ment with said first opening and a screw-threaded mem-ber closing said opening.

10. In a device of the class described, a boiler wall having an opening therein, a member having a continuous wall in contact with and welded to said boiler wall, said member having an opening in alinement with said first opening and a cap closing said opening whereby the pres-sure within the inclosure thus formed results in a tensile stress on the welded joint with substantially no bending stress.

11. In a stay bolt construction, the combination with a boiler wall having an opening therein, of a cap having a continuous wall in contact with and welded to said boiler wall whereby the pressure within said cap results in a tensile stress on the welded joint with substantially no bending stress, and a stay bolt having a head seated within said cap.

12. In a stay bolt connection for a boiler, the combina-tion of a boiler plate having a depressed seat for the head of the stay bolt, and a bolt opening at the bottom of the depression, a housing welded to said plate around the depression and open to render the bolt head accessible, a bolt, the head of which is seated in said depression, and means for closing the opening in the housing.

13. The combination with a boiler wall having an open-ing therein, of a member surrounding said opening and welded to said wall and means for closing the outer end of said member.

14. In a stay bolt construction, the combination with an outer and inner boiler sheet, and a stay bolt secured to the inner sheet and connected with the outer sheet by a universal joint, of a cap inclosing the outer end of the stay bolt and welded around its edge to the face of the sheet, whereby the pressure within said cap results in a tensile stress on the welded joint with substantially no bending stress.

15. In a stay bolt construction, the combination with an inner and outer boiler sheet, of a staybolt secured to the inner sheet and connected with the outer sheet by a universal joint, and a cap inclosing the outer end of the stay bolt and having its butt welded to the outer sheet, whereby the pressure within its welded joint with substantially no bending stress

16. In a stay bolt construction, the combination with an inner and outer boiler sheet, of a stay bolt secured to the inner sheet and connected with the outer sheet by a universal joint, and a cap inclosing the outer end of the staybolt and having its butt end secured to the outer sheet, solely by a welded joint, whereby the pressure within said cap results in a tensile stress on the welded joint with substantially no bending stress.

14,797. WHEEL-BRAKE. CHESTER B. MILLS, East Mc-Keesport, Pa., and JOHN P. NIKONOW, New York, N. Y., assignors to Westinghouse Electric and Manufacturing Company, a Corporation of Pennsylvania. Filed July 22, 1918. Serial No. 246,253. Original No. 1,204,471, dated Nov. 14, 1916, Serial No. 752,635, filed Mar. 7, 1913. 31 Claims. (Cl. 74—70.)

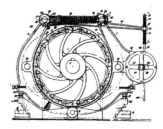

1. In combination, a wheel, brake shoes adapted for fric-tional engagement with said wheel, a motor having sup-porting means in common with one of said brake shoes, and means for operatively connecting said motor to said brake shoes, said means comprising a rack and pinion and a plurality of levers.

The following trade-marks are published in compliance with section 6 of the act of February 20, 1905, as amended March 2, 1907. Notice of opposition must be filed within thirty days of this publication.

Marks applied for "under the ten-year proviso" are registrable under the provision in clause (b) of section 5 of said act as amended February 18, 1911.

As provided by section 14 of said act, a fee of ten dollars must accompany each notice of opposition.

Ser. No. 98,890. (CLASS 50. MERCHANDISE NOT OTHERWISE CLASSIFIED.) PETERS MANUFACTURING Co., Boston, Mass. Filed Oct. 25, 1916.

Particular description of goods.—Shoe Fabrics Consisting of Waterproofed, Reinforced, and Decorated Cotton Cloth.

Claims use since Aug. 16, 1916.

Ser. No. 106,212. (CLASS 39. CLOTHING.) THE MARATHON TIRE & RUBBER Co., Cuyahoga Falls, Ohio. Filed Sept. 12, 1917.

Particular description of goods.—Rubber and Composition Soles and Heels.

Claims use since Feb. 10, 1917.

Ser. No. 107,018. (CLASS 46. FOODS AND INGREDIENTS OF FOODS.) AMERICAN POP CORN WORKS, INC., Boston, Mass. Filed Oct. 30, 1917.

Particular description of goods.—Popcorn Confections.

Claims use since Feb. 1, 1917.

Ser. No. 110,254. (CLASS 6. CHEMICALS, MEDICINES, AND PHARMACEUTICAL PREPARATIONS.) MALONE & HYDE, Memphis, Tenn. Filed Apr. 16, 1918.

Particular description of goods.—Castor-Oil, Epsom Salts, and Sulfur.

Claims use since Jan. 15, 1918.

Ser. No. 110,418. (CLASS 49. DISTILLED ALCOHOLIC LIQUORS.) VALLE, BALLINA Y FERNANDEZ, S. A., Villaviciosa, Spain. Filed Apr. 24, 1918. Under ten-year proviso.

Wherein the apparel upon the figure is colored as follows: the waistcoat in red, the hat and coat in green, the trousers brown, the stockings blue, the shoes of a bluish tint, and the bag of the bagpipe red.

Particular description of goods.—Champagne Cider.

Claims use since about April, 1878.

Ser. No. 111,270. (CLASS 38. PRINTS AND PUBLICATIONS.) THE HENDERSON LITHOGRAPHING COMPANY, Cincinnati, Ohio. Filed May 31, 1918.

Particular description of goods.—Printed and Decorated Tops for Blotters, Folders, Message-Cards in the Nature of Post-Cards: Hangers—Namely, Mottoes and Resolutions; Pictures, Directories, Printed and Decorated Service-Cards, Advertising-Cards, Advertising-Prints, Printed and Decorated Labels; Fan-Backs—Namely, Prints Used as Heads or Tops for Fans and Calendar-Backs.

Claims use since May 1, 1894.

Ser. No. 113,670. (CLASS 46. FOODS AND INGREDI-
ENTS OF FOODS.) WM. T. REYNOLDS & CO., Poughkeepsie, N. Y. Filed Oct. 10, 1918.

Particular description of goods.—Butter, Olive-Oil, Rice,
Dried Fruits, Coffee.
Claims use on butter since Aug. 24, 1918 ; on olive-oil
since Aug. 1, 1910 ; on rice since June 1, 1912 ; on dried
fruits since Mar. 1, 1906, and on coffee since June, 1902.

Ser. No. 114,057. (CLASS 46. FOODS AND INGREDI-
ENTS OF FOODS.) LEONARD G. PAGE, St. Joseph, Mo.
Filed Nov. 5, 1918.

LOYALTY

CHILLO

No claim being made in this application to the word
" Chillo."
Particular description of goods.—A Mixture Which
Comprises Chilli Peppers, Comino, Oregano, Garlic, and
other Spices, Which Mixture is Known as Chillo.
Claims use since Oct. 8, 1915.

Ser. No. 114,103. (CLASS 19. VEHICLES, NOT IN-
CLUDING ENGINES.) THE PEERLESS MOTOR CAR
COMPANY, Cleveland, Ohio. Filed Nov. 8, 1918.

Particular description of goods.—Automobiles and Motor-Trucks.
Claims use since and including the year 1902.

Ser. No. 115,190. (CLASS 39. CLOTHING.) O. L.
STANARD DRY GOODS COMPANY, Huntington, W. Va.
Filed Jan. 14, 1919.

No claim being made to the exclusive use of the word
" Mills " apart from the other features of the mark.
Particular description of goods.—Knitted Hosiery,
Underwear, and Sweaters for Men, Women, and Children
and Work-Shirts for Men and Boys.
Claims use since Sept. 1, 1918.

Ser. No. 115,306. (CLASS 6. CHEMICALS, MEDI-
CINES, AND PHARMACEUTICAL PREPARATIONS.)
PAUL ZATYKO, Divernon, Ill. Filed Jan. 18, 1919.

Zatyko

No claim being made to the name " Zatyko " except in
the fanciful form shown.
Particular description of goods.—A Salve Used in the
Treatment of Sores, Burns, &c.
Claims use since 1893.

Ser. No. 115,801. (CLASS 1. RAW OR PARTLY-PRE-
PARED MATERIALS.) HORACE E. CONKLIN, Binghamton, N. Y. Filed Feb. 12, 1919.

EARLY WONDER

Particular description of goods.—Seed-Corn, Grass-
·Seeds, and Field-Seeds.
Claims use since Mar. 28, 1917.

Ser. No. 115,916. (CLASS 46. FOODS AND INGREDI-
ENTS OF FOODS.) THE INTERNATIONAL PRESERVING
CORPORATION, New York, N. Y. Filed Feb. 17, 1919.

No claim being made to the word " Brand " nor to the
words " Trade-Mark Registered U. S. Patent Office " apart
from the mark shown in the drawing.
Particular description of goods.—Preserved or Partially
or Wholly Prepared Foods—Namely, Cooked Pork and
Beans, Pork Cassoulet, Clams à la Créole, Bœuf Jardinière,
Haricot de Mouton, Orange Marmalade, and Grape-Fruit
Marmalade.
Claims use since Jan. 20, 1919.

Ser. No. 116,223. (CLASS 44. DENTAL, MEDICAL,
AND SURGICAL APPLIANCES.) UNITED DRUG COM-
PANY, Boston, Mass. Filed Feb. 28, 1919.

Particular description of goods.—Rubber Goods—
Namely, Water-Bottles, Syringe-Bags, Ice-Bags, Atomizers,
Nursing-Nipples, Air-Pump Atomizers, Operating-Gloves,

Douches for the Administration of Medicaments, Inhalers; Hard-Rubber Pipes and Soft-Rubbber Tubing Peculiarly Adapted to Use with Dental, Medical, and Surgical Appliances; Air-Cushions for Surgical Use, Air and Water Cushions for Invalid Use, Bulb-Syringes, Nasal and Ear Syringes, Breast-Pumps, Nipple-Shields, Invalid-Rings, Face-Bottles, Combination Attachment Sets for Use in Converting a Hot-Water Bottle into a Fountain-Syringe, Medicine-Droppers, Baby-Comforters, Hard-Rubber Infant Rectal Syringes, Hard-Rubber Uterine Syringes, Surgeons' Rubber Aprons, Absorbent Linen and Gauze, Absorbent Cotton, Medicated Cotton and Wool, Absorbent Pads, Suspensories, Abdominal Bands and Surgical Bandages, Trusses, Eye-Cups, Bed-Pans, Sterilizers Specially Adapted for Use with Surgical and Dental Apparatus and Instruments, Babies' Nursing-Bottles, Orange-Wood Sticks and Nail-Boards, Emery-Boards, Nail-Cleaners, Nail-Clippers, Nail-Files, Nail-Polishers, and Manicure-Tweezers.
Claims use since Mar. 1, 1914.

Ser. No. 116,795. (CLASS 6. CHEMICALS, MEDICINES, AND PHARMACEUTICAL PREPARATIONS.) THE REMILLER COMPANY, New York, N. Y. Filed Mar. 21, 1919.

Mirimbi
Lily

Particular description of goods.—Toilet Waters, Tooth and Mouth Preparations, Liquid and Dry Rouges, Bath-Salts, Smelling-Salts, Hair-Treatment Preparations—Namely, Hair-Tonics and Shampoo-Pastes; Compact Face-Powders, Talcum Powders, Vegetais, (an Alcoholic Preparation Used on the Face Like Toilet Water;) Bandoline, Complexion-Creams, Skin-Beautifiers, Nail Preparations, Brilliantine, Cold-Creams, (for the Face, Used as a Cleanser or Massage;) Perfumes, Face-Powders, Sachet-Powders, and Eyebrow-Crayons.
Claims use since October, 1917.

Ser. No. 117,184. (CLASS 46. FOODS AND INGREDIENTS OF FOODS.) ALEXANDER GREWE, New York, N. Y. Filed Apr. 5, 1919.

LAURA

Particular description of goods.—Candy.
Claims use since April, 1918.

Ser. No. 117,270. (CLASS 19. VEHICLES, NOT INCLUDING ENGINES.) DAFOE-EUSTICE COMPANY, Detroit, Mich. Filed Apr. 8, 1919.

Particular description of goods.—Automobile-Curtains.
Claims use since Dec. 1, 1918.

Ser. No. 117,394. (CLASS 40. FANCY GOODS, FURNISHINGS, AND NOTIONS.) WHITEHOUSE BROTHERS, Newark, N. J. Filed Apr. 11, 1919.

Particular description of goods.—Buckles for Personal Wear and Not Made of Precious Metal.
Claims use since Dec. 30, 1918.

Ser. No. 117,450. (CLASS 50. MERCHANDISE NOT OTHERWISE CLASSIFIED.) DYMALKON METALS CORPORATION, New York, N. Y. Filed Apr. 14, 1919.

Particular description of goods.—Honor-Rolls, Bas-Reliefs, and Memorial Tablets, All Made of Metal.
Claims use since the 1st day of April. 1919.

Ser. No. 117,723. (CLASS 39. CLOTHING.) BARIN, LEHRMAN & BERLER, INC., New York, N. Y. Filed Apr. 22, 1919.

No claim being made to the use of the words " Supreme Fashion Clothes " apart from the mark shown in the drawing.
Particular description of goods.—Men's Clothing, Such Clothing Consisting of Men's Wearing-Apparel—Namely, Coats, Pants, Vests, and Overcoats Manufactured from Cloth Fabrics by the Applicant.
Claims use since Jan. 15, 1919.

Ser. No. 118,157. (CLASS 42. KNITTED, NETTED, AND TEXTILE FABRICS.) M. LOWENSTEIN & SONS, INC., New York, N. Y. Filed May 5, 1919.

Wear-Ever

Particular description of goods.—Unbleached, Dyed, and Printed Drills, Twills, and Sheeting.
Claims use since Apr. 15, 1919.

Ser. No. 118,239. (CLASS 39. CLOTHING.) ROSEN-BERG BROS. & CO., Rochester, N. Y. Filed May 7, 1919.

Fashion Park Clothes

The word "Clothes" as it appears in the trade-mark is hereby disclaimed apart from the mark shown on the drawing.
Particular description of goods.—Men's Coats, Vests, Pants, and Overcoats.
Claims use since on or about the 1st day of January, 1915.

Ser. No. 118,409. (CLASS 46. FOODS AND INGREDI-ENTS OF FOODS.) EUGENE A. TUCHSCHMIDT, St. Louis, Mo. Filed May 12, 1919.

No claim being made for the exclusive use of the words "I stand for quality."
Particular description of goods.—Candies.
Claims use since Apr. 4, 1919.

Ser. No. 118,441. (CLASS 40. FANCY GOODS, FUR-NISHINGS, AND NOTIONS.) LION MANUFACTURING COMPANY, Omaha, Nebr. Filed May 13, 1919.

Particular description of goods.—Suspenders, Waist-Belts for Supporting Wearing-Apparel, Garters, Armbands, and Children's Supporters.
Claims use since Apr. 30, 1915.

Ser. No. 118,501. (CLASS 46. FOODS AND INGREDI-ENTS OF FOODS.) LILLIAN W. SMITH, Cape Charles, Va. Filed May 14, 1919.

No claim is made herein to the exclusive use of the words "Smith Distributing Co.," the word "Potatoes," the words "Honest Grade," or the word "Brand."
Particular description of goods.—Fresh Potatoes.
Claims use since Apr. 16, 1919.

Ser. No. 118,588. (CLASS 46. FOODS AND INGREDI-ENTS OF FOODS.) BUCKEYE NURSERIES, Tampa, Winterhaven, Lucerne Park, and Howey, Fla. Filed May 17, 1919.

Temple

Particular description of goods.—Fresh Oranges.
Claims use since the 12th day of May, 1919.

Ser. No. 118,790. (CLASS 46. FOODS AND INGREDI-ENTS OF FOODS.) THE NULOMOLINE COMPANY, New York, N. Y. Filed May 22, 1919.

GLUCOLINE

Particular description of goods.—Syrups for Table Purposes.
Claims use since Apr. 10, 1919.

Ser. No. 118,935. (CLASS 40. FANCY GOODS, FUR-NISHINGS, AND NOTIONS.) RICE-STIX DRY GOODS COMPANY, St. Louis, Mo. Filed May 26, 1919.

WONDERWEB

Particular description of goods.—Suspenders, Garters, Hose-Supporters, Armbands, and Woven Elastic Belts for Personal Wear.
Claims use since May 7, 1919.

Ser. No. 118,969. (CLASS 46. FOODS AND INGREDI-ENTS OF FOODS.) McCORMICK & CO., Baltimore, Md. Filed May 27, 1919.

RESOLEUM

Particular description of goods.—Spices and Extracts of Spices, Allspice, Cinnamon, Cloves, Ginger, Mace, Nutmeg, Paprika, Cayenne Pepper, Sage, Celery, Coriander, Black Pepper, Onion, Garlic, Flavors for Foods.
Claims use since Apr. 25, 1919.

Ser. No. 119,029. (CLASS 43. THREAD AND YARN.) DEXTER YARN COMPANY, Pawtucket, R. I. Filed May 29, 1919.

NUSILK

Particular description of goods.—Mercerized Cotton Thread and Yarn for Embroidery, Knitting, and Crocheting.
Claims use since Apr. 1, 1905.

Ser. No. 119,132. (CLASS 46. FOODS AND INGREDI-
ENTS OF FOODS.) PENDLETON CREAMERY COMPANY,
Pendleton, Ind. Filed June 2, 1919.

The word " Eversweet " is hereby disclaimed apart from
the trade-mark as shown herein.
Particular description of goods.—Butter.
Claims use since March, 1918.

Ser. No. 119,183. (CLASS 4. ABRASIVE, DETERGENT,
AND POLISHING MATERIALS.) CHARLES C. CUM-
MINGS, St. Louis, Mo. Filed June 4, 1919.

The trade-mark consists of the arbitrary word " Sizz "
written within the left-hand end of a panel, as shown.
Particular description of goods.—Laundry Soaps and
Soap Tablets and Rug-Cleaners.
Claims use since the 15th day of April, 1916.

Ser. No. 119,262. (CLASS 1. RAW OR PARTLY-PRE-
PARED MATERIALS.) ARMIN RICHARD BRUNS, Washington, Iowa. Filed June 6, 1919.

No claim being made of the words " Quality Seeds "
apart from the mark shown in the drawing.
Particular description of goods.—Field, Garden, and
Flower Seeds.
Claims use since 1913.

Ser. No. 119,591. (CLASS 46. FOODS AND INGREDI-
ENTS OF FOODS.) C. F. BLANKE TEA & COFFEE COM-
PANY, St. Louis, Mo. Filed June 14, 1919.

Particular description of goods.—Salad-Dressing, Peanut-Butter, and Salted Peanuts.
Claims use since June 5, 1919.

Ser. No. 119,841. (CLASS 42. KNITTED, NETTED,
AND TEXTILE FABRICS.) TAYLOR, CLAPP & BEALL,
New York, N. Y. Filed June 21, 1919.

No claim being made to the exclusive use of the words
" Crea Catalana De Hilo Redondo " except the arrange-
ment of the mark as shown.
Particular description of goods.—Cotton Piece Goods.
Claims use since Aug. 30, 1916.

Ser. No. 119,858. (CLASS 46. FOODS AND INGREDI-
ENTS OF FOODS.) LAWRENCE T. MALONE, San Antonio, Tex. Filed June 23, 1919.

CANDYFOOD

The language " Candy That's Food " and " Food That's
Candy " is hereby disclaimed.
Particular description of goods.—A Taffy and Cream
Candy Containing Assorted Fruits and Nuts, Made from
Sugar, Corn-Syrup, Butter, Eggs, and Milk and Put Up in
Kisses, Bars, and Balls.
Claims use since Jan. 2, 1918.

Ser. No. 119,859. (CLASS 46. FOODS AND INGREDI-
ENTS OF FOODS.) LAWRENCE T. MALONE, San Antonio, Tex. Filed June 23, 1919.

DIVINITY BALL

The language " Chocolate Coated " and " One's a Meal,"
which has been declared descriptive, is hereby disclaimed.
Particular description of goods.—A Chocolate - Coated
Candy Containing the Following Ingredients, viz: Egg-
Whites, Sugar, Corn-Syrup, and Pecan-Meats, Made into a
Ball, Each Ball Being About Two Inches in Diameter and
Weighing Two Ounces and Being Coated with Chocolate.
Claims use since Sept. 1, 1917.

Ser. No. 119,920. (CLASS 46. FOODS AND INGREDI-
ENTS OF FOODS.) B. F. TRAPPEY, Jeanerette, La.
Filed June 24, 1919.

Particular description of goods.—Tabasco Sauce, Peppers in Vinegar, Extract of Pepper, Ground Pepper.
Claims use in the specific form shown in the drawing
since January, 1912; but a trade-mark consisting of a

shield such as shown in the drawing has been used continuously in my business since some time in the year 1898 upon pepper-pulp.

Ser. No. 119,988. (CLASS 24. LAUNDRY APPLIANCES AND MACHINES.) ROCHESTER WASHING MACHINE CORP., Rochester, N. Y. Filed June 26, 1919.

Particular description of goods.—Clothes-Washing Machines.
Claims use since August, 1914.

Ser. No. 119,990. (CLASS 39. CLOTHING.) FLOYD J. STEWART, Centerville, Iowa. Filed June 26, 1919.

No claim is made to the exclusive right to the use of the word "Legging" or the representation of the same apart from the mark shown. The signature is the facsimile signature of applicant.
Particular description of goods.—Leather and Fabric Leggings.
Claims use since July 1, 1912.

Ser. No. 120,005. (CLASS 46. FOODS AND INGREDIENTS OF FOODS.) HARVARD COMPANY, Lowell, Mass. Filed June 27, 1919.

Grapespread

Said trade-mark consists of the word "Grapespread" ordinarily displayed as appears on the drawing, which is a part of this application. This is used as a single, not as a compound word, and no claim is made to the ownership either of the word "Grape" or the word "Spread," which constitute the different portions of the name, or the exclusive right to use either the word "Grape" or the word "Spread" apart from its use in the combination for which this application is made.
Particular description of goods.—Jellies, Jams, Marmalades, and Crushed Fruits.
Claims use since Apr. 1, 1919.

Ser. No. 120,023. (CLASS 46. FOODS AND INGREDIENTS OF FOODS.) ASPEGREN & COMPANY, New York, N. Y. Filed June 28, 1919.

GOLDTOP

Consisting of the words "Gold Top."
Particular description of goods.—Edible Oils—viz., Peanut-Oil, Cotton-Seed Oil, Soy-Bean Oil—and Lard Substitute.
Claims use since February, 1919.

Ser. No. 120,024. (CLASS 46. FOODS AND INGREDIENTS OF FOODS.) ASPEGREN & COMPANY, New York, N. Y. Filed June 28, 1919.

DIAMOND

TOP

Consisting of the words "Diamond Top."
Particular description of goods.—Edible Oils—viz., Peanut-Oil, Cotton-Seed Oil, Soy-Bean Oil—and Lard Substitute.
Claims use since Mar. 12, 1919.

Ser. No. 120,441. (CLASS 40. FANCY GOODS, FURNISHINGS, AND NOTIONS.) LEONARD WOODS, St. Louis, Mo. Filed July 10, 1919.

The word "Wood's" and the words "Aluminum Suspenders" are not claimed aside from the trade-mark here with presented.
Particular description of goods.—An Article of Men's Furnishings in the Form of Aluminum-Plate Supporters for Trousers.
Claims use since July 24, 1917.

Ser. No. 120,968. (CLASS 46. FOODS AND INGREDI-ENTS OF FOODS.) NORMAN BROS. & BERLIANT, INC., Chicago, Ill. Filed July 26, 1919.

No claim is made to the words "Brand" and "Pre-serves" apart from the arrangement.

Particular description of goods.—Fruit Preserves, In-cluding Peach, Pineapple, Strawberry, Raspberry, Black-berry, Currant, and Plum Preserves.

Claims use since a date prior to May 1, 1917.

Ser. No. 121,062. (CLASS 40. FANCY GOODS, FUR-NISHINGS, AND NOTIONS.) WALDES & Co., Prague, Bohemia. Filed July 29, 1919.

SOMESNAP

No claim is made herein to the exclusive use of the word "Snap" except in connection with the mark as shown.

Particular description of goods. — Placket - Fasteners, Glove-Fasteners, Buttons Not Made of Precious Metal, Snap-Fasteners, and Clasps for Personal Wear Not Made of Precious Metal.

Claims use since December, 1915.

Ser. No. 121,065. (CLASS 40. FANCY GOODS, FUR-NISHINGS, AND NOTIONS.) WALDES & Co., Prague, Bohemia. Filed July 29, 1919.

FIVERSNAPS

No claim is made herein to the exclusive use of the word "Snaps" except in connection with the mark as shown.

Particular description of goods. — Placket - Fasteners, Glove-Fasteners, Buttons Not Made of Precious Metal, Snap-Fasteners, and Clasps for Personal Wear Not Made of Precious Metal.

Claims use since December, 1915.

Ser. No. 121,146. (CLASS 40. FANCY GOODS, FUR-NISHINGS, AND NOTIONS.) JULIUS KAYSER & Co., New York, N. Y. Filed July 31, 1919.

Marvelstraps

Particular description of goods.—Short Narrow Strips of Fabric for Use as Trimmings for Underwear.

Claims use since May 20, 1919.

Ser. No. 121,182. (CLASS 42. KNITTED, NETTED, AND TEXTILE FABRICS.) PARISTYLE NOVELTY Co. INC., New York, N. Y. Filed Aug. 1, 1919.

The lining on the drawing being for the purpose of shading only.

Particular description of goods.—Hair-Nets.

Claims use since the 1st day of August, 1910.

Ser. No. 121,382. (CLASS 46. FOODS AND INGREDI-ENTS OF FOODS.) MITCHEL BECK, Brooklyn, N. Y. Filed Aug. 8, 1919.

DORIO

Particular description of goods.—Canned Fish—Namely, Canned Salmon.

Claims use since July 26, 1919.

Ser. No. 121,494. (CLASS 1. RAW OR PARTLY-PRE-PARED MATERIALS.) R. T. VANDERBILT COMPANY, INC., New York, N. Y. Filed Aug. 9, 1919.

No claim is made for registration of the words "R. T. Vanderbilt Co., N. Y., Whiting, American Products."

Particular description of goods.—Whiting, a Carbonate of Lime and Used as a Filler in Rubber Goods.

Claims use since March, 1919.

Ser. No. 121,691. (CLASS 29. BROOMS, BRUSHES, AND DUSTERS.) THE C. & K. MFG. Co., New Haven, Conn. Filed Aug. 15, 1919.

ROSE

Particular description of goods.—Powder-Puffs.

Claims use since July 1, 1919.

Ser. No. 121,700. (CLASS 1. RAW OR PARTLY-PRE-PARED MATERIALS.) PHILIP A. SINGER & BRO., Newark, N. J. Filed Aug. 15, 1919.

Particular description of goods.—Dressed Furs for Use in Apparel.
Claims use since July 20, 1919.

Ser. No. 121,800. (CLASS 24. LAUNDRY APPLIANCES AND MACHINES.) GUSTAVE WENZELMANN, Galesburg, Ill. Filed Aug. 18, 1919.

SUPREME

Particular description of goods.—Clothes-Washing Machines, Clothes-Wringers, and Combinations, as Well as Parts of Same.
Claims use since March, 1918.

Ser. No. 121,805. (CLASS 46. FOODS AND INGREDIENTS OF FOODS.) WALTER L. GEER, New York, N. Y. Filed Aug. 19, 1919.

The lines in the drawing merely representing shading.
Particular description of goods.—Olive-Oil.
Claims use since May 18, 1919.

Ser. No. 121,819. (CLASS 23. CUTLERY, MACHINERY, AND TOOLS, AND PARTS THEREOF.) UNION CUTLERY CO., Olean, N. Y. Filed Aug. 19, 1919.

MAG-NAM

Consisting of the word "Mag-Nam."
Particular description of goods.—Pocket-Cutlery, Razors, Shears, and Butcher-Knives.
Claims use since June 12, 1918.

Ser. No. 121,915. (CLASS 6. CHEMICALS, MEDICINES, AND PHARMACEUTICAL PREPARATIONS.) PERCIVAL B. ZEVELY, Pittsburgh, Pa. Filed Aug. 22, 1919.

Particular description of goods.—A Liquid Vegetable Laxative of Prunes and Senna with Carminatives and Aromatics.
Claims use since Aug. 14, 1919.

Ser. No. 121,947. (CLASS 19. VEHICLES, NOT INCLUDING ENGINES.) STEWART MOTOR CORPORATION, Buffalo, N. Y. Filed Aug. 23, 1919.

No claim being made for the word "Stewart" apart from the mark shown in the drawing, but without waiving any common-law or other rights incident thereto other than the disclaimer specifically set forth.
Particular description of goods.—Motor-Trucks and Passenger-Automobiles.
Claims use since about Aug. 11, 1919.

Ser. No. 122,016. (CLASS 6. CHEMICALS, MEDICINES, AND PHARMACEUTICAL PREPARATIONS.) THE INTRAVENOUS PRODUCTS COMPANY, Denver, Colo. Filed Aug. 26, 1919.

Ven

Particular description of goods.—Preparations Used for Intramuscular, Intravenous, Subcutaneous, or Local Administration for the Treatment of Diseases of the Blood and Tissues of the Different Organs, Such as Brain, Heart, Lung, Spleen, Pancreas, Stomach, Intestines, and Genito-Urinary Tract in General, Such as Kidneys, Ureters, Bladder, Urethra, and, in the Male, the Prostate Gland; in the Female, Vagina, Uterus, Fallopian Tubes, and Ovaries; also for the Destruction and Elimination of the Different Micro-Organisms, Bacteria, and Toxins That the Tissues and Blood are Host to or Become Infected with.
Claims use since June 10, 1919.

Ser. No. 122,135. (CLASS 48. MALT BEVERAGES, EXTRACTS, AND LIQUORS.) EDGAR L. ROPKINS, Hartford, Conn. Filed Aug. 29, 1919.

Bunny

Particular description of goods.—Non-Intoxicating Cereal Beverages Made of Malt and Hops and Containing Less Than One-Half of One Per cent. of Alcohol, by Weight.
Claims use since Apr. 1, 1919.

Ser. No. 122,144. (CLASS 37. PAPER AND STATIONERY.) WHITING PAPER COMPANY, Holyoke, Mass. Filed Aug. 29, 1919.

WHEN YOU THINK OF WRITING THINK OF
WHITING

Particular description of goods.—Ledger-Paper, Bond and Linen Writing-Paper, and Mailing-Envelops.
Claims use since about the year 1909.

Ser. No. 122,227. (CLASS 46. FOODS AND INGREDI-ENTS OF FOODS.) PILLSBURY FLOUR MILLS COM-PANY, Minneapolis, Minn. Filed Sept. 2, 1919.

The curved blades or zones of the main design are in white and red, while the background in the central portion is in blue, and these colors are indicated by the conventional lines.

Particular description of goods.—Buckwheat Pancake-Flour, Wheat Cereal, Pancake-Flour, and Health-Bran.
Claims use since on or about Apr. 15, 1914.

Ser. No. 122,247. (CLASS 46. FOODS AND INGREDI-ENTS OF FOODS.) GERTRUDE H. FORD TEA COM-PANY, INC., New York, N. Y. Filed Sept. 3, 1919.

Particular description of goods.—Teas.
Claims use since July 14, 1919.

Ser. No. 122,257. (CLASS 2. RECEPTACLES.) PAT-RICK H. KELLY, Philadelphia, Pa. Filed Sept. 3, 1919.

Particular description of goods.—Burial-Boxes, Burial-Caskets, and Burial-Vaults.
Claims use since May, 1919.

Ser. No. 122,284. (CLASS 14. METALS AND METAL CASTINGS AND FORGINGS.) CRUCIBLE STEEL COM-PANY OF AMERICA, Pittsburgh, Pa. Filed Sept. 4, 1919.

SENECA

Particular description of goods.—Steel Bars, Rods, Billets, Blooms, Sheets, Plates, Slabs, Strips, Blocks, and Forgings.
Claims use since May, 1915.

Ser. No. 122,304. (CLASS 39. CLOTHING.) KAPLAN BROTHERS CO., New York, N. Y. Filed Sept. 4, 1919.

No claim is made to the words "Made by" or "Trade-Mark."
Particular description of goods.—Collars and Shirts for Men.
Claims use since June, 1919.

Ser. No. 122,317. (CLASS 46. FOODS AND INGREDI-ENTS OF FOODS.) STROHMEYER & ARPE COMPANY, New York, N. Y. Filed Sept. 4, 1919.

R. U.

Particular description of goods.—Olive-Oil, Salad-Oil, Preserved Vegetables, Preserved Fish, Rice, Macaroni, Cheese, Coffee, Tea, Olives, Preserved Fruit, Pickles, Candy, Preserved Meat, Jams and Jellies, Fruit-Syrups, and Caviar.
Claims use since 1909.

Ser. No. 122,354. (CLASS 39. CLOTHING.) HARRY HINDLEMANN, INC., New York, N. Y. Filed Sept. 5, 1919.

Particular description of goods.—Men's Suits and Over-coats.
Claims use since Feb. 15, 1919.

Ser. No. 122,384. (CLASS 6. CHEMICALS, MEDI-
CINES, AND PHARMACEUTICAL PREPARATIONS.)
HARRY BELL, Chicago, Ill. Filed Sept. 6, 1919.

Particular description of goods.—Roach-Powder.
Claims use since Mar. 15, 1909.

Ser. No. 122,585. (CLASS 46. FOODS AND INGREDI-
ENTS OF FOODS.) A. & C. BUSCAGLIA CO., Buffalo,
N. Y. Filed Sept. 12, 1919.

TRINACRIA

Particular description of goods.—Olive-Oil and Tomato
Paste.
Claims use since about Jan. 1, 1904.

Ser. No. 122,657. (CLASS 12. CONSTRUCTION MA-
TERIALS.) PYRO PRODUCTS COMPANY, Chicago, Ill.
Filed Sept. 13, 1919.

Particular description of goods.—Fire-Brick.
Claims use since Nov. 4, 1913.

Ser. No. 122,678. (CLASS 12. CONSTRUCTION MA-
TERIALS.) AMERICAN POZZOLANA COMPANY, Indianapolis, Ind. Filed Sept. 15, 1919.

POZZO

Particular description of goods.—Cement, Stucco, and
Plaster.
Claims use since Aug. 1, 1919.

Ser. No. 122,679. (CLASS 38. PRINTS AND PUBLICA-
TIONS.) AMERICAN CARPENTER AND BUILDER CO., Chicago, Ill. Filed Sept. 15, 1919.

AMERICAN BUILDER

Particular description of goods.—A Monthly Magazine.
Claims use since Feb. 1, 1917.

Ser. No. 122,718. (CLASS 36. MUSICAL INSTRU-
MENTS AND SUPPLIES.) THE MUSIC TABLE COM-
PANY, Greenfield, Ohio. Filed Sept. 15, 1919.

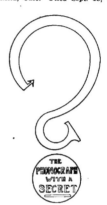

Particular description of goods.—Phonographs.
Claims use since May 1, 1919.

Ser. No. 122,788. (CLASS 2. RECEPTACLES.) CHARLES
ROSENTHAL, New York, N. Y. Filed Sept. 16, 1919.

No claim being made to the exclusive use of the words
" Sanitary Drinking Cups " apart from the mark as shown
in the drawing.
Particular description of goods.—Sanitary Paper Drink-
ing-Cups.
Claims use since May, 1914.

Ser. No. 122,822. (CLASS 40. FANCY GOODS, FUR-
NISHINGS, AND NOTIONS.) GERTRUDE R. BONE-
BRIGHT, Grand Rapids, Mich. Filed Sept. 18, 1919.

DI. DE. TITE

Particular description of goods.—Supporters for Diapers.
Claims use since June 24, 1919.

Ser. No. 122,842. (CLASS 23. CUTLERY, MACHINERY,
AND TOOLS, AND PARTS THEREOF.) LONGHORN
DRILLING & DEVELOPMENT ASSOCIATION, Fort Worth,
Tex. Filed Sept. 18, 1919.

Particular description of goods.—Well-Drilling Machinery and Tools Comprising Temper-Screws, Rope-
Clamps, Bits, Rope-Sockets. Tool-Wrenches. Clutch-Boxes,

Tool-Wrench Liners, Gripping Devices, Chain Tongs, Underreamers, Cutters for Underreamers, Sand-Pumps, Valve-Bailers, Round Reamers, Derrick-Cranes, Casing-Hooks, Snatch-Blocks, Link-Elevators, Spiders, Tongs, Fishing-Tool Sockets, Casing-Bowls, Casing-Spears, Casing-Splitters, Casing-Cutters, Rope-Sinkers, Rope-Grabs, Hydraulic Swivel, Side Rasps, Casing-Swages, and Well Equipment Comprising Casing-Shoes, Floating Plugs, Die and Casing Nipples, Casing-Heads, Drive-Heads, Drive-Clamps, Anchor-Clamps, Sucker-Rods, Rod-Grips, and Casing-Swabs.

Claims use since May 1, 1919.

Ser. No. 122,871. (CLASS 19. VEHICLES, NOT IN-CLUDING ENGINES.) AMERICAN COMMERCIAL CAR Co., Detroit, Mich. Filed Sept. 18, 1919.

No claim is made to the word "Truck" apart from the mark shown in the drawing.
Particular description of goods.—Automobile-Trucks.
Claims use since March, 1918.

Ser. No. 122,872. (CLASS 40. FANCY GOODS, FUR-NISHINGS, AND NOTIONS.) NU-WAY STRECH SUS-PENDER COMPANY, Adrian, Mich. Filed Sept. 18, 1919.

Particular description of goods.—Suspenders and Garters.
Claims use since 1912.

Ser. No. 122,895. (CLASS 6. CHEMICALS, MEDI-CINES, AND PHARMACEUTICAL PREPARATIONS.) DAVID KIEBANOFF, Philadelphia, Pa. Filed Sept. 19, 1919.

No claim being made to the words "Cold Capsules."
Particular description of goods.—A Remedy for La Grippe, Colds, and Headache.
Claims use since Aug. 1, 1917.

Ser. No. 122,916. (CLASS 6. CHEMICALS, MEDI-CINES, AND PHARMACEUTICAL PREPARATIONS.) F. AD. RICHTER & Co, New York, N. Y. Filed Sept. 19, 1919.

MADONA

Particular description of goods.—Medicinal Prepara-tions—Namely, a Vegetable Preparation for Constipation, Diarrhea, and Fever Resulting from Indigestion.
Claims use since Aug. 12, 1919.

Ser. No. 122,995. (CLASS 46. FOODS AND INGREDI-ENTS OF FOODS.) OWENSBORO PRODUCTS COMPANY, Owensboro, Ky. Filed Sept. 22, 1919.

BLUE GRASS

Particular description of goods.—Stock Feed.
Claims use since the 25th day of June, 1919.

Ser. No. 123,016. (CLASS 17. TOBACCO PRODUCTS.) THE AMERICAN TOBACCO COMPANY, New York, N. Y. Filed Sept. 23, 1919.

LIBERTY

Particular description of goods.—Smoking and Chewing Tobacco.
Claims use since about February, 1891.

Ser. No. 123,017. (CLASS 17. TOBACCO PRODUCTS.) THE AMERICAN TOBACCO COMPANY, New York, N. Y. Filed Sept. 23, 1919.

Particular description of goods.—Smoking and Chewing Tobacco and Cigarettes.
Claims use since about February, 1894.

Ser. No. 123,049. (CLASS 6. CHEMICALS, MEDI-CINES, AND PHARMACEUTICAL PREPARATIONS.) ALBANY CHEMICAL COMPANY, Albany, N. Y. Filed Sept. 24, 1919.

AUTO ETHER

No claim is made to the exclusive use of the words "Auto Ether" apart from the other exclusive features of the mark shown in the drawing.
Particular description of goods.—Fluid for Priming and Starting Internal-Combustion Engines.
Claims use since Sept. 1, 1919.

Ser. No. 123,055. (CLASS 46. FOODS AND INGREDI-ENTS OF FOODS.) HALLER BAKING COMPANY, Pittsburgh, Pa. Filed Sept. 24, 1919.

No claim is made to the words "Special" or "Bread."
Particular description of goods.—Bread.
Claims use since about Mar. 1, 1914.

Ser. No. 123,081. (CLASS 17. TOBACCO PRODUCTS.) WARD P. ROBERTS, Milford, Mass. Filed Sept. 24, 1919.

Particular description of goods.—Cigars.
Claims use since about Jan. 1, 1894.

Ser. No. 123,083. (CLASS 17. TOBACCO PRODUCTS.) WARD P. ROBERTS, Milford, Mass. Filed Sept. 24, 1919. Under ten-year proviso.

Particular description of goods.—Cigars.
Claims use since about Jan. 1, 1894.

Ser. No. 123,183. (CLASS 6. CHEMICALS, MEDICINES, AND PHARMACEUTICAL PREPARATIONS.) NARM S. SUE, Modesto, Calif. Filed Sept. 26, 1919.

Particular description of goods.—A Medicinal Preparation for the Treatment of Influenza.
Claims use since Sept. 1, 1918.

Ser. No. 123,189. (CLASS 19. VEHICLES, NOT INCLUDING ENGINES.) HOWARD W. WEED, Stamford, Conn. Filed Sept. 26, 1919.

Particular description of goods.—An Awning in the Nature of Wind-Shield Protector.
Claims use since Aug. 15, 1919.

Ser. No. 123,273. (CLASS 6. CHEMICALS, MEDICINES, AND PHARMACEUTICAL PREPARATIONS.) EVA ADAMS, Sparta, Ill. Filed Sept. 30, 1919.

Particular description of goods.—Hair-Tonics and Hair-Straighteners.
Claims use since May 15, 1919.

Ser. No. 123,291. (CLASS 19. VEHICLES, NOT INCLUDING ENGINES.) PIEDMONT MOTOR CAR COMPANY., INC., Lynchburg, Va. Filed Sept. 30, 1919.

Particular description of goods.—Passenger-Automobiles and Motor-Trucks.
Claims use since February, 1917.

Ser. No. 123,304. (CLASS 46. FOODS AND INGREDIENTS OF FOODS.) F. B. CHAMBERLAIN COMPANY, St. Louis, Mo. Filed Oct. 1, 1919.

Particular description of goods.—Farina, Pearl-Barley, Yellow Cornmeal, White Cornmeal, Hominy-Grits, Pearl-Hominy, and Oatmeal.
Claims use since about Nov. 9, 1918.

Ser. No. 123,314. (CLASS 6. CHEMICALS, MEDICINES, AND PHARMACEUTICAL PREPARATIONS.) ARTHUR M. FLOOD, San Francisco, Calif. Filed Oct. 1, 1919.

Particular description of goods.—A Medicinal Preparation to be Used as a Dentifrice, Such as Tooth-Powder, Tooth-Paste, Tooth-Wash, Mouth-Wash, or Gargle, and for the Treatment of Pyorrhea, Tender, Spongy, and Receding Gums.
Claims use since Jan. 1, 1916.

Ser. No. 123,324. (CLASS 6. CHEMICALS, MEDI-CINES, AND PHARMACEUTICAL PREPARATIONS.) VICTOR VIVAUDOU, New York, N. Y. Filed Oct. 1, 1919.

JEUNESSE

Particular description of goods.—Face-Powders, Face-Creams, Perfumes, Toilet Waters, Rouges. Hair-Tonics, Dentifrices, Tooth-Powders, Nail-Polishes, Deodorizing Preparations, Brilliantines, and Sachet-Powders.
Claims use since Sept. 24, 1919.

Ser. No. 123,333. (CLASS 6. CHEMICALS, MEDI-CINES, AND PHARMACEUTICAL PREPARATIONS.) EDWARD BEALL, Los Angeles, Calif. Filed Oct. 2, 1919.

Particular description of goods.—A Combination of Herbs for Use in the Treatment of Bright's Disease, Diabetes, Rheumatism, Constipation, Liver, Bladder, Kidney, and Stomach Troubles.
Claims use since Nov. 15, 1910.

Ser. No. 123,358. (CLASS 6. CHEMICALS, MEDI-CINES, AND PHARMACEUTICAL PREPARATIONS.) THE MALTBIE CHEMICAL COMPANY, Newark, N. J. Filed Oct. 2, 1919.

Creo-Tussin

Particular description of goods.—A Preparation for Use in the Treatment of Whooping-Cough.
Claims use since May, 1919.

Ser. No. 123,364. (CLASS 6. CHEMICALS, MEDI-CINES, AND PHARMACEUTICAL PREPARATIONS.) JOSEPH M. PIERRE, Fort Wayne, Ind. Filed Oct. 2. 1919.

Particular description of goods.—A Preparation for the Treatment of Asthma, Bronchitis, Catarrh. Burns, Rheumatism, and Itching Piles.
Claims use since Aug. 7, 1919.

Ser. No. 123,372. (CLASS 6. CHEMICALS, MEDI-CINES, AND PHARMACEUTICAL PREPARATIONS.) THE TILDEN COMPANY, New Lebanon, N. Y., and St. Louis, Mo. Filed Oct. 2, 1919.

EUPINOL

Particular description of goods.—An Anodyne, Antiseptic, and Local Anesthetic.
Claims use since 1912.

Ser. No. 123,418. (CLASS 6. CHEMICALS, MEDI-CINES, AND PHARMACEUTICAL PREPARATIONS.) GEORGE BORGFELDT & Co., New York, N. Y. Filed Oct. 4, 1919.

Splashme

Particular description of goods.—Toilet Powder.
Claims use since Sept. 8, 1919.

Ser. No. 123,437. (CLASS 34. HEATING, LIGHTING, AND VENTILATING APPARATUS, NOT INCLUDING ELECTRICAL APPARATUS.) JOSEPH N. KLEMA, Austin, Minn. Filed Oct. 4, 1919.

Particular description of goods.—Lanterns.
Claims use since the 22d day of September, 1919.

Ser. No. 123,477. (CLASS 19. VEHICLES. NOT IN-CLUDING ENGINES.) ELBE MOTOR Co., Los Angeles, Calif. Filed Oct. 6, 1919.

SPEEDASCOPE

Particular description of goods.—Rear-Sight Mirrors for Vehicles.
Claims use since Sept. 1, 1919.

Ser. No. 123,481. (CLASS 46. FOODS AND INGREDI-ENTS OF FOODS.) GIBBS PRESERVING Co., Baltimore. Md. Filed Oct. 6, 1919.

Particular description of goods.—Pure Fruit Jams.
Claims use since Sept. 22, 1919.

Ser. No. 123,509. (CLASS 6. CHEMICALS. MEDI-CINES, AND PHARMACEUTICAL PREPARATIONS.) THOMAS A. WALSH, Yonkers, N. Y. Filed Oct. 6, 1919.

CULTINE

Particular description of goods.—A Bacteriological Culture of *Bacillus Bulgaricus* for Diarrhea in Chicks and Fowls.
Claims use since Sept. 15, 1919.

Ser. No. 123,550. (CLASS 45. BEVERAGES, NON-ALCOHOLIC.) CONSTANTINE G. MANGOS, Davenport, Iowa. Filed Oct. 8, 1919.

Particular description of goods.—Carbonated Water.
Claims use since about Aug. 15, 1919.

Ser. No. 123,600. (CLASS 40. FANCY GOODS, FURNISHINGS, AND NOTIONS.) AMERICAN HARD RUBBER CO., Hempstead and New York, N. Y. Filed Oct. 10, 1919.

Particular description of goods.—Combs for Dressing, Ornamenting, and Cleaning the Hair and Buttons for Wearing-Apparel.
Claims use since Oct. 7, 1919.

Ser. No. 123,601. (CLASS 40. FANCY GOODS, FURNISHINGS, AND NOTIONS.) AMERICAN HARD RUBBER COMPANY, Hempstead and New York, N. Y. Filed Oct. 10, 1919.

ACE

Particular description of goods.—Combs for Dressing, Ornamenting, and Cleaning the Hair and Buttons for Wearing-Apparel.
Claims use since Oct. 7, 1919.

Ser. No. 123,602. (CLASS 40. FANCY GOODS, FURNISHINGS, AND NOTIONS.) AMERICAN HARD RUBBER COMPANY, Hempstead and New York, N. Y. Filed Oct. 10, 1919.

SPADE

Particular description of goods.—Combs for Dressing, Ornamenting, and Cleaning the Hair and Buttons for Wearing-Apparel.
Claims use since Oct. 7, 1919.

Ser. No. 123,637. (CLASS 46. FOODS AND INGREDIENTS OF FOODS.) GRAND UNION TEA CO., Brooklyn, N. Y. Filed Oct. 10, 1919.

Particular description of goods.—Tea.
Claims use since about 1910.

Ser. No. 123,638. (CLASS 46. FOODS AND INGREDIENTS OF FOODS.) GRAND UNION TEA CO., Brooklyn, N. Y. Filed Oct. 10, 1919.

Particular description of goods.—Plain Ground Cocoa, Sweet Ground Cocoa, Plain Chocolate, Sweet Chocolate, Flavoring Extracts for Food ; Spices, Whole and Ground ; Prepared Mustard, Salad-Dressing, Celery-Salt, Vinegar, White Pepper, Black Pepper, Cane-Syrup for Food, Shredded Cocoanut, Turmeric, Paprika, and Tea.
Claims use since about 1888.

Ser. No. 123,639. (CLASS 39. CLOTHING.) GAGE BROTHERS & COMPANY, Chicago, Ill. Filed Oct. 10, 1919. Under ten-year proviso.

The lining on the drawing is for shading only, not for color.
Particular description of goods.—Ladies' Hats.
Claims use for upward of twenty-five years last past.

Ser. No. 123,692. (CLASS 7. CORDAGE.) THE HOOVEN & ALLISON COMPANY, Xenia, Ohio. Filed Oct. 11, 1919.

The trade-mark consists of an elongated lineal white marker or label separate from the structural part of the rope, but located in the interior of the rope and inclosed by the rope-strands. No claim is made herein for the representation of the rope or of the hands shown in the drawing, these being shown merely to illustrate the method by which the white lineal marker or label may be detected at an intermediate point in the rope.
Particular description of goods.—Hemp Rope.
Claims use since June 6, 1919.

Ser. No. 123,738. (CLASS 6. CHEMICALS, MEDI-
CINES, AND PHARMACEUTICAL PREPARATIONS.)
CHAS. A. HARRIS, Dawson, Ga. Filed Oct. 13, 1919.

HARRIS'

(121)

(signature: Chas. A. Harris)

The name "Chas. A. Harris" being the facsimile signa-
ture of the applicant.
Particular description of goods.—A Blood Remedy.
Claims use since 1903.

Ser. No. 123,828. (CLASS 46. FOODS AND INGREDI-
ENTS OF FOODS.) GEORGE WALLACE, New York,
N. Y. Filed Oct. 15, 1919.

Particular description of goods.—Chocolates.
Claims use since June 24, 1919.

Ser. No. 123,829. (CLASS 46. FOODS AND INGREDI-
ENTS OF FOODS.) W. B. WOOD MFG. CO., St. Louis,
Mo. Filed Oct. 15, 1919.

Fairy Powder

No claim being made to the word "Powder" apart
from the mark shown on the drawing.
Particular description of goods.—A Powder for the
Manufacture of Ice-Cream, Fruit Sherbet, Frozen Pud-
ding, and Frozen Punches.
Claims use since Nov. 1, 1914.

Ser. No. 123,830. (CLASS 40. FANCY GOODS, FUR-
NISHINGS, AND NOTIONS.) JOSEPH ZIFF, Detroit,
Mich. Filed Oct. 15, 1919.

Premier

Particular description of goods.—Suspenders and Men's
Garters.
Claims use since Jan. 1, 1917.

Ser. No. 123,906. (CLASS 2. RECEPTACLES.) HARRY
R. RADIN, Newark, N. J. Filed Oct. 17, 1919.

Particular description of goods.—Containers and Steri-
lizers for Tooth-Brushes, Usually Made Tubular and
Equipped with an End Closure.
Claims use since the latter part of May, 1919.

Ser. No. 123,947. (CLASS 19. VEHICLES, NOT IN-
CLUDING ENGINES.) ARGONNE MOTOR CAR COM-
PANY, Jersey City, N. J. Filed Oct. 18, 1919.

Particular description of goods.—Automobiles, Automobile Radiators and Wheel-Hub Caps.
Claims use since Feb. 15, 1919.

Ser. No. 123,960. (CLASS 45. BEVERAGES, NON-
ALCOHOLIC.) CHILL-O COMPANY, Chicago, Ill. Filed
Oct. 20, 1919.

PEP-FORD

Particular description of goods.—Non-Alcoholic Non-
Intoxicating Maltless Non-Cereal Beverage and Sold as a
Soft Drink.
Claims use since July 1, 1919.

Ser. No. 123,982. (CLASS 48. MALT BEVERAGES,
EXTRACTS, AND LIQUORS.) BRUNO A. HOEHL,
Wheeling, W. Va. Filed Oct. 20, 1919.

BRUNOLA

Particular description of goods.—Malt and Hop Extract for Non-Alcoholic Beverages.
Claims use since Sept. 26, 1919.

Ser. No. 124,045. (CLASS 46. FOODS AND INGREDIENTS OF FOODS.) D. A. P. CONFECTIONERY, INC., New York, N. Y. Filed Oct. 21, 1919.

Particular description of goods.—Candies and Chocolates.
Claims use since about Sept. 10, 1919.

Ser. No. 124,060. (CLASS 46. FOODS AND INGREDIENTS OF FOODS.) THE WOOLSON SPICE CO., Toledo, Ohio. Filed Oct. 21, 1919.

HOUSEWIFE

Particular description of goods.—Coffee.
Claims use since Oct. 3, 1919.

Ser. No. 124,064. (CLASS 23. CUTLERY, MACHINERY, AND TOOLS, AND PARTS THEREOF.) THE WOOD SHOVEL & TOOL CO., Piqua, Ohio. Filed Oct. 21, 1919.

Particular description of goods.—Shovels, Spades, Scoops, and Drainage-Tools.
Claims use since Oct. 1, 1919.

Ser. No. 124,082. (CLASS 34. HEATING, LIGHTING, AND VENTILATING APPARATUS, NOT INCLUDING ELECTRICAL APPARATUS.) DELAWARE ELECTRIC & SUPPLY CO., Wilmington, Del. Filed Oct. 20, 1919.

Particular description of goods.—Coal-Stoves.
Claims use since about 1889.

Ser. No. 124,155. (CLASS 7. CORDAGE.) TATE MANUFACTURING COMPANY, Boston, Mass. Filed Oct. 24, 1919.

TATESPUN

The word "Tate" is disclaimed apart from the mark shown in the drawing.
Particular description of goods.—Braided Rope.
Claims use since Aug. 26, 1919.

Ser. No. 124,169. (CLASS 46. FOODS AND INGREDIENTS OF FOODS.) CHERI, INC., Philadelphia, Pa. Filed Oct. 25, 1919.

CHÉRI

Particular description of goods.—Raw and Cooked Sea Food—Namely, Oysters, Clams, Lobsters, Scallops, and Fish ; Cooked Meats—Namely, Poultry, Beef, Lamb, Pork, and Game ; Uncooked and Cooked Vegetables, Uncooked and Cooked Fruit, Bread, Butter, Salads ; Cereals—Namely, Oatmeal, Hominy, and All Kinds of Breakfast Cereals ; Cooked and Uncooked Nuts, and Desserts—Namely, Pies, Cakes, Puddings, and Frozen Desserts.
Claims use since about September, 1918.

Ser. No. 124,176. (CLASS 46. FOODS AND INGREDIENTS OF FOODS.) E. GREENFIELD'S SONS, New York and Brooklyn, N. Y. Filed Oct. 25, 1919.

Country Club

Particular description of goods.—Chocolate and Candies.
Claims use since May 1, 1911.

Ser. No. 124,189. (CLASS 23. CUTLERY, MACHINERY, AND TOOLS, AND PARTS THEREOF.) SAMUEL W. PRUSSIAN, Cambridge, Mass. Filed Oct. 25, 1919.

GUARANTY

Particular description of goods.—Power-Hoists.
Claims use since Jan. 1, 1918.

Ser. No. 124,298. (CLASS 12. CONSTRUCTION MATERIALS.) DYMALKON METALS CORPORATION, New York, N. Y. Filed Oct. 29, 1919.

Particular description of goods.—Architectural Bronzework for Building Exteriors and Interiors, Including Banks, Court-Houses, Libraries, Railings, and Stairs.
Claims use since the 1st day of April, 1919.

Ser. No. 124,340. (CLASS 17. TOBACCO PRODUCTS.) WILLIAM J. FISHER & CO., Boston, Mass. Filed Oct. 30, 1919.

FISHER'S W.J.F.

The name "Fisher's" being disclaimed apart from the mark shown.
Particular description of goods.—Cigars.
Claims use since Oct. 24, 1919.

Ser. No. 124,414. (CLASS 38. PRINTS AND PUBLICA-TIONS.) M-C Syndicate, Philadelphia, Pa. Filed Oct. 31, 1919.

Uncle Harry Talks

Particular description of goods.—Articles on Current Events for Children, Printed from Time to Time.
Claims use since Oct. 14, 1915.

Ser. No. 124,535. (CLASS 48. MALT BEVERAGES, EXTRACTS, AND LIQUORS.) Adam Scheidt Beverage Company, Norristown, Pa. Filed Nov. 4, 1919.

ALEIKE

Particular description of goods.—A Beverage Made of Malt and Cereals and Containing Less Than One-Half of One Per Cent. of Alcohol, by Volume.
Claims use since October, 1919.

Ser. No. 124,592. (CLASS 46. FOODS AND INGREDI-ENTS OF FOODS.) Cloud-Thomas Co., Yakima, Wash. Filed Nov. 6, 1919.

Particular description of goods.—Fresh Fruits—Namely, Apples.
Claims use since June 1, 1919.

Ser. No. 124,600. (CLASS 46. FOODS AND INGREDI-ENTS OF FOODS.) Fresno Brewing Co., Fresno, Calif. Filed Nov. 6, 1919.

Particular description of goods.—Ice-Cream and Ices.
Claims use since Oct. 15, 1919.

Ser. No. 124,612. (CLASS 46. FOODS AND INGREDI-ENTS OF FOODS.) Lawrence Canning Co., Rockland, Me. Filed Nov. 6, 1919.

Particular description of goods.—Canned Fish—Namely, Canned Sardines.
Claims use since Oct. 20, 1916.

Ser. No. 124,620. (CLASS 46. FOODS AND INGREDI-ENTS OF FOODS.) Petersburg Food Products Cor-poration, Petersburg, Va. Filed Nov. 6, 1919.

VIRGINIA DARE

Particular description of goods.—Apple and Grain Vine-gar, Vegetable Oil for Food Purposes, and Table-Syrups.
Claims use since Aug. 1, 1919.

Ser. No. 124,621. (CLASS 46. FOODS AND INGREDI-ENTS OF FOODS.) Rueckheim Bros. & Eckstein, Chicago, Ill. Filed Nov. 6, 1919.

PELICANS

Particular description of goods.—Chocolate Candies.
Claims use since Apr. 27, 1914.

Ser. No. 124,636. (CLASS 46. FOODS AND INGREDI-ENTS OF FOODS.) Alma R. Alfoth, Chicago, Ill. Filed Nov. 7, 1919.

Roselma

Particular description of goods.—Candies.
Claims use since September, 1911.

Ser. No. 124,642. (CLASS 46. FOODS AND INGREDI-ENTS OF FOODS.) The Corno Mills Company, St. Louis, Mo. Filed Nov. 7, 1919.

Particular description of goods.—Rolled Oats.
Claims use since Sept. 18, 1919.

Ser. No. 124,659. (CLASS 46. FOODS AND INGREDI-ENTS OF FOODS.) Mason City Candy Co., Mason City, Iowa. Filed Nov. 7, 1919.

Handkraft

Particular description of goods.—Candies.
Claims use since Sept. 18, 1909.

Ser. No. 124,670. (CLASS 46. FOODS AND INGREDI-
ENTS OF FOODS.) SAMOSET CHOCOLATES Co., Boston,
Mass. Filed Nov. 7, 1919.

Particular description of goods.—Candies.
Claims use since 1911.

Ser. No. 124,676. (CLASS 23. CUTLERY, MACHINERY,
AND TOOLS, AND PARTS THEREOF.) LOUIS BUR-
LASKY, New York, N. Y. Filed Nov. 8, 1919.

Particular description of goods.—Sewing-Machines and
Parts Thereof.
Claims use since about Jan. 1, 1910.

Ser. No. 124,687. (CLASS 46. FOODS AND INGREDI-
ENTS OF FOODS.) KEHOE PRESERVING Co., Clay City
and Terre Haute, Ind. Filed Nov. 8, 1919.

Particular description of goods.—Canned Vegetables.
Claims use since Sept. 29, 1919.

Ser. No. 124,706. (CLASS 17. TOBACCO PRODUCTS.)
THE AMERICAN TOBACCO COMPANY, New York, N. Y.
Filed Nov. 10, 1919.

NAVY

Particular description of goods.—Smoking and Chewing
Tobacco.
Claims use since about October, 1865.

Ser. No. 124,708. (CLASS 17. TOBACCO PRODUCTS.)
THE AMERICAN TOBACCO COMPANY, New York, N. Y.
Filed Nov. 10, 1919.

Particular description of goods.—Smoking and Chewing
Tobacco and Cigarettes.
Claims use since about July, 1904.

Ser. No. 124,766. (CLASS 46. FOODS AND INGREDI-
ENTS OF FOODS.) SMART & FINAL Co., Santa Ana,
Calif. Filed Nov. 11. 1919.

ORANGE
BLOSSOM

Particular description of goods.—Roasted Coffee in
Packages.
Claims use since July 1, 1919.

Ser. No. 124,792. (CLASS 46. FOODS AND INGREDI-
ENTS OF FOODS.) EARLE GERNERT, Billings, Mont.
Filed Nov. 12, 1919.

The cross being lined for blue.
Particular description of goods.—Canned Vegetables.
Claims use since June, 1919.

Ser. No. 124,802. (CLASS 46. FOODS AND INGREDI-
ENTS OF FOODS.) JOHN MORRELL & Co., Ottumwa,
Iowa. Filed Nov. 12, 1919.

Particular description of goods.—Eggs.
Claims use since Aug. 8, 1919.

Ser. No. 124,816. (CLASS 46. FOODS AND INGREDI-
ENTS OF FOODS.) THE SEARS AND NICHOLS CANNING
COMPANY, Chillicothe, Ohio. Filed Nov. 12, 1919.

SUPERBA

Particular description of goods.—Canned Vegetables.
Claims use since 1899.

Ser. No. 124,825. CLASS 46. FOODS AND INGREDI-
ENTS OF FOODS.) WILLIAMS CHOCOLATE COMPANY,
Scranton, Pa. Filed Nov. 12, 1919.

MIL-DAR

Particular description of goods.—Chocolate Candy.
Claims use since Sept. 9, 1919.

Ser. No. 124,873. (CLASS 17. TOBACCO PRODUCTS.) D. A. SCHULTE INC., New York, N. Y. Filed Nov. 13, 1919.

BELLEFAIR

Particular description of goods. — Cigars, Cigarettes, Cheroots, Smoking and Chewing Tobacco, and Snuff.
Claims use since Nov. 29, 1910.

Ser. No. 124,878. (CLASS 46. FOODS AND INGREDI-ENTS OF FOODS.) ARCHBOLD MANUFACTURING COR-PORATION, Rochester, N. Y. Filed Nov. 14, 1919.

AR-CANE

Particular description of goods. — Syrup Made of Cane-Sugar to be Used as a Food or as an Ingredient of Foods.
Claims use since Mar. 1, 1919.

Ser. No. 124,995. (CLASS 46. FOODS AND INGREDI-ENTS OF FOODS.). R. F. KEPPEL & BRO. INC., Lancas-ter, Pa. Filed Nov. 17, 1919.

HY-GLOSS

Particular description of goods. — Candies.
Claims use since Mar. 15, 1918.

Ser. No. 125,001. (CLASS 50. MERCHANDISE NOT OTHERWISE CLASSIFIED.) THE MARATHON TIRE AND RUBBER CO., Cuyahoga Falls, Ohio. Filed Nov. 17, 1919.

FLEXYDE

The word "Flexyde."
Particular description of goods. — Imitation Leather.
Claims use since Sept. 3, 1919.

Ser. No. 125,027. (CLASS 48. MALT BEVERAGES, EX-TRACTS, AND LIQUORS.) THE F. & M. SCHAEFER BREWING CO., New York. N. Y. Filed Nov. 17, 1919.

Particular description of goods. — A Soft Drink Contain-ing Less Than One-Half of One Per Cent. Alcohol and Ap-proximately Three Per Cent. Malt.
Claims use since Dec. 6, 1917.

Ser. No. 125,070. (CLASS 46. FOODS AND INGREDI-ENTS OF FOODS.) THE ALASKA SALMON & HERRING PACKERS, INC., Seattle, Wash. Filed Nov. 19, 1919.

Particular description of goods. — Canned Salmon, Canned Herring.
Claims use since July, 1919.

Ser. No. 125,080. (CLASS 46. FOODS AND INGREDI-ENTS OF FOODS.) JOHN A. DE LUCA, St. Helena, Md. Filed Nov. 19, 1919.

De-Lite

Particular description of goods. — Mayonnaise Dressing, Chilli-Chow, and a Marshmallow Preparation for Use in Making Icings, Coatings, and Fillers for Pastry and Con-fectionery.
Claims use since on or about Feb. 1, 1919.

Ser. No. 125,143. (CLASS 46. FOODS AND INGREDI-ENTS OF FOODS.) WM. WRIGLEY JR. COMPANY, Chi-cago, Ill. Filed Nov. 20, 1919.

Particular description of goods. — Chewing-Gum.
Claims use since Sept. 10, 1914.

Ser. No. 125,159. (CLASS 45. BEVERAGES, NON-ALCOHOLIC.) LONDON 'O-T' LIMITED, Blackfriars, London, England, and Prahran, Victoria, Australia. Filed Nov. 21, 1919.

KIA-ORA

Particular description of goods. — Lemon - Squash and Lime-Juice.
Claims use since May, 1910.

Ser. No. 125,175. (CLASS 1. RAW OR PARTLY-PRE-PARED MATERIALS.) JOHN R. EVANS & COMPANY, Philadelphia, Pa. Filed Nov. 22, 1919.

Consists of the word "Del Phia."
Particular description of goods. — Leather.
Claims use since March, 1919.

Ser. No. 125,258. (CLASS 46. FOODS AND INGREDI-
ENTS OF FOODS.) Isaac M. Simonin, Philadelphia,
Pa. Filed Nov. 24, 1919.

BANQUET

Particular description of goods.—Edible Vegetable Oils.
Claims use since about Mar. 1, 1919.

Ser. No. 125,277. (CLASS 46. FOODS AND INGREDI-
ENTS OF FOODS.) W. W. Doane, Cincinnati, Ohio.
Filed Nov. 25, 1919.

No claim is made to the word " Sweets " except in the
connection shown.
Particular description of goods.—Candy.
Claims use since Oct. 6, 1919.

Ser. No. 125,387. (CLASS 1. RAW OR PARTLY-PRE-
PARED MATERIALS.) Kullman, Salz & Co., San
Francisco, Calif. Filed Nov. 28, 1919. Under ten-year
proviso.

Particular description of goods.—Hides and Leather.
Claims use since Aug. 20, 1892.

Ser. No. 125,573. (CLASS 1. RAW OR PARTLY-PRE-
PARED MATERIALS.) David J. Lindner, New York,
N. Y. Filed Dec. 4, 1919.

GOLD BRAND

No claim is herein made to the exclusive use of the word
" Brand " apart from the word " Gold."
Particular description of goods.—Chamois-Skins.
Claims use since Nov. 1, 1918.

TRADE-MARK REGISTRATIONS GRANTED

JANUARY 27, 1920.

129,110. LIMBURGER CHEESE. Joseph Acherman & Co., Monroe, Wis.
Filed July 8, 1919. Serial No. 120,342½. PUBLISHED NOVEMBER 11, 1919.

129,111. IRON PLATES, BILLETS, BLOOMS, AND SLABS AND STEEL PLATES, BILLETS, BLOOMS, AND SLABS. Alan Wood Iron & Steel Company, Philadelphia, Pa.
Filed August 8, 1919. Serial No. 121,431. PUBLISHED NOVEMBER 11, 1919.

129,112. HOSIERY. Ambridge Knitting Co., Ambridge, Pa.
Filed July 26, 1919. Serial No. 120,948. PUBLISHED NOVEMBER 4, 1919.

129,113. SEEDS. American Mutual Seed Company, Chicago, Ill.
Filed August 15, 1918. Serial No. 112,723. PUBLISHED NOVEMBER 4, 1919.

129,114. CERTAIN NAMED IRON, STEEL, AND SHEET-METAL PRODUCTS AND FORGINGS. American Steel Export Company, New York, N. Y.
Filed April 30, 1918. Serial No. 110,555. PUBLISHED NOVEMBER 4, 1919.

129,115. CERTAIN NAMED MACHINERY AND TOOLS AND PARTS THEREOF. American Steel Export Company, New York, N. Y.
Filed April 30, 1918. Serial No. 110,559. PUBLISHED NOVEMBER 4, 1919.

129,116. HOSIERY. American Trading Company, New York, N. Y.
Filed August 25, 1919. Serial No. 121,957. PUBLISHED NOVEMBER 4, 1919.

129,117. HOSIERY. American Trading Company, New York, N. Y.
Filed August 25, 1919. Serial No. 121,958. PUBLISHED NOVEMBER 4, 1919.

129,118. MEN'S, WOMEN'S, AND CHILDREN'S HOSIERY MADE OF SILK AND MIXTURE OF SILK AND LISLE. Apex Hosiery Company, Philadelphia, Pa.
Filed March 8, 1919. Serial No. 116,398. PUBLISHED NOVEMBER 4, 1919.

129,119. STEEL OF ALL KINDS. The Apex Steel Co. Ltd., Sheffield, England.
Filed July 9, 1919. Serial No. 120,363. PUBLISHED NOVEMBER 4, 1919.

129,120. STEEL OF ALL KINDS. The Apex Steel Co. Ltd., Sheffield, England.
Filed July 9, 1919. Serial No. 120,365. PUBLISHED NOVEMBER 4, 1919.

129,121. INTERNAL-COMBUSTION ENGINES. Arrol-Johnston Limited, Heathhall, Dumfries, Scotland.
Filed May 23, 1919. Serial No. 118,820. PUBLISHED NOVEMBER 11, 1919.

129,122. CERTAIN NAMED PIPE FITTINGS, VALVES AND NOZZLES AND COCKS AND TUBES. M H— Aterite Company Inc., New York, N. Y.
Filed June 28, 1919. Serial No. 120,025. PUBLISHED NOVEMBER 11, 1919.

129,123. CATTLE FOOD, PARTICULARLY FOR MILK-PRODUCING ANIMALS AND THEIR YOUNG. J. J. Badenoch Co., Chicago, Ill.
Filed January 8, 1919. Serial No. 115,044. PUBLISHED NOVEMBER 11, 1919.

129,124. MOTION - PICTURE - PRODUCING APPARATUS—NAMELY, MOTION-PICTURE CAMERAS AND MOTION-PICTURE-FILM PRINTERS. Bell & Howell Co., Chicago, Ill.
Filed September 16, 1918. Serial No. 113,186. PUBLISHED NOVEMBER 11, 1919.

129,125. OVERALLS AND WORK-SHIRTS. Blubuck Manufacturing Co., Hopkinsville, Ky.
Filed June 10, 1919. Serial No. 119,385. PUBLISHED AUGUST 26, 1919.

129,126. CERTAIN NAMED CLOTHING. Blum Brothers, Chicago, Ill.
Filed June 19, 1919. Serial No. 119,758. PUBLISHED NOVEMBER 4, 1919.

129,127. BUILDERS' HARDWARE—NAMELY, SPRING-HINGES, SPRING-PIVOTS, DOOR-CHECKS, DOOR-SPRINGS, DOOR - STOPS, AND BUTT - HINGES. Emil Bommer, Brooklyn, N. Y.
Filed December 13, 1918. Serial No. 114,611. PUBLISHED NOVEMBER 11, 1919.

129,128. TRACTOR-CABS. Henry V. Browne, Tonkawa, Okla.
Filed June 10, 1919. Serial No. 119,397. PUBLISHED NOVEMBER 11, 1919.

129,129. PROTECTING-TUBES FOR PYROMETERS. The Brown Instrument Company, Philadelphia, Pa.
Filed July 12, 1919. Serial No. 120,473. PUBLISHED NOVEMBER 11, 1919.

129,130. LEATHER SHOES USED FOR WOMEN'S, MISSES', AND CHILDREN'S FOOTWEAR. The C and E Shoe Company, Columbus, Ohio.
Filed June 30, 1919. Serial No. 120,096. PUBLISHED NOVEMBER 4, 1919.

129,131. CANNED VEGETABLES, CANNED FRUITS, DRIED FRUITS, JELLIES, PRESERVES, CATSUP. California Packing Corporation, San Francisco, Calif.
Filed April 24, 1918. Serial No. 110,405. PUBLISHED NOVEMBER 11, 1919.

129,132. NECKTIE FORMER AND HOLDER FOR AIDING IN THE ADJUSTMENT OF THE TIE WHEN WORN. Leon F. Caumont, New York, N. Y.
Filed January 14, 1919. Serial No. 115,169. PUBLISHED OCTOBER 7, 1919.

129,133. BARS, PLATES, AND BOLTS FOR SECURING ANTISKID - CHAINS TO VEHICLE - WHEELS. Challoner Company, Oshkosh, Wis.
Filed June 11, 1919. Serial No. 119,471. PUBLISHED NOVEMBER 4, 1919.

129,134. HOSIERY. Chipman Knitting Mills, Easton, Pa.
Filed July 26, 1919. Serial No. 120,952. PUBLISHED NOVEMBER 4, 1919.

129,135. CASTINGS AND FORGINGS OF CERTAIN NAMED ALLOYS. The Cleveland Brass Manufacturing Co., Cleveland, Ohio.
Filed April 18, 1919. Serial No. 117,590. PUBLISHED NOVEMBER 4, 1919.

129,136. CERTAIN NAMED ENAMELED STEEL WARE. The Cleveland Metal Products Company, Cleveland, Ohio.
Filed April 15, 1918. Serial No. 110,200. PUBLISHED OCTOBER 28, 1919.

129,137. LADIES' BLOUSES. COBDEN CO. INC., New York, N. Y.
Filed May 28, 1919. Serial No. 118,986. PUBLISHED OCTOBER 28, 1919.

129,138. STEEL BARS, RODS, BILLETS, BLOOMS, SHEETS, PLATES, SLABS, STRIPS, BLOCKS, AND FORGINGS. CRUCIBLE STEEL COMPANY OF AMERICA, Pittsburgh, Pa.
Filed September 4, 1919. Serial No. 122,283. PUBLISHED NOVEMBER 11, 1919.

129,139. STEEL BARS, RODS, BILLETS, BLOOMS, SHEETS, PLATES, SLABS, STRIPS, BLOCKS, AND FORGINGS. CRUCIBLE STEEL COMPANY OF AMERICA, Pittsburgh, Pa.
Filed September 4, 1919. Serial No. 122,285. PUBLISHED NOVEMBER 11, 1919.

129,140. STEEL BARS, RODS, BILLETS, BLOOMS, SHEETS, PLATES, SLABS, STRIPS, BLOCKS, AND FORGINGS. CRUCIBLE STEEL COMPANY OF AMERICA, Pittsburgh, Pa.
Filed September 4, 1919. Serial No. 122,286. PUBLISHED NOVEMBER 11, 1919.

129,141. STEEL BARS, RODS, BILLETS, BLOOMS, SHEETS, PLATES, SLABS, STRIPS, BLOCKS, AND FORGINGS. CRUCIBLE STEEL COMPANY OF AMERICA, Pittsburgh, Pa.
Filed September 4, 1919. Serial No. 122,291. PUBLISHED NOVEMBER 11, 1919.

129,142. STEEL BARS, RODS, BILLETS, BLOOMS, SHEETS, PLATES, SLABS, STRIPS, BLOCKS, AND FORGINGS. CRUCIBLE STEEL COMPANY OF AMERICA, Pittsburgh, Pa.
Filed September 4, 1919. Serial No. 122,294. PUBLISHED NOVEMBER 11, 1919.

129,143. FINISHED SAILS AND FOR TRUCK AND AUTO COVERS FORMING PART OF SUCH VEHICLES. JOHN CURTIN CORP., New York, N. Y.
Filed June 13, 1919. Serial No. 119,549. PUBLISHED OCTOBER 7, 1919.

129,144. GRATE-BAR FOR USE WITH FURNACES AND STOVES. CYCLONE GRATE-BAR CO., Buffalo. N. Y.
Filed July 12, 1919. Serial No. 120,476 PUBLISHED OCTOBER 7, 1919.

129,145. BAR-STEEL AND STEEL CASTINGS. DARWIN & MILNER, INC., New York, N. Y.
Filed September 13, 1919. Serial No. 122,631. PUBLISHED NOVEMBER 11, 1919.

129,146. BREAD. EUGENE A. DEXTER, Springfield, Mass.
Filed July 12, 1919. Serial No. 120,478. PUBLISHED NOVEMBER 11, 1919.

129,147. THREADS AND YARNS MADE OF WOOL. DOLLFUS-MIEG & CIE. SOCIETE ANONYME, Mulhouse, Germany.
Filed June 16, 1919. Serial No. 119,636. PUBLISHED OCTOBER 7, 1919.

129,148. ELECTRIC-CURRENT GENERATING AND DISTRIBUTING SYSTEM FOR LIGHTING AND POWER PURPOSES THE DOMESTIC ENGINEERING COMPANY. Dayton, Ohio.
Filed June 4, 1919. Serial No. 119,187. PUBLISHED OCTOBER 14, 1919.

129,149. WHEAT-FLOUR. DONMEYER, GARDNER CO., Peoria, Ill.
Filed August 30, 1919. Serial No. 122,157. PUBLISHED NOVEMBER 11, 1919.

129,150. BAROMETERS. DOURDE ET CIE., Paris, France.
Filed May 29, 1919. Serial No. 119,030. PUBLISHED NOVEMBER 11, 1919.

129,151. DOUGH-MIXERS THE EAST IRON & MACHINE CO., Lima, Ohio.
Filed July 25, 1919. Serial No. 120,911. PUBLISHED NOVEMBER 11, 1919

129,152. INGOTS OF BRONZE; INGOTS OF AN ALLOY OF BRONZE AND COPPER; AND BABBITT METAL. EASTWOOD WIRE MANUFACTURING COMPANY, Belleville, N. J.
Filed July 10, 1919. Serial No. 120,415. PUBLISHED NOVEMBER 4, 1919.

129,153. [WITHDRAWN.]

129,154. CERTAIN NAMED STEEL TOILET PARTITIONS AND DRAINAGE-FITTINGS. FIAT METAL MANUFACTURING COMPANY, Chicago, I.l.
Filed September 16, 1919. Serial No. 122,768. PUBLISHED NOVEMBER 11, 1919.

129,155. MEN'S OVERALLS. FINCH, VAN SLACK & McCONVILLE, St. Paul. Minn.
Filed June 4, 1917. Serial No. 104,246. PUBLISHED JULY 16, 1918.

129,156. CERTAIN NAMED NON ALCOHOLIC BEVERAGES. FRANK J. FISHER, Oconto, Wis.
Filed September 7, 1917. Serial No. 106,112. PUBLISHED OCTOBER 16, 1917.

129,157. CERTAIN NAMED CANNED FRUITS AND VEGETABLES, VANILLA AND LEMON EXTRACTS FOR FOOD-FLAVORING PURPOSES FLAHERTY & URBANOWSKI CO., Peru, Ill.
Filed November 25, 1918. Serial No. 114,339. PUBLISHED NOVEMBER 11, 1919.

129,158. CATERPILLAR TYPE OF PAVING-MIXERS. THE FOOTE COMPANY, Nunda, N. Y.
Filed September 16, 1919. Serial No. 122,762. PUBLISHED NOVEMBER 11, 1919.

129,159. CERTAIN NAMED MEN'S, YOUNG MEN'S, YOUTHS', AND BOYS' OUTER GARMENTS. GONZALEZ PADIN CO., San Juan, Porto Rico.
Filed February 27, 1917. Serial No. 101,737. PUBLISHED NOVEMBER 4, 1919.

129,160. WHEAT FLOUR. GOERZ FLOUR MILLS CO., Newton, Kans.
Filed September 10, 1919. Serial No. 122,587. PUBLISHED NOVEMBER 11, 1919.

129,161. NON-ALCOHOLIC NON-CEREAL MALTLESS BEVERAGE. WILBERT E. GOULD. Denver, Colo.
Filed June 28, 1919. Serial No. 120,053. PUBLISHED NOVEMBER 18, 1919.

129,162. CERTAIN NAMED CLOTHING. HALL, HARTWELL & CO., Troy, N. Y.
Filed July 25, 1919. Serial No. 120,918. PUBLISHED NOVEMBER 4, 1919.

129,163. CEREAL NON-INTOXICATING MALT BEVERAGE. HARVARD COMPANY, Lowell. Mass.
Filed June 12, 1919. Serial No. 119,513. PUBLISHED NOVEMBER 18, 1919.

129,164. LADIES' HATS. JAMES A. HEARN & SON INC., New York, N. Y.
Filed June 13, 1919. Serial No. 119,558. PUBLISHED NOVEMBER 4, 1919.

129,165. COAL. WILLIAM W. HEIDELBAUGH, Lancaster, Pa.
Filed July 2, 1919. Serial No. 120,211. PUBLISHED OCTOBER 7, 1919.

129,166. CONDENSED MILK. HOLLAND FOOD CORPORATION, New York, N. Y.
Filed October 24, 1918. Serial No. 113,873. PUBLISHED NOVEMBER 11, 1919.

129,167. PHOTOGRAPHIC SHUTTERS AND PHOTOGRAPHIC LENSES. ILEX OPTICAL COMPANY, Rochester, N. Y.
Filed August 29, 1919. Serial No. 122,121. PUBLISHED NOVEMBER 11, 1919.

129,168. HOSE-COUPLINGS. INDEPENDENT PNEUMATIC TOOL COMPANY, Chicago, Ill.
Filed September 5, 1919. Serial No. 122,358. PUBLISHED NOVEMBER 11, 1919

129,169. MEN'S, WOMEN'S, AND CHILDREN'S FOOT-
WEAR MADE WHOLLY OR IN PART OF LEATHER
OR TEXTILE MATERIAL. THE IRVING DREW COM-
PANY, Portsmouth, Ohio.
Filed January 23, 1919. Serial No. 115,389. PUB-
LISHED OCTOBER 28, 1919.

129,170. MEN'S, BOYS', AND CHILDREN'S CAPS.
JACKOWAY AND KATZ CAP CO., St. Louis, Mo.
Filed May 19, 1919. Serial No. 118,677. PUBLISHED
OCTOBER 28, 1919.

129,171. METAL ROLL-SCREENS FOR WINDOWS,
DOORS, AND FOOD-SAFES. CHAS. H. JACKSON,
Philadelphia, Pa.
Filed March 24, 1919. Serial No. 116,839. PUBLISHED
NOVEMBER 11, 1919.

129,172. STILL AND EFFERVESCENT TABLE-
WATER. JACOB RIES BOTTLING WORKS, INC.,
Shakopee, Minn.
Filed September 3, 1919. Serial No. 122,267. PUB-
LISHED NOVEMBER 11, 1919.

129,173. WATER-FLOW-CONTROLLING VALVES FOR
CARBID-LAMPS. JUSTRITE MFG. CO., Chicago, Ill.
Filed April 2, 1919. Serial No. 117,118. PUBLISHED
OCTOBER 7, 1919.

129,174. LADIES', MISSES', AND CHILDREN'S HATS.
HENRY KANE, Brooklyn, N. Y.
Filed April 1, 1919. Serial No. 117,131. PUBLISHED
NOVEMBER 4, 1919

129,175. GINGER-ALE. RUSSELL B. KINGMAN, West
Orange, N. J.
Filed September 13, 1919. Serial No. 122,645. PUB-
LISHED NOVEMBER 18, 1919.

129,176. WORK-CLOTHES IN ONE, TWO, AND THREE
PIECE GARMENTS. THE H. D. LEE MERCANTILE
Co., Salina, Kans., and Kansas City, Mo.
Filed May 15, 1919. Serial No. 118,520. PUBLISHED
OCTOBER 28, 1919.

129,177. THREAD AND YARN. H. E. LOCKE & COM-
PANY, INC., Boston, Mass.
Filed August 9, 1919. Serial No. 121,514. PUBLISHED
OCTOBER 7, 1919.

129,178. NURSES' UNIFORMS AND ELEMENTS
THEREOF. HERBERT A. LOEB, New York, N. Y.
Filed June 26, 1919. Serial No. 119,979. PUBLISHED
NOVEMBER 4, 1919.

129,179. COOKIES. LOOSE-WILES BISCUIT COMPANY,
Chicago, Ill.
Filed June 13, 1919. Serial No. 119,560. PUBLISHED
NOVEMBER 11, 1919

129,180. DECORATED HAND-PAINTED GARMENT
HANGERS, SHOE - TREES, WINDOW - WEDGES,
CURTAIN PULLS, TELEPHONE - DOLLS, DOOR
PORTERS. LOWE & LOWE, Washington, D. C.
Filed January 18, 1917. Serial No. 100,716. PUB-
LISHED NOVEMBER 4, 1919.

129,181. CERTAIN NAMED PIPE-FITTINGS, VALVES,
AND NOZZLES. THE LUNKENHEIMER COMPANY,
Cincinnati, Ohio.
Filed October 21, 1918. Serial No. 113,832. PUB-
LISHED OCTOBER 28, 1919.

129,182. TIRE-VENTILATING VALVES. THOMAS
COLDEN MCEWEN, Belleville, N. J., assignor to Mc-
Ewen Tire Ventilator Company, Inc., of New York,
N. Y., a Corporation of New York.
Filed June 11, 1919. Serial No. 119,487. PUBLISHED
NOVEMBER 11, 1919.

129,183. WEIGHING-SCALES. MASON, DAVIS & COM-
PANY, Chicago, Ill.
Filed July 1, 1919. Serial No. 120,174. PUBLISHED
NOVEMBER 4, 1919.

129,184. NON-ALCOHOLIC NON-CEREAL MALTLESS
BEVERAGES SOLD AS SOFT DRINKS. FERD
MESSMER MFG. CO., St. Louis, Mo.
Filed April 26, 1919. Serial No. 117,889. PUBLISHED
NOVEMBER 18, 1919.

129,185. TRACTORS. MIDWEST ENGINE COMPANY, In-
dianapolis, Ind.
Filed June 30, 1919. Serial No. 120,120. PUBLISHED
NOVEMBER 4, 1919.

129,186. AUTO-COATS, RAIN-COATS, DRESS-COATS,
UTILITY-COATS. THE MILLER CLOAK CO., Cleve-
land, Ohio.
Filed March 19, 1918. Serial No. 109,653. PUBLISHED
JULY 29, 1919.

129,187. MALTLESS NON-ALCOHOLIC FRUIT BEV-
ERAGES. MONOPOLE VINEYARDS CORP., New York,
N. Y.
Filed September 9, 1919. Serial No. 122,492. PUB-
LISHED NOVEMBER 18, 1919.

129,188. MALTLESS NON-ALCOHOLIC FRUIT BEV-
ERAGES. MONOPOLE VINEYARDS CORP., New York,
N. Y.
Filed September 9, 1919. Serial No. 122,493. PUB-
LISHED NOVEMBER 18, 1919.

129,189. CERTAIN NAMED MACHINERY AND PARTS
THEREOF. THE MURRAY COMPANY, Dallas, Tex.
Filed July 23, 1919. Serial No. 120,839. PUBLISHED
NOVEMBER 11, 1919.

129,190. AIR-COMPRESSORS, VACUUM HEATING-
PUMPS, BOILER FEED-PUMPS, TURBINES, AND
TURBINE-ENGINES. NASH ENGINEERING COMPANY,
South Norwalk, Conn.
Filed July 19, 1919. Serial No. 120,712. PUBLISHED
NOVEMBER 4, 1919.

129,191. CERTAIN NAMED STEAM-ENGINEERING
APPLIANCES AND FLEXIBLE COUPLINGS FOR
MACHINERY. NASH ENGINEERING CO., South Nor-
walk, Conn.
Filed August 8, 1919 Serial No. 121,405. PUBLISHED
NOVEMBER 4, 1919.

129,192. OIL OF PEPPERMINT USED AS A FLAVOR
FOR SOFT DRINKS. NATIONAL ANILINE & CHEM-
ICAL COMPANY, INCORPORATED, New York, N. Y.
Filed May 20, 1919. Serial No. 118,740. PUBLISHED
NOVEMBER 11, 1919.

129,193. CERTAIN NAMED ENAMELED METAL
WARE. NATIONAL ENAMELING & STAMPING CO.,
New York, N. Y.
Filed February 5, 1918. Serial No. 108,840. PUB-
LISHED NOVEMBER 11, 1919.

129,194. HACKSAWS AND SCREW-DRIVERS. NEW
ENGLAND TOOL CO. INC., Boston, Mass.
Filed May 15, 1919. Serial No. 118,522. PUBLISHED
NOVEMBER 11, 1919.

129,195. BIAS SEAM-TAPE. THE OMO MFG. CO., Mid-
dletown, Conn.
Filed May 29, 1919. Serial No. 119,043. PUBLISHED
OCTOBER 7, 1919.

129,196. BIAS SEAM-TAPE. THE OMO MFG. CO., Mid-
dletown, Conn.
Filed May 29, 1919. Serial No. 119,044. PUBLISHED
OCTOBER 7, 1919.

129,197. MINERAL WATER. ORANGE CITY MINERAL
SPRING COMPANY, Orange City, Fla.
Filed August 12, 1919 Serial No. 121,601. PUBLISHED
NOVEMBER 11, 1919.

129,198. SAFETY - RAZORS AND RAZOR - BLADES.
WILLIAM EDMUND O'REILLY, London, England.
Filed June 25, 1919. Serial No 119,959. PUBLISHED
NOVEMBER 11, 1919.

129,199. WHEAT-FLOUR. OTTAWA MILLING COMPANY,
Kansas City, Mo., and Ottawa, Kans.
Filed September 10, 1919. Serial No. 122,543. PUB
LISHED NOVEMBER 11, 1919

129,200. STARCH-GLUE MATERIAL. PERKINS GLUE
COMPANY, Lansdale, Pa.
Filed July 24, 1919. Serial No. 120,877. PUBLISHED
NOVEMBER 18, 1919.

129,201. MALT BEVERAGE COMMONLY KNOWN AS NEAR BEER. PITTSBURGH BREWING COMPANY, Pittsburgh, Pa. Filed January 6, 1919. Serial No. 115,010. PUBLISHED NOVEMBER 18, 1919.

129,202. FRESH CITRUS FRUITS—VIZ., ORANGES AND GRAPE-FRUIT. POLK COUNTY CITRUS SUB-EXCHANGE, Bartow, Fla. Filed July 23, 1919. Serial No. 120,846. PUBLISHED NOVEMBER 11, 1919.

129,203. OVERALLS AND ONE-PIECE GARMENTS COMPRISING JACKETS AND TROUSERS COMBINED. THE POWERS MANUFACTURING COMPANY, Waterloo, Iowa. Filed July 31, 1919. Serial No. 121,155. PUBLISHED NOVEMBER 4, 1919.

129,204. CANNED FRUITS AND CANNED VEGETABLES. ALFRED PUTNAM & COMPANY, New York, N. Y. Filed June 13, 1919. Serial No. 119,577. PUBLISHED NOVEMBER 11, 1919.

129,205. MEN'S AND BOYS' COATS, VESTS, PANTS, OVERCOATS, AND OVERALLS. PUTNAM OVERALL MFG. CO., Cookeville, Tenn. Filed April 26, 1919. Serial No. 117,899. PUBLISHED NOVEMBER 4, 1919.

129,206. SELF-RISING WHEAT-FLOUR. QUAKER CITY FLOUR MILLS COMPANY, Philadelphia, Pa. Filed July 16, 1919. Serial No. 120,620. PUBLISHED NOVEMBER 11, 1919.

129,207. STOCK FOODS, POULTRY FOODS, AND DOG FOODS. RANDALL-MCLOUGHLIN CO., Seattle, Wash. Filed August 13, 1919. Serial No. 121,640. PUBLISHED NOVEMBER 11, 1919.

129,208. CANDY. REYNOLDS-LINDHEIM CIGAR COMPANY, Nashville, Tenn. Filed August 23, 1919. Serial No. 121,945. PUBLISHED NOVEMBER 11, 1919.

129,209. TURNBUCKLES, METAL NAME-PLATES, AND METAL INSTRUCTION-PLATES. A. V. ROE & CO. LTD, Manchester, England. Filed November 30, 1918. Serial No. 114,433. PUBLISHED NOVEMBER 11, 1919.

129,210. TURNBUCKLES, METAL NAME-PLATES, AND METAL INSTRUCTION-PLATES. A. V. ROE & CO., LTD., Manchester, England. Filed September 3, 1919. Serial No. 122,263. PUBLISHED NOVEMBER 11, 1919.

129,211. CERTAIN NAMED ACCESSORIES FOR AUTOMOBILES, CLOTHESLINE-REELS, AND BLOW-GUNS. ROMORT MANUFACTURING COMPANY, Oakfield, Wis. Filed December 9, 1918. Serial No. 114,571. PUBLISHED NOVEMBER 4, 1919.

129,212. WHEAT-FLOUR. JACOB ROSENSTEIN, New York, N. Y. Filed September 10, 1919. Serial No. 122,549. PUBLISHED NOVEMBER 11, 1919.

129,213. LADIES' HATS. CHAS. ROTH, New York, N. Y. Filed June 17, 1919. Serial No. 119,718. PUBLISHED NOVEMBER 4, 1919.

129,214. LADIES', MEN'S, AND CHILDREN'S ONE AND TWO PIECE UNDERWEAR MADE FROM COTTON YARNING. J. C. ROULETTE AND SONS, Hagerstown, Md. Filed June 5, 1919. Serial No. 119,250. PUBLISHED NOVEMBER 4, 1919.

129,215. BLOOMERS. SAUL GELARIE & COMPANY, Brooklyn and New York, N. Y. Filed August 2, 1919. Serial No. 121,201. PUBLISHED NOVEMBER 4, 1919.

129,216. BALL-BEARINGS AND PARTS THEREOF, ROLLER-BEARINGS AND PARTS THEREOF. JAKOB SCHMID-ROOST, Oerlikon, Switzerland. Filed December 31, 1918. Serial No. 114,930. PUBLISHED NOVEMBER 11, 1919.

129,217. NON-ALCOHOLIC NON-CEREAL MALTLESS BEVERAGE AND A SYRUP FOR MAKING THE SAME. SCHOENHOFEN COMPANY, Chicago, Ill. Filed July 10, 1919. Serial No. 120,437. PUBLISHED NOVEMBER 18, 1919.

129,218. MUFFINS. FREDERICK A. SCHULLER, Boston, Mass. Filed July 29, 1918. Serial No. 112,417. PUBLISHED NOVEMBER 11, 1919.

129,219. CANNED FISH AND CLAMS. SIDNEY CANNING CO., LTD., Sidney, British Columbia, Canada. Filed October 10, 1918. Serial No. 113,679. PUBLISHED NOVEMBER 11, 1919.

129,220. BICYCLES. SIMMONS HARDWARE COMPANY, St. Louis, Mo. Filed March 15, 1919. Serial No. 116,629. PUBLISHED SEPTEMBER 30, 1919.

129,221. OPHTHALMIC-LENS BLANKS AND OPHTHALMIC LENSES. SIMPSON-WALTHER LENS COMPANY INCORPORATED, Rochester, N. Y. Filed July 18, 1919. Serial No. 120,680. PUBLISHED NOVEMBER 11, 1919.

129,222. COTTON-SEED-OIL SHORTENING COMPOUND COMPOSED OF FATTY OLEAGINOUS OR UNCTUOUS FOOD SUBSTANCES. THE SOUTHERN COTTON OIL COMPANY, Jersey City and Bayonne, N. J.; New York, N. Y.; Gretna, La.; Savannah, Ga., and Chicago, Ill. Filed May 24, 1919. Serial No. 118,897. PUBLISHED NOVEMBER 11, 1919.

129,223. IRON TUBES AND STEEL TUBES. SPANG, CHALFANT & CO. INCORPORATED, Pittsburgh, Pa. Filed July 25, 1919. Serial No. 120,936. PUBLISHED NOVEMBER 11, 1919.

129,224. VEHICLE-WHEELS. THE STOPSHOK WHEEL CO., INC., Washington, D. C. Filed February 17, 1919. Serial No. 115,932. PUBLISHED OCTOBER 7, 1919.

129,225. CANNED FRUITS—NAMELY, CANNED PEACHES, CANNED APRICOTS. CHARLES STERN & SONS INC., Los Angeles, Calif. Filed August 18, 1919. Serial No. 121,789. PUBLISHED NOVEMBER 11, 1919.

129,226. ICE-CREAM CONES. SUPERIOR CONE COMPANY, St. Louis, Mo. Filed June 2, 1919. Serial No. 119,138. PUBLISHED NOVEMBER 11, 1919.

129,227. LADIES' HATS. J. TENENBAUM & SONS, New York, N. Y. Filed May 16, 1919. Serial No. 118,574. PUBLISHED OCTOBER 28, 1919.

129,228. CEREAL MALT BEVERAGE CONTAINING LESS THAN ONE-HALF OF ONE PER CENT. ALCOHOL. TERRE HAUTE BREWING COMPANY, Terre Haute, Ind. Filed June 30, 1919. Serial No. 120,135. PUBLISHED NOVEMBER 18, 1919.

129,229. OIL-CLOTH, LINOLEUMS, AND FELT-BASE FLOOR-COVERINGS OF THE NATURE OF LINOLEUM OR OILED CLOTH, CONSISTING OF STAIR AND PASSAGE CLOTHS, MATS, AND RUGS. TEXOLEUM CO. OF N. Y. INC., New York, N. Y. Filed May 21, 1919. Serial No. 118,770. PUBLISHED SEPTEMBER 30, 1919.

129,230. DOUGH-BALLING MACHINES. ROUNDING-UP MACHINES, AND DOUGH-PROOFING MACHINES. THOMSON MACHINE COMPANY, Belleville, N. J. Filed July 8, 1919. Serial No. 120,357. PUBLISHED OCTOBER 28, 1919.

129,231. TIRE-REMOVING TOOLS. TREXLER RIM COMPRESSOR CO., Philadelphia, Pa. Filed June 30, 1919. Serial No. 120,137. PUBLISHED NOVEMBER 11, 1919.

129,232. BABBITT METAL. UNITED AMERICAN METALS CORPORATION, Brooklyn, N. Y. Filed August 28, 1919. Serial No 122,094. PUBLISHED NOVEMBER 11, 1919.

129,233. HOSIERY FOR WOMEN, MEN, AND CHILDREN. UNITED HOSIERY MILLS CORPORATION, East Chattanooga, Tenn. Filed July 19, 1919. Serial No. 120,728. PUBLISHED OCTOBER 28, 1919

129,234. CERTAIN NAMED CHEMICALS. U. S. INDUSTRIAL CHEMICAL CO. INCORPORATED, New York, N. Y. Filed August 31, 1918. Serial No. 112,960. PUBLISHED JANUARY 21, 1919.

129,235. RUBBER MATS AND RUBBER MATTINGS. UNITED STATES RUBBER COMPANY, New Brunswick. N. J., and New York, N. Y. Filed July 5, 1919. Serial No. 120,296. PUBLISHED OCTOBER 7, 1919.

129,236. CYLINDER-REBORING TOOLS AND KITS FOR REPAIRING AND REPLACING BEARINGS. THE UNIVERSAL TOOL CO., Detroit, Mich. Filed May 17, 1919. Serial No. 118,629. PUBLISHED NOVEMBER 11, 1919.

129,237. LUBRICATING-OILS. VACUUM OIL COMPANY, Rochester, N. Y. Filed May 6, 1918. Serial No. 110,723. PUBLISHED APRIL 22, 1919.

129,238. STOCK AND POULTRY FEED. VOIGT MILLING COMPANY, Grand Rapids, Mich. Filed September 8, 1919. Serial No. 122,452 PUBLISHED NOVEMBER 11, 1919.

129,239. SLEEPING - GARMENTS — VIZ., NIGHTDRESSES. WACHUSETT SHIRT CO., Leominster, Mass. Filed July 31, 1919. Serial No. 121,166. PUBLISHED NOVEMBER 4, 1919.

129,240. FEATHERS. WAHLERT & GUNTZLER, St. Louis, Mo. Filed June 4, 1919. Serial No. 119,221. PUBLISHED OCTOBER 7, 1919.

129,241. BOYS' OUTER CLOTHING — NAMELY, COATS, VEST - COATS, TROUSERS, AND OVER COATS. PHIL. WALCOFF & CO., INC., New York, N. Y. Filed June 3, 1919. Serial No. 119,177. PUBLISHED NOVEMBER 11, 1919.

129,242. SNAP-FASTENERS. DAVID WARSHAWSKY, New York, N. Y. Filed June 19, 1919. Serial No. 119,786. PUBLISHED OCTOBER 7, 1919.

129,243. FINE GRITS, PEARL-HOMINY, CREAMMEAL, AND WHITE CORN-FLOUR. WATHEN MILLING COMPANY, Louisville, Ky. Filed September 10, 1919. Serial No. 122,562. PUBLISHED NOVEMBER 11, 1919.

129,244. [WITHDRAWN.]

129,245. TRACTORS. THE WELLMAN - SEAVER - MORGAN COMPANY, Cleveland, Ohio. Filed April 17, 1919. Serial No. 117,585. PUBLISHED NOVEMBER 11, 1919.

129,246. TRACTOR-WHEELS. WILLIAM WHARTON, JR., & CO., INCORPORATED, Philadelphia and Easton, Pa. Filed August 4, 1919. Serial No. 121,269. PUBLISHED NOVEMBER 11, 1919.

129,247. GINGER - BEER. JOSEPH VLADIMIR WILLIS, New York, N. Y. Filed August 6, 1919. Serial No. 121,325. PUBLISHED NOVEMBER 11, 1919.

129,248. SHOE STRINGS AND LACINGS, TAPES, AND GALLOONS. WHAT CHEER BRAID COMPANY, Providence. R. I. Filed June 27, 1919. Serial No. 120,022. PUBLISHED OCTOBER 7, 1919.

129,249. FABRIC SHOES FOR CHILDREN. ROWENA L WHITNEY, Springfield, Mass. Filed June 30, 1919. Serial No. 120,138. PUBLISHED NOVEMBER 4, 1919.

129,250. MACHINES FOR GRINDING, CRUSHING, AND PULVERIZING CERTAIN NAMED MATERIALS. WILLIAMS PATENT CRUSHER AND PULVERIZER COMPANY, St. Louis, Mo. Filed February 15, 1918. Serial No. 109,016. PUBLISHED JULY 16, 1918.

129,251. NECKTIES. WILSON BROTHERS, Chicago. Ill. Filed May 28, 1919. Serial No. 119,010. PUBLISHED OCTOBER 28, 1919

129,252. KID OR LEATHER GLOVES AND KID OR LEATHER MITTENS. RAYMOND K. WILSON, Gloversville, N. Y. Filed May 22, 1919. Serial No. 118,814. PUBLISHED OCTOBER 21, 1919.

129,253. NON-ALCOHOLIC NON-CEREAL MALTLESS BEVERAGE SOLD AS A SOFT DRINK AND SYRUP FOR MAKING THE SAME. W. B. WOOD MFG. CO., St. Louis, Mo. Filed August 11, 1919. Serial No. 121,554. PUBLISHED NOVEMBER 11, 1919.

129,254. NON-ALCOHOLIC NON-CEREAL MALTLESS BEVERAGE SOLD AS A SOFT DRINK AND SYRUP FOR MAKING THE SAME. W. B. WOOD MFG. CO., St. Louis, Mo. Filed August 11, 1919. Serial No. 121,555 PUBLISHED NOVEMBER 11, 1919.

129,255. CARBONATED BEVERAGE MADE FROM AN APPLE BASE, NON - ALCOHOLIC, NON - CEREAL, AND MALTLESS. YONKERS BREWERY, Yonkers, N. Y., assignor to Bittersweet Products Corporation, Yonkers, N Y., a Corporation of New York. Filed May 21, 1919. Serial No. 118,772. PUBLISHED NOVEMBER 11, 1919.

129,256. HACKSAWS. YOUNG, CORBEY & DOLAN, INC., New York, N. Y. Filed May 6, 1919. Serial No. 118,216. PUBLISHED NOVEMBER 11, 1919.

TRADE-MARK REGISTRATIONS RENEWED.

17,641. HYDRAULIC HOSE, (RUBBER-LINED, SEAMLESS, ONE-PLY, AND COTTON FABRIC.) EUREKA FIRE HOSE COMPANY, New York, N. Y.; Eureka Fire Hose Manufacturing Company. successor. Registered March 11, 1890. Renewed March 11, 1920.

LABELS

REGISTERED JANUARY 27, 1920.

21,646.—*Title:* " CONTINENTAL PEANUT BAG." (For Paper Bags.) CONTINENTAL PAPER BAG CO., New York, N. Y. Filed March 21, 1919.

21,647.—*Title:* " HAIRFOREVER." (For a Hair-Tonic.) MANGAN & CO., New York, N. Y. Filed August 26, 1919.

21,648.—*Title:* " NEUPRO." (For Ginger-Ale) JOSEPH S. ROTH, Carroll township, Washington county, Pa. Filed May 24, 1919.

21,649.—*Title:* " SEA SIDE." (For Canned Sardines.) STANDARD EXPORT-IMPORT CO. LTD., Stavanger, Norway. Filed July 24, 1919

PRINTS

REGISTERED JANUARY 27, 1920.

5,194.—*Title:* " WEAR B. V. D. ON YOUR VACATION." (For Athletic Underwear.) THE B. V. D. COMPANY, New York, N. Y. Filed June 6, 1919.

5,195.—*Title:* " SAMSON MOTOR FUEL." (For Motor-Fuel.) GREAT SOUTHERN PRODUCING & REFINING CO., Indianapolis, Ind. Filed September 7, 1918.

5,196.—*Title:* "ASTOUNDING GROWTH OF THE WORLD WIDE RIT INDUSTRY." (For Rit Dye-Soap.) SUNBEAM CHEMICAL COMPANY, Chicago, Ill. Filed June 9, 1919.

5,197.—*Title:* " MAKE YOUR OWN COLORS SUCCESS-FULLY." (For Rit Dye-Soap.) SUNBEAM CHEMICAL COMPANY, Chicago, Ill. Filed June 13, 1919.

5,198.—*Title:* " TRY HER BEAUTY SECRET." (For Rit Dye-Soap.) SUNBEAM CHEMICAL COMPANY, Chicago, Ill. Filed July 11, 1919.

DECISIONS

OF THE

COMMISSIONER OF PATENTS

AND OF

UNITED STATES COURTS IN PATENT CASES.

DECISIONS OF THE U. S. COURTS.

U. S. Circuit Court of Appeals—Third Circuit.

PARAMOUNT HOSIERY FORM DRYING CO. *v.* MOORHEAD KNITTING CO.

Decided October 13, 1919.

[260 Fed. Rep., 841.]

PROCESS OF DRYING AND SHAPING HOSIERY ARTICLES—FUNCTION OF APPARATUS.

The claim of the Collis patent, No. 1,204,945, reading as follows: "A method of treating hosiery articles, con sisting in heating, from within, and to a predetermined fabric-drying temperature, a metallic form having its sides relatively narrow in cross-section and converging into substantially reduced, crease-producing edges ; then superposing upon said form a hosiery article and subjecting the same to the action of heat imparted internally thereto by the form for producing a substantially flattened and creased article," *Held* void as covering nothing more than the function of an apparatus which was the subject of a separate patent which had been held invalid because of prior invention and use. " The process in this case is as clearly the whole value, the sole purpose of the apparatus," as in the case of *Busch v. Jones* (184 U. S., 598) " the process was the whole value, the sole purpose of the press."

APPEAL from the District Court of the United States for the Middle District of Pennsylvania ; Charles B. Witmer, judge.

Suit in equity by the Paramount Hosiery Form Drying Company against the Moorhead Knitting Company. Decree for defendant, (251 Fed. 897,) and complainant appeals. Affirmed.

Mr. Robert F. Rogers, Mr. Charles H. Howson, and *Mr. Edmund H. Parry* for the appellant.

Mr. Henry N. Paul and *Mr. Joseph C. Fraley* for the appellee.

Before BUFFINGTON, WOOLLEY. and HAIGHT. Circuit Judges.

HAIGHT, *Cir. J.*:

In the court below the appellant sued the appellee for an alleged infringement of two patents, numbered 1,114,966 and 1,204,945, granted to it as assignee of one George Collis, on October 27, 1914, as November 14, 1916, respectively. The last patent was issued on a division of the application for the first. The earlier patent will hereafter, for convenience, be referred to as " the apparatus patent," and the later one as " the process patent." Generally speaking, one covers an apparatus for simultaneously drying and finishing hosiery articles, in the sense of stretching, shaping, smoothing, and creasing, and the other a method for accomplishing the same purpose.

In the court below, the claims in suit of both patents were held to be invalid, and a decree dismissing the bill was entered. The appellant has acquiesced in the decree so far as its effect was to invalidate the apparatus patent, and appeals from only that part which dismissed the bill as to the process patent. Infringement is not seriously denied. Some question as to an estoppel was presented in the court below, and decided adversely to the appellant, as was likewise decided adversely to the appellee a counter-claim interposed by it. The appellant has abandoned its claim that the appellee is estopped to deny the validity of the process patent, and the appellee has not appealed from the decree dismissing its counter-claim. The only question, therefore, to be considered on this appeal, is the validity of the process patent.

The original application for apparatus patent was filed on June 27, 1911. After a rather stormy career in the Patent Office, a patent containing forty-five claims was issued on October 27, 1914. Three days before its issue a division of the original application was filed, which eventuated on November 14, 1916. in the process patent, containing five claims, the last three of which are in the suit. The learned judge of the court below accepted the month of September, 1910, as the date of the Collis invention. We shall do likewise. Passing for the moment the exact state of the art at the time Collis made his alleged invention, we will refer briefly to what Collis assumed that he had invented.

It had been for many years the custom to remove as much as possible of the moisture, with which dyed or bleached hosiery and other similar textile articles become saturated in the dyeing or bleaching process, by means of a centrifugal machine known as a " whizzer," and to finish the drying by drawing the articles over wooden forms or boards and then depositing them in dry-boxes. The latter were compartments supplied with interior heating-coils and fans to insure circulation of the air. After the articles had been thus thoroughly dried, they were removed from the boards, and finally shaped, smoothed, and given the crease necessary to make them marketable, by placing them in a press and there subjecting them to pressure for various periods of time, depending upon the character of press used. The apparatus described in the Collis patents was designed to, and in practice actually did, accomplish the ultimate drying and finishing in one operation.

Without referring to the supplemental housing or casing described in the patents (which is of no materiality in this case), the Collis apparatus consists of hollow metal forms, similar in shape to the wooden forms before mentioned, and internally heated by steam or other means. Over these the wet hosiery article is drawn. The forms are narrow relatively to their width, and have their opposite narrow edges substantially sharp. The forms being heated internally, the hosiery mounted on them is dried, and the sharp edges produce the before-mentioned finish. The utility of the apparatus of the first patent, and the advance which its use in the art of finishing hosiery made, were fully recognized by the court below, and is not, as indeed it could not very well be, disputed. The court below found, however (and, as before stated, the appellant accepts such finding), that Collis was not the first to conceive and practically develop the apparatus covered by his patent, and therefore the apparatus patent was held to be invalid. Indeed, as appears from the opinion of the learned judge of the court below, appellant abandoned during the trial any claim to the validity of that patent.

The patented prior art, as Collis admitted during the prosecution of his application for the apparatus patent, exhibits several examples of hollow metal forms designed to dry hosiery and textile articles by the application of internal heat. The evidence also abundantly demonstrates that, long prior to the earliest date claimed for the Collis invention, internally-heated metal forms with sharp edges, to produce the necessary creases, had been designed and used, although not patented, by several concerns for the finishing of silk gloves and silk hosiery. The proof of the prior uses of an apparatus similar to, if not identical in all respects with, that covered by the patent, in a suit instituted by the present appellant against one Walter Snyder and the Walter Snyder Company, was so overwhelming as to cause the appellant to voluntarily abandon that suit, although the forms manufactured and sold by the alleged infringers unquestionably infringed the Collis apparatus patent.

The process patent, in the language of the specification, describes the method sought to be covered by it as follows:

A method of treating hosiery articles, consisting in heating, from within, and to a predetermined fabric-drying temperature, a metallic form having its sides relatively narrow in cross-section and converging into substantially reduced, crease-producing edges; then superposing upon said form a hosiery article and subjecting the same to the action of heat imparted internally thereto by the form for producing a substantially flattened and creased article.

Notwithstanding the invalidity of the apparatus patent because of anticipation, it is sought to avoid a like result as to the process patent on the theory that, although it was old in the finishing of silk gloves and silk hosiery to smooth and crease them on internally-heated metallic forms with sharp

edges, and although the prior art exhibited internally-heated metal forms for the drying of hosiery, the method or process of simultaneously drying (in the sense of extracting the excess moisture acquired during the dyeing or bleaching process and not removed by the "whizzer" and ordinary evaporation) and finishing (in the sense of stretching, smoothing, and creasing) hosiery through the use of internally-heated metallic forms, with crease-producing edges, had not been conceived by any one before Collis.

It will be noted that the court below based its judgment that the process patent was invalid, both upon the ground that it covered nothing more than the function of the patented apparatus, and that the before-mentioned prior use of the forms covered by the apparatus patent anticipated the method or process of the process patent. If it be true, as appellant contends, that these sharp-edge, crease-producing forms of the prior art were not designed or used for drying hosiery in the sense before mentioned, although capable of performing that function, but only for finishing and creasing silk gloves and hosiery from which all moisture had been extracted, and which it was necessary to again dampen before the finishing, and that the process patent was not, therefore, anticipated by their prior use, (*Carnegie Steel Co.* v. *Cambria Iron Co.*, 185 U. S., 403, 424 ; 22 Sup. Ct., 698 ; 46 L. Ed., 968,) it is apparent that the invention of that patent, if any there is, resides simply in taking that part of the prior art which exhibits apparatus for drying wet hosiery and coupling it with that part of the prior art which used the same forms, different only in that their edges were sharp, to produce the necessary crease or finish on articles which had already been dried.

We shall not pause to consider whether this constituted patentable invention, or whether the use of the prior-art crease-producing forms to finish textile articles which had already been dried, but which proper practice required should again be moistened, in order that they could be properly finished, was the practising of the process or method of the Collis process patent, or whether the process patent can relate back to the date of the filing of the original application for the apparatus patent, and thus avoid anticipation due to the use of Ermentrout's forms, because we think that the decree of the court below must be affirmed on the other ground, namely, that the process patent covers merely the function of the apparatus described and covered by the apparatus patent. In this connection, it may be well to briefly review some of the circumstances surrounding the acquisition of the Collis application by the appellant, and some of the events that transpired thereafter.

It appears that one Ermentrout, of Reading, Pa., having seen a circular put out by a concern known as the Curtin-Hebert-Anthony Company, which had before the earliest date claimed for the Collis invention manufactured and sold internally-heated, sharp-edged, crease-producing metal forms, to certain

tain concerns engaged in manufacturing silk gloves and silk hosiery, began in the autumn of 1911 the manufacture of internally-heated hosiery-forms, substantially identical with those shown in the two Collis patents. They were designed to be used for the same purpose as the forms of the patent. Some of them found their way into the factory of the Paramount Hosiery Company, and worked so well that the officers of that concern determined to purchase Ermentrout's business and a limited patent, relating to a specific type of coupling between the form and a steam-supply pipe, which he had secured. A company was subsequently formed for the purpose of carrying on the business which had been begun by Ermentrout. In the course of selling some of such forms, the original Collis application, which was then pending in the Patent Office, was discovered. The appellant thereupon, on December 24, 1913, in order to protect itself, purchased the same for a comparatively small sum, and thereafter prosecuted the original application and the subsequent division thereof. It was not until the following June, although the application had then been pending for three years, that the division was suggested. In the meanwhile, the prior act, so far as it was accessible to the Patent Office, had been quite thoroughly reviewed, and the slight field of invention left open to Collis made manifest. In the early or middle part of 1914, Walter S. Snyder, who was engaged in manufacturing laundry machinery in Philadelphia, began the manufacture of drying-forms for laundry purposes, and subsequently extended his business to the manufacturing of these forms for hosiery manufacturers.

In 1916, the present appellant began suit against Snyder and the Walter Snyder Company, alleging that the forms which were thus being manufactured by them infringed the apparatus patent in suit in this case. That suit was voluntarily discontinued under the circumstances before mentioned. Most of the forms manufactured by the appellant are distributed to those who use them, under license agreements which provide for the payment of certain royalties, based on the amount of hosiery articles dried on the forms. The appellee had acquired, under such an agreement, a number of the appellant's forms. Subsequently it acquired some of the forms manufactured by the Walter Snyder Company, and used both in its business. After the appellant abandoned its suit against the Snyder Company, it began this suit, basing the alleged infringement upon the appellee's use of the forms which it had purchased from the Snyder Company. It is thus apparent that the appellant is attempting in this suit by means of the process patent to secure a monopoly in the use of an apparatus which admittedly could not be the subject-matter of a valid patent at the earliest date at which it is claimed that Collis invented it, because the only way shown in the patent, or otherwise, for practising the method covered by the process patent, is the use of the particular apparatus described and covered by the apparatus patent.

ent. The process is, in reality, nothing but the use of the apparatus. That is manifest by reference to the before-quoted portion of the specification of the process patent, as well as the following extract therefrom, viz:

From the foregoing, it will be seen that the procedure followed, in treating hosiery articles under my improved method, is first to effect a heating (from within and to a predetermined drying temperature) of a hollow form, preferably constructed of metal, and having its sides narrow in cross-section and converging into substantially reduced-edge portions; then manually stretching a hosiery article longitudinally thereon and retaining the same on the form for the fabric-drying period, during which the fabric of the article is simultaneously dried, shaped, and creased at two oppositely disposed portions, and then removing or stripping the article from the form.

Moreover, the apparatus patent specifies, and in fact claims, the function of the apparatus as the simultaneous drying, creasing, and finishing of the textile article mounted on the exterior thereof. It is impossible for us to perceive how this process can be considered in any other light than the mere function of the apparatus. The inevitable result of any other conclusion would be to give validity to a patented process which consists solely in the use of an apparatus which cannot be the subject-matter of a valid patent.

It would serve no useful purpose, and would unduly burden this opinion, to review the authorities which have differentiated between the mere function of a machine or apparatus and a patentable process, which could be practised by the use of the apparatus or machine, and to attempt to distinguish those cases from this. It is sufficient, we think, to refer to *Busch* v. *Jones*, (184 U. S., 598,) and particularly to the remarks of Mr. Justice McKenna on page 607, (22 Sup. Ct., 511; 46 L. Ed., 707.) In the case at bar, the dependence is the process upon the apparatus, and not the apparatus upon the process, just as the process in that case was dependent upon the press. It is equally true that the process in this case is as clearly the whole value, the sole purpose of the apparatus, as in that case "the process was the whole value, the sole purpose of the press." We are accordingly of the opinion that the claims in suit of the process patent cover nothing but the mere function of a machine or apparatus, and hence are invalid.

The decree appealed from is therefore affirmed, with costs.

Interference Notices.

DEPARTMENT OF THE INTERIOR,
UNITED STATES PATENT OFFICE,
Washington, D. C., January 5, 1920.

Nicholas R. Bartz, his assigns or legal representatives, take notice:
An interference having been declared by this Office between the application of Griffith Alverson Co., care of Campholatum Co., Mason City, Iowa, for registration of a trade-mark and trade-mark registered October 8, 1912, No. 88,611, to Nicholas B. Bartz, 84 Adams street, Chicago, Ill., and a notice of such declaration sent by registered mail to said Nicholas B. Bartz at the said address having been returned by the post-office undeliverable, notice is hereby given that unless said Nicholas B. Bartz, his assigns or legal representatives, shall enter an appearance therein within thirty days from the first publication of this order the interference will be proceeded with as in case of default.
This notice will be published in the OFFICIAL GAZETTE for three consecutive weeks.
M. H. COULSTON,
Assistant Commissioner.

DEPARTMENT OF THE INTERIOR,
UNITED STATES PATENT OFFICE,
Washington, D. C., January 5, 1920.

Moki Herb Remedy Company, its assigns or legal representatives, take notice:

An interference having been declared by this Office between the application of Edwin R. Mohler, No. 900 Penn street, Reading, Pa., for registration of a trade-mark and trade-mark registered November 1, 1892, No. 21,922, to Moki Herb Remedy Company, Tempe, Ariz., and a notice of such declaration sent by registered mail to said Moki Herb Remedy Company at the said address having been returned by the post-office undeliverable, notice is hereby given that unless said Moki Herb Remedy Company, its assigns or legal representatives, shall enter an appearance therein within thirty days from the first publication of this order the interference will be proceeded with as in case of default.

This notice will be published in the OFFICIAL GAZETTE for three consecutive weeks.

M. H. COULSTON,
Assistant Commissioner.

DEPARTMENT OF THE INTERIOR,
UNITED STATES PATENT OFFICE,
Washington, D. C., January 9, 1920.

Murphy Wall Bed Co. of California, its assigns or legal representatives, take notice:

An interference having been declared by this Office between the application of Murphy Wall Bed Company, of 422 Crocker Building, San Francisco, Calif., for registration of a trade-mark and trade-mark registered December 23, 1913, No. 94,655, to Murphy Wall Bed Co. of California, of 809–10–11 Longacre Building, New York, N. Y., and a notice of such declaration sent by registered mail to said Murphy Wall Bed Co. of California at the said address having been returned by the post-office undeliverable, notice is hereby given that unless said Murphy Wall Bed Co. of California, its assigns or legal representatives, shall enter an appearance therein within thirty days from the first publication of this order the interference will be proceeded with as in case of default.

This notice will be published in the OFFICIAL GAZETTE for three consecutive weeks.

R. F. WHITEHEAD,
First Assistant Commissioner.

DEPARTMENT OF THE INTERIOR,
UNITED STATES PATENT OFFICE,
Washington, D. C., January 9, 1920.

George T. Robie, his assigns or legal representatives, take notice:

An interference having been declared by this Office between the application of Boston Belting Corporation, of 80 Elmwood street, Boston, Mass., for registration of a trade-mark and trade-mark registered March 21, 1899, No. 32,623, to George T. Robie, of 88 and 90 Lake street, Chi-

cago, Ill., and a notice of such declaration sent by registered mail to said George T. Robie at the said address having been returned by the post-office undeliverable, notice is hereby given that unless said George T. Robie, his assigns or legal representatives, shall enter an appearance therein within thirty days from the first publication of this order the interference will be proceeded with as in case of default.

This notice will be published in the OFFICIAL GAZETTE for three consecutive weeks.

R. F. WHITEHEAD,
First Assistant Commissioner.

DEPARTMENT OF THE INTERIOR,
UNITED STATES PATENT OFFICE,
Washington, D. C., January 13, 1920.

Dodge & Starkel, their assigns or legal representatives, take notice:

An interference having been declared by this Office between the application of the Globe Canning Co., Eastport and North Lubec, Me., for registration of a trade-mark and trade-mark registered March 10, 1908, No. 68,135, to Dodge & Starkel, 42 River street, Chicago, Ill., and a notice of such declaration sent by registered mail to said Dodge & Starkel at the said address having been returned by the post-office undeliverable, notice is hereby given that unless said Dodge & Starkel, their assigns or legal representatives, shall enter an appearance therein within thirty days from the first publication of this order the interference will be proceeded with as in case of default.

This notice will be published in the OFFICIAL GAZETTE for three consecutive weeks.

R. F. WHITEHEAD,
First Assistant Commissioner.

DEPARTMENT OF THE INTERIOR,
UNITED STATES PATENT OFFICE,
Washington, D. C., January 17, 1920.

Eggoline Manufacturing Co., their assigns or legal representatives, take notice:

An interference having been declared by this Office between the application of Mountain States Manufacturing Co., Provo, Utah, for registration of a trade-mark and trade-mark registered January 2, 1894, No. 23,974, to Eggoline Manufacturing Co., of 126 Bleecker street, New York, N. Y., and a notice of such declaration sent by registered mail to said Eggoline Manufacturing Co. at the said address having been returned by the post-office undeliverable, notice is hereby given that unless said Eggoline Manufacturing Co., their assigns or legal representatives, shall enter an appearance therein within thirty days from the first publication of this order the interference will be proceeded with as in case of default.

This notice will be published in the OFFICIAL GAZETTE for three consecutive weeks.

R. F. WHITEHEAD,
First Assistant Commissioner.

CHANGES IN CLASSIFICATION.

(ORDER No. 2,543.)

DEPARTMENT OF THE INTERIOR,
UNITED STATES PATENT OFFICE,
Washington, D. C., December 31, 1919.

The following changes in the classification of inventions are hereby directed, to take effect immediately:

In class 2, Apparel, (Division XXIV,) establish subclass—

Body-garments—
Corset-stiffeners—
198.   Formed wire.

The patents contained in this subclass have been taken for the most part from class 267, Spring Devices, subclass 33.5, Bending, Leaf, Structure, Formed wire, hereinafter abolished.

In class 24, Buckles, Buttons, Clasps, Etc., (Division XXXV,) abolish the following subclass, with its definition:

268.   Resilient connections.

The patents formerly contained in this subclass have

267.—SPRING DEVICES.
1.   Miscellaneous.
2.   Vehicle—
3.   Railway—
4.   Coil,
5.   Perambulator,
6.   Bolster—
7.   Leaf,
8.   Springs and retarders—
9.   Friction—
10.   Flexible strap,
11.   Parallel depression—
12.   Positive connections—
13.   Duplex—
14.   Single point,
15.   Lever—
16.   Leaf and coil—
17.   Leaf - end - connecting lever,
18.   Leaf and fluid-pressure,
19.   Leaf,
20.   Coil,
21.   Deformable,
22.   Compound—
23.   Leaf, coil, and fluid-pressure,
24.   Leaf, fluid-pressure and liquid,
25.   Leaf and torsion—
26.   Torsion-coil—
27.   Leaf-end connecting,

been placed for the most part in class 267, Spring Devices, hereinafter established.

In class 54, Harness, (Division XI,) abolish the following subclass, with its definition:

86.   Elastic connections.

The patents formerly contained in this subclass have been placed for the most part in class 267, Spring Devices, hereinafter established.

In class 241, Garment-Supporters, (Division XXIV,) abolish subclass—

Waist-line body-garment—
Shoulder suspension —
Connections—
21.   Resilient.

The patents formerly contained in this subclass have been placed for the most part in class 267, Spring Devices, hereinafter established.

In class 267, Spring Devices, (Division XI,) abolish the existing subclasses and establish in lieu thereof the following subclasses and definitions:

267.—SPRING DEVICES—Continued.
Vehicle—
Compound—
28.   Leaf and coil—
29.   Leaf-end connecting.
30.   Leaf and deformable,
31.   Leaf and fluid - pressure—
32.   Leaf-end connecting,
33.   Coil and deformable,
34.   Coil and fluid-pressure,
35.   Deformable and fluid-pressure,
36.   Leaf—
37.   Covering and lubricating,
38.   Twin, axle interposed.
39.   Side-bar,
40.   Longitudinal,
41.   Cantaliver,
42.   Elliptic,
43.   Elliptic and leaf,
44.   Semi-elliptic,
45.   Semi-elliptic and leaf—
46.   End-to-end connected
47.   Structure—
48.   Auxiliary tensioning elements,
49.   Antifriction,
50.   Lubrication.

267.—SPRING DEVICES—Continued.
Vehicle—
Structure—
51.   Broken-spring supports,
52.   Intermediate supports,
53.   Clips,
54.   End connections—
55.   Elliptic,
56.   Sliding,
57.   Torsion—
58.   Coil—
59.   Volute,
60.   Coil—
61.   Structure—
62.   Volute,
63.   Deformable,
64.   Fluid-pressure and liquid,
65.   Fluid-pressure,
66.   Braces—
67.   Yielding,
68.   Sliding.
69.   Elastic extension devices—
70.   Compression-spring—
71.   Single—
72.   Drawbars inclosed.
73.   Tension-spring—
74.   Single.
75.   Reciprocating-bed-cushioning devices.

J. T. NEWTON, *Commissioner.*

Changes in Classification.

(ORDER No. 2,544.)

DEPARTMENT OF THE INTERIOR,
UNITED STATES PATENT OFFICE,
Washington, D. C., December 31, 1919.

The following changes in the classification of inventions are hereby directed, to take effect immediately:

In class 16, Builders' Hardware, (Division XX,) abolish subclass—

37.   Till-alarms.

The patents formerly contained in this subclass have been placed for the most part in class 116, Signals and Indicators, subclass 76, Alarms, Burglar, Till, hereinafter established.

In class 40, Card, Picture, and Sign Exhibiting, (Division XXXV,) establish the following subclass and definition:

Checks, labels, and tags—
Holders—
19.5.   Check boards or racks.

19.5.   CHECKS, LABELS, AND TAGS, HOLDERS, CHECK BOARDS OR RACKS. Boards or racks provided with means—such as pins, hooks, clips, chutes, etc.—to detachably hold groups of checks, labels, tags, or cards.

The patents contained in this subclass have been taken for the most part from class 116, Signals, subclasses 31, Indicators; 45, Indicators, Barbers' turns, and 48, Indicators, Peg, hereinafter abolished.

In class 83, Mills, (Division XXV,) abolish subclass—

Grinding-mills—
16.   Grist-alarms.

The patents formerly contained in this subclass have been placed for the most part in class 116, Signals and Indicators, subclass 71, Alarms, Grist-mill, hereinafter established, and class 177, Electric Signaling, subclass 311, Alarms.

In class 116, Signals, (Division XXV,) change the title of the class to read *Class 116.—Signals and Indicators*, abolish the existing subclasses, and establish in lieu thereof the following subclasses and definitions:

116.—SIGNALS AND INDICATORS.
1. Miscellaneous.
2. Combined functions—
3. Horns with lamps,
4. Alarms with indicators—
5. Burglar or fire.
6. Burglar-alarms—
7. Light-producing,
8. Locks—
9. Door - knob controlled—
10. Combined knob and bell,
11. Detonating,
12. Door-securing—
13. Braces,
14. Chain or link,
15. Detonating,
16. Sash-fastening—
17. Detonating.
18. Code-signaling—
19. Ship's course,
20. Heliographic.
21. Ships' telegraphs.
22. Periodic—
23. Detonating,
24. Horns and whistles,
25. Bells.
26. Nautical—
27. Submarine.
28. Vehicle—
29. Station-indicators,
30. Car and train markers,
31. Steering - wheel - position indicators.
32. Collision-released identification-tags.
33. Theft-preventing,
34. Tire inflation or deflation,
35. Motion and direction—
36. Combined with vehicle control,
37. Speed-controlled—
38. Governor-actuated,
39. Pneumatically operated,
40. Lazy-tong operated,
41. Fan type,
42. Window-exhibited sign or shutter—
43. Rotatable,
44. Sliding,
45. Movable cover or screen,
46. Rotatable—
47. Pointer—
48. Illuminated,
49. Illuminated casing,
50. Sliding,
51. Pivoted—
52. Laterally - swinging arm—
53. Multiple arms,
54. Illuminated.
55. Pneumatic train-pipe,
56. Vehicle-energy actuated—
57. Speed limit,
58. Pneumatic,
59. Diaphragm-horns,

116.—SIGNALS AND INDICATORS—
Continued.
Vehicle—
Vehicle-energy actuated—
60. Bells—
61. Friction-wheel,
62. Bicycle-pedal.
63. Street traffic.
64. Elevator.
65. Pneumatic.
66. Learners' telegraph instruments.
67. Alarms—
68. Elevator or hoist,
69. Rain,
70. Fluid-pressure variation.
71. Grist-mill,
72. Poison-container,
73. Operation-counting.
74. Speed limit,
75. Burglar—
76. Till,
77. Portable—
78. Drop detonating,
79. Knob-attached,
80. Key or keyhole,
81. Cord-controlled,
82. Floor-supported,
83. Detonating,
84. Pickpocket,
85. Closure-operated—
86. Door and window—
87. Detonating—
88. Reciprocating hammer—
89. Rotary release.
90. Gear and friction wheel,
91. Clockwork-bell—
92. Door-knob,
93. Automatic wind,
94. Cable control,
95. Single-stroke bell—
96. Door-knob,
97. Door-knob,
98. Tread-operated,
99. Portable receptacle,
100. Closure-operated,
101. Thermal—
102. Expansion control—
103. Fluid,
104. Ignition control—
105. Explosive,
106. Fusible control,
107. Buoy—
108. Whistling,
109. Liquid-level—
110. Float,
111. Clockwork-bell,
112. Fluid-flow,
113. Shoal water.
114. Indicators—
115. Shaft rotation,
116. Speed limit,
117. Fluid-flow,

116.—SIGNALS AND INDICATORS—
Continued.
Indicators—
118. Liquid-level,
119. Book,
120. Game,
121. Medicine-dose,
122. Elevator position,
123. Tube - guided signal element,
124. Position—
125. Valve,
126. Ship's rudder,
127. Brake-piston,
128. Grouped annunciators,
129. Rotary,
130. Hand-set—
131. Combined with changeable exhibitor,
132. Semaphore type,
133. Rotary,
134. Pivoted,
135. Sliding,
136. Peg.
137. Horns and whistles—
138. Motor exhaust or suction,
139. Manually - actuated air-compressor,
140. Variable tone,
141. Chime,
142. Diaphragm-horns—
143. Rotary striker—
144. Toothed wheel—
145. Parallel diaphragm,
146. Ball-contacts.
147. Sirens.
148. Bells—
149. Sound modification,
150. Swinging,
151. Pneumatic actuation,
152. Gong type—
153. Door-knob contained,
154. Rotary,
155. Pivoted striker—
156. Multiple,
157. Multiple stroke—
158. Rotary striker—
159. Lever-operated,
160. Plunger-operated,
161. Escapement—
162. Clockwork type,
163. Double,
164. Spring-impact,
165. Pull cord or rod,
166. Bicycle-clamp,
167. Fixed, with pivoted striker,
168. Spiral-spring type,
169. Tube or rod type,
170. Animal and sleigh type,
171. Hand,
172. Bell pulls, cranks, and push-buttons.
173. Flags and flagstaffs—
174. Non-fouling,
175. Metallic flags.

J. T. NEWTON, *Commissioner.*

Changes in Classification.

(ORDER NO. 2,545.)

DEPARTMENT OF THE INTERIOR,
UNITED STATES PATENT OFFICE,
Washington, D. C., December 31, 1919.

The following changes are hereby directed in the Manuel of Classification, revised to January 1, 1916:

On page 10, in the table of "Examiners in Charge of Examining Divisions," cancel the names of Disney, I. P.; Lovett, G. A., and Milburn, J. W.; change Glascock, E. S., to Division 46, Room 332, and add the names of Cutting, H. O., Division 42, Room 114; Mead, T. L., Jr., (acting) Trade-Marks and Designs, Room 163; Pierce, P. P., Division 12, Room 322; Ragan, E. T., Division 31, Room 172, and Shaffer, C. H., (acting,) Division 44, Room 253.

J. T. NEWTON,
Commissioner.

ALPHABETICAL LIST OF PATENTEES

TO WHOM

PATENTS WERE ISSUED ON THE 27TH DAY OF JANUARY, 1920.

NOTE.—Arranged in accordance with the first significant character or word of the name. (In accordance with city and telephone directory practice.)

Aaron, Solomon E., Boston, Mass. Pliers. No. 1,329,155; Jan. 27; v. 270; p. 554.

Aeolian Company, The. (See Callender, Romaine, assignor.)

Allegretti, Benedetto E., Chicago, Ill. Candy-making machine. No. 1,329,282; Jan. 27; v. 270; p. 578.

American Bank Note Company. (See Marquardt, Frank C., assignor.)

American Steel Foundries. (See Peycke, Armand H., assignor.)

American Tap Bush Co. (See Rice, Frank E., assignor.)

American Warp Drawing Machine Company. (See Lea, Charles, assignor.)

Allesina, John, Portland, Oreg. Umbrella. No. 1,329,219; Jan. 27; v. 270; p. 566.

Andersen, Peter C., Medford, Wis. Crushing - machine. No. 1,328,806; Jan. 27; v. 270; p. 487.

Anderson, Arvid R., assignor to The Automatic Reclosing Circuit Breaker Company, Columbus, Ohio. Attachment for electric controllers. No. 1,328,804; Jan. 27; v. 270; p. 487.

Anderson, Frank, Denver, Colo., and A. Wild, Loveland, Colo. Dumping-body for automobile-trucks, wagons, freight-cars, and other vehicles. No. 1,328,805; Jan. 27; v. 270; p. 487.

Anderson, Gideon, assignor to W. West, New York, N. Y. Tilting bed. No. 1,328,802; Jan. 27; v. 270; p. 487.

Anderson, Harry T., Butler, Pa., assignor to Harry Vissering & Company, Chicago, Ill. Manufacture of railway draft-gear yokes. No. 1,328,975; Jan. 27; v. 270; p. 521.

Anderson, Harry T., Crafton. Pa., assignor to Harry Vissering & Company, Chicago, Ill. Draft-gear yoke. No. 1,329,318; Jan. 27; v. 270; p. 584.

Anderson, Lee S., Detroit, Mich. Device for turning sheet-music. No. 1,328,976; Jan. 27; v. 270; p. 521.

Andrew, William P., Mount Pleasant, Pa. Nut-lock. No. 1,328,939; Jan. 27; v. 270; p. 514.

Araan Company, The. (See Roberts, Fred T., assignor.)

Arnold, Harold D., Maplewood, N. J., assignor to Western Electric Company, Incorporated, New York, N. Y. Thermionic amplifier. No. 1,329,283; Jan. 27; v. 270; p. 578.

Ashby, Bert A., El Paso, Tex. Spark - arrester. No. 1,328,868; Jan. 27; v. 270; p. 500.

Ashby, Bert, El Paso, Tex. Packet-holder. No. 1,328,869; Jan. 27; v. 270; p. 500.

Austin, Herbert, Bromsgrove, England. Mounting an aeroplane-propeller and carrying a gun which fires axially through the propeller. No. 1,328,866; Jan. 27; v. 270; p. 555.

Automatic Electric Company. (See Campbell, Wilson L., assignor.)

Automatic Reclosing Circuit Breaker Company, The. (See Anderson, Arvid R., assignor.)

Automatic Straight Air Brake Company. (See Neal, Spencer G., assignor.)

Avery Company. (See Bartholomew, John B., assignor.)

Babcock & Wilcox Company, The. (See Jacobus, David S., assignor.)

Badger Meter Manufacturing Company. (See Krueger, Emil M., assignor.)

Badoian, Vartan K., Lawrence. Mass. Shuttle-guard for looms. No. 1,329,157; Jan. 27; v. 270; p. 555.

Bagley, Charles H. F., Stockton-upon-Tees, England. Making basic steel in open - hearth steel - furnaces. No. 1,328,803; Jan. 27; v. 270; p. 487.

Baker, Arthur F., Sedro Woolley, assignor to The Perfecto Gear Differential Co., Seattle, Wash. Driving mechanism for motor-cars. No. 1,329,319; Jan. 27; v. 270; p. 584.

Bakke, Bjarne, assignor to Norsk Hydro-Elektrisk Kvaelstofaktieselskab, Christiania, Norway. Treatment of liquids to effect crystallization therefrom while the liquid is kept in motion. No. 1,329,158; Jan. 27; v. 270; p. 555.

Baldon, J. L., et al. (See Shreibman, Abram, assignor.)

Ballin, Hugo, New York, N. Y. Bird-house. No. 1,329,104; Jan. 27; v. 270; p. 545.

Balzer, Fritz, assignor to Troy Laundry Machinery Company, Ltd., Chicago, Ill. Shirt-bosom-ironing machine. No. 1,328,807; Jan. 27; v. 270; p. 488.

Barnes, Peter, et al. (See de Esparya, Timoteo R., assignor.)

Bartholomew, John B., assignor to Avery Company, Peoria, Ill. Steering mechanism for tractors. No. 1,328,808; Jan. 27; v. 270; p. 488.

Bartz, Adolph J., Crandall. Tex. Stalk - chopper. No. 1,329,220; Jan. 27; v. 270; p. 566.

Basford, Harold R., San Francisco, Calif. Foldable bed. No. 1,328,977; Jan. 27; v. 270; p. 521.

Bateman, Ernest, Madison, Wis. Bleaching wood. No. 1,329,284; Jan. 27; v. 270; p. 578.

Bates, Albert J., Chicago, Ill., assignor to Bates Expanded Steel Truss Co., Wilmington, Del. Discharging mechanism. No. 1,328,809; Jan. 27; v. 270; p. 488.

Bates Expanded Steel Truss Co. (See Bates, Albert J., assignor.)

Baum, William F. (See Greco, Vito B., assignor.)

Beach, Milo D., Litchfield, Conn. Wheel-indicator. No. 1,328,978; Jan. 27; v. 270; p. 521.

Beaman, Albert W., Pittsboro, Ind. Pig-brooder. No. 1,328,810; Jan. 27; v. 270; p. 488.

Beatty, Harry W., Oilfields, Calif. Casing-cutter. No. 1,328,940; Jan. 27; v. 270; p. 514.

Beccari, Giuseppe, Florence, Italy. Apparatus for working garbage and refuse of towns. No. 1,329,105; Jan. 27; v. 270; p. 545.

Becker, Benjamin, St. Louis, Mo. Door - opener. No. 1,328,979; Jan. 27; v. 270; p. 522.

Benjamin, Edward O., Newark, N. J. Closure and tap for tanks, &c. No. 1,328,980; Jan. 27; v. 270; p. 522.

Benjamin, Edward O., Newark, N. J. Electrolytic apparatus. No. 1,328,981; Jan. 27; v. 270; p. 522.

Berger, Joseph, Utica, N. Y., assignor to Union Special Machine Company, Chicago, Ill. Sewing - machine. No. 1,329,221; Jan. 27; v. 270; p. 567.

Bernier, Henry N., Iroquois Falls, Ontario, assignor of one-half to J. De Froy, Timmins, Canada. Lamp-burner. No. 1,329,222; Jan. 27; v. 270; p. 567.

Betts, Arthur L. (See Davis and Betts.)

Bevier, Henry R., assignor to Johnson Automatic Sealer Co., Ltd., Battle Creek, Mich. Wrapping-machine. No. 1,329,069; Jan. 27; v. 270; p. 538.

Binder, Richard L., Philadelphia, Pa. Chain. No. 1,329,034; Jan. 27; v. 270; p. 532.

Birkigt, Marc, Bois-Colombes, France. Mechanism for synchronizing machine-gun fire. No. 1,328,811; Jan. 27; v. 270; p. 488.

Bissinger, John B., Jr., Lancaster, Pa. Means for carrying out systems for savings-accounts. No. 1,329,106; Jan. 27; v. 270; p. 545.

Blackmer Rotary Pump Co. (See Oldham, John H., assignor.)

Blaisdell, Sidney S. (See Cook and Blaisdell.)

Blake, John R., Rolling Prairie, Ind. Shock-absorber. No. 1,328,812; Jan. 27; v. 270; p. 489.

Blakemore, James R., assignor to G. B. Sawyer, Murfreesboro, Tenn. Egg-tester. No. 1,329,223; Jan. 27; v. 270; p. 567.

Blanchard, Herbert C., assignor to The A. I. Root Company, Medina, Ohio. Honeycomb-foundation machine. No. 1,328,813; Jan. 27; v. 270; p. 489.

Bobst, Charles A., Brooklyn, assignor to National Binding Machine Company, New York, N. Y. Label-detaching device. No. 1,328,814; Jan. 27; v. 270; p. 489.

Bolton, James, Council Bluffs, Iowa. Road-maintainer. No. 1,328,910; Jan. 27; v. 270; p. 509.

Bombardie, Charles H., South Bend, Ind., assignor to Wirebounds Patents Company, Kittery, Me. Box. No. 1,329,332; Jan. 27; v. 270; p. 586.

Bombardie, Charles H., South Bend, Ind., assignor to Wirebounds Patents Company, Kittery, Me. Box. No. 1,329,333; Jan. 27; v. 270; p. 586.

Bosch, Robert, Aktiengesellschaft. (See Kratz, Franz, assignor.)

Boulton, William W. (See McClure and Boulton.)

Bowen, Charles, assignor of one-third to F. Gaskins and one-third to A. G. Niebergall, Fort Wayne, Ind. Bumper for automobiles. No. 1,329,334; Jan. 27; v. 270; p. 586.

Bowness, George A. (See Jardine, Dickie, and Bowness.)

Brady, Francis M. (See Richard and Brady.)

Brazil, Harry D., Montgomery, Ala. Fluid - fuel burner. No. 1,329,224; Jan. 27; v. 270; p. 567.

Brewer, Griffith, London, England. Adjustable dial for pressure-gages and like dial instruments. No. 1,328,941; Jan. 27; v. 270; p. 515.

Dawson, Arthur T., and G. T. Buckham, assignors to Vickers Limited, Westminster. London, England. Ordnance-sighting apparatus. No. 1,328,914; Jan. 27; v. 270; p. 509.

Dean, John S., Winkinsburg. Pa., assignor to Westinghouse Electric and Manufacturing Company. Commutator-cylinder. No. 1,329,267; Jan. 27; v. 270; p. 575.

De Esparza, Timoteo R., assignor of two-fifths to P. Barnes and one-tenth to F. Defoy, Calexico, Calif. Marine propulsion. No. 1,329,228; Jan. 27; v. 270; p. 508.

Defoy, Fred. et al. (See de Esparza, Timoteo R., assignor.)

De Froy, Jules. (See Bernier, Henry N., assignor.)

Dehuff, Walter F., Glen Rock, Pa. Dough-mixer No. 1,329,164; Jan. 27; v. 270; p. 556.

De Lavaud, Dimitri S., New York, N. Y. Rotary casting. No. 1,329,295; Jan. 27; v. 270; p. 580.

De Lavaud, Dimitri S., New York, N. Y. Rotary casting. No. 1,329,296; Jan. 27; v. 270; p. 580.

Derrom, Donald L., Chicago, Ill. Lathe. No. 1,329,042; Jan. 27; v. 270; p. 533.

De Sibour, Jules II., Washington, D. C. Hatband. No. 1,328,823; Jan. 27; v. 270; p. 491.

De Waele, René E., Paris, France. Submarine toy. No. 1,328,867; Jan. 27; v. 270; p. 500.

Diamond Match Company, The (See Paridon, Michael, assignor.)

Dickelmann, Lawrence II., and J. Kuchler, Milwaukee, Wis. Pipe-clip and forming same. No. 1,329,268; Jan. 27; v. 270; p. 576.

Dickie, James. (See Jardine, Dickie, and Bowness.)

Diemer, Charles P., Sapulpa, Okla. Indicating device for vehicles. No. 1,329,043; Jan. 27; v. 270; p. 533.

Diver, Daniel, Calgary, Alberta, Canada. Machine for the separation of gold, silver, and platinum from sand. No. 1,329,113; Jan. 27; v. 270; p. 547.

Dixon, Amos F., Newark, N. J., assignor to Western Electric Company, Incorporated, New York, N. Y. Selecting system. No. 1,328,986; Jan. 27; v. 270; p. 523.

Donaldson, Harry R. (See Donaldson, Robert M. and H. R.)

Donaldson, Robert M. and H. R., Claysville, Pa. Carbureter-adjuster. No. 1,328,946; Jan. 27; v. 270; p. 515.

Donovan, Michael L., Omaha, Nebr. Lubricator. No. 1,329,229; Jan. 27; v. 270; p. 568.

Dorrell, Harry, Peoria, Ill. Violin peg. No. 1,328,824; Jan. 27; v. 270; p. 491.

Dover, George W., Cranston, R. I. Lathe tool. No. 1,328,947; Jan. 27; v. 270; p. 516.

Dover, George W., Cranston, R. I. Setting for jewelry. No. 1,328,948; Jan. 27; v. 270; p. 516.

Dover, George W., Cranston, R. I. Setting for jewelry. No. 1,328,949; Jan. 27; v. 270; p. 516.

Dover, George W., Incorporated. (See Peterson, Erick B., assignor.)

Draper Corporation. (See Stimpson, Edward S., assignor.)

Drew, John W., assignor to Moon Brothers Manufacturing Company, St Louis, Mo. Pump-packing. No. 1,329,165; Jan. 27; v. 270; p. 556.

Drysdale, Charles V., Dumbartonshire, Scotland. Alternating-current relay. No. 1,328,825; Jan. 27; v. 270; p. 491.

Dudley, Howard M., Philadelphia, Pa. Fiber-treating machine. No. 1,328,987; Jan. 27; v. 270; p. 523.

Duncombe, Tyrrell II., Romeo, Mich. Change-speed-power-transmitting mechanism. No. 1,329,297; Jan. 27; v. 270; p. 580.

Dürsteler, Wilhelm, Switzerland. Apparatus for treating hanks of textile fabrics with liquids. No. 1,329,166; Jan. 27; v. 270; p. 556.

Eaton, George M., Pittsburgh, Pa., assignor to Westinghouse Electric & Manufacturing Company. Locomotive-transmission system. No. 1,329,269; Jan. 27; v. 270; p. 576.

Ebeling, Robert W., Oakland, Calif., assignor to R. W. Ebeling Company, Incorporated. Rheostat. No. 1,329,167; Jan. 27; v. 270; p. 557.

Ebeling, Robert W., Oakland, Calif., assignor to R. W. Ebeling Company, Incorporated. Multiple - circuit - resistance control. No. 1,329,168; Jan. 27; v. 270; p. 557.

Ebeling, R. W. Company. (See Ebeling, Robert W., assignor.)

Eberle, John A., St. Louis, Mo. Baby-walker No 1,328,826; Jan. 27; v. 270; p. 491.

Eckert, Carl J., and P J. Richman, Chicago, Ill. Waterproof combination cigarette, match, and coin case. No. 1,328,988; Jan. 27; v. 270; p. 523.

Eckert, Joseph, Dayton, Ohio. Bottle-cap remover. No. 1,328,827; Jan. 27; v. 270; p. 492.

Eclipse Stove Company. (See Robinson, Harry A., assignor.)

Edward Valve & Manufacturing Co., The. (See Oleson, Olaf E., assignor.)

Eggleston, William II., Grandville, assignor of one-half to D. Ritzema, Grand Rapids, Mich. Extension angle-square No. 1,329,337; Jan. 27; v. 270; p. 587.

Ehrhart, Raymond M., Edgewood Park, Pa., assignor to Westinghouse Electric & Manufacturing Co. Condenser. No. 1,328,828; Jan. 27; v. 270; p. 492.

Eisenhauer, Charles P., assignor to The Burnett-Larsh Manufacturing Company, Dayton, Ohio. Water-pumping system. No. 1,328,989; Jan. 27; v. 270; p. 523.

Elevator Supplies Company. (See Parsons, Levi L., assignor.)

Elevator Supply & Repair Company. (See Parsons, Levi L., assignor.)

Elias, Perfecto M., and F. F. Llera, Tucson, Ariz. Soldering and melting apparatus. No. 1,329,270; Jan. 27; v. 270; p. 576.

Ellis, Arthur L., et al. (See Golata and Roberts, assignors.)

Ellis, Arthur T., assignor of one-half to H. A. Hands, London, England. Valve of internal-combustion engines. No. 1,329,321; Jan. 27; v. 270; p. 584.

Ellis, Carleton, Montclair, N. J. Making powdered metals and reduced metallic compounds. No. 1,329,322; Jan. 27; v. 270; p. 584.

Ellis, Carleton, Montclair, N. J. Making catalytic material No 1,329,323; Jan. 27; v. 270; p. 585.

Elliot, William D., Big Timber, Mont. Paper-bag holder No. 1,328,950; Jan. 27; v. 270; p. 516.

Ely, Frank D., Tientsin, China. Firearm control. No. 1,329,230; Jan. 27; v. 270; p. 568.

Engle, Isaiah G., Philadelphia, Pa. Valve. No. 1,329,231; Jan. 27; v. 270; p. 569.

Enochs, C. D., trustee. (See Thomasson, Hiram S., assignor.)

Enslin, Herbert E., Malden, Mass., assignor to United Shoe Machinery Corporation, Paterson, N. J. Lacing-machine. No. 1,329,298; Jan. 27; v. 270; p. 580.

Erler, William C., Terre Haute, Ind. Bituminous composition. No. 1,329,232; Jan. 27; v. 270; p. 569.

Escholz, Otto II., Wilkinsburg. Pa., assignor to Westinghouse Electric & Manufacturing Company. Arc-welding system. No. 1,329,233; Jan. 27; v. 270; p. 569.

Estberg, William T., assignor to Penn Pressed Metal Co., Camden, N. J. Automobile-lock. No. 1,329,114; Jan. 27; v. 270; p. 547.

Evans, Edgar A., Victoria, British Columbia, Canada. Spark arrester and quencher. No. 1,329,115; Jan. 27; v 270; p. 547.

Evans, Franklin J., West Hazleton, Pa. Positioning-button. No. 1,329,234; Jan. 27; v. 270; p. 569.

Exley, William II. (See Leitner, Henry, assignor.)

Eyles, Anton G., Cedar Rapids, Iowa, assignor of one-half to J. H. Lee, Oak Park, Ill. Tempo-control device. No. 1,328,870; Jan. 27; v. 270; p. 501.

Fairbanks, James J., Gardner, Mass., assignor to The U. S. Toy & Novelties Mfg. Co., Templeton, Mass. Toy Ferris wheel. No. 1.328,829; Jan. 27; v. 270; p. 492.

Fairbanks, Morse & Co. (See Thompson, Harry E., assignor.)

Fairmont Gas Engine & Railway Motor Car Co. (See Kasper, Walter F., assignor.)

Farnam, Elvin, Los Angeles, Calif. Scarecrow. No. 1,329,044; Jan. 27; v. 270; p. 534.

Fawcett, Charles II., assignor to Interstate Ever-license Company, Independence, Iowa. License-holder for motor-vehicles. No. 1,328,915; Jan. 27; v. 270; p. 510.

Fehan, John, Buffalo, N. Y. Reserve device for fuel-tanks. No. 1,329,074; Jan. 27; v. 270; p. 579.

Felten & Guilleaume Fabrik Elektrischer Kabel, Stahl- und Kupferwerke Aktiengesellschaft. (See Knaur, Richard, assignor.)

Ferguson, Milford B., and E. Haas, Brooklyn, N. Y. Wrapping mechanism for candy. No. 1,329,236; Jan. 27; v. 270; p. 569.

Fig-nsbn, William L., assignor of one-half to O Heymann, Philadelphia, Pa. Bowling-alley. No. 1,329,235; Jan. 27; v. 270; p. 569.

Flanagan, John, Davenport, Iowa. Lifting-jack. No. 1,329,116; Jan. 27; v. 270; p. 547.

Flannery Bolt Company. (See Mennie, Robert S., assignor.)

Fleming, James C., Denver, Colo. Key system for clarinets. No. 1,328,831; Jan. 27; v. 270; p. 492.

Formonzini, Gervaso, Lanzada, Italy. Sighting means for firearms, optical apparatus, and the like. No. 1,329,075; Jan. 27; v. 270; p. 539.

Forster, Andrew, and J. H. Brown, Cowes, assignors to J. Samuel White & Company, Limited, East Cowes, Isle of Wight. England. Air-valve. No. 1,328,951; Jan. 27; v. 270; p. 516.

Foster, George W., assignor of one-half to G. Mayer, New York, N. Y. Flush-valve. No. 1,329,169; Jan. 27; v. 270; p. 557.

Foster, George D., assignor to Union Land & Power Company, North Yakima, Wash. Power-windmill. No. 1,329,299; Jan. 27; v. 270; p. 581.

Fourneaux, Emile A., Manchester, England. Production of black upon vegetable textile fibers, silk fibers, or mixtures of same. No. 1,329,117; Jan. 27; v. 270; p. 548.

Fow, Raymond S. C., assignor of seventy-nine one-hundredths to R T Frush and twenty-one one-hundredths to W. Thompson, Philadelphia, Pa. Slicing-machine. No. 1,328,916; Jan. 27; v. 270; p. 510.

Franke, Johan F., Santa Ana, Calif. Toy. No. 1,329,045; Jan. 27; v. 270; p. 534.

Frey, George E., Steubenville, assignor of one-half to R. E. Snider, Mingo Junction, Ohio. Rail-chair. No. 1,328,917; Jan. 27; v. 270; p. 510.

Frick, Gilbert V. H. (See Henry and Fricke.)

Friedman, Mitchell J., Washington, D. C. Calendar. No. 1,328,830; Jan. 27; v. 270; p. 492.

Frisbie, Howard I., Anaconda, Mont. Electric precipitator. No. 1,329,237; Jan. 27; v. 270; p. 569.

Frohner, Edward H., Youngstown, Ohio, assignor to Standard Oilcloth Co., New York, N. Y. Method of and apparatus for treating oil and obtaining by-products therefrom. No. 1,329,076; Jan. 27; v. 270; p. 539.

Fronczak, Antoni, Wilkes-Barre, Pa. Harrow. No. 1,329,118; Jan. 27; v. 270; p. 548.

Frush, Roland T., et al. (See Fow, Raymond S. C., assignor.)

Fugina, Arthur R., Louisville, Ky. Renitent railway-rail support. No. 1,329,077; Jan. 27; v. 270; p. 540.

Fuld, Katherine B., Baltimore, Md. Toy. No. 1,329,338; Jan. 27; v. 270; p. 587.

Fulda, Edward, New York, N. Y. Metal door construction. No. 1,328,918; Jan. 27; v. 270; p. 510.

Fulda, Edward, New York, N. Y. Uniting vertical plates by electric welding. No. 1,328,919; Jan. 27; v. 270; p. 510.

Funahashi, Jo, Kobe, Japan. Manufacture of floor-covering. No. 1,329,170; Jan. 27; p. 270; p. 557.

Furstenberg, Paul W., New York, N. Y. Advertising device or the like. No. 1,329,078; Jan. 27; v. 270; p. 540.

Fynn, Valère A., assignor to Wagner Electric Manufacturing Company, St. Louis, Mo. Ignition-switch. No. 1,328,990; Jan. 27; v. 270; p. 523.

Gammeter, John R., Akron, Ohio, assignor to The B. F. Goodrich Company, New York, N. Y. Bumper. No. 1,329,339; Jan. 27; v. 270; p. 587.

Gardner, Florinda, Salt Lake City, Utah. Speed-indicator. No. 1,329,046; Jan. 27; v. 270; p. 534.

Garfield, Elva R., New York, N. Y. Method and apparatus for teaching manuscript-form. No. 1,828,952; Jan. 27; v. 270; p. 516.

Garrison, Orlando, Dayton, Ohio. Grinding-machine. No. 1,328,953; Jan. 27; v. 270; p. 517.

Garry, Jerome G. (See Garry, Robert S. and J. G.)

Garry, Robert S. and J. G., Jenks, Okla. Strainer for pumps. No. 1,329,171; Jan. 27; v. 270; p. 557.

Gaskins, Fred, et al. (See Bowen, Charles, assignor.)

General Fireproofing Company, The. (See Herbert, Arthur W., assignor.)

General Motors Company. (See Sweet, Ernest E., assignor.)

Genett, Levi E. (See Miles, Edward L., assignor.)

George, Maude S., St. Louis, Mo. Baby-pants. No. 1,329,119; Jan. 27; v. 270; p. 548.

Gesell, Frank A., Los Angeles, Calif. Controlling means for saving systems combined with insurance protection. No. 1,329,120; Jan. 27; v. 270; p. 548.

Gilson, John P. (See Gilson, Michael and J. P.) (Reissue.)

Gilson, Michael and J. P., Fredonia, Wis. Concrete-mixer. (Reissue.) No. 14,795; Jan. 27; v. 270; p. 590.

Gluck, Marcus. New York, N. Y. Spoon. No. 1,329,172; Jan. 27; v. 270; p. 558.

Golata, Andrew J., and L. L. Roberts, assignors of one-tenth to W. W. Carswell and one-tenth to A. L. Ellis, Detroit, Mich. Piston. No. 1,329,238; Jan. 27; v. 270; p. 570.

Goldthwaite, Helen A., Saco, Me. Conducting-cord holder. No. 1,329 173; Jan. 27; v. 270; p. 558.

Goodrich, B. F., Company, The. (See Gammeter, John R., assignor.)

Goulet, Delphine. (See Goulet, Omer C., assignor.)

Goulet, Omer C., assignor to D. Goulet, Fall River, Mass. Lever-chocking device. No. 1,329,079; Jan. 27; v. 270; p. 540.

Graham, Joshua S., Detroit, Mich. Hatpin-guard. No. 1,328,954; Jan. 27; v. 270; p. 517.

Granger, William S., Duluth. Minn. Gas-mixer. No. 1,329,324; Jan. 27; v. 270; p. 585.

Graybill, Bird M., Chicago, Ill. Apparatus for indicating fuel consumption. No. 1,328,920; Jan. 27; v. 270; p. 511.

Greco, Vito B., assignor of one-half to W. F. Baum, Waterloo, Iowa. Heel for boots and shoes. No. 1,328,991; Jan. 27; v. 270; p. 524.

Green, Walter R., Chicago, Ill. Extra-tire carrier. No. 1,329,174; Jan. 27; v. 270; p. 558.

Griffin Wheel Company. (See Vial, Frederick K., assignor.)

Griscom-Russell Company. (See Jones, Russell C., assignor.)

Gunchick, Frank, Blanchard, Idaho. Combined card-container and table. No. 1,329,080; Jan. 27; v. 270; p. 540.

Haas, Edward. (See Ferguson and Haas.)

Hachmann, Frederick, St. Louis, assignor of one-half to D. M. Hutchinson, Ferguson, Mo. Hose-mender. No. 1,329,121; Jan. 27; v. 270; p. 548.

Hackleman, William H., Appleton, Wis. Gear-cutting attachment. No. 1,329,175; Jan. 27; v. 270; p. 558.

Hadjisky, Joseph N. (See Heldeman and Hadjisky.)

Hafner, Edward P., and J. T. Roberts, St. Louis, Mo. Tire-peeling machine. No. 1,329,239; Jan. 27; v. 270; p. 570.

Hahn, Louis C., Cincinnati, Ohio. Drafting device. No. 1,328,871; Jan. 27; v. 270; p. 501.

Hamilton, Clifford C. (See Hutchinson and Hamilton.)

Hamlyn, George A. (See Weizmann and Hamlyn.)

Hammerstrom, Arthur, Deerfield, N. H. Sled-brake. No. 1,329,047; Jan. 27; v. 270; p. 534.

Hands, Harry A. (See Ellis, Arthur T., assignor.)

Hanrath, Theodore W., Chicago, Ill. Baby-carrier. No. 1,328,832; Jan. 27; v. 270; p. 493.

Harley, Melvin G., South Bend, Ind. Headlight. No. 1,328,992; Jan. 27; v. 270; p. 524.

Harpman, Albert J., Owatonna, Minn. Propeller-drive for aeroplanes. No. 1,329,081; Jan. 27; v. 270; p. 540.

Harris, James W., Turbeville, S. C. Corn-cleaner. No. 1,328,872; Jan. 27; v. 270; p. 501.

Hartog, S. D., Manufacturing Company. (See Hartog, Stephen D., assignor.)

Hartog, Stephen D., assignor to S. D. Hartog Manufacturing Company, St. Louis, Mo. Manufacturing piston-rings. No. 1,329,271; Jan. 27; v. 270; p. 576.

Hasburg, John W., Chicago, Ill. Staining glass. No. 1,328,883; Jan. 27; v. 270; p. 493.

Haugen, Henry, Stoughton, Wis. Lawn - edge trimmer. No. 1,329,176; Jan. 27; v. 270; p. 558.

Haugh, Frank A., Winfield, Kans. Underreamer. No. 1,328,955; Jan. 27; v. 270; p. 517.

Hayden, Don H., Cleveland, Ohio. Switch - box. No. 1,328,993; Jan. 27; v. 270; p. 524.

Hayes, Robert D., assignor to Index Visible, Incorporated, New Haven, Conn. Index or file. No. 1,328,956; Jan. 27; v. 270; p. 517.

Hays, Charles F., Cottagegrove, Tenn. Grass-rope reel. No. 1,329,240; Jan. 27; v. 270; p. 570.

Heany, John A., Jersey City, N. J., assignor, by mesne assignments, to Industrial Research Corporation. Dynamo-electric starting, lighting, and ignition mechanism for automobiles. No. 1,328,873; Jan. 27; v. 270; p. 501.

Heath, Wilfrid P. (See Kirkpatrick, Swordling, and Heath.)

Heldeman, Fred J., and J. N. Hadjisky, Detroit, Mich., assignors to Kelvinator Corporation, Wilmington, Del. Means and method of regulating automatic mechanical refrigerators. No. 1,329,350; Jan. 27; v. 270; p. 589.

Heldeman, Fred J., and J. N. Hadjisky, Detroit, Mich., assignors to Kelvinator Corporation, Wilmington, Del. Pressure-operated-regulating apparatus. No. 1,329,351; Jan. 27; v. 270; p. 589.

Hellmund, Rudolf E., Swissvale, and B. S. Moore, Wilkinsburg, Pa., assignors to Westinghouse Electric and Manufacturing Company. Shaft-bearing. No. 1,329,241; Jan. 27; v. 270; p. 570.

Hellmund, Rudolf E., Swissvale, Pa., assignor to Westinghouse Electric and Manufacturing Company. Coil-supporting device for dynamo - electric machines. No. 1,329,242; Jan. 27; v. 270; p. 570.

Hellmund, Rudolf E., Pittsburgh, Pa., assignor to Westinghouse Electric and Manufacturing Company. System of control. No. 1,329,243; Jan. 27; v. 270; p. 571.

Heltzel, John N., Warren, Ohio. Concrete-form. No. 1,329,177; Jan. 27; v. 270; p. 559.

Henault, Lewis N., Albany, N. Y. Deck-sash support. No. 1,328,874; Jan. 27; v. 270; p. 501.

Henry, Albert, and G. V. B. Fricke, Hoboken, N. J. Shoe-protector. No. 1,328,957; Jan. 27; v. 270; p. 518.

Herbert, Arthur W., Youngstown, Ohio, assignor to The General Fireproofing Company. Safety-tread structure. No. 1,328,875; Jan. 27; v. 270; p. 502.

Hermann, Oscar. (See Figenshu, William L., assignor.)

Hill, Alfred N., Lund, Sweden. Measuring instrument. No. 1,328,876; Jan. 27; v. 270; p. 502.

Hilley, William P., Des Moines, Iowa. Operating device for window-sashes. No. 1,329,178; Jan. 27; v. 270; p. 559.

Hillman, Herbert H., assignor to Challenge Refrigerator Company, Grand Haven, Mich. Refrigerator. No. 1,329,340; Jan. 27; v. 270; p. 588.

Hilty, Frederick, Waukegan, assignor to L. R. Wilder, Chicago, Ill. Centrifugal valve-casting machine. No. 1,329,179; Jan. 27; v. 270; p. 559.

H-K Toy & Novelty Co., The. (See McDaniel, Walter O., assignor.)

Hobbs, William I. (See Hudgins, Iverson D., assignor.)

Hodge, William B. (See Cramer and Hodge.)

Hodgman, Willis K., Taunton, Mass. Apparatus for operating alarms or other devices. No. 1,328,994; Jan. 27; v. 270; p. 524.

Hoe, Robert, New York, N. Y. Sheet-feeding mechanism for printing-presses. No. 1,328,877; Jan. 27; v. 270; p. 502.

Hoge, Joseph F. D., New York, N. Y. Thermostat. No. 1,329,122; Jan. 27; v. 270; p. 548.

Holland, Walter E., and J. M. Skinner, assignors to Philadelphia Storage Battery Company, Philadelphia, Pa. Storage-battery separator. No. 1,329,180; Jan. 27; v. 270; p. 559.

Holland, Walter E., Philadelphia, and L. J. Pearson, Wyncote, assignors to Philadelphia Storage Battery Company, Philadelphia, Pa. Storage battery and preparing same. No. 1,329,181; Jan. 27; v. 270; p. 560.

Holt Auto Devices Company. (See Holt, Edward E., assignor.)

Holt, Edward E., assignor to Holt Auto Devices Company, Chicago, Ill. Valve-cap. No. 1,329,182; Jan. 27; v. 270; p. 560.

Holt Manufacturing Company, The. (See Norelius, Emil F., assignor.)

Holt Manufacturing Company, The. (See Turnbull, William, assignor.)

Holt Manufacturing Company, The. (See Wickersham, Elmer E., assignor.)

Hoover, Howard E., Chicago, Ill., assignor to Hoover Suction Sweeper Company, New Berlin, Ohio. Cleaner. No. 1,329,048 ; Jan. 27 ; v. 270 ; p. 534.

Hoover Suction Sweeper Company. (See Hoover, Howard E., assignor.)

Hopkins, Alfred, Boston, Mass. Curtain-stretcher. No. 1,328,995 ; Jan. 27 ; v. 270 ; p. 524.

Horschmann, Mary E., Springfield, Mo. Belt or girdle support. No. 1,328,958 ; Jan. 27 ; v. 270 ; p. 518.

Houskeeper, William G., Philadelphia, Pa., assignor to Western Electric Company, Incorporated, New York, N. Y. Transmitter. No. 1,328,996 ; Jan. 27 ; v. 270 ; p. 525.

Howe, Dale E., assignor of one-half to J. M. Newton, Sioux Falls, S. D. Toy-furniture set. No. 1,328,921 ; Jan. 27 ; v. 270 ; p. 511.

Howell, Robert R., Minneapolis, Minn. Device for grinding-mills. No. 1,328,834 ; Jan. 27 ; v. 270 ; p. 493.

Höyberg, Hans M., Frederiksberg, near Copenhagen, Denmark. Ascertaining the quantity of fat in milk and cream. No. 1,329,183 ; Jan. 27 ; v. 270 ; p. 560.

Hudgins, Iverson D., Kirkwood, assignor of one-third to W. I. Hobbs, Gainesville, Ga. Water-motor. No. 1,329,244 ; Jan. 27 ; v. 270 ; p. 571.

Hughes, Robert R., Jr., New York, N. Y., assignor to Union Special Machine Company, Chicago, Ill. Sewing-machine. No. 1,329,245 ; Jan. 27 ; v. 270 ; p. 571.

Hunt, William H. (See Macintosh and Hunt.)

Hurt, Henry H., Yonkers, assignor to Robeson Process Company, New York, N. Y. Burning fuel. No. 1,329,300 ; Jan. 27 ; v. 270 ; p. 581.

Hutchinson, David M. (See Hachmann, Frederick, assignor.)

Hutchinson, Joseph, and C. C. Hamilton, Gull Lake, Saskatchewan, Canada, Wheel - lubricator. No. 1,328,959 ; Jan. 27 ; v. 270 ; p. 518.

Hyde, Claude C., Otisville, N. Y. Snowplow. No. 1,329,123 ; Jan. 27 ; v. 270 ; p. 548.

Ilyams, Herbert B., St. Paul, Minn. Dispensing-receptacle. No. 1,329,184 ; Jan. 27 ; v. 270 ; p. 560.

Index, Visible. (See Hayes, Robert D., assignor.)

Industrial Research Corporation. (See Heany, John A., assignor.)

Interstate Ever-license Company. (See Fawcett, Charles H., assignor.)

Irwin, De Witt D., assignor of one-half to E. M. Knowles, East Liverpool, Ohio. Drying-machine. No. 1,329,082 ; Jan. 27 ; v. 270 ; p. 540.

Iverson, Eric, Omaha, Nebr. Cuspidor. No. 1,329,124 ; Jan. 27 ; v. 270 ; p. 549.

Jackson, Corwill, Kalamazoo, Mich. Tamper. No. 1,329,049 ; Jan. 27 ; v. 270 ; p. 534.

Jacobus, David S., Jersey City, assignor to The Babcock & Wilcox Company, Bayonne, N. J. Superheat-limiting device. No. 1,328,997 ; Jan. 27 ; v. 270 ; p. 525.

Jakora-Merturi, Gaspard, Paris, France. Directly and completely transforming and reducing iron ores into iron, steel, or cast-iron. No. 1,329,055 ; Jan. 27 ; v. 270 ; p. 536.

James Manufacturing Company. (See Shodron, John G., assignor.)

Jamin, Cornelis D. J., Rotterdam, Netherlands. Electro-mechanical chronometer driving mechanism. No. 1,329,083 ; Jan. 27 ; v. 270 ; p. 541.

Jardine, James C. J. Dickie, and G. A. Bowness, Summer-side, Prince Edward Island, Canada. Cart-saddle. No. 1,328,922 ; Jan. 27 ; v. 270 ; p. 511.

Jarry, Frederick, New Bedford, Mass. Tension device for spooling-machines. No. 1,329,341 ; Jan. 27 ; v. 270 ; p. 588.

Jasper, Joseph H., Philadelphia, Pa. Dump-wagon. No. 1,328,923 ; Jan. 27 ; v. 270 ; p. 511.

Johnson Automatic Sealer Co. (See Bevier, Henry R., assignor.)

Jones, George H. (See Wilbur, Burt, assignor.)

Jones, Russell C., Garden City, N. Y., assignor to Gris-com-Russell Company. High - heat - level evaporator system. No. 1,328,998 ; Jan. 27 ; v. 270 ; p. 525.

Kangas Pappersbruks Aktiebolag. (See Suursalmi, Onni, assignor.)

Kaplan, Nathan, Covington, Ga. Bed-slat. No. 1,328,878 ; Jan. 27 ; v. 270 ; p. 502.

Kasley, Alexander T., Swissvale, Pa., assignor to Westinghouse Electric & Manufacturing Company. Turbine. No. 1,328,835 ; Jan. 27 ; v. 270 ; p. 493.

Kasper, Walter F., assignor to Fairmont Gas Engine & Railway Motor Car Co., Fairmont, Minn. Cutter-bar control for weed-mowers. No. 1,328,836 ; Jan. 27 ; v. 270 ; p. 493.

Kawashima, Haruo, North Platte, Nebr. Track lifter and liner. No. 1,329,185 ; Jan. 27 ; v. 270 ; p. 560.

Kees, Homer R., and E. F. Thomas, Pampa, Tex. Portable elevator. No. 1,329,084 ; Jan. 27 ; v. 270 ; p. 541.

Kelvinator Corporation. (See Copeland, Edmund J., assignor.)

Kelvinator Corporation. (See Heideman and Hadjisky, assignors.)

Kennedy, Lawrence F., St. Paul, Minn. Resilient recoil-pad for gun-stocks. No. 1,328,924 ; Jan. 27 ; v. 270 ; p. 511.

Kenner, Nettie C. (See Osgood, Samuel W., assignor.)

Kern, Walter C., and W. Young, Leavenworth, Kans. Dump-body hoist. No. 1,328,837 ; Jan. 27 ; v. 270 ; p. 494.

270 O. G.—41a

Kimberly Clark Company. (See Mahler, Ernst, assignor.)

Kime, George F., Eldorado, Kans. Wagon-body. No. 1,328,999 ; Jan. 27 ; v. 270 ; p. 525.

Kindig, Samuel C., assignor of one-half to W. C. Ludwig, Baltimore, Md. Broom-holder. No. 1,329,186 ; Jan. 27 ; v. 270 ; p. 560.

King, Rufus, Plainville, assignor to Bugbee and Niles Company, North Attleboro, Mass. Slide for buckles or clasps. No. 1,329,085 ; Jan. 27 ; v. 270 ; p. 541.

Kirk, Walter L., assignor to Lyon & Healy, Chicago, Ill. Tuning-fork. No. 1,328,838 ; Jan. 27 ; v. 270 ; p. 494.

Kirkpatrick, Robert J., S. M. Swordling, and W. P. Heath, Spokane, Wash. Ice-cream-freezing process. No. 1,329,246 ; Jan. 27 ; v. 270 ; p. 571.

Kleckler, Henry, Buffalo, N. Y., assignor to Curtiss Aeroplane and Motor Corporation. Aeroplane construction. No. 1,329,342 ; Jan. 27 ; v. 270 ; p. 588.

Kline, Charles D., Cleveland, Ohio. Light-shade. No. 1,329,187 ; Jan. 27 ; v. 270 ; p. 561.

Kuapp, Charles P., Rochester, Ohio. Automatic crossing-gate. No. 1,329,188 ; Jan. 27 ; v. 270 ; p. 561.

Knaur, Richard, assignor to Firm of Felten & Guilleaume Fabrik Elektrischer Kabel, Stahl- und Kupferwerke Aktiengesellschaft, Vienna, Austria. Wire fence. No. 1,329,189 ; Jan. 27 ; v. 270 ; p. 561.

Knopp, Julius W., Toledo, Ohio. Pawl-and-ratchet means. No. 1,329,000 ; Jan. 27 ; v. 270 ; p. 525.

Knowles, Edwin M. (See Irwin, De Witt D., assignor.)

Koppelman, Harold I. (See Bruder, Edmund, assignor.)

Kornstein, Ulrich, New York, N. Y. Hair-drying comb. No. 1,329,301 ; Jan. 27 ; v. 270 ; p. 581.

Kratz, Franz, assignor to Robert Bosch Aktiengesellschaft, Stuttgart, Germany. Rolled condenser for sparking apparatus. No. 1,328,925 ; Jan. 27 ; v. 270 ; p. 512.

Kratz, Roy G., Omaha, assignor to L. C. Sharp, Plattsmouth, Nebr. Releasing cup-pastry from molds. No. 1,329,086 ; Jan. 27 ; v. 270 ; p. 541.

Kring, Levi, Westerville, Ohio. Tractor. No. 1,328,839 ; Jan. 27 ; v. 270 ; p. 494.

Krueger, Emil M., assignor to Badger Meter Manufacturing Company, Milwaukee, Wis. Water-meter spindle. No. 1,328,879 ; Jan. 27 ; v. 270 ; p. 503.

Kuchler, John. (See Dickelmann and Kuchler.)

Kusuda, Takejiro, Osaka, Japan. Belt. No. 1,329,190 ; Jan. 27 ; v. 270 ; p. 561.

Kuyser, Jan A., Sale, England, assignor to Westinghouse Electric and Manufacturing Company. Dynamo-electric machine. No. 1,329,247 ; Jan. 27 ; v. 270 ; p. 571.

Lachman, Maurice, assignor to Universal Electric Welding Company, New York, N. Y. Fencepost. No. 1,328,926 ; Jan. 27 ; v. 270 ; p. 512.

Lachman, Maurice, assignor to Universal Electric Welding Company, New York, N. Y. Pole or post. No. 1,328,927 ; Jan. 27 ; v. 270 ; p. 512.

Lallié, Norbert, Nantes, France. Typewriter. No. 1,329,087 ; Jan. 27 ; v. 270 ; p. 541.

Lammers, Matthew, Sheboygan Falls, Wis. Milker-head. No. 1,328,880 ; Jan. 27 ; v. 270 ; p. 503.

Lams, William R. (See Snelling and Lams.)

Larkin, Francis C., Rutherford, N. J. Closure for milk-bottles. No. 1,329,248 ; Jan. 27 ; v. 270 ; p. 572.

Lathrop, Edward K. (See Myers, Charles D., assignor.)

Lawes, William F., Bedford, N. H. Dumping device. No. 1,328,928 ; Jan. 27 ; v. 270 ; p. 512.

Lazarus, Willis H., assignor to S. Pfeiffer Manufacturing Company, St. Louis, Mo. Can or container. No. 1,328,881 ; Jan. 27 ; v. 270 ; p. 503.

Lea, Charles, assignor to American Warp Drawing Machine Company, Boston, Mass. Tube-frame for looms. No. 1,329,302 ; Jan. 27 ; v. 270 ; p. 581.

Lea, Charles, assignor to American Warp Drawing Machine Company, Boston, Mass. Tube-frame. No. 1,329,303 ; Jan. 27 ; v. 270 ; p. 581.

Leach, William H., Childress, Tex. Shade-roller and curtain-pole bracket. No. 1,329,249 ; Jan. 27 ; v. 270 ; p. 572.

Lee, John H. (See Eyles, Anton G., assignor.)

Lefax. (See Parker, John J., assignor.)

Lehmann, Karl A. A., Biel, and C. Schindler, Pfäfers, Switzerland. Machine for stamping workmen's individual cards. No. 1,328,840 ; Jan. 27 ; v. 270 ; p. 495.

Leitner, Emil, Hoboken, N. J., assignor to Powers Photo Engraving Company, New York, N. Y. Making printing-plates. No. 1,329,188 ; Jan. 27 ; v. 270 ; p. 541.

Leitner, Henry, London, and W. H. Exley, Pontefract, England. Manufacture of electric accumulators. No. 1,329,125 ; Jan. 27 ; v. 270 ; p. 549.

Leming, Frank, Hingham, Mass. Adjustable dust-cap for valve-stems. No. 1,329,126 ; Jan. 27 ; v. 270 ; p. 549.

Levine, William. (See Rubin and Levine.)

Lewis, Lloyd W., Edgewood borough, assignor to The Union Switch & Signal Company, Swissvale, Pa. Railway-signal. No. 1,328,960 ; Jan. 27 ; v. 270 ; p. 518.

Libbey-Owens Sheet Glass Company, The. (See Colburn, Irving W., assignor.) (Reissue.)

Libbey-Owens Sheet Glass Company, The. (See Whittemore, James, assignor.)

Lindmann, Konrad W., assignor, by mesne assignments, to Nordiska Kullager Aktiebolaget, Gottenborg, Sweden. Ball-holder for ball-bearings. No. 1,329,089 ; Jan. 27 ; v. 270 ; p. 542.

Lindström, Carl, Berlin, Germany. Stamp-affixing machine. No. 1,329,090 ; Jan. 27 ; v. 270 ; p. 542.

Oleson, Olaf E., assignor to The Edward Valve & Manufacturing Co., Chicago, Ill. Separator for steam and oil. No. 1,328,889; Jan. 27; v. 270; p. 505.

Ollard, James C. (See Seabury and Ollard.)

Olleo, Ralph, assignor to Frederick Ossann Company, New York, N. Y. Dust-collector for beating-machines. No. 1,329,138; Jan. 27; v. 270; p. 551.

Olsen, Simon D., Leeds, England. Machine for making hollow glassware. No. 1,329,253; Jan. 27; v. 270; p. 573.

Omen, Charles A., Princeton, Ill. Automobile dump-body. No. 1,328,890; Jan. 27; v. 270; p. 505.

Ormiston, John A., Calgary, Alberta, assignor of one-third to A. G. Slaght and one-third to W. P St. Charles, Toronto, Canada. Locomotive exhaust-nozzle. No. 1,329,093; Jan. 27; v. 270; p. 543.

Osgood, Samuel W., assignor, by mesne assignments, to N. C. Kenner, Chicago, Ill. Producing flake graphite. No. 1,328,845; Jan. 27; v. 270; p. 496.

Ossann, Frederick, Company. (See Olleo, Ralph, assignor.)

Ouzoun-Boghossian, Sissak K., Washington, D. C. Workbench for watchmakers and jewelers. No. 1,328,891; Jan. 27; v. 270; p. 505.

Overgaard, Christen, Skovshoved, near Copenhagen, Denmark. Lathe. No. 1,328,962; Jan. 27; v. 270; p. 518.

Page, Frederick H., assignor to Handley Page Limited, London, England. Connection for members of aircraft-frames. No. 1,328,963; Jan. 27; v. 270; p. 519.

Page, Handley, Limited. (See Page, Frederick H., assignor.)

Paige, Jason, Chicago, Ill. Track-switch. No. 1,329,007; Jan. 27; v. 270; p. 527.

Paridon, Michael, Barberton, Ohio, assignor to The Diamond Match Company, Chicago, Ill. Assembling-machine for matches and splints. No. 1,329,060; Jan. 27; v. 270; p. 536.

Paridon, Michael, Barberton, Ohio, assignor to The Diamond Match Company, Chicago, Ill. Assembling machine for matches and splints. No. 1,329,061; Jan. 27; v. 270; p. 537.

Parker, Arthur C., assignor to Lefax, Philadelphia, Pa. Filing-case. No. 1,329,189; Jan. 27; v. 270; p. 551.

Parkin, Henry, assignor of one-half to G. G. Meeley, Philadelphia, Pa. Starter applicable to magnetos. No. 1,328,892; Jan. 27; v. 270; p. 505.

Parks-Cramer Company. (See Cramer and Hodge, assignors.)

Parry, Arthur, Port Orchard, Wash. Handle attachment. No. 1,329,203; Jan. 27; v. 270; p. 563.

Parsons, Levi L., New York, N. Y., assignor to Elevator Supply & Repair Company. Door-hanger. No. 1,329,326; Jan. 27; v. 270; p. 585.

Parsons, Levi L., New York, N. Y., assignor to Elevator Supplies Company, Inc. Door-hanger. No. 1,329,327; Jan. 27; v. 270; p. 585.

Patrick, Robert A., assignor to Columbian Bronze Corporation, Freeport, N. Y. Flexible coupling for propeller-shafts. No. 1,328,893; Jan. 27; v. 270; p. 505.

Patterson, Ralph J., Berlin, N. H. Electrical water-heater. No. 1,329,204; Jan. 27; v. 270; p. 564.

Patterson, Warren C., Tamaqua, Pa. Metallic railway-tie. No. 1,329,205; Jan. 27; v. 270; p. 564.

Paulson, John E., Minneapolis, Minn. Seed spacing and dropping mechanism for planters. No. 1,328,846; Jan. 27; v. 270; p. 496.

Pearson, Arthur E., Muskegon Mich. Grinding-machine. No. 1,328,894; Jan. 27; v. 270; p. 506.

Pearson, Lawrence J. (See Holland and Pearson.)

Pense, Charles H., Canaan, Conn. License-tag bracket. No. 1,329,206; Jan. 27; v. 270; p. 564.

Pedley, W. P. (See Moors, Walter C., assignor.)

Peerless Album Company. (See Uffner, Hyman, assignor.)

Penn, Harry J., Madison, N. C. Tobacco-extractor. No. 1,328,964; Jan. 27; v. 270; p. 519.

Penn Pressed Metal Co. (See Estberg, William T., assignor.)

Pentecost, Arthur, East Orange, N. J., assignor to Wales Adding Machine Company, Wilkes-Barre, Pa. Calculating-machine. No. 1,328,847; Jan. 27; v. 270; p. 496.

Peppers, Thomas H., Nashville, Ark. Display-basket. No. 1,329,207; Jan. 27; v. 270; p. 564.

Perfecto Gear Differential Co., The. (See Baker, Arthur F., assignor.)

Pernot, Henri A., assignor to Compagnie des Bouchages Hermatiques Simplex, Paris, France. Apparatus for closing containers by pressure. No. 1,329,140; Jan. 27; v. 270; p. 552.

Peterson, Erick B., assignor to George W. Dover, Incorporated, Providence. R. I. Ball safety-catch for brooches and articles of a similar nature. No. 1,328,965; Jan. 27; v. 270; p. 519.

Peycke, Armand H., assignor to American Steel Foundries, Chicago, Ill. Slack-adjuster. No. 1,329,008; Jan. 27; v. 270; p. 527.

Peycke, Armand H., assignor to American Steel Foundries, Chicago, Ill. Brake mechanism. No. 1,329,009; Jan. 27; v. 270; p. 527.

Peycke, Armand H., assignor to American Steel Foundries, Chicago, Ill. Brake mechanism. No. 1,329,010; Jan. 27; v. 270; p. 527.

Pfeiffer, S., Manufacturing Company. (See Lazarus, Willis H., assignor.)

Philadelphia Storage Battery Company. (See Holland and Pearson, assignors.)

Philadelphia Storage Battery Company. (See Holland and Skinner, assignors.)

Phillips, John E., Birmingham, England. Guard for power-presses. No. 1,329,011; Jan. 27; v. 270; p. 527.

Pick, Albert, & Company. (See Pick, Hugo, assignor.)

Pick, Hugo, assignor to Albert Pick & Company, Chicago, Ill. Match-box. No. 1,329,012; Jan. 27; v. 270; p. 527.

Pieper, Alphonse F. (See Pieper, Oscar H. and A. F.)

Pieper, Oscar H. and A. F., Rochester, N. Y. Indicator mechanism. No. 1,328,895; Jan. 27; v. 270; p. 506.

Pierce, Percy, Philadelphia, Pa. Toy. No. 1,329,062; Jan. 27; v. 270; p. 537.

Pneumatic Process Flotation Company. (See Callow, John M., assignor.)

Pogue, Homer C., Chicago, Ill. Spark-gap attachment for spark-plugs. No. 1,329,013; Jan. 27; v. 270; p. 527.

Pollard, George, assignor to The Menco-Elma Syndicate Limited, London, England. Electromagnetic brake for motor road-vehicles. No. 1,328,966; Jan. 27; v. 270; p. 519.

Poole, Arthur F., Kenilworth, Ill., assignor to The Wahl Company, Wilmington, Del. Gear-shift for cross-actuators. No. 1,329,014; Jan. 27; v. 270; p. 528.

Poseon, Edward, Chicago, Ill. Trap and drain for railway-cars. No. 1,329,015; Jan. 27; v. 270; p. 528.

Powell, Peter, assignor of one-half to J. Rosenfield, Boston, Mass. Air-bag. No. 1,329,208; Jan. 27; v. 270; p. 564.

Powers Photo Engraving Company. (See Leitner, Emil, assignor.)

Prentiss, Augustin M., Fort Caswell, N. C., assignor of one-half to D. E. Bulloch, Washington, D. C. Carbureter. No. 1,329,308; Jan. 27; v. 270; p. 582.

Prentiss, Augustin M., Rock Island, Ill., assignor of one-half to D. E. Bulloch, Washington, D. C. Carburetor. No. 1,329,309; Jan. 27; v. 270; p. 582.

Purdy, Fred P., Sharon, Mass. Bowling game. No. 1,329,254; Jan. 27; v. 270; p. 573.

Quigley Furnace Specialties Co. (See Renkin, William O., assignor.)

Raba, Ernest, Valley, Okla. Combined gasket and oil-gasifier. No. 1,329,343; Jan. 27; v. 270; p. 588.

Ramauge, Adalberto, Buenos Aires, Argentina. Parachute comprising pneumatic means. No. 1,328,848; Jan. 27; v. 270; p. 496.

R. & C. Engineering Company, The. (See Reed, Chase C., assignor.)

Reaben, George B., New York, N. Y. Arrow. No. 1,328,967; Jan. 27; v. 270; p. 519.

Reed, Chase C., assignor to The R. & C. Engineering Company, Toledo, Ohio. Plowing-machine. No. 1,328,896; Jan. 27; v. 270; p. 506.

Renkin, William O., Oradell, N. J., assignor to Quigley Furnace Specialties Co., Inc. Valve. No. 1,329,016; Jan. 27; v. 270; p. 528.

Renkin, William O., Oradell, N. J., assignor to Quigley Furnace Specialties Co., Inc. Valve-operating mechanism. No. 1,329,017; Jan. 27; v. 270; p. 528.

Renkin, William O., Oradell, N. J., assignor to Quigley Furnace Specialties Co., Inc. Apparatus for automatically controlling flowing materials. No. 1,329,018; Jan. 27; v. 270; p. 528.

Riccio, Pasquale A., Brooklyn, N. Y. Foot-operated valve. No. 1,329,209; Jan. 27; v. 270; p. 564.

Rice, Frank E., assignor to American Tap Bush Co., Detroit, Mich. Tap-attaching thimble. No. 1,329,141; Jan. 27; v. 270; p. 552.

Rice, Otis D., Winthrop, Mass. Method of and apparatus for drying material. No. 1,328,897; Jan. 27; v. 270; p. 506.

Richard, François, and F. M. Brady, Cleveland, Ohio, Plastic composition. No. 1,329,094; Jan. 27; v. 270; p. 543.

Richardson, John R., Madera, Calif. Mold for constructing hollow walls of concrete. No. 1,329,095; Jan. 27; v. 270; p. 543.

Richman, Philip J. (See Eckert and Richman.)

Ricketts, William C., Dayton, Ohio. Scouring soap cake, to be used in general scouring and cleaning purposes. No. 1,328,898; Jan. 27; v. 270; p. 506.

Rickon, Harold J., assignor of one-half to J. A. Sandal, San Francisco, Calif. Automatic air-release. No. 1,329,210; Jan. 27; v. 270; p. 565.

Riedele, Philip, Los Angeles, Calif. Bumper-bracket holder. No. 1,329,019; Jan. 27; v. 270; p. 529.

Ritter, Thomas J., Jr., and B. M. Warn, Lairdsville, Pa. Lever-holding mechanism for automobiles. No. 1,329,142; Jan. 27; v. 270; p. 506.

Ritter, Thomas J., Jr., and B. M. Warn, Lairdsville, Pa. Lever-holding mechanism for automobiles. No. 1,329,142; Jan. 27; v. 270; p. 552.

Ritzema, David. (See Eggleston, William H., assignor.)

Roberts, Fred T., assignor to The Aranar Company, Cleveland, Ohio. Inflated golf-ball and making. No. 1,329,310; Jan. 27; v. 270; p. 582.

Roberts, Fred T., Cleveland Heights, assignor to The Aranar Company, Cleveland, Ohio. Making balls. No. 1,329,311; Jan. 27; v. 270; p. 583.

Roberts, Fred T., Cleveland Ohio. Mold for making rubber articles. No. 1,329,312; Jan. 27; v. 270; p. 583.

Roberts, John T. (See Hafner and Roberts.)

Roberts, Louis L. (See Golata and Roberts.)

Robeson Process Company. (See Hurt, Henry H., assignor.)

Robinson, Harry A., assignor to Eclipse Stove Company, Mansfield, Ohio. Gas burner. No. 1,329,096; Jan. 27; v. 270; p. 543.

Rockford Milling Machine Company. (See Sundstrand, Gustaf D., assignor.)

Rodger, Joseph B., Independence, Mo. Automatic time-controlled trip mechanism. No. 1,329,020; Jan. 27; v. 270; p. 529.

Rogers, Harry M., Petersburg, Va. Humidifier. No. 1,329,143; Jan. 27; v. 270; p. 552.

Root, A. I., Company, The. (See Blanchard, Herbert C., assignor.)

Rosebourne, Mostyn, Manchester, and F. A. Couse, Urmston, England, assignors to Westinghouse Electric and Manufacturing Company. Automatic protective gear for electrical systems. No. 1,329,255; Jan. 27; v. 270; p. 573.

Rosenfield, James. (See Powell, Peter, assignor.)

Ross, William H., Washington, D. C. Removal of Hydrofluoric acid from phosphoric acid. No. 1,329,273; Jan. 27; v. 270; p. 576.

Rownd, Annie K., Rochester, N. Y. Nursery-seat. No. 1,328,900; Jan. 27; v. 270; p. 507.

Rubin, Morris, and W. Levine, New York, N. Y. Soap-holder. No. 1,329,097; Jan. 27; v. 270; p. 543

Rumsey, Ernest. (See Upp, William M., assignor.)

Russell, Bertrom R., Sheridan, Nev. Match-safe. No. 1,328,968; Jan. 27; v. 270; p. 519.

Ryder, Ambrose, New York, N. Y. Umbrella. No. 1,328,901; Jan. 27; v. 270; p. 507.

Ryder, Ambrose, New York, N. Y. Umbrella. No. 1,328,902; Jan. 27; v. 270; p. 507.

Rypinski, Albert B., Brooklyn, assignor to T. E. Murray, New York, N. Y. Connecting plates by electrical riveting. No. 1,329,144; Jan. 27; v. 270; p. 552.

Sandal, John A. (See Rickon, Harold J., assignor.)

Sanders, J. Wofford, et al. (See Theriot, Charles, assignor.)

Santoro, Harry, New York, N. Y. Chenille scarf. No. 1,328,903; Jan. 27; v. 270; p. 507.

Sartain, Isaac M., Tracy City, Tenn. Spring-tire. No. 1,329,021; Jan. 27; v. 270; p. 529.

Saurer, Hippolyt, Arbon, Switzerland. Embroidering-machine. No. 1,328,969; Jan. 27; v. 270; p. 520.

Sawyer, Green B. (See Blakemore, James R., assignor.)

Schein, Charles F. (See Nickol and Schein.)

Schenck, John F., Jr., Shelby, N. C. Attachment for cotton-pickers. No. 1,328,904; Jan. 27; v. 270; p. 507.

Schieman, Paul W., Rockville Center, N. Y., assignor to The A. Dewes Company, New York, N. Y. Jack. No. 1,329,098; Jan. 27; v. 270; p. 543.

Schindler, Conrad. (See Lehmann and Schindler.)

Schindler & Cie. (See Schneider, Eugene, assignor.)

Schneider, Eugene, assignor to Schneider & Cie., Paris, France. Gun - carriage with endless tracks. No. 1,328,849; Jan. 27; v. 270; p. 496.

Schneider, Michael J. N., Black River Falls, Wis. Rail-way-gate. No. 1,329,022; Jan. 27; v. 270; p. 529.

Scott, Barton W., San Jose, Calif. Prune-pitting machine. No. 1,329,023; Jan. 27; v. 270; p. 529.

Scott, William M., Sullivan, Ill. Hen's nest. No. 1,329,024; Jan. 27; v. 270; p. 530.

Seabury, Benjamin H. and J. C. Ollard, Tacoma, Wash. Buffer for doors. No. 1,329,313; Jan. 27; v. 270; p. 583.

Seclig, Joseph, Lead, S. D. Metallic bed - bottom. No. 1,329,145; Jan. 27; v. 270; p. 553.

Seiss, George J., Toledo, Ohio. Mechanically - operated horn. No. 1,329,275; Jan. 27; v. 270; p. 576.

Sellers, J. E., et al. (See Shreibman, Abram, assignor.)

Sexton, Isaac E., Boston, Mass. Riveting-machine. No. 1,328,905; Jan. 27; v. 270; p. 508.

Sharp, L. C. (See Kratz, Roy G., assignor.)

Shodron, John G., assignor to James Manufacturing Company, Fort Atkinson, Wis. Feed-trough for pigs and other animals. No. 1,328,970; Jan. 27; v. 270; p. 520.

Shreibman, Abram, Keokuk, Iowa, assignor of one-third to J. L. Baldon and one-third to J. E. Sellers, Elvaston, Ill. Radiator. No. 1,329,256; Jan. 27; v. 270; p. 573.

Singer Manufacturing Company, The. (See Corrall, Herbert, assignor.)

Skelton, John W., Douglas, Ariz. Flytrap. No. 1,328,850; Jan. 27; v. 270; p. 497.

Skinner, James M. (See Holland and Skinner.)

Skinner, Perry R., Amsterdam, N. Y. Dental tool. No. 1,329,274; Jan. 27; v. 270; p. 576.

Slaght, Arthur G., et al. (See Ormiston, John A., assignor.)

Slater, Horace G., Los Angeles, Calif. Dust-cap valve. No. 1,329,146; Jan. 27; v. 270; p. 553.

Smith, Burns L., Syracuse, N. Y. Heat treatment for castings. No. 1,328,851; Jan. 27; v. 270; p. 497.

Smith, Burns L., Syracuse, N. Y. Apparatus for casting hollow one-piece spoke-wheels. No. 1,328,852; Jan. 27; v. 270; p. 497.

Smith, Irwin J., Menands, N. Y. Garment. No. 1,329,025; Jan. 27; v. 270; p. 530.

Snelling, Walter O., and W. R. Lams, Allentown, Pa., assignors by mesne assignments, to Trojan Powder Company, New York, N. Y. Nitrostarch explosive and manufacturing same. No. 1,329,211; Jan. 27; v. 270; p. 565.

Snelling, Walter O., and W. R. Lams, assignors to Trojan Powder Company, Allentown, Pa. Manufacturing nitrostarch explosives. No. 1,329,212; Jan. 27; v. 270; p. 565.

Snider, R. E. (See Frey, George E., assignor.)

Snyder, Daniel H., Snyderville, Ohio. Post. No. 1,329,026; Jan. 27; v. 270; p. 530.

Soemer, Joseph C., Newark, N. J. Desk-basket paper holder and clip. No. 1,328,971; Jan. 27; v. 270; p. 520.

Sparrow, Simon, assignor to Wagner Electric Manufacturing Company, St. Louis, Mo. Coil for dynamo-electric machines. No. 1,329,027; Jan. 27; v. 270; p. 530.

Spencer, Ira H., West Hartford, assignor to The Spencer Turbine Company, Hartford, Conn. Valve. No. 1,329,099; Jan. 27; v. 270; p. 544.

Spencer Turbine Company, The. (See Spencer, Ira H., assignor.)

Spreckels, Diedrich H., Dexter, Minn. Poultry-crate. No. 1,329,344; Jan. 27; v. 270; p. 588.

Sprong, Severn D., Brooklyn, N. Y. Apparatus for adding to the output of a main power station, the output of one or more distant sources. No. 1,329,276; Jan. 27; v. 270; p. 577.

Standard Oilcloth Co. (See Frohner, Edward H., assignor.)

St. Charles, William P., et al. (See Ormiston, John A., assignor.)

Stefferud, Leonard C., Brandt, S. D. Steam-jacket for oil-pumps. No. 1,328,906; Jan. 27; v. 270; p. 508.

Stein, Noah S., Bristol, Ind. Engine. No. 1,328,972; Jan. 27; v. 270; p. 520.

Stern, Louis J., Boston, Mass. Mirror-mounting. No. 1,328,930; Jan. 27; v. 270; p. 512.

Stevens, William H., New York, N. Y. Garter. No. 1,329,931; Jan. 27; v. 270; p. 513.

Steward, Archie L., Chicago, Ill. Strainer for vacuum gasolene systems. No. 1,328,853; Jan. 27; v. 270; p. 497.

Stimpson, Edward S., assignor to Draper Corporation, Hopedale, Mass. Feeler-motion for looms. No. 1,328,907; Jan. 27; v. 270; p. 508.

Stimpson, Edward S., assignor to Draper Corporation, Hopedale, Mass. Feeler-motion for looms. No. 1,328,908; Jan. 27; v. 270; p. 508.

Stimpson, Edward S., assignor to Draper Corporation, Hopedale, Mass. Feeler with concave teeth. No. 1,329,325; Jan. 27; v. 270; p. 585.

Stimpson, Edwin B., Brooklyn, N. Y. Cartridge-belt. No. 1,329,346; Jan. 27; v. 270; p. 589.

Stowell, Lawrence H., Litchville, N. D. Snowplow. No. 1,328,973; Jan. 27; v. 270; p. 521.

Straub, Anselm, Jr., Magnolia, N. J., assignor of one-half to W. F. Tosney, Philadelphia, Pa. Union-suit. No. 1,329,329; Jan. 27; v. 270; p. 585.

Strauss, Ernest H., Chicago, Ill. Lamp-shade and light-diffuser. No. 1,329,147; Jan. 27; v. 270; p. 553.

Strobel, Carl W. F., Lima, Ohio. Railway-crossing signal. No. 1,328,854; Jan. 27; v. 270; p. 497

Sulzberger, Nathan, New York, N. Y. Iodin dusting-powder and making same. No. 1,329,148; Jan. 27; v. 270; p. 553.

Sundstrand, Gustaf D., assignor to Rockford Milling Machine Company, Rockford, Ill. Listing and adding machine. No. 1,329,028; Jan. 27; v. 270; p. 530.

Suursalmi, Onni, assignor to Kangas Pappersbruks Aktiebolag, Jyväskylä, Finland. Making lines and water-marks on paper and apparatus therefor. No. 1,329,100; Jan. 27; v. 270; p. 544.

Sweet, Ernest E., assignor to General Motors Company, Detroit, Mich. Hydrocarbon-motor. No. 1,328,855; Jan. 27; v. 270; p. 498.

Swordling, Severn M. (See Kirkpatrick, Swordling, and Heath.)

Tamura, Shinkichi, Kobe, and M. Watanabe, Tokyo, Japan; said Watanabe assignor to said Tamura. Motor-car of small type. No. 1,328,909; Jan. 27; v. 270; p. 508.

Taylor, Walter M., London, England. Gas-fired water-heater or steam-generator. No. 1,328,856; Jan. 27; v. 270; p. 498.

Terry, Ellis L., Los Angeles, Calif. Folding ironing-board. No. 1,329,257; Jan. 27; v. 270; p. 574.

Thamm, Rosle, Berkeley, Calif. Napkin-fastener. No. 1,329,149; Jan. 27; v. 270; p. 553.

Theriot, Charles, assignor of one-third to J. W. Sanders and one-third to P. R. Burke, New Iberia, La. Railway-crossing signal. No. 1,328,932; Jan. 27; v. 270; p. 513.

Thomas, Elbert F. (See Kees and Thomas.)

Thomas, George B., assignor to The Bryant Electric Company, Bridgeport, Conn. Electric fitting. No. 1,329,330; Jan. 27; v. 270; p. 586.

Thomas, Raymond G., Monticello, Iowa. Method of and apparatus for measuring the heights of superposed liquids of varying specific gravities. No. 1,329,150; Jan. 27; v. 270; p. 553.

Thomasson, Hiram S., assignor, by mesne assignments, of two-thirds to C. D. Enochs, trustee, Minneapolis, Minn. Tank-heater. No. 1,329,063; Jan. 27; v. 270; p. 537.

Thompson, Earl A., Gresham, Oreg. Hydraulic engine. No. 1,328,974; Jan. 27; v. 270; p. 521.

Thompson, Peter E., Three Rivers, Mich., assignor to Fairbanks, Morse & Co., Chicago, Ill. Standpipe. No. 1,328,857; Jan. 27; v. 270; p. 498.

ALPHABETICAL LIST OF REGISTRANTS OF TRADE-MARKS.

Monopole Vineyards Corp., New York, N. Y. Maltless non-alcoholic fruit beverages. Nos. 129,187–8 ; Jan. 27 ; v. 270 ; p. 615.

Murray Company, Dallas, Tex. Machinery and parts thereof. No. 129,189 ; Jan. 27 ; v. 270 ; p. 615.

Nash Engineering Company, South Norwalk, Conn. Air-compressors, vacuum heating-pumps, &c. No. 129,190 ; Jan. 27 ; v. 270 ; p. 615.

Nash Engineering Co., South Norwalk, Conn. Steam-engineering appliances, &c. No. 129,191 ; Jan. 27 ; v. 270 ; p. 615.

National Aniline & Chemical Company, Incorporated, New York, N. Y. Oil of peppermint used as a flavor for soft drinks. No. 129,192 ; Jan. 27 ; v. 270 ; p. 615

National Enameling & Stamping Co., New York, N. Y. Enameled metal ware. No. 129,193 ; Jan. 27 ; v 270 ; p. 615.

New England Tool Co. Inc., Boston, Mass. Hacksaws and screw-drivers. No. 129,194 ; Jan. 27 ; v. 270 ; p. 615.

Ono Mfg. Co., Middletown, Conn. Bias seam-tape. Nos. 129,195–6 ; Jan. 27 ; v. 270 ; p. 615.

Orange City Mineral Spring Company, Orange City, Fla. Mineral water. No. 129,197 ; Jan. 27 ; v. 270 ; p. 615.

O'Reilly, William E., London, England. Safety-razors and razor-blades. No. 129,198 ; Jan. 27 ; v. 270 ; p. 615.

Ottawa Milling Company, Kansas City, Mo., and Ottawa, Kans. Wheat-flour. No. 129,199 ; Jan. 27 ; v. 270 ; p 615.

Perkins Glue Company, Lansdale, Pa. Starch-glue material. No. 129,200 ; Jan. 27 ; v. 270 ; p. 615.

Pittsburgh Brewing Company, Pittsburgh, Pa. Malt beverage. No. 129,201 ; Jan. 27 ; v. 270 ; p. 616.

Polk County Citrus Sub-Exchange, Bartow, Fla. Fresh citrus fruits. No. 129,202 ; Jan. 27 ; v. 270 ; p. 616.

Powers Manufacturing Company, The, Waterloo, Iowa. Overalls and one-piece garments. No. 129,203 ; Jan. 27 ; v. 270 ; p. 616.

Putnam, Alfred, & Company, New York, N. Y. Canned fruits and canned vegetables. No. 129,204 ; Jan. 27 ; v. 270 ; p. 616.

Putnam Overall Mfg. Co., Cookeville, Tenn. Men's and boys' coats, pants, &c. No. 129,205 ; Jan. 27 ; v. 270 ; p. 616.

Quaker City Flour Mills Company, Philadelphia, Pa. Self-rising wheat-flour. No. 129,206 ; Jan. 27 ; v. 270 ; p. 616.

Randall-McLoughlin Co., Seattle, Wash. Stock foods, poultry and dog foods. No. 129,207 ; Jan. 27 ; v. 270 ; p. 616.

Reynolds - Lindheim Cigar Company, Nashville, Tenn. Candy. No. 129,208 ; Jan. 27 ; v. 270 ; p. 616.

Ries, Jacob, Bottling Works, Inc., Shakopee, Minn. Still and effervescent table-water. No. 129,172 ; Jan. 27 ; v. 270 ; p 615.

Roe, A. V., & Co. Ltd., Manchester, England. Turnbuckles, metal name-plates, &c. Nos. 129,209–10 ; Jan. 27 ; v. 270 ; p. 616.

Romort Manufacturing Company, Oakfield, Wis. Automobile, &c., accessories. No. 129,211 ; Jan. 27 ; v. 270 ; p. 616.

Rosenstein, Jacob, New York, N Y. Wheat-flour. No. 129,212 ; Jan. 27 ; v. 270 ; p. 616.

Roth, Charles, New York, N. Y. Ladies' hats. No. 129,213 ; Jan. 27 ; v. 270 ; p. 616.

Roulette, J. C. and Sons, Hagerstown, Md. Underwear. No. 129,214 ; Jan. 27 ; v. 270 ; p. 616.

Gelarie, Saul, & Company, Brooklyn and New York, N. Y. Bloomers. No. 129,215 ; Jan. 27 ; v. 270 ; p. 616

Schmid, Roost Jakob, Oerlikon. Switzerland. Ball and roller bearings and ports. No. 129,216 ; Jan. 27 ; v. 270 ; p. 616.

Schoenhoffen Company, Chicago, Ill. Non-alcoholic non-cereal maltless beverage. No. 129,217 ; Jan. 27 ; v. 270 ; p. 616.

Schuller, Frederick A., Boston, Mass. Muffins. No. 129,218 ; Jan. 27 ; v. 270 ; p. 616.

Sidney Canning Co., Ltd., Sidney, British Columbia, Canada. Canned fish and clams. No. 129,219 ; Jan. 27 ; v. 270 ; p. 616.

Simmons Hardware Company, St. Louis, Mo. Bicycles. No. 129,220 ; Jan. 27 ; v. 270 ; p. 616.

Simpson-Walther Lens Company, Inc., Rochester, N. Y. Ophthalmic - lens blanks and ophthalmic lenses. No. 129,221 ; Jan. 27 ; v. 270 ; p. 616.

Southern Cotton Oil Company, Jersey City and Bayonne, N. J. ; New York, N. Y. ; Gretna, La. ; Savannah, Ga., and Chicago, Ill. Cotton-seed-oil shortening compound. No. 129,222 ; Jan. 27 ; v. 270 ; p. 616.

Spang, Chalfant & Co. Incorporated, Pittsburgh, Pa. Iron and steel tubes. No. 129,223 ; Jan. 27 ; v. 270 ; p. 616

Stern, Charles, & Sons Inc., Los Angeles, Calif. Canned fruits. No. 129,225 ; Jan. 27 ; v. 270 ; p. 616.

Stopshok Wheel Co., Inc., Washington, D. C. Vehicle-wheels. No. 129,224 ; Jan. 27 ; v. 270 ; p. 616.

Superior Cone Company, St. Louis, Mo. Ice-cream cones. No 129,226 ; Jan. 27 ; v. 270 ; p. 616.

Tenenbaum, J., & Sons, New York, N. Y. Ladies' hats. No. 129,227 ; Jan. 27 ; v. 270 ; p. 616.

Terre Haute Brewing Company, Terre Haute, Ind. Cereal malt beverage. No. 129,228 ; Jan. 27 ; v. 270 ; p. 616.

Texoleum Co. of N Y. Inc., New York, N. Y. Oil-cloth, linoleums, &c. No. 129,229 ; Jan. 27 ; v. 270 ; p. 616.

Thomson Machine Company, Belleville, N. J. Dough balling and proofing machine, rounding-up machines. No. 129,230 ; Jan. 27 ; v. 270 ; p. 616.

Trexler Rim Compressor Co., Philadelphia, Pa. Tire-removing tools. No. 129,231 ; Jan. 27 ; v. 270 ; p. 616.

United American Metals Corporation, Brooklyn, N Y. Babbitt metal. No. 129,232 ; Jan. 27 ; v. 270 ; p. 616.

United Hosiery Mills Corporation, East Chattanooga, Tenn. Hosiery. No. 129,233 ; Jan. 27 ; v. 270 ; p. 617.

U. S. Industrial Co., New York, N. Y. Chemicals. No. 129,234 ; Jan. 27 ; v. 270 ; p. 617.

United States Rubber Company, New Brunswick, N. J., and New York, N. Y. Rubber mats and mattings. No. 129,235 ; Jan. 27 ; v. 270 ; p. 617.

Universal Tool Co., Detroit, Mich. Cylinder-reboring tools and kits, &c. No. 129,236 ; Jan. 27 ; v. 270 ; p 617.

Vacuum Oil Company, Rochester, N. Y. Lubricating-oils. No. 129,237 ; Jan. 27 ; v. 270 ; p. 617.

Voigt Milling Company, Grand Rapids, Mich. Stock and poultry feed. No. 129,238 ; Jan. 27 ; v. 270 ; p. 617.

Wachusett Shirt Co., Leominster, Mass. Sleeping-garments—viz., night-dresses. No. 129,239 ; Jan. 27 ; v. 270 ; p. 617.

Wahlert & Guntzler, St. Louis, Mo. Feathers. No. 129,240 ; Jan. 27 ; v 270 ; p. 617.

Walcoff, Phil., & Co., Inc., New York, N. Y. Boys' outer clothing. No. 129,241 ; Jan. 27 ; v. 270 ; p. 617.

Warshavsky. David, New York, N. Y. Snap-fasteners. No. 129,242 ; Jan. 27 ; v. 270 ; p. 617.

Wathen Milling Company, Louisville, Ky. Fine grits, pearl-hominy, &c. No. 129,243 ; Jan. 27 ; v. 270 ; p. 617.

Wellman-Seaver-Morgan Company, Cleveland, Ohio. Tractors. No. 129,245 ; Jan. 27 ; v. 270 ; p. 617.

Wharton, William, Jr., & Co., Incorporated, Philadelphia and Easton, Pa. Tractor-wheels. No. 129,246 ; Jan. 27 ; v. 270 ; p. 617

Willis, Joseph V., New York, N. Y. Ginger-beer. No. 129,247 ; Jan. 27 ; v. 270 ; p. 617.

What Cheer Braid Company. Providence, R. I. Shoe strings and lacings, tapes, galloons. No. 129,248 ; Jan. 27 ; v. 270 ; p. 617.

Whitney, Rowena L., Springfield, Mass. Fabric shoes for children. No. 129,249 ; Jan. 27 ; v. 270 ; p. 617.

Williams Patent Crusher and Pulverizer Company, New York, N. Y. Grinding, crushing, and pulverizing machines. No. 129,250 ; Jan 27 ; v. 270 ; p. 617.

Wilson Brothers, Chicago, Ill. Neckties. No. 129,251 ; Jan. 27 ; v. 270 ; p. 617.

Wilson, Raymond K., Gloversville, N. Y. Gloves and mittens No. 129,252 ; Jan. 27 ; v. 270 ; p. 617.

Wood, W. B., Mfg. Co., St. Louis, Mo. Non-alcoholic non-cereal maltless beverage and syrup for making same. Nos. 129,253–4 ; Jan. 27 ; v. 270 ; p. 617.

Yonkers Brewery, assignor to Bittersweet Products Corporation, Yonkers, N. Y. Carbonated beverage. No. 129,255 ; Jan. 27 ; v. 270 ; p. 617.

Young, Corley & Dolan, Inc., New York, N. Y. Hacksaws. No. 129,256 ; Jan. 27 ; v. 270 ; p. 617.

ALPHABETICAL LIST OF REGISTRANTS OF LABELS.

Continental Paper Bag Co., New York, N. Y. "Continental Peanut Bag." (For Paper Bags.) No. 21,646; Jan. 27; v. 270; p. 618.

Mangan & Co., New York, N. Y. "Hairforever." (For a Hair-Tonic.) No. 21,647; Jan. 27; v. 270; p. 618.

Roth, Joseph S., Carroll township, Washington county, Pa. "Neupro." (For Ginger-Ale.) No. 21,648; Jan. 27; v. 270; p. 618.

Standard Export-Import Co. Ltd., Stavanger, Norway. "Seaside." (For Canned Sardines.) No. 21,649; Jan. 27; v. 270; p. 618.

ALPHABETICAL LIST OF REGISTRANTS OF PRINTS.

B. V. D. Company, The, New York, N. Y. "Wear B. V. D. On Your Vacation." (For Athletic Underwear.) No. 5,194; Jan. 27; v. 270; p. 618.

Great Southern Producing & Refining Co., Indianapolis, Ind. "Samson Motor Fuel." (For Motor-Fuel.) No. 5,195; Jan. 27; v. 270; p. 618.

Sunbeam Chemical Company, Chicago, Ill. "Astounding Growth of The World Wide Rit Industry." (For Rit Dye-Soap.) No. 5,196; Jan. 27; v. 270; p. 618.

Sunbeam Chemical Company, Chicago, Ill. "Make Your Own Colors Successfully." (For Rit Dye-Soap.) No. 5,197; Jan. 27; v. 270; p. 618.

Sunbeam Chemical Company, Chicago, Ill. "Try Her Beauty Secret." (For Rit Dye-Soap.) No. 5,198; Jan. 27; v. 270; p. 618.

ALPHABETICAL LIST OF REGISTRANTS OF TRADE-MARKS.

(REGISTRATION APPLIED FOR.)

Adams, Eva, Sparta, Ill. Hair-tonic and hair-straighteners. No. 123,273 ; Jan. 27 ; v. 270 ; p. 604.

Alaska Salmon & Herring Packers, Inc., Seattle, Wash. Canned salmon and herring. No. 125,070 ; Jan. 27 ; v. 270 ; p. 611.

Albany Chemical Company, Albany, N. Y. Fluid for priming and starting internal-combustion engines. No 123,049 ; Jan. 27 ; v. 270 ; p. 603.

Alfoth, Alma R., Chicago, Ill. Candies. No. 124,636 ; Jan. 27 ; v. 270 ; p. 609.

American Carpenter and Builder Co., Chicago, Ill. Monthly magazine. No. 122,679 ; Jan. 27 ; v. 270 ; p. 602.

American Commercial Car Co., Detroit, Mich. Automobile-trucks. No. 122,871 ; Jan. 27 ; v. 270 ; p. 603.

American Hard Rubber Co., Hempstead and New York, N. Y. Combs for dressing, ornamenting, and cleaning the hair and buttons for wearing-apparel. Nos. 123,600–2 ; Jan. 27 ; v. 270 ; p. 606.

American Pop Corn Works, Inc., Boston. Mass. Popcorn confections. No. 107,018 ; Jan. 27 ; v. 270 ; p. 593.

American Pozzolana Company, Indianapolis, Ind. Cement, stucco, and plaster. No. 122,678 ; Jan. 27 ; v. 270 ; p. 602.

American Tobacco Company, The, New York, N. Y. Smoking and chewing tobacco. No. 123,016 ; Jan. 27 ; v. 270 ; p. 603.

American Tobacco Company, The, New York, N. Y. Smoking and chewing tobacco. No. 124,706 ; Jan. 27 ; v. 270 ; p. 610.

American Tobacco Company, The, New York, N. Y. Smoking and chewing tobacco and cigarettes. No. 124,708 ; Jan. 27 ; v. 270 ; p. 610.

American Tobacco Company, The, New York, N. Y. Smoking and chewing tobacco and cigarettes. No. 123,017 ; Jan. 27 ; v. 270 ; p. 603.

Archbold Manufacturing Corporation, Rochester, N. Y. Syrup. No. 124.878 ; Jan. 27 ; v. 270 ; p. 611.

Argonne Motor Car Company, Jersey City, N. J. Automobiles, automobile-radiator and wheel-hub caps. No. 123,947 ; Jan. 27 ; v. 270 ; p. 607.

Aspegren & Company, New York, N. Y. Edible oils. Nos. 120,023–4 ; Jan. 27 ; v. 270 ; p. 598

Baren, Lehrman & Berler, Inc., New York, N. Y. Men's clothing. No. 117,723 ; Jan. 27 ; v. 270 ; p. 595.

Beall, Edward, Los Angeles, Calif. Combination of herbs for use in the treatment of Bright's disease, diabetes, &c. No. 123,333 ; Jan. 27 ; v. 270 ; p. 605.

Beck, Mitchel, Brooklyn, N. Y. Canned fish. No. 121,382 ; Jan. 27 ; v. 270 ; p. 599.

Bell, Harry, Chicago, Ill. Roach-powder. No. 122,384 ; Jan. 27 ; v. 270 ; p. 602.

Blanke. C. F., Tea & Coffee Company. St. Louis, Mo. Salad-dressing, peanut-butter, and salted peanuts. No. 119,591 ; Jan. 27 ; v. 270 ; p. 597.

Bonebright, Gertrude R., Grand Rapids, Mich. Supporters for diapers. No. 122,822 ; Jan. 27 ; v. 270 ; p. 603.

Borgfeldt, George, & Co., New York, N. Y. Toilet powder. No. 123,418 ; Jan. 27 ; v. 270 ; p. 605.

Bruns, Armin R., Washington, Iowa. Field, garden, and flower seeds. No. 119,262 ; Jan. 27 ; v. 270 ; p. 597.

Buckeye Nurseries, Tampa, Winterhaven. Lucerne Park, and Howey, Fla. Fresh oranges. No. 118,588 ; Jan. 27 ; v. 270 ; p. 596.

Burlasky. Louis, New York. N. Y. Sewing-machines and parts thereof. No. 124,676 ; Jan. 27 ; v. 270 ; p. 610.

Buscaglia, A. & C., Co., Buffalo. N. Y. Olive-oil and tomato paste. No. 122,585 ; Jan. 27 ; v. 270 ; p. 602.

C. & K. Mfg. Co., The, New Haven, Conn Powder-puffs. No. 121,691 ; Jan. 27 ; v. 270 ; p 599.

Chamberlain, F. B., Company, St. Louis, Mo. Farina, pearl-barley, cornmeal, &c. No. 123,304 ; Jan. 27 ; v. 270 ; p. 604.

Cheri, Inc., Philadelphia, Pa. Raw and cooked sea food, cooked meats, cooked and uncooked vegetables, &c. No. 124,169 ; Jan. 27 ; v. 270 ; p. 608.

Chili-O Company, Chicago, Ill. Non-alcoholic non-intoxicating maltless non-cereal beverage. No. 123,960 ; Jan. 27 ; v. 270 ; p. 607.

Cloud-Thomas Co.. Yakima, Wash. Fresh fruits. No. 124,592 ; Jan. 27 ; v. 270 ; p. 609.

Conklin, Horace E., Binghamton, N. Y. Seed-corn, grass and field seeds. No. 115,801 ; Jan. 27 ; v. 270 ; p. 594.

Corno Mills Company, St. Louis. Mo. Rolled oats. No. 124,642 ; Jan. 27 ; v. 270 ; p. 609.

Crucible Steel Company of America, Pittsburgh, Pa. Steel bars, rods, billets, blooms, sheets, &c. No. 122,284 ; Jan. 27 ; v. 270 ; p. 601.

Cummings. Charles C., St. Louis, Mo. Laundry soaps, soap tablets, and rug-cleaners. No. 119,183 ; Jan. 27 ; v. 270 ; p. 597.

D. A. P. Confectionery, Inc., New York, N. Y. Candies and chocolates. No. 124,045 ; Jan. 27 ; v. 270 ; p. 608.

Dafoe-Eustice Company, Detroit, Mich. Automobile-curtains. No. 117,270 ; Jan. 27 ; v. 270 ; p. 595.

De Luca. John A., St. Helena, Md. Mayonnaise dressing, chilli-chow, and marshmallow preparation. No. 125,080 ; Jan. 27 ; v. 270 ; p. 611.

Delaware Electric & Supply Co., Wilmington, Del. Coal-stoves. No. 124,082 ; Jan. 27 ; v. 270 ; p. 608.

Dexter Yarn Company, Pawtucket, R. I. Mercerized cotton thread and yarn. No. 119,029 ; Jan. 27 ; v. 270 ; p. 596.

Doane. W. W., Cincinnati, Ohio. Candy. No. 125,277 ; Jan. 27 ; v. 270 ; p. 612.

Dymalkon Metals Corporation, New York, N. Y. Architectural bronzework for building exteriors and interiors. No. 124,298 ; Jan. 27 ; v. 270 ; p. 608.

Dymalkon Metals Corporation. New York, N. Y. Honor-rolls, bas-reliefs, and memorial tablets. No. 117,450 ; Jan. 27 ; v. 270 ; p. 595.

Elbe Motor Co., Los Angeles, Calif. Rear-sight mirrors for vehicles. No. 123,477 ; Jan. 27 ; v. 270 ; p. 605.

Evans, John R., & Company, Philadelphia, Pa. Leather. No. 125,175 ; Jan. 27 ; v. 270 ; p. 611.

Fisher, William J., & Co., Boston, Mass. Cigars. No. 124,340 ; Jan. 27 ; v. 270 ; p. 608.

Flood. Arthur M., San Francisco, Calif. Medicinal preparation to be used as a dentifrice, &c. No. 123,314 ; Jan. 27 ; v. 270 ; p. 604.

Ford, Gertrude H., Tea Company, New York, N. Y. Teas. No 122,247 ; Jan. 27 ; v. 270 ; p. 601.

Fresno Brewing Co., Fresno. Calif. Ice-cream and ices. No. 124,600 ; Jan. 27 ; v. 270 ; p. 609.

Gage Brothers & Company, Chicago, Ill. Ladies' hats. No. 123.639 ; Jan. 27 ; v. 270 ; p. 606.

Geer, Walter L., New York, N. Y. Olive-oil. No. 121,805 ; Jan. 27 ; v. 270 ; p. 600.

Gernert, Earle, Billings, Mont. Canned vegetables. No. 124.792 ; Jan. 27 ; v. 270 ; p. 610.

Gibbs Preserving Co., Baltimore, Md. Pure fruit jams. No. 123,481 ; Jan. 27 ; v. 270 ; p. 605.

Grand Union Tea Co., Brooklyn, N. Y. Plain ground cocoa, flavoring extracts, prepared mustard, celery-salt, &c. No. 123 638 ; Jan. 27 ; v. 270 ; p. 606.

Grand Union Tea Co.. Brooklyn, N. Y. Tea. No. 123,637 ; Jan. 27 ; v. 270 ; p. 606.

Greenfield's. E., Sons. New York and Brooklyn, N. Y. Chocolate and candies. No. 124,176 ; Jan. 27 ; v. 270 ; p. 608.

Growe, Alexander, New York, N. Y. Candy. No. 117,184 ; Jan. 27 ; v. 270 ; p. 595.

Haller Baking Company, Pittsburgh, Pa. Bread. No. 123,055 ; Jan. 27 ; v. 270 ; p. 604.

Harris, Chas A., Dawson. Ga. Blood remedy. No. 123,738 ; Jan. 27 ; v. 270 ; p. 607.

Harvard Company, Lowell, Mass. Jellies, jams, marmalades, and crushed fruits. No. 120,005 ; Jan. 27 ; v. 270 ; p. 598.

Henderson Lithographing Company, The, Cincinnati, Ohio. Printed and decorated tops for blotters, folders, and message-cards, hangers, &c. No. 111,270 ; Jan. 27 ; v. 270 ; p. 593.

Hindlemann, Harry, Inc., New York, N. Y. Men's suits and overcoats. No. 122,354 ; Jan. 27 ; v. 270 ; p. 601.

Hoehl, Bruno A., Wheeling, W. Va. Malt and hop extract. No. 123,982 ; Jan. 27 ; v. 270 ; p. 607.

Hooven & Allison Company, Xenia, Ohio. Hemp rope. No. 123,692 ; Jan. 27 ; v. 270 ; p. 606.

International Preserving Corporation, New York, N. Y. Preserved or prepared foods. No. 115,916 ; Jan. 27 ; v. 270 ; p. 594.

Intravenous Products Company, Denver, Colo. Preparations used for intramuscular, intravenous, subcutaneous, or local administration. No. 122,016 ; Jan. 27 ; v. 270 ; p. 600.

Kaplan Brothers Co., New York, N. Y. Collars and shirts for men. No. 122,304 ; Jan. 27 ; v. 270 ; p. 601.

Kayser, Julius, & Co., New York, N. Y. Short narrow strips of fabric for use as trimmings for underwear. No. 121,146 ; Jan. 27 ; v. 270 ; p. 599.

Kehoe Preserving Co., Clay City and Terre Haute, Ind. Canned vegetables. No. 124,687 ; Jan. 27 ; v. 270 ; p. 610.

Kelly, Patrick H., Philadelphia, Pa. Burial boxes, caskets. and vaults. No. 122,257 ; Jan. 27 ; v. 270 ; p. 601.

Keppel, R. F., & Bro., Lancaster, Pa. Candies. No. 124,995; Jan. 27; v. 270; p. 611.

Klebanoff, David, Philadelphia, Pa. Remedy for la grippe, colds, and headache. No. 122,895; Jan. 27; v. 270; p. 603.

Klema, Joseph U., Austin, Minn. Lanterns. No. 123,437; Jan. 27; v. 270; p. 605.

Kuliman, Salz & Co., San Francisco, Calif. Hides and leather. No. 125,387; Jan. 27; v. 270; p. 612.

Lawrence Canning Co., Rockland, Me. Canned fish. No. 124,612; Jan. 27; v. 270; p. 609.

Lindner, David J., New York, N. Y. Chamois-skins. No. 125,573; Jan. 27; v. 270; p. 612.

Lion Manufacturing Company, Omaha, Nebr. Suspenders, waist-belts, garters, &c. No. 118,441; Jan. 27; v. 270; p. 596.

London, 'O-T.' Limited, Blackfriars, London, England, and Prahran, Victoria, Australia. Lemon-squash and lime-juice. No. 125,159; Jan. 27; v. 270; p. 611.

Longhorn Drilling & Development Association, Fort Worth, Tex. Well-drilling machinery and tools and well equipment. No. 122,842; Jan. 27; v. 270; p. 603.

Lowenstein, M., & Sons, Inc., New York, N. Y. Unbleached, dyed, and printed drills, twills, and sheeting. No. 118,157; Jan. 27; v. 270; p. 595.

M-C Syndicate, Philadelphia, Pa. Articles on current events for children. No. 124,414; Jan. 27; v. 270; p. 609.

Malone & Hyde, Memphis, Tenn. Castor-oil, Epsom salts, and sulfur. No. 110,234; Jan. 27; v. 270; p. 593.

Malone, Lawrence T., San Antonio, Tex. Chocolate-coated candy. No. 119,859; Jan. 27; v. 270; p. 597.

Malone, Lawrence T., San Antonio, Tex. Taffy and cream candy. No. 119,858; Jan. 27; v. 270; p. 597.

Maltbie Chemical Company, Newark, N. J. Preparation for use in the treatment of whooping-cough. No. 123,358; Jan. 27; v. 270; p. 605.

Mangos, Constantine G., Davenport, Iowa. Carbonated water. No. 123,550; Jan. 27; v. 270; p. 606.

Marathon Tire & Rubber Co., The, Cuyahoga Falls, Ohio. Rubber and composition soles and heels. No. 106,212; Jan. 27; v. 270; p. 593.

Marathon Tire and Rubber Co., Cuyahoga Falls, Ohio. Imitation leather. No. 125,001; Jan. 27; v. 270; p. 611.

Morrell, John, & Co., Ottumwa, Iowa. Eggs. No. 124,802; Jan. 27; v. 270; p. 610.

Mason City Candy Co., Mason City, Iowa. Candies. No. 124,659; Jan. 27; v. 270; p. 609.

McCormick & Co., Baltimore, Md. Spices and extracts of spices, allspice, cinnamon, cloves, &c. No. 118,969; Jan. 27; v. 270; p. 596.

Music Table Company, The, Greenfield, Ohio. Phonographs. No. 122,718; Jan. 27; v. 270; p. 603.

Norman Bros. & Berliant, Inc., Chicago, Ill. Fruit preserves. No. 120,968; Jan. 27; v. 270; p. 599.

Nu-Way Strech Suspender Company, Adrian, Mich. Suspenders and garters. No. 122,872; Jan. 27; v. 270; p. 603.

Nulomoline Company, The, New York, N. Y. Table-syrups. No. 118,790; Jan. 27; v. 270; p. 596.

Owensboro Products Company, Owensboro, Ky. Stock feed. No. 122,995; Jan. 27; v. 270; p. 603.

Page, Leonard G., St. Joseph, Mo. Mixture which comprises chili peppers, comino, &c. No. 114,057; Jan. 27; v. 270; p. 594.

Paristyle Novelty Co., Inc., New York, N. Y. Hair-nets. No. 121,182; Jan. 27; v. 270; p. 599.

Peerless Motor Car Company, The, Cleveland, Ohio. Automobiles and motor-trucks. No. 114,103; Jan. 27; v. 270; p. 594.

Pendleton Creamery Company, Pendleton, Ind. Butter. No. 119,132; Jan. 27; v. 270; p. 597.

Peters Manufacturing Co., Boston, Mass. Shoe fabrics. No. 98,890; Jan. 27; v. 270; p. 593.

Petersburg Food Products Corporation, Petersburg, Va. Apple and grain vinegar, vegetable oil for food purposes, &c. No. 124,620; Jan. 27; v. 270; p. 609.

Piedmont Motor Car Company, Inc., Lynchburg, Va. Passenger-automobiles and motor-trucks. No. 123,291; Jan. 27; v. 270; p. 604.

Pierre, Joseph M., Fort Wayne, Ind. Preparation for the treatment of asthma, bronchitis, burns, &c. No. 123,364; Jan. 27; v. 270; p. 605.

Pillsbury Flour Mills Company, Minneapolis, Minn. Buckwheat pancake-flour, wheat cereal, pancake-flour, and health-bran. No. 122,227; Jan. 27; v. 270; p. 601.

Prussian, Samuel W., Cambridge, Mass. Power-hoists. No. 124,189; Jan. 27; v. 270; p. 608.

Pyro Products Company, Chicago, Ill. Fire-brick. No. 122,657; Jan. 27; v. 270; p. 602.

Radin, Harry R., Newark, N. J. Containers and sterilizers for tooth-brushes. No. 123,906; Jan. 27; v. 270; p. 607.

Remiller Company, The, New York, N. Y. Toilet waters, tooth and mouth preparations, liquid and dry rouges, &c. No. 116,795; Jan. 27; v. 270; p. 595.

Reynolds, Wm. T., & Co., Poughkeepsie, N. Y. Butter, olive-oil, rice, dried fruits, coffee. No. 113,670; Jan. 27; v. 270; p. 594.

Rice-Stix Dry Goods Company, St. Louis, Mo. Suspenders, garters, hose-supporters, &c. No. 118,935; Jan. 27; v. 270; p. 596.

Richter, F. Ad., & Co., New York, N. Y. Medicinal preparation. No. 122,916; Jan. 27; v. 270; p. 603.

Roberts, Ward P., Milford, Mass. Cigars. No. 123,081; Jan. 27; v. 270; p. 604.

Roberts, Ward P., Milford, Mass. Cigars. No. 123,083; Jan. 27; v. 270; p. 604.

Rochester Washing Machine Corp., Rochester, N. Y. Clothes-washing machines. No. 199,988; Jan. 27; v. 270; p. 598.

Ropkins, Edgar L., Hartford, Conn. Non-intoxicating cereal beverages. No. 122,185; Jan. 27; v. 270; p. 600.

Rosenberg Bros. & Co., Rochester, N. Y. Men's coats, vests, pants, and overcoats. No. 118,239; Jan. 27; v. 270; p. 596.

Rosenthal, Charles, New York, N. Y. Sanitary paper drinking-cups. No. 122,788; Jan. 27; v. 270; p. 603.

Rueckheim Bros. & Eckstein, Chicago, Ill. Chocolate candies. No. 124,621; Jan. 27; v. 270; p. 609.

Samoset Chocolates Co., Boston, Mass. Candies. No. 124,670; Jan. 27; v. 270; p. 610.

Scars and Nichols Canning Company, Chillicothe, Ohio. Canned vegetables. No. 124,816; Jan. 27; v. 270; p. 610.

Schaefer, F. & M., Brewing Co., New York, N. Y. Soft drink. No. 125,027; Jan. 27; v. 270; p. 611.

Scheidt, Adam, Beverage Company, Norristown, Pa. Beverage. No. 124,535; Jan. 27; v. 270; p. 609.

Schulte, D. A., Inc., New York, N. Y. Cigars, cigarettes, cheroots, &c. No. 124,873; Jan. 27; v. 270; p. 611.

Simonin, Isaac M., Philadelphia, Pa. Edible vegetable oils. No. 125,258; Jan. 27; v. 270; p. 612.

Singer, Philip A., & Bro., Newark, N. J. Dressed furs for use in apparel. No. 121,700; Jan. 27; v. 270; p. 600.

Smart & Final Co., Santa Ana, Calif. Roasted coffee in packages. No. 124,766; Jan. 27; v. 270; p. 610.

Smith, Lillian W., Cape Charles, Va. Fresh potatoes. No. 118,501; Jan. 27; v. 270; p. 596.

Stannard, O. L., Dry Goods Company, Huntington, W. Va. Knitted hosiery, underwear, and sweaters, work-shirts for men and boys. No. 115,190; Jan. 27; v. 270; p. 594.

Stewart, Floyd J., Centerville, Iowa. Leather and fabric leggings. No. 119,990; Jan. 27; v. 270; p. 598.

Stewart Motor Corporation, Buffalo, N. Y. Motor-trucks and passenger-automobiles. No. 121,947; Jan. 27; v. 270; p. 600.

Strohmeyer & Arpe Company, New York, N. Y. Olive and salad oils, preserved vegetables and fish, rice, cheese, fruit, &c. No. 122,317; Jan. 27; v. 270; p. 601.

Sue, Narm S., Modesto, Calif. Medical preparation for the treatment of influenza. No. 123,183; Jan. 27; v. 270; p. 604.

Tate Manufacturing Company, Boston, Mass. Braided rope. No. 124,155; Jan. 27; v. 270; p. 608.

Taylor, Clapp & Beall, New York, N. Y. Cotton piece goods. No. 119,841; Jan. 27; v. 270; p. 597.

Tilden Company, New Lebanon, N. Y., and St. Louis, Mo. Anodyne, antiseptic, and local anesthetic. No. 123,372; Jan. 27; v. 270; p. 605.

Trappey, B. F., Jeanerette, La. Tabasco sauce, peppers in vinegar, extract of pepper, ground pepper. No. 119,920; Jan. 27; v. 270; p. 597.

Tuchschmidt, Eugene A., St. Louis, Mo. Candies. No. 118,409; Jan. 27; v. 270; p. 596.

Union Cutlery Co., Olean, N. Y. Pocket-cutlery, razors, shears, and butcher-knives. No. 121,819; Jan. 27; v. 270; p. 600.

United Drug Company, Boston, Mass. Rubber goods, &c. No. 116,223; Jan. 27; v. 270; p. 594.

Valle, Ballina y Fernandez, S. A., Villaviciosa, Spain. Champagne cider. No. 110,418; Jan. 27; v. 270; p. 593.

Vanderbilt, R. T., Company, Inc., New York, N. Y. Whiting used as a filler in rubber goods. No. 121,494; Jan. 27; v. 270; p. 599.

Vivaudou, Victor, New York, N. Y. Face-powders, face-creams, toilet waters, &c. No. 123,324; Jan. 27; v. 270; p. 605.

Waldes & Co., Prague, Bohemia. Placket, glove, and snap fasteners, buttons, &c. No. 121,062; Jan. 27; v. 270; p. 599.

Waldes & Co., Prague, Bohemia. Placket, glove, and snap fasteners, buttons, clasps, &c. No. 121,065; Jan. 27; v. 270; p. 599.

Wallace, George, New York, N. Y. Chocolates. No. 123,828; Jan. 27; v. 270; p. 607.

Walsh, Thomas A., Yonkers, N. Y. Bacteriological culture of Bacillus Bulgaricus for diarrhea in chicks and fowls. No. 123,509; Jan. 27; v. 270; p. 605.

Weed, Howard W., Stamford, Conn. Awning in the nature of wind-shield protector. No. 123,189; Jan. 27; v. 270; p. 604.

Wenzelmann, Gustave, Galesburg, Ill. Clothes-washing machines, clothes-wringers, and combinations and parts of same. No. 121,800; Jan. 27; v. 270; p. 600.

Whitehouse Brothers, Newark, N. J. Buckles. No. 117,394; Jan. 27; v. 270; p. 595.

Whiting Paper Company, Holyoke, Mass. Ledger-paper, bond and linen writing paper, and mailing-envelops. No. 122,144; Jan. 27; v. 270; p. 600.

(REGISTRATION APPLIED FOR.)

Williams Chocolate Company, Scranton, Pa. Chocolate candy. No. 124,825; Jan. 27; v. 270; p. 610.

Wood Shovel & Tool Co., Piqua, Ohio. Shovels, spades, scoops, &c. No. 124,064; Jan. 27; v. 270; p. 608.

Wood, W. B., Mfg. Co., St. Louis, Mo. Powder for the manufacture of ice-cream, fruit sherbet, &c. No. 123,829; Jan. 27; v. 270; p. 607.

Woods, Leonard, St. Louis, Mo. Article of men's furnishings in the form of aluminum-plate supporters for trousers. No. 120,441; Jan. 27; v. 270; p. 598.

Woolson Spice Co., Toledo, Ohio. Coffee. No. 124,060; Jan. 27; v. 270; p. 608.

Wrigley, Wm., Jr., Company, Chicago, Ill. Chewing-gum. No. 125,143; Jan. 27; v. 270; p. 611.

Zatyko, Paul, Divernon, Ill. Salve for sores, burns, &c. No. 115,306; Jan. 27; v. 270; p. 594.

Zevely, Percival B., Pittsburgh, Pa. Liquid vegetable laxative. No. 121,915; Jan. 27; v. 270; p. 600.

Ziff, Joseph, Detroit, Mich. Suspenders and men's garters. No. 123,830; Jan. 27; v. 270; p. 607.

ALPHABETICAL LIST OF INVENTIONS

TO WHOM

PATENTS WERE ISSUED ON THE 27TH DAY OF JANUARY, 1920.

xvii

Lifting-jack. J. Flanagan. No. 1,329,116; Jan. 27; v. 270; p. 547.
Light: See—
  Headlight.
Light-shade. C. D. Kline. No. 1,329,187; Jan. 27; v. 270; p. 561.
Lighting-fixture. A. A. Wohlauer. No. 1,329,280; Jan. 27; v. 270; p. 577.
Liquids to effect crystallization therefrom while the liquid is kept in motion, Treatment of. B. Bakke. No. 1,329,158; Jan. 27; v. 270; p. 555.
Listing and adding machine. G. D. Sundstrand. No. 1,329,028; Jan. 27; v. 270; p. 530.
Lock: See—
  Automobile-lock.   Shade-roller lock.
  Nut-lock.   Steering-wheel lock.
  Permutation-lock.
Locomotive transmission system. G. M. Eaton. No. 1,329,269; Jan. 27; v. 270; p. 576.
Loom shuttle-guard. V. K. Badolan. No. 1,329,157; Jan. 27; v. 270; p. 555.
Loom tube-frame. C. Lea. No. 1,329,302; Jan. 27; v. 270; p. 581.
Looms, Feeler-motion for. E. S. Stimpson. No. 1,328,907; Jan. 27; v. 270; p. 508.
Looms, Feeler-motion for. E. S. Stimpson. No. 1,328,908; Jan. 27; v. 270; p. 508.
Lubricator: See—
  Wheel-lubricator.
Lubricator. M. L. Donovan. No. 1,329,229; Jan. 27; v. 270; p. 568.
Luggage-carrier. F. T. Wentworth. No. 1,328,863; Jan. 27; v. 270; p. 499.
Magnetos, Starter applicable to. H. Parkin. No. 1,328,892; Jan. 27; v. 270; p. 505.
Manhole. A. Davis, Jr. No. 1,329,040; Jan. 27; v. 270; p. 533.
Manuscript form, Method and apparatus for teaching. E. R. Garfield. No. 1,328,952; Jan. 27; v. 270; p. 516.
Marine propulsion. T. R. de Esparza. No. 1,329,228; Jan. 27; v. 270; p. 568.
Match-box. H. Pick. No. 1,329,012; Jan. 27; v. 270; p. 527.
Match-safe. B. R. Russell. No. 1,328,968; Jan. 27; v. 270; p. 519.
Matches for splints, Assembling-machine for. M. Paridon. No. 1,329,060; Jan. 27; v. 270; p. 536.
Matches and splints, Assembling-machine for. M. Paridon. No. 1,329,061; Jan. 27; v. 270; p. 537.
Measuring instrument. A. N. Hill. No. 1,328,876; Jan. 27; v. 270; p. 502.
Measuring the heights of superposed liquids of varying specific gravities, Method of and apparatus for. R. G. Thomas. No. 1,329,150; Jan. 27; v. 270; p. 553.
Metals and reduced metallic compounds, Making powdered. C. Ellis. No. 1,329,322; Jan. 27; v. 270; p. 584.
Milk and cream, Ascertaining the quantity of fat in. H. M. Höyberg. No. 1,329,183; Jan. 27; v. 270; p. 560.
Milk-carrier, Sanitary. B. Wilbur. No. 1,328,937; Jan. 27; v. 270; p. 514.
Milker-head. M. Lammers. No. 1,328,880; Jan. 27; v. 270; p. 503.
Mill: See—
  Windmill.
Mirror-mounting. L. J. Stern. No. 1,328,930; Jan. 27; v. 270; p. 512.
Mixer: See—
  Dough-mixer.   Gas-mixer.
Mold: See—
  Asbestos-flange mold.
Molding apparatus. J. Nitzgen. No. 1,328,887; Jan. 27; v. 270; p. 504.
Molds, Releasing cup-pastry from. R. G. Kratz. No. 1,329,086; Jan. 27; v. 270; p. 541.
Motion mechanism, Differential-. W. H. Brown. No. 1,329,159; Jan. 27; v. 270; p. 555.
Motor: See—
  Aeroplane-motor.   Water-motor.
  Hydrocarbon-motor.   Weight-motor.
Motors, Lubricating system for traveling. G. H. Curtiss. No. 1,329,038; Jan. 27; v. 270; p. 532.
Mowers, Cutter-bar control for weed-. W. F. Kasper. No. 1,328,836; Jan. 27; v. 270; p. 493.
Multiple-circuit-resistance control. R. W. Ebeling. No. 1,329,108; Jan. 27; v. 270; p. 557.
Music, Device for turning sheet-. L. S. Anderson. No. 1,328,976; Jan. 27; v. 270; p. 521.
Music-sheet. R. Callender. No. 1,329,286; Jan. 27; v. 270; p. 578.
Napkin-fastener. R. Thamm. No. 1,329,149; Jan. 27; v. 270; p. 553.
Nest, Hen's. W. M. Scott. No. 1,329,024; Jan. 27; v. 270; p. 530.
Nozzle, Locomotive exhaust-. J. A. Ormiston. No. 1,329,093; Jan. 27; v. 270; p. 543.
Nursery-seat. A. K. Rownd. No. 1,328,900; Jan. 27; v. 270; p. 507.
Nut-lock. W. P. Andrew. No. 1,328,939; Jan. 27; v. 270; p. 514.
Oil and obtaining by-products therefrom, Method of and apparatus for treating. E. H. Frohner. No. 1,329,076; Jan. 27; v. 270; p. 539.
Ordnance-sighting apparatus. A. A. Dawson and G. T. Buckham. No. 1,328,914; Jan. 27; v. 270; p. 509.

Ores, Method of and apparatus for concentrating. J. M. Callow. No. 1,329,385; Jan. 27; v. 270; p. 587.
Ores, Separation of. A. A. Lockwood. No. 1,329,127; Jan. 27; v. 270; p. 549.
Packet-holder. B. Ashby. No. 1,328,869; Jan. 27; v. 270; p. 500.
Pan: See—
  Seed-pan.
Pants, Baby-. M. S. George. No. 1,329,119; Jan. 27; v. 270; p. 548.
Paper, Apparatus for making ornamental. E. Mahler. No. 1,329,130; Jan. 27; v. 270; p. 550.
Paper and apparatus therefor, Making lines and watermarks on. O. Suursalmi. No. 1,329,100; Jan. 27; v. 270; p. 544.
Paper-bag holder. W. D. Elliot. No. 1,328,950; Jan. 27; v. 270; p. 516.
Paper box. F. M. Wade. No. 1,328,935; Jan. 27; v. 270; p. 513.
Paper holder and clip, Desk-basket. J. C. Soemer. No. 1,328,971; Jan. 27; v. 270; p. 520.
Parachute comprising pneumatic means. A. Ramauge. No. 1,328,848; Jan. 27; v. 270; p. 496.
Pawl-and-ratchet means. J. W. Knopp. No. 1,329,000; Jan. 27; v. 270; p. 525.
Peas from wheat, Machine for separating wild. C. W. Carter. No. 1,328,819; Jan. 27; v. 270; p. 490.
Permutation-lock. D. J. Davis. No. 1,329,041; Jan. 27; v. 270; p. 533.
Picker: See—
  Cotton-picker.
Picture apparatus, Motion-. N. T. Whitaker. No. 1,329,216; Jan. 27; v. 270; p. 566.
Pile-cutting mechanism. A. F. McCollum. No. 1,329,251; Jan. 27; v. 270; p. 572.
Pins, hinge-pins, coupling-pins, &c., Locking means for joint-. E. Mepsted. No. 1,329,131; Jan. 27; v. 270; p. 550.
Pipe: See—
  Standpipe.
Pipe-clip and forming same. L. H. Dickelmann and J. Kuehler. No. 1,329,268; Jan. 27; v. 270; p. 576.
Piston. A. J. Golata and L. R. Roberts. No. 1,329,238; Jan. 27; v. 270; p. 570.
Piston-rings, Manufacturing. S. D. Hartog. No. 1,329,271; Jan. 27; v. 270; p. 576.
Planters, Seed spacing and dropping mechanism for. J. E. Paulson. No. 1,328,846; Jan. 27; v. 270; p. 496.
Plastic composition. F. Richard and F. M. Brady. No. 1,329,094; Jan. 27; v. 270; p. 543.
Pliers. S. E. Aaron. No. 1,329,155; Jan. 27; v. 270; p. 554.
Plow, Shovel or spade. I. Cohen. No. 1,328,913; Jan. 27; v. 270; p. 509.
Plowing-machine. C. C. Reed. No. 1,328,896; Jan. 27; v. 270; p. 506.
Pocket for garments, Safety-. C. M. Miller, Jr. No. 1,328,884; Jan. 27; v. 270; p. 504.
Pole or post. M. Lachman. No. 1,328,927; Jan. 27; v. 270; p. 512.
Portable elevator. H. R. Kees and E. F. Thomas. No. 1,329,044; Jan. 27; v. 270; p. 541.
Post: See—
  Fencepost.
Post. D. H. Snyder. No. 1,329,026; Jan. 27; v. 270; p. 530.
Power-converter. C. C. Butler. No. 1,329,037; Jan. 27; v. 270; p. 532.
Power-press guard. J. E. Phillips. No. 1,329,011; Jan. 27; v. 270; p. 527.
Power station, the output of one or more distant sources, Apparatus for adding to the output of a main. S. D. Sprong. No. 1,329,276; Jan. 27; v. 270; p. 577.
Power-transmitting-mechanism, Change-speed. T. H. Duncombe. No. 1,329,297; Jan. 27; v. 270; p. 580.
Printing-machine. G. W. Mascord. No. 1,329,325; Jan. 27; v. 270; p. 585.
Printing-machines, Lock-bearing for the composition rollers of. C. Winkler. No. 1,329,217; Jan. 27; v. 270; p. 566.
Printing machines, Registering mechanism for form or plate cylinders of multicolor-. F. C. Marquardt. No. 1,328,842; Jan. 27; v. 270; p. 495.
Printing-plates, Making. E. Leitner. No. 1,329,088; Jan. 27; v. 270; p. 541.
Printing-presses, Sheet-feeding mechanism for. R. Hoe. No. 1,328,877; Jan. 27; v. 270; p. 502.
Propeller-shafts, Flexible coupling for. R. A. Patrick. No. 1,328,893; Jan. 27; v. 270; p. 505.
Protractor. J. Neumaier. No. 1,329,005; Jan. 27; v. 270; p. 526.
Prune-pitting machine. B. W. Scott. No. 1,329,023; Jan. 27; v. 270; p. 529.
Pump-base. F. W. Zingsheim. No. 1,329,281; Jan. 27; v. 270; p. 578.
Pump-packing. J. W. Drew. No. 1,329,165; Jan. 27; v. 270; p. 556.
Pump-strainer. R. S. and J. G. Garry. No. 1,329,171; Jan. 27; v. 270; p. 557.
Pumps, Hand-operating attachment for. J. H. Oldham. No. 1,329,137; Jan. 27; v. 270; p. 551.
Pumps, Steam-jacket for oil-. L. C. Stefferud. No. 1,328,906; Jan. 27; v. 270; p. 508.

Wheels, Apparatus for casting hollow one-piece spoke-. B. L. Smith. No. 1,328,852 ; Jan. 27 ; v. 270 ; p. 497.
Wheels, Spoke and tire for automobile and truck. A. Collier. No. 1,329,111 ; Jan. 27 ; v. 270 ; p. 546.
Window. B. S. McClellan. No. 1,329,003 ; Jan. 27 ; v. 270 ; p. 526.
Window-sashes, Operating device for. W. P. Hilley. No. 1,329,178 ; Jan. 27 ; v. 270 ; p. 559
Windmill, Power-. G. D. Foster. No. 1,329,299 ; Jan. 27 ; v. 270 ; p. 581.
Wire fence. R. Knaur. No. 1,329,189 ; Jan. 27 ; v. 270 ; p. 561.
Wood, Bleaching. E. Bateman. No. 1,329,284 ; Jan. 27 ; v. 270 ; p. 578.

Workbench, Watchmaker's and Jeweler's. S. K. Ouzoun-Boghossian. No. 1,328,891 ; Jan. 27 ; v. 270 ; p. 505.
Wrapper. R. H. Mester. No. 1,329,056 ; Jan. 27 ; v. 270 ; p. 536.
Wrapping-machine. H. R. Bevier. No. 1,329,069 ; Jan. 27 ; v. 270 ; p. 538.
Wrapping mechanism. Candy-. M. B. Ferguson and E. Haas. No. 1,329,236 ; Jan. 27 ; v. 270 ; p. 569.
Wrench. R. J. Colson. No. 1,329,161 ; Jan. 27 ; v. 270 ; p. 557.
Yoke. Draft-gear. H. T. Anderson. No. 1,329,318 ; Jan. 27 ; v. 270 ; p. 584.
Yokes, Manufacture of railway draft-gear. H. T. Anderson. No. 1,328,975 ; Jan. 27 ; v. 270 ; p. 521.

ALPHABETICAL LIST OF TRADE-MARKS.

Air-compressors, Vacuum heating-pumps, &c. Nash Engineering Company. No. 129,190 ; Jan. 27 ; v. 270 ; p. 615.
Automobile, &c., accessories. Romort Manufacturing Company. No. 129,211 ; Jan. 27 ; v. 270 ; p. 616.
Babbitt metal. United American Metals Corporation. No. 129,232 ; Jan. 27 ; v. 270 ; p. 617.
Barometers. Dourde et Cie. No. 129,150 ; Jan. 27 ; v. 270 ; p. 614.
Bearings and parts, Ball and roller. J. Schmid-Roost. No. 129,216 ; Jan. 27 ; v. 270 ; p. 616.
Beverage and syrup for making same, Non-alcoholic. W. B. Wood Mfg. Co. Nos. 129,253-4 ; Jan. 27 ; v. 270 ; p. 617.
Beverage. Carbonated. Yonkers Brewery. No. 129,255 ; Jan. 27 ; v. 270 ; p. 617.
Beverage. Cereal malt. Terre Haute Brewing Company. No. 129,228 ; Jan. 27 ; v. 270 ; p. 616.
Beverage. Malt. Pittsburgh Brewing Company. No. 129,201 ; Jan. 27 ; v. 270 ; p. 616.
Beverage. Maltless non-alcoholic fruit. Monopole Vineyards Corp. Nos. 129,187-8 ; Jan. 27 ; v. 270 ; p. 615.
Beverage, Non-alcoholic non-cereal maltless. W. E. Gould. No. 129,161 ; Jan. 27 ; v. 270 ; p. 614.
Beverage. Non-alcoholic non-cereal maltless Schoenhofen Company. No. 129,217 ; Jan. 27 ; v. 270 ; p. 616.
Beverage. Non-intoxicating malt. Harvard Company. No. 129,168 ; Jan. 27 ; v. 270 ; p. 614.
Beverages, Non-alcoholic. F. J. Fisher. No. 129,156 ; Jan. 27 ; v. 270 ; p. 614.
Beverages, Non-alcoholic maltless. Fred Messmer Mfg. Co. No. 129,184 ; Jan. 27 ; v. 270 ; p. 615.
Bicycles. Simmons Hardware Company. No. 129,220 ; Jan. 27 ; v. 270 ; p. 616.
Bloomers. Saul Gelarie & Company. No. 129,215 ; Jan 27 ; v. 270 ; p. 616.
Blouses. Cobden Co. No. 129,137 ; Jan. 27 ; v. 270 ; p. 614.
Bread. E. A. Dexter. No. 129,146 ; Jan. 27 ; v. 270 ; p. 614.
Bronze ingots. Babbitt metal, &c. Eastwood Wire Manufacturing Company. No. 129,152 ; Jan. 27 ; v. 270 ; p. 614.
Candy. Reynolds-Lindhelm Cigar Company. No. 129,208 ; Jan 27 ; v. 270 ; p. 616.
Canned fish and clams. Sidney Canning Co. No. 129,219 ; Jan. 27 ; v. 270 ; p. 616.
Canned fruits. Charles Stern & Sons. No. 129,225 ; Jan. 27 ; v. 270 ; p. 616.
Canned fruits and vegetables. Alfred Putnam & Company. No. 129,204 ; Jan. 27 ; v. 270 ; p. 616
Canned fruits and vegetables and vanilla and lemon extracts. Flaherty & Urbanowski Co. No. 129,157 ; Jan. 27 ; v. 270 ; p. 614.
Canned vegetables and fruits, dried fruits, jellies, &c. California Packing Corporation. No. 129,131 ; Jan. 27 ; v. 270 ; p. 615.
Caps. Jackoway and Katz Cap Co. No. 129,170 ; Jan. 27 ; v. 270 ; p. 615.
Castings and forgings. The Cleveland Brass Manufacturing Co. No. 129,135 ; Jan. 27 ; v. 270 ; p. 613.
Chains to vehicle-wheels, Bars, &c., for securing antiskid-. Challoner Company. No. 129,133 ; Jan. 27 ; v. 270 ; p. 613.
Cheese, Limburger. Joseph Acherman & Co. No. 129,110 ; Jan. 27 ; v. 270 ; p. 613.
Chemicals. U. S. Industrial Chemical Co. No. 129,234 ; Jan. 27 ; v. 270 ; p. 617.
Clothes. Work-. The H. D. Lee Mercantile Co. No. 129,176 ; Jan. 27 ; v. 270 ; p. 615.
Clothing. Blum Brothers. No. 129,126 ; Jan. 27 ; v. 270 ; p. 613.
Clothing. Hall. Hartwell & Co. No. 129,162 ; Jan. 27 ; v. 270 ; p. 614.
Clothing, Boys' outer. Phil. Walcoff & Co., Inc. No. 129,241 ; Jan. 27 ; v. 270 ; p. 617.
Coal. W. W. Heidelbaugh. No. 129,165 ; Jan. 27 ; v. 270 ; p. 614.
Coats, Auto. rain. dress, and utility. The Miller Cloak Co. No. 129,186 ; Jan. 27 ; v. 270 ; p. 615.
Coats, vests, &c., Men's and boys'. Putnam Overall Mfg. Co. No. 129 205 ; Jan. 27 ; v. 270 ; p. 616.
Cookies. Loose Wiles Biscuit Company. No. 129,179 ; Jan. 27 ; v. 270 ; p. 615.
Cylinder-reboring tools and kits. Universal Tool Co. No. 129,236 ; Jan. 27 ; v. 270 ; p. 617.

Dough balling and proofing machine, &c. Thomson Machine Company. No. 129,230 ; Jan. 27 ; v. 270 ; p. 616.
Dough-mixers. The East Iron & Machine Co. No. 129,151 ; Jan. 27 ; v. 270 ; p. 614.
Enameled metal ware. National Enameling & Stamping Co. No. 129,193 ; Jan. 27 ; v. 270 ; p. 615.
Enameled steelware. Cleveland Metal Products Company. No. 129,136 ; Jan. 27 ; v. 270 ; p. 613.
Engines. Internal-combustion. Arrol-Johnston. No. 129,121 ; Jan. 27 ; v. 270 ; p. 613.
Feathers. Wahlert & Guntzler. No. 129,240 ; Jan. 27 ; v. 270 ; p. 617.
Feed. Voigt Milling Company. No. 129,238 ; Jan. 27 ; v. 270 ; p. 617.
Flour. Self-rising wheat-. Quaker City Flour Mills Company. No. 129,206 ; Jan. 27 ; v. 270 ; p. 616.
Flour. Wheat-. Donmeyer, Gardner Co. No. 129,149 ; Jan. 27 ; v. 270 ; p. 614.
Flour. Wheat-. Goerz Flour Mills Co. No. 129,160 ; Jan. 27 ; v. 270 ; p. 614.
Flour. Wheat-. Ottawa Milling Company. No. 129,199 ; Jan. 27 ; v. 270 ; p. 615.
Flour. Wheat-. J. Rosenstein. No. 129,212 ; Jan. 27 ; v. 270 ; p. 616.
Food, Cattle. J. J. Badenoch Co. No. 129,123 ; Jan. 27 ; v. 270 ; p. 613.
Foods, Stock poultry, and dog. Randall-McLoughlin Co. No. 129,207 ; Jan. 27 ; v. 270 ; p. 616.
Footwear. The Irving Drew Company. No. 129,169 ; Jan. 27 ; v. 270 ; p. 614.
Fruits, Fresh citrus. Polk County Citrus Sub-Exchange. No. 129,202 ; Jan. 27 ; v. 270 ; p. 616.
Garment-hangers, shoe-trees, &c., Decorated hand-painted. Lowe & Lowe. No. 129,180 ; Jan. 27 ; v. 270 ; p. 615.
Garments. Men's and boys' outer. Gonzalez Padin Co. No. 129,159 ; Jan. 27 ; v. 270 ; p. 614.
Ginger-ale. R. B. Kingman. No. 129,175 ; Jan. 27 ; v. 270 ; p. 615.
Ginger-beer. J. V. Willis. No. 129,247 ; Jan. 27 ; v. 270 ; p. 617.
Gloves and mittens. R. K. Wilson. No. 129,252 ; Jan. 27 ; v. 270 ; p. 617.
Grate-bar for furnaces and stoves. Cyclone Grate-Bar Co. No. 129 144 ; Jan. 27 ; v. 270 ; p. 614.
Grinding. crushing. and pulverizing machines. Williams Patent Crusher and Pulverizer Company. No. 129,250 ; Jan. 27 ; v. 270 ; p. 617.
Grits, pearl-hominy, &c. Wathen Milling Company. No. 129,243 ; Jan. 27 ; v. 270 ; p. 617.
Hacksaws. Young. Corley & Dolan. No. 129,256 ; Jan. 27 ; v. 270 ; p. 617.
Hacksaws and screw-drivers. New England Tool Co. Inc. No. 129 194 ; Jan. 27 ; v. 270 ; p. 615.
Hardware. Builders'. E. Bommer. No. 129,127 ; Jan. 27 ; v. 270 ; p. 613.
Hats. Ladies'. James A. Hearn & Sons. No. 129,164 ; Jan. 27 ; v. 270 ; p. 614.
Hats. Ladies'. C. Roth. No. 129,213 ; Jan. 27 ; v. 270 ; p. 616.
Hats, Ladies'. J. Tenenbaum & Sons. No. 129,227 ; Jan. 27 ; v. 270 ; p. 616.
Hats Ladies'. and children's. H. Kane. No. 129.174 ; Jan. 27 ; v. 270 ; p. 615.
Hose-couplings. Independent Pneumatic Tool Company. No. 129,168 ; Jan. 27 ; v. 270 ; p. 614.
Hosiery. Ambridge Knitting Co. No. 129,112 ; Jan. 27 ; v. 270 ; p. 613.
Hosiery. American Trading Company. Nos. 129,116-17 ; Jan. 27 ; v. 270 ; p. 613.
Hosiery. Apex Hosiery Company. No. 129,118 ; Jan. 27 ; v. 270 ; p. 613.
Hosiery. Chipman Knitting Mills. No. 129,134 ; Jan. 27 ; v. 270 ; p. 613.
Hosiery. United Hosiery Mills Corporation. No. 129,233 ; Jan. 27 ; v. 270 ; p. 617.
Ice-cream cones. Superior Cone Company. No. 129,226 ; Jan. 27 ; v. 270 ; p. 616.
Iron and steel plates. &c. Alan Wood Iron & Steel Company. No. 129,111 ; Jan. 27 ; v. 270 ; p. 613.
Iron. steel. and sheet-metal products and forgings. American Steel Export Company. No. 129,114 ; Jan. 27 ; v. 270 ; p. 613.
Lens blanks and lenses. Ophthalmic. Simpson-Walther Lens Company. No. 129,221 ; Jan. 27 ; v. 270 ; p. 616.

ALPHABETICAL LIST OF LABELS.

ALPHABETICAL LIST OF PRINTS.

ALPHABETICAL LIST OF TRADE-MARK TITLES.

(REGISTRATION APPLIED FOR.)

Laxative, Liquid vegetable. P. B. Zevely. No. 121,915 ; Jan. 27 ; v. 270 ; p. 600.
Leather. John R. Evans & Company. No. 125,175 ; Jan. 27 ; v. 270 ; p. 611.
Leather Imitation. Marathon Tire and Rubber Co. No. 125,001 ; Jan. 27 ; v. 270 ; p. 611.
Leggings. Leather and fabric. F. J. Stewart. No. 119,990 ; Jan. 27 ; v. 270 ; p. 598.
Lemon-squash and lime-juice. London ' O-T ' Limited. No. 125,159 ; Jan. 27 ; v. 270 ; p. 611.
Machines and parts thereof. Sewing. L. Burlasky. No. 124,676 ; Jan. 27 ; v. 270 ; p. 610.
Magazine Monthly. American Carpenter and Builder Co. No. 122,679 ; Jan. 27 ; v. 270 ; p. 602.
Mayonnaise dressing, chilli-chow, and a marshmallow preparation. J. A. De Luca. No. 125,080 ; Jan. 27 ; v. 270 ; p. 611.
Medicinal preparation. A. M. Flood. No. 123,314 ; Jan. 27 ; v. 270 ; p. 604.
Medicinal preparation for influenza. N. S. Sue. No. 123,183 ; Jan. 27 ; v. 270 ; p. 604.
Medicinal preparations. F. Ad. Richter & Co. No. 122,916 ; Jan. 27 ; v. 270 ; p. 603.
Mirrors for vehicles, Rear-sight. Elbe Motor Co. No. 123,477 ; Jan. 27 ; v. 270 ; p. 605.
Mixture which comprises chilli peppers, comino, &c. L. G. Page. No. 114,057 ; Jan. 27 ; v. 270 ; p. 594.
Oats, Rolled. Corno Mills Company. No. 124,642 ; Jan. 27 ; v. 270 ; p. 609.
Oil and tomato paste, Olive-. A. & C. Buscaglia Co. No. 122,585 ; Jan. 27 ; v. 270 ; p. 602.
Oil, Epsom salts, and sulfur, Castor-. Malone & Hyde. No. 110,254 ; Jan. 27 ; v. 270 ; p. 593.
Oil, Olive-. W. L. Geer. No. 121,805 ; Jan. 27 ; v. 270 ; p. 600.
Oil, preserved vegetables and fish, cheese, tea, pickles, candy, &c., Olive. Strohmeyer & Arpe Company. No. 122,317 ; Jan. 27 ; v. 270 ; p. 601.
Oils, Edible. Aspegren & Company. Nos. 120,023-4 ; Jan. 27 ; v. 270 ; p. 598.
Oils, Edible vegetable. I. M. Simonin. No. 125,258 ; Jan. 27 ; v. 270 ; p. 612.
Oranges, Fresh. Buckeye Nurseries. No 118,588 ; Jan. 27 ; v. 270 ; p. 596.
Paper, bond and linen writing paper, and envelops. Ledger-Whiting Paper Company. No. 122,144 ; Jan. 27 ; v. 270 ; p. 600.
Paper drinking-cups, Sanitary. C. Rosenthal. No. 122,788 ; Jan. 27 ; v. 270 ; p. 602.
Phonographs. Music Table Company. No. 122,718 ; Jan. 27 ; v. 270 ; p. 602.
Placket, glove, and snap fasteners, buttons, clasps. Waldes & Co. No. 121,062 ; Jan. 27 ; v. 270 ; p. 599.
Placket, glove, and snap fasteners, buttons, clasps. Waldes & Co. No. 121,065 ; Jan. 27 ; v. 270 ; p. 599.
Popcorn confections. American Pop Corn Works. No. 107,018 ; Jan. 27 ; v. 270 ; p. 593.
Potatoes, Fresh. L. W. Smith. No. 118,501 ; Jan. 27 ; v. 270 ; p. 596.
Power-hoists. S. W. Prussian. No. 124,189 ; Jan. 27 ; v. 270 ; p. 608.
Powder-puffs. C. & K. Mfg. Co. No. 121,691 ; Jan. 27 ; v. 270 ; p. 599.
Powder, Toilet. George Borgfeldt & Co. No. 123,418 ; Jan. 27 ; v. 270 ; p. 605.
Powders and creams, perfumes, &c., Face. V. Vivaudou. No. 123,324 ; Jan. 27 ; v. 270 ; p. 605.
Preparation for asthma. &c. J. M. Pierre. No. 123,364 ; Jan. 27 ; v. 270 ; p. 605.
Preparation for use in the treatment of whooping-cough. Malthe Chemical Company. No. 123,358 ; Jan. 27 ; v. 270 ; p. 605.
Preparation used for intramuscular intravenous, subcutaneous, or local administration. Intravenous Products Company. No. 122,016 ; Jan. 27 ; v. 270 ; p. 600.
Preserves, Fruit. Norman Bros. & Berliant. No. 120,968 ; Jan. 27 ; v. 270 ; p. 599.
Remedy, Blood. C. A. Harris. No. 123,738 ; Jan. 27 ; v. 270 ; p. 607.
Remedy for la grippe, colds, and headache. D. Klebanoff. No. 122,895 ; Jan. 27 ; v. 270 ; p. 603.

Roach-powder. H. Bell. No. 122,384 ; Jan. 27 ; v. 270 ; p. 602.
Rope, Braided. Tate Manufacturing Company. No. 124,155 ; Jan. 27 ; v. 270 ; p. 608.
Rope, Hemp. Hooven & Allison Company. No. 123,692 ; Jan. 27 ; v. 270 ; p. 606.
Rubber and composition soles and heels. Marathon Tire & Rubber Co. No. 106,212 ; Jan. 27 ; v. 270 ; p. 593.
Rubber goods, &c. United Drug Company. No. 116,223 ; Jan. 27 ; v. 270 ; p. 594.
Sand-dressing, peanut-butter, and salted peanuts. C. F. Blanke Tea & Coffee Company. No. 119,591 ; Jan. 27 ; v. 270 ; p. 597.
Salve. P. Zatyko. No. 115,306 ; Jan. 27 ; v. 270 ; p. 594.
Seeds, Corn, grass, and field. H. E. Conklin. No. 115,801 ; Jan. 27 ; v. 270 ; p. 594.
Seeds, Field, garden, and flower. A. R. Bruns. No. 119,262 ; Jan. 27 ; v. 270 ; p. 597.
Shoe fabrics. Peters Manufacturing Co. No. 98,890 ; Jan. 27 ; v. 270 ; p. 593.
Shovels, spades, scoops, and drainage-tools. Wood Shovel & Tool Co. No. 124,064 ; Jan. 27 ; v. 270 ; p. 608.
Skins, Chamois-. D. J. Lindner. No. 125,573 ; Jan. 27 ; v. 270 ; p. 612.
Soaps, soap tablets, and rug-cleaners, Laundry. C. C. Cummings. No. 119,183 ; Jan. 27 ; v. 270 ; p. 597.
Spices and extracts. McCormick & Co. No. 118,969 ; Jan. 27 ; v. 270 ; p. 596.
Steel bars, rods, billets, &c. Crucible Steel Company of America. No. 122,284 ; Jan. 27 ; v. 270 ; p. 601.
Stoves, Coal-. Delaware Electric & Supply Co. No. 124,082 ; Jan. 27 ; v. 270 ; p. 608.
Suits and overcoats, Men's. Harry Hindlemann, Inc. No. 122,354 ; Jan. 27 ; v. 270 ; p. 601.
Suspenders and garters. Nu-Way Strech Suspender Company. No. 122,872 ; Jan. 27 ; v. 270 ; p. 603.
Suspenders and men's garters. J. Ziff. No. 123,830 ; Jan. 27 ; v. 270 ; p. 607.
Suspenders, garters, hose-supporters, &c. Rice-Stix Dry Goods Company. No. 118,935 ; Jan. 27 ; v. 270 ; p. 596.
Suspenders, waist-belts for supporting wearing-apparel, &c. Lion Manufacturing Company. No. 118,441 ; Jan. 27 ; v. 270 ; p. 596.
Syrup made of cane-sugar. Archbold Manufacturing Corporation. No. 124,878 ; Jan. 27 ; v. 270 ; p. 611.
Syrups, Table-. Nulomoline Company. No. 118,790 ; Jan. 27 ; v. 270 ; p. 596.
Tabasco sauce, peppers in vinegar, &c. B. F. Trappey. No. 119,920 ; Jan. 27 ; v. 270 ; p. 597.
Tea. Grand Union Tea Co. No. 123,637 ; Jan. 27 ; v. 270 ; p. 606.
Teas. Gertrude H. Ford Tea Company. No. 122,247 ; Jan. 27 ; v. 270 ; p. 601.
Tobacco. American Tobacco Company. No. 123,016 ; Jan. 27 ; v. 270 ; p. 603.
Tobacco and cigarettes. American Tobacco Company. No. 123,017 ; Jan. 27 ; v. 270 ; p. 603.
Tobacco. Smoking and chewing. American Tobacco Company. No. 124,706 ; Jan. 27 ; v. 270 ; p. 610.
Tobacco and cigarettes, Smoking and chewing. American Tobacco Company. No. 124,708 ; Jan. 27 ; v. 270 ; p. 610.
Toilet waters, tooth and mouth preparations, &c. Remiller Company. No. 116,795 ; Jan. 27 ; v. 270 ; p. 595.
Trousers-supporters. L. Woods. No. 120,441 ; Jan. 27 ; v. 270 ; p. 598.
Trucks and passenger-automobiles, Motor-. Stewart Motor Corporation. No. 121,947 ; Jan. 27 ; v. 270 ; p. 600.
Trucks, Automobile-. American Commercial Car Co. No. 122,871 ; Jan. 27 ; v. 270 ; p. 603.
Vinegar, vegetable oil, and table-syrups. Petersburg Food Products Corporation. No. 124,620 ; Jan. 27 ; v. 270 ; p. 609.
Washing-machines. Rochester Washing Machine Corp. No. 119,988 ; Jan. 27 ; v. 270 ; p. 598.
Water, Carbonated C. G. Mangos. No. 123,550 ; Jan. 27 ; v. 270 ; p. 606.
Well-drilling machinery and tools and well equipment. Longhorn Drilling & Development Association. No. 122,842 ; Jan. 27 ; v. 270 ; p. 602.
Whiting. R. T. Vanderbilt Company. No. 121,494 ; Jan. 27 ; v. 270 ; p. 599.

CLASSIFICATION OF PATENTS

ISSUED JANUARY 27, 1920.

NOTE.—First number—class, second number—subclass, third number—patent number.

2— 15: 1,328,884
42: 1,328,958
109: 1,328,823
131: 1,329,119
144: 1,329,025
1,329,329
4— 2: 1,329,058
5: 1,329,109
18: 1,328,900
1,329,339
39: 1,329,124
5— 5: 1,328,977
8: 1,329,202
12: 1,328,802
25: 1,328,878
40: 1,329,145
6— 11: 1,328,813
8— 2: 1,329,284
5: 1,329,117
18: 1,328,987
19: 1,329,166
9— 21: 1,329,073
15— 60: 1,329,048
16— 77: 1,329,313
90: 1,329,326
1,329,327
100: 1,328,961
106: 1,329,059
142: 1,328,874
17— 24: 1,328,916
18— 5: 1,328,887
43: 1,329,208
47: 1,329,312
19— 8: 1,328,704
20— 16: 1,329,310
69: 1,329,003
79: 1,328,875
83: 1,329,290
21— 46: 1,329,047
69: 1,329,210
150: 1,329,307
63: 1,329,316
22— 65: 1,329,179
1,329,296
130: 1,328,852
209: 1,329,295
23— 1: 1,329,273
3: 1,329,183
1,329,183
13: 1,328,938
1,329,072
24: 1,329,214
1,329,272
28: 1,329,322
1,329,323
24— 7: 1,329,149
18: 1,328,869
77: 1,329,085
155: 1,328,954
156: 1,328,965
201: 1,328,945
234: 1,329,071
257: 1,329,186
25— 118: 1,328,817
1,329,095
28— 21: 1,328,943
29— 99: 1,328,947
156.1: 1,329,271
167: 1,328,975
30 - 3: 1,329,133
22: 1,328,772
31— 98: 1,328,880
33— 1: 1,328,881
48: 1,328,911
52: 1,329,075
75: 1,329,005
98: 1,329,337
145: 1,329,196
1,329,197
169: 1,329,234
34— 12: 1,329,082
63: 1,328,807
26: 1,329,301
35— 12: 1,328,818
1,328,952
36— 38: 1,328,816
40: 1,329,064
62: 1,329,064
63: 1,328,957
37— 7: 1,328,910
57: 1,329,123
62: 1,328,973

38— 22: 1,328,850
39— 1: 1,329,022
66: 1,329,263
40— 7: 1,329,207
10: 1,328,915
53: 1,329,216
77: 1,329,218
107: 1,328,830
125.6: 1,329,206
152: 1,329,078
42— 70: 1,329,280
74: 1,328,924
43— 20: 1,329,128
22: 1,328,936
44— 1: 1,329,300
45— 2: 1,329,139
21: 1,328,995
28: 1,329,097
93: 1,328,891
119: 1,329,070
46— 14: 1,329,044
35: 1,328,867
37: 1,328,867
40: 1,329,201
45: 1,328,820
1,329,045
59: 1,329,291
66: 1,329,254
1,329,254
48— 171: 1,329,129
180: 1,329,210
49— 9: 1,329,253
12: 1,328,864
17: R.14,794
17.1: 1,329,065
51— 4: 1,328,894
1,328,953
52— 3: 1,329,131
1,329,212
39: 1,328,922
54— 39: 1,329,102
55— 61: 1,329,154
80: 1,329,118
118: 1,329,220
56— 32: 1,329,067
207: 1,329,266
232: 1,328,836
57— 18: 1,329,057
58— 28: 1,329,083
60— 66: 1,328,951
61— 42: 1,329,317
62— 4: 1,329,350
63— 28: 1,328,948
1,328,949
64— 24: 1,329,241
30: 1,328,983
52: 1,329,217
59: 1,329,089
79: 1,328,877
96: 1,328,893
65— 13: 1,329,203
47: 1,328,827
79: 1,329,222
87— 9: 1,328,807
68— 10: 1,329,257
69— 9.5: 1,329,294
70: 1,329,041
129: 1,328,882
1,329,114
71— 1: 1,329,105
72— 68: 1,329,160
73— 51: 1,329,160
54: 1,329,000
109: 1,328,895
110: 1,328,934
74— 7: 1,328,934
1,329,159
21: 1,328,966
34: 1,329,297
39: 1,328,809
1,329,079
1,329,142
45: 1,329,050
46: 1,329,011
54: 1,329,000
63: 1,329,190
70: R.14,797
1,328,966
99: 1,329,319
106: 1,329,037
75— 14: 1,329,055
76— 40: 1,329,036

78— 49: 1,328,905
81— 9.5: 1,329,155
195: 1,328,940
179: 1,329,161
82— 2: 1,328,962
11: 1,329,042
35: 1,329,265
83— 53: 1,328,806
67: 1,329,113
73: R.14,795
85: 1,329,127
1,329,335
84— 7: 1,328,831
16: 1,328,976
43: 1,328,848
78: 1,328,844
100: 1,328,870
162: 1,329,286
85— 1.5: R.14,776
5: 1,329,131
11: 1,328,911
87— 3: 1,328,898
12: 1,328,076
89— 35: 1,429,346
40: 1,428,811
1,328,849
90— 1: 1,329,175
91— 14.5: 1,328,814
72: 1,328,883
92— 40: 1,429,130
48: 1,329,100
93— 2: 1,329,069
1,429,256
81: 1,328,912
95— 5.7: 1,329,098
97— 25: 1,328,913
28: 1,329,176
72: 1,328,876
91: 1,328,898
19— 6: 1,329,223
8: 1,329,246
101— 216: 1,329,325
248: 1,328,812
102— 26: 1,328,967
29: 1,329,154
103— 62: 1,329,137
64: 1,329,171
65: 1,328,980
1,329,281
67: 1,328,983
104— 13: 1,329,049
118: 1,329,304
1,329,305
105— 49: 1,329,289
406: 1,329,006
106— 21: 1,329,004
31: 1,329,232
107— 58: 1,329,094
110— 41: 1,328,883
111— 9: 1,328,848
112— 3: 1,329,298
7: 1,328,821
86: 1,328,760
100: 1,329,221
113— 14: 1,329,250
30: 1,329,140
116: 1,329,268
114— 51: 1,329,225
79: 1,328,841
218: 1,329,085
115— 28: 1,329,228
116— 1: 1,329,053
1,329,275
31: 1,328,978
49: 1,329,046
65: 1,329,046
119— 23: 1,329,104
25: 1,328,861
48: 1,329,024
61: 1,329,288
63: 1,329,970
121— 63: 1,328,972
122— 250: 1,328,856
123— 58: 1,329,343
58: 1,329,033
131: 1,328,844
148: 1,329,152
149: 1,328,892

123— 165: 1,328,960
169: 1,329,013
1,329,3.0
174: 1,328,815
1,328,875
180: 1,329,345
193: 1,329,238
124— 13: 1,328,929
360: 1,329,063
367: 1,329,035
128— 105: 1,328,944
286: 1,329,195
129— 1: 1,328,971
16: 1,328,956
20: 1,329,030
130— 16: 1,328,872
18: 1,328,819
30: 1,329,113
59: 1,328,961
131— 17: 1,329,162
1.5— 20: 1,328,501
23: 1,328,902
31: 1,329,219
134— 75: 1,329,285
139: 1,328,9 6
1,329,017
1,329,170
139— 1: 1,329,251
23: 1,329,251
30: 1,329,157
66: 1,329,302
1,329,303
85: 1,328,907
1,328,908
1,329,3.8
140— 123: 1,329,026
143— 133: 1,328,682
144— 61: 1,329,061
191: 1,329,060
304: 1,328,862
146— 5: 1,329,023
148— 13: 1,328,831
150— 8: 1,328,879
1,328,688
151— 8: 1,328,939
152— 8: 1,329,021
1,329,217
1,329,331
12: 1,329,126
1,329,116
1,329,182
14: 1,429,200
21: 1,329,289
31: 1,329,213
1,328,838
50: 1,329,111
154— 9: 1,329,239
17: 1,329,310
1,329,311
155— 8: 1,329,261
45: 1,328,826
156— 24: 1,329,243
35: 1,329,092
158— 1.5: 1,329,279
36: 1,329,079
46.5: 1,329,074
64: 1,329,066
65: 1,329,224
116: 1,329,096
179: 1,329,068
161— 8: 1,329,020
162— 4: 1,329,093
167— 9: 1,329,148
169— 23: 1,328,994
170— 67: 1,329,209
150: 1,329,104
171— 206: 1,329,027
252: 1,329,242
321: 1,329,247
1,329,277
172— 129: 1,329,247
274: 1,329,243
175— 294: 1,329,193
176— 103: 1,329,132
177— 337: 1,329,043

178— 17: 1,328,186
179— 17: 1,329,287
73: 1,329,004
84: 1,329,001
156: 1,329,029
157: 1,329,031
190: 1,328,996
180— 9: 1,329,314
53: 1,328,839
89: 1,328,809
182— 13: 1,329,015
183— 7: 1,329,237
10: 1,329,115
72: 1,329,138
74: 1,328,868
111: 1,328,880
184— 6: 1,329,038
18: 1,328,959
103: 1,328,843
104: 1,328,906
185— 41: 1,329,091
188— 1: 1,328,886
24: 1,329,000
1,329,010
51: 1,329,008
189— 24: 1,328,976
1,328,927
28: 1,329,026
46: 1,328,918
190— 12: 1,329,080
49: 1,329,194
193— 10: 1,329,018
195— 1: 1,328,888
197— 6.1: 1,329,087
200— 91: 1,328,825
142: 1,329,122
153: 1,329,347
204— 2: 1,329,315
5: 1,328,981
29: 1,329,125
1,329,180
1,329,181
206— 20: 1,328,968
28: 1,329,012
91: 1,329,056
210— 16: 1,328,853
211— 2: 1,328,950
214— 12: 1,329,318
32: 1,329,293
46: 1,329,084
77: 1,328,923
91: 1,328,809
215— 52: 1,329,248
100: 1,328,860
216— 44: 1,329,290
217— 12: 1,329,032
1,329,332
1,329,333
64: 1,329,344
219— 2: 1,329,144
10: 1,329,135
1,329,136
15: 1,329,233
39: 1,329,204
55: 1,329,167
56: 1,329,168
220— 1: 1,328,937
39: 1,329,040
221— 39: 1,329,184
27: 1,328,881
47: 1,329,229
78: 1,329,199
224— 29: 1,329,028
1,329,174
225— 19: 1,329,110
229— 39: 1,328,935
230— 27: 1,329,185
1,329,348
234— 31: 1,328,840
235— 59: 1,329,014
60: 1,328,822
1,328,847
82: 1,329,090
91: 1,329,000
236— 44: 1,329,112
237— 32: 1,328,820

238— 3: 1,329,264
262: 1,329,227
272: 1,328,917
286: 1,329,205
295: 1,329,163
302: 1,329,077
311: 1,329,153
240— 53: 1,329,051
61: 1,328,902
78: 1,329,330
93: 1,329,147
108: 1,329,187
115: 1,329,280
241— 6: 1,328,931
242— 77: 1,329,240
155: 1,329,341
244— 2: 1,329,336
12: 1,329,082
14: 1,329,342
21: 1,328,848
25: 1,329,156
31: 1,328,963
245— 6: 1,329,199
246— 34: 1,328,865
125: 1,329,188
126: 1,328,854
200: 1,329,258
223: 1,328,960
294: 1,328,932
301: 1,329,054
428: 1,329,007
247— 5: 1,325,993
248— 20: 1,328,930
30: 1,329,173
27: 1,329,151
249— 20: 1,328,933
250— 27: 1,329,283
41: 1,328,925
251— 51: 1,329,009
109: 1,329,016
137: 1,329,209
114: 1,329,321
159: 1,329,231
252— 1,328,845
253— 19: 1,329,244
65: 1,328,835
254— 43: 1,329,185
111: 1,329,068
131: 1,329,116
135: 1,329,107
255— 75: 1,328,951
257— 24: 1,328,818
30: 1,328,908
259— 129: 1,329,256
151: 1,329,198
134: 1,329,164
261— 16: 1,329,309
52: 1,329,308
121: 1,329,252
135: 1,329,278
263— 41: 1,329,278
265— 13: 1,329,192
266— 57: 1,328,812
267— 27: 1,328,812
4: 1,329,175
9: 1,328,979
271— 2: 1,329,108
32: 1,328,877
279— 77: 1,329,274
280— 5: 1,329,039
283— 6: 1,329,260
57: 1,329,106
58: 1,329,002
60: 1,329,120
40: 1,329,141
77: 1,329,121
4: 1,329,776
285— 37: 1,328,873
287— 1: 1,328,911
290— 37: 1,328,873
293— 53: 1,329,019
1,329,334
294— 22: 1,328,800
296— 10: 1,328,999
8: 1,329,163
298— 13: 1,328,805
19: 1,328,837
1,328,928
30: 1,329,101
83: 1,328,942
299— 97: 1,329,103

INDEX

TO THE

DECISIONS OF THE COMMISSIONER OF PATENTS AND OF THE UNITED STATES COURTS.

JANUARY, 1920.

[Decisions of the Court of Appeals of the District of Columbia are indicated by a star (*) and of the United States Circuit Court of Appeals by the letter d.]

TABLE OF CASES.

SUBJECT-MATTER INDEX.

DIGEST

OF THE

DECISIONS OF THE COMMISSIONER OF PATENTS AND OF THE UNITED STATES COURTS.

JANUARY, 1920.

[Decisions of the Court of Appeals of the District of Columbia are indicated by a star (*) and of the United States Circuit Court of Appeals by the letter d.]

ANTICIPATION.

See Construction of Specifications and Patents, 1; Particular Patents, 4; Suits for Infringement, 2.

BROAD CLAIMS.

See Particular Patents, 2.

BURDEN OF PROOF.

See Priority of Invention.

CLAIMS.

See Construction of Specifications and Patents, 1; Jurisdiction of the Court of Appeals of the District of Columbia; Particular Patents, 1, 2, 3, 4, 6.

1. LIMITATION.
   Where a claim defines an element in terms of its form, material, location, or function, thereby apparently creating an express limitation, and the limitation pertains to the inventive step rather than to its environment and imports a substantial function which the patentee considered of importance, forms excluded cannot be considered covered by the patent under the doctrine of equivalency.
   [d D'Arcy Spring Co. et al. v. Marshall Ventilated Mattress Co., 347.

2. MEASURE OF INVENTION.
   A patent is sustained not for what the inventor may have done, in effect, but for what is pointed out clearly and distinctly in his claims. As much as is not so claimed belongs to the public.
   [d Knight Soda Fountain Co. v. Walrus Mfg. Co., 350.

3. LIMITATION.
   A patent claim may be limited by reference to the specifications.
   [d Bisight Co. et al. v. Onepiece Bifocal Lens Co., 479.

COMMERCIAL SUCCESS.

See Construction of Specifications and Patents, 1.

COMMISSIONER OF PATENTS.

See Jurisdiction of the Court of Appeals of the District of Columbia.

CONSTRUCTION OF CLAIMS.

See Particular Patents.

CONSTRUCTION OF SPECIFICATIONS AND PATENTS.

See Infringement, 2; Particular Patents.

1. DESCRIPTION—SUFFICIENCY.
   Though the patentee did not anticipate the use to which the patented article could be and was put, he is entitled to protection for such use where the adaptability was inherent in the structure shown and described in claims and specifications.
   [d D'Arcy Spring Co. et al. v. Marshall Ventilated Mattress Co., 347.

2. INSTRUCTION—LIMITATIONS.
   The Marshall patent, No. 685,160, for a mattress comprising a cover and a plurality of transversely-extending strips of material stitched at intervals to form pockets, the pocket of one strip alternating with those of adjacent strip, and spiral springs arranged in such pockets, Held limited therein to that form of arrangement and not to be infringed by a mattress similarly constructed where the pockets were arranged with centers equidistant in right-angled directions, so that there was no nesting of the springs.
   [d Id.

3. PRESUMPTION OF INVENTIVE NOVELTY FROM USE—ATTRIBUTION TO PRODUCT.
   Though brick of a certain type, which have gone on the market and had a large sale, are the product of the patentee's patented machine, which has been manufactured by him and sold to brick-makers, such credit and such presumption of inventive novelty as arise from public use should be given to the product—the bricks—and not to the machine.
   [d Dunn Wire-Cut Lug Brick Co. v. Toronto Fire Clay Co. et al., 480.

CORPORATIONS.

See Infringement, 1; Suits for Infringement, 1.

DAMAGES AND PROFITS.

See Infringement, 1.

DELAY IN FILING EVIDENCE.

See Suits for Infringement, 2.

DESCRIPTION.

See Construction of Specifications and Patents 1, 2.

DESCRIPTIVE TERMS.

See Registration of Trade-Marks, 1, 2.

EARLIER AND LATER PATENTS.

See Infringements, 2.

ELEMENTS.

See Claims, 1.

EQUIVALENTS.

See Claims, 1.

EVIDENCE.

See Priority of Invention; Suits for Infringement, 2.

FOREIGN PATENTS.

See Suits for Infringement, 2.

FORMER DECISIONS CITED.

See Particular Patents, 1.

FUNCTION.

See Claims, 1; Particular Patents, 1.

INDEFINITENESS.

See Claims, 3; Particular Patents, 6.

INFRINGEMENT.

See Construction of Specifications and Patents, 2; Particular Patents, 3, 6; Suits for Infringement.

1. DAMAGES.
The president and general manager of a corporation which infringed a patent is not individually liable for damages and profits on infringement unless he inflicted the damages or received the profits otherwise than through the usual relations between officer and corporation.
[d D'Arcy Spring Co. et al. v. Marshall Ventilated Mattress Co., 347.

2. WHAT CONSTITUTES.
As between plaintiff's earlier and defendant's later patent a finding that the earlier device, if later, would not have infringed the later patent is not helpful in deciding whether defendant's device infringes plaintiff's patent.
[d Dunn Wire-Cut Lug Brick Co. v. Toronto Fire Clay Co. et al., 480.

INTERFERENCE.

See Jurisdiction of the Court of Appeals of the District of Columbia; Priority of Invention.

INTERLOCUTORY DECREE.

See Suits for Infringement, 2.

INVENTION.

See Claims, 3; Construction of Specifications and Patents, 3; Particular Patents, 5, 7.

JURISDICTION OF THE COURT OF APPEALS OF THE DISTRICT OF COLUMBIA.

INTERFERENCE PROCEEDING.
The Court of Appeals of the District of Columbia is without authority in an interference proceeding to review the Commissioner's ruling that the claims of one of the parties are not patentable because barred by the statute of public use (or printed publication).
[* Cowles v. Rody, 191.

LIABILITY.

See Infringement, 1; Suits for Infringement, 1.

LIMITATION OF CLAIMS.

See Claims; Particular Patents, 2.

LIMITED PATENTS.

See Particular Patents, 2.

MACHINE.

See Construction of Specifications and Patents, 3; Particular Patents, 1, 2, 3, 4.

MECHANICAL SKILL.

See Particular Patents, 4, 5.

METHOD AND PRODUCT.

1. NEW PRODUCT—VARIATIONS IN METHOD OF MAKING.
The inventor of a new and useful product or article of manufacture may have a patent covering it and giving a monopoly upon it regardless of great variations in the method of making.
[d Dunn Wire-Cut Lug Brick Co. v. Toronto Fire Clay Co. et al., 480.

2. SEPARATE PATENTS.
In the ordinary and typical case the method of manufacture and the product manufactured are separable inventions supporting separate patents, one of which may be valid and the other not.
[d Id.

MONOPOLY.

See Method and Product, 1.

NEW USE.

See Construction of Specifications and Patents, 1.

NOVELTY.

See Construction of Specifications and Patents, 3.

OFFICER OF CORPORATION.

See Infringement, 1; Suits for Infringement, 1.

PARTICULAR PATENTS.

1. COLLIS—No. 1,204,905—PROCESS FOR DRYING AND SHAPING HOSIERY ARTICLES—VOID.
The claim of the Collis patent, No. 1,204,945, reading as follows: "A method of treating hosiery articles, consisting in heating, from within, and to a predetermined fabric-drying temperature, a metallic form having its sides relatively narrow in cross-section and converging into substantially reduced, crease-producing edges; then superposing upon said form a hosiery article and subjecting the same to the action of heat imparted internally thereto by the form for producing a substantially flattened and creased article," Held void as covering nothing more than the function of an apparatus which was the subject of a separate patent which had been held invalid because of prior invention and use. "The process in this case is as clearly the whole value, the sole purpose of the apparatus," as in the case of Busch v. Jones (184 U. S., 598) "the process was the whole value, the sole purpose of the press."
d Paramount Hosiery Form Drying Co. v. Moorhead Knitting Co., 619.

2. CONNOR—No. 836,486—BIFOCAL LENS—I IMITATION.
The Connor machine patent, No. 836,486, claim 1, for making bifocal lenses, as limited by its reference to the specifications, is not invalid because too broad.
[d Bisight Co. et al v. Onepiece Bifocal Lens Co., 479.

3. SAME—INFRINGEMENT.
No. 836,486, claim 1, for making bifocal lenses, Held infringed.
[d Id.

4. SAME—ANTICIPATION.
No. 836,486, claim 1, for producing bifocal lenses, is not anticipated by grinding-machines in remote arts, such as grinding buttons, since more than mechanical skill was required to apply the grinding process to lenses.
[d Id.

5. DUNN—No. 918,980—WIRE-CUT PAVING-BRICK—VALIDITY.
Dunn's patent, No. 918,980, for wire-cut paving-brick having wire-cut ribs on the side, Held valid because the concept had inventive character, as distinguished from mere skill.
[d Dunn Wire-Cut Lug Brick Co. v. Toronto Fire Clay Co. et al., 480.

6. FARIES—No. 779,271—JAR AND DIPPER—VALIDITY—INDEFINITENESS.
The Faries patent, No. 779,271, for a jar and dipper for serving crushed fruit, etc., claim 3 Held not infringed. Claims 4 and 5 Held invalid for indefiniteness in view of the prior art.
[d Knight Soda Fountain Co. v. Walrus Mfg. Co., 350.

7. MARSHALL—No. 685,160—MATTRESS—INVENTION.
The Marshall patent, No. 685,160, for a mattress comprising a cover and a plurality of transversely-extending strips of material stitched at intervals to form pockets, etc., and spiral springs arranged in such pockets, Held valid, showing invention.
[d D'Arcy Spring Co. et al. v. Marshall Ventilated Mattress Co., 347.

PRESUMPTION.

See Construction of Specifications and Patents, 3.

PRIORITY OF INVENTION.

See Particular Patents, 1.

AWARD—EVIDENCE.
Evidence reviewed and *Held* insufficient to establish that the junior party, on whom the burden of proof rested heavily as an applicant against a patentee, was the first inventor.
[*Bader v. Burroughs, 190.

PROCESS AND APPARATUS

See Particular Patents, 1.

PRODUCTS.

See Construction of Specifications and Patents, 3; Method and Product; Suits for Infringement, 2.

PUBLIC PROPERTY.

See Claims, 2.

PUBLIC USE.

See Construction of Specifications and Patents, 3; Jurisdiction of the Court of Appeals of the District of Columbia.

RECORD OF CASE.

See Suits for Infringement, 2.

REGISTRATION OF TRADE-MARKS.

See Similarity of Trade-Marks.

1. DESCRIPTIVENESS—"SAFETSEAL," FOR ENVELOPS.
The mark "SafeTseal" as applied to envelops *Held* descriptive, as indicating either safety-seal envelops or safe-seal envelops.
[*In re Alvah Bushnell Company, 189.

2. "EVERLASTING, FOR VEHICLE-WHEELS—DESCRIPTIVE.
The word "Everlasting" *Held* descriptive, and therefore not registrable as a trade-mark for vehicle-wheels. This word expresses aptly the idea that applicant's wheels will last a very long time, and therefore cannot be monopolized.
[*Ex parte* Smith Wheel, Inc., 479.

SEPARATE PATENTS.

See Method and Product, 2; Particular Patents, 1.

SIMILARITY OF TRADE-MARKS.

See Registration of Trade-Marks.

1. "BIG CHIEF" AND "ARAB."
A mark consisting of the words "Big Chief," associated with the representation of a man on horseback, inclosed within a circle, *Held* deceptively similar to a mark consisting of the word "Arab," associated with the representation of a man on horseback, inclosed within two circles.
[*American Feed Milling Co. v. M. C. Peters Mill Co., 189.

2. "FROM THE LAND OF SUNSHINE" AND "BLOSSOM AND SUNSHINE."
A mark consisting of the words "From the Land of Sunshine" *Held* not deceptively similar to a mark consisting of the words "Blossom and Sunshine," associated with the representation of blossoms and a sunburst.
[*L. Otsen & Co. v. The J. K. Armsby Co., 191.

SPECIFICATIONS.

See Claims, 3; Construction of Specifications and Patents, 1; Infringement, 2; Particular Patents, 2.

STATE OF THE ART.

See Particular Patents, 6.

STATUTORY BAR.

See Jurisdiction of the Court of Appeals of the District of Columbia.

SUFFICIENCY OF DESCRIPTION.

See Construction of Specifications and Patents, 1.

SUITS FOR INFRINGEMENT.

1. DEFENDANT.
In a suit against a corporation for infringement of patent the president and general manager, in active control of the corporate affairs, may be made defendant, so that he may be personally bound and enjoined.
[d D'Arcy Spring Co. et al. v. Marshall Ventilated Matiress Co., 347.

2. LATE INTRODUCTION OF EVIDENCE—CONDITIONS OF PERMISSION.
In suit for infringement of patent where, after direction of the usual interlocutory decree on finding of infringement, defendants present foreign patents said to anticipate plaintiff's product and ask leave to apply to reopen the case and put them into the record on account of the public interest and the interest of the courts the proposed evidence will be permitted to be brought into the record on defendants' meeting additional expenses of another trial, their showing to excuse failure to put in the evidence in due time not being satisfactory.
[d Dunn Wire-Cut Lug Brick Co. v. Toronto Fire Clay Co. et al., 480.

USE OF INVENTION.

See Construction of Specifications and Patents, 1, 3; Particular Patents, 1.

VALID PATENTS.

See Method and Product, 2; Particular Patents, 2, 5, 7.

VOID PATENTS.

See Particular Patents, 1, 6.

CPSIA information can be obtained
at www.ICGtesting.com
Printed in the USA
LVHW081420250522
719731LV00003B/102